31.99

PAGE 48 ON THE ROAD

YOUR COMPLETE DESTINATION GUIDE
In-depth reviews, detailed listings
and insider tips

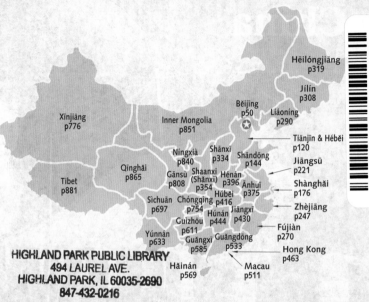

W9-BTB-465

Hēilóngjiāng p319

Jílín p308

Běijīng p50

Liáoníng p290

Xīnjiāng p776

Inner Mongolia p851

Tiānjīn & Héběi p120

Níngxià p840

Shǎnxī p334

Shāndōng p144

Jiāngsū p221

Qīnghǎi p865

Gānsù p808

Shaanxi (Shǎnxī) p354

Hénán p396

Ānhuī p375

Shànghǎi p176

Tibet p881

Húběi p416

Zhèjiāng p247

Sìchuān p697

Chóngqìng p754

Húnán p444

Jiāngxī p430

Guìzhōu p611

Fújiàn p270

Yúnnán p633

Guǎngxī p585

Guǎngdōng p533

Hong Kong p463

HIGHLAND PARK PUBLIC LIBRARY
494 LAUREL AVE.
HIGHLAND PARK, IL 60035-2690
847-432-0216

Hǎinán p569

Macau p511

PAGE 981 SURVIVAL GUIDE

VITAL PRACTICAL INFORMATION TO
HELP YOU HAVE A SMOOTH TRIP

Directory A-Z 982
Transport 996
China by Train................ 1004
Health............................ 1010
Language....................... 1016
Index 1030
Map Legend 1046

Transport

THIS EDITION WRITTEN AND RESEARCHED BY
Damian Harper
Piera Chen, Chung Wah Chow, David Eimer,
Tienlon Ho, Robert Kelly, Michael Kohn, Shawn Low,
Bradley Mayhew, Daniel McCrohan, Christopher Pitts

welcome to
China

Awe-Inspiring Antiquity

China is modernising at a head-spinning pace, but slick skyscrapers, Lamborghini showrooms and Maglev trains are little more than dazzling baubles. Let's face it: the world's oldest continuous civilisation is bound to pull an artefact or two out of its hat. You won't find history at every turn – three decades of full-throttle development and socialist iconoclasm have taken their toll – but travel selectively in China and rich seams of antiquity pop into view. With tumble-down chunks of the Great Wall, mist-wreathed, temple-topped mountains, quaint villages, water towns and eye-catching ethnic borderlands, China is home to one of the world's oldest and most remarkable civilisations. You'll need a well-made pair of travelling shoes and a strong stomach for long-distance wayfaring: China's artefacts are strewn about, so put some serious mileage under your soles.

Stupendous Scenery

China is vast. Off-the-scale massive. You simply have to get outside: island-hop in Hong Kong, gaze over the epic grasslands of Inner Mongolia or squint up at the mind-blowing peaks of the Himalayas. Expect to trek, cycle between fairy-tale karst pinnacles, or merely stand and ponder the desiccated enormity of the northwestern deserts or the preternatural mists of China's sacred mountains. Swoon before the rice terraces of the

Antique yet up-to-the-minute, familiar yet unrecognisable, outwardly urban but quintessentially rural, conservative yet path-breaking, space-age but old-fashioned, China is a land of mesmerising contradictions.

(left) Watchtowers along the Great Wall near Běijīng (p113)
(below) Canals of Zhūjiājiǎo (p220)

south, size up some awesome sand dunes in Gānsù, trace the Great Wall as it meanders across mountain peaks, get lost in forests of bamboo, sail through dramatic river gorges or, when your energy fails you, flake out for a tan on a distant beach. China's sublime scenery is also richly flecked with seasonal shades, from the crimson leaves of autumn maples to the colourful azaleas of spring in Huángshān and the ice-encrusted roofs of mountaintop Buddhist temples. Your camera will be glued to your hand.

Cuisine

China may be fixated with food but treat yourself by swapping your meagre local Chinatown menu for the lavish Middle Kingdom cookbook. Wolf down Peking duck, size up a sizzling lamb kebab in Kāifēng or gobble down a bowl of Lánzhōu noodles on the Silk Road. Spicy Húnán or Sìchuān dishes really raise the temperature but don't forget about what's cooking along China's frontier lands – always an excellent excuse to get off the beaten path. Impress your friends as you *gānbēi* (down-in-one) the local firewater, sip an ice-cold beer in a slick Běijīng bar or survey the Shànghǎi skyline through a raised cocktail glass. Culinary exploration is possibly the most enticing aspect of Middle Kingdom travel: you'll return with stimulated taste buds and much cherished gastronomic memories.

China

0 ───── 500 km
0 ───── 250 miles

RUSSIA

KAZAKHSTAN

Silk Road
Camels, deserts and
vanished cities (p798)

Dūnhuáng
Silk Road oasis town (p829)

TASHKENT

★ **BISHKEK**

KYRGYZSTAN

Yīníng

Ürümqi

MONGOLIA

TAJIKISTAN

Kashgar

Kuqa

XĪNJIĀNG

Dūnhuáng

GĀNSÙ

Zhāngyè

Dégé

PAKISTAN

Tashkurgan

Qinghai Hú

Xīníng

Jiǔzhàigōu National Park
Hiking in the beautiful wilds
of Sìchuān (p742)

Changtang
Nature
Preserve

QĪNGHǍI

Xiàl

Aldan Gu

Shílín

DELHI

Lake Manasarovar

TIBET

Milam
Glacier

Silíng-tso

Ngu-Chu

SÌCHUĀ

NEPAL

Nam-tso

Mt Everest
(8488m)

Thimphu
Valley

○ **Lhasa**

Téngchōng

Měnglà

KATHMANDU

☆ **THIMPHU**

Zhōngdiàn
(Shangri-la)

Měngyǎ

BHUTAN

Shíbǎoshān

Lhasa
The land of snows (p884)

INDIA

BANGLADESH

Xiàguān
(Dàlǐ City)

angzi Riv

**MYANMAR
(BURMA)**

Kūnmíng

DHAKA ☆

YÚNNÁ

Tiger Leaping Gorge
Stunning
Yúnnán scenery (p667)

Jǐnghóng

Jǐngzhēn

ELEVATION

| 6000m |
| 5000m |
| 4000m |
| 3000m |
| 2000m |
| 1000m |
| 500m |
| 0 |

20°N

Yuányáng Rice Terraces
For beautiful, iconic
views (p648)

LAO

*Bay of
Bengal*

85°E

90°E

THAILAND

Great Wall
Walking on the mother of all walls (p113)

Forbidden City
Imperial seat of two dynasties (p55)

Píngyáo
China's most charming walled town (p346)

Terracotta Warriors
Astonishing artistry from ancient China (p364)

Shànghǎi
The Paris of the East (p176)

Huángshān
China's mountain of mists (p385)

Yangzi River Cruise
China's greatest river journey (p770)

Labrang Monastery
Suffused with Buddhist mystery (p816)

Cycling Yángshuò
Pedalling through gorgeous karst scenery (p595)

30
TOP
EXPERIENCES

Forbidden City

1 Not a city and no longer forbidden, Běijīng's enormous palace (p55) is the be-all-and-end-all of dynastic grandeur with its vast halls and splendid gates. No other place in China teems with so much history, legend and good old-fashioned imperial intrigue. You may get totally lost here but you'll always find something to write about on the first postcard you can lay your hands on. The complex also heads the list with one of China's most attractive admission prices and almost endless value-for-money sightseeing.

Great Wall

2 Spotting it from space is both tough and pointless: the only place you can truly put the Great Wall (p113) under your feet is in China. Select the Great Wall according to taste: perfectly chiselled, dilapidated, stripped of its bricks, overrun with saplings, coiling splendidly into the hills or returning to dust. The fortification is a fitting symbol of those perennial Chinese traits: diligence, mass manpower, ambitious vision and engineering skill (coupled with a distrust of the neighbours). Part of the wall at Mùtiányù, northeast of Běijīng

1

ROEUN / GETTY IMAGES ©

Tiger Leaping Gorge

3 Picture snowcapped mountains rising on either side of a gorge so deep that you can be 2km above the river rushing across the rocks far below. Then imagine winding up and down trails that pass through tiny farming villages, where you can rest while enjoying views so glorious they defy superlatives. Cutting through remote northwest Yúnnán for 16 kilometres, Tiger Leaping Gorge (p667) is a simply unmissable experience. Hikers returning from the gorge invariably give it glowing reviews.

The Bund, Shànghǎi

4 More than just a city, Shànghǎi is the country's neon-lit beacon of change, opportunity and sophistication. Its sights set squarely on the not-too-distant future, Shànghǎi offers a taste of all the superlatives China can dare to dream up, from the world's highest observation deck to its largest underground theatre. Whether you're just pulling in after an epic 40-hour train trip from Xīnjiāng or it's your first stop, you'll find plenty to indulge in here. Start with the Bund (p180), Shànghǎi's iconic riverfront area where it all began.
View across to Pǔdōng from the Bund

Yangzi River Cruise

5 Snow melting from the world's 'third pole' – the high-altitude Tibet–Qīnghǎi plateau – is the source of China's mighty, life-giving Yangzi. The country's longest river, the Yangzi surges west–east across the nation before pouring into the Pacific Ocean. It reaches a crescendo with the Three Gorges, carved out throughout the millennia by the inexorable persistence of the powerful waters. The gorges are a magnificent spectacle and a Yangzi River cruise (p770) is a rare chance to hang up your travelling hat, take a seat and leisurely watch the drama unfold. Little Three Gorges, Húběi

Mt Kailash, Western Tibet

6 Worshipped by more than a billion Buddhists and Hindus, Asia's most sacred mountain (p903) rises from the Barkha plain like a giant four-sided 6714m-high *chörten* (stupa). Throw in stunning nearby Lake Manasarovar and a basin that forms the source of four of Asia's greatest rivers, and it's clear that this place is special. Travel here to one of the world's most beautiful and remote corners brings a bonus: the three-day pilgrim path around the mountain erases the sins of a lifetime.

Hiking Dragon's Backbone Rice Terraces

7 After a bumpy bus ride to northern Guǎngxī, you'll be dazzled by one of China's most archetypal and photographed landscapes: the splendidly named Dragon's Backbone Rice Terraces (p593). The region is a beguiling patchwork of minority villages, with layers of waterlogged terraces climbing the hillsides. You'll be enticed into a game of village-hopping. The most invigorating walk between Píng'ān and Dàzhài villages offers the most spine-tingling views. Visit after the summer rains when the fields are glistening with reflections.

GREG ELMS / GETTY IMAGES ©

MICHAEL COYNE / GETTY IMAGES ©

LONELY PLANET / GETTY IMAGES ©

China's Cuisine

8 Say *zàijiàn* (goodbye) to that Chinatown schlock and *nǐhǎo* (hello) to a whole new world of food and flavour (see p941). You'll certainly find dim sum, noodles and dumplings aplenty, but there's also the liquid fire of a Chóngqìng hotpot, Tibetan cuisine, or the adventurous flavours of Kāifēng's night market. You'll see things you've never seen before, eat things you've never heard of and drink things that could lift a rocket into space. And that's just for starters.

Wonton soup and dumplings

Diāolóu in Kāipíng

9 If you only have time for one attraction in Guǎngdōng, Kāipíng's *diāolóu* (p552) should be it. Approximately 1800 outlandishly designed watchtowers and fortified residences scatter higgledy-piggledy in the farmland in Kāipíng, a town not far from Guǎngzhōu. These sturdy bastions built in the early 20th century may not be what you'd typically expect in the Middle Kingdom, but they inspire awe with their eccentric fusion of foreign and domestic architectural styles. Greek, Roman, Gothic, Byzantine and baroque – you name it, they've got it.

French Concession, Shànghǎi

10 Once home to the bulk of Shànghǎi's adventurers, revolutionaries, gangsters, prostitutes and writers, though ironically many of them weren't French, the former concession (also called Frenchtown) is the most graceful part of Pǔxī. The Paris of the East turns on its European charms to maximum effect here, where leafy streets and 1920s villas meet art deco apartment blocks, elegant restaurants and chic bars. The French Concession (p185) is Shànghǎi sunny side up, at its coolest, hippest and most alluring. Xīntiāndì shopping precinct (p191)

Huángshān & Hui Villages

11 Shrouded in mist and light rain more than 200 days a year, and maddeningly crowded most of the time, Huángshān (p385) has an appeal that attracts millions of annual visitors. Perhaps it's the barren landscape, or an otherworldly vibe on the mountain. Mist – a fickle mistress – rolls in and out at will; spindly bent pines stick out like lone pins across sheer craggy granite faces. Not far from the base are the perfectly preserved Hui villages including Xīdì (p380) and Hóngcūn (p381). Unesco, Ang Lee and Zhang Yimou were captivated – you will be too. Mercy Light Temple, Huángshān

Grand Buddha, Lèshān

12 You can read all the stats you like about Lèshān's Grand Buddha statue (p718) – yes, its ears really are 7m long! – but until you descend the steps alongside the world's tallest Buddha statue and stand beside its feet, with its toenails at the same level as your eyes, you can't really comprehend just how massive it is. Still not impressed? Consider then that this wonderful, riverside stone statue was carved painstakingly into the cliff face above you more than 1200 years ago.

Terracotta Warriors

13 Standing silent guard over their emperor for more than 2000 years, the terracotta warriors (p364) are one of the most extraordinary archaeological discoveries ever made. It's not just that there are thousands of the life-sized figures lined up in battle formation; it's the fact that no two of them are alike, with every single one of them wearing a distinct expression. This is an army, but it's one made up of individuals. Gazing at these superbly sculpted faces brings the past alive in a unique way.

The Lí River & Cycling Yángshuò

14 It's hard to exaggerate the beauty of Yángshuò (p595) and the Lí River (p599) area, renowned for classic images of mossy-green jagged limestone peaks providing a backdrop for weeping willows leaning over bubbling streams, wallowing water buffaloes and farmers sowing rice paddies. Ride a bamboo raft along the river and you'll understand why this stunning rural landscape has inspired painters and poets for centuries. Another popular way to appreciate the scenery is a bike tour along the Yùlóng River (p599). Lí River

Lhasa

15 The holy city of Lhasa (p884) is the perfect introduction to Tibet, and just arriving here can make the hairs stand up on the back of your neck. The spectacular prayer halls of the Potala Palace, the medieval Jokhang Temple and the monastic cities of Drepung and Sera are the big draws, but don't miss the less-visited chapels and pilgrim paths. The whitewashed alleys of the old town hold the real heart of the Tibetan quarter, and you could spend hours here wandering around backstreet handicraft workshops, hidden temples and local teahouses. Potala Palace

KEREN SU / GETTY IMAGES ©

CHRISTIAN KOBER / GETTY IMAGES ©

The Silk Road

16 There are other Silk Road cities in countries such as Uzbekistan and Turkmenistan, but it's in China where you get the feeling of stepping on the actual 'Silk Road', with its pervasive Muslim heritage and fragments from ancient Buddhist civilisations. Travel by bus and experience the route as ancient traders once did – mile by mile, town by town. Kashgar (p790) is the ultimate Silk Road town and remains a unique melting pot of peoples, but Hotan (p800) is equally special: a rough-and-tumble town still clinging to bygone days. Tadjik camel driver, Xīnjiāng

Píngyáo

17 Time-warped Píngyáo (p346) is a true gem: an intact, walled Chinese town with an unbroken sense of continuity to its Qing-dynasty heyday. Píngyáo ticks most of your China boxes with a flourish: imposing city walls, atmospheric alleys, ancient shopfronts, traditional courtyard houses, some excellent hotels, hospitable locals and all in a compact area. You can travel the length and breadth of China and not find another town like it. In fact, when you discover Píngyáo, you may never want to leave. The intact Ming-dynasty city walls of Píngyáo

KRZYSZTOF DYDYNSKI / GETTY IMAGES ©

Labrang Monastery

18 If you can't make it to Tibet, visit the Gānsù province town of Xiàhé, a more accessible part of the former Tibetan region of Amdo. One moment you are in Han China, the next you are virtually in Tibet. Here, Labrang Monastery (p816) attracts legions of sun-tanned Tibetan pilgrims who perambulate single-mindedly around the huge monastery's prayer-wheel-lined *kora* (pilgrim path). As a strong source of spiritual power, the monastery casts its spell far and wide, and with great hiking opportunities plus an intriguing ethnic mix, it's a fascinating corner of China.

Běijīng's Hútòng

19 To get under the skin of the capital, you need to get lost at least once in its enchanting, ancient alleyways (p96). *Hútòng* are Běijīng's heart and soul; it's in these alleys that crisscross the centre of the city that you'll discover the capital's unique street life. Despite its march into the 21st century, Běijīng's true charms – heavenly courtyard architecture, pinched lanes and a strong sense of community – are not high-rise. It's easy to find that out; just check into a courtyard hotel and true Běijīng will be right on your doorstep.

Yúngāng Caves

20 Buddhist art taken to sublime heights, these 5th-century caves (p338) house some of the most remarkable statues in all of China. Carved out of the harsh yellow earth of Shānxī and surrounded by superb frescoes, the statues inside the caves represent the highpoint of the Tuoba people's culture and draw on influences from as far away as Greece and Persia. Marvel at how the pigment on some of them has miraculously survived 1500-odd years, and respect how potent they remain to followers of Buddhism.

Taichi

21 An ethereal form of moving meditation to some, an awesome arsenal of martial-arts techniques to others, taichi (p977) is quintessentially Chinese. Daily practice could add a decade or more to your lifespan or give you some handy moves for getting on those crowded buses. And it's not all slow-going: Chen style has snappy elements of Shàolín boxing and it'll give you a leg-busting workout. Find a teacher – in Běijīng, Shànghǎi, Yángshuò, Wǔdāngshān – and put some magic and mystery into your China adventure.

Yuányáng Rice Terraces

22 Hewn out of hills that stretch off into the far distance, the rice terraces of Yuányáng (p648) are testimony to the wonderfully intimate relationship the local Hani people have with the sublime landscape they live in. Rising like giant steps, the intricate terraces are a stunning sight at any time of year. But when they are flooded in winter and the sun's rays are dancing off the water at sunrise or sunset, they're absolutely mesmerising. Just make sure you have enough space on your camera's memory card.

21

HUW JONES / GETTY IMAGES ©

22

WILLIAM YU PHOTOGRAPHY / GETTY IMAGES ©

DIANA MAYFIELD / GETTY IMAGES ©

Cruising up Victoria Harbour

23 A buzzer sounds, you bolt for the gangplank. A whistle blows, your boat chugs forward. Beyond the waves, one of the world's most famous views unfolds – Hong Kong's skyscrapers in their steel and neon splendour, against a backdrop of mountains. You're on the Star Ferry (p475), a legendary service that's been carrying passengers between Hong Kong Island and Kowloon Peninsula since the 19th century. Ten minutes later, a hemp rope is cast, then a bell rings, and you alight. At only HK$2, this is possibly the world's best-value cruise. Star Ferry

Tǔlóu Roundhouses

24 Rising up in colonies from the hilly borderlands of Fújiàn, Guǎngdōng and Jiāngxī, the stupendous *tǔlóu* roundhouses house entire villages, even though occupant numbers are way down these days. The imposing and well-defended bastions of wood and earth – not all circular it must be added – were once mistaken by the CIA for missile silos. Do the right thing and spend the night in one: this is a vanishing way of life, the pastoral setting is quite superb and the architecture is unique.

Hiking in Jiǔzhàigōu National Park

25 Strolling the forested valleys of Jiǔzhàigōu National Park (p742) – past bluer-than-blue lakes and small Tibetan villages, in the shadow of snow-brushed mountains – was always a highlight of any trip to Sìchuān province, but an excellent new ecotourism scheme means travellers can now hike and even camp their way around this stunning part of southwest China. Guides speak English and all camping equipment is provided, so all you need to bring is your sense of adventure and a spare set of camera batteries. Pearl Shoals Waterfall

ZOU YANJU / GETTY IMAGES ©

Tài Shān

26 A visit to China just isn't complete without scaling a sacred mountain or two, and antediluvian Tài Shān (p153) in Shāndōng province is the granddaddy of them all. Climb the Taoist mountain and you'll live to 100, they say, even if you feel you are going to drop dead with exhaustion on the gruelling Path of 18 Bends (lightweights can hitch a ride on the cable car instead). The views are standout and with Tài Shān's mountainous aspect in the east, summit sunrises are the order of the day.

Dūnhuáng

27 Where China starts transforming into a lunar desertscape in the far west, the handsome oasis town of Dūnhuáng (p829) is a natural staging post for dusty Silk Road explorers. Mountainous sand dunes swell outside town while Great Wall fragments lie scoured by abrasive desert winds, but it is the magnificent caves at Mògāo (p833) that truly dazzle. Mògāo is the cream of China's crop of Buddhist caves, and its statues are ineffably sublime and some of the nation's most priceless cultural treasures. Mògāo Caves

Kashgar's Sunday Market

28 Avoid lunchtime, and arrive at the tail end of the Livestock Market (p790), when the crowds are vanishing and the tour buses have rolled on. Wander around and peek over the shoulders of traders as they inspect sheep, goats, camels and other beasts for sale. Amid the dust, heaving crowds and animal odours, you'll find yourself on the very western edge of China, where the local culture takes on more pronounced Central Asian shades and Běijīng is further away than Baghdad.

Fènghuáng

29 Houses perched precariously on stilts, ancestral halls, crumbling temples and gate towers set amidst a warren of back alleys full of shops selling mysterious foods and medicines – it's enough on its own to make the ancient town of Fènghuáng (p458) an essential stop. Add in the seductive setting on either side of the Tuó River and the chance to stay at an inn right by the water, and you have one of the most evocative towns in China. *Hóng Bridge and stilt houses*

Cycling Hǎinán

30 The same blue skies and balmy weather that make China's only tropical island (p569) ideal for a do-nothing holiday, make it superb for exploring on a bicycle. Hit the east for picturesque rice-growing valleys, spectacular bays and some of Asia's finest beaches. And don't miss the sparsely populated central highlands, a densely forested region that's home to the island's original settlers, the Li and the Miao. Here, even the road more taken is still not taken by many at all. *Sānyà Bay*

DIANA MAYFIELD / GETTY IMAGES ©

VINNY P IMAGES / ALAMY ©

need to know

Currency
» The yuan (¥)

Language
» Mandarin
» Cantonese

When to Go

Warm to hot summers, mild winters
Mild to hot summers, cold winters
Mild summers, very cold winters
Desert, dry climate
Cold climate

Běijīng GO Sep–Oct

Shànghǎi GO Oct

Chéngdū GO Mar–May

Kūnmíng GO Dec–Jan

Hong Kong GO Nov–Feb

High Season
(May–Aug)
» Prepare for crowds at traveller hot spots and summer downpours.
» Accommodation prices peak during the first week of the May holiday period.

Shoulder
(Feb–Apr, Sep & Oct)
» Expect warmer days in spring, cooler days in autumn.
» In the north this is the optimum season, with fresh weather and clear skies.
» Accommodation prices peak during holidays in early October.

Low Season
(Nov–Feb)
» Domestic tourism is at a low ebb, but things are busy and expensive for Chinese New Year.
» Weather is bitterly cold in the north and at altitude, and only warm in the far south.

Your Daily Budget

Budget less than
¥200
» Dorm Beds: ¥40–60
» Food markets, hole-in-the-wall restaurants and street food: ¥40
» Affordable internet, bike hire or other transport: ¥20
» Some free museums

Midrange
¥200–1000
» Double room in mid-range hotel: ¥200–600
» Lunch/dinner in local restaurant: ¥80–100
» Drinks in a bar: ¥60
» Riding by taxi: ¥60

Top end over
¥1000
» Double room in a top-end hotel: ¥600+
» Lunch and dinner in excellent restaurants: ¥300
» Shopping at top-end shops: ¥300
» Two tickets to Chinese opera: ¥300

Money

» ATMs in big cities and towns. Credit cards less widely used; always carry cash.

Visas

» Needed for all visits to China except Hong Kong and Macau. Additional permit required for Tibet and a few other areas.

Mobile Phones

» Inexpensive pay-as-you-go SIM cards can be bought locally for most mobile phones. Buying a local mobile phone is also cheap.

Transport

» The train and bus network is extensive, domestic and air routes are plentiful. Cars can be hired in Běijīng, Shànghǎi, Hong Kong and Macau, for local use.

Websites

» **Lonely Planet** (www. lonelyplanet.com/china) Destination information, hotel bookings, traveller forum and more.

» **Ctrip** (www.english. ctrip.com) Hotel booking, air ticketing.

» **Danwei** (www.danwei. org) Perspectives into the real China.

» **Chinasmack** (www. chinasmack.com) Human-interest stories and videos.

» **Tea Leaf Nation** (www.tealeafnation. com) Chinese social media pickings.

» **Popupchinese** (www. popupchinese.com) Excellent podcasts (great to learn Chinese).

Exchange Rates

Australia	A$1	¥6.32
Canada	C$1	¥6.70
Euro zone	€1	¥10.36
Hong Kong	HK$1	¥0.98
Japan	¥100	¥6.50
New Zealand	NZ$1	¥5.58
UK	UK£1	¥15.22
USA	US$1	¥7.72

For current exchange rates see www.xe.com.

Important Numbers

Ambulance	☑120
Fire	☑119
Police	☑110
Country code (China/Hong Kong/Macau)	☑86/852/853
International access code	☑00
Directory assistance	☑114

Arriving in China

» **Běijīng Capital Airport**
Airport Express – Every 15 minutes
Airport Bus – To central Běijīng every 10 to 20 minutes
Taxi – ¥80–100

» **Shànghǎi Pǔdōng International Airport**
Maglev – Every 20 minutes
Metro – Line 2 to Hóngqiáo Airport
Airport Bus – Every 15 to 25 minutes
Taxi – ¥160

» **Hong Kong International Airport**
Airport Express – Every 12 minutes
Taxi – About HK$300 to Central

Internet Access in China

Pack a wi-fi equipped mobile phone, tablet or laptop for use in wi-fi zones in hotels, restaurants, cafes and other hotspots in large cities and towns to access the internet. Be warned that internet cafes in a large number of towns and cities across China do not permit users to get online without Chinese ID. Plan ahead and don't be caught out: if you don't have a wi-fi equipped mobile phone, tablet or laptop, you may need to find a hotel or cafe with a terminal you can use, or a hotel room equipped with a computer. Wi-fi enabled hotels in this book carry the 🛜 wi-fi icon; hotels equipped with internet access display the @ internet icon. Social networking sites such as Facebook and Twitter are banned and therefore inaccessible in China.

first time

Everyone needs a helping hand when they visit a country for the first time. There are phrases to learn, customs to get used to and etiquette to understand. The following section will help demystify China so your first trip goes as smoothly as your fifth.

Language

It is entirely possible to travel around China hardly hearing any English at all. Tourist industry employees across the land are more likely to speak English; in the big cities such as Shànghǎi, Běijīng and of course Hong Kong, English is more widely spoken and understood, but generally only among educated Chinese. In smaller towns and the countryside, English is often of little or no use (the vast majority of Chinese do not speak the language at all). See the language section of this book (p1016) for some phrases you'll need.

Booking Ahead

Reserving a room, even if only for the first night of your stay, is the best way to ensure a smooth start to your trip. These phrases should see you through a call if English isn't spoken.

Hello	你好	Nǐhǎo
I would like to book a room	我想订房间	Wǒ xiǎng dìng fángjiān
a single room	单人间	dānrén jiān
a double room	双人间	shuāngrén jiān
My name is...	我叫…	Wǒ jiào...
from... to... (date)	从…到…	cóng... dào...
How much is it per night/person?	每天/人多少钱?	Měi tiān/rén duōshǎo qián?
Thank you	谢谢你	Xièxie nǐ

What to Wear

You can pretty much wear casual clothes throughout your entire journey in China, unless dining in a smart restaurant in Shànghǎi, Běijīng or Hong Kong, when you may need to dress less casually. In general, trousers (pants) and shirts or tees for guys; dresses, skirts or trousers for women will serve you well nationwide; shorts and short sleeves are generally fine in summer, but don long trousers and long sleeves in the evenings to keep mosquitoes at bay. A sunhat can be invaluable. A thin waterproof coat and sturdy shoes are a good idea for all-weather hiking and sightseeing. Winter is a different ball game up north and especially at altitude: you'll need several layers, thick shirts, jerseys and warm coats, jackets, gloves, socks and a hat.

What to Pack

» Passport
» Credit card
» Phrasebook
» Money belt
» Travel plug
» Medical kit
» Insect repellent
» Mobile (cell) phone charger
» Clothes
» Earplugs
» Toiletries
» Sunscreen
» Sunhat and shades
» Tissues
» Waterproof clothing
» Padlock
» Torch
» Pocketknife
» Camera
» Pen
» Novel

Checklist

» Check the validity of your passport

» Make any necessary bookings (for accommodation and travel)

» Work out your itinerary (p34)

» Secure your visa and additional permits well in advance

» Check what clothing you will need

» Check the airline baggage restrictions

» Inform your credit/ debit card company

» Organise travel insurance (see p988)

» Check if you can use your mobile/cellphone (see p992)

Etiquette

China is a pretty relaxed country regarding etiquette, but there are a few things you need to be aware of:

» Greetings & Goodbyes

Shake hands, but never kiss someone's cheek. Say 'Nǐhǎo' as you greet someone and 'Zàijiàn' to say goodbye.

» Asking for Help

To ask for directions start by saying 'Qǐng wèn....' ('Can I ask...'); say 'Duìbuqǐ...' (sorry) to apologise.

» Religion

Dress sensitively when visiting Buddhist (especially in Tibet) and Taoist temples, churches and mosques.

» Eating & Drinking

Help fill your neighbour's plate or bowl at the dinner table; toast the host and others at the table; at the start of dinner, wait till toasting starts before drinking from your glass; offer your cigarettes around if you smoke; always offer to buy drinks in a bar but never fight over the drink/ food tab if someone else wants to pay.

» Gestures

Don't use too many hand movements or excessive body language.

Money

» **Credit Cards** Credit/ debit cards are increasingly accepted in tourist towns/big cities, particularly Visa and MasterCard. Ask if bars and restaurants take cards before ordering.

» **ATMs** 24-hour ATMs are available at Bank of China and ICBC branches.

» **Changing Money** Change money at hotels, large Bank of China branches, some department stores and international airports. Some towns don't have money-change facilities: carry enough cash.

» **Tipping** Don't tip taxi drivers or restaurants. Some restaurants add a service charge.

Tours

The vast majority of sights in China can be visited independently. Tours (easy to arrange through your hotel or travel agent) may use mediocre English speakers and can be expensive and uninspiring so avoid taking them to places you can easily visit on your own (eg some sections of the Great Wall or the water towns around Shànghǎi). Note some tours are Chinese-language only, and watch out for predatory tours that drag you to shops or commercial diversions en route. Always consider hiring a taxi driver to ferry you around, as it may be a lot cheaper and offer more flexibility. Arranged tours can be helpful though, for difficult-to-reach sights, for overnight or multiday/week expeditions to more inaccessible regions, or for lassoing together a disparate array of sights. Recommended individual tour guides and outfits are listed throughout the destination chapters of this book.

if you like...

Imperial Architecture

If ancient monuments are your cup of *chá*, you can't go far wrong in China. Crumbling dynasties have scattered an imposing trail of antiquity across north China from vast imperial palaces to the noble ruins of the Great Wall and altars reserved for the emperor. Běijīng should be your first port of call, before turning to the ancient dynastic cities of Kāifēng, Xī'ān and Dàtóng.

Forbidden City China's standout imperial residence in Běijīng, home to two dynasties of emperors and their concubines (p55)

Summer Palace An epic demonstration of traditional Chinese aesthetics with all essential ingredients: hills, lakes, bridges, pavilions and temples (p84)

Imperial Palace Manchu splendour in Shěnyáng within the former Manchurian heartland of Liáoníng province (p292)

Xī'ān Shaanxi home of the Terracotta Warriors, an imposing Ming city wall and traces of the city's famous Tang apogee (p356)

Chéngdé Summer bolt hole of the Qing emperors, with palatial remains and a riveting brood of Tibetan-style temples (p133)

The Great Wall

There's far more to the wall than Bādálǐng's crowds and over-restored masonry; get off the beaten path and unearth the real brickwork. The wall most famously belongs to Běijīng, but fragments create a ragged band across a lot of north China, trailing from the North Korean border to the windswept deserts of China's wild west.

Jiànkòu Běijīng's prime chunk of Great Wall ruin, a sublime portrait of disintegrating brickwork, overgrown with trees and set against a magnificent mountain panorama (p115)

Zhuàngdàokǒu Little-visited length of wall near Běijīng packing supreme views and hiking opportunities (p117)

Huánghuā Chéng Excellent hiking opportunities along some of the most authentic sections of wall to be found around Běijīng (p116)

Jiāyùguān Fort Confront weathered slogans from Mao's Cultural Revolution scoured by the Gānsù desert winds (p827)

Sīmǎtái Embark on the leg-busting four-hour trek between Jīnshānlǐng and Sīmǎtái outside Běijīng and admire the awesome Great Wall panorama unfold before you (p117)

Modern Architecture

Befitting its ascendancy on the world stage, China has reached for the stars with some dazzling and funky newfangled architecture. And you don't have to be a building buff to get a buzz from the sleek skyline of Shànghǎi or Hong Kong; all you need is a taste for the up-to-the-minute, the unexpected and high-altitude observation decks.

Shànghǎi World Financial Center Reigning supreme over Lùjiāzuǐ, but soon to be eclipsed by the even more titanic Shànghǎi Tower (p194)

CCTV Building 'Big Underpants' to Běijīng locals, a masterclass in engineering complexity to others (p75)

National Centre for the Performing Arts The opinion-dividing Běijīng edifice drops jaws whatever your perspective or persuasion (p81)

HSBC Building Hong Kong's most elaborate and precision engineered building and a masterclass in feng shui design (p467)

Shànghǎi Tower Still forming in Shànghǎi's Lùjiāzuǐ district, but already beginning to overshadow its soaring rivals (p176)

KRZYSZTOF DYDYNSKI / GETTY IMAGES ©

» City Tower in Píngyáo, China's best-preserved ancient walled town (p346)

Ancient Settlements

China's traditional livelihoods can be glimpsed in its picturesque, ancient villages and towns. Here Ming- and Qing-dynasty architecture, pinched, narrow lanes and superlative feng shui combine to create a pastoral aesthetic complemented by a relaxed rural tempo. Some settlements are home to ethnic minorities and their distinctive building styles.

Píngyáo China's best-looking, best-preserved walled town – by a long shot – warrants thorough exploration (p346)

Hóngcūn Within easy reach of Huángshān, this delightful Ānhuī village is a primer in the Huīzhōu style (p381)

Wùyuán Take time off to village-hop in the gorgeous Jiāngxī countryside and dream of abandoning urban China for good (p435)

Tǔlóu earth buildings Explore the fortress-like earthen 'round-houses' of the Guǎngdōng, Fújiàn and Jiāngxī borderlands, distinctive for their imposing enormity (p280)

Zhènyuǎn Gorgeous Guìzhōu riverside town, a good-looking spectacle of cliff-side temples, history and charm (p621)

Urban Extravaganzas

China's most dynamic and stylish environments belong to cities like Shànghǎi, where glittering skyscrapers overlook Maglev trains, and hard-working, hard-playing middle-class consumers shop in chic malls, drink at elegant cocktail bars and dine at fashionable restaurants. China's unfathomable reservoirs of energy and manpower are sucked up by its leading cities for transmutation into iconic skylines.

Shànghǎi The city that somehow single-handedly achieved the repositioning of China in the global psyche (p176)

Hong Kong Poised between China and the West, the ex-British colony continues to plough its own lucrative furrow on the south China coastline (p463)

Běijīng Engaging blend of ancient capital and modern metropolis, China's leading city matches its newfound guise with a bevy of historical sights (p50)

Hángzhōu One of China's most attractive cities with the sublime and romantic West Lake at its heart (p249)

Boat Trips

China is cut by some dramatic and breathtaking rivers, including the mighty Yangzi River, which snakes across the width of the land from its high-altitude source as snowmelt on the Tibet-Qīnghǎi plateau. Occasionally it's time to unplug from travel on the road and ease into to a totally different experience of China's landscapes. Hopping on a riverboat to explore riverine panoramas slots you into a lower gear for enjoyment of the landscape drifting leisurely by.

Three Gorges China's most awesome river panorama (p770)

Lí River The dreamlike karst landscapes of northeast Guǎngxī (p587)

Star Ferry, Hong Kong The short but iconic ferry hop across Victoria Harbour from Tsim Sha Tsui (p475)

Evening river cruise, Chóngqìng Before getting all misty through the Three Gorges, experience Chóngqìng's nocturnal, neon performance (p765)

Qīngyuǎn boat trip, Guǎngdōng Lazily float along the Běi River from Qīngyuǎn past secluded Fēilái Temple and Fēixiá monastery (p557)

» Mt Everest from Everest Base Camp, Tibet (p899)

Great Food

With its novel flavours, and unexpected aromas and tastes, China is a culinary travel adventure. Běijīng, Shànghǎi and Hong Kong are stuffed with Chinese and international dining options, but it could be a meal in a village tucked away up a distant mountainside that is most memorable. Head west for zing, zest and spice, north for hearty and salty flavours, east for fresh and lightly flavoured seafood, and south for dim sum. Don't forget the border regions where the culinary recipes of neighbouring lands permeate into China.

Peking duck Once bitten, forever smitten, and only in Běijīng (p93)

Chóngqìng hotpot Sweat like never before over China's most volcanic culinary creation (p761)

Xiǎolóngbāo Shànghǎi's bite-sized snack packs a lot of flavour (but watch out for the super-heated meat juice) (p205)

Street food Everywhere you go, street snacks fill in between meals and cost a pittance

Museums

Urbanisation means that museum collections can be the clearest window onto China's past, and they are ubiquitous, covering everything from ethnic clothing to Běijīng tap water or Buddhist artefacts. And with a growing number of museums waiving admission fees, museums are an affordable and comprehensive inroad into local culture and history.

Palace Museum The official and highly prosaic name for the Forbidden City, China's supreme link to its dynastic past (p55)

Shànghǎi Museum A dazzling collection of ceramics, paintings, calligraphy and much more at the heart of Shànghǎi (p181)

Poly Art Museum Bronzes and Bodhisattvas in Běijīng (p66)

Hong Kong Museum of History Entertaining, resourceful and informative leafing through the pages of Hong Kong history (p477)

Cultural Revolution Museum One-of-a-kind in China and a testament to an almost forgotten decade (p566)

Sacred China

Modern China's modern overlays – an amalgam of communism, Yves Saint Laurent and epic traffic jams – cannot hide the nation's compelling spiritual seam. From the esoteric mysteries of Tibetan Buddhism to the palpable magic of its holy Taoist mountains and the country's disparate collection of Christian churches, mosques and shrines, China's sacred realm is the point at which the supernatural and natural worlds converge.

Pǔníng Temple, Chéngdé Be rendered speechless by China's largest wooden statue, a towering effigy of the Buddhist Goddess of Mercy (p136)

Labrang Monastery Tap into the ineffable rhythms of south Gānsù's place of pilgrimage for legions of Tibetans (p816)

Gyantse Kumbum An overwhelming sight and monumental experience, the nine-tiered *chörten* is Tibet's largest stupa (p895)

Qīnglóng Dòng Climb through Taoist, Buddhist and Confucian realms in this cliffside labyrinth in riverside Zhènyuǎn (p621)

Wǔdāng Shān Commune with the spirit of Taoist martial arts in the birthplace of taichi (p425)

If you like... communist collectives
Spend a day exploring Nánjiēcūn, China's last Maoist collective (p401)

If you like... beer
Head to seaside Dàlián for its International Beer Festival in July (p300)

Hiking

Despite urban encroachment, China is one of the world's most geographically varied and largest nations, with stupendous hiking opportunities amid breathtaking scenery. With its combination of physical exertion, stunning backdrops, ethnic minority life and unexpected discoveries, trekking is perhaps the best way to experience China. As a rule, the further west and southwest you travel from Běijīng, the more exhilarating the opportunities.

Tiger Leaping Gorge Yúnnán's best-known and most enticing hike is not for the faint-hearted (p667)

Dragon's Backbone Rice Terraces Work your way from Dàzhài to Píng'ān through some of China's most delicious scenery (p593)

Wùyuán Follow the old postal roads from village to village in the drop-dead gorgeous Jiāngxī countryside (p435)

Lángmùsì Excellent trekking options radiate in most directions from the charming monastic town on the Gānsù–Sìchuān border (p821)

Ganden to Samye Go all out on this 80km, four- to five-day high-altitude hike between Ganden and Samye monasteries in Tibet (p894)

Ethnic Minorities

Han China hits the buffers around its far-reaching borderlands, where a colourful patchwork of ethnic minorities preserves distinct cultures, languages, architectural styles and livelihoods. From Yúnnán, Guìzhōu and the southwest to Tibet, Xīnjiāng, Inner Mongolia and the hardy northeast, China is a vibrantly rich nation of contrasting peoples and traditions.

Tibet Explore this vast region in the west of China or jump aboard our itinerary (p40) through the easier-to-access regions outside the Tibetan heartland (p881)

Déhāng This Miao village in Húnán finds itself delightfully embedded in some breathtaking scenery (p457)

Lìjiāng Yúnnán's famous home of the blue-clothed Naxi folk affords glorious views across to the stunning slopes of Yùlóng Xuěshān (p659)

Kashgar Dusty Central Asian outpost and Uighur China's most famous town, on the far side of the Taklamakan Desert (p790)

Stunning Scenery

You haven't really experienced China until you've had your socks blown off by one of its scenic marvels. China's man-made splendours have lent cities such as Shànghǎi head-turning cachet, but Mother Nature steals the show. Shoulder your backpack and make a break for the hills (but don't forget that extra pair of socks).

Yángshuò You've probably seen the karst topography before in picture-perfect photographs; now see the real thing (p595)

Huángshān When suffused in their spectral mists, China's Yellow mountains enter a different dimension of beauty (p385)

Jiǔzhàigōu National Park Turquoise lakes, waterfalls, snow-capped mountains and green forests: all this and more (p742)

Chìshuǐ Trek past waterfalls and through ancient forests dating to the Jurassic (p630)

Everest Base Camp Rise early for dramatic images of the mountain in the morning sun (p899)

Yuányáng Rice Terraces Be transfixed by the dazzling display of light and water (p648)

month by month

Top Events

1 **Monlam Great Prayer Festival,** February or March

2 **Naadam,** July

3 **Běijīng International Literary Festival,** March

4 **Spring Festival,** January, February or March

5 **Luòyáng Peony Festival,** April

January

North China is a deep freeze but the south is far less bitter; preparations for the Chinese New Year get under way well in advance of the festival, which arrives any time between late January and March.

✷ Spring Festival

The Chinese New Year is family-focused, with dining on dumplings and gift-giving of *hóngbāo* (red envelopes stuffed with money). Most families feast together on New Year's Eve, then China goes on a big week-long holiday. Expect fireworks, parades, temple fairs and lots of colour.

✷ Hā'ěrbīn Ice & Snow Festival

Hēilóngjiāng's good-looking capital Hā'ěrbīn is all aglow with rainbow lights refracted through fanciful buildings and statues carved from blocks of ice. It's outrageously cold, but that's the whole point. (p325)

◉ Yuányáng Rice Terraces

The watery winter is the optimum season for the rice terraces' spectacular combination of liquid and light. Don't forget your camera, or your sense of wonder. (p648)

February

North China remains shockingly icy and dry but things are slowly warming up in Hong Kong and Macau. The Chinese New Year could well be firing on all cylinders but sort out your tickets well in advance.

✷ Monlam Great Prayer Festival

Held during two weeks from the third day of the Tibetan New Year and celebrated with spectacular processions across the Tibetan world, huge silk *thangka* (Tibetan sacred art) is unveiled and, on the last day, a statue of the Maitreya Buddha is conveyed around towns and monasteries; catch it in Xiàhé. (p815)

✷ Lantern Festival

Held 15 days after the spring festival, this celebration was traditionally a time when Chinese hung out highly decorated lanterns. Lantern-hung Píngyáo in Shānxī (p346) is an atmospheric place to soak up the festival (sometimes held in March).

March

China comes back to life after a long winter, although high-altitude parts of China remain glacial. The mercury climbs in Hong Kong and abrasive dust storms billow into Běijīng. Admission prices are still low-season.

✷ Běijīng Book Bash

Curl up with a good book at the Bookworm cafe (p103) for Běijīng's international literary festival, and lend an ear to lectures from international and domestic authors. Also earmark Shànghǎi for its international literary festival in the Bund-side Glamour Bar (p209) or the Man Hong Kong International Literary Festival.

◉ Fields of Yellow

Delve into south Chinese countryside to be bowled over by a landscape saturated in bright yellow rapeseed. In some parts of China, such as lovely Wùyuán (p435) in Jiāngxī province, it's a real tourist draw.

April

Most of China is warm so it's a good time to be on the road, ahead of the May holiday period and before China's summer reaches its full power. The Chinese take several days off to pass the Qīngmíng festival, a traditional date for honouring their ancestors.

 A Good Soaking
Flush away the dirt, demons and sorrows of the old year and bring in the fresh at the Dai New Year, with its vast amount of water at the water-splashing festival in Xīshuāngbǎnnà (p687). Taking an umbrella is pointless.

 Paeon to Peonies
Wángchéng Park in Luòyáng (p405) bursts into full-coloured bloom with its peony festival: pop a flower garland on your head and join in the floral fun (but don't forget your camera).

 Third Moon Festival
This Bai ethnic minority festival is an excellent reason to pitch up in the lovely north Yúnnán town of Dàlǐ (p651). It's a week of horse racing, singing and merrymaking at the end of April and the beginning of May.

 Formula One
Petrol heads and aficionados of speed, burnt rubber and hairpin bends flock to Shànghǎi for some serious motor racing at the track near Āntíng. Get your hotel room booked early: it's one of the most glamorous events on the Shànghǎi calendar.

May

China is in full bloom in mountain regions such as Sìchuān's Wòlóng Nature Reserve. The first four days of May sees China on vacation for one of the three big holiday periods, kicking off with Labour Day (1 May).

 Walking Around the Mountain Festival
On Pǎomǎ Shān, Kāngdìng's famous festival celebrates the birthday of Sakyamuni, the historical Buddha, with a magnificent display of horse racing, wrestling and a street fair. (p727)

🏃 **Great Wall Marathon**
Experience the true meaning of pain (but get your Great Wall sightseeing done and dusted at the same time). Not for the infirm or unfit (or the cable car fraternity). See www.greatwall-marathon.com for more details.

June

Most of China is hot and getting hotter. Once-frozen areas, such as Jílín's Heaven Lake, are accessible – and nature springs instantly to life. The great peak season is cranking up.

 Dragon Boat Festival
Find yourself the nearest large river and catch all the waterborne drama of dragon boat racers in this celebration of one of China's most famous poets. The Chinese traditionally eat *zòngzi* (triangular glutinous rice dumplings wrapped in reed leaves).

Shangri-la Horse Racing Festival
In mid- to late June, the north Yúnnán town of Shangri-la (p671) lets go of the reins with this celebration of horse racing, coupled with singing, dancing and merriment, on the southeastern fringes of Tibet.

July

Typhoons can wreak havoc with travel itineraries down south, lashing the Guǎngdōng and Fújiàn coastlines. Plenty of rain sweeps across China: the big 'plum rains' give Shànghǎi a serious soaking and the grasslands of Inner Mongolia and Qīnghǎi turn green.

Mongolian Merrymaking
Mongolian wrestling, horse racing, archery and more during the week-long Naadam festival on the grasslands of Inner Mongolia at the end of July, when the grasslands are at their summer best.

Dàlián International Beer Festival
Xīnghǎi Square in the Liáoníng port city is steeped

in the aroma of hops and ale and strewn with beer tents in this 12-day celebration of more than 400 international and Chinese beers from a plethora of breweries. (p300)

August

The temperature gauge of the 'three ovens' of the Yangzi region – Chóngqìng, Wǔhàn and Nánjīng – gets set to blow. Rainstorms hit Běijīng, which is usually way hotter than 40°C; so is Shànghǎi. So head uphill: Lúshān, Mògānshān, Huángshān or Guōliàngcūn.

 Lǐtáng Horse Festival

Occasionally cancelled in recent years (restrictions on travel may suddenly appear) and also shrunk from one week to one day, this festival in West Sìchuān is a breathtaking display of Tibetan horsemanship, archery and more.

 **Qīngdǎo International Beer Festival**

Slake that chronic summer thirst with a round of beers and devour a plate of mussels in Shāndōng's best-looking port town, home of the Tsingtao beer brand.

September

Come to Běijīng and stay put – September is part of the fleetingly lovely *tiāngāo qìshuǎng* ('the sky is high and the air is fresh') autumnal season – it's an event in itself.

(above) Yùyuán Bazaar, Shànghǎi (p185) during the lantern festival
(below) Musicians performing during the celebrations for Chinese New Year

Mid-Autumn Festival

Also called the moon festival, locals celebrate by devouring daintily prepared moon cakes – stuffed with bean paste, egg yolk, walnuts and more. With a full moon, it's a romantic occasion for lovers and a special time for families. It's on the 15th day of the eighth lunar month.

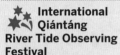

International Qiántáng River Tide Observing Festival

The most popular time to witness the surging river tides sweeping at up to 40km per hour along the Qiántáng River in Yánguān is during the mid-autumn festival, although you can catch the wall of water during the beginning and middle of every lunar month. (p260)

Confucius' Birthday

Head to the Confucius Temple in Qūfù (p157) for the 28 September birthday celebrations of axiom-quipping philosopher, sage and patriarch Confucius.

October

The first week of October can be hellish if you're on the road: the National Day week-long holiday kicks off, so everywhere is swamped. Go mid-month instead, when everywhere is deserted.

Kurban Bairam (Gu'erbang Jie)

Catch the four-day festivities of the Muslim festival of sacrifice in communities across China; the festival is at its liveliest and most colourful in Kashgar.

Hairy Crabs in Shànghǎi

Now's the time to sample delicious hairy crabs in Shànghǎi; they are at their best – male and female crabs eaten together with shots of lukewarm Shàoxīng rice wine – between October and December.

Miao New Year

Load up with rice wine and get on down to Guìzhōu for the ethnic festivities in the very heart of the minority-rich southwest.

November

Most of China is getting pretty cold as tourist numbers drop and holidaygoers begin to flock south for sun and the last pockets of warmth.

Surfing Hǎinán

Annual surfing competition in Shíméi Bay and Sun and Moon Bay in Hǎinán (p580) as the surfing season gets under way and hordes of Chinese flee the cold mainland for the warmer climes of the southern island.

itineraries

Whether you have six days or 60, these itineraries provide a starting point for the trip of a lifetime. Want more inspiration? Head online to lonelyplanet. com/thorntree to chat with other travellers.

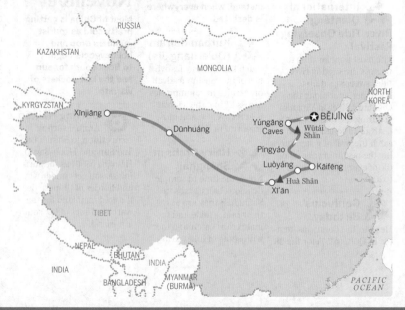

Four Weeks
Northern Tour

> **Běijīng** is fundamental to this tour, so you'll need at least five days to do the Forbidden City, size yourself up against the Great Wall, wander like royalty around the Summer Palace and lose your bearings amid the city's *hútòng* (narrow alleyways). The splendour of the **Yúngāng Caves** outside Dàtóng should put you in a Buddhist mood, heightened by a few nights on monastic **Wǔtái Shān**. We recommend a three-day stopover in **Píngyáo**, an age-old walled town you imagined China *should* look like. The historic walled city of **Kāifēng** in Hénán was the traditional home of China's small community of Chinese Jews and has a remarkable night market; move on to **Luòyáng** and the Buddhist spectacle of the Lóngmén Caves and the Shàolín Temple, also within reach. Four days' sightseeing in **Xī'ān** brings you face-to-face with the Army of Terracotta Warriors and gives you time for the Taoist mountain of **Huà Shān**. Xī'ān traditionally marked the start of the Silk Road which you can follow through Gānsù province all the way to the oasis-town of **Dūnhuáng**. From Dūnhuáng continue into **Xīnjiāng** for a taste of the mighty northwest.

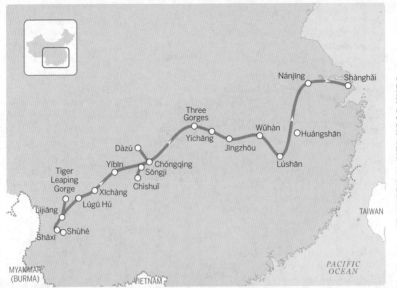

Three to Four Weeks
Yangzi River Tour

After exploring north Yúnnán's ancient Naxi town of **Lìjiāng**, pick up the trail of the Jīnshā River (Gold Sand River, which spills down from Tibet and swells into the Yangzi River) on a breathtaking multiday hike along **Tiger Leaping Gorge**. Rest your worn-out legs before discovering the scattered villages and old towns around Lìjiāng, including **Shāxī** and **Shùhé** on the old Tea-Horse Road, and being blown away by the magnificent views of Yùlóng Xuěshān. Also consider (warmer months only) a trip from Lìjiāng northeast towards west Sìchuān and the gorgeous **Lúgū Hú** on the provincial border, where you can spend several days unwinding by the lakeside. During the winter months this entire area is snowbound, so you may have to fly on from Lìjiāng. A morning bus from Lúgū Hú runs to **Xīchāng** in Sìchuān, from where you can reach **Yíbīn** and then **Chóngqìng**; alternatively, return to Lìjiāng to fly to Chóngqìng, home of the spicy and searing Chóngqìng hotpot and gateway to the Three Gorges. Detour by backtracking by bus to the stunning landscapes and natural beauty of **Chìshuǐ** on the Guìzhōu border to relax, unwind and explore the region before returning by bus to urban Chóngqìng. You'll need around three days in Chóngqìng for the sights in town and for a journey to the Buddhist Caves at **Dàzú** and a trip to the Yangzi River village of **Sōngji** to keep a perspective on historic, rural China. Then hop on a cruise vessel or passenger boat (or even a bus followed by hydrofoil) to **Yíchāng** in Húběi through the magnificent **Three Gorges**. Journey from Yíchāng to the Yangzi River city of **Wǔhàn** via the walled town of **Jīngzhōu**, where it's worth spending the night. After two days in Wǔhàn, hop on a bus to **Lúshān** in Jiāngxī province, from where you can reach **Nánjīng** or make your way to **Huángshān** in the Yangzi River province of Ānhuī. Alternatively, travel direct to Nánjīng and thread your way to **Shànghǎi** via a delightful string of canal towns – Sūzhōu, Tónglǐ, Lùzhí and Zhūjiājiǎo. Explore Shànghǎi and consider launching yourself into the East–South Rural Tour (p38).

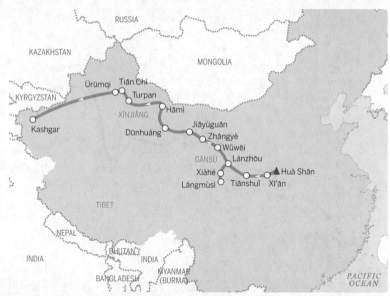

Three Weeks
Silk Road Tour

Overlapping with the end of the Northern Tour (p34), this breathtaking journey takes you on an epic journey along the ancient Silk Road. From the southernmost extents of the Silk Road at **Xī'ān**, discover one of imperial China's most iconic remains at the Army of Terracotta Warriors and, for a major workout, climb the precipitous Taoist mountain of **Huà Shān** – just don't look down. Back in Xī'ān, explore the Muslim Quarter to feast on local Hui specialities – one of the culinary highpoints of China travel – and climb atop the imposing city walls. Hop aboard the train to **Lánzhōu** but get off in southeast Gānsù at **Tiānshuǐ** for the remarkable Buddhist grottoes at verdant Màijī Shān. From Lánzhōu you have the option of disembarking temporarily from the Silk Road to ramble along the fringes of the Tibetan world (see the Tibet Fringes Tour, p40) in the Buddhist monastic settlements of **Xiàhé** and **Lángmùsì**. The Hèxī Corridor draws you on to the ancient Great Wall outpost of **Jiāyùguān**, via the Silk Road stopover town of **Wǔwēi**, and the Great Buddha Temple with its outsize effigy of a reclining Sakyamuni in **Zhāngyè**. Stand on the wind-blasted ramparts of Jiāyùguān Fort, the last major stronghold of imperial China, and tramp alongside westerly remnants of the Great Wall. The delightful oasis outpost of **Dūnhuáng** is one of China's tidiest and most pleasant towns, with the mighty sand dunes of the Singing Sands Mountains pushing up from the south, a scattered array of sights in the surrounding desert and some excellent food. The town is the hopping-off point for China's splendid hoard of Buddhist art, the spellbinding Mògāo Caves. From Dūnhuáng you can access the mighty northwestern Uighur province of Xīnjiāng via the melon-town of **Hāmì** before continuing to **Turpan** and **Ürümqi**; consider also spending the night in a yurt or camping on the shores of mountainous **Tiān Chí**. Thread your way through a string of Silk Road towns by rail to the Central Asian outpost of **Kashgar**, or reach the distant Uighur town via the Marco Polo–journeyed Southern Silk Road along the cusp of the Taklamakan Desert. From Kashgar, hatch exciting plans to conquer the Karakoram Highway or, in the other direction, work out how to get back into China proper.

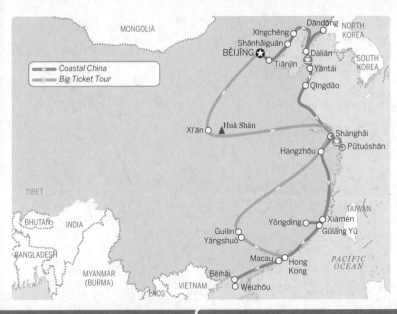

Coastal China
Big Ticket Tour

Three to Four Weeks
Coastal China

From **Běijīng**, hop on the high-speed train to face-lifted **Tiānjīn** en route to the Ming dynasty garrison town of **Shānhǎiguān** on the edge of Manchuria. Beyond the ancient port town of **Xīngchéng** and on around the coast is urbane **Dàlián**, where you can weigh up trips to the North Korean border at **Dāndōng**, or the ferry crossing to **Yāntái** en route to a two-day sojourn around breezy **Qīngdǎo**, the eye-catching Shāndōng port city. Cashing in on dashing **Shànghǎi** is crucial – allow four to five days to tick off surrounding sights, including a mid-week expedition over the waves to insular **Pǔtuóshān** and a trip to the cultured former southern Song dynasty capital of **Hángzhōu**. Work your way south around the coast to **Xiàmén** (Amoy) to capture some of the magic of **Gǔlàng Yǔ**, using the port town as a base to explore the Hakka roundhouses around **Yǒngdìng**. Conclude the tour feasting on dim sum and getting in step with the rhythms of **Hong Kong** before surrendering to the Portuguese lilt of **Macau**, or go further along the coast to the sleepy port town of **Běihǎi** in Guǎngxī and bounce over the sea in a boat to the volcanic island of **Wéizhōu**.

Two Weeks
Big Ticket Tour

After four days satiating yourself on **Běijīng's** mandatory highlights – the Forbidden City, Tiān'ānmén Square, the Summer Palace, the Great Wall and the city's charming *hútòng* (alleyways) – hop on the overnight high-speed Z class sleeper across north China from Běijīng West to **Xī'ān** to inspect the famed Terracotta Warriors, walk around the city's formidable Ming dynasty walls and climb the granite peaks of Taoist **Huà Shān**. Climb aboard the late-afternoon high-speed Z class sleeper to pulsating **Shànghǎi**, which pulls into town before breakfast. After three days sightseeing, museum-going, shopping and sizing up the sizzling skyscrapers of Pǔdōng, detour for a day to the former southern Song dynasty capital of **Hángzhōu**, before flying from either Hángzhōu or Shànghǎi to **Guìlín** for some of China's most serene and ageless panoramas, the breathtaking karst landscapes of **Yángshuò**. For a fitting and natural conclusion to your journey, fly straight from Guìlín to **Hong Kong**, or to Guǎngzhōu or Shēnzhèn to make your way south across the border to the former British territory. Squeeze in a day for exploring **Macau** to add a Portuguese complexion to your voyage.

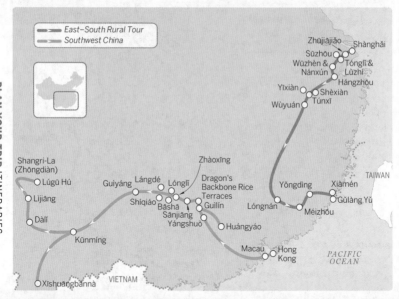

East–South Rural Tour
Southwest China

Zhūjiājiǎo   Shànghǎi
Sūzhōu   Tónglǐ &
Wūzhèn &   Lùzhí
Nánxún   Hángzhōu
Yīxiàn   Shèxiàn
Wùyuán   Túnxī

Zhàoxīng

Shangri-La
(Zhōngdiàn)
Lúgū Hú   Guìyáng   Lángdé   Lónglǐ
Dragon's
Lìjiāng   Backbone Rice
Shíqiáo   Terraces   Yǒngdìng   Xiàmén
Bāshā   Guìlín   Gǔlàng Yǔ
Dàlǐ   Sānjiāng   Lóngnán   Méizhōu
Yángshuò
Kūnmíng   Huángyáo
Macau   Hong
Kong   PACIFIC
OCEAN
Xīshuāngbǎnnà   VIETNAM

TAIWAN

Two Weeks
East–South Rural Tour

From **Shànghǎi**, head to **Zhūjiājiǎo** in the municipality's rural west to catch its canal-side charms; if you find yourself in a canal-town mood, the water towns of Jiāngsū and north Zhèjiāng – including **Tónglǐ**, **Lùzhí**, **Wūzhèn** and **Nánxún** – are easy to get to. From either **Sūzhōu** or **Hángzhōu**, take a bus to **Túnxī** in Ānhuī province to spend several days exploring the delightful clusters of ancient Huīzhōu villages of **Yīxiàn** and **Shèxiàn**. Bus it across the border to Jiāngxī province for two or three days' fabulous hiking from village to village in the gorgeous rural landscape around **Wùyuán**. Work your way to the south of the province to enter Hakka country – a hilly region dotted with fortified villages around **Lóngnán** – and give yourself four days to ramble around the neighbouring roundhouse areas of **Méizhōu** and **Yǒngdìng** in Guǎngdōng and Fújiàn, where you can spend the night in an earth building and fully tap into the local rhythms. Round off the tour at coastal **Xiàmén**, spending a night or two amid the colonial remains of **Gǔlàng Yǔ**.

Three Weeks
Southwest China

Four days' wining and dining in **Hong Kong** and **Macau** should whet your appetite, before you head inland to **Guìlín** and three days' immersing yourself in the dreamy karst landscape of **Yángshuò**. Jump on a bus to delightful **Huángyáo** before backtracking to Guìlín and journeying north to the **Dragon's Backbone Rice Terraces** and the wind-and-rain bridges and ethnic hues of **Sānjiāng**. Creep over the border to explore the minority-rich villages of eastern Guìzhōu, including **Lángdé**, **Shíqiáo**, **Lónglǐ**, **Bāshā** and **Zhàoxīng**, before continuing to **Guìyáng** and on by train to the capital of Yúnnán province, **Kūnmíng**. Spend a few days in Kūnmíng before penetrating north Yúnnán to explore **Dàlǐ**, **Lìjiāng** and **Shangri-la (Zhōngdiàn)**. Consider exploring the border area with Sìchuān at the remote **Lúgū Hú**, from where you can head into Sìchuān. In the other direction, the fertile **Xīshuāngbǎnnà** region lies in the deep south of the province, where Yúnnán's Southeast Asian complexion comes to the fore. You will be rewarded with a profusion of ethnic villages and countless hiking opportunities around China's southwest borders.

» (above) Buddha statues at the Unesco World Heritage site of the Lóngmén Caves (p407)
» (left) Grand (Sunday) bazaar in the old Silk Road town of Kashgar (p790)

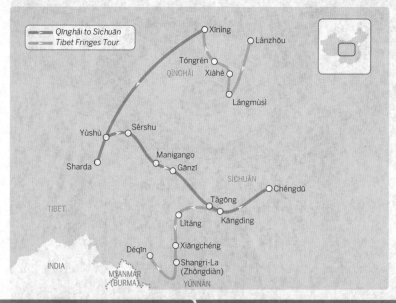

Legend:
- Qīnghǎi to Sìchuān
- Tibet Fringes Tour

Map locations: Xīníng, Lánzhōu, Tóngrén, QĪNGHǍI, Xiàhé, Lángmùsì, Yùshù, Sêrshu, Manigango, Sharda, Gānzī, SÌCHUĀN, Chéngdū, Tǎgōng, Lǐtáng, Kāngdìng, Déqīn, Xiāngchéng, Shangri-La (Zhōngdiàn), INDIA, TIBET, MYANMAR (BURMA), YÚNNÁN

10 Days
Qīnghǎi to Sìchuān

This colossal, rough-and-ready journey draws you through stunning landscapes from Xīníng to Chéngdū. The scenery is sublime but do this trip only in summer (it's too cold even in spring), and take cash and lots of food with you (you won't be able to change money). Prepare also for bus breakdowns, irregular transport connections, simple accommodation and the effects of high altitude. The epic bus journey from **Xīníng** to **Sharda** in the former Tibetan kingdom of Nangchen, where monasteries and dramatic scenery await, takes 20 to 24 hours. From Nangchen you can continue to Sìchuān via the Tibetan trading town of **Yùshù** (Jyekundo). You can also fly direct (or take the bus) from Xīníng to Yùshù to continue to Sìchuān direct from there, but we don't recommend staying in Yùshù as it is still recovering from the 2010 earthquake. Buses from Yùshù run to **Sêrshu** (Shíqú Xiàn) in northwest Sìchuān, where bus connections run through some stunning scenery past **Manigango** (perhaps with a side trip to Dege), the Tibetan town of **Gānzī** and on past **Tǎgōng** to **Kāngdìng** (Dardo) along the Sìchuān–Tibet Hwy, from where you can head west in the direction of Tibet or east to **Chéngdū**.

Three to Four Weeks
Tibet Fringes Tour

Travel permits are required for the Tibet Autonomous Region (TAR), a land that is periodically inaccessible to foreigners and always an arduous undertaking. This tour immerses you in more accessible areas, rich with the colour of Tibet. Only undertake the tour in the warmer summer months; other times can be dangerous. From **Lánzhōu** in Gānsù province, go southwest to **Lángmùsì** and **Xiàhé**, before passing awesome scenery by bus or taxi into **Qīnghǎi** via the monastery town of **Tóngrén**. Pick up a *thangka* (Tibetan sacred art) and continue by bus to **Xīníng**, then fly to **Chéngdū** in Sìchuān and take the bus to **Kāngdìng**, or fly to Kāngdìng via Chéngdū. The long, overland bus route from Xīníng to Kāngdìng is also possible via Yùshù in south Qīnghǎi. While Yùshù is still recovering from the 2010 earthquake, transport connections are possible. From Kāngdìng you can journey by bus west to the stupendous scenery around **Lǐtáng**, with some breathtaking hiking opportunities, or travel south to **Xiāngchéng** and on to **Shangri-la (Zhōngdiàn)** and the gorgeous Tibetan region of north Yúnnán. From Zhōngdiàn take a bus to high-altitude **Déqīn**, enveloped in gorgeous mountain scenery.

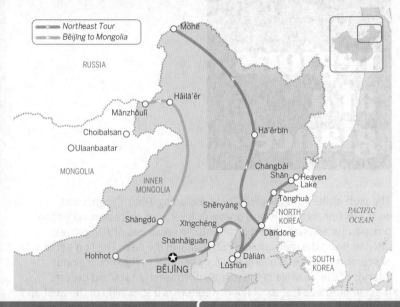

Northeast Tour
Běijīng to Mongolia

RUSSIA
Mòhé
Hǎilā'ěr
Mǎnzhōulǐ
Choibalsan
Ulaanbaatar
MONGOLIA
INNER MONGOLIA
Hā'ěrbīn
Chángbái Shān — Heaven Lake
Tōnghuà
Shěnyáng
Shàngdū
Xīngchéng
Shānhǎiguān
Dāndōng
Hohhot
Dàlián
Lǚshùn
BĚIJĪNG
NORTH KOREA
SOUTH KOREA
PACIFIC OCEAN

---

10 Days
Northeast Tour

With **Běijīng** as a start point, hop on a train to stylish **Dàlián**, but plan to spend a few days exploring the historic walled coastal towns of **Shānhǎiguān** and **Xīngchéng** en route. You'll need several days for Dàlián's sights, including the historic port of **Lǚshùn** and an adorable coastline. Border watchers will be keen to get to **Dāndōng**, on the border with North Korea, for its peculiar frisson. Take a boat trip along the Yālù River, dine on North Korean food and visit Tiger Mountain Great Wall. Consider a trip by rail and bus to **Heaven Lake** in **Chángbái Shān** (the largest nature reserve in China) via **Tōnghuà**. Straddling the North Korea border, the volcanic lake is a stunning sight (only accessible mid-June to September). Alternatively, take the train to **Shěnyáng** and visit its Qing dynasty Imperial Palace and the tomb of Huang Taiji, founder of the Qing dynasty. Hop on a bus or a train to **Hā'ěrbīn** to Dàolǐqū district and wonder at the city's Russian and Jewish ancestry. If you've really picked up momentum and can't stop, make a full meal by journeying to China's 'North Pole Village' to try to catch the *aurora borealis* in **Mòhé**.

One Week
Běijīng to Mongolia

After exhausting the superb sightseeing, and wining and dining choices, in **Běijīng**, jump aboard a train to **Hohhot** in Inner Mongolia where a late-July arrival should coincide with the Naadam festivities at Gegentala to the north, when the grasslands are turning green. Explore Hohhot's lamaseries and temples and make a trip to the grasslands outside town for a taste of the epic Inner Mongolian prairie. From Hohhot you can either take the train direct to **Ulaanbaatar** in Mongolia; or an alternative route to Mongolia is to first journey by train from Hohhot to **Shàngdū** – vanished site of Kublai Khan's celebrated palace at Xanadu – and then on to **Hǎilā'ěr** in the far north of Inner Mongolia, towards the border with Mongolia and Russia. The grasslands outside Hǎilā'ěr are a real highlight, so consider spending the night under the stars in a yurt on the prairie. If you are Russia-bound, you can enter the country via the nearby trading town of **Mǎnzhōulǐ** on the border. Alternatively, hop on a train from Hǎilā'ěr to Hā'ěrbīn in Hēilóngjiāng (to hook up with the Northeast Tour) or jump aboard a flight to **Choibalsan** in eastern Mongolia.

regions at a glance

The high-altitude, far west of China, including Tibet, Qīnghǎi and west Sìchuān, gradually and unevenly levels out as it approaches the prosperous and well-watered canal-town provinces of Jiāngsū and Zhèjiāng, and the metropolis of Shànghǎi in the east. The lion's share of scenic marvels and hiking territory belongs to the mountainous interior of China, while in the mighty northwest, peaks and deserts meet in dramatic fashion. Minority culture is a speciality of the west and southwest, and of the remote border regions. Different cuisines range across the entire nation, from the hardy northeast to the warm jungles of the far southwest.

Běijīng

History ✓✓✓
Temples ✓✓✓
Food ✓✓✓

Běijīng's imperial pedigree assures it a rich vein of dynastic history, balanced by splendid seams of temple and *hútòng* (narrow alley-way) architecture. Wining and dining is a further attraction as the capital is home to a resourceful restaurant scene. **p50**

Tiānjīn & Héběi

History ✓✓✓
Temples ✓✓✓
Outdoors ✓✓✓

Tiānjīn's spruced-up foreign concession streetscapes echo stylish Shànghǎi, and some standout pagodas and temples can be found in Héběi, where the rural side of China – brimming with rustic village getaways – comes to the fore. **p120**

Shāndōng

History ✓✓✓
Tsingtao ✓✓✓
Mountains ✓✓

Shāndōng groans under the weight of its historical heavy-hitters: the revered Confucian home and tomb at Qūfù, and sacred Tài Shān. Then, of course, there is the home of Tsingtao beer, Qīngdǎo, today a breezy, laid-back port city. **p144**

Shànghǎi

Architecture ✓✓✓
Food ✓✓✓
Urban Style ✓✓✓

Shànghǎi exudes a unique style unlike anywhere else in China. There's plenty to do, from nonstop shopping and skyscraper-hopping to standout art, fantastic eats and touring the city's elegant art deco heritage. **p176**

Jiāngsū

Canal Towns ✓✓✓
Outdoors ✓✓
History ✓✓

Jiāngsū is awash with cute-as-pie canal towns – from Tónglǐ to Sūzhōu – all reachable as day trips from neighbouring Shànghǎi. The provincial capital, Nánjīng, has history in spades, with its fabulous Ming wall and epic past as former national capital. **p221**

Zhèjiāng

Canal Towns ✓✓✓
Outdoors ✓✓✓
Islands ✓✓

Flushed with water and vaulted with bridges, Zhèjiāng's water towns are full of traditional charm. Pastoral escapes abound further south; Hángzhōu is one of China's most appealing cities; and the Buddhist island of Pǔtuóshān makes a breezy escape off the coast. **p247**

Fújiàn

Architecture ✓✓✓
Food ✓✓
Islands ✓✓

Fújiàn is Hakka heartland and home to the intriguing *tǔlóu* – massive packed stone, wood and mud structures once housing hundreds of families. Gǔlàng Yǔ, a tiny and hilly island off Xiàmén, is decorated with crumbling colonial villas, each one distinctive. **p270**

Liáoníng

Festivals ✓✓✓
History ✓✓✓
Minority Culture ✓✓✓

In history-rich Liáoníng, imperial relics contend with the legacy of Russian and Japanese colonialism. The North Korean border at Dāndōng is a sobering contrast to the wild beer festival at Dàlián. **p290**

Jílín

Landscapes ✓✓✓
Culture ✓✓✓
Skiing ✓✓

Boasting China's largest nature reserve, and a top ski destination, Jílín exerts a pull on the nature lover. On the trail of the exotic? Head to Jí'ān for the ruins of an ancient Korean empire. **p308**

Hēilóngjiāng

Festivals ✓✓
Culture ✓✓
Nature ✓✓✓

Fire and ice are the highlights in this province where volcanic explosions have left one of China's most mesmerising landscapes, and the winter's bitter climate provides the raw materials for a spectacular ice sculpture festival. **p319**

Shānxī

History ✓✓✓
Culture ✓✓✓
Mountains ✓✓✓

Repository of one of China's most superlative Buddhist grottoes, Shānxī also brings you one of its most magical Buddhist mountains. History is on all sides: the walled city of Píngyáo is the most intact of its kind. **p334**

Shaanxi

Historic Sites ✓✓✓
Museums ✓✓✓
Mountains ✓✓

A treasure trove of archaeological sites is scattered across the plains surrounding Shaanxi's capital, Xī'ān, where there are museums galore. Blow off all that ancient dust with a trip to Huá Shān, one of China's five holy Taoist peaks. **p354**

Ānhuī

Villages ✓✓✓
Mountains ✓✓✓
Outdoors ✓✓

The amazing Unesco-listed Hui villages of Hóngcūn and Xīdì are some of China's best-preserved. But let's not forget *that* mountain, Huángshān. Its soaring granite peaks have inspired a legion of poets and painters. **p375**

Hénán

History ✓✓✓
Temples ✓✓✓
Mountains ✓✓

Hénán's overture of dynastic antiquity is balanced by some excellent mountain escapes and the quirky allure of Nánjiēcūn, China's last Maoist collective. The province's *wǔshù* (martial arts) credentials come no better: the Shàolín Temple is here. **p396**

Húběi

Scenic Wonders ✓✓✓
History ✓✓✓
Rivers ✓✓✓

Slashed by the mighty Yangzi River, history-rich Húběi is one of the gateways to the Three Gorges, but Taoist martial artists may find themselves mustering on Wǔdāng Shān, home of taichi and scenic views. **p416**

Jiāngxī

Scenery ✓✓✓
Mountains ✓✓✓
Ancient Villages ✓✓✓

Communists herald it as the mythic starting point of the Long March, but it's the spectacular mountain scenery and hiking trails past preserved villages and terraced fields that should pop Jiāngxī into your travel plans. **p430**

Húnán

Ancient Towns ✓✓✓
Minority Villages ✓✓
Mountains ✓✓

Home to one of China's most noteworthy ancient towns, Fènghuáng, as well as the sacred mountain of Héng Shān, the other-worldly karst peaks of Wǔlíngyuán, and secluded Miao and Dong villages. **p444**

Hong Kong

Food ✓✓✓
Shopping ✓✓✓
Scenery ✓✓✓

This culinary capital offers the best of China and beyond, while a seductive mix of vintage and cutting-edge fashion attracts armies of shoppers. Meanwhile, leafy mountains, shimmering waters, skyscrapers and tenements make an unlikely but poetic match. **p463**

Macau

Food ✓✓✓
Architecture ✓✓✓
Casinos ✓✓✓

Marrying flavours from five continents, Macanese cooking is as unique as the cityscape, where Taoist temples meet baroque churches on cobbled streets with Chinese names. It's also a billionaire's playground where casino-resorts and other luxuries vie for space. **p511**

Guǎngdōng

Food ✓✓✓
History ✓✓
Architecture ✓✓

A strong gastronomic culture offers travellers the chance to savour world-renowned Cantonese cuisine. Guǎngdōng's seafaring temperament has brought the region diverse, exotic architectural styles, including the World Heritage–listed watchtowers. **p533**

Hǎinán

Beaches ✓✓✓
Cycling ✓✓✓
Surfing ✓✓

When it comes to golden-sand beaches and warm clear waters, this tropical island doesn't disappoint. An ideal cycling destination, Hǎinán attracts in-the-know adventurers with its good roads, balmy winters and varied landscape. **p569**

Guǎngxī

Scenery ✓✓✓
Outdoors ✓✓✓
Cycling ✓✓

Much famed for its out-of-this-world karst landscape, Guǎngxī offers the adventure-loving traveller lush green valleys, charming folksy villages and countless walking, cycling and rafting opportunities. **p585**

Guìzhōu

Festivals ✓✓✓
Minority Villages ✓✓✓
Waterfalls ✓✓✓

With more than a third of the population made up of minorities, and more folk festivals than anywhere else in China, you can party here with the locals year-round. For nature lovers, there's an abundance of waterfalls; for old-town watchers, there's lovely Zhènyuán. **p611**

Yúnnán

Ancient Towns ✓✓✓
Mountains ✓✓✓
Minority Villages ✓✓✓

Yúnnán is the province that has it all: towering Himalayan mountains, tropical jungle, sublime rice terraces and over half of China's minority groups. And did we mention gorgeous historic towns like Lìjiāng, the fantastic trekking and the great food? **p633**

Sìchuān

Mountains ✓✓✓
Scenery ✓✓✓
Cuisine ✓✓✓

One province: three regions. Stay in central or southern Sìchuān for steamy bamboo forests and cute Ming-dynasty villages. Head north for stunning lakes set among alpine-esque mountain scenery. Venture west for remote Tibetan-plateau grasslands. **p697**

Chóngqìng

Cuisine ✓✓✓
Ancient Villages ✓✓✓
River Trips ✓✓✓

A unique city with a unique location, hilly Chóngqìng hugs cliffs overlooking the Yangzi, bursts with old-China energy, offers some fascinating day trips and is home to hotpot – the spiciest dish on the planet. **p754**

Xīnjiāng

History ✓✓✓
Minority Culture ✓✓✓
Nature ✓✓

Bazaars, kebabs and camels are just a few of the icons that hint at your arrival in Central Asia. Ancient Silk Road towns include Turpan, Kashgar and Hotan, while hikers gravitate to Kanas Lake and the Tiān Shān. **p776**

Gānsù

Silk Road ✓✓✓
Tibetan Areas ✓✓✓
Buddhism ✓✓✓

Gānsù is all about diversity: colourful Tibetan regions in the southwest, Inner Mongolia alongside the north, and a rich accumulation of Silk Road culture through the middle. Think deserts, mountains, Buddhist artefacts, camels, yaks, pilgrims and nomads. **p808**

Níngxià

History ✓✓✓
Minority Culture ✓✓✓
Activities ✓✓

In the designated homeland of the Hui, visit the great tombs of the Xixia, nomadic rock art and the enormous Buddhas of Xūmí Shān. For camel trekking or sliding down the sand dunes, head for the Tengger Desert. **p840**

Inner Mongolia

Remote Journeys ✓✓✓
Food ✓✓
Activities ✓✓

Ride a famed Mongolian horse at a yurt camp near Hohhot and Hǎilā'ěr and sit down to a Mongolian hotpot (a delicious stew of meat and vegies). Further-flung western Inner Mongolia is a hard-to-reach landscape of towering sand dunes, desert lakes and ancient sites. **p851**

Qīnghǎi

Monasteries ✓✓✓
Scenery ✓✓✓
Culture ✓✓

Vast and remote, the best parts of Qīnghǎi – way up on the Tibetan plateau – are for those who like their travel rough. Need a hot shower and a coffee every morning? Go somewhere else. **p865**

Tibet

Monasteries ✓✓✓
Scenery ✓✓✓
Culture ✓✓

The 'Roof of the World' is a stunningly beautiful high plateau of turquoise lakes, desert valleys and Himalayan peaks, dotted with monasteries, yaks and sacred Buddhist sites. Tight and ever-changing travel regulations can easily derail travel plans. **p881**

Every listing is recommended by our authors, and their favourite places are listed first

Look out for these icons:

 Our author's top recommendation

 A green or sustainable option

 No payment required

BĚIJĪNG **50**
AROUND BĚIJĪNG 110

THE GREAT WALL . . . **113**

TIĀNJĪN & HÉBĚI . . . **120**
TIĀNJĪN 122
HÉBĚI 128
Shíjiāzhuāng 128
Chéngdé 133
Shānhǎiguān 139
Jīmíngyì 141

SHĀNDŌNG **144**
Jǐ'nán 146
Tài'ān 150
Tài Shān 153
Qūfù 156
Qīngdǎo 161
Láo Shān 170
Yāntái 171

SHÀNGHǍI **176**
AROUND SHÀNGHǍI 220

JIĀNGSŪ **221**
Nánjīng 223
Sūzhōu 234

ZHÈJIĀNG **247**
Hángzhōu 249
Wūzhèn 261
Nánxún 262
Wǔyì 264
Pǔtuóshān 265

FÚJIÀN **270**
Xiàmén 272
Gǔlàng Yǔ 277
Fújiàn Tǔlóu 280
Quánzhōu 284
Fúzhōu 287
Wǔyí Shān 288

LIÁONÍNG **290**
Shěnyáng 292
Dàlián 296
Dāndōng 303
Xīngchéng 306

JÍLÍN **308**
Chángbái Shān 310
Jí'ān 313
Chángchūn 316

HĒILÓNGJIĀNG **319**
Hā'ěrbīn 321
Mǔdānjiāng 328
Wǔdàlián Chí 330

SHĀNXĪ **334**
Dàtóng 336
Wǔtái Shān 340
Tàiyuán 343
Píngyáo 346
Qìkǒu 350
Jìnchéng 352

SHAANXI (SHǍNXĪ) **354**
Xī'ān 356
Huà Shān 368

Hánchéng 370
Yán'ān 372
Yúlín 373
Mǐzhǐ 374

ĀNHUĪ **375**
Túnxī 377
Huīzhōu Villages 380
Huángshān 385
Jiǔhuá Shān 390
Héféi 392

HÉNÁN **396**
Zhèngzhōu 398
Sōng Shān & Dēngfēng 401
Luòyáng 404
Guōliàngcūn 409
Kāifēng 410
Zhūxiān Zhèn 415

HÚBĚI **416**
Wǔhàn 418
Jīngzhōu 422
Wǔdāng Shān 424
Shénnóngjià 427
Yíchāng 428

JIĀNGXĪ **430**
Nánchāng 432
Wùyuán 435
Sānqīng Shān 438
Lónghǔ Shān 440
Lúshān 441

HÚNÁN **444**
Chángshā 446

On the Road

Sháoshān............451
Héng Shān............452
Wǔlíngyuán &
Zhāngjiājiè............453
Déhāng............457
Fènghuáng............458
Hóngjiāng Old Town.....462

HONG KONG.......463

MACAU............511

GUǍNGDŌNG......533
Guǎngzhōu............535
Fóshān............550
Kāipíng............552
Yángjiāng............554
Zhàoqìng............555
Nánlǐng National
Forest Park............557
Shēnzhèn............558
Zhūhǎi............561
Cháozhōu............563
Méizhōu............566

HǍINÁN............569
Hǎikǒu............571
Central Highlands............576
Around Wǔzhǐshān............577
The East Coast............578
Sānyà............581

GUǍNGXĪ............585
Guìlín............587
Dragon's Backbone
Rice Terraces............593
Yángshuò............595

Nánníng............601
Běihǎi............605
Wéizhōu Island............607
Détiān Waterfall............608
Lèyè............609

GUÌZHŌU..........611
CENTRAL GUÌZHŌU......613
EASTERN GUÌZHŌU......616
WESTERN GUÌZHŌU......624
NORTHERN GUÌZHŌU....630

YÚNNÁN..........633
CENTRAL YÚNNÁN......635
NORTHWEST YÚNNÁN...659
NÙ JIĀNG VALLEY......679
BǍOSHĀN REGION......681
DÉHÓNG PREFECTURE...684
XĪSHUĀNGBǍNNÀ
REGION............687

SÌCHUĀN..........697
CENTRAL SÌCHUĀN......701
SOUTHERN SÌCHUĀN....722
WESTERN SÌCHUĀN.....726
NORTHERN SÌCHUĀN....739

CHÓNGQÌNG......754
Chóngqìng City..........756
Dàzú Buddhist Caves....766
Zhōngshān............767

CRUISING THE
YANGZI............770

XĪNJIĀNG.........776
CENTRAL XĪNJIĀNG.....779
SOUTHWEST XĪNJIĀNG –
KASHGARIA............790
SOUTHERN SILK ROAD...798
NORTHERN XĪNJIĀNG....803

GĀNSÙ............808
LÁNZHŌU &
SOUTHERN GĀNSÙ......810
HÉXĪ CORRIDOR.........823
EASTERN GĀNSÙ.......836

NÍNGXIÀ..........840
Yínchuān............842
Zhōngwèi............847
Gùyuán & Around.......850

INNER MONGOLIA..851
Hohhot............853
Shàngdū (Xanadu).......857
Bāotóu............858
Hǎilā'ěr............860
Mǎnzhōulǐ............863

QĪNGHǍI..........865
Xīníng............867
Tóngrén (Repkong)......873
Guìdé............875
Yùshù (Jyekundo)......877
Golmud............880

TIBET............881
Lhasa............884
The Friendship Highway...894
Western Tibet............902

Běijīng

♪010 / POP 19.6 MILLION

Includes »

Sights 54
Activities........................ 87
Courses 88
Sleeping......................... 88
Eating 93
Drinking......................... 99
Entertainment.............. 100
Shopping 102
Getting There & Away .. 105
Around Běijīng.............. 110
Ming Tombs 110
Chuāndǐxià 111

Best Places to Eat

» Zuǒ Lín Yòu Shè (p93)

» Dàlǐ Courtyard (p94)

» 4Corners (p98)

» Yáojì Chǎogān (p94)

» Nàjiā Xiǎoguǎn (p97)

Best Places to Stay

» Peking Youth Hostel (p90)

» Courtyard 7 (p90)

» Red Capital Residence (p89)

» Opposite House Hotel (p91)

» DùGé (p90)

Why Go?

Not only is Běijīng (北京) one of China's true ancient citadels, it's also a confident and increasingly modern capital seemingly assured of its destiny to rule over China till the end of time.

Through its magnificent architecture – including numerous stretches of the Great Wall – visitors can trace every historical mood swing from Mongol times to the present day. Reminders of epic imperial grandeur and of imposing socialist realism stand strong amidst an emerging global powerhouse preparing to dominate the 21st century.

The city's denizens chat in Běijīnghuà – the gold standard of Mandarin – and marvel at their good fortune for occupying the centre of the known world. And yet for all its gusto, Běijīng dispenses with the persistent pace of Shànghǎi or Hong Kong. The remains of its historic *hútòng* (alleyways) still exude a unique village-within-a-city vibe, and it's in these neighbourhoods that locals shift down a gear and find time to sit out front, play chess and watch the world go by.

When to Go
Běijīng

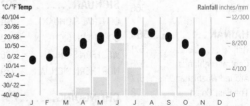

Oct–Nov Gorgeously fresh after the scorching summer, with blue skies and fewer tourists.

Apr–May Warming up after the winter freeze. Windy, but usually dry and clear.

Dec–Feb Dry as a bone and brutally cold, but clear skies and quiet streets.

History

Although seeming to have presided over China since time immemorial, Běijīng (literally, Northern Capital) – positioned outside the central heartland of Chinese civilisation – only emerged as a cultural and political force that would shape the destiny of China with the 13th-century Mongol occupation of China.

Chinese historical sources identify the earliest settlements in these parts from 1045 BC. In later centuries Běijīng was successively occupied by foreign forces: it was established as an auxiliary capital under the Khitan, nomadic Mongolic people who formed China's Liao dynasty (AD 907–1125). Later the Jurchens, Tungusic people originally from the Siberian region, turned the city into their Jin-dynasty capital (1115–1234) during which time it was enclosed within fortified walls, accessed by eight gates.

But in 1215 the army of the great Mongol warrior Genghis Khan razed Běijīng, an event that was paradoxically to mark the city's transformation into a powerful national capital. Apart from the first 53 years of the Ming dynasty and 21 years of Nationalist rule in the 20th century, it has enjoyed this status to the present day.

The city came to be called Dàdū (大都; Great Capital), also assuming the Mongol name Khanbalik (the Khan's town). By 1279, under the rule of Kublai Khan, grandson of Genghis Khan, Dàdū was the capital of the largest empire the world has ever known.

The basic grid of present-day Běijīng was laid during the Ming dynasty, and Emperor Yongle (r 1403–24) is credited with being the true architect of the modern city. Much of Běijīng's grandest architecture, such as the Forbidden City and the iconic Hall of Prayer for Good Harvests in Temple of Heaven Park, date from his reign.

The Manchus, who invaded China in the 17th century to establish the Qing dynasty, essentially preserved Běijīng's form. In the last 120 years of the Qing dynasty, Běijīng, and subsequently China, was subjected to power struggles and invasions and the ensuing chaos. The list is long: the Anglo-French troops who in 1860 burnt the Old Summer Palace to the ground; the corrupt regime of Empress Dowager Cixi; the catastrophic Boxer Rebellion; General Yuan Shikai; the warlords; the Japanese occupation of 1937; and the Kuomintang. Each and every period left its undeniable mark, although the shape and symmetry of Běijīng was maintained.

Modern Běijīng came of age when, in January 1949, the People's Liberation Army (PLA) entered the city. On 1 October of that year Mao Zedong proclaimed a 'People's Republic' from the Gate of Heavenly Peace to an audience of some 500,000 citizens.

Like the emperors before them, the communists significantly altered the face of Běijīng. The *páilóu* (decorative archways) were destroyed and city blocks pulverised to widen major boulevards. From 1950 to 1952, the city's magnificent outer walls were levelled in the interests of traffic circulation. Soviet experts and technicians poured in, bringing their own Stalinesque touches.

The past quarter of a century has transformed Běijīng into a modern city, with skyscrapers, shopping malls and an ever-expanding subway system. The once flat skyline is now crenellated with vast apartment blocks and office buildings. Recent years have also seen a convincing beautification of Běijīng: from a toneless and unkempt city to a greener, cleaner and more pleasant place.

But as Běijīng continues to evolve, it is shedding its increasingly tenuous links with its ancient past one fibre at a time. Even the old-school newspaper *China Daily* has observed that 4.43 million sq metres of old courtyards have been demolished in Běijīng's historic *hútòng* neighbourhoods since 1990; around 40% of the total area of the city centre. Preservation campaign groups have their work cut out to save what's left.

Climate

In winter, it's glacial outside (dipping as low as -20°C) and the northern winds cut like a knife through bean curd. But the air is clear

---

PRICE INDICATORS

The following price indicators are used in this chapter:

Sleeping

$ less than ¥400 (for a standard twin room)

$$ ¥400 to ¥1000

$$$ more than ¥1000

Eating

$ less than ¥40 (for a meal for one)

$$ ¥40 to ¥100

$$$ more than ¥100

Běijīng Highlights

❶ Hike your way along an unrestored 'wild' section of China's most famous icon; the **Great Wall** (p113)

❷ Marvel at the might and splendour of the awe-inspiring **Forbidden City** (p55), the world's largest palace complex and one-time home of 24 emperors of China

❸ Lose yourself in the city's warren of historic **hútòng** (alleyways, p96), or follow our absorbing *hútòng* walking tour (p72)

❹ Běijīng is blessed with a host of splendid royal parks, but the higlight is unmissable **Temple of Heaven Park** (p72)

❺ Enjoy a taste of imperial high life by wandering the sumptuous gardens, temples, pavilions and corridors of the **Summer Palace** (p84)

❻ Scoff **Peking duck** (p97), the capital's signature dish, in the restaurants where it originated

❼ Climb the magnificent **Drum Tower** (p67) or its charming counterpart, the **Bell Tower** (p67), and look over the grey-tiled rooftops in the alleys below

❽ Down a beer or catch some live music in one of Běijīng's **back-alley bars**. Jiāng Hú (p101) is a good place to start

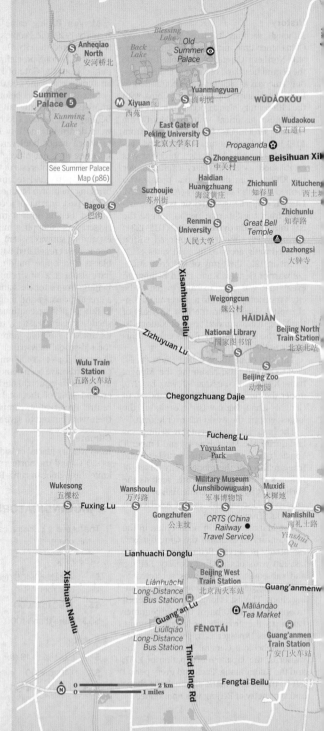

To The Great Wall (70km)

Olympic Forest Park

Badaling Expwy

South Gate of Forest Park 森林公园南门

China Science & Technology Museum

Chengfu Lu

Happy Magic Water Park

Olympic Green 奥林匹克公园

National Stadium (Bird's Nest)

Datunlu East 大屯路东

Wangjingxi 望京西

Guangshan Beidajie

Huixinxijie Beikou 惠新西街北口

North Fourth Ring Rd

Olympic Sports Center 奥体中心

Mudanyuan 牡丹园

Anzhenmen 安贞门

Huixinxijie Nankou 惠新西街南口

Shaoyaoju 芍药居

798 Art District

Jiandemen 健德门

Beitucheng 北土城

Guangximen 光熙门

Taiyanggong 太阳宫

Beisihuan Donglu

Beisanhuan Zhonglu (Third Ring Rd)

Hepingxiqiao 和平西桥

Xiba River

Airport Expwy

Beisanhuan Donglu

Sanyuanqiao 三元桥

See Drum Tower & Dōngchéng North Map (p68)

See Běihǎi Park & Xīchéng North Map (p80)

Andingmen Dongdajie (Second Ring Rd)

See Sānlǐtún & Cháoyáng Map (p76)

SĀNLǏTÚN EMBASSY AREA

Cháoyáng Park

XĪCHÉNG

Bell Tower & Drum Tower 7

Hútòng 3

Back-alley bars 8

CHÁOYÁNG

Xindong Lu

Nongzhanguan Nanlu

XĪDĀN

Chaoyang Dajie

Forbidden City 2 DŌNGCHÉNG

See Forbidden City Map (p56)

Tiananmen Square

Express Bus Line 3 to Capital Airport

Beijing Train Station 北京火车站

Tonghui River

Bawangfen Long-Distance Bus Station

Beijing East Train Station 北京东站

Peking duck 6

See Dōngchéng Central Map (p62)

Guangqumenwai Dajie

Shuangjing 双井

...ajie

CHÓNGWÉN

Tiyuguan Lu

Jinsong 劲松

See Dashilar & Xīchéng South Map (p83)

Taoranting Park

Temple of Heaven Park 4

Pānjiāyuán Market

Dongsanhuan Nanlu

Longtan Park

Beijing South 北京南站

Beijing South Train Station 北京南站

Zuo'anmen Xibīnhe Lu

See Temple of Heaven Park & Dōngchéng South Map (p73)

Puhuangyu 蒲黄榆

BĚIJĪNG IN...

Two Days

Stroll around the incense smoke–filled courtyards of the **Lama Temple** before hopping over the road to the even more laid-back **Confucius Temple**. Grab a coffee and lunch at **Confucius Cafe** before walking through the **hútòng alleys** to the ancient **Drum and Bell Towers** and finishing off the day with a meal in **Dàlǐ Courtyard**.

Get up early to enjoy the **Temple of Heaven Park** at its magical, early-morning best: filled with opera-singing locals rather than photo-snapping tourists. Grab a bite to eat in historic **Dashilar** before walking across **Tiān'ānmén Square** en route to exploring the awe-inspiring **Forbidden City**. Finish the day by tucking into Běijīng's signature dish – roast duck – at China's most famous restaurant **Quánjùdé Roast Duck Restaurant**.

Four Days

Follow the itinerary above, but save plenty of energy for the trip of a lifetime on day three; your journey to **The Great Wall**. There are plenty of options, from a quick half-day jaunt at touristy **Bādálǐng** to a strenuous hike along wild, unrestored sections such as **Huánghuā Chéng** or **Jiànkòu**. **Mùtiányù** makes a good option for families. Pack a picnic and don't expect to get back to the city until nightfall.

Hop on the subway on day four to visit the **Summer Palace**. You could spend the day here or make side trips to the **Botanic Gardens**, **Old Summer Palace** or **Fragrant Hills Park**, all of which are close. Return for an early evening meal so that you have time to catch a show, the **Peking Opera** or **acrobatics**, on your final evening.

and fresh at this time and the city unusually quiet. Arid spring is much more comfortable (unless there is a sand storm in town), but it only lasts for a month or so (April to May). Spring also sees the *liǔxù* (willow catkins) wafting through the air like snowflakes. From May onwards the mercury surges above 30°C, reaching the 40s in late summer. Sporadic downpours help clear the air for a day or two – this is often a smog-filled time of the year. Běijīng becomes cooler and clearer in autumn (end of September to early November), which is the best time to visit.

Language

Běijīnghuà (北京话), the Chinese spoken in the capital, is seen by purists as the finest variety of the Chinese language. Although the standard Mandarin is based on the Běijīng dialect, the two are very different in both accent and colloquialisms. Běijīnghuà is under threat from migrants who flock to town, bringing their own dialects in tow.

⊙ Sights

Historic **Dōngchéng District** (东城区; Dōngchéng Qū) is the largest of Běijīng's central districts and by far the most interesting for visitors. For convenience, we've split it into North, Central and South neighbourhoods. Dōngchéng Central has the lion's share of top-name sights, including the immense Forbidden City. A fascinating network of imperial *hútòng* (alleyways) fans out north and east from here. Dōngchéng North is also a fabulously historic, *hútòng*-rich neighbourhood, and arguably the most pleasant area in which to base yourself while in Běijīng. Dōngchéng South is dominated by the wonderful Temple of Heaven Park.

Cháoyáng District (朝阳区; Cháoyáng Qū) sprawls east from Dōngchéng and is home to the majority of Běijīng's foreign embassies, as well as most of its expat population. The area lacks history and character, but it does contain some of the capital's best modern restaurants, bars and shops, many of which are in the area known as Sānlǐtún.

West of Dōngchéng, **Xīchéng District** (西城区; Xīchéng Qū) has strong historical links. We've split it into north and south neighbourhoods. The north includes the city's lovely central lakes – at Hòuhǎi and within the centuries-old Běihǎi Park. The south includes the backpacker-central neighbourhood of Dashilar.

Outlying **Hǎidiàn** (海淀区; Hǎidiàn Qū), is the capital's main university district – head to Wǔdàokǒu to tap into student life in Běijīng – but it also includes some great day-trip destinations, including the hugely attractive Summer Palace.

FORBIDDEN CITY & DŌNGCHÉNG CENTRAL

Forbidden City HISTORIC SITE
(紫禁城; Zǐjīn Chéng; Map p56; www.dpm.org.cn; admission Nov-Mar/Apr-Oct ¥40/60, audio guide ¥40; ☉ 8.30am-4pm May-Sep, 8.30am-3.30pm Oct-Apr; ⑤Tian'anmen West or Tian'anmen East)
Ringed by a 52m-wide moat at the very heart of Běijīng, the Forbidden City is China's largest and best-preserved collection of ancient buildings, and the largest palace complex in the world. So called because it was off limits for 500 years, when it was steeped in stultifying ritual and Byzantine regal protocol, the otherworldly palace was the reclusive home to two dynasties of imperial rule until the Republic overthrew the last Qing emperor.

Today, the Forbidden City is prosaically known as the Palace Museum (故宫博物馆; Gùgōng Bówùguǎn), although most Chinese people simply call it *gùgōng* (故宫; former palace).

In former ages the price for uninvited admission was instant execution; these days ¥40 or ¥60 will do. Allow yourself the best part of a day for exploration or several trips if you're an enthusiast.

Guides – many with mechanical English – mill about the entrance, but the automatically activated audio tours are cheaper (¥40; more than 40 languages) and more reliable. Restaurants, a cafe, toilets and even ATMs can be found within the palace grounds. Wheelchairs (¥500 deposit) are free to use, as are pushchairs (¥300 deposit).

Entrance

Tourists must enter through **Meridian Gate** (午门; Wǔ Mén), a massive U-shaped portal at the south end of the complex, which in former times was reserved for the use of the emperor. Gongs and bells would sound imperial comings and goings, while lesser mortals used lesser gates: the military used the west gate, civilians the east gate. The emperor also reviewed his armies from here, passed judgement on prisoners, announced the new year's calendar and oversaw the flogging of troublesome ministers.

Through Meridian Gate, you enter an enormous courtyard, and cross the **Golden Stream** (金水; Jīn Shuǐ) – shaped to resemble a Tartar bow and spanned by five marble bridges – on your way to the magnificent **Gate of Supreme Harmony** (太和门; Tàihé Mén). This courtyard could hold an imperial audience of 100,000 people. For an idea of the

size of the restoration challenge, note how the crumbling courtyard stones are stuffed with dry weeds, especially on the periphery.

First Side Galleries

Before you pass through the Gate of Supreme Harmony to reach the Forbidden City's star attractions, veer off to the east and west of the huge courtyard to visit the Calligraphy and Painting Gallery inside the **Hall of Martial Valor** (武英殿; Wǔ Yīng Diàn) and the particularly good Ceramics Gallery, housed inside the creaking **Hall of Literary Glory** (文化殿; Wén Huà Diàn).

Three Great Halls

Raised on a three-tier marble terrace with balustrades are the Three Great Halls (三大殿; Sān Dàdiàn), the glorious heart of the Forbidden City. The recently restored **Hall of Supreme Harmony** (太和殿; Tàihé Diàn) is the most important and largest structure in the Forbidden City. Built in the 15th century and restored in the 17th century, it was used for ceremonial occasions, such as the emperor's birthday, the nomination of military leaders and coronations. Inside the Hall of Supreme Harmony is a richly decorated **Dragon Throne** (龙椅; Lóngyǐ), from which the emperor would preside over trembling officials. The entire court had to touch the floor nine times with their foreheads (the custom known as kowtowing) in the emperor's presence. At the back of the throne is a carved Xumishan, the Buddhist paradise, signifying the throne's supremacy.

Behind the Hall of Supreme Harmony is the smaller **Hall of Middle Harmony** (中和殿; Zhōnghé Diàn), which was used as the emperor's transit lounge. Here he would make last-minute preparations, rehearse speeches and receive close ministers. On display are two Qing-dynasty sedan chairs, the emperor's mode of transport around the Forbidden City. The last of the Qing emperors, Puyi, used a bicycle and altered a few features of the palace grounds to make it easier to get around.

FORBIDDEN CITY WALKING TOUR

Don't miss our full-colour 3D illustration of the Forbidden City on p58. It's brand new for this edition and includes our author's recommended walking tour of the complex.

Forbidden City

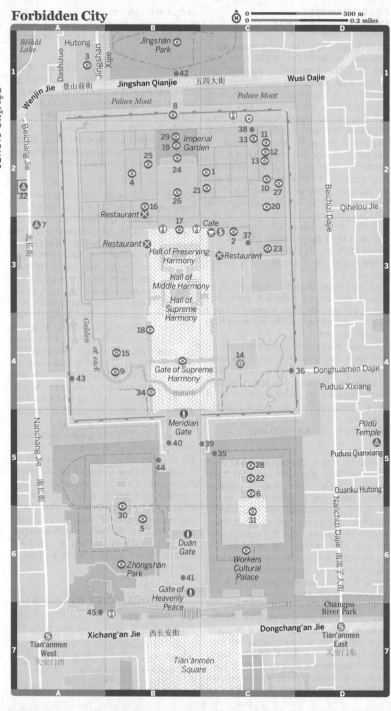

Forbidden City

◉ Sights

1 Chéngqiáng Hall..C2
2 Clock Exhibition Hall................................C3
3 Dàgāoxuán Temple...................................A1
4 Eternal Spring Palace...............................B2
5 Forbidden City Concert Hall.................B6
6 Front Hall C5
7 Fúyòu Temple A3
8 Gate of Divine Prowess (exit
    only)...B1
9 Gate of Heavenly Purity B3
10 Gate of Military Prowess.......................B4
    Hall for Ancestral Worship............(see 2)
11 Hall of Character Cultivation................C2
12 Hall of Harmony C2
13 Hall of Jewellery C2
14 Hall of Joyful Longevity C2
15 Hall of Literary Glory C4
16 Hall of Martial Valor B4
17 Hall of Mental Cultivation B2
18 Hóngyì Pavilion.......................................B4
19 Imperial Peace Hall................................B2
20 Imperial Supremacy Hall.......................C2
21 Jǐngrén Hall...B2
22 Middle Hall C5
23 Nine Dragon Screen C3
24 Palace of Earthly Tranquility B2
25 Palace of Gathered Elegance B2
26 Palace of Heavenly Purity B2
27 Pavilion of Cheerful Melodies C2
28 Rear Hall C5
29 Shùnzhēn Gate B2
30 Square Altar B6
31 Supreme Temple.....................................C6
32 Wánshòu Xīnglóng Temple....................A2
33 Well of Concubine Zhen.........................C2
34 Xīhé Gate B4

ℹ Information

35 Cultural Workers Palace
    northwest entrance................................C5
36 Donghua Gate (exit only) C4
37 Entrance to Complete Palace
    of Peace and Longevity C3
38 Exit of Complete Palace of
    Peace and Longevity.............................C2
39 Forbidden City ticket office...................C5
40 Forbidden City ticket office...................B5
41 Gate of Heavenly Peace
    ticket office...B6
42 Jǐngshān Park south entrance..............B1
43 Xīhuá Gate (closed)...............................A4
44 Zhōngshān Park northeast
    entrance B5
45 Zhōngshān Park south
    entrance A7

The third of the Great Halls is the **Hall of Preserving Harmony** (保和殿; Bǎohé Diàn), used for banquets and later for imperial examinations. The hall has no support pillars. To its rear is a 250-tonne **marble imperial carriageway** carved with dragons and clouds, which was transported into Běijīng on an ice path. The emperor used to be carried over this carriageway in his sedan chair as he ascended or descended the terrace. The outer housing surrounding the Three Great Halls was used for storing gold, silver, silks, carpets and other treasures.

A string of side halls on the eastern and western flanks of the Three Great Halls usually, but not always, house a series of excellent exhibitions, ranging from scientific instruments and articles of daily use to objects presented to the emperor by visiting dignitaries. One contains an interesting diorama of the whole complex.

Lesser Central Halls

The basic configuration of the Three Great Halls is echoed by the next group of buildings. Smaller in scale, these buildings were more important in terms of real power, which in China traditionally lies at the back door.

The first structure is the **Palace of Heavenly Purity** (乾清宫; Qiánqīng Gōng), a residence of Ming and early Qing emperors, and later an audience hall for receiving foreign envoys and high officials.

Immediately behind it is the **Hall of Union** (交泰殿; Jiāotài Diàn), which contains a clepsydra – a water clock made in 1745 with five bronze vessels and a calibrated scale. There's also a mechanical clock built in 1797 and a collection of imperial jade seals on display. The **Palace of Earthly Tranquility** (坤宁宫; Kūnníng Gōng) was the imperial couple's bridal chamber and the centre of operations for the palace harem.

Imperial Garden

At the northern end of the Forbidden City is the Imperial Garden (御花园; Yù Huāyuán), a classical Chinese garden with 7000 sq metres of fine landscaping, including rockeries, walkways, pavilions and ancient cypresses.

Forbidden City

WALKING TOUR

After entering through the imperious Meridian Gate, resist the temptation to dive straight into the star attractions and veer right for a peek at the excellent **1 Ceramics Gallery** housed inside the creaking Hall of Literary Glory.

Walk back to the central complex and head through the magnificent Gate of Supreme Harmony towards the Three Great Halls: first, the largest – the **2 Hall of Supreme Harmony**, followed by the **3 Hall of Middle Harmony** and the **4 Hall of Preserving Harmony**, behind which slopes the enormous Marble Imperial Carriageway.

Turn right here to visit the fascinating **5 Clock Exhibition Hall** before entering the **6 Complete Palace of Peace & Longevity**, a mini Forbidden City constructed along the eastern axis of the main complex. It includes the beautiful **7 Nine Dragon Screen** and, to the north, a series of halls, housing some excellent exhibitions and known collectively as The Treasure Gallery. Don't miss the **8 Pavilion of Cheerful Melodies**, a wonderful three-storey opera house.

Work your way to the far north of this section, then head west to the **9 Imperial Garden**, with its ancient cypress trees and pretty pavilions, before exiting via the garden's West Gate (behind the Thousand Year Pavilion) to explore the **10 Western Palaces**, an absorbing collection of courtyard homes where many of the emperors lived during their reign.

Exit this section at its southwest corner before turning back on yourself to walk north through the Gate of Heavenly Purity to see the three final Central Halls – the **11 Palace of Heavenly Purity**, the **12 Hall of Union** and the **13 Palace of Earthly Tranquility** – before leaving via the North Gate.

Water Vats
More than 300 copper and brass water vats dot the palace complex. They were used for fighting fires and in winter were prevented from freezing over by using thick quilts.

Entrance/Exit
You must enter through the south gate (Meridian Gate), but you can exit via south, north or east.

ticket offices

Guardian Lions
Pairs of lions guard important buildings. The male has a paw placed on a globe (representing the emperor's power over the world). The female has her paw on a baby lion (representing the emperor's fertility).

Kneeling Elephants

At the northern entrance of the Imperial Garden are two bronze elephants kneeling in an anatomically impossible fashion, which symbolise the power of the emperor; even elephants kowtowed before him.

Nine Dragon Screen

One of only three of its type left in China, this beautiful glazed dragon screen served to protect the Hall of Imperial Supremacy from evil spirits.

Forbidden City North Gate (exit only)

Thousand Year Pavilion

10

9

13

12

11

Marble Imperial Carriageway

Gate of Heavenly Purity

4

5

8

2

3

6

7

The Treasure Gallery

NORTH →

Gate of Supreme Harmony

1

Meridian Gate

Forbidden City East Gate (exit only)

Off-Limits

Only part of the Forbidden City is open to the public. The shaded areas you see here are off-limits.

Opera House

The largest of the Forbidden City's opera stages; look out for the trap doors, which allowed supernatural characters to make dramatic entrances and exits during performances.

Dragon-Head Spouts

More than a thousand dragon-head spouts encircle the raised marble platforms at the centre of the Forbidden City. They were – and still are – part of the drainage system.

Roof Guardians

The imperial dragon is at the tail of the procession, which is led by a figure riding a phoenix followed by a number of mythical beasts. The more beasts, the more important the building.

DON'T MISS

CLOCK EXHIBITION HALL

The **Clock Exhibition Hall** (钟表馆; Zhōngbiǎo Guǎn; Map p56; admission ¥10; ⊗8.30am-4pm summer, 8.30am-3.30pm winter) is one of the unmissable highlights of the Forbidden City. Located in the **Hall for Ancestral Worship** (Fèngxiàn Diàn) – just off to the right after the Three Great Halls – the exhibition contains an astonishing array of elaborate timepieces, many of which were gifts to the Qing emperors from overseas. Many of the 18th-century examples are crafted by James Cox or Joseph Williamson (both of London) and imported through Guǎngdōng from England; others are from Switzerland, America and Japan. Exquisitely wrought and fashioned with magnificently designed elephants and other creatures, they all display astonishing artfulness and attention to detail. Standout clocks include the 'Gilt Copper Astronomy Clock' equipped with a working model of the solar system, and the automaton-equipped 'Gilt Copper Clock with a robot writing Chinese characters with a brush'. Time your arrival for 11am or 2pm to see the **clock performance** in which choice timepieces strike the hour and give a display to wide-eyed children and adults.

Before you reach the **Gate of Divine Prowess** (神武们; Shénwǔ Mén), the Forbidden City's north exit, and **Shùnzhēn Gate** (顺贞门; Shùnzhēn Mén), which leads to it, note the pair of **bronze elephants** whose front knees bend in an anatomically impossible fashion, signifying the power of the emperor; even elephants would kowtow before him.

Complete Palace of Peace and Longevity

A mini Forbidden City, known as the Complete Palace of Peace and Longevity (宁寿全宫; Níng Shòu Quán Gōng) was built in the northeastern corner of the complex, mimicking the structure of the great halls of the central axis. During the Ming dynasty this was where the empress dowager and the imperial concubines lived. Now it houses a series of quieter courtyard buildings, which contain a number of fine museum exhibitions, known collectively as the **Treasure Gallery** (珍宝馆; Zhēn Bǎo Guǎn; entrance ¥10).

The complex is entered from the south – not far from the Clock Exhibition Hall. Just inside the entrance, you'll find the beautiful glazed **Nine Dragon Screen** (九龙壁; Jiǔlóng Bì), one of only three of its type left in China.

Visitors then work their way north, exploring a number of peaceful halls and courtyards before being popped out at the northern end of the Forbidden City. Don't miss the **Pavilion of Cheerful Melodies** (畅音阁; Chàngyīn Gé), a three-storey wooden opera house, which was the palace's largest theatre. Note the trap doors that allowed actors to make dramatic stage entrances.

Western & Eastern Palaces

About half a dozen smaller palace courtyards lie to the west and east of the Lesser Central Halls. They should all be open to the public, although at the time of research many of the eastern ones were closed for extensive renovation. It was in these smaller courtyard buildings that most of the emperors actually lived and many of the buildings, particularly those to the west, are decked out in imperial furniture. The **Hall of Mental Cultivation** (养心殿; Yǎng Xīn Diàn) is a highlight, while the **Palace of Gathered Elegance** (储秀宫; Chǔ Xiù Gōng) contains some interesting photos of the last emperor Puyi, who lived here as a child ruler at the turn of the 20th century.

FREE **Tiān'ānmén Square** SQUARE (天安门广场; Tiān'ānmén Guǎngchǎng; Map p62; ⓢTian'anmen West, Tian'anmen East or Qianmen) Flanked by stern 1950s Soviet-style buildings and ringed by white perimeter fences, the world's largest public square (440,000 sq metres) is an immense flatland of paving stones at the heart of Běijīng.

Here one stands at the symbolic centre of the Chinese universe. The rectangular arrangement, flanked by halls to both east and west, to some extent echoes the layout of the Forbidden City: as such, the square employs a conventional plan that pays obeisance to traditional Chinese culture, but many of its ornaments and buildings are Soviet-inspired. Mao conceived the square to project the enormity of the Communist Party, and during the Cultural Revolution he reviewed parades of up to a million people here. The 'Tiān'ānmén Incident', in 1976, is the term given to the near-riot in the square that accompanied the death of Premier Zhou Enlai. Another million people jammed the square to pay their last respects to Mao in the same year. Most infamously, in 1989 the army forced prodemocracy demonstrators out of the square. Hundreds lost their lives in the surrounding streets, although contrary to widespread belief, it is unlikely that anyone was killed in the square itself.

Despite being a public place, the square remains more in the hands of the government than the people; it is monitored by closed circuit TV cameras, Segway-riding policemen and plain-clothes officers. The designated points of access, security checks on entry and twitchy mood cleave Tiān'ānmén Square from the city. A tangible atmosphere of restraint and authority reigns.

All this – plus the absence of anywhere to sit – means the square is hardly a place to chill out (don't whip out a guitar), but such is its iconic status that few people leave Běijīng without making a visit. In any case, there's more than enough space to stretch a leg and the view can be breathtaking, especially on a clear blue day or at nightfall when the area is illuminated.

If you get up early, you can watch the **flag-raising ceremony** at sunrise, performed by a troop of People's Liberation Army (PLA) soldiers drilled to march at precisely 108 paces per minute, 75cm per pace. The soldiers emerge through the Gate of Heavenly Peace to goosestep impeccably across Chang'an Jie; all traffic is halted. The same ceremony in reverse is performed at sunset.

Gate of Heavenly Peace   HISTORIC SITE

(天安门; Tiān'ānmén; Map p62; admission ¥15, bag storage ¥2-6; ⊘8.30am-4.30pm; ⑤Tian'anmen West or Tian'anmen East) Hung with a vast likeness of Mao Zedong, and guarded by two pairs of Ming stone lions, the double-eaved Gate of Heavenly Peace (天安门; Tiān'ānmén), north of Tiān'ānmén Square, is a potent national symbol. Built in the 15th century and restored in the 17th century, the gate was formerly the largest of the four gates of the Imperial City Wall, and it was from this gate that Mao proclaimed the People's Republic of China on 1 October 1949. Today's political coterie watches mass troop parades from here.

Climb the gate for excellent views of the square, and peek inside at the impressive beams and overdone paintwork; in all there are 60 gargantuan wooden pillars and 17 vast lamps suspended from the ceiling. Within the gate tower there is also a fascinating photographic history of the gate and Tiān'ānmén Square, although captions are in Chinese only.

There's no fee for walking through the gate, en route to the Forbidden City, but if you climb it you'll have to pay. The ticket office is on the north side of the gate. For Forbidden City tickets, keep walking about 600m further north.

Front Gate   HISTORIC SITE

(前门; Qián Mén; Map p62; admission ¥20, audio guide ¥20; ⊘9am-4pm Tue-Sun; ⑤Qianmen) Front Gate actually consists of two gates. The northernmost is the 40m-high **Zhèngyáng Gate** (正阳门城楼; Zhèngyáng Mén Chénglóu) which dates from the Ming dynasty and which was the largest of the nine gates of the Inner City Wall separating the inner, or Tartar (Manchu) city from the outer, or Chinese city. Partially destroyed in the Boxer Rebellion around 1900, the gate was once flanked by two temples that have since vanished. With the disappearance of the city walls, the gate sits out of context, but it can be climbed for decent views of the square and of Arrow Tower, immediately to the south.

Inside the upper levels are some fascinating **historical photographs**, showing the area as it was at the beginning of the last century, before the city walls and many of the surrounding gates and temples were demolished. Explanatory captions are in English as well as Chinese.

Zhèngyáng Gate Arrow Tower (正阳门箭楼; Zhèngyángmén Jiànlóu), directly south, can't be climbed. It also dates from the Ming dynasty and was originally connected to Zhèngyáng Gate by a semicircular enceinte (demolished last century).

FREE National Museum of China   MUSEUM

(中国国际博物馆; Zhōngguó Guójì Bówùguǎn; Map p62; en.chnmuseum.cn; admission with passport only, audio guide ¥30; ⊘9am-5pm Tue-Sun; ⑤Tian'anmen East; 🟦) After years of renovation, China's premier museum, housed in the immense 1950s building on the eastern side of Tiān'ānmén Square, finally reopened in 2011. It was still a work in progress at the time of research, with some halls closed, but much of what was open was well worth visiting. The Ancient China exhibition on the basement floor is outstanding. It contains dozens and dozens of stunning pieces, from

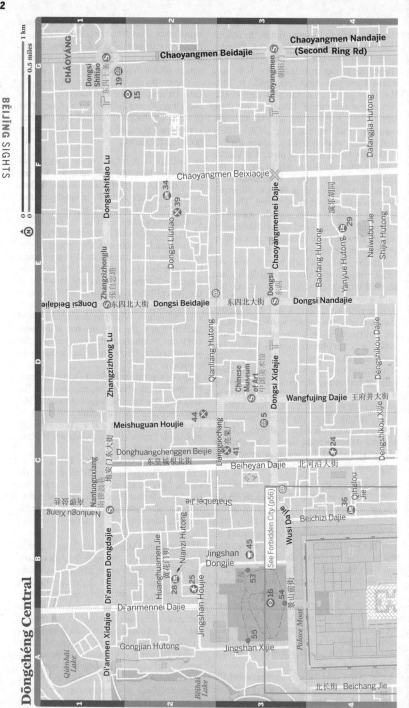

Dōngchéng Central

Chaoyangmen Beidajie

Chaoyangmen Nandajie (Second Ring Rd)

CHÁOYÁNG

Dongsi Shitiao

19

15

Dongsishitiao Lu

Chaoyangmen Beixiaojie

34

39

Dongsi Liutiao

Chaoyangmennei Dajie

Dongsi

29

Yanyue Hutong

Baofang Hutong

Neiwubu Jie

Shijia Hutong

Datangjia Hutong

Zhangzizhonglu

Zhangzizhong Lu

Dongsi Beidajie 东四北大街

东四北大街

Dongsi Nandajie

Dengshikou Dajie

Qianliang Hutong

Chinese Museum of Art 中国美术馆

Dongsi Xidajie

Wangfujing Dajie 王府井大街

Dengshikou Xijie

44

Meishuguan Houjie

Liangguochang

5

Donghuangchenggen Beijie 东皇城根北街

41

Beiheyan Dajie 北河沿大街

24

Nanluoguxiang 南锣鼓巷

Nanluoguxiang 南锣鼓巷

Shatanbei Jie

See Forbidden City (p56)

36

Qihelou Jie

Beichizi Dajie

Di'anmen Dongdajie

Huanghuamen Jie 黄花门街

Nianzi Hutong

25

28

Jingshan Dongjie

45

Jingshan Houjie

Di'anmennei Dajie

53

16

54

景山前街

Wusi Dajie

Qiánhǎi Lake

Di'anmen Xidajie

Gongjian Hutong

Jingshan Xijie

55

Běihǎi Lake

Palace Moat

北长街 Beichang Jie

1 km

0.5 miles

0

0

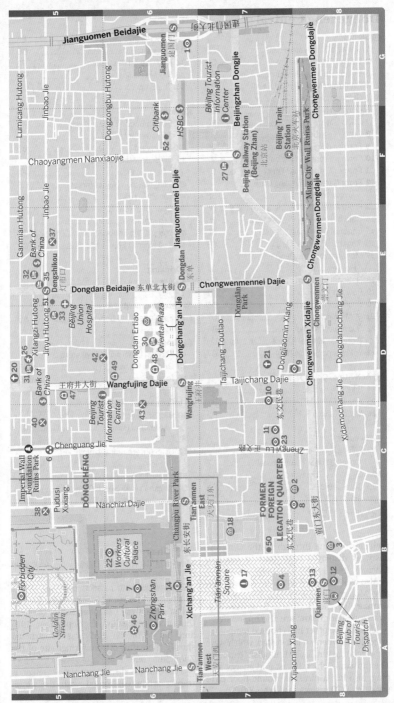

Jianguomen Beidajie

Lumicang Hutong

Jinbao Jie

Dongzongbu Hutong

Jianguomen
建国门

Beijing Tourist
Information
Center
Beijingzhan Dongjie

Beijing Train
Station
北京火车站

Chongwenmen Dongdajie

Chaoyangmen Nanxiaojie

Ganmian Hutong

Bank of
China
32 35
Dengshikou
灯市口

Jinbao Jie

37

Citibank

52

HSBC

Beijing Railway Station
(Beijing Zhan)
北京站

27

Ming City Wall Ruins Park

Chongwenmen Dongdajie

Jianguomennei Dajie

Dongdan
东单

Chongwenmennei Dajie

Dongdan Beidajie 东单北大街

Xitangzi Hutong 51
Jinyu Hutong
Beijing
Union
Hospital
33

Dongdan
Park

26
31
Bank of
China

42 49
Wangfujing Dajie

Dongdan Ertiao
Oriental Plaza

30
48

Dongchang'an Jie

Taijichang Toutiao

Dongjiaomin Xiang

21

9

Chongwenmen Xidajie
Chongwenmen
崇文门

Dongdamochang Jie

王府井大街

Beijing
Tourist
Information
Center
47

Wangfujing
王府井

Taijichang Dajie

40
43

Chenguang Jie

10

11
23

Zhengyi Lu 正义路

Xidamochang Jie

DŌNGCHÉNG

Imperial Wall
Foundation
Ruins Park

Pudusi
Xixiang

Nanchizi Dajie

38

Changpu River Park

Tian'anmen
East
天安门东

FORMER
FOREIGN
LEGATION QUARTER

2

前门东大街

18

50

东交民巷

3

Xichang'an Jie

Tian'anmen
Square

Workers
Cultural
Palace
22

7
14

Zhongshan
Park

17

4

13

12

Forbidden
City

46

Qianmen
前门

Beijing
Hub of
Tourist
Dispatch

Golden
Stream

Tian'anmen
West
天安门西

Nanchang Jie

Nanchang Jie

Xijiaomin Xiang

Dōngchéng Central

◎ **Sights**
1 Ancient Observatory G6
2 Běijīng Police Museum..........................C8
3 Běijīng Railway Museum B8
4 Chairman Mao Memorial Hall B7
5 China Art Museum.................................C3
6 Dōng'ān Mén Remains C5
7 Duān Gate B6
8 Dutch Legation......................................B7
9 Former Belgian Legation D8
10 Former French Legation D7
11 Former French Post Office.....................C7
12 Front Gate (Zhèngyáng Gate
    Arrow Tower) B8
13 Front Gate (Zhèngyáng Gate)..............B8
14 Gate of Heavenly Peace B6
15 Imperial Granaries................................G2
16 Jǐngshān Park..B3
17 Monument to the People's
    Heroes...B7
18 National Museum of China B7
19 Poly Art Museum G1
20 St Joseph's Church D5
21 St Michael's Church D7
22 Supreme Temple B6
    Workers Cultural Palace..............(see 22)
23 Yokohama Specie Bank C7

◎ **Activities, Courses & Tours**
24 Bike Běijīng C4
25 Jǐngshān Table Tennis Park B2
26 Mǐlún Kungfu School D5

◎ **Sleeping**
27 Běijīng City Central
    International Youth Hostel F7
28 City Walls Courtyard B2
29 Côté Cour E4
30 Grand Hyatt D6
31 Jìngyuán Hotel D5

32 Park Plaza..E5
33 Peninsula...D5
34 Red Capital Residence..........................F2
35 Regent Běijīng.......................................E5
36 The Emperor C4

◎ **Eating**
37 Běijīng Dàdǒng Roast Duck
    Restaurant..E5
38 Courtyard...B5
39 Crescent Moon Muslim
    Restaurant..F2
40 Dōnghuámén Night Market C5
41 Lǎo Zhái Yuán C3
42 Quánjùdé Roast Duck
    Restaurant..D5
43 Wángfǔjǐng Snack Street......................C6
44 Zuǒ Lín Yòu Shé....................................C2

◎ **Drinking**
45 Alley Coffee...B3

◎ **Entertainment**
46 Forbidden City Concert Hall A6

◎ **Shopping**
47 Foreign Languages Bookstore D5
48 Oriental Plaza..D6
49 Ruìfùxiàng..D6

◎ **Information**
50 Bag Storage for Chairman Mao
    Memorial Hall...................................B7
51 CITS..E5
52 CITS (international train ticket
    office)..F6
53 Jǐngshān Park East Gate B3
54 Jǐngshān Park South Gate.....................B3
55 Jǐngshān Park West Gate A3

prehistoric China through to the Qing dynasty, all displayed beautifully in modern, spacious, low-lit exhibition halls.

Also worth seeking out is the Ancient Chinese Money exhibition on the top floor. The **Bronze Art and Buddhist Sculpture** galleries, one floor below, are also impressive.

Many of the other halls housed temporary art galleries when we last visited, which were eye-catching, but lacked English captions. The museum, which is vast and energy sapping, also has a pleasant ground-floor **cafe** (coffee from ¥20, pastries/sandwiches ¥10-20).

FREE **Chairman Mao Memorial Hall**   MAUSOLEUM
(毛主席纪念堂; Máo Zhǔxí Jìniàntáng; Map p62; admission with passport only; bag storage ¥2-10, camera storage ¥2-5; ◎8am-noon Tue-Sun; ⓢTian'anmen West, Tian'anmen East or Qianmen) Chairman Mao died in September 1976 and his Memorial Hall was constructed shortly thereafter on the former site of the Zhōnghuá Gate.

The Chinese display an almost religious respect when confronted with the physical presence of Mao. The Great Helmsman's mummified corpse lies in a crystal cabinet, draped in a red flag emblazoned with hammer and sickle while impatient guards in white gloves brusquely wave the hoi polloi on towards further rooms housing Mao memorabilia. Bags must be deposited at a building east of the memorial hall across the road.

Former Foreign Legation Quarter

HISTORIC SITE

(Map p62; S Qianmen or Tian'anmen East) For grand shades of Europe, the former Foreign Legation Quarter where the 19th-century foreign powers flung up embassies, schools, churches, post offices and banks is worth a quick stroll if you are in the Tiān'ānmén Square area.

Access the area walking up the steps east from Tiān'ānmén Sq into Dongjiaomin Xiang (东交民巷), once called Legation St and renamed 'Anti-Imperialism Road' during the iconoclastic Cultural Revolution. You'll soon reach an archway on your right, through which is the **Legation Quarter** (23 Qianmen Dongdajie), a classy cluster of elegantly restored legation buildings, now home to several exclusive restaurants, shops and an art gallery. Back on Dongjiaomin Xiang, the excellent **Police Museum** is at No 36, while the attractive green-roofed, orange brick building further east at No 40 is the stately former **Dutch Legation**.

The domed building at 4a Zhengyi Lu, on the corner of Zhengyi Lu (正义路) and Dongjiaomin Xiang, is the former **Yokahama Specie Bank**. The grey building at No 19 Dongjiaomin Xiang is the former **French post office**, now housing the low-key Sichuanese restaurant Jīngyuán Chuāncài. Nearby is the former **French Legation** (法国使馆旧址; Fǎguó Shǐguǎn Jiùzhǐ) at No 15.

Backing onto a small school courtyard, the twin spires of the Gothic **St Michael's Church** (东交民巷天主教堂; Dōngjiàomínxiàng Catholic Church) rise ahead at No 11, facing the green roofs and ornate red brickwork of the former **Belgian Legation**.

North along Taijichang Dajie is a brick street sign embedded in the northern wall of **Tǎijīchǎng Tóutiáo** (台基厂头条), carved with the old name of the road, Rue Hart.

Běijīng Police Museum

MUSEUM

(北京警察博物馆; Běijīng Jǐngchá Bówùguǎn; 36 Dongjiaomin Xiang; Map p62; admission ¥5, through ticket ¥20; ⊗9am-4pm Tue-Sun; S Qianmen) Propaganda-filled it may be, but some riveting exhibits make this museum a fascinating peek into Běijīng's police force. Learn how Běijīng's first Public Security Bureau college operated from the Dōngyuè Temple in 1949, and how the Běijīng PSB was destroyed during the 'national catastrophe' of the Cultural Revolution. Upstairs gets to grips with morbid crimes and their investigations; for police weapons, head to the 4th floor. The 'through ticket' includes laser shooting practice and a souvenir. The building was once the First National City Bank of New York.

Jīngshān Park

PARK

(景山公园; Jǐngshān Gōngyuán; Map p62; summer/winter ¥5/2; ⊗6am-9.30pm; S Tian'anmen West, then bus 5) The dominating feature of Jīngshān – one of the city's finest parks – is one of central Běijīng's few hills; a mound that was created from the earth excavated to make the Forbidden City moat. Called Coal Hill by Westerners during Legation days, Jīngshān also serves as a feng shui shield, protecting the palace from evil spirits – or dust storms – from the north. Clamber to the top for a magnificent panorama of the capital and princely views over the russet roofing of the Forbidden City. On the eastern side of the park a locust tree stands in the place where the last of the Ming emperors, Chongzhen, hung himself as rebels swarmed at the city walls. The rest of the park is one of the best places in Běijīng for people watching. Come early to see (or join in with) elderly folk going about their morning routines of dancing, singing, performing taichi or playing keepie-uppies with oversized shuttlecocks. In April and May the park bursts into bloom with fabulously colourful peonies and tulips forming the focal point of a very popular flower fair.

Alley Coffee (cnr of Jingshan Dongjie & Shatan Houjie; ⊗8.30am-11pm), a cute courtyard cafe near the east gate, makes a decent lunch stop here.

Zhōngshān Park

PARK

(中山公园; Zhōngshān Gōngyuán; Map p62; admission ¥3; ⊗6am-9pm summer, 6.30am-7pm winter; S Tian'anmen West) This lovely little park, west of the Gate of Heavenly Peace, has a section hedging up against the Forbidden City moat. Formerly the sacred Ming-style Altar to the God of the Land and the God of Grain (Shìjìtán), where the emperor offered sacrifices, it's tidy and tranquil and, like Jīngshān Park to the north, it bursts into bloom in April and May for its **Spring Flower and Tulips Show** (¥10).

Workers Cultural Palace PARK

(劳动人民文化宫; Láodòng Rénmín Wénhuà Gōng; Map p62; admission ¥2; ◎6.30am-7.30pm; S Tian'anmen East) Sounding like a social centre for Leninist labourers, this haven of peace was actually the emperor's premier place of worship, centred on the magnificent **Supreme Temple** (太庙; Tài Miào; admission ¥10). The often-overlooked temple halls, cloaked in imperial yellow tiles and hunched over expansive courtyards, are like a mini version of the Forbidden City, only without the crowds.

Poly Art Museum MUSEUM

(保利艺术博物馆; Bǎolì Yìshù Bówùguǎn; Map p62; ☑6500 8117; www.polymuseum.com; 9th fl, Poly Plaza, 14 Dongzhimen Nandajie; admission ¥20, audio guide ¥10; ◎9.30am-4.30pm; S Dongsishitiao) This small, but exquisite museum displays a glorious array of ancient bronzes from the Shang and Zhou dynasties, a magnificent high-water mark for bronze production. In an attached room are four of the Western-styled 12 bronze animals plundered with the sacking of the Old Summer Palace (p85) that have been acquired by the museum. The last room is populated with a sublime collection of standing bodhisattva statues, most of which date from the Northern Qi, Northern Wei and Tang dynasties.

Those interested in Ming-dynasty architecture should check out the nearby **Imperial Granaries** (南新仓; Nán Xīn Cāng). Nine of the storehouses, dating from 1409, have been lovingly restored. They once contained grain and rice for Běijīng's royalty; they now house posh wine bars and members' clubs.

FREE St Joseph's Church CHURCH

(东堂; Dōng Táng; Map p62; 74 Wangfujing Dajie; ◎6.30-7am Mon-Sat, to 8am Sun; S Dengshikou) A crowning edifice on Wangfujing Dajie, and one of Běijīng's four principal churches, St Joseph's was originally built during the reign of Shunzhi in 1655, but was damaged by an earthquake in 1720 and reconstructed. The luckless church also caught fire in 1807, was destroyed again in 1900 during the Boxer Rebellion and restored in 1904, only to be shut in 1966. Now fully repaired, the church is a testament to the long history of Christianity in China. A large piazza in front swarms with children playing, elderly folk resting and newlyweds posing for photographs. Mass is held in Chinese at 6.30am and 7am from Monday to Saturday, and at 6.15am, 7am and 8am on Sundays. An English version is held every Sunday at 4pm.

Ancient Observatory HISTORIC SITE

(古观象台; Gǔ Guānxiàngtái; Map p62; admission ¥20; ◎9.30am-4.30pm Tue-Sun; S Jianguomen) This unusual former observatory is mounted on the battlements of a watchtower lying along the line of the old Ming City Wall and originally dates back to Kublai Khan's days, when it lay north of the present site. Khan, like later Ming and Qing emperors, relied heavily on astrologers to plan military endeavours. The present observatory – the only surviving example of several constructed during the Jin, Yuan, Ming and Qing dynasties – was built between 1437 and 1446 to facilitate both astrological predictions and seafaring navigation.

BĚIJĪNG MUSEUM PASS

If you're staying in the capital for a while, the Běijīng Museum Pass (博物馆通票; Bówùguǎn Tōngpiào) is a great investment that will save you both money and queuing for tickets. For ¥120 you get either complimentary access or discounted admission (typically 50%) to 65 museums, temples and tourist sights in and around Běijīng. Attractions covered include the **Great Wall at Bādàlǐng** (p118), **Front Gate** (p61), the **Drum Tower**, the **Bell Tower**, the **Confucius Temple** (p69), the **Botanic Gardens** (p84), the **Běijīng Railway Museum** (p75) and **Dōngyuè Temple** (p75). Not all museums are worth visiting, but many are, and you only have to visit a small selection to get your money back. The pass comes in the form of a booklet (Chinese with minimal English), valid from 1 January to 31 December in any one year. The pass, which is harder to obtain as the year goes on, can be picked up from participating museums and sights, from some post offices or, most easily, from the huge bookstore known as **Běijīng Books Building** (Map p80; 西单图书大厦; Xīdān Túshū Dàshà; 17 Xichang'an Jie; 西长安街17号; ◎9am-9pm; S Xidan). Go to the service desk to your far right as you enter the bookstore.

The scheme has a website (www.bowuguan.bj.cn), but it's in Chinese only, as is the phone service (☑6222 3793).

Clamber the steps to the roof of the watchtower to admire a mind-boggling array of Jesuit-designed astronomical instruments, embellished with sculptured bronze dragons and other particularly Chinese flourishes – a kind of East meets West astronomical fusion.

FREE **China Art Museum** ART GALLERY
(中国美术馆; Zhōngguó Měishùguǎn; Map p62; 1 Wusi Dajie; ⊙9am-5pm, last entry 4pm; ⑤Chinese Museum of Art) This revamped museum has received a shot of imagination and flair, with absorbing exhibitions from home and abroad. For something more cutting edge, though, consider a trip to 798 Art District (p67). Lifts allow for wheelchair access. Note, you must bring your passport along to gain entry.

DRUM TOWER & DŌNGCHÉNG NORTH

Drum Tower HISTORIC SITE
(鼓楼; Gǔlóu; Map p68; Gulou Dongdajie; admission ¥20, both towers through ticket ¥30; ⊙9am-5pm, last tickets 4.40pm; ⑤Shichahai or Gulou Dajie) Along with the older-looking Bell Tower, which stands behind it, the magnificent red-painted Drum Tower used to be the city's official timekeeper, with drums and bells beaten and rung to mark the times of the day; effectively the Big Ben of Běijīng.

Originally built in 1272, the Drum Tower was once the heart of the Mongol capital of Dàdū, as Běijīng was then known. That structure was destroyed in a fire before a replacement was built, slightly to the east of the original location, in 1420. The current structure is a Qing-dynasty version of that 1420 tower.

You can climb the steep inner staircase for views of the grey-tiled rooftops in the surrounding *hútòng* alleys. But, you can't view the Bell Tower as the north-facing balcony has been closed. It's well worth climbing the tower, though, especially if you can time it to coincide with one of the regular drumming performances, which are played out on reproductions of the 25 Ming-dynasty watch drums, which used to sound out across this part of the city. One of the original 25 drums, the **Night Watchman's Drum** (更鼓; Gēnggǔ), is also on display; dusty, battered and worn. Also on display is a replica of a Song-dynasty water clock, which was never actually used in the tower, but is interesting nonetheless.

The times of the **drumming performances**, which only last for a few minutes, are posted by the ticket office. At the time of research they were: 9.30am, 10.30am, 11.30am, 1.30pm, 2.30pm, 3.30pm and 4.45pm.

REDEVELOPMENT PLANS

In late 2012 controversial plans to redevelop the *hútòng*-rich area around the Drum and Bell Towers looked like they were back on the table. At press time it was not clear if, when and how much of the area might be demolished.

Bell Tower HISTORIC SITE
(钟楼; Zhōnglóu; Map p68; Gulou Dongdajie; admission ¥20, both towers through ticket ¥30; ⊙9am-5pm, last tickets 4.40pm; ⑤Shichahai or Gulou Dajie) The more modest, grey-stone structure of the Bell Tower is arguably more charming than the resplendent Drum Tower, after which this area of Běijīng is named.

Along with the Drum Tower's drums, the bells in the Bell Tower were used as Běijīng's official timekeepers throughout the Yuan, Ming and Qing Dynasties, and until 1924. The Bell Tower looks older, perhaps because it isn't painted, but both are of similar age.

The Bell Tower can also be climbed, up an incredibly steep inner staircase (take care), but the views from the top are even better here, partly because the structure is set back more deeply into the surrounding *hútòng*, and partly because you can view the Drum Tower from the balcony. Marvel too at the huge, **63-tonne bell** that is suspended in the pleasantly unrestored interior. Note how Chinese bells have no clappers but are instead struck with a stout pole.

The **Drum & Bell Square**, which lies between the two towers, is a great people-watching space, especially during the evening when locals congregate for formation dancing. There is a handful of excellent bars and cafes here too, some with rooftop views over the square. Both towers are lit up beautifully come evening.

Lama Temple BUDDHIST TEMPLE
(雍和宫; Yónghé Gōng; Map p68; 28 Yonghegong Dajie; admission ¥25, English audioguide ¥50; ⊙9am-4.30pm; ⑤Yonghegong-Lama Temple) This exceptional temple is a glittering attraction in Běijīng's Buddhist firmament. If you only have time for one temple (the Temple of Heaven isn't really a temple) make it this one, where riveting roofs, fabulous frescoes, magnificent decorative arches, tapestries, eye-popping carpentry, Tibetan prayer wheels, Tantric statues and a superb pair of Chinese lions mingle with dense clouds of incense.

Drum Tower & Dōngchéng North

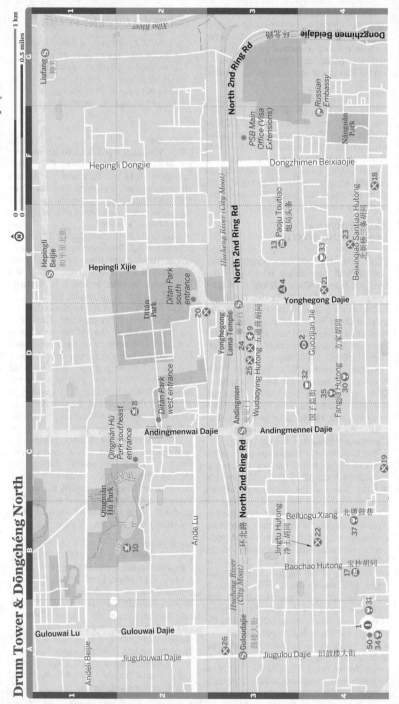

0 — 0.5 miles
0 — 1 km

Xiba River

Dōngzhímén Běidàjiē 东直门北大街

North 2nd Ring Rd

Russian Embassy

PSB Main Office (Visa Extensions)

Nánguǎn Park

Hepingli Dongjie

Dongzhimen Beixiaojie

Liufang 柳芳

Hepingli Beijie 和平里北街

Hepingli Xijie

Huicheng River (City Moat)

North 2nd Ring Rd

Paoju Toutiao 炮局头条

13

Běixīnqiáo Santiao Hutong 北新桥三条胡同

18

33

23

Dǐtán Park south entrance

Dǐtán Park

4

21

Yonghegong Dajie

Yonghegong Lama Temple

Yonghegong 雍和宫

20

24

25

Andingmen 安定门

Wudaoying Hutong 五道营胡同

Guozijian Jie

2

32

35

国子监街

Fangjia Hutong 方家胡同

30

Dǐtán Park west entrance

8

Andingmenwai Dajie

Andingmennei Dajie

Qīngnián Hú Park southeast entrance

Qīngnián Hú Park

10

19

Ande Lu

Beiluogu Xiang 北锣鼓巷

Jingtu Hutong 净土胡同

22

37

Baochao Hutong 宝抄胡同

17

North 2nd Ring Rd 二环北路

Huicheng River (City Moat)

31

Gulouwai Lu

Gulouwai Dajie

Guloudajie 鼓楼大街

26

Jiuguloulou Dajie 旧鼓楼大街

50

34

1

Jiugulouwai Dajie

Andeli Beijie

Jiugulou Dajie 旧鼓楼大街

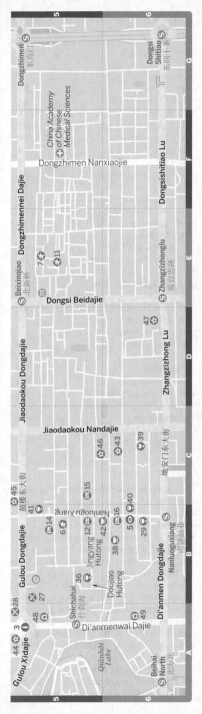

The most renowned Tibetan Buddhist temple outside Tibet, the Lama Temple was converted to a lamasery in 1744 after serving as the former residence of Emperor Yong Zheng. Today the temple is an active place of worship, attracting pilgrims from afar, some of whom prostrate themselves in submission at full length within its halls.

Resplendent within the **Hall of the Wheel of the Law** (Fălún Diàn), the fourth hall you reach from the entrance, is a substantial bronze statue of a benign and smiling Tsong Khapa (1357–1419), founder of the Gelugpa or Yellow Hat sect, robed in yellow and illuminated by a skylight.

The fifth hall, the **Wànfú Pavilion** (Wànfú Gé), houses a magnificent 18m-high statue of the Maitreya Buddha in his Tibetan form, clothed in yellow satin and reputedly sculpted from a single block of sandalwood. Each of the Bodhisattva's toes is the size of a pillow. Behind the statue is the Vault of Avalokiteshvara, from where a diminutive and blue-faced statue of Guanyin peeks out. The Wànfú Pavilion is linked by an overhead walkway to the Yánsuí Pavilion (Yánsuí Gé), which encloses a huge lotus flower that revolves to reveal an effigy of the Longevity Buddha.

Don't miss the collection of bronze Tibetan Buddhist statues within the **Jiètái Lóu**, a small side hall. Most effigies date from the Qing dynasty, from languorous renditions of Green Tara and White Tara to exotic, Tantric pieces (such as Samvara) and figurines of the fierce-looking Mahakala. Also peruse the collection of Tibetan Buddhist ornaments within the **Bānchán Lóu**, another side hall, where an array of *dorje* (Tibetan sceptres), mandalas and Tantric figures are displayed along with an impressive selection of ceremonial robes in silk and satin.

The street outside the temple entrance heaves with shops piled high with statues of Buddha, talismans, Buddhist charms, incense and keepsakes, picked over by a constant stream of pilgrims.

Confucius Temple & Imperial College CONFUCIAN TEMPLE

(孔庙、国子监; Kǒng Miào; Map p68; 13 Guozijian Jie; admission ¥20, audio guide ¥30; ⊙8.30am-5.30pm; ⑤Yonghegong-Lama Temple) An incense stick's toss away from the Lama Temple, the desiccated Confucius Temple had a pre-Olympics spruce up that failed to shift its indelible sense of otherworldly detachment. Like all Confucian shrines, China's second-largest Confucian temple feels

Drum Tower & Dōngchéng North

⊙ **Sights**
1 Bell Tower A4
2 Confucius Temple & Imperial
   College.................................... D4
3 Drum Tower.............................. A5
4 Lama Temple............................ E3
5 Nanluogu Xiang B6

⊕ **Activities, Courses & Tours**
6 Black Sesame Kitchen B5
7 Culture Yard E5
8 Dìtán Sports Centre C2
9 Natooke D3
10 Qīngnián Hú Park Swimming
   Pool.. B2
11 The Hutong.............................. E5

🛏 **Sleeping**
12 Běijīng Downtown Backpackers........... B5
13 Běijīng P-Loft Youth Hostel E3
14 Courtyard 7.............................. B5
15 DùGé C5
16 Peking Youth Hostel B6
17 The Orchid B4

✖ **Eating**
18 Bǎihé Vegetarian Restaurant................F4
19 Dàlǐ Courtyard C4
20 Jīn Dǐng Xuān.......................... D2
21 Qí Shān Miàn E4
22 Róng Tiān Sheep Spine B4
23 Tàn Huā Lamb BBQ................. E4
24 Veggie Table D3
25 Vineyard Cafe.......................... D3
26 Xīnmín Food Market A3

27 Yáng Fāng Lamb Hotpot B5
28 Yáojí Chǎogān.......................... A5

🍷 **Drinking**
29 12SQM....................................... B6
30 46 Fangjia Hutong D4
31 Ball House A4
32 Cafe Confucius D4
33 Courtyard No 28 .... E4
34 Drum & Bell A4
35 El Nido D4
36 Great Leap Brewing B5
37 If B4
38 Irresistible Café B6
39 Mao Mao Chong....................... C6
40 Passby Bar B6
41 Reef Bar B5
   Sculpting in Time ....(see 44)
42 Xiǎoxīn's Café B6

✦ **Entertainment**
43 Jiāng Hú C6
44 Jiāng Jín Jiǔ............................ A5
45 MAO Livehouse........................ C5
46 Pénghǎo Theatre..................... C5
47 Yúgōng Yíshān........................ D6

🛍 **Shopping**
48 Ruìfúxiáng............................... A5
49 Tiān Yí Goods Market............. A6

ℹ **Information**
50 Cycle Rickshaw tours ticket
   office A4

rather like a mausoleum, so expect peace and quiet. Some of Běijīng's last remaining *páilóu* (decorative archways) survive in the *hútòng* outside (Guozijian Jie) while antediluvian *bìxì* (tortoise-like dragons) glare inscrutably from repainted pavilions. Lumpy and ossified ancient cypresses claw stiffly at the sky, while at the rear a 'stone' forest of 190 stelae (upright slabs etched with figures or inscriptions) records the 13 Confucian classics in 630,000 Chinese characters.

A footnote lies unrecorded behind the tourist blurb. Běijīng writer Lao She was brought here in August 1966, forced to his knees in front of a bonfire of Běijīng opera costumes to confess his 'antirevolutionary crimes', and beaten. The much-loved writer drowned himself the next day in Taiping Lake.

Next to the Confucius Temple, but within the same grounds, is the **Imperial College** (国子监; Guózǐjiàn), where the emperor expounded the Confucian classics to an audience of thousands of kneeling students, professors and court officials – an annual rite. Built by the grandson of Kublai Khan in 1306, the former college was the supreme academy during the Yuan, Ming and Qing dynasties. On the site is a marvellous glazed, three-gated, single-eaved decorative archway. The Bìyōng Hall beyond is a twin-roofed structure with yellow tiles surrounded by a moat and topped with a shimmering gold knob.

The surrounding streets and *hútòng* are ideal for browsing, harbouring a charming selection of cafes and boutique shops.

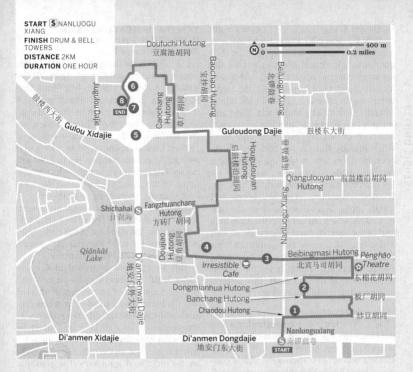

START Ⓢ NANLUOGU
XIANG
FINISH DRUM & BELL
TOWERS
DISTANCE 2KM
DURATION ONE HOUR

Walking Tour
Hútòng

❯ This easy tour explores some of the historic alleyways that branch off Běijīng's most famous *hútòng*, Nanluogu Xiang.

Exit Nanluoguxiang subway station and turn right into Chaodou Hutong (炒豆胡同). Starting at No 77, the next few courtyards once made up the ❶ **former mansion of Seng Gelinqin**, a Qing-dynasty army general. Note the enormous *bǎogǔshí* (drum stones) at the entranceway to No 77, followed by more impressive gateways at Nos 75, 69, 67 and 63. After No 53 turn left up an unmarked winding alleyway before turning left onto Banchang Hutong (板厂胡同).

At No 19, turn right through a ❷ **hallway gate**, a connecting passageway leading to Dongmianhua Hutong (东棉花胡同). Turn right here, then left down an unnamed alley, signposted to Pénghāo Theatre Cafe.

Turn left onto Beibingmasi Hutong (北兵马司胡同) and continue across Nanluogu Xiang into particularly historic ❸ **Mao'er Hutong** (帽儿胡同). Stop for a drink at Irresistible Cafe or just admire the entranceways to the charming old courtyards at Nos 5 and 11; both worth a peek if the gates are open.

Further on, No 37 was the ❹ **former home of Wan Rong**, who would later marry China's last emperor Puyi.

Next, turn right down Doujiao Hutong (豆角 胡同) and wind your way to Fangzhuanchang Hutong (方砖厂胡同) then Nanxia-wazi Hutong (南下洼子胡同). Just before the end turn right onto Qiangulouyan Hutong (前鼓楼沿胡同), then immediately left down Houguloulouyuan Hutong (后鼓楼湖同) and work your way north to busy Guloudong Dajie (鼓楼东大街). Turn left here and then, just before you reach the imperious red-painted ❺ **Drum Tower**, turn right into Caochang Hutong (草厂胡同). Continue down the lane beside Sea View Cafe, then take the second left, where you'll see the magnificent grey-brick ❻ **Bell Tower** in front of you. Follow this wonderfully winding alley to the back of the Bell Tower then walk around the tower to ❼ **Drum & Bell Square**, a great place for people-watching, where you can end your walk with a drink on the rooftop terrace at ❽ **Drum & Bell**.

Nanluogu Xiang

(南锣鼓巷; Map p68) Once neglected and ramshackle, strewn with spent coal briquettes in winter and silent except for the hacking coughs of shuffling old-timers and the jangling of bicycle bells, the funky north–south alleyway of Nanluogu Xiang (literally 'South Gong and Drum Alley', and roughly pronounced 'nan-law-goo-syang') has been undergoing evolution since 1999 when **Passby Bar** (at No 108) first threw open its doors, and it was the subject of a complete makeover in 2006. Today, the alley is an insatiably bubbly strip of bars, wi-fi cafes, restaurants, courtyard hotels and trendy shops. Don't miss exploring the quieter alleys, which fan out from the main lane and house Qing-dynasty courtyards as well as hidden cafes, restaurants and bars. Our Hútòng Walking Tour (p72) can help here. See our Sleeping section (p88) for recommendations on how to make this historic area your home while in Běijīng.

Wudaoying Hutong

(五道营胡同; Map p68; Ⓢ Yonghegong Lama Temple) Following the huge success of the Nanluogu Xiang renovation project, Wudaoying Hutong was given a massive facelift a couple of years back, and this once-residential back-alley is now another wannabe trendy lane packed with wi-fi cafes, cute restaurants, boutique shops and a couple of bars. It's nowhere near as popular, or historic as Nanluogu Xiang, but there are some decent places worth visiting; namely Veggie Table (p95), Běijīng's first vegan restaurant, **Natooke** (at No 19-1), the capital's coolest bike shop, and **Vineyard Cafe** (at No 31), every expat's favourite brunch stop.

Dìtán Park

(地坛公园; Dìtán Gōngyuán; Map p68; park admission ¥2, altar ¥5; ☺6am-9pm; Ⓢ Yonghegong-Lama Temple) Directly north of the Lama Temple, but cosmologically juxtaposed with the likes of Temple of Heaven Park and Rìtán Park (p75), Dìtán is the Temple of the Earth. The park, site of imperial sacrifices to the Earth God, lacks the splendour of Temple of Heaven Park but is a popular spot for kite-flying, badminton and morning exercises, and is certainly worth a stroll if you've just been to nearby Lama Temple. During Chinese New Year a huge temple fair is held here. The park's large altar (*fāngzé tán*) is square in shape, symbolising the earth.

TEMPLE OF HEAVEN PARK & DŌNGCHÉNG SOUTH

Temple of Heaven Park

(天坛公园; Tiāntán Gōngyuán; Map p73; Tiantan Donglu; admission park/through ticket ¥15/35, audio tour available at each gate ¥40; ☺park 6am-9pm, sights 8am-6pm; Ⓢ Tiantandongmen) A tranquil oasis of peace and methodical Confucian design in one of China's busiest urban landscapes, the 267-hectare Temple of Heaven Park is encompassed by a long wall with a gate at each compass point. Although not strictly speaking a temple – the Chinese name means 'Altar of Heaven', so don't expect burning incense or worshippers – it originally served as a vast stage for solemn rites performed by the Son of Heaven (a title bestowed on the emperor of the time), who prayed here for good harvests and sought divine clearance and atonement.

The arrangement is typical of Chinese parks, with the imperfections, bumps and wild irregularities of nature largely deleted and the harmonising hand of man accentuated in obsessively straight lines and regular arrangements. This effect is magnified by Confucian objectives, where the human intellect is imposed on the natural world, fashioning order and symmetry. The resulting balance and harmony have an almost haunting – but slightly claustrophobic – beauty. Police whir about in electric buggies as visitors stroll among old buildings, groves of ancient trees and birdsong. Around 4000 ancient, knotted cypresses (some 800 years old, their branches propped up on poles) poke towards the Běijīng skies within the grounds.

Seen from above, the temple halls are round and the bases square, in accordance with the notion 'Tiānyuán Dìfāng' (天圆地方) – 'Heaven is round, Earth is square'. Also observe that the northern rim of the park is semicircular, while its southern end is square. The traditional approach to the temple was from the south, via **Zhāohēng Gate** (昭亨门; Zhāohēng Mén); the north gate is an architectural afterthought.

Central Structures

The highlight of the park, and an icon of Běijīng in its own right, is the **Hall of Prayer for Good Harvests** (祈年殿; Qínián Diàn; admission ¥20), an astonishing structure with a triple-eaved purplish-blue umbrella roof mounted on a three-tiered marble terrace. The wooden pillars (made from Oregon fir) support the ceiling without nails or cement – for a building 38m high and 30m in diam-

Temple of Heaven Park & Dōngchéng South

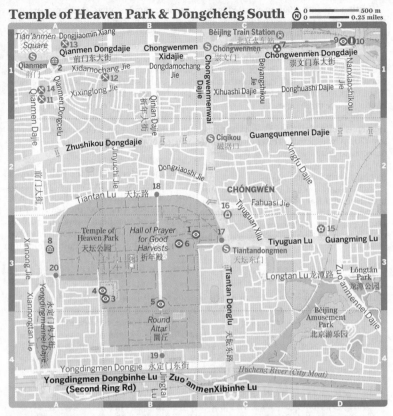

Temple of Heaven Park & Dōngchéng South

⊙ Sights

1 Animal Killing Pavilion	B3
2 Běijīng Railway Museum	A1
3 Divine Music Administration	B3
4 Fasting Palace	A3
5 Imperial Vault of Heaven	B3
6 Long Corridor	B3
7 Ming City Wall Ruins Park	C1
8 Natural History Museum	A3
9 Red Gate Gallery	D1
10 Southeast Corner Watchtower	D1

⊗ Eating

11 Dūyīchù	A1
12 Liqún Roast Duck Restaurant	B1

13 Lost Heaven	A1
14 Qiánmén Quánjùdé Roast Duck Restaurant	A1

☆ Entertainment

15 Red Theatre	D3

⊙ Shopping

16 Hóngqiáo (Pearl) Market	C2

ⓘ Information

17 Temple of Heaven East Gate	C3
18 Temple of Heaven North Gate	B2
19 Temple of Heaven South Gate	B4
20 Temple of Heaven West Gate	A3

eter, that's quite an accomplishment. Embedded in the ceiling is a carved dragon, a symbol of the emperor. Built in 1420, the hall was reduced to carbon after being zapped by

a lightning bolt during the reign of Guangxu in 1889; a faithful reproduction based on Ming architectural methods was erected the following year.

Continuing south along an elevated imperial pathway, you soon reach the octagonal **Imperial Vault of Heaven** (皇穹宇; Huáng Qióngyǔ), which was erected at the same time as the Round Altar, but with its shape echoing the lines of the Hall of Prayer for Good Harvests. The hall contained tablets of the emperor's ancestors, employed during winter solstice ceremonies.

Wrapped around the Imperial Vault of Heaven is **Echo Wall** (回音壁; Huíyīnbì; admission ¥20). A whisper can travel clearly from one end to your friend's ear at the other – unless a cacophonous tour group joins in (get here early for this one).

Immediately south of Echo Wall, the 5m-high **Round Altar** (圜丘; Yuánqiū; admission ¥20) was constructed in 1530 and rebuilt in 1740. Consisting of white marble arrayed in three tiers, its geometry revolves around the imperial number nine. Odd numbers possess heavenly significance, with nine the largest single-digit odd number. Symbolising heaven, the top tier is a huge mosaic of nine rings, each composed of multiples of nine stones, so that the ninth ring equals 81 stones. The stairs and balustrades are similarly presented in multiples of nine. Sounds generated from the centre of the upper terrace undergo amplification from the marble balustrades (the acoustics can get noisy when crowds join in).

Other Notable Structures

Off to the eastern side of the Hall of Prayer for Good Harvests, and with a green-tiled tow-tier roof, the **Animal Killing Pavilion** (宰牲亭; Zǎishēng Tíng) was the venue for the slaughter of sacrificial oxen, sheep, deer and other animals. Today it stands locked and passive but can be admired from the

---

BĚIJĪNG CITY WALLS

Had they been preserved – or even partially protected, Nánjīng-style – rather than almost entirely obliterated in the ideological 1950s and '60s, Běijīng's mighty city walls and imposing gates would rank among China's top sights. Their loss is visceral, for they were once a central part of Běijīng's identity and the city's geographic rationale owed so much to their existence. Many Běijīngers over the age of 50 lament their destruction in the same way they might deplore the devastation of Běijīng's *hútòng*. A disparate collection of original gates (Front Gate, Déshèngmén, the Gate of Heavenly Peace) survive and the occasional portal, such as Yǒngdìng Mén, has been rebuilt, but otherwise the lion's share of Běijīng's grand gates is at one with Nineveh and Tyre.

An epitaph for the city walls, the **Ming City Wall Ruins Park** (明城墙遗志公园; Míng Chéngqiáng Yízhǐ Gōngyuán; Chóngwénmén Dongdajie; Map p73; admission free; ⏰24hr; Ⓢ Chóngwénmén;) runs next to a section of the Ming inner-city wall along the entire length of the northern flank of Chongwenmen Dongdajie. The part-restored wall stretches for around 2km, rising to a height of around 15m and interrupted every 80m with *dūn tái* (buttresses), which extend south from the wall.

The park extends from the former site of Chóngwén Mén (one of the nine gates of the inner city wall) to the **Southeast Corner Watchtower** (东南角楼; Dōngnán Jiǎolóu; Dongbianmen; Map p73; admission ¥10; ⏰8am-5.30pm; Ⓢ Jiànguómén or Chōngwénmén;). Its green-tiled, twin-eaved roof rising up imperiously, this splendid Ming-dynasty fortification is punctured with 144 archer's windows. The highly impressive interior has some staggering carpentry: huge red pillars surge upwards, topped with solid beams. On the 1st floor is the superb **Red Gate Gallery** (红门画廊; Hóngmén Huàláng; www.redgate gallery.com; admission free; ⏰10am-5pm); say you are visiting the Red Gate Gallery and the ¥10 entry fee to the watchtower is waived. An exhibition on the 2nd floor details the history of Běijīng's city gates and includes some fascinating old photographs.

Humble counterpart of the Southeast Corner Watchtower, the **Southwest Corner Watchtower** (西便门角楼; Xībiànmén Jiǎolóu; Map p80) is not as impressive as its famous sibling, but you can climb up onto a section of the old city wall amid the roaring traffic.

In an excavated pit on Beiheyan Dajie, east of the Forbidden City, sits a pitiful stump – all that remains of the magnificent **Dōng'ān Mén** (Map p62), the east gate of the Imperial City. The remains are located in the **Imperial Wall Foundation Ruins Park** (Map p62), a slender strip of park following the footprint of the eastern side of the vanished Imperial City Wall.

outside. Stretching out from here runs a **Long Corridor** (Chángláng), where locals sit out and deal cards, listen to the radio, play keyboards, practise Běijīng opera, try dance moves and kick hacky-sacks. Just north of here is a large and very popular exercise park.

In the west of the park, sacrificial music was rehearsed at the **Divine Music Administration** (Shényuè Shǔ), while wild cats inhabit the dry moat of the green-tiled **Fasting Palace**.

Běijīng Railway Museum
MUSEUM
(北京铁路博物馆; Běijīng Tiělù Bówùguǎn; Map p73; ☑6705 1638; 2A Qianmen Dongdajie; 前门东大街2A号; admission ¥20; ☉9am-5pm Tue-Sun; ⑤Qianmen) Located in the historic former Qiánmén Railway Station, which once connected Běijīng to Tiānjīn, this museum offers an engaging history of the development of the capital and China's railway system, with plenty of photos and models. Its size, though, means it doesn't have many actual trains. But there is a life-size model of the cab of one of China's new high-speed trains which you can clamber into (¥10). Hardcore trainspotters should make tracks for the **China Railway Museum** (中国铁道博物馆; Zhōngguó Tiědào Bówùguǎn; ☑6438 1519; Jiuxianqiao North Rd, Chaoyang District; 朝阳区酒仙桥北路1号院北侧; ¥20; ☉9am-4pm Tue-Sun) on the far northeastern outskirts of Běijīng, which is vast and has far more loco action.

Natural History Museum
MUSEUM
(自然博物馆; Zìrán Bówùguǎn; Map p73; 126 Tianqiao Nandajie; admission ¥10; ☉8.30am-5pm Tue-Sun, last tickets 4pm; ⑤Qiánmén or Tiantandongmen) The main entrance hall to the recently restored Natural History Museum is hung with portraits of the great natural historians, including Darwin and Linnaeus. Escort kiddies to the revamped dinosaur hall facing you as you enter, which presents itself with an overarching skeleton of a *Mamenchisaurus jingyanensis* – a vast sauropod that once roamed China – and a much smaller *protoceratops*.

SĀNLǏTÚN & CHÁOYÁNG

Dōngyuè Temple
TAOIST TEMPLE
(东岳庙; Dōngyuè Miào; Map p76; 141 Chaoyangmenwai Dajie; adult ¥10, with guide ¥40; ☉8.30am-4.30pm Tue-Sun; ⑤Chaoyangmen) Dedicated to the Eastern Peak (Tài Shān) of China's five Taoist mountains, the morbid Taoist shrine of Dōngyuè Temple is an unsettling albeit fascinating experience. With its roots poking deep into the Yuan dynasty, what's above ground level has been revived with care and investment. Dōngyuè Temple is an active place of worship where Taoist monks attend to a world entirely at odds with the surrounding glass-and-steel high-rises. Note the temple's fabulous *páifāng* (memorial archway) lying to the south, divorced from its shrine by the intervention of the busy main road, Chaoyangmenwai Dajie.

FREE Rìtán Park
PARK
(日坛公园; Rìtán Gōngyuán; Ritan Lu; Map p76; ☉6am-9pm; ⑤Chaoyangmen) Meaning 'Altar of the Sun', Rìtán (pronounced 'rer-tan') is arguably the most pleasant area to spend time in this part of Běijīng. One of a set of imperial parks, which covers each compass point, Rìtán dates from 1530 and is the eastern counterpart to the likes of Temple of Heaven (p72) and Temple of Earth (Dìtán Park; p72). The altar is now little more than a raised platform, but the surrounding park is beautifully landscaped and a popular city-centre escape. Activities include dancing, singing, kite flying, rock-climbing (¥30 to ¥50), table tennis and pond fishing (¥5 per hour). Otherwise, just stroll around and enjoy the flora, or head to one of the park's pleasant cafes; the standout one is **Stone Boat** (石舫咖啡; Shífǎng Kāfēi; beer & coffee from ¥25, cocktails from ¥35; ☉10am-10pm), located by a large landscaped pond.

CCTV Building
ARCHITECTURE
(央视大楼; Yāngshì Dàlóu; Map p76; 32 Dongsanhuan Zhonglu; ⑤Jintaixizhao) Shaped like an enormous pair of trousers, and known locally as Dà Kùchǎ (大裤衩), or Big Underpants, the astonishing CCTV Tower is an architect's wet dream. Its overhang (the bum in the pants) seems to defy gravity and is made possible by an unusual engineering design which creates a three-dimensional cranked loop, supported by an irregular grid on its surface. Designed by Rem Koolhaas and Ole Scheeren of OMA, the building is an audacious statement of modernity (despite its nickname) and has created a unique addition to the Běijīng skyline.

Bird's Nest & Water Cube
ARCHITECTURE
(国家体育场、国家游泳中心; Guójiā Tǐyùchǎng & Guójiā Yóuyǒng Zhōngxīn; Map p52; Bird's Nest ¥50; ☉9am-5.30pm; Water Cube ¥30; ☉9am-6.30pm; ⑤Olympic Sports Centre) So quiet and desolate these days, it's hard to imagine that this was the scene of such great sporting exultation in 2008, but such is the fate of most

Sānlǐtún & Cháoyáng

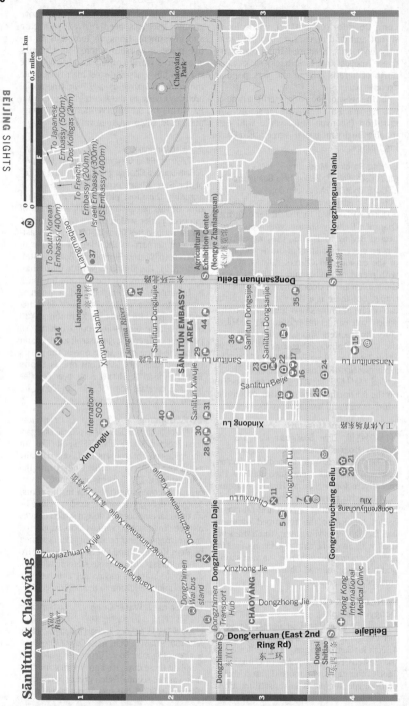

Ch\u00e1oy\u00e1ng Park

To Japanese
Embassy (500m);
Dos Kolegas (2km)

To French
Embassy (200m);
Israeli Embassy (300m);
US Embassy (400m)

To South Korean
Embassy (400m)

Liangmaqiao
Lu

Liangmaqiao

Liangma River

Xinyuan Nanlu

International
SOS

Xin Donglu

Zuojiazhuang Xijie

Zuojiazhuang Lu

Xiliu River

Dongzhimenwai Xiejie
新东门外斜街

Dongzhimenwai Xie jie

Xiangheyuan Xijie

Dongzhimen
Wai bus stand

Dongzhimenwai Dajie

Dongzhimen
Transport
Hub

Xinzhong Jie

CHÁOYÁNG

Dongzhong Jie

Dongzhimen

Dong'erhuan (East 2nd
Ring Rd)
东二环

Dongsi
Shitiao
东四十条

Agricultural
Exhibition Center
(Nongye Zhanlanguan)
农业展览馆

Dongsanhuan Beilu

Nongzhanguan Nanlu

Tuanjiehu
团结湖

Sanlitun Donglujie

SANLITUN EMBASSY
AREA

Sanlitun Dongsijie

Sanlitun Dongsanjie

Sanlitun Xiwujie

Sanlitun
Lu

SANLITUN EMBASSY
AREA

Sanlitun Beijie

Xindong Lu

Nansanlitun Lu

Xingfucun Lu

Chunxiu Lu

Xingfucun Lu

Gongrentiyuchang Beilu

Gongrentiyuchang
Xilu

Hong Kong
International
Medical Clinic

Beidajie

14

37

41

44

29

36

23

22

17

16

9

35

15

24

25

19

40

31

30

28

5

11

7

10

20

21

0   0.5 miles
0   1 km
N

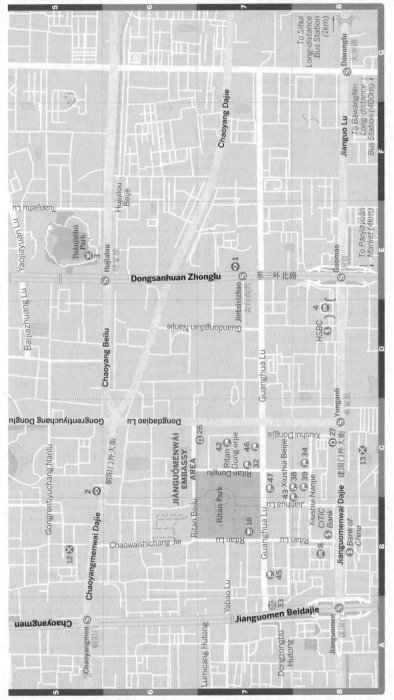

To Sìhuì
Long-distance
Bus Station
(1km)

Dawanglu 大望路 S

Jianguo Lu

To Bāwángfén
Long-distance
Bus Station (400m)

To Panjiāyuán
Market (4km)

Dawanglu 大望路

Tuānjiéhú
Park

Tuānjiéhú
Park 3

Hujialou
呼家楼

Hujialou
Beijie

Chaoyang Dajie

Yaojiayuan Lu

Baijiazhuang Lu

Chaoyang Beilu

Gongrentiyuchang Donglu

Gongrentiyuchang Nanlu

Chaoyangmenwai Dajie

Chaoyangmen S
朝阳门

Chaoyang Dajie

Hujialou S

Dongsanhuan Zhonglu 东三环北路

1

Jintaixizhao
金台夕照 S

Guandongdian Nanjie

Guanghua Lu

Dongdaqiao Lu

JIÀNGUÓMÉNWÀI
EMBASSY
AREA

Rìtán Park

Ritan Beilu

Chaowaishichang Jie

Yabao Lu

Lumicang Hutong

Dongzongbu
Hutong

Jianguomen Beidajie

Jianguomen S
建国门

Ritan Lu

Guanghua Lu

Jianhua Lu

Ritan Lu

Xiushui Nanjie

CITIC
Bank

Bank of
China

Jianguomenwai Dajie 建国门外大街

Guomao 国贸 S

HSBC S
4

Yonganli 永安里 S

Xiushui Dongjie

建国门外大街 27

13

26

42

Ritan
Dong erjie

46

32

47

43 Xiushui Beijie

38

39

34

18

12

45

33

8

2

Sānlǐtún & Cháoyáng

◎ Sights
1 CCTV Building.............................E7
2 Dōngyuè Temple.....................C5

✚ Activities, Courses & Tours
3 Tuánjiéhú Park swimming pool.............E5

🛏 Sleeping
4 China World Hotel....................D8
5 Holiday Inn Express..................B3
6 Opposite House Hotel...............D3
7 Sānlǐtún Youth Hostel..............C4
8 St Regis....................................B8
9 Yoyo Hotel D3

✖ Eating
10 Bàodǔ Huáng...........................B2
  Běi.....................................(see 6)
11 Jīngzūn Peking Duck................C3
12 Jíxiángniǎo Xiāngcài...............B5
13 Nájiā Xiǎoguǎn........................C8
14 Sānyuánlǐ Market.....................D1

🍸 Drinking
  Apothecary ....(see 17)
15 Bookworm D4
16 First Floor D3
  Migas ....(see 17)
17 Nali Patio...............................D3
  Saddle Cantina ....(see 16)
18 Stone Boat B7
19 Tree..D3

✦ Entertainment
20 Mix C4

21 Vics..C4

🛍 Shopping
22 3.3 Shopping Centre...............D3
23 Sānlǐtún Village (North)...........D3
24 Sānlǐtún Village (South) D4
25 Sānlǐtún Yashow Clothing
  Market................................D4
26 Shard Box Store.....................C7
27 Silk Market.............................C8

ℹ Information
28 Australian Embassy.................C2
29 Cambodian Embassy................D2
30 Canadian Embassy..................C2
31 German Embassy.....................C2
32 Indian Embassy.......................C7
33 International Post Office A7
34 Irish Embassy.........................C8
35 Italian Embassy.......................E3
36 Laotian Embassy.....................D3
37 Lufthansa Centre.....................E1
38 Mongolian Embassy................C8
39 Mongolian Embassy (visa
  section)..............................C8
40 Nepalese Embassy..................C2
41 Netherlands Embassy..............E2
42 New Zealand Embassy.............C7
43 Singapore Embassy.................C8
44 South African Embassy............D2
45 Thai Embassy..........................B7
46 UK Embassy............................C7
47 Vietnamese Embassy...............C7

Olympics projects. Squinting in the sun, guards in ill-fitting black combat gear point the occasional group of map-clutching domestic tourists to the signature National Stadium, known colloquially as the Bird's Nest (鸟巢; Niǎocháo). Occasional events are held here, but it's generally empty. Nevertheless, it's still an iconic piece of architecture, as is the bubble-covered National Aquatics Centre (aka the Water Cube) next door, which is at least being put to some use, now housing Happy Magic Water Park (p87).

**China Science &
Technology Museum** MUSEUM
(中国科技馆; Zhōngguó Kējìguǎn; Map p52; 5 Beichendong Lu; 北辰东路5号; adult/child ¥30/20; ◎9.30am-5pm Tue-Sun; ⑤South Gate of Forest Park) About 8km north of the city centre, and a big favourite with kids, this huge facility has an array of hands-on scientific exhibitions, a science playground and state-of-the-art 3D and '4D' cinemas. Walk east from South Gate of Forest Park subway station, then take the second right (10 minutes).

BĚIHǍI PARK & XĪCHÉNG NORTH
Běihǎi Park PARK
(北海公园; Běihǎi Gōngyuán; Map p80; admission high/low season ¥10/5, through ticket high/low season ¥20/15; ◎6am-9pm, sights until 5pm; ⑤Xisi or Nanluogu Xiang) Běihǎi Park, northwest of the Forbidden City, is largely occupied by the North Sea (běihǎi), a huge lake that freezes in winter and blooms with lotuses in summer. Old folk dance together

outside temple halls and come twilight, young couples cuddle on benches. It's a restful place to stroll around, rent a rowing boat in summer and watch calligraphers practising characters on paving slabs with fat brushes and water.

The site is associated with Kublai Khan's palace, Běijīng's navel before the arrival of the Forbidden City. All that survives of the Khan's court is a large jar made of green jade in the **Round City** (团城; Tuánchéng), near the southern entrance. Also within the Round City is the **Chengguang Hall** (Chéngguāng Diàn), where a white jade statue of Sakyamuni from Myanmar (Burma) can be found, its arm wounded by the allied forces that swarmed through Běijīng in 1900 to quash the Boxer Rebellion. At the time of writing, the Round City was closed to visitors.

Attached to the North Sea, the South (Nánhǎi) and Middle (Zhōnghǎi) Seas to the south lend their name to **Zhōngnánhǎi** (literally 'Middle and South Seas'), the heavily-guarded compound less than a mile south of the park where the Chinese Communist Party's top leadership live.

Topping **Jade Islet** (琼岛; Qióngdǎo) on the lake, the 36m-high Tibetan-style **White Dagoba** (白塔; Báitǎ) was built in 1651 for a visit by the Dalai Lama, and was rebuilt in 1741. Climb up to the dagoba via the **Yǒng'ān Temple** (永安寺; Yǒng'ān Sì).

WORTH A TRIP

798 ART DISTRICT

A vast area of disused factories built by the East Germans, **798 Art District** (798艺术区; Qī Jiǔ Bā Yìshù Qū; Map p52;), also known as **Dà Shānzi** (大山子), is Běijīng's leading concentration of contemporary art galleries.

The industrial complex celebrates its proletarian roots in the communist heyday of the 1950s via retouched red Maoist slogans decorating gallery interiors and statues of burly, lantern-jawed workers dotting the lanes. The voluminous factory workshops are ideally suited to art galleries that require space for multimedia installations and other ambitious projects.

You could easily spend half a day wandering around the complex. Signboards with English-language maps on them dot the lanes.

Galleries

Some are more innovative than others. Highlights include:

BTAP (Ceramics Third St; ☺Tue-Sun) One of 798's original galleries.

UCCA (798 Rd) Big-money gallery with exhibition halls, a funky shop and a small cinema screening films (¥15) most days. Thursday is free.

Pace (797 Rd) Wonderfully large space holding some top-quality exhibitions.

Galleria Continua (just south of 797 Rd) Another large space; below a towering, hard-to-miss, brick chimney.

Eating & Drinking

Most places have fresh coffee, free wi-fi, Western food and English menus.

At Cafe (798 Rd; ☺10am-11pm) 798's first cafe and a popular hangout for artists.

Timezone 8 (798 Rd; ☺8.30am-8pm) Cool cafe attached to the best art bookshop in Běijīng.

Happy Rooster (cnr 7 Star Rd & Ceramics First St; ☺9.30am-9pm) Cheapest decent Chinese restaurant in 798. Has picture menu, plus coffee and wi-fi.

Getting There & Away

From Exit C of Dongzhimen subway station, take Bus 909 (¥2) for about 6km northeast to Dashanzi Lukou Nan (大山子路口南), where you'll see the big red 798 sign. Buses run until 8.30pm.

A further extensive colony of art galleries can be found around 3km northeast of 798 Art District at **Cǎochǎngdì** (草场地). Bus 909 continues here.

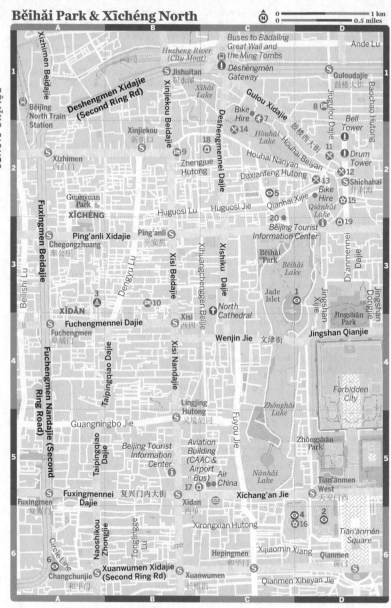

Xītiān Fánjìng (西天梵境; Western Paradise), situated on the northern shore of the lake, is a lovely temple (admission to which is included in the park ticket). The nearby **Nine Dragon Screen** (九龙壁; Jiǔlóng Bì), a 5m-high and 27m-long spirit wall, is a glimmering stretch of coloured glazed tiles depicting coiling dragons, similar to its counterpart in the Forbidden City. West, along the shore, is the pleasant **Little Western Heaven** (小西天; Xiǎo Xītiān), a further shrine.

Běihǎi Park & Xīchéng North

◎ Sights
1 Běihǎi Park.................................D3
2 Great Hall of the People..............D6
3 Miàoyīng Temple White Dagoba..........A3
4 National Centre for the
   Performing Arts.......................D6
5 Prince Gong's Residence.............C2
6 Southwest Corner Watchtower..........A6

◎ Activities, Courses & Tours
7 Hòuhǎi Exercise Ground...............C1

◎ Sleeping
8 Drum Tower Youth Hostel.............D1
9 Red Lantern East Courtyard..........B2
10 Red Lantern House West Yard........B3

◎ Eating
11 4Corners...............................D2

12 Běipíngjū...............................D2
13 Hutong Pizza..........................D2
14 Kǒng Yǐjǐ..............................C2

◎ Entertainment
15 East Shore Jazz Café.................D2
   Grand Opera House ....(see 5)
16 National Centre for the
   Performing Arts.....................D6

◎ Shopping
17 Běijīng Books Building...............B5
18 Rùndélì Food Market.................C2
19 Three Stone Kite Shop..............D3

◎ Information
20 Cycle Rickshaw tours ticket
   office................................C3

FREE Capital Museum   MUSEUM
(中国首都博物馆; Zhōngguó Shǒudū Bówùguǎn; 6337 0491; www.capitalmuseum.org.cn; 16 Fuxingmenwai Dajie; 9am-5pm; Muxidi) Behind the riveting good looks of the Capital Museum are some first-rate galleries, including a mesmerising collection of ancient Buddhist statues and a lavish exhibition of Chinese porcelain. There is also an interesting chronological history of Běijīng, an exhibition that is dedicated to cultural relics of Peking opera, a fascinating Běijīng Folk Customs exhibition, and displays of ancient bronzes, calligraphy and paintings. Bring your passport for free entry. The museum is 400m east of Muxidi station.

Hòuhǎi Lakes   LAKES
(后海; Hòuhǎi; Map p80; Shichahai, Nanluogu Xiang or Jishuitan) Also known as Shíchàhǎi (什刹海) but mostly just referred to collectively as 'Hòuhǎi', the Hòuhǎi Lakes are compromised of three lakes: Qiánhǎi ('Front Lake'), Hòuhǎi ('Back Lake') and Xīhǎi ('West Lake'), two of which (Qiánhǎi and Hòuhǎi) are linked. They are one of the capital's favourite outdoor spots and provide great people-spotting action.

During the day, people fish, fly kites or just meander along. In the evening, the area turns into one of the more popular nightlife areas, as the restaurants, bars and cafes that surround the lakes spring into life and the lakes become a mass of pedalos circling round and round.

Numerous places by the lakeshores hire out bikes by the hour (¥10 per hour, ¥200 deposit). There are many spots to rent pedalos too (¥80 per hour, ¥300 deposit), if you want to take to the water (some locals swim in the lakes, but we wouldn't advise that).

The lakes look majestic in the winter, when they freeze over and become the best place in Běijīng to ice skate. Local vendors appear magically at this time of year, with all the gear you'll need.

Prince Gong's Residence   HISTORIC RESIDENCE
(恭王府; Gōngwáng Fǔ; Map p80; 8328 8149; 14 Liuyin Jie; admission ¥40, guided tours incl tea & opera performance ¥70; 7.30am-4.30pm summer, 8am-4pm winter; Pinganli or Shichahai) Reputed to be the model for the mansion in Cao Xueqin's 18th-century classic *Dream of the Red Mansions*, this huge courtyard is one of Běijīng's largest private residential compounds. If you can, get here ahead of the tour buses and admire the rockeries, plants, pools, pavilions, corridors and elaborately carved gateways. Arrive with the crowds and you won't want to stay. Performances of Běijīng opera are held regularly in the Qing-dynasty **Grand Opera House** (大戏楼; Dàxì Lóu) in the east of the grounds.

National Centre for the
Performing Arts (NCPA)   THEATRE
(国家大剧院; Guójiā Dàjùyuàn; Map p80; 2 Xichang'an Jie; 西长安街2号; www.chncpa.org/ens; admission ¥40; 9am-5pm Tue-Sun;

S Tian'anmen West) Critics have compared it to an egg, but it looks more like a massive mercury bead, an ultramodern missile silo, or the futuristic lair of a James Bond villain. Sometimes known as the National Grand Theatre, and now one of Běijīng's key cultural hubs, the NCPA rises like some huge reflective mushroom nosing up from the ground.

Examine the bulbous interior, including the titanic steel ribbing of interior bolsters (each of the 148 bolsters weighs 8 tonnes). Inside, you can tour the three halls, although individual ones are occasionally shut. Check the website for upcoming performances (tickets ¥80-800).

Great Hall of the People
HISTORIC SITE

(人民大会堂; Rénmín Dàhuítáng; Map p80; adult ¥30, bag deposit ¥5; ⊗8.30am-3pm; S Tian'anmen West) On the western side of Tiān'ānmén Sq – on a site previously occupied by Taichang Temple, the Jinyiwei (Ming-dynasty secret service) and the Ministry of Justice – the Great Hall of the People is the venue of the legislature, the National People's Congress (NPC). The 1959 architecture is monolithic, and a fitting symbol of China's political inertia. The tour parades visitors past a choice of 29 of its lifeless rooms named after the provinces of the Chinese universe. Also here is the 10,000-seat auditorium with the familiar red star embedded in a galaxy of ceiling lights. The Hall is closed to the public when the NPC is in session. The ticket office is down the south side of the building. Bags must be checked in but cameras are admitted.

Miàoyīng Temple
White Dagoba
BUDDHIST TEMPLE

(妙应寺白塔; Miàoyīng Sì Báitǎ; Map p80; 171 Fuchengmennei Dajie; admission ¥20; ⊗9am-5pm Tue-Sun; S Fuchengmen) Towering over the surrounding *hútòng*, the Miàoyīng Temple slumbers beneath its distinctive chalk-white Yuan-dynasty pagoda, which was being refurbished at the time of writing. The highlight of a visit here is its diverse collection of Buddhist statuary: pop into the Hall of the Great Enlightened One (大觉宝殿; Dàjué Bǎodiàn), which glitters splendidly with hundreds of Tibetan Buddhist effigies. In other halls reside a four-faced effigy of Guanyin (Goddess of Mercy, and here called Parnashavari), as well as a trinity of the past, present and future Buddhas and a population of bronze *luóhàn* fig-

ures. After you finish here, exit the temple and wander the tangle of local alleyways for earthy shades of *hútòng* life.

White Cloud Temple
TAOIST TEMPLE

(白云观; Báiyún Guàn; Baiyunguan Jie; admission ¥10; ⊗8.30am-4.30pm May-Sep, to 4pm Oct-Apr; S Muxidi) Founded in AD 739, White Cloud Temple is a lively complex of shrines and courtyards, tended by distinctive Taoist monks with their hair twisted into topknots. Today's temple halls principally date from Ming and Qing times.

Near the temple entrance, a queue snakes slowly through the gate for a chance to rub a polished stone carving for good fortune. Drop by the White Cloud Temple during Chinese New Year for a magnificent *miàohuì* (temple fair).

To find the temple, walk east from Muxidi subway station on Fuxingmenwai Dajie for 400m and then turn right on Baiyun Lu and walk south until you reach Baiyunguan Jie. Turn left there and the temple is 50m ahead on the left.

DASHILAR & XĪCHÉNG SOUTH
Dashilar
HISTORIC SHOPPING STREET

(大栅栏; Dàshílán'er; Map p83; S Qianmen) Just west of Qianmen Dajie is this centuries-old shopping street. While it has been given a makeover, which has sadly robbed it of much of its charm, many of the shops are the same ones which have been here for hundreds of years and are well worth a browse for the sometimes esoteric goods – ancient herbal remedies, handmade cloth shoes – they sell.

Nuí Jiē Mosque
MOSQUE

(牛街礼拜寺; Niújiē Lǐbài Sì; off Map p83; 88 Niu Jie; admission ¥10, Muslims free; ⊗8am-sunset; S Caishikou) Dating back to the 10th century and lively with worshippers on Fridays (it's closed to non-Muslims at prayer times), Běijīng's largest mosque is the centre of the community for the 10,000 or so Huí Chinese Muslims who live nearby. The Chinese-styled mosque is pleasantly decorated with plants and flourishes of Arabic – look out for the main prayer hall (note that only Muslims can enter), women's quarters and the Building for Observing the Moon (望月楼; Wàngyuèlóu), from where the lunar calendar was calculated. Remember to dress appropriately (no shorts or short skirts). The mosque is about 1km from Caishikou subway station. Walk west out of the station then turn left down Niu Jie (牛街) and the mosque will soon be on your left.

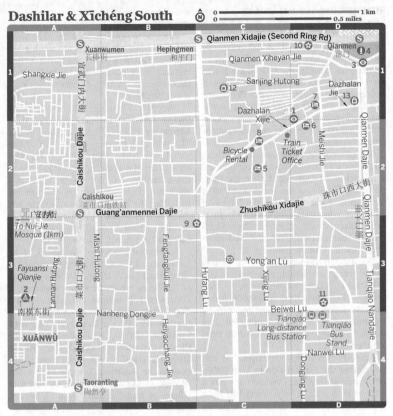

Dashilar & Xīchéng South

⊙ Sights
1 Dashilar	D1
2 Fǎyuán Temple	A3
3 Qiánmén Decorative Arch	D1
4 Zhèngyáng Gate Arrow Tower	D1

🛏 Sleeping
5 Leo Courtyard	C2
6 Leo Hostel	D2
7 Qiánmén Hostel	D1
8 Three-Legged Frog Hostel	C2

✪ Entertainment
9 Húguǎng Guild Hall	C3
10 Lao She Teahouse	D1
11 Tiānqiáo Acrobatics Theatre	D3

🛍 Shopping
12 Liulichang Xijie	C1
13 Ruìfúxiáng	D1

Fǎyuán Temple　　　　BUDDHIST TEMPLE
(法源寺; Fǎyuán Sì; Map p83; 7 Fayuansi Qianjie; admission ¥5; ⊙8.30-5pm; ⑤Caishikou) With its air of monastic reverence and busy monks, this bustling temple east of Niú Jiē Mosque was originally constructed in the 7th century. Now the China Buddhism College, the temple follows a typical Buddhist layout, but make your way to the fourth hall for its standout copper **Buddha** seated atop four further Buddhas, themselves atop a huge bulb of myriad effigies. Within the Guanyin Hall is a Ming-dynasty Thousand Hand and Thousand Eye Guanyin, while a huge supine Buddha reclines in the rear hall.

SUMMER PALACE & HǍIDIÀN

Summer Palace   HISTORIC SITE

(颐和园; Yíhé Yuán; Map p86; 19 Xinjian Gongmen; ticket ¥30, through ticket ¥60, audio guide ¥40; ◎8:30am-5pm; ⑤Xiyuan or Beigongmen) Virtually as mandatory a Běijīng sight as the Great Wall or the Forbidden City, this former playground for emperors fleeing the suffocating summer torpor of the old imperial city easily merits an entire day's exploration, although a (high-paced) morning or afternoon may suffice.

The grounds, temples, gardens, pavilions, lakes, bridges, gate-towers and corridors are a marvel of landscaping. Unlike the overpowering flatland of the Forbidden City or the considered harmonies of the Temple of Heaven, the Summer Palace – with its huge lake, hilltop views and energising walks – offers a pastoral escape into the landscapes of traditional Chinese painting.

The domain had long been a royal garden before being considerably enlarged and embellished by Emperor Qianlong in the 18th century. He marshalled a 100,000-strong army of labourers to deepen and expand **Kūnmíng Lake** (昆明湖; Kūnmíng Hú), and reputedly surveyed imperial navy drills from a hilltop perch.

Anglo-French troops vandalised the palace during the Second Opium War (1856–60). Empress Dowager Cixi launched into a refit in 1888 with money earmarked for a modern navy; the marble boat at the northern edge of the lake was her only nautical, albeit quite unsinkable, concession.

Foreign troops, angered by the Boxer Rebellion, had another go at torching the Summer Palace in 1900, prompting further restoration work. By 1949 the palace had once more fallen into disrepair, eliciting a major overhaul.

Glittering Kūnmíng Lake swallows up three-quarters of the park, overlooked by **Longevity Hill** (万寿山; Wànshòu Shān). The principal structure is the **Hall of Benevolence and Longevity** (仁寿殿; Rénshòu Diàn; Map p86), by the east gate, housing a hardwood throne and attached to a courtyard decorated with bronze animals, including the mythical *qílín* (a hybrid animal that only appeared on earth at times of harmony). Unfortunately, the hall is barricaded off so you will have to peer in.

An elegant stretch of woodwork along the northern shore, the **Long Corridor** (长廊; Cháng Láng) is trimmed with a plethora of paintings, while the slopes and crest of Longevity Hill behind are adorned with Buddhist temples. Slung out uphill on a north-south axis, the **Buddhist Fragrance Pavilion** (佛香阁; Fóxiāng Gé) and the **Cloud Dispelling Hall** (排云殿; Páiyún Diàn) are linked by corridors. Crowning the peak is the **Buddhist Temple of the Sea of Wisdom** (智慧海; Zhìhuì Hǎi), tiled with effigies of Buddha, many with obliterated heads.

WORTH A TRIP

BOTANIC GARDENS

Exploding with blossom in spring, the well-tended **Botanic Gardens** (北京植物园; Běijīng Zhíwùyuán; Map p110; adult ¥10, through ticket ¥45; ◎6am-9pm summer, last entry 7pm, 7am-7pm winter, last entry 5pm; ⑤Xiyuan or Yuanmingyuan, then ▣331), set against the backdrop of the Western Hills and about 1km northeast of Fragrant Hills Park, make for a pleasant outing among bamboo fronds, pines, orchids, lilacs and China's most extensive botanic collection. Containing a rainforest house, the standout **Běijīng Botanical Gardens Conservatory** (admission with through ticket; ◎8.30am-4pm) bursts with 3000 different varieties of plants.

About a 15-minute walk from the front gate (follow the signs), but within the grounds of the gardens, is the **Sleeping Buddha Temple** (Wòfó Sì; adult ¥5, or entry with through ticket; ◎8am-5pm). The temple, first built during the Tang dynasty, houses a huge reclining effigy of Sakyamuni weighing 54 tonnes.

On the eastern side of the gardens is the **Cao Xueqin Memorial** (Cáo Xuěqín Jìniànguǎn; 39 Zhengbaiqi; admission ¥10, or entry with through ticket; ◎8.30am-4.15pm), where Cao Xueqin lived in his latter years. Cao (1715–63) is credited with penning the classic *Dream of the Red Mansions*, a vast and lengthy family saga set in the Qing period. Making a small buzz in the west of the gardens is the little **China Honey Bee Museum** (☑8.30am-4.30pm Mar-Oct).

THE HUTONG

Hidden down a maze of narrow alleys, **The Hutong** (Map p68; ☑159 0104 6127, www. thehutong.com; 1 Jiudaowan Zhongxiang Hutong, off Shique Hutong; 北新桥石雀胡同九道弯中巷胡同1号; ⊗9am-9pm; ⑤Beixinqiao) is a highly recommended Chinese-culture centre, run by a group of extremely knowledgeable expats and skilled locals. Classes are held in a peaceful converted courtyard, and focus on three main areas:

Cookery (¥250; ⊗10.30am, 2.30pm & 7pm) Hugely popular, and run three times a day, the focus is on cuisine from around China, but other Asian-cuisine classes are also run. Some classes include trips to a local food market.

Chinese Tea (☑135 0112 6093; www.t-journeys.com; tea tasting/tea-market tours ¥160/250) The Hutong's 'Tea Journeys' are a wonderfully accessible way to learn about this ancient Chinese tradition. They also sell beautifully packaged own-brand teas (¥110–¥180).

Traditional Chinese Medicine (☑150 1151 0363; www.straightbamboo.com; ⊗8am-6pm Sun-Thu) Run by Alex Tan, an Australian-Chinese TCM expert, classes range from introductions to qi gōng, yoga and Taoism as well as to Chinese medicine itself.

Getting There & Away

Come out of Exit C of Beixinqiao subway station and turn left onto Shique Hutong. Take the second right down the very narrow Jiudaowanxi Xiang (九道弯西巷), then take the first left followed by the first right and you'll see The Hutong on your right.

Cixi's **marble boat** (清晏船; Qīngyàn Chuán) sits immobile on the north shore, south of some fine Qing **boathouses** (船坞; Chuán Wù). When the lake is not frozen, you can traverse Kūnmíng Lake by ferry to **South Lake Island** (南湖岛; Nánhú Dǎo), where Cixi went to beseech the **Dragon King Temple** (龙王庙; Lóngwáng Miào) for rain in times of drought. A graceful **17-arch bridge** (十七孔桥; Shíqīkǒng Qiáo) spans the 150m to the eastern shore of the lake. In warm weather, **pedal boats** (4-/6-person boat per hr ¥40/60; ⊗8.30am-4.30pm in summer) are also available from the dock.

Try to do a circuit of the lake along the **West Causeway** (Xīdī) to return along the east shore (or vice versa). It gets you away from the crowds, the views are gorgeous and it's a great cardiovascular workout. Based on the Su Causeway in Hángzhōu, and lined with willow and mulberry trees, the causeway kicks off just west of the boathouses. With its delightful hump, the grey and white marble **Jade Belt Bridge** (Yùdài Qiáo) dates from the reign of emperor Qianlong and crosses the point where the Jade River (Yùhé) enters the lake (when it flows).

Towards the North Palace Gate, **Sūzhōu Street** (苏州街; Sūzhōu Jiē) is an entertaining and light-hearted diversion of riverside walkways, shops and eateries, whcih are designed to mimic the famous Jiāngsū canal town.

Old Summer Palace HISTORIC SITE
(圆明园; Yuánmíng Yuán; Map p86; admission ¥10, palace ruins ¥25, map ¥6; ⊗7am-7pm; ⑤Yuanmingyuan) Forever etched on China's national consciousness for its sacking and destruction by British and French forces during the Second Opium War, the old Summer Palace was originally laid out in the 12th century. Resourceful Jesuits were later employed by Emperor Qianlong to fashion European-style palaces for the gardens, incorporating elaborate fountains and baroque statuary. During its looting, much went up in flames and considerable booty was sent abroad, but a melancholic tangle of broken columns and marble chunks from the hardier Jesuit-designed stone palace buildings remain.

The subdued marble ruins of the **Palace Buildings Scenic Area** (Xīyánglóu Jǐngqū) can be mulled over in the **Eternal Spring Garden** (Chángchūn Yuán) in the northeast of the park, near the east gate. There were once over 10 buildings here, designed by Giuseppe Castiglione and Michael Benoist.

The **Great Fountain Ruins** (大水法遗址; Dàshuǐfǎ Yízhǐ) themselves are considered the best-preserved relics. Built in

Summer Palace

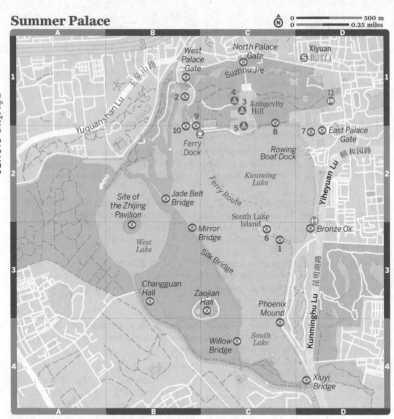

1759, the main building was fronted by a lion-head fountain. Standing opposite is the **Guānshuǐfǎ** (观水法), five large stone screens embellished with European carvings of military flags, armour, swords and guns. The screens were discovered in the grounds of Peking University in the 1970s and later restored to their original positions.

West of the Great Fountain Ruins are the vestiges of the **Hǎiyàntáng Reservoir** (海宴堂蓄水池台基; Hǎiyàntáng Xùshuǐchí Tǎijī), where the water for the impressive fountains was stored in a tower and huge water-lifting devices were employed. Also known as the Water Clock, the **Hǎiyàntáng**, where 12 bronze human statues with animal heads jetted water in 12 two-hour sequences, was constructed in 1759. The 12 animal heads from this apparatus were distributed among collections abroad, and Běijīng is attempting to retrieve them (four animal heads can be seen at the Poly Art Museum (p66). Just

west of here is the **Fāngwàiguàn**, a building turned into a mosque for an Imperial concubine; an artful reproduction of a former labyrinth called the **Garden of Yellow Flowers** (迷宫; Mígōng) is also nearby.

The gardens cover a huge area – some 2.5km from east to west – so be prepared for some walking. Bus 331 goes from the south gate (which is by Exit B of Yuanmingyuan subway station) to the east gate of the **Summer Palace** (p84) before continuing to the **Botanic Gardens** (p84) and eventually terminating at **Fragrant Hills Park** (p88).

Great Bell Temple
BUDDHIST TEMPLE
(大钟寺; Dàzhōng Sì; Map p52; 31a Beisanhuan Xilu; admission ¥20; ⊙9am-4.30pm Tue-Sun; ⑤Dazhongsi) Once a shrine where Qing emperors prayed for rain, the temple today is named after its gargantuan Ming-dynasty bell: 6.75m tall and weighing a hefty 46.5 tonnes, the colossal bell was cast in 1406 and is inscribed with Buddhist sutras, compris-

Summer Palace

◉ Sights

1	17-Arch Bridge	C3
2	Boathouses	B1
3	Buddhist Fragrance Pavilion	C1
4	Buddhist Temple of the Sea of Wisdom	C1
5	Cloud Dispelling Hall	C2
6	Dragon King Temple	C3
7	Hall of Benevolence & Longevity	D2
8	Long Corridor	C1
9	Marble Boat	B1
10	Rowing Boat Dock	B2

◉ Sleeping

11	Aman at Summer Palace	D1

ing more than 227,000 Chinese characters and decorated with Sanskrit incantations. Also on view are copies of the bells and chimes of the Marquis of Zeng and a collection of Buddhist and Taoist bells including *vajra* bells and the wind chimes (*fēnglíng*) that tinkle from temple roofs and pagodas across China. The temple is 500m west of Dazhongsi subway station.

🏃 Activities

Cycling

Běijīng is flat as a pancake and almost every road has a dedicated cycle lane, meaning cycling is easily the best way to see the city; it's especially fun to explore *hútòng* areas by bike. Most hostels rent bikes. There are also bike rental depots around the Hòuhǎi Lakes (p81). Look out for the new bike-sharing scheme which was about to be unveiled as this book was being researched.

The scheme was only open to Chinese nationals when it launched, but there were plans to open it to foreigners at a later stage. To use the bikes you first needed to get an ordinary travel card (p109) which you had to activate for bike rental use. The two most convenient places to activate the cards were Exit A2 of Tiantandongmen station and by Exit A of Dongzhimen station. You could only activate the cards from Monday to Friday (9am to 11am and 2pm to 4pm), but once activated they could be used any time for renting bikes.

Bike Běijīng　　　　　　　　　CYCLING
(康多自行车租赁; Kāngduō Zìxíngchē Zūlín; Map p62; ☑6526 5857; www.bikebeijing.com; 34 Donghuangchenggen Nanjie; 东皇城根南街34号; ☉9am-7pm; Ⓢ China Museum of Art) Rents a range of good quality bikes (per day ¥50–100) and equipment, and runs guided bike tours around the city and beyond, including trips to the Great Wall. Guides and shop assistants speak English.

Kite Flying

The quintessential Chinese pastime, kite flying is hugely popular in Běijīng. Top spots include the northeast portion of Temple of Heaven Park (p72) and the east gate of Dìtán Park (p72). Note, you are no longer allowed to fly kites in Tiān'ānmén Square.

Three Stone Kite Shop　　　　　　KITES
(三石斋风筝; Sānshízhāi Fēngzhēng; Map p80; 25 Dianmen Xidajie; ☉9am-9pm; Ⓢ Nanluogu Xiang) Kites by appointment to the former Qing emperors; the great-grandfather of the owner of this friendly store used to make the kites for the Chinese royal family. There's a tremendous selection of handmade, hand-painted kites in all sizes.

Swimming

Locals swim daily in the Hòuhǎi Lakes (p81) – even in icy midwinter! If that's not clean enough for you, head to the outdoor leisure pools at Qīngnián Hú Park (青年湖公园; Qīngniánhú Gōngyuán; Map p68), Tuánjiéhú Park (团结湖公园; Tuánjiéhú Gōngyuán; Map p76) or Cháoyáng Park (朝阳公园; Cháoyáng Gōngyuán; Map p76) or the indoor pool at Dìtán Sports Centre (地坛体育馆; Dìtán Tǐyùguǎn; Map p68; admission ¥30; ☉8.30am-3.30pm & 6.30-10pm Mon-Fri, noon-10pm Sat & Sun).

Happy Magic Water Park　　　SWIMMING
(水立方嬉水乐园; Shuǐlìfāng Xīshuǐ Lèyuán; Map p52; Olympic Green, off Beichen Lu; 北辰路奥林匹克公园内; water park entrance adult/child ¥200/160, swimming only ¥50; ☉10am-9pm; Ⓢ Olympic Green) The 2008 Běijīng Olympics National Aquatics Centre, aka the Water Cube, is now China's largest indoor water park.

Table Tennis

China's national sport can be played all over the capital at free-to-use, outdoor tables in parks, squares and housing estates. If you fancy being on the wrong end of a ping-pong thrashing, head to Jīngshān Table Tennis Park (Map p62). Hòuhǎi Exercise Ground (Map p80) also has tables. Pick up a cheap table tennis bat on the 2nd floor of Tiān Yì Goods Market (Map p68).

FRAGRANT HILLS PARK

Easily within striking distance of the Summer Palace are Běijīng's Western Hills (西山; Xī Shān), another former villa-resort of the emperors. The section closest to Běijīng is known as Fragrant Hills Park (香山公园; Xiāng Shān Gōngyuán; Map p110; summer/winter ¥10/5; ☻6am-7.30pm; ⓢXiyuan or Yuanmingyuan, then ☐331).

Scramble up the slopes to the top of **Incense-Burner Peak** (Xiānglú Fēng), or take the **chairlift** (one way/return ¥30/50; ☻8.30am-5pm). From the peak there's an all-embracing view of the countryside, and you can leave the crowds behind by hiking further into the Western Hills. Běijīngers flock here in autumn when the maple leaves saturate the hillsides in great splashes of red.

Near the north gate of Fragrant Hills Park, but still within the park, is the excellent **Azure Clouds Temple** (Bìyún Sì; adult ¥10; ☻8am-5pm), which dates back to the Yuan dynasty. The **Mountain Gate Hall** contains two vast protective deities: Heng and Ha, beyond which is a small courtyard and the drum and bell towers, leading to a hall with a wonderful statue of Milefo; bronze, but coal-black with age. Only his big toe shines from numerous inquisitive fingers.

The **Sun Yatsen Memorial Hall** contains a statue and a glass coffin donated by the USSR on the death of Mr Sun in 1925. At the very back is the marble **Vajra Throne Pagoda**, where Sun Yatsen was interred after he died, before his body was moved to its final resting place in Nánjīng. The **Hall of Arhats** is well worth visiting; it contains 500 *luóhàn* statues, each crafted with an individual personality.

Southwest of the Azure Clouds Temple is the Tibetan-style **Temple of Brilliance** (Zhāo Miào), and not far away is a glazed-tile pagoda. Both survived visits by foreign troops intent on sacking the area in 1860 and 1900.

There are dozens of cheap **restaurants** and snack stalls on the approach road to the north gate of the park, making this your best bet for lunch out of any of the sights in this part of the city.

Note, sometime after 2013, the subway will extend all the way out here, via the Summer Palace and Botanic Gardens.

🎓 Courses

Language & Culture

Culture Yard CULTURAL PROGRAMMES
(天井越洋; Tiānjǐng Yuèyáng; Map p68; ☑8404 4166; www.cultureyard.net; 10 Shique Hutong; 石雀胡同10号; ☻10am-7pm; ⓢBeixinqiao) Tucked away down a *hútòng,* this cultural centre focuses on language classes (Chinese, English, French, Spanish, Portuguese), including crash-course beginners' Chinese, but also does Chinese culture workshops (tea, calligraphy, *hútòng* photography).

Martial Arts

Mílún Kungfu School MARTIAL ARTS
(北京弥纶传统武术学校; Běijīng Mílún Chuántǒng Wǔshù Xuéxiào; Map p62; ☑138 1170 6568; www.kungfuinchina.com; 33 Xitangzi Hutong; 西堂子胡同33号; drop-in rate per class ¥100, 8-class card ¥600; ☻7pm-8.30pm Mon & Thu, 5pm-6.30pm Sat & Sun; ⓢDengshikou) Runs classes in various forms of traditional Chinese martial arts (including taichi) from an historic courtyard near Wángfǔjǐng shopping district. In summer, typically in August, all classes are held in Rìtán Park (p75). Class times listed above are for drop-in group classes, but private classes can be arranged. Instruction is in Chinese, but with an English translator.

Cookery

Black Sesame Kitchen COOKERY
(Map p68; www.blacksesamekitchen.com; ☑136 9147 4408; 3 Heizhima Hutong) Runs popular cooking classes with a variety of recipes from across China; just off Nanluogu Xiang.

🛏 Sleeping

Hútòng-rich Dōngchéng North is Běijīng's most pleasant neighbourhood to stay in, although Dōngchéng Central has some great digs too. Dashilar, in Xīchéng South, is ground zero for budget backpackers, although there are good hostels throughout the capital.

Frustratingly, some of the very cheapest hotels still do not accept foreigners.

If you want to splash the cash, **Peninsula** (Map p62; www.peninsula.com), **Grand Hyatt** (Map p62; www.beijing.grand.hyatt.com) and **China World Hotel** (Map p76; www.shangri-la.com) are three of the city's better five-star options, offering familiar international-standard top-end facilities.

FORBIDDEN CITY & DŌNGCHÉNG CENTRAL

TOP CHOICE Red Capital Residence   COURTYARD HOTEL **$$$**

(新红资客栈; Xīnhóngzī Kèzhàn; Map p62; ☎8403 5308; www.redcapitalclub.com.cn; 9 Dongsi Liutiao; 东四六条9号; s/d ¥1150/1500; **S**Zhangzizhonglu; ❋@🛜) Dressed up with Liberation-era artefacts and established in a gorgeous Qing-dynasty courtyard, this tiny but unique guest house – owned by American activist and author Laurence Brahm – offers a heady dose of nostalgia for a vanished age. Make your choice from four rooms which, though small, are decked out with paraphernalia that wouldn't look out of place in a museum. Don't miss the unique cigar bar, housed in an underground bomb shelter below the courtyard. There's no sign on the front door; just a number. It also has a sister branch – the Red Capital Ranch – within a 20-acre estate near the Great Wall; see boxed text below.

City Walls Courtyard   HÚTÒNG HOSTEL **$$**

(城墙旅舍; Chéngqiáng Lǚshè; Map p62; ☎6402 7805; www.beijingcitywalls.com; 57 Nianzi Hutong; 碾子胡同57号; 8-/4-bed dm ¥100/120, d ¥420; **S**Nanluoguxiang; ❋@🛜) Expensive for a hostel, and staff could do with smiling a bit more often, but this is still an attractive choice because of its peaceful courtyard atmosphere and fabulous *hútòng* location – authentically hidden away in one of the city's most historic areas. The maze-like web of alleyways can be disorientating: from Jingshan Houjie, look for the *hútòng* opening just east of Jǐngshān Table Tennis Park. Walk up the *hútòng* and follow it around to the right and then left; the hostel is then on the left-hand side.

Jìngyuán Hotel   COURTYARD HOTEL **$$**

(靖园雅筑宾馆; Jìngyuán Yǎzhù Bīnguǎn; Map p62; ☎6525 9259; jyyz2008@yahoo.com.cn; 35 Xitangzi Hutong; 西堂子胡同35号; r with shared bathroom ¥486, r ¥988-1398; **S**Dengshikou; ❋@🛜) Once the home of the Qing-dynasty painter Pu Jin – a cousin of China's last emperor Puyi – this peaceful, good-value courtyard hotel is tucked away beside St Joseph's Church. Rooms are fairly ordinary – like those of a standard midrange Chinese hotel – but are situated around two pleasant courtyards, and come with good discounts. The ones with shared bathrooms were going

---

ESCAPE TO THE GREAT WALL

As well as the usual accommodation options in our special Great Wall chapter (p113), the following luxury digs offer some exclusivity beside more remote parts of China's best-known icon.

Commune by the Great Wall   LUXURY HOTEL **$$$**

(长城脚下的公社; Chángchéng Jiǎoxià de Gōngshè; ☎8118 1888; www.communebythegreatwall.com; r from ¥2500; ❋@🛜🚅) The Commune is seriously expensive but the cantilevered geometric architecture, location and superb panoramas are simply standout. Positioned at the Shuǐguān Great Wall, off the Badaling Hwy, the Kempinski-managed Commune may have a proletarian name but the design and presentation are purely for the affluent. Take out another mortgage and treat yourself – this is the ultimate view, with a room. There is a kid's club to boot.

Red Capital Ranch   HERITAGE HOTEL **$$$**

(新红资避暑山庄; Xīnhóngzī Bìshǔshānzhuāng; ☎8403 5308; www.redcapitalclub.com.cn; 28 Xiàguāndì Village, Yanqi Town, Huáiróu County; 怀柔县雁栖镇下关地村28号; r from ¥1500; ❋@🚅) Doing its own thing miles from civilisation, Red Capital Ranch is *the* Běijīng escapist option. Ten individually styled villas are housed in a Manchurian hunting lodge on a 20-acre estate. If the mountain setting – complete with Great Wall remains running through the estate – doesn't dissolve your stress, the Tibetan Tantric Space Spa will. Free transport is laid on daily from its city-centre sister branch, Red Capital Residence (p89).

for ¥298 when we were here, while those with private bathrooms could be had for ¥680. English-language skills are limited.

Côte Cour
COURTYARD HOTEL $$$

(北京演乐酒店; Běijīng Yǎnyuè Jiǔdiàn; Map p62; ☑6523 3958; www.hotelcotecourbj.com; 70 Yanyue Hutong; 演乐胡同70号; d ¥1150-2000; S Dengshikou; ✲@☎) With a calm, serene atmosphere and a lovely magnolia courtyard, this 14-room *hútòng* hotel makes a charming place to rest your head. Like all courtyard hotels, rooms and bathrooms are petite, but the decor in some of them is exquisite and there's plenty of space to relax in the courtyard.

The Emperor
BOUTIQUE HOTEL $$

(皇家驿栈酒店; Huángjiā Yìzhàn Jiǔdiàn; Map p62; ☑6526 5566; www.theemperor.com.cn; 33 Qihelou Jie, off Beichizi Dajie; 北池子大街骑河楼33号; r from ¥1000; S Dengshikou; ⊖✲@☎) Attempting to capitalise on a majestic position just east of the Forbidden City, the Emperor's lofty ambitions were undermined by height restrictions so upper-floor rooms merely graze the rooftops of the imperial palace. Nonetheless you can't question the excellent feng shui this locale brings. The un-numbered rooms are named after emperors and come with funky, albeit slightly weird fitted furniture with lots of smooth curves and strange cubbyholes. It's quirky, but cool and the views from the rooftop bar are simply imperial.

Park Plaza
HOTEL $$

(北京丽亭酒店; Běijīng Lìtíng Jiǔdiàn; Map p62; ☑8522 1999; www.parkplaza.com/beijingcn; 97 Jinbao Jie; 金宝街97号; d from ¥900; S Dengshikou; ⊖✲@☎) A good-value riposte to the overblown top-flight hotels in the area (see the gaudy Legendale across the road for what *not* to do), the Park Plaza is a treasured find. If you can't or don't want to stretch to a five-star hotel, this friendly place has a strong location and a comfortable, modern and well-presented four-star finish. It's hidden away behind its glitzier sister hotel, the excellent **Regent Běijīng** (北京丽晶大酒店; Běijīng Lìjīng Dàjiǔdiàn; ☑8522 1888; www.regenthotels.com; 99 Jinbao Jie; 金宝街99号; r from ¥1600; S Dengshikou; ⊖✲@☒☎).

Běijīng City Central International Youth Hostel
HOSTEL $

(北京城市国际青年旅社; Běijīng Chéngshì Guójì Qīngnián Lüshè; Map p62; ☑6525 8866, 8511 5050; www.centralhostel.com; 1 Beijingzhan Xijie; 北

京站街1号; 4-8 bed dm ¥60, s/d with shared bathroom ¥128/160, d from ¥298-368; S Beijing Railway Station; ✲@☎) The first youth hostel you hit after exiting Běijīng Train Station, this place is a decent choice if you can't be bothered to lug your heavy rucksack to nicer parts of the city. Rooms are pretty basic, but clean and spacious enough, and there's a large bar-cafe area with free wi-fi, internet terminals, pool tables and Western food.

DRUM TOWER & DŌNGCHÉNG NORTH

TOP CHOICE Peking Youth Hostel
HÚTÒNG HOSTEL $$

(北平国际青年旅社; Běipíng Guójì Qīngnián Lüshè; Map p68; ☑8403 9098; pekinghostel@yahoo.com.cn; 113 Nanluogu Xiang; 南锣鼓巷113号; dm/tw from ¥120/450; S Nanluoguxiang; ✲@☎) Fabulous, flower-filled youth hostel located on trendy Nanluogu Xiang, an historic *hútòng* that's been transformed into a lively lane of bars, cafes, restaurants and boutique shops. In keeping with its fashionable location, this is more of a boutique hostel than a backpackers' haven, with a beautifully renovated building including a quaint, country cottage-like restaurant and a wonderful rooftop cafe-bar. All the usual youth hostel services are dished up, though, including bike hire and trips to the Great Wall.

TOP CHOICE Courtyard 7
COURTYARD HOTEL $$$

(四合院酒店; Sìhéyuàn Jiǔdiàn; Map p68; ☑6406 0777; www.courtyard7.com; 7 Qianggulou Yuan Hutong, off Nanluogu Xiang; 鼓楼东大街南锣鼓巷前鼓楼苑胡同7号; r ¥900-1500; S Nanluoguxiang; ✲@) Immaculate rooms, decorated in traditional Chinese furniture face on to two, 300-year-old courtyards, which over the years have been home to government ministers, rich merchants and even an army general. Despite the historical narrative, rooms still come with modern comforts such as underfloor heating, broadband internet (but no wi-fi) and cable TV, and the *hútòng* location – down a quiet alley, but very close to trendy Nanluogu Xiang – is a winner. Breakfast included.

TOP CHOICE DùGé
COURTYARD HOTEL $$$

(杜革四合院酒店; Dùgé Sìhéyuàn Jiǔdiàn; Map p68; ☑6406 0686; www.dugecourtyard.com; 26 Qianyuan Ensi Hutong; 交道口南大街前园恩寺胡同26号; r ¥1800-2500; S Nanluoguxiang or Beixinqiao; ✲@☎) This 19th-century former residence was originally home to a Qing-dynasty minister but was recently converted by a Belgian–Chinese couple into an exquisite designer courtyard hotel. Each of the six rooms is decorated uniquely with modern and artistic touches blended with overall themes of traditional China. Some of the wood furniture – four-poster beds, decorative Chinese screens – is simply beautiful. Rooms are set around small, romantic, bamboo-lined courtyards. The only downside is that, as with most courtyard hotels, space is at a premium, so rooms are far smaller than you'd expect from similarly priced top-end hotels.

TOP CHOICE **Běijīng Downtown Backpackers**   HÚTÒNG HOSTEL $
(东堂客栈; Dōngtáng Kèzhàn; Map p68; ☑8400 2429; www.backpackingchina.com; 85 Nanluogu Xiang; 南锣鼓巷85号; dm/s/tw/tr from ¥75/160/170/270, sq/tr per bed ¥75/85, d ¥150-190, ste ¥300; ⑤Beixinqiao; ❉@☎) A cheaper option than the excellent Peking International Youth Hostel, but still with the same wonderful *hútòng* location, Downtown Backpackers is Nanluogu Xiang's original youth hostel and it hasn't forgotten its roots. Rooms are basic, therefore cheap, but are kept clean and tidy, and staff members are fully plugged in to the needs of Western travellers. Rents bikes and runs recommended hiking trips to the Great Wall (¥280) plus a range of other city trips. Rates include breakfast.

The Orchid   COURTYARD HOTEL $$
(兰花宾馆; Lánhuā Bīnguǎn; Map p68; ☑8404 4818; www.theorchidbeijing.com; 65 Baochao Hutong; 鼓楼东大街宝钞胡同65号; d ¥700-1200; ⑤Gulou Dajie; ❉@☎) Opened by a Canadian guy and a Tibetan girl, this place may lack the history of other courtyard hotels, but it's been renovated into a beautiful space, with a peaceful courtyard and some rooftop seating with distant views of the Drum and Bell Towers. Rooms are doubles only, and are small, but are tastefully decorated and all come with an Apple TV home entertainment system. Hard to spot, The Orchid is down an unnamed, shoulder-width alleyway opposite Mr Shi's Dumplings.

Běijīng P-Loft Youth Hostel   HÚTÒNG HOSTEL $
(跑局工厂青年旅舍; Pàojú Gōngchǎng Qīngnián Lǚshè; Map p68; ☑6402 7218; ploft@yahoo.cn; 29 Paoju Toutiao; 炮局头条29号; dm/r from ¥56/195; ⑤Yonghegong-Lama Temple; ❉@☎) First an 18th-century artillery factory, then a prison; now a hidden gem of a youth hostel with a distinctly urban feel to it. Embedded in a *hútòng* warren behind the Lama Temple, P-Loft seems to be on the fringe of things, but it's only a short meander to the subway system. Dorms are fine, as are the private rooms with en suite, and a degree on anonymity is guaranteed by the hard-to-find-location. Facilities include bar, bike hire and a roomy sports area for table tennis and pool.

SĀNLǏTÚN & CHÁOYÁNG

TOP CHOICE **Opposite House Hotel**   BOUTIQUE HOTEL $$$
(瑜舍; Yúshè; Map p76; ☑6417 6688; www.theoppositehouse.com; Bldg 1, Village, 11 Sanlitun Lu; 三里屯路11号院1号楼; r from ¥2500; ❉❋@☎⑥) With see-all open-plan bathrooms, American oak bath tubs, lovely mood lighting, underfloor heating, sliding doors, complimentary beers, TVs on extendable arms and a metal basin swimming pool, this trendy Swire-owned boutique hotel is top-drawer chic. Chinese motifs are muted: this is an international hotel with prices to match. It's not the sort of place to take the kids, but couples can splash out or sip drinks in its trendy bar, Mesh. The location is great for shopping, restaurants and drinking. No obvious sign, or reception area. Just walk into the striking green glass cube of a building and ask.

Sānlǐtún Youth Hostel   HOSTEL $
(三里屯青年旅馆; Sānlǐtún Qīngnián Lǚguǎn; Map p76; ☑5190 9288; www.itisbeijing.com; Chunxiu Lu; 春秀路南口往北250米路东; dm/tw from ¥60/220; ⑤Dongsishitiao or Dongzhimen; ❉@☎) Sānlǐtún's only decent youth hostel, this place is very well run and extremely popular. It has added an outdoor terrace to its good-value bar-restaurant area, and still offers its usual trustworthy travel advice. Rooms are functional, but clean, and there's internet, wi-fi, a pool table, table football, bike rental (¥30) and friendly staff.

St Regis   LUXURY HOTEL $$$
(北京国际俱乐部饭店; Běijīng Guójì Jùlèbù Fàndiàn; Map p76; ☑6460 6688; www.stregis.com/beijing; 21 Jianguomenwai Dajie; 建国门外大街21号; r from ¥2600; ⑤Jianguomen; ❉❋@☎⑥) Its extravagant foyer, thorough professionalism and tip-top location make the St Regis a marvellous, albeit costly, five-star choice. Sumptuous and soothing rooms ooze comfort, 24-hour butlers are at hand to fine-

tune your stay and a gorgeous assortment of restaurants steers you into one of Běijīng's finest dining experiences. Wi-fi costs ¥80 per day.

Holiday Inn Express
HOTEL $$

(智选假日酒店; Zhìxuǎn Jiàrì Jiǔdiàn; Map p76; ☑6416 9999; www.holidayinnexpress.com.cn; 1 Chunxiu Lu; 春秀路1号; r ¥598; ⑤Dongsishitiao or Dongzhimen; ✳@🛜) Brand new 350-room hotel with bright, clean, comfortable rooms (we love the big puffy pillows!) that come equipped with wide-screen TV, free wi-fi and internet access via a cable. The lobby has Apple computers for the use of guests. Staff members are friendly and speak some English.

Yoyo Hotel
HOTEL $$

(优优客酒店; Yōuyōu Kèjiǔdiàn; Map p76; ☑6417 3388; www.yoyohotel.cn; Bld 10 Dongsanjie Erjie, off Sanlitun Lu; 三里屯北路东三街二街中10楼; r from ¥310; ⑤Tuanjiehu; ✳@🛜) Has a modern, boutique feel to it, but rooms here are tiny. Nevertheless, they are excellent value for the location and are kept clean and tidy. Staff members speak some English and are friendly considering how rushed off their feet they usually are. There's internet via a cable inside rooms. Wi-fi is in the lobby only.

BĚIHǍI PARK & XĪCHÉNG NORTH

TOP CHOICE Red Lantern House
West Yard
COURTYARD HOTEL $

(红灯笼; Hóng Dēnglong; Map p80; ☑6617 0870; 12 Xisi Beiertiao; 西斜北二条12号; s ¥280, d & tw ¥360, ste ¥450; ⑤Xisi; ✳@🛜) Set around two lovely, quiet courtyards, the rooms here are thoughtfully and comfortably furnished in an old Běijīng style – wooden beds and fittings – and the staff are efficient and unobtrusive. There's also a honeymoon suite for those in the mood for love. It's essential to book ahead here. To find it, walk north on Xisi Beidajie from Xisi subway and it's two *hútòng* up on the left.

Drum Tower Youth Hostel
HOSTEL $

(鼓韵青年旅舍; Gǔyùn Qīngnián Lǚshè; Map p80; ☑8401 6565; www.24hostel.com; 51 Jiugulou Dajie; 旧鼓楼大街51号; 6-bed dm without/with bathroom ¥60/80, d & tw without/with bathroom ¥200/280; ⑤Gulou Dajie; ✳@🛜) A few years ago, this place had a deservedly bad rep amongst travellers. Now, it has upped its game with staff who are actually interested in helping people and clean, if uninspired,

dorms and rooms. The added bonuses are a cool roof terrace and the attached next-door bar Lakers, which serves up reasonably-priced Western comfort food and standard Chinese dishes. Bike hire is ¥35 a day.

DASHILAR & XĪCHÉNG SOUTH

Qiánmén Hostel
HOSTEL $

(前门客栈; Qiánmén Kèzhàn; Map p83; ☑6313 2370/2369; www.qianmenhostel.com; 33 Meishi Jie; 煤市街33号; 6-8/4-bed dm ¥60/70, tw/d/ tr without/with bathroom ¥200-240/240-300; ⑤Qianmen; ✳@🛜) This heritage hostel combines a relaxing environment with high-ceilinged original woodwork, charming antique buildings and able staff. Affable hostel owner Genghis Kane may show off his environmentally sound heating equipment (fired with dried pellets of plant matter). Heritage rooms are simple; purpose-built rooms are more modern with less character. Western breakfasts, bike hire nearby, laundry available.

Three-Legged Frog Hostel
HOSTEL $

(京一食青年旅舍; Jīngyī Shí Qīngnián Lǚshè; Map p83; ☑6304 0749, 6304 3721; 3legs@three leggedfroghostel.com; 27 Tieshu Xiejie; 铁树斜街 27号; 6-bed dm with bathroom ¥70, 10-bed dm ¥60, d & tw ¥220, tr ¥300, q ¥420; ⑤Qianmen) The name is a mystery but this is a welcome addition to the growing band of hostels along and off Dazhalan Xijie. The six-bed dorms are an excellent deal, while the rooms are compact but clean and all are set around a cute courtyard. There's a communal area out front which does Western breakfasts and beers in the evening and a sardonic, but helpful, owner.

Leo Hostel
HOSTEL $

(广聚元饭店; Guǎngjùyuán Fàndiàn; Map p83; ☑8660 8923, 6303 1595; www.leohostel.com; 52 Dazhalan Xijie; 大栅栏西街52号; 10-12-bed dm ¥50, 8-bed dm with toilet ¥70, 6-bed dm ¥60, q ¥60-80, tr ¥210-300, d & tw ¥240; ⑤Qianmen; ✳@🛜) Far less atmosphere than its venerable cousin Leo Courtyard, but the dorms and rooms are more modern and frankly better, even if the overall vibe is rather sterile. But there's a fair-sized communal area which does OK food and it's close to Tiān'ānmén Sq and the surrounding sights. Always busy, it's worth booking ahead.

Leo Courtyard
HOSTEL $

(上林宾馆; Shànglín Bīnguǎn; Map p83; ☑8316 6568, 6303 4609; www.leohostel.com; 22 Shanxi Xiang; 陕西巷胡同22号; 6-bed dm ¥50, tw ¥160;

tr ¥270; Ⓢ Qianmen; ❄@🛜) It's a superb, historic building with a racy past featuring courtesans and the imperial elite, but the rooms themselves are a little tatty and the bathrooms nothing to write home about. Nor do the sleepy staff inspire confidence. That said, the small dorms and communal showers are clean and the attached bar/restaurant next door is a good place for a libation come sundown. It's down an alley off Dazhalan Xijie.

SUMMER PALACE & HǍIDIÀN

TOP CHOICE Aman at Summer Palace   HERITAGE HOTEL $$$

(颐和安缦; Yíhé Ānmàn; Map p86; 📞5987 9999; www.amanatsummerpalace.com; 1 Gongmen Qianjie; 宫门前街1号; r US$650, courtyard r US$750, ste US$950; Ⓢ Xiyuan; ❄@🛜) Hard to fault this exquisite hotel, which is a true candidate for best in Běijīng. From the location around the corner from the Summer Palace – part of the hotel buildings date back to the 19th century and were used to house distinguished guests waiting for audiences with Empress Cixi – to the superbly appointed rooms in a series of picture-perfect pavilions set around courtyards, to step through the imposing red gates here is to enter a very different, very hushed and very privileged world. Choice restaurants, a spa, a library, a cinema, pool, squash courts and, of course, silky-smooth service round off the refined picture.

✕ Eating

Eating out will almost certainly be a highlight of your trip here. Běijīng has a staggering 60,000 restaurants, and between them they cater to all tastes and all budgets. True to its north China roots, Běijīng cuisine is warming, fatty and filling, with generous amounts of garlic finding its way into many dishes. The adventurous can sample some unusual stuff here – boiled tripe, tofu paste, sour soy milk... Just be sure to leave your table manners at home; Běijīngers like mealtimes to be raucous affairs, with plenty of drinking, smoking and shouting to accompany their hearty platters.

Every cuisine from every corner of China finds its way onto the tables of Běijīng's restaurants, and there's also plenty of snacks and street food to eat on the go. If you're missing home, you'll find the whole gamut of international options too, including some decent Western food in some of Běijīng's excellent independent coffee shops.

FORBIDDEN CITY & DŌNGCHÉNG CENTRAL

TOP CHOICE Zuǒ Lín Yòu Shè   CHINESE BĚIJĪNG $

(左邻右舍褡裢火烧; Map p62; 50 Meishuguan Houjie; 美术馆后街50号; dumplings per liǎng ¥4-6, dishes ¥5-20; ⏱11am-9.30pm; Ⓢ Chinese Museum of Art; 📶) This small, no-nonsense and often noisy restaurant focuses on Běijīng cuisine. The speciality is *dālian huǒshāo* (褡裢火烧), golden-fried finger-shaped dumplings stuffed with all manner of savoury fillings; we prefer the pork ones, but there are lamb, beef and vegie choices too. They are served by the *liǎng* (两), with one *liǎng* equal to three dumplings, and you must order at least two *liǎng* (二两; *èr liǎng*) of each filling to make it worth their while cooking a batch. Other specialities include the pickled fish (酥鲫鱼; *sū jì yú*), the spicy tofu paste (麻豆腐; *má dòufu*) and the deep-fried pork balls (干炸丸子; *gān zhá wánzi*), while filling bowls of millet porridge (小米粥; *xiǎo mǐ zhōu*) are served up for free. There's no English sign (look for the wooden signboard), and no English spoken, but there is an English translation of the menu available (*yīngwén càidān*).

TOP CHOICE Courtyard   FUSION $$$

(四合院; Sìhéyuàn; Map p62; 📞6526 8883; 95 Donghuamen Dajie; 东华门大街95号; mains ¥130-300, set menu ¥488; ⏱6-10pm; Ⓢ Tian'anmen East or Dengshikou; ➔) Classy Courtyard enjoys a peerless location perched by the side of the moat surrounding the Forbidden City. Romantics will need to book ahead to ensure they have one of the cosy window tables that offer the best views. The menu is small but sumptuous and the wine list impressive, while the basement houses a small art gallery.

Crescent Moon Muslim Restaurant   CHINESE XĪNJIĀNG $

(新疆弯弯月亮维吾尔穆斯林餐厅; Xīnjiāng Wānwānyuèliàng Wéiwú'ěr Mùsīlín Cāntīng; Map p62; 16 Dongsi Liutiao Hutong; 东四六条胡同 16号(东四北大街); dishes from ¥18; ⏱10am-midnight; Ⓢ Dongsishitiao; 📶) Located down a *hútòng* off Dongsi Beidajie, and owned and staffed by Uighur Muslims from Xīnjiāng province, this place attracts many Běijīng-based Uighurs and people from Central Asia, plus a lot of Western expats. It's more expensive than most other Muslim-food restaurants in Běijīng, but the food is consistently good, and it has an English menu. The speciality is the leg of lamb (¥128).

Lǎo Zhái Yuàn   ROAST DUCK $$
(老宅院; Map p62; 14 Liangguochang, off Meishuguan Houjie; 美术馆后街亮果厂14号; mains ¥30-50; ⊙10am-1.30pm & 4.30pm-8.30pm; ⑤Chinese Museum of Art; 回) Good-value Běijīng roast duck in a small courtyard restaurant. The duck on the English menu costs ¥135, and is the better quality of the two types available. If you want the cheaper, but still tasty version, which costs ¥98, ask for *pǔtōng kǎo yā* (普通烤鸭; ordinary roast duck).

Běijīng Dàdǒng
Roast Duck Restaurant   PEKING DUCK $$$
(北京大董烤鸭店; Běijīng Dàdǒng Kǎoyādiàn; Map p62; ☑8522 1111; 5th fl Jinbaohui Shopping Centre, 88 Jinbao Jie; 东城区金宝街88号金宝汇购物中心5层; roast duck ¥238; ⊙11am-10pm; ⑤Dengshikou) Ultra modern Dàdǒng sells itself on being the only restaurant which serves Běijīng roast duck with all the flavour of the classic imperial dish, but none of the fat; the leanest roast duck in the capital. For some it's hideously overpriced and far from authentic. For others it's the best roast duck restaurant in China.

Dōnghuámén Night Market   STREET FOOD $
(东华门夜市; Dōnghuámén Yèshì; Map p62; Dong'anmen Dajie; 东安门大街; snacks ¥5-15; ⊙4-10pm; ⑤Wangfujing) A sight in itself, the bustling night market near Wangfujing Dajie is a veritable food zoo: lamb, beef and chicken skewers, corn on the cob, smelly *dòufu* (tofu), cicadas, grasshoppers, kidneys, quail's eggs, snake, squid, fruit, porridge, fried pancakes, strawberry kebabs, bananas, Inner Mongolian cheese, stuffed eggplants, chicken hearts, pitta bread stuffed with meat, shrimps – and that's just the start. Prices are all marked and in English. The daytime version can be found nearby at **Wángfǔjǐng Snack Street** (王府井小吃街; Wángfǔjǐng Xiǎochījiē; off Wangfujing Dajie; 王府井大街西侧; ⊙9.30am-10pm; Ⓜ Wangfujing).

DRUM TOWER & DŌNGCHÉNG NORTH

⊕TOP CHOICE Yáojì Chǎogān   CHINESE BĚIJĪNG $
(姚记炒肝店; Map p68; 311 Gulou Dongdajie; 鼓楼东大街311号; mains ¥5-20; ⊙6am-10.30pm; ⑤Shichahai) Proper locals joint, serving proper Běijīng dishes in a noisy, no-nonsense atmosphere. The house speciality is *chǎogān* (炒肝; pig's liver stew; ¥5-8). This is also a good place to try *zhá guànchang* (炸灌肠; garlic-topped deep-fried crackers; ¥6) and *má dòufu* (麻豆腐; spicy tofu paste; ¥10).

Their steamed pork dumplings (包子; *bāozi*; per dumpling ¥1) are excellent, and are perfect for breakfast with a bowl of *xiǎomǐ zhōu* (小米粥; millet porridge; ¥2) or local favourite *dòuzhī* (豆汁; soy milk; ¥2). It also does a decent bowl of Běijīng's best-known noodle dish *zhájiàng miàn* (炸酱面; ¥10). No English menu or English sign.

⊕TOP CHOICE Dàlǐ Courtyard   CHINESE YÚNNÁN $$$
(大理; Dàlǐ; Map p68; ☑8404 1430; 67 Xiaojingchang Hutong, Gulou Dongdajie; 鼓楼东大街小经厂胡同67号; set menus from ¥128; ⊙11am-3pm & 6pm-11pm; ⑤Andingmen) The beautiful setting in a restored open-air *hútòng* courtyard makes this one of Běijīng's more idyllic places to eat, especially in summer. Specialising in the subtle flavours of the cuisine of southwestern Yúnnán province, it's also one of Běijīng's more creative restaurants. There's no menu. Instead, you pay ¥128, ¥200 or ¥300 per head (drinks are extra) and the chef decides what to give you, depending on what inspires him and what ingredients are fresh. It's the first left down Xiaojingchang Hutong; look for the red lanterns.

Yáng Fāng Lamb Hotpot   MONGOLIAN HOTPOT $
(羊坊涮肉; Yáng Fāng Shuàn Ròu; Map p68; 270 Guloudong Dajie; 鼓楼东大街270号; broth ¥6-10, dips ¥2-4, raw ingredients ¥5-20; ⊙11am-11pm; ⑤Shichahai) There are two main types of hotpot in China: the ridiculously spicy one that comes from the fire-breathing southwestern city of Chóngqìng, and the milder version which is cooked in an unusual conical brass pot and which originally hails from Mongolia, but has been adopted as a Běijīng speciality. Yáng Fāng is a salt-of-the-earth version of the latter, and is a real favourite with the locals round here. First order the broth you want in your pot – clear (清汤锅底; *qīng tāng guōdǐ*), or spicy (辣锅底; *là guōde*). Then choose your dipping sauce – sesame (麻酱; *má jiàng*) or chilli oil (辣椒油; *là jiāo yóu*) – before finally selecting the raw ingredients you want to cook. Our favourites include wafer-thin lamb slices (鲜羊肉; *xiān yáng ròu*), lotus root slices (藕片; *ǒu piàn*), tofu slabs (鲜豆腐; *xiān dòufu*), sweet potato (红薯; *hóng shǔ*) and spinach (菠菜; *bō cài*). No English sign; no English menu; no English spoken.

Róng Tiān Sheep Spine   HOTPOT $
(容天土锅羊羯子馆; Róngtiān Tǔguō Yángjiézi Guǎn; Map p68; 8 Jingtu Hutong, off Beiluogu Xiang;

LOCAL KNOWLEDGE

BĚIJĪNG MENU

The following are all classic Běijīng dishes, many of which you'll only find at places specialising in Běijīng cuisine. Try Zuǒ Lín Yòu Shè (p93), Yáojì Chǎogān (p94) or Bàodǔ Huáng (p98). Many roast duck restaurants will have some of the other Běijīng specialities as well as roast duck.

Roast Duck (烤鸭; *kǎo yā*) Běijīng's most famous dish, the duck here is fattier but much more flavoursome than the roast duck typically served in Chinese restaurants in the West. Like back home, though, it also comes with pancakes, cucumber slices and plum sauce.

Zhá Jiàng Miàn (炸酱面) Very popular noodle dish found in many regions, but a favourite in Běijīng; thick wheat noodles with ground pork and cucumber shreds mixed together in a salty fermented soybean paste. Chilli oil (辣椒油; *là jiāo yóu*) is a popular optional extra.

Dālian Huǒshāo (褡裢火烧) Finger-shaped fried dumplings with a savoury filling.

Má Dòufu (麻豆腐) Spicy tofu paste.

Zhá Guànchang (炸灌肠) Deep-fried crispy crackers served with a very strong garlic dip.

Chǎo Gānr (炒肝) Sauteed liver served in a gloopy soup.

Bào Dǔ (爆肚) Boiled tripe, usually lamb. Sometimes served in a seasoned broth.

Yáng Zá (羊杂) Similar to *bào dǔ*, but includes an assortment of sheep's innards, not just tripe, and is always served in a broth.

Ròu Bǐng (肉饼) Meat patty, usually filled with pork or beef, before being lightly fried.

Jiāo Quān (焦圈) Deep-fried dough rings, usually accompanied with a cup of *dòu zhī*.

Dòu Zhī (豆汁) Sour-tasting soy milk drink.

北锣鼓巷净土胡同8号; sheep spine per jīn ¥29, other ingredients ¥5-10; ⏱10.30am-10pm; Ⓢ Gulou Dajie) Rough-and-ready locals favourite serving mouth-wateringly good sheep-spine hotpot. Order your sheep-spine chunks by the *jīn* (500g). Two *jīn's* worth (二斤; *èr jīn*) is normally about right. They will then come ready-cooked in a boiling broth – the longer you leave them to simmer, the juicier they get. You then add other raw ingredients to cook in the broth like a standard Chinese hotpot. Our favourite extras include sweet potato (红薯; *hóng shǔ*), tofu blocks (鲜豆腐; *xiān dòufu*), mushrooms (木耳; *mù'ěr*), Oriental raddish (白萝卜; *bái luóbo*) and Chinese spinach (油麦菜; *yóu mài cài*). Complimentary fresh noodles are thrown in at the end, to soak up the juices. When you're ready for them, say '*fàng miàn*' (put the noodles in). There's no English sign, no English menu and no English spoken. Some outdoor seating.

Bǎihé Vegetarian Restaurant VEGETARIAN $$
(百合素食; Bǎihé Sùshí; Map p68; 23 Caoyuan Hutong; 东直门内北小街草园胡同甲23号; dishes from ¥25; ⏱11.30am-3pm & 5-9.30pm, tea-drinking only ⏱2-5pm; Ⓢ Dongzhimen or Beixinqiao; ➌) Set around a large courtyard and specialising in vegetarian dishes that masquerade as meat or fish. Courteous service, an excellent tea menu and non-smoking throughout.

Veggie Table VEGETARIAN $$
(吃素的; Map p68; 19 Wudaoying Hutong; 五道营胡同19号; mains ¥50-70; ⏱11.30am-2pm & 5.30-9.30pm; Ⓢ Yonghegong-Lama Temple; ➌) Běijīng's first fully vegan restaurant and the most organic-focused restaurant in the capital.

Qí Shān Miàn CHINESE SHAANXI $
(岐山面; Map p68; 32 Yonghegong Dajie; 雍和宫大街32号; noodles ¥10-18, ⏱10.30am-10pm; Ⓢ Yonghegong Lama Temple; ➌) This very popular restaurant specialises in dishes from Shaanxi province. The badly translated English menu includes delicious noodle dishes – try the 'particular handmade noodle with hot oil and seasoner' or the 'Qi Shan Mian (dry style with pork)' – as well as the house speciality, *ròujiāmò* (肉夹馍; ¥7), a baked bun filled with juicy shreds of pork, and China's answer to the burger. It's translated onto the English menu as 'traditional

BĚIJĪNG'S HÚTÒNG

Běijīng's medieval genotype is most discernible down the city's leafy *hútòng* (胡同; narrow alleyways). The spirit and soul of the city lives and breathes among these charming and ragged lanes where a warm sense of community and hospitality survives. Crisscrossing chunks of Běijīng within the Second Ring Rd, the *hútòng* link up into a huge and enchanting warren of one-storey dwellings and historic courtyard homes. Hundreds of *hútòng* survive but many have been swept aside in Běijīng's race to build a modern city. Identified by white plaques, historic homes are protected, but for many others a way of life hangs in a precarious balance.

After Genghis Khan's army reduced the city of Běijīng to rubble, the new city was redesigned with *hútòng*. By the Qing dynasty more than 2000 such passageways riddled the city, leaping to around 6000 by the 1950s; now the figure has drastically dwindled to somewhere above 1000. Today's *hútòng* universe is a hotchpotch of the old and the new: Qing-dynasty courtyards are scarred with socialist-era conversions and outhouses while others have been assiduously rebuilt.

Hútòng nearly all run east–west so that the main gate faces south, satisfying feng shui (wind/water) requirements. This south-facing aspect guarantees sunshine and protection from negative principles amassing in the north.

Old walled *sìhéyuàn* (courtyards) are the building blocks of this delightful universe. Many are still lived in and hum with activity. From spring to autumn, men collect outside their gates, drinking beer, playing chess, smoking and chewing the fat. Inside, scholar trees soar aloft, providing shade and a nesting ground for birds. Flocks of pigeons whirl through the Běijīng skies overhead, bred by locals and housed in coops often buried away within the *hútòng*.

More venerable courtyards are fronted by large, thick red doors, outside of which perch either a pair of Chinese lions or drum stones. To savour Běijīng's courtyard ambience, down a drink at Irresistible Cafe (p100), devour a meal at the Dàlǐ Courtyard (p94) and sleep it all off at Courtyard 7 (p90). Alternatively, follow our leisurely Hútòng Walking Tour (p72).

Organised tours are easy to find: *hútòng* rickshaw riders lurk in packs around the Drum and Bell Square (p67) and Qiánhǎi Lake (p81), charging between ¥60 and ¥120 per person for a 45-minute or one-hour tour. Alternatively, Bike Běijīng (p87) does guided cycle tours of *hútòng* areas.

Chinese pork (beef) pancake (Xi'an style)'. The bowls of hot noodle juice (面汤; *miān tāng*) are free, and the friendly manager keeps a strict no-smoking policy; very rare for a budget restaurant in China. No English spoken.

Tàn Huā Lamb BBQ LAMB BARBECUE **$**
(碳花烤羊腿; Tàn Huā Kǎo Yángtuǐ; Map p68; 63 Beixintiao Santiao Hutong; 北新桥三条胡同63号; lamb per jīn ¥32, side dishes ¥1-12; ☉11am-midnight; ⑤Beixinqiao) Meat-loving Běijīngers flock to this raucous joint where you roast a leg of lamb on your own personal tabletop barbecue spit before hacking away at the meatiest bits with a rudimentary, long-handled knife and fork. Tables spill out onto the lively *hútòng*, creating a party atmosphere of multi-barbecue revelry. Order your leg of lamb (羊腿; *yáng tuǐ*) by the *jīn* (500g). Three *jīn* (三斤; *sān jīn*) is enough

for two or three people. You'll then be given a selection of free cold dishes as accompaniments, plus a cumin-based dry dip to roll your lamb slices in. Other popular side dishes include barbecued naan bread (烤馕; *kǎo náng*), soy fried rice (酱油炒饭; *jiàng yóu chǎo fàn*) and noodle-drop soup (疙瘩汤; *gēda tāng*). Outdoor seating.

Jīn Dǐng Xuān CHINESE CANTONESE **$$**
(金鼎轩; Map p68; 77 Hepingli Xijie; 地坛南门和平里西街77号; dim sum ¥8-20, mains ¥30-100; ☉24hr; ⑤Yonghegong-Lama Temple; ⓘ) By the south gate of Dìtán Park (p72), this giant, busy, neon-lit, 24-hour restaurant on three floors serves up good-value dim sum, as well as a host of other mostly Cantonese dishes. Note there is a separate menu for dim sum (点心; *diǎn xin*). Menus are in English and have photos, but not much English is spoken.

Ghost Street FOOD STREET

(簋街; Guǐ Jiē; Map p68) Hopping at weekends and one of Běijīng's busiest and most colourful restaurant strips at virtually any hour, Ghost Street is the English nickname of this spirited section of Dongzhimennei Dajie, where scores of restaurants converge to feed legions of locals and out-of-towners. Splendidly lit with red lanterns from dusk to dawn, Ghost Street is lined with vocal restaurant staff enticing passersby into hotpot eateries, spicy seafood restaurants and other heaving outfits. It's always open so you'll always be able to get fed. Take the subway to Běixīnqiáo, and walk east.

TEMPLE OF HEAVEN PARK & DŌNGCHÉNG SOUTH

TOP CHOICE Lost Heaven CHINESE YÚNNÁN $$$

(花马天堂; Huāmǎ Tiāntáng; Map p73; ☎8516 2698; 23 Qianmen Dongdajie; 前门东大街23号; dishes from ¥40; ⊙lunch & dinner; Ⓢ Qianmen; ⊖📋) The latest addition to the restaurants clustered in this former section of the Legation Quarter, Lost Heaven specialises in the subtle and light, but sometimes spicy, folk cuisine of Yúnnán province. Try the Dai-style roast pork in banana leaf (¥68), or one of their many splendid salads such as the marinated beef salad and peppers or the Burmese tea leaves salad. There's an elegant outside area and attentive service. Book ahead.

TOP CHOICE Lìqún Roast Duck Restaurant PEKING DUCK $$$

(利群烤鸭店; Lìqún Kǎoyādiàn; Map p73; ☎6702 5681, 6705 5578; 11 Beixiangfeng Hutong; 前门东大街正义路南口北翔凤胡同11号; roast duck ¥220; ⊙lunch & dinner; Ⓢ Qianmen; ⊖📋) The approach to this compact courtyard restaurant is through a maze of crumbling *hútòng* that have somehow survived total demolition; look for the signs pointing the way. The delectable duck on offer here is so in demand that it's essential to call ahead to reserve both a bird and a table (otherwise, turn up off-peak and be prepared to wait an hour). Inside, it's a little tatty (no prizes for the toilets), but walk by the ovens with their rows of ducks on hooks, squeeze past the scurrying, harried waiters and then sit back and enjoy some of the finest duck in town.

Dūyīchù CHINESE DUMPLINGS $$

(都一处; Map p73; ☎6702 1555; 38 Qianmen Dajie; 前门大街38号; dumplings from ¥42; ⊙9am-9pm; Ⓢ Qianmen; 📋) Now back on the newly spiffy street where it started business during the mid-Qing dynasty, Dūyíchù specialises in the delicate dumplings called *shāomài*. The shrimp and leek (¥42) are especially good, but they also do a nice line in seasonal variations, such as sweet corn and bean (¥42) in the summer, or beef and yam (¥48) in the winter.

Qiánmén Quánjùdé Roast Duck Restaurant PEKING DUCK $$$

(前门全聚德烤鸭店; Qiánmén Quánjùdé Kǎoyādiàn; Map p73; ☎6701 1379, 6511 2418; 30 Qianmen Dajie; 前门大街30号; roast duck ¥228; ⊙lunch & dinner; Ⓢ Qianmen; 📋) The most popular branch of Běijīng's most famous destination for duck, which is roasted here in ovens fired by fruit-tree wood. Another popular branch is by Wángfǔjǐng shopping street (Map p62).

SĀNLǏTÚN & CHÁOYÁNG

Nàjiā Xiǎoguǎn CHINESE MANCHU $$

(那家小馆; Map p76; ☎6567 3663; 10 Yong'an Xili, off Jianguomenwai Dajie; Chunxiu Lu; 建国门外大街永安西里10号; mains ¥40-70; ⊙11am-9.30pm; Ⓢ Yonganli; 📋) There's a touch of the traditional Chinese teahouse to this excellent restaurant, housed in a reconstructed two-storey interior courtyard, and bubbling with old-Peking atmosphere. The menu is based on an old imperial recipe book known as the Golden Soup Bible, and the dishes are consistently good. No English sign, and not much English spoken, but the menu is in English.

Jīngzūn Peking Duck PEKING DUCK $$

(京尊烤鸭; Jīngzūn Kǎoyā; Map p76; ☎6417 4075; 6 Chunxiu Lu; 春秀路6号; mains ¥30-50; ⊙11am-10pm; Ⓢ Dongzhimen or Dongsishitiao; 📋) Very popular place to sample Běijīng's signature dish. Not only is the duck here extremely good value at ¥128 including all the trimmings but, unusually for a roast duck restaurant, you can also sit outside, on the wooden decking overlooking the street. The rest of the menu is a mix of Chinese cuisines, rather than Běijīng specialities, but the food here is all decent.

Jíxiángniǎo Xiāngcài CHINESE HÚNÁN $$

(吉祥鸟湘菜; Map p76; Jishikou Donglu; 吉市口东路; mains ¥20-50; ⊙11am-9.30pm; Ⓢ Chaoyangmen; 📋) There aren't enough places in Běijīng that serve up *xiāng cài* (湘菜), the name given to the notoriously spicy cuisine of Húnán province, but this large, fiery restaurant is arguably the best of them.

PICNIC SUPPLIES

Western-style supermarkets are on the rise, but thankfully there are still some atmospheric food markets in Běijīng where you can stock up on fresh fruit and unusual snacks as you watch locals pick their favourite frogs and fish.

Rùndélì Food Market (润得立菜市场; Rùndélì Càishìchǎng; Map p80; ⊙7am-7pm), also known as Sìhuán Market (四环市场; Sìhuán Shìchǎng), is close to the Hòuhǎi Lakes, while **Xīnmín Food Market** (Map p68; 新民菜市场; Xīnmín Càishìchǎng; ⊙5am-noon) is north of the Drum Tower.

For more familiar foodstuffs, **Sānyuánlǐ Market** (Map p76; 三源里菜市场; Sānyuánlǐ Càishìchǎng; Shunyuan Jie; 朝阳区东三环顺源街; ⊙5am-7pm) has a great range of imported products alongside all the usual Chinese favourites.

The braised pork with brown sauce (¥38), known in China as *hóngshāo ròu* (红烧肉), is understandably popular – it's well known for being the favourite dish of Mao Zedong, who hailed from Húnán. But the fish head with chopped pepper (¥68) is also sumptuous. Not much English spoken here, but the menu has photos and English translations. No English sign; look for the red neon Chinese characters.

Bàodǔ Huáng   CHINESE BĚIJĪNG $
(爆肚皇; Map p76; 15 Dongzhimenwai Dajie; 东直门外大街15号; mains ¥10-30; ⊙11am-2pm & 5-9pm; ⓈDongzhimen) In-the-know locals pile into this no-nonsense apartment-block restaurant to gobble and slurp their way through its authentic Běijīng-grub menu. The speciality is *bàodǔ* (爆肚; boiled lamb tripe; from ¥13). If that's something you feel you can't, er, stomach, then plump instead for a delicious *niúròu dàcóng ròubǐng* (牛肉大葱肉饼; beef and onion fried patty; ¥8). The blanched vegetables are popular side dishes; choose from *chāo báicài* (焯白菜; blanched cabbage; ¥4), *chāo fěnsī* (焯粉丝; blanched glass noodles; ¥4) or *chāo dòng dòufu* (焯冻豆腐; blanched tofu; ¥4). And if you haven't ordered a meat patty, grab a *zhīma shāobing* (芝麻烧饼; roasted sesame-seed bun; ¥1.50) instead. True Běijīngers will also nibble on *jiāo quān* (焦圈; deep-fried dough rings; ¥1), washed down with gulps of *dòu zhī* (豆汁; sour soy milk). But you may prefer to go for a bottle of local beer (啤酒; *píjiǔ*; ¥5). No English spoken, no English menu, no English sign.

Běi   EAST ASIAN $$$
(北; Map p76; ☑6410 5230; Opposite House, Bldg 1, 11 Sanlitun Lu; 三里屯路11号院1号楼; mains ¥150-400; ⊙6pm-10pm; ⓈTuanjiehu; ▣) Located in the nightclub-like basement below

ultra-trendy boutique hotel Opposite House (p91), this achingly cool Asian restaurant specialises in Korean and Japanese cuisine. The sushi is top-notch, the tuna outstanding, and there's a strong selection of *saki* and *soju* to keep you in high spirits. Booking recommended.

BĚIHǍI PARK & XĪCHÉNG NORTH

TOP CHOICE **4Corners**   VIETNAMESE $$
(四角餐吧; Sìjiǎo Cānbā; Map p80; ☑6401 7797; www.these4corners.com; 27 Dashibei Hutong; 大石碑胡同27号; dishes from ¥34; ⊙11am-3am; ⓈShichahai; ⊝☏🔊▣) A laid-back spot with a cosy outside area, 4Corners serves up a medley of zingy Vietnamese, and some Thai, dishes. There's a tremendous selection of spring rolls for those who just want to graze while imbibing one of their excellent martinis (¥40), and live music some nights too. It's hidden down a *hútòng* just off Gulou Xidajie.

Kǒng Yǐjǐ   CHINESE ZHÈJIĀNG $$
(孔乙己酒店; ☑6618 4915; Deshengmennei Dajie, Shichahai, Houhai Nan'an; 德胜门内大街什刹海后海南岸; dishes from ¥28; ⊙lunch & dinner; ⓈJishuitan) Zhèjiāng Province is famous for Shàoxīng, a sherry-like wine, so it's entirely appropriate that this lively restaurant with a nice outdoor area right by Hòuhǎi Lake serves some dishes – such as drunken shrimp (醉虾; *zuìxiā*) and drunken chicken (醉鸡; *zuìjī*) – swimming in the stuff. There's no English or picture menu; take a look at what other people are eating and point.

Hútòng Pizza   PIZZA $$
(胡同比萨; Hútòng Bǐsà; Map p80; 9 Yindingqiao Hutong Hou; pizzas from ¥65; ⊙11am-11pm; ⓈShichahai; ▣) The Chinese accuse Marco Polo of stealing pizza from China, and it's

come back again. This relaxing, but busy spot just off Hòuhǎi Lake fires up some enormous pizzas (although they can be slow in coming). The *hútòng* house interior is funky and the attic room is handsome, with old painted beams.

Běipíngjū ROAST DUCK $$

(北平居烤鸭店; Map p80; 29 Di'anmenwai Dajie; 地安门外大街29号; mains ¥20-40; ⏰11am-9.30pm; Ⓢ Shichahai; ▣) One of the best-value duck restaurants in the city, this bright, clean, family-friendly restaurant does delicious, authentic roast duck, plus a small range of other Běijīng specialities, as well as dishes from other parts of China. The standard whole duck (单店烤鸭; *dāndiàn kǎoyā*) costs ¥98. You then choose the trimmings: cucumber (瓜条; *guātiáo*; ¥2), spring onion (葱; *cōng*; ¥2), pancakes (鸭饼; *yābǐng*; ¥6), plum sauce (甜面酱; *tiánmiànjiàng*; ¥2). It has an English menu with photos.

Drinking

There are three top spots for a night out in Běijīng (and others you can explore). **Sānlǐtún** (三里屯; Map p76), loud, brash and relatively expensive, is where expats and Chinese party-goers come when they want to drink all night long. Here you'll find the city's best cocktail bars, biggest night clubs and seediest dives. Head to Sanlitun Lu or the Workers Stadium.

Nanluogu Xiang (南锣鼓巷; Map p68), in Dōngchéng North, is far more laid back than Sānlǐtún. This historic *hútòng,* and the network of lanes branching off it, houses smaller bars – some are in converted courtyards – that are better for a drink and a chat, rather than a dance. The city's coolest live-music venues are in this area too. Head to Nanluogu Xiang, Beiluogu Xiang or the square between the Drum & Bell Towers.

At **Hòuhǎi Lakes** (后海; Map p80) there's a noisy but undoubtedly fun strip of bars, located attractively on the banks of Hòuhǎi and Qiánhǎi Lakes in Xīchéng North and specialising in neon-lit guitar bars with karaoke on tap. More popular with Chinese drinkers than foreigners, and dead in winter.

At the time of research **Fangjia Hutong** (方家胡同; Map p68), a largely residential lane, south of the Confucius Temple, was fast developing into another drinking hotspot with quirky, laid-back bars similar to those found in the Nanluogu Xiang area.

DRUM TOWER & DŌNGCHÉNG NORTH

Great Leap Brewing BAR

(大跃啤酒; Dàyuè Píjiǔ; Map68; www.greatleapbrewing.com; 6 Doujiao Hutong; 豆角胡同6号; beer per pint ¥25-50; ⏰7pm-midnight Tue-Fri, 3pm-midnight Sat, 2pm-9pm Sun; Ⓢ Shichahai) A hidden gem to beat all hidden gems, this micro-brewery, run by American beer enthusiast Carl Setzer, is housed in a hard-to-find, 100-year-old Qing-dynasty courtyard and serves up a wonderful selection of unique ales made largely from locally sourced ingredients. Sip on familiar favourites such as pale ales and porters or choose from China-inspired tipples such as the one made with lip-tingling Sìchuān peppercorns. From Nanluogu Xiang, walk west down Jingyang Hutong (景阳胡同), bearing right, then left, then right again before turning left down Doujiao Hutong.

El Nido BAR

(59号酒吧; Wǔshíjiǔ Hào Jiǔbā; Map p68; 59 Fangjia Hutong Dongdajie; 方家胡同59号; beers from ¥10; ⏰6pm-late; Ⓢ Andingmen) Friendly pint-sized bar, with some outdoor seating and more than 100 types of imported beer. There's no drinks menu; just dive into the fridge and pick out whichever bottles take your fancy. If it gets too packed (it really is tiny) then try walking up the road to No 46, where there's a bunch of bars and cafes in a small cul-de-sac.

Reef Bar BAR

(触礁; Chùjiāo; Map p68; 14-1 Nanluogu Xiang; 南锣鼓巷14-1号; beers from ¥20, cocktails from ¥25; ⏰2pm-late; Ⓢ Nanluoguxiang) Much more of a bar for locals than many others in the area, Reef, run by a cheerful husband-and-wife team, has a friendly vibe and stays open into the wee hours on busy nights.

Ball House BAR

(波楼酒吧; Bōlóu Jiǔbā; Map p68; Lǎo Mó; 40 Zhonglouwan Hutong; 钟楼湾胡同40号; ⏰2pm-late; Ⓢ Gulou Dajie) A bar for those in the know, Ball House is impossible to stumble across; there's no sign and it's set back from the main *hútòng* (which circumnavigates the Bell Tower) at the end of a narrow pathway. Inside, though, it's an enormous, beautifully restored split-level room with pool tables (¥30 per hour) and table football tables (free) dotted around the place – hence the name – but enough nooks and crannies to find your own quiet spot. Beers from ¥15.

LOCAL KNOWLEDGE

HÚTÒNG CAFES

Cute wi-fi cafes have been all the rage in Běijīng for some time now and these days there are dozens of excellent ones, particularly in and around the *hútòng* of North Dōngchéng. Some are housed in converted courtyards, most have free wi-fi, fresh coffee (from ¥20), well-priced local beer (from ¥10) and a limited choice of mostly Western food (dishes from ¥30). They are also among the cheapest places in Běijīng to sample Chinese tea (from ¥20 per cup, with unlimited refills).

Irresistible Cafe (诱惑咖啡厅; Yòu Huò Kāfēitīng; Map p68; 14 Mao'er Hutong; 帽儿胡同14号; ⏰11am-midnight, closed Mon & Tue; 📶) Large courtyard. Czech beers. Good, healthy food.

Cafe Confucius (秀冠咖啡; Xiù Guàn Kāfēi; Map p68; 25 Guozijian Jie; 国子监街25号; ⏰8.30am-8.30pm; 📶) Buddhist themed. Very friendly.

Xiǎoxīn's Cafe (小新的店; Xiǎoxīnde Diàn; Map p68; 103 Nanluogu Xiang; 南锣鼓巷103号; ⏰9.30am-midnight; 📶) Quiet retreat from the Nanluogu Xiang shopping frenzy.

Sculpting in Time (雕刻时光咖啡; Diāokè Shíguāng Kāfēi; Map p68; 2 Zhongku Hutong, Drum & Bell Square; 钟鼓楼文化广场,钟库胡同2号; ⏰10am-10pm; 📶) Rooftop terrace with views of the Drum and Bell Towers.

Courtyard No 28 (28号院; Èrshíbā Hào Yuàn; Map p68; Xilou Hutong; 戏楼胡同; 📶) Lovely courtyard. Cheap beer.

Mao Mao Chong　　　　BAR
(毛毛虫; Máomao Chóng; Map p68; 12 Banchang Hutong; 板厂胡同12号; beers from ¥25, cocktails from ¥40; ⏰7pm-midnight, closed Mon & Tue; Ⓢ Nanluoguxiang; ✈) This small but lively expat favourite has a rustic interior, good-value cocktails and a no-smoking policy. Its pizzas get rave reviews.

If　　　　BAR
(如果酒吧; Rúguǒ Jiǔbā; Map p68; 67 Beiluogu Xiang; 北锣鼓巷67号; beers from ¥15; ⏰1pm-2am; Ⓢ Gulou Dajie) Housed on three small levels, this quirky bar includes strangely shaped furniture, cheese-like wall panelling punctured with holes, and floors with rather disconcerting glass sections that allow you to view the level below.

Drum & Bell　　　　BAR
(鼓钟咖啡馆; Gǔzhōng Kāfēiguǎn; Map p68; 41 Zhonglouwan Hutong; 钟楼湾胡同41号; beers from ¥15, cocktails from ¥35; ⏰1pm-2am; Ⓢ Gulou Dajie) Located in between the Drum and Bell Towers, from whom it takes its name, the main attraction of this bar is its splendid roof terrace. It's a great spot to catch some rays on lazy Sunday afternoons, or to wile away a summer evening. In winter, retreat downstairs, where there are comfy sofas to sink into.

SĀNLǏTÚN & CHÁOYÁNG
Nali Patio　　　　BAR AREA
(那里花园; Nàlǐ Huāyuán; Map p76; off Sanlitun Lu; 三里屯路) Sānlǐtún's current drinking hotspot, Nali Patio is a small square surrounded and overlooked by clusters of hugely popular bars and restaurants. The big favourite is **Migas** (米家思; Mǐ Jiā Sī; 6th fl), a three-in-one venue which houses a good-quality Spanish restaurant, a cosy indoor bar and a wildly popular roof terrace bar. **Apothecary** (酒术; Jiǔ Shù; www.apothecarychina.com; 3rd fl) is Běijīng's best cocktail bar, while **Saddle Cantina** (1st & 2nd fl) offers a decent pub vibe, and terrace seating. Most places are open from around midday until the early hours.

Just round the corner from Nali Patio, behind Saddle Cantina, is **First Floor** (壹楼; Yī Lóu; Ground fl Tongli Studios, Sanlitun Houjie; 三里屯后街同里1层), which is another popular pub-like venue, and **Tree** (树酒吧; Shù Jiǔbā; 43 Sanlitun Beijie; 三里屯北街43号), which does dozens of Belgian beers plus great pizza.

⭐ Entertainment

FORBIDDEN CITY & DŌNGCHÉNG CENTRAL
Forbidden City Concert Hall　　CLASSICAL MUSIC
(中山公园音乐堂; Zhōngshān Gōngyuán Yīnyuè Táng; Map p62; ☎6559 8285; Zhongshan Park; 中山公园内; tickets ¥30-880; ⏰performances 7.30pm; Ⓢ Tian'anmen West) Located on the eastern side of Zhōngshān Park, this is a wonderfully romantic venue for performances of classical and traditional Chinese music. It's also one of the best acoustically.

DRUM TOWER & DŌNGCHÉNG NORTH

TOP CHOICE **Jiāng Hú** LIVE MUSIC

(江湖酒吧; Jiāng Hú Jiǔbā; Map p68; 7 Dongmianhua Hutong; 东棉花胡同7号; admission from ¥30; ⊙7pm-2am; ⑤Nanluoguxiang) One of the coolest places to hear Chinese indie and rock bands, Jiāng Hú, run by a trombone-playing, music-loving manager, is housed in an old courtyard and packs in the punters on a good night. Intimate, cool, and a decent spot for a drink in a courtyard, even when no bands are playing. Beers from ¥20.

TOP CHOICE **Jiāng Jìn Jiǔ** LIVE MUSIC

(疆进酒吧; Jiāngjìn Jiǔbā; Map p68; 2 Zhongku Hutong; 钟库胡同2号(鼓楼北口); admission from ¥20; ⊙1pm-2am; ⑤Gulou Dajie or Shichahai) This tiny, laidback venue is the best place to hear Chinese folk music from the country's ethnic minorities, particularly Uighur and Mongolian. Live music is Thursday to Sunday and is usually free, although there's sometimes a small cover charge on Fridays and Saturdays if a more popular act is playing. Beers from ¥15. Cocktails from ¥25.

Yúgōng Yíshān LIVE MUSIC

(愚公移山; Map p68; ☑6404 2711; www.yugongyishan.com; West Courtyard, 3-2 Zhangzizhong Lu; 张自忠路3-2(号段祺瑞执政府旧址西院); admission from ¥50; ⊙7pm-2am; ⑤Zhangzizhonglu) Reputedly one of the most haunted places in Běijīng, this historic building has been home to Qing dynasty royalty, warlords and the occupying Japanese army in the 1930s. You could probably hear the ghosts screaming if it wasn't for the array of local and foreign bands, solo artists and DJs who take to the stage here every week. With a very sound booking policy and a decent space to play with, this is one of the best places in town to listen to live music.

Mao Livehouse LIVE MUSIC

(光芒; Guāngmáng; Map p68; 111 Gulou Dongdajie; 鼓楼东大街111号; admission from ¥50; ⊙8pm-late; ⑤Shichahai) Large enough to give the many gigs it hosts a sense of occasion, but small enough to feel intimate.

Pénghāo Theatre CONTEMPORARY THEATRE

(蓬蒿剧场; Pénghāo Jùchǎng; Map p68; ☑6400 6452; www.penghaoren.com; in an alley beside 35 Dongmianhua Hutong; 东棉花胡同35号; tickets from ¥50; ⑤Nanluoguxiang) Students from the nearby drama academy sometimes perform here, in this small informal non-profit theatre, tucked away down a narrow, unnamed alleyway between Dongmianhua Hutong and Beibinmasi Hutong. The venue, which doubles as a cafe, is enchanting, and has some lovely rooftop seating areas, shaded by a 200-year-old tree which slices through part of the building. Performances are mostly modern drama, and are often held in English as well as Chinese.

TEMPLE OF HEAVEN PARK & DŌNGCHÉNG SOUTH

Red Theatre ACROBATICS

(红剧场; Hóng Jùchǎng; ☑6714 2473, 6714 8691; 44 Xingfu Dajie; tickets ¥180-680; ⊙performances 5.15pm & 7.30pm; ⑤Tiantandongmen) The daily show is *The Legend of Kung Fu* and it follows one boy's journey to becoming a warrior monk. Look for the all-red exterior set back from the road.

SĀNLǏTÚN & CHÁOYÁNG

Vics NIGHTCLUB

(威克斯; Wēikèsī; Map p76; Workers' Stadium, Gongrentiyuchang Beilu, 工人体育场; Fri & Sat ¥50; ⊙7pm-late; ⑤Dongsishitiao) Vics is not the most sophisticated nightclub, but has remained a favourite with the young crowd for many years now. The tunes are mostly

RED LIGHT PEKING

These days, Dazhalan Xijie and the surrounding *hútòng* just to the west of Dashilar are Běijīng's backpacker central. But for hundreds of years, these innocuous-looking alleys were infamous for being old Peking's red-light district (红灯区; *hóngdēngqū*).

Centered around Bada Hutong, a collection of eight alleys, the area had already acquired a raunchy reputation in the 18th century. By the time of the fall of the Qing dynasty in 1911, there were reckoned to be more than 300 brothels lining the lanes. The working girls ranged from cultivated courtesans whose clients were aristocrats and court officials, to more mundane types who served the masses.

Many of the eight alleys that made up Bada Hutong have been demolished and/or rebuilt and show no sign of what went on there in the past. Shanxi Xiang, though, is still standing and the historic building that is now the hostel Leo Courtyard (p92) was once one of the most upmarket knocking shops in the capital. But it didn't do dorm beds back then.

CON 'ARTISTS' & TEA MERCHANTS

Beware pesky 'art students' and English students around Wangfujing Dajie, Tiān'ānmén Sq and other tourist areas. They drag Western visitors to exhibitions of overpriced art or extortionate tea ceremonies; the latter may cost ¥2000 or more. If approached by over-friendly girls wanting to speak English, refuse to go to a place of their choosing.

standard R&B and hip-hop, there's an infamous ladies night on Wednesdays (free drinks for women before midnight), and weekends see it crammed with the footloose and fancy free. If you can't score here, you should give up trying. Entry is free from Monday to Thursday; located inside the Workers Stadium north gate, opposite **Mix**, a very similar, equally popular venue.

BĚIHǍI PARK & XĪCHÉNG NORTH

TOP CHOICE East Shore Jazz Café LIVE MUSIC
(东岸; Dōng'àn; Map p80; 2nd fl, 2 Shichahai Nanyan; beers from ¥35, cocktails from ¥40; ☉3pm-2am; ⑤Shichahai) Fine views over Qiánhǎi Lake and the place to hear the best local jazz bands, with live performances from Wednesdays to Sundays (from 10pm) in a laid-back atmosphere.

DASHILAR & XĪCHÉNG SOUTH

Húguǎng Guild Hall PEKING OPERA
(湖广会馆; Húguǎng Huìguǎn; Map p83; 3 Hufang Lu; tickets ¥180-680; ☉performances 6.30pm; ⑤Caishikou) With a magnificent red, green and gold interior and balconies surrounding the canopied stage, this theatre dates from 1807 and is a great spot to catch a Běijīng opera show. There's also a small **opera museum** (admission ¥10; ☉9am to 5pm) opposite the theatre.

Lao She Teahouse TEAHOUSE
(老舍茶馆; Lǎo Shě Cháguǎn; Map p83; 3rd fl, 3 Qianmen Xidajie; evening tickets ¥180-380; ☉performances 7.50pm; ⑤Qianmen) This popular teahouse has nightly shows, largely in Chinese. Performances include folk music, tea ceremonies, theatre, puppet shows and matinée Běijīng opera, as well as acrobatics and magic. Prices depend on the type of show and your seat option.

Tiānqiáo Acrobatics Theatre ACROBATICS
(天桥杂技剧场; Tiānqiáo Zájì Jùchǎng; Map p83; ☑6303 7449; 95 Tianqiao Shichang Lu Jie; tickets ¥180-380; ☉performances 5.30pm; ⑤Taoranting) West of the Temple of Heaven Park, this 100-year-old theatre offers one of Běijīng's best acrobatic displays. The entrance is down the eastern side of the building.

SUMMER PALACE & HǍIDIÀN

Propaganda CLUB
(Map p52; Huaqing Jiayuan; 华清嘉园; ☉8.30pm-late; ⑤Wudaokou) Wǔdàokǒu's student crew are drawn like moths to this long-running club, thanks to cheap drinks, hip-hop sounds and the chance for cultural exchange with the locals. Entry is free. To find it, walk 50m west of Wudaoku subway station and turn left onto Huaqing Jiayuan.

 Shopping

With much of the nation's wealth concentrated in Běijīng, shopping has become the favourite pastime of the young and the rising middle class in recent years. Whether you're a diehard shopaholic or just a casual browser, you'll be spoiled for choice with shiny shopping malls, markets, specialist shopping streets, pavement vendors and itinerant hawkers all doing their best to part you from your cash.

FORBIDDEN CITY & DŌNGCHÉNG CENTRAL

Wangfujing Dajie SHOPPING STREET
(王府井; Map p62; ⑤Wangfujing) Prestigious, but these days rather old-fashioned, this part-pedestrianised shopping street not far from Tiān'ānmén Sq, is generally known as Wángfǔjǐng. It boasts a strip of stores selling well-known, midrange brands, and a number of tacky souvenir outlets. At its south end, **Oriental Plaza** is a top-quality, modern shopping mall. Further north, just before the pedestrianised section ends, is the well-stocked **Foreign Languages Bookstore**.

DRUM TOWER & DŌNGCHÉNG NORTH

TOP CHOICE Nanluogu Xiang SHOPPING STREET
(南锣鼓巷; Map p68; ⑤Nanluoguxiang) The wildly popular historical *hútòng* of Nanluogu Xiang contains an eclectic mix of clothes and gifts, sold in trendy boutique shops, alongside dozens of cute cafes, bars and restaurants. It's an extremely pleasant place to shop for souvenirs, but avoid summer weekends if you can, when it gets unfeasibly busy.

TEMPLE OF HEAVEN & DŌNGCHÉNG SOUTH

Hóngqiáo Pearl Market   SOUVENIR MARKET

(红桥市场; Hóngqiáo Shìchǎng; Map p73; Tiantan Donglu; ◎9am-7pm; §Tiantandongmen) The cosmos of clutter across from the east gate of Temple of Heaven Park ranges from shoes, leather bags, jackets, jeans, silk by the yard, electronics, Chinese arts, crafts and antiques to a galaxy of pearls (freshwater and seawater, white and black) on the 3rd floor. Prices for the latter vary incredibly depending on the quality; the more expensive specimens are on the 4th and 5th floors.

SĀNLǏTÚN & CHÁOYÁNG

TOP CHOICE Pānjiāyuán Market   ANTIQUES MARKET

(潘家园古玩市场; Pānjiāyuán Gǔwán Shìchǎng; Map p52; West of Panjiayuan Qiao; 潘家园桥西侧; ◎8.30am-6pm Mon-Fri, 4.30am-6pm Sat & Sun; ◎Jinsong) The best place in Běijīng to shop for arts, crafts and antiques, Pānjiāyuán hosts around 3000 dealers and up to 50,000 visitors a day, all scoping for treasures. Make a few rounds to compare prices before forking out for something.

The market is about 1km south of Jinsong subway station on Line 10. Come out of Exit D and keep walking straight. Turn right at the flyover and you'll see the market on your left. At the time of research, Line 10 was due to be extended south and will eventually include a Panjiayuan station.

TOP CHOICE Sānlǐtún Village   SHOPPING MALL

(Map p76; 19 Sanlitun Lu; 三里屯路19号; ◎10am-10pm; §Tuanjiehu) This ultra modern, eye-catching collection of midsized malls is a shopping and architectural highlight of this part of the city. The Village looms over what was once a seedy strip of dive bars (there are still a few of those left, mind) and has transformed the area into a hangout hotspot for locals and foreigners alike. The complex is in two sections, which book-end the slightly older **3.3 Shopping Centre**. The **South Village** was completed a few years back and is home to Běijīng's first Apple store, the world's largest Adidas shop and a number of midrange Western clothing stores. Nearby **North Village** is home to more high-end labels and local designer boutiques.

TOP CHOICE Bookworm   BOOKSHOP & CAFE

(书虫; Shūchóng; Map p76; ☑6586 9507; www. beijingbookworm.com; Bldg 4, Nansanlitun Lu; 南三里屯路4号楼; mains from ¥70; ◎9am-2am; §Tuanjiehu; ◎☻) A combination of a bar, cafe, restaurant and library, the Bookworm is a Běijīng institution. There are 16,000-plus books you can browse whilst sipping your coffee, or working your way through the extensive wine list, but this is also one of the epicentres of Běijīng cultural life, hosting lectures, poetry readings and a very well-regarded annual book festival.

Shard Box Store   JEWELLERY

(慎德阁; Shèndégé; Map p76; 4 Ritan Beilu; 日坛北路4号; ◎9am-7pm; §Yonganli) Using porcelain fragments from Ming- and Qing-dynasty vases that were destroyed during the Cultural Revolution, this fascinating family-run store creates beautiful and unique shard boxes (from ¥30), bottles and jewellery.

Silk Market   SOUVENIR MARKET

(秀水市场; Xiùshuǐ Shìchǎng; Map p76; 14 Dongdaqiao Lu; 东大桥路14号; ◎10am-8.30pm; §Yonganli) The six-storey Silk Market continues to thrive despite some vendors being hit by lawsuits from top-name brands tired of being counterfeited on such a huge scale. Not that the legal action has stopped the coach loads of tourists who descend on this place every day. Their presence makes effective bargaining difficult. But this is a good place for cashmere, T-shirts, jeans, shirts, skirts and, of course, silk, which is one of the few genuine items you will find here.

Sānlǐtún Yashow Clothing Market   SOUVENIR MARKET

(三里屯雅秀服装市场; Sānlǐtún Yǎxiù Fúzhuāng Shìchǎng; Map p76; 58 Gongrentiyuchang Beilu; 工体北路58号; ◎10am-9pm; §Tuanjiehu) Five floors of virtually anything you might need and a favourite with expats and visitors. Bargain hard.

> **WORTH A TRIP**
>
> ## MǍLIÁNDÀO TEA MARKET
>
> The largest tea market in Běijīng, **Mǎliándào** (马连道茶城; Mǎliándào Cháchéng; Map p52; 6 Maliandao Lu; 马连道路6号; ◎9am-7pm; §Beijing West Railway Station), a few minutes walk south of Běijīng West Train Station, is home to, if not all the tea in China, then an awful lot of it. Although it's mostly for wholesalers, this is a great place to wander for anyone interested in tea and the vendors are normally happy to let you sample some.

DASHILAR & XĪCHÉNG SOUTH

Liulichang Xijie
ANTIQUES

(琉璃厂; Liúlíchǎng) Běijīng's premier antique street, not far west of Dashilar, is worth delving along for its quaint, albeit dressed-up, age-old village atmosphere and (largely fake) antiques. Alongside ersatz Qing mono- chrome bowls and Cultural Revolution kitsch, you can also rummage through old Chinese books, paintings, brushes, ink and paper. Prepare yourself for pushy sales staff and stratospheric prices. If you want a chop (carved seal) made, you can do it here. At the western end of Liulichang Xijie, a collection of ramshackle stalls flog bric-a-brac, Buddhist statuary, Cultural Revolution pamphlets and posters, fake Tang-dynasty *sāncǎi* (three-colour porcelain), shoes for bound feet, silks, handicrafts, Chinese kites, swords, walking sticks, door knockers etc.

Ruìfúxiáng
CLOTHING

(瑞蚨祥丝绸店; Ruìfúxiáng Sīchóudiàn; Map p83; 5 Dazhalan Jie; ☺9.30am-8.30pm; ⑤Qianmen) Housed in a historic building on Dashilar, this well-renowned clothing store is one of the best places in town to browse for silk. It starts at ¥98 a metre, although most of the fabric is more expensive. On the 2nd floor ready-made, traditional Chinese clothing is sold. Also has an outlet on Wangfujing Dajie (p102) and one just south of the Drum Tower, at No 50 Di'anmenwai Dajie (Map p68).

ⓘ Information

Internet Access

Internet cafes (网吧; wǎngbā) are everywhere, although some are tucked away down side streets and above shops. They rarely have English signs, so memorise the characters 网吧. They are generally open 24 hours. Standard rates are ¥3 to ¥5 per hour. You must show your passport, and you may be photographed at the front desk. We've marked some handy internet cafes on our Běijīng maps with the @ icon.

All hotels and hostels we've reviewed in this chapter provide internet access of some sort, and numerous bars and cafes around Běijīng have free wi-fi.

Maps

English-language maps of Běijīng can be grabbed for free at most big hotels and branches of the Běijīng Tourist Information Center. The Foreign Languages Bookstore and other bookshops with English-language titles have maps. Pushy street vendors hawk cheap Chinese character maps near subway stations around Tiān'ānmén Sq and Wangfujing Dajie. The Běijīng Tourist Map, labelled in both English and Chinese, has little detail but is quite useful.

Medical Services

Pharmacies (药店; yàodiàn) are identified by a green cross and are widespread.

Běijīng Union Hospital (协和医院; Xiéhé Yīyuàn; Map p62; ☏6529 6114, emergency 6529 5284; 53 Dongdan Beidajie, Dōngchéng; ☺24hr) A recommended Chinese hospital with a full range of facilities for inpatient and outpatient care, plus a pharmacy. Head for **International Medical Services** (国际医疗部; Guójì Yīliáo Bù; ☏6915 4270; 6529 5284), a wing reserved for foreigners which has English-speaking staff and telephone receptionists.

Hong Kong International Medical Clinic (北京香港国际医务诊所; Běijīng Xiānggǎng Guójì Yīwù Zhěnsuǒ;Map p76; ☏6553 2288; www.hkclinic.com; 9th fl, Office Tower, Hong Kong Macau Center, Swissôtel, 2 Chaoyangmen Beidajie, Cháoyáng; ☺9am-9pm, dental ☺9am-7pm) Well trusted dental and medical clinic with English-speaking staff. Prices are more reasonable than at International SOS. Medical consultations cost ¥680. Has night staff on duty too, so you can call for advice round the clock.

International SOS (国际SOS医务诊所; Guójì SOS Yīwù Zhěnsuǒ; Map p76; www.internationalsos.com; ste 105, Wing 1, Kunsha Bldg, 16 Xinyuanli, Cháoyáng; ☺9am-8pm Mon-Fri, 9am-6pm Sat & Sun; ☏clinic appointments 6462 9199, dental appointments 6462 0333, 24hr alarm centre 6462 9100) Offering 24-hour emergency medical care, with a high-quality clinic with English-speaking staff. Dental check up ¥900; medical consultation ¥1160.

Money

ATMs (取款机; qǔkuǎnjī) taking international cards are in abundance, including at the airport. Carry cash at all times as credit cards are much less widely accepted than you'd expect.

Foreign currency and travellers cheques can be changed at large branches of Bank of China, CITIC Industrial Bank, Industrial & Commercial Bank of China (ICBC), HSBC, the airport and hotel moneychanging counters.

For international money transfers, branches of **Western Union** (www.westernunion.com) can be found in the **International Post Office** and the Cháoyáng branch of **China Post** (3 Gongrentiyuchang Beilu).

Useful banks with money-changing facilities include:

Bank of China (中国银行; Zhōngguó Yínháng) Lufthansa Center (Map p76; 1st fl, Lufthansa Center Yǒuyì Shopping City, 50 Liangmaqiao Lu); Novotel Peace Hotel (Map p62; foyer,

Novotel Peace Hotel, 3 Jinyu Hutong); Oriental Plaza (Map p62; Oriental Plaza, cnr Wangfujing Dajie & Dongchang'an Jie); Sūndōngān Plaza (Map p62; next to main entrance of Sūndōngān Plaza, Wangfujing Dajie); Swissôtel (Map p76; 2nd fl, Swissôtel, 2 Chaoyangmen Beidajie)

Citibank (花旗银行; Huāqí Yínháng; Map p62; ☑6510 2933; 6th fl, Tower 2, Bright China Cháng'ān Bldg, 7 Jianguomennei Dajie)

HSBC (汇丰银行; Huìfēng Yínháng; ☑6526 0668, 800 820 8878) China World Hotel (Map p76; ste L129, Ground fl, China World Hotel, 1 Jianguomenwai Dajie); COFCO Plaza (Map p76; Ground fl, Block A, COFCO Plaza, 8 Jianguomennei Dajie); Lufthansa Center (Map p76; Ground fl, Lufthansa Center, 50 Liangmaqiao Lu)

Industrial & Commercial Bank of China (ICBC; 工商银行; Gōngshāng Yínháng; Map p62; Wangfujing Dajie) Opposite Bank of China ATM at entrance to Sūndōngān Plaza.

China Post

Large offices (邮局; yóujú) are generally open daily between 8.30am and 6pm. We've marked some on our Běijīng maps.

Letters and parcels marked 'Poste Restante, Běijīng Main Post Office' will arrive at the **International Post Office** (国际邮电局; Guójì Yóudiàn Jú; Map p76; ☑6512 8114; Jianguomen Beidajie, Cháoyáng; ☑8.30am-6pm). Outsized parcels going overseas should be sent from here (parcels can be bought at the post office); smaller parcels (up to around 20kg) can go from smaller post offices. Both outgoing and incoming packages will be opened and inspected. If you're sending a parcel, don't seal the package until you've had it inspected.

Express Mail Service (EMS; 快递; kuàidì) is available for registered deliveries to domestic and international destinations from most post offices around town. Prices are very reasonable. Alternatively, **Federal Express** (联邦快递; Liánbāng Kuàidì; FedEx; Map p76; ☑6561 2003, 800 810 2338; 1217, Tower B, Hanwei Bldg, 7 Guanghua Lu) is near the CBD, and also has a branch at Wangfujing Dajie (Map p62; Room 107, No 1 Office Bldg, Oriental Plaza).

Public Security Bureau

PSB (公安局; Gōng'ānjú; Map p68; ☑8402 0101, 8401 5292; 2 Andingmen Dongdajie; ☑8.30am-4.30pm Mon-Sat) The Foreign Affairs Branch of the PSB handles visa extensions; see p992 for further information. The visa office is on the 2nd floor.

Tourist Information

Hotels often have tourist information desks, but the best travel advice for independent travellers is usually dished out at youth hostels.

Běijīng Tourist Information Center (北京旅游咨询服务中心; Běijīng Lǚyóu Zīxún Fúwù Zhōngxīn; ☑9am-5pm) Beijing Train Station (Map p62; ☑6528 4848; 16 Laoqianju Hutong); Capital Airport (Map p110; ☑6459 8148); Hòuhǎi Lakes (Map p80; 49 Di'anmenxi Dajie; 地安门西大街49号); Wangfujing Dajie (Map p62; 269 Wangfujing Dajie; 王府井大街269号; ☑9am-9pm). English skills are limited and information is basic, but you can grab free maps. The detailed map of the *hútòng* surrounding Hòuhǎi Lakes, which is given out at the Hòuhǎi branch, is particularly useful.

Travel Agencies

China International Travel Service (CITS; 中国国际旅行社; Zhōngguó Guójì Lǚxíngshè; Map p62; ☑8511 8522; www.cits.com.cn; Room 1212, CITS Bldg, 1 Dongdan Beidajie) Useful for booking tours, although aimed mostly at domestic tourists.

ⓘ Getting There & Away

As the nation's capital, getting to Běijīng is straightforward. Rail and air connections link the city to virtually every point in China, and fleets of buses head to abundant destinations from Běijīng. Using Běijīng as a starting point to explore the rest of the country makes perfect sense.

Air

Běijīng has direct air connections to most major cities in the world. For more information, see p996.

Daily flights connect Běijīng to every major city in China. There should be at least one flight a week to smaller cities throughout China. Prices vary depending on when you fly and when you book, but as a rough guide, expect to be able to find seats for between ¥600 and ¥1200 for any internal one-way flight from Běijīng.

For good deals, check the following websites:

C-trip (www.ctrip.com)

eLong (www.elong.net)

Travel Zen (www.travelzen.com)

eBookers (www.ebookers.com)

Expedia (www.expedia.com)

If for some reason you can't get online, you can also purchase tickets in person at the **Civil Aviation Administration of China** (中国民航; CAAC; Zhōngguó Mínháng; Aviation Bldg; 民航营业大厦; Mínháng Yíngyè Dàshà; Map p80; ☑6656 9118, domestic 6601 3336, international 6601 6667; 15 Xichang'an Jie; ☑7am-midnight).

You can make enquiries for all airlines at Běijīng's **Capital Airport** (PEK; Map p110; ☑from Běijīng only 962 580). Call ☑6454 1100 for information on international and domestic arrivals and departures.

Bus

No international buses serve Běijīng; however, there are plenty of long-distance domestic routes from the city's numerous long-distance bus stations. **Bāwángfén long-distance bus station** (八王坟长途客运站; Bāwángfén chángtú kèyùnzhàn; Map p52; 17 Xidawang Lu) is in the east of the city, 500m south of Dawanglu subway station. Destinations include:

Bāotóu sleeper ¥181, 12 hours, one daily (6pm)

Chángchūn ¥320, 12 hours, one daily (6pm)

Dàlián ¥326, 8½ hours, two daily (noon and 10pm)

Hā'ěrbīn ¥301, 14 hours, once daily but only if enough passengers (5.30pm)

Shěnyáng ¥165, nine hours, regular (8am–10pm)

Tiānjīn ¥35, two hours, regular (9.30am–6.30pm)

Sìhuì long-distance bus station (四惠长途汽车站; Sìhuì chángtú qìchēzhàn; Map p52) is in the east of town, 200m east of Sihui subway station. Destinations include:

Bāotóu ¥180, 12 hours, one daily (10.30am)

Chéngdé ¥85, four hours, regular (7am–4pm)

Dāndōng ¥220, 12 hours, one daily (4pm)

Jìxiàn ¥30, two hours, regular (6.40am–7.20pm)

Liùlǐqiáo long-distance bus station (六里桥长途站; Liùlǐqiáo chángtúzhàn; Map p52) is in the southwest of the city, one subway stop from Běijīng West Train Station. Destinations include:

Dàtóng ¥133, 4½ hours, regular (7.10am–6pm)

Héféi ¥380, 13 hours, one daily (1.45pm)

Luòyáng ¥148, 10 hours, one daily (7.30pm)

Shíjiāzhuāng ¥83, 3½ hours, two daily (8am and 5.30pm)

Xiàmén ¥580, 30 hours, every other day (11am)

Xī'ān ¥298, 12 hours, one daily (5.45pm)

Zhèngzhōu seat/sleeper ¥128/158, 8½ hours, seat 8.30am, sleeper 7pm and 9pm

Liánhuāchí long-distance bus station (莲花池长途汽车站; Liánhuāchí chángtú qìchēzhàn; Map p52) is a short walk north of Liùlǐqiáo long-distance bus station. Destinations include:

Ānyáng ¥120, 6½ hours, 8am-7pm (regular)

Luòyáng ¥150, 11 hours, one daily (6.30pm)

Yán'ān ¥251, 14 hours, one daily (2.30pm)

Zhàogōngkǒu long-distance bus station (赵公口汽车站; Zhàogōngkǒu qìchēzhàn; Map p52) is in the south, 10 minutes walk west of Liujiayao subway station. Destinations include:

Jǐ'nán ¥129, 5½ hours, four daily (6am, 8am, 11am and 12.40pm)

Shànghǎi ¥340, 16 hours (4.30pm)

Tiānjīn ¥30–35, two hours, regular (7am–6pm)

Train

There are no longer dedicated ticket offices for foreigners at the main stations in Běijīng, although there is sometimes a ticket window with a temporary 'for foreigners' sign attached to it. Look out for this. Otherwise, join any queue, but arm yourself with a few key Chinese phrases, or better still have a Chinese person write down what you want so you can show the ticket seller. Increasingly, ticket sellers at the three main stations speak a bit of English, but don't bank on it.

Almost all hotels and hostels, can buy train tickets for you, for a small commission, of course. Official **train ticket offices** (火车票代售处; huǒchēpiào dàishòuchù) are dotted around town and charge a very reasonable ¥10 commission per ticket. But although they have an English sign, English-language skills are usually nonexistent.

For more on trains and train travel in China, see p1004.

Běijīng Train Station (北京站; Běijīng Zhàn; Map p62) is the most central of Běijīng's four main train stations, and is linked to the subway system. It's mainly for T class trains (tèkuài), slow trains and trains bound for the northeast; most fast trains heading south now depart from Běijīng South Train Station and Běijīng West Train Station. Slower trains to Shànghǎi still leave from here, though.

Typical fares (hard-sleeper unless indicated) include:

Dàlián Z series train, soft sleeper ¥390, 10½ hours (8.46pm)

Dàlián T & K series, ¥260, 12 hours (6.07pm and 8.06pm)

Dàtóng K series, ¥108, six hours (regular)

Hā'ěrbīn D series, soft seat ¥267, 10 hours (7.13am, 1.51pm and 2.18am)

Hā'ěrbīn T series, ¥281, 12 hours (4.50pm and 9.26pm)

Jílín T series, ¥263, 12 hours (7.10pm)

Shànghǎi T series, soft-sleeper ¥327, 14 hours (4.56pm and 7.28pm)

Běijīng West Train Station (西站; xī zhàn; Map p52) is gargantuan. At the time of research, it was on the disconnected subway Line 9, so it was better to use Military Museum station on Line 1 (turn left out of Exit D of the station, then left again and keep walking; 15 minutes). By the time you read this, though, Line 9 should be connected to the rest of the subway network.

Běijīng West accommodates fast Z series trains, such as the following (fares are soft-sleeper unless indicated):

Chángshā ¥529, 13 hours (6.16pm)

Fúzhōu ¥458, 20 hours (3.08pm)

TRAIN TO TIBET

For Lhasa (拉萨; Lāsà) in Tibet (西藏; Xīzàng), the **T27** (hard seat/hard-sleeper/soft-sleeper ¥389/766/1189, 44 hours) leaves Běijīng West Train Station at 8.09pm, taking just under two days. In the return direction, the T28 departs Lhasa at 1.45pm and arrives at Běijīng West at 8.07am.

You will, of course, need all your Tibet permits in order before taking this train.

Hànkǒu (Wǔhàn) ¥429, 10 hours (8.54pm and 9.12pm)

Kowloon (Hong Kong) ¥488, 24 hours (train Q97, 1.08pm)

Lánzhōu Z & T series, hard-sleeper ¥345, 17 hours (2.31pm and 8.09pm)

Nánchāng hard sleeper ¥319, 11½ hours (7.45pm, 8pm and 8.06pm)

Wǔchāng (Wǔhàn) hard sleeper ¥281, 10 hours (9pm and 9.06pm)

Xī'ān hard sleeper ¥270–290, 11–12 hours (8.03pm and 8.48pm)

Other typical train fares for hard-sleeper tickets include:

Chángshā T & K series, ¥345, 14 hours (regular)

Chéngdū T & K series, ¥418–469, 26–31 hours (9am, 11.08am, 6.29pm and 9.52pm)

Chóngqìng T & K series, ¥409–458, 25-30 hours (five daily)

Guǎngzhōu T & K series, ¥458, 21 hours (five daily)

Guìyáng T series, ¥490, 29 hours (3.58pm and 4.57pm)

Kūnmíng T series, ¥578, 38 hours (4.37pm)

Shēnzhèn T & K series, ¥467, 24–29 hours (8.12pm and 11.45pm)

Shíjiāzhuāng D series, 2nd-class seat, ¥82, two hours (regular)

Ürümqi T series, ¥569, 34 hours (10.08am)

Xī'ān T series, ¥274, 13–14 hours (regular from 2pm onwards)

Xīníng T series, ¥379–430, 20–24 hours (1.59pm and 8.09pm)

Yíchāng K series, ¥319–333, 21½ hours (1.35pm and 11.11pm)

Běijīng South Train Station (南站; nán zhàn; Map p52) is ultra modern, and is linked to the subway system on Line 4. It accommodates very high speed 'bullet' trains to destinations such as Tiānjīn, Shànghǎi, Hángzhōu and Qīngdǎo. Sample fares:

Fúzhōu D series, second-class seat ¥676, 15 hours (7.50am)

Hángzhōu G series, second-class seat ¥631, six hours (regular)

Jǐ'nán G series, second-class seat ¥185, 1½ hours (regular)

Nánjīng G series, second-class seat ¥445, four hours (regular)

Qīngdǎo G & D series, second-class seat ¥250–315, five hours (regular)

Shànghǎi (Hóngqiáo Station) G class trains, second-class seat, ¥555, 5½ hours (regular)

Sūzhōu G series, second-class seat ¥525, five hours (regular)

Tiānjīn C series, ¥55, 30 minutes (regular)

Běijīng North Train Station (北站; běi zhàn; Map p52) is a short walk north of Xizhimen subway station, and is much smaller. Destinations include:

Bādálǐng Great Wall hard/soft seat ¥7/10, 75 minutes (regular)

Hohhot K series, hard-sleeper ¥137, nine hours (11.47pm)

ⓘ Getting Around

To/From Capital Airport

The **Airport Express** (机场快轨; Jīchǎng Kuàiguǐ; one-way ¥25; 30 minutes), also written as ABC (Airport Běijīng City), is quick and convenient and links Terminals 2 and 3 to Běijīng's subway system at Sanyuanqiao station (Line 10) and Dongzhimen station (Lines 2 and 13). Trains leave every few minutes. Train times are as follows: Terminal 3 (6.21am–10.51pm); Terminal 2 (6.35am–11.10pm); Dongzhimen (6am–10.30pm).

A **taxi** (using its meter) should cost ¥80–100 from the airport to the city centre, including the ¥15 airport expressway toll; bank on 30 minutes to one hour to get into town. Join the taxi ranks and ignore approaches from drivers. When you get into the taxi, make sure the driver uses the meter (打表; dǎ biǎo). It is also useful to have the name of your hotel written down in Chinese to show the driver. Very few drivers speak English.

There are 10 different routes for the airport **shuttle bus** (机场巴士; jīchǎng bāshì; one-way ¥16) including those listed below. They all leave from all three terminals and run from around 5am to midnight.

Line 1 To Fāngzhuāng (方庄), via Dàběiyáo (大北窑) for the CBD (国贸; guó mào)

Line 3 To Běijīng Train Station (北京站; Běijīng Zhàn), via Dōngzhímén (东直门), Dōngsìshítiáo (东四十条) and Cháoyángmén (朝阳门)

Line 7 To Běijīng West Train Station (西站; xī zhàn)

INTERNATIONAL TRAINS

Mongolia

Two, sometimes three direct weekly trains leave from Běijīng Train Station to the Mongolian capital of Ulaanbaatar (乌兰巴托; Wūlánbātuō). The **Trans-Mongolian (K3)** (hard-sleeper/soft-sleeper/delux ¥1430/2056/2241, 30 hours, 7.45am) to Moscow goes via Ulaanbaatar, and leaves every Wednesday. Meanwhile the **K23** train has a Tuesday service (¥1430/2056/2241, 30 hours, 8.05am) and a Saturday service (¥1472/2056/2202, 30 hours, 8.05am). During the summer, both trains usually run, but at other times of the year it is only one or the other. Double check at the CITS international train ticket office.

In the other direction, the **K4** leaves Ulaanbaatar at 7.15am on Tuesday and arrives in Běijīng at 2.04pm on Wednesday. The **K24** departs from Ulaanbaatar at 8.05am on either Thursday, Friday or both days, and reaches Běijīng the following day at 2.04pm.

Russia

The Trans-Siberian Railway runs from Běijīng to Moscow (莫斯科; Mòsīkē) via two routes: the **Trans-Mongolian (K3)** (¥4049/5962/6527, see Mongolia above) and the **Trans-Manchurian (K19)** (hard-sleeper/delux ¥4473/6953). The K19 leaves Běijīng Train Station every Saturday at 11pm, arriving in Moscow on Friday at 5.58pm.

The return **K20** leaves Moscow at 11.55pm on Saturday and arrives in Běijīng on Friday at 5.32am.

Vietnam

There are two weekly trains from Běijīng to Hanoi (河内; Hénèi). The **T5** (M2 in Vietnam) leaves Běijīng West Train Station at 3.45pm on Thursday and Sunday, arriving in Hanoi at 8.10am on Saturday and Wednesday.

In the other direction, the **T6** (M1 in Vietnam) leaves Hanoi at 6.30pm on Tuesday and Friday and arrives at Běijīng West at 12.07pm on Friday and Monday. Only soft-sleeper tickets (¥2390) are available.

North Korea

There are four weekly services to Pyongyang (平壤; Píngrǎng; hard-sleeper ¥1164-1214, soft-sleeper ¥1692-1737). The **K27** and **K28** both leave twice a week from Běijīng Train Station, meaning there's a train on Monday, Wednesday, Thursday and Saturday. Each train leaves at 5.30pm and arrives the following day at 7.30pm.

Return trains leave from Pyongyang at 10.10am on Monday, Wednesday, Thursday and Saturday and arrive the following day in Běijīng at 8.31am.

Visas, Tickets & Tours

Visas aren't available at these border crossings. Ensure you arrange yours beforehand.

You can't buy international tickets at Běijīng train stations without going through a travel agency. For Mongolia, Russia and Vietnam, buy tickets at the helpful **CITS** (China International Travel Service; 中国国际旅行社; Zhōngguó Guójì Lǚxíngshè; Map p62; ☎6512 0507; Běijīng International Hotel, 9 Jianguomennei Dajie, Dōngchéng; ☺9am-noon & 1.30-5pm Mon-Fri, 9am-noon Sat & Sun), at the rear of the left side of the hotel lobby, one block north of Běijīng Train Station

For North Korea, buy tickets at the office of **CRTS** (China Railway Travel Service; 中国铁道旅行社; Zhōngguó Tiědào Lǚxíngshè; Map p52; ☎5182 6541; 20 Beifengwo Lu; 北蜂窝路20号; ☺9am-4pm). There's no English sign, but it's opposite the easy-to-spot Tiānyòu Hotel (天佑大厦; Tiānyòu Dàshà). Walk straight out of Exit C1 of Military Museum subway station, take the first right and CRTS will be on your left (10 minutes).

Trans-Siberian/Mongolian/Manchurian tickets can be bought from home, using **Intourist Travel** (www.intourist.com), which has branches in the UK, the USA, Canada, Finland and Poland.

For help with booking a tour to North Korea, Běijīng's leading tour company for the area is **Koryo Tours** (www.koryogroup.com).

Line 10 To Běijīng South Train Station (南站; nán zhàn)

Coach service to Tiānjīn (天津; ¥80, 2½ hours, 8am–10pm hourly)

To/From Nányuàn Airport

The very small **Nányuàn Airport** (南苑机场; Nányuàn Jīchǎng; NAY; Map p110; ☑6797 8899; Jingbeixi Lu, Nányuàn Zhèn, Fēngtái District; 丰台区南苑镇警备西路(警备路口)) feels more like a provincial bus station than an airport, but it does service quite a few domestic routes. Airport facilities are limited to a few shops and snack stalls, and English-language skills are minimal.

The **shuttle bus** (机场巴士; jīchǎng bāshì) goes to Xīdān (西单; ¥16; two hours; 11.15am–12.50am), from where you can pick up the subway.

A **taxi** costs around ¥60 to the Tiān'ānmén Square area. Ignore drivers who approach you. Use the official taxi queue. And make sure the driver uses the meter (打表; dǎ biǎo).

Bicycle

See Activities (p87).

Subway

Massive, and getting bigger every year, the **Běijīng subway system** (地铁; dìtiě; www.bjsubway.com; per trip ¥2; ☑6am-11pm) is modern, easy to use and cheap. Get hold of a **travel card** (交通一卡通; jiāotōng yīkǎtōng; refundable deposit ¥20) if you don't fancy queuing for tickets each time you travel. The card won't make subway trips any cheaper, although it will get you a 60% discount on all bus journeys within the municipality of Běijīng. You'll find a pull-out subway map in the back of this book.

Taxi

Taxis (出租车; chūzūchē) are everywhere, although finding one can be a problem during rush hour and rainstorms. It can also take longer than usual to flag down a taxi between around 8pm and 10pm – prime time for people heading home after eating out at a restaurant.

Flag fall is ¥10, and lasts for three kilometres. After that it's ¥2 per kilometre. Drivers also add a small flat-rate fuel surcharge (usually ¥3). Rates increase slightly at night.

Drivers rarely speak any English so it's important to have the name and address of where you want to go written down in Chinese characters. And always remember to keep your hotel's business card on you so you can get home at the end of the night.

By law, taxi drivers must use the meter (打表; dǎ biǎo). If they refuse, get out and find another cab. The exception is for long, out-of-town trips to, say, the Great Wall, where prices are agreed (but not paid for!) beforehand.

TAKEN FOR A RIDE

A well-established illegal taxi operation at the airport attempts to lure weary travellers into a ¥300-plus ride to the city, so be on your guard. If anyone approaches you offering you a taxi ride, ignore them and join the queue for a taxi outside.

For taxi companies in Běijīng, see our Great Wall chapter (p116).

Car

See our Great Wall chapter (p116) for more on car rentals.

The **Vehicle Administration Office** (车管所; Chēguǎnsuǒ; Map p110; ☑6453 0010; ☑9am-6pm) on the 1st floor of Terminal 3 at Capital Airport – look for the 'Traffic Police' sign – issues temporary driving licences for use in Běijīng municipality. Applicants must be between the ages of 18 and 70 and must hold a temporary Chinese visa (three months or less). The straightforward procedure takes about 30 minutes and costs ¥10.

Bus

Běijīng's buses (公共汽车; gōnggòng qìchē) have always been numerous and dirt cheap (from ¥1), but they're now becoming easier to use for non-Chinese-speaking visitors, with swipe cards, announcements as English, and bus stop signs written in Pinyin as well as Chinese characters. Nevertheless, it's still a challenge to get from A to B successfully, and the buses are still as packed as ever, so you rarely see foreigners climbing on board.

If you use a travel card (see subway section), you get 60% discount on all journeys. Useful routes include:

4 Runs along Chang'an Jie, Jianguomenwai Dajie and Jianguomennei Dajie: Gongzhufen, Junshi Bowuguan, Muxidi, Xidan, Tiān'ānmén West, Dongdan, Yong'anli, Bawangfen, Sihuizhan

5 Deshengmen, Di'anmen, Běihǎi Park, Xihuamen, Zhongshan Park, Qianmen

20 Běijīng South Train Station, Tianqiao, Dashilar, Tiān'ānmén Sq, Wangfujing, Dongdan, Běijīng Train Station

52 Běijīng West Train Station, Muxidi, Fuxingmen, Xidan, Gate of Heavenly Peace, Dongdan, Běijīng Train Station, Jianguomen

103 Běijīng Train Station, Dengshikou, China Art Gallery, Forbidden City (north entrance), Běihǎi Park, Fuchengmen, Běijīng Zoo

332 Běijīng Zoo, Weigongcun, Renmin Daxue, Zhongguancun, Haidian, Běijīng University, Summer Palace

2 Qianmen, north on Dongdan Beidajie, Dongsi Nandajie, Dongsi Beidajie, Lama Temple, Zhonghua Minzu Yuan (Ethnic Minorities Park), Asian Games Village

AROUND BĚIJĪNG

The Great Wall 长城

See our dedicated Great Wall chapter (p113) for trips to the Great Wall.

Ming Tombs 十三陵

The Unesco-protected Ming Tombs (十三陵; Shísān Líng; Map p110) are the resting place for 13 of the 16 Ming-dynasty emperors, and makes a fascinating half-day trip. The scattered tombs – each a huge temple-like complex, guarding an enormous burial mound at its rear – back onto the southern slopes of Tiānshòu Mountain. Only three of the 13 tombs are open to the public, and only one has had its underground burial chambers excavated. But what you do see is impressive, and leaves you wondering just how many priceless treasures must still be buried here.

Cháng Líng (长陵; admission ¥45, audio guide ¥50), the resting place of the first of the 13 emperors to be buried here, contains the body of Emperor Yongle (1402–1424), his wife and 16 concubines, and is the largest, most impressive and most important of the tombs. Seated upon a three-tiered marble terrace, the standout structure in this complex is the **Hall of Eminent Favours** (灵恩殿; Líng'ēn Diàn), containing a recent statue of Yongle, various artefacts excavated from Dìng Líng, and a breathtaking interior with vast *nánmù* (cedar wood) columns. As with all three tombs here, you can climb the **Soul Tower** (明楼; Míng Lóu) at the back of the complex for fine views of the surrounding hills.

Běijīng Municipality

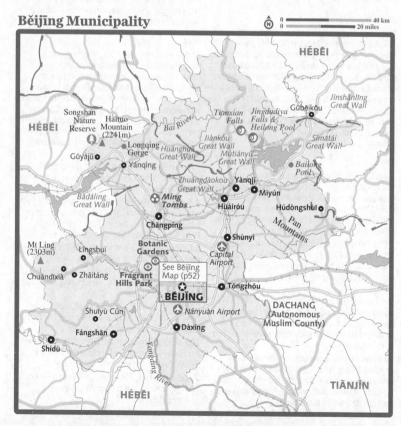

Dìng Líng (定陵; admission ¥65, audio guide ¥50), the final resting place of Emperor Wanli (1572–1620) and his wife and concubines, is at first less impressive than Cháng Líng because many of the halls and gateways have been destroyed. A number of the priceless artefacts were ruined after being left in a huge, unsealed storage room that leaked water, and what treasures that were left – including the bodies of Emperor Wanli and his entourage – were looted and burned by red guards during the Cultural Revolution. However, this is the only tomb where you can climb down into the burial chambers. Learn from signs dotted around the tomb how archaeologists found their way in, à la Indiana Jones, after following instructions they discovered on a carved tablet.

Zhāo Líng (昭陵; admission ¥35) is the smallest of the three, and many of its buildings are recent rebuilds. But it's much less visited than the other two, so is more peaceful, and the **fortified wall** (宝成; *bǎo chéng*) surrounding the burial mound at the back is unusual in both its size and form. The tomb, which is the resting place of Emperor Longqing (1537–1572), is located at the end of the small and eerily quiet village of Zhāolíng Cūn (昭陵村).

Spirit Way (神道; Shén Dào; admission ¥35) is the original road leading up to the tombs. Commencing from the south with a triumphal triple archway, known as the **Great Palace Gate** (大宫门; Dàgōng Mén), the road (now a pedestrianised pathway) passes through **Stele Pavilion** (碑亭; Bēi Tíng), which contains a giant *bìxì* bearing the largest stele in China. A guard of 12 sets of giant stone animals and officials awaits.

✖ Eating

There's a small restaurant (Chinese menu) in the car park at Dìng Líng, and a cafe further towards the tomb entrance.

ℹ Getting There & Away

Bus 872 (¥9, one hour, 7.10am–7.10pm) leaves regularly from the north side of the **Déshèngmén Gateway** (德胜门; Map p80) and passes all the sights, apart from Zhāo Líng, before terminating at Cháng Líng, the main tomb. Last bus back is at 6pm.

It's easy to bus hop around. Start at Cháng Líng, the main tomb, then take bus 872 (¥2) or 314 (¥1) to Dìng Líng, then bus 67 (¥1) to Zhāo Líng. Take bus 67 again to Hu Zhuang

(胡庄) bus stop, from where you either catch bus 872 back to Běijīng, or walk along Spirit Way to see the stone statues. At the other end of Spirit Way is Da Gong Men (大宫门) bus stop, from where you can also catch the 872 back to Běijīng.

Chuāndǐxià 爨底下

Nestled in a valley 90km west of Běijīng and overlooked by towering peaks, the Ming-dynasty village of Chuāndǐxià (entrance ¥35) is a gorgeous cluster of historic courtyard homes with old-world charm. The backdrop is lovely: terraced orchards and fields with ancient houses and alleyways rising up the hillside. Two hours is more than enough to wander around the village because it's not big, but staying the night allows you to soak up its historic charms without the distraction of all those day-trippers.

There are **Maoist slogans** to track down, and **temples** in the surrounding hills, but the main attraction here is the **courtyard homes** and the steps and alleyways that link them up. Many of the homes are Qing-dynasty, some remain from Ming times, and some have been turned into small restaurants or guesthouses, meaning you can eat, drink tea or even stay the night in a 500-year-old Chinese courtyard.

✖ Eating & Sleeping

Restaurant and guesthouse signs are clearly labelled in English, so places are easy to spot. Most restaurants have English menus.

Cuan Yun Inn INN
(爨韵客栈; Chuànyùn Kèzhàn; 23 Chuāndǐxià Village; 爨底下村23号; mains ¥20-40; ☺6.30am-8.30pm) Best place to sample the village speciality roast leg of lamb (烤羊腿; *kǎo yáng tuǐ*; ¥150). On the right of main road as you enter the village.

Chéng Bǎo Inn INN
(城堡客栈; Chéngbǎo Kèzhàn; bed ¥20, r ¥80-100; mains ¥20-40) Translated as Castle Inn, this 400-year-old building is perched high above most of the rest of the village and enjoys fine views from its terrace restaurant. Rooms are simple but charming. Two of the four rooms have traditional stone *kàng* beds, which can be fire-heated in winter. The shared bathroom has no shower, but you can use their neighbour's. Chéng Bǎo Inn is located in the top left-hand corner of the village.

ⓘ Getting There & Away

Bus 892 leaves from a bus stop 200m west of Pingguoyuan subway station (come out of Exit D and turn right) and goes to Zhāitáng (斋堂; ¥16, two hours, 6.30am–5.50pm), from where you'll have to take a taxi (¥20) for the last 6km to Chuāndǐxià. The last bus back leaves Zhāitáng at 5pm. If you miss that you're looking at around ¥200 for a taxi back to Pingguoyuan.

Other Historic Villages

If the enchanting Chuāndǐxià is a bit too touristy for you, these three lesser-known gems might just do the trick. If you fancy staying the night in Língshuǐ or Shuǐyù, look out for signs for 农家院 (nóngjiāyuàn; village guesthouse). There's nowhere to stay at Gǔyájū, although some travellers have camped in the caves. This is almost certainly not allowed, though.

Língshuǐ   VILLAGE

Packed with history, the alluring village of Língshuǐ (灵水村) is home to Běijīng's oldest temple; **Língquánchán Temple** (灵泉禅寺; Língquánchán Sì). It's in ruins, with the main gate pretty much all that has survived, but it dates from the Han dynasty (206 BC–AD 220). Also seek out the **Dragon King Temple** (龙王庙; Lóngwáng Miào) and the **Goddess Temple** (娘娘庙; Niángniáng Miào), which are joined together, and complimented by a pair of ancient intertwining trees.

Língshuǐ is famed for being a village of scholars. No less than 22 former residents passed the notoriously hard imperial exams back in the day, and the village marks their achievements each year with small celebrations on 6 and 7 August. Doors marked '举人' (jǔrén; graduate) show where scholars here used to live.

To get here, turn right out of Exit D of Pingguoyuan subway station and walk 200m to a bus stop. Take bus 829 to Jūnxiǎng (军响; ¥12, 90 minutes, 6.30am–5.30pm) from where you can take a taxi (¥10–20) for the final 5km.

Shuǐyù Cūn   VILLAGE

Shuǐyù Cūn (水峪村) is one of Běijīng's most attractive ancient villages (entrance ¥20). Head to the west side of the more modern half of town for your fix of charming cobble-stoned alleys and Ming- and Qing-dynasty courtyards (there are more than 100 old courtyards). Hunt down the weathered **Goddess Temple** (娘娘庙; Niángniáng Miào) – yes, this village has one too! – and keep an eye out for the numerous Qing-dynasty millstones dotted around the place. Try not to miss the traditional flagpole ceremony carried out each morning and afternoon by women of the village.

To get here, from Tiānqiáo long-distance bus station (天桥长途汽车站; Tiānqiáo chángtú qìchēzhàn; Map p83), take bus 836 to Fángshàn Gòuwù Zhōngxīn bus stop (房山购物中心, ¥11, 90 minutes, 5.40am–8pm) then cross the road to find Fángshān bus station (房山客运站; Fángshān kèyùnzhàn) and take bus 房23 (fáng èrshísān) to Shuǐyù Cūn (水峪村; ¥11, two hours). Returning, the last 房23 bus leaves Shuǐyù at 4.20pm.

Gǔyájū   CAVE VILLAGE

Gǔyájū (古崖居; entrance ¥40) is an enigma; an ancient abandoned cave village of unknown origin, it pokes out from rocks in the water-starved hills of Yánqìng District and is the stuff of storybook legends. More than a dozen cave dwellings, spanning five or six levels of an open rockface, look out over the surrounding barren landscape. Steps carved into the side of the rock allow you to climb up and explore the pleasingly cool caves, some of which have two or three rooms. Some of the caves on the upper levels have been cordoned off, but there's still plenty of scope for exploration. Pack some food, and picnic in one of the strangest spots in Běijīng.

To get here, from Déshèngmén gateway (德胜门; Map p80), take bus 919 (¥12, two hours, 6am–6pm) to Yánqìng Dōngguān (延庆东关) then take bus 920 (¥5, 40 minutes, 6am–6pm) to Dōngményíng (东门营), which is about a 2km walk from Gǔyájū. The last 919 back to Déshèngmén Gate leaves Yánqìng Dōngguān at 5.30pm.

The Great Wall

Includes »

Great Wall History..........113
Visiting the Wall.............114
Mùtiányù.........................115
Jiànkòu...........................115
Huánghuā Chéng...........116
Zhuàngdàokǒu...............117
Jīnshānlǐng.....................117
Bādálǐng.........................118

He who has not climbed the Great Wall is not a true man.

Mao Zedong

China's greatest engineering triumph and must-see sight, the Great Wall (万里长城; Wànlǐ Chángchéng) wriggles haphazardly from its scattered Manchurian remains in Liáoníng province to wind-scoured rubble in the Gobi desert and faint traces in the unforgiving sands of Xīnjiāng.

The most renowned and robust examples undulate majestically over the peaks and hills of Běijīng municipality – and these are the sections we focus on in this chapter – but the Great Wall can be realistically visited in many north China provinces. See the relevant regional chapters for details. It is mistakenly assumed that the wall is one continuous entity; in reality, the edifice exists in chunks interspersed with natural defences (such as precipitous mountains) that had no need for further bastions.

Great Wall History

The 'original' wall was begun more than 2000 years ago during the Qin dynasty (221–207 BC), when China was unified under Emperor Qin Shi Huang. Separate walls that had been constructed by independent kingdoms to keep out marauding nomads were linked together. The effort required hundreds of thousands of workers – many of whom were political prisoners – and 10 years of hard labour under General Meng Tian. An estimated 180 million cubic metres of rammed earth was used to form the core of the original wall, and legend tells that one of the building materials used was the bones of deceased workers.

Its beacon tower system, using gunpowder explosions or smoke signals from burning wolves' dung, quickly conveyed news of enemy movements back to the capital. To the west was Jiāyùguān, an important link on the Silk Road, where a customs post of sorts existed and where unwanted Chinese were ejected through the gates to face the terrifying wild west.

The Great Wall

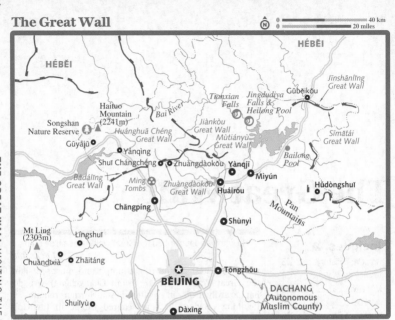

Ming engineers made determined efforts to revamp the eroding bastion, facing it with some 60 million cubic metres of bricks and stone slabs. This project took more than a century, and the cost in human effort and resources was phenomenal. The picture-postcard brick-clad modern day manifestations of the Great Wall date from Ming times.

The wall occasionally served its impractical purpose but ultimately failed as an impenetrable line of defence. Genghis Khan dryly noted, 'The strength of a wall depends on the courage of those who defend it'. Sentries could be bribed. Despite the wall, the Mongol armies managed to impose foreign rule on China from 1279 to 1368 and the bastion failed to prevent the Manchu armies from establishing two and a half centuries of non-Chinese rule on the Middle Kingdom. The wall did not even register with the 19th-century European 'barbarians' who simply arrived by sea, and by the time the Japanese invaded, it had been outflanked by new technologies (such as the aeroplane).

The wall was largely forgotten after that. Mao Zedong encouraged the use of the wall as a source of free building material, a habit that continues unofficially today. Its earthen core has been pillaged and its bountiful sup-

ply of shaped stone stripped from the ramparts for use in building roads, dams and other constructions.

Without its cladding, lengthy sections have dissolved to dust and the barricade might have vanished entirely without the tourist industry. Several important sections have been rebuilt, kitted out with souvenir shops, restaurants, toboggan rides and cable cars, populated with squads of hawkers and opened to the public.

Visiting the Wall

Bādálǐng is the most touristy part of the wall, followed by **Mùtiányù**. Part-renovated and much less commercial are **Sīmǎtái**, **Jīnshānlǐng** and, to a lesser extent, **Huánghuā Chéng**. Unrenovated sections of 'wild wall' include **Jiànkòu** and **Zhuàngdàokǒu**, but there are many others. Most of the above can be reached using public transport. Some require a taxi/minivan ride for the last part of the journey.

Tours run by hostels, or by specialist tour companies, are far preferable to those run by ordinary hotels or state-run travel companies, as they tend to cater more to the needs of adventurous Western travellers and don't come with any hidden extras, such as a side-trip to the Ming Tombs (a common add-on) or a tiresome diversion to gem factory or a traditional Chinese medicine centre.

Almost all the hostels reviewed in the Běijīng chapter (p88) of this guide run Great Wall trips that we recommend.

Independent companies, which run trips to the wall that we like, include the following:

Běijīng Sideways (www.beijingsideways.com) For trips in a motorbike sidecar.

Bespoke Běijīng (www.bespokebeijing.com)

Bike Běijīng (www.bikebeijing.com) For cycling trips.

Dandelion Hiking (www.chinahiking.cn)

SnapAdventures (www.snapadventures.com)

Mùtiányù 慕田峪

Like Bādálǐng, **Mùtiányù** (adult/student ¥45/25; ⏰7am-6.30pm, winter 7.30am-5.30pm), 90km northeast of Běijīng, is a recently renovated stretch of wall, which sees a lot of tourists and is fairly easy to reach from Běijīng. It's also well set up for families, with a cable car, a chair lift and a hugely popular toboggan ride. Far fewer tour groups come here than go to Bādálǐng, though, so the crowds are much more manageable, and there is the opportunity to do some good hiking.

Famed for its Ming-era guard towers and excellent views, this 3km-long section of wall is largely a recently restored Ming dynasty structure that was built upon an earlier Northern Qi-dynasty edifice. With 26 watchtowers, the wall is impressive and manageable, and although it can get crowded, most souvenir hawking is reserved to the lower levels.

From the ticket office, there are three or four stepped pathways leading up to the wall, plus a **cable car** (缆车; lǎn chē; one-way/return ¥60/80, children half price), a **chair lift** (索道; suǒdào; one-way ¥50) and a **toboggan ride** (滑道; huá dào; adult/child ¥60/50), making this ideal for those who can't manage too many steps, or who have young kids in tow.

🛏 Sleeping & Eating

As with Bādálǐng, Mùtiányù has a branch of Subway (just down from the car park). There are also lots of fruit stalls here. Up by the main entrance is **Yì Sōng Lóu Restaurant** (翼松楼餐厅; Yì Sōng Lóu Cāntīng; mains ¥20-50; 🍴), which does OK Chinese food.

The Schoolhouse HOLIDAY HOMES $$$
(小园; Xiǎoyuán; ☎6162 6505; www.theschool houseatmutianyu.com; Mutianyu Village; houses per night ¥2600-5000; ❄🛜) The main building is a former primary school, about 1km down from the Mùtiányù car park, but accommodation is in a collection of lovingly restored buildings dotted around the area, each comprising luxury self-contained multi-roomed accommodation, which can sleep families or small groups. Excellent food.

Getting to Mùtiányù

From **Dongzhimen Wai bus stand** (Map p76; 东直门外车站; Dōngzhímén Wài chēzhàn), bus 867 makes a special detour to Mùtiányù twice every morning (¥16, 2½ hours, 7am and 8.30am, 15 March to 15 November only) and returns from Mùtiányù twice each afternoon (2pm and 4pm).

Otherwise, you need to go via the town of Huáiróu (怀柔). From **Dongzhimen transport hub** (Map p76; Dōngzhímén shūniǔzhàn) take bus 916快 (the character is 'kuài', and means 'fast') to Huáiróu (¥12, one hour, 6.30am to 7.30pm). Get off at Míngzhu Guangchang (明珠广场) bus stop (ignore touts that try to lure you off the bus before that), then take the first right to find a bunch of minivans waiting to take passengers to Mùtiányù (per person ¥15, 30 minutes).

Return minivans start drying up from around 6pm. The last 916快 back to Běijīng leaves Huáiróu at around 7pm.

Jiànkòu 箭扣

For stupefyingly gorgeous hikes along perhaps Běijīng's most incomparable section of 'wild wall', head to the rear section of the **Jiànkòu Great Wall** (后箭扣长城; Hòu Jiànkòu Chángchéng; admission ¥20), accessible from the town of Huáiróu. Tantalising panoramic views of the Great Wall spread out in either direction from here, as the crumbling brickwork meanders dramatically along a mountain ridge; the setting is truly sublime. But this is completely unrestored wall, so it is both dangerous and, strictly speaking, illegal to hike along it. Make sure you wear footwear with very good grips, and never attempt to traverse this section in the rain, particularly during thunderstorms. When the weather is fine, though, the Jiànkòu area offers fabulous opportunities to hike and camp along the wall.

From the drop off at Xīzhàzi Village (西栅子村; Xīzhàzi Cūn), it's a one-hour walk uphill to the wall, along a narrow dirt path, which climbs through a beautiful pine forest. From here turn east (left) to hike all the way to Mùtiányù (two hours), from where you can easily pick up transport back to Huáiróu, or even to Běijīng. Note, there are different parts, or *duì* (队) to Xīzhàzi Village. All have paths that lead up to the wall, but for the sake of ease, head to the first part of the village (一队; yī duì), which is down a lane to your left immediately after the ticket office.

Sleeping & Eating

The following are friendly but basic, have no English signs, and no English is spoken.

Jiǎnkòu Chángchéng Nóngjiāyuàn
GUESTHOUSE $

(箭扣长城农家院; ☑6161 1794, 136 9307 0117; r ¥80-100; ❄ ❋) The first *nóngjiāyuàn* (农家院; farmers-style courtyard) you come to as you enter Xīzhàzi Village, rooms here are set around a vegetable-patch courtyard, and are simple, but have private bathrooms. Does food.

Guóhuái Dàyuàn
GUESTHOUSE $

(国槐大院; ☑137 1698 2205, 136 2136 2662; r ¥80-120; ❋) Further into the village, this place has similarly clean but simple rooms. Meals here cost a set-price ¥30.

Getting to Jiànkòu

As with getting to Mùtiányù, take bus 916快 from the **Dongzhimen transport hub** (Map p76; Dōngzhímén shūniǔzhàn) to Huáiróu (¥12, one hour, 6.30am to 7.30pm). Get off at Mingzhu Guangchang (明珠广场) bus stop, then start negotiating for a taxi to Xīzhàzi Village (西栅子村; Xīzhàzi Cūn; one-way ¥100-130, one hour).

Huánghuā Chéng   黄花城

Strikingly free of crowds, **Huánghuā Chéng**, 77km north of Běijīng, allows visitors to admire this classic and well-preserved example of Ming defence, with high and wide ramparts, intact parapets and sturdy beacon towers, in relative isolation. The patchy and periodic restoration work on the wall here has left its crumbling nobility and striking authenticity largely intact, with the ramparts occasionally dissolving into rubble and some of the steps in ruins.

From the road, you can go either west (left) towards Zhuàngdàokǒu, or east (right) up the stupidly steep section that rises up from the reservoir and which eventually leads to Jiànkòu and Mùtiányù (if you've got three days on your hands). Not only is it very steep, the stonework here has been worn smooth, making it very slippery. You need shoes with very good grip. There are also no guardrails around.

To head west, it's easiest to climb the path that leads up to the wall from behind the guesthouse Ténglóng Fàndiàn. The wall on this side of the road is almost as steep and, in places, equally smooth and slippery. The views from the top, looking down on the reservoir and at the opposite section of the wall stretching over the mountain, are simply stunning.

Sleeping & Eating

Ténglóng Fàndiàn
GUESTHOUSE $

(滕龙饭店; ☑6165 1929; r without/with attached bathroom ¥50/80) One of a number of small guesthouses here. Most are on the river side

---

TAXIS AND CAR HIRE

Miles Meng (☑137 1786 1403; www.beijingtourvan.blog.sohu.com) is a friendly, reliable, English-speaking driver with a variety of decent-quality vehicles at his disposal. Prices for day-long trips to the Great Wall start at ¥600 to ¥700 per vehicle (for the Mùtiányù Great Wall area), and he is happy to drop you at one part of the wall and pick you up at another to allow you to hike from A to B. See his blog for a full list of prices.

Mr Sun (孙先生; Sūn Xiānsheng; ☑136 5109 3753) only speaks Chinese but is very reliable and can find other drivers if he's busy. Does round trips to the Great Wall from around ¥600.

Xīn Lǚchéng (新旅程; ☑6235 5003) is a local Běijīng taxi company. He does round trips to the Great Wall for around ¥500. No English spoken.

Hertz (赫兹; Hèzī; ☑800 988 1336, 5739 2000; www.hertzchina.com; ◷8am-8am Mon-Fri, 9am-6pm Sat & Sun) has an office at Terminal 3 of Běijīng airport. Self-drive hire cars (自驾; zìjià) start from ¥230 per day (up to 150km per day), with a ¥20,000 deposit. See p1002 for details on getting a temporary driving licence. A car-with-driver service (代驾; dàijià) is also available from ¥660 per day.

of the road, but this friendly place, accessed via steps on your left just before the wall, clings to the hillside on the other side of the road and sports fine views of the wall. Rooms are basic, but clean and sleep two to three people. No English spoken, but the restaurant, with terrace seating, has an English menu (mains ¥15 to ¥35).

Getting to Huánghuā Chéng

From **Dongzhimen transport hub** (Map p76; Dōngzhímén shūniǔzhàn) take bus 916快 to Huáiróu (¥12, one hour, 6.30am to 7.30pm). Get off at Nanhuayuan Sanqu (南花园三区) bus stop, then walk straight ahead about 200m (crossing one road), until you get to the next bus stop, called Nanhuayuan Siqu (南花园四区). A bus to Huánghuā Chéng (¥8, one hour, until 6.30pm) stops here, but it doesn't have a number. Instead look for a placard in the front windscreen reading: '怀柔—黄花城', which means 'Huáiróu to Huánghuā Chéng'. It only runs about once an hour, though, so if you get bored waiting, hop in one of the minivans (¥10), which regularly trawl the bus stop for passengers.

The last 916快 from Huáiróu back to Běijīng leaves Huáiróu at around 7pm.

Zhuàngdàokǒu   撞道口

The small village of **Zhuàngdàokǒu**, 80km north of Běijīng, and just over the hill from Huánghuā Chéng, has access to a rarely visited and completely unrestored section of 'wild wall'. It's also possible to hike over to Huánghuā Chéng on a restored section from here, although surprisingly few people do this, considering how straightforward it is.

The bus should drop you off at the far end of Zhuàngdàokǒu Village, where the road crosses a small stream. Pick up some water and snacks at the small shop near here, then turn right and follow the lane along the stream and then up behind the houses until it meets a rocky pathway that leads up the wall. Once at the wall (20 minutes), turn right for a one-hour walk along a restored, but very steep section of wall which eventually leads down to the road at Huánghuā Chéng, via some fabulous viewpoints. Or turn left to commence a two-hour hike along a crumbling stretch of shrub-covered wall towards Shuǐ Chángchéng. You'll see almost no one on this unrestored section and the going can get tricky, so take extra care here. See p119 for more details.

🍴 Sleeping & Eating

Zǎoxiāng Tíngyuàn   GUESTHOUSE **$**
(枣香庭院; ☎135 2208 3605; r ¥40-100) On your right, just before the stream at the end of the village, this modest guesthouse – one of a few here – is housed in a 70-year-old courtyard building. A couple of rooms have TV, a couple have air-conditioning, and one has a private bathroom. No English sign, no English spoken. Does home-cooked meals, but the menu is in Chinese only. Dishes we've enjoyed here include stewed pork with roast chestnuts (栗子肉; lìzi ròu), pork fried with chillies (炒肉尖椒; chǎoròu jiānjiāo), braised pork belly (红烧肉; hóng shāo ròu), barbecued fish (烤鱼; kǎo yú) and beef and potato stew (土豆牛肉; tǔdòu niúròu).

Getting to Zhuàngdàokǒu

Same as getting to Huánghuā Chéng, but once you've arrived at the bus stop in Huáiróu called Nanhuayuan Siqu (南花园四区), board a bus to Shuǐ Chángchéng, which stops at Zhuàngdàokǒu (¥8, one hour, every 30 minutes until 6.30pm). It doesn't have a number. Instead look for a placard in the front windscreen reading: 怀柔—水长城, which means Huáiróu to Shuǐ Chángchéng.

Jīnshānlǐng   金山岭

The **Jīnshānlǐng** (Jīnshānlǐng Chángchéng; summer/winter ¥65/55) section of the Great Wall, near the small town of Gǔběikǒu (古北口), is 142km northeast of Běijīng and marks the starting point of an exhilarating 7km hike to **Sīmǎtái** (司马台; admission ¥40; ☺8am-5pm). The adventure – winding through stunningly remote mountainous terrain – takes three to four hours as the trail is steep and parts of the wall have collapsed, but it can be traversed without too much difficulty, provided you are reasonably fit. Note that the watchtowers are in various states of preservation and some have been stripped of their bricks. The scenery is perhaps less picturesque than at, say, Jiànkòu – here the landscape is drier and more stark – but arguably more powerful and it leaves you with a feeling that you're hiking through genuinely remote territory.

Autumn is the best season for hiking here; in summer you'll be sweating gallons, so load up with water before you go (ever-present hawkers on the wall sell pricey water for around ¥10 a bottle or more, depending on how thirsty you appear).

To commence the hike to Sīmǎtái, turn left when you reach the wall and keep going. If you need it, there's a **cable car** (缆车; lǎn chē; one way/return trip ¥30/50) by the west gate ticket office.

Sīmǎtái, which is more touristy than Jīnshānlǐng, was closed for renovations at the time of research, but should be open again when you read this. Arriving at Sīmǎtái, having walked from Jīnshānlǐng, you used to have to buy another ticket to cross a rope bridge (¥5), as well as the entrance ticket to the Sīmǎtái section.

🛏 Sleeping & Eating

It can be a long trip out here, so take the stress out of having to rush back the same day by arriving mid-afternoon and hunting around near the West Gate (西门; Xīmén) for some lodgings. Rooms range from ¥50 to ¥100; meals from ¥30. Look for signs on buildings saying 农家院 (nóngjiāyuàn; farmers-style courtyard). You can then mount your assault on the wall the next morning.

The East Gate entrance (东门; Dōngmén), about 2km up from the West Gate, has a hotel-lobby–like cafe, with an English menu.

Getting to Jīnshānlǐng

Local Bus

There are two options: catch a bus to Chéngdé (承德; ¥85, 2½ hours) from **Sìhuì long-distance bus station** (四惠长途汽车站; Sìhuì chángtú qìchēzhàn), 200m walk southeast of Sihui subway station, and tell the driver you want to get off at Jīnshānlǐng. You'll be dropped at a service station on the highway, about 1km from the east gate ticket office (walk back under the highway and keep going. Note, you have to pay the full price ¥85 ticket to Chéngdé, even though you get off early at Jīnshānlǐng.

Your second option is to catch Bus 980 from **Dongzhimen transport hub** (Dōngzhímén shūniǔzhàn; Map p76) to the town of Mìyún (¥15), and then take a taxi to Jīnshānlǐng (one-way ¥50).

The last bus 980 back to Běijīng leaves Mìyún at 7pm. Chéngdé-to-Běijīng buses run along the main highway until mid-evening and usually have spare seats if you flag one down at the service station.

If you're returning from Sīmǎtái after the hike from Jīnshānlǐng, you should be able to catch a shared minivan or taxi to Mìyún from where you can pick up bus 980.

Tourist Bus

A special tourist bus (金山岭长城旅游班车专线; jīnshānlǐng chángchéng lǚyóu bānchē zhuānxiàn; ¥120, two hours) leaves once a day for Jīnshānlǐng from **Dongzhimen Wai bus stand** (Map p76; 东直门外车站) at 8am and returns from Jīnshānlǐng at 3pm.

Tours

Before renovation work began on the Sīmǎtái section of the wall, youth hostels in Běijīng used to run highly recommended early-morning trips by minibus (excluding/including ticket ¥180/260) to Jīnshānlǐng for the four-hour hike to Sīmǎtái. Buses usually left at around 6am or 7am. They would drop you at Jīnshānlǐng, then pick you up four hours later in Sīmǎtái. The entire journey from Běijīng and back would take up to 12 hours. Běijīng Downtown Backpackers (p91) said at the time of research that it was planning to restart the trip once Sīmǎtái had opened again. Check with staff there, or with other hostels, for details.

Bādálǐng　　　　八达岭

The mere mention of its name sends a shudder down the spine of hardcore Great Wall walkers, but **Bādálǐng** (Bādálǐng Chángchéng; adult/student ¥45/25; ☉6am-7pm summer, 7am-6pm winter), 70km northwest of Běijīng, is the easiest part of the wall to get to and as a result, if you are really pushed for time, this may be your only option. It ticks all the iffy Great Wall boxes in one flourish: souvenir stalls, T-shirt–flogging hawkers, restaurants, heavily restored brickwork, little authenticity, guardrails and mobs of sightseers. However, on the plus side, the scenery is raw and striking and the wall, which snakes off in classic fashion into the hills, is extremely photogenic. It dates back to Ming times (1368–1644), although it underwent particularly heavy restoration work during the 1950s and 1980s when it was essentially rebuilt.

There is a **cable car** (缆车; lǎn chē; one-way/return ¥60/80; ☉8am-4.30pm) as well as disabled access. You'll find a Bank of China ATM near the west car park.

🍴 Eating

There are dozens of restaurants on the main drags leading up to the entrance to the wall. Most lead up from the west car park, and most are fast-food outlets or snack stalls. Give KFC and Subway a miss and go next door instead, to **Yong He King** (永和大王; Yǒnghé Dàwáng; mains ¥10-20; ☉10am-9pm; 🖥), for the Chinese version of fast food: rice meals, dumplings, noodles.

TOP GREAT WALL HIKES

Jīnshānlǐng to Sīmǎtái

Three to four hours Very popular with youth hostel groups before Sīmǎtái closed for renovation, but should be open again by the time you read this, the three- to four-hour hike from Jīnshānlǐng is straightforward, but breathtaking. Scenery is vast, rugged and remote and the wall is a photogenic mix of part-restored and unrestored sections. Access the wall from the East Gate at Jīnshānlǐng (20-minute climb up steps), then turn left when you hit the wall.

Jiànkòu to Mùtiányù

Two hours Unrivalled for pure 'wild-wall' scenery, this stretch of the wall at Jiànkòu is very tough to negotiate, but soon links up with the easier, restored section at Mùtiányù. Access the wall from the back of Jiànkòu Great Wall (后箭扣; Hòu Jiànkòu) at the first part of Xīzhàzi Village (西栅子村一队; Xīzhàzi Cūn Yīduì). It takes an hour to reach the wall from the village; from the sign that says the Great Wall here is closed, follow a narrow dirt path uphill and through a lovely pine forest. Go straight on at the abandoned wooden hut, rather than right, and then when you hit the wall, turn left.

Zhuàngdàokǒu to Huánghuā Chéng

One hour This very steep climb on a restored section of the wall offers fabulous views of Huánghuā Chéng Great Wall once you reach the top. Access the wall from Zhuàngdàokǒu Village; turn right at the end of the village, by the small river, then follow the river (keeping it on your left) before turning right up the hill behind the houses, to climb a stony pathway. When you reach the wall (20 minutes), turn right and keep climbing before eventually descending to the main road by the reservoir, from where you can pick up buses back to Huáiróu.

Zhuàngdàokǒu to Shuǐ Chángchéng

Two hours Climb up to the wall from Zhuàngdàokǒu Village, only this time turn left at the wall to be rewarded with this dangerous, but fabulous stretch of crumbling bastion. When the wall eventually splits at a corner tower; turn left. Soon after, you reach another tower from where you can see the reservoir far below you, and the wall crumbles down the mountain and is impassable. Take the path that leads down to your left, just before the tower. This path links up with the wall again, but if you follow it all the way down to the road from here, you'll be able to pick up a bus back to Huáiróu from the lower of the two large car parks.

Getting to Bādálǐng

Local Bus
The 877 (¥12, one hour, 6am-5pm), 919 (¥12, 1½ hours, 6am-6.30pm) and 880 (¥12, 1½ hours, 7am-5pm) all leave for Bādálǐng from the northern side of the Déshèngmén Gateway (Map p80; 德胜门), about 500m east of Jishuitan subway station. Bus 877 goes to the east car park, the 919 and 880 go to the west car park. The main entrance, beside two large archways, is between the two car parks and uphill from both.

Tour Bus
Tour buses to Bādálǐng depart from the beautifully named **Běijīng Hub of Tourist Dispatch** (Map p76; 北京旅游集散中心; Běijīng Lǚyóu Jísàn Zhōngxīn; ☎8353 1111), by Arrow Tower, south of Tiān'ānmén Sq. Line C runs to Bādálǐng (¥120 return, price includes entry to Great Wall, departs 9.30am to 11am); Line A runs to Bādálǐng and the Ming Tombs (¥180, includes entrance tickets and lunch, departs 7am to 9.30am). Plan about nine hours for the whole trip. The tours are primarily aimed at Chinese domestic tourists, so don't expect much English to be spoken.

Train
Bādálǐng Train Station is a short walk down from the west car park. Morning trains (hard/soft seat ¥7/11, 75 minutes) leave from Běijīng North Station (Map p52; 北京北站; Běijīng Běizhàn) – which is beside Xizhimen subway station – at these times: 6.12am, 7.58am, 8.34am, 9.02am and 10.57am. Afternoon trains return at 1.02pm, 3.19pm, 3.52pm, 4.21pm, 5.33pm and 7.55pm.

Tiānjīn & Héběi

POP 110 MILLION

Includes »

Tiānjīn 122
Around Tiānjīn 127
Héběi.............................128
Shíjiāzhuāng 128
Around Shíjiāzhuāng 130
Chéngdé........................133
Shānhǎiguān.................139
Jìmíngyì 141

Best Ancient Towns

» Chéngdé (p133)

» Jìmíngyì (p141)

» Yújiācūn (p132)

» Zhèngdìng (p130)

Best Temples

» Lóngxīng Temple (p130)

» Monastery of Deep Compassion (p123)

» Pǔníng Temple (p136)

» Tàishān Temple (p142)

Why Go?

A slow-moving panorama of grazing sheep, brown earth and fields of corn and wheat, Héběi (河北) is Běijīng's back garden. Cosmopolitan Tiānjīn (天津) may put on a dazzling show, and providential economic feng shui from Běijīng lends a sparkle here and there, but arid Héběi's main charms are its timeworn and earthy textures. More than anything, Héběi offers the chance to disengage from Běijīng's modernity and frantic urban tempo, and experience a more timeless China. Wander through ancient settlements and walled towns, skirt the wild edges of the former Manchuria and journey to the majestic 18th-century summer retreat of the Qing emperors in Chéngdé. There are temples galore to explore, or just head for the hills and little-visited towns whose ancient rhythms and rural seclusion make them the perfect retreats.

When to Go
Tiānjīn

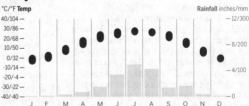

Mar & Apr
Avoid the intense summer crush and roasting north China weather.

Jun & Jul
Get bronzed on the beaches of Běidàihé.

Sep & Oct
Catch the fresh Héběi autumnal weather (not too hot, not too cold).

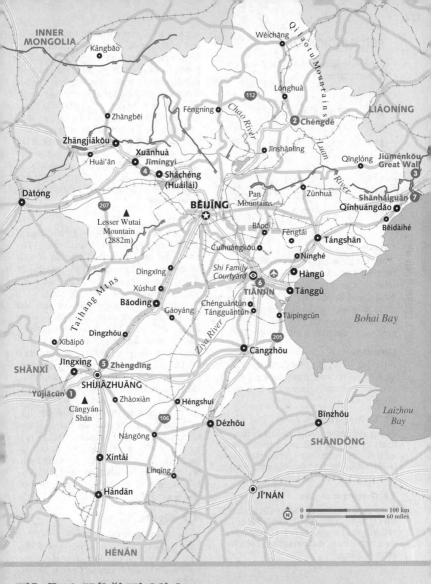

Tiānjīn & Héběi Highlights

1 Say *zàijiàn* (goodbye) to China's growing urban sprawl in the centuries-old stone village of **Yújiācūn** (p132)

2 Be rendered speechless by the colossal multiarmed occupant of **Pǔníng Temple** (p136) in Chéngdé

3 Steal across the Liáoníng border to see **Jiǔménkǒu**

Great Wall (p141) plunging into the Jiǔjiāng River

4 Step back in time in the ancient walled town of **Jīmíngyì** (p141), China's oldest surviving postal station

5 Explore the temple town of **Zhèngdìng** (p130) and size up the giant metal statue

of Guanyin in the Lóngxìng Temple

6 Wander the grand, European-inspired streets of the former foreign concession areas in **Tiānjīn** (p122)

7 See where the Great Wall meets the sea in **Shānhǎiguān** (p139)

PRICE INDICATORS

The following price indicators are used in this chapter:

Sleeping

$	less than ¥400
$$	¥400 to ¥1000
$$$	more than ¥1000

Eating

$	less than ¥50
$$	¥50 to ¥100
$$$	more than ¥100

Climate

Considerable temperature differences exist between the mountainous north and the south of the province, as well as between coastal and inland regions, but Héběi generally gets very hot in summer and freezing cold in winter, with dust fallout in spring and heavy rain in July and August.

Language

Although Héběi is a Mandarin-speaking region, areas furthest from Běijīng have pronounced regional accents and a distinctive argot.

ⓘ Getting There & Away

Běijīng and Tiānjīn are the most convenient bases for exploring the province and the two cities are connected by high-speed express train. Héběi is also linked to numerous other domestic destinations by both bus and rail.

ⓘ Getting Around

The provincial rail hub is Shíjiāzhuāng, with rail links to all major towns and cities in Héběi. Travel to Chéngdé, Jīmíngyì and Shānhǎiguān is best done from Běijīng. Bus connections cover the entire province.

TIĀNJĪN

Tiānjīn 天津

♪ 022 / POP 4.57 MILLION

Stepping out of the long shadow cast by its near neighbour Běijīng at a rate of knots, the ambitious and booming port of Tiānjīn is a special municipality that sits in the east of Héběi. Its past as a foreign concession and impressive European architecture is redolent of Shànghǎi. Now, after a facelift of its historic quarters and riverfront, Tiānjīn's potential as a tourist destination is finally being realised. Some stunning modern architecture pushes towards the sky here, dramatic new bridges span the Hǎi River and luxury hotels are opening all the time. And with the local economy growing faster than anywhere else in China, at a dizzying rate of 16.7% a year according to the city government, Tiānjīn clearly means business. Best of all, slick and very speedy trains link Tiānjīn to Běijīng, making day trips supremely easy.

History

Tiānjīn rose to prominence as a grain-storage point during the Mongol Yuan dynasty. The city found itself at the intersection of both inland and port navigation routes, and by the 15th century the town had become a walled garrison.

During the foreign concession era, the British and French settled in, joined by the Japanese, Germans, Austro-Hungarians, Italians and Belgians between 1895 and 1900. Each concession was a self-contained world, with its own prison, school, barracks and hospital. During the Boxer Rebellion, the foreign powers levelled the walls of the old Chinese city.

The Tángshān earthquake of 28 July 1976 registered 8.2 on the Richter scale and killed nearly 24,000 people in the Tiānjīn area. The city was badly rocked, but escaped the devastation that virtually obliterated nearby Tángshān, where (according to government estimates) some 240,000 residents died.

◉ Sights

The grandiose vista that greets visitors as they exit Tiānjīn train station signals the city's intent to rise even further. To the west the glittering **Tiānjīn World Financial Centre** (Jīnróng Dàshà), a singularly bold statement of glass and steel, towers over the river. Facing you across **Liberation Bridge** (解放桥; Jiěfàng Qiáo) is a lengthy and ostentatious sweep of rebuilt red and orange Sino-European pomposity in brick, splendidly illuminated at night. A huge and rather surreal mechanical clock tells the time just north of Liberation Bridge, while a bizarre collection of erotic statues do their thing west of the bridge on the south side of the water.

Treaty Port Area
HISTORIC SITE

South of the station across Liberation Bridge was the British concession, on and around Jiefang Lu. Cross over the bridge to walk around the newly revamped concession district near the river. You need to walk a fair distance south along **Jiefang Beilu** (解放北路) to delve behind the rebuilt riverside facade, an impressive sight at night from the north side of the river, .

Buildings of note include the **former French Municipal Administration Council Building** (原法国公议局大楼; Yuán Fǎguó Gōngyìjú Dàlóu), built in 1924, on Chengde Dao; the **Sino-French Industrial and Commercial Bank** (中法工商银行; Zhōngfǎ Gōngshāng Yínháng), dating from 1932; and the **Yokohama Specie Bank Ltd** (横滨正金银行; Héngbīn Zhèngjīn Yínháng), dating from 1926.

Next door at No 82 is the former **Hongkong & Shanghai Bank Building** (汇丰银行遗址; Huìfēng Yínháng), a pompous creation, now housing the Bank of China. Look out also for the former address of **Jardine Matheson & Co** (怡和洋行; Yíhé Yángháng), decorated with vast pillars, at No 157.

Old Town
HISTORIC SITE

(老城区) Originally enclosed by a wall, Tiānjīn's old town centres on the restored **Drum Tower** (鼓楼; Gǔ Lóu; Chengxiang Zhonglu; admission free; ☉9am-4.30pm Tue-Sun). Decorated with *páilóu* (ornate archways), the pedestrianised shopping street to the north of the Drum Tower is excellent for buying items such as calligraphy brushes, kites, paper cuts, snuff bottles, fans, silk, ceramics, jade, taichi swords, chops, jewellery, candy floss and sugarcane juice.

Opposite the Drum Tower you'll find the **Guǎngdōng Guild Hall** (广东会馆; Guǎngdōng Huìguǎn; ☏2727 3443; 31 Nanmenli Dajie; admission ¥10; ☉9am-4.30pm Tue-Sun), built in 1907 and also known as the Museum of Opera; it's a lovely old ornate hall with lavishly carved woodwork and performances of traditional music from old-timers. The historic **Confucius Temple** (文庙; Wén Miào; ☏2727 2812; 1 Dongmennei Dajie; admission ¥30; ☉9am-4.30pm Tue-Sun) is also nearby.

Monastery of Deep Compassion
BUDDHIST TEMPLE

(大悲禅院; Dàbēi Chányuàn; 40 Tianwei Lu; admission ¥5; ☉9am-6.30pm Apr-Oct, 9am-5pm Nov-Mar) Tiānjīn's most important Buddhist temple is noted for its **Shìjiā Bǎo Hall** (Shìjiā

Bǎodiàn) and the subsequent large hall where a huge and golden multiarmed statue of Guanyin awaits, her eyes following you around the hall. The covered alleys to the side of the temple house an extraordinary market of religious paraphernalia: from prayer mats to books, Buddhist rosaries, talismans, statues and incense.

Italian Concession
HISTORIC AREA

(意式风景区; Yìshì Fēngjīngqū) Like a well-cut suit discovered hanging in the back of a wardrobe, Tiānjīn's newly spruced up Italian Style District aims to dress up the city as a cosmopolitan and elegant destination. It's more for domestic visitors, who come here to dine at Italian and French restaurants and daydream they are in Europe. While it's an attractive quadrant for exploration, prices are stratospheric and the blatant commercial bent reduces its charm.

Ancient Culture Street
HISTORIC STREET

(古文化街; Guwenhua Jie) Ancient Culture Street is stuffed with vendors flogging Chinese calligraphy, paintings, tea sets, paper cuts, clay figurines, chops and goods from all over China. The fascinating **Tiānhòu Temple** (天后宫; Tiānhòu Gōng; admission free; ☉8.30am-4.30pm Tue-Sun), Tiānjīn's version of the shrine dedicated to the goddess of sailors that is found in every Chinese seaport, is also here, as well as a shoe museum.

Wǔdàdào
HISTORIC SITE

(五大道; Five Large Roads) The area of Wǔdàdào is rich in the villas and pebble-dash former residences of the well-to-do of the early 20th century. Consisting of five roads in the south of the city – Machang Dao, Changde Dao, Munan Dao, Dali Dao and Chengdu Dao – the streetscapes are European, lined with charming houses dating from the 1920s and before. Some scream of English suburbia; others are art deco. Hop on a horse and carriage for ¥50 tours or jump on an electric buggy (¥20 per person).

St Joseph's Church
CHURCH

(西开天主教堂; Xīkāi Tiānzhǔ Jiàotáng; Binjiang Dao; ☉5.30am-4.30pm Mon-Sat, 5am-8pm Sun) Erected by the French in 1917, this Catholic church is the largest church in Tiānjīn and its fine brick exterior is a marked contrast to the shopping malls surrounding it. Inside, it's rather more decorative than most Chinese churches. English Mass is at 11.30am on Sundays.

Central Tiānjīn

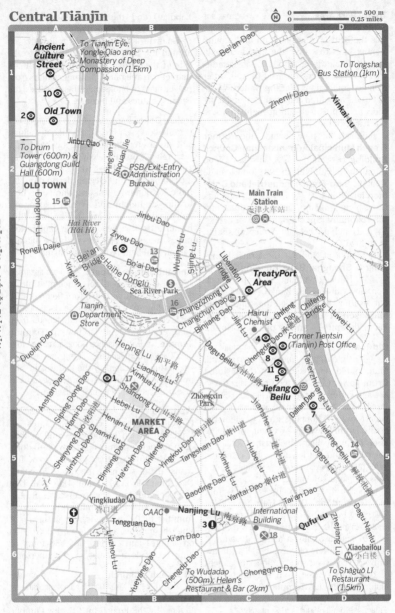

500 m
0.25 miles

Ancient Culture Street

To Tianjin Eye, Yongle Qiao and Monastery of Deep Compassion (1.5km)

10

Old Town

2

To Drum Tower (600m) & Guangdong Guild Hall (600m)

Jinbu Qiao

Ping'an Jie

Shouan Jie

PSB/Exit-Entry Administration Bureau

OLD TOWN

15

Dongma Lu

Hǎi River (Hǎi Hé)

Jinbu Dao

Rongji Dajie

Ziyou Dao

6

Bei'an Bridge

13

Bo'ai Dao

Sea River Park

Xing'an Lu

Haihe Donglu

Winjing Lu

Sijing Lu

16

Zhangzizhong Lu

Changchun Dao

Binjiang Dao

Tianjin Department Store

Duolun Dao

Heping Lu 和平路

Liaoning Lu

Xinhua Lu

17

1

Shandong Lu 山东路

Anshan Dao

Siping Dong Dao

Hami Dao

Shenyang Dao 沈阳道

Jinzhou Dao

Hebei Lu

Henan Lu

Shanxi Lu

Binjiang Dao

Ha'erbin Dao

Chifeng Dao

MARKET AREA

Zhongxin Park

Jianshe Lu 建设道

Yingkou Dao

Tangshan Dao 唐山道

Xinhua Lu

Hubei Lu

Baoding Dao

Yantai Dao 烟台道

Yingkiudào

CAAC

Tongguan Dao

9

Xi'an Dao

Nanjing Lu 南京路

3

18

International Building

Xueyang Lu

Chengdu Dao

Liuzhou Lu

To Wudaodao (500m); Helen's Restaurant & Bar (2km)

Chongqing Dao

Qufu Lu

Zhejiang Lu

Dagu Nanlu

Xiaobailou 小白楼

To Shāguō Lǐ Restaurant (1.5km)

Bei'an Dao

Zhenli Dao

Xinkai Lu

To Tongsha Bus Station (1km)

Main Train Station 天津火车站

Liberation Bridge

TreatyPort Area

Hairui Chemist

Chifeng

Chifeng Bridge

Liuwei Lu

承德道 Chengde Dao

Former Tientsin (Tianjin) Post Office

4

8

11

5

Jin Lu

Dagu Beilu 大沽北路

Chengde Dao

Jiefang Beilu

Taierzhuang Lu

7

Dalian Dao

Jiefang Beilu 解放北路

14

Dagu Lu

Tai'an Dao

Qufu Lu

Tianjin Eye

FERRIS WHEEL

(天津之眼; Tiānjīn Zhǐ Yǎn; Yongle Qiao; adult/child ¥70/35; ⊙9.30am-9.30pm Tue-Sun, 5-9.30pm Mon) To get the city's transformation in perspective, or for a night-time angle on Tiānjīn, ride this Ferris wheel situated slap on the Hǎi River.

Antique Market

MARKET

(古玩市场; Gǔwán Shìchǎng; cnr Shenyang Dao & Shandong Lu; ⊙9am-5pm Sat & Sun) Best visited on Sunday, the antique market is great for a rifle through its stamps, silverware, porcelain, clocks, Mao badges and Cultural Revolution memorabilia.

Central Tiānjīn

◎ **Top Sights**

Ancient Culture Street A1
Jiefang Beilu C4
Old Town A1
Treaty Port Area C3

◎ **Sights**

1 Antique Market B4
2 Confucius Temple.................................... A1
3 Earthquake Memorial............................. C6
4 Former French Municipal
   Administration Council
   Building C4
5 Hongkong & Shanghai Bank Building . C4
6 Italian Concession B3
7 Jardine Matheson & Co Building D4

8 Sino-French Industrial and
   Commercial Bank.................................... C4
9 St Joseph's Church A6
10 Tiānhòu Temple...................................... A1
11 Yokohama Specie Bank Ltd.................. C4

🛏 **Sleeping**

12 Astor Hotel D5
13 Home Inn C3
14 Home Inn B3
15 Orange Hotel A2
16 St Regis Tianjin B3

✖ **Eating**

17 Gǒubùlǐ.. B4
18 YY Beer House C6

👉 Tours

A variety of pleasure boats cruise the Hǎi River. Night trips are especially popular. **Fine Line Hai Cruises** (☑5878 9911) has a number of different boats leaving from Yongle Qiao on the hour every hour from 9am to 5pm during the summer (¥80). Night cruises depart at 7.30pm and 8.30pm (¥100).

🛏 Sleeping

TOP CHOICE St Regis Tianjin HOTEL $$$

(天津瑞吉金融街酒店; Tiānjīn Ruìjí Jīnróngjiē Jiǔdiàn; ☑5830 9999; www.stregis.com/tianjin; 158 Zhangzizhong Lu; 张自忠路158号; d ¥1035-1298; ❄✳@🛜🏊) A vast, hulking, hollowed-out square of a building that is the most eye-catching of all the recent additions to the riverfront, the St Regis is the last word in luxury in Tiānjīn. Super-comfy beds, huge bathrooms and splendid service cocoon weary travellers and there are great river views too. European and Chinese restaurants are onsite as well.

Orange Hotel HOTEL $

(桔子酒店; Júzi Jiǔdiàn; ☑2734 8333; 7 Xing'an Lu; 兴安路7号; d/tw ¥258-358; ✳🛜) That rare beast, a boutique hotel outside of Běijīng and Shànghǎi, this quirky place attracts a younger clientele to its stylish and unfussy rooms, some of which have river views. Bicycle hire is available, with the first two hours free. At the time of research, roadworks meant the hotel could only be accessed from the rear via an alley running off Xing'an Lu. Look for the big sign with an orange on it to direct you.

Astor Hotel HOTEL $$$

(利顺德大饭店; Lìshùndé Dàfàndiàn; ☑2331 1688; www.luxurycollection.com/astor; 33 Tai'erzhuang Lu; 台儿庄路33号; d ¥1035; ❄✳@🛜🏊) Staying in this elegant hotel steeped in history is to travel back in time to the foreign concession era. From the imposing, marbled lobby and solid and traditional wooden furniture, to the staff dressed in formal morning coats, there's an old school charm to the place that makes it special. Like all historic hotels, the rooms and bathrooms are huge.

Home Inn HOTEL $

(如家; Rújiā; d ¥209-229; ✳@) Binjiang Dao (☑5899 6888; 32 Binjiang Dao; 滨江道32号); Xinkai Lu (☑8469 9999; 225 Xinkai Lu; 新开路225号); Ziyou Dao (☑5819 9388; 5 Ziyou Dao; 自道5号) The Binjiang Dao location on the south side of Liberation Bridge, off Jiefang Beilu, has bright bedrooms and fresh bathrooms and makes this a decent choice. Free broadband; ground-floor restaurant. Other branches are southwest and east of the train station.

✖ Eating & Drinking

TOP CHOICE Shāguō Lǐ NORTHERN CHINESE $$

(砂锅李; ☑2326 0075; 46 Jiujiang Lu; 九江路46号; dishes ¥10-88; ⊙11.30am-2.30pm & 5.30-8.30pm; 🚇) Of all Tiānjīn's restaurants, this is the one the locals recommend. They flock here in droves for the speciality pork spare ribs in a sweet barbecue sauce; so tender that they pull apart at the touch of a chopstick. The small portion (¥58) is easily enough for two people. There are many other classic northern Chinese dishes on the menu too.

YY Beer House
THAI $$

(粤园泰餐厅; Yuèyuán Tàicāntíng; ☑2339 9634; 3 Aomen Lu; 澳门路3号; dishes ¥40-80; ☺11am-midnight; ☺🍴) Despite its name, this atmospheric place is actually a Thai restaurant with a wide range of flavoursome dishes from the land of smiles. But it does have an excellent selection of foreign beers too. It's tucked away down a quiet street behind Nanjing Lu. Perennially popular with expats, as well as well-heeled locals, reservations are essential at weekends.

Helen's Restaurant & Bar
INTERNATIONAL $

(海伦餐厅; Hǎilún Cāntīng; ☑2334 0071; 116 Heyan Lu; 河沿路116号; dishes ¥25-45; ☺10am-3am; 🛜🍴) Heaving most evenings with an enthusiastic crowd downing cheap beers (¥10) and scoffing Western comfort food (pizza, pasta and hamburgers), Helen's is more sedate during the day when it becomes a decent place for a coffee or an all-day breakfast (¥25).

Gǒubùlǐ
DUMPLINGS $$

(狗不理; ☑2730 2540; 77 Shandong Lu; 山东路77号; dishes ¥26-70; ☺9am-10pm) Tiānjīn's most famous restaurant is a mixed bag. The trademark *bāozi* (steamed dumplings), including vegie options, are big, juicy and delicious. They're also seriously overpriced, but the place is always packed which may explain the prices. The set meal (¥70), available at the ground-floor cafeteria and including dumplings, soup and a cold dish, is more reasonable than the upstairs restaurant. Picture menu.

ℹ Information

A handful of 24-hour internet cafes can be found above the shops around the train station concourse.

Try to score a copy of the magazine *Jin*, which has listings of restaurants, bars and cultural events in town; it also publishes an annual guidebook. A useful expat community website is www.tianjinexpats.net.

Agricultural Bank of China (农业银行; Nóngyè Yínháng; Jiefang Beilu) Has a 24-hour ATM.

Bank of China (中国银行; Zhōngguó Yínháng; 80-82 Jiefang Beilu) The 24-hour ATM takes international cards.

China Post (中国邮政; Zhōngguó Yóuzhèng; 153 Jiefang Beilu)

Hairui Chemist (海瑞药店; Hǎiruì Yàodiàn; 22 Chifeng Dao; ☺7.30am-10.30pm)

HSBC (汇丰银行; Huìfēng Yínháng; Ocean Hotel, 5 Yuanyang Guangchang) There's an ATM at the International Building, 75 Nanjing Lu.

Public Security Bureau (PSB; 公安局出入境管理局; Gōng'ānjú/Chūrùjìng Guǎnlǐjú; ☑2445 8825; 19 Shouan Jie)

Tianjin International SOS Clinic (天津国际紧急救援诊所; Tiānjīn Guójì Jǐnjí Jiùyuán Yīliáo Zhěnsuǒ; ☑2352 0143; Sheraton Tianjin Hotel, Zijinshan Lu)

ℹ Getting There & Away

Air

Tiānjīn Bīnhǎi International Airport (Tiānjīn Bīnhǎi Guójì Jīchǎng; ☑2490 2950) is 15km east of the city centre. Destinations include Shànghǎi (¥620), Guǎngzhōu (¥1700), Shēnzhèn (¥930), Xī'ān (¥430) and Chéngdū (¥1230). Tickets can be bought from the **Civil Aviation Administration of China** (CAAC; 中国民航; Zhōngguó Mínháng; ☑2490 6296; 10 Baoding Lu; ☺8.30am-7pm) or www.elong.com or www.ctrip.com

Boat

Tiānjīn's harbour is Tánggū, 50km (30 minutes by train or one hour by bus) from Tiānjīn. See the boxed text opposite for details of arriving and departing by boat.

Bus

Tiānjīn-bound buses run from Běijīng's Zhàogōngkǒu bus station (¥30, 1½ hours, every 45 minutes), the Sìhuì bus station (¥23, hourly) or regularly from the Bāwángfén bus station (¥41, every 40 minutes). A shared taxi to Běijīng from the main train station will cost around ¥60 per person.

TŌNGSHĀ BUS STATION Tiānjīn's **Tōngshā bus station** (通莎客运站; Tōngshā kèyùnzhàn; ☑6053 3950; 43 Zhenli Dao) is closest to the centre of town and has regular buses to:

Běijīng (Bāwángfén, Sìhuì and Zhàogōngkǒu long-distance bus stations) ¥30, 1½ hours, hourly 7.45am to 5.45pm

Hohhot ¥212, 5pm

Qīngdǎo ¥181, 8pm

Qínhuángdǎo ¥99, hourly 9.30am to 6pm

Shěnyáng ¥182, 6pm

Shíjiāzhuāng ¥117, 8am, 11.30am and 1pm

TIĀNHUÁN BUS STATION Bus services from **Tiānhuán bus station** (天环客运站; Tiānhuán kèyùnzhàn; ☑2305 0530; cnr Hongqi Lu & Anshan Xidao).

Běijīng ¥37, 7am to 4.30pm

Dalian ¥288, 3pm

Shànghǎi ¥317, 6pm

Xī'ān ¥308, 3.30pm

TIĀNJĪN WEST STATION Bus services from **Tiānjīn West Station** (天津西站客运站; Tiānjīn Xīzhàn Kèyùnzhàn; ☑2732 1282; Xiqing Dao):

Jǐ'nán ¥120, 2pm and 8.50pm

Qínhuángdǎo ¥100, 9am, 2pm and 4.30pm

Shíjiāzhuāng ¥120, every half-hour from 6.30am to 6.30pm

GETTING TO JAPAN, SOUTH KOREA OR DÀLIÁN

After not running for almost a year, ferries to Dàlián (¥290 to ¥1590, 13 hours) now depart every day from Tánggū (塘沽), about 50km east of Tiānjīn. Weekly boats to Kōbe (Japan; ¥1540 to ¥4500, 51 hours, departs Monday) and Incheon (South Korea; ¥888 to ¥1930, 25 hours, departing Thursday and Sunday) also sail from Tánggū.

In Tiānjīn, buy tickets from the **ticket office** (2339 2455; 1 Pukou Dao); in Tánggū, tickets can be bought from the **Passenger Ferry Terminal** (天津港客运站; Tiānjīngǎng Kèyùnzhàn; 2587 3261).

Frequent minibuses and buses to Tánggū (¥10) leave from Tiānjīn's main train station; bus 835 (¥5) also runs to Tánggū. In Tánggū, minibuses to Tiānjīn run from outside the train station. A light rail system runs between Zhōngshānmén station in southeast Tiānjīn and Dōnghǎilù station in Tánggū (¥5, 50 minutes, roughly every 15 minutes, from 7am to 7pm).

Train

Tiānjīn has four train stations: main, north, south and west. Most trains leave from the **Main Train Station** (Tiānjīn Zhàn; 6053 6053). If you have to alight at the **West Train Station** (2618 2662), bus 24 runs to the main train station. The far-off **South Train Station** (2421 0073) is solely for high-speed trains to Shànghǎi.

C class trains connect Tiānjīn with Běijīng, making day trips feasible. Regular trains (¥55, every 20 to 30 minutes) take around 30 minutes to cover the 120km journey. The first and last trains leaving Běijīng South Train Station at 6.30am and 9.40pm. The last train to Běijīng leaves Tiānjīn at 10.20pm. Slower trains also link the two cities.

Tiānjīn is a major north–south train junction:

Hā'ěrbīn hard seat/sleeper ¥154/281

Jǐ'nán express train ¥90, two hours; hard seat ¥52

Nánjīng express train ¥405 , three hours 40 minutes; hard seat/sleeper ¥130/239

Qīngdǎo express train ¥260, four hours; hard seat/sleeper ¥103/191

Shànghǎi express train ¥510, four hours 50 minutes; hard seat/sleeper ¥165/301

Shānhǎiguān express train ¥88, two hours 40 minutes; hard seat ¥24

Shěnyáng express train ¥202, five hours; hard seat/sleeper ¥83/164

Shíjiāzhuāng hard seat/sleeper ¥63/118

Xī'ān hard seat/sleeper ¥170/309

Zhèngzhōu hard seat/sleeper ¥113/209

ⓘ Getting Around

To/From the Airport

Taxis ask ¥60 to the airport from the city centre. Airport buses for Běijīng's Capital Airport leave from the Tiānhuán bus station every hour from 4am to 6am, then half-hourly to 6pm (¥70, 2½ hours). From Běijīng Capital Airport terminal 2 to Tiānjīn buses run hourly from 7am to 9am, then every 30 minutes to 11pm. Bus 689 (¥3) leaves from the main train station from 6am to 7pm.

Public Transport

Tiānjīn's metro has three lines and trains run from around 6.30am to just after 10pm (tickets ¥2 to ¥5). Chargeable transport cards (chéngcì piào) are available. Another four lines are under construction, while a light rail (Metro Line 9) connects Tiānjīn with the port of Tánggū.

Buses run from 5am to 11pm. Useful routes include:

Bus 600 Runs from the square behind Tiānjīn train station to stops for the Tianjin Eye, Ancient Culture Street, the Old Town, St Joseph's Church, Wǔdàdào, Binjiang Dao, Da Guangming Qiao (for Jiefang Beilu and the concession districts) and back again.

Bus 24 Runs between the main and west train stations.

Bus 8 Starts at the main train station then zigzags down to the southwest of town.

Taxi

Flag fall is ¥9 for the first 3km, then ¥1.70 per kilometre thereafter.

Around Tiānjīn

SHI FAMILY COURTYARD

In Yángliǔqīng, in the far western suburbs of Tiānjīn, is the marvellous **Shi family residence** (石家大院; Shí Jiā Dàyuàn; 47 Yangliuqing Guyi Jie; 杨柳青估衣街 47号; admission ¥27; ⊙9am-5pm Apr-Oct, 9am-4.30pm Nov-Mar), a vast warren of courtyards and enclosed gardens.

Formerly belonging to a prosperous merchant family, the restored residence contains a theatre and 278 rooms, some of which are furnished. From Tiānjīn, take bus 153 (¥2) from the west train station or bus 672 from the Tiānjīn Department Store to Yángliǔqīng. A taxi costs around ¥120 return.

HÉBĚI

Shíjiāzhuāng 石家庄

📞 0311 / POP 2.65 MILLION

Until relatively recently a small hamlet – the quaint name literally means village of the Shi family – Shíjiāzhuāng is today an archetypal Chinese city and the provincial capital of Héběi: a frantic, prosperous and sprawling railway junction town with little sensation of history. But Shíjiāzhuāng's nearby sights – including historic Zhèngdìng and rural Yújiācūn – are more than enough to warrant the short hop down from Běijīng.

👁 Sights

FREE **Héběi Provincial Museum**   MUSEUM
(河北省博物馆; Héběi Shěng Bówùguǎn; Zhongshan Donglu; ⏱9am-5pm Tue-Sun) It's a colossus of a building; a shame that inside there are far more photos than there are exhibits. That might change in the future if the museum ever gets round to putting its real treasures on display: the finds from the Mancheng Western Han tombs, including two jade Han burial suits, one of which is sewn with 1.1kg of gold thread. Bring your passport for free entry.

FREE **Revolutionary Martyrs' Mausoleum**   PARK
(烈士陵园; Lièshì Língyuán; 343 Zhongshan Xilu; ⏱6am-5.30pm) With its emphasis on patriotic education, this mausoleum is located in a pleasant tree-shaded park and contains the tomb of Canadian doctor Norman Bethune (1890–1939), a surgeon with the Eighth Route Army in the war against Japan.

🛏 Sleeping

Like other cities in Héběi, foreigners are barred from staying in many of the cheaper hotels here. Shíjiāzhuāng takes that policy to extremes by banning foreign travellers from the one hostel in town and the chain hotels.

World Trade Plaza Hotel   HOTEL $$
(世贸广场酒店; Shìmào Guǎngchǎng Jiǔdiàn; 📞8667 8888; www.wtphotels.com; 303 Zhongshan Donglu; 中山东路303号; d/tw ¥818-918, ste ¥1318; ❄@🌐) Shíjiāzhuāng's finest hotel wouldn't rate five stars in Běijīng, but is still impressively efficient and comfortable. Rooms are big and spick and span; it's worth shelling out the extra ¥100 for the deluxe rooms which come with excellent bathrooms. There are Chinese and Western restaurants onsite and small discounts are available in quiet periods.

Huiwen Hotel   HOTEL $
(汇文大酒店; Huìwén Dàjiǔdiàn; 📞8786 5999; www.hwhotel.cn; 6 Zhanqian Jie; 站前街6号; s ¥358, d/tw ¥483; ❄@) Directly opposite the train station, this busy, big place makes a decent base. Reasonably sized, bright and clean rooms for the price, especially with the generous discounts, but go for the quieter ones at the back. The staff, though, is nonplussed by foreign guests. Discounts of 50%.

🍴 Eating

Nan Xiaojie (南小街), south of the train station, is good in the summer for outdoor *shāokǎo* (barbecue) places, as well as hotpot restaurants, while nearby Minzu Lu (民族路) has a whole crop of noodle and dumpling restaurants.

TOP CHOICE **Chéngdé Huìguǎn**   HÉBĚI $
(承德会馆; 12 Zhanqian Jie; 站前街12号; dishes ¥20-40; ⏱10am-9pm) Specialising in northern Héběi cuisine, this place is actually two restaurants in one. Go through the flash entrance for the posh one with stone floors, a water feature and wooden booths; right next door is the more proletarian *cāntīng* where the prices are much more reasonable. But the food is still good, even if the setting is mundane. Picture menu.

Tudari   KOREAN $
(土大力; Tǔdàlì; www.tudari.com.cn; 2 Jinqiao Beijie; dishes from ¥18; ⏱11am-3pm & 6-11pm; 🚪) A bustling, spotless Korean eatery that's open later than most Shíjiāzhuāng restaurants. Tasty hotpots, including the ever-popular *shíguō bànfàn* (¥25; meat, rice, vegetables and egg served in a claypot), spicy salads and many different barbecued skewer options. There's a picture menu and it's just to the side of the Dōngfāng City Plaza Shopping Centre (东方大厦; Dōngfāng Dàshà).

Quánjùdé   PEKING DUCK $$
(全聚德; 9 Jianshe Nandajie; roast duck ¥198; ⏱10am-2pm & 5-9pm) If you didn't manage your full fix of Peking duck in the capital, this big and swish branch of the Běijīng chain fires up its duck traditional-style over fruit wood. A half-duck with all the trimmings is ¥99. Picture menu.

Shíjiāzhuāng

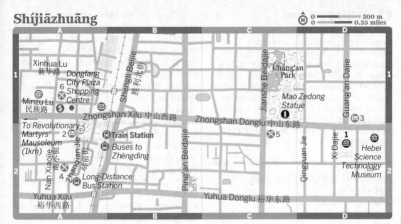

ⓘ Information

At the time of writing, foreigners were barred from using Shíjiāzhuāng's internet cafes.

Bank of China (中国银行; Zhōngguó Yínháng; Jinqiao Beidajie) Through the west door of the Dōngfāng City Plaza Shopping Centre.

China Post (中国邮政; Zhōngguó Yóuzhèng; cnr Gongli Jie & Zhongshan Xilu; ⏲24hr)

Měijué Internet Cafe (美爵网吧; Měijué Wǎngbā; Zhanqian Jie; per hr ¥3; ⏲24hr) Just to the side of the Huiwen Hotel.

Public Security Bureau (PSB; 公安局; Gōng'ānjú; Dongfeng Lu)

ⓘ Getting There & Away

Air

Flights from Shíjiāzhuāng:

Chéngdū ¥900

Guǎngzhōu ¥780

Kūnmíng ¥1020

Shànghǎi ¥500

Xī'ān ¥600

Bus

Most buses depart from the **long-distance bus station** (石家庄客运总站; shíjiāzhuāng kèyùn zǒngzhàn):

Běijīng ¥83, 3½ hours, every 30 minutes (7am to 6.30pm)

Chéngdé ¥160, seven hours, four daily

Jǐ'nán ¥115, four hours, every 40 minutes (7.20am to 5.30pm)

Kāifēng ¥140, eight hours, one daily (11am)

Tiānjīn ¥120 to ¥130, four hours, every 40 minutes (6.30am to 6.30pm)

Zhèngzhōu ¥121, six hours, nine daily (9am to 6.30pm)

Shíjiāzhuāng

◎ Sights

1 Héběi Provincial Museum D2

🛏 Sleeping

2 Huiwen Hotel A2

3 World Trade Plaza Hotel D1

🍴 Eating

4 Chéngdé Huìguǎn A2

5 Quánjùdé C2

6 Tudari A1

Train

Shíjiāzhuāng is a major rail hub with D series express trains from the **train station** (☑8760 0111) to/from Běijīng West (¥88, two hours), Zhèngzhōu and Ānyáng. The speed of connections to Běijīng makes Shíjiāzhuāng possible as a day trip. Most trains heading south from Běijīng come via Shíjiāzhuāng.

Chángchūn hard sleeper ¥309, 15½ hours

Chéngdé hard sleeper ¥134, 11 hours

Dàtóng hard sleeper ¥149, 8½ hours

Guǎngzhōu hard sleeper ¥409, 18½ hours

Jǐ'nán hard seat ¥47, 4½ hours

Luòyáng express ¥162, 4½ hours; hard seat ¥76, five hours

Nánjīng hard sleeper ¥231, 8½ hours

Shànghǎi hard sleeper ¥290, 11 hours

Shānhǎiguān express ¥178, 5½ hours; hard sleeper ¥175, 7½ hours

Tiānjīn hard seat ¥55, four hours

Zhèngzhōu hard seat ¥63, 3½ hours

Some trains also stop at or depart from Shíjiāzhuāng North Train Station (Shíjiāzhuāng Běizhàn).

❶ Getting Around

Shíjiāzhuāng's international airport is 40km northeast of town. Airport buses (¥25, 35 minutes, 6am to 8pm) to the airport depart from the Civil Aviation Hotel next to the **CAAC office** (中国民航; Zhōngguó Mínháng; ☎8505 4084; 471 Zhongshan Donglu); the office can be reached on bus 1. There are numerous buses per day, with departures depending on flights. A taxi to the airport will take about an hour and cost ¥130. Taxis are ¥5 at flag fall, then ¥1.60 per kilometre.

Around Shíjiāzhuāng

ZHÈNGDÌNG   正定

☏ 0311 / POP 130,300

Its streets littered with needy Taoist soothsayers and temple remains, walled Zhèngdìng is an appetising – albeit incomplete – slice of old China. From atop Zhèngdìng's South Gate, you can see the silhouettes of four distinct pagodas jutting above the sleepy town. Nicknamed the town of 'nine buildings, four pagodas, eight great temples and 24 golden archways', Zhèngdìng has tragically lost many of its standout buildings and archways – Píngyáo it isn't – but enough remains to lend the townscape an air of faded grandeur.

◉ Sights

All attractions are either off the east–west Zhongshan Lu or the north–south Yanzhao Nandajie. Beginning with Lóngxīng Temple, you can see almost everything by walking west until reaching Yanzhao Nandajie, then continuing south to the city gate.

No through ticket (通票; *tōngpiào*) was available at the time of writing. Opening hours are from 8am to 5.30pm.

Lóngxīng Temple   BUDDHIST TEMPLE

(隆兴寺; 109 Zhongshan Donglu; adult/student ¥40/30, guide ¥40) Of Zhèngdìng's temple tribe, the most notable is this impressive site, more popularly known as **Dàfó Temple** (大佛寺; Dàfó Sì) or 'Big Buddha Temple', in the east of town.

The time-worn bridge out front constitutes a handsome historical prelude. Dating way back to AD 586, the temple has been much restored and stands divided from its spirit wall by Zhongshan Donglu.

You are greeted in the first hall by the jovial Milefo, chubby enough that temple caretakers have pluralised him – he's now the 'Monks with a Bag'. The four Heavenly Kings flanking him in pairs are disconcertingly vast.

Beyond is the **Manichaean Hall**, an astonishingly voluminous hall flagged in smoothed stone with amazing carpentry overhead, a huge gilded statue of Sakyamuni and delectable Ming frescoes detailing Buddhist tales. At the rear of the hall is a distinctly male statue of the goddess Guanyin, seated in a lithe pose with one foot resting on her/his thigh (a posture known as *lalitāsana*) and surrounded by *luóhàn* (those freed from the cycle of rebirth).

The **Buddhist Altar** behind houses an unusual bronze Ming-dynasty two-faced Buddha, gazing north and south. Signs say 'no touching' but it's evident that its fingers and thumb have been smoothed by legions of worshippers. There are two halls behind the Buddhist Altar. On the left is the **Revolving Library Pavilion** (Zhuǎnlúnzàng Gé), which contains a revolving octagonal wooden bookcase for the storing of sutras and a stele on the back of a snarling *bìxì* (a mythical tortoiselike dragon). Opposite stands the **Pavilion of Kindness**, containing a 7.4m-high statue of Maitreya, one hand aloft.

The blurb introducing the **Pavilion of the Imperial Library** (Yùshū Lóu) draws your attention to a statue of Guanyin and 18 *luóhàn* but they are nowhere to be found. The library is connected by a walkway to the immense **Pavilion of Great Mercy** (大悲阁; Dàbēi Gé), where a bronze colossus of Guanyin rises. At 21.3m high, cast in AD 971 and sporting a third eye, the effigy is wonderful, standing on a magnificently carved base from the Northern Song. Examine the carvings which include myriad characters and musicians, including Buddhist angels and a woman blowing a conch. Overhead towers the dusty goddess with a litter of smaller Guanyin statues at her feet: clamber up into the galleries surrounding Guanyin for free, but the third level is often out of bounds. The wooden hall in which the goddess is housed was rebuilt in 1999 with reference to Song-dynasty architecture manuals.

Circumambulated by worshippers, the **Hall of Vairocana** at the rear contains a four-faced Buddha (the Buddha of four directions), crowned with another four-faced Buddha, upon which is supported a further set. The entire statue and its base contain 1072 statues of Buddha.

Tiānníng Temple   BUDDHIST TEMPLE

(天宁寺; Tiānníng Sì; admission ¥15) About 10 minutes' walk west (right as you exit) of Dàfó Temple are the remains of this temple, whose 41m-high Tang-dynasty **Lofty Pagoda** (凌霄塔; Língxiāo Tǎ) – also called Mùtǎ or Wooden Pagoda – originally dates from AD 779; it was later restored in 1045. The octagonal, nine-eaved and spire-topped pagoda is in fine condition and typical of Tang brickwork pagodas. Sadly, it is not possible to climb it.

The half-finished shell of a building to the right of the temple is supposed eventually to become the **Zhèngdìng Museum** (正定博物馆; Zhèngdìng Bówùguǎn). No one knows when it will be finished, though.

Further west on Zhongshan Xilu from Tiānníng Temple, about 250m past the intersection with Yanzhao Nandajie and down an alley, is the unassuming **Confucius Temple** (文庙; Wén Miào; admission ¥15), though there is little to see here.

Kāiyuán Temple
BUDDHIST TEMPLE

(开元寺; Kāiyuán Sì; admission ¥15) South on Yanzhao Nandajie this temple originally dates from AD 540 but was destroyed in 1966, the first year of the Cultural Revolution. Little remains apart from some leftover good vibes (it's a popular spot for qì gōng and taichi practitioners), the **Bell Tower** and the drawcard dirt-brown **Xumi Pagoda**, a well-preserved and unfussy early-Tang-dynasty brickwork, nine-eaved structure, topped with a spire. Its round arched doors and carved stone doorway are particularly attractive, as are the carved figures on the base.

Also displayed is a colossal stone *bìxì* statue – China's largest – near the entrance, with a vast chunk of its left flank missing and its head propped up on a plinth. Dating from the late Tang era, the creature was excavated in 2000 from a street in Zhèngdìng.

FREE Línjì Temple
BUDDHIST TEMPLE

(临济寺; Línjì Sì; Linji Lu) This active monastery, around 500m southeast of Kāiyuán Temple, is notable for its tall, elegant, carved brick **Chénglíng Pagoda** (澄灵塔; also called the Green Pagoda), topped with an elaborate lotus plinth plus ball and spire. The main hall behind has a large gilt effigy of Sakyamuni and 18 golden *luóhàn*. At the rear of the hall is Puxian astride an elephant, Wenshu on a lion and a figure of Guanyin. In the Tang dynasty, the temple was home to one of Chan (Zen) Buddhism's most eccentric and important teachers, Linji Yixuan, who penned the now famous words, 'If you meet the Buddha on the road, kill him!'

Guǎnghuì Temple
BUDDHIST TEMPLE

(广惠寺; Guǎnghuì Sì; admission ¥15) Nothing remains of this temple a little further south, except its unusual Indian-style pagoda decorated with lions, elephants, sea creatures, *púsà* (Bodhisattvas; those worthy of nirvana who remain on earth to help others attain enlightenment) and other figures (some missing). With a brick base and four doors, the pagoda has stone-carved upper storeys and a brickwork cap.

City Walls
HISTORIC SITE

(城墙; Chéngqiáng) Much of Zhèngdìng's main street (Yanzhao Dajie) has been restored and is now a pleasant stretch of traditional Chinese roofing, brickwork and willows called the **Zhèngdìng Historical Culture Street** (正定历史文化街; Zhèngdìng Lìshǐ Wénhuà Jiē). At the southern end of the street is **Chánglè Gate** (长乐门; Chánglè Mén; admission ¥15), also known as Nánchéngmén or South Gate. The original wall (which dates back to the Northern Zhou) was made up of an outer wall (*yuèchéng*) and an inner wall (*nèichéng*), with enceintes (*wèngchéng*), and had a total length of 24km. You can climb onto Chánglè Gate and view a few dilapidated remains of the wall.

🛏 Sleeping & Eating

For a town with such a strong Buddhist heritage, Zhèngdìng has a significant Hui population (their modern mosque is to the side of Guǎnghuì Temple) and there are many Muslim noodle restaurants on Yanzhao Dajie. Zhongshan Donglu has loads of eateries too, including Sìchuān places and cake outlets.

Huayang Vacation Hotel
HOTEL $

(华阳假日酒店; Huáyáng Jiàrì Jiǔdiàn; ☑8801 1470; 2 Shanxi Lu; 山西路2号; tw/d ¥268/288; ✳@) One of a handful of places that will take foreigners, the Huayang has attractive and modern rooms and bathrooms. The staff are friendly, but speak no English.

ℹ Information

Industrial & Commercial Bank of China (ICBC; 工商银行; Gōngshāng Yínháng; cnr Zhongshan Donglu & Yanzhao Nandajie)

Internet cafe (网吧; wǎngbā; Yanzhao Nandajie; per hr ¥3; ⊙24hr) Just down an alley a few metres south of the intersection between Yanzhao Nandajie and Zhongshan Donglu.

ℹ Getting There & Away

From Shíjiāzhuāng, buses 131 and 132 (¥2, 45 minutes, 6.30am to 6.30pm) run regularly to Zhèngdìng's bus station from the main bus stop in the train station square. Regular train services also run through Zhèngdìng from Shíjiāzhuāng.

ℹ Getting Around

Zhèngdìng is not huge and walking is easy as sights are largely clustered together. Taxi flagfall within Zhèngdìng is ¥5; three-wheel motorcycles cost ¥4 for anywhere in town. Bus 177 runs past Dàfó Temple down Zhongshan Donglu and then Yanzhao Nandajie.

YÚJIĀCŪN 于家村
POP 1600

Also known as **Stone Village** (石头村; Shítou Cūn) and hidden in the hills near the Héběi–Shānxī border is the peaceful little settlement of **Yújiācūn** (admission ¥20). Nearly everything, from the houses to furniture inside, was originally made of stone. As such, Yújiācūn is remarkably well preserved: bumpy little lanes lead past traditional Ming- and Qing-dynasty courtyard homes, old opera stages and tiny temples. Actually, 'traditional' doesn't quite describe it: this is a model Chinese clan village, where 95% of the inhabitants all share the same surname of Yu (于).

One of the more unusual sights is inside the **Yu Ancestral Hall** (于氏宗祠; Yúshì Zōngcí), where you'll find the 24-generation family tree, reaching back over 500 years. There are five tapestries, one for the descendants of each of the original Yu sons who founded the village.

Another oddity is the three-storey **Qīngliáng Pavilion** (清凉阁; Qīngliáng Gé), completed in 1581. Supposedly the work of one thoroughly crazed individual (Yu Xichun, who wanted to be able to see Běijīng from the top), it was, according to legend, built entirely at night, over a 16-year period, without the help of any other villagers. It was certainly built by an amateur architect: there's no foundation, and the building stones (in addition to not being sealed by mortar) are of wildly different sizes (some as large as 2m), giving it a higgledy-piggledy look that's quite uncommon in Chinese architecture.

Other buildings worth hunting down are the **Guānyīn Pavilion** (观音阁; Guānyīn Gé) and the **Zhēnwǔ Temple** (真武庙; Zhēnwǔ Miào). Near the primary school is the **Stone Museum** (石头博物馆; Shítou Bówùguǎn) displaying local items made of stone.

🛏 Sleeping

The Mandarin accent here is as thick as the coal dust that settles everywhere in the Héběi–Shānxī borderlands, but mercifully Yújiācūn is free of the pollution and it's definitely worth spending the night here. As the sun sets, the sounds of village life – farmers chatting after a day in the fields, clucking hens, kids at play – are miles away from the raging pace of modern Chinese cities.

Villagers rent out rooms for ¥15 per person; home-cooked meals are another ¥15 each, a bottle of beer is ¥2. One friendly place is the **Chūnyīng Yuàn** (春英院; ☑0311 8237 6583), which has simple rooms for around ¥15. It's very close to the Zhēnwǔ Temple.

ℹ Getting There & Away

All roads to Yújiācūn pass through Jǐngxíng (井陉), about 35km west of Shíjiāzhuāng. The quickest and easiest way to get there is to catch one of the many buses (¥11, one hour, every 30 minutes 7am to 6pm) to Jǐngxíng from Shíjiāzhuāng's **Xīwáng bus station** (西王客运站; Xīwáng kèyùnzhàn). Take bus 9 (¥1) to Xīwáng from Shíjiāzhuāng train station. A taxi will cost ¥17 to ¥20.

From Jǐngxíng you can catch buses through a landscape blackened with coal dust to Yújiācūn (¥5, one hour, regular departures 7.30am to 5.15pm) and Cāngyán Shān (¥5, one hour, departures 9am to 1pm, returns noon to 5pm). Buses arrive at and depart from various intersections in town; tell the bus driver where you are going and he will drop you at the right place. Alternatively, hire a taxi for one destination (¥80 return) or for the day (¥200). Be warned that the roads in these parts can be full of coal trucks so journeys can take longer. To reach Cāngyán Shān from Yújiācūn, take a bus to Bǎishān (柏山; ¥2) and change.

CĀNGYÁN SHĀN 苍岩山

Cāngyán Shān (admission ¥50) – literally 'Green Crag Mountain' – is the site of the transcendent cliff-spanning Hanging Palace, a Sui-dynasty construction perched halfway up a precipitous gorge. If you think you've seen it before, you probably have; this was one of the locations for the hit movie *Crouching Tiger, Hidden Dragon*.

Given its dramatic setting, it must have been an impressive temple complex at one time, though these days the best views after the main hall are of the surrounding canyons. It is a quick, steep jaunt up to the palace, and then another 45 minutes past scattered pagodas and shrines to the new temple at the mountain's summit. The standard lunar festivals see a lot of worshippers and are a good time to visit if you don't mind crowds.

Morning buses (¥26, two hours) for Cāngyán Shān leave from Shíjiāzhuāng's Xīwǎng station at 7am, returning in the late afternoon. It can also be combined with a trip to Yújiācūn and Jǐngxíng.

ZHÀOZHŌU BRIDGE 赵州桥

China's oldest-standing **bridge** (Zhàozhōu Qiáo; admission ¥30) has spanned the Jiāo River (Jiǎo Hé) for 1400 years. In Zhàoxiàn County, about 40km southeast of Shíjiāzhuāng and 2km south of Zhàoxiàn town, this is the world's first segmental bridge (ie its arch is a segment of a circle, as opposed to a complete semicircle) and predates other bridges of its type throughout the world by 800 years. In fine condition, it is 50.82m long and 9.6m wide, with a span of 37m. Twenty-two stone posts are topped with carvings of dragons and mythical creatures, with the centre slab featuring a magnificent *tāotiè* (an offspring of a dragon). The bridge is also known as (安济桥; Ānjì Qiáo) or 'Safe Crossing Bridge'.

To reach the bridge from Shíjiāzhuāng's long-distance bus station, take bus 30 to the **south bus station** (南焦客运站; nánjiāo kèyùnzhàn; ✆8657 3806), then take a minibus to Zhàoxiàn town (赵县; ¥10, one hour). There are no public buses from Zhàoxiàn to the bridge, but a *sānlúnchē* (three-wheeled pedicab) can oblige for ¥3.

Chéngdé 承德

📱 0314 / POP 479,703

Chéngdé might look like an unremarkable provincial town at first glance, but it has an extraordinary history as the summer playground of the Qing-dynasty emperors. In the early 18th century, it evolved into both the Qing rulers' holiday resort and Manchu headquarters of foreign affairs. Beginning with Kangxi, the Qing emperors fled here to escape the torpid summer heat of the Forbidden City (and occasionally foreign armies) and for closer proximity to the hunting grounds of their northern homelands.

The Bìshǔ Shānzhuāng (Fleeing-the-Heat Mountain Villa) is a grand imperial palace and the walled enclosure behind houses China's largest regal gardens. Beyond the grounds is a remarkable collection of politically chosen temples, built to host dignitaries such as the sixth Panchen Lama. Autumn visits are recommended, as tourists swarm like termites during summer while winters are face-numbingly cold.

History

In 1703, when an expedition passed through the Chéngdé valley, Emperor Kangxi was so enamoured with the surroundings that he had a hunting lodge built, which gradually grew into the summer resort. Rèhé – or Jehol (Warm River; named after a hot spring here) – as Chéngdé was then known, grew in importance and the Qing court began to spend more time here, sometimes up to several months a year, with some 10,000 people accompanying the emperor on his seven-day expedition from Běijīng.

The emperors also convened here with the border tribes – undoubtedly more at ease here than in Běijīng – who posed the greatest threats to the Qing frontiers: the Mongols, Tibetans, Uighurs and, eventually, the Europeans. The resort reached its peak under Emperor Qianlong (1735–96), who commissioned many of the outlying temples to overawe visiting leaders.

In 1793 British emissary Lord Macartney arrived to open trade with China. The well-known story of Macartney refusing to kowtow before Qianlong probably wasn't the definitive factor in his inevitable dismissal (though it certainly made quite an impression on the court) – in any case, China, it was explained, possessed all things and had no need for trade.

The Emperor Xianfeng died here in 1861, permanently warping Chéngdé's feng shui and tipping the Imperial Villa towards long-term decline.

🔆 Sights

Bìshǔ Shānzhuāng   HISTORIC SITE

(避暑山庄; admission Apr-Oct ¥120, Nov-Mar ¥90; ☉palace 7am-6pm Apr-Oct, 8am-5.30pm Nov-Oct)
The imperial summer resort is composed of a main palace complex and vast park-like gardens, all enclosed by a good-looking 10km-long wall. The peak season entrance price is steep, but the gardens provide splendid walks away from the crowds.

A huge spirit wall shields the resort entrance from the bad spirits and traffic fumes of Lizhengmen Dajie. Through **Lizhèng Gate** (丽正门; Lìzhèng Mén), the **Main Palace** (正宫; Zhèng Gōng) is a series of nine courtyards and five elegant, unpainted halls, with a rusticity complemented by towering pine trees. The wings in each courtyard have various exhibitions (porcelain, clothing, weaponry), and most of the halls are decked out in period furnishings.

Chéngdé

0 — 600 m
0 — 0.4 miles

To Shuxiang Temple (1km)

Pǔtuózōngchéng Temple

Temple of Sumeru, Happiness & Longevity

To Pǔníng Temple & Puyou Temple (500m); Guǎngyúan Temple (300m)

Huancheng Beilu 环城北路

Shizi Gouche

Puning Lu 普宁路

Guodao 国道

Xibei Gate

Ancient Pavilion

Beizhen Twin Peaks

Huidiji Gate

7

Bìshǔ Shānzhuāng

Chairlift to Hammer Rock

1

4

Pushan Temple

5

Shanzhuang Donglu 山庄东路

Huancheng Donglu 环城东路

6

3

Ruyi Island

Fragrant Garden House (Fangyuanju)

2

Main Palace

Dehui Gate

Bifeng Gate

Xi Dajie 西大街

Guāndì Temple

Lizheng Gate

Lizhengmen Dajie

15 10-13

Dutongfu Dajie 都统府大街

Zhonggulou Dajie

Shaanxiyling Jie 陕西营街

Chaichang Hutong 柴场胡同

Wulie Lu 武烈路

Wuli River

14

Zhonggulou Dajie 钟鼓楼大街

Nanyingzi Dajie 南营子大街

8

Arhat Hill

Xinhua Lu

Nanyuan Donglu

11

Banbishan Lu 半壁山路

Cuiqiao Lu 翠桥路

9

Chezhan Lu 车站路

12

Train Station 火车站

To East Bus Station (8km)

Chéngdé

⊙ Top Sights

Guāndì Temple.....................................B5
Main Palace C5
Pŭtuózōngchéng Temple B1
Temple of Sumeru, Happiness &
   Longevity C1

⊙ Sights

1 Ānyuan Temple...............................D2
2 Boat Rental....................................C4
3 Misty Rain Tower C4
4 Pŭlè Temple...................................D2
5 Pŭrén Temple.................................D3
6 Wénjīn Pavilion.............................B3
7 Yŏngyòusì Pagoda.........................C3

⊜ Sleeping

8 Chéngdé Bīnguǎn.........................B6
9 Ming's Dynasty Hostel C7
10 Mountain Villa Hotel C5
11 Yúnshān Hotel...............................C7

⊗ Eating

12 Dà Qīng Huā...................................D7
13 Dà Qīng Huā...................................C5
14 Night Food Market.......................B5
15 Xiăo Féiyáng C5

ⓘ Information

Bank of China............................ (see 13)

The first hall is the refreshingly cool **Hall of Simplicity and Sincerity**, built of an aromatic cedar called *nánmù,* and displaying a carved throne draped in yellow silk. Other prominent halls include the emperor's study (Study of Four Knowledges) and living quarters (Hall of Refreshing Mists and Waves). On the left-hand side of the latter is the imperial bedroom. Two residential areas branch out from here: the empress dowager's **Pine Crane Palace** (松鹤斋; Sōnghè Zhāi), to the east, and the smaller Western Apartments, where the concubines (including a young Cixi) resided.

Exiting the Main Palace brings you to the gardens and forested hunting grounds, with landscapes borrowed from famous southern scenic areas in Hángzhōu, Sūzhōu and Jiāxīng, as well as the Mongolian grasslands. The 20th century took its toll on the park, but you can still get a feel for the original scheme of things.

The double-storey **Misty Rain Tower** (烟雨楼; Yānyǔ Lóu), on the northwestern side of the main lake, served as an imperial study.

Further north is the **Wénjīn Pavilion** (文津阁; Wénjīn Gé), built in 1773 to house a copy of the *Siku Quanshu,* a major anthology of classics, history, philosophy and literature commissioned by Qianlong. The anthology took 10 years to compile, and totalled an astounding 36,500 chapters. Four copies were made, only one of which has survived (now in Běijīng). In the east, elegant **Yŏngyòusì Pagoda** (永佑寺塔; Yŏngyòusì Tǎ) soars above the fragments of its vanished temple.

About 90% of the compound is taken up by lakes, hills, forests and plains, with the odd vantage-point pavilion. In the northern part of the park, the emperors reviewed displays of archery, equestrian skills and fireworks.

Just beyond the Main Palace are electric carts that whiz around the grounds (¥50); further on is a **boat-rental area** (出租小船; Chūzū Xiǎochuán; per hr ¥30-40, deposit ¥300). Almost all of the forested section is closed from November through May because of fire hazard in the dry months, but fear not, you can still turn your legs to jelly wandering around the rest of the park.

Guāndì Temple
TAOIST TEMPLE
(关帝庙; Guāndì Miào; 18 Lizhengmen Dajie; admission ¥20; ⊙7am-7pm Apr-Oct, 8am-5pm Nov-Oct) The heavily restored Taoist Guāndì Temple was first built during the reign of Yongzheng, in 1732. For years the temple housed residents but is again home to a band of Taoist monks, garbed in distinctive jackets and trousers, their long hair twisted into topknots.

Eight Outer Temples
BUDDHIST TEMPLES
(外八庙; wài bā miào) Skirting the northern and eastern walls of the Bìshǔ Shānzhuāng, the eight outer temples were, unusually, designed for diplomatic rather than spiritual reasons. Some were based on actual Tibetan Buddhist monasteries but the emphasis was on appearance: smaller temple buildings are sometimes solid, and the Tibetan facades (with painted windows) are often fronts for traditional Chinese temple interiors. The surviving temples and monasteries were all built between 1713 and 1780; the prominence given to Tibetan Buddhism was as much for the Mongols (fervent Lamaists) as the Tibetan leaders.

Bus 6 taken to the northeastern corner will drop you in the vicinity and bus 118 runs along Huancheng Beilu, though pedalling the 12km (round trip) by bike is an excellent idea.

Pǔníng Temple
BUDDHIST TEMPLE

(普宁寺; Pǔníng Sì; Puningsi Lu; admission Apr-Oct ¥80, Nov-Mar ¥60; ☺8am-6pm Apr-Oct, 8.30am-5pm Nov-Mar) With its squeaking prayer wheels and devotional intonations of its monks, Chéngdé's only active temple was built in 1755 in anticipation of Qianlong's victory over the western Mongol tribes in Xīnjiāng. Supposedly modelled on the earliest Tibetan Buddhist monastery (Samye), the first half of the temple is distinctly Chinese (with Tibetan buildings at the rear).

Enter the temple grounds to a stele pavilion with inscriptions by the Qianlong emperor in Chinese, Manchu, Mongol and Tibetan. The halls behind are arranged in typical Buddhist fashion, with the **Hall of Heavenly Kings** (天王殿; Tiānwáng Diàn) and beyond, the **Mahavira Hall** (大雄宝殿; Dàxióng Bǎodiàn), where three images of the Buddhas of the three generations are arrayed. Some very steep steps rise up behind (the temple is arranged on a mountainside) leading to a gate tower, which you can climb.

On the terrace at the top of the steps is the dwarfing **Mahayana Hall**. On either side are stupas and square blocklike Tibetan-style buildings, decorated with attractive water spouts. Some buildings have been converted to shops, while others are solid, serving a purely decorative purpose.

The mind-bogglingly vast gilded statue of **Guanyin** (the Buddhist Goddess of Mercy) towers within the Mahayana Hall. The effigy is astounding: over 22m high, it's the tallest of its kind in the world and radiates a powerful sense of divinity. Hewn from five different kinds of wood (pine, cypress, fir, elm and linden), Guanyin has 42 arms, with each palm bearing an eye and each hand holding instruments, skulls, lotuses and other Buddhist devices. Tibetan touches include the pair of hands in front of the goddess, below the two clasped in prayer, the right one of which holds a sceptre-like *dorje* (*vajra* in Sanskrit), a masculine symbol, and the left a *dril bu* (bell), a female symbol. On Guanyin's head sits the Teacher Longevity Buddha. To the right of the goddess stands a huge male guardian and disciple called Shàncái, opposite his female equivalent, Lóngnǚ (Dragon Girl). Unlike Guanyin, they are both coated in ancient and dusty pigments. On the wall on either side are hundreds of small effigies of Buddha.

If you're fortunate, you may be able to clamber up to the first gallery (¥10) for a closer inspection of Guanyin; torches are provided to cut through the gloom. Sadly, higher galleries are often out of bounds, so an eye-to-eye with the goddess may be impossible. To climb the gallery, try to come in the morning, as it is often impossible to get a ticket in the afternoon, and prepare to be disappointed, as the gallery may simply be shut.

Pǔníng Temple has a number of friendly lamas who manage their domain, so be quiet and respectful at all times. The ticket price includes admission to the Pǔyòu Temple. Take bus 6 from in front of the Mountain Villa Hotel.

Pǔtuózōngchéng Temple
BUDDHIST TEMPLE

(普陀宗乘之庙; Pǔtuózōngchéng Zhīmiào; Shizigou Lu; admission Apr-Oct ¥80, Nov-Mar ¥60; ☺8am-6pm Apr-Oct, 8.30am-5pm Nov-Mar) Chéngdé's largest temple is a not-so-small replica of Lhasa's Potala Palace and houses the nebulous presence of Avalokiteshvara (Guanyin). A marvellous sight on a clear day, the temple's red walls stand out against its mountain backdrop. Enter to a huge stele pavilion, followed by a large triple archway topped with five small stupas in red, green, yellow, white and black. In between the two gates are two large stone elephants whose knees bend impossibly.

Fronted by a collection of prayer wheels and flags, the **Red Palace** (also called the Great Red Platform) contains most of the main shrines and halls. Continue up past an exhibition of *thangka* (sacred Tibetan paintings) in a restored courtyard and look out for the marvellous sandalwood pagodas in the front hall. Both are 19m tall and contain 2160 effigies of the Amitabha Buddha.

Among the many exhibits on view are displays of Tibetan Buddhist objects and instruments, including a *kapala* bowl, made from the skull of a young girl. The main hall is located at the very top, surrounded by several small pavilions and panoramic views.

The admission ticket includes the neighbouring Temple of Sumeru, Happiness and Longevity. Bus 118 (¥1) runs along Huancheng Beilu past the temple.

Temple of Sumeru, Happiness & Longevity
BUDDHIST TEMPLE

(须弥福寿之庙; Xūmífúshòu Zhīmiào; Shizigou Lu; admission Apr-Oct ¥80, Nov-Mar ¥60; ☺8am-6pm Apr-Oct, 8.30am-5pm Nov-Mar) East of the Pǔtuózōngchéng Temple, this huge temple was built in honour of the sixth Panchen Lama, who stayed here in 1781. Incorporating Tibetan and Chinese architectural elements, it's an imitation of the Panchen's home monastery Tashilhunpo in Shigatse, Tibet. Note the eight huge, glinting dragons (each said to weigh over 1000kg) that adorn the roof of the main hall. The admission price includes Pǔtuózōngchéng Temple. Bus 118 (¥1) runs along Huancheng Beilu past the temple.

Pǔlè Temple   BUDDHIST TEMPLE
(普乐寺; Pǔlè Sì; admission incl Hammer Rock ¥50; ⊙8am-5.30pm Apr-Oct, 8.30am-4.30pm Nov-Mar) This peaceful temple was built in 1776 for the visits of minority envoys (Kazakhs among them). At the rear of the temple is the unusual Round Pavilion, reminiscent of the Hall of Prayer for Good Harvests at Běijīng's Temple of Heaven. Inside is an enormous wooden mandala (a geometric representation of the universe).

It's a 30-minute walk to **Hammer Rock** (磐锤峰; Qìngchuí Fēng) from Pǔlè Temple – the club-shaped rock is visible for miles around and is said to resemble a kind of musical hammer. There is pleasant hiking and commanding views of the area. Bus 10 will take you to the chairlift (return ¥50) for Hammer Rock.

Pǔyòu Temple   BUDDHIST TEMPLE
(普佑寺; Pǔyòu Sì; ⊙8am-6pm) Just east of Pǔníng Temple, this temple is dilapidated and missing its main hall, but it has a plentiful contingent of merry gilded *luóhàn* in the side wings, although a fire in 1964 incinerated many of their confrères. Admission is included in the ticket for Pǔníng Temple.

Guǎngyuán Temple   BUDDHIST TEMPLE
(广缘寺; Guǎngyuán Sì) Unrestored and inaccessible, the temple's rounded doorway is blocked up with stones and its grounds are seemingly employed by the local farming community. The temple is a couple of hundred metres southeast of Pǔníng Temple.

Ānyuǎn Temple   BUDDHIST TEMPLE
(安远庙; Ānyuǎn Miào; admission ¥20; ⊙8am-5.30pm Apr-Oct, 8.30am-4.30pm Nov-Mar) Closed for repairs at the time of writing, this is a copy of the Gurza Temple in Xīnjiāng. Only the main hall remains, which contains deteriorating Buddhist frescoes. Take bus 10.

Pǔrén Temple   BUDDHIST TEMPLE
(普仁寺; Pǔrén Sì) Built in 1713, this is the earliest temple in Chéngdé, but is not open to the public.

Shūxiàng Temple   BUDDHIST TEMPLE
(殊像寺; Shūxiàng Sì) Surrounded by a low red wall, with its large halls rising on the hill behind and huge stone lions parked outside, this temple is almost permanently closed. Just to the west of Shūxiàng Temple is a military zone which foreigners are not allowed to access, so don't go wandering around.

🛌 Sleeping

Chéngdé has an unremarkable and expensive range of tourist accommodation. At the time of writing, foreigners were barred from many hotels, both cheap and midrange. Hotel room prices increase at the weekend and during the holiday periods.

TOP CHOICE Ming's Dynasty Hostel   HOSTEL $
(明朝国际城市青年酒店; Míngcháo Guójì Chéngshì Qīngnián Jiǔdiàn; ☑761 0360; www.mingsdynastyhostel.com; Huilong Plaza, Xinjuzhai, Chezhan Lu; 车站路新居宅会龙大厦; dm ¥70, tw without/with bathroom ¥160/300; ☺❄@🖤) A lifesaver for budget travellers in Chéngdé, this family-run hostel has shifted location to a more hotel-like building while retaining its friendly, homely feel. The dorms and rooms are simple, clean and comfortable and the staff solicitous, handing out advice, free maps and booking transport. Turn right out of the train station and it's a five-minute walk.

Mountain Villa Hotel   HOTEL $$
(山庄宾馆; Shānzhuāng Bīnguǎn; ☑209 1188; www.hemvhotel.com; 11 Lizhengmen Dajie; 丽正门路11号; d ¥680-780, tr ¥400; ❄@) The cavernous Mountain Villa has a plethora of rooms and offers pole position for a trip inside the Bìshǔ Shānzhuāng. The rooms are a little dreary and functional for the price, but with the big discounts on offer at slack times they are a decent deal for pricy Chéngdé. Take bus 7 from the train station and from there it's a short walk. All major credit cards are accepted. Discounts of 50%.

Yúnshān Hotel   HOTEL $$
(云山大酒店; Yúnshān Dàjiǔdiàn; ☑205 5588; 6 Nanyuan Donglu; 南园东路6号; d ¥880-980; ❄@) The dirty white tile exterior makes it resemble a towering public convenience, but inside the rooms at this four-star hotel are comfortable enough, albeit a little faded. The bathrooms are small. Good location, though. Discounts of 35%.

Chéngdé Hotel HOTEL $$
(承德宾馆; Chéngdé Bīnguǎn; ☑590 1888; 19 Nanyingzi Dajie; 南营子大街19号; d/tw ¥780-880, discounts of 35%; ✳@) Another big hotel that could do with an upgrade, but a prime position in the centre of town, big rooms with reasonable bathrooms and efficient staff.

✕ Eating

Chéngdé is famous for wild game –notably *lùròu* (venison) and *shānjī* (pheasant), a reminder of its past as an imperial hunting base, but don't expect to see too much on the menus these days. On summer nights, do as the locals do and head for Shaanxiying Jie (northern end of Nanyingzi Dajie) to a night food market for a good choice of *shāokǎo* and Muslim noodle restaurants, as well as a few bars. Nanxinglong Jie is good for *ròujiāmó* (肉夹馍; meat in a bun) and other snacks. Dongxing Lu (东兴路) is full of big, brash hotpot restaurants.

⌐TOP CHOICE⌐ Dà Qīng Huā DUMPLINGS $
(大清花; ☑208 2222; 241 Chezhan Lu; 车站路241号; dishes from ¥12; ☉11.30am-9pm) The finest dumpling house in Chéngdé, this excellent establishment has a big choice of juicy *jiǎozi*, with vegie options such as pumpkin and egg (¥18), as well as a huge range of other dishes. The fresh, pine wood interior is a delight to eat in, and all orders come with a selection of free cold nibbles. There is another branch at Lizhengmen Dajie. Picture menu.

Xiǎo Féiyáng HOTPOT $
(小肥羊; Xīnyìfùlái Hotel; ☑202 2166; Lizhengmen Dajie; meals ¥50; ☉10am-late) Right across the way from Lìzhèng Gate, this hotpot restaurant is excellent for post–Imperial Summer Resort ramblings. The two-flavour, spicy and mild *yuānyāng* (鸳鸯锅; ¥20) base is best, into which you fling plate loads of lamb (羊肉; *yángròu*; ¥18), cabbage (白菜; *báicài*; ¥4), potatoes (土豆片; *tǔdòupiàn*; ¥4), eggs (鸡蛋; *jīdàn*; ¥1) and more. No English menu but the waitresses will help you tick the form. It's on the ground floor of the Xīnyìfùlái Hotel (新意富来酒店).

ⓘ Information

Bank of China (中国银行; Zhōngguó Yínháng; 4 Dutongfu Dajie) Also on Xinsheng Lu and Lizhengmen Dajie; 24-hour ATMs.

China Post (中国邮政; Zhōngguó Yóuzhèng; cnr Lizhengmen Dajie & Dutongfu Dajie; ☉8am-6pm)

A smaller branch is on Lizhengmen Dajie, east of the Main Gate of the Imperial Summer Resort.

Public Security Bureau (PSB; 公安局; Gōng'ānjú; ☑202 2352; 9 Wulie Lu; ☉8.30am-5pm Mon-Fri)

Xiàndài Internet Cafe (现代网吧; Xiàndài Wǎngbā; Chezhan Lu; per hr ¥3; ☉24hr) West of the train station.

ⓘ Getting There & Away

Bus

Buses for Chéngdé leave Běijīng hourly from Liùlǐqiáo bus station (¥50, four hours); buses also run from Běijīng's Sihuì long-distance station (¥50, four hours, 6am to 4pm). Buses from Chéngdé leave every half-hour for Běijīng (¥85, three hours, last bus 6.30pm) from the train station car park.

Buses also leave from Chéngdé's **east bus station** (dōng qìchēzhàn; ☑212 3566), 8km south of town:

Běijīng ¥87, four hours, every 20 minutes (6am to 6pm)

Dálián ¥221, 13 to 14 hours, 3pm

Jìxiàn ¥57, four hours, 9.30am and 7.30pm

Qínhuángdǎo ¥112, five hours, six daily (for Shānhǎiguān)

Tiānjīn ¥122, six hours, 8.50am and 10pm

Train

The fastest regular trains from Běijīng Train Station take over four hours (hard/soft seat ¥41/61); slower trains take much longer. The first train from Běijīng departs at 8.05am, arriving in Chéngdé at 12.31pm. Alternatively, catch the 12.15am train from Běijīng and reach Chéngdé at 6.31am. In the other direction, the 1.53pm service from Chéngdé is a useful train, arriving in Běijīng at 6.19pm. The first train to Běijīng is at 4.19am, arriving at 10.09am.

Shěnyáng hard seat/hard sleeper ¥45/100, 12/13 hours, two daily (6.53am and 5.31pm)

Shíjiāzhuāng hard seat/hard sleeper ¥67/134, 10 hours

Tiānjīn hard seat/hard sleeper ¥31/71, seven hours, one daily (10.50pm)

ⓘ Getting Around

Taxis are ¥7 at flag fall (then ¥1.40 per kilometre); on the meter, a taxi from the train station to the Bìshǔ Shānzhuāng should cost around ¥9. There are several minibus lines (¥1), including minibus 5 from the train station to Lizhengmen Dajie, minibus 1 from the train station to the east bus station and minibus 6 to the Eight Outer Temples, grouped at the northeastern end of town. Bus 11 also runs from the train station to the Bìshǔ Shānzhuāng. To reach the east bus station, take bus 118 or a taxi (¥20).

Shānhǎiguān 山海关

📞 0335 / POP 19,500

A possible day trip from Běijīng or pit stop on the way to the northeast Manchurian heartland, the drowsy walled town of Shānhǎiguān marks the point where the Great Wall snakes out of the hills to meet the sea.

In recent years, Shānhǎiguān has sold some of its soul for a rebuild of the old town's central sections. Thoughtful restoration of Shānhǎiguān's rundown buildings would have been desirable, but their replacement with faux traditional buildings is the typical default mode of tourist developers keen to make a fast buck. The effect has been to render Shānhǎiguān more than a little sterile, although thankfully a few pockets of original buildings remain in the *hútòng* (alleys) running off the main streets.

Shops along Nan Dajie and Bei Dajie have been rebuilt (with lashings of carefully concealed concrete) along with the Drum Tower, rows of *páilóu* and a smattering of temples. The old town is still a pleasant place for a wander; just bear in mind that what you are seeing is a recreation.

History

Guarding the narrow plain leading to northeastern China, the Ming garrison town of Shānhǎiguān and its wall were developed to seal off the country from the Manchu, whose troublesome ancestors ruled northern China during the Jin dynasty (AD 1115–1234). This strategy succeeded until 1644, when Chinese rebels seized Běijīng and General Wu Sangui opted to invite the Manchu army through the impregnable pass to help suppress the uprising. The plan worked so well that the Manchus proceeded to take over the entire country and establish the Qing dynasty.

An ironic footnote: in 1681 Qing rulers finished building their own Great Wall, known as the Willow Palisade (a large ditch fronted by willow trees), which stretched several hundred kilometres from Shānhǎiguān to Jílín, with another branch forking south to Dāndōng from Kāiyuán. The purpose of the Palisade, of course, was to keep the Han Chinese and Mongols out of Manchuria.

👁 Sights

First Pass Under Heaven HISTORIC SITE
(天下第一关; Tiānxià Dìyī Guān; cnr Dong Dajie & Diyiguan Lu; adult/student ¥40/20; ⊙7am-5.30pm) A restored section of wall studded with watchtowers and tourist paraphernalia, the First Pass Under Heaven is also called East Gate (东门; Dōng Mén). The 12m-high wall's principal watchtower – two storeys with double eaves and 68 arrow-slit windows – is a towering 13.7m high.

The calligraphy at the top (attributed to the scholar Xiao Xian) reads 'First Pass Under Heaven'. Several other watchtowers can also be seen and a *wèngchéng* (enceinte) extends out east from the wall. To the north, decayed sections of battlements trail off into the hills; to the south you can walk to the ramp just east of the South Gate.

FREE Great Wall Museum MUSEUM
(长城博物馆; Chángchéng Bówùguǎn; Diyiguan Lu; ⊙9am-4pm Tue-Sun) The most worthwhile sight in Shānhǎiguān, this impressive museum, housed in a geometric block of grey stone, provides a comprehensive history of the wall's evolution from mud embankment to permanent barrier. Plenty of photos and artefacts, as well as decent English captions.

Shānhǎiguān

◎ Top Sights

First Pass Under Heaven	B1
Great Wall Museum	B1

◎ Sights

1 Dàbēi Pavilion	A1
2 Drum Tower	A1
3 Wang Family Courtyard House	A1
4 West Gate	A1

⊟ Sleeping

5 Friendly Cooperate Hotel	B2
6 Shānhǎi Holiday Hotel	A1

Jiǎo Shān
HISTORIC SITE

(角山; admission ¥30; ⊙7am-sunset) Closed at the time of research (expect some changes and an increase in the ticket price), Jiǎo Shān offers an excellent hike up the Great Wall's first high peak; a telling vantage point over the narrow tongue of land below and one-time invasion route for northern armies. For something more adventurous, follow the wall's unrestored section indefinitely past the watchtowers or hike over to the secluded **Qīxián Monastery** (栖贤寺; Qīxián Sì; admission ¥5).

Jiǎo Shān is a 3km bike ride north of town or a half-hour walk from the north gate; otherwise take a *sānlúnchē* (¥10). It's a steep 20-minute clamber from the base, or a cable car can yank you up for ¥20.

Old Dragon Head
HISTORIC SITE

(老龙头; Lǎolóngtou; admission ¥30; ⊙7.30am-6.30pm) The mythic origin/conclusion of the Great Wall at the sea's edge, Old Dragon Head is 4km south of Shānhǎiguān. What you see now was reconstructed in the late 1980s – the original wall crumbled away long ago. The name derives from the legendary carved dragon head that once faced the waves; as attractions go, it's essentially a lot more hype than history. Buses 25 and 21 (¥1) go to Old Dragon Head from Shānhǎiguān's South Gate.

Other Sights
HISTORIC SITE

The vaguely interesting 18th-century **Wang Family Courtyard House** (王家大院; Wángjiā Dàyuàn; 29-31 Dongsantiao Hutong; admission ¥25; ⊙7.30am-5.30pm) is a large residence with an amateur display of period furnishings.

The wall attached to **North Gate** (北门; Běi Mén) has been partially restored. The city gates once had circular enceintes attached to them, as you can see at the East Gate. The excavated outlines outside the **West Gate** (西门; Xī Mén) are discernible, as are slabs of the original Ming-dynasty road lying 1m below the current level of the ground.

The **Dàbēi Pavilion** (大悲阁; Dàbēi Gé; Bei Dajie; admission ¥15; ⊙7am-6pm) in the northwest of town has been rebuilt, as has the Taoist **Sānqīng Temple** (三清观; Sānqīng Guàn; Beihou Jie; admission free; ⊙8am-5pm), which is a half-mile walk outside the walls from the west gate. Shānghǎiguān's **Drum Tower** (鼓楼; Gǔlóu) has been similarly rebuilt, with a liberal scattering of newly constructed *páilóu* running off east and west along Xi Dajie and Dong Dajie.

The Taoist **Mèngjiāngnǚ Temple** (孟姜女庙; Mèngjiāngnǚ Miào; admission ¥25; ⊙7am-7pm) is a large and handsome Song–Ming reconstruction 6km east of Shānhǎiguān. A round trip in a taxi is ¥50.

🛏 Sleeping & Eating

Most hotels close to the old town do not accept foreigners and it's best to do Shānhǎiguān as a day trip from Běijīng. The other alternative is to stay in nearby Qínhuángdǎo, where there are far more hotel and restaurant options. The **Qinfa Holiday Hotel** (秦发假日酒店; Qínfā Jiàrì Jiǔdiàn; 📞385 1428; www.qinfa.com.cn; 123 Yingbin Rd; 迎宾路123号; d/tw ¥438-518, discounts of 50%; ✳@) has reasonable, if dull, rooms and is handy for the train and bus stations and buses to Shānhǎiguān.

In the summer, *shāokǎo* and noodle stalls line the sides of the market opposite the south gate.

Shānhǎi Holiday Hotel
HOTEL $$

(山海假日酒店; Shānhǎi Jiàrì Jiǔdiàn; 📞535 2888; www.shanhai-holiday.com; Bei Madao; 北马道; d/tw ¥880-1280, discounts of 50%; ✳@) A traditional-style four-star hotel with attractive courtyard rooms, pleasant staff and a good location near the West Gate. It's a tourist vision of old China, but done in a tasteful way.

Friendly Cooperate Hotel
HOTEL $$

(谊合酒店; Yìhé Jiǔdiàn; 📞593 9777; 4-1 Nanhai Xilu; 南海西路4-1号; d/tw/tr ¥380/420/560, discounts of 40%; ✳@) This well-maintained two-star hotel is the only realistic option close to the old town. Clean rooms with broadband access. The attached restaurant has an outside area and is good for *shāokǎo* in the summer. It's next door to the post office.

ℹ Information

There are no internet cafes in or close to the old town. In Qínhuángdǎo, a few cluster near the bus and train stations.

Bank of China (中国银行; Zhōngguó Yínháng; Nanhai Xilu; ⊙8.30am-5.30pm) Foreign exchange facilitiy, but small amounts of US dollars only.

China Post (中国邮政; Zhōngguó Yóuzhèng; Nanhai Xilu; ⊙8.30am-6pm) Next door to the Friendly Cooperate Hotel.

Kodak Express (柯达; Kēdá; Nanhai Xilu) CD burning costs ¥15 per disc. Next to the Bank of China.

JIǓMÉNKǑU GREAT WALL

In a mountain valley 15km north of Shānhǎiguān stretches **Jiǔménkǒu Great Wall** (九门口长城; Jiǔménkǒu; admission ¥60), the only section of the Great Wall ever built over water. Normally the wall stopped at rivers, as they were considered natural defence barriers all on their own. At Jiǔménkǒu Great Wall, however, a 100m span supported by nine arches crosses the Jiǔjiāng River, which we can only guess flowed at a much faster and deeper rate than it does today (or else the arches would function more like open gates).

Much effort has gone into restoring this formidable-looking bridge and on both sides the wall continues its run up the steep, rocky hillsides. Heading left, you can quickly see where the wall remains unrestored on the opposite side. Sadly, access to this area is blocked but the distant sight of crumbling stone watchtowers truly drives home the terrible isolation that must have been felt by the guardians of frontier regions such as this.

No buses head to the wall from Shānhǎiguān but the taxis that gather beyond the South Gate will make the return trip for ¥100 to ¥120. Don't expect to have this place to yourself any more though. The crowds have found their way, as have the hawkers and the cheap amusement attractions, though they're not too hard to escape.

Public Security Bureau (PSB; 公安局; Gōng'ānjú; ☑505 1163) Opposite the entrance to First Pass Under Heaven, on the corner of a small alleyway.

Zhōngxing Pharmacy (中兴药店; Zhōngxing Yàodiàn; Nan Dajie; ◷7am-9pm) You'll find it just south of Dōngwǔtiáo Hútòng (东五条胡同).

ⓘ Getting There & Around

The fastest and most convenient train from Běijīng train station is the D 21 soft-seat express to Shěnyáng, which leaves Běijīng Train Station at 7am, arriving in Shānhǎiguān at 9.32am (¥93). The D 19 leaves at 10.02am and gets in at 12.38pm. Other slower trains also pass through Shānhǎiguān from Běijīng and Tiānjīn. Alternatively, trains from Běijīng stop in the larger city of Qínhuángdǎo (¥39 to ¥88, two to four hours), from where bus 33 (¥2, 30 minutes) connects with Shānhǎiguān. Buses from Běijīng's Bāwángfén station also run to Qínhuángdǎo (秦皇岛; ¥81, 3½ hours regularly from 7.30am to 6pm).

In the return direction, buses leave for Běijīng's Bāwángfén station (¥75, 3½ hours, regularly from 7.30am to 6pm) and Běijīng's Capital Airport (¥140, four hours, hourly 5am to 3pm) from Qínhuángdǎo. There are also direct buses from Qínhuángdǎo to Chéngdé (¥110, five hours), departing hourly from 7am to 11am, and at 5pm. From Chéngdé, you can take a bus from the east bus station for Qínhuángdǎo (¥112, five hours).

Cheap taxis are ¥5 flag fall and ¥1.40 per kilometre after that. Shānhǎiguān has a vast miscellany of motor tricycles, which cost ¥2 for trips within town.

Near Shānhǎiguān, Qínhuángdǎo's little airport has flights from Dàlián, Shànghǎi, Tàiyuán, Hā'ěrbīn and Chángchūn.

Jīmíngyì 鸡鸣驿

POP 1000

An ancient snapshot of China, the very sleepy hamlet of Jīmíngyì is a delightful surprise to find amidst the scruffy northern Héběi countryside. China's oldest surviving post station, the walled town of Jīmíngyì is a historic reminder of a system that endured for 2000 years and enabled the officials in the Forbidden City to keep in touch with their far-flung counterparts around China. Whipped by dust storms in the spring and with archaic, fading Mao-era slogans still visible on the walls, Jīmíngyì sees few visitors and feels a long, long way from the gleaming capital – much further than the 140km distance would suggest.

During the Ming and Qing dynasties, Jīmíngyì was a place of considerably more bustle and wealth, as evidenced in the numerous surviving temples and its town wall. Many of its courtyard houses remain too, albeit in dilapidated condition. Their residents are a friendly lot, even if their thick Mandarin accents are a struggle to comprehend, and will help find the gatekeepers to the various temples if they are locked.

There has been a flurry of activity in Jīmíngyì recently, with the town walls and gates newly restored, as the local government attempts to boosts its appeal as a tourist destination. There is now also an **admission fee** (¥40), although the ticket does provide access to all the principal sites. Jīmíngyì is likely to change more in the near future, so get here before it does finally move into the modern world.

BĚIDÀIHÉ

The breezy seaside resort of Běidàihé (北戴河) was first stumbled upon by English railway engineers in the 1890s. To this day it retains a kitsch atmosphere reminiscent of Brighton or Margate (without the fish and chips), even though these days it's flooded with vacationing Russians, as well as senior CCP officials on their hols.

During the May to October high season, Běidàihé comes alive with holiday-goers who crowd the beaches and feast on seafood. During the low season, however, the town is a freezing dead zone. Wandering the streets and seafront is enjoyable, or you can hire a bike to wheel around the beachfront roads. Otherwise, fork out for a rubber ring or inner tube from one of the street vendors and plunge into the sea (after elbowing through the crowds).

Běidàihé can be reached by direct bus or train from Běijīng, or by bus from Qínhuángdǎo. From Shānhǎiguān, the beach resort is a short journey away via Qínhuángdǎo: catch bus 33 (¥2, 30 minutes) to Qínhuángdǎo and then bus 34 to Běidàihé (¥2, 30 minutes) from in front of the train station on Yingbin Lu. Buses to Běijīng's Bāwángfén long-distance bus station (¥100, three hours) from Běidàihé leave from Haining Lu (海宁路) and Bao'er Lu (保二路) three times a day – at 8am, 1pm and 4pm.

History

For more than 2000 years, imperial China employed a vast network of postal routes for conveying official correspondence throughout the land. Post stations, where couriers would change horses or stay the night, were often fortified garrison towns that also housed travelling soldiers, merchants and officials. Marco Polo estimated there were some 10,000 post stations and 300,000 postal-service horses in 13th-century China. While Marco clearly recognised that a little embellishment makes for a good story, there is little doubt the system was well developed by the Yuan dynasty (AD 1206–1368). Jīmíngyì was established at this time under Kublai Khan as a stop on the Běijīng–Mongolia route. In the Ming dynasty, the town expanded in size as fortifying the frontiers with Chinese soldiers became increasingly important.

◉ Sights

The infamous Empress Dowager Cixi passed through here on her flight from Běijīng in 1900; you can see the room she slept in but it's decidedly unimpressive.

Confucius Temple   CONFUCIAN TEMPLE

(文昌宫; Wénchāng Gōng) Meandering along the baked-mud-wall warren of Jīmíngyì's courtyard houses takes you past scattered temples, including this simple Ming-dynasty temple which, like many Confucius temples, also doubled as a school.

Tàishān Temple   TEMPLE

(泰山行宫; Tàishān Xínggōng) Not far away is this larger temple, whose simply stunning Qing murals depicting popular myths (with the usual mix of Buddhist, Taoist and Confucian figures) were whitewashed – some say for protection – during the Cultural Revolution. A professor from Qīnghuá University helped to uncover them; you can still see streaks of white in places.

Other Temples   HISTORIC SITES

Other small temples that can be visited include the **Temple of the God of Wealth** (财神庙; Cáishén Miào) and the **Temple of the Dragon King** (龙王庙; Lóngwáng Miào). You will find the occasional *yǐngbì* (spirit wall) standing alone, its courtyard house demolished, and a few ancient stages. Adding to the time-capsule feel are the numerous slogans from the Cultural Revolution daubed on walls that seem to have been simply left to fade.

City Walls   HISTORIC SITE

Jīmíngyì's walls have been restored so you can promenade all around them. Ascend the **East Gate** (东门; Dōng Mén) for fine views of the town, surrounding fields and **Jīmíng Mountain** (鸡鸣山; Jīmíng Shān) to the north. Across town is the **West Gate**; the **Temple of the Town Gods** (城隍庙; Chénghuáng Miào), overgrown with weeds and in ruins, stands nearby. There are a few intriguing Qing caricatures of Yuan-dynasty crime fighters remaining on the chipped walls. The largest and oldest temple in the area is the **Temple of Eternal Tranquility** (永宁寺; Yǒngníng Sì), located 12km away on Jīmíng Mountain.

🛏 Sleeping & Eating

Most people visit Jīmíngyì as a day trip, but spending the night is a great way to experience rural life once others have returned to Běijīng's luxuries. Ask around and you'll soon find a local willing to host you for ¥25; a home-cooked meal will cost the same. There are a few restaurants outside the north wall; bear in mind they eat a lot of donkey in these parts.

ℹ Getting There & Away

Jīmíngyì can be reached by bus (¥3, 30 minutes, 8.30am to 5pm) from the town of Shāchéng (沙城). You'll be dropped off along the north wall. Direct buses (¥50, 11.50am and 2pm) to Shāchéng run from Běijīng's Liùlǐqiáo Station; otherwise, regular buses run past Shāchéng (¥60, three hours, hourly from 7.40am to 4pm). Ask to be dropped off at the Jīmíngyì turn-off, then scramble up to the overpass and head towards the toll gate. Jīmíngyì is a 2km walk away. From Shāchéng, buses return to Běijīng from 8.30am to 4pm, but it is much quicker to walk back to the expressway and flag down any Běijīng-bound bus.

Frequent trains run to Shāchéng from Běijīng West and Běijīng Train Station (hard seat ¥19, 2½ to three hours). You can also catch a train on to Dàtóng (hard seat ¥41, four hours, eight trains a day).

You'll need to take a taxi (¥6) or motor tricycle between Shāchéng's train and bus stations. You can store luggage at the bus station for a fee of ¥1.

Shāndōng

POP 96.8 MILLION

Includes »

Jǐ'nán	146
Around Jǐ'nán	149
Tài'ān	150
Tài Shān	153
Qūfù	156
Qīngdǎo	161
Láo Shān	170
Yāntái	171

Best Historical Sights

» Tài Shān (p153)

» Confucius Mansion (p158)

» Zhūjiāyù (p149)

» Pénglái Pavilion (p174)

Best Places for a Dip

» Shílǎorén Beach (p164)

» Nos 2 and 3 Bathing Beach, Qīngdǎo (p164)

» Wángfǔ Pool (p146)

» No 1 Beach, Yāntái (p173)

Why Go?

Steeped in myth and supernatural allure, the Shāndōng (山东) peninsula on China's northeastern coast is the stuff of legends. Its captivating landscape – a fertile flood plain fed by rivers and underground springs capped by granite peaks and framed in wild coastline – can't help but inspire wonder.

A lumpy-headed boy named Confucius was born here and grew up to develop a philosophy of virtue and ethics that would reach far beyond his lectures under an apricot tree. Three centuries later China's first emperor Qin Shi Huang would climb Tài Shān, Shandong's highest peak, to proclaim a unified empire in 219 BC.

But this place is more than its past. The gorgeous seaside city of Qīngdǎo ranks among the best places to live in Asia. This is the Shāndōng's real draw: you can climb mountains, explore the legacies of kingdoms of old, and still have time to hit the beach.

When to Go
Qīngdǎo

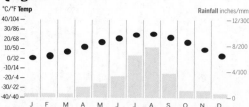

Jun–Jul Cool sea breezes and warm waters make summer the time to explore Qīngdǎo.

Sep–Oct Sacred Tài Shān is gloriously shrouded in mist for part (not all) of the day.

Dec–Jan Dress warmly and ascend Shāndōng's frosted peaks in winter.

History

Shāndōng's tumultuous history is tied to the capricious temperament of the Yellow River, which crosses the peninsula before emptying into the Bo Sea. The 'Mother River' nurtured civilisation but when unhinged left death, disease and rebellion in its wake. In 1898 the river flooded the entire Shāndōng plain, capping a decade of floods and droughts. The disaster also followed a long period of economic depression and unrest, and an influx of demobilised troops and refugees in 1895 after Japan defeated China in Korea.

The Europeans had also arrived. After two German missionaries died in a peasant uprising in western Shāndōng in 1897, Germany seized Qīngdǎo and Britain forced a lease of Wēihǎi. The Europeans' ensuing railroad projects and feverish missionary work emboldened a band of superstitious nationalists. In the closing years of the 19th century, the Boxers rose out of Shāndōng, armed with magical spells and broadswords to lead a rebellion against the eight-nation alliance. After the foreign powers violently seized Běijīng in 1900, the Empress Cixi effectively surrendered and Boxer and other resistance leaders were executed. The Qing dynasty would soon collapse.

Emerging from decades of war, Shāndōng recovered its cities following Japan's surrender in WWII.

Today Jǐ'nán, the provincial capital, and the prospering coastal cities of Yāntái and Wēihǎi, all play a supporting role to Qīngdǎo, the province's headliner.

Climate

Temperatures average 26°C in summer (May to August), down to -3°C in winter (November to March). Temperatures on the coast stay at least a few degrees cooler in the summer and warmer in the winter than in the interior.

Language

Standard Mandarin is the primary language spoken in Shāndōng, but regional varieties of northern Mandarin often pop up in casual conversation. The characteristic drawls of the three most common dialects, Jǐlǔ (冀鲁), Zhōngyuán (中原) and Jiāoliáo (胶辽), are

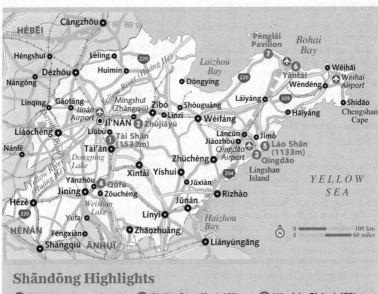

Shāndōng Highlights

❶ Climb the slopes of **Tài Shān** (p153), where stones speak the wisdom of millennia

❷ Be charmed by village life in venerable **Zhūjiāyù** (p149)

❸ Chill in **Qīngdǎo** (p161) with a pitcher of China's most famous beer

❹ Visit ancient **Qūfù** (p156), hometown of the sage Confucius

❺ Hike **Láo Shān** (p170), with its hidden springs

❻ Escape to the port city of **Yāntái** (p171)

❼ Discover the legends of immortals and pirates at **Pénglái Pavilion** (p174)

PRICE INDICATORS

The following price indicators are used in this chapter:

Sleeping

$	less than ¥200
$$	¥200 to ¥500
$$$	more than ¥500

Eating

$	less than ¥75
$$	¥75 to ¥200
$$$	more than ¥200

each distinctive but tend to condense syllables and merge Mandarin's standard four tones into three.

ⓘ Getting There & Around

Shāndōng is linked to neighbouring and distant provinces by both bus and rail. The provincial transportation hub is Ji'nán, with rail connections to all major towns and cities in Shāndōng. The express rail now links Ji'nán, Tàishān, Qūfù and Qīngdǎo to Běijīng and Shànghǎi. Buses also reach every corner of the province.

With South Korea and Japan just across the water, there are direct international flights through the Ji'nán, Qīngdǎo and Yāntái airports. Ferries also sail from Qīngdǎo to South Korea (Incheon and Gunsan) and Japan (Shimonoseki), and from Yāntái to Incheon.

Ji'nán 济南

☎0531 / POP 2.37 MILLION

Ji'nán is a busy capital city serving as a transit hub to other destinations around Shāndōng. On its surface, the city is in flux, but beneath the construction and sprawl are 72 artesian springs, which gently roil in azure pools and flow steadily into Dàmíng Lake (Dàmíng Hú).

The train stations are to the west. The heart of the city, encircled by the Húchéng River, is more tourist friendly with the major shopping zone on Quancheng Lu and Quancheng Sq.

◉ Sights

Parks PARKS

(公园; Gōngyuán) Strolling through the willows is a pleasant escape from Ji'nán's din. The most central include the sprawling **Bàotū Spring** (趵突泉; Bàotū Quán; Gongqingtuan Lu; admission ¥40); **Black Tiger Spring**

(黑虎泉; Hēihǔ Quán; Heihuquan Donglu; admission free) along the Húchéng River and **Five Dragon Pool** (五龙潭; Wǔlóngtán; Gongqingtuan Lu; admission ¥5), a serene study of local life, where residents paint calligraphy with water on the steps. In a quiet alleyway off Furong Jie (turn east at the police stand), the neighbourhood comes to soak in the spring-fed **Wángfǔ Pool** (王府池子, Wángfǔ Chi; admission free).

Thousand Buddha Mountain BUDDHIST MOUNTAIN

(千佛山; Qiānfó Shān; 18 Jingshi Yilu; admission ¥30; ⊙5am-9pm; 🚌K51) Beginning in the Sui dynasty (581–618), the pious carved Buddhas into this hillside southeast of the city centre. The oldest are at **Xīnguóchán Temple** (兴国禅寺; admission ¥5; ⊙7.30am-4.30pm), the golden-roofed complex near the **cable car** (one way/return ¥20/30) and **luge** (¥25/30) drop-off on the mountaintop. On the rare clear day looking south, you can spot Tài Shān, the anthill in the distance.

FREE **Ji'nán Museums** MUSEUMS

North of Thousand Buddha Mountain's main entrance, the **Ji'nán Museum** (济南博物馆; Ji'nán Bówùguǎn; ☎8295 9204; 3 Jing Shiyilu; audio tour ¥10; ⊙8.30am-4.30pm Tue-Sun) has a small but distinctive collection including paintings, calligraphy, ceramics, Buddhist figures from the Tang dynasty and a delightful boat carved from a walnut shell.

The enormous, new **Provincial Museum** (省博物馆; Shěng Bówùguǎn; 11899 Jingshi Donglu; audio tour ¥30; ⊙9am-4pm Tue-Sun; 🚌115, 51) – a 7km slog east of the city centre – surveys Shāndōng's culture from the Mesolithic age to the present. On display are oracle bone fragments, Qi and Lu kingdom pottery, Han tomb murals and clothing worn by the Kong clan (Confucius's descendants).

FREE **Great Southern Mosque** MOSQUE

(清真南大寺; Qīngzhēn Nán Dà Sì; 47 Yongchang Jie) Ji'nán's oldest mosque has stood in the centre of town since 1295. Cover arms and remove hats before entering. A lively Hui (Muslim Chinese) neighbourhood is to the north.

🛏 Sleeping

Budget hotels are clustered around the main train station, though not all cater to foreigners. Look first.

Silver Plaza Quancheng Hotel HOTEL $$

(银座泉城大酒店; Yínzuò Quánchéng Dàjiǔdiàn; ☎8629 1911; 2 Nanmen Jie; incl breakfast d/tr

Jǐ'nán

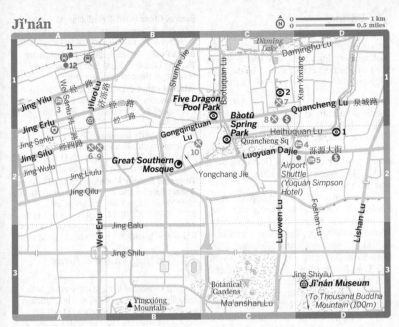

Jǐ'nán

◎ Top Sights

Bàotū Spring Park C2
Five Dragon Pool Park............................ C1
Great Southern Mosque B2
Jǐ'nán Museum D3

◎ Sights

1 Black Tiger Spring Park D2
2 Wángfǔ Pool C1

🛏 Sleeping

3 Shāndōng Hotel A1
4 Silver Plaza Quancheng Hotel.............. D2
5 Sofitel Silver Plaza D2

✖ Eating

6 Dàguān Gardens......................................A2
7 Fúróng Jiē... C1
Fúshúnjūjiācháng Restaurant........ (see 7)
Lǔxǐ'nán Flavor Restaurant............ (see 6)
8 Seasons Mínghú C1
9 Wěi Èrlù...A2
10 Yǐnhǔchí Jiē..B2

ℹ Transport

11 Jǐ'nán Railway Hotel A1
12 Shèngxiángyuán Plane/Train
   Ticket Office A1

¥478/680; ⊖ ❄ @) You know this is a Chinese-business hotel from the blinding Euro-style bling in the lobby. Professional staff and a good location overlooking Quancheng Sq makes up for that and the compact rooms with stained tile ceilings. Shell out for an upgrade in the renovated B-wing.

Shāndōng Hotel   HOTEL $

(山东宾馆; Shāndōng Bīnguǎn; ☑ 8606 7000; 92 Jing Yilu; d/tr ¥179/209; ❄ @) On the corner of Jing Yīlù and Wei Sanlu across from the train station, this old-timer hosted Mao and other dignitaries in its heyday, but today is used to dealing with budget travellers.

Sofitel Silver Plaza   HOTEL $$$

(索菲特银座大饭店; Suǒfēitè Yínzuò Dàfàndiàn; ☑ 8981 1611; 66 Luoyuan Dajie; r from ¥1101, plus 10% service charge; ⊖ ❄ @ ≋) The city's first five-star is in the commercial district and still the best option, though we wish standard rooms were as spacious as the lobby promises. Discounts up to 50% often available.

✖ Eating

Jǐ'nán is a famed centre of Lǔ cuisine, characterised by bold flavours brought out by cooking over high heat with plenty of oil. Most of the best eating is had in the city's alleyways.

Food Streets
STREET FOOD $

Evenings are smoky on **Yǐnhǔchí Jie** (饮虎池街) in the Hui district near the Great Southern Mosque. Hawkers fan the flames of charcoal grills lining the street, roasting up all manner of *shāokǎo* (barbecue on a stick). They make crisp, scallion pancakes and fresh noodles too.

Off Quancheng Lu's shopping strip, **Fúróng Jie** (芙蓉街) is a pedestrian alley crammed with restaurants and food stalls. **Fúshúnjūjiācháng Restaurant** (福顺居家常饭馆; Fúshùnjūjiācháng Fànguǎn; ✎188 0640 9638; 112 Furong Jie; most dishes ¥8–28; ⊙9.30am-10.30pm) has Lǔ cuisine's greatest hits pictured on its menu.

About 1km south of the main train station, **Dàguān Gardens** (大观园; Dàguān Yuán; Jing Silu) is a dandified enclave of modern eateries. The alley next to it, **Wěi Èrlu** (纬二路) is a messy strip of noodle, *shāokǎo* and lamb soup carts that buzzes until late. Beers are ¥4!

Lǔxī'nán Flavor Restaurant
SHANDONG $

(鲁西南老牌坊; Lǔxī'nán Lǎopáifang; ✎8605 4567; 2 Daguan Yuan; dishes ¥28-98; ⊙11am-2.30pm & 5-10pm) Just inside Dàguān Gardens' north gate, this is the place for a refined take on Lǔ cuisine. Order the down-home classics like sweet and spicy cabbage with glass noodles (¥18) and lamb (braised or sautéed, from ¥38), accompanied with sesame cakes (¥2) – not rice. Chinese menu with pictures.

Seasons Mínghú
CANTONESE $$$

(四季明湖; Sìjì Mínghú; ✎6666 9898; 188 Quancheng Lu, Parc66, 7th fl; ⊙11am-10pm; ◍) The dandy waiters at this elegant restaurant on the top of the Parc66 (恒隆广场) don gloves when serving southern Chinese classics such as steamed lily and pumpkin (¥32), salt-baked chicken (¥48) and black bean spareribs (¥58). Steamed fish can be pricey – up to ¥998 per *jīn*!

ℹ Information

ATMs (自动取款机; Zìdòng Qǔkuǎn Jī) Available in the lobbies of the Sofitel and Crowne Plaza hotels. There are plenty of full-service banks in town.

Bank of China (中国银行; Zhōngguó Yínháng; 22 Luoyuan Dajie; ⊙9am-5pm Mon-Fri) Currency exchange/24-hour ATMs accepting foreign cards.

China Post (中国邮政; Zhōngguó Yóuzhèng; 162 Jing Erlu; ⊙8.30am-6pm) A red-brick building on the corner of Wei Erlu.

Internet cafes Often restricted to Chinese nationals, but if open to foreigners will require a passport. Look around the train station (¥2 to ¥5 per hour).

Public Security Bureau (PSB; 公安局; Gōng'ānjú; ✎8508 1088 ext 2, visa inquiries ext 2459; 145 Jing Sanlu; ⊙8-11.40am & 2-4.40pm Mon-Fri) On the corner of Wei Wulu.

Thousand Buddha Mountain Hospital International Clinic (千佛山医院国际医疗中心; Qiānfó Shān Yīyuàn Guójì Yīliáo Zhōngxīn; ✎8926 8018, 8926 8017; 16766 Jinshi Lu; ⊙8-11am & 2-5pm) English and Japanese spoken. Take bus K51 or K68 to *nǎnkóu* (南口) stop on Lishan Lu.

ℹ Getting There & Away

Air

Jǐ'nán is connected to most major cities, with daily flights to Běijīng (¥760, one hour), Dàlián (¥1050, two hours), Guǎngzhōu (¥1790, 2½ hours), Hā'ěrbīn (¥1330, two hours), Shànghǎi (¥960, 80 minutes), Xī'ān (¥1080, 1½ hours) and Yāntái (¥790, 50 minutes).

Lines at the station's ticket office can be slow. Book tickets at **Shèngxiángyuán plane/train ticket office** (盛祥源航空铁路售票处; Shèngxiángyuán hángkōng tiělù shòupiàochù; ✎8610 9666; 115 Chezhan Jie, 1st fl, Quánchéng Bīnguǎn; ⊙plane 7.30am-10pm, train 8am-8pm) immediately south of the train station, or in the lobby of the **Jǐ'nán Railway Hotel** (济南铁道大酒店; Jǐ'nán Tiědào Dàjiǔdiàn; 19 Chezhan Jie; ⊙8am-midnight), immediately east of the train station. Both take ¥5 commission.

Bus

Jǐ'nán's most convenient station is the **main long-distance bus station** (长途总汽车站; chángtú zóngqìchēzhàn; ✎8594 1472; 131 Jiluo Lu;) about 3km north of the train station, though buses to destinations within the province also leave from the **bus station** (✎8830 3030; 22 Chezhan Jie) directly across from the train station.

Some buses departing regularly from the main long-distance bus station:

Běijīng ¥124, 5½ hours, hourly

Qīngdǎo ¥113, 4½ hours, every 40 minutes

Qūfù ¥44, two hours, every 50 minutes

Shànghǎi ¥266, 12 hours, four daily (9am, 3pm, 5pm and 6pm)

Tài'ān ¥25, two hours, every 30 minutes

Tiānjīn ¥120, 4½ hours, hourly

Yāntái ¥120, 5½ hours, hourly

Train

Jǐ'nán is a major hub in the east China rail system and has several busy train stations. Most travellers can rely on the **Main Train Station** (火车总站; Huǒchē Zǒngzhàn) and the **West Train Station** (火车西站; Huǒchē Xī Zhàn), about 20km west of the city centre. Bus K156 (¥2) connects these two stations.

Some regular trains (seat/hard sleeper) departing from the Main Train Station:

Qīngdǎo ¥65/109, 4½ to five hours, nine daily

Qūfù ¥17/71, 2½ hours, three daily (5.13am, 8.11am and 4pm)

Tài Shān ¥12/103, one hour, frequently

Xī'ān ¥150/274, 15 to 18 hours, four daily (3.45pm, 4.32pm, 6.56pm and 10.41pm)

Yāntái ¥76/143, 6½ to eight hours, five daily (1.27am, 6.45am, 7.20am, 11.12am and 2.53pm)

Zhèngzhōu ¥92/170, 8½ to 10 hours, regularly

Some express D trains (hard/soft seat only) departing from the West Train Station (G trains also available):

Běijīng ¥125/150, two to three hours, eight daily

Nánjīng ¥190/228, 4½ hours, seven daily

Qīngdǎo ¥121/146, 2½ hours, regularly

Qūfù ¥40/48, 40 minutes, regularly

Shànghǎi ¥281/338, five to 6½ hours, six daily

ⓘ Getting Around

To/From the Airport

Jǐ'nán's Yáoqiáng **airport** (☑8208 6666) is 40km from the city. Airport shuttles (¥20) run from the **Yùquán Simpson Hotel** (玉泉森信大酒店; Yùquán Sēnxìn Dàjiǔdiàn; ☑96888; Luoyuan Dajie) and from the main train station hourly from 6am to 7pm. A taxi costs about ¥100.

Public Transport

Bus 84 (¥1) connects the main long-distance bus station with the main train station. Bus K51 (¥2) runs from the main train station through the city centre and then south past Bàotū Spring Park to Thousand Buddha Mountain.

Taxi

Taxis cost ¥7.50 for the first 3km then ¥1.75 (slightly more at night) per kilometre thereafter.

Water Taxi

Open-air, motorised **boats** (☑8690 5886; per stop ¥10; ☺every 20 min, 8am-8pm) circle clockwise around the scenic Húchéng River and the south side of Dàmíng Lake, making 10 stops at attractions including Bàotū Spring Park, Black Tiger Spring, Five Dragon Pool Park and Quancheng Sq. It takes about 1½ hours for the full circuit.

Around Jǐ'nán

ZHŪJIĀYÙ 朱家峪
☑0531

Eighty kilometres east of Jǐ'nán, **Zhūjiāyù** (admission ¥15) is one of Shāndōng's oldest intact hamlets, dating back as far as the Xia dynasty (2070–1600 BC). Most of Zhūjiāyù's buildings are from the more recent Ming and Qing dynasties, and many have been spruced up to serve as Chinese movie and soap opera sets, but strolling the narrow streets is still a journey back in time. Wander on your own or hire one of the elderly residents playing tour guide (¥10 to ¥20, Chinese-speaking only) inside the city walls.

Flanked by bucolic panoramas of rolling hills, Zhūjiāyù can be explored in half a day. Pay at the main gate in the restored wall on the village's northern end and then walk along the Ming-dynasty, **double-track ancient road** (双轨古道; *shuānggǔi gǔdào*) to the Qing-dynasty **Wénchāng Pavilion** (文昌阁; Wénchāng Gé), an arched gate topped by a single-roofed shrine where teachers would take new pupils to make offerings to Confucius before their first lesson. On your left is **Shānyīn Primary School** (山阴小学; Shānyīn Xiǎoxué), a series of halls and courtyards with exhibits on local life. Further along the road looms a wall with two fading portraits of Chairman Mao dating from 1966.

Wander to see the many ancestral temples, including the **Zhu Family Ancestral Hall** (朱氏家祠; Zhūshì Jiācí), packed mud-brick homesteads (many are deserted and collapsing), and delightful, arched *shíqiáo* (stone bridges). The **Lìjiāo Bridge** (立交桥; Lìjiāo Qiáo) is an early form of traffic overpass dating from 1671. A further 30-minute climb past the last drystone walls of the village will take you to the gleaming white **Kuíxīng Pavilion** (魁星楼; Kuíxīng Lóu; admission ¥2) crowning the hill.

If you want to spend the night, look for flags posting 农家乐 (*nóngjiālè*; a guesthouse or homestay). The basic **Gǔcūn Inn** (古村酒家; Gǔcūn Jiǔjiā; ☑8380 8135; d with bath ¥100) is a lovely old courtyard home with a spirit wall decorated with a peacock, 80m past the Lìjiāo Bridge. The owners will also cook up dinner (dishes from ¥12). At **Lǎo Jiā Restaurant** (老家菜馆), next to the Mao portraits, the genial owners take their sleepy yellow dog hunting for wild rabbit and forage for fresh mushrooms and greens in the hills (¥35 per *jīn* for rabbit and vegie dishes from ¥10).

To reach Zhūjiāyù from Jǐnán, catch the Zhāngqiū bus (章丘; ¥21, 1½ hours, from 7am to 6.30pm) from the bus station directly across from the train station; ask for the village drop off. From there, it's a further 2km walk (locals offer lifts for ¥10). Returning to Jǐnán, flag down a bus across from the massive gate on the main road. Buses are rare after 6pm.

Tài'ān 泰安

☑ 0538 / POP 1.05 MILLION

Gateway to Tài Shān's sacred slopes, Tài'ān's tourist industry has been in full swing since before the Ming dynasty. In the 17th-century, historian Zhang Dai described package tours that included choice of lodging (enormous inns with more than 20 kitchens and hundreds of servants, opera performers and courtesans) and post-summit congratulatory banquet, plus an optional sedan chair upgrade. (Special mountain-climbing tax of eight fén silver not included in the advertised price.)

Today's tourist scene in Tài'ān is much more subdued in comparison. Though there's not much to see outside of the magnificent Dài Temple, you will need the better part of a day for the mountain, so spending the night here or at the summit is advised.

◉ Sights

Dài Temple TEMPLE

(岱庙; Dài Miào; Daimiao Beijie Lu; adult/child ¥30/15; ◉8am-6pm summer, to 5pm winter) This magnificent Taoist temple complex is the place in town where all the roads lead, being the traditional first stop on every pilgrimage route up the mountain. It is dedicated to the Lord of Tài Shān, whose responsibilities include deciding the length of every person's life. The grounds are an impressive example of Song-dynasty (960–1127) temple construction with features of an imperial palace, though other structures stood here a millennium before that.

Most visitors enter from the north through the **Hòu Zài gate** (候载门) at the end of Hongmen Lu. Entering from the south through the **Zhèngyáng gate** (正阳门) allows you to follow the traditional passage through the temple and up Hongmen Lu to **Red Gate Palace**, and the start of the Tài Shān ascent.

From the south end, two lions flank a memorial gate and watch cars pass by on Dongyue Dajie. Beyond is the **Yáocān Pavilion** (遥参亭; Yáocān Tíng; ◉6.30am-6pm) containing a hall dedicated to the grandmother of Tài Shān (Taishan Laomu), Bixia, and Songzi Niangniang, a deity to whom

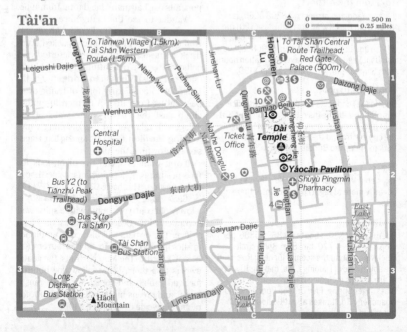

Tài'ān

couples wanting children dutifully pay their respects. The splendid **Dàimiào Fāng**, a *páifāng* (ornamental arch) decorated with four pairs of weathered lions and dragon and phoenix motifs, towers just before the Zhèngyáng gate.

Inside the complex, the courtyards are filled with prized examples of poetry and imperial records. Fossilised-looking *bìxì* (the mythical tortoise son of the dragon), dating from the 12th century onward, carry stelae (stone slabs or columns decorated with figures or inscriptions) on their backs documenting everything from the civil exam process to emperors' birthdays. Across the way, the Han Emperor Wudi is said to have planted some of the massive, twisting trees in the **Han Cypress Tree Pavilion** 2100 years ago. The main hall is the colossal, twin-eaved, nine-bay-wide **Hall of Heavenly Blessing** (天贶殿; Tiānkuàng Diàn; shoe covers ¥1), which dates to AD 1009. The dark interior houses a marvellous 62m-long Song-dynasty fresco depicting Emperor Zhenzong as the god of Tài Shān. Take time to scale the walls over the Hòu Zài gate to see what's in store for your pilgrimage up the mountain.

🛏 Sleeping

There are many midrange options in town, mostly clustered around the train station. Ask for discounts. The **Tài'ān Tourist Information Centre** in front of the train station can help you book a room.

Tài'ān

◎ **Top Sights**
Dài Temple...C2
Yáocān Pavilion C2

◎ **Sights**
1 Hòu Zài Gate..C1
2 Zhèngyáng Gate..................................C2

🛏 **Sleeping**
3 Roman Holiday.....................................C1
4 Tàishān International Youth
   Hostel...C2
5 Yùzuò Hotel C1

🍴 **Eating**
6 Ǎ Dōng de Shuǐjiǎo.............................C1
7 Běixīn Snack Street............................C1
8 Dài Běi Market....................................D1
9 Night Market..C2
10 Shèngtáoyuán Coffee & Tea.............C1

Tàishān International Youth Hostel
HOSTEL **$**

(太山国际青年旅舍; Tàishān Guójì Qīngnián Lǚshè; ☑ 628 5196; 65 Tongtian Jie; dm ¥40-60, d/tw/tr ¥228/160/180; ❄@ 🛜) Tài'ān's first youth hostel has clean spartan rooms with pine furnishings and old propaganda posters. Bike rental, free laundry and a bar on the 3rd floor make this a pleasant experience. Dorms are a bargain. Look for the pair of arches just off Tongtian Jie.

Yùzuò Hotel
HOTEL **$$$**

(御座宾馆; Yùzuò Bīnguǎn; ☑ 826 9999; 50 Daimiao Beilu; tw/d/ste ¥360/780/1680; ❄@) This pretty hotel next to the Dài Temple's north gate was purposely kept to two storeys out of respect for its neighbour. Deluxe rooms are decked out imperial style; cheaper rooms are rather ordinary. The attached bakery and restaurants serve Taoist food (12-course set menu ¥168 per person). Discounts of 20%.

Roman Holiday
HOTEL **$$**

(罗马假日商务酒店; Luómǎ Jiàrì Shāngwù Jiǔdiàn; ☑ 627 9999; 18 Hongmen Lu; incl breakfast s/d ¥298/358; ❄@) This oddly named hotel's location along the sacred route to Tài Shān can't be beat. Discounts get singles down to ¥168. Small, neat rooms with see-through showers and worn carpeting, but no Audrey Hepburn.

Ramada Plaza Tai'an
HOTEL **$$$**

(东尊华美达大酒店; Dōngzūn Huáměidá Dàjiǔdiàn; 16 Ying Sheng Donglu; 迎胜东路; s/d ¥1160-1400, ste ¥1960-3360; ⊕❄🛜🏊) The town's only five-star is on the northwest side of town and has all the usual comforts plus fantastic views of the main attraction.

🍴 Eating

There are three busy food streets. The **night market** (yè shì; ⏰5.30pm-late) on the Nai River's east bank has many hotpot stalls. Pick your ingredients (thinly sliced meats, fish balls, vegetables, tofu etc) and take a seat at a low table. Meals cost about ¥25, and a large jug of beer is ¥6. Vendors on **Běixīn Snack Street** (北新小吃步行街; Běixīn Xiǎochī Bùxíng Jiē) set up carts for lunch (except Saturday) and dinner. Look for *mántóu* (馒头, steamed buns), various meats on skewers, fried chicken and more. Hawkers serve similar delights by the temple at **Dài Běi Market** (贷北市场; Dàibei Shìchǎng) but expect tourist prices.

Ā Dōng de Shuǐjiǎo
CHINESE $

(阿东的水饺; 31 Hongmen Lu; meals from ¥12; 9am-10pm; 🚇) This centrally located restaurant serves up northern Chinese staples including *shuǐjiǎo* (水饺; dumplings). There are a wide range of fillings including lamb (¥24 per *jīn* – enough for two) and vegetable (¥18 per *jīn*). The English menu is incomprehensible so be prepared to point.

Shèngtáoyuán Coffee & Tea
INTERNATIONAL $$

(圣淘缘休闲餐厅; Shèngtáoyuán Xiūxián Cāntīng'; 33 Hongmen Lu; dishes ¥25-150; ⊗8.30am-midnight; 🚇🛜) The ivory baby grand piano beside the toilet may be overkill but the comfy couches and 41-page menu (with photos) are lovely. Decent pizzas (from ¥25), salads (from ¥12) and spaghetti (¥25).

Dōngzūn Court
CHINESE $$

(东尊阁, Dōng Zūngé; ☎836 8222; 16 Yingsheng Donglu; ⊗11.30am-2.30pm & 5.30-8.30pm; mains from ¥48; 🚇) This tablecloth affair at the Ramada Plaza has an entire room dedicated to live seafood (priced by the *jīn*) and freshly made spring-water bean curd (¥38).

ⓘ Information

Agricultural Bank of China (22 Daizong Jie; ⊗8.30am-4pm Mon-Fri) Currency exchange and 24-hour ATM accepts foreign cards.

Bank of China (中国银行; Zhōngguó Yínháng; 116 Tongtian Jie; ⊗8.30am-4.30pm) Currency exchange 24-hour ATM accepts foreign cards.

Central Hospital (中心医院; Zhōngxīn Yīyuàn; ☎822 4161; 29 Longtan Lu) Limited English.

China Post (中国邮政; Zhōngguó Yóuzhèng; 232 Daizong Dajie; ⊗8.30am-5.30pm)

Public Security Bureau (PSB; 公安局; Gōng'ānjú; ☎827 5264; cnr Dongyue Dajie & Qingnian Lu). The **visa office** (出入境管理处; ⊗8.30am-noon & 1-5pm Mon-Fri, or by appointment) is on the east side of the shiny grey building.

Shùyù Píngmín Pharmacy (漱玉平民大药房; Shùyù Píngmín Dàyàofáng; 38 Shengping Jie; ⊗7.30am-9pm)

Tài'ān tourist information centre (泰安市旅游咨询中心; Tài'ānshì Lǚyóu Zīxún Zhōngxīn; ☎info hotline 12301) Hongmen Lu (☎bookings 218 7989; 22 Hongmen Lu; ⊗8am-6pm); Train station (☎bookings 688 7358; ⊗8.30am-7.30pm) Can book hotels, train tickets (¥20 fee per ticket), and air tickets. Limited English. Internet cafes are often restricted to Chinese customers and always require a passport.

Wànjīng Internet Cafe (万景网吧; Wànjīng Wǎngbā; 180 Daizong Dajie; per hr ¥2; ⊗7am-midnight)

World Net Bar Internet (大世界网吧; Dàshìjiè Wǎngbā; 2nd fl, 6-1 Hongmen Lu; per hr ¥2; ⊗24hr) Nonsmoking room available.

ⓘ Getting There & Away

Most travel routes pass through Jǐ'nán, 80km north. Keep in mind that bus and train agents sometimes refer to Tài'ān and Tài Shān interchangeably.

Buy tickets west of the temple at **train and plane ticket bookings** (火车票代售处, 空售票处; ☎train 611 1111, plane 218 3333; 111 Qingnian Lu; ⊗8.30am-5.30pm). Tickets sell out quickly so book early.

Bus

The **long-distance bus station** (长途汽车站; chángtú qìchēzhàn; ☎218 8777; cnr Tài'shān Dalu & Longtan Lu), also known as the old station (lǎo zhàn), is just south of the train station. Buses regularly depart for these destinations:

Běijīng ¥140, six hours, one daily (2.30pm)

Jǐ'nán ¥25, 1½ hours, every 30 minutes (6.30am to 6pm)

Qīngdǎo ¥126, 5½ hours, four daily (6am, 8am, 2.30pm and 3.30pm)

Qūfù ¥21, one hour, hourly

Shànghǎi ¥205, 12 hours, two daily (3.20pm and 4.30pm)

Wēihǎi ¥165, seven hours, one daily (7.20am)

Train

Two train stations service this region. **Tài Shān Train Station** (泰山火车站; ☎688 7358; cnr Dongyue Dajie & Longtan Lu) is the most central, but express trains only pass through **Tài'ān Train Station** (泰安火车站; ☎138 0538 5950; Xingaotiezhan Lu), sometimes referred to as the new station (xīn zhàn), about 9km west of the town centre.

Some regular trains (prices for seat/hard sleeper) departing from Tài Shān Train Station:

Běijīng ¥79/149, seven to 9½ hours, five daily

Jǐ'nán ¥8 to ¥14/¥67 to ¥109, one hour, regularly

Nánjīng ¥82/155, seven to 8½ hours, regularly

Qīngdǎo ¥70/131, five to seven hours, regularly

Shànghǎi ¥102 to ¥120/¥201 to ¥222, 8½ to 13 hours, regularly

Some express D trains (prices for hard/soft seat only) departing from Tài'ān Train Station (G trains also available):

Běijīng ¥143/172, two to three hours, four daily

Nánjīng ¥172 to ¥254/¥207 to ¥432, three to four hours, six daily

Qīngdǎo (G train only) ¥207/353, three hours, one daily (5.55pm)

Shànghǎi ¥263/316, five to six hours, five daily

❶ Getting Around

Buses connect the Tài Shān Train Station with access points to the mountain. Bus 3 (三路汽车; ¥2) reaches both the central route trailhead and the western route trailhead at Tiānwài Village (Tiānwài Cūn). Bus Y2 (游二路汽车(往天烛峰景区)) runs to the Tiānzhú Peak trailhead. Bus 16 reaches Peach Blossom Park. Bus 4 reaches Dài Temple.

Taxis cost ¥6 for the first 3km and ¥1.50 (slightly more at night) per kilometre thereafter.

Tài Shān 泰山

☎ 0538

Sacred mountains are a dime a dozen in China, but in the end the one that matters most is **Tài Shān** (admission Feb-Nov ¥127, Dec-Jan ¥102). Its fellow Unesco World Heritage sites Éméi Shān may be higher and Huángshān more photogenic, but Tài Shān has been worshipped since at least the 11th century BC.

Qin Shi Huang, the First Emperor, chose its summit to proclaim the unified kingdom of China in 219 BC. Seventy-one other emperors and countless figures including Du Fu and Mao Zedong also left their marks on the mountain. Their poetry and prose are inscribed into tablets, boulders, caves and cliffs all over the slopes. Pilgrims still make their way up the steps as a symbol of their devotion to Taoist and Buddhist teachings.

Autumn, when humidity is low, is the best time to visit; early October onwards has the clearest weather. In winter temperatures dip below freezing and most summit hotels have no hot water. Tourist season peaks from May to October, with climbers converging for the **International Climbing Festival** (www.mt taishan.com) every September. Avoid major holidays.

◉ Sights & Activities

There are three routes up the mountain to its highest peak, 1532m above sea level, that can be followed on foot: the **central route** (御道; *yù dào*), historically the Emperor's Route winding 7.5km from base to summit, gaining 1400m of elevation; the **western route**, which follows the bus route; and the less travelled **Tiānzhú Peak** trail up the back of the mountain. The central and western routes converge at the halfway point (Midway Gate to Heaven), from where it's another 3.5km up steep steps to the summit.

SHĀNDŌNG TÀI SHĀN

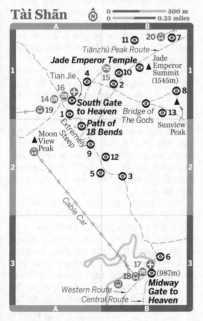

Tài Shān

◉ Top Sights

Jade Emperor Temple	B1
Midway Gate to Heaven	B3
Path of 18 Bends	A2
South Gate to Heaven	A1

◉ Sights

1	Archway to Immortality	A1
2	Azure Clouds Temple	B1
3	Cloud Step Bridge	B2
4	Confucius Temple	A1
5	Five Great Pines	A2
6	God of Wealth Temple	B3
7	North Gate to Heaven	B1
8	North Pointing Rock	B1
9	Opposing Pines Pavilion	A2
10	Qīngdi Palace	B1
11	Rear Rocky Recess	B1
12	Ten-Thousand Zhang Tablet	B2
13	Zhānlǔ Terrace	B1

⌂ Sleeping

14	Nán Tiān Mén Bīnguǎn	A1
15	Shénqì Hotel	B1
16	Xiānjū Bīnguǎn	A1
17	Yùyèquán Hotel	B3

❶ Transport

18	Cable Car to Moon View Peak	B3
19	Cable Car to Peach Blossom Park	A1
20	Cable Car to Rear Rocky Recess	B1

If this sounds like too much for your knees, take a minibus to Midway Gate to Heaven and then a cable car to South Gate to Heaven near the summit, and then a bus back down.

Keep in mind that sights at the summit close around 5.15pm. Weather can change suddenly and the summit can be very cold, windy and wet, so bring warm layers and rain gear. You can buy rain ponchos and at the top, rent overcoats (¥20).

As with all Chinese mountain hikes, viewing the sunrise is considered an integral part of the experience. Stay overnight at one of the summit guesthouses to greet the first rays of dawn.

CENTRAL ROUTE 中路

This has been the main route up the mountain since the 3rd century BC, and over the past two millennia a bewildering number of bridges, trees, rivers, gullies, inscriptions, caves, pavilions and temples have become famous sites in their own right. Although the central route is well paved, don't underestimate the challenge of its 7000 steps. Figure on at least four hours to get to the top.

Tài Shān functions as an outdoor museum of calligraphic art. Prize works include the **Rock Valley Scripture** (经石峪; Jīngshí Yù), in the first part of the climb, a massive inscription of a Buddhist text that was once hidden behind a waterfall, and **North Prayer Rock** (拱北石; Gǒngběi Shí) commemorating an imperial sacrifice to heaven at the summit.

Purists can begin with a south–north perambulation through Dài Temple in Tài'ān, 1.7km south of the trailhead, in accordance with imperial tradition, but there is no shame in starting at the bus stop by **Guandi Temple** (关帝庙; Guāndì Miào; admission ¥10), the first of many dedicated to the Taoist protector of peace. Passing **First Gate of Heaven** (一天门; Yītiān Mén) marks the start of the actual ascent, though the **ticket office** (售票处; Shòupiào Chù; ☑806 6077; ⊙24hr) is still a way further. The **Red Gate Palace** (红门宫; Hóng Mén Gōng; admission ¥5; ⊙8am-5pm) is the first of a series of temples dedicated to Bixia, the compassionate daughter of the god of Tài Shān. She wears a headdress adorned with phoenixes and is accompanied by nine attendants including the Goddesses of Children and of Eyesight.

Take a detour into the **Geoheritage Scenic Area** (地质园区; Dìzhì Yuánqū) for a look at unusual radial rock formations that mesmerised Confucius himself. Back on the main path is the Buddhist **Dǒumǔ Hall** (斗母宫; Dǒumǔ Gōng), first constructed in 1542 under the more magical name 'Dragon Spring Nunnery'. The back of the temple yard offers a quiet view of a triple waterfall, best seen in July and August. Prayers are written on the ribbons festooning the pines. Continue through the tunnel of cypresses known as **Cypress Cave** (柏洞; Bódòng) to **Balking Horse Ridge** (回马岭; Huímǎ Lǐng), which marks the point where Emperor Zhenzong had to dismount and continue by litter because his horse refused to go further.

The **Midway Gate to Heaven** (中天门; Zhōng Tiān Mén) marks the point where some travellers, seeing the stairway disappearing into the clouds, turn heel for the cable car. Don't give up! Rest your legs, visit the small and smoky **God of Wealth Temple** (财神庙; Cáishén Miào), and stock up on snacks. (If you need them, 24-hour **first aid stations** are at both the Midway and South Gate.)

If you decide to catch a ride, the **main cable car** (空中索道; kōngzhōng suǒdào; one way/return ¥80/140; ⊙7.30am-6.30pm 16 Apr-15 Oct, 8.30am-5pm 16 Oct-15 Apr) is near the Midway Gate to Heaven. The 15-minute ride is to Moon View Peak (Yuèguān Fēng), near the South Gate to Heaven. Be warned: peak season and weekend queues can take two hours. Also, the cable car stops when there is any risk of lightning.

If you continue on foot you'll come next to **Cloud Step Bridge** (云步桥; Yúnbù Qiáo), once a modest wooden bridge spanning a torrent of waterfalls, and the withered and wiry **Wǔdàfū Pine** (五大夫松; Wǔdàfū Sōng), under which Emperor Qin Shi Huang, overtaken by a violent storm, sought shelter. Across the valley each character carved in the **Ten-Thousand Zhàng Tablet** (万丈碑), dated 1748, measures 1m across.

You'll pass **Opposing Pines Pavilion** (对松亭; Duìsōng Tíng) and then finally reach the arduous **Path of 18 Bends** (十八盘; Shíbāpán), a 400m near-vertical ascent to the mountain's false summit; climbing it is performed in slow motion as legs turn to lead. If you have the energy, see if you can spot the small shrine dedicated to the Lord of Tài Shān's grandmother along the way. There is an alternate route to the Azure Clouds Temple here via a steep, narrow staircase to the right. If you continue on the main route, at the top is the **Archway to Immortality** (升仙坊; Shēngxiān Fāng), once believed to bestow immortality on those dedicated enough to reach it. From here to the summit, emperors were carried on huge litters.

The final stretch takes you to the **South Gate to Heaven** (南天门; Nán Tián Mén), the third celestial gate, which marks the beginning of the summit area. Bear right along Tian Jie, the main strip, and pass through the gate to reach the sublimely perched **Azure Clouds Temple** (碧霞祠; Bìxiá Cí; admission ¥5; ☉morning-5.15pm). The iron tiling of the temple buildings is intended to prevent damage by strong winds, and *chīwěn* (ornaments meant to protect against fire) decorate their bronze eaves.

You have to climb higher to get to the **Confucius Temple** (孔庙; Kǒng Miào), where statues of Confucius (Kongzi), Mencius (Mengzi), Zengzi and other Confucian luminaries are venerated. The Taoist **Qīngdì Palace** (青帝宫; Qīngdì Gōng) is right before the fog- and cloud-swathed **Jade Emperor Temple** (玉皇顶; Yùhuáng Dǐng), which stands at the summit, the highest point of the Tài Shān plateau. Inside is an effigy of the Jade Emperor, who governs all mortal realms.

The main sunrise vantage point is the **North Pointing Rock** (拱北石; Gǒngběi Shí); if you're lucky, visibility extends over 200km to the coast. At the rear of the mountain is the tranquil **Rear Rocky Recess** (后石坞; Hòu Shíwù), where ruins are hidden in the pine forests and brush.

You can descend to another side of the reserve by taking the **Peach Blossom Park cable car** (桃花源索道; Táohuā Yuán suǒdào; ☎833 0763; one way/return ¥80/140; ☉8am-5.30pm) to Peach Blossom Park, a scenic area that explodes with colour in late spring. This cable car operates infrequently, so call ahead. From the Peach Blossom Park cable car drop-off it is another 10km on foot or by minibus (one way ¥25) to reach the park exit and buses to Tài Shān train station.

WESTERN ROUTE   西路

The most popular way to descend the mountain is by bus (¥30) via the western route. If you walk, the poorly marked footpath and road often intercept or coincide. You may decide to hop on a bus rather than inhale its fumes, but buses will not stop once they leave the Midway Gate to Heaven.

The western route treats you to a variety of scenic orchards and pools. The main attraction along this route is **Black Dragon Pool** (黑龙潭; Hēilóng Tán), just below **Longevity Bridge** (长寿桥; Chángshòu Qiáo). Mythical tales swarm about the pool, which

SHĀNDŌNG TÀI SHĀN

CONFUCIUS: THE FIRST TEACHER

Born into a world of violent upheaval, Confucius (551–479 BC) spent his life trying to stabilise society according to traditional ideals. By his own measure he failed, but over time he became one of the most influential thinkers the world has known. Confucius' ideals remain at the core of values in east Asia today.

Confucius was born Kǒng Qiū (孔丘), earning the honorific Kǒngfūzǐ (孔夫子), literally 'Master Kong', after becoming a teacher. His family was poor but of noble rank, and eventually he became an official in his home state of Lǔ (in present-day Shandong). At the age of 50, he put a plan into action to reform government that included routing corruption. This resulted in his exile, and he spent 13 years travelling from state to state, hoping to find a ruler who would put his ideas into practice. Eventually, he returned to his hometown of Qūfù and spent the remainder of his life expounding the wisdom of the Six Classics (*The Book of Changes, Songs, Rites, History, Music* and the *Spring and Autumn Annals*). Taking on students from varied backgrounds, he believed that everyone, not just aristocracy, has a right to knowledge. This ideal became one of his greatest legacies.

Confucius' teachings were compiled by his disciples in *The Analects* (*Lúnyǔ*), a collection of 497 aphorisms. Though he claimed to be merely transmitting the ideals of an ancient golden age, Confucius was in fact China's first humanist philosopher, upholding morality (humaneness, righteousness and virtue) and self-cultivation as the basis for social order. 'What you do not wish for yourself,' he said, 'do not do to others.' For more on Confucian philosophy, see p938.

is fed by a small waterfall and said to conceal grand carp palaces and herbs that turn humans into beasts.

At the mountain's base, **Pervading Light Temple** (普照寺; Pǔzhào Sì; admission ¥5; ☺8am-5.30pm), a Buddhist temple dating from the Southern and Northern dynasties (420–589), offers a serene end to the hike.

TIĀNZHÚ PEAK ROUTE 天烛峰景区

The route up the back of the mountain from the **Tiānzhú Peak Scenic Area** (Tiānzhú Fēng Jǐngqū) offers a rare chance to ascend Tài Shān without crowds. It's mostly ancient forest and peaks back there, so take the central route down for the manmade sights.

Get an early start; the bus ride takes 45 minutes, and the climb itself can take upwards of five hours.

It's 5.4km from the trailhead to the **Rear Rocky Recess cable car** (后石坞索道; Hòu Shíwù suǒdào; ☎833 0765; one way ¥20; ☺8.30am-4pm Apr-Oct, closed 16 Oct-15 Apr), which takes you from the back of the mountain to the **North Gate to Heaven cable car stop** (北天门索道站; Běi Tiānmén suǒdào zhàn) and views of Tiānzhú Peak – when it's running. Call in advance.

Sleeping & Eating

Look for signs posting 如家 (*rújiā*) or 宾馆 (*bīngguǎn*) at the summit area along Tian Jie for inns starting from ¥120 and going *way* up on weekends. Rates provided below don't apply to holiday periods, when they can triple. At other times, ask for discounts.

There is no food shortage on Tài Shān; the central route is dotted with stalls and restaurants, but prices rise as you do. Expect food to cost double the usual.

Nán Tiān Mén Bīnguǎn HOTEL $$
(南天门宾馆; ☎833 0988; 1 Tian Jie; tw ¥300-400, with private bath ¥680, tr ¥600-800; ❄@) Located smack bang before you turn onto Tian Jie, this is the easiest place to reach on weary legs. Rooms are a bit beaten up but still clean and airy.

Shénqì Hotel HOTEL $$$
(神憩宾馆; Shénqì Bīnguǎn; ☎822 3866; fax 826 3816; s/d ¥1000-1800, ste ¥6000; ❄@) As the only hotel on the actual summit, prices reflect that. The priciest mountain-view, standard rooms have new everything and are the only rooms on the mountain with hot water in the winter. The restaurant serves 'Taoist banquet' fare.

Xiānjū Bīnguǎn HOTEL $$
(仙居宾馆; ☎823 9984; 5 Tian Jie; tw ¥100-360, d/tr ¥420-700; ❄) By the South Gate to Heaven, this two-star hotel has decent rooms. Some even have large windows overlooking greenery.

Yùyèquán Hotel HOTEL $
(玉夜泉兵宾; ☎822 6740, Midway Gate to Heaven; s/d ¥200-300, ste ¥760-1200; ❄) The only thing going at the Midway Gate to Heaven has drab but tidy rooms facing an inner courtyard. Plenty of food options next door.

🛈 Getting There & Away

Bus 3 (¥2) connects the Tài Shān central route trailhead to the western route trailhead at Tiānwài Village via the Tài Shān train station. Bus Y2 (¥3) and bus 19 (¥2) connect from Caiyuan Dajie across from the train station to the Tiānzhú Peak trailhead. Bus 16 connects the train station to Peach Blossom Park. The last bus returns to Tài'ān at 5pm.

🛈 Getting Around

From Tiānwài Village, minibuses (¥30 each way) depart every 20 minutes (or when full) for the 13km journey to Midway Gate to Heaven, halfway up Tài Shān, from 4am to 8pm in peak season and from 7am to 7pm in low season. Frequent buses come down the mountain. Cable cars reach the summit area from Midway Gate to Heaven, Peach Blossom Park and Rear Rocky Recess.

Qūfù 曲阜

☎ 0537 / POP 88,905

Hometown of the great sage Confucius and his descendants the Kong clan, Qūfù is a testament to the importance of Confucian thought in imperial China. Viewing the main sights within the city walls of ancient Qūfù will take a full day.

◉ Sights

The principal sights – Confucius Temple, Confucius Mansion and Confucius Forest – are known collectively as 'Sān Kǒng' ('Three Kongs'). The **main ticket office** (售票处; *shòupiàochù*) is at the corner of Queli Jie and Nanma Dao, east of the Confucius Temple's main entrance. You can buy admission to individual sights, but the **combination ticket** (per person ¥150), grants access to all three plus free or half-price entry to a number of other Confucius-related sights, including **Confucius Cave** (夫子洞; Fūzǐ Dòng) about

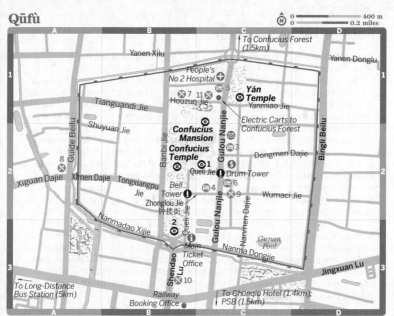

Qūfù

◎ Top Sights

Confucius Mansion	C1
Confucius Temple	B2
Yán Temple	C1

◎ Sights

1	Entrance to Confucius Mansion	C2
2	Entrance to Confucius Temple	B3

🛏 Sleeping

3	Mingya Confucianist Hotel	C2
4	Quèlǐ Hotel	C2
5	Qūfù International Youth Hostel	C1
6	Rúguāngé Business Hotel	C2

✕ Eating

7	Mùèn Lóu Halal Food and Drink	B1
8	Muslim Quarter	A2
9	Night Market	C2
10	Shendao Lu	B3
11	Yù Shū Fáng	C1

30km southeast of Qūfù on Ni Shān. This is where, according to legend, a frighteningly ugly Confucius was born, abandoned, and cared for by a tiger and an eagle before his mother realised he was sent from heaven and decided to care for him.

From 16 November to 14 February, admission is ¥10 cheaper than listed (combined ticket stays the same) and sights close about a half-hour earlier.

Confucius Temple TEMPLE

(孔庙; Kǒng Miào; admission ¥90, included in combination ticket; ◎8am-5.10pm) China's largest imperial building complex after the Forbidden City began as Confucius' three-room house. After his death in 478 BC, the Duke of the Lu state consecrated his simple house as a temple. Everything in it, including his clothing, books, musical instruments and a carriage, was perfectly preserved. The house was rebuilt for the first time in AD 153, kicking off a series of repairs, expansions and renovations in subsequent centuries. By 1012, it had four courtyards and over 300 rooms. An imperial palace-style wall was added. After a fire in 1499, it was rebuilt to its present scale.

Like shrines to Confucius throughout Asia, this is more museum than altar. Over 1000 stelae documenting imperial gifts and sacrifices from the Han dynasty onwards as well as treasured examples of calligraphy and stone reliefs are preserved on the grounds. Look for a *bìxì*, mythical tortoise, bearing the **Chéng Huà stele** (成化碑), dedicated by the Ming emperor in 1468, which

WORTH A TRIP

HOME OF THE SECOND SAGE

Twenty-three kilometres south of Qūfù is **Zōuchéng** (邹城；also called Zōuxiàn, 邹县), where the revered Confucian scholar Mencius (孟子；c 372–289 BC) was born. Like Confucius, Mencius was raised by a single mother and as an adult travelled the country trying to reform government. His belief that humanity is by nature good formed the core of all his teachings, including his call to overthrow self-serving rulers. Though unpopular among his contemporaries, a thousand years after his death Mencius' work was elevated a step below Confucius'.

Zōuchéng today is a relaxed town with fewer tourist hassles than Qūfù. Combined tickets are sold for ¥40 at either of the adjacent main attractions from 8am to 6pm. **Mencius Temple** (孟庙；Mèng Miào) originally dates to the Song dynasty and bears the marks of past anti-Confucian mood swings, though restoration is in progress. With few visitors around to cut in, you can stand in the shade of ancient gnarled cypresses and absorb the serene surroundings. The twin-roofed Hall of the Second Sage (亚圣殿；Yàshèng Diàn) looms in the centre of the grounds. A small shrine next to it is dedicated to Mencius' mother, the 'model for all mothers'. West of the Temple, **Mencius Family Mansion** (孟府；Mèng Fǔ) exhibits the family's living quarters, including teacups and bedding left by Mencius' 74th-generation descendant, who lived there into the 1940s.

Zōuchéng is any easy day trip from Qūfù. Buses make the 40-minute journey from Qūfù (¥7) every 15 minutes from 6.50am to 6pm. A taxi will cost about ¥60. From Zōuchéng's bus station, bus 20 (¥1) stops within a 10-minute walk of the sights, or just catch a motorcycle (¥5) or taxi (¥7).

praises Confucius in a particularly bold, formal hand. The characters are so perfect that copies were made to teach script. The **Shèngjì temple** (圣迹殿) houses 120 famed Tang-dynasty paintings depicting Confucius' life immortalised as carvings.

The temple has nine courtyards arranged on a central axis. Halfway along rises the triple-eaved **Great Pavilion of the Constellation of Scholars** (奎文阁；Kuíwén Gé), an imposing Song-dynasty wooden structure. A series of gates and colossal, twin-eaved stele pavilions lead to the **Apricot Altar** (杏坛；Xìng Tǎn), which marks the spot where Confucius taught his students under an apricot tree.

The core of the complex is the huge yellow-eaved **Dàchéng Hall** (大成殿；Dàchéng Diàn), which in its present form dates from 1724. Craftspeople carved the 10 dragon-coiled columns so expertly that they were covered with red silk when Emperor Qianlong visited, lest he feel that the Forbidden City's Hall of Supreme Harmony (p55) paled in comparison. Inside is a huge statue of Confucius resplendent on a throne. Above him are the characters for '*wànshì shībiǎo*', meaning 'model teacher for all ages'.

South of **Chóngshèng Hall** (崇圣祠；Chóngshèng Cí), which was once the site of the original, modest family temple, the **Lǔ Wall** (鲁壁；Lǔ Bì) stands where Confucius' ninth descendant hid Confucius' writings in the walls of his house during Emperor Qin Shi Huang's book-burning campaign around 213 BC. The texts were uncovered during an attempt to raze the grounds in 154 BC, spurring new schools of Confucian scholarship and long debates over what Confucius really said.

Confucius Mansion   MUSEUM
(孔府；Kǒng Fǔ; admission ¥60, included in combination ticket; ◷8am-5.15pm) Adjacent to Confucius Temple is this maze of 152 buildings and 480 halls, rooms and side passages. The mansion buildings were moved from the temple grounds to the present site in 1377 and expanded in 1503 into nine courtyards and 560 rooms. More remodelling followed, including reconstruction following a fire in 1885.

The mansion was for centuries the most sumptuous private residence in China, thanks to imperial sponsorship and the Kong clan's rule, which included powers of taxation and execution, over Qūfù as an autonomous estate. They indulged in 180-course meals, and kept servants and consorts. Male heirs successively held the title of Duke Yan Sheng from the Song dynasty until 1935.

Confucius Mansion is built on an 'interrupted' north–south axis with administrative offices (taxes, edicts, rites, registration and examination halls) at the entrance (south) and private quarters at the back (north). The **Ceremonial Gate** (重光门; Chóngguāng Mén) was opened only when emperors dropped in for visits. The central path passes a series of halls, including the **Great Hall** (大堂; Dà Tǎng) and **Nèizhái Gate** (内宅门; Nèizhái Mén), which separated the private and public parts of the residence and was guarded at all times.

The large '*shòu*' character (寿; longevity) within the single-eaved **Upper Front Chamber** (前上房; Qián Shàng Fáng) north of Nèizhái Gate was a gift from Qing Empress Cixi. The Duke lived in the two-storey **Front Chamber** (前堂楼; Qián Tǎng Lóu).

East just before the Nèizhái Gate is the **Tower of Refuge** (奎楼; Kuí Lóu), not open to visitors, where the Kong clan could gather if the peasants turned nasty. It has an iron-lined ceiling on the ground floor and a staircase that could be yanked up.

Confucius Forest CEMETERY
(孔林; Kǒng Lín; admission ¥40, included in combination ticket; ⏰7.30am-6pm) About 2km north of town on Lindao Lu is the peaceful Confucius Forest, a cemetery of pine and cypress covering 200 hectares bounded by a 10km-long wall. Confucius and more than 100,000 of his descendants have been buried here for the past 2000 years, a tradition still ongoing.

When Confucius died in 479 BC he was buried on the bank of the Si River beneath a simple marker. In the Western Han dynasty, Emperor Wudi deemed Confucianism the only worthy school of thought, and the **Tomb of Confucius** (孔子墓; Kǒngzǐ Mù) became a place of pilgrimage. Today the tomb is a simple grass mound enclosed by a low wall and faced with a Ming-dynasty stele. Pairs of stone guardians stand at the ready. The sage's son and grandson are buried nearby, and scattered through the forest are dozens of temples and pavilions.

A slow walk through the parklike cemetery can take a couple of hours, though Confucius' tomb is just a 15-minute walk from the entrance (turn left after the carts). **Sightseeing carts** (¥20) allow you to hop on and off at the main attraction.

To get to the Confucius Forest, take an **electric cart** (电动旅游车; Diàndòng Lǚyóu Chē; one way/return ¥10/15) from the corner of Houzuo Jie and Gulou Dajie. Otherwise take a pedicab (¥5) or bus 1 (¥2) from Gulou Beijie. Walking takes about 30 minutes.

Yán Temple TEMPLE
(颜庙; Yán Miào; Yanmiao Jie; admission ¥50, included in combination ticket; ⏰8am-5.30pm) This tranquil temple northeast of Confucius Mansion is dedicated to Confucius' beloved disciple Yan Hui, whose death at age 32 caused the understated Confucius 'excessive grief'. The main structure, **Fùshèng Hall** (复圣殿; Fùshèng Diàn), has a magnificent ceiling decorated with a dragon head motif. Outside a *bìxì* carries a stele that posthumously granted Yan the title of Duke of Yanguo (in both Han and Mongol script) in AD 1331.

✫✫ Festivals & Events

Confucius Temple holds two major festivals a year, **Tomb Sweeping Day** (usually 5 April; celebrations may last all weekend) and the **Sage's Birthday** (28 September). The city also comes alive with crafts people, healers, acrobats and peddlers during annual fairs in the spring and autumn.

🛏 Sleeping

TOP CHOICE **Qūfù International Youth Hostel** HOSTEL $
(曲阜国际青年旅舍; Qūfù Guójì Qīngnián Lǚshè; ☑441 8989; www.yhaqf.com; Gulou Beijie; 鼓楼北街北首路西; dm/tw/tr ¥45/110/130; ❄@🅿) A fantastic hostel at the north end of Gulou Beijie with rooms so clean you can smell the fresh linen. Bike rental, ticket bookings, and a cafe/bar (cocktails are ¥15 to ¥18) serving Chinese and Western fare. Dorms have five to eight beds with a shared bathroom. Only fault? Hot water can be scarce in the mornings.

Chūnqiū Hotel HOTEL $$
(春秋大酒店; Chūnqiū Dà Jiǔdiàn; ☑505 1888; 13 Chunqiu Lu; 春秋路13号; incl breakfast s ¥398-788, d ¥298-788; ❄❄@) Just outside the city walls, this rather subdued business hotel is a favourite of bureaucrats (government buildings are next door). Standard rooms have plush beds, views of the park, and bathrooms sized for an airplane. Discounts available.

Mingya Confucianist Hotel HOTEL $$
(名雅儒家大饭店; Míngyǎ Rújiā Dàfàndiàn; ☑505 0888; 8 Gulou Beijie; incl breakfast s ¥128, d ¥218-238, tr ¥338; ❄@) While we're pretty sure the great sage would not approve of his name on a hotel banner, we are sure he

would like the efficient location (smack-bang in the middle of town) and the courteous staff. Avoid the stuffy, windowless economy rooms. Discounts up to 40%.

Quèlǐ Hotel
HOTEL $$$

(阙里宾舍; Quèlǐ Bīnshè; ☎486 6400; 15 Zhonglou Jie; 钟楼街15号; s/d/ste ¥498/568/2288; ✳@⊛) The four-star Quèlǐ was once the fanciest hotel in town, but the photos of visiting dignitaries on the walls are fading. A refurb is in progress, so some rooms look great while others are musty. Look first.

Rúguānggé Business Hotel
HOTEL $

(儒光阁商务宾馆; Rúguānggé Shāngwù Bīngguǎn; ☎446 0688; 12 Gulou Nanjie; 鼓楼大街中段12号; incl breakfast s/d ¥258-588; tr ¥468; ⊜✳@) The best rooms in this new, fauxMing building overlook Gulou Nanjie. The entrance is in an alley off Wumaci Jie. Discounts of up to 50% make this a good economy choice. No smoking on the premises.

✗ Eating

The local speciality is Kong-family cuisine (孔家菜), which despite its name is the furthest thing from home cooking since it developed as a result of all the banquets the family threw.

Restaurants skip the pageantry nowadays but for still less formal fare, head to the area around **Shendao Lu** (south of Confucius Temple) or the **night market** (夜市; yèshì), off Wumaci Jie, east of Gulou Nanjie. Vendors make noodles, grill skewers of meat, and jiānbǐng guǒzi (煎饼裹子; ¥3 to ¥5), a steaming parcel of egg, vegetables and chilli sauce in a crêpe. Stalls displaying raw meat and produce cook it to order. Just point at what you want. At night, the **Muslim Quarter** comes alive outside the western gate on Xiguan Dajie (西关大街).

Yù Shū Fáng
CHINESE BANQUET $$$

(御书房; ☎441 9888; 2nd fl, Houzuo Jie; set meals ¥128-500; ⊙9am-1.30pm & 5-8.30pm) With private rooms overlooking the Confucius Mansion, this is a fantastic place to take a breather after following kilometres of courtyards. Recharge with some very fine teas (铁观音; tiě guānyīn) from ¥38 per pot (壶), or shell out for the banquet meal (套餐; tào cān). The most basic serves eight to 10 Kong-family dishes in quick succession. No English spoken; enter by the door beside the furniture store (the owner is also a woodcarver).

Mù'ēn Lóu Halal Food and Drink
CHINESE MUSLIM $

(穆恩楼清真餐飲; Mùēn Lóu, Qīngzhēn Cānyǐn; ☎448 3877; Houzuo Jie; mains ¥15-48; ⊙8.30am-1.30pm & 5-8.30pm) A friendly Huí family has run this place by the Confucius Mansion's exit for decades, serving house specialities like beef spiced with cumin, star anise and turmeric (南前牛肉片; nánqián niúròu piàn; ¥68) and tongue-numbing, spicy tofu (麻辣豆腐; málà dòufu; ¥12).

ⓘ Information

ATMs accepting foreign cards are along or just off Gulou Beijie.

Internet cafes are often restricted to Chinese nationals or always require a passport. Look for signs posting '网吧' around Wumaci Jie (per hour ¥2 to ¥5), or surf at **Qūfù International Youth Hostel** (per hour ¥5).

Bank of China (中国银行; Zhōngguó Yínháng; 96 Dongmen Dajie; ⊙8.30am-4.30pm) Foreign exchange and ATM.

China Post (中国邮政; Zhōngguó Yóuzhèng; Gulou Beijie, 鼓楼门分理处; ⊙8am-6pm summer, 8.30am-5.30pm winter) In front of the Drum Tower.

People's No 2 Hospital (第二人民医院; Dì'èr Rénmín Yīyuàn; ☎448 8120; 7 Gulou Beijie) Next to the Qūfù International Youth Hostel.

Public Security Bureau (PSB; 公安局; Gōng'ānjú; ☎443 0007; 1 Wuyutai Lu; ⊙8.30am-noon & 2-6pm Mon-Fri) South of the city walls.

ⓘ Getting There & Away

Bus

Qūfú's **long-distance bus station** (长途汽车站; chángtú qìchēzhàn; ☎441 2554; Yulong Lu) is 6km southwest of the city walls. **Left luggage** (¥2; ⊙6am-6pm) is available here.

Běijīng ¥160 to ¥180, six hours, two daily (8.10am and 11.20am)

Jǐ'nán ¥44, three hours, every 30 minutes

Qīngdǎo ¥125, five hours, five daily (8.30am, 9.30am, 1.30pm, 2.20pm and 4.40pm)

Tài'ān ¥23, 1½ hours, every 30 minutes

Yǎnzhōu ¥5, 20 minutes, frequently

Train

The newly built **East train station** (高铁东火车站; ☎442 1571), 12km east of the walled city, offers convenient access to the express rail. The **Yǎnzhōu Train Station** (兖州火车站; ☎346 2965; Beiguan Jie), 16km west of Qūfù, is also convenient for destinations on the Běijīng to Shànghǎi line. The **Huódōng Train Station** (火东火车站; ☎442 1571; Dianlan Lu) is closest to the walled city (6km east) but only slow trains stop there.

Buy tickets at the **railway booking office** (火车售票处; huǒchē shòupiào chù; ☑ 335 2276; 8 Jingxuan Lu; ⊙ 7.30am-6pm); ¥5 commission. The Qūfù International Youth Hostel also books tickets (¥15 to ¥20 commission).

Some regular trains (seat/hard sleeper) departing from Yǎnzhōu Train Station:

Jǐ'nán ¥15/67, two to three hours, frequently

Qīngdǎo ¥76/143, six to 8½ hours, frequently

Yāntái ¥43/76, nine to 10½ hours, six daily

Some express D trains (hard/soft seat only; G trains also available) departing from East Train Station:

Běijīng ¥165/198, three to four hours, six daily

Jǐ'nán ¥40/48, one hour, eight daily

Nánjīng ¥151/181, 2½ to 3½ hours, five daily

Shànghǎi ¥242/290, 4½ to 5½ hours, three daily

Tiānjīn ¥127/153, two to three hours, four daily

ⓘ Getting Around

Bus K01 (¥3) connects the long-distance bus station to Qūfù's south gate and the east train station. A taxi from within the wall is about ¥30 to the east train station and ¥15 to the long-distance bus station. Bus 1 travels along Gulou Beijie and Lindao Lu between the bus station and Confucius Forest.

Minibuses (¥5 to ¥7, every 15 minutes) connect Yǎnzhōu train station to the walled city from 6.30am to 5.30pm. Otherwise, a taxi costs about ¥50.

Persistent pedicabs (¥5 to ¥6 within Qūfù; ¥10 to ¥20 outside the walls) chase all and sundry. Decorated horse carts take short tours (¥30 to the Confucius Forest from Queli Jie).

Qīngdǎo 青岛

☑ 0532 / POP 1.83 MILLION

Offering a breath of fresh air to those emerging from the polluted urban interior, Qīngdǎo is a rare modern city that has managed to preserve some of its past. Its blend of concession-era and modern architecture puts China's standard, white-tile and blue-glass developments to shame.

The city's beauty, the local saying goes, is in its red roofs, green trees, cerulean sea and azure sky. In truth, the beaches are overhyped and trees are rare in the new neighbourhoods, but Qīngdǎo is right to take pride in its mixed heritage, including its mostly intact German concession structures. The winding cobbled streets and red-capped hillside villas are captivating. There is also plenty to enjoy in the city's diverse food scene, headlined by the ubiquitous hometown beer Tsingtao.

Qīngdǎo is rapidly expanding into a true multidistrict city, but for now, most of the fun is in or around Shì'nán district (市南区), the strip of land along the sea.

History

Before catching the acquisitive eye of Kaiser Wilhelm II, Qīngdǎo was a harbour and fishing village known for producing delicious sea salt. Its excellent strategic location was not lost on the Ming dynasty, which built a defensive battery – nor on the Germans who wrested it from them in 1897. China signed a 99-year concession, and under German rule during the next decade the future Tsingtao Brewery was opened, electric lighting installed, missions and a university established, and the railway to Jǐ'nán built.

In 1914 the Japanese took over after a successful joint Anglo-Japanese naval bombardment of the city. The Treaty of Versailles strengthened Japan's occupation in 1919, sparking fervent student demonstrations in Běijīng that came to be known as the May 4th Movement. The city reverted to Chinese rule in 1922 but the Japanese seized it again in 1938 in the Sino-Japanese War and held it until the end of WWII.

In peacetime, Qīngdǎo became one of China's major ports and a flourishing centre of trade and manufacturing (home to both domestic and international brands). It hosted the Olympic sailing events in 2008. All this and the clean air keep it at the top of the list of Asia's most liveable cities.

◉ Sights

Most sights are squeezed into the Old Town (the former concession area), with the train and bus stations, historic architecture and budget accommodation, and Bādàguān, a serene residential area of parks, spas and old villas. East of Shandong Lu rises the modern city with the central business district (CBD) to the north and the latest in retail and dining in Dōngbù, closer to the water to the south. Further east still is the developing Láo Shān (崂山区) district, anchored by the Municipal Museum, Grand Theatre and International Beer City (site of the annual festival).

The Qīngdǎo Municipal Government has put up plaques identifying notable historic buildings and sites throughout the city.

Qīngdǎo

SHĀNDŌNG QĪNGDǍO

500 m
0.25 miles

TAIDŌNG

SHINAN DISTRICT

SHIBEI DISTRICT

BADAGUAN

OLD TOWN

Governor's House Museum

Protestant Church

Tianhou Temple

Signal Hill Park

Qingdaoshan Park

Zhongshan Park

Lu Xun Park

Guanhaishan Park

Taiping Shan

Jiaozhou Bay

Huiquan Bay

Qingdao Bay

Fushan Bay

Train Station

To Huashi Lou (300m)
To Culture Street (500m)

To Café Yum (1km);
Carrefour (1km);
Jusco (2km)

Airport Shuttle
(Haitian Hotel)

To No 2 Bathing Beach;
Huashi Lou (300m)

Airport Shuttle
(Green Tree Inn)

Ningxia Lu

Yan'an Sanlu 延安三路

Yan'an Lu

Dengzhou Lu 登州路

Huangtai Lu 黄台路

Rehe Lu 热河路

Jiangsu Lu

Liaocheng Lu 聊城路

Jining Lu

Zhifu Lu

Jiaozhou Lu

Hubei Lu 湖北路

Feicheng Lu

Feixian Lu

Tai'an Lu

Dagu Lu 大沽路

Tianjin Lu 天津路

Zhongshan Lu

Guangxi Lu

Hunan Lu

Anhui Lu

Taiping Lu

Hongdao Lu

Jiangsu Lu

Longshan Lu

Changzhou Lu

Daxue Lu

Fushan Lu

Qixia Lu

Yan'an Yilu

Wendeng Lu

Rongcheng Lu

Nanhai Lu 南海路

Zhengyangguan Lu

Laiyang Lu 莱阳路

Qinyu Lu

Huangdao Lu

Guantao Lu

Xianggang Xilu

Donghai Xilu

Taidong Yilu

1 2 3 4 5 6 7 8 9 10 11 12 13 14 15 16 17 18 19 20 21 22 23 24 25 26 27 28 29 30 31

Qīngdǎo

⊙ **Top Sights**
Governor's House Museum...................C2
Protestant Church...............................C3
Tianhou Temple...................................B3

⊙ **Sights**
1 Chinese Navy Museum.....................C4
2 Huílán Pavilion................................B3
3 Little Fish Hill..................................D3
4 Little Qīngdǎo.................................B4
5 Little Qīngdǎo Lighthouse..............B4
6 No 1 Bathing Beach........................D4
7 No 3 Bathing Beach........................G4
8 No 6 Bathing Beach........................A3
9 Qīngdǎo Underwater World.............C4
10 St Michael's Cathedral...................B2
11 Tàipíng Shān...................................F2
12 Tsingtao Beer Museum...................E1
13 TV Tower..F2
Zhàn Bridge..............................(see 2)
14 Zhànshān Temple...........................G3

🛏 **Sleeping**
15 Hǎilóng Castle Hotel.......................C3
16 Hengshan No. 5 Hostel...................C3
17 Kǎiyuè Hostelling International.......B2
18 Nordic Osheania Youth Hostel........B1
19 Oceanwide Elite Hotel....................B3

20 Qīngdǎo International Youth
Hotel...D3
21 Starway Hotel, Pǐcháiyuán.............B2
22 YHA Old Observatory......................C2

🍴 **Eating**
23 Chūn Hé Lóu...................................B2
Firewood Court.........................(see 21)
24 Huángdǎo Market...........................B2
25 Ma Jia Lā Miàn...............................B2
26 Wángjiě Shāokǎo............................B2

🍷 **Drinking**
27 Beer Street.....................................E1
Mamahuhu Lounge....................(see 22)
Old Church Lounge....................(see 17)

🛍 **Shopping**
28 Jímòlù Market.................................B1
29 Parkson..B2

ℹ **Information**
Qīngdǎo Shìnán Tourist Information
Center....................................(see 21)
30 Ticket Office...................................A2

ℹ **Transport**
31 Dōngshēng Air Ticket Office...........B2

Governor's House Museum MUSEUM
(青岛德国总督楼旧址博物馆; Qīngdǎo Déguó Zǒngdū Lóu Jiùzhǐ Bówùguǎn; 26 Longshan Lu; admission summer/winter ¥20/15, multilingual audio tour ¥10; ◷8.30am-5.30pm; 🚇1, 221) East of Xìnhàoshān Park stands one of Qīngdǎo's best examples of concession-era architecture – the former German governor's residence constructed in the style of a German palace. It was built in 1903 at a cost of 2,450,000 taels of silver by an indulgent governor, whom Kaiser Wilhelm II immediately sacked when he saw the bill. In 1957 Chairman Mao stayed here with his wife and kids on holiday. So did defence minister Lin Biao, who would later attempt to assassinate him (supposedly, Lin had an aversion to sunlight and kept the curtains drawn). The building's interior is characteristic of *Jugendstil*, the German arm of art nouveau, with some Chinese furnishings.

Protestant Church CHURCH
(基督教堂; Jīdū Jiàotáng; 15 Jiangsu Lu; admission ¥7; ◷8.30am-5pm, weekend services; 🚇1, 221, 367) On a street of German buildings, this

copper-capped church was designed by Curt Rothkegel and built in 1908. The interior is simple and Lutheran in its sparseness, apart from some carvings on the pillar cornices. You can climb up to inspect the clock mechanism (Bockenem 1909).

FREE **Tianhou Temple** TEMPLE
(天后宫; Tiānhòu Gōng; 19 Taiping Lu; ◷8am-6pm; 🚇25, 220) This small restored temple dedicated to the patron of seafarers has stood by the shore since 1467. The main hall contains a colourful statue of Tianhou, flanked by fearsome guardians. There is also Dragon King Hall (龙王殿; Lóngwáng Diàn), where a splayed pig lies before the ruler of oceans, and a shrine to the God of Wealth. Vendors in the alley adjacent (21 Taiping Lu) sell handicrafts.

St Michael's Cathedral CHURCH
(天主教堂; Tiānzhǔ Jiàotáng; 15 Zhejiang Lu; 🚇1, 221, 367) Up a hill off Zhongshan Lu looms this grand Gothic- and Roman-style edifice. It is closed for renovation until 2014, but you can still wander the exterior. Completed in 1934, the church spires were supposed to

MADE IN TSINGTAO

The beer of choice in Chinese restaurants around the world, Tsingtao is one of China's oldest and most respected brands. Established in 1903 by a joint German–British corporation, the Germania-Brauerei began as a microbrewery of sorts using spring water from nearby Láo Shān to brew a Pilsener Light and Munich Dark for homesick German troops. In 1914 the Japanese occupied Qīngdǎo and confiscated the plant, rechristening it Dai Nippon and increasing production to sell under the 'Tsingtao,' 'Asahi' and 'Kirin' labels. In 1945 the Chinese took over and gave the brewery its current name. At first, only China's elite could afford to drink it, but advertisements touting Tsingtao as a health drink boosted its appeal ('It's not only harmless, it strengthens the body!'). In 2011 China's beer consumption topped 766 million kegs, enough to convince Tsingtao's distant cousin Asahi Breweries to invest in a minority stake.

be clock towers but Chancellor Hitler cut funding of overseas projects and the plans were scrapped. The church was badly damaged during the Cultural Revolution and the crosses capping its twin spires torn off. Devout locals rescued the crosses and buried them in the hills. Workers uncovered them while repairing pipes in 2005.

Huāshí Lóu
CONCESSION BUILDING

(花石楼; Huāshí Lóu; 18 Huanghai Lu; admission ¥8.50; ◎8am-5pm; 📌26, 231, 604) This granite and marble villa built in 1930 was first the home of a Russian aristocrat, and later the German governor's hunting lodge. It is also known as the 'Chiang Kaishek Building' as the generalissimo secretly stayed here in 1947. While most of the rooms are closed, you can clamber up two narrow stairwells to the turret for views of the hills and bay. Located on the east end of No 2 Bathing Beach at the southern tip of Zijingguan Lu in Bādàguān.

Tsingtao Beer Museum
MUSEUM

(青岛啤酒博物馆; Qīngdǎo Píjiǔ Bówùguǎn; 56-1 Dengzhou Lu; admission ¥60, English guide ¥60; ◎8.30am-4.30pm; 📌1, 205, 221) For a self-serving introduction to China's iconic beer, head to the original and still operating brewery. On view are old photos, preserved brewery equipment and statistics, but there are also a few fascinating glimpses of the modern factory line. The aroma of hops is everywhere. Thankfully, you get to sample brews along the way. Alternatively, skip the tour and head straight for Beer St just outside. If you're taking a bus, get off at the '15中' (shíwǔ zhōng) stop. A taxi from Old Town costs ¥10.

Qīngdǎo Beaches
BEACHES

(青岛沙滩; Qīngdǎo Shātān) Qīngdǎo is famed for its beaches, which are pleasant enough, but don't expect the French Riviera.

Chinese beach culture is low-key, though swimming season (June to September) attracts hordes of sun-seekers fighting for towel space. Shark nets, lifeguards, lifeboat patrols and medical stations are on hand.

There are ways to enjoy the water without jumping in. If you give in to touts, rides around the bay are ¥10 to ¥40 depending on the boat. Or stroll the **Bīnhǎi boardwalk** (滨海步行道), which stretches 40km along the city's shoreline from Tuándǎo Bay to **Shílǎorén Beach** (石老人海水浴场) on the far east of town in the Láo Shān district.

Shílǎorén, a 2.5km-long strip of clean sand and polished seashells, is Qīngdǎo's largest. There's been heavy development, but the rocky outcrop, the 'Old Stone Man' from which the beach gets its name, still stands on its eastern end. Take bus 304 from Zhàn Bridge (Zhàn Qiáo; ¥2.50, 45 minutes) or catch a taxi (¥40).

Closest to the train station is the **No 6 Bathing Beach** and neighbouring **Zhàn Bridge** (栈桥; Zhàn Qiáo), a pier that reaches out into the bay. At its tip, the eight-sided **Huílán Pavilion** (回澜阁; Huílán Gé; admission ¥4; ◎8am-9pm) is constantly packed to the rafters. If the pavilion looks familiar, that's because it's on every Tsingtao beer label.

South of Bādàguān, the sand at **No 1 Bathing Beach** is coarse-grained and littered with seaweed. The prettier, sheltered coves of **Nos 2 and 3 Bathing Beaches** are just east of Bādàguān. Take bus 214 directly, or bus 26 to the wǔshèngguān (武胜关) stop to wander past the exquisite villas, spas and guesthouses scattered within Bādàguān's wooded headlands down to the sea.

For wide open spaces of sand, sea and sky, there's **Golden Sand Beach** (金沙滩) on the western peninsula of Huángdǎo district (团岛区). An undersea tunnel linking Huángdǎo and Shìnán puts it within easy reach of Old Town. Take the red double-decker sightseeing bus 2 (¥15, 30 minutes) by the train station at 9am or 10am, or tunnel bus 3 (隧道3; ¥2) from in front of the Municipal Hospital (市立医院) on Jiaozhou Lu in Old Town to the terminus and then transfer to bus 18 (¥1). A taxi costs ¥70 including toll.

Qīngdǎo Parks   PARKS

Within central Qīngdǎo, **Zhōngshān Park** (中山公园; Zhōngshān Gōngyuán; ⏰24hr; 🚌26, 202, 501) is a vast 69 hectares of lakes and trees. There's an amusement park, botanical gardens and walking paths, and the park hosts lively festivals in the spring and summer. In the park's northeast rises hilly **Tàipíng Shān** (太平山; Tàipíng Shān). Reach the **TV Tower** (Diànshì Tǎ; admission depending on view ¥45/80/100) on top by **cable car** (one way/return ¥60/80; ⏰7.30am-6.30pm). Free admission to the tower with reservations at its lacklustre **restaurant** (📞8635 4020; set meal ¥108; ⏰8am-7pm).

Also within the park is Qīngdǎo's largest temple, **Zhànshān Temple** (湛山寺; Zhànshān Sì; admission ¥10; ⏰8am-4pm), an active Buddhist sanctuary. When you get off the cable car at the temple, look for a round concrete dome on the right. This is the entrance to a bunker, which the Germans used as a wine cellar, and today houses a wine bar. Fantastic!

Many parks with ticket booths, including **Little Fish Hill** (小鱼山公园; 24 Fushanzi Lu; admission ¥15; ⏰6.30am-6.30pm) by No 1 Bathing Beach and **Signal Hill Park** (信号山; 16 Longshan Lu; viewing platform ¥15; ⏰7.30am-6pm) in Old Town, are free to wander in after 6.30pm.

Little Qīngdǎo   LIGHTHOUSE

(小青岛; Xiǎo Qīngdǎo; 26 Qinyu Lu; admission summer/winter ¥15/10; ⏰7am-6.30pm; 🚌6, 26, 202, 231, 304) In the shape of a *qín* (a stringed instrument) jutting into Qīngdǎo Bay, this former island was connected to the mainland in the 1940s. The Germans built the white lighthouse in 1900 on the leafy promontory. It is an excellent spot for watching the city come to life in the morning.

Chinese Navy Museum   MUSEUM

(中国海军博物馆; Zhōngguó Hǎijūn Bówùguǎn; admission ¥80; ⏰8.30am-5.30pm; 🚌6, 26, 304) Just adjacent to Little Qīngdǎo, this museum's main attractions are the rusty submarine and destroyer anchored in the harbour. There are also, of course, displays on Chinese naval history.

Qingdao Underwater World   AQUARIUM

(青岛海底世界; Qīngdǎo Hǎidǐ Shìjiè; 1 Laiyang Lu; summer/winter ¥120/100, 6yr & under free, students ¥60/50; ⏰8am-5.30pm; 🚌6, 26, 304, 321, 501) Kids will love this long-standing aquarium's spectacular 82m underwater glass-enclosed tunnel, jellyfish tanks and various underwater performances. Try to avoid weekends.

FREE **Municipal Museum**   MUSEUM

(青岛市博物馆; Qīngdǎo Shì Bówùguǎn; 📞8889 6286; 51 Meiling Lu; 梅岭东路51号; ⏰9am-4.30pm, closed Mon; 🚌230, 321) This massive collection of relics anchors the budding cultural zone about 13km east of Old Town in Láo Shān district. It has the usual broad span of exhibits expected in a big city museum. This does not make them any less impressive.

✸✸ Festivals & Events

Lantern Festival   SPRING

The city glows at the end of the Chinese New Year/Spring Festival in February/March.

Cherry Blossom Festival   CHERRY BLOSSOM

The cherry blossoms explode with colour in Zhōngshān Park around April.

International Beer Festival   BEER

(www.qdbeer.cn) The city's premier party draws more than three million tipplers every August.

International Sailing Week   SPORTS

(www.qdsailing.org) Watch (or join) the regattas and windsurfing by the Olympic Sailing Center every August/September.

🛏 Sleeping

Old Town has excellent budget and mid-range options. The CBD and Dōngbù have the top-end international chains but a lot less soul. Rates increase as much as 30% in July and August.

TOP CHOICE **Kǎiyuè Hostelling International**   HOSTEL **$**

(凯悦国际青年旅馆; Kǎiyuè Guójì Qīngnián Lǚguǎn; 📞8284 5450; www.yhaqd.com; 31 Jining Lu; 济宁路31号; dm ¥25-30, f ¥100-179, r ¥80-100, with private bath from ¥189; ✱@🖥🛜) This hostel in a historic church at Sifang Lu and Jining Lu has a lively congregation. The sociable staff create a real community in the great bar and restaurant (Old Church Lounge), and cosy public spaces. They offer thoughtful services like bike rental (¥10) and a free beer each night. Clean dorms are large; doubles vary in quality. Book in advance.

YHA Old Observatory
HOSTEL **$**

(奥博维特国际青年旅舍; Àobówèitè Guójì Qīngnián Lǚshè; ☑8282 2626; www.hostelqingdao.com; 21 Guanxiang Erlu; 观象二路21号; dm ¥40-50, r with private bath ¥138-238; ❄@🖥) Perched on a hill in a working observatory, this happy hostel has unbeatable views of the city and bay. Take them in with a beer in hand at the rooftop Mamahuhu Lounge. Staff (and resident pooch Wilson) provide all the usual plus organise group outings. Comfort level varies – revamped doubles have swank bathrooms. Some dorms are huge. A private car service (¥25) is handy for late-night arrivals. Book in advance.

China Community Art and Culture
HOTEL **$$**

(老转村公社文华艺术酒店; Lǎozhuǎncūn Gōngshè Wénhuá Yìshù Jiǔdiàn; ☑8576 8776; 8 Minjiang Sanlu; s ¥198-498, d ¥298-398, ste ¥598-980) With silk lanterns illuminating the hallways, ceramic bowls serving as sinks, wood-floor showers and antique furnishings, each sumptuously decorated room in this polished hotel in the heart of Dōngbù has the feel of a courtyard residence. There's a fantastic restaurant next door.

Starway Hotel, Pīcháiyuàn
HOTEL **$$**

(劈柴院民俗主题酒店; Pīcháiyuàn Mínsú Zhǔtí Jiǔdiàn; ☑8280 7288; 34 Jiangning Lu, inside Firewood Court; s ¥189, d ¥239-309; ❄@) Set in a conserved *lǐyuàn*, apartment complexes once common in old Qīngdǎo, this 'folk-custom theme' hotel has TVs and modern bathrooms. Everything else is a throwback, down to the neighbours who have been here for generations. Upgrade to rooms with traditional bed rolls (褥子; *rùzi*; ¥239) or a Chinese wedding bed (¥309). Look for the wooden door and round blue sign.

Hengshan No. 5 Hostel
HOSTEL **$**

(恒山5号, Héngshān Wǔ Hào; ☑8288 9888; 5 Hengshan Lu; dm/r ¥60/175; ❄@) On a short street south of the Governor's Mansion Museum, this new arrival boasts a primo location in a three-storey, white stuccoed German mansion. Beds are all the same (pine frame, reasonably soft) but rooms with private baths are like small apartments, while some bunk rooms are windowless closets. There's a small bar and cafe across the garden.

Oceanwide Elite Hotel
HOTEL **$$$**

(泛海名人酒店; Fànhǎi Míngrén Jiǔdiàn; ☑8299 6699; 29 Taiping Lu; d without/with sea view ¥1160/1560, ste ¥2800 plus 10% service charge; ❄@) This pretty five-storey hotel benefits from a superb seafront location overlooking (if you opt for the pricier sea-view rooms) Zhàn Bridge and Qīngdǎo Bay. Little touches like complimentary snacks put it leagues ahead of its neighbours. Low-season prices for doubles drop to ¥700.

Sea View Garden Hotel
HOTEL **$$$**

(海静花园大酒店; Hǎijìng Huāyuán Jiǔdiàn; ☑8587 5777; 2 Zhanghua Lu; r ¥1017-1491, ste ¥2043; ❄@🖥) With all the five-star competition, this hotel on the water in Dōngbú distinguishes itself with beyond professional (dare we say, neo-imperial) service. Refreshments, hot towels and even unsolicited delivery of homemade soup to ease a cough – we could get used to this assuming our credit cards don't max out. Fortunately, the 10% service charge is already included, and discounts up to 40% are available.

Hǎilóng Castle Hotel
HOTEL **$$**

(青岛海龙古堡酒店; Qīngdǎo Hǎilóng Gǔbǎo Jiǔdiàn; ☑8289 2626; 23 Changzhou Lu; s ¥300-438, d/tr ¥338/438; ❄@) This recently redone beachside hotel, off Taiping Lu near Bādàguān, occupies the police offices of the former Qīngdǎo Prison and shares the grounds with the current museum, but 'Prison Hotel' doesn't have much of a ring to it. Spartan rooms with standard pine furniture.

Qīngdǎo International Youth Hotel
HOTEL **$$**

(青岛国际青年旅舍; Qīngdǎo Guójì Qīngnián Lǚshè; ☑8286 5177; www.youthtaylor.com; 7a Qixia Lu; 栖霞路7号甲; dm ¥60, s/d/tr ¥260-480; ❄@🖥) Despite the name, this hotel in Bādàguān feels more like a B&B/hostel. Rooms (and bathrooms) are cavernous. There's some dust on the yesteryear charm, but there is a shared kitchen.

Nordic Osheania Youth Hostel
HOSTEL **$**

(青岛巢城青年旅舍; Qīngdǎo Cháochéng Qīngnián Lǚshè; ☑8282 5198; www.nordicosheania.com; 28 Guantao Lu; 馆陶路28号; dm ¥40-65, s/d ¥168-178, tr ¥228; ❄🖥) This hive of basic rooms is on the north edge of Old Town. Management prioritised putting in a great bar and a huge movie room over revamping the crummy bathrooms (all shared).

✖ Eating

Qīngdǎo's kitchens have no problem satisfying all tastes. The waterfront area from No 6 to No 1 Bathing Beach is brimming with restaurants – priced for tourists. The Dōngbù neighbourhood of **Hong Kong Garden** (香港花园; Xiānggǎng Huāyuán; ☐222, 501) around Xianggang Zhonglu is jam-packed with hip eateries: Korean, Japanese, Thai, Italian and Russian are just some of the cuisines.

For the city's staple seafood, stick to the streets. The **Táidōng** neighbourhood between Taidong Yilu (台东一路) and Taidong Balu (台东八路) in Shìběi district (市北区) north of Old Town is packed with restaurants, street markets and carts. Take bus 2, 222 or 217. For the quintessential Qīngdǎo meal, buy a *jīn* of clams – in local-speak *gálá* (蛤蜊; from ¥16) – and take it to a streetside stall with '加功' (*jiā gōng*) on its sign. They'll cook up your catch for ¥5, and pour a bag of fresh Tsingtao beer for ¥6 more. (Pints and pitchers available if you want to be fancy.)

TOP
CHOICE **China Community**

Art and Culture CHINESE $$$
(老转村公社文华艺术酒店; Lǎozhuǎncūn Gōngshè Wénhuá Yìshù Jiǔdiàn; ☐8077 6776; 8 Minjiang Sanlu; mains from ¥48; ☺11.30am-2.30pm & 5.30-10pm; ☐222, 304) This gorgeous restaurant next to its namesake hotel in Hong Kong Garden is set in a stylised Hakka roundhouse (the sort once mistaken by the CIA for missile silos). The kitchen turns out sophisticated regional cuisine from Shāndōng and Sìchuān. Everything from the mushrooms to water for the tea is locally sourced from Láo Shān.

Huángdǎo Market STREET MARKET $
(黄岛路市场; Huángdǎo Lù Shìchǎng; meals from ¥5; ☺8am-9pm; ☐228, 231) In the heart of Old Town, this long-standing, frenetic street market is chock-a-block with stalls selling squirming seafood, fried chicken, pancakes, fruit, soymilk...it's all cheap, so just stop when something catches your fancy. Nearby Zhifu Lu has sit-down curbside joints such as No 17 with the red awning that will prepare whatever you bring for ¥5.

Firewood Court STREET MARKET $
(劈柴院; Pīcháiyuàn; meals from ¥10; ☺6am-10pm; ☐2, 228) Off Zhongshan Lu, an archway with a plaster motif '1902' leads to a vast warren of food stalls and the Jiāngníng Assembly Hall (江宁会馆), a long-time draw for renowned performers that still puts on musical acts. The whole place is rather done up, but at least that means prices are labelled and eateries have picture menus.

Chūn Hé Lóu CHINESE $$
(春和楼; ☐8282 4346; 146 Zhongshan Lu; meals from ¥40; ☺11am-3pm & 5-9.30pm; ☐2, 228) This Lǔ cuisine institution, which was founded in 1891, makes legendary pot-stickers (锅贴; *guōtiē*) and crispy, fragrant chicken (香酥鸡; *xiāngsū jī*). The top-floor tables have the most atmosphere and get the full attention of the chefs. Downstairs is a fast-food version and a take-out counter for dumplings.

Mǎ Jiā Lā Miàn NOODLES $
(马家拉面; Yizhou Lu near Gaomi Lu; noodles ¥7-12; ☺9am-11pm; ☐222, 308) This no-frills restaurant, run by a Muslim family in the Old Town, makes a variety of handmade noodles. The beef noodle soup (牛肉面; *niúròu miàn*) is savoury and good, but you can't go wrong with any choice and it's all cheap. Bottomless refills of soup and raw garlic for accompaniment.

Wángjiě Shāokǎo ROAST GRILL $
(王姐烧烤; 113 Zhongshan Lu & Dexian Lu; skewers ¥2-12; ☺10am-9.30hpm) Qīngdǎo's famous meat skewers will require your undivided attention. Join the throng outside this streetside stand gorging on lamb (羊肉; *yángròu*), cuttlefish (鱿鱼; *yóuyú*) and chicken hearts (鸡心; *jīxīn*), and toss your spent skewers in the bucket. There's a sit-down restaurant around the corner.

Cafè Yum INTERNATIONAL $$$
(☐8388 3838, ext 6008; 9 Xianggang Zhonglu; buffet lunch/dinner ¥198/228; ☺noon-2.30pm & 6-9.30pm) This all-you-can-eat buffet in the swish Shangri-La Hotel is pricey but the spread is a glutton's paradise. Did we mention the all-you-can-drink beer? Reservations recommended.

The Canvas INTERNATIONAL $$
(☐8565 5688; 63B Zhangzhou Yilu; 漳州一路63号乙; meals from ¥48; ☺9am-midnight Sun-Thu, 9am-2am Fri & Sat) The owners' craving for al dente pasta inspired this stylish bistro in Hong Kong Garden. The pasta is great, but the burger with blue cheese, rocket and tomato (¥55) hits the spot. Decent wines from ¥30 per glass.

♟ Drinking & Entertainment

Qīngdǎo wouldn't be Qīngdǎo without Tsingtao, the beer that bears its name. The first stop for any committed tipplers should probably be the many drinking holes along **Beer Street** (啤酒街; Píjiǔ Jiē) where you can sample the delicious dark, unfiltered *yuánjiāng* (原浆啤酒), which is hard to find elsewhere. The youth hostel bars are pleasant, particularly **Mamahuhu Lounge** on the top of YHA Old Observatory and **Old Church Lounge** in Kǎiyuè Hostelling International. Check out *Red Star* (online or magazine racks in hostels and foreign restaurants) for the latest.

Club New York BAR
(纽约吧; Niǔyuē Bā; 2nd fl, 41 Xianggang Zhonglu; beer from ¥35; ⏰7pm-2am; 🚌208, 216) Despite the overpriced drinks, this expat favourite overflows with revellers and sports fans when there's a match on. There's a cover band most nights (9pm to 1am) and an incongruously classy sushi bar (5pm to 9pm, meals from ¥250) adjoining. Above the lobby of the Overseas Chinese International Hotel in Dōngbù.

Spark Café and Brewery BAR $$
(咖啡、酿酒厂; ☑8578 2296; Qingdao Beer Bldg, 35 Donghai Xilu Rd; 东海西路35号, 五四广场、青皮大厦; 🍺) Grab a seat on a long wooden bench in this crowded watering hole on the east edge of the Municipal Government square. There's all manner of drinks – beer (including the house 'dark' and 'light' microbrews at ¥35 a pint), cocktails, coffee, tea and milkshakes. For more than pizza and sausage platters (¥65 to ¥88), move next door to the sister restaurant.

☆ Entertainment

Broadway Cinemas CINEMA
(百老汇影城; Bǎilǎohuì Yǐngchéng; 88 Aomen Lu; 澳门路88号; tickets from ¥40) Domestic and Hollywood blockbusters on the 3rd floor of Marina City shopping mall, in the CBD. Half-price Tuesdays and Thursdays.

Qīngdǎo Grand Theatre THEATRE
(青岛大剧院; ☑8066 5555; www.qingdaograndtheatre.com; 5 Yunling Lu; 云岭路5号; 🚌230, 321) North of Shílǎorén in the Láo Shān district, the city's grand performing arts centre puts world-class theatre, music, dance, comedy and kiddie acts on its three stages. Check the website or www.qingdaonese.com for dates.

🛍 Shopping

Qīngdǎo's main shopping drags are in Dōngbù, around Xianggang Zhonglu, but there are plenty of places to spend.

Book City BOOKS
(书城; Shū Chéng; 67 Xianggang Zhonglu at Yan'erdao Lu; ⏰9am-7pm) Vast aisles of Chinese media and some in English.

Carrefour HYPERMART
(家乐福; Jiālèfú; ⏰8.30am-10pm) Massive general store at Nanjing Lu and Xianggang Zhonglu.

Culture Street ANTIQUES
(文化路; Wénhuà Lù; Changle Lu btwn Lijin Lu & Huayang Lu; ⏰8am-4pm) 'Antiques' and handicrafts sold in front of a tidy row of concession architecture north of Old Town.

Jímòlù Market MALL
(即墨路小商品市场; Jímòlù Xiǎoshàngpǐn Shìchǎng; 45 Liaocheng Lu; ⏰9am-5.30pm) A four-storey bargain bonanza north of Old Town. Pearls, purses, clothing, shoes, backpacks, jade, wigs for the haggling.

Jusco SUPERMARKET
(佳世客; Jiāshìkè; Xianggang Zhonglu; ⏰9am-11pm) Food court and supermarket at Fuzhou Nanlu and Xianggang Zhonglu.

Marina City MALL
(百丽广场; ☑6606 1177; 88 Aomen Rd; ⏰10am-10pm) International brands plus an ice rink.

Parkson MALL
(百盛; 44 Zhongshan Lu; ⏰9.30am-9pm) Multi-level shopping and a supermarket.

ℹ Information

Internet Access

Internet cafes (网吧) abound in the city and often are restricted to Chinese nationals or always require a passport. Hostels have terminals for use.

Hǎodú Wǎngbā (好读网吧; 2 Dagu Lu; per hr ¥2; ⏰24hr) Near the train station.

Yìjiéyù Wǎngbā (义杰玉网吧; 120 Zhangzhou Lu; per hr ¥2; ⏰24hr) In Hong Kong Garden, on the north end of the plaza.

Medical Services

Qīngdǎo Municipal Hospital, International Clinic (青岛市立医院国际门诊; Qīngdǎoshì Shìlì Yīyuàn, Guójì Ménzhěn; ☑International clinic 8593 7690, ext 2266; emergency 8278 9120; 5 Donghai Zhonglu; ⏰8am-noon & 1.30-5.30pm Mon-Sat)

BORDER CROSSING: JAPAN & SOUTH KOREA

International boats depart from Qīngdǎo's **passenger ferry terminal** (青岛港客运站; Qīngdǎogǎng kèyùnzhàn; ☑8282 5001; 6 Xinjiang Lu). **Orient Ferry** (☑389 7646; www.orientferry.co.jp; Haitian Hotel, 48 Xianggang Xilu) sells tickets for the twice-weekly boats to Shimonoseki, Japan (¥1100, 26 hours, 3.30pm Mon and Thu). **Weidong Ferry Company** (☑8280 3574; www.weidong.com; 4 Xinjiang Lu) operates boats regularly departing for South Korea, via Incheon (from ¥750, 17 hours, 5pm Mon, Wed and Fri) and Gunsan (¥920, 16 hours, 2.30pm Mon, Wed and Sat). Boats sail from Yāntái and Wēihǎi for Incheon.

Money

ATMs are easy to find in Qīngdǎo.

Bank of China (中国银行; Zhōngguó Yínháng; 66 & 68 Zhongshan Lu; ☺8.30am-5pm Mon-Fri, 9.30am-4pm Sat & Sun) On the corner of Feicheng Lu in Old Town. Also 59 Xianggang Zhonglu; ☺ 8.30am to 5pm; in the tower at the intersection of Fuzhou Nanlu in the CBD. Branches have currency exchange and 24-hour ATMs.

Post

China Post (中国邮政; Zhōngguó Yóuzhèng; 23-1 Taidong Yilu; ☺8.30am-6pm) On the west edge of Táidōng, north of Old Town. Also 119 Nanjing Lu; ☺9am-5pm Mon-Fri, 9am-4.30pm Sat & Sun; by the ICBC tower in the CBD.

Public Security Bureau

(PSB; 公安局; Gōng'ānjú; 272 Ningxia Lu; ☺9am-noon & 1.30-5pm Mon-Fri) Take bus 301 from the train station to the terracotta-coloured building (stop 14). Visa inquiries (出入境管理处); ☑6657 3250, ext 2860. The general police hotline is ☑6657 0000.

Tourist Information

Qīngdǎo Shì'nán tourist information centre (青岛市南旅游信息咨询中心; Qīngdǎo Shì'nán Lǚyóu Xìnxī Zīxún Zhōngxīn; ☑8287 2787; 56 Jiangning Lu) Free maps and travel info in Firewood Court.

Travel Agencies

China International Travel Service (CITS; 中国国际旅行社; Zhōngguó Guójì Lǚxíngshè; ☑8389 5022, booking hotline 400 600 8888; 33 Lianyungang Lu; 万达广场商务楼B座5层(连云港路33号); ☺8.30am-5pm Mon-Fri, 9am-4pm Sat & Sun) On 5th flr, Wanda Plaza, Bldg B in CBD.

Websites

Qingdaonese (www.qingdaonese.com) Listings and active forums.

Red Star (www.myredstar.com) Online entertainment guide and monthly magazine – pick it up in hostels, bars, foreign restaurants or at their offices at 100 Nanjing Lu, Creative 100 building in the CBD.

That's Qīngdǎo (www.thatsqingdao.com) Listings and news clips.

ⓘ Getting There & Away

A handy ticket office sells air, train and boat tickets in the ground floor of the **Tiānqiáo Hotel** (青岛新天桥兵官售票处; Qīngdǎo Xīn Tiānqiáo Bīngguǎn Shòupiàochù; ☑train 8612 0111, air & boat 8612 0222; 47 Feicheng Lu; ☺7.30am-9pm), near the train station.

Air

Qīngdǎo's **Liúting International Airport** (☑8471 5139, booking & flight status hotline 96567; www.qdairport.com) is 30km north of the city. There are flights to most large cities in China, including daily services to Běijīng (¥710, 1¼ hours), Shànghǎi (¥740, 1¼ hours) and Hong Kong (¥1220, three hours). International flights include daily flights to Seoul (¥570), Tokyo (¥1660) and four weekly flights to Osaka (¥1660).

Book tickets directly through the airport's hotline or airline offices (many are on Xianggang Zhonglu). These ticket offices book for no additional fee:

Civil Aviation Administration of China (CAAC; 中国民航; Zhōngguó Mínháng) Domestic (☑8289 5577; 29 Zhongshan Lu; ☺8am-5pm); Domestic & International (☑8578 2381, 8577 5555; 30 Xianggang Lu; ☺8am-5pm) Book domestic tickets in person to save yourself grief.

Dōngshēng Air Ticket Office (东升航空售票处; Dōngshēng Hángkōng Shòupiào Chù; ☑8069 0169; 140 Jiaozhou Lu; ☺8am-6pm) Below the KFC. Book by phone 24 hours.

Boat

Boats regularly depart for Dàlián across the bay from Yāntái (¥168 to ¥300, six to eight hours) or Wēihǎi (¥180 to ¥320, eight to 10 hours); tickets from CITS or Dōngshēng Air Ticket Office.

Bus

Among Qīngdǎo's many bus stations, the **long-distance bus station** (长途汽车站; chángtú qìchēzhàn; ☑400 691 6916; 2 Wenzhou Lu) in the Sìfāng (四方区) district, north of most tourist sights, best serves most travellers. A limited number of buses also depart for provincial destinations including Yāntái (¥81, four hours, every 20 to 30 minutes, 6am to 5.30pm) directly across from the train station.

Daily buses from the long-distance bus station:

Běijīng ¥195 to ¥230, nine hours, seven daily

Hángzhōu ¥310, 12 hours, four daily (10.45am, 11.30am, 6pm and 6.30pm)

Héféi ¥219, 10 hours, seven daily

Jǐ'nán ¥84 to ¥113, 4½ hours, every 30 minutes

Qūfù ¥127, six hours, four daily

Shànghǎi ¥200 to ¥286, 11 hours, six daily

Tài'ān ¥116 to ¥125, six hours, six daily

Wēihǎi ¥94, 3½ hours, hourly

Yāntái ¥67, four hours, every 30 minutes

Train

All trains from Qīngdǎo pass through Jǐ'nán except the direct Qīngdǎo to Yāntái and Wēihǎi trains. Buy tickets at the **train station** (☑9510 5175; 2 Tai'an Lu), which has a hectic 24-hour ticket office on the east side (bring your passport). Booking offices around town collect a service charge, typically ¥5. Tickets sell out quickly so buy early.

Regular trains (seat/hard sleeper):

Běijīng ¥113/209, 13½ hours, one daily (12.42pm)

Jǐ'nán seat ¥28 to ¥65, hard sleeper ¥67 to ¥109, 4½ to six hours, regularly

Qūfù ¥32/74, eight hours, one daily (7.28am)

Tài'shān ¥70/131, five to seven hours, 11 daily

Xī'ān ¥191/345, 21 to 24 hours, three daily (9.45am, 11.12am and 1.42pm)

Yāntái ¥22/71, four hours, one daily (6.15am)

Zhèngzhōu seat ¥123 to ¥140, hard sleeper ¥249 to ¥257, 13½ to 16 hours, six daily

Except where noted, express D (hard/soft seat only) trains (G trains also available) regularly depart for:

Běijīng ¥253/303, five to 5½ hours, six daily

Jǐ'nán ¥121/146, 2½ to three hours, hourly

Qūfù ¥239/407, three hours, one daily (1.55pm)

Shànghǎi G train ¥596/1014, 6½ hours, four daily (6.55am, 9.26am, 1.55pm and 4.35pm)

Tài'ān ¥207/353, three hours, one daily (6.55am)

ⓘ Getting Around

To/From the Airport

Bright blue **airport shuttles** (机场巴士; Jīchǎng Bāshì; ☑8286 0977; ¥20) follow three routes through town. Shuttles leave hourly from the **Green Tree Inn** (77 Zhongshan Lu) in Old Town from 5.40am to 7.40pm, and every half-hour from **Haitian Hotel** (48 Xianggang Xilu) near No 3 Bathing Beach from 6am to 8pm and the CBD's

Century Mandarin Hotel (10 Haijiang Lu) from 6.10am to 5.45pm. A taxi to/from Shìnán district is ¥80 to ¥100.

Public Transport

From the train station, buses 26 and 501 head east past Zhōngshān Park and continue north on Nanjing Lu and east along Xianggang Lu, respectively. From the long-distance bus station, buses 221 and 366 go to Old Town and Dōngbù, respectively. Bus 5 connects the long-distance bus and train stations. Most city buses cost ¥1 to ¥2, but onboard conductors issue tickets for further destinations. Plan your trip with www. qdjyjt.com, in Chinese.

Outside the train station, red double-decker **sightseeing buses** (unlimited ¥30, per stop ¥10; hourly) head to all the biggies: bus 1 passes sights along the water going east to Láo Shān from 9am to 3pm, last return at 5pm. Bus 3 swings by Firewood Court, Beer Street, Culture Street and Táidōng from 7pm onward. Bus 2 (¥15) goes to Huángdǎo district.

The highly anticipated underground metro, scheduled to open in late 2014, will hopefully ease Qīngdǎo's gridlock.

Taxi

Flag fall is ¥9 or ¥12 for the first 6km and then ¥2.10 (slightly more at night) per kilometre thereafter, plus a ¥1 fuel surcharge. If your driver takes detours, it's because many city streets are restricted from 7am to 10pm.

Láo Shān   崂山

A short ride from Qīngdǎo, an arresting jumble of sun-bleached granite and hidden freshwater springs rises over the sea. It's easy to understand why Láo Shān has attracted spiritual seekers throughout the centuries.

In his quest for immortality, Emperor Qin Shi Huang ascended these slopes (with the help of a litter party of course), and the Buddhist pilgrim Faxian landed here upon returning from India in the 5th century with the first set of Buddhist scriptures. Láo Shān has its share of religious sites, but it is most steeped in Taoist tradition. Adepts of the Quanzhen sect, founded near Yāntái in the 12th century, cultivated themselves in hermitages scattered all over the mountain.

Paths wind past ancient temples (and ruins), bubbling springs trickling into azure pools, and inscriptions left by Chinese poets and German alpinists. For the most part, routes are paved but there are plenty of opportunities to off-road as well (look for red flags tied to branches marking trails).

The loop through **Běijiǔshuǐ Scenic Area** (北九水景区; admission peak ¥95, off-peak ¥70) on the north end of the park is mostly flat and takes a couple of hours. The path winds besides and across limpid waters before reaching **Cháoyīn Waterfall** (潮音瀑), which in the wet season roars like the ocean tide. (In drier months, the water falls in pieces, hence its ancient name, Fish Scales Waterfall.)

To the south, the picturesque hike to **Jùfēng** (巨峰; admission peak ¥95, off-peak ¥65), the highest point at 1133m above sea level, can start with a **cable car** (suǒ dào; one way/return ¥40/80) partway up the mountain. From there, it takes another four hours to hike up steps past temples and a spring to the stone terrace at the peak for awe-inspiring views of mountains, sky and sea.

On the east side, the **Yǎngkǒu Scenic Area** (仰口景区; admission Apr-Oct ¥130, Nov-Mar ¥100, includes admission to Tàiqīng Palace) offers an opportunity to ascend by foot or **cable car** (one way ¥60) past wind- and water-carved granite. There's a 30m scramble in total darkness up a crevice to the top of **Looking for Heaven Cave** (觅天洞) and then upward still for views of the sea. The hike takes about three hours.

Of Láo Shān's temples, **Tàiqīng Palace** (太清宫; Tàiqīng Gōng; admission ¥20 or included with Yǎngkǒu ticket; ⊙closes 5.30pm) is the oldest and grandest, established by the first Song emperor around AD 960 to perform Taoist rites to protect the souls of the dead. Devotees in blue and white still live here, and many credit their good health to drinking from the **Spring of the Immortals** (神水泉), which feeds into the grounds. The massive, hoary gingkoes, cedars and cypress trees apparently also benefit.

If you want to extend your stay, pick-your-own seafood restaurants and a range of guesthouses line the main road hugging the coast. The Yǎngkǒu branch of the **Qingdao Old Observatory Youth Hostel** (仰口度假酒店; ☑0532 8282 2626; dm ¥50, r with private bath ¥168-268) overlooks a picturesque fishing village and organises off-trail day trips into the park. To the south in Liúqīnghé, **Bàoyúdǎo Hotel** (崂山流清河鲍鱼岛酒店; ☑8882 0333; r ¥398) has a handful of simple rooms above an excellent seafood restaurant.

From Qīngdǎo, catch red sightseeing bus 2 (¥10) by the train station or bus 304 (¥7, one hour, from 6.30am) from the Zhàn Qiáo stop by No 6 Bathing Beach. The ride ends at the Dàhédòng Tourist Service Center on the park's south end, where you can pay admission and catch a park bus (included with ticket). Private cars aren't allowed within park boundaries. Tour buses to Láo Shān (around ¥40 return, excluding entrance fees) ply Qīngdǎo's streets from 6am onwards but stop at 'sights' on the way to the mountain and back.

Yāntái 烟台

☑ 0535 / POP 878,981

The sleepy portside town of Yāntái somehow has one of the fastest-developing economies in China – no small feat in a country of exponential growth. It managed to court foreign investment in its high-tech industry while building itself into a popular beach resort. A new tunnel connects the old district of Zhīfú with the developing Láishān district to the southeast. With Pénglái Pavilion not far away, the town makes for a relaxing two-day sojourn.

History

Starting life as a defence outpost and fishing village, Yāntái's name literally means 'Smoke Terrace'; wolf-dung fires were lit on the headlands during the Ming dynasty to warn villagers of Japanese marauders. Yāntái was thrust under the international spotlight in the late 19th century when the Qing government, reeling from defeat in the Opium War, surrendered it to the British. The British established a treaty port here and named it Chefoo (Zhīfú). The eight national alliance of Austria-Hungary, France, Germany, Italy, Japan, Russia, the UK and the USA set up trading establishments and the town became a resort area.

⊙ Sights

Yāntái Hill Park PARK
(烟台山公园; Yāntáishān Gōngyuán; admission ¥30; ⊙7am-6pm) This quaint park of stone paths, leafy gardens and ocean vistas is also a museum of Western treaty port architecture. The former **American Consulate Building** retains some original interior features and contains an exhibit on Yāntái's port days. Nearby, the former **Yāntái Union Church** dates from 1875, and now serves as the office for a wedding-planning company. The former **British Consulate** overlooks the bay with its **Annexe** surrounded by an overgrown English garden. At the top of the hill is the Ming-dynasty **Dragon King Temple**, which in 1860

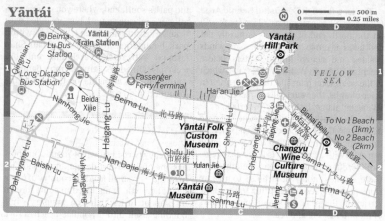

Yāntái

◎ Top Sights

Changyu Wine Culture Museum D2
Yāntái Folk Custom Museum C2
Yāntái Hill Park C1
Yāntái Museum C2

◎ Sights

1 Amber Coastal City Walk.................. D2

◎ Sleeping

2 Golden Gulf Hotel............................ C1
3 Karen Bayview Hotel........................ C1
4 Shandong Machinery Hotel.............. D2
5 Waitinn A1

◎ Eating

6 Brazil Barbecue C1
7 Parkson... A2
8 Shìdè Wū C1

◎ Information

9 Yāntáishān Hospital C2

◎ Transport

China Travel Service .... (see 1)
10 Shāndōng Airlines B2
11 Yāntái International Airport
    Group Air Travel Agency A1

was co-opted as military headquarters for French troops. Wolf-dung fires burned continuously along the smoke terrace above, beginning in the 14th-century reign of Emperor Hongwu. Behind the temple, the **lighthouse** (admission ¥5) houses a maritime museum in progress at the time of writing. In the west of the park, the 1930s-built **Japanese Consulate** is an austere brick structure with a 'torture inquisition room'.

FREE **Yāntái Folk Custom Museum** MUSEUM (烟台民俗博物馆; Yāntái Mínsú Bówùguǎn; 2 Yulan Jie; ⏱8.30-11.30am & 1.30-4.30pm) About 200m east of the Yāntái Museum stands this museum housed in a guild hall constructed between 1884 and 1906 by arrivals from Fújiàn. In the centre of the courtyard is a spectacularly intricate, decorated gate. Supported by 22 pillars, the portal is adorned

with hundreds of carved and painted figures, flowers, beasts, phoenixes and animals depicting folk legends, including *The Eight Immortals Crossing the Sea*. In the **Hall of Heavenly Goddess**, Tianhou the patron of seafarers is surrounded by a set of tin instruments in the shapes of gourds and tiny mice, crawling dragons and dragon heads.

FREE **Yāntái Museum** MUSEUM (烟台市博物馆; Yāntái Shì Bówùguǎn; ☑623 2976; 61 Nan Dajie; ⏱9am-4pm, closed Mon) The sparkling new museum traces the historical development of the Jiāodōng peninsula, where Yāntái currently stands, from the prehistoric age and successive kingdoms to the present. There's a display on the Shell Mound culture (a glimpse at a Neolithic civilisation's trash) and a wonderful collection of rare porcelain. English descriptions.

Changyu Wine Culture Museum MUSEUM
(张裕酒文化博物馆; Zhāngyù Jiǔwénhuà Bówùguǎn; 56 Dama Lu; admission ¥50; ⊙8am-5.30pm) The unexpected Changyu Wine Culture Museum introduces the history of China's oldest and largest Western-style winery, which produces grape wines as well as brandy and a Chinese 'health liquor'. Cheong Fatt-Tze, dubbed 'China's Rockfeller' by the *New York Times*, founded the winery in 1894, supposedly after overhearing that the Yāntái climate might grow good grapes at a party at the French Consulate. Tastings of the (mostly so-so) wines are in the old wine cellar and included in admission.

Beaches BEACHES
Yāntái has two main beaches, **No 1 Beach** (第一海水浴场; Dìyī Hǎishuǐ Yùchǎng), a long stretch of soft sand in a calm bay, is much nicer than **No 2 Beach** (第二海水浴场; Dì'èr Hǎishuǐ Yùchǎng), which is less crowded but more polluted. Bus 17 passes both.

Amber Coastal City Walk HISTORIC AREA
(广仁步行街; Guǎng Rén Búxíngjiē) East of the Changyu Wine Culture Museum is an attractive (but rather soulless) cluster of restored concession buildings, housing a variety of restaurants, clubs and bars.

🛏 Sleeping

Many hotels are clustered around the train and bus stations where it's noisy and dull. It's much more pleasant staying around the charming northern end of Chaoyang Jie.

Golden Gulf Hotel HOTEL $$$
(金海湾酒店; Jīnhǎiwān Jiǔdiàn; ☑663 6999; fax 663 2699; 34 Haian Lu; 海安路34号; s/d incl breakfast ¥920-1200; ✳@) The city's first five-star has a superb sea and parkside location and bright, well-maintained rooms. Barbecue on the seaside patio in the evenings.

Karen Bayview Hotel HOTEL $$
(凯琳海景酒店; Kǎilín Hǎijǐng Jiǔdiàn; ☑622 6600; 30 Dongtaiping Jie; 东太平街30号; s/d ¥160/260; ✳@) Jutting out at a striking angle to allow a few rooms a view of the bay, this hotel also has its share of drab, windowless rooms. Sea-view rooms are the same price but come with clean carpets, new furniture and a better floorplan.

Shandong Machinery Hotel HOTEL $$
(山东机械宾馆; Shāndōng Jīxiè Bīnguǎn; ☑621 6469; 162 Jiefang Lu; s/d ¥320-480, ste ¥580; ✳@) With a Korean, Japanese and Cantonese restaurant, and an Asiana Airlines office on the premises, staff here know how to cater to non-Mandarin–speaking guests. The Asian-decor rooms have nicer details (wooden soaking tubs) than the Western-style ones, but all are comfy. Discounts up to 70% make this a bargain.

Waitinn HOTEL $
(维特风尚酒店; Wéitè Fēngshàng Jiǔdiàn; ☑212 0909; 73 Beima Lu; tw & d ¥88-228, tr ¥258; ✳@) Opposite the train station, this refurbished hotel is a good place to, as it were, wait in. Rooms are large, comfortable and equipped with flat-screen TVs. Add breakfast for ¥8 and ask for a discount, up to 20%.

🍴 Eating & Drinking

South of Yāntái Hill Park, the pedestrian streets Chaoyang Jie and Hai'an Jie have a range of bars, cafes and even an Irish pub, though outside of summer some places are closed. The area surrounding the train station also has plenty of options, including late night joints dishing up noodle soups (拉面) for ¥15. There's a small strip of street food stalls on the east side of the **Parkson** (☑6293322; 166 Nan Dajie, near Qingnian Lu, ⊙9am-8pm) in the heart of the shopping district. If you crave tablecloths, the Korean, Latin and Chinese restaurants in the

---

MAKING COPIES

For millennia, everything from imperial decrees to poetry, religious scriptures and maps were preserved by carving them into stone. This was done either as an inscription (yin-style) or a relief (yang-style). Copies could then be made by applying ink to the stone and pressing rice paper onto it, or by tamping a damp sheet of paper into the crevices and allowing it to dry, before patting ink onto the paper's surface. Over time, even stone would wear and the clearest, best-made prints became works of art themselves. Unfortunately, this prompted unscrupulous collectors to damage carvings to ensure they had the very best copy. These are the gouges and scratches you see in many of the most prized tablets and stelae.

Crowne Plaza (☑689 9999; Gangcheng Donglu) may be worth the 50-minute ride to Láishān district. Take bus 50 (¥2) or a taxi (¥50) from the town centre.

Shìdé Wū   JAPANESE $$

(食德屋; Shídé Wū; ☑621 6676; 23 Hai'an Jie; meals ¥120; ⏰lunch & dinner 11am-1pm & 5-9.30pm) Chef Hao lived in Japan for a decade before opening up this place with his wife. Now it's a popular spot for sashimi (from ¥38), fried pork cutlets (¥30), and udon and ramen (¥25 to ¥36). The soothing wood decor balances out the Japanese TV turned up full blast.

Brazil Barbecue   BARBECUE $$

(巴西烤肉主题餐厅; Bāxī Kǎoròu Zhǔtí Cāntīng; ☑661 0185; 23 Hai'an Jie; buffet ¥58; ⏰11.30am-2pm & 5.30am-9pm) The Chinese take on Brazilian *churrascaria* (barbecue) includes pork seasoned with garlic, sliced beef tongue and chicken giblets. The accompanying all-you-can-eat buffet has everything from French fries to scallops in the shell. Staff offering grilled meats come round once, so don't feel shy to call out for more.

Information

There are numerous internet cafes (网吧; *wǎngbā*) along Chaoyang Jie, south of Yāntái Hill Park, and across from the train station on Beima Lu (from ¥2 per hour). Many are restricted to Chinese nationals or always require a passport.

Bank of China (中国银行; Zhōngguó Yínháng; 166 Jiefang Lu) ATM accepts all cards. Full-service branch at Beima Lu and Dahaiyang Lu opens from 8.30am to 4.20pm.

China International Travel Service (CITS; 中国国际旅行社; Zhōngguó Guójì Lǚxíngshè; ☑626123; 180 Jiefang Lu; ⏰9-11.30am & 2-5.30pm) Guided Chinese day tours to Wēihǎi (from ¥170) and Pénglái (from ¥220). Ticket bookings including the boat (¥30 per ticket).

China Post (中国邮政; Zhōngguó Yóuzhèng; Beima Lu & Dahaiyang Lu, across from the train station) Another branch is at 28 Hai'an Jie.

China Travel Service (中国旅行社总社; ☑668 8777; 26 Guangren Lu; ⏰8.30am-5.30pm) In Amber Coastal City Walk. Books tours and tickets including boat.

Public Security Bureau (PSB; 公安局; Gōng'ānjú; ☑629 7050; 78 Shifu Jie; ⏰8-11.30am & 2-5.30pm Mon-Sat) On the corner of Chaoyang Jie. **Entry-exit visas** (出入境管理处; ☑629 7050; 7 Chang'an Jie; 长安路7号; ⏰8.30-11.30am & 2-5.30pm Mon-Sat) are available in Láishān district.

Yāntáishān Hospital (烟台山医院; Yāntáishān Yīyuàn; ☑660 2001; 91 Jiefang Lu)

WORTH A TRIP

PÉNGLÁI PAVILION

About 75km northwest of Yāntái perched on a bluff overlooking the waves, the 1000-year-old **Pénglái Pavilion** (蓬莱阁; Pénglái Gé; admission ¥140; ⏰7am-5.30pm summer, to 5pm winter) is closely entwined with Chinese mythology and the Taoist legend of the *Eight Immortals Crossing the Sea*.

The route up to the pavilion passes the grounds of an ancient naval base and a series of temples. The pavilion itself is unassuming as its restored exterior is rather similar to surrounding structures. Inside is a collection of prized inscriptions left by famous visitors since the Song dynasty, and a beautiful modern rendering of the *Eight Immortals*, by Zhou Jinyun. There are many versions of the story, but in this one the immortals, who came from different walks of life, shared drinks at the pavilion before crossing the Bo Sea using unique superpowers.

After the pavilion, zip across the bay by **cable car** (¥30/50 return, 8am to 5.10pm) for cliffside walks overlooking the Bo and Yellow Seas. There are also museums (open 7.30am to 5.30pm) dedicated to ancient shipbuilding, regional relics and Qi Jiguang, a Ming-dynasty general who battled pirates.

If you arrive after a heavy rain, keep an eye on the marine layer where mirages appear every few years. Long ago, this earned Pénglái a reputation as a gateway to immortal lands and compelled Emperor Qin Shi Huang to send ships in search of islands of immortality further east.

Pénglái is an easy day trip by bus from Yāntái (¥24, 1½ hours, every 20 minutes, 5.30am to 6pm), with the last returning at 7.45pm. The bus station (166 Zhonglou Beilu) is a 15-minute walk to the park. Taxi drivers will go for ¥7 but sometimes stop elsewhere first.

BORDER CROSSING: SOUTH KOREA

International boats depart from Yāntái's **passenger ferry terminal** (烟台港客运站; Yāntáigǎng kèyùnzhàn; ☏624 2715; 155 Beima Lu) for Incheon (from ¥960, 16 hours, 5pm Mon, Wed and Fri) in South Korea. **Weidong Ferry Company** (www.weidong.com) Incheon (☏8232 777 0490; International Passenger Terminal, 71-2 Hang-dong); Seoul (☏822 3271 6710; 10th fl, 1005 Sungji Bldg, 585 Dohwa-dong, Mapo-gu) also operates boats to Incheon (deluxe/1st/2nd/economy ¥1370/1090/890/750, 15 hours, 5pm Tue, Thur and Sun). From Wēihǎi, buy at the **ticket office** (☏522 6173; 48 Haibin Beilu) south of the passenger ferry terminal (威海港客运码头; Wēihǎigǎng kèyùnmǎtóu). Boats also sail from Qīngdǎo for Incheon and Gunsan.

 Getting There & Away

Air

Yāntái **Láishān International Airport** (☏624 1330) is 20km south of town. Book tickets near the train station at **Yāntái International Airport Group Air Travel Agency** (航空国际旅行有限公司; Yāntái Gúojì Lǚxiàngshè Yǒuxiàngōngsī; ☏625 3777; 6 Dahaiyang Lu; ◷8am-5.30pm); the Civil Aviation Hotel **ticket centre** (烟台国际机场售票中心; Yāntái Guójì Jīchǎng Shòupiào Zhōngxīn; ☏658 3366; 78 Dahaiyang Lu; 大海阳路78号); or **Shāndōng Airlines** (山东航空公司; Shāndōng Hángkōng; ☏662 2737; 236 Nan Dajie, Bihai Dàshà; ◷8.30am-5.30pm) in the Bihai Hotel.

There are regular flights to Běijīng (¥690, one hour), Shànghǎi (¥790, 1½ hours), Guǎngzhōu (¥1930, three hours), Seoul (¥1116, one hour) and Osaka (¥2388, 1½ hours).

Boat

Purchase tickets for fast boats to Dàlián (seat ¥160, bed ¥200 to ¥800, six to seven hours, 9am, 10am, 12.30pm, 3.30pm, 8.30pm and 10pm) at the **Yāntái Harbour passenger transit terminal** (烟台港客运站; Yāntáigǎng Kèyùnzhàn; ☏650 6666; www.bohaiferry.com; 155 Beima Lu) or from numerous ticket offices east of the train station.

Bus

Minibuses to Pénglái (¥24, 1½ hours, 5.15am to 6.30pm) depart every 20 minutes from **Beima Lu bus station** (北马路汽车站; Běimǎlù qìchē zhàn; ☏665 8714; cnr Beima Lu & Qingnian Lu).

From the **long-distance main bus station** (长途总汽车站; chángtú zǒng qìchē zhàn; ☏666 6111; cnr Xi Dajie & Qingnian Lu;) there are buses to numerous destinations:

Běijīng ¥246, 13 hours, one daily (3pm)

Jǐ'nán ¥175, 5½ hours, hourly

Qīngdǎo ¥85, four hours, every 30 minutes

Shànghǎi ¥320, 12 hours, one daily (5pm), every other day (8.15pm)

Tiānjīn ¥184, 11 hours, one daily (7.30pm), every other day (10am)

Wēihǎi ¥25 to ¥31, one hour, hourly

Train

Trains from **Yāntái Train Station** (火车站; huǒchēzhàn; Beima Lu):

Běijīng hard seat/soft sleeper ¥130/365, 13½ hours, one daily (11.25pm)

Jǐ'nán hard seat/soft sleeper ¥76/215, 7½ hours, eight daily

Qīngdǎo hard/soft seat ¥22/31, 4½ hours, one daily (2.58pm)

Shànghǎi hard seat/soft sleeper ¥182/511, 20½ hours, one daily (9.40am)

Xī'ān hard seat/soft sleeper ¥200/554, 24 hours, one daily (3.30pm)

 Getting Around

Airport shuttles (机场巴士; ☏1510 659 0123, 666 6111; ¥10) depart from the long-distance main bus station from 6am to 7.30pm, and the Civil Aviation Hotel at 78 Dahaiyang Lu and Xinshi Nanlu from 6.15am to 8pm. Bus 17 connects the city's two beaches. Buses 10 and 50 connect Zhīfú and Láishān district's main streets.

Taxi flag fall is ¥7 or ¥8 for the first 6km and ¥2.25 (slightly more at night) per kilometre thereafter.

Shànghǎi

♩021 / POP 23 MILLION

Includes »

Sights 177
Courses 198
Tours 198
Festivals & Events 199
Sleeping 199
Eating 205
Drinking 209
Entertainment 211
Shopping 213
Getting There & Away ... 217
Around Shànghǎi 220

Best Places to Eat

» Huanghe Rd food street (p205)

» Yīn (p206)

» Din Tai Fung (p206)

» Lost Heaven (p205)

» Fu 1039 (p208)

Best Places to Stay

» Fairmont Peace Hotel (p200)

» Urbn (p203)

» Ritz-Carlton Shanghai Pudong (p204)

» Magnolia Bed & Breakfast (p203)

» Le Tour Traveler's Rest Youth Hostel (p204)

Why Go?

You can't see the Great Wall from space, but you'd have a job missing Shànghǎi (上海). One of the country's largest and most vibrant cities, Shànghǎi somehow typifies modern China while being unlike anywhere else in the land. Shànghǎi *is* real China, but – rather like Hong Kong or Macau – just not the China you had in mind.

This is a city of action, not ideas. You won't spot many Buddhist monks contemplating the dharma, oddball bohemians or wild-haired poets handing out flyers, but skyscrapers will form before your eyes. Shànghǎi is best seen as an epilogue to your China experience: submit to its debutante charms after you've had your fill of dusty imperial palaces and bumpy 10-hour bus rides. From nonstop shopping to skyscraper-hopping to bullet-fast Maglev trains and glamorous cocktails – this is Shànghǎi.

When to Go
Shànghǎi

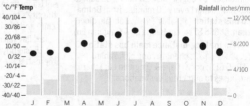

Feb Visit Yùyuán Gardens for the lantern festival, two weeks after Chinese New Year.

Apr & May March is chilly and 1 May is chaos, but otherwise spring is ideal.

Oct The optimal season: neither too hot nor too rainy.

History

As the gateway to the Yangzi River (Cháng Jiāng), Shànghǎi (the name means 'by the sea') has long been an ideal trading port. However, although it supported as many as 50,000 residents by the late 17th century, it wasn't until after the British opened their concession here in 1842 that modern Shànghǎi really came into being.

The British presence in Shànghǎi was soon followed by the French and Americans, and by 1853 Shànghǎi had overtaken all other Chinese ports. Built on the trade of opium, silk and tea, the city also lured the world's great houses of finance, which erected grand palaces of plenty. Shànghǎi also became a byword for exploitation and vice; its countless opium dens, gambling joints and brothels managed by gangs were at the heart of Shànghǎi life. Guarding it all were the American, French and Italian marines, British Tommies and Japanese bluejackets.

After Chiang Kaishek's coup against the communists in 1927, the Kuomintang cooperated with the foreign police and the Shànghǎi gangs, and with Chinese and foreign factory owners, to suppress labour unrest. Exploited in workhouse conditions, crippled by hunger and poverty, sold into slavery, excluded from the high life and the parks created by the foreigners, the poor of Shànghǎi had a voracious appetite for radical opinion. The Chinese Communist Party (CCP) was formed here in 1921 and, after numerous setbacks, 'liberated' the city in 1949.

The communists eradicated the slums, rehabilitated the city's hundreds of thousands of opium addicts, and eliminated child and slave labour. These were staggering achievements; but when the decadence went, so did the splendour. Shànghǎi became a colourless factory town and political hotbed, and was the power base of the infamous Gang of Four during the Cultural Revolution.

Shànghǎi's long slumber came to an abrupt end in 1990, with the announcement of plans to develop Pǔdōng, on the eastern side of the Huángpǔ River. Since then Shànghǎi's burgeoning economy, leadership and intrinsic self-confidence have put it miles ahead of other Chinese cities. Its bright lights and opportunities have branded Shànghǎi a mecca for Chinese (and foreign) economic migrants. In 2010, 3600 people squeezed into every square kilometre, compared with 2588 per sq km in 2000 as the city's population leaped to a staggering 23 million. Around nine million migrants live in Shànghǎi, colouring the local complexion with a jumble of dialects, outlooks, lifestyles and cuisines.

Language

Spoken by more than 13 million people, the Shanghainese dialect (Shànghǎihuà in Mandarin) belongs to the Wú dialect. Due to the spread of Mandarin and the absence of a standard form of Shanghainese, fewer and fewer young people are able to speak it properly.

Climate

Shànghǎi's winters are cold and damp while summers are hot, humid and sapping, with sudden epic rains. Try to catch the weather in between: April to mid-May is probably the best time to visit, along with autumn (late September to mid-November).

◉ Sights

Shànghǎi municipality covers a vast area, but the city proper is more modest. Broadly, central Shànghǎi is divided into two areas: Pǔxī (west of the Huángpǔ River) and Pǔdōng (east of the Huángpǔ River). The historical attractions and charm are in Pǔxī, where Shànghǎi's personality lives: the Bund (officially called East Zhongshan No 1 Rd) and the former foreign concessions, the principal shopping districts, and Shànghǎi's trendiest clusters of bars, restaurants and nightclubs. Pǔdōng – the location of the financial district and the famous Shànghǎi skyline – is a very recent creation, with sights falling in the observation deck/skyscraping towers/museums arena.

The last entrance to many Shànghǎi museums is one hour before closing.

PRICE INDICATORS

The following price indicators are used in this chapter:

Sleeping

$	less than ¥500
$$	¥500 to ¥1300
$$$	more than ¥1300

Eating
(based on meal)

$	less than ¥60
$$	¥60 to ¥160
$$$	more than ¥160

Shànghǎi Highlights

1 Stroll down the **Bund** promenade (p180) or raise a glass to the Pǔdōng lights

2 Contemplate the masterpieces of traditional Chinese art in the **Shànghǎi Museum** (p181)

3 Admire the curvature of the earth from atop the **Shànghǎi World Financial Center** (p194)

4 Treat your taste buds: from fusion cuisine to Sichuanese peppercorns, **French Concession restaurants** (p206) have you covered

5 Delve into the old alleyways and quirky boutiques at **Tiánzǐfáng** (p191)

6 Put on your best shoes and step out into the **Shànghǎi night** (p211)

7 Bargain hunt for faux antiques and tailormade clothes in the **Old Town** (p209)

8 Test your aesthetic boundaries with the latest in Chinese art at **M50** (p192)

9 Escape the big city for the canal-town vistas of **Zhūjiājiǎo** (p220)

10 Find yourself a quiet pocket and sit down within the **Yùyuán Gardens** (p185)

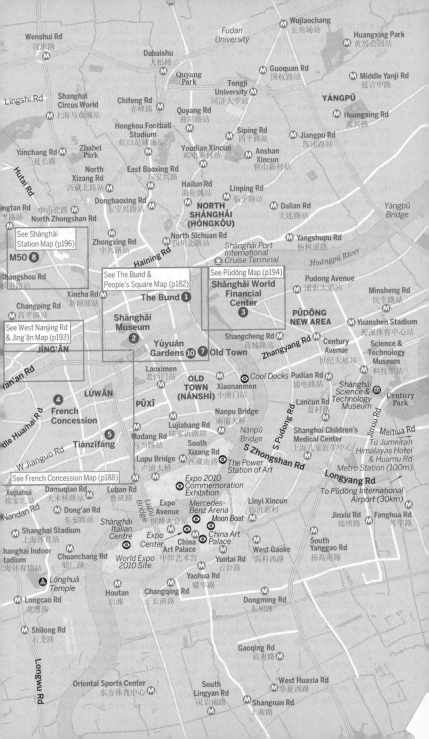

THE BUND 外滩

The area around the Bund is the tourist centre of Shànghǎi and is the city's most famous mile.

The Bund ARCHITECTURE

Symbolic of colonial Shànghǎi, the **Bund** (Wàitān; Map p182) was the city's Wall St, a place of feverish trading and fortunes made and lost. Coming to Shànghǎi and missing the Bund is like visiting Běijīng and bypassing the Forbidden City or the Great Wall. Originally a towpath for dragging barges of rice, the Bund (an Anglo-Indian term for the embankment of a muddy waterfront) was gradually transformed into a grandiose sweep of the most powerful banks and trading houses in Shànghǎi. The majority of art deco and neoclassical buildings here were built in the early 20th century and presented an imposing – if strikingly un-Chinese – view for those arriving in the busy port.

Today it has emerged as a designer retail and restaurant zone, and the city's most exclusive boutiques, restaurants and hotels see the Bund as the only place to be. The optimum activity here is to simply stroll, contrasting the bones of the past with the futuristic geometry of Pǔdōng's skyline. Evening visits are rewarded by electric views of Pǔdōng and the illuminated grandeur of the Bund. Other options include taking a boat tour on the Huángpǔ River or relaxing at some fabulous bars and restaurants. Huángpǔ Park, at the north end of the promenade, features the modest **Bund History Museum** (外滩历史纪念馆; Wàitān Lìshǐ Jìniànguǎn; Map p182; admission free; ⊗9am-4pm Mon-Fri), which contains a collection of old photographs and maps. See the illustrated highlight (p186) for a rundown of the area's most famous buildings.

East Nanjing Rd ARCHITECTURE

Once known as Nanking Rd, East Nanjing Rd (南京东路; Map p182) was where the first department stores in China were opened in the 1920s, and where the modern era – with its new products and the promise of a radically different lifestyle – was ushered in. A glowing forest of neon at night, it's no longer the cream of Shànghǎi shopping, but it's still one of the most famous and crowded streets in China. Shànghǎi's reputation as the country's most fashionable city was forged in part here, through the new styles and trends introduced in department stores such as the Sun Sun (1926), today the

Shànghǎi No 1 (First) Food Store (p213), and the Sun Company (1936), now the **Shànghǎi No 1 Department Store** (上海第一百货商店; Shànghǎi Dìyī Bǎihuò Shāngdiàn; Map p182; 800 East Nanjing Rd; Ⓜ People's Square).

Guard against English-speaking Chinese women and students shanghaiing you towards extortionate 'tea ceremonies'.

Rockbund Art Museum MUSEUM

(上海外滩美术馆; Shànghǎi Wàitān Měishùguǎn; Map p182; www.rockbundartmuseum.org; 20 Huqiu Rd; 虎丘路20号; adult ¥15; ⊗10am-6pm Tue-Sun; Ⓜ East Nanjing Rd) Housed in the former Royal Asiatic Society building (1933), this private museum behind the Bund focuses on contemporary art, with rotating exhibits year-round. Opened in 2010 to mark the opening of the Rockbund (north Bund) renovation project – funded by the Rockefeller Group – the museum has since become one of the city's top modern-art venues.

In addition to the art museum, there are a number of other architectural gems in this area that are part of the project, including the **former British Consulate**, which can be accessed at the Bund's northern tip. The most extensively renovated section is along **Yuanmingyuan Rd** (圆明园路), a magnet for the latest crop of high-profile restaurants and luxury brands to come to Shànghǎi. Additional landmark buildings in the area are slated for redevelopment, including the wonderful curved facade of the art deco Capitol Theatre (1928), at the north end of Huqiu Rd.

FREE Shànghǎi Post Museum MUSEUM

(上海邮政博物馆; Shànghǎi Yóuzhèng Bówùguǎn; Map p182; 250 North Suzhou Rd; 北苏州路250号; ⊗9am-5pm Wed, Thu, Sat & Sun; Ⓜ Tiantong Rd) It may sound like a yawner, but this is actually a pretty good museum, where you can learn about postal history in imperial China and view rare pre- and post-Liberation stamps (1888–1978). It's located in a magnificent 1924 post office, with panoramic views from the rooftop garden (garden closed at time of writing).

Bund Sightseeing Tunnel TUNNEL

(外滩观光隧道; Wàitān Guānguāng Suìdào; Map p182; The Bund; one way/return ¥50/60; ⊗8am-10pm; Ⓜ East Nanjing Rd) The weirdest way to get to Pǔdōng, where train modules convey speechless passengers through a tunnel of garish lights between the Bund and the opposite shore. The entrance is behind the Tourist Information & Service Centre.

SHÀNGHĂI IN...

One Day

Rise with the sun for early morning riverside scenes on **the Bund** as the vast city stirs from its slumber. Then stroll down East Nanjing Rd to **People's Sq** and either the **Shànghăi Museum** or the **Shànghăi Urban Planning Exhibition Hall**. After a dumpling lunch on Huanghe Rd food street, hop on the metro at People's Sq to shuttle east to Pŭdōng. Explore the fun and interactive **Shànghăi History Museum** or contemplate the Bund from the breezy Riverside Promenade, then take a high-speed lift to the world's highest observation deck, in the **Shànghăi World Financial Center**, to put Shànghăi in perspective. Stomach rumbling? Time for dinner in the French Concession, followed by a nightcap on the Bund if you want to go full circle.

Two Days

Beat the crowds with an early start at the Old Town's **Yùyuán Gardens** before poking around for souvenirs on Old St and wandering the alleyways. Make your next stop **Xīntiāndì** for lunch and a visit to the **Shíkùmén Open House Museum**. Taxi it to **Tiánzǐfáng** for the afternoon, before another French Concession dinner. Caught a second wind? Catch the acrobats, hit the clubs or unwind with a traditional Chinese massage.

PEOPLE'S SQUARE   人民广场

Once the site of the Shànghăi Racecourse, People's Sq is the modern city's nerve centre. Overshadowed by the dramatic form of **Tomorrow Sq** (明天广场; Míngtiān Guǎngchǎng; Map p182), the open space is peppered with museums, performing arts venues and leafy People's Park. Beneath it all, the city's frenetic energy reaches full crescendo amid the tunnels of Shànghăi's busiest subway interchange.

Shànghăi Museum   MUSEUM

(上海博物馆; Shànghăi Bówùguǎn; Map p182; www.shanghaimuseum.net; 201 Renmin Ave; 人民大道201号; admission free; ⊙9am-5pm; ⍨People's Square) This must-see museum guides you through the craft of millennia while simultaneously escorting you through the pages of Chinese history. Expect to spend half, if not most of, a day here (note that entrance is from East Yan'an Rd).

Designed to resemble the shape of an ancient Chinese *dǐng* vessel, the building is home to one of the most impressive collections in China. Take your pick from the archaic green patinas of the **Ancient Chinese Bronzes Gallery** through to the silent solemnity of the **Ancient Chinese Sculpture Gallery**, and from the exquisite beauty of the porcelain and pottery in the **Ceramics Gallery** to the measured and timeless flourishes captured in the **Chinese Calligraphy Gallery**. Chinese painting, seals, jade,

Ming and Qing furniture, coins and ethnic costumes are also on offer in this museum, intelligently displayed in well-lit galleries. Seats are provided outside galleries on each floor for when lethargy strikes.

Photography is allowed in some galleries. The audio guide (available in eight languages) is well worth the ¥40 (deposit ¥400 or your passport). The excellent **museum shop** sells postcards, a rich array of books, and faithful replicas of the museum's ceramics and other pieces. There is an overpriced teahouse and restaurant inside the museum; you're better off eating at nearby **Yunnan Rd food street** (see the boxed text, p205).

Shànghăi Urban Planning Exhibition Hall   MUSEUM

(上海城市规划展示馆; Shànghăi Chéngshì Guīhuà Zhǎnshìguǎn; Map p182; 100 Renmin Ave; 人民大道100号; adult ¥30; ⊙9am-5pm Tue-Sun, last entry 4pm; ⍨People's Square) Some cities romanticise their past, others promise good times in the present, but only in China are you expected to visit places that haven't even been built yet. The third floor features Shànghăi's idealised future (c 2020), with an incredible model layout of the megalopolis-to-come plus a dizzying Virtual World 3D wrap-around tour complete with celebratory fireworks. Balancing it all out are photos and maps of historic Shànghăi. Entrance is from Xizang Rd.

The Bund & People's Square

Wuzhen Rd

Jinyuan Rd 晋元路

Qipu Rd

N Fujian Rd

Tiantong Rd

Ⓜ Qufu Rd 曲阜路站

Qufu Rd

N Suzhou Rd 苏州北路

S Suzhou Rd 南苏州路

To Soho People's Square Youth Hostel (200m)

Guangfu Rd

Xiamen Rd 厦门路

Ⓜ Xinzha Rd 新闸路站

E Beijing Rd 北京东路

Ningbo Rd

Xinzha Rd 新闸路

W Beijing Rd 北京西路

Middle Zhejiang Rd

Guizhou Rd

N Guangxi Rd

Huanghe Rd

Fengyang Rd

7

Ⓞ 10

62

66 ⓘ

E Nanjing Rd 南京西路

44 Ⓧ 37

Jiujiang Rd

Hubei Rd

36

Hankou Rd

Fengyang Rd

People's Square Ⓜ 人民广场站

People's Square

21

40

54

People's Park

People's Square Ⓜ 人民广场站

34

Fuzhou Rd 福州路

Xinchang Rd

49

9

56

W Nanjing Rd 南京西路

Shànghăi Urban Planning Exhibition Hall

14

8

N Huangpi Rd 黄陂北路

Middle Xizang Rd

Hubei Rd

Jiangyin Rd

24

55

People's Square

E Yan'an Rd 延安东路

Weihai Rd

Wusheng Rd 武胜路

Shànghăi Museum

S Yunnan Rd

30

43

45

61

S Xizang Rd

23

Dagu Rd

Dashijie 大世界站

N Chengdu Rd 成都北路

E Yan'an Rd

Middle Huaihai Rd

S Huangpi Rd

68

Middle Jinling Rd

Putuo Rd

To Dongtai Rd Antique Market (100m)

58

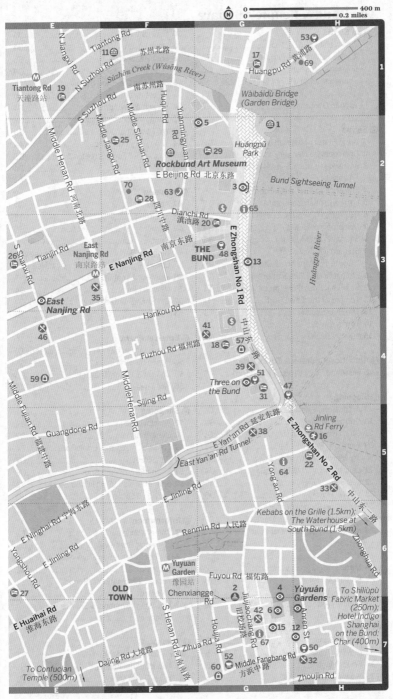

The Bund & People's Square

◎ **Top Sights**

East Nanjing Rd..................................E3
Rockbund Art Museum........................F2
Shànghǎi Museum..............................C6
Shànghǎi Urban Planning Exhibition
　Hall...C5
Yùyuán Gardens................................H7

◎ **Sights**

1　Bund History Museum.......................G2
2　Chénxiānggé Nunnery.......................G6
3　Entrance to Bund Sightseeing
　　Tunnel..G2
4　Entrance to Yùyuán Gardens..............G6
5　Former British Consulate...................G2
6　Húxīntíng Teahouse.........................G7
7　Madame Tussaud's..........................B4
8　Shànghǎi Art Museum......................B5
9　Shànghǎi Museum of
　　Contemporary Art..........................B5
10　Shànghǎi No 1 Department Store........C4
11　Shànghǎi Post Museum....................F1
12　Temple of the Town God..................H7
13　The Bund....................................G3
14　Tomorrow Sq................................A5
15　Yùyuán Bazaar..............................G7

◎ **Activities, Courses & Tours**

16　Huángpǔ River Cruise (The Bund).......H5

◎ **Sleeping**

17　Astor House Hotel..........................G1
18　Captain Hostel..............................G4
19　Chai Living Residences....................E1
20　Fairmont Peace Hotel......................G3
　　JW Marriott Tomorrow Square....(see 14)
21　Langham Yangtze Boutique...............C4
22　Les Suites Orient...........................H5
23　Marvel Hotel.................................D6
24　Mingtown Etour Youth Hostel............A6
25　Mingtown Hiker Youth Hostel............F2
26　Mingtown Nanjing Road Youth
　　Hostel..E3
27　Motel 168....................................E6
28　Motel 268....................................F2
29　Peninsula Hotel.............................G2
30　The Phoenix.................................D6
31　Waldorf Astoria.............................G4

◎ **Eating**

32　Din Tai Fung.................................H7
33　el Willy.......................................H5
34　Food Republic...............................C5
35　Hóngyī Plaza................................E3

36　Huanghe Rd Food Street...................B4
37　Jiājiā Soup Dumplings......................B4
38　Lost Heaven..................................G5
39　M on the Bund...............................G4
40　Nánxiáng Steamed Bun
　　Restaurant..................................D5
41　Shànghǎi Grandmother....................G4
42　Sōngyuèlóu...................................G7
43　Wǔ Fāng Zhāi................................D6
44　Yang's Fry Dumplings......................A4
45　Yunnan Rd Food Street.....................D6
46　Yúxìn Chuāncài..............................E4

◎ **Drinking**

47　Atanu...G4
48　Bar Rouge....................................G3
49　Barbarossa...................................B5
　　Captain's Bar........................(see 18)
　　Glamour Bar.........................(see 39)
　　Long Bar.............................(see 31)
50　Moonlight Teahouse........................H7
51　New Heights.................................G4
52　Old Shànghǎi Teahouse....................G7
53　Vue...H1

◎ **Entertainment**

　　Fairmont Peace Hotel Jazz Bar...(see 20)
54　Peace Cinema................................C5
55　Shànghǎi Grand Theatre....................B6
56　Yìfū Theatre.................................C5

◎ **Shopping**

57　Annabel Lee..................................G4
58　Cybermart....................................D7
59　Foreign Languages Bookstore.............E4
60　Old Street....................................G7
61　Shànghǎi Museum Shop....................C6
62　Shànghǎi No 1 (First) Food Store.........C4
　　Sūzhōu Cobblers....................(see 18)

◎ **Information**

63　China Mobile.................................F2
64　Domestic Boat Tickets shop................G5
65　Tourist Information & Service
　　Centre.......................................G2
66　Tourist Information & Service
　　Centre.......................................D4
67　Tourist Information & Service
　　Centre.......................................G7

◎ **Transport**

68　Pu'an Rd Bus Station.......................C7
69　Train Ticket Office..........................H1
70　Train Ticket Office..........................F2

Shànghǎi Museum of Contemporary Art
MUSEUM

(Moca Shànghǎi; 上海当代艺术馆; Shànghǎi Dāngdài Yìshùguǎn; Map p182; www.mocashanghai.org; People's Park; 人民公园; adult ¥30; ☺10am-9.30pm; Ⓜ People's Square) This nonprofit contemporary art centre has an all-glass construction to maximise Shànghǎi's often dismal sunlight and a tip-top location in People's Park. Temporary exhibits range from urban dystopia sculptures to Japanese ecodesign and multimedia instalments.

FREE Shànghǎi Art Museum
MUSEUM

(上海美术馆; Shànghǎi Měishùguǎn; Map p182; www.sh-artmuseum.org.cn; 325 West Nanjing Rd; 南京西路325号; ☺9am-5pm; Ⓜ People's Square) The exhibits of modern Chinese art are hit-and-miss, but the building (the former Shànghǎi Racecourse Club) and its period details are simply gorgeous. English captions are sporadic.

OLD TOWN & SOUTH BUND
南市

Known to locals as Nán Shì (Southern City), the Old Town is the most traditionally Chinese part of Shànghǎi, bar Qībǎo. Its oval layout still reflects the footprint of its 16th-century walls, erected to keep marauding Japanese pirates at bay. Sections of the Old Town have been bulldozed over the past decade to make room for developments but tatty charm survives along the neighbourhood's narrow and pinched alleyways. On the South Bund, the **Cool Docks** (时尚老码头; Shíshàng Lǎomǎtou) is a kind of riverside Xīntiāndì-lite, with *shíkùmén* (low-rise tenement buildings built in the early 1900s) and converted warehouses.

Yùyuán Gardens & Bazaar
GARDENS, BAZAAR

(豫园、豫园商城; Yùyuán & Yùyuán Shāngchéng; Map p182; admission gardens ¥40, bazaar free; ☺gardens 8.30am-5.30pm, last entry 5pm; Ⓜ Yuyuan Garden) With their shaded alcoves, glittering pools churning with carp, pavilions, pines sprouting wistfully from rockeries and roving packs of Japanese tourists, these **gardens** are one of Shànghǎi's premier sights – but are overpoweringly crowded on weekends.

The Pan family, rich Ming-dynasty officials, founded the gardens, which took 18 years (1559–77) to be nurtured into existence before bombardment during the Opium War in 1842. The gardens took another trashing during French reprisals for attacks on their nearby concession by Taiping rebels. Restored, they are a fine example of Ming

garden design. The spring and summer blossoms bring a fragrant and floral aspect to the gardens, especially in the heavy petals of its *Magnolia grandiflora,* Shànghǎi's flower. Other trees include the Luohan pine, willows, towering gingkos, cherry trees and fine-needled dawn redwoods.

Next to the garden entrance is the **Húxīntíng Teahouse** (湖心亭; Húxīntíng; Map p182; ☺8.30am-9.30pm), once part of the gardens and now one of the most famous teahouses in China.

The adjacent **bazaar** may be tacky and crowded, but it's good for a browse if you can handle the crowds and fake Rolex vendors. The nearby Taoist **Temple of the Town God** (城隍庙; Chénghuáng Miào; Map p182; Yùyuán Bazaar; admission ¥10; ☺8.30am-4.30pm) is also worth visiting. Just beyond the bazaar is **Old Street** (老街; Lǎo Jiē), known more prosaically as Middle Fangbang Rd, a busy street lined with curio shops and teahouses.

Chénxiānggé Nunnery
BUDDHIST

(沉香阁; Chénxiāng Gé; Map p182; 29 Chenxiangge Rd; 沉香阁路29号; admission ¥10; ☺7am-5pm; Ⓜ Yuyuan Garden) Sheltering a community of dark-brown-clothed nuns, this gorgeous yellow-walled temple is a tranquil portal to a devout existence far from the city's frantic temporal realm. Climb the **Guanyin Tower** (观音楼; Guānyīn Lóu; admission ¥2) at the rear hall to view an exquisite statue of Guanyin, the Buddhist goddess of compassion; the original vanished during the Cultural Revolution.

Confucian Temple
CONFUCIAN

(文庙; Wén Miào; off Map p182; 215 Wenmiao Rd; 文庙路215号; admission ¥10; ☺9am-5pm; Ⓜ Laoximen) This well-tended temple to the dictum-coining sage-cum–social theorist is a cultivated acreage of maples, pines, magnolias and birdsong. Originally dating from 1294, the temple was moved to its current site in 1855. There's a **secondhand book market** (☺7.30am-4pm; admission ¥1) here on Sundays.

FRENCH CONCESSION
法租界

Once home to the bulk of Shànghǎi's adventurers, revolutionaries, gangsters, prostitutes and writers, the French Concession is the most graceful part of the city. Today a residential, retail and restaurant district with atmospheric tree-lined streets, the French Concession is a name you won't find appearing on any Chinese maps, but it ranges elegantly through the districts of Lúwān and Xúhuì, also taking in slices of Chángníng and Jìng'ān.

The Bund

The best way to get acquainted with Shànghǎi is to take a stroll along the Bund. The waterfront was the seat of colonial power from the mid-19th century onward, and the city's landmark hotels, banks and trading houses all established themselves here, gradually replacing their original buildings with even grander constructions as the decades passed.

The Bund had its golden age in the 1920s and '30s before the turmoil of war and occupation brought an end to the high life enjoyed by Shànghǎi's foreign residents. Mothballed during the communist era, it's only in the past 15 years that the strip has sought to rekindle its past glory, restoring one heritage building after another. Today, it has become China's showcase lifestyle destination, and many of the landmarks here house designer restaurants, swish cocktail bars and the flagship stores of some of the world's most exclusive brands.

Once you've wandered the promenade and ogled at the Pǔdōng skyline opposite, return to

CHRIS MELLOR/GETTY/©

Hongkong & Shanghai Bank Building (1923)

Head into this massive bank (🕙9am-4.30pm Mon-Fri) to marvel at the beautiful mosaic ceiling, featuring the 12 zodiac signs and the world's (former) eight centres of finance.

North China Daily News Building (1924)

Known as the 'Old Lady of the Bund', the *News* ran from 1864 to 1951 as the main English-language newspaper in China. Look for the paper's motto above the central windows.

Russo-Chinese Bank Building (1902)

Custom House (1927)

One of the most important buildings on the Bund, Custom House was capped by the largest clock face in Asia and 'Big Ching', a bell modelled on London's Big Ben.

Former Bank of Communications (1947)

Bund Public Service Centre (2010)

KEITH LEVIT/ALAMY ©

Top Tip

The promenade is open around the clock, but it's at its best in the early morning, when locals are out practising taichi, or in the early evening, when both sides of the river are lit up and the majesty of the waterfront is at its grandest.

examine the Bund's magnificent facades in more detail and visit the interiors of those buildings open to the public.

This illustration shows the main sights along the Bund's central stretch, beginning near the intersection with East Nanjing Road. The Bund is 1km long and walking it should take around an hour. Head to the area south of the Hongkong & Shanghai Bank Building to find the biggest selection of prominent drinking and dining destinations.

FACT FILE

» Number of remaining heritage buildings on the Bund: 22

» Date the first foreign building on the Bund was constructed: 1851

» The year in which M on the Bund, the first high-profile Bund restaurant, opened: 1999

» Approximate number of wooden piles supporting the Fairmont Peace Hotel: 1600

CHRISTOPHER PITTS

Bank of China (1942)

This unusual building was originally commissioned to be the tallest building in Shànghǎi, but, probably because of Victor Sassoon's influence, wound up being one metre shorter than its neighbour.

Former Palace Hotel (1909)

Now known as the Swatch Art Peace Hotel (an artists' residence and gallery, with a top-floor restaurant and bar), this building hosted Sun Yatsen's 1911 victory celebration following his election as the first president of the Republic of China.

rmer Bank of aiwan (1927)

Former Chartered Bank Building (1923)

Reopened in 2004 as the upscale entertainment complex Bund 18, the building's top-floor Bar Rouge is one of the Bund's premier late-night destinations.

Fairmont Peace Hotel (1929)

Originally built as the Cathay Hotel, this art deco masterpiece was *the* place to stay in Shànghǎi and the crown jewel in Sassoon's real estate empire.

ASIATRAVELCOLLECTION/ALAMY ©

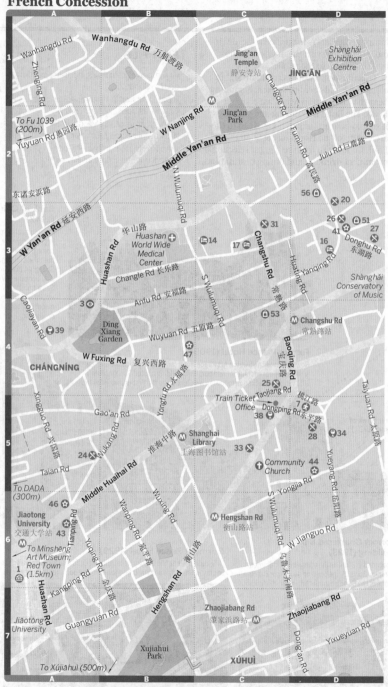

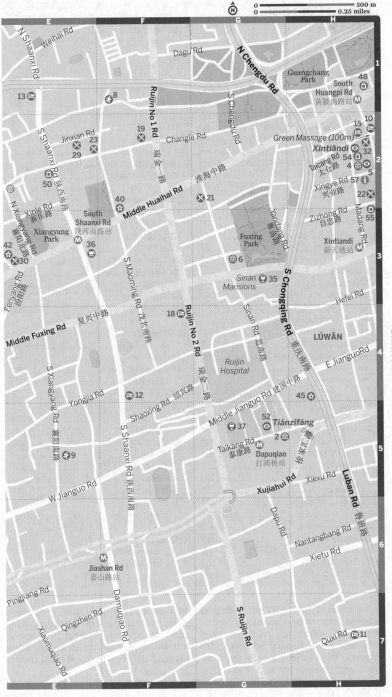

French Concession

◉ Top Sights

Tiánzǐfáng G5
Xīntiāndì H2

◉ Sights

Beaugeste ....(see 52)
1 CY Tung Maritime Museum A6
Deke Erh Art Centre ....(see 52)
2 Liúlí China Museum G5
3 Propaganda Poster Art Centre A4
4 Shíkùmén Open House Museum H2
5 Site of the 1st National Congress
of the CCP H2
6 Sun Yatsen's Former Residence G3

◉ Activities, Courses & Tours

7 Chinese Cooking Workshop D5
8 Lóngwǔ Kungfu Center F1
9 The Kitchen at E5

◉ Sleeping

10 Andaz H2
11 Blue Mountain Youth Hostel H7
12 Hàntíng Hotel F4
13 Héngshān Moller Villa E1
14 Kevin's Old House C3
15 Langham Xīntiāndì H2
16 Magnolia Bed & Breakfast D3
17 Quintet C3
18 Ruìjīn Hotel F4

◉ Eating

19 Bankura F2
20 Bǎoluó Jiǔlóu D2
21 Chá's G2
22 Crystal Jade H2
23 Dī Shuǐ Dòng E2
Din Tai Fung ....(see 22)
24 Ferguson Lane A5
25 Haiku C4
26 Noodle Bull D3
27 Sìchuān Citizen D3
28 Simply Thai D5
29 Southern Barbarian E2
30 Spicy Joint E3
31 Xībó Grill C3

32 Xīnjíshì H2
33 Yīn C5

◉ Drinking

34 Abbey Road D5
Apartment ....(see 47)
Bell Bar ....(see 52)
35 Boxing Cat Brewery G3
36 Cafe 85°C E3
37 Kāibā G5
Kommune ....(see 52)
38 Shànghǎi Brewery C5
39 Time Passage A4

◉ Entertainment

40 Cathay Theatre F2
41 Dragonfly D3
42 Dragonfly E3
43 Eddy's Bar A6
44 Lola D5
45 MAO Livehouse H4
No 88 ....(see 41)
46 Shànghǎi Studio A6
47 Shelter B4

◉ Shopping

Annabel Lee ....(see 54)
48 Apple Store H1
49 Brocade Country D2
Chouchou Chic ....(see 52)
50 Garden Books E2
51 NuoMi D3
Shànghǎi 1936 ....(see 52)
Shànghǎi Tang ....(see 54)
52 Tiánzǐfáng G5
Woo ....(see 52)
53 XinleLu.com C4
54 Xīntiāndì H2
55 Xīntiāndì Style H3
56 Yú D2
Zhenchalin Tea ....(see 52)

◉ Information

57 Shanghai Information Centre for
International Visitors H2

The cream of Shànghǎi's old residential buildings and art deco apartment blocks, hotels and edifices are preserved here, while commercial Huaihǎi Rd teems with shoppers. The district naturally tends towards gentrification, but it's also a trendy and happening enclave, excellent for random exploration in a slow progression or by full immersion in Tiánzǐfáng, a hip quadrant of lane housing overflowing with shops and cafes, which has overtaken Xīntiāndì as one of the latest retail and entertainment hot spots.

Tiánzǐfáng   SHOPPING PRECINCT
(田子坊; Map p188; Lane 210, Taikang Rd; 泰康路
210弄; MDapuqiao) Xīntiāndì and Tiánzǐfáng
are based on a similar idea – an entertainment
complex housed within a warren of traditional *lòngtáng* (alleyways) – but when it comes
to genuine charm and vibrancy, Tiánzǐfáng is
the one that delivers. A community of design
studios, wi-fi cafes and boutiques, this is the
perfect antidote to Shànghǎi's oversized malls
and skyscrapers. With some families still re-
siding in neighbouring buildings, a community mood survives.

There are three main north–south lanes
(Nos 210, 248, 274) criss-crossed by irregular
east–west alleyways, which makes exploration slightly disorienting and fun. On
the main lane is the **Deke Erh Art Centre**
(尔冬强艺术中心; Ěr Dōngqiáng Yìshù Zhōngxīn;
Map p188; No 2, Lane 210), owned by a local
photographer and author. An even better
gallery is the tiny **Beaugeste** (比极影像;
Bǐjí Yǐngxiàng; Map p188; www.beaugeste-gallery.
com; 5th fl, No 5, Lane 210; ⏱10am-6pm), with
exhibits that feature contemporary Chinese
photographers.

Of course, the real activity here is shopping, and the recent explosion of creative
start-ups makes for some interesting finds,
from ethnic embroidery and hand-wrapped
pu-erh teas to retro communist dinnerware.
Elsewhere, a growing band of cool cafes,
such as Kommune (p210), can sort out meals
and drinks and take the weight off your feet.
Don't bother looking for Chinese food here;
there isn't any.

Xīntiāndì   SHOPPING PRECINCT
(新天地; Map p188; www.xintiandi.com; cnr Taicang & Madang Rds; 太仓路与马当路路口;
MSouth Huangpi Rd or Xintiandi) Xīntiāndì has
only been around for a decade and already

it's a Shànghǎi icon. An upmarket retail and
dining complex consisting of largely rebuilt
shíkùmén houses, this was the first development in the city to prove that historic architecture does, in fact, have economic value.
Well-heeled shoppers and al fresco diners
keep the place busy until late, while two museums add a dash of culture to the mix.

The north block is where most of the
action is. The small **Shíkùmén Open
House Museum** (屋里厢石库门民居陈列
馆; Wūlǐxiāng Shíkùmén Mínjū Chénlièguǎn; Map
p188; admission ¥20; ⏱10.30am-10.30pm) depicts traditional life in a 10-room Shànghǎi
shíkùmén. Beyond this, it's best for strolling
the prettified alleyways and enjoying a summer's evening over drinks or a meal.

Liúlí China Museum   MUSEUM
(琉璃艺术博物馆; Liúlí Yìshù Bówùguǎn; Map
p188; www.liulichinamuseum.com; 25 Taikang Rd;
泰康25号; admission ¥20; ⏱10am-5pm Tue-Sun;
MDapuqiao) Founded by Taiwanese artists
Loretta Yang and Chang Yì, the Liúlí China
Museum is dedicated to the art of glass
sculpture. Peruse the collection of ancient
artefacts – some of which date back over
2000 years – to admire the early craftsmanship of pieces such as earrings, belt buckles
and even a Tang-dynasty crystal *wéiqí* (go)
set.

The collection transitions fluidly to more
contemporary creations from around the
world, before moving on to Yang's serene
Buddhist-inspired creations, including a
sublime 1.6m-high 1000-armed Guanyin.

FREE Site of the 1st National
Congress of the CCP   MUSEUM
(中共一大会址纪念馆; Zhōnggòng Yīdà Huìzhǐ;
Map p188; 76 Xingye Rd; 兴业路76号; ⏱9am-5pm;
MSouth Huangpi Rd or Xintiandi) The CCP was

SEDUCTION & THE CITY

Shànghǎi owes its reputation as the most fashionable city in China to the calendar
poster, whose print runs once numbered in the tens of millions and whose distribution
reached from China's interior to Southeast Asia. The basic idea behind the poster –
associating a product with an attractive woman to encourage subconscious desire and
consumption – today sounds like Marketing 101, but in the early 20th century it was
revolutionary. Calendar posters not only introduced new products to Chinese everywhere, their portrayal of Shànghǎi women – wearing make-up and stylish clothing,
smoking cigarettes and surrounded by foreign goods – set the standard for modern
fashion that many Chinese women would dream of for decades. Today reproduction
posters are sold throughout the Old Town for as little as ¥10, though finding a bona fide
original is quite a challenge. For an in-depth look at calendar posters and Shànghǎi's
role in shaping modern China, see Wen-hsin Yeh's *Shanghai Splendor*.

founded in July 1921 in this French Concession *shíkùmén* building in one fell swoop, converting an unassuming block into one of Chinese communism's holiest shrines. Now a museum, its dizzying Marxist spin and communist narcissism is a bit much, but you can nonetheless visit the room where the Party began. Passport required for entry.

Propaganda Poster Art Centre   GALLERY
(宣传画年画艺术中心; Xuānchuánhuà Niánhuà Yìshù Zhōngxīn; Map p188; www.shanghaipropagandaart.com; Room B-OC, President Mansion, 868 Huashan Rd; 华山路868号B-OC室; admission ¥20; ⊙10am-5pm; MShanghai Library or Jiangsu Rd) If phalanxes of red tractors, bumper harvests, muscled peasants and lantern-jawed proletariat get you going, this small gallery in the bowels of a residential block will truly fire you up. Go weak-kneed at the cartoon world of anti-US defiance, and size up a collection of 3000 original posters from the 1950s, '60s and '70s – the golden age of Maoist poster production. The centre divides into a showroom and a shop featuring posters and postcards for sale. Once you find the main entrance, a guard will point the way.

Sun Yatsen's
Former Residence   HISTORIC BUILDING
(孙中山故居; Sūn Zhōngshān Gùjū; Map p188; 7 Xiangshan Rd; 香山路7号; admission ¥20; ⊙9am-4.30pm; MSouth Shaanxi Rd or Xintiandi) China is stuffed to the gills with Sun Yatsen memorabilia, and this former residence, on what was previously rue Molière, is where the founder of modern China (posthumously dubbed Guófù, Father of the Nation) lived for six years. After Sun's death, his wife Song Qingling (1893–1981) remained here until 1937, watched by plainclothes Kuomintang and French police. The two-storey house is decorated with period furnishings, despite looting by the Japanese.

WEST NANJING ROAD & JÌNG'ĀN
南京西路、静安
Lined with sharp top-end shopping malls, clusters of foreign offices and a dense crop of embassies and consulates, West Nanjing Rd is where Shànghăi's streets are paved with gold, or at least Prada and Gucci.

But head north of West Nanjing Rd and you're plunged into a grittier and more absorbing section of Jìng'ān, which extends until reaching the Shànghăi Railway Station. Like Hóngkǒu (north of the Bund), this area is primed for development.

Jade Buddha Temple   BUDDHIST
(玉佛寺; Yùfó Sì; Map p196; 170 Anyuan Rd; 安远路170号; adult ¥20; ⊙8am-4.30pm; MChangshou Rd) One of Shànghăi's few active Buddhist monasteries, this temple was built between 1918 and 1928. The centrepiece is the 1.9m-high pale green **Jade Buddha**, seated upstairs in his own hall. It is said that Hui Gen (Wei Ken), a Pǔtuóshān monk, travelled to Myanmar (Burma) via Tibet, shipped five jade Buddhas back to China and then sought alms to build a temple for them. The beautiful effigy of Sakyamuni, clearly Southeast Asian in style, gazes ethereally from a cabinet. Visitors are not able to approach the statue, but can admire it from a distance. An additional charge of ¥10 is levied to see the statue (no photographs).

An equally elegant **reclining Buddha** is downstairs, opposite a much more substantial copy in marble. A large **vegetarian restaurant** (素菜餐厅; sùcài cāntīng; 999 Jiangning Rd) is attached to the temple around the corner.

In February the temple is very busy during the Lunar New Year, when some 20,000 Chinese Buddhists throng to pray for prosperity.

FREE **M50**   GALLERIES
(M50创意产业集聚区; M Wǔshí Chuàngyì Chǎnyè Jíjùqū; Map p196; 50 Moganshan Rd; 莫干山路50号; ⊙10am-6pm Tue-Sun; MShanghai Railway Station) Běijīng may dominate the art scene in China, but Shànghăi has its own thriving gallery subculture, centred on this complex of industrial buildings down dusty Moganshan Rd in the north of town. Although most of the artists who originally established the enclave are long gone, it is well worth putting aside a half-day to poke around the many galleries here.

Like most galleries, cutting-edge work is often surrounded by mediocrity, so be prepared to sift. The best of the bunch include old-timer **ShanghART** (香格纳画廊; Xiānggénà Huàláng; Map p196; www.shanghartgallery.com; Bldg 16 & 18), the collaborative and provocative **island6** (Map p196; www.island6.org; 2nd fl, Bldg 6), and photography from **OFoto** (Map p196; www.ofoto-gallery.com; 2nd fl, Bldg 13) and **m97** (Map p196; www.m97gallery.com; 2nd fl, 97 Moganshan Rd), the latter of which is across the street. When your legs finally give way, flop down at **Bāndù Cabin** (p210) or at the **Roof Club**, a cafe located on the roof of Building 17.

West Nanjing Rd & Jìng'ān

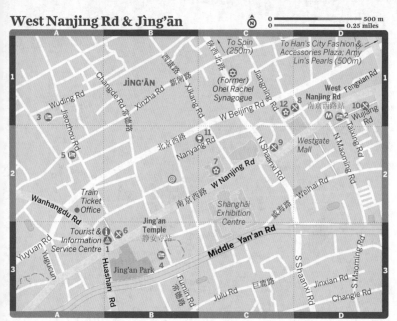

West Nanjing Rd & Jìng'ān

◎ Sights
1 Jìng'ān Temple..................................B3

🛏 Sleeping
2 Jia Shànghǎi....................................D1
3 Le Tour Traveler's Rest Youth
    Hostel..A1
4 Púlì..B3
5 Urbn..A2

✕ Eating
6 Gǔyì Húnán Restaurant......................B3
7 Shànghǎi Centre...............................C2

8 Vegetarian Lifestyle..........................D1
9 Wagas..C2
10 Wujiang Rd Food Street....................D1

◎ Drinking
11 Big Bamboo.....................................C2

◎ Entertainment
Green Massage...............................(see 7)
Shànghǎi Centre Theatre.............(see 7)
12 Shànghǎi Cultural Information
    & Booking Centre..........................C1

Jìng'ān Temple BUDDHIST
(静安寺; Jìng'ān Sì; Map p193; 1686-1688 West Nanjing Rd; 南京西路1686-1688号; admission ¥30; ◎7.30am-5pm; Ⓜ Jing'an Temple) After over a decade of restoration, Jìng'ān Temple is finally coming together as one of the city's most eye-catching temples. Although it lacks an air of venerability and there are fewer devotees than at the Jade Buddha Temple, there can be no denying its spectacular location among the district's soaring skyscrapers.

PǓDŌNG NEW AREA 浦东新区
On the east side of the Huángpǔ River, the colossal concrete and steel Pǔdōng New Area (Pǔdōng Xīnqū) is best known for the skyscraper-stuffed skyline of Lùjiāzuǐ, one of China's most photographed panoramas. The best time to visit is at night when the neon effect is intoxicating and towers are lit up like TV screens. Pǔdōng's multilane roads and unyielding expanses can turn pedestrians' legs to concrete, but the main attractions are around Lujiazui station.

Pǔdōng

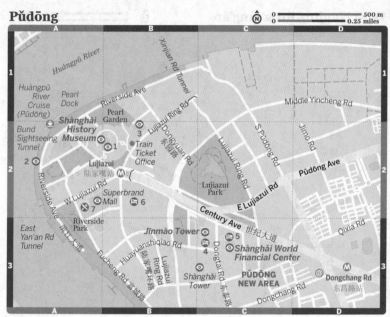

Shànghǎi World Financial Center
ARCHITECTURE

(SWFC; 上海环球金融中心; Shànghǎi Huánqiú Jīnróng Zhōngxīn; Map p194; www.swfc-observ atory.com; 100 Century Ave; 世纪大道100号; observation deck 94th/94th, 97th & 100th/exclusive tour ¥120/150/300, concessions for children, seniors & students; ⏰8am-11pm, last admission 10pm; Ⓜ Lujiazui) Awaiting displacement by the nearby **Shànghǎi Tower** (completion date 2014) as the city's tallest building, the neck-craning 492m-high Shànghǎi World Financial Center is an astonishing sight, even more so come nightfall when its 'bottle opener' top dances with lights. There are three observation decks in total (94th, 97th and 100th floors), with head-spinning, altitude-adjusted ticket prices and wow-factor elevators thrown in. Clear, smog-free day are be imperative; the 100th-floor Skywalk includes sections of transparent glass walkways. To make a meal (or a cocktail) of it, there's always the option of sashaying into the restaurant/bar on the 91st floor of the Park Hyatt instead (but it's not cheap).

Jīnmào Tower
ARCHITECTURE

(金茂大厦; Jīnmào Dàshà; Map p194; 88 Century Ave; 世纪大道88号; adult/student/child ¥120/90/60; ⏰8.30am-9.30pm; Ⓜ Lujiazui) The deco-esque Jīnmào Tower is Pǔdōng's most

graceful and second (soon-to-be third) tallest (420.5m) tower. An observation deck is on the 88th floor (no admittance for those 'drunk or not properly dressed'), or contemplate sinking a drink in the Cloud 9 bar (p211) on the 87th floor (time your visit for dusk for both day and night views).

Shànghǎi History Museum
MUSEUM

(上海城市历史发展陈列馆; Shànghǎi Chéngshì Lìshǐ Fāzhǎn Chénlièguǎn; Map p194; www.his torymuseum.sh.cn; Oriental Pearl Tower basement; adult ¥35, audio tour ¥30; ⏰8am-9.30pm; Ⓜ Lujiazui) In the basement of the Oriental Pearl Tower, this informative museum has fun multimedia presentations and imaginative displays re-creating the history of Shànghǎi, with an emphasis on the pre-1949 era. Life-sized models of traditional shops are peopled by realistic wax figures, and the museum abounds with a wealth of historical detail.

World Expo 2010 Site
ARCHITECTURE

(世博会区; Shìbó Huì Qū; Map p178; Ⓜ Yaohua Rd, Lines 7 & 8) Most of the pavilions at the 2010 World Expo site were dismantled. However, at least five structures on the Pǔdōng side remain standing and continue to host exhibits and events, including the iconic **China Pavilion** (中国国家馆; Zhōngguó Guójiā Guǎn; Map p178), **Expo Center** (世博中心; Shìbó

Pǔdōng

◎ **Top Sights**
Jīnmào Tower...C3
Shànghǎi History Museum.................A2
Shànghǎi World Financial
    Center..C3

◎ **Sights**
1 Oriental Pearl Tower........................B2
2 Riverside Promenade.......................A2
3 Shànghǎi Ocean Aquarium B2

🛏 **Sleeping**
4 Grand Hyatt.......................................C3
5 Park Hyatt..C3
6 The Ritz-Carlton Hotel Pudong
    Shanghai..B2

✖ **Eating**
100 Century Avenue....................(see 5)
7 Element Fresh A2

◎ **Drinking**
Cloud 9..(see 4)
Flair...(see 6)

◎ **Shopping**
IFC Mall...(see 6)
South Beauty..................................(see 7)

Zhōngxīn; Map p178) and the galactically styled UFO **Mercedes-Benz Arena** (梅赛德斯奔驰文化中心; Méisàidésī Bēnchí Wénhuà Zhōngxīn; Map p178; www.mercedes-benzarena.com).

At the time of writing a handful of structures were open on the Pǔdōng side: the underwhelming **Moon Boat** (月亮船; Yuèliàng Chuán; Map p178; admission Mon-Fri ¥60, Sat & Sun ¥80, holiday ¥100; ⊙9am-6pm Tue-Sun) – the former Saudi Pavilion – and the **Shànghǎi Italian Centre** (Map p178; admission ¥60; ⊙9am-5pm Tue-Sun) in the former Italian World Expo Pavilion.

With 6000 sq metres of exhibition space, the China Pavilion was relaunched in 2012 as the **China Art Palace** (⊙9am-5pm Tue-Sun; Ⓜ China Art Palace) and was set to become a landmark art museum. Hosting the Shànghǎi Biennale, the **Power Station of Art** (Lane 20 Huayuangang Rd; ⊙9am-5pm Tue-Sun; Ⓜ South Xizang Rd) also opened in late 2012 on the far side of the Huángpǔ River in the disused Nanshi power station (the former Pavilion of the Future).

Engaging highlights of the Expo are on display at the **Expo 2010 Commemoration Exhibition** (上海世博会纪念展; Shànghǎi Shìbóhuì

Jìniànzhǎn; Map p178; admission ¥30; ⊙9am-5pm Tue-Sun; Ⓜ Luban Rd) on the Pǔxī side, including exhibits and parts of the original pavilions. Sadly there are no English captions.

Oriental Pearl Tower   SKYSCRAPER
(东方明珠电视塔; Dōngfāng Míngzhū Diànshì Tǎ; Map p194; 1 Century Ave; 世纪大道1号; tickets ¥120-298; ⊙8am-10pm; Ⓜ Lujiazui) Best viewed when illuminated at night, this poured-concrete, atomic age retro rocket tower is one of Lùjiāzuǐ's unmissable structures. The Shànghǎi History Museum in the basement is well worth exploring, and not just because it's the one part of Pǔdōng where you can't see the tower itself.

Science & Technology Museum   MUSEUM
(上海科技馆; Shànghǎi Kējìguǎn; Map p178; www.sstm.org.cn; 2000 Century Ave; 世纪大道2000号; adult ¥60; ⊙9am-5.15pm Tue-Sun; Ⓜ Science & Technology Museum) You need to do a huge amount of walking to get around this spaced-out museum but there are some fascinating exhibits, from Rubik's-cube–solving robots to taking penalty kicks against a computerised goalkeeper. There are also four theatres (two IMAX, one 4D and one outer space) that show themed 15- to 40-minute films (tickets ¥20 to ¥40) throughout the day.

Riverside Promenade   PROMENADE
(滨江大道; Bīnjiāng Dàdào; Map p194; ⊙6.30am-11pm; Ⓜ Lujiazui) The best stroll in Pǔdōng, the promenade alongside Riverside Ave offers splendid Bund photo-ops across the water and some choicely positioned riverfront cafes.

Shànghǎi Ocean Aquarium   AQUARIUM
(上海海洋水族馆; Shànghǎi Hǎiyáng Shuǐzúguǎn; Map p194; www.sh-aquarium.com; 1388 Lujiazui Ring Rd; 陆家嘴环路158号; adult/child ¥160/110; ⊙9am-6pm; Ⓜ Lujiazui) Education meets aquatic entertainment in this slick and intelligently designed aquarium.

NORTH SHÀNGHǍI (HÓNGKǑU) 虹口
More off the beaten trail, the gritty northeast districts of Hóngkǒu and Zháběi have some interesting backstreets and a few minor sights. Originally the American Settlement before the Japanese took over, Hóngkǒu also welcomed thousands of Jewish refugees fleeing persecution.

Ohel Moishe Synagogue   MUSEUM
(摩西会堂; Móxī Huìtáng; 62 Changyang Rd; 长阳路62号; admission ¥50; ⊙9am-4.30pm; Ⓜ Dalian Rd) Built by the Russian Ashkenazi Jewish

Shànghǎi Railway Station

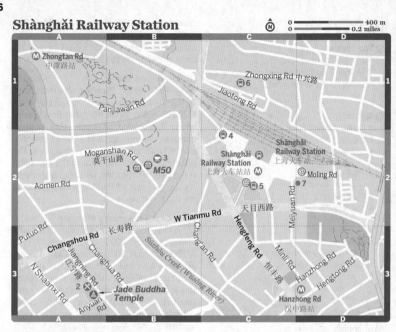

Shànghǎi Railway Station

◎ **Top Sights**
Jade Buddha Temple A3
M50...B2

◎ **Sights**
island6 .... (see 3)
1 m97..B2
OFoto .... (see 3)
ShanghART....................................... (see 3)

✖ **Eating**
2 Jade Buddha Temple
   Vegetarian Restaurant......................A3

◉ **Drinking**
3 Bǎndù Cabin B2

ℹ **Transport**
4 Bus 941 to Hóngqiáo
   Airport C2
5 Bus to Pǔdōng International
   Airport C2
6 Shànghǎi Long-Distance
   Bus Station C1
7 Train Ticket Office D2

community in 1927, this synagogue lies in the heart of the 1940s Jewish ghetto. Today it houses the synagogue and the Shànghǎi Jewish Refugees Museum, with exhibitions on the lives of the approximately 20,000 Central European refugees who fled to Shànghǎi to escape the Nazis. There are English-language tours every 45 minutes (9.30am to 4.15pm).

Duolun Road Cultural Street ARCHITECTURE
This restored **street** (多伦文化名人街; Duōlún Wénhuà Míngrén Jiē; M Dongbaoxing Rd) of fine old houses was once home to several of China's most famous writers (as well as Kuomintang generals). Today it has a few excellent antique shops (Dàshǎnghǎi at No 181 is fascinating to browse), some historic architecture (the brick Hóngdé Temple at No 59 is a Christian church) and a few cafes, including the **Old Film Cafe** (No 123; ◎10am-midnight), by the bell tower at the bend in the road. The **Shànghǎi Duōlún Museum of Modern Art** (上海多伦现代美术馆; Shànghǎi Duōlún Xiàndài Měishùguǎn; No 27; admission ¥10; ◎10am-6pm Tue-Sun) puts on exhibits of contemporary Chinese art. The street ends in the north at the Moorish-looking **Kong Residence** (No 250), built in 1924, with its Middle Eastern tiles and windows.

SOUTH SHÀNGHǍI (XÚJIĀHUÌ)   徐家汇

Originally a Jesuit settlement dating back to the 17th century, Xújiāhuì was known to 1930s expat residents as Ziccawei or Sicawei. Today it's more characterised by shopping malls, including the massive Grand Gateway.

Lónghuá Temple
BUDDHIST

(龙华寺; Lónghuá Sì; Map p178; 2853 Longhua Rd; 龙华路2853号; admission ¥10; ⊙7am-4.30pm; MLongcao Rd) Southwest of central Shànghǎi, this is the oldest and largest temple in the city; said to date from the 10th century, it's much restored. Opposite the temple rises a seven-storey pagoda, originally built in AD 977 and also rebuilt. From Longcao Rd station head east along North Longshui Rd for about 1km.

FCY Tung Maritime Museum
MUSEUM

(董浩云航运博物馆; Dǒng Hàoyún Hángyùn Bówùguǎn; Map p188; 1954 Huashan Rd, Jiāotōng University campus; 华山路1954号交通大学内; ⊙1.30-5.30pm Tue-Sun; MJiaotong University) This small but fascinating museum features exhibits on the legendary explorer Zheng He and the often overlooked world of Chinese maritime history.

Bibliotheca Zi-Ka-Wei
LIBRARY

(徐家汇藏书楼; Xújiāhuì Cángshūlóu; ☑6487 4095, ext 208; 80 North Caoxi Rd; 漕溪北路 80号; ⊙library tour 2pm Sat; MXujiahui) This former Jesuit library has a free 15-minute group tour of the main library and its stunning collection of antiquarian tomes on Saturdays. Reservations are essential.

St Ignatius Cathedral
CATHEDRAL

(天主教堂; Tiānzhǔ Jiàotáng; 158 Puxi Rd; 蒲西路158号; ⊙1-4.30pm Sat & Sun; MXujiahui) This dignified twin-spired cathedral (1904) has some stunning recently installed stained glass inscribed with archaic Chinese. Across the road stands the former St Ignatius Convent, now a restaurant.

Tousewe Museum
MUSEUM

(土山湾博物馆; Tǔshānwān Bówùguǎn; 55-1 Puhuitang Lu; 蒲汇塘路55-1号; admission ¥10; ⊙9am-4.30pm Tue-Sun; MShanghai Indoor Stadium/Xujiahui) Next to a middle school along Puhuitang Rd, this magnificent museum is dedicated to the Sino-Western arts and crafts of the former red-brick Tousewe Orphanage, established here by the resourceful Jesuits in 1864. Audio tours available.

WEST SHÀNGHǍI

West Shànghǎi includes a large area made up of the districts of Mǐnháng (闵行) and Chángníng (长宁), which envelops the smaller residential community of Gǔběi (古北). It is mainly of interest for long-term expats and those on business. That said, there are a few sites in the area, as well as Hóngqiáo Airport.

Qībǎo
HISTORIC VILLAGE

(七宝; Map p178; Mǐnháng district; admission ¥45; MQibao) When you tire of Shànghǎi's incessant quest for modernity, this tiny town is only a hop, skip and metro ride away. An ancient settlement that prospered during the Ming and Qing dynasties, it is littered with traditional historic architecture, threaded by small, busy alleyways and cut by a picturesque canal. If you can somehow blot out the crowds, Qībǎo brings you the flavours of old China along with huge doses of entertainment.

There are nine official sights included in the through ticket, though you can also skip the ticket and just pay ¥5 to ¥10 per sight as you go. The best of the bunch include the **Cotton Textile Mill**, the **Shadow Puppet Museum** (performances from 1pm to 3pm Wednesday and Sunday) and the **Old Trades House**. Half-hour **boat rides** (per person ¥10; ⊙8.30am-5pm) along the canal slowly ferry passengers from Number One Bridge to Dōngtángtān (东塘滩) and back. Also worth ferreting out is the 19th-century **Catholic Church** (天主教堂; 50 Nanjie), adjacent to a convent off Qibao Nanjie, south of the canal.

Wander along Bei Dajie north of the canal for souvenirs; Nan Dajie south of the canal is full of snacks and small eateries such as No 26, which sells sweet *tāngyuán* (dumplings) and No 9, which is a rarely seen traditional **teahouse** (storytelling ⊙12.20-2.30pm).

Mǐnshēng Art Museum & Red Town
MUSEUM

(民生现代美术馆、红坊; Mǐnshēng Xiàndài Měishùguǎn, Hóng Fāng; off Map p188; Bldg F, 570 West Huaihai Rd; 淮海西路570号F座; admission ¥20; ⊙10am-9pm Tue-Sun; MHongqiao Rd) Although sponsored mainly by the Mǐnshēng Bank, this edgy art space also counts the Tate, Centre Pompidou, MoMA and Guggenheim among its partners, so it should come as no surprise that the exhibits (about three per year) are generally excellent. Adding to its street cred is artistic director Zhou Tiehai, one of Shànghǎi's most well-known artists. It's located in the sculpture-dotted Red Town complex (formerly the No 10 Steel Factory).

Courses

Learn how to balance your yin and yang with the following courses.

The Kitchen at... COOKING

(Map p188; ☎6433 2700; www.thekitchenat.com; Bldg 20, 3rd fl, 383 South Xiangyang Rd; 襄阳南路383弄20号3楼; Ⓜ South Shanxi Rd) Great culinary school offering courses in regional Chinese and Western cuisines; good for both long-term residents and short-term visitors.

Chinese Cooking Workshop

(Map p188; www.chinesecookingworkshop.com) Learn different Chinese cooking styles from dim sum to Sichuanese. It also offers market tours and courses for kids.

Lóngwǔ Kungfu Center MARTIAL ARTS

(龙武功夫馆; Lóngwǔ Gōngfū Guǎn; Map p188; ☎6287 1528; www.longwukungfu.com; 1 South Maoming Rd; 茂名南路1号; Ⓜ South Shaanxi Rd) The largest centre in the city, with classes in Chinese, Japanese and Korean martial arts, children's classes and lessons in English.

Tours

From boats to bikes to buses, organised tours offer a great introduction to Shànghǎi.

BOHDI CYCLING TOUR

(☎5266 9013; www.bohdi.com.cn; tours ¥220) Night-time cycling tours on Tuesdays (March to November) and trips around the region.

Huángpǔ River Cruise (The Bund) BOAT TOUR

(黄浦江游览船; Huángpǔjiāng Yóulǎnchuán; Map p182; 219-239 East Zhongshan No 2 Rd; 中山东二路219-239号; tickets ¥128; ⊙11am-8.30pm) Ninety-minute cruises run from the south end of the Bund (near East Jinling Rd) up to the Shànghǎi Port International Cruise Terminal and back – and then they do it all over again. Try to find a rarer 40- to 60-minute cruise (¥100), which only makes the trip once.

Huángpǔ River Cruise (Pǔdōng) BOAT TOUR

(黄浦江游览船; Huángpǔjiāng Yóulǎnchuán; Map p194; Pearl Dock; 明珠码头; tickets ¥100; ⊙10am-1.30pm; Ⓜ Lujiazui) Six 40-minute cruises depart from Pǔdōng.

Shanghai Sideways MOTORCYCLE TOUR

(www.shanghaisideways.com; tours from ¥800) Unusual motorcycle-sidecar tours of the city for up to two passengers, setting off from the Peninsula Hotel.

SHÀNGHĂI FOR CHILDREN

Shànghǎi isn't exactly at the top of most kids' holiday wish lists, but the new Disney theme park in Pǔdōng (estimated completion date 2015) will no doubt improve its future standing. In the meantime, if you're passing through the city with children, the following sights should keep the entire family entertained.

» Shànghǎi World Financial Center (p194) or Jīnmào Tower (p194)

» Shànghǎi History Museum (p194)

» Shànghǎi Ocean Aquarium (p195)

» Science & Technology Museum (p195)

» Acrobatics show (p211)

» Bus tours (see the boxed text, p199)

Note that, in general, 1.4m (4ft 7in) is the cut-off height for children's tickets. Children under 0.8m (2ft 7in) normally get in for free.

If sightseeing mutiny strikes, also check out the following:

» **Happy Valley** (欢乐谷; Huānlè Gǔ; http://sh.happyvalley.cn; adult/child 1.2-1.4m ¥200/100; Linyin Ave, Sheshan, Songjiang County; 松江区佘山林荫大道; ⊙9am-6pm; Ⓜ Sheshan, Line 9) Popular national amusement park an hour from Shànghǎi by metro.

» **Dino Beach** (热带风暴; Rèdài Fēngbào; off Map p178; www.dinobeach.com.cn; 78 Xinzhen Rd; 新镇路78号; admission ¥100-200; ⊙10am-11pm Tue-Sun, 2-11pm Mon Jun-Sep; Ⓜ Xinzhuang, Line 1, then bus No 763 or 173) Way down in south Shànghǎi, this water park has a beach, a wave pool and water slides.

» **Shànghǎi Zoo** (上海动物园; Shànghǎi Dòngwùyuán; Map p178; www.shanghaizoo.cn; 2381 Hongqiao Rd; 虹桥路2381号; adult/child ¥40/20; ⊙6.30am-6pm Apr-Sep, to 5pm Oct-Mar; Ⓜ Shanghai Zoo) As Chinese zoos go, this is just about the best there is.

GOING FOR A RIDE

Tickets for the handy hop-on, hop-off open-top **City Sightseeing Buses** (📞6252 0000; www.springtour.com; tickets ¥30; ⏰9am-8.30pm summer, 6pm winter) last 24 hours and are, besides touring Shànghǎi's highlights, a great way to get around the city centre and Pǔdōng. A recorded commentary runs in eight languages: just plug in your earphones (supplied). Buses have their own stops across central Shànghǎi, including the Bund, the Old Town and People's Sq. **Big Bus Tours** (📞6351 5988; www.bigbustours.com; adult/child US$44/29) also operate hop-on, hop-off bus services, lassoing in the top sights along 22 stops across two routes. Tickets are valid for 48 hours and include a one-hour boat tour of the Huángpǔ River plus admission to the 88th-floor observation tower of the Jīnmào Tower.

Shànghǎi Sightseeing Buses BUS TOUR
(上海旅游集散中心; Shànghǎi Lǚyóu Jísàn Zhōngxīn; www.chinassbc.com; Ⓜ Shanghai Stadium) Daily tours from Shànghǎi Stadium to nearby canal towns (eg Tónglǐ, Nánxún and Zhōuzhuāng). Convenient, but less fun than visiting on your own. For more bus tours, see the boxed text (p199).

SISU CYCLING TOUR
(📞5059 6071; www.sisucycling.com; tour ¥150) Night-time cycling tours on Wednesdays, and trips out of town.

Sūzhōu Creek Boat Tours BOAT TOUR
(苏州河游览船; Sūzhōuhé Yóulǎnchuán; Changhua Rd Dock, 1250 Yichang Rd; 昌化路码头宜昌路1250; Danba Rd Dock, 2690 West Guangfu Rd; 丹巴路码头光复西路2690号; tickets ¥80-150; ⏰1.30-8.15pm; Ⓜ Changshou Rd, then taxi) One-way or 1¾-hour round trips along newly dredged Suzhou Creek from Changhua Rd Dock to Danba Rd Dock near Changfeng Park in Putuo district. You can board the boat from either dock. Plans are to extend the trip east to Waibaidu Bridge north of the Bund. Charter boats are also available.

✦✦ Festivals & Events

Lantern Festival TRADITIONAL
A colourful time to visit Yùyuán Gardens. People make *yuánxiāo* or *tāngyuán* (glutinous rice dumplings with sweet fillings) and some carry paper lanterns on the streets. The lantern festival (元宵节; Yánxiāo Jié) falls on the 15th day of the first lunar month (14 February 2014 and 5 March 2015).

Shànghǎi International Literary Festival LITERARY
Held in March or April, this massively popular **festival** (上海国际文学艺术节; Shànghǎi Guójì Wénxué Yìshù Jié) for bibliophiles is staged in the Glamour Bar (p209), with international and local authors in attendance.

Lónghuá Temple Fair TRADITIONAL
This **fair** (龙华寺庙会; Lónghuá Sì Miàohuì) at Lónghuá Temple, held for several weeks during the third lunar month (late March, April or early May), is eastern China's largest and oldest folk gathering, with all kinds of snacks, stalls, jugglers and stilt walkers.

Formula 1 SPORT
(www.formula1.com; 2000 Yining Rd, Jiādīng; Ⓜ Shanghai International Circuit, Line 11) The slick Shànghǎi International Circuit hosts several high-profile motor-racing competitions, including the hotly contested Formula 1 in April.

Dragon Boat Festival SPORT
Celebrated on the fifth day of the fifth lunar month (12 June 2013, 2 June 2014, 20 June 2015), this **festival** (端午节; Duānwǔ Jié) sees dragon boats raced along Sūzhōu Creek.

China Shànghǎi International Arts Festival ARTS
(中国上海国际艺术节; Zhōngguó Shànghǎi Guójì Yìshù Jié; www.artsbird.com) A month-long program of cultural events held in October and November, including the Shànghǎi Art Fair, international music, dance, opera, acrobatics and the Shànghǎi Biennale.

🛏 Sleeping

Shànghǎi's sleeping options are excellent at either end of the spectrum, though quality in the midrange market remains in short supply – it's best to do your homework and secure a room well ahead of time. Don't forget top-end hotels, however, as discounts often make them considerably affordable. In general, hotels fall into five main categories: luxury skyscraper hotels, historic old villa and apartment block hotels, boutique hotels, Chinese chain hotels, and hostels. There's also a handful of B&Bs, though these are relatively scarce.

WANT MORE?

For in-depth information, reviews and recommendations at your fingertips, head to the Apple App Store to purchase Lonely Planet's *Shànghǎi City Guide* iPhone app.

Alternatively, head to **Lonely Planet** (www.lonelyplanet.com/china/shanghai) for planning advice, author recommendations, traveller reviews and insider tips.

The most central neighbourhoods are the Bund and People's Sq. If you'd rather be based in a more residential area, consider the French Concession and Jìng'ān, where unique choices exist. Pǔdōng is perfect for panoramas and high-altitude rooms, with a price tag.

Rack rates are listed here, but discounts are standard outside holiday periods. Four- and five-star hotels add a 10% or 15% service charge (sometimes negotiable).

For hotel bookings, the online agencies **CTrip** (☏400 619 9999; http://english.ctrip.com) and **Elong** (☏400 617 1717; www.elong.net) are good choices.

THE BUND & PEOPLE'S SQUARE

TOP CHOICE **Astor House Hotel** HISTORIC HOTEL $$
(浦江饭店; Pǔjiāng Fàndiàn; Map p182; ☏6324 6388; www.astorhousehotel.com; 15 Huangpu Rd; 黄浦路15号; d/ste ¥1280/2800; ❀@☎; Ⓜ East Nanjing Rd) Stuffed with history (and perhaps a ghost or two), this august old-timer shakes up an impressive cocktail from select ingredients: a location just off the Bund, old world Shànghǎi charm, great discounts and colossal rooms. There's enough wood panelling to build an ark, and you could shove a bed in the capacious bathrooms, while the original polished wooden floorboards, corridors and galleries (the forlorn-looking Richard's Bar and massage parlours aside) pitch the mood somewhere between British public school and Victorian asylum. Only partial wi-fi cover; broadband is ¥60 per day. Discounts of 40%.

Fairmont Peace Hotel HISTORIC HOTEL $$$
(费尔蒙和平饭店; Fèi'ěrméng Hépíng Fàndiàn; Map p182; ☏6321 6888; www.fairmont.com; 20 East Nanjing Rd; 南京东路20号; d ¥2200-3400; Ⓜ East Nanjing Rd; ❀❀☎☎) If anywhere in town fully conveys the swish sensations of 1930s Shànghǎi, it's the old Cathay rising majestically from the Bund (see the boxed text, p201).

Reopened in 2010 after years of renovations, it's since reasserted its claim as one of the city's most iconic hotels. Rooms are decked out in art deco style, from the light fixtures on down to the coffee tables, and the entire hotel is cast in the warm, subdued tints of a bygone era. Wi-fi access is an extra ¥99 per day.

Marvel Hotel HOTEL $$
(商悦青年会大酒店; Shāngyuè Qīngniánhuì Dàjiǔdiàn; Map p182; ☏3305 9999; www.marvelhotels.com.cn; 123 South Xizang Rd; 西藏南路123号; d ¥1080-1580; ❀@; Ⓜ Dashijie) Occupying the former YMCA building (1931) just south of People's Sq, the Marvel is one of the city's standout midrange hotels. The successful mix of history, central location and modern comfort (broadband access via the TV, soundproofed windows, comfy down pillows) makes it one of Shànghǎi's best-value hotels. Wi-fi in the lobby only.

Chai Living Residences APARTMENT $$$
(Map p182; ☏3366 3209; www.chailiving.com; Embankment Building, 400 North Suzhou Rd; 苏州北路400号; apt 3 days/1 week/1 month from ¥3300/6000/13500; Ⓜ Tiantong Rd; ❀☎) If you need a stylish Shànghǎi address for three days or more (minimum stay), you can't get much better than these swish individually-styled apartments in the art deco Embankment Building, a living, breathing residential block (bumping into local tenants merely adds authentic charm). Apartments range from 40 to 200 sq metres, with daily maid service, underfloor heating, kitchens and tantalising river views.

Langham Yangtze Boutique BOUTIQUE HOTEL $$$
(朗廷扬子精品宾馆; Lǎngtíng Yángzǐ Jīngpǐn Bīnguǎn; Map p182; ☏6080 0800; www.langhamhotels.com; 740 Hankou Rd; 汉口路740号; d ¥1300-1800; Ⓜ People's Square; ❀❀☎) Originally built in the 1930s, this art deco beauty was refurbished and reopened in 2010. In addition to period decor, rooms feature deep baths, glass-walled bathrooms (with Venetian blinds) and even tiny balconies – a rarity in Shànghǎi. The hammam and sauna in the fabulous Chuan spa are complimentary for guests; breakfast is served in the Italian restaurant Ciao. Wi-fi costs extra.

JW Marriott Tomorrow Square LUXURY HOTEL $$$
(明天广场JW万怡酒店; Míngtiān Guǎngchǎng JW Wànyí Jiǔdiàn; Map p182; ☏5359 4969; www.marriotthotels.com/shajw; 399 West Nanjing Rd; 南京

西路399号; d ¥2180-3330; ❄✳@⊜✉; Ⓜ People's Square) Victor Sassoon probably would have traded in his old digs in a heartbeat if he could have stayed in the chairman's suite here. Housed across the upper 24 floors of one of Shànghǎi's most dramatic towers, the JW Marriott boasts marvellously appointed rooms with spectacular vistas (the view over People's Sq from the 38th-floor lobby cafe is something in itself) and showers with hydraulic massage functions to soak away the stress. Wi-fi access is an extra ¥120 per day.

Les Suites Orient
LUXURY HOTEL $$$

(东方商旅酒店; Dōngfāng Shānglǔ Jiǔdiàn; Map p182; ☑6320 0088; www.hotelsuitesorient.com; 1 East Jinling Rd; 金陵东路1号; d ¥1580-2280; Ⓜ Yuyuan Garden; ❄✳@⊜✉) Located at the southern edge of the Bund, Les Suites Orient is notable as the only hotel on the strip with standard rooms (Bund Studio) that have fantastic river and Bund views – in some rooms even the bathtub has a view. It's housed in a modern 23-storey tower, with hardwood floors and minimalist design adding to the appealingly chic interior. Excellent service.

Peninsula Hotel
LUXURY HOTEL $$$

(上海半岛酒店; Shànghǎi Bàndǎo Jiǔdiàn; Map p182; ☑2327 2888; www.peninsula.com; 32 East Zhongshan No 1 Rd; 中山东一路32号; d ¥2300-4600; ❄✳@⊜✉; Ⓜ East Nanjing Rd) This luxury hotel at the Bund's northern end combines art deco motifs with Shànghǎi modernity, but it's the little touches that distinguish it from the numerous other five-star places in the neighbourhood: a TV in the bathtub, valet box, Nespresso machine, and fabulous views across the river or out onto the gardens of the former British consulate.

Waldorf Astoria
LUXURY HOTEL $$$

(华尔道夫酒店; Huáěr Dàofū Jiǔdiàn; Map p182; ☑6322 9988; www.waldorfastoriashanghai.com; 2 East Zhongshan No 1 Rd; 中山东一路2号; d ¥2500-3500; Ⓜ East Nanjing Rd; ❄✳@⊜✉) Marking the southern end of the Bund is the stately Shànghǎi Club (1910), once the Bund's most exclusive gentlemen's club. The 20 original rooms here were reconverted in 2010 to house the Waldorf Astoria's premium suites, six of which look out onto Huángpǔ River. Behind this heritage building is a new hotel tower, which holds 252 state-of-the-art rooms, each featuring luxuries such as touch digital controls, espresso machine, walk-in closet and even a TV in the mirror.

Motel 268
MOTEL $

(莫泰连锁旅馆; Mòtài Liánsuǒ Lǚguǎn; Map p182; ☑5179 3333; www.motel168.com; 50 Ningbo Rd; 宁波路50号; d ¥268-308; ✳@⊜; Ⓜ East Nanjing Rd) The ever-dependable Motel 268 comes through with modern doubles near the Bund, with huge beds, wood-trimmed furnishings, and smartly tiled chrome and glass bathrooms. Check the website for other locations around Shànghǎi, including the **Motel 168** (Map p182; ☑5153 3333; 531 East Jinling Rd; 金陵东路531号; d ¥311-338; ✳@; Ⓜ Dashijie) near People's Sq.

Mingtown Nanjing Road Youth Hostel
HOSTEL $

(明堂上海南京路青年旅舍; Míngtáng Shànghǎi Nánjīng Lù Qīngnián Lǚshè; Map p182; ☑6322 0939; 258 Tianjin Rd; 天津路258号; dm ¥55, s/d ¥150/220; Ⓜ East Nanjing Rd; ❄@⊜) This new Mingtown hostel is located halfway between the Bund and People's Sq and is just a short hop away from the nearest metro station.

SHÀNGHǍI SLEEPING

DON'T MISS

KEEPING THE PEACE

Lording it over the corner of East Nanjing and East Zhongshan Rds is the most famous building on the Bund, the landmark **Fairmont Peace Hotel**, constructed between 1926 and 1929. It was originally built as the Sassoon House, with Victor Sassoon's famous Cathay Hotel on the 4th to the 7th floors. It was not a hotel for the hoi polloi, with a guest list running to Charlie Chaplin, George Bernard Shaw and Noel Coward, who penned *Private Lives* here in four days in 1930 when he had the flu. Sassoon himself spent weekdays in his personal suite on the top floor, just beneath the green pyramid.

You don't have to be a guest to admire the wonderful art deco lobby and magnificent rotunda or listen to the old jazz band (p211) in the evening. It's also possible to arrange an hour-long tour (¥100) of the premises through the **Peace Gallery** (☑6321 6888, ext 6751; ⊙10am-7pm), a small museumlike space that contains hotel memorabilia and is hidden up a flight of stairs near the main entrance. It's recommended you book a half-day in advance.

The six-bed dorms each have a private bathroom, laminated wood flooring and simple particleboard decor; perks include laundry, a real kitchen, bar-restaurant, DVD room and pool table.

Mingtown Etour Youth Hostel HOSTEL $

(上海新易途国际青年旅舍; Shànghǎi Xīnyìtú Guójì Qīngnián Lǚshè; Map p182; ☑6327 7766; 55 Jiangyin Rd; 江阴路55号; dm ¥55, d without/with bathroom ¥160/260; ❄@🛜; Ⓜ People's Square) The Etour has a choice location just behind People's Sq, and pleasant rooms (many with reproduction antique furniture) to boot. But it's the tranquil courtyard with fish pond and split-level bar-restaurant that really sells this one. The superb communal area comes with computers, a projector-screen DVD player, free pool table and plenty of outdoor seating.

Mingtown Hiker Youth Hostel HOSTEL $

(上海旅行者青年旅舍; Shànghǎi Lǚxíngzhě Qīngnián Lǚshè; Map p182; ☑6329 7889; 450 Middle Jiangxi Rd; 江西中路450号; dm without/with window ¥50/55, s/d ¥160/220; ❄@; Ⓜ East Nanjing Rd) A short hike from the Bund, this is a well-located and friendly hostel. Rooms include tidy four- and six-bed dorms (some with shower, cheapest without windows) and a handful of good-value luxury doubles, decorated in a Chinese style. There's a bar with pool table, free movies, and internet access. Wi-fi in the lobby only.

Soho People's Square
Youth Hostel HOSTEL $

(苏州河畔国际青年旅舍; Sūzhōu Hépàn Guójì Qīngnián Lǚshè; off Map p182; ☑5888 8817; 1307 South Suzhou Rd; 南苏州路1307号; dm without/with bathroom ¥55/65, d ¥200-300, tr ¥400; ❄@🛜; Ⓜ Xinzha Rd) Set in a former warehouse along Sūzhōu Creek, this spacious hostel features high ceilings, painted murals on the walls and oodles of laid-back common space. It's a bit out of the way, but only a five-minute walk from the Xinzha Rd metro station on Line 1, which runs direct through People's Sq and the French Concession. Laundry and some kitchen facilities (microwave, fridge) available.

The Phoenix HOSTEL $

(老陕客栈; Lǎoshǎn Kèzhàn; Map p182; ☑6328 8680; www.thephoenixshanghai.com; 17 South Yunnan Rd; 云南南路17号; dm/d ¥55/230; ❄@🛜; Ⓜ Dashijie) Although the corridors are a bit grotty, the rooms at this friendly place are actually in pretty good shape. Dorms sleep eight people, and doubles are more appealing than similar choices in more expensive midrange hotels. The rooftop bar and ground-floor Shaanxi dumpling restaurant adds to the appeal. Good location close to People's Sq.

Captain Hostel HOSTEL $

(船长青年酒店; Chuánzhǎng Qīngnián Jiǔdiàn; Map p182; ☑6323 5053; www.captainhostel.com.cn; 37 Fuzhou Rd; 福州路37号; dm ¥65, r ¥358-458; ❄@) Hands down the least-friendly youth hostel in Shànghǎi, this state-run place still reels in punters by the boatload with its fantastic location off the Bund and spot-on rooftop bar. Wi-fi in the lobby area only.

OLD TOWN & SOUTH BUND
The Waterhouse
at South Bund BOUTIQUE HOTEL $$

(off Map p182; ☑6080 2988; www.waterhouseshanghai.com; 1-3 Maojiayuan Rd, Lane 479, South Zhongshan Rd; 中山南路479弄毛家园路1-3; d ¥1100-2800; Ⓜ Xiaonanmen; 🌐🛜) This 19-room, four-storey South Bund converted 1930s warehouse right by the Cool Docks has excellent views, with natty guestrooms (some with terrace) dressed with swish designer furniture. The ethos is industrial chic, capped by a lovely rooftop bar.

Hotel Indigo
Shanghai on the Bund HOTEL $$$

(英迪格酒店; Yīngdígé Jiǔdiàn; off Map p182; www.hotelindigo.com; 585 East Zhongshan No 2 Rd; 中山东二路585号; d ¥4546-5006; @🛜❄; Ⓜ Xiaonanmen) With its creatively conceived lobby, the towering Hotel Indigo is a stylish South Bund arrival overlooking the Huángpǔ River. The chic and playful rooms are all colourful cushions, whimsical design, lovely rugs and spotless shower rooms, while the infinity pool is a dream. Regular discounts reach up to 60%.

FRENCH CONCESSION
Langham Xīntiāndì LUXURY HOTEL $$$

(新天地朗廷酒店; Xīntiāndì Lǎngtíng Jiǔdiàn; Map p188; ☑2330 2288; http://xintiandi.langhamhotels.com; 99 Madang Rd; 马当路99号; r ¥1550-2900; Ⓜ Changshu Rd; 🌐❄🛜) Xīntiāndì has become a magnet for luxury hotels and they don't come much nicer than this one. Its 357 rooms all feature huge floor-to-ceiling windows, plenty of space to spread out and an attention to minute details: Japanese-style wooden tubs in suites, heated bathroom floors and white orchids in bloom year-round.

Andaz

LUXURY HOTEL $$$

(安达仕酒店; Ăndáshì Jiŭdiàn; Map p188; ☑2310 1234; http://shanghai.andaz.hyatt.com; 88 Songshan Rd; 嵩山路88号; r ¥1820-2820; Ⓜ South Huangpi Rd; ☺✲✱☎) Housed in one of the twin skyscrapers just north of Xīntiāndì, Andaz brought in Japanese interior designer Super Potato to lay out the rooms, and the result is a hip, modern space, with clean lines, natural materials (hardwood floors, granite bathrooms) and the signature LED lighting, which can be customised to suit your mood. Discounts of up to 35% online.

TOP CHOICE ★ Magnolia Bed & Breakfast

B&B $$

(Map p188; www.magnoliabnbshanghai.com; 36 Yanqing Rd; 延庆路36号; r ¥650-1200; ☺✲☎; Ⓜ Changshu Rd) Opened by the duo that started the cooking school The Kitchen at... (p198), this cosy little B&B is located in a 1927 French Concession home. It's Shànghǎi all the way, with an art deco starting point followed by a stylish quest for modernity in both comfort and design. While the five rooms are on the small side, the place is a true labour of love and you couldn't ask for a better neighbourhood to base yourself.

Quintet

B&B $$

(Map p188; ☑6249 9088; www.quintet-shanghai. com; 808 Changle Rd; 长乐路808号; d ¥850-1200; ☺✲☎; Ⓜ Changshu Rd) This chic B&B has six beautiful double rooms in a 1930s townhouse that's not short on character. Some of the rooms are on the small side, but each is decorated with style, incorporating modern luxuries such as big-screen satellite TV, wifi and laptop-sized safes, with more classic touches such as stripped-wood floorboards and deep porcelain bathtubs. No elevator.

Kevin's Old House

B&B $$

(老时光酒店; Lǎoshíguāng Jiŭdiàn; Map p188; ☑6248 6800; www.kevinsoldhouse.com; No 4, Lane 946, Changle Rd; 长乐路946弄4号; ste ¥1180-1280; Ⓜ Changshu Rd; ✲☎) Housed in a secluded 1927 French Concession villa, this lovely boutique hotel has been lovingly restored to create an elegant yet affordable place to stay. Six suites are spread throughout the house; each is decorated with care and comes with wooden floorboards, traditional Chinese furniture, stylish artwork and a few antiques.

Héngshān Moller Villa

HISTORIC HOTEL $$$

(衡山马勒别墅饭店; Héngshān Mǎlè Biéshù Fàndiàn; Map p188; ☑6247 8881; www.moller villa.com; 30 South Shaanxi Rd; 陕西南路30号; r ¥1500-2800; Ⓜ South Shaanxi Rd; ✲@) This fairy-tale castle lookalike, built by Swedish businessman and horse-racing fanatic Eric Moller, was a family home until 1949 when the Communist Youth League took it over. One of Shànghǎi's strangest buildings, it's nonetheless a gorgeous place, with parquet floors in the lobby and a lush garden in the back. Wi-fi in the lobby only.

Ruìjīn Hotel

HISTORIC HOTEL $$$

(瑞金宾馆; Ruìjīn Bīnguǎn; Map p188; ☑6472 5222; www.ruijinhotelsh.com; 118 Ruijin No 2 Rd, French Concession East; 瑞金二路118号; d standard/executive ¥1320/2310; Ⓜ South Shaanxi Rd; ✲@) There are four buildings in this lovely garden estate, but the one you want is building No 1, a 1919 red-brick mansion and the former residence of Benjamin Morris, one-time owner of *North China Daily News*. Expect discounts of 20%.

Blue Mountain Youth Hostel

HOSTEL $

(蓝山国际青年旅舍; Lánshān Guójì Qīngnián Lǔshě; Map p188; ☑6304 3938; www.bmhostel. com; Bldg 1, 2nd fl, 1072 Quxi Rd; 瞿溪路1072号1 号甲2楼; dm ¥55-65, d ¥190; ✲@☎; Ⓜ Luban Rd) A good hostel that's not exactly in the thick of things, but it is next to a metro station so transport is at least convenient. Rooms are simple but clean, and there are women-only, men-only and mixed dorms. The communal facilities are excellent, including a bar-restaurant area with free pool table, internet and films, plus a kitchen and washing machines.

Hàntíng Hotel

HOTEL $

(汉庭酒店; Hàntíng Jiŭdiàn; Map p188; ☑5465 6633; www.htinns.com; 233 South Shaanxi Rd, French Concession East; 陕西南路233号; d from ¥339; ✲@☎; Ⓜ South Shaanxi Rd or Jiashan Rd) Although rooms are a bit on the small side at this midrange chain, they're nonetheless spotless and in good condition, with a sprig of plastic ivy on the air conditioner to add that special touch. English is limited.

WEST NANJING ROAD & JÌNG'ĀN

★ Urbn

BOUTIQUE HOTEL $$$

(Map p193; ☑5153 4600; www.urbnhotels.com; 183 Jiaozhou Rd; 胶州路183号; r from ¥1500; ☺✲☎; Ⓜ Changping Rd) China's first carbon-neutral hotel not only uses recyclable materials and low-energy products where possible, it also calculates its complete carbon footprint – including staff commutes and delivery journeys – then offsets it by donating money to environmentally friendly projects. The 26 open-plan rooms are beautifully designed with low furniture and sunken living areas exuding space.

TOP CHOICE Le Tour Traveler's Rest Youth Hostel
HOSTEL $

(乐途静安国际青年旅舍; Lètú Jìng'ān Guójì Qīngnián Lǔshè; Map p193; ☑6267 1912; www.le tourshanghai.com; 36, Alley 319, Jiaozhou Rd; 胶州路319弄36号; dm/d ¥70/260; ❋@❄; MJìng'ān Temple) Housed in a former towel factory, this fabulous youth hostel leaves most others out to dry. Sitting quietly in a *lòng* (alleyway), this great place has bundles of space, and the old-Shànghǎi textures continue once inside, with red-brick interior walls and reproduced stone gateways above doorways. Internet, laundry, kitchen, free umbrella loan, table tennis and a pool table.

Jia Shànghǎi
BOUTIQUE HOTEL $$$

(Map p193; ☑6217 9000; www.jiashanghai.com; 931 West Nanjing Rd; 南京西路931号; studio ¥2500; ❄❋@❄) It's easy to miss the understated and anonymous front door of this chic boutique hotel (entrance down Taixing Rd), announced with an unassumingly minute plaque. Offbeat, fun and modish, the lobby ornaments (funky birdcages, amusingly designed clocks) and dapper staff prepare you for the colourful studio rooms in this 1920s building. Discounts of up to 50%.

Pǔlì
LUXURY HOTEL $$$

(璞丽酒店; Pǔlì Jiǔdiàn; Map p193; ☑3203 9999; www.thepuli.com; 1 Changde Rd; 常德路1号; d from ¥3380; ❄❋@❄❄; MJìng'ān Temple) A future-forward Shànghǎi edifice, with open-space rooms divided by hanging screens, and an understated beige and mahogany colour scheme accentuated by the beauty of a few well-placed orchids. Twenty-five storeys high, the Pǔlì makes a strong case for stylish skyscrapers. Book ahead for discounts of up to 60%.

PǓDŌNG NEW AREA

TOP CHOICE The Ritz-Carlton Shanghai Pudong
LUXURY HOTEL $$$

(上海浦东丽思卡尔顿酒店; Shànghǎi Pǔdōng Lìsī Kǎ'ěrdùn Jiǔdiàn; Map p194; ☑2020 1888; www. ritzcarlton.com; Shanghai IFC, 8 Century Ave; 世纪大道8号; d from ¥2400; ❋@❄❄; MLujiazui) From the stingray skin effect wallpaper in the lift to its exquisite accommodation and stunning alfresco bar, the deliciously styled

285-room Ritz-Carlton in the Shanghai IFC seizes the much-contested Pǔdōng hotel crown with aplomb. The beautifully designed rooms – a blend of feminine colours, eye-catching art deco motifs, chic elegance and dramatic Bund-side views – are a stylistic triumph. Divided from the room by a screen, delightful open plan bathrooms feature deep and inviting freestanding bathtubs.

Park Hyatt
LUXURY HOTEL $$$

(柏悦酒店; Bóyuè Jiǔdiàn; Map p194; ☑6888 1234; www.parkhyattshanghai.com; 100 Century Ave; 世纪大道100号; d from ¥3600; ❋@❄❄; MLujiazui) Spanning the 79th to 93rd floors of the towering Shànghǎi World Financial Center, this stratospheric hotel is cool. Beyond the ample windows, the huge towers below dwarf into Lego blocks while from the lobby your view grazes the tip of the Jīnmào Tower. The 174-room hotel is modern and subdued with deco touches: high-walled corridors with beige and brown fabric and tranquilising grey-stone hues lead to luxurious rooms where in-room espresso machines, mist-free bathroom mirrors (containing a small TV screen) and automatically opening toilet seats await. The Park Hyatt is accessed from the south side of the tower. Discounts of up to 20%.

Jumeirah Himalayas Hotel
LUXURY HOTEL $$$

(卓美亚喜玛拉雅酒店; Zhuóměiyà Xǐmǎlāyǎ Jiǔdiàn; ☑3858 0888; www.jumeirah.com; 1108 Meihua Rd; 梅花路1108号; d ¥4149, ste ¥5989-6564; ❋@❄❄; MHuama Rd) Its awesome lobby is festooned with traditional Chinese paintings as an overhead screen swarms with hypnotic images above a Chinese pavilion – this hotel is jaw-dropping. Feng shui–planned rooms are gorgeous and spacious, designed with a strong accent on traditional Chinese aesthetics, given a highly contemporary twist. Discounts are good, but book ahead. The hotel is located south of Century Park, at the junction of Huama Rd and Fangdian Rd, very near Huama Rd metro station.

Grand Hyatt
LUXURY HOTEL $$$

(金茂凯悦大酒店; Jīnmào Kǎiyuè Dàjiǔdiàn; Map p194; ☑5049 1234; www.shanghai.grand. hyatt.com; 88 Century Ave; 世纪大道88号; d from ¥2500; ❋@❄❄; MLujiazui) Commencing on the 54th floor of the Jīnmào Tower, the 555-room Grand Hyatt is still one of Shànghǎi's finest. Its once unimpeachable standard for quality high-rise hotel living in Shànghǎi drew inevitable competition, but an ongoing floor-by-floor refurbishment has pepped up rooms, with eye-catching calligraphic Tang-dynasty poems above beds, espresso-making machines and smart tan leather work desks. Corner rooms are coveted, and the neck-craning 33-storey atrium is always astonishing, while service remains highly attentive and restaurants outstanding.

✗ Eating

In true Shànghǎi style, today's restaurant scene is a reflection of the city's craving for outside trends and tastes, whether it's Hunanese spice or French foie gras. Most visitors will gravitate to the Chinese end of the spectrum, of course, for that's where the best cooking is.

While a dinner overlooking the Huángpǔ River or safe in the Xīntiāndì bubble makes for a nice treat, real foodies know that the best restaurants in China are often where you least expect to find them. Part of the fun of eating out in Shànghǎi is stumbling across those tiny places in malls, metro stations or down backstreets that offer an inimitable dining experience. Don't be put off by eating in chain restaurants; many of Shànghǎi's better eateries have branches scattered across town.

Shànghǎi cuisine itself is generally sweeter than other Chinese cuisines, and is heavy on fish and seafood. Classic dishes and snacks to look for include *xūnyú* (熏鱼; smoked fish), *hóngshāo ròu* (红烧肉; braised pork belly), *shēngjiān* (生煎; fried dumplings) and the *xiǎolóngbāo* (小笼包; Shànghǎi's steamed dumpling) copied everywhere else in China but only true to form here. Make sure to reserve at fancier places.

THE BUND & PEOPLE'S SQUARE

Lost Heaven   CHINESE YÚNNÁN $$$
(花马天堂; Huāmǎ Tiāntáng; Map p182; ☑6330 0967; www.lostheaven.com.cn; 17 East Yan'an Rd; 延安东路17号; dishes ¥38-180; ☺◉回; ⓂEast Nanjing Rd) Lost Heaven might not have the views that keep its rivals in business, but why go to the same old Western restaurants when you can get sophisticated Bai, Dai and Miao folk cuisine from China's mighty southwest? Specialities are flowers (banana and pomegranate), wild mushrooms, chillies, Burmese curries, Bai chicken and superb pu-erh teas, all served in gorgeous Yúnnán-meets-Shànghǎi surrounds.

ᴛᴏᴘ ᴄʜᴏɪᴄᴇ **Hóngyī Plaza**   CHINESE $
(宏伊国际广场; Hóngyī Guójì Guǎngchǎng; Map p182; 299 East Nanjing Rd; 南京东路299号; meals from ¥30; 回; ⓂEast Nanjing Rd) Not all malls are created equal: the Hóngyī effortlessly slices and dices the competition with its star-studded restaurant line-up, and the whole shebang is a mere stone's throw from the waterfront. Top picks here are South Memory (6th floor), which specialises in spicy Hunanese; Dolar Hotpot (5th floor), whose delicious sauce bar makes it popular even outside of winter; Charme (4th floor), a rip-roarin' Hong Kong–style tea restaurant; Wagas (ground floor), Shànghǎi's own wi-fi cafe chain; and Ajisen (basement), king of Japanese ramen.

Yúxin Chuāncài   SICHUANESE $$
(渝信川菜; Map p182; 5th fl, Huasheng Tower, 399 Jiujiang Rd; 九江路399号华盛大厦5楼; dishes ¥18-98; ⓂEast Nanjing Rd; ☺回) A regular contender for Shànghǎi's best Sichuanese, Yúxìn pulls no punches when it comes to the blistering chillies and numbing peppercorns.

SHÀNGHǍI EATING

FOOD STREETS

Shànghǎi's food streets are great spots for gourmands to search for something new. It's not really street food like elsewhere in Asia, but rather a collection of tiny restaurants, each specialising in a different Chinese cuisine.

With a prime central location near People's Park, **Huanghe Rd** (黄河路美食街; Huánghé Lù Měishí Jiē; Map p182; ⓂPeople's Square) covers all the bases from cheap lunches to late-night post-theatre snacks. It's best for dumplings – get 'em fried at **Yang's Fry Dumplings** (小杨生煎馆; No 97) or served up in bamboo steamers across the road at **Jiājiā Soup Dumplings** (佳家汤包; No 90).

Yunnan Rd (云南路美食街; Yúnnán Lù Měishí Jiē; ⓂDashijie) has some interesting speciality restaurants and is just the spot for an authentic meal after museum-hopping at People's Sq. Look out for Shaanxi specialities at No 15 and five-fragrance dim sum at **Wǔ Fāng Zhāi** (五芳斋; Map p182; No 28). You can also find *yán shuǐ yā* (盐水鸭; salted duck) – it's better than it sounds – and Mongolian hotpot here.

Nánxiáng Steamed Bun Restaurant
DUMPLINGS $

(南翔馒头店; Nánxiáng Mántou Diàn; Map p182; 2nd fl, 666 Fuzhou Rd; 豫园商城福佑路666号2楼; steamer 8 dumplings ¥25-50; MPeople's Square; 🚇) Pleasant branch of Shànghǎi's most famous *xiǎolóngbāo* restaurant near People's Sq.

el Willy
SPANISH $$$

(Map p182; ☎5404 5757; www.el-willy.com; 5th fl, 22 East Zhongshan No 2 Rd; 中山东二路22号5楼; tapas ¥45-165, rice for 2 ¥195-265; ⊗Mon-Sat; 🚇; MYuyuan Garden) The unstoppable energy of colourful sock-wearing Barcelona chef Willy fuels this new South Bund space, which ups its charms with cool river views through the 5th-floor arched windows. Take a taxi from the metro station.

M on the Bund
CONTINENTAL $$$

(米氏西餐厅; Mǐshì Xīcāntīng; Map p182; ☎6350 9988; www.m-onthebund.com; 7th fl, 20 Guangdong Rd; 广东路20号7楼; mains ¥188-288, 2-course lunches ¥186; 🚇; MEast Nanjing Rd) With table linen flapping in the breeze alongside exclusive rooftop views to Pǔdōng, the grand dame of the Bund still elicits applause from Shànghǎi's gastronomes.

Shànghǎi Grandmother
CHINESE $

(上海姥姥; Shànghǎi Lǎolao; Map p182; 70 Fuzhou Rd; 福州路70号; dishes ¥20-52; 🚇; MEast Nanjing Rd) This packed home-style eatery is within easy striking distance of the Bund and handy for a casual lunch or dinner. You can't go wrong with the classics, like Grandma's braised pork and fried tomato and egg.

Food Republic
FOOD COURT $

(大食代; Dàshídài; Map p182; 6th fl, Raffles City, 268 Middle Xizang Rd; 西藏中路268号; meals from ¥40; MPeople's Square) King of the food courts, Food Republic offers Asian cuisines in abundance for busy diners, with handy branches around town – this one overlooks the nonstop action on People's Sq. Prepay, grab a card (¥10 deposit) and head to the stall of your choice for on-the-spot service.

OLD TOWN & SOUTH BUND

Din Tai Fung
SHANGHAINESE $$

(鼎泰丰; Map p182; www.dintaifungsh.com.cn; 2nd fl, Yu Fashion Garden, 168 Middle Fangbang Rd; 方浜中路168号豫龙坊2楼; dumplings from ¥29; ⊗10.30am-10pm; 🚇; MYuyuan Garden) This brightly lit and busy Taiwan-owned chain – one of six branches in town – delivers

scrummy Shànghǎi *xiǎolóngbāo* at the apex of flavour – not cheap, but worth every jiǎo. Service is top-notch.

Kebabs on the Grille
INDIAN $$

(off Map p182; ☎6152 6567; No 8, The Cool Docks, 479 South Zhongshan Rd; 中山南路479号; mains from ¥45, steamed rice ¥25, naan ¥20; ⊗11am-10.30pm; 🚇; MXiaonanmen) This very popular Cool Docks restaurant is a real crowd-pleaser. The Boti Mutton (barbecued lamb pieces) is adorable, and there's a delicious range of tandoori dishes, live table-top grills, an excellent range of vegetarian options, and an all-you-can-eat Sunday brunch (¥150).

Char
STEAKHOUSE $$$

(怡餐厅; off Map p182; ☎3302 9995; www.char-thebund.com; 29-31 fl, Hotel Indigo Shanghai on the Bund, 585 East Zhongshan No 2 Rd; steaks from ¥390, burger ¥290, other mains from ¥140; ⊗6-10pm; 🚇; MXiaonanmen) Park yourself on a sofa and size up your Tajima Wagyu rib-eye steak, grilled black cod, seafood tower and stirring views of Lùjiāzuǐ. The views continue in spectacular fashion from the terrace of the supremely chilled-out upstairs bar. Book ahead.

Sōngyuèlóu
VEGETARIAN, CHINESE $

(松月楼; Map p182; 99 Jiujiaochang Rd; dishes ¥25-48; ⊗7am-10pm; 🚇; MYuyuan Garden) This humble spot is Shànghǎi's oldest vegie restaurant, with the usual mix of tofu masquerading as meat. English menu on the 2nd floor.

FRENCH CONCESSION

TOP CHOICE Yīn
CHINESE $$

(音; Map p188; ☎5466 5070; 2nd fl, 4 Hengshan Rd; 衡山路4号2楼; dishes ¥38-108; 🚇; MHengshan Rd) A throwback to the 1930s, Yīn emanates soft, jazzy decadence with its antique furnishings, Song dynasty–style tableware and Ella Fitzgerald on the stereo. It has standout regional dishes from across China, including the superbly named 'squid lost in a sandstorm'.

Dī Shuǐ Dòng
HÚNÁN $$

(滴水洞; Map p188; ☎6253 2689; 2nd fl, 56 South Maoming Rd; 茂名南路56号2层; dishes ¥25-88; 🚇; MSouth Shaanxi Rd) Shànghǎi's oldest Hunanese restaurant is surprisingly down-home, but the menu is sure-fire, albeit mild for one of China's spiciest culinary traditions. The spicy bean curd and *zīrán* (cumin) ribs hit the mark; flesh out the meal with Mao's stewed pork.

Xīnjíshì SHANGHAINESE $$

(新吉士; Map p188; 6336 4746; Xīntiāndì North Block, Bldg 9; 新天地北里9号楼; dishes ¥38-88; South Huangpi Rd or Xintiandi) Delectable Shanghainese home cooking in swish surrounds: specialities include crab dumplings, stuffed red dates and the classic Grandma's braised pork. Several branches.

Spicy Joint SICHUANESE $

(辛香汇; Xīnxiānghuì; Map p188; 3rd fl, K Wah Center, 1028 Middle Huaihai Rd; 淮海中路1028号嘉电中心3楼; dishes ¥12-58; South Shaanxi Rd) The blistering heat at this Sichuanese joint is matched only by its scorching popularity. Dishes are inexpensive by the city's standards; favourites include massive bowls of spicy catfish in hot chilli oil, smoked tea duck and chilli-coated lamb chops. They may ask for a mobile number to secure a place in the queue.

Southern Barbarian CHINESE YÚNNÁN $

(南蛮子; Nánmánzi; Map p188; 5157 5510; 2nd fl, 169 Jinxian Rd; 进贤路169号2楼; dishes ¥25-68; South Shaanxi Rd) Despite the alarming name, there's nothing remotely barbaric about the food here. Instead you get superb MSG-free Yúnnán cuisine: barbecued snapper, beef and mint casserole, chicken wings and the famous Yúnnán goat cheese. Enter through the mall.

Bǎoluó Jiǔlóu SHANGHAINESE $

(保罗酒楼; Map p188; 6279 2827; 271 Fumin Rd; 富民路271号; dishes ¥20-68; 11am-3am; Changshu Rd or Jing'an Temple) Gather up a boisterous bunch of friends for a fun-filled meal at this typically chaotic and cavernous Shànghǎi institution, which has lines out the door late into the night. Try the excellent lion's head meatballs, lotus-leaf roasted duck or the *bǎoluó kǎomàn* (保罗烤鳗; baked eel).

Crystal Jade DIM SUM $

(翡翠酒家; Fěicuì Jiǔjiā; Map p188; 6385 8752; Xīntiāndì South Block, 2nd fl, Bldg 6; 兴业路123弄新天地南里6号2楼; noodles & dim sum ¥16-40; South Huangpi Rd or Xintiandi) What distinguishes Crystal Jade from other dim sum restaurants is the dough: dumpling wrappers are perfectly tender, steamed buns come out light and airy, and the fresh noodles have been pulled to perfection. Go for lunch, when both Cantonese and Shanghainese dim sum are served. It's located in the mall, on the same floor as an equally popular branch of Din Tai Fung (p206).

Sìchuān Citizen SICHUANESE $$

(龙门陈茶屋; Lóngmén Chénchá Wū; Map p188; 5404 1235; 30 Donghu Rd; 东湖路30号; dishes ¥28-98; South Shaanxi Rd) Citizen has opted for the 'rustic chic' look: the wood panelling and ceiling fans conjure up visions of an old-style Chéngdū teahouse that's been made over for an *Elle* photoshoot. But the food is the real stuff, prepared by a Sìchuān kitchen crew to ensure no Shanghainese sweetness creeps into the peppercorn onslaught.

Simply Thai THAI $$

(天泰餐厅; Tiāntài Cāntīng; Map p188; 6445 9551; 5c Dongping Rd; 东平路5号C座; dishes ¥48-68; Changshu Rd) Everyone raves about this place for its delicious MSG-free curries and salads, and crisp decor. There's nice outdoor seating, a decent wine list and good-value lunch specials. Another branch is in Xīntiāndì.

Ferguson Lane ITALIAN, FRENCH $$

(武康庭; Wǔkāng Tíng; Map p188; 376 Wukang Rd; 武康路376号; meals ¥48-130; Shanghai Library or Jiaotong University) On those rare days when Shànghǎi's skies are cloud free, the elegant Ferguson Lane courtyard fills up in the blink of an eye with sun-starved diners. There are several tempting options, including **Coffee Tree** (9am-10pm;), which features panini, salads and organic coffee, and French bistro fare at **Franck** (6437 6465; Tue-Sun, lunch Sat & Sun only).

Noodle Bull NOODLES $

(狠牛面; Hěnniú Miàn; Map p188; 3b, 291 Fumin Rd; 富民路291号1F3b室; noodles ¥28-35; Changshu Rd or South Shaanxi Rd) Far cooler than your average street-corner noodle stand (minimalist concrete chic and funky bowls), Noodle Bull's secret ingredient is the super-slurpable MSG-free broth. Entrance is on Changle Rd.

Chá's CANTONESE $

(查餐厅; Chá Cāntīng; Map p188; 30 Sinan Rd; 思南路30号; dishes ¥20-50; South Shaanxi Rd) Busy, retro Hong Kong–style diner (sweet and sour pork, baked salt chicken, noodles). Plan on a minimum 15-minute wait.

Bankura JAPANESE $

(万藏; Wànzàng; Map p188; 6215 0373; 344 Changle Rd; 长乐路344号; noodles ¥30-45; South Shaanxi Rd) Underground Japanese noodle bar, with delectable extras such as grilled fish, curried prawns and fried shiitake mushrooms.

SHÀNGHǍI EATING

Haiku
JAPANESE $$

(隐ways之语; Yínquán Zhī Yǔ; Map p188; ☑6445 0021; 28b Taojiang Rd; 桃江路28号乙; maki rolls ¥68-98; 😊🍴🅳; Ⓜ Changshu Rd) Wacky maki rolls from the Ninja (prawns, crab and killer spicy sauce) and the Philly (cream cheese and salmon) to the Pimp My Roll (everything).

Xībó Grill
CENTRAL ASIAN $$

(锡伯餐厅; Xībó Cāntīng; Map p188; ☑5403 8330; 3rd fl, 83 Changshu Rd; 常熟路83号3楼; dishes ¥52-98; 🅳; Ⓜ Changshu Rd) If you're in need of a mutton fix, try out the 3rd-floor terrace of this stylish Xīnjiāng joint.

WEST NANJING ROAD & JÌNG'ĀN

Fu 1039
SHANGHAINESE $$$

(福一零三九; Fú Yāo Líng Sān Jiǔ; off Map p188; ☑5237 1878; 1039 Yuyuan Rd; 愚圆路1039号; dishes ¥48-108; 🅳; Ⓜ Jiangsu Rd) Set in a three-storey 1913 villa, Fu is upmarket Shanghainese all the way, with an unusual old-fashioned charm in a city hell-bent on modern design. Not easy to find, it rewards the persistent with succulent standards such as the smoked fish starter and stewed pork in soy sauce.

To get here, follow Yuyuan Rd west from the metro station for about 200m (after crossing Jiangsu Rd) and then turn south down an alley. The unmarked entrance will be the first on your left. There's a minimum charge of ¥200 per person.

[TOP CHOICE] Wujiang Road Food St
FOOD STREET $

(Map p193; Wujiang Rd; 吴江路; meals from ¥30; Ⓜ West Nanjing Rd) This two-block pedestrian snack strip has still got the goods, with plenty of cafes, Japanese and Korean noodle joints, and ice-cream vendors. For Shanghainese, head into the mall at No 269 (above the metro station exit) and look for Yang's Fry Dumplings or Nánxiáng Steamed Bun on the 2nd floor.

Gǔyì Húnán Restaurant
HÚNÁN $$

(古意湘味浓; Gǔyì Xiāngwèinóng; Map p193; ☑6232 8377; 8th fl, City Plaza, 1618 West Nanjing Rd; 南京西路1618号8楼久百城市广场; dishes ¥28-98; Ⓜ Jing'an Temple; 🅳) Classy Húnánese dining and mouth-watering cumin ribs right next to Jìng'ān Temple (in the mall).

[🌿] Vegetarian Lifestyle
CHINESE $$

(枣子树; Zǎozi Shù; Map p193; ☑6215 7566; 258 Fengxian Rd; 奉贤路258号; dishes ¥22-68; 😊🍴🅳; Ⓜ West Nanjing Rd) For light and healthy organic vegetarian Chinese food, with zero meat and precious little oil, this welcoming place has excellent fare. The health-conscious, eco-friendly mentality extends all the way to the toothpicks, made of cornflour.

Shànghǎi Centre
DUMPLINGS, PIZZERIA $$

(上海商城; Shànghǎi Shāngchéng; Map p193; 1376 West Nanjing Rd; 南京西路1376号; pizza ¥58-88; 😊🍴🚭🅳; Ⓜ Jing'an Temple or West Nanjing Rd) You can't beat the Shànghǎi Centre for gourmet offerings: to-die-for dumplings from Din Tai Fung, super smoothies from Element Fresh, thin-crust pies from Pizza Marzano, and carrot cake and sandwiches from Baker & Spice.

Wagas
CAFE $

(沃歌斯; Wògēsī; Map p193; www.wagas.com.cn; 11a, Citic Sq, 1168 West Nanjing Rd; 南京西路1168号下一层11a室; meals from ¥48; ⊙7am-10pm; 😊🍴🅳; Ⓜ West Nanjing Rd) Breakfasts are 50% off before 10am, pasta is ¥38 after 6pm, you can hang out here for hours with your laptop and no one will shoo you away – need we say more? Locations abound.

PǓDŌNG NEW AREA

South Beauty
SICHUANESE, CANTONESE $

(Map p194; 俏江南; Qiào Jiāngnán; ☑5047 1817; 10th fl, Superbrand Mall, 168 West Lujiazui Rd; 陆家嘴西路168号10楼; dishes from ¥18; ⊙11am-10pm; Ⓜ Lujiazui) Views, views and more views – while everyone else is gazing at Pǔdōng's lights, you can stare back at them with loaded chopsticks from this elegant Sìchuān-Cantonese combo. Reserve for window seats.

Element Fresh
SANDWICHES $

(新元素; Xīnyuánsù; Map p194; www.elementfresh.com; 1st fl, Superbrand Mall, 168 West Lujiazui Rd; 陆家嘴西路168号; breakfast ¥38-88; 🅳😊🚭; Ⓜ Lujiazui) This funky Pǔdōng outpost of the Element Fresh chain provides healthy eats through the day from endless coffee refills on breakfasts for early starters to terrific salads, hefty sandwiches, pastas, smoothies and a kid's menu through the day.

NORTH SHÀNGHǍI (HÓNGKǑU)

[TOP CHOICE] Guǒyuán
HÚNÁN $

(果园; 520 Dongjiangwan Rd; 东江湾路520号; meals from ¥30; Ⓜ Hongkou Football Stadium) The cool lime-green tablecloths do little to prepare you for the serious red-hot, chilli-infused flavours of this fantastic Húnán restaurant not too far north of Hongkou Football Stadium metro station. The *tiěbǎn niúròu* (铁板牛肉; sizzling beef platter;

¥30) is a magnificent dish, but its fiery flavours are almost eclipsed by the enticing *xiāngwèi qiézibāo* (湘味茄子煲; Húnán flavour aubergine hotpot).

SOUTH SHÀNGHǍI (XÚJIĀHUÌ)

1001 Noodles House
NOODLES $

(Unit 502, 5th fl, Grand Gateway; 港汇广场5楼502室; noodles from ¥22; 🖻; ⏰10am-10pm; ⓜXujiahui) The *yúxiāng* shredded pork noodles (¥22) or pork chop noodles (¥26) are served in ample and comely bowls at this spotless, sophisticated but cheap noodle house for the dapper dining set in Grand Gateway.

Xīnjiāng Fēngwèi Restaurant
UIGHUR $

(维吾尔餐厅; Wéiwú'ěr Cāntīng; 280 Yishan Rd; 宜山路280号; dishes from ¥15; ⏰10am-2am; 🖻; ⓜYishan Rd or Xujiahui) Kashgar kitsch is the name of the game at this raucous upstairs Uighur restaurant with the bright brass grill out the front, tinsel on the banisters and a menu of tasty Xīnjiāng grilled lamb dishes. Things start buzzing from early evening when the music and dance kick in.

 Drinking

Shànghǎi is awash with watering holes, their fortunes cresting and falling with the vagaries of the latest vogue. Drinks are pricier here than in the rest of China, retailing from around ¥30 (beer) or ¥60 (cocktails) at most places, so happy-hour visits (typically 5pm to 8pm) can be crucial. Bars open either for lunch or in the late afternoon, calling it a night at around 2am.

THE BUND & PEOPLE'S SQUARE

Glamour Bar
COCKTAIL BAR

(魅力酒吧; Mèilì Jiǔbā; Map p182; www.m-glamour. com; 6th fl, 20 Guangdong Rd; 广东路20号6楼; ⏰5pm-late; ⓜEast Nanjing Rd) Michelle Garnaut's stylish bar is set in a splendidly restored space just beneath M on the Bund. In addition to mixing great drinks, it hosts an annual literary festival, music performances and China-related book launches.

Long Bar
BAR

(廊吧; Láng Bā; Map p182; ☎6322 9988; 2 East Zhongshan No 1 Rd; 中山东一路2号; ⏰4pm-1am; ⓜEast Nanjing Rd; 🛜) For a taste of colonial-era Shànghǎi's elitist trappings, you'll do no better than the gorgeous Long Bar inside the Waldorf Astoria. This was once the members' only Shànghǎi Club, whose most spectacular accoutrement was a 34m-long wooden bar, said to be the longest in Asia.

Captain's Bar
BAR

(船长青年酒吧; Chuánzhǎng Qīngnián Jiǔbā; Map p182; 6th fl, 37 Fuzhou Rd; 福州路37号6楼; ⏰11am-2am; 🛜; ⓜEast Nanjing Rd) There's the odd drunken sailor and the crummy lift needs a rethink, but this is a fine Bund-side terrace-equipped bar atop the Captain Hostel. Come for cheap drinks and phosphorescent nocturnal Pǔdōng views, with pizza and without wall-to-wall preening sophisticates.

Barbarossa
BAR

(芭芭露莎会所; Bābālùshā Huìsuǒ; Map p182; People's Park, 231 West Nanjing Rd; 南京西路231号人民公园内; ⏰11am-2am; 🛜; ⓜPeople's Square) Bringing a whiff of Middle Eastern promise to the Pearl of the Orient, this Moroccan-styled bar-restaurant sits pondside in People's Park like something from a mirage. It's more than a mere novelty: there's excellent music, outside seating and evening views.

New Heights
BAR, CAFE

(新视角; Xīn Shìjiǎo; Map p182; 7th fl, Three on the Bund, 3 East Zhongshan No 1 Rd; 中山东一路3号7楼; ⏰11am-1.30am; 🛜; ⓜEast Nanjing Rd) The terrace of this casual Three on the Bund bar pretty much has *the* definitive angle on Lùjiāzuǐ's neon nightfall overture.

Bar Rouge
BAR

(Map p182; 7th fl, Bund 18, 18 East Zhongshan No 1 Rd; 中山东一路18号7楼; ⏰6pm-2am Sun-Thu, to 4.30am Fri & Sat; ⓜEast Nanjing Rd) Bar Rouge attracts a cashed-up party crowd who come for the fantastic views from the terrace and the all-night DJ parties.

Atanu
BAR, CAFE

(阿塔努咖啡酒吧; Ātǎnǔ Kāfēi Jiǔbā; Map p182; 1 Zhongshan East No 2 Rd; 中山东二路1号; ⏰10am-2am; ⓜEast Nanjing Rd) Located on the top two floors of the former signal tower at the Bund's southern terminus, this is an ideal pit stop.

OLD TOWN

Old Shànghǎi Teahouse
TEAHOUSE

(老上海茶馆; Lǎo Shànghǎi Cháguǎn; Map p182; 385 Middle Fangbang Rd; 方浜中路385号; ⏰9am-9pm; ⓜYuyuan Garden) Heading up here is like barging into someone's attic, where ancient gramophones, records, typewriters, fire extinguishers and even an ancient Frigidaire refrigerator share space with the aroma of Chinese tea and tempting snacks.

Moonlight Teahouse TEAHOUSE

(耕月人茶馆; Gēngyuèrén Cháguǎn; Map p182; 4th fl, 235 Middle Fangbang Rd; 方浜中路235号4楼; ⏰10am-11pm; ⓜYuyuan Garden) Squirreled away on the 4th floor, the Qing-dynasty setting of stone carvings, Chinese lions and antiques is unrepentently faux, but this is a relaxing place caressed with traditional Chinese music and infused with the aroma of tea. It's next to the Temple of the Town God, on the corner of Anren St (安仁街); take the lift.

FRENCH CONCESSION

TOP CHOICE **Abbey Road** BAR

(艾比之路; Àibǐ Zhī Lù; Map p188; 45 Yueyang Rd; 岳阳路45号; ⏰4pm-late Mon-Fri, 8.30am-late Sat & Sun; ☎; ⓜChangshu Rd) The cheap beer-classic rock combination works its stuff again, attracting plenty of regulars to this French Concession favourite.

Apartment BAR

(Map p188; 3rd fl, 47 Yongfu Rd; 永福路47号; ⏰11-2am; ☎; ⓜShanghai Library) This trendy loft-style bar has a dance space located across from the bar and a top-level terrace for summer BBQ action.

Bell Bar BAR, CAFE

(Map p188; http://bellbar.cn; Tiánzǐfáng, No 11 (back door) Lane 248, Taikang Rd; 泰康路248弄11号后门田子坊; ⏰11am-2am; ☎; ⓜDapuqiao) Perhaps the most discreet of Tiánzǐfáng's drinking options, this dimly lit hookah-equipped den is the perfect spot to chill for an hour or three. It's located in the second alley (Lane 248) on the right.

Kommune CAFE

(公社酒吧; Gōngshè Jiǔbā; Map p188; Tiánzǐfáng, No 7, Lane 210, Taikang Rd; 泰康路210弄7号田子坊; ⏰8am-midnight; ☎; ⓜDapuqiao) The original Tiánzǐfáng cafe, Kommune is a consistently packed hang-out with outdoor courtyard seating, drinks, big breakfasts and sandwiches on the menu.

Kāibā BAR

(开巴; Map p188; www.kaiba-beerbar.com; Tiánzǐfáng, 2nd fl, 169 Middle Jianguo Rd; 建国中路169号2楼田子坊; ⏰11am-2am; ⓜDapuqiao; ☎) The Kāibā beer specialists run one of Tiánzǐfáng's most popular bars. You'll need to explore to find it.

Boxing Cat Brewery BAR

(拳击猫啤酒屋; Quánjīmāo Píjiǔwū; Map p188; www.boxingcatbrewery.com; Unit 26A, Sinan Mansions, 519 Middle Fuxing Rd; 复兴中路519号思南

公馆26A; ⏰11am-2am; ⓜXintiandi) Deservedly popular microbrewery in the Sinan Mansions complex with Southern-style grub.

Cafe 85°C CAFE

(85度咖啡店; Bāshíwǔ Dù Kāfēidiàn; Map p188; 117 South Shaanxi Rd; 陕西南路117号; ⏰24hr; ⓜSouth Shaanxi Rd) The cheapest caffeine fix (and breakfast) in town, with quality coffee, tea and never-before-seen Taiwanese pastries. Dozens of branches in town.

Shànghǎi Brewery BREWERY

(Map p188; www.shanghaibrewery.com; 15 Dongping Rd; 东平路15号; ⏰10am-2am; ⓜChangshu Rd, Hengshan Rd; ☎) Hand-crafted microbrews, a huge range of comfort food, pool tables and sports on TV...this massive two-storey hang-out might have it all.

Time Passage BAR

(昨天今天明天; Zuótiān Jīntiān Míngtiān; Map p188; No 183, Lane 1038, Caojiayan Rd; 曹家堰路1038弄183号; ⏰5.30pm-2am; ☎; ⓜJiangsu Rd) If you like cheap beer, an undemanding, lived-in ambience and John and Yoko posters, this businessman-free bar has been charting its passage since 1994.

JÌNG'ĀN

Big Bamboo SPORTS BAR

(Map p193; 132 Nanyang Rd; 南阳路132号; ⏰9.30am-2am; ☎; ⓜJing'an Temple) Huge sports bar ranging over two floors with mammoth sports screen backed up by a constellation of TV sets, Guinness, pool and darts.

Bàndù Cabin CAFE

(半度音乐; Bàndù Yīnyuè; Map p196; ☑6276 8267; Bldg 11, 50 Moganshan Rd; 莫干山路50号11号楼; ⏰10am-6.30pm; ☎; ⓜShanghai Railway Station) A welcoming low-key Moganshan Rd Art Centre enclave with pine tables, low-cost menu (noodles, coffee) and traditional Chinese musical events on Saturday evenings at 7.30pm (reserve).

PǓDŌNG NEW AREA

Flair BAR

(Map p194; 58th fl, The Ritz-Carlton Shanghai Pudong, 8 Century Ave; 世纪大道8号58楼; ⏰5.30pm-2am; ⓜLujiazui) To wow your date (and your bank manager), take the lift to Flair, the highest alfresco terrace in town, for ringside seats onto some of the most sublime neon-scape views of nocturnal Shànghǎi. Clear evenings are crucial, but drink prices can be sky scraping on the terrace itself (although the bar inside is almost as knock-out).

Cloud 9

BAR

(九重天酒廊; Jiǔchóngtiān Jiǔláng; Map p194; 87th fl, Jinmào Tower, 88 Century Ave; 世纪大道88号金茂大厦87; ⊙5pm-1am Mon-Fri, 11am-2am Sat & Sun; Ⓜ Lujiazui) Atop the Grand Hyatt, this is no longer the highest bar in the city, but it's still cool.

NORTH SHÀNGHǍI (HÓNGKǑU)

Vue

BAR

(非常时髦; Fēicháng Shímáo; Map p182; 32nd & 33rd fl, Hyatt on the Bund, 199 Huangpu Rd; 外滩茂悦大酒店黄浦路199号32-33楼; ⊙6pm-1am; Ⓜ Tiantong Rd) Extra-sensory nocturnal views of the Bund and Pǔdōng with an outdoor Jacuzzi to go with your glasses of bubbly or Vue martinis (vodka and mango purée).

☆ Entertainment

There's something for most moods in Shànghǎi: opera, rock, hip-hop, techno, salsa and early-morning waltzes in People's Sq. None of it comes cheap, however (except for the waltzing, which is free). Expect a night on the town in Shànghǎi to be comparable to a night out in Hong Kong or Taipei.

Traditional Performances

The Shànghǎi acrobatics troupes are among the best in the world, and spending a night watching them spinning plates on poles and contorting themselves into unfeasible anatomical positions never fails to entertain.

Yìfū Theatre

OPERA

(逸夫舞台; Yìfū Wǔtái; Map p182; ☑6322 5294; 701 Fuzhou Rd; tickets ¥30-280; Ⓜ People's Square) A block east of People's Sq, this is the main opera theatre in town, staging a variety of regional operatic styles, including Běijīng opera, Kunqu opera and Yue opera, with a Běijīng opera highlights show several times a week at 1.30pm and 7.15pm.

Shànghǎi Centre Theatre

ACROBATICS

(上海商城剧院; Shànghǎi Shāngchéng Jùyuàn; Map p193; ☑6279 8948; www.pujiangqing.com; 1376 West Nanjing Rd; 南京西路1376号; tickets ¥100-280; Ⓜ Jing'an Temple) The Shànghǎi Acrobatic Troupe has short but entertaining performances here most nights at 7.30pm. The ticket office is on the right-hand side at the entrance to the Shànghǎi Centre.

Live Music

Fairmont Peace Hotel Jazz Bar

LIVE MUSIC

(Map p182; ☑6138 6883; 20 East Nanjing Rd; 南京东路20号; ⊙5.30pm-1am; Ⓜ East Nanjing Rd) Shànghǎi's most famous hotel features

TICKETS

Tickets for all of Shànghǎi's performing-arts events can be purchased at the venues where the performances take place. Tickets are also available from **Smart Ticket** (www.smartshanghai.com/smartticket) and the **Shànghǎi Cultural Information & Booking Centre** (上海文化信息票务中心; Shànghǎi Wénhuà Xìnxī Piàowù Zhōngxīn; Map p193; ☑6217 2426; www.culture.sh.cn; 272 Fengxian Rd; 奉贤路272号; ⊙9am-7pm; Ⓜ West Nanjing Rd), which is directly behind the Westgate Mall on West Nanjing Rd. It often has tickets available when other places have sold out.

Shànghǎi's most famous jazz band, a septuagenarian sextet that's been churning out nostalgic covers like 'Moon River' and 'Summertime' since time immemorial. The original band takes the stage from 7pm to 9.45pm; afterwards it's Theo Croker's smokin' contemporary group (from 10pm to 1am Tuesday to Saturday). Entrance is ¥100; reserve on weekends.

Yùyīntáng

ROCK

(育音堂; www.yuyintang.org; 1731 West Yan'an Rd, 延安西路1731号; admission ¥40; ⊙8pm-midnight Thu-Sun; Ⓜ West Yan'an Rd) Small enough to feel intimate, but big enough for a sometimes pulsating atmosphere, Yùyīntáng has long been the place in the city to see live music. Rock is the staple diet, but anything goes, from hard punk to gypsy jazz. It's west of the city, on Lines 3 and 4. The entrance is on Kaixuan Rd.

MAO Livehouse

LIVE MUSIC

(Map p188; www.mao-music.com; 3rd fl, 308 South Chongqing Rd; 重庆南路308号3楼; Ⓜ Madang Rd) One of the city's best and largest music venues, MAO is a stalwart of the Shànghǎi music scene, with acts ranging from rock to pop to electronica. Check the website for upcoming shows.

Nightclubs

Shànghǎi's swift transition from dead zone to party animal and its reputation as a city on the move forges an inventive clubbing attitude and a constant stream of clubbers. There's a high turnover, so check listings websites and magazines for the latest on the club scene.

ACUPRESSURE MASSAGE

Shànghǎi's midrange massage parlours are a must – for the price of a cocktail or three, you get your own set of PJs, some post-therapy tea and Chinese flute music to chill out with. Just don't expect the masseuses to be gentle. As they say: no pain, no gain. Reserve in advance.

Dragonfly (悠庭保健会所; Yōutíng Bǎojiàn Huìsuǒ; Map p188; www.dragonfly.net.cn; massages ¥168-420; ⏱10am-2am); Donghu Rd (☎5405 0008; 20 Donghu Rd; 东湖路20号; Ⓜ South Shaanxi Rd); Xinle Rd (☎5403 9982; 206 Xinle Rd; 新乐路206号; Ⓜ South Shaanxi Rd) Offers hour-long Chinese body massages, Japanese-style shiatsu and traditional foot massages in soothing surroundings. There are several branches around town.

Green Massage (青专业按摩; Qīng Zhuānyè Ànmó; www.greenmassage.com.cn; massages ¥118-528; ⏱10.30am-2am) French Concession (off Map p188; ☎5386 0222; 58 Taicang Rd; 太仓路58号; Ⓜ South Huangpi Rd); Jing'an (Map p193; ☎6289 7776; 2nd fl, Shànghǎi Centre, 1376 West Nanjing Rd; 南京西路1376号2楼; Ⓜ Jing'an Temple) Has 45-minute *tuīná* and shiatsu massages with Chinese cupping and hour-long foot massages.

Shelter
CLUB

(Map p188; 5 Yongfu Rd; 永福路5号; ⏱9pm-4am Wed-Sun; Ⓜ Shanghai Library) The darling of the underground crowd, Shelter is a converted bomb shelter where you can count on great music and cheap drinks. A good line-up of DJs and hip-hop artists pass through; admission for big shows is around ¥30.

No 88
CLUB

(搜浩88酒吧; Sōuhào Bābā Jiǔbā; Map p188; www.no88bar.com; 2nd fl, 291 Fumin Rd; 富民路291号; ⏱9pm-6am; Ⓜ South Shaanxi Rd or Changshu Rd) One of the city's most popular party spots, this is the place to go when you're ready to get down China style. The interior is totally over the top – you have to see it to believe it.

Lola
CLUB

(Map p188; www.lolaclubshanghai.com; Bldg 4, Surpass Ct, 570 Yongjia Rd; 永嘉路570号4号楼; ⏱10pm-3am Tue-Sat; Ⓜ Hengshan Rd) A superior sound system and wall-to-ceiling video projections that sync with the beat pull in the crowds at this first-rate club, opened by a trio of Catalan DJs.

DADA
CLUB

(off Map p188; 115 Xingfu Rd; 幸福路115号; ⏱8pm-late; Ⓜ Jiaotong University) This friendly no-frills place out by Jiaotong University is one of Shànghǎi's most popular dives, specialising in cheap drinks, Tuesday-night slasher flicks (free popcorn) and popular weekend dance parties.

Gay & Lesbian Venues

Shànghǎi Studio
GAY

(嘉浓休闲; Jiānóng Xiūxián; Map p188; No 4, Lane 1950, Middle Huaihai Rd; 淮海中路1950弄4号; ⏱9pm-2am; Ⓜ Jiaotong University) This hip addition to the Shànghǎi gay scene has transformed the cool depths of a former bomb shelter into a laid-back bar, art gallery and men's underwear shop.

Eddy's Bar
GAY

(嘉浓咖啡; Jiānóng Kāfēi; Map p188; 1877 Middle Huaihai Rd; ⏱8pm-2am; Ⓜ Jiaotong University) A gay-friendly bar-cafe attracting a slightly more mature Chinese and international gay crowd with inexpensive drinks and neat decor.

Classical Music, Opera & Theatre

Shànghǎi Grand Theatre
PERFORMING ARTS

(上海大剧院; Shànghǎi Dàjùyuàn; Map p182; ☎6386 8686; www.shgtheatre.com; 300 Renmin Ave; 人民大道300号; tickets ¥50-2280; Ⓜ People's Square) This state-of-the-art venue is in People's Sq and features both national and international opera, dance, music and theatre performances.

Cinemas

Only a limited (and generally late) selection of foreign-language films makes it to cinemas, and they are often dubbed into Chinese, so ensure your film is *yīngwénbǎn* (英文版; English-language version). Tickets generally cost ¥70 to ¥100; you could also look out for free movie screenings in bars around town.

Peace Cinema
CINEMA

(和平影都、巨幕影院; Hépíng Yǐngdū; Map p182; 290 Middle Xizang Rd; 西藏中路290号; Ⓜ People's Square) A useful location at People's Sq, with an IMAX cinema.

Cathay Theatre — CINEMA

(国泰电影院; Guótài Diànyǐngyuàn; Map p188; 870 Middle Huaihai Rd; 淮海中路870号; ⓂSouth Shaanxi Rd) Landmark 1932 art deco theatre in the French Concession.

Shopping

It is no exaggeration to say that there are some people who come to Shànghǎi specifically to shop. What the city lacks in terms of historical sights, it makes up for with its fashion-forward attitude and great bargains. From megamalls to independent boutiques and haute couture, Shànghǎi is once again at the forefront of Chinese fashion and design.

THE BUND & PEOPLE'S SQUARE

Annabel Lee — FASHION

(安梨家居; Ānlí Jiājū; Map p182; www.annabellee.com; No 1, Lane 8, East Zhongshan No 1 Rd; ⏰10am-10pm; ⓂEast Nanjing Rd) On the Bund, Annabel Lee sells a lovely range of playfully designed, soft-coloured accessories in silk, linen and cashmere, many of which feature delicate embroidery. There's another branch in Xīntiāndì.

Shànghǎi Museum Shop — ART

(上海博物馆商店; Shànghǎi Bówùguǎn Shāngdiàn; Map p182; 201 Renmin Ave; ⏰9am-5pm; ⓂPeople's Square) This shop sells excellent but expensive imitations of museum pieces, which are far superior to the mediocre clutter in tourist shops.

Sūzhōu Cobblers — SHOES

(上海起越艺术品; Shànghǎi Qǐxiǎng Yìshùpǐn; Map p182; www.suzhou-cobblers.com; Room 101, 17 Fuzhou Rd; ⏰10am-6pm; ⓂEast Nanjing Rd) For hand-embroidered silk slippers and shoes, pop into this minute shop just off the Bund.

Cybermart — ELECTRONICS

(赛博数码广场; Sàibó Shùmǎ Guǎngchǎng; Map p182; 1 Middle Huaihai Rd; 淮海中路1号; ⏰10am-8pm; ⓂDashijie) Cybermart is the most central and reliable location for all sorts of gadgetry, including laptops, digital cameras and memory sticks. You can try to bargain, but don't expect enormous discounts.

Foreign Languages Bookstore — BOOKS

(外文书店; Wàiwén Shūdiàn; Map p182; 390 Fuzhou Rd; ⏰9.30am-6pm Sun-Thu, to 7pm Fri & Sat; ⓂEast Nanjing Rd) Hit the 1st floor for guidebooks and China-related material, and the 4th floor for imported non-fiction and novels.

Shànghǎi No 1 (First) Food Store — FOOD

(上海市第一食品商店; Shànghǎishì Dìyī Shípǐn Shāngdiàn; Map p182; 720 East Nanjing Rd; ⏰9.30am-10pm; ⓂEast Nanjing Rd) It's bedlam, but this is how the Shanghainese shop and it's a lot of fun. Trawl the ground floor for egg tarts, moon cakes, dried mushrooms, ginseng and dried seafood, or pop a straw into a thirst-quenching coconut.

OLD TOWN

Yùyuán Bazaar is a frantic sprawl of souvenir shops with some choice gift-giving ideas and quality handicrafts, from painted snuff bottles to paper and leather silhouette cuttings, delightful Chinese kites, embroidered paintings, and clever palm and finger paintings, but sadly the hard sale is off-putting. Shops along nearby **Old Street** (老街; Middle Fangbang Rd; Map p182) are more ye olde, selling everything under the Shànghǎi sun from calligraphy to teapots, memorabilia, woodcuts, reproduction 1930s posters and surreal 3D dazzle photos of kittens.

SHÀNGHǍI SHOPPING

WHERE CAN I FIND...

» **Faux antiques and souvenirs?** Old St or the Dongtai Rd Antique Market in the Old Town.

» **Local fashion?** Tiánzǐfáng and the French Concession (Xinle and Changle Rds).

» **Tailormade clothing and fabric?** Shíliùpù Fabric Market in the Old Town.

» **Discount (OK, fake) clothing and accessories?** Han City Fashion & Accessories Plaza in Jìng'ān or the AP Xīnyáng Fashion & Gifts Market in Pǔdōng.

» **Real pearls?** Amy Lin's Pearls in Jìng'ān.

» **Handicrafts?** Brocade Country, Yú or Sūzhōu Cobblers.

» **Electronics? My laptop crashed in Sìchuān!** Cybermart or the Apple Store in the French Concession.

Shíliùpù Fabric Market

FABRIC

(十六铺面料城; Shíliùpù Miánliào Chéng; off Map p182; 2 Zhonghua Rd; 中华路2号; ⊙8.30am-6.30pm; MXiaonanmen) Expats and travellers line up for made-to-measure clothing at this market, popular for its bolts of cheap silk, cashmere, wool, linen and cotton. Follow Middle Fangbang Rd from the Yùyuán Bazaar east towards the river and you'll reach it after about 10 minutes (500m).

Dongtai Rd Antique Market

SOUVENIRS

(东台路古商品市场; Dōngtáilù Gǔshāngpǐn Shìchǎng; off Map p182; Dongtai Rd; 东台路; ⊙8.30am-6pm; MLaoximen) West of the Old Town towards Xīntiāndì, the Dongtai Rd Antique Market is a long sprawl of miniature terracotta warriors, Guanyin figures, imperial robes, walnut-faced *luóhàn* (arhat) statues, twee lotus shoes, fake old tin cars, helicopter pilot helmets and Mao-era knick-knacks; generally only recent stuff such as art deco ornaments are genuine. Get haggling.

FRENCH CONCESSION

The French Concession is where it's at for shoppers; there are boutiques on almost every corner. For a one-stop trip head to Tiánzǐfáng. With more time, start near the South Shaanxi metro station and try South Maoming Rd for tailormade *qípáo* (a tight-fitting Chinese-style dress that came into fashion in 1920s Shànghǎi), and Xinle and Nanchang Rds (between Ruijin No 1 and S Chengdu Rds) for more contemporary fashion. Afternoon and evening are the best hours for browsing: some smaller shops don't open their doors until noon, but most stay open until 10pm.

Tiánzǐfáng

FASHION, SOUVENIRS

(田子坊; Map p188; Taikang Rd; 泰康路; ⊙10am-8pm; MDapuqiao) Burrow into the *lòng* here for a rewarding haul of creative boutiques, selling everything from hip jewellery and yak-wool scarves to retro communist dinnerware. Stores get shuffled around about as regularly as mahjong tiles, but keep your eyes peeled for **Shànghǎi 1936** (Unit 110, No 3, Lane 210) offering tailored Chinese clothing, **Woo** (Unit 7, No 10, Lane 210) for scarves and shawls, and **Chouchou Chic** (No 47, Lane 248) for kid's clothes, as well as artsy tea shop **Zhenchalin Tea** (No 13, Lane 210).

Xīntiāndì

FASHION

(Map p188; 新天地; cnr Taicang & Madang Rds; 太仓路与马当路路口; ⊙11am-11pm; MSouth Huangpi Rd or Xintiandi) Browse the north block for upmarket boutiques, from the fluorescent chic of **Shanghai Tang** (Bldg 15) to embroidered accessories at **Annabel Lee** (Bldg 3), and the mall **Xīntiāndì Style** (新天地时尚; Xīntiāndì Shíshàng; 245 Madang Lu; 马当路245号), which features a handful of local designers including la vie, Heirloom, The Thing and Shànghǎi Trio. It's the second mall at the end of the South Block.

NuoMi

CLOTHING, JEWELLERY

(糯米; Nuòmǐ; Map p188; 196 Xinle Rd; 新乐路196号; MChangshu Rd) This Shànghǎi-based label seems to do everything right: gorgeous dresses made from organic cotton, silk and bamboo, eye-catching jewellery fashioned from recycled materials, and a sustainable business plan that gives back to the community.

XinleLu.com

CLOTHING, VINTAGE

(Map p188; www.xinlelu.com; 87 Wuyuan Rd; 五原路87号; ⊙noon-10pm Tue-Sun; MChangshu Rd) Local style mavens XinleLu.com have finally ventured out into the offline world with this original showroom, displaying the best of its handpicked bags, shoes and dresses from local designers. Also sharing the space is vintage store William the Beekeeper.

Yú

CERAMICS

(萸; Map p188; 164 Fumin Rd; 富民路164号; ⊙11am-9pm; MChangshu Rd) Man Zhang and her husband create the personable porcelain at this tiny shop, the latest link in the Shànghǎi-Jǐngdézhèn connection, which is an excellent place to browse for handmade and handpainted teaware, bowls and vases.

Brocade Country

HANDICRAFTS

(锦绣纺; Jǐnxiù Fǎng; Map p188; 616 Julu Rd; 巨鹿路616号; ⊙10.30am-7pm; MChangshu Rd) Exquisite collection of minority handicrafts from China's southwest, personally selected by owner, Liu Xiaolan a Guìzhōu native.

Garden Books

BOOKS

(韬奋西文书局; Tāofèn Xīwén Shūjú; Map p188; 325 Changle Rd; 长乐路325号; ⊙10am-10pm; ☎; MSouth Shaanxi Rd) Ice-cream parlour or bookshop? You decide.

Apple Store

ELECTRONICS

(Map p188; Hong Kong Plaza North Block, 282 Middle Huaihai Rd; 淮海中路282号香港广场北座; ⊙10am-10pm; ☎; MSouth Huangpi Rd) Stop by the Genius Bar for advice or troubleshooting, get online or browse the latest wonders of the tech world in this two-floor Apple outlet.

JÌNG'ÀN

Spin
CERAMICS

(旋; Xuán; off Map p193; 360 Kangding Rd; 康定路 360号; ⊙11am-9.30pm; MChangping Rd) New-wave and snazzy Jīngdézhèn ceramics, from cool celadon tones and oblong teacups to 'kung-fu' vases, presented in a sharp and crisp showroom.

Amy Lin's Pearls
PEARLS

(艾敏林氏珍珠; Àimǐn Línshì Zhēnzhū; off Map p193; Room 30, 3rd fl, 580 West Nanjing Rd; 南京西路580号3楼30号; ⊙10am-8pm; MWest Nanjing Rd) Shànghǎi's most reliable retailer of pearls of all colours and sizes, which come for a fraction of the price that you'd pay back home.

Han City Fashion
& Accessories Plaza
CLOTHING, SOUVENIRS

(韩城服饰礼品广场; Hánchéng Fúshì Lǐpǐn Guǎngchǎng; off Map p193; 580 West Nanjing Rd; 南京西路580号; ⊙9am-9pm; MWest Nanjing Rd) This unassuming-looking building is one of the best locations to pick up bargain T-shirts, jackets, bags and so on, with hundreds of stalls spread across several floors. Bargain hard.

PǓDŌNG

IFC Mall
MALL

(Map p194; IFC, 8 Century Ave; www.shanghaiifcmall.com.cn; ⊙10am-10pm; MLujiazui) This incredibly glam and glitzy six-storey mall beneath the Cesar Pelli–designed twin towers of the Shànghǎi International Finance Center (IFC) hosts a swish coterie of top-name brands from Armani and Prada to Vivienne Westwood, along with some dining options.

AP Xīnyáng Fashion
& Gifts Market
CLOTHING, SOUVENIRS

(亚大新阳服饰礼品市场; Yàdà Xīnyáng Fúshì Lǐpǐn Shìchǎng; ⊙10am-8pm; MScience & Technology Museum) Well worth a trip, this mammoth underground market by the Science & Technology Museum metro station is Shànghǎi's largest collection of shopping stalls, with a separate market devoted to pearls. Shop vendors are persistent and clawing, with scouts at metro exit turnstiles to turn shoppers their way. Haggling is the *lingua franca*.

HÓNGKǑU

Qīpǔ Market
CLOTHING, SHOES

(七浦服装市场; Qīpǔ Fúzhuāng Shìchǎng; 168 & 183 Qipu Rd; 七浦路168 & 183号; ⊙7am-5pm; MTiantong Rd) One big 'everything must go

now' sale, this is Shànghǎi's cheapest and most full-on clothes and shoes market. Haggle hard.

 Information

Free English and bilingual maps of Shànghǎi are available at airports, tourist information & service centres, bookshops and many hotels. Metro maps (地铁线路图; dìtiě xiànlùtú) are usually available at all stations.

Internet Access

Internet cafes are now scarce in touristy areas – it's more convenient to get online at your hotel or at a wi-fi hotspot. Otherwise, ask your hotel for the closest *wǎngba* (网吧; internet cafe) and take your passport.

Bùlè Internet Cafe (布乐网吧; Bùlè Wǎngba; Map p196; 2nd fl, Moling Rd; per hr ¥3; ⊙24hr) Corner of Moling Rd by main Shànghǎi Train Station.

Eastday Bar (东方网点; Dōngfāng Wǎngdiǎn; 30 East Yuyuan Rd; per hr ¥4; ⊙24hr)

Internet Cafe (网吧; Wǎngbā; Map p194; 3rd fl, 565 Dongchang Rd; per hr ¥4; ⊙8am-midnight) Just off South Pudong Rd.

Internet Cafe (网吧; Wǎngbā; Map p196; per hr ¥5; ⊙24hr) Down the escalator, across the road opposite the main Shànghǎi Train Station.

Internet Cafe (网吧游艺城; Wǎngbā Yóuyìchéng; 5th fl, eastern entrance to Duolun Rd; per hr ¥3; ⊙24hr)

Jidu Internet Cafe (极度网络; Jídù Wǎngluò; Map p188; 2nd fl, cnr Changle & North Xiangyang Rds; per hr ¥3; ⊙24hr)

Tàshí Internet Cafe (拓实网吧; Tàshí Wǎngbā; 3rd fl, 18 Yuyuanzhi Rd; 愚园支路18号3楼; per hr ¥4; ⊙24hr)

Xīwàng Internet Cafe (夕旺网吧; Xīwàng Wǎngbā; Map p182; 515 Fuzhou Rd; per hr ¥4; ⊙24hr)

Media

Grab free copies of *That's Shanghai*, *City Weekend* and *Time Out Shanghai* from an expat-centric restaurant or bar and for a plug into what's on in town, from art exhibitions and club nights to restaurant openings.

Medical Services

Huashan World Wide Medical Center (Map p188; ☑6248 3986; www.sh-hwmc.com.cn; 12 Middle Wulumuqi Rd; 乌鲁木齐中路12号; MChangshu Rd) Hospital treatment and outpatient consultations are available at the 8th-floor foreigners' clinic in Building 1 (open 8am to 10pm daily) of Huàshān Hospital (华山医院; Huàshān Yīyuàn), with 24-hour emergency treatment on the 15th floor in Building 6.

Parkway Health (以极佳医疗保健服务; Yījíjiā Yīliáo Bǎojiàn Fúwù; ☑24hr hotline 6445 5999; www.parkwayhealth.cn) Seven locations around Shànghǎi, including at the **Shànghǎi Centre** (上海商城; Shànghǎi Shāngchéng; Ste 203-204, Shànghǎi Centre, 1376 West Nanjing Rd; 南京西路1376号203室; ⓜWest Nanjing Rd). Private medical care by expat doctors, dentists and specialists.

Watson's (屈臣氏; Qūchénshì) French Concession (787 Middle Huaihai Rd; 淮海中路787号; ⓜSouth Shaanxi Rd); West Nanjing Rd (Westgate Mall, 1038 West Nanjing Rd; 南京西路1038号; ⓜWest Nanjing Rd) For Western cosmetics, over-the-counter medicines and health products, with numerous outlets around the city.

Money

Almost every hotel has money-changing counters. Most tourist hotels, upmarket restaurants and banks accept major credit cards. Twenty-four hour ATMs are everywhere; most accept major cards.

Bank of China (中国银行; Zhōngguó Yínháng; Map p182; The Bund; ◷9am-noon & 1.30-4.30pm Mon-Fri, 9am-noon Sat) Right next to the Fairmont Peace Hotel. Tends to get crowded, but is better organised than Chinese banks elsewhere around the country (it's worth a peek for its grand interior). Take a ticket and wait for your number. For credit-card advances, head to the furthest hall (counter No 2).

Citibank (花旗银行; Huāqí Yínháng; Map p182; The Bund; ◷24hr) Useful ATM.

Hongkong & Shanghai Bank (汇丰银行; HSBC; Huìfēng Yínháng) Shànghǎi Centre (West Nanjing Rd); The Bund (15 East Zhongshan No 1 Rd) Has ATMs in the above locations; also an ATM at Pǔdōng International Airport arrivals hall.

Post

Larger tourist hotels have post offices where you can mail letters and small packages – the most convenient option. China Post offices and post-boxes are green. The **International Post Office** (国际邮局; Guójì Yóujú; 276 North Suzhou Rd; 苏州北路276号; ◷7am-10pm; ⓜTiantong Rd) is just north of Sūzhōu Creek.

Public Security Bureau

(PSB; 公安局; Gōng'ānjú; ☑2895 1900, ext 2; 1500 Minsheng Rd; 民生路1500号; ◷9am-4.30pm Mon-Sat; ⓜScience & Technology Museum) Handles visas and registrations; 30-day visa extensions cost around ¥160. In Pǔdōng.

Telephone

After **Skype** (www.skype.com) and **Viber** (www.viber.com), internet phone (IP) cards are the cheapest way to call internationally (¥1.80 per minute to the US), but may not work with some hotel phones. Using a mobile phone is naturally the most convenient option. For mobile phone SIM cards, China Mobile shops are ubiquitous; cards can also be bought from newspaper kiosks with the China Mobile sign.

China Mobile (中国移动通信; Zhōngguó Yídòng Tōngxìn; Map p182; 21 Yuanmingyuan Rd; 圆明园路21号; ◷8.30am-6.30pm; ⓜEast Nanjing Rd)

Tourist Information

Your hotel should be able to provide you with maps and most of the tourist information you require. For other helpful websites, see p216.

Shànghǎi Call Centre (☑962 288; ◷24hr) This toll-free English-language hotline is possibly the most useful telephone number in Shànghǎi – it can even give your cab driver directions if you've got a mobile phone.

Shànghǎi Information Centre for International Visitors (Map p188; ☑6384 9366; No 2, Alley 123, Xingye Rd) Xīntiāndì information centre with currency exchange and free brochures.

Tourist Information & Service Centres (旅游咨询服务中心; Lǚyóu Zīxún Fúwù Zhōngxīn) The Bund (Map p182; beneath the Bund promenade, opposite the intersection with East Nanjing Rd); East Nanjing Rd (Map p182; Century Sq, 518 Jiujiang Rd); Jing'an (Map p193; Lane 1678, 19 West Nanjing Rd); Old Town (Map p182; 149 Jiujiaochang Rd) These centres are conveniently located near major tourist sights. The standard of English varies from good to nonexistent, but free maps and some information are available.

Travel Agencies

For details on train and ferry ticket agencies, see p218 and p217.

CTrip (☑400 619 9999; http://english.ctrip.com) Helpful online agency for hotel and flight bookings.

Elong (☑400 617 1717; www.elong.net) Online agency good for hotel and flight bookings.

STA Travel (☑2281 7723; www.statravel.com.cn; Room 1609, Shanghai Trade Tower, 188 Siping Rd; ◷9.30am-6pm Mon-Fri, 9.30am-12.30pm Sat; ⓜHailun Rd) Sells train and air tickets, and can issue international student identity cards.

Websites

City Weekend (www.cityweekend.com.cn) Listings website.

Shanghai Daily (www.shanghaidaily.com) (Censored) coverage of local news.

Shanghai Expat (www.shanghaiexpat.com) A must-see if you are thinking of relocating to Shànghǎi; useful forum.

Shanghaiist (www.shanghaiist.com) Local entertainment and news blog.

SmartShanghai (www.smartshanghai.com) For food, fun and frolicking. Good entertainment coverage.

That's Shanghai (www.thatsmags.com/shanghai) Listings website.

Time Out Shanghai (www.timeoutshanghai.com) Excellent listings and reviews.

Virtual Shanghai (www.virtualshanghai.net) Amazing database of old photos, maps and texts plus blog.

❶ Getting There & Away

Shànghǎi is straightforward to reach. With two airports, rail and air connections to places all over China, and buses to destinations in adjoining provinces and beyond, it's a handy springboard to the rest of the land.

Air

Shànghǎi has international flight connections to most major cities, many operated by China Eastern, which has its base here.

All international flights (and a few domestic flights) operate out of **Pǔdōng International Airport** (浦东国际机场; Pǔdōng Guójì Jīchǎng; ✈ flight information 96990; www.shairport.com; Ⓜ Pudong International Airport), with most (but not all) domestic flights operating out of **Hóngqiáo Airport** (虹桥机场; Hóngqiáo Jīchǎng; ✈ flight information 96990; www.shairport.com; Ⓜ Hongqiao Airport) on Shànghǎi's western outskirts. If you are making an onward domestic connection in Pǔdōng, it is essential that you find out whether the domestic flight leaves from Pǔdōng or Hóngqiáo, as the latter will require *at least* an hour to cross the city.

Daily (usually several times) domestic flights connect Shànghǎi to major cities in China:

Běijīng ¥1220, 1½ hours

Chéngdū ¥1700, two hours and 20 minutes

Guǎngzhōu ¥1280, two hours

Guìlín ¥1200, two hours

Qīngdǎo ¥740, one hour

Xī'ān ¥1260, two hours

You can buy air tickets almost anywhere, including at major hotels, travel agencies and online websites such as ctrip.com and elong.net. Discounts of up to 40% are standard.

Boat

Domestic boat tickets can be bought from travel agents in the **domestic boat tickets shop** (Map p182; ✆ 6336 8600; 21 East Jinling Rd; 金陵东路21号; ◷ 9am-6pm; Ⓜ East Nanjing Rd) on East Jinling Rd.

Overnight boats (¥109 to ¥499, 10½ hours) to Pǔtuóshān depart daily at 8pm from the **Wúsōng Wharf** (吴淞码头; Wúsōng Mǎtou; Ⓜ Songbing Rd), almost at the mouth of the Yangzi River; to reach Wúsōng Wharf take metro Line 3 to Songbing Rd and then walk or hail a taxi.

A high-speed ferry service (¥255 to ¥340, three hours, 9.30am) to Pǔtuóshān departs twice daily from Xiǎo Yáng Shān (小洋山). A bus (price included in ferry ticket; two hours, departs 7.20am and 8am) runs to Xiǎo Yáng Shān from Nánpǔ Bridge (南浦大桥; by the bridge).

Bus

Shànghǎi has several long-distance bus stations, though given the traffic gridlock it's best to take the train when possible.

The vast **Shànghǎi south long-distance bus station** (上海长途客运南站; Shànghǎi chángtú kèyùn nánzhàn; Map p178; www.ctnz.net; ✆ 5436 2835; 666 Shilong Rd; Ⓜ Shanghai South Railway Station) serves cities in south China, including:

Hángzhōu (Jiǔbǎo, Hángzhōu north bus station and Hángzhōu south bus station) ¥68, two hours, regular (7.10am to 7.20pm)

Nánjīng ¥105, four hours

Nánxún ¥47, 2½ hours, eight daily, take the bus for Húzhōu (湖州; 6.50am to 7.28pm)

Níngbō ¥99, three hours, regular

Shàoxīng ¥80, three hours, regular (7.10am to 7.55pm)

Shěnjiāmén ¥130

Sūzhōu (south and north bus stations) ¥38, 1½ hours, regular (6.27am to 7.30pm)

Túnxī/Huáng Shān ¥135, six hours, eight daily

Wùyuán ¥194, five hours, two daily (9.28am & 6.45pm)

Wūzhèn ¥49, two hours, eight daily (7.44am to 6.17pm)

Xītáng ¥32, 1½ hours, 12 daily

The massive **Shànghǎi long-distance bus station** (上海长途汽车客运总站; Shànghǎi chángtú qìchē kèyùn Zǒngzhàn; Map p196; 1666 Zhongxing Rd; Ⓜ Shanghai Railway Station), north of Shànghǎi train station, has buses to destinations as far away as Gānsù province and Inner Mongolia. Regular buses run to Sūzhōu (frequent) and Hángzhōu (frequent), as well as Nánjīng (12 daily) and Běijīng (¥311, 4pm). Although it appears close to the train station, it is a major pain to reach on foot. It's easiest to catch a cab here.

Shànghǎi Sightseeing Buses run to the canal towns outside Shànghǎi; see p199 for details.

Train

Many parts of the country can be reached by direct train from Shànghǎi. The city has three useful stations: the main **Shànghǎi Train Station** (Shànghǎi Zhàn; Map p196; Ⓜ Shanghai Railway Station), the **Shànghǎi South Train Station** (Shànghǎi Nánzhàn; Map p178; Ⓜ Shanghai South Railway Station) and the **Hóngqiáo Train Station** (上海虹桥站; Shànghǎi Hóngqiáo Zhàn; Ⓜ Hong-qiao Railway Station) near Hóngqiáo Airport. Most trains depart from the main station, though for some southern destinations, like Hángzhōu, they leave from Shànghǎi South. International trains for Kowloon in Hong Kong leave from the main train station. The Hóngqiáo Train Station is for new express trains (many Nánjīng and Sūzhōu trains leave from here) and serves as the terminus for the Shànghǎi–Běijīng G class express. Wherever you're going, make sure to get your tickets as early as possible. If you're arriving in Shànghǎi, don't get off at **Shànghǎi West Train Station** (上海西站; Shànghǎi Xīzhàn; Map p178) which is inconvenient for travellers.

There are several ways to purchase tickets: at the station (generally stressful), via your hotel or a travel agency (much easier but expect a commission charge), or at train ticket offices around town.

At the main station there are two ticket halls (售票厅; shòupiàotīng): one in the main building (same-day tickets) and another on the east side of the square (advance tickets). One counter will claim to have English speakers. The **bilingual automated machines** (自助售票处; zìzhù shòupiàochù) require Chinese ID. You will need your passport to buy tickets.

Alternatively, tickets can be purchased for a small commision (¥5) from one of the numerous **train ticket offices** (火车票预售处; huǒchēpiào yùshòuchù) Bund (Map p182; 384 Middle Jiangxi Rd; 江西中路384号; ⊗8am-8pm); Hóngkǒu (Map p182; 106 Huangpu Lu; 黄浦路106号; ⊗8-11.30am & 12.30-6pm); Jìng'ān (Map p193; 77 Wanhangdu Rd; 万航渡路77号; ⊗8am-5pm); French Concession (Map p188; 12 Dongping Rd; ⊗8am-noon & 1-6pm Mon-Fri, 9am-noon & 1-5.30pm Sat & Sun); Pǔdōng (Map p194; 1396 Lujiazui Ring Rd; 陆家嘴环路1396号; ⊗8am-7pm) around town.

Prices and times listed following are always for the fastest train. Slower, less expensive trains have not been listed. Some trains leaving from Shànghǎi Train Station:

Běijīng (D class) seat/sleeper ¥311/698, eight to 11½ hours, three daily

Chéngdū seat/hard sleeper ¥267/467, 35 hours, four daily

Hángzhōu (G class) 2nd/1st class ¥93/148, 1½ hours, four daily

Hong Kong seat/hard sleeper ¥226/409, 18½ hours, one daily (6.24pm)

Huángshān seat/hard sleeper ¥94/175, 11½ hours, two daily

Lhasa hard/soft sleeper ¥845/1314, 48 hours, one every other day (7.28pm)

Nánjīng (G class) 2nd/1st class ¥140/220, two hours, frequent

Sūzhōu (G class) 2nd/1st class ¥40/60, 30 minutes, frequent

Ürümqi hard/soft sleeper ¥699/1079, 44 hours, one daily (8.32pm)

Xī'ān seat/hard sleeper ¥182 to ¥333, 16 to 20 hours, 10 daily

Some trains leaving from Shànghǎi South Train station:

Guìlín hard/soft sleeper ¥353/539, 22 hours, four daily

Hángzhōu ¥29, 2½ to three hours, frequent

Kūnmíng hard/soft sleeper ¥536/825, 38 hours, three daily

Yùshān (Sānqīng Shān) ¥130, six hours, six daily

Some trains leaving from Hóngqiáo Train Station:

Běijīng (G class) 2nd/1st class ¥555/935, 5½ hours, very regular (7am to 7.55pm)

Hángzhōu (G class) 2nd/1st class ¥78/124, one hour, very regular (6.38am to 9.32pm)

Qīngdǎo (G class) 2nd/1st class ¥520/820, 6½ hours, four daily

Shàoxīng (G class) 2nd/1st class ¥65/78, two hours, 10 daily

Sūzhōu (D class) 2nd/1st class seat ¥26/31, 30 minutes, regular

Xiàmén (D class) 2nd/1st class ¥339/408, nine hours, 10 daily

Zhèngzhōu (D class) 2nd/1st class ¥238/381, seven hours, three daily

❶ Getting Around

The best way to get around Shànghǎi is the metro, which now reaches most places in the city, followed by cabs. Buses (¥2) are tricky to use unless you are a proficient Mandarin speaker. Whatever mode of transport you use, try to avoid rush hours between 8am and 9am, and 4.30pm and 6pm.

Although there are some fascinating areas to stroll around, walking from A to B is generally an exhausting and sometimes stressful experience.

To/From the Airport

Pǔdōng International Airport handles most international flights and some domestic flights. There are four ways to get from the airport to the city: taxi, Maglev train, metro and bus.

Taxi rides into central Shànghǎi cost around ¥160 and take about an hour; to Hóngqiáo Airport costs around ¥200. Most Shànghǎi taxi drivers are honest, though ensure they use the meter; avoid monstrous overcharging by using the regular taxi rank outside the arrivals hall. Regular buses run to Sūzhōu (¥84) and Hángzhōu (¥100).

The bullet-fast and time-saving **Maglev train** (www.smtdc.com) runs from Pǔdōng International Airport to its terminal in Pǔdōng in just eight minutes, from where you can transfer to the metro (Longyang Rd station) or take a taxi (¥40 to People's Sq). Economy single/return tickets cost ¥50/80, but show your same-day air ticket and it's ¥40 one way. Children under 1.2m travel free (taller kids are half-price). Trains depart every 20 minutes from roughly 6.45am to 9.40pm.

Metro Line 2 runs from Pǔdōng International Airport to Hóngqiáo Airport, passing through central Shànghǎi. It is convenient, though not for those in a hurry. From Pǔdōng Airport, it takes about 75 minutes to People's Sq (¥7) and 1¾ hours to Hóngqiáo Airport (¥8).

There are also numerous **airport buses**, which take between one and 1½ hours to run to their destinations in Pǔxī. Buses leave from the airport roughly every 15 to 25 minutes from 6.30am to 11pm; they go to the airport from roughly 5.30am to 9.30pm (bus 1 runs till 11pm). The most useful buses are airport bus 1 (¥30), linking Pǔdōng International Airport with Hóngqiáo Airport, and airport bus 2 (¥22), linking Pǔdōng International Airport with the Airport City Terminal (上海机场城市航站楼; Shànghǎi Jīchǎng Chéngshì Hángzhàn Lóu) on West Nanjing Rd, east of Jìng'ān Temple. Airport bus 5 (¥22) links Pǔdōng International Airport with Shànghǎi train station via People's Sq.

Hóngqiáo Airport is 18km from the Bund, a 30- to 60-minute trip. Most flights now arrive at Terminal 2, connected to the city centre via metro Lines 2 and 10 (30 minutes to People's Sq). If you arrive at Terminal 1, you can also catch the airport shuttle bus (¥4, 7.50am to 11pm) to the Airport City Terminal on West Nanjing Rd. Airport bus 1 (¥30, 6am to 9.30pm) runs to Pǔdōng International Airport; bus 941 (¥6) links Hongqiao Airport with Shànghǎi main train station. Taxis cost ¥70 to ¥100 to central Shànghǎi.

Major hotels run airport shuttles to both airports (generally free to Hóngqiáo; ¥30 to Pǔdōng).

Public Transport

FERRY The **Jinling Rd Ferry** (金陵路轮渡站; Jīnlíng Lù Lúndù Zhàn) runs between the southern end of the Bund and the Dongchang Rd dock in Pǔdōng. Ferries (¥2) run roughly every 15 minutes from 7am to 10pm. The Fuxing Rd Ferry

TRANSPORT CARD

If you are going to be doing a lot of travelling in Shànghǎi, it's worth investing in a *jiāotōng kǎ* (交通卡; transport card), as it can save you queuing. Sold at metro stations and some convenience stores, cards can be topped up with credit and used on the metro, most buses and in taxis. Credits are electronically deducted from the card as you swipe it over the sensor at metro turnstiles and near the door on buses; when paying your taxi fare, hand the card to the driver, who will swipe it for you. You'll need to pay a deposit of ¥20, which can be refunded before you leave at the East Nanjing Rd metro station.

(复兴路轮渡站; Fùxīng Lù Lúndù Zhàn) runs from Fuxing Rd north of the Cool Docks in the South Bund to Dongchang Rd as well. Ferries (¥2) run every 10 to 20 minutes from around 5am to 11pm.

METRO The **Shànghǎi metro system** (www.shmetro.com), indicated by a red M, currently runs to 11 lines after huge expansion; two additional lines (13 and 22) were expected to open by this book's publication and a further two lines are expected (12 and 16) in 2013. Lines 1, 2 and 10 are the most useful for travellers. Tickets cost ¥3 to ¥10 depending on distance, sold from coin and note-operated bilingual automated machines (and from booths at some stations); keep your ticket until you exit. Transport cards are available from information desks for ¥50 and ¥100; they don't offer any savings, but are useful for avoiding queues and can also be used in taxis and on most buses. A one-day metro pass is also sold from information desks for ¥18.

Metro maps are available at most stations; the free tourist maps also have a small metro map printed on them. Check out www.shmetro.com for a map of the metro network.

Taxi

Shànghǎi's taxis are reasonably cheap, hassle-free and easy to flag down outside rush hour, although finding a cab during rainstorms is impossible. Flag fall is ¥14 (for the first 3km) and ¥18 at night (11pm to 5am). A new 4000-strong fleet of more spacious and comfortable white Volkswagen Touran taxis was introduced for the World Expo (same flag fall).

Major taxi companies:

Bàshì (☏96840)

Dàzhòng (☏96822)

Qiángshēng (☏6258 0000)

BORDER CROSSING: GETTING TO JAPAN

The **China-Japan International Ferry Company** (☑6595 6888, 6325 7642; www.chinajapanferry.com; 18th fl) has staggered departures weekly to either Osaka or Kobe in Japan on Saturdays at 12.30pm. The **Shànghǎi International Ferry Company** (☑6595 8666; www.shanghai-ferry.co.jp; 15th fl) has departures to Osaka on Tuesdays at 11am. Both ferry companies are located in the Jin'an Building (908 Dongdaming Rd; 东大明路908号金岸大厦), north of the Bund. Fares on all boats (44 hours) range from ¥1300 in an eight-bed dorm to ¥6500 in a deluxe twin cabin. Reservations are recommended in July and August. Passengers must be at the harbour three hours before departure to get through immigration. All vessels depart from the **Shànghǎi Port International Cruise Terminal** (Map p178; 上海港国际客运中心; Shànghǎi Gǎng Guójì Kèyùn Zhōngxīn; 800 Dongdaming Rd; 东大明路908号).

At the time of writing, a recently opened, weekly 26-hour **ferry route** (http://htbc.co.jp; from ¥1160) between Shànghǎi and Nagasaki had been suspended but may run again.

AROUND SHÀNGHǍI

The most popular day trips from Shànghǎi are probably to Hángzhōu (a quick zip away on the train) and Sūzhōu.

Zhūjiājiǎo 朱家角

Thirty kilometres west of Shànghǎi, **Zhūjiājiǎo** (optional ticket incl entry to 4/9 sights ¥30/90) is easy to reach and charming – as long as your visit does not coincide with the arrival of phalanxes of tour buses.

What survives of this historic canal town today is a charming tableau of Ming- and Qing-dynasty alleys, bridges and *gǔzhèn* (古镇; old town) architecture, its alleyways steeped in the aroma of *chòu dòufu* (stinky tofu).

On the west side of the recently built City God Temple bridge stands the **City God Temple** (城隍庙; Chénghuáng Miào; admission ¥10; ☉7.30am-4pm), moved here in 1769 from its original location in Xuějiābāng. Further north along Caohe St (漕河街), running alongside the canal, is the **Yuánjīn Buddhist Temple** (圆津禅院; Yuánjīn Chányuàn; admission ¥5; ☉8am-4pm) near the distinctive **Tài'ān Bridge** (泰安桥; Tài'ān Qiáo). Pop into the temple to climb the **Qīnghuá Pavilion** (清华阁; Qīnghuá Gé) at the rear, a towering hall visible from many parts of town.

Earmark a detour to the **Zhūjiājiǎo Catholic Church of Ascension** (朱家角耶稣升天堂; Zhūjiājiǎo Yēsū Shēngtiāntáng; No 317 Alley, 27 Caohe Jie; 漕河街27号317弄), a gorgeous church with its belfry rising in a detached tower by the rear gate. Also hunt down the **Qing dynasty Post Office** (admission ¥5).

Of Zhūjiājiǎo's quaint ancient bridges, the standout **Fàngshēng Bridge** (放生桥; Fàngshēng Qiáo) is the most photogenic. First built in 1571, the five-arched bridge was originally assembled with proceeds from a monk's 15 years of alms gathering. You can jump on boats for comprehensive tours of town at various points, including Fàngshēng Bridge. Tickets are ¥60/120 per boat for the short/long tour; speed boats (¥40) also run from the bridge for 30-minute trips.

Food sellers line Bei Dajie, flogging everything from pig's trotters to plump coconuts, above which flail plastic bags of fans to fend off flies. Plentiful cafes have squeezed in along Caohe Jie, Xihu Jie and Donghu Jie, and even a creperie has set up shop near Yongquan Bridge. Top pick for overnighting is the lovely old courtyard **Uma Hostel** (☑189 1808 2961; umahos tel@gmail.com; 103 Xijing Jie; 西井街103号; dm/d ¥80/240), near the Kèzhí Gardens (课植园; Kèzhí Yuán). Book ahead.

To get to Zhūjiājiǎo, head to the **Pu'an Rd Bus Station** (普安路汽车站; Pǔ'ān Lù Qìchē Zhàn; Map p182; ⓂDashijie) just south of People's Sq, and hop on the pink and white Hùzhū Gāosù Kuàixiàn bus (沪朱高速快线; ¥12, one hour, every 20 minutes from 6am to 10pm, less frequently in low season) direct to the town. If you're pushed, take a Shànghǎi Sightseeing Bus day tour (¥85, departs 9am and 10am) from the Shànghǎi Sightseeing Bus Center at the Shànghǎi Stadium; it returns to Shànghǎi at 3.45pm and 4.45pm. The price includes admission to the town. Zhūjiājiǎo can also be reached from the bus station in Tónglǐ (¥15, 1½ hours).

Jiāngsū

POP 78.9 MILLION

Includes »

Nánjīng 223
Around Nánjīng 233
Sūzhōu 234
Around Sūzhōu 242

Best Classical Gardens

» Garden of the Master of the Nets (p234)
» Humble Administrator's Garden (p234)
» Presidential Palace (p227)

Best Museums

» Sūzhōu Museum (p234)
» Nánjīng Museum (p228)
» Memorial Hall of the Nánjīng Massacre (p225)

Why Go?

Jiāngsū (江苏) is alluring, especially to sedentary travellers. The province, which owed its historical wealth to silk and salt production, boasts the Grand Canal as well as elaborate waterways that thread through the Yangzi River (Cháng Jiāng). It's known throughout China for its cute canal towns, enchanting gardens and sophisticated opera and folk arts.

The charms of the province are so well known that it has attracted domestic tourists in large numbers since the 1990s, much earlier than most other places in the country. Package tourists flock to Sūzhōu anytime of the year, and you're likely to be rubbing elbows with them in the gardens or any of the famous water towns. But don't be put off. Kick start your day early, go slightly off the main streets, and you'll see the old-world charm and have the place to yourself. In the provincial capital and university town of Nánjīng there's a lot that remains relatively undiscovered by outsiders: Ming-dynasty heritage, leafy parks and fantastic museums.

When to Go
Nánjīng

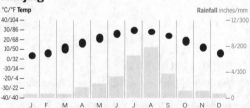

Mar & Apr Best time to visit the gardens when flowers bloom in early spring.

Oct Mist-shrouded vistas of gardens and canals in autumn.

Dec Snow-covered views of the pretty canal towns of Sūzhōu in winter.

Jiāngsū Highlights

1 Come face-to-face with Chinese history in the **Memorial Hall of the Nánjīng Massacre** (p225)

2 Feast your eyes on the historical artefacts at **Sūzhōu Museum** (p234)

3 Indulge in the beauty of the **gardens of Sūzhōu** (p234)

4 Sūzhōu's 'Venice of the East' moniker becomes clear along **Píngjiāng Lù** (p235)

5 Enjoy tea-tasting and a traditional píngtán performance at the **Pingtan Teahouse** (p239)

6 Lose yourself in the alleys and canals of **Tónglǐ** (p242)

7 Four words: **Chinese Sex Culture Museum** (p243)

8 Relax in the charming towns of **Lùzhí** (p243), **Mùdú** (p244) or **Zhōuzhuāng** (p245)

9 Get some highbrow culture at a **Kūnqǔ opera performance** (p231)

10 Scenic **Míng Xiàolíng Tomb** (p226) and **Línggǔ Temple Scenic Area** (p227) are perfect for a stroll

History

Jiāngsū was a relative backwater until the Song dynasty (960–1279), when it emerged as an important commercial centre because of trading routes opened up by the Grand Canal. In particular, the south of the province flourished: the towns of Sūzhōu and Yángzhōu played an important role in silk production and began to develop a large mercantile class.

Prosperity continued through the Ming and Qing dynasties, and with the incursion of Westerners into China in the 1840s, southern Jiāngsū opened up to Western influence. During the Taiping Rebellion (1851–64), the Taiping established Nánjīng as their capital, calling it Tiānjīng (Heavenly Capital).

Jiāngsū was also to play a strong political role in the 20th century when Nánjīng was established as the capital by the Nationalist Party until taken over by the communists in 1949, who moved the capital to Běijīng.

Today, because of its proximity to Shànghǎi, southern Jiāngsū benefits from a fast-growing economy and rapid development, although northern Jiāngsū still lags behind.

Climate

Jiāngsū is hot and humid in summer (May to August), yet has temperatures requiring coats in winter (December to February, when visibility can drop to zero because of fog). Rain or drizzle can be prevalent in winter, adding a misty touch to the land. The natural colours can be brilliant in spring (March and April). Heavy rains fall in spring and summer; autumn (September to November) is the driest time of year, and the best time to visit.

ℹ Getting There & Around

Jiāngsū is well connected to all major cities in China. There are numerous flights daily from Nánjīng to points around the country, as well as frequent bus and train connections.

Jiāngsū has a comprehensive bus system that allows travellers to get to most destinations within the province without difficulty. Travelling by train is straightforward.

Nánjīng 南京

♫ 025 / POP 3.7 MILLION

Many visitors only pass through Nánjīng when travelling from Shànghǎi to Běijīng (or vice versa), missing out on so much. This underrated capital city of Jiāngsū, lying on the lower stretches of the Yangzi

---

PRICE INDICATORS	
The following price indicators are used in this chapter:	
Sleeping	
$	less than ¥250
$$	¥250 to ¥800
$$$	more than ¥800
Eating	
$	less than ¥30
$$	¥30 to ¥70
$$$	more than ¥70

River, boasts a surprisingly rich and impressive historical heritage that survived the Cultural Revolution. The major attractions are the reminders of the city's brief, former glory as the nation's capital under the Ming dynasty (1368–1644) and then as the capital of the Republic of China in the early years of the 20th century. Solid evidence includes a magnificent city wall that still encloses most of the city, and the elegant republican-era buildings that dot the centre.

Today the city is sprawling, but its relaxed atmosphere remains intact even when the day is hazy. This famous university town has wide, tree-lined boulevards, chic cafes and wonderful museums, set in a beautiful landscape of lakes, forested parks and rivers. And the city's pleasant *wutong* trees afford glorious shade in the summer and lend the city a leafy complexion.

History

During the Qin dynasty (221–207 BC), Nánjīng prospered as a major administrative centre. Nánjīng fell during the Sui dynasty (AD 589–618) and later enjoyed a period of prosperity under the long-lived Tang dynasty, before slipping into obscurity.

In 1356 a peasant rebellion led by Zhu Yuanzhang against the Mongol Yuan dynasty was successful. In 1368 it became capital under Zhu Yuanzhang's Ming dynasty, but its glory was short-lived. In 1420 the third Ming emperor, Yongle, moved the capital back to Běijīng. From then on Nánjīng's fortunes variously rose and declined as a regional centre, but it wasn't until the 19th and 20th centuries that the city again entered the centre stage of Chinese history.

Nánjīng

2 km
1 miles
0

To Yangzi River Bridge (3km)

Nanjing Train Station
南京火车站
Nanjing Huochezhan

Shanshan Lu

Xuánwǔ Lake Park

Ming City Walls

Ziijn Mountain (448m)

Zǐxiá Lake

Ming Xiàolíng Tomb

Qián Lake

Hu-Ning Expwy

Língyuán Lu

Cable Car

Minggugong Donglu

Minggugong

Muxuyuan

Xi'anmen

Daxinggong

Huangpu Lu

Zhu Jiang Lu 珠江路

Taiping Beilu

Beijing Donglu

Hongwu Lu

Zhongyang Lu

Xuanwu

Hunan Lu

Yunnan Lu

Zhongshan Beilu 中山北路

Xinmofan Malu

Jianning Lu

Caochang Lu

Huju Beilu

Beijing Xilu

Ninghai Lu

Jiangsu Lu

Nánjīng Huochezhan

Shanghai Lu

Nanxiu Cun

Nanjing Normal University

Qínhuái Shān

Guangzhou Lu

Hanzhongmen

Mochou Lu

Wanfu Dajie

Xinjiekou

Changjiang Lu

Zhongshan Nanlu

Huaqiao Lu

Shanghai Lu

Mochouhu

Yunjin Lu

Mingguguong Dongu

CITS

Zhongshan Beilu

Zhongyang Lu

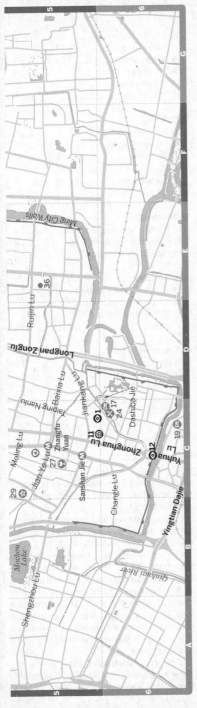

In the 19th century the Opium Wars brought the British to Nánjīng and it was here that the first of the 'unequal treaties' was signed, opening several Chinese ports to foreign trade, forcing China to pay a huge war indemnity, and officially ceding the island of Hong Kong to Britain. Just a few years later Nánjīng became the Taiping capital during the Taiping Rebellion, which succeeded in taking over most of southern China.

In 1864 the combined forces of the Qing army, British army, and various European and US mercenaries surrounded the city. They laid siege for seven months, before finally capturing it and slaughtering the Taiping defenders.

The Kuomintang made Nánjīng the capital of the Republic of China from 1928 to 1937. But in the face of advancing Japanese soldiers, the capital was moved to Chóngqìng in 1937. Nánjīng was again capital between 1945 and 1949, when the communists 'liberated' the city and made China their own.

⊙ Sights

Dominating the eastern fringes of Nánjīng is Zǐjīn Mountain (紫金山; Zǐjīn Shān), or 'Purple-Gold Mountain', a heavily forested area of parks and the site of most of Nánjīng's historical attractions – Sun Yatsen Mausoleum, Míng Xiàolíng Tomb, Línggǔ Temple Scenic Area and the Botanic Gardens (植物园; Zhíwù yuán). It's also one of the coolest places to escape from the steamy summers. There are discounts if tickets to various sights are purchased together.

TOP CHOICE Memorial Hall of the Nánjīng Massacre MEMORIAL

(南京大屠杀纪念馆; Nánjīng Dàtúshā Jiniànguǎn; 418 Shuiximen Dajie; admission free; ⊙8.30am-4.30pm Tue-Sun; Ⓜ Yunjin Lu) In the city's southwestern suburbs, the unsettling exhibits in the Memorial Hall of the Nánjīng Massacre document the atrocities committed by Japanese soldiers against the civilian population during the occupation of Nánjīng in 1937. They include pictures of actual executions – many taken by Japanese army photographers – and a gruesome viewing hall built over a mass grave of massacre victims. Detailed captions are in English, Japanese and Chinese, but the photographs, skeletons and displays tell their own haunting stories without words. At times it feels overwhelming but

Nánjīng

◎ Top Sights
Míng Xiàolíng Tomb F3
Xúanwǔ Lake Park D2

◎ Sights
1 Fūzǐ Temple C5
Imperial Examinations History
Museum .... (see 1)
2 Jīmíng Temple D3
3 Jiǔhúashān Park D3
4 Línggǔ Temple G3
5 Memorial Hall of the Nánjīng
Massacre A4
6 Ming Palace Ruins E4
7 Míng Xiàolíng Scenic Area F3
8 Nánjīng Museum E4
9 Presidential Palace D4
10 Sun Yatsen Mausoleum G3
11 Taiping Heavenly Kingdom
History Museum C5
12 Zhōnghuá Gate C6
13 Zhōngshān Gate E4
14 Zhōngyāng Gate C1

🛏 Sleeping
15 Nánjīng Time International
Youth Hostel D4
16 Nánjīng Zhōngfáng Service
Apartment C4
17 Orange Hotel C6
18 Sheraton Nánjīng Kingsley B4
19 Travelers' Soul Inn Nanjing C6

✴ Eating
20 A Simple Diet C3

21 Cosima Restaurant C3
22 Mǎxiángxīng C2
23 Nanjing 1912 .... D4
24 Sculpting in Time C6
25 Sìchuān Jiǔjiā D4
Yǒnghéyuán .... (see 1)

◎ Drinking
26 Behind the Wall C3
27 Finnegans Wake C5
28 Florentina B3

✪ Entertainment
29 Lányuàn Theatre C5

◎ Shopping
30 Foreign Languages Bookstore C4
31 Librairie Avant-Garde C4
32 Popular Book Mall C4

ⓘ Information
33 Jiāngsū People's Hospital B4
34 Jīnsuǒ Internet Cafe B3
35 Nánjīng International SOS
Clinic E4

ⓘ Transport
36 CAAC E5
37 Dragonair C4
38 East Bus Station E1
39 Nánjīng Long-Distance Bus
Station C1
40 Train Ticket Office D4
41 Train Ticket Office C3

visitors might begin to understand the link between the massacre and the identity of the city. Get there early to beat the surge of people.

Míng Xiàolíng Tomb
TOMB

(明孝陵; Míng Xiàolíng; admission ¥70; ⊙8am-5.30pm, to 6.30pm summer; Ⓜ Muxuyuan) Zhu Yuanzhang (1328–1398), the founding emperor of the Ming dynasty, was buried in the tomb of Míng Xiàolíng, and he was the only Ming emperor buried outside of Běijīng. The first section of this magnificent mausoleum is a 618m 'spirit path', lined with stone statues of lions, camels, elephants and horses that drive away evil spirits and guard the tomb. Among them lurks two mythical animals: a *xiè zhì*, which has a mane and a single horn on its head, and a *qílín*, which has a scaly body, a cow's tail, a deer's hooves and one horn.

As you enter the first courtyard, a paved pathway leads to a pavilion housing several stelae. The next gate leads to a large courtyard with the **Línghún Pagoda** (Línghún Tǎ), a mammoth rectangular stone structure. Look for the stalactites and stalagmites formed by years of water dripping down the walls. Walk through a long tunnel and up a wall, 350m in diameter, to get to a huge earth mound. Beneath this mound is the unexcavated tomb vault of the emperor.

The area surrounding the tomb is the **Míng Xiàolíng Scenic Area** (明孝陵风景区; Míng Xiàolíng Fēngjǐngqū). A tree-lined pathway winds around pavilions and picnic grounds and ends at scenic **Zǐxiá Lake** (Zǐxiá Hú; admission ¥10), ideal for strolling. A combo ticket of the tomb and Línggǔ Temple Scenic Area (below) is ¥115.

From Muxuyuan metro station (line 2), it's a 1.6km walk uphill. Bus Y3 from the city centre also takes you there.

FREE **Sun Yatsen Mausoleum**   MEMORIAL
(中山陵; Zhōngshān Líng; ⊗6.30am-6.30pm; M Xiamafang) Dr Sun is recognised by the communists and Kuomintang alike as the father of modern China. He died in Běijīng in 1925, and had wished to be buried in Nánjīng, no doubt with greater simplicity than the Ming-style tomb his successors built for him. Despite this, less than a year after his death, construction of this mausoleum began.

The tomb itself lies at the top of an enormous stone stairway – a breathless 392 steps. At the start of the path stands a dignified marble gateway, with a roof of blue-glazed tiles. The blue and white of the mausoleum symbolise the white sun on the blue background of the Kuomintang flag.

The crypt lies at the top of the steps at the rear of the memorial chamber. A tablet hanging across the threshold is inscribed with the 'Three Principles of the People', as formulated by Dr Sun: nationalism, democracy and people's livelihood. Inside is a statue of a seated Dr Sun. The walls are carved with the complete text of the Outline of Principles for the Establishment of the Nation put forward by the Nationalist government. A prostrate marble statue of Dr Sun seals his copper coffin.

Buses 9, Y2 or Y3 go from the city centre to the Sun Yatsen Mausoleum. A shuttle bus (¥5) resembling a red steam train goes to the Línggǔ Temple Scenic Area.

Línggǔ Temple Scenic Area   TEMPLE
(灵谷寺风景区; Línggǔ Sì Fēngjǐng Qū; admission ¥80; ⊗7am-6.30pm; M Zhonglingjie) The large Ming Línggǔ Temple complex has one of the most interesting buildings in Nánjīng – the **Beamless Hall** (Wúliáng Diàn), built in 1381 entirely out of brick and stone and containing no beam supports. Buildings during the Ming dynasty were normally constructed of wood, but timber shortages meant that builders had to rely on brick. The structure has a vaulted ceiling and a large stone platform where Buddhist statues once sat. In the 1930s the hall was turned into a memorial to those who died resisting the Japanese.

A road runs on both sides of the hall and up two flights of steps to the graceful **Pine Wind Pavilion** (Sōngfēng Gé), originally dedicated to Guanyin as part of **Línggǔ Temple**. The temple itself and a memorial hall to Xuan Zang (the Buddhist monk who travelled to India and brought back the Buddhist scriptures) are close by; after you pass through the Beamless Hall, turn right and then follow the pathway. Inside the memorial hall is a golden scale model of a 13-storey wooden pagoda that contains part of Xuan Zang's skull, a sacrificial table and a portrait of the monk.

Nearby is the colourful **Línggǔ Pagoda** (Línggǔ Tǎ). This nine-storey, 60m-high, octagonal pagoda was finished in 1933 under the direction of a US architect, to remember those who died during the Kuomintang revolution. Tour buses Y2 and Y3 run to the Línggǔ Temple from Nánjīng Train Station. A free shuttle bus connects the area to the Sun Yatsen Mausoleum.

Ming Palace Ruins   PARK
(明故宫; Míng Gùgōng; M Minggugong) The Ming Palace Ruins are scattered around peaceful but maudlin **Wǔcháomén Park** (Wǔcháomén Gōngyuán; Zhongshan Donglu; admission free; ⊗6.30am-9.30pm). Built by Zhu Yuanzhang, the imperial palace is said to have been a magnificent structure after which the Imperial Palace in Běijīng was modelled. Anyone familiar with the layout of the Forbidden City will see similarities in the arrangement.

You can clamber into the ruined **Meridian Gate** (Wǔ Mén), which once had huge walls jutting out at right angles from the main structure, along with watchtowers. Today, the park is filled with locals practising ballroom dancing.

You can reach the Ming Palace Ruins by catching bus Y1 from Nánjīng Train Station or bus 9 from Zhongyang Lu.

Presidential Palace   HISTORICAL BUILDING
(总统府; Zǒngtǒng Fǔ; 292 Changjiang Lu; admission ¥40; ⊗8am-6pm; M Daxinggong) After the Taiping took over Nánjīng, they built the **Mansion of the Heavenly King** (Tiānwáng Fǔ) on the foundations of a former Ming-dynasty palace. This magnificent palace did not survive the fall of the Taiping, but there is a reconstruction and a classical Ming garden, now known as the Presidential Palace. Other buildings on the site were used briefly as presidential offices by Sun Yatsen's government in 1912 and by the Kuomintang from 1927 to 1949. Bus Y1 travels here.

THE RAPE OF NÁNJĪNG

In 1937, with the Chinese army comparatively weak and underfunded and the Japanese army on the horizon, the invasion into, and occupation of, Nánjīng by Japan appeared imminent. As it packed up and fled, the Chinese government encouraged the people of Nánjīng to stay, saying, 'all those who have blood and breath in them must feel that they wish to be broken as jade rather than remain whole as tile.' To reinforce this statement, the gates to the city were locked, trapping more than half a million citizens inside.

What followed in Nánjīng was six weeks of continuous, unfathomable victimisation of civilians to an extent unwitnessed in modern warfare. According to journalists and historians such as Iris Chang and Joshua Fogel, during Japan's occupation of Nánjīng between 200,000 and 300,000 Chinese civilians were killed, either in group massacres or individual murders. Within the first month, at least 20,000 women between the ages of 11 and 76 were raped. Women who attempted to refuse or children who interfered were often bayoneted or shot.

The Japanese, however, underestimated the Chinese. Instead of breaking the people's will, the invasion fuelled a sense of identity and determination. Those who did not die – broken as jade – survived to fight back.

Iris Chang's highly acclaimed *The Rape of Nanjing* details the atrocities suffered by Chinese civilians under the occupation of the Japanese. The dark nature of the massacre seemed to have played heavily on Chang and she later committed suicide. But Chang wasn't the first suicide linked to the massacre: Minnie Vautrin, an American missionary in Nánjīng, felt responsible for not being able to save more Chinese civilians' lives and killed herself after the massacre.

Jīmíng Temple
TEMPLE

(鸡鸣寺; Jīmíng Sì; admission ¥5; ⏰7.30am-5pm winter, to 5.30pm summer) Close to the Ming walls and Xuánwǔ Lake (Xuánwǔ Hú) is the Buddhist Jīmíng Temple, which was first built in AD 527 during the Three Kingdoms period. It's been rebuilt many times since, but has retained the same name (which literally translates as 'rooster crowing') since 1387. This temple is the most active temple in Nánjīng and is packed with worshippers during the Lunar New Year. The seven-storey-tall Yàoshīfó Pagoda (药师佛塔) offers views over Xuánwǔ Lake. Walk up to the rear of the temple and out onto the **city wall** (admission ¥15). Tufts of grass poke out from between the stones and you can embark on a lengthy and fabulous jaunt east along the overgrown ramparts; see the boxed text on p229. Buses Y1 and 304 can get you here.

Fūzǐ Temple
TEMPLE

(夫子庙; Fūzǐ Miào; Gongyuan Jie; admission ¥30; ⏰9am-10pm; Ⓜ Sanshan Jie) The Confucian Fūzǐ Temple, in the south of the city in a pedestrian zone, was a centre of Confucian study for more than 1500 years. But what you see here today are newly restored, late-Qing-dynasty structures or wholly new buildings reconstructed in traditional style.

Today the area surrounding Fūzǐ Temple has become Nánjīng's main shopping quarter and is a particularly crowded and fairly unattractive place. The whole area is lit up at night, adding to the kitsch ambience. **Tour boats** (*yóuchuán*) leave from the dock across from the temple itself for 30-minute day (¥60) and evening (¥80) trips along the Qínhuái River (秦淮河; Qínhuái Hé). Catch bus 1 or Y2 from Xīnjiēkǒu here.

Imperial Examinations History Museum
MUSEUM

(江南贡院历史陈列馆; Jiāngnán Gòngyuàn Lìshǐ Chénlièguǎn; 1 Jinling Lu; admission ¥20; ⏰8.30am-10pm) Across from the Fūzǐ temple complex to the east is this museum. It's a recent reconstruction of the building where scholars once spent months – or years – in tiny cells studying Confucian classics in preparation for civil-service examinations.

FREE Nánjīng Museum
MUSEUM

(南京博物馆; Nánjīng Bówùguǎn; 321 Zhongshan Donglu; ⏰9am-4.30pm; Ⓜ Minggugong) Just west of Zhōngshān Gate, modern China's first national museum displays artefacts from Neolithic times right through to the communist period...when it's not under renovation. The main building was constructed in 1933 in the style of a

Ming temple. While this building is being tinkered with, a small collection has moved to the **Art Gallery** (艺术陈列馆; Yìshùchénlièguǎn) building next door.

The limited offerings include a haphazardly arranged collection of porcelain, textiles, bronze ware, earthen ware and folk art. Some of the 500-plus-year-old porcelain, with striking colours, looks startlingly contemporary, while a large wooden weaving machine boggles the imagination. Some displays are labelled in (bad) English.

Xuánwǔ Lake Park   PARK

(玄武湖公园; Xuánwǔhú Gōngyuán; admission 1 Mar-1 May & 1 Sep-30 Nov ¥30, 1 Dec-29 Feb & 1 Jun-31 Aug ¥20; ⊙7am-9pm) This verdant 530-hectare park, backing onto the Ming-dynasty city wall, has a connected network of five isles spread across its lake. Scattered on the isles are bonsai gardens, camphor and cherry-blossom trees, temples and bamboo forests. The entire lake circuit is 9.5km for those inclined to a long jaunt. For the lazy, take a languid boat ride (¥70 per hour) around the lake – just make sure your boat steers properly before taking off.

Taiping Heavenly Kingdom
History Museum   MUSEUM

(太平天国历史博物馆; Tàipíng Tiānguó Lìshǐ Bówùguǎn; 128 Zhonghua Lu; admission ¥30; ⊙8am-5pm; Ⓜ Sanshan Jie) Hong Xiuquan, the leader of the Taiping, had a palace built in Nánjīng, but the building was completely destroyed when Nánjīng was taken in 1864.

The museum (no English sign) was originally a garden complex, built in the Ming dynasty, and housed some of the Taiping officials before their downfall. There are displays of maps showing the progress of the Taiping army from Guǎngdōng, Hong

MING CITY WALLS

Běijīng will be forever haunted by the communists' destruction of its awe-inspiring city walls. Xī'ān's mighty Tang-dynasty wall – which was far, far larger than its current wall – is a mere memory. Even Shànghǎi's modest city wall came down in 1912.

The same story is repeated across China, but Nánjīng's fabulous surviving city wall is a constant reminder of the city's former glories. The wall may be overgrown, but this neglect – in a land where historical authenticity has too often courted destruction – has helped ensure its very survival.

Perhaps the most impressive remnant of Nánjīng's Ming-dynasty golden years, the impressive, five-storey Ming bastion, which measures over 35km, is the longest city wall ever built in the world. About two-thirds of it still stands.

Built between 1366 and 1393, by more than one million labourers, the layout of the wall is irregular, an exception to the usual square format of these times; it zigzags around Nánjīng's hills and rivers, accommodating the local landscape. Averaging 12m high and 7m wide at the top, the fortification was built of bricks supplied from five Chinese provinces. Each brick had stamped on it the place it came from, the overseer's name and rank, the brick-maker's name and sometimes the date. This was to ensure that the bricks were well made; if they broke, they had to be replaced. Many of these stamps remain intact.

Some of the original 13 Ming city gates remain, including the **Zhōngyāng Gate** (中央门; Zhōngyāng Mén) in the north, **Zhōnghuá Gate** (中华门; Zhōnghuá Mén; admission ¥20) in the south and **Zhōngshān Gate** (中山门; Zhōngshān Mén) in the east. The city gates were heavily fortified; built on the site of the old Tang-dynasty wall, Zhōnghuá Gate has four rows of gates, making it almost impregnable, and could house a garrison of 3000 soldiers in vaults in the front gate building. When walking through, observe the trough in either wall of the second gate, which held a vast stone gate that could be lowered into place. The gate is far more imposing than anything that has survived in Běijīng.

You can climb onto the masonry for exploration at several points. Long walks extend along the wall from Zhōngshān Gate in the east of the city and it's quite common to see locals walking their dogs or taking post-dinner walks along the weathered path; there is no charge for climbing the wall here.

One of the best places to access the gate is from the rear of Jīmíng Temple. Walk to Jiǔhuáshān Park off Taiping Beilu, looking out over huge **Xuánwǔ Lake Park** (玄武湖公园) and passing crumbling hillside pagodas along the way.

Xiuquan's seals, Taiping coins, weapons and texts that describe the Taiping laws on agrarian reform, social law and cultural policy. Bus Y2 goes to the museum from the Ming Palace Ruins or Taiping Nanlu.

Yangzi River Bridge
BRIDGE

(南京长江大桥; Nánjīng Chángjiāng Dàqiáo) Opened on 23 December 1968, the Yangzi River Bridge is one of the longest bridges in China – a double-decker with a 4.5km-long road on top and a train line below. Wonderful socialist-realist sculptures can be seen on the approaches. Odds are that you'll probably cross the bridge if you take a train from the north. Probably the easiest way to get up on the bridge is to go through the **Bridge Park** (Dàqiáo Gōngyuán; adult/child ¥12/10; ⏱7.30am-6.30pm). Catch bus 67 from Jiangsu Lu, northwest of the Drum Tower (鼓楼; Gǔlóu), to its terminus opposite the park.

✸✸ Festivals & Events

Nánjīng International Plum Blossom Festival
PLUM BLOSSOM

Held yearly from the last Saturday of February to early March, it takes place on Zǐjīn Mountain near the Míng Xiàolíng Tomb when the mountain bursts with pink and white blossoms.

🛏 Sleeping

Most of Nánjīng's accommodation is midrange to top end in price. All rooms have broadband internet, and most places can help to book air and train tickets.

Orange Hotel
HOTEL $$

(桔子酒店; Júzi Jiǔdiàn; ☎8696 8090; www.orangehotel.com.cn; 26 Dashiba Jie; 大石坝街26号; r ¥298-328; ✲@) A great riverside location, this reliable chain is big bang for the buck. The ultra-modern rooms, with good bedding and lighting, have every gizmo and gadget your computer, PDA or mobile phone might ever need. It's worth paying a few more bucks for the rooms with river-facing balconies. Other pluses include complimentary fruit and free use of the hotel's bikes.

Nánjīng Time International Youth Hostel
HOSTEL $

(南京时光国际青年旅舍; Nánjīng Shíguāng Guójì Qīngnián Lǚshè; ☎8556 9053; www.yhachina.com/ls.php?id=271; 6-5 Yongyuan, Méiyuán Xīncūn; 梅园新村雍园6-5号; dm ¥60, r ¥180-260; ✲@) Time – for atmosphere alone it's the best in town – is in a republican-era mansion not far

from the Presidential Palace. The salubrious neighbourhood guarantees you a good sleep at night. Dorms are spotless and the rooms have a simplistic charm. There's a lot of common area, including a relaxing rooftop terrace. The hostel is hidden in an alley with lots of twists and turns in the Méiyuán Xīncūn district. Download a map from the hostel website for directions.

Nánjīng Zhōngfáng Service Apartment
SERVICE APARTMENT $$

(南京中房酒店公寓; Nánjīng Zhōngfáng Jiǔdiàn Gōngyù; ☎6867 8188; www.njmyhome.com; 88 Wangfu Dajie; 王府大街88号; r ¥328-368; ✲@) All rooms at this central service apartment come with a kitchenette, fridge and washing machine/dryer, and they are immaculately clean and extremely comfortable. Enter via 118 Moling Lu (秣陵路118号), turn right and head to the last building. The reception is on the 4th floor.

Travelers' Soul Inn Nanjing
HOSTEL $

(南京心之旅国际青年旅舍; Nánjīng Xīnzhīlǚ Guójì Qīngnián Lǚshè; ☎8329 2888; www.nanjinginn.com; Bldg B7/B5, 1865 Creativity Industrial Park; 1865创意园区B7幢; 4-/6-bed dm ¥55/45, d ¥180-668; ✲@) This spanking new digs is both a hostel and a hotel, with a plethora of rooms to suit your budget. The dorms and simpler (cheaper) rooms are on the ground floor. All basic but clean. Above, the rooms are decorated with themes, ranging from kitschy to quirky. The location is a bit out of the way (it's outside the southern city wall). From the Zhonghuamen metro, it's a 1km walk east along Yingtian Dajie.

Sheraton Nánjīng Kingsley
HOTEL $$$

(南京金丝利喜来登酒店; Nánjīng Jīnsīlì Xǐláidēng Jiǔdiàn; ☎8666 8888, 800 810 3088; www.sheraton.com/nanjing; 169 Hanzhong Lu; 汉中路169号; d ¥1580-2080) The centrally located Sheraton is a safe bet for business travellers, with four restaurants and two bars, indoor pool and tennis court. Discounts of almost 50% are available.

🍴 Eating

The two main eating quarters in Nánjīng are at Fūzǐ Temple and Shīziqiáo (狮子桥) off Hunan Lu. Both are lively pedestrian areas that come alive at night, packed with people, snack stands and small eateries. Shanghai Lu is home to a strip of restaurants popular with the university crowd. Near the

Presidential Palace, **Nánjīng 1912** (cnr Taiping Beilu & Changjiang Lu) is a compound of shiny neon-lit bars, coffee houses and upscale chain restaurants.

Mǎxiángxīng   HALAL, CHINESE JIĀNGSŪ $$

(马祥兴; 32 Yunnan Beilu; dishes ¥12-158; ⊙ground fl 6.30am-7pm, 2nd fl 6.30am-9pm) On the ground floor of this 172-year-old institution is a canteen, and you'll encounter beef at every repast. Try the hearty *niúròu miàn* (牛肉面; beef noodles), or the crispy *niúròu guōtiē* (牛肉锅贴; beef potstickers). Diners flock to the pricier restaurant upstairs for its carefully prepared *huí* dishes with a Jiāngsū twist. Among the offerings are *měirén gān* (美人肝; duck liver with turnip and celeries) and *dàn shāomài* (蛋烧卖; egg dumplings stuffed with shrimps). There's a picture menu.

Sìchuān Jiǔjiā   SICHUANESE, CHINESE JIĀNGSŪ $

(四川酒家; 171 Taiping Nanlu; meals from ¥15; ⊙10.30am-10.30pm) Rub shoulders with locals in the cheap, local dining area on the ground floor: there's *yánshuǐ yā* (盐水鸭; Nánjīng pressed duck), *dàndànmiàn* (担担面; spicy noodles), *chā shāo* (叉烧; pork slices; ¥10), *jiānjiǎo* (煎饺; fried dumplings); *Suāncàiyú* (酸菜鱼; fish and cabbage soup). Other Sìchuān dishes are on the smarter and dearer 2nd floor. There's no English sign, so look for the bright-red building and the sign with dancing chilli peppers.

Cosima Restaurant   PIZZA, TAPAS $$

(120 Shanghai Lu; pizza ¥48-80, tapas ¥12-48; ⊙10am till late; 🖳) Wash down the authentically made tapas with glasses of sangria in this teeny weeny Spanish joint, and you might soon forget you're in China. Pizzas are also served here. There are only three tables and no bookings are accepted.

A Simple Diet   CHINESE JIĀNGSŪ $$

(粗茶淡饭; Cūchá Dànfàn; 32 Shiziqiao; mains ¥8-20; ⊙11am-9pm) This busy restaurant serves excellent *xiǎolóng tāngbāo* (小笼汤包; soup dumplings) and is by far the best place in the Shízíqío strip to grab a cheap bite.

Yǒnghé Yuán   CHINESE JIĀNGSŪ, SHANGHAINESE $

(永和园; 122 Gongyuan Jie; mains ¥15; ⊙8.30am-9pm) Not far from the decorative arch roughly halfway along Gongyuan Jie, this long-serving food court is low on decor but that doesn't stop the crowds from packing in. It serves a great range of tasty snacks, from *páigǔ miàn* (排骨面; spare ribs and noodles) and *xiānròu húntun* (鲜肉馄饨; meat dumplings) to *wǔxiāng dàn* (五香蛋; five-flavour eggs), *xiaolong* dumplings and the local favourite *yāxiě fěnsī tāng* (鸭血粉丝汤; mung bean vermicelli with duck blood pudding). Grab a tray, order your dishes, take them to the cashier and pay.

Sculpting in Time   WESTERN, CAFE $$

(雕刻时光; Diāokè Shíguāng; 32 Dashiba Jie; mains ¥50; ⊙9am-11pm; 🖳) This branch of the excellent Taiwanese cafe chain is an appealing, relaxed spot with an outdoor terrace overlooking the river. It's a favourite eating and drinking place for a cool but unpretentious crowd. The pastries and cakes make a good afternoon treat.

🍷 Drinking

Nánjīng's nightlife scene is not as vibrant as Shànghǎi's. There are bars and clubs in **Nánjīng 1912** (cnr Taipei Beilu & Changjiang Lu).

Behind the Wall   BAR

(答案; Dá'àn; 150 Shanghai Lu; pint ¥30; 🕾) Very laid-back outside seating, convivial atmosphere and draught beer. A talented guitar duo performs most nights. The bar doubles as a Mexican restaurant. It's literally 'behind the wall'.

Finnegans Wake   BAR

(芬尼根酒吧; Fēnnígēn Jiǔbā; ☑5220 7362; 400 Zhongshan Nanlu; Guinness draft pint ¥70; ⊙5pm-late Mon-Fri, 10.30am-late Sat & Sun) After relocating to an alley off Zhongshan Nanlu in a rebuilt historical neighbourhood, this pricey expats' bar has gone even pricier. Guinness on tap and an Irish bartender also belts out the tunes. Phone if you can't find the bar. Don't try the chilli vodka unless you want to spend the night writhing on the ground.

Florentina   BAR

(cnr Nanyingyangying Xiang & Shanghai Lu; beer from ¥20) In an alley just off Shanghai Lu, this studenty bar has 40+ Belgian and US beers, hookahs, and a young garrulous crowd. Feeling peckish? Feel free to order food from eateries next door.

☆ Entertainment

Lányuàn Theatre   CHINESE OPERA

(兰苑剧场; Lányuàn Jùchǎng; ☑8446 9284; 4 Cháotiangong) *Kūnqǔ*, an extant form of Chinese opera originating from Jiāngsū, is staged here every Saturday evening. There are English subtitles and tickets are ¥80.

🏠 Shopping

The area surrounding **Fūzǐ Temple** is a pedestrian zone with souvenirs, clothing, shoes, antiques and even animals for sale.

Librairie Avant-Garde BOOKS
(先锋书店; Xiānfēng Shūdiàn; 173 Guangzhou Lu; ⏰10am-9.30pm; Ⓜ Shanghai Lu) Housed in a disused bomb shelter, this mammoth indie bookshop has zero foreign-language books, but the ambience and the decor alone certainly deserve a visit. You'll see what we mean when you go and inspect it yourself. Students and literati alike love the sizeable collection of social science and humanities books in this Nánjīng cultural landmark, and the fine selection of postcards and handmade accessories draws in the shoppers. There's also a nice cafe and plenty of comfortable seating areas. From Shanghai Lu metro station, it's a 15-minute walk to the bookshop.

Foreign Languages Bookstore BOOKS
(外文书店; Wàiwén Shūdiàn; 218 Zhongshan Donglu; ⏰9am-7pm) This bookshop has English maps and pricey, imported English bestsellers.

Popular Book Mall BOOKS
(大众书局; Dàzhòng Shūjú; Xīnjiēkǒu; ⏰9am-9pm) A range of English fiction can be found on the 4th floor.

ℹ️ Information

Internet Access
Jīnsuǒ Internet Cafe (金锁网洛; Jīnsuǒ Wǎngluò; 85 Shanghai Lu; per hr ¥3; ⏰24hr)

Internet Resources
Nanjing Expats (www.nanjingexpat.com) Active forum, events and listings in Nánjīng. It also distributes a magazine around the city.

Media
Map (www.mapmagazine.com.cn) Expat listings magazine.

Nanjing Expats (www.nanjingexpat.com) Another expat listings magazine available at restaurants and bars.

Medical Services
Jiāngsū People's Hospital (江苏省人民医院; Jiāngsū Shěng Rénmín Yīyuàn; ☏8371 8836; 300 Guangzhou Lu; ⏰8am-noon & 2-5.30pm) Runs a clinic for expats and has English-speaking doctors available.

Nánjīng International SOS Clinic (南京国际 SOS 紧急救援诊所; Nánjīng Guójì SOS Jǐnjí Jiùyuán Zhěnsuǒ; ☏8480 2842, 24hr alarm centre 010 6462 9100) On the ground floor of the Grand Metropark Hotel. The staff speaks English.

Money
An ATM taking international cards can be found in the Sheraton Nánjīng Kingsley. Most bank ATMs are open 24 hours and take international cards. The banks listed below change major currency and travellers cheques.

Bank of China (中国银行; Zhōngguó Yínháng; 29 Hongwu Lu; ⏰8am-5pm Mon-Fri, to 12.30pm Sat)

Bank of China (中国银行; Zhōngguó Yínháng; 148 Zhonghua Lu; ⏰8am-5pm Mon-Fri, to 12.30pm Sat)

Post
China Post (中国邮政; Zhōngguó Yóuzhèng; 2 Zhongshan Nanlu; ⏰8am-6.30pm) Postal services and international phone calls.

Public Security Bureau
PSB (公安局; Gōng'ānjú) On a small lane called Sanyuan Xiang down a nest of streets west off Zhongshan Nanlu.

Travel Agencies
Most hotels have their own travel agencies and can book tickets for a service charge. They can also arrange tours around town and to neighbouring sights.

China International Travel Service (CITS; 中国国际旅行社; Zhōngguó Guójì Lûxíngshè; ☏8342 1125; 202 Zhongshan Beilu; ⏰9am-4pm) Across from the Nánjīng Hotel; arranges tours, and books air and train tickets.

ℹ️ Getting There & Away

Air
Nánjīng has regular air connections to all major Chinese cities. The main office for the **Civil Aviation Administration of China** (CAAC; 中国民航; Zhōngguó Mínháng; ☏8449 9378; 50 Ruijin Lu) is near the terminus of bus 37, but you can also buy tickets at most top-end hotels.

Dragonair (港龙航空; Gǎnglóng Hángkōng; ☏8471 0181; Room 751-53, World Trade Centre, 2 Hanzhong Lu) has daily flights to Hong Kong.

Bus
Of Nánjīng's numerous long-distance bus stations, **Nánjīng long-distance bus station** (南京门长途汽车站; Nánjīng chángtú qìchēzhàn; ☏8533 1288), aka Zhōngyángmén long-distance station, is the largest, located southwest of the wide-bridged intersection with Zhongyang Lu. Regular buses departing from here:

Héféi ¥50, 2½ hours

Shànghǎi ¥88, four hours

Sūzhōu ¥64, 2½ hours

Wúxī ¥52, two hours

Buses departing the **east bus station** (长途汽车东站; chángtú qìchē dōngzhàn):

Hángzhōu ¥125, four hours

Huángshān ¥120, four hours

Yángzhōu ¥37, 1½ hours

Zhènjiāng ¥24, 1½ hours

From Nánjīng Train Station, take bus 13 north to Zhōngyāngmén long-distance bus station. Bus 2 from Xīnjiēkǒu goes to the east bus station. A taxi from town will cost ¥20 to ¥25 to either station.

Train

Nánjīng Train Station (☎ 8582 2222) is a major stop on the Běijīng–Shànghǎi train line. Heading eastward from Nánjīng, the line to Shànghǎi connects with Zhènjiāng, Wúxī and Sūzhōu. Most G trains terminate at the new **Nánjīng South Train Station** (南京南站; Nánjīng Nánzhàn), so check when you buy your ticket.

Frequent high-speed G trains run between Nánjīng and Shànghǎi (¥135, ½ hour), stopping at Sūzhōu (¥100, 50 minutes). G trains to Běijīng (¥274, five hours) run almost every 20 minutes from Nánjīng South Train Station; the station also has 15 G trains to Hángzhōu (¥211, 2½ hours). Regular trains go to Huángshān City in Ānhuī province (¥54 to ¥159, seven hours) from Nánjīng Train Station.

A slow train to Guǎngzhōu (¥208 to ¥658, 28 hours, two daily) goes via Shànghǎi.

Try to get tickets via your hotel or the **train ticket office** (火车票售票处; huǒchēpiào shòupiàochù; ⊗ 8.30am-5pm) on the 3rd floor of the post office, or the **train ticket office** (35 Taiping Beilu) on Taiping Beilu.

ℹ️ Getting Around

To/From the Airport

Nánjīng's Lùkǒu airport is approximately one hour south of the city. Buses (¥25) run to the airport every 30 minutes between 6am and 9pm from the square east of Nánjīng Train Station. Most hotels have hourly shuttle buses to and from the airport. A taxi will cost around ¥130.

Public Transport

Nánjīng has an efficient **metro system** that cuts through the city centre. Line No 1 runs north to south and links both train stations. Line No 2 goes east from Jǐngtiānlù to Yóufāngqiáo in the west and makes getting to some sights more convenient. Six more lines are under construction and are expected to be in service by 2015. Tickets are ¥2 to ¥4.

You can get to Xīnjiēkǒu, in the heart of town, by jumping on bus 13 from Nánjīng Train Station or from Zhōngyāng Gate. There are also tourist bus routes that visit many of the sights:

Bus Y1 Goes from Nánjīng Train Station and Nánjīng long-distance bus station through the city to the Sun Yatsen Mausoleum.

Bus Y2 Starts in the south at the Martyrs' Cemetery (烈士墓地; Lièshì Mùdì), passes Fūzǐ Temple and terminates halfway up Zǐjīn Mountain.

Bus Y3 Passes by Nánjīng Train Station en route to the Míng Xiàolíng Tomb and Línggǔ Temple.

Many local maps contain bus routes. Normal buses cost ¥1 and tourist buses cost ¥2.

Taxi

Taxi fares start at ¥9 and it's ¥2.40 for each 3km thereafter. Trips to most destinations in the city are ¥10 to ¥14. Taxis are easy to flag down anywhere in the city.

Around Nánjīng

On Qīxiá Mountain, 22km northeast of Nánjīng, **Qīxiá Temple** (栖霞寺; Qīxiá Sì; admission ¥20; ⊗ 7am-5.30pm) was founded by the Buddhist monk Ming Sengshao during the Southern Qi dynasty, and is still an active place of worship. It's long been one of China's most important monasteries, and even today it's still one of the largest Buddhist seminaries in the country. Relics believed to be part of the skull of Gautama Buddha were unveiled and interred here. There are two main temple halls: the Maitreya Hall, with a statue of the Maitreya Buddha sitting cross-legged at the entrance; and the Vairocana Hall, housing a 5m-tall statue of the Vairocana Buddha.

Behind Qīxiá Temple is the **Thousand Buddha Cliff** (Qiānfó Yá). Several grottoes housing stone statues are carved into the hillside, the earliest of which dates as far back as the Qi dynasty (AD 479–502). There is also a small stone pagoda, **Shělì Pagoda** (舍利; Shělì Tǎ), which was built in AD 601, and rebuilt during the late Tang period. The upper part has engraved sutras and carvings of Buddha; around the base, each of the pagoda's eight sides depicts Sakyamuni.

The temple is built in a scenic area. Continue northwards to admire a whole heap of views behind the temple. The steep path meanders along an array of pavilions and rocky outcrops. The entire area is rather serene and you could bring your lunch and spend the better part of your day here.

You can reach the temple from Nánjīng by a public bus (南上, Nán Shàng, ¥2.50, one hour) that departs from a stop beside the Nánjīng Train Station. When you get off the bus, you will be approached by motorcycle taxis that will offer to take you into the temple the 'back' way for ¥10. Be warned, it's an arduous hike up and down a large hill to the temple if you take this option.

Sūzhōu 苏州

✓ 0512 / POP 1.3 MILLION

Historically, Sūzhōu was synonymous with high culture and elegance, and generations of artists, scholars, writers and high society in China were drawn by its exquisite art forms and the delicate beauty of its gardens. Communist rule has spawned some mightily unattractive cities and disfigured many more, and like all modern Chinese towns, Sūzhōu has had to contend with the destruction of its heritage and its replacement with largely arbitrary chunks of modern architecture.

Having said that, the city still retains enough pockets of charm to warrant two to three days' exploration. Sūzhōu is one of the few (relatively) bike-friendly cities in China. And the gardens, Sūzhōu's main attraction, are a symphonic combination of rocks, water, trees and pavilions that reflects the Chinese appreciation of balance and harmony. You could easily spend an enjoyable several days wandering through gardens, visiting some excellent museums, and exploring some of Sūzhōu's surviving canal scenes, pagodas and humpbacked bridges.

History

Dating back some 2500 years, Sūzhōu is one of the oldest towns in the Yangzi Basin. With the completion of the Grand Canal during the Sui dynasty, Sūzhōu began to flourish as a centre of shipping and grain storage, bustling with merchants and artisans.

By the 14th century, Sūzhōu had become China's leading silk-producing city. Aristocrats, pleasure seekers, famous scholars, actors and painters arrived, constructing villas and garden retreats.

The town's winning image as a 'Garden City' or a 'Venice of the East' drew from its medieval blend of woodblock guilds and embroidery societies, whitewashed housing, cobbled streets, tree-lined avenues and canals. The local women were considered the most beautiful in China, largely thanks to the mellifluous local accent, and the city was home to a variety of rich merchants and bookish scholars...no doubt drawn by the beautiful women.

In 1860 Taiping troops took the town without a blow and in 1896 Sūzhōu was opened to foreign trade, with Japanese and other international concessions. Since 1949 much of the historic city, including its city walls, has vanished (yes, blame development and the Cultural Revolution).

◉ Sights & Activities

High-season prices listed are applicable from March to early May and September to October. Gardens and museums stop selling tickets 30 minutes before closing, and are best visited early in the mornings before they get too crowded.

FREE **Sūzhōu Museum** MUSEUM
(苏州博物馆; Sūzhōu Bówùguǎn; 204 Dongbei Jie; audioguide ¥30; ⊙9am-5pm) An architectural triumph in Sūzhōu, this IM Pei–designed museum is an inspirational interpretation of a Sūzhōu garden, with a creative combination of water, bamboo and straight lines. Inside is a fascinating array of jade, ceramics, wooden carvings, textiles and other displays, all with good English captions. Look out for the boxwood statue of Avalokiteshvara (Guanyin), dating from the republican period. Draconian entry rules apply: flip-flops wearers get turned away.

Garden of the Master of the Nets GARDENS
(网师园; Wǎngshī Yuán; high/low season ¥30/20; ⊙7.30am-5pm) Off Shiquan Jie, this pocket-sized garden is considered one of the best preserved in the city. It was laid out in the 12th century, went to seed and was later restored in the 18th century as part of the home of a retired official turned fisherman (hence the name). The central section is the main garden. The western section is an inner garden where a courtyard contains the master's study.

The most striking feature of this garden is its use of space: the labyrinth of courtyards, with windows framing other parts of the garden, is ingeniously designed to give the illusion of a much larger area. Trivia nuts: the **Peony Study** is used as the model for the Astor Court and Ming Garden in the Museum of Modern Art, New York.

There are two ways to the entry gate, with English signs and souvenir stalls marking the way: you can enter from the alley on Shiquan Jie; or via Kuòjiātóu Xiàng (阔家头巷), an alley off Daichengqiao Lu.

Humble Administrator's Garden GARDENS
(拙政园; Zhuōzhèng Yuán; 178 Dongbei Jie; high/low season ¥70/50, audioguide free; ⊙7.30am-5.30pm) First built in 1509, this 5.2-hectare garden is clustered with water features, a museum, a teahouse and at least 10 pavilions such as 'the listening to the sound of rain' and 'the faraway looking' pavilions – hardly humble, we know. It is the largest of all the gardens and considered by many to

be the most impressive. With its zigzagging bridges, pavilions, bamboo groves and fragrant lotus ponds, it should be an ideal place for a leisurely stroll...sadly you'll have to battle with crowds for right of way!

Lion's Grove Garden
GARDENS

(狮子林; Shīzi Lín; 23 Yuanlin Lu; high/low season ¥30/20; ⊙7.30am-5.30pm) The garden was constructed in 1342 by the Buddhist monk Tianru to commemorate his master, who lived on Lion Cliff on Zhèjiāng's Tiānmú Mountain. The legion of curiously shaped rocks in the garden was meant to resemble lions, protectors of the Buddhist faith. If the Humble Administrator's Garden was crowded, get ready to be pushed along by the tide of tourists here.

Garden to Linger In
GARDENS

(留园; Liú Yuán; 79 Liuyuan Lu; high/low season ¥40/30; ⊙7.30am-5pm) One of the largest gardens in Sūzhōu, this 3-hectare garden was originally built in the Ming dynasty by a doctor as a relaxing place for his recovering patients. It's easy to see why the patients took to the place: the winding corridors are inlaid with calligraphy from celebrated masters, their windows and doorways opening onto unusually shaped rockeries, ponds and dense clusters of bamboo. Stone tablets hang from the walls, inscribed by patients recording their impressions of the place. The teahouse is a fantastic place to recover from crowd overload. Order a cup of *lóngjǐng* (龙井; dragon well tea; ¥15) and relax.

The garden is about 3km west of the city centre and can be reached on tourist bus Y1 from the train station or Renmin Lu.

West Garden Temple
GARDENS

(西园寺; Xīyuán Sì; Xiyuan Lu; admission ¥25; ⊙8am-5pm) The West Garden Temple, with its mustard-yellow walls and gracefully curved eaves, was burnt to the ground during the Taiping Rebellion and rebuilt in the late 19th century.

Greeting you on entry to the magnificent **Arhat Hall** (罗汉堂; Luóhàn Táng) in the temple is a stunning four-faced and thousand-armed statue of Guanyin. Beyond this lies mesmerising and slightly unnerving rows of 500 glittering Arhat statues (Arhats are monks who have achieved enlightenment and pass to nirvana at death), each one unique and near life-size. There's also a vegetarian restaurant serving noodles.

The temple is 400m west of the Garden to Linger In. Take Y1 or Y3 from the train station to get there.

Soochow University
HISTORIC BUILDINGS

Before the communists took over the nation, this college (苏州大学; Sūzhōu Dàxué) was the oldest private university of the land, having been founded by missionaries of the Methodist church in 1900. The university is still in operation and its beautiful old campus is accessible from the west gate (西门; xīmén) where you'll see **St Joseph Church**, built in 1881, standing right outside. Inside the leafy campus there are ivy-clad colonial buildings, and the most notable ones include the imposing **Clock Tower** and the **Laura Haygood Memorial Hall**.

The Xiangmen metro stop (exit 1) is next to the north gate of the campus, or bus 8 from the train station will drop you off at the west gate.

Píngjiāng Lù
STREET

While most of the canals in the city have been sealed and paved into roads, the pedestrianised **Píngjiāng Lù** (平江路) would give you some clue to the Sūzhōu of yesteryear. On the eastern side of the city, this road (watch out for electric bikes!) is set alongside a canal. Whitewashed local houses, most now converted to guesthouses, teahouses or trendy cafes selling overpriced beverages, sit comfortably side-by-side. Had enough of makeover studios and Tsingtao-swilling tourists? Duck down some of the side streets that jut out from the main path for a glimpse at the slow-paced local life.

Blue Wave Pavilion
GARDENS

(沧浪亭; Cānglàng Tíng; Renmin Lu; high/low season ¥20/15; ⊙7.30am-5pm) Instead of attracting hordes of tourists, this wild, overgrown garden around the Blue Wave Pavilion is one of those where the locals actually go to chill and enjoy a leisurely stroll. Originally the home of a prince, the oldest garden in Sūzhōu was first built in the 11th century, and has been repeatedly rebuilt since.

Lacking a northern wall, the garden creates the illusion of space by borrowing scenes from the outside. A double verandah out the front pavilion wends its way along a canal. From the outer path, you'll see green space inside and from the inner path you can see views of the water. Look out for a 'temple' whose dark walls are carved with the portraits of more than 500 sages, and the 'pure fragrance house' has some impressive furniture made from the gnarled roots of banyan trees.

Sūzhōu

0 — 1 km
0 — 0.5 miles

Train Station

32

33

Guangji Lu

Píngqí Lu

Qimen Lu

Humble Administrator's Garden

35

Sūzhōu Museum

12

7

Dongbei Jie

22

Panru Xiang

6

Baita Donglu

Cang Jie

3

Baita Xilu

Dong Zhongshi

31

Daicheng Fang
大成坊

Lindun Lu

Pingjiang Lu

Qiaosikong Xiang

24

Yinguo Xiang

9

Daru Xiang

21

5

Zhongzhangjia Xiang

Ping'an Fang

14

13

34

17

18

Pingjiāng Lù

Jingde Lu

Guanqian Jie

Taijian Long

20

25

Xiangmen

Jia Yu Fang

Furen Fang

15

Ganjiang Lu

Lindun Lu

Twin Pagodas

29

Leqiao

Wuzhou Lu

Yangyu Xiang

Dashitou Xiang

19

11

Shizi Jie

28

Daoqian Jie

23

Fenghuang Jie

Dong Dajie 东大街

Shiquan Jie 十全街

26

27

Suzhou Tourism Information Center

Daichengqiao Lu

4

2

1

Renmin Lu 人民路

Wuquequiao Lu

Zhuhui Lu

Xiangwang Lu

Changxu Lu

Xinshi Lu

16

10

30

8

Wumen Bridge

Renmin Bridge

To South Long-Distance Bus Station (0.5km); Train Ticket Office (0.5km)

Waicheng River

Sūzhōu

◎ **Top Sights**

Humble Administrator's Garden C2
Píngjiāng Lù D4
Sūzhōu Museum C2

◎ **Sights**

1 Blue Wave Pavilion C6
2 Confucian Temple B6
3 Couple's Garden D3
4 Garden of the Master of the
   Nets C6
5 Kūnqǔ Opera Museum D3
6 Lion's Grove Garden C2
7 North Temple Pagoda B2
8 Pán Gate A7
9 Píngtán Museum D3
10 Ruìguāng Pagoda B7
11 Soochow University D5
12 Suzhou Silk Museum B2
13 Temple of Mystery C3

🛏 **Sleeping**

14 Hotel Soul B3
15 Marco Polo Suzhou C4
16 Pan Pacific Sūzhōu B6
17 Píngjiāng Lodge C4
18 Sūzhōu Mingtown Youth Hostel D4
19 Sūzhōu Watertown Youth
    Hostel B5

🍴 **Eating**

20 Déyuè Lóu C4
21 Pingvon C3
22 Wúmén Rénjiā C2
23 Xīshèngyuán C5
24 Yǎbā Shēngjiān C3
25 Zhūhóngxīng Miànguǎn C4

🍷 **Drinking**

26 Bookworm C5

🎭 **Entertainment**

Garden of the Master of the Nets .. (see 4)
Kūnqǔ Opera Museum .... (see 5)
Píngtán Museum .... (see 9)
27 Pingtan Teahouse C5

ⓘ **Information**

28 No 1 Hospital C5

ⓘ **Transport**

29 China Eastern Airlines B4
30 Grand Canal Boat Ticket Office C7
31 Liánhé Ticket Centre B3
32 Local Buses A1
33 North Long-Distance Bus Station B1
34 Train Ticket Office (Guanqian Jie) C4
35 Yángyáng Bike Rental Shop B2

JIĀNGSŪ SŪZHŌU

FREE **Confucian Temple** TEMPLE
(文庙; Wénmiào; 613 Renmin Lu; ⊙8.30am-4.30pm) The main building of this former Confucian Temple is still under renovation and should look stunning when complete. The highlight now is the fabulous stelae carved during the Southern Song dynasty (1137–1279). One features a map of old Sūzhōu – it details the canal system (much of which is now paved over and blocked), old roads and the city walls dating back to 1229. Surprisingly, the whole city grid is relatively unchanged from 800 years ago. There's also an astronomy stelae from 1190 – one of the oldest astronomy charts in the world.

Sūzhōu Silk Museum MUSEUM
(苏州丝绸博物馆; Sūzhōu Sīchóu Bówùguǎn; 2001 Renmin Lu; admission ¥15; ⊙9am-5pm) Sūzhōu was renowned for silk production and weaving, and the Sūzhōu Silk Museum houses a number of fascinating exhibitions that detail the history of Sūzhōu's 4000-year-old silk industry. Exhibits include a section on silk-weaving techniques and a room with live silk worms munching away on mulberry leaves and spinning cocoons. There are many functioning looms and its not uncommon to see staff at work on a large brocade. Many of the captions are in English. Adjacent to the museum is the new Sūzhōu Arts Museum, but the exhibitions are a bit hit and miss.

North Temple Pagoda PAGODA
(北寺塔; Běisì Tǎ; 1918 Renmin Lu; admission ¥25; ⊙7.45am-5.30pm) The tallest pagoda south of the Yangzi, at nine storeys North Temple Pagoda dominates the northern end of Renmin Lu. Climb it for sweeping views of hazy modern-day Sūzhōu.

The temple complex goes back 1700 years and was originally a residence; the current reincarnation dates back to the 17th century. Off to the side is **Nánmù Guānyīn Hall** (Nánmù Guānyīn Diàn), which was rebuilt in the Ming dynasty with some features imported from elsewhere.

THE GRAND CANAL

The world's longest canal, the Grand Canal (大运河; Dàyùnhé) once meandered for almost 1800km from Běijīng to Hángzhōu, and is a striking example of China's engineering prowess. Sections of the canal have been silted up for centuries and today perhaps half of it remains seasonally navigable.

The Grand Canal's construction spanned many centuries. The first 85km were completed in 495 BC, but the mammoth task of linking the Yellow River (Huáng Hé) and the Yangzi River (Cháng Jiāng) was undertaken between AD 605–609 by a massive conscripted labour force during Sui times. It was developed again during the Yuan dynasty (1271–1368). The canal enabled the government to capitalise on the growing wealth of the Yellow River basin and to ship supplies from south to north.

The Jiāngnán section of the canal (Hángzhōu, Sūzhōu, Wúxī and Chángzhōu) is a skein of canals, rivers and branching lakes. There are boat rides along certain sections of the canal in Sūzhōu – with all the surrounding modernity, though, the grandness of the project seems to have all but faded.

Pán Gate
LANDMARK

(盘门; Pán Mén; 1 Dong Dajie; admission Pán Gate only/with Ruìguāng Pagoda ¥25/31; ⏲7.30am-6pm) This stretch of the city wall straddling the outer moat in the southwest corner of the city has Sūzhōu's only remaining original coiled gate, Pán Gate, which dates from 1355. This overgrown double-walled water gate was used for controlling waterways and has many defensive positions at the top. From the gate, you can spy the exquisite arched Wúmén Bridge (Wúmén Qiáo) to the east and there are great views of the moat and the crumbling **Ruìguāng Pagoda** (瑞光塔; Ruìguāng Tǎ), constructed in 1004. The gate is also connected to 300m of the ancient city wall, which visitors can walk along. To get there, take tourist bus Y5 from the train station or Changxu Lu.

Temple of Mystery
TEMPLE

(玄妙观; Xuánmiào Guàn; Guanqian Jie; admission ¥10, incl performance ¥30; ⏲7.30am-5.30pm) The Taoist Temple of Mystery stands in what was once Sūzhōu's old bazaar, a rowdy entertainment district with travelling showmen, acrobats and actors. The temple's present surroundings of Guanqian Jie are just as boisterous, but the current showmen are more likely to sell you a fake designer watch, and blasphemously, the front hall of the temple is now selling gold and jewellery!

The temple was founded in the 3rd century AD, and restored many times over its long history. The complex contains several elaborately decorated halls, including **Sānqīng Diàn** (Three Purities Hall), which is supported by 60 pillars and capped by a double roof with upturned eaves. The temple dates from 1181 and is the only surviving example of Song architecture in Sūzhōu.

Tiger Hill
PARK

(虎丘山; Hǔqiū Shān; Huqiu Lu; admission high/low season ¥60/40; ⏲7.30am-6pm, to 5pm winter) In the far northwest of town, Tiger Hill is popular with local tourists. The hill itself is artificial and is the final resting place of He Lu, founding father of Sūzhōu. He Lu died in the 6th century BC and myths have coalesced around him – he is said to have been buried with a collection of 3000 swords be guarded by a white tiger.

The beacon drawing the visitors is the leaning **Cloud Rock Pagoda** (云岩塔; Yúnyán Tǎ) atop Tiger Hill. The octagonal seven-storey pagoda was built in the 10th century entirely of brick, an innovation in Chinese architecture at the time. The pagoda began tilting over 400 years ago, and today the highest point is displaced more than 2m from its original position. Tourist buses Y1 and Y2 from the train station go to Tiger Hill.

Couple's Garden
GARDENS

(耦园; Ǒu Yuán; high/low season ¥20/15; ⏲8am-4.30pm) The tranquil Couple's Garden is off the main tourist route and sees fewer visitors (a relative concept in China), though the gardens, pond and courtyards are quite lovely. Surrounding the garden on Pingjiang Lu are some fine examples of traditional Sūzhōu architecture, bridges and canals.

FREE Kūnqǔ Opera Museum
MUSEUM

(戏曲博物馆; Xìqǔ Bówùguǎn; 14 Zhongzhangjia Xiang; ⏲8.30am-4pm) Down a warren of narrow lanes, the small Kūnqǔ Opera Museum is dedicated to *kūnqǔ*, the opera style of the region. The beautiful old theatre houses a stage, musical instruments, costumes and photos of famous performers. It also puts on occasional performances of *kūnqǔ*.

Píngtán Museum   MUSEUM
(评弹博物馆; Píngtán Bówùguǎn; 3 Zhongzhangjia Xiang; admission ¥4; ⊙8.30am-noon, 3.30-4.30pm) Almost next to the Kūnqǔ Opera Museum is the Píngtán Museum, which puts on wonderful performances of *píngtán*, a singing and storytelling art form sung in the Sūzhōu dialect. Shows are at 1.30pm daily.

☞ Tours

Evening boat tours wind their way around the outer canal leaving nightly from 6pm to 8.30pm (¥120, 55 minutes, half-hourly). The trips, usually with *píngtán* performance on board, are a great way to experience old Sūzhōu. Remember to bring bug repellent as the mosquitoes are tenacious. Tickets can be bought at the port near Rénmín Bridge, which shares the same quarters with the Grand Canal boat ticket office (划船售票处; Huáchuán Shòupiàochù).

✿ Festivals & Events

Sūzhōu Silk Festival   SILK
Every September Sūzhōu hosts a silk festival. There are exhibitions devoted to silk history and production, and silk merchants get to show off their wares to crowds of thousands.

🛏 Sleeping

Hotels in general are terribly overpriced in Sūzhōu. Get ready to hone your bargaining skills.

TOP CHOICE Píngjiāng Lodge   BOUTIQUE HOTEL $$$
(苏州平江客栈; Sūzhōu Píngjiāng Kèzhàn; ☑6523 2888; www.pingjianglodge.com; 33 Niujia Xiang; 钮家巷33号; r ¥988-2588; ❀@) This 17th-century, traditional courtyard building has well-kept gardens and 51 rooms bedecked in traditional furniture (we love the wooden bathtub!). Rooms at the pointy end are suites with split-level living spaces. Services are attentive. Discounts of up to 50% are available.

Sūzhōu Watertown Youth Hostel   HOSTEL $
(苏州浮生四季国际青年旅舍; Sūzhōu Sìjìfúshēng Qīngnián Lǚshè; ☑6521 8885; www.watertownhostel.com; 27 Dashitou Xiang, Renmin Lu; 人民路大石头巷27号; 6-/4-bed dm ¥50/60, r ¥130-220; ❀@) Tucked away in an alley off Renmin Lu, this 200-year-old courtyard complex now houses a lovely, serene hostel with 18 rooms, every one of which is different. Rooms on the 2nd floor are quieter while ground-floor rooms have better wi-fi reception. Most rooms have attached bathrooms but you may find more intimacy than privacy (no doors, shower curtain only). Dorms are compact but clean enough. The cosy Sūzhōu-styled patio invites you to chill. Another plus is that the airport bus station is just a stone's throw away.

PÍNGTÁN: TRADITIONAL STORYTELLING IN SŪZHŌU'S HEART

Savouring tea in a Sūzhōu teahouse while indulging in a *píngtán* performance is the local equivalent of whiling away an evening in a jazz bar in the West.

Unlike *kūnqǔ* opera, an extant Chinese opera that also originated in Jiāngsū and a dominant form of high culture in China, *píngtán* is more of a folk art. It combines exquisite storytelling and ballad singing in the local dialect, and is often accompanied by traditional instruments like *gǔzhēng* (zither) and *pípá* (lute). The stories tend to revolve around Chinese classics such as *The Three Kingdoms* (a warring period from AD 220 to 280) and *The Legend of the White Snake*. Instead of a chamber group playing music in a theatre, *píngtán* is often a one-man (or a maximum of two) show in a teahouse. Done well, it's an enchanting blend of singing and strings that emotes the themes behind most of these tunes. Done poorly? Think wailing cats.

Most teahouses have Sūzhōu's version of 'live music' on the weekend, and reservation is essential. A handful of them have a *píngtán* master take the stage every night, for example, the delightful **Pingtan Teahouse** (评弹茶馆; Píngtán Cháguǎn; 2nd fl, 626 Shiquan Jie), where *píngtán* enthusiasts get together to keep the traditions alive. The music usually starts between 8pm and 10pm. Order some tea (the speciality is Yunnan pu'erh, unlimited serves from ¥100), and pick songs (from ¥45, some lyrics have English translations) for the master to play. Enjoy!

Sūzhōu Mingtown Youth Hostel
HOSTEL $

(苏州明堂青年旅舍; Sūzhōu Míngtáng Qīngnián Lǚshè; ☑6581 6869; 28 Pingjiang Lu; 平江路28号; 6-bed dm ¥50, r ¥160-180; ❊@) Across the canal from Píngjiāng Lodge is this well-run youth hostel, whose rooms and dorms come with dark wooden 'antique' furniture, and the hot water is finally 24/7. The only downside is the rooms aren't soundproof in this compound. There's free internet, free laundry, and bike rental.

Pan Pacific Sūzhōu
HOTEL $$$

(苏州吴宫泛太平洋酒店; Sūzhōu Wúgōng Fàntàipíngyáng Dàjiǔdiàn; ☑6510 3388; www.pan pacific.com/Suzhou; 259 Xinshi Lu; 新市路259号; d ¥1268; ❊@) There's a kitschy feel to the exterior of this former Sheraton Hotel, which looks like a faux Forbidden City. But once you step into the lobby, you'll know this is truly a five-star luxury. The 500+ rooms are spacious and stylish, fitted with all the latest gadgets to make you happy. Services are simply impeccable. A bonus is guests get to enjoy free access to the adjacent Gán Gate Garden.

Hotel Soul
HOTEL $$$

(苏哥李酒店; Sūgēlǐ Jiǔdiàn; ☑6777 0777; www.hotelsoul.com.cn; 27-33 Qiaosikong Xiang; 乔司空巷27-33号; d & tw ¥1080-1680; ❊🛜) This Philippe Starck–wannabe has a lot of sharp angles and neon blue lights but not much soul. It is, however, very good value. Rooms are huge with textured wallpaper, plush beds and tones that make you want to order a martini. Staff are eager and attentive.

Marco Polo Suzhou
HOTEL $$

(苏州玄妙马可波罗大酒店; Sūzhōu Xuánmiào Mǎkěbōluó Dàjiǔdiàn; ☑6801 9888; www.marco polohotels.com; 818 Ganjiang Donglu; 干将东路818号; d ¥1250-2200; ❊@) Right in the heart of Sūzhōu, this former Sofitel has been re-branded and still makes the grade. Its 314 rooms are tailored to suit the needs of the business traveller. Leisure visitors also like the spacious rooms with modern furnishings. Discounts knocked rooms down to ¥500 during time of research.

✗ Eating

Plentiful restaurants can be found along Guanqian Jie, especially down the road from the Temple of Mystery.

Some local delicacies to try are *sōngshǔ guìyú* (松鼠桂鱼; sweet-and-sour mandarin fish), *xiāngyóu shànhú* (香油鳝糊; stewed shredded eel) and *xīguā jī* (西瓜鸡; chicken placed in watermelon rind and steamed).

Wúmén Rénjiā
CHINESE JIĀNGSŪ $$

(吴门人家; ☑6728 8041; 31 Panru Xiang; dishes from ¥40; 🍴) Hidden in a quiet alley north of Lion's Grove Garden, this courtyard restaurant attracts a mix of locals and well-informed visitors who enjoy the subtle flavours of traditional Sūzhōu cooking. It's said that only locally sourced natural ingredients are used. Service can sometimes be a bit slow. Reservation essential.

Pingvon
TEAHOUSE $

(品芳; Pǐnfāng; 94 Pingjiang Lu; dishes from ¥4; 🍴) A cute little teahouse perched beside one of Sūzhōu's most popular canal-side streets. Pingvon serves up excellent dumplings and delicate little morsels on small plates. The tea rooms upstairs are more atmospheric.

Xīshèngyuán
DUMPLINGS $

(熙盛源; 43 Fenghuang Jie; dumplings from ¥8) Crowds pay and gather near the entrance to wait for the steaming fresh *xiǎolóng bāo* (小龙包; soup dumplings) to come out of the kitchen. If you don't want to jostle, grab a seat and order several other great dishes including assorted *húntūn* (馄饨; dumplings; ¥6 to ¥10).

Yǎba Shēngjiān
DUMPLINGS $

(哑巴生煎; 12 Lindun Lu; dumplings ¥10; ☺5.30am-7.30pm) This 60-year-old institution also sells noodles but all hail its uber-fresh handmade *shēnjiān bāo* (生煎包; pan-fried dumplings) stuffed with juicy pork. During lunch hours expect to queue for 30 minutes just to order! Join the line, snag a table and enjoy your trophy. No English menu.

Zhūhóngxīng
NOODLES $

(朱鸿兴; Taijian Long; mains ¥20-47) Popular with locals, this eatery, with several branches across town, has a long history and wholesome, filling noodles – try the scrummy *xiàrén miàn* (虾仁面; noodles with baby shrimps) or the *bàoshànmiàn* (爆鳝面, eel noodles, ¥10). There's no English menu.

Déyuè Lóu
CHINESE JIĀNGSŪ $$$

(得月楼; ☑6523 8940; 43 Taijian Long; mains ¥30-120; ☺24hr; 🍴) It's hard to know what to start with in this institution, with a menu featuring over 300 items! The star is the freshwater fish. The restaurant is a popular stop for tour groups and for large wedding parties, and feels a little over the top at times.

Drinking

There are stacks of trendy cafe-bars scattered along Pingjiang Lu. The nightlife scene on Shiquan Jie is dying as most of the expats' watering holes have moved to the new Suzhou Industrial Park, 9km east of the centre of town.

Bookworm CAFE, BAR
(老书虫; Lǎo Shūchóng; 77 Gunxiu Fang; ⊙9am-1am) Běijīng's Bookworm has wormed its way down to Sūzhōu, although the selection isn't as good as Běijīng's. The food is crowd pleasers (lots of Western options) and the cold beers include Tsingtao and Erdinger. There are occasional events and books you can borrow or buy. Just off Shiquan Jie.

☆ **Entertainment**

Regular performances of *kūnqǔ* opera and *píngtán*, two of the exquisite performance arts sung in local dialects, are regularly scheduled at the following places.

Kūnqǔ Opera Museum CHINESE OPERA
(昆曲博物馆; Kūnqǔ Bówùguǎn; 14 Zhongzhangjia Xiang; tickets ¥30) This place puts on performances of *kūnqǔ* at 2pm on Sundays.

Garden of the Master of the Nets MUSIC
(网师园; Wǎngshī Yuán; tickets ¥100) From March to November, music performances are held nightly from 7.30pm to 9.30pm for tourist groups at this garden. Don't expect anything too authentic.

Píngtán Museum TRADITIONAL SINGING
(评弹博物馆; Píngtán Bówùguǎn; 3 Zhongzhangjia Xiang; tickets ¥4-5) This museum has traditional *shuōshū* (storytelling, in Chinese only) at 1.30pm daily. Tickets on sale at noon.

 Shopping

Sūzhōu-style embroidery, calligraphy, paintings, sandalwood fans, writing brushes and silk underclothes are for sale nearly everywhere. For good-quality items at competitive rates, shop along Shiquan Jie, east off Renmin Lu, which is lined with shops and markets selling souvenirs. The northern part of Renmin Lu has a number of silk stores (丝绸商店; Sīchóu Shāngdiàn).

Xīnhuá Bookshop BOOKS
(新华书店; Xīnhuá Shūdiàn; 166 Guanqian Jie; ⊙9am-9pm) This bookshop sells a variety of English- and Chinese-language maps. Stodgy English novels on the 4th floor.

ⓘ **Information**

Major tourist hotels have foreign-exchange counters.

Bank of China (中国银行; Zhōngguó Yínháng; 1450 Renmin Lu) Changes travellers cheques and foreign cash. There are ATMs that take international cards at most larger branches of the Bank of China.

China Post (中国邮政; Zhōngguó Yóuzhèng; cnr Renmin Lu & Jingde Lu)

Hóng Qīngtíng Internet Cafe (红蜻蜓网吧; Hóng Qīngtíng Wǎngbā; 916 Shiquan Jie; per hr ¥2.50; ⊙24hr)

Industrial & Commercial Bank of China (工商银行; Gōngshāng Yínháng; 222 Guanqian Jie) It has 24-hour ATM facilities.

No 1 Hospital (苏大附一院; Sūdà Fùyīyuàn; 96 Shizi Jie) There are other hospitals in Sūzhōu.

Public Security Bureau (PSB; 公安局; Gōng'ānjú; ✆6522 5661, ext 20593; 1109 Renmin Lu) Can help with emergencies and visa problems. The visa office is about 200m down a lane called Dashitou Xiang.

Sūzhōu Tourism Information Center (苏州旅游咨询中心; Sūzhōu Lǚyóu Zīxún Zhōngxīn; ✆6530 5887; www.classicsuzhou.com; 345 Shiquan Jie) Several branches in town including at bus stations. Can help with booking accommodation and tours. Festival listings and general information on website.

ⓘ **Getting There & Away**

Air

Sūzhōu does not have an airport, but **China Eastern Airlines** (东方航空公司; Dōngfāng Hángkōng Gōngsī; ✆6522 2788; 115 Ganjiang Lu) can help with booking flights out of Shànghǎi. Buses leave here frequently for Hóngqiáo Airport in Shànghǎi. Tickets are ¥53.

Bus

Sūzhōu has three long-distance bus stations and the two listed are the most useful. Tickets for all buses can also be bought at the **Liánhé ticket centre** (Liánhé shòupiàochù; 1606 Renmin Lu; ⊙bus tickets 8.30-11.30am & 1-5pm).

The principal station is the **north long-distance bus station** (汽车北站; qìchē běizhàn; ✆6577 6577) at the northern end of Renmin Lu, next to the train station:

Hángzhōu ¥71, two hours, regular services

Nánjīng ¥75, 2½ hours, regular services

Níngbō ¥130, four hours, seven daily

Yángzhōu ¥75, three hours, regular services

The **south long-distance bus station** (汽车南站; qìchē nánzhàn; cnr Yingchun Lu & Nanhuan Donglu) has buses to the following:

Hángzhōu ¥71, two hours, every 20 minutes

Nánjīng ¥75, two hours, every 20 minutes

Shànghǎi ¥35, 1½ hours, every 30 minutes

Yángzhōu ¥75, two hours, hourly

Train

Sūzhōu is on the Nánjīng–Shànghǎi express G line. Trains stop at either the more centrally located **Sūzhōu Train Station** (苏州站; Sūzhōu Zhàn) or the new **Sūzhōu North Train Station** (苏州北站; Sūzhōu Běizhàn), 12km north of the city centre. Book train tickets on the 2nd floor of the **Liánhé ticket centre** (Liánhé shòupiàochù; 1606 Renmin Lu; train tickets 7.30-11am & noon-5pm). There's also a ticket office along Guanqian Jie across from the Temple of Mystery. Another ticket office can be found on the other side of the road from the south bus station.

Běijīng ¥525, five hours, 15 daily

Nánjīng ¥100, 50 minutes, frequent services

Shànghǎi ¥40, 25 minutes, frequent services

Wúxī ¥20, 15 minutes, frequent services

ⓘ Getting Around

Bicycle

Riding a bike is the best way to see Sūzhōu, though nutty drivers and traffic in the city centre can be nerve jangling. Search out the quieter streets and travel along the canals to get the most of what this city has to offer.

You can rent a bike from most hostels in Sūzhōu. The **Yángyáng Bike Rental Shop** (洋洋车行; Yángyáng Chēháng; 2061 Renmin Lu; 7am-6pm), a short walk north of the Silk Museum, offers bike rentals (¥25 per day plus ¥200 deposit). Check out the seat and brakes carefully before you pedal off.

Public Transport

Sūzhōu has some convenient tourist buses that visit all sights and cost ¥2. They all pass by the train station.

Bus Y5 Goes around the western and eastern sides of the city and has a stop at Sūzhō Museum.

Bus Y2 Travels from Tiger Hill, Pán Gate and along Shiquan Jie.

Buses Y1 & **Y4** Run the length of Renmin Lu.

Bus 80 Runs between two train stations.

The new Sūzhōu metro line runs along Ganjiang Lu. The second line will link Sūzhōu north station with downtown when it enters service (hopefully) in 2014.

Taxi

Fares start at ¥10 and drivers generally use their meters. A trip from Guanqian Jie to the train station should cost around ¥15. From Sūzhōu north station to downtown, the fare is around ¥50 to ¥60. Pedicabs hover around the tourist areas and can be persistent (¥5 for short rides is standard).

Around Sūzhōu

Sūzhōu's tourist brochures offer a mind-boggling array of sights around the town. Sadly, not all are great, and noteworthy ones are often overrun by tourists. Go early to avoid the crowds.

TÓNGLǏ 同里
☑ 0512

This lovely **Old Town** (老城区; Lǎochéngqū; ☑ 6333 1140; admission ¥100, free after 5.30pm), only 18km southeast of Sūzhōu, boasts rich, historical canal-side atmosphere and weather-beaten charm. Many of the buildings have kept their traditional facades, with stark whitewashed walls, black-tiled roofs, cobblestone pathways and willow-shaded canal views adding to a picturesque allure. The town is best explored the traditional way: aimlessly meandering along the canals and alleys until you get lost. It doesn't really matter where you go, as long as you can elude the crowds.

You can reach Tónglǐ from either Sūzhōu or Shànghǎi, but aim for a weekday visit.

The admission fee to the town includes access to the following sights, except the Chinese Sex Culture Museum.

⊙ Sights & Activities

Gēnglè Táng HISTORIC BUILDING
(耕乐堂; 9am-5.30pm) There are three old residences that you'll pass at some point, the best of which is this sprawling Ming-dynasty estate with 52 halls spread out over five courtyards in the west of town. The buildings have been elaborately restored and redecorated with paintings, calligraphy and antique furniture to bring back the atmosphere of the original buildings.

Pearl Pagoda PAGODA
(珍珠塔; Zhēnzhū Tǎ; 9am-5.30pm) In the north of town is this pagoda, which dates from the Qing dynasty but has recently been restored. Inside, you'll find a large residential compound decorated with Qing-era antiques, an ancestral hall, a garden and an opera stage. The place gets its name from a tiny pagoda draped in pearls.

Tuìsī Garden GARDENS
(退思园; Tuìsī Yuán; 9am-5.30pm) This beautiful 19th-century garden in the east of the old town delightfully translates as the 'Withdraw and Reflect Garden', so named because it was a Qing government official's retirement home. The Tower of Fanning

Delight served as the living quarters, while the garden itself is a lovely portrait of pond water churning with outsized goldfish, rockeries and pavilions, caressed by traditional Chinese music.

Chinese Sex Culture Museum MUSEUM

(中华性文化博物馆; Zhōnghuá Xìngwénhuà Bówùguǎn; admission ¥20; ⊙9am-5.30pm) This private museum, located east of Tuìsī Garden, is quietly housed in a historic but disused girls' school campus and you won't miss it. If you thought Confucius was a prude, think again.

☞ Tours

Slow-moving **six-person boats** (¥90 for 25 minutes) ply the waters of Tónglǐ's canal system. The boat trip on Tónglǐ Lake is free, though of no particular interest.

🛏 Sleeping & Eating

Guesthouses are plentiful, with basic rooms starting at about ¥100. Restaurants are everywhere, and food prices here are much higher than Sūzhōu. Some local dishes to try include *méigāncàishāoròu* (梅干菜烧肉; stewed meat with dried vegetables), *yínyúchǎodàn* (银鱼炒蛋; silver fish omelette) and *zhuàngyuángtí* (状元蹄; stewed pig's leg).

Zhèngfú Cǎotáng BOUTIQUE HOTEL $$$

(正福草堂; ☏6333 6358; www.zfct.net; 138 Mingqing Jie; 明清街138号; d ¥380-1380; ※@) *The* place to stay in town. The 14 deluxe rooms and suites are all aesthetically set with Qing-style furniture and antiques. The rooms wouldn't be out of place in a *Wallpaper* spread, and each one is unique. Facilities like bathrooms and floor heating are ultramodern.

Tongli International Youth Hostel HOSTEL $

(同里国际青年旅舍; Tónglǐ Guójì Qīngnián Lǔshè; ☏6333 9311; 210 Zhuhang Jie; 竹行街210号; dm ¥45, r ¥120-150; ※@⊚) This youth hostel has two locations. The main one, slightly off Zhongchuan Beilu, is 300m west of Zhèngfú Cǎotáng. Rooms are decked out in traditional furniture, and the wooden pillars and stone courtyard ooze an old-China charm. The alternative location beside Taiping bridge has compact dorms, and all doubles have shared bathroom only.

ⓘ Getting There & Away

From Sūzhōu, take a bus (¥8, 50 minutes, every 30 minutes) at the south long-distance bus station for Tónglǐ. Grab an electric cart (¥2) from

beside the Tónglǐ bus station to the Old Town, or you can walk it in about 15 minutes.

Twelve daily buses (¥36) leave Tónglǐ bus station for Shànghǎi and there are frequent buses to Zhōuzhuāng (¥6, 30 minutes).

LÙZHÍ 角直

This minute, relatively less commercialised canal town, only a 25km public bus trip east of Sūzhōu, has bundles of charm. The entrance ticket of ¥78 can be skipped if you just want to wander the streets, alleys and bridges – you only have to pay if you enter the **tourist sights** (⊙8am-5pm), such as the **Wànshèng Rice Warehouse** (万盛米行; Wànshèng Mǐháng), the **Bǎoshèng Temple** (保圣寺; Bǎoshèng Sì) and a handful of museums, but these can be missed without detracting from the overall experience.

The humpbacked bridges here are delightful. Check out the centuries-old **Jìnlì Bridge** (进利桥; Jìnlì Qiáo) and **Xīnglóng Bridge** (兴隆桥; Xīnglóng Qiáo). Taking a half-hour **boat ride** (¥40) is an excellent way to sample the canal views. Boats depart from several points, including the **Yǒng'ān Bridge** (永安桥; Yǒng'ān Qiáo).

The newest attraction here is the **Lùzhí Cultural Park** (角直文化园), a huge, faux Ming-dynasty complex filled with tourist shops and a couple of exhibition halls.

FIVE THOUSAND YEARS OF EROTICA

Overall, there's not a whole lot distinguishing one canal town from another, and which ever one you choose to visit is ultimately a matter of either convenience or fate (or both). Tónglǐ, however, does have an X-rated trump card up its sleeve, it's the **Chinese Sex Culture Museum**. Unfortunately, the name deters most people from even considering a visit (visitors tentatively approach, see the sign, giggle, blush and turn around), though in reality it is not that racy.

Founded by sociology professors Liu Dalin and Hu Hongxia against all odds, the museum's aim is not so much to arouse, but rather to reintroduce an aspect of the country's culture that, ironically, has been forcefully repressed since China was 'liberated' in 1949. The pair have collected several thousand artefacts relating to sex, from the good (erotic landscape paintings, fans and teacups) to the bad (chastity belts and saddles with wooden dildos used to punish 'licentious' women and 'zoophilia' statues), and the humorous (satirical Buddhist statues) to the unusual (a pot-bellied immortal with a penis growing out of his head topped by a turtle). This is also one of the only places in the country where homosexuality is openly recognised as part of Chinese culture.

Though some of the exhibits seem a little forced (a stone pillar displayed represents a 'penis'? That's stretching it), and the one-too-many pictures of penis- and vagina-shaped rocks will elicit schoolboy giggles, it's worth a visit simply to support this endeavour; and there isn't anything like this anywhere else in China.

Admission is free and the landscaped gardens, ponds, pavilions and an opera stage make it a nice area to amble.

To get to Lùzhí, take bus 518 from Sūzhōu's train station (¥4, one hour, first/last bus 6am/8pm) or from the bus stop on Pingqi Lu (平齐路) to the last stop. When you get off, take the first right along Dasheng Lu (达圣路) to the decorative arch; crossing the bridge takes you into the back of the old town in five minutes. Hordes of pedicabs will descend upon you offering to take you to the main entrance. Pay no more than ¥5.

The last bus back from Lùzhí is at 7.30pm. If you want to continue to Shànghǎi from Lùzhí, buses (¥18, two hours) from the Lùzhí bus station run between 6.20am and 5pm.

MÙDÚ 木渎

Dating back to the Ming dynasty, Mùdú was once the haunt of wealthy officials, intellectuals and artists, and later even attracted the Qing Emperor Qianlong to come and visit six times. Today, the village of Mùdú has been swallowed up by Sūzhōu's growing urban sprawl. While it is neither the largest nor the most appealing of Jiāngsū's canal towns, it makes for a convenient half-day tour.

Mùdú is free if you merely want to soak up the atmosphere – the entrance fees are for the top sights. Sadly, as most of the buildings along the canal are now modern structures, it's actually worth shelling out the admission fees.

⊙ Sights

Bǎngyǎn Mansion   HISTORIC BUILDING
(榜眼府第; Bǎngyǎn Fǔdi; Xiatang Jie; admission ¥10; ⊙8am-4.30pm) This dignified complex was the home of the 19th-century writer and politician Feng Guifen. It has a rich collection of antique furniture and intricate carvings of stone, wood and brick – it often does part-time duty as a movie set. The surrounding garden is pretty but fairly typical – lotus ponds, arched bridges, bamboo – and can't compare to the more ornate gardens of Sūzhōu.

Hóngyǐn Mountain Villa   HISTORIC BUILDING
(虹饮山房; Hóngyǐn Shānfáng; Shantang Jie; admission ¥30; ⊙8am-4.30pm) By far the most interesting place in Mùdú is this villa, with its elaborate opera stage, exhibits and even an imperial pier where Emperor Qianlong docked his boat. The stage in the centre hall is impressive; honoured guests were seated in front and the galleries along the sides of the hall were for women. The emperor was a frequent visitor and you can see his uncomfortable-looking imperial chair, which faces the stage. Said chair is more than 1000 years old, worn smooth in spots where hands have touched it. Operas are still performed here during the day. Surrounding the stage are some carefully arranged gardens, criss-crossed with dainty arched bridges and walkways. The old residence halls have been wonderfully pre-

served and have some interesting exhibits, including displays of dusty hats and gowns worn by imperial officers. Look out for the display on the Manchu-Han imperial feast: 111 faux, plastic dishes are on display.

Ancient Pine Garden   HISTORIC BUILDING
(古松园; Gǔsōngyuán; Shantang Jie; admission ¥20; ⊙8am-4.30pm) In the middle of Shantang Jie is this courtyard complex known for its intricately carved beams. Look out for wooden impressions of officials, hats, phoenixes, flowers and stuff most people can't identify.

Yan Family Garden   HISTORIC BUILDING
(严家花园; Yánjiā Huāyuán; cnr Shantang Jie & Mingqing Jie; admission ¥30; ⊙8am-4.30pm) In the northwest corner of the Old Town is this beautiful complex, which dates back to the Ming dynasty and was once the home of a former magistrate. The garden, with its rockeries and a meandering lake, is separated into five sections and divided by walls, with each section meant to invoke a season. Flowers, plants and rocks are arranged to create a 'mood'. If you come during the weekend, the only mood the crowds might invoke is exasperation.

👉 Tours
The most pleasurable way to experience Mùdú is by **boat**. You'll find a collection of traditional skiffs docked outside the Băngyăn Mansion. A ride in one of these will take you along the narrow canals, shaded by ancient bridges and battered stone walls. A 10-minute boat ride is ¥10 per person (¥30 per boat minimum charge).

ℹ Getting There & Away
From Sūzhōu, tourist bus Y4 runs from the train station to Mùdú (¥3). Get off at Mùdú Yánjiā Huāyuán Zhàn (木渎严家园站), across from a small road (明清街; Míngqīng Jiē) leading to the main entrance. You'll see a big sign and a car park full of tour buses. The ride takes about 45 minutes.

Or you can take the metro and get off at the eponymous last stop. Take exit 1 and then board bus 38. Get off at Mùdú Gŭzhèn zhàn (木渎古镇站, four stops).

TĪANPÍNG SHĀN & LÍNGYÁN SHĀN   天平山、灵岩山
These two hill areas are along the bus route to Mùdú and can be combined in one long day trip. Scenic **Tiānpíng Shān** (Lingtian Lu; admission ¥20; ⊙7.30am-5pm) is a low, forested hill about 13km west of Sūzhōu. It's a wonderful place for hiking or just meandering

along one of its many wooded trails. It's also famous for its medicinal spring waters.

Eleven kilometres southwest of Sūzhōu is **Língyán Shān** (Lingtian Lu; admission ¥20; ⊙8am-4.30pm winter, to 5pm summer), or 'Cliff of the Spirits', once the site of a palace where Emperor Qianlong stayed during his inspection tours of the Yangzi River valley. Now the mountain is home to an active Buddhist monastery. The climb to the peak is exhausting but it offers panoramic views of the city of Sūzhōu. On the way up, take the path on the left for an exciting clamber over rough-hewn stone and paths.

Tourist bus 4 goes to Língyán Shān and Tiānpíng Shān from Sūzhōu's train station.

ZHŌUZHUĀNG   周庄
Some 30km southeast of Sūzhōu, the 900-year-old water village of **Zhōuzhuāng** (admission ¥100, free access after 8pm) is probably the most commercialised canal town and often invaded by tour groups, thanks to Chen Yifei, the late renowned Chinese painter whose works of the once idyllic village are its claim to fame.

It is not impossible, though, to catch a glimpse of the old-world charm that still exists in Zhōuzhuāng. Get up early or take an evening stroll, before the crowds arrive or when they begin to thin out. Zhōuzhuāng boasts some appealing architectural delights, which makes a trip to this 'Venice of the East' worthwhile.

◉ Sights
Twin Bridges   BRIDGE
There're a total of 14 bridges in Zhōuzhuāng, but the most attractive is this pair of Ming-dynasty bridges (双桥; Shuāngqiáo) gorgeously standing at the intersection of two waterways in the heart of this canal town. **Shìdé Bridge** (世德桥; Shìdé Qiáo) is a humpbacked bridge while the connecting **Yŏngān Bridge** (永安桥; Yŏngān Qiáo) is the one with a square arch. The bridges were depicted in Chen Yifei's *Memory of Hometown*, which shot the whole town to fame from the 1980s onwards.

It's fun to go under bridge after bridge by **boat**. A one-hour boat ride is ¥100 per boat (six people).

Zhang's House   HISTORICAL BUILDING
(张厅; Zhāngtīng; ⊙8.30am-5.30pm) To the south of the Twin Bridges, this magnificent 70-room, three-hall structure was built in the Ming-era and bought by the Zhang clan

in the early Qing dynasty as their residence. There's an opera stage in the house to keep the ladies entertained as they were not supposed to leave home or seek entertainment outside. Note the chairs in the main hall. The unmarried women could only sit on those with a hollow seatback, symbolising that they had nobody to rely on! The servants' walkways, a long narrow lane with sharp zigzagging turns, are for the kid in you.

Shen's House
HISTORIC BUILDING

(沈厅; Shěntīng; Nanshi Jie; ⊙8.30am-5.30pm) Near another famous bridge of Fú'ān Qiáo, this property of the Shen clan is a piece of lavish Qing-style architecture that boasts three halls and more than 100 rooms. The first hall is particularly interesting, as it has a water gate and a wharf where the family moors their private boats.

Quánfú Temple
TEMPLE

(全福寺; Quánfú Sì; ⊙8.30am-5.30pm) It's hard to miss this eye-catching amber-hued temple complex. The 'full fortune' temple was founded during the Song dynasty and has been rebuilt numerous times since then. The structure you see today is an incarnation from 1995, when a handful of halls and gardens were added to the mix. The setting is simply stunning. Surrounded by crisscrossing waterways, the whole complex appears to float on water, while there are ponds and lakes between each building, with bridges linking all of them. The gardens provide a nice retreat from the bustling streets throughout the village.

🛏 Sleeping & Eating

There're a handful of guesthouses in town. Expect to pay ¥80 for a basic room. With eateries at almost every corner, you won't starve.

Zhèngfú Cǎotáng
BOUTIQUE HOTEL $$$

(正福草堂; ☑5721 9333; www.zfct.net; 90 Zhongshi Jie; 中市街90号; d ¥480-1080; ❀@) Again, kudos goes to this five-room boutique accommodation for beautifully combining antique furniture with top-notch facilities to create the best hotel in this water town. The courtyard gives a cosy feel where you can chill and sip tea.

Zhōuzhuāng
International Youth Hostel
HOSTEL $

(周庄国际青年旅舍; ☑5720 4566; 86 Beishi Jie; 北市街86号; dm ¥45, r ¥100-140; ❀@🛜) Near the old opera stage is this new youth hostel in a converted courtyard. It has a selection of tidy rooms and a clean (but dim) dorm, and offers free laundry. The hostel owner is a barista, so enjoy a perfect brew in the trendy cafe on the ground floor.

❶ Getting There & Away

From the north long-distance bus station in Sūzhōu, half-hourly buses (¥20, 1½ hours) leave for Zhōuzhuāng between 6.55am and 5.20pm. From the bus station in Zhōuzhuāng, turn left and walk till you see the bridge. Cross the bridge and you'll see the gated entrance to the village of Zhōuzhuāng. The walk is about 20 minutes. A taxi ride from the bus station is no more than ¥10.

Zhèjiāng

POP 47 MILLION

Includes »

Hángzhōu 249
Around Hángzhōu 260
Wūzhèn 261
Nánxún 262
Wǔyì 264
Around Wǔyì 264
Pǔtuóshān 265

Best Hikes

» Mògānshān (p260)

» Guódòng (p264)

» Pǔtuóshān (p265)

Best Places to Stay

» Mògānshān House 23 (p260)

» Le Passage Mohkan Shan (p261)

» Four Seasons Hotel Hángzhōu (p255)

Why Go?

Zhèjiāng's trump card is its handsome and much-visited capital, Hángzhōu. But while Hángzhōu – a quick zip away on the train from Shànghǎi – is the front-running highlight, Zhèjiāng is no one-trick pony. There are the arched bridges and charming canal scenes of Wūzhèn and Nánxún, water towns that typify the lushly irrigated north of Zhèjiāng (浙江) with its sparkling web of rivers and canals. The Buddhist island of Pǔtuóshān is the best known of the thousands of islands dotting a ragged and fragmented shoreline. The mist- and tree-cloaked slopes of Mògānshān provide refreshing natural air-conditioning when the thermostat in Shànghǎi is set to blow in the steamy summer months. Zhèjiāng's rural aspect comes even more to the fore in the less-visited ancient villages of Guódòng and Yúyuán outside the town of Wǔyì.

When to Go
Hángzhōu

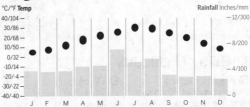

Late Mar–early May Spring sees low humidity and vegetation turning a brilliant green.

Aug & Sep Flee the simmering lowland heat to the cooler heights of Mògānshān.

Late Sep–mid-Nov Steal a march on winter and evade the sapping summer in Hángzhōu.

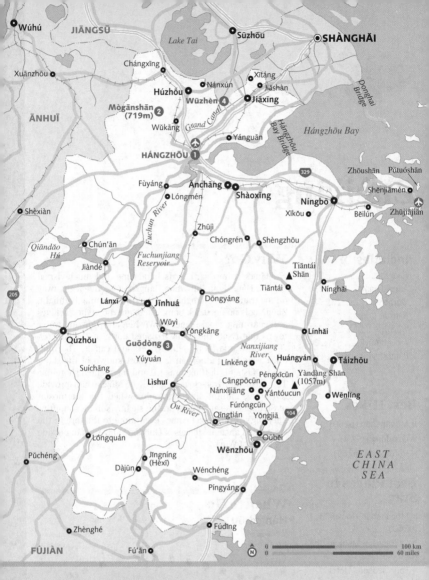

Zhèjiāng Highlights

1 Hop on a bike for a leisurely circuit of Hángzhōu's inimitable **West Lake** (p251)

2 Turn your back on urban China and explore the forested inclines of lush **Mògānshān** (p260)

3 Escape to the small village charms and pastoral shades of **Guōdòng** (p264)

4 Discover Zhèjiāng's picturesque canal-town culture at **Wūzhèn** (p261)

History

By the 7th and 8th centuries Hángzhōu, Níngbō and Shàoxīng had emerged as three of China's most important trading centres and ports. Fertile Zhèjiāng was part of the great southern granary from which food was shipped to the depleted areas of the north via the Grand Canal (Dà Yùnhé), which commences here. Growth accelerated when the Song dynasty moved court to Hángzhōu in the 12th century after invasion from the north. Due to intense cultivation, northern Zhèjiāng has lost a lot of natural vegetation and much of it is now flat, featureless plain.

Climate

Zhèjiāng has a humid, subtropical climate, with hot, sticky summers and chilly, clammy winters. Rain lashes the province in May and June (and typhoons can make landfall in summer) but slows to a drizzle for the rest of the year.

Language

Zhèjiāng residents speak a variation of the Wu dialect, also spoken in Shànghǎi and Jiāngsū. As the dialect changes from city to city, Mandarin is also widely used.

❶ Getting There & Away

Zhèjiāng is well connected to the rest of the country by plane, high-speed train and bus. The provincial capital Hángzhōu is effortlessly reached by train from Shànghǎi and Sūzhōu, and serves as a useful first stop in Zhèjiāng. Hángzhōu and Pǔtuóshān are both served by nearby airports.

❶ Getting Around

The province is quite small and getting around is straightforward. Travelling by high-speed train is fast and efficient but buses (and boats) are needed for some destinations; flying to the larger cities is also possible.

Hángzhōu　杭州

📞 0571 / POP 6.16 MILLION

One of China's most illustrious tourist drawcards, Hángzhōu's dreamy West Lake panoramas and fabulously green and hilly environs can easily lull you into long sojourns. Eulogised by poets and applauded by emperors, the lake has intoxicated the Chinese imagination for aeons. Religiously cleaned by armies of street sweepers and litter collectors, its scenic vistas draw you into a classical Chinese watercolour of willow-lined banks, ancient pagodas, mist-covered

---

PRICE INDICATORS

The following price indicators are used in this chapter:

Sleeping

$	less than ¥200
$$	¥200 to ¥500
$$$	more than ¥500

Eating

$	less than ¥40
$$	¥40 to ¥100
$$$	more than ¥100

---

hills and the occasional *shíkùmén* building and old *lìlòng* alleyway. Despite vast tourist cohorts, West Lake is a delight to explore, either on foot or by bike. You'll need about three days to fully savour the picturesque Jiāngnán ('south of the Yangzi River') ambience, but the inclination is to take root – like one of the lakeside's lilting willows – and stay put.

History

Hángzhōu's history dates to the start of the Qin dynasty (221 BC). Marco Polo passed through in the 13th century, calling Hángzhōu Kinsai and noting in astonishment that Hángzhōu had a circumference of 100 miles (161km), its waters vaulted by 12,000 bridges.

Hángzhōu flourished after being linked with the Grand Canal in AD 610 but fully prospered after the Song dynasty was overthrown by the invading Jurchen, who captured the Song capital Kāifēng, along with the emperor and the leaders of the imperial court, in 1126. The remnants of the Song court fled south, finally settling in Hángzhōu and establishing it as the capital of the Southern Song dynasty. Hángzhōu's wooden buildings made fire a perennial hazard; among major conflagrations, the great fire of 1237 reduced some 30,000 residences to piles of smoking carbon.

When the Mongols swept into China they established their court in Běijīng, but Hángzhōu retained its status as a prosperous commercial city. With 10 city gates by Ming times, Hángzhōu took a hammering from Taiping rebels, who besieged the city in 1861 and captured it; two years later the imperial armies reclaimed it. These

ZHĚJIĀNG HÁNGZHŌU

Hángzhōu

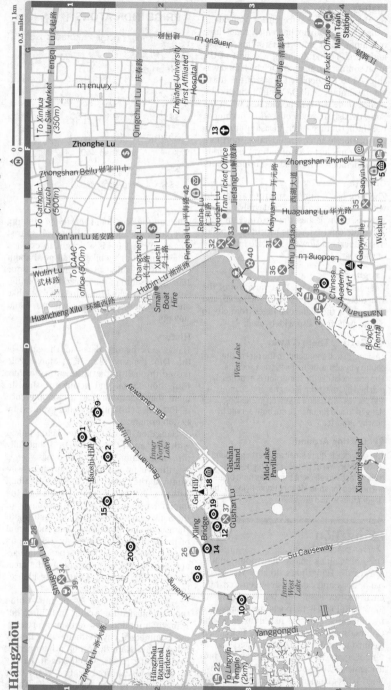

1 km
0.5 miles

G — **F** — **E** — **D** — **C** — **B** — **A**

To Xinhua Lu Silk Market (350m)

Fengqi Lu 凤起路

Xinhua Lu 新华路

Qingchun Lu 庆春路

Zhejiang University First Affiliated Hospital

Jiangon Lu

Zhongshan Beilu 解放北路中

Zhonghe Lu

To Catholic Church (500m)

Zhongshan Zhonglu

Zhongshan Zhonglu

13

Gaoyin Lu

30

5

Zhongshan Beilu 解放北路中

Yan'an Lu 延安路

Changsheng Lu 长生路

Xueshi Lu 学士路

Renhe Lu 仁和路

Pinghai Lu 平海路

Youdian Lu 邮电路

Train Ticket Office 解放路

Kaiyuan Lu 开元路

西湖大道 Xihu Dadao

Huaguang Lu 华光路

35

42

32

33

31

Gaoyin Jie

To CAAC office (500m)

Wulin Lu 武林路

Hubin Lu 湖滨路

40

36

Xihu Lu

Laodong Lu

4

Chinese Academy of Art

Huancheng Xilu 环城西路

Small Boat Hire

Wushan

Nanshan Lu

24

25

38

Bicycle Rental

West Lake

Bai Causeway

Inner North Lake

Beishan Lu 北山路

9

1

2

Baoshi Hill

15

Gushan Island

Gushan Lu

Mid-Lake Pavilion

Xiaoying Island

18

19

37

Gu Hill

Xiling Bridge

12

14

Xixiaing

26

8

200

Su Causeway

Inner West Lake

28

34

39

Shuguang Lu 曙光路

Zheda Lu 浙大路

10

Yanggongdi

Hángzhōu Botanical Gardens

22

To Lingyin Temple (2km)

Main Train Station

Bus Ticket Office

Qingtai Jie

Jiefanglu

41

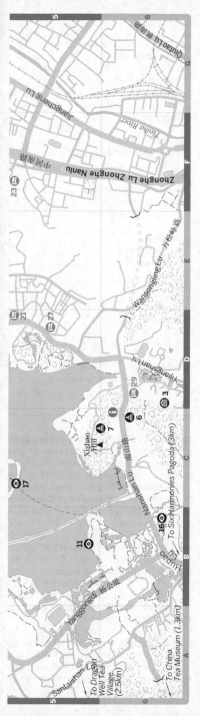

campaigns reduced almost the entire city to ashes, led to the deaths of over half a million of its residents through disease, starvation and warfare, and finally ended Hángzhōu's significance as a commercial and trading centre.

Few monuments survived the devastation; much of what can be seen in Hángzhōu today is of fairly recent construction.

◉ Sights & Activities

Hángzhōu grants free admission to all museums and gardens. Other sights offer half-price tickets for children between 1m to 1.3m, free for those under 1m.

West Lake   LAKE
(西湖; Xīhú) The saccharine tourist brochure hyperbole extolling West Lake is almost justified in its cloying accolades. The very definition of classical beauty in China, West Lake continues to mesmerise and methodical prettification has worked a cunning magic. Pagoda-topped hills rise over willow-lined waters as boats drift slowly through a vignette of leisurely charm. With history heavily repackaged, it's not that authentic – not by a long shot – but it's still a grade-A cover version of classical China.

Originally a lagoon adjoining the Qiántáng River, the lake didn't come into existence until the 8th century, when the governor of Hángzhōu had the marshy expanse dredged. As time passed, the lake's splendour was gradually cultivated: gardens were planted, pagodas built, and causeways and islands were constructed from dredged silt.

Celebrated poet Su Dongpo himself had a hand in the lake's development, constructing the **Sū Causeway** (苏堤; Sūdī) during his tenure as local governor in the 11th century. It wasn't an original idea – the poet-governor Bai Juyi had already constructed the **Bái Causeway** (白堤; Báidī) some 200 years earlier. Lined by willow, plum and peach trees, today the traffic-free causeways with their half-moon bridges make for restful outings, particularly on a bike.

Connected to the northern shores by the Bái Causeway is **Gūshān Island** (孤山岛; Gūshān Dǎo), the largest island in the lake and the location of the **Zhèjiāng Provincial Museum** (浙江省博物馆; Zhèjiāng Shěng Bówùguǎn; 25 Gushan Lu; admission free, audioguide ¥10; ◷8.30am-4.30pm Tue-Sun) and **Zhōngshān Park** (中山公园; Zhōngshān Gōngyuán). The island's buildings and

Hángzhōu

◎ Sights
1	Bǎochù Pagoda	C1
2	Bàopǔ Taoist Temple	C1
3	China Silk Museum	D6
4	Confucius Temple	E4
5	Húqìngyú Táng Chinese Medicine Museum	F4
6	Jìngcí Temple	C6
7	Léifēng Pagoda	C6
8	Mausoleum of General Yue Fei	B2
9	Ming Dynasty Effigies	C1
10	Qūyuàn Garden	A3
11	Red Carp Pond	B5
12	Seal Engravers' Society	B3
13	Sìchéng Church	F3
14	Su Xiaoxiao's Tomb	B3
15	Sunrise Terrace	B1
16	Tàizǐwān Park	B6
17	Three Pools Mirroring the Moon	C5
18	Zhèjiāng Provincial Museum	C3
19	Zhōngshān Park	B3
20	Zǐyún Cave	B2

◎ Sleeping
21	Crystal Orange Hotel	D5
22	Four Seasons Hotel Hángzhōu	A3
23	Hofang International Youth Hostel	F5
24	In Lake Youth Hostel	E4
25	Mingtown Youth Hostel	D4
26	Shangri-La Hotel	B2
27	Starway Jǐngshàng Youth Hostel	D5
28	Tea Boutique Hotel	B1
29	West Lake Youth Hostel	D6
30	Wúshānyì International Youth Hostel	F4

◎ Eating
31	Carrefour	E3
32	Grandma's Kitchen	E3
33	Green Tea Restaurant	E3
	Jīn Shā	(see 22)
34	La Pedrera	B1
35	Lǎo Hángzhōu Fēngwèi	E4
36	Lǎomǎjiā Miànguǎn	E3
37	Lóuwàilóu Restaurant	B3

◎ Drinking
38	Eudora Station	E4
39	Maya Bar	B1

◎ Entertainment
40	JZ Club	E3

◎ Shopping
41	Huíchūn Táng	F4
42	Wúshān Lù Night Market	F2

◎ Information
	Hángzhōu Tourist Information Centre	(see 35)

gardens were once the site of Emperor Qianlong's 18th-century holiday palace and gardens. Also on the island is the intriguing **Seal Engravers' Society** (西泠印社; Xīlíng Yìnshè), dedicated to the ancient art of carving the name seals (chops) that serve as personal signatures.

On the northwest of the lake is the lovely **Qūyuàn Garden** (曲院风荷; Qūyuàn Fēnghé), a collection of gardens spread out over numerous islets and renowned for their fragrant spring lotus blossoms. Near Xīlíng Bridge (Xīlíng Qiáo) is the tomb of **Su Xiaoxiao** (苏小小墓; Sū Xiǎoxiǎo Mù), a 5th-century courtesan who died of grief while waiting for her lover to return. It's been said that her ghost haunts the area and the tinkle of the bells on her gown can be heard at night.

The smaller island in the lake is **Xiǎoyíng Island** (小瀛洲; Xiǎoyíng Zhōu), where you can look over at **Three Pools Mirroring the Moon** (三潭印月; Sāntán Yìnyuè), three small towers in the water on the south side of the island; each has five holes that release shafts of candlelight on the night of the mid-autumn festival. From Lesser Yíngzhōu Island, you can gaze over to **Red Carp Pond** (花港观鱼; Huāgǎng Guānyú), home to a few thousand red carp.

Impromptu opera singing and other cultural activities may suddenly kick off around the lake, and if the weather's fine don't forget to earmark the east shore for sunset over West Lake photos. Walking around West Lake at night is also gorgeous and very romantic, with loads of benches and seats facing the still waters.

The best way to get around the lake is by bike. **Buggies** (⊙8am-6.30pm) speed around West Lake (just raise your hand to flag one down). A complete circuit is ¥40, otherwise ¥10 takes you to the next stop. Tourist buses Y1 and Y2 also run around West Lake.

Mausoleum of General Yue Fei TEMPLE

(岳庙; Yuè Fēi Mù; Beishan Lu; admission ¥25; ⏰7am-6pm) Commander of the southern Song armies, General Yue Fei (1103–42) led a series of successful battles against Jurchen invaders from the north in the 12th century. Despite his initial successes, he was recalled to the Song court, where he was executed, along with his son, after being deceived by the treacherous prime minister Qin Hui. In 1163 Song emperor Gao Zong exonerated Yue Fei and had his corpse reburied at the present site.

Léifēng Pagoda PAGODA

(雷峰塔; Léifēng Tǎ; adult/child ¥40/20; ⏰8am-8.30pm Mar-Nov, 8am-5.30pm Dec-Feb) Topped with a golden spire, the eye-catching Léifēng Pagoda can be climbed for fine views of the lake. The original pagoda, built in AD 977, collapsed in 1924. During renovations in 2001, Buddhist scriptures written on silk were discovered in the foundations, along with other treasures.

Jìngcí Temple BUDDHIST

(净慈寺; Jìngcí Sì; admission ¥10; ⏰6.30am-5pm) The serene Chan (Zen) Jìngcí Temple was originally built in AD 954 and is now fully restored. The splendid first hall is home to the massive and foreboding Heavenly Kings and a magnificent red and gold case encapsulating Milefo (the future Buddha) and Weituo. The main hall – the **Great Treasure Hall** –contains a simply vast seated effigy of Sakyamuni. Hunt down the awesome **1000-arm Guanyin** (千手观音) in the Guanyin Pavilion, with her huge fan of arms. The temple's enormous bronze bell is struck 108 times for prosperity on the eve of the Lunar New Year. Vegetarian restaurant attached.

Língyǐn Temple BUDDHIST

(灵隐寺; Língyǐn Sì; Lingyin Lu; grounds ¥35, grounds & temple ¥65; ⏰7am-5pm) Hángzhōu's most famous Buddhist temple, Língyǐn Temple was built in AD 326. Due to episodes of war and calamity, it has been destroyed and restored no fewer than 16 times. During the time of the Five Dynasties (907–60) about 3000 monks lived in the saffron-walled temple.

The main temple buildings are restorations of Qing-dynasty structures. The Hall of the Four Heavenly Kings is astonishing, with its four vast guardians and a beautifully elaborate cabinet housing Milefo. The **Great Hall** contains a magnificent 20m-high statue of Siddhartha Gautama (Sakyamuni), sculpted from 24 blocks of camphor wood in 1956 and based on a Tang-dynasty original. Behind the giant statue is a startling montage of Guanyin surrounded by 150 small figures, including multiple arhat (luóhàn), in a variety of poses. The Hall of the Medicine Buddha is beyond.

The walk up to the temple skirts the flanks of **Fēilái Peak** (Fēilái Fēng; Peak Flying from Afar), magically transported here from India according to legend. The Buddhist carvings (all 470 of them) lining the riverbanks and hillsides and tucked away inside grottoes date from the 10th to 14th centuries. To get a close-up view of the best carvings, including the famed 'laughing' Maitreya Buddha, follow the paths along the far (east) side of the stream.

There are several other temples near Língyǐn Temple that can be explored, including Yǒngfú Temple and Tāoguāng Temple.

Behind Língyǐn Temple is the **Northern Peak** (Běi Gāofēng), which can be scaled by cable car (up/down/return ¥30/20/40). From the summit there are sweeping views across the lake and city.

Bus K7 and tourist bus Y2 (both from the train station), and tourist bus Y1 from the roads circling West Lake, go to the temple.

Qīnghéfāng Old Street STREET

(清河坊历史文化街; Qīnghéfāng Lìshǐ Wénhuà Jiē) At the south end of Zhongshan Zhonglu is this fun, crowded and bustling pedestrian street, stuffed with all manner of shops, stalls and gift shops while snacking alleys branching off from it swarm with diners. It's an entertaining place to browse and there are several traditional medicine shops, including the atmospheric **Húqìngyú Táng Chinese Medicine Museum** (中药博物馆; Zhōngyào Bówùguǎn; 95 Dajing Xiang; admission ¥10; ⏰8.30am-5pm), which is an actual dispensary and clinic. **Huíchūn Táng** (回春堂; 117 Hefang Jie) is another delightful old medicine shop with a swallow's nest inside, high above the entrance.

FREE Confucius Temple TEMPLE

(文庙; Wénmiào; cnr Fuxue Xiang & Laodong Lu; ⏰9am-4.30pm Tue-Sun) A repository of silence and calm, Hángzhōu's Confucius Temple is worth exploring for the main hall and the fabulous painted woodwork of its beams and ceiling. Seated within are imposing figures of Confucius and other Confucian philosophers, including Mencius.

SOUTH OF WEST LAKE

The hills south of West Lake are a prime spot for walkers, cyclists and green tea connoisseurs.

FREE China Silk Museum
MUSEUM

(中国丝绸博物馆; Zhōngguó Sīchóu Bówùguǎn; 73-1 Yuhuangshan Lu; audioguide ¥100; ⊙8.30am-4.30pm, closed Mon morning) Close to the lake, this museum has absorbing displays of silk samples, and exhibits explain (in English) the history and processes of silk production.

FREE China Tea Museum
MUSEUM

(中国茶叶博物馆; Zhōngguó Cháyè Bówùguǎn; 88 Longjing Lu; ⊙9am-4.30pm Tue-Sun) Not far into the hills, you'll begin to see fields of tea bushes planted in undulating rows, the setting for the China Tea Museum – 3.7 hectares of land dedicated to the art, cultivation and tasting of tea. Further up are several tea-producing villages, all of which harvest China's most famous variety of green tea, *lóngjǐng* (dragon well), named after the spring where the pattern in the water resembles a dragon. You can enjoy one of Hángzhōu's most famous teas at the **Dragon Well Tea Village** (龙井问茶; Lóngjǐng Wènchá; ⊙8am-5.30pm), near the first pass. Tourist bus Y3 or K27 will take you to the museum and the village.

Tàizǐwān Park
PARK

(太子湾公园; Nanshan Lu; ⊙24hr) This lovely and serene park just south of the Sūdī Causeway off West Lake offers quiet walks

---

CRUISING WEST LAKE

Cruise boats (游船; yóuchuán; incl entry to Three Pools adult/child ¥45/22.50; ⊙7am-4.45pm) shuttle frequently from four points (Húbīn Park, Red Carp Pond, Zhōngshān Park and the Mausoleum of General Yue Fei) to the Mid-Lake Pavilion (Húxīn Tíng) and Xiǎoyíng Island (Xiǎoyíng Zhōu). Trips take 1½ hours and depart every 20 minutes. Alternatively, hire one of the six-person boats (小船; xiǎo chuán; ¥80 per person or ¥160 per boat) rowed by boatmen. Look for them across from the Overseas Chinese Hotel or along the causeways. Paddle boats (¥15 per 30 minutes, ¥200 deposit) on the Bái Causeway are also available for hire.

---

among lush woodland, ponds, lakes, rose gardens and lawns along a wooden walkway. Just take off and explore.

Six Harmonies Pagoda
PAGODA

(六和塔; Liùhé Tǎ; 16 Zhijiang Lu; grounds ¥20, grounds & pagoda ¥30; ⊙6am-6.30pm) Three kilometres southwest of the lake, an enormous rail and road bridge spans the Qiántáng River. Close by rears up the 60m-high octagonal Six Harmonies Pagoda, first built in AD 960. Stout (rather than the usual slender Chinese pagoda form), the pagoda also served as a lighthouse, and was said to possess magical powers to halt the 6.5m-high tidal bore that thunders up Qiántáng River. You can climb the pagoda, while behind stretches a charming walk through terraces dotted with sculptures, bells, shrines and inscriptions. Take bus K4 or 504 from Nanshan Lu.

OTHER SIGHTS

Catholic Church
CHURCH

(天主堂; Tiānzhǔ Táng; 415 Zhongshan Beilu; admission free) Hidden away behind sheet-metal gates, the blue-and-white Catholic church is a lovely old building, with a compassionate effigy of Mary above the door. Knock on the gate and the gatekeeper may let you in.

Sīchéng Church
CHURCH

(思澄堂; Sīchéng Táng; 132 Jiefang Lu; admission free) Chinese-built, the brick Protestant Sīchéng Church is more Chinese-style than the Catholic church, with a loyal and welcoming congregation; if it looks shut, try the entrance along Jueyuansi Alley (觉苑寺巷) down the east side of the church.

☞ Tours

Just about every midrange and top-end hotel offers tours to West Lake and the surrounding areas. Frequent tours also run from the Hángzhōu Tourist Information Centre.

✬ Festivals & Events

The international Qiántáng River tide observing festival every autumn in Yánguān, outside Hángzhōu, is a top event. See p260 for more details.

🛏 Sleeping

Hángzhōu's hotels have expanded in recent years across all budgets; youth hostels are now plentiful. Book well ahead in the summer months, at weekends and during the busy holiday periods. Room prices at hos-

WEST LAKE WALK

For a breathtaking trek into the hills above the lake, take Xixialing Lu (栖霞岭路; also called Qixialing Lu) just west of the Mausoleum of General Yue Fei. The road runs past the west wall of the temple before entering the shade of towering trees to climb stone steps. At Zǐyún Cave (紫云洞; Zǐyún Dòng), the road forks; take the right-hand fork towards Bàopǔ Taoist Temple (Bàopǔ Dàoyuàn) 1km away and the Bǎochù Pagoda (保俶塔; Bǎochù Tǎ). At the top of the steps turn left and, passing the Sunrise Terrace (初阳台; Chūyáng Tái), again bear left. Down the steps bear right to the **Bàopǔ Taoist Temple** (抱朴道院; admission ¥5; ⊙6am-5pm), whose first hall contains a statue of Guanyin (Buddhist goddess nonetheless) before a yin-yang diagram; an effigy of Taoist master Gehong (葛洪) – who once smelted cinnabar here – resides in the next hall, behind a fabulously carved altar decorated with figures. Return the way you came to continue east to the Bǎochù Pagoda and after hitting a confluence of three paths, take the middle track. Squeeze into a gap between some huge boulders and you will spot the Bǎochù Pagoda rising up ahead. Repeatedly restored, the seven-storey brick pagoda was last rebuilt in 1933, although its spire tumbled off in the 1990s. Continue on down and you will pass through a *páilóu* – or decorative arch – erected during the Republic (with some of its characters scratched off) to a series of cliff-side Ming-dynasty effigies, all of which were vandalised in the tumultuous 1960s, apart from two effigies on the right which were left untouched. Bear right and head down to Beishan Lu (北山路), emerging from Baochutaqianshan Lu (保俶塔前山路).

tels and some hotels get a weekend hike when there's an inflow of travellers from all compass points. Look out for 住宿 and 客房 signs (meaning 'rooms available'), which identify cheap guesthouses that may take foreigners.

Four Seasons Hotel Hángzhōu HOTEL $$$
(杭州西子湖四季酒店; Hángzhōu Xīzíhú Sìjì Jiǔdiàn; ☏8829 8888; www.fourseasons.com/hangzhou; 5 Lingyin Lu; 灵隐路5号; d ¥3048-3738, ste from ¥6693; ❀❀@☎❀) More of a resort than a hotel, the fabulous 78-room, two-swimming pool Four Seasons enjoys a seductive position in lush grounds next to West Lake. Low-storey buildings and villas echo traditional China, a sensation amplified by the osmanthus trees, ornamental shrubs, ponds and tranquillity. Checking into the gorgeously appointed and very spacious ground-floor deluxe premier rooms throws in a garden; rooms have lovely bathrooms, walk-in wardrobe and hugely inviting beds. The infinity pool alongside West Lake is a dream, as is the outstanding spa. Charge for wi-fi.

Tea Boutique Hotel HOTEL $$$
(杭州天伦精品酒店; Hángzhōu Tiānlún Jīngpǐn Jiǔdiàn; ☏8799 9888; www.teaboutiquehotel.com; 124 Shuguang Lu; 曙光路124号; d ¥988-1280, ste ¥2688; ❀@☎) The simply but effectively done wood-sculpted foyer area with its sinuously shaped reception is a presage to the lovely accommodation at this hotel where a Japanese-minimalist mood holds sway among celadon teacups, muted colours and – interestingly for China – a Bible in each room. Double-glazed windows roadside keep the traffic noise low while the wide corridors convey a sense of space the boutique label often lacks. Service is excellent and healthy discounts run between 20% and 40%.

Hofang International Youth Hostel HOSTEL $
(荷方国际青年旅社; Héfāng Guójì Qīngnián Lǚshè; ☏8706 3299; 67 Dajing Xiang; 大井巷67号; dm ¥50-55, tw ¥100, d ¥99-119; ❀@☎) Very pleasantly tucked away from the noise down a historic alley off Qīnghéfāng Old Street, this hostel has an excellent location and exudes a pleasant and calm ambience, with attractive tatami loft rooms.

Wúshānyì International Youth Hostel HOSTEL $
(吴山驿国际青年旅社; Wúshānyì Guójì Qīngnián Lǚshè; 22 Zhongshan Zhonglu; 中山中路22号; d/tr ¥248/320; ❀@☎) With a healthy mix of Chinese and Western travellers, this quiet, unhurried and comfy hostel has clean and well-looked-after rooms and excellent, very helpful staff plus a charmingly tucked-away location off Qinghefang Jie (and not too far from West Lake either). Three computers (first half-hour free) are at hand in the (wi-fi-equipped) lobby.

Mingtown Youth Hostel HOSTEL $

(明堂杭州国际青年旅社; Míngtáng Hángzhōu Guójì Qīngnián Lǚshè; ☎8791 8948; 101-11 Nanshan Lu; 南山路101-11号; dm ¥60, s/d ¥185/265; ❉) With its pleasant lakeside location, this friendly hostel is often booked out so reserve well ahead. It has a relaxing cafe/bar, offers ticket booking, internet access, and rents bikes and camping gear.

In Lake Youth Hostel HOSTEL $

(柳湖小筑青年旅社; Liǔhú Xiǎozhù Qīngnián Lǚshè; ☎8682 6700; 5 Luyang Lu; 绿杨路5号; 6-bed dm with shower ¥70, tw & d ¥368-448; ❉☎) Ideally located a few steps from picturesque West Lake off Nanshan Lu, this friendly and amenable hostel radiates a peaceful ambience, with a flower-bedecked courtyard, clean dorms (all with shower), smart doubles and twins, a roof terrace for barbecues, downstairs cafe and bar, and welcoming staff.

West Lake Youth Hostel HOSTEL $

(杭州过客青年旅社; Hángzhōu Guòkè Qīngnián Lǚshè; ☎8702 7027; www.westlakehostel.com; 62-3 Nanshan Lu; 南山路62-3号; dm ¥50-55, s ¥170, tw ¥210-220; ❉@) Set back off the road amid trees and foliage east of Jìngcí Temple, this is a good bet with decent rooms and comfy lounge-bar area hung with lanterns, and a good sense of character and seclusion; reserve ahead. The kindergarten next door may be noisy in the morning. From the train station take bus Y2 and get off at the Chángqiáo (长桥) stop.

Crystal Orange Hotel HOTEL $$$

(桔子水晶酒店; Júzi Shuǐjīng Jiǔdiàn; ☎2887 8988; www.orangehotel.com; 122 Qingbo Jie; 清波街122号; tw/ste ¥788/1388; ❉@☎) Uncluttered and modern business hotel with a crisp and natty interior, Warhol prints in the lobby, glass lift and only four floors, but sadly no views of West Lake from the neat rooms. Discounts of 50%.

Shangri-La Hotel HOTEL $$$

(杭州香格里拉饭店; Hángzhōu Xiānggélǐlā Fàndiàn; ☎8797 7951; www.shangri-la.com; 78 Beishan Lu; 北山路78号; d ¥1650, with lake view ¥2500; ❉@☎❉) Surrounded by forest on the north shore of the lake, this hotel enjoys a winning, picturesque location. The hotel has been around for a long time, so view rooms first, as quality varies. Wireless connection, swimming pool, health club and discounts of 30%.

Starway Jīngshàng Youth Hostel HOSTEL $

(景上南山; Jīngshàng Nánshān; ☎2806 9000; 148-5 Nanshan Lu; 南山路148-5号; dm ¥50, d/ tw ¥255/235; ❉@☎) Starway is an OK place with so-so dorms and doubles set back from the road near West Lake; there's little character, but it could be handy if other places are booked out.

✗ Eating

Hángzhōu cuisine emphasises fresh, sweet flavours and makes good use of freshwater fish, especially eel and carp. Dishes to watch for include *dōngpō ròu* (东坡肉; braised pork), named after the Song-dynasty poet Su Dongpo, and *jiàohuā tóngjī* (叫花童鸡; chicken wrapped in lotus leaves and baked in clay), known in English as 'beggar's chicken'. Bamboo shoots are a local delicacy, especially in the spring when they're most tender. Hángzhōu's most popular restaurant street is **Gaoyin Jie**, parallel to Qīnghéfáng Old St, a long sprawl of restaurants brashly lit up like casinos at night and aimed at visitors. On top of vegie options listed here, the Jìngcí Temple has a vegetarian restaurant that is open till 10pm.

⬥ TOP CHOICE Green Tea Restaurant HÁNGZHŌU $$

(绿茶; Lǜchá; 250 Jiefang Lu; 解放路250号; meals ¥70; ▣) Doing a brisk trade, this excellent Hángzhōu restaurant has superb food and should be one of your first stops. With a bare brick finish and decorated with rattan utensils and colourful flower-patterned cushions, the dining style is casual. The long paper menu (tick what you want) includes clam soup (¥19) – a plate of mussels – a salty and moreish dish, spiced up with chilli. The eggplant clay pot (¥20) is simply gorgeous while the Green Tea roast chicken (half/whole ¥25/48) is tasty. Avoid the coffee unless you like super-sweet creamer added automatically. Further four branches in town.

La Pedrera SPANISH, TAPAS $$$

(巴特洛西班牙餐厅; Bātèluò Xībānyá Cāntīng; ☎8886 6089; 4 Baishaquan, Shuguang Lu; 曙光路白沙泉4号; tapas from ¥30, meals ¥200; ⊙11am-11pm) This fine two-floor Spanish restaurant just off Shuguang Lu bar street has tapas diners in a whirl, seafood paella-aficionados applauding and Spanish wine fans gratified. Prices may take a sizeable bite out of your wallet, but the convivial atmosphere and assured menu prove popular and enjoyable.

Grandma's Kitchen
HÁNGZHŌU $

(外婆家; Wàipójiā; 3 Hubin Lu; mains ¥6-55; ⊙lunch & dinner; 🖼) Highly popular with locals, this chain restaurant cooks up classic Hángzhōu favourites; try the *hóngshāo dōngpō ròu* (红烧东坡肉). There are several other branches in town.

Jīn Shā
CHINESE $$$

(金沙厅; Jīn Shā Tīng; Four Seasons Hotel Hángzhōu; 📞8829-8888; www.fourseasons.com /hangzhou; 5 Lingyin Lu; meals ¥300; ⊙lunch & dinner) For fine waterside Hángzhōu, Shànghǎi and Cantonese cuisine in a particularly elegant and well-presented ambience, you can't go far wrong with this signature restaurant at the Four Seasons Hotel Hángzhōu; there's alfresco seating on the terrace outside and a fine selection of teas and wines.

Lǎo Hángzhōu Fēngwèi
HÁNGZHŌU $

(老杭州风味; 141 Gaoyin Jie; mains from ¥20; ⊙11.30am-9pm; 🖼) This overlit restaurant is one of several along Gaoyin Jie selling traditional Hángzhōu cuisine. Try the flavoursome diced chicken and eggplant pot (*lǎo hángzhōu jīlì qiézi bāo*; ¥28) and the salty and fatty Hángzhōu-style lamb chops (*lǎo hángzhōu kǎoyángpái*; ¥68) or the *dōngpō* pork (¥15 per chunk).

Lóuwàilóu Restaurant
HÁNGZHŌU $$$

(楼外楼; Lóuwàilóu; 30 Gushan Lu; mains ¥30-200; ⊙10.30am-3.30pm & 4.30-8.45pm; 🖼) Founded in 1838, this is Hángzhōu's most famous restaurant. The local speciality is *xīhú cùyú* (西湖醋鱼; sweet and sour carp) and *dōngpō* pork, but there's a good choice of other well-priced standard dishes.

Lǎomǎjiā Miànguǎn
NOODLES $

(老马家面馆; 232 Nanshan Lu; meals ¥15; ⊙7am-10.30pm) Simple, popular and unfussy Muslim restaurant stuffed into an old *shíkùmén* tenement building with a handful of tables and spot-on *niúròu lāmiàn* (牛肉拉面; beef noodles; ¥7) and super-scrummy *ròujiāmó* (肉夹馍; meat in a bun; ¥5).

Carrefour
SUPERMARKET $

(家乐福; Jiālèfú; 135 Yan'an Lu; 延安路135号; ⊙9am-9pm) On Yan'an Lu in between Xihu Dadao and Kaiyuan Lu.

🍷 Drinking

For drinking, Shuguang Lu north of West Lake is the place; a brash clutch of lesser bars also operates opposite the China Academy of Art on Nanshan Lu (南山路). For a comprehensive list of Hángzhōu bars and restaurants, grab a copy of *More – Hangzhou Entertainment Guide* (www.morehangzhou. com), available from bars and concierge desks at good hotels.

Maya Bar
BAR

(玛雅酒吧; Mǎyǎ Jiǔbā; 94 Baishaquan, Shuguang Lu; ⊙noon-2am) Jim Morrison, Kurt Cobain, Mick Jagger, Bob Dylan and the Beatles watch on approvingly from the walls of this darkly lit, solid and rock-steady bar. Almost as importantly, the drinks are seriously cheap; happy hour sees draught beer costing a risible ¥10 (¥20 at other times). Staff may be morose, but so what?

Eudora Station
BAR

(亿多瑞站; Yìduōruìzhàn; 101-107 Nanshan Lu; ⊙9am-2am) A fab location by West Lake, roof terrace aloft, strong menu and a sure-fire atmosphere conspire to make this welcoming watering hole a great choice. There's sports TV, live music, a ground-floor terrace, and a good range of beers; barbecues fire up on the roof terrace in the warmer months.

☆ Entertainment

JZ Club
CLUB

(黄楼; Huáng Lóu; 📞8702 8298; 6 Liuying Lu, by 266 Nanshan Lu; ⊙6.30pm-2.30am) The folk that brought you JZ Club in Shànghǎi have the live jazz scene sewn up in Hángzhōu with this neat and cultured three-floor venue near West Lake. There's live jazz nightly with international names on the billing.

🔒 Shopping

Hángzhōu is famed for its tea, in particular *lóngjǐng* green tea, as well as silk, fans and, of all things, scissors. All of these crop up in the **Wúshān Lù night market** (吴山路夜市; Wúshān Lù Yèshì), now on Huixing Lu (惠兴路) between Youdian Lu (邮电路) and Renhe Lu (仁和路), where fake ceramics jostle with ancient pewter tobacco pipes, Chairman Mao memorabilia, silk shirts and pirated CDs. Qīnghéfāng Old Street (see p253) has loads of possibilities, from Chinese tiger pillows to taichi swords.

Xinhua Lu Silk Market
SILK

(新华路丝绸市场; Xīnhuá Lù Sīchóu Shìchǎng; Xinhua Lu; ⊙8am-5pm) For silk, try this string of silk shops strung out along the north of Xinhua Lu. Check out the Ming-dynasty residence (明宅; Míng Zhái), now a silk emporium, at 227 Xinhua Lu.

ⓘ Information

Internet Access

Twenty-four-hour internet cafes are in abundance around the train station (typically ¥4 or ¥5 per hour); look for the neon signs '网吧'. There is free internet access at some Hángzhōu Tourist Information Centres, such as the branch at 10 Huaguang Lu.

Yēzitóu Internet Cafe (椰子头网吧; Yēzitóu Wǎngbā; 2nd fl, east end of Gaoyin Jie; per hr ¥4; ⊘24hr) Just west of intersection with Zhonghe Nanlu.

Medical Services

Zhèjiāng University First Affiliated Hospital (浙江大学医学院附属第一医院; Zhèjiāng Dàxué Yīxuéyuàn Fùshǔ Dìyī Yīyuàn; 79 Qingchun Lu)

Money

Bank of China (中国银行; Zhōngguó Yínháng; 177 Laodong Lu) Offers currency exchange plus 24-hour ATM.

HSBC (汇丰银行; Huìfēng Yínháng; cnr Qingchun Lu & Zhonghe Lu) Has a 24-hour ATM.

Industrial & Commercial Bank of China (ICBC; 工商银行; Gōngshāng Yínháng; 300 Yan'an Lu) Has a 24-hour ATM.

Post

China Post (中国邮政; Zhōngguó Yóuzhèng; Renhe Lu) Close to West Lake.

Public Security Bureau

Public Security Bureau Exit & Entry Administration Service Center (PSB; 公安局; Gōng'ānjú Bànzhèng Zhōngxīn; ☑8728 0600; 35 Huaguang Lu; ⊘8.30am-noon & 2-5pm Mon-Fri) Can extend visas.

Tourist Information

Asking at, or phoning up, your hostel or hotel for info can be very handy.

Hángzhōu Tourist Information Centre (杭州旅游咨询服务中心; Hángzhōu Lǚyóu Zīxún Fúwù Zhōngxīn; ☑hotline 96123; Hángzhōu Train Station) Provides basic travel info, free maps and tours. Other branches include Léifēng Pagoda, 228 Yan'an Lu and 10 Huaguang Lu, just off Qīnghéfáng Old Street.

Tourist Complaint Hotline (☑8796 9691)

Travellers Infoline (☑96123) Helpful 24-hour information with English service from 6.30am to 9pm.

Websites

Hángzhōu City Travel Committee (www. gotohz.com) Current information on events, restaurants and entertainment venues around the city.

Hángzhōu News (www.hangzhou.com.cn/english) News-oriented website with travel info.

More Hángzhōu (www.morehangzhou.com) Handy website with restaurant and nightlife reviews, forums and classifieds.

ⓘ Getting There & Away

Air

Hángzhōu has flights to all major Chinese cities (bar Shànghǎi) and international connections to Hong Kong, Macau, Tokyo, Singapore and other destinations. Several daily flights connect to Běijīng (¥1050) and Guǎngzhōu (¥960).

One place to book air tickets is at the **Civil Aviation Administration of China** (CAAC; 中国民航; Zhōngguó Mínháng; ☑8666 8666; 390 Tiyuchang Lu; ⊘7.30am-8pm). Most hotels will also book flights, generally with a ¥20 to ¥30 service charge.

Bus

All four bus stations are outside the city centre; tickets can be conveniently bought for all stations from the **bus ticket office** (长途汽车售票处; chángtú qìchē shòupiàochù; ⊘6.30am-5pm) right off the exit from Hángzhōu's main train station.

Buses from the huge **Jiǔbǎo bus station** (九堡客运中心; Jiǔbǎo kéyùn zhōngxīn) in the far northeast of Hángzhōu:

Níngbō ¥60, two hours

Shànghǎi ¥69, 2½ hours, regular

Shàoxīng ¥26, one hour

Sūzhōu ¥60, two hours

Wūzhèn ¥30, one hour

Until the metro line direct to Jiǔbǎo bus station opens, hop on bus K21 to Xīhú Tīyùguǎn and change for bus K101 (1½ hours). A taxi will cost around ¥60 from West Lake, while bus K508 runs from Jiǔbǎo bus station to Hángzhōu Main Train Station.

Buses from the **south bus station** (汽车南站; qìchē nánzhàn; 407 Qiutao Lu):

Níngbō ¥60, two hours, every 20 minutes

Shàoxīng ¥26, one hour, every 20 minutes

Wǔyì ¥60, six daily

Buses from the **north bus station** (汽车北站; qìchē běizhàn; 766 Moganshan Lu):

Nánxún ¥40, 1½ hours, regular

Sūzhōu ¥72, two hours, regular

Tónglǐ ¥15, two hours, three daily

Wūkāng ¥15, one hour, hourly

From Shànghǎi, buses leave frequently for Hángzhōu's various bus stations (¥65, 2½ hours) from the Shànghǎi south bus station. Buses to Hángzhōu also run every 30 minutes between 10am and 9pm from Shànghǎi's Hóngqiáo airport (¥85, two hours). Regular buses also run to Hángzhōu from Shànghǎi's Pǔdōng International Airport (¥100, three hours).

Buses for Huángshān (¥100, four hours) leave from the **west bus station** (汽车西站; qìchē xīzhàn; 357 Tianmushan Lu).

Train

The easiest way to travel to Hángzhōu from Shànghǎi is on the high-speed G class train to **Hángzhōu Main Train Station** (杭州火车站; Hángzhōu Huǒchēzhàn) east of West Lake. The overnight Z10 (¥194 to ¥539) departs Hángzhōu Main Train Station for Běijīng at 6.16pm, arriving at 7.28am. Also handy, the T32 (¥194 to ¥539) departs Hángzhōu Main Train Station for Běijīng at 6.25pm, arriving shortly after 10am the next day. Daily G class high-speed trains from Hángzhōu Train Station:

Běijīng South Train Station 2nd/1st class ¥631/1058, 6½ hours, seven daily

Nánjīng South Train Station 2nd/1st class ¥211/353, two hours 20 minutes, 10 daily

Shànghǎi Hóngqiáo Train Station 2nd/1st class ¥78/124, 55 minutes, first/last 6.14am/9.10pm, regular

Sūzhōu 2nd/1st class ¥111 to ¥188, 1½ hours, four daily

Daily D class high-speed trains from Hángzhōu Train Station:

Níngbō East Train Station 2nd/1st class ¥52/62, two hours, eight daily

Shànghǎi Hóngqiáo Train Station 2nd/1st class ¥49/60, 70 minutes, eight daily

Shàoxīng 2nd/1st class ¥19/22, 40 minutes, six daily

Sūzhōu 2nd/1st class ¥75/91, two hours, three daily

Xiàmén North Train Station 2nd/1st class ¥284/341, 7½ hours, two daily

Wēnzhōu South Train Station 2nd/1st class ¥131/158, four hours, seven daily

Regular D class trains (2nd/1st class ¥54/65, 1½ hours) also run to **Shànghǎi Hóngqiáo Train Station** (杭州火车南站; Hángzhōu Huǒchē Nánzhàn), south of the Qiántáng River. Due for completion by 2013, Hángzhōu East Train Station (杭州东站; Hángzhōu Dōngzhàn) is being rebuilt to accommodate high-speed trains and will be linked to the metro system.

Booking sleepers can be difficult at Hángzhōu Train Station, especially to Běijīng. Most hotels can do this for you for a service charge. A handy **train ticket office** (火车票售票处; huǒchēpiào shòupiàochù; 147 Huansha Lu) is north of Jie-fang Lu, just east of West Lake. Other offices are at 72 Baochu Lu (near turning with Shengfu Lu) and 149 Tiyuchang Lu. Train tickets are also available at certain China Post branches including 10 Desheng Lu and 60 Fengqi Lu.

Getting Around
To/From the Airport

Hángzhōu's airport is 30km from the city centre; taxi drivers ask around ¥100 to ¥130 for the trip. Shuttle buses (¥20, one hour) run every 15 minutes from 5.30am and 9pm from the CAAC office (also stopping at the train station).

Bicycle

The best way to hire a bike is to use the public **bike hire scheme** (8533 1122; www.hzzxc.com.cn, in Chinese). Stations are dotted in large numbers around the city. You can apply at one of the **booths** (6.30am-9pm Apr-Oct, 6am-9pm Nov-Mar) at certain bike stations (marked on the Hángzhōu map) where you will need ¥300 (¥200 for the deposit and ¥100 as credit) and your passport as ID. You will then get a swipe card to hop aboard one of the bright red bikes which you can return to any other station. The first hour on each bike is free, so if you switch bikes within the hour, the rides are free. The second hour on the same bike is ¥1, the third is ¥2 and after that it's ¥3 per hour. Your deposit and unused credit is refunded to you when you return your swipe card. Note you cannot return bikes outside booth operating hours as the swipe units deactivate (you will be charged a whole night's rental). Youth hostels also rent out bikes, but these are more expensive.

Public Transport

BUS Hángzhōu has a clean, efficient bus system and getting around is easy (but roads are increasingly gridlocked). 'Y' buses are tourist buses; 'K' is simply an abbreviation of 'kōngtiáo' (air-con). Tickets are ¥2 to ¥5. Following are popular bus routes:

Bus K7 Usefully connects the main train station to the western side of West Lake and Língyǐn Temple.

Tourist bus Y1 Circles West Lake in a return loop to Língyǐn Temple.

Tourist bus Y2 Goes from the main train station, along Beishan Lu and up to Língyǐn Temple.

Tourist bus Y3 Travels around West Lake to the China Silk Museum, China Tea Museum, Dragon Well Tea Village and the Southern Song–dynasty Guan Kiln.

Bus K56 Travels from the east bus station to Yan'an Lu.

Buses 15 & K15 Connects the north bus station to the northwest area of West Lake.

Bus K95 Links Hángzhōu Train Station with the north bus station.

Bus K518 Connects the East Train Station with the main train station, via the east bus station.

METRO Line 1 of Hángzhōu's new metro system was due to open by 2012 and will run through the main train station, Hángzhōu East Train Station and Jiǔbǎo bus station.

Taxi

Metered Hyundai taxis are ubiquitous and start at ¥10; figure on around ¥20 to ¥25 from the main train station (queues can be horrendous though) to Hubin Lu.

Around Hángzhōu

QIÁNTÁNG RIVER
TIDAL BORE   钱塘江潮

A spectacular natural phenomenon occurs when the highest tides of the lunar cycle sweep a wall of water up the narrow mouth of the Qiántáng River from Hángzhōu Bay (Hángzhōu Wān) at thundering speeds of up to 40km per hour.

Although the tidal bore can be viewed from the riverbank in Hángzhōu, the best place to witness this amazing phenomenon is on either side of the river at **Yánguān** (盐官), a lovely ancient town about 38km northeast of Hángzhōu. The most popular viewing time is during the mid-autumn festival, around the 18th day of the eighth month of the lunar calendar, when the **international Qiántáng River tide observing festival** takes place. However, you can see it throughout the year when the highest tides occur at the beginning and middle of each lunar month. For tide times, check with the Hángzhōu Tourist Information Centre.

Hotels and travel agencies offer tours to see the bore during the mid-autumn festival, but you can visit just as easily on your own. To reach Yánguān, take a bus (¥25, one hour) from Hángzhōu's Jiǔbǎo bus station to Hǎiníng and change to bus 106 (¥8) to Yánguān; alternatively, take a bus from Hángzhōu Train Station (45 minutes) and change to bus 109 to Yánguān.

MÒGĀNSHĀN   莫干山
📞 0572

A blessed release from the suffocating summer torpor roasting north Zhèjiāng, this delightful **hilltop resort** (admission ¥80) was developed by 19th-century Europeans from Shànghǎi and Hángzhōu during the concession era, in the style of Lúshān and Jīgōngshān in Hénán. Refreshingly cool in summer and sometimes smothered in spectral fog, Mògānshān is famed for its scenic vistas, forested views, towering bamboo and stone villa architecture; the mountain remains a weekend bolt hole for expat *tàitai* (wives) fleeing the simmering lowland heat.

👁 Sights & Activities

The best way to enjoy Mògānshān is just to wander the winding forest paths and stone steps, taking in some of the architecture en route. There's Shànghǎi gangster **Du Yuesheng's old villa** (杜月笙别墅; Dù Yuèshēng Biéshù) – now serving as a hotel – Chiang Kaishek's lodge, a couple of churches (375 Moganshan and 419 Moganshan) and many other villas linked (sometimes tenuously) with the rich and famous, including the **house** (毛主席下榻处; Máo Zhǔxí Xiàtàchù; 126 Moganshan) where Chairman Mao rested his chubby limbs.

Apart from the gaunt villa architecture, more recent construction has flung up less attractive villas made of more regular blocks; the genuine older villas are made of irregularly shaped stone. Sadly, many of the original interiors have been ripped out, so much of the period charm is absent. Mock classical porticos have been bolted on to other villas in a clumsy Chinese interpretation of European style. The blue and red corrugated-iron roofing looks new, but is actually the original roofing material.

Containing **Tǎ Mountain** (塔山; Tǎshān) in the northwest, the **Dà Kēng Scenic Area** (大坑景区; Dàkēng Jǐngqū) is great for rambling. You can pick up a Chinese map (¥4) at your hotel for some sense of orientation, otherwise there are billboard maps dotted about.

For information on **hikes** or for suggestions for activities on Mògānshān, contact well-informed Mark Kitto, author of the riveting *China Cuckoo,* at Mògānshān Lodge (he may appreciate it if you bought a coffee there).

🛏 Sleeping

Mògānshān is full of hotels of varying quality, most housed in crumbling villas; room prices peak at weekends (Friday to Sunday). Don't expect to find any backpacker spots, but haggle your socks off to drive prices down; if you come off-season (eg early spring) you can expect good rates, but be warned that many hotels either shut up shop or close for renovation over the winter.

TOP CHOICE Mògānshān House 23   HOTEL $$$
(莫干山杭疗23号; Mògānshān Hángliáo 23 Hào; 📞803 3822; www.moganshanhouse23.com; 23 Moganshan; 莫干山23号; weekday d & tw ¥900, weekend 2 nights Y2400; ❀@�) This exquisitely restored villa hits the Mògānshān nail squarely on the head, bursting with period charm, from art deco–style sinks

black-and-white tiled bathroom floors, wooden floorboards and the original staircase to a lovely English kitchen. It's also kid friendly with a family room, baby chairs and swings in the garden. With only six rooms, book well in advance, especially for weekend stays (when it's a minimum two-night stay). Breakfast is included in room price. Also ask about the two other Mògānshān properties run by the same owners, House 2 and House 25.

📷 **Naked Home Village**   FARM HOUSES $$
(☎021-6431 8901; www.nakedretreats.cn; 329 Moganshan; 莫干山329号; per person weekday lodge/bungalow ¥350/520, weekend ¥450/750; ❄) Naked Retreats is at the top of a gully below the village, offering a selection of eco-lodges, farm houses and bungalows enveloped in bamboo forest sleeping anything from a couple to a crowd; lovely views. A range of activities is also organised, from biking to fishing, hiking, star gazing, yoga and massage. Rates are for a minimum double occupancy.

📷 **Naked Stables
Private Reserve**   VILLAS $$$
(☎021-6431 8901; www.nakedretreats.cn; earth hut ¥2600, tree-top villas ¥5800; ❄@❄) For further unbridled escapism, Naked Retreats also runs these luxurious and beautifully situated mod-con-equipped tree-top villas and earth huts within a 24-hectare resort in Mògānshān; expect serene forest views, infinity pools, a spa and wellness centre, and heaps of eco brownie points.

📷 **Le Passage Mohkan Shan**   HOTEL $$$
(莫干山里法国山居; Mògānshānlǐ Fǎguóshānjū; ☎805 2958; www.lepassagemoganshan.com; Xiānrénkēng Tea Plantation, Zǐlíng Village; 紫岭村仙人坑茶厂; per person r ¥1500-2100; ❄❄❄) A Gallic bid to cash in on the mountain's escapist colonial magic, Le Passage is a lovely and kid-friendly 38-room country house hotel ensconced within a Mògānshān tea plantation. Rooms and bathrooms are high on period charm, with high ceilings. Rates are calculated on a two-night stay basis; add ¥1000 surcharge for a one-night stay. Pricy pick-up service from Shànghǎi and Hángzhōu provided. There's a wine cellar, of course.

✕ **Eating**

Yinshan Jie has a number of restaurants and hotels with restaurants.

TOP CHOICE **Mògānshān Lodge**   INTERNATIONAL $$
(马克的咖啡厅; Mǎkè de Kāfēitīng; ☎803 3011; www.moganshanlodge.com; Songliang Shanzhuang, off Yinshan Jie; ❄9am-11pm; ❄) English Mògānshān resident Mark Kitto can cook up a treat, brew up a fine coffee and give you the low-down on Mògānshān's charms at this elegantly presented villa up some steps from Yinshan Jie.

ℹ **Information**

The main village (Mògānshān Zhèn) is centred around Yinshan Jie (荫山街), where you will find the **China Post** (40 Moganshan; ❄8.30-11am & 1-4pm), a branch of the PSB (opposite the post office) and several hotels.

ℹ **Getting There & Away**

From Hángzhōu, buses leave from the north bus station to Wǔkāng (武康; ¥15, 40 minutes, every 30 minutes) from 6.20am to 7pm; in the other direction, buses run every 30 minutes from 6.30am till 7pm; note that Wǔkāng is also known as Déqīng (德清).

From Wǔkāng minivans run to the top of Mògānshān for around ¥50; a taxi will cost around ¥70 to ¥80. Buses from Shànghǎi run to Wǔkāng (¥53, four hours) and leave from the old north bus station near Baoshan Rd metro, at 80 Gongxing Rd. Buses depart from Shànghǎi at 6.30am, 11.50am and 12.50pm; buses depart from Wǔkāng for Shànghǎi at 6.30am, 7.40am, 1pm and 3.30pm. Buses also run between Shànghǎi north bus station and Wǔkāng (¥60).

Wūzhèn   乌镇

☎0573

Like Zhōuzhuāng and other water towns in southern Jiāngsū, Wūzhèn's charming network of waterways and access to the Grand Canal once made it a prosperous place for its trade and production of silk.

◎ **Sights**

With its old bridges, ancient temples, age-old residences, museums and canal-side Ming and Qing-dynasty architecture, Wūzhèn (www.wuzhen.com.cn) is an appetising and photogenic if over-commercialised slice of old China. It's a lovely place to overnight, although you can easily make it a day trip from either Shànghǎi or Hángzhōu.

The old town is divided into two areas: **Dōngzhà** (东栅; east scenic zone; admission ¥100) and **Xīzhà** (西栅; west scenic zone; admission ¥120, ¥80 after 5pm) with a combined ticket for both areas (¥150). Buy your ticket at the

main visitor centre (入口; rùkǒu; Daqiao Lu; through ticket ¥150; ⏱8am-5.30pm), where money exchange and an ATM can be found; you can also take a boat from here across the lake.

The main street of Dōngzhà scenic zone, Dongda Jie, is a narrow path paved with stone slabs and flanked by wooden buildings. Some of these are workshops, such as the **Sānbái Wine Workshop** (三白酒坊; Sānbái Jiǔfáng), an actual distillery churning out a pungent rice wine ripe for the sampling. Along here are many other workshops, embracing all trades from cloth dying to bamboo weaving and tobacco making.

Mao Dun's Former Residence
HISTORIC BUILDING

(茅盾故居; Máo Dùn Gùjū) Mao Dun's Former Residence is also in the Dōngzhà scenic zone. Revolutionary writer Mao Dun was a contemporary of Lu Xun and the author of *Spring Silkworms* and *Midnight*. His great-grandfather, a successful merchant, bought the house in 1885 and it's a fairly typical example from the late Qing dynasty. There are photographs, writings and other memorabilia of Mao Dun's life, though not much explanation in English.

Hundred Beds Museum
MUSEUM

(210 Dongzha Dajie) The Hundred Beds Museum has an intriguing collection of historic beds from the region, while at the western end of the Dōngzhà scenic zone, around the corner on Changfeng Jie, is an interesting exhibit many visitors miss.

Huìyuán Pawn House
HISTORIC BUILDING

(汇源当铺; Huìyuán Dàngpù) The Huìyuán Pawn House was once a famous pawnshop that eventually expanded to branches in Shànghǎi.

🛏 Sleeping

Wūzhèn Guesthouse
GUESTHOUSE

(☎873 1666; 137 Xizha Jie; r from ¥340; 🌑) This is a centralised collection of canal-side B&Bs on either side of the water run by families where you are then given a well-presented room with air-con, telephone and bathroom.

☆ Entertainment

One of the best reasons to visit Wūzhèn is for the regular live performances of local **Flower Drum opera** (Huāgǔ xì) held throughout the day in the village square, and shadow puppet shows *(píyǐngxì)* in the small theatre beside the square. The puppet shows in particular

are great fun and well worth watching. You can hire a boat at the main gate (¥80 per person) for a ride down the canal.

ℹ Getting There & Away

From Hángzhōu, buses run from the Jiǔbǎo bus station to Wūzhèn (¥30, one hour) leaving every hour or so from 6.25am to 6.25pm.

From Shànghǎi, buses (¥49, two hours, eight daily) run from the Shànghǎi south bus station. Tour buses (¥165 return, ticket includes the entrance fee to Wūzhèn and a Chinese-speaking guide, 9am and 9.30am, two hours) also leave from Shànghǎi Stadium. Minibuses (¥10) connect Wūzhèn with the canal town of Nánxún.

Nánxún   南浔

📋0572

Nestled on the border with Jiāngsū province, about 125km from Hángzhōu and only 20km from Wūzhèn, Nánxún is a water town whose contemporary modest appearance belies its once glorious past. Established more than 1400 years ago, the town came to prominence during the Southern Song dynasty due to its prospering silk industry. By the time the Ming rolled around, it was one of Zhèjiāng's most important commercial centres. The town shares the typical features of other southern water towns – arched bridges, canals, narrow lanes and old houses – but what sets it apart is its intriguing mix of Chinese and European architecture, introduced by affluent silk merchants who once made their homes here.

⊙ Sights

Since **Nánxún** (adult/student through ticket ¥100/50; ⏱8am-5pm summer, to 4.30pm winter) isn't large, it won't take more than a couple of hours to see everything. The entrance fee includes all sights. On the back of your ticket is a small map to help you find your way around.

100 Room Pavilion
HISTORIC BUILDING

(百间楼; Bǎijiān Lóu) Nánxún's most famous structure is the rambling 100 Room Pavilion in the northeast corner of town. It was built 400 years ago by a wealthy Ming official to supposedly house his servants. It's a bit creaky but in amazingly good shape for being so old.

Little Lotus Villa
GARDENS

(小莲庄; Xiǎolián Zhuāng) Nánxún has some attractive gardens; the loveliest is

Little Lotus Villa, once the private garden of a wealthy Qing official. The villa gets its name from its pristine lotus pond surrounded by ancient camphor trees. Within the garden are some elaborately carved stone gates and a small family shrine.

Jiāyè Library
LIBRARY
(嘉业堂藏书楼; Jiāyètáng Cángshūlóu) Jiāyè Library was once one of the largest private libraries in southeast China. It was home to more than 30,000 books, some dating back to the Tang dynasty. Inside is a large woodblock collection and displays of manuscripts. The library is surrounded by a moat – an effective form of fire prevention in the Qing.

Zhang Family Compound
HISTORIC BUILDING
(张石铭旧宅; Zhāng Shímíng Jiùzhái) The Zhang Family Compound is one of the more interesting old residences in Nánxún. Once owned by a wealthy silk merchant, it was the largest and most elaborate private residence in southeastern China during the late Qing dynasty. The home was constructed with wood, glass, tiles and marble, all imported from France. The buildings are an intriguing combination of European and Chinese architecture surrounded by delicate gardens, fish ponds and rockeries. Most incongruous is a French-style mansion with red-brick walls, wrought-iron balconies and louvred shutters. Amazingly there's even a ballroom inside, complete with bandstand. This fondness for Western architecture is also seen in the Liu Family Compound (刘氏梯号; Liúshì Tīhào) with its imported stained glass, heavy wooden staircases and red-brick exterior.

 Eating

It's pleasant after a day of walking to relax at one of the small restaurants facing the canal for a snack or some tea. You'll need to bargain for your meal; don't accept the first price you're given.

Getting There & Away

Buses leave hourly from Hángzhōu's north bus station for Nánxún (¥40, 10 daily). Buses also link Nánxún and Wūzhèn (¥10). Regular buses run from Shànghǎi south bus station (¥47, 2½ hours, eight per day). Buses also run from the main Shànghǎi bus station (¥48).

Nánxún has two bus stations: the Tài'ān Lù station (Tài'ān Lù chēzhàn) and another station (Nánxún qìchēzhàn) by the expressway. Both stations have buses from 5.50am to 5pm:
Shànghǎi ¥30 to ¥50, 2½ hours
Sūzhōu ¥21, one hour

ZHĒJIĀNG NÁNXÚN

SHÀOXĪNG

With its winding canals, arched bridges and antiquated homesteads, Shàoxīng (绍兴) is a large water town 67km southeast of Hángzhōu. The town has been the birthplace of many influential and colourful figures, including mythical 'flood tamer' the Great Yu, painter and dramatist Xu Wei, female revolutionary hero Qiu Jin and China's first great modern novelist, Lu Xun, who lived here until he went abroad to study. He later returned to China, but was forced to hide out in Shànghǎi's French Concession when the Kuomintang decided his books were too dangerous.

Sights linked to Lu Xun are clustered along Lu Xun Zhonglu (鲁迅中路), including **Lu Xun's Former Residence** (鲁迅故居; Lǔ Xùn Gùjū; 393 Lu Xun Zhonglu; ⏱8.30am-5pm); the **Lu Xun Memorial Hall** (鲁迅纪念馆; Lǔ Xùn Jìniànguǎn; ⏱8am-5pm), at the same location; and the **Lu Xun Ancestral Residence** (鲁迅祖居; Lǔxùn Zǔjū; 237 Lu Xun Zhonglu). Opposite is the one-room school (Sānwèi Shūwū) the writer attended as a young boy. All sights are free but you need to register by showing your passport at the nearby **Tourist Centre Ticket Office** (免费领票处; Miǎnfèi Lǐngpiàochù; ⏱8.30am-5pm).

Shàoxīng can easily be done as a day trip from Hángzhōu, where accommodation options are superior and more enjoyable. For eats, the **Āpó Miànguǎn** (阿婆面馆; ☎8513 0826; 100 Lu Xun Zhonglu; meals ¥20; ⏱9am-11pm) does excellent noodle dishes.

The quickest way to reach Shàoxīng is by D class train (¥19 to ¥22, 40 minutes, six daily) from Hángzhōu Main Train Station, but plentiful long-distance buses run to Hángzhōu south bus station (¥26, one hour, every 20 minutes) and Shànghǎi south long-distance bus station (¥80, three hours, regular). Shàoxīng taxis start at ¥7.

Wǔyì 武义

☎ 0579

Located far inland, Wǔyì is itself an uninspiring city, but it is the gateway to the two villages of Yúyuán and Guōdòng in the surrounding scenic hilly countryside. It is preferable to spend the night in Guōdòng, which has more character and charm, but if you wish to stay in Wǔyì, hotels can be found near the long-distance bus station.

The **Hóngdá Hotel** (鸿达大酒店; Hóngdá Dàjiǔdiàn; ☎ 8762 2001; 2 Jiefang Beilu; 解放北路 2号; s & tw with computer ¥218, d ¥258; ❊ @) has a grim lift but rooms are pleasant and clean with wood flooring, some with computer and discounts of around 60%; ask for the slightly pricier refurbished rooms.

Several popular fish restaurants can be found by the Shúxī River next to Jiěfàng Bridge on Shuxi Beilu (熟溪北路).

ℹ Information

Several internet cafes are stuffed into the Zǐjīn Wǔshèng Shāngyè Zhōngxīn (紫金五圣商业中心) block on the corner of Shang Jie (上街) and Jiefang Zhonglu (解放中路), opposite KFC.

Bank of China (中国银行; Zhōngguó Yínháng; 71 Hushanxia Jie) In the south of town; has foreign currency exchange.

ICBC (工商银行; Gōngshāng Yínháng; Wuyang Lu) Has a 24-hour ATM.

Péngkè Wǎngbā (朋客网吧; Jiefang Beijie; per hr ¥2.50; ⊙24hr) For internet access.

ℹ Getting There & Around

Buses 2 and 302 connect the train station and the main bus station.

Bus

Buses run to and from Wǔyì's **main bus station** (客运中心; kèyùn zhōngxīn; ☎ 8851 5959) from Hángzhōu south bus station (¥76, six per day from 7.10am to 4.40pm), Níngbō (¥85, three per day) and Wēnzhōu (8.30am).

Train

Wǔyì is easy to reach by train from a number of destinations:

Hángzhōu hard/soft seat ¥38/57, 3½ to four hours, six daily

Nánjīng hard/soft sleeper ¥159/244, 9½ to 13 hours, four daily

Shànghǎi South Train Station hard/soft sleeper ¥101/156, six hours, one daily

Wēnzhōu hard/soft seat ¥38/57, four to five hours, 12 daily

Around Wǔyì

GUŌDÒNG 郭洞

Embraced by bamboo-clad hills and dating to the Song dynasty, this lovely old Zhèjiāng village (through ticket ¥30) is miles away from it all south of Wǔyì. Exquisite in parts, Guōdòng offers ample opportunity for threading through ancient and cramped Ming-dynasty lanes with their even brickwork and mud-packed walls, past washer women, ancient wells and antique shops, and trekking in the surrounding scenery. Note the lovely brickwork along Qingyuan Lu (清源路), which is where you also find a small church (in a courtyard, next to 20 Qingyuan Lu). The **Ancestral Hall of the He Clan** (何氏宗祠; Héshì Zōngcí) is a huge affair at the heart of the village, originally dating to the Ming dynasty. Also worth looking out for are the Fányù Hall (凡豫堂) and the Rènlán Hall (纫兰堂; Rènlán Táng).

Beware if you've a fear of canines, Guōdòng has a large population of barking dogs.

Some homesteads are graced with Christian posters on their doors, while others are decorated with lovely poetic couplets celebrating the rhythms of nature, such as '近山识鸟音、临水知鱼性' (Enter the mountains to know the sounds of birds, face the water to know the nature of fish). After you have explored the village, wander along Longshan Lu (龙山路) and up into the bamboo and woods in the hill above the village (admission included in ticket).

A highlight is the **Dàwān Lake Scenic Area** (大弯湖景区; Dàwānhú Jǐngqū; admission ¥5), a 30-minute walk out of the village (follow the signs) past the Wénchāng Pavilion (文昌阁; Wénchāng Gé) and a vast, 600-year-old fir tree. At the lake, cross over the dam and wander round the lake with its dark pine-green waters picturesquely surrounded by forests of bamboo.

It's well worth spending the night in Guōdòng (rather than Wǔyì) and the village has more character than Yúyuán. Near the bus drop-off is the small **Qīngyuán Hotel** (清源旅馆; Qīngyuán Lǚguǎn; ☎ 6890 3801; d ¥80; ❊), with clean and modern rooms with flat-screen TVs.

All hotels either have restaurants or can fix you a meal, but avoid being pushed towards *tǔjī* (free-range chicken) unless you really want it, as it is expensive. A small plate of *xiǎo xīyú* (小溪鱼; grilled river fish) should cost around ¥18.

To reach Guódòng, take bus 5 (¥1.50) to the east bus station (客运东站; *kèyùn dōngzhàn*) in Wǔyì and hop on a Guódòng-bound bus (¥3.50, one hour, every 30 minutes) collecting passengers across the road. Returning to Wǔyì, the first/last bus from Guódòng is at 7am/5.50pm.

YÚYUÁN   俞源

Around 20km away through the glittering Zhèjiāng countryside from Wǔyì, past mountains, fields of tea bushels, yellow and green bamboo, old bridges and fields of rapeseed is the riverside village of Yúyuán. The **ancient village** (admission ¥30) is famously based on the arrangement of the Taoist Taiji (twin fish) diagram, although this can be hard to discern if you don't have a definitive interest in feng shui.

◎ Sights

With its whitewashed residences, ancient halls, old doorways decorated with hanging red couplets, carved woodwork, cobbled lanes, crowing cocks and waddling geese, the village has an abundance of historic charm.

Old Buildings   HISTORIC BUILDINGS

Hidden away behind towering trees, the **Hall of Bowen** (伯温草堂; *Bówēn Cǎotáng*) is an attractive old structure, decorated with Taiji symbols. Originally dating to 1374, the **Ancestral Hall of the Yu Clan** (俞氏宗祠; *Yúshì Zōngcí*) is a lovely and unrestored collection of halls around a magnificently carved stage daubed at the rear with a conspicuous slogan from the Cultural Revolution. At the rear is the **Qín Táng** (寝堂), where the tablets of the ancestors resided. The hall once burned down and was rebuilt, a battalion camped in the hall in 1930 and it served as a grain storage depot in 1951. Also track down the **Ancestral Hall of the Li Clan** (李氏宗祠; *Lǐshì Zōngcí*) – in need of repair – with its light well (*tiānjǐng*) courtyard and side halls bedecked with folk articles.

Several of the village's **old residences** – many in need of restoration – are still occupied, such as Dūnhòu Táng (敦厚堂) and the Xiàtài Lóu (下态楼). Also look out for the lovely wood-fronted Hóngbīn Lóu (鸿宾楼) by the Yín River (银河; Yín Hé), the lovely Jīngshēn Lóu (精深楼), the ample Yùhòu Táng (裕后堂) – occupying 2560 sq m – and the **Shēngyuǎn Táng** (声远堂; also called Liùfēng Hall), one of the most ambitious

and best-preserved of Yúyuán's halls. A fair amount of Yúyuán's feng shui charm has been irreversibly ruined by modern eyesore attachments thrown up willy-nilly and white-tile buildings with aluminium shuttering that overlook old residences.

Temple of the Cave Host   TAOIST, TEMPLE

(洞主庙; *Dòngzhǔ Miào*) Next to a bridge and by a large camphor tree by the river on the outskirts of Yúyuán, the lovely Taoist Temple of the Cave Host originally dates to the Northern Song and is seemingly one of the best preserved buildings in the village.

❶ Getting There & Away

To reach Yúyuán, take a direct bus (¥4.50, 30 minutes, every 30 minutes, first/last bus 6.30am/5.30pm) from the west bus station (西站; *Xīzhàn*) in Wǔyì. Bus 5 (¥1.50) runs between the main bus station in Wǔyì and the west bus station.

Pǔtuóshān   普陀山

✓ 0580

The lush and well-tended Buddhist island of Pǔtuóshān – the Zhōushān Archipelago's most celebrated isle – is the abode of Guanyin, the eternally compassionate Goddess of Mercy. One of China's four sacred Buddhist mountains, Pǔtuóshān is permeated with the aura of the goddess and the devotion of her worshippers. Endless boatloads of visitors, however, frequently upset the island's sacred nimbus, especially as access has improved in recent years. During holiday periods and weekends things can get rampant (aim for a midweek visit). Commercialism long ago ensnared Pǔtuóshān: Buddhist chants emerge from speakers camouflaged as rocks and something has been lost in the deliberate prettification of the island. To underline this, the island was reportedly considering a multimillion-dollar stock market flotation in 2012. Guanyin's three birthdays (19 February, 19 June and 19 September) are celebrated with gusto across the island.

◎ Sights

A crippling **entrance fee** (summer/winter ¥160/140) is payable when you arrive; entry to some other sights is extra.

Images of Guanyin are ubiquitous and Pǔtuóshān's temples are all shrines for the merciful goddess. Besides the three main

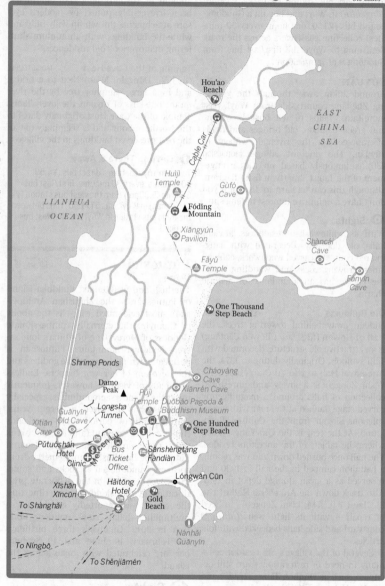

0 ——— 1 km
0 ——— 0.5 miles

Hou'ao Beach

EAST CHINA SEA

Cable Car

Huìjì Temple

Gùfó Cave

LIANHUA OCEAN

Fódīng Mountain

Xiāngyún Pavilion

Shàncái Cave

Fǎyǔ Temple

Fànyīn Cave

One Thousand Step Beach

Shrimp Ponds

Cháoyáng Cave

Damo Peak

Pǔjì Temple

Xiānrén Cave

Duōbǎo Pagoda & Buddhism Museum

Guānyīn Old Cave

Longsha Tunnel

Xītiān Cave

One Hundred Step Beach

Pǔtuóshān Hotel

Clinic

Bus Ticket Office

Sānshèngtáng Fàndiàn

Xīshān Xīncūn

Hǎitōng Hotel

Lóngwān Cūn

To Shànghǎi

Gold Beach

Nánhǎi Guānyīn

To Níngbō

To Shěnjiāmén

temples, you will stumble upon nunneries and monasteries everywhere you turn, while decorative archways may suddenly appear from the sea mist.

The central part of the island is around Pǔjì Temple about 1km north of the ferry terminal, reachable by taking the roads leading east or west from the ferry terminal; either way takes about 20 minutes. Alternatively, minibuses from the ferry terminal run to Pǔjì Temple and to other points of the island.

Pǔjì Temple TEMPLE

(普济禅寺; Pǔjì Sì; admission ¥5; ⊙5.30am-6pm) Fronted by large ponds and over-looked by towering camphor trees and Luóhàn pines, and undergoing restora-tion at the time of writing, this temple stands by the main square and dates to at least the 17th century. Past chubby Milefo sitting in a red, gold and green burnished cabinet in the Hall of Heavenly Kings, throngs of worshippers stand with flaming incense in front of the stunning main hall. Buses leave from the west side of the temple to various points around the island. South-west of the temple is the enchanting and tranquil **Pǔtuó Mountain Botanical Garden** (admission free).

FREE Buddhism Museum MUSEUM

(佛教博物馆; Fójiào Bówùguǎn; ⊙9am-3pm Tue-Sun) A short walk from Pǔjì temple is the five-storey **Duōbǎo Pagoda** (多宝塔; Duōbǎo Tǎ), built in 1334. Next door stands the brand-new and ambitiously cre-ated Buddhism Museum which affords an intriguing glimpse at the culture of Bud-dhism by way of displays of ritual imple-ments, Buddhist objects, ceramics and artefacts.

Fǎyǔ Temple TEMPLE

(法雨禅寺; Fǎyǔ Chánsì; admission ¥5; ⊙5.30am-6pm) Colossal camphor trees and a huge gingko tree tower over this temple, where a vast glittering statue of Guanyin is seated in the main hall, flanked by rows of historic *luóhàn* effigies. In the hall behind stands a 1000-arm Guanyin. Get to the temple by bus from the ferry terminal (¥6).

Fódǐng Mountain MOUNTAIN

(佛顶山; Fódǐng Shān; admission ¥5) A fantas-tic, shaded half-hour climb can be made from Fǎyǔ Temple to Fódǐng Mountain – Buddha's Summit Peak – the highest point on the island. This is also where you will find the less elaborate **Huìjì Temple** (慧济禅寺; Huìjì Chánsì; admission ¥5; ⊙5.30am-6.30pm). In summer the climb is much cooler in the late afternoon; watch devout pilgrims and Buddhist nuns stop every three steps to either bow or kneel in supplication. The less motivated take the **cable car** (one way/return ¥30/50; ⊙6.40am-5pm). The Xiāngyún Pavilion (香云亭; Xiāngyún Tíng) is a pleasant spot for a breather.

Nánhǎi Guānyīn STATUE

(南海观音; admission ¥6) The first thing you see as you approach Pǔtuóshān by boat is this 33m-high glittering statue of Guanyin, overlooking the waves at the southernmost tip of the island.

Beaches BEACHES

Pǔtuóshān's two large beaches, **One Hun-dred Step Beach** (百步沙; Bǎibùshā; ⊙6am-6pm) and **One Thousand Step Beach** (千步沙; Qiānbùshā) on the east of the island are attractive and largely unspoilt, although periodically you may have to pay for access; swimming (May through August) is not permitted after 6pm, but it's lovely to plonk down on the sand in the early evening in warm weather.

Caves CAVES

Fànyīn Cave (梵音洞; Fànyīn Dòng; admis-sion ¥5; ⊙5.30am-6pm), on the far eastern tip of the island, has a temple dedicated to Guanyin perched between two cliffs with a seagull's view of the crashing waves below. The sound of the roaring waves in **Cháoyáng Cave** (朝阳洞; Cháoyáng Dòng; ad-mission ¥12), which overlooks the sea, is said to imitate the chanting of the Buddha. A fully fledged temple has been assembled around the small grotto of the Guānyīn Old Cave (观音古洞; Guānyīn Gǔdòng). Other natural wonders include the **Shàncái Cave** (善财洞; Shàncái Dòng; admission ¥5), **Gǔfó Cave** (古佛洞; Gǔfó Dòng; admission ¥5), **Xiānrén Cave** (仙人洞; Xiānrén Dòng; admission ¥5) and **Xītiān Cave** (西天洞; Xītiān Dòng; admission ¥5).

🛏 Sleeping

Most hotels on Pǔtuóshān are squarely aimed at tour groups and holidaying Chi-nese, so prices are not cheap. Room rates are generally discounted from Sunday to Thursday; prices given here refer to Friday and Saturday and holiday periods.

As you leave the arrivals building, local hotel touts flapping plastic photo sheets of their hotels will descend; these rooms are generally at the cheaper end in a nearby village, not luxurious, but serviceable and more affordable than many other hotels on the island. Alternatively, turn left upon exiting the arrivals building and walk to the cheap hotels clustering off Meicen Lu in Xīshān Xīncūn (西山新村), a short walk over the hill to the west from the ferry ter-minal. They are all very similar, with stand-ard singles, twins and perhaps triples. Some hotels may not take foreigners, but others should (speaking Chinese helps); rooms go for around ¥100 to ¥150 on a weekday but will rise considerably at weekends; bargain for your room. Look for the characters '内有住宿', which means rooms are available. Several of the larger hotels have shuttle buses to and from the pier.

Pǔtuóshān Hotel
HOTEL $$$

(普陀山大酒店; Pǔtuóshān Dàjiǔdiàn; ☑609 2828; www.putuoshanhotel.com; 93 Meicen Lu; 梅岑路93号; d ¥1668-2268, ste from ¥2568; ❀@) Maximising its feng shui by backing onto a green hill, Pǔtuóshān's finest hotel has a pleasant and uncluttered feel, with agreeable rooms and service to match. Many other Pǔtuóshān hotels are overwhelmed with Buddhist kitsch, avoided here. Discounts of up to 70% are regular midweek.

Sānshèngtáng Fàndiàn
HOTEL $$$

(三圣堂饭店; ☑609 3688; 121 Miaozhuang Yanlu; 妙庄严路121号; d ¥800-1040, tr ¥1020; ❀) Often full, this traditional-style place is attractively set among trees off a small path near Pǔjì Temple. Rooms are rather musty but generally go for around ¥300 during slack times.

Hǎitōng Hotel
HOTEL $$$

(海通宾馆; Hǎitōng Bīnguǎn; ☑609 2569; r ¥780-1180; ❀) Across the road as you exit the ferry terminal, this agreeable place has helpful staff and a tempting traditional feel. Midweek discounts are as high as 60% to 70%; weekend discounts of 30% sometimes available.

✖ Eating

With a focus on seafood and hotel dining, eating on Pǔtuóshān is expensive, unless you eat at places such as the noodle restaurants in small villages such as Xīshān Xīncūn (eateries are off Meicen Lu) and also in Lóngwān Cūn (龙湾村), the village east of the Citic Putuo Hotel (22 Jinsha Lu). Some of the best places to eat are in the temples, where vegetarian lunches are usually served and sometimes breakfast and dinner for ¥2 to ¥10.

❶ Information

Bank of China (中国银行; Zhōngguó Yínháng; 85-7 Meicen Lu; ⊙8-11am & 2-5pm) Forex currency exchange. ATMs (24-hour) taking international cards for the Bank of China and other banks are down the side of the block (which is called 'Financial Street').

China Mobile (中国移动; Zhōngguó Yídòng; Meicen Lu) For mobile phone SIM cards. Located near the banks.

China Post (中国邮政; Zhōngguó Yóuzhèng; 124 Meicen Lu) Southwest of Pǔjì Temple.

Clinic (诊所; Zhěnsuǒ; ⊙8am-5pm) Situated down the side of the block behind the Bank of China.

ICBC (工行; Gōngshāng Yínháng; 85-15 Meicen Lu; ⊙8-11am & 2-5pm) Forex currency exchange.

Left-luggage office (寄存处; jìcúnchù; per luggage piece ¥4; ⊙6.30am-5pm) At the ferry terminal.

Tourist Service Centre (旅游咨询中心; Lǚyóu Zīxún Zhōngxīn; ☑609 4921; ⊙9am-6pm) Near Pǔjì Temple.

❶ Getting There & Away

The shortest and fastest ferry crossing to Pǔtuóshān is from Shěnjiāmén (沈家门) on the neighbouring island of Zhōushān (舟山岛), from where fast boats (¥28, 15 minutes) head every 10 minutes between 6.20am and 5.30pm for the short hop to Pǔtuóshān. Slower boats (¥22) also run, but less frequently. The recent construction of bridges lashing the principle islands of the Zhōushān archipelago to the mainland means you can largely make the trip by bus from Shànghǎi or Hángzhōu.

Tickets for buses to Hángzhōu (¥95, first/last bus 6.20am/6.50pm, regular) and Shànghǎi Nánpǔdàqiáo (¥138, five hours, first/last bus 6.30am/6pm, regular) from Shěnjiāmén are available from the **passenger ferry terminal ticket office** (☑609 1186), from the **bus ticket office** (74 Meicen Lu; ⊙8-10.40am & 1.20-4.15pm) opposite the Pǔtuóshān Hotel or at the bus station by the wharf in Shěnjiāmén.

The nearest airport is Zhōushān (Pǔtuóshān) airport on the neighbouring island of Zhūjiājiān (朱家尖), linked to Pǔtuóshān by regular fast boats (¥24) between 6.30am and 5.30pm.

A more sedate way to journey is on the night boat that leaves Pǔtuóshān at 4.40pm for the 12-hour voyage to Shànghǎi's Wúsōng Wharf. Offering numerous grades of comfort from 4th class to special class, tickets cost ¥109 to ¥499 (or ¥998 for your own room); it's easy to upgrade (bǔpiào) once you're on board. From Shànghǎi, the boat leaves Wúsōng Wharf at 8pm, with an extra two services on Friday at 7.20pm and 8.40pm. To reach Wúsōng Wharf, take metro line 3 to Songbin Rd, from where it's a 15-minute walk. Cross the eight-lane highway and follow the signs to the wharf. Bank on a 1½-hour journey from People's Square.

A fast boat (¥255 to ¥340) departs Pǔtuóshān for the port of Xiǎo Yáng Shān (小洋山) south of Shànghǎi at 1.30pm, where passengers are then bussed to Nánpǔ Bridge; the whole trip takes four hours. The twice-daily bus/ferry from Shànghǎi to Pǔtuóshān departs from Xiǎo Yáng Shān; shuttle buses depart Nánpǔ Bridge in Shànghǎi at 7.20am and 8am to connect with them.

Tickets for all of the above boats can either be bought at the ticket office at the jetty/arrivals halls or from the office at 74 Meicen Lu, opposite the Pǔtuóshān Hotel.

Other boats from Pǔtuóshān include fast ferries to Níngbō (¥83, first/last boat 7.40am/5.20pm, 10 per day) on the Zhèjiāng coast; the trip takes about 2½ hours, including the bus ride to the fast boat wharf outside Níngbō. Buses (¥60, three hours, every 30 minutes) from the **Níngbō north bus station** (qìchē běizhàn; ☑ 8735 5321; 122 Taodu Lu) run to Shěnjiāmén.

Tickets for both ferry and bus/ferry services are available at the travel agents in the **shop** (☑ 6336 8600; 21 East Jinling Rd; 金陵东路 21号; ⊙ 9am-6pm; Ⓜ East Nanjing Rd) on East Jinling Rd in Shànghǎi.

ℹ Getting Around

Walking around Pǔtuóshān is the most relaxing option if you have time. In recent years, wooden walkways have been added to sections of the island in an ongoing program which makes it easier on the knees and feet for pedestrians, and safer than walking on the roads. Minibuses zip from the passenger ferry terminal to various points around the island, including Pǔjì Temple (¥5), One Thousand Step Beach (¥6), Fǎyǔ Temple (¥6), Fànyīn Cave (¥8) and the cable car station (¥10). Bus stop signs are in English and Chinese. There are more bus stations at Pǔjì Temple, Fǎyǔ Temple and other spots around the island serving the same and other destinations.

ZHÈJIĀNG PǓTUÓSHĀN

Fújiàn

POP 36.8 MILLION

Includes »

Xiàmén	272
Gǔlàng Yǔ	277
Fújiàn Tǔlóu	280
Quánzhōu	284
Around Quánzhōu	286
Fúzhōu	287
Wǔyí Shān	288

Best Temples

» Nánpǔtuó Temple (p273)

» Kāiyuán Temple (p284)

» Cǎo'ān Manichean Temple (p287)

» Guāndì Temple (p284)

Best Tǔlóu Clusters

» Tiánluókēng Tǔlóu Cluster (p282)

» Gāoběi Tǔlóu Cluster (p282)

» Hóngkēng Tǔlóu Cluster (p281)

» Yúnshuǐyáo Tǔlóu Cluster (p282)

Why Go?

If you talk to Chinese descendents in Southeast Asia or in Taiwan, you're likely to find that many of them have roots that go back several centuries in Fújiàn (福建) on China's southern coast. With a seafaring mentality, Fújiàn used to be one of the windows that connected China to the outside world. Its multicultural heritage still stands beautifully in Xiàmén and Quánzhōu, where you can glimpse the region's glorious maritime past.

Moving inland, rolling hills are dotted with some of the quirkiest buildings in China. Rising like castles, the marvellous *tǔlóu* (roundhouses) in Fújiàn's southwest will add delight to your China experience. Heading northwest, the mountainous Wǔyí Shān offers hiking opportunities galore.

The slow-tempo harbour city of Xiàmén is a useful first port of call. From here, you can drift to the popular isle of Gǔlàng Yǔ, or the more enchanting Taiwanese island of Kinmen.

When to Go
Xiàmén

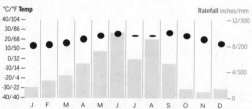

Mar & Apr Beat the summer heat with a springtime visit to the World Heritage–listed *tǔlóu*.

Jun & Sep Visit the breezy coast of Xiàmén and island-hop in summer or autumn.

Oct Low-season prices and clear mountain air coalesce in the rugged, lush Wǔyí Shān.

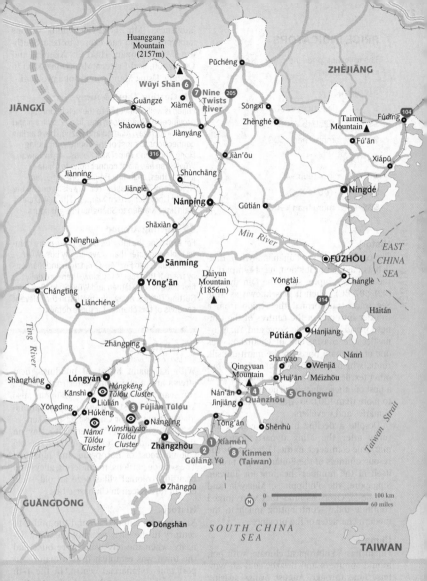

Fújiàn Highlights

① Wander around the breezy **Xiàmén** (p272), one of China's most attractive cities

② Lose yourself in the warren of back lanes in **Gǔlàng Yǔ** (p277), an island packed with colourful colonial villas

③ Explore the region's World Heritage Site, **Fújiàn tǔlóu** (p280), massive, semi-enclosed earthen edifices that are the ancient equivalents of modern-day condos

④ Conjure up the vanished era of China's maritime glory in **Quánzhōu** (p284)

⑤ Amble down the alleys and ramparts of the walled city of **Chóngwǔ** (p286), one of the best preserved in China

⑥ Hike and marvel at some of Fújiàn's most magnificent terrain at **Wǔyí Shān** (p288)

⑦ Float on a raft down the **Nine Twists River** (p288) and look for boat-shaped coffins in cavities along the rock faces

⑧ Detour to pretty **Kinmen** (p279), Taiwan's closest island outpost to China

PRICE INDICATORS

The following price indicators are used in this chapter:

Sleeping

$	less than ¥250
$$	¥250 to ¥500
$$$	more than ¥500

Eating

$	less than ¥40
$$	¥40 to ¥90
$$$	more than ¥90

History

The coastal region of Fújiàn, known in English as Fukien or Hokkien, has been part of the Chinese empire since the Qin dynasty (221–207 BC), when it was known as Min. Sea trade transformed the region from a frontier into one of the centres of the Chinese world. During the Song and Yuan dynasties the coastal city of Quánzhōu was one of the main ports on the maritime silk route, which transported not only silk but other textiles, precious stones, porcelain and a host of other valuables. The city was home to more than 100,000 Arab merchants, missionaries and travellers.

Despite a decline in the province's fortunes after the Ming dynasty restricted maritime commerce in the 15th century, the resourcefulness of the Fújiàn people proved itself in the numbers heading for Taiwan, Singapore, the Philippines, Malaysia and Indonesia. Overseas links that were forged continue today, contributing much to the modern character of the province.

Climate

Fújiàn has a subtropical climate, with hot, humid summers and drizzly, cold-ish winters. June through August brings soaring temperatures and humidity, and torrential rains and typhoons are common. In the mountainous regions, winters can be fiercely cold. The best times to visit are spring (March to May) and autumn (September to October).

Language

Fújiàn is one of the most linguistically diverse provinces in China. Locals speak variations of the Min dialect, which includes Taiwanese. Min is divided into various subgroups – you can expect to hear Southern Min (Mǐnnán Huà) in Xiàmén and Quánzhōu, and Eastern Min (Dōng Mǐn) in Fúzhōu. Using Mandarin is not a problem.

ⓘ Getting There & Away

Fújiàn is well connected to the neighbouring provinces of Guǎngdōng and Jiāngxī by train and coastal highway. Xiàmén and Fúzhōu have airline connections to most of the country, including Hong Kong, and Taipei and Kaohsiung in Taiwan. Wǔyí Shān has flight connections to China's larger cities, including Běijīng, Shànghǎi and Hong Kong. The coastal freeway also goes all the way to Hong Kong from Xiàmén. The new D class train links Xiàmén to Shànghǎi in eight hours.

ⓘ Getting Around

For exploring the interior, D trains are more comfortable and safer than travelling by bus. Wǔyí Shān is linked to Fúzhōu, Quánzhōu and Xiàmén by train. If the train is too slow, there are daily flights between Xiàmén and Wǔyí Shān. See the Getting There & Away information in the relevant sections of this chapter for more details.

Xiàmén 厦门

☏ 0592 / POP 668,000

With its quaint historical buildings, neat streets and a charming waterfront district, you can understand why Xiàmén, also known to the West as Amoy, is a popular holiday destination for Chinese flashpackers.

The highlight of Xiàmén is to stay on the tiny island of Gǔlàng Yǔ, once the old colonial roost of Europeans and Japanese. The seaside gardens, meandering alleys and beautiful colonial villas ooze an old-world charm rarely seen in Chinese cities.

History

Xiàmén was founded around the mid-14th century in the early years of the Ming dynasty, when the city walls were built and the town was established as a major seaport and commercial centre. In the 17th century it became a place of refuge for the Ming rulers fleeing the Manchu invaders. Xiàmén and nearby Jīnmén were bases for the Ming armies who, under the command of the general Koxinga, raised their anti-Manchu battlecry, 'resist the Qing and restore the Ming'.

The Portuguese arrived in the 16th century, followed by the British in the 17th century, and later by the French and the Dutch, all attempting, rather unsuccessfully, to establish Xiàmén as a trade port. The port was closed to foreigners in the 1750s and it was not until the Opium Wars that the tide turned. In August 1841 a British naval force of 38 ships carrying artillery and soldiers sailed into Xiàmén harbour, forcing the port to open. Xiàmén then became one of the first treaty ports.

Japanese and Western powers followed soon after, establishing consulates and making Gǔlàng Yǔ a foreign enclave. Xiàmén turned Japanese in 1938 and remained that way until 1945.

Sights & Activities

The town of Xiàmén is on the island of the same name. It's connected to the mainland by a 5km-long causeway bearing a railway, a Bus Rapid Transit (BRT) line, road and footpath. The most absorbing part of Xiàmén is near the western (waterfront) district, directly opposite the small island of Gǔlàng Yǔ. This is the old area of town, known for its colonial architecture, parks and winding streets.

FREE Nánpǔtuó Temple   BUDDHIST

(南普陀寺; Nánpǔtuó Sì; Siming Nanlu; admission ¥3; ☺8am-6pm) This Buddhist temple complex on the southern side of Xiàmén is one of the most famous temples among the Fujianese, and is also considered a pilgrimage site by dedicated followers from Southeast Asia. The temple has been repeatedly destroyed and rebuilt. Its latest incarnation dates to the early 20th century, and today it's an active and busy temple with chanting monks and worshippers lighting incense.

The temple is fronted by a huge lotus lake. In front of the courtyard is the twin-eaved **Big Treasure Hall** (Dàxióng Bǎodiàn), presided over by a trinity of Buddhas representing his past, present and future forms. Behind rises the eight-sided **Hall of Great Compassion** (Dàbēi Diàn), in which stands a golden 1000-armed statue of Guanyin, facing the four directions.

The temple has an excellent **vegetarian restaurant** (dishes ¥20-50; ☺10.30am-4pm) in a shaded courtyard where you can dine in the company of resident, mobile phone-toting monks. Round it all off with a hike up the steps behind the temple among the rocks and the shade of trees.

Take bus 1 from the train station or bus 21, 45, 48 or 503 from Zhongshan Lu to reach the temple.

Xiàmén University   HISTORIC BUILDING

(厦门大学; Xiàmén Dàxué) Next to Nánpǔtuó Temple and established with overseas Chinese funds, the university has beautiful republican-era buildings and an attractive lake. It's a good place for a pleasant stroll. The **anthropology museum** (人类学博物馆; Rénlèixué Bówùguǎn) in the campus boasts two large 'boat coffins' unearthed from a cliff in Wǔyí Shān. The campus entrance is next to the stop for bus 1.

Húlǐ Shān Fortress   MILITARY BUILDING

(胡里山炮台; Húlǐ Shān Pàotái; admission ¥25; ☺7.30am-5.30pm) Across Daxue Lu, south of the university, is this gigantic German gun artillery built in 1893. You can rent binoculars to peer over the water to the Taiwanese-occupied island of Kinmen (金门; Jīnmén; see boxed text, p279), formerly known as Quemoy and claimed by both mainland China and Taiwan. Boats (¥126) do circuits of Jīnmén from the **passenger ferry terminal** (客运码头; kèyùn mǎtóu; ☎298 5551) off Lujiang Lu.

FREE Overseas Chinese Museum   MUSEUM

(华侨博物馆; Huáqiáo Bówùguǎn; 73 Siming Nanlu; ☺9.30am-4.30pm Tue-Sun) An ambitious celebration of China's communities abroad, with dioramas, street scenes, photos and props.

Kāihé Lù Fish Market   MARKET

(开禾路菜市场; Kāihélù Càishìchǎng; Kaihe Lu) In the old district of Xiàmén, this tiny but lively market sells various (weird) sea creatures with historical covered balcony buildings and a church as a backdrop. Access from Xiahe Lu.

Tours

China International Travel Service (CITS; p276) and many larger hotels can also help with tours.

Apple Travel   TRAVEL AGENCY

(☎505 3122; www.appletravel.cn; Shop 20, Guanren Lu) Pricey but can help arrange tours to the Hakka *tǔlóu* and Wǔyí Shān. Also organises English-speaking guides.

Festivals & Events

Xiàmén International Marathon   MARATHON

(www.xmim.org) Held in January, and draws local and international participants. Runners race around the coastal ring road that circles the island.

Xiàmén & Gǔlàng Yǔ

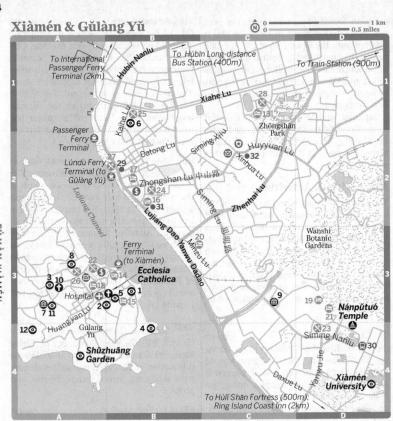

Dragon Boat Races   DRAGON BOATING
Held in Xiàmén at the Dragon Pool (龙舟池;
Lóngzhōu Chí) in Jíměi (集美) every June,
they are quite a sight.

🛏 Sleeping

Xiàmén is a popular, year-round destination in China, so making a reservation well
in advance is essential. Hotels are clustered
around the harbour and most are midrange,
shading top end.

There's a wide range of top-end accommodation in Xiàmén, but much of it is badly
located in the eastern part of town. Most
places offer 40% discounts.

TOP CHOICE **21 Howtel**   HOTEL **$$**
(☑205 0321; www.21howtel.com, in Chinese; 21
Huaxin Lu; 华新路21号; s¥238, tw¥268-388; ❄@)
Tucked away in a tranquil neighbourhood of
1950s mansions, this quaint old villa has 14
rooms, every one of which is different. The

whole place is a combination of clean and
homey. Booking is a pain though. Walk in and
try your luck, or reserve at least three weeks
in advance. Not all the staffers speak English.

Hotel Indigo Xiàmén Harbour   HOTEL **$$$**
(厦门海港英迪格酒店; Xiàmén Hǎigǎng Yīndígé
Jiǔdiàn; ☑226 1666; www.hotelindigo.com; 16 Lujiang Dao; 鹭江道16号; d¥2600-3600, discounts
around 50%; ❄❄@) This newest chain hotel addition to the waterfront district has
found a balance between funky and kitschy
in its design and decor. Both business travellers and tourists will appreciate the central location and the generous number of
rooms with sweeping harbour views. Staff
are attentive.

Xiàmén International Youth Hostel   HOSTEL **$**
(厦门国际青年旅舍; Xiàmén Guójì Qīngnián
Lǚshè; ☑208 2345; www.yhaxm.com; 41 Nanhua
Lu; 南华路41号; dm from ¥55, s ¥80-160, d ¥160-
240; ❄@) With clean dorms and doubles,

Xiàmén & Gǔlàng Yǔ

◎ Top Sights

Ecclesia Catholica	B3
Nánpǔtuó Temple	D4
Shūzhuāng Garden	A4
Xiàmén University	D4

◎ Sights

1	Bo'ai Hospital	B3
	Former British Consulate	(see 1)
2	Former Japanese Consulate	B3
3	Former Law Court	A3
	Former Spanish Consulate	(see 2)
	Guāncǎi Lóu	(see 3)
4	Hàoyuè Garden	B4
5	Huang Rongyuan Villa	B3
6	Kāihé Lù Fish Market	B1
7	Koxinga Memorial Hall	A3
8	Organ Museum	A3
9	Overseas Chinese Museum	C3
10	Sanyi Church	A3
	Statue of Koxinga	(see 4)
	Sunlight Rock	(see 11)
11	Sunlight Rock Park	A3
12	Yīngxióng Hill	A4
	Yìzú Shānzhuāng	(see 3)

🛏 Sleeping

13	21 Howtel	C1
	46Howtel	(see 5)
14	Gǔlàng Yǔ International Youth Hostel	B3
15	Gǔlàng Yǔ Lù Fēi International Youth Hostel	B3
16	Hotel Indigo Xiàmén Harbour	B2
17	Lùjiāng Harbourview Hotel	B2
18	Mogo Cafe Hotel	A3
19	Xiàmén International Youth Hostel	D3
20	Xiàmén Locanda International Youth Hostel	B3
21	Xiàmén Locanda International Youth Hostel	D3

✖ Eating

22	Babycat Café	A3
	Cherry 32 Café	(see 13)
23	Dàfāng Sùcàiguǎn	D4
24	Huángzéhé Peanut Soup Shop	B2
25	Kāihé Shāchámiàn	B1
26	Líjì Mùdān Fishball	A3
27	Lucky Full Seafood City	B2
	Seaview Restaurant	(see 17)
28	Tiānhé Xīmén Túsǔndòng	C1

ⓘ Transport

29	Chūnguāng Hotel (Airport Shuttle Buses)	B2
30	Public Bus Terminal	D4
31	Silk Air	B2
	Thai Airways International	(see 31)
32	Train Ticket Booking Office	C2

this famous hostel is run by an efficient and helpful staff. There's also bike rental, a ticket-booking service, computer stations with internet access (¥2.50 per hour) and the cosy Anywhere Pub. Reservations essential.

Lùjiāng Harbourview Hotel   HOTEL $$$
(鹭江宾馆; Lùjiāng Bīnguǎn; ☎202 2922; www. lujiang-hotel.com; 54 Lujiang Dao; 鹭江道54号; s ¥1345-1450, sea-view d ¥1955-2300, discounts 30%; ❄@) Finally, the rooms in this 1940s structure have received a complete makeover, giving them the modern facilities and quite tasteful furnishings that befit the hotel's four-star billing. It's worth paying more for the spacious sea-view rooms, some of which also boast balconies.

Xiàmén Locanda International Youth Hostel   HOTEL $
(厦门卢卡国际青年旅舍; Xiàmén Lúkǎ Guójì Qīngnián Lǚshè; ☎208 2918; www.locandahostel. com; 35 Minzu Lu; 民族路35号; 4-/6-bed dm ¥60/55, s ¥208, d & tw ¥258; ❄@) This amicable hostel can be easily identified by its ochre walls and a lovely courtyard. All rooms are clean and amber-hued. The dorms are compact, though. It has a **branch** (☎209 9053; 12 Nanhua Lu; 4-/6-bed dm ¥55/50, r ¥198-238; ❄@) not far from Xiàmén International Youth Hostel, which, while being less attractive, offers more spacious rooms.

Ring Island Coast Inn   GUESTHOUSE $$
(环岛海岸客栈; Huándǎo Hǎiàn Kèzhàn; ☎219 6677; www.xm-inn.com; 20 Zeng Cuo An, Huandao Nanlu; 环岛南路曾厝安20号; r ¥150-350; ❄@) Further southeast of Xiàmén University is the fishing village of Zēng Cuō Ān, where family-run guesthouses are mushrooming. This nine-room guesthouse (aka the Blue House) has two cosy rooms with beautiful balcony views of the sea. The cheapest rooms have no attached bathroom. To get there, catch bus 29 from Siming Nanlu.

✖ Eating

Being a port city, Xiàmén is known for its fresh seafood, especially oysters and shrimp. The alleys on both sides of Zhongshan Lu teem with eateries of all shapes and sizes. Yundang Lu (筼筜路), near Marco Polo Hotel, has a long strip of cafes and restaurants popular with expats and trendy locals.

Seaview Restaurant
DIM SUM, FUJIANESE $$
(鹭江宾馆观海厅; Lùjiāng Bīnguǎn Guānhǎitīng; 7th fl, 54 Lujiang Dao; meals from ¥80; ⊘10am-10pm; 🖥) What's better than sipping tea and enjoying freshly made dim sum on a sun-kissed terrace with sweeping harbour views? This rooftop restaurant in Lùjiāng Harbourview Hotel is a choice place to savour Fujianese street snacks in a comfy setting. No English dim sum menu, but you can pick what you want from the cooking stations.

Kāihé Shāchámiàn
NOODLES $
(开禾沙茶面; 126 Xiahe Lu; noodles from ¥12; ⊘24hr) This absolutely no-frills eatery is a perennial favourite of the locals for its *Shāchámiàn* (satay-inspired noodles). The ingredients can be customised but a typical bowl will include shellfish, meatballs and pig innards. Let your fingers do the talking. The shop is identifiable by the yellow characters on the green front panel.

Huángzéhé Peanut Soup Shop
SNACKS $
(黄则和花生汤店; Huángzéhé Huāshēng Tāngdiàn; 20 Zhongshan Lu; snacks ¥4-10; ⊘6.30am-10.30pm) Very popular restaurant with basic service and seating, famed for its delectably sweet

---

NOT FOR THE SQUEAMISH!

Fancy aspic dishes, or some jelly with a difference? *Tǔsǔndòng* (土笋冻), or sandworm jelly, is one of the best loved appetisers in Fújiàn. The sandworms are boiled into a jelly mould and the crunchy end product, an aspic dish, is said to be rich in collagen. Locals love eating them with mustard, cilantro and turnip slices. You'll find the jelly sold in any street food joints, but Amoyers all recommend **Tiānhé Xīmén Tǔsǔndòng** (天河西门土笋冻; 33 Douxi Lu; snacks from ¥10; ⊘8am-10pm) near the west gate of Zhōngshān Park. If the idea of eating worms is too gross for you, the restaurant also serves delicious octopus and ark clams.

---

huāshēng tāng (花生汤; peanut soup) and popular snacks including *hǎlìjiān* (海蛎煎; oyster omelette) and *zhūròu chuàn* (猪肉串; pork kebabs). You need to purchase coupons that you hand over when you order food.

Lucky Full City Seafood
DIM SUM $$
(潮福城; Cháofú Chéng; 28 Hubin Beilu; dim sum from ¥12, meals from ¥70; ⊘10am-10pm; 🖥) Priding itself on MSG-free dim sum and dishes, this extremely popular restaurant is where you'll have to try your luck or wait at least 30 minutes to get a table. Catch a taxi here: the driver will know where it is. It now has a **branch** (33 Lujiang Dao; ⊘8am-2.30am) next to Lúndù Ferry Terminal.

Cherry 32 Cafe
CAFE $$
(32 Huaxin Lu; coffee from ¥45; ⊘11am-11pm; 🖥) Run by 21 Howtel and just a stone's throw from it, Cherry 32 serves arguably the best coffee in town. The very delicate porcelains, the retro phones and clocks on the wall, together with the lovely courtyard, all evoke the mood in a grandma's home. It has a decent selection of wines, too.

Dàfāng Sùcàiguǎn
VEGETARIAN $$
(大方素菜馆; ☎209 3236; 3 Nanhua Lu; dishes ¥28-68; ⊘9am-9.30pm; 🅿🖥) This cheerfully furnished vegetarian restaurant has a very wide range of delicious dishes including hotpots and mock meat.

🛍 Shopping

Zhongshan Lu is essentially a long shopping strip filled with souvenir shops and the latest fashion brands.

ℹ Information

Pickpockets operate around the popular areas in Xiàmén. This includes Zhongshan Lu and the ferry to/from Gǔlàng Yǔ.

Bank of China (中国银行; Zhōngguó Yínháng; 6 Zhongshan Lu) The 24-hour ATM accepts international cards.

China International Travel Service (CITS; 中国国际旅行社; Zhōngguó Guójì Lǚxíngshè; 335 Hexiang Xilu) There are several offices around town. This branch near Yundang Lake is recommended.

China Post (中国邮政; Zhōngguó Yóuzhèng; cnr Xinhua Lu & Zhongshan Lu) Telephone services available.

Life Line Medical Clinic (Mǐfú Zhěnsuǒ; ☎532 3168; 123 Xidi Villa Hubin Beilu; ⊘8am-5pm Mon-Fri, to noon Sat) English-speaking doctors; expat frequented. Telephone-operated 24 hours.

Public Security Bureau (PSB; 公安局; Gōng'ānjú; ☑226 2203; 45-47 Xinhua Lu) Opposite the main post and telephone office. The visa section (*chūrùjìng guǎnlǐchù*; open 8.10am to 11.45am and 2.40pm to 5.15pm Monday to Saturday) is in the northeastern part of the building on Gongyuan Nanlu.

What's On Xiamen (www.whatsonxiamen.com) Up-to-date information on Xiàmén.

Getting There & Away

Air

Air China, China Southern, Xiàmén Airlines and several other domestic airlines operate flights to/from Xiàmén to all major domestic airports in China. There are innumerable ticket offices around town, many of which are in the larger hotels, such as the Millennium Harbourview Hotel. There are international flights to/from Bangkok, Hong Kong, Jakarta, Kuala Lumpur, Los Angeles, Manila, Osaka, Penang, Singapore and Tokyo.

All Nippon Airways (☑573 2888; 12-8 Zhenhai Lu) In Millennium Harbourview Hotel.

Apple Travel (☑505 3122; www.appletravel.cn; Shop 20, Guanren Lu) Flight and tour bookings. Located behind Marco Polo Hotel.

Silk Air (胜安航空; Shèng'ān Hángkōng; ☑205 3280; International Plaza, 15th fl, Unit H, 8 Lujiang Dao)

Thai Airways International (泰国航空公司; Tàiguó Hángkōng Gōngsī; ☑226 1688) In the International Plaza.

Boat

Fast boats (¥10, 20 minutes) leave for the nearby coastal Fújiàn town of Zhāngzhōu (漳州) from the passenger ferry terminal (客运码头; *kèyùn mǎtóu*). Boats run every 15 minutes between 6.30am and 9.30pm. There are also ferry services to Kinmen (Jīnmén), Taiwan (¥180, one hour, hourly). For details, see boxed text, p280.

Bus

Buses to the following destinations leave from **Húbīn long-distance bus station** (湖滨长途汽车站; Húbīn chángtú qìchēzhàn; 58 Hubin Nanlu) and tickets can also be bought two days in advance at the ticket booth in the local bus terminal adjacent to Xiàmén University at the end of Siming Nanlu.

Fúzhōu ¥75, four hours, every 10 minutes
Guǎngzhōu ¥200, nine hours, two daily
Guìlín ¥240, one daily (8.30am)
Lóngyán ¥58, three hours, regular services
Nánjìng (in Fújiàn) ¥35, two hours, regular services
Quánzhōu ¥37, two hours, every 20 minutes
Wǔyí Shān ¥124, nine hours, one daily (11.10am)
Yǒngdìng ¥65, four hours, four daily

Train

Book tickets at the train station or through the **train ticket booking office** (☑203 8565; cnr Xinhua Lu & Zhongshan Lu) behind the Gem Hotel (Jīnhòu Jiǔdiàn). Most trains leave from Xiàmén's main train station on Xiahe Lu, and all northbound D trains stop at the new Xiàmén north station 25km north of the city centre (prices range from hard seat to soft sleeper tickets):

Běijīng (west) ¥253 to ¥705, 33 hours
Hángzhōu (D train) ¥285, seven hours
Kūnmíng ¥266 to ¥783, 41 hours
Nánjīng (in Jiāngsū) ¥150 to ¥452, 30 hours
Shànghǎi (D train) ¥237, 7½ hours
Wǔyí Shān ¥149 to ¥232, 13½ hours

Getting Around

To/From the Airport

Xiàmén airport is 15km from the waterfront district. Taxis cost about ¥45. Bus 27 travels from the airport to Dìyī ferry terminal (but not vice versa). From the city centre, airport shuttle buses leave from **Chūnguāng Hotel** (春光酒店; Chūnguāng Jiǔdiàn; cnr Datong Lu & Lujiang Dao; ¥10), opposite the Lúndù ferry terminal.

Public Transport

Bus Rapid Transit (BRT) line 1 links the waterfront to both train stations via Xiahe Lu (¥1). Bus 19 runs to the train station from the ferry terminal (¥1). Buses to Xiàmén University leave from the train station (bus 1) and from the ferry terminal (bus 2). Taxis start at ¥8 plus ¥3 fuel surcharge.

Gǔlàng Yǔ　　　鼓浪屿
☑0592

The small island of Gǔlàng Yǔ is the trump card of Xiàmén. It's not hard to see why it attracts droves of visitors every year. Just a five-minute boat ride away, you'll find yourself on a breezy islet with warrens of backstreets, set in the architectural kaleidoscope of more than 1000 colonial villas, imposing mansions and ancient banyan trees. The area near the ferry terminal tends to get very crowded, but the higher and further you go, the more you have the island to yourself, and it's worth spending a few days here to soak up its charms.

The foreign community was well established on Gǔlàng Yǔ by the 1880s, with a daily English newspaper, churches, hospitals, post and telegraph offices, libraries, hotels and consulates. In 1903 the island was officially designated an International Foreign Settlement, and a municipal council with a police force of Sikhs was established to govern it. Today, memories of the settlement linger in the many charming colonial buildings and the sound of classical piano wafting from speakers (the island is nicknamed 'piano island' by the Chinese). Many of China's most celebrated musicians have come from Gŭlàng Yŭ, including the pianists Yu Feixing, Lin Junqing and Yin Chengzong.

The best way to enjoy the island is to wander along the streets, peeking into courtyards and down alleys to catch a glimpse of colonial mansions seasoned by local life before popping into one of the many cute cafes for a beer or milk tea.

Sights

Historic Buildings
HISTORIC BUILDINGS

Old colonial residences and consulates are tucked away in the maze of streets leading from the pier, particularly along Longtou Lu and the back lanes of Huayan Lu. Some of Gŭlàng Yŭ's buildings are deserted and tumbledown, with trees growing out of their sides, as residents cannot afford their upkeep.

Southeast of the pier you will see the two buildings of the **former British Consulate** (原英国领事馆; 14-16 Lujiao Lu) above you, while further along at 1 Lujiao Lu (鹿礁路) is the cream-coloured former Japanese **Bo'ai Hospital**, built in 1936. Residents have now barred access to the public via a warning near the entrance. Up the hill on a different part of Lujiao Lu at No 26 stands the redbrick **former Japanese Consulate**, just before you reach the magnificent snow-white **Ecclesia Catholica** (天主堂; Roman Catholic Church; Tiānzhǔtáng; 34 Lujiao Lu), dating from 1917. The white building next to the church is the **former Spanish Consulate**. Just past the church on the left is the **Huáng Róngyuǎn Villa** (admission adult/child ¥60/30); a marvellous pillared building, now the Puppet Art Center. There is also some art deco architecture. Take a look at the building at **28 Fujian Lu.** Other buildings worth looking at include the Protestant **Sānyī Church** (三一堂), a red-brick building with a classical portico and cruciform-shaped interior on the corner of Anhai Lu (安海路) and Yongchun Lu (永春路). Where Anhai Lu meets Bishan Lu (笔山路) is the former **Law Court** (1-3 Bishan Lu), now inhabited by local residents.

Doing a circuit of Bishan Lu will take you past a rarely visited part of the island. **Guāncǎi Lóu** (观彩楼; 6 Bishan Lu), a residence built in 1931, has a magnificently dilapidated interior with a wealth of original features and, like so many other buildings

here, is crying out to be preserved. The building stands in stark contrast next to the immaculate **Yìzú Shānzhuāng** (亦足山庄; 9 Bishan Lu), a structure dating from the 1920s.

Organ Museum
MUSEUM

(风琴博物馆; Fēngqín Bówùguǎn; admission ¥20; ⏱8.40am-5.30pm) The highly distinctive **Bāguà Lóu** (八卦楼) at No 43 Guxin Lu (鼓新路) is now the Organ Museum, with a fantastic collection including a Norman & Beard organ from 1909.

Hàoyuè Garden
GARDEN

(皓月园; Hàoyuè Yuán; admission ¥15; ⏱6am-7pm) Hàoyuè Garden is a rocky outcrop containing an imposing **statue of Koxinga** in full military dress.

Sunlight Rock Park
PARK

(日光岩公园; Rìguāng Yán Gōngyuán; admission ¥60; ⏱8am-7pm) **Sunlight Rock** (Rìguāng Yán), in Sunlight Rock Park, is the island's highest point at 93m. At the foot of Sunlight Rock is a large colonial building known as the **Koxinga Memorial Hall** (郑成功纪念馆; Zhèng Chénggōng Jìniànguǎn; ⏱8-11am & 2-5pm). Also in the park is **Yīngxióng Hill** (Yīngxióng Shān), near the memorial and connected via a free cable-car ride. It has an **open-air aviary** (admission free) with chattering egrets and parrots, and a terrible bird 'show'.

Shūzhuāng Garden
GARDEN

(菽庄花园; Shūzhuāng Huāyuán; admission ¥30) The waterfront Shūzhuāng Garden on the southern end of the island is a lovely place to linger for a few hours. It has a small *pénzāi* (bonsai) garden and some delicate-looking pavilions. The piano theme is in full effect at the piano museum housed within the grounds. One piano has its original bill of sale from Melbourne at the turn of the 20th century.

Sleeping

There's a plethora of accommodation choices in Gŭlàng Yŭ, but its popularity means booking in advance is a must. Cars aren't allowed on the island, so try to book a hotel close to he ferry terminal if you've got a lot of luggage.

46Howtel
HOTEL $$$

(🖉206 5550; www.46howtel.com; 46 Fujian Lu; 福建路46号; r ¥365-780; ❄@) The 17 rooms in this luxury boutique hotel are spacious, sleek and cutting-edge modern. Expect rooms straight out of a *Wallpaper* spread: sharp lines, glossy surfaces and plush carpets. Service is top notch too.

KINMEN, TAIWAN

If you have a multiple-entry China visa, it's worth making a detour to the island of Kinmen (金门; Jīnmén) in Taiwan. Lying only 2km off the coast of Xiàmén, this peaceful islet was once part of a five-decade political tug-of-war between the mainland and Taiwan, and was subjected to incessant bombings from the mainland throughout the 1950s and 1960s. It wasn't until 1993 that martial law was lifted and people living on this once off-limit frontier island were allowed to travel freely to and from the mainland and Taiwan. In 2000, the government of Taiwan removed the ban on travel and trade between the mainland and the Strait Islands, and ferry crossings between the two sides have thrived ever since.

Today, Kinmen is fairly developed and visitor-friendly. The former battlefields and military bunkers are now opened up for tourism. In addition to war relics, the island has tree-lined streets, lakes, a national park and a cluster of beautiful villages dotted with colourful temples and Fújiàn-style houses (ironically, most of their counterparts back in Fújiàn have been demolished in the past 30 years). Attractions include **Chukuang Tower** (莒光楼; Jǔguāng Lóu), built in 1952 to honour the fallen soldiers of Kinmen; the historical **Shuǐtóu Village** (水头村; Shuǐtóu Cūn) and **Jhushan Village** (珠山; Zhūshān); and the meandering alleys and market streets in **Kincheng** (金城; Jīnchéng), the largest city on Kinmen. All these are within reachable distance from the ferry terminal and ideal for a day trip.

The size of Kinmen (153 sq km) suggests that a multiday excursion is possible. It's rewarding to further venture to the cute **Lièyǔ Island** (列屿乡; Lièyǔ Xiāng), less than 2 sq km in area and a 10-minute boat ride from Kinmen.

Cycling is the best way to see the island. Bikes can be borrowed free-of-charge for a maximum of three days from most visitor information centres, with a handy one in Kincheng bus station (金城车站; Jīnchéng chēzhàn). Bike lanes as well as all sights are well-marked in both Chinese and English. Free Chinese maps are available in all visitor information centres, and the Chinese-speaking staff can recommend accommodation. Shuǐtóu and Jhushan villages have lots of B&Bs (民宿; mínsù), and we love **Qin Inn** (水头一家亲; Shuǐtóu Yijiāqīn; ☑886-910-395565; http://qininn.tumblr.com; 63-64 Qian Shuitou; s NT$1200, d NT2400-3600; ❈🙾). In Kincheng, the brand-new **In99 Hotel** (☑886-082-3248; www.in99hotel.com; 60 Minsheng Lu, Jīnchéng Township; d NT$1800-3000) is the place to stay.

To get there, see the boxed text, p280. On Kinmen island, bus 7 links the ferry terminal with Shuǐtóu village and Kincheng, and bus 3 runs between Kincheng, Jhushan and the airport. Ferries to Lièyǔ Island depart from the dock diagonally opposite to the ferry terminal every 30 minutes between 6.30am and 8.30pm.

A friendly reminder: you need a multiple-entry China visa if you want to go back to Fújiàn. Otherwise you have to fly to Taipei or Kaohsiung to get one through a travel agent.

Free luggage storage is available at the departure hall in the ferry terminal. The money changers in the terminal only accept rénmínbì at the time of research.

Mogo Cafe Hotel HOTEL $$
(蘑菇旅馆; Mógū Lǚguǎn; ☑208 5980; www.mogo-hotel.com; 3-9 Longtou Lu; 龙头路3-9号; r ¥280-650; ❈@) Every one of the 19 rooms in this fabulous option is a distinctive statement of designer flair: think textured wallpaper, mood lighting, rain showers. The hotel is just a short walk from the ferry terminal, though you'll have to lug your bags up three flights of stairs when you arrive.

**Gǔlàng Yǔ
International Youth Hostel** HOSTEL $
(鼓浪屿国际青年旅馆; Gǔlàng Yǔ Guójì Qīngnián Lǚguǎn; ☑206 6066; 18 Lujiao Lu; 鹿礁路18号; 6-/4-bed dm ¥50/75, s ¥110, d ¥270 & ¥370; ❈@🙾) Housed in a revamped old building, this well-located hostel features large rooms with high beamed ceilings and a relaxing courtyard. We think it's the best value for money on the island. There's internet access, a laundry and lots of company.

**Gǔlàng Yǔ Lù Fēi
International Youth Hostel** HOSTEL $
(鼓浪屿鹭飞国际青年旅舍; Gǔlàng Yǔ Lù Fēi Guójì Qīngnián Lǚshè; ☑208 2678; www.yhalf.cn; 20 Guxin Lu; 鼓新路20号; dm ¥60, s & d ¥290-370; ❈@🙾) Rooms are cute and sparkling clean, and each has a theme. We love its pastel hues and wrought-iron beds. It's 400m west of the ferry terminal.

✗ Eating

You'll find small eateries and trendy cafes aplenty, especially in the streets off Longtou Lu. Try the shark fishballs and the Amoy pie (a sweet filled pastry).

Babycat Café   CAFE **$$**
(☎206 3651; 143 Longtou Lu; ⏲10.30am-11pm; 🛜)
This trendy cafe has attracted foodies from all corners of China for its Amoy handmade pies. Additionally, there's a large range of coffees and free wi-fi.

Líjì Mùdān Fishball   SEAFOOD **$**
(林记木担鱼丸; Línjì Mùdān yúwán; 56 Longtou Lu; meals from ¥15; ⏲10am-9pm) Pull up a bench and order some local specialities: shark fishball noodles (鲨鱼丸粉丝) and a serve of oyster omelette (海蛎煎). Slurp it down and order a second serve.

ℹ Information

There are different maps for sale (¥10). The flavour of the month seems to be a hand-drawn Chinese version printed on brown paper; while it lists all the sights of interest, it's not to scale and useless when you get lost.

Bank of China (中国银行; Zhōngguó Yínháng; 2 Longtou Lu; ⏲9am-7pm) Forex and 24-hour ATM.

China Post (中国邮政; Zhōngguó Yóuzhèng; 102 Longtou Lu)

Hospital (Yīyuàn; 60 Fujian Lu) Has its own miniature ambulance for the small roads.

Xiàmén Gǔlàng Yǔ Visitor Center (Xiàmén Gǔlàng Yǔ Yóukè Zhōngxīn; Longtou Lu) Left luggage ¥3 to ¥5.

ℹ Getting There & Around

Ferries for the five-minute trip to Gǔlàng Yǔ leave from Lúndù ferry terminal (轮渡) just west of Xiàmén's Lùjiāng Harbourview Hotel. The round-trip fare is ¥8 (getting on the upper deck costs an additional ¥1). Boats run between 5.30am and midnight. Waterborne circuits of the island can be done by boat (¥15), with hourly departures from the passenger ferry terminal off Lujiang Lu between 7.45am and 8.45pm.

Fújiàn Tǔlóu   福建土楼

☏0597 / POP 40,200

Scattered all over the pretty, rolling countryside in southwestern Fújiàn, the remarkable tǔlóu (土楼) are vast, fortified earthen edifices that have been home to both the Hakka and the Mǐnnán (Fujianese) people since the year dot. Today, more than 3000 survive, many still inhabited and open to visitors.

Since Unesco status was conferred on 46 tǔlóu in 2008, the local government has been in a flap revamping. New roads were added to link the tǔlóu areas to the nearest counties and new hotels erected. Some tǔlóu are more than eager to convert the family properties into guesthouses to meet the tourism demand. Needless to say, entry fees have increased. You'll see a convoy of tour buses bringing droves of visitors to some of the most popular tǔlóu clusters, but don't be deterred by that. The setting and architectural structure of the tǔlóu are simply stunning, and each one is unique. If you venture off the beaten path, crowds thin out consider-

---

BORDER CROSSINGS: GETTING TO TAIWAN

Eighteen ferries ply between Xiàmén and Kinmen (金门; Jīnmén) Island in Taiwan roughly between 8am and 7pm. You can catch the boat from the International Passenger Ferry Terminal (¥150/NT$750, one hour), more commonly known as Dōngdù Mǎtóu (东渡码头), 4km north of Lúndù ferry terminal; or from Wǔtōng ferry terminal (五通码头; Wǔtōng Mǎtóu; 20 minutes), 8km east of the airport. Check www.kma.gov.tw for the schedule.

Tickets can only be bought an hour before departure time. In Kinmen, visas are issued on the spot for most nationalities. But you need a multiple-entry China visa if you want to return to Fújiàn.

Both ferry terminals can only be reached by taxi. Expect to pay ¥15 to get to the International Passenger Ferry Terminal from the waterfront district; and ¥20 to go from the airport to Wǔtōng ferry terminal.

At the time of research, Rénmínbì is the only currency accepted in the money exchange counters in Kinmen's ferry terminal. There are no ATM machines in the pier area. From Kinmen, there are flights to other major cities in Taiwan.

Alternatively, you can catch a ferry (¥300, 90 minutes, 9.15am) from Fúzhōu's Máwěi ferry terminal (马尾码头; Máwěi Mǎtóu) to Taiwan's archipelago of Matzu (马祖; Mázǔ). From there, you'll find boats to Keelung and flights to other cities in Taiwan.

JUST WHAT IS A TǓLÓU?

Tǔlóu, literally mud houses, are outlandish, multistorey, fortified mud structures built by the inhabitants of southwest Fújiàn to protect themselves from bandits and wild animals.

Tǔlóu were built along either a circular or square floor plan. The walls are made of rammed earth and glutinous rice, reinforced with strips of bamboo and wood chips. These structures are large enough to house entire clans, and they did, and still do! They are a grand exercise in communal living. The interior sections are enclosed by enormous peripheral structures that could accommodate hundreds of people. Nestled in the mud walls were bedrooms, wells, cooking areas and storehouses, circling a central courtyard. The later *tǔlóu* had stone fire walls and metal-covered doors to protect against blazes.

The compartmentalised nature of the building meant that these structures were the ancient equivalent of modern apartments. A typical layout would be the kitchens on the ground floor, storage on the next level and accommodation on the floors above this. Some *tǔlóu* have multiple buildings built in concentric rings within the main enclosure. These could be guest rooms and home schools. The centre is often an ancestral hall or a meeting hall used for events such as birthdays and weddings. For defence purposes, usually there is only one entrance for the entire *tǔlóu* and there are no windows on the first three storeys.

It was once believed that these earthen citadels were inhabited solely by the Hakka. They are the people who migrated from northwest China during the Jin dynasty (AD 265–314) to the south to escape persecution and famine, and they eventually settled in Jiāngxī, Fújiàn and Guǎngdōng. While most *tǔlóu* in the vicinity of Yǒngdìng County are inhabited by the Hakka, there are far more *tǔlóu* in other counties like Nánjìng and Huá'ān populated by the indigenous Mǐnnán (Fujianese) people. A key distinguishing feature between the Hakka and Mǐnnán *tǔlóu* is that the former has communal corridors and staircases, as well as a central courtyard, while the latter *tǔlóu* puts more emphasis on privacy, ie each unit has its own staircases and patio.

No matter what type or shape of *tǔlóu* you're looking at, many of them are still inhabited by a single clan, and residents depend on a combination of tourism and farming for a living. The *tǔlóu* are surprisingly comfortable to live in, being '*dōng nuǎn, xià liáng*' (冬暖夏凉), or 'warm in winter and cool in summer'. These structures were built to last.

ably and some little-known or even nameless *tǔlóu* are the most authentic reflection of rural life in these packed-earth chateaux.

⊙ Sights

The most notable of the 3000-odd *tǔlóu* are lumped into various clusters, and they are in the vicinity of two main counties: Nánjìng (南靖) and Yǒngdìng (永定). If you rely solely on public transport to see the *tǔlóu*, you can base yourself in the small village of Liùlián (六联), aka the Tǔlóu Mínsú Wénhuàcūn (土楼民俗文化村). The village is 800m south of the Hóngkē Tǔlóu Cluster and is reachable by bus from Xiàmén or Yǒngdìng. It consists of a small bus station, some hotels and restaurants. If you hire a vehicle, the scenic Tǎxià village (p282), 55km northeast of Nánjìng county, is an ideal base.

See p283 for details on how to get to the various *tǔlóu*.

HÓNGKĒNG TǓLÓU CLUSTER
洪坑土楼群

Cluster admission is ¥90.

Zhènchéng Lóu
TǓLÓU

(振成楼) A short walk from Liùlián, this most visited *tǔlóu* is a grandiose structure built in 1912, with two concentric circles and a total of 222 rooms. The ancestral hall in the centre of the *tǔlóu* is complete with Western-style pillars. The locals dub this *tǔlóu wángzǐ* (土楼王子), the prince *tǔlóu*.

Kuíjù Lóu
TǓLÓU

(奎聚楼) Near Zhènchéng Lóu, this much older, square *tǔlóu* dates back to 1834.

Rúshēng Lóu
TǓLÓU

(如升楼) The smallest of the roundhouses, this late-19th-century, pea-sized *tǔlóu* has only one ring and 16 rooms.

Fúyù Lóu
TŬLÓU

(福裕楼) Along the river, this five-storey square *tǔlóu* boasts some wonderfully carved wooden beams and pillars. Rooms are available here for ¥100.

TIÁNLUÓKĒNG TŬLÓU CLUSTER
田螺坑土楼群

A pilgrimage to the earthen castles is not complete if you miss **Tiánluókēng** (田螺坑), which is 37km northeast of Nánjìng and home to arguably the most picturesque cluster of *tǔlóu* in the region. The locals affectionately call the five noble buildings 'four dishes with one soup' because of their shapes: circular, square and oval. All of them were upgrading their guest rooms at the time of research. Wénchāng Lóu (文昌楼), for example, has fan rooms with wi-fi for ¥70. Expect more facilities to be available by the time you read this book.

There's one direct bus (¥55, 3½ hours) to the cluster from Xiàmén, leaving at 8.30am. Make sure your driver, if you've hired one, takes you up the hill for a postcard-perfect view of Tiánluókēng. Cluster admission is ¥100.

Yùchāng Lóu
TŬLÓU

(裕昌楼) The tallest roundhouse in Fújiàng, this vast five-floor structure has an observation tower to check for marauding bandits and 270 rooms. Interestingly, this 300-year-old property's pillars bend at an angle on the 3rd floor, and at the opposite angle on the 5th floor, and each room and kitchen on the ground floor has its own well.

Tǎxià
VILLAGE

(塔下村) This nearby village is a delightful river settlement, with several *tǔlóu*, including the **Qìngdé Lóu**, where you can spend the night in a modern *tǔlóu* room (¥160). Another highlight of the village is the **Zhang Ancestral Hall**. It's surrounded by 23 elaborately carved spearlike stones, which celebrate achievements of prominent villagers. The bus station in Nánjìng runs six buses (¥17, 1½ hours) to the village between 8am and 4.30pm.

Bùyún Lóu
TŬLÓU

(步云楼) At the heart of the Tiánluókēng cluster is this square building. First built in the 17th century, it burnt down in 1936 and was rebuilt in the 1950s.

Wénchāng Lóu
TŬLÓU

(文昌楼) The Tiánluókēng cluster's oval-shaped building.

GĀOBĚI TŬLÓU CLUSTER
高北土楼群

Cluster admission is ¥50.

Chéngqǐ Lóu
TŬLÓU

(承启楼) In the village of Gāoběi (高北), this 300-year-old *tǔlóu* has 400 rooms and once housed 1000 inhabitants. It's built with elaborate concentric rings, with circular passageways between them and a central shrine. It's one of the most iconic and photographed *tǔlóu* and we're not surprised that it has been dubbed the king *tǔlóu*.

Wǔyún Lóu
TŬLÓU

(五云楼) Deserted and rickety, this square building took on a slant after an earthquake in 1918.

Qiáofú Lóu
TŬLÓU

(侨福楼) A modern *tǔlóu* constructed in 1962, housing 90 rooms across three levels. Decent rooms are available for ¥100.

Yíjīng Lóu
TŬLÓU

(遗经楼) The largest rectangular *tǔlóu* found in Fújiàn. The crumbling structure has 281 rooms, two schools and 51 halls. Built in 1851.

YÚNSHUǏYÁO TŬLÓU CLUSTER
云水谣土楼群

The cluster, 48km northeast of Nánjìng, is set in idyllic surrounds with rolling hills, verdant farms and babbling streams. There are six buses (¥20) to Yúnshuǐyáo (云水谣) that leave from the bus station in Nánjìng. The admission is ¥90.

Héguì Lóu
TŬLÓU

(和贵楼) The tallest rectangular *tǔlóu* in Fújiàn has five storeys and was built on a swamp. It boasts 120 rooms, a school, two wells, and a fortified courtyard in front of the entrance. The mammoth structure was built in 1732.

Huáiyuǎn Lóu
TŬLÓU

(怀远楼) This relatively young *tǔlóu* (built in 1909) has 136 equally sized rooms and a concentric ring that houses an ancestral hall and a school.

Chángjiào
VILLAGE

(长教村) Between the above two *tǔlóu* is this beautiful village (now also called Yúnshuǐyáo) where you can sip tea under the big banyan trees and watch water buffalo frolic in the river. The village has a few guesthouses that offer rooms from ¥200 (see p283).

NÁNXĪ TǓLÓU CLUSTER 南溪土楼群

Cluster admission is ¥70.

Huánjí Lóu
TǓLÓU

(环极楼) Sitting midway between Yǒngdìng and Nánjìng, this four-storey building is a huge roundhouse with inner concentric passages, tiled interior passages and a courtyard. It also sports a *huíyīnbì* (回音壁) – a wall that echoes and resonates to sharp sounds. Some villagers may ask you for a 'sanitation fee'. It's not legal. Don't pay.

Yǎnxiāng Lóu
TǓLÓU

(衍香楼) This four-storey *tǔlóu* rises up beautifully next to a river, and is in the same direction as Huánjí Lóu.

Lìběn Lóu
TǓLÓU

(立本楼) To the rear of Yǎnxiāng Lóu is this derelict *tǔlóu* with crumbling walls. It was burnt down during the civil war and stands without its roof.

Qìngyáng Lóu
TǓLÓU

(庆洋楼) Also not far from Yǎnxiāng Lóu, this huge, rectangular, semi-decrepit structure was built between 1796 and 1820.

🛏 Sleeping & Eating

There are many hotels in Yǒngdìng and Nánjìng, but neither town is attractive. We recommend you base yourself in a *tǔlóu*, which will give you a glimpse of a vanishing dimension of life in China. Bring a flashlight and bug repellent. Most families can cook up meals for you. Expect to pay ¥30 upwards for a dish and always ask the price before ordering.

You will be able to find a room in most of the *tǔlóu* you visit as many families have now moved out. Some *tǔlóu* have upgraded their rooms with modern facilities, but most are still very basic – a bed, a thermos of hot water and a fan. You might also find that the toilets are on the outside, and the huge gates to the *tǔlóu* shut around 8pm.

Most *tǔlóu* owners can also organise a pick-up from Xiàmén and transport for touring the area.

Qìngdé Lóu
TǓLÓU $

(庆德楼; ☎777 1868, 1386 0800 101; www.qingde lou.com, in Chinese; d ¥100-160; ❄🛜) The 30 rooms in this rectangular *tǔlóu* are modern with air-con and wi-fi. Some rooms on the 2nd and 3rd floors have shared bathrooms only, but they are clean and comfy. Rooms with attached bathroom have a strong shower and heat lights. Located in the village of Tàxià.

Fúyù Lóu Chángdì Inn
TǓLÓU $

(福裕楼常棣客栈; ☎553 2800, 1379 9097 962; www.fuyulou.net, in Chinese; d incl breakfast ¥100-150; 🛜) Rooms are basic but comfy doubles complete with fan and TV. The owners are friendly and speak some English.

Tǔlóu Club
GUESTHOUSE $

(土楼会所; Tǔlóu Huìsuǒ'; ☎777 3888, 1396 0090 178; www.tulou168.com; d ¥200; ❄🛜) This wooden-cottage is neither a *tǔlóu* nor a club, but its riverside location in the idyllic village of Chángjiào makes it a pleasant place to stay and chill. Windows in some rooms are small, but the whole place is neat and tidy. The kitchen dishes out delicious Hakka food.

ℹ Getting There & Away

Bus

NÁNJÌNG From Xiàmén long-distance bus station, take a bus headed to Nánjìng (¥35, two hours, 12 daily between 7am and 5.30pm). Upon arrival, you can either take the respective buses as mentioned on p280 to some of the clusters, or hire a private vehicle to take you there.

YǑNGDÌNG Xiàmén has eight daily buses to Yǒngdìng (永定县; ¥72, four hours) from 7.10am to 4pm. They pass Liùlián and the Gāoběi *tǔlóu* cluster. In the other direction, check with local bus stops for timings closer to departure. Yǒngdìng can also be accessed by bus from Guǎngdōng and Lóngyán (¥20, one hour, regular).

Train

The new D trains that run to the *tǔlóu* areas came into service in 2011. Eleven high-speed trains link Xiàmén and Lóngyán via Nánjìng (¥30, one hour) daily. Local buses 1 and 2 link the train and bus stations. But by the time you read this, buses to Tiánluókēng and Yúnshuǐyáo should be available from the train station.

ℹ Getting Around

The easiest way to see the *tǔlóu* is to book a tour, or hire a vehicle either from Xiàmén, Nánjìng or Yǒngdìng. You'll most probably need to find transport at the *tǔlóu* areas, so it makes fiscal sense to just get transport from Xiàmén (haggle but expect to pay ¥600 a day to/from Xiàmén).

If you book a place to stay in one of the *tǔlóu*, most owners can help with transport and they usually arrange pick-up from Nánjìng or Yǒngdìng.

You'll find taxi drivers in Yǒngdìng, Liùlián or Nánjìng offering their services for around ¥450 a day (¥300 if you hire more than one day), setting off early morning and returning late afternoon. Expect to see two clusters per day.

Apple Travel (p276) can organise English-speaking guided tours.

Quánzhōu 泉州

📞0595 / POP 648,000

While Gŭlàng Yŭ and the *tŭlóu* get all the limelight in Fújiàn, the underrated small town of Quánzhōu is actually an enchanting place to delve into for China's maritime past. The city was once a great trading port and an important stop on the maritime silk route. Back in the 13th century, Marco Polo informed his readers that 'it is one of the two ports in the world with the biggest flow of merchandise'. The city reached its zenith as an international port during the Song and Yuan dynasties, drawing merchants from all over the world to its shores. By the Qing, however, it was starting to decline and droves of residents began fleeing to Southeast Asia to escape the constant political turmoil.

Though its heyday is long gone, much of Quánzhōu's impressive heritage has been preserved, and evidence of its multiculturalism, especially some fine lingering traces of Islamic presence, can still be detected among the city's residents and buildings.

👁 Sights

The centre of town lies between Zhongshan Nanlu, Zhongshan Zhonglu and Wenling Nanlu. This is where you'll find most of the tourist sights. The oldest part of town is to the west, where many narrow alleys and lanes that still retain their traditional charm are waiting to be explored.

Kāiyuán Temple
BUDDHIST

(开元寺; Kāiyuán Sì; 176 Xi Jie; admission ¥10; ⊙7.30am-7pm) In the northwest of the city is one of the oldest temples in Quánzhōu, dating back to AD 686. Surrounded by trees, Kāiyuán Temple is famed for its pair of rust-coloured five-storey stone pagodas, stained with age and carved with figures, which date from the 13th century. Behind the eastern pagoda is a **museum** containing the enormous hull of a Song dynasty seagoing junk, which was excavated near Quánzhōu in 1974. The temple's **Great Treasure Hall** (Dàxióng Băodiàn) and the hall behind are decorated with marvellous overhead beams and brackets. The main courtyard is flanked by a row of wizened banyan trees; one is 800 years old! Take bus 2 (¥2) from Wenling Nanlu.

FREE Maritime Museum
MUSEUM

(泉州海外交通史博物馆; Quánzhōu Hăiwài Jiāotōngshǐ Bówùguǎn; Donghu Lu; ⊙8.30am-5.30pm Tue-Sun) On the northeast side of town, this fabulous museum explains Quánzhōu's trading history, the development of Chinese shipbuilding, and the kaleidoscope of religions in the port's heyday. There are wonderfully detailed models of Chinese ships, from junks to pleasure boats. The brand-new Religious Stone Hall and the Islamic Culture Hall are highlights, which boast a beautiful collection of gravestones and reliefs of different religions dated from the Yuan dynasty. Take bus 7 or 203 and alight at Qiáoxiāng Tǐyùguǎn (侨乡体育馆).

Qīngjìng Mosque
MOSQUE

(清净寺; Qīngjìng Sì; 108 Tumen Jie; admission ¥3; ⊙8am-5.30pm) Built by the Arabs in 1009 and restored in 1309, this stone edifice is one of China's only surviving mosques from the Song dynasty. Only a few sections (mainly walls) of the original building survive, largely in ruins. The adjacent brand-new mosque is a donation from the government of Saudi Arabia.

Língshān Islamic Cemetery
CEMETERY

(灵山伊斯兰教圣墓; Língshān Yīsīlán Shèngmù; cnr Donghu Lu & Lingshan Lu) Set at the foot of the mountain of Língshān, this leafy 'oasis' is truly a hidden gem in Quánzhōu and is one of the most intact historic cemeteries in China. Two of Mohammed's disciples are said to be buried here, and you'll also find some granite stelea dated from the Míng dynasty. Take bus 7 or 203 and hop off at Shèngmùzhàn (圣墓站).

Guāndì Temple
TAOIST TEMPLE

(关帝庙; Guāndì Miào; Tumen Jie) This smoky and magnificently carved temple is southeast of the mosque. It's dedicated to Guan Yu, a Three Kingdoms hero and the God of War, and inside the temple are statues of the god and wall panels that detail his life.

FREE Jīnxiùzhuāng Puppet Museum
MUSEUM

(锦绣庄木偶艺术馆; Jīnxiùzhuāng Mù'ǒu Yìshùguǎn; 10-12 Houcheng; ⊙9am-9pm) Has displays of 3000 puppet heads, intricate 30-string marionettes and comical hand puppets.

🛏 Sleeping

Quánzhōu can be visited as a day trip from Xiàmén. If you want to stay here, there are plenty of nondescript midrange Chinese hotels along Wenling Nanlu heading north, in addition to the following options.

Tíhò Cafe & Hostel
HOSTEL $

(堤后咖啡客栈; Tíhòu Kāfēi Kèzhàn; ☎2239 0800, 1865 9009 055; caimj@126.com; 114 Tihou Lu; 堤后路114号; dm ¥50, s & d ¥98-158; ❈@) A cheery new hostel-cum-cafe and the best budget option in town. The six-bed mixed dorm is small but clean, the rooms have no attached bathrooms but are cosy and relaxing. Catch bus 29 (westbound) from the long-distance bus station and alight at Shūcàigōngsī (蔬菜公司). A taxi from the centre of town is around ¥20.

Jǐnjiāng Hotel
HOTEL $

(锦江之星旅馆; Jǐnjiāng Zhīxīng Lǚguǎn; ☎2815 6355; 359 Wenling Beilu; 温陵北路359号; tw/d ¥169/179; ❈@) Located right across a park, this midrange chain has decently sized rooms and clean bathrooms. It's a notch above similar Chinese hotel chains in the midrange category.

Quánzhōu Yeohwa Hotel
HOTEL $$$

(泉州悦华酒店; ☎2801 9999; www.yeohwahotels.com; 129 Citong Xilu; 刺桐西路129号; d¥1650-2200, discount 40%; ❈@) This 378-room giant is arguably the best hotel in Quánzhōu and is a favourite of many business travellers.

🍴 Eating & Drinking

You can find the usual noodle and rice dishes served in the back lanes around Kāiyuán Temple and also along the food street close to Wenling Nanlu.

Lánshì Zhōnglóu
HAKKA $

(蓝氏钟楼肉粽; 19-21 Dong Jie; meals from ¥20; ⊙11am-9.30pm) Be prepared to sit elbow to elbow with the next table for the famous glutinous rice dumplings in this unpretentious joint. No English menu but there are pictures of the dishes on the wall. The signature black rice dumplings (黑米粽; *hēimǐzòng*) and rice dumpling with yolk (蛋黄粽; *dànhuángzòng*) are recommended.

Gǔcuò Cháfáng
TEA $$

(古厝茶坊; 44 Houcheng Xiang; tea ¥46-480, snacks from ¥20; ⊙9am-1am; 🄳) This quaint teahouse in the alley behind the Guāndì Temple has a refreshing old-time courtyard ambience, paved with flagstones and laid out with traditional wooden halls and bamboo chairs.

ℹ️ Information

You'll find internet cafes near the PSB on Dong Jie and in the small lanes behind Guāndì Temple. Most charge ¥4 to ¥5 an hour.

Bank of China (中国银行; Zhōngguó Yínháng; 9-13 Jiuyi Jie; ⊙9am-5pm) Has a 24-hour ATM.

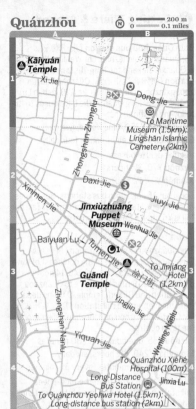

Quánzhōu

FÚJIÀN QUÁNZHŌU

Quánzhōu

◎ Top Sights
Guāndì Temple B3
Jǐnxiùzhuāng Puppet Museum B3
Kāiyuán Temple A1

◎ Sights
1 Qīngjìng Mosque B3

⊗ Eating
2 Gǔcuò Cháfáng B3
3 Lánshì Zhōnglóu B1

China Post (中国邮政; Zhōngguó Yóuzhèng; cnr Dong Jie & Nanjun Lu; ⊙8.30am-6pm)

Public Security Bureau (PSB; 公安局; Gōng'ānjú; ☎2218 0323; 62 Dong Jie; ⊙visa section 8-11.30am & 2.30-5.30pm)

Quánzhōu Xiéhé Hospital (Quánzhōu Xiéhé Yīyuàn; Tian'an Nanlu) In the southern part of town.

❶ Getting There & Around

Bus

Both **Quánzhōu bus station** (泉州汽车站; Quánzhōu qìchēzhàn; cnr Wenling Nanlu & Quanxiu Jie) and the **long-distance bus station** (泉州客运中心站; Quánzhōu kèyùn zhōngxīnzhàn; cnr Quanxiu Jie & Pingshan Lu) further east along Quanxiu Jie have buses to the following destinations:

Guǎngzhōu ¥250, nine hours, five daily

Shēnzhèn ¥250, eight hours, four daily

Regular deluxe buses:

Fúzhōu ¥70, 3½ hours

Xiàmén ¥37, 1½ hours

Local bus 15 links both bus stations. Bus 2 goes from the bus station to Kāiyuán Temple. Taxi flag fall is ¥6, then ¥1.60 per kilometre.

Train

The Quánzhōu East Train Station (泉州东站; Quánzhōu Dōngzhàn) is in the northeast of town for Wǔyí Shān (hard sleeper ¥149, 14 hours, 3.38pm). Bus 19 runs from here to Quánzhōu bus station and Guāndì Temple. D trains depart from the high-speed rail station (高铁泉州火车站; Gāotiě Quánzhōu huǒchēzhàn), 15km from the town centre:

Fúzhōu ¥55, one hour, every 30 minutes

Shànghǎi ¥240, 8½ hours, six daily

Xiàmén ¥30, 45 minutes, every 30 minutes

Buses 17 and K1 run from the high-speed rail station to Quánzhōu bus station and the long-distance bus station respectively. Bus 203 links both train stations, with stops at the Maritime Museum and Islamic Cemetery. A taxi from the centre of town to this station is ¥40. In town, train tickets can be bought at the Wenling Nanlu **ticket office** (铁路火车票代售点; tiělù huǒchēpiào dàishòudiǎn; 166 Wenling Nanlu; ◷9am-6pm) or from the **ticket office** (火车售票亭; huǒchē shòupiàotíng; 675 Quanxiu Jie; ◷7am-6pm) just east of the long-distance bus station. There's a ¥5 booking fee.

Around Quánzhōu

Not far from Quánzhōu there are a few oft-overlooked sights worth exploring.

CHÓNGWǓ   崇武

One of the best-preserved city walls in China can be found in the ancient 'stone city' of Chóngwǔ (admission free), about 50km east of Quánzhōu. The granite walls date back to 1387, stretch over 2.5km and average 7m in height. Scattered around the walls are 1304 battlements and four gates into the city.

The town wall was built by the Ming government as a frontline defence against marauding Japanese pirates, and it must be said that it has survived the past 600 years remarkably well. Meander and peruse the old halls and courtyard residences, where you'll find the warren of lanes and cul-de-sacs are maddeningly unique. You can also walk along the top of the wall at some points.

Next to the stone city is **Chóngwǔ Stone Arts Expo Park** (崇武石雕工艺博览园; Chóngwǔ shídiāo Gōngyì Bólǎnyuán; admission ¥45), which boasts a large park filled with 500 stone sculptures made by local crafts-people, a small beach, a lighthouse and some seafood restaurants. You won't miss much if you skip it.

Frequent minibuses depart Quánzhōu's long-distance bus station (¥12, 1½ hours), taking you past arrays of stone statues (the area is famed for its stone-carving work-shop) before ending up in Chóngwǔ.

Motorbikes (¥3 to ¥5) will take you from the bus drop-off to the Chóngwǔ Stone Arts Expo Park. From here, walk along the stone wall away from this entrance to find access to the stone city via a city gate.

XÚNPǓ VILLAGE   蟳埔村

The fishing village of Xúnpǔ at the estuary of Jìnjiāng River, some 10km southeast of the city centre of Quánzhōu, was on the old trade route of the maritime silk road and was perhaps the Arabs' first port of call when they set foot in Quánzhōu during the Song dynasty. The village, now under en-croaching urbanisation, is still fascinating and you'll find some old houses built with oyster shells, while the grannies are still wearing the flamboyant traditional head ornaments that they love to brag about.

The descendents in this village are said to have traces of Arab blood, but they cer-tainly observe more Chinese than Islamic customs these days. The **Mazǔ Temple** (妈祖庙; Māzǔ Miào) in the village, dedicated to the goddess of seafarers, turns very lively on the 29th day of the first lunar calendar month, the birthday of the protector. All the women in the village will turn out in traditional costumes to join in the annual Māzǔ procession.

Take bus 1 or 8 from the long-distance bus station, and alight at Gélín Gōngsī (格林公司). Then it's a 1km walk to the south. A taxi ride from the bus station is about ¥20.

CǍO'ĀN MANICAHEAN TEMPLE 草庵摩尼教寺

Perched on the hill of Huábiǎo, 19km south of Quánzhōu, this quirky **temple** (Cǎo'ān Mōníjiào Miào; Sūnēicūn, Shēdiàn, Jìnjiāng; 晋江佘店苏内村; admission ¥20; ⏱8am-6pm) is dedicated to Manichaeism, a religion originating in Persia in the third century, combining elements of Zoroastrian, Christian and Gnostic thought, that reached China in the seventh century.

The original temple was a straw hut, and the well-restored stone complex you see today was a rebuild dating to the Yuan dynasty (14th century). The most remarkable relic in the temple is the 'Buddha of Light', a sitting stone statue in the main hall, which is actually the prophet Mani, founder of Manichaeism, in a Buddhist disguise. Manichaeism was considered an illegal religion during the Song period and the religion had to operate in the guise of an esoteric Buddhist group. Take a closer look at the statue, and you'll find its hairstyle (straight instead of curly), hand gestures and colour combinations are distinctly different from most representations of the Buddha.

From the long-distance bus station in Quánzhōu, board bus to Ānhǎi (安海; ¥10) and tell the driver to drop you off at Cǎo'ān Lùkǒu (草庵路口). Then look for the English signage saying Grass Temple and it's a 2km walk uphill. The road is not well-marked so taking a taxi is a recommended alternative. A taxi from Quánzhōu is around ¥40.

Fúzhōu 福州

TRANSPORT HUB / ☎0591

Fúzhōu, capital of Fújiàn, is one of the major transport hubs in southern China. You'll find flights, inter-city/province trains and buses to most of the destinations you're likely to go to, especially the coastal provinces.

🛏 Sleeping

Fúzhōu accommodation falls mainly in the midrange and top-end categories. Many hotels offer discounts. If you're stranded in the city, the following are decent options near the train or bus stations.

Shangri-La Hotel HOTEL $$$

(香格里拉大酒店; Xiānggélǐlā Dàjiǔdiàn; ☎8798 8888; www.shangri-la.com; 9 Xinquan Nanlu; 新权南路9号; d ¥1250; ⏱❄✳@) Top-notch service is expected in every Shangri-La, and this classy tower at the heart of town overlooking Wuyi Sq is no exception. A cab from the south long-distance bus station is around ¥15.

Jīnhuī Hotel HOTEL $$

(金辉大酒店; Jīnhuī Dàjiǔdiàn; ☎8759 9999; www.hoteljh.com; 492 Hualin Lu; 华林路492号; d ¥395-520; ✳) Good discounts that take prices down to around ¥250 (including breakfast) make this a good-value option, though the rooms are a bit tired. Directly opposite the train station, north of town. The airport bus also leaves from here.

7 Days Inn HOTEL $

(7天; Qītiān; ☎8803 8377; www.7daysinn.cn; 98 Wuyi Nanlu; 五一南路98号; d & tw ¥147-247; ✳@) This budget chain was opened in 2011, so all rooms are sparking clean. The cheapest rooms are windowless. It's 500m south of the south long-distance bus station.

🍴 Eating

The pedestrianised **Sānfāng Qīxiàn** (三坊七巷) is a popular dining and shopping area lined with Ming-style houses and lanterns. You'll find small eateries on both sides of **Nanhou Jie** (南后街), the main street of the area. Take a cab and ask to be dropped off at the intersection of Yangqiao Donglu and Nanhou Jie. The fare is around ¥15 from the south long-distance bus station.

The area north of town around the train station is home to many fast-food restaurants and local noodle joints.

ℹ Getting There & Away

Air

The **Civil Aviation Administration China** (CAAC; 中国民航; Zhōngguó Mínháng; ☎8334 5988; 18 Wuyi Zhonglu) sells tickets for daily flights to Běijīng (¥1500, 2½ hours), Guǎngzhōu (¥1000, one hour), Shànghǎi (¥1200, 70 minutes), Hong Kong (¥2000, 80 minutes), and Xiàmén (¥900, 35 minutes).

Airport buses leave from two locations in town: the Apollo Hotel (Ābōluó Dàjiǔdiàn; ¥25) on Wuyi Zhonglu, 400m north of the south long-distance bus station, has departures every 20 minutes between 5.30am and 10pm; Jīnhuī Hotel (¥30) near the North Rail Station has departures every hour between 6am and 8pm. The 50km trip takes about an hour.

Bus

The **north long-distance bus station** (长途汽车北站; chángtú qìchē běizhàn; 317 Hualin Lu) is 400m south of the North Rail Station. Services include the following:

Guǎngzhōu ¥258, 12 hours, 14 daily

Quánzhōu ¥63, two hours, regular

Shànghǎi ¥398, 10 hours, three daily

Wēnzhōu ¥125, four hours, seven daily

Wǔyí Shān ¥86 to ¥90, eight hours, night bus

Xiàmén ¥75, 3½ hours, every 15 minutes

The **south long-distance bus station** (长途汽车南站; chángtú qìchē nánzhàn; cnr Guohuo Xilu & Wuyi Zhonglu) services the following destinations:

Guǎngzhōu ¥180 to ¥258, 13 to 15 hours, 10 daily

Hong Kong ¥358, 15 hours, four daily (6.30pm, 6.50pm, 7pm and 8pm)

Shēnzhèn ¥260, 12 hours, six daily

Xiàmén ¥85, 3½ hours, every 15 minutes

Train

Fúzhōu has a good network of trains to most many major cities. D trains leave from either the more centrally located North Rail Station (福州北站; Fúzhōu Běizhàn) or the new South Rail Station (福州南站; Fúzhōu Nánzhàn) 17km southeast of the centre of town:

Quánzhōu ¥55, one hour, every 30 minutes

Shànghǎi ¥264, 6½ hours, 16 daily

Xiàmén ¥81, 1½ hours, every 15 minutes

The North Rail Station also has regular trains to Wǔyí Shān (¥47 to ¥141, 4½ to 6½ hours, eight daily) and one direct D366 express to Běijīng (soft sleeper ¥1165, 15 hours, 7am).

The **train ticket booking office** (火车票售票处; huǒchēpiào shòupiàochù; ⊙8am-5pm) is on the west side of the Xīnhuádū Bǎihuò (新都百货) at the corner of Bayiqi Lu and Dong Jie.

Wǔyí Shān   武夷山

☑0599 / POP 22,000

With crisp climes and unspoilt scenery, Wǔyí Shān is a popular mountain retreat in the northwest corner of Fújiàn where many a Chinese from the plains goes to beat the heat. The rivers, waterfalls, mountains and protected forests combine to make it a great place for day hikes and short treks. Try to come midweek or in low season (November, March and April) and you might have the area to yourself. Avoid the area during heavy rain (especially during summer months) even if the hotels and tour organisers advise otherwise.

The scenic part lies on the west bank of Chóngyáng Stream (Chóngyáng Xī), and some accommodation is located along its shore. Most of the hotels are concentrated in the *dù jià qū* (resort district) on the east side of the river. The main settlement is Wǔyí Shān city, about 10km to the northeast, with the train station and airport roughly halfway between.

⊙ Sights & Activities

Wǔyí Shān Scenic Area   MOUNTAIN PARK

(武夷宫; 1-/2-/3-day access ¥140/150/160; ⊙6am-8pm) The entrance to the area is at Wǔyí Gōng, about 200m south of the Wǔyí Mountain Villa, near the confluence of the Chóngyáng Stream and the Nine Twists River. Trails within the scenic area connect all the major sites. Good walks include the 530m **Great King Peak** (大王峰; Dàwáng Fēng), accessed through the main entrance, and the 410m **Heavenly Tour Peak** (天游峰; Tiānyóu Fēng), where an entrance is reached by road up the Nine Twists River. It's a moderate two-hour walk to Great King Peak among bamboo groves and steep-cut rock walls. The trail can be slippery and wet, so bring suitable shoes.

The walk to Heavenly Tour Peak is more scenic, with better views of the river and mountain peaks. But the path is also the most popular with tour groups. At the northern end of the scenic area, the **Water Curtain Cave** (水帘洞; Shuǐlián Dòng) is a cleft in the rock about one-third of the way up a 100m cliff face. In winter and autumn, water plunges over the top of the cliff, creating a curtain of spray.

Nine Twists River   RIVER

(九曲溪; Jiǔqū Xī; boat rides ¥100; ⊙7am-5pm) One of the highlights for visitors is floating down the river on **bamboo rafts** (*zhúpái*) fitted with rattan chairs. Departing from Xīngcūn (星村), a short bus ride west of the resort area, the trip down the river takes over an hour and brings you through some magnificent gorge scenery, with sheer rock cliffs and lush green vegetation.

One of the mysteries of Wǔyí Shān is the cavities, carved out of the rock faces at great heights, which once held boat-shaped coffins. Scientists have dated some of these artefacts back 4000 years. If you're taking a raft down the river, it's possible to see some remnants of these coffins on the west cliff face of the fourth meander, also known as **Small Storing Place Peak** (小藏山峰; Xiǎozàngshān Fēng).

Xiàméi   ANCIENT VILLAGE

(下梅; admission ¥26) This village dates to the Northern Song dynasty and boasts some spectacular Qing dynasty architecture from its heyday as a wealthy tea-trading centre. To reach Xiàméi, hop on a minibus (¥4) from Wǔyí Shān city for the 12km journey. Minibuses also run to Xiàméi (¥3) from the Wǔyí Shān Scenic Area.

Wǔfū

ANCIENT VILLAGE

(五夫; admission ¥60) Sixty kilometres southeast of Wǔyí Shān Scenic Area, this 1700-year-old village got its fame as the hometown of Zhu Xi, a Confucian scholar in the Song dynasty. It's best visited when the lotus in the giant ponds, which are back-dropped by some quaint Ming-era architecture, are in full bloom. Minibuses to Wǔfū (¥13, two hours) leave from the small bus station next to the long-distance bus station.

Sleeping

Most of the accommodation in Wǔyí Shān is in the midrange category and most is overpriced unless you come here during low season. Hotels are mostly on the east side of the river. On the quieter west side, family-run guesthouses are mushrooming in the village of Sángū (700m north of Wǔyí Mountain Villa).

Wǔyí Mountain Yeohwa Resort

HOTEL $$$

(武夷山悦华酒店; ☏523 8999; www.yeohwahotels.com; Dawangfeng Lu; 大王峰路; s/d ¥748/848; ❀◉) This high-end Chinese chain in the resort district features 204 spacious, luxurious rooms with wickerwork furniture, good beds and great views of the Great King Peak. The F&B outlets here are recommended.

Wǔyíshān Shāncháhuā Youth Hostel

HOSTEL $

(武夷山山茶花青年旅舍; Wǔyíshān Shāncháhuā qīngnián lǚshè; ☏523 2345, 1890 5093 345; wulifang21@yahoo.com.cn; 27 Sangu Lantangcun; 三菇兰汤村27号; 8-/4-bed dm ¥35/50, d ¥118-190; ◉) The 'Camellia' hostel is located in the village of Sángū Lántāng on the west bank. The dorms are passable and the rooms have a cosy feeling without being claustrophobic. The laidback courtyard invites a quiet, lazy afternoon. To get there, take bus 5, or pay about ¥30 to ¥40 for a taxi ride from the train station.

Wǔyí Mountain Villa

HOTEL $$$

(武夷山庄; Wǔyí Shānzhuāng; ☏525 1888; www.513villa.com; Wuyi Gong; 武夷宫; d ¥888-988, ste ¥1388-2888; ❀) Located at the foot of Great King Peak, the villa is considered by the Chinese to be the most prestigious place to stay in Wǔyí Shān. Buildings are chalet-style and surrounded by peaceful gardens, a swimming pool and a waterfall. Some rooms are dated, but the views are fine. Discounts of 40% available.

Eating

Frogs, mushrooms, bamboo rice and bamboo shoots are the specialities of Wǔyí Shān's cuisine. In town, there are food stalls along the streets in the evening. As to be expected, restaurants are overpriced.

Information

Chinese maps of the Wǔyí Shān area are available in bookshops and hotels in the resort district. There are some grubby internet cafes in the back alleys south of Wangfeng Lu (望峰路), charging ¥2 to ¥4 an hour.

Bank of China (中国银行; Zhōngguó Yínháng; Wujiu Lu; ◷9am-5pm) In Wǔyí Shān city, this branch has an ATM.

China International Travel Service (CITS; 中国国际旅行社; Zhōngguó Guójì Lǚxíngshè; ☏5134 666; Guolu Dalou, Sangu Jie; ◷9am-4pm Mon-Sat) The staff can arrange train tickets and tours.

Getting There & Away

Air

Wǔyí Shān has air links to several cities.

Běijīng ¥1350, two hours

Guǎngzhōu ¥890, 2½ hours

Hong Kong ¥1300, two hours

Shànghǎi ¥660, one hour

Xiàmén ¥720, 50 minutes

Bus

Buses run from the long-distance bus station in Wǔyí Shān city.

Fúzhōu ¥86 to ¥90, eight hours

Nánpíng ¥44, three hours

Shàngráo ¥30, two hours

Shàowǔ ¥22, 1½ hours

Xiàmén regular/deluxe ¥159, nine hours

Train

Direct trains go to Wǔyí Shān from Quánzhōu (¥145 to ¥232, 13 hours) and Xiàmén (¥149 to ¥232, 12 hours).

Getting Around

Bus 6 runs between the long-distance bus station, the train station, the airport, the resort area and Wǔyí Mountain Villa. Bus 5 links the train station, the airport and Sángū village. The resort area is small enough for you to walk everywhere.

Expect to pay about ¥15 for a motorised trishaw from the resort district to most of the scenic area entrances. A ride from the train station or airport to the resort district will cost ¥15 to ¥25.

Liáoníng

POP 43.1 MILLION

Includes »

Shěnyáng 292
Dàlián. 296
Around Dàlián 301
Dāndōng 303
Xīngchéng 306

Best Walks

» Dàlián's southwest coastline (p297)
» Expo Garden Shěnyáng (p293)
» North Korean Border (p303)
» Xīngchéng beaches (p307)

Best Historical Sites

» Imperial Palace (p292)
» North Tomb (p293)
» Tiger Mountain Great Wall (p304)
» Xīngchéng Old City (p306)
» Soviet Martyrs Cemetery (p302)

Why Go?

History and hedonism run side by side in Liáoníng (辽宁). Walled Ming-dynasty cities rub up against booming beach resorts, while imperial palaces sit in the centre of bustling modern cities. Nothing quite captures the fun and distinction, however, as much as seaside Dàlián with its golden coastline and summer beer festival (or is that bacchanalia?), and former battlegrounds where Russian and Japanese armies wrestled for control of the region in the early 20th century.

Outside of the major cities, Liáoníng is largely an expanse of farmland, forest and smokestack towns. The North Korean border runs alongside the province and is an intriguing area, not simply because it's as close as you can get to the Democratic People's Republic of Korea (DPRK) without actually going there. The large Korean population and easy mix of cultures provide a ready example that China is only a land of stereotypes if you never venture far into it.

When to Go
Dàlián

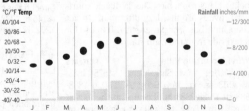

May & Jun Catch deals on a seaside hotel.

Jun & Jul Enjoy fresh cherries, mulberries and blueberries at roadside stands everywhere.

Jul & Aug Have fun at the Dàlián International Beer Festival.

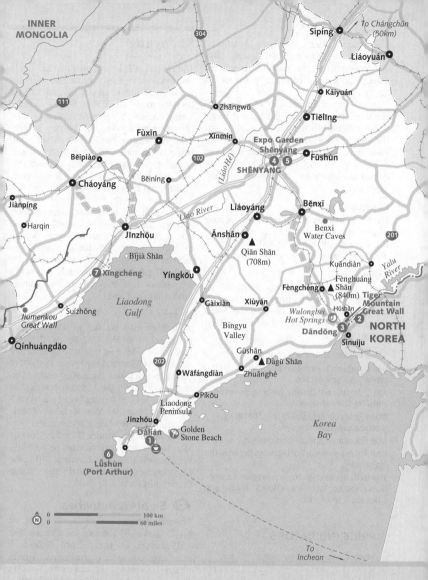

Liáoníng Highlights

1 Kick back in **Dàlián** (p296) and enjoy the beaches, coastal walkways and beer festival

2 Climb the easternmost stretch of the Great Wall at **Tiger Mountain Great Wall** (p304), near Dāndōng

3 Cruise the Yālù River close to North Korea and experience the mix of Korean and Chinese culture in **Dāndōng** (p303)

4 Explore the tomb of Huang Taiji, founder of the Qing dynasty, in **Shěnyáng** (p293)

5 Lose yourself in nature at the enormous **Expo Garden Shěnyáng** (p293)

6 Wander the old battlefields and graves of **Lǔshùn** (p302), fought over by rival Japanese and Russian Empires

7 Laze on the beach and stroll the old walled city of historic, little-visited **Xīngchéng** (p306)

History

The region formerly known as Manchuria, including the provinces of Liáoníng, Jílín and Hēilóngjiāng, plus parts of Inner Mongolia, is now called Dōngběi, which means 'the northeast'.

The Manchurian warlords of this northern territory established the Qing dynasty, which ruled China from 1644 to 1911. From the late 1800s to the end of WWII, when Western powers were busy carving up pieces of China for themselves, Manchuria was occupied alternately by the Russians and the Japanese.

Climate

Liáoníng's weather is cold and dry in the long winter, with temperatures dipping to -15°C. It's warm (tending to hot) and wet in summer. Heavy afternoon showers are frequent.

Language

Nearly everyone in Liáoníng speaks standard Mandarin, albeit with a distinct accent. In Dāndōng and areas close to the North Korean border, it's quite common to hear Korean spoken.

ℹ Getting There & Around

Getting around Liáoníng is easy. Shěnyáng is the province's transport hub.

AIR Shěnyáng and Dàlián have busy domestic and international airports.

BOAT Boats connect Dàlián with Shāndōng province and South Korea.

BUS Buses are a speedy alternative to trains.

CAR There's a network of highways between the major cities.

TRAIN Rail lines criss-cross the region; connections (including fast D trains) link Shěnyáng with cities south and north.

PRICE INDICATORS

The following price indicators are used in this chapter:

Sleeping

$	less than ¥200
$$	¥200 to ¥400
$$$	more than ¥400

Eating

$	less than ¥40
$$	¥40 to ¥80
$$$	more than ¥80

Shěnyáng 沈阳

♪ 024 / POP 5.7 MILLION

The capital of Liáoníng province has made enormous strides in overcoming its reputation as an industrial city that could have been the model for William Blake's vision of 'dark satanic mills'. True, Shěnyáng is still a sprawling metropolis, but the new subway lines are easing traffic, the urban landscape is fast improving, and there's a buzz on the streets these days that suggests this city's people are growing confident, secure, positive and even a touch urbane.

For the traveller, Shěnyáng boasts its very own Imperial Palace, a tomb complex and two decent museums, as well as several fine parks, including an expansive botanical garden on the outskirts of town. Given its strategic location as a transport hub for the north of China, Shěnyáng is well worth a couple of days' stopover on your journey further north or south.

History

Shěnyáng's roots go back to 300 BC, when it was known as Hou City. By the 11th century it was a Mongol trading centre, before reaching its historical high point in the 17th century when it was the capital of the Manchu empire. With the Manchu conquest of Běijīng in 1644, Shěnyáng became a secondary capital under the Manchu name of Mukden, and a centre of the ginseng trade.

Throughout its history Shěnyáng has rapidly changed hands, dominated by warlords, the Japanese (1931), the Russians (1945), the Kuomintang (1946) and finally the Chinese Communist Party (CP; 1948).

◉ Sights & Activities

Imperial Palace   HISTORIC SITE

(故宫; Gùgōng; 171 Shenyang Lu; admission ¥60; ⊘8.30am-6pm, last entry 5.15pm) Shěnyáng's main attraction is an impressive palace complex resembling a small-scale Forbidden City. Constructed between 1625 and 1636 by Manchu emperor Nurhachi (1559–1626) and his son, Huang Taiji, the palace served as the residence of the Qing-dynasty rulers until 1644.

The central courtyard buildings include ornate ceremonial halls and imperial living quarters, including a royal baby cradle. In all, there are 114 buildings, not all of which are open to the public.

Don't miss the double-eaved octagonal **Dàzhèng Hall** (at the rear of the complex), which has two gold dragons curled around the pillars at the entrance, a deep interior plafond ceiling and an elaborate throne, where Nurhachi's grandson, Emperor Shunzhi, was crowned. At **Chóngzhèng Hall**, the first large building as you enter, the beams over the entrance portico are all carved in the shape of five-fingered dragons.

The palace is in the oldest section of the city. Zhong Jie metro station (exit B) drops you off a few minutes north.

North Tomb HISTORIC SITE
(北陵; Běi Líng; 12 Taishan Lu; park/tombs ¥6/50; ⊘7am-6pm) Another Shěnyáng highlight is this extensive tomb complex, the burial place of Huang Taiji (1592–1643), founder of the Qing dynasty. The tomb's animal statues lead up to the central mound known as the Luminous Tomb (Zhāo Líng).

In many ways a better-preserved complex than the Imperial Palace, the tomb site is worth a few hours examining the dozens of buildings with their traditional architecture and ornamentation. **Lóng'ēn Hall** is a particularly fine structure, and as you circumambulate the base observe the richness of traditional symbols (peonies, vases, lucky clouds) carved in relief.

The North Tomb sits a few kilometres north of town inside expansive **Běi Líng Park**. With its pine trees and large lake, the park is an excellent place to escape Shěnyáng's hubbub. Locals come here to promenade, sing or just kick back. Beiling Gongyuan metro station is directly outside the park.

Expo Garden Shěnyáng GARDENS
(沈阳世博园; Shěnyáng Shìbó Yuán; admission ¥50; ⊘9am-5pm, last entry 3.30pm) These vast gardens on the eastern outskirts of Shěnyáng have dozens of elaborate exhibition gardens featuring plants and flowers from almost every region of China, as well as some from overseas. Trains to the Expo ground were no longer running at the time of research but bus 168 (¥5, frequent) ran from the **Shenyang bus station** just across from the wide intersection of Zhonghua Lu and Heping Dajie. A taxi to the grounds costs ¥50 to ¥70.

FREE **Liáoníng Provincial Museum** MUSEUM
(辽宁省博物馆; Liáoníng Shěng Bówùguǎn; SE cnr Government Sq; ⊘9am-noon & 1-5pm, last entry 3.30pm, closed Mon & public holidays) Three floors of exhibits highlight the region's art and history, from prehistoric times through the late Qing dynasty. The 3rd floor is the

---

THE 'MUKDEN INCIDENT'

By 1931 Japan was looking for a pretext to occupy Manchuria. The Japanese army took matters into its own hands by staging an explosion on the night of 18 September at a tiny section of a Japanese-owned railway outside Mukden, the present-day city of Shěnyáng. Almost immediately, the Japanese attacked a nearby Chinese army garrison and then occupied Shěnyáng the following night. Within five months, they controlled all of Manchuria and ruled the region until the end of WWII.

---

most interesting, with a rich collection of antiquities. English explanations accompany most displays.

FREE **18 September History Museum** MUSEUM
(九一八历史博物馆; Jiǔ Yī Bā Lìshǐ Bówùguǎn; 46 Wanghua Nanjie; ⊘9am-5pm, last entry 4pm) There's an obvious propagandic purpose to this museum, but the hundreds of photographs, sculptures, paintings and dioramas are informative on this notorious part of China's modern history. English captions are limited. Bus 325 from the North Train Station stops across the street. The museum is about 2km northeast from the town centre.

🛏 Sleeping

The main train station area is modern and vibrant, and near overloaded with glossy shopping malls, to say nothing of restaurants and cafes of all stripes. With several metro stations nearby it's also convenient for getting around town.

The Imperial Palace area has more of a neighbourhood feel, but accommodation is limited for foreign travellers.

TOP CHOICE **Liáoníng Bīnguǎn** HOTEL $$$
(辽宁宾馆; Liaoning Hotel; ☑2383 9104; 97 Zhongshan Lu; 中山路97号; r incl breakfast from ¥458; ❄@) This grand old Japanese-built hotel dates back to 1927. Recently refurbished, it retains many of its period details – the marbled lobby is particularly impressive – but also offers comfortable modern rooms, as well as a restaurant and outdoor patio for when the sun deigns to shine. Discounts usually available.

Shěnyáng

Home Inn
HOTEL $$

(如家快捷酒店; Rújiā Kuàijié Jiǔdiàn; ☑2401 7777; 7 Donghua Nan Lane, Shenyang Lu; 沈阳路东华南巷7号; r ¥149-229; ⊜❄@🛜) While the hallways are getting a little bit scuffed, the rooms at this chain are still bright and spotless, and include free broadband (wifi in the lobby), and quiet nights facing a back alley. The location's just a stone's throw from the Imperial Palace, rows of good small restaurants and lively shopping on Zhong Jie.

Traders Hotel
HOTEL $$$

(商贸饭店; Shāngmào Fàndiàn; ☑2341 2288; www.tradershotel.com; 68 Zhonghua Lu; 中华路68号; r from ¥698; ⊜❄@🛜) Owned by the Shangri-La chain, this is one of Shěnyáng's best luxury hotels, with big rooms and efficient, English-speaking staff delivering top-notch service. Room rates vary depending on the season. Book online for good deals. Add a 15% service charge to room rates.

Sanpi Youth Hostel
HOSTEL $

(三皮青年旅社; Sānpí Qīngnián Lǚshè; ☑2251 1133; www.gjqnls.com; 21 Yalu Jiang Jie; 鸭绿江街21号; dm/tw with shared bathroom ¥45/100; ❄@🛜) To the east of the North Tomb is this laid-back hostel which may remind you of a best friend's basement suite in the sub-urbs. Which is a bit odd as it's on the 5th floor of an otherwise unpromising-looking building next to a KTV. The location's not great, but there's laundry and internet and the rooms are organised and clean. From the South Train Station take bus 162 to Jianyuanxiaoqu stop.

Peace Hotel
HOTEL $

(和平宾馆; Hépíng Bīnguǎn; ☑2349 8888; www.hpbg.com.cn; 104 Shengli Beijie; 胜利北街104号; tw with shared bathroom ¥100, tw with bathroom ¥200-280; ❄@) Rooms can be a bit smoky but this clean, friendly hotel tower just 200m north of the train station is a good budget option. There are discounts of 20%.

Shěntiě Shěnzhàn Bīnguǎn
HOTEL $

(沈铁沈站宾馆; Shěnyáng Railway Station Hotel; ☑2358 5888; 2 Shengli Dajie; 胜利大街2号; r without bathroom ¥120, tw with bathroom ¥168-188; ❄@) A convenient if ageing place next to the South Train Station. Note that some of the cheaper rooms have no windows.

🍴 Eating

Both the North and South Train Stations are cheap-restaurant zones. You'll also find lots of reasonably priced restaurants around the Imperial Palace. Most have picture menus.

Shěnyáng

◎ Top Sights

Imperial Palace..............................D2
Liáoníng Provincial Museum..............C2

🛏 Sleeping

1 Home Inn.....................................D3
2 Liáoníng Bīnguǎn A3
3 Peace Hotel A3
4 Shěntiě Shěnzhàn Bīnguǎn................A3
5 Traders Hotel A3

✖ Eating

6 Carrefour Supermarket C1
7 Lǎobiān Dumplings.........................D2
8 Qīnzǐ Shāngmiàn...........................D3
9 View & World Vegetarian
    Restaurant................................B3
10 Yúfū Mǎtóu Shāokǎo.......................C2

◎ Drinking

11 Stroller's..................................B3

🏬 Shopping

12 Taiyuan Jie.................................A3
13 Zhong Jie...................................D2

Lǎobiān Dumplings   DUMPLINGS $$
(老边饺子馆; Lǎobiān Jiǎoziguǎn; 3f 208 Zhong Jie; dumplings ¥12-30; ⊙10am-10pm; 📶) Shěnyáng's most famous restaurant has been packing in the locals since 1829, and they continue to flock here for the fine boiled, steamed and fried dumplings in an array of flavours: from staid cabbage to mandarin duck and even curry. The restaurant is on the 3rd floor of the Lǎobiān Hotel which is just across from the B1 exit of Zhong Jie metro station.

 View & World Vegetarian Restaurant   VEGETARIAN $
(宽巷子素菜馆; Kuān Xiàngzi Sùcàiguǎn; 202 Shiyi Wei Lu; dishes ¥8-36; ⊙10am-10.30pm; 🖉📶) Peking duck and meatballs are on the menu here, but there won't be any actual meat on your plate. Everything is meat-free at this classy nearly vegan paradise, which claims to be the only non-MSG restaurant in all of northeast China (an astonishing claim if true). The fruit and vegie drinks pair up nicely with the main courses.

View & World is on one of Shěnyáng's busy eating streets and you'll find much to sample nearby, including real Peking duck, if you so desire.

Yúfū Mǎtóu Shāokǎo   SEAFOOD $
(沈阳渔夫码头烧烤; Fisherman's Harbour Barbecue; 75 Huigong Jie; dishes ¥15-36; ⊙11.30am-midnight) A friendly, fun, three-floor restaurant with a nautical theme. The seafood platter (¥118) arrives in a boat-shaped dish and satisfies two or three people easily. Plenty of meat is available, plus hotpot, meat skewers, and some very filling and cheap noodle and vegie dishes with an emphasis on spice.

Qīnzǐ Shāngmiàn   DŌNGBĚI $
(亲子商面; Shenyang Lu; dishes ¥8-18; ⊙8.30am-midnight) At the end of a short row of good restaurants is this family-run place serving simple cold noodle, meat and vegetable dishes. There's a picture menu.

Carrefour Supermarket   SUPERMARKET $
(家乐福; Jiālèfú; Beizhan Lu) Near the long-distance bus station. You can pack a picnic for your travels here or grab a quick bite from the decent food court.

🍷 Drinking

Liáoníng Bīnguǎn has a pleasant patio bar facing Zhongshan Lu that's open when the weather cooperates.

Stroller's   BAR
(流浪者餐厅; Liúlàngzhě; 36 Beiwu Jing Jie) This long-running ground floor pub is popular with both locals and expats and has a decent imported beer selection. The pub's street is not signed but if you take Exit B of Nanshichang Station, just cross the road and head north up the side street one block and you'll hit it.

🔒 Shopping

Near the South Train Station is **Taiyuan Jie**, one of Shěnyáng's major shopping streets, with high-end department stores and an extensive underground shopping street (mostly small clothing boutiques) that's the perfect place to feel the energy of modern Shěnyáng.

Zhong Jie, near the Imperial Palace, is another popular pedestrianised shopping zone that hopefully will one day get the resurfaced ground it deserves.

ℹ Information

ATMs can be found all over the city.
Bank of China (中国银行; Zhōngguó Yínháng) Government Sq (253 Shifu Dalu); South Train Station area (96 Zhonghua Lu; ⊙8.30am-5pm

Mon-Fri) South station area branch has 24-hour ATM. Government Sq branch has ATM and changes travellers cheques.

Internet cafe (网吧; wǎngbā; main level, South Train Station; per hr ¥4; ⊘24hr) May let you use computers without a Chinese ID, but there is no guarantee of this.

Public Security Bureau (PSB; 公安局; Gōng'ānjú; ☎2253 4850; Zhongshan Sq)

ⓘ Getting There & Away

Large hotels can book airline and train tickets, as can **China Travel Service of Shenyang** (沈阳市中国旅行社; Shěnyáng Shì Zhōngguó Lǚxíngshè; ☎137 0000 0681; 1 Shifu Lu; ⊘8.30am-5pm).

Air

Shenyang Taoxian International Airport has flights to South Korea and Russia as well as the following domestic cities:

Běijīng ¥700
Hā'ěrbīn ¥510
Shànghǎi ¥1380

Bus

The **long-distance express bus station** (长途汽车快速客运站; chángtú qìchē kuàisù kèyùnzhàn; 120 Huigong Jie) is south of Beizhan Lu, about a five-minute walk from the North Train Station and close to the Carrefour Supermarket. Current schedules are available at the information counter as you walk in. Buses service the following destinations:

Běijīng ¥149-166, 7½ hours, eight daily (from 8am to 9pm)
Chángchūn ¥85, 4½ hours, seven per day (8.30am to 5pm)
Dāndōng ¥82, 3½ hours, every 30 minutes (6am to 7pm)
Hā'ěrbīn ¥122, 6½ hours, two daily (11am and 2.30pm)
Xīngchéng ¥83, 4½ hours, two daily (8.50am and 3.40pm)

Train

Shěnyáng's major train stations are the North and South Stations. Many trains arrive at one station, stop briefly, then travel to the next; it may be different when departing – always confirm which station you need. Buy sleeper or D train tickets (to Běijīng or Shànghǎi) as far in advance as possible. Bus 262 runs between the North and South Train Stations, or take the metro.

SOUTH STATION TRAINS

Báihé (for Chángbáishān) hard/soft sleeper ¥100/156, three daily (departs 9.13am, 7.28pm and 8.18pm), 13 hours
Dàlián hard/soft seat ¥55/87, four to seven hours

Dāndōng hard/soft seat ¥42/64, five hours
Hā'ěrbīn hard/soft seat ¥44/72, seven hours
Xīngchéng hard/soft seat ¥54/84, four to six hours

NORTH STATION TRAINS

Běijīng (D train) ¥207, five hours, frequent
Běijīng hard seat/sleeper ¥99/172, 10 hours
Hā'ěrbīn (D train) ¥161, four hours, five daily
Chángchūn (D train) ¥88, 2½ hours, four morning trains

ⓘ Getting Around

TO/FROM THE AIRPORT The airport is 25km south of the city. Shuttle buses (¥15, hourly) leave from an alley just before the intersection of Zhonghua Lu and Heping Dajie. Taxis cost ¥80.

BUS Buses are cheap, frequent and cover the city but the subway covers most areas travellers want to visit. Maps of the routes (¥5) are sold at train stations.

SUBWAY With only two lines (Line 1 running east–west and Line 2 running north–south) and one connecting station, Shěnyáng's clean and relaxed subway system is easy to figure out. There are stops along both the North and South Train Stations as well as the North Tomb and Zhong Jie (for the Imperial Palace). The average ride costs ¥2 to ¥4. Stations have public toilets.

TAXI Taxis cost ¥8 for the first 3km, and ¥9 if air-conditioned.

Dàlián　　　　大连

☎0411 / POP 3.6 MILLION

Perched on the Liáodōng Peninsula and bordering the Yellow Sea, Dàlián is one of the most relaxed and liveable cities in the northeast, if not all of China. Tree-lined hilly streets with manageable traffic and fresh air, a surfeit of early-20th-century architecture, and an impressive coastline, complete with swimming beaches, just begins the list of its charms. Toss in a decent restaurant and bar scene, some serious shopping, and the buzz of a town growing more and more prosperous by the year, and that frequent Dàlián epithet, the 'Hong Kong of the North', looks like more than just bluster.

Dàlián is a fine place to unwind for a few days. But after lazing on the beaches, and strolling along the southwest coastline (on one of the world's longest continuous boardwalks), do pay a visit to the historic port town of Lǚshùn. The old battlefields and cemeteries offer a rare firsthand glimpse into some of the north's most turbulent days.

THE DÀLIÁN OIL DISASTER

It's still regarded as the worst oil spill in Chinese history. On 16 July 2010, two pipelines in the Xingang oil terminal burst as high-sulphur crude was being unloaded from an oil tanker. Within days, overwhelmed officials had acknowledged that over 400 sq km of ocean had been affected. They called on volunteers to help, and offered US$44 for every barrel of oil they recovered from the sea. That was all that was needed to unleash the entrepreneurial valour of the Chinese. Within three weeks 8000 workers on 800 fishing boats (with the help of a few specialist clean-up vessels) had removed almost all traces of the spill. Small fortunes were made, but volunteers were lucky if they had rubber gloves to work with. Some became seriously ill even before the clean-up was over.

Officially the government is sticking to its story that 1500 tonnes (about 11,000 barrels) were released into the Yellow Sea. Rick Steiner, a respected marine conservationist who has spent years working on oil spills around the world, visited the affected area not long after the spill and reported that several hundred thousand barrels of leaked oil is a more likely figure. This would place the Dàlián spill on a comparable scale with the Exxon Valdez disaster (which Steiner studied) off Alaska in 1989.

Two years later, the Dàlián coastline shows no signs of the spill, and swimmers have long gone back to enjoying the gold-sand beaches and warm waters. The long-term effects on the coastal environment, the fisheries and the locals, who suffered both from direct contact with the oil and from the toxic air that hung over the city for days, remains uncertain. No official studies were ever undertaken or released.

👁 Sights & Activities

TOP CHOICE Southwest Coastline OUTDOORS

Dàlián's southwest coastline (Map p302) is the city's most alluring natural destination. Dramatic headlands, deep bays and sandy beaches are the obvious attraction, but there are also parks, lighthouses and quaint villages, and the longest continuous boardwalk (reportedly at 20.9km) in the world joining them all.

Start your exploration either by taking the tram from downtown to **Xīnghǎi Sq**, or a bus to **Fùjiāzhuāng Beach** (傅家庄海滨; Fùjiāzhuāng Hǎitān). The square, which is sporting some heady architecture these days, is the site of Dàlián's popular beer festival, and is a good place to people watch, fly a kite, or just stroll about. Nearby is a small beach and amusement park.

Fùjiāzhuāng is a popular beach set in a deep bay. Junks float just offshore, small broken islands dot the horizon, and loads of families come here for no other reason than to have fun. Bus 5 leaves from Jiefang Lu (¥1, 20 to 30 minutes) and drops you off across from the beach.

A very pleasant boardwalk joins Fùjiāzhuāng and Xīnghǎi Sq. From the beach you can continue on this same walkway another 8km to **Lǎohǔtān Ocean Park** (老虎滩海洋公园; Lǎohǔ Tān Hǎiyáng Gōngyuán; www.lao hutan.com.cn; admission ¥210; ⏰7.30am-5.30pm), a family-friendly theme park with a **Polar Aquarium**. At Laohutan you can catch bus 30 (¥1) to Sanba or Zhongshan Square in central Dàlián.

But more spectacular coastline awaits along yet another stretch of the boardwalk. In a few kilometres you reach **Fisherman's Wharf** (漁人码头; Yúrén Mǎtóu), which is actually a seaside community built in the style of an early-20th-century American east coast village. The village makes a great backdrop for photos, has a pleasant square to enjoy a coffee, and features rather oddly a perfect replica of the 1853 German **Bremen Port Lighthouse**, built with bricks from razed local villages.

The boardwalk continues east along the coast past Fisherman's Wharf, but public transport is sparse so remember you will likely have to retrace your steps to Laohutan for a bus or taxi back to the city.

Golden Stone Beach BEACH

The coast around Golden Stone Beach (Jīnshítān), 60km north of the city, is in the process of being turned into a domestic tourism mecca with a number of theme parks, and rock formations commanding inflated entrance fees. The long pebbly beach itself is free and quite pretty, set in a wide bay with distant headlands.

Dàlián

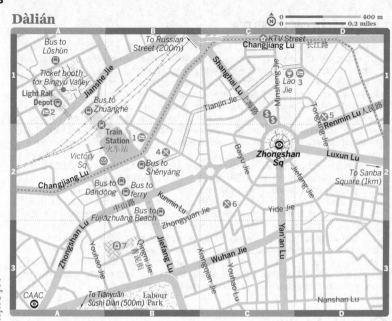

To get here take the light rail, known by the locals as Line 3 (轻轨三号线; Qīngguǐ Sānhàoxiàn), from the depot on the east side of Triumph Plaza, behind the Dàlián Train station (¥8, 50 minutes). From the beach station it's a 10-minute walk to the beach, or catch a tourist shuttle bus (¥20, 30 minutes), which winds round the coast first before dropping you off at the beach. There's a **visitor centre** to the right of the train station as you exit, with English-speaking staff if you need help.

Zhongshan Sq   HISTORIC BUILDINGS

(Map p298; 中山广场; Zhōngshān Guǎngchǎng) This is Dàlián's hub, a 223m wide square with 10 lanes radiating out from a centre first designed by the Russians in 1889. With the exception of the Dalian Financial Building, all the other grand structures hail from the early 20th century when Dàlián was under the control of the Japanese. Styles range from art deco to French Renaissance. The **Dàlián Bīnguǎn**, a dignified hotel built in 1914 and called then the Dalian Yamato Hotel, appeared in the movie *The Last Emperor*.

🛏 Sleeping

Reservations are highly recommended in the summer months, when prices may be 50% more than listed below. The train station area has a number of budget hotels but it's best to sleep elsewhere as it's a noisy, frenetic place. Touts will find you if you do need a room: rates are around ¥140 to ¥180 a night (add another ¥100 in high summer season).

Dalian South Mountain Youth Hostel   HOSTEL $

(Map p302; 大连南山国际青年旅舍; Dàlián Nánshān Guójì Qīngnián Lǚshè; 114 Minze St; 明泽街114号; ☎8263 1189; froh@163.com; dm ¥60-70, d/tw 178/188; ❀@🛜) Tucked away in a quiet hillside neighbourhood is this friendly little hostel with clean comfortable dorms and private rooms. Facilities include self-service laundry and kitchen, as well as computer use and wi-fi. The southwest coastline is a 15-minute bus ride away, numerous parks are within walking distance, and even the train station can be reached quickly by taxi (¥10). If you want to catch a bus here contact the hostel for directions.

Ibis Dalian Sanba Hotel   HOTEL $$

(Map p302; 大连三八宜必思酒店; Dàlián Sānbā Yíbìsī Jiǔdiàn; ☎3986 5555; www.ibishotel.com. cn; 49 Wuwu Rd; 中山区五五路49号; d & tw ¥219; ❀@) This European-style business hotel is in an ideal location surrounded by

Dàliàn

◎ **Top Sights**
 Zhongshan Sq C2

◎ **Sleeping**
 1 Bóhǎi Pearl Hotel B2
 2 Hanting Express A1
 3 Home Inn D1

◎ **Eating**
 4 Night Market B2
 5 Tiāntiān Yúgáng D1
 6 Xiǎo Yǎogǔ Shǎnxī Miàn
  Zhuāng C2

◎ **Shopping**
 7 New Mart Shopping Mall B3

restaurants and markets, but is also a five-minute walk to parks and quiet tree-lined streets. Rooms are slick and modern and the English-speaking staff are fairly attentive. For best rates book online.

Tian Tong Hotel　　　　　　　　　HOTEL $$
(Map p302; 天通大酒店; Tiān Tōng Dà Jiǔdiàn; 58 Luxun Lu; 鲁迅路58号; d/tw ¥518/497; ❉@) The off-season rates (up to 60% off) for this behemoth near Sanba Sq make it a solid choice, as does the location across from shops and restaurants, barbecue stalls and fruit stands. The southwest coast is just 10 minutes away by taxi, and you can walk the 1km to Zhongshan Sq in no time. Single travellers should ask for the Japanese-style rooms, which go for ¥168 during the off season.

Home Inn　　　　　　　　　　　　HOTEL $$
(Map p298; 如家快捷酒店; Rújiā Kuàijié Jiǔdiàn; ☑8263 9977; www.homeinns.com; 102 Tianjin Jie; 天津街102号; d/tw ¥189/209; ❉@) With its brightly coloured and tidy little rooms, free broadband and in-house restaurant serving cheap but tasty dishes, this is a good choice for the city centre. Recently the square around the hotel has seen some impressive urban regeneration, with a fake but good 'old street' opening just 100m away with a number of high-end cafes and bars. There's also a continuous pedestrian-only street/night market extending all the way to the train station.

Bóhǎi Pearl Hotel　　　　　　　　HOTEL $$$
(Map p298; 渤海明珠酒店; Bóhǎi Míngzhū Jiǔdiàn; ☑8812 8888; www.bohaipearl.com; 8 Vic-

tory Sq; 胜利广场8号; r from ¥867; ⊝❉@❉) This 30-storey tower with a kitschy revolving restaurant faces the train station, but the large lobby area means you are spared the madness of the outside world. Rooms are in need of an update, but with discounts of 40% they're good value, especially in summer. A few unexpected facilities include a spa and pool.

Hanting Express　　　　　　　　　HOTEL $$
(Map p298; 汉庭快捷酒店; Hàntíng kuàijié Jiǔdiàn; ☑6666 2888; 32 Yunyang Jie; 云阳街32号; r from ¥209; ❉@❉) Just behind the train station, overlooking the light-rail square, is this tidy business hotel. There's broadband internet in every room and wi-fi in the lobby. The hotel entrance is to the back of the building away from the light-rail square.

Dàlián Bīnhǎi Hotel　　　　　　　HOTEL $$$
(Map p302; 大连滨海大厦; Dàlián Bīnhǎi Dàshà; ☑8240 6666; fax 8240 6668; 2 Binhai Xilu; 滨海西路2号; r/ste ¥460/620; ❉@) A favourite with visiting Russians, this high-rise hotel could be better maintained, but it's got a great location literally across the road from Fùjiāzhuāng Beach. Discounts of 30% in the off season.

✗ Eating

There are plenty of small restaurants on the roads leading off Zhongshan Sq and Friendship Sq. The upscale New Mart Shopping Mall has a spiffy food court (dishes from ¥8 to ¥38) on the 5th floor with a huge range of eating and drinking options. It's a good choice for a single traveller in a city where most restaurants are set up for groups. There's also a well-provisioned supermarket on the lower level. Note that Friendship Sq has numerous buildings and malls on it, so look for the big mall directly across from Starbucks. The food court in the nearby underground mall in Victory Sq is a bit cheaper but not as nice in atmosphere.

Both sides of the plaza outside the train station are lined with fruit vendors and shops selling cheap *bāozi* (包子; steamed dumplings). Zhongyuan Jie and Kunmin Jie are loaded with restaurants serving stir-fries and stews with the heavy flavours of the north.

Xúncǎi Lāmiàn　　　　　　　　DUMPLINGS $
(Map p302; 旬采拉面; Chaoyang Jie; dishes ¥12-20; ◷8am-8.30pm) If you're staying in the Sanba Sq area this popular little eatery

one block southeast of the square is a great venue for starting your day or for a light meal any time. In addition to its delicious *xiǎolóngbāo* (小笼包; steamed dumplings) look for wonton soup and smoked chicken leg. There's a picture menu on the wall.

Xiǎo Yáogǔ

Shǎnxī Miàn Zhuāng   SHAANXI $

(Map p298; 小腰鼓陕西面庄; dishes ¥5-22; ⊙8am-9pm) At the end of Zhongyuan Jie is this Shaanxi restaurant that serves great dishes such as *jiāmó* (羊肉夹馍; lamb in pita bread) or *pàomó* (泡馍; bread stew) at a ridiculously low price. A light meal will set you back under ¥15. Look for the red lanterns outside and place your order at the front desk beside the picture menu.

Tiāntiān Yúgǎng   SEAFOOD $$$

(Map p298; 天天鱼港; 10 Renmin Lu; dishes ¥12-88; ⊙11am-10pm) Choose your meal from the near museum-level variety of aquatic creatures at this upscale seafood restaurant. Most dishes are set out in refrigerated displays, making this a rare easy seafood-eating experience in China.

Tiānyuán Sùshí Diàn   VEGETARIAN $

(off Map p298; 天缘素食店; Tangshan Jie; dishes ¥12-38; ⊙8.30am-8pm) Close to Labour Park is this tiny Buddhist vegetarian place popular with worshippers at the nearby temple. To find the entrance head up Tangshan Jie about 30m past the intersection with Tongshan Jie.

Night market   MARKET $

Stretching from the train station to the Home Inn off Tianjin Jie, this outdoor market (Map p298), open during the evenings, offers near endless outdoor venues to eat barbecued seafood with a beer. There's also a smaller market around Sanba Sq with outdoor barbecue stalls and seating, in addition to an abundance of fruit stands.

 Drinking & Entertainment

Dàlián has the most happening bar and club scene of any city in the northeast. Check out *Focus on Dalian* magazine for the latest.

Changjiang Lu is home to a host of upscale KTVs, clubs and bars. A fake, but still very pleasant **Lǎo Jiē** (Map p298; Old Street) sits off the plaza near the Tianjin Jie Home Inn and has several upscale cafes and bars with indoor and outdoor seating.

I-55 Coffee Stop & Bakery   CAFE

(Map p302; Àiwǔwǔ Měishì Kāfēizhàn; 67 Gao'erji Lu; ⊙8.30am-midnight; ☎◉) For coffee, cakes and sandwiches, try the I-55. There's a cosy upscale atmosphere here with throw-cushion-decked lounges, jazzy music and a nice leafy outdoor patio.

Lenbach Beer House   PUB

(Map p302; 兰巴赫西餐 &啤酒坊; Lán Bāhè Xīcān & Píjiǔ Fáng; 49 Gao'erji Lu) This two-storey, upscale Bavarian beer pub serves a fantastic range of German beers, including several darks and whites on tap (¥35 for 0.5l). There is outdoor seating so you can enjoy the quiet neighbourhood atmosphere on Gao'erji Lu, and there's a selection of sausage dishes if quenching your thirst builds up a hunger.

Noah's Ark   BAR

(Map p302; Nuòyà Fāngzhōu; 32 Wusi Lu; ⊙12.30pm-2am; ☎) A laid-back, long-standing place to catch local musicians and grab a beer. There's indoor and outdoor seating and a good mix of locals and expats in the crowd.

 Shopping

There are malls all over Dàlián. The **New Mart Shopping Mall** (Map p298), which is south of Victory Sq, is a pedestrian plaza lined with upscale department stores. Across from the train station there's an

---

BEER MANIA

For 12 days every July and spilling over into August, Dàlián stages the **Dàlián International Beer Festival**, its very own version of Munich's Oktoberfest. Beer companies from across China and around the world set up tents at the vast Xīnghǎi Sq (Map p302), near the coast, and locals and visitors flock (more than two million in 2012) to sample the brews, gorge on barbecue and snacks from around China, listen to live music and generally make whoopee. Entrance tickets are a low ¥10 and in 2012 there were 30 beer vendors offering more than 400 brands for sampling. See the festivals page on the China Highlights (www.chinahighlights.com) website for the dates each year.

enormous underground shopping centre below Victory Sq. Dàlián's **Russian Street** (off Map p298), a pedestrianised street with some of the city's oldest buildings, is a good spot for souvenir hunting.

Information

There are ATMs all around town. Zhongshan Sq has a number of large bank branches including **Bank of China** (中国银行; Zhōngguó Yínháng; 9 Zhongshan Sq), where you can change currency and travellers cheques.

Dàlián Xpat (www.dalianxpat.com) An excellent source of English-language information about restaurants, bars and clubs in Dàlián.

Focus on Dalian (www.focusondalian.com) Bilingual magazine with good articles and restaurant and bar recommendations.

Getting There & Away

Air

Dàlián International Airport is 12km from the city centre and well connected to most cities in China and the region. Tickets can be purchased at the **Civil Aviation Administration of China** (CAAC; 中国民航; Zhōngguó Mínháng; 8361 2888; www.tickets.dlairport.com; Zhongshan Lu) or any of the travel offices nearby. In addition to the domestic destinations below, there are also flights to Khabarovsk, Vladivostok and Tokyo.

Běijīng ¥710, one hour
Hā'ěrbīn ¥840, 1½ hours
Hong Kong ¥2640, 3½ hours

Boat

There are several daily boats to Yāntái (¥160 to ¥600, five to eight hours) and Wēihǎi (¥170 to ¥600, seven to eight hours). Buy tickets at the passenger ferry terminal in the northeast of Dàlián or from one of the many counters in front of the train station. To the ferry terminal, take bus 13 (¥1) from the southeast corner of Shengli Guangchang and Zhongshan Lu near the train station.

Bus

Long-distance buses leave from various points around the train station. It can be tricky to find the correct ticket booths, and they do occasionally move.

Dāndōng ¥100, four hours, seven daily, 6.20am to 2.30pm. Buses leave from stand No 2 on Shengli Guangchang just south of Changjiang Lu.

Lǚshùn 旅顺; ¥8, one hour, every 10 minutes. Buses leave from the back of the train station, across the square.

BORDER CROSSING: DÀLIÁN TO SOUTH KOREA

The Korean-run **Da-in Ferry** (Dàlián 8270 5082, Incheon 032-891 7100, Seoul 822-3218 6500; www.dainferry.co.kr) to Incheon in South Korea departs from Dàlián on Monday, Wednesday and Friday at 4.30pm (¥920 to ¥1848, 16 hours).

Shěnyáng 沈阳; ¥128, five hours, every 30 minutes. Buses depart from the northeast corner of Victory Sq.

Zhuānghé 庄河; ¥47, 2½ hours, frequent. Buses leave from in front of the ticket booth on Jiangshe Jie, the first street behind the train station.

Train

Buy your ticket as early as possible for long-distance trains.

Běijīng hard seat/sleeper ¥140/240, 10 to 12 hours

Chángchūn hard seat/sleeper ¥83/164, nine to 10 hours

Hā'ěrbīn hard seat/sleeper ¥110/201, nine to 13 hours

Shěnyáng seat ¥28 to ¥55, five to six hours

Getting Around

Dàlián's central district is not large and can be covered on foot.

TO/FROM THE AIRPORT A taxi from the city centre costs ¥30 to ¥60 depending on the time of day. No shuttle buses.

BUS Buses are plentiful and stops have English signboards explaining the route.

TAXI Fares start at ¥8; most trips are less than ¥15.

TRAM Dàlián has a very slow but stylish tram, with two lines – the 201 and the 202 (¥1 to ¥2 each). No 201 runs past the train station on Changjiang Lu, while 202 runs out to the ocean and Xīnghǎi Sq (you must take 201 first and transfer).

Around Dàlián

LǙSHÙN 旅顺

With its excellent port, and strategic location on the northeast coast, Lǚshùn (formerly Port Arthur) was the focal point of both Russian and Japanese expansion in the late 19th and early 20th centuries. The bloody 1904–05 Russo-Japanese War finally saw the area fall under Japanese colonial rule, which would continue for the next 40 years.

Greater Dàlián

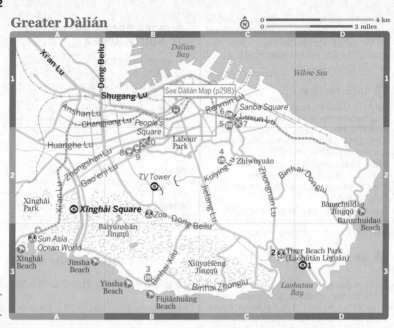

Greater Dàlián

◎ Top Sights
Xīnghǎi Square.....................................A2

◎ Sights
1 Fisherman's Wharf D3
2 Polar Aquarium C3

◎ Sleeping
3 Dàlián Bīnhǎi Hotel B3
4 Dalian South Mountain Youth
   Hostel C2
5 Ibis Dalian Sanba Hotel......................C1
6 Tian Tong Hotel..................................C1

◎ Eating
7 Xúncǎi Lāmiàn....................................C1

◎ Drinking
8 I-55 Coffee Stop & Bakery..................B2
9 Lenbach Beer House...........................B2
10 Noah's Ark B2

Lǔshùn is a must-see during any visit to Dàlián. It's a relaxed town built on the hills and, while most sites are related to military history, there's an excellent museum on Liáoníng, as well as a number of scenic lookouts and parks.

As soon as you exit the bus station at Lǔshùn, taxis will cry out for your business. A few hours touring the sights will cost ¥150 to ¥200. Pick up a bilingual English–Chinese map at the station newsstand to help you negotiate.

◎ Sights

TOP CHOICE Soviet Martyrs Cemetery CEMETERY
(苏军烈士陵园; Sūjūn Lièshì Língyuán; ◎8.30-4.30pm) The largest cemetery in China for foreign-born nationals honours Soviet soldiers who died in the liberation of northeast China at the end of WWII, as well as pilots killed during the Korean War (known as the War Against US Aggression). Designed by Soviet advisers, the cemetery is heavy with communist-era iconography. A giant rifle-holding soldier guards the front, while inside are memorials to the sacrifice of Soviet soldiers and rows of neatly tended gravestones.

Lǔshùn Museum MUSEUM
(旅顺博物馆; Lǔshùn Bówùguǎn; admission ¥20; ◎9am-4pm Tue-Sun) The history of Liáoníng province is covered in this stylish old museum in a building erected in 1917. Among the thousands of artefacts on display are ancient bronzes, coins and paintings, as well as several mummies. The area around

the museum has a number of other old buildings from the Japanese colonial era and is a great spot for photographs.

Hill 203
WAR MEMORIAL
(二0三景区; Èr Líng Sān Jǐngqū; admission ¥30) During the 1904–05 Russo-Japanese War, troops fought like wildcats for control of this strategic hill (when you get to the top you'll see why). More than 5000 Russian and 10,000 Japanese soldiers lost their lives in the battle, which eventually went to the Japanese. Afterwards the victors erected a 10m-high bullet-shaped memorial (constructed from shell casings) and, remarkably, it still stands to this day.

Lǔshùn Railway Station
HISTORIC BUILDING
(旅顺火车站; Lǔshùn Huǒchēzhàn) Built in 1903 during Russia's brief control of the area, the handsome station was rebuilt in 2005 following the original design. It's worth a pop by on your way to other sights.

❶ Getting There & Away

Buses to Lǔshùn (¥8, one hour) leave every 10 minutes from a stop across the square at the back of the Dàlián Train Station (see Map p296). Buy your ticket from the booth before lining up. Buses run from early morning to evening.

BĪNGYÙ VALLEY
冰峪沟
If you can't travel south to Guìlín (p587), Bīngyù Valley (Bīngyù Gōu) offers a taste of what you're missing. About 250km northeast of Dàlián, the valley has tree-covered limestone cliffs set alongside a river; it's similar to Guìlín, if not nearly as dramatic. From the entrance a boat takes you along a brief stretch of the river, where rock formations rise steeply along the banks, before depositing you at a dock. From there, you can hire your own little boat and paddle around the shallow waters, or follow some short trails along the river and up to some lookouts.

The park is increasingly popular with big tour groups, who come for the zip lines, tame amusement-park rides, and even jet-skiing. Given the rather small area that you can explore, it can be tough to find any tranquility in this otherwise lovely environment.

In summer, day trips run from the train station area, leaving at 7.30am and returning around 7pm. Buy your ticket (¥238) the day before from the tourism vans across from the light-rail depot in the back train station area. It's not really worth coming out here on your own.

Dāndōng
丹东

☎0415 / POP 780,400

The principal gateway to North Korea (Cháoxiǎn) from China, Dāndōng has a buzz that's unusual for a Chinese city of its size. Separated from the Democratic People's Republic of Korea (DPRK) by the Yālù River (Yālù Jiāng), Dāndōng thrives on trade, both illegal and legal, with North Korea.

For most visitors to Dāndōng, this is as close as they will get to the DPRK. While you can't see much, the contrast between Dāndōng's lively, built-up riverfront and the desolate stretch of land on the other side of the Yālù River speaks volumes about the dire state of the North Korean economy and the restrictions under which its people live.

Although China International Travel Service (CITS) runs tours to the DPRK, they are aimed at Chinese nationals. If you want to visit, you'd do better to travel with the reputable Běijīng-based **Koryo Tours** (☎010-6416 7544; www.koryogroup.com; 27 Beisanlitun Nan, Běijīng), which can help you organise visas and offers trips designed for Westerners. At the time of writing, US citizens could fly into North Korea but could not take the train from Dāndōng to North Korea.

Dāndōng is relatively compact and easy to walk around. The river is about 800m southeast of the train station while the main shopping district is just east of the station.

◉ Sights & Activities

North Korean Border
BORDER, PARK
(北朝鲜边界; Běi Cháoxiǎn Biānjiè) For views of the border, stroll along the riverfront **Yālùjiāng Park** that faces the North Korean city of Sinuiju.

The area's most intriguing sight is the shrapnel-pockmarked **Broken Bridge** (Yālùjiāng Duànqiáo; admission ¥30; ⊙7am-6.30pm). In 1950, during the Korean War, American troops 'accidentally' bombed the original steel-span bridge between the two countries. The North Koreans dismantled the bridge less than halfway across the river, leaving a row of support columns. You can wander along the remaining section and get within the distance of a good toss of a baseball to the North Korean shoreline. The Sino–Korean Friendship Bridge, the official border crossing between China and North Korea, is next to the old one, and trains and trucks rumble across it on a regular basis.

To get closer to North Korea, take a 30- to 40-minute **boat cruise** (guānguāng chuán; ⏱7am-6pm) from the tour-boat piers on either side of the bridges. The large boats (¥60) are cheaper than the smaller speedboats (¥80), but you have to wait for the former to fill up with passengers (on average 30 minutes). In the summer you can sometimes see kids splashing about in the river, as well as fishermen and the crews of the boats moored on the other side.

Jīnjiāng Pagoda
PAGODA

(锦江塔; Jǐnjiāng Tǎ) The highest point around for miles, this pagoda sits atop Jǐnjiāng Shān in a park of the same name. The views across to North Korea are unparalleled and the park itself (a former military zone) is a well-tended expanse of forested slopes. You can take a taxi to the entrance or easily walk there in 20 minutes from the train station, though it's another steep kilometre uphill to the pagoda.

FREE Museum to Commemorate US Aggression
MUSEUM

(抗美援朝纪念馆; Kàngměi Yuáncháo Jìniànguǎn; ⏱9am-4pm Tue-Sun) With everything from statistics to shells, this comprehensive museum offers Chinese and North Korean perspectives – they won it! – on the war with the US-led UN forces (1950–53). There are good English captions here. The adjacent North Korean War Memorial Column was built 53m high, symbolising the year the Korean War ended.

A taxi to the museum will cost ¥8 from downtown, or you can walk as part of a trip to the Jīnjiāng Pagoda. From the entrance to the park on Shanshang Jie, it's about 1.5km to the entrance of the memorial.

Tiger Mountain Great Wall
GREAT WALL

(虎山长城; Hǔshān Chángchéng; admission ¥60; ⏱8am-dusk) About 12km northeast of Dāndōng, this steep, restored stretch of the wall, known as Tiger Mountain Great Wall, was built during the Ming dynasty and runs parallel to the North Korean border. Unlike other sections of the wall, this one sees comparatively few tourists.

The wall ends at a small **museum** (admission ¥10, buy ticket at main entrance booth) with a few weapons, vases and wartime dioramas. From here two routes loop back to the entrance. Heading straight ahead on the road is the easy way back. But there's nothing to see. Better is to climb back up the stairs a short way and look for a path on the right

FREE TRADE AMONG COMMUNIST ALLIES

It's no exaggeration to say that, without China, the North Korean regime would not survive. China has been trading with the Democratic People's Republic of Korea (DPRK) since the 1950s and is now the country's largest trading partner. Almost half of all the DPRK imports come directly from China, and the Hermit Kingdom is the direct beneficiary of more than half of all Chinese foreign aid. That China supports its neighbour for its own geopolitical reasons is no surprise – that it does so for economic reasons probably is. However, put simply, Chinese leaders in the northern provinces insist they need market reforms across the border if they are to see their own long-term development plans fully realised.

Dāndōng is the hub of Sino–North Korean trade, and the site of a possible free-trade zone between the two countries. Yes, you read that right. In early June 2011, China and the DPRK announced plans to establish a joint manufacturing, tourism and IT zone on North Korea's Hwanggumpyong and Wihwa Islands. As with Dāndōng not so many years ago, these islands are currently little more than farmland, and turning the area into what Pyongyang has called the 'Hong Kong of North Korea' is going to take some doing. While Dāndōng's economic zones have seen impressive development these past five years, satellite images show that so far the only changes to the North Korean side are piles of dumped construction waste – from China.

But one area where the two nations have made progress is in expanding working visas. In 2012 some 40,000 North Korean seamstresses, construction workers, technicians and miners were granted industrial training visas for employment in China. (Some analysts believe the program, which has not officially been announced, could see numbers go higher than 100,000.) While most of the workers' wages will be remitted directly back to the near-bankrupt DPRK government, North Koreans are still rushing to take advantage of the program.

that drops and then literally runs along the cliff face. There are some good scrambles and in 20 minutes or so you'll get to a point called Yībùkuà – 'one step across' – marking an extremely narrow part of the river between the two countries. Not far past this you'll reach an area where you can walk back to the entrance gate in a minute or take a short boat ride along the river.

Buses to the wall (¥6.50, 40 minutes) run about every hour from the Dāndōng's long-distance bus station.

📖 Sleeping

There are many hotels in Dāndōng, most for around ¥200 a night. High-summer rates may be 30% to 50% more than the prices given below.

Huá Xià Cūn Bīnguǎn HOTEL $$
(华夏村宾馆; ☑212 1999; 11 Bajing Jie; 八经街11号; d incl breakfast from ¥200; ✳@) This is a good budget option, with rooms sporting comfort far above their price level, broadband internet, and a location smack in the middle of town. The restaurant on the ground floor serves a range of tasty northern dishes (¥15 to ¥60) and has a picture menu wall. Portions are large. The hotel is on the corner of Bajing Jie and Qiwei Lu. Discounts of 25% are usual.

Zhong Lian Hotel HOTEL $$$
(中联大酒店; Zhōng Lián Dà Jiǔdiàn; ☑233 3333; www.zlhotel.com; 62 Binjiang Zhong Lu; 滨江中路62号; d/tw incl breakfast ¥478/578; ✳@✇) Directly across from the Broken Bridge is this solid midrange option with large rooms, an even larger marble lobby (with wi-fi) and English-speaking staff. Discounts available.

Lǜyuàn Bīnguǎn HOTEL $
(绿苑宾馆; ☑212 7777; fax 210 9888; cnr Shiwei Lu & Sanjing Jie; 三经街十纬路交界处; dm with shared bathroom ¥50-60, s with shared bathroom ¥128, d & tw with bathroom from ¥168; ✳@) There are reasonable singles and three- and four-bed dorms at this long-running guesthouse on busy Shiwei Lu. The more expensive doubles and twins (which include internet) are a bit overpriced.

🍴 Eating & Drinking

On summer nights, the smoke from hundreds of barbecues drifts over Dāndōng as street corners become impromptu restaurants serving up fresh seafood and bottles of Yālù River beer, the refreshing local brew.

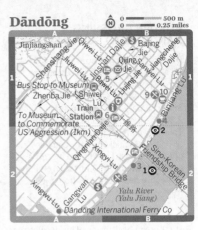

Dāndōng

◎ Sights
1 Broken Bridge B2
2 Yālùjiāng Park B2

⊕ Activities, Courses & Tours
3 Tour-Boat Piers B2
4 Tour-Boat Piers B1

📖 Sleeping
5 Huá Xià Cūn Bīnguǎn B1
6 Lǜyuàn Bīnguǎn B1
7 Zhong Lian Hotel B2

⊗ Eating
8 Píngrǎng Sōngdǎoyuán Fàndiàn B2
9 Tesco's B1

⊖ Drinking
10 Peter's Coffee House B1

One of the best places for barbecue is in the tents on the corner of Bawei Lu and Qijing Jie. More conventional restaurants, including a range of Korean, hotpot and DIY barbecue, as well as comfortable cafes where you can sip coffee and watch how the other half lives, line the riverfront on either side of the bridges. There's also a big **Tesco's** (Lègòu; cnr Liuwei Lu & Sanjing Jie) supermarket in the east part of town.

**Píngrǎng
Sōngdǎoyuán Fàndiàn** NORTH KOREAN $$
(平壤松涛园饭店; Jinjiang Lu; dishes ¥10-48; ⊙dinner) A big part of the experience for many travellers to this region is eating at a North Korean restaurant with reputedly real

BORDER CROSSING: DĀNDŌNG TO SOUTH KOREA

Dāndōng International Ferry Co (丹东国际航运有限公司: www.dandong ferry.co.kr; cnr Xingwu Lu & Gangwan Lu; ⊙8am-5pm) runs a boat to Incheon in South Korea, with a boarding time of 2.20pm (4pm departure) on Tuesday, Thursday and Sunday (¥1010 to ¥1710, 16 hours). Buy tickets at the company's office on Xingwu Lu. A bus to the ferry terminal leaves at 1.50pm (¥20) on the respective departure days from the train station.

North Korean waitresses. This locally recommended place sits appropriately enough just a few hundred metres from the Broken Bridge (directly beside SPR Coffee) and has a range of traditional dishes, from pickled vegies to hotpot to fish stews that can cost hundreds of yuán. There's a full picture menu to help you decide.

Peter's Coffee House CAFE, WESTERN $$
(彼得咖啡室; Bǐde Kāfēi Shì; www.peterscoffee house.com; Binjiang Lu; ⊙9am-9pm; 🛜) Down by the riverfront is this friendly cafe run by a long-term Canadian expat family. In addition to its excellent coffees, Peter's serves milkshakes and sodas (¥25), authentic Western baked goods, a fine all-day breakfast (¥30; great hash browns), burgers and sandwiches. This is also the place to go for local information and recommendations on the latest North Korean eatery in town.

❶ Information

Bank of China (中国银行; Zhōngguó Yínháng; 60 Jinshan Dajie) Has ATM and will change travellers cheques. Also an ATM closer to the river at 77-1 Binjiang Zhong Lu.

China International Travel Service (CITS; 中国国际旅行社; Zhōngguó Guójì Lǚxíngshè; ☑213 2196; 20 Shiwei Lu, at Jiangcheng Dajie; ⊙8am-5.30pm) Can arrange DPRK visits with Chinese tours. Email English-speaking Jackie Zhang (jacky790117@hotmail.com) for details.

Public Security Bureau (PSB; 公安局; Gōng'ānjú; 15 Jiangcheng Dajie)

❶ Getting There & Away

Dāndōng airport has infrequent flights to a few cities in China, but most travellers arrive by bus or train.

Bus

The **long-distance bus station** (98 Shiwei Lu) is near the train station.

Dàlián ¥100, 3½ hours, seven daily (7.50am to 2.50pm)

Jí'ān ¥80, seven hours, one daily (8.30am)

Shěnyáng ¥82, three hours, every 30 minutes (5.10am to 6.30pm)

Tōnghuà ¥82, seven hours, two daily (6.30am and 8.50am)

Train

The train station is in the centre of town, north of the river. A lofty Mao statue greets arriving passengers.

Shěnyáng seat ¥24 to ¥44, four hours

Xīngchéng   兴城

☑0429 / POP 140,000

Despite being one of only four Ming-dynasty cities to retain their complete outer walls and boasting the oldest surviving temple in all of northeastern China, as well as an up-and-coming beach resort, Xīngchéng has stayed well off the radar of most travellers. In truth it's still a bit dusty and rough round the edges, and the old city is as notable for its rows of jeans shops as Ming gates, but conditions are improving and historians and aficionados will have a field day here.

Xīngchéng's main drag is Xinghai Lu Er duan (兴海路二段), where you'll find hotels, a **Bank of China** (中国银行; Zhōngguó Yínháng) with a 24-hour ATM, and restaurants. From the train station head right, take the first left, and then a quick right to get onto Xinghai Lu Yi Duan. This merges into Er Duan (Section 2) in a kilometre.

◎ Sights

Old City HISTORIC SITE
(老城; Lǎo Chéng) The walled city, dating back to 1430, is the principal reason to visit Xīngchéng. Modern Xīngchéng has grown up around it, but it's still home to around 3000 people. You can enter by any of the four gates, but the easiest one to find is the **south gate** (南门; nánmén), which is just off Xinghai Lu Er Duan. There are signs in English and Chinese pointing the way.

In addition to the **City Walls** (城墙; Chéngqiáng; admission ¥25; ⊙8am-5pm), the **Drum Tower** (鼓楼; Gǔlóu; admission ¥20; ⊙8am-5pm), which sits slap in the middle of the Old City, and the watchtower on the southeastern corner of the city are all intact.

You can do a complete circuit of the walls in around an hour.

Also inside the Old City is the **Gao House** (将军府; Jiāngjūn Fǔ; admission ¥10; ⊙8am-5pm), the former residence of General Gao Rulian, who was one of Xīngchéng's most famous sons. The impressive and well-maintained **Confucius Temple** (文庙; Wénmiào; admission ¥35; ⊙8am-5pm), built in 1430, is reputedly the oldest temple in northeastern China. Don't miss the incredibly incongruous **dinosaur museum** at the back of the grounds.

If you plan on seeing all the above, buy the ¥80 pass that grants admission to every paid site within the walled town.

BEACHES

Xīngchéng's imaginatively named **Beach 1** (第一浴场), **Beach 2** (第二浴场) and **Beach 3** (第三浴场) are pretty enough, with groomed golden sands and calm waters, but are not particularly special.

At Beach 1 look for a statue honouring **Juhua Nu** (the Chrysanthemum Woman). According to local legend, she changed herself into an island to protect Xīngchéng from a sea dragon. This island, **Júhuā Dǎo**, lies 9km off the coast and is home to a fishing community, a small beach and a couple of temples. Daily **ferries** (round trip ¥175; ⊙depart 8.30am & 10am, return noon, 2pm & 5.30pm) leave from the northern end of Beach 1.

Bus 1 (¥1) travels from Xinghai Lu to Beach 1 (9km from the city centre) in about 30 minutes, and then further north to Beach 2 and Beach 3. A taxi to the area costs ¥15 to ¥20.

🛏 Sleeping

Cheap hotels around the train station won't accept foreigners. Small hotels line the street across from Beach 1, but again, the budget places won't accept foreigners. Rooms in ordinary beach hotels go for hundreds a night even in the off season.

Jīn Zhǒng Zi Dà Shà   HOTEL $$
(金种子宾馆; ☑352 1111; 9 Xinghai Lu Yi Duan; 兴海路一段9号; r from ¥398; ❄@) Right in the heart of the city on a busy intersection, this hotel offers comfortable rooms, free broadband internet and a good attached restaurant (dishes from ¥16 to ¥36). With the standard discount a double goes for around ¥200.

Yǎ Yí Xuān Bīnguǎn   HOTEL $
(雅宜轩宾馆; Xinghai Lu Yi Duan; ☑513 4488; d ¥158-188, tw ¥228; ❄@) Rooms are spacious though somewhat cheaply furnished in this new hotel, a five-minute walk from the train station heading into town. The pricier doubles and twins come with computers and broadband internet.

🍴 Eating

Unsurprisingly, seafood is big here. Restaurants line the beachfront at Beach 1, where you can pick your crustacean or fish from the tanks in which they await their death.

The restaurant in the **Jīn Zhǒng Zi Dà Shà** (dishes ¥16-36; ⊙breakfast, lunch & dinner) serves an excellent range of seafood, meat and vegetable dishes. There's a picture menu and also display items you can point to. Around the hotel you'll find other seafood and stir-fry places, many also with picture menus.

In the evenings, head to the tents outside the South Gate for barbecued meats and vegetables served with plenty of beer.

ℹ Getting There & Away

Xīngchéng is a stop for many trains between Běijīng and Hā'ěrbīn (and all cities in between). It can be easier to get a bus out than a train, but head to **Jǐnzhōu South Station** for comfortable D trains to major cities. Note that buses and trains from Xīngchéng go to the main station in Jǐnzhōu first; there are buses (¥5, 30 minutes) out the front of the South Station.

Bus

Xīngchéng's bus station (兴城市客运站; Xīngchéng shì kèyùn zhàn) is just to the left of the train station.

Běijīng ¥131, one daily (8.10am)

Jǐnzhōu ¥18, two hours, every 30 minutes (6.30am-3.30pm)

Shānhǎiguān ¥20.50, two hours, two daily (6.50am and 7.40am)

Shěnyáng ¥81, 3½ hours, five daily

Train

Běijīng hard/soft seat ¥63/110, six to seven hours, six daily

Jǐnzhōu seat ¥13, one hour, several morning trains then again late afternoon

Shānhǎiguān hard/soft seat ¥17/27, 1½ hours

Shěnyáng hard/soft seat ¥47/72, four hours

LIÁONÍNG XĪNGCHÉNG

Jílín

POP 27.1 MILLION

Includes »

Chángbái Shān............. 310
Yánjí 313
Ji'ān 313
Běidàhú Ski Resort 316
Chángchūn 316

Best Landscapes

» Heaven Lake (p310)
» Yánjí to Báihé (p314)
» Wandu Mountain City (p315)

Best Historical Sights

» Puppet Emperor's Palace (p316)
» Koguryo Kingdom (p314)
» Bānruò Temple (p316)

Why Go?

A flirty province, Jílín (吉林) teases with the ancient and the modern, the artificial and the supernatural. Travellers tired of great walls and imperial facades can explore Western-influenced palaces and the ruins of an ancient Korean kingdom. In fact much of the far-eastern region comprises the little-known Korean Autonomous Prefecture, home to more than one million ethnic Koreans. Kimchi and cold noodles dominate the menu here and there's an easy acceptance of outsiders.

Known for its motor cities and smokestack towns, Jílín is also a popular ski destination and boasts China's largest nature reserve. So go for the contrasts? No, go for the super-latives. Heaven Lake, a stunning, deep-blue volcanic crater lake within the country's largest reserve, is one of China's most mesmerising natural wonders. Jílín can be a little rough around the edges at times, but its rewards are pure polished jewels.

When to Go
Chángchūn

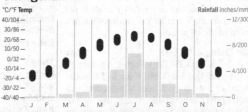

Jun–Sep Best months to visit Chángbái Shān.

Jul–Aug Country-side around the Korean Autonomous Prefecture at its most bucolic.

Nov–Mar Ski season at Běidàhú Ski Resort.

History

Korean kings once ruled parts of Jílín and the discovery of important relics from the ancient Koguryo kingdom (37 BC–AD 668) in the small southeastern city of Jí'ān has resulted in the area being designated a World Heritage Site by Unesco.

The Japanese occupation of Manchuria in the early 1930s pushed Jílín to the world's centre stage. Chángchūn became the capital of what the Japanese called Manchukuo, with Puyi (the last emperor of the Qing dynasty) given the role of figurehead of the puppet government. In 1944 the Russians wrested control of Jílín from the Japanese and, after stripping the area of its industrial base, handed the region back to Chinese control. For the next several years Jílín would pay a heavy price as one of the frontlines in the civil war between the Kuomintang and the Chinese Communist Party (CCP).

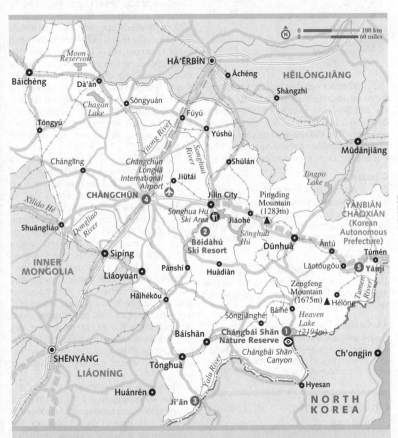

Jílín Highlights

❶ Visit China's largest nature reserve, **Chángbái Shān** (p310), with its waterfalls, birch forests and aptly named **Heaven Lake** (p311)

❷ Hit the slopes at the **Běidàhú Ski Resort** (p316),

one of China's premier skiing spots

❸ Explore the mysterious remains of the ancient Koguryo kingdom in **Jí'ān** (p314), just across the Yālù River from North Korea

❹ Go on the trail of Puyi, the last emperor of China, at the Imperial Palace of Manchu State in **Chángchūn** (p316)

❺ See China's ethnic Korean culture in **Yánjí** (p313)

PRICE INDICATORS

The following price indicators are used in this chapter:

Sleeping

$	less than ¥200
$$	¥200 to ¥400
$$$	more than ¥400

Eating

$	less than ¥30
$$	¥30 to ¥80
$$$	more than ¥80

Jílín's border with North Korea has dominated the region's more recent history. Since the mid-1990s, thousands of North Koreans have fled into China to escape extreme food shortages. The Chinese government has not looked favourably on these migrants, refusing to grant them protected refugee status.

Climate

Jílín is bitterly cold during its long winter, with heavy snow, freezing winds and temperatures as low as -20°C. In contrast, summer is pleasantly warm, especially along the coastal east, but short. Rainfall is moderate.

Language

Mandarin is the standard language across Jílín. Korean is widely spoken in the Korean Autonomous Prefecture in the east of the province.

❶ Getting There & Around

The rail and bus network connects all major cities and towns, but not many daily trains head east. The new airport connects Chángbái Shān with Chángchūn and other major Chinese cities.

Chángbái Shān　　长白山

BÁIHÉ/NORTHERN SLOPE 📞 0433
SŌNGJIĀNGHÉ/WESTERN SLOPE 📞 0439

Chángbái Shān (Ever-White Mountains), China's largest nature reserve, covers 2100 sq km (densely forested) on the eastern edge of Jílín. By far the region's top attraction, the park's greenery and open space offers a very welcome contrast to Jílín's industrial cities.

The centrepiece of Chángbái Shān is the spellbinding Heaven Lake, whose blue waters stretch across an outsized volcanic crater straddling the China–North Korea border. Heaven Lake's beauty and mystical reputation, including its Loch Ness–style monster *(guàiwu)*, lures visitors from all over China, as well as many South Koreans. For the latter, the area is known as Mt Paekdu, or Paekdusan. North Korea claims that Kim Jung-il was born here (although he's believed to have entered the world in Khabarovsk, Russia).

At lower elevations, the park's forests are filled with white birch, Korean pines and hundreds of varieties of plants, including the much-prized Chángbái Shān ginseng. Above 2000m the landscape changes dramatically into a subalpine zone of short grasses and herbs. Giant patches of ice cover parts of the jagged peaks even in mid-June, and mountain streams rush down the treeless, rocky slopes. With the lake at an altitude of nearly 2200m, visitors should be prepared for lower temperatures. It might be sunny and hot when you enter the reserve, but at higher altitudes strong winds, rain and snow are possible.

Chángbái Shān has two main recreation areas: the northern slope (Běi Pō) and the western slope (Xī Pō), and the entrance areas are separated by 100km of road. Visitors to either slope area are limited to a few sights and a few short walks. Chángbái Shān is unfortunately geared towards Chinese tour groups rather than independent travellers, and a multibillion-yuán project is under way to turn the park into a luxury sightseeing zone – a Banff of sorts, with hot springs resorts, skiing and golf courses but little hiking or camping. In late 2012 a new ski resort area was about to open west of Chángbái Shān, and with 20 runs over two mountains this area might offer some decent hiking in summer. Certainly the skiing should be superlative in the winter. Ask around when you arrive.

Though you can visit most of the year, unless you are coming to ski the best time to see the crater (and be assured the roads are open) is from June to early September. Accommodation is widely available, including within the park, but most travellers stay in the respective gateway towns of Báihé and scruffy Sōngjiānghé.

NORTHERN SLOPE　　北坡

The views of Heaven Lake from the **northern slope** (Běi Pō; admission ¥125, transport fee ¥85; ⏰7am-6pm) are the best. The gateway town for this area, where most travellers spend the night, is **Báihé** (白河).

You can see all the sights below in half a day.

◉ Sights & Activities

Heaven Lake   CRATER LAKE
(天池; Tiān Chí) This two-million-year-old crater lake, 13km in circumference, sits at an altitude of 2194m and is surrounded by rock outcrops and 16 mountainous peaks. The highest, **White Rock Peak** (Báiyán Fēng), soars to 2749m and can be climbed if you have permits and are with a Chinese tour group. Legend has it that the lake is home to a large, but shy, beastie that has the magical power to blur any photo taken of him.

Hiking to the lakeside area is prohibited but you can enjoy panoramic views from the crater lip. To get here take a 4WD vehicle from the park's main transport junction. Note that the ride costs an extra ¥80 over the regular park transport and admission fee.

Changbai Waterfall   WATERFALL
(长白瀑布; Chángbái Pùbù) The first park bus you take will drop you off at a junction/parking lot (lùkǒu). From here you can either catch a 4WD vehicle to Heaven Lake, or a shuttle up to Yuèhuà Plaza (岳桦广场; Yuèhuà Guǎngchǎng), in essence another big parking lot. On the edge of the lot is a small area of **hot springs** where you can soak your feet, or boil an egg, and past that a short trail leads quickly to the viewpoint for the magnificent 68m Changbai Waterfall. In the past you could follow the dramatic-looking caged trail beside the falls up the back canyon, but that route is now officially sealed. And don't bother trying to sneak in; park staff will quickly call you back.

If you want to get in a short hike, follow the road 1.5km up from the junction, and at the Green Deep Pool area join the 3.5km-long boardwalk running through birch forests to the falls.

Green Deep Pool   POOL
(绿渊潭; Lǜ Yuān Tán) At the beginning (or end) of the boardwalk from Changbai Waterfall, cross the lot and head up the stairs to this aptly named river pool. Buses run from here down to the junction and the Underground Forest.

Underground Forest   FOREST PARK
(地下森林; Dìxià Sēnlín) Lying between the park entrance and junction, this verdant woodland area, also known as the Dell Forest (谷底森林; Gǔdǐ Sēnlín), has a few trails

with an hour's worth of hiking. Buses run from here back to the junction and north gate. If the trail is opened you can also hike here from the junction. The path is just over 3km and starts across the parking lot past the bathrooms.

⌂ Sleeping & Eating

There are overpriced hotels and restaurants inside the park, but most people stay in Èrdào Báihé, generally called Báihé, about 20km north of the reserve. The town is divided into three rather distinct sections: the train station area, the dusty main drag (Baishan Jie) a few kilometres away, and the pleasant riverside strip (Baihe Dajie) which is gradually being turned into a modern luxury village. There's lodging and small restaurants in all areas. Baishan Jie has a fruit street just around the corner from the Xìndá Hotel. In the evenings the second half of the street hosts a row of barbecue stalls.

A taxi from the train station into town costs ¥10.

BÁIHÉ

On your arrival at the train or bus station, touts for cheap guesthouses will likely approach. Many of these guesthouses can be found in the small lane just past the Woodland Youth Hostel. Private rooms without bathroom go for ¥30 to ¥80. The more expensive rooms sometimes have their own computer.

TOP
CHOICE **Woodland Youth Hostel**   HOSTEL $
(望松国际青年旅舍; Wàngsōng Guójì Qīngnián Lǚshè; ☑571 0800; www.cbshan.net; dm/tw ¥45/190; ❄@☎) This friendly hostel offers male and female separated dorms, as well as basic, clean twins, and the usual hostel amenities such as restaurant (which faces a wooded park), laundry, wi-fi and travel information. The hostel runs its own shuttle to the North and Western slopes (¥30 and ¥70 respectively) and also offers overnight **camping trips** (¥350–1800) in the park.

To get here from the train station, exit and turn right, then left and walk to the main road. Turn right here, walk about 150m and look for the hostel sign.

Yǎjūgé Shíshàng Bīnguǎn   GUESTHOUSE $
(雅居阁时尚宾馆; ☑139 4475 7965; d/tw ¥80/100) Set inside its own courtyard is this quaint guesthouse with a few small but tidy rooms. The guesthouse is about 600m up the main road from the bus station as

THE WESTERN SLOPE

Chángbái Shān's **western slope** (西坡; Xī Pō; admission ¥125, transport fee ¥85; ☉7am-6pm) offers much the same experience as the northern. The setup is a little fancier, but as in the north you have little chance of getting away from the crowds here. Once again the view from the crater is the main attraction, though the **Chángbái Shān Canyon** (长白山大峡谷; Chángbái Shān Dàxiágǔ), a 200m wide and 100m deep gorge filled with dramatic rock formations, is also worth a look.

The **Woodland Youth Hostel** (☎571 0800; www.cbshan.net) in Báihé has a shuttle to the western slope for ¥70 per person return. Taxis also run the route for ¥200 one way.

The gateway town for the western slope is the dusty traffic-snarled town of **Sōngjiānghé** 40km to the northwest, from where there are buses and trains to Tōnghuà and Shěnyáng. **Changbaishan Airport**, halfway between the park and Sōngjiānghé, has flights to/from Shànghǎi (¥1830, 3½ hours), Chángchún (¥850, 40 minutes) and Běijīng (¥1130, two hours).

Sōngjiānghé offers midrange accommodation similar to Báihé, while closer to the park a number of new resorts have popped up in recent years including **Days Hotel Landscape Resort** (蓝景戴斯度假酒店; Lánjǐngdàisī Dùjià Jiǔdiàn; ☎0433-633 7999; r from ¥850), a stylish lodge with a lobby fireplace, high-end eating and drinking venues, and wood, glass and stone decor that wouldn't look out of place at Lake Louise in Canada.

you head towards town. Look for a massive modern log-cabin-style restaurant; Yǎjùgé Shíshàng is just to the right of that.

Zōu Xián Jū Shíshàng Bīnguǎn
HOTEL $$

(聚闲居时尚宾馆; ☎574 9555; Baihe Dajie; d/tw ¥398/498; ❀⃝) In the most modern district of town, and facing the pretty Baihe River, is this spotless hotel with bright stylish rooms and friendly management. The hotel is currently at the end of a strip of shops and small hotels, though by the time you read this the row may have been extended. Expect discounts of 30% to 40%.

Xìndá Bīnguǎn
HOTEL $$

(信达宾馆; ☎572 0444; Baishan Jie; d/tw incl breakfast ¥480/360; ❀) On Báihé's main drag, at the north end of town across from the woods, this hotel offers a pleasant environment, cosy rooms as well as an attached restaurant. Small discounts are sometimes available.

Héshèngyuán Yěshēng Xiǎoyúguǎn
SEAFOOD $$

(合盛源野生小鱼馆; dishes ¥18-48) Next to the Woodland Hostel in Báihé is this primarily seafood restaurant matching flashy lights and good food. Staff are friendly but speak no English.

NORTHERN SLOPE

Lanjing Spa Holiday Inn
LUXURY HOTEL $$$

(蓝景温泉度假酒店; Lánjǐng Wēnquán Dùjià Jiǔdiàn; ☎505 2222, 574 5555; r from ¥1702; ❀@)

The top accommodation in the area, this 200-room European-style lodge (with obligatory touches of Chinese kitsch) is just 300m from the north gate entrance but quiet enough in its wooded setting off the main road. In addition to multiple food and beverage outlets, the inn features a high-end hot spring spa with indoor and outdoor facilities.

ⓘ Information

The **Bank of China** (中国银行; Zhōngguó Yínháng; Baishan Jie) is on the main street in Báihé towards the end of town and has an ATM.

ⓘ Getting There & Away

Public transport only goes as far as Báihé.

BUS Buses leave from the **long-distance bus station** (kèyùnzhàn). From the train station head to the main road; the station is across and to the left.

Mǔdānjiāng ¥96, eight hours, one daily (6.55am)

Yánjí ¥47, 3½ hours, five daily

TRAIN Trains from Báihé:

Jí'ān hard/soft sleeper ¥64/98, eight hours, one daily at 10.25am

Shěnyáng hard/soft sleeper ¥100/156, 14 hours, three daily (6.47am, 5.35pm and 7.10pm)

Sōngjiānghé seat ¥8, two hours, seven daily

Tōnghuà hard seat/sleeper ¥24/58, six to seven hours, six daily (6.40am to 7pm)

ℹ Getting Around

Hotels and hostels in Báihé can organise cheap, shared transport to the reserve (¥20 to ¥30), which usually leaves early morning and returns around 4pm. Taxis charge ¥60 to ¥70 (per car) for the one-way trip. Returning, it's usually easy to share a taxi back (per person ¥20).

Once you've entered the reserve's north gate, a park bus will take you to a junction/parking lot (lùkǒu) where you can board a 4WD for the final 16km trek to Heaven Lake or take other park buses to the waterfall, the Green Deep Pool and Underground Forest. The park bus rides are all included in your ticket, but the 4WD is another ¥80.

Yánjí 延吉

📞0433 / POP 375,000

The relaxed and attractive capital of China's Korean Autonomous Prefecture has one foot across the nearby border with North Korea. About a third of the population is ethnic Korean and it's common to hear people speaking Korean rather than Mandarin, and to see Korean written on official road signs. The Bù'ěrhǎtōng River (Bù'ěrhǎtōng Hé) bisects the city and has pleasant parks and walkways running alongside. ATMS are all over the city including a 24-hour ATM at the Industrial & Commercial Bank of China (ICBC; 中国工商银行; Zhōnguó Gōngshāng Yínháng) three blocks up from the train station at the corner of Changbaishan Xilu and Zhanqian Jie.

🛏 Sleeping & Eating

There are a few budget hotels around the train station but it's a sleazy area and male travellers may find themselves directly solicited for sex.

Diànlì Dàshà HOTEL $
(电力大厦; 📞291 1881; 399 Guangming Lu; 光明街399号; tw ¥148-188, tr ¥225; ❄☎) Even the cheaper rooms here are spacious, clean and cosy, and that goes for the bathrooms too. With a great restaurant on the ground floor, wireless internet, and a good location near restaurants, shopping malls and the river, this hotel is an ideal spot to hang out in if you need a bit of time to unwind after a long haul on the road.

The hotel's **restaurant** (dishes ¥18-48; ☺6am-9pm) is packed every meal with outside guests devouring a range of excellent Korean dishes. There's a big picture-menu wall and plenty of side dishes (¥4 to ¥8) you can point to.

ℹ Getting There & Away

The train and bus stations are south of the river, while the commercial district is north. Taxi fares start at ¥5, and most rides cost less than ¥10.

Buses to Chángchūn or Jílín leave from in front of the train station. Yánjí's long-distance **bus station** (客运站; kèyùn zhàn; 2319 Changbaishan Xilu) services:

Èrdào Báihé ¥45, four hours, six daily (6.40am to 2.40pm)

Húnchūn ¥28, two hours, every 30 minutes (7am to 3.30pm)

Mǔdānjiāng ¥71, five hours, four daily (6.30am, 9.50am, 12.10pm and 4.30pm)

Train services:

Chángchūn hard seat/sleeper ¥70/124, eight to nine hours

Jílín hard seat/sleeper ¥52/98, six to eight hours

Jí'ān 集安

📞0435 / POP 240,000

This small city, just across the Yālù River from North Korea, was once part of the Koguryo (高句丽; Gāogōulí) kingdom, a Korean dynasty that ruled areas of northern China and the Korean peninsula from 37 BC to AD 668. Jí'ān's extensive Koguryo pyramids, ruins and tombs resulted in Unesco designating it a World Heritage Site in 2004. Archaeologists have unearthed remains of three cities plus some 40 tombs around Jí'ān and the town of Huánrén (in Liáoníng province).

With a drive to capitalise on its Korean heritage's tourism potential, modern-day Jí'ān has transformed itself into one of northern China's more pleasant towns, with well-tended parks, leafy streets and a beautiful new riverfront area where you can gaze across to North Korea. Add in the town's 360-degree mountain backdrop, excellent Korean food, friendly locals and scenic train or bus rides getting here, and it's a great little stopover on a loop through Dōngběi.

Shengli Lu runs east–west through town, with the long-distance bus station at the west end. The main north–south road is Li Ming Jie, which ends at the river park. It's easy to walk around town and you can pick up a good English-language map (¥5) of Jí'ān and the surrounding area at any hotel. There's a **Bank of China** (中国银行; Zhōngguó Yínháng; Shengli Lu) just east of the junction of Shengli Lu and Li Ming Jie with a 24-hour ATM.

THE LITTLE-KNOWN KOREAN AUTONOMOUS PREFECTURE

Ask people to list some of China's ethnic minorities and you will hear talk of Tibetans, Uighur, Mongolians, Hui and perhaps the Li or Dai. Mention that China also has almost two million ethnic Koreans, and that the majority live in their own autonomous prefecture along the North Korean border, and you'll likely get some astonished looks.

The **Yánbiān Korean Autonomous Prefecture** (延边朝鲜族自治州; Yánbiān Cháoxiǎnzú Zìzhìzhōu) is the only minority prefecture in the north of China. While established in 1955, in part as a reward for Koreans who fought on the side of the communists in the Civil War, the region has in fact been settled by Koreans since the 1880s. These days, street signs are officially bilingual; much of the population is also bilingual thanks to state-sponsored Korean-language schools; TV shows and newspapers are in Korean; and ethnic food is ubiquitous.

Over the past decades, however, the percentage of ethnic Koreans has dropped steadily: from 60% in the 1950s to 38% today. In part this reflects the Chinese government's desire to stamp out any potential for irredentism (many Koreans refer to Yánbiān as the 'third Korea', after the South and North) by encouraging Han migrants. More positively, it seems to indicate that the well-educated ethnic population experiences little to no discrimination in seeking employment or advancement outside the prefecture. Yánbiān may occupy a quarter of all Jílín province (it's about half the size of South Korea), but the population is little more than two million, and opportunities are limited.

Major tourist attractions are also surprisingly scarce. The most famous sight in fact may be the sliver of land at the very eastern edge of the prefecture. Here, from a platform vantage point, you can see Russia to the north, North Korea to the south, China to the west, and sometimes the Sea of Japan to the east. If this sounds appealing, catch a bus from Yánjí east to Húnchūn (混春; ¥23, two hours, every 30 minutes), and then grab a taxi to Fángchuān (防川) about 70km away. Tell the driver (if he hasn't already guessed) you want to go to **Yī Yǎn Wàng Sān Guó** (一眼望三国; admission $20), the name of the platform where you can see the three countries.

For those doing an extensive tour of northern China, consider looping up through Yánbiān as you go from Dāndōng or Chángbáishān to Hā'ěrbīn. The regional capital, Yánjí, is an attractive laid-back place, loaded with excellent Korean food, and the routes in and out run hour after hour through a bucolic landscape of corn fields, rolling forested hills and little brick villages.

Summer evenings are lively in Jí'ān, both at the riverside and the park across from the Cuìyuán Bīnguǎn (hotel) where live amateur performances of traditional song and dance are held most nights.

◉ Sights

The main sights other than the river park are scattered on the outskirts of the city. You could cover them on foot in a long day, but most people hire a taxi. Expect to pay at least ¥100 for a three- to four-hour tour.

The **Koguryo sites** (☉8am-5pm) are spread around the very lovely green hills surrounding Jí'ān. Despite their historical significance, most sites don't have a terrible amount of detail to examine. Many of the tombs are cairns – essentially heaps of stones piled above burial sites – while others are stone pyramids. But there is something magical about the open fields and high terraces they were constructed on that makes you want to linger. The most impressive site, Wandu Mountain City, needs a couple of hours to cover its expansive grounds. It's best to get your taxi to drop you off here at the end (negotiate a lower rate if you do). You can easily walk back to Jí'ān on Shancheng Rd in less than an hour, following the river down the valley.

A ¥100 ticket gets you into the four most important sites; you can also buy separate tickets for each sight for ¥30.

Jiāngjūnfén (General's Tomb)　　TOMB
(将军坟) One of the largest pyramid-like structures in the region, the 12m-tall Jiāngjūnfén was built during the 4th century for a Koguryo ruler. The nearby smaller tomb is the resting place of a family member. The site is set among the hills 4km northeast of town.

Hǎotàiwáng Stele
STELE

(好太王碑; Hǎotàiwáng Bēi) Inscribed with 1775 Chinese characters, the Hǎotàiwáng Stele, a 6m-tall stone slab that dates to AD 415, records the accomplishments of Koguryo king Tan De (374–412), known as Hǎotàiwáng. Tan De's tomb (labelled 'Tài-wáng Tomb') is on the same site, and you can enter and see the stone burial slabs.

Cemetery of Noblemen at Yushan
TOMBS

(禹山贵族墓地; Yǔshān Guìzú Mùdì) Scattered about a small gated park lie the stone crypts of various Koguryo-kingdom noblemen. You can enter and explore Tomb No 5 (wait for the guide) via a creepy descent underground. As your eyes adjust to the light in the chilly stone chamber look, for paintings of dragons, white tigers, black tortoises and lotus flowers on the walls and ceilings.

TOP CHOICE Wandu Mountain City
RUIN

(丸都山城; Wándū Shānchéng) First built in AD 3, the city became capital of the Koguryo kingdom in 209, after the fall of the first capital, Guonei city (on the site of present-day Jí'ān). There's little left of the original buildings, but the layout has been cleared and it's still immensely enjoyable scrambling about the terraces and taking in the views that surely must have been a deciding factor in establishing the capital here.

Down on the plains below the city, on a large shelf above the river, sits Jí'ān's largest collection of giant stone **cairns**. Erected after the destruction of Wandu, this vast cemetery for the city's noblemen is so far unaffected by many tourists or tourism infrastructure. The sight of the massive rock piles in fields of Spanish needle (Bidens pilosa) is probably the most photogenic in all Jí'ān.

Riverside Plaza
WATERFRONT

This lively modern waterfront park features stone fountains, landscaped gardens, cobbled walkways, carp pools, lotus ponds, statues and riverside decks where you can view North Korea across the Yālù River. The centrepiece, the very sleek **Jí'ān Museum** (集安博物馆; Jí'ān Bówùguǎn), sports a brown stone base and glass top with sails that open up like leaves. The museum has existed in a state of limbo for several years now, but locals believe it will finally open in 2013. Naturally, it will display artefacts from the Koguryo era.

To get to the park, walk east on Shengli Lu to the corner of Jian She Jie.

🛏 Sleeping & Eating

Lùmíng Bīnguǎn
HOTEL $

(鹿鸣宾馆; ☑625 6988; 653 Shengli Lu; 胜利路653号; s/tw without bathroom ¥40/60, d with bathroom & incl breakfast ¥138-158; ❀@) Friendly staff and well-kept rooms make this Jí'ān's best budget option. It's three blocks east of the bus station on the north side of Shengli Lu just before you reach Liming Jie. Look for the English sign reading 'Guesthouse' above the entrance. Some rooms have their own computer.

Cuìyuán Bīnguǎn
HOTEL $$

(翠园宾馆; ☑622 2123; www.jiancy.com; 888 Shengli Lu; 胜利路888号; d/tw ¥488/344) Two blocks east of the bus station, and across from a cute park with a cobbled stream running through it, Cuìyuán Bīnguǎn offers good midrange comfort. Rooms usually go for around ¥200 after discounts.

Pū Jiā Gǒuròu Lěngmiàn Chéng
KOREAN $$

(扑家狗肉冷面城; cnr Shengli Lu & Dongsheng Lu; dishes ¥6-38) The speciality here, as in many restaurants around town, is dog meat, but it also serves great lěngmiàn (冷面; cold noodles) and shuǐjiǎo (水饺; dumplings). The characters for dog meat are 狗肉 in case you want to ensure that you don't eat any.

Head to the markets east and west of Liming Jie for fruit, dumplings, bread and barbecue. Dongsheng Lu has dumpling and barbecue restaurants, Tuanjie Lu is home to cafes and Chinese fast-food joints, while Liming Jie offers a number of hotpot and barbecue spots.

ℹ Getting There & Away

The main routes to Jí'ān are via Tōnghuà and Báihé (gateway to Chángbái Shān) to the north, or Shěnyáng and Dāndōng in Liáoníng province to the west and south. If you're travelling to Báihé by bus, you need to change in Tōnghuà. If travelling up to Chángchūn it's probably faster to take a bus, as by train you'll need to change at Tōnghuà.

The **long-distance bus station** (客运站; kèyùn zhàn; Shengli Lu) is in the west part of town.

Chángchūn ¥109, 5½ hours, two daily (5.30am and 2.50pm)

Dāndōng ¥73, six hours, two daily (7.30am and 9.20am)

Shěnyáng ¥97, six hours, three daily (6.20am, 11.20am and 2.55pm)

Tōnghuà ¥28, two hours, every two hours (5am to 5pm)

The **train station** (Yanjiang Lu) is in the northeast part of town. There's one slow but scenic train ride a day to Báihé (hard/soft sleeper ¥64/98, eight hours) departing at 9am.

JÍLÍN JÍ'ĀN

Běidàhú Ski Resort 北大湖滑雪场

Since it hosted the 2007 Asian Winter Games, **Běidàhú** (Běidàhú Huáxuěchǎng; www .beidahuski.com) has established itself as one of China's premier ski resorts. Located in a tiny village 53km south of Jílín, the resort has runs on two mountains ranging from beginner to advanced. Though it hasn't turned a profit since 2009, Běidàhú is seeing renewed investment resulting in an additional 10km of runs being added each year. For more on skiing here, including tour, transport and accommodation information, see the **China Ski Tours** (www. chinaskitours.com/home.html) website and the box text p329.

Chángchūn 长春

☑ 0431 / POP 2.93 MILLION

The Japanese capital of Manchukuo between 1933 and 1945, Chángchūn was also the centre of the Chinese film industry in the 1950s and '60s. Visitors expecting a Hollywood-like backdrop of palm trees and beautiful people will be disappointed, though. Chángchūn is now better known as China's motor city, the largest automobile-manufacturing base in the country.

But for people on the trail of Puyi, China's last emperor, it's an essential stop. There are also a fair few historic buildings dating back to the early days of the 20th century, mostly along and off Renmin Dajie.

Chángchūn sprawls from north to south. The long-distance bus station and the train station are in the north end of the city and surrounded by budget hotels. If you plan on more than an overnight in Chángchūn, however, the southern end is by far a more pleasant neighbourhood to stay.

◎ Sights

TOP CHOICE **Imperial Palace of Manchu State (Puppet Emperor's Palace)** MUSEUM

(伪满皇宫博物院; Wěimǎn Huánggōng Bówùyuàn; 5 Guangfu Lu; admission ¥80; ◎8.30am-4.20pm, last entry 40min before closing) Chángchūn's main attraction is the former residence of Puyi, the Qing dynasty's final emperor. His story was the basis for the 1987 Bernardo Bertolucci film *The Last Emperor*.

In 1908, at age two, Puyi became the 10th Qing emperor. His reign lasted just over three years, but he was allowed to remain in the Forbidden City until 1924. Subsequently, he lived in Tiānjīn until 1932, when the Japanese installed him at this palace as the 'puppet emperor' of Manchukuo. After Japan's defeat in 1945, Puyi was captured by Russian troops. In 1950 he was returned to China, where he spent 10 years in a re-education camp before ending his days as a gardener in Běijīng. Puyi died in 1967.

Puyi's study, bedroom and temple, as well as his wife's quarters (including her opium den) and his concubine's rooms, have all been elaborately re-created. His American car is also on display, but it's the exhibition on his extraordinary life, told in part with a fantastic collection of photos, that is most enthralling. A taxi from the train station here costs ¥7.

Bānruò Temple BUDDHIST

(般若寺; Bānruò Sì; 137 Changchun Lu) One of the largest Buddhist temples in the northeast, Bānruò is a lively place of worship for locals and pilgrims alike. After touring the inner grounds, wander the back alleys to observe the merchants peddling all manner of charms, statues, shrines and incense to the faithful.

To get here take bus 281 or 256 from the train-station area bus station. You can also walk in about 30 minutes, passing by the attractive grounds of Shengli Park on the way.

Jìngyuètán PARK

(净月潭旅游区; Jìngyuètán Lǚyóuqū; admission ¥30; ◎24hr) This massive lakeside park on the southeast outskirts of Chángchūn encompasses more than 90 sq km and is a most welcome break if you have to spend any time in the motor city. Established in 1934, it features well-tended gardens, pavilions, lookouts and a 20km round-the-lake bike path. Shuttle buses (¥10) take you to the dam, where you can take boat rides. At the front gate there are bike rentals (¥30 per hour) but note that shuttle buses, boats and bikes are only available from 9am to 6pm.

The easiest way to get here is to take the light rail from the station on Liaoning Lu (¥4, 55 minutes) to Jingyue Gongyuan Station.

🛏 Sleeping

There are half a dozen budget hotels within walking distance of the train station, with rooms (most with broadband internet) going for between ¥140 and ¥180.

Chángchūn

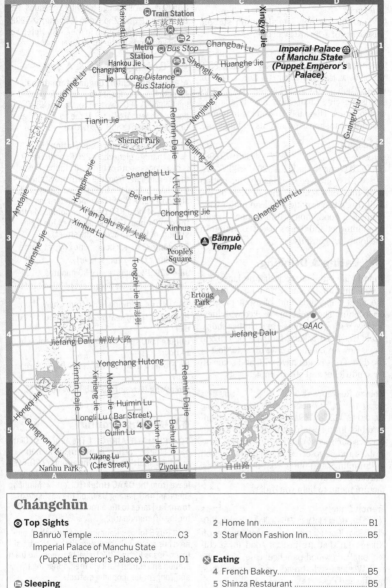

Chángchūn

◉ Top Sights
Bānruò Temple C3
Imperial Palace of Manchu State
(Puppet Emperor's Palace)................D1

🛏 Sleeping
1 Chūnyì Bīnguǎn......................................B1

2 Home Inn B1
3 Star Moon Fashion Inn...........................B5

🍴 Eating
4 French Bakery..B5
5 Shinza Restaurant B5

Chūnyì Bīnguǎn HOTEL **$$$**
(春谊宾馆; ☏8209 6888; www.chunyihotel.com;
80 Renmin Dajie; 人民大街80号; r incl breakfast
from ¥680; ❄@) The old-school charm has
diminished a little since this place was built
back in 1909; however, it retains a gorgeous
marble staircase and foyer, and is arguably
a more comfortable place to stay now. The

rooms and bathrooms are huge, and as a sop to modern times feature broadband internet.

The hotel is opposite the train station. Discounts of 40% are available.

Star Moon Fashion Inn
HOTEL $

(星月时尚酒店; Xīngyuè Shíshàng Jiǔdiàn; ☑8509 0555; www.starmoon.inn.com.cn; 1166 Longli Lu; 隆礼路1166号; d from ¥148; ❋@) For a grey industrial city, Chángchūn has its share of fashion inns. This modern hotel is in a great location near shops, restaurants and nightlife.

Home Inn
HOTEL $

(如家快捷酒店; Rújiā Kuàijié Jiǔdiàn; ☑8986 3000; 20 Changbai Lu; 长白路20号; r ¥159-209; ❸❋@) If you need a nonsmoking option near the train station, this branch of the well-run, always spotlessly clean nationwide chain is a good choice. Rooms have broadband internet and there's also a computer in the lobby for guest use.

✕ Eating & Drinking

Tongzhi Jie (and all the radiating lanes) between Huimin Lu and Ziyou Lu is one of the most happening and pleasant parts of Chángchūn. The streets are packed with inexpensive restaurants, music and clothes shops, while tree-lined Xikang Lu (west of Tongzhi Jie) is now an unofficial **cafe street**. Most of the dozen or so cafes have wi-fi and some offer sandwiches and other simple meals.

Shinza Restaurant
KOREAN $$

(延边信子饭店; Yánbiān Xìnzǐ Fàndiàn; 728 Xikang Lu; dishes ¥12-38; ⊙9am-midnight) This comfortable dining establishment offers Korean classics such as *shí guō bàn fàn* (rice, vegetables and eggs served in a clay pot) as well as dumplings and filling cold noodle dishes. Korean beers are also available and there's a picture menu to help you order.

French Bakery
BISTRO $

(红磨坊; Hóng Mòfáng; 745 Guilin Lu; dishes ¥10-25; ⊙9am-10pm) There are places nearby on Xikang Lu that are just as good for a coffee but this wood-panelled cafe also sells real Western-style bread loafs, sandwiches, quiche and desserts.

ⓘ Information

There are 24-hour ATMs all over town. Most hotels have in-room broadband internet and you'll find wi-fi at the cafes on Xikang Lu.

Bank of China (中国银行; Zhōngguó Yínháng; 1296 Xinmin Dajie) Near Nánhú Park (Nánhú Gōngyuán). Will change travellers cheques.

CAAC (中国民航; Zhōngguó Mínháng; ☑8298 8888; 480 Jiefang Dalu) In the CAAC Hotel. For air tickets and shuttle buses to airport.

ⓘ Getting There & Away

AIR The **Chángchūn Lóngjiā International Airport** has daily flights to major cities including Běijīng (¥960, two hours), Dàliǎn (¥580, 1½ hours), Shànghǎi (¥1600, three hours) and also Chángbái Shān (¥850, 2½ hours).

BUS The **long-distance bus station** (长途汽车站; chángtú qìchēzhàn; 226 Renmin Dajie) is two blocks south of the train station. Buses to Hā'ěrbīn leave from the north bus station (běizhàn) behind the train station. Facing the station, head left and take the underpass just past the 24-hour KFC (not to be confused with the non-24-hour KFC to the right of the train station, or the two across the street).

Dàndōng ¥130, six hours, one daily at 9am
Hā'ěrbīn ¥77, 3½ hours, hourly
Jílín ¥29, 1½ hours, every 30 minutes
Shěnyáng ¥83, 4½ hours, every 30 minutes

TRAIN The following leave from Chángchūn:
Běijīng (D train) seat ¥227, seven hours, seven daily
Běijīng hard seat/sleeper ¥130/224, nine to 14 hours
Hā'ěrbīn (D train) seat ¥72, two hours, five daily
Shěnyáng (D train) seat ¥88, 2½ hours, 12 daily

ⓘ Getting Around

TO/FROM THE AIRPORT The airport is 20km east of the city centre, between Chángchūn and Jílín. Shuttle buses to the airport (¥20, 50 minutes, every 30 minutes from 6am to 7pm) leave from the **CAAC Hotel** (民航宾馆; Mínháng Bīnguǎn; 480 Jiefang Dalu) on the east side of town. Taxi fares to the airport are ¥80 to ¥100 for the 40-minute trip.

BUS Bus 6 follows Renmin Dajie from the train-area bus station all the way to the south part of town. Buses 62 and 362 travel between the train station and Nánhú Park via the Chongqing Lu and Tongzhi Jie shopping districts.

LIGHT RAIL The **Chángchūn Light Rail** (⊙6.30am-9pm) service is only useful for getting to Jīngyuètán park. The station is just west of the train station.

TAXI Fares start at ¥5.

Hēilóngjiāng

POP 37.3 MILLION

Includes »

Hā'ěrbīn 321
Mǔdānjiāng 328
Around Mǔdānjiāng 329
Wǔdàlián Chí 330
Russian Borderlands.... 332

Best Landscapes

» Lǎohēi Shān (p331)
» Běijícūn (p332)
» Jìngpò Hú (p329)

Best Activities

» Skiing (p329)
» Watching the Northern Lights (p332)
» Ice and Snow Festival (p325)

Why Go?

It's cold in China's northernmost province, sub-Arctic cold – but that frigid weather is put to good use. Winter is peak tourist season, and with a world-renowned ice sculpture festival and some of China's finest ski runs it's worth swaddling yourself in layers and joining the crowds.

Hēilóngjiāng (黑龙江) means Black Dragon River, and this particular coiling dragon is the separating line between China and Russia. Across the province a neighbourly influence is evident in architecture, food and even souvenirs. Hā'ěrbīn's famed cobblestoned streets and European-style facades are just the beginning.

Outside the cities, Hēilóngjiāng is a rugged, beautiful landscape of forests, lakes, mountains and dormant volcanoes. In Mòhé, China's most northerly village, the meadows and marshes have a magnetic pull all their own, and the bragging rights to say you have stood at the very top of the Middle Kingdom may in fact be worth the 21-hour train ride to get there.

When to Go
Hā'ěrbīn

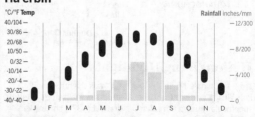

Jan Hā'ěrbīn hosts the ice and snow festival.

Jun Mòhé holds the northern lights festival.

Dec–Mar Ski season at Yàbùlì.

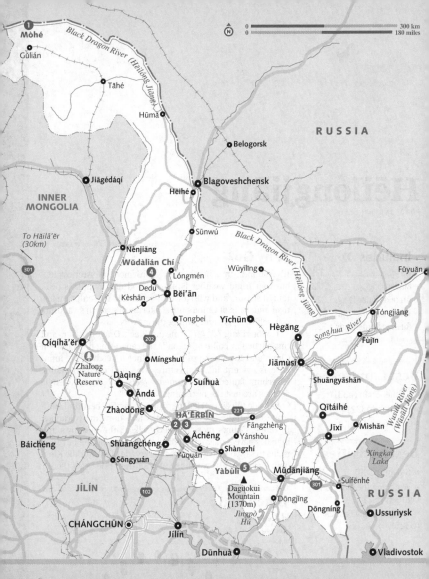

Hēilóngjiāng Highlights

1 Visit China's 'North Pole Village' and see the spectacular **aurora borealis** (p332) in Mòhé

2 Brave the cold and join the crowds who flock to Hā'ěrbīn's world-famous **ice and snow festival** (p325)

3 Walk the brick-lined streets of the historic **Dàolǐqū district** (p321) and explore Hā'ěrbīn's Russian and Jewish past

4 Hike to the top of a dormant volcano and through the lava fields of **Wǔdàlián Chí** (p331)

5 Ski and snowboard at **Yàbùlì** (p329), one of China's finest ski resorts

6 Go on the search for **rare cranes** (p327) in nature reserves all across the north.

History

Hēilóngjiāng forms the northernmost part of Dōngběi, the region formerly known as Manchuria. Its proximity to Russia has long meant strong historical and trade links with its northern neighbour. In the mid-19th century, Russia annexed parts of Hēilóngjiāng, while in 1897 Russian workers arrived to build a railway line linking Vladivostok with Hā'ěrbīn. By the 1920s well over 100,000 Russians resided in Hā'ěrbīn alone.

Like the rest of Manchuria, Hēilóngjiāng was occupied by the Japanese between 1931 and 1945. After the Chinese Communist Party (CCP) took power in 1949, relations with Russia grew steadily frostier, culminating in a brief border war in 1969. Sino-Russian ties have improved much in recent years and the two sides finally settled on the border in July 2008, after 40-odd years of negotiation.

Climate

The region experiences long, freezing winters, with temperatures dropping below -30°C. Short summers are warm and humid, especially in the south and east. Mid- to high 30s temperatures are possible and afternoon showers are common.

Language

The vast majority of people in Hēilóngjiāng speak northeast Mandarin, which is the same as standard Mandarin, apart from the accent. You're also likely to hear a lot of Russian. In the far northwest, tiny numbers of the Oroqen, Daur, Ewenki and Hezhen ethnic minorities still speak their own languages. A handful of people can speak Manchu, once the dominant tongue of the region.

ℹ Getting There & Around

Hā'ěrbīn is the logistical hub for the region and has extensive links with the rest of China. Buses are often a quicker way of getting around, rather than the slow local trains. If you're headed for Inner Mongolia, direct trains run from Hā'ěrbīn to the cities of Hǎilā'ěr and Mǎnzhōulǐ.

Hā'ěrbīn 哈尔滨

✉ 0451 / POP 3.72 MILLION

For a city of its size, Hā'ěrbīn is surprisingly easygoing. Cars (and even bicycles) are barred from Zhongyang Dajie, the main drag of the historic Dàolǐqū district, where most of Hā'ěrbīn's old buildings can be found. The long riverfront also provides sanctuary for walkers, as does Sun Island on the other side.

PRICE INDICATORS

The following price indicators are used in this chapter:

Sleeping

$	less than ¥150
$$	¥150 to ¥300
$$$	more than ¥300

Eating

$	less than ¥30
$$	¥30 to ¥80
$$$	more than ¥80

The city's sights are as varied as the architectural styles on the old street. Temples, old churches and synagogues coexist, while deep in the southern suburbs a former Japanese germ-warfare base is a sobering reminder of less harmonious times. Hā'ěrbīn's rich Russian and Jewish heritage makes it worth visiting at any time of year, but winter is tops with the world-class ice sculpture festival turning the frosty riverfront, and other venues, into a multicoloured wonderland.

History

In 1896 Russia negotiated a contract to build a railway line from Vladivostok to Hā'ěrbīn, then a small fishing village, and Dàlián (in Liáoníng province). The subsequent influx of Russian workers was followed by Russian Jews and then by White Russians escaping after the 1917 Russian Revolution.

These days, Hā'ěrbīn, whose name comes from a Manchu word meaning 'a place to dry fishing nets', is an ever-expanding, largely industrial city, and while Chinese are the majority, because Russia is so close foreign faces are still common on the streets.

◉ Sights

Old Harbin   HISTORIC BUILDINGS

The Dàolǐqū district, in particular the brick-lined street of **Zhongyang Dajie**, is the most obvious legacy of Russia's involvement with Hā'ěrbīn. Now a pedestrian-only zone, the street is lined with buildings that date back to the early 20th century. Some are imposing, others distinctly dilapidated, but the mix of architectural styles is fascinating. Other nearby streets lined with handsome old buildings include **Shangzhi Dajie** and **Zhaolin Jie**.

Hā'ěrbīn

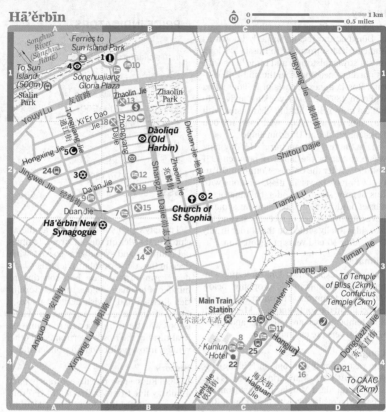

Elsewhere in the city, **Hongjun Jie**, heading south from the train station, and **Dongdazhi Jie** also feature rows of stately old buildings, including a few churches. The latter street, and some of its arteries, also have the dubious reputation of sporting some heady postmodern Russian-style architecture of questionable taste.

In all of these areas the city has erected plaques on the most worthy buildings giving short English and Chinese descriptions of the date of construction, the architect and the former usage.

Church of St Sophia RUSSIAN CHURCH
(圣索菲亚教堂; Shèng Suǒfēiyà Jiàotáng; cnr Zhaolin Jie & Toulong Jie; admission ¥20; ⊙8.30am-5pm) The red-brick Russian Orthodox Church of St Sophia, with its distinctive green 'onion' dome, is Hā'ěrbīn's most famous landmark. Built in 1907, the church is now home to the **Hā'ěrbīn Architecture Arts Centre**, which displays charming black and white photographs of Hā'ěrbīn from the early 1900s. It's interesting to note that the captions display a very positive attitude towards the foreign influence on the city.

Stalin Park PARK
(斯大林公园; Sīdàlín Gōngyuán) Locals and visitors alike congregate year-round in Stalin Park. The tree-lined promenade, dotted with statues, playgrounds and cafes, runs along a 42km-long embankment built to curb the unruly Sōnghuā River. The odd **Flood Control Monument** (防洪胜利纪念塔; Fánghóng Shènglì Jìniàntǎ), from 1958, commemorates the thousands of people who died in years past when the river overflowed its banks.

Sun Island Park PARK
(太阳岛公园; Tàiyángdǎo Gōngyuán) Across the river from Stalin Park is Sun Island Park, a 38-sq-km recreational zone with landscaped gardens, miniforests, a 'water world', a 'Russian-style' town, and various small gal-

Hā'ěrbīn

⊙ Top Sights
Church of St Sophia B2
Dàolǐqū (Old Harbin) B2
Hā'ěrbīn New Synagogue B3

⊙ Sights
1 Flood Control Monument B1
2 Hā'ěrbīn Architecture Arts
   Centre.. C2
   Jewish Middle School.................(see 3)
3 Old Main Synagogue A2
4 Stalin Park.................................... A1
5 Turkish Mosque A2

🛏 Sleeping
6 Běiběi Hotel C4
7 Central Old Street Hotel B2
8 Hanting Express........................... C4
9 Haolin Business Hotel A2
10 Jīndì Bīnguǎn B1
   Kazy International Youth Hostel....(see 3)
11 Lungmen Grand Hotel................. C4
12 Modern Hotel.............................. B2

✪ Eating
13 Cafe Russia 1914........................ B1
14 Dǐng Dǐng Xiāng B3
15 Dōngfāng Jiǎozi Wáng............... B2
16 Dōngfāng Jiǎozi Wáng............... D4
17 Food Market............................... B2
18 Lǎo Chāng Chūnbǐng B2
19 Xiǎochī Jiē B2

☕ Drinking
   Àogǔ Yǎba ....(see 3)
20 Ming Tien B1

🛍 Shopping
21 Hóngbó Century Square D4

ℹ Information
22 Hā'ěrbīn Railway International
   Travel Service C4

ℹ Transport
23 Bus stop..................................... C4
24 Bus stop to Siberian Tiger Park........... A2
25 Long-Distance Bus Station C4

leries and museums. It's a pleasant place to walk around, though as usual you need to pay extra to get into many areas.

You can boat across (¥10) from the dock directly north of the Flood Control Monument or catch the nearby **cable car** (one way/return ¥50/100; ⊙8.30am-6.30pm).

Siberian Tiger Park   WILDLIFE RESERVE
(东北虎林园; Dōngběihǔ Línyuán; 88 Songbei Jie; admission ¥90; ⊙8.30am-4.30pm, last tour 4pm) At the Siberian Tiger Park, visitors get the chance to see one of the world's rarest animals (and largest felines) close-up. This breeding centre and urban park is not the most edifying spectacle, however, with the tigers fenced in and visitors, who tour safari-style in buses, encouraged to buy (live!) chickens (¥60), ducks and even cows (¥2800) to throw to the animals. The feeding takes place during the ride around the park, so if you don't think you can handle the spectacle (of cheering locals as much as well-fed tigers indifferently mauling their prey), consider not taking the ride.

The park is located roughly 15km north of the city. Bus routes seem to change yearly so ask at your hotel or hostel for the latest. A taxi from the city centre is ¥30 to ¥40 one way.

Jewish Hā'ěrbīn   HISTORIC BUILDINGS
The Jewish influence on Hā'ěrbīn was surprisingly long lasting; the last Jewish resident of the city died in 1985. In the 1920s Hā'ěrbīn was home to some 20,000 Jews, the largest Jewish community in the Far East at the time.

If you're on the trail of Hā'ěrbīn's Jews, then the **Hā'ěrbīn New Synagogue** (哈尔滨犹太新会堂; Hā'ěrbīn Yóutài Xīnhuìtáng; 162 Jingwei Jie; admission ¥25; ⊙8.30am-5pm) is the place to start. The synagogue was built in 1921 by and for the community, the vast majority of which had emigrated from Russia. Restored and converted into a museum in 2004, the 1st floor is an art gallery with pictures and photos of old Hā'ěrbīn. The 2nd and 3rd floors feature photos and exhibits that tell the story of the history and cultural life of Hā'ěrbīn's Jews. From all accounts they had a splendid life centred on sports, music and business.

Tongjiang Jie was the centre of Jewish life in the city till the end of WWII, and many of the buildings on the street are from the early 20th century. The museum can clue you in to the former location of bakers, kosher butchers and furriers. The old **Main Synagogue** (Yóutài Jiùhuìtáng; 82 Tongjiang Jie),

THE GREAT CATS

As with many of the world's powerful wild creatures, size did not give the amur (Siberian tiger), much of an advantage during the 20th century. The largest feline in the world, topping 300kg for males and capable of taking down a brown bear in a fair fight, was no match for poachers, wars, revolutions, railway construction and economic development in its traditional territory across Russia, China and Korea. These days fewer than 400 of the great cats are believed to still prowl the wilds of Russia, none in Korea, and perhaps 20 divided between Hēilóngjiāng and Jílín provinces in China.

It's a dismal figure, and in 1986 the Chinese government set about boosting numbers by establishing the world's largest tiger breeding centre in Hā'ěrbīn. Beginning with only eight tigers, the centre has been so successful that the worldwide number of Siberian tigers may now exceed 1000.

The majority of these are in captivity, which makes any wild sighting a cause for celebration. In April 2012 the figurative champagne flowed when a wild Siberian tiger was captured on film for the first time in Wangqing Nature Reserve in Jílín province. Speculation had it that the cat was one of several that appeared in March in Húnchūn along the border with Russia. If true it may be evidence the cats are expanding their range south – back into traditional Chinese territory.

built in 1909, now houses a cafe, shops and an excellent little hostel. Close by is the former **Jewish Middle School** (犹太中学; Yóutài Zhōngxué).

Further up Tongjiang Jie is the interesting **Turkish Mosque** (土耳其清真寺; Tǔ'ěrqí Qīngzhēn Sì); built in 1906, it's no longer operating and is closed to visitors.

In the far eastern suburbs of Hā'ěrbīn is the **Huángshān Jewish Cemetery**, the largest in the Far East. There are more than 600 graves here, all well maintained. A taxi here takes around 45 minutes and costs about ¥100.

FREE **Japanese Germ Warfare Experimental Base**   MUSEUM
(侵华日军第731部队遗址; Qīnhuá Rìjūn Dì 731 Bùduì Yízhǐ; Xinjiang Dajie; ⊙9-11am & 1-3.30pm Tue-Sun) There are museums highlighting Japanese wartime atrocities all over Dōngběi, but this one is actually set in the notorious Japanese Germ Warfare Experimental Base – 731 Division used to inflict some of those atrocities. Between 1939 and 1945, Chinese prisoners of war and civilians were frozen alive, subjected to vivisection or infected with bubonic plague, syphilis and other virulent diseases. Three to four thousand people died here in the most gruesome fashion, including Russians, Koreans, Mongolians and, it is believed, a few American airmen.

The main building of the base is now a museum complete with photos, sculptures and exhibits of the equipment used by the Japanese. There are extensive English captions and an audio guide is available for ¥15.

The base is in the far south of Hā'ěrbīn and takes about an hour to get to by bus. In the alley beside China Post on Tielu Jie (just southwest of the train station), catch bus 343 (¥2). Get off at the stop called Xinjiang Dajie just after the bus turns the corner leaving Xinjiang Dajie itself. Walk back 500m along Xinjiang Dajie and look for the base on the left-hand side of the road. If you get lost, just ask the locals the way to 'Qi San Yi' or '731'.

Temples

The following temples are within walking distance of each other. The first sits off a pedestrian-only street reachable by taxi from the Dàolǐqū district for ¥10. For the Confucius Temple, look for an arch down to the right at the start of the pedestrian street. Pass through this and then a second arch on the left. The temple is a 10-minute walk along Wen Miao Jie.

Temple of Bliss   BUDDHIST
(吉乐寺; Jí Lè Sì; 9 Dongdazhi Jie; admission ¥10; ⊙8.30am-4pm) Hēilóngjiāng's largest temple complex has an active Buddhist community in residence, giving it a genuine religious atmosphere despite the ticket sales. There are many large statues here including Milefo (Maitreya), the Buddha yet-to-come, and the Sakyamuni Buddha, and the **Seven-Tiered Buddhist Pagoda** (七级浮屠塔; Qījí Fútú Tǎ), from 1924. The entrance to the temple is to the left at the start of the pedestrian street.

FREE Confucius Temple   CONFUCIAN
(文庙; Wén Miào; 25 Wen Miao Jie; ☉9am-3.30pm)
This peaceful temple complex was first built
in 1929 and is said to be the largest Confucian temple in northeastern China. Most of
what you see now, though, is from a recent
restoration. You need a passport to enter.

Other Sights

Hēilóngjiāng Science & Technology Museum   MUSEUM
(黑龙江省科技馆; Hēilóngjiāngshěng Kējìguǎn;
adult/child ¥24/12; ☉9am-4pm Tue-Sun, last ticket sale 3pm) This children's museum is west
of Sun Island Park and features excellent
hands-on displays highlighting the principles of aviation, acoustics, transportation,
energy and aeronautics. The museum can
be reached either by taxi or by following
the road west about 4km after you get off
the boat to the island. It makes for a pleasant walk.

Festivals & Events

Ice & Snow Festival   ICE SCULPTURE
(冰雪节; Bīngxuě Jié; www.chinahighlights.com/fes
tivals/harbin-ice-and-snow-festival.htm; ☉9.30am-
9.30pm) Hā'ěrbīn's main claim to fame these
days is this festival. Every winter, from December to February (officially the festival
opens 5 January), Zhāolín Park (照林公
园) and Sun Island Park become home to
extraordinarily detailed, imaginative and
downright wacky snow and ice sculptures.
They range from huge recreations of iconic
buildings, such as the Forbidden City and
European cathedrals, to animals and in-
terpretations of ancient legends. At night
they're lit up with coloured lights to create
a magical effect.

It might be mind-numbingly cold and the
sun disappears mid-afternoon, but the festival, which also features figure-skating shows
and a variety of winter sports, is Hā'ěrbīn's
main tourist attraction – and prices jump
accordingly.

The festival takes place in multiple locations. The main venue, **Harbin Ice and
Snow World** (admission ¥300) and the **Snow
Sculpture Art Exhibition** (admission ¥240)
are both held on **Sun Island**. The Ice and
Snow World exhibits are held in the west
end of the island on the north bank of the
Sōnghuā River. They are best seen at night,
so note that a daytime ticket (good from
9.30am to 1.30pm) does not grant admission
to the venue at night.

The **Ice Lantern Venue** is held in **Zhaolin Park** (admission ¥200) and many consider
it the least interesting venue. If you do go,
again, get along at night when the lanterns
are lit.

Taxis are expensive and often hard to flag
down during the festival times but you can
ride horse carriages, or even use your own
feet: the Sun Island venues are actually
reachable by crossing the frozen Sōnghuā
River (plan on one to two hours). Note that
prices for the festival have been skyrocket-
ing recently so don't be surprised if they are
even higher than quoted above.

Sleeping

The most convenient places to stay are along
Zhongyang Dajie in Dàolǐqū district or in
one of the many hotels that surround the
train station. During the ice and snow festival expect hotel prices to go up by at least
20%.

TOP CHOICE Kazy International
Youth Hostel   HOSTEL $
(卡兹国际青年旅舍; Kǎzī Guójì Qīngnián Lǚshè;
☎8469 7113; kazyzcl@126.com; 82 Tongjiang Jie;
通将街82号; dm/s/tw with shared bathroom
¥40/60/80, d with bathroom ¥140; ☎) This hostel has taken over the lower floors of the old
Main Synagogue, giving it the largest and
highest ceiling lobby of any hostel we've
seen. Dorm rooms are bright and clean, but
the rooms in the garret with Star of David
frame windows are a treat to stay in, even if
(or maybe because) they lack air-con. Staff
are friendly and a great source of travel information around the city and province. The
hostel, with its laundry, cafe and ticket booking services, is popular with Chinese travellers, so book ahead.

Century Old Street Hotel   HISTORIC HOTEL $$
(百年老街酒店; Bǎinián Lǎojiē Jiǔdiàn; ☎8463
8888; fax 8468 1157; 32 Zhongyang Dajie; 中央
大街32-40号; d & tw ¥198-298; ✳@) With a
prime location on Zhongyang Dajie, and
comfortable rooms with dark panelling,
this heritage hotel is your best budget/mid-
range choice in Hā'ěrbīn. Corners rooms
are tops, their sweeping windows flooding
the interior with light and offering views
over Zhongyang Dajie. Windowless rooms
go for around ¥130, a steal for this location.
The hotel is about one block up from the
start of Zhongyang Dajie. Discounts of 30%
are usual.

Modern Hotel HISTORIC HOTEL **$$$**
(马迭尔宾馆; Mǎdié'ěr Bīnguǎn; ☎8488 4000; www.hrbmodern.com; 89 Zhongyang Dajie; 中央大街89号; r from ¥680; ❋@❊) One of the more imposing buildings on Zhongyang Dajie, this 1906 construction still features some of its original marble, blond-wood accents and art nouveau touches. All rooms include free broadband, and a breakfast buffet in the classy dining hall. Note that the entrance to the hotel is around the back. Discounts available.

Lungmen Grand Hotel HISTORIC HOTEL **$$$**
(龙门贵宾楼酒店; Lóngmén Guìbīn Lóu Jiǔdiàn; ☎8679 1999; 85 Hongjun Jie; 红军街86号; d/tw ¥480/680; ❋@) With its turn of the century old-world styling almost entirely intact (including the marble staircase, dark wood-panelled hallways, and the copper revolving door), the Lungmen is one of the best top-end options in the city. Though technically across from the train station, the hotel lobby opens onto Hongjun Jie and its rows of heritage buildings. A quick walk up the street's wide pavements takes you into the shopping heart of Hā'ěrbīn. Discounts available.

Jīndì Bīnguǎn HOTEL **$$**
(金地宾馆; ☎8461 8013; 16 Dongfeng Jie; 东风街16号; s & d ¥150, tw ¥230-280; ❋@) If you're looking for a river view on the cheap, then this is the place. Rooms are spacious, and there's broadband available in most, with computers in the more expensive twins. To get to the hotel, turn right at the very end of Zhongyang Dajie before the park. Jīndì sits just past the Gloria Plaza Hotel.

Haolin Business Hotel HOTEL **$$**
(昊麟商务连锁酒店; Hàolín Shāngwù Liánsuǒ Jiǔdiàn; ☎400-060 6530; 26 Tongjiang Jie; 通将街26号; d/tw ¥218/268; ❋@) In the centre of Jewish Hā'ěrbīn, a neighbourhood now loaded with restaurants and barbecue stalls at night, is this new business-style express hotel with surprisingly comfortable rooms sporting high ceilings, bright interiors and good modern bathrooms. It's a two-minute walk to Zhongyang Dajie from Haolin. Expect discounts of 30%.

Hanting Express HOTEL **$$**
(汉庭快捷酒店; Hàntíng kuàijié Jiǔdiàn; ☎5180 1177; www.htinns.com; Huochezhan Guangchang Dian; 火车站广场店; d/tw ¥289/299; ❋@☎) This tidy, friendly business-style hotel is to the right of the train station square (as you exit the station) on the 23rd floor. The entrance is next to a KFC (one of many in the train station area). Rooms have broadband internet and there's wi-fi in the lobby.

Běiběi Hotel HOTEL **$$**
(北北大酒店; Běiběi Dàjiǔdiàn; ☎8257 0960; www.bblsjd.com; 2 Chunshen Jie; 春申街2号; d/tw ¥198-228; ❋@) Just to the left of the bus station as you face the entrance, Běiběi is a little worn with traffic but a good deal if you have an early bus or train to catch. Look for room deals each day that go for as low as ¥168.

✕ Eating

Hā'ěrbīn dishes tends to be heavy, with thick stewlike concoctions commonly found on the picture menus of a thousand eateries. You'll also find delicious hotpot, barbecued meats and Russian dishes in the tourist areas. Zhongyang Dajie and its side alleys are full of small restaurants and bakeries. Tongjiang Jie has fruit stands, sit-down restaurants and an abundance of outdoor barbecue stalls (with ad hoc seating) set up in the evenings.

In summer, the streets off Zhongyang Dajie come alive with open-air food stalls and beer gardens, where you can sip a Hāpí (the local beer), while chewing squid on a stick, or *yángròu chuàn* (lamb kebabs) and all the usual street snacks.

The year-round indoor **food market** (小吃城; xiǎochī chéng; 96 Zhongyang Dajie; ◷8.30am-8pm) has stalls selling decent bread, smoked meats, sausages, wraps and fresh dishes, as well as nuts, cookies, fruits and sweets. It's a great place to grab a quick breakfast or to stock up on food for a long bus or train ride.

Just south of the market, on the opposite side of the street, look for the underground **Xiǎochī Jiē** (小吃街; Snack Street; dishes ¥8-15), a clean modern food court with a range of inexpensive noodle and rice dishes, as well as kebabs, curries and pasta dishes.

Dōngfāng Jiǎozi Wáng DUMPLINGS **$**
(东方饺子王; Orient King of Eastern Dumplings; dumpling plate ¥8-20; ◷10.30am-9.30pm; ☎🍴) Dàolǐqū district (51 Zhongyang Dajie); train station area (72 Hongjun Jie) It's not just the cheap *jiǎozi* (饺子; stuffed dumplings) that are good at this always busy chain: there are plenty of tasty vegie dishes, too, and excellent fresh fruit drinks. The Hongjun Jie branch is a 10-minute walk southeast of the train station, next to the Overseas Chinese Hotel down the alley. Both branches have English

menus. More surprisingly, all branches have good password-free wi-fi, which you can also usually access just outside the front door.

Cafe Russia 1914
RUSSIAN $$

(露西亚咖啡西餐厅; Lùxīyà kāfēi Xīcān Tīng; 57 West Ist Rd; dishes ¥18-48; ☉10am-midnight) Step back in time at this tranquil, ivy-covered teahouse-cum-restaurant and cafe. Black and white photos illustrating Hā'ěrbīn's Russian past line the walls, while the old school furniture and fireplace evoke a different era. The food is substantial Russian fare, such as borscht and *piroshki* (cabbage, potato and meat puffs). Russian vodka is available, too.

The restaurant is off Zhongyang Dajie in a little courtyard.

Dǐng Dǐng Xiāng
HOTPOT $$

(鼎鼎香; Hotpot Paradise; 58 Jingwei Jie; hotpot starter from ¥20, dishes ¥12-68; ☉9.30am-9pm) In winter, Hā'ěrbīn and hotpot go together like strawberries and cream, and in summer, well, what else are you going to do with a well-prepared broth, a stack of vegies and thinly sliced meat? This three-storey hotpot restaurant, which looks like a karaoke TV palace, can get very pricey if you order some of the face-giving seafood and Japanese beef dishes, but you can also dine well on normal beef, lamb and seafood for a modest outlay. Just make sure you order the special sauces (from ¥10) to accompany your hotpot. There's a picture menu to make things easy.

Lǎo Chāng Chūnbǐng
SPRING ROLLS $

(老昌春饼; Old Chang's Spring Rolls; 180 Zhongyang Dajie; dishes ¥12-38; ☉10.30am-9pm; 🖫) At this well-known basement spring roll shop, order a set of roll skins (per roll ¥1), a few plates of meat and vegetable dishes, and then wrap your way to one enjoyable repast.

🍷 Drinking & Entertainment

Hā'ěrbīn has the usual collection of karaoke TV (KTV) joints. If communal singing isn't your bag, there are a few bars on and off Zhongyang Dajie and Tiandi Lu. Zhongyang Dajie and Stalin Park also have beer gardens in the summer with cheap draft and plenty of snack food to enjoy as you watch sports on the big screens. Ask around for the latest nightclubs.

Àogǔ Yǎbā
CAFE

(傲古雅吧; 82 Tongjiang Jie; drinks ¥18-35; ☉10am-midnight; 🕿🖫) Excellent coffee and a delightful old world design make this cafe in a side chamber of the old Jewish Main Synagogue one of the nicest places in Hā'ěrbīn to enjoy a beverage. The food is rather mediocre, however.

Ming Tien
CAFE

(名典西餐; Míngdiǎn Xīcān; www.hrbmingdian.com; 214 Shangzhi Dajie; drinks ¥35-60) For afternoon tea or coffee head to this slightly over-the-top cafe occupying two floors of a heritage building on Shangzhi Dajie. Enter via the subdued parlour, wind your way up the tree-enshrouding staircase and ease into a big brown leather booth with views of Zhāolín Park – and some very odd wallpaper. Ming Tien has an equally eclectic menu ranging from borscht to pizza if you get hungry.

🛍 Shopping

There's a distinctly martial-arts bent to some of the shops along Zhongyang Dajie, with imitation Russian and Chinese camouflage uniforms on sale alongside the sort of fearsome-looking knives you shouldn't attempt to take on a plane. But there are also department stores, boutiques and many Western clothes chains here. Souvenir shops selling Russian knick-knacks, dolls, binoculars, and also vodka and other spirits can be found all over the city.

Locals head to Dongdazhi Jie for their shopping needs, as well as the **Hóngbó Century Square** (红博世纪广场; Hóngbó Shìjì Guǎngchǎng; ☉6.30am-5pm), a huge subterranean shopping complex for men's and women's clothing.

❶ Information

There are ATMs all over town. Most large hotels will also change money. Many midrange and top-end hotels have travel services that book tickets and arrange tours throughout the province.

Bank of China (中国银行; Zhōngguó Yínháng; Xi'Er Dao Jie) Has a 24-hour ATM and will cash travellers cheques. Easy to spot on a side road as you walk up Zhongyang Dajie.

Civil Aviation Administration of China (CAAC; Zhōngguó Mínháng; 101 Zhongshan Lu) In the CAAC Hotel; for flight tickets and airport shuttle buses.

Harbin Modern Travel Company (哈尔滨马迭尔旅行社; Hā'ěrbīn Mǎdié'ěr Lǚxíngshè; http:hotel.hrbmodern.com; 89 Zhongyang Dajie) This travel agency on the 2nd floor of Modern Hotel offers one- and two-day ski trips to Yàbùlì and can handle flight tickets to Mòhé and other regions.

❶ Getting There & Away

Air

Harbin Taiping International Airport has flights to Russia and South Korea as well as the following domestic routes:

Běijīng ¥960, one hour and 50 minutes

Dàlián ¥840, 1½ hours

Mòhé ¥1610, 2½ hours, two flights daily (8.20am and 1pm)

Bus

The main long-distance bus station is directly opposite the train station. Buy tickets on the 2nd floor.

Chángchūn ¥76, four hours, hourly from 8am to 5pm

Mŭdānjiāng ¥96, 4½ hours, hourly from 8am to 5pm

Wŭdàlián Chí ¥67 to ¥79, five to six hours, three daily (9am, 11.30am and 1.30pm). The 1.30pm bus is the most comfortable.

Běi'ān ¥65 to ¥82.5, five hours, four daily (7.10am, 8.30am, 2.20pm and 4.30pm)

Train

Hā'ěrbīn is a major rail transport hub with routes throughout the northeast and beyond. If you don't want to brave the lines in the station, buy tickets at the nearby **train booking office** (Tiělù Jie; ⏰8am-5pm) to the left of the Kunlun Hotel.

Běijīng hard seat/sleeper ¥158/270, 10 to 16 hours

Běijīng (D train) seat ¥267, nine hours

Chángchūn (D train) seat ¥72, two hours, six daily

Mòhé hard/soft sleeper ¥246/400, 21 hours

Mŭdānjiāng hard seat/sleeper ¥48/94, five to seven hours

BORDER CROSSING: GETTING TO RUSSIA

As of May 2012, trains no longer depart from Hā'ěrbīn East to Vladivostok. Trains do run as far as Suífēnhé, however, from where you can make an onward connection to Vladivostok.

Travellers on the Trans-Siberian Railway to or from Moscow can start or finish in Hā'ěrbīn (six days). Contact the **Hā'ěrbīn Railway International Travel Service** (哈尔滨铁道国际旅行社; Hā'ěrbīn Tiědào Guójì Lüxíngshè; ☎5361 6717; www.ancn.net; Kunlun Hotel, 7th fl, 8 Tielu Jie) for information on travelling through to Russia.

Shěnyáng hard seat/sleeper ¥76/134, six to seven hours

Shěnyáng (D train) seat ¥161, four hours, five daily

❶ Getting Around

To/From the Airport

Hā'ěrbīn's airport is 46km from the city centre. From the airport, shuttle buses (¥20) will drop you at the railway station or the CAAC office. To the airport, shuttles leave every 30 minutes from the CAAC office from 5.30am to 7.30pm. A taxi (¥100 to ¥125) takes 45 minutes to an hour.

Public Transport

Buses 101 and 103 run from the train station to Shangzhi Dajie, dropping you off at the north end of Zhongyang Dajie (the old street). Buses leave from a stop across the road and to the left as you exit the train station (where Chunshen Jie and Hongjun Jie meet).

Hā'ěrbīn's long-awaited metro began trial runs of its first line at the end of 2012.

Taxi

Taxis are fairly plentiful though they fill up quickly when it's raining. Taxi flag-fall is ¥8.

Mŭdānjiāng 牡丹江

☎0453 / POP 764,000

A pleasant and surprisingly modern small city surrounded by some lovely countryside, Mŭdānjiāng is the jumping-off point for nearby Jìngpò Hú (Mirror Lake) and the Underground Forest. Tàipíng Jie is the main drag in town and runs directly south of the train station. There's a **Bank of China** (中国银行; Zhōngguó Yínháng) two blocks where you can (very slowly) cash travellers cheques and access a 24-hour ATM.

🛏 Sleeping & Eating

The train station area has a number of good hotels and there is no reason to look further into town. For budget accommodation head right as you exit the station. Just past the station square on Guanghua Jie runs a row of guesthouses. There are at least half a dozen to choose from, all offering similar prices and surprisingly decent digs: dorm beds go for ¥20, rooms with shared bathroom for around ¥40 and rooms with their own bathroom (and sometimes even a computer) for ¥80.

There are plenty of cheap restaurants around as well, and also in the alleys off Qixing Jie, which intersects with Taiping Jie half a kilometre up from the train station. Dongyi-

SKIING IN CHINA

China's ski industry has all the appearance of a success story. From 20,000 visits to the slopes in 1996, numbers have grown to around 15 million in 2012. There are now over 20 large resorts across the country in areas as diverse as Jílín, Hēilóngjiāng, Yúnnán and Héběi provinces.

But industry insiders say that most resorts have been in the red for years because the average visitor tries the sport once and then never again. Building slopes and resorts has been easy: maintaining them while a ski culture develops has not been. In 2012 there was renewed hope, however, as another round of investment hit the industry. This time the focus would be on upping the luxury quotient, and also opening more runs and facilities for absolute beginners.

In China's north, the largest resorts are Jílín's **Běidàhú Ski Resort** (see p316) and Hēilóngjiāng's **Yàbùlì Ski Resort** (亚布力滑雪中心; Yàbùlì Huáxuě Zhōngxīn; www.yabuliski. com), 200km southeast of Hā'ěrbīn. Yàbùlì was China's first destination ski resort, and remains the training centre for the Chinese Olympic ski team. Since 2009 the resort has expanded to cover two mountains and now has a good division of advanced, intermediate and beginner runs, as well as a four-star lodge that can reasonably cater to Western guests.

The latest slopes to be developed in the region are at **Chángbái Shān** on the China–North Korean border. In the winter of 2012–13 an as yet unnamed resort was set to open about 20km from the new airport. Expect to find 20 runs on two mountains as well as a luxury alpine village offering hotels, restaurants and private condos.

Lift tickets in the north average around ¥500 per day on weekends, and a little less on weekdays. Clothing and equipment rental comes to another ¥140. For up-to-date information on all the major ski areas of China, as well as transport and tour advice, see the excellent **China Ski Tours** (www.chinaskitours.com/home.html) website.

---

tiao Lu (off Qixing Jie) is a lively pedestrian-only street with a wide range of BBQ, noodle and snack venues open in the evening.

Home Inn   HOTEL **$$**
(如家快捷酒店; Rújiā Kuàijié Jiǔdiàn; ☑6911 1188; 651 Guanghua Jie; 光花街651号; r ¥129-179; ➋❈@☎) Probably the best-value rooms around the train station are in this well-managed chain just to the right as you exit. Top floors are nonsmoking and very quiet despite the location.

Shuānglóng Jiǎozi Wáng   DUMPLINGS **$**
(双龙饺子王; cnr Qixing Jie & Taiping Jie; dumplings ¥12-25; ◷9am-9pm) There's a wide selection of *jiǎozi* here, as well as the usual Dōngběi classics. As you turn left off Taiping Jie, the restaurant is the big glass building on the right. There's an English sign out front and a partial picture menu inside to help you order.

➊ Getting There & Away
Bus
Long-distance buses usually drop you off near the train station and depart from a station (客车站; kè chēzhàn) a few kilometres away. A taxi to the station costs ¥6.

Dōngjīng Chéng ¥15, 1¼ hours
Hā'ěrbīn ¥70, 4½ hours, every 40 minutes (5am to 6pm)
Yánjí ¥71, five hours, 6.30am and 11.30am

Train
Mǔdānjiāng has rail connections:
Hā'ěrbīn hard seat/sleeper ¥54/100, five to seven hours, frequent services
Suífēnhé seat ¥30 to ¥47, five hours
Yánjí hard seat/sleeper ¥22/56, six hours, one daily (4.26pm)

Around Mǔdānjiāng
JÌNGPÒ HÚ
Formed on the bend of the Mǔdān River 5000 years ago by the falling lava of five volcanic explosions, **Jìngpò Hú** (镜泊湖; Mirror Lake; www.jingpohu.com.cn; admission ¥80), 110km south of Mǔdānjiāng, gets its name from the unusually clear reflections of the surrounding lush green forest in its pristine blue water.

Hugely popular in summer with Chinese daytrippers who come to paddle or picnic by the lakeside, it's a pleasant spot if you hike along the lake to escape the crowds. Shuttle buses (¥12 per trip) run to various sights, and ferries (¥80) make leisurely tours of the lake.

◎ Sights

Diàoshuǐlóu Waterfall
WATERFALL

One of the area's biggest attractions is this **fall** (吊水楼瀑布; Diàoshuǐlóu Pùbù) with a 12m drop and 300m span. During the rainy season (from June to September), when Diàoshuǐlóu is in full throttle, it's a spectacular raging beauty, but during spring and autumn it's little more than a drizzle.

You can walk to the waterfall from the north gate entrance in about five minutes. Just stay on the main road and follow the English signs.

Underground Forest
FOREST

(地下森林; Dìxià Sēnlín; admission ¥40) Despite its name, the Underground Forest isn't below the earth; instead it has grown within volcano craters that erupted some 10,000 years ago. Hiking around the thick pine forest and several of the 10 craters takes about an hour.

The forest is 50km from Jìngpò Hú. Some day tours include it in their itinerary. Otherwise, you have to take a bus from the north gate of Jìngpò (one hour), which is not really viable if you only have a day at the lake.

⌘ Sleeping & Eating

It's pleasant to spend the night in the park and enjoy the lake when the crowds return to their hotels in Mǔdānjiāng.

Jìngpò Hú Shānzhuāng Jiǔdiàn
HOTEL $$

(镜泊湖山庄酒店; ☎627 0039, 139 0483 9459; r¥200-300) This hotel sits just back from the water at the first lakeside drop-off point for the shuttle buses. Rooms are very basic but there's a small beach where you can swim, and the hotel's restaurant has decent food (if a little overpriced).

❶ Getting There & Away

The easiest way to get to Jìngpò Hú is on the one-day tours (call ☎139 4533 1797) that leave from the train station in Mǔdānjiāng from 6.30am to 7.30am. Tours cost ¥235 and include transport, admission, a boat tour, and two shuttle bus tickets (to the ferry dock and back).

If you want to head out here under your own steam, first get to dusty Dōngjīng Chéng (东京城). Buses to Dōngjīng Chéng (¥15, 1½ hours, frequent) leave from Mǔdānjiāng's bus station (客车站; kè chēzhàn); take a taxi here (¥6). Minibuses (¥10, 40 to 60 minutes) to the lake either leave from outside Dōngjīng Chéng's train station (about 0.5km down the road from where the bus from Mǔdānjiāng drops you off) or directly across the street. In the late afternoon you can usually get a seat on one of the tour buses directly back to Mǔdānjiāng from the lake (¥30).

❶ Getting Around

The ticket centre for the lake is at the North Gate (Běimén). From here walk about five minutes to a car park for shuttle buses to the lake and ferry dock (get a ticket to the stop 'Jìngpò Shānzhuāng'; 镜泊山庄) and other sights (¥12 per ride). Diàoshuǐlóu Waterfall is just behind this car park.

Wǔdàlián Chí 五大连池

☑0456

Formed by a series of volcanic eruptions, the Wǔdàlián Chí nature reserve boasts one of northern China's most mesmerising landscapes. It's a genuine Lost World with vast fields of hardened lava, rivers of basalt, volcanic peaks, azure lakes and the odd little reed-lined pond. You could spend days exploring.

The last time the volcanoes erupted was in 1720, and the lava flow blocked the nearby North River (Běi Hé), forming the series of five interconnected lakes that give the area its name. Wǔdàlián Chí is about 250km northwest of Hā'ěrbīn, and in addition to the volcanic landscape is home to mineral springs that draw busloads of Chinese and Russian tourists to slurp the allegedly curative waters. So many Russians roll up that the town's street signs are in both Chinese and Russian.

There's no real town here, just a long, pleasant tree-lined street called Yaoquan Lu. Everything you want is on a section that runs west of the bus station. The intersection of Yaoquan Lu and Shilong Lu (about 3km from the bus stop) is the main crossroad and is smack in the middle of the hotel area. Taxis make the trip from the bus station to the hotel area for ¥5 to ¥10.

Recently, some travellers have also started to base themselves in Wǔdàlián Chí Shì (五大连池市), a real town about 20km away and where most buses drop you off from Hā'ěrbīn.

It's only really viable to visit Wǔdàlián Chí between May and October.

◎ Sights & Activities

A bike is the perfect way to take in the sights in this flat landscape. You can rent cheap ones for puttering around town at Gōngrén Liáoyǎngyuàn (per hour ¥20). For a half-day loop taking in the lakes, volcanoes and caves most people hire a taxi (¥150). Negotiate beforehand whether the fee covers parking at each sight (¥5 to ¥10).

CRANE COUNTRY

Northeastern China is home to several nature reserves established to protect endangered species of wild cranes. **Zhālóng Nature Reserve** (扎龙自然保护区; Zhālóng Zìrán Bǎohùqū) near Qíqíhā'ěr is the most accessible and most visited of these sanctuaries. The reserve is home to some 260 bird species, including several types of rare cranes. Four of the species that migrate here are on the endangered list: the extremely rare red-crowned crane, the white-naped crane, the Siberian crane and the hooded crane.

The reserve comprises some 2100 sq km of wetlands that are on a bird migration path extending from the Russian Arctic down into Southeast Asia. Hundreds of birds arrive in April and May, rear their young from June to August and depart in September and October. Unfortunately, a significant percentage of the birds you can see live in zoolike cages and are released once a day so that visitors can take photos.

The best time to visit Zhālóng is in spring. In summer the mosquitoes can be more plentiful than the birds – take repellent!

Xiànghǎi National Nature Reserve (向海; Xiànghǎi Guójiā Zìrán Bǎohùqū), 310km west of Chángchūn in Jílín province, is on the migration path for Siberian cranes, and the rare red-crowned, white-naped and demoiselle cranes breed here. More than 160 bird species, including several of these cranes, have been identified at the **Horqin National Nature Reserve** (科尔沁; Kē'ěrqín Guójiā Zìrán Bǎohùqū), which borders Xianghai in Inner Mongolia. The **Mòmògé National Nature Reserve** (莫莫格; Mòmògé Guójiā Zìrán Bǎohùqū) in northern Jílín province is also an important wetlands area and bird breeding site.

For more information about China's crane population and these nature reserves, contact the **International Crane Foundation** (www.savingcranes.org) or see the website of the **Siberian Crane Wetland Project** (www.scwp.info).

If your time is short, just visit Lǎohēi Shān and you will get most of what the area has to offer.

TOP CHOICE Lǎohēi Shān
VOLCANO

(老黑山; admission ¥80 plus ¥25 shuttle fee; ⊙7.30am-7pm May-Oct) It's a mostly uphill 1km stair climb to the summit of Lǎohēi Shān, one of the area's 14 volcanoes. From the lip of the crater you will have panoramic views of the lakes and other volcanoes.

Taxis drop you at the ticket booth from where park shuttle buses take you to a large car park. To the left is the trail up the mountain; to the right is a boardwalk to the aptly named **Shí Hǎi** (石海; Stone Sea), a magnificent lava field.

Back in the car park smaller green shuttle buses take you to **Huǒshāo Shān** (火烧山) and the end of the road at another collection of weirdly shaped lava stones. This stretch is one of Wǔdàlián Chí's most enchanting, with lava rock rivers, **birch forests**, grassy fields, ponds and more wide stretches of lava fields. It's about 5km from the start to the end, meaning you could walk it back, but be careful as the shuttle drivers go fast.

Lóngmén 'Stone Village'
LAVA FIELD

(龙门后塞奇观观光区; Lóngmén Hòusài Qíguān Guānguāngqū; admission ¥50; ⊙7am-6pm May-Oct) At this impressive lava field, walk through a forest of white and black birch trees on a network of boardwalks, with the lava rocks stretching away in the distance on both sides.

Ice Caves
CAVES

(熔岩冰洞; Róngyán Bīngdòng; admission ¥30; ⊙7.30am-6pm May-Oct) Families with small kids might enjoy the simple ice sculptures and chilly year-round -5°C environment in the **Lava Ice Cavern** and the nearby **Lava Snow Cavern** (熔岩雪洞; Róngyán Xuědòng; admission ¥30; ⊙7.30am–6pm). At both you can rent a warm coat (¥10) if you don't have your own.

Sleeping & Eating

Yaoquan Lu, the main east–west drag in Wǔdàlián Chí, has a dozen or more hotels operating from May to October. Book in advance to avoid getting stranded without a room.

The area caters to group tours – single travellers who aren't staying at a hotel with a restaurant will have to go for the local places just south of the main intersection at Yaoquan and Shilong Lu. There are two dozen greasy-spoon choices (dishes ¥5 to ¥48), largely serving the same five types of local fish the area is famous for. You can also get cheap jiǎozi and BBQ. Several grocery stores sell fruit and imported snacks including real chocolate.

Staying in Wǔdàlián Chí Shì is a decent alternative to Wǔdàlián Chí. The town is not as pleasant but there is steady work at building wide pavements and greening the streets. Within a short walk of the bus station there are half a dozen hotels and plenty of restaurants.

Gōngrén Liáoyǎngyuàn
HOTEL $$

(工人疗养院; Workers Sanatorium; ☑722 1569; www.hljwdlc.com; d/tw ¥180/360; ✿) This cavernous complex in Wǔdàlián Chí has long corridors reminiscent of *The Shining* and is popular with Russian tourists. The parklike grounds are pleasant and the restaurant, which serves both Chinese and Russian food, is decent value (but will only serve guests). You can rent bikes (per hour ¥20) at the shops off the path leading from the gate to the main building.

Kèyùn Bīnguǎn
HOTEL $

(客运宾馆; ☑261 6666; d/tw ¥100; ✿) In Wǔdàlián Chí Shì, directly beside the bus station, is this cheerful, reasonably clean hotel that's a good option if you're looking to do Wǔdàlián Chí on the cheap. There's a row of inexpensive restaurants across the street, and taxis offering day trips to Wǔdàlián Chí (¥150) line up outside the hotel in the morning.

❶ Information

There's a visitor centre between the bus station and hotel area with good English maps (¥5) of the area. There are no banks or ATMs accepting foreign cards in Wǔdàlián Chí.

❶ Getting There & Away

Bus

Both Wǔdàlián Chí and Wǔdàlián Chí Shì have bus stations. Direct buses from Hǎ'ěrbīn (¥67 to ¥79, six hours, three daily at 9am, 11.30am and 1.30pm) may drop you off at Wǔdàlián Chí Shì despite assurances from the ticket office in Hǎ'ěrbīn to the contrary. A taxi the rest of the way will cost ¥40.

Buses leave for Hǎ'ěrbīn from Wǔdàlián Chí (¥67 to ¥79, six hours, 5.40am and 8.10am) and Wǔdàlián Chí Shì (6.50am and 8.20am). There are also buses to Hēihé and Běi'ān, the nearest train station, which has connections on to Hǎ'ěrbīn.

Russian Borderlands

Much of the remote northeastern border between China and Siberia follows the Black Dragon River (Hēilóng Jiāng), known to the Russians as the Amur River. In this region it's possible to see Siberian forests and dwindling settlements of northern minorities, such as the Daur, Ewenki, Hezhen and Oroqen.

Major towns in the far north include Mòhé and Hēihé, the latter a popular shopping destination for people in the province. On the eastern border, Suífēnhé is a gateway to Vladivostok.

MÒHÉ & BĚIJÍCŪN (NORTH POLE VILLAGE)
北极村, 漠河
☑0457

China's a big place, if you haven't noticed. And that vastness contains a multitude of landscapes, ecosystems and climates. China's northernmost town, Mòhé, standing amid spindly pine forests and vast bogs, holds the record for the lowest plunge of the thermometer: -52.3°C, recorded in 1956. That same day in the southern extreme at Sānyà, a tropical beach paradise of azure waters and coconut palms, the temperature was likely in the high 20s.

Mòhé is one of China's most intriguing outliers, sharing not just a border with Russia, but architecture as well. In 1985 the town burned to the ground in a raging forest fire and when it came time for rebuilding, a curious decision was made: given the town's proximity to Russia, and Hēilóngjiāng's long close relations with that country, the main streets would be rebuilt in an imperial-era style with spired domes, pillared entrances and facades with rows of narrow windows.

These days, Mòhé is best known for its midnight sun, visible for as long as 22 hours during the annual **Festival of Aurora Borealis** (北极光节; Běijíguāng Jié), held in late June. Oddly, this is one of the few times you can see the lights, according to locals. Later in the summer, when there are more hours of darkness, the lights don't appear.

Even more northerly than Mòhé is Běijícūn (北极村; North Pole Village) a sprawling village/recreation area on the very banks of the Hēilóng Jiāng River separating China and Russia. There's nowhere to go but back south here and one house has even been labelled **China No 1** (中国最北一家), ie China's first house. To visit this area you need to hire a taxi from Mòhé. Expect to pay around ¥250 to ¥300 return.

Běijícūn covers an area of forest, meadow-land and bog, with the occasional hamlet, log cabin or Russian-style structure dotting the pretty surroundings. If the mood strikes, you can stand at the top of a **map of China** that has been etched into a square. Step up on the podium and you are at the most northerly point one can be within 9,671,018 sq km of the earth's surface.

Between Běijícūn and Mòhé is the somber **Prostitutes Graveyard** (胭脂沟妓女坟; Yānzhī Gōu Jìnǚ Fén), reachable by a 30-minute drive down a side road to the **source of the Hēilóng Jiāng River** (黑龙江源头; Hēilóngjiāng Yuántóu). The grave-yard contains the burial mounds of dozens of destitute women who worked as prosti-tutes during Mòhé's gold rush in the late 19th century.

There are a number of hotels and guest-houses in Mòhé, including the comfortable and well-run **Mòhé Jiā Xīn Bīnguǎn** (漠河佳鑫宾馆; ☏287 0666; r ¥180-220). Rooms go for ¥120 in the low season. There is also a number of cheap **guesthouses** and restau-rants down the alleys off Fanrong Xiang. To get here from the **North Pole Star Park** (北极星公园; Běijí Xīng Gōngyuán) at the top end of town, head down Zhenxing Jie (the main street) two blocks and turn right.

There are four flights a day from Hā'ěrbīn to Mòhé (¥1610, 2½ hours). Trains (hard/soft sleeper ¥256/400, 9.55pm) take 21 hours to reach the northern town. Heading back, a train leaves at 7.46pm.

Mòhé's train station is about 2km from the centre of town and it costs ¥10 to get here by taxi. To/from the airport, taxis charge ¥20.

Shānxī

POP 36.3 MILLION

Includes »

Dàtóng 336
Around Dàtóng 338
Wǔtái Shān 340
Tàiyuán 343
Píngyáo 346
Around Píngyáo 350
Qīkǒu 350
Jìnchéng 352
Around Jìnchéng 352

Best Ancient Towns & Villages

» Píngyáo (p346)
» Guōyù (p352)
» Lǐjiāshān (p351)
» Qīkǒu (p350)

Best Temples

» Xiǎntōng Temple (p341)
» Tǎyuàn Temple (p341)
» Huáyán Temple (p336)
» Shuānglín Temple (p350)

Why Go?

Waist-deep in handsome history, Shānxī (山西) meets virtually all your China travel expectations – and throws in a few surprises. If you only visited Píngyáo and jetted home, you might assume China was bursting with picture-perfect ancient walled settlements oozing character and charm from each nook and adorable cranny. For sure, basing yourself here and jumping to Píngyáo's surrounding sights is practically all you need, with time-worn temples, traditional Qing-dynasty courtyard architecture and some of the warmest people in the Middle Kingdom.

The mountain vastness of Wǔtái Shān, however, reveals Shānxī's other great source of magic, a Buddhist leaning that fashions magnificent monastic architecture, a disposition further concentrated in the astonishing Buddhist cave sculptures at Yúngāng. Add in the time-warp walled village of Guōyù and the still-inhabited cave dwellings of Lǐjiāshān, and you'll find yourself spending more time here than you imagined.

When to Go
Dàtóng

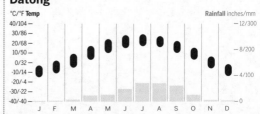

| May Get a jump on the sapping summer months. | Late May–early Sep For trips to cooler, mountainous Wǔtái Shān. | Late Sep Enjoy the comfortable start of the lovely Shānxī autumn. |

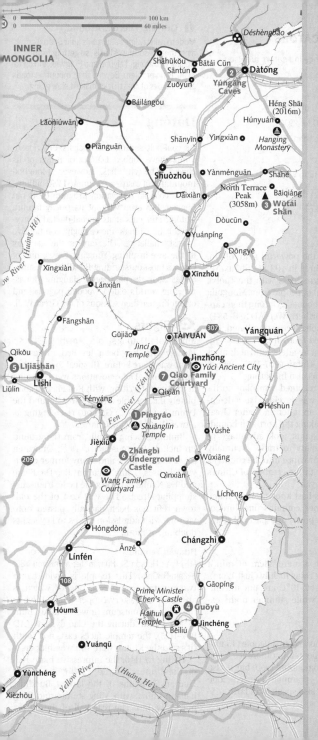

Shānxī Highlights

1 Fall head over heels for time-warped **Píngyáo** (p346)

2 Discover the indescribable beauty of the Buddhist statues at the **Yúngāng Caves** (p338)

3 Hang up your traveller's hat in the monastic enclave of **Wǔtái Shān** (p340)

4 Journey to the still-inhabited historical walled village of **Guōyù** (p352) in Shānxī's remote southeast

5 Head back in time with an overnight stay in the ancient cave village of **Lǐjiāshān** (p351)

6 Go subterranean at the fascinating **Zhāngbì Underground Castle** (p350)

7 Explore some of China's best-preserved courtyard architecture at the **Qiao Family Courtyard** (p345)

PRICE INDICATORS

The following price indicators are used in this chapter:

Sleeping

$	less than ¥200
$$	¥200 to ¥500
$$$	more than ¥500

Eating

$	less than ¥50
$$	¥50 to ¥100
$$$	more than ¥100

History

Though home to the powerful state of Jin, which split into three in 403 BC, Shānxī really only rose to greatness with the Tuoba, a clan of the Xianbei people from Mongolia and Manchuria who made Dàtóng their capital during the Northern Wei (AD 386–534). Eventually the Tuoba were assimilated, but as China weakened following the Tang collapse, the northern invaders returned; most notable were the Khitan (907–1125), whose western capital was also in Dàtóng.

After the Ming regained control of northern China, Shānxī was developed as a defensive outpost, with an inner and outer Great Wall constructed along the northern boundaries. Local merchants took advantage of the increased stability to trade, eventually transforming the province into the country's financial centre with the creation of China's first banks in Píngyáo.

Today Shānxī is best known for its many mines; the province contains one-third of all China's coal deposits and parts of it are heavily polluted.

Climate

Dry as dust, with a mere 35cm of rain a year. It only really rains in July (just 12cm). In Tàiyuán, lows of -10°C are not uncommon in January, while summer highs exceed 30°C.

Language

Jin is spoken by most Shānxī people (45 million speakers). The main difference from Mandarin is its final glottal stop, but it also features complex grammar-induced tone shifts. Most locals also speak Mandarin.

ℹ️ Getting There & Around

Modern railway lines and roads split Shānxī on a northeast–southwest axis, so getting from Běijīng to Dàtóng, Tàiyuán and Píngyáo, and on to Xī'ān, is no problem. Beyond that, mountain roads and convoys of coal trucks make it slow going.

Dàtóng   大同

📞0352 / POP 1.1 MILLION

Its coal-belt setting and socialist-era refashioning have robbed Dàtóng of much of its charm. The city has, however, ploughed mountains of cash – an estimated ¥50 billion – into a colossal renovation program of its old quarter. But even without its pricey facelift, Dàtóng still cuts it as a coal-dusted heavyweight in China's increasingly competitive tourist challenge. The city is the gateway to the awe-inspiring Yúngāng Caves, one of China's most outstanding Buddhist treasures, and close to the photogenic Hanging Monastery, the world's oldest wooden pagoda, and crumbling earthen sections of the Great Wall.

⊙ Sights

Much of Dàtóng's **old town** (老城区; *lǎochéngqū*) has been levelled to restore what was there before. Illogical for sure, but this is China. The renovations were ongoing at the time of writing, with Red Flag Sq completely inaccessible and the area around the Drum Tower (鼓楼; Gǔ Lóu) re-emerging as a twee 'Ye Olde Qing Quarter'.

Buildings being rebuilt from the ground up include the mosque (清真寺; Qīngzhēn Sì), a Taoist temple and many former courtyard houses, while Huayan Jie, Da Beijie and Da Nanjie have become pedestrian-only shopping streets. The vast cost of the old-town refit has been partially passed onto visitors, with admission prices to key sights doubling or more.

Huáyán Temple   BUDDHIST
(华严寺; Huáyán Sì; Huayan Jie; admission ¥80; ☉8am-6.30pm) This temple is divided into two separate complexes, one of which is an active monastery (upper temple), while the other is a museum (lower temple). Built by the Khitan during the Liao dynasty (AD 907–1125), the temple faces east, not south (it's said the Khitan were sun worshippers).

Dating to 1140, the impressive main hall of the **Upper Temple** (上华严寺; Shàng Huáyán Sì) is one of the largest Buddhist halls in China, with Ming statues and Qing murals within. The rear hall of the **Lower**

Temple (下华严寺; Xià Huáyán Sì) is the oldest building in Dàtóng (1038), containing some remarkable Liao-dynasty wooden sculptures. Side halls contain assorted relics from the Wei, Liao and Jin dynasties.

Take bus 4 (¥1) from the train station to get here.

Nine Dragon Screen   WALL
(九龙壁; Jiǔlóng Bì; Da Dongjie; admission ¥10; ☉8am-7pm) With its nine beautiful multicoloured coiling dragons, this 45.5m-long, 8m-high and 2m-thick Ming-dynasty spirit wall was built in 1392. It's the largest glazed-tile wall in China and an amazing sight; the palace it once protected burnt down years ago.

Shànhuà Temple   BUDDHIST
(善化寺; Shànhuà Sì; Nansi Jie; admission ¥50; ☉8.30am-6.30pm) Originally constructed in AD 713; Shànhuà was rebuilt by the Jin. The grand wooden-bracketed rear hall contains five beautiful central Buddhas and expressive statues of celestial generals in the wings.

🛌 Sleeping

Jiahe Hotel   HOTEL $$
(嘉和宾馆; Jiāhé Bīnguǎn; ☎555 9555; 1 Zhanqian Jie; 站前街1号; d & tw ¥268; ❄@) By the train station, this place has reasonably sized, comfortable rooms (with double beds raised off the floor in an imitation of the traditional *kàng*-style), modern showers and a strong broadband connection. The location is ideal for restaurants and transport to Dàtóng's surrounding sites, and beyond. Discounts bring the room prices down well below ¥200.

Datong Youth Hostel   HOSTEL $
(大同青年旅舍; Dàtóng Qīngnián Lûshè; ☎242 7788/7766; www.doyouhike.net; 2 Huayan Jie; 华严寺街2号; dm ¥50, d & tw ¥158; ❄@☎) The sole hostel in town is aimed at Chinese travellers, but foreigners will get a warm welcome (in broken English), too. The dorms and doubles are clean and fresh, and all come with bathrooms. Not much of a communal area, and there's no food here, but it makes a decent enough base if you avoid the rooms facing noisy Huayan Jie. The hostel is located above a tiny kids' clothes store; look for the English sign and then go through the shop and climb the stairs to the 3rd floor.

Garden Hotel   HOTEL $$$
(花园大饭店; Huāyuán Dàfàndiàn; ☎586 5888; www.huayuanhotel.com.cn; 59 Da Nanjie; 大南街59号; d & tw ¥1080-1380; ❄@☎) Impeccable rooms at this intimate hotel feature goose-

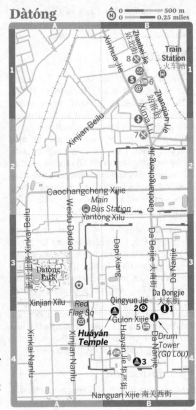

Dàtóng

Dàtóng

◎ **Top Sights**
Huáyán Temple B4

◎ **Sights**
1 Nine Dragon Screen B3
2 Old Town B3
3 Shànhuà Temple B4

🛌 **Sleeping**
4 Datong Youth Hostel B4
5 Garden Hotel B4
6 Jiahe Hotel B1

🍴 **Eating**
7 Hàoxuān Huǒguō B2
8 Tónghé Dàfàndiàn B1

down quilts, carved pear-wood bed frames, reproduction antique furnishings and lovely bathrooms. It has an attractive atrium, Latin American and Chinese restaurants, plus excellent staff and a Bank of China ATM. You can sometimes score very significant discounts here, even in high season.

 Eating

TOP CHOICE **Tónghé Dàfàndiàn** CHINESE $
(同和大饭店; Zhanqian Jie; meals ¥16-40; 11am-2pm & 6-9pm;) This very popular, bright and cheery spot next to the Hongqi Hotel may look a little intimidating with its big round tables, but solo diners can also pull up a chair. There's a huge range of tasty, well-presented dishes on the menu, suiting all budgets. Try the excellent beef rice noodles (¥16), or pick from a selection of dumplings, soups and vegie dishes, as well as the pricier fish and duck options.

Hàoxuān Huǒguō HOTPOT, BARBECUE $
(浩轩火锅; Bldg 1, Xinghuayuan, Xima Lu; hotpot for 1 ¥25; 9.30am-11pm) A friendly place with a split personality. Inside, it's a clean and modern hotpot palace serving hotpot for individuals (砂锅; *shāguō*) and groups (火锅; *huǒguō*). Outside, it's a raucous joint for spicy *shāokǎo* (barbecue). It has big vats of beer for ¥55, handy if there's a few of you, but it also comes by the glass (¥6). No English or picture menu, but the waitresses will help you out.

❶ Information

Bank of China (中国银行; Zhōngguó Yínháng; Da Nanjie) ATM; for travellers cheques, you need the Yingbin Xilu branch (open 8am to noon and 2.30pm to 6pm Monday to Friday). There's another branch close to the train station on Xima Lu.

China Construction Bank (中国建设银行; Zhōngguó Jiànshè Yínháng; Xinjian Beilu) ATM near the train station.

China Post (中国邮政; Zhōngguó Yóuzhèng; Xinjian Beilu; 8am-6.30pm) Opposite the train station.

Internet cafe (网吧; wǎngbā; Xinjian Beilu; per hr ¥4; 24hr) West of the Jiahe Hotel (Jiāhé Bīnguǎn).

Public Security Bureau (PSB; 公安局出入境接待处; Gōng'ānjú Chūrùjìng Jiēdàichù; Weidu Dadao; 9am-noon & 3-5.30pm Mon-Fri)

❶ Getting There & Away

Air

Located 20km east of the city, Dàtóng's small airport has flights to Běijīng (¥400), Shànghǎi (¥1450) and Guǎngzhōu (¥1630). Buy tickets at www.ctrip.com or www.elong.net. No public transport goes to the airport. A taxi costs around ¥50.

Bus

Note that minibuses run to many of the destinations listed below from outside the train station. Buses from the **south bus station** (新南站; xīnnán zhàn):

Běijīng ¥125, four hours, hourly (7.10am to 4.10pm)

Mùtǎ ¥25, two hours, half-hourly (7.40am to 7pm)

Tàiyuán ¥120, 3½ hours, every 20 minutes (6.50am to 7.30pm)

Wǔtái Shān ¥75, 3½ hours, two daily (8.30am and 2.10pm; summer only)

Buses from the **main bus station** (大同汽车站; Dàtóng qìchēzhàn; 20 Yantong Xilu):

Jíníng (for Déshèngbǎo) ¥15, one hour, hourly (7.30am to 5.30pm)

Hanging Monastery ¥30, two hours, half-hourly (6.30am to 6.30pm)

Hohhot ¥80, 3½ hours, hourly (7.30am to 5.50pm)

Train

Train departures from Dàtóng include the following:

Běijīng hard seat/sleeper ¥54/108, six hours, 12 daily

Hohhot hard seat ¥44, four hours, 11 daily

Píngyáo hard seat/sleeper ¥62/123, seven to eight hours, four daily

Tàiyuán hard seat ¥46, six hours, seven daily

Xī'ān hard seat/sleeper ¥115/224, 16½ hours, one daily

❶ Getting Around

Bus 4 (¥1) runs from the train station through the centre of town, down Da Beijie before turning west along Da Xijie. Bus 30 (¥1, 30 minutes) runs from the train station to the new south bus station. Buses 2 and 15 (¥1, 10 minutes) run from the train station to the main bus station.

Taxi flagfall is ¥6.

Around Dàtóng

YÚNGĀNG CAVES 云冈石窟
One of China's best examples of Buddhist cave art, these 5th-century **caves** (Yúngāng Shíkū; admission ¥150; 8.30am-5.30pm summer) are ineffably sublime. With 51,000 ancient statues, they put virtually everything else in the Shānxī shade.

Carved by the Turkic-speaking Tuoba, the Yúngāng Caves draw their designs from Indian, Persian and even Greek influences that swept along the Silk Road. Work began in AD 460, continuing for 60 years before all 252 caves, the oldest collection of Buddhist carvings in China, had been completed.

At the time of writing, caves 9 to 13 were shut for restoration. That still leaves 40 showcasing some of the most precious and elegant Buddhist artwork in China. Despite weathering, many of the statues at Yúngāng still retain their gorgeous pigment, unlike the slightly more recent statues at Lóngmén (p407). Note that worshippers still pray here, too. A number of the caves were once covered by wooden structures, but many of these are long gone, although Caves 5, 6, 7 and 8 are fronted by wooden temples.

Some caves contain intricately carved square-shaped pagodas, while others depict the inside of temples, carved and painted to look as though made of wood. Frescos are in abundance and there are graceful depictions of animals, birds and angels, some still brightly painted, and almost every cave contains the 1000-Buddha motif (tiny Buddhas seated in niches).

Eight of the caves contain enormous Buddha statues; the largest can be found in Cave 5, an outstanding 17m-high, seated effigy of Sakyamuni with a gilded face. The frescos in this cave are badly scratched, but note the painted vaulted ceiling. Bursting with colour, Cave 6 is also stunning, resembling a set from an *Indiana Jones* epic with legions of Buddhist angels, Bodhisattvas and other figures. In the middle of the cave, a square block pagoda connects with the ceiling, with Buddhas on each side over two levels. Most foreign visitors are oblivious to the graffiti in bright red oil paint on the right-hand side of the main door frame within the cave, which reads 大同八中 (Dàtóng Bāzhōng; Datong No 8 Middle School), courtesy of pupils probably during the Cultural Revolution. On the priceless fresco to the right is further graffiti in red paint, left by what appears to be a contingent from Píngyáo.

Further damage is much in evidence. Chronic weathering has afflicted Cave 7 (carved between AD 470 and 493) and Cave 8, both scoured by the Shānxī winds. Atmospheric pollution has also taken its toll.

Caves 16 to 20 are the earliest caves at Yúngāng, carved under the supervision of monk Tanyao. Examine the exceptional quality of the carvings in Cave 18; some of the faces are perfectly presented. Cave 19 contains a vast 16.8m-high effigy of Sakya-muni. The Maitreya Buddha is a popular subject for Yúngāng's sculptors, for example in the vast seated forms in Cave 17 and Cave 13; the latter statue has been defaced with graffiti by workers from Hohhot and other miscreants.

Cave 20 is similar to the Ancestor Worshipping Cave at Lóngmén, originally depicting a trinity of Buddhas (the past, present and future Buddhas). The huge seated Buddha in the middle is the representative icon at Yúngāng, while the Buddha on the left has somehow vanished. Many caves in the western end of Yúngāng have Buddhas with their heads smashed off, as in Cave 39. Buddhist figures exposed to the elements, especially near doorways, have been almost totally weathered away.

Most of the caves come with good English captions, but there's also a free audio guide in English (¥100 deposit). Note that photography is permitted in some caves but not in others.

❶ Getting There & Away

Take bus 4 (¥1, 30 minutes) from outside the post office opposite Dàtóng's train station to its terminus (tell the driver you're headed for the caves). Then cross the road and catch bus 3 (¥1, 30 minutes), which goes to the main gate. Buses run every 10 to 15 minutes. A taxi is ¥40 each way.

GREAT WALL 长城

The Great Wall (Chángchéng) is far less spectacular here than the restored sections found near Běijīng. Its Ming bricks – too useful for local farmers to leave alone – have all but disappeared, so just picture rammed earthen mounds, parts of which have crumbled away into nothing.

A good place to see some raw wall is little-visited **Déshèngbǎo** (得胜堡), a 16th-century walled fort almost on the border with Inner Mongolia that is now a small farming village. The fort's north and south gates are still standing, as are parts of its walls. Walk through the village (many of its houses are built out of Great Wall bricks) to the north gate and beyond it you'll see wild wall; 10m-high sections of it.

To get here, buy a ticket to Fēngzhèn (丰镇; ¥15, one hour) on any bus to Jíníng (集宁) from Dàtóng's main bus station. The bus will drop you at the turn-off for Déshèngbǎo, from where it's a 1km walk to the south gate. Heading back, return to the highway and flag down any Dàtóng-bound bus.

HANGING MONASTERY 悬空寺

Built precariously into the side of a cliff, the Buddhist **Hanging Monastery** (Xuánkōng Sì; admission ¥130; ⊙8am-7pm summer) is made all the more stunning by its long support stilts. The halls have been built along the contours of the cliff face, connected by rickety catwalks and narrow corridors, which can get very crowded in summer.

Buses travel here from Dàtóng's main bus station (¥30, two hours). Most will transfer passengers to the monastery into a free taxi for the last 5km from Húnyuán (浑源). Heading back, you'll be stung for ¥20 for a taxi (per person) to Húnyuán. If you want to go on to Mùtǎ, there are frequent buses from Húnyuán (¥14, one hour), or shared taxis make the run from the monastery car park for ¥50 per person.

MÙTĂ 木塔

Built in 1056, this charming five-storey **tower** (admission ¥60; ⊙7.30am-7pm summer, 8am-5.30pm winter) is the world's oldest and tallest (67m) wooden pagoda. The clay Buddhist carvings it houses, including an 11m-high Sakyamuni on the 1st floor, are as old as the pagoda itself. Due to its fragile state, visitors can no longer climb the pagoda, but there are photos of the higher floors to the side of the pagoda.

Mùtǎ is located in unlovely Yìngxiàn (应县). Buses from Dàtóng's south bus station (¥25, two hours) run to its west bus station (西站; *xīzhàn*). Hourly buses return to Dàtóng until 6pm, or you can travel onto Tàiyuán (¥85, 3½ hours, last bus 3.30pm). From the east bus station (东站; *dōngzhàn*), which is really just a crossroads, there are two buses a day to Wŭtái Shān (¥55, 2½ hours, 10.30am and 3.30pm).

Wŭtái Shān 五台山

📱0350

The gorgeous mountainous, monastic enclave of Wŭtái Shān (Five Terrace Mountains) is Buddhism's sacred northern range and the earthly abode of Manjusri (文殊; Wénshū), the Bodhisattva of Wisdom. Chinese students sitting the ferociously competitive *gāokǎo* (university entrance) exams troop here for a nod from the learned Bodhisattva, proffering incense alongside saffron-robed monks and octogenarian pilgrims. A powerful sense of the divine holds sway in Wŭtái Shān, emanating from the port-walled monasteries – the principal sources of spiritual power – and finding further amplification in the sublime mountain scenery.

The forested slopes overlooking the town eventually give way to alpine meadows where you'll find more temples and great hiking possibilities. Wŭtái Shān is also famed for its mysterious rainbows, which can appear without rain and are said to contain shimmering mirages of Buddhist beings, creatures and temple halls.

There's a steep ¥218 entrance fee for the area – including a mandatory ¥50 'sightseeing bus' ticket (旅游观光车票; *lǚyóu guānguāng chēpiào*) for transport within the area, which is valid for three days. Some of the more popular temples charge an additional small entrance fee.

Avoid Wŭtái Shān during the holiday periods and high-season weekends; temperatures are often below zero from October to March and roads can be impassable.

History
It's believed that by the 6th century there were already 200 temples in the area, although all but two were destroyed during the official persecution of Buddhism in the 9th century. During the Ming dynasty, Wŭtái Shān began attracting large numbers of Tibetan Buddhists (principally from Mongolia) for whom Manjusri holds special significance.

Climate
Wŭtái Shān is at high altitude and powerful blizzards can sweep in as late as May and as early as September. Winters are freezing and snowbound; the summer months are the most pleasant, but always pack a jacket, as well as suitable shoes or boots for rain, as temperatures fall at night. If you are climbing up the peaks to see the sunrise, warm coats can be hired.

⦿ Sights

Enclosed within a lush valley between the five main peaks is an elongated, unashamedly touristy town, called **Táihuái** (台怀) but which everyone simply calls Wŭtái Shān. It's here that you'll find the largest concentration of temples, as well as all the area's hotels and tourist facilities. The five main peaks are north (北台顶; *běitái dǐng*), east (东台顶; *dōngtái dǐng*), south (南台顶; *nántái dǐng*), west (西台顶; *xītái dǐng*) and central (中台顶; *zhōngtái dǐng*).

Wŭtái Shān

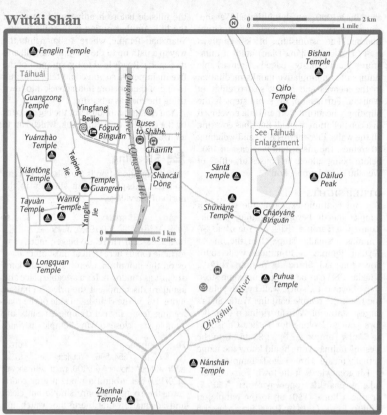

More than 50 temples lie scattered in town and across the surrounding countryside, so knowing where to start can be a daunting prospect. Most travellers limit themselves to what is called the **Táihuái Temple Cluster** (台怀寺庙群; Táihuái Sìmiàoqún), about 20 temples around Táihuái itself, among which Tǎyuàn Temple and Xiǎntōng Temple are considered the best. Many temples in Táihuái contain a statue of Manjusri, often depicted riding a lion and holding a sword used to cleave ignorance and illusion. You could spend weeks exploring the mountain area, investigating temple after temple.

Tǎyuàn Temple
BUDDHIST TEMPLE

(塔院寺; Tǎyuàn Sì; admission ¥10) At the base of **Spirit Vulture Peak** (灵鹫峰; Língjiù Fēng), the distinctive white stupa rising above, Tǎyuàn Temple is the most prominent landmark in Wŭtái Shān and virtually all pilgrims pass through here to spin the prayer wheels at its base or to prostrate

themselves, even in the snow. Beyond the **Devaraja Hall** (Hall of Heavenly Kings), with its candlelit gilded statue of Avalokitesvara (instead of Milefo, who you usually find in this position), at the rear of the **Dàcí Yánshòu Hall** is an altar where worshippers leave tins of instant coffee to Guanyin. Hung with small yellow bells chiming in the Wŭtái Shān winds, the marvellous **Great White Stupa** (大白塔; Dàbái Tǎ) dates originally from 1301 and is one of 84,000 dagobas built by King Asoka, 19 of which are in China. The **Great Sutra-Keeping Hall** is a magnificent sight; its towering 9th-century revolving Sutra case originally held scriptures in Chinese, Mongolian and Tibetan.

Xiǎntōng Temple
BUDDHIST TEMPLE

(显通寺; Xiǎntōng Sì; admission ¥10) Xiǎntōng Temple – the largest and most captivating temple in town with around 150 monks in residence – embraces more than 100 halls and rooms. The **Qiānbō Wénshū Hall** contains a 1000-armed, multifaced Wenshu, whose every palm supports a miniature Buddha. The astonishing brick **Beamless Hall** (无梁殿; Wúliáng Diàn) holds a miniature Yuan-dynasty pagoda, remarkable statues of contemplative monks meditating in the alcoves and a vast seated effigy of Wenshu. Further on, up some steps is the blindingly beautiful **Golden Hall**, enveloped in a constellation of small Buddhas covering all the walls. Five-metres high and weighing 50 tonnes, the metal hall was cast in 1606 before being gilded; it houses an effigy of Wenshu seated atop a lion.

OTHER SIGHTS

You can continue exploring the cluster of temples north beyond Xiǎntōng Temple. **Yuánzhào Temple** (圆照寺; Yuánzhào Sì) contains a smaller stupa than the one at Tǎyuán Temple. A 10-minute walk south down the road, **Shūxiàng Temple** (殊像寺; Shūxiàng Sì) can be reached up some steep steps beyond its spirit wall by the side of the road; the temple contains Wǔtái Shān's largest statue of Wenshu riding a lion. Before you go looking for Father Christmas at **Sāntǎ Temple** (三塔寺; Sāntǎ Sì) to the west of Tǎihuái, you should know the name actually means Three Pagoda Temple.

For great views of the town, you can trek, take a chairlift (one-way/return ¥50/85) or ride a horse (¥50) up to the temple on **Dàiluó Peak** (黛螺顶; Dàiluó Dǐng; admission ¥8), on the eastern side of Qīngshuǐ River (清水河; Qīngshuǐ Hé). For even better views of the surrounding hills, walk 2.5km south to the isolated, fortress-like **Nánshān Temple** (南山寺; Nánshān Sì), which sees far fewer tour groups than the other temples and has beautiful stone carvings. **Wànfó Temple** (万佛阁; Wànfó Gé) is perfect for a pit stop. During summer there are fabulous, free performances of Shānxī opera on its outdoor stage that run all morning and from 3pm to 6pm.

🏃 Activities

Opportunities for hiking are immense, but there are no good maps, no marked trails and no locals with any interest in hiking to show you the way. You're on your own here, so take food and plenty of water. A good place to start is Shūxiàng Temple. Walk past the temple on the small road leading to the central and western peaks, and turn left immediately after the small bridge. You'll find a trail behind the houses that leads up

the hillside before heading west on top of the hill. Another option is the hills behind Yuánzhào Temple, where a sign points the way to a path up to the surrounding hill and its pagoda. Roads lead to the summits of the five main peaks, so you could take a taxi up to one of them before hiking back into town using the road as a bearing.

You can find minibuses at the big car park by the chairlift to Dàiluó Peak, which run to all five peaks for ¥350.

🛏 Sleeping

Most accommodation is fairly basic. You can find real cheapies without showers in the north of the village.

Cháoyáng Bīnguǎn   HOTEL **$$**
(朝阳宾馆; ☏180 3500 9567; Wayao Jie; 瓦窑街; tw/tr ¥388/528) There are bigger, more comfortable rooms here than at most other places on the mountain, even if the bathrooms are just as rundown. It's a sizeable place and standard discounts cut the prices in half or more. It's on the right-hand side of the road leading from Tǎyuán Temple to Shūxiàng Temple, very close to Wǔyé Temple (五爷庙).

Fóguó Bīnguǎn   HOTEL **$**
(佛国宾馆; ☏654 5962; Yingfang Jie; 营坊街; tw/tr without shower ¥60/100, tw/tr with shower ¥120/180) Set around a modern grey courtyard, the rooms here are simple but clean and adequate, while there's hot water and the staff are used to dealing with foreigners. Walk to the end of Yingfang Beijie alley, turn left and it's on your left (opposite the bridge).

🍴 Eating

Loads of small family-run restaurants are tucked away behind hotels and down small alleys off the main strip. *Táimó* (台蘑), the much-revered Wǔtái Shān mushroom, is the local treat and you will be steered towards it. Try *táimódùn jīkuài* (台蘑炖鸡块; *táimó* stewed chicken) or *táimódùn tǔ jī* (台蘑炖土鸡; *táimó* stewed wild chicken). Also look out for *táimódùn dòufu* (台蘑炖豆腐; *táimó* stewed tofu). Bear in mind, though, that *táimó* dishes are pricey, and that there are plenty of other options available.

ℹ Information

Bring cash, as there's nowhere to change money and ATMs only accept Chinese cards. There are no proper hiking maps available, but you can pick up an OK tourist map (¥5) from many shops.

China Post (中国邮政; Zhōngguó Yóuzhèng; ⏰8am-7pm) By the bus station, a half-hour walk south, just north of a China Mobile shop.

Internet cafe (网吧; wǎngbā; per hr ¥4; ⏰24hr) Almost next door to the Fóguó Bīnguǎn.

ℹ️ Getting There & Away

Bus

Buses to Shāhé (¥25, 1½ hours, hourly, 8am to 6pm) leave from the car park by the chair lift to Dàiluó Peak.

Buses from **Wǔtái Shān bus station** (汽车站; qìchē zhàn):

Běijīng ¥145, 6½ hours, four daily

Dàtóng ¥75, four hours, four daily (7.30am to 2.30pm, summer only)

Hanging Monastery ¥65, three hours, one daily (8am)

Tàiyuán ¥74, three to four hours, hourly (6am to 4pm)

To get here in winter, first go to Shāhé from Dàtóng (¥43, 3½ hours, two daily, 6.30am and 7am) and then take a minibus taxi (around ¥70).

Train

The station known as **Wǔtái Shān** is actually 50km away in the town of Shāhé (砂河). An example route and fare is for Běijīng (¥63, five to seven hours, 10 daily).

Tàiyuán 太原

📞0351 / POP 2.85 MILLION

Most travellers pass through Shānxī's capital en route to Píngyáo, but the city has enough to keep you occupied for a day with its excellent museum and a few handsome temples.

👁 Sights

FREE **Shānxī Museum** MUSEUM
(山西博物馆; Shānxī Bówùguǎn; Binhe Xilu Zhongduan; ⏰9am-5pm Tue-Sun, last entrance 4pm) This top-class museum has three floors that walk you through all aspects of Shānxī culture, from prehistoric fossils to detailed local opera and architecture exhibits. All galleries are imaginatively displayed and most contain good English captions. Take bus 6 (¥1) from the train station, get off at Yifen Qiaoxi (漪汾桥西) bus stop across the river and look for the inverted pyramid.

Twin Pagoda Temple/
Yǒngzuò Temple BUDDHIST TEMPLE
(双塔寺/永祚寺; Shuāngtǎ Sì/Yǒngzuò Sì; admission ¥30; ⏰8.30am-5.30pm) This gorgeous pair of namesake twin pagodas rises up south

of the Nansha River in Tàiyuán's southwest. Not much of the temple itself is left but the area is well tended with shrubs and greenery; with the wind in their tinkling bells, the highlight brick pagodas are lovely. The 13-storey **Xuānwén Pagoda** (宣文塔; Xuānwén Tǎ) dates from the reign of Ming emperor Wanli and can be climbed. The adjacent pagoda dates from the same period but cannot be climbed. Take bus 820 or 812 from the train station.

Chóngshàn Temple BUDDHIST
(崇善寺; Chóngshàn Sì; Dilianggong Jie; admission ¥2; ⏰8am-4.30pm) Lovely and cool in summer, the double-eaved wooden hall in this Ming temple contains three magnificent statues: Samanthabhadra (the Bodhisattva of Truth), Guanyin (the Goddess of Mercy with 1000 arms) and Manjusri (the Bodhisattva of Wisdom with 1000 alms bowls). The other halls were being renovated at the time of writing. The entrance is down an alley off Dilianggong Jie behind the **Confucius Temple** (文庙; Wén Miào; 3 Wen Miao Xiang; admission free; ⏰9am-5pm Tue-Sun), which still has its spirit wall standing guard, as well as a calligraphy exhibition and posh tea house.

🛏 Sleeping

There are very basic guesthouses offering rooms for around ¥40 on Wuyi Dongjie.

World Trade Hotel HOTEL $$$
(山西国贸大饭店; Shānxī Guómào Dàfàndiàn; 📞868 8888; www.sxwtc.com; 69 Fuxi Jie; 府西街69号; d ¥1258-1578, ste ¥2478; 🅿️❄️@📶☕🏊) Its marbled lobby a vast atrium-lit space slung between its two towers (named after and resembling New York's former World Trade Center), this dapper, efficient five-star hotel has the finest rooms and facilities in town, including a gym and spa. You need to pay extra for a view not looking straight into the neighbouring tower. Discounts of 25% available.

Jiaotong Dasha Business Hotel HOTEL $$
(交通大厦; Jiāotōng Dàshà; 📞826 7008; 50 Yingze Dajie; 迎泽大街50号; d & tw ¥428; ❄️@) Slightly weary rooms for the price at this big hotel south of the train station, but they're a reasonable size and the bathrooms are modern. The staff are helpful and the discounts of 40% decent.

Taiyuan Wanming Hotel HOTEL $
(太原万明宾馆; Tàiyuán Wànmíng Bīnguǎn; 📞494 8888; 23 Wuyi Dongjie; 五一东街23号; tw ¥158-198; ❄️@) A blast from the past with its

Tàiyuán

SHĀNXĪ TÀIYUÁN

Tàiyuán

◎ Top Sights
Chóngshàn Temple C1
Confucius Temple C1

☐ Sleeping
1 Jiaotong Dasha Business Hotel..........C2
2 Taiyuan Wanming Hotel.......................C2

⊗ Eating
3 Food St A1
4 Tàiyuán Noodle House A2

old-school *fúwùyuán* (attendants) on each floor, the rooms here are battered and noisy but clean. There's a decent internet connection and an attached restaurant, while the location is fine for the train and main bus stations. Discounts of 10% available.

✗ Eating

Shānxī is famed for its noodles – including *dāoxiāo miàn* (刀削面; knife-pared noodles) and *lāmiàn* (拉面; hand-pulled noodles) – and vinegar, both in abundance in Tàiyuán. Mutton soup is lapped up by locals for breakfast.

TOP CHOICE ⟩ Tàiyuán Noodle House   NOODLES $
(太原面食店; Tàiyuán Miànshí Diàn; 7 Jiefang Lu; noodles from ¥8; ⏰11am-9.30pm) Great, bustling locals' joint and *the* place to try Shānxī's famous vinegar/noodle combo. Classic forms (named after their shape, not ingredients) include *māo'ěrduo* (猫耳朵; cat's ears; ¥10) and *cuōyú* (搓鱼; rolled fish; ¥10). Garnishes include *ròuzhàjiàng*

(肉炸酱; pork) and *yángròu* (羊肉; mutton). It also does fine *shāomài* (烧麦; ¥12). No English menu, but there are pictures of the dishes on the wall.

Food Street   CHINESE $
(食品街; Shipin Jie; meals from ¥7; ⏰11am-2am) For a change from noodles, head to this street lined with all manner of restaurants and outdoor *shāokǎo* (barbecue) places. You can get noodles here, of course, but also hotpot, dumplings and fried dishes. It gets lively late in the evening, when it's a good place for a beer and a bit of chat with the locals. The street runs north off Zhonglou Jie; look for the Qing-era arch and go through it.

ℹ Information

There are internet cafes all around the train station, but many won't accept foreigners.

Bank of China (中国银行; Zhōngguó Yínháng; 169 Yingze Dajie; ⏰8.30am-5.30pm) ATM accepts foreign cards. Can change travellers cheques (Monday to Friday).

China Post (中国邮政; Zhōngguó Yóuzhèng; ⏰8am-7pm) Opposite the train station.

Industrial & Commercial Bank of China (ICBC; 工商银行; Gōngshāng Yínháng; Yingze Dajie) The 24-hour ATM accepts foreign cards.

Internet cafe (网吧; wǎngbā; Wuyi Dajie; per hr ¥3; ⏰24hr) Down an alley to the right of Taiyuan Wanming Hotel.

Public Security Bureau (PSB; 公安局; Gōng'ānjú; ☎895 5355; Wuyi Dongjie; ⏰8-11.30am & 2.30-5.30pm Mon-Fri winter, 8-11.30am & 3-5.30pm summer) Can extend visas.

ⓘ Getting There & Away

Air

Shuttle buses to the airport (¥15, 40 minutes, hourly from 6am to 8.30pm) run from the side of the Sanjin International Hotel on Wuyi Guangchang. The airport is 15km southeast of downtown Tàiyuán; a taxi costs around ¥50.

Destinations include Běijīng (¥590), Hángzhōu (¥580), Hong Kong (¥1400), Kūnmíng (¥1640), Nánjīng (¥700), Shànghǎi (¥920) and Shēnzhèn (¥1090).

Bus

Tàiyuán's **long-distance bus station** (长途汽车站; chángtú qìchēzhàn) is 500m south of the train station on Yingze Dajie. Buses travel to the following destinations:

Běijīng ¥146, seven hours, three daily (8.30am, 10.30am and 2.30pm)

Dàtóng ¥117, 3½ hours, every 20 minutes (6.40am to 7pm)

Shànghǎi ¥409, 17 hours, one daily (2.30pm)

Shíjiāzhuāng ¥65, 3½ hours, two daily (10.30am and 2.30pm)

Xī'ān ¥180, eight hours, five daily (8am to 6pm)

Zhèngzhōu ¥156, seven hours, five daily (7am to 5pm)

Buses from the **Jiànnán bus station** (建南站; Jiànnán zhàn), 3km south of the train station:

Jièxiū ¥42, two hours, half-hourly (7.30am to 7pm)

Jìnchéng ¥114, four hours, every 40 minutes (6.50am to 7pm)

Píngyáo ¥26, two hours, half-hourly (6am to 7.30pm)

Qíxiàn ¥23, two hours, half-hourly (7.30am to 7pm)

The **east bus station** (东客站; dōng kèzhàn) has buses to Wǔtái Shān (¥74, three to four hours, every 50 minutes, 6.40am to 6.30pm).

The **west bus station** (客运西站; kèyùn xīzhàn) has the following services:

Líshí ¥70, two hours, frequent (7am to 7.30pm)

Qìkǒu ¥79, four hours, one daily (10.30am)

Train

Direct routes from **Tàiyuán Train Station** (火车站; huǒchē zhàn):

Běijīng D express train ¥149, three hours 40 minutes; normal train ¥73, five to six hours, 22 daily

Dàtóng hard seat/sleeper ¥46/100, five to seven hours, seven daily

Jìnchéng hard seat/sleeper ¥48/108, seven hours, four daily

Píngyáo ¥15, 1½ hours, frequent

Wǔtái Shān ¥54, five hours, one daily

Xī'ān hard seat/sleeper ¥103/191, nine to 11 hours, nine daily

ⓘ Getting Around

Bus 1 (¥1) runs the length of Yingze Dajie. For the Jiànnán bus station and the west bus station, take bus 611 (¥1.50) from the train station. For the east bus station take any bus (¥1.50) heading east from Wulongkou Jie.

Taxi flagfall is ¥8.

DON'T MISS

QIAO FAMILY COURTYARD

This 18th-century complex of courtyards at the **Qiao Family Courtyard** (乔家大院; Qiáojiā Dàyuàn; admission ¥72; ⊙8am-7pm) is one of the finest remaining examples of a traditional private residence in northern China. Once home to a celebrated merchant, it's an austere maze of doorways and courtyards that lead onto seemingly endless rooms (there are over 300 of them).

The complex is famous in China for being where Zhang Yimou's lush fifth-generation tragedy *Raise the Red Lantern* was filmed. Appropriately, there are red lanterns hanging everywhere, but there are also many fascinating exhibits of Qing-era furniture and clothes, as well as Shānxī opera costumes and props.

Souvenir and food stalls surround the compound, which is extremely popular with domestic tour groups (get here as early as you can). But the residence is still big enough to escape the crowds; you can step through one of the many doorways and they magically disperse.

To get here, catch any bus going to Qíxiàn (祁县; ¥23, 1½ hours) from Tàiyuán's Jiànnán bus station. Tell the driver where you're headed and they'll drop you at the main gate. You can also visit from Píngyáo.

Píngyáo 平遥

☑ 0354 / POP 450,000

China's best-preserved ancient walled town, Píngyáo is fantastic. Anyone with any China mileage under their belt will be bewitched by the town's age-old charms; charms squandered away – or forever lost – elsewhere across the Middle Kingdom. While other 'ancient' cities in China will rustle together an unconvincing display of old city walls, sporadic temples or the occasional ragged alley thrust beneath an unsightly melange of white-tile architecture and greying apartment blocks, Píngyáo has managed to keep its beguiling narrative largely intact. This is the China of your dreams: red-lantern–hung lanes set against night-time silhouettes of imposing town walls, elegant courtyard architecture, ancient towers poking into the north China sky, and an entire brood of creaking temples and old buildings.

Píngyáo is also a living and breathing community where the 30,000-odd locals who reside in the old town hang laundry in courtyards, career down alleyways on bicycles, sun themselves in doorways or chew the fat with neighbours. If you've been doing some hard travelling in the hinterlands, it's a great place to catch your breath and kick back for a few days, while Píngyáo is also a fine base for day trips to the Wang Family Courtyard and Zhāngbì Cūn and its 1400-year-old underground castle.

History

Already a thriving merchant town during the Ming dynasty, Píngyáo's ascendancy came in the Qing era when merchants created the country's first banks and cheques to facilitate the transfer of silver from one place to another. The city escaped the shocking reshaping much loved by communist town planners, and almost 4000 Ming- and Qing-dynasty residences remain within the city walls.

Píngyáo

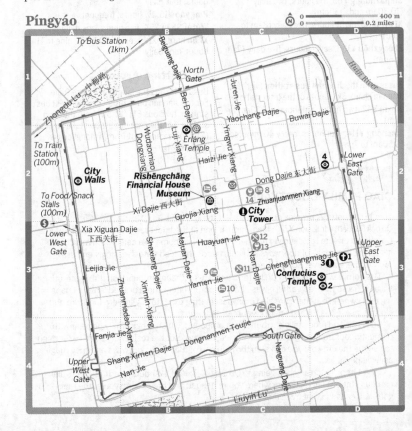

◉ Sights & Activities

Bounded by an intact city wall, gates access the old town at various points in the east, west, north and south. The main drag is Nan Dajie (南大街), where you'll find guesthouses, restaurants, museums, temples and souvenir shops galore. If you have even the remotest interest in Chinese history, culture or architecture, you could easily spend a couple of days wandering the pinched lanes of Píngyáo, stumbling across hidden gems while ticking off all the well-known sights. It's free to walk the streets, but you must pay ¥150 to climb the city walls or enter any of the 18 buildings deemed historically significant. Tickets are valid for three days; electronic audio tours are ¥40 (¥100 deposit). Opening hours for the sights are from 8am to 7pm in summer and 8am to 6pm in winter.

City Walls
WALLS

A good place to start is the magnificent city walls (城墙; *chéng qiáng*), which date from 1370. At 10m high and more than 6km in circumference, they are punctuated by 72 watchtowers, each containing a paragraph from Sunzi's *The Art of War*. Part of the southern wall, which collapsed in 2004, has been rebuilt, but the rest is original. Píngyáo's **city gates** (城门; *chéngmén*) are fascinating and are some of the best preserved in China; the **Lower West Gate** (Fèngyì Mén; Phoenix Appearing Gate) has a section of the original road, deeply grooved with the troughs left by cartwheels (also visible at the South Gate).

Rìshēngchāng Financial House Museum
MUSEUM

(日升昌; Rìshēngchāng; 38 Xi Dajie; 西大街38号) Not to be missed, this museum began life as a humble dye shop in the late 18th century before its tremendous success as a business saw it transform into China's first draft bank (1823), eventually expanding to 57 branches nationwide. The museum has nearly 100 rooms, including offices, living quarters and a kitchen, as well as several old cheques.

Confucius Temple
CONFUCIAN

(文庙; Wén Miào) Píngyáo's oldest surviving building is **Dàchéng Hall** (大成殿; Dàchéng Diàn), dating from 1163 and found in the Confucius Temple, a huge complex where bureaucrats-to-be came to take the imperial exams.

City Tower
TOWER

(市楼; Shì Lóu; Nan Dajie; admission ¥5; ◷8am-7pm) Tallest building in the old town. Climb its smooth stone steps for fine views over Píngyáo's magnificent rooftops and inspect its ragged and forlorn shrine to a severe-looking Guandi.

Qīngxū Guàn
TAOIST

(清虚观; Dong Dajie) Shānxī dust has penetrated every crevice of the 10 halls that make up this impressive Taoist temple. But that only adds to its ancient aura; it dates back to the Tang dynasty.

Slogans
HISTORIC SITE

Pop into 153 Xi Dajie for two red-blooded slogans from the Cultural Revolution that have survived on buildings within the courtyard. The one on the left intones: 工业学大庆 ('Industry should learn from Dàqìng'); the rarer slogan on the right proclaims: 认真搞好斗批改 ('Earnestly undertake struggle, criticism and reform').

Nine Dragon Screen
MONUMENT

(九龙壁; Jiǔlóng Bì; Chenghuangmiao Jie) In front of the old Píngyáo Theatre (大戏堂; Dàxìtáng).

SHĀNXĪ PÍNGYÁO

Píngyáo

◉ Top Sights
City Tower...C2
City Walls A2
Confucius Temple................................D3
Rìshēngchāng Financial House
  Museum B2

◎ Sights
1 Catholic Church D3
2 Dàchéng Hall D3
3 Nine Dragon Screen D3
4 Qīngxū Guàn D2

🛏 Sleeping
5 Cuì Chénghǎi Hotel..........................C3
6 Déjūyuán Guesthouse.......................B2
7 Harmony Guesthouse........................C3
8 Jing's Residence C2
9 Yámén Youth Hostel B3
10 Zhèngjiā Kèzhàn C3

✖ Eating
11 Bĕibăokè...C3
12 Déjūyuán C3

☕ Drinking
13 Sakura Café.....................................C3
14 Sakura Café.....................................C2

Catholic Church CHURCH

(天主堂; Tiānzhǔ Táng; 2 Anjia Jie) With a snow-white statue of the Virgin Mary outside, this historic, if dilapidated, church is the focal point for Píngyáo's Catholics.

☞ Tours

Mr Deng, who runs the Harmony Guest-house, gives reader-recommended day-long tours of the city for ¥150. He's a great source of local knowledge and can also point you towards some little-visited sites outside town.

🛏 Sleeping

Most of the old-town hotels are conversions of old courtyard homes, and finding a bed for the night is not hard. Píngyáo courtyards differ from their squarer Běijīng equivalents; courtyards in Píngyáo are 目字形, meaning 'shaped like the character 目', and are more rectangular in shape. Píngyáo hoteliers are increasingly tuned in to the needs of Western travellers, which means some English is spoken and they can make a passable Western breakfast. Most hotels and hostels will do pick-ups from the train or bus stations.

TOP CHOICE Harmony Guesthouse COURTYARD HOTEL $

(和义昌客栈; Héyìchāng Kèzhàn; 2 568 4952; www.py-harmony.com; 165 Nan Dajie; 南大街165号; dm ¥40-60, s ¥140, d & tr ¥180-210; ❈@?) Justifiably popular, Harmony Guesthouse offers rooms off two beautifully preserved courtyards in a lovely 300-year-old Qing building, as well as in a smaller courtyard down a neighbouring alley. The unflagging English-speaking husband and wife team have created a hospitable environment and most rooms come with traditional stone *kàng* beds, wooden bed-top tea tables and delightful wooden inlaid windows. Dorm accommodation is in the original guest-house, as well as in the bar just up the road. Also offers tours, ticketing, bike rental (¥10 per day), laundry, internet, wi-fi and pick-up.

Dejuyuan Guesthouse COURTYARD HOTEL $$

(德居源客栈; Déjúyuán Kèzhàn; 2 568 5266; www.pydjy.net; 43 Xi Dajie; 西大街43号; d ¥280, tw ¥368-580, ste ¥1480; ❈@?) Very well-maintained rooms are set around two of the oldest courtyards in Píngyáo (400 years old) at this efficient and friendly place. The cheapest rooms are excellent value, while the suites are luxurious and come with tip-top bathrooms. Its restaurant is a fine place to try high quality local dishes at reasonable prices. Staff can arrange train tickets and tours as well.

TOP CHOICE Jing's Residence COURTYARD HOTEL $$$

(锦宅; Jǐn Zhái; 2 584 1000; www.jingsresidence.com; 16 Dong Dajie; 东大街16号; r ¥1438; ❈@?) With the super-hushed atmosphere that's unique to the most exclusive (and expensive) hotels, Jing's is a soothing blend of old Píngyáo and modern flair that's squarely aimed at upmarket Western travellers. At 260 years old the former home of a Qing-dynasty silk merchant is sleek and well finished: the themed courtyards are picture-perfect, rooms are elegant and stylish (the vast upstairs suites have views over Píngyáo's rooftops), while the upstairs bar must be the most sophisticated in all of Shānxī. Its restaurant serves high-priced Western fusion cuisine. There are only 19 rooms here and it's essential to book ahead.

Yámén Youth Hostel HOSTEL $

(衙门官舍青年旅社; Yámén Guānshè Qīngnián Lüshè; 2 568 3539; 69 Yamen Jie; 衙门街69号; 7-/3-bed dm ¥40/60, d & tw ¥180-240; ❈@?) Set around a series of courtyards, rooms are larger than many in Píngyáo but rather done in; the bathrooms could do with an upgrade. Dorms under the eaves are clean, with OK showers and toilets downstairs. The staff are obliging and all the usual hostel favourites are here: DVD room, ticketing, laundry, free internet, wi-fi, bike hire, pool table and pick-up. Discounts of 30% available.

Zhèngjiā Kèzhàn COURTYARD HOTEL $

(郑家客栈; 2 568 4466; 68 Yamen Jie; 衙门街68号; dm ¥35-40, d ¥168-218; ❈@?) With two locations virtually next door to each other, head to the one closest to the Listen to the Rain Pavilion for decent doubles with *kàng* beds set around a very pleasant courtyard. The cramped but fresh and clean dorms are under the eaves at the neighbouring courtyard (which also has doubles). There's a good communal area and it sees more Chinese travellers than the other guesthouses, making it a good place to meet the locals.

Cuì Chénghǎi Hotel COURTYARD HOTEL $

(翠成海客栈; Cuì Chénghǎi Kèzhàn; 2 577 7888; www.pycch.com; 178 Nan Dajie; 南大街178号;

d & tw ¥168; 🌀@🛜) Rooms are spacious, with big *kàng* beds, but rather stark. The restored Ming-dynasty courtyard setting, though, is lovely.

🍴 Eating & Drinking

Most guesthouses can rustle up (Western or Chinese) breakfast, lunch and dinner. Píngyáo's lanes are stuffed with *xiǎochī* (小吃; hole-in-the-wall restaurants), almost all offering the same dishes at similar prices. For something cheaper and less touristy, head to Xia Xiguan Jie (下西关街) just outside the lower west gate, where food stalls offer different varieties of noodles for ¥4 and up, as well *ròujiāmó* (肉夹馍; fried pork or beef with green peppers in bread) and meat and vegie skewers.

Píngyáo doesn't have many worthwhile bars, but courtyard hotels provide virtually all you need: bottles of chilled beer, a gorgeous courtyard to sit in, a chair and table, some grilled peanuts, the Shānxī night sky above your head, a book and some candlelight. Look out for heart-warming, soothing alcoholic infusions such as the pink *nǚ'er hóng* (女儿红) or the clear *méiguì* (玫瑰), which are available at most guesthouses and restaurants.

Déjūyuán
SHĀNXĪ $

(德居源; 82 Nan Dajie; ⊙8.30am-10pm; 🖋) Traveller friendly, but no worse for that, this welcoming and popular little restaurant has a simple and tasty menu of northern Chinese dishes, such as dumplings (¥15), as well as all the local faves. Try the famed Píngyáo beef or the mountain noodles (¥12). Cold dishes start at ¥8.

Bēibāokè
SHĀNXĪ $

(背包客; 37 Yamen Jie; dishes from ¥12; ⊙7am-10.30pm) Despite its name ('backpacker' in Mandarin), this cubbyhole restaurant sees fewer foreign faces than many places in Píngyáo. It also has a rather more esoteric kitchen, with the likes of spicy mini-hotpot (*shāguō niúròu*; 沙锅牛肉) and sweet and sour meatballs (¥28) available, as well as the inevitable noodle options. No English menu, but there are pictures on the wall.

Sakura Cafe
BAR $

(樱花屋西餐酒吧; Yīnghuāwū Xīcān Jiǔbā; 6 Dong Dajie; dishes from ¥35, beers from ¥10; ⊙9.30am-midnight; 🛜) Always busy, this lively, fun cafe-bar attracts both locals and foreigners with its daily food and drink specials. It does

decent pizzas (¥55), as well as breakfasts, coffee, beers and cocktails. There's another equally popular branch at 86 Nan Dajie.

🛍 Shopping

Part of Píngyáo's charms lie in its peeling and weatherbeaten shopfronts, yet to be mercilessly restored. Nan Dajie is stuffed with wood-panelled shops selling ginger sweets (marvel at vendors pulling the golden sugary ginger mass into strips), moon cakes, Píngyáo snacks, knick-knacks, Cultural Revolution memorabilia, jade, shoes and slippers, and loads more. Look out for red and black Shānxī paper cuts, which make excellent presents.

ℹ Information

All guesthouses and hostels have internet and wi-fi access.

China Post (中国邮政; Zhōngguó Yóuzhèng; Xi Dajie; ⊙8am-6pm)

Industrial & Commercial Bank of China (ICBC; 工商银行; Gōngshāng Yínháng; Xia Xiguan Dajie) Has an ATM that accepts Visa but, like all other Píngyáo banks, does not change money or travellers cheques.

Internet cafe (网吧; wǎngbā; per hr ¥3; ⊙24hr) Down a scruffy alley opposite the Èrláng Temple on Bei Dajie. Turn left into the first courtyard and go up to the 2nd floor.

Public Security Bureau (PSB; 公安局; Gōng'ānjú; 🖂563 5010; Shuncheng Lu; ⊙8am-12pm & 3-6pm Mon-Fri) Around 3km south of the train station, on the corner of the junction with Shuguang Lu. Cannot extend visas.

ℹ Getting There & Away

Bus

Píngyáo's **bus station** (汽车新站; qìchēxīnzhàn) has buses to Tàiyuán (¥26, two hours, frequent, 6.30am to 7.40pm), Líshí (¥44, two hours, 8.30am to 12.30pm) and Chángzhì (¥68, three hours, 7.50am and 1.40pm). Catch buses to local destinations such as Jiéxiū (¥9, 40 minutes) from the train station.

Train

Tickets for trains (especially to Xī'ān) are tough to get in summer, so plan ahead. Your hotel/hostel should be able to help. Trains depart for the following destinations:

Běijīng hard seat/sleeper ¥92/170, 11 to 14 hours, three daily

Dàtóng hard seat/sleeper ¥62/123, seven to eight hours, four daily

Tàiyuán ¥15, 1½ hours, frequent

Xī'ān hard seat/sleeper ¥67/134, 8½ to 10½ hours, five daily

ⓘ Getting Around

Píngyáo can be easily navigated on foot or bicycle (¥10 per day). Bike rental is all over the place; most guesthouses offer it and there are many spots along Nan Dajie and Xi Dajie. Rickshaws run to the train and bus stations for ¥10.

Around Píngyáo

Most hostels and guesthouses will arrange transport to the surrounding sights. Day tours including the Wang Family Courtyard and Zhāngbì Underground Castle are typically ¥80 per person (excluding the admission price or food).

ZHĀNGBÌ UNDERGROUND CASTLE 张壁古堡

This 1400-year-old network of defence tunnels (Zhāngbì Gǔbǎo; admission ¥60; ⊙8am-6.30pm) are the oldest and longest series of such tunnels in all China. Built at the end of the Sui dynasty and stretching underground for 10km, they were never employed for their intended use against possible attack from Tang-dynasty invaders and subsequently fell into disrepair. Now, 1500m of tunnels on three levels have been restored. You descend as low as 26m in places and tour narrow and stooped subterranean passageways, which were once storage rooms, guardhouses and bedrooms. Holes cut into the side of shafts leading to the surface indicate escape routes and places where the soldiers stood sentry to spy on would-be attackers.

Guides are compulsory and essential; you don't want to get lost here. They are included in the ticket price and foreigners are normally assigned someone who can speak English.

The tour includes a visit to fascinating Zhāngbì Cūn (张壁村), a still-occupied Yuan-dynasty farming village above the tunnels. You can wander its cobblestoned streets and temples for free if you don't mind skipping the underground castle.

You can only get here on a tour or by taxi. To cut the cost, take a bus halfway to Jièxiū (介休; ¥9, 40 minutes). A return taxi from Jièxiū, including waiting time, is around ¥150.

WANG FAMILY COURTYARD 王家大院

More castle than cosy home, this Qing-dynasty former residence (Wángjiā Dàyuàn; admission ¥66; ⊙7.30am-7pm) is grand and has been very well maintained (note the wooden galleries still fronting many of the courtyard buildings). Its sheer size, though, means that the seemingly endless procession of courtyards (123 in all) becomes a little repetitive. Behind the castle walls are interesting and still-occupied cave dwellings (窑洞; yáodòng), while in front of the complex is a Yuan-dynasty Confucius Temple (文庙; Wén Miào; admission ¥10), with a beautiful three-tiered wooden pagoda.

Two direct buses (¥17, one hour, 8.50am and 1.10pm) leave from Píngyáo's bus station, returning at 12.40pm and 4pm. Regular buses go to Jièxiū (介休; ¥9, 40 minutes), where you can change to bus 11 (¥5, 40 minutes), which terminates at the complex. The last bus back to Jièxiū leaves at 6pm.

SHUĀNGLÍN TEMPLE 双林寺

Within easy reach of Píngyáo, this Buddhist temple (Shuānglín Sì; admission ¥40; ⊙8.30am-6.30pm) surrounded by cornfields, houses a number of rare, intricately carved Song and Yuan painted statues. Rebuilt in 1571, it's an impressive complex of halls and rather more authentic than many restored temples. The interiors of the Sakyamuni Hall and flanking buildings are especially exquisite. A rickshaw or taxi from town will cost ¥40 to ¥50 return, or you could cycle the 7km here (although expect to swallow coal truck dust if you do).

Qìkǒu 碛口

☏0358 / POP 32,000

Separated from neighbouring Shaanxi (Shǎnxī) province (p354) by the fast-flowing and muddy Yellow River (黄河; Huáng Hé), this tiny Ming River port found prosperity during its Qing heyday when hundreds of merchants lived here, only to lose it when the Japanese army arrived in 1938. It's well worth visiting for its evocative stone courtyards and cobbled pathways. All wind their way, eventually, up to the Black Dragon Temple, which overlooks the town. Some of the houses have English captions revealing their former official roles, such as the pawnshop and chamber of commerce. The weekly market on Saturday is a good time to visit, when people from the surrounding villages arrive by tractor and electric cart for a day of shopping and revelry.

The main draw, though, is the nearby ancient village of Lìjiāshān, a seemingly long-forgotten settlement of hundreds of cave dwellings (窑洞; yáodòng), some of which remain inhabited today.

CAVE DWELLINGS

People have been living in cave houses (窑洞; *yáodòng*) in Shānxī for almost 5000 years; it's believed that at one stage a quarter of the population lived underground. Shānxī's countryside is still littered with *yáodòng*, especially around the Yellow River area, and Lǐjiāshān is a wonderful example. These days most lie abandoned, but almost three million people in Shānxī (and around 30 million in total in China) still live in caves. And who can blame them? Compared to modern houses, they're cheaper, far better insulated against freezing winters and scorching summers, much more soundproof, while they also afford better protection from natural disasters such as earthquakes or forest fires. Furthermore, with far fewer building materials needed to construct them, they're a lot more environmentally friendly. So why isn't everyone living in them? Well, although most are now connected to the national grid, the vast majority of cave communities have no running water or sewerage system, turning simple daily tasks like washing or going to the toilet into a mission and suddenly making even the ugliest tower block seem a whole lot more attractive.

👁 Sights

Lǐjiāshān   CAVES
(李家山) An absolute dream for travellers wanting to experience Shānxī's **cave houses** (窑洞; *yáodòng*), this remote, supremely peaceful 550-year-old village, hugging a hillside with terraces of crops running up it, has hundreds of cave dwellings scaling nine storeys. Once home to more than 600 families, most surnamed Li, today's population is around 45. Almost all inhabitants are elderly: the local school, with caves for classrooms, has just four pupils. People here speak Jin, although most understand Mandarin. Some of the stone paths and stairways that twist up the hill date from Ming times; note the rings on some walls that horses were tied to.

To get here, cross the bridge by Qìkǒu's bus stop and follow the river for about 30 minutes until you see a blue sign indicating Lǐjiāshān. Walk on for about 100m and then take the road up the hill for another 30 minutes and you'll reach the old village.

Black Dragon Temple   TAOIST
(黑龙庙; Hēilóng Miào) They say the acoustics of this Ming Taoist temple, with wonderful views of the Yellow River, were so excellent that performances held on its stage were audible on the other side of the river in Shaanxi (Shǎnxī) province. On Saturday afternoons, there are often fantastic, free Shānxī opera shows, which attract a crowd of knowledgeable senior citizens. From Qìkǒu's bus stop, follow the road to the river, then take any number of old cobbled pathways up the hill, via the odd courtyard or two.

🛏 Sleeping & Eating

Some locals offer functional beds for around ¥50. There are basic noodle joints on the 'main' street behind the bus stop.

TOP CHOICE Qìkǒu Kèzhàn   GUESTHOUSE $
(碛口客栈; ☑446 6188; d/tw/tr ¥188/218/388; @) Overlooking the river in Qìkǒu, this historic (the Red Army used it as a base in WWII) and friendly place has comfortable and very large, *yáodòng*-style rooms (all with internet connections) with *kàng* beds set off two 300-year-old courtyards. Climb the stone stairs and there's a wonderful terrace that has great views over the Yellow River. It's a fine place to enjoy a beer, or the tasty meals cooked up here, under the starry sky. Discounts of 10% available.

Sìhéyuàn Lǚdiàn   COURTYARD GUESTHOUSE $
(四合院旅店; ☑138 3583 2614; r per person incl meals ¥50; @) This 180-year-old rustic courtyard has a handful of cave bedrooms burrowed into the hill behind it. Run by the genial Mr Li, and his welcoming wife, whose family have lived here for six generations, rooms come with huge, chunky, stone *kàng* beds, traditional Chinese paper window panes and computers. There's electricity and running water (most of the time). Give Mr Li a call when you're on the way and he'll come and meet you. Otherwise, wander down the path through the village from the road and look for the big sign displaying 四合院旅店.

ℹ Getting There & Away

One bus runs from Tàiyuán to Qìkǒu (¥79, four hours, 10.30am). If you miss it, or are coming from Píngyáo, you will have to go through Líshí (离石).

Regular buses go from Tàiyuán to Líshí (¥70, three hours, half-hourly from 7.35am to 7pm). There are five daily buses from Píngyáo (¥44, two hours, 7.30am to 12.30pm). From Líshí's long-distance bus station (长途汽车站; chángtú qìchēzhàn), take bus 1 (¥1, 15 minutes) to the crossroads where buses to Qìkǒu (¥17, 1½ hours, 6.30am to 3.30pm) depart.

There's one daily bus from Qìkǒu to Tàiyuán, but it leaves at 5.30am. There are regular buses to Líshí from Qìkǒu until around 3pm. From Líshí, there are many buses back to Tàiyuán (¥70, from 7am to 8pm), two to Píngyáo (¥44, 7.30am and 11.40am) and three to Xī'ān (¥180, eight hours, 7am, 11.30am and 2.30pm).

Jìnchéng 晋城

☎0356 / POP 505,115

One snug, 470-year-old pagoda aside, Jìnchéng has few sights, but this small, little-visited city is the launch pad for a historical adventure into Shānxī's southeast. The surrounding countryside hides some very impressive ancient architecture, making this a rewarding stop, particularly if you are continuing south into Hénán.

The only sight of note in town is **Bǐfēng Temple** (笔峰寺; Bǐfēng Sì; ◎6am-6pm), which sits atop a hill close to the train station. The temple itself is newly built but the nine-storey pagoda dates back to the Ming dynasty. You can climb its dark and very narrow steps for views over Jìnchéng.

Most hotels in town are either overpriced or won't accept foreigners. The best option is the eccentric **Venice Water City** (威尼斯水城; Wēinísī Shuǐchéng; ☎888 3600; 978 Wenchang Dongjie; 文昌东街978号; tw/d ¥205/215; ❄@), a spa-cum-hotel close to the People's Hospital (人民医院; Rénmín Yīyuàn). You take your shoes off in the lobby (and pad around in slippers), while the staff hover unnervingly, but the rooms are modern, clean and comfortable, and all come with computers.

On Wenchang Dongjie you can also find a branch of the Bank of China with an ATM (there are many more around town), plenty of restaurants and an internet cafe (¥2 per hour; open 24 hours), although foreigners were barred from using it at the time of writing.

Buses to Tàiyuán (¥114, four hours, hourly, 6.30am to 6.30pm) and Chángzhì (¥38, half-hourly, 6.30am to 6.30pm), where you can change for Píngyáo, depart from the central bus station (客运总站; kèyùn

zǒngzhàn) close to the train station. If you're heading south to Hénán, you need the long-distance bus station (长途汽车站; chángtú qìchēzhàn) on Jianshe Lu. There are buses to Zhéngzhōu (¥63, every 40 minutes, 5.40am to 6.20pm) and Luòyáng (¥50, hourly, 7.20am to 6pm), as well as to Xī'ān (¥176 to ¥196, three daily, 8.30am, 10am, 6.20pm) and Běijīng (¥261, 10 hours, 6.20pm).

The few trains that pass Jìnchéng shuttle between Tàiyuán (hard seat/sleeper ¥54/108, seven hours, four daily) and Zhèngzhōu (¥30, 3½ hours, two daily).

Bus 2 (¥1) connects the train station with the central and long-distance bus stations. Taxi flagfall is ¥5.

Around Jìnchéng

GUŌYÙ 郭峪古城

This atmospheric walled village (Guōyù Gǔchéng) is the highlight of a trip to this part of Shānxī. There's no entrance fee and no tourist nonsense (amazingly, many of the domestic tour groups skip the village); just the genuine charm of a historic and still-inhabited Ming-dynasty settlement.

The crumbling remains of this one-time fort's south gate and some of its old walls still stand sentry at the entrance to the village close to the road. Walk 200m and it's as if you've stepped back in time. Narrow alleys and stone streets run past courtyard houses, where the locals sit and chatter in their native dialect.

It's best to wander Guōyù aimlessly. But don't miss **Tāngdì Miào** (汤帝庙), a 600-year-old Taoist temple and the village's oldest building. Make sure to climb up to the stage, where there are two very rare Cultural Revolution–era paintings adorned with slogans exhorting the locals to work harder (the temple was a government building during that time). It's also worth looking inside the former courtyard **residence** of Minister Chen's grandfather at 1 Jingyang Beilu (景阳北路1号).

To get here, catch one of the frequent buses headed to Prime Minister Chen's Castle (¥15, 1½ hours, 6am to 6.30pm) from Jìnchéng's long-distance station. Guōyù is a 10-minute walk south of the castle. Return transport is scarce, so it's best to take a mini-bus to the small town of Běiliú (北留; ¥3, 15 minutes), then catch an ordinary bus back to Jìnchéng (¥12).

FOR REFERENCE – PRIME MINISTER CHEN'S DICTIONARY

Prime Minister Chen Tingjing was undoubtedly a man of many talents. Outside his governmental responsibilities he also inspired as a teacher, poet and musician. His surviving legacy, however, was not one of China's great works of creativity, but a dictionary. Not just any dictionary, mind. China's most famous and most comprehensive, and the last one ever to be commissioned by an emperor. Named after that emperor, the *Kangxi Dictionary* was a mammoth undertaking put together by Chen and Zhang Yushu, both of whom died before its completion in 1716. Multi-volumed, and containing 49,030 characters, it was, until 1993, the largest Chinese dictionary ever compiled.

Appropriately enough, Chen's former residence now houses China's only dictionary museum. Among the exhibits are 39 versions of the *Kangxi Dictionary*, the oldest being a 42-volume, 47,035-character edition of 1827. Modern reprints can be bought in the small dictionary shop, although you might need a spare rucksack to get one back to the hotel!

PRIME MINISTER CHEN'S CASTLE
皇城相府

This beautifully preserved Ming-dynasty **castle** (Huángchéng Xiàngfǔ; admission ¥100; ⊙8am-6.30pm) is the former residence of Chen Tingjing, prime minister under Emperor Kangxi in the late 17th century, and co-author of China's most famous dictionary. The Chen family rose to prominence as senior officials in the 16th century and the castle walls were originally constructed to keep revolting peasants out.

The castle now comes with all the tourist trappings – souvenir sellers, flag-waving guides with microphones – but it remains an attractive maze of battlements, courtyards, gardens and stone archways. It's also home to China's only dictionary museum.

Regular buses (¥15) run to the ticket office from Jìnchéng's long-distance bus station.

HǍIHUÌ TEMPLE
海会寺

Closed at the time of writing, but normally open, this Buddhist **temple** (Hǎihuì Sì; admission ¥30), where Minister Chen used to study, is dominated by its two magnificent brick pagodas. The 20m-high **Shělì Tǎ** (舍利塔) is almost 1100 years old. Towering above it is the octagonal **Rúlái Tǎ** (如来塔), built in 1558, which can be climbed for an extra ¥10. To get here, take the bus to Prime Minister Chen's Castle but tell the driver you want to get off at Hǎihuì. To continue to the castle or Guōyù, take a minibus from the main road (¥2) or walk (45 minutes).

Shaanxi (Shǎnxī)

POP 37.3 MILLION

Includes »

Xī'ān.............................356
Around Xī'ān................364
Huà Shān.....................368
Hánchéng....................370
Yán'ān.........................372
Yúlín............................373
Mǐzhǐ...........................374

Best Historic Sites

» Army of Terracotta Warriors (p364)

» Tomb of Emperor Jingdi (p367)

» Big Goose Pagoda (p359)

» Yángjiālǐng Revolution Headquarters Site (p372)

Best Museums

» Forest of Stelae Museum (p357)

» Shaanxi History Museum (p359)

» Xiányáng City Museum (p366)

» Yán'ān Revolution Museum (p372)

Why Go?

Shaanxi (陕西) is where it all started for China. As the heartland of the Qin dynasty, whose warrior emperor united much of China for the first time, Shaanxi was the cradle of Chinese civilisation. Later on, Xī'ān was the beginning and end of the Silk Road and a buzzing, cosmopolitan capital long before anyone had heard of Běijīng.

Shaanxi's archaeological sites makes it an essential destination. Around Xī'ān there's an excavated Neolithic village and numerous royal graves; chief among them the tomb of Qin Shi Huang and his private army of terracotta warriors. Shaanxi has its share of contemporary history too; the caves around Yán'ān were the Chinese Communist Party's (CCP) base in the 1930s and '40s.

Xī'ān is an emergent travellers hub, with good nightlife, museums, ancient pagodas and a fascinating Muslim Quarter. Set aside time to get into the rural areas, with its fascinating villages barely touched by modern life and mountains that were once home to hermits and sages.

When to Go

Xī'ān

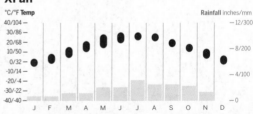

Apr & May Spring breezes and the ideal time to climb Huà Shān.

Sep & Oct The rain's stopped and it's still warm, so hit Xī'ān's sights.

Dec Avoid the crowds and maybe get the Terracotta Warriors all to yourself.

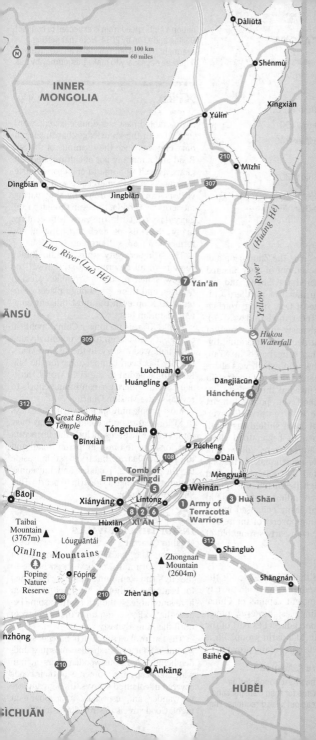

Shaanxi Highlights

1 See what an emperor takes with him to the grave at the extraordinary **Army of Terracotta Warriors** (p364)

2 Admire Xī'ān's distinctively named **Big Goose Pagoda** (p359), the centrepiece for a stunning sound and light show

3 Watch the sun rise over the Qínlǐng Mountains from atop Taoism's sacred western peak, **Huà Shān** (p368)

4 Explore the old town of **Hánchéng** (p370), a quaint quarter of buildings that date from the Yuan, Ming and Qing eras

5 Take a different look at China's past by gazing down on the enthralling excavations at the **Tomb of Emperor Jingdi** (p367)

6 Get lost wandering the backstreets of Xī'ān's ancient **Muslim Quarter** (p356)

7 Check out the **cave** (p372) where Mao Zedong lived in Yán'ān and the red tourists who flock to see it

8 Hop on a bike and ride atop Xī'ān's glorious **city walls** (p373), a pretty 14km loop of the city

PRICE INDICATORS

The following price indicators are used in this chapter:

Sleeping

$	less than ¥190
$$	¥190 to ¥400
$$$	more than ¥400

Eating

$	less than ¥30
$$	¥30 to ¥60
$$$	more than ¥60

History

Around 3000 years ago, the Zhou people of the Bronze Age moved out of their Shaanxi homeland, conquered the Shang and became dominant in much of northern China. Later the state of Qin, ruling from its capital Xiányáng (near modern-day Xī'ān), became the first dynasty to unify much of China. Subsequent dynasties, including the Han, Sui and Tang, were based in Xī'ān, then known as Cháng'ān, which was abandoned for the eastern capital of Luòyáng (in Hénán) whenever invaders threatened.

Shaanxi remained the political heart of China until the 10th century. However, when the imperial court shifted eastward, the province's fortunes began to decline. Rebellions and famine were followed in 1556 by the deadliest earthquake in history, when an estimated 830,000 people died (the unusually high death toll was attributed to the fact that millions were living in cave homes which easily collapsed in the quake). The extreme poverty of the region ensured that it was an early stronghold of the CCP.

Language

Locals like to joke that Xī'ān's dialect is the 'real' standard Mandarin – after all, the city was one of the ancient capitals of China. Those pedantic linguists, however, prefer to classify the Shaanxi dialect as part of the central Zhōngyuán Mandarin group. Jin is also spoken in some parts of the province.

❶ Getting There & Around

Xī'ān has one of China's best-connected airports. Xī'ān is also a hub for road transport and mega-highways spread out in all directions. The nation's high-speed train is expected to connect Běijīng and Xī'ān by 2014. Note that getting overnight trains from Yúlín to Xī'ān is difficult so it may be necessary to make this journey by bus.

Xī'ān 西安

♪ 029 / POP 6.5 MILLION

Xī'ān's fabled past is a double-edged sword. Primed with the knowledge that this legendary city was once the terminus of the Silk Road and a melting pot of cultures and religions, as well as home to emperors, courtesans, poets, monks, merchants and warriors, visitors can feel let down by the roaring, modern-day version. But even though Xī'ān's glory days ended in the early 10th century, many elements of ancient Cháng'ān, the former Xī'ān, are still present.

The Ming-era city walls remain intact, vendors of all descriptions still crowd the narrow lanes of the warrenlike Muslim Quarter, and there are enough places of interest to keep even the most diligent amateur historian busy.

While Xī'ān is no longer China's political capital, it's woken up to the potential value of its hallowed history. In the last few years, the city has been campaigning for the Silk Road to be added to the UN's World Heritage List, and there are continuing efforts to revitalise the Muslim Quarter.

Most people only spend two or three days in Xī'ān; history buffs could easily stay busy for a week. Must-sees include the Terracotta Warriors, the Tomb of Emperor Jingdi and the Muslim Quarter, but try to set time aside for the city walls, pagodas and museums. Better still, arrange a side trip to nearby Huà Shān or Hánchéng.

⊙ Sights

INSIDE THE CITY WALLS

Muslim Quarter   HISTORIC SITE

(回族区) The backstreets leading north from the Drum Tower have been home to the city's Hui community (Chinese Muslims) for centuries. Although Muslims have been here since at least the 7th century, some believe that today's community didn't take root until the Ming dynasty.

The narrow lanes are full of butcher shops, sesame-oil factories, smaller mosques hidden behind enormous wooden doors, men in white skullcaps and women with their heads covered in coloured scarves. It's a great place to wander and especially atmospheric at night. Good streets to stroll down are Xiyang

Shi, Dapi Yuan and Damaishi Jie, which runs north off Xi Dajie through an interesting Islamic food market.

Great Mosque
MOSQUE

(清真大寺; Qīngzhēn Dàsì; Huajue Xiang; admission Mar-Nov ¥30, Dec-Feb ¥15, Muslims free; ⊙8am-7.30pm Mar-Nov, to 5.30pm Dec-Feb) One of the largest mosques in China, the Great Mosque is a fascinating blend of Chinese and Islamic architecture. Facing west (towards Mecca) instead of the usual south, the mosque begins with a classic Chinese temple feature, the spirit wall, designed to keep demons at bay. The gardens, too, with their rocks, pagodas and archways are obviously Chinese, with the exception of the four palm trees at the entrance. Arab influence, meanwhile, extends from the central minaret (cleverly disguised as a pagoda) to the enormous turquoise-roofed Prayer Hall (not open to visitors) at the back of the complex, as well as the elegant calligraphy gracing most entryways. The present buildings are mostly Ming and Qing, though the mosque was founded in the 8th century.

To get here, follow Xiyang Shi several minutes west and look for a small alley leading south past a gauntlet of souvenir stands.

Forest of Stelae Museum
MUSEUM

(碑林博物馆; Bēilín Bówùguǎn; 15 Sanxue Jie; admission Mar-Nov ¥75, Dec-Feb ¥50; ⊙8am-6.15pm Mar-Nov, to 5.15pm Dec-Feb) Housed in Xī'ān's Confucius Temple, this museum holds more than 1000 stone stelae (inscribed tablets), including the nine Confucian classics and some exemplary calligraphy. The second gallery holds a Nestorian tablet (AD 781), the earliest recorded account of Christianity in China. (The Nestorians professed that Christ was both human and divine, for which they were booted out of the Church in 431.) The fourth gallery holds a collection of ancient maps and portraits, and is where rubbings (copies) are made, an interesting process to watch.

The highlight, though, is the fantastic sculpture gallery (across from the gift shop), which contains animal guardians from the Tang dynasty, pictorial tomb stones and Buddhist statuary.

To get to the museum, follow Shuyuan Xiang east from the South Gate.

Bell Tower & Drum Tower
HISTORIC SITES

Now marooned on a traffic island, the Bell Tower (钟楼; Zhōng Lóu; admission ¥27, combined Drum Tower ticket ¥40; ⊙8.30am-9.30pm Mar-Nov, to 6pm Dec-Feb) sits at the heart of Xī'ān and originally held a large bell that was rung at dawn, while its alter ego, the Drum Tower (鼓楼; Gǔ Lóu; Beiyuanmen; admission ¥27, combined Bell Tower ticket ¥40; ⊙8.30am-9.30pm Mar-Nov, to 6pm Dec-Feb), marked nightfall. Both date from the 14th century and were later rebuilt in the 1700s (the Bell Tower initially stood two blocks to the west). Musical performances, included in the ticket price, are held inside each at 9am, 10.30am, 11.30am, 2.30pm, 4pm and 5pm. Enter the Bell Tower through the underpass on the north side.

Folk House
HISTORIC SITE

(高家大院; Gāojiā Dàyuàn; 144 Beiyuanmen; admission ¥15, with tea ¥20; ⊙8.30am-11pm) This well-rounded historic residence also serves as an art gallery, entertainment centre and teahouse. Originally the home of the Qing bureaucrat Gao Yuesong, it's a fine example of a courtyard home and has been tastefully restored. There are reception rooms, bedrooms, servants' quarters, an ancestral temple and a study (now the teahouse).

Tours start with an optional marionette or shadow-puppet demonstration (¥10). As the complex currently belongs to the Shaanxi Artists Association, there's an art gallery here where you can pick up reasonably priced traditional Chinese art. Confusingly, despite the address, this place isn't at No 144, but is about 20m down the street.

> **DON'T MISS**
>
> ## CITY WALLS
>
> Xī'ān is one of the few cities in China where the old **city walls** (城墙; Chéngqiáng; admission ¥40; ⊙8am-8.30pm Apr-Oct, to 7pm Nov-Mar) are still standing. Built in 1370 during the Ming dynasty, the 12m-high walls are surrounded by a dry moat and form a rectangle with a perimeter of 14km.
>
> Most sections have been restored or rebuilt, and it is now possible to walk the entirety of the walls in a leisurely four hours. You can also cycle from the South Gate (bike hire ¥40 for 100 minutes, ¥200 deposit). Access ramps are located inside the major gates.
>
> To get an idea of Xī'ān's former grandeur, consider this: the Tang city walls originally enclosed 83 sq km, an area seven times larger than today's city centre.

SHAANXI (SHĂNXĪ) XĪ'ĀN

Xī'ān

SHAANXI (SHĂNXĪ) XĪ'ĀN

1 km
0.5 miles

Yongle Lu

Changle Lu

5

Huancheng Donglu

East Gate

北新街

To Big Goose Pagoda &
Da Ci'en Temple (4km)

Train Station

Long-Distance
Bus Station

Dong Balu
Dong Qilu
Dong Liulu

Dong Wulu

Dong Silu
Dong Santu
Dong Erlu

21

Jiefang Lu 解放路

Heping Lu 和平路

10

19

To Shaanxi Grand
Opera House (550m)

Huancheng Beilu

Xi-Balu

China
Eastern
Geming
Park

China Eastern Airlines

Shangde Lu

Dong Xinjie

12

Dong Yilu

Dong Dajie

Juhuayuan

Dong Lu

An Yuanmen
安远门

North
Gate

Houzaimen

Xi Wulu 西五路

Bei Dajie 北大街

Beixin Jie 北新街

Nanxin jie
南新街

Xi Xinjie
Nancheng
Xiang
南长巷

Zhong Lu

钟楼站

7

8

16

Duanlümen

15

Dongmutou Shi

Shuyuan Xiang
书院巷

4

9

To CITS; Tang
Dynasty (2km)

Nan Dajie 南大街

1

6

14

Beiyuanmen

Dapi Yuan

Muslim
Quarter

3

2

Great
Mosque

17

Beiguangji Jie

Airport
Shuttle Bus

20

18

Detu Xiang
创福巷

13

11

Advance Train Ticket
Booking Office

Xiyang Shi

Xi Dajie 西大街

Damaishi Jie

Hongguang Jie

Shuyacheng Xixiang

South Gate

Yong Ningmen 永宁门

Xi Qilu

Xi Qilu

Lianhu
Park

Lianhu Lu

Qianwei Jie

Huancheng Beilu

Xiguan
Zhengjie

Daqing Lu

City
Walls

Huancheng Xilu 环城西路

West Gate

Taibai Beilu

Xī'ān

◎ Top Sights
City Walls	A2
Great Mosque	C3
Muslim Quarter	C2

◎ Sights
1	Bell Tower	D3
2	Drum Tower	C3
3	Folk House	C3
4	Forest of Stelae Museum	D4
5	Temple of the Eight Immortals	G2

🛏 Sleeping
6	Bell Tower Hotel	D3
7	Hàn Táng House	D3
8	Hàn Táng Inn	D3
9	Jano's Backpackers	D4
10	Jǐnjiāng Inn	F3
11	Shūyuàn Youth Hostel	D4
12	Sofitel	E2

13	Xiāngzǐmén Youth Hostel	C4

◎ Eating
14	Défǎcháng Jiǎoziguǎn	D3
15	First Noodle Under the Sun	D4
	Jamaica Blue	(see 7)
16	Lǎo Sūn Jiā	E3
17	Muslim Family Restaurant	C3

◎ Drinking
18	Old Henry's Bar	C4
	Park Qin	(see 11)
	The Belgian	(see 9)

◎ Entertainment
19	1+1	E3
20	Song & Song	D4

◎ Shopping
21	Northwest Antique Market	F3

OUTSIDE THE CITY WALLS

FREE **Shaanxi History Museum**　MUSEUM
(陕西历史博物馆; Shǎnxī Lìshǐ Bówùguǎn; 91 Xiaozhai Donglu; ⏰8.30am-6pm Tue-Sun Apr-Oct, last admission 4.30pm, 9.30am-5pm Tue-Sun Nov-Mar, last admission 4pm) Shaanxi's museum is often touted as one of China's best, but if you come after visiting some of Xī'ān's surrounding sights you may feel you're not seeing much that is new. Nevertheless, the museum makes for a comprehensive and illuminating stroll through ancient Cháng'ān, and most exhibits include labels and explanations in English.

Look out for the four original terracotta warrior statues on the ground floor. In the Sui and Tang section there are unique murals depicting a polo match; and a series of painted pottery figurines with elaborate hairstyles and dress, including several bearded foreigners, musicians and braying camels.

The number of visitors is limited to 4000 a day (2500 tickets are distributed in the morning starting at 8.30am and another 1500 in the afternoon starting at 1.30pm), so get here early and expect to queue for at least 30 minutes. Make sure you bring your passport to claim your free ticket. Take bus 610 from the Bell Tower or bus 701 from the South Gate.

Big Goose Pagoda　BUDDHIST TEMPLE
(大雁塔; Dàyàn Tǎ; Yanta Nanlu; admission to grounds ¥50, entry into pagoda ¥30; ⏰8am-7pm Apr-Oct, to 6pm Nov-Mar) Xī'ān's most famous landmark, this pagoda dominates the surrounding modern buildings. One of China's best examples of a Tang-style pagoda (squarish rather than round), it was completed in AD 652 to house the Buddhist sutras brought back from India by the monk Xuan Zang. Xuan spent the last 19 years of his life translating scriptures with a crack team of linguist monks; many of these translations are still used today. His travels also inspired one of the best-known works of Chinese literature, *Journey to the West.*

Surrounding the pagoda is **Dà Cí'ēn Temple** (大慈恩寺; Dàcí'ēn Sì), one of the largest temples in Tang Cháng'ān. The buildings today date from the Qing dynasty. To the south of the pagoda is a newly developed open-air mall of shops, galleries, restaurants and public art; well-worth a wander. The area also includes a cinema and monorail.

Bus 610 from the Bell Tower and bus 609 from the South Gate drop you off at the pagoda square; the entrance is on the south side. An evening fountain show is held on the square.

FREE **Xī'ān Museum**　MUSEUM
(西安博物馆; Xī'ān Bówùguǎn; 76 Youyi Xilu; ⏰8.30am-7pm, closed Tue) Housed in the pleasant grounds of the Jiànfú Temple is this museum featuring relics unearthed in Xī'ān over the years. There are some exquisite ceramics from the Han dynasty, as well as figurines, an exhibition of Ming-dynasty

MONKEY BUSINESS

Buddhist monk Xuan Zang's epic 17-year trip to India, via Central Asia and Afghanistan, in search of Buddhist enlightenment was fictionalised in *Journey to the West*, one of Chinese literature's most enduring texts. The Ming-dynasty novel gives the monk Xuan three disciples to protect him along the way, the best-loved of which is the Monkey King.

The novel, attributed to the poet Wu Cheng'en, has inspired many films, plays and TV shows, including the cult '70s series *Monkey*. More recently, the Gorillaz team of Damon Albarn and Jamie Hewlett collaborated with opera director Chen Shi-Zheng on a popular 2007 stage version.

seals and jade artefacts. Don't miss the basement, where a large-scale model of ancient Xī'ān gives a good sense of the place in its former pomp and glory.

Also in the grounds is the **Little Goose Pagoda** (小雁塔; Xiǎoyàn Tǎ; ☉8.30am-7pm, closed Tue). The top of the pagoda was shaken off by an earthquake in the middle of the 16th century, but the rest of the 43m-high structure is intact. Jiànfú Temple was originally built in AD 684 to bless the afterlife of the late Emperor Gaozong. The pagoda, a rather delicate building of 15 progressively smaller tiers, was built from AD 707 to 709 and housed Buddhist scriptures brought back from India by the pilgrim Yi Jing. Admission to the grounds is free but climbing up the pagoda requires a Y30 ticket.

Bus 610 runs here from the Bell Tower; from the South Gate take bus 203.

Temple of the Eight Immortals TAOIST TEMPLE
(八仙庵; Bāxiān Ān; Yongle Lu; admission ¥5; ☉7.30am-5.30pm Mar-Nov, 8am-5pm Dec-Feb) Xī'ān's largest Taoist temple dates back to the Song dynasty and is still an active place of worship. Supposedly built on the site of an ancient wine shop, it was constructed to protect against subterranean divine thunder. Scenes from Taoist mythology are painted around the courtyard. Empress Cixi, the mother of the last emperor, stayed here in 1901 after fleeing Běijīng during the Boxer Rebellion. The small **antique market** opposite is busiest on Sundays and Wednesdays. Bus 502 runs close by the temple (eastbound from Xi Xinjie).

🛏 Sleeping

If you're arriving by air and have not yet booked accommodation, keep in mind that touts at the shuttle-bus drop-off (outside the Melody Hotel) can often get you discounted rooms at a wide selection of hotels.

All hostels in the city offer a similar range of services, including bike hire, internet, laundry, restaurant and travel services. Ask about free pick-up from the train station and book ahead at the most popular places. In low season (January–March) you can usually get 20 percent off at the hostels.

Hàn Táng Inn HOSTEL $
(汉唐驿; Hàntáng Yì; ☎8728 7772, 8723 1126; www.hostelxian@yahoo.com.cn; 7 Nanchang Xiang; 南长巷7号; dm ¥30-50, s & d ¥160-200; ❀❋@◗) This popular hostel has a friendly and helpful staff with loads of information and tours of Xī'ān. The dorms are compact but spotless and come with en suite bathrooms. There's a pleasant rooftop terrace, ping pong table and even a sauna! Activities are organised too, including an occasional free dumplings night. It's tucked down an alley off Nanxin Jie; look for the two terracotta warriors standing guard outside.

TOP CHOICE ☞ Hàn Táng House HOSTEL $$
(汉唐居; Hàntáng Jū; ☎8738 9765; www.itisxian.com; 32 Nanchang Xiang; 南长巷32号; dm/s/d/tr ¥50/120/180/240; ❀❋@◗) A hybrid of sorts, this place has dorms and the vibe of a youth hostel but the look and feel of a three-star hotel. The spotless rooms are decked out with high-quality dark-wood furnishings, slab floors and some of the most comfortable beds in China. It's a nice option for travellers looking for something upscale and also traveller friendly. There's a cafe on the ground floor where you can get good Western food. It's located down an alley off Nanxin Jie.

Xiāngzǐmén Youth Hostel HOSTEL $
(湘子门国际青年旅舍; Xiāngzǐmén Guójì Qīngnián Lǚshè; ☎6286 7999/7888; www.yhaxian.com; 16 Xiangzimiao Jie; 南门里湘子庙街16号; dm ¥40-50, r ¥180-240; ❋@◗) Set around a series of interconnected courtyards, this hostel is a big, sprawling place with an ever-busy pub known for its smoky and noisy atmosphere. Rooms are clean, modern and warm in winter but avoid the stuffy windowless basement rooms. Staff can organise tours but aren't great for independent travel info. Take bus 603 from opposite the train station to the South Gate and walk 100m west.

Sofitel
HOTEL $$$

(索菲特人民大厦; Suǒfēitè Rénmín Dàshà; ☑8792 8888; sofitel@renminsquare.com; 319 Dong Xinjie; 东新街319号; d/ste ¥1150/3150; ☺✳@⊛) Xī'ān's self-proclaimed 'six-star' hotel is undoubtedly the most luxurious choice in the city and has a soothing, hushed atmosphere. The bathrooms are top-notch. Cantonese, Japanese and Moroccan restaurants are onsite, as well as a South American–themed bar. Reception is in the east wing and room rates change daily, so you can score a deal when business is slow.

Shūyuàn Youth Hostel
HOSTEL $

(书院青年旅舍; Shūyuàn Qīngnián Lǚshè; ☑8728 7721; www.hostelxian.com; 2a Shuncheng Xixiang; 南门里顺城西巷甲2号; dm ¥30-50, s/d ¥160/180; ✳@⊛) The longest-running hostel in Xī'ān and still one of the most amenable, the Shūyuàn is located in a converted courtyard residence near the South Gate. The cafe serves excellent food and there's an atmospheric bar in the basement (guests get a free beer voucher). Rooms are simple but clean and the staff is switched onto the needs of travellers. The hostel is 20m west of the South Gate along the city walls and bus 603 runs close to it.

Jǐnjiāng Inn
HOTEL $$

(锦江之星; Jǐnjiāng Zhīxīng; ☑8745 2288; www.jj-inn.com; 110 Jiefang Lu; 解放路110号; d/tw/ste ¥179/199/219; ✳@) By Xī'ān's standards, the prices are close to budget, but the clean and bright modern rooms, all with ADSL internet connections, make this a better option than most three-star places in town. There's a cheap restaurant here, too.

Bell Tower Hotel
HOTEL $$$

(西安钟楼饭店; Xī'ān Zhōnglóu Fàndiàn; ☑8760 0000; www.belltowerhtl.com; 110 Nan Dajie; 南大街110号; d ¥850-1080; ✳@) Slap in the centre of downtown, this state-owned four-star place is comfortable and handy for the airport bus stop. Some rooms have a bird's-eye view of the Bell Tower and all are spacious and comfortable with cable TV and ADSL internet connections. Discounts of 15%.

Jano's Backpackers
HOSTEL $$

(杰诺庭背包旅舍; Jiénuò Tíngyuàn Bēibāo Lǚshè; ☑8725 6656; www.xian-backpackers.com; 69 Shuncheng Nanlu Zhongduan, South Gate; 南门顺城南路中段69号; dm ¥50-60, r without bathroom ¥120, with bathroom ¥200-260, ste ¥320-390; ✳@⊛) Set in a little faux *hútòng* located about 200m east of the South Gate, and with artist galleries, cafes and pubs nearby, this is a pleasant place to escape the bustling boulevards of Xī'ān. Rooms are brand new and decorated in traditional style, including some with *kang* beds. Despite the name, it feels more like a small boutique hotel rather than a hangout for backpackers, and as a bonus, the staff speak English.

✕ Eating

Hit the Muslim Quarter for fine eating in Xī'ān. Common dishes here are *májiàng liángpí* (麻酱凉皮; cold noodles in sesame sauce), *fěnzhēngròu* (粉蒸肉; chopped mutton fried in a wok with ground wheat), *ròujiāmó* (肉夹馍; fried pork or beef in pitta bread, sometimes with green peppers and cumin), *càijiāmó* (菜夹馍; the vegetarian version of *ròujiāmó*) and the ubiquitous *ròuchuàn* (肉串; kebabs).

Best of all is the delicious *yángròu pàomó* (羊肉泡馍), a soup dish that involves crumbling a flat loaf of bread into a bowl and adding noodles, mutton and broth. You can also pick up mouth-watering desserts such as *huāshēnggāo* (花生糕; peanut cakes) and *shìbǐng* (柿饼; dried persimmons), which can be found at the market or in Muslim Quarter shops.

A good street to wander for a selection of more typically Chinese restaurants is Dongmutou Shi, east of Nan Dajie.

All the hostels serve up Western breakfasts and meals with varying degrees of success.

Muslim Family Restaurant
CHINESE MUSLIM $

(回文人家; Huiwen Renjia; Damaishi Jie; dishes ¥6-58; ⊙9am-10.30pm; ⓐ) Deep in the heart of the Muslim Quarter, this fine establishment serves all the classic Muslim dishes and quick dishes for solo travellers like soups and dumplings. There's no English sign so look out for the noodle chef in the streetside open-air kitchen. Picture menu.

First Noodle Under the Sun
NOODLES $

(天下第一面酒楼; Tiānxià Dìyī Miàn Jiǔlóu; 19 Dongmutou Shi; dishes ¥16-58; ⊙9am-10.30pm; ⓐ) This is a chain of restaurants with an unusual name and a nonsensical English-language menu. The speciality is *biáng biáng miàn,* a giant, 3.8m strip of noodle that comes folded up in a big bowl with two soup side dishes (¥10). But all sorts of excellent noodle, meat and vegie dishes are available here.

Lǎo Sūn Jiā
SHAANXI $

(老孙家; 5th fl, cnr Dong Dajie & Duanlumen; dishes ¥12-40; ⊙8am-9pm; ⊜) Xī'ān's most famous restaurant (with more than a hundred years of history) is well known for its specialty dish – steaming bowls of *yángròu pàomó*. The catch here is that the patron is responsible for ripping up the bread before the chefs add the soup. The soup is an acquired taste for most people but the experience is fun nonetheless. It's located on the 5th floor of a large black glass building.

Jamaica Blue
CAFE $$

(藍色牙買加; Lánsè Yámǎijiā; 32 Nanchang Xiang; 南长巷32号; dishes ¥32-49; @🛜🖶) This Australia-based café has washed up in a little alley in Xī'ān, serving up excellent sandwiches, wraps, Western-style breakfast, pastas, desserts and reliable coffee. Has a friendly English-speaking staff, wi-fi, games and quasi-Irish pub atmosphere. Live music is played here nightly from 9pm to 11pm.

Défācháng Jiǎoziguǎn
DUMPLINGS $$

(德发长饺子馆; Bell & Drum Tower Sq; dishes ¥22-34; ⊙10am-9pm) Dumpling fanatics will want to try this 100-year-old restaurant, famed for its dumplings stuffed with beef, pork, mushrooms and other fillings. It's double the price of other places but you are paying for the atmosphere and history of the place. Order from the counter on the 1st floor and avoid the pricey upstairs dining hall. It's tucked into a building behind the pyramid plaza, look for the gigantic golden dumpling in the entrance.

🍷 Drinking

Xī'ān's nightlife options range from bars and clubs to cheesy but popular tourist shows.

The main bar strip is Defu Xiang, close to the South Gate. The top end of the street has coffee shops and teahouses. The bars get more raucous the closer to the South Gate you get, but it's still fairly tame.

Old Henry's Bar
BAR

(老亨利酒吧; Lǎohēnglì Jiǔbā; 48 Defu Xiang; ⊙8pm-3am) Always busy and has outside seating.

Park Qin
BAR

(琴文化吧; Qín Wénhuà Jiǔbā; 2a Shuncheng Xixiang; beers ¥20-25; ⊙7pm-3am) Andy Warhol meets Emperor Qin Shi Huang at this cosy bar, decorated with terracotta warriors art-fully rendered with playful colour schemes. There's a mix of young Chinese patrons and Westerners who all come for the Belgian beers, low prices and live music. Disregard the sign outside that says 'members only' as this only applies to local Chinese (tourists are welcome without membership).

The Belgian
BAR

(比利时咖啡酒吧; Bǐlìshí Kāfēi Jiǔbā; ⊙7pm-3am) A laid-back Western-style bar stocked with around 40 types of imported Belgian beers and pub grub (burgers and fries). The little alley where it sits is developing as a pub street so its fun to hang out on the patio and people-watch.

☆ Entertainment

Clubs get going early in Xī'ān, in part because they're as much places to drink as to dance. They are free to get into, but expect to pay at least ¥30 for a beer. Most are located along or off Nan Dajie.

Some travellers enjoy spending the evening at the **fountain and music show** (⊙9pm Mar-Nov, 8pm Dec-Feb) on Big Goose Pagoda Sq; it's the largest such 'musical fountain' in Asia. Xī'ān also has a number of dinner-dance shows, which are normally packed out with tour groups. They can be fun if you're in the mood for a bit of kitsch.

Song & Song
CLUB

(上上酒吧乐巢会; Shàngshàng Jiǔbā Lècháohuì; 109 Ximutou Shi; ⊙7pm-late) More of a big bar with DJs than a genuine club.

1+1
CLUB

(壹加壹俱乐部; Yījiāyī Jùlèbù; 2nd fl, Heping Yinzuo Bldg, 118 Heping Lu; ⊙7pm-late) The ever-popular 1+1 is a neon-lit maze of a place that pumps out party hip-hop tunes well into the early hours.

Tang Dynasty
DINNER SHOW

(唐乐宫; Tángyuè Gōng; ☑8782 2222; www.xiantangdynasty.com; 75 Chang'an Beilu; performance with/without dinner ¥500/220) The most famous dinner theatre in the city stages an over-the-top spectacle with Vegas-style costumes, traditional dance, live music and singing. It's dubbed into English.

Shaanxi Grand Opera House
DINNER SHOW

(陕歌大剧院; Shǎngē Dàjùyuàn; ☑8785 3295; 165 Wenyi Lu; performance with/without dinner ¥298/198) Also known as the Tang Palace Dance Show, this is a cheaper, less flashy alternative to the Tang Dynasty show. Wenyi

Lu starts south of the city walls. You can get a better price by buying your ticket through a reputable hostel or hotel.

Shopping

Stay in Xī'ān for a couple of days and you'll be offered enough sets of miniature terracotta warriors to form your own army. A good place to search out gifts is the Muslim Quarter, where prices are generally cheaper than elsewhere.

Xiyang Shi is a narrow, crowded alley running north of the Great Mosque where terracotta warriors, Huxian farmer paintings, shadow puppets, lanterns, tea ware, Mao memorabilia and T-shirts are on offer.

Near the South Gate is the Qing-style Shuyuan Xiang, the main street for art supplies, paintings, calligraphy, paper cuts, brushes and fake rubbings from the Forest of Stelae Museum. Serious shoppers should also visit the **Northwest Antique Market** (西北古玩城; Xīběi Gǔwán Chéng; Dong Xinjie; ⊙10am-5.30pm), by the Zhongshan Gate. This three-storey warren of shops selling jade, seals, antiques and Mao memorabilia sees far fewer foreign faces than the Muslim Quarter.

There's a much smaller antique market by the Temple of the Eight Immortals on Sunday and Wednesday mornings.

Information

Pick up a copy of the widely available *Xi'an Traffic & Tourist Map* (¥12), a bilingual publication with listings and bus routes. It's available at the airport and some bookshops. Chinese-language maps with the bus routes are sold on the street for ¥5. The English-language magazine *Xianese* (www.xianese.com) is available in some hotels and restaurants that cater to tourists.

All hostels and most hotels offer internet access. You can burn digital photos onto CDs at the youth hostels (per disc ¥10).

In the event of an emergency, call ☑120.

Bank of China (中国银行; Zhōngguó Yínháng) Juhuayuan Lu (38 Juhuayuan Lu; ⊙8am-8pm) Nan Dajie (29 Nan Dajie; ⊙8am-6pm) You can exchange cash and travellers cheques and use the ATMs at both of these branches.

China International Travel Service (CITS; 中国国际旅行社; Zhōngguó Guójì Lǚxíngshè) Branch office (2nd fl, Bell Tower Hotel, 110 Nan Dajie); Main office (48 Chang'an Beilu) The Bell Tower Hotel office is best for organising tours but the better deals are usually with the hostels.

China Post (中国邮政; Zhōngguó Yóuzhèng; Bei Dajie; ⊙8am-8pm)

Internet cafe (网吧; wǎngbā; 21 Xi Qilu; per hr ¥3; ⊙24hr) Around the corner from the long-distance bus station. There are also other internet cafes in this area.

Public Security Bureau (PSB; 公安局; Gōng'ānjú; 2 Keji Lu; 科技路2号 ⊙8.30am-noon & 2-6pm Mon-Fri) This is on the southeast corner of Xixie 7 Lu. Visa extensions take five working days. To get there from the Bell Tower, take bus K205 and get off at Xixie 7 Lu.

Getting There & Away

Air

Xī'ān's Xiányáng Airport is one of China's best connected – you can fly to almost any major Chinese destination from here, as well as several international ones. Most hostels and hotels and all travel agencies sell airline tickets.

China Eastern Airlines (中国东方航空公司; Zhōngguó Dōngfāng Hángkōng; ☑8208 8707; 64 Xi Wulu; ⊙8am-9pm) Operates most flights to and from Xī'ān. Daily flights include Běijīng (¥840), Chéngdū (¥630), Guǎngzhōu (¥890), Shànghǎi (¥1260) and Ürümqi (¥2060). On the international front, China Eastern has flights from Xī'ān to Hong Kong (¥1640), Seoul, Bangkok, Tokyo and Nagoya.

Bus

The long-distance **bus station** (长途汽车站; chángtú qìchēzhàn) is opposite Xī'ān's train station. It's a chaotic place. Note that buses to Huà Shān (6am to 8pm) depart from in front of the train station.

Other bus stations around town where you may be dropped off include the **east bus station** (城东客运站; chéngdōng kèyùnzhàn; Changle Lu) and the **west bus station** (城西客运站; chéngxī kèyùnzhàn; Zaoyuan Donglu). Both are located outside the Second Ring Rd. Bus K43 travels between the Bell Tower and the east bus station, and bus 103 travels between the train station and the west bus station. A taxi into the city from either bus station costs between ¥15 and ¥20.

Buses from Xī'ān's long-distance bus station:

Luòyáng ¥107.50, five hours (10am, noon, 1pm, 3pm)

Píngyáo ¥160, six hours (8am, 9.30am, 10.30am, 12.30pm, 4.30pm)

Zhèngzhōu ¥133, six hours, hourly (7am to 4pm)

Buses from Xī'ān's east bus station:

Hánchéng ¥69, four hours, every 30 minutes (8am to 6.30pm)

Huà Shān one way ¥40.50, two hours, hourly (7.30am to 7pm)

Yán'ān ¥92.50, five hours, every 40 minutes (8.30am to 5.35pm)

Train

Xī'ān's main train station (huǒchē zhàn) is just outside the northern city walls. It's always busy. Buy your onward tickets as soon as you arrive. Xī'ān's North Train Station (běi huǒchē zhàn) is used by D and G class high-speed trains. High-speed trains from Běijīng, Shànghǎi, Lánzhōu and other destinations are expected to start running in the next several years but for now the only destination is Luòyáng (1st class/2nd class ¥280/175).

Most hotels and hostels can get you tickets (¥40 commission); there's also an **advance train ticket booking office** (代售火车票; dàishòu huǒchēpiào; Nan Dajie; ☺8.30am-noon & 2-5pm) in the ICBC Bank's south entrance. Or brave the crowds in the main ticket hall.

Xī'ān is well connected to the rest of the country. Deluxe Z trains run to/from Běijīng west (soft sleeper only ¥417, 11½ hours), leaving Xī'ān at 7.23pm and Běijīng at 9.24pm. Several express trains also make the journey (¥265, 12½ hours); departures begin late afternoon. The Z94 to Shànghǎi departs 5.12pm and arrives 7.42am (hard/soft sleeper ¥333/511, 14½ hours).

All prices listed below are for hard/soft sleeper tickets.

Chéngdū ¥209/316, 16½ hours
Chóngqìng ¥191/286, 14 hours
Guìlín ¥399/613, 27 hours
Lánzhōu ¥175/264, 7½ to nine hours
Luòyáng ¥109/162, five hours
Píngyáo ¥134/206, nine hours
Shànghǎi ¥333/511, 15 to 22 hours
Tàiyuán ¥191/286, 10 to 12 hours
Ürümqi ¥287/467, 27 to 39 hours
Zhèngzhōu ¥137/205 six to eight hours

Within Shaanxi, there are five trains (including two night trains) to Yúlín (hard/soft sleeper ¥155/232, 12 to 14 hours) via Yán'ān (hard/soft sleeper ¥102/128, five to nine hours). Buy tickets in advance. There is also an early morning train to Hánchéng (¥33, 4½ hours).

ⓘ Getting Around

Xī'ān's Xiányáng Airport is about 40km northwest of Xī'ān. Shuttle buses run every 20 to 30 minutes from 5.40am to 8pm between the airport and the Melody Hotel (¥26, one hour). Taxis into the city charge over ¥100 on the meter.

If you're itching to try out the public buses, they go to all the major sights in and around the city. Bus 610 is a useful one: it passes the train station, then onto the Bell Tower, Little Goose Pagoda, Shaanxi History Museum and Big Goose Pagoda. Remember that packed buses are a pickpocket's paradise, so watch your wallet.

Taxi flagfall is ¥6. It can be very difficult to get a taxi in the late afternoon, when the drivers change shifts. If you can cope with the congested roads, bikes are a good alternative and can be hired at the youth hostels.

The new Xī'ān metro system (西安地铁; Xī'ān dìtiě) went into action in 2011 with the completion of Line 2. Line 1 is expected to open in September 2013 and Line 3 is planned for 2015. Rides cost ¥2 to ¥4 depending on distance. Useful stations on Line 2 include Běihuǒchē Zhàn (North Train Station) and Xiǎozhai (near the Shaanxi History Museum). Line 1 has a stop at the Bànpō Neolithic Village.

Around Xī'ān

The plains surrounding Xī'ān are strewn with early imperial tombs, many of which have not yet been excavated. But unless you have a particular fascination for burial sites, you can probably come away satisfied after visiting a couple of them.

The Army of Terracotta Warriors is obviously the most famous site, but it's really worth the effort to get to the Tomb of Emperor Jingdi as well.

Tourist buses run to almost all of the sites from in front of Xī'ān Train Station, with the notable exception of the Tomb of Emperor Jingdi.

◉ Sights

EAST OF XĪ'ĀN

Army of Terracotta Warriors MUSEUM
(兵马俑; Bīngmǎyǒng; www.bmy.com.cn; admission Mar-Nov ¥150, students ¥75, Dec-Feb ¥120, students ¥60; ☺8.30am-5.30pm Mar-Nov, to 5pm Dec-Feb) The Terracotta Army isn't just Xī'ān's premier site, but one of the most famous archaeological finds in the world. This subterranean life-size army of thousands has silently stood guard over the soul of China's first unifier for more than two millennia. Either Qin Shi Huang was terrified of the vanquished spirits awaiting him in the afterlife, or, as most archaeologists believe, he expected his rule to continue in death as it had in life – whatever the case, the guardians of his tomb today offer some of the greatest insights we have into the world of ancient China.

The discovery of the army of warriors was entirely fortuitous. In 1974, peasants drilling a well uncovered an underground vault that eventually yielded thousands of terracotta soldiers and horses in battle formation. Throughout the years the site became so fa-

Around Xī'ān

mous that many of its unusual attributes are now well known, in particular the fact that no two soldier's faces are alike.

The on-site theatre gives a useful primer on how the figures were sculpted. You could also employ a guide (¥150) or try the audio-guide (¥40, plus ¥200 deposit), although the latter is somewhat useless, being difficult to understand and not very compelling. Then visit the site in reverse, which enables you to build up to the most impressive pit for a fitting finale.

Start with the smallest pit, **Pit 3**, containing 72 warriors and horses, which is believed to be the army headquarters due to the number of high-ranking officers unearthed here. It's interesting to note that the northern room would have been used to make sacrificial offerings before battle. In the next pit, **Pit 2**, containing around 1300 warriors and horses, you get to examine five of the soldiers up close: a kneeling archer, a standing archer, a cavalryman and his horse, a mid-ranking officer and a general. The level of detail is extraordinary: the expressions, hairstyles, armour and even the tread on the footwear are all unique.

The largest pit, **Pit 1**, is the most imposing. Housed in a building the size of an aircraft hangar, it is believed to contain 6000 warriors (only 2000 are on display) and horses, all facing east and ready for battle. The vanguard of three rows of archers (both crossbow and longbow) is followed by the main force of soldiers, who originally held spears, swords, dagger-axes and other long-shaft weapons. The infantry were accompanied by 35 chariots, though these, made of wood, have long since disintegrated.

Almost as extraordinary as the soldiers is a pair of bronze chariots and horses unearthed just 20m west of the Tomb of Qin Shi Huang. These are now on display, together with some of the original weaponry, in a small **museum** to the right of the main entrance.

The Army of Terracotta Warriors is easily reached by public bus. From Xī'ān Train Station's carpark, take one of the green Terracotta Warriors minibuses (¥8, one hour) or bus 306 (¥8, one hour), both of which travel via Huáqīng Hot Springs and the Tomb of Qin Shi Huang. The carpark for all vehicles is a 15-minute walk from the Terracotta Warriors site, with the ticket kiosk near the parking lot. Electric carts do the run for ¥5. If you want to eat here, go for the restaurants across from the car park. To get back to Xī'ān, buses leave from the parking lot.

Huáqīng Hot Springs
HISTORIC SITE

(华清池; Huáqīng Chí; admission Mar-Nov ¥110, Dec-Feb ¥50; ⏰7am-7pm Mar-Nov, 7.30am-6.30pm Dec-Feb) The natural hot springs in this park were once the favoured retreat of emperors and concubines during the Tang dynasty.

An obligatory stop for Chinese tour groups, who pose for photos in front of the elaborately restored pavilions and by the ornamental ponds, it's a pretty place but not really worth the high admission price. You can, though, hike up to the **Taoist temple** on Black Horse Mountain (Lí Shān). The temple is dedicated to Nuwa, who created the human race from clay and also patched up cracks in the sky. There's also a **cable car** (one way/return ¥45/70) to the temple, but note that the stop is outside the park, so you won't be able to get back in unless you buy another ticket.

Tomb of Qin Shi Huang   HISTORIC SITE
(秦始皇陵; Qín Shǐhuáng Líng; admission free with Terracotta Warrior ticket; ⊘8am-6pm Mar-Nov, to 5pm Dec-Feb) In its time, this tomb must have been one of the grandest mausoleums the world had ever seen.

Historical accounts describe it as containing palaces filled with precious stones, underground rivers of flowing mercury and ingenious defences against intruders. The tomb reputedly took 38 years to complete, and required a workforce of 700,000 people. It is said that the artisans who built it were buried alive within, taking its secrets with them.

Archaeologists have yet to enter the tomb but probes and sensors have been sent inside. Levels of mercury inside exceed 100 times the normal occurring rate, which seems to substantiate some of the legends. Since little has been excavated there isn't much to see but you can climb the steps to the top of the mound for a fine view of the surrounding countryside. The tomb is about 2km west of the Army of Terracotta Warriors. Take bus 306 from Xī'ān Train Station.

Bànpō Neolithic Village   ANCIENT VILLAGE
(半坡博物馆; Bànpō Bówùguǎn; admission Mar-Nov ¥65, Dec-Feb ¥45; ⊘8am-6pm) This village is of enormous importance for Chinese archaeological studies, but unless you're desperately interested in the subject it can be an underwhelming visitor experience.

Bànpō is the earliest example of the Neolithic Yangshao culture, which is believed to have been matriarchal. It appears to have been occupied from 4500 BC until around 3750 BC. The excavated area is divided into three parts: a pottery manufacturing area, a residential area complete with moat, and a cemetery. There are also two exhibition halls that feature some of the pottery, including strange shaped amphorae, discovered at the site.

The village is in the eastern suburbs of Xī'ān. Bus 105 (¥1) from the train station runs past (ask where to get off); it's also often included on tours.

NORTH & WEST OF XĪ'ĀN

Fǎmén Temple   BUDDHIST TEMPLE
(法门寺; Fǎmén Sì; admission Mar-Nov ¥120, Dec-Feb ¥90; ⊘8am-6pm) This temple dating back to the 2nd century AD was built to house parts of a sacred finger bone of the Buddha, presented to China by India's King Asoka. In 1981, after torrential rains had weakened the temple's ancient brick structure, the entire western side of its 12-storey pagoda collapsed. The subsequent restoration of the temple produced a sensational discovery. Below the pagoda in a sealed crypt were over 1000 sacrificial objects and royal offerings – all forgotten for over a millennium.

Sensing a cash cow, the local authorities began enlarging the temple complex and it now includes a sprawling modern section featuring a 1.6km long walkway lined with 10 golden Buddhas, eccentric modern sculptures and outsized gates. Shuttle buses (¥20) are on hand to whisk the pious to the main temple, which is topped with an enormous replica of the box in which the finger bone was kept.

Although it may feel like a Cecil B DeMille Hollywood movie set, the older section is still worth a visit and you can join the queue of pilgrims who shuffle past the finger bone. The real reason to make the trip out here is the superb **museum** and its collection of Tang-dynasty treasures. There are elaborate gold and silver boxes (stacked on top of one another to form pagodas) and tiny crystal and jade coffins that originally contained the four separated sections of the holy finger.

Other notable exhibits are ornate incense burners, glass cups and vases from the Roman Empire, statues, gold and silver offerings, and an excellent reproduced cross-section of the four-chamber crypt, which symbolised a tantric mandala (a geometric representation of the universe).

Fǎmén Temple is 115km northwest of Xī'ān. Tour bus 2 (¥25, 8am) from Xī'ān Train Station runs to the temple and returns to Xī'ān at 5pm. The temple is also generally included on Western Tours.

FREE **Xiányáng City Museum**   MUSEUM
(咸阳市博物馆; Xiányáng Shì Bówùguǎn; Zhongshan Jie; ⊘9am-5.30pm) More than 2000 years ago, Xiányáng was the capital of the Qin dynasty. These days, it's just a dusty satellite of Xī'ān. Its chief attraction is this museum, which houses a remarkable collection of 3000 50cm-tall terracotta soldiers and horses, excavated from the tomb of Liu Bang, the first Han emperor, in 1965. Set in an attractive courtyard, the museum also has bronze and jade exhibits and good English captions.

Buses run every 15 minutes to Xiányáng (¥8.50, one hour) from Xī'ān's long-distance bus station. Ask to be dropped off at the museum. To get back to Xī'ān, just flag down buses going in the opposite direction.

TOMB OF EMPEROR JINGDI

This tomb (汉阳陵; Hàn Yánglíng; admission Mar-Nov ¥90, Dec-Feb ¥65; ⊙8.30am-7pm Mar-Nov, to 6pm Dec-Feb), which is also referred to as the Han Jing Mausoleum, Liu Qi Mausoleum and Yangling Mausoleum, is easily Xī'ān's most underrated highlight. If you only have time for two sights, then it should be the Army of Terracotta Warriors and this impressive museum and tomb. Unlike the warriors, though, there are relatively few visitors here so you have the space to appreciate what you're seeing.

A Han-dynasty emperor influenced by Taoism, Jingdi (188–141 BC) based his rule upon the concept of *wúwéi* (nonaction or noninterference) and did much to improve the life of his subjects: he lowered taxes greatly, used diplomacy to cut back on unnecessary military expeditions and even reduced the punishment meted out to criminals. The contents of his tomb are particularly interesting, as they reveal more about daily life than martial preoccupations – a total contrast with the Terracotta Army.

The site has been divided into two sections: the museum and the excavation area. The **museum** holds a large display of expressive terracotta figurines (more than 50,000 were buried here), including eunuchs, servants, domesticated animals and even female cavalry on horseback. The figurines originally had movable wooden arms (now gone) and were dressed in colourful silk robes.

Inside the **tomb** are 21 narrow pits, some of which have been covered by a glass floor, allowing you to walk over the top of ongoing excavations and get a great view of the relics. In all, there are believed to be 81 burial pits here.

Unfortunately, getting here by public transport isn't easy. First, take bus 4 (¥1) from Xī'ān's North Gate. After 30 minutes, it reaches the end of its line at the Zhang Jiabu roundabout. Get off and walk 100m right of the roundabout, where another bus, also numbered 4 (¥2), leaves for the tomb. The catch is that while there are many buses to the roundabout, only a few do the second leg to the tomb. At the time of writing, they were leaving at 8.30am, 10.50am, 2.50pm and 4.30pm, returning to Xī'ān at 9.10am, 12.10pm, 3.10pm and 5.20pm.

Alternatively, you can take a tour (around ¥160), usually arranged by the guesthouses. The tomb is close to the airport, so you can stop here on your way to or from there.

Imperial Tombs

HISTORIC SITES

A large number of imperial tombs (皇陵; *huáng líng*) dot the Guānzhōng plain around Xī'ān. They are sometimes included on tours from Xī'ān, but most aren't so remarkable as to be destinations in themselves. By far the most impressive is the **Qián Tomb** (乾陵; Qián Líng; admission Mar-Nov ¥45, Dec-Feb ¥25; ⊙8am-6pm), where China's only female emperor, Wu Zetian (AD 625–705), is buried together with her husband Emperor Gaozong, whom she succeeded. The long **Spirit Way** (Yù Dào) here is lined with enormous, lichen-encrusted sculptures of animals and officers of the imperial guard, culminating with 61 (now headless) statues of Chinese ethnic group leaders who attended the emperor's funeral. The mausoleum is 85km northwest of Xī'ān. Tour bus 2 (¥25, 8am) runs close to here from Xī'ān Train Station and returns in the late afternoon.

Nearby are the **tomb of Princess Yong Tai** (永泰幕; Yǒng Tài Mù) and the **tomb of Princess Zhang Huai** (章怀幕; Zhāng Huái Mù), both of whom fell foul of Empress Wu, before being posthumously rehabilitated. Other notable tombs are the **Zhao Tomb** (昭陵; Zhāo Líng), where the second Tang emperor Taizhong is buried, and the **Mao Tomb** (茂陵; Mào Líng), the resting place of Wudi (156–87 BC), the most powerful of the Han emperors.

☞ Tours

One-day tours allow you to see all the sights around Xī'ān more quickly and conveniently than if you arranged one yourself. Itineraries differ somewhat, but there are two basic tours: an Eastern Tour and a Western Tour.

Most hostels run their own tours, but make sure you find out what is included (admission fees, lunch, English-speaking guide) and try to get an exact itinerary, or you could end up being herded through the Terracotta Warriors before you have a chance to get your camera out.

Eastern Tour

The Eastern Tour (Dōngbù Zhīlǔ – 东线游览) is the most popular as it includes the Army of Terracotta Warriors, as well as the Tomb of Qin Shi Huang, Bànpō Neolithic Village, Huáqīng Hot Springs and possibly the Big Goose Pagoda. Most travel agencies and hostels charge around ¥300 for an all-day, all-in excursion, including admission fees, lunch and guide, although sometimes the hostel tours skip Bànpō. Tours to the Terracotta Warriors only are also available for around ¥160.

It's perfectly possible to do a shortened version of the Eastern Tour by using the tourist buses or bus 306, all of which pass by Huáqīng Hot Springs, the Terracotta Warriors and the Tomb of Qin Shi Huang. If you decide to do this, start at the hot springs, then travel to Qin Shi Huang's tomb and end at the Terracotta Warriors.

Western Tour

The longer Western Tour (Xībù Zhīlǔ – 西线游览) includes the Xiányáng City Museum, some of the imperial tombs, and possibly also Fǎmén Temple and (if you insist) the Tomb of Emperor Jingdi. It's far less popular than the Eastern Tour and consequently you may have to wait a couple of days for your hostel or agency to organise enough people. It's also more expensive; expect to pay ¥600.

A tour of the Tomb of Emperor Jingdi, usually done by itself without any other sights, will cost around ¥160.

Huà Shān 华山

One of Taoism's five sacred mountains, the granite domes of Huà Shān used to be home to hermits and sages. These days, though, the trails that wind their way up to the five peaks are populated by droves of day-trippers drawn by the dreamy scenery. And it is spectacular. There are knife-blade ridges and twisted pine trees clinging to ledges as you ascend, while the summits offer transcendent panoramas of green mountains and countryside stretching away to the horizon. Taoists hoping to find a quiet spot to contemplate life and the universe will be disappointed, but everyone else seems to revel in the tough climb and they're suitably elated once they reach the top. So forget all that spiritual malarkey and get walking.

◉ Sights & Activities

There are three ways up the mountain to the **North Peak** (北峰; Běi Fēng), the first of five summit peaks. Two of these options start from the eastern base of the mountain, at the cable-car terminus. The first option is handy if you don't fancy the climb: an Austrian-built **cable car** (one way/return ¥80/150; ⊙7am-7pm) will lift you to the North Peak in eight scenic minutes.

The second option is to work your way to the North Peak under the cable-car route. This takes a sweaty two hours, and two sections of 50m or so are quite literally vertical, with nothing but a steel chain to grab onto and tiny chinks cut into the rock for footing. Not for nothing is this route called the 'Soldiers Path'.

The third option is the most popular, but it's still hard work. A 6km path leads to the North Peak from the village of Huà Shān, at the base of the mountain (the other side of the mountain from the cable car). It usually takes between three and five hours to reach the North Peak via this route. The first 4km up are pretty easy going, but after that it's all steep stairs.

The village at the trailhead is a good place to stock up on water and snacks. Snacks are also available at shops on the trail but prices double and triple the further you head up the mountain. Curiously, you'll also see old ladies selling cotton gloves, the purpose of which becomes obvious at the steepest sections where you need to grab onto rusty chains for support.

If you want to carry on to the other peaks, then count on a minimum of eight hours in total from the base of Huà Shān. If you want to spare your knees, then another option is to take the cable car to the North Peak and then climb to the other peaks, before ending up back where you started. It takes about four hours to complete the circuit in this fashion and it's still fairly strenuous. In places, it can be a little nerve-racking, too. Huà Shān has a reputation for being dangerous, especially when the trails are crowded, or if it's wet or icy, so exercise caution.

But the scenery is sublime. Along **Blue Dragon Ridge** (苍龙岭; Cānglóng Lǐng), which connects the North Peak with the **East Peak** (东峰; Dōng Fēng), **South Peak** (南峰; Nán Fēng) and **West Peak** (西峰; Xī Fēng), the way has been cut along a narrow rock ridge with impressive sheer cliffs on either side.

Huà Shān

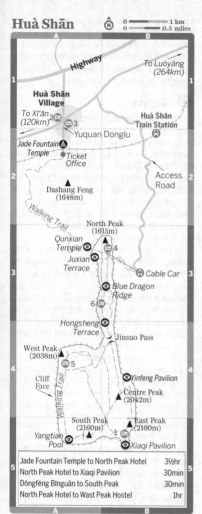

Huà Shān

🛏 Sleeping

1	Dōngfēng Bīnguǎn	B5
2	Huáyuè Kuài Jié Jiǔdiàn	A1
3	Míngzhū Jiǔdiàn	A1
4	North Peak Hotel	B3
5	West Peak Hostel	A4
6	Wǔyúnfēng Fàndiàn	A3

Jade Fountain Temple to North Peak Hotel	3½hr
North Peak Hotel to Xiaqi Pavilion	30min
Dōngfēng Bīnguǎn to South Peak	30min
North Peak Hotel to Wast Peak Hostel	1hr

There is accommodation on the mountain, most of it basic and overpriced, but it does allow you to start climbing in the afternoon, watch the sunset and then spend the night, before catching the sunrise from either the East Peak or South Peak. Some locals make the climb at night, using torches (flashlights). The idea is to start around 11pm and be at the East Peak for sunrise; you get to see the scenery on the way down.

Admission is ¥180 (students ¥90). To get to the cable car *(suŏdào),* take a taxi from the village to the ticket office (¥10) and then a shuttle bus (one way/return ¥20/40) the rest of the way.

🛏 Sleeping & Eating

You can either spend the night in Huà Shān village or on one of the peaks. Take your own food or eat well before ascending, unless you like to feast on instant noodles and processed meat – proper meals are very pricey on the mountain. Don't forget a torch and warm clothes. Bear in mind that prices for a bed triple during public holidays. The hotels on the mountain are basic; there are no showers and only shared bathrooms.

In the village, there are a number of dingy, shabby hotels along Yuquan Lu, the road leading up to the trailhead, that offer beds from ¥50 upwards. Pretty much every shop has rooms and the owners will find you. There are smarter places on Yuquan Donglu.

In Huà Shān village:

Míngzhū Jiǔdiàn
HOTEL $$

(明珠酒店; ☑0913-436 9899; Yuquan Donglu; 玉泉東路; s & d ¥238-281; ❄🛜) Located in Hua Shan village at the main intersection, this Chinese two-star hotel has clean and modern rooms with wi-fi. Discounts of 30% available outside peak holiday travel times.

Huáyuè Kuài Jié Jiǔdiàn
HOTEL $

(华岳快捷酒店; ☑0913-436 8555; Yuquan Donglu; 玉泉路; s & d ¥120; 🛜) Clean and simple rooms with OK bathrooms make this an

The South Peak is the highest at 2160m and the most crowded. The East Peak is less busy, but all three rear peaks afford great views when the weather cooperates. If possible, avoid weekends when foot traffic is heaviest.

At the South Peak thrillseekers can try the **Plank Walk** (admission ¥30), which consists of a metal ladder that leads down to a path made from wooden boards that hover above a 2000m vertical drop. Thankfully, the admission fee includes a harness and carabineers that you lock onto cables, but even with these safety features it's scary as hell.

obvious option for budget travellers. It's on Yuquan Lu at the bottom of the hill near the main intersection.

On the mountain:

Wŭyúnfēng Fàndiàn　　　HOTEL $$
(五云峰饭店; dm ¥100-180, tr/d ¥220/300) If you're planning on doing a circuit of the rear peaks the next day, or want to catch the sunrise at the East or South Peak, this is a good choice.

Dōngfēng Bīnguǎn　　　HOTEL $$
(东峰宾馆; dm ¥150-220, tr/d ¥280/340) The top location for watching the sun come up and the best restaurant.

West Peak Hostel　　　HOSTEL $
(西峰旅社; Xīfēng Lǚshè; dm ¥100) Rustic and basic, but also the friendliest place on the mountain. It shares its premises with an old Taoist temple.

North Peak Hotel　　　HOTEL $$
(北峰饭店; Běifēng Fàndiàn; ☑157 1913 6466; dm ¥95, d ¥240-260) The busiest of the peak hotels.

ⓘ Getting There & Away

From Xī'ān to Huà Shān, catch one of the private buses (¥36, two hours, 6am to 8pm) that depart when full from in front of Xī'ān Train Station. You'll be dropped off on Yuquan Lu, which is also where buses back to Xī'ān leave from 7.30am to 7pm. Coming from the east, try to talk your driver into dropping you at the Huà Shān highway exit if you can't find a direct bus. Don't pay more than ¥10 for a taxi into Huà Shān village. There are few buses (if any) going east from Huà Shān; pretty much everyone catches a taxi to the highway and then flags down buses headed for Yùnchéng, Tàiyuán or Luòyáng. If you can't read Chinese, try to find someone to help you out.

Hánchéng　　　韩城

☑ 0913 / POP 59,000

Hánchéng is best known for being the home-town of Sima Qian (145–90 BC), China's legendary historian and author of the *Shǐjì* (Records of the Grand Historian). Sima Qian chronicled different aspects of life in the Han dynasty and set about arranging the country's already distant past in its proper (Confucian) order. He was eventually castrated and imprisoned by Emperor Wudì, after having defended an unsuccessful general.

Hánchéng makes for a good side trip from Xī'ān. Built upon a hill, the new town (新城; *xīnchéng*) located at the top is dusty and unremarkable and is where you'll find hotels, banks and transport. But the more atmospheric old town (古城; *gǔchéng*) at the bottom of the hill boasts a handful of historic sights. The unique Ming-dynasty village of Dǎngjiācūn is 9km further east.

◉ Sights

Confucius & Chénghuáng Temples　　　CONFUCIAN TEMPLES
In the heart of the old town, the tranquil **Confucius Temple** (文庙; Wén Miào; admission ¥15; ☻8am-5.30pm) is the pick of the sights in Hánchéng itself. The dilapidated Yuan, Ming and Qing buildings could do with a fresh coat of paint, but there's a half-moon pool, towering cypress trees and glazed dragon screens. The city museum holds peripheral exhibits in the wings.

At the back of the Confucius Temple is the **Chénghuáng Temple** (城隍庙; Chénghuáng Miào; admission ¥15; ☑8am-5.30pm), in a lane lined with Ming-dynasty courtyard houses. There has been a temple here since the Zhou dynasty, but the whole site has undergone extensive renovation in recent years. The main attraction is the **Sacrificing Hall**, with its intricate roof detail, where gifts were offered to the gods to protect the city.

Buying a ticket to either temple gets you into the other as well. Bus 102 (¥1) runs here from the southwest corner of Huanghe Dajie, close to the bus station. A taxi is ¥10.

Yuánjué Pagoda　　　MONUMENT
(园觉寺塔; Yuánjué Sìtǎ; ☻6am-6pm) Looming over the old town and dating back to the Tang dynasty, but rebuilt in 1958, this pagoda also acts as a memorial to Red Army soldiers killed fighting the KMT. It's impossible to climb the pagoda itself, but the steep ascent to it offers panoramic views over the old town. To get here, turn sharp right when leaving the Chénghuáng Temple and take the first major right you come to. The walk takes you through the most evocative part of the old town; exit the pagoda through the park on the other side and you're back in the new town.

Dǎngjiācūn　　　ANCIENT VILLAGE
(党家村; admission ¥40; ☻7.30am-6.30pm) This perfectly preserved, 14th-century village nestles in a sheltered location in a loess valley. Once the home of the Dang clan, successful merchants who ferried timber and other goods across the Yellow River (黄河; Huáng Hé), it's since evolved into a quintessential farming community. The village is

THE MAN BEHIND THE ARMY

History is written by the winners. But in China, it was penned by Confucian bureaucrats and for Qin Shi Huang that was a problem, because his disdain for Confucianism was such that he outlawed it, ordered almost all its written texts to be burnt and, according to legend, buried 460 of its top scholars alive. As a result, the first emperor went down in history as the sort of tyrant who gives tyrants a bad name.

At the same time, though, it's hard to overstate the magnitude of his accomplishments during his 36 years of rule (which began when he was just 13). A classic overachiever, he created an efficient, centralised government that became the model for later dynasties; he standardised measurements, currency and, most importantly, writing. He built over 6400km of new roads and canals and, of course, he conquered six major kingdoms before turning 40.

The fact that Qin Shi Huang did all this by enslaving hundreds of thousands of people helped ensure that his subsequent reputation would be as dark as the black he made the official colour of his court. But in recent years, there have been efforts by the China Communist Party (CCP) to rehabilitate him, by emphasising both his efforts to unify China and the far-sighted nature of his policies.

Nevertheless, he remains a hugely controversial figure in Chinese history, but also one whose presence permeates popular culture. The first emperor pops up in video games, in literature and on TV shows. He's also been the subject of films by both Chen Kaige and Zhang Yimou (*The Emperor and the Assassin* and *Hero*), while Jet Li played a thinly disguised version of him in the 2008 Hollywood blockbuster *The Mummy: Tomb of the Dragon Emperor*. See the Army of Terracotta Warriors on p364 for info on his famous tomb.

home to 125 grey-brick courtyard houses, which are notable for their carvings and mix of different architectural styles. The elegant six-storey tower is a **Confucian pagoda** (Wénxīng gé). Unfortunately, many of the families have moved out and their homes are now exhibition showrooms, so the village feels a little lifeless. Still, it's worth a wander to explore the old alleys and admire the architecture.

Dǎngjiācūn is 9km northeast of Hánchéng. To get here, take a minibus (¥3, 20 minutes) from the bus station to the entrance road, from where it's a pleasant 2km walk through fields to the village. Otherwise, you can take a taxi from Hánchéng (¥30).

🛏 Sleeping

For something completely different, spend the night in Dǎngjiācūn, where basic dorm beds in some of the courtyard houses are available for ¥30. If a local doesn't approach you, just ask and you'll be pointed in the right direction. They also offer simple and cheap home cooking.

If you'd prefer to spend the night in town, try one of the following options.

Tiānyuán Bīnguǎn HOTEL $
(天园宾馆; ☎529 9388; Longmen Dajie Beiduan; 龙门大街北段; s & d ¥120-130; ❄@) A few

doors down from the main bus station, this place has simple but perfectly functional rooms.

Yínhé Dàjiǔdiàn HOTEL $$
(银河大酒店; ☎529 2555; Longmen Dajie Nanduan; 龙门大街南段; r ¥398; ❄@) This is an upmarket option. From the bus station turn left and walk on the main road for about 10 minutes. Discounts of 30% available.

ℹ Information

There's a branch of the **Bank of China** (中国银行; Zhōngguó Yínháng; cnr Huanghe Dajie & Jinta Zhonglu; ☺8am-6pm) close to the bus station that has a 24-hour ATM and will change cash.

ℹ Getting There & Away

Buses leave Xī'ān's east bus station for Hánchéng (¥68, three hours, seven daily) from 7am onwards. Buses back to Xī'ān run until 6.30pm. There are two buses per day to Huà Shān (¥40.50, two hours) at 7am and 12.30pm. There are also two daily buses to Yán'ān (¥79.50, eight hours) at 6.50am and 8am.

A middle-of-the-night train runs from Xī'ān to Hánchéng (¥33, 4½ hours) at 2.50am. From Hánchéng, the daily local train No 1164 rumbles towards Běijīng (hard sleeper ¥224, 18 hours) via Píngyáo (¥96, five hours) and Tàiyuán (¥115, seven hours), departing at 4.10pm.

Yán'ān 延安

📞 0911 / POP 107,000

When the diminished communist armies pitched up here at the end of the Long March, it signalled the beginning of Yán'ān's brief period in the sun. For 12 years, from 1935 to 1947, this backwater town was the CCP headquarters, and it was in the surrounding caves that the party established much of the ideology that was put into practice during the Chinese revolution.

These days, Yán'ān's residents seem to be more interested in consumerism than communism; for a small place, there are a surprising number of shopping malls. But its livelihood is still tied to the CCP; endless tour groups of mostly middle-aged 'red tourists' pass through each year on the trail of Mao and his cohorts. Few foreigners make it here, so expect some attention.

◉ Sights

FREE **Yán'ān Revolution Museum**   MUSEUM
(延安革命简史陈列馆; Yán'ān Gémìng Jiǎnshǐ Chénlièguǎn; Shengdi Lu; ⊙8.30am-5pm) By far the most flash building in town is the **Yán'ān Revolutionary Memorial Hall** (延安革命纪念馆; Yán'ān Gémìng Jìniànguǎn), fronted by a statue of Mao and housing this museum. It offers an excellent, if obviously one-sided, account of the CCP's time in Yán'ān and the Sino-Japanese War. More English captions would be nice, but there are plenty of photos of the good old days and other exhibits that are self-explanatory. Bus 1 (¥1) runs here.

FREE **Wángjiāpíng Revolution Headquarters Site**   HISTORIC SITE
(王家坪革命旧址; Wángjiāpíng Gémìng Jiùzhǐ; Wangjiaping Lu; ⊙8am-5.30pm Mar-Nov, 8.30am-5pm Dec-Feb) During an extended stay, the communist leadership moved around Yán'ān, resulting in numerous former headquarters sites. Adjacent to the Revolution Museum is the last site occupied by the communist leadership in Yán'ān. The improved living conditions at the site, houses rather than dugouts, indicate the way the CCP's fortunes were rising by the time it moved here.

FREE **Yángjiālǐng Revolution Headquarters Site**   HISTORIC SITE
(杨家岭革命旧址; Yángjiālǐng Gémìng Jiùzhǐ; Yangjialing Lu; ⊙8am-6pm Mar-Nov, 8.30am-5pm Dec-Feb) Perhaps the most interesting site, this is located 3km northwest of the town centre. Here you can see the assembly hall where the first central committee meetings were held, including the seventh national plenum, which formally confirmed Mao as the leader of the party and the revolution. It's fun watching the red tourists pose in old CCP uniforms in front of the podium.

Nearby are simple **dugouts** built into the loess earth where Mao, Zhu De, Zhou Enlai and other senior communist leaders lived, worked and wrote.

FREE **Zǎoyuán Revolution Headquarters Site**   HISTORIC SITE
(枣园革命旧址; Zǎoyuán Gémìng Jiùzhǐ; Yangjialing Lu; ⊙8am-6pm Mar-Nov, 8.30am-5pm Dec-Feb) The Communist leadership took refuge here between 1943 and 1947, on land allocated by a wealthy merchant. The leafy grounds are perhaps the most attractive of the revolutionary sites. It is located 4km past the Yángjiālǐng site.

FREE **Fènghuángshān Revolution Headquarters Site**   HISTORIC SITE
(凤凰山革命旧址; Fènghuángshān Gémìng Jiùzhǐ; ⊙8am-5pm Mar-Nov) More accessible from town, this Revolution Headquarters Site is about 100m west of China Post. This was the first site occupied by the communists after their move to Yán'ān, before being abandoned because it was too exposed to enemy aircraft fire. There's a photo exhibit about Norman Bethune, the Canadian doctor who became a hero in China for treating CCP casualties in the late 1930s.

Treasure Pagoda   MONUMENT
(宝塔; Bǎo Tǎ; admission ¥65; ⊙6.30am-9pm Mar-Nov, to 8pm Dec-Feb) Yán'ān's most prominent landmark, Treasure Pagoda dates back to the Song dynasty. For an extra ¥10, you can climb the very narrow steps and ladders of the pagoda for an unrestricted view of the city.

Qīngliáng Mountain   PARK
(清凉山; Qīngliáng Shān; admission ¥31; ⊙8am-7pm Mar-Nov, to 5.30pm Dec-Feb) This was the birthplace of the CCP propaganda machine; *Xinhua* News Agency and the *Liberation Daily* started life here when the place was known as 'Information Mountain'. Now, it's a pleasant hillside park with some nice trails and a few sights, including **Ten Thousand Buddha Cave** (万佛洞; Wànfó Dòng) dug into the sandstone cliff beside the river. The cave has relatively intact Buddhist statues.

🛏 Sleeping & Eating

There are few budget options in Yán'ān. Most hotels, though, offer discounts. It's also not a gourmet's paradise, though the night market, just off the small square in the centre of town, is a fine spot for eating al fresco and meeting the locals. Try the very tasty handmade noodles.

Hǎishèng Jiǔdiàn　　　　　HOTEL $$$
(海盛酒店; ☑821 3333; Daqiaojie; 大桥街; s/d ¥438/698; ❄@) This midrange hotel has excellent rooms with computers and the price includes breakfast. In a town of overpriced hotels this is not a bad option, with rooms usually going for around ¥268. Discounts of 50% available outside peak travel times.

Yàshèng Dàjiǔdiàn　　　　HOTEL $$
(亚圣大酒店; ☑266 6000; Erdaojie Zhongduan; 二道街中段; tw ¥328-368; ❄) Located in the centre of town, the rooms here are clean and comfortable, if a bit gloomy. There's a decent restaurant (dishes ¥14 to ¥40) on the top floor. Discounts of 40%.

ℹ Information

Bank of China (中国银行; Zhōngguó Yínháng; Daqiao Jie; ⏰8am-5pm) On the corner of Daqiao Jie and Erdao Jie, this branch has a 24-hour ATM. There are other ATMs around town, too.

China Post (中国邮政; Zhōngguó Yóuzhèng; Yan'anshi Dajie) Post and telephone office.

Internet cafe (wǎngbā; per hr ¥3; ⏰24hr) On the 2nd floor, down an alley just to the left of the Yàshèng Dàjiǔdiàn.

ℹ Getting There & Away

Bus

From Xī'ān's east bus station, there are buses to Yán'ān (¥92.50, four hours) every 40 minutes from 8.30am to 5.35pm. The schedule back to Xī'ān is essentially the same. Buses arrive and depart from the south bus station (汽车南站; qìchē nánzhàn).

At Yán'ān's east bus station (qìchē dōngzhàn), there are buses to Yúlín (¥80, five hours) every 50 minutes from 7.25am to 5.30pm. Local buses to Mǐzhǐ (¥53.50, four hours) depart at 9.15am, 1.10pm and 2.20pm.

Heading west, there are departures to Yínchuān in Níngxià (¥127, eight hours); buses leave at 8am, 9.30am and 10.30am, while sleepers leave at 4pm and 5.30pm. You can also get into Shānxī and Hénán from here.

Train

An overnight train back to Xī'ān leaves at 10.28pm (hard/soft sleeper ¥102/128, eight hours). Advance tickets in Yán'ān can be hard to come by – consider taking the bus instead. A taxi from the train station into town costs ¥10.

ℹ Getting Around

The Revolution Headquarters sites can be reached by taking bus 1, which runs along the road east of the river and then heads up Shengdi Lu. This bus starts at the train station. Bus 8 also passes by these places and can be caught from Da Bridge (大桥). The taxi flag fall is ¥5.

Yúlín　　　　　　　　　榆林

☑ 0912 / POP 92,000

Thanks to extensive coal mining and the discovery of natural gas fields nearby, this one-time garrison town on the fringes of Inner Mongolia's Mu Us Desert is booming. Despite all the construction, there's still enough of interest to make this a good place to break a trip if you're following the Great Wall or heading north on the trail of Genghis Khan.

Parts of the earthen **city walls** are still intact, while the main north–south pedestrian street in the elongated old town (divided into Beidajie and Nandajie) has several restored buildings, including a **Bell Tower** (钟楼; Zhōng Lóu) first erected in 1472 and destroyed several times (the current tower dates to the early 20th century). With several restaurants and antique shops, it's a nice street to wander at night, when it's lit by lanterns.

Seven kilometres north of the Yúlín bus station, on the outskirts of town, are some badly eroded sections of the Great Wall and a Ming-era four-storey **beacon tower** (镇北台; zhènběitái; admission ¥20; ⏰7.30am-7.30pm) that dates to 1607. Bus 11 (¥1) runs here from Changcheng Nanlu, about 200m west of the main bus station.

🛏 Sleeping

Jīnyù Hotel　　　　　　　HOTEL $$
(金域大酒店; Jīnyù Dàjiǔdiàn; ☑233 3333; 6 Xinjian Nanlu; 新建南路6号; tw/d ¥238/298; ❄@) This midrange place has large comfortable rooms and cable internet access. It's across the street from the main train station. Discounts of 30% available.

Jiāyuán Shāngwù Bīnguǎn　　HOTEL $
(嘉源商务宾馆; ☑326 8958; 2nd fl, 5 Yuyang Zhonglu; 榆扬中路5号二楼; r with shared bathroom ¥60) Five minutes' walk west from the main bus station, this cheapie has a filthy staircase but the rooms are OK. A massive internet cafe is located on the 2nd floor.

FROM FARM BOY TO EMPEROR

Li Zicheng enjoyed a remarkable rise from shepherd to sitting on the imperial throne and led the most successful of the many peasant rebellions that took place in the dying days of the Ming dynasty. Born in 1606, Li drew tens of thousands of followers in famine-racked, 1630s Shaanxi by advocating equal shares of land for all and no taxes. Having taken over large parts of Shaanxi, Shānxī and Hénán, Li and his army sacked Běijīng and, after the suicide of the last Ming emperor, Li proclaimed himself Emperor of the Shun dynasty in April 1644.

His reign was short-lived. Less than two months later, the invading Manchu forces defeated his army and Li retreated back to Shaanxi and subsequently to Húběi, where he either committed suicide or was killed in 1645. Four centuries later, Li's impeccable socialist credentials made him an ideal role model for the CCP, who continue to laud his exploits as an early revolutionary.

❶ Getting There & Around

There are several daily flights from Yúlín to Xī'ān (¥850).

Yúlín has two bus stations. If you get off the bus inside the town walls (near the south gate), you are at the main (south) bus station (汽车站; qìchē zhàn); the regional (north) bus station (客运站; kèyùn zhàn) is located 3.5km northwest on Yingbin Dadao.

The main bus station has regular buses to Xī'ān (¥170 to ¥181, seven to eight hours) from 7.25am to 7.30pm. You can also get frequent buses to Yán'ān (¥80, five hours, 7.25am to 5pm every 30 minutes), and buses to Tàiyuán (¥136, eight hours, 6.50am and 12.50pm) and Yínchuān (¥142, five to six hours, eight daily).

The regional bus station has hourly buses to Bāotóu in Inner Mongolia (¥94, four hours) and half-hourly buses to Dàliùtǎ (¥49, two hours), from where you can travel on to Dōngshèng. Note that the buses to Dōngshèng pass by Genghis Khan's Mausoleum.

The train station is 4km west of the main bus station. There are two trains a day to Xī'ān (hard/soft sleeper ¥155/232, 12 to 14 hours) via Yán'ān, but sleeper tickets are pretty much impossible to grab on short notice.

Bus 1 (¥1) runs between the two bus stations. Taxis around town and to the train station will cost you ¥6.

Mǐzhǐ 米脂

☑ 0912

About 70km south of Yúlín, Mǐzhǐ is best known as the hometown of Li Zicheng, proto-communist and would-be emperor, as well as for the alleged beauty of its female residents.

Despite those twin draws, it's a sleepy place with a small Hui presence and way off the tourist circuit; you will be the sole foreigner in town and likely the only visitor of any description. Some of the local population still live in caves and homes carved out of the surrounding hillsides, while the small old quarter, with its narrow alleys and dilapidated courtyard homes, is a fascinating place to wander.

The principal sight, though, is the **Li Zicheng Palace** (李自成行宫; Lǐ Zichéng Xínggōng; Xinggong Lu; admission ¥20; ⊙8am-5pm). This well-preserved and compact palace was built in 1643 at the height of Li's power. Set against a hillside, there's a statue of the man himself, as well as pavilions, which house exhibits about Li and notable Mǐzhǐ women, and a pagoda. There's also a fine theatre, where music performances and plays were held, sometimes for three days at a time, to celebrate Li's victories. To reach the palace, walk east on Xinggong Lu. It's a 10- to 15-minute walk from the bus station.

Turn left immediately after leaving the palace and you are in the heart of the **old quarter** of Mǐzhǐ. Many of the original, late-Ming-dynasty courtyard homes survive, albeit in a rundown condition.

Mǐzhǐ makes an easy day trip from Yúlín or you could stop here to/from Yán'ān. Frequent buses (¥20, two hours) run from Yúlín's main, or south, bus station. Ask to get off at Jiulong Qiao (which is a little closer to the palace). From Mǐzhǐ to Yán'ān (¥53.50, 3½ hours) there are three daily buses at 7.40am, 8.20am and 1.30pm.

Ānhuī

POP 64.1 MILLION

Includes »

Túnxī 377
Around Túnxī 380
Huīzhōu villages 380
Huángshān 385
Jiǔhuá Shān 390
Héféi 392

Best Mountains

» Huángshān (p385)
» Jiǔhuá Shān (p390)
» Qíyún Shān (p380)

Best Villages

» Xīdì (p380)
» Hóngcūn (p381)
» Chéngkǎn (p383)

Why Go?

Well-preserved villages and fantastical mountain scapes are the principal draw for visitors to Ānhuī (安徽). The main attraction of this southern Huīzhōu region is unquestionably Huángshān, a jumble of sheer granite cliffs wrapped in cottony clouds that inspired an entire school of ink painting during the 17th and 18th centuries. But the often-overlooked peaks of nearby Jiǔhuá Shān, where Buddhists bless the souls of the recently departed, are much quieter, with a hallowed aura that offers a strong contrast to Huángshān's stunning natural scenery.

At the foot of these ranges are strewn the ancient villages of Huīzhōu; their distinctive whitewashed walls and black-tiled roofs stand out against a verdant backdrop of green hills and terraced tea gardens. Ānhuī's lush mountains and slower pace of life are the perfect antidote to the brashness of China's larger cities.

When to Go

Túnxī

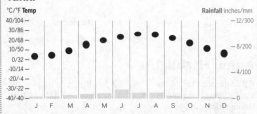

Mar Summer days are best for climbing ethereal Huángshān.

Oct The terrain is awash with autumn colours – Tǎchuān is particularly pretty.

Dec The snow-capped rooftops of Xīdì's Hui houses make the bitter winter worthwhile.

Ānhuī Highlights

1 Climb and stay on the iconic Chinese mountain, **Huángshān** (p385)

2 Explore the grottoes and dilapidated temples at Taoist **Qíyún Shān** (p380)

3 Soak up the Ming-dynasty vibe along Túnxī's **Old Street** (p377)

4 Join the Buddhist pilgrims at fog-shrouded **Jiǔhuá Shān** (p390)

5 Don't miss the World Heritage village of **Hóngcūn** (p381)

6 Eschew crowds and enjoy authentic village life at **Chéngkǎn** (p383)

7 Soar across heavy plumes of feathery bamboo in Mùkēng...on a **zipline** (p382)

8 Seek out the unmarked **Pig's Heaven Inn** (p382) in Xīdì for a fantastic meal

9 Make a movie pilgrimage to where Ang Lee and Zhang Yimou shot films, in **Guānlù** (p382)

History

The provincial borders of Ānhuī were defined by the Qing government, bringing together two disparate geographic regions and cultures: the arid, densely populated North China Plain and the mountainous terrain south of the Yangzi River (Cháng Jiāng), which wasn't settled until the late Tang dynasty.

Traditionally impoverished, Ānhuī's fortunes have begun to reverse. Some say the massive infrastructure improvements in the hitherto remote areas are partly due to president Hu Jintao, whose ancestral clan hails from Jìxī County. Hu comes from a long line of Huīzhōu merchants, who for centuries left home to do business or fill official posts elsewhere, but would never fail to complete their filial duty and send their profits back home (much of it by way of large homes and ceremonial structures).

These days, locals often leave the region to seek work and fortune elsewhere (no different from their ancestors). However, they are never ashamed to declare their origins. And rightly so.

Climate

Ānhuī has a warm-temperate climate, with heavy rain in spring and summer that brings plenty of flooding. Winters are damp and very cold. When travelling through Ānhuī at any time of year, bring rain gear and a warm jacket for the mountain areas.

ⓘ Getting There & Away

The historical and tourist sights of Ānhuī are concentrated in the south around the town of Túnxī and are easily accessible by bus, train or plane from Hángzhōu, Shànghǎi and Nánjīng.

Túnxī   屯溪

☏ 0559 / POP 77,000

Ringed by low-lying hills, the old trading town of Túnxī (also called Huángshān Shì) is the main springboard for trips to Huángshān and the surrounding Huīzhōu villages. If you stay in the old town, it's an agreeable place with good transport connections to the Yangzi River delta area. Compared with the region's capital, Héféi, Túnxī makes for a better base from which to explore southern Ānhuī.

◉ Sights

The oldest and most interesting part of town is in the southwest, along Old St (Lao Jie). The newer part of town is in the northeast, near the train station.

PRICE INDICATORS

The following price indicators are used in this chapter:

Sleeping

$	less than ¥200
$$	¥200 to ¥550
$$$	more than ¥550

Eating

$	less than ¥25
$$	¥26 to ¥60
$$$	more than ¥60

Old Street   STREET

(老街; Lao Jie) Running a block in from the river, Old St is a souvenir street lined with wooden shops and restored Ming-style Huīzhōu buildings open till late. Duck into the side alleys for a glimpse at the local life and to find small eateries.

Wàncuìlóu Museum   MUSEUM

(万粹楼博物馆; Wàncuìlóu Bówùguǎn; 143 Lao Jie; admission ¥50; ◷8.30am-9.30pm) On Lao Jie, Wàncuìlóu Museum displays a private antiques collection, offering an introduction to Huīzhōu architecture and furniture over four floors.

☞ Tours

Youth hostels offer a day-long village tour to Xīdì and Hóngcūn (¥210 including transport, admission fees and lunch) and a direct bus to Huángshān (¥18, one hour, 6.15am).

Huángshān Tourist Distribution Center   BUS TOURS

(黄山市旅游集散中心; Lǚyóu Jísàn Zhōngxīn; ☏255 8358; ◷7.30am-6pm) Huángshān Tourist Distribution Center – located in a connecting building beside the long-distance bus station – offer tours and discounted tickets.

⌂ Sleeping

Ancient Town Youth Hostel   HOSTEL $

(小镇国际青年旅舍; Xiǎozhèn Guójì Qīngnián Lǚshè; ☏252 2088; www.yhahs.com; 11 Sanma Lu; 三马路11号; dm ¥40-45, d & tw ¥145-198; ✳@☏) Started by some former tour guides, this hostel ticks all the right boxes, with a well-stocked bar, movie room, good lounging areas, friendly English-speaking staff, bike rental, organised tours and so on. Dorm beds are huge

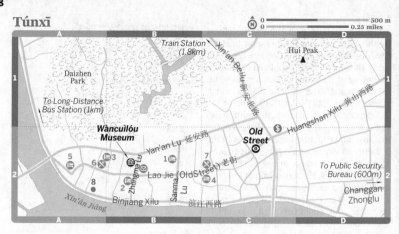

Túnxī

◎ Top Sights

Old Street..C2
Wàncuìlóu Museum...........................B2

⊟ Sleeping

1 Ancient Town Youth Hostel...............B2
2 Harbour Inn & Bar...............................B2
3 Hui Boutique Hotel B2
4 Old Street Hostel C2
5 Túnxī Lodge A2

⊗ Eating

6 Gāotāng Húndún...................................A2
7 Měishí Rénjiā C2

⊙ Transport

8 Huángshān Air Travel Agency A2

and comfy, while the cheaper twin rooms are clean, though lacking in natural light. The more expensive doubles are hotel quality.

Old Street Hostel   HOSTEL $

(老街国际青年旅舍; Lǎojiē Guójì Qīngnián Lǚshè; ☑254 0386; www.hiourhostel.com; 266 Lao Jie; 老街266号; dm ¥35-45, tw ¥159-169, d/ tr/f ¥139/199/219; ❋@⊛) With its convenient location and decent rooms – the four-person dorms come with proper mattresses and private bathrooms, while the private rooms sport wood-lattice decor and flat-screen TVs – this place clearly has an appeal that extends beyond the backpacking crowd. The 2nd floor houses a cafe overlooking Lao Jie with couches, pricey beer and a balcony. Staff speak English, though they tend to be efficient rather than warm.

ⓉⓄⓅ CHOICE ⊛ Hui Boutique Hotel   BOUTIQUE HOTEL $$$

(黄山徽舍品酒店; Huángshān Huīshèpǐn Jiǔdiàn; ☑235 2003; www.huistylehotel.com; 3 Lihong Xiang; 老街利洪巷3号; r incl breakfast ¥588-1080; ❋⊛) Tucked down an alley off Old St, this hotel, housed in a restored Qing-dynasty building, is boutique chic meets traditional style. Dark rooms are decked out with antique furnishings and modern toilets. There are 40% discounts online.

Harbour Inn & Bar   HOTEL $$

(夜泊客栈; Yèbó Kèzhàn; ☑252 2179; 29 Zhongma Lu; 中马路29号; d & tw ¥200; ❋@⊛) We're not sure where to set sail from, but the rooms in this renovated traditional building in Túnxī's old town are a notch above the typical midrange options. Get a twin that overlooks the street or splash out for the deluxe room for a chance to sleep in a traditional wooden Chinese canopy bed. A bar is located downstairs, for when you get bored looking at the floral wallpaper and matching bed sheets in the rooms.

Túnxī Lodge   HOTEL $$

(屯溪客栈; Túnxī Kèzhàn; ☑258 0388; 15 Lao Jie; 老街口15号; r incl breakfast ¥368-680; ❋) At the western end of Lao Jie, this stylish hotel gets guests in the right mood with its Huīzhōu interior. The traditionally styled rooms have lovely wooden beds and clean, bright showers. There's a decent attached restaurant serving Chinese and Western cuisine. Discounts knock a double down to ¥200.

🍴 Eating & Drinking

There are cheap street eats and a variety of local restaurants in the area just east of the eastern end of Old St. There are restaurants galore on Old St and the streets abutting it. Zhongma Lu off Old St has a string of cute coffee shops and bars, all with free wi-fi, ¥12 to ¥20 coffees and ¥10 to ¥25 beers.

TOP CHOICE Měishí Rénjiā — CHINESE HUI $

(美食人家; Lao Jie; dishes ¥7-56; ⊙lunch & dinner) At the official entrance to Lao Jie, this bustling restaurant – spread over two floors and hung with traditional Chinese *mǎdēng* lanterns – seethes with satisfied customers. Peruse the counter for the range of dishes on display – *húndūn* (wontons; dumpling soup), *jiǎozi* (stuffed dumplings), *bāozi* (steamed buns stuffed with meat or vegetables), noodles, claypot and more – then have them cooked fresh to order. If you want to linger over a meal, a more expensive version is located next door.

Gāotāng Húndūn — WONTON $

(高汤馄饨; 1 Haidi Xiang; húndūn ¥8-12; ⊙10am-late) Duck down a little alley opposite 120 Lao Jie to enjoy a warming bowl of *húndūn* (wonton) made by a 12th-generation seller. The secret is in the superthin *húndūn* skins, meat minced from whole lean pork, and the tasty soup. No room on the skinny benches outside? Grab a seat in the owner's living room: it's set in an atmospheric Qing-era Hui home. Also sells *dà húndūn* (larger, vegie-filled dumplings).

ℹ️ Information

The hostels have PCs for internet (¥4 per hour).

Bank of China (中国银行; Zhōngguó Yínháng; cnr Xin'an Beilu & Huangshan Xilu; ⊙8am-5.30pm) Changes travellers cheques and major currencies; 24-hour ATM.

China Post (中国邮局; Zhōngguó Yóuqū; 183 Lao Jie)

Public Security Bureau (PSB; 公安局; Gōng'ānjú; ☑232 3093; 1st fl, 108 Changgan Zhonglu; ⊙8am-noon & 2.30-5pm)

ℹ️ Getting There & Away

Air

Daily flights from Huángshān City Airport (黄山市飞机场; Huángshānshì Fēijīchǎng):

Běijīng ¥990, 2½ hours, one daily
Guǎngzhōu ¥800, 1½ hours, two daily
Hong Kong ¥2250, 1¾ hours, three times a week
Shànghǎi ¥500, one hour, one daily

You can buy tickets at the **Huángshān Air Travel Agency** (黄山航空旅游公司; Huángshān Hángkōng Lǚyóu Gōngsī; ☑251 7373; 1-1 Binjiang Xilu; ⊙8am-5.30pm).

Bus

The **long-distance bus station** (客运总站; kèyùn zǒngzhàn; Qiyun Dadao) is roughly 2km west of the train station on the outskirts of town. Destinations include the following:

Hángzhōu ¥89, three hours, hourly (6.50am to 5.50pm)
Jǐngdézhèn ¥61, 3½ hours, three daily (9.15am, noon and 2.10pm)
Nánjīng ¥120, 5½ hours, three daily (7.25am, 12.10pm and 4.20pm)
Shànghǎi ¥135, five hours, five daily (last bus 5pm)
Sūzhōu ¥132, six hours, two daily (6am and 6.50am)
Wùyuán ¥40, two hours, two daily (8.30am and 12.30pm)

Within Ānhuī, buses go to these destinations:
Héféi ¥144, four hours, hourly
Jiǔhuá Shān ¥59, 3½ hours, one daily (1.30pm)
Shèxiàn ¥6, 45 minutes, frequent services
Yīxiàn ¥12.50, one hour, frequent services (6am to 5pm)

Buses to Huángshān go to the main base at Tāngkǒu (¥13, one hour, frequent, 6am to 5pm) and on to the north entrance, Tàipíng (¥20, two hours). There are also minibuses to Tāngkǒu (¥15) from in front of the train station.

Inside the bus station (to the right as you enter) is the separate **Huángshān Tourist Distribution Centre** (黄山市旅游集散中心; Lǚyóu Jísàn Zhōngxīn; ☑255 8358; ⊙7.30am-6pm) with special tourist buses to popular destinations. Return buses operate hourly from 8am to 4pm, with a break from noon to 1pm. Destinations include the following:

Hóngcūn ¥14.50, 1½ hours
Qíyún Shān ¥8.50, 40 minutes
Xīdì ¥12.50, one hour

Train

Train connections are abysmal. Trains from Běijīng (¥195 to ¥500, 20 hours, 9.21am), Shànghǎi (¥110 to ¥265, 13 hours, 8.45pm and 10.06pm) and Nánjīng (¥70 to ¥159, six to 7½ hours, nine daily) stop at Túnxī (generally called Huángshān). There is also service to Jǐngdézhèn (¥25 to ¥115, three to five hours, 11 daily). For better connections to southern destinations, first go to Yīngtán (¥55 to ¥153, five to eight hours, nine daily) in Jiāngxī and change trains there.

ℹ️ Getting Around

Taxis are ¥5 at flag fall, with the 5km taxi ride to the airport costing about ¥30. Competition among pedicab drivers is fierce, so they are the cheapest way of getting around, costing approximately ¥4 for a trip to Old St from the train station area. Short rides start at ¥2. Bus 9 (¥1) runs between the bus station and train station; otherwise, a taxi should cost ¥7 to ¥10.

Around Túnxī

QÍYÚN SHĀN   齐云山

A 40-minute bus trip west of Túnxī brings you to the lush mountain panoramas of **Qíyún Shān** (admission 1 Mar-30 Nov ¥75, 1 Dec-28 Feb ¥55; ⏲8am-5pm Mon-Fri, 7.30am-5.30pm Sat & Sun). Long venerated by Taoists, the reddish sandstone rock provides a mountain home to the temples and the monks who tend to them, while mountain trails lead hikers through some stupendous scenery.

From the bus drop-off, cross the **Dēngfēng Bridge** (登封桥; Dēngfēng Qiáo) – dwelling on the luxuriant river views – and turn right through the village at the foot of the mountain for a 75-minute clamber up stone steps to the ticket office. Or ask the driver to drop you at the cable car (索道; Suǒdào; up ¥26, down ¥14) station ahead and do the circuit in reverse.

Beyond the ticket office, the **Zhēnxiān Cave** (真仙洞府; Zhēnxiān Dòngfǔ) houses a complex of Taoist shrines in grottoes and niches gouged from the sandstone cliffs. Seated within the smoky interior of the vast and dilapidated **Xuán Tiān Tàisù Gōng** (玄天太素宫) further on is an effigy of Zhengwu Dadi, a Taoist deity. A further temple hall, the **Yùxū Gōng** (玉虚宫), is erected beneath the huge brow of a 200m-long sandstone cliff, enclosed around effigies of Zhengwu Dadi and Laotzu.

There's a completely charming village, **Qíyún Village** (Qíyún Cūn), seemingly plonked in the middle of the mountain range. Its whitewashed buildings are home to a variety of restaurants, souvenir stalls and friendly residents.

ℹ️ Getting There & Away

Tourist buses run directly to Qíyún Shān (¥8.50, 45 minutes) from the Túnxī long-distance bus station tourist centre, leaving hourly from 8am to 4pm. This bus can drop you at the Dēngfēng Bridge or the cable-car station. Otherwise, take any Yīxiàn-bound bus

from Túnxī and ask the driver to stop at Qíyún Shān. Returning to Túnxī, wait at the side of the road for buses coming from Yīxiàn, but note that the last bus from Yīxiàn to Túnxī departs at 5pm. The last tourist bus departs at 4pm.

Huīzhōu Villages

📞 0559

The home of highly successful merchants who dealt in lumber, tea and salt – in addition to running a string of lucrative pawnshops throughout the empire – Huīzhōu was a double-edged sword: the inhabitants were often quite wealthy, but they were also mostly absent. At age 13, many young men were shunted out the door for the remainder of their lives to do business elsewhere, sometimes returning home only once per year. Rather than uproot their families and disrespect their ancestral clans, these merchants remained attached to the home towns they rarely saw, funnelling their profits into the construction of lavish residences and some of China's largest ancestral halls.

Consequently, the villages scattered throughout southern Ānhuī (also known as Wǎnnán; 皖南) and northern Jiāngxī are some of the country's loveliest, augmented by the fact that they are often set in the lush surroundings of buckling earth and bamboo and pine forest, the silhouettes of stratified hills stacked away into the distance.

WESTERN VILLAGES (YĪXIÀN)   黟县

Yīxiàn is home to the two most picturesque communities in Ānhuī: Xīdì and Hóngcūn. Even with soaring ticket prices and when spilling over with crowds (most of the time), these are, hands down, the most impressive sights in the Huīzhōu area.

◎ Sights & Activities

Xīdì   HISTORIC VILLAGE
(西递; admission ¥104) Dating to AD 1047, the village of Xīdì has for centuries been a stronghold of the Hu (胡) clan, descended from the eldest son of the last Tang emperor who fled here in the twilight years of the Tang dynasty. Typical of the elegant Huīzhōu style (see boxed text, p384), Xīdì's 124 surviving buildings reflect the wealth and prestige of the prosperous merchants who settled here.

Xīdì's Unesco World Heritage status means it enjoys a lucrative tourist economy. The village nevertheless remains a picturesque tableau of slender lanes, cream-coloured walls topped with horse-head gables, roofs capped with dark tiles, and doorways ornately decorated with carved lintels.

Wander around the maze of flagstone lanes, examining lintel carvings above doorways decorated with vases, urns, animals, flowers and ornamental motifs, and try to avoid tripping over hordes of high-school artists consigning scenes of stone bridges spanning small streams to canvas.

Xīdì's magnificent three-tiered Ming-dynasty decorative arch, the **Húwénguāng Páifāng** (胡文光牌坊), at the entrance to the village, is an ostentatious symbol of Xīdì's former standing. Numerous other notable structures are open to inspection, including the **Díjí Hall** (迪吉堂; Díjí Táng) and the **Zhuīmù Hall** (追慕堂; Zhuīmù Táng), both on Dalu Jie (大路街). **Jìng'ài Hall** (敬爱堂; Jìng'ài Táng), is the town's largest building and was used for meetings, weddings and, of course, meting out punishment. Back in the day, women weren't allowed in the hall; oh, how things have changed. **Xīyuán** (西园) is a small house known for its exquisite stone carvings on the windows. Unlike regular carvings, these are carved on both sides. The owner is said to have previously rejected offers of US$10,000 (each!) for them.

When you're done with the village, pop out on paths leading out to nearby hills where there are suitable spots for your picture-postcard panoramas of the village (though a mobile-phone tower now blights the landscape). If you want to avoid the crowds, you'll have to start early or hang out late: tour groups start roaming around at 7am and only trickle out at 5pm or so.

Hóngcūn

HISTORIC VILLAGE

(宏村; admission ¥104) Dating to the southern Song dynasty, the delightful village and Unesco World Heritage site of Hóngcūn, 11km northeast of Yìxiàn, has at its heart the crescent-shaped Moon Pond (月沼; Yuè Zhǎo) and is encapsulated by South Lake (南湖; Nán Hú), West Stream (西溪; Xī Xī) and Léigǎng Mountain (雷岗山; Léigǎng Shān). Founding village elders of the Wang (汪) clan consulted a feng shui guru and the village was remodelled to resemble an ox, with its still-functioning waterway system representing the entrails. Wealth soon followed, though the descendants of the Wang clan now trade in tourism rather than goods.

Today, the village is a charming and unhurried portrait of bridges, lakeside views, narrow alleys and traditional halls. Alleyway channels flush water through the village from West Stream to Moon Pond and from there on to South Lake, while signs guide visitors on a tour of the principal buildings. Lost? Just follow the waterflow.

If the bridge at the entrance to the village looks familiar, it's because it featured in the opening scene from Ang Lee's *Crouching Tiger, Hidden Dragon*. The picturesque Moon Lake also features in the film. The **Chéngzhì Hall** (承志堂; Chéngzhì Táng; Shangshuizhen Lu; 上水圳路) dates from 1855 and was built by a salt merchant. It has 28 rooms, adorned with fabulous woodcarvings, 2nd-floor balconies and light wells. Peepholes on top-floor railings are for girls to peek at boy visitors and the little alcove in the mahjong room was used to hide the concubine. The now-faded gold-brushed carvings are said to have required 100 taels of the expensive stuff and took over four years to be completed.

Other notable buildings include the **Hall of the Peach Garden** (桃源居; Táoyuán Jū), with its elaborate carved wood panels, and the **South Lake Academy** (南湖书院; Nánhú Shūyuàn), which enjoys an enviable setting beside tranquil South Lake. Overlooking Moon Pond is a gathering of further halls, chief among which is the dignified **Lèxù Hall** (乐叙堂; Lèxù Táng), a hoary Ming antique from the first years of the 15th century. Turn up bamboo carvings, trinkets and a large selection of tea at the **market** west of Moon Pond. The busy square by **Hóngjì Bridge** (宏际桥; Hóngjì Qiáo) on the West Stream is shaded by two ancient trees (the 'horns' of the ox), a red poplar and a gingko.

Admission to the village includes a guide with limited English-speaking skills – you'll have to engage one at the main entrance in case you enter by the side gate.

Tǎchuānǎ

HISTORIC VILLAGE

(塔川; admission ¥20) Located 3km northwest of Hóngcūn is the tiny little village of Tǎchuānǎ. It's set at the base of a valley and noted for its stunning autumn scenery. Each year, the leaves on old-growth trees in and around the village change colours for anywhere between 10 to 30 days. The entire valley comes ablaze in shades of orange, green and brown, much to the delight of photographers. On other days, the villagers eke out their living by planting rice and tea. From afar, the village looks like a pagoda as it's built across the steps of foothills. New management was not providing guides or house visits when we called, but in case the service is reinstated, house 18 has some of the most exquisite wooden carvings in the region. Otherwise, you could look out for dilapidated house 25 where you'll find empty antique furnishing and other bits and pieces strewn across a traditional Hui house.

Nánpíng
HISTORIC VILLAGE

(南屏; admission ¥43) With a history of more than 1100 years, this intriguing and labyrinthine village, 5km to the west of Yīxiàn town, is famed as the setting of Zhang Yimou's 1989 tragedy *Judou* and, of course, scenes from *Crouching Tiger, Hidden Dragon*. Numerous ancient ancestral halls, clan shrines and merchant residences survive within Nánpíng's mazelike alleys, including the **Chéngshì Zōngcí** (程氏宗祠) and the **Yèshì Zōngcí** (叶氏宗祠). The **Lǎo Yáng Jiā Rǎnfáng** (老杨家染坊) residence that served as the principal household of dyer Gongli and her rapacious husband in *Judou* remains cluttered with props, and faded stills from the film hang from the walls. Admission includes a guide with limited English-speaking skills.

Guānlù
HISTORIC VILLAGE

(关麓; admission ¥35) Around 8km west of Yīxiàn and further along the road beyond Nánpíng, this small village's drawcard sights are the fabulous households – **Bādàjiā** (八大家) – of eight rich brothers. Each Qing-dynasty residence shares similar elegant Huīzhōu features, with light wells, interior courtyards, halls, carved wood panels and small gardens. Each an independent entity, the households are interconnected by doors and linked together into a systemic whole. A distinctive aspect of the residences is their elegantly painted ceilings, the patterns and details of which survive. The houses have now been subdivided among the descendants' families, and many wings are in disrepair as many of the younger villagers have left for more modern abodes. Admission includes a guide with limited English-speaking skills.

Mùkēng Zhúhǎi
FOREST

(木坑竹海; admission ¥30) A hike through Mùkēng's **bamboo forest** is an excellent way to escape the megaphones and roving packs of art students in the nearby towns. Remember *Crouching Tiger, Hidden Dragon's* breathtaking bamboo-top fight scenes? Yep, they were filmed here. The two-hour circuit along a ridgeline leads past the top-

heavy plumes of feathery bamboo, trickling streams and hillside tea gardens, past a small village where you can get a filling meal and a clean room with bathroom for ¥60 to ¥120, and eventually to a small hamlet where you can break for a cup of *chá* (tea). Perhaps inspired by the movie, a **zipline** (¥40) has been built near the highest point in the trail; it's a 40-second zip to the bottom from more than 75m above the ground! The forest is 5km northeast of Hóngcūn.

🛏 Sleeping & Eating

Due to local regulations, it's not possible to just turn up and find simple homestay-style accommodation (住农家; *zhù nóngjiā*) in Xīdì and Hóngcūn. Each of the villages has 'approved' accommodation for foreigners, most listed below. You can visit local homes to sample some excellent cooking (meals are generally around ¥20, unless you have a chicken slaughtered, which will cost ¥50 to ¥100). Restaurants abound; in spring, succulent bamboo shoots (竹笋; *zhúsǔn*) figure prominently in many dishes.

XĪDÌ

Pig's Heaven Inn
BOUTIQUE HOTEL $$$

(猪栏酒吧; Zhūlán Jiǔbā; ☑515 4555; http://blog.sina.com.cn/zhulanjiuba; Renrang Li; 西递镇仁让里; d incl breakfast ¥360, ste ¥460-880; ❀⊚) This is a 400-year-old house in Xīdì that has been restored, with a study, two terraces and five distinctive rooms. Reservations are essential (the entrance is unmarked); gourmet sleuths can seek it out for a fantastic lunch (dishes from ¥20) in the courtyard. The owners have developed a larger, pricier property in Bìshān (碧山), several kilometres away. This is a great place to just unwind for a day or three; grab one of their bicycles and explore the surrounding area. Transfers to both properties are available. Limited English.

Xīdì Travel Lodge
HOTEL $$

(西递行馆; Xīdì Xíngguǎn; ☑515 6999; www.xidilodge.com; 西递; d incl breakfast ¥368-488, ste ¥608-1288; ❀⊚) This can't-miss-it property just behind the main gate to the Xīdì village, is a sprawling, multibuilding affair complete with comfortable rooms and its own restaurant and alfresco cafe. All rooms have modern showers, flat-screen TVs and faux antique furnishing, while some have balconies. Get a room facing the small tea garden. The restaurant serves local fare (dishes ¥18 to ¥108) and there's cheap ¥10 beer at the cafe. Discounts of 30% available.

HÓNGCŪN

TOP CHOICE **Long Lane Inn** BOUTIQUE HOTEL **$$$**
(宏村一品更楼; Hóngcūn Yīpǐn Gēng Lóu; ☑554 2001; www.hcno-1.com; 1 Shangshui Quan; 宏村上水圳1号; r incl breakfast ¥380-1280; ❀☎) Sitting in a quiet corner of Hóngcūn, this 10-room Taiwanese-run boutique hotel is a welcome addition to the village. Visitors have a choice of rooms: traditionally styled with rosewood Chinese four-posted beds (or splash out for the suite with a cute garden and sunken bath) or simple tatami rooms, each one comfortable and immaculate. In-house meals are great too. Iris, the owner, speaks good English and can help with travel plans and private-vehicle hire.

Hóngdá Tíngyuàn HOMESTAY **$**
(宏达庭院; ☑554 1262; 5 Shangshui Zhen; 宏村上水圳5号; r¥100) The draw of this Hóngcūn home is the verdant courtyard filled with potted daphne, heavenly bamboo and other flowering shrubs, all set around a small pool and pavilion. Its rooms are unadorned, but the peaceful location in the upper part of the village is ideal. You can stop by for lunch (dishes from ¥20), space permitting. No English spoken.

ℹ️ **Getting There & Around**

BUS Tourist buses run directly to Xīdì (¥12.50, one hour) and then to Hóngcūn (¥14.50, 1½ hours) from the Túnxī long-distance bus station's tourist centre, leaving hourly from 8am to 4pm, with a break at noon. Otherwise, catch a local bus from the long-distance bus station to Yīxiàn (¥13, one hour, frequent, 6am to 5pm), the transport hub for public transport to the surrounding villages.

From Yīxiàn there are green minibuses (¥2, half-hourly, 7am to 5pm) to Xīdì (15 minutes), Nánpíng (15 minutes), Guānlù (20 minutes) and Hóngcūn (20 minutes). You will need to return to Yīxiàn to get between the different villages, with the exception of Nánpíng and Guānlù, which are both in the same direction. From Yīxiàn, it's possible to travel on to Tāngkǒu (¥15, one hour, four daily) and Qīngyáng (¥38, 2½ hours, three daily).

BICYCLE A great way to explore the surrounding countryside is on **bikes** (出租自行车; chūzū zìxíngchē; per 4hr ¥5-15), found on the modern street opposite Hóngcūn's Hóngjì Bridge (宏际桥; Hóngjì Qiáo).

TAXI Taxis and pedicabs go to Xīdì (¥10), Hóngcūn (¥15), Nánpíng (¥20) and Guānlù (¥25) from Yīxiàn. Booking a pedicab to take you to all four villages from Yīxiàn can cost as little as ¥150 for the day, depending on your bargaining

skills. A minivan for the day will cost ¥300 to ¥400. Most accommodation places can help with transport bookings. From Hóngcūn, get a pedicab to Tǎchuān (¥10) and Mùkēng Zhúhǎi (¥15). You'll need to negotiate for the driver to wait for you as returning pedicabs are rare.

NORTHERN VILLAGES

Rarely visited by individual travellers, the villages north of Túnxī can serve as a quieter antidote to the much-hyped and crowded towns to the west.

👁 **Sights**

Chéngkǎn HISTORIC VILLAGE
(呈坎; admission ¥80; ⏰8am-5pm) A real working community, Chéngkǎn presents a very different picture from its more affluent cousins in Shèxiàn – farmers walk through town with hoes slung over their shoulders, tea traders dump baskets of freshly picked leaves straight out onto the street, quacking ducks run amok in streams and there's the unmistakable smell of pig manure in the air: a bona fide slice of life in rural China. Most visitors come to see southern China's largest **ancestral temple** (罗东舒祠; Luó Dōngshū Cí), a massive wooden complex several courtyards deep that took 71 years (1539–1610) to build. It has a mixed bag of architectural styles: from Greco-Roman columns to Persian patterns on overhead beams. There are other venerable structures in town, such as the three-storey **Yànyì Táng** (燕翼堂), which is nearly 600 years old; however, many residences are in poor condition. Look out for a house where the owner still gives haircuts (¥2) on his 100-year-old-plus chair. The mirror is just as old. Another big appeal lies in the lush panoramas of the surrounding Ānhuī countryside.

Tángmó HISTORIC VILLAGE
(唐模; admission ¥80, incl electronic guide deposit ¥300; ⏰8am-5pm) A narrow village that extends 1km along a central canal, Tángmó was originally established during the late Tang dynasty. A pathway follows the waterway from the entrance at the east gate (东门; dōng mén) into the village, leading past the large **Tán'gàn Garden** (檀干园; Tán'gàn Yuán), which was modelled after Hángzhōu's West Lake. Here you'll enter the village proper, passing canalside Qing residences along **Shui Jie** (水街) before coming to the covered **Gāoyáng Bridge** (高阳桥; Gāoyáng Qiáo), built in 1733 and now home to a small teahouse. At the end of town is the **Shàngyì Ancestor Hall** (尚义堂; Shàngyì Táng), with 199 peony blossoms carved into the entrance

HUĪZHŌU STYLE

Huīzhōu architecture is the most distinctive ingredient of the regional personality, representative of the merchant class that held sway in this region during the Ming and Qing dynasties. The residences of Yīxiàn and Shèxiàn are the most typical examples of Huīzhōu architecture, their whitewashed walls topped on each flank by horse-head gables, originally designed to prevent fire from travelling along a line of houses, and later evolving into decorative motifs. Strikingly capped with dark tiles, walls are often punctured by high, narrow windows, designed to protect the residence from thieves (and lonely wives from illicit temptations).

Exterior doorways, often overhung with decorative eaves and carved brick or stone lintels, are sometimes flanked by drum stones (*gǔshí*) or mirror stones (*jìngshí*) and lead onto interior courtyards delightfully illuminated by light wells (*tiānjǐng*), rectangular openings in the roof. The doors are a talking point in themselves. It's said that an owner would spend 1000 taels of silver on the decorative archway and carvings but only four taels on the actual door!

Many Huīzhōu houses are furnished with intricately carved wood panels and extend to two floors, the upper floor supported on wooden columns. Even the furnishing holds much meaning. The main hall for taking visitors has several elements worth keeping an eye out for. You might notice semicircle half-tables against the walls: if the master of the house is in, the tables would be combined; if they are split, it's a subtle hint for male visitors to not intrude upon the wife. There might also be a mantelpiece where you will see a clock, vase and mirror. This symbolises peace and harmony in the house. The Chinese words for these items translate as: *zhōng shēng* (钟声; hourly chiming on clock), *píng* (平; harmony) and *jìng* (静; peace).

Another characteristic element of regional architecture is the obsession with decorative archways (*páifāng* or *páilóu*), which were constructed by imperial decree to honour an individual's outstanding achievement. Examples include becoming a high official (for men; *páifāng*) or leading a chaste life (for women; *páilóu*). Archways are common throughout China and don't always carry symbolic meaning, but in Huīzhōu they were of great importance because they gave the merchants – who occupied the bottom rung of the Confucian social ladder (under artisans, peasants and scholars) – much-desired social prestige. Roads were built to pass under a *páifāng* but around a *páilóu*, so that a man would never feel that his status was beneath that of a woman's.

beam. A hotel complex is being developed nearby. There's a string of traditional workshops and stalls near the east gate. Sample homemade *dòujiāng* (豆浆; soya bean milk; ¥1.50) and pick up a traditional Ānhuī ink stone (砚台; *yàntái*) and brushes.

Note that the public bus will probably drop you off at the west gate (meaning you'll see the sights listed above in reverse), but there should be onward transport of some kind to the east gate, or just backtrack.

ⓘ Getting There & Around

There's a tourist bus from the Túnxī long-distance bus station that stops at Tángmó (¥14, 1½ hours, every two hours). It runs from 8am to 4pm with a break from noon to 1pm.

Getting to Chéngkǎn is slightly complicated. Start by taking a bus to Yánsì (岩寺; ¥4.50, 30 minutes, frequent) from the Túnxī long-distance bus station. From the Yánsì bus terminus, you'll need to proceed to the town's north bus station (北站; *běi zhàn*) by public bus (¥1) or a pedicab (¥4). From the north bus station, you can take another bus to Chéngkǎn (¥3.50, 20 minutes, hourly). You can also get to Tángmó (¥2.50, 20 minutes, hourly).

It's also possible to hire a pedicab from the Yánsì bus terminus to Chéngkǎn (¥30) or Tángmó (¥20). Decent bargainers can get one for a day for ¥80 to ¥100. To get between the villages on public transport, you'll need to return to Yánsì. Note that the last buses are at 5pm, and transport stops for an hour around noon.

EASTERN VILLAGES

The appeal of the eastern villages is also in their less-touristy vibe. Shèxiàn is a decent-sized provincial town that hides some interesting historic sights, while the neighbouring port of Yúliáng presents an architectural heritage entirely different from the other Huīzhōu villages.

⊙ Sights

Shèxiàn

HISTORIC VILLAGE

Historic seat of the Huīzhōu prefecture, Shèxiàn (歙县) is 25km east of Túnxī and can be visited as a day trip. The town was formerly the grand centre of the Huīzhōu culture, serving as its capital. Today, the **Ancient City** (徽州古城; Huīzhōu Gǔchéng; admission incl entry to Yúliáng & Chinese-speaking guide ¥80, without entry to Yúliáng ¥60) serves as the town's main sight.

From the Shèxiàn bus station, cross the bridge over the river, hang right and go through a gate tower and along to **Yánghé Mén** (阳和门), a double-eaved gate tower constructed of wood. Get your admission ticket and climb the gate to examine a Ming-dynasty stone *xièzhì* (獬豸; a legendary beast) and elevated views of the magnificent **Xǔguó Archway** (许国石坊; Xǔguó Shífáng) below. Fabulously decorated, this is China's sole surviving four-sided decorative archway, with 12 lions (18 in total if you count the cubs) seated on pedestals around it and a profusion of bas-relief carvings of other mythical creatures.

Continue in the same direction to reach the alleyway (on left) to the old residential area of **Doushan Jie** (斗山街古民居; Dòushānjiē Gǔmínjū), a street of Huīzhōu houses, with several courtyard residences open to visitors and decorated with exquisitely carved lintels, beautiful interiors and occasional pairs of leaping-on blocks for mounting horses. Look out for the *páifāng* (decorative archway) that has been filled in and incorporated into a wall.

At the time of research, massive construction in the Ancient City was under way. When complete (expected to be 2013), a replica of the original capital city complex will be open to the public.

Yúliáng

HISTORIC VILLAGE

(渔梁; admission ¥30) Little-visited Yúliáng is a historic riverine port village on the Liàn River (Liàn Jiāng). Cobbled **Yuliang Jie** (渔梁街) is a picturesque alley of buildings and former transfer stations for the wood, salt and tea that plied the Liàn River and was shipped to north China; the **teashop** at No 87 is an example. Note the firewalls separating the houses along the road. Examine the traditional Huīzhōu arrangement of the **Bāwèizǔ Museum** (巴慰祖纪念馆; Bāwèizǔ Jìniànguǎn), also on Yuliang Jie.

The **Lion Bridge** (狮子桥; Shīzǐ Qiáo) dates to the Tang dynasty, a time when the 138m-long granite **Yúliáng Dam** (渔梁坝; Yúliáng Bà) across the river was first constructed. Boats can ferry you from the dam for short 20-minute return river trips (¥10 to ¥20).

Tranquil Yúliáng is a good place to recharge your batteries. There are rooms with lovely views at a small **inn** (☑0559-653 9731; 147 Yuliang Jie; 渔梁街147号; d with bathroom ¥50-60; ❀). There's another similar **inn** (☑0559-653 8024; 145 Yuliang Jie; 渔梁街145号; d with bathroom ¥80-100; ❀) two doors along. Both serve meals with dishes starting at ¥15. The innkeepers will take you into the village if you book ahead.

ⓘ Getting There & Away

Buses from Túnxī's long-distance bus station run regularly to Shèxiàn (¥6.50, 45 minutes, frequent). To reach Yúliáng, take a pedicab (¥5) from Shèxiàn's bus station (by the bridge), or hop on bus 1, which runs to Yúliáng (¥1) from outside the bus station and also along the road opposite Shèxiàn Ancient City. The last bus back to Túnxī departs at 6pm.

Huángshān 黄山

☑0559

When its archetypal granite peaks and twisted pines are wreathed in spectral folds of mist, Huángshān's idyllic views easily nudge it into the select company of China's top 10, nay, top five, sights. Legions of poets and painters have drawn inspiration from Huángshān's iconic beauty. Yesterday's artists seeking an escape from the hustle and bustle of the temporal world may have been replaced by crowds of tourists, who bring the hustle and bustle with them, but Huángshān still rewards visitors with moments of tranquility, and the unearthly views can be simply breathtaking.

Climate

Locals claim that it rains more than 200 days a year up on the mountain. Allow yourself several days and head to the mountain when the forecast is best. Spring (April to June) generally tends to be misty, which means you may be treated to some stunning scenery, but you're just as likely to encounter a thick fog that obscures everything except for a line of yellow ponchos extending up the trail. Summer (July to August) is the rainy season, though storms can blow through fairly quickly. Autumn (September to October) is generally

Huángshān

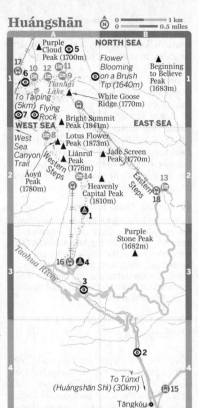

⊙ Sights

1 Bànshān Temple	A2
2 Front Gate	B4
3 Hot Springs	A3
4 Mercy Light Temple	A3
Mt Huángshān Visitors Centre	(see 4)
5 Refreshing Terrace	A1
6 West Sea Canyon (Ring Road 1)	A1
7 West Sea Canyon (Ring Road 2)	A1

⊟ Sleeping

8 Báiyún Hotel	A2
9 Běihǎi Hotel	A1
Běihǎi Hotel (three-star wing)	(see 9)
10 Páiyúnlóu Hotel	A1
11 Shílín Hotel	A1
12 Xīhǎi Hotel	A1
13 Yúngǔ Hotel	B2
14 Yùpínglóu Hotel	A2

ⓘ Information

Bank of China	(see 9)
Police Station	(see 9)

ⓘ Transport

15 East Long-Distance Bus Station	B4
16 Mercy Light Temple Station	A3
17 Tàipíng Cable Car Station	A1
18 Yúngǔ Station	B2

considered to be the best travel period. Even at the height of summer, average temperatures rarely rise above 20°C at the summit, so come prepared.

⊙ Sights & Activities

Buses from Túnxī (Huángshān Shì) drop you off in Tāngkǒu, the sprawling town at the foot of Huángshān. A base for climbers, this is the place to stock up on supplies (maps, raincoats, food, money), store your excess luggage and arrange onward transport. It's possible to spend time in Tāngkǒu, but unless you're on a tight budget, you might as well stay on the mountain.

The town consists of two main streets, the larger Feicui Lu – a strip of restaurants, supermarkets and hotels – and the more pleasant Yanxi Jie, which runs along the river perpendicular to Feicui Lu and is accessed by stairs leading down from the bridge.

ASCENDING & DESCENDING THE MOUNTAIN

Regardless of how you ascend **Huángshān** (admission 1 Mar-30 Nov ¥230, 1 Dec-29 Feb ¥130, seniors year-round ¥60, child 1.1-1.3m ¥60), you will be stung by the dizzying entrance fee. You can pay at the eastern steps near the Yúngǔ Station (云谷站; Yúngǔ Zhàn) or at the Mercy Light Temple Station (慈光阁站; Cíguāng Gé Zhàn), where the western steps begin. Shuttle buses (¥13) run to both places from Tāngkǒu.

Three basic routes will get you up to the summit: the short, hard way (eastern steps); the longer, harder way (western steps); and the very short, easy way (cable car). The eastern steps lead up from the Yúngǔ Station; the western steps lead up from the parking lot near Mercy Light Temple. It's possible to do a 10-hour circuit going up the eastern steps and then down the western steps in one day, but you'll have to be slightly insane, in good shape and you'll definitely miss out on some of the more spectacular, hard-to-get-to areas.

A basic itinerary would be to take an early-morning bus from Túnxī, climb the eastern steps, hike around the summit area, spend the night at the top, catch the sunrise and then hike back down the western steps the next day, giving you time to catch an afternoon bus back to Túnxī. Most travellers do opt to spend more than one night on the summit to explore all the various trails. Don't underestimate the hardship involved; the steep gradients and granite steps can wreak havoc on your knees, both going up and down.

Most sightseers are packed (and we mean *packed*) into the summit area above the upper cable car stations, consisting of a network of trails running between various peaks. The highlight of the climb for many independent travellers is the lesser-known West Sea Canyon hike (p388), a more rugged, exposed section where most tour groups do not venture.

Make sure to bring enough water, food, warm clothing and rain gear before climbing. Bottled water and food prices increase the higher you go. As mountain paths are easy to follow and English signs plentiful, guides are unnecessary.

Hot Springs
HOT SPRINGS

(黄山温泉; Huángshān Wēnquán; admission ¥238; ⊙10.30am-10.30pm) The hot springs area, with renovations complete, is the place to soak after the strenuous climb. It offers a mind-boggling variety of themed springs. Soak in a coffee-infused pool or get heady in the wine- or alcohol-infused spring. There's also a pool with fish that nibble away dead skin on your feet. Follow it all up with a foot massage. Entry includes complimentary snacks and tea.

The best way to get to the springs is to arrange for a free transfer and pick-up via your hotel. Shuttle buses (¥7) run to the Yúngǔ Station, from where it's a short walk downhill to the hot springs.

Eastern Steps
TRAIL

A medium-fast climb of the 7.5km eastern steps from Yúngǔ Station (890m) to **White Goose Ridge** (白鹅峰; Bái'é Fēng; 1770m) can be done in 2½ hours. The route is pleasant, but lacks the awesome geological scenery of the western steps. In spring wild azalea and weigela add gorgeous splashes of colour to the wooded slopes of the mountain.

Much of the climb is comfortably shaded and although it can be tiring, it's a doddle compared with the western steps. Slow-moving porters use the eastern steps for ferrying up their massive, swaying loads of food, drink and building materials, so considerable traffic plies the route. While clambering up, note the more ancient flight of steps that makes an occasional appearance alongside the newer set.

Purists can extend the eastern steps climb by several hours by starting at the **Front Gate** (黄山大门; Huángshān Dàmén), where a stepped path crosses the road at several points before linking with the main eastern steps trail.

Western Steps
TRAIL

The 15km western steps route has some stellar scenery, but it's twice as long and strenuous as the eastern steps, and much easier to enjoy if you're clambering down rather than gasping your way up. If you take the cable car up, just do this in reverse.

The western steps descent begins at the **Flying Rock** (飞来石; Fēilái Shí), a boulder perched on an outcrop half an hour from Běihǎi Hotel, and goes over **Bright Summit Peak** (光明顶; Guāngmíng Dǐng; 1841m). Look out from Bright Summit Peak to **Áoyú Peak** (鳌鱼峰; Áoyú Fēng; 1780m): you'll notice that it looks like two turtles!

South of Áoyú Peak en route to Lotus Flower Peak, the descent funnels you down through a **Gleam of Sky** (一线天; Yīxiàn Tiān), a remarkably narrow chasm – a vertical split in the granite – pinching a huge rock suspended above the heads of climbers. Further on, **Lotus Flower Peak** (莲花峰; Liánhuā Fēng; 1873m) marks the highest point, but is occasionally sealed off, preventing ascents. **Liánruǐ Peak** (莲蕊峰; Liánruǐ Fēng; 1776m) is decorated with rocks whimsically named after animals, but save some energy for the much-coveted and staggering climb – 1321 steps in all – up **Heavenly Capital Peak** (天都峰; Tiāndū Fēng; 1810m) and the stunning views that unfold below. As elsewhere on the mountain, young lovers bring padlocks engraved with their names up here and lash them for eternity to the chain railings. Successful ascents can be commemorated with a gold medal engraved with your name (¥15). Access to Heavenly Capital Peak (and other peaks) is sometimes restricted for maintenance and repair, so keep those fingers crossed when you go!

Further below, the steps lead to **Bànshān Temple** (半山寺; Bànshān Sì) and below that the **Mercy Light Temple** (慈光阁; Cíguāng Gé), where you can pick up a mini-bus back to Tāngkǒu (¥13) or continue walking to the hot springs area.

Huángshān is not one of China's sacred mountains, so little religious activity is evident. The Cíguāng Temple at the bottom of the western steps is one of the few temples on the mountain whose temple halls survive, although they have been converted to more secular uses. The first hall now serves as the **Mt Huángshān Visitors Centre** (黄山游人中心; Huángshān Yóurén Zhōngxīn), where you can pore over a diorama of the mountain ranges. Now head to Tāngkǒu to find yourself some beer as a reward.

Yúngǔ Cable Car CABLE CAR

(云谷索道; Yúngǔ Suǒdào; one way 1 Mar-20 Nov ¥80, 1 Dec-29 Feb ¥65; ⊙7am-4.30pm) Shuttle buses (¥13) ferry visitors from Tāngkǒu to the cable car. Either arrive very early or late (if you're staying overnight) as long queues are the norm. Thankfully, a new cable-car station has shortened the three-hour queues to nothing more than 45 minutes.

Shuttle buses (¥13) also run from Tāngkǒu to Mercy Light Temple, which is linked by the **Yùpíng Cable Car** (玉屏索道; Yùpíng Suǒdào; one way 1 Mar-20 Nov ¥80, 1 Dec-29 Feb ¥65; ⊙7am-4.30pm) to the area just below the Yùpínglóu Hotel.

ON THE SUMMIT

The summit is essentially one huge network of connecting trails and walks that meander up, down and across several different peaks. More than a few visitors spend several nights on the peak, and the North Sea (北海; Běihǎi) sunrise is a highlight for those staying overnight. **Refreshing Terrace** (清凉台; Qīngliáng Tái) is five minutes' walk from Běihǎi Hotel and attracts sunrise crowds. Lucky visitors are rewarded with the luminous spectacle of *yúnhǎi* (literally 'sea of clouds'): idyllic pools of mist that settle over the mountain, filling its chasms and valleys with fog.

The staggering and otherworldly views from the summit reach out over huge valleys of granite and enormous formations of rock, topped by gravity-defying slivers of stone and the gnarled forms of ubiquitous Huángshān pine trees (*Pinus taiwanensis*). Many rocks have been christened with fanciful names by the Chinese, alluding to figures from religion and myth. **Beginning to Believe Peak** (始信峰; Shǐxìn Fēng; 1683m), with its jaw-dropping views, is a major bottleneck for photographers. En route to the North Sea, pause at the **Flower Blooming on a Brush Tip** (梦笔生花; Mèngbǐ

Shēnghuā; 1640m), a granite formation topped by a pine tree. Clamber up to **Purple Cloud Peak** (丹霞峰; Dānxiá Fēng; 1700m) for a long survey over the landscape and try to catch the sun as it descends in the west. Aficionados of rock formations should keep an eye out for the poetically named **Mobile Phone Rock** (手机石; Shǒujī Shí), located near the top of the western steps. Continue on to sights en route to the Western Steps (p387).

WEST SEA CANYON 西海大峡谷

A strenuous and awe-inspiring 8.5km hike, this route descends into a gorge (Xīhǎi Dàxiágǔ) and has some impressively exposed stretches (it's not for those afraid of heights), taking a minimum four hours to complete. You can access the canyon at either the northern entrance (near the Páiyúnlóu Hotel) or the southern entrance (near the Báiyún Hotel aka White Clouds Hotel).

A good option to start would be at the northern entrance. From there, you'll pass through some rock tunnels and exit onto the best bits of the gorge. Here, stone steps have been attached to the sheer side of the mountain! Peer over the side for some serious butt-clenching views down. Don't worry, there are handrails. If you're pressed for time or don't have the energy to stomach a long hike, do a figure-eight loop of Ring Road 1 (一环上路口) and Ring Road 2 (二环上路口), and head back to the northern entrance. Sure, you'll miss some stunning views across lonely, mist-encased peaks, but you'll also miss the knee-killing dip into the valley and the subsequent thigh-killing climb out to the southern entrance.

At the time of research, construction of a new cable car up to this area was in full swing so you may be restricted to Ring Rds 1 and 2. When complete, expect the area to get a lot busier. Avoid the area in bad weather.

🛏 Sleeping & Eating

Huángshān has various locations where hotels can be found. Prices and availability vary according to season; it's a good idea to book ahead for summit accommodation, especially so for dorms. Prices for hotels tend to cost at least double what you'd pay in a nonmountain setting. If you're on a tight budget, make sure to take plenty of food to the summit. You won't be able to get a hot meal there for under ¥50. Summit hotels usually offer warm jackets for sunrise watchers.

TĀNGKŎU 汤口

Mediocre midrange hotels line Tāngkŏu's main strip, Feicui Lu; remember to look at rooms first and ask for discounts before committing. There are also a host of budget choices along Tiandu Lu. Restaurants cluster along Yanxi Jie, which runs along the river perpendicular to Feicui Lu.

Pine Ridge Lodge HOTEL $

(黄山天客山庄; Huángshān Tiānkè Shānzhuāng; ☑1377-761 8111; www.hstksz.com; Scenic Area South Gate; 风景区南门; r incl breakfast ¥120-150; ✻) Wayne, the friendly English-speaking owner likens it to a lodge in Aspen...in reality, the place isn't so much a ski lodge but a very decent midrange hotel. Book a cosy room in the charming outhouse for privacy. The inhouse restaurant serves great local food. Rooms include return transfers to/from the Tāngkŏu bus station.

Huáyì Bīnguǎn HOTEL $$

(华艺宾馆; ☑556 6888; South Gate; 南大门; tw ¥480-680; ✻) A large white edifice on the west side of the river on the Huángshān access road, this four-star hotel offers the priciest and nicest (the word being relative in this context) accommodation in Tāngkŏu. Prices in the three-star building are lower. Staff can help with bus and flight bookings.

YÚNGǓ STATION 云谷索道站

Yúngǔ Hotel山庄 HOTEL $$

(云谷山庄; Yúngǔ Shānzhuāng; ☑558 6444; s & d ¥580; ✻) With a lovely but inconveniently located setting looking out onto bamboo and forest, this traditionally styled hotel has fine, clean rooms, with 35% discounts frequently given. Walk down from the car park in front of the cable-car station.

WESTERN STEPS 西线台阶

Yùpínglóu Hotel HOTEL $$$

(玉屏楼宾馆; Yùpínglóu Bīnguǎn; ☑558 2288; www.hsyplhotel.com; d/q/tr ¥1480/1600/1680; ✻@) A 10-minute walk from the Yùpíng cable car (go to your right), this four-star hotel is perched on a spectacular 1660m-high lookout just above the Welcoming Guest Pine Tree. Aim for the doubles with the good views at the back, as some rooms have small windows with no views. Discounted doubles are ¥880.

Báiyún Hotel HOTEL $$$

(白云宾馆; Báiyún Bīnguǎn; ☑558 2708; www.baiyunhotel.com; dm ¥280-360, d/tr ¥1480/1680; ✻@) Dorms come with TV and shower, but are a bit old and worn; doubles (with private bathroom) pass muster but the hotel is sorely lacking compared with its competition. No English sign, but well signposted in English as White Clouds Hotel. Discounts knock dorms to ¥200 and doubles to ¥980.

THE SUMMIT 山顶

Ideally, Huángshān visits include nights on the summit. Note that room prices rise on Saturday and Sunday, and are astronomical during major holiday periods. Most hotel restaurants offer buffets (breakfast ¥60, lunch and dinner ¥100 to ¥140) plus a selection of standard dishes (fried rice ¥40), though it can be difficult to get service outside meal times. Hotels in Tāngkŏu can arrange tents (帐篷; zhàngpéng; ¥180) for camping at selected points on the summit.

Shílín Hotel HOTEL $$

(狮林饭店; Shílín Fàndiàn; ☑558 4040; www.shilin.com; dm with bathroom ¥300, d & tw ¥1680-1980; @) Cheaper rooms are devoid of views, but the pricier doubles are bright and clean and have flat-screen TVs. Cramped nine-bed dorms are also well kept, with bunk beds and shared bathroom; the block up the steps from the hotel has good views, as do some of the newer rooms in the main block and the villa behind. Discounted doubles are ¥1280.

Běihǎi Hotel HOTEL $$$

(北海宾馆; Běihǎi Bīnguǎn; ☑558 2555; www.hsbeihaihotel.com; dm ¥180, s & d ¥1880; @🛜) The four-star Běihǎi comes with professional service, money exchange, a mobile-phone charging point, cafe and 30% discounts during the week. Larger doubles with private bathroom have older fittings than the smaller, better-fitted-out doubles (same price). There are ¥1000 doubles in the three-star compound on a hill across the main square. Although it's the best-located hotel, it's also the busiest and lacks charm.

Páiyúnlóu Hotel HOTEL $$

(排云楼宾馆; Páiyúnlóu Bīnguǎn; ☑558 1558; www.paiyunlou.com; dm/d/tr ¥300/1480/1680; @) With an excellent location near Tiānhǎi Lake (Tiānhǎi Hú) and the entrance to the West Sea Canyon, plus three-star comfort, this place is recommended for those who prefer a slightly more tranquil setting. None of the regular rooms has any views, but the newer dorms are unobstructed and come with attached showers and TVs. Discounted dorms are ¥160 and doubles ¥780.

Xīhǎi Hotel HOTEL $$
(西海饭店; Xīhǎi Fàndiàn; ☎558 8888; www.
hsxihaihotel.cn; dm/d ¥380/1680; ❄@) Regular
rooms are tired but clean with heating and
hot water, but take a look at the doubles
first, as some face inwards. Discounts knock
dorms to ¥280 and doubles to ¥1280. A new
five-star block was under construction at the
time of research. It will be completed in 2013.

ℹ Information

Tāngkǒu

Bank of China (中国银行; Zhōngguó Yínháng;
☺8am-5pm) Southern end of Yanxi Jie.

Internet cafe (网吧; wǎngbā; per hr ¥3;
☺8am-midnight) On the west side of the river,
2nd floor.

Public Security Bureau (PSB; 公安局;
Gōng'ānjú; ☎556 2311) Western end of the
bridge.

On the Mountain

Most hotels on the mountain have internet
access areas for guests and nonguests, with
hourly rates of ¥15 to ¥20. Some have free wi-fi.

Bank of China (中国银行; Zhōngguó Yínháng;
☺8-11am & 2.30-5pm) Opposite Běihǎi Hotel.
Changes money. ATM that accepts international
cards.

Police station (派出所; pàichūsuǒ; ☎558
1388) Beside the bank.

ℹ Getting There & Away

Buses from Túnxī (aka Huángshān Shì) take
around one hour to reach Tāngkǒu from either
the long-distance bus station (¥18, one hour,
frequent, 6am to 5pm) or the train station (¥18,
departures when full, 6.30am to 5pm, may leave
as late as 8pm in summer). Buses back to Túnxī
from Tāngkǒu are plentiful, and can be flagged
down on the road to Túnxī (¥18). The last bus
back leaves at 5.30pm.

Tāngkǒu has two bus stations. When getting
into Tāngkǒu, you will be dropped at the south
long-distance bus station (南门换乘分中心;
nándàmén huànchéng fēnzhōngxīn). When
coming down the mountain, you may be dropped
at the east long-distance bus station (东岭换乘
分中心; dōnglǐng huànchéng fēnzhōngxīn) east
of the town centre and within walking distance
from Feicui Lu. Your hotel should be able to help
with bookings and pick-up or transfers. Major
destinations include:

Hángzhōu ¥100, 3½ hours, seven daily

Héféi ¥91, four hours, seven daily

Jiǔhuá Shān ¥47, 2½ hours, two daily (6.30am
and 2.20pm)

Nánjīng ¥93, five hours, three daily

Shànghǎi Y140, 6½ hours, five daily

Wǔhàn ¥235, nine hours, two daily (8.40am
and 5.30pm)

Yīxiàn ¥15, one hour, four daily (stops at
Hóngcūn and Xīdì)

ℹ Getting Around

Official tourist shuttles run between the two long-
distance bus stations and the hot springs area
(¥7), Yúngǔ station (云谷站; Yúngǔ zhàn; eastern
steps; ¥13) and Mercy Light Temple station (慈
光阁站; Cíguānggé zhàn; western steps; ¥13),
departing every 20 minutes from 6am to 5.30pm,
though they usually wait until enough people are
on board. A taxi to the eastern or western steps
will cost ¥50; to the hot springs area ¥30.

Jiǔhuá Shān 九华山

☎0566

The Tang-dynasty Buddhists who deter-
mined Jiǔhuá Shān to be the earthly abode
of the Bodhisattva Dizang (Ksitigarbha),
Lord of the Underworld, chose well. Often
shrouded in a fog that pours in through
the windows of its cliff-side temples, Jiǔhuá
Shān exudes an aura of otherworldliness,
heightened by the devotion of those who
come here to pray for the souls of the de-
parted. At times, though, it seems that the
commerce that drives the religion – religious
trinkets, good-luck charms and overpriced
joss sticks abound – detracts from the overall
experience. However, true believers seem to be
able to brush it all off with their fervency.
With its yellow-walled monasteries, flicker-
ing candles and the steady drone of Buddhist
chanting emanating from pilgrims' MP3
players, the mountain is an entirely different
experience from neighbouring Huángshān.

History

One of China's four Buddhist mountain
ranges, Jiǔhuá Shān was made famous by
the 8th-century Korean monk Kim Kiao Kak
(Jin Qiaojue), who meditated here for 75
years and was posthumously proclaimed to
be the reincarnation of Dizang. In temples,
Dizang is generally depicted carrying a staff
and a luminous jewel, used to guide souls
through the darkness of hell.

◉ Sights & Activities

Buses will let you off at Jīhuáshān
Xīnqūzhàn (九华山新区站). It's the local
bus terminus and main ticket office where
you purchase your ticket for the **mountain**
(admission 1 Mar-30 Nov ¥190, 1 Dec-29 Feb ¥140).
You'll also then need to buy a return shuttle

bus ticket (¥50, 20 minutes, every 30 minutes) from the counters on the left of the admission-ticket windows. The bus goes to **Jiǔhuájiē village**, the main accommodation area that is about halfway up the mountain (or, as locals say, at roughly navel height in a giant Buddha's potbelly). The shuttle terminates at the bus station just before the gate (大门; *dàmén*) leading to the village, from where the main street (芙蓉路; Furong Lu) heads south past hotels and restaurants. The main square is on the right off Furong Lu as you proceed up the street.

FREE **Zhīyuán Temple** TEMPLE
(祇园寺; Zhīyuán Sì; ⊘6.30am-8.30pm) Just past the village's main entrance on your left, worshippers hold sticks of incense to their foreheads and face the four directions at this enticingly esoteric yellow temple. There are chanting sessions in the evening that pilgrims can join.

FREE **Huàchéng Sì** TEMPLE
(化成寺; ⊘6.30am-8.30pm) The largest, most elaborate temple in town. Ornately carved dragons serve as handrails up the main steps. The eaves and beams of the buildings are painted in every colour imaginable and the icing on the cake is the three huge golden bodhisattvas that greet visitors: each one sits at least 25m tall and provides quite the setting come evening prayer time.

Mountain Summit TRAIL
The real highlight is walking up the mountain alongside the pilgrims, following a trail (天台正顶) that passes waterfalls, streams and countless nunneries, temples and shrines. The summit is on a mountain range behind the village. The hike up takes a leisurely four hours; count on about two to three hours to get back down to the village.

You can begin just after the village's main entrance, where a 30-minute hike up the ridge behind Zhīyuán Temple leads you to **Bǎisuì Gōng** (百岁宫; admission free; ⊘6am-5.30pm), an active temple built into the cliff in 1630 to consecrate the Buddhist monk Wu Xia, whose shrunken, embalmed body is coated in gold and sits shrivelled within an ornate glass cabinet in front of a row of pink lotus candles. If you don't feel like hiking, take the **funicular** (express/ordinary return ¥150/100, one way ¥55; ⊘7am-5.30pm) to the ridge.

From the top, walk south along the ridge past the **Dōngyá Temple** (东崖禅寺; Dōngyá Chánsì) to the **Huíxiāng Pavilion** (回香阁; Huíxiāng Gé), above which towers the seven-storey **10,000 Buddha Pagoda** (万佛塔; admission ¥10; ⊘6am-5.30pm), fashioned entirely from bronze and prettily lit at night. A western path leads to town, while the eastern one dips into a pleasant valley and continues past the **Phoenix Pine** (凤凰松; Fènghuáng Sōng) and the **cable car station** (one-way/return ¥75/140) to **Tiāntái Peak** (天台正顶; Tiāntái Zhèng Dǐng; 1304m). The two-hour walk to the summit is tough going, passing small temples and nunneries. The cable car ride takes 15 minutes each way. Note that there's still a 1km walk up flights of stairs even if you take the cable car!

The summit is slightly damp, with incense-like mist shrouding the area. Within the faded **Tiāntái Temple** (天台寺; Tiāntái Sì) on Tiāntái Peak, a statue of the Dizang Buddha is seated within the **Dìzàng Hall** (Dìzàng Diàn), while from the magnificent **10,000 Buddha Hall** (Wànfó Lóu) above, a huge enthroned statue of the Dizang Buddha gazes at the breathless masses appearing at his feet. Note the beams above your head that glitter with rows of thousands of Buddhas.

There's another trail to your right before the main stairs to the Tiāntái Temple. This one leads you to one of the highest and quietest points of the mountain, **Shíwáng Peak** (十王峰; Shíwáng Fēng; 1344m), where you can stop and let the rolling fog sweep past you.

An easier route is to take a bus (return trip included with the ¥50 bus ticket) from Jiǔhuájiē village up to the **Phoenix Pine area** (凤凰松; Fènghuáng Sōng) to take the cable car. You can also walk to the summit in two hours from here. The bus option does not pass Bǎisuì Gōng.

🛏 Sleeping & Eating

There are a large number of hotels in Jiǔhuájiē village along Furong Lu. Outside of major holiday periods, most dorm beds go for ¥30, while basic twins can be had from ¥80. Prices often double during weekends and public holidays. Cheap guesthouses can be found along Jiuhua Lao Jie.

There are numerous restaurants in the village around the main square and along Furong Lu and Huacheng Lu, which serve local dishes (from ¥10 to ¥100). The Zhīyuán Temple serves good ¥8 vegetarian meals (5.30am, 10.40am and 4.40pm). Food is plentiful on the way up; stop at one of the reasonable restaurants near the Phoenix Pine (about halfway up). Food costs rise the higher you climb.

Jùlóng Hotel
HOTEL $$$

(聚拢大酒店; Jùlóng Dàjiǔdiàn; ☑283 1368; Furong Lu; 芙蓉路; d & tw ¥1280-1480; ❋@) The long-standing Jùlóng's recent facelift has resulted in quality rooms decked out with easy-on-the-eyes hues of brown and gold. Flat-screen TVs, good bathrooms and friendly staff round out the experience. Discounts knock rooms down to ¥680 on weekdays, ¥880 on weekends. It's opposite Zhīyuán Temple, off Furong Lu as you enter the main gate.

Lóngquán Hotel
HOTEL $$

(龙泉饭店; Lóngquán Fàndiàn; ☑328 8888; Furong Lu; d & tw incl breakfast ¥780-880; ❋@) Located at the end of Furong Lu, this corner hotel has compact but smartly renovated rooms. Comfy beds, modern showers that don't choke, Chinese cable TV and terrible breakfast. Don't pay rack rate: weekend discounts are 50% and soar to 70% on weekdays. Walk to the end of Furong Lu and it's on the right as the road curves.

Shàngkètáng Hotel
HOTEL $$$

(上客堂; Shàngkètáng Bīnguǎn; ☑283 3888; Furong Lu; 芙蓉路; d & tw ¥1280; ❋@) Keeping in tune with the mountain, this prime-located hotel has gone with a Buddhist theme. Rooms are splashed out in rosewood furniture, flatscreen TVs and plush carpets (some rooms have a wet carpet smell though). Weekday discounts knock rooms down to ¥580, ¥780 on weekends. The inhouse vegetarian restaurant (dishes from ¥22) is very good.

Bǎisuìgōng Xiàyuàn Hotel
HOTEL $$

(百岁宫下院; Bǎisuìgōng Xiàyuàn; ☑283 3118; dm ¥30, d ¥200-240, tr ¥260-300; ❋) Pleasantly arranged around an old temple, this hotel has the right atmosphere and a good location. Standard rooms are just that – lino floors, small showers, but comfortable enough. The dorms (common shower) are appropriately priced. It's right beside Jùlóng Hotel.

❶ Information

Bank of China (中国银行; Zhōngguó Yínháng; 65 Huacheng Lu; ◷9am-5pm) Foreign exchange and 24-hour international ATM. West of the main square.

China Post (中国邮政; Zhōngguó Yóuzhèng; 58 Huacheng Lu; ◷8am-5.30pm) Off the main square.

Jiǔhuáshān Red Cross Hospital (九华山红十字医院; Jiǔhuáshān Hóngshízì Yīyuàn; ☑283 1330) After the pond on Baima Xincun.

❶ Getting There & Away

Buses from the Jiǔhuáshān xīnqūzhàn (九华山新区站) – the bus terminus and main Jiǔhuá Shān ticket office – run to/from the following destinations:

Héféi ¥75, 3½ hours, 10 daily

Huángshān ¥50, three hours, one daily (7am)

Nánjīng ¥75, three hours, four daily (6.20am, 7.20am, 8.40am and 1pm)

Qīngyáng ¥7, 30 minutes, frequent services (6.30am to 5pm)

Shànghǎi ¥115, six hours, two daily (7am and 2pm)

Tónglíng ¥21, one hour, two daily (10am and 12.40pm)

Túnxī ¥60, 3½ hours, one daily (7am)

Wǔhàn ¥129, six hours, one daily (7am)

More frequent buses leave from nearby Qīngyáng:

Hángzhōu ¥85, five hours, hourly

Héféi ¥70, two to three hours, hourly

Huángshān ¥55, three hours, three daily (7.30am, 9.30am and 2pm)

Nánjīng ¥70, three hours, hourly

Shànghǎi ¥110, six hours, hourly

Túnxī ¥60, two hours, two daily (7.30am and 2pm)

Yīxiàn ¥60, 2½ hours, two daily (8.30am and 1.30pm)

❶ Getting Around

The ¥50 shuttle ticket includes four bus rides: from the main ticket office to Jiǔhuájiē village (base for the mountain ascent), from the village to Phoenix Pine (cable car station) and back to the village, and from the village back to the main ticket office (first bus 6am, last bus 5pm).

To get to Phoenix Pine, catch the bus (every 30 minutes or when full) from the bus station north of the main gate (cross the bridge on the right after the Jùlóng Hotel). On busy days, you may need to queue for more than two hours for the cable car to/from the peak.

Héféi 合肥

☑0551 / POP 1.37 MILLION

The provincial capital, Héféi is a pleasant and friendly city with lively markets, pleasant lakes and parks but few other attractions. It's better used as a transport hub to the rest of Ānhuī.

Héféi

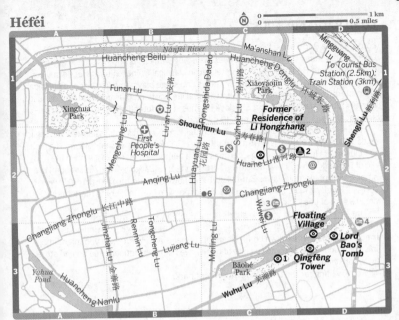

☉ Sights

Shengli Lu leads from the train station down to the Nánfēi River (Nánfēi Hé) then meets up with Shouchun Lu. Changjiang Zhonglu is the main commercial street and cuts east–west through the city. Between Suzhou Lu and Huancheng Donglu is Huaihe Lu Buxing Jie, a busy pedestrian shopping street.

Parks
PARKS

Among Héféi's green spaces, **Xiǎoyáojīn Park** (Xiǎoyáojīn Gōngyuán; Shouchun Lu; admission free; ☉6am-7pm) and **Bāohé Park** (Bāohé Gōngyuán; admission free; ☉6am-10pm) are the most pleasant and great places to relax and people watch. Bāohé Park contains various sights (see the boxed text, p394) worth paying for.

Former Residence of Li Hongzhang
HOUSE

(李鸿章故居; Lǐ Hóngzhāng Gùjū; Huaihe Lu; admission ¥20; ☉8.30am-6.30pm) Located along the Huaihe Lu Buxing Jie, this restored home of a local official from the late Qing dynasty sits stoically amid the hubbub of commercial activity all around.

Míngjiào Temple
TEMPLE

(明教寺; Míngjiào Sì; Huaihe Lu; admission ¥10; ☉6am-6pm) Small, atmospheric and looking out of place, this temple sits 5m above ground on the pedestrianised section of Huaihe Lu.

Héféi

☉ Top Sights
Floating Village	D3
Former Residence of Li Hongzhang	C2
Lord Bao's Tomb	D3
Qīngfēng Tower	D3

☉ Sights
1	Bǎo Gōng Temple	C3
2	Míngjiào Temple	D2

⊟ Sleeping
3	Green Tree Inn	C2
4	Westin	D3

✕ Eating
5	Lúzhōu Kǎoyā	C2

ⓘ Transport
6	China Eastern Airlines	C2

⊟ Sleeping & Eating

The city is awash with a range of hotels (but there are no hostels!). The area around the train station has Chinese budget- and midrange-category places (from ¥70; look for the characters 宾馆; *bīnguǎn*) and the main commercial street of Changjiang

LORD BAO: FAIR & JUST

Lord Bao, aka Bao Zheng, was an official in the Northern Song dynasty (960–1279). Owing to his sense of filial piety, fairness in dealing with cases and his stance against corruption, Lord Bao has been immortalised in classical Chinese literature. He still continues to be the subject of movies, TV shows and stage plays. And like all good classical characters, the line between fiction and his real life has been blurred. The Ming-dynasty interpretation made him into a Sherlock Holmes–type detective with several martial-arts capable sidekicks. He even has his own video game.

Héféi is his birthplace and Bāohé Park contains four **sights** (admission ¥50, incl English guide ¥200; ◷8am-6pm). The **floating village** (浮庄; Fúzhuāng; ◷8am-5.45pm) is a pleasant cluster of Hui-style buildings, gardens and a teahouse built on an island in the middle of the park's river. The **Bāo Gōng Temple** (包公祠; Bāogōng Cí; ◷7.30am-6pm) is a small memorial temple with a 3m-tall statue of Lord Bao, and the **Qīngfēng Tower** (清风园; Qīngfēng Yuán; ◷7.30am-6pm) is a 42m pavilion built in 1999 to mark the 1000th anniversary of Lord Bao's birth.

The most interesting of these sights is undoubtedly **Lord Bao's Tomb** (包公墓园; Bāogōng Mùyuán; ◷8am-5.45pm). A sombre stone tunnel leads you under his burial mound and to a large brown coffin where his remains are interred. As you might imagine, not much is left and various bits of bone have been hermetically sealed and stored away for scientific purposes.

We're waiting for the Lord Bao amusement park...

ĀNHUĪ HÉFÉI

Zhonglu is where you'll find the midrange hotel chains such as 7 Days, Home Inn and Hanting. For food, head to the pedestrianised Huaihe Lu Buxing Jie. The side streets have cheap eats and there's everything from fast-food chains to noodle shops. A night market sets up in the area too.

Westin
HOTEL $$$
(合肥万达威斯汀酒店; Héféi Wàndáwēisītīng Jiǔdiàn; ☎298 9888; www.westin.com/hefeibaohe; 150 Ma'anshan Lu; 马鞍山路150号; d from ¥1500; ✳@⌗≋) The nicest choice in the city, with a full range of modern facilities including a fitness centre, swimming pool, spa and good restaurants. Rooms have flat-screen TVs and soft bedding. There's a megamall across the street where you can shop at Gucci before watching an IMAX movie. Bāohé Park is just round the corner. There's 35% discount online.

Green Tree Inn
HOTEL $
(格林豪泰; Géli'n Háotài; ☎225 8188; www.998.com; 34 Hogxing Lu; 红星路34号; tw¥199, d¥169-189; ✳@) This reliable, modern midrange chain hotel offers compact, cheap and clean accommodation in a 24-room branch along a quiet residential street. More expensive rooms have a PC. There's food and shopping within walking distance.

Lúzhōu Kǎoyā
ROAST DUCK $
(庐州烤鸭店; 107 Suzhou Lu; dishes from ¥8) Sample some of Ānhuī's traditional roast duck (烤鸭; ¥20 per 500g), plus plenty of other noodle and dumpling dishes (from ¥8) at this buzzy eatery. Order at the counter and show the slip to the server, then take a seat. Grab some of the savoury roasted biscuits (¥1.70; look for the queue outside) to go.

Information

Bank of China (中国银行; Zhōngguó Yínháng) Wuwei Lu (Wuwei Lu); Shouchun Lu (Shouchun Lu) Currency exchange and international ATMs.

China Post (中国邮政; Zhōngguó Yóuzhèng; Changjiang Zhonglu) There's also a branch beside the train station.

First People's Hospital (第一人民医院; Dìyī Rénmín Yīyuàn; ☎265 2893; 322 Huaihe Lu)

Internet cafes (网吧; wǎngbā; per hr ¥2; ◷8am-midnight) A cluster is located about 80m west of Motel 168, off Huaihe Lu Buxing Jie. You'll need to show a passport.

Public Security Bureau (PSB; 公安局; Gōng'ānjú) On the northwest corner of the intersection of Shouchun Lu and Liu'an Lu.

Getting There & Away

Air

Daily flights include the following:

Běijīng ¥890, two hours
Guǎngzhōu ¥750, two hours
Shànghǎi ¥550, one hour
Xiàmén ¥600, 1½ hours

Bookings can be made at **China Eastern Airlines/Lanyu Travel** (东方航空售票处/兰宇旅行社; Dōngfāng Hángkōng Shòupiàochù; ☑262 9955; 158 Changjiang Zhonglu), situated next to the Húadū Hotel, and at the train station's ticket booking office.

Bus

Héféi has numerous bus stations for its relatively small size, but the following are the most useful ones.

The **Héféi long-distance bus station** (合肥长途汽车站; Héféi chángtú qìchēzhàn; 168 Mingguang Lu) has buses to numerous destinations in the surrounding provinces:

Hángzhōu ¥140, 5½ hours, six daily

Nánjīng ¥55, 2½ hours, every 30 minutes

Shànghǎi ¥180, seven hours, 12 daily (including sleeper)

Wǔhàn ¥185, 6½ hours, eight daily

The **east bus station** (汽车东站; qìchē dōngzhàn; Changjiang Donglu) runs buses to most destinations in Ānhuī:

Huángshān ¥115, four hours, four daily

Túnxī ¥115, four hours, hourly

Buses to Jiǔhuá Shān (¥88, 3½ hours, every 40 minutes) leave from the **tourist bus station** (旅游汽车站; lǚyóu qìchēzhàn; Zhanqian Jie) 500m west of train station. The so-called **main bus station** (客运总站; kèyùn zǒngzhàn; Zhanqian Jie), just outside the train station, is for local buses only.

Train

The train station is 4km northeast of the city centre. Express D trains:

Nánjīng ¥61, one hour, 27 daily

Shànghǎi Hóngqiáo ¥151 to ¥218, 3½ hours, 15 daily

Regular service destinations:

Běijīng ¥145 to ¥411, 10 to 16 hours, six daily

Shànghǎi ¥116 to ¥183, 6½ to 8½ hours, eight daily

Túnxī ¥66 to ¥162, six to seven hours, three daily

❶ Getting Around

Metered taxis are cheap, starting at ¥6. Taking a taxi (¥35, 30 minutes) is the best way to the airport, 11km south of the city centre. Rides from the city to the train station should cost ¥10.

ĀNHUĪ HÉFÉI

Hénán

POP 100 MILLION

Includes »

Zhèngzhōu 398
Nánjiēcūn 401
Sōng Shān &
Dēngfēng 401
Luòyáng 404
Around Luòyáng 407
Guōliàngcūn 409
Kāifēng 410
Zhūxiān Zhèn 415

Best Villages

» Guōliàngcūn (p409)
» Zhūxiān (p415)
» Nánjiēcūn (p401)

Best Historic Sites

» Shàolín Temple (p402)
» Kāifēng (p410)
» Luòyáng (p404)

Why Go?

Affluent Chinese roll their eyes at the mention of impoverished and land-locked Hénán (河南), yet the province's heritage takes us back to the earliest days of Chinese antiquity. Ancient capitals rose and fell in Hénán's north, where the capricious Yellow River (Huáng Hé) nourished the flowering of a great civilisation. Hénán is home to China's oldest surviving Buddhist temple and one of the country's most astonishing collections of Buddhist carvings, the Lóngmén Caves. There is also the Shàolín Temple, that legendary institution where the martial way and Buddhism found an unlikely and effective alliance. Hénán's inability to catch up with the rest of the land perhaps helps explain why the unusual village of Nánjiēcūn still sees a future in Maoist collectivism. Hénán is also home to the excellent walled town of Kāifēng and the 1000-year-old craft of woodblock printing in Zhūxiān.

When to Go
Zhèngzhōu

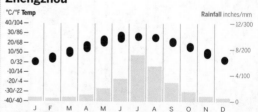

Apr Wángchéng Park in Luòyáng is a blaze of floral colour during the peony festival.

Jun Trips to cool Guōliàngcūn up in the Ten Thousand Immortals Mountains.

Sep & Oct Catch the lovely and fleeting north China autumn.

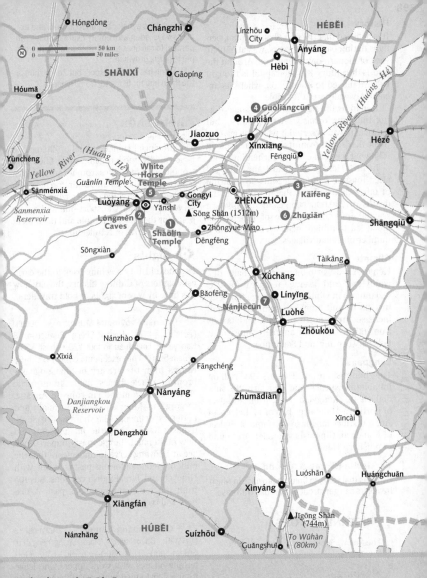

Hénán Highlights

① Fathom the martial mysteries of Shàolín boxing at the **Shàolín Temple** (p402)

② Seek enlightenment among the carved Bodhisattvas at the **Lóngmén Caves** (p407)

③ Take a trip back in time to **Kāifēng** (p410) and engage in some adventurous snacking at the night market

④ Hide away in cliff-top **Guōliàngcūn** (p409) – don't forget your sketchpad

⑤ Explore China's oldest Buddhist shrine: the **White Horse Temple** (p409) outside Luòyáng

⑥ Get acquainted with the ancient craft of Chinese woodblock printing in **Zhūxiān** (p415)

⑦ Rediscover communism with Chinese characteristics at **Nánjiēcūn** (p401)

History

It is believed that the first Shang capital, perhaps dating back 3800 years, was at Yǎnshī, west of modern-day Zhèngzhōu. Around the mid-14th century BC, the capital is thought to have moved to Zhèngzhōu, where its ancient city walls are still visible.

Hénán again occupied centre stage during the Song dynasty (AD 960–1279), but political power deserted it when the government fled south from its capital at Kāifēng following the 12th-century Juchen invasion.

In 1975 Hénán's Bǎnqiáo Dam collapsed after massive rainfall, leading to a string of other dam failures that resulted in the deaths of 230,000 people. In the 1990s a scandal involving the sale of HIV-tainted blood led to a high incidence of AIDS in a number of Hénán villages.

Climate

Hénán has a warm-temperate climate: dry, windy and cold (average temperature -2°C in January) in winter, hot (average temperature 28°C) and humid in summer. Rainfall increases from north to south and ranges from 60cm to 120cm annually; most of it falls between July and September.

Language

The lion's share of Hénán's 93 million inhabitants speaks one of nearly 20 sub-dialects of Zhōngyuán Huà, itself a dialect of northern Mandarin. Two of 15 dialects of Jin, a distinct language or simply a dialect of Mandarin (linguists wrangle), are found in northern Hénán.

❶ Getting There & Around

Hénán is that rarity in China: a province in which travellers can get in, out and around with ease.

PRICE INDICATORS

The following price indicators are used in this chapter:

Sleeping

$	less than ¥200
$$	¥200 to ¥500
$$$	more than ¥500

Eating

$	less than ¥35
$$	¥35 to ¥100
$$$	more than ¥100

Zhèngzhōu is a major regional rail hub, and expressways laden with comfy express buses run parallel to rail lines and stretch into southern parts of the province.

Luòyáng has a small airport but Zhèngzhōu is the main hub for flying to/from Hénán.

Zhèngzhōu 郑州

♪0371 / POP 2.03 MILLION

The provincial Hénán capital of Zhèngzhōu is a rapidly modernising smog-filled metropolis with few relics from its ancient past (courtesy of the Japanese air force, which bombed the city flat). Zhèngzhōu largely serves as a major transport hub and access point for the Shàolín Temple and the offbeat Maoist collective of Nánjiēcūn.

◉ Sights

Despite a history reaching back to the earliest chapters of Chinese history, the city now has little by way of sights to hold travellers.

FREE **Hénán Provincial Museum** MUSEUM
(河南省博物馆; Hénán Shěng Bówùguǎn; 8 Nongye Lu; English audio tour ¥20, deposit ¥200; ☺9am-5pm) The excellent collection here ranges from the artistry of Shang-dynasty bronzes, oracle bones made from turtle shells, relics from the Yīn ruins in Ānyáng, to gorgeous Ming and Qing porcelain and pottery specimens. The dioramas of Song-dynasty Kāifēng and the magnificent, and now obliterated, Tang-dynasty imperial palace at Luòyáng serve to underscore that the bulk of Hénán's glorious past is at one with Nineveh and Tyre. English captions. Bus 105 from the train station comes past. A taxi here will cost ¥18.

FREE **Chénghuáng Temple** TAOIST TEMPLE
(城隍庙; Chénghuáng Miào; Shangcheng Lu; ☺9am-6pm) This 600-year-old City God temple bustles with worshippers who leave its trees festooned with red ribbons and its entrances swirling with incense smoke. Take bus 2 from the train station.

FREE **Confucius Temple** TEMPLE
(文庙; Wén Miào; 24 Dong Dajie; ☺8.30am-5pm) Massively restored (at a cost of 30 million yuan!) into a pretty, photo-worthy temple replete with colourfully painted eves and ornate carvings. Take bus 60 or 85 from the train station.

Zhèngzhōu

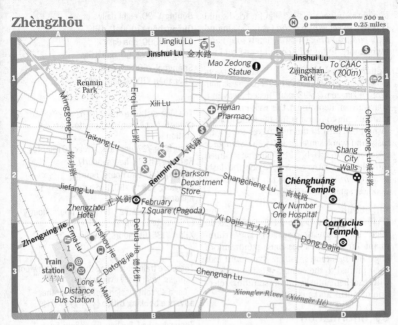

Sleeping

Your best bet for a cheap bed (¥60 to ¥150) is at one of the numerous guesthouses (宾馆, *bīnguǎn*) around the train station. Better digs are northeast of the train station at Jinshui Lu where a cluster of chains such as Crowne Plaza and Holiday Inn reside.

Sofitel HOTEL $$$
(索菲特国际饭店; Suǒfēitè Guójì Fàndiàn; ☑6595 0088; www.sofitel.com; 289 Chengdong Lu; d incl breakfast ¥2722; ☺✳@☎☲) Rooms at the five-star Sofitel are excellent as expected. The funky atrium area bathes the cafe (with a popular afternoon-tea buffet), bar and restaurants below in natural light. Other facilities include a health club. Discounts of 40%.

Jǐnjiāng Inn MOTEL $$
(锦江之星; Jǐnjiāng Zhīxīng; ☑6693 2000; 77 Erma Lu; s & d ¥189-219) Modern and swish looking, with crisp, sharp and well looked-after rooms (work desks, flat-screen TVs) in a block set back from the road.

Eating & Drinking

Five hundred metres north of the train station is the busy February 7 Sq, aka Èrqī Guǎng Chǎng (二七广场). Nearby are shops, restaurants and a night market.

Zhèngzhōu

◉ Top Sights
Chénghuáng Temple..........................D2
Confucius Temple...............................D3

⊜ Sleeping
1 Jǐnjiāng Inn.....................................A3
2 Sofitel...D1

⊗ Eating
3 Guǎngcǎi Market.............................B2
4 Hénán Shífǔ....................................B2

⊖ Drinking
5 Target Pub.......................................C1

Look out for the large white pagoda. Bus 26 from the train station takes you past listed options.

Guǎngcǎi Market MARKET $
(光彩市场; Guǎngcǎi Shìchǎng; snacks ¥1-5; ☺8am-9pm) Gritty, perhaps, but this crowded warren of food and clothes stalls in the block northeast of Èrqī Tǎ is always packed. Try *málà tàng* (麻辣烫; spicy soup with skewered vegies and meat), *chūn juǎn* (春卷; spring rolls), *ròujiāmó* (肉夹馍; spicy meat in a bun), *càijiābǐng* (菜夹饼; vegetables in a bun); *guōtiē* (锅贴; fried dumplings),

bàokǎo xiān yóuyú (爆烤鲜鱿鱼; fried squid kebabs), sweet *xìngrén chá* (杏仁茶; almond tea), *yángròu tāng* (羊肉汤; lamb soup) and much more. Enter via Remin Lu or Erqi Lu.

Hénán Shífǔǔ   CHINESE HENAN $
(河南食府; ☑6622 2108; 25 Renmin Lu; meals from ¥25; ⊙10am-2pm & 5-9.30pm) Tucked away in a courtyard off Renmin Lu, this well-known restaurant's photo menu is full of exotic-looking dishes, but turn to the rear pages for cheap, tasty and wholesome fare. Try the *Shànghǎi xiǎolóngbāo* (上海小笼包; Shànghǎi steamed dumplings; meat/vegie ¥12/10) or the tasty *yángròu huìmiàn* (羊肉烩面; lamb-braised noodles; small/large ¥8/12).

Target Pub   PUB
(目标酒吧; Mùbiāo Jiǔbā; ☑138 0385 7056; 10 Jingliu Lu; ⊙8pm-last customer) The triumphant Target Pub, a seasoned panorama of flags, old banknotes, rattan chairs and half a car pinned to the ceiling, hits the bullseye with excellent music, an outstanding selection of spirits and a laid-back vibe.

ℹ Information

Bank of China (中国银行; Zhōngguó Yínháng; 8 Jinshui Lu; ⊙9am-5pm)

China Post (中国邮政; Zhōngguó Yóuzhèng; ⊙8am-8pm) South end of train station concourse.

City Number One Hospital (市一院; Shì Yīyuàn; Dong Dajie)

Hénán Pharmacy (河南大药房; Hénán Dàyàofáng; ☑6623 4256; 19 Renmin Lu; ⊙24hr)

Industrial & Commercial Bank of China (ICBC; 工商银行; Gōngshāng Yínháng; Renmin Lu) 24-hour ATM.

Internet cafes (网吧; per hour ¥3 to ¥5) clustered near the train station.

Public Security Bureau (PSB; 公安局出入境管理处; Gōng'ānjú Chūrùjìng Guǎnlǐchù; ☑6962 0350; 90 Xihuanghe Donglu; ⊙8.30am-noon & 3-6.30pm Jun-Aug, 2-5.30pm Mon-Fri Sep-May) For visa extensions; take bus 135 or 114.

ℹ Getting There & Away

Air

The **Civil Aviation Administration of China** (CAAC; 中国民航; Zhōngguó Mínháng; ☑6599 1111; 3 Jinshui Lu, at Dongmin Lu), east of the city centre, sells flight tickets, as does the **ticket office** (售票处; shòupiàochù; ☑6677 7111) at the **Zhèngzhōu Hotel** (郑州大酒店; Zhèngzhōu Dàjiǔdiàn; 8 Xinglong Jie). Look for the sign that reads Zhengzhou Airport ticket office. Flights include the following:

Běijīng ¥790, eight daily

Guǎngzhōu ¥1000, 11 daily

Guìlín ¥1300, one daily

Hong Kong ¥2200, one daily

Shànghǎi ¥600, 12 daily

Shēnzhèn ¥1000, nine daily

Bus

The long-distance bus station (长途汽车站; chángtú qìchēzhàn) is opposite the train station.

Dēngfēng ¥27, one hour, every 30 minutes

Kāifēng ¥16, 1½ hours, hourly

Línyǐng ¥40, two hours, hourly

Luòyáng ¥38 to ¥50, two hours, every 15 minutes

Shàolín Temple ¥27, 1½ to 2½ hours, hourly (7.40am to 11.40pm)

Xī'ān ¥135, 6½ hours, hourly

Train

There are trains, including the Běijīng–Kowloon express, to virtually everywhere.

For a ¥5 commission, get tickets at the **advance booking office** (火车预售票处; huǒchē yùshòupiàochù; ☑6835 6666; cnr Zhengxing Jie & Fushou Jie; ⊙8am-5pm).

Ānyáng D train, hard/soft seat ¥55/65, 1½ hours, five daily

Běijīng West D train, hard/soft seat ¥202/243, 5½ hours, six daily

Jǐ'nán D train, hard/soft seat ¥194/273, 5½ hours, 12.28pm

Kāifēng D train, hard/soft seat ¥19/24, 30 minutes, three daily

Luòyáng ¥17 to ¥20, 2½ hours, regular

Luòyáng Lóngmén G train, hard/soft seat ¥60/90, 35 minutes, 10 daily

Nánjīng D train, hard/soft seat ¥205/288, 5½ hours, three daily

Shànghǎi D train, hard/soft seat ¥238/381, 6½ hours, three daily

Xī'ān G train, hard/soft seat ¥230/370, 2½ hours, regular

ℹ Getting Around

Buses for the airport (¥15, one hour, from 6.30am to 7pm) leave every hour from the Zhèngzhōu Hotel. A taxi (40 minutes) costs around ¥100.

Bus 26 travels from the train station past 7 February Sq, along Renmin Lu and Jinshui Lu to the CAAC office. Local buses cost ¥1 to ¥2.

Metro Line 1 along Renmin Lu and the north–south Line 2 following Zijingshan Lu are under construction.

Taxi fares start at ¥6 (¥8 at night).

Nánjiēcūn 南街村

South of Zhèngzhōu, **Nánjiēcūn** (www.nanjie cun.cn; admission free) is China's very last Maoist collective (*gōngshè*). There are no Buddhist temples or mist-wreathed mountain panoramas, but a trip to Nánjiē is nonetheless one back in time: a journey to the puritanical and revolutionary China of the 1950s, when Chairman Mao was becoming a supreme being, money was yesterday's scene and the menace of karaoke had yet to be prophesied by even the most paranoid party faithful.

The first inkling you are stepping into an entirely different world appears when you notice the streets: perfectly clean willow tree-lined streets run in straight lines with a kind of austere socialist beauty, past noodle factories, schools and rows of identikit blocks of workers' flats emblazoned with vermillion communist slogans. Beatific portraits of Chairman Mao gaze down on all.

From the main entrance, continue along the main drag, Yingsong Dadao (颍松大道). The oddity continues when you drop your bag off at the Nánjiēcūn Supermarket (南街村超市; Nánjiēcūn Chāoshì), where smiling young girls in revolutionary greens accept no fee for bag storage. Wow.

Make your way along Yingsong Dadao to **East is Red Square** (东方红广场; Dōngfānghóng Guǎngchǎng), where guards maintain a 24-hour vigil at the foot of a statue of Chairman Mao, and portraits of Marx, Engels, Stalin and Lenin (the original 'Gang of Four') rise up on all four sides. The square is deluged with shrill propaganda broadcast from speakers in true 1950s style. A short stroll to the left brings you to **Cháoyáng Gate Square** (朝阳门广场; Cháoyángmén Guǎngchǎng) and the rebuilt, traditional architecture of **Cháoyáng Gate** (朝阳门; Cháoyáng Mén).

However, once you look closer, you'll realise that all is not well. Stroll to the edges of the town and you'll see dilapidated buildings with broken windows. A strong whiff of sewage permeates the northeastern section. Walk into a public toilet and you'll find the taps locked. The Culture Garden where 'tourists can seek for the pioneering and developing history of people in Nanjiecun by watching video tapes, pictures and material objects', is closed. Still, it's a relief to find a hermetically sealed bubble of space, cleanliness and quietness against the messy backdrop of frenetic China.

Eating

A clutch of restaurants can be found along the western end of Zhongyuan Lu (中原路), to the south of and parallel with Yingsong Dadao. There's also a large workers' eating house on the right near the main entrance. Look for the sign 清真快餐. It shuts at 1.30pm. Alternatively, head through Cháoyáng Gate to the boisterous market street in real China, which is peppered with restaurants.

Information

Avoid the **Tourist Service Centre** (旅游接待处; Yóukè Jiēdàichù; 7.30am-5.30pm) at the west end of Yingsong Dadao as they'll ask you to buy an admission ticket for ¥80. If you do take the offer up, it comes with a Chinese-speaking guide and a jaunt around town on an electric cart.

Getting There & Away

From Zhèngzhōu bus station, buses (¥40, two hours) run south every hour between 6.20am and 6.20pm to the bus station at Línyíng (临颍), from where it's a ¥3 *sānlúnchē* (pedicab) journey south to Nánjiēcūn.

Sōng Shān & Dēngfēng 嵩山、登封

☑ 0371

In Taoism, Sōng Shān is regarded as the central mountain, symbolising earth (*tǔ*) among the five elements and occupying the axis directly beneath heaven. Despite this Taoist affiliation, the mountains are also home to one of China's most famous and legendary Zen (Chan) Buddhist temples, the Shàolín Temple. There are two main ranges in the area, the 1494m-high **Tàishì Shān** (太室山) and the 1512m-high **Shàoishì Shān** (少室山) whose peaks compose Sōng Shān about 80km west of Zhèngzhōu. Both peaks can be ascended.

At the foot of Tàishì Shān, 12km southeast of the Shàolín Temple and 74km from Zhèngzhōu, sits the squat little town of **Dēngfēng**. Tatty in parts, it is used by travellers as a base for trips to surrounding sights or exploratory treks into the hills.

The main bus station is in the far east of town. Most hotels and restaurants are strung out on or near Zhongyue Dajie (中岳大街), the main east-west street, and Shaolin Dadao (少林大道), parallel to the south. The Shàolín Temple is a 15-minute bus ride northwest of town.

👁 Sights & Activities

Shàolín Temple
BUDDHIST TEMPLE

(少林寺; Shàolín Sì; ☎6370 2503; admission ¥100; ⏰8am-6.30pm) The largely rebuilt Shàolín Temple is a victim of its own success. A frequent target of war, the temple was last torched in 1928, and the surviving halls – many of recent construction – are today besieged by marauding tour groups. Accounts vary but the temple seems to have been founded in approximately AD 500. Its claim to fame, the *gōngfū* (kung fu) based on varying animals and insects, was reputedly the result of a later monk Damo developing a set of exercises for monks to keep fit. The rest is (mainly celluloid) history.

A visit to Shàolín Temple requires a certain Zen mentality to manage the visiting hordes. You could spend an entire day or two as there are quite a few smaller temples to visit and peaks to hike up and around. Coming through the main entrance, you'll pass several *gōngfū* schools. On the right about 500m in, is a square showcasing impressive daily 30-minute outdoor **martial arts performances**. Next door is the **Wushu Training Centre** also with shows featuring monks tumbling around and breaking sticks and metal bars over their heads.

The main temple itself is another 600m along. Many buildings such as the main **Daxiong Hall** (大雄宝殿; Dàxióng Bǎodiàn; reconstructed in 1985) – were levelled by fire in 1928. Some halls only date back as far as 2004. Among the oldest structures at the temple are the **decorative arches** and **stone lions**, both outside the main gate.

At the rear, the **West Facing Hall** (西方圣人殿; Xīfāng Shèngrén Diàn) contains the famous depressions in the floor, apocryphally the result of generations of monks practising their stance work, and huge colour frescos. Always be on the lookout for the ubiquitous Damo (Bodhidharma), whose bearded Indian visage gazes sagaciously from stelae or peeks out from temple halls.

Across from the temple entrance, the Arhat Hall within the **Shífāng Chányuàn** (十方禅院) contains legions of crudely fashioned *luóhàn* (monks who have achieved enlightenment and passed to nirvana at death). The **Pagoda Forest** (少林塔林; Shàolín Tǎlín), a cemetery of 248 brick pagodas including the ashes of an eminent monk, is well worth visiting if you get here ahead of the crowds. Sadly, where visitors were once allowed to wander amongst the pagodas, the area is now only viewable via a wooden fence circuit.

As you face the Shàolín Temple, paths on your left lead up **Wǔrǔ Peak** (五乳峰; Wǔrǔ Fēng). Flee the tourist din by heading towards the peak to see the **cave** (达摩洞; Dámó Dòng) where Damo meditated for nine years; it's 4km uphill. From the base, you may spot the peak and the cave, marked by a large bodhisattva figure. En route to the cave, detour to the **Chūzǔ Temple** (初祖庵; Chūzǔ Ān), a quiet and battered counterpoint to the main temple. Its main structure is the oldest wooden one in the province (c AD 1125).

At 1512m above sea level and reachable on the Sōngyáng Cableway (Sōngyáng Suǒdào; ¥40 return, 20 minutes), **Shàoshì Shān** (少室山) is the area's tallest peak. The area beyond the cable car is home to the peak and **Èrzǔ Nunnery** (二祖庵; Èrzǔ Ān) with four wells where you can sample its various tasting waters (sour, sweet, peppery and bitter).

There's also a scenic trek to neighbouring Sānhuángzhài. The trek takes about six hours return, covers 15km and goes past craggy rock formations along a path that often hugs the cliff to the 782-step **Rope Bridge** (连天吊桥; Lián Tiān Diào Qiáo). To begin the hike, look for the small Chinese sign which leads to **Sānhuángzhài** (三皇寨). It's a long and hard-going hike, so for safety reasons, monks recommend trekking with a friend.

If you'd prefer an easier hike, head to the newer Shàolín Cableway (Shàolín Suǒdào; ¥60 return, 40 minutes) which takes you to Sānhuángzhài. From there, it's a shorter hike to the bridge. Both cableways can be found just beyond the Pagoda Forest. Note that the bridge may be closed at times for repair or during inclement weather. Start hikes early, as you don't want to be caught out in the dark.

To reach the Shàolín Temple, take a bus (¥3, 15 minutes) from Dēngfēng's west bus station (西站; xīzhàn) on Zhongyue Dajie to the drop-off point. The temple compound office is across the road. Within the compound, you can choose to take a buggy (¥10, from 8am to 6pm) to the main temple entrance, or walk (20 minutes). Alternatively, take a minibus from either Luòyáng or Zhèngzhōu (¥19.50 to ¥27, 1½ to 2½ hours) to the drop-off. From the temple, return buses leave from the drop-off point (last bus at around 8pm). A taxi to the temple from Dēngfēng will cost ¥30 (unofficial fare, no meter).

Sōngyáng Academy
ACADEMY

(嵩阳书院; Sōngyáng Shūyuàn; admission ¥30; ⊙7am-6pm) At the foot of Tàishì Shān sits one of China's oldest academies, the lush and well-tended Sōngyáng Academy, a building complex that dates to AD 484 and rises up the hill on a series of terraces. In the courtyard are two cypress trees believed to be around 4500 years old – and they're still alive!

Both bus 2 and bus 6 (¥1) from Dēngfēng run to the Sōngyáng Academy.

Mt Tàishì
MOUNTAIN

(太室山; Tàishì Shān; admission ¥50; ⊙8am-6pm) A 2km walk from the Sōngyáng Academy, the pretty **Sōngyuè Pagoda** (嵩岳塔; Sōngyuè Tǎ), built in AD 509, is China's oldest brick pagoda. Nearby is the **Fǎwáng Temple** (法王寺; Fǎwáng Sì), ringed by mountains and first established in AD 71. Most visitors however, come here to ascend Mt Tàishì. To begin the climb, look for the large stone path just beyond the Sōngyáng Academy. The Junji Peak is 1470m high and isn't much more than a viewing point (sorry, no temple here!). The challenging climb up stone steps takes three to four hours (one way).

Zhōngyuè Temple
TAOIST TEMPLE

(中岳庙; Zhōngyuè Miào; admission ¥30; ⊙6.30am-6.30pm) A few kilometres east of Dēngfēng, the ancient and hoary Zhōngyuè Miào is a colossal active Taoist monastery complex that originally dates back to the 2nd century BC. Less visited, the complex – set against a mountainous background and with its monks wearing traditional dress and top knots – exudes a more palpable air of reverence than its Buddhist sibling, the Shàolín Temple. Besides attending the main hall dedicated to the Mountain God, walk through the **Huàsān Gate** (化三门; Huàsān Mén) and expunge *pengju, pengzhi* and *pengjiao* – three pestilential insects that respectively inhabit the brain, tummy and feet. Drop by the four **Iron Men of Song**, rubbed by visitors to cure ailments and pay a visit to the **Sixty Gods Hall**, where visitors pay respects to the God corresponding to their birth year. From Dēngfēng, take the green bus 2 along Zhongyue Dajie.

🛏 Sleeping & Eating

The stretch of Chonggao Lu (崇高路) around the Shàolín Travelers Hostel has eating options galore. You'll also find plenty of restaurants in town along Zhongyue Dajie (中岳大街) between Jiming Jie (鸡鸣街) and Songshan Lu (嵩山路) – ¥5 to ¥7 taxi rides from most hotels. At night, look for barbecue stalls set up outside restaurants. Local specialities are thickly cut handmade noodles in broth (烩面; *huì miàn*; ¥6 to ¥8) and barbecue lamb skewers (羊肉串; *yángroù chuàn*; ¥2).

Shàolín Travelers Hostel
HOSTEL **$**

(旅行家青年旅舍; Lǚxíngjiā Qīngnián Lǚshè; ☑159 8188 3801; www.shaolintravelershostel.hostel.com; 308 Chonggao Luxi; 崇高路西308号; dm ¥30, d & tw with/without bathroom ¥160/100; ✳@🛜) The 10-bed dorms are roomy, but basic with no lockers, while the private rooms are large with foam mattresses and an odd stone-slab decor. The owner Coco speaks English and can help with recommendations. The massage shop (¥60, one hour) next door can work out the kinks after a hard day's hike. It's a ¥7 taxi ride from the main bus station or take bus 1 (¥1) and stop along Shaosi Lu (少室路).

Shàolín Hotel
HOTEL **$$**

(少林宾馆; Shàolín Bīnguǎn; ☑6016 1616; 66 Zhongyue Dajie; 中岳大街66号; d/tr ¥320/500; ✳) Bright and cheery staff, good discounts and clean rooms make this neat and trim hotel on Zhongyue Dajie a good choice. There's no English sign, so look for the four-storey white building east of Dicos (a fast-food restaurant) with the yellow and red sign. Take bus 1 from the main bus station or a ¥7 taxi ride. Discounts of 50%.

Shàolín International Hotel
HOTEL **$$$**

(少林国际大酒店; Shàolín Guójì Dàjiǔdiàn; ☑6285 6868; www.shaolinhotel.com; 20 Shaolin Dadao; 少林大道20号; s/d/ste ¥680/780/1180; ✳) Calling itself a four-star hotel, this is more like a smartish three-star, with the obligatory scads of black Buicks parked outside. Jiang Zemin stayed here, leaving his photo in the lobby and making the hotel popular with visiting Chinese. A taxi from the main bus station will cost ¥7. Discounts of 40%.

ℹ Information

Bank of China (中国银行; Zhōngguó Yínháng) 52 Zhongyue Dajie (⊙9am-5pm Mon-Fri); 186 Shaolin Dadao (⊙9am-noon & 2-5pm Mon-Fri) 24-hour ATM and forex.

HÉNÁN SŌNG SHĀN & DĒNGFĒNG

China International Travel Service (CITS; 中国国际旅行社; Zhōngguó Guójì Lǚxíngshè; ☑6288 3442; Beihuan Lu Xiduan) Helpful, English-speaking staff.

China Post (中国邮政; Zhōngguó Yóuzhèng; cnr Zhongyue Dajie & Wangji Lu)

No 2 People's Hospital (第二人民医院; Dì'èr Rénmín Yīyuàn; ☑6289 9999; 189 Shaolin Dadao) On the main road.

ⓘ Getting There & Around

The **Dēngfēng bus station** (总站; zǒng zhàn) is in the east of town; jump on bus 1 (¥1) to reach Zhongyue Dajie and the town centre. There's also a **west bus station** (西站; xī zhàn) which some buses head to after dropping people off at the main station. Buses to and from Zhèngzhōu (¥27, 1½ hours) and Luòyáng (¥19.50, two hours) run every 30 minutes from the main station. To purchase tickets for trains departing from Zhèngzhōu, go to the **train ticket office** (☑8am-noon & 2-5pm) at the gate of the **Sōngyáng Yingbin Hotel** (130 Shaolin Dadao). Taxis are a cheap and easy way to get around. Fares start at ¥5 but use those with meters.

Luòyáng   洛阳

☑0379 / POP 1.4 MILLION

The capital of 13 dynasties, until the Northern Song dynasty shifted its capital to Kāifēng in the 10th century instead, Luòyáng was one of China's true dynastic citadels. Charted on maps of the town, the mighty Sui- and Tang-dynasty walls sat in an imposing rectangle north and south of the Luò River, while the city boasted 1300 Buddhist temples. It's hard today to conceive that Luòyáng was once the very centre of the Chinese universe and the eastern capital of the great Tang dynasty. The heart of the magnificent Sui-dynasty palace complex was centred on the point where today's Zhongzhou Lu and Dingding Lu intersect in a frenzy of traffic.

On the surface, Luòyáng may look like any fume-laden modern Chinese town, but spend some time here and you'll find the people more patient and the streets actually less frantic than Zhèngzhōu. Nearby, the magnificently sculpted Lóngmén Caves by the banks of the Yī River remain one of China's most prized Buddhist treasures and the annual **peony festival**, centred on Wángchéng Park in April, is colourful fun. The buzzy old town, where the bulk of Luòyáng's history survives, is in the east.

◉ Sights & Activities

FREE **Luòyáng Museum**   MUSEUM
(洛阳市博物馆; Luòyáng Shì Bówùguǎn; Nietai Lu; ☑9am-4.30pm Tue to Sun) The location, in the south of town, is inconvenient, but where else in the city is there space to build such an imposing new building that stands toe to toe with both Shànghǎi and Běijīng's best? The museum houses an exhausting number of displays across two huge floors and is one of the few places you can get your finger on the pulse of ancient Luòyáng. It has an absorbing collection of Tang-dynasty three-colour *sāncǎi* porcelain and traces the city's rise through the various dynasties' pottery, bronzeware and other resplendent objects. There's also an incongruently stark room with a massive collection of material on Mao Zedong – there are hundreds of books and magazines, each one carefully wrapped in cellophane. Take bus 77 from the train station. A taxi from town will cost ¥20.

Old Town   HISTORIC AREA
Any Chinese city with any sense of history has its old town (老城区; *lǎochéngqū*). Luòyáng's old town lies east of the rebuilt **Lijīng Gate** (丽京门; Lìjīng Mén), where a maze of narrow and winding streets rewards exploration, and old courtyard houses survive amid modern outcrops. From the gate, stroll down Xi Dajie (西大街) along a stone pathway. Look out for an indoor **antique market** (文博城古玩字画玩中心; Wénbóchéng Gǔwán Zìhuàwán Zhōngxīn) on your left. There are three storeys of antique stalls stocking everything from Tang-era pottery, Mao busts, old bank notes, pipes, jades and other dusty trinkets. Further along and originally dating to 1555, the old **Drum Tower** (鼓楼; Gǔ Lóu) rises up at the east end of Dong Dajie (东大街), itself lined with traditional rooftops. The rest of Dong Dajie is a hubbub of local life: hairdressers, noodle stalls and tradesmiths all cluster within crumbling old houses.

Wángchéng Square & Around SQUARE, MUSEUM
(王城广场; Wángchéng Guángchǎng; Zhongzhou Zhonglu) This square is the meeting place for locals who come to play chess and cards under fluttering red country flags. At night, there's line dancing, and enterprising individuals set up makeshift massage beds along the stone seating ledges. Across Zhongzhou Zhonglu and marked with a huge statue of six rearing horses is the underground

Luòyáng

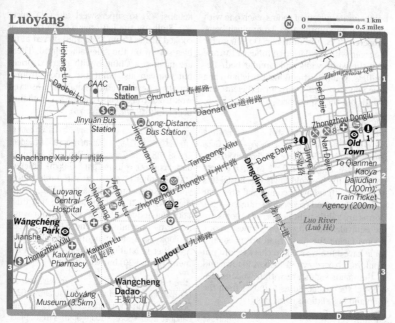

Eastern Zhou Royal Horse and Carriage Museum (admission ¥30; 9am-5pm winter, 8.30am-7pm summer). The principal draw is the unearthed remains of a former emperor's royal horses. These carriage-bearing horses were buried alive when the emperor passed on. The exhibition is filled out with dioramas of the former imperial city and with other archaeological finds.

Wángchéng Park   PARK
(王城公园; Wángchéng Gōngyuán; Zhongzhou Zhonglu; admission park & zoo ¥25, park, zoo & cable car ¥30, after 7pm ¥15, peony festival ¥50-55) One of Luòyáng's indispensable green lungs, this park is the site of the annual **peony festival**; held in April, the festival sees the park flooded with colour, floral aficionados, photographers, girls with garlands on their heads and hawkers selling huge bouquets of flowers. Unfortunately, the park is home to a decrepit zoo for which you're forced to pay an admission charge. There's also an amusement park (rides ¥15 to ¥20). Artists ply their trade along the walls on the left as your turn into the park.

🛏 Sleeping

Luòyáng has a large range of hotels in every budget bracket dotted all over the city.

Luòyáng

⊙ Top Sights
Old Town D2
Wángchéng Park A3

⊙ Sights
1 Drum Tower D2
2 Eastern Zhou Royal Horse &
   Carriage Museum B2
3 Lìjīng Gate D2
4 Wángchéng Square B2

🛏 Sleeping
5 Christian's Hotel B2
   Lìjīngmén Hotel .... (see 3)
6 Luòyáng Yijia International
   Youth Hostel D1

✗ Eating
7 Carrefour B2
8 Old Town Market D2
9 Zhēn Bù Tóng Fàndiàn D2

TOP CHOICE **Christian's Hotel**   BOUTIQUE HOTEL $$$
(克丽司汀酒店; Kèlìsītīng Jiǔdiàn; ☎6326 6666; www.5xjd.com; 56 Jiefang Lu; 解放路56号; d & tw ¥819-919; ❀@) We have no idea who Christian is, but he sure knows how to deck out a hotel room. This boutique hotel scores

points for its variety of rooms, each one with a kitchen and dining area, large plush beds, flat-screen TVs, and mini-bar. Do you go for the room with the dark rich tones or the one with the white walls and circular bed? Regardless, you'll be thanking Christian each time you step into the room. Efficient staff rounds out the experience.

Luòyáng Yijia International Youth Hostel
HOSTEL $

(洛阳易家国际青年旅舍; Luòyáng Yìjiā Guójì Qīngnián Lûshè; ☏6526 0666; 329 Zhongzhou Donglu; 中州东路329号; dm ¥40, d & tw ¥130; ❋@☎) Located in the busy old town, this hostel hits its stride with its lively communal area, bar and excellent food (pizzas ¥32, burgers ¥26). Dorms are a little tight but private rooms are the equivalent of a two-star Chinese room. Rooms facing the main road are noisy and some have a funky smell, so check before you plonk your bags down. Transport to town and all the major sights are within walking distance of the hostel. Buses 5 and 41 from the train and bus stations come past.

Lìjīngmén Hotel
HOTEL $$

(丽京门宾馆; Lìjīngmén Bīnguǎn; ☏6350 3381; Lìjīng Gate; 丽京门; s & d ¥240-320; ❋@) With an enviable position within the restored Lìjīng Gate and facing a canal, one might overlook the compact rooms and showers. Decor is *de rigueur* Chinese two-star standard: hard beds, flat-screen TV, kettle and clean sheets. The more expensive rooms are larger, have windows facing the canal and are equipped with internet-enabled PCs. Discounts of 50%.

✗ Eating

Luòyáng's famous 'water banquet' (水席; *shuǐxí*) resonates along China's culinary grapevine. The main dishes of this 24-course meal are soups and are served up with the speed of flowing water – hence the name.

A handy branch of the **Carrefour** (家乐福; Jiālèfú) supermarket can be found near the corner of Tanggong Xilu and Jiefang Lu in the **Today mall** (新都汇; Xīndòuhuì) where you can also find a wide variety of things to eat. The old town is also rife with everything from noodles to dumplings, hotpot and more.

Old Town Market
MARKET $

(南大街夜市; Nándàjiē yèshì; cnr Xi Dajie & Dong Dajie & north to Zhongzhou Donglu; ☻5-10pm) Lively night market with a cornucopia of snacks from *yángròu chuàn* (羊肉串; lamb kebabs; ¥2) to super-sweet *zhī* (汁; juice; ¥3). Stalls on the left offer a wide range of cooked dishes (from ¥8 to ¥58) served at tables set up on the sidewalk behind. There are menus in Chinese with marked prices but you can just point and choose from a variety of seafood and vegetables, all served wok-fried. You can also ask for a pint of draft beer (生啤酒; *shēngpíjiǔ*; ¥5).

Qianmen Kaoya Dajiudian
ROAST DUCK $$

(前门烤鸭大酒店; Qiánménkǎoyá Dàjiǔdiàn; ☏636 0188; cnr Zhongzhou Donglu & Minzu Jie; duck from ¥60; ☻10am-2pm & 5-9pm) Efficient staff shepherd you to a stiff table where you'll be presented with a tome-like picture menu. Order a roast duck (烤鸭; half duck ¥60, whole duck ¥110) served up four ways. An army of white-clad chefs then proceed to cook up a storm in the kitchen. There are other vegetable and meat dishes on the menu (from ¥20) but why bother?

Zhēn Bù Tóng Fàndiàn
CHINESE HENAN $$

(真不同饭店; One of a Kind Restaurant; ☏6399 5080; 369 Zhongzhou Donglu; dishes ¥15-45, water banquet from ¥688; ☻10am-9pm) Huge place behind a colourful green, red, blue and gold traditional facade. If you can rustle up a large group, this is the place to come for a water-banquet experience; if 24 courses and ¥688 seems a little excessive, you can opt to pick individual dishes from the menu.

ℹ Information

Internet cafes (per hour ¥3) are scattered around the train station and sprinkled along nearby Jinguyang Lu.

Bank of China (中国银行; Zhōngguó Yínháng; ☻8am-4.30pm) The Zhongzhou Xilu office exchanges travellers cheques and has an ATM that accepts MasterCard and Visa. There's also a branch on the corner of Zhongzhou Lu and Shachang Nanlu. Another branch just west of the train station has foreign-exchange services.

China Post (中国邮政; Zhōngguó Yóuzhèng; Zhongzhou Zhonglu)

Industrial & Commercial Bank of China (ICBC; 工商银行; Gōngshāng yínháng; 228 Zhongzhou Zhonglu) Huge branch; forex and 24-hour ATM.

Kāixīnrén Pharmacy (开心人大药房; Kāixīnrén Dàyàofáng; ☏6392 8315; Zhongzhou Zhonglu; ☻24hr)

Luòyáng Central Hospital (洛阳市中心医院; Luòyáng Shì Zhōngxīn Yīyuàn; ☏6389 2222; 288 Zhongzhou Zhonglu) Works in cooperation with SOS International; also has a 24-hour pharmacy.

Public Security Bureau (PSB; 公安局; Gōng'ānjú; ☎6393 8397; cnr Kaixuan Lu & Tiyuchang Lu; ⊙8am-noon & 2-5.30pm Mon-Fri) The exit-entry department (Chūrùjìng Dàtīng) is in the south building.

Getting There & Away

Air

You would do better to fly into or out of Zhèngzhōu. The **CAAC** (中国民航; Zhōngguó Mínháng; ☎6231 0121, 24hr 6539 9366; 196 Chundu Lu) is in a white-tile building north of the railway line, but tickets can be obtained through hotels. Daily flights operate to Běijīng (¥810, 1½ hours), Shànghǎi (¥990, 1½ hours) and other cities.

Bus

Regular departures from the **long-distance bus station** (一远汽车站; yīyuǎn qìchēzhàn; Jinguyuan Lu) diagonally across from the train station include the following:

Dēngfēng ¥20, two hours, hourly

Kāifēng ¥55, three hours, hourly

Shàolín Temple ¥19.50, 1½ hours, every 30 minutes (5.20am to 4pm)

Xī'ān ¥90, four hours, hourly

Zhèngzhōu ¥40, 1½ hours, hourly

Buses to similar destinations also depart from the friendly and less frantic **Jǐnyuǎn bus station** (锦远汽车站; Jǐnyuǎn qìchēzhàn), just west of the train station.

Train

Luòyáng's new **Luòyáng Lóngmén Station** (洛阳龙门站; Lùoyáng Lóngmén Zhàn) over the river in the south of town has D and G trains to Zhèngzhōu and Xī'ān. The regular **train station** (洛阳火车站; Lùoyáng Huǒchē Zhàn) has regional and long-distance trains.

You can get tickets for a ¥5 commission from a **train ticket agency** (火车票代售处; huǒchēpiàodàishòuchù; 249 Zhongzhou Donglu).

Regional destinations include Kāifēng (hard seat ¥35, three hours, regular) and Zhèngzhōu (hard seat ¥25, 1½ hours, regular).

Hard-sleeper destinations:

Běijīng West seat/sleeper ¥110/197, seven to 10 hours, eight daily

Nánjīng seat/sleeper ¥113/316, eight to 12 hours, six daily

Shànghǎi seat/sleeper ¥153/263, 12 to 17 hours, five daily

Wǔhàn seat/sleeper ¥90/170, nine hours, regular

From Lùoyáng Lóngmén Station:

Xī'ān 2nd/1st class ¥120/190, two hours, eight daily

Zhèngzhōu 2nd/1st class ¥61/97, 40 minutes, 10 daily

Getting Around

The airport is 12km north of the city. Bus 83 (¥1, 30 minutes) runs from the parking lot to the right as you exit the train station. A taxi from the train station costs about ¥35.

Buses 5 and 41 go to the Old Town from the train station, running via Wángchéng Sq. Buses 26, 28, 33, 65 and 66 run to Lùoyáng Lóngmén station. A taxi from town costs about ¥20.

Taxis are ¥5 at flag fall, making them good value and a more attractive option than taking motor-rickshaws, which will cost you around ¥4 from the train station to Wángchéng Sq.

Around Luòyáng

LÓNGMÉN CAVES   龙门石窟

A Unesco World Heritage site, the ravaged grottoes at Lóngmén constitute one of China's handful of surviving masterpieces of Buddhist rock carving. A Sutra in stone, the epic achievement of the **Lóngmén Caves** (Dragon Gate Grottoes; Lóngmén Shíkū; admission ¥120, English-speaking guide ¥150; ⊙day 7.30am-4.30pm summer, 8am-4pm winter, night 7-10.30pm) was first undertaken by chisellers from the Northern Wei dynasty, after the capital was relocated here from Dàtóng in AD 494. During the next 200 years or so, more than 100,000 images and statues of Buddha and his disciples emerged from over a kilometre of limestone cliff wall along the Yī River (Yī Hé).

A disheartening amount of decapitation disfigures the statuary. In the early 20th century, many effigies were beheaded by unscrupulous collectors or simply extracted whole, many ending up abroad in such institutions as the Metropolitan Museum of Art in New York, the Atkinson Museum in Kansas City and the Tokyo National Museum. A noticeboard at the site lists significant statues that are missing and their current whereabouts. Some effigies are returning and severed heads are gradually being restored to their bodies, but many statues have clearly just had their faces crudely bludgeoned off, vandalism that dates to the Cultural Revolution and earlier episodes of anti-Buddhist fervour. Weather has also played its part, wearing smooth the faces of many other statues.

The caves are scattered in a line on the west and east sides of the river. Most of the significant Buddhist carvings are on the west side, but a notable crop can also be admired after traversing the bridge to the east side. Admission also includes entry to a temple and garden on the east side. English captions are rudimentary despite the caves being a major tourist drawcard. The caves are numbered and illuminated at night (aficionados and those seeking a different experience can opt for night tickets). Whether you visit in the day or night, allow your eyes to adjust to the light inside the cave and details will start to pop out. We list some of the major caves below.

The Lóngmén Caves are 13km south of Luòyáng and can be reached by taxi (¥30) or bus 81 (¥1.50, 40 minutes) from the east side of Luòyáng's train station. The last bus 81 returns to Luòyáng at 8.50pm. Buses 53 and 60 also run to the caves.

From the west side, you can take a boat (¥20 to ¥25) back to the main entrance to get a riverside view of the grottoes. Note that you can't re-enter the west side once you leave. From the east side, there are electric carts (¥5 to ¥10) to take you back to the main entrance.

WEST SIDE

Three Bīnyáng Caves CAVE
Work began on the Three Bīnyáng Caves (宾阳三洞; Bīnyáng Sān Dòng) during the Northern Wei dynasty. Despite the completion of two of the caves during the Sui and Tang dynasties, statues here all display the benevolent expressions that characterised Northern Wei style. Traces of pigment remain within the three large grottoes and other small niches honeycomb the cliff walls. Nearby is the Móyá Three Buddha Niche (摩崖三佛龛; Móyá Sānfó Kān), with seven figures that date to the Tang dynasty.

Ten Thousand Buddha Cave CAVE
South of Three Bīn-yáng Caves (万佛洞; Wànfó Dòng), the Tang-dynasty Ten Thousand Buddha Cave dates from 680. In addition to its namesake galaxy of tiny bas-relief Buddhas, there is a fine effigy of the Amitabha Buddha. Note the red pigment on the ceiling.

Losana Buddha Statue Cave CAVE
The most physically imposing and magnificent of all the Lóngmén caves, this vast cave (奉先寺; Lúshě) was carved during the Tang dynasty between 672 and 675; it contains the best examples of sculpture, despite evident weathering and vandalism.

Nine principal figures dominate the Ancestor Worshipping Temple. Tang figures tend to be more three-dimensional than the Northern Wei figures, while their expres-

sions and poses also seem more natural. In contrast to the other-worldly effigies of the Northern Wei, many Tang figures possess a more fearsome ferocity and muscularity, most noticeable in the huge guardian figure in the north wall.

The 17m-high seated central Buddha is said to be Losana, whose face is allegedly modelled on Tang empress and Buddhist patron Wu Zetian, who funded its carving.

The final stretch of caves scattered along a maze-like set of stone steps have suffered the most damage and many grottoes are empty, so much so that staff sometimes discourage visitors from checking them out. There are gems to be found if you take the time to wander around. From the base, look up to see six pagodas carved at the top of the rock face.

EAST SIDE
When you have reached the last cave on the west side, cross the bridge and walk back north along the east side. The lovely Thousand Arm and Thousand Eye Guanyin (千手千眼观音龛; Qiānshǒu Qiānyǎn Guānyīn Kān) in Cave 2132 is a splendid bas-relief dating to the Tang dynasty, revealing the Goddess of Mercy framed in a huge fan of carved hands, each sporting an eye. Two Tang-dynasty guardian deities stand outside the sizeable Lord Gāopíng Cave (高平郡王洞; Gāopíng Jùnwáng Dòng). Further is the large Reading Sutra Cave (看经寺洞; Kàn Jīng Sìdòng), with a carved lotus on its ceiling and 29 luóhàn around the base of the walls. There is also a large viewing terrace for sizing up the Ancestor Worshipping Temple on the far side of the river.

Xiangshan Temple TEMPLE
(香山寺; Xiāngshān Sì) Past the caves on the eastern side and up a steep flight of steps is this restored temple nestled against the hill. First built in AD 516 and restored on various occasions, the temple is filled with bronze Buddhist images and a villa which once belonged to former president Jiang Jieshi, built in 1936 to celebrate his 50th birthday (what a present, what a view!). Look out for a stele with a poem written by Emperor Qianlong who visited and was moved by the temple's beauty.

Bai Juyi's Graveyard GARDEN, TOMB
The final stop at the site is a lovely garden built around Tang-dynasty poet Bai Juyi's tomb (白居易墓地; Bái Jūyì Mùdì). It's a peaceful,

leafy place to rest your tired feet. There's a cute alfresco teahouse inside where you can get tea (from ¥38), snacks and instant noodles.

WHITE HORSE TEMPLE　　　白马寺

Although its original structures have largely been replaced and it is likely older temples have vanished, this active **monastery** (Báimǎ Sì; admission ¥50; ⊙7am-6pm) is regarded as the first surviving Buddhist temple erected on Chinese soil, originally dating from the 1st century AD.

When two Han-dynasty court emissaries went in search of Buddhist scriptures, they encountered two Indian monks in Afghanistan; the monks returned to Luòyáng on two white horses carrying Buddhist Sutras and statues. The impressed emperor built the temple to house the monks; it is also their resting place. Ironically, the tombs are now overgrown and neglected and set off on the sides of the compound.

In the **Hall of the Heavenly Kings**, Milefo laughs from within an intricately carved cabinet featuring more than 50 dragons writhing across the structure. Other buildings of note include the **Hall of Great Heroes** with its two-level carved wooden structure and the **Pilu Hall** at the very rear. Also look out for peony gardens in bloom come April/May. The standout **Qíyún Pagoda** (齐云塔; Qíyún Tǎ), an ancient 12-tiered brick tower, is a pleasant five-minute walk through a garden and across a bridge.

The temple is 13km east of Luòyáng, around 40 minutes away on bus 56 from the Xīguān (西关) stop. Bus 58 runs from Zhongzhou Donglu in the old town also runs here.

Guōliàngcūn　　　郭亮村

📞 0373 / POP 300

On its clifftop perch high up in the Wànxiàn (Ten Thousand Immortals) Mountains in north Hénán, this delightful high-altitude stone hamlet was for centuries sheltered from the outside world by its combination of inaccessibility and anonymity. Guōliàngcūn shot to fame as the bucolic backdrop to a clutch of Chinese films, which firmly embedded the village in contemporary Chinese mythology.

Today, the village attracts legions of artists, who journey here to capture the unreal mountain scenery on paper and canvas. Joining them are weekend Chinese tourists who get disgorged by the busloads. For a true rustic mountaintop experience, come on a weekday when it's tranquil. New hotels have sprung up at the village's foot, but the original dwellings – climbing the mountain slope – retain their simple, rustic charms. Long treks through the lovely scenery more than compensate for the hard slog of journeying here.

Approximately 6°C colder than Zhèngzhōu, Guōliàngcūn is cool enough to be devoid of mosquitoes year-round (some locals say), but pack warm clothes for winter visits, which can be bone-numbing. Visiting in low season may seem odd advice, but come evening the village can be utterly tranquil, and moonlit nights are intoxicating. Pack a small torch as lights beyond the hotels are scarce.

Several kilometres before the village, you will be meant to get off the bus to purchase a ticket (¥80) to the Wànxiàn Mountains Scenic Area. There are no ATMs and nowhere to change money in Guōliàngcūn. A small **medical clinic** (📞671 0303) can be found in the village.

◉ Sights & Activities

All of the **village dwellings**, many hung with butter yellow *bàngzi* (sweetcorn cobs), are hewn from the same local stone that paves the slender alleyways, sculpts the bridges and fashions the picturesque gates of Guōliàngcūn. Walnut-faced old women peek from doorways and children scamper about, but locals are well used to outsiders.

You will have passed by the **Precipice Gallery** (绝壁长廊; Juébì Chángláng), also referred to on some signs as 'Long Corridor in the Cliffs' en route to the village, but backtrack down for a closer perspective on these plunging cliffs, with dramatic views from the tunnel carved through the rock. Before this tunnel was built (between 1972 and 1978) by a local man called Shen Mingxin and others, the only way into the village was via the **Sky Ladder** (天梯; Tiān Tī), Ming-dynasty steps hewn from the local pink stone, with no guard rails but amazing views.

To get to the Sky Ladder, take the left fork of the road heading towards the tunnel and walk for 2.5km. Another 500m along the road takes you to the charming village of **Huìtáo Zhài** (会逃寨), with its cliff-top cottages.

Over the bridge on the other side of the precipice from the village, walk past the small row of cottages almost on the edge of the cliff called **Yáshàng Rénjiā** (崖上人家) and you can step onto a platform atop a pillar of rock for astonishing views into the canyon.

Head through the strip of street stalls, past the hotels to get to the start of a bracing 5km circuit through the mountain valley. From the end of the street, you can walk or take an electric cart (¥15 return) 1.3km to the starting point of the loop. Sadly, the mood of the area has been spoilt with the addition of several man-made oddities; a cable ride and a drain-like slide from the top of the mountain. If you start on the left-hand set of steps, you'll first go past the awe-inspiring curtain of rock above the **Shouting Spring** (喊泉; Hǎn Quán). According to local lore, its flow responds to the loudness of your whoops (it doesn't). You'll also pass the peaceful **Old Pool** (老潭; Lǎo Tán), whose banks are sadly littered with bottles and cake wrappers. Further along, you'll pass the **Red Dragon Cave** (红龙洞; Hónglóng Dòng), now closed, and after a few steep flights of stairs, the slide ride (¥30) and then the **White Dragon Cave** (白龙洞; Báilóng Dòng; admission ¥20). The last sight is a set of steps which lead up **Pearl Spring** (珍珠泉; Zhēnzhū Quán), a fissure in the mountain from which pours out cool, clear spring water. You can of course, do the loop in the opposite direction (it's easier).

Once you've seen the big sights, get off the beaten trail and onto one of the small paths heading into the hills (such as the boulder-strewn brookside trail along the flank of Guōliàngcūn that leads further up into the mountain), but take water.

🛏 Sleeping & Eating

There are hotels galore in Guōliàngcūn though they offer identical two-star quality with hot showers and TVs (no toiletries or towels though). There's a strip of hotels at the foot of the village and another strip on the precipice facing the tunnel. The latter has better views though you'll have to contend with roosters crowing at odd hours. Rooms cost ¥40 to ¥100 depending on the size and orientation. Prices are a bit higher during the summer but negotiable in the low season and on weekdays. There are no restaurants, but hoteliers have kitchens and Chinese menus offering a wide variety of vegie and meat-based dishes, rice and noodles. There are simple noodle stalls near the hotels at the foot of the village and at the start of the mountain circuit. A couple of shops sell snacks and essentials.

ℹ Getting There & Away

Reach Guōliàngcūn from Xīnxiāng (新乡), between Ānyáng and Zhèngzhōu. Fast trains run to Xīnxiāng from Zhèngzhōu (¥24, 45 minutes), as do regular buses (¥20, 1½ hours). Exit Xīnxiāng Train Station, head straight ahead and take the first left and cross the road onto Ziyou Lu (自由路) to flag down buses to Huīxiàn (辉县; ¥6.50, 50 minutes, regular). The bus also departs from the bus station.

Five buses (¥12, one hour 40 minutes, first/last bus 7am/4.30pm) from Huīxiàn's bus station (辉县站; Huīxiàn zhàn) pass by the mountain road to Guōliàngcūn. Buses may have the characters for Guōliàng (郭亮) on the window, but may head straight to the final stop Nánpíng (南坪), a village beyond the base of the road to Guōliàngcūn, depending on passenger numbers. If the bus isn't going up the mountain, you can either ask to be dropped at the bottom of the Guōliàngcūn road and ask a local to bring you up the 4km steep winding road for a wallet-gouging ¥50 or head on to Nánpíng where there are green buses (¥15) that do a circuit to Guōliàngcūn. The green buses run regularly on the weekends but on weekdays will only go when there are enough passengers. The last bus leaves at 5.30pm.

In the other direction, Huīxiàn-bound minibuses (¥12) run from the bottom of the mountain road from Guōliàngcūn at 6.30am, 9am, noon, 1pm and 3pm. Guesthouse owners should be able to run you down to the drop-off point for around ¥40 if you spend the night in their lodgings. Otherwise, take the green bus to Nánpíng to catch a bus to Huīxiàn.

Kāifēng   开封

☑0378 / POP 594,000

More than any other of Hénán's ancient capitals, Kāifēng has preserved a semblance of its original grandeur. Kāifēng has character: you may have to squint a bit and learn to sift the fakes from the genuine historical fragments, but the city still offers up a riveting display of age-old charm, magnificent market food, relics from its long-vanished apogee and colourful chrysanthemums (the city flower; Kāifēng is also known as Júchéng, or 'Chrysanthemum Town'). One reason you won't see soaring skyscrapers here is because buildings requiring deep foundations are prohibited, for fear of destroying the ancient northern Song-dynasty city below.

History

Once the prosperous capital of the Northern Song dynasty (960–1126), Kāifēng was established south of the Yellow River, but not far enough to escape the river's capricious wrath.

After centuries of flooding, the city of the Northern Song largely lies buried 8m to 9m deep. Between 1194 and 1938 the city flooded 368 times, an average of once every two years.

Kāifēng was also the first city in China where Jewish merchants settled when they arrived, along the Silk Road, during the Song dynasty. A small Christian and Catholic community also lives in Kāifēng alongside a much larger local Muslim Hui community.

◉ Sights

Most travellers should base themselves within the walls of the old town. For ancient Kāifēng architecture, wander along small streets off the main drag within the city walls, where you can find old, tumbledown, one-storey buildings with misshapen tiled roofs.

Temple of the Chief Minister BUDDHIST TEMPLE
(大相国寺; Dà Xiàngguó Sì; Ziyou Lu; admission ¥30; ☺8am-6pm) First founded in AD 555, this frequently rebuilt temple was destroyed along with the city in the early 1640s when rebels breached the Yellow River's dykes. During the Northern Song, the temple covered a massive 34 hectares and housed over 10,000 monks.

Within the **Hall of the Revarajas** (天王殿; Tiānwáng Diàn), the mission of chubby Mílefo (the Laughing Buddha) is proclaimed in the attendant Chinese characters: 'Big belly can endure all that is hard to endure in the world.' But the temple showstopper is the mesmerising **Four-Faced Thousand Hand Thousand Eye Guanyin** (四面千手千眼观世音), towering within the octagonal Arhat Hall (罗汉殿; Luóhàn Diàn), beyond the **Hall of Tathagata** (大雄宝殿; Dàxióng Bǎodiàn). Fifty-eight years in the carving, the 7m-tall gold-gilded, four-sided statue bristles with giant fans of 1048 arms, an eye upon each hand; the arhats themselves are presented with considerably less artistry. On the left of the **Hall of Tripitaka** (Cángjīng Lóu) is a small hall (大师堂; Dàshītáng) where a master calligrapher works and plies his craft (works from ¥100). A huge pagoda and hall is under construction at the rear. Elsewhere in the temple you can divine your future by drawing straws (chōuqiān) or dine at the pleasant onsite **vegetarian restaurant** (素斋部; sùzhāibù).

Shānshǎngān Guild Hall GUILDHALL
(山陕甘会馆; Shānshǎn'gān Huìguǎn; 85 Xufu Jie; admission ¥30; ☺8.30am-6.30pm summer, 8.20am-5pm winter) Here's proof that good things come in small packages. The tiny, elaborately styled guild hall was built as a lodging and meeting place during the Qing dynasty by an association of merchants from Shānxi, Shǎnxi (Shaanxi) and Gānsù provinces. Note the ornate carvings on the roofs, and delve into the exhibition on historic Kāifēng. Check out the fascinating diorama of the old Song city – with its palace in the centre of town – and compare it with a model of modern Kāifēng. Look out for the scale-model recreation of Zhang Zeduan's famed Qingming painting.

Kāifēng Fú HISTORIC SITE
(开封府; 85 Xufu Jie; admission ¥50; ☺7am-7pm summer, 7.30am-5.30pm winter) Local tour groups flock to this site by the Baogong Lake for a bit of a historical kick. The drama

HÉNÁN KĀIFĒNG

'THAT' PAINTING: ZHANG ZEDUAN'S MASTERPIECE

These days, you'll see it most everywhere in Kāifēng. Museums and parks have it in carved wood and stone bas-relief, there are scale dioramas, souvenir posters, advertising (it's on the Kaifeng Hostel's poster) and even a historical theme park modelled on it. 'It' being a scroll painting from the Song dynasty. Now held in the Forbidden City and widely acknowledged as China's first *shén* (Godly) painting, *Along the River during the Qingming Festival* was completed by Zhang Zeduan (张择端) in the early 12th century.

The long 24.8cm x 528.7cm painting depicts life in a city which experts have attributed as Kāifēng. It's packed to the gills with details of the period: boats unloading goods at a harbour, an inn crowded with customers, children playing on the streets etc. As you would imagine, it offers valuable insight into the life and times of a large Song dynasty town. The piece has been likened in importance to the Mona Lisa and was toted by the last emperor Puyi to Manchukuo. When the original gets displayed in Beijing, queues to see it last hours.

Several places in Kāifēng to see versions of it include the Riverside Scenic Park, the scale diorama in the Shānshǎngān Guild Hall, the replica version in the museum and the paper cutting in Zhūxiàn's Qingzhen Mosque (p415). There's even a large-scale version on one of the train station walls!

Kāifēng

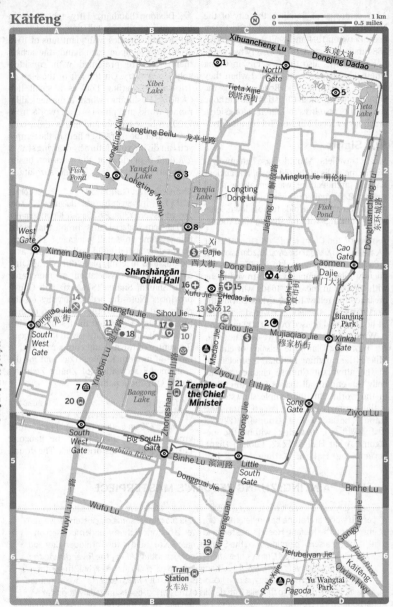

Xihuancheng Lu 东京大道

Dongjing Dadao

North Gate

铁塔西街 Tieta Xijie

Xibei Lake

Tieta Lake

Longting Beilu 龙亭北路

Longting Xilu

Fish Pond

Yangjia Lake

Longting Namlu

Minglun Jie 明伦街

Panjia Lake

Longting Dong Lu

Fish Pond

West Gate

Cao Gate

Ximen Dajie 西门大街 Xinjiekou Jie

Xi Dajie 西大街

Dong Dajie 东大街

Caomen Dajie 曹门大街

Shānshāngān Guild Hall

Xufu Jie

Shudian Jie

Hedao Jie

Caoshi Jie 草市街

Bianjing Park

Shengfu Jie

Sihou Jie

Gulou Jie

Mujiaqiao Jie 穆家桥街

Xinkai Gate

Dinghao Jie 丁角街

Yingbin Lu 迎宾路

Madao Jie

Ziyou Lu 自由路

South West Gate

Temple of the Chief Minister

Zhongshan Lu 中山路

Wolong Jie

Baogong Lake

Song Gate

Ziyou Lu

South West Gate

Huangbian River

Big South Gate

Binhe Lu 滨河路

Little South Gate

Binhe Lu

Dongguai Jie

Xinmenguan Jie

Wufu Lu 五福路 一路

Wufu Lu

Tielubeiyan Jie

Kaifeng Qixian Hwy

Train Station 火车站

Pota Xijie

Pó Pagoda

Yu Wangtai Park

Gongyuan Lu

HÉNÁN KĀIFĒNG

starts outside the gates at 9am daily – the doors get thrown open and out troops a bunch of costumed actors, playing a period scene complete with cracking whips and the sound of gongs. They then retreat inside to continue the play (in Chinese). Drama aside, the site, encased within tall walls, is a recreation of Song imperial life. There are a number of buildings from ye olde times including the armoury, distillery, a vinegar workshop, a pagoda and a 'Building of Mental Cultivation'.

Kāifēng

◎ Top Sights

Shānshǎngān Guild Hall C3

Temple of the Chief Minister................ C4

◎ Sights

1 City Walls C1

2 Dōngdà Mosque......................................C4

3 Dragon Pavilion B2

4 Former Site of Kāifēng
  Synagogue C3

5 Iron Pagoda Park D1

6 Kāifēng Fú B4

7 Kāifēng Museum A4

8 Lóngtíng Park B3

9 Riverside Scenic Park Qīngmíng
  Garden B2

◎ Sleeping

10 Jīnjiāng Inn...B4

11 Kāifēng International Youth
  Hostel..B4

12 Soluxe Hotel Kāifēng............................C4

◎ Eating

13 Gǔlóu Night Market................................C3

14 Xīsī Night Market....................................A3

◎ Information

15 Kaifeng No 1 People's Hospital C3

16 Zhāngzhòngjǐng Pharmacy...................B3

◎ Transport

17 IATA Air Ticket Office B4

18 Railway Ticket office..............................B4

19 South Long-Distance Bus
  Station C6

20 West Long-Distance Bus
  Station A4

21 Xiàngguósì Bus Station B4

Iron Pagoda Park PARK

(铁塔公园; Tiě Tǎ Gōngyuán; 210 Beimen Dajie; admission ¥50; ◎7am-7pm) Rising up within Iron Pagoda Park is a magnificent 55m, 11th-century pagoda, a gorgeous, slender brick edifice wrapped in glazed rust-coloured tiles (hence the name); it's narrow stairs are climbable for ¥30. Take bus 1 from Zhongshan Lu.

FREE Kāifēng Museum MUSEUM

(开封博物馆; Kāifēng Bówùguǎn; 26 Yingbin Lu; ◎9am-noon & 2.30-5.30pm Tue-Sun) Houses a couple of rooms with archaeological finds, woodblock prints and odd historical bits and pieces. There are two notable Jewish stelae on the 4th floor, managed by the **Kāifēng Institute for Research on the History of Chinese Jews** (◎393 2178, ext 8010), but you will have to pay ¥50 to see them. Buses 1, 7, 9, 16, 20 and 23 all travel past here.

Riverside Scenic Park Qīngmíng Garden PARK

(Millennium City Park; 清明上河园; Qīngmíng Shànghéyuán; Longting Nanlu; admission day/night ¥80/199; ◎9am-6pm) High on historical kitsch, this theme park is a recreation of Zeduan's famous Qingming painting. It's brought to life with roving staff in Song-era costumes, cultural performances, folk art and music demonstrations. If you can get over the number of souvenir stalls, there's fun to be had (there's a wedding ceremony and even a mock naval battle with pyrotechnics, out on the lake).

The night ticket allows entry during the day and a seat for a colourful night performance (8.10pm) out on the lake.

Lóngtíng Park PARK

(龙亭公园; Lóngtíng Gōngyuán; ◎566 0316; Zhongshan Lu; admission ¥35; ◎7am-6.30pm) Site of the former imperial palace, this park is largely covered by lakes, into which hardy swimmers dive in winter. Cross a bridge and climb the **Dragon Pavilion** (龙亭; Lóng Tíng) for town views.

City Walls HISTORIC SITE

Kāifēng is ringed by a relatively intact, much-restored Qing-dynasty wall (城墙). Encased with grey bricks, rear sections of the ramparts have been recently buttressed unattractively with concrete. Today's bastion was built on the foundations of the Song-dynasty **Inner Wall** (内城; Nèichéng). Rising up beyond was the mighty, now buried **Outer Wall** (外城; Wàichéng), a colossal construction containing 18 gates, which looped south of the Pó Pagoda, while the **Imperial Wall** (皇城; Huángchéng) protected the imperial palace.

Kāifēng Synagogue RUINS

(开封犹太教堂; Kāifēng Yóutài Jiàotáng Yízhǐ; 59 Beitu Jie) Sadly, nothing remains of the synagogue except a well with an iron lid in the boiler room of the Kaifeng Traditional Chinese Medicine Hospital. Under renovation at the time of research, visitors may need to check if the new hospital will allow visitors

HÉNÁN KĀIFĒNG

to the site. The spirit of it lingers, however, in the name of the brick alley immediately south of the hospital – Jiaojing Hutong (教经胡同; Teaching the Torah Alley). In the house with the blue sign (yisrael-kaifeng@hotmail.com) lives a local English-speaking guide familiar with local Jewish history. Send an email prior to visiting if you intend to engage her guide services or want an extended chat.

Dōngdà Mosque   MOSQUE
(东大寺; Dōngdà Sì; 39 Mujiaqiao Jie) South in Kāifēng's main Muslim district, whose landmark place of worship is this Chinese temple-styled mosque. Streets have colourful names, such as Shaoji Hutong (Roast Chicken Alley).

🛏 Sleeping

Kāifēng International Youth Hostel   HOSTEL $
(开封国际青年旅舍; Kāifēng Guójì Qīngnián Lǚshè; ☎255 2888; 30 Yingbin Lu; 迎宾路30号; dm ¥50, s ¥120, d & tw ¥140; ❇@🛜) On the edge of Baogong Lake, the town's first and only hostel has helpful English-speaking staff and a location close to buses. Bunk-bed dorms have an ensuite shower while private rooms have flat-screen TVs, AC and an internet cable. Cold beer, an extensive Chinese and Western food menu, and a pool table help while the hours away. Bike rental cost ¥20 daily.

Soluxe Hotel Kāifēng   HOTEL $$$
(开封阳光酒店; Kāifēng Yángguāng Jiǔdiàn; ☎595 8888; 41 Gulou Jie; 鼓楼街41号; s & d ¥518; ❇@) The smart Soluxe Hotel offers compact but modern business-style rooms in shades of brown out the features list. Discounts of 40%. On the ground floor is an attractive and plush-looking roast-duck restaurant.

Jǐnjiāng Inn   HOTEL $
(锦江之星; Jǐnjiāng Zhīxīng; ☎399 6666; 88 Zhongshan Lu; 中山路88号; s & d ¥159-179; ❇@) In a star location on the intersection of Zhongshan Lu, this chain hotel's branch ticks the right boxes: efficient staff, clean rooms, modern furnishing, flat-screen TVs and good plumbing.

🍴 Eating & Drinking

Xīsī Night Market   STREET MARKET $
(西司夜市; Xīsī Yèshì; Dingjiao Jie; snacks from ¥2; ⏱6.30pm-late) Join the scrum weaving between stalls busy with red-faced popcorn sellers and hollering Hui Muslim chefs cooking up kebabs and náng bread. There are loads of vendors from whom you can buy cured meats, hearty jiānbǐng guǒzi (煎饼裹子; pancake with chopped onions), sweet potatoes, roast rabbit, xiǎolóngbāo (Shànghǎi-style dumplings), peanut cake (花生糕; huāshēng gāo), and cups of sugarcane juice. Look for yángròu kàngmó (羊肉炕馍; lamb in a parcel of bread), a local Kāifēng Muslim speciality. Or opt for yángròu chuàn (羊肉串; lamb kebabs). Look out for noodle vendors who pull and twist fresh niú ròu lā miàn (牛肉拉面; noodles in beef broth).

Among the flames and clouds of steam erupting from the ovens slave vocal vendors of xìngrén chá (杏仁茶; almond tea), a sugary paste made from boiling water thickened with powdered almond, red berries, peanuts, sesame seeds and crystallised cherries.

Gǔlóu Night Market   STREET MARKET $
(鼓楼夜市; Gǔlóu Yèshì; off Sihou Jie; snacks from ¥2; ⏱6.30pm-late) Kāifēng's steaming, bustling and bellowing night market has been sanitised and relocated. While the food stays the same, authenticity has been traded for faux antique tables and benches, and stalls are now housed in wooden huts. This hasn't stopped the locals from having a good time. Visit the Tsingtao stall serving jugs (壶; hú; ¥15 to ¥18) of draught lager (黄扎; huáng zhā), ale (红扎; hóng zhā) and stout (黑扎; hēi zhā). East on Shudian Jie and around are more food stalls and others selling clothes, toys and books.

ℹ Information

The area around Zhongshan Lu has internet cafes but at the time of research, you need local ID for surfing though some shops may let you get online for an hour or so.

Bank of China (中国银行; Zhōngguó Yínháng; cnr Xi Dajie & Zhongshan Lu) 24-hour ATM (MasterCard and Visa).

China Construction Bank (中国建设银行; Zhōngguó Jiànshè Yínháng; Gulou Jie) 24-hour ATM (Cirrus, Maestro, Visa and MasterCard).

China Post (中国邮政; Zhōngguó Yóuzhèng; Ziyou Lu; ⏱8am-5.30pm)

Kāifēng No 1 People's Hospital (开封第一人民医院; Kāifēng Dìyī Rénmín Yīyuàn; ☎567 1288; 85 Hedao Jie)

Public Security Bureau (PSB; 公安局; Gōng'ānjú; ☎532 2242; 86 Zhongshan Lu; ⏱8.30am-noon & 2.30-6pm Mon-Fri) Visa renewals.

Zhāngzhòngjǐng Pharmacy (张仲景大药房; Zhāngzhòngjǐng Dàyàofáng; ⏱7.30am-10pm summer, 8am-9pm winter) Next to Shānshǎngǎn Guild Hall.

ℹ Getting There & Away

Air

The nearest airport is at Zhèngzhōu. Tickets can be bought at the **IATA Air Ticket Office** (☑595 5555; Hángkōng Dàshà) next to the PSB; two free daily buses (8am and 2pm) run to Zhèngzhōu airport from here. There's also an airport shuttle from the corner of Gulou Jie and Jiefang Lu (¥40, 1½ hours, 10 daily).

Bus

Buses run from the **west long-distance bus station** (长途汽车西站; chángtú qìchē xīzhàn):

Dēngfēng ¥35, three hours, two daily (9.30am and 1.20pm)

Luòyáng ¥57, three hours, two daily (9am and 2pm)

Xīnxiāng ¥26, two hours, six daily

Zhèngzhōu ¥8, 1½ hours, every 20 minutes (6.20am to 7.30pm)

Buses also leave from the **south long-distance bus station** (长途汽车南站; chángtú qìchē nánzhàn), opposite the train station:

Ānyáng ¥54, four hours, regular services

Luòyáng ¥57, three hours, hourly

Xīnxiāng ¥32, two hours, every 40 minutes

Zhèngzhōu ¥8, 1½ hours, every 15 minutes

Train

Buy tickets at the **railway ticket office** (火车票代售; huǒchēpiào dàishòu; Yingbin Lu; ⊘8am-noon & 1.30-5.30pm) diagonally opposite the Kāifēng Hostel.

Běijīng West seat/sleeper ¥99/185, 12 hours

Luòyáng ¥40-80, 2½ hours, eight daily

Shànghǎi hard/soft seat ¥235/375, seven hours, 8.59am & 3.53pm

Xī'ān seat/sleeper ¥85/155, eight hours, regular

Zhèngzhōu ¥25-30, 45 minutes

ℹ Getting Around

Zhongshan Lu is a good place to catch buses to most sights (¥1). Taxis (flag fall ¥5) are the best way to get about; a journey from the train station to Zhongshan Lu should cost ¥7. Avoid pedicabs as they frequently rip off tourists.

Zhūxiān Zhèn　朱仙镇

Twenty-three kilometres north of Kāifēng is **Zhūxiān** (Vermillion Immortal). Some say it's one of China's four 'ancient' towns – the other three are Hánkǒu (trade), Jǐngdézhèn (porcelain) and Fóshān (silk). Here, the 1000-year-old craft of woodblock printing (木板年画; hànkǒu) is still practised.

Traditionally come spring festival, families plaster their door fronts and houses with these prints (though many now use commercially printed ones) to usher in luck and prosperity for the year ahead. Five or so families have continued the craft. Sets of wooden blocks are painstakingly carved and each print requires anywhere from five to seven blocks, one for the base black outline and one for each other colour. Pigments (generally red, blue, yellow, black and green), made from natural materials such as seeds and plants, are then applied via handmade brushes onto rice paper. The outline in black is first printed, the paper left to dry and the process is repeated for each colour required. The prints feature Chinese characters from folklore, gods and others related to luck and blessings. These luridly coloured prints are embarrassingly cheap (¥5 to ¥30 for an A4/letter-size prints to ¥100 for a print made from 150-year-old blocks).

Visit **Tiānchéng Niánhuà Lǎodiàn** (天成年画老店), 100m north of the Yuèfēi Temple. The artist and owner Mr Yin (尹) is a 5th-generation artisan, and his family has been in business for more than 200 years, 'excluding a period of 30 years or so because of the Cultural Revolution'. His work has been represented at the 2008 Beijing Olympics and the 2010 Shanghai World Expo. You can pick up a beautifully bound book of prints with English explanations, housed in a wooden presentation box for ¥200 (if you're nice, he'll sell it for ¥180). There are several other workshops along the canal at the end of town.

Exploring the town further, you'll find two temples on the main drag: the **Yuèfēi Temple** (岳飞庙; Yuèfēi Miào; admission ¥20) and **Guānyǔ Temple** (关羽庙; Guānyǔ Miào; admission ¥1). Heading 700m or so south off the main road along a wide stone path, you'll get to the **Qīngzhēn Temple** (清真寺; Qīng Zhēn Sì; free admission). This is a mosque housed in a traditional Chinese temple compound with a pretty rose garden. Look for a stall featuring elaborate paper-cutting art by Mr Hu (胡). The artist is listed in the *Guinness World Records* for cutting 10,000 (!) paper butterflies. On the wall is a paper-cut version of Zeduan's famed Qingming painting.

Head to the **Xiàngguó Sì** bus station (相国寺汽车站) on Zhongshan Lu where buses (¥6, 45 minutes, every 12 minutes) run all the way to Zhūxiān. The last bus from Zhūxiān leaves at 5.50pm. You'll pass through a busy thoroughfare where you should get off.

Húběi

POP 61.8 MILLION

Includes »

Wǔhàn.............................418
Jīngzhōu.........................422
Around Jīngzhōu...........424
Wǔdāng Shān...............424
Shénnóngjià...................427
Yíchāng..........................428

Best for Scenery

» Shénnóngjià (p427)
» Wǔdāng Shān (p424)
» Three Gorges (p770)

Best for History

» Jīngzhōu (p422)
» Wǔdāng Shān (p424)
» Wǔhàn (p418)

Why Go?

Vast hordes of travellers find themselves drifting into Húběi (湖北) through the magnificent Three Gorges, the precipitous geological marvel that begins in neighbouring Chóngqìng and concludes here. It's a once-in-a-lifetime trip which perfectly introduces Húběi's dramatic natural beauty.

Sliced by rivers (including, of course, the mighty Yangzi) and dappled with lakes, Húběi is largely lush and fertile, but its western regions are dominated by stunning mountain scenery. National parks such as Shénnóngjià are jaw-droppingly spectacular, while the sacred peaks of Wǔdāng Shān add a strong cultural significance to the awe-inspiring landscape.

Húběi's central location ensured it played a key role in Chinese history, with plenty of evidence around the ancient city of Jīngzhōu of the great Chu kingdom that ruled this part of China more than 2000 years ago. China's modern history, meanwhile, is woven into the fabric of Wǔhàn, Húběi's monstrous, battle-scarred capital city.

When to Go

Wǔhàn

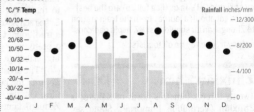

Mar & Apr Get in ahead of the draining Yangzi summer, but bring an umbrella.

Sep–Nov The stupefying summer heat has finally lifted.

Nov–Mar Wǔdāng Shān at its prettiest, snowiest best. Pack your thermals.

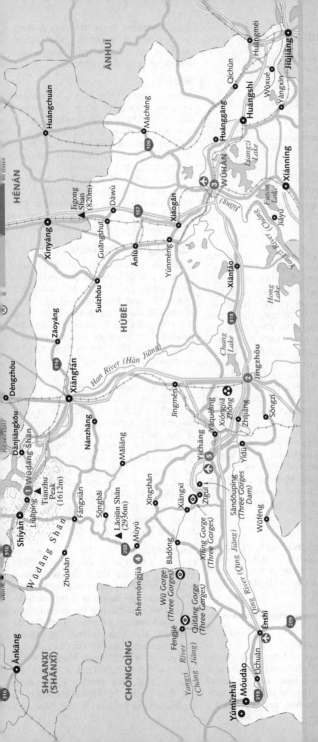

Húběi Highlights

① Study taichi where it all began, on the awe-inspiring mountain slopes of **Wǔdāng Shān** (p424)

② Explore the historic gates, city walls and ruined temples of ancient **Jīngzhōu** (p422)

③ Find a bar and knock back a beer in the riverside concession district of mighty **Wǔhàn** (p418)

④ Flee China's urban sprawl and camp out in the wilds of stunning **Shénnóngjià** (p427)

⑤ Go against the tourist tide and start your Three Gorges cruise in **Yíchāng** (p428) rather than Chóngqìng

PRICE INDICATORS

The following price indicators are used in this chapter:

Sleeping

$	less than ¥200
$$	¥200 to ¥500
$$$	more than ¥500

Eating

$	less than ¥40
$$	¥40 to ¥100
$$$	more than ¥100

History

The Húběi area first came to prominence during the Eastern Zhou (700–221 BC), when the powerful Chu kingdom, based in present-day Jīngzhōu, was at its height. Húběi again became pivotal during the Three Kingdoms (AD 220–280). The Chinese classic *The Romance of the Three Kingdoms (Sān Guó Yǎnyì)* makes much reference to Jīngzhōu. The mighty Yangzi River ensured prosperous trade in the centuries that followed, especially for Wǔhàn, China's largest inland port and stage of the 1911 uprising, which led to the fall of the Qing and the creation of the Republic of China.

Climate

Even Húběi's 'furnace', Wǔhàn, is only seriously hot in July and August. Other months are much more pleasant, while the western mountains are more temperate, generally. Rainfall is heavy in the southeast but decreases north and west. Expect most of it from April to July.

Language

Húběi has two dialects of northern Mandarin – southwest Mandarin and lower-mid Yangzi Mandarin – while in the southeast many people speak Gàn, a Mandarin dialect from Jiāngxī.

Wǔhàn 武汉

 027 / POP 4.26 MILLION

A gargantuan alloy of three formerly independent cities (Wǔchāng, Hànkǒu and Hànyáng), Wǔhàn is huge. But the Yangzi River thrusts its way through the centre, carving the city in two and allowing for some breathing space between towering buildings and gnarling traffic, while numerous lakes and a smattering of decent sights provide more welcome retreats.

History

Although not actually named Wǔhàn until 1927, the city's three mighty chunks trace their influential status back to the Han dynasty, with Wǔchāng and Hànkǒu vying for political and economic sway. The city was prised open to foreign trade in the 19th century by the Treaty of Nanking.

The 1911 uprising sparked the beginning of the end for the Qing dynasty. Much that wasn't destroyed then was flattened in 1944 when American forces fire-bombed the city after it had fallen under Japanese control.

◉ Sights & Activities

In Hànkǒu, the area west of Yanjiang Dadao remains a hodgepodge of **concession-era architecture** and old consulate buildings.

A stroll along **Hànkǒu Bund** (汉口海滩; Hànkǒu Hǎitān) is a popular way to spend the early evening. It's essentially an elongated park, running along the western bank of the Yangzi, and is where locals come to exercise, chat and fly kites.

FREE **Húběi Provincial Museum**   MUSEUM
(湖北省博物馆; Húběi Shěng Bówùguǎn; 156 Donghu Lu; 东湖路156号; ⊙9am-5pm, no admission after 3.30pm, closed Mon) The centrepiece of this fabulous museum is the exhibition of the tomb of Marquis Yi of Zeng, which includes one of the world's largest musical instruments, a remarkable five-tonne set of 64 double-tone bronze bells. Next door, the **Húběi Museum of Art**, also free, often holds worthwhile exhibitions. Both museums lie beside the enormous **East Lake** (东湖; Dōng Hú). Take bus 402 or 411.

Guīyuán Temple   BUDDHIST
(归元寺; Guīyuán Sì; 20 Cuiweiheng Lu; 翠微横路20号; admission ¥10; ⊙8am-5pm) Pass a large rectangular pond where turtles cling like shipwrecked survivors to two metal lotus flowers and examine the magnificently burnished cabinet housing Milefo in the first hall. Also seek out this 350-year-old Buddhist temple's collection of more than 500 statues of enlightened disciples in the Hall of Arhats (罗汉堂; Luóhàn Táng). Completed in 1890, after nine years in the making, they remain in pristine condition. In the Mahasattva Pavilion (大士阁; Dàshì Gé),

the 2m-high Tang-dynasty tablet carved with an image of Guanyin holding a willow branch is impressive, and a jade Buddha can be found in the **Cángjīng Pavilion** (藏经阁; Cángjīng Gé). Buses 401 and 402 both go here.

Yellow Crane Tower HISTORIC SITE
(黄鹤楼; Huánghè Lóu; Wuluo Lu; admission ¥80; ⏱7.30am-5.30pm, to 6.30pm summer) Wǔhàn's magical dancing crane, immortalised in the poetry of Cui Hao, has long flown but the city's pride and joy remains perched on top of Snake Hill. The tower has had its history rebuilt out of it since the original was constructed in AD 223, and today's beautiful five-storey, yellow-tiled version is a 1980s remake of the Qing tower that combusted in 1884. Buses 401, 402 and 411, and trolley buses 1 and 10, all go here.

Chángchūn Temple TAOIST
(长春观; Chángchūn Guàn; admission ¥10; ⏱8am-5pm) This charming Taoist temple dates back to the Han dynasty, although much building restoration has gone on in the past couple of years. The Hall of Supreme Purity (Tàiqīng Diàn), containing a white-bearded statue of Laotzu, is the centrepiece. Other halls lead up the steep steps behind it. There's a well-regarded vegetarian restaurant next door (p421). Buses 411, 401 and 402 all go here.

FREE The Revolution of 1911 Museum MUSEUM
(辛亥革命博物馆; Xīnhài Gémìng Bówùguǎn; Shouyi Guangchang (Uprising Square); 首义广场; ⏱9am-5pm, closed Mon) Chinese Communist Party propaganda machine in full tilt, but includes some interesting old photos. Housed in an eye-catching red rock–like building.

East Lake SWIMMING
(东湖游泳池; Dōnghú Yóuyǒngchí; entrance ¥10; ⏱9am-10pm) In summer, escape the sweltering city and head to this section of East Lake, which has been cordoned off for swimming. Take bus 402 to Donghu Donglu Youyongchi (东湖东路游泳池).

🛏 Sleeping

TOP CHOICE Pathfinder Youth Hostel HOSTEL $
(探路者国际青年旅社; Tànlùzhě Guójì Qīngnián Lǔshè; ☎8884 4092; yhawuhan@hotmail.com; 368 Zhongshan Lu; 中山路368号; dm/r from ¥40/138; ✲@🛜) Next to the Húběi Art Gallery (湖北美术馆; Húběi Měishùguǎn), Wǔhàn's best budget option has an art-warehouse feel to it where guests add graffiti to the walls. Pinewood-decorated rooms are smart and clean; bathrooms are small with squat loos (communal bathrooms have sit-down versions), but the rest of the place oozes space. There's internet, travel advice, real coffee and very helpful, English-speaking staff. Walk south from exit A2 of Pangxiejia (螃蟹岬) metro station along Zhongshan Lu, and it's on your right.

Tomolo BOUTIQUE HOTEL $$$
(天美乐饭店; Tiānměilè Fàndiàn; ☎8275 7288; 56 Jianghan Sanlu; 江汉三路56号; r ¥698, discounted to ¥348; ✲@🛜) Tucked away in a lane off a modern pedestrianised shopping street, this excellent-value boutique hotel has a prime location and a natty finish throughout. Big rooms come with sofas, wide-screen TVs, internet access and lush carpets, while the bathrooms, complete with mosaic tiling and power showers, are in pristine condition; staff make a real effort. Excellent discounts.

Wànkě Bīnguǎn HOTEL $
(万可宾馆; ☎8271 9922; 315 Shengli Jie; 胜利街315号; r from ¥178, discounted to ¥128; ✲@) Wooden stairs and floorboards make this basic cheapie more stylish than most. Good location on the fringes of the pleasant former concession area, and close to the river. Internet connection for laptop users. No English sign; no English spoken.

Zhōng Huì Hotel HOTEL $
(中惠宾馆; Zhōnghuì Bīnguǎn; ☎8805 9288; 188 Shouyi Xincun; 首义新村188号; d without/with window ¥118/208; ✲@) This three-star hotel has well-kept rooms with clean bathrooms. The cheapies are smaller and have no windows, but are still comfortable, and you'll have fun getting to them in the exterior brass lift. Rates include breakfast. Some rooms have a computer. Others have internet connection. The ¥208 rooms usually go for ¥168.

Marco Polo HOTEL $$$
(马哥孛罗酒店; Mǎgē Bóluó Jiǔdiàn; ☎8277 8888; www.marcopolohotels.com; 159 Yanjiang Dadao; 沿江大道159号; r from ¥850, with river view ¥1050; ✲@🛜) The best-located five-star hotel in Wǔhàn, Marco Polo offers sweeping views of the Yangzi River and is backed by the tree-lined former concession area, which is dotted with bars, cafes and restaurants.

Wǔhàn

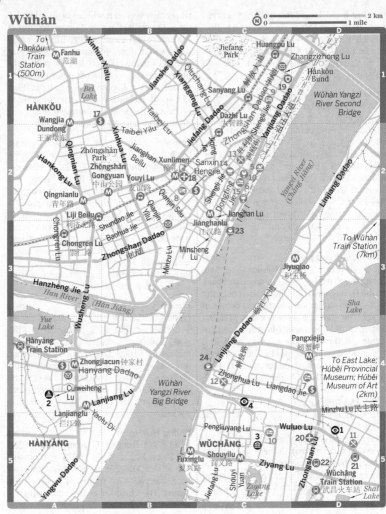

To Hànkǒu Train Station (500m)

Fanhu 范湖

Jiefang Park

Huangpú Lù

Zhangzizhong Lù

Xinhua Xialu

Jianshe Dadao

Xiangganglu

Qiuchang Lu

解放大道

Hànkǒu Bund

Sanyang Lù

19

Wǔhàn Yangzi River Second Bridge

Bei Lake

HÀNKǑU

17

Taibei Lu

Jiefang Dadao

Dazhi Lù 大智路

中山大道

Zhongshan Dadao

Yanjiang Dadao

沿江大道

Wangjia Dundong 王家墩东

Qingnian Lu

Zhōngshān Park Zhōngshān Gōngyuán 中山公园

Taibei Yilu

Jianghan Beilu

Xunlimen 循礼门

Zhongshan Shanglu Jie

Jiqing 吉庆

13

街

Yangzi River (Cháng Jiāng)

Hankong Lu

Xinhua Lu

Youyi Lù 友谊路

Sanxin Hengjie

14

18

5

Qingnianlu 青年路

Shundao Jie

Qianjin Silu

Shenqi Jie

Dongting

16

15

Liji Beilu 利济北路

Baohua Jie

Qianjin Yilu

Jianghanlu 江汉路

Jianghan Lù

Linjiang Dadao

Chongren Lù 崇仁路

Chongren Lu

Minzu Lu

Zhongshan Dadao 中山路

Minsheng Lù

23

To Wǔhàn Train Station (7km)

Hanzheng Jie

Wusheng Lu

Han River (Hàn Jiāng)

Jiyuqiao 积玉桥

Sha Lake

Yue Lake

Hanzhong Jie

Pangxiejia 螃蟹岬

Hànyáng Train Station

Zhongjiacun 钟家村 Hanyang Dadao

24

Linjiang Dadao

沿江大道

To East Lake; Húběi Provincial Museum; Húběi Museum of Art (2km)

Cuiweiheng Lu

Zhonghua Lù

Liangdao Jie

7

2

Lanjiang Lu

Yaolu Di

Lanjianglu 拦江路

Wǔhàn Yangzi River Big Bridge

12

4

Minzhu Lu 民主路

HÀNYÁNG

Pengliuyang Lu

Wuluo Lù

1

11

Yingwu Dadao

WǓCHĀNG

3

10

20

22

21

Fuxinglu

Shouyilu 首义路

Ziyang Lù

Wǔchāng Train Station 武昌火车站

Shouyi Yuan

Ziyang Lake

Zhongshan Lu

Shai Lake

✕ Eating

In Hànkǒu, the alleyways north of Zhong-shan Dadao, between Qianjin Yilu and Qianjin Silu, are particularly lively. **Jiqing Jie** (吉庆街) has numerous *dàpáidǎng* (open-air food stalls or restaurants) selling seafood and duck, especially at the Dazhi Lu end. **Cai'e Lu** (才俄路), the road which Xiǎo Bèiké restaurant is on, is littered with *shāokǎo* ((烧烤; barbecues).

In Wǔchāng, follow your nose to the hugely popular **Hùbù Xiàng Snack Street** (户部巷小吃; Hùbù Xiàng Xiǎochī).

Breakfast – called *guòzǎo* (过早) in Wǔhàn – is all about *règān miàn* (热干面; literally 'hot-dry noodles'; ¥4).

TOP CHOICE **Xiǎo Bèiké**   CHINESE $$

(小贝壳; 129 Dongting Jie; 洞庭街129号; mains ¥20-50; ⏱9.30am-10.30pm) This stylish res-taurant, with lovely tree-shaded terrace seating, offers an excellent range of pan-Chinese cuisine, with dishes from Húběi, Sìchuān and Chóngqìng featuring highly. Also does a number of fish dishes, includ-ing Yangzi River catfish and delicious

Wǔhàn

◎ Sights
1 Chángchūn Temple D5
2 Guīyuán Temple A4
3 The Revolution of 1911
   Museum C5
4 Yellow Crane Tower C4

⚙ Activities, Courses & Tours
5 Public Swimming Pool C2

🛏 Sleeping
6 Marco Polo C2
7 Pathfinder Youth Hostel D4
8 Tomolo B2
9 Wànkě Bīnguǎn C1
10 Zhōng Huì Hotel C5

✴ Eating
Chángchūn Temple
   Vegetarian Restaurant .... (see 1)
11 Crown Bakery D5

12 Hùbù Xiàng Snack Street C4
13 Xiǎo Bèiké C2

🍷 Drinking
14 Cafes C2
15 Nightclubs C2
16 York Teahouse C2

ℹ Information
17 HSBC ATM A1
18 Pǔ'ān Pharmacy B2
19 Public Security Bureau C1
20 Zhōnglián Pharmacy D5

ⓘ Transport
21 Fùjiāpō Long-Distance Bus
   Station D5
22 Hóngjī Long-Distance Bus
   Station D5
23 Wǔhàn Guān Dock C3
24 Zhonghua Lu Dock C4

scallops. No English sign – it's in the yellow building on the corner of Dongting Jie and Cai'e Lu (蔡锷路) – but has an English menu with photos.

Chángchūn Temple Vegetarian Restaurant　　　VEGETARIAN $$
(长春观素菜餐厅; Chángchūnguān Sùcài Cāntīng; 145 Wuluo Lu; 武珞路145号; mains ¥20-50; ⊙9.30am-9pm; 🖉) Housed next door to a Taoist temple, this place prides itself on bizarre mock-meat creations but also serves fish dishes. Photo menu.

Crown Bakery　　　BAKERY $
(皇冠蛋糕; Huángguān Dàngāo; 345 Wuluo Lu; 武珞路345号; ⊙7am-9pm) Fabulously located in an old cruciform church built in 1907, with its original wood ceiling intact along with loads of portraits of Jesus, come here for the ambience, take a seat in the apse to break bread and order egg tarts (¥4), tea (¥5), instant coffee (¥5) or loads of cakes (¥2 to ¥5).

🍷 Drinking & Entertainment

Hànkǒu is the place to go for a night out; Yanjiang Dadao (沿江大道) and its surrounding lanes are the best place to start. There are neon-tastic **nightclubs** towards the ferry port, while Lihuangpi Lu (黎黄陂路) is one of a number of lanes here with cutesy **Western-style cafes**.

York Teahouse　　　BAR
(约克英式茶馆; Yuēkè Yīngshì Cháguǎn; 162 Yanjiang Dadao; ⊙1pm-3am) Run by 'Mr Sugar' (Tang Xiansheng), this old-timer has been doing its thing on the riverfront since 2001. Inside is a warren of rooms, but there's plenty of outdoor seating. Beers and coffee from ¥20.

ℹ Information

Most ATMs accept foreign cards. We've marked a few on our map, along with some handy branches of China Post. Internet cafes (网吧; wǎngbā) here may be reluctant to accept foreigners because they need to swipe a Chinese ID card to register their users. All hotels we list have internet access of some sort.

Pǔ'ān Pharmacy (普安大药房; Pǔ'ān Dàyàofáng; 148 Jianghan Lu; 江汉路148号; ⊙24hr)

Public Security Bureau (PSB; 公安局; Gōng'ānjú; ☎8539 5351; 7 Zhangzizhong Lu; 张自忠路7号; ⊙8.30am-noon & 2.30-5.30pm) Can extend visas.

Zhōnglián Pharmacy (中联大药店; Zhōnglián Dàyàodiàn; 404 Zhongshan Lu; 中山路404号; ⊙24hr)

ⓘ Getting There & Away

Air

Tiānhé International Airport (天河飞机场; Tiānhé Fēijīchǎng; ☎8581 8888) is 30km northwest of town and has direct flights to the likes of Běijīng (¥800), Chéngdū (¥600) and Hong Kong (¥1000). Use elong.net or ctrip.com to book flights.

Regular airport shuttle buses go to and from Hànkǒu Train Station (¥15, 45 minutes) and Fùjiāpō long-distance bus station (¥30, one hour). A taxi is about ¥100.

Bus

There is a number of long-distance bus stations, all of which run very similar services. In Hànkǒu, the main one is beside Hànkǒu Train Station. In Wǔchāng, the main two are Fùjiāpō long-distance bus station (傅家坡汽车客运站; Fùjiāpō qìchē kèyùnzhàn) and Hóngjī long-distance bus station (宏基长途汽车站; Hóngjī chángtú qìchēzhàn).

You can get buses to most major cities, even as far away as Shànghǎi and Běijīng. The following are sample services from Hóngjī long-distance bus station:

Jīngzhōu ¥75 to ¥89, three hours, every 45 minutes (7am to 8pm)

Mùyú (for Shénnóngjià) ¥150, eight hours, one daily (8.50am)

Shíyàn (for Wǔdāng Shān) ¥145, six hours, three daily (8.40am, 11.40am and 1.30pm)

Yíchāng ¥115 to ¥142, four hours, every 30 minutes (6.50am to 6pm)

Train

Wǔhàn has three major train stations: Hànkǒu Train Station (汉口火车站; Hànkǒu Huǒchēzhàn), Wǔchāng Train Station (武昌火车站; Wǔchāng Huǒchēzhàn) and Wǔhàn Train Station (武汉火车站; Wǔhàn Huǒchēzhàn), all of which should be linked up to the metro system by the time you read this.

Services include:

Běijīng D train 2nd-/1st-class seat ¥267/333, 10 hours, three daily (8.06am*, 9.05am* and 11.57am***)

Běijīng Z train hard/soft sleeper ¥263/411, 10 hours, four daily (8.24pm*, 9.03pm**, 9.09pm** and 9.12pm*)

***Chángshā** G train 2nd-/1st-class seat ¥165/265, 1½ hours, more than 40 daily (7am to 7.55pm)

***Guǎngzhōu** G train 2nd-/1st-class seat ¥465/740, four hours, more than 40 daily (7am to 7.55pm)

Kūnmíng hard/soft sleeper ¥380/600, 26 to 30 hours, three daily (5.07am, 10.55am and 10.46pm)

*Shànghǎi D train 2nd-/1st-class seat ¥264/317, five to six hours, 11 daily (7.05am to 5.23pm)

*Wǔdāng Shān hard seat ¥70, six to seven hours, two daily (10.35am and 4pm)

*Xī'ān D train 2nd-/1st-class seat ¥307/432, 7½ hours (9.15am)

**Yíchāng hard seat ¥54, five hours, four daily (7.36am, 11.26am, 12.10pm and 5.35pm)

*(*Hànkǒu Station; **Wǔchāng Station; ***Wǔhàn Station)*

ⓘ Getting Around

Bus

Bus 10 (¥1.50) Connects Hànkǒu and Wǔchāng Train Stations.

Bus 401 (¥2) From Hànyáng past Guīyuán Temple, Yellow Crane Tower and Chángchūn Temple to East Lake.

Bus 402 (¥2) From Wǔchāng Train Station to Chángchūn Temple and Yellow Crane Tower, then via Hànyáng to Yanjiang Dadao in Hànkǒu before returning over the river for the provincial museum and half a circuit of East Lake.

Bus 411 (¥1.50) Travels a more direct route from the museum to Yellow Crane Tower and Chángchūn Temple before carrying on to Hànkǒu Train Station.

Ferry

Ferries (¥1.50, 6.30am to 8pm) make swift daily crossings of the Yangzi between Zhonghua Lu Dock (中华路码头; Zhōnghuá Lù Mǎtóu) and Wǔhàn Guān Dock (武汉关码头; Wǔhàn Guān Mǎtóu).

Metro

Wǔhàn's fledgling metro system (地铁; dìtiě) includes Line 1, an aboveground light-rail line in Hànkǒu, and Lines 2 and 4, which tunnel under the river, linking the main train stations. Other lines are on the way.

Jīngzhōu　荆州

📋 0716 / POP 1.5 MILLION

Capital of the Chu kingdom during the Eastern Zhou, Jīngzhōu has an ancient history and a homely small-town feel. One of the few Chinese cities still ringed by an intact city wall, Jīngzhōu has also managed to cling on to some of its ancient temples, and boasts a noteworthy museum. The surrounding farmlands are home to several ancient burial sites, including Xióngjiā Zhǒng, the largest collection of Chu kingdom tombs ever discovered.

⊙ Sights

The walled section of Jīngzhōu is approximately 3.5km from east to west and 2.5km from north to south, with impressive city gates at each cardinal point, as well as several lesser gates. Passing through the wall at New East Gate (新东门; *Xīn Dōngmén*), as you will if you're on the bus from the main stations, you'll have Jingzhou Nanlu (荆州南路) stretching out in front of you, and you'll see the older East Gate (东门; *Dōngmén*) off to your right. Zhangjuzheng Jie (张居正街) leads away from East Gate and runs parallel to Jingzhou Nanlu.

FREE **Jīngzhōu Museum** MUSEUM
(荆州博物馆; Jīngzhōu Bówùguǎn; Jingzhou Zhonglu; 荆州中路; audio tour ¥20, English tour guide ¥200; ⊙9am-5pm Tue-Sun) The highlight of this excellent museum, which showcases some wonderful artefacts unearthed from Chu tombs around the area, is the incredibly well-preserved 2000-year-old body of a man found in his tomb with ancient tools, clothing and even food; the airtight mud seal around his crypt helped preserve him. It's in one of the buildings around the large pond behind the main building. Take bus 12, 19 or 101 to West Gate (西门; *Xīmén*), then backtrack 200m.

City Wall HISTORIC SITE
Jīngzhōu's original **city wall** (城墙; *chéngqiáng*) was a mud wall dating from the Eastern Han dynasty. The first stone version came during the Five Dynasties and Ten Kingdoms. Today, the oldest surviving sections, around **South Gate** (南门; *Nánmén*), are Song, but most of what you'll see is Ming and Qing. The South Gate, with its enceinte still attached, is best for flavours of medieval Jīngzhōu and swarms with Taoist soothsayers, outdoor hairdressers offering cutthroat shaves and vegetable sellers. A similar carnival feel accompanies **East Gate** (老东门; *Lǎo Dōngmén*), which also has an enceinte and a fairground feel with bouncing castles and costume hire. You can walk on parts of the wall, sometimes for a small fee (¥7 to ¥27), but the best way to see it is to rent a bike and cycle around the outside (1½ hours) between the wall and the city moat. This path also makes a lovely walk.

Kāiyuán Temple TAOIST
(开元观; Kāiyuán Guàn) Explore the fascinating empty remains attached to the Jīngzhōu Museum.

Guāndì Temple TAOIST
(关帝庙; Guāndì Miào) Up the road from the South Gate.

Tiěnǚ Temple BUDDHIST
(铁女寺; Tiěnǚ Sì; off Jingbei Lu) The intriguingly named Iron Girl Temple.

Xuánmiào Temple TAOIST
(玄妙观; Xuánmiào Guàn; north of Jingbei Lu) This Taoist temple, just north of New North Gate (新北门; *xīnběimén*), literally translates as the 'Temple of Mystery'.

Confucian Temple CONFUCIAN
(文庙; Wén Miào) Now part of Shíyàn Zhōngxué (Experimental Middle School), a short walk east of the museum. Smile sweetly to be let in.

🛏 Sleeping

Jiǔgē Holiday Hotel HOTEL $$
(九歌假日酒店; Jiǔgē Jiàrì Jiǔdiàn; ☎885 7777; 13 Jingzhou Nanlu; 荆州南路13号; r from ¥380, discounted to ¥198; ❀❂⑤) Good-quality, modern, midrange hotel offering large, comfortable, wi-fi–enabled rooms, a restaurant and a cafe. It's about 200m inside the New East Gate.

Bāyī Bīnguǎn HOTEL $
(八一宾馆; ☎152 7248 2879; 14-4 Zhangju Zhengjie; 张居正街14-4号; r from ¥70; ❀) One of several cheap hotels on Zhangju Zhengjie. Was undergoing wholesale renovation when we last visited. Expect newly decorated rooms, wi-fi and slightly higher prices by the time you read this. It's 200m inside the older East Gate.

🍴 Eating

Come evening, locals head to the East Gate end of Zhangju Zhengjie for *shāokǎo*. See p761 for more on *shāokǎo*.

Bàyú Rénjiā CHINESE HÚBĚI $$
(巴渝人家; New East Gate, Donghuan Lu; 东环路新东门外; mains ¥20-50; ⊙11am-9pm) Great location by the moat, outside New East Gate. Grab a table overlooking the city wall and moat and tuck into the restaurant speciality, *gānguō* (干锅), an iron pot of spicy delights, kept bubbling hot with a small candle burner. Varieties include chicken (干锅仔鸡; *gānguō zǐjī*; ¥38), bullfrog (干锅牛蛙; *gānguō niúwā*; ¥48), tofu (干锅千叶豆腐; *gānguō qiānyè dòufu;* ¥32) and pig intestine (干锅肥肠; *gānguō féicháng*; ¥38). One pot is enough for two or three people with rice (米饭; *mǐfàn*), which is free. Exit New East Gate, cross the moat and the restaurant is on your right.

ⓘ Information

There's a China Construction Bank (中国建设银行; Zhōngguó Jiànshè Yínháng) with a foreign-friendly ATM between New East Gate and Jiǔgē Holiday Hotel. There are 24-hour internet cafes opposite both hotels that we've reviewed. Look for the characters 网吧 (wǎngbā).

ⓘ Getting There & Around

Bicycle

The **bicycle rental place** (per hr/day ¥7/50) by East Gate is one of many around the walled section of the city.

Bus

You'll probably arrive at either Shāshì long-distance bus station (沙市长途汽车站; Shāshì chángtú qìchēzhàn) or Shāshì central bus station (沙市中心客运站; Shāshì zhōngxīn kèyùnzhàn). Turn right out of either, walk to the first bus stop and take bus 101 (¥2) to East Gate (东门; dōngmén). Get off at the first stop after passing through the gate. For Jiǔgē Holiday Hotel, keep walking straight and the hotel will be on your left after 200m. For Bāyī Bīnguǎn, walk back, take the first left, then left again down Zhangju Zhengjie and the hotel will be on your right.

Buses from Shāshì long-distance bus station:

Wǔdāng Shān ¥120, five hours (7.45am and 1pm)

Wǔhàn ¥80, four hours (6.30am to 8pm)

Yíchāng ¥44, two hours (7am to 6pm)

Train

Jīngzhōu should be linked up by rail to Wǔhàn and Yíchāng by the time you read this. Bus 49 (¥2) will connect the train station (火车站; huǒchē zhàn) with East Gate.

Around Jīngzhōu

When we first visited the 2300-year-old tombs of Xióngjiā Zhǒng (熊家冢; admission ¥30; ⊙9.30am-4.30pm) back in 2008, they had only just begun excavation here (see boxed text, p427), and tourists were allowed a rare opportunity to witness archaeology in progress, as most of the tombs, including the main tomb itself, had yet to be opened. Artefacts that had already been excavated included a large collection of jade (now on display at the Jīngzhōu Museum) and the fascinating skeletal remains of two horses pulling a chariot, which had been left in their small, open tomb for visitors to see. When we revisited the site most recently it was closed to the public, but was due to re-open as part of a modern hangerlike museum (à la the Terracotta Warriors) towards the end of 2012. Expect a much more informative experience, but also a price hike.

The tombs are 40km north of Jīngzhōu. Buses (¥9, 70 minutes) leave hourly from the back of the bus station called Chǔdū Kèyùn Zhàn (楚都客运站). Bus 24 links this station with Jīnfēng Guǎngchǎng (金凤广场) bus stop, just outside East Gate (over the moat and turn left). A taxi will be at least ¥100 return.

Wǔdāng Shān 武当山

☑0719

Wǔdāng Shān may not be one of China's five sacred Taoist mountains but it's paradoxically known as the No 1 Taoist Mountain in the Middle Kingdom. Sacrosanct in martial arts circles, it is acknowledged that 'in the north they esteem Shàolín, in the south they revere Wǔdāng'. The Unesco World Heritage Site of Wǔdāng Shān is the apocryphal birthplace of taichi, and possesses supernaturally good-looking vistas and an abundance of medicinal plants that naturally find their way into a panoply of Taoist medicinal potions. The mountain is also sadly overpriced and overcommercialised, with new developments afoot, so expect the magic of Taoist chanting to be occasionally perforated by the squeal of buzz saws.

⊙ Sights & Activities

The town's main road, Taihe Lu (太和路) – which at various sections is also labelled Taihe Donglu (太和东路; Taihe East) and Taihe Zhonglu (太和中路; Taihe Central) – runs east–west on its way up towards the main gate of the mountain. Everything of interest in town is either on or near this road and road numbers are clearly labelled. Buses often drop you at the junction by the main expressway, a 1km walk east of the town centre. From here, turn left to the mountain entrance (100m) or right into town.

You can buy Chinese (¥3) or English (¥8) maps at the main gate of the mountain or at Jīnlóngdiàn Hotel, which is between the two hotels we recommend here.

[FREE] **Wǔdāng Museum of China** MUSEUM (武当博物馆; Wǔdāng Bówùguǎn; Culture Sq; 文化广场; audio tour ¥20, deposit ¥200; ⊙9-11am & 2.30-5pm) This is a great opportunity to get to grips with Wǔdāng Shān history, lore and architecture. There's a whole pantheon of gods, including the eminent Zhenwu (patriarch of the mountain) and a section on Taoist medicine including the fundamentals of *nèidān Xué* (内丹学; internal alchemy). There are also some stunning bronze pieces. Turn right out of either of the hotels listed here, then right down Bowuguan Lu (博物馆路), which leads to Culture Sq (文化广场; Wenhua Guangchang).

Wǔdāng Shān TAOIST MOUNTAIN

(admission ¥140, bus ¥100, audio guide ¥30) The mountain attracts a diverse array of climbers: Taoist nuns with knapsacks, workers shouldering paving slabs and sacks of rice, businessmen with laptops and bright-eyed octogenarians hopping along. Take bus 1 (¥1) or walk from Taihe Lu to the Main Gate (山门口; Shān Ménkǒu) and ticket office. The bus ticket you must buy with your admission gives you unlimited use of shuttle buses (from 6am to 6.30pm). Note that everything added together (including buses and temple tickets) will cost you ¥245; presumably this funded the construction of the expensive-looking ticket hall. The ticket-checking guards in black quasi-military outfits and red berets are curious in such a sacred place. Before buying your ticket you are funnelled mercilessly past shops selling Wǔdāng swords and the like.

One bus – often only leaving when full – runs to the start of the **cable car** (索道; suǒdào; up/down ¥50/45). For those who don't mind steps, take the bus to South Cliff (南岩; Nányán), where the trail to 1612m **Heavenly Pillar Peak** (天柱峰; Tiānzhù Fēng), the highest peak, begins. Consider disembarking early at the beautiful, turquoise-tiled **Purple Cloud Temple** (紫霄宫; Zǐxiāo Gōng; admission ¥20), from where a small stone path leads up to South Cliff (45 minutes). From South Cliff it's an energy-sapping, two-hour, 4km climb to the top, but the scenery is worth every step and there are plenty of Taoist temples en route where you can take contemplative breathers. Note the occasional Taoist cairn and trees garlanded with scarlet ribbons weighed with small stones.

The enchanting red-walled **Cháotiān Temple** (朝天宫; Cháotiān Gōng) is about halfway up, housing a statue of the Jade Emperor and standing on an old, moss-hewn stone base with 4m-high tombstones guarding its entrance. From here you have a choice of two ascent routes, via the 1.4km Ming-dynasty route (the older, Back Way)

WŬHÀN WORDS

Wǔhàn locals speak Hànqiāng (汉腔) or 'Wǔhàn speak', a local speciality. To locals, shoes are *haizi* (sounding like the word for 'child') rather than the more standard *xiézi*, so Wǔhàn's ubiquitous shoe cleaners shout '*ca haizi*' ('clean shoes') instead of '*cā xiézi*' (in this respect the word is similar to the Cantonese). Another lovely peculiarity you don't hear in many other parts of China is the word *fúzi* (服子) for towel and *mámù* (麻木) for a pedicab, more prosaically called a *sānlúnchē* (三轮车) elsewhere across the land. To show off is to *fapao* (create a froth) while 'inside' (里面) is inexplicably '*dòulǐ*' (豆里; literally 'inside the bean'). 'Clean' in Wǔhàn is not '*gānjìng*' but '*línxīn*' (林新). Wǔhàn folk end their sentences with a *sa* (撒) particle, instead of the far more usual *a* (啊) sound you hear elsewhere in China.

or the 1.8km Qing-dynasty path (the 'Hundred Stairs'). The shorter but more gruelling Ming route ascends via the **Three Heaven's Gates**, including the stupefying climb to the **Second Gate of Heaven** (二天门; Èrtiān Mén). You can climb by one route and descend by the other. Temple ruins, fallen trees, shocking inclines and steep steps misshapen by centuries of footslogging await you, but the climb is hugely rewarding.

Near the top, beyond the cable-car exit, is the magnificent **Forbidden City** (紫金城; Zǐjīn Chéng; admission ¥20) with its 2.5m-thick stone walls hugging the mountainside and balustrades festooned with lovers' locks. From here you can stagger to magnificent views from the **Golden Hall** (金殿; Jīn Diàn; admission ¥20), constructed entirely from bronze, dating from 1416 and in dire need of some buffing up. A small statue of Zhenwu – Ming emperor and Wǔdāng Shān's presiding Taoist deity – is enclosed within. On the way down, note how some pilgrims descend backwards!

Courses

Wǔdāng Taoist Kungfu Academy TAICHI
(武当道教功夫学院; Wǔdāng Dàojiào Gōngfu Xuéyuàn; ☑568 9185; www.wudang.org; fees per day classes/accommodation/meals ¥250/120/50) There are dozens of taichi schools (太极拳;

THE BIRTH OF TAICHI

Zhang San Feng (张三丰), a semi-legendary Wŭdāng Shān monk from the 10th or 13th century (depending on what source you read), is reputed to be the founder of the martial art *tàijíquán*, or taichi. Zhang had grown dissatisfied with the 'hard' techniques of Shaolin boxing and searched for something 'softer'. Sitting on his porch one day, he became inspired by a battle between a huge bird and a snake. The sinuous snake used flowing movements to evade the bird's attacks. The bird, exhausted, eventually gave up and flew away. Taichi is closely linked to Taoism, and many priests on Wŭdāng Shān practise some form of the art.

tàijíquán) in these parts, but this one stands out in terms of its location, its qualities as a school and its accessibility to foreigners. The setting is magical; in a large, secluded courtyard surrounded by pine trees halfway up the mountain. Classes, which follow a strict regime (including 5.30am starts!), are held either in and around the courtyard or at various scenic spots on the mountain. One member of the admin staff speaks excellent English and is very helpful. You can sign up for anything from a few days to one year; the longer you study, the cheaper the rates. You'll have to find, and fund, your own way here the first time (it's down the steps to your left, just past Purple Cloud Temple; no English sign). After that, the school will arrange a pass for you so you can come and go without having to pay the hefty entrance fees to the mountain each time. There are no classes on Thursdays.

🛏 Sleeping

IN TOWN

Xuán Yuè Hotel HOTEL $$
(玄岳饭店; Xuányuè Fàndiàn; ☎566 5111; 27 Yuxu Lu; 玉虚路27号; r from ¥428, discounted to ¥160; ❈@) Very smart, recently refurbished midrange hotel, with carpeted rooms and spotless bathrooms. Some rooms have computers, some have internet connection for laptops. It's on the corner of Yuxu Lu and Taihe Zhonglu and is accessed through an entranceway to the right of the one with the English sign for the hotel (the one with the English sign leads to the restaurant).

Shèngjǐngyuàn Bīnguǎn HOTEL $$
(圣景苑宾馆; ☎566 2118; 7 Taihe Zhonglu; 太和中路7号; r without/with bathroom ¥258/288, discounted to ¥80/120; ❈@) Simple, bright, pleasant rooms come with firm mattresses and spacious bathrooms. Internet connection for laptop users. Next door but one to the hard-to-miss Bank of China.

ON THE MOUNTAIN

There are about a dozen hotels and guesthouses by South Cliff. The cheapest rooms go for around ¥80.

Nányán Hotel HOTEL $$
(南岩宾馆; Nányán Bīnguǎn; ☎568 9182; r ¥380-486, discounted to ¥150-200; ❈@) This hotel right by the bus stop at South Cliff has large, clean, comfortable rooms and welcoming staff. Cheaper rooms have squat loo and no internet connection.

Taichi Hotel HOTEL $$
(太极会馆; Tàijí Huìguǎn; ☎568 9888; r without/with window ¥288/498; ❈@) The best-quality hotel on the mountain, although discounts aren't as good as elsewhere. Rooms with windows go for ¥348, and have fabulous mountain views. Rooms without windows are identical (apart from the views) but are generally not discounted. Internet connection for laptops is in all rooms. It's 200m downhill from the bus stop at South Cliff.

🍴 Eating

IN TOWN

A few *shāokǎo* stalls set up every evening in an alley off Taihe Lu. Look for the neon-lit archway with the characters 鱼羊鲜, beside No 14.

Taìhé Xuánwǔ Dàjiǔdiàn CHINESE $$
(太和玄武大酒店; 35 Taihe Zhonglu; 太和中路35号; mains ¥20-50; ⏰6.30am-11.30pm) Large bustling restaurant with half its menu helpfully translated into English. Various regional cuisines are represented, from Sichuanese to Cantonese; even Běijīng roast duck! No English sign. Turn right out of either hotel we list here, and it's on your right.

ON THE MOUNTAIN

There are plenty of food options by South Cliff, although not many English menus. **Taste of Wŭdāng** (味道武当; Wèidao Wŭdāng; mains ¥15-32), a fast-food-style restaurant right by the bus stop, does noodles and rice meals and has an English menu.

⭐ Entertainment

Wǔdāng Grand Theatre THEATRE
(武当大剧院; Wǔdāng Dàjùyuàn; ☏506 2366; Culture Sq) Modern theatre opposite the museum. Hosts the **Wǔdāng Taichi Show** (tickets ¥200-280; ⊙8-9pm) every Thursday, Friday and Saturday.

❶ Information

Bank of China (中国银行; Zhōngguó Yínháng; 1 Taihe Zhonglu; 太和中路1号; ⊙8.30am-5.30pm) Foreign friendly ATM and money-exchange facility. Next door but one to Shèngjīngyuàn Bīnguǎn.

Jísù Internet (极速网吧; Jísù Wǎngbā; 2nd fl, 20 Taihe Lu; 太和路20号; per hr ¥3; ⊙24hr) Through a round archway. No English sign.

❶ Getting There & Away
Bus

The new bus station (客运汽车站; kèyùn qìchēzhàn), 200m downhill from the expressway, on the right of the road leading into town, was still being built when we were here, but buses were already running from it. Expect schedules to change once the bus station is completed.

Jīngzhōu ¥120, five hours (9am)
Wǔhàn ¥150, five hours (8.30am and 11am)
Xī'ān ¥110, four hours (8.30am)
Yíchāng ¥110, five hours (9.30am)

A fleet of small green buses shuttles between the two nearest train stations – Wǔdāngshān and Shíyàn (十堰; ¥8, one hour, 5.10am to 8pm) – via Liùlǐpíng (六里坪; ¥4, 20 minutes). They leave from outside Taìhé Xuánwǔ Dàjiǔdiàn restaurant.

Train

Wǔdāng Shān no longer has a train station, although the train station at Liùlǐpíng is often referred to as Wǔdāng Shān. You can buy train tickets from the **train ticket agency** (铁路客票代售; tiělù piàodàishòu; ⊙8.30am-6pm), beside Wǔdāng Shān's old train station on Chezhan Lu (车站路), a road opposite Xuánwǔ Dàjiǔdiàn restaurant. For Yíchāng, you need to change trains at Xiāngyáng (襄阳), a train station in the city of Xiāngfán (襄樊), from where there are also regular trains to places such as Xī'ān, Chéngdū and Luòyáng.

Liùlǐpíng trains:

Wǔhàn (Wǔchāng) hard seat ¥70, six to 6½ hours, three daily (12.56pm, 1.11pm and 4.21pm)
Xiānyáng hard seat ¥24, two hours, regular (6am to 11.30pm)

Shíyàn trains:

Wǔhàn (Wǔchāng) hard seat ¥73, six to seven hours, regular (9am to 11.30pm)

Xiāngyáng trains:

Yíchāng hard seat ¥33 to ¥38, three hours, hourly (7am to noon, then 8.48pm and 8.55pm)

Shénnóngjià 神农架

☏0719

Famed for its medicinal plants and legendary ape-man (野人; yěrén), Shénnóngjià forms a significant chunk of the most spectacular region of Húběi province. Thickly forested peaks with part-exposed rock faces rise up dramatically from a small network of Yangzi River tributaries; the bus journey here alone will leave you gobsmacked. Foreigners are only allowed into one of the four sections of

---

LYING IN WAIT

Despite being discovered 30 years ago, when canal diggers dug up the remains of a horse and chariot, mystery still surrounds the potentially momentous tomb site at Xióngjiā Zhǒng. Fears of insufficient preservation techniques meant excavation only began in 2006, and only a fraction of its more than 100 tombs have been opened. Finds already unearthed include one of China's finest collections of jade, but potentially there's a lot more to come. Work began in 2008 on excavating the huge, 130m-long horse and chariot tomb, while the main tomb itself, which is believed to contain the largest royal coffin ever discovered in China (248 sq metres, if estimates are accurate), still hasn't been touched. Exactly whose body is lying in it, waiting to be discovered, is unknown. The site is believed to be named after the surname of the person buried in it (Xióng; 熊). No accounts specify who that person is, but Xióng was a royal family name of the Chu kingdom (722–221 BC) so it's widely assumed the tomb belongs to one of the 20 Chu kings who used to rule the area. If so, it would be the first Chu king tomb ever discovered. Experts date the site at around 2300 years old, which points to the last Chu king, Chu Zhaowang (楚昭王), also known as Xiong Zhen (熊珍). No documents link him with the site, but he was known to have been so popular that people were willing to die for him, which is perhaps why the main tomb comes with at least 92 accompanying tombs, all thought to contain human remains.

the national park, at **Yāzikǒu** (鸭子口; admission ¥140), but the area is big enough for good walking. You can also camp here. Once inside the park, you can board shuttle buses (¥90) to various points of interest. Worth checking out are **Xiǎolóngtán** (小龙潭), about 10km from the entrance, and a good place to spot monkeys (Shénnóngjià is home to the rare golden snub-nosed monkey; 川金丝猴; *chuān jīnsīhóu*), and **Shénnóngdǐng** (神农顶), 20km from the entrance and the highest peak here (3105m). There's a camping area (¥30) at the base of Shénnóngdǐng, called **Shénnóngyíng** (神农营). Winter is bitterly cold and snow often blocks roads.

Yāzikǒu is accessed from **Mùyú** (木鱼), a small but well-developed tourist village about 14km down the mountain. All buses drop you in Mùyú.

The modest **Shuānglín Hotel** (双林酒店; Shuānglín Jiǔdiàn; ☑345 2803; 25 Muyu Lu; 木鱼路25号; r from ¥88, with computer ¥128; ❄@), where buses drop you off, has tidy rooms and welcoming management, though there are flashier hotels, too. You can normally rent tents (帐篷; *zhàngpeng*; ¥100 to ¥200) once inside the park, or buy them (¥700 to ¥800) from a couple of camping shops in Mùyú.

The coolest place to eat in Mùyú is **Piān Qiáo Wān** (偏桥湾; 53 Muyu Lu; 木鱼路53号; mains ¥20-40; ☉10am-9pm), which is accessed via a wobbly bridge and which backs onto a small tea plantation (you can buy tea here). The menu is in Chinese only. Try the *huíguō niúròu* (回锅牛肉; spicy fried beef; ¥48), the *cháshùgū chǎolàròu* (茶树菇炒腊肉; wild mushrooms and cured pork; ¥38) or the *xiānggū ròusī* (香菇肉丝; shiitake mushrooms with pork shreds; ¥38). Don't forget to leave room for the *qiáomài bìng* (荞麦并; flatbread made with buckwheat and wild herbs and served with a honey dip).

ⓘ Information

The ICBC Bank at the top of Mùyú village has an ATM that accepts foreign cards. Internet cafes are simply marked with the characters 网吧 (*wǎngbā*; per hour ¥4).

Shared minibuses to Yāzikǒu (per person ¥10) leave from the top end of Mùyú.

ⓘ Getting There & Away

Buses leave from outside Shuānglín Hotel, where you can also buy tickets. Foreigners aren't allowed to continue north to Wǔdāng Shān from Mùyú.

Bādōng ¥55, three hours, one daily (9.30am)

Yíchāng ¥60, 2½ hours, five daily (7am to 3.30pm)

Yíchāng 宜昌

☑0717 / POP 4 MILLION

A young vibrant city of four million souls, Yíchāng lacks tourist sights but is on the map as a gateway to the magnificent Three Gorges (p770).

◉ Sights

Three Gorges Dam ARCHITECTURE

(三峡大坝; Sānxiá Dàbà; admission ¥105) The huge Three Gorges Dam hulks away upstream. The world's largest dam due to its length (2.3km) rather than its height (101m), it isn't the most spectacular dam, but is worth a peek. You can't walk on it, but there's a tourist viewing area to the north. The view from the south is much the same, and free. Take a bus from the long-distance station to Máopíng (茅坪; ¥15, 8.30am to 3pm), but get off at Bālù Chēzhàn (八路车战). Alternatively, bus 8 (¥20, one hour, 8am to 4pm) leaves from Yíchāng's East Train Station.

Day trips can also be taken by boat (¥280 including entrance fee and lunch) from the old ferry port (老码头; *lǎo mǎtóu*). They leave at 7.30am and return around 5pm. Buy tickets from Yangtze River International Travel (p775) at the port.

⌂ Sleeping

Yíchāng Hotel HOTEL $$

(宜昌饭店; Yíchāng Fàndiàn; ☑644 1616; 113 Dongshan Dadao; 东山大道113号; r from ¥268, discounted to ¥198; ❄@) This jolly place has an elegant foyer, and large and pleasant carpeted rooms (some with a computer; ¥20 extra). English is limited but it's all smiles. Diagonally opposite the long-distance bus station.

Yíling Hotel HOTEL $$

(夷陵饭店; Yíling Fàndiàn; ☑886 7199; 41 Yunji Lu; 云集路41号; r from ¥528, discounted to ¥260; ❄@) Large bright rooms with laminated wood flooring. Not as friendly as Yíchāng Hotel, but well located; close to the river and opposite a number of restaurants, bars and cafes. Bus 4 from the old dock; bus 6 from the long-distance bus station.

✕ Eating

Opposite Yíling Hotel there's a **Korean restaurant** and a **Western-style cafe**, which both have English menus.

For something more local, hop on bus 2 or 6 (¥1) or into a taxi (¥7) to Běimén (北门), where you can eat *xiāo yè* (宵夜; literally 'midnight snacks') at a number of stalls and restaurants which spill out onto the streets each evening (5pm to 2am). You'll see skewers (串; *chuàn*), dumplings (饺子; *jiǎozi*) and noodles (面; *miàn*) as well as places doing barbecued fish (烤鱼; *kǎoyú*). Look out for the **pancake stall** making *fēi bǐng* (飞饼; 'flying pancakes'; ¥12 to ¥15); the banana ones (香蕉; *xiāngjiāo*) are delicious.

Xiǎo Hú Niú
CHINESE HÚBĚI $

(小胡牛; Běimén; 北门; ingredients ¥8-20; ⏱5pm-2am) Our favourite restaurant in Běimén, this one specialises in a local beef hot-plate called *xiǎo hú niú*; order that first, stipulating how spicy you want your beef; mild (微辣; *wēi là*), medium (中辣; *zhōng là*) or hot (麻辣; *má là*), before ordering other raw ingredients to fry with it on your hot plate. Choices include *qīngjiāo* (青椒; green peppers), *xiānggū* (香菇; shiitake mushrooms), *tǔdòu piàn* (土豆片; potato slices) and *ǒu piàn* (藕片; lotus root slices).

ℹ️ Information

There are 24-hour **internet cafes** (per hr ¥3) opposite both hotels that we have reviewed. Look for the characters 网吧 (wǎngbā). Foreign-friendly ATMs are also everywhere. For information on booking Three Gorges cruises, see p775.

ℹ️ Getting There & Around

Local buses cost ¥1.

Bus 4 Old ferry port (三码头; sān mǎtóu)–Yílíng Hotel (夷陵饭店; Yílíng Fàndiàn)–old train station (火车站; huǒchē zhàn; for Yíchāng Hotel or long-distance bus station).

Bus 6 Long-distance bus station (长途汽车站; chángtú qìchēzhàn; for Yíchāng Hotel) to Běimén (北门).

Bus 9 East Train Station (火车东站; huǒchē dōngzhàn) to the long-distance bus station (长途汽车站; chángtú qìchēzhàn).

Air

Daily flights from Three Gorges Airport (三峡机场; Sānxiá Jīchǎng) include Běijīng (¥1300), Chéngdū (¥740), Shànghǎi (¥1080) and Xī'ān (¥880).

Airport shuttle buses (¥20, 50 minutes) run to and from the Qīngjiāng building (清江大厦; Qīngjiāng dàshà). They leave two hours before outward bound flights and meet all incoming flights. Flight tickets can be bought from the Air China office in the Qīngjiāng building. Turn right out of Yíchāng Hotel and it's on your right after about 1km.

Boat

For Three Gorges details, see p773.

Bus

There are three main long-distance bus stations – Yíchāng long-distance bus station (长途汽车站; chángtú qìchēzhàn), plus ones at the East Train Station and the old ferry port. All are modern and well run, and offer very similar bus services. Services from the Yíchāng long-distance bus station include:

Jīngzhōu ¥40, two hours, every 30 minutes (6.40am to 6.30pm)

Lǎoyíng (for Wǔdāng Shān) ¥130, six hours, regular (8am to 1pm)

Mùyú (for Shénnóngjià) ¥70, five hours, seven daily (7.45am to 3.30pm)

Wǔdāng Shān ¥135, six hours, one daily (either 7.45am or 1.45pm)

Wǔhàn (Wǔchāng) ¥110 to ¥157, 4½ hours, every hour (7am to 8pm)

Train

Yíchāng's East Train Station (火车东站; huǒchē dōngzhàn) is the one almost all trains use now. Train tickets (¥5 service charge) can also be bought at window 1 of Yíchāng long-distance bus station. Trains include:

Běijīng hard sleeper ¥300, 21 hours, two daily (12.34am and 6.12pm)

Chéngdū hard sleeper ¥239, 13 to 16 hours, seven daily

Chóngqìng hard sleeper ¥179, 10 to 12 hours, six daily

Shànghǎi hard sleeper ¥290 and ¥365, 18 and 23 hours, two daily (1.17am and 1.54pm)

Wǔhàn hard seat ¥55, four to six hours, regular

Xī'ān hard sleeper ¥224, 15 hours, one daily (3.50pm)

Xiāngyáng (for Wǔdāng Shān) hard seat ¥22 to ¥38, three hours, eight daily (8.23am to 8.20pm)

Jiāngxī

POP 45.2 MILLION

Includes »

Nánchāng 432
Around Nánchāng 434
Wùyuán 435
Around Wùyuán 436
Sānqīng Shān 438
Lónghǔ Shān 440
Lúshān 441

Best Hikes

» Sānqīng Shān (p438)
» Wùyuán (p435)
» Lúshān (p441)
» Wǔdāng Shān (p443)
» Lónghǔ Shān (p440)

Best Villages

» Little Lǐkēng (p437)
» Sīxī (p438)
» Luótiáncūn (p434)

Why Go?

An interconnected web of rivers, lakes and shimmering rice paddies, Jiāngxī (江西) is defined by its water. Farmers in ponchos and heavy boots till the fields in drizzling rain as snow-white herons whirl overhead, and off at the edges of the province, low-lying hills of pencil-thin pines give way to more substantial mountain ranges, seemingly shrouded in perpetual mist. At the northern border is Poyang Lake, a wetlands area that swells to become the country's largest freshwater lake in summer.

While it certainly doesn't wind up on many people's must-see list, the province has its surprises, and it can be just the spot if you're after a more remote corner of the country. Hikers should lace up their boots immediately; almost all of the major attractions are off in the mountains or verdant rolling countryside. And with several high-speed train connections from Shànghǎi and Hángzhōu, getting here has never been easier.

When to Go
Nánchāng

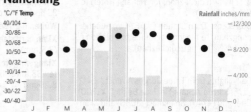

Mid-Mar Terraced rapeseed fields bloom in Wùyuán, drawing amateur photographers from across China.

Late May–early Jun Rhododendrons add splashes of pink to the Sānqīng Shān canopy.

Sep–Nov Less rainfall and moderate temperatures; best time to visit Jiāngxī.

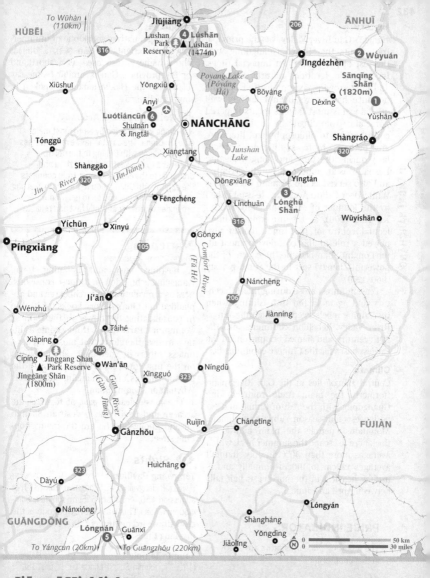

Jiāngxī Highlights

1 Look out over a forest of granite spires in **Sānqīng Shān** (p438), one of eastern China's most underrated national parks

2 Walk the ancient postal roads linking the Huīzhōu-style villages around **Wùyuán** (p435)

3 Discover a forgotten Taoist cultural centre at **Lónghǔ Shān** (p440)

4 Seek out China's literary muse, unravel political scandals or wait for the ethereal mists to clear on **Lúshān** (p441)

5 Explore Hakka country around **Lóngnán** (p443), where fortified villages and subtropical forest await

6 Escape the urban greys of Nánchāng in the traditional alleyways of **Luótiáncūn** (p434)

History

Jiāngxī's Gan River Valley was the principal trade route that linked Guǎngdōng with the rest of the country in imperial times. Its strategic location, natural resources and long growing season ensured that the province has always been relatively well off. Jiāngxī is most famous for its imperial porcelain (from Jǐngdézhèn), although its contributions to philosophy and literature are perhaps more significant, particularly during the Tang and Song dynasties. Lúshān was an important Buddhist centre, and also served as the home to the famous White Deer Grotto Academy, re-established by the founder of neo-Confucianism, Zhu Xi (1130–1200), as the pre-eminent intellectual centre of the time. Taoism also played a role in Jiāngxī's development after Lónghǔ Shān became the centre of the powerful Zhèngyī sect in the Song dynasty (960–1279).

Peasant unrest arose during the 16th century and again in the 19th century when the Taiping rebels swept through the Yangzi River Valley. Rebellion continued into the 20th century, and Jiāngxī became one of the earliest bases for the Chinese communists.

Climate

Central Jiāngxī lies in the Gan River plain (formerly the main trade route linking Guǎngdōng with the rest of China) and experiences a four-season, subtropical climate. Mountains encircle the plain and locals flock here to escape the summer heat, which averages more than 30°C in July. Rainfall averages 120cm to 190cm annually and is usually heaviest in the northeast; half falls between April and June.

PRICE INDICATORS

The following price indicators are used in this chapter:

Sleeping

$	less than ¥100
$$	¥100 to ¥400
$$$	more than ¥400

Eating

$	less than ¥30
$$	¥30 to ¥60
$$$	more than ¥60

Language

Most Jiāngxī natives speak one of innumerable local variants of Gàn (赣), a dialect whose name is also used as a shorthand for the province. Gàn is similar (some say related) to the Hakka language, spoken in southern Jiāngxī.

ⓘ Getting There & Around

Nánchāng is connected by air to most major cities in China. The capital has several express trains linking it with Běijīng to the north, Chángshā to the west, and Hángzhōu and Shànghǎi to the east. A sleeper train connects the capital with Guǎngzhōu to the south. Getting around the province and on to neighbouring provinces by bus is generally fast and reliable.

Nánchāng 南昌

🕿 0791 / POP 2.5 MILLION

A bustling, busy and booming town, Nánchāng is branded on Chinese consciousness as a revolutionary torchbearer and applauded in China's history books for its role in consolidating the power of the Chinese Communist Party (CCP). It may come as little surprise, therefore, that most travellers, unless otherwise detained, should jump on the first connection out of town to the bucolic charms of Luótiáncūn, stupendous Wùyuán or Sānqīng Shān.

The most pleasant part of town is the area around Bayi Park; pedestrian Shengli Lu and Zhongshan Lu are the main shopping streets.

◉ Sights

Téngwáng Pavilion MONUMENT
(腾王阁; Téngwáng Gé; Rongmen Lu; 榕门路; admission ¥50; ⊗7.30am-6.15pm summer, 8am-4.50pm winter) This nine-storey pagoda is the city's drawcard monument, first erected during Tang times.

Yòumín Temple BUDDHIST
(佑民寺; Yòumín Sì; 181 Minde Lu; 民德路181号; admission ¥2; ⊗9am-5pm) This huge temple was heavily damaged during the Cultural Revolution, but contains some notable statuary.

FREE **Former Headquarters of the Nánchāng Uprising** MUSEUM
(八一南昌起义纪念馆; Bāyī Nánchāng Qǐyì Jìniànguǎn; 380 Zhongshan Lu; 中山路380号; ⊗9-11.30am & 1-4pm) Wartime paraphernalia for rainy days and enthusiasts of the CCP. Admission free with passport.

Nánchāng

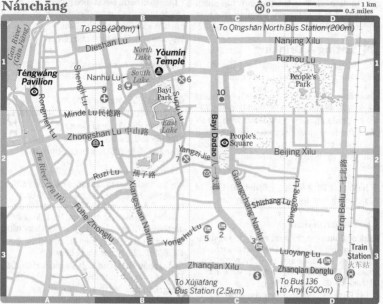

Sleeping

7 Days Inn HOTEL **$$**
(七天连锁酒店; Qītiān Liánsuǒ Jiǔdiàn; ☑8885 7688; www.7daysinn.cn; 142 Bayi Dadao; 八一大道142号; r ¥162-218; ❋@) This popular hotel, done up in pastel orange and yellow, is one of the most reliable of Nánchāng's midrange chains. Some of the rooms could use a fresh coat of paint, but it's still both comfortable and convenient. Wi-fi in the lobby and ¥7 Chinese breakfasts.

Hàntíng Inn HOTEL **$$**
(汉庭连锁酒店; Hàntíng Liánsuǒ Jiǔdiàn; ☑8885 5556; www.htinns.com; 8 Yongsu Lu; 永叔路8号; d ¥199-239; ❋) The Hàntíng is a reasonably classy, midrange option, with hardwood floors, flat-screen TVs and newer rooms. There's wi-fi in the lobby, but breakfast is for members only.

There's another **branch** (☑8622 1000; Train Station Sq; 火车站广场; d ¥199-229; ❋) across from the train station. Book ahead.

Galactic Peace Hotel HOTEL **$$$**
(嘉莱特和平国际酒店; Jiālàitè Hépíng Guójì Jiǔdiàn; ☑8611 1118; www.glthp.com; 10 Guangchang Nanlu; 广场南路10号; d incl breakfast ¥1080-1580; ❀❋@☎❄) Though there's no particular charm here, this is as comfortable as it

Nánchāng

◎ Top Sights
Téngwáng Pavilion..............................A1
Yòumín Temple...................................B1

◎ Sights
1 Former Headquarters of the
Nánchāng Uprising.........................B2

🛏 Sleeping
2 7 Days Inn C3
3 Galactic Peace Hotel C3
4 Hàntíng Inn D3
5 Hàntíng Inn C3

⊗ Eating
6 Xiánhēng Jiǔdiàn..................................B1
7 Yangzi Jie...B2

◉ Drinking
8 Bossa Nova B1

ℹ Information
9 Nánchāng No 1 People's
Hospital..B1

ℹ Transport
10 Advance Rail Ticket Office...................C1
Nánchāng Railway International
Ticket Office ....(see 10)

gets in Jiāngxī. The facilities are top-notch and the refurbished rooms spacious (the best are in Block B). Discounts of 35% available.

 Eating & Drinking

The western end of Yangzi Jie (羊子街) is lined with tiny inexpensive restaurants.

Xiánhēng Jiǔdiàn SOUTHERN CHINESE **$$**
(咸亨酒店; 48 Minde Lu; 民德路48号; dishes ¥16-58; 🖲) Contemporary restaurant, with a mix of southern cuisines (Jiāngxī, Cantonese and Zhèjiāng); try the spicy, peanut-laden 'alcoholic beef' (酒鬼牛肉; *jiǔguǐ niúròu*).

Bossa Nova BAR
(5 Nanhu Lu; 南湖路5号; ⊙6pm-1am) One of Nánchāng's best foreigner-friendly bars.

① Information

Bank of China (中国银行; Zhōngguó Yínháng; Zhanqian Xilu; 站前西路) The main branch has foreign exchange and an ATM (open office hours only). ATMs throughout Nánchāng accept all major cards.

China Post (中国邮政; Zhōngguó Yóuzhèng; cnr Bayi Dadao & Ruzi Lu)

http://verynanchang.com Useful listings website.

Nánchāng No 1 People's Hospital (南昌市第一人民医院; Nánchāng Shì Dìyī Rénmín Yīyuàn; 128 Xiangshan Beilu; 象山北路128号)

Public Security Bureau (PSB; 公安局; Gōng'ānjú; ☑8728 8493; 131 Yangming Lu; 阳明路131号; ⊙8am-noon & 2.30-6pm)

Xīntiě Wǎngchéng (鑫铁网城; Train Station Sq; per hr ¥3; ⊙24hr) One of several internet cafes on the Train Station Sq.

① Getting There & Away

Air

Chāngběi airport is 28km north of the city, with flights to the following destinations:

Běijīng ¥1490, two hours
Guǎngzhōu ¥850, 1½ hours
Shànghǎi ¥830, one hour
Xī'ān ¥1200, 1½ hours

Air tickets can be purchased from the **Nánchāng railway international ticket office** (南铁国旅; Nántiě Guólǚ; 393 Bayi Dadao; ⊙8.30am-6pm), next to the advance rail ticket office.

Bus

Nánchāng has a number of long-distance bus stations scattered about town, but in most cases you're better off taking the train, which is faster and more convenient.

The **Qīngshān north bus station** (青山北站; Qīngshān běizhàn) serves the following:

Lúshān ¥50, 2½ hours, 9.30am
Wùyuán ¥95, 3½ hours, four daily

The **Xújiāfāng bus station** (徐家坊客运站; Xújiāfāng kèyùnzhàn) serves the following destinations:

Gànzhōu ¥102, 5½ hours, hourly
Jiǔjiāng ¥30, two hours, every 40 minutes
Shàngráo ¥58, 3½ hours, hourly
Yīngtán ¥50, 2½ hours, hourly
Yùshān ¥70 to ¥95, four hours, three daily

Train

Buy train tickets at the **advance rail ticket office** (铁路售票处; huǒchē shòupiàochù; 393 Bayi Dadao; ⊙8am-noon & 12.30-5pm) or brave the crowds at the main train station. The following destinations have rail connections with Nánchāng:

Běijīng West Z series train, hard/soft sleeper ¥298/466, 11½ hours, three daily

Guǎngzhōu East hard/soft sleeper ¥260/404, 12 to 14 hours, four daily

Hángzhōu D series train, hard/soft seat ¥185/222, five hours, four daily

Hángzhōu hard/soft sleeper ¥153/234, nine hours, five daily

Jiǔjiāng from ¥40, one to two hours, frequent

Shànghǎi (Hóngqiáo) D series train, hard/soft seat ¥239/287, 6½ hours, three daily

Shànghǎi South K series train, hard/soft sleeper ¥185/286, nine to 13 hours, four daily

① Getting Around

Airport buses (¥10, 45 minutes, half-hourly from 6am to 8pm) leave from in front of the train station. A taxi to the airport costs around ¥100.

Nánchāng is in the process of constructing five new (and urgently needed) metro lines. There's no definite completion date, but some lines may be running as early as 2014 or 2015. The most useful for travellers will be Line 2, which passes the train station and follows Bayi Dadao north. Line 3 should pass by the Qīngshān north and Xújiāfāng bus stations, while Line 1 will run east–west, following Beijing Xilu and Zhongshan Lu.

From the train station, bus 2 goes up Bayi Dadao past People's Sq. Taxis are ¥6 to ¥8 at flag fall; some levy a ¥1 fuel surcharge.

Around Nánchāng

Northwest of town and faced on all sides by imposing ornamental gateways (*ménlóu*), the 1120-year-old village of **Luótiáncūn** (罗田村; admission ¥30), its uneven stone-flagged alleys etched with centuries of wear, makes an ideal day out and rural escape from urban Nánchāng. A disorientating labyrinth of tight, higgledy-piggledy lanes, disued halls and ancient homesteads assembled from dark stone, Luótiáncūn is set among a picturesque landscape of fields and hills that maximise its pastoral charms.

A self-guided tour (beginning at the square with the pond) will take you through a tight maze of lanes, past hand-worked pumps, ancient wells, stone steps, scattering chickens, lazy water buffaloes and conical haystacks. There are some lovely buildings here, including the former residence **Dàshìfūdì** (大世夫第) on Hengjie (横街; Cross St). On the fringes of the village is a fat old camphor tree dating from Tang days; also hunt down the **old well** (古井; *gǔjǐng*), which locals swear is 1000 years old.

From the waterwheel at the foot of Qianjie, a flagstone path links Luótiáncūn with its sibling village, **Shuǐnán** (水南). In Shuǐnán, follow the signs to the **Shuǐnán Folk Museum** (水南民俗馆; Shuǐnán Mínsúguǎn), another old residence consisting of bedchambers and threadbare exhibits. Towards the edge of the village, the **Guīxiù Lóu** (闺秀楼) is another notable building.

A further 500m down the stone path (and across the road) is forlorn **Jīngtái** (京台), whose gap-toothed and largely non-Mandarin-speaking denizens are all surnamed either Liu (刘) or Li (李).

Simple, peasant-family (农家; *nóngjiā*) **accommodation** (bed ¥50) is available in Luótiáncūn, but all three villages can be done as a day trip from Nánchāng. Avoid eating on the main square – seek out one of the two family-run restaurants within Luótiáncūn itself.

Getting here is somewhat complicated. You'll need to take bus 136 to Ānyì (安义; ¥10, one hour, frequent from 6am to 6pm) from the north *tánzikǒu* bus stop (坛子口北; *tánzikǒubĕi*) in Nánchāng; a taxi here should be ¥10 to ¥20, depending on where you're coming from. Try to double-check the location first, however, as the Ānyì service has changed in recent years. At the Ānyì bus station, transfer to a bus to Shíbí (石鼻; ¥4, 30 minutes, frequent), from where *sānlúnchē* (a pedicab) muster for bone-jarring trips to Luótiáncūn (¥8, 15 minutes). Alternatively, you can take a cab direct to Luótiáncūn from Ānyì for about ¥50.

Wùyuán 婺源

📞 0793 / POP 81,200

The countryside around Wùyuán is home to some of southeastern China's most immaculate views. Parcelled away in this hilly pocket is a scattered cluster of picturesque Huīzhōu villages, where old China remains preserved in enticing panoramas of ancient bridges, glittering rivers and stone-flagged alleyways.

Despite lending its name to the entire area, Wùyuán itself is a far-from-graceful town and most travellers will need no excuses before immersing themselves in the region's tantalising bucolic charms way out beyond the shabby suburbs.

Wengong Lu (文公路) is the main north–south drag.

👉 Tours

Hire an English-speaking guide (¥200 per day) and driver at the **CITS office** (中国国际旅行社; Zhōngguó Guójì Lǚxíngshè; 📞 0798-862 9999) in nearby Jǐngdézhèn.

🛏 Sleeping

It's preferable to stay in one of the villages, but if you arrive in the middle of the night there are several hotels along Wengong Lu.

Yíngdū Bīnguǎn   HOTEL $
(迎都宾馆; 📞 734 8620; 13 Wengong Nanlu; 文公南路13号; s & tw ¥100; ❄@) Centrally located hotel in reasonable condition. More expensive rooms come with a computer.

Tiānmǎ Hotel   HOTEL $$
(天马大酒店; Tiānmǎ Dàjiǔdiàn; 📞 736 7123; www.wytm.cn; 119 Wengong Beilu; 文公北路119号; d week/weekend ¥188/228; ❄🛜) This smart hotel is the most comfortable option in the area; room rates can jump up to ¥688 during high season (March, April and major holidays).

ℹ Information

Bank of China (中国银行; Zhōngguó Yínháng; 1 Dongxi Lu) The 24-hour ATM accepts international cards.

China Post (中国邮政; Zhōngguó Yóuzhèng; cnr Tianyou Donglu & Lianxi Lu)

People's Hospital (人民医院; Rénmín Yīyuàn; Wengong Nanlu)

Public Security Bureau (PSB; 公安局; Gōng'ānjú; 2 Huancheng Beilu; ⏰ 8-11.30am & 2.30-5.30pm)

Qǐháng Wǎngbā (启航网吧; Wengong Nanlu; per hr ¥3; ⏰ 24hr) Internet cafe; located next to the People's Hospital.

ℹ Getting There & Away

The Wùyuán **main bus station** (婺源汽车站; Wùyuán qìchēzhàn) is located west of town. A motorbike or taxi here should cost you ¥5; public buses are ¥1. Note that buses that arrive at night (such as the Shànghǎi one) will drop you off at the north end of town, not at the station. Buses depart for the following destinations:

Hángzhōu ¥130, 3½ hours, four daily

Jiǔjiāng ¥90, 2½ hours, three daily

Nánchāng (Qīngshān north bus station) ¥105, 3½ hours, four daily

Shànghǎi south ¥194, six hours, two daily

Shàngráo ¥58, four hours, frequent

Túnxī ¥45, 2½ hours, three daily

Yùshān (Sānqīng Shān) ¥47, 2½ hours, two daily

Around Wùyuán

Wùyuán has become a massively popular destination with domestic tourists in the past few years, but as it's such a large area, it's possible to escape the tour buses with a little bit of determination. However, do not underestimate the number of visitors that can squeeze into these villages during high season (particularly when the rapeseed flowers are in bloom). If you visit during a holiday, expect mega crowds and book your hotel as far as possible in advance.

There are two main ticketing options: either a **five-day pass** (adult/student ¥180/126), which grants you admission to 12 sights, or **single tickets** (per ticket ¥60) at each village. The pass covers a number of villages (only the most interesting are listed here), including Sīxī/Yáncūn, Little Lǐkēng (Xiǎo Lǐkēng) and Xiǎoqǐ, plus various other sights such as Wòlóng Valley.

Big Lǐkēng (Dà Lǐkēng) has a separate admission fee. The lesser-known outer villages – including Guānkēng, Lǐngjiǎo, Qìngyuán and Chángxī – were free at the time of writing. They are best visited in two days.

ℹ Getting Around

Transport throughout the region can be frustrating as villages are spaced apart and are not always linked by reliable bus connections. Hiring a motorbike (摩的; módī) taxi or minivan in either Wùyuán or Qīnghuá is easier than getting a bus. Motorbikes can go as low as ¥120 (plus lunch for your driver) for a full day, which should give you enough time to get to four or five villages. Taxis and minivans generally start out asking around ¥300 for a full day, but they may go as low as ¥200 when business is slow. Drivers may baulk if you ask them to visit a mix of the eastern and northern villages; shop around if necessary.

If you're spending the night in a village, you can also haggle for one-way trips. Individual trips by motorbike from Wùyuán include Qīnghuá (¥20), Little Lǐkēng (¥15) or outer villages (¥60).

If you take the bus, be aware there are three possible departure points, depending on where you want to go. From Wùyuán's main bus station you can get to the northern villages:

Big Lǐkēng ¥16, one hour, two daily

Guānkēng ¥23, 50 minutes, two daily

Lǐngjiǎo ¥19, two hours, two daily

From in front of Wùyuán's old north bus station (老北站; lǎo běizhàn), at the northern end of Wengong Beilu, frequent buses run to Qīnghuá and various eastern villages:

Around Wùyuán

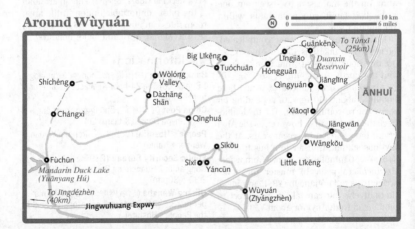

Little Lǐkēng ¥5, 20 minutes, frequent (6.40am to 4.20pm)

Qīnghuá ¥10, 30 minutes, frequent (6.30am to 5.30pm)

Xiǎoqǐ ¥15, one hour, frequent (6.40am to 4.20pm)

To catch transport to Qìngyuán, you need to go to the fruit market (水果市场; *shuǐguǒ shìchǎng*) and ask around – it should cost about ¥30. Before you actually go to any of these places, make sure to confirm first, as departure points change.

EASTERN VILLAGES

LITTLE LǏKĒNG   李坑

The most picturesque village in the area, Little Lǐkēng (Xiǎo Lǐkēng) enjoys a stupendous riverside setting, hung with lanterns, threaded by tight alleys and tightly bound together by quaint bridges. Come nighttime, Little Lǐkēng is even more serene, its riverside lanes glowing softly under red lanterns and old-fashioned street lamps.

Little Lǐkēng's highly photogenic focal point hinges on the confluence of its two streams, traversed by the bump of the 300-year-old **Tōngjì Bridge** (通济桥; Tōngjì Qiáo) and signposted by the **Shēnmíng Pavilion** (申明亭; Shēnmíng Tíng), one of the village's signature sights, its wooden benches polished smooth with age.

Among the *báicài* (Chinese cabbage) draped from bamboo poles and chunks of cured meat hanging out in the air from crumbling, mildewed buildings, notable structures include the **Patina House** (铜录坊; Tónglù Fáng), erected during Qing times by a copper merchant, the rebuilt **old stage** (古戏台; *gǔxìtái*), where Chinese opera and performances are still held during festivals, and spirit walls erected on the riverbank to shield residents from the sound of cascading water.

Cross one of the bridges just beyond the old stage and take the stone-flagged path up the hill, past an old camphor tree and terraced fields, through bamboo and firs, and down to the river and the **Li Zhicheng Residence** (李知诚故居; Lǐ Zhīchéng Gùjū), the residence of a military scholar from the Southern Song. Walk in any direction and you will hit the countryside.

Accommodation is easy to find; try the helpful **Brook Hotel** (小桥驿栈; Xiǎoqiáo Yizhàn; ☎138 7934 9519; d ¥100; ❂@🖘) near the Tōngjì Bridge, where at least one person

speaks English, or the teahouse **Guāngmíng Chálóu** (光明茶楼; ☎0793-737 0999; d ¥80; ❂🖘), overlooking the river and just past Shēnmíng Pavilion.

Buses drop you off at the village turn-off, from where it's a five-minute walk to the ticket office.

XIǍOQǏ   晓起

About 36km from Wùyuán, Xiǎoqǐ dates back to 787. There are actually two villages here: the tacky and overcrowded lower Xiǎoqǐ (下晓起) and the more pleasant upper Xiǎoqǐ (上晓起), where you'll find a fascinating old **tea factory** (传统生态茶作坊; *chuántǒng shēngtài chá zuòfang*).

QÌNGYUÁN   庆源

If you've had enough of the jostling tour groups, the isolated village of Qìngyuán is a good place to escape to. It doesn't have the architectural beauty of the other villages in the Huīzhōu area; it's quite poor and looks like it always has been. But unlike most of the surrounding villages, it is entirely undeveloped and has never been repackaged for the tour bus crowd. Infinitely more peaceful, a trip here will nonetheless help you to appreciate the benefits of organised tourism – namely the economic ones for local villagers – in China. A popular destination for independent Chinese travellers, you can easily find **accommodation** (homestay per person ¥20) here; otherwise hire a driver and visit as a day trip.

NORTHERN VILLAGES

QĪNGHUÁ   清华

Qīnghuá is the largest and least-captivating place in Wùyuán, but because of its central location, it can make a good base. The main sight is the 800-year-old southern Song-dynasty **Rainbow Bridge** (彩虹桥; Cǎihóng Qiáo), which is somewhat underwhelming, but you can also wander along the old street **Qinghua Laojie** (清华老街), a dilapidated portrait of time-worn stone architecture with carved wood shopfronts, lintels, decorative architraves and old folk stripping bamboo. The hospitable **Lǎojiē Kèzhàn** (老街客栈; ☎0793-724 2359; 355 Qinghua Laojie; 清华老街355号; s/d ¥50/60, ❂) has basic, clean rooms.

Buses here depart for Sīkǒu (¥3, 10 minutes), Wùyuán (¥6, 30 minutes) and Jǐngdézhèn (¥22, two hours, two daily), among other places.

WALKING WÙYUÁN

Many of Wùyuán's villages are linked by timeworn **postal roads** (驿道; *yìdào*) that today provide hikers with the perfect excuse to explore the area's gorgeous backcountry: imagine wild azalea, wisteria and iris blooms dotting steep hills cut by cascading streams and you're off to the right start. You'll have to find a villager willing to guide you, and be forewarned that it can be quite difficult – but not impossible – to arrange without Chinese-language skills. For a half-/full-day hike, figure on spending about ¥60/120, including meal(s) for your guide, and ¥20 for accommodation (if you strand him). Note: do not hike from one village to another without a guide; you will get lost.

You can start by asking around for a guide in the village you're staying in. (我要步行去 X. 这里有没有一个人可以带我去?/*Wǒ yào bùxíng qù X. Zhèlǐ yǒu méiyǒu yī gè rén kěyǐ dài wǒ qù?*/I want to hike to X. Can someone here guide me?)

Recommended hikes:

» **Guānkēng to Lǐngjiǎo** (官坑-岭脚; 8km, minimum three hours) A straightforward hike over a high ridge, from one remote village to another. You'll need at least two days. A 9am bus leaves Wùyuán for Guānkēng (¥20, two hours). That night you can arrange a simple homestay (住农家; *zhù nóngjiā*; about ¥20) in either Lǐngjiǎo or Hóngguān, 30 minutes' walk down the road. Buses leave the next morning for Wùyuán (¥16, two hours).

» **Qìngyuán to Xiǎoqī** (庆源-晓起; 12km, minimum four hours) This walk follows a river valley and passes a mixture of terraced fields and secluded backcountry. It can be done either way, though public transport to Xiǎoqī is easiest.

If all this sounds too complicated for your tastes, remember that you can simply walk into the tea terraces or rapeseed fields outside any of the villages for a much shorter and equally beautiful day hike.

SĪXĪ & YÁNCŪN　　思溪、延村

The village of Sīxī is a delightful little place favoured by film crews, with the prow-shaped, covered wooden **Tōngjì Bridge** (通济桥; Tōngjì Qiáo) at its entrance, dating back to the 15th century and adorned with a large *bāguà* (eight trigrams) symbol. Follow the self-guided tour past the numerous Qing residences, many of which are open to the public, and make sure not to miss the large **Jìngxù Hall** (敬序堂; Jìngxù Táng) upstream. A 15-minute walk downstream (back towards Sīkǒu) brings you to Yáncūn, Sīxī's more homely sibling. To get here, take any Wùyuán–Qīnghuá bus (¥3) and get off at Sīkǒu (思口). Motorbikes (if you can find one) will take you the rest of the way for ¥5.

WÒLÓNG VALLEY　　卧龙谷

A 1½-hour hiking trail through Wòlóng Valley (Wòlóng Gǔ) follows a boulder-strewn stream up into the hills past waterfalls and pretty scenery until you reach the main sight: two giant waterfalls (White Dragon and Big Dragon), cascading down sheer cliff faces. Although it can quickly get crowded, it's a nice spot for an easy hike. Two to four buses run here daily from Wùyuán (¥16, one hour), but it's easiest to reach with your own driver.

BIG LǏKĒNG　　理坑

This riverside hamlet of around 300 homesteads is popularly called **Dà Lǐkēng** (admission ¥60), not to be confused with Little Lǐkēng to the east. Perhaps the most splendid aspect of a visit here is traversing the hilly countryside from Qīnghuá, a beautiful landscape of fields and valleys cut by shimmering streams.

The village itself is only of moderate interest and is a private enterprise that exists outside the official Wùyuán network; however, because of this, it is less crowded. As in Qìngyuán, several local households have opened their doors to travellers, with simple beds available from around ¥30 per night.

Sānqīng Shān　　三清山
♪ 0793

Imagine a hiking trail built into a sheer rock face, looking out onto a forest of fantastical granite spires and a gorgeous canopy sprinkled with white rhododendron blooms.

This is one of the many walks you can do at **Sānqīng Shān** (www.sanqingshan.com.cn; adult/student ¥150/80), one of the most underrated national parks in eastern China. It's underrated not just because of the unique scenery, but also because it's relatively unknown and less crowded than other Chinese mountains.

Unlike its more famous neighbour to the north, Huángshān, Sānqīng Shān has a spiritual legacy and has been a place of retreat for Taoist adepts for centuries. The name Sānqīng means 'The Three Pure Ones', in reference to the three main peaks, which are believed to resemble Taoism's three most important deities. Views are spectacular in any season, reaching a climax when the rhododendrons start to bloom in late May.

There are enough trails that you could easily spend two days up here, though a long day hike (roughly 13km) is definitely doable. There are two main access points: the southern route (南部; *nán bù*) and the eastern route (东部; *dōng bù*). Yùjīng Peak is the highest point in the area, with an altitude of 1820m. Maps (¥5) are easy to find in the summit area.

Sights & Activities

Nánqīng Garden   HIKING
(南清苑; Nánqīng Yuàn) The main summit area is known as the Nánqīng Garden, a looping trail that wends beneath strange pinnacles and connects the southern and eastern routes.

West Coast Trail   HIKING
(西海岸; Xī Hǎi'àn) From the Nánqīng Garden loop you can take the spectacularly exposed West Coast Trail, which was built into the cliff face at an average altitude of 1600m. This trail eventually leads to the secluded **Taoist Sānqīng Temple** (三清宫; Sānqīng Gōng), established during the Ming dynasty. It's one of the few Taoist temples in Jiāngxī to have survived the Cultural Revolution.

Sunshine Coast Trail   HIKING
(阳光岸; Yángguāng Àn) Returning from the temple, the Sunshine Coast Trail winds through a forest of ancient rhododendrons, sweet chestnut, bamboo, magnolia and pine, and even features a glass-floored observation platform. There are lots of steps here; make sure you take it on the way back from the temple.

Sleeping

You can sleep in three areas: on the summit, at the trailheads (south or east) or in the town of Yùshān. Prices rise on weekends; reserve if you want to sleep at the trailheads or on the summit.

YÙSHĀN

Fāngfāng Bīnguǎn   HOTEL $
(芳芳宾馆; 255 5909; off Renmin Dadao; 人民大道日景现代城; s/d ¥60/88; ✳@) The best of the simple family-run guesthouses near the bus station; some rooms even come with computers. Signs outside advertise prices as low as ¥30; however, you'll first get quotes closer to ¥90. It's on a side street on the left if you're coming from the bus station.

Péngfā Hotel   HOTEL $$
(蓬发宾馆; Péngfā Bīnguǎn; 220 6666; Xiufeng Lu; 秀峰路; tw from ¥130; ✳@) Dependable midrange rooms, though you may need to haggle on the rate. Make two lefts after you exit the Yùshān bus station; it's about a five-minute walk.

AT THE TRAILHEADS

Sānqīngshān International Resort HOTEL $$$
(三清山国际度假酒店; Sānqīngshān Guójì Dùjià Jiǔdiàn; 223 3333; www.sqshotel.com; tw from ¥2000; ✳) Located at the southern trailhead, this is by far the nicest hotel in the Sānqīng Shān area, with satellite TV and modern decor. Wi-fi in the lobby. Discounts of up to 50%.

Dìwáng Shānzhuāng   HOTEL $$
(地王山庄; 213 7999; d from ¥280) Convenient rooms at the eastern trailhead.

ON THE SUMMIT

If you have your own equipment, you can pitch tents near Sānqīng Temple (a minimum 3km walk from the southern chairlift).

Rìshàng Bīnguǎn   HOTEL $$$
(日上宾馆; 218 9377; r from ¥480) One of several summit hotels; a 10-minute walk past the top of the southern chairlift.

Nǚshén Hotel   HOTEL $$$
(女神酒店; Nǚshén Jiǔdiàn; 218 9366; r from ¥480) One of several summit hotels; a 20-minute walk past the top of the eastern chairlift.

Information

Agricultural Bank of China (中国农业银行; Zhōngguó Nóngyè Yínháng; Renmin Dadao) Twenty-four hour ATM about a 10-minute walk from the Yùshān bus station.

JĬNGDÉZHÈN: CHINA'S CHINA

Jĭngdézhèn (景德镇) is a name known to many: it's where China's much-coveted porcelain is fired up, although the imperial kilns that manufactured ceramics for the occupants of the Forbidden City were long ago extinguished. With more china here than the rest of China put together, travellers can rapidly feel glazed: Jĭngdézhèn is hardly an oil painting and is strictly for those in the business. If you're a porcelain buff, visit Shànghǎi instead: the collection at the Shànghǎi Museum is China's best, and shops such as Spin and Yú sell standout pieces in all styles.

ⓘ Getting There & Away

Sānqīng Shān is accessed via the town of Yùshān (玉山), accessible by both bus and train. If you can't get to Yùshān directly, go to the nearby city of Shàngráo (上饶) instead and then take a connecting train or bus (note that buses to Yùshān do not leave from Shàngráo's long-distance bus station – you'll need to catch a cab or motorcycle to the drop-off point).

Bus

Yùshān bus station (汽车站; qìchēzhàn) connections:

Hángzhōu ¥90, four hours, four daily
Nánchāng ¥72, four to five hours, two daily
Shàngráo ¥14, one hour, frequent
Wùyuán ¥45, 2½ hours, two daily

Train

Yùshān is on the Shànghǎi–Nánchāng line. A taxi to the train station (火车站; huǒchēzhàn) costs ¥10. Destinations from Sānqīng Shān include the following:

Hángzhōu South from ¥45, 4½ hours, six daily
Nánchāng ¥22 to ¥44, 4½ hours, four daily
Shànghǎi South hard seat/sleeper ¥76/134, seven hours, five daily
Shàngráo ¥3.50 to ¥10, 20 minutes, seven daily
Yīngtán ¥12 to ¥24, two hours, seven daily

ⓘ Getting Around

Minibuses (¥15, 80 minutes, 6.30am to 5.20pm) run from the Yùshān bus station to the start of both the eastern route (东部) and southern route (南部) – make sure you specify your destination. A **chairlift** (索道; one way/return ¥70/125) leaves from both places.

Otherwise, the porter's trail – a sweaty 1½-hour walk (2.5km) that snakes under the chairlift – ascends the southern route.

The eastern route has a more spectacular chairlift but is further from the West Coast Trail; if you're walking, the southern route is a much shorter hike.

Lónghǔ Shān 龙虎山
🗺 0701

From powerful Taoist priests to the opening scenes of the martial-arts novel *Outlaws of the Marsh*, Lónghǔ Shān (Dragon and Tiger Mountain) left a distinct mark on traditional Chinese culture in its heyday during the Song, Yuan and Ming dynasties. The Cultural Revolution may have wiped clean the physical traces of this past, but with a setting reminiscent of a landscape painting – a winding river, cluster of red sandstone peaks, grazing water buffaloes and solitary herons – this is as good a place as any to discover the lush Jiāngxī countryside.

During the Song dynasty (960–1279), Lónghǔ Shān became the centre of the emergent Zhèngyī sect, which claimed to represent the teachings of religious Taoism's founder, Zhang Daoling (34–156). Together with the Quánzhēn sect, Zhèngyī Taoism was one of the most prominent schools of Taoism in late imperial China, and there were once over 100 temples and monasteries here. Zhèngyī Taoists were active in society, selling protective talismans (still for sale) and performing religious services for the general populace. The head of the Zhèngyī sect was known as the Celestial Master, a lineage that was traced back to Zhang Daoling.

◎ Sights & Activities

The Lónghǔ Shān scenic area encompasses 200 sq km, most of which is located along the eastern bank of the Lúxī River. A **ticket** (www.longhushan.com.cn; without/with raft trip ¥175/225) includes admission to seven sites and a raft ride, as well as transport on miniature trains (main entrance to Zhèngyī Temple) and shuttle buses (from Zhèngyī Temple to the Residence of the Celestial Masters). To get the most out of your visit, narrow your sightseeing options to two main areas: the Residence of the Celestial Masters and Elephant's Trunk Hill.

At the main entrance are two small museums, the **Taoist Museum** (◷8am-5pm), with information in Chinese only, and the **Geology Museum** (☺8am-5pm), with detailed explanations of Lónghǔ Shān's formation.

Residence of the Celestial Masters
TAOIST TEMPLE

(天师府; Tiānshī Fǔ) About 28km from Lónghǔ Shān's main entrance, this is the largest and best-preserved temple in the area. It was originally built in the Song dynasty as Zhèngyī's main temple complex, thoroughly renovated in the Qing dynasty and then again in the 1990s. The oldest building still standing is the **Sanctuary of Triple Introspection** (三省堂; Sān Xǐng Táng), which dates to 1865. To get here, walk 15 minutes through old Shàngqīng village from the shuttle drop-off. Another 500m along Fuqian Jie (府前街) is an abandoned **Catholic church** (天主教堂; Tiānzhǔjiào Táng), a wonderfully bizarre building and strange relic of colonial missionary days.

Shàngqīng Palace
TAOIST TEMPLE

(大上清宫; Dà Shàngqīng Gōng) Five hundred metres past the Catholic church, this temple complex was almost entirely destroyed by fire; only the entrance gate, first courtyard (with the drum and bell tower) and a few side halls remain. A mythic spot, Shàngqīng Palace is both the alleged site of the residence of the first Celestial Master (Zhang Daoling) as well as the place from which the 108 spirits were accidentally released in *Outlaws of the Marsh*.

Elephant's Trunk Hill
SCENIC AREA

(象鼻山; Xiàngbí Shān) Close to Lónghǔ Shān's main entrance, this is the first stop you'll reach on the miniature train. Here you can hike a loop past rock formations and rebuilt temples, then descend to the river from where you'll be able to spy Lónghǔ Shān's **hanging coffins** (悬棺; xuán guān) on the opposite side of the bank. About 2500 years ago, the original inhabitants of the area, the Guyue, buried their dead in grottoes located high up on the cliff face. A hanging coffin performance (it's a liberal reinterpretation) is staged four times a day here at 10am, noon, 2pm and 4pm; a ferry also crosses the river for free.

🛏 Sleeping & Eating

Hotels and restaurants are conveniently based near the main entrance. There are smaller restaurants in Shàngqīng village, at the opposite end of the scenic area.

Róngshèng Bīnguǎn
HOTEL $$

(荣盛宾馆; Róngshèng Bīnguǎn; ☎665 7666; 龙虎山新大门对面; tw week/weekend ¥130/160; ✳@) Tasteful and surprisingly sophisticated, the Róngshèng has hardwood floors, flat-screen TVs and traditional Chinese-style sinks in the bathrooms. It's opposite the park entrance.

Lónghǔ Shān Nóngjiālè
HOTEL $

(龙虎山农家乐; ☎665 9506; 39 Xianrencheng Lu; 仙人城路39号; d/tw ¥60/80; ✳) Down a side street, this clean and friendly place is more a homestay than a hotel.

ℹ Information

There are **internet cafes** (网吧; wǎngbā) and a 24-hour ATM across from the train station in Yīngtán.

ℹ Getting There & Around

Lónghǔ Shān is near the city of Yīngtán (鹰潭), which is on the Shànghǎi–Nánchāng railway line. To get to Lónghǔ Shān from Yīngtán, take bus K2, which runs from in front of the train station, past the bus station and on to the main entrance (¥3, 25 minutes, 6.15am to 6.30pm).

Services from Yīngtán Train Station (火车站; huǒchē zhàn) include the following:

Hángzhōu D series train, hard/soft seat ¥142/171, 3½ to four hours, five daily

Hángzhōu hard seat ¥70, five to seven hours, frequent

Nánchāng ¥12 to ¥43, one to two hours, frequent

Shànghǎi Hóngqiáo D series train, hard/soft seat ¥197/236, 5½ hours, four daily

Shànghǎi South ¥94 to ¥164, 7½ to 9½ hours, frequent

Shàngráo ¥19 to ¥34, one to two hours, frequent

Services from the bus station (客运站; kèyùn zhàn) are less practical:

Nánchāng (Xújiāfāng bus station) ¥50, two hours, hourly

Shàngráo ¥36, two hours, hourly

Wùyuán ¥73, 3½ hours, four daily

Lúshān 庐山

☎0792

One of the great early cultural centres of Chinese civilisation, the dramatic fog-enshrouded cliffs of **Lúshān** (adult/student ¥180/135) attracted large numbers of monastics and thinkers for some 1500 years.

The monk Hui Yuan, one of the first Chinese teachers to emphasise the importance of meditation, founded Pure Land Buddhism here in the 4th century AD. His contemporary and acquaintance, Tao Yuanming, who lived at the foot of the mountain, is generally regarded as China's first landscape poet.

Numerous other writers resided on Lúshān's slopes in the centuries that followed – notably Bai Juyi, Zhu Xi and Su Dongpo – but unfortunately the Taiping Rebellion destroyed almost everything of note in the mid-19th century. Western colonialists and missionaries followed in the rebels' wake and built the retreat town of Gǔlíng (Kuling; altitude 1167m), where Nobel Prize-winner Pearl S Buck spent her childhood summers and Mervyn Peake (author of the *Gormenghast* novels) was born.

Following the CCP's rise to power, the European-style villas of Gǔlíng were subsequently transformed into an infamous political conference centre, which, together with the stunning scenery, is what most visitors today come to see.

👁 Sights & Activities

The main attraction here is exploring the mountain roads and paths on your own – generally, any place you have to walk to will be significantly less crowded. The **Xīnhuá Bookshop** (新华书店; Xīnhuá Shūdiàn; 11 Guling Zhengjie) sells detailed maps showing roads and walking paths.

Lúshān's old places of worship include the **Protestant Church** (基督教堂; Jīdūjiào Táng; 23 Hexi Lu) and **Catholic Church** (天主教堂; Tiānzhǔjiào Táng; 12 Xiangshan Lu).

Měilú Villa   HISTORIC BUILDING
(美庐别墅; Měilú Biéshù; 180 Hedong Lu; admission ¥25, incl with Zhōu Ēnlái Residence; ⏰8am-6pm) Built by Chiang Kaishek in the 1930s and named after his wife, Song Meiling.

Zhōu Ēnlái Residence   HISTORIC BUILDING
(周恩来纪念室; Zhōu Ēnlái Jìniàn Shì; admission incl with Měilú Villa) The former premier's residence stands defiantly across the stream from the Měilú Villa.

Site of the Lúshān Conference   MUSEUM
(庐山会议旧址; Lúshān Huìyì Jiùzhǐ; 504 Hexi Lu; admission ¥50; ⏰8am-5pm) Also called the People's Hall, this was the venue for the CCP's historic confabs in 1959 and 1970.

FREE **Lúshān Museum**   MUSEUM
(庐山博物馆; Lúshān Bówùguǎn; 1 Lulin Lu; ⏰8am-5.30pm) Mao's former residence, littered with paraphernalia detailing the Lúshān communist connection.

Hiking

One excellent destination for hikers is **Wǔ Lǎo Fēng** (五老峰; Five Old Men Peak; 1358m). A bit less remote but a favourite with photographers is the **Three Step Waterfall** (三叠泉; Sāndié Quán).

At Lúshān's northwestern rim, the land falls away abruptly to spectacular views across Jiāngxī's densely settled plains. A long walking track south (about one hour from Gǔlíng) around these precipitous slopes leads to **Dragon Head Cliff** (龙首崖; Lóngshǒu Yá), a natural rock platform tilted above an eye-popping vertical drop.

🛏 Sleeping

July and August is the Lúshān peak season, and if you are coming then – particularly on a weekend – you should book in advance. Outside of this time period, it's quite possible to just show up and find a room.

Lúshān Yúntiān Villa   HOTEL $$
(庐山云天别墅; Lúshān Yúntiān Biéshù; ☎829 3555; www.lsytbs.com; Guling Zhengjie; d Jul & Aug ¥760, rest of year ¥240; ❄@🖧) A move away from Lúshān's typically musty and worn lodging options, this place offers old-villa atmosphere with roomy, fresh accommodation and a crisp finish.

Youth Hostel   HOSTEL $
(大自然青年旅社; Dàzìrán Qíngnián Lǚshè; ☎829 6327; www.yhalushan.com; 1 Hubei Lu; 湖北路1号; dm/d ¥35/120; ❄@🖧) The only decoration here is the graffiti on the walls, but the secluded hillside location is ideal. It's about a 1km walk from the bus station; from Guling Zhengjie turn left onto Henan Lu and continue for about 600m.

ℹ Information

Bank of China (中国银行; Zhōngguó Yínháng; 13 Hemian Jie) Change money or use the 24-hour ATM here.

Internet cafe (极速网吧; Jísù Wǎngbā; Guling Zhengjie; per hr ¥3; ⏰8am-midnight) Near the intersection with Dalin Lu, at the far end of Guling Zhengjie.

Public Security Bureau (PSB; 公安局; Gōng'ānjú; 20 Guling Zhengjie)

LÓNGNÁN

In the deep south of Jiāngxī lies the rarely visited Hakka country, a region of lush hills peppered with fortified villages, unusually built in rectangular shapes, unlike the mostly circular *tǔlóu* (roundhouse) of Fújiàn. Although there are estimates of some 370 such dwellings in Lóngnán (龙南) County, travellers can safely narrow down the choices to two main areas, both of which can be visited from the busy town of Lóngnán.

Built by a lumber merchant in the early 19th century, **Guānxī New Fort** (关西新围; Guānxī Xīn Wéi; admission ¥10) is the largest and most ornate fortified village in the county. Nearby is the **Hakka Wine Castle** (客家酒堡; Kèjiā Jiǔbǎo; admission ¥15), built at the same time by a rich wine producer. A bus from Binjiang Sq in Lóngnán runs to Guānxī (¥5, 40 minutes, hourly), passing by the Hakka Wine Castle (¥3).

A number of crumbling old fortified villages lie in the vicinity of Yángcūn (杨村) town, including the 350-year-old **Yànyì Wéi** (燕翼围; admission ¥10), the tallest such residence in the county (four storeys). However, more striking is nearby **Wǔdāng Shān** (武当山; admission ¥15; ☉8am-6pm), a group of weathered sandstone domes poking above subtropical forest (not to be confused with Húběi's Wǔdāng Shān). To get to Yángcūn, take a bus (¥11, 1¼ hours, frequent) from 99 Longding Dadao (龙鼎大道99号) in Lóngnán. Buses in both directions pass Wǔdāng Shān on the way; drivers will let you off at the entrance.

Trains to Lóngnán run from Nánchāng (¥134, 7½ hours) and Guǎngzhōu (seat/hard sleeper ¥87/177, 5½ to 6½ hours); otherwise take a bus from Nánchāng to Gànzhōu (¥120, 4½ hours), where you can transfer to a Lóngnán-bound bus (¥49, two hours). Two daily buses run to Guǎngzhōu (¥90, five hours). Bus 1 (¥1.5) runs from the train station past the bus station to the centre of town. If you're interested in getting to/from the *tǔlóu* in Fújiàn, it won't be easy. You can transfer to a Fújiàn-bound bus in Gànzhōu (eg heading to Yǒng'ān), but after a minimum five-hour trip across the border, you'll need to transfer again to get to Yǒngdìng.

In Lóngnán, you can stay at the **Xīnxìng Bīnguǎn** (新兴宾馆; ☎353 6288; Binjiang Sq; 滨江广场; r ¥70-138; ✳@).

ℹ Getting There & Around

Travellers generally arrive in Lúshān from the city of Jiǔjiāng (九江). Buses (¥15, one hour, 6.50am to 4.30pm) run hourly to Lúshān from Jiǔjiāng's long-distance bus station, dropping off passengers in front of a small ticket office on Guling Jie. In summer it's a good idea to book your return seat upon arrival.

There is also one bus to Nánchāng's Qīngshān north bus station (¥50, 2½ hours, 2.30pm) that leaves from the Lúshān bus station on Hexi Lu; sometimes there are more in summer.

Jiǔjiāng is easily accessible from Nánchāng by both bus and train. Jiǔjiāng's long-distance bus station (长途汽车站; chángtú qìchē zhàn) has connections to the following cities:

Nánchāng ¥30, two hours, half-hourly

Nánjīng ¥149, 6½ hours, hourly

Shànghǎi ¥218, 10 hours, three daily

Wǔhàn ¥90, four hours, hourly

Wùyuán ¥90, three hours, six daily

Lúshān's myriad footpaths and bus-bound tour groups make explorations on foot the most enjoyable way to go. However, there is also a hop-on, hop-off **shuttle service** (旅游观光车; lǚyóu guānguāng chē; 7-day pass ¥80) that goes to most sights and can be convenient – the main drawback is that you won't escape the crowds. Buy the pass at the bus station that serves Nánchāng. Taxi service is of no use here as private vehicles are barred from entering most roads. Lúshān has several cable cars (return ¥80).

Húnán

POP 66 MILLION

Includes »

Chángshā.....................446
Sháoshān.....................451
Héng Shān...................452
Wǔlíngyuán &
Zhāngjiājiè...................453
Déhāng.........................457
Fènghuáng...................458
Hóngjiāng Old Town......462

Best Walks

» Golden Whip Stream
Scenic Route (p455)

» Tiānzǐ Shān Nature
Reserve (p455)

» Nine Dragon Stream
Scenic Area (p458)

» Fànyīn Valley (p452)

Best Architecture

» Fènghuáng's *diàojiǎolóu*
(stilt houses) (p460)

» Hóngjiāng Old Town
(p462)

» Mao's childhood house
(p451)

» Tiānxīn Gé (p447)

Why Go?

Communist Party cadres might wax lyrical about the sacred standing of Húnán (湖南) in the annals of Chinese history, being as it is the birthplace of Mao Zedong, but it is Húnán's dramatic scenery that is the real draw.

An astonishing landscape of massive, isolated mountain ranges and jagged, karst peaks covers more than 80% of the province. These geological spectacles rise up from the impossibly green vales fed by the tributaries in the fertile Yangzi River basin. People have long made a home amid these natural wonders, taming the rocky slopes into terraces of lush fields. Their distinctive cultures live on in charming hillside villages and lively riverside towns.

Native sons and scenery aside, let's not forget the food. Húnán's fiery cuisine has mouths (and eyes) watering all over the world, and it tastes even better on its home turf.

When to Go
Chángshā

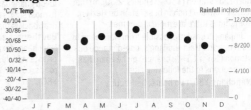

Apr–May
Spring awakens in Wǔlìngyuán's subtropical forest and karst peaks.

Sep & Oct
The waters flow from Héng Shān's stunning vistas.

Nov–Dec
Tour groups thin out on Fèng-huáng's ancient streets.

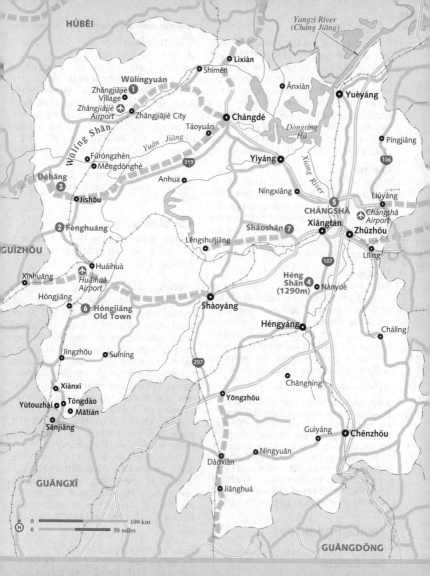

Húnán Highlights

1 Enter another geological dimension in **Wǔlíngyuán** (p453)

2 Absorb the crumbling charms of ancient **Fènghuáng** (p458)

3 Hike into the extraordinary karst scenery surrounding the Miao village of **Déhāng** (p457)

4 Ascend sacred slopes through forests and waterfalls to **Héng Shān** (p452)

5 Dance like nobody's watching in Chángshā's **bars** and **clubs** (p449)

6 Wander the age-old merchant streets in **Hóngjiāng Old Town** (p462)

7 Join the masses paying homage to Mao in **Sháoshān** (p451)

History

During the Ming and Qing dynasties, Húnán was one of the empire's granaries, transporting vast quantities of rice to the embattled north. By the 19th century, land shortages and feudalism caused widespread unrest among farmers and hill-dwelling minorities. These economic disparities galvanised the Taiping Rebellion in the 1850s, ensuring widespread support by the 1920s for the Chinese Communist Party (CCP) and Húnán's Mao Zedong.

Climate

Subtropical Húnán's mostly temperate climate averages 28°C in summer, and 6°C in its brief winter season. Monsoon rains fall from April to June, followed by high temperatures and humidity in July and August. The province's northern region sees more fickle weather and even winter snow.

Language

Xiāng (湘语; Hunanese) is a northern Mandarin dialect with six to eight sub-dialects of its own commonly spoken in central and southwest Húnán. Gàn (赣语; Jiangxinese), another northern Mandarin dialect, is used in the east and south. In the border regions, you will hear a mosaic of other dialects and minority languages, such as Xiāngyǔ and Gànyǔ.

ⓘ Getting There & Around

A high-speed rail line connecting Húnán to its provincial neighbours Húběi and Guǎngdōng now runs along Húnán's eastern length through Yuèyáng, Chángshā, Héngshān and Chēnzhōu. (Urban planners must be anticipating major sprawl judging by the often remote stations.) A network of convenient, older rail lines and expressways spans the entire province. Airports at Chángshā, Zhāngjiājiè and Huáihuà bring every major city within a two-hour flight of the sights.

PRICE INDICATORS

The following price indicators are used in this chapter:

Sleeping

$	less than ¥200
$$	¥200 to ¥550
$$$	more than ¥550

Eating

$	less than ¥75
$$	¥75 to ¥200
$$$	more than ¥200

Chángshā 长沙

☏0731 / POP 2.5 MILLION

For 3000 years, this city flourished steadily on the Xiāng River's banks as a centre of agriculture and intellect. In the 1920s, it was still so much as it always had been that British philosopher Bertrand Russell compared it to 'a mediaeval town', but not long after, the Sino–Japanese War and a massive fire in 1938 consumed virtually all of old Chángshā, leaving little of its early history. Chángshā today is known mainly for sights relating to a revolutionary by the name of Mao.

◉ Sights

Most of Chángshā's sights lie east of the river and close a half-hour early from late August through April.

FREE **Chángshā Municipal Museum** MUSEUM
(市博物馆; Shì Bówùguǎn; ☏8224 2209; 538 Bayi Lu; ⊙9am-5pm Tue-Sun; 🚌1, 501) A colossal statue of Mao Zedong cast out of aluminium-magnesium alloy in Hēilóngjiāng in 1968 affably greets you at the entrance. (Compare his carriage – arm aloft, heralding a new dawn – with more subdued statues erected post-reform.) It's the first clue that despite the paintings, ceramics and jade on display, this museum is really a shrine. Check out the huge portrait of a young Mao with shafts of light emanating from his head above the entrance.

The museum also houses the former site of the **Húnán CCP Committee** (中共湘区委员会旧址; Zhōng Gòng Xiāngqū Wěiyuánhuì Jiùzhǐ), where Mao lived from 1921 to 1923 with his first wife and mother-in-law while secretly running the local CCP. Bring a picture ID.

Húnán County No 1 Teachers' Training School HISTORIC SITE
(第一师范学校旧址; Dìyī Shīfàn Xuéxiào Jiùzhǐ; ☏8515 7430; 356 Shuyuan Lu; admission ¥15; ⊙8.30am-5.30pm; 🚌1, 122) Between 1913 and 1918, Mao studied here and returned to teach classics from 1920 to 1922. It's still a working college, and sometimes students keen to practise English will show you around Mao's dormitory and classrooms, the halls where he held his first political meetings, and the well where he drew water for his cold baths. Otherwise, there are a few English captions.

Chángshā

Tiānxīn Gé
HISTORIC SITE

(天心阁; Heart of Heaven Pavilion; ☑8489 1389; 3 Tianxin Lu; park admission free, pavilion ¥16; ⏰8am-6pm, pavilion 7.30am-6pm; ☐202) The old city walls were built of rammed earth in 202 BC, reinforced with stone in AD 1372, and finally demolished in 1928 save for this section. It's a popular place to escape the summer heat.

Yuèlù Academy
HISTORIC SITE

(岳麓书院; Yuèlù Shūyuàn; ☑8882 3764; Lushan Nanlu; admission ¥30; ⏰7.30am-6pm; ☐202) Students have been cramming for exams at the base of Yuèlù Mountain west of the river since AD 976, when the academy was established as one of China's four institutions of higher learning. The Song-era grounds are now part of Húnán University. By the entrance is **Hèxī Pavilion** (Hèxī Tǎi), once on Yuèlù's summit, which assembles the writings of some of China's great minds, including a poem of conversing sonnets collaboratively composed by the Confucian scholars Zhu Xi and Zhang Shi.

Orange Isle
PARK

(橘子洲; Júzi Zhōu; ☑8861 4640; ⏰24hr; ☐3) The most famous of the city's parks is a 5km-long sliver in the Xiāng River. A reflective 32-year-old Mao immortalised it in 'Changsha', probably his best regarded poem, after standing at its southern tip and looking west towards Yuèlù Mountain one autumn day. A towering granite bust of a youthful Chairman with flowing locks now stands at the spot – but faces in a new direction. Catch a **sightseeing trolley** (guānguāng diàndòng chē; ticket ¥20; ⏰7.30am-8.30pm) at the entrance and skip the run up of manicured lawns before the main attraction.

Chángshā

◎ Top Sights
Chángshā Municipal Museum............B1

◎ Sights
1 Orange Isle.................................A1
2 Tiānxīn Gé..................................B2

⬤ Sleeping
3 Guǎngshèng Fēngjǐng Hotel............D1
4 Jǐnjiāng Inn.................................B1
5 Lotus Huátiān Hotel.....................C1
6 Sheraton Chángshā Hotel.............B1

⊗ Eating
7 Carrefour...................................B1
8 Huǒgōngdiàn...............................C2
9 Huǒgōngdiàn...............................A2
10 Sunriver Dumpling Restaurant........C1
11 Xīnhuá Lóu.................................D2

◎ Drinking
12 Hualongchi Xiang.........................B2
13 Jiefang Xilu................................A2
14 Taiping Jie.................................A2

ℹ Transport
15 Enjoy Going...............................B1
Gump's Teahouse ....(see 14)

TOP CHOICE Húnán Provincial Museum MUSEUM
(湖南省博物馆; Húnán Shěng Bówùguǎn; ☑8451 4630; www.hnmuseums.com; 50 Dongfeng Lu; admission free; ⏰9am-5pm Tue-Sun; ☐113, 136) This first-rate, not-to-be-missed museum is closed for renovations through the end of 2015. Until then, select pieces,

MAO: THE GREAT HELMSMAN

Mao Zedong was born in the village of Sháoshān in 1893, the son of 'wealthy' peasants. Mao worked beside his father on the 8-hectare family farm from age six and was married by 14.

His life appeared settled. He later credited a pamphlet a teacher gave him describing the colonisation of Asia as awakening his political consciousness. At 16, he convinced his father to let him attend middle school in Chángshā. In the city, Mao discovered Sun Yatsen's revolutionary secret society. When the Qing dynasty collapsed that year, Mao joined the republican army but soon quit, thinking the revolution was over.

At the Húnán County No 1 Teachers' Training School (p446), Mao began following the Soviet socialism movement. He put an ad in a Chángshā newspaper 'inviting young men interested in patriotic work to contact me', and among those who responded were Liu Shaoqi, who would become president of the People's Republic of China (PRC), and Xiao Chen, who would be a founding member of the Chinese Communist Party (CCP).

Mao graduated in 1918 and went to work as an assistant librarian at Peking University, where he befriended more future major CCP figures. By the time he returned to teach in Chángshā, Mao was active in communist politics. Unlike orthodox Marxists, Mao saw peasants as the lifeblood of the revolution. The CCP formed in 1921, and soon included unions of peasants, workers and students. Vengeful warlords compelled Mao to flee to Guǎngzhōu.

In April 1927, following Kuomintang leader Chiang Kaishek's attack on communists, Mao was dispatched to Chángshā to organise what became the 'Autumn Harvest Uprising'. Mao's army scaled Jǐnggāng Shān to embark on a guerrilla war. The campaign continued until the Long March in October 1934, a 9600km retreat from which Mao emerged the CCP leader.

Mao forged a fragile alliance with the Kuomintang to expel the Japanese, and from 1936 to 1948 the two sides engaged in betrayals, conducting a civil war simultaneously with WWII. Mao's troops eventually won, and the PRC was established 1 October 1949.

As chairman of the PRC, Mao embarked on radical campaigns to repair his war-ravaged country. In the mid-1950s he began to implement peasant-based and decentralised socialist developments. The outcome was the ill-fated Great Leap Forward and later the chaos of the Cultural Revolution (for details, see p924).

China saw significant gains in education, women's rights, and average life expectancy under Mao's rule; however, by most estimates between 40 and 70 million people died during that era of change. Five years after Mao's death, Deng Xiaoping famously announced Mao had been 70% right and 30% wrong in an effort, some say, to tear down Mao's cult of personality. Yet today, Mao remains revered as the man who united the country, and he is still commonly referred to as the 'Great Leader', 'Great Teacher' and 'supremely beloved Chairman'. His image hangs everywhere – in schools, taxis and living rooms – but as a symbol of exactly what is the question with which China now grapples.

including some from the astounding collection of relics uncovered from the 2100-year-old Western Han tombs of Mǎwángduī, will tour national museums.

🛏 Sleeping

Chángshā is short on decent budget options. You can find basic rooms clustered around the train station, but you get what you pay for.

Chángshā – Húnán International Youth Hostel
HOSTEL $

(长沙国际青年旅舍; Chángshā Guójì Qīngnián Lǚshè; ☏8299 0202; www.hnhostel.com; 61 Gong-shang Xiang; 东风路下大垅工商巷61号; dm ¥35-45, s/d/tr ¥108/138/168; ⊜❉@) Tucked away down a quiet, tree-lined street, the only centrally located hostel in town has clean, airy dorm rooms and doubles. There's a nice garden area and knowledgable staff. The main downside is the limited hours for hot showers. Take bus 136 from the train station to the Xiàdàlǒng (下大垅) stop on Dongfeng Lu and follow the YHA signs. Similarly priced but much more compact rooms can be found at the hostel's new branch west of the river, Yuèlù Mountain International Youth Hostel (☏8536 8418; 50 Xinmin Lushan Huaqiao Cun; 新民路50号麓山华侨村).

Lotus Huátiān Hotel   HOTEL $$

(芙蓉华天大酒店; Fúróng Huátiān Dàjiǔdiàn; ✆8440 1888; fax 8440 1889; 176 Wuyi Dadao; s/d ¥398/498, ste ¥988 plus 10% service charge; **P**✽@) The ageing concrete and glass exterior fails to impress but inside is a spick-and-span, well-run hotel. Discounts of 25% make this a comfortable midrange option, especially if you get a room on the newly fixed up 7th or 8th floors.

Sheraton Chángshā Hotel   LUXURY HOTEL $$$

(喜来登酒店; Xǐláidēng Jiǔdiàn; ✆8488 8888; 478 Furong Zhonglu; 芙蓉中路一段478号运达国际广场; s & d ¥1238 plus 15% service charge; ☺✽@☎) The finest hotel in Chángshā offers top-notch service and stylish rooms with plush beds. There's also a spa, gym, pool, and Cantonese, Húnán and Italian restaurants. Rates change daily, so you might catch a deal in slack periods.

Guǎngshèng Fēngjǐng Hotel   HOTEL $$

(广圣风景酒店; Guǎngshèng Fēngjǐng Jiǔdiàn; ✆8217 9999; 309 Chezhan Zhonglu; s & d ¥288-348, tr ¥388; ✽@) A standard Chinese cheapie popular with domestic tour groups. The tiny bathrooms have seen better days but the rooms are clean and the location opposite the train station handy. Discounts up to 50%.

Jǐnjiāng Inn   HOTEL $$

(锦江之星宾馆; Jǐnjiāng Zhīxīng Bīnguǎn; ✆8828 1888; 1 Dongfeng Lu; 东风路1号; s/d ¥169/209; ✽@) Generic but in a good way. Near the centre of town with leafy Lièshì Park steps away.

✗ Eating

Zhaoyang Lu and the lanes off the major shopping zone Huangxing Zhonglu are good places for street food. **Carrefour** (家乐福; Jiālèfú; 238 Furong Zhonglu; ☺8am-10.30pm) is a lifesaver for those in search of Western provisions. Stick to sit-down restaurants for a taste of Hunan's regional cuisine, Xiāngcài.

TOP CHOICE Huǒgōngdiàn   CHINESE HÚNÁN $$

(火宫殿; ✆8581 4228; 127 Pozi Jie; dishes ¥5-78; ☺6am-2am) There's a great buzz at this landmark eatery, established in 1747. In 1958, Mao tried the housemade choù dòufu (臭豆腐; stinky tofu; ¥58), and praised it as both 'stinky and delicious'. A huge selection of small dishes are wheeled around, but there are menu items too, including Máoshì hóngshāoròu (毛氏红烧肉; Mao-

style braised pork; ¥78). A less atmospheric branch is near the train station at 93 Wuyi Dadao (✆8412 0580).

Xī Hú Lóu Jiǔ Jiā   CHINESE $$

(西湖楼酒家; Xī Hú Lóu Jiǔ Jiā; ✆8425 8188; Jīnmǎ Food City; 金马美食城内, 省广电中心斜对面; vegetable dishes from ¥58, clay pots from ¥78; ☺11am-2pm & 5-9pm; 🚌158) About 9km northeast of the city centre, the world's biggest Chinese restaurant, according to the *Guinness Book of World Records* and a plaque on the wall, is a village of five kitchens, staff of 1000, and banquet halls, stages, courtyards and gardens to entertain 5000 guests. The picture menu is a textbook on regional cuisines, plus there's an alley of street food. Escape the pomp in a private room. Book in advance.

Sunriver Dumpling Restaurant   DUMPLINGS $

(松花江饺子馆; Sōnghuājiāng Jiǎoziguǎn; www.songhuajiang.net; 102 Wuyi Dadao; dumplings from ¥4; ☺9am-1.20am; 🏮) If you need a break from chillies, this bustling eatery specialises in the deliciously mellow cuisine of northern China. Dumplings (jiǎozi) are the speciality and come in many varieties, including vegie.

Xīnhuá Lóu   CHINESE HÚNÁN $

(新华楼; 35 Wuyi Dadao; dishes ¥4-25; ☺6.30am-2am) The harried ladies at this longtime favourite for xiāng cuisine push trolleys of cold and hot dishes from which to pick and choose. They also have great noodles (from ¥7). Two other branches at 54 Sudong Zhonglu (✆8552 1000) and Pozi Jie (✆8599 6705).

🍷 Drinking & Entertainment

Chángshā comes alive after dark. The following is just a guide; places open and shut quicker than you can down a green tea–whisky. Check the online entertainment guide *Changshahua* (www.changshahua.com) for the latest.

A good place to start the night is **Taiping Jie**, a cobbled walking street between Wuyi Dadao and Jiefang Xilu, west of the shopping district on Huangxing Zhonglu. One of Chángshā's oldest surviving streets, it has a mix of bars, boutiques and souvenir shops. From there, it's a short walk around the corner to **Jiefang Xilu**, Chángshā's club central with all manner of KTV (karaoke) joints and discos. There are no covers but drinks are expensive.

There's another a busy enclave of bars down an ancient alley off Huangxing Zhonglu. Turn down the alley marked Dagudao Xiang (大古道巷) and walk 100m to **Hualongchi Xiang** (化龙池巷).

ⓘ Information

ATMs all over town take foreign cards. The train station area is densely populated with internet cafes.

Bank of China (中国银行; Zhōngguó Yínháng; 43 Wuyi Dadao) Next door to the Civil Aviation Hotel with an exchange and 24-hour ATM.

China International Travel Service (CITS; 中国国际旅行社; Zhōngguó Guójì Lǚxíngshè; ☑8446 8929; http://hnguolv.com; 160 Wuyi Dadao; ◷8am-8pm) On the corner of Changdao Lu, east of Lotus Huátiān Hotel. Smaller branch at 54 Wuyi Dadao (☑8229 0512).

China Post (中国邮政; Zhōngguó Yóuzhèng; 460 Chezhan Lu; ◷9am-5pm) To the right exiting the train station.

HSBC (汇丰银行; Huìfēng Yínháng; 159 Shaoshan Lu) Inside the Dolton Hotel with a 24-hour ATM.

Liányíng Internet Cafe (联赢网吧; Liányíng Wǎngbā; 446 Chezhan Lu; per hr ¥4-5; ◷8am-8pm) To the right exiting the train station concourse.

Provincial People's Hospital (省人民医院; Shěng Rénmín Yīyuàn; ☑8227 8071; 61 Jiefang Xilu)

Public Security Bureau (PSB; 公安局; Gōng'ānjú; ☑8589 5023; 1 Dianli Lu) Entry-exit visas are handled here, 20km south of the city centre. Take bus 705 and get off at the Yǒuyìshè (友谊社) stop on Furong Nanjie.

ⓘ Getting There & Away

Air

Chángshā's **Huánghuā International Airport** (黄花国际机场; Huánghuā Guójì Jīchǎng; ☑8479 8777; www.hncaac.com) has multiple daily flights to major cities including Běijīng (¥1210, two hours), Chéngdū (¥910, two hours), Kūnmíng (¥950, two hours), Qīngdǎo (¥1040, two hours), Shànghǎi (¥890, two hours), Xiàmén (¥860, 1½ hours) and Xī'ān (¥890, two hours). One daily flight to Huáihuà (¥810, one hour) and Zhāngjiājiè (¥850, 50 minutes).

Book tickets at the **Civil Aviation Administration of China** (CAAC; 中国民航售票处; Zhōngguó Mínháng Shòupiàochù; ☑8411 2222; 49 Wuyi Dadao; ◷8.30am-5.30pm), a five-minute walk west of the train station in the Civil Aviation Hotel. International Desk speaks English.

Bus

As a major transport hub, Chángshā has multiple bus stations connecting to many of the same destinations. Most travellers will find what they need at the **south bus station** (汽车南站; qìchē nánzhàn; ☑8280 5051; Zhong Yilu). To get there, take bus 107 or bus 7 (¥2) from the train station; a taxi is about ¥40. Buses clustered in the train station square are mostly for guided tours.

Buy bus tickets at the stations or the bus ticket office in the train station square. Below are only some of the south bus station's regular routes.

Chángníng ¥68, four hours, 10 daily

Guǎngzhōu ¥162 to ¥182, seven hours, two daily (10am and 8.30pm)

Guìlín ¥190, six hours, two daily (8.30am and 4pm)

Héng Shān ¥19 to ¥38, three hours, seven daily

Héngyáng ¥51, two hours, frequently

Huáihuà ¥132, six hours, eight daily

Shànghǎi ¥282, 16 hours, one daily (5pm)

Zhāngjiājiè ¥109, four hours, four daily (8.40am, 9.40am, 10.40am and 12.10pm)

Train

The central **Chángshā Train Station** (火车站; huǒchēzhàn; ☑9510 5105; Chezhan Zhonglu) has two trains daily to Běijīng (from ¥506, 13 hours), and one daily to Guǎngzhōu (from ¥99, 8½ hours), Jíshǒu (¥76, 6½ hours), Shànghǎi (from ¥260, 9½ hours) and Zhāngjiājiè (¥99, 11 hours). If you're heading to Hong Kong, you can take the overnight, air-conditioned train to Shēnzhèn (¥147, 11 hours).

Counter 7 in the train station booking hall is staffed with English speakers, or buy tickets from any of the ticket booking offices (火车售票处; huǒchē shòupiàochù) populating the train station square. In town, **Enjoy Going** (亲和力旅游; Qīnhélì Lǚyóu; ☑8222 7222; 25 Yingpan Donglu; ◷8am-9pm) or **Gump's Teahouse** (阿甘茶馆; Āgān Cháguǎn; ☑8258 9999; 133 Taiping Lu; ◷9am-11pm) are reliable and charge ¥5 commission per ticket.

Express trains depart daily from the **South Rail Station** (南火车站; nán huǒchēzhàn; ☑280505; Huaqiao Lu), about 8km southeast of the city centre, for Wǔhàn (D train, hard/soft seat ¥112/134, two hours; G train, hard/soft seat ¥165/281, 1½ hours) and Guǎngzhōu (D train, hard/soft seat ¥204/244, 4½ hours; G train, hard/soft seat ¥322/516, 2½ hours).

ⓘ Getting Around

To/From the Airport

Chángshā's Huánghuā International Airport is 26km from the city centre. **Shuttle buses** (长沙黄花国际机场-机场巴士; ☑8479 8076; ¥20) depart from the Civil Aviation Hotel, next to the

CAAC on Wuyi Dadao, every 15 minutes between 5.30am and 10pm; the west bus station every 40 minutes between 9am and 5pm; the south bus station every 30 minutes from 9am to 6.10pm; and Hèlóng Stadium on Furong Zhonglu hourly from 7am to 8pm. Buses take about an hour. A taxi from the city centre will cost about ¥60.

Public Transport

Chángshā public buses reach every inch of the city. You can plan trips with the **online bus network** (http://changsha.8684.cn, in Chinese). Tourist bus 1 (旅1路; ¥1) runs east–west along Wuyi Dadao, connecting the train station and Yuèlù Mountain.

Taxi

Flag fall is ¥6 for the first 2km and then ¥1.80 (slightly more at night) per kilometre thereafter.

Sháoshān 韶山

☎ 0732

More than three million make the pilgrimage each year to Mao Zedong's hometown, a pretty hamlet frozen in time 130km southwest of Chángshā. The swarms of young and old drop something to the tune of ¥1.8 billion annually. Mao statues alone are such big business that each must pass inspection by no fewer than five experts checking for features, expression, hairstyle, costume and posture. The 6m-high bronze statue of Mao erected in 1993 in Mao Zedong Square is considered a model example.

An overall resurgence in queuing at revolutionary sights is due in part to a government-sponsored Red Tourism campaign, which encourages young Chinese to reconnect with China's past. Some arrive sceptical, but others whisper prayers, asking the founder of New China for health, prosperity and help with exams.

◉ Sights & Activities

Sháoshān has two parts: the modern town with the train and bus stations, and the original village about 5km away, where all the sights are clustered. Only a handful of the designated sights have a genuine connection to the man.

FREE **Mao's Childhood House**   HISTORIC SITE
(毛泽东故居; Máo Zédōng Gùjū; ⊙8.30am-5pm) Surrounded by lotus ponds and rice paddies, this modest mud-brick house is like millions of other country homes except that Mao was born here in 1893. By most accounts, his childhood was relatively normal

though he tried to run away at age 10. He returned briefly in 1921 as a young revolutionary. On view are some original furnishings, photos of Mao's parents and a small barn. No photography inside.

FREE **Nán'àn School**   HISTORIC SITE
(南岸私塾; Nán'àn Sīshú; ⊙8.30am-5pm) Mao began his education in this simple country school, just steps from his childhood home. Its interior is illuminated by *tiān jǐng* (天井), light wells, about which a precocious Mao wrote a poem. It's on display along with Mao's classroom and the teacher's quarters. Some English captions.

FREE **Museum of Comrade Mao**   MUSEUM
(毛泽东同志纪念馆; Máo Zédōng Tóngzhì Jìniànguǎn; ⊙9am-4.30pm) The life of Mao (minus some of the controversial years) in photos, clothing and life-sized figures. To the right as you face the museum and opposite the bronze statue of Mao Zedong (decorated with calligraphy by Jiang Zemin) is the **Mao Family Ancestral Hall** where you can trace the family's genealogy.

Dripping Water Cave   PARK
(滴水洞; Dī Shuǐ Dòng; admission ¥50; ⊙8am-5.30pm) Mao secluded himself for 11 days in June 1966 here, 3km outside of Sháoshān village, to contemplate the start of the Cultural Revolution. His retreat was actually a low-slung, cement and steel bunker (not the cave, which was a few kilometres away). Members of the Mao clan are entombed nearby.

Sháo Peak   MOUNTAIN
(韶峰; Sháo Fēng; admission ¥80, cable car included; ⊙8.30am-5pm) This cone-shaped mountain is visible from the village. The summit has a lookout pavilion, and on the lower slopes, the **forest of stelae** has stone tablets engraved with Mao's poems. Hiking to the top takes about an hour.

🛏 Sleeping & Eating

Sháoshān can be easily done as a day trip from Chángshā, so there's little reason to spend the night here. Close to the bus station in the new town are nondescript hotels with rooms for ¥140 after discounts. In the village itself, touts can lead you to a *nóngjiālè* (农家乐), a local family's guesthouse.

Restaurants are all over the village, all serving Mao's favourite dish, *Máo jiā hóngshāoròu* (Mao family red-braised pork) for ¥45 and up.

Shàoshān Bīnguǎn HOTEL $$
(韶山宾馆; ☎5568 5262; 16 Guyuan Lu; 故园路16号; s/d ¥368/398 plus 10% service charge; ❇@) The rooms are clean and bright – four-star standard issue. You're paying for location and the fact that Mao and various CCP bigwigs slept in the building next door in June 1959. (It's ¥20 more to glimpse the actual rooms where they stayed – not worth it.)

❶ Getting There & Away

Daily buses (¥26) depart every 30 minutes from 8am to 5.30pm for the 1½-hour drive from Chángshā's south bus station to Shàoshān. Buses return to Chángshā from Shàoshān's **long-distance bus station** (长途汽车站; chángtú qìchēzhàn; Yingbin Lu), just north of the train station, until about 5.30pm. Guided tour buses also depart from the Chángshā train station square (day tour ¥150).

A daily train (hard/soft seat ¥11/17, 2½ hours) from Chángshā to Shàoshān departs at 6.40am; the return from Shàoshān departs at 4.38pm.

❶ Getting Around

A tourist minibus (中巴; ¥10) lets you hop on and off at the key sights with one ticket from 7am to 6pm. Pick it up in front of sights and the Shàoshān Bīnguǎn. Local minibuses (¥2.50) also circle the sights starting from the train station. Expect to pay ¥100 for a taxi to take you around.

Héng Shān 衡山

☎0734

About 127km south of Chángshā rises the southernmost of China's five sacred Taoist mountains, to which emperors came to make sacrifices to heaven and earth. The ancients called it Nányuè (南岳; Southern Mountain), a name it now shares with the town at its base. The imperial visits left a legacy of sublime scenery of Taoist temples and ancient inscriptions scattered amid gushing waterfalls, dense pine forests and terraced fields cut from lush canyons. Bring extra layers, as the weather can turn quickly and the summit is often cold and wet.

◉ Sights & Activities

Héng Shān MOUNTAIN
Seventy-two peaks spanning 400km comprise Héng Shān, but most visitors focus on **Zhùróng Peak** (祝融峰; Zhùróng Fēng; admission ¥100), rising 1290m above sea level.

The challenging, continuous 13km ascent up winding paths, busy roads and steep staircases can fill a day. A bus and then a cable car can take you two-thirds of the way.

If you want a lift, buy the combined ticket on the 2nd floor of the **Tourist Centre** (Lǚkè fùwù zhōngxīn; Yanshou Lu; admission & one way/return ¥40/70; ◷7am-5.30pm). Buses depart directly from there and stop at various sights up to the mountain's halfway point, **Bànshān Tíng** (半山亭). From there, it's a short ride on the **cable car** (every 30min; ◷7am-6pm) to **Nántiānmén** (南天门). It's an 18km bus ride (7am to 6pm) back down from Nántiānmén to the Tourist Centre.

If you decide to hike, start up the tree-lined road 300m east of the Tourist Centre marked by the stone **Shènglì Archway** (胜利坊). The road leads to the **entrance** (jìnshān ménpiàochù; ☎567 3377; ◷24hr), where you can pay admission, and then to a tranquil path that winds 5km past lakes, waterfalls and streams in **Fànyīn Valley** (Fànyīn Gǔ) to almost the cable car departure point at Bànshān Tíng. Along the way, you can stop to see the colourful figures of Taoist and Buddhist scripture on display in **Shénzhōu Temple** (Shénzhōu Zǔmiào), the grand and dignified **Nányuè Martyrs Memorial Hall** (Nányuè Zhōnglièci), dedicated to the anti-Japanese resistance, and a **stele** inscribed with a dedication from Kuomintang leader Chiang Kaishek celebrating the pine forest. Before you jump on the cable car, take a break and reconsider at **Xuándōu Guàn** (玄都观), an active Taoist temple. The couplet carved at the entry reminds weary climbers that the path of righteousness is long, so don't give up halfway through!

The next 4.5km up to Nántiānmén frequently takes the busy road and scattered staircases, but there are more inspiring temples along the way. Once you reach Nántiānmén, it's a chilly (outside of July and August) 3km ascent to the peak. You can rent coats (¥20) before heading up to **Zhù Róng Palace** (Zhù Róng Diàn), an iron-tiled temple built for Zhu Rong, an ancient official who devised a method of striking stones to create sparks. After his death, he became revered as the god of fire.

Nányuè Temple TEMPLE
(南岳大庙; Nányuè Dàmiào; ☎567 3658; admission ¥50; ◷7am-6pm) This sprawling Taoist and Buddhist temple was moved from Héng Shān summit to its foot in the Sui dynasty

and then rebuilt many times, most recently in the Qing dynasty. Each carved panel in the main pavilion's balustrade tells a legend of one of Héng Shān's peaks.

Zhùshèng Temple
TEMPLE

(祝圣寺; Zhùshèng Sì; 67 Dong Jie; admission ¥5; ⏰5am-6pm) A 10-minute walk east of Nányuè Temple, this Zen Buddhist temple dates back to the Tang dynasty.

FREE Dàshàn Chán Temple
MONASTERY

(大善禅寺; Dàshàn Chánsì; Zhurong Beilu; ⏰7.30am-6pm) This active Taoist nunnery is on the west side of Nányuè.

🛏 Sleeping & Eating

The cheapest rooms are ¥70 (¥90 with air-con and shower) in Nányuè's small family-run inns (客栈; *kèzhàn*). Ask at the bus station; many restaurants also offer rooms. Otherwise, look along Zhurong Beilu (祝融北路). It's best to stay on the mountain to catch the sunrise. Many basic hotels are clustered at Bànshān Tíng and Nántiānmén.

Nányuè has more than its share of restaurants though they're pricey and mostly similar. Food on the mountain is even costlier; take snacks and water with you.

TOP CHOICE Vegetarian Meal and Tea
HOTEL $$

(素语茶绿; ☎568 7222; 1 Jiyang Jie; 吉祥街1号; s/d ¥260, ste ¥360, ¥50 surcharge on weekends; main courses from ¥25; P🅿🌐@🍴) The nine, elegant rooms in this boutique hotel next to Nányuè Temple are beautifully decorated with Chinese wood furniture and Buddhist antiques, though everything else is decidedly modern. Saffron-hued walls give the whole place a peaceful temple feel. The rooms are above a delicious vegetarian restaurant and traditional teahouse.

Zǔshī Diàn
GUESTHOUSE $$

(祖师殿; Zǔshī Diàn; ☎568 7181; inside Nántiānmén Temple; d ¥460; @) The spartan rooms in this Taoist temple are the nicest this high on the mountain. It's a convenient launching pad for early morning hikes. Prices rocket during holiday periods, otherwise discounts of 20% are available. Vegetarian meals for ¥20 per plate.

Cohere Hotel
LUXURY HOTEL $$$

(枕岳楼大酒店; ☎539 8888; 8 Jinsha Lu; 金沙路8号; s/d/ste ¥688/888/1088; P🅿🌐🛜🏊) The nicest hotel in Nányuè is a health resort that doesn't serve soda in the lobby bar. It has everything else – foot massages, gym, pool, roof garden, ping-pong room, three restaurants and an ATM. Rooms discounted by 40% in slow periods.

Nányuè Telecom Hotel
HOTEL $$

(南岳电信宾官; ☎567 8888; 173 Zhurong Lu; 祝融路173号; s/d/tr ¥328/438/488; P🅿🌐@) A standard three-star with clean enough bathrooms. Close to the bus station. A good deal when discounted by 40%.

ℹ Information

Near the bus station, there's a branch of the **Bank of China** (中国银行; Zhōngguó Yínháng; 270 Hengshan Lu) with currency exchange and a 24-hour ATM. There is a PSB (公安局; Gōng'ānjú) on Xijie (西街) at Furong Jie.

ℹ Getting There & Around

The long-distance bus station is a few minutes north of the archway (牌坊; *páifāng*) at the intersection of Zhurong Beilu and Hengshan Lu. There are seven daily buses to Chángshā (¥45) departing every 40 minutes between 7.20am and 3.40pm for the three-hour journey.

The express train from Chángshā (¥42) takes half an hour, departing every 30 minutes from 7.27am and 9.20pm and arriving 10km from town at Héng Shān west station (西站). Buy tickets in town next to the bus station at the **Nányuè Héng Shān ticket centre** (南岳衡山代票点; 167 Zhurong Lu; 祝融路167号; ¥5 commission; ⏰8am-9pm).

Free minibuses (电瓶车) pass all the sights between the bus station to Nányuè Temple and the Héng Shān entrance between 7am and 7pm. Taxis usually charge ¥10 to each sight.

Wǔlíngyuán & Zhāngjiājiè
武陵源、张家界

☎0744

Rising from the misty subtropical and temperate forests of northwest Húnán is a concentration of quartzite-sandstone formations found nowhere else in the world. Some 243 peaks and more than 3000 karst pinnacles and spires dominate the landscape of this designated Unesco World Heritage Site. For thousands of years, this was a remote landscape known mainly to three minority peoples: Tujia, Miao and Bai. Today more than 20 million visitors annually come to the Wǔlíngyuán Scenic and Historic Interest Area. The park is also home to more than 3000 distinct plant species

Wǔlíngyuán

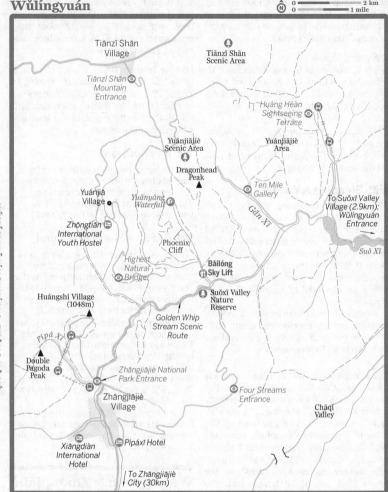

0 — 2 km
0 — 1 mile

Tiānzǐ Shān Village

Tiānzǐ Shān Scenic Area

Tiānzǐ Shān Mountain Entrance

Huáng Héàn Sightseeing Terrace

Yuánjiājiè Scenic Area

Yuánjiājiè Area

Dragonhead Peak

Ten Mile Gallery

Yuánjiā Village

Yuānyāng Waterfall

Gān Xī

To Suǒxī Valley Village (2.9km); Wǔlíngyuán Entrance

Zhōngtiān International Youth Hostel

Phoenix Cliff

Suǒ Xī

Highest Natural Bridge

Bǎilóng Sky Lift

Huángshí Village (1048m)

Suǒxī Valley Nature Reserve

Golden Whip Stream Scenic Route

Pípá Xī

Double Pagoda Peak

Zhāngjiājiè National Park Entrance

Zhāngjiājiè Village

Four Streams Entrance

Cháqī Valley

Xiāngdiàn International Hotel

Pípáxī Hotel

To Zhāngjiājiè City (30km)

as well as diverse fauna. Macaques gambol and dangle along paths, while endangered species like the Chinese giant salamander, Chinese water deer and the elusive clouded leopard (only their tracks have been seen) lurk deep in the park.

Tourist season peaks from July to September but each season presents a unique beauty. Avoid the national holidays. Your ticket is valid for three consecutive days, a good estimate of the time it will take to enjoy the main sections of the park. Expect to pay additional fees for cable cars and some sights within the park.

Sights & Activities

WǓLÍNGYUÁN SCENIC & HISTORIC INTEREST AREA

The **park** (武陵源风景区; Wǔlíngyuán Fēngjǐngqū; adult/student ¥245/168) is divided into the Zhāngjiājiè, Tiānzǐ Shān, Yuánjiājiè and Suǒxī Valley scenic areas covering a vast 264 sq km.

There are access points on all sides of the park, but most enter from the south, passing through Zhāngjiājiè village to the **Zhāngjiājiè National Park entrance** (张家界公园门票站; Zhāngjiājiè Gōngyuán ménpiàozhàn). Otherwise, many enter from the east through **Wǔlíngyuán en-**

trance (武陵源门票站; Wǔlíngyuán ménpiàozhàn), which sits on Suǒxī Lake (索溪湖; Suǒxī Hú).

Locals often refer to the collective area as Zhāngjiājiè, though this is also the name of the city (张家界市; Zhāngjiājiè *shì*) 30km south of the park with useful transport links and shopping, and the village (张家界村; Zhāngjiājiè *cūn*).

Zhāngjiājiè National Forest Park & Suǒxī Valley Nature Reserve SCENIC AREA

(张家界国家森林公园) From the south entrance, this is the first opportunity for a birds'-eye view of the spires from **Huángshí Village** (黄石寨), a 3km loop on a plateau 1048m up. It's a two-hour slog up 3878 stone steps, or a half hour by bus (one way/return ¥96/50; 6.30am to 6pm) and then cable car (one way ¥50).

Back on the canyon floor, the **Golden Whip Stream Scenic Route** (金鞭溪精品游览线) is a flat path meandering 7.5km east along its namesake stream and past its namesake crag to the **Suǒxī Valley Nature Reserve** (索溪峪自然保护区). From there, it's less than 1km to the **Bǎilóng Sky Lift** (百龙天梯; each way ¥56), a cliff-side elevator rising 335m in under two minutes to the Yuánjiājiè Scenic Area in the heart of the park.

Yuánjiājiè Scenic Area SCENIC AREA

(袁家界风景区) Touring here means manoeuvring around particularly large crowds, but the vistas, including the **Highest Natural Bridge** (天下第一桥), a wind- and water-carved structure spanning two peaks 357m above the canyon floor, are worth it. The path also passes the newly renamed 'Avatar Hallelujah Mountain', a tie in to the record-breaking film *Avatar*. Though director James Cameron mentioned only Huángshān, the ethereal mountains in Ānhuī province, on promotional tours, park officials are convinced Wǔlíngyuán's karst peaks inspired Pandora's Hallelujah Mountains. You'll have to wait until 2014 to see whether Yuánjiājiè gets a cameo in the sequels.

A short walk from the west entrance of the scenic area is **Yuánjiā Village** (袁家寨子; admission ¥85, performance ¥25), a once remote Tujia community that now offers a packaged but still interesting glimpse into marriage, farming and trading traditions. Look for the wooden archway hung with ox skulls.

Tiānzǐ Shān Nature Reserve SCENIC AREA

About 20km northwest of the Wǔlíngyuán Entrance rises **Tiānzǐ Shān** (天子山自然保护区), including the West Sea (西海), Emperor Pavilion (天子阁), the Gathering of the Invincible Army (神兵聚会) and many other landscapes of angular spires often featured on postcards. A cable car (one way ¥52; 6.50am to 5.10pm) can take you up to the **Huáng Hé'àn Sightseeing Terrace** (黄河岸观景台) for the sky-high paths overlooking the range. The routes here are more challenging than in other parts of the park. (At one point, an optional foray crosses chain bridges and ladders pinned precariously to the cliffs.) For mellower views, take the sightseeing tram (each way ¥40) along the **Ten Mile Gallery** (十里画廊) on the canyon floor.

Caves & Rafting OUTDOORS

With more than 40 limestone caves hidden along the banks of the Suǒxī River and the southeast side of Tiānzǐ Shān, the region offers ample opportunities to raft (漂流; *piāoliú*) and tour caves.

Just inside the Wǔlíngyuán Entrance, **Jīliú Huíxuán** (激流回旋; ☑150 7441 9596; www.jiliuhuixuan.com, in Chinese; trips ¥168; ☺8am-7pm) offers a 3km, one-hour rafting trip down a section of the Suǒxī River used for Olympic training events. After that, check out **Yellow Dragon Cave** (黄龙洞; Huánglóng Dòng; admission ¥80), the longest in Asia, 10km east of the Wǔlíngyuán Entrance.

Tour companies offer combination cave and rafting trips further afield. Tour **Jiǔtiān Cave** (九天洞; Jiǔtiān Dòng; admission ¥76; ☺8am-6pm) about 160km northwest of the park, and then ride the currents 20km down the **Máoyán River** (茅岩河; Máoyán Hé; from ¥188; ☺8am-6pm). The Máoyán's pretty tame, but the scenery is fantastic. The actual rafting lasts about three hours.

Day trips down the **Měngdòng River** (猛洞河; Měngdòng Hé; www.mdh.cn, in Chinese; from ¥200) are also possible. The best white water is near the Húběi border, but you'll have to make special arrangements for equipment and transport.

ZHĀNGJIĀJIÈ CITY

Tiānmén Shān SCENIC AREA

(天门山; admission ¥258; ☺8am-5pm) Visible from anywhere in Zhāngjiājiè city, this distinctive range features Tiānmén Dòng (天门洞), a prominent keyhole cut through the mountainside. The 7km-long **cable car** (return ¥52) presents scenes of the verdant mountainside. A riveting 60m, glass plank road a short walk from the upper cable station will test your belief in human engineering.

HÚNÁN WǓLÍNGYUÁN & ZHĀNGJIĀJIÈ

☞ Tours

You can join tours of the park and rafting trips, or arrange your own, through hotels and travel agencies in Zhāngjiājiè city. A typical three-day park tour costs ¥798 (be sure to clarify what sights and transportation are not included). Both the Zhōngtiān International Youth Hostel and **CITS** (中国国际旅行社; Zhōngguó Guójì Lǚxíngshè; ☏ 820 0885; 631 Ziwu Lu; ⊙ 8am-6pm) arrange tours.

🛏 Sleeping & Eating

Staying near the park's south entrance in Zhāngjiājiè village keeps you in the middle of the Wǔlíng foothills, but the gorgeous setting will cost you. You can find cheap inns (客栈; kèzhàn) by the eastern entrance of the park. The widest selection of hotels is in Zhāngjiājiè city. You'll find cheapies starting at ¥80 around the bus station and on Bei Zhengjie (北正街).

As for eats, small restaurants are scattered around Zhāngjiājiè village cooking up Tujia dishes; servers may try to steer you towards expensive tǔjī (土鸡; free-range chicken; from ¥180). In Zhāngjiājiè city, there are many choices in the shopping area along Renmin Lu. In the park, snack stalls are everywhere but expensive.

ZHĀNGJIĀJIÈ VILLAGE   张家界村

Staying cheaply in the park overnight is tricky as most options are family-run inns. Some only house tour groups, and others only Chinese nationals. If you can find a bed, expect to pay ¥80 to ¥120. The locals manning the food, drink and souvenir stalls can offer good tips.

There are standard hotels along the popular trail routes, including a Yuánjiājiè outpost of the **Zhōngtiān International Youth Hostel** (☏ 590 3315; dm ¥40-50, s & d ¥150). Tiānzǐ Shān and Suǒxī Valley have a bewildering choice of hotels and hostels. All of the following are on the main road, Jinbian Lu (金鞭路), which has many other options.

TOP CHOICE ☆ Xiāngdiàn International Hotel   HOTEL $$$

(湘电国际酒店; Xiāngdiàn Guójì Jiǔdiàn; ☏ 571 2999; s & d ¥1080-1280, ste ¥3380, plus 10% service charge; ☀❄📶) This serene four-star mountain lodge has courtyard gardens almost pretty enough to distract you from the incredible surroundings. Most rooms have balconies and at least partial mountain views. Discounts of 40% to 60% make this a great deal.

Pípaxī Hotel   HOTEL $$

(琵琶溪宾馆; Pípaxī Bīnguǎn; ☏ 571 8888; s & d ¥580-680, ste ¥2680; ☀❄📶) This quiet hotel set in Tujia-style buildings is beautifully maintained and surrounded by longan trees and the mountains. The rooms are surprisingly luxurious. Request a balcony and the 20% discount.

ZHĀNGJIĀJIÈ CITY   张家界市

Zhōngtiān International Youth Hostel   HOSTEL $

(中天国际青年旅舍; Zhōngtiān Guójì Qīngnián Lǚshè; ☏ 832 1678; www.zjjzthostel.com; Room 4 A1, Zhōngtiān Bldg, Ziwu Lu; 子午路中天大厦4楼A1室; dm ¥35-40, dm with private bathroom ¥45-50, d ¥138-148; ❄@) Despite the location in an anonymous office block, this pleasant hostel has a rooftop garden, small bar and restaurant, and cosy rooms. The four tatami rooms are a bargain but hard to snag (¥110 with private bathroom). Helpful staff speak some English. There's a more basic branch in the Yuánjiājiè area of the park.

Dàchéng Shānshuǐ Hotel   HOTEL $$$

(大城山水国际大酒店; Dàchéng Shānshuǐ Guójì Jiǔdiàn; ☏ 888 9999; cnr Dayong Xilu & Airport Rd; 大庸西路、机场路; s & d ¥1688-2688, ste ¥3288 incl breakfast; ❄@) One of a few five-star choices, this one overdoes it with the gold decor but distinguishes itself with spacious rooms and particularly attentive staff. There's 24-hour room service and a travel office in the lobby. Discounts of 50% to 75%.

Jīnjiāng Inn   HOTEL $$

(锦江之星; Jīnjiāng Zhīxīng; ☏ 839 8777; 51 Ziwu Lu; 子午路51号; d/tw ¥269/229; ❄@) The Jīnjiāng shows some grey hairs, but it has the usual setup and dependable internet access.

ⓘ Information

Maps (some English) of the scenic area and Zhāngjiājiè city are available at ticket offices and major hotels for ¥5.

2 in 1 Internet Cafe (二合一网吧; Èrhéyī Wǎngbā; per hr ¥2; ⊙ 24hr) On the corner of Bei Zhengjie and Ziwu Lu in Zhāngjiājiè city.

Bank of China (中国银行; Zhōngguó Yínháng; Ziwu Lu, Zhāngjiājiè city) Close to the Zhōngtiān International Youth Hostel, with a currency exchange and 24-hour ATM. There's also a 24-hour ATM at the park's south entrance.

China Post (中国邮政; Zhōngguó Yóuzhèng; ⊙ 8am-5.30pm) On Guyong Lu and Daqiao Lu in Zhāngjiājiè city.

MINORITIES & MISSILES

In southwest Húnán near the Guǎngxī and Guìzhōu borders is the Tōngdào Dong Minority Autonomous County (通道侗族自治区; Tōngdào Dòngzú Zìzhìqū), the heartland of the Dong tribe. In the hills surrounding nondescript Tōngdào city are picturesque villages famed for their distinctive wood architectural tradition – as well as a sizeable proportion of China's intercontinental ballistic missiles. While you won't see the missile silos, as they're buried or semi-camouflaged as wind and rain bridges, the area is officially closed to foreigners at the time of writing. Visiting status may have changed by the time you read this, so check with the **Tōngdào PSB** (☏0745-5862 2322).

Industrial & Commercial Bank of China (ICBC; 工商银行; Gōngshāng Yínháng; Huilong Lu, Zhāngjiājiè city) It's 250m east of the bus station.

People's Hospital (市人民医院; Shì Rénmín Yīyuàn; ☏822 7836; 208 Guyong Lu) In Zhāngjiājiè city.

Public Security Bureau (PSB; 公安局; Gōng'ānjú; ☏571 2329; Jinbian Lu, Zhāngjiājiè village)

For visa questions go to Nanzhuang Lu, Zhāngjiājiè city (☏824 8129).

Getting There & Away

Air

Zhāngjiājiè Héhuā Airport is 6km southwest of Zhāngjiājiè city and about 40km from the Zhāngjiājiè National Park entrance; a taxi costs about ¥100 to the park. Flights connect Zhāngjiājiè city with Běijīng (¥1340, 2½ hours), Chángshā (¥850, one hour), Chóngqìng (¥580, one hour), Guǎngzhōu (¥860, 1½ hours), Shànghǎi (¥1100, 1½ hours) and Xī'ān (¥690, 1½ hours).

Bus

Buses leave from the **long-distance bus station** (☏822 2417) on Huilong Lu in Zhāngjiājiè city.

Chángshā ¥83/96, four hours, every half hour

Fènghuáng ¥42/45, four hours, four daily (two at 8.30am, 2pm and 2.30pm)

Jíshǒu ¥35, two hours, hourly

Shànghǎi ¥309, 20 hours, two daily (6.30am and 9.30am)

Wǔhàn ¥135/155, 12 hours, three daily (8.30am, 5.30pm and 6.30pm)

Xī'ān ¥292, 20 hours, one daily (1.30pm)

Train

The **station** (☏214 5182) is 8km southeast of the city; buy tickets well in advance. There are five morning trains from Chángshā between 2.39am to 8.29am (hard/soft seat ¥65/87, 4½ to six hours). In the other direction, there

are six trains during the day (hard/soft seat ¥32/81) from 1.16pm to 6.18pm and one overnight one (hard/soft sleeper ¥183/276, 11 hours) at 7pm. Some other services include:

Běijīng hard/soft sleeper ¥307/353, 25 hours, two daily (12.47pm and 6.18pm)

Guǎngzhōu hard/soft sleeper ¥164/383, 14 to 21 hours, three daily (6.40am, 3.27pm and 4.52pm)

Huáihuà hard/soft seat ¥19/31, 3½ to six hours, frequent

Jíshǒu hard/soft seat ¥11/17, two to four hours, frequent

Yíchāng hard/soft seat ¥25 to ¥62, five hours, three daily (4.53am, 9.23am and 6.36pm)

Getting Around

Minibuses travel between Zhāngjiājiè village (¥10, 50 minutes) – also called Forest Park (森林公园; Sēnlín Gōngyuán) – and the long-distance bus station every 15 minutes from 6am to 7pm. Make sure to get on the right bus, as some go east to the Wǔlíngyuán entrance and others to Tiānzǐ Shān (¥13, every hour). Buses run between the park entrances and are free with a ticket.

Taxi flag fall in Zhāngjiājiè city is ¥5. A taxi from the city to the village costs around ¥120.

Déhāng　　

☏0743

The Miao hamlet of Déhāng (admission ¥60; ⊙7am-10pm, performances at 10am, 3pm & 7.30pm), northwest of Jíshǒu in western Húnán, offers a rare chance to step into astonishing countryside landscapes of terraced valleys and waterfalls framed by towering columns of stone.

Pleasant, affordable inns make Déhāng an attainable getaway. The village is dolled up for tourists, but in the narrow lanes along the river beyond the arched **Jiēlóng Bridge** (接龙桥; Jiēlóng Qiáo), the Miao culture still flourishes.

◉ Sights & Activities

Déhāng is located within a huge 164 sq km geological park threaded with delightful treks. Look for signs posted by Jiēlóng Bridge for the trailheads.

Nine Dragon Stream Scenic Area   HIKING
(九龙溪景区; Jiǔlóngxī Jǐngqū) This beautiful riverside hike cuts through the village, past Miao peasants tilling their fields, and into a landscape of peaks and vales carpeted in green. The main path leads to **Liúshā Waterfall** (流沙瀑布; Liúshā Pùbù) China's longest, where sprays of water drop a dramatic 216m. You can climb behind the waterfall for views through the curtain of water. Backtrack to the bend in the path. The turnoff there leads to a 1.5km clamber up gullies and falls to the **Nine Dragon Waterfall** (九龙瀑布; Jiǔlóng Pùbù; admission ¥15). The walk to the Liúshā Waterfall takes about an hour from Jiēlóng Bridge. The sights are particularly beautiful after a rainfall, though this makes the journey slippery.

Yùquánxī Scenic Area   HIKING
(玉泉溪景区; Yùquánxī Jǐngqū) The 2.6km-long path along Yùquán Stream stretches along the valley, passing haystacks and terraced fields, before ducking into a small gorge and crisscrossing the river and finally entering a thick profusion of green. Cross the **Jade Fountain Gate** (玉泉门; Yùquán Mén) and follow the path to the sinuous waterfall. Then climb the steps up to the **Tiānwèn Platform** (天问台; Tiānwèn Tái) for fabulous views of the gorge and Miao homesteads.

Jiēlóng Bridge   VIEWPOINT
This short walk leads from Jiēlóng Bridge up flagstone steps and through the bamboo to lovely views of the village.

🛏 Sleeping & Eating

Simple inns (客栈; *kèzhàn*) are around the square and suspended over the river. Travellers wanting midrange comfort can find it in nearby (soulless) Jíshǒu.

    Restaurants are clustered around the square and main road. The inns also have restaurants, though their meals are more expensive than their rooms. Hawkers in the alleys proffer small bites, including skewers of grilled fish (*táohuāyú; ¥3*) and tiny crabs (*xiǎo pángxiè; ¥5*).

Jiēlóngqiáo Inn   INN $
(接龙桥客店; Jiēlóngqiáo Kèdiàn; ☑135 1743 0915; s/d ¥40/50) This small varnished wood inn by Jiēlóng Bridge has the best-kept rooms, with fan and TV, in the village. The downside is the shared bathroom, two flights down in the dank basement.

Fēngyǔqiáo Inn   INN $
(风雨桥客栈; Fēngyǔqiáo Kèzhàn; ☑135 1743 0915; dm/d ¥30/60) This newly done-up inn is across the river from the square by the Yùquánxī Scenic Area trailhead.

Jiēlóng Inn   INN $
(接龙客栈; Jiēlóng Kèzhàn; ☑135 7432 0948; s/d ¥40/60; 🏠) Next to Jiēlóng Bridge, this popular spot has rooms with shared bathroom and a restaurant overlooking the river.

Miáojiěcānguǎn   CHINESE $
(苗姐餐馆; ☑152 7435 8239; dishes from ¥40; ⊙6am-9pm) Perch on a low stool at a table on the balcony overlooking the square, and wash down the tasty local dishes with the village firewater.

ℹ Getting There & Away

You can reach Déhāng via Jíshǒu, a rail town to the southeast. Buses (¥7, 50 minutes) depart when full from Jíshǒu Train Station for Déhāng's square from 6am to 6.30pm. Keep your eye on the scenery for the last third of the journey. The driver will wait while you pay admission at the park entrance.

Fènghuáng   凤凰

☑0743

Fènghuáng was once a frontier town, marking the boundary between the Han civilisations of the central plains and the Miao (苗), Tujia (土家) and Dong (侗) minorities of the southwest mountains. Protective walls went up in the Ming dynasty, but despite the implications Fènghuáng prospered as a centre of trade and cultural exchange. Its diverse residents built a breathtaking riverside settlement of winding alleys, temples and rickety stilt houses. Today, tourist development is taking precedence over careful preservation efforts, so see it before it crumbles away.

◉ Sights & Activities

Wandering aimlessly is the best way to experience the charms of **old town Fènghuáng** (凤凰古城; Fènghuáng Gǔchéng). The back alleys are a trove of shops, temples, ancestral halls and courtyard homes.

    Much of Fènghuáng can be seen for free, but the **through ticket** (tōngpiào; ☑322 3315; ¥148) allows two days' access to major sights

Fènghuáng

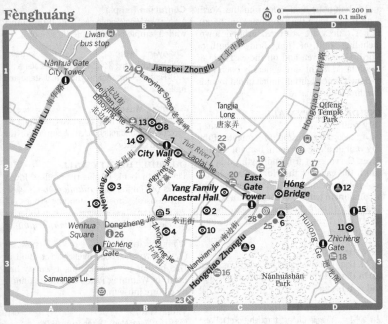

HÚNÁN FÈNGHUÁNG

Fènghuáng

⊙ Top Sights

City Wall	B2
East Gate Tower	C2
Hóng Bridge	C2
Yang Family Ancestral Hall	C2

⊙ Sights

1	Cháoyáng Temple	A2
2	Chóngdé Hall	C2
3	Confucian Temple	B2
4	Former Home of Shen Congwen	B3
5	Gǔchéng Museum	B2
6	Jiāngxīn Buddhist Temple	C3
7	North Gate Tower	B2
8	Stepping Stones	B2
9	Three Kings Temple	C3
10	Tiānhòu Temple	C3
11	Wànmíng Pagoda	D3
12	Wànshòu Temple	D2
13	Wooden Footbridge	B2
14	Xiong Xi Ling Former Residence	B2
15	Yíngxī Gate	D2

🛏 Sleeping

| 16 | Border Town International Youth Hostel | C3 |

17	Fènghuáng International Youth Hostel	D2
18	Koolaa's Small Room – A Good Year	D3
19	Phoenix Jiāngtiān Holiday Village	C2
20	Túoshuǐ Rénjiā Kèzhàn	C2

⊗ Eating

21	Night Market	C2
22	Soul Cafe	C2
23	Wànmù Zhāi	B3

🍷 Drinking

| 24 | Laoying Shao | B1 |

ℹ Information

| 25 | Ticket office | C3 |
| 26 | Tourism Administrative Bureau of Fènghuáng | B3 |

ℹ Transport

| 27 | North Gate Boat Dock | B2 |
| 28 | Train Ticket Booking Office | C3 |

and a half-hour boat ride from the North Gate Tower down the Tuó River (Tuó Jiāng). Ticket offices are scattered around town, including south of Hóng Bridge, south of North Gate Tower, and on the east side of Wenhua Sq. Sights are generally open 8am to 6pm. Come nightfall, much of old town is dazzlingly illuminated.

INSIDE THE CITY WALL

City Wall
HISTORIC SITE

(城墙; chéngqiáng) Restored fragments of the city wall lie along the south bank of the Tuó River. Carvings of fish and mythical beasts adorn the eaves of the **North Gate Tower** (北门城楼; Běimén Chénglóu), one of four original main gates. Another, the **East Gate Tower** (东门城楼; Dōngmén Chénglóu; through ticket), is a twin-eaved tower of sandstone and fired brick.

Hóng Bridge
BRIDGE

(虹桥; Hóng Qiáo; through ticket for upstairs galleries) In the style of the Dòng minority's wind and rain bridges.

Yang Family Ancestral Hall
HISTORIC SITE

(杨家祠堂; Yángjiā Cítáng; through ticket) West of East Gate Tower, built in 1836. Its exterior is covered with slogans from the Cultural Revolution.

Xiong Xi Ling
Former Residence
HISTORIC SITE

(熊希龄故居; Xióng Xī Líng Gùjū; through ticket) The home of a former Premier and Finance Minister.

Jiāngxīn Buddhist Temple
TEMPLE

(江心禅寺; Jiāngxīn Chánsì) On Huilong Ge, a narrow alley.

Three Kings Temple
TEMPLE

(三皇庙; Sānhuáng Miào) Great views of town await up the temple's steps off Jianshe Lu.

Tiānhòu Temple
TEMPLE

(天后宫; Tiānhòu Gōng) Off Dongzheng Jie, dedicated to the patron of seafarers.

Former Home of Shen Congwen
HISTORIC SITE

(沈从文故居; Shěn Cóngwén Gùjū; through ticket) The famous modern novelist was born here in 1902. (His tomb is east of town.)

Chóngdé Hall
HISTORIC SITE

(崇德堂; Chóngdé Táng; through ticket) The town's wealthiest resident Pei Shoulu's personal collection of antiques is on display in his former residence on Shijialong.

Confucian Temple
TEMPLE

(文庙; Wén Miào; Wenxing Jie) This 18th-century walled temple is now a middle school.

Cháoyáng Temple
TEMPLE

(朝阳宫; Cháoyáng Gōng; 41 Wenxing Jie; admission ¥10) Features an ancient theatrical stage and hall.

Gǔchéng Museum
MUSEUM

(古城博物馆; Gǔchéng Bówùguǎn; Dengying Jie; ⊙6.30am-6pm; through ticket) A survey of the old town's history.

OUTSIDE THE CITY WALL

The north bank of the river offers lovely views of Fènghuáng's *diàojiǎolóu* (吊脚楼; stilt houses). Cross by stepping stones (跳岩; *tiàoyán*), best navigated when sober, or wooden footbridge (木头桥; *mùtóu qiáo*).

Wànshòu Temple
HISTORIC SITE

(万寿宫; Wànshòu Gōng; through ticket) Built in 1755 by Jiāngxī arrivals, this assembly hall north of Wànmíng Pagoda houses a minority culture museum.

Yíngxī Gate
GATE

(迎曦门; Yíngxī Mén) Dates from 1807.

Southern Great Wall
ARCHITECTURE

(南长城; Nán Chángchéng; admission ¥45) The Ming-dynasty defensive wall, 13km from town, once stretched to Guìzhōu.

Huángsī Bridge Old Town
VILLAGE

(黄丝桥古城; Huángsī Qiáo Gǔchéng; admission ¥20) A Tang-dynasty military outpost 5km outside town. Motorcycles will take you for ¥4.

Qíliáng Dòng
CAVE

(奇梁洞; Qíliáng Dòng; admission ¥60) A cave of underground rivers and waterfalls 7km north of town. Take the Lìwān tourist bus.

🛏 Sleeping

Inns (客栈; *kèzhàn*) are easy to find in Fènghuáng. The river's east bend is good for digs with river views away from the noisy bars. Prepare for rudimentary dwellings with squat toilets. Some rooms can be damp, so check first. In July and August, rates triple and rooms go quickly, so book ahead. Signs with '今日有房' mean vacancy.

TOP CHOICE Koolaa's Small Room – A Good Year
INN $

(考拉小屋的一年好时光; Kǎolā Xiǎowū de Yī Nián Hǎo Shíguāng; ☑322 2026; 89 Huilong Ge; 迴龙阁89号; d ¥120; ✱🐾) There are just 10 rooms in this sweet, wood-framed inn on the river; all have balconies, showers and TVs but six have fantastic river views. Air-con is ¥20 extra. The kindly staff of aunties live on the premises, just past Zhìchéng Gate (志城关). Book ahead.

Border Town International Youth Hostel
HOSTEL $

(边城国际青年旅舍; Biānchéng Guójì Qīngnián Lǚshè; ☑322 8698; 45 Hongqiao Zhonglu; dm/s ¥30/80, d ¥100-130, tr ¥188; ❀@) Named for a novel by Fènghuáng's famous son Shen Congwen, this hostel is a five-minute walk south of the Hóng Bridge. The pricier doubles are especially spacious, and those on the top floor have great views of the old town. Squat toilets.

Phoenix Jiāngtiān Holiday Village
HOTEL $$$

(凤凰江天旅游度假村; Fènghuáng Jiāngtiān Lǚyóu Dùjiàcūn; ☑326 1998; Jiangtian Sq; 虹桥路江天广场; s & d ¥588, tr ¥668; ❀@) The aging Phoenix is ready for a rebirth, but for now these are good-sized rooms with so-so bathrooms. There are 40% discounts outside of peak periods, but no river views. Turn right at the arch on Laoying Shao.

Fènghuáng International Youth Hostel
HOSTEL $

(凤凰国际青年旅馆; Fènghuáng Guójì Qīngnián Lǚguǎn; ☑326 0546; yhaphoenix@163.com; 11 Shawan; 沙湾11号; dm ¥35-50, s & d ¥148-238; ❀@) Situated on the river's northeast bank next to Dōngguān Mén (东关门) are these quaint rooms. Shared bathrooms have squat toilets.

Túoshuǐ Rénjiā Kèzhàn
INN $

(沱水人家; ☑350 1690; 12 Beibian Jie; dm ¥100-120, s/d ¥200/300, discounts of 50%; ❀@) The wood-finished rooms, four of which have balconies with river views and computers, are quite nice until the neighbourhood bars open up. Bring earplugs.

✖ Eating & Drinking

Fènghuáng's restaurants can be pricey; the ones west of the North Gate Tower are less touristy and sometimes cheaper. Fortunately, there is plenty of cheap, tasty street food – everything from kebabs to spicy *dòufu* (tofu) and cooling bowls of *liángfěn* (jellies made from grasses or starchy roots).

There are few mellow watering holes. Bars wake up with a shout at nightfall along Laoying Shao (老营哨; Lǎoyíng Shào) on the river's north bank, and opposite along Beibian Jie and the north end of Huilong Ge. Tip back local Miao spirits *(Miáo jiǔ)*, 53-proof, mind-warping alcohol at ¥12 per glass.

TOP CHOICE Night Market
MARKET $

(虹桥夜市; Hóngqiáo Yèshì; Hongqiao Donglu; ☺5pm-1am) Lively vendors set up shop in the late afternoon just north of the Hóng Bridge, ready to grill all manner of meat and vegies or slice up ripe fruits. Everything is on display, so just pick what you want, grab a beer from the shops across the way, and take a seat at the covered tables.

Wànmù Zhāi
CHINESE HÚNÁN $

(万木斋; ☑322 1589; Hongqiao Beilu; dishes from ¥25; ☺10am-9pm) The Yang family serves up generous portions of Tujia dishes as well as regional *xiāng* cuisine at this popular local spot. The waiters make good suggestions such as loquat duck and sweet rice (皿杷鸭子; ¥68).

Soul Cafe
WESTERN $$

(亦素咖啡; Yìsù Kāfēi; ☑326 0396; 18 Laoying Shao; ☺8am-midnight) This upmarket north bank cafe serves proper coffee (from ¥29), pizza (from ¥48) and chocolate cake (¥20). It's not cheap, but then again how many places have an extensive list of foreign wines and Cuban cigars?

ℹ Information

The main bank branches are on Nanhua Lu. China Construction Bank (中国建设银行; Zhōngguó Jiànshè Yínháng) has a currency exchange and 24-hour ATM.

China Post (中国邮政; Zhōngguó Yóuzhèng; cnr Sanwangge Lu & Hongqiao Zhonglu; ☺8am-5.30pm)

Kāimíng Pharmacy (开明大药房; Kāimíng Dàyàofáng; ☑322 8578; Hongqiao Xilu; ☺7.30am-10.30pm) Near intersection with Sanwangge Lu.

Mènghuàn Internet Cafe (梦幻网城; Mènghuàn Wǎng Chéng; Hongqiao Donglu; per hr ¥3; ☺24hr)

New People's Hospital (新人民医院; Xīn Rénmín Yīyuàn; ☑322 1199; Hongqiao Xilu) Southwest of town at the Jiensu Lu intersection.

Tourism Administrative Bureau of Fènghuáng (凤凰旅游中心; Fènghuáng Lǚyóu Zhōngxīn; ☑322 8365; ☺6.30am-6pm) Off Wenhua Sq.

Xīndònglì Internet Cafe (新动力网吧; Xīndònglì Wǎngbā; 2nd fl, Jianshe Lu; per hr ¥2-3; ☺24hr)

ℹ Getting There & Around

Long-distance buses to/from Jíshǒu Train Station (¥20, 1½ hours) frequently stop outside the old town from 6am to 8pm. Motorcycles (¥5) will ferry you in.

Buses come from:

Chángshā ¥130, five hours, eight daily

Huáihuà ¥35, three hours, every 20 minutes

Wǔhàn ¥200, eight hours, one daily (4.30pm)

Zhāngjiājiè ¥70, 4½ hours, four daily (8.30am, 9.30am, 2.30am and 4.30pm)

There's no train station in Fènghuáng, but you can book tickets at the **train ticket booking office** (火车代票处; huǒchē dàipiàochù; ☎322 2410; Hongqiao Zhonglu; ☺8am-10pm) south of Hóng Bridge.

The interior of the old town is closed to traffic. A minibus makes the circuit to the Southern Great Wall and Qíliáng Dòng from the Liwān bus stop (栗湾停车场; ¥30, every 10 minutes, 8am to 10pm) at Fènghuáng Bridge and Jiang Beixilu. Taxis start at ¥3 but try going off-meter.

Hóngjiāng Old Town 洪江古商城

☎0745 / POP 60,783

This little-known town 55km south of Huáihuà boasts an extraordinary history as a Qing-dynasty financial and trading centre, due to its fortuitous location at the confluence of the Yuán (沅江; Yuán Jiāng) and Wū (巫水; Wū Shuǐ) Rivers. At one time, it was the main opium-distribution hub in southwest China. Dating as far back as the Northern Song dynasty, the surrounding city is mostly modern now, but the past lives on in the remarkable old town (Hóngjiāng Gǔshāngchéng), which is still home to a few thousand people.

◎ Sights

The old town is the principal reason to come here and can be visited in half a day. The city's main roads, Xinmin Lu (新民路), Yuanjiang Lu (沅江路) and Xiongxi Lu (雄溪路), which turns into Xingfu Lu (幸福路), mark its borders.

There's an official **ticket office** (☎763 2579; admission ¥120; ☺8am-5pm) marked with red lanterns in an alley off Yuanjiang Lu. Admission includes guided two-hour tours in Chinese featuring entertaining re-enactments of merchants' daily life. You need not pay admission if you enter via any of the other alleys connecting to the main roads. You won't be allowed into the buildings without a ticket.

The old town undulates in a delightful, higgledy-piggledy, often steep, maze of narrow stone-flagged alleys and lanes. English and Chinese signposts point the way to the notable buildings, some of which have been fully restored, including the tax office, opium shop, brothel, newspaper office, ancestral halls, and courtyard homes of prominent merchants. Most are of the *yìnzǐwū* (窨子屋) style, characterised by a series of adjoining courtyards, high exterior walls and concave roofs with *tiān jǐng* (light wells). Make sure to check out the ruins of **Tàipíng Temple** (太平宫; Tàipíng Gōng), built in 1723 as part of an assembly hall for Shàoyáng traders and destroyed during the Cultural Revolution. Getting lost is inevitable, but neighbours living in and among the 380 historic structures can point the way.

🛏 Sleeping & Eating

Hotels are along the roads bordering the old town. For restaurants, food stalls cook up the catch of the day on the riverbank by Hóng Bridge. Sit-down restaurants are along Xinmin Lu and Yuanjiang Lu.

Wǔlíngchéng Hotel HOTEL $$
(武陵城酒店; Wǔlíngchéng Jiǔdiàn; ☎766 6677; Xinmin Lu; 新民路、武陵广场; s/d ¥238/288, ste ¥438; ✹@) Less than 1km from Hóng Bridge, this high-rise has the polished decor and buttoned-up staff you'd expect in a big city. Out front, Wǔlíng plaza is the town community centre. There's a travel office in the lobby. Discounts of 20%.

Hóngjiāng Hotel HOTEL $
(洪江大酒店; Hóngjiāng Dàjiǔdiàn; ☎766 2999; 50 Xinmin Lu; 新民路50号; s/d ¥138/158, ste ¥248; ✹@) Despite the decrepit lobby, this hotel is well maintained and comfortable. It's just across the road from the old town and the steps from Hóng Bridge. Discounts of 20%.

❶ Information

Bank of China (中国银行; Zhōngguó Yínháng; Xinmin Lu) Has a 24-hour ATM and changes currency. Next to Hóngjiāng Hotel.

❶ Getting There & Away

Don't confuse Hóngjiāng old town with Hóngjiāng city (洪江市; Hóngjiāng shì), the town on the railway 30km west. The old town is most easily reached via Huáihuà (怀化). Buses leave Huáihuà's south bus station (¥25, 1½ hours, every 40 minutes) between 6.40am and 6.20pm for the **bus station** (Yuanjiang Lu), opposite the main entrance to the old town. Taxis charge a flat fee of ¥140 to/from Huáihuà.

Hóngjiāng train ticket booking office (洪江火车票代售点; Huǒchēpiào dàishòuchù; ☎266 3111; 81 Xinmin Lu; ☺7.30am-5.30pm) Across from Wǔlíngchéng Hotel.

Hong Kong

☎ 852 / POP 7 MILLION

Includes »

Sights 467
Activities.......................482
Tours............................484
Festivals & Events 484
Sleeping........................484
Eating 489
Drinking........................493
Entertainment..............494
Shopping.......................496
Getting There & Away...500
Getting Around 501

Best Places to Eat

» Dong Lai Shun (p491)
» Kowloon Tang (p491)
» Luk Yu Teahouse (p489)
» Yin Yang (p490)
» Pure Veggie House (p490)

Best Places to Stay

» Peninsula Hong Kong (p486)
» Espace Elastique (p488)
» Hotel Icon (p487)
» Helena May (p485)
» Upper House (p485)

Why Go?

Like a shot of adrenalin, Hong Kong quickens the pulse. Skyscrapers march up jungle-clad slopes by day and blaze neon by night across a harbour crisscrossed by freighters and motor junks. Above streets teeming with traffic, five-star hotels stand next to ageing tenement blocks.

The very acme of luxury can be yours, though enjoying the city need not cost the earth. The HK$2 ride across the harbour must be one of the world's best-value cruises. A meander through a market offers similarly cheap thrills. You can also escape the crowds – just head for one of the city's many country parks.

It's also a city that lives to eat, offering diners the very best of China and beyond. Hong Kong, above all, rewards those who grab experience by the scruff of the neck, who'll try that jellyfish, explore half-deserted villages or stroll beaches far from neon and steel.

When to Go
Hong Kong

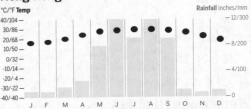

Mar–May Asia's top film festival, rugby and deities' birthdays beckon beyond a sea of umbrellas.

Jun–Sep Get hot (beach, new wardrobe), get wet (dragon boat, beer): antidotes to sultry summers.

Nov–Feb Hills by day, arts festival by night, celebrate Chinese New Year under Christmas lights.

Hong Kong Highlights

1 Cross Victoria Harbour on the legendary **Star Ferry** (p475)

2 Take the steep ascent to Victoria Peak on the **Peak Tram** (p467)

3 Yum cha under whirling fans at **Luk Yu Teahouse** (p489)

4 Soak up the incensed air at **Man Mo Temple** (p467)

5 Feel the chug of the world's last **double-decker trams**

6 Indulge in the visual feast of **Tsim Sha Tsui East Promenade** (p477)

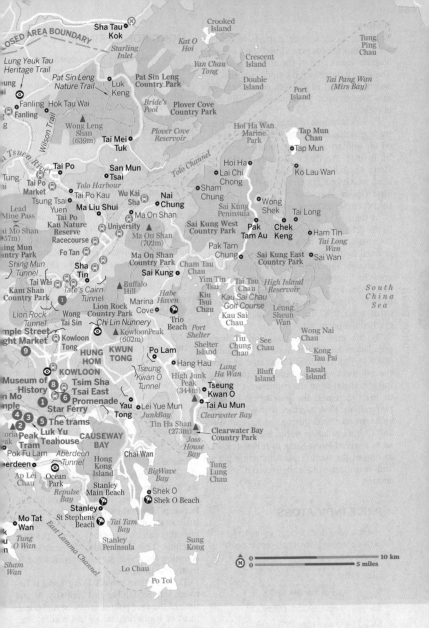

7 Lose yourself in a walled village on the **Ping Shan Heritage Trail** (p480)

8 Get some context for it all at the **Museum of History** (p477)

9 The indigenous sights, sounds and smells of **Temple Street Night Market** (p478)

10 Pay your respects to the magnificent **Tian Tan Buddha** (p482)

History

Until European traders started importing opium into the country, Hong Kong was an obscure backwater in the Chinese empire. The British developed the trade aggressively and by the start of the 19th century traded this 'foreign mud' for Chinese tea, silk and porcelain.

China's attempts to stamp out the opium trade gave the British the pretext they needed for military action. Gunboats were sent in. In 1841, the Union flag was hoisted on Hong Kong Island and the Treaty of Nanking, which brought an end to the so-called First Opium War, ceded the island to the British crown 'in perpetuity'.

At the end of the Second Opium War in 1860, Britain took possession of Kowloon Peninsula, and in 1898 a 99-year lease was granted for the New Territories.

Through the 20th century Hong Kong grew in fits and starts. Waves of refugees fled China for Hong Kong during times of turmoil. Trade flourished as did British expat social life, until the Japanese army crashed the party in 1941.

By the end of the war Hong Kong's population had fallen from 1.6 million to 610,000. But trouble in China soon swelled the numbers again as refugees (including industrialists) from the communist victory in 1949 increased the population beyond two million. This, together with a UN trade embargo on China during the Korean War and China's isolation in the next three decades, enabled Hong Kong to reinvent itself as one of the world's most dynamic ports and manufacturing and financial service centres.

HONG KONG PRIMER

Partly owing to its British colonial past, Hong Kong's political and economic systems are still significantly different from those of mainland China. See p989 for information on money and p994 for visas. Prices in this chapter are quoted in Hong Kong dollars (HK$).

In 1984 Britain agreed to return what would become the Special Administrative Region (SAR) of Hong Kong to China in 1997, on the condition it would retain its free-market economy and its social and legal systems for 50 years. China called it 'One country, two systems'. On 1 July 1997, in pouring rain, outside the Hong Kong Convention & Exhibition Centre, the British era ended.

In the years that followed, Hong Kong weathered major storms – an economic downturn, the outbreak of the SARS virus and a nagging mistrust of the government.

In March 2012, Leung Chun-ying, a former property surveyor, became Hong Kong's fourth chief executive. Though a seemingly more decisive man than his predecessors, Leung's unsubstantiated 'red' connections have many Hong Kongers worried, something not helped by spiralling living costs and China's treatment of its dissidents.

Climate

Hong Kong rarely gets especially cold, but it's worth packing something at least a little bit warm between November and March. Between May and mid-September temperatures in the mid-30s combined with stifling humidity can turn you into a walking sweat machine. This time is also the wettest, accounting for about 80% of annual rainfall, partly due to typhoons.

The best time to visit Hong Kong is between mid-September and February. At any time of the year pollution can be diabolical, most of it pouring across the border from the coal-powered factories of Guǎngdōng, many of which are Hong Kong owned.

Language

Almost 95% of Hong Kongers are Cantonese-speaking Chinese, though Putonghua (Mandarin) is increasingly used. Visitors should

PRICE INDICATORS

The following price indicators are used in this chapter. Note that prices for eating are per meal.

Sleeping

$	less than HK$900
$$	HK$900 to HK$1500
$$$	more than HK$1500

Eating

$	less than HK$200
$$	HK$200 to HK$400
$$$	more than HK$400

have few problems, however, because English is widely spoken and the street signs are bilingual, as are most restaurant menus. Written Chinese in Hong Kong uses traditional Chinese characters, which tend to be more complicated than the simplified Chinese used on the mainland.

◉ Sights

Hong Kong comprises four main areas: Hong Kong Island, Kowloon, the New Territories and the Outlying Islands. Most sights are distributed in the northwestern part of Hong Kong Island, southern Kowloon Peninsula and throughout the New Territories.

More than 70% of Hong Kong is mountains and forests, most of it in the New Territories (NT). The area has seen plenty of urbanisation, but there remain traditional villages, mountain walks and beaches, all within an hour or so of the urban area by public transport. The suburbs in the NT are connected by the MTR, which links Kowloon to Lo Wu (East Rail) in the north and Kowloon to Tuen Mun (West Rail) in the west.

Of Hong Kong's 234 islands, only Lantau, Cheung Chau, Lamma and Peng Chau have easy access by ferry.

Admission charges for children and seniors at many sights are roughly half the regular price.

HONG KONG ISLAND

Central is where high finance meets haute couture, and mega deals are closed in towering skyscrapers. To the west is historically rich Sheung Wan, while Admiralty with its few but excellent offerings lies to the east. The 800m-long **Central–Mid-Levels Escalator** (Map p468; ⊙down 6-10am, up 10.30am-midnight), which begins on Queen's Rd Central and finishes at Conduit Rd, is useful for negotiating the slopes of Sheung Wan.

East of Admiralty is Wan Chai which features skyscrapers in the north and old neighbourhoods in the south. Neon-clad Causeway Bay lies to the east.

TOP
CHOICE **Peak Tram**   FUNICULAR
(www.thepeak.com.hk; one-way/return HK$28/40; ⊙7am-midnight; MCentral, exit J2) The gravity-defying Peak Tram was the first funicular railway in Asia and is also one of Hong Kong's most memorable attractions.

Rising steeply above skyscrapers, the funicular runs every 10 minutes from the lower terminus (Map p468) up the side of 552m **Victoria Peak** (Map p468). On clear days and at night, the view from the top is spectacular.

HSBC Building   BUILDING
(匯豐銀行大廈; Map p468; 1 Queen's Rd, Central; MCentral, exit K) The stunning headquarters of the HSBC, designed by British architect Sir Norman Foster, is a masterpiece of precision, sophistication and innovation. And so it should be. On completion in 1985 it was the world's most expensive building (it cost upward of US$1 billion). The ground floor is public space; from there, escalators rise to the main banking hall. It's worth taking the **escalator** (⊙9am-4.30pm Mon-Fri, 9am-12.30pm Sat) to the cathedral-like atrium on the 3rd floor.

TOP
CHOICE **Man Mo Temple**   TEMPLE
(文武廟; Map p468; 124-126 Hollywood Rd, Sheung Wan; ⊙8am-6pm; ☐bus 26) The temple was the centre of civil life on the island in the 19th century. It was built between 1847 and 1862 by Chinese merchants and dedicated to the gods of literature ('man') and of war ('mo'). Besides a place of worship, it was a court of arbitration for local disputes. Back in the early colonial days, the government only accepted oaths taken here, rather than in a court of law.

Not far from Man Mo Temple, **Pak Sing Ancestral Hall** (百姓廟; Map p468; 42 Tai Ping Shan St; ⊙8am-6pm) was a clinic for Chinese patients refusing treatment by Western medicine and a storeroom for bodies awaiting

EXCHANGE RATES		
Australia	A$1	HK$8.04
Canada	C$1	HK$7.76
China	¥1	HK$1.24
Euro zone	€1	HK$10.04
Japan	¥1	HK$0.097
Macau	MOP$1	HK$1.03
New Zealand	NZ$1	HK$6.36
UK	UK£1	HK$12.47
USA	US$1	HK$7.75

For current exchange rates see www.xe.com.

HONG KONG SIGHTS

Sheung Wan, Central & Admiralty

Western Harbour Crossing

Connaught Rd West
To Courtyard
by Marriott (650m)

Hong Kong-
Macau Ferry
Terminal

Government
Pier

Des Voeux Rd West

West Fire
Service St

Chung Kong Rd

Pier Rd

Tramway **32**

26

Wilmer St

Ko Shing St

Queen St

Bonham Strand West

New Market St

Western
Market
27

Sheung
Wan
20

Man Wa La

Tramway

CTS
(Main
Branch)

Queen's Rd West

New St

Hollywood
Road
Park

66

48

Wing Lok St

Morrison St

Bonham Strand East

Wing Lok St

Wing Wo St

Gilman

King George V
Memorial Park

High St

Hospital Rd

Bonham
Rd

Po Yan St

Possession St

Wa La

SHEUNG WAN
MID-LEVELS

Cleverly St

Burd St

Jervois St

Queen's Rd Central

Dragonair

Wing Kut St

Gilman's
Bazaar

The
Centre

Park Rd

15

11

19

Ta Ping Shan St

53 Lok Ku Rd

54

Hillier St

Gough St

Wing Wo St

36 Jubilee
St

Breezy Path

Blake
Gardens

Pound La

Po Hing Fong

37

12

Ladder St

39

Hollywood Rd

Aberdeen St

Peel St

Gage St

Wellington St

Stanley
St

Conduit Rd

Castle Rd

Seymour Rd

14

Bridges St

Wing Lee St

Shing Wong St

Staunton St

46 **41**

52

Graham St

43

Lyndhurst Tce

47

Caine Rd

5

34

49

SOHO

4

Robinson Rd

Prince's Tce

Shelley St

Elgin St

31

Old Bailey St

Victoria
Prison

Wyndham St

45

50

Central-Midlevels
Escalator

Chancery La

25

Arbuthnot Rd

51

Glenealy

Albert
Rd

Mosque St

Mosque Jct

10

7

21

Glenealy Lower

Robinson
Rd

Pok Fu Lam
Country
Park

Hornsey Rd

Old Peak Rd

▲ Victoria Peak
(552m)

Lugard Rd

Mt Austine Rd

THE PEAK

Tregunter Path

May Rd

Brewin Path

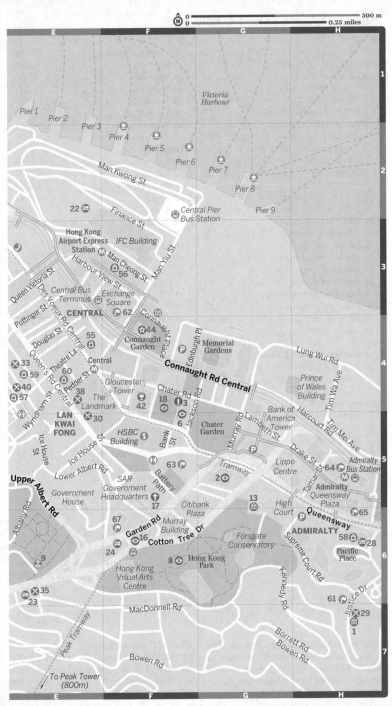

N
0 — 500 m
0 — 0.25 miles

Victoria Harbour

Pier 1
Pier 2
Pier 3
Pier 4
Pier 5
Pier 6
Pier 7
Pier 8
Pier 9

Man Kwong St

22

Finance St

Central Pier Bus Station

Hong Kong Airport Express Station

IFC Building

Man Yiu St

Man Cheong St

56

Harbour View St

Queen Victoria St
Des Voeux Rd Central
Central Bus Terminus

Exchange Square

Connaught Pl

62

CENTRAL

Pottinger St

Douglas St

55

Connaught Garden

44

Edinburgh Pl

Memorial Gardens

Connaught Rd Central

33
59
40
57

Theatre La
Queen's Rd Central
Pedder St

Central

60

Gloucester Tower

Chater Rd

18
3

Jackson Rd

Lung Wui Rd

Prince of Wales Building

Tim Wa Ave

38

The Landmark

42

6

Chater Garden

Bank of America Tower

Harcourt Rd

Tim Mei Ave

LAN KWAI FONG

30

Wyndham St

Ice House St

HSBC Building

Bank St

Murray Rd

Lambeth St

Drake St

Admiralty Bus Station

64

Ice House St

Lower Albert Rd

63

Battery Path

Tramway

2

Lippo Centre

Admiralty Queensway Plaza

Upper Albert Rd

Government House

SAR Government Headquarters

17

Citibank Plaza

13

High Court

Queensway

65

ADMIRALTY

67

Garden Rd

Murray Building

Cotton Tree Dr

Forsgate Conservatory

Supreme Court Rd

58
28

Pacific Place

Albany Rd

16

24

8

Hong Kong Park

9

Hong Kong Visual Arts Centre

Kennedy Rd

61

Justice Dr

35
23

MacDonnell Rd

Borrett Rd

29
1

Bowen Rd

Bowen Rd

Peak Tramway

To Peak Tower (800m)

Sheung Wan, Central & Admiralty

◎ Sights

1 Asia Society Hong Kong Centre H7
2 Bank of China Building........................... G5
3 Cenotaph...F4
4 Central Police Station
    Compound...D4
5 Dr Sun Yatsen Museum........................C4
6 Former Legislative Council
    Building...F5
7 Hong Kong Catholic Cathedral of
    the Immaculate
    Conception..D5
8 Hong Kong Park......................................F6
9 Hong Kong Zoological &
    Botanical Gardens.............................E6
10 Jamia Mosque.......................................C5
11 Kwun Yam Temple.................................B3
12 Man Mo Temple C3
13 Museum of Tea Ware G5
14 Ohel Leah Synagogue B4
15 Pak Sing Ancestral Hall.........................B3
16 Peak Tram Lower Terminus...................F6
17 St John's Cathedral...............................F5
18 Statue Square.......................................F4
19 Tai Sui Temple.......................................B3

◎ Activities, Courses & Tours

20 Wan Kei Ho International
    Martial Arts Association C2

◎ Sleeping

21 Bishop Lei International House............ D5
22 Four Seasons...E2
23 Garden View E6
24 Helena May F6
25 Hotel LKF D5
26 Ibis B2
27 Mandarin Oriental.................................C2
28 Upper House H6

◎ Eating

29 AMMO...H7
    city'super ....(see 56)
30 L'Atelier de Joël Robuchon....................E5
31 Life Cafe D4
32 Lin Heung Kui B2
33 Luk Yu Tea House...................................E4
    Lung King Heen ....(see 22)

34 Posto Pubblico.......................................C4
35 Pure Veggie House.................................E6
    San Xi Lou ....(see 35)
36 Sing Kee...D3
37 Teakha..B3
38 ThreeSixty..E4
39 Yardbird..C3
40 Yung Kee...E4

◎ Drinking

    Amo Eno ....(see 56)
41 Club 71...D4
    Gecko Lounge ....(see 47)
42 Sevva..F4
    T:me..(see 41)
43 The Globe D4

◎ Entertainment

44 Grappa's Cellar F4
45 Makumba...D4
46 Peel Fresco...D4
47 Propaganda..D4
48 Sheung Wan Civic Centre......................B2
49 TakeOut Comedy Club D4
50 Tivo...D4
51 Works..D5

◎ Shopping

52 Arch Angel Antiques D4
53 Cat Street B3
    Fook Ming Tong Tea Shop ....(see 56)
54 Hollywood Road......................................B3
55 Hong Kong Book Centre.........................E4
56 IFC Mall..F3
57 Mountain Folkcraft.................................E4
58 Pacific Place...H6
59 Photo Scientific.....................................E4
60 Shanghai Tang..E4

◎ Information

61 British Consulate....................................H6
62 Canadian Consulate................................F3
63 Dutch Consulate.....................................F5
64 French Consulate...................................H5
65 German Consulate H6
    Japanese Consulate.......................(see 62)
66 Lao Consulate...B2
67 US Consulate..F6

burial in China. **Kwun Yam Temple** (觀音堂; Map p468; 34 Tai Ping Shan St) honours the Goddess of Mercy. **Tai Sui Temple** (太歲廟; Map p468; 9 Tai Ping Shan St; ◎8am-6pm) houses statues of animals of the Chinese zodiac.

Bank of China Building BUILDING
(中國銀行大楼; Map p468; 1 Garden Rd; Ⓜ Central, exit K) The awe-inspiring Bank of China Tower designed by IM Pei rises from the ground like a cube, and is successively re-

duced until the south-facing side is left to rise upward on its own. The **public viewing gallery** (⊙8am–6pm Mon–Fri) on the 43rd floor offers panoramic views of Hong Kong.

TOP
CHOICE **Happy Valley Racecourse** RACECOURSE
(跑馬地馬場; Map p472; www.hkjc.com/home/english/index.asp; 2 Sports Rd, Happy Valley; admission HK$10; ⊙7-10.30pm Wed Sep-Jun; 🚇Happy Valley) An evening at the races here is one of the quintessential Hong Kong things to do, if you happen to be around during one of the weekly Wednesday evening races. The punters pack into the stands and trackside, cheering and drinking, and the atmosphere is electric. Check the website for details on betting and tourist packages.

Asia Society
Hong Kong Centre BUILDING, GALLERY
(亞洲協會香港中心; Map p468; The Hong Kong Jockey Club Former Explosives Magazine; ☎2103 9511; http://asiasociety.org/hong-kong; 9 Justice Dr, Admiralty; ⊙gallery 11am-5pm Tue–Sun, to 8pm last Thu of the month; ⓂAdmiralty, exit F) This magnificent site integrates 19th-century British military buildings, including two explosives magazines, and transforms them into a sublime-looking complex comprising an exhibition gallery, a theatre and a restaurant (p489). The centre is an easy walk from the hotels in Admiralty.

Dr Sun Yatsen Museum MUSEUM
(孫中山紀念館; Map p468; 7 Castle Rd, Mid-Levels, Central; admission HK$10; ⊙10am-6pm Mon-Wed, Fri & Sat, to 7pm Sun; 🚌buses 3B, 12) Housed in a marvellous Edwardian-style building, the museum is dedicated to the father of modern China and his time in Hong Kong. The mansion was built in 1914 as the residence of a tycoon from an influential Eurasian family. It was converted into a Mormon Church in 1960, and became the museum that it is today in 2006.

Dr Sun Yatsen was a key figure in modern Chinese history. Unfortunately, the dull exhibition here does not really do justice to his legendary life, though the architecture of the repurposed building is a delight.

Central Police Station
Compound HISTORIC BUILDING
(前中區警署; Map p468; 10 Hollywood Rd; ⓂCentral, exit D1) This enormous disused colonial compound, together with the adjacent former magistracy and Victoria Prison, were built between 1841 and 1919. There are plans to revitalise the buildings as an art gallery, cinema, museum and boutique shopping mall. The whole renovation is expected to be completed in 2014.

Hong Kong Park PARK
(香港公園; Map p468; 19 Cotton Tree Dr, Admiralty; ⊙park 6am-11pm; ⓂAdmiralty, exit C1) The artificial waterfalls and swan-graced ponds in this 8-hectare park may be a tad too picture-perfect unless you're a bride (or groom), but the dramatic views of skyscrapers facing off mountains should lure anyone to snap away. Highlights here are the **Edward Youde Aviary** (尤德觀鳥園; ⊙9am–5pm), which has a wooden bridge suspended at eye level with tree branches where 600 birds reside, and the **Museum of Tea Ware** (茶具文物館; Map p468; www.lcsd.gov.hk/ce/Museum/Arts/en/tea/tea01.html; 10 Cotton Tree Dr, Admiralty; admission free; ⊙10am-5pm Wed-Mon).

HONG KONG IN...

One Day

Catch a tram up to **Victoria Peak** for great views of the city, stopping in **Central** for lunch on the way down. Head to **Man Mo Temple** for a taste of history before boarding the **Star Ferry** to Kowloon. Enjoy the views along **Tsim Sha Tsui East Promenade** as you stroll over to the **Museum of History**. After dinner in Tsim Sha Tsui, take the MTR to **Soho** for drinks.

Two Days

In addition to the above, you could go to **Aberdeen** for a boat ride, then seafood and shopping in **Ap Lei Chau**. Alternatively, go hiking and swimming in **Sai Kung** followed by seafood on the waterfront. After dark, head to the **Temple Street Night Market** for sightseeing, shopping and street food. If you're still game, check out the **Yau Ma Tei Wholesale Fruit Market**.

Wan Chai & Causeway Bay

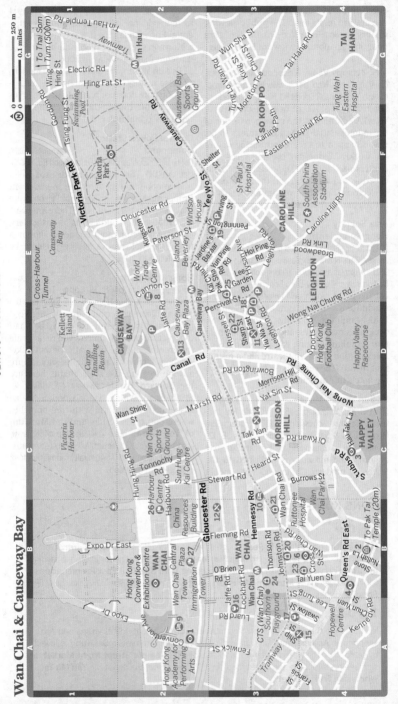

Wan Chai & Causeway Bay

◎ Sights

1	Hong Kong Arts Centre	A2
2	Hong Kong House of Stories (Blue House)	B4
3	Khalsa Diwan Sikh Temple	C4
4	Old Wan Chai Post Office	B4
5	Victoria Park	F1
6	Wan Chai Market	B4

◎ Activities, Courses & Tours

7	South China Athletic Association	E4

◎ Sleeping

8	Alisan Guest House	E2
9	Harbour View	A2
10	Regal iClub Hotel	C3

◎ Eating

11	Irori	D3
12	Joon Ko Restaurant	B3
13	Manor Seafood Restaurant	D2
14	Old Bazaar Kitchen	C3
15	Yin Yang	A4

◎ Drinking

16	Delaney's	A3
	Executive Bar	(see 11)
17	Pawn	A3

◎ Shopping

	Daydream Nation	(see 1)
18	G.O.D.	E3
19	Jardine's Bazaar	E3
20	Johnston Road	B3
21	Kung Fu Supplies	B3
22	Page One	D3
23	Tai Yuen Toy Shops	B4
24	Wan Chai Computer Centre	B3
25	Yiu Fung Store	E3

◎ Information

26	Australian Consulate	B2
27	New Zealand Consulate	B2

Hong Kong Zoological & Botanical Gardens
PARK

(香港動植物公園; Map p468; Albany Rd, Central; ☉terrace gardens 6am-10pm, zoo & aviaries to 7pm, greenhouse 9am-4.30pm; 🚌buses 3B, 12) Built more than a century ago in the style of an English park, the gardens feature a pleasant collection of arboured paths, fountains, aviaries and a zoo. It's ideal for a walk, if you can ignore the smell of flamingo droppings.

Statue Square
MONUMENT, HISTORIC BUILDING

(皇后像廣場;Map p468; Edinburgh Pl, Central; Ⓜ Central, exit K) This leisurely square used to house effigies of British royalty. Now it pays tribute to a single sovereign – the founder of HSBC, the banking giant that owns the square. To the east is the **Former Legislative Council Building** (前立法會大樓; Map p468; 8 Jackson Rd), a neoclassical edifice. To the north is the **Cenotaph** (和平紀念碑; Map p468; Chater Rd), a memorial to Hong Kong residents killed during the two world wars.

Old Wan Chai
NEIGHBOURHOOD

(Map p472; Ⓜ Wan Chai, exit A3, 🚌6 or 6A) The area around Queen's Rd E is filled with pockets of local culture that are best explored on foot. The mini-museum **Hong Kong House of Stories** (香港故事館; Map p472; ☎enquiries 2117 5850, tour enrolment (Suki Chau) 2835 4376; wctour@gmail.com; http://houseofstories.sjs.org.

hk; 74 Stone Nullah Lane, Wan Chai; ☉11am-5pm) occupies the historic **Blue House** (藍屋) a pre-war building with cast-iron Spanish balconies reminiscent of New Orleans, and no toilet flushing facilities. It runs tours of Wan Chai in English (HK$600, two hours). Email a month in advance to arrange.

The **Old Wan Chai Post Office** (舊灣仔郵政局; Map p472; 221 Queen's Rd E; ☉10am-5pm Wed-Mon) is Hong Kong's oldest post-office building. The area sandwiched by Queen's Rd E and Johnston Rd is a lively outdoor bazaar. **Wan Chai market** (Map p472; ☉7.30am-7pm) vendors flaunt their wares on Cross St and Stone Nullah Lane. **Tai Yuen Street** has goldfish, plastic flowers and granny underwear for sale but is best known for its **toy shops** (Map p472; 14-19 Tai Yuen St; ☉10am-8.30pm) selling collectibles such as clockwork tin.

Pak Tai Temple
TEMPLE

(北帝廟; off Map p472; 2 Lung On St, Wan Chai; ☉8am-5pm; Ⓜ Wan Chai, exit A3) A short stroll up Stone Nullah Lane takes you to a majestic Taoist temple built in 1863 to honour a god of the sea, Pak Tai. The temple – the largest on Hong Kong Island – is quite impressive and contains a 3m-tall copper likeness of Pak Tai cast in the Ming dynasty in its main hall.

Yau Ma Tei

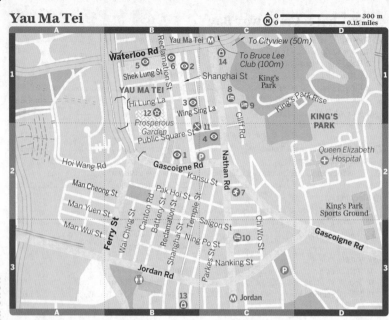

Yau Ma Tei

◎ Sights
1	Jade Market	B2
2	Red Brick House	B1
3	Temple Street Night Market	B1
4	Tin Hau Temple	C2
5	Wholesale Fruit Market	B1
6	Yau Ma Tei Theatre	B1

✪ Activities, Courses & Tours
7	Map Publications Centre	C2

🛏 Sleeping
8	Booth Lodge	C1
9	Caritas Bianchi Lodge	C1
10	Madera Hong Kong	C3

✕ Eating
11	Mido Café	B2

✪ Entertainment
12	Broadway Cinematheque	B1

🛍 Shopping
13	Chan Wah Kee Cutlery Store	B3
14	Protrek	C1

Victoria Park　　　　　　　　　　PARK

(維多利亞公園; Map p472; Causeway Rd, Causeway Bay; admission free; ⊗6am or 7am-11pm; MTin Hau, exit B) Hong Kong's largest patch of public greenery is best visited on weekday mornings, when it becomes a slow-motion forest of taichi practitioners, and during the **mid-autumn festival**, when people turn out en masse carrying lanterns.

Hong Kong Film Archive　　FILM ARCHIVE

(香港電影資料館; ☎2739 2139, bookings 2734 9009, 2119 7383; www.filmarchive.gov.hk; 50 Lei King Rd, Sai Wan Ho; ⊗box office noon-8pm, closed Thu, resource centre 10am-7pm Mon-Wed & Fri, to 5pm Sat, 1-5pm Sun; MSai Wan Ho, exit A) With more than 6300 reels in the vaults and 30,000 pieces of related materials, this excellent archive dedicated to Hong Kong cinema is well worth a visit for film buffs.

St John's Cathedral　　　　　CHURCH

(聖約翰座堂; Map p468; www.stjohnscathedral.org.hk; 4-8 Garden Rd, Central; ⊗7am-6pm; MCentral, exit J2) Services have been held at this elegant Anglican cathedral since it opened in 1849, except in 1944, when the Japanese army used it as a social club.

Khalsa Diwan Sikh Temple　　TEMPLE

(Map p472; ☎2572 4459; www.khalsadiwan.com; 371 Queen's Rd E, Wan Chai; ⊗4am-9pm; 🚇) Hong Kong's largest Sikh temple welcomes people of any creed, caste or colour to partake of their prayer services (4 to 8am and

6 to 8pm Monday to Saturday, 9am to 1pm Sunday) and free vegetarian meals (11.30am to 8.30pm).

Hong Kong Catholic Cathedral of the Immaculate Conception
CHURCH
(天主教聖母無原罪主教座堂; Map p468; http://cathedral.catholic.org.hk; 16 Caine Rd, Central; ⊙7am-7pm) Hong Kong's most important Catholic building, built in 1888.

Jamia Mosque
MOSQUE
(回教清真禮拜堂; Map p468; ☎2523 7743; 30 Shelley St, Central) Erected in 1849, this oldest mosque in Hong Kong is not open to non-Muslims, but you can admire the facade from the terrace out front.

Ohel Leah Synagogue
SYNAGOGUE
(猶太教莉亞堂; Map p468; ☑2589 2621; www.ohelleah.org; 70 Robinson Rd, Mid-Levels; ⊙10.30am-7pm Mon-Thu) This Moorish-looking temple is the territory's earliest synagogue. Bring ID if you want to visit the interior. Visit by appointment only.

Stanley Beach & Market
MARKET, BEACH
This crowd pleaser is best visited on weekdays. The **Stanley Market** (Map p464; Stanley Village Rd; ⊙10am-6pm) is a maze of alleyways which has bargain clothing (haggling a must!). **Stanley Main Beach** (Map p464) is for beach-bumming and windsurfing. With graves dating back to 1841, **Stanley Military Cemetery** (Map p464), 500m south of Stanley Market, is worth a visit.

Aberdeen
HARBOUR
(Map p464) Aberdeen's main attraction is the typhoon shelter it shares with sleepy **Ap Lei Chau**, where the sampans of the boat-dwelling fisherfolk used to moor. A half-hour tour of the typhoon shelter by sampan costs about HK$68 per person. You can also hop on the commuter boats plying the waters between Aberdeen Promenade and Ap Lei Chau (HK$1.80, five minutes).

Repulse Bay
BEACH
(Map p464) At the southeastern end of Hong Kong's most popular beach stand the eccentric **Kwun Yam shrine** (觀音廟) and a garish gallery of deities – from goldfish and a monkey god to the more familiar Tin Hau. Crossing Longevity Bridge (長壽橋) is supposed to add three days to your life.

Ocean Park
AMUSEMENT PARK
(香港海洋公園; Map p464; www.oceanpark.com.hk; Ocean Park Rd; admission HK$250; ⊙10am-6pm) Ocean Park, the worthy nemesis of Hong Kong Disneyland, is a massive marine-themed amusement park complete with white-knuckle rides, giant pandas and the very rare red pandas, an atoll reef and an amazing aquarium. Kidults will have a blast at the park's annual **Halloween Bash** (⊙5.30pm-midnight late Sep-Oct). Bus 629 from Admiralty MTR Station or Central Pier No 7 takes you there.

Shek O
BEACH
(Map p464) Shek O is the kind of place where villagers drying algae on clotheslines live alongside Vespa-riding 'bourgeois bohemians'. Ragged cliffs and a laid-back vibe complete the picture.

KOWLOON

Tsim Sha Tsui, known for its variety of dining and shopping options, is Hong Kong's most eclectic district, with the glamorous

---

THE STAR FERRY

You can't say you've 'done' Hong Kong until you've taken a ride on a **Star Ferry** (天星小輪; Map p468; www.starferry.com.hk; ⊙Central–Tsim Sha Tsui every 6-12min, 6.30am-11.30pm, Wan Chai–Tsim Sha Tsui every 8-20 min, 7.20am-11pm), that legendary fleet of electric-diesel vessels with names like *Morning Star* and *Twinkling Star*. At any time of the day, the HK$2.50 ride with its riveting views of skyscrapers and jungle-clad hills, must be one of the world's best-value cruises. At the end of the 10-minute journey, a hemp rope is cast and caught with a billhook, the way it was in 1888 when the first boat docked.

The Star Ferry was founded by Dorabjee Nowrojee, a Parsee from Bombay. Parsees believe in Zoroastrianism, and the five-pointed star on the Star Ferry logo is an ancient Zoroastrian symbol – in fact the same as the one followed by the Three Magi (who may have been Zoroastrian pilgrims) to Bethlehem in the Christmas tale.

Zoroastrians consider fire a medium through which spiritual wisdom is gained, and water is considered the source of that wisdom. No wonder that on an overcast day, the only stars you'll see over Victoria Harbour are those of the Star Ferry.

Kowloon

200 m
0.1 miles

0
0

N

To Elements (150m); Kowloon
Tang (150m); Ozone (200m);
Ritz Carlton Hong Kong (200m);
Tin Lung Heen (200m)

HUNG HOM

Hung
Hom

Hong Kong
Coliseum

Cheong Wan Rd

Hong Chong Rd

Hung Hom Bypass

Cross-Harbour Tunnel

Yuk Choi Rd

Concordia
Plaza

Cheong Wan Rd

Science Museum Rd

Chinachem
Golden Plaza

TSIM SHA
TSUI EAST

Salisbury Rd

Tsim Sha Tsui
East Ferry Pier

Victoria
Harbour

Hong Kong Polytechnic
University

Granville Rd

Energy
Plaza

Peninsula

Avis

Empire
Centre

Centre

Houston
Centre

Tsim Sha Tsui
East Centre

Wing On
Plaza

Chatham Rd South

Centenary
Gardens

East Tsim Sha Tsui
(KCR East Rail
Terminus)

Observatory Rd

Kimberley St

Kimberley Rd

Granville Rd

Carnarvon Rd

Cameron Rd

Prat Ave

Hart Ave

Minden Ave

Minden Row

Salisbury
Gardens

Austin Ave

Austin Rd

Hillwood Rd

Humphreys Ave

Cornwall
Ave

Canton Rd

Hanoi Rd

Nathan Rd

Haiphong Rd

Tsim Sha
Tsui

Lock
Rd

Hankow Rd

Ashley Rd

Middle Rd

Salisbury Rd

Chinese
Garden

Kowloon Park

Kowloon Park Dr

Peking Rd

Ocean
Centre

Star
House

Star Ferry

China Hong Kong City

HARBOUR
CITY

Canton Rd

China Ferry
Terminal

Ocean
Terminal

Kowloon

◉ Sights

1 Avenue of the Stars D4
2 Fook Tak Ancient Temple C3
3 Former Kowloon British School
   (Antiquities and
   Monuments Office) C1
4 Former Marine Police
   Headquarters (Heritage
   1881) C4
5 Hong Kong Cultural Centre C4
6 Hong Kong Museum of Art C4
7 Hong Kong Museum of History E1
8 Kowloon Mosque and Islamic
   Centre C2
9 Kowloon Park C2
10 Kowloon-Canton Railway Clock
   Tower C4
11 Middle Road Children's
   Playground D3
12 Signal Hill Garden & Blackhead
   Point Tower D3
13 St Andrew's Anglican Church D1
14 Tsim Sha Tsui East Promenade E4
15 Tsim Sha Tsui East Waterfront
   Podium Garden E3

⊜ Sleeping

16 BP International Hotel C1
17 Chungking Mansions D3
18 Hop Inn C3
19 Hop Inn on Carnarvon D2
20 Hotel Icon F2
21 Hyatt Regency Tsim Sha Tsui D3

22 Mirador Mansion D3
23 Peninsula Hong Kong C3
24 Salisbury C4

⊗ Eating

25 city'super B2
26 Din Tai Fung C3
27 Dong Lai Shun E2
28 Kimberley Chinese Restaurant D2
29 Spring Deer D3
   Stables Grill .... (see 4)
30 Typhoon Shelter Hing Kee
   Restaurant C1
31 Woodlands E3
32 Yè Shanghai B3
33 Ziafat C3

◉ Drinking

34 Butler D3
35 Ned Kelly's Last Stand C3
36 Tapas Bar E3

⊜ Shopping

37 Harbour City B4
38 Initial D2
39 Premier Jewellery D3
40 Rise Shopping Arcade D2
41 Swindon Books C3
42 Yue Hwa Chinese Products
   Emporium C1

ⓘ Information

43 Phoenix Services Agency D1

only a stone's throw from the pedestrian, and a population comprising Chinese, South Asians, Africans, Filipinos and Europeans.

To the north, buzzing with local life, is down-at-heel Yau Ma Tei. Traffic- and pedestrian-choked Mong Kok is the world's most densely populated place.

TOP CHOICE **Tsim Sha Tsui East Promenade**   HARBOUR
(尖沙嘴東部海濱花園; Map p476; Salisbury Rd; ⓜ Tsim Sha Tsui, exit E) The resplendent views of Victoria Harbour make this walkway one of the best strolls in Hong Kong. Begin your journey at the old **Kowloon–Canton Railway clock tower**, a landmark of the Age of Steam, near the **Star Ferry concourse**. To your left is the windowless **Hong Kong Cultural Centre** (香港文化中心), passing

which you'll arrive at the **Avenue of the Stars** (星光大道), Hong Kong's unoriginal tribute to its brilliant film industry. It's the vantage point for watching the **Symphony of Lights** (☺8-8.20pm), a laser-light show projected from atop skyscrapers.

TOP CHOICE **Hong Kong Museum of History**   MUSEUM
(香港歷史博物館; Map p476; 100 Chatham Rd South; admission HK$10; ☺10am-6pm Mon & Wed-Sat, to 7pm Sun; ⓜ Tsim Sha Tsui, exit B2) If you only have time for one museum, do make it this one. It will take you on a fascinating journey through Hong Kong's past, from prehistoric times to 1997. The 'Hong Kong Story' has interesting artefacts showing the customs of the territory's earliest inhabitants and the development of its urban culture.

HONG KONG MUSEUMS

The **Hong Kong Museum Pass** (seven days HK$30), which allows multiple entries to all museums mentioned in this chapter, is available from the participating museums – see www.discoverhongkong.com/eng/attractions/museum-major.html.

Museums are free on Wednesday.

Former Marine Police Headquarters
HISTORIC BUILDING

(前水警總部; Map p476; www.1881heritage.com; 2A Canton Rd, Tsim Sha Tsui; admission free; ⊙exhibition hall 10am-10pm; ⊛Star Ferry) Built in 1884, this gorgeous Victorian-style complex is one of Hong Kong's four oldest government buildings. Much to some Hong Kongers' chagrin, it was converted into a nakedly commercial property featuring shops, restaurants and a hotel in 2009. The developer felt the number '4' in the founding date was unlucky as it has a similar pronunciation to 'death' in Chinese, so the site was named 'Heritage 1881'.

TOP CHOICE St Andrew's Anglican Church
CHURCH

(聖安德烈堂; Map p476; www.standrews.org.hk; 138 Nathan Rd, Tsim Sha Tsui; ⊙7.30am-10.30pm; ⓂTsim Sha Tsui, exit B1) Hidden on a knoll behind the Former Kowloon British School is Kowloon's oldest Protestant church. The charming complex was built in 1905 in red brick and granite in an English Gothic style, and served briefly as a Shinto shrine during the Japanese occupation.

Former Kowloon British School
HISTORIC BUILDING

(前九龍英童學校; Map p476; www.amo.gov.hk; 136 Nathan Rd, Tsim Sha Tsui; ⓂTsim Sha Tsui, exit B1) The oldest surviving school building for the children of Hong Kong's expat community is a listed Victorian-style building that now houses the **Antiquities and Monuments Office** (古物古蹟辦事處). Constructed in 1902, it was subsequently modified to incorporate breezy verandas and high ceilings, prompted possibly by the fainting spells suffered by its young occupants.

Hong Kong Museum of Art
MUSEUM

(香港藝術博物館; Map p476; www.lcsd.gov.hk; 10 Salisbury Rd, Kowloon; admission HK$10, free Wed; ⊙10am-6pm Fri-Wed, to 8pm Sat; ⓂTsim Sha Tsui, exit J) The museum's six floors of Chinese antiquities, paintings, calligraphy and contemporary Hong Kong art are a must if you're remotely interested in art. Thematic exhibitions featuring modern works by local and overseas artists are also inspiring. Free English-language tours at 11am.

TOP CHOICE Temple Street Night Market
MARKET

(廟街夜市; Map p474; ⊙6pm-midnight; ⓂYau Ma Tei, exit C) Extending from Man Ming Lane to Nanking St, this famous bazaar hawks everything under the moon from pirated designer bags to sex toys. Remember to bargain. There are also Cantonese opera performances, and fortune-tellers, many of whom are English-speaking. Night owls should saunter over to the historic **wholesale fruit market** (Map p474; cnr Shek Lung & Reclamation Sts; ⊙midnight-dawn; ⓂYau Ma Tei, exit B2) nearby with its spectacle of trucks off-loading fresh fruit and workers manoeuvring boxes in front of century-old stalls.

Jade Market & Shanghai Street
MARKET, STREET

(玉器市場和上海街; Map p474; cnr Kansu & Battery Sts, Yau Ma Tei; ⊙10am-5pm; ⓂYau Ma Tei, exit C) Some 450 stalls sell all varieties and grades of jade, but unless you know your nephrite from your jadeite, it's wise not to buy expensive pieces here. Walking down **Shanghai Street** (上海街) on the other side of Kansu St, however, is free. Once Kowloon's main drag, it's lined with stores selling embroidered Chinese wedding gowns, sandalwood incense, kitchenware and Buddhist provisions; there's a pawn shop at the junction with Saigon St, and mahjong parlours (you can go in, but refrain from taking photos).

Tin Hau Temple
TEMPLE

(天后廟; Map p474; cnr Temple & Public Square Sts; ⊙8am-5pm; ⓂYau Ma Tei, exit C) This large, incense-filled sanctuary built in the 19th century is one of Hong Kong's most famous Tin Hau temples. The square in front is Yau Ma Tei's communal heart, where fishermen once laid out their hemp ropes to sun next to banyans that today shade chess players, retirees and gangsters.

Chi Lin Nunnery
TEMPLE

(志蓮淨苑; Map p464; www.chilin.org; 5 Chin Lin Dr, Diamond Hill; ⊙9am-4.30pm; ⓂDiamond Hill, exit C2) This beautiful replica of a Tang dynasty monastery comes complete with temples, lotus ponds, Buddhist relics and timber structures assembled without the use of a single iron nail. It's the world's largest cluster of handcrafted timber buildings. Connected to the nunnery is **Nan Lian Garden** (www.nanliangarden.org; ⊘10am-6pm), a Tang-style garden featuring a pagoda, a tea pavilion, a koi pond and a bizarre collection of petrified wood.

Sik Sik Yuen Wong Tai Sin Temple TEMPLE
(嗇色園黃大仙祠; www.siksikyuen.org.hk; Lung Cheung Rd, Wong Tai Sin; admission by donation HK$2; ⊘7am-5.30pm; MWong Tai Sin, exit B3) This Taoist temple is dedicated to Wong Tai Sin, who was said to have transformed boulders into sheep. In fact, the whole area, an MTR station and a residential property near the temple are all named after this poor immortal who was supposed to have been a hermit.

Middle Road Children's Playground PARK
(中間道遊樂場; Map p476; Middle Rd; ⊘7am-11pm; MEast Tsim Sha Tsui) On weekends, this hidden gem with play facilities, shaded seating, abundant greenery and views of the waterfront attracts children and picnickers of as many ethnicities as there are ways to go down a slide (if you're 12). The park sits on the podium of the MTR Tsim Sha Tsui East station. Its eastern exit is connected to the handsome **Tsim Sha Tsui East Waterfront Podium Garden** (尖沙咀東海濱平台花園; Map p476).

Signal Hill Garden & Blackhead Point Tower PARK, TOWER
(訊號山公園和訊號塔; Map p476; Minden Row; ⊘tower 9-11am & 4-6pm) The views at the top of this knoll are quite spectacular, though if this were the 1900s all the ships in the harbour could be returning your gaze – a copper ball in the handsome Edwardian-style tower here was dropped at 1pm daily so seafarers could adjust their chronometers. Enter from Minden Row (off Mody Rd).

Kowloon Park PARK
(九龍公園; Map p476; 22 Austin Rd; ⊘6am-midnight; MJordan, exit E) This green oasis is great for people-watching, particularly on Sunday when it's packed with migrant domestic workers enjoying their day off, singing, dancing and socialising. Sunday is also the day for Kung Fu Corner, a display of martial arts.

Yau Ma Tei Theatre HISTORIC BUILDING
(油麻地戲院; Map p474; ☑enquiries 2264 8108, tickets 2374 2598; www.lcsd.gov.hk/ymtt; MYau Ma Tei, exit B2) Two historic buildings have been converted into a centre for Cantonese opera. For decades, the art deco interiors of the YMT Theatre kept many a coolie and rickshaw driver entertained, but losing business to modern cinemas in the '80s, it began showing porn to stay afloat. The neoclassical **Red Brick House** (紅磚屋; Map p474) was the Engineer's Office of the former **Pumping Station** (前水務署抽水站工程師辦公室; 8 Waterloo Rd) built in 1895.

Jockey Club Creative Arts Centre ARTS CENTRE
(賽馬會創意藝術中心; www.jccac.org.hk; 30 Pak Tin St, Shek Kip Mei; ⊘10am-10pm; MShek Kip Mei, exit C) More than 150 artists have moved into these factory premises that used to churn out shoes and watches. Many studios are closed on weekdays, but you can visit the

HONG KONG SIGHTS

FRED YEUNG: ROCK CLIMBER, GRAFFITI ARTIST

Best Rock Climbing

On Tung Lung Chau (Map p464), where there's a technical wall, a sea gully and a big wall. Follow the path to the fort on the island and you'll see Holiday Store. The folks there will show you. A **ferry** (☑2560 9929) leaves Sai Wan Ho typhoon shelter for the island four to six times a day on weekends. On weekdays you can just show up at the typhoon shelter and haggle with sampan operators. Tai Tau Chau, near Shek O beach, also has excellent granite, some with bolted routes.

Best Graffiti

Hong Kong's graffiti hall of fame is a lane close to a school and one of the exits of Mong Kok East MTR station. You'll see throw-ups, stencils, pieces and wildstyle. There's also a pavilion at Hong Kong's most popular surf spot, **Big Wave Bay** (Map p464; MShau Kei Wan station, exit A3, Shek O-bound minibus) featuring works that change every year. The Jockey Club Creative Arts Centre has graffiti on the 5th and 6th levels.

SIGHTS WEBSITES

Handy websites for sights listed in this chapter are:

Antiquities & Monuments Office (http://amo.gov.hk) All villages, heritage trails and some historic structures.

Chinese Temple Committee (www.ctc.org.hk) Most temples.

Leisure & Cultural Services Department (www.lcsd.gov.hk) All public parks, beaches and museums.

breezy communal areas and **G.O.D. Street Culture Museum & Store** (Unit L2-09; ⏰12.30-6.30pm, closed Mon & Tue), which has an attractive 'old Hong Kong' display and regular opening hours.

Yuen Po St Bird Garden   GARDENS
(園圃街雀鳥花園; Flower Market Rd, Mong Kok; ⏰7am-8pm; MPrince Edward, exit B1) To the east of the Prince Edward MTR station is this delightful place where birds are preened, bought, sold and fed bugs with chopsticks by their fussy owners (usually men). Nearby is the **flower market**, which keeps the same hours but is busiest after 10am.

Fook Tak Ancient Temple   TEMPLE
(福德古廟; Map p476; 30 Haiphong Rd; ⏰6am-8pm; MTsim Sha Tsui, exit A1) Built in 1900, Tsim Sha Tsui's only temple is a smoky hole-in-the-hall with a hot tin roof. Most incense offerers are white-haired octogenarians – Fook Tak specialises in longevity.

Kowloon Mosque & Islamic Centre MOSQUE
(九龍清真寺暨伊斯蘭中心; Map p476; 105 Nathan Rd; ⏰5am-10pm; MTsim Sha Tsui, exit A1) This edifice with its gleaming dome accommodates up to 2000 worshippers. Non-Muslims should ask for permission to enter.

NEW TERRITORIES

Occupying 747 sq km of Hong Kong's land mass, the New Territories is a combination of housing estates and some unspoiled rural areas.

The New Towns of Tsuen Wan, Tuen Mun, Fanling, Sheung Shui, Tai Po and Sha Tin are all worth visiting for their temples and museums. They are accessible via their eponymous MTR stations, and Tuen Mun is served by the Light Rail network.

Yuen Long boasts Hong Kong's most historical walled villages and a world-class nature reserve. It's on both the West Rail and the Light Rail Transit networks.

The Sai Kung Peninsula is great for hiking, sailing and seafood. The New Territories' best beaches are here.

Mai Po Marsh Nature Reserve   WILDLIFE RESERVE
(米埔自然保護區; Map p464; ☎2471 3480; www.wwf.org.hk; San Tin, Yuen Long; ⏰9am-5pm Mon-Fri) This 380-hectare area in Deep Bay is home to a plethora of flora and fauna, including 380 species of migratory and resident birds. Three-hour English tours ($70) leave the visitor centre at 9.30am, 10am, 2pm and 2.30pm on weekends and public holidays. Online registration is now available. Remember to bring your binoculars, or you can rent some at the visitor centre for HK$20. Take bus 76K from Fanling or Sheung Shui MTR East Rail stations.

Ping Shan Heritage Trail   OUTDOORS
(屏山文物徑; Map p464; MWest Rail Tin Shui Wai, exit E) The 1km trail through three partially walled villages will lead you down the memory lane of pre-colonial Hong Kong. The trail boasts 12 well-restored historic buildings, including two magnificent **ancestral halls** (⏰9am-1pm & 2-5pm), a **study hall**, the territory's **oldest pagoda** (⏰9am-1pm & 2-5pm, closed Tue) and a **museum** about the powerful Tang clan, among the first immigrants to settle in Hong Kong in the 11th century. Cross Tsui Sing Rd from the ground floor of the West Rail MTR station and you'll see the pagoda.

Tai Fu Tai Mansion   HISTORIC BUILDING
(大夫第; Map p464; ⏰9am-1pm & 2-5pm Wed-Mon; MSan Tin, Yuen Long; 🚌76K) This splendid Mandarin-style building complex from 1865 used to be the dwelling of the Man clan, another powerful family in the New Territories, until they moved out in 1980. The courtyard is encircled by stone walls with a formerly guarded checkpoint. Inside, auspicious Chinese symbols are found in the woodcarvings along with art-nouveau glass panels. Board bus 76K in Sheung Shui and get off at the San Tin stop.

Lung Yeuk Tau Heritage Trail   OUTDOORS
(龍躍頭文物徑; Map p464; MEast Rail Fanling, then bus 54K or 56K) This 4.5km-long trail northeast of Fanling meanders through five

walled villages. The most attractive of the lot is the oldest (800 years) but most intact **Lo Wai**, identifiable by its 1m-thick fortified wall. Other attractions here include the **Tang Chung Ling Ancestral Hall** (⊘9am-5pm Wed-Mon) and the stone mansion of **Shek Lo**.

Kat Hing Wai
VILLAGE

(吉慶圍; Map p464) This tiny (100m by 90m), once-moated hamlet on Kam Tin Rd is another domicile of the Tang clan, though some Hakka villagers also live here. Visitors are asked to make a donation as they enter the walled village. For HK$10, you can take pictures of the old Hakka ladies near the entrance. If you don't pay, they'll hide their faces.

Tai Po Market & Man Mo Temple
MARKET, TEMPLE

(大埔街市 & 文武廟; Map p464; Fu Shin St; ⊘6am-8pm; MEast Rail Tai Wo) This busy outdoor wet market is one of the most interesting markets in the New Territories. Towards the northern end of the same street, the double-hall **Man Mo Temple** (文武廟; ⊘8am-6pm) from the late 19th century is a centre of worship for the Tai Po area.

Hong Kong Wetland Park
PARK

(香港濕地公園; Map p464; www.wetlandpark. com; Wetland Park Rd, Tin Shui Wai; admission HK$30; ⊘10am-5pm) The natural trails, bird hides and viewing platforms make this 60-hectare ecological park an excellent spot for bird-watching. Take the West Rail line to Tin Shui Wai and board MTR Light Rail line 705 or 706.

Fung Ying Seen Temple
TEMPLE

(蓬瀛仙館; 66 Pak Wo Rd, Fanling; ⊘8am-6pm; MEast Rail Fan Ling) For all its cheerful colours, this Taoist temple is a little morbid. It contains a dozen columbaria for cremated ancestral remains. If you venture into the hills behind the complex, you'll see graves flung all over the slopes, Tim Burton style.

TOP CHOICE Hong Kong Heritage Museum
MUSEUM

(香港文化博物館; 1 Man Lam Rd; admission HK$10; ⊘10am-6pm Mon & Wed-Sat, to 7pm Sun; MEast Rail Sha Tin) There are impressive displays on Cantonese opera and New Territories heritage here, which feature replicas of traditional villages and bamboo theatres, and stunning costumes once worn by opera artists. Kids will love the large **Children's Discovery Gallery** on the ground floor. There are free **Cantonese opera** performances every Saturday from 3pm to 5.30pm.

Tsing Shan Monastery
BUDDHIST

(青山禪院; Map p464; ☑2461 8050; Tsing Shan Monastery Path; ⊘24hr; ⓡline 610, 615, 615P) Founded 1500 years ago, the oldest temple in Hong Kong you see today was rebuilt in 1926. There are a cluster of quirky shrines for different saints and bodhisattvas. The temple was one of the shooting locations for the Bruce Lee classic *Enter the Dragon*. Alight at Tsing Shan Tsuen Light Rail station. The steep path to the entrance of the monastery is a 30-minute walk.

Ten Thousand Buddhas Monastery
MONASTERY

(萬佛寺; 221 Pai Tau Village; ⊘9am-5pm; MSha Tin, exit B) Some 12,800 miniature statues line the walls of the main temple and dozens of life-sized golden statues of Buddha's followers flank the steep steps leading to the monastery complex. There are several temples and pavilions split over two levels, as well as a nine-storey pagoda. From the MTR exit, walk down the ramp, turning left onto Pai Tau St. After a short distance, turn right onto Sheung Wo Che St, walk to the end and follow the signs up the 400 steps.

RENT-A-CURSE GRANNIES

Under the Canal Rd Flyover (Map p472) between Wan Chai and Causeway Bay, you can hire little old ladies to beat up your enemy. From their perch on plastic stools, these rent-a-curse grannies will pound paper cut-outs of your romantic rival, office bully or a whiny celeb with a shoe (their orthopaedic flat or your stilettos) while rapping curses. All for only HK$50.

Villain hitting (打小人; *da siu yan*) is a practice related to folk sorcery. It's performed throughout the year but the most popular date for it is on the Day of the Awakening of Insects when the sun is at an exact celestial longitude of 345 degrees (usually between 5 and 20 March on the Gregorian calendar).

It's believed to bring reconciliation or resolution, though that too could be symbolic.

Dragon Garden
GARDENS

(龍圃; http://dragongarden.hk; Sham Tseng) Hong Kong's largest remaining private garden has gorgeous faux-ancient architecture inspired by period styles of the Song, Ming and Qing dynasties. A philanthropist's weekend villa, it appeared in the Bond classic *Man with the Golden Gun* (1974) and the mini-series *Noble House* starring Pierce Brosnan (1988).

Hoi Ha Wan Marine Park
OUTDOORS, BEACH

(海下灣海岸公園; Map p464; ☎hotline 1823; Hoi Ha, Sai Kung; ☐green minibus 7) The marine park is a 260-hectare protected area and is one of the few places in Hong Kong waters where coral still grows in abundance. Snorkels, masks and kayaks can be rented from the store on the beach. The 1½-hour tours of the marine park are available at 10.30am and 2.15pm on Sunday and public holidays. You must register with the **Agriculture, Fisheries & Conservation Department** (AFCD; ☎1823) in advance.

OUTLYING ISLANDS

Lantau is the largest island in Hong Kong and is ideal for a multiday excursion to explore its trails, villages and to enjoy the beaches. Mui Wo is the arrival point for ferries from Central, and Tung Chung is connected by MTR.

Laid-back **Lamma** (Map p464) has decent beaches, excellent walks and a cluster of restaurants in **Yung Shue Wan** and **Sok Kwu Wan**. A fun day involves taking the ferry to Yung Shue Wan, walking the easy 90-minute trail to Sok Kwu Wan and settling in for lunch at one of the seafood restaurants beside the water.

Dumbbell-shaped **Cheung Chau** (Map p464), with a harbour filled with fishing boats, a windsurfing centre, several temples and some waterfront restaurants, also makes a fun day out. Not far away is **Peng Chau** (Map p464), the smallest and most traditional of the easily accessible islands.

TOP CHOICE ▸ Po Lin Monastery
MONASTERY

(寶蓮禪寺; Map p464; Lantau; ⊙9am-6pm) Lording over Ngong Ping plateau, 500m above sea level, this enormous temple complex contains the 26m-tall **Tian Tan Buddha statue** (天壇大佛; ⊙10am-5.30pm), the world's tallest seated bronze Buddha statue. From Mui Wo, board bus 2 to Ngong Ping; alternatively, a cable-car system called **Ngong Ping 360** (昂平360纜車; www.np360.com.hk; adult/child/concession one way HK$86/44/70, return HK$125/62/98; ⊙10am-6pm Mon-Fri, 9am-6.30pm Sat, Sun & public holidays) links Ngong Ping with Tung Chung, and whizzes you past breathtaking views to the monastery. The lower terminal in Tung Chung is next to Tung Chung MTR station.

Tai O
VILLAGE

(大澳; Map p464; Lantau) For a fascinating glimpse of the life of a traditional fishing village, head to this far-flung part of Lantau. The stilt houses, the canals and temples dedicated to water deities and the God of War are still there, as well as the recently repurposed colonial-era police station. Tai O is reachable by bus 1 from Mui Wo, bus 11 from Tung Chung or bus 21 from Ngong Ping.

Activities

The Hong Kong Tourism Board (HKTB) offers a range of fun and free activities, from feng shui classes through sunset cruises to taichi sessions. For a list of what's on, visit www.discoverhongkong.com. The **Map Publications Centre** (香港地圖銷售處; Map p474) sells excellent maps detailing hiking and cycling trails; buy online (www.landsd.gov.hk/mapping/en/pro&ser/products.htm) or at major post offices (www.landsd.gov.hk/mapping/en/pro&ser/outlet.htm). Sporting buffs should contact the **South China Athletic Association** (南華體育會; Map p472; ☎2577 6932; www.scaa.org.hk; 5th fl, South China Sports Complex, 88 Caroline Hill Rd, Causeway Bay; visitor membership HK$50), which has facilities for any number of sports. Another handy website is www.hkoutdoors.com.

Martial Arts

Wan Kei Ho International Martial Arts Association
MARTIAL ARTS SCHOOL

(Map p468; ☎2544 1368; www.kungfuwan.com; 3rd fl, Yue's House, 304 Des Voeux Rd Central, Sheung Wan; Ⓜ Sheung Wan, exit A) This place is popular with locals and foreigners alike.

Hiking

Hong Kong is an excellent place to hike and the numerous trails on offer are all very attractive. The four main ones are **MacLehose Trail**, **Wilson Trail**, **Lantau Trail** and **Hong Kong Trail**. The famous **Dragon's Back Trail** is scenic and relatively easy.

For more information check out www.hkwalkers.net.

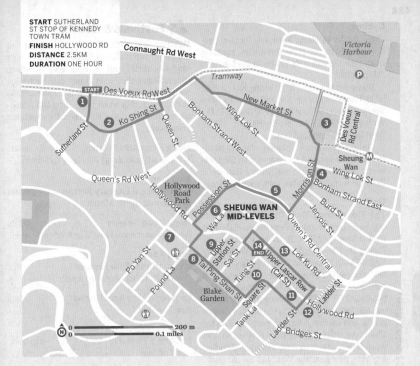

START SUTHERLAND ST STOP OF KENNEDY TOWN TRAM
FINISH HOLLYWOOD RD
DISTANCE 2.5KM
DURATION ONE HOUR

Walking Tour
Sheung Wan

❯ A one-hour walk through Sheung Wan will lead you down the memory lane of Hong Kong's past. Begin the tour at the Sutherland St stop of the Kennedy Town–bound tram. Have a look at Des Voeux Rd West's **❶ dried seafood shops**, then turn up Ko Shing St, where there are **❷ herbal medicine wholesalers**. At the end of the street, walk northwest along Des Voeux Rd West and turn right onto New Market St, where you'll find **❸ Western Market**. Walk south along this street past Bonham Strand, which is lined with **❹ ginseng root sellers**, and turn right on Queen's Rd Central. To the right you'll pass **❺ traditional shops** selling bird's nests (for soup) and paper funeral offerings (for the dead).

Cross Queen's Rd Central and turn left onto **❻ Possession St**, where the British flag was first planted in 1841.

Climbing Pound Lane to where it meets Tai Ping Shan St, look right to see **❼ Pak Sing Ancestral Hall**, then turn left to find **❽ Kwun Yam Temple** and **❾ Tai Sui Temple**.

A bit further on, turn left into Square St, where you'll pass **❿ Cloth Haven** (43-45 Square St), a weaving workshop, and **⓫ funeral shops**. Turn left into Ladder St and you'll see **⓬ Man Mo Temple**. Descend Ladder St to Upper Lascar Row, home of the **⓭ Cat Street bazaar**. Go down the length of Cat St, then turn left into Lok Ku Rd. Another left takes you to **⓮ Hollywood Road**, with its antique shops and art galleries.

Cycling

Cycle tracks in Hong Kong are located predominantly in the New Territories, running from Sha Tin through Tai Po to Tai Mei Tuk (Map p464).

Bikes can be rented from **Wong Kei** (📞2662 5200; Ting Kok Rd, Tai Mei Tuk) and **Friendly Bike Shop** (老友記單車; 📞2984 2278; Shop B, 13 Mui Wo Ferry Pier Rd, Lantau; per day HK$30; ⊙10am-7pm Mon-Fri, to 8pm Sat & Sun).

Online resources include the **Agriculture, Fisheries and Conservation Department** (www.afcd.gov.hk) and **Crazy Guy on a Bike** (www.crazyguyonabike.com/doc/Hongkong).

Golf

The **Hong Kong Golf Club** (www.hkgolfclub.org) welcomes nonmembers on weekdays at its **Fanling** (📞2670 1211; Lot No 1, Fan Kam Rd, Sheung Shui; Ⓜ Fanling) and **Deep Water Bay** (📞2812 7070; 19 Island Rd, Deep Water Bay; 🚌bus 6, 6A) venues. The scenic 36-hole **Jockey Club Kau Sai Chau Public Golf Course** (Map p464; 📞2791 3388; www.kscgolf.org.hk/index-e.asp; Kau Sai Chau, Sai Kung) is the territory's only public golf course. A ferry departs for Kau Sai Chau (every 20 minutes from 6.40am to 7pm weekdays, 6.40am to 9pm Friday to Sunday) from the pier near the Wai Man Rd car park.

 Tours

Star Ferry (📞2118 6201; www.starferry.com.hk) runs a 60-minute **Harbour Tour** (HK$80-200; ⊙11.55am-8.55pm) covering calling points at Tsim Sha Tsui, Central and Wan Chai. Get tickets at the piers.

Tours run by the **HKTB** (📞2508 1234; www.discoverhongkong.com; ⊙9am-6pm):

Island Tour   BUS TOUR
(half-/full day HK$350/490) Includes Man Mo Temple, the Peak, Aberdeen, Repulse Bay and Stanley Market.

Hong Kong Dolphinwatch   DOLPHIN CRUISE
(📞2984 1414; www.hkdolphinwatch.com) Offers 2½-hour cruises to see the native Chinese pink dolphins every Wednesday, Friday and Sunday year-round.

Water Sports

Hong Kong's government-run **water-sports centres** (www.lcsd.gov.hk/watersport/en/index.php) have canoes, windsurfing boards and other equipment for hire by certificate-holders. For wakeboarding, try **Tai Tam Wakeboarding Centre** (📞3120 4102; www.wakeboard.com.hk).

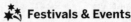 **Festivals & Events**

Western and Chinese culture combine to create an interesting mix of cultural events and about 20 public holidays. However, determining the exact times can be tricky: some follow the Chinese lunar calendar, so the dates change each year. For a full schedule with exact dates see www.discoverhongkong.com.

Hong Kong Arts Festival   ARTS
(www.hk.artsfestival.org) February to March.

Man Hong Kong International Literary Festival   LITERARY
(www.festival.org.hk) March.

Hong Kong Sevens   SPORTS
(www.hksevens.com) Late March or early April.

Hong Kong International Film Festival   FILM
(www.hkiff.org.hk) March to April.

Le French May Arts Festival   ARTS
April to May.

Tin Hau Festival & Buddha's Birthday   TRADITIONAL
April or May.

Art Basel Hong Kong   ART
(hongkong.artbasel.com) May.

International Dragon Boat Races   SPORTS
(www.hkdba.com.hk) June or July.

Summer International Film Festival   FILM
(www.hkiff.org.hk) August to September.

Hong Kong International Jazz Festival   MUSIC
(http://hkja.org/blog) November.

Hong Kong Photo Festival   ART
(www.hkphotofest.org) Biennial. Dates change; check the website.

Clockenflap Outdoor Music Festival   MUSIC
(www.clockenflap.com) December.

🛌 Sleeping

Hong Kong offers the full gamut of accommodation, from cell-like spaces to palatial suites in some of the world's finest hotels. Compared with those in other cities in China, rooms are relatively expensive, though they can still be cheaper than their US or European counterparts. The rates listed here are the rack rates.

Most hotels are on Hong Kong Island between Central and Causeway Bay, and either side of Nathan Rd in Kowloon, where you'll also find the largest range of budget places. All hotels and some budget places add 13% in taxes to the listed rates.

Prices fall sharply outside the peak seasons, particularly in the midrange and top-end categories, when you can get discounts of up to 50% if you book online, or through an agency such as the **Hong Kong Hotels Association** (HKHA; ☑2383 8380; www.hkha.org).

High seasons are March to early May, October to November, and Chinese New Year (late January or February). Check the exact dates on www.discoverhongkong.com.

Unless specified otherwise, all rooms listed here have private bathrooms and air-conditioning. Almost all places offer broadband and/or wi-fi access, as well as computers for guests' use. All hotels that are midrange and above and some budget places have nonsmoking floors, or are nonsmoking.

HONG KONG ISLAND

Most of Hong Kong Island's top-end hotels are in Central and Admiralty, while Wan Chai and Sheung Wan cater to the midrange market. Causeway Bay has quite a few budget guesthouses that are a step up (in both price and quality) from their Tsim Sha Tsui counterparts.

⭑ TOP CHOICE Helena May HOSTEL $

(梅夫人婦女會主樓; off Map p468; ☑2522 6766; www.helenamay.com; 35 Garden Rd, Central; s/d HK$400/580, monthly HK$9900/13,100, studios HK$13,860-18,060, minimum 1 month; ☐12A from ⓜAdmiralty) If you like the Peninsula's colonial setting but not its price tag, this dowager might just be your cup of tea. Opened in 1916 by a governor's wife as a club for single European women for whom the colony had little to offer by way of respectable pastimes such as tea parties and ballet lessons, HM is now a private club and a hostel with 43 smallish but decent rooms. Those in the main building are women-only with shared bathrooms, while the studio flats in an adjacent building welcome both genders. You have to be 18 or above to live here.

If you just want to visit, there are 20-minute tours in English once every two months (10am to noon Saturday). Reservations – compulsory – are accepted a month in advance. The website has dates.

⭑ TOP CHOICE Upper House BOUTIQUE HOTEL $$$

(Map p468; ☑2918 1838; www.upperhouse.com; 88 Queensway, Pacific Place, Admiralty; r from HK$4000, ste from HK$9000; ⓜAdmiralty, exit F; @ ☎) Every corner of this boutique hotel oozes zenlike serenity – the understated lobby, the sleek eco-minded rooms, the elegant sculptures, the warm and discreet service, and the manicured lawn where guests can join free yoga classes. Other pluses include a free minibar, and easy access to the Admiralty MTR station.

Hotel LKF HOTEL $$$

(蘭桂芳酒店; Map p468; ☑3518 9688; www.hotel-lkf.com.hk; 33 Wyndham St, Central; r from HK$3500, low-season discounts up to 50%; ⓜCentral, exit D2; @) Hotel LKF is arguably the best gateway to the Lan Kwai Fong action, but is far enough above it so you get your peace and quiet when you need it. It has high-tech rooms in muted tones, and they brim with all the trimmings you'll need: fluffy bathrobes, espresso machines and free bedtime milk and cookies.

⭑ TOP CHOICE Y-Loft Youth Square Hostel HOSTEL $$

(☑3721 8989; http://youthsquare.hk; 238 Chai Wan Rd, Chai Wan; tw/tr low season HK$600/900, high season HK$1200/1800, ste HK$3000; ⓜChai Wan, exit A; @ ☎) If you don't mind trading off 20 extra minutes on the MTR for an excellent budget option, you'll be rewarded with large, clean and cheerful rooms in Chai Wan (not Wan Chai!). Stanley market is only 15 minutes away by bus from the 16X bus stop opposite the MTR station. To reach the hostel from exit A, go straight through the mall to the footbridge and take the first exit on your right. Reception's on the 12th floor.

Garden View HOTEL $$

(女青年會園景軒; Map p468; ☑2877 3737; http://the-garden-view-ywca.hotel-rn.com; 1 MacDonnell Rd, Central; r HK$880-1760, ste HK$2500-2900, weekly per day from HK$1500, per month from HK$19,500; ☐green minibus 1A; @ ☎ ✦) Straddling the border of Central and the Mid-Levels, the YWCA-run Garden View has 133 plain, quiet and functional rooms overlooking the Zoological & Botanical Gardens. The outdoor swimming pool is a delight. Daily rates drop substantially in the low season.

Bishop Lei International House HOTEL $

(宏基國際賓館; Map p468; ☑2868 0828; www.bishopleihtl.com.hk; 4 Robinson Rd, Mid-Levels; s/d/ste from HK$650/700/1250; ☐23 or 40; @ ☎)

This 203-room hotel provides a lot of bang for the buck: good service, a swimming pool and a gym, and proximity to the Zoological & Botanical Gardens. Rooms are small and it's worth paying a little more for the larger, harbour-facing rooms.

Harbour View
HOTEL $$

(香港灣景國際酒店; Map p472; ☎2802 0111; www.theharbourview.com.hk; 4 Harbour Rd, Wan Chai; r HK$2000, fortnightly/monthly packages from HK$10,500/21,000, ☐18, Ⓜ Wan Chai, exit A5; @☒) Right next door to the Hong Kong Arts Centre and a mere stroll to the Hong Kong Convention & Exhibition Centre and Wan Chai ferry terminal, this 320-room, YMCA-run hotel is excellent value. It offers simply furnished but adequate rooms, and friendly staff. Rooms drop by 45% in the low season.

TOP CHOICE Mandarin Oriental
LUXURY HOTEL $$$

(文華東方酒店; ☎2522 0111; www.mandarin oriental.com/hongkong; 5 Connaught Rd, Central; r HK$3800-6000, ste HK$6500-45,000, Landmark Oriental d from HK$5200, ste HK$9300; Ⓜ Central, exit J3; @☎☒) The venerable Mandarin has historically set the standard in Asia and continues to be a contender for the top spot, despite the competition from the likes of the Four Seasons. The styling, service, food and atmosphere are stellar throughout and there's a sense of gracious, old-world charm.

Four Seasons
LUXURY HOTEL $$$

(四季酒店; Map p468; ☎3196 8888; www.fourseasons.com/hongkong; 8 Finance St, Central; r HK$4500-6500, ste HK$9300-63000; Ⓜ Hong Kong, exit F; @☎☒☒) The Four Seasons arguably edges into top place on the island for its amazing views, its location close to the Star Ferry, Hong Kong station, the inland and Sheung Wan, its palatial rooms, glorious pool and spa complex, and its stellar restaurants Lung King Heen and Caprice. Service is pristine and personable.

The T Hotel
HOTEL $$

(酒店; ☎3717 7388; www.vtc.edu.hk/thotel; 6/F, VTC Pokfulam Complex, 145 Pokfulam Rd, Pok Fu Lam; r HK$1030, ste HK$1880; ☐7 or 91 from Central, 973 from Tsim Sha Tsui; @☎☒) The 30-room T Hotel on the island's southwest shore is entirely run by students of the local hospitality training school. Expect cheerful and attentive services. Rooms are sparkling new and spacious, and offer either ocean or mountain views. The culinary school in the complex provides excellent Chinese and Western meals.

Courtyard by Marriott Hong Kong
BUSINESS HOTEL $$$

(香港萬怡酒店; off Map p468; ☎3717 8888; www.marriott.com/hotel-search/china; 167 Connaught Rd W; r HK$1560-2440, ste HK$3450; ☐5 or 5B from Central; @☎) This hotel juggles luxury with limited space and it works. Most rooms offer harbour views and are smartly done up with modern furnishings. The plump beds and high thread-count sheets guarantee you a good night's sleep. There's an Airbus stop across the street.

Regal iClub Hotel
BUSINESS HOTEL $$

(Map p472; ☎3669 8668; www.regalhotel.com; 211 Johnston Rd, Wan Chai; d HK$800-1100, ste HK$1900; Ⓜ Wan Chai, exit A3; @☎) This modern 99-room hotel in the heart of Wan Chai is a good choice if you don't mind small rooms and sometimes cavalier service.

Ibis
HOTEL $$

(上環宜必思酒店; Map p468; ☎2252 2929; www.ibishotel.com; 18-30 Des Voeux Rd W; r HK$1500-1800; ☐5B from Central; @) Opened in 2012, this 550-room Ibis has small but spanking-clean rooms and is a more affordable option in this expensive part of town.

Alisan Guest House
GUESTHOUSE $

(阿里山賓館; Map p472; ☎2838 0762; http://home.hkstar.com/~alisangh; Flat A, 5th fl, Hoito Ct, 23 Cannon St, Causeway Bay; s/d/tr HK$320/440/660; Ⓜ Causeway Bay, exit D1; ☎) This spotless place has 21 rooms with air-con, bathrooms and free internet. The multilingual owners can organise China visas. There's a computer, and a communal fridge and microwave oven in the tiny kitchen. Enter from 23 Cannon St. Prices increase by 10% during the peak season.

KOWLOON

Kowloon has an incredible array of accommodation: from the Peninsula, the 'grand dame' of hotels, to its infamous neighbour, Chungking Mansions, plus plenty in between.

TOP CHOICE Peninsula Hong Kong
LUXURY HOTEL $$$

(香港半島酒店; Map p476; ☎2920 2888; www.peninsula.com; Salisbury Rd, Tsim Sha Tsui; r HK$5000-7000, ste from HK$8200; Ⓜ Tsim Sha Tsui, exit E; @☎☎☒) Lording it over the southern tip of Kowloon, Hong Kong's finest hotel evokes colonial elegance. Your main dilemma will be how to get here: landing on the rooftop helipad or arriving in one of the hotel's 14-strong fleet of Rolls Royce Phantoms. Some 300 classic European-style rooms boast wi-fi, CD and DVD players, as well as marble bathrooms. Many rooms in the Pen's 20-storey annexe offer spectacular harbour views; in the original building you'll have to make do with the glorious interiors. There's a top-notch spa and swimming pool.

Hyatt Regency Tsim Sha Tsui
LUXURY HOTEL $$$

(尖沙咀凱悅酒店; Map p476; ☎2311 1234; http://hongkong.tsimshatsui.hyatt.com; 18 Hanoi Rd, Tsim Sha Tsui; r HK$1800-2900, ste from HK$3500; MTsim Sha Tsui, exit D2; @🛜🏊🐾) Top marks to this Tsim Sha Tsui classic which exudes understated elegance and composure. Staff are warm and knowledgeable. The well-appointed rooms are relatively spacious with those on the upper floors commanding views over the city. The photos of Tsim Sha Tsui add a thoughtful touch to the decor.

Salisbury
HOSTEL, HOTEL $

(香港基督教青年會; Map p476; ☎2268 7888; www.ymcahk.org.hk; 41 Salisbury Rd, Tsim Sha Tsui; dm HK$260, s/d/ste from HK$850/950/1600; MTsim Sha Tsui, exit E; @🛜🏊🐾) If you can manage to book a room here, you'll be rewarded with professional service and excellent exercise facilities, including a swimming pool and a climbing wall. The rooms are comfortable but simple, so keep your eyes on the harbour: that view would cost you five times as much at the Peninsula next door. The four-bed dormitory rooms are a bonus, but restrictions apply: check-in is at 2pm, no one can stay more than seven consecutive nights, and walk-in guests aren't accepted if they've been in Hong Kong for more than seven days.

TOP CHOICE Hotel Icon
LUXURY HOTEL $$$

(唯港薈; Map p476; ☎3400 1000; www.hotel-icon.com; 17 Science Museum Rd, Tsim Sha Tsui; r HK$2200-4100, ste HK$3000-5100; MEast Tsim Sha Tsui, exit P1; 🛜🏊🐾) The rooms at this teaching hotel are clean, modern and spacious, and the staff are attentive. Though not all rooms have harbour views and children are not allowed into the terrace lounge, it still offers solid value for money. Icon is a 10-minute walk to the MTR station and the History Museum, and a shuttle service takes guests to the more central parts of Tsim Sha Tsui.

MECCA OF CHEAP SLEEPS

Chungking Mansions (重慶大廈; Map p476) has been synonymous with budget accommodation in Hong Kong for decades. The crumbling block on Nathan Rd is stacked with the city's cheapest hostels and guesthouses. Rooms are usually minuscule and service rudimentary. But standards have risen in recent years and several guesthouses positively sparkle with new fittings. Even the lifts have been upgraded, though they're still painfully slow.

Mirador Mansion (美麗都大廈; Map p476), its neighbour just up the street, also has a fair number of cheap sleeps.

Hop Inn
HOSTEL $

(Map p476; ☎2881 7331; www.hopinn.hk; Flat A, 2nd fl, Hanyee Bldg, 19-21 Hankow Rd, Tsim Sha Tsui; s HK$410-510, d & tw HK$520-740, tr HK$650-930; MTsim Sha Tsui, exit A1; @🛜) This nonsmoking guesthouse has a youthful vibe and nine spotless but tiny rooms, each featuring illustrations by a different Hong Kong artist. Some rooms have no windows, but they're quieter than the ones that do. The new **Hop Inn on Carnarvon** (Map p476; 9th fl, James S Lee Mansion, 33-35 Carnarvon Rd) has spanking-new rooms, including our favourite one designed by Sim Chan. Both branches have free in-room wi-fi and help to organise China visas.

Madera Hong Kong
HOTEL $$

(Map p474; ☎2121 9888; www.hotelmadera.com.hk; 1-9 Cheong Lok St, Yau Ma Tei; d & tw HK$1400-$1800, ste HK$2800; MJordan, exit B1) A spirited addition to Kowloon's midrange options, Madera is close to the Temple Street Night Market and a brisk 20-minute walk from the Star Ferry. The decent-sized rooms come in neutral tones with bright accents. There's also a women-only floor and a tiny workout room.

Ritz-Carlton Hong Kong
LUXURY HOTEL $$$

(麗思卡爾頓; off Map p476; ☎2263 2263; www.ritzcarlton.com; 1 Austin Rd West, Jordan; r HK$6000-7800, ste from HK$8000; 🛜🏊🐾) Sitting atop the Airport Express Kowloon Station, this off-the-way luxury address was the tallest hotel on earth at the time of writing (the lobby's on the 103rd floor). The only thing taller is the over-the-top decor featuring heavy furniture and a superfluity of shiny services. That said, the service is pristine, Tin Lung Heen is an excellent restaurant and the views on clear days are stunning.

BP International Hotel HOTEL $$

(龍堡國際酒店; Map p476; ☎2376 1111; www.bpih.com.hk; 8 Austin Rd; r from HK$1450, ste from HK$5200; Ⓜ Jordan, exit C; @☎🏊🛏) This enormous hotel overlooking Kowloon Park has rooms of a reasonable standard with the more expensive ones commanding views of the harbour. There are also family rooms with bunk beds available. Depending on the season and day of the week, prices are often reduced by 50%.

Cityview HOTEL $$$

(城景國際; off Map p474; ☎2771 9111; www.thecityview.com.hk; 23 Waterloo Rd, Yau Ma Tei; r HK$1880, tr HK$2400, ste from HK$3080; Ⓜ Yau Ma Tei, exit A2; @☎🏊🛏) All 413 rooms at this YMCA-affiliated hotel are clean, smart and come in mellow tones. The service is also excellent. The hotel is a short stroll away from the Yau Ma Tei Theatre.

Caritas Bianchi Lodge GUESTHOUSE $

(明愛白英奇賓館; Map p474; ☎2388 1111; www.caritas-chs.org.hk/eng/bianchi_lodge.asp; 4 Cliff Rd; s from HK$750, d & tw from HK$870, f from HK$1080; Ⓜ Yau Ma Tei, exit D) This 90-room hotel-cum-guesthouse just off Nathan Rd (and a goalie's throw from Yau Ma Tei MTR station) has clean rooms with private bathrooms. The rear ones are quiet and some have views of King's Park. Breakfast is included in the rates.

Booth Lodge GUESTHOUSE $$

(卜維廉賓館; Map p474; ☎2771 9266; http://boothlodge.salvation.org.hk; 11 Wing Sing La, Yau Ma Tei; r HK$620-1500; Ⓜ Yau Ma Tei, exit D; @☎) Run by the Salvation Army, this 53-room place is spartan but clean and comfortable. Promotional rates for rooms can drop to HK$500. Rates include breakfast.

Nic & Trig's GUESTHOUSE $

(☎6333 5352; rooms@nostalgic.org; 705 Shanghai St, Mong Kok; r with shared bathroom from HK$400; Ⓜ Prince Edward, exit C1; ☎) This place inside a 'walk-up' tenement building has three rooms inspired respectively by Hong Kong of the '60s, the '70s (with Bruce Lee posters) and the '80s. The English-speaking owners are friendly and helpful. Email and they'll tell you how to get there.

NEW TERRITORIES

Good-value accommodation in the New Territories is sparse, but there are both official and independent hostels, usually in remote areas. The **Country & Marine Parks Authority** (☎1823) maintains 40 no-frills campsites in the New Territories. Go to www.afcd.gov.hk and click on 'Country & Marine Parks'.

Tao Fong Shan Pilgrim's Hall HOSTEL $

(道風山雲水堂; ☎2691 2739; www.tfssu.org/pilgrim.html; 33 Tao Fong Shan Rd, Sha Tin; s/d with shared bathroom HK$260/400; Ⓜ East Rail Sha Tin station, exit B) Peacefully perched on a hillside, this Lutheran Church–affiliated hostel has 18 basic but clean rooms. Getting there is a pain, though. Follow the directions from the website carefully or take a cab (about HK$30) from Sha Tin MTR station.

Hyatt Regency Hong Kong LUXURY HOTEL $$$

(☎3723 1234; www.hongkong.shatin.hyatt.com; r HK$2500-3100, ste HK$3700-12700; Ⓜ East Rail University station, exit B; @☎🏊🛏) The Hyatt lives up to its name of being the poshest hotel in the New Territories. Rooms are nicely appointed, with most commanding views of the harbour or the hills. The Chinese restaurant Sha Tin 18 (p493) is excellent.

Bradbury Jockey Club Youth Hostel HOSTEL $

(☎2662 5123; www.yha.org.hk; 66 Tai Mei Tuk Rd; dm members under/over 18yr HK$65/95, d/q members HK$290/420; 🅿75K) This HKYHA's flagship hostel is open daily year-round. Take bus 75K (or 275R on Sundays and public holidays) from Tai Po Market East Rail station to the Tai Mei Tuk bus terminus. The hostel is on the road leading to the reservoir.

OUTLYING ISLANDS

Lantau, Lamma and Cheung Chau all have decent accommodation with a holiday vibe. For campers, the **Country & Marine Parks Authority** (☎1823) maintains 11 sites on Lantau. Camping is prohibited on Hong Kong beaches.

TOP CHOICE Espace Elastique B&B $$

(歸田園居; ☎2985 7002; www.espaceelastique.com.hk; 57 Kat Hing St, Tai O; r Sun-Thu HK$600-1400, Fri & Sat HK$800-2230; 🚌 Lantau; @☎🏊) This cosy B&B has four tastefully decorated rooms, two with balcony overlooking the main Tai O waterway. The polyglot owner Veronica provides useful travel advice and hearty breakfasts in the downstairs cafe.

Bali Holiday Resort
STUDIOS, APARTMENTS $

(優閒渡假屋; ☎2982 4580; 8 Main St, Lamma; r HK$280-380, apt HK$560-760; ☎) An agency rather than a resort as such, Bali has about 30 studios and apartments sprinkled around the island. All have TVs, fridges and air-con, and some have sea views. Prices double on weekends. Only the apartments get wi-fi.

✖ Eating

One of the world's greatest food cities, Hong Kong offers culinary excitement whether you're spending HK$20 on a bowl of noodles or megabucks on haute cuisine.

The best of China is well represented, be it Cantonese, Shanghainese, Northern or Sichuanese. What's more, the international fare on offer – French, Italian, Spanish, Japanese, Thai, Indian, fusion – is the finest and most diverse in all of China.

Hong Kong is an expensive place to dine by regional Chinese standards, but cheaper than Sydney, London or New York, and with more consistent quality of food and service than most eateries in mainland China.

At most of the eateries listed here, reservations are strongly advised, especially for dinner.

HONG KONG ISLAND

The island's best range of cuisines is in Central, Sheung Wan and Wan Chai.

TOP CHOICE Manor Seafood Restaurant
CANTONESE $$$

(富瑤酒家; Map p472; ☎2836 9999; Shop F-G, 440 Jaffe Rd, Causeway Bay; meals from HK$300-2000; ☉lunch & dinner; Ⓜ Causeway Bay, exit B) Upscale Manor does most Cantonese dishes well, but is best known for a now-rare classic. *Gum chin gai* (金錢雞; literally 'gold coin chicken', although it has no chicken meat) is a succulent 'cholesterol sandwich' of chicken liver, barbecued pork and lard – all marinaded in Chinese wine, roasted to perfection and eaten between pancakes. It's guilt-laden, melt-in-your-mouth goodness.

Old Bazaar Kitchen
SINGAPOREAN MALAYSIAN $

(老巴剎廚房; Map p472; ☎2893 3998; 207 Wan Chai Rd, Wan Chai; lunch from HK$50, dinner from HK$150; ☉lunch & dinner Mon-Sat; Ⓜ Wan Chai, exit A2) The tasty Singaporean, Malaysian and Chinese dishes at this unpretentious eatery are executed with more flair than authenticity, but they're convincing. The chef's knack for working magic with culinary influences has won him a following among foodies.

TOP CHOICE AMMO
EUROPEAN $$

(Map p468; ☎2537 9888; Asia Society Hong Kong Centre, 9 Justice Dr, Admiralty; lunch set from HK$188, dinner from HK$400; ☉11.30am-11.30pm Sun-Thu, to 12.30pm Fri & Sat; Ⓜ Admiralty) Awash in light the colour of bullets, this sleek cafe at the Asia Society Centre has chandeliers and metallic panels evoking the site's past as an explosives magazine. The pricey menu is well thought out, with a selection of mostly Italian mains, and tapas available at cocktail hour (from HK$58). Bookings essential.

TOP CHOICE Luk Yu Teahouse
CANTONESE $$

(陸羽茶室; Map p468; ☎2523 5464; 24-26 Stanley St, Central; mains HK$100-350; ☉7am-10pm; Ⓜ Central, exit D2; ☷) This elegant establishment is arguably the most famous teahouse in Hong Kong. With Eastern art deco interiors featuring ceiling fans and stained-glass windows, it could almost be the setting of a mystery novel. Dim sum is available till 5.30pm.

Sing Kee
DAI PAI DONG $

(盛記; Map p468; ☎2541 5678; 9-10 Stanley St, Central; dishes from HK$50; ☉ lunch & dinner; Ⓜ Central, exit D2) This is one of the few surviving *dai pai dongs* (open-air food stalls) on the island that has withstood the tide of gentrification and still retains a working-class character. There's no English signage; look for the crammed tables and steam billowing out from the cooking station at the end of Stanley St.

Lin Heung Kui
CANTONESE $

(蓮香居; Map p468; ☎2156 9328; 2-3/F, 46-50 Des Voeux Rd West; meals HK$120-250; ☉6am-11pm, dim sum to 3.30pm; ⓑbus 5B from Des Voeux Rd Central) This old-school dim sum restaurant is where you can pick dim sum from the strolling carts or the cooking stations. The grandfatherlike waiters still wear their traditional white tunics and serve you tea from huge brass kettles. The place is no-frills, so service charge isn't expected.

TOP CHOICE Life Cafe
VEGETARIAN, WESTERN $

(Map p468; www.lifecafe.com.hk; 10 Shelley St, Central; salads HK$80-90, mains HK$80-105; ☉9am-10pm; ☷☷) Life is a vegetarian's dream, serving organic vegan food and dishes free of gluten, wheat, onion and garlic. Housed in a three-storey, pre-war building, it is filled with intimate seatings; the ground-floor deli has guilt-free goodies for takeaway.

SELF-CATERING

Hong Kong's two main supermarket chains **Park'nShop** (www.parknshop.com) and **Wellcome** (www.wellcome.com.hk) have so many outlets you're bound to run into a few. **ThreeSixty** (Map p468; www.threesixtyhk.com; Landmark, Central; ☺8am-7.30pm Mon-Sat) has more organic choices but is on the pricey side. The gourmet **city'super** (Map p476; www.citysuper. com.hk; Shop 3001, Gateway Arcade, 25-27 Canton Rd, Harbour City, Tsim Sha Tsui; ☺10am-10.30pm) has attractive but expensive produce. Branches include one in the **IFC Mall** (Map p468; www.citysuper.com.hk; Shop 1041-1049, IFC Mall, 8 Finance St, Central; ☺10.30am-9.30pm).

Lung King Heen   CANTONESE, DIM SUM $$$
(龍景軒; Map p468; ☑3196 8888; www.fourseasons.com/hongkong; Four Seasons Hotel, 8 Finance St; lunch set HK$450, dinner set HK$1280; ☺lunch & dinner; ⓜHong Kong, exit E1) The world's first Chinese restaurant to receive three stars from the Michelin people still keeps them. The Cantonese food here is excellently prepared, and when combined with the harbour views and the smooth service, it makes for a truly stellar dining experience.

Posto Pubblico   ITALIAN, ORGANIC $$
(Map p468; ☑2577 7160; 28 Elgin St, Soho; set lunch from HK$130, meals from HK$150, cocktails from HK$75; ☺breakfast, lunch & dinner; ⓠ26) A New York–style Italian bistro, the 'Public Place' serves delicious and sustainable seafood, all-natural meats, and handpicked vegetables from local organic farms. No service charge.

TOP
CHOICE **Yin Yang**   CHINESE $$$
(鴛鴦飯店; Map p472; ☑2866 0868; www.yinyang.hk; 18 Ship St; lunch HK$180-280, dinner from HK$680; ☺lunch & dinner Mon-Sat; ⓜWan Chai, exit B2) Margaret Xu, the chef of Yin Yang, grows organic vegetables and uses old-fashioned tools such as stone-grinds and terracotta ovens to create Hong Kong classics with a contemporary twist. Yin Yang is housed in a gorgeous heritage building (c 1930s). Dinner is a tasting menu, and you need to book at least five days in advance. The website mentions a deposit but that's negotiable.

San Xi Lou   SICHUANESE $$
(三希樓; Map p468; ☑2838 8811; 7th fl Coda Plaza, 51 Garden Rd, Admiralty; meals HK$200-450; ☺11am-10.30pm; ⓠ12A from ⓜAdmiralty) If the fresh ingredients and the complexity of the spices don't tell you this is Hong Kong's finest Sichuanese kitchen, the large number of Sichuanese expats among its repeat customers should.

TOP
CHOICE **Pure Veggie House**   VEGETARIAN, CHINESE $$
(Map p468; ☑2525 0556; 3rd fl, Coda Plaza, 51 Garden Rd, Admiralty; meals HK$200-400; ☺11am-10pm; ⓠbus 12A from ⓜAdmiralty; ⓟ) This Buddhist place cooks up some of the best vegetarian fare around. Tasty MSG-free dim sum and an assortment of creative Chinese dishes are served by well-mannered staff in a setting resembling a rustic inn.

Joon Ko Restaurant   KOREAN $$
(純子餐廳; Map p472; 209 Jaffe Rd, Wan Chai; lunch from HK$11, dinner from HK$200; ☺lunch & dinner; ⓜWan Chai, exit A1; ⓟ) This small family-run shop comes recommended by Korean friends. Carnivores must try the beef ribs and ox tongue, while vegetarians shouldn't miss the cold noodles.

L'Atelier de Joël Robuchon   MODERN FRENCH $$$
(Map p468; ☑2166 9000; www.joel-robuchon.com; Shop 401, Landmark, Queen's Rd Central, Central; lunch set from HK$398, dinner set from HK$980; ☺lunch & dinner; ⓜCentral, exit G) This red and black workshop of the celebrity chef's three-part wonder in Hong Kong has a tantalising list of tapas. For the haute version, visit **Le Jardin** next door, which also serves breakfast (7.30am to 10am Monday to Saturday). **Le Salon de The** (☺8am-8pm), one floor down, has some of the best sandwiches, pastries and cakes in town for dine-in or takeaway.

Yung Kee   CANTONESE $$
(鏞記酒家; Map p468; www.yungkee.com.hk; 32-40 Wellington St, Central; meals HK$300-600; ☺11am-11.30pm; ⓜCentral, exit D2) The goose roasting in the coal-fired ovens here has been the talk of the town since 1942. During lunch hours, it's a popular dim sum place for the Central workforce.

Yardbird   JAPANESE $$
(Map p468; ☑2547 9273; 33-35 Bridges St; meals from HK$300; ☺6pm-late Mon-Sat; ⓠ26) This

Japanese bistro with a New York touch is the place to see and to be seen. The bar table at centre stage ignites a festive, social space. The yakitori and sake are first-rate. No reservations are accepted.

Piccolo Pizzeria & Bar ITALIAN $$
(☑2824 3000; Shop 1E, Davis St, Kennedy Town; meals from HK$150; ☺dinner Mon, lunch & dinner Tue-Sat; ☒ 5B or 5X from Central) Located at the west end of the island, Piccolo serves arguably the best pizzas in town. The open kitchen design allows diners to view the giant gas oven through a glass wall at the back.

TOP CHOICE Irori JAPANESE $$
(酒處; Map p472; ☑2838 5939; 2nd fl, Bartlock Centre, Yiu Wa St, Causeway Bay; lunch from HK$150, dinner from HK$300; ☺lunch & dinner; ⓂCauseway Bay, exit A) Irori's versatile kitchen turns out raw and cooked delicacies of an equally impressive standard. Seasonal fish flown in from Japan is carefully crafted into sushi. To warm the stomach, there's a creative selection of tasty tidbits, such as fried beef roll and yakitori.

Thai Som Tum THAI $
(泰爽甜; off Map p472; ☑3622 1795; Shop C1, 2/F, Electric Road Municipal Services Bldg, 229 Electric Rd, North Point; meals HK$50-100; ☺lunch Mon-Fri, dinner Mon-Sun; ⓂFortress Hill, exit B; ☑) Feisty food stall that has perfected the demonic art of frying and grilling. The 'neck of pork', sliced into luscious slivers, is grilled à la minute; down a Singha while you wait. The tasty Thai-style fried fish, presented like a tribal headdress, is a wonder to behold.

Teakha TEAHOUSE $
(茶家; Map p468; ☑2858 9185; Shop B, 18 Tai Ping Shan St, Sheung Wan; ☺11am-6pm Wed-Fri, noon-7pm Sat & Sun; ☒26) Organic milk teas, be it the Indian chai or Hojicha latte, are best enjoyed with a homemade scone in this oasis just off the main street. The tea wares are so cute that you can't help buying them as souvenirs.

KOWLOON
There's plenty of choice in both cuisine and budget, especially in Tsim Sha Tsui. More local places can be found further north.

TOP CHOICE Dong Lai Shun NORTHERN CHINESE $$
(東來順; Map p476; ☑2733 2020; www.rghk. hk; B2, The Royal Garden, 69 Mody Rd, Tsim Sha Tsui; lunch set HK$200-400, dinner set HK$300-450; ☺lunch & dinner; ⓂEast Tsim Sha Tsui, exit P2; ☑)

While the mainland outlets of this Běijīng chain are of varying quality, this Hong Kong branch is outstanding. Besides Northern Chinese dishes, which are superbly executed, its phonebook of a menu also features Cantonese, Sichuanese and Shanghainese favourites, served in an elegant setting.

Tin Lung Heen CANTONESE $$$
(天龍軒; off Map p476; ☑2263 2270; www.ritz carlton.com/hongkong; 102nd fl, Ritz-Carlton Hong Kong, International Commerce Centre, 1 Austin Rd W, West Kowloon; meals HK$300-1800; ☺lunch & dinner; ⓂKowloon, exit U3) The atmosphere here is imposing – you'd expect Hu Jintao to walk in any minute for his fried rice. But the service is personable, and we were floored by the sweeping views of West Kowloon. The famous *char siu* (barbecued meat), at HK$218, is the costliest plate of barbecued swine in town, but it's made from Spanish Iberico pork, and you can taste the difference.

TOP CHOICE Kowloon Tang CHINESE $$$
(九龍廳; off Map p476; ☑2811 9398; www.kow loontang.com; Shop R002-003, Civic Square, 3rd fl, Elements Mall, 1 Austin Rd, West Kowloon; meals HK$300-2000; ☺noon-10.30pm; ⓂKowloon, exit U3) Located atop the Elements Mall, Kowloon Tang serves excellent Cantonese classics, a mean Peking duck (order 24 hours in advance) and sumptuous European-style desserts in a fashionably retro setting. They have great cocktails too!

Ziafat ARABIC, INDIAN $
(Map p476; ☑2312 1015; 6th fl, Harilela Mansion, 81 Nathan Rd, Tsim Sha Tsui; meals HK$120-200; ☺11am-midnight; ⓂTsim Sha Tsui, exit R; ☑) This halal restaurant serves up tasty Arabic and Indian dishes. It's located in an old building along with budget hostels, but the restaurant itself is clean and humbly furnished with Arabic art. Tables near the entrance are reserved for hookah smokers.

Typhoon Shelter Hing Kee Restaurant CANTONESE $$$
(避風塘興記; Map p476; ☑2722 0022; 1st fl Bowa House, 180 Nathan Rd, Tsim Sha Tsui; meals HK$300-1000; ☺6pm-5am; ⓂJordan, exit D) This celebrity haunt is run by a feisty fisherman's daughter who's known for her brilliant dishes prepared the way they were on sampans. Service can be a little edgy though. Be sure you know the prices of all 'seasonal' items you order.

Yè Shanghai
SHANGHAINESE, DIM SUM $$$

(夜上海; Map p476; ☑2376 3322; www.elite
-concepts.com; 6th fl, Marco Polo Hotel, Harbour
City, Canton Rd, Tsim Sha Tsui; meals HK$300-
600; ☺lunch & dinner; ⓂEast Tsim Sha Tsui, exit
L4) The name means 'Shanghai Nights'.
Dark woods and subtle lighting inspired by
1920s Shanghai fill the air with romance.
The modern Shanghainese dishes are also
exquisite. The only exception to this Jiang-
nan harmony is the Cantonese dim sum
being served at lunch (though that too is
wonderful).

Woodlands
INDIAN, VEGETARIAN $

(活蘭印度素食; Map p476; ☑2369 3718; Upper
ground fl, 16 & 17 Wing On Plaza, 62 Mody Rd; meals
HK$55-130; ☺noon-3.30pm & 6.30-10.30pm;
ⓂEast Tsim Sha Tsui, exit P1; ☑) Located above
a department store, good old Woodlands of-
fers excellent-value Indian vegetarian food
to compatriots and the odd local. Dithering
gluttons should order the *thali* meals, which
are served on a round metal plate with 10
dishes, dessert and bread.

Kimberley
Chinese Restaurant
CANTONESE $$

(君怡閣中菜廳; Map p476; ☑2369 8212; M fl,
Kimberley Hotel, 28 Kimberley St, Tsim Sha Tsui;
meals from HK$400; ⓂTsim Sha Tsui, exit B1) This
restaurant is famous for the Kimberley Pig –
a 30-day-old piglet stuffed with sticky rice
cooked with shallots and garlic, then roasted whole. Each piglet (HK$900) will feed at
least five hungry people. You need to order it
two days in advance, and pay a (negotiable)
deposit of HK$200.

Wo Mei Restaurant
CANTONESE $$

(和味館; ☑2748 0002; ground fl, 29-33 Shun
Ning Rd, Cheung Sha Wan; meals HK$100-400;
☺lunch & dinner; ⓂCheung Sha Wan, exit A2; ☑)
Ingredients here are carefully sourced and
served piping hot. But there's another rea-
son Wo Mei is popular with food critics but
not vegetarians – it's famous for creepy-
crawlies such as bamboo worms and
honeybee pupae, which are fried and
sprinkled with salt and pepper.

Stables Grill
EUROPEAN $$$

(Map p476; ☑3988 0104; www.hulletthouse.com;
1881 Heritage, Hullett House, 2A Canton Rd, Tsim
Sha Tsui; meals from HK$400; ☺noon-10.30pm;
☒Star Ferry; ☑) The home of horses of the
Former Marine Police Headquarters is now
an atmospheric restaurant with tables spilling out on to a beautiful garden. The menu

features grilled foods and a variety of tapas
and pastas. Service can be so-so, but the setting makes that easy to overlook.

Din Tai Fung
TAIWANESE, NOODLES $

(鼎泰豐; Map p476; www.dintaifung.com.tw; Shop
130, 3rd fl, 30 Canton Rd, Tsim Sha Tsui; meals
HK$120-300; ☺11.30am-10.30pm; ⓂTsim Sha
Tsui, exit C1; ☑) Whether it's comfort food or
a carb fix you're craving, the dumplings and
noodles at this Michelin-starred Taiwanese
chain will do the trick. Expect to queue; they
don't take reservations.

Spring Deer
NORTHERN CHINESE $$

(鹿鳴春飯店; Map p476; ☑2366 4012; 1st fl, 42
Mody Rd, Tsim Sha Tsui; meals HK$80-550; ☺lunch
& dinner; ⓂTsim Sha Tsui, exit N2) Hong Kong's
most authentic Northern-style roasted lamb
is served here, and the Peking duck is de-
cent, but the service can be about as wel-
coming as a Běijīng winter c 1967. Booking
essential.

Mido Café
TEA CAFE, CHINESE $

(美都餐室; Map p474; 63 Temple St; meals HK$25-
80; ☺9am-10pm; ⓂYau Ma Tei, exit B2) Opened
in 1950, this vintage *cha chaan tang* (local
'tea cafe') with its mosaic tiles and metal lat-
ticework stands astride a street corner that
comes to life at sundown. Ascend to the up-
per floor and take a seat next to a wall of
iron-framed windows overlooking Tin Hau
Temple.

NEW TERRITORIES

Cuisines are less diverse in the New
Territories than Kowloon and Hong Kong but
this area has an abundance of seafood and
local eateries.

TOP CHOICE Loaf On
CANTONESE, SEAFOOD $$

(六福菜館; ☑2792 9966; 49 Market St; meals
from $200; ☺lunch & dinner) This Michelin-star
restaurant is where fish freshly caught from
the Sai Kung waters in the morning lands
on customer plates by midday. There is no
English signage, but it's identifiable by a
lone dining table marooned outside. Reservations recommended.

Dah Wing Wah
CANTONESE, DIM SUM $

(大榮華酒樓; ☑2476 9888; 2nd fl, Koon Wong
Mansion, 2-6 On Ning Rd; dim sum HK$14, meals
from HK$150; ☺6am-midnight; ☒Tai Tong Rd Light
Rail Station) This Michelin-recommended old-
ie is *the* place to go for the walled-village cuisine of the New Territories. Cantonese dim
sum is served throughout the day.

Ho To Tai Noodle Shop　　　CANTONESE $
(好到底麵家; ☎2476 2495; 67 Fau Tsoi St; meals from HK$30; ◷8am-8pm; ⓡTai Tong Rd Light Rail Station) One of the world's cheapest Michelin restaurants, this 60-year-old Yuen Long institution is best known for the fresh Cantonese egg noodles and shrimp roe noodles.

Sha Tin 18　　　NORTHERN CHINESE $$$
(沙田18; ☎3723 1234; www.hongkong.shatin .hyatt.com; Hyatt Regency Hong Kong, 18 Chak Cheung St, Sha Tin; meals HK$280-800; ◷11.30am-3pm & 5.30-10.30pm; ⓜEast Rail University station; ⚄♪) The Peking duck here has put this hotel restaurant in the gastronomic spotlight since its opening in 2009. Book your prized fowl 24 hours in advance.

TOP
CHOICE **Honeymoon Dessert**　　　DESSERTS $
(滿記甜品; www.honeymoon-dessert.com; 9-10A, B&C Po Tung Rd, Sai Kung; dishes HK$30; ◷1pm-2.45am; ⓜEast Rail Sha Tin station, then bus 299; ♪) This shop specialising in Chinese desserts such as sweet walnut soup and durian pudding is so successful that it's got branches all over China and in Indonesia, not to mention some 20 locations in Hong Kong.

OUTLYING ISLANDS
Lamma boasts the biggest choices in Yung Shue Wan and Sok Kwu Wan. There are also some decent choices on Lantau and fewer on Cheung Chau.

Bookworm Cafe　　　CAFE, VEGETARIAN $
(南島書蟲; ☎2982 4838; bookwormcafe.com.hk; 79 Main St, Yung Shue Wan; ◷10am-9pm Mon-Fri, 9am-10pm Sat, 9am-9pm Sun; @; ♪) Vegie foodies are in heaven in Bookworm, the granddaddy of healthy and eco-conscious eating in the Hong Kong dining scene. The cafe doubles as a secondhand bookshop.

Solo　　　CAFE $
(☎9153 7453; 86 Kat Hing St, Tai O; meals from HK$40; ◷11am-6pm Mon-Sat; ⓡ1 from Mui Wo) Framed by a backdrop of stilt houses and lush mountains, this sun-kissed terrace right on the water invites lazy afternoons spent enjoying coffee. The cakes and pies are as tempting as its fresh roasted coffee.

🍸 **Drinking**

Lan Kwai Fong (LKF) in Central is synonymous with nightlife in Hong Kong, attracting everyone from expat and Chinese suits to travellers. In general, watering holes in Wan Chai are cheaper and more relaxed (some say seedier), though sleek new spots

STUBBED OUT

In Hong Kong, smoking is banned in all restaurants, bars, shopping malls and museums – even at beaches and public parks – but you can light up in 'alfresco' areas. Some bars, however, risk getting fined to attract more customers during nonpeak hours. You'll know which ones they are by the ashtray they nonchalantly place on your table.

have been fast emerging around Star St. Drinking places in Kowloon tend to attract more locals. Most places offer discounts on drinks during happy hour, usually from late afternoon to early evening – 4pm to 8pm, say – but times vary from place to place.

HONG KONG ISLAND

TOP
CHOICE **The Globe**　　　BAR
(Map p468; 45-53 Graham St, Soho; ◷happy hour 9am-8pm; ⓜCentral, exit D1) In addition to the impressive imported wine and beer list, gastropub Globe is one of the few bars in town that serves Typhoon, the first caskconditioned ale brewed in Hong Kong. Occupying an enviable space, the bar has a huge dining area with long wooden tables and comfy banquettes, where comfort food is served.

Club 71　　　BAR
(七一吧; Map p468; Basement, 67 Hollywood Rd, Central; ◷3pm-2am Mon-Sat, 6pm-1am Sun; ⓡbus 26) Named after a huge protest march held on 1 July 2003, this friendly bar is a haven for artists, bohemians and the socially conscious. Find it by taking a sharp right down a narrow alley off Hollywood Rd or via a small footpath running west off Peel St.

Gecko Lounge　　　LOUNGE, WINE BAR
(Map p468; ☎2537 4680; lower ground fl, 15-19 Hollywood Rd; ◷4pm-2am Mon-Thu, 4pm-4am Fri & Sat, happy hour 6-9pm; ⓜCentral, exit D1) Entered from narrow Ezra's Lane off Cochrane or Pottinger Sts, Gecko is an intimate lounge and wine bar run by a friendly French sommelier with a penchant for absinthe. The well-hidden DJ mixes good sounds with kooky Parisian tunes.

8th Estate Winery　　　WINE BAR $
(☎2518 0922; www.the8estatewinery.com; Room 306, 3rd fl, Harbour Industrial Centre, 10 Lee Hing St, Ap Lei Chau; admission HK$100; ◷2-5pm Sat, by

appointment Mon-Fri; ⬚90 from Exchange Square in Central) This winery has no chateaux or vineyards, but you can enjoy 'Made in Hong Kong' wines out on the terrace, which affords sweeping ocean views, or in the rustic barrel rooms. To get there from Ap Lei Chau bus terminus, take a taxi (UK$20).

Amo Eno WINE BAR
(Map p468; Shop 3027, Podium Level 3, IFC Mall, 1 Harbour View St; ⓂHong Kong, exit E) 'Love wine' delivers a sophisticated wine experience, whether you're a debutant or a connoisseur. You can browse by colour, grape and price on a table with a touch-screen top, then pick your poison, and the size of pour from 72 bottles kept in enomatic machines.

TOP CHOICE **Sevva** COCKTAIL BAR
(Map p468; ☑2537 1388; www.sevva.hk; 25th fl, Prince's Bldg, 10 Chater Rd, Central; ⊙noon-midnight Mon-Thu, to 2am Fri & Sat; ⓂCentral, exit H) If there was a million-dollar view in Hong Kong, it'd be the one from the balcony of stylish Sevva – skyscrapers so close you see their arteries of steel, with the harbour and Kowloon in the distance. At night, it takes your breath away, and Sevva's cocktails are a wonderful excuse to let it.

TOP CHOICE **Executive Bar** LOUNGE BAR
(Map p472; ☑2893 2080; 7th fl, Bartlock Centre, 3 Yiu Wa St, Causeway Bay; ⊙5pm-1am Mon-Sat; ⓂCauseway Bay, exit A) You won't be served if you just turn up at this clubby, masculine bar high above Causeway Bay – it's by appointment only. Odd perhaps, but worth the trip if you are serious about whisky and bourbon. Several dozen varieties are served here, in large brandy balloons with large orbs of ice hand-chipped by the Japanese bartender.

Delaney's BAR, PUB
(Map p472; Ground & 1st fl, One Capital Place, 18 Luard Rd, Wan Chai; ⊙happy hour noon-9pm; ⓂWan Chai, exit C) At this popular Irish watering hole you can choose between the black and white tiled pub on the ground floor and a sports bar and restaurant on the 1st floor. The food is good and plentiful.

Pawn BAR, PUB
(Map p472; www.thepawn.com.hk; 62 Johnston Rd, Wan Chai; ⓂWan Chai, exit A3) This handsome three-storey gastropub used to house tenement houses and a century-old pawn shop. Now it contains a restaurant and a bar. The

slouchy sofas, shabby-chic interiors, and terrace spaces overlooking the tram tracks, make it a pleasant location to sample the great selection of lagers, bitters and wine.

KOWLOON

TOP CHOICE **Butler** BAR
(Map p476; 5th fl, Mody House, 30 Mody Rd, Tsim Sha Tsui; cover charge HK$200; ⓂEast Tsim Sha Tsui (exit N2) A cocktail and whisky heaven hidden in the residential part of TST. You can flip the whisky magazines as you watch the bartender, Uchida, create his magical concoctions with the flair and precision of a master mixologist in Ginza.

Ozone BAR
(off Map p476; ☑2263 2263; 118th fl, ICC, 1 Austin Rd, West Kowloon; ⊙5pm-2am; ⓂKowloon, exit U3) Asia's highest bar is imaginatively decorated with pillars resembling chocolate fountains in a hurricane, myriads of refracted glass and colour-changing illumination. Equally dizzying is the superfluous wine list, with the most expensive bottle selling for HK$150,000. A once-in-a-lifetime experience, in more ways than one.

Ned Kelly's Last Stand PUB
(Map p476; ☑2376 0562; 11A Ashley Rd, Tsim Sha Tsui; ⊙happy hour 11.30am-9pm; ⓂTsim Sha Tsui, exit L5) Named after an Australian bushranger, Ned's is one of Hong Kong's oldest pubs. Many customers who come here are attracted by the laid-back vibe and the Dixieland jazz band that cracks jokes between sets. The bar is filled with old posters and other Oz-related paraphernalia.

Tapas Bar TAPAS BAR
(Map p476; www.shangri-la.com; Lobby, Kowloon Shangri-La, 64 Mody Rd, Tsim Sha Tsui East; ⊙3.30pm-1am; ⓂEast Tsim Sha Tsui, exit P1) An intimate vibe and bistro-style decor make this a good place to unwind over champagne and tapas after a day of sightseeing.

☆ Entertainment

Hong Kongers work hard and play harder. To find out what's on, pick up a copy of *HK Magazine* (http://hk-magazine.com), an entertainment listings magazine. It's free, appears on Friday and can be found in restaurants, bars and hotels. For more comprehensive listings buy the fortnightly *Time Out* (www.timeout.com.hk) from newsstands. Also worth checking out is the free *bie bc magazine* (www.bcmagazine.net).

DANCE, DANCE!

Opportunities to kick up your heels abound in town.

Tango

Hong Kong has a zealous community of tango dancers. **Tango Tang** (www.tangotang.com), the most prominent of all the schools, has all tango events, including those by other organisers, posted on its website. You can join any of the *milongas* (dance parties) held every week all over town. The **Hong Kong Tango Festival** (www.hktangofest.com), held at the end of the year, features classes, workshops and more parties. The website has details.

Salsa

Hong Kong's vibrant salsa community has weekly club nights that are open to anyone in need of a good time. See www.dancetrinity.com or www.hongkong-salsa.com. The annual **Hong Kong Salsa Festival** (http://hksalsafestival.com), held around February, features participants from the world over.

Swing

If you like swing, there are socials with live jazz bands (and free beginners' classes) at least six times a month. See the calendar on www.hongkongswings.com.

Queer Tea Dance

Party with lovely drag hostesses every first and third Sunday of the month at gay-friendly bar **Tivo** (p468; 43-55 Wyndham St, Central; ⊘closed Sun; Ⓜ Central, exit D2). The frolicking starts at 7pm.

The main ticket providers, **Urbtix** (☑2734 9009; www.urbtix.hk; ⊘10am-8pm), **Cityline** (☑2317 6666; www.cityline.com.hk) and **Hong Kong Ticketing** (☑3128 8288; www.hkticketing.com; ⊘10am-8pm), have among them tickets to every major event in Hong Kong. Book online or by phone.

Cinema

Tickets can be bought through Cityline (for mainstream films) and Urbtix (for alternative screenings). If you're into arthouse films, don't miss **Broadway Cinematheque** (Map p474; ☑2338 3188; www.cinema.com.hk (click 'Cinematheque'); Prosperous Garden, 3 Public Square St, Yau Ma Tei; ⊘11.30am-10.30pm).

Cantonese Opera

Hong Kong is one of the best places to watch Cantonese opera. **Sunbeam Theatre** (www.ua-sunbeam.com; 423 King's Rd, North Point) and Yau Ma Tei Theatre (see p479) are dedicated to the art form. You can book through Urbtix or Cityline.

Live Music

TOP CHOICE **Street Music Series** LIVE MUSIC
(☑2582 0280; www.hkac.org.hk; ⊘6.30-9pm 1 Fri a month) One Friday a month, musician Kung Chi-sing throws a free outdoor concert outside the **Hong Kong Arts Centre** (Map p472; 香港藝術中心; 2 Harbour Rd, Wan Chai; Ⓜ Admiralty, exit E2). The colourful line-ups have included anything from indie rock and jazz to Cantonese opera and Mozart. Followers of this excellent, professional-quality music (Kung trained in classical music) performed in an electrifying atmosphere have included the Venezuelan and Canadian consuls-general in Hong Kong. Check the website's calendar for dates.

TOP CHOICE **Peel Fresco** LIVE MUSIC
(Map p468; www.peelfresco.com; 49 Peel St, Central; ⊘5pm-late Mon-Sat) A classy jazz venue with massive paintings taking centre stage. It's also famed for the pop stars who come in and out. Soul and reggae are also played here.

Grappa's Cellar LIVE MUSIC
(Map p468; ☑2521 2322; www.elgrande.com.hk/outlets/HongKong/GrappasCellar; 1 Connaught Pl, Central; Ⓜ Hong Kong, exit B2) For at least two weekends a month, this underground Italian restaurant morphs into a jazz or rock music venue. Call or check website for event and ticketing details.

HONG KONG'S HIDDEN AGENDA

Founded in a clandestine band room in the gritty industrial hub of Kwun Tong, **Hidden Agenda** (☎9170 6073; www.hiddenagendahk.com; 2A, Wing Fu Industrial Bldg, 15-17 Tai Yip St, Kwun Tong; Ⓜ Ngau Tau Kok, exit B6) has become synonymous with underground music in Hong Kong. It now occupies a warehouse-turned-venue that accommodates 300 people. While the music started out with a raucous, head-banging focus, the mix of genres now include post-rock, reggae, jazz, folk, techno and punk.

Bands both local (Chochukmo, Hungry Ghosts) and foreign (Tahiti 80, The Chariot, Anti-Flag, Two Gallants, Alcest, Pitchtuner) have performed here. There are shows every week. Check the website for the latest.

Sheung Wan Civic Centre LIVE MUSIC
(Map p468; 上環文娛中心; ☑booking 2853 2678, enquiries 2853 2689; 5th fl, Sheung Wan Municipal Services Bld, 345 Queen's Rd Central, Sheung Wan; ☺9am-11pm, box office 10am-6.30pm; Ⓜ Sheung Wan, exit A2) This government-run performance venue, which shares a building with a wet market and cooked food centre, has programmes all year round that lean towards drama by local theatre troupes, some engagingly experimental, and concerts by independent musicians and bands.

Makumba Africa Lounge LIVE MUSIC
(Map p468; ☑2522 0544; http://makumbahk.com; 2nd fl, Ho Lee Commercial Bldg, 38-44 D'Aguilar St, Lan Kwai Fong, Central; ☺5pm-late) This is the premier club for African and reggae music.

Gay & Lesbian Venues

For the latest, try **Utopia Asia** (www.utopia -asia.com/hkbars.htm), **Gay HK** (www.gayhk.com) or the free, monthly magazine **Dim Sum** (http://dimsum-hk.com).

Hong Kong's premier lesbian organisation, **Les Peches** (☑9101 8001; lespechesinfo@ yahoo.com) has monthly events for lesbians, bisexual women and their friends.

Propaganda CLUB
(Map p468; lower ground fl, 1 Hollywood Rd, Central; weekend cover HK$160; ☺9pm-late Tue-Sat) Hong Kong's premier gay dance club. The weekend cover charge gets you into Works below on Friday. Enter from Ezra's Lane.

T:me BAR
(Map p468; ☑2332 6565; www.time-bar.com; ☺6pm-2am Mon-Sat) A small and chic gay bar located in a back alley off Hollywood Rd, close to Club 71; drinks are a bit on the pricey side but they have happy hour throughout the week.

Comedy Venues
TakeOut Comedy Club COMEDY
(Map p468; ☑6220 4436; www.takeoutcom edy.com; Basement, 34 Elgin St, Soho; ☑26) Hong Kong's first comedy club will blow your socks off with consistently good stand-up and improvised acts in English, Cantonese and Mandarin.

🔒 Shopping

It's not the bargain destination it was, but Hong Kong is crammed with retail space, making it a delight for shoppers. If you prefer everything under one roof, some of the sleeker options are: **IFC Mall** (國際金 融商場; Map p468; www.ifc.com.hk; 1 Harbour View St, Central; Ⓜ Hong Kong), **Pacific Place** (太古廣場; Map p468; 88 Queensway, Admiralty; Ⓜ Admiralty), **Elements** (圓方; off Map p476; www.elementshk.com; 1 Austin Rd W, West Kowloon; Ⓜ Kowloon, exit U3) and **Harbour City** (海港城; Map p476; Canton Rd, Tsim Sha Tsui; ⛴Star Ferry). This last is an enormous complex.

If you're looking for antiques and curios, Central's Hollywood Road (Map p468) should be your first stop, while cheaper Cat Street (Map p468), also in Central, specialises in younger (ie retro) items such as Mao paraphernalia.

For cheap attire, browse at Jardine's Bazaar (渣甸街; Map p472) in Causeway Bay, Johnston Road (Map p472) in Wan Chai or the **Ladies Market** (女人街; Tung Choi St, Fa Yuen St & Sai Yeung Choi St, Mong Kok; ☺noon-10.30pm; MTR Mong Kok, exit B2) in Mong Kok, Kowloon.

Hong Kong is one of the best places in Asia to buy English-language books and the city's computer malls have some of the lowest prices on earth. Similarly, there are some fantastic camera stores, though most are *not* on Nathan Rd in Tsim Sha Tsui.

HONG KONG ISLAND

Central and Causeway Bay are the main shopping districts on Hong Kong Island.

TOP CHOICE Horizon Plaza
FURNITURE

(海怡工貿中心; 2 Lee Wing St, Ap Lei Chau, Aberdeen; ⊙10am-7pm) This industrial citadel now boasts more than 150 shops and outlets over 28 storeys, selling furniture and designer clothing at knock-down prices. Most shops will pack and ship too. Bus 90 from Central's Exchange Sq terminus takes you to Ap Lei Chau Estate bus terminus; from there take a cab.

Arch Angel Antiques
ANTIQUES

(Map p468; 53-55 Hollywood Rd, Central; ⊙9.30am-6.30pm; ⊒bus 26) This well-respected shop has knowledgeable staff and a wide selection of antiques and curios, including many at affordable prices. Everything is authenticated.

TOP CHOICE G.O.D.
HOMEWARES, GIFTS

(Map p472; www.god.com.hk; Leighton Centre, Sharp St E, Causeway Bay; MCauseway Bay, exit A) If you only have time for one souvenir place, make it G.O.D. This cheeky lifestyle store sells retro-with-a-twist home and office accessories, and clothing designed in-house. It's fun, chic and very Hong Kong. G.O.D. has five branches, including one at JCCAC (p479).

Photo Scientific
CAMERAS

(攝影科學; Map p468; 6 Stanley St, Central; ⊙9am-7pm Mon-Sat; MCentral) Photo Scientific has a rock-solid reputation among professional photographers, with labelled prices, no bargaining, no arguing and no cheating.

Mountain Folkcraft
CRAFTS

(高山民藝; Map p468; 12 Wo On Lane, Central; ⊙9.30am-6.30pm Mon-Sat; MCentral, exit D1) This place sells bolts of batik, clothing, wood carvings and paper cuts made by ethnic minorities in Asia.

TOP CHOICE Shanghai Tang
CLOTHING, ACCESSORIES

(上海灘; Map p468; ☑2525 7333; www.shanghaitang.com; Shanghai Tang Mansion, 1 Duddell St; MCentral, exit D1) If you fancy a *cheongsam* (a body-hugging Chinese dress) with a modern twist, a Chinese-style clutch or a lime-green mandarin jacket, this is the place to go. Shanghai Tang also stocks a range of lifestyle products – everything from cushions to picture frames, teapots, even mahjong-tile sets – designed in a modern *chinoiserie* style.

Fook Ming Tong Tea Shop
FOOD, DRINK

(福茗堂; Map p468; ☑2295 0368; Shop 3006, IFC Mall, 8 Finance St; MCentral, exit A) Tea-making accoutrements and carefully chosen teas of various ages and grades, from gunpowder to Nanyan Ti Guan Yin Crown Grade – costing anything from HK$10 to HK$9000 per 100g.

Hong Kong Book Centre
BOOKS

(Map p468; ☑2522 7046; www.hongkongbookcentre.com; Basement, On Lok Yuen Bldg, 25 Des Voeux Rd, Central; ⊙9am-6.30pm Mon-Fri, to 5.30pm Sat; MCentral) Basement shop with a vast selection of English-language books and magazines, particularly business titles.

Wan Chai Computer Centre
ELECTRONICS

(灣仔電腦城; Map p472; 1st fl, Southorn Centre, 130-138 Hennessy Rd, Wan Chai; ⊙10am-8pm Mon-Sat; MWan Chai, exit B2) A reliable mall for computers, peripherals and most things electronic and digital.

TOP CHOICE Daydream Nation
CLOTHING

(Map p472; ☑3741 0758; www.daydream-nation.com; 2nd fl, Hong Kong Arts Centre, 2 Harbour Rd, Wan Chai; ⊒⊒) A 'Vogue Talent 2010' brand founded by two of the most creative local designers around – Kay Wong and her brother Jing who's also a musician. DN is known for its highly wearable fashion and accessories that come with a touch of theatricality. Check the website for the latest opening hours.

Kung Fu Supplies
SPORTS

(功夫用品公司; Map p472; ☑2891 1912; Room 6A, 6th fl, Chuen Fung House, 188-192 Johnston Rd, Wan Chai; ⊙Mon-Sat; ⊒6, 6A or 6X) If you need to stock up on martial-arts accessories, including uniforms, nunchakus and safety weapons for practice, or just want to thumb through a decent collection of books and DVDs, this is the place to go.

Yiu Fung Store
FOOD

(么鳳; Map p472; 3 Foo Ming St, Causeway Bay; MCauseway Bay, exit A; ☑) Hong Kong's most famous store (c 1960s) for Chinese pickles and preserved fruit features sour plum, liquorice-flavoured lemon, tangerine peel, pickled papaya and dried longnan.

WANT MORE?

For in-depth information, reviews and recommendations at your fingertips, head to the Apple App Store to purchase Lonely Planet's *Hong Kong City Guide* iPhone app.

Alternatively, head to **Lonely Planet** (www.lonelyplanet.com/china/hong-kong) for planning advice, author recommendations, traveller reviews and insider tips.

KOWLOON

Shopping in Kowloon is a mix of the down-at-heel and the glamorous; you can find just about anything – especially in Tsim Sha Tsui.

Page One   BOOKS
(Map p472; Shop LG1 30, lower ground fl, Festival Walk, 80-88 Tat Chee Ave, Kowloon Tong; ⓂKowloon Tong, exit C2) A chain, yes, but a good one. Page One has Hong Kong's best selection of art and design magazines and books; it's also strong on photography, literature, film and children's books. There's another branch in **Causeway Bay** (☑2506 0381; Shop 922, Time's Square, 1 Matheson St, Causeway Bay; ⊙10.30am-10pm; ⓂCauseway Bay, exit A).

Premier Jewellery   JEWELLERY
(愛寶珠寶有限公司; Map p476; ☑2368 0003; Shop G14-15, ground fl, Holiday Inn Golden Mile Shopping Mall, 50 Nathan Rd; ⊙10am-7.30pm Mon-Sat, 10.30am-4pm Sun; ⓂTsim Sha Tsui, exit G) This family firm directed by a qualified gemologist has a small but attractive range of jewellery. If you're looking for something particular, give them a day's notice and a selection will be ready in time for your arrival.

Initial   CLOTHING
(Map p476; www.initialfashion.com; Shop 2, 48 Cameron Rd, Tsim Sha Tsui; ⊙11.30am-11.30pm; ⓂTsim Sha Tsui, exit B2) This attractive shop carries stylish, multifunctional urban wear with European and Japanese influences. The clothes, created by inhouse designers, are complemented by imported shoes, bags and costume jewellery.

TOP CHOICE **Ap Liu St Flea Market**   ELECTRONICS
(Ap Liu St, Sham Shui Po; ⊙noon-midnight; ⓂSham Shui Po, exit A2) Shops and stalls selling every electronic/electrical appliance you can imagine, including exotic batteries and satellite dishes. It's very local.

Swindon Books   BOOKS
(Map p476; www.swindonbooks.com; 13-15 Lock Rd, Tsim Sha Tsui; ⓂTsim Sha Tsui, exit A1) This is one of the best 'real' (as opposed to 'supermarket') bookshops. An excellent range and knowledgeable staff. Strong on local books and history in particular.

Rise Shopping Arcade   CLOTHING
(利時商場; Map p476; www.rise-hk.com; 5-11 Granville Circuit, Tsim Sha Tsui; ⓂTsim Sha Tsui, exit B2) Bursting at the seams of this mini-mall is cheap streetwear from Korea and Japan, with a few knock-offs chucked in for good measure. Patience and a good eye could land you purchases fit for a *Vogue* photo shoot. Best visited between 4pm and 8.30pm when most of the shops are open.

Yue Hwa Chinese Products Emporium   DEPARTMENT STORE
(裕華國貨; Map p476; ☑2384 0084; 301-309 Nathan Rd; ⓂYau Ma Tei, exit D) An enormous place with seven floors of ceramics, furniture, souvenirs and clothing for the old-school souvenir-hunting tourist.

Bruce Lee Club   SPORTS
(李小龍會; off Map p474; www.bruceleeclub.com; Shop 160-161, In's Point, 530 Nathan Rd; ⊙1-9pm; ⓂYau Ma Tei, exit A1) A small martial-arts museum and souvenir shop dedicated to Bruce Lee.

Chan Wah Kee Cutlery Store   HOMEWARES
(陳華記刀莊; Map p474; ☑2730 4091; 278D, Temple St, close to Bowring St, Yau Ma Tei; ⊙11am-6pm, closed Wed; ⓂJordan, exit C2) Kitchen weaponry sharpened the ancient way by an 80-year-old guru. Need a chopper that can julienne tofu? Here's the place to go.

Protrek   OUTDOOR EQUIPMENT
(Map p474; www.protrek.com.hk; 522 Nathan Rd, Yau Ma Tei; ⊙noon-8pm Mon-Sat, 11.30am-9.30pm Sun; ⓂYau Ma Tei, exit C) Arguably your best bet for outdoor gear that will see you through from sea to summit.

ⓘ Information

Emergency
Fire, police & ambulance (☑999)

Internet Access
Internet cafes are hard to come by, but wi-fi is widely available. It's free at Hong Kong International Airport, and at parks, public libraries, sports centres, museums, cooked-food markets, community halls and government premises listed at www.gov.hk/en/theme/wifi/location.

McDonald's (www.mcdonalds.com.hk), **Pacific Coffee** (www.pacificcoffee.com) and **Starbucks** (www.starbucks.com.hk) outlets have free wi-fi with purchase.

A 60-minute PCCW wi-fi pass is available at HKTB visitor centres. A 3G rechargeable SIM card (from HK$48) will connect your phone to the internet and these are available at PCCW and SmarTone shops, PCCW provides some 10,000 wi-fi hot spots. Check service plans at www.pccwwifi.com.

Media

Local and Asian editions of printed newspapers and journals locally include *South China Morning Post, The Standard, HK Magazine, BC Magazine, Time Out, USA Today, International Herald Tribune, Financial Times* and *Wall Street Journal Asia*.

English-language TV (terrestrial) and radio include TVB Pearl, ATV World; BBC World Service, RTHK 3 and 4.

Medical Services

Medical care is of a high standard in Hong Kong, though private hospital care is costly.

Ambulance (☑999)
General inquiry number for hospitals (☑2300 6555)

Hospitals with 24-hour emergency services:
Matilda International (明德國際醫院; ☑2849 0111; 41 Mt Kellett Rd, Peak) Pricey private hospital atop Victoria Peak.

Prince of Wales (威爾斯親王醫院; ☑2632 2211; 30-32 Ngan Shing St, Sha Tin) Public hospital in the New Territories.

Queen Elizabeth (伊利沙伯醫院; ☑2958 8888; 30 Gascoigne Rd, Yau Ma Tei) Public hospital in Kowloon.

Money

ATMs are available throughout Hong Kong, including at the airport. Most are available 24 hours. Banks have the best exchange rates, but some levy commissions of HK$50 or more per transaction. Opening hours are 9am to 4.30pm or 5.30pm Monday to Friday, 9am to 12.30pm Saturday.

Licensed moneychangers are abundant in tourist districts, the ground floor of Chungking Mansions and at **Wing Hoi Money Exchange** (ground fl, Shop No 9b, Mirador Mansion, 58 Nathan Rd, Tsim Sha Tsui; ☺8.30am-8.30pm Mon-Sat, to 7pm Sun). Rates at the airport are poor.

Post

Hong Kong Post (www.hongkongpost.com) offices:
General post office (中央郵政局; 2 Connaught Pl, Central; ☺8am-6pm Mon-Sat, 9am-5pm Sun)

Tsim Sha Tsui post office (尖沙咀郵政局; ground & 1st fl, Hermes House, 10 Middle Rd, Tsim Sha Tsui; ☺9am-6pm Mon-Sat, to 2pm Sun)

Telephone

All phone numbers have eight digits (except ☑800 toll-free numbers) and no area codes. Local calls are free on private phones and cost HK$1 for five minutes on pay phones.

A phonecard, available at convenience stores, will let you make international direct-dial calls. A SIM card (from HK$50) with prepaid call time will connect you to the local mobile phone network.

Tourist Information

HKTB (香港旅遊發展局; ☑visitor hotline 2508 1234; www.discoverhongkong.com; ☺hotline 9am-6pm) runs a website, visitor hotline and several visitor information and service centres:

Hong Kong International Airport (Halls A & B, Arrivals Level, Terminal 1; ☺7am-11pm)

Hong Kong Island (The Peak Piazza; ☺9am-9pm)

Kowloon (Star Ferry Concourse, Tsim Sha Tsui; ☺8am-8pm)

Lo Wu border (2nd fl, Arrival Hall, Lo Wu Terminal Bldg; ☺8am-6pm)

Travel Agencies

China Travel Service (中國旅行社; CTS; ☑2522 0450; www.ctshk.com; ground fl, China Travel Bldg, 77 Queen's Rd, Central; ☺9am-7.30pm Mon-Fri, to 5pm Sat, 9.30am-5pm Sun)

HSBC'S GEOMANCY

The 52-storey HSBC building is supposedly full of examples of good feng shui (Chinese geomancy). Care is taken to ensure nothing blocks its view of Victoria Harbour, because water is associated with wealth and prosperity. The escalators are believed to symbolise the whiskers of a dragon sucking wealth into its belly; and they are built at an angle to the entrance, which supposedly disorients evil spirits which can only travel in a straight line. Care was also taken not to locate the banking hall on the ground floor, because doing so would block off the flow of the 'dragon's vein' from Victoria Harbour to the mountains at the back, creating bad feng shui.

HKIA TO CHINA THE FAST WAY

You can head straight from Hong Kong International Airport (HKIA) to Macau and airports in Shēnzhèn and Guǎngzhōu. The following companies (all with counters at HKIA Terminal 2) have buses going to points in southern China (Fóshān HK$230, Guǎngzhōu HK$250 and Shēnzhèn airport HK$180):

CTS Express Coach (☎2261 2147, 3559 1474)

Eternal East Cross Border Coach (☎2261 0176)

Trans-Island Limousine Service (☎3193 9333)

A fast ferry service, **Skypier** (☎2215 3232) links HKIA with Macau and six Pearl River delta destinations. Travellers can board ferries without clearing Hong Kong customs and immigration. Book a ticket prior to boarding from ticketing desks located in the transfer area at Arrivals (Level 5, close to immigration counters).

Chu Kong Passenger Transportation Co (☎2858 3876; www.cksp.com.hk) Has ferries from HKIA to Shēnzhèn airport (HK$295, 40 minutes, eight daily, 10.15am to 6.30pm) and to Macau, Shékǒu, Dōngguǎn, Zhūhǎi and Zhōngshān.

TurboJet (☎2859 3333; www.turbojet.com.hk) Has services to Macau (HK$233, one hour, eight daily, 10am to 10pm).

Phoenix Services Agency (峯寧旅運社; Map p476; ☎2722 7378; info@phoenixtrvl.com; Room 1404-5, 14th fl, Austin Tower, 22-26A Austin Ave, Tsim Sha Tsui; ⏱9am-6pm Mon-Fri, to 4pm Sat)

Websites
Lonely Planet (www.lonelyplanet.com/hong-kong) Destination information, bookings, traveller forum and more.

Discover Hong Kong (www.discoverhongkong.com) Official tourist board website.

Time Out Hong Kong (www.timeout.com.hk) Live entertainment listings and more.

ℹ Getting There & Away

Air

Over 100 airlines operate between **Hong Kong International Airport** (HKG; ☎2181 8888; www.hkairport.com) and some 160 destinations around the world. Fares are relatively low and you can find quite a number of discounted tickets.

That said, bargain airfares between Hong Kong and mainland China are few, as the government regulates the prices. The volume of business travellers and Chinese tourists is enormous, so book well in advance. If you're prepared to travel to Guǎngzhōu or Shēnzhèn, in Guǎngdōng province, you can find much cheaper flights. Shēnzhèn airport (see p560) has flights to just about everywhere in China (see www.elong.net).

See p996 for international airlines flying to/from Hong Kong.

Airline offices in Hong Kong:

Air China (www.airchina.hk)

Cathay Pacific (www.cathaypacific.com)

China Airlines (www.china-airlines.com)

China Southern (www.cs-air.com)

Dragonair (www.dragonair.com)

Hong Kong Airlines (www.hongkongairlines.com)

Boat

Regular ferries link the **China Ferry Terminal** (中港碼頭; China Hong Kong City, 33 Canton Rd, Tsim Sha Tsui) in Kowloon and the **Hong Kong–Macau Ferry Terminal** (港澳碼頭; Shun Tak Centre, 200 Connaught Rd, Sheung Wan) on Hong Kong Island with towns and cities on the Pearl River delta – but not central Guǎngzhōu or Shēnzhèn. For sea transport to/from Macau, see p531. You'll find left-luggage lockers (HK$20 to HK$30 per hour) in both terminals.

Chu Kong Passenger Transportation Co (☎2858 3876; www.cksp.com.hk) provides regularly scheduled ferries to Zhūhǎi (HK$190, 70 minutes), Zhōngshān (HK$210, 1½ hours), Shùndé (HK$228, two hours), Zhàoqìng (HK$220, four hours), Kāipíng (HK$180, four hours) and Shékǒu (HK$110, one hour).

Bus

For information on buses from the airport to mainland China, see the boxed text. You can reach virtually any major destination in Guǎngdōng province by bus (HK$100 to HK$220):

CTS Express Coach (☎2764 9803; http://ctsbus.hkcts.com) The most extensive cross-border bus services to Guǎngdōng.

Trans-Island Limousine Service (☎3193 9333; www.trans-island.com.hk) Buses to a dozen destinations in the province.

Train

For schedules and ticket prices, see www.mtr.com.hk.

Immigration formalities at Hung Hom must be completed before boarding, including checking your visa for China; arrive at the station 45 minutes before departure.

Tickets can be booked at CTS, East Rail stations in Hung Hom, Mong Kok, Kowloon Tong and Sha Tin, and MTR Travel at Admiralty Station; tickets booked with credit card by phone (☑2947 7888) must be collected at least one hour before departure.

Trains to Guǎngzhōu, Shànghǎi, Běijīng and Zhàoqìng Daily from Hung Hom station (HK$230 to HK$1191).

Trains to Shēnzhèn The East Rail train takes you to Lo Wu or Lok Ma Chau; from Shēnzhèn you can take a local train or bus to Guǎngzhōu and beyond.

❶ Getting Around

Hong Kong's public transport system is fast, convenient, relatively inexpensive and easy to use with the Octopus card payment system.

To/From the Airport

The **Airport Express** (www.mtr.com.hk; HK$100/90/60 per 24/21/13min from Central/Kowloon/Tsing Yi; ⊙every 12min from Hong Kong station, Central) Fastest and costliest public route to the airport; most airlines allow Airport Express passengers to check in at Central or Kowloon stations between 5.30am and 12.30am one day to 90 minutes before departure; at Hong Kong International Airport there is a **left-luggage office** (☑2261 0110; HK10/120 per hr/day; ⊙5.30am-1.30am) on Level 3 of Terminal 2.

Bus fares to the airport are HK$21 to HK$45. See 'Transport' on the www.hkairport.com website for details.

A taxi to Central is about HK$300 plus luggage charge of HK$5 per item.

For details on the ferry to Shēnzhèn airport, see the boxed text.

Bicycle

In quiet areas of the Outlying Islands or New Territories, a bike can be a lovely way of getting around. For rental info, see p484.

Car & Motorcycle

Driving in Hong Kong isn't for the faint-hearted. But if you are determined to see Hong Kong under your own steam try **Avis** (☑2890 6988; www.avis.com.hk; per day/week HK$970/3700, with chauffeur per hr HK$350, minimum 3hr) which has Honda Civics with unlimited kilometres.

Public Transport

No more rummaging in your purse for small change:

Airport Express Travel Pass ($220/300) Three consecutive days of unlimited travel on the MTR and one/two trips on the Airport Express.

MTR Tourist Day Pass (HK$55) Unlimited travel on the MTR for 24 hours.

Octopus card (www.octopuscards.com; HK$150, plus refundable deposit HK$50) Reusable 'smart cards' that are accepted on most forms of public transport, available at convenience stores, supermarkets and fast-food chains. You can add money on your card at MTR stations and 7-Eleven stores.

BUS Hong Kong's **bus system** (fares HK$2.50-52; ⊙5.30/6am-midnight/12.30am) will get you almost anywhere. Exact change or an Octopus card is required. The HKTB has leaflets on major bus routes. Bus companies:

City Bus and First Bus (www.nwstbus.com.hk)

Kowloon Motor Bus (www.kmb.hk)

New Lantau Bus (www.newlantaobus.com)

Major bus stops and stations:

Central Bus Terminus (Exchange Sq) Gets you to southern side of the island; buses 6, 6A and 260 leave for Stanley and Repulse Bay; buses 70 and 70P for Aberdeen.

Admiralty Above Admiralty MTR station; gets you to the southern side of the island.

Star Ferry Pier Has buses to Hung Hom station and points in eastern and western Kowloon.

PUBLIC LIGHT BUS Better known as 'minibuses', these 16-seaters come in two varieties:

With red roof/stripe Fares HK$2 to HK$22; supplement bus services. Get on or off almost anywhere – just yell 'ni do, m gói' (here, please); Octopus card accepted on certain routes.

With green roof/stripe Operate on more than 350 set routes and make designated stops; Octopus card accepted on all routes.

BEWARE: FAKE MONKS

Real monks in Hong Kong never solicit money. However, you may be approached in temples and even bars and shops by con artists in monks' habits who try to make you part with your money. The more aggressive may offer fake Buddhist amulets for sale, or force 'blessings' on you and then pester you for a donation. When accosted, just say 'no' and ignore them.

For more on scams, see p992.

CROSS-HARBOUR FERRY The **Star Ferry** (www.starferry.com.hk; from HK$2) operates on two routes: Central–Tsim Sha Tsui and Wan Chai–Tsim Sha Tsui.

OUTLYING ISLANDS FERRIES See schedules at ferry piers and ferry company websites, or ask for a pocket-sized timetable. Most ferries depart from the Outlying Islands Piers close to the IFC building in Central. The main companies are:

Hong Kong & Kowloon Ferry Co (www.hkkf.com.hk) Serves Lamma.

New World First Ferry (NWFF; www.nwff.com.hk) Services to Cheung Chau, Peng Chau and Lantau; an inter-island service connects the three.

TRAIN The **Mass Transit Railway** (MTR; www.mtr.com.hk; fares HK$4-25) runs 10 lines; buy tickets or use the Octopus card (slightly cheaper). Once past the turnstile, you must complete the journey within 150 minutes.

The MTR also runs overland services on two main lines and two smaller lines, offering transport to the New Territories:

East Rail From Hung Hom station in Kowloon to Lo Wu (HK$35) and Lok Ma Chau (HK$35), gateway to Shēnzhèn; a spur runs from Tai Wai to Wu Kai Sha.

Light Rail Fares HK$4 to HK$5.50; routes in western New Territories between Tuen Mun and Yuen Long, and feeds the West Rail.

West Rail From Hung Hom station to Tuen Mun (HK$20) via Yuen Long.

There are left-luggage lockers in major MTR train stations, including Hung Hom station.

TRAM Hong Kong's century-old **trams** (www.hktramways.com; fares HK$2.50) represent the only all double-decker wooden-sided tram fleet in the world. They operate on six overlapping routes running east–west along the northern side of Hong Kong Island.

Taxi

Hong Kong is served by taxis of three colours:

Blue Serving Lantau; HK$15 flag fall, then HK$1.30 for every 200m.

Green Serving the New Territories; HK$16.50 flag fall, then HK$1.30 for every 200m.

Red Serving Hong Kong Island and Kowloon; HK$20 flag fall for the first 2km, then HK$1.50 for every additional 200m.

Essential China

**Cuisine »
The Great Wall »
Temples »
Hiking »
Festivals »**

Cormorant fisherman on the Lí River near Xīngpíng (p599)

GLOWINGEARTH / GETTY IMAGES ©

Cuisine

To the Chinese, food is life. Dining is the cherished high point of the daily social calendar and often the one occasion to stop work and fully relax. The only problem is knowing where to begin: the sheer variety on offer can have your head spinning and your tummy quivering.

Noodles

1 Marco Polo may have nicked the recipe to make spaghetti (so they say), but he didn't quite get the flavouring right. Noodles range across an exciting spectrum of taste, from the wincingly spicy *dàndan miàn* (spicy noodles) through to the supersalty *zhájiàng miàn* (fried sauce noodles).

Dim Sum

2 Dim sum is steamed up across China, but like the Cantonese dialect, it's best left to the masters of the south to get it right. Hong Kong (p463), Macau (p511) and Guǎngzhōu (p535) should be your first stops – they set the dim sum benchmark.

Dumplings

3 Set your compass north and northeast for the best *jiǎozi* (dumplings) – leek, pork, lamb, crabmeat wrapped in an envelope of dough. If you like them crispy, get them *guōtiē* (fried). Shànghǎi's interpretation is *xiǎolóngbāo* – scrummy and steamed.

Peking Duck

4 Purists insist you must be in Běijīng for true Peking duck roasted to an amber hue over fruit tree wood. You might as well take their advice as that's where you'll find the best Peking duck restaurants (p93).

Hotpot

5 An all-weather meal, hotpot is ideal for banishing the bitter cold of a northern winter, while in steaming Chóngqìng (p761) old folk devour the spiciest variety in the height of summer.

Clockwise from top left
1 Rice noodles 2 Dim sum 3 Steamed dumplings
4 Peking duck

The Great Wall

China's elongated bastion ranges in fragments from the North Korean border, vaulting rivers, down to the sea, snaking over mountains around Běijīng, disappearing here and reappearing there before being ground down by the remorseless desert winds of the northwest.

Jīnshānlǐng

1 The hike from Jīnshānlǐng (p119) towards Sìmǎtái is ideal in late autumn, when Běijīng's weather is at its best; in the hammering heat of summer you'll need a lot of water and an effective sunhat.

Jiāyùguān Fort

2 Jiāyùguān Fort (p827) in Gānsù offers the unique image of a wind-blasted desert fort set against snowcapped mountains. China's Wild West kicks off here and you can explore vestiges of the wall running between ancient watchtowers.

Jiànkòu

3 Běijīng's most authentic part of the wall is not the easiest to reach, but it's worth the effort: Jiànkòu (p115) provides the best experience, the finest photos, an excellent workout and almost certainly unforgettable memories.

Huánghuā Chéng

4 A much-needed alternative to overdone and over-commercialised sections of wall, Huánghuā Chéng (p116) is an authentic rendition of the Great Wall. Excellent hiking awaits if you have time, shoes with a good grip and a sense of exploration.

Zhuàngdàokǒu

5 Great Wall purists will swoon at the unrestored brickwork at Zhuàngdàokǒu (p117), where images of the wall in varying stages of distress, dilapidation and restoration meet supreme views.

Clockwise from top left
1 Jīnshānlǐng 2 Jiāyùguān Fort
3 Jiànkòu unrestored section

Temples

Divided between Buddhist, Taoist and Confucian faiths, China's temples are places of introspection, peace and absolution. Find them on mountain peaks, in caves, on side streets, hanging from cliffsides or occupying the epicentre of town, from Tibet to Běijīng and beyond.

Temple of Heaven, Běijīng

1 Not really a temple, but let's not quibble. Běijīng's Temple of Heaven (p72) was China's graceful place of worship for the Ming and Qing emperors, encapsulating the Confucian desire for symmetry and order, and harmony between heaven and earth.

Pǔníng Temple, Chéngdé

2 On a clear day this temple (p136) stands out against the hills around Chéngdé, while in the Mahayana Hall is the Guanyin statue, a 22m-high, multiarmed embodiment of Buddhist benevolence – this is perhaps China's most astonishing statue.

Confucius Temple, Qūfù

3 This is China's largest and most important Confucius Temple (p157). The Shāndōng sage has had an immeasurable influence on the Chinese persona through the millennia – visit the town where it began and try to put his teachings in perspective.

Labrang Monastery, Xiàhé

4 If it's a hassle to rustle up a Tibet travel permit, pop down to this gargantuan Tibetan monastery (p816) in the scenic southwest corner of Gānsù. Its aura of devotion is amplified by the nonstop influx of Tibetan pilgrims and worshippers.

Jokhang Temple, Lhasa

5 Tibet's holiest place of worship, the Jokhang Temple (p886) in Lhasa is a place of pilgrimage for every Tibetan Buddhist at least once in their lifetime.

Right
1 Hall of Prayer for Good Harvests, Temple of Heaven Park, Běijīng 2 Pǔníng Temple, Chéngdé

Hiking

If you're keen to escape the cities into the great outdoors, China's dramatic variety of landscapes is the perfect backdrop for bracing walks – whether island-hopping in Hong Kong, exploring the foothills of the Himalayas or trekking through gorges in Yúnnán province.

Huángshān, Ānhuī

1 Sooner or later you'll have to hike uphill, and where better than up China's most beautiful mountain (p385). The steps may be punishing, but just focus on the scenery: even if the fabled mists are nowhere to be seen, the views are incredible.

Hong Kong's Outlying Islands & New Territories

2 A whopping 70% of Hong Kong is hiking territory, so fling off your Gucci loafers, lace up your hiking boots and go from island to island or make a break for the New Territories, where fantastic hiking trails await (p482).

Ganden to Samye, Tibet

3 You'll need four to five days for this glorious high-altitude hike connecting two of Tibet's most splendid monasteries (p894). The landscape is beautiful, but the trek requires preparation both physically and mentally, plus a Tibet travel permit.

Tiger Leaping Gorge, Yúnnán

4 The mother of all southwest China's treks, this magnificently named Yúnnán hike (p667) is at its most picturesque in early summer. It's not a walk in the park, so plan ahead and give yourself enough time.

Yángshuò, Guǎngxī

5 Yángshuò's karst topography (p595) is truly astonishing. Base yourself in town, give yourself three or four days, and walk your socks off (or hire a bike). Adventurous types can even try rock climbing.

Left
1 The archetypal Chinese mountain, Huángshān
2 Hiking the trails crossing Hong Kong Island

Festivals

China is a nation of hard workers and entrepreneurs, but considerable energy is reserved for its festivals and celebrations. Festivals can be religious, fun-filled, commemorative or seasonal. Locals don their best clothes and get seriously sociable. Join in and be part of the party.

Dragon Boat Festival

1 Commemorating the death of Qu Yuan, the celebrated third century BC poet and statesman, dramatic dragon boat races can be seen in May or June churning up the waterways across China, including in Shànghǎi, Hong Kong and Tiānjīn.

Ice and Snow Festival, Hā'ěrbīn

2 The arctic temperatures may knock the wind from your lungs, but in January the frost-bitten capital of Hēilóngjiāng province (p325) twinkles with an iridescent collection of carved ice sculptures.

Third Moon Fair, Dàlǐ

3 One of China's many ethnic minority festivals, and usually held in April, this Bai festival (p651) commemorates the appearance of Guanyin, the Bodhisattva of Mercy, to the people of the Nanzhao kingdom.

Spring Festival

4 China's most commercially driven and full-on celebration takes the entire nation by storm at midnight on the first day of the first lunar month. The fuse is lit on a nationwide arsenal of fireworks.

Monlam (Great Prayer) Festival, Xiàhé

5 Celebrated across Tibet, the highlight of this Buddhist festival (in February or March) is easiest to witness in the monastic town of Xiàhé (p818), where a host of celebrations include the unfurling of a huge *thangka* (sacred painting) on the hillside.

Right

1 Dragon boat racing during the dragon boat festival, Hong Kong Island 2 Ice and snow festival, Hā'ěrbīn

Macau

☎ 853 / POP 549,500

Includes »

Sights	512
Activities	523
Festivals & Events	523
Sleeping	523
Eating	526
Drinking	527
Entertainment	528
Shopping	529
Getting There & Away	531
Getting Around	531

Best Places to Eat

» Antonio (p526)

» Robuchon Au Dôme (p526)

» Tim's Kitchen (p526)

» Alfonso III (p526)

» Lung Wah Tea House (p527)

Best Sights

» Ruins of the Church of St Paul (p513)

» Guia Fort (p518)

» Mandarin's House (p513)

» St Lazarus District (p513)

Why Go?

The Chinese people have stood up and they're off to Macau. Chairman Mao (who coined the first half of that sentence) must be spinning in his glass coffin. Mainlanders can't get enough of this once Portuguese-administered backwater-turned-gambling-megaresort.

Such has been its explosive growth since 2002 that it is commonplace to refer to Macau as the Vegas of the East. It might be more appropriate to put that the other way round, since Macau has eclipsed its American rival in gambling income. And there are many other things that Macau does better. Beyond the gaming halls, it offers cobblestoned streets punctuated with Chinese temples and baroque churches, pockets of (natural) greenery, a historic centre of Unesco World Heritage status and balmy beaches.

Macau's history has also created a one-of-a-kind cuisine that celebrates the marriage of European, Latin American, African and Asian flavours.

When to Go

Macau

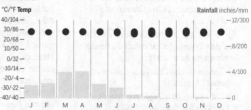

Mar–May Celebrate the arts, a sea goddess and a dragon as mist hangs over the harbour.

Jun–Sep Days in the shade of temples and dragon boats; nights aglow with fireworks.

Oct–Feb Music and Grand Prix in a high-octane run-up to Christmas and New Year.

History

Portuguese galleons first visited southern China to trade in the early 16th century, and in 1557, as a reward for clearing out pirates endemic to the area, they obtained a leasehold for Macau and were allowed to establish a tiny enclave here. The first Portuguese Governor of Macau was appointed in 1680, and as trade with China grew, so did Macau, which became the principal centre for Portuguese trade with China, Japan and Southeast Asia. However, after the Opium Wars between the Chinese and the British, and the subsequent establishment of Hong Kong, Macau went into a long decline.

China's Cultural Revolution spilled over into the territory as riots broke out in 1966. The Portuguese government tried to hand Macau back to China, but the latter, fearing the economic shock that would have on Hong Kong, refused the offer.

In 1999, under the Sino–Portuguese Joint Declaration, Macau was returned to China and designated a Special Administrative Region (SAR). Like Hong Kong, the pact ensures Macau a 'high degree of autonomy' in all matters (except defence and foreign affairs) for 50 years. The handover, however, did not change Macau as much as the termination of gambling monopoly in 2001 (see p528). Casinos mushroomed, transforming the skyline of the city, and tourists from mainland China surged.

Language

Cantonese and Portuguese are the official languages of Macau, though few people speak Portuguese. English is harder to find here than in Hong Kong, but in most midrange and top-end hotels, casinos, restaurants and tourist zones you should be able to get by. Mandarin is reasonably well understood, though note that most written Chinese is in traditional characters, not the simplified forms used on the mainland.

☉ Sights

For a small place (just 29 sq km), Macau is packed with important cultural and historical sights, including eight squares and 22 historic buildings, which have collectively been named the Historic Centre of Macau World Heritage site by Unesco. Most of the sights are on the peninsula. At many of these sites, seniors aged over 60 years and children 11 years or under are admitted free. The **Macau Museums Pass** (MOP$25) allows entry to a half-dozen museums over a five-day period.

CENTRAL MACAU PENINSULA

Running from Avenida da Praia Grande to the Inner Harbour, Avenida de Almeida Ribeiro – or San Ma Lo (新馬路; New Thoroughfare) in Cantonese – is the peninsula's

Macau Highlights

① Get context for your impressions at the **Macau Museum** (p513)

② Explore the ethereal ruins of the very symbol of Macau at the **Church of St Paul** (p513)

③ Take a stroll in the old quarter around **Rua dos Ervanários** and **Rua de Nossa Senhora do Amparo** (p529)

④ Sample Macau's unique cuisine at **Alfonso III** (p526)

⑤ Lose yourself in mazelike spaces at **Lou Lim Ioc Garden** (p519) and the **Mandarin's House** (p513)

⑥ Take the cable car to handsome **Guia Fort** (p518) and its gorgeous chapel

⑦ Mingle with artists on the cobbled paths of the charming **St Lazarus district** (p513)

main thoroughfare and home to the charming **Largo do Senado** (Map p520), a black and white tiled square close to major sights.

Ruins of the Church of St Paul RUINS
(大三巴牌坊; Map p516; Ruinas de Igreja de São Paulo; Rua de São Paulo; ☐8A, 17) A gateway to nowhere in the middle of the city is all that remains of the Church of St Paul, considered by some to be the greatest monument to Christianity in Asia. The church was designed by an Italian Jesuit and built in 1602 by Japanese Christian exiles and Chinese craftsmen. In 1835 a fire destroyed everything except the facade. Like much of Macau's colonial architecture, its European appearance belies the fascinating mix of influences (in this case, Chinese, Japanese, Indochinese) that contributed to its aesthetics. Behind the ruins, there's a small **Museum of Sacred Art** (天主教藝術博物館; Map p516; Museu de Arte Sacra; Rua de São Paulo; ⊙9am-6pm), and a crypt and ossuary.

Monte Fort &
Macau Museum   FORT, MUSEUM
(大炮台; Fortaleza do Monte; Map p520; admission free; ⊙7am-7pm Mon-Sun; ☐7, 8) Built by the Jesuits between 1617 and 1626, Monte Fort's barracks and storehouses were designed to allow the fort to survive a long siege, but the cannons were fired only once: during an aborted invasion by the Dutch in 1622. Now the ones on the south side are trained at Grand Lisboa Casino.

On the outside of the southeastern wall, under a cannon about 6m from the ground, is a (sealed) rectangular opening. This was a former door used by soldiers patrolling the old city wall, which was connected to the fort at a right angle. Housed in the fort is the remarkable **Macau Museum** (澳門博物館; Museu de Macau; Map p520; ☑2835 7911; www.macaumuseum.gov.mo; admission MOP$15; ⊙10am-5.30pm Tue-Sun), with exhibits on the history and traditions of Macau.

Mandarin's House   HISTORIC BUILDING
(鄭家大屋; Caso do Mandarim; Map p516; www.wh.mo/mandarinhouse; 10 Travessa de Antonio da Silva; admission free; ⊙10am-5.30pm Fri-Tue; ☐28B, 16) Built in 1869, this sprawling complex with more than 60 rooms was the ancestral home of Zheng Guanying, an author-merchant whose readers included emperors, Dr Sun Yatsen and Chairman Mao. The stunning compound features a moon gate, courtyards and halls, in a labyrinthine arrangement.

EXCHANGE RATES

Australia	A$1	MOP$ 8.27
Canada	C$1	MOP$ 8.02
China	¥1	MOP$ 1.28
Euro zone	€1	MOP$ 10.24
Hong Kong	HK$1	MOP$1.03
Japan	¥1	MOP$ 0.099
New Zealand	NZ$1	MOP$ 6.59
UK	UK£1	MOP$ 12.795
USA	US$1	MOP$ 7.98

For current exchange rates see www.xe.com.

St Lazarus
Church District   NEIGHBOURHOOD
(瘋堂斜巷; Calcada da Igreja de Sao Lazaro; Map p520; ☐7, 8) A lovely neighbourhood with quiet houses and cobbled streets. Artists, designers and independents have been setting up shop here during the past few years.

The **St Lazarus Church District Creative Industries Promotion Association** (望德堂區創意產業促進會; www.cipa.org.mo) lines up tenants and organises the weekly **Sun Never Left – Public Art Performance** (p528). Check the website for updates. Following are some of the neighbourhood's highlights.

The **Old Ladies' House** (仁慈堂婆仔屋; Map p520; www.albcreativelab.com; 8 Calcada da Igreja de Sao Lazaro; ⊙noon-7pm Wed-Mon) sheltered Portuguese refugees from Shànghǎi in WWII and later housed homeless, elderly women. It is now run by a group of avant-garde designers. Out front, there's a poetic courtyard with old trees. Fashion boutique **Lines Lab** (p529) and Portuguese grocery shop **Mercearia Portuguesa** (p529) are also here.

G32 (Map p520; ☑2834 6626; 32 Rua de Sao Miguel; free guided tours 3-5pm Sat & Sun) is a restored tenement building that's been refurbished as a Macanese home from the 1960s

PRICE INDICATORS

The following price indicators are used in this chapter and are quoted in patacas (MOP$) unless otherwise stated. Note that prices for eating are per meal:

Sleeping

$	less than MOP$700
$$	MOP$700 to MOP$2000
$$$	more than MOP$2000

Eating

$	less than MOP$200
$$	MOP$200 to MOP$400
$$$	more than MOP$400

and '70s. The three-storey structure with a narrow staircase features wooden floorboards and retro furniture.

Tai Fung Tong Art House (大瘋堂藝社; Map p520; ☑2835 3537; 7 Calcada da Igreja de Sao Lazaro; ☑2-6pm, closed Mon) is a gorgeous historical building featuring a mix of Chinese and European architectural styles. Built almost a century ago by a philanthropist, it's now occupied by a group that promotes Chinese heritage. The house has displays of traditional Chinese artefacts and calligrapher Carlos Choi is sometimes seen demonstrating his art.

G17 (p529) is a new exhibition space for pottery artists and Jabber Cafe (p528), run by a fashion designer, is also here.

Church of St Dominic   CHURCH
(聖母堂; Igreja de São Domingos; Map p520; Largo de São Domingos; ☑10am-6pm; ☐3, 6) This lovely 17th-century baroque church occupies the site of a convent built by the Spanish Dominicans in 1587. It contains the **Treasury of Sacred Art** (聖物寶庫; Tresouro de Arte Sacra; Map p520; admission free; ☑10am-6pm), an Aladdin's cave of ecclesiastical art, including dismembered relics and a skull.

FREE **Lou Kau Mansion**   HISTORIC BUILDING
(盧家大屋; Casa de Lou Kau; Map p520; 7 Travessa da Sé; ☑9am-7pm Tue-Sun; ☐2, 3) Built in 1889, this elegant Cantonese-style mansion with southern European elements belonged to a merchant. Behind the grey facade, a maze of open and semi-enclosed spaces mesmerise with stained-glass windows.

St Joseph's Seminary Church   CHURCH
(聖若瑟修院及聖堂; Capela do Seminario São Jose; Map p520; Rua do Seminario; ☑10am-5pm; ☐9, 16) One of Macau's most beautiful buildings and the best example of tropicalised baroque, the church was consecrated in 1758 as part of the Jesuit seminary. It has a lemon-meringue facade and the first dome to be built in all of China.

Leal Senado   NOTABLE BUILDING
(民政總署大樓; Map p520; 163 Avenida de Almeida Ribeiro; ☐3, 6) The 'Loyal Senate' is home to Macau's main municipal administrative body. If you walk through, there's a peaceful courtyard and the stately **Senate Library** (☑1-7pm) out the back. Inside, the **IACM Gallery** (☑9am-9pm Tue-Sun) holds well-curated exhibitions.

Na Tcha Temple   TEMPLE
(哪咤古廟; Templo de Na Tcha; Map p516; Rua de São Paulo; ☑8am-5pm; ☐8A, 17) There's no better symbol of Macau's cultural diversity than this Chinese temple (c 1888), sitting quietly in the compound of the Ruins of the Church of St Paul. It's dedicated to the child god of war to halt the plague that was occurring at the time. Incidentally, the wall outside the temple, often said to be a section of the old city walls, is in fact the wall of the former St Paul's College.

Ox Warehouse   CULTURAL BUILDING
(牛房倉庫; Map p516; http://oxwarehouse.blogspot.com; cnr Avenida do Coronel Mesquita & Almirante Lacerda; ☑noon-7pm Wed-Mon; ☐1A, 12) This atmospheric former slaughterhouse is a happening art space featuring engagingly experiential exhibitions and performances.

Pawnshop Museum   MUSEUM
(典當業展示館; Espaço Patrimonial – Uma Casa de Penhores Tradicional; Map p520; 396 Avendia de Almeida Ribeiro; admission MOP$5; ☑10.30am-7pm, closed 1st Mon of month; ☐3, 6) Occupying

MACAU PRIMER

Like Hong Kong's, Macau's political and economic systems are still significantly different from those of mainland China. See p989 for information on money, and p994 for details on visas. The term 'Macanese' refers specifically to people of Portuguese descent who were born in Macau, or their traditions.

the premises of a former pawnshop (c 1917), this quaint museum shows how this once-thriving business was run in Macau.

FREE **AFA (Art for All Society)** GALLERY
(全藝社; Map p516; ☑ 2836 6064; www.afamacau .com; 10th fl Edificio da Fabrica de Baterias NE National, 52 Estrada da Areia Preta; ⊗ noon-7pm Mon-Sat) Macau's very best contemporary art can be seen at this nonprofit gallery founded in 2007 by a local artist. There are monthly exhibitions by Macau's artists. The gallery is located near the Mong Ha Multi-sport Pavilion (望廈體育館). Take bus 8, 8A or 7 and get off at Rua Da Barca or Rua De Francisco Xavier Pereira. Alternatively, it's a 20-minute walk from Largo do Senado.

SOUTHERN MACAU PENINSULA
The southern Macau Peninsula features a number of old colonial houses and baroque churches that are best visited on foot.

Colonial Macau HISTORIC NEIGHBOURHOOD
From Avenida de Almeida Ribeiro, follow Calçada do Tronco Velho to the **Church of St Augustine** (聖奧斯定教堂; Igreja de Santo Agostinho; Map p520; Largo de Santo Agostinho; ⊗ 10am-6pm; ☐ 3,6), dating from 1814. Facing the church is China's first Western theatre, the **Dom Pedro V Theatre** (崗頂劇院; Teatro Dom Pedro; Map p520; Calçada do Teatro; ☐ 9, 16). This 19th-century pastel-green building is not open to the public.

Next up is the **Church of St Lawrence** (聖老楞佐教堂; Igreja de São Lourenço; Map p516; Rua da Imprensa Nacional; ⊗ 10am-6pm Tue-Sun, 1-2pm Mon; ☐ 3, 6) with its magnificent painted ceiling. Walk down Travessa do Padre Narciso to the pink **Government House** (特區政府總部; Sede do Goberno; Map p516; cnr Avenida da Praia Grande & Travessa do Padré Narciso), the headquarters of the Macau SAR government.

The oldest section of Macau is a short distance southwest of here, via the waterfront promenade **Avenida da República** (Map p516). Along this stretch you'll see several colonial villas and civic buildings. These include the **residence of the Portuguese consul-general** (葡國駐澳門領事官邸; Consulado-Geral de Portugal em Macau; Map p516; Rua do Boa Vista), which was once the Hotel Bela Vista, one of the most storied hotels in Asia. Nearby is the ornate **Santa Sancha Palace** (禮賓府; Palacete de Santa Sancha; Map p516; Estrada de Santa Sancha), once the residence of Macau's Portuguese governors.

MACAU IN ONE DAY

Start in the **Largo do Senado** and wander up to the **Ruins of the Church of St Paul**. Spend an hour or so in the **Macau Museum** to give it all some context, before getting a feel for Macau's living history as you wander back through the tiny streets towards the Inner Harbour port and lunch at **Litoral**. After lunch take a look around the **A-Ma Temple** before jumping on a bus to sleepy **Coloane Village**. Take an easy stroll around here and bus it back via the **Cotai Strip** for an awe-inspiring look at the megaresorts. Have dinner at unpretentious **Alfonso III**, then, for contrast, head for the gaudy magnificence of the **Grand Lisboa casino**, before enjoying rooftop drinks at **Corner's Wine Bar & Tapas Cafe**. If you've still got the energy, saunter over to **Macau Soul** for live jazz.

TOP CHOICE **Macau Museum of Art** MUSEUM
(澳門藝術博物館; Museu de Arte de Macau; Map p516; www.mam.gov.mo; Macau Cultural Centre, Avenida Xian Xing Hai; admission MOP$5, ⊗ 10am-6.30pm Tue-Sun; ☐ 1A, 8) This vast, excellent museum houses rotating exhibits as well as permanent collections of works by established Chinese and Western artists such as George Chinnery (1774–1852), who spent most of his adult life in Macau painting.

A-Ma Temple TEMPLE
(媽閣廟; Templo de A-Ma; Map p516; Rue de São Tiago da Barra; ⊗ 7am-6pm; ☐ 1, 5) The A-Ma Temple is dedicated to A-Ma (better known as Tin Hau, the goddess of the sea), from which the name Macau is derived. Many believe that when the Portuguese asked the name of the place, they were told 'A-Ma Gau' (bay of A-Ma). In modern Cantonese, 'Macau' is Ou Mun (澳門), meaning 'gateway of the bay'.

Penha Hill SCENIC AREA
(主教山; Colina da Penha; Map p516; ☐ 6, 9) The views here are excellent, as are buildings such as Bishop's Palace, the Chapel of Our Lady of Penha (Capela de Nostra Senora da Penha) and modernist villas.

Moorish Barracks HISTORIC BUILDING
(港務局大樓; Capitania dos Portos; Map p516; Barra Hill; ☐ 2, 5) Italian-designed, this lovely neoclassical building with Moorish

Macau Peninsula

Rotunda da
Amizade

0   500
0   0.25 miles

Av do Nordeste

48

Rua de Maio

Av Leste do Hipódromo

Rua do Canal
Novo

Reservoir

Rua dos Pescadores

Cemetery

Estrada de Ferreira do amaral

Montanha
Russa
Garden

6

4
Guia
Hill

Flora
Garden

9

Guanshan Waterway

Rua de Terminal
Marítimo

Rua de Malaca

49

50

1

38

Mong Ha
Multi-sport
Pavilion

Travessa
de Praia

E do Arco
Lin
Fung Temple

32

Av do Coronel
Mesquita

Ferreira de
Almeida

Rua de Silva Mendes

Travessa
do Túnel

8

10

Rua de Conselheiro Xavier Pereira

26
Av do

11

Colonial
Buildings

27

Tap
Seac
Square

Macau
Peninsula

Calçada do Gaio

E do Almirante Lacerda

41

20

2

23

39

Rua de Brás
da Rosa

Av Horta e Costa

Rua de Almirante Costa Cabral

Rua do Coelho do Amaral

Estrada de Adolfo
de Loureiro

40

Rua du Campo

Av do Conselheiro Borja

Av do General
Castelo Branco

Ribeira do Patane

Rua da

37

Travessa
Corda

Entre Campos

Rua de Tomás Vieira

18 24

Rua de
São Paulo

Ilha
Verde

Inner
Harbour

12

Luis de Camões
Garden &
Grotto

17

19

Praça de
Luís de Camões

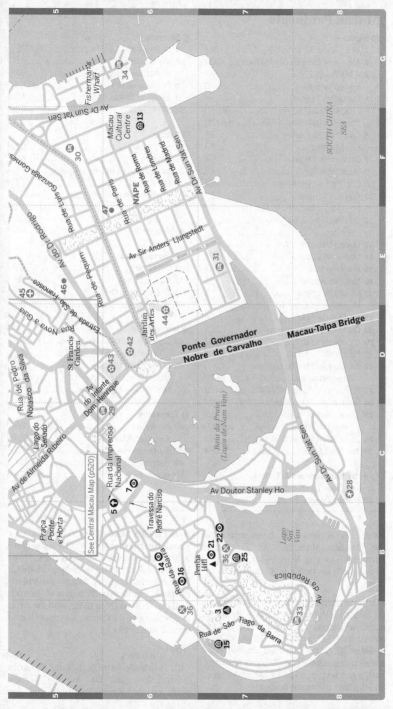

Macau Peninsula

⊙ Sights

1 AFA (Art for All Society) E2
2 Almirante Lacerda (Red Market)..........D2
3 A-Ma Temple...A7
   Bishop's Palace............................ (see 21)
4 Cable Car Terminus..............................F4
   Chapel of Our Lady of Guia.............(see 9)
   Chapel of Our Lady of Penha ...... (see 21)
5 Church of St Lawrence B6
6 Flora Garden..F3
7 Government House C6
8 Guia Cable Car.......................................E3
9 Guia Fort & Lighthouse.........................E4
10 Kun Iam Temple.....................................E2
11 Lou Lim Ioc Garden................................E3
12 Luís de Camões Garden &
   Grotto C3
13 Macau Museum of Art............................F6
14 Mandarin's House..................................B6
15 Maritime Museum A7
16 Moorish Barracks B6
17 Museu do Oriente C3
   Museum of Sacred Art................ (see 24)
18 Na Tcha Temple.....................................C4
19 Old Protestant Cemetery C3
20 Ox Warehouse D2
21 Penha Hill...B7
22 Residence of the Portuguese
   Consul General....................................B7
23 Rotunda de Caros da Maia D3
24 Ruins of the Church of St Paul..............C4
25 Santa Sancha Palace B7
   Sr Wong Ieng Kuan Library.......... (see 12)
26 Sun Yatsen Memorial House.................E3
27 Tap Seac Square....................................E4

⊙ Activities, Courses & Tours

   Gray Line Tours............................ (see 50)
28 Macau Tower...C8

⊙ Sleeping

29 Hotel Sintra...C6
30 Mandarin Oriental F5
31 MGM Grand Macau E7
32 Pousada de Mong Há.............................E2
33 Pousada de São Tiago...........................A8
34 Rocks Hotel G6

⊗ Eating

35 Henri's Galley...B7
36 Litoral...A6
37 Lung Wah Tea House.............................C2
38 O Porto...E2
   Robuchon Au Dôme..................... (see 43)
   Tim's Kitchen .... (see 42)
39 Toung King D3
40 Xina Cafe D4

⊗ Entertainment

41 Canidrome D1
42 Casino Lisboa..D6
43 Grand Lisboa Casino.............................D6
44 Wynn Macau D6

⊙ Information

45 Centro Hospitalar Conde São
   Januário.. E5
46 China Travel Service E5
   MGTO (Ferry Terminal)................(see 50)
   MGTO (Guia Lighthouse) ....(see 9)

⊙ Transport

47 Air Macau E6
   Avis Rent A Car...........................(see 50)
48 Burgeon Rent A Car G1
49 Heliport..G4
50 Macau Ferry Terminal G4

influences is now the headquarters of the Macau Maritime Administration. Turn right as you leave A-Ma Temple; a 10-minute walk uphill will take you to the barracks.

Maritime Museum MUSEUM
(海事博物館; Museu Marítimo; Map p516; www.museumaritimo.gov.mo; 1 Largo do Pagode da Barra; admission MOP$10, Sun MOP$5; ☺10am-5.30pm Wed-Mon; ☒2, 5) The Maritime Museum has interesting artefacts from Macau's seafaring past, a mock-up of a Hakka fishing village, and displays of dragon boats.

NORTHERN MACAU PENINSULA
The northern peninsula is quite a good area to just wander around in. The historic **Three Lamps** (三盞燈; *saam jaan dang*) district is known for its Southeast Asian – particularly Burmese – influences. It begins at Rotunda de Caros da Maia (Map p516), with the street lamps that give it its name, and sprawls over several square blocks.

TOP CHOICE Guia Fort FORT
(東望洋山堡壘; Fortaleza de Guia; Map p516; ☺9am-5.30pm; ☒2, 17) As the highest point on the Macau Peninsula, this fort

MACAU'S INNER BEAUTIES

Lovely Libraries

Macau's libraries show how tiny proportions can be beautiful.

Sir Robert Ho Tung Library (何東圖書館; Map p520; ☎2837 7117; 3 Largo de St Agostinho; ⊙10am-7pm Mon-Sat, 11am-7am Sun; @) is a stunner comprising a 19th-century villa and a glass and steel extension rising above a back garden, with Piranesi-like bridges shooting out between the two.

Chinese Reading Room (八角亭; Map p520; Rua de Santa Clara; ⊙9am-noon & 7pm-midnight) is a former drinks booth, known as 'Octagonal Pavilion' (c 1926) in Chinese.

Sr Wong Ieng Kuan Library (白鴿巢公園黃營均圖書館; Map p516; ☎2895 3075; Praça de Luís de Camões; ⊙8am-8pm, closed Mon; @) is an oasis of calm between a boulder (which juts into its interior) and a banyan tree (which frames its entrance) in the Luís de Camões Garden.

Coloane Library (路環圖書館; Map p524; ☎2888 2254; Av de Cinco de Outubro, Coloane; ⊙1-7pm Mon-Sat; @), a mini Grecian temple c 1917, has a pediment and too-fat columns.

Modernist Marvels

Pier 8 (8號碼頭; Map p520; Rua do Dr Lourenco Pereira Marquez) is a fine example of Chinese modernism in grey, 50 paces south from Macau Masters Hotel; best views are from the **South Sampan Pier** (南舢板碼頭; Cais de Sampanas Sul; Map p520) next door.

East Asia Hotel (東亞酒店; Map p520; cnr Rua do Guimares & Rua da Madeira) has Chinese art deco in mint green; it's a little shabby, very chic; and **Almirante Lacerda** (紅街市大樓; Mercado Almirante Lacerda; Map p516; cnr Avs do Almirante Lacerda & Horta e Costa; ⊙7.30am-7.30pm) is an art deco 'Red Market' that houses a wet market.

---

affords panoramic views of the city and, on a clear day, across to the islands and China. At the top you'll find a **lighthouse**, built in 1865 and the oldest on the China coast, and the lovely **Chapel of Our Lady of Guia** (聖母雪地殿聖堂; Capela de Nossa Señora da Guia; Map p516; ⊙10am-5pm Tue-Sun), built in 1622 and retaining almost 100% of its original features, including one of the most valuable mural paintings in East Asia. Walk up or take the **Guia Cable Car** (東望洋山纜車; Teleférico da Guia; Map p516; one way/return MOP$3/5; ⊙8am-6pm Tue-Sun) that runs from the entrance to **Flora Garden** (二龍喉公園; Jardim da Flora; Map p516; Travessa do Túnel; ⊙7.30am-8.30pm), Macau's largest public park.

Lou Lim Ioc Garden　　　　GARDEN
(盧廉若公園; Jardim Lou Lim Ioc; Map p516; 10 Estrada de Adolfo Loureiro; ⊙6am-9pm; ☐12, 16) A cool and shady Sūzhōu-style garden with pavilions, lotus ponds, bamboo groves, grottoes and a bridge with nine turns (to escape from evil spirits, who can only move in straight lines). You'll see locals practising taichi or playing Chinese musical instruments here.

Luís de Camões Garden & Grotto　　GARDEN
(白鴿巢公園(賈梅士公園; Jardim e Gruta de Luís de Camões; Map p516; free admission; ⊙6am-10pm; ☐8A, 17) This relaxing park is dedicated to the one-eyed poet Luís de Camões (1524–80), who is said to have written part of his epic *Os Lusíadas* in Macau, though there is little evidence that he ever reached the city. **Sr Wong Leng Kuan Library** is inside the garden.

TOP CHOICE **Kun Iam Temple**　　TEMPLE
(觀音廟; Templo de Kun Iam; Map p516; Avenida do Coronel Mesquita; ⊙10am-6pm) Dating back four centuries, Kun Iam Temple is Macau's oldest and most interesting temple. The likeness of Kun Iam, the Goddess of Mercy, is in the main hall; to the left of the altar and behind glass is a statue of a bearded arhat rumoured to represent Marco Polo. The first treaty of trade and friendship between the USA and China was signed in the temple's terraced gardens in 1844.

Tap Seac Square　　SQUARE
(塔石廣場; Map p516; ☐7,8) Bold and beautiful, this square lined with important historic architecture was designed by Macanese

Central Macau

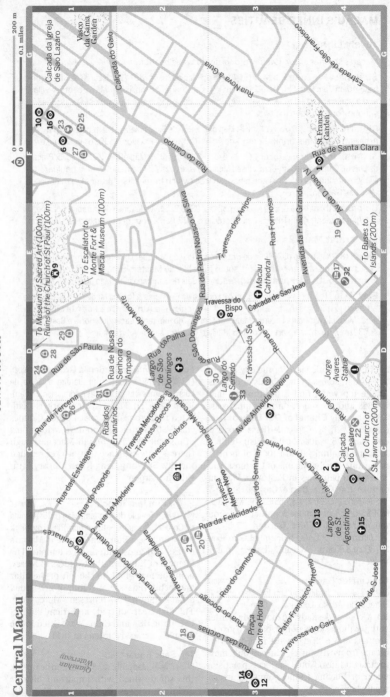

MACAU SIGHTS

Central Macau

◎ Sights

1 Chinese Reading Room...........................F4
2 Church of St Augustine..........................C4
3 Church of St Dominic............................D2
4 Dom Pedro V Theatre C4
5 East Asia Hotel..B1
6 G32 ....F1
  IACM Gallery.................................(see 7)
7 Leal Senado...C3
8 Lou Kau Mansion D3
  Macau Museum..............................(see 9)
9 Monte Fort E1
10 Old Ladies' House...................................F1
11 Pawnshop Museum.................................C2
12 Pier 8 ....A3
  Senate Library...............................(see 7)
13 Sir Robert Ho Tung Library B4
14 South Sampan Pier A3
15 St Joseph's Seminary Church..............B4
16 Tai Fung Tong Art House......................F1
  Treasury of Sacred Art..................(see 3)

◎ Sleeping

17 Augusters Lodge.....................................E4
18 Macau Masters Hotel.............................A2
19 New Nam Pan Hotel E4
20 San Va Hospedaria.................................B2
21 Vila Universal...B2

◎ Eating

22 Alfonso III..C4

◎ Drinking

23 Jabber F1

◎ Entertainment

24 Macau Soul..D1
25 Sun Never Left - Public Art
  Performance.......................................F1

◎ Shopping

26 Flea Market..C1
27 G17..F1
  Lines Lab ....(see 10)
28 Macau Creations D1
  Mercearia Portuguesa.................(see 10)
29 MOD Design Store D1
30 Pinto Livros..D3
31 Traditional Shops D1

◎ Information

32 Companhia de
  Telecomunicações de
  Macau (CTM).......................................E4
33 MGTO (Largo do Senado).....................D3

MACAU SIGHTS

architect Carlos Marreiros, who also created Tap Seac Health Centre (adjacent to Cultural Affairs Bureau), a contemporary interpretation of Macau's neoclassical buildings featuring wavy glass suggestive of windblown *cheongsams* (Chinese dress for women).

FREE Sun Yatsen Memorial House MUSEUM
(國父紀念館; Casa Memorativa de Doutor Sun Yat Sen; Map p516; ☑2857 4064; 1 Rua de Silva Mendes; ⊗10am-5pm Wed-Mon; ☐2, 9) This neo-Moorish house commemorates Dr Sun Yatsen (1866–1925), founder of the Chinese republic, though he never lived in it.

Museu do Oriente GALLERY
(東方基金會　博物館; Map p516; www.foriente. pt; 13 Praça de Luís de Camões; ⊗10am-5.30pm Mon-Fri, 10am-7pm daily during exhibitions) Housed in Casa Garden, the former headquarters of the British East India Company, this gallery mounts some of the best exhibitions of contemporary and ancient art in Macau.

Old Protestant Cemetery CEMETERY
(基督教墳場; Antigo Cemitério Protestante; Map p516; 15 Praça de Luís de Camões; ⊗8.30am-5.30pm; ☐8A, 17) This cemetery was established in 1821 as the last resting place of (mostly Anglophone) Protestants. Among those interred here is Irish-born artist George Chinnery.

THE ISLANDS

Connected to the Macau mainland by three bridges and joined together by an ever-growing area of reclaimed land called Cotai, Coloane and, to a lesser extent, Taipa are oases of calm and greenery. By contrast, the Cotai Strip is development central, with megacasinos sprouting up.

TOP CHOICE Taipa ISLAND
(氹仔; Tam Chai in Cantonese; Map p522) Traditionally an island of duck farms and boat yards, Taipa is rapidly becoming urbanised and now houses hotels, a university, a racecourse, a stadium and an airport.

The Islands – Taipa

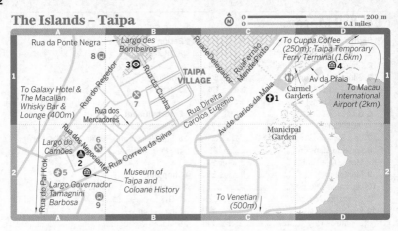

The Islands – Taipa

◎ Sights
1 Church of Our Lady of Carmel............C1
2 Pak Tai Temple.................................A2
3 Taipa Flea Market.............................B1
4 Taipa House Museum.........................D1

◑ Activities, Courses & Tours
5 Aluguer de Bicicletas.........................A2

⊗ Eating
6 Antonio...A2
7 O Santos...B1

❶ Transport
Bicycle Rental..............................(see 9)
8 Bus Stop...A1
9 Main Bus Stop..................................A2

But a parade of baroque churches, temples, overgrown esplanades and lethargic settlements mean it's still possible to experience the traditional charms of the island.

Taipa Village, in the north-central part of the island, is a window to the island's past. Here you'll find the **Taipa House Museum** (龍環葡韻; Casa Museum da Taipa; Map p522; Avenida da Praia; admission MOP$5; ⊙10am-5.30pm Tue-Sun; ⊡22, 26), housed in five waterfront villas that give a sense of how the Macanese middle-class lived in the early 20th century. Also in the village is the **Church of Our Lady of Carmel** (嘉模聖母堂; Igreja de Nossa Senhora de Carmo; Map p522; Avenida de Carlos da Maia; ⊡22, 26) and temples including **Pak Tai Temple** (北帝廟; Templo Pak Tai; Map p522; Largo do Camões).

The small **Taipa Flea Market** (Map p522; www.iacm.gov.mo; Bombeiros Square, Rua do Regedor & Rua das Gaivotas; ⊙11am-8pm Sun), organised for most parts of the year, is a good place to shop for souvenirs.

You can rent bicycles in Taipa Village from **Aluguer de Bicicletas** (Map p522; ☎2882 7975; 36 Largo Governador Tamagnini Barbosa); there's no English sign but it's next to the Don Quixote restaurant.

Coloane ISLAND
(路環; Lo Wan in Cantonese; Map p524) A haven for pirates until the start of the 20th century, Coloane, considerably larger than Taipa, is the only part of Macau that doesn't seem to be changing at a head-spinning rate, which is a relief.

All buses stop at the roundabout in Coloane Village, which overlooks mainland China across the water. The main attractions here are the **Chapel of St Francis Xavier** (聖方濟各教堂; Capela de São Francisco Xavier; Map p524; Avenida de Cinco de Outubro; ⊙10am-8pm; ⊡21, 25), built in 1928 and which contains a relic of the saint's arm bone, and **Tam Kong Temple** (譚公廟; Templo Tam Kong; Map p524; Largo Tam Kong Miu; ⊙8.30am-6pm; ⊡21A, 25), which has a dragon boat made of whale bone.

About 1.5km southeast of Coloane Village is **Cheoc Van Beach** (Map p524; Bamboo Bay; ⊡21A, 25), while larger and more popular **Hác Sá Beach** lies to the northeast.

Atop **Alto de Coloane** (170m), the 20m-high **A-Ma Statue** (媽祖像及媽閣廟; Estátua da Deusa A-Ma; Estrada do Alto de Coloane) represents the goddess who gave Macau its name.

Hewn from white jade, it stands beside the enormous **Tian Hou Temple** (天后廟; ⊗8am-6pm), which forms the core of the touristy **A-Ma Cultural Village** (媽祖文化村). A free shuttle runs every 30 minutes (9am to 6pm) from the ornamental gate on Estrada de Seac Pai Van.

🏃 Activities

While Macau is no adventure paradise, it offers a taste of everything from spectator sport to extreme sport. For more ways to get those endorphins flowing, visit www.iacm. gov.mo (click 'facilities').

AJ Hackett ADVENTURE CLIMBS
(☑8988 8875; http://macau.ajhackett.com) New Zealand–based AJ Hackett organises all kinds of adventure climbs up and around the Macau Tower.

Macau Motor Sports Club GO-KARTING
(☑2888 2126; Estrada de Seac Pai Van, Coloane; per 10/20min MOP$100/180; ⊗11:30am-7pm Mon-Fri, 11am-8pm Sat & Sun; ☐21A, 25) This club has a picturesque 1.2km professional go-karting circuit at the southern end of the Cotai Strip.

Macau Formula 3 Grand Prix CAR RACING
(☑2855 5555; www.macau.grandprix.gov.mo) Macau's biggest sporting event of the year is the Macau Formula 3 Grand Prix, held in the third week of November. The 6.2km Guia circuit starts near the Lisboa Hotel and follows the shoreline along Avenida da Amizade, going around the reservoir and back through the city.

Cycling

There are two cycling trails in Taipa. The longer **Taipa Grande trail** (☐21A, 26) can be accessed via a paved road off the Estrada Colonel Nicolau de Mesquita, near the United Chinese Cemetery; whereas the **Taipa Pequena Trail** (☐21A, 33) is reachable by way of Estrada Lou Lim Ioc, behind the Regency Hotel. Bicycles can be rented from a kiosk near the bus stop adjacent to the Museum of Taipa and Coloane History in Taipa Village.

Hiking

Macau's hiking trails are not difficult and you can quickly get to a road to flag down a taxi if necessary. The longest one is the 8100m **Coloane Trail**, which begins in the mid-section of Estrada do Alto de Coloane and winds around the island.

You can also make a detour to **Alto de Coloane** (170m) to see the A-Ma Statue. **Guia Hill** on the peninsula has a popular pedestrian trail. As you leave the fort, turn right on Estrada do Engenheiro Trigo.

👉 Tours

Quality Tours, coach trips organised by the MGTO (Macau Government Tourist Office) and tendered to such agents as **Gray Line** (錦倫旅行社; Map p516; ☑2833 6611; Room 1015, ground fl, Macau Ferry Terminal; adult MOP$880-1800, child MOP$810-1470), take about 10 hours.

🎉 Festivals & Events

The mixing of two very different cultures for more than 400 years has left Macau with a unique collection of festivals and cultural events. For exact dates, check www.macau tourism.gov.mo or the individual event's website.

Lunar new year is in late January or early February; **Procession of the Passion of Our Lord** takes place in February; and both the **Macau Arts Festival** (www.icm.gov.mo/fam), which sees local and overseas music ensembles and dance and theatre troupes performing in Macau, and the **A-Ma Festival**, which honours the Goddess of the Sea, are held in May.

A **feast of the drunken dragon**, arguably the most unique festival and featuring a dragon dance performed by intoxicated men through markets and lanes, is in May or June.

The **dragon boat festival** takes place in June; an **international fireworks display contest** is held in September; and an **international music sestival** (www.icm.gov.mo/fimm) is in October and November.

The end of the year is greeted by the **Macau Formula 3 Grand Prix** (www.macau.grandprix. gov.mo) during the third weekend in November; and the **Macau International Marathon** (www.sport.gov.mo) takes place on the first Sunday of December.

🛏 Sleeping

Most of Macau's hotels are aimed at moneyed visitors rather than budget travellers.

For those with the cash, there are some world-class options. Rates shoot up on Friday or Saturday, while during the week you can find some incredible deals at travel agencies, hotel websites and specialist sites such as www.macau.com, and booths

The Islands – Coloane

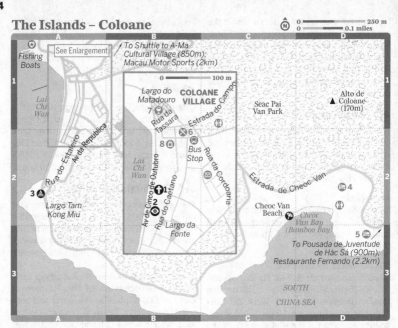

The Islands – Coloane

⦿ Sights
1 Chapel of St Francis Xavier B2
2 Coloane Library..................................B2
3 Tam Kong Temple A2

🛏 Sleeping
4 Pousada de Coloane............................D2
5 Pousada de Juventude de
   Cheoc Van..D3

✘ Eating
6 Café Nga Tim.......................................B2

🍸 Drinking
7 Lord Stow's Cafe B1

🛍 Shopping
8 Asian Artefacts...................................B2

at Hong Kong's **Shun Tak Centre** (200 Connaught Rd, Sheung Wan) from where the Macau ferries depart, and the arrivals hall of the Macau Ferry Terminal.

All rooms listed here have air-conditioning and bathroom unless otherwise stated. Most midrange and top-end hotels have shuttle buses from the ferry terminal.

MACAU PENINSULA

Cheap guesthouses occupy central Macau, on and around Rua das Lorchas and Avenida de Almeida Ribeiro, with options aplenty on Rua da Felicidade, the hub of the former red-light district, while the top-end casino-hotels generally occupy the southeast and centre of town.

TOP **Mandarin Oriental**   LUXURY HOTEL **$$$**
(文華東方酒店; Map p516; ☑8805 8888; www.mandarinoriental.com/macau; Avenida Dr Sun Yat Sen; r MOP$3500-4500, ste from MOP$6200; 🐕@🛜🏊) A great high-end option, the Mandarin has everything associated with the brand – understated elegance, superlative service, comfortable rooms and excellent facilities. A refreshing contrast to the glossy casino-hotels.

San Va Hospedaria   GUESTHOUSE **$**
(新華旅店; Map p520; ☑2857 3701; www.sanvahotel.com; 65-67 Rua da Felicidade; r MOP$150-270; 🖃3, 6) Built in 1873, San Va is about the cheapest and most atmospheric lodging in town (Wong Kar-wai filmed parts of the classic 2004 film, *2046* here). It is, however, very basic, with tiny rooms and shared bathrooms.

TOP CHOICE **Pousada de Mong Há** INN $$

(望廈賓館; Map p516; ☑2851 5222; www.ift.edu.mo; Colina de Mong Há; r MOP$600-1200, ste from MOP$1200; ◯@☎; ☑5, 22, 25) This attractive Portuguese-style inn atop Mong Há Hill is an old barracks and is now run by tourism students. The rooms are simple, homely and squeaky clean. The rates are among the best in the city.

Pousada de São Tiago LUXURY HOTEL $$$

(聖地牙哥酒店; Map p516; ☑2837 8111; www.saotiago.com.mo; Fortaleza de São Tiago da Barra, Avenida de República; ste MOP$3000-4200); ◯@☎; ☑6, 9, 28B) The 'St James Inn', built into the ruins of a 17th-century fort, has 12 balconied suites with splendid views of the harbour. It's romantic, old-fashioned and expensive.

MGM Grand Macau LUXURY HOTEL $$$

(澳門美高梅酒店; Map p516; ☑8802 1888; www.mgmgrandmacau.com; Avenida Dr Sun Yat Sen, NAPE; r from MOP$3200, ste from MOP$7800; ◯@☎≋; ☑8, 3A, 12) This casino-hotel has a youthful vibe and contemporary architecture featuring a baroque-inspired wave motif that's repeated inside the stylish rooms.

Hotel Sintra HOTEL $$

(新麗華酒店; Map p516; ☑2871 0111; www.hotelsintra.com; Avenida de Do João IV; r MOP$1250-1900, ste from MOP$2360; ☑3, 11, 22) This centrally located three-star hotel is great value. The rooms are spotless and the staff polite. Our only complaint was the slow lift.

Rocks Hotel BOUTIQUE HOTEL $$$

(萊斯酒店; Map p516; ☑2295 6528; www.rockshotel.com.mo; Macau Fisherman's Wharf; r MOP$1880-2980, ste from MOP$4080; ◯☎; ☑3A, 5, 23) This elegant Victorian-style boutique hotel is set amid a tribal-hut African restaurant and casino. The rooms are decent and most have a view of the waterfront.

New Nam Pan Hotel GUESTHOUSE $

(新南濱賓館; Map p520; ☑2848 2842; www.cnmacauhotel.com; 2nd fl, 8 Avenida de D. Joao IV; s/d/tr/q MOP$380/580/780/880, with increases of MOP$100-200 on weekends; ☎; ☑3, 5, 10) Central location, a rustic vibe and eight spotless rooms make New Nam Pan a good budget option.

Vila Universal GUESTHOUSE $

(大利迎賓館; Map p520; ☑2857 3247/5602; Cheng Peng Bldg, 73 Rua Felicidade; s/d from MOP$280/350; ☎; ☑3, 6, 26) Fish tanks, seashell displays and yellow sofas in the lobby impart a homely atmosphere, but the 32 rooms, though clean and decent, are more impersonal.

Augusters Lodge GUESTHOUSE $

(Map p520; ☑2871 3242, 6664 5026; www.augusters.de; Flat 3J, Block 4, Kam Loi Bldg, 24 Rua do Dr Pedro Jose Lobo; dm per person from MOP$130; ☎; ☑6, 11, 19;) Something of a backpackers' hub, this tiny, friendly guesthouse has basic but clean rooms with shared bathrooms and a kitchen. It's located above the CTM shop.

Macau Masters Hotel HOTEL $

(萬事發酒店; Map p520; ☑2893 7572; www.mastershotel-macau.com; 162 Rua das Lorchas; s/d from MOP$680/980; ◯☎; ☑1, 2, 10) A shabby exterior hides a smartly maintained hotel with small, well-equipped, if somewhat outmoded, rooms. Electricity supply is sometimes unstable.

THE ISLANDS

Taipa is changing fast, with several high-end international hotel chains opening up along the Cotai Strip. Coloane offers some great budget options, including two HI-affiliated hostels.

TOP CHOICE **Pousada de Coloane** HOTEL $$

(竹灣酒店; Map p524; ☑2882 2143; www.hotelpcoloane.com.mo; Estrada de Cheoc Van, Coloane; r from MOP$750; ≋; ☑21A, 25) This 30-room hotel with its Portuguese-style rooms (all with balconies and sea views) is excellent value. And the location above Cheoc Van Beach is about as chilled as you'll find. Discounts of 20% to 40% available in the low season.

Grand Hyatt Macau LUXURY HOTEL $$$

(澳門君悅酒店; ☑8868 1234; http://macau.grand.hyatt.com; City of Dreams, Estrada do Istmo, Cotai; r MOP$1300-3200, ste from MOP$2300; ◯@☎≋; ☑35, 50) The most tasteful of the casino-hotels on the Cotai Strip, the Grand Hyatt is part of the City of Dreams casino-shopping-performance complex. The massive rooms come with glass and marble showering areas and a full battery of technology.

Banyan Tree Luxury HOTEL $$$

(☑8883 8833; www.banyantree.com/en/macau; Galaxy, Avenida Marginal Flor de Lotus, Cotai; ste MOP$2880-63800, villas MOP$23,600-35,100; ☑25, 25X) This extravagant resort recreates tropical-style luxury in Macau. All 10 villas come with private gardens and swimming pools, while the suites have huge baths set by the window. If you need more pampering, there's a spa with state-of-the-art facilities. The other hotel at the Galaxy, **Okura** (www.hotelokuramacau.com; r MOP$2200-5600, ste MOP$3000-20,000) offers luxury with a Japanese twist.

Hostels

Beachside Youth Hostels HOSTEL $
(☑2855 5533; www.dsej.gov.mo/~webdsej; dm/ tw/q from MOP$100/160/120; 🚌21A, 25, 26A) These two beachside hostels under the government's Education and Youth Affairs Bureau are excellent value, but you need to book three months in advance and show an International Youth Card or International Youth Hostel Card upon check-in. Men and women are separated. Other conditions apply – please check the website. Other hostels include **Pousada de Juventude de Cheoc Van** (Map p524; ☑2888 2024; Estrada de Cheoc Van, Coloane) and **Pousada de Juventude de Hác Sá** (off Map p524; ☑2888 2701; Rua de Hác Sá Long Chao Kok, Coloane).

✖ Eating

Browse a typically Macanese menu and you'll find an enticing stew of influences from Chinese and Asian cuisines, as well as from those of former Portuguese colonies in Africa, India and Latin America. Coconut, tamarind, chilli, jaggery (palm sugar) and shrimp paste can all feature. A famous Macanese speciality is *galinha africana* (African chicken), made with coconut, garlic and chillies. Other Macanese favourites include *casquinha* (stuffed crab), *minchi* (minced meat cooked with potatoes, onions and spices) and *serradura,* a milk pudding.

You'll find Portuguese dishes here too; popular ones include *salada de bacalhau* (dried salted cod salad), *arroz de pato* (rice with duck confit) and *leitão assado no forno* (roast suckling pig). While Macau's Chinese cuisine is excellent, most people come here to sample Macanese or Portuguese food.

Alfonso III MACANESE $
(亞豐素三世餐廳; Map p520; ☑2858 6272; 11a Rua Central; MOP$70-200; ⊙lunch & dinner Mon-Sat; 🚌3, 6) With a diverse menu featuring liver and tripe dishes in addition to popular classics, all fabulously executed, it's clear this unpretentious eatery doesn't just cater for the weekend crowds. It's always packed with Macanese families, so book ahead.

TOP CHOICE Antonio PORTUGUESE $$$
(安東尼奧; Map p522; ☑2899 9998; www.an toniomacau.com; 3 Rua dos Negociantes, Taipa; MOP$250-1200; ⊙lunch & dinner Mon-Fri, noon-10.30pm Sat & Sun; 🚌22, 26) Dark mahogany set off by blue and white *azulejo* tiles prepare you for an authentic Portuguese meal at this Michelin-recommended restaurant known for whipping up a mean goat's cheese with honey and a lavish seafood stew.

TOP CHOICE Tim's Kitchen CHINESE $$$
(桃花源小廚; Map p516; ☑8803 3682; Shop F25, East Wing, Hotel Lisboa, Avenida de Lisboa, Praia Grande; lunch from MOP$200, dinner from MOP $400; ⊙lunch & dinner; 🚌3, 6, 26A) Tim's, with one Michelin star, captures some of the best of Cantonese cooking. Fresh ingredients are meticulously prepared using methods that highlight their original flavours, resulting in dishes that look simple but taste divine – a giant 'glass' prawn shares a plate with a sliver of Chinese ham; a crab claw lounges on a cushion of winter melon in a sea of broth.

Robuchon Au Dôme MODERN FRENCH $$$
(Map p516; ☑8803 7878; 43rd fl, Grand Lisboa, Avenida de Lisboa; lunch/dinner set from MOP$400/1588; ⊙lunch & dinner; 🚌3, 10) Macau's only restaurant with three Michelin stars has everything you'd associate with the Robuchon name: elegant decor, fine Gallic creations, and impeccable service. The wine cellar with 8000 bottles is one of Asia's best.

O Santos MACANESE $
(山度士葡式餐廳; Map p522; ☑2882 7508; 20 Rua da Cunha, Taipa; MOP$150-250; ⊙lunch & dinner; 🚌22, 26) Despite its location on the touristy Rua da Cunha, charming O Santos keeps its standards up. Patrons come back for the chicken and rice in blood (*arroz de cabidela*) and friendly banter with the owner, a former naval chef, for 20 years.

Litoral MACANESE $$
(海灣餐廳; Map p516; ☑2896 7878; http://restau rante-litoral.com; 261A Rua do Almirante Sérgio; from MOP$250; ⊙lunch & dinner; 🚌1, 5, 7) This famous joint serves solid Macanese and Portuguese fare, including delicious stews and baked rice dishes – many spun from the heirloom recipes of the matron Manuela, who runs the place.

Henri's Galley MACANESE $$
(美心亨利餐廳; Map p516; ☑2855 6251; www. henrisgalley.com.mo; 4G-H Avenida da República; MOP$130-350; ⊙11am-10pm; 🚌6,9,16) Macanese

chef Henri Wong is the soul of this 34-year-old institution. Mr Wong expertly prepares Macanese specialities like African chicken and Macau sole with unique recipes containing secret ingredients. The Sai Van Lake setting, though a little out of the way, is superb.

Xina Cafe
MEDITERRANEAN $

(Map p516; ☎2835 0489; 72b Rua Tomas Vieira; lunch from MOP$35, dinner MOP$250; ☉11.30am-6.30pm Tue-Sun; ☏; ☐7, 8) 'China' serves simple salads and tapas during the day. In the evening, owner Pedro cooks superb, Mediterranean-style dinners for the lucky few who manage to land a seat at his table (bookings of at least six people, two days in advance). Family friendly.

O Porto
MACANESE $

(內港餐廳; Map p516; ☎2859 4643; 17 Travessa da Praia; MOP$110; ☉lunch & dinner, closed Wed; ☐2, 10, 12) Not to be confused with O Porto Interior on Rua do Almirante Sérgio, this modest place near the steps leading to Mong Há Hill serves reasonably priced Macanese dishes, with a few luxuries: chequered tablecloth, football paraphernalia and homely service.

Lung Wah Tea House
CANTONESE $

(龍華茶樓; Map p516; http://lungwahteahouse. com; Avenida do Almirante Lacerda; MOP$70; ☉breakfast & lunch; ☐23, 32) There's grace in the retro furniture and the casual way it's thrown together in this airy Cantonese teahouse (c 1963) with a Michelin Bib Gourmand. Take a booth by windows overlooking the Almirante Lacerda, where the teahouse buys its produce. There's no English menu; let your fingers do the talking.

Restaurante Fernando
MACANESE $

(法蘭度餐廳; off Map p524; www.fernando restaurant.com; 9 Praia de Hác Sá, Coloane; MOP$120; ☉noon-9.30pm) A Macau institution famed for seafood and the perfect place for a protracted, boozy lunch by the sea. Take bus 25, 26A or 21A and get off at the Hac Sa beach stop. Walk in the direction of the bus for one minute and the restaurant is on your right.

Café Nga Tim
MACANESE $

(雅憩花園餐廳; Map p524; 8 Rua do Caetano, Coloane; MOP$100; ☉noon-1am; ☐21A, 25) We love the Chinese-Portuguese food, the small-town atmosphere, the prices and the owner – a guitar- and erhu-strumming ex-cop named Feeling Wong.

Toung King
BURMESE, CHINESE $

(東京小食館; Map p516; 1c Rotunda da Carlos Da Maia, Santo Antonio; MOP$15-40; ☉10am-10pm; ☐23, 32) The Burmese-style snacks here are much raved about by foodies, many of whom make a trip from Hong Kong just for the noodles with pig's brain (tastes just like tofu, the owner assures). If that's too heady, you might like the dry tossed egg noodles with dried shrimp, chilli and peanuts.

🍷 Drinking

Macau's unique and atmospheric drinking places are far removed from the glitz of the Outer Harbour.

TOP CHOICE The Macallan Whisky Bar & Lounge
WHISKY BAR

(off Map p522; 203, 2nd fl, Galaxy Hotel; ☐25, 25X) Arguably the best whisky bar in Macau (and Hong Kong), this handsome establishment features lots of oak panels, Jacobean rugs and a real fireplace. The 400-plus whisky labels include representatives from Ireland, France, Sweden and India, and a 1963 bottle of Glemorangie, besides the usual suspects. It opens at 5pm.

Club Cubic
CLUB

(www.cubic-cod.com; 2105-02, City of Dreams, Estrada do Istmo, Cotai; ☐50, 35) Spanning some 30,000 sq ft, the flashy, two-level Club Cubic, located at the Hard Rock Hotel, features themed rooms, a champagne bar, and a large 'disco' ball that can hold up to four people. There are DJs mixing a variety of tunes including hip hop, techno, and Korean pop. The City of Dreams (新濠天地) is a massive, hard-to-miss casino-hotel complex on the Cotai Strip, between Coloane and Taipa.

Lord Stow's Cafe
CAFE

(澳門澳門安德魯餅店; Map p524; www.lord stow.com; Largo do Matadouro, Coloane Village; ☉10am-6pm) This cosy cafe serves baked goodies from the famous bakery around the corner, including the deservedly popular *pastéis de nata* (scrumptious egg-custard tarts with a flaky crust).

McSorley's Ale House
PUB

(麥時利愛爾蘭酒吧; Shop 1038, Venetian Macao Resort Hotel, Estrada da Baía de Nossa Senhora da Esperança, Taipa; ☐25, 25X) This cosy tavern-style watering hole in the Venetian is a genial spot that attracts rugby and soccer fanatics with its live-satellite broadcasts of European matches. Its extensive selection of imported beers is reasonably priced. Take bus 25 or 26A and get off at the City of Dreams stop. Walk in the direction of the bus for five minutes and the Venetian is on the right.

Jabber   CAFE

(Map p520; 34-38 Rua de São Roque; ⊙noon-7pm Tue-Fri, 3-7pm Sat & Sun; ☐7, 8) Located in the St Lazarus district, this sexy subterranean cafe with hot-pink walls belongs to Venessa Cheah, a fashion designer, who also lends her talent to the tasty and creative menu.

Cuppa Coffee   CAFE

(104 Rua Fernão Mendes Pinto, Taipa; ⊙8am-8pm; ☎; ☐25, 26) Expect freshly baked bread, yummy sandwiches, great smoothies and decent coffees at this nifty cafe. The cafe is right next to a zebra crossing, at the junction with Avenida Olimpica (奧林柏克大馬路).

★ Entertainment

Macau's nightlife may be dominated by the ever-expanding casino scene, but a number of interesting live-music venues have also sprung up about town. For entertainment/ cultural events listings, check out the bi-monthly CCM+ and monthly Destination Macau available for free at MGTO outlets and larger hotels.

Canidrome   SPECTATOR SPORT

(逸園狗場; Map p516; www.macauyydog.com; Avenida do General Castelo Branco; admission MOP$10; ☐1, 3) Asia's only facility for greyhound racing, the Canidrome has races every Monday, Thursday, Saturday and Sunday at 7.30pm.

Sun Never Left – Public Art Performance   FAIR

(Map p520; ☑2834 6626; www.cipa.org.mo; Rua de São Roque, St Lazarus District; admission free; ⊙3-6pm Sat & Sun; ☐7, 8) Every Saturday and Sunday afternoon, this fair in the lovely St Lazarus District features stalls selling art and crafts, live music, food and drinks. Participants are mostly artists in the neighbourhood.

Macau Soul   BAR, LIVE MUSIC

(澳感廊; Map p520; ☑2836 5182; www.macausoul.com; 31a Rua de São Paulo; ⊙9.30am-8.30pm Mon-Thu, 9.30am-midnight Fri-Sun; ☐8A, 17) Huddled in the shadows of the Ruins of St Paul, Macau Soul is elegantly decked out in woods and stained-glass windows, with a basement where blues bands perform to packed audiences. Opening hours vary, so phone ahead.

Wynn Macao   CASINO

(永利澳門; Map p516; www.wynnmacau.com; Rua Cidade de Sintra; ☐8, 10A) A gentlemen's club for punters, Wynn features interiors in solid browns interrupted impatiently by reds and golds. Presumably feng shui had a say too – the hotel sports a chip on its shoulder that's pointed at Grand Lisboa.

Grand Lisboa Casino   CASINO

(新葡京; Map p516; www.grandlisboa.com; Avenida de Lisboa; ☐3, 10) This flaming torch-shaped megastructure has become the landmark you navigate the streets by, out-shining its sister next door, **Casino Lisboa** (葡京; Map p516; 2-4 Avenida de Lisboa), once the best-known casino in Asia for its faded '60s glamour.

BRIGHT LIGHTS, SIN CITY

Macau's seafront has turned into King Kong's playground, a space occupied by gargantuan monuments whose size makes it easy to imagine their downfall. Casinos are no stranger to a city known as 'the Vegas of the East', but while previously there was only one landmark house of cards, now the sky's the limit. The change began when casino mogul Stanley Ho's monopoly ended in 2002 and Las Vegas operators set up shop in competition. There are at present some 30 casinos in Macau.

More than 80% of gamblers and 95% of high rollers come from mainland China. The latter play in members-only rooms where the total amount wagered on any given day can exceed a country's GDP, and where money allows you to do wonderful things like smash a chandelier with an ashtray and not pay for it.

For recreational players, your closest brush with a casino's seedy side will probably be harassment by tip hustlers – scam artists who hang around tables acting like your new best friend. They can steal your chips, nag you for a cut or try to lure you to a casino that'll tip them for bringing clients.

All casinos operate 24 hours a day. Punters must be at least 18 years old and properly dressed (no shorts or flipflops).

FREELOADING IN MACAU

So you've lost the shirt off your back but you still want to travel. Well, you probably can, if you're in Macau.

All big-name casinos have free shuttle service to and from the Macau Ferry Terminal, Taipa Ferry Terminal, the Border Gate, even the airport, with Venetian boasting an enormous fleet. Anyone can use these buses – no questions asked. What's more, some casinos have buses to each other. Combine that with walking and you're pretty much set.

Operating hours of these services fall between 9.30am and 11pm, and buses depart every three to 15 minutes. Check the casino websites or at the front desk.

If you're on a casino-bound route, don't forget to pick up your complimentary chip. A free spin may be just what's needed to land you a bed for the night. If it doesn't, don't lose heart. You can leave your bags at any casino-hotel for free even if your real pad is the pavement.

You know what they say: you find out who your real friends are when you're down and out.

Shopping

Browsing through the shops in the old city, specifically on crumbly **Rua dos Ervanários** and **Rua de Nossa Senhora do Amparo** (Map p516) near the Ruins of St Paul, can be a great experience. There are shops selling stamps, jade, incense and goldfish. In the afternoon, flea-market vendors spread their wares on the ground.

You can also look for antiques or replicas at shops on or near **Rua de São Paulo**, **Rua das Estalagens** and **Rua de São António**. **Rua de Madeira** and **Rua dos Mercadores**, which lead up to **Rua da Tercena** and its **flea market** (Map p520), have stores selling mah jong tiles and bird cages. With their humble, one- or two-storey houses dating from agricultural times, these are lovely streets to walk along, even if you don't buy anything.

TOP CHOICE **Mercearia Portuguesa** FOOD, JEWELLERY
(Map p520; ☑2856 2708; www.merceariaportuguesa.com; 8 Calçada da Igreja de Sao Lazaro; ⊙noon-8pm; ☑7, 8) The charming Portuguese shop opened by a film director and actress has a small but well-curated selection of provisions, such as jams and honeys, soaps and chinaware, gold jewellery, wooden toys and bath products from Portugal, all gorgeously packaged and reasonably priced.

TOP CHOICE **Macau Creations** LIFESTYLE
(澳門佳作; Map p520; ☑2835 2954; www.macaucreations.com; 5a Rua da Ressurreicao; ⊙10am-10pm; ☑3, 6) Excellent Macau-themed clothes, stationery and memorabilia designed by 30 artists living in the city, including Russian Konstantin Bessmertny and Macanese Carlos Marreiros.

G17 Gallery CERAMICS
(陶藝廊; Map p520; ☑2834 6626; 17a Rua de Sao Miguel; ⊙10am-7pm Mon-Sat, 2-6pm Sun; ☑7, 8) A small, new gallery that displays and sells ceramics and pottery produced by Macau's artists.

MOD Design Store CLOTHING, ACCESSORIES
(Map p520; www.mod-store.com; B1, Macau Tourism & Cultural Activity Centre, Ruins of St Paul & Companhia de Jesus Square; ⊙9am-7pm; ☑3, 6, 26) The new Mod shop next to the Ruins of the Church of St Paul sells souvenirs from Portugal and T-shirts created by Macau's designers.

Pinto Livros BOOKS
(邊度有書; Map p520; http://blog.roodo.com/pintolivros; 1a Veng Heng Bldg, 31 Largo do Senado; ⊙11.30am-11pm; ☑3, 6, 26A) This upstairs reading room overlooking Largo do Senado has a decent selection of books on art and culture, esoteric CDs and two resident cats.

Lines Lab CLOTHING
(Map p520; www.lineslab.com; Shop A3, 8 Calçada da Igreja de São Lazaro; ⊙1-8pm, closed Mon; ☑7, 8) Edgy Macau-inspired clothes and accessories by two designers from Lisbon.

Asian Artefacts ANTIQUES
(Map p524; 9 Rua dos Negociantes, Coloane; ⊙10am-7pm) If you're serious about antiques, this shop in Coloane Village, with its before and after photos of restored pieces, is recommended.

MACAU'S SWORD MASTER

Want a really special memento of your trip? One of Macau's most respected artists Antonio Conceição Junior custom designs swords (www.arscives.com/bladesign) inspired by Macau, ancient mythology and the modern world.

The charismatic artist has designed Eastern blades such as katana, tanto and dhakris, Western sabres, hand-and-a-halves, and cutlasses, as well as hybrids featuring, say, a Western-style blade with a sword guard inspired by the Harley Davidson wheel. Sleek, precise and original, they're works of contemporary art, rather than imitations of 'real' weaponry.

After he finishes the design, Antonio will recommend bladesmiths in North America who will deal directly with the customers and ship them the finished products.

Interested parties should start by emailing him (antonio.cejunior@gmail.com). Expect about one to two weeks for the design and a design fee of about US$3000.

Formerly director of the Museum of Macau, Antonio is a versatile artist with a mile-long repertoire spanning fashion, stamps, jewellery, medallions and book covers.

His website (www.arscives.com) includes a section called 'How to Work with a Designer'. Yes, Antonio is a meticulous man.

❶ Information

The Macau Government Tourist Office (MGTO) distributes the excellent (and free) *Macau Tourist Map*, with tourist sights and streets labelled in Portuguese and Chinese. Small inset maps highlight the Taipa and Coloane areas and show bus routes.

Emergency
24-hour Tourists' Emergency Hotline (☏112) English-speaking staff.
Police, Fire & Ambulance (☏999)

Internet Access
Macau's few internet cafes come and go quickly. The good news is that wi-fi coverage is expanding. Most libraries, museums, touristy and busy areas have free wi-fi daily from 8am to 1am the following day. User name and password are 'wifigo'. Each session lasts 45 minutes but you can reconnect again. See the website www.wifi.gov.mo/en/index.php for an updated list.

To enjoy mobile wi-fi, you can buy a prepaid phonecard (MOP$50 to MOP$130) or a mobile wireless broadband pass (MOP$120/220 for one/five days) from CTM.

Medical Services
Centro Hospitalar Conde São Januário (山頂醫院; ☏2831 3731; Estrada do Visconde de São Januário) Southwest of Guia Fort; 24-hour emergency service.
University Hospital (☏2882 1838; www. uh.org.mo; Block H, Macau University of Science & Technology, Avenida Wai Long, Taipa; ◷9am-9pm Mon-Sat, to 5pm Sun) Western and Chinese medical services available.

Money
ATMs are everywhere, with half a dozen just outside the Hotel Lisboa. Most allow you to choose between patacas and Hong Kong dollars.

You can change cash and travellers cheques at the **banks** (◷9am-5pm Mon-Fri, to 1pm Sat) lining Avenida da Praia Grande and Avenida de Almeida Ribeiro.

Hong Kong bills and coins (except the $10 coins) are accepted everywhere in Macau, but your change will be returned in patacas.

Post
Macau Post (澳門郵政; www.macaupost. gov.mo) ferry terminal branch (☏2872 8079; ◷10am-7pm Mon-Sat); main post office (☏2832 3666; 126 Avenida de Almeida Ribeiro; ◷9am-6pm Mon-Fri, to 1pm Sat) Little red vending machines dispense stamps throughout Macau. Poste restante service is available at counters 1 and 2 of the main post office.

Telephone
Local calls Free from private phones and most hotel telephones; calls from public payphones cost MOP$1 for five minutes.
Prepaid IDD/local cards (from MOP$50) Can be used in most mobile phones; purchase from CTM stores or the ferry terminal.
International directory assistance (☏101)
Local directory assistance (☏181)

Tourist Information
Macau Government Tourist Office (MGTO; Map p520; 澳門旅遊局; ☏2831 5566; www.macau tourism.gov.mo) has themed leaflets on Macau's sights and bilingual maps at its outlets:
Guia Lighthouse (旅遊局東望洋燈塔分局; ☏2856 9808; ◷9am-1pm & 2.15-5.30pm)

Hong Kong (澳門政府旅遊局; ☑2857 2287; Room 336-337, Shun Tak Centre, 200 Connaught Rd, Sheung Wan; ⊙9am-10pm)

Largo do Senado (旅遊諮詢處; ☑8397 1120; ⊙9am-6pm)

Macau Ferry Terminal (旅遊局外港碼頭分局; ☑2872 6416; ⊙9am-10pm)

Travel Agencies

China Travel Service (CTS; 中國旅行社; Map p516; 中國國際旅行社; ☑2870 0888; cts@cts.com.mo; Avenida do Dr Rodrigo 207, Edifício Nam Kuong; ⊙9am-5pm) China visas (MOP$285 plus photos) are available to most passport holders in one day.

Websites

Cityguide (www.cityguide.gov.mo) Practical information (eg transport).

Macau Cultural Institute (www.icm.gov.mo) Macau's cultural offerings month by month.

Macau Government Tourist Office (www.macautourism.gov.mo) The best source of information for visiting Macau.

ⓘ Getting There & Away

Macau International Airport is connected to limited destinations in Asia. If you are coming from outside Asia, your best option is to fly to Hong Kong International Airport and take a ferry to Macau without going through Hong Kong customs.

Air

MACAU INTERNATIONAL AIRPORT (☑2886 1111; www.macau-airport.com) Located on Taipa Island, 20 minutes from the city centre.

FREQUENT SERVICES To destinations including Bangkok, Chiang Mai, Kaohsiung, Kuala Lumpur, Manila, Osaka, Seoul, Singapore, Taipei and Tokyo.

REGULAR FLIGHTS Between Macau and Běijīng, Hángzhōu, Nánjīng, Níngbō, Shànghǎi and Xiàmén and less frequent flights to Chéngdū, Chóngqìng, Fúzhōu and Wǔhàn). Check www.macau-airport.com for timetable and airlines.

LEFT LUGGAGE COUNTER Departures level of the **Macau International Airport** (per hr/day MOP$10/80; ⊙24hr).

HELICOPTER Sky Shuttle (www.skyshuttle hk.com; HK$3700; ⊙9am-11pm) Runs a 15-minute helicopter shuttle between Macau and Hong Kong up to 27 times daily.

Boat

TO CHINA TurboJet (☑3628 3628; www.turbo jet.com.hk) has departures daily to Shékǒu, in Shēnzhèn (MOP$210, one hour, 10 between 9.45am and 8.45pm) It also has departures to Shēnzhèn airport (MOP$210, one hour, five

from 11.30am to 7.30pm), and to Nánshà, near Guǎngzhōu (MOP$180, two between 10.45am and 4.15pm).

Yuet Tung Shipping Co (☑2893 9944; www.ytmacau.com) has ferries connecting Macau's Taipa temporary ferry terminal (MOP$155, 1½ hours, 11am, 2pm, 7pm) with Shékǒu. Ferries also leave from Macau maritime ferry terminal (MOP$12, every half-hour, 8am to 4.15pm) for Wanzai of Zhūhǎi.

TO HONG KONG Two ferry companies operate services to/from Hong Kong virtually 24 hours a day.

CotaiJet (☑2885 0595; www.cotaijet.com.mo) Runs between Taipa temporary ferry terminal and Hong Kong's Hong Kong–Macau ferry terminal (economy/first class Monday to Friday HK$151/201, 10% more for weekends, 20% more after 6pm; every half hour, 6.30am to midnight). A feeder shuttle bus service drops off at destinations on the Cotai Strip. See website for services to Hong Kong International Airport.

TurboJet (☑3628 3628; www.turbojet.com.hk) has the most frequent sailings, departing for Macau from the Hong Kong–Macau ferry terminal (economy/superclass Monday to Friday HK$151/291, 10% more for weekends and 20% more from 6.15pm to 6.30am; every 15 minutes, 7am-midnight); and China ferry terminal (every 30 minutes, 7am to midnight, less frequent after midnight). See website for services to Hong Kong International Airport.

Lockers (MOP$20/25 for first two hours, MOP$25/30 for each additional 12 hour period) are on both arrival and departure levels of the Macau ferry terminal.

Bus

Macau is an easy gateway into China.

Border gate (Portas de Cerco; ⊙7am-midnight) Take bus 3, 5, 9 and walk across.

Cotai frontier post (⊙9am-8pm) On the causeway linking Taipa and Coloane; allows visitors to cross Lotus Bridge by shuttle bus (MOP$4) to Zhūhǎi; buses 15, 21 and 26 drop you off at the crossing.

Macau International Airport (info ☑2888 1228) Buses to Guǎngzhōu and Dōngguǎn (both MOP$155, four hours).

Underground bus terminal near border gate (☑2893 3888) Kee Kwan Motor Rd Co has buses to Guǎngzhōu (MOP$80, 2½ hours, every 15 minutes from 8am to 9.40pm) and to Zhōngshān (MOP$23, 1½ hours, every 20 minutes from 8am to 6.30pm).

ⓘ Getting Around

To/From the Airport

Airport bus AP1 Airport to Macau Ferry Terminal and Border Gate (MOP$4.20, every five to 12 minutes, 6.30am-midnight); stops at major hotels en route. Extra charge of MOP$3 for each large piece of luggage.

Airport buses MT1 and MT2 Airport to Praça de Ferreira do Amaral near Casino Lisboa (MOP$4.20, every 12 to 20 minutes, 7am-10.30pm).

Buses 21 and 26 Airport to Coloane.

Bus 21 Airport to A-Ma Temple.

Taxi Airport to town centre about MOP$40.

Bicycle

Bikes can be rented in Taipa Village. You are not allowed to cross the Macau–Taipa bridges on a bicycle.

Car

Avis Rent A Car (www.avis.com.mo; Room 1022, ground fl, Macau Ferry Terminal) hires out cars (MOP$700 to 1400 per day; with chauffeur from MOP$300 per hour, 20% more on weekends).

Burgeon Rent A Car (Map p516; www.burgeon rentacar.com; Shop O,P & Q, Block 2, La Baie Du Noble, Avenida Do Nordeste) hires out Kia cars (from MOP$190/270/390 for 6/11/24 hours; with chauffeur from MOP$160 per hour, minimum two hours)

Public Transport

ROUTES Macau has about 50 public bus and minibus routes running from 6am to midnight.

FARES MOP$3.20 on the peninsula, MOP$4.20 to Taipa, MOP$5 to Coloane Village, MOP$6.40 to Hác Sá Beach

DESTINATIONS Displayed in Portuguese and Chinese.

INFORMATION Macau Transmac Bus Co (www.transmac.com.mo), **Macau TCM Bus Co** (www.tcm.com.mo) and **REOLIAN** (www.reolian.com.mo) have info on routes and fares. The *Macau Tourist Map,* available at MGTO outlets, has a list of both bus routes and a pamphlet listing all bus routes.

USEFUL SERVICES Buses 3 and 3A (between ferry terminal and city centre); buses 3 and 5 (to the Border Gate); and bus 12 (from ferry terminal, past Hotel Lisboa to Lou Lim Ioc Garden and Kun Iam Temple). Buses 21, 21A, 25 and 26A go to Taipa and Coloane.

Taxi

LANGUAGE Not many taxi drivers speak English, so it can help to have your destination written in Chinese.

COST Flag fall is MOP$13 (first 1.6km); then it's MOP$1.50 for each additional 230m.

SURCHARGE MOP$5/2 surcharge to Coloane from Macau peninsula/Taipa; MOP$5 surcharge for journeys from the airport; large bags cost an extra MOP$3.

HANDY NUMBERS Call ☎2851 9519 or ☎2893 9939 for yellow radio taxis.

Guǎngdōng

POP 93 MILLION

Includes »

Guǎngzhōu 535
Fóshān 550
Kāipíng 552
Yángjiāng 554
Zhàoqìng 555
Qīngyuǎn 557
Nánlǐng National
Forest Park 557
Shēnzhèn 558
Zhūhǎi 561
Cháozhōu 563
Shàntóu 566
Méizhōu 566

Best Views

» Nánlǐng National Forest Park (p557)
» White Cloud Hills (p550)
» Fēixiá (p557)
» Jǐnjiānglǐ (p552)

Best Walks

» Dōngshān (p541)
» West Lake (p564)
» Chìkǎn (p553)
» Shāmiàn Island (p541)

Why Go?

Sometimes hiding under the traveller's radar, Guǎngdōng's unique culture and natural beauty have yet to be discovered by most visitors, so you may have a plethora of sublime sights (not to mention great dim sum) all to yourself.

Northern Guǎngdōng (广东) is home to some wild and wondrous landscapes. In the blue pine forests of Nánlǐng, the music of waterfalls and windswept trees boomerangs in your direction. Or if it's Unesco-crowned heritage you're after, Kāipíng's flamboyant watchtowers, Cháozhōu's intricate woodcarvings and the stylised poses of Cantonese opera will leave you riveted.

Historically Guǎngdōng was the starting point of the Maritime Silk Road and the birthplace of revolution. On the scenic byways of the Pearl River Delta, you'll uncover the glory of China's revolutionary past. While on the surf-beaten beaches of Hǎilíng Island, an ancient shipwreck and its treasures await.

When to Go
Guǎngzhōu

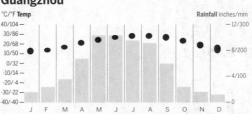

Apr–Jun Verdant paddy fields against the man-made wonders of Kāipíng and Méizhōu.

Jul–Sep Blue pines and stained-glass windows offer respite from summer.

Oct–Dec The typhoons and heat are gone; this is the best time to visit.

Guǎngdōng Highlights

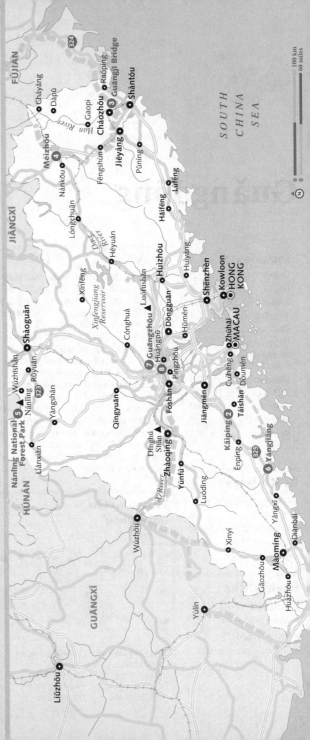

1 Experience the vestiges of rich and vibrant **Lingnán culture** (p544)

2 Climb dramatic Unesco-listed watchtowers at **Kāipíng** (p552)

3 Cross the **Guǎngjì Bridge** (p563) in Cháozhōu with its 18 boats and 24 piers

4 Town-hop in **Méizhōu** (p566) to see earthen roundhouses and old mansions

5 After a day's hike, fall asleep to the whispered symphony of an ancient forest in **Nánlíng National Forest Park** (p557)

6 Visit silken beaches and an 800-year-old shipwreck in **Yángjiāng** (p554)

7 Lunch in a garden-restaurant in **Guǎngzhōu** (p543) while listening to an operatic aria

8 Join the pilgrims at the **Memorial Museum of Generalissimo Sun Yatsen's Mansion** (p539) in Guǎngzhōu

9 Food, glorious (Cantonese) food!

History

Guǎngdōng has had contact with the outside world for nearly two millennia. Among the first outsiders to arrive were the Romans, who appeared in the 2nd century AD. By the Tang dynasty (AD 618–907), a sizeable trade with the Middle East and Southeast Asia had developed.

The first Europeans to settle here were the Portuguese in 1557, followed by the Jesuits who established themselves in Zhàoqìng. The British came along in the 17th century and by 1685 merchant ships from the East India Company were calling at Guǎngzhōu. In 1757 an imperial edict gave the *cohong,* a local merchants' guild, a monopoly on China's trade with foreigners, who were restricted to Shāmiàn Island. Trade remained in China's favour until 1773, when the British shifted the balance by unloading 1000 chests of Bengal opium in Guǎngzhōu. Addiction spread in China like wildfire, eventually leading to the Opium Wars.

In the 19th century Guǎngdōng was a hotbed of reform and revolt. Among the political elites who sowed revolutionary ideas here was Sun Yatsen, who later became the first president of the Republic of China.

The 20th century saw Guǎngdōng serving as the headquarters of both the Nationalist and Communist parties, and enduring great suffering during the Cultural Revolution. After the implementation of the 'open door' policy in 1978, it became the first province to embrace capitalism. The province's continued economic success has made it a leading export centre for consumer goods.

Language

The vast majority of the people of Guǎngdōng speak Cantonese, a dialect distinct from Mandarin. Though it enjoys a less exalted status than the national dialect, Cantonese is older and far better suited than Mandarin for the reading of classical poetry.

Guǎngzhōu 广州

♩020 / POP 12 MILLION

Guǎngzhōu, known to many in the West as Canton, is China's busiest transport and trade hub. You are likely to pass through it at least once to get to other parts of the country. Avoid visiting during Chinese New Year, which sees the largest annual human migration in the world.

PRICE INDICATORS

The following price indicators are used in this chapter:

Sleeping

$	less than ¥250
$$	¥250 to ¥600
$$$	more than ¥600

Eating

$	less than ¥70
$$	¥70 to ¥150
$$$	more than ¥150

History

Guǎngzhōu's history is one dominated by trade and revolution. Since the Tang dynasty (AD 618–907), it had been China's most important southern port and the starting point for the Maritime Silk Road, a trade route to the West. It became a trading post for the Portuguese in the 16th century, and later the British.

After the fall of the Qing dynasty in 1911, the city was a stronghold of the republican forces led by Sun Yatsen and, subsequently, a centre of activity also of the Chinese Communist Party (CCP) led by Mao Zedong.

During the post-1949 years of China's self-imposed isolation, the Canton Trade Fair was the only platform on which China did business with the West.

In 2010 Guǎngzhōu held the Asian Games, resulting in major expansion of the city's transport network.

◉ Sights & Activities

ZHŪJIĀNG XĪNCHÉNG (ZHŪJIĀNG NEW TOWN)

FREE New Guǎngdōng Museum   MUSEUM
(广东省博物馆新馆; Guǎngdōngshěng Bówùguǎn Xīnguǎn; Map p540; ☑3804 6886; www.gdmuseum. com; 2 Zhujiang Donglu; ⊙9am-5pm Tue-Sun; Ⓜ Line 3, Zhūjiāng Xīnchéng, exit B1) This ultramodern museum resembling a Chinese lacquer box occupies almost the entire block by the waterfront. The highlights are exhibits on Cantonese art, in particular ancient Cháozhōu woodcarvings. Displays on the human and natural history of Guǎngdōng seem to have fallen short of the museum's ambitions.

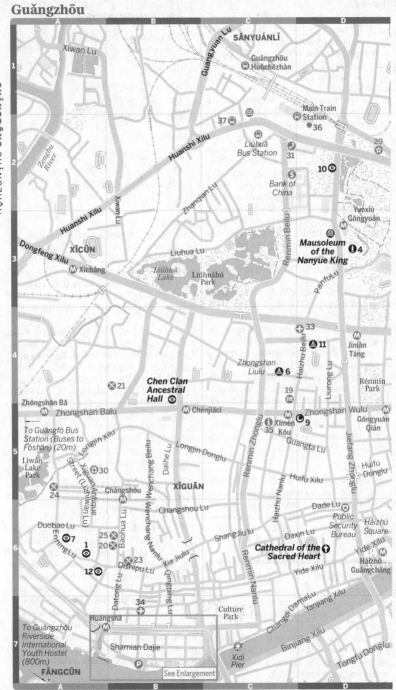

SĀNYUÁNLÍ

Xiwan Lu

Guǎngyuan Lu

Guǎngzhōu
Huǒchēzhàn

Main Train
Station
36

29

37

Liúhuā
Bus Station

31

Huanshi Xilu

Zhanqian Lu

Bank of
China

10

Xiwan Lu

Yuèxiù
Gōngyuán

Huanshi Xilu

Liuhua Lu

Renmin Beilu

Mausoleum
of the
Nanyue King

4

Dongfeng Xilu

XĪCŪN

Liúhuā
Lake

Liúhuāhú
Park

Panfu Lu

Xīchǎng

33

11

Jìniàn
Táng

Haizhu Beilu

Zhongshan
Liulu

6

Liurong Lu

Rénmín
Park

21

Chen Clan
Ancestral
Hall

19

Zhōngshān Bā

Chénjiācí

Zhongshan Wulu

Gōngyuán
Qián

Zhongshan Balu

35

Xīmén
Kǒu

9

Renmin Zhonglu

Guangta Lu

To Guǎngfó Bus
Station (Buses to
Fóshān) (20m)

Longjin Xilu

Longjin Donglu

XĪGUĀN

Huifu
Donglu

Jiefang Zhonglu

Lìwān
Lake Park

30

Daihe Lu

Huifu Xilu

24

Chángshòu

Xiguan Antique
Street (Lìzhiwan Lu)

Wenchang Beilu

Changshou Lu

Haizhu Nanlu

Dade Lu

Public
Security
Bureau

Hàizhū
Square

Duobao Lu

7

Enning Lu

25

20

Baohua Lu

Shang Jiu lu

Daxin Lu

Yide Xilu

1

Datong Lu

Wenchang Nanlu

Xia Jiulu

Cathedral of the
Sacred Heart

Hàizhū
Guǎngchǎng

12

23

Dishipu Lu

Qingping Lu

Renmin Nanlu

Yide Xilu

34

Culture
Park

Changdī DamaLu

Yanjiang Xilu

Tongfú Donglu

To Guǎngzhōu
Riverside
International
Youth Hostel
(800m)

Huángshā

Shamian Dajie

P

Xidi
Pier

Binjiang Xilu

FĀNGCŪN

See Enlargement

Guǎngzhōu

◎ Top Sights

Cathedral of the Sacred Heart	D6
Chen Clan Ancestral Hall	B4
Guǎngzhōu City Museum	E3
Guǎngzhōu Museum of Art	F2
Mausoleum of the Nanyue King	D3
Spring Garden	H6

◎ Sights

	Ancestral home of Bruce Lee	(see 7)
1	Bāhé Academy	A6
2	Church of Our Lady of Lourdes	H1
3	Dōngshān Area	H5
4	Five Rams Statue	D3
5	Goelia Concept 225	E5
6	Guāngxiào Temple	C4
	Kuí Garden	(see 3)
7	Luányú Táng	A6
8	Memorial Museum of Generalissimo Sun Yatsen's Mansion	F7
9	Mosque Dedicated to the Prophet	D5
	Old Muslim Grave	(see 10)
10	Orchid Garden	D2
11	Temple of the Six Banyan Trees	D4
12	Zhāntiānyòu House	A6
13	Zhènhǎi Tower	E3

🛌 Sleeping

14	Garden Hotel	G3
15	Guǎngdōng Victory Hotel	G1
16	Guǎngdōng Victory Hotel (New Annexe)	G1
17	Guǎngzhōu Youth Hostel	G1
	Old Canton Youth Hostel	(see 3)
18	White Swan Hotel	G1
19	Zhūhǎi Special Economic Zone Hotel	C4

✗ Eating

20	Chén Tiānjì	B6
21	Fó Yǒu Yuán	B4
22	Lucy's	G1
23	Nánxìn	B6
24	Pànxī Restaurant	A5
25	Shùnjì Bīngshì	B6
26	Wilber's	H4

🍷 Drinking

	Kuí Garden	(see 3)
27	Shāmiàn Clubhouse	H1
28	Ten Cafe	H5

🎭 Entertainment

29	Guǎngzhōu Tekkuan Live House	D2

🛍 Shopping

	Benshop	(see 5)
30	Xīguān Antique Street	A5

ℹ Information

31	China Telecom	C2
32	China Travel Service	E6
33	Guǎngzhōu First Municipal People's Hospital	D4
34	Guangzhou Hospital of Traditional Chinese Medicine	B7
35	Tourist Information Centre	C5

ℹ Transport

36	China Southern Airlines	D2
37	Guǎngdōng Long-Distance Bus Station	C2
38	Hotel Landmark Canton–buses to Hong Kong & Macau	E6
39	Malaysia, Thai International, United and Vietnam Airlines	G3

Guǎngzhōu Opera House CULTURAL BUILDING (广州大剧院; Guǎngzhōu dà jù yuàn; Map p540; ☑3839 2888 2666; www.chgoh.org; 1 Zhujiang Xilu; ☺9am-4.30pm, closed Mon; Ⓜ Line 3, Zhūjiāng Xīnchéng, exit B1) Designed by Zaha Hadid, the biggest performance venue in southern China has transformed the area with its other-worldly appearance. But equally surreal was the speed with which the ¥1300-million structure was built – five years. Composed of glass panels knitted together to form subtle curves, the complex has been described as pebbles on the bed of the Pearl River. Erosion has apparently come too soon – panels have been falling off the roof.

To enter the opera house, you have to join one of five 45-minute daily **tours** (per person ¥30; ☺10am, 11am, 2pm, 3pm and 4pm). Tours in English require advance booking and a ¥200 deposit paid the day before. Inside, you'll see the ethereally beautiful opera hall with 4200 LED lights and floor planks from Russia, as well as state-of-the-art rehearsal halls.

HǍIZHŪ DISTRICT

FREE **Memorial Hall of the Lǐngnán School of Painting** MUSEUM
(岭南画派纪念馆; Lǐngnán Huàpài Jìniànguǎn; off Map p536; 8401 7167; www.lingnans.org; 257 Changgang Donglu; 9am-5pm Tue-Sun; Xiǎogǎng, exit A) This small but excellent museum on the leafy campus of the Guǎngzhōu Academy of Fine Arts (广州美术学院; Guǎngzhōu Měishù Xuéyuàn) pays tribute to the founders of the Lǐngnán school of painting such as Gao Jianfu, and shows the colourful ink and brush works of contemporary artists versed in the Lǐngnán style.

Memorial Museum of Generalissimo Sun Yatsen's Mansion HISTORIC SITE
(孙中山大元帅府; Sūn Zhōngshān Dàyuánshuài Fǔ; Map p536; 8901 2366; www.dyshf.com; 18 Dongsha Jie, Fangzhi Lu; admission ¥10; 9am-5pm Tue-Sun; Line 2, Shì Èrgōng) This Victorian mansion was where Sun Yatsen lived when he established governments in then Canton in 1917 and 1923. After exiting the metro, take a cab (¥10) or walk for 20 minutes.

Canton Tower TOWER
(广州电视观光塔; Guǎngzhōu Diànshì Guānguāng Tǎ; off Map p540; 8933 8222; 222 Yuejiang Xilu; admission ¥50-150; 9am-10pm; Line 3, Chìgǎngtǎ, exit D) The ¥150 admission gets you all the way to the top of the world's second-tallest TV tower (610m) and the views are riveting.

LÌWĀN DISTRICT

Chen Clan Ancestral Hall HISTORIC SITE
(陈家祠; Chénjiā Cí; Map p536; 8181 4559; 34 Enlong Li, Zhongshan Qilu; admission ¥10; 8.30am-5.30pm; Line 1, Chénjiācí) This enormous compound is an ancestral shrine, a Confucian school and a 'chamber of commerce' for the Chen clan, built in 1894 by the residents of 72 villages in Guǎngdōng, where the Chen lineage is predominant. The complex encompasses 19 buildings in the traditional Lǐngnán style. All feature exquisite carvings, statues and paintings, and are decorated with ornate scrollwork throughout.

Enning Road STREET
(恩宁路; Ēnníng Lù; Map p536; Chángshòu Lù) No trip to Guǎngzhōu is complete without a stroll down century-old Ēnníng Rd. Located in the area known traditionally as Xīguān (西关), the western gate and commercial hub of old Canton, it still retains a few cultural relics, despite earnest urban renewal efforts.

The highlight is **Bāhé Academy** (八和会馆; Bāhé Huì Guǎn; Map p536; 8170 1877; 117 Ēnníng Lu; admission free; 9am-noon), a guild hall for Cantonese opera practitioners. The original academy opened in 1889 to provide lodging, schooling, medical and funeral services to Cantonese opera troupes. There are Bāhé Academies in some 20 countries worldwide, but this one is the mother house. It's now a gathering place for retired artists, and you'll likely meet a couple during your visit.

LOCAL KNOWLEDGE

KǑNG XIÀNZHŪ (孔宪珠), VETERAN CANTONESE OPERA ACTOR, 87

How did you get into Cantonese opera?

In the 1930s after the Japanese had seized Guǎngzhōu, I was a kid living in the country. I followed an opera troupe around. They were performing for the Japanese army so they could have food to eat. They let me in as a sidekick; eventually I came to play comedic characters.

Why do Cantonese opera people worship the Fire God?

According to legend, the Fire God (华光师傅; Huāguāng Shīfù) was sent by the emperor of the heavens to burn down an opera house that was making too much noise. But the god was so moved by the performance that he asked the audience to burn incense instead to fool the emperor. He protects us from fire, poverty, tricky negotiations and other mishaps. Many actors came from the grassroots, you see.

Are there special festivals?

Every year on the birthday of the Fire God (the 28th day of the ninth month of the lunar calendar usually around November, Bāhé throws a banquet for those in the industry. From early morning, you'll hear gongs and drums and ceremonies are performed at Luányú Táng. More than 500 people will show up for the feasting that takes place both indoors and on the sidewalk.

East Guǎngzhōu

N 0 —— 200 m
0 —— 0.1 miles

East Guǎngzhōu

◎ Top Sights
Guǎngzhōu Opera House A6
New Guǎngdōng Museum................B6

✕ Eating
1 Bǐngshèng Restaurant B6

◎ Drinking
2 Brew A6
3 McCawley's.......................................A5
4 Rebel Rebel B4
5 Tavern A6

◎ Entertainment
6 Guǎngzhōu Opera House A6

ⓘ Transport
7 Guǎngzhōu Dōngzhàn Coach
   Station..A1
8 Singapore Airlines A2

grey walls are photos of well-known artists and librettists, and at the far end of the hall, incense glows on a shrine dedicated to the Fire God.

Turn right as you leave the academy and walk for about a block before making another right into a lane called Yongqing Erxiang (永庆二巷). The second-last unit in the lane is **Luányú Táng** (銮舆堂; Map p536; ◎10am-3pm), a 200-year-old union for actors playing martial and acrobatic roles in Cantonese opera. The union still gives free training in martial arts for the stage to children on weekends. Every Monday, Wednesday and Friday, after 2pm, members come here for an opera 'jamming' session on the 2nd floor. Visitors may be let in at their discretion.

Interestingly, the last unit in this lane used to be the **ancestral home of Bruce Lee** (Map p536), the kung fu (gōngfū) icon, whose father Lǐ Hǎiquán (李海泉) was – you guessed it – a Cantonese opera actor and a member of that union. There's now a wall in its place, but if you retrace your steps out of the alley, turn right and head up Enning Rd, you'll pass the gates of a school. In the right corner, just past the entrance, you can see that shuttered house.

Other highlights on Enning Rd include **Zhāntiānyòu House** (詹天佑故居; Zhāntiānyòu Gùjū; Map p536; 43 Yacai Xiang; 芽菜巷43號; admission free; ◎10am-noon & 2.30-5.30pm Tue-Sun), a modest Xīguān house with a humble exhibition on the life of the Father of Chinese Railroad.

Don't miss the original 3m-tall wooden door from 1889. The only item that survived a bombing by the Japanese in 1937, it was used during the Great Leap Forward as a parking plank for 4-tonne vehicles, and clearly survived that as well. Gracing the

ISLANDS

Shāmiàn Island
HISTORIC AREA

(沙面岛; Shāmiàn Dǎo; Map p536; M Line 1, Huángshā) This leafy oasis, acquired as a foreign concession in 1859, offers a peaceful respite from the city. In the 19th century, the British and French were granted permission to set up their warehouses here. Major renovation has restored some of the buildings to their original splendour. Shamian Dajie is a tranquil stretch of gardens and trees. The **Church of Our Lady of Lourdes** (天主教露德圣母堂; Tiānzhǔjiào Lùdé Shèngmǔ Táng; Map p536; 14 Shamian Dajie; ⊙8am-6pm) was built by the French in 1892.

FREE Whampoa Military Academy
MUSEUM

(黄埔军校; Huángpǔ Jūnxiào; ⊘8820 1082; ⊙9am-5pm Tue-Sun) Located on Chángzhōu Island (长洲岛; Chángzhōu Dǎo), the academy, established in 1924 by the Kuomintang (KMT), trained military elites for both the KMT and the CCP. It was destroyed by the Japanese in 1938 and the present structure was restored in 1965. The complex has a museum dedicated to the military history of modern China.

Take metro Line 2 to Chìgǎng station, then exit C1. Board bus 262 on Xingang Zhonglu to Xīnzhōu pier (新洲码头; Xīnzhóu Mǎtou). Ferries (¥1.50) to the academy depart every hour from 7.40am to 7.40pm, and every 20 minutes from 7.50am to 9.30am. Private boats will also make the 10-minute trip there for about ¥15.

FREE Xīnhài Revolution Museum
MUSEUM

(辛亥革命纪念馆; Xīnhàigémìng Jiniànguǎn; ⊘8252 5897; Junxiao Lu, Huángpǔ Qū; ⊙9am-5pm Tue-Sun) Also on Chángzhōu Island is this handsome 18,000 sq m museum that was opened to commemorate the centenary of the Xinhai Revolution in 1911.

Costing some ¥320 million to build, it tells the story of the revolution, its important players, and the literary trends that emerged around that time. Though the narrative tends towards propaganda, the exhibits are interesting and well put together.

Take bus 383 or 430 and disembark at Chángzhōujie, or take Line 4 of the metro and get off at Dàxuéchéng Běi, then take bus 383 to Chángzhōujie, and walk for five minutes.

Guǎngdōng Museum of Art
MUSEUM

(广东美术馆; Guǎngdōng Měishùguǎn; off Map p536; ⊘8735 1468; www.gdmoa.org; 38 Yanyu Lu; admission ¥15; ⊙9am-5pm Tue-Sun; ⊒89, 194, 131A) At the southern end of Èrshā Island (Èrshā Dǎo), this worthy museum showcases the works of important Cantonese artists and has been the site of the Guǎngzhōu Triennale, first held in 2003.

Guǎngdōng Overseas Chinese Museum
MUSEUM

(广东华侨博物馆; Guǎngdōng Huáqiáo Bówùguǎn; off Map p536; ⊘8735 3707; 32 Yanyu Lu; ⊙9.30am-noon & 1.30-4.30pm Tue, Thu and Sat; ⊒89, 194, 131A) This museum opposite the Guǎngdōng Museum of Art toots the horn of overseas Chinese of Cantonese descent with its tiny collection on the history and contributions of this group of people.

YUÈXIÙ DISTRICT

Mausoleum of the Nanyue King
MAUSOLEUM

(南越王墓; Nányuèwáng Mù; Map p536; ⊘3618 2475; www.gznywmuseum.org/nanyuewang/index. html; 867 Jiefang Beilu; admission ¥15; ⊙9am-5.30pm; M Line 2, Yuèxiù Gōngyuán) This superb mausoleum from the 2000-year-old Nányuè kingdom is one of China's best museums. It houses the tomb of Zhao Mo, second king of Nányuè, who was sent south by the emperor in 214 BC to quell unrest and established a sovereign state with Guǎngzhōu as its capital. Don't miss Zhao Mo's jade burial suit – jade was thought to preserve the body.

Dōngshān Area
HISTORIC AREA

(东山区; Dōngshān Qū; Map p536) Tree-lined Xinhepu Lu (新河浦路), Xuguyuan Lu (恤孤院路) and Peizheng Lu (培正路) and the vicinity in the historic Dōngshān area offer a welcome respite from the city. You'll see schools and churches raised by American missionaries in the 1900s, and exquisite villas built by overseas Chinese and military bigwigs of the Kuomintang. To get here, take metro Line 1 to Dōngshān Kǒu station, exit A. Walk along Shuqian Lu to the south and follow the signs.

The most beautifully restored building is the three-storey **Kuí Garden** (逵园; Kuí Yuán; Map p536; ⊘8765 9746; 9 Xuguyuan Lu; admission free; ⊙10am-midnight), built in 1922 by an overseas Chinese in America. Surrounded by a lush garden, it features a reddish facade, portico, colonnaded verandahs and the original fireplace. It now houses an art gallery and a cafe, both lovely.

Spring Garden (春园; Chūnyuán; Map p536; 22-26 Xinhepu Lu; admission free; ⊙9am-5pm, closed Mon) was the former headquarters of the central committee of the CCP in 1923, and Mao Zedong lived here during the party's third national congress.

Yuèxiù Park PARK

(越秀公园; Yuèxiù Gōngyuán; Map p536; 988 Jiefang Beilu; admission ¥5; ⏱6am-9pm; Ⓜ Line 2, Yuèxiù Gōngyuán) You'll find gardens, shaded paths, historical monuments and museums in this vast urban park. **Zhènhǎi Tower** (Zhènhǎi Lóu; Map p536), built in 1380, was used as a watchtower to keep out the pirates who once pillaged China's coastal cities. It contains **Guǎngzhōu City Museum** (广州市博物馆; Guǎngzhōushì Bówùguǎn; Map p536; www.guangzhoumuseum.cn/en/main.asp; admission ¥10; ⏱9am-5.30pm), which has an excellent collection tracing the history of Guǎngzhōu from the Neolithic period, and sweeping views from the top storey.

Orchid Garden GARDENS

(兰圃; Lán Pǔ; Map p536; 901 Jiefang Beilu; admission ¥5, with tea tasting ¥20; ⏱8am-6pm; Ⓜ Line 2, Yuèxiù Gōngyuán) Across from Yuèxiù Park is this charming orchid garden. On the western edge of the park is an **old Muslim grave** (清真先贤古墓; Qīngzhēn Xiānxián Gǔmù; Map p536; admission ¥5; ⏱8am-6pm) that's supposedly the burial site of Abu Waqas, who is credited with bringing Islam to China.

Guǎngzhōu Museum of Art MUSEUM

(广州艺术博物院; Guǎngzhōu Yìshù Bówùyuàn; Map p536; ☎8350 6255; 13 Luhu Lu; admission ¥20; ⏱9am-5pm Tue-Fri, 9.30am-4.30pm Sat & Sun; 🚌10, 63) The museum has an extensive collection of works, ranging from ancient to contemporary Chinese art and sculpture, and a collection of rare Tibetan tapestries on the top floor.

Temple of the Six Banyan Trees BUDDHIST

(六榕寺; Liùróng Sì; Map p536; ☎8339 2843; 87 Liurong Lu; admission ¥5, pagoda ¥10; ⏱8am-5pm; 🚌56) This Buddhist temple was built in AD 537 to enshrine Buddhist relics brought over from India. They were placed in the octagonal Decorated Pagoda (Huā Tǎ). The temple was given its current name by the exiled poet Su Dongpo in 1099, who waxed lyrical over the banyans in the courtyard. The trees are long gone but you can see the characters *(liùróng)* he wrote above the temple gates.

Guǎngxiào Temple BUDDHIST

(光孝寺; Guǎngxiào Sì; Map p536; ☎8108 7421; 109 Guangxiao Lu; admission ¥5; ⏱6am-5.30pm; Ⓜ Line 1, Xīmén Kǒu) The 'Bright Filial Piety Temple' is the oldest temple in Guǎngzhōu, dating back to the 4th century. By the Tang dynasty it was well established as a centre of Buddhist learning in southern China. Bodhidharma, the founder of Zen Buddhism, taught here. Most of the current buildings date from the 19th century, including a main hall with double eaves and a 10m-tall Buddha statue.

Mosque Dedicated to the Prophet MOSQUE

(怀圣寺; Huáishèng Sì; Map p536; ☎8333 3593; 56 Guangta Lu; Ⓜ Line 1, Xīmén Kǒu) The original building is believed to have been founded here in 627 by Abu Waqas, an uncle of the Prophet Mohammed, making it the first of its kind in China. The present mosque dates from the Qing dynasty.

Cathedral of the Sacred Heart CHURCH

(石室教堂; Shíshì Jiàotáng; Map p536; 368 Yide Lu; Ⓜ Line 2, Hǎizhū Guǎngchǎng) The French were granted permission to build this cathedral after the second Opium War. The twin-spired Roman Catholic cathedral was designed in the neo-Gothic style and built entirely of granite, with massive towers reaching a height of 48m.

FREE Goelia Concept 225 BUILDING

(歌莉娅225概念会所; Gēlìyà Èrèrwǔ Gàiniàn Huìsuǒ; Map p536; ☎8336 0050; 225 Beijing Lu; ⏱11am-11pm Tue-Sun; 🚌106, 544) Behind the orange facade of this charming restored building (c 1949) are five floors of narrow, mazelike spaces containing an indoor garden, a flower shop and exhibition galleries. On the top floor is cafe and store Benshop (see p548).

Pearl River Cruises BOAT TRIP

The **Guǎngzhōu Star Cruises Company** (☎8333 2222) has eight evening cruises on the Pearl River (¥48 to ¥88, two hours) between 6pm and 11pm. Boats leave from the **Tiānzì Pier** (Tiānzì Mǎtou; Map p536; Beijing Lu), just east of Hǎizhū Bridge (Hǎizhū Qiáo; catch metro Line 2 from Hǎizhū Guǎngchǎng station), and head down the river as far as Èrshā Island (Èrshā Dǎo) before turning back.

TIĀNHÉ DISTRICT

Redtory VILLAGE

(红砖厂; Hóngzhuān Chǎng; ☎8557 8470; www.redtory.com.cn/english/redtory.php; 128 Yuancun Sihenglu; 员村四横路128号; ⏱10.30am-9pm; Ⓜ Line 3, Yúncūn, exit B) Occupying the former premises of Guǎngdōng Canned Food Factory (c 1958) is this pleasant artist village featuring galleries, bookstores and cafes. **Cultural** (有文化; Yǒuwénhuà; http://

travelideas.taobao.com; ⊙11am-8pm) sells attractive souvenirs created by designers in Guǎngdōng. Redtory is about 600m from the metro exit.

✰✰✰ Festivals & Events

Canton Trade Fair
TRADE FAIR
(Zhōngguó Chūkǒu Shāngpǐn Jiāoyì Huì; ☑2608 8888; www.cantonfair.org.cn) The 15-day Canton Trade Fair is held twice yearly, usually in April and October, on Pázhōu Island (Pázhōu) south of the river.

🛏 Sleeping

Guǎngzhōu's choices in the budget and lower midrange are dreary. For those who want to splurge, there are plenty of excellent top-end and upper-midrange hotels. They're expensive, especially during the Canton Trade Fair (usually in April and October). All hotels offer in-room broadband internet access.

HǍI ZHŪ, YUÈXIÙ & TIĀNHÉ DISTRICTS

⌜TOP CHOICE⌟ Garden Hotel
HOTEL $$$
(花园酒店; Huāyuán Jiǔdiàn; Map p536; ☑8333 8989; www.thegardenhotel.com.cn; 368 Huanshi Donglu; 环市东路368号; r/ste from ¥3200/5200; Ⓜ Line 5, Táojīn; ❋ @ 🛜 🌊) One of the most popular upmarket hotels in Guǎngzhōu with waterfalls and lovely gardens at the back and on the 4th floor. Rooms are as classy as its lobby. Bookings essential.

Zhūhǎi Special Economic Zone Hotel
HOTEL $$
(珠海特区大酒店; Zhūhǎi Tèqū Dàjiǔdiàn; Map p536; ☑61276888; fax 8108 3542; 11-15 Haizhu Beilu; 海珠北路11-15号; d/ste from ¥580/828; Ⓜ Line 1, Xīmén Kǒu, exit C; ❋ @ 🛜) This designated hotel for the reception of government officials has 170 clean and spacious rooms, and very good service. There's a nonsmoking floor and wi-fi in the lobby. It's next to a large seafood restaurant owned by the same group.

Old Canton Youth Hostel
HOSTEL $
(广州古粤东山青年旅舍; Guǎng zhōu Gǔyuè Dōngshān Qīngnián Lǚshè; Map p536; ☑8730 4485; 22 Xuguyuan Lu; 恤孤院路22号; dm ¥50, s with bathroom ¥120-150, d without bathroom ¥150; ❋ @ 🛜) Located close to Kuí Garden in the leafy Dōngshān area (东山) of Yuèxiù (越秀) district, this new hostel is a good budget option. Rooms are clean and come with free wi-fi.

SHĀMIÀN ISLAND & FĀNGCŪN DISTRICTS

Shāmiàn Island is by far the quietest and most attractive area to stay in Guǎngzhōu.

Guǎngdōng Victory Hotel
HOTEL $$$
(胜利宾馆; Shènglì Bīnguǎn; Map p536; ☑8121 6688; www.vhotel.com; 53 & 54 Shamian Beijie; 沙面北街53、54号; r from ¥800, tr ¥1180, ste from ¥1380; ❋ @) There are two branches of the Victory Hotel on Shāmiàn Island: an older one at 54 Shamian Beijie (enter from 10 Shamian Sijie) and a newer wing (胜利宾馆 (新楼); Map p536) at 52 Shamian Nanjie. Both offer decent value for money.

White Swan Hotel
HOTEL $$$
(白天鹅宾馆; Báitiān'é Bīnguǎn; Map p536; ☑8188 6968; www.whiteswanhotel.com; 1 Shamian Nanjie; r ¥1600-1800, ste from ¥4100; @ 🛜) One of the city's most prestigious hotels, it has a waterfall and fish pond in the lobby and an excellent range of rooms and outlets. It's was renovated in September 2012.

Guǎngzhōu Riverside International Youth Hostel
HOSTEL $
(广州江畔国际青年旅舍; Guǎngzhōu Jiāngpàn Guójì Qīngnián Lǚshè; off Map p536; ☑2239 2500; www.yhachina.com; 15 Changdi Jie; 长堤街15号; dm ¥50, s ¥108-138, d ¥148-198, ste from ¥268; Ⓜ Line 1, Fāngcūn, exit B1; @ 🛜) Located in Fāngcūn next to a bar street, this YHA-affiliated hostel has spotless rooms and a welcoming vibe.

As you exit the metro station, turn right and walk through the back lane next to the hospital and you'll reach tree-lined Luju Lu (陆居路). Turn left and walk until you see the river. Then make a right and it's another five minutes' walk. Ferries depart frequently from Huángshā pier on Shāmiàn Island to Fāngcūn pier right in front of the hostel.

Guǎngzhōu Youth Hostel
HOSTEL $
(广东鹅潭宾馆; Guǎngdōng Étán Bīnguǎn; Map p536; ☑8121 8298; www1.gzyhostel.com; 2 Shamian Sijie; 沙面四街2号; dm/s ¥60/240, d ¥260-320, tr ¥390; @) For the cheapest beds on Shāmiàn Island, head to this nondescript hostel. Backpacker ambience is nonexistent, but rooms are moderately clean.

🍴 Eating

Guǎngzhōu is home to some excellent Cantonese restaurants. Dim sum (点心; diǎnxīn), or yum cha (饮茶; yǐnchá; tea-drinking), may be the best-known form of Cantonese cuisine to foreigners, but in fact, noodles, congee and desserts are equally popular locally.

LĬNGNÁN CULTURE

Lǐngnán (岭南), literally, South of the Ranges, refers to that region to the south of the five mountain ranges (see p557) that separate the Yangzi River (central China) from the Pearl River (southern China). Traditionally Lǐngnán encompassed several provinces, but today, it's become almost synonymous with Guǎngdōng.

The term Lǐngnán was traditionally used by men of letters on the Yangzi side as a polite reference to the boonies, where 'mountains were tall and emperors out of sight'. These northerners regarded their southern cousins as less robust (physically and morally), more romantic and less civilised. But being far-flung had its benefits. Lǐngnán offered refuge to people not tolerated by the Middle Kingdom (see Hánwén Temple, p564); and played host in various diasporas in Chinese history to migrants from the north, such as the Hakkas in Méizhōu. This also explains why some Cantonese words are closer in pronunciation to the ancient speech of the Chinese.

Culturally Lǐngnán was a hybrid and a late bloomer that often went on to reverse-influence the rest of the country. Its development was also fuelled by the ideas of the revolution to end feudalism. Boundaries between refined and pedestrian are relaxed and there's an open-mindedness towards modernity. For a long time in the Qing dynasty, Guǎngzhōu was the only legal port for trade between China and the world. Interactions with the outside world infused the local culture with the foreign and the modern. Some of the most important political thinkers in modern China came from Lǐngnán, such as Kang Youwe and, of course, Sun Yatsen.

Lǐngnán culture is an important part of Cantonese culture and it manifests itself most notably in food, art and architecture, and Cantonese opera.

Lǐngnán School of Painting (1900–50)

The Lǐngnán painters were an influential lot who ushered in a national movement in art in the first half of the 20th century.

Traditionally, Chinese painters were literati well-versed in calligraphy, poetry and Confucian classics. These scholar-artists would later become imperial bureaucrats, and as they were often stationed somewhere far away from home, they expressed their nostalgia by recreating the landscapes of their childhood villages from memory.

The founding masters of the Lǐngnán School of Painting, however, studied abroad where they were exposed to Japanese and European art. China, during the Qing dynasty, was being carved up by Western powers. Sharing the ideals of the revolutionaries, these artists devoted themselves to a revolution in art by combining traditional techniques with elements of Western and Japanese realist painting.

The New National Painting, as it came to be called, featured a bolder use of colours, more realism and a stronger sense of perspective – a style that was more accessible to the citizenry of China's new republic than the literati painting of the past.

You can see Lǐngnán paintings at the Guǎngdōng Museum of Art (p541) and Memorial Hall of the Lǐngnán School of Painting (p539).

Lǐngnán Architecture

The Lǐngnán school of architecture is one of three major schools of modern Chinese architecture, alongside the Běijīng and Shànghǎi schools. It was founded in the 1950s, though earlier structures exhibiting a distinctive local style had existed since the late Ming dynasty (1600s). The features of the Lǐngnán school are lucidity, openness and an organic incorporation of nature into built environments.

ANCIENT

Examples of this style of architecture include schools, ancestral halls and temples of the Ming and Qing dynasties. The Chen Clan Academy (p539) in Guǎngzhōu and Zǔmiào in Fóshān are prime illustrations of this style.

Vernacular Lǐngnán-style houses are more decorative than their austere northern cousins. The 'wok-handle' houses (锅耳屋) in Líchá Cūn (p557) near Zhàoqìng have distinctive wok-handle-shaped roofs that also serve to prevent the spread of fire. You'll also see in Líchá Cūn bas-relief sculpting and paintings (浮雕彩画), intricate and colourful, above windows or doors, portraying classical tales, birds, flowers and landscapes.

MODERN

Appearing in the late Qing dynasty an excellent example of of this style of architecture are the Xīguān houses on Enning Road (p539) in Guǎngzhōu, with their grey bricks and stained-glass windows. These windows were products of the marriage between Manchurian windows (simple contraptions consisting of paper overlaid with wood) and coloured glass introduced to Guǎngzhōu by Westerners. It's said that when a foreign merchant presented the Empress Dowager with a bead of coloured glass, she was so dazzled by its beauty that she reciprocated with a pearl. Pànxī Restaurant(p546) in Guǎngzhōu has Manchurian windows embedded with coloured glass.

Another example of modern Lǐngnán architecture are shophouses with arcades or qílóu (骑楼) on the ground floor, a style which evolved from the arcades of southern Europe. You see them on Enning Rd and in Chìkǎn (p553) in Kāipíng.

CONTEMPORARY

The garden-restaurants and garden-hotels that proliferated between the 1950s and 1990s are examples of contemporary architecture. Guǎngzhōu's Garden Hotel (p543), White Swan Hotel (p543) and Pànxī Restaurant all contain elaborate indoor gardens complete with trees and waterfalls, and make use of glass to blur the boundary between built and natural environments.

These indoor Edens were fashioned after the private Lǐngnán-style gardens of wealthy families, such as Liáng Garden (p550) in Fóshān, which together with the imperial gardens of Peking and the scholars' gardens of Jiāngnán, constituted the three main types of Chinese gardens. Thanks to these architects, the privilege of having gardens in the interior was now available to all.

Cantonese Opera

Cantonese opera is a regional form of Chinese opera that evolved from theatrical forms of the north and neighbouring regions. Like Peking opera, it involves music, singing, martial arts, acrobatics and acting. There's elaborate face painting, glamorous period costumes and, for some of the roles, high-pitched falsetto singing. But compared to its northern cousin, it tends to feature more scholars than warriors in its tales of courtship and romance.

You don't have to understand or even like Cantonese opera to appreciate it as an important aspect of Cantonese culture – there's no shortage of related attractions, such as Bāhé Academy (p539) and Luányú Táng (p539) in Guǎngzhōu, a festival (see boxed text, p539), and a props speciality shop in Cháozhōu (see p564).

If you do decide to catch a show at Culture Park in Guǎngzhōu, those exotic strains could years later become the key that unlocks your memory of your travels in China.

Cantonese Cuisine

There's a saying 'Good food is in Guǎngzhōu' (食在广州). Regional chauvinism aside, Cantonese food is very good. The most influential of the eight major regional cuisines of China, it's known for complex cooking methods, an obsession with freshness and the use of a wide range of ingredients.

Many Cantonese dishes depend on quick cooking over high heat – these require skills (versus patience over a stew) that are less common in other regional cuisines. Cantonese chefs are also masters at making new techniques sizzle in their language. Dishes like sweet and sour pork, crab shell au gratin and tempura-style prawns show an open-mindedness to foreign ideas.

When it comes to haute cuisine, even northern cooks would acknowledge the superiority of their Cantonese colleagues in making the best of expensive items like abalone. Also, many of the costliest marine life to grace the Cantonese table, such as deep-sea fish and large prawns, simply don't grow in inland rivers.

TOP CHOICE Pànxī Restaurant DIM SUM $$

(泮溪酒家; Pànxī Jiǔjiā; Map p536; ☎8172 1328; 151 Longjin Xilu; dishes from ¥40; ☺7.30am-midnight; MChángshòu Lù; 🅿) Set in a majestic garden and embracing another one within its walls, Pànxī is the most representative of Guǎngzhōu 's garden-restaurants. Corridors, courtyards, ponds, bridges and bushes have been brought together to give the effect of 'every step, a vista' (一步一景). Seniors come for the solid dim sum and to sing an operatic aria or two when the mood is right. It's impossible to get a table after 8.30am.

Bǐngshèng Restaurant CANTONESE $$

(炳胜品味; Bǐngshèng Hǎixiān Jiǔjiā; Map p540; ☎3803 5888; 2 Xiancun Lu; dishes from ¥48; ☺11am-midnight; 🚌293, 886) One of the top restaurants in town in terms of food quality, this flagship of the Bǐngshèng chain in Zhūjiāng New Town has classy decor to boot. Its signature dish is the crispy barbecued pork (脆皮叉烧; cuìpí chāshāo).

Táng Lì Yuán CANTONESE $$

(唐荔园; Táng Lì Yuán; ☎8181 8002; mains ¥18-200; ☺7.30am-3pm & 5pm-3am; MLine 1, Huángshā) This garden-restaurant, known for its roast pigeon (金牌乳鸽; jīnpái rǔgē), is located inside Lìwān Lake Park (荔湾湖公园; Lìwān Hú Gōngyuán; Map p536). A highlight are the tables on boats that you can reserve for dinner. They're inspired by Zǐdòng Chuán (紫洞船), aka 'drinking boats' or 'whore boats' used in the Qing dynasty by Xīguān merchants to entertain with banquets, opera and women.

Each boat here seats six. There's a cover charge and a 'seat fee' of respectively ¥150 and ¥20 per person. The restaurant sits at the junction of Huangsha Dadao (黄沙大道) and Ruyi Fang (如意坊).

Wilber's EUROPEAN $$$

(Map p536; ☎3761 1101; www.wilber.com.cn; 62 Zhusigang Ermalu; mains ¥30-180; ☺11am-4pm & 5-9pm; MDōngshān Kǒu; 🛜🅿) Hidden on the edge of Yuèxiù district, gay-friendly Wilber's gets top marks for drinks and atmosphere, and the food is not far behind. It's housed in a restored colonial villa with whitewashed walls and a leafy patio.

Chén Tiānjì CANTONESE $

(陈添记; Map p536; ☎8182 8774; 59 Baohua Lu; dishes ¥7-32; ☺9.30am-10.30pm; MChángshòu Lù) This famous old hole-in-the-wall serves three things – crunchy blanched fish skin (鱼皮; yúpí) tossed with peanuts and parsley, sampan congee (艇仔粥; tǐngzǎi zhōu) and riceflour rolls (肠粉; chángfěn). At 59 Baohua Lu, turn into an alley, and it's the second eatery.

Shùnjì Bīngshì CANTONESE, DESSERTS $

(顺记冰室; Map p536; ☎8181 4287; 85 Baohua Lu; dishes ¥6-20; ☺7am-1am; MChángshòu Lù; 🍴) Steamed rice-flour rolls come in many varieties here, including vegetarian such as plain (净斋肠; zhèngzhāi cháng), with crullers (炸面肠; zhámiàn cháng), monk's way (罗汉素肠; luóhàn sùzhāi cháng) or with eggs (鸡蛋肠; jīdàn cháng). There's also a selection of desserts.

Nánxìn DESSERTS $

(南信; Map p536; 47 Dishipu Lu; desserts ¥7-15; ☺10am-midnight; MChángshòu Lù) Popular stop for Cantonese desserts, including steamed egg white with milk (双皮奶; shuāngpínǎi).

Fó Yǒu Yuán VEGETARIAN $

(佛有缘; Map p536; 1 Fu'er Rd, Liwan district; dishes from ¥18; ☺7am-3pm & 5-10pm; MChénjiācí) An unpretentious vegetarian restaurant hidden in the Xìngfú Xīncūn (幸福新村) residential quarter.

Lucy's WESTERN $$

(Lùsī Jiǔbā Cāntīng; Map p536; 3 Shamian Nanjie; mains ¥23-118; ☺11am-2am; MHuángshā; 🛜🅿) This Tex Mex place is popular with expats seeking comfort food. It's located in a park on Shāmiàn.

🍷 Drinking

Guǎngzhōu's next party hub is looking to be Zhūjiāng Pátí (珠江琶醍; off Map p536), a strip of land by the river that houses the massive Zhūjiāng Brewery. The brewery, however, has been slowly evacuating from the premises and should finish relocating by 2015. Abandoned facilities have been taken over by trendy bars and clubs. With the brewery still visibly in operation, it's the city's most surreal (and boozy) party place.

As well as the entries listed below, you can try the upmarket Yánjiāng Lù Bar Street.

Shāmiàn Clubhouse BAR

(Shāmiàn Dàjiē; Map p536; ☺11am-11pm; MHuángshā; 🛜) The 'Red Mansion' (c 1907) houses a hotel reserved for customs officials and a clubby bar with long teak flooring that's open to the public. Once known as 'Shāmiàn's grandest mansion', the building fuses features of British colonial architecture such as conical pinnacles, colonnades and louvre windows, with the Lǐngnán fondness for skylight.

TOP CHOICE Kuí Garden
CAFE

(逵园; Kuí Yuán; Map p536; ☑8765 9746; 9 Xuguyuan Lu; ⊙10am-midnight; Ⓜ Line 1, Dōngshān Kǒu; ☎) Housed in the gorgeous Kuí Garden, in the Dōngshān (东山) area, this cafe serves decent coffees and teas, as well as canapés and alcoholic beverages. The rooms and verandah of the original house have been turned into stylish, warm-toned seating areas.

Ten Cafe
CAFE

(十号咖啡店; Shíhào Kāfēidiàn; Map p536; ☑8766 9918; 105 Yandun Lu; ⊙8pm-2am; Ⓜ Line 1, Dōngshān Kǒu; ☎) With large hanging mirrors, marble-topped tables and leather couches, this upmarket lounge in the Dōngshān area resembles a cosy living room, with hints of a 19th-century French salon. It has a good selection of imported beer and wine, and decent cocktails.

Rebel Rebel
BAR

(Map p540; ☑8520 1579; www.rebelrebelgz.com; 42 Tiyu Donglu; ⊙10am-2am, happy hour 3-9pm; Ⓜ Shípáiqiáo) Located within the Tiānhé District, this new bar with open frontage is easy to spot with its rows of coloured bottles stacked up against a white wall. It has a nice urban vibe, good wines, and beer on tap. See the website for special events. Exiting the metro station, walk down Tiyu Donglu on the One Link Plaza side of the road. After about 300m turn left down a side road. You'll see a light box showing directions.

Sun's
LOUNGE

(☑8977 9056; www.sunsgz.com; B25-26 Yuejiang Xilu; ☐779, 765) The best of the lot in Zhūjiāng Pátí Sun's is packed with trendy expats and moneyed locals. You can choose to sip cocktails on couches by the river or dance to electronic music inside the design-oriented bar. Take bus 779 or 765 and disembark at the final stop, Zhūjiāng Beer Brewery (珠江啤酒厂总站).

There are a number of exuberant pubs in Zhūjiāng New Town (Ⓜ Zhūjiāng Xīnchéng) offering live sports broadcasts, free wi-fi and beer on tap that have recently sprung up, all within five minutes' walk of each other.

Tavern
PUB

(Map p540; ☑8550 3038; www.taverngz.com; Poly 108, 6 Huaju Lu; ⊙11am-2am, happy hour 4-8pm, all day Mon; ☎) English sports bar Tavern offers a selection of premium beers including Paulaner and Strongbow, and a pool table.

Brew
PUB

(Map p540; ☑3804 9549; www.thebrew-china.com; 105, 106 Huaxun Jie; ⊙happy hour 4-8pm, all day Mon; ☎) Canadian-American bar that has table taps that let you pour your own beer and pay with a 'VIP' card; it holds beer-pong contests.

McCawley's
PUB

(Map p540; ☑3801 7000; www.mccawleys.com; Shop 101, 16 Huacheng Dadao; ⊙10am-2am, happy hour 10am-10pm; ☎) Spacious McCawley's has more than 50 Irish whiskies on offer, in addition to Irish cider, Irish beer and a Filipino band.

☆ Entertainment

Your best resource for entertainment in Guǎngzhōu is www.gzstuff.com.

TOP CHOICE Guǎngzhōu

Tekkuan Live House
LIVE MUSIC

(广州踢馆; Guǎngzhōu Tīguǎn; Map p536; www.gztekkwun.com; 201 Huan Shi Zhonglu; Ⓜ Xiǎoběi, exit B) The most professional live house venue in Guǎngzhōu, Tekkuan only opens three or four nights a week when there are gigs on (check its website for exact times). Professional bands from Russia, the Netherlands, France and Hong Kong have performed there, playing jazz, rock, fusion and pop.

Tell the cab driver to go to Xisheng Jie (西胜街) on Huāguǒ Shān (花果山), which is 150m away from Guǎngzhōu TV Station (广州电视台; Guǎngzhōu Diànshì Tái). Walk to the end of Xisheng Jie and you'll see it. Alternatively, take Line 5 of the metro to Xiǎoběi (小北), leaving by exit B. Go down Tongxin Lu (童心路) and turn left at the first traffic lights into Xisheng Jie.

C Union
LIVE MUSIC

(喜窝 (城市会); Xǐwō; off Map p536; ☑3584 0144; 115 Shuiyin Lu; ⊙7pm-2am) An unpretentious and busy boozer, C Union attracts a good mix of college students and expats with its live R&B and reggae. It's behind the Chéngshìhuì (城市会) building, in the Yuèxiù District. Only accessible by taxi.

Guǎngzhōu Opera House
THEATRE

(广州大剧院; Guǎngzhōu dàjùyuàn; Map p540; ☑3839 2888-2666; www.chgoh.org; 1 Zhujiang Xilu; ⊙9am-4.30pm, closed Mon; Ⓜ Line 3, Zhūjiāng Xīnchéng, exit B1) This new opera house in Zhūjiāng New Town is Guǎngdōng's premier performance venue.

Xīnghǎi Concert Hall — THEATRE
(星海音乐厅; Xīnghǎi Yīnyuè Tīng; off Map p536; ☎8735 2766; 33 Qingbo Lu; 🚌 89, 194, 131A) Home to the Guǎngzhōu Symphony Orchestra, the city's venue for classical music is on Èrshā Island.

🛍 Shopping

Xīguān Antique Street — ANTIQUES
(西关古玩城; Xīguān Gǔwán Chéng; Map p536; Lizhiwan Lu; Ⓜ Line 5, Zhōngshān Bālù) This street, in the Xīguān area, has shops which sell everything from ceramic teapots to Tibetan rugs. Even if you're not in the market for loading up your pack with ceramic vases, it's still a wonderful place in which to wander and browse.

Fāngcūn Tea Market — TEA
(芳村茶叶市场; Fāngcūn Cháyè Shìchǎng; Fangcun Dadao; Ⓜ Fāngcūn, exit C) A sprawling market with block after block of tea shops, along with malls selling tea and teaware. Most target wholesale traders but retail is often possible.

Fāng Suǒ Commune — BOOKS
(方所; Fāngsuǒ; ☎3868 2327; MU35, Tai Koo Hui, 383 Tianhe Lu; ⊙10am-10pm; Ⓜ Line 1, Shípáiqiáo) Occupying some 2000 sq m in a classy mall, this elegant bookstore also sells clothes, homewares and coffee. There are more than 90,000 titles, mostly Chinese, including many on art, literature and culture, as well as books from Taiwan. The fashion and lifestyle items on sale have a clean, minimalist feel, but they're pricey.

Benshop — SOUVENIRS
(Map p536; www.benshop.net) A trendy souvenir store and cafe on the top floor of Goelia Concept 225.

ℹ Information

Good maps of Guǎngzhōu in both English and Chinese can be found at newsstands and bookshops.

Emergency
Ambulance (☎120)
Fire (☎119)
Police (☎110)

Internet Access
Most hotels provide free broadband internet access. Free wi-fi is available at all Guǎngdōng branches of Starbucks, Fairwood (大快活; dàkuàihuó) and Cafe de Coral (大家乐; dàjiālè).

Medical Services
Can-Am International Medical Centre (加美国际医疗中心; Jiāměi Guójì Yīliáo Zhōngxīn; ☎8386 6988; www.canamhealthcare.com; 5th fl, Garden Tower, Garden Hotel, 368 Huanshi Donglu) Has English-speaking doctors, but you'll need to call ahead.

Guǎngzhōu First Municipal People's Hospital (广州第一人民医院; Guǎngzhōu Dìyī Rénmín Yīyuàn; ☎8104 8888; 1 Panfu Lu) Medical clinic for foreigners on 1st floor.

Guǎngzhōu Hospital of Traditional Chinese Medicine (广州市中医医院; Guǎngzhōu shì Zhōngyī Yīyuàn; ☎8122 6288; 16 Zhuji Lu) Acupuncture, herbal medicine and other traditional Chinese remedies.

Money
ATMs are available – most 24 hours – throughout Guǎngzhōu.

American Express Guǎngzhōu (美国运通广州; Měiguó Yùntōng Guǎngzhōu; ☎8331 1611; fax 8331 1616; Room 1004, Main Tower, Guǎngdōng International Hotel, 339 Huanshi Donglu; ⊙9am-5.30pm Mon-Fri) Cashes/sells Amex travellers cheques.

Bank of China (中国银行; Zhōngguó Yínháng; ☎8334 0998; 686 Renmin Beilu; ⊙9am-5.30pm Mon-Fri, to 4pm Sat & Sun) Most branches change travellers cheques.

Post
China Post (中国邮政; Zhōngguó Yóuzhèng; 151 Huanshi Xilu; ⊙8am-8pm) Located next to the train station.

Telephone
China Telecom (中国电信; Zhōngguó Diànxìn; ☎10000; 196 Huanshi Xilu; ⊙9am-6pm) Main branch is opposite the train station (eastern side of Renmin Beilu).

Tourist Information
Tourism Administration of Guǎngzhōu (www.visitgz.com) has 19 tourist information centres, including the airport, train station and at 325 Zhongshan Liu Rd (open 9am to 6pm).
Tourist Complaint Hotline (☎8666 6666)

Travel Agencies
Most hotels offer travel services that, for a small charge, can help you book tickets and tours.

China Travel Service (CTS; 广州中国旅行社; Zhōngguó Lǚxíngshè; ☎8333 6888; 8 Qiaoguang Lu; ⊙8.30am-6pm Mon-Fri, 9am-5pm Sat & Sun) Located next to Hotel Landmark Canton (华夏大酒店; Huáxià Dàjiǔdiàn).

Websites
Delta Bridges Guǎngzhōu (www.deltabridges.com/users/guangzhou) Listings of events around town.

Guǎngzhōu Stuff (www.gzstuff.com) Entertainment listings, forums and classifieds.

Life of Guǎngzhōu (www.lifeofguangzhou.com) Yellow pages for visitors and expats.

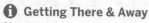 Getting There & Away

Air

China Southern Airlines (中国南方航空; Zhōngguó Nánfāng Hángkōng; ☑95539; www.cs-air.com; 181 Huanshi Xilu; ⊘24hr) The office of the major airline serving Guǎngzhōu is southeast of the main train station. Frequent flights to major cities in China include Guìlín (¥660), Shànghǎi (¥1280) and Běijīng (¥1700); also numerous international destinations.

Bus

Guǎngzhōu has many long-distance bus stations with services to destinations in Guǎngdōng, southern Fújiàn, eastern Guǎngxī and further afield. The following have frequent buses to Fóshān (¥18, 45 minutes), Kāipíng (¥62, two hours), Shēnzhèn (¥65, two hours) and Zhūhǎi (¥85, two hours). Some useful stations:

Tiānhé passenger station (Tiānhé kèyùnzhàn; Huadi Dadao; Ⓜ Tiānhé) Most frequent departures to destinations in Guǎngdōng; accessible by metro (Tiānhé Kèyùnzhàn station).

Fāngcūn passenger station (Fāngcūn kèyùnzhàn; Huadi Dadao) Accessible by metro (Kēngkǒu station).

Guǎngzhōu dōngzhàn coach station (广州东站客运站; Guǎngzhōu dōngzhàn kèyùnzhàn; Linhe Xilu) Behind Guǎngzhōu East Train Station. Good for destinations within Guǎngdōng; departures aren't as frequent as from other stations.

Guǎngdōng long-distance bus station (广东省汽车客运站; Guǎngdōng shěng qìchē kèyùnzhàn; Huanshi Xilu) Right of train station. There's a smaller long-distance bus station (Guǎngzhōu shìqìchēzhàn) over the footbridge.

Liúhuā bus station (流花车站; Liúhuā chēzhàn) Across Huanshi Xilu in front of train station.

Destinations include:

Cháozhōu ¥160 to ¥180, six hours, hourly from Tiānhé station

Guìlín ¥170, 10 hours, five daily from Guǎngdōng long-distance bus station (9.10am, 11.30am, 8.30pm, 9.30pm and 10.30pm)

Hǎikǒu ¥250 to ¥280, 13 hours, seven daily from Guǎngdōng long-distance bus station

Nánníng ¥180, 10 hours, nine daily from Guǎngdōng long-distance bus station

Qīngyuǎn ¥20 to ¥40, two hours, hourly from Liúhuā bus station

Shàntóu ¥180, five hours, every 30 minutes from Tiānhé station

Sháoguān ¥70 to ¥80, four hours, every 45 minutes from Guǎngdōng long-distance bus station

Xiàmén ¥220, nine hours, every 45 minutes from Tiānhé station

Zhàoqìng ¥45, 1½ hours, every 15 minutes from Fāngcūn station

To Hong Kong deluxe buses ply the Guǎngzhōu–Shēnzhèn freeway and this is the easiest way. Buses (¥100 to ¥110) to Hong Kong and its airport leave from Hotel Landmark Canton near Hǎizhū Square station every 30 minutes.

Buses through Zhūhǎi to Macau (¥75, 2½ hours) leave frequently from Tiānhé station (7.40am to 8pm).

Train

Guǎngzhōu's three major train stations serve destinations all over China. CTS, next to Hotel Landmark Canton, books train tickets up to five days in advance for ¥20.

From **Guǎngzhōu Main Train Station** (Guǎngzhōu Zhàn; Huanshi Xilu; Ⓜ Line 2, Guǎngzhōu Huǒchēzhàn):

Lhasa ¥818, 54 hours, one daily (12.19pm)

Sháoguān ¥57, 2½ hours, frequent services

Zhàoqìng ¥29, two hours, 14 daily

High-speed trains leave from **Guǎngzhōu South Station** (Guǎngzhōu Nánzhàn; Shibi, Pānyú) in Pānyú:

Chángshā ¥322, 2½ hours, frequent

Qīngyuǎn ¥38, 30 minutes, 12 daily (7.40am to 8.30pm)

Sháoguān ¥104, 50 minutes, frequent

Shēnzhèn North Station ¥47, 50 minutes

Wǔhàn ¥330 to ¥490, four hours, frequent

Light rail goes to Zhūhǎi (¥34, one hour).

To get to Guǎngzhōu South Station, take metro Line 2 from the Main Train Station (45 minutes) or one of the express buses (¥15, 50 minutes) from the South Station (南站快线; Nánzhàn Kuàixiàn) that leave from Liúhuā bus station, Garden Hotel and Hotel Landmark Canton.

Tickets for trains leaving from the south station can be bought in other stations, but not vice versa.

From **Guǎngzhōu East** (Guǎngzhōu Dōngzhàn; Ⓜ Line 1, Guǎngzhōu Dōngzhàn):

Běijīng ¥443, 21½ hours, two daily (3.08pm and 6.05pm)

Shànghǎi ¥367, 17 hours, one daily (6.11pm)

The station is used more for bullet trains to Shēnzhèn (¥45, 1½ hours, 6.07am to 10.40pm) and a dozen direct trains to Hong Kong (¥186, HK$190, 1¾ hours, 8.19am to 9.32pm). The **ticketing booths** (⊘7.30am-9pm) for trains to Hong Kong are on the 2nd floor.

❶ Getting Around

Greater Guǎngzhōu extends some 20km east to west and north to south. The metro is the speediest way to get around.

To/From the Airport

Báiyún International Airport (Báiyún Guójì Jīchǎng; www.baiyunairport.com) is 28km north of the city. Airport shuttle buses (¥17 to ¥28, one hour, every 15 to 30 minutes, 5am to 11pm) leave from a half-dozen locations, including the China Southern Airlines office near the Main Train Station; Tiānhé passenger station; and Fāngcūn bus station. A taxi to/from the airport will cost about ¥150.

Metro Line 3 links the airport's south terminal (Airport South station; Jīchǎng Nán) and Guǎngzhōu east station. The ride takes 45 minutes (¥7).

Bus

Guǎngzhōu has a large network of motor buses and bus rapid transport (BRT) (¥2 to ¥5).

Metro

Guǎngzhōu has eight metro lines in full service, all with free maps available. Operating hours are approximately 6.20am to 11pm and fares are ¥2 to ¥14.

Transit passes (羊城通; yáng chéng tōng; from ¥50, deposit ¥30) are available at metro stations. The deposit is refundable in designated stations, including Dōngshān Kǒu and Gōngyuán Qián. The pass can be used on all public transport, including yellow taxis.

Taxi

Taxis are abundant but demand is high. Peak hours are 8am to 9am, also around lunch and dinner. Yellow or red cabs are driven by local drivers; others by migrant drivers who may not know the city well. Flag fall is ¥10 for the first 2.3km; ¥2.6 for every additional kilometre, with a ¥1 fuel surcharge.

Around Guǎngzhōu

WHITE CLOUD HILLS 白云山

White Cloud Hills (Báiyún Shān; admission ¥5), in the northern suburbs of Guǎngzhōu, are an adjunct of **Dàyú Range** (大庾岭; Dàyú Lǐng). There are more than 30 peaks that were once dotted with temples and monasteries. It's a good hike up to the top. **Star Touching Peak** (摩星岭; Móxīng Lǐng), at 382m, is the highest point in the hills.

Take bus 24 from Zhongshan Wulu, just south of Rénmín Gōngyuán, and alight at the terminal. The trip takes between 30 to 60 minutes.

Fóshān 佛山

☑ 0757 / POP 5.9 MILLION

An hour-long bus ride will take day-trippers from Guǎngzhōu to this city. Fóshān (literally 'Buddha Hill') was famous for its ceramics in the Ming dynasty. Today, it's better known as the birthplace of two kung fu icons.

◉ Sights

Zǔ Miào TAOIST TEMPLE
(祖庙; 21 Zumiao Lu; admission ¥20; ☺8.30am-6pm; ☒101, 105, 106) Founded in the 11th century, this complex is the premier temple in Guǎngdōng dedicated to Běidì (北帝) or God of the North – his imposing likeness graces the main hall. The temple is also believed to be the place where Cantonese opera flourished, and it's still performed on Saturday and Sunday (1.50pm to 3.30pm), and during festivals to entertain the gods (and the tourists). There are also daily performances of kung fu (10.15am and 3pm) and lion dance (10.30am, 1.30pm and 3.30pm).

Besides these, the complex has two exhibition halls dedicated to Fóshān-born kung fu icons, Ip Man and Wong Fei Hung.

Liáng Garden GARDENS
(梁园; Liáng Yuán; ☑8224 1279; Songfeng Lu; admission ¥10; ☺8.30am-5.30pm) This gorgeous residence of a wealthy family that produced painters and calligraphers was built during the Qing dynasty. Designed in a Lǐngnán style (see also boxed text, p544), it delights with tranquil ponds, willow-lined pathways and, in the summer, trees heavy with wax apple, mangoes and jackfruit. From Rénshòu Temple, walk north until you see a branch of the Bank of China across the road. Liáng Garden is another 300m north of the bank.

Nánfēng Ancient Kiln CERAMICS
(南风古灶; Nánfēng Gǔzào; ☑8271 1798; 6 Gaomiao Lu, Shíwān; admission ¥25; ☺9am-5.30pm) Shíwān (石湾), 2km from downtown Fóshān, was once China's most important ceramics production centre – much of the Ming-dynasty pottery you see at museums come from this place (those sold in shops near the kiln, however, are mass-produced copies). Two ancient 'dragon kilns' of more than 30m long are set in this lovely complex with meandering stone-paved paths and the air of an ancient town. It's 17 stops from Zǔ Miào on bus 137.

THE MAKING OF A NATIONAL LEGEND

Fóshān-born Wong Fei Hung (1847–1924) is one of China's best-known folk heroes. Although a consummate kung fu (gōngfū) master in his lifetime, he didn't become widely known until his story was combined with fiction in countless movies made since 1949, most by Hong Kong directors. These, including Jet Li's *Once Upon a Time in China*, portray him as a hero who fought villains in defence of justice and national pride. Sadly, Wong spent his later years in desolation, after his son was murdered and his martial-arts school was destroyed by fire. Regardless, an astonishing 106 movies (and counting!) have celebrated this son of Fóshān, resulting in the world's longest movie series and a national legend.

Another Fóshān hero is Ip Man (1893–1972), who rose to fame as a Wing Chun master at the outset of WWII (see also p979). He fled to Hong Kong in 1949 where he founded the first-ever Wing Chun school. His most famous student was Bruce Lee. Ip Man was recently immortalised by a series of semibiographical movies starring Donnie Yen.

FREE **Rénshòu Temple** BUDDHIST
(仁寿寺; Rénshòu Sì; ☑8225 3053; 9 Zumiao Lu; ◎8am-5pm; 🚍1, 2B, 5, 11) A short walk north of Zǔ Miào Temple is this former Míng monastery, which remains an active place of worship today. Inside, you'll find a pagoda built in 1656, and the Fóshān Folk Arts Studio, featuring pretty papercut art.

Fóshān Lǐngnán Tiāndì HISTORIC BUILDINGS
(Tiandi Lu, Chánchéng Qū; ◎11am-9pm; 🚍101, 105) Photogenic and gentrified, Fóshān's latest attraction is this collection of restored medicinal shops, Chinese liquor stores and old villas, that have been turned into upmarket boutiques and imported restaurants. The brand-new **Fóshān Marco Polo** (马哥孛罗酒店; Mǎgē Bóluó Jiǔdiàn; ☑757 82501888; www.marcopolohotels.com; 97 Renmin Lu, Chánchéng Qū; r/ste from ¥2380/3080; @🛜🏊❄️), under the same project, has spacious rooms, excellent service, and gives up to 50% discount off-season.

✕ Eating

Yīngjì Noodle Shop NOODLES $
(应记面家; Yīngjì Miànjiā; 116 Lianhua Lu; 莲花路116号; noodles ¥5-10; ◎7am-11pm) This excellent noodle shop opposite Liánhuā Supermarket (莲花超市; Liánhuā Cháoshì) is the go-to place in Fóshān for noodles with shrimp wonton (鲜虾云吞面; *xiānxiā yúntūnmiàn*).

Healthy Buddha Vegetarian CANTONESE, VEGETARIAN $
(健康菩提素食; Jiànkāng Pútí Sùshí; ☑8230 2836; mains ¥18-35; 🚍1, 2b, 5, 10, 11; ◎lunch & dinner; 🅿️🈲) This vegetarian restaurant on the property of Rénshòu Temple offers great value for money.

☆ Entertainment

AD Livehouse LIVE MUSIC
(西元 Livehouse; Xīyuán Livehouse; ☑139 2991 1129; Bldg 5, Xijie, Poly Canal Plaza, Denghu Xilu, Nánhǎi District; 水岸长廊,南海区,灯湖西路,保利水成西街5栋1号; ◎8.30am-2am; 🛜) This large and out-of-the-way bar with a wonderful sound system has live music on offer from 10pm every night. Performances are usually by a local band, but every month or so there are overseas acts in pop, hip hop, jazz, indie or rock who come and play. A cab here from Fóshān Lǐngnán Tiāndì costs under ¥30.

ℹ Getting There & Around

From **Zǔmiào bus station** (Zǔmiào chēzhàn; Jianxin Lu) there are buses (¥15, every 20 minutes, 6.45am to 11pm) to Guǎngzhōu's long-distance bus station, Guǎngfó bus station (Guǎngfó qìchēzhàn; Zhongshan Balu) and Fāngcūn bus station in Kēngkǒu.

Services from the **long-distance bus station** (fóshān shěng qìchēzhàn; Fenjiang Beilu), 400m south of the train station:

Shēnzhèn ¥90 to ¥100, 2½ hours, every 20 to 60 minutes

Zhūhǎi ¥60 to ¥70, three hours, every 15 to 40 minutes

Trains go to Guǎngzhōu Main Train Station (¥8 to ¥27, 30 minutes, 19 daily).

The metro runs between Guǎngzhōu and Fóshān's Zǔmiào station (¥5, 30 minutes). There's a direct express train to Hong Kong (¥210, three hours; 4.13pm) and at 10.42pm from Kowloon.

Buses 101 and 109 (¥2) link the train station to Zǔ Miào and Shíwān. Taxis start at ¥7.

Kāipíng 开平

♪0750 / POP 680,000

Kāipíng, 140km southwest of Guǎngzhōu, is home to one of the most arresting manmade attractions in Guǎngdōng – the Unesco-crowned *diāolóu* (碉楼), eccentric watchtowers featuring a fusion of Eastern and Western architectural styles. Out of the approximately 3000 original *diāolóu,* only 1833 remain.

Downtown Kāipíng is pleasant, especially the section near the Tǎnjiāng River (谭江), where you'll see people fishing next to mango and wampee trees.

Kāipíng is also the home of many overseas Chinese. Currently, 720,000 people from the country are living overseas – 40,000 more than its local population.

◉ Sights

A combo ticket to Lì Garden and the villages of Mǎjiànglóng and Zìlì costs ¥180; if you just visit Lì Garden and one of the villages, it's ¥150. Jīnjiānglǐ Village alone is ¥50.

Zìlì HISTORIC VILLAGE
(自力村; Zìlì Cūn; ◷8.30am-5.30pm) The pretty village of Zìlì, 11km west of Kāipíng, has the largest collection of *diāolóu*. Fifteen towers rise beautifully amid the paddy fields but only a few are open to the public. The most stunning is **Míngshí Lóu** (铭石楼) which has

a verandah with Ionic columns and baroque embellishments, and a hexagonal pavilion supported by European columns on its roof. It appeared in the 2010 film *Let the Bullets Fly*. **Yúnhuàn Lóu** (云幻楼) has four towers known as 'swallow nests', each with embrasures, cobblestones and a water cannon.

Next to the village is **Fang Clan's Dēng Lóu** (方氏灯楼; admission free), aka Light Tower, because of its powerful searchlight.

Jīnjiānglǐ HISTORIC VILLAGE
(锦江里; Jīnjiānglǐ Cūn; ◷9am-5pm) The highlights in this village, 20km south of Kāipíng, are the privately run **Ruìshí Lóu** (瑞石楼; admission ¥20) and **Shēngfēng Lóu** (升峰楼). The former (c 1923) is Kāipíng's tallest *diāolóu* and comprises nine storeys, topped off with a Byzantine-style roof and Roman dome. The latter was one of the few *diāolóu* that had a European architect.

In nearby Nánxìng Village, **Nánxìng Xié Lóu** (南兴斜楼; Leaning Tower; admission free) tilts severely to one side, with its central axis over 2m off-centre.

Lì Garden HISTORIC SITE
(立园; Lì Yuán; ◷8.30am-5.30pm) About 15 minutes by taxi from Kāipíng, Lì Garden has a fortified mansion constructed in 1936 by a wealthy Chinese-American born in Chicago. The interiors featuring Italianate motifs and the gardens with their manmade canals, footbridges and dappled pathways are delightful.

KĀIPÍNG'S BIZARRE TOWERS

Scattered across Kāipíng's 20km periphery are *diāolóu* – multistorey watchtowers and fortified residences displaying a flamboyant mix of European, Chinese and Moorish architectural styles. The majority were built in the early 20th century by villagers who had made a fortune working as coolies overseas. They brought home fanciful architectural ideas they'd seen in real life and on postcards, and built the towers as fortresses to protect their families from bandits, flooding and Japanese troops.

The oldest *diāolóu* were communal watchtowers built by several families in a village. Each family was allocated a room within the citadel, where all its male members would go to spend the night to prevent kidnapping by bandits. These narrow towers had sturdy walls, iron gates and ports for defence and observation. The youngest *diāolóu* were also watchtowers, but equipped with searchlight and alarm, and located at entrances to villages.

More than 60% of *diāolóu*, however, combined residential functions with defence. Constructed by a single family, they were spacious and featured a mix of decorative motifs. As the builders had no exposure to European architectural traditions, they took liberties with proportions, resulting in outlandish buildings that seem to have leapt out of an American folk art painting or a Miyazaki cartoon.

These structures would retain a towerlike form for the first few floors, then like stoic men who have not forgotten to dream, let loose a riot of arches and balustrades, Egyptian columns, domes, cupolas, corner turrets, Chinese gables and Grecian urns.

PIGLETS FOR SALE

The mid-19th century saw Guǎngdōng in a state of despair, stalked by famine and revolt. Meanwhile, slavery was outlawed in most Western countries, creating a need to recruit cheap manpower for the exploitation of the New World. Conditions were ripe for many unskilled workers from Táishān (where Kāipíng was located) to seek opportunities for a better life overseas.

Disingenuous recruiters promised good pay and working conditions, but in reality the workers were made to work as coolies under deplorable conditions on the sugar-cane fields of South America, on farms in Southeast Asia, and in goldmining and rail construction in North America. The coolie trade was known in Cantonese as *maai ju jai* – 'selling piglets'.

Of the nine million Chinese workers who left home in the mid-19th to early 20th centuries, many died, but a handful made a fortune, becoming wealthy 'overseas Chinese', a powerful community that often brought home wealth and exotic ideas that were assimilated into the local culture.

Other *diāolóu* include the oldest tower, Yínglóng Lóu (迎龙楼) which is found in Sānménlǐ Village (三门里) and the fortified villas of Mǎjiànglóng Village (马降龙; Mǎjiànglóng).

Chìkǎn
HISTORIC VILLAGE

The charming old town of Chìkǎn (赤坎), 10km southwest of Kāipíng, has streets of shophouses with an arcade on the ground floor flanking the Tánjiāng River (潭江). These distinctive *qílóu* (骑楼) buildings were built by overseas Cantonese merchants in the 1920s. Bus 6 from Yìcí bus station takes you to Chìkǎn.

Fēngcǎi Hall
HISTORIC SITE

(风采堂; Fēngcǎi Táng; admission ¥5; ◷9am-4.30pm) Not a typical ancestral hall, this compound built in 1906 retains an exquisite southern Chinese architectural style, but with Western elements eccentrically blended. The complex is hidden inside a school 1.5km south of Chángshā bus station. Bus 2 from either bus station takes you to Fēngcǎi Zhōngxué (风采中学).

🛏 Sleeping & Eating

Staying overnight in Kāipíng would allow you to give its unique sights the attention they deserve.

Tribe of Diāomín
HOTEL $

(碉民部落; Diāomín Bùluò; ☑0750 261 6222; 126 Henan Lu, Chìkǎn; 赤坎镇河南路126号; dm per person ¥40-50, r without bathroom ¥80, q/f with bathroom ¥200-300; 🛜) A historic building right by Tánjiāng River in Chìkǎn has been turned into this pleasant hostel with a backpackers' vibe by a bicycle club. There are more than 100 bikes for hire. You can rent one for a full day of sightseeing for ¥80.

Pan Tower Hotel
HOTEL $$

(潭江半岛酒店; Tánjiāng Bàndǎo Jiǔdiàn; ☑233 3333; www.pantower.com; 2 Zhongyin Lu; 中银路2号; r ¥800; 🌡@) *The* place to stay in Kāipíng. It's on an islet on the Tánjiāng River and only accessible by taxi (¥12 from Chángshā bus station, five minutes). Offers discounts of 50% to 60%.

Kāipíng Hotel
HOTEL $$

(☑223 3333; Kaipinghotel@126.com; 19-21 Changsha Wenxin Rd; 长沙文新路19-21号; r ¥588-688, ste ¥688-1688; @🛜) This refurbished hotel has clean rooms, some overlooking the lovely Tánjiāng River. Take bus 2 or 3 from Yìcí bus station. From Chángshā bus station, it's a five-minute walk.

Home Restaurant
CHINESE $

(农家饭; Nóngjiā Fàn) Many villagers in Zìlì Village serve rustic dishes cooked with home-grown ingredients in their homes. Popular items include free-range chicken (走地鸡; *zǒudìjī*) ¥25 a catty (斤; *jīn*), and rice cooked with baby eel (黄鳝饭; *huángshàn fàn*; ¥60).

Cháojiāngchūn Restaurant
CHINESE $

(潮江春酒楼; Cháojiāngchūn Jiǔlóu; ☑0750 2219963; mains ¥25-60; ◷11am-10.30pm) This excellent restaurant serves the local speciality – braised wild-grown goose (狗仔鹅; *gǒuzǎi é*). The steamed tofu with shredded taro and ground pork (肉碎芋丝蒸豆腐; *ròusuì yùsī zhēng dòufu*) and salt-baked chicken (手撕鸡; *shǒusījī*) are also delicious.

ℹ️ Getting There & Around

Kāipíng has two bus stations that are linked by local buses 7 and 13: **Yìcí bus station** (义祠总站; Yìcí zǒngzhàn; ☑221 3126; Mucun Lu) and **Chángshā bus station** (长沙汽车站; Chángshā qìchēzhàn; ☑233 3442; Musha Lu). Both run frequent services to:

Guǎngzhōu ¥60, two hours, every 40 minutes (7am to 7.30pm)

Hong Kong (from Yìcí station only) HK$150, four hours, four times daily

Shēnzhèn ¥90, 2½ hours, every 45 minutes (7.30am to 9pm)

Zhūhǎi ¥50 to ¥72, 2½ hours, every 30 to 40 minutes (7am to 7.40pm)

Opposite Chángshā station, local buses (¥4 to ¥5) go to Chìkǎn and some of the *diāolóu*. But as these are scattered over several counties, your best bet would be to hire a taxi for the day. A full day will cost around ¥600, but you can negotiate.

Yángjiāng 阳江

☑0662 / POP 2.3 MILLION

Yángjiāng is a city on the southwestern coast of Guǎngdōng. While downtown Yángjiāng has little to jump up about, picturesque Hǎilíng Island (海陵岛; Hǎilíng Dǎo), located 50km or an hour's drive away, is home to the Maritime Silk Road Museum and some of the finest beaches in the province.

If money is not an issue, stay on Hǎilíng Island – in the up-and-coming resort area near the museum, or the livelier Zhápō (闸坡) resort town. Downtown Yángjiāng has the cheapest sleeping options.

👁 Sights

Maritime Silk Road Museum of Guǎngdōng   MUSEUM

(广东海上丝绸之路博物馆; Guǎngdōng Hǎishàng Sīchóu Zhīlù Bówùguǎn; ☑368 1111; admission ¥80, free English audioguide; ⊗9.30am-5.30pm, closed 1st & 2nd Mar & Nov) Sitting right on Shílǐ Yíntān (十里银滩) beach is this museum, purpose-built to house an 800-year-old Song-dynasty shipwreck that was wholly salvaged near the island. The remains of the 30m-long merchant vessel (Nanhai No. 1; 南海一号), and much of the 70,000 pieces of merchandise on board, now rest in a sealed glass tank. The ship is believed to have been headed for the Middle East or Africa when it sank.

The wreckage has significant archaeological value, though only 200 pieces of the porcelain, gold and copper treasures have been put on display. That said, full excavation has been planned starting in early 2013.

Beaches   BEACHES

The most beautiful with the longest stretch of coastline is **Shílǐ Yíntān** (十里银滩; literally, 10 'miles' of silver beach) where the museum is, and it's free of charge. More centrally located, however, is **Dàjiǎowān** (大角湾) beach in the lively Zhápō (闸坡) area, 10 minutes away from Shílǐ Yíntān by pedicab or a balmy 45-minute walk. It's attractive and close to restaurants and a water world. A ¥50 ticket gives you two days' unlimited entry to the beach and water world from 8am to 7pm. Tickets sold at water world are good for only a day.

🛏 Sleeping & Eating

Days Hotel & Suites   LUXURY HOTEL $$$

(☑369 8888; www.haiyundayshotel.com; Hǎilíng Island National Resort District; 海陵岛国家旅游度假区; s ¥1688-2688, d ¥1388-2388, ste ¥3288-4688; @🛜🏊) Yángjiāng's best hotel has 368 bright and spacious rooms with plush bedding, stylish lamps and, for sea-facing units, balconies. It's right by the museum.

Sunshine Peninsula International Hotel   LUXURY HOTEL $$$

(阳光半岛国际酒店; Yángguāng Bàndǎo Guójì Jiǔdiàn; ☑389 7777; www.sunshine369.com; Zhápō Lǚyóu Dàdào Nán; 闸坡旅游大道南; r ¥1380-1880, ste ¥2280-2580, villas ¥2880-8880; 🛜) A family-friendly upmarket option right by the beach in Zhápō.

Jīnhǎilì Hotel   HOTEL $

(金海利大酒店; Jīnhǎilì Dàjiǔdiàn; ☑389 6688; fax 389 5599; 23 Haibin Lu, Zhápō Town; 闸坡市海滨路23号; r ¥220-280) This affordable option in the upmarket Zhápō area has a gloomy lobby and big decent rooms. In July and August, prices go up by 30% on Friday, and double on Saturday.

7 Days Inn   HOTEL $

(☑321 7888; www.7daysinn.cn; 37 Dongfeng Erlu, Yángjiāng; 阳江市,东风二路37号; r ¥140-195; 🛜) If you want to stay in Yángjiāng, this place has cheerful rooms, and wi-fi in the lobby.

Seafood Restaurants   SEAFOOD $$

In Zhápō, there are seafood restaurants galore. Pick out what you want from the tanks full of swimming marine life, agree on the price, and they'll cook it for you. Generally, seafood items cost ¥28 to ¥200 per 500g/1 catty (斤; *jīn*). Nonseafood dishes fall between ¥18 and ¥90.

ℹ️ Getting There & Away

Yángjiāng has two bus stations. The **main bus station** (阳江汽车客运总站; Yángjiāng qìchē kèyùn zǒngzhàn; ✆316 6593; cnr Xiping Belu & Jinshan Gonglu) has direct services to:

Fóshān ¥55, four daily (9.10am to 4pm)

Guǎngzhōu ¥65 to ¥88, 30 daily (8am to 9pm)

Hong Kong ¥220 to ¥230, two daily (9am and 2.30pm)

Shēnzhèn ¥90 to ¥100, five daily (8.30am to 3.30pm)

Zhūhǎi ¥60, nine daily (8am to 5pm)

No. 2 bus station (阳江二运车站; Yángjiāng èryùn chēzhàn; ✆365 0888; 666 Shiwan Beilu) has daily direct services to:

Guǎngzhōu 17 daily (6.30am to 4.40pm)

Kāipíng one daily (3pm)

Shēnzhèn nine daily (7.30am to 11pm)

Kāipíng's Yìcí bus station has two buses daily (12.55pm and 5.15pm) to Yángjiāng's main bus station and six (8.45am to 4.10pm) to its No 2 station (¥36).

ℹ️ Getting Around

Local buses run every 10 to 20 minutes to Zhápō from No 2 station (¥13, one hour, 6.30am to 9pm) and the main station (6am to 7.30pm).

Zhápō and the museum area are connected by pedicabs (¥15, 10 minutes). A taxi from downtown Yángjiāng to the museum costs ¥100 (one hour).

Zhàoqìng 肇庆

✆0758 / POP 3.9 MILLION

Bordered by lakes and limestone formations, the leisurely town of Zhàoqìng in western Guǎngdōng province was where Jesuit Mateo Ricci first set foot in China in 1583.

👁️ Sights

Seven Star Crags Park PARK

(七星岩公园; Qīxīng Yán Gōngyuán; ✆230 2838; admission ¥60; ⊙8am-5.30pm) The landscape of limestone hills, grottoes and willow-graced lakes in this massive park is beautiful, so it's a pity the authorities try so hard – limestone caves are illuminated like nightclubs and boat rides cost extra (¥10 to ¥60). The easiest way to navigate between sights is to use the battery-operated carts (¥10 to ¥25 per person).

FREE **Plum Monastery** BUDDHIST TEMPLE

(梅庵; Méián; ✆283 3284; Mei'an Lu, Duānzhōu Qū; ⊙8.30am-4pm) This dignified, state-protected temple is dedicated to the Father of Chinese Zen Buddhism – Master Huineng (六祖慧能). Born in Zhàoqìng during the Tang dynasty, Master Huineng was said to be fond of plum blossoms, and during a sojourn here, he planted plum trees all over the hillside. This temple was built by a disciple to commemorate his teacher.

Don't miss the ancient well, with petals carved into its parapet, that's said to have been dug by Master Huineng to irrigate his trees. The temple's plum trees bloom between winter and spring. A pedicab from downtown Zhàoqìng costs ¥15.

City Walls HISTORIC SITE

Zhàoqìng's city walls (古城; *gǔ chéng*) were built during several periods – the lowest part with large mud bricks are Song dynasty; above that is Ming; then a Qing extension featuring smaller bricks. Anything above that was built yesterday. River View Tower and Cloud-Draped Tower were closed for repairs at the time of writing.

🛏️ Sleeping & Eating

Blue Palace Hotel HOTEL $$

(南宫宾馆; Nángōng Bīnguǎn; ✆227 8020; fax 227 2085; 76 Tianning Beilu; 天宁北路76号; r ¥438-468, ste ¥888; @) This centrally located hotel has 106 refurbished rooms that are clean, smart and comfortable. Walls are thick too, so it's very quiet at night even if your neighbours are partying.

Bōhǎilóu CHINESE $

(波海楼; ✆230 2708; Xinghu Xilu; dim sum ¥4-22; ⊙lunch&dinner) This restaurant with lake views serves Zhàoqìng delicacies including sticky rice dumplings (裹蒸粽; *guǒzhēngzòng*), containing beans, pork, chestnuts and egg yolk, and fox nuts buns (茨实包; *císhí bāo*). It's a 10-minute walk from the western entrance of Seven Star Crags Park. Bus 19 (¥2) from the entrance passes here (波海楼; Bōhǎilóu).

ℹ️ Information

Bank of China (中国银行; Zhōngguó Yínháng; Duanzhou Wulu; ⊙9am-5pm Mon-Sat)

China Post (中国邮政; Zhōngguó Yóuzhèng; Jianshe Sanlu; ⊙9am-8pm)

China Travel Service (CTS; 肇庆中国旅行社; Zhàoqìng Zhōngguó Lǚxíngshè; ✆226 8090; Duanzhou Wulu; ⊙8am-9pm)

Zhàoqìng

ℹ Getting There & Away

Bus

The **long-distance bus station** (汽车客运总站; qìchē kèyùn zǒngzhàn; Duanzhou Silu) runs frequent services to:

Guǎngzhōu ¥46, 1½ hours

Shēnzhèn ¥100, three hours

Zhūhǎi ¥75, four hours

The **east bus station** (城东客运站; chéngdōng kèyùnzhàn; Duanzhou Sanlu), 1.5km east of the long-distance bus station, has services to Kāipíng (¥42, 2½ hours).

Train

The fastest train to Guǎngzhōu (¥17 to ¥36) takes two hours. The direct express train to Hong Kong (HK$235, 4½ hours) departs at 3.10pm.

ℹ Getting Around

Bus 12 links the train and long-distance bus stations with the ferry pier. A taxi to the train station from the centre costs about ¥15.

Around Zhàoqìng

DĬNGHÚ SHĀN   鼎湖山

This 11.3 sq km **reserve** (Mt Dingu; ☎0758-262 2510; 21 Paifang Lu; admission ¥60), 18km northeast of Zhàoqìng, offers great walks among lush vegetation, rare trees and roaring waterfalls, among other attractions.

A boat (¥30) will ferry you to the tiny wooded island in Dǐng Lake (Dǐng Hú), where there's a butterfly preserve. You can do an hour-long hike through a scenic forest with ponds and waterfalls, to emerge near Bǎodǐng Garden (宝鼎园) which contains the world's largest *dǐng*, a three-legged cauldron.

Qìngyún Temple (庆云寺; Qìngyún Sì) is a gaudy complex, but it's where you'll find a good upmarket **vegetarian restaurant** (☎0758-262 1585; mains ¥38-118; ⊗breakfast, lunch & dinner) that serves the famous monk invention Dǐnghú vegetarian dish (鼎湖上素; Dǐnghú Shàngsù).

Zhàoqìng

◎ **Top Sights**
City Walls B4
River View Tower C4
Seven Star Crags Park C1

◎ **Sights**
1 Cloud-Draped Tower B4
2 Plum Monastery B4

◎ **Sleeping**
3 Blue Palace Hotel C4

◎ **Eating**
4 Bōhǎilóu B1

◎ **Transport**
5 Boats to Seven Star Crags Park ...C3
6 Ferry C1
7 Local Bus Station (Buses to
   Dǐnghú Shān) C3
8 Long-Distance Bus Station C3
9 Qiáoxī Bus Station A3

Bus 21 (¥2) goes to Dǐnghú Shān from the **local bus station** (Duanzhou Silu) in Zhàoqìng. Battery-operated carts (¥20) are useful for navigating the reserve.

BĀGUÀ VILLAGES   八卦村

Two villages, exceptional for their shape and feng shui, make great excursions from Zhàoqìng.

Known as Bāguà Cūn (八卦村), **Líchá Cūn** (黎槎村; admission ¥20; ⊙8.15am-5.30pm), 21km east of Zhàoqìng, is a 700-year-old octagonal village, built according to *bāguà*, a Taoist symbol in an octagonal shape that has eight trigrams representing different phases in life.

Houses, many with wok-handle roofs, radiate from a taichi (a symbol of yin and yang) on a central terrace, turning the village into a maze. Most villagers have emigrated to Australia and only the elders remain. Bus 315 (¥9, 40 minutes) leaves for Líchá behind **Qiáoxī bus station** (Qiáoxī kèyùnzhàn; Duanzhou Qilu) in Zhàoqìng every 15 minutes.

To the southeast of Zhàoqìng, **Xiǎngǎng Cūn** (蚬岗村) is another Ming-dynasty Bāguà village. It's larger and livelier than Líchá, and has a market at its entrance. Its 16 ancestral halls, some opulent, only open on the first and 15th day of the lunar month. Board bus 308 (¥9, one hour) at Qiáoxī station to get here.

Qīngyuǎn   清远

📞0763 / POP 3.9 MILLION

The industrial town of Qīngyuǎn is where to set off for a scenic jaunt down the Běijiāng River (北江). The secluded temple in Fēilái and the monastery in Fēixiá are the main attractions. Boats (¥380, four hours) leave from Qīngyuǎn's **Wǔyī dock** (五一码头; Wǔyī Mǎtóu).

The first part of the trip takes you past ancient pagodas to the Buddhist complex of **Fēilái** (飞来; admission ¥15). Though it has been around for more than 1400 years, the whole complex was destroyed by a landslide in 1997 and subsequently rebuilt. The mountaintop pavilion offers terrific views of the river gorge below.

The admission fee to the monastery at **Fēixiá** (飞霞; admission ¥50), 4km upstream, also includes an eight-minute van ride up to the Taoist relics. **Cángxiá Ancient Cave** (藏霞古洞; c 1863) is a maze of whispering shadows, abandoned courtyards and crumbling alleys connected by arboured paths.

You can buy seafood from the floating market at Fēixiá and your boatman will cook it for you at no extra charge.

❶ Getting There & Around

To visit Fēilái and Fēixiá on a day trip from Guǎngzhōu, catch one of the 10 high-speed trains from Guǎngzhōu South Station that stop in Qīngyuǎn (¥40, 22 minutes). On arrival, it's a 15-minute walk to Wǔyī dock. Turn right as you leave the station.

Buses run every 15 minutes from Guǎngzhōu's long-distance bus stations near the train station (¥35, two hours, 6.30am to 9pm).

Nánlǐng National Forest Park   南岭国家森林公园

📞0751 / POP 2000

Lying 285km north of Guǎngzhōu, the Nánlǐng (Southern Mountains) ranges stretch from Guǎngxī to Jiāngxī provinces, separating the Pearl River from the Yangzi River.

The range in Guǎngdōng, home to the only ancient forests in the province, is a **reserve** (Nánlǐng Guójiā Sēnlín Gōngyuán; 📞523 2038; www.eco-nanling.com; admission ¥60; ⊙6am-6pm) for old-growth blue pines, a species unique to this part of Guǎngdōng.

◉ Sights & Activities

Come here with your walking boots. There are four trails, most of which can be completed within two to three hours. The easiest, 6km trail follows a stream and leads you through the steep-sided gorges and crystalline pools of **Water Valley** (亲水谷; Qīnshuǐgǔ). The shorter but more interesting 3.5km trail takes you past roaring **waterfalls** (瀑布长廊; Pùbù Chángláng).

The 12km-long trail to **Little Yellow Mountain** (小黄山; Xiǎo Huángshān) is a more challenging hike through a forest of blue pines. The view of rolling mountain ranges from the crest (1608m) is spectacular.

The longest (28km) and least difficult is the No 4 Trail (四号林道; Sìhào Líndào) to **Shíkēngkōng** (石坑空). At 1902m, Shíkēngkōng is the highest peak in Guǎngdōng and straddles the boundary between Guǎngdōng and Húnán.

The park entrance is at the southern end of the village of **Wǔzhǐshān** (五指山), which is small enough to cover on foot. Farmers nearby do their weekly shopping and stock clearance at Wǔzhǐshān's lively Sunday market. Staying in Orange House here will give you access to the park the next day. Just get your ticket and receipt stamped at the hotel.

From Wǔzhǐshān it's 6km to the start of the trails to the waterfalls and Water Valley, and another 6km to Little Yellow Mountain. The best way is to hire a taxi from Wǔzhǐshān. For between ¥180 and ¥250 you can hire one for the whole day. The driver can drop you at one end of the trail and wait for you at the other. A one-way trip to the lower entrance of the trail to Little Yellow Mountain is ¥90.

⌕ Sleeping & Eating

As camping inside the park is prohibited, the only option is to stay in Wǔzhǐshān. There are a couple of zhāodàisuǒ (招待所; basic lodgings) where you can get a room from ¥80.

Orange House   BOUTIQUE HOTEL $$
(橙屋; Chéngwū; ☎523 2929; d ¥398-489, high season ¥500-600; ❋ @) Orange House is a cheery boutique hotel with 32 comfortable rooms, though those on the 1st floor have a musty smell. Bookings essential. The hotel also manages an air-con-free **Ranger House** (林舍; Línshè; tr ¥198), equipped with eight spotless triple rooms right behind Orange House. Discounts of 30% to 40% via www.ctrip.com.

Feng's Kitchen   CANTONESE $
(冯家菜; Féngjiācài; ☎523 2107; mains ¥8-14) Mr Feng serves delectable meals in his courtyard. Reservations necessary.

❶ Getting There & Away

Bus

Sháoguān (韶关) is your gateway to Nánlǐng. Buses (¥70, four hours) leave Guǎngzhōu's long-distance bus stations for Sháoguān's Xīhé bus station every 40 minutes (6.50am to 8.30pm).

If you miss the bus to Wúzhǐshān, catch a bus to Rǔyuán (乳源; ¥10, one hour, every 15 minutes). From Rǔyuán, three buses to Wǔzhǐshān (¥10) leave at 9.05am, 12.45pm and 4.30pm, or you can hire a taxi (¥80).

In Wǔzhǐshān, buses to Sháoguān leave at 7.30am, 12.30pm and 3.30pm.

Train

High-speed trains (¥105, one hour) leave from Guǎngzhōu South Station for Sháoguān Train Station (韶关高铁站; Sháoguān Gāotiézhàn). From there, board bus 22 or 26 and get off at **Xīhé bus station** (西河汽车站; Xīhé qìchēzhàn; Gongye Donglu). Buses to Wúzhǐshān (¥20, two hours) depart at 8am, 11.45am and 3.30pm.

Guǎngzhōu's Main Train Station has trains that stop over at **Sháoguān East Station** (韶关东站; Sháoguān Dōngzhàn; ¥38, 2½ hours). Buses to Wúzhǐshān leave at 7.45am, 11.15am and 3.15pm.

Shēnzhèn   深圳
☎0755 / POP 14 MILLION

One of China's wealthiest cities and a Special Economic Zone (SEZ), Shēnzhèn draws a mix of businessmen, investors and migrant workers to its golden gates. It's also a useful transport hub to other parts of China.

You can buy a five-day, Shēnzhèn-only visa (¥160 for most nationalities, ¥469 for Brits; cash only) at the **Luóhú border** (Lo Wu; ⊘9am-10.30pm), **Huánggǎng** (⊘9am-1pm & 2.30-5pm) and **Shékǒu** (⊘8.45am-12.30pm & 2.30-5.30pm). US citizens must buy a visa in advance in Macau or Hong Kong.

◉ Sights

FREE **Shēnzhèn Museum**   MUSEUM
(深圳博物馆新馆; Shēnzhèn Bówùguǎn Xīnguǎn; ☎8201 3036; www.shenzhenmuseum.com.cn; East Gate, Citizens' Centre, Fuzhong Sanlu, Fútián district; ⊘10am-6pm Tue-Sun; Ⓜ Line 4, Shìmín Zhōngxīn, exit B) With life-sized dioramas and interactive multimedia presentations, the museum showcases the city's short but dynamic history of social transformation.

FREE OCT Contemporary

Art Terminal MUSEUM
(华侨城当代艺术中心; Huáqiáochéng Dāngdài Yìshù Zhōngxīn; ☑2691 1976; Enping Jie, Overseas Chinese Town; ☺10am-5.30pm Tue-Sun; Ⓜ Line 1, Qiáochéng Dōng station, exit A) This is an excellent museum with exhibits of international and local contemporary Chinese artists.

Art Galleries GALLERIES
Just one metro stop from the OCT Art Terminal are two galleries worth a visit. He Xiangning Art Gallery (何香凝美術館; Héxiāngníng Měishúguǎn; ☑2660 4540; www.hxnart.com; 9013 Shennan Lu; admission ¥20, Fri free; ☺10am-5.30pm Tue-Sun; Ⓜ Huáqiáochéng, exit C) has an esoteric collection of hybrid Japanese/Chinese water paintings by the late master, He Xiangning. Adjacent to it is the OCT Art & Design Gallery (华美术馆; Huá Měishúguǎn; ☑3399 3111; www.oct-and.com; 9009 Shennan Lu; admission ¥18; ☺10am-5.30pm Tue-Sun) featuring works by China's avant-garde designers.

🛏 **Sleeping**

Hotels in Shēnzhèn regularly slash up to 50% off the regular rack rates on weekdays, though you should always ask for a discount. This is also partially offset by the 10% or 15% tax/service charge levied by many places. All hotels provide in-room broadband.

Shēnzhèn Loft Youth Hostel HOSTEL $
(深圳侨城旅友国际青年旅舍; Shēnzhèn Qiáochéng Lǚyǒu Guójì Qīngnián Lǚshè; ☑8609 5773; www.yhachina.com; 3 Enping Jie, Huáqiáochéng; 华侨城恩平街3栋; dm ¥60, d from ¥158; Ⓜ Qiáochéngdōng, exit A; ✳@) The hostel by which all hostels in China should be judged. It's located in the OCT Contemporary Art Terminal.

**Shēnzhèn Vision
Fashion Hotel** BOUTIQUE HOTEL $$
(深圳视界风尚酒店; Shēnzhèn Shìjiè Fēngshàng Jiǔdiàn; ☑2558 2888; www.visionfashionhotel.com; 5018 Shennan Donglu; 深南东路5018号; d ¥486-1880, discounts of 50-70%; Ⓜ Dàjùyuàn, exit B; ✳@) Its prime location and quiet environment make this boutique hotel inside a theatre complex very good value.

🍴 **Eating**

Laurel CANTONESE $$
(丹桂轩; Dānguì Xuān; ☑8232 1888; 2nd fl, Century Plaza Hotel, 1 Chunfeng Lu; meals ¥50-180; ☺7am-11pm) Located in the Century Plaza Hotel and serving some of the best dim sum in town. A hit with day-trippers from Hong Kong.

Summer Tea House VEGETARIAN, DIM SUM $
(静颐茶馆; Jìngyí Cháguǎn; ☑2557 4555; 7th & 8th fl, Jīntáng Dàxià, 3038 Bao'an Nanlu; dishes ¥50-80; ☺10am-1am; ♦☑) Tucked away in an office building is this vegies' favourite with healthy dim sum (available all day) and a relaxing tea-tasting area.

🍷 **Drinking & Entertainment**

Citic City Plaza (中信城市广场; Zhōngxìn Chéngshì Guǎngchǎng; Ⓜ Kēxué Guǎn) and **COCO Park** (Ⓜ Gòuwù Gōngyuán) are happening areas. The free That's PRD (http://shenzhen.urbanatomy.com) has monthly events listings.

Yīdù Táng LIVE MUSIC
(一渡堂; ☑8610 6046; Block F3, OCT-LOFT Art Terminal, Enping Lu, Huáqiáochéng; ☺10am-2am; Ⓜ Qiáochéngdōng, exit A) A warehouse turned bohemian den where local bands jam every night after 10pm.

True Color CLUB
(本色; Běnsè; ☑8230 1833; 4th fl, Golden World, 2001 Jiefang Lu; ☺9am-1am; Ⓜ Lǎojiē, exit A) A longtime local favourite that attracts city slickers and trendy young adults alike with its watering-hole-plus-dance-floor formula.

🛍 **Shopping**

Die-hard shoppers won't leave Shēnzhèn empty-handed, though the quality may vary. Remember to bargain!

Dàfēn Village PAINTINGS
(大芬村; Dàfēncūn; ☑8473 2633; www.dafenvillageonline.com; Dafen, Buji, Lónggǎng District) This eye-opener has 600 studios-cum-stores, churning out thousands of Rembrandt and Renoir copies every week, with prices starting from ¥300. There are original works too, and art supplies costing about half of what they'd cost downtown. Bus 306 from Luóhú station takes you here in an hour. A taxi ride costs around ¥70.

**Century Furnishings
Central Mall** HOMEWARES
(世纪中心家居广场; Shìjìzhōngxīn jiājùguǎngcháng; www.sz-sjzx.com; Shennan Dadao, west of Xiāngmì Hú Water Park, Fútián District; ☺9.30am-8pm Mon-Fri, to 8.30pm Sat & Sun; Ⓜ Chēgōngmiào, exit A) This mall has a whopping 30,000 sq m of retail space for homewares. Zones A and B sell tiles, sinks, showers and mirrors C specialises in lamps and furniture. A cab from Luóhú station costs ¥30.

Shēnzhèn

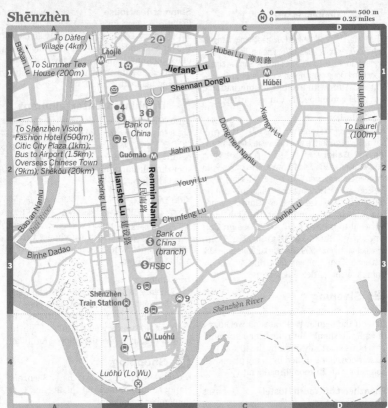

Dōngmén Market MARKET
(东门市场; Dōngmén Shìchǎng; ⊗10am-10pm; MLǎojiē, exit A) This chaotic market is popular for tailored suits, skirts, curtains and beddings. Same-day pick-up is possible if you place your order early. Be careful of pickpockets.

ⓘ Information

Bank of China (中国银行分行; Zhōngguó Yínháng; 2022 Jianshe Lu; ⊗9am-5.30pm Mon-Fri, to 4pm Sat & Sun)

China Post (中国邮政; Zhōngguó Yóuzhèng; 3040 Shennan Donglu; ⊗8am-8pm)

China Travel Service (CTS; 深圳中国旅行社; Zhōngguó Lǚxíngshè; ☎8228 7644; 3023 Renmin Nanlu; ⊗9am-6pm)

Great Land International Travel Service (巨邦国际旅行社; Jùbāng Guójì Lǚxíngshè; ☎2515 5555; 3rd fl, Jùntíng Hotel, 3085 Shennan Donglu; ⊗10am-6pm) Good for air tickets.

HSBC (汇丰银行; Huìfēng Yínháng; Ground fl, Shangri-La Hotel; 香格里拉大酒店; Xiānggélǐlā Dàjiǔdiàn; 1002 Jianshe Lu; ⊗9am-5pm Mon-Fri, 10am-6pm Sat)

Internet cafe (网吧; 3023 Renmin Nanlu; per hr ¥5) Adjacent to CTS.

Public Security Bureau (PSB; 公安局; Gōng'ānjú; ☎2446 3999; 4018 Jiefang Lu)

SZ Party (www.shenzhenparty.com) For current events in Shēnzhèn.

ⓘ Getting There & Away

Air

Shēnzhèn airport (Shēnzhèn Jīchǎng; ☎2345 6789; eng.szairport.com) has flights to most major destinations around China.

Boat

Shékǒu port (☎2669 1213) has services to Hong Kong:

Hong Kong International Airport ¥260, 30 minutes, 14 daily (7.45am to 9pm)

Shēnzhèn

⊙ **Entertainment**
1 True Color B1

⊜ **Shopping**
2 Dōngmén Market B1

ℹ **Information**
3 China Travel Service B1
4 Great Land International Travel
 Service B1

ℹ **Transport**
5 Buses to Shékǒu B2
6 Local Bus Station B3
7 Local Minibuses B4
8 Luóhú Bus Station B3
9 Taxi Stands B3

Macau ferry pier, Central ¥110, one hour, six daily (7.45am, 10.15am, 11.45am, 2pm, 4.30pm and 7.15pm)

To Macau:

Macau ferry terminal ¥180, one hour, 10 daily (8.15am to 7.30pm)

Taipa ¥180, one hour, four daily (9.30am, 11am, 12.15pm and 5.30pm)

To Zhūhǎi:

Jiǔzhōu Port ¥100, one hour, every 30 minutes (7.30am to 8.30pm)

Fúyǒng ferry terminal (Fúyǒng kèyùnzhàn; ☑2345 5107) in Shēnzhèn airport runs ferries to Hong Kong and Macau:

Macau ferry terminal ¥210, 70 minutes, six daily (9.30am to 6pm)

Skypier, Hong Kong International Airport ¥298, 40 minutes, four daily (8.30am, 11.30am, 3.30pm and 6.30pm)

Bus

Regular intercity buses leave from **Luóhú bus station** (罗湖汽车站; Luóhú qìchēzhàn):

Cháozhōu ¥150, 5½ hours, three daily (8.30am, 1.40pm and 8pm)

Guǎngzhōu ¥60, two hours, every 10 minutes (6am to 10pm)

Shàntóu ¥170, five hours, every 30 minutes (7.30am to 9.30pm)

Xiàmén ¥240 to ¥303, eight hours, six daily (9.30am, 11am, 7.30pm, 8.30pm, 9.30pm and 9.50pm)

Train

Services to Guǎngzhōu and Hong Kong leave from Luóhú Train Station to Guǎngzhōu East Station (Y45, 1½ hours); and from Shēnzhèn North Station (深圳北站; Shēnzhèn Běizhàn) in Lónghuá to Guǎngzhōu South Station (¥47, 40 minutes).

The Mass Transit Railway (MTR) links Shēnzhèn with Hong Kong (see p501).

ℹ **Getting Around**

To/From the Airport

Shēnzhèn's airport, 36km west of the city, is connected to Lónghuá by the metro Line 1 (¥9, one hour). A taxi costs ¥140 to ¥160. Airport bus departures are from **Huálián Hotel** (华联大厦; Huálián Dàshà; Shennan Zhonglu; Ⓜ Kēxué Guǎn, exit B2, ☐ 101), costing ¥20 (35 minutes, every 15 minutes, 5.30am to 9pm), and Shenzhen Train Station in Luóhú (¥20, one hour, every 15 minutes, 6.30am to 10pm). Buses leave from the local bus station east of the train station.

Public Transport

Shēnzhèn has a good public transport network, with five metro lines (¥2 to ¥11). Transit passes (Shēnzhèn Tōng; 深圳通) can be bought in metro stations and are good for all except taxis. Bus and minibus fares cost ¥2 to ¥4.

Taxi

Flag fall is ¥10 (¥16 from 11pm to 6am), ¥4 fuel surcharge and ¥2.40 every additional kilometre.

Around Shēnzhèn

Dàpéng Fortress (大鹏所城; Dàpéng Suǒchéng; ☑0755-8431 5618; Dàpéng Town, Lónggǎng District; adult/student & senior ¥20/10; ⊙10am-6pm), a fortified town to the east of Shēnzhèn, was a key battle site in the Opium Wars of the 19th century. Today it's a lively home to locals and migrants.

From Shēnzhèn, board bus 360 at Yínhú bus terminal (银湖汽车总站). After about 90 minutes, alight at Dàpéng bus station (大鹏总站) and change to minibus 966. A taxi from Luóhú costs ¥170.

Zhūhǎi 珠海

☑0756 / POP 1.5 MILLION

Zhūhǎi, Shēnzhèn's little SEZ sister, is close enough to Macau for a day trip. It's laid-back and has the fewest maniacal drivers in China.

Gǒngběi in the south is the main tourist district. Ferries connecting to Hong Kong, Shēnzhèn and Guǎngdōng stop at Jídàin in the northeast.

Visas (¥160 for most nationalities, ¥469 for Brits) valid for three days are available at the border (8.30am to 12.15pm, 1pm to 6.15pm, and 7pm to 10.30pm). US citizens must buy a visa in advance in Macau or Hong Kong.

Zhūhǎi

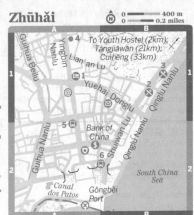

Zhūhǎi

🛏 **Sleeping**
1 Yindo Hotel A1

✗ **Eating**
2 Jīn Yuè Xuān B1
3 Rosa Chinensis B1

ⓘ **Information**
  Bank of China ....(see 1)
4 China Travel Service A1

ⓘ **Transport**
5 Airport Shuttle Bus.................................A2
6 Gǒngběi Long-Distance Bus
  Station...B2

◉ Sights

FREE **Zhūhǎi City Museum**   MUSEUM
(珠海市博物馆; Zhūhǎishì Bówùguǎn; ☏332 4708; 191 Jingshan Lu; ⊙9am-5pm Tue-Sun) The City Museum in Jídà has 13 exhibition halls showing old photos of Zhūhǎi, as well as cannon batteries and stelae excavated around the city. From Gǒngběi take bus 2 on Yingbin Nanlu.

Tángjiā Public Garden   GARDENS
(唐家共乐园; Tángjiā Gònglèyuán; ☏338 8896; Eling, Tángjiāwān; adult/student ¥10/5; ⊙8.30am-5.30pm) Thirteen kilometres north of Zhūhǎi is the labyrinthine town of Tángjiāwān (唐家湾), where you'll find the former estate of the first premier of the Republic of China, Tong Shaoyi, now a garden with old-growth and rare trees. From Zhūhǎi take the K3, 3A, 69 or 3 bus (40 minutes) at the

bus stop near the junction of Fenghuang Nanlu and Dongfeng Lu, and exit at Tángjiā Shìchǎngzhàn (唐家市场站; Tangjia Market station).

FREE **Tángjiā Temple**   BUDDHIST TEMPLE
(唐家三庙; Tángjiā Sānmiào; cnr Datong Lu & Xindizhi Jie, Tángjiāwān; ⊙8.30am-6pm) On your way to Tángjiā Public Garden, detour to this 300-year-old temple with a grim-looking Buddha statue brought from India. Board bus 10 on Yingbin Nanlu and alight at Tángjiā Market (Tángjiāshìchǎng).

🛏 Sleeping

There's little demand for budget accommodation as very few travellers stay in Zhūhǎi.

Youth Hostel   HOSTEL **$**
(国际青年学生旅馆; Guójì Qīngnián Xuéshēng Lǚguǎn; ☏7711 7712; www.zhuhai-holitel.com; 9 Shihua Donglu; 石花东路9号; dm ¥60; 🖥99) Hidden away inside the Zhūhǎi Holiday Resort (珠海度假村; Zhūhǎi Dùjiàcūn) in Jídà, this hostel has two eight-bed dorms.

Yindo Hotel   HOTEL **$$**
(银都酒店; Yíndū Jiǔdiàn; ☏888 3388; fax 888 3311; cnr Yingbin Nanlu & Yuehai Donglu; 迎宾大道与粤海东路交界; s & d ¥780-1440, discounts of 40-50%; ❈@) A good-value midrange option close to the border.

✗ Eating & Drinking

Gǒngběi near the Macau border has restaurants, bars and street hawkers.

Jīn Yuè Xuān   DIM SUM **$$**
(金悦轩; ☏813 3133; 1st-3rd fl, Block B, 265 Rihua Commercial Sq, Qinglu Nanlu; meals ¥100-130; ⊙9am-10pm) For the best dim sum and Cantonese cuisine in Zhūhǎi, head to this elegant restaurant before 11am to land a table.

Rosa Chinensis   DIM SUM **$$**
(月桂轩; Yuèguì Xuān; ☏818 3382; 2nd fl, 305 Qinglu Nanlu; dim sum ¥8-28, dishes ¥48-188; ⊙8am-5pm) A good, affordable alternative to Jīn Yuè Xuān.

ⓘ Information

Bank of China (中国银行; Zhōngguó Yínháng) Gǒngběi (cnr Yingbin Nanlu & Yuehai Donglu; ⊙9am-5.30pm Mon-Fri, to 4pm Sat & Sun); Lianhua Lu (⊙9am-5.30pm Mon-Fri, to 4pm Sat & Sun)
China Post (中国邮政; Zhōngguó Yóuzhèng; 1041-1043 Yuehai Donglu; ⊙8am-8pm)

China Travel Service (CTS; 中国旅行社; Zhōngguó Lǚxíngshè; ☏889 9228; 2nd fl, Overseas Chinese Hotel, 2016 Yingbin Nanlu; ⏱8am-8pm)

Internet cafe (E霸网吧; E-bar; 1155 Yingbin Nanlu; per hr ¥5)

Public Security Bureau (PSB; 公安局; Gōng'ānjú; ☏888 5277; 1038 Yingbin Nanlu)

ⓘ Getting There & Away

Air

Zhūhǎi's airport serves various destinations in China, including Běijīng (¥1400), Shànghǎi (¥700) and Chéngdū (¥1460).

Boat

Hong Kong–bound jetcats from **Jiǔzhōu Harbour** (九州港码头; Jiǔzhōu Gǎng Mǎtóu; ☏333 3359):

China ferry terminal, Kowloon ¥175, 70 minutes, six times daily (8am to 5pm)

Hong Kong International Airport ¥280, one hour (9.30am, 12.40pm, 3.30pm and 6.30pm)

Macau ferry pier, Central nine times daily (9am to 9.30pm)

Ferries leave Jiǔzhōu Harbour for Shēnzhèn's port of Shékǒu (¥100, one hour, every half-hour, 8am to 9.30pm); they leave Shékǒu for Jiǔzhōu Harbour every half-hour (7.30am to 9.30pm).

Local buses 3, 23, 25 and 26 go to Jiǔzhōu Harbour.

Bus

Gǒngběi long-distance bus station (拱北长途汽车站; Gǒngběi chángtú qìchēzhàn; ☏888 5218; Youyi Lu) at Gǒngběi Port runs regular buses between 6am and 10pm:

Fóshān ¥55, three hours

Guǎngzhōu ¥55, 2½ hours

Kāipíng ¥40, three hours

Shàntóu ¥180, five hours

Shēnzhèn ¥75, three hours

Zhàoqìng ¥65, 4½ hours

Light Rail

Light-rail trains serve Zhūhǎi North Station (珠海北站) and Guǎngzhōu South Station (¥34, one hour). The light-rail station can be reached by buses K1, 3A and 65.

ⓘ Getting Around

Zhūhǎi's airport, 43km southwest of the centre, runs a shuttle service (¥25) to the city centre (every hour, 6.30am to 9.30pm) from outside the **Zhōngzhū Building** (Zhōngzhū Dàshà; cnr Yuehua Lu & Yingbin Nanlu). A taxi to the centre costs about ¥150.

Flag fall for taxis is ¥10 for the first 3km, then ¥0.60 for each additional 250m.

Cháozhōu 潮州

☏0768 / POP 2.5 MILLION

Charming Cháozhōu was once a thriving trading and cultural hub in southern China, rivalling Guǎngzhōu. Today, it still preserves its distinct dialect, cuisine and opera. Cháozhōu is best appreciated at a leisurely pace, so do consider spending a night here.

Paifang Jie (牌坊街; Street of Memorial Arches), running 1948m from north to south in the old quarter, has signage to the main sights and is a good place to orient yourself. It's made up of Taiping Lu (太平路; 1742m) and Dongmen Jie (东门街; 206m).

⊙ Sights

Sights abound in Cháozhōu but admission charges can add up. Before you go sightseeing, buy a combo ticket (¥80) from **Jīnlóng Travel Service** (金龙旅行社; Jīnlóng Lǚxíngshè; ☏222 8900; 39 Huangcheng Nanlu; ⏱9am-9pm) located across Huangcheng Nanlu from the southern entrance of Street of Memorial Arches.

There are two types of combo tickets, both good for two days: one with 10 sights, and one with 11.

Guǎngjǐ Bridge
TOP CHOICE | BRIDGE

(广济桥; Guǎngjǐ Qiáo; ☏222 2683; admission ¥50; ⏱10am-5.30pm) Originally a 12th-century pontoon bridge with 86 boats straddling the Hán River, Guǎngjǐ Bridge suffered repeated destruction over the centuries. The current version, opened in 2007, is a brilliant, faux-ancient passageway with 18 wooden boats hooked up afresh every morning and 24 stone piers with pagodas.

A ticket allows you one crossing. If you want to come back, tell the staff 'I want to come back' (我要回来; 'wǒyào huílai') before leaving the bridge and they'll make a note of it.

Jǐluè Huáng Temple
TEMPLE

(己略黄公祠; Jǐluè Huánggōngcí; ☏225 1318; 2 Tie Xiang, Yian Lu; admission ¥10; ⏱8.30am-5pm) The highlights here are the ancient Cháozhōu woodcarvings decorating the walls and thresholds. The Unesco-crowned art form is famous for its rich and subtle details, intricate designs and exquisite craftsmanship. Born 1000 years ago, it was in the Qing dynasty when this temple (1887) was built that the art flourished. The temple is about ¥8 by pedicab from Paifang Jie.

Cháozhōu

Cháozhōu

⊙ Top Sights

Guǎngjǐ Bridge.................................B2

⊙ Sights

1 Cháozhōu Opera Costumes &
   Props...B2
2 Emperor Xu's Son-in-Law's
   Mansion....................................B1
3 Hánbì Building..............................A1
4 Jao Tsung I Petite Ecole..............B2
5 Jīluè Huáng Temple......................B1
6 Kāiyuán Temple............................B2
7 Paifang Jie...................................B2
8 Phoenix Building...........................A1
  Sìwàng Lóu.............................(see 8)

⊙ Sleeping

9 Cháozhōu Hotel............................A2
10 Chéngfǔ Inn................................B2
11 Zàiyáng Inn................................B2

⊙ Eating

12 Hú Róng Quán..............................B1
13 Liánhuā Vegetarian......................B2
14 Rúyǎ Jū......................................B2

⊙ Transport

15 West Bus Station.........................A1

TOP CHOICE **West Lake** PARK

(西湖; Xīhú; ☑222 0731; Huancheng Xilu; admission ¥8; ⊙8am-11pm) The moat of ancient Cháozhōu is a tranquil lake inside a park that marks the boundary between the old city and the new. Well-loved by locals, the leafy park is blessed with a mixed but har-

monious collection of buildings. **Hánbì Building** (涵碧楼; Hánbì Lóu), which served as a military office during antiwarlord expeditions in 1925, has a free exhibition showcasing weaponry and the achievements of Zhou Enlai.

Phoenix Building (凤楼; fènglóu; admission ¥4; ⊙6am-6pm) is a fantastical rendition of the symbol of Cháozhōu that sits on a knoll a five-minute walk uphill. Inside the bird, stairs take you past an iron moongate and gourd-shaped ceiling openings, to quirky spaces shaped by the fowl's anatomy – abdomen tapering into tail, chest sweeping up into neck, openings patterned like wings...you get the idea. It's attached to a shuttered building (四望楼; Sìwàng Lóu) in a period style reminiscent of '70s kung fu movies.

West Lake is about ¥10 by pedicab from Paifang Jie.

Kāiyuán Temple BUDDHIST TEMPLE

(开元寺; Kāiyuán Sì; admission ¥5; ⊙6am-5.30pm) Built in AD 738, Cháozhōu's most famous temple has old bodhi trees and an embarrassment of statues, including one of a 1000-arm Guanyin.

Cháozhōu Opera Costumes & Props OPERA

(吉元戏剧歌舞用品; ☑222 6041; 12 Kaiyuan Lu; ⊙9am-10.30pm) Diagonally across the road from Kāiyuán Temple is this tiny shop that makes gowns, headdresses, swords, sedans and shoes for the Cháozhōu operatic stage.

Hánwén Temple TEMPLE

(韩文公祠; Hánwéngōng Cí; admission ¥20; ⊙8am-5.30pm) On the east bank of the Hán, this is the oldest and best-preserved temple dedicated to the Tang-dynasty philosopher Han Yu, who was banished to 'far-flung' Guǎngdōng for his anti-Buddhist views.

Emperor Xu's Son-in-Law's Mansion HISTORIC BUILDING

(许驸马府; Xǔfùmǎ Fǔ; ☑225 0021; 4 Dongfucheng, Putao Xiang, Zhongshan Lu, Xiāngqiáo District; admission ¥20; ⊙9am-5.30pm) This breezy mansion originally built in 1064 retains some of the ancient stonework and wall coverings. The high door saddles, unique to southern China, were used to protect doors from humidity.

Confucian Academy TEMPLE, GARDENS

(海阳县儒学宫; Hǎiyángxiàn Rúxué Gōng; cnr of Changli Lu & Wenxing Lu, Xiāngqiáo District; admission ¥10; ⊙8am-5pm) This 4000-sq-m compound has lily ponds teeming with koi and a main temple dedicated to Confucius that is supported by 48 pillars.

Jao Tsung I Petite Ecole — MUSEUM
(饶宗颐学术馆; Ráozōngyí Xuéshùguǎn; ☑222 8966; admission ¥10; ☉9am-5pm) Located near the eastern gate of the old city wall is this museum and exquisite Cháozhōu-style garden dedicated to the sinologist Jao Tsung I.

🛏 Sleeping

Zàiyáng Inn and Chéngfǔ Inn are in alleys off Paifang Jie, ¥10 by pedicab from the main bus station (汽车总站).

Zàiyáng Inn — HOTEL $
(载阳客栈; Zàiyáng Kèzhàn; ☑223 1272; www. czdafudi.com; 15 Zaiyang Xiang, Taiping Lu; 太平路, 载阳巷15号; r ¥100-250; 🛜) This classy Qing-style inn with graceful courtyards and antique wood carvings (that were smothered in lime during the Cultural Revolution to prevent looting) is *the* place to stay in Cháozhōu. Rooms are small, but clean and very quiet. Prices more than double during holidays.

Chéngfǔ Inn — HOTEL $
(城府客栈; Chéngfǔ Kèzhàn; ☑222 8585; 9 Fensi Houxiang, Taiping Lu; 太平路, 分司后巷9号; r ¥98-158) Also located in an old building, but a few notches down from Zàiyáng Inn in terms of atmosphere and service.

Cháozhōu Hotel — HOTEL $$$
(潮州宾馆; Cháozhōu Bīnguǎn; ☑233 3333; www. chaozhouhotel.com; cnr Chaofeng Lu & Yonghu Lu; 潮枫路与永护路交界; r ¥618-758, discounts of 50%; ❄@) A solid option if you want to stay in the new part of town. The excellent restaurant has an English menu.

🍴 Eating & Drinking

Food is generally good in Cháozhōu. On Paifang Jie, there are eateries serving local specialities like beef balls with noodles (牛丸粉; *niúwán fěn*) and oyster omelette (蚝烙; *háolào*). Hú Róng Quán (☉8am-late), with three branches close to each other, sells pastries and sweet soups. There are also a number of bars and cafes here, all offering free wi-fi.

TOP CHOICE Rúyǎ Jū — CHINESE $$
(茹雅居; ☑225 9326; Xingning Xiang, Taiping Lu; 太平路, 兴宁巷; meals per person ¥80-100; ☉lunch & dinner) If there are at least five of you, book a table (at least a day in advance)

with Mr Wong to enjoy an authentic multi-course Cháozhōu meal in the sunset splendour of a private kitchen in a once-regal mansion.

Liánhuā Vegetarian — CHINESE $
(莲华素食府; Liánhuā Sùshífǔ; ☑223 8033; 9 Kaiyuan Sq; mains ¥15-30; ☉lunch & dinner; 🖈) An excellent vegetarian restaurant opposite Kāiyuán Temple. The menu includes some Cháozhōu specialities, such as the desserts on the last page.

ℹ Getting There & Away

Bus
Services from Cháozhōu's **main bus station** (2 Chaofeng Lu):

Guǎngzhōu ¥110 to ¥170, 5½ hours, nine daily (8am to 11.55pm)

Méizhōu ¥60, two hours, two daily (8.30am and 3pm)

Raópíng ¥20, one hour, 32 daily (6.30am to 6.30pm)

Shànghǎi ¥380, 15 hours, one daily, (3.15pm)

Shàntóu ¥17, one hour, 48 daily (7am to 6.40pm)

Shēnzhèn ¥120 to ¥140, 4½ hours, seven daily (8am to 11pm)

Xiàmén ¥80 to ¥120, 3½ hours, four daily (7am to 2pm)

Zhūhǎi ¥140, two daily (8.30am and 9.10pm)

Train
Services from Cháozhōu's Train Station, 8km west of the centre:

Guǎngzhōu ¥137 to ¥167, seven hours, two daily (9.23am and 1.13pm)

Shàntóu ¥8, 30 minutes, four daily (8.50am, 4.28pm, 9.15pm and 10.50pm)

Shēnzhèn ¥76, seven hours, one daily (7.15pm)

Around Cháozhōu

Located in Raópíng (饶平), 53km from downtown Cháozhōu, is China's largest octagonal Hakka earthen house, **Dàoyùnlóu** (道韵楼; admission ¥20; ☉8.30am-5.30pm). Six hundred villagers once resided in this stunning complex built in 1587; now only 100 remain. Ascend to the upper floors from unit 18 to admire the views and frescoes.

Buses to Raópíng (¥20, one hour) leave from the main bus station. Change to a bus to the village of Sānráo (三饶; ¥11), another 50km away. From there, motorrickshaws will take you to Dàoyùnlóu (¥5, 10 minutes).

Shàntóu 汕头

📞 0754 / POP 4.9 MILLION

Polluted Shàntóu has a couple of interesting sights on its outskirts that can be covered on a day trip from Cháozhōu.

👁 Sights

Cultural Revolution Museum MUSEUM
(文革博物馆; Wéngé Bówùguăn; admission ¥10; ⏱9.30am-5.30pm) The only museum in China that honours the victims of the revolution sits atop Tăshān Park (塔山风景区; Tăshānfēngjǐngqū), 25km north of the city centre. Names and inscriptions are engraved on the walls.

Take eastbound bus 18 on Jinsha Lu (¥6) to Túchéng Tăshān (涂城塔山), or bus 102 outside the long-distance bus station to Tăshān Lùkŏu (塔山路口). After the 45-minute ride, cross the road and walk 800m to the entrance, then another 3.5km uphill (take the path on the left).

Chen Cihong Memorial Home BUILDING
(陈慈黉故居; Chén Cíhóng Gùjū; admission ¥25; ⏱8am-5.30pm) This attractive complex was built by a businessman who made his fortune in Thailand in the 19th century. He famously had the region's best raw materials shipped here and assembled in imaginative ways that incorporated Asian, Western and Moorish motifs. The ground-floor souvenir shops are worth checking out. Board bus 103 from People's Sq (eastern edge) in Shàntóu.

🍴 Eating & Sleeping

The streets behind the hotel are teeming with stalls and hawkers selling noodles, congee and local dishes.

Jīnguān Hotel HOTEL $$
(金冠酒店; Jīnguān Jiŭdiàn; 📞8989 8882; fax 8989 8989; 6 Rongjiang Lu; 榕江路6号; r ¥488; @🛜) Reasonably priced with spacious rooms and helpful, English-speaking staff who can recommend reliable taxi drivers.

LA Music Cafe WESTERN $$
(5 Rongjiang Lu; mains ¥35-158; ⏱11am-2am; 🛜) Just across the road from Jīnguān Hotel is this gay-friendly bar with nice decor and a decent Western menu.

ℹ Getting There & Away
Bus

Shàntóu's **central bus station** (Shàntóu zhōngxīngzhàn; Taishan Lu), **long-distance bus station** (Shàntóu qìchē zŏngzhàn; Huoche Lu) and **CTS bus station** (Zhōnglǚ Chēzhàn; cnr Shangzhang Lu & Changping Lu) run regular services:

Cháozhōu ¥17, one hour, every hour (8am to 6.10pm)

Guăngzhōu ¥150, six hours, around every hour (8am to 6.40pm)

Méizhōu ¥35 to ¥98, 2½ hours, two daily (6.25am and 8.45pm)

Shēnzhèn ¥140, five hours, four daily (9.20am, 1pm, 2pm, 5pm)

Minibus

Minibuses leave from a small office south of CTS station for:

Cháozhōu ¥12, one hour, every hour (7am to 8pm)

Méizhōu ¥45, three hours, every hour (8am to 5pm)

Train

The station is 5km east of the city centre.
Cháozhōu ¥10 to ¥31, 30 minutes, three daily (8.50am, 12.40pm and 5.20pm)

Guăngzhōu ¥92 to ¥168, seven hours, two daily (8.50am and 12.40pm)

Méizhōu ¥29, two hours, three daily (7.15am, 10.22am and 6.26pm)

Méizhōu 梅州

📞 0753 / POP 5 MILLION

Méizhōu, populated by the Hakka (Kèjiā in Mandarin; 客家) people, is home to China's largest cluster of 'coiled dragon houses' or *wéilóngwū* (围龙屋). Specific to the Hakka, these are dwellings arranged in a horseshoe shape evocative of a dragon napping at the foot of a mountain. You'll also see *tŭlóu* (roundhouses) dotting the fields like mysterious flying saucers, in addition to a jumble of architectural wonders.

👁 Sights

FREE **Hakka Museum** MUSEUM
(客家博物馆; Kèjiā Bówùguăn; Dongshan Dadao; ⏱9am-5pm; 🚌1, 6) This museum in Hakka Park (客家公园; Kèjiā Gōngyuán) on the north bank of the Méijiāng River is a good warm-up to the culture of Hakkaland. The park itself with its pebbled paths and willow-fringed ponds is a delight to stroll in.

Tài'ān Lóu HISTORIC SITE
(泰安楼; admission ¥20) Further afield in Dàpu County (大埔), 70km east, is this three-storey square citadel, a cousin of the roundhouse.

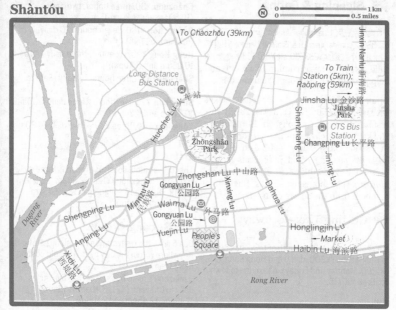

Built in 1764, it comprises four square brick and stone structures with 220 rooms, sitting northeast to southeast. Only eight families live here now.

Cháyáng Old Town
TOWN

(茶阳古镇; Cháyáng Gǔzhèn) People still take long siestas in lazy Cháyáng, 27km from Dàpu County. Its old streets (老街; *lǎojiē*) with pillared arcades are nice to lose yourself in for a couple of hours. **Memorial Arch of the Father and Son Graduates** (父子进士牌坊; Fùzǐ Jìnshì Páifāng; Dàpu High School, Xueqian Jie; 学前街,大埔中学), a granite edifice from 1610, stands, aptly, before a school. Ageing gracefully, **Xuán Villa** (旋庐; Xuánlú; 115 Dahua Lu; 大华路115号), c 1936, was built by a Malaysian-Chinese who was a member of a secret society tied to Sun Yatsen. Parts of the building used to double up as air-raid shelters. If the owners let you in, you'll see tea fields from the roomy balconies.

Nánkǒu
HISTORIC SITES

The quiet village of Nánkǒu (南口), about 16km west of Méizhōu, is where you'll see *wéilóngwū* (围龙屋) dwellings nestled between paddy fields and the hills like dragons in repose. It's derelict, but interesting to wander around in, and there are a few

formerly glorious dwellings that you can request to enter, if they're open.

Bus 9 from the **local bus terminal** (市公共汽车总站; Shì Gōnggòng Qìchēzhàn; cnr Meijiang Dadao & Xinzhong Lu) and buses to Xìng-níng (兴宁; ¥10, every 20 minutes) from the main bus station go to Nánkǒu. Once you get off, walk 1km to the village entrance. The last bus back leaves at 4.30pm. A taxi ride costs around ¥35.

Liánfāng Lóu
HISTORIC SITE

(联芳楼) Hidden in a village near the town of Báigōng (白宫), 14km east of Méizhōu, this magnificent three-storey mansion (c 1930s) owned by an Indonesian Hakka family has 100 rooms arranged around indoor courtyards lush with tropical greenery. Domes crown the roof garden; balconies are guarded by mythical creatures of mixed pedigree. Following a recent theft, the family is wary of visitors, so ask politely to enter.

Huā'è Lóu
HISTORIC SITE

(花萼楼; admission ¥10) The 400-year-old 'house of calyx', 33km east of Liánfāng Lóu and 20km south of Meizhou, is the largest circular earthen castle in Guǎngdōng. It comes complete with three rings and stone walls more than 1m thick.

✕ Sleeping & Eating

Ramada   HOTEL $$

(华美达酒店; Huáměidá Jiŭdiàn; ☑611 3828; fax 611 3800; cnr Meiyuan Lu & Binfang Dadao; 梅园路口、彬芳大道; r ¥238-710, ste ¥810-2180; @ 🛜) A solid hotel with large, comfortable rooms and helpful staff. The 8th floor is nonsmoking.

Chéngdé Lóu   CHINESE HAKKA $

(承德楼; ☑233 1315; Fuqi Lu; mains ¥28-68) This restaurant inside a polished 19th-century Hakka house close to the airport excels in Hakka classics like salt-baked chicken (盐局鸡; *yánjú jī*) and pork braised with preserved vegetables (梅菜扣肉; *méicài kòuròu*). The manager speaks English. A taxi here from the centre costs ¥12.

ℹ Getting There & Away

Air

Méizhōu's airport, 9km south of town, has flights to Guăngzhōu (¥800, daily) and Hong Kong (¥1200, Monday and Friday). A taxi ride to town costs about ¥15.

Bus

There are two bus stations: the **main bus station** (汽车总站; qìchē zŏngzhàn; Meizhou Dadao), north of the river, and **Jiāngnán bus station** (江南汽车站; Jiāngnán qìchēzhàn; Binfang Dadao) to the south. Most buses to Méizhōu drop you off at the former.

Cháozhōu ¥30, three hours, two daily (10.50am and 3.30pm)

Guăngzhōu ¥130, seven hours, 20 daily (6.50am to 11pm)

Hong Kong ¥90, six hours, three daily (7.40am, 10.05am and 2.40pm)

Shàntóu Y60, three hours, 13 daily (8am to 5.20pm)

Shēnzhèn ¥26, two hours, three daily (7.15am, 10.22am and 6.26pm)

Yŏngdìng ¥40, three hours, two daily (6.30am and 4pm)

Train

The train station, south of town, has three daily trains to Guăngzhōu (¥120, 12.56am, 1.12am and 12.38pm) and Yŏngdìng (¥18, 12.43am, 1.04am and 3.01am).

ℹ Getting Around

Bus 6 links the train station to both bus stations. Anywhere within the city by taxi should cost no more than ¥15.

Méizhōu's main bus station has five buses daily to Cháyáng (¥21, 6.40am, 8.15am, 11.10am, 12.45pm and 2.10pm).

Apart from Nánkŏu and Cháyáng, the sights listed here are scattered in different villages, and almost inaccessible by public transport. It makes more sense to hire a taxi for a day. Expect to pay about ¥400.

Hǎinán

POP 8.8 MILLION

Includes »

Hǎikǒu 571
Around Hǎikǒu 575
Central Highlands 576
Around Wǔzhǐshān 577
The East Coast 578
Sānyà 581

Best Beaches

» Sānyà Bay (p581)

» Yàlóng Bay (p581)

» Bó'áo (p578)

» Yuè Liàng Wān (p576)

» Hòuhǎi (p581)

Best Activities

» Climb Wǔzhǐshān & Seven Fairy Mountain (p577)

» Cycle the Central Highlands (p572)

» Explore Xīncūn fishing harbour (p580)

» Wander through Hǎinán Museum (p571)

» Visit Hǎikǒu Volcanic Cluster Geopark (p575)

Why Go?

China's largest tropical island boasts all the balmy weather, coconut palms and gold-sand beaches you could ask for. Down at Sānyà it's see-and-be-seen on the boardwalks or escape altogether at some of Asia's top luxury resorts. Thatched huts and banana pancakes haven't popped up anywhere yet, but there's a whiff of funkiness coming from the east coast beachside towns, and the budding surf scene is helping to spread the gospel of chill-out.

Money is pouring into Hǎinán (海南) these days to ramp up the luxury quotient. You can cruise on the new high-speed rail, but cycling is still the better way to get around. When you've had enough of a lathering on the coast, the cool central highlands are an ideal place to be on two wheels. The good roads, knockout mountain views, and concentration of Li and Miao, the island's first settlers, give the region an appealing distinction from the lowlands.

When to Go

Sānyà

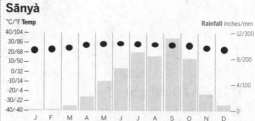

| Apr–Oct The best months to grab a hotel bargain. | Nov–Mar The best time of the year for cycling. | Nov–Jan This is the prime surfing season. |

HĂINÁN

History

Until the economic boom of the last 30 years, Hăinán had been a backwater of the Chinese empire since the first Han settlements appeared on the coast almost 2000 years ago. Largely ignored by a series of dynasties, Hăinán was known as the 'tail of the dragon', 'the gate of hell', and a place best used as a repository for occasional high-profile exiles such as the poet Su Dongpo and the official Hai Rui.

More recently, China's first communist cell was formed here in the 1920s, and the island was heavily bombarded and then occupied by the Japanese during WWII. Li and Han Chinese guerrillas waged an effective campaign to harass the Japanese forces but the retaliation was brutal – the Japanese executed a third of the island's male population. Even today resentment over Japanese atrocities lingers among the younger generation.

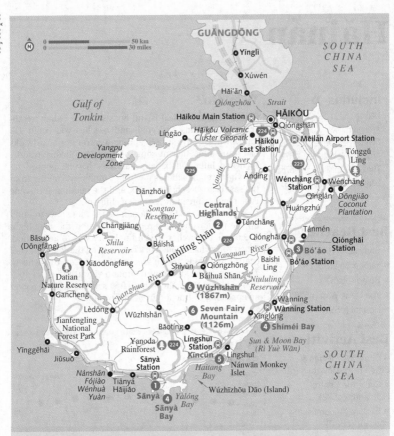

Hăinán Highlights

① Soak up the sun, sand and cocktails at **Sānyà** (p581), China's top beach resort

② Cycle the **Central Highlands** (p576), home of the Li and Miao

③ Explore the traditional villages and empty beaches around **Bó'áo** (p578)

④ Surf China's best waves at **Sānyà Bay** (p581) and **Shíméi Bay** (p580)

⑤ Wander a classic south seas fishing port at **Xīncūn** (p580)

⑥ Climb **Wǔzhǐshān** (p577) and **Seven Fairy Mountain** (p577), the most famous peaks on Hăinán

⑦ Enjoy **fresh seafood** at markets all over the island

In 1988 Hǎinán was taken away from Guǎngdōng and established as its own province and Special Economic Zone (SEZ). After years of fits and starts, development is now focused on turning tropical Hǎinán into an 'international tourism island' by 2020. What this really means, besides developing every beach, and building more golf courses and mega-transport projects (such as a high-speed rail service round the island, a cruise ship terminal and even a space station), is not entirely clear.

Climate

The weather on Hǎinán is largely warm in autumn and winter, and hot and humid in spring and summer. The mountains are always cooler than the coast, and the north is cooler than the south. Hǎinán is hit by at least one typhoon a year, usually between May and October.

Language

Hǎinánese is a broad term for the baker's dozen local dialects of Hǎinán Mǐn (it's known by many other names), most of which are also spoken in Guǎngdōng. While the Li and Miao can usually speak Mandarin, they prefer to use their own languages.

ⓘ Getting Around

Getting around most of Hǎinán is both cheap and easy. Hǎikǒu and Sānyà are linked by three main highways: the eastern expressway along the coast (only 3½ hours by bus); the central and much slower highway via Wǔzhǐshān; and the less popular western expressway. The main roads are great, bus services comfortable and departures regular.

A high-speed rail system runs from Hǎikǒu to Sānyà along the east coast. Tickets cost only slightly more than buses, but most stations are not centrally located.

For cycling around Hǎinán, see the boxed text, p572.

Hǎikǒu　　　　海口

☏0898 / POP 724,000

Hǎikǒu means 'Mouth of the Sea', and while sea trade remains important, the buzzing provincial capital at the northern tip of Hǎinán is most notable for its booming construction. New and restarted projects are everywhere.

While poor in sights, Hǎikǒu makes a good base for exploring the north of the island. There are some decent beaches a short bike or bus ride away, the air is fresh

PRICE INDICATORS

The following price indicators are used in this chapter:

Sleeping

$	less than ¥200
$$	¥200 to ¥400
$$$	more than ¥400

Eating

$	less than ¥30
$$	¥30 to ¥80
$$$	more than ¥80

and clean (though worsening yearly because of traffic), and some visitors find themselves quite satisfied just hanging out here for a few days.

Travellers tend to stay around Hǎikǒu Park or north of the river on Hǎidiàn Island (海甸岛; Hǎidiàn Dǎo). These are both older, slightly run-down neighbourhoods (especially compared with the western sections of the city), but all your life-support systems, including banks, food and travel agents, can be found here.

To the northwest are the main railway station, port area and the city's beach zone. The main bus station and high-speed rail terminal are in the southeast of town. The airport is about 25km to the east.

⊙ Sights & Activities

A few kilometres west of the city centre is a long stretch of sandy beaches. Take bus 37 (¥2) from Értóng Park and get off anywhere; alternatively, rent a bike in town. Cycling Hǎidiàn Island is also rewarding; look for news of the completion of a network of routes out to reservoirs and the Hǎikǒu Volcanic Cluster Geopark.

Hǎinán Museum　　　　　　　MUSEUM
(海南省博物馆; Hǎinán Shěng Bówùguǎn; 68 Guoxing Dadao; ⊙9am-5pm, closed Mon) This large complex of exhibition rooms should be your first stop when you arrive in Hǎinán. The displays on ethnic minorities, as well as Hǎinán's 20th-century history, which included fierce resistance against the Japanese and later Nationalists, are particularly informative (and in English, too!). Buses 43 and 48 from downtown stop outside the museum. A taxi will cost around ¥30.

CYCLING HĂINÁN

Hăinán is a great destination for recreational touring. You're rarely more than an hour from a village with food and water, and never more than a few hours from a town with a decent hotel. At the same time, you'll find most of your riding is out in nature or through pretty farming valleys, not urban sprawl. Preparation time for a tour can be minimal.

Some popular routes include the following:

Hăidiàn Island – plenty of fishing villages and rural landscapes and so close to Hăikŏu.

North Coast – ride alongside kilometre after kilometre of sand beaches and down side routes into the interior.

Wénchāng County – ride 100km out to Dōngjiāo Coconut Plantation and spend the night at a quiet beachside cabin. The next day head to Tónggŭ Lĭng, one of Hăinán's best undeveloped beaches.

The most popular multiday ride is the 250km journey from Hăikŏu to Wŭzhĭshān and on to Sānyà. The highway has a good shoulder most of the way, and allows for endless side trips up small country roads and stops in tiny villages. After a day riding through the lush Túnchāng County valley, the route climbs into some fine hill country around **Shíyùn** (什运). The village, 32km southwest of Qióngzhōng (琼中), sits on a grassy shelf above a river and is worth a look around. Local cyclists recommend the 42km side trip from here up a wooded canyon to **Báishā** (白沙). The major towns in this area are **Túnchāng** (屯昌) and **Qióngzhōng**, the latter a major settlement for the Miao.

After Shíyùn you can look forward to a long climb (at least 10km), followed by a long fast descent into Wŭzhĭshān. If you are continuing on to Sānyà, the road is one long, steep downhill after the turn-off to Băotíng.

If you're not bringing your own wheels, you can rent decent-quality mountain bikes at the **Hăikŏu Banana Youth Hostel** (www.haikouhostel.com) for ¥50 a day. Check out the hostel's websites for detailed information on cycling Hăinán. There's also a **Giant Bicycles** (☑6865 5598; www.hncycling.com; 26 Jinmao Xilu; 金贸西路26号) shop in Hăikŏu that does rentals. It's worth noting that people in Hăinán call bikes *dānchē*.

Five Officials Memorial Temple TEMPLE
(五公祠; Wŭgōng Cí; 169 Haifu Dadao; admission ¥20; ⏰8am-6pm) This Ming temple and surrounding gardens are dedicated to five officials who were banished to Hăinán in earlier times. Famous Song dynasty poet, Su Dongpo, also banished to Hăinán, is commemorated here as well.

🛏 Sleeping

Unlike in the more seasonal Sānyà, prices in Hăikŏu tend to be greatly discounted from the published rates pretty much year-round. Only during major holidays might you get a rude shock.

Hăikŏu Banana Youth Hostel HOSTEL $
(海口巴纳纳国际青年旅舍; Hăikŏu Bānànà Qīngnián Lûshè; ☑6628 6780; www.haikouhostel.com; 3 Dong, 6 Bieshu Liyuan Xiaoqu, 21 Renmin Dadao; 海甸岛人民大道21号梨园小区6号别墅3栋; dm/s/tw/tr ¥45/80/120/150; ❋@🅰) The Banana's back. Back as one Hăinán's best hostels that is, with good dorms, bright

and spiffy en suite rooms (including a family room for ¥160), and a new menu at its patio **restaurant** (dishes ¥35-60; ⏰8am-1pm & 6-9pm) that includes excellent pizza and other backpacker favourites. Hostel amenities include laundry, internet and common areas, as well as a super-informative bulletin board and website. Bicycle rentals range from day-trip beaters (per day ¥20) to solid Giant mountain bikes for multiday trips (per day ¥50; book in advance).

Golden Sea View Hotel HOTEL $$$
(黄金海景大酒店; Huángjīn Hăijǐng Dà Jiǔdiàn; ☑6851 9988; www.goldenhotel.com.cn; 67 Binhai Dajie; r from ¥825) With discounts of 40% to 50%, rooms in this well-run three-star hotel are priced similarly to those stuck deep in the city. The Sea View, however, sits across from a large park at the start of the beaches to the west of town. The hotel's revolving restaurant has excellent views over Hăikŏu and the ocean, and is well regarded for its breakfast buffet.

Redbud Flower
International Youth Hostel HOSTEL $
(紫荆花墅国际青年旅舍; Zǐjīng Huā Shù Guójì Qīngnián Lǔshè; ☑3661 1352; zjhsyha@163.com; 13 Bilin Ge, Ye Hai Shanzhuang, Jinmao Xilu; 龙华区金贸西路椰海山庄碧林阁13幢; dm/d ¥45/110; ❈@⧄) Popular with Chinese back-packers, this hostel moved in the summer of 2012 from the south part of town to a more central location near the Xiùyíng Battery. There are dorms and ensuite private rooms available (which include free breakfast and coffee), a restaurant and bar, rooftop terrace, laundry, help with bike rentals and tour routes, and a decent amount of English information on trans-port and things to do.

Hǎinán Mínháng Bīnguǎn HOTEL $
(海南民航宾馆; Hǎinán Civil Aviation Hotel; ☑6650 6888; www.mhbghotel.com; 9 Haixiu Dong-lu; r from ¥190; ❈@) The hotel isn't setting any trends, but the inoffensive modern decor of-fers a cosy environment to unwind. There's an attached restaurant and coffee shop and the surrounding zone is loaded with cheap eateries and good hotel restaurants. As a bo-nus, the airport shuttle bus (¥15) starts and ends here.

✗ Eating

A lot of evening eating is done in the re-freshingly cool outdoors on practically every major street. Haixiu Donglu between the Hǎikǒu Bīnguǎn and Hǎinán Mínháng Bīnguǎn is chock-a-block full of cheap food stalls and fast-food joints. For a proper sit-down meal try the hotel restaurants around the park. The Banana Youth Hostel is the place for good Western favourites like pizza and breakfast.

On the corner of Haidian 3 Donglu and Renmin Dadao you'll find a stack of cafes, fruit stalls, supermarkets and restaurants with picture menus. Haidian 2 Donglu is one long row of barbecue stalls at night with tables set up from Renmin Dadao to Heping Dadao.

There's a **Carrefour** (家乐福; Jiālèfú) on Haifu Dadao with a large selection of pre-pared and fresh goods; a second branch is across the road from the Mǐlǐ Cafe.

Bǎnqiáo Road
Seafood Market SEAFOOD MARKET $$
(板桥路海鲜市场; Bǎn Qiáo Lù Hǎixiān Shì Cháng; Banqiao Lu) For a fresh seafood dinner with lots of noise, smoke and toasting head to the hectare of tables at the Bǎnqiáo Road Seafood Market, known island-wide. It's best to go with a group; prices average ¥50 per person (not including beer). A taxi to the market from downtown costs ¥15.

Hǎikǒu Qílóu Snack Street MARKET $
(海口骑楼小街; Hǎikǒu Qílóu Xiǎo Jiē; cnr Da-tong Lu & Jiefang Lu) The Hǎikǒu Qílóu is a veritable coliseum-sized food court with two floors, a large open interior and a stage where opera and other traditional perform-ances are sometimes shown in the evening. Almost next door to the left is a more typical snack street winding down a covered lane. There are all manner of inexpensive things

Hǎikǒu

🛏 Sleeping
1 Hǎikǒu Banana Youth Hostel A1
2 Hǎinán Mínháng Bīnguǎn A3

✗ Eating
3 Carrefour B3
4 Hǎikǒu Qílóu Snack Street A2

🍸 Drinking
5 Red's Pub B1

ℹ Transport
6 China Southern Airlines A3

HĂINÁN FARE

There is a huge variety of Chinese cuisine available in Hăinán. Fresh fruit and vegies are available everywhere, and, unlike much of China, they are grown under blue skies and in red soil mostly free from industrial contamination. There are myriad seafood dishes available, but most of them use imported or locally farmed fish and crustaceans.

Don't forget to try Hăinán's own famous four dishes.

» **Dōngshān mutton** (东山羊; *dōngshān yáng*) A black-wool mountain goat fed camellias and orchids, and stewed, roasted or cooked in coconut milk, or used in soups.

» **Hélè crab** (和乐蟹; *hélè xiè*) Juicy crab, usually steamed but also roasted, from Hélè near Wànníng; it's best eaten in autumn.

» **Jiāji̇̄ duck** (加积鸭; *jiāji̇̄ yā*) To-die-for roast duck from Jiāji̇̄ (the alternative name for Qiónghăi).

» **Wénchāng chicken** (文昌鸡; *wénchāng ji̇̄*) Most famous of all and originally cooked up in coastal Wénchāng, this is succulent chicken raised on a diet of rice and peanuts.

to munch on here: from shaved ice fruit plates to dumplings to corn on the cob to barbecued everything. The snack street ends oddly at a popular Buddhist shrine that fills the air with sweet incense.

Drinking

Small stands selling lemon drinks and teas are plentiful. *Liángchá* (cool tea) is a little medicinal in taste but locals swear it helps cool the body's fires on a hot day. Heping Dadao, north of Haidian 2 Donglu, hosts a number of friendly bars, including **Red's Pub** (红蜘蛛), home of the Hăikŏu Hash House Harriers.

Mĭlì Cafe   CAFE

(米粒咖啡; Mĭlì Kāfēi; http://millicafe.niwota.com; 8 Jinlong Lu; 金龙路8号嘉华城市广场美景苑101房; drinks ¥16-36; ☺10am-midnight; 🛜📶) This stylish hang-out offers good coffee, free wireless internet and great desserts. The cafe is off Jinlong Lu just east of Yu Sha Lu and accessed by going through the central opening in the Jiāhuá Plaza. The only downside is that smoking is allowed indoors and it can get pretty thick at times.

Information

The annually published *Hăinán Island Guide Map* (¥6) has a good city map of Hăikŏu, which includes a map of all of Hăinán Island on the back in addition to smaller maps of Sānyà and Bó'áo. **Xīnhuá Bookstore** (新华书店; Xīnhuá Shūdiàn; 10 Jiefang Xilu; ☺9am-10pm) has good maps if you are biking.

Many cafes around Guomao and Jinlong Lu have wireless internet access. The **Bank of China** (中国银行; Zhōngguó Yínháng; Datong Lu) changes money and travellers cheques. ATM outlets are plentiful around town.

Getting There & Away

Air

Hăikŏu's **Mĕilán Airport** (www.mlairport.com) is well connected to most of China's major cities, including Hong Kong and Macau, with international flights to Bangkok, Singapore, Kuala Lumpur and Taipei. Low-season one-way domestic fares are cheap. Destinations include Bĕijīng (¥2250), Guăngzhōu (¥700) and Shànghăi (¥1660).

Bus

Buses from Xiùyíng Harbour Station (海口秀英港客运站; Hăikŏu Xiùxīnggăng Kèyùn Zhàn) run to Guăngzhōu (¥280, 10 hours, hourly) and Guìlín (¥280, 15 hours, hourly).

The station is far to the west of town. Catch bus 37 from Értóng Park. A taxi costs about ¥25 from downtown.

Buses from the **south bus station** (汽车南站; 32 Nanhai Dadao) go to:

Qióngzhōng ¥33, three hours, hourly buses via the central highway

Sānyà ¥73, 3½ hours

Wŭzhĭshān ¥75, four hours via the east highway, hourly

Buses from the **east bus station** (汽车东站; 148 Haifu Lu) go to:

Qiónghăi ¥26, 1½ hours, frequent

Wénchāng ¥19, 1½ hours, frequent services

Sānyà ¥75, 3½ hours

Train

The main train station is far west of the city. Bus 37 (¥2) connects the train station and Értóng Park. Bus 40 (¥2) connects the southern part of the city with the train station.

Trains to/from Guǎngzhōu (hard/soft sleeper ¥197/298, 12 hours, two daily at 8.42pm and 10.53pm) are shunted onto a ferry to cross the Qióngzhōu Strait. Buy tickets (¥5 service fee) at the train station or from the dedicated counter in the **China Southern Airlines** (中国南方航空; Zhōngguó Nánfāng Hángkōng; 9 Haixiu Donglu) office.

High-speed train

Running from Hǎikǒu to Sānyà via the east coast, the new high-speed rail stops in Hǎikǒu at the main train station (Hǎikǒu Railway Station) to the west of the city, the east train station (Hǎikǒu East Railway Station), and Měilán Airport. Note that many trains do not go all the way to Hǎikǒu Railway Station. Services:

Qiónghǎi ¥41, one hour, irregular schedule

Sānyà ¥90, two hours, frequent

ⓘ Getting Around

To/From the Airport

Měilán Airport is 25km southeast of the city centre. A shuttle bus (¥15, every 30 minutes) runs to/from Hǎinán Mínháng Bīnguǎn. A taxi costs around ¥80 (negotiated price) to downtown. The high-speed rail also has a stop at the airport.

Public Transport

Hǎikǒu's centre is easy to walk around. The bus system (¥1 to ¥2) is decent, though it often takes transfers to get around.

Taxi

Taxis charge ¥10 for the first 3km. They're easy to spot, but difficult to catch on large roads because of barriers.

START YOUR DAY THE HǍINÁN WAY

Getting started in the morning with a decent and cheap breakfast is often a challenge in China. On Hǎinán, in nearly every city, town and hovel, look for a local institution called *lǎobà chá* where you can get fresh coffee (¥4 a pot), meat-filled buns (包子; *bāozi*) and a host of sweet snacks. OK, healthwise it's not exactly muesli and yoghurt, but you can always supplement it with some fresh fruit picked up from the stall down the street.

Lǎobà chá are easily recognised by their large bare interiors, or in smaller towns by their outdoor seating (usually under shady trees). If you can't find one, just ask a local.

Around Hǎikǒu

HǍIKǑU VOLCANIC CLUSTER GEOPARK 海口火山群世界地质公园

The geopark (Hǎikǒu Huǒshānqún Shìjiè Dìzhì Gōngyuán) encompasses about 108 sq km of rural countryside in Shíshān township and features dozens of extinct volcanoes, lava tunnels and even an abandoned village made of lava stones. Minibuses from Hǎikǒu will drop you off outside a spiffy **tourist park** (admission ¥60; ◷8.30am-5.30pm) that's worth a visit if you want to walk into a volcanic crater overgrown with lush vegetation.

From the park, catch a motorcycle taxi 2km to the **Seventy-Two Cave Lava Tunnel Protected Area** (七十二洞熔岩隧道保护区), which is more commonly known as Huǒshān Dòng (Volcanic Cave). The tunnel is several hundred metres long, about 20m wide and 15m high. While there isn't an official ticket booth outside, the local elders will ask you to pay ¥10, plus another ¥2 for a torch that will burn out long before you reach the end.

Just a few metres away from the trailhead to the tunnel entrance is **Huǒshān Cūn** (火山村; Volcanic Village). The abandoned village is made entirely out of lava stones and is very photogenic. You may also be asked to pay to enter here.

ⓘ Getting There & Away

The geopark is about 15km from Hǎikǒu. To get here, first take a taxi to the T-intersection of Xiuying Xiaojie and Xiuying Dadao (秀英小街、秀英大道) and then catch one of the frequent minibuses (¥4, 30 minutes) to Shíshān County (石山镇; Shíshān Zhèn) from the bus stop on the far side of Xiuying Dadao.

A taxi to the park costs ¥60. Given the size of the area, and its proximity to Hǎikǒu, exploring by bicycle is best.

DŌNGJIĀO COCONUT PLANTATION 东郊椰林

The coconut plantation (Dōngjiāo Yēlín) takes up a big chunk of Wénchāng County on the northeast coast. It's more like a large farming community than a single plantation, and the cool palm-lined lanes and traditional villages give the region a lot of character. Add in kilometres of long sandy beaches and you have a great place to hang out for a few days, exploring or relaxing. In the low season you'll have the beaches virtually to yourself unless a student group has shown up to conquer the land.

Accommodation is provided by a couple of resorts. The **Hǎinán Prima Resort** (海南百莱玛度假酒店; ☎0898-6353 8222; www.hainanprimaresort.com; r/cabins from ¥289/498) has bare rooms, and comfortable one- and two-storey wood chalets priced by size and proximity to the beach. All signs, menus and instruction boards are in English, though the staff speak little English. If the Prima isn't your bag, wander into the nearby village, where locals offer homestays.

❶ Getting There & Away

From Hǎikǒu's east station catch a high-speed train to Wénchāng (¥27, 30 minutes, hourly). Then catch bus 6 (¥2) to the Xinhua Chu Dian stop (about five minutes' ride), cross the street and catch a bus on to Jiànhuáshān (建华山; ¥8.50), the last stop. The beach is just ahead through the gate of the Hǎinán Prima Resort.

TÓNGGǓ LǏNG & YUÈ LIÀNG WĀN 铜鼓岭、月亮湾

Tónggǔ Lǐng is the name of a small mountain and nature reserve on the northeast coast just north of the Dōngjiāo Coconut Plantation. There are great views up and down the coast from the top, and to the north is the long gorgeous stretch of Yuè Liàng Wān's beach. There's no public transportation to the area but motorcycle rentals might be available in the village around the Hǎinán Prima Resort. If you cycle from the coconut plantation, expect to take around two hours. It's a pleasant ride through the rural backwaters of Hǎinán.

Central Highlands

☎0898

Hǎinán's reputation rests on its tropical beaches, but for many travellers it's in this region of dark green mountains and terraced rice-growing valleys that they make genuine contact with the island's culture.

Until recently, Han Chinese had left almost no footprint here, and even today visible signs of Chinese culture, such as temples or shrines, are very rarely seen. Instead, the region is predominantly Li and Miao – minority ethnic groups who have lived a relatively primitive subsistence existence for most of their time on the island. Indeed, groups of Li living as hunter-gatherers were found in the mountainous interior of Hǎinán as recently as the 1930s. Today, they are by far the poorest people on Hǎinán.

Travelling in the region is easy, as a decent bus system links major and minor towns. Most buses from Hǎikǒu reach Wǔzhǐshān in a few hours via the east coast highway. If you want to ply the central highway, head first to Qióngzhōng and from there catch a bus onward to Wǔzhǐshān.

Cycling is also a great way to get around this region – see boxed text, p572.

WǓZHǏSHĀN CITY (TÓNGSHÍ) 五指山市(通什)

Once called Tōngzhá or Tōngshí, Wǔzhǐshān Shì was renamed after the famous nearby mountain, the highest point on the island and a symbol of Hǎinán. Though the size of a large town, Wǔzhǐshān is actually China's smallest city, having been given such status when it became the capital of the short-lived Li and Miao Autonomous Prefecture back in the 1980s.

Most travellers here are heading out to climb the mountain, or using the town as a base for exploring the region. Note that there's nowhere to change or withdraw money in Wǔzhǐshān, so bring what you need. There's an **internet cafe** (per hr ¥2.50; ⊙24hr) on the 2nd floor of the Jīnyuán Dàjiǔdiàn but you'll need Chinese ID to use it.

🛏 Sleeping & Eating

There are cheap restaurants all around the bus station area, as well as countless fruit stalls, bakeries and cafes. Barbecue stalls are set up in the evenings all around town and, if you have a group, these are an excellent dining option. Off Buxing Jie, the wide riverside promenade with more than one kilometre of old spreading banyan trees, sit rows of *lǎobà chá* (places selling coffee and snacks), teahouses and barbecue joints.

Holiday Inn of Jadeite Mountain City HOTEL $$

(五指山翡翠山城假日酒店; Wǔzhǐshān Fěicuì Shānchéng Jiàrì Jiǔdiàn; ☎8663 08888; 1 Shanzhuang Lu; s/d ¥298/368; ❄🔇🛜) The clean, bright upper-floor rooms command wide views over the town and nearby mountains. The spacious mezzanine-level **restaurant** (average dish ¥28-58, set meals ¥18-25; ⊙7am-midnight) serves excellent Chinese food including a reasonably priced dim sum breakfast. To get here from the bus station, turn left as you exit and follow the road as it bends right with the river. The hotel is about 500m further down. Expect discounts of up to 40%.

THE LI & MIAO

Four main ethnic groups live on Hăinán (though the government lists 39 in total). These include the first settlers of the island, the Li and Miao (H'mong), who today are found mostly in the forested areas covering the Límŭlĭng Shān (Mother of the Lí Mountain) range that stretches down the centre of the island. The Li probably migrated to Hăinán from Fújiàn 3000 years ago and today they number more than one million.

Despite a long history of rebellion against the Chinese, the Li aided communist guerrillas on the island during the war with the Japanese. Perhaps for this reason the island's centre was made an 'autonomous' region after the communist takeover. The region hereafter would be self-governing, giving the marginalised Li and Miao communities a degree of control. That situation, however, proved short-lived after newly empowered local politicians were done in for corruption and money-wasting.

Like the Li, the Miao spread from southern China and now can be found across northern Vietnam, Laos and Thailand. Today there are some 60,000 Miao living on Hăinán, occupying some of the most rugged terrain on the island.

Tōng Shí Guó Jì Hotel HOTEL **$**
(通什国际大酒店; Tōngshí Guójì Dàjiŭdiàn; ☎8663 3158; Haiyu Lu; d/tw ¥180/258) The larger 2nd-floor twins are cheap in the off season and offer more light and more open views than the doubles. The hotel is a few blocks down from Jīnyuán Dàjiŭdiàn, on the corner just as the road starts to swing to the right to follow the river. There are discounts of up to 60%.

Zhèngzōng Lánzhōu Lāmiàn NOODLES **$**
(正宗兰州拉面; Authentic Lanzhou Noodles; 海榆路; Haiyu Lu; dishes ¥7-15; ⌚6.30am-10pm) Just a few doors down from the Jīnyuán Dàjiŭdiàn, this Hui Muslim restaurant sells a wide range of cheap but excellent noodle and lamb dishes. Try the *gānbànmiàn* (干伴面; ¥8), a kind of stir-fried spaghetti bolognaise with hand-pulled noodles.

Getting There & Away

Buses from Wŭzhĭshān include the following:

Băotíng ¥9, 40 minutes, hourly
Hăikŏu ¥86, four hours, seven daily
Qióngzhōng ¥28, two hours, hourly
Sānyà ¥23, 1½ hours, frequent
Shuĭmăn ¥8, one hour, hourly

Around Wŭzhĭshān

WŬZHĬSHĀN (FIVE FINGER MOUNTAIN) 五指山

The **mountain** (admission ¥50; ⌚24hr) after which Wŭzhĭshān is named rises 1867m out of the centre of Hăinán in a reserve 30km northeast of the city. As the highest peak in the land, it's naturally steeped in local lore: the five peaks, for example, are said to represent the Li people's five most powerful gods. Despite the name, however, from most angles the summit looks like a single volcanic peak or a cleft hoof.

The reserve is the source of the Wànquán (万泉河) and Chānghuà (昌化江) rivers and protects a mixed forest containing 6.5% of all vascular plant species in China. It's a rich (though threatened) ecosystem and receives the highest rainfall in Hăinán. *Average* humidity is more than 90% and the mountaintop is often shrouded in fog and mist.

It's pretty much an all-day event to get out here and climb the mountain, so leave as early as possible if you hope to enjoy clear views from the peak. Most people can reach the top of the first finger (the second is highest) in three hours. The path is clear but very steep and includes a number of ladder climbs further up. Coming down is not much faster than going up, so give yourself six to eight hours.

Wŭzhĭshān sits about 4km from the village of **Shuĭmăn** (水满). There is no fixed schedule to Shuĭmăn but buses (¥8, one hour, 35km) run about every hour. In Wŭzhĭshān, buy your ticket on the bus, which leaves across the street from the station front. Make sure to get a bus going to Shuĭmăn via Nánshèng.

In Shuĭmăn, motorcycle taxis will take you the remaining 4km for ¥15. The last bus back to Wŭzhĭshān leaves Shuĭmăn around 6pm.

QĪ XIĀN LĬNG (SEVEN FAIRY MOUNTAIN) 七仙岭

About 39km southeast of Wŭzhĭshān lies the small and conspicuously orderly Li town of **Băotíng** (保亭). While that orderliness may strike you as noteworthy after a few weeks spent travelling in China, the main reason to come here is to climb the 1126m **Seven Fairy Mountain** (Qī Xiān Lǐng), comprising an eye-catching ridge of jagged spear-like crags. The area is perhaps more famous among Chinese, however, for the hot-spring resorts popping up in the tropical forest.

The mountain entrance and hot springs area are 9km off the main road from Bǎotíng in what is ostensibly now a **national hot springs and forest park** (七仙岭温泉国家森林公园; Qī Xiān Lǐng Wēnquán Guójiā Sēnlín Gōngyuán; admission ¥48). Tickets to climb the Seven Fairy Mountain can be purchased at the new national park office at the start of the 2.4km long trail. It's three hours to the top and back along a stepped path through a dense, healthy rainforest buzzing with bird and insect life. The final 100m climb to the peak runs up a pitted slope with chains and railings in place to aid your near-vertical climb. The views from the top are worth the effort.

There are frequent buses to Bǎotíng from Wūzhīshān (¥9, 40 minutes) and also Sānyà (¥22, 1½ hours). From Bǎotíng's bus station, catch a motorcycle to the national park entrance (¥30). Make sure not to catch a motorcycle with a side car as they lack the power to make it the last 4km from the hot springs area up to the trailhead.

If you want to spend the night in Bǎotíng, **Jīn Zhōu Dù Jià Xiūxián Bīnguǎn** (金洲度假休闲宾馆; ☏0898-8366 3888; tw from ¥130) has surprisingly comfortable modern rooms with great extras like wide-screen TVs and computers with broadband internet. The hotel is literally to the right of the bus station as you exit.

The East Coast

☏0898

Hǎinán's east coast is a series of spectacular palm-lined beaches, long bays and headlands most of which are, unfortunately, not usually visible from the main roads, not even at bicycle level. With the best beaches developed or being developed, there is little reason to make a special trip out here (to Bó'áo being the exception) unless you are surfing or wish to stay at a resort. Biking or motorcycling is another story, however, as there are endless small villages and rural roads to explore and even a few near-deserted bays.

In the past, the east coast was the centre of Han settlement. If you are coming from the highlands you will start to notice temples, gravesites, shrines and other signs of Chinese culture dotting the landscape.

BÓ'ÁO   博鳌

This attractive little coastal town at the confluence of three rivers is famous as the site of the Bó'áo Forum for Asia (BFA), a yearly meet-up of top-level officials, academics and economists exclusively from the Asia region. For cyclists, Bó'áo is a natural stop along the coast, offering good accommodation and food. For all travellers, it's an unpretentious little beach town (with a usually deserted beach), surrounded by some of the prettiest countryside on Hǎinán.

Like much of Hǎinán or China for that matter, during the past few years Bó'áo has been under the spell of the construction fairy, and in the north of town luxury villas and resorts continue to pop up. Officially Bó'áo is starting to cover a large area, but the 'downtown' blocks, where most travellers both stay and eat are tiny, in essence being two streets that intersect at a T-junction: Haibin Lu (海滨路) runs north–south and Zhaobo Lu (朝博路) runs east–west. The beach is a five-minute walk from here.

Avoid planning a trip to Bó'áo either during the forum or the week before as the town is pretty much closed off under the scrutiny of high-level security (there are even warships in the harbour).

◉ Sights & Activities

Despite hosting the BFA every year, and despite over-construction giving parts of town the look of a small Dubai, Bó'áo is still a rather rural place. Even a few blocks from the main junction are small villages of stone and brick buildings where locals dry rice in the middle of the lanes, and burn incense in small shrines to their local folk deities. Some good examples are **Dà Lù Pō Village** (大路坡村; Dà Lù Pō Cūn) and **Nánqiáng Village** (南强村; Nánqiáng Cūn) off the main road about 2km west of the downtown junction. About 20km northeast of Bó'áo look for the little fishing village of **Tánmén** (潭门), where the local multicoloured wooden junks are made and repaired.

Beaches   BEACHES

Bó'áo's beach is a few hundred metres east of the main road. Head south down Haibin Lu, turn left at the Jinjiang Hot Spring

Hotel and follow the road as it swings right to drop you off at a **Matsu Temple**. The river hits the sea here and a long thin sandbar at the mouth is for very dubious reasons (go ahead and ask the locals) a popular place to boat out to.

If you plan to swim, head at least 500m north to avoid dangerous currents.

Cài Family Former Residence HISTORIC SITE
(蔡家宅; Càijiā Zhái) For a rewarding half-day trip, grab a bike, or rent a motorcycle taxi (¥60), and head to this sprawling old mansion built in 1934 by several brothers who made their fortune in the Indonesian rubber industry. The building was abandoned in 1937 after the Japanese invaded Hǎinán, and later became a guerrilla outpost for resistance fighters. In 2006 it was declared a heritage site and these days you can wander around inside for a look if the caretaker is about.

To reach the house, head west out of town and when the road ends at a junction turn left (south) and cross two long bridges. Head right after crossing the second bridge at the English sign. In a couple of blocks stay left and enjoy a sumptuous ride through green fields and collections of handsome old and new houses alongside the road.

Courtyard of Eastern Culture MONASTERY
(东方文化苑; Dōngfāng Wénhuàyuàn) This modern Buddhist temple complex is not being maintained well, and the excellent Lotus Museum seems permanently closed, but it's still worth a visit to see the enormous statue of the many-armed and many-headed Guanyin, the stunning pagoda, and the views over the delta which show just how pretty and rural Bó'áo can still be.

A motorcycle taxi costs ¥10 from the centre of Bó'áo. You can easily walk back and take in some of the traditional villages along the way.

Sleeping

TOP CHOICE **Bó'áo Inn** B&B $$
(博鳌客栈; Bó'áo Kèzhàn; ☎138 7627 1007; www.hainan-letsgo.com; r incl breakfast from ¥395; ✳☎) The owner of this great little inn, an American expat, started it in part just to meet more travellers. So expect to be treated like family during your stay and to be doted on and plied with homemade meals and fresh-baked goodies (her banana bread is fantastic and becoming the stuff of backpacker legend). The inn offers tours to

Miao villages and bicycle rentals for local rides (with an accompanying map), and has arrangements with a local motorcycle taxi driver to take you to the sights around town at fixed rates. Reservations must be made in advance.

Hǎi Jǐng Wān Hotel HOTEL $
(海景湾宾馆; Hǎijǐng Wān Bīnguǎn; ☎6277 9558; r ¥90-130) Just 150m west of the main junction in town is this friendly family-run hotel with large rooms facing towards the sea and river, and more boxy offerings with little to no natural light. Staff tend to steer foreigners to the large topmost room, the priciest but also the best of the lot.

Eating

Because of its international status as thesite of the BFA, the town has a good range of Chinese restaurants dedicated to regional cuisine (Hui Muslim, Húnán and Sìchuān are just the start; dishes ¥8 to ¥60) as well as plenty of barbecue stalls that set up in the evenings. You'll see English signs out the front and even some English or picture menus within. On the main streets there are grocery stores, and abundant fruit stands.

Around 4pm each day head north about 150m from the main intersection on Haibin Lu and look for stalls on either side of the road near the Hainan Bank selling succulent Jiājī duck (¥10 for a leg), a Hǎinán speciality. Don't be tardy as it sells out quickly.

Colourful Noodles VEGETARIAN $
(七彩面馆; Qīcǎi Miànguǎn; Zhaobo Lu; dishes ¥13-15; ☯8am-late; ✐◱) Though a few meat dishes are on offer at this warm family-run place, it's otherwise a true vegetarian set-up serving vegie-flavoured noodle dishes, as well as dumplings, fresh fruit and juices. To get here head west along Zhaobo Lu almost to the end of the two-storey row of whitewashed buildings.

TOP CHOICE **Sea Story** SEAFOOD, CAFE $$
(海的故事; Hǎide Gùshì; dishes ¥18-38; ☯9.30am-1am; ☎◱) The ocean-facing Sea Story has an open driftwood frame with a funky beach-comber design: an old wood fishing junk even sits as the centrepiece inside the lobby. Outside, the breezy deck is an ideal spot for cocktails or an extended lunch or dinner. Loud music, karaoke and other intrusive noises or activities are banned. Sea Story is about 1km north from the Matsu Temple along the seaside lane.

THE COLOURFUL FISHING PORT OF XĪNCŪN

This classic south seas fishing port (新村; Xīncūn) is one of the most authentic, and authentically picturesque, destinations on Hăinán. Among the hubbub, the clutter, the filth and the flotsam of a typical fishing port float hundreds of painted wooden ships in a deep blue tropical bay ringed with emerald green hills. Fish dry on the docks, women weave nets, men weld old scraps of metal together, and a whole community thrives, including the hundreds of families who live on permanent floating houseboats across the bay.

Most people come to this area simply to see the rather dull **Nánwān Monkey Islet** (南湾猴岛; Nánwān Hóudǎo) across the bay and reached by China's longest **gondola** (¥163; ⏰8am-4.50pm, last gondola 4.20pm). Some 1000 macaque monkeys (*Macaca mulatta*) live on the hilly islet, and while most of the area is now off limits to tourists, monkeys are still made to perform for visitors, are said to be beaten by staff and show clear signs of stress.

If you just want to see the monkeys and ride the gondola the best way is to go on a tour from Sānyà. Otherwise, to visit the fishing port, catch a bus from Sānyà to Língshuǐ (陵水; ¥18, 1½ hours, 79km, hourly). In Língshuǐ, after leaving the station's main exit, cross the road and head right. Walk a few blocks and catch a minibus in front of the Bank of China to Xīncūn (¥3, 40 minutes). In Xīncūn, catch a motorcycle taxi or walk the 1km to the harbour.

Áozhuāng Hǎixiān Chéng SEAFOOD $$
(熬庄海鲜城) For seafood, head north out of town to this collection of seaside cafes, which are famous across the island. Just choose and then point to what you want cooked up but make sure to ask the price before sitting down. Restaurants open around 9.30am and close when the last customers leave. You can walk here on the main road, or better yet along the seaside lane starting at the Matsu Temple, in about 30 minutes.

Drinking

Lao Wood Coffee Rest Area CAFE
(老房子; Lǎo Fángzi; 61 Haibin Lu; drinks from ¥18, ⏰9am-2am; 🛜) The owner of this cafe, a local dancer and art administrator, literally had an old traditional stone house taken apart and reassembled on Bó'áo's main street to make his dream of opening a stylish cafe come true. The inside is chock-full of antiques and *objets d'art*, while out the back is a small leafy garden.

Information

You can buy high-speed train tickets from Yuantong International Travel Agency (64 Haibin Lu; ⏰8am-10pm) about 200m north of the main intersection across from an ABC Bank. In the same area is a Bank of China (中国银行; Zhōngguó Yínháng) with an ATM. A decent map of the Bó'áo area can be found at the bottom of the general Hǎinán Tourism Guide Map.

Getting There & Away

HIGH-SPEED TRAIN

The nearest station to Bó'áo is actually Qiónghǎi and from there you'll need to catch a taxi (¥40) the rest of the way. Alternatively, catch bus 6 or 7 outside the rail station to Qiónghǎi East Station (琼海东站) and then follow the directions below.

Sānyà ¥49, one hour, hourly

Hǎikǒu ¥41, one hour, hourly

BUS

From Hǎikǒu's east bus station catch a bus to the main station in Qiónghǎi (琼海; ¥26, 1½ hours, 102km) then cross the street to the Kentucky Fried Chicken side, and look for the bus stop just down the road to the left. Catch minibus 2 to Bó'áo (¥4, 30 minutes, frequent). Passengers get dropped off at the main junction in Bó'áo.

SHÍMÉI BAY & SUN & MOON BAY 石梅湾、日月湾

Shíméi Bay (Shíméi Wān) and Sun and Moon Bay (Rì Yuè Wān) are among the most stunning stretches of coastline on Hǎinán. Development of major resorts is proceeding apace but the beaches are still open to the public and offer some of China's best surfing waves, especially from November to January (see boxed text, p581). Some hostels and hotels in Sānyà offer day trips to the bays and you can ride out to them if you are biking the east coast.

Sānyà 三亚

📞 0898 / POP 685,400

China's premier beach community is a modern construction in every way – which makes the claim that it is the Hawaii of China a little suspect. Certainly, if you are hoping to be charmed by an indigenous culture closely tied to the sea – in addition to enjoying your beer, golden sand beaches and clear tropical blue waters, of course – you will be a bit disappointed. Sānyà is built just for fun.

While the full 40km or so of coastline dedicated to tourism is usually referred to as Sānyà, the region is actually made up of three distinct zones. Sānyà Bay is home to the bustling city centre and a long stretch of beach and hotels aimed at locals and mainland holidaymakers. Dàdōnghǎi Bay, about 3km southeast, beyond the Lùhuítóu Peninsula, is where most Western travellers stay. In fact, it receives such a steady influx of Russian vacationers these days that almost all signs are in Cyrillic as well as Chinese. A further 15km east, at exclusive Yàlóng Bay, the beach is first-rate, as is the line of plush international resorts.

You'll find the bus station in the Sānyà Bay area on Jiefang Lu, the main drag. This road morphs into Yuya Lu as it heads into Dàdōnghǎi Bay and Yàlóng Bay. The *Sānyà Tour Guide* map (¥6) is worth buying from hostels and hotels to get an overview of the area. Also check out the What's On Sanya website (www.whatsonsanya.com) for events, as well as eating and drinking recommendations.

◉ Sights & Activities

Unsurprisingly for a beach resort, the vast majority of things to see and do revolve around sand, sea, shopping and after-hours entertainment. Strolling along the riverfronts is pleasant in the cool evenings. Banyan trees shade the boulevards, healthy looking mangroves line the shore, and a modern glitzy skyline dominates the background.

If you want to scuba or snorkel, May to August, before typhoon season, is the best time though locals will tell you honestly that there is not that much to see in the water. Surfing is possible all year round if you alternate between Dàdōnghǎi, Hòuhǎi and nearby Sun and Moon Bay.

Beaches
BEACHES

The long sandy strip off the city centre at **Sānyà Bay** (三亚湾; Sānyà Wān) is the most relaxed of the three main beaches, and the one place you will really see people kicking back, laughing, playing and having a beachy old time. In little covered areas you'll find locals playing music, singing, engaged in conspiracy, writing characters in the sand,

---

HITTING THE WAVES ON HǍINÁN

Surfing is slowly gaining a following in China, and Hǎinán is without question the centre of that budding scene. While the majority of people out on the waters are still Westerners, the number of Chinese trying the sport grows each year. Conditions are never going to make this the next Indonesia, as surf shop owner Brendon Sheradon says, but every level, from beginner to advanced, can find suitable waves. In recognition of the growing interest, two annual competitions are now held each year in the Shímēi Bay and Sun and Moon Bay area (see p578): the **Hainan Surf Open**, in November, organised by Sheradon's **Surfing Hǎinán** (冲浪海南; Chōnglàng Hǎinán; www.surfinghainan.com); and the **Hainan Classic**, in January, sponsored by ASP (the Association of Surfing Professionals).

If you want to try your hand at the sport, Dàdōnghǎi and Hòuhǎi get decent waves from May to September and are suitable for absolute novices (especially quiet Hòuhǎi). Shímēi Bay/Sun and Moon Bay are prime from November to January but it's possible to surf all year. With up to five breaks, the area is suitable for all levels; advanced surfers can try their luck on the Ghost Hotel waves. Unlike further south, Shímēi Bay and Sun and Moon Bay get a bit chilly and overcast in the winter months, so light wetsuits are recommended.

You can find rentals and basic lessons in Sānyà at **Sānyà Backpackers** (www.sanyabackpackers.com), but if you want professional instructions contact Surfing Hainan, which offers two-hour lessons for ¥400 and rentals for ¥100 per day. It also has wetsuits for rent at ¥50 per day.

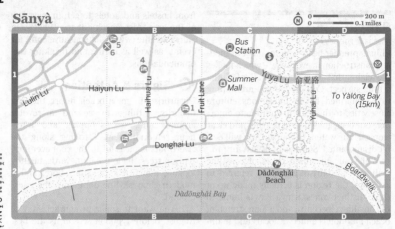

Sānyà

🛏 Sleeping

1 Blue Sky International Youth
  Hostel B1
2 Golden Beach Villa.........................C2
3 Resort Intime.................................B2
4 Sānyà Backpackers.........................B1
5 Sānyà Lùxiáng Shāngwù
  Zhōngxīn B1

✕ Eating

6 Casa Mia Italian Restaurant B1

ℹ Transport

7 Air Ticket Office D1

and so on. There's a long pathway for strolling in the cool evenings, and if the tide is out a little you can walk on the sand for many kilometres. In the evenings it's fun to watch the lights on Phoenix Island (the awesome cruise ship terminal) turn on.

Dàdōnghǎi Bay (大东海湾; Dàdōnghǎi Wān) sports a wider beach than Sānyà and has a shaded boardwalk running along most of its length. The setting, in a deep blue bay with rocky headlands, is simply gorgeous but it does get busy here, and sometimes people do seem to be trying just a little too hard to enjoy themselves.

Some consider **Yàlóng Bay** (亚龙湾; Yàlóng Wān; Asian Dragon Bay) to have the best beach but it can seem the least relaxing of all with a lot of frenetic activity.

Both Dàdōnghǎi and Yàlóng Bays offer a wide range of activities, including jet-skiing, snorkelling and parasailing, but instruction is usually substandard and lifeguards on duty are not properly trained and may be of little use in an emergency. See Sānyà Backpackers for scuba lessons and rentals and also surfing.

Hòuhǎi (后海), a crescent-shaped sandy beach about 45 minutes northeast out of Dàdōnghǎi, is popular with those looking to get away from the crowds (though ironically it lies in the southern reach of Hǎitáng Bay where the scale of development must be seen to be believed). Sānyà-based hostels take people here to surf and scuba while Chinese tourists are shuttled to the pier for a boat ride out to Wúzhīzhōu Dǎo (Island). Bus 28 from the main road in Dàdōnghǎi (¥11) takes you to the beach. There's a small village here with plenty of small restaurants and fruit stands.

🛏 Sleeping

Dàdōnghǎi Bay is the place to head for mid-range and budget lodgings. The top-end resorts are off the beach at Yàlóng Bay in a private area of palm-lined roads and landscaped grounds. Outside peak periods 30% to 60% discounts are common everywhere and even hostel bed prices fluctuate with the season and the midweek/weekend divide.

DÀDŌNGHǍI

TOP CHOICE **Sānyà Backpackers** HOSTEL $
(三亚背包度假屋; Sānyà Bēibāo Dùjià Wū; ☎8821 3963; www.sanyabackpackers.com; No 1 Type 1 Villa, Lu Ming Community, Haihua Lu, Dàdōnghǎi Bay; dm ¥75, d/tw ¥280/220; ❋@◎) Run by a Singaporean diving instructor and his charming wife, this spick-and-span

hostel is a more intimate and friendly place than others in town. Set in a whitewashed building in a quiet residential compound it's also an oasis. Simple backpacker dishes are available, and there's a new bar for hanging out in the evenings. In addition to open water certification and refresher courses (per day ¥500 including lunch and transport), the hostel offers surfing lessons and rentals (per day ¥380) and some customised trips out to waterfalls and jungle hiking trails.

Resort Intime   RESORT $$$

(湘投银泰度假酒店; Xiāngtóu Yíntái Dùjià Jiǔdiàn; ☑8821 0888; www.resortintime.com; Dàdōnghǎi Bay; r from ¥1688; ☺✳@☀) It feels a bit like you are entering a busy bus terminal when you walk in the lobby and head up the elevator to reception, but that's about the only thing pedestrian about this great little resort that's right by the beach. The hotel grounds are surprisingly large and leafy, and feature a barbecue area near the pool. The rooms aren't the most spacious but those with sea views are set at a perfect angle to take in the bay. Nonsmoking floors are available.

Blue Sky
International Youth Hostel   HOSTEL $

(蓝天国际青年旅舍; Lántiān Guójì Qīngnián Lûshè; ☑133 2209 8659; www.sanyahostel.com; 1 Lanhai Alley, Haiyun Lu, Dàdōnghǎi Bay; dm ¥60-70, tw/d ¥190/220; ☎) This long-running backpacker hang-out in Dàdōnghǎi is a bit impersonal but well set up for foreign travellers. There's wi-fi, bike rentals, laundry and an informative bulletin board, as well as a decent restaurant (when it's open). The hostel is in a lane running off to the left just past the fruit stands as you head down Haiyun Lu.

Golden Beach Villa   HOTEL $$$

(金沙滩海景度假别墅; Jīn Shātān Hǎijǐng Dùjià Biéshù; ☑8821 2220; www.jinshatan888.com; 21 Haihua Lu; r from ¥1088; ✳) Despite the address, the front office and the suites are actually on Donghai Lu facing the beach. Rooms, which are enclosed in a walled-off garden, face the sea, and the upper floors have excellent views. Despite being so close to the seaside action this is a fairly quiet part of Dàdōnghǎi.

Sānyà Lùxiáng
Shāngwù Zhōngxīn   GUESTHOUSE $

(三亚鹿翔商务中心; ☑8822 4771; 17 Lulin Lu; r ¥100; ✳☎) There are many grubby guesthouses in the high-rises around Dàdōnghǎi, which makes this place, with its clean modern rooms set in a bright garden villa, such a great deal. There's no English name but look for the English sign at the front gate announcing there are rooms inside.

LOVER'S BAY

With prices rising in Dàdōnghǎi, hostels are starting to pop up outside the busy areas. Most are too far out to be recommended, but on the west side of Lùhuítóu Cape sits Lover's Bay (情人湾; Qíngrén Wān), a quiet fishing village with a row of low-rise hostels, open-air restaurants and guesthouses, literally spilling back from the edge of the sand. You can swim in the bay here but you need to wear sandals in the water because of shells.

Lover Bay Beach Cafe Hostel   HOSTEL $

(情人湾沙滩度假屋; Qíngrén Wān Shātān Dùjià Wū; ☑8883 8855; http://loverbayhostel.taobao.com; 175 Lùhuítóu Village; 三亚鹿回头村一组175号,居委会后面; dm/tw ¥60/220; ✳☎) Run by a friendly English-speaking former Shanghainese, this beachfront hostel has clean basic dorms and private rooms. Simple hostel foods are available or you can prepare your own in the kitchen. A stone's throw away are a number of outdoor seafood and Chinese restaurants. Contact the owner about getting to the hostel the first time as it's a bit tricky.

✗ Eating

The entire beachfront at Dàdōnghǎi is one long strip of restaurants, bars and cafes, most of which are overpriced and not terribly good, even if the overall atmosphere is cool, shady and scenic.

Haihua Lu is lined with restaurants featuring outdoor seating for barbecue and seafood at night, while in the alley leading to the Blue Sky hostel look for inexpensive dumpling shops and barbecue, also at night.

Hóng Shǎo Mǎ Tóu   SEAFOOD $$$

(红少码头) The floating seafood restaurants at Hóng Shǎo Mǎ Tóu won't be to everyone's taste, but it you enjoy a rustic, loud, convivial atmosphere when you eat then take bus 17 (¥1) from Yuya Lu in Dàdōnghǎi to the last stop. Around the corner you'll find a row of wooden junks ready to take you out to the floating restaurant base just a few hundred metres offshore. Make sure you agree on the fixed price for your set of seafood dishes (usually under ¥100 per person) before you start eating.

Lì Guó Cāntīng
HĀINĀN $$

(利国餐厅; Wenming Lu, Sānyà; 文明路; ☏8825 9099; dishes ¥20-40; ☻11am-8.30pm) This well-established local restaurant serves excellent Hāinán fare such as Wénchāng chicken (文昌鸡; *Wénchāng jī*; per *jīn* ¥40, good for one or two people). Also try its *tiěbǎn niúròu* (铁板牛肉; beef on a hot plate). It's best to take a taxi here as it's hard to find on your own.

Casa Mia Italian Restaurant
ITALIAN $$

(卡萨米亚意大利餐厅; Kǎsà Mǐyà Yìdàlì Cāntīng; 15 Lulin Lu; mains ¥48-78; ☏回) This branch of a long-running Sānyà Bay restaurant serves top-of-the-line Italian dishes such as pastas, raviolis, pizzas and appetisers. There's a decent wine list to help make a visit here a long lunch or evening out.

🍷 Drinking

Most of the after-hours fun is in Sānyà and Dàdōnghǎi Bay. There's a bar and karaoke TV (KTV) street on Yuya Lu near the river.

TOP CHOICE Bud
CAFE, BAR

(早苗岩烧; Zǎomiáo Yánshāo; www.syzaomiao.com; 11f Shèngshìxīndì Bldg, cnr Sanyawan Lu & Jixiang Lu, Sānyà; 三亚市三亚晚路吉祥路口盛世新大楼十一楼; drinks from ¥25; ☻1pm-1am) Overlooking Sānyà Bay from its inimitable rooftop location, Bud serves fruit drinks, teas, coffees and alcoholic drinks (also light meals). Enter to the left of the shop with the sign 'Mu Wu Health Preservation Center'.

🛈 Information

There is the full gamut of internet cafes (Chinese ID needed), banks, travel agencies etc in Sānyà city as well as Dàdōnghǎi Bay. Wi-fi is widely available in restaurants and cafes. The **Bank of China** (中国银行; Zhōngguó Yínháng; Yuya Lu) in Dàdōnghǎi changes travellers cheques and has an ATM.

🛈 Getting There & Away

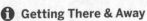

Air

Sānyà's **Phoenix Airport** (www.sanyaairport.com) has international flights to Singapore, Hong Kong, Malaysia, Thailand, Taiwan and Japan, as well as to Běijīng (¥2310), Guǎngzhōu (¥800) and Shànghǎi (¥1890).

Bus

Frequent buses and minibuses to most parts of Hǎinán depart from the **long-distance bus station** (Sānyà qìchēzhàn; Jiefang Lu, Sānyà).

Bǎotíng ¥22, 1½ hours, hourly

Hǎikǒu ¥75, 3½ hours, regular services

Língshuǐ ¥18, 1½ hours, hourly

Wànníng ¥30, two hours, hourly

Wǔzhǐshān ¥23, two hours, regular services

High-Speed train

Tickets can be purchased in Dàdōnghǎi from the **air ticket office** (蓝色海航空售票中心; Yuya Lu) two bus stops east of Summer Mall (the stop is called Bayi Zhongxue). You can also order tickets online (at least a week in advance) from **Apple Travel** (www.appletravel.cn/china-trains).

Hǎikǒu ¥90, two hours, frequent

Qiónghǎi ¥49 one hour, hourly

🛈 Getting Around

Phoenix Airport is 25km from Dàdōnghǎi Bay. Shuttle bus 8 (¥5, one hour) leaves for the airport from Yuya Lu. A taxi costs ¥60 to ¥70. The high-speed train station is far out of town. Bus 4 (¥1) runs there from Dàdōnghǎi but takes over an hour. A taxi will cost ¥40 for a 20-minute ride.

Buses 2 and 8 (¥1, frequent) travel from Sānyà bus station to Dàdōnghǎi Bay.

From Dàdōnghǎi Bay to Yàlóng Bay, catch bus 15 (¥5).

Taxis charge ¥8 for the first 2km. A taxi from Sānyà to Dàdōnghǎi Bay costs ¥10 to ¥15, and from Dàdōnghǎi Bay to Yàlóng Bay it's ¥60.

Guǎngxī

POP 50 MILLION

Includes »

Guìlín 587
Dragon's Backbone
Rice Terraces...............593
Sānjiāng........................594
Yángshuò......................595
Huángyáo 601
Nánníng 601
Yángměi........................604
Běihǎi............................605
Wéizhōu........................607
Zuǒ River Scenic Area..607
Píngxiáng......................608
Détiān Waterfall...........608
Míngshì Tiányuán.........609
Lèyè 610

Why Go?

Tell someone you're heading to Guǎngxī (广西) and they'll seethe with envy. The star attraction is the karst scenery in Guìlín and Yángshuò, where travellers can venture by bicycle or hike through lush valleys. It's hard not to fall for this achingly beautiful province, which offers endless rewards for those with an outdoors temperament.

Expect the mighty rush of the Détiān Waterfall, and the marvellous Chéngyáng Wind and Rain Bridge, to dazzle you. A trek through the villages of the lofty Dragon's Backbone Rice Terraces gives you a glimpse into the distinct traditions of diverse minority groups like the Zhuang, Yao and Dong.

Less-active travellers can discover the 2000-year-old Huāshān cliff murals in a peaceful boat journey on the Zuǒ River; or simply wander along the quaint old settlements in Běihǎi and savour their wonderful human landscape.

Best Non-Karst Sights

» Dragon's Backbone Rice Terraces (p593)

» Huángyáo (p601)

» Détiān Waterfall (p608)

» Chéngyáng Wind and Rain Bridge (p594)

Best Mountain Scenery

» Yangshuo (p595)

» Xīngpíng (p599)

» Míngshì Tiányuán (p609)

» Lèyè (p609)

When to Go

Guìlín

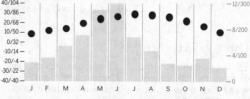

Apr & May The karst scenery in Guìlín and Yángshuò turns lushly green.

Jun–Sep Summer rains give the fields on Dragon's Backbone Rice Terraces full sparkle.

Sep & Oct The cool gulf breeze caresses as you stroll on Wéizhōu Island.

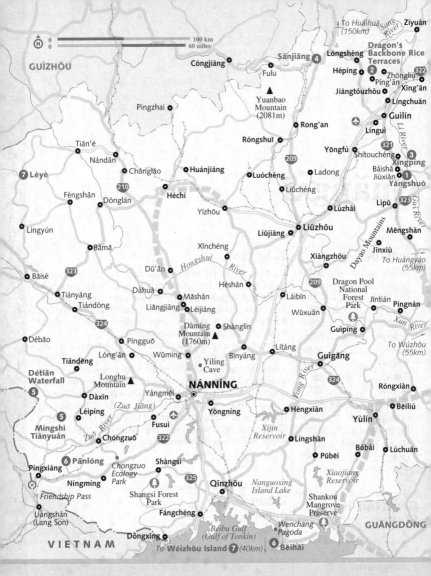

Guǎngxī Highlights

1 Lose yourself among the dramatic limestone scenery when cycling alongside the Yùlóng River in **Yángshuò** (p595)

2 Trek through China's most spectacular highland vistas at **Dragon's Backbone Rice Terraces** (p593)

3 Hike, bike or climb around **Xīngpíng** (p599), and enjoy a taste of Yángshuò circa 15 years ago

4 Admire the striking **Chéngyáng Wind and Rain Bridge** (p594) near Sānjiāng and experience the rural pleasure around nearby paddies

5 Feel the spray of the **Détiān Waterfall** (p608) before village-hopping to rustic **Míngshì Tiányuán** (p609)

6 Enjoy the boat journey from Pànlóng to the 2000-year-old **Huāshān cliff murals** (p607)

7 Gawp at the mist-covered, yawning chasm of the sky pits at **Lèyè** (p609)

History

In 214 BC a Qin-dynasty army attempted to assimilate the Zhuang people, living in what is now called Guǎngxī, into their newly formed Chinese empire. But while the eastern and southern parts submitted, the western extremes remained largely controlled by hill-tribe chieftains.

Major tribal uprisings occurred in the 19th century, the most significant being the Taiping Rebellion (1850–64), which began in Guìpíng and became one of the bloodiest civil wars in human history.

Communist bases were set up in Guǎngxī following the 1929 Baise Uprising led by Deng Xiaoping, although they were eventually destroyed by Kuomintang forces. And much of Guǎngxī fell briefly under Japanese rule following highly destructive WWII invasions.

Today the Zhuang, China's largest minority group, make up 32% of Guǎngxī's population, which led to the province being reconstituted in 1955 as the Guǎngxī Zhuang Autonomous Region. As well as Zhuang, Miao and Yao, Guǎngxī is home to significant numbers of Dong people.

Language

Travellers with a grasp of Mandarin (Pǔtōnghuà) will have few problems navigating Guǎngxī's vast sea of languages. Cantonese (Guǎngdōnghuà), known as Báihuà in these parts, is the language of choice in Nánníng, Píngxiáng and Dàxīn, but most people also understand Mandarin. Visitors will also hear a number of minority languages being spoken, such as Zhuang, Dong, Xiang, Hmong, Sui, Hakka, Jing (Vietnamese) and Yi.

The Zhuang romanisation system, looking like badly spelled Pinyin, is prominently displayed, while bilingual Chinese/Vietnamese signs can be seen in areas nearing Vietnam.

In Guìlín and Yángshuò, you'll come across locals with an excellent knowledge of English.

Guìlín 桂林

☑ 0773 / POP 826,640

Whether you're going north to the highlands, or south to Yángshuò and beyond, Guìlín is a place you're likely to spend a night or two. Set off alongside the tranquil Lí River (漓江; Lí Jiāng) it is a good introduction to Guǎngxī's dreamlike scenery, with its otherworldly karst topography as a backdrop.

PRICE INDICATORS

The following price indicators are used in this chapter:

Sleeping

$	less than ¥150
$$	¥150 to ¥400
$$$	more than ¥400

Eating

$	less than ¥40
$$	¥40 to ¥100
$$$	more than ¥100

The city's complete reliance on tourism means that it's well managed and clean, but you'll have to share it with the crowds, and there are touts and high admission fees to sights. With modern facilities and a high percentage of English-speaking locals, Guìlín is a convenient base to plan trips to the rest of the province.

◉ Sights

Guìlín's sights are built around scraggly karst peaks dotted around the bustling city, and owing to recent price hikes can be easily skipped. You'll save 10% to 20% by buying a combined ticket. A stroll along the Róng and Shān Lakes and along the Lí River offers a wallet-friendly alternative to the pricey sights.

Lakes & City Wall LAKES, RUIN

On the northern shore of Róng Lake (榕湖; Róng Hú), and strikingly illuminated at night, the South Gate (南门; Nán Mén) is the only surviving section of the original Song-dynasty city wall (城墙; chéng qiáng). The area is a buzzing hub of activity and a good place to watch locals practising taichi, calligraphy and dancing.

About 1km north of Folded Brocade Hill is the East Gate (东镇门; Dōngzhèn Mén), a part-reconstructed gateway flanked by crumbling sections of the original wall. Take bus 1 or 2 and get off at the Dōngzhèn Lù stop, then turn right down the road of the same name. Alternatively, it's a short walk or cycle north along the riverbank, just east of the entrance to Folded Brocade Hill.

The gate lies on the northeast edge of Mùlóng Lake Park (木龙湖; Mùlóng Hú; admission ¥90; ◉9am-10pm), which houses a

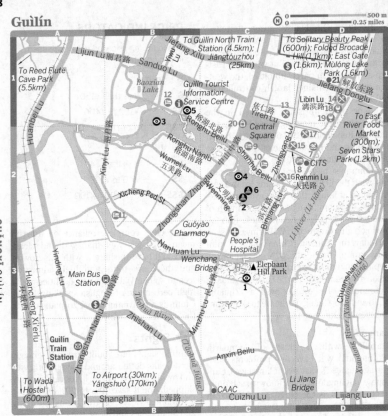

reconstruction of a Song-dynasty pagoda (木龙塔; Mùlóng Tǎ) and is a picturesque setting for Chinese classical music performances, held at 8pm every evening.

Sun & Moon Twin Pagodas   PAGODAS
(日月双塔; Rìyuè Shuāng Tǎ; admission ¥30; ⏰8.30am-10.30pm) Elegantly embellishing the scenery of **Shān Lake** (杉湖; Shān Hú), the Sun and Moon Twin Pagodas, beautifully illuminated at night, are the highlight of a stroll around Guìlín's two central lakes. The octagonal, seven-storey **Moon Pagoda** (月塔; Yuè Tǎ) is connected by an underwater tunnel to the 41m-high **Sun Pagoda** (日塔; Rì Tǎ), the world's tallest copper pagoda and one of the few pagodas anywhere in the world with a lift.

Solitary Beauty Peak   PARK
(独秀峰; Dúxiù Fēng; 1 Wangcheng; 王城1号; admission ¥88; ⏰7.30am-6pm) A peaceful, leafy retreat from the city centre, the entrance fee for this famous lone pinnacle includes admission to a 14th-century Ming prince's mansion (oversold as a 'palace'), and a recreation of a Qing-dynasty examination hall. The 152m peak is a steep climb, but affords fine views of Guìlín. Buses 1 and 2 both stop nearby.

Seven Stars Park   PARK
(七星公园; Qīxīng Gōngyuán; admission ¥55, Seven Star Caves ¥60; ⏰park 6am-9.30pm, caves 8am-5.30pm) One of China's original tourist attractions, first opening to sightseers during the Sui dynasty, the 137-hectare Seven Stars Park makes for some pleasant strolls. There are peaks to climb, caves to explore, lawns to picnic on and even wild monkeys to see; early evening on Moon Tooth Hill (月牙山; Yuèyá Shān) is your best bet.

To get here, walk, cycle or catch bus 10 or 11 from the train station. From the park, free bus 58 runs to Wave-Subduing Hill, Folded Brocade Hill and Reed Flute Cave.

Guìlín

⊙ **Sights**
1 Elephant Trunk Hill C3
2 Moon Pagoda C2
3 Róng Lake B1
4 Shān Lake C2
5 South Gate B1
6 Sun Pagoda C2

⊙ **Activities, Courses & Tours**
7 Sheraton D2

⊙ **Sleeping**
8 Backstreet Youth Hostel D2
9 Lakeside Inn C2
10 Lijiang Waterfall Hotel C2
11 Riverside Hostel B2
12 This Old Place Hostel B1

⊗ **Eating**
13 Amani C1
14 Amani D1
Chóngshàn Mǐfěn Diàn ....(see 17)
15 Lǎo Chén Jì C2
16 Tasty Castle C2
17 Zhèngzōng Yóuzháwáng D2

⊙ **Drinking**
18 G+ Cafe & Wine Bar D1
19 Little Italian D1
Steam Coffee ....(see 19)

⊙ **Shopping**
20 Night Market C1

ⓘ **Transport**
21 Ride Giant D1

Other Hills
HILLS

Just west of Solitary Beauty Peak is **Wave-Subduing Hill** (伏波山; Fúbō Shān; admission ¥25; ⊙7am-6pm), which offers more great views as well as the chance to see Song- and Tang-dynasty Buddhist carvings etched into the walls of **Returned Pearl Cave** (还珠洞; Huánzhū Dòng). A short walk further north is **Folded Brocade Hill** (叠彩山; Diécǎi Shān; admission ¥35; ⊙7am-6pm), where you can find arguably the best views of the city, some restored Ming-dynasty pavilions and, inside **Wind Cave** (风洞; Fēngdòng), another fine collection of Buddhist sculptures. Just south of the city centre is **Elephant Trunk Hill** (象鼻山; Xiàngbí Shān; admission ¥75; ⊙7am-6.30pm), perhaps best viewed from one of the bamboo rafts (about ¥15) that float down the Lí River.

⚡ Activities

Swimming in the Lí River is very popular in summer. If that's not clean enough for you, the **Sheraton** (喜来登酒店; Xǐláidēng Jiǔdiàn; ☏282 5588; 15 Binjiang Lu; 滨江路15号) has an outdoor pool (admission ¥30).

☞ Tours

The popular **Lí River trip** from Guìlín to Yángshuò lasts about 4½ hours and includes a wonderfully scenic boat trip to Yángshuò, lunch and a bus ride back to Guìlín. Expect to pay ¥350 to ¥450 for a boat with an English-speaking guide or ¥245 for the Chinese version. There's also the 'Two Rivers Four Lakes' (二江四湖) boat ride around Guìlín that does a loop of the Lí River and the city's lakes. Prices vary from ¥80 to ¥180 depending on time of day (it costs more at night). China International Travel Service (p591), can arrange these two tours, as can pretty much every Guìlín hotel and tourist information service centre.

🛏 Sleeping

Wada Hostel
HOSTEL $

(瓦当旅舍; Wǎdāng Lǚshè; ☏215 4888; www.wadahostel.com; 212 Huanchengxi Yilu; 环城西一路212号; dm ¥25-35, d ¥110; ❋@🖥) This hostel is a bit out of the city centre but the useful bus 10 will connect you to most of the attractions. All buses to Yángshuò stop at its main entrance (ask the driver). It has a comfortable bar and cafe, and dorms with huge bunk beds. To get there from the train station, take the first right on Shanghai Lu. Go under the bridge and turn left at the intersection onto Huanchengxi Yilu. From there it's a 10-minute walk (600m) and the hostel is on the left.

This Old Place Hostel
HOSTEL $

(老地方国际青年旅舍; Lǎodìfāng Guójì Qīngnián Lǚshè; ☏281 3598; www.topxingping.com; 2 Yiwu Lu; 翊武路2号; dm ¥35, d ¥120-130, tr ¥150; ❋@🖥) Run by the owners of This Old Place in Xīngpíng, this hostel has an enviable position facing Róng Lake and is a 10-minute walk to eating and shopping areas. Three-bed dorms are single beds with an ensuite while regular rooms are similar, albeit less cramped. The communal area has a movie corner and pool table. You can also dine on a mix of Western and Chinese dishes. A taxi here from the train/bus station costs ¥8 to ¥10.

Backstreet Youth Hostel
HOSTEL $

(后街国际青年旅舍; Hòujiē Qīngnián Lǚshè; ☏281 9936; www.guilinhostel.com; 3 Renmin Lu, Xiùfēng district; 秀峰区人民路3号; dm ¥30-40, d ¥120; ❂@❖) Run by the same owner as the Wada Hostel, rooms here are big (even the dorms) and are decorated tastefully with wood furnishings. The location is superb, with bars, restaurants and shops just a stone's throw away. Staff are friendly, the communal area is roomy and cafe fare is available.

Shangri-La Hotel HOTEL $$$
(香格里拉大酒店; Xiānggélǐlā Dàjiǔdiàn; ☑269 8888; www.shangrila.com/guilin; 111 Huancheng Bei Erlu; 环城北二路111号; d from ¥950; ❂❂❖) If you're tired of Chinese-style hotels, splash out on the money-no-object, local branch of the Shang. Sure, it's location is slightly out of town but the views of the karst scenery along the Lí River and classy service make it a winner.

Riverside Hostel INN $$
(九龙商务旅游酒店; Jiǔlóng Shāngwù Lǚyóu Jiǔdiàn; ☑258 0215; www.guilin-hostel.com; 6 Zhumu Xiang, Nánmén Qiáo; 南门桥竹木巷6号; s & d ¥100-220; ❂@❖) This cosy inn by the Táohuā River (桃花江) comes highly recommended by travellers (especially couples). Staff are attentive and rooms are comfy. Its centrally located three-room branch, **Lakeside Inn** (背包驿站; Bēibāo Yìzhàn; ☑280 6806; 1-1-2 Shanhu Beilu; 杉湖北路杉湖综合楼1-1-2; d & tw ¥180-200, ste ¥260; ❂@❖) by Shān Lake is equally good. Advance bookings by phone or via the website are essential.

Lìjiāng Waterfall Hotel HOTEL $$$
(漓江大瀑布饭店; Lìjiāng Dàpùbù Fàndiàn; ☑282 2881; www.waterfallguilin.com; 1 Shanhu Beilu; 杉湖北路1号; d without/with river view ¥1320/1480; ❂❂@❖) This hotel has first-class facilities, accommodating staff and a general feeling of grandeur. Splash out for a room with stunning views of the river, lakes and Elephant Trunk Hill. It's also the proud owner of the world's tallest man-made waterfall (45m high), turned on daily from 8.30pm to 8.45pm and best viewed from Central Sq. It has become something of a tourist attraction! Discounts of 10% to 40%.

✗ Eating

Local specialities include Guìlín rice noodles (桂林米粉; Guìlín *mǐfěn*), beer duck (啤酒鸭; *píjiǔ yā*) and Guìlín snails (桂林田螺; Guìlín *tiánluó*), while the ubiquitous *chǎoguō fàn* (炒锅饭; claypot rice dishes; from ¥6) make a great snack.

Cantonese and Western food are not uncommon in the city. The pedestrianised Zhengyang Lu and its surrounding lanes are the busiest dining area, while there's a cluster of fish restaurants on Nanhuan Lu, just east of Wenchang Bridge.

Chóngshàn Mǐfěn Diàn NOODLES $
(崇善米粉店; Yiren Lu; dishes from ¥3-8; ❂6pm-midnight) Wildly popular Guìlín rice noodle store with a cheap and delish array of noodle and rice dishes. Order at the front, and take your docket to the cook. Soup for your noodles is in a DIY dispenser on the side. It's right next to Zhèngzōng Yóuzháwáng, which is next to KFC.

Zhèngzōng Yóuzháwáng SNACKS $
(正宗油炸王; Yiren Lu; skewers from ¥1.50; ❂10.30am-2am) For late-night spicy, and we mean spicy, *má là chuàn* (麻辣串; spicy kebabs), you could do worse than this busy hole-in-the-wall near the corner of Zhengyang Lu and Yiren Lu. No menu. No need. Just point, pay and eat. It's next to KFC.

Tasty Castle INTERNATIONAL $$
(好吃保; Binjiang Lu; dishes from ¥20; ❂10am-midnight) There's nothing aristocratic about this place but the food here sure is tasty. Grab a seat on the breezy alfresco deck and order from a thick picture menu chock-a-block with everything from sashimi to pizza to a range of local favourites. Located at the start of Zhengyang Lu next to Shanhu Beilu.

Amani PIZZA $$
(阿玛尼; Āmǎní; ☑210 6351; Binjiang Lu; pizzas from ¥38; ❂10am-1am) Customers flock here for the tasty thin-crust pizza. The laid-back setting makes this an easy place to while away the hours. It has a more hectic **branch** (☑280 9351; 159 Zhengyang Lu; ❂10am-2am) on the pedestrianised street.

Lǎo Chén Jì NOODLES $
(老陈记; Zhengyang Lu; dishes ¥5-10; ❂10am-midnight) Here's a twist on the local noodles... they are served with horse meat (马肉米粉; *mǎròumǐfěn*). If you like your meat conventional, there's also beef (牛肉; *niúròu*) and pork (猪肉; *zhūròu*).

♟ Drinking & Entertainment

Guìlín's streets are dotted with trendy little cafes, while Zhengyang Lu has a short stretch of bars with outdoor seating. Binjiang Lu has a slew of cute cafes and bars, most with free wi-fi.

G+ Cafe & Wine Bar
BAR

(18 Binjiang Lu; drinks from ¥20; ⊙4pm-1.30am; 🛜) Small, cosy bar serving up a neat list of wine, beer and coffee. Next to Amani pizza.

Little Italian
CAFE

(这里; Zhèlǐ; 18 Binjiang Lu; drinks from ¥20; ⊙10am-midnight; 🛜) A pleasant, studenty place that offers great coffee and breakfast goodies.

Steam Coffee
CAFE

(爱上咖啡; Àishàng Kāfēi; 10 Binjiang Lu; drinks from ¥20; ⊙10am-midnight; 🛜) One of several trendy cafes on this stretch of street that serve equally good coffee.

🛍 Shopping

Night Market
MARKET

(夜市; Yèshì; Zhongshan Zhonglu; ⊙from 7pm) For souvenirs, check out Guìlín's night market, which runs along Zhongshan Zhonglu from Ronghu Beilu to Sanduo Lu.

Bird Flower Market
MARKET

(花鸟市场; Huāniǎo Shìchǎng; ⊙8am-5pm Sat & Sun) This local flea market is awash with everything from electronics to vintage magazines, calligraphy brushes, dogs and, of course, birds and flowers. Bus 51 comes here.

East River Food Market
MARKET

(东江市场; Dōngjiāng Shìchǎng; ⊙6am-8pm) On the way to Seven Stars Park, this bustling undercover market sells everything from fresh fruit and vegetables to live eels.

ℹ Information

Buy a map of Guìlín (桂林地图; Guìlín dìtú) from bookshops or kiosks (¥6).

Bank of China (中国银行; Zhōngguó Yínháng) Branches on Zhongshan Nanlu (near the main bus station) and Jiefang Donglu change money, give credit-card advances and have 24-hour ATMs.

China International Travel Service (CITS; 中国国际旅行社; Zhōngguó Guójì Lǚxíngshè; www.guilintrav.com; Binjiang Lu) Helpful staff.

China Post (中国邮政; Zhōngguó Yóuzhèng; Zhongshan Beilu; ⊙8am-7pm) Just 500m north of the roundabout of Jiefang Donglu. Another branch by the train station.

Guìlín Tourist Information Service Centre (桂林旅游咨询服务中心; Guìlín Lǚyóu Zīxún Fúwù Zhōngxīn; ☑280 0318; South Gate, Ronghu Beilu; ⊙8am-10pm) These helpful centres dot the city. There's a good one by the South Gate on Róng Lake.

Guóyào Pharmacy (国药大药房; Guóyào Dàyàofáng; 19 Nanhuan Lu; ⊙8am-8pm) Around the corner from the People's Hospital.

People's Hospital (人民医院; Rénmín Yīyuàn; Wenming Lu)

Public Security Bureau (PSB; 公安局; Gōng'ānjú; ☑582 3492; 16 Shijiayan Lu; ⊙8.30am-noon & 3-6pm Mon-Fri) Visa extensions. Located by Xiǎodōng River and 500m south of the Seven Stars Park. A taxi from downtown will cost around ¥18.

ℹ Getting There & Away

Air

Air tickets can be bought from the **Civil Aviation Administration of China** (CAAC; 中国民航; Zhōngguó Mínháng; ☑384 7252; cnr Shanghai Lu & Anxin Beilu; ⊙7.30am-8.30pm). Direct flights include Běijīng (¥1470), Chéngdū (¥980), Chóngqìng (¥790), Hǎikǒu (¥850), Guǎngzhōu (¥890), Hong Kong (Xiānggǎng; ¥1575), Kūnmíng (¥840), Shànghǎi (¥1200) and Xī'ān (¥970).

International destinations include Seoul, Korea (Hànchéng; ¥2200), and Osaka, Japan (Dàbǎn; ¥3200).

Bus

Guìlín's **main bus station** (客运总站; Guìlín kèyùn zǒngzhàn; ☑382 2666; Zhongshan Nanlu) is north of the train station. There are regular buses to the following destinations:

Běihǎi ¥172, seven hours, three daily (8.30am, 9.20am and 9pm)

Guǎngzhōu ¥169, 9½ hours, six daily

Huángyáo ¥60, five hours, three daily (9.10am, 1.10pm and 2.20pm)

Lóngshèng ¥30, two hours, every 40 minutes

Nánníng ¥100 to ¥120, five hours, every 15 minutes

Sānjiāng ¥33, four hours, hourly

Shēnzhèn ¥210, 12 hours, two daily (6pm and 9.20pm)

Yángshuò ¥18, 1½ hours, every 15 minutes

Train

Few trains start in Guìlín, so it's often tough to find tickets, especially for sleepers. Get tickets a few days in advance. Most trains leave from Guìlín Station (桂林站; Guìlín Zhàn), but some may leave from Guìlín North Train Station (桂林北站; Guìlín Běizhàn), 9km north of the city centre.

Direct services include:

Běijīng ¥416, 23 hours, four daily (1.57am, 1.05pm, 3.40pm and 6.55pm)

Chóngqìng ¥272, 19 hours, two daily (12.38pm and 12.58pm)

GREAT GUĂNGXĪ BIKE RIDES

Ancient Village Pursuit

Guìlín to Jiāngtóuzhōu (25km, three hours) Leave the city behind and take this relaxing, countryside spin to the 1000-year-old village of Jiāngtóuzhōu. From the west gate of Solitary Beauty Peak, head north along Zhongshan Beilu for 1km, then turn left onto Huancheng Beiyilu (环城北一路) before taking the first right. Keep cycling north until you leave the suburb town of Dìngjiāng Zhèn (定江镇), then continue along the country lane for about 15km. When the road forks, bear right towards Tánxià Zhèn (潭下镇). At the Tánxià Zhèn junction, turn left then follow signs to Jiǔwū (九屋). Jiāngtóuzhōu is down a track on the right, just past Jiǔwū.

Yùlóng River Loop

Yángshuò to Dragon Bridge & back (20km round trip, four hours) Soak up rural charm as you follow the beautiful Yùlóng River past rice paddies, fish farms and water buffalo to the 600-year-old Dragon Bridge (遇龙桥; Yùlóng Qiáo; p600). From Yángshuò, cycle along Pantao Lu and take the first main road on the left after the Farmers Trading Market. Continue straight, past the hospital on your right, and through the village of Jìmǎ (骥马), before following the road round to the right to reach the start of a bumpy track. Follow this all the way to Dragon Bridge. Note: the last few hundred metres are on a main road. Cross the bridge and follow another track south for 20 minutes (around 8km) until it becomes a small, paved road, which eventually stops at the river's edge. Take a bamboo raft across the river (¥5), then turn left off a small paved road down a tiny pathway, which leads you back to the Jìmǎ village road.

Guǎngzhōu ¥207, 12 hours, two daily (6.28pm and 9.18pm)

Kūnmíng ¥298, 18½–24 hours, three daily (9.50am, 10.09am and 3.23pm)

Nánníng ¥116, six hours, regular

Shànghǎi ¥330, 22 hours, four daily (11.58am, 3pm, 5.13pm and 7.11pm)

Xī'ān ¥375, 27 hours, one daily (5.49pm)

ⓘ Getting Around

To/From the Airport

Guìlín's Liǎngjiāng International Airport (两江国际机场; Liǎngjiāng Guójì Jīchǎng) is 30km west of the city. Half-hourly shuttle buses (¥20) run from the CAAC office between 6.30am and 9pm. From the airport, shuttle buses meet every arrival. A taxi costs about ¥80 (40 minutes).

Bicycle

Guìlín's sights are all within cycling distance. Many hostels rent bicycles (about ¥20 per day). For decent bikes, head to **Ride Giant** (捷安特自行车; Jié'àntè Zìxíngchē; ☑286 1286; 16 Jiefang Donglu; 解放东路16号; ⊙9am-8.30pm). Rental is ¥30 per day, with a ¥500 deposit.

Bus

Buses numbered 51 to 58 are all free but run very infrequently. Regular buses cost ¥1. The following are the most useful:

Bus 2 Runs past Elephant Trunk Hill and Folded Brocade Hill.

Bus 10 Goes from Wada Hostel to the train and bus stations, and Seven Stars Park.

Bus 51 Starts at the train station and heads north along the length of Zhongshan Lu, the Bird Flower Market and beyond.

Bus 58 Goes to Elephant Trunk Hill, Seven Stars Park, Wave-Subduing Hill, Folded Brocade Hill and Reed Flute Cave.

Around Guìlín

The fascinating 1000-year-old village of **Jiāngtóuzhōu** (江头洲), whose 800 inhabitants are all surnamed Zhōu (周), is tucked away among farmland about 25km north of Guìlín. There's an unmistakable rustic charm, with dogs and chickens running freely through narrow, cobblestone alleyways, which in turn house weathered, grey-brick courtyard homes fronted by huge wooden gates. As you approach the village, you'll notice the ancient and misshapen arched **Hùlóng Bridge** (护龙桥; Hùlóng Qiáo), opposite which are a cluster of old buildings. Duck along an alleyway and just keep wandering.

You can also visit the nearby **Jīnshān Miào** (金山庙), roughly 1km on the left off the main road leading to Jiāngtóuzhōu.

The temple itself is new and impressively perched on top of a large hill. The main attraction here is renting a **rowboat** (¥30 a day) and paddling out along the river and under an atmospheric gaping hole in a karst mountain.

The only place to stay is the basic **Láishānlí Fànzhuāng** (来山里饭庄; ☎0773-633 1676; tw without/with air-con ¥50/70; ❄) on the corner of the main road from Jiǔwū, about 500m back from the village. You can also eat here.

Jiāngtóuzhōu is a two- to three-hour bike ride from Guìlín (see boxed text). Alternatively, take an orange minibus on the stretch of Zhongshan Beilu near Guìlín north train station to Língchuān (灵川; ¥3, 30 minutes), then change to a bus to Jiǔwū (九屋; ¥4, 35 minutes), from where it's a 15-minute walk to the village. Buses stop running around 5.30pm.

Dragon's Backbone Rice Terraces 龙脊梯田

☎0773

This part of Guǎngxī boasts stunning views of terraced paddy fields, and the clear standout is **Dragon's Backbone Rice Terraces** (Lóngjǐ Tītián; adult ¥80). The rice fields rise up to 1000m high and are an amazing feat of farm engineering on hills dotted with minority villages.

The best time to visit is after the summer rains in May, which leave the fields glistening with reflections. The fields turn golden just before harvesting (October), and become snow-white in winter (December). Avoid early spring (March), when the mountains are shrouded in mist.

There are several villages to visit. **Píng'ān** (平安), a sprawling 600-year-old Zhuang village, is the biggest settlement and the most popular among tourists. It has the best facilities, but expect to share your experience with Chinese tour groups.

Further along is **Dàzhài** (大寨), a laid-back Yao village that has an idyllic rural allure with a bubbling stream. Continue uphill to the village of **Tiántóuzhài** (田头寨) atop the mountain. It's a sublime place to marvel at the panoramic views of the terraces, the sunrise or the starry night sky. Tourism is picking up here and new hotels are mushrooming, each trying to outdo the other in height and views (including a concrete five-star at the peak). Construction for

a cable car up the mountain was under way at the time of research. This will save you the challenging but inspiring two-hour hike up to the viewing points.

Most locals here are Zhuang or Yao, but you'll also find Dong and Miao people in the area. Many wear ethnic clothing and will sell you postcards and handmade souvenirs.

As all of the villages are perched on hills, bring a daypack and leave your luggage at the hotel in Guìlín or at left luggage in the main ticket office. Otherwise porters can help lug your luggage up for ¥40. There's nowhere in this area to change money.

🏃 Activities

You can take a number of short **walks** from each village to fabulous viewing points with Chinglish names such as 'Music from Paradise'. These are clearly marked by signs. To really get among the terraces there are great **hiking** opportunities, taking anywhere from 30 minutes to several hours. The four- to five-hour trek between the villages of Dàzhài and Píng'ān, passing through the villages of Tiántóuzhài and Zhōngliù (中六), is highly recommended. The route is clearly signposted, but if you want a local to guide you, there will be plenty of offers. Expect to pay ¥40.

🛏 Sleeping & Eating

You can stay in traditional wooden homes in minority villages (¥30 to ¥40 for a simple bed), but three in particular – Dàzhài, Tiántóuzhài and Píng'ān – are set up for tourists.

Nearly all guesthouses offer food, and many guesthouses and restaurants have English menus. Look out for *zhútǒng fàn* (竹筒饭; ¥15), a rice meal barbecued inside bamboo sticks.

PÍNG'ĀN

TOP CHOICE **Lóngjǐ One Hotel**   HOTEL $$
(龙脊一木楼; Lóngjǐ Yìmùlóu; ☎758 3597; www. zljyl.com; r ¥168-228; ❄@⊛) This guesthouse is filled with character, friendly staff and is a great pick among the ski-resort chalet lookalikes elsewhere in Píng'ān. Corridors are adorned with framed photographs and rooms are comfortable with tasteful modern plumbing and beds with unobstructed views out to the rice terraces.

Lóngjǐ International Youth Hostel   HOSTEL $
(龙脊国际青年旅舍; Lóngjǐ Guójìqīngnián Lǚshè; ☎758 3265; dm ¥30, tw ¥60-120, tr ¥99-160; ❄@⊛) The location at the base of the village

may not have views, but the private rooms are clean with flat-screen TVs. Four-bed dorms are compact but you'll find that the roomy terrace, facing a rushing stream, is a great place to nurse a beer.

DÀZHÀI

Minority Cafe & Inn   GUESTHOUSE **$**
(龙脊咖啡店; Lóngjǐ Kāfēidiàn; ☑ 758 5605; r ¥80) Perched above the Dàzhài village on the trail leading up to Tiántóuzhài, this small guesthouse has a terrace and an English menu (dishes from ¥25). It's about a 20-minute walk (1km) uphill from the main gate.

TIÁNTÓUZHÀI

Dàzhài Dragon's Den Hostel   HOSTEL **$**
(大寨青年旅舍; Dàzhài Qīngnián Lǚshè; ☑ 758 5780; www.dragonsdenhostel.com; dm ¥30-35, r ¥70-100) The first youth hostel in the village has a fabulous lounge area (good library, comfy couches, espresso and beer). Rooms are OK: wooden walls are paper-thin and the Western toilets are covered in vinyl sheeting. Dorms are good value as they're essentially spacious triples! The hostel is a tough 40-minute climb from Dàzhài to Tiántóuzhài via rice terraces. When you see another youth hostel (Mr Liao Cafe & Bar, in itself a decent place to stay), turn right and go another 150m.

Méijǐnglóu   INN **$**
(美景楼; ☑ 758 5678; www.meijinglou.com, in Chinese; r ¥100-120; ❋ @) This excellent guesthouse is located above Tiántóuzhài. Rooms at the front have sweeping, unobstructed views to the fields. After you leave the village of Tiántóuzhài, take the path up to the right (the left is to Píng'ān). From there it's another 15-minute walk (about 800m) and the guesthouse is above the Wángjǐnglóu Hotel. There's a set of concrete steps leading up to the entrance. It can arrange direct shuttle buses to/from Guìlín.

ⓘ Getting There & Away

Hotels including **Méijǐnglóu** (☑ 758 5678), **Dàzhài Dragon's Den Hostel** (☑ 758 5780) and **Quánjǐng Lóu** (全景楼; ☑ 758 5688) arrange direct shuttle service between Guìlín and Dàzhài for their guests. They also take other passengers if seats are available.

The bus (¥50, three hours) leaves Guìlín train station at 9am. Reservations are a must. Buses return to Guìlín at 11.30am.

All hotels in Píng'ān provide a similar service. The bus (¥50) leaves Guìlín train station at 1pm

and returns at 10am. Again, reservations are necessary. Times may change so ring to check.

For public transport, head to Qíntán bus station (琴潭汽车总站) in the south of Guìlín via public bus 1. From there, take a bus to Lóngshèng (龙胜; ¥24 to ¥31, 1½ hours, every 30 minutes) and ask to get off at Héping (和平). From the road junction (or the ticket office three minutes' walk away), minibuses trundle between Lóngshèng and the rice terraces, stopping to pick up passengers to Dàzhài (¥8, 45 minutes, every 30 minutes, 7am to 6pm) and Píng'ān (¥7, 30 minutes, every 30 minutes, 7.40am to 5pm).

Buses to Guìlín (¥30, 1½ hours, 6.30am to 6pm) also stop over here. To continue to Sānjiāng you have to catch a bus from Lóngshèng bus station.

Sānjiāng   三江

☑ 0772 / POP 350,000

Sānjiāng is notoriously humdrum, but it's a jumping-off point to get to the idyllic Dong villages and the exquisite, 78m-long **Chéngyáng Wind and Rain Bridge** (程阳桥; Chéngyáng Qiáo; admission ¥60). This is the grandest of more than 100 nail-less bridges in the area built by the Dong (they are renowned carpenters) at the turn of the last century from fir logs. It took 12 years to knock together and is a picture of poetic engineering.

Once you get a ticket, you'll be allowed access across the bridge into the village of **Mǎān** (马鞍). From here, there are signs pointing you to the surrounding network of villages. These paths make for great **walks** past rice fields, historic old wooden buildings and several other wind and rain bridges. Possible **bike rides** include the tough, three-hour climb to the remote hilltop village of Gāoyǒu (高友; see boxed text, p599).

There are a plenty of places to stay in, with many offering food, some with basic English menus. Just inside Mǎān, **Yang's Guesthouse** (程阳客栈; Chéngyáng Kèzhàn; ☑ 858 3126; r ¥60; @ ☎) has bikes (¥30 per day), friendly staff, food and free internet.

For its great location facing lush rice fields, the **Chéngyáng Āsī Hotel** (程阳阿思宾馆; Chéngyáng Āsī Bīnguǎn; ☑ 852 3311; r ¥100-120) is hard to beat. Get a room facing the fields. Walk past Yang's Guesthouse on the left path, head to the end and turn left. Continue another 150m to find the hotel on the right past the Hélóng Bridge.

ℹ️ Getting There & Away

Most buses go to/from Sānjiāng's east bus station (河东车站; hédōng chēzhàn), but buses to Chéngyáng bridge go from the west bus station (河西车站; héxī chēzhàn), a 10-minute walk (about 500m, or a ¥2 pedicab ride) across the river. To get to the west bus station, turn right from the east bus station, right again over the river and right once more after you cross the river. The ticket office is up a slope on the left.

For Chéngyáng bridge, take the half-hourly bus bound for Línxī (林溪) from Sānjiāng west bus station (¥6, 30 minutes, 7.30am to 5.30pm). If you miss the last bus, private minivans to Línxī wait on the main road outside the west bus station. The fare is the same as the buses but they won't leave until they're full. If you're late or in a hurry, expect to pay ¥40 to ¥50 to get the bus going.

Buses depart regularly from Sānjiāng east bus station for Lóngshèng (¥8, 1½ hours, 6.30am to 5.50pm) and Guìlín (¥45, three to four hours, last bus at 4.15pm), and four daily depart for Tōngdào in Húnán (¥25, 2½ hours, 7.20am, 8.30am, 12.35pm and 1.45pm).

Yángshuò 阳朔

☑ 0773 / POP 310,000

Seasoned travellers to Guǎngxī spend little time in Guìlín, preferring to make Yángshuò their base, though many of these veterans will gripe about Yángshuò's lack of authenticity – 'too many tourists', they complain. And they're right: the town, once peaceful, is now a messy, smoggy collage of Chinese tour groups, bewildered Westerners, discos, pole-dancing bars, bad traffic and the glue that binds any tourist hot spot together – touts.

Outside of town however, Yángshuò's dramatic karst landscape is surreal and the stuff of Chinese landscape paintings. Take a bamboo-raft ride or cycle through the dreamy valleys and you'll see. There's s host of well-run courses and activities to keep you occupied far beyond your original intended length of stay. Travelling with kids is easy here. It's one of the more family-friendly Chinese destinations, with English-speaking locals, well set-up hostels and food for the finicky.

👁️ Sights

Peaks & Hills HILLS

Yángshuò is surrounded by towering, leafy, limestone peaks. The most accessible is **Bìlián Peak** (碧莲峰; Bìlián Fēng; admission ¥30), which overlooks Xijie (West St) and the Lí River, and can be climbed in about half an hour for some excellent views. Look for the signboard that says 山水园. **Yángshuò Park** (阳朔公园; Yángshuò Gōngyuán) is a short walk west of Xijie and where you'll find **Man Hill** (西郎山; Xīláng Shān), which supposedly resembles a young man bowing to a shy young girl represented by **Lady Hill** (小姑山; Xiǎogū Shān). **Dragon Head Hill** (龙头山; Lóngtóu Shān) is a short walk north of the town centre.

🏃 Activities

Yángshuò is one of the hottest climbing destinations in Asia. There are eight major peaks in regular use, already providing more than 250 bolted climbs (and climbing!).

Insight Adventures Climb ROCK CLIMBING

(☑ 881 1033; www.insight-adventures.com; 45 Xianqian Jie; ☉ 9am-9pm) Offers local advice for experienced climbers and fully guided, bolted climbs for beginners. Prices start at ¥300 per person for a half-day climb, with everything included. Kayaking and other activities (from ¥150) are also organised.

Bike Asia CYCLING

(☑ 882 6521; www.bikeasia.com; 42 Guihua Lu; 桂花路42号; ☉ 9am-6pm) There's no shortage of places to rent bikes (from ¥15 per day), but for the best equipment and advice on possible trips, try Bike Asia. Bikes are ¥70 per day (deposit ¥300), including safety helmet and map. English-speaking guides (from ¥300) are available.

🕮 Courses

Yángshuò is a premier place to expand your skills with a course or two.

Yángshuò Taichi Health Centre TAICHI

(阳朔太极拳健康中心; Yángshuò Tàijíquán Jiànkāng Zhōngxīn; ☑ 890 0125; www.chinasouthtaichi.com; Baoquan Lu; classes per week/month ¥1500/4000; ☉ office 8-11.30am & 2.30-5.30pm) Runs classes for both the Yang and Chen styles of taichi. Cheap accommodation available for students.

Omeida Chinese Academy CHINESE LANGUAGE

(欧美达书院; Ōuměidá Shūyuàn; ☑ 881 2233; www.omeida.com.cn; Pantao Lu) Has reader-recommended Chinese-language classes. Offers all-inclusive two- to 24-week classes (15 hours per week) from ¥2920 and also hires English teachers.

V.E.T Project VOLUNTEERING

(☑ 881 1420; www.vet-china.org) V.E.T China organises volunteers to teach English in and around Yángshuò.

Yángshuò

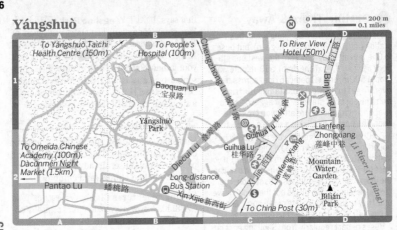

Yángshuò

● Activities, Courses & Tours
1 Bike Asia...C2
2 Cloud 9 Restaurant C2
3 Insight Adventures Climb..................D1

● Sleeping
4 Hóngfú Palace Hotel...........................C2
 Magnolia Hotel ....(see 5)

● Eating
 Le Vôtre...(see 4)
5 Pure Lotus Vegetarian
 Restaurant.......................................D1

Cloud 9 Restaurant COOKING
(聚福楼; Jùfúlóu Fàndiàn; ☑881 3686; cloud9rest
urant03@yahoo.com; 1 Chengzhong Lu) Runs two
three-hour cooking courses a day, for around
¥120 per person including a market tour and
lunch. Would-be chefs receive printouts of
the recipes they've just messed up.

Yángshuò Cooking School COOKING
(www.yangshuocookingschool.com) This is another classy cooking school worth checking out.

⌂ Sleeping

Yángshuò is overrun with hotels run by
English-speaking staff, and all provide internet access. While the Xijie neighbourhood
has abundant options, some of the best lodgings are on the outskirts of Yángshuò.

TOP CHOICE Secret Garden BOUTIQUE HOTEL $$
(旧县村老房子花园酒店; Jiuxiàn Cūn Lǎofángzǐ
Huāyuánjiǔdiàn; ☑877 1932; www.yangshuosecret

garden.com; Jiuxiàn Village; 旧县村; r ¥388 &
¥488; ❄@⊛) A Welsh architect nicknamed
'Crazy One' by the locals spent five months
negotiating a lease on a cluster of Ming-
dynasty houses in the village of Jiuxiàn. He
then spent many more months renovating it
into a gorgeous boutique hotel...all in an at-
tempt to preserve the architectural heritage
of the village. He succeeded: where many
neighbours are knocking down old houses
and replacing them with concrete monstros-
ities, this cluster makes for a picturesque
photograph from across the rice fields. A
taxi from town costs ¥40.

⌖ Yángshuò Village Inn BOUTIQUE HOTEL $$
(听月楼; Tīngyuè Lóu; ☑159 7736 4111;
www.yangshuoguesthouse.com; Moon Hill Village; Yuèliàng
Shān Lìcūn; 月亮山历村; d ¥380-390, ste ¥500;
❄@⊛) Located opposite Moon Hill (9km
south of Yángshuò centre), the Village Inn
touts ecofriendly practices. Rooms with local
handmade bamboo furniture provide rustic
creature comforts. Choose the renovated
mudbrick farmhouse out the back. Staff are
attentive and speak excellent English. The
rooftop houses an Italian restaurant, Luna.
From Yángshuò bus station, take a minibus
to Gāotián (高田) and tell the driver to drop
you at Lì Cūn (历村; ¥5, every 15 minutes). A
taxi from Xijie costs around ¥30.

**Yángshuò
Mountain Retreat** BOUTIQUE HOTEL $$$
(阳朔胜地; Yángshuò Shèngdì; ☑877 7091; www.
yangshuomountainretreat.com; Gāotián Zhèn
Fēnglóu Cūnwěi Wánggōng Shānjiǎo; 高田镇凤
楼村委王公山脚; s ¥280, d & tw ¥350-550, ste

¥550-680; ❄@🛜) Yángshuò Village Inn's sister hotel, facing the beautiful Yùlóng River (遇龙河; Yùlóng Hé), is an affordable luxury and a better option for those who want a more relaxing stay. A taxi from town costs ¥30. Free twice-daily shuttle buses link the two properties to town.

Yángshuò Outside Inn
HOTEL $

(荷兰饭店; Hélán Fàndiàn; 📞881 7109; www.yangshuo-outside.com; Cháolóng Village, Jìmǎ; 骥马朝龙村; dm/s ¥50/100, d ¥120-200, f ¥300-500; ❄@) Run by a friendly Dutchman, this fabulous farmhouse-turned-guesthouse surrounded by rural vistas is 4km southwest of Yángshuò. The adobe complex has a communal rustic charm – enjoy a glimpse of rural life in China (minus poor plumbing). The modern-furnished family suites sleep five. Staff speak English and guests can get help with activities including taichi lessons! It's close to the Yùlóng River; a taxi here will cost ¥25, or it's 20 minutes by bike. Check the website for directions and bookings.

Magnolia Hotel
HOTEL $$

(百酒店; Bǎi Jiǔdiàn; 📞881 9288; magnoliahotel@hotmail.com; 7 Diecui Lu; 叠翠路7号; tw/d/tr ¥480/680/880; ❄@🛜) The tastefully fitted out Magnolia Hotel, with flat-screen TVs, dark wooden Chinese aesthetics and comfy beds just manages to mask the hubbub of the surrounding streets. Rooms are regularly discounted by ¥200 to ¥300. Ask for rooms facing away from noisy Xijie. If you *have* to stay in town, this is a great choice.

Trippers Carpe Diem
HOSTEL $

(山景假日酒店; Shānjǐng Jiàrì Jiǔdiàn; 📞882 2533; www.guesthouseyangshuo.com; 35 Shibanqiaocun; 石板桥村35号; dm/s ¥40/160, d ¥180-300; ❄@🛜) This hostel run by a Belgian–Chinese family is recommended by travellers. In addition to views of rice fields and karst peaks, excellent staff and clean pinewood rooms, the hostel has an MSG-free cafe with Western and Chinese favourites and Belgian beer. It's out of town but close enough to walk to. From Xijie, it's a 1.5km walk along the river (upstream) for 25 minutes to Shíbǎnqiáo Village. A taxi from the bus station costs no more than ¥20 or ring the hostel to arrange transport.

Yángshuò Culture House
GUESTHOUSE $

(阳朔文化小屋; Yángshuò Wénhuà Xiǎowū; 📞882 7750; www.yangshuo-study-travel.com; 110 Beisan Xiang, Chengxi Lu; 城西路北三巷110号; d & tw ¥90; ❄@🛜) The pinewood rooms are nothing to write home about but they are bright and spacious. Owner Mr Wei can help organise activities and classes, but best of all he throws in three meals a day for free. It's about a 10-minute walk west of the bus station, along Chengxi Lu. Look out for the yellow sign on the right. This place gets booked up, so it's well worth making an online reservation.

River View Hotel
HOTEL $$

(望江楼酒店; Wàngjiānglóu Jiǔdiàn; 📞882 2688; www.riverview.com.cn; 11 Binjiang Lu; 滨江路11号; s ¥168, d & tw ¥268-388; ❄@) If you prefer staying in downtown but want to avoid the hubbub of Yángshuò's nightlife, this hotel around the corner from Xijie is good value for money. The balcony rooms overlooking the Lí River are bright and spacious, and they fill up fast. The restaurant-bar in the new wing is a good spot to watch the world go by.

Hóngfú Palace Hotel
HOTEL $$

(鸿福饭店; Hóngfú Fàndiàn; 📞137 3739 7888; www.yangshuohongfuhotel.com; 79 Xijie; 西街79号; d ¥380-480, tw/ste ¥660/880; ❄) Cracking location, set back from Xijie in the historical Jiāngxī Guild Hall and sharing its premises with Le Vôtre. Roomy doubles, regularly discounted to ¥250, overlook a Qing-style courtyard. Identical rooms without the courtyard view go for ¥200.

✗ Eating & Drinking

Local specialities include *píjiǔ yú* (啤酒鱼; beer fish) and *tiánluóniàng* (田螺酿; stuffed snails). From wood-fired pizza to that most famous of fast foods, you'll now find it in and around Xijie. Bars come and go like flowing water and the best place to bar hop is on Guìhua Lu (桂花路) just off Xijie where you might find German beer gardens sitting next to a generic Western-style cafe-bar.

TOP CHOICE Pure Lotus

Vegetarian Restaurant
CHINESE, VEGETARIAN $$

(暗香蔬影素菜馆; Ànxiàng Shūyǐng Sùcàiguǎn; Diecui Lu; dishes ¥22-48; ⏱11am-10pm; ✍) Buddhist music tinkles across the antique furniture to create an enchanting atmosphere in which to delve into Lotus' sumptuous menu. The modern English menu has pictures of all the dishes and staff speak English. Though you don't have to be all goody two-shoes here: there's beer and wine in case you don't want your karma fully restored.

Luna

ITALIAN $$

([☎]139 7836 9849; Moon Hill Village; Yuèliàng Shān Lícūn; 月亮山历村; dishes from ¥38; ⊙7.30am-midnight) Sure, there's organic salad and a list of Italian staples from pasta to pizza, but what really seems to keep customers coming to Luna is the spectacular views of Moon Hill. The accompanying wine list will almost remind you of home. It's on the rooftop of Yángshuò Village Inn.

Le Vôtre

FRENCH $$

(乐德法式餐厅; Lèdé Fǎshì Cāntīng; 79 Xijie; dishes from ¥40; ⊙8am-midnight) Pretenders may come and go but the town's first French restaurant remains standing. This one shares its historic premises with the Hóngfú Palace Hotel and the interior, flanked by a creepy array of Christian and Buddhist statues and hung with portraits of Chairman Mao, oozes a certain eccentric charm. The huge outdoor seating area draws big crowds, as do the fine menu and home-brewed beer (from ¥20).

Dàcūnmén Night Market

MARKET $

(大村门夜市; Dàcūnmén Yèshì; Pantao Lu; ⊙5pm-late) This night market is a culture-filled slice of nontourist Yángshuò life. Watch locals sniffing out the best spices or bartering for their snails, but be warned: it's not for the squeamish. Exotic tastes such as beer fish, dog hotpot, fish-head soup, frogs and snails can be found here. It's a 30-minute walk from Xijie. After you pass the gas station on Pantao Lu, look for the fire station on the left. Behind it is the night market.

☆ Entertainment

Impressions Liú Sānjiě

PERFORMING ARTS $$

(印象刘三姐; Yìnxiàng Liú Sānjiě; [☎]881 7783; tickets ¥198-680; ⊙7.30-8.30pm & 9.30-10.30pm) The busiest show in town is directed by moviemaker Zhang Yimou, the man who also directed the opening ceremony at the Běijīng Olympics in 2008 and several acclaimed films such as *Hero*. Six hundred performers, including local fishermen, take to the Lí River each night with 12 illuminated surrounding karst peaks serving as a backdrop. The cheapest tickets give you great front-row seats but be prepared for smoking Chinese tourists who sing and chatter during the performance.

Book at your hostel or hotel for slight discounts and transport to/from the venue (1.5km from town).

Shopping

Souvenir shops run the length of Xijie, while stalls set up daily along Binjiang Lu. You'll find silk scarves, trinkets, knitted shoes and all manner of things here. Bargain your socks off.

Information

Travel agencies are all over town, while backpacker-oriented cafes and bars, as well as most hotels, can often dispense good advice. Shop around for the best deals.

Touts are an almost constant nuisance in Yángshuò, but with perhaps a greater percentage of English speakers here than in any other place in China, there's little need for their services. Fend them off firmly but politely.

Bank of China (中国银行; Zhōngguó Yínháng; Xijie; ⊙9am-5pm) Foreign exchange and 24-hour ATM.

Café Too & Hostel (自游人旅店; Zìyóurén Lǚdiàn; [☎]882 8342; 7 Chengzhong Lu; ⊙8am-midnight) Cafe, free internet and an impressive range of foreign-language books that you can swap.

China Post (中国邮政; Zhōngguó Yóuzhèng; Pantao Lu; ⊙8am-5pm) English-speaking staff and long-distance phone services.

People's Hospital (人民医院; Rénmín Yīyuàn; 26 Chengzhong Lu) English-speaking doctors.

Public Security Bureau (PSB; 公安局; Gōng'ānjú; Chengbei Lu; ⊙8am-noon & 3-6pm summer, 2.30-5.30pm winter) Has several English speakers. Doesn't issue visa extensions. It's 100m east of People's Hospital.

Getting There & Away

Air

The closest airport is in Guìlín; see p591 for details of available flights. Your hotel should be able to organise taxi rides directly to the airport (about ¥240, one hour).

Bus

Direct bus links:

Guìlín ¥20, one hour, every 10 to 20 minutes (6.45am to 8.30pm)

Nánníng ¥166, 6½ hours, two daily (8am and 11.30am)

Shēnzhèn ¥236, 13 hours, four daily (5.30pm, 7pm, 7.30pm and 9pm)

Xīngpíng ¥8, one hour, every 15 minutes (6.30am to 6pm)

Yángdī ¥11, 30 minutes, every 20 minutes (6.30am to 6pm)

The bus from Guìlín to Huángyáo only stops in Yángshuò (¥50, two hours, one daily) erratically, so check.

MORE GREAT GUĂNGXĪ BIKE RIDES

Lí Valley Boat 'n' Bike Combo

Yángshuò to Xīngpíng & back (15km boat, 20km cycle, half-day) Combine a river cruise from Yángshuò to Xīngpíng with a bike ride back along this glorious valley. Put your bike on a bamboo raft (¥170 to ¥250, 1½ hours), then sit back and enjoy the view to the historic village of Xīngpíng. From here, cycle south, following the trail past the villages of Gūpí Zhài (古皮寨), Qiáotóu Pù (桥头铺) and Dòngxīn (洞心) before reaching Fúlì (福利), 4km east of Yángshuò. Just past Fúlì take your bike on a ferry (¥5) across the Lí River, then continue past Dùtóu (渡头) and back to Yángshuò, crossing the river once more, this time over a bridge.

Dong Village Lung Buster

Chéngyáng Bridge to Găoyŏu Village (16km, three hours) This challenging trip starts at the elegant Chéngyáng Wind and Rain Bridge and ends with a muscle-stretching 6km climb to the hilltop village of Găoyŏu (高有). From the bridge, follow the river along the 10km road to Línxī (林溪), passing the villages of Píngzhài (平寨), Dōngzhài (东寨), Dàzhài (大寨), Píngpŭ (平埔) and Guàndòng (冠洞). If you don't have the time or energy for the climb up to Găoyŏu, lunch here and head back to Chéngyáng Bridge (two to three hours round trip). If your thighs are up to it, turn right in the village centre, soon leaving the paved road behind you, and after 1.5km, by a small wind and rain bridge, turn sharply right to begin the big ascent. The mountain views are stunning, but even without stopping for photos it will take about 1½ hours to reach Găoyŏu, where, just before the drum tower, on your right, you'll find the family-run **Găoyŏu Guesthouse** (高有客栈; Găoyŏu Kèzhàn; r ¥30). Meals (¥30) are available, but no English is spoken. The freewheel back to Chéngyáng takes about two hours.

Train

Yángshuò has no train station, but train tickets for services from Guìlín and Nánníng can be bought from hotels and travel agencies around town. Expect to pay ¥50 commission.

❶ Getting Around

The best way to get around is by bicycle; you can rent one at almost all hostels, and from streetside outlets for ¥15 per day. A deposit of ¥200 is standard, but don't hand over your passport. For better-quality bikes, and sound advice on bike trips, head to Bike Asia (see p595).

Around Yángshuò

The countryside of Yángshuò offers weeks of exploration by bike, boat, foot or any combination thereof. Cycle along the Lí River (漓江) and you'll find a number of picturesque, ancient villages to visit. Classic rural scenes of wallowing water buffalo and farmers tending to crops are dominated by a backdrop of prominent limestone peaks.

In addition, there are a myriad other activities to cater to those with a penchant for the outdoors – from rafting down the Lí River to caving to rock climbing up karst peaks,

you'll find it here. The villages in the vicinity of Yángshuò, especially Xīngpíng, come alive on **market days**, which operate on a three-, six- and nine-day monthly cycle.

XĪNGPÍNG & AROUND

Xīngpíng (兴坪), the location of the photo on the back of ¥20 banknotes, is more than 1000 years old and houses a number of historic residences. For years, it was on the cusp of being the 'next' Yángshuò but it doesn't really matter that this hasn't come true because there's still lots of charm, without the tourist hordes.

The town itself is compact, with the old town around Lao Jie particularly atmospheric. Most travellers base themselves here to explore the beautiful surrounding countryside and many end up staying longer than they originally intended.

The HI-affiliated **This Old Place** (老地方; Lăo Dìfang; ☑870 2887; www.topxingping.com; 5 Rongtan Lu; dm ¥30-40, s ¥60, d ¥80-190; ❉@☎) is an excellent place to stay, with a cosy, large lounge area, helpful English-speaking staff and great wood-fired pizza. Stay in the new wing or ask for the balcony room 305 in the old wing. The hostel owners have explored the area in-depth and have plenty of

Around Yángshuò

Around Yángshuò

Sleeping

1 Trippers Carpe Diem B2
2 Yángshuò Mountain Retreat A3
3 Yángshuò Outside Inn A3
4 Yángshuò Village Inn A3

suggested itineraries and activities for guests. It also has a **cafe** (Lao Jie) which serves yummy Chinese and Western dishes.

You can hike the mountain behind Xīngpíng, past pomelo and orange groves, to the sleepy old **Fish Village** (鱼村; Yúcūn). This tiny village is awash with historic homes, friendly residents and was visited by Bill Clinton and family back in the '90s... something it still takes pride in today. Hike back or, better yet, organise to take a bamboo raft back to Xīngpíng (¥100).

Another fun option in this area is the boat and bike trip from Yángshuò to Xīngpíng and back (see boxed text, p599).

The stunning 16km **hiking trail** between Xīngpíng and Yángdī (扬堤) takes around four to five hours to complete, crossing the river three times. The admission fee is ¥16, which includes two ferry crossings. The last crossing is an extra ¥4.

You can take a bus (¥8) from Yángshuò to Yángdī, then walk the trail to Xīngpíng before getting a raft (¥170) or bus (¥7, until 7pm) back.

A raft between Xīngpíng and Yángdī is ¥120. A bus from Yángshuò to Xīngpíng takes an hour (¥7, every 15 minutes).

FÚLÌ · 副利

Also very popular, and much closer to Yángshuò (about 9km east), is the historic village of Fúlì with its stone houses and cobbled lanes. Fúlì is famous in these parts for its handmade fans. You'll see them everywhere. It takes about an hour to get here by bike. First cycle south from Yángshuò before turning east over the bridge that takes you on towards Dùtou Village (渡头村; Dùtou Cūn). There, take your bike on the ferry (¥5) across the river to Fúlì. There are also regular buses from Yángshuò to a drop-off point within walking distance of Fúlì (¥3, 15 minutes).

YÙLÓNG RIVER · 遇龙河

The scenery along this smaller, quieter river, about 6km southwest of Yángshuò, is breathtaking. There are a number of great swimming spots and countless exploring possibilities. Just rent a bike and get out there.

One option is to aim for **Dragon Bridge** (遇龙桥; Yùlóng Qiáo), about 10km upstream. This 600-year-old stone arched bridge is among Guăngxī's largest and comes with higgledy-piggledy steps and sides that lean inwards with age. It's certainly a great spot for a swim. For details of how to get here by bike, see boxed text, p599. Alternatively, take a bus to Jīnbăo (金宝) and ask to get off at the bridge (¥5, 35 minutes), just after Báishā (白沙).

Along the same route to the Dragon Bridge is the bucolic village of Jiùxiàn (旧县村; Jiùxiàn Cūn), about 9km from Yángshuò. Have lunch at one of the many *nóngjiā* (农家乐; homestays) that pepper the paths between rice paddies. Most have English menus with prices, and dishes start from ¥12. If you're taken by the village's charm, stay the night at the Secret Garden (p596).

MOON HILL · 月亮山

For mind-blowing views of the surrounding countryside, head to the surreal limestone pinnacle **Moon Hill** (Yuèliàng Shān; admission ¥15), famed for its moon-shaped hole. To get here by bike, take the main road south of

Yángshuò towards the river and turn right onto the road about 200m before the bridge. Moon Hill is another 8km down the road on your right.

SHÍTOUCHÉNG 石头城

A visit to this fascinating Qing-dynasty village, perched on top of a limestone peak, is an unusual foray into the countryside and makes a great day trip for those looking for an off-the-beaten-track adventure. The village was once a garrison town and the ancient gates and walls are mostly still intact. It's a steep 30- to 50-minute climb up the hill from the village's 'new town' to the 'old town' where the wall begins. Once at the top, it will take another four to five hours to walk around to all four of the main gates. Locals will show you around the stone ruins for about ¥30.

To get here from Yángshuò, take any Guìlín-bound bus to Pútáo (¥5), from where a motorbike taxi (¥20) will take you the rest of the way to Shítouchéng. You should be able to arrange a motorbike ride back to Pútáo through one of the villagers. From there, you can flag down a southbound bus back to Yángshuò.

Huángyáo 黄姚

☑ 0774

Huángyáo is one of China's most high-profile villages, with many movies and TV dramas filmed here; Edward Norton's *The Painted Veil* is possibly the most well known of the lot. The lovingly preserved 900-year-old **village** (admission ¥100) is dotted with two dozen temples, a number of pavilions and clan halls, and an old stage (古戏台; *gǔ xìtái*). Bucolic charm permeates the place when you amble along the stone pathways: dogs and chickens roam the streets, villagers hang their laundry along the river...though roving tour groups take a little shine off. Two 500-year-old banyan trees wind their way up from the river's edge to the side of the village and make a lovely place to rest after wandering the streets.

Chance (偶然间; Ǒuránjiān; ☑ 672 2046; 33 Zhongxing Jie; 中兴街38号; d ¥100; ❈ ☞), on the other side of the river, has comfortable rooms, with the best facing the river. On the left past the banyan trees is the cute **Yanimu** (一念一梦; Yīniànyīmèng; ☑ 672 2477; 66 Anle Jie; 安乐街8号; d ¥100-120; ❈ ☞). Along the main cobblestone street is **Happiness**

Inn (幸福里; Xìngfúlǐ; ☑ 672 2805; 8 Yingxiu Jie; 迎秀街8号; d ¥100-130; ❈ ☞), popular with young Chinese travellers. All these have wood furnishing, free wi-fi and a communal area though you'll need to bring your own towel.

Huángyáo is famed for its *dòufu* (豆腐; tofu). Dine in the courtyard of **Guōjiā Dàyuàn** (郭家大院; 44 An Dongjie; 安东街44号), which does simply delicious *dòufu niàng* (豆腐酿; tofu slabs stuffed with minced pork and vegetables; ¥20). There are plenty of restaurants around town. Look for signs saying 农家乐 (*nóngjiālè*).

There are two direct buses daily from Guìlín (¥60, three hours, 8.30am and 1.30pm). The return buses from Huángyáo leaves at 8.10am and 2.20pm though the service is erratic, meaning you may have to take a bus to Hèzhōu (贺州; ¥18, two hours) and change to a Guìlín service (¥60 to ¥80, 2½ to four hours, regular). The bus service from Yángshuò is erratic so ask at the ticket counter (¥50, two hours, one daily).

Nánníng 南宁

☑ 0771 / POP 7.1 MILLION

Like many provincial capitals in China, Nánníng is a bog-standard city with few sights of note. But at heart it's a fairly relaxed place to recharge your batteries before leaving for, or coming back from, Vietnam. Travel agencies and hostels can arrange Vietnam visas in one to three days and there's just about enough to keep you occupied while you wait.

◎ Sights & Activities

FREE **Guǎngxī Provincial Museum** MUSEUM (广西省博物馆; Guǎngxī Shěng Bówùguǎn; www.gxmuseum.com; cnr Minzu Dadao & Gucheng Lu; ⊙9am-5pm Tue-Sun) The Zhuang-romanised sign on the building says 'Gvangsusaih Bouxcuengh Swcigih Bozvuzgvanj'. Thankfully, the exhibits inside actually have English signs that make sense, which is great because the collection of pottery, ceramics and bronze ware, some dating back more than 200 years, is superb.

The leafy back garden showcases minority culture, with daily dance performances, some full-size examples of Dong and Miao houses, and a nail-less wind and rain bridge, which now houses a restaurant, Āmóu Měishí (p603).

Nánníng

Nánníng

🛏 Sleeping
1 High-Class Hotel A1
2 Lotusland Hostel (Train Station)..........A2
3 Yōngjiāng Hotel......................................B3

🍴 Eating
4 Farmers Market B1
5 Xù Courtyard Restaurant B3
6 Zhongshan Lu Food Stalls....................B3

Guǎngxī Medicinal
Herb Botanical Garden   GARDEN

(广西药用植物园; Guǎngxī Yàoyòng Zhíwùyuán; admission ¥10; ⊙dawn-dusk) The fascinating subtropical Guǎngxī Medicinal Herb Botanical Garden on the eastern side of the city is the largest medicinal botanical garden in China. More than 4000 medicinal plants from more than 20 countries can be found here. Buses 22 and 81 from Cháoyáng Garden stop by the main gate. Buses 7 and 66 from the train station also go there. It's a 20- to 30-minute bus ride.

Alleyways   ARCHITECTURE

East along Linjiang Lu look out for small networks of alleyways. Here you'll find some of Nánníng's older, low-rise housing, a stark contrast from the shiny shopping centres of nearby Chaoyang Lu, and an interesting place for a quiet stroll. Rampant development means these houses might soon become a condominium complex.

Yōng River Bridge   SWIMMING

(邕江桥; Yōngjiāng Qiáo) The green river at the southwestern end of the modern Yōng River Bridge is a very popular swimming spot, particularly on summer evenings. Amusingly, swimmers sometimes do their laundry post-swim...all to the roar of traffic from the bridge.

🛏 Sleeping

There's a cluster of budget hotels around the train station, displaying the price of their cheapest discounted rooms on signs in the windows. Prices are ¥60 upwards.

Lotusland Hostel (Train Station)   HOSTEL $

(荷逸居; Héyì Jū; ☑243 2592; lotuslandhostel @163.com; 64 Shanghai Lu; 上海路64号; d/tw ¥50/120; ❋@☎) Lotusland is a hostel pioneer in Nánníng and its relative age shows. Rooms seem clean until you look closely (marked walls, dusty floors). Shared bathrooms only, but they are sparkling. It's a relatively easy 15-minute walk (about 900m) from the train station. A Vietnam visa application service is provided here with no additional costs. From Lángdōng bus station, take bus 6 or 213.

Lotusland Hostel
(Lángdōng Station)   HOSTEL $

(荷逸居 琅东客运站; Héyì Jū Lángdōng kèyùnzhàn; ☑677 3664; newlotuslandhostel@163.com; 155 Minzu Dadao; 民族大道155号; d/tw ¥50/100; ❋@☎) Lotusland's new branch at the Lángdōng long-distance bus station. Spiffy fitout and cleaner because it's newer.

Nánníng City Hostel   HOSTEL $

(南宁市青年旅舍; Nánníngshì Qīngniáng Lǚshè; ☑152 7771 7217; www.nanningcityhostel.bravehost. com; Apartment 102, Block 12, Ou Jing Ting Yuan Community, 63-1 Minzu Dadao; 民族大道63-1号阳光一百欧景庭园E座12单元1102号; dm from ¥50, s without bathroom ¥80, d with bathroom per person ¥80; ❋@☎) This tidy hostel on the penthouse floor of an apartment block has the feel of a friendly boarding house. Dorms have large beds and one has an ensuite. Self-caterers will appreciate the communal kitchen but everyone will have to overlook the orange walls. It's hard to find, though. Look for the residential complex Sunshine 100 (阳光一百; Yángguāng

Yībái), an orange building on Minzu Dadao. The complex of 欧景庭园 (Ōu Jǐng Tíng Yuán) is behind it on the right-hand side. Enter the gated area and head to block 12 near the end of the compound. You can download a map from the hostel's website. Bus 6 from Lángdōng bus station and the train station stop along Minzu Dadao.

High-Class Hotel　　　　　　HOTEL $$

(海格拉斯大酒店; Hǎigélāsī Dàjiǔdiàn; ☑579 6888; 76 Zhonghua Lu; 中华路76号; d & tw ¥388; ❈☎) Spacious doubles with spotless wooden floors, smart furniture, supportive mattresses and accommodating staff make this well-presented hotel the best choice in the train station area. Discounts bring rooms down to ¥168 (¥178 with computer). All rooms have wi-fi.

Yōngjiāng Hotel　　　　　　HOTEL $$$

(邕江宾馆; Yōngjiāng Bīnguǎn; ☑218 0888; www. yongjianghotel.com; 1 Linjiang Lu; 临江路1号; standard/deluxe d ¥780/980; ❈@☎) If you get the discounted rate of 50%, this welcoming five-star hotel overlooking the river (and an unsightly traffic bridge) is worth the splurge. Decor is smart Chinese-hotel chic with lots of brown hues. There's a small, kidney-shaped outdoor pool.

✗ Eating

The place to eat is Zhongshan Lu, a bustling street jam-packed with food stalls and small restaurants selling all manner of tasty fare including squid kebabs, barbecued oysters topped with garlic, roasted pigeon, crocodile skewers, *chòu dòufu* (臭豆腐; stinky tofu) and *lǎoyǒumiàn* (老友面; literally 'old friend' noodles). Street food costs ¥5 to ¥10 and seafood at sit-down restaurants starts at ¥20.

You'll find simple restaurants around the train station selling breakfast *bāozi* (包子; dumplings; ¥3) or Guìlín *mǐfěn* (桂林米粉; Guìlín noodles; ¥3.50). For familiar Western fare and a sip of coffee or beer, there are a few cafes and bars in the Sunshine 100 complex on Minzu Dadao. The lane beside it, Shangye Jie (商业街), has a bunch of cheap local eats.

Closer to the train station, on the north side of Cháoyáng Stream, is the small **Farmers Market** (农贸市场; Nóngmào Shìchǎng; ⊙5am-11pm), another excellent place for fresh fruit.

TOP CHOICE **Āmóu Měishí**　　　CHINESE GUĂNGXĪ $$

(阿谋美食; 21 Gucheng Lu; ⊙9am-9pm) Housed on the picturesque wind and rain bridge behind Guǎngxī Provincial Museum,

this restaurant has a beautiful, leafy garden as its backdrop. The ethnic-minority food it serves is as good as the stellar locale. Try the Miao *zhūxiāng* fish (苗家竹香鱼; *miáojiā zhūxiāngyú;* ¥78). Other mouthwatering dishes include roasted eggplant in Tai style (傣家茄子; *dǎijiā qiézi;* ¥25) and shredded Lí River duck (手撕漓江鸭; *shǒusī líjiāngyā;* ¥38). Chinese picture menu.

Xù Courtyard Restaurant　　　SOUTHERN CHINESE $$

(旭园; Xù Yuán; Linjiang Lu; ⊙10.30am-9.30pm) This friendly restaurant is housed in a converted courtyard that dates back to 1892. It whips up some scrumptious dishes, including orange-peel-flavoured pork-rib wraps (橙皮纸包骨; *chéngpí zhǐbāogǔ;* ¥52), secret recipe roast duck (密制丁香鸭; *mìzhì dīngxiāngyā;* ¥42 per half duck) and plum marinated *huángfēng* fish (梅子黄蜂鱼; *méizi huángfēngyú;* ¥42). Chinese picture menu, but basic English is spoken.

❶ Information

The useful *Street Map of Nanning* (南宁街道图; Nánníng Jiēdào Tú; ¥4), in English and Chinese, can be found at bookshops and kiosks around town.

Bank of China (中国银行; Zhōngguó Yínháng; Chaoyang Lu; ⊙9am-5pm Mon-Fri) Changes travellers cheques and gives credit-card advances. Other Bank of China branches around town have 24-hour ATMs that accept international cards.

China International Travel Service (CITS; 中国国际旅行社; Zhōngguó Guójì Lǚxíngshè; ☑232 3330; 76 Chaoyang Lu; ⊙7am-11pm) Has some English-speaking staff, issues one-month Vietnam visas (¥420) and sells bus tickets (¥150) to Hanoi (Hénèi).

China Post (中国邮政; Zhōngguó Yóuzhèng; Zhonghua Lu; ⊙8am-6pm) Across from the train station.

Public Security Bureau (PSB; 公安局; Gōng'ānjú; ☑289 1260; 10 Xiuling Lu Xierli; 秀灵路西二里10号; ⊙9am-4.30pm Mon-Fri) Located 2km north of the train station, off Xiuling Lu (秀灵路).

❶ Getting There & Away

Air

Direct daily flights from Nánníng include Běijīng (¥1850), Shànghǎi (¥1550), Xī'ān (¥1800), Kūnmíng (¥730), Guǎngzhōu (¥650) and Hong Kong (¥1850). You can also fly to a number of other countries in Asia, including Vietnam (Yuènán; ¥1950).

BORDER CROSSING: GETTING TO VIETNAM FROM NÁNNÍNG

There are seven daily buses to Hanoi (Hénèi, Vietnam; ¥150, 7½ hours) via the Friendship Pass (友谊关; Yǒuyì Guān). Two departures (8am and 8.20am) leave from the Nánníng International Tourism Distribution Centre (南宁国际旅游集散中心; Nánníng Guójì Lǚyóu Jísàn Zhōngxīn), and four departures (8.40am, 9am, 10am and 1.40pm) leave from Lángdōng bus station. One bus run by CITS (¥150, 7.30am) leaves from Nánfāng Hotel (南方酒店; Nánfāng Jiǔdiàn). Note that you'll have to get off the bus and walk across the border at Friendship Pass before boarding another bus to Hanoi. There's a daily train from Nánníng train station to Hanoi (1st/2nd class ¥248/160, 6.20pm, 11 hours).

The border is open from 8am to 8pm Chinese time; however, travellers have reported that passports aren't always stamped after around 4.30pm. China is one hour ahead of Vietnam.

Local hostels are also great places to get information on Vietnamese visas and border crossings. All will help organise visas (free, pay for visa only) and transport (¥30 fee).

The **Civil Aviation Administration of China** (CAAC; 中国民航; Zhōngguó Mínháng; ☎243 1459; 82 Chaoyang Lu; ☉24hr) sells tickets. The twice-hourly airport shuttle bus (¥20, 40 minutes, 5.30am to 10.30pm) leaves from outside this office. A taxi to the airport is about ¥120.

Bus

All long-distance bus stations are inconveniently located on the outskirts of the city. The main **Lángdōng long-distance bus station** (琅东客运站; Lángdōng kèyùnzhàn; ☎550 8333) is 5km east of the city centre. Buses to pretty much everywhere leave from there, although you may be dropped at one of the other bus stations when arriving. There's a ticketing office in town on Chaoyang Lu near CAAC.

There are frequent daily services:

Běihǎi ¥65, three hours, every 10 to 20 minutes (7am to 10.40pm)

Guǎngzhōu ¥160 to ¥210, nine hours, 12 daily (9am to 10.40pm)

Guìlín ¥75 to ¥128, 4½ hours, every 15 to 30 minutes (7.30am to 10pm)

Píngxiáng ¥68, 2½ hours, 16 daily (7.30am to 8.30pm)

There is one direct bus daily to Détiān Falls (Détiān Pùbù; ¥50, 3½ hours, 7.40am). Other daily routes include Chóngqìng, Chéngdū, Hǎinán Dǎo, Shànghǎi and Hong Kong (Xiānggǎng).

Local buses 6 and 213 (45 minutes) go from Chaoyang Lu and Minzu Dadao to Lángdōng bus station.

Train

Some daily services:

Běihǎi ¥35 to ¥45, three hours, two daily (12.55pm and 1.40pm)

Běijīng West ¥276, 27 hours, two daily (8am and 10.30am)

Chéngdū ¥199, 36½ hours, one daily (7.38pm)

Chóngqìng ¥152, 27 hours, one daily (12.50pm)

Guǎngzhōu ¥94 to ¥106, 11½ to 14 hours, three daily (12.27am, 5.12am and 6.50pm)

Guìlín ¥57 to ¥1183, 4½ to 6½ hours, over 20 daily

Shànghǎi ¥199/231, 31/28 hours, two daily (6am and 9am)

Xī'ān ¥223, 33 hours, one daily (11.20am)

Two daily trains go to Píngxiáng (¥17/15, 3½/5½ hours, 7.40am/11.45am) near the Vietnam border. Both stop at Chóngzuǒ (¥10/9, two/three hours) and Níngmíng (¥13/11, 2½ to four hours), but only the slow one stops at Píngxiáng's north train station.

Booth 16 in the train station sells international tickets to Hanoi.

ℹ Getting Around

Buses 6 and 213 run the length of Chaoyang Lu and Minzu Dadao until around 11pm (¥2 per ride). A taxi ride from Lángdōng bus station to downtown is around ¥35. Taxis start at ¥7 and short pedicab rides cost ¥5.

Yángměi 扬美

A rambling, barf-inducing bus ride 26km west of central Nánníng takes you to this half-preserved **17th-century town** (admission ¥10) on the Yōng River (邕江; Yōng Jiāng). Join curious city locals and spend a couple of hours wandering the cobbled streets and historic buildings. While many parts of the town have been subject to modern renovations, the pace is slow and you're free to peep into some of the crumbling and musty Ming- and Qing-dynasty homes. Have lunch on a river boat (dishes from ¥15) or buy some fried fish kebabs (¥5) or noodles (¥2) from street-side vendors.

Buses leave from behind Huátiān Guójì (华天国际), an office-block building on Huaqiang Lu (华强路) just west of Nánníng's train station, from around 8.30am to 4.30pm (¥13, 1½ hours, every 50 minutes) and return between the same times. The last bus gets packed so wait early for a seat.

Běihǎi 北海

📞 0779 / POP 427,000

Běihǎi (literally 'North Sea') is famed among Chinese tourists for its Silver Beach, dubbed 'the Number One beach on earth' in tourism brochures (it's not). Much more charming is Běihǎi's quaint old quarter of colonnaded streets, where crumbling colonial-era architectural heritage has escaped the demolition ball.

👁 Sights & Activities

Old Town HISTORIC AREA

Běihǎi's old town (老城; *lǎochéng*) used to be a trading hub of old Běihǎi but is now a sleepy home of the city's older residents. It spreads east away from Sichuan Lu, with recently restored 19th-century *qílóu* buildings (Chinese arcade houses) straddling the streets housing an alarming number of pearl shops.

The best place to start your stroll is at the western end of Zhuhai Lu (珠海路), off Sichuan Lu, just before the Wàishā Island bridge. Look for the small white arch inscribed with the Chinese characters 升平街 (Shengping Jie), the road's former name. This street has been paved over and offers visitors an atmospheric, slightly contrived, walk.

A few buildings of note include the attractive **former post office** (大清邮政北海分局旧址; Dàqīng Yóuzhèng Běihǎi Fēnjú Jiùzhǐ; cnr Zhongshan Donglu & Haiguan Lu; admission ¥5), which now serves as a simple museum devoted to relics of the Qing-dynasty postal system; and the **Maruichi Drugstore** (丸一药房; Wányī Yàofáng; 📞 203 9169; 104 Zhuhai Lu; ◎ 8.30am-5.30pm), a site in the disguise of a pharmacy that allowed the Japanese to carry on espionage activities in the 1930s, which now houses a tiny national security museum (no English captions).

The **former British Consulate Building** (英国领事馆旧址; Yīngguó Lǐngshìguǎn Jiùzhǐ), within the grounds of a high school, is a white-washed edifice built in 1885.

Silver Beach BEACH

This is what most Chinese tourists come to Běihǎi for: Silver Beach (银滩; *yíntān*), a long stretch of silvery-yellow sand with so-so waters, about 8km south of the city centre. There's a host of midrange, doll's house–lookalike hotels and a number of places to eat, serving expensive but very fresh seafood. Take bus 3 (¥1.50) from the central bus station; it runs until 10pm.

🛏 Sleeping

From the central bus station, cross Sichuan Lu (四川路), which leads north to Wàishā Island (外沙岛; Wàishā Dǎo), to reach Běihǎi's cheapest accommodation, on Huoshaochuang Wuxiang (火烧床五巷), a small alley off Beibuwan Xilu, jam-packed with *zhāodàisuǒ* (招待所), simple guesthouses offering doubles and twins from ¥30.

Most budget and midrange options in town are of a low standard so look before you decide.

Běihǎi Seahouse Hostel HOSTEL $
(北海国际青年旅舍; Běihǎi Guójìqīngnián Lǔshè; 📞 221 0555; Beibuwan Lu; 北部湾路; dm ¥50-60, d ¥130-160; ❄@⑨) This hostel may be inconveniently located several kilometres south of town but it doesn't stop Chinese backpackers from flocking here like seagulls to chips. Friendly staff can help with onward travel. Rooms are clean and unremarkable but it's sitting on the doorstep of a local beach. Take bus 5 from Beibuwan Lu opposite the central bus station to the last stop (20 minutes) and look for the red building.

Shangri-La Hotel HOTEL $$$
(香格里拉大饭店; Xiānggélǐlā Dàfàndiàn; 📞 206 2288; 33 Chating Lu; 茶亭路33号; d with city/sea view from ¥529/609; ❄@⑨) Běihǎi's best hotel has top-class facilities, including a pool, tennis courts and several good restaurants. Rooms are large and luxurious, and staff can be very helpful. It's about 2km northeast of the central bus station.

Gofar Huálián Hotel HOTEL $$
(国发花联酒店; Guófā Huálián Jiǔdiàn; 📞 308 7888; Beibuwan Xilu; 北部湾西路; d/tw ¥258/358; ❄@) A midrange hotel close to the central bus station and shopping action. Its brown-carpeted rooms are spacious with dark-wood furniture. Doubles and twins drop to ¥118 and ¥138, offering good value but blaring karaoke might make you wish to 'gofar'. Turn left from the bus station and walk 700m.

Běihǎi

Běihǎi

⊙ Top Sights
Former Post Office C1
Maruichi Drugstore B1

⊙ Sights
1 Former British Consulate
    Building C2

⊗ Eating
2 Old Town Coffee, Bar and
    Restaurant A1
3 Seafood Restaurants A1

✗ Eating

Wàishā Island, just northwest of the old town, is awash with fish restaurants. It's not cheap – expect to pay at least ¥70 per *jīn* (600g) for fish – but the seafood is fresh and the seaside location is hard to beat. Walk along Sichuan Lu and cross the bridge onto the island.

A growing number of Western-style cafes and bars, housed in renovated 19th-century buildings, have sprung up in the heart of the old town. Most are at the western end of Zhuhai Lu, off Sichuan Lu.

You can also find street food (and shopping) at a night market (夜市; *yèshì*) on the left off Beibuwan Lu, about 700m southwest of the central bus station.

Old Town Coffee,
Bar and Restaurant   CAFE **$**
(老道咖啡; Lǎodào Kāfēi; ☑203 6652; 80 Zhuhai Lu; 珠海路80号; dishes from ¥20; ⊙2.30pm-1.30am; ☎) Serves Chinese and Western food including noodles, steaks and pasta, fresh coffee (¥18) and beer (¥6), and has free wi-fi and English-speaking staff.

ⓘ Information

China Post (中国邮政; Zhōngguó Yóuzhèng; ⊙8am-6pm)

Dōnghǎng Internet (东航网吧; Dōnghǎng Wǎngbā; Sichuan Lu; per hr ¥1.50; ⊙24hr)

ICBC (中国工商银行; Zhōngguó Gōngshāng Yínháng) Has a 24-hour ATM for international cards.

Public Security Bureau (PSB; 公安局; Gōng'ānjú; 213 Zhongshan Donglu; ⊙8am-noon & 2.30-5.30pm, 3-6pm summer) At the eastern end of the old town; can extend visas.

ⓘ Getting There & Away

Air
There are daily flights to Běijīng (¥1950) and Shànghǎi (¥1650). The airport is 21km northeast of the centre of town.

Boat
The international ferry terminal (国际客运码头; guójì kèyùn mǎtou) is on the road to Silver Beach (bus 3; ¥1.50). One ferry daily (¥120 to ¥280, 12 hours, 6pm) leaves for Hǎikǒu on Hǎinán Dǎo.

Three express ferries (¥120 to ¥180, one hour 10 minutes, 8.30am, 11.15am and 4pm) leave daily for the nearby volcanic island of Wéizhōu. Ferries return to Běihǎi at 9.40am, 2.30pm and 5.15pm. Services double on the weekend.

Bus
Direct bus routes include Nánníng (¥65, three hours, regular) and Guìlín (¥180, seven hours, seven daily).

Train

Two trains leave daily to Nánníng from Běihǎi Train Station (¥40 to ¥60, three hours), at 9.24am and 11.50am. Tickets to onward destinations can be bought from the **train station ticket office** (⊙8.10am-noon & 2-5pm) for a ¥5 fee.

ℹ Getting Around

To/From the Airport

Airport shuttle buses (¥10, 30 minutes) leave from outside the **Civil Aviation Administration of China** (CAAC; 中国民航; Zhōngguó Mínháng; ☑303 3757; Beibuwan Xilu; 北部湾西路; ⊙8am-10pm), a few hundred metres beyond Huoshaochuang Wuxiang, and connect with every flight. Flight tickets can also be bought here.

Bus

There are two main bus stations, a central long-distance (客运总站; kèyùn zǒngzhàn) one on Beibuwan Lu (北部湾路) and a newer, inconveniently located one (北海南珠汽车站; Běihǎi nánzhū qìchē zhàn). Most buses drop you at the latter station. You'll need to take public bus 15 (¥1.5) to Beibuwan Lu or a taxi (¥25)

From the central bus station, bus 2 (¥1.5) goes to the train station.

Pedicab & Motorcycle Taxi

There are three-wheeled pedicabs and motorcycle taxis. From the central long-distance station expect to pay ¥5 to Huoshaochuang Wuxiang, ¥8 to Wàishā Island, Zhuhai Lu or the Shangri-La Hotel, and ¥10 to the train station.

Wéizhōu Island   涠洲岛

With its friendly fishing families, the island of Wéizhōu (admission ¥90) is not yet overwhelmed by throngs of tourists. The island is 124km from Běihǎi and is China's largest volcanic island. Make this 6.5km-long and 6km-wide island a day trip. Pick up a free map with your admission.

Boats from Běihǎi pull into the new ferry pier in the northwest of the island. The main settlement **Nánwān Port** (南湾港; Nánwān Gǎng) is 5km south of the pier. The waters around Wéizhōu contain some of the most diverse coral communities in the area; ask in Nánwān Port about motorboat rides and diving opportunities, though instructions will be in Chinese.

Beyond the island's beaches, caves, corals and dormant volcanic scenery, visitors will find a handful of historic sights awaiting exploration. Within Nánwān Port – the former

volcanic nucleus of the island – is the **Three Old Women Temple** (三婆庙; Sānpó Miào), dedicated to the goddess Mazu. Of more interest are the two French-built churches on Wéizhōu. Built in 1853, the whitewashed **Catholic Church** (天主堂; Tiānzhǔ Táng) in Shèngtáng (盛塘) in the northeast of the island still attracts worshippers and has a nativity scene built out of corals.

The ticket also includes admission to the **Crocodile Mountain Scenic Area** (鳄鱼山景区; Èyúshān Jǐngqū) at the island's southwest point. Walk 1.8km from the entrance or take an electric cart (¥20 return) to trails leading to spots along the coast such as 'Listen to the Sea on the Platform' (a platform by the sea), 'Underwater Adventure' (a hole in the ground) and 'Old Fort' (a WWII gun).

The HI-affiliated **Piggybar** (猪仔吧; Zhūzǎibā; ☑601 3610; http://weibo.com/piggybar, in Chinese; Nánwān Port; dm ¥35-40, r ¥80-120) has basic rooms and facilities. Bike rental (¥20 per day) is available and there's an attached restaurant serving Chinese and Western food. You can also ask around to stay at local **homestays** (农家乐; nóngjiālè; r ¥60-80).

You can find some east-meets-west cafes and bars at the eastern end of Nánwān Port and there's a fresh-food market behind the docks at the end of Nánwān Port. Vendors sell barbecue seafood and fried noodles on the colourful beach (彩色滩; Cǎisètān) in the southeast portion of the island. Pedicabs will take you to overpriced seafood restaurants. The food is fresh, but ask for prices before committing.

ℹ Getting There & Around

To get from the ferry pier to Nánwān Port, it's ¥10 by pedicab. If you're planning a day trip, negotiate hire of a pedicab (roughly ¥100 for four to five hours). At the time of writing, the official electric carts (¥40 per person) that toured the island were not in use.

Tickets for boats to Wéizhōu Island can be purchased from the international ferry terminal in Běihǎi. For the schedule, see opposite;

Zuǒ River Scenic Area   左江风景区

The chance of catching a glimpse of white-headed leaf monkeys in the wild, gaping at 170m-high ancient rock murals and puttering along a spectacular section of the Zuǒ River in a small wooden boat make this area, on the train line between Nánníng and Píngxiáng, well worth checking out.

The village of **Pánlóng** (攀龙) is the launch pad. It's commonly referred to as **Huāshān Shānzhài** (花山山寨). Behind it, you'll find **Lǒngruì Nature Reserve** (陇瑞自然保护区; Lǒngruì Zìrán Bǎohùqū), home to forest-covered karst peaks, elusive monkeys and hiking opportunities. But be sure to get a permit (许可证; xúkězhèng) from the police in the village before you head off into the hills. You might not be allowed to wander off on your own unless you hire a local guide (向导; xiàngdǎo) to accompany you as there's a danger of getting lost. Expect to pay ¥100 or so for a couple of hours.

Up the hill to the right of the ticket booth, you'll find a whitewashed hotel with decent accommodation for ¥180. The staff are very helpful (limited English) and there's a small restaurant on site with a basic English menu (dishes from ¥25).

The main reason to come here, though, is to take a one-hour (one-way) boat trip past stunning, karst-rock scenery to the **Huāshān cliff murals** (花山岩画; Huāshān yánhuà). These crudely drawn depictions of ancient people and animals, painted in red on sheer cliff faces up to 172m above the river, are almost 2000 years old. They are apparently the work of the Luoyue people, ancestors of the Zhuang, but why they were painted is still a mystery. For an idea of scale, the largest painted figure is 30m tall. Conservation works were ongoing at the time of research so there may be scaffolding covering portions of the cliff. The admission fee (¥80) includes the boat ride, which leaves at 10am and 2pm; outside these times, you'll have to pay an extra ¥400 to hire the boat.

ⓘ Getting There & Away

To get to Pánlóng, first catch a train or bus to Níngmíng (宁明). From the train station, take a pedicab (¥20 to ¥40, 30 minutes) to Huāshān Shānzhài (花山山寨). From Níngmíng bus station, take a pedicab (¥30 to ¥50, 40 minutes).

Regular buses leave Níngmíng for Píngxiáng (¥12, one hour), Chóngzuǒ (¥20, 1½ hours) and Nánníng (¥65, three hours), the last buses leaving at 6.30pm, 6pm and 7.50pm, respectively.

Trains to Píngxiáng leave at 10.57am (¥56, 55 minutes) and 4.44pm (¥38, one hour 13 minutes). Trains to Chóngzuǒ (¥38/46, 1½ hours/ one hour) and Nánníng (¥72/46, three hours/ four hours 40 minutes) leave at 9.50am (slow train) and 1.07pm (fast train).

Píngxiáng 凭祥

☏0771 / POP 182,000

Guǎngxī's gateway to Vietnam (越南; Yuènán) is a neat and pleasant market town with a dusty, end-of-the-world feel. If you stay the night, wandering the streets at night offers an eye-popping (literally!) look at a town obsessed with flashing LED-lit buildings.

Turn right out of the bus station's front entrance onto Yingxing Lu (银兴路) to find the Bank of China (中国银行; Zhōngguó Yínháng), and a couple of internet cafes (网吧; wǎngbā). For a bite to eat, turn left from the bus station, where there are a handful of shops selling rice and noodle dishes. There's a local market with fresh produce two streets across from the bus station.

If you need accommodation, there are numerous hotels located behind the bus station on Beida Lu (北大路) with air-con and internet ranging from ¥50 to ¥148. Look out for the Chinese characters 宾馆 (bīnguǎn).

Trains leave for Níngmíng (¥56) and Nánníng (¥72, 3½ hours) from the train station, Píngxiáng Zhàn (凭祥站) from 10.25am. The station is 3km south of the bus station and pedicabs (about ¥5) link the two.

From Píngxiáng bus station there are regular buses to Níngmíng (¥12, one hour) until 7pm, to Chóngzuǒ (¥33, one hour 20 minutes) until 6.40pm and to Nánníng (¥77, three hours) until 8pm.

Détiān Waterfall 德天瀑布

☏0771

It's no Niagara Falls, but **Détiān Waterfall** (Détiān Pùbù; www.detian.com; admission ¥80), Asia's largest and the world's second-largest transnational waterfall, is quite picturesque. There's the added buzz of being surrounded by karst peaks and being able to legally cross the Vietnamese border.

The falls drop in three stages to create casades and small pools. Swimming is not allowed, but bamboo rafts (¥20) will take you up to the spray. Follow the signs past the falls to the '53rd mere stone'. After running the gauntlet of Chinese souvenir stalls, you'll hit a market of Vietnamese traders hawking snacks and smokes, and thronged with Chinese tourists getting their photo taken in front of the weathered stone as proof that they crossed into Vietnam without a passport.

Outside the entrance gates there are guesthouses offering doubles with air-con for

BORDER CROSSING: GETTING TO/FROM VIETNAM FROM PÍNGXIÁNG

The Friendship Pass (友谊关; Yǒuyì Guān) border is located about 10km south of Píngxiáng on the Chinese side, and a few kilometres from the obscure town of Dong Dang on the Vietnamese side; the nearest Vietnamese city (Liàngshān; Lang Son in Vietnamese) is 18km from Friendship Pass. The border is open from 8am to 8pm Chinese time (China is one hour ahead of Vietnam), but some travellers have reported that passports aren't always stamped after around 4.30pm.

To get to the border crossing, take a pedicab or taxi (about ¥35) from Píngxiáng. From there it's a 600m walk to the Vietnamese border post. Onward transport to Hanoi, located 164km southwest of the border, is by bus or train via Lang Son.

If you're heading into China from the Friendship Pass, catch a minibus to Píngxiáng bus station, from where there are regular onward buses to Nánníng and beyond. A word of caution: because train tickets to China are more expensive in Hanoi, some travellers buy a ticket to Dong Dang, walk across the border and then buy a train ticket on the Chinese side. This isn't the best way, because it's several kilometres from Dong Dang to Friendship Pass, and you'll need someone to take you by motorbike. If you're going by train, it's best to buy a ticket from Hanoi to Píngxiáng, and then in Píngxiáng buy a ticket to Nánníng or beyond.

There are still reports of Lonely Planet's *China* being confiscated by border officials at Friendship Pass. We advise copying vital information and putting a cover over your guidebook just in case. Note that all bags are searched as you walk into the train station. Once you leave Píngxiáng, you won't have a problem.

around ¥70. **Détiān Kèzhàn** (德天客栈; ☑377 5201) is a decent option. There are a number of very similar restaurants with very similar menus (¥30 per dish) just outside the gates.

Unless you catch the one direct bus, which departs from Nánníng's International Tourism Distribution Centre (one way/return ¥50/90, 3½ hours, 7.40am) and stops en route at Lángdōng bus station (8.30am), you will have to come via Dàxīn (大新) from Nánníng. At Dàxīn, switch to a bus headed to Détiān (德天; ¥20, two hours, hourly).

The last bus leaves for Dàxīn at around 5.30pm. There are regular buses from Dàxīn to Nánníng (¥55, 2½ hours) until 8.30pm. The direct bus from the falls to Nánníng leaves at 3.20pm. The road from Dàxīn to Détiān was being upgraded at the time of research, while it should be completed by the time the book is printed, you might have to head to Míngshì Tiányuán and ask around to hire a private van to go to the waterfalls for ¥150.

Míngshì Tiányuán 明仕田园

Míngshì Tiányuán, a succession of scenic Zhuang settlements 100km southwest of Nánníng, is an unspoiled version of Yángshuò. **Ming Shi Mountain Village** (明仕山庄; Míngshì Shānzhuāng; ☑0771 375 5028; gxmingshi@ yahoo.cn; Kānxú Village; Kānxú Xiāng; 堪圩乡; d from ¥1180) is a landmark and resort with rooms housed in faux Zhuang-style buildings. Discounts of 40% available.

The best way to explore the area is via bicycle (free for hotel guests, otherwise ¥40 for four hours). Bikes come with a touring route map but the best views are via the back roads which take you past flitting dragonflies and rice paddies nestled at the foot of soaring karst peaks. The resort has enclosed its own landscaped area and asks ¥80 (free if you stay) entry. There's nothing worth seeing except for a few replica traditional Zhuang buildings.

There are some cheap *nóngjiālè* in the area with decent doubles (¥80) and fresh homemade meals (dishes from ¥30). One is located 100m before the resort's entrance. No English spoken. The resort also runs spick-and-span **Míng Shì Express Business Hotel** (明仕便捷酒店; Míngshì Biànjié Jiǔdiàn; ☑0771 375 5028; Kānxú Village; Kānxú Xiāng; 堪圩乡; r ¥180) next to the *nóngjiālè*. A new hotel complex was being built opposite the road at the time of research.

To get there, take a bus to Dàxīn (大新) and switch to an hourly bus (¥10, one hour). The bus also continues to Détiān Waterfall (¥20, two hours). To leave, flag down the same hourly bus from where you get dropped off.

Lèyè 乐业

🎵 0776

This tidy little town on the western edge of the province is keen to promote itself as a base for visiting underground caves, primeval forests hidden in collapsed mountains and cute little local villages. While many of the sights have been featured prominently in Chinese tourism and geographic magazines, its remote location keeps tourist numbers low – 30,000 a year!

👁 Sights & Activities

The city is compact though it's of little interest. Next to the Luómèi Lotus Cave is a staircase that takes you up the mountain overlooking the town for great views of the area. Most of the sights listed below can be visited in a day or two. Public transport was patchy at the time of research and you'll have to hire a pedicab for the day (¥150 to ¥200) in order to get around. Ask the driver: *Bāochē yìtiān yào duō shǎo?* 包车一天要多少?

Lèyè Geopark   NATURE RESERVE

(世界地质公园; Shìjiè Dìzhì Gōngyuán; ⊙8am-5pm) The geopark encompasses a variety of sinkholes (天坑; *tiānkēng;* collapsed portions of karst mountains which are now home to primeval forests) but there are two which are must-visits. The former allows you access into the forest at a sinkhole base and the latter, butt-clenching vistas over a 600m deep drop. Together, they give you a great overview of this peculiar regional topology.

The first, the **Chuāntóng Tiānkēng** (穿洞天坑; admission ¥60) is 8km southwest of town. From the top, turn left and do a two-hour circuit of the eerily lush forest. There's a large cave not far from the starting point: come noon on a sunny day, a beam of sunlight shines down from a hole through the darkness...very Indiana Jones–esque.

Another 4km along the same road is the region's most popular sinkhole, **Dàshíwéi Tiānkēng** (大石围天坑; admission ¥98). From the ticket office, you'll be transferred to an electric cart for the final 25 minutes to the actual sinkhole. Follow the path to one of three viewing platforms at the top for stunning views of, yes, more karst ranges. The sinkhole looks like a deep crater carved out by a meteor. At the time of research, there were plans for building a large platform that would extend out across the top of the drop below. There was even talk of building an elevator to take visitors to the forest below.

Luómèi Lotus Cave   CAVE

(罗妹莲花洞; Luómèi Liánhuā Tòng; Tongle Lu; admission ¥25; ⊙8.30am-5.30pm) This otherworldly 970m-long cave, once an underground river, now boasts the largest collection of lotus-shaped limestone formations in the world. It also claims to have the largest, at 9.2m in diameter. As it's a Chinese obsession to attach real-life examples to rocks, the guide points out (in Chinese) formations that look like an elephant, parrot, a Buddha and more. The cave isn't entirely dry and there's still a portion near the end which links a dark underground cavern to a river flowing out of the exit. You'll need to arrange for transport to meet you at the exit or go back with the guide to the main entrance. The cave is 200m north of the bus station.

Huǒmài Village   VILLAGE

Heading 8km southwest, you'll come to the local 'eco' village of **Huǒmài** (火卖村; Huǒmài Cūn). Once teeming with rustic wooden houses, today it houses small restaurants and walking trails. There are plans to launch a boat ride into local water caves. While the 'eco' term is marketing guff, it's a real treat to lunch and wander around this unspoilt village.

🛏 Sleeping & Eating

There are hotels along Xingle Lu (兴乐路), a ¥5 pedicab ride from the train station. Rooms start at ¥70, are decent and come with air-con and ensuite bathrooms. You'll find several restaurants along the same street selling cheap noodles (粉; *fěn*) though avoid any with 狗 unless you really want to eat Fido. From Xingle Lu, it's a ¥3 ride or a 10-minute walk west towards Tongle Zhonglu (同乐中路). This is the city's old quarter where you'll find street vendors selling fruit and other snacks. Come night time, ask around for *shāokǎo* (烧烤) restaurants for barbecued kebabs.

ℹ Getting There & Around

Lèyè is far from everywhere else and buses are the only way to get here. There are four daily buses from Nánníng (¥135, six hours). The main station is on the southern end of Tongle Lu (同乐路) and the town is 1km north. The best way to get around is via pedicab – short rides costs about ¥5. Regular daily buses depart for:

Bǎisè (the regional hub where you can connect to southern destinations such as Dàxīn and Guǎngdōng) ¥50, 4½ hours, regular

Nánníng ¥135, six hours (9.10am, 10.50am, 6.30pm and 7pm)

Guìzhōu

POP 36.7 MILLION

Includes »

Guìyáng 613
Qīngyán 616
Kǎilǐ 616
Zhènyuǎn 621
Ānshùn 624
Wēiníng 628
Chìshuǐ 630

Best Views

» Yúnjiù Temple (p628)
» Huángguǒshù Falls (p627)
» Shízhàngdòng Waterfall (p631)
» Tiāntáishān (p627)

Best Historic Towns & Villages

» Zhènyuǎn (p621)
» Yúnshān (p628)
» Zhàoxīng (p620)
» Tiānlóng (p627)

Why Go?

Poor old Guìzhōu (贵州), always the short-end-of-the-stick southwest China province. A much-quoted proverb describes it as a place 'without three *lǐ* of flat land, three days of fine weather, or three cents to rub together'. Ouch.

Certainly, pockets of Guìzhōu are desperately poor and you'll see cloud cover more often than the sun. The upside is that there's plenty of elbow room out in the simply stunning countryside, a sublime mix of undulating hills and carpets of forest, riven with rivers tumbling into magnificent waterfalls and down into spooky-thrilling karst cave networks.

As big a draw as the landscapes is Guìzhōu's extraordinary human mosaic. Almost 35% of the province's population consists of more than 18 ethnic minorities. They all contribute to Guìzhōu's social-butterfly calendar, which enjoys more folk festivals than any other province in China, and the welcome you'll get from the people more than makes up for the weather.

When to Go
Guìyáng

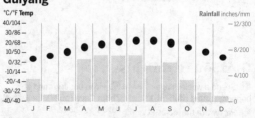

°C/°F Temp — Rainfall inches/mm

Jan Brave the chill for the wondrous sight of thousands of rare birds wintering at Cǎohǎi Lake.

Jun Hope for some summer sunshine as you village-hop around the southeast.

Oct & Nov See in the Miao New Year in Xījiāng with gallons of rice wine.

Guìzhōu Highlights

1 Spend a week village-hopping around **Kǎilǐ** (p616)

2 Party with the locals at one of the thousand-odd **festivals** (p631) held in Guizhōu each year

3 Get way off the beaten track in the prehistoric fern forests around **Chìshuǐ** (p631)

4 Head underground at **Zhījīn Cave** (p627), the largest cavern in China

5 Soak yourself in the mists at the thundering **Huángguǒshù Falls** (p627), China's largest waterfall

6 Escape the madding crowds and get up close with rare black cranes at remote **Cǎohǎi Lake** (p629)

7 Amble in low gear around the charming old town of **Zhènyuǎn** (p621), on either bank of the Wuyang River

History

Chinese rulers set up an administration in this area as far back as the Han dynasty (206 BC–AD 220), but it was merely an attempt to maintain some measure of control over Guìzhōu's non-Han tribes.

It wasn't until the Sino-Japanese war, when the Kuomintang made Chóngqìng their wartime capital, that the development of Guìzhōu began. Most of this activity ceased at the end of WWII and industrialisation of the area wasn't revived until the Chinese Communist Party (CCP) began construction of the railways.

Despite an expanding mining industry, Guìzhōu's GDP per capita remains the lowest in all China.

Climate

Guìzhōu has a temperate climate with an annual average temperature of 15°C. The coldest months are January and February, when temperatures dip to around 1°C. It usually feels damp, mists are heavy and the sun rarely shines.

Language

Mandarin Chinese is spoken by the Han majority, although with a distinctive local accent. Thai and Lao are spoken by some, and Miao-Yao (Hmong-mien) dialects by the Miao and Yao.

ⓘ Getting There & Away

AIR You can fly to more than 40 destinations within China from Guìyáng Lóngdòngbǎo International Airport, including all major Chinese cities plus direct flights to Taipei in Taiwan.

BUS Guìyáng and Chóngqìng are linked by an expressway. Another expressway links Guìyáng with Kūnmíng, via Huángguǒshù Falls. Yúnnán is also accessible – less comfortably – by bus via Wēiníng in the west. Reach Guǎngxī through Cóngjiāng in the southeastern part of the province from Guǎngxī.

Within the province, many of the major sites are accessible via OK roads. However, secondary roads in the northeast, west and southeast are uniformly poor.

TRAIN Sleepers to Chéngdū, Kūnmíng and Guìlín are popular. Guìyáng is due to be linked by high-speed rail with Chéngdū, Guìlín, Lèshān and Guǎngzhōu by 2015. You can enter Guìzhōu by train from Húnán through the back door from Huáihuà to Zhènyuǎn.

ⓘ Getting Around

Buses are useful for much of Guìzhōu, but the train is very handy for Kǎilǐ, Zhènyuǎn,

---

the east of the province and major cities. New expressways access the more remote western areas of the province. However, roads between smaller cities and villages remain a work in progress – and there are many mountains and hills out there to wind around – so bring bags of patience.

CENTRAL GUÌZHŌU

The capital city, Guìyáng, dominates the central portion of the province.

Guìyáng   贵阳

✉ 0851 / POP 1.2 MILLION

Guìzhōu's capital serves as a jumping-off point to Ānshùn and its surrounding sights, Huángguǒshù Falls, Kǎilǐ, Zhènyuǎn and other destinations in the province.

◉ Sights

Hóngfú Temple   BUDDHIST
(弘福寺; Hóngfú Sì; admission ¥2; ⊙7am-6pm) Located in **Qiánlíng Park** (黔灵公园; Qiánlíng Gōngyuán; admission ¥5; ⊙24hr) in the north of the city, Hóngfú Temple is perched near the top of 1300m Qiánlíng Shān and dates back to the 17th century. It's an easy 40-minute walk to the temple, or there's a **cable car** (up/down ¥15/20; ⊙9am-5pm). The monastery has a vegetarian restaurant in the rear courtyard. From the train station area, take bus 2.

Other Sights   HISTORIC SITES
Walk north across the river, turn right (east) onto Yangming Lu, cross a roundabout, descend to the river and follow it to

Guìyáng

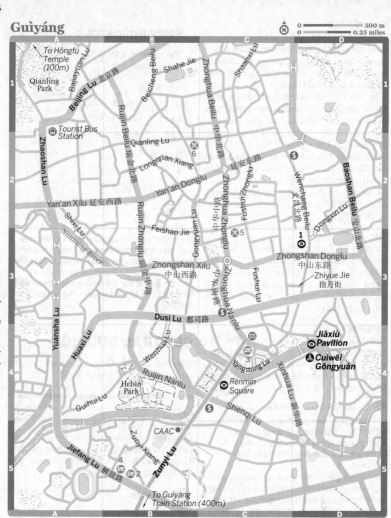

the triple-roofed **Jiǎxiù Pavilion** (甲秀楼; Jiǎxiù Lóu; admission ¥2; ⊙8.30am-11pm), Guìyáng's most famous landmark.

Across the river stands **Cuìwēi Gōngyuán** (翠微公园; admission ¥2; ⊙9am-11pm), an erstwhile Ming-dynasty temple which has picturesque pavilions and some pricey Miao souvenirs.

Backtrack across the bridge and walk north along Wenchang Beilu to another Ming-dynasty speciality: **Wénchāng Pavilion** (文昌阁; Wénchāng Gé), restored along with the city walls. There are always plenty of locals lounging around, chatting and snacking here.

☞ Tours

Organised tours (in Chinese) to Huángguǒshù Falls and Lónggōng Caves leave daily from a special tourist bus station (旅游客运站; lǚyóu kèyùnzhàn) opposite Qiánlíng Park. Many hotels also organise day tours, with fewer tours (if at all) in the low season.

🛏 Sleeping

Hanting Express   HOTEL **$**
(汉庭连锁酒店; Hàntíng Liánsuǒ Jiǔdiàn; www.htinns.com; ☎855 1888; 188 Jiefang Lu; 解放路188号; d/ste ¥219/259; ❄@🛜) Very ably run

Guìyáng

◉ **Top Sights**
Cuìwēi Gōngyuán D4
Jiǎxiù Pavilion D4

◉ **Sights**
1 Wénchāng Pavilion D3

🛏 **Sleeping**
2 Hanting Express.....................................B5
3 Sheraton Hotel C4
4 Star Hotel...B5

🍴 **Eating**
5 Kaili Sour Fish Restaurant....................C3
6 Sìhéyuàn B2

and super-clean express hotel with excellent rooms and efficient service. Free coffee awaits guests in the lounge, there are three internet terminals and a lift. Walk north up Zunyi Lu and turn left along Jiefang Lu; it's on the far side of the road.

Sheraton Hotel HOTEL **$$$**
(喜来登贵航酒店; Xǐláidēng Guìháng Jiǔdiàn; ☑588 8280; www.sheraton.com/guiyang; 49 Zhonghua Nanlu; 中华南路49号; d ¥1580; ☀✳@☻) Sitting astride a central intersection like a colossus, the rooms here are Guìyáng's top digs. Huge, comfy beds, as well as a spa, gym, pool, and Western and Chinese restaurants. Discounts of up to 50% available.

Star Hotel HOTEL **$**
(兴瑜商务宾馆; Xīngyú Shāngwù Bīnguǎn; ☑595 2588; 192 Jiefang Lu; 解放路192号; s & d ¥158; ✳@) This upstairs hotel a short walk north of the train station has so-so partially refurbed rooms just west of the Hanting Express.

🍴 Eating

North of the train station and Jiefang Lu, Zunyi Xiang (遵义巷) is a lively and busy food street of hotpot, Sichuan and Jiāchángcài restaurants. It shuts around 10pm.

TOP CHOICE Kaili Sour Fish Restaurant ETHNIC MINORITY **$$**
(老凯俚酸汤鱼; Lǎo Kǎilǐ Suāntāngyú; ☑584 3665; 55 Shengfu Lu; mains from ¥38; ☻9.30am-midnight) Locals come here for the best *suāntāngyú* (酸汤鱼; sour fish soup) in town. A Miao delicacy that's Guìzhōu's most

famous dish, fish are chopped up or dumped whole in a bubbling hotpot. Fling in vegies of your choice and you're all set.

Sìhéyuàn GUÌZHŌU **$**
(四合院; ☑682 5419; Qianling Xilu; mains from ¥15; ☻9am-10pm) Every Guìyáng local (and expat) knows this place – a rowdy, riotous and labyrinthine spot with very tasty local dishes. It's tough to find – walk west along Qianling Xilu off Zhonghua Beilu and keep your eyes peeled for a Protestant church on the right; the restaurant is down a small alley opposite. No English menu.

ℹ Information

Bank of China (中国银行; Zhōngguó Yínháng; near cnr Dusi Lu & Zhonghua Nanlu) Has an ATM and offers all services you need. Other branches can be found on the corner of Wenchang Beilu and Yan'an Donglu, and on Zunyi Lu near Rénmín Sq.

Internet Access At the time of writing, internet cafes in Guìyáng were not accepting foreigners.

Public Security Bureau (PSB; 公安局; Gōng'ānjú; ☑590 4509; Daying Lu; ☻8.30am-noon & 2.30-5pm Mon-Fri)

ℹ Getting There & Around

Air

The **Civil Aviation Administration of China** (CAAC; 中国民航; Zhōngguó Mínháng; 264 Zunyi Lu; ☻8.30am-8.30pm) is around 1km north of the train station, on the corner with Qingyun Lu.

Destinations include Běijīng (¥1730), Shànghǎi (¥1280), Guǎngzhōu (¥770), Chéngdū (¥630), Xī'ān (¥840), Kūnmíng (¥440), Chóngqìng (¥620) and Hong Kong (¥1570).

Guìyáng Lóngdòngbǎo International Airport is around 10km east of the city. Airport buses depart from the CAAC office every 30 minutes (¥10, 20 minutes, 8.30am to 6.30pm). A taxi from the airport will cost around ¥60.

Bus

The **Jīnyáng long-distance bus station** (金阳客运站; Guìyáng kèchēzhàn) is in the western suburbs on Jinyang Nanlu, a long haul from central Guìyáng. Take bus 219 (¥2, 6.30am to 10pm) from the train station; a taxi will cost ¥40. Destinations include the following:

Ānshùn ¥35, 1½ hours, hourly (7am to 10pm)
Cóngjiāng ¥140, seven hours (9am and 11am)
Huángguǒshù ¥50, 2½ hours, eight daily (8am to 3pm)
Kǎilǐ ¥60, 2½ hours, hourly (7am to 8.30pm)
Wēiníng ¥90, six hours, 9am and noon
Zhènyuǎn ¥100, five hours, 9.10am and 2.10pm

Taxi

Taxi flagfall is ¥10; late at night it increases to ¥12.

Train

Guìyáng's train station in the south of town has been upgraded; trains are useful for reaching Kǎilǐ, Ānshùn and Zhènyuǎn. Destinations include the following:

Ānshùn seat/hard sleeper ¥16/70, 1½ hours, regular

Chéngdū hard/soft sleeper ¥191/286, 11 to 20 hours, seven daily (12.38am, 4.10pm, 4.30pm, 4.59pm, 5.27pm, 6.08pm and 8.15pm)

Chóngqìng hard/soft sleeper ¥131/195, nine to 12 hours, 10 daily (12.38am to 10.47pm)

Guǎngzhōu (K66, fastest train) hard/soft sleeper ¥345/588, 20 hours, one daily (3.21pm)

Kǎilǐ seat/hard sleeper ¥29/¥83, three hours, regular

Kūnmíng hard/soft sleeper ¥162/245, 10 hours, 14 daily

Zhènyuǎn seat/hard sleeper ¥42/96, four hours, 16 daily

Qīngyán 青岩

With its winding, stone-flagged streets and restored city walls, **Qīngyán** (admission ¥30) makes a pleasant diversion from modern Guìyáng. A former Ming-era military outpost dating back to 1378, Qīngyán was once a traffic hub between the southwest provinces, leaving the village with Taoist temples and Buddhist monasteries rubbing up against Christian churches and menacing watchtowers.

Some of the places of worship are still active; make sure to visit the tranquil **Yíng xiáng Temple** (迎祥寺; Yíngxiáng Sì), on a side street populated by fortunetellers, and to compare the current, minimalist **Catholic Church** (天主教堂; Tiānzhǔ Jiàotáng) with the now disused but much more impressive 19th-century original. Opposite the **church** (基督教堂; Jīdū Jiàotáng) north of **Dìngguǎng Gate** (定广门; Dìngguǎngmén) and **Bǎisuì Fáng** (百岁坊) – an elaborately carved but recent gate – is the **Gǔdào Kèzhàn** (古道客栈; ☏139 8540 8581; d ¥128), with simple rooms.

Qīngyán is about 30km south of Guìyáng and makes an easy day trip. Take bus 207 from the Hébīn Bus Depot to Huāxī (¥2, 45 minutes, every 20 minutes from 6.30am) and get off at the last stop. Then take bus 210 (¥2, 20 minutes), which will drop you outside the north gate and the ticket office.

EASTERN GUÌZHŌU

More than a dozen minority groups live in the gorgeous misty hills and river valleys east of Kǎilǐ; this area is truly a rare window on atypical life in China. Sure, some villages have been discovered big time, but there are still endless places to lose yourself here. Booming country markets and festivals are held almost weekly.

China's largest Miao village, Xījiāng, and the remote Dong village of Zhàoxīng, in the southeast, are particularly popular. If you have time, consider visiting them as part of the back-door route into Guǎngxī. Outside Kǎilǐ there are no places to change money, so bring plenty of renminbi with you.

Kǎilǐ 凯里

☏0855 / POP 153,000

About 195km east of Guìyáng, Kǎilǐ is a compact, friendly town but little more than a base for visiting minority villages or planning a back-door trip into Guǎngxī or Húnán.

Sights & Activities

If you have time, visit **Dàgé Park** (大阁公园; Dàgé Gōngyuán; Big Pagoda Park) or **Jīnquánhú Park** (金泉湖公园; Jīnquánhú Gōngyuán; Big Pagoda Park), which has a Dong-minority drum tower (dating from – whoa! – two decades ago). Also check out the **Minorities Museum** (贵州民族博物馆; Guìzhōu Mínzú Bówùguǎn; Ningbo Lu; admission free; ⏰9am-5pm) in the south of town, which has some displays of minority clothing and artefacts.

Wu Min, also known as Louisa, a local Miao woman, runs **treks** to remote Miao and Dong villages that come highly recommended. She can also organise homestays, as well as arrange for visitors to study the Miao and Dong languages and learn local dances. She speaks good English. Contact her via email at wuminlouisa@gmail.com.

Festivals & Events

Markets and festivals are one of Guìzhōu's major attractions, and the profusion of them around Kǎilǐ makes this sleepy town the best place to base yourself for exploring them. For more festival details, see the boxed text, p631.

Sleeping

The huge and ostentatious development of Kaili Century City (under construction at the time of writing) on Wenhua Beilu will comprise what is billed as a 'five-star hotel'.

Yíngpánpō Mínzú Bīnguǎn HOTEL $$
(营盘坡民族宾馆; ☑382 7779; 53 Yingpan Dong-lu; 营盘东路53号; s ¥288, tw ¥218-288, ste ¥688-1300; ❄) This pleasant place has very well-presented rooms and a secluded location up the hill, with a lovely garden decorated with *Magnolia grandiflora*. Discounts of around 50% are common.

Dálī'ān Hotel HOTEL $
(达里安宾馆; Dálī'ān Bīnguǎn; ☑823 9688; 4 Yingpan Donglu; 营盘东路4号; s ¥128-138, tw ¥148; ❄) You can get a bright clean and uncluttered room in the grey block tucked away on your right up the hill just east of the Xinhua Bookstore and through the gates. Pricier singles and twins come with computer.

New Century Hotel HOTEL $$
(新世纪大酒店; Xīnshìjì Dàjiǔdiàn; ☑826 0333; 1 Shaoshan Nanlu; 韶山南路1号; s ¥238-288, tw ¥348-398, tr ¥458; ❄@) With decent-sized rooms, this place in the middle of town is strong on flock wallpaper and purple reclining couches, but it's comfy. Avoid the noisy rooms at the front. Breakfast is included. Discounts of up to 60% are possible, so you could get a room for ¥150 to ¥190.

✗ Eating

Kǎilǐ's streets are lined with some fantastic snack stalls. Savoury crepes, potato patties, barbecues, tofu grills, noodles, hotpot, *shuǐjiǎo* (boiled dumplings) and wonton soup overflow at reasonable prices. Look out for *guōtiēdiàn* (锅贴店; dumpling snack restaurants), which sell scrummy *guōtiē* (锅贴; fried dumplings) and Shànghǎi-style *xiǎolóngbāo;* there are several on Wenhua Beilu, including a tasty outfit just north of the long-distance bus station. Also make tracks for the **night market** (夜市; yèshì; off Beijing Donglu), very close to the **Guotai Hotel** (Guótài Dàjiǔdiàn; 6 Beijing Donglu), which is usually packed with locals and open til the wee hours, though it was shut at the time of writing.

Lǐxiǎng Miànshídiàn NOODLES $
(理想面食店; Wenhua Nanlu; dishes from ¥5; ⏱7.30am-7.30pm; 🍴) This friendly eatery, with blue plastic furniture, serves simple dishes such as spare ribs soup (¥7), and is handy for a morning meal or coffee prior to village-hopping. Try the *bīngyín'ěr tāng* (冰银耳汤; ¥5), a cooling and sweet dessert (containing a nutritious fungus).

Kǎilǐ

◎ Top Sights

Dàgé Park...B1
Minorities Museum.............................B3

🛏 Sleeping

1 Dálī'ān Hotel.....................................B2
2 New Century Hotel.........................A2
3 Yíngpánpō Mínzú Bīnguǎn..........B1

✗ Eating

4 Lǐxiǎng Miànshídiàn.......................B2
5 Night Market....................................B2

❶ Information

Every other shop in Kǎilǐ is a chemist.

Bank of China (中国银行; Zhōngguó Yínháng; Shaoshan Nanlu) This main branch has all services and an ATM. A second branch on Beijing Donglu will also change cash. Many other ATMs around town accept foreign cards.

Bóyǔ Internet Cafe (博宇网吧; wǎngbā; Wenhua Beilu; per hr ¥2; ⏱24hr) There are loads of other internet cafes on Wenhua Beilu.

China International Travel Service (CITS; 中国国际旅行社; Zhōngguó Guójì Lǚxíngshè; ☑822 2506; 53 Yingpan Donglu; ⏱9am-5.30pm) Tucked just behind Yingpan Donglu and by the Yíngpánpo Mínzú Bīnguǎn, this place has the most up-to-date information on minority villages, festivals, markets and organised tours. Staff here are helpful, with English, French and Japanese speakers among them.

China Post (中国邮政; Zhōngguó Yóuzhèng; cnr Shaoshan Beilu & Beijing Donglu)

Kǎilǐ People's Hospital (Kǎilǐshì Dìyī Rénmín Yīyuàn; 28 Yingpan Xilu)

Public Security Bureau (PSB; 公安局; Gōng'ānjú; ☑ 853 6113; Beijing Donglu; ◔ 8.30-11.30am & 2.30-5.30pm Mon-Fri) Deals with all passport and visa enquiries.

Getting There & Away

Air

If arriving or leaving from Guìyáng Lóngdòngbǎo International Airport, airport buses (¥60, 2½ hours, 7am to 6pm) leave regularly from the **airport office** (☑ 836 3868; 73 Jinjing Lu), where you can also check-in before your flight. You can also buy air tickets here.

Bus

Kǎilǐ is served by five bus stations. The **long-distance bus station** (长途客运站; ☑ 825 1025; Wenhua Beilu) has departures to most destinations.

Cóngjiāng ¥83 to ¥98, five hours, six daily (7am to 2.30pm)

Guìyáng ¥62 to ¥73, 2½ hours, every 20 minutes (7am to 8.30pm)

Jǐnpíng (锦屏; for Lónglǐ) ¥85, five hours, 10 daily (8am to 4pm)

Léishān ¥14, one hour, every 25 minutes (7am to 7pm)

Lípíng ¥99, five hours, eight daily (7.30am to 3.30pm)

Májiāng ¥17.5

Róngjiāng ¥62 to ¥3, 4½ hours, every 40 minutes (7.20am to 6.20pm)

Xījiāng ¥13.5, 80 minutes, five daily (7.30am, 8.50am, 10.20am, 1.20pm, 2.30pm and 3pm)

Zhènyuǎn ¥33 to ¥39

If you can't find what you are looking for, try the **local bus station** (客运站; ☑ 806 3925; Shiyi Lu), off Yingpan Lu, where several buses a day run to most surrounding villages, including Chóng'ān (¥13, one hour) and Huángpíng (¥17 to ¥25, one hour, 7am to 4pm). Buses also run to Guìyáng (¥50, 2½ hours, 6am to 4.40pm) from here.

For Shíqiáo (¥16, 1½ hours, several from 7am to 7pm), head to the **small local bus station** (往石桥的公交车; Wenhua Nanlu), south of the long-distance bus station.

Still another is located north of the first mentioned local bus station. This **local bus station** (往麻塘、舟溪的公交车; Huancheng Beilu) has departures for points north such as Mátáng (but also, inexplicably, south, such as Zhōuxī).

Train

Kǎilǐ's train station is a couple of kilometres north of town but departures are infrequent and the service slow (but cheap), apart from regular trains to Guìyáng (¥14 to ¥29, two to three hours), Zhènyuǎn (¥7 to ¥15, 1½ hours) and Huáihuà (¥21 to ¥42, four hours). A handy **train ticket office** (火车票代售处; huǒchēpiào dàishòuchù; ☑ 381 7920; 38 Wenhua Beilu; ◔ 8.30am-6.30pm) is in town; another **train ticket office** (◔ 8am-6pm) is next to the post office.

For longer distances, it's worth stopping in Guìyáng to secure a reservation.

Getting Around

Bus fares cost ¥1 in Kǎilǐ and almost all of the buses departing from the train station follow the same route: up Qingjiang Lu, past the long-distance bus station, along Beijing Donglu and down Shaoshan Nanlu to the Minorities Museum. For the train station, take bus 2.

Taxi flagfall is ¥5. A taxi to the train station from the centre of town will cost around ¥10.

Around Kǎilǐ

If you are village-hopping into Guǎngxī, which is lovely wherever you go, plan on spending about a week. Note that some of these villages charge entrance fees. An extraordinary number of markets are held in the villages surrounding Kǎilǐ. Check with the CITS in Kǎilǐ for the latest information.

XĪJIĀNG 西江

Snugly ensconced in the pretty Léigōng Hills, Xījiāng (admission ¥100) is thought to be the largest Miao village (its full name in Chinese is 西江千户苗寨; Xījiāng Qiānhù Miáozhài – Xījiāng 1000-Household Miao Village) and is famous for its embroidery and silver ornaments (the Miao believe that silver can dispel evil spirits). Now firmly embedded on the tourist trail, commercialisation has cheapened its allure but it still flings together a pastoral picture of paddies, wooden *diàojiǎolóu* (traditional handcrafted houses), water buffalo and mists.

After arriving at the bus stop by the ticket office it's another ¥5 to convey you to the main entrance. The tourist infrastructure runs to a performance square, English signposts, souvenir shops, an ATM taking foreign cards and a post office. But old men still squat on the streets smoking pipes, women do their washing in the river, pigs grunt and chickens scatter while the pace of life remains that of a traditional village. There are, furthermore, some charming places to overnight.

When the sun obliges, Xījiāng is lovely and you can do yourself a favour by departing the main drag and climbing to the top of the village where the herringbone stone lanes are more tranquil. Head away from the village on paths that weave through rice paddies, sidestepping farmers and water buffalo, and recharge your soul in the surrounding hills. A lovely trek is the 50-minute hike past terraced fields and rice paddies over the hills to **Kāijué Miao Village** (开觉苗寨; Kāijué Miáozhài) and **Kāijué Waterfall** (开觉瀑布; Kāijué Pùbù) a bit further beyond.

There's also a three-day trek from Xījiāng to **Páiyáng** (排羊), a Miao village north of Xījiāng. This trail winds its way through some remote minority villages and lush scenery. You will probably find accommodation with locals en route, but you shouldn't expect it so come prepared to sleep under the stars. Also ask about the largely uphill 27km trek from Xījiāng to gorgeous Léigōngpíng through a lushly green and forested landscape; you can continue on to Léishān from Léigōngpíng.

Many families in Xījiāng offer rooms with dinner for around ¥50. Quite a clamber up the hill just before the river in the south of Xījiāng, **998** (☑0855-334 871; dm/r ¥25/40) has lavish views, attractive rooms, a boho air in a fantastic *diàojiǎolóu* plus a friendly, guitar-playing owner. Quite a hefty walk to the top of the village is rewarded with further excellent views from the undisturbed **Gǔzàngtóujiā** (鼓藏头家; ☑136 3809 5568; tw/d/tr/q ¥80/100/100/120), where clean and fresh wooden rooms occupy a traditional building opposite the historic **Gǔzàngtáng**. It's run by an old man who speaks nary a word of English.

From Kǎilǐ, buses depart on the hour from 8am to 5pm (¥13.5, 80 minutes). Returning to Kǎilǐ, buses leave at 8am, 9.30am, 11am, 1.30pm and 3.30pm. Alternatively, if you're heading south and east towards Guǎngxī, there are 12 buses a day to Léishān (¥10, 1½ hours, 6.30am to 5.40pm), from where you can head south towards Róngjiāng (榕江). A taxi to Kǎilǐ from Xījiāng should cost in the region of ¥100.

LÁNGDÉ 郎德

Superb extant Miao architecture and cobbled pathways naturally draw loads of tour buses for elaborate singing, dancing and reed flute performances in this village. But the commercialisation can't overcome the wondrousness of the locals. There's a terrific 15km trail along the Bālā River that will take you through several Miao villages.

About 20km outside Kǎilǐ, buses pass by Lángdé (¥10) on the way to Léishān. The village is 2km from the main road. Getting away, get out on the street and flag down a bus back to Kǎilǐ.

LÉISHĀN 雷山

This village is usually used as a transit point, but you can also head to **Léigōng Shān** (雷公山; Leigong Mountain; admission ¥50), at 2178m, which offers some interesting hiking opportunities and some charming settlements, including the attractive Miao village of Wūdōngzhài. Other nearby Miao villages include Páikǎ (Páikǎ Miáozhài), around 3km south of Léishān, where *lúshēng* bamboo and reed musical instruments have been handmade for centuries. Either walk or hop on a Dàtáng-bound bus (¥3) from Léishān bus station. The road from Léishān continues towards Róngjiāng. From Kǎilǐ, there are numerous buses to Léishān (¥14, one hour).

SHÍQIÁO 石桥

Shíqiáo means 'stone bridge' and you'll know why when you spy the lovely ones in this beautiful Miao town southwest of Kǎilǐ. The town was famed for its handmade paper, which, though not so apparent today, can still be seen. Even if you're not into paper, it's a great place to visit.

Shíqiáo buses (¥16, two hours) depart from a local bus station on Wenhua Nanlu in Kǎilǐ, south of the long-distance bus station.

MÁTÁNG 麻塘

This village around 20km from Kǎilǐ is home to the Gejia. Officially classified as a subgroup of the Miao minority, the Gejia have different customs, dress and language, and are renowned batik artisans; their traditional dress often features batik and embroidery. Mátáng has been dolled up for tourism – the inevitable performance square has materialised – and the women hawkers can be persistent. A worthwhile 30-minute walk from Mátáng brings you to the village of Shílóngzhài, populated by another subbranch of the Miao called the Xijia.

GUIZHŌU AROUND KǍILǏ

Mátáng is 2km from the main road and buses regularly run past the drop-off point in the direction of Chóng'ān (¥6) and Kăilĭ (¥8). Just stand on the side of the road and flag down anything that comes your way.

LÓNGLĬ   隆里

Stranded in splendid isolation amid fields and rice paddies near the Húnán border, Lónglĭ (admission ¥15) is a former garrison town populated by the descendants of Han soldiers sent to protect the empire from the pesky Miao. One of the province's 'eco-museums' (read, real-live village), it's fascinating for its extant architecture.

Enter via the East Gate (Dōngmén) and savour its warren of narrow cobblestone streets – you'll only need about an hour – and mostly wooden houses, lovely courtyards, pavilions, temples and town walls. The surrounding area looks prime for bike exploration, too.

Just outside the old town, Lónglĭ Gǔchéng Jiǔdiàn (隆里古城酒店; ☑0855-718 0018, 136 3855 4888; r with/without bathroom ¥60/40) offers basic rooms with Chinese-style toilets.

Coming from Kăilĭ is rather arduous as there's no direct bus. First take a bus to Jǐnpíng (锦屏; ¥85, five hours, 10 buses daily, 8am to 4pm), then switch to another bus (¥15, 1½ hours, half-hourly or so from 7.30am to around 5pm) to Lónglĭ.

BĀSHĀ   岜沙

Wander up the hill from Cóngjiāng (从江) and you'd swear Bāshā (admission ¥12) is a movie set reproducing Tang or Song eras – the local men wear period clothes with daggers secured to their belts, their heads shaved with a sickle, leaving only a stylish topknot. When not farming, they can be found hunting with antique rifles. Meanwhile, the women parade in full Miao rig with their hair twisted into a curl on the top of their heads.

Quite why Bāshā is stuck in a timewarp is a mystery, as it's only 7.5km from very modern Cóngjiāng. Not even the locals can explain why they've retained their ancient customs so well. Nor is Bāshā undiscovered. A collection of six hamlets that sprawls across a beautiful valley, Chinese-English signs point the way to the various places of interest. It's best seen during a festival, even if that means more visitors, because most of the year the men are out in the fields during the day. But at any time,

the surrounding countryside is superb. You might also be able to arrange a hunting trip with the men.

Some rudimentary inns in the village offer beds for ¥20 but water cuts are common. The Gǔfēngzhài Qīngnián Lǚguǎn (古风寨青年旅馆; ☑138 8554 9720; s/d ¥80/120; @) on the main street has a pretty courtyard and pleasant enough rooms. Alternatively, you can spend the night in Cóngjiāng. The Xīngyuè Bīnguǎn (星月宾馆; ☑0855-641 8598; Jiangnan Lu; 江南路; d ¥128; ✱@✿) has clean, spacious rooms and is just to the left of the bus station.

There's no bus to Bāshā and it's a very steep walk up to the village. Taxis in Cóngjiāng will try and sting you for ¥40 for a one-way journey, but you should pay ¥50 for a round-trip. It's best to get the driver to wait for you, as very little transport hangs around the village.

ZHÀOXĪNG   肇兴

Perhaps the quintessential Dong village and packed with traditional wooden structures, several wind and rain bridges and five remarkable drum towers, Zhàoxīng is no longer the little-known paradise it once was. Its sheer uniqueness makes for a powerful draw, and the locals are certainly not complaining about the increase in visitors.

But the essential, amazing nature of Zhàoxīng hasn't changed. Yes, the restaurants on the main street have English menus, which is just as well as they eat rat (老鼠肉; lǎoshǔ ròu) in these parts, and there are now any number of quasi-inns and guesthouses offering rooms from ¥50. But Zhàoxīng remains a working farming village, where most people still speak only their native Dong language and are extremely welcoming. The tour groups might swoop in, but Zhàoxīng remains a very easy place to while away a few days.

Nearby, too, are tourist-free Dong villages. Hike west out of Zhàoxīng from the bus station for an hour, up a steep hill and past some splendid rice terraces, and you're in equally friendly Jītáng (基塘), which has its own drum tower. Head the other way out of Zhàoxīng through the fields and two hours later you reach Tǎng'ān (堂安), a village so essentially Dong it's been named a living museum.

The Wangjiang Lou Hostel (望江楼客栈; Wàngjiānglóu Kèzhàn; ☑0855-613 0269; d/tr ¥60/80; ✱@) isn't a hostel, but is a family-run place by the river with nice wooden rooms featuring hot showers and sit-down toilets. The most modern digs in the village can be found at the **Zhàoxīng Bīnguǎn** (肇兴宾馆; ☎0855-613 0899; s & d ¥228-398; ✳), where rooms are spotless, with tiny gleaming bathrooms. It's a tour-group haunt, so it's often booked out.

Getting here from Kǎilǐ is still a slog. First you have to travel to Cóngjiāng (¥87, five hours, six buses daily from 7.10am to 2pm) and then change for a bus to Zhàoxīng (¥18, 2½ hours, 7.30am and 1pm). From Lípíng (黎平) there are five buses daily (¥18, 3½ hours, 8.20am to 2.50pm). Alternatively, take a bus from Kǎilǐ to Luòxiāng (洛香; four hours) followed by a bus (30 minutes) to Zhàoxīng.

Heading out of Zhàoxīng, there are two morning buses (¥18, 7.30am and noon) to Cóngjiāng and two buses daily to Sānjiāng (三江) in Guǎngxī (¥35, four hours, 8.30am and 11.30am). From there you can catch an onward bus to Guìlín. There are at least five buses daily to Lípíng.

Zhènyuǎn · 镇远

☑0855 / POP 60,000

Plunging into the far east of the province from Kǎilǐ to Zhènyuǎn, the train traverses an astonishing panorama of surging peaks and hills densely cloaked with trees. The delightful riverine town of Zhènyuǎn sits picturesquely astride the Wuyang River (Wǔyáng Hé), pinched between towering cliffs and peaks. Making its name as a garrison outpost on the trade route from Yúnnán to Húnán, Zhènyuǎn's trump card is its riverine old town, in contrast to its unattractive new-build district. Largely off the Western traveller radar, the old town is a delightful place for a few days temple hunting before framing the enchanting nighttime river scenes through your hotel window.

◎ Sights

Qīnglóng Dòng   TEMPLE
The epic vertical warren of temples, grottoes, corridors and caves of **Qīnglóng Dòng** (青龙洞; Green Dragon Cave; admission ¥60; ◷8am-4.30pm) rises up against **Zhōnghéshān** (中和山) on the far side of Zhusheng Bridge. It is flooded with lights at night to form a sublime backdrop to the town. Put aside a good hour to explore the grottoes: it's labyrinthine and there's a lot to see, including some choice panoramas.

The intriguing complex was commenced in the Ming dynasty, its temples dedicated to the three faiths of Buddhism, Taoism and Confucianism. At the far entrance to Zhōngyuán Dòng (中元洞) is a stone table allegedly used by the eccentric founder of taichi, Zhang Sanfeng. The exterior of the splendid **Wànshòu Gōng** (万寿宫) – once the Jiāngxī Guildhall – is still bedecked with slogans, its interior a prime example of *jiāngnán*-style architecture with delightful woodcarvings. The unruffled Jade Emperor presides over everything – and some fine views – from the Yùhuáng Gé (玉皇阁; Jade Emperor Pavilion), his namesake pavilion at the top. Watch out when walking, as some of the stone steps are super slippery.

Zhùshèng Bridge   BRIDGE
Zhènyuǎn's old **bridge** (祝圣桥; Zhùshèng Qiáo), a gorgeous and robust span of arches topped with a three-storey pavilion, is an impressive sight, leading visitors across the water to Qīnglóng Dòng. River views along the river from the bridge at night are serene, with Qīnglóng Dòng splendidly lit up.

Alleys   ALLEYS
Four old and well-preserved **alleys** (古巷; *gǔxiàng*) lead north away from Xinglong Jie: Sifangjing Xiang, Fuxing Xiang, Renshou Xiang and Chongzikou Xiang. Wander along Sifangjing Xiang and peek at its namesake **Sìfāngjǐng** (Four Directions Well), with its three deities overlooking the water, capped with red cloths. Note the magnificently made stone steps of this alley and the gorgeous old residences. Look out for the **Fùshì Mínzhái** (付氏民宅; Fu Family Residence; admission ¥3), where the knowledgeable owner will give you a tour and show off his antiques. The alleyways are a picture at night, dressed with red lanterns.

Miáojiāng Great Wall   WALL
There's an energetic half-hour climb past the **Four Officials Temple** (四官殿; Sìguān Diàn) to the top of **Shípíng Shān** (石屏山) above town to the remains of this **wall** (苗疆长城; Miáojiāng Chángchéng; Miao Border Great Wall; admission ¥30). Get up really early or leave it late in the day and you could get a jump on ticket collectors. Undulating across peaks, the wall is quite substantial and glorious views range over town.

Zhènyuǎn

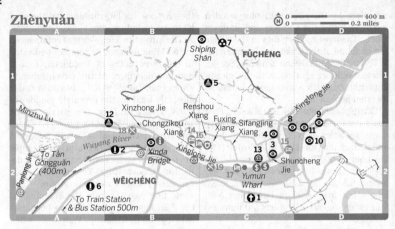

Zhènyuǎn

⊙ Sights
1 Catholic Church C2
2 City Walls B2
3 Confucius Temple C2
4 Fire God Temple C2
5 Four Officials Temple C1
6 Hépíng Cūn A2
7 Miáojiāng Great Wall C1
8 Pavilion C2
9 Qīnglóng Dòng Entrance D1
10 Qīnglóng Dòng Exit D2
11 Qīnglóng Dòng Ticket Office D2
12 Tiānhòu Temple B1

13 Zhènyuǎn Museum C2
Zhusheng Bridge ....(see 8)

⊙ Sleeping
14 Bóhǎiyì Zhàn B2
15 Dàhéguān Hotel C2
16 Héjiā Dàyuàn Kèzhàn B2
17 Liúhúlán Jiǔdiàn C2
Yuántàichāng Gǔmínjū ....(see 3)

⊗ Eating
18 Cola Cat B2
19 Gǔchéng Zhēngjiāo C2

Tán Gōngguǎn HISTORIC BUILDING
Just north of Wuyanghe Bridge (Wǔyánghé Dàqiáo), the splendid Tán Gōngguǎn (谭公馆) is sadly shut, inaccessible and unrestored. Festooned with Mao-era slogans, the building is a remarkably solid piece of historic architecture and remains unconverted. Note the carvings on the door pillars.

⊙ Other Sights

The small **Fire God Temple** (炎帝宫; Yándì Gōng) backs onto the green cliffs, housing the fearsome deities Yandi and the fiery-faced Huǒshén (Fire God). Now pretty much a block of flats from the 1960s, little remains of the **Confucius Temple** (文庙; Wénmiào) on Shuncheng Jie save its main facade and the Lǐ Mén (Gate of Rites). The **Zhènyuǎn Museum** (镇远展览馆; Zhènyuǎn Zhǎnlǎnguǎn; ☺8.30am-5.30pm) displays items relating to the history of the town. The old **city walls**

on the south side of the Wuyang River have been restored and you can walk a considerable way along them towards the train station. The **Tiānhòu Temple** (天后宫; Tiānhòu Gōng) – a temple dedicated to the goddess Tianhou – can be found along Minzhu Jie to the west of the old town. It's worth hunting out the welcoming **Catholic Church** (天主教堂; Tiānzhǔ Jiàotáng) south of the river. Further along the road from the church, the compound and watchtowers of **Hépíng Cūn** (和平村; ☺8.30am-5.30pm) was Kuomintang HQ during the war against Japan.

☞ Tours

Buy tickets for the riverborne cruises (¥80 per hour) at the office next to **Yumun Wharf** (禹门码头; Yǔmén Mǎtóu), identified by the decorative arch. Travel agents line Xinglong Jie; you should also be able to book tours through your hotel.

✈ Festivals & Events

On the fifth day of the fifth lunar month **dragon boat festival** races churn the waters of the Wuyang River. In the high season, **dragon boat races** take place most Saturdays at around 1pm from Xinda Bridge (新大桥; Xīn Dàqiáo).

🛏 Sleeping

There are rooms everywhere in the old town and even the old Tiānhòu Temple has accommodation overlooking its roof. Don't expect any spoken English. Rooms south of the river get the amplified sound of trains rumbling by. Ask for discounts.

Liúhúlán Jiǔdiàn   HOTEL $
(刘胡兰酒店; ☎572 0586; Shuncheng Jie; 顺城街; r ¥180-260; ✴@) This handy place has several rooms overlooking the river, including a pleasant ground-floor double with big sliding windows and an upstairs terrace. Note that locals pronounce this place 'Liufulan'.

Dàhéguān Hotel   HOTEL $
(大河关宾馆; Dàhéguān Bīnguǎn; ☎571 0188; Shuncheng Jie; 顺城街; tw ¥150; ✴) Clean and spacious place on the corner with river rooms, some with Western toilets, and a ping-pong table.

Héjiā Dàyuàn Kèzhàn   HOTEL $$
(何家大院客栈; ☎572 3770; Chongzikou Xiang; 冲子口巷囗号; s/d ¥388/428; ✴) For a measure of comfort, this traditional courtyard hotel has pleasant rooms in a lovely old property tucked away up an alley away from the river. Expect discounts of around 30%.

Bóhǎiyì Zhàn   HOTEL $
(渤海驿栈; ☎572 1636; 8 Chongzikou Xiang; 冲子口巷囗号; s/d ¥120/128; ✴@) There's not much English (and no river views) at this friendly, small place tucked away opposite the Héjiā Dàyuàn Kèzhàn on the left-hand side of historical Chongzikou (Chongzikou Xiang). Rooms are nothing special but come with showers (and squat toilets). It's quiet and you can talk room prices down.

Yuántàichāng Gǔmínjū   HOTEL $
(圆泰昌古民居; ☎573 4511; Shuncheng Jie; 顺城街; s/d/ste ¥188/298/298; ✴) For a dose of historic charm and the aroma of *nánmù* wood, check into this hotel in an old converted courtyard house, once the residence of the Lu family. Expect discounts of around 30% or more.

🍴 Eating & Drinking

The main drag is full of restaurants, many of them aimed at tourists. Look out for local men wielding hefty wooden mallets to pound *mùchuí xiāngsū*, a kind of sweet, crispy and brittle biscuit made from walnut, sesame seeds, sugar and honey (it's delicious). A handful of places along Xinglong Jie sell cheap plates of fried *jiǎozi* (stuffed dumplings). One or two rowdy bars dotted along Xinglong Jie see local bands step up on stage to an audience of largely empty tables.

Gǔchéng Zhēngjiǎo   DUMPLINGS $
(古城蒸饺; Xinglong Jie; 兴隆街; mains ¥7; ⊙noon-2am) Right next to Yumun Wharf, this very simple restaurant does lovely *jiānjiǎo* (fried dumplings) and is a cheap place for a beer.

Cola Cat   ICE CREAM $
(可乐猫; Kělè Māo; Xinzhong Jie; 新中街; milk shakes from ¥8; ⊙9.30am-midnight) This ice-cream bar along Xinzhong Jie does fine milkshakes (*nǎixī*) and ice creams.

ℹ Information

Agricultural Bank of China (农业银行; Nóngyè Yínháng; Xinglong Jie; ⊙24hr) ATM taking foreign cards; opposite Zhěnyuǎn Museum.

Industrial and Commercial Bank of China (ICBC; 工商银行; Gōngshāng Yínháng; Xinglong Jie; ⊙24hr) ATM taking foreign cards.

Public Security Bureau (PSB; 公安局; Gōng'ānjú; Xinglong Jie) Across from Yumun Pier.

China Post (中国邮政; Xinglong Jie)

Shénzhōu internet cafe (神舟网吧; Shénzhōu wǎngbā; per hr ¥3; ⊙24hr) On south side of the Xinda Bridge by the wall.

Xīnshíkōng internet cafe (新时空网吧; Xīnshíkōng wǎngbā; Panlong Jie; per hr ¥3; ⊙24hr)

Zhěnyuǎn Tourist & Information Centre (镇远旅游咨询服务中心; Zhènyuǎn Lǚyóu Zīxún Fúwù Zhōngxīn; Xinzhong Jie; ⊙8am-8pm) Good for maps of Zhěnyuǎn. Short rickshaw rides around town (¥10).

ℹ Getting There & Around

The best way to reach Zhěnyuǎn from Guìyáng is by train (the tracks thunder south of the old town). The **train station** (huǒchēzhàn) is on the south of the river in the southwest of town, not far from Wuyanghe Bridge (Wǔyánghé Dàqiáo). A taxi to the old town from the train station is ¥4. It's a good 15-minute walk to the old town from the train station, so either book your ticket out of Zhènyuǎn when you arrive or ask your hotel owner to book one for you (they will need to take your passport, however). You can book tickets more than three days in advance at the post office for a commission (¥15). Trains from Zhènyuǎn include the following:

Ānshùn ¥48 to ¥54, 5½ hours, five per day
Guìyáng ¥37 to ¥42, 3¾ hours, regular
Huáihuà ¥29, 2½ hours, regular
Kǎilǐ ¥15, 75 minutes, regular
Yùpíng ¥13, one hour, regular

The **bus station** (chángtú qìchēzhàn) is opposite the train station. There are no direct buses to Tóngrén (铜仁), first take a train to Yùpíng (玉屏; ¥13), then change for a bus to Tóngrén (¥26). Buses run to the following:

Bàojīng ¥13, four daily (8.30am, 12.50pm, 1pm and 3pm)
Kǎilǐ ¥33, five daily (8am, 9.30am, 11am, 1pm and 3pm)

Around Zhènyuǎn

Tiěxī   铁溪
Once you have seen all the sights, this attractive **gorge** (admission ¥50) is a pleasant diversion from town. From the main entrance you can hike to **Dragon Pool** (龙潭; Lóngtán) and **Jīguān Lǐng** (鸡冠岭) along a scenic route. Reach the gorge by buggy (¥6, 20 minutes) from the western end of Zhusheng Bridge; vehicles depart when full.

Bàojīng   报京
This well-preserved Dong minority village around 40km from Zhènyuǎn has some fine examples of diàojiǎolóu architecture. The **seed sowing festival** (播种节; bōzhǒngjié) on the third day of the third lunar month is Bàojīng's best-known minority festival where dancing and courtship rituals meet in lively celebration. Four buses (¥13, 8.30am, 12.50pm, 1pm and 3pm) run to Bàojīng daily from the bus station in Zhènyuǎn.

WESTERN GUÌZHŌU

Birds, caves and waterfalls are the main attractions of this region. Outside Ānshùn, the thundering Huángguǒshù Falls is Guìzhōu's premier tourist attraction, while Zhījīn Cave is one of the largest in the world. Way out west, the town of Wēiníng has one of China's top birdwatching locations in Cǎohǎi Lake, and also offers a backdoor route into Yúnnán.

Ānshùn   安顺

☎0853 / POP 449,000

Once a centre for tea and opium trading, Ānshùn remains the commercial hub of western Guìzhōu and is now most famous as a producer of batik, kitchen knives and the lethal Ānjiǔ brand of alcohol. Once a marvellous historical city ringed by a town wall, the city's heritage has largely vanished and it's surrounding sights that are the real draws.

◉ Sights

A modest chunk of the former Ānshùn city walls (安顺城墙遗址; Ānshùn chéngqiáng yízhǐ) stands opposite the Fènghuángshān Dàjiǔdiàn on Tashan Donglu, where a revealing photo on the wall depicts Ānshùn during Republican days, before the advent of concrete, road widening and Socialist aesthetics.

Fǔwén Miào   CONFUCIAN
(府文庙; admission ¥10; ⊙8.30am-6pm) Check out this charming Confucian temple in the north of town with some stunningly intricate cloud-scrolling carvings on the twin stone pillars before the main hall.

Dōnglín Temple   BUDDHIST
(东林寺; Dōnglín Sì; ⊙7.30am-6pm) The resident Buddhist monks welcome visitors warmly to this temple, built in AD 1405 (during the Ming dynasty) and restored in 1668.

Lóngwáng Miào   BUDDHIST
(龙王庙; ⊙7.30am-5.30pm) A working Buddhist temple, just off Zhonghua Beilu.

🛏 Sleeping

If your Chinese is up to it, try one of the guesthouses (lǚguǎn) in the train station area for a cheap room.

Jūngòng Ruìqí Jiǔdiàn
(军供瑞琪酒店; ☑333 0666; 121 Zhonghua Nanlu; 中华南路121号; s & d ¥110-150; ❀) On your right as you exit the train station, this affordable and convenient place has decent rooms and friendly staff. No English sign.

Xīxiùshān Bīnguǎn   HOTEL $$
(西秀山宾馆; ☑333 7888; fax 333 7668; 63 Zhonghua Nanlu; 中华南路63号; s/d ¥288/328, ste ¥388; ❀@) Pleasantly different from the competition, set back from the road with a garden in the main courtyard at the rear.

FÀNJÌNGSHĀN

Accessed via the gateway town of Tóngrén in the northeast of Guìzhōu, the 2572m-high Buddhist-named mountain of **Fànjìngshān** (梵净山; ¥120) is a must for fans of Buddhist culture, nature lovers or those en route to Húnán or Chóngqìng from Zhènyuǎn or Kǎilǐ. The reserve provides a home to more than half the province's protected plants and two-thirds of its animals, including the very rare (and even more rarely glimpsed) golden monkey (*jīnsīhóu*).

To reach the mountain, hop on a bus (¥29, hourly, first/last bus 7.30am/4.30pm, 90 minutes) to Jiāngkǒu (江口) from the north bus station (北站; běizhàn) around the corner from the train station in Tóngrén; ignore minivan taxis offering to take you for ¥500 return. It's possible to walk the extra 9.5km to the start of the climb proper from the drop-off but you will be bushwhacked upon arrival, so most travellers jump on a waiting minibus (¥20 return) to then take the **cable car** (¥160 return), which takes 20 minutes to ascend the mountain from where you can climb to the summit (金顶; jīndǐng). As it is both pricey and a soft option, it's tempting to skip the cable car, but it is worth every penny; climbing the entire route is a marathon on the legs.

Spring and autumn are the best seasons to visit Fànjìngshān, but check on the weather before you go as it can be fogged out; clear days are rewarded with spectacular views. In Tóngrén, the **Fólúnbèisī Liánsuǒ Jiǔdiàn** (佛伦贝斯连锁酒店; ☎0856 691 8001; 清水大道; Qīngshuǐ Dàdao; r from ¥279; ❄@) is a handy and serviceable hotel very near the train station. Tóngrén itself is an unremarkable town, although it has an intriguing tumbledown **Old Town** (古城区; Gǔchéng Qū) around Zhongshan Lu near the Jin River (锦江) in the south of town.

To reach Tóngrén from Zhènyuǎn, first take a train (¥13) to Yùpíng and then jump on a bus (¥26). Other buses from Tóngrén bus station run to Huáihuà (¥45, three daily), Kǎilǐ (¥80 to ¥90, six daily) and Guìyáng (¥125, eight daily); bus 4 (¥1) links the bus station and the train station. Trains run southeast from Tóngrén to Huáihuà and north to Chóngqìng and Chéngdū.

Rooms are very clean, considering the high occupancy. Singles are quite a lot smaller, with shower not bath. Discounts of up to 50% available.

Fènghuángshān Dàjiǔdiàn HOTEL $$
(凤凰山大酒店; Golden Phoenix Mountain Hotel; ☎322 5724; 58 Tashan Donglu; 塔山东路58号; d r¥228-398; ❄@) There's loads of brass and faded marble here, bathrooms are cramped and rooms have seen better days, but staff are pleasant enough. Look for a building that looks like a bank, with two lions standing guard outside. Big discounts of around 40% are normally available.

Eating

Local speciality *qiáoliángfěn* (乔凉粉) is a spicy dish made from buckwheat noodles and preserved bean curd. A good on-the-run snack is *chōngchōng gāo* (冲冲糕), a cake made from steamed sticky rice with sesame and walnut seeds and sliced wax gourd. Also look out for plates of fried potatoes, hawked at the roadside, which taste like chips; local call them *yángyì*. The teahouse at the rear of the Wǔmiào is a serene place for a cup of *chá* (from ¥28).

By far the best place to eat is the **night market** (夜市; yèshì; Gufu Jie). It's the most happening spot in Ānshùn, with the locals crowding out the many food tents and stalls that set up here. The speciality is barbecued fish (*kǎoyú*), while Uighur chefs, snails sizzling up in woks and proudly displayed pigs' trotters fill out the picture.

Liúyìshǒu Kǎoyú FISH $
(留一手烤鱼; Hongqi Lu; 红旗路; fish per jīn from ¥20; ⏰6pm till late) Packed during night-market hours, when the restaurant fills its premises on Hongqi Lu and spills onto tables flung out on Gufu Jie, this heaving eatery specialises in tasty grilled fish. It's best to dine as a group, as fish weights start at around three *jīn*.

ℹ Information

Bank of China (中国银行; Zhōngguó Yínháng; cnr Tashan Xilu & Zhonghua Nanlu) Offers all services and has an ATM. There are many other ATMs around town.

Ānshùn

GUÌZHŌU AROUND ĀNSHÙN

Getting There & Around

The **north bus station** (安顺客车北站; Ānshùn kèyùnzhàn) has buses (¥30, four hours, every 45 minutes) to Zhījīn town (for Zhījīn Cave). The **west bus station** (客运西站; kèyùn xīzhàn) has some handy buses:

Guìyáng ¥42, every 20 minutes (7am to 7pm)

Lónggōng Caves ¥10, every 25 minutes (7.30am to 6pm), via Shítouzhài (¥5).

Yúnfēng ¥5, 40 minutes, every 25 minutes (7am to 6pm)

The **south bus station** (客车南站; kèchē nánzhàn; ☎ 322 2169; cnr Huangguoshu Dajie & Zhonghua Nanlu) has a handful of useful destinations:

Guìyáng ¥35, 1½ hours, every 20 minutes (6.50am to 7.10pm)

Huángguǒshù ¥15, one hour, every 20 minutes (8am to 6pm)

Kūnmíng sleeper ¥150, 11 hours, four daily (9am, 10.40am, 1pm and 4pm)

Píngbà ¥13, 30 minutes, every 20 minutes (7.20am to 7pm)

Shuǐchéng ¥55, 3½ hours, every 50 minutes (8am to 5.30pm)

Wēiníng ¥90, 10am

Buses from the **Xīxiù long-distance bus station** (Xīxiù kèyùnzhàn) near the train station has buses for provinces in the southeast and southwest of China and hourly buses to Shítouzhài (¥6).

Most trains from the **train station** (huǒchēzhàn) heading east stop in Guìyáng (¥8 to 16, 1½ hours, regular). It is still hard to get sleeper reservations for trains from here; pick them up in Guìyáng instead. A train ticket office can be found just north of the Jūngòng Ruìqí Jiǔdiàn. Destinations include the following:

Guìyáng ¥8 to ¥16, 1½ hours, regular

Kǎilǐ ¥44, four hours, nine daily

Kūnmíng ¥76 to ¥215, nine hours, regular

Liùpánshuǐ ¥24, 2½ hours, regular

Bus 1 zips around town from the train station and up Tashan Donglu. Bus 2 travels between the train station and the north bus station. Bus 6 runs from the train station to the south bus station. Buses cost ¥1. Taxi flagfall is ¥6.

Ānshùn

◎ Top Sights
Dōnglín Temple.................................B2
Fǔwén Miào.....................................A2
Lóngwáng Miào.................................A2

🛏 Sleeping
1 Fènghuángshān Dàjiǔdiàn..................B2
2 Jūngòng Ruìqí Jiǔdiàn.....................B4
3 Xīxiùshān Bīnguǎn.........................B3

🍴 Eating
4 Liúyìshǒu Kǎoyú............................A2
5 Night Market................................B2

China Post (中国邮政; Zhōngguó Yóuzhèng; cnr Zhonghua Nanlu & Tashan Donglu) Look for it tucked next to the China Telecom building.

China Travel Service (CTS; 中国旅行社; Zhōngguó Lǚxíngshè; ☎ 322 4537; Tashan Donglu; ☺9am-6pm Mon-Fri) Look for a blue sign with white Chinese characters.

Around Ānshùn

LÓNGGŌNG CAVES
龙宫洞

The vast **Lónggōng Cave** (Lónggōng Dòng; Dragon Palace; admission ¥120; ☺8.30am-5.30pm) network snakes through 20 hills. While some travellers enjoy drifting through the caves on rowboats with their subdued guides, others find the whole experience – coloured lights, cheesy music, tour groups – kitschy.

An easy day trip, Lónggōng is 27km south of Ānshùn. Local buses (¥8, 40 minutes, 5.30am to 6pm) – ask for the *lónggōng zhuānxiànchē* (龙宫专线车) – depart hourly from Ānshùn's west bus station from 7.30am. Returning, buses leave hourly until about 5pm.

ZHĪJĪN CAVE   织金洞

As the largest cave in China, and one of the biggest in the entire world at 10km long and up to 150m high, Zhījīn Cave (Zhíjīn Dòng; admission ¥135; ◷8.30am-5.30pm) gets tourist accolades. *Lord of the Rings* has been invoked to describe the abstract landscape of spectacular shapes and spirals, often cathedral-like, reaching from floor to ceiling.

Tickets to the cave, which is 15km outside Zhíjīn and 125km north of Ānshùn, include a compulsory 2½-hour Chinese-only tour (minimum 10 people). The tour covers some 6km of the cave, up steep, slippery steps at times, and there are English captions at the main points along the way. Solo travellers visiting outside peak summer months or Chinese holidays should be prepared for a possibly tedious wait for enough people to roll up to form a group.

A long day trip from Ānshùn is just possible, but you need to be on the 7.25am bus to Zhíjīn (¥30, 3½ hours), which leaves from Ānshùn's north bus station. Once there, hop in a taxi (¥4) to the local bus station on Yuping Jie and catch one of the minibuses that leave regularly for the cave entrance (¥7, 50 minutes). Returning from the caves, buses leave regularly. The last bus back to Ānshùn heads out of Zhíjīn at 5.30pm.

From Guìyáng, regular buses (return ¥98, four hours) depart every 30 minutes to Zhíjīn from the long-distance bus station from 6.30am in the morning until 5.20pm.

HUÁNGGUǑSHÙ FALLS   黄果树大瀑布

Disgorging from endless buses, a friendly invasion of frenetic tourists from all over China come to see the 77.8m-tall, 81m-wide Huángguǒshù Falls (Huángguǒshù Dàpùbù; Yellow Fruit Tree Falls; admission Mar-Oct ¥180, Nov-Feb ¥160; ◷7.30am-6pm), making this Guìzhōu's number-one natural attraction. From May to October in particular, these falls really rock the local landscape with their cacophony, while rainbows from the mist dance about Rhinoceros Pool below and colourful peacocks show off their dazzling plumage.

The cascades are actually part of a 450 sq km cave and karst complex discovered when engineers explored the area in the 1980s to gauge the region's hydroelectric potential. Although there are paths around the falls, the entire area is vast and sights so spread out you'll really need to board one of the sightseeing cars (guānguāngchē; ¥50). They link the main areas, which include Dǒupōtáng Waterfall, Lúosītān Waterfall, Tiānxīng Qiáo Scenic Zone and the Main Waterfall Scenic Zone. Hiring a cab from the entrance for a tour will cost around ¥100 or expect to pay around ¥20 for a single journey.

In the main waterfall area, don't miss groping your way through the dripping natural corridor in the rock face of the 134m-long Water Curtain Cave (水帘洞; Shuǐlián Dòng), behind the waterfall.

Going underground into the colossal caves within the geological Tiānxīng Qiáo Scenic Zone (天星桥景区; Tiānxīng Qiáo Jǐngqū) is a quite awe-inspiring sideshow, especially if you do not have time for the Lónggōng or Zhíjīn Caves.

The bus back to Ānshùn from Huángguǒshù Falls passes the drop-off for the riverside village of Shítouzhài (石头寨; admission ¥40), around 6km north of the falls, its stone houses and bridges picturesquely set next to a hill amid paddy fields. Famed for its batik, which you can see Buyi women making by hand, the village is a joy to explore. It's around a 2km walk from the main road to the village. The bus from Lónggōng Caves also passes by.

You can do Huángguǒshù Falls in a day trip from Guìyáng at a push, while it's an easy one from Ānshùn. There are accommodation options everywhere in Huángguǒshù village, but there is little need to overnight.

From Ānshùn, buses (¥15, one hour, 8am to 6pm) run every 20 minutes from the south bus station. There are eight buses a day from Guìyáng to Huángguǒshù (¥50, 2½ hours, every 30 minutes from 8am) from the long-distance bus station on Jinyang Nanlu. The last bus returns to Guìyáng at 4pm. Buses (¥35, two hours) also regularly leave from Guìyáng train station to Huángguǒshù.

TIĀNLÓNG &
TIĀNTÁISHĀN   天龙、天台山

You only need around an hour or so to explore this delightful village cut with a sparkling stream not far outside Ānshùn. Tiānlóng (admission ¥35) is a well-preserved

Túnpǔ village (屯堡), its settlements erected by Ming-dynasty garrison troops posted here during the reign of Hongwu to help quell local uprisings and consolidate control. Coming from the middle and lower reaches of the Yangzi River, the soldiers brought their customs and language with them. Han descendants of these 14th-century soldiers live in Tiānlóng today, and the women are notable for their turquoise tops with embroidered hems. Gorgeous-looking embroideries are on sale everywhere (bargain hard), while local women sit sewing small and exceptionally colourful embroidered shoes, in all sizes.

Complementing its dry stonewalls and narrow alleyways, the architectural highlight of the village is the **Tiānlóng Xuétáng** (天龙学堂), an impressive and distinctive building. The **Sānjiào Temple** (三教寺; Sānjiào Sì) is a creakingly dilapidated shrine dedicated to Taoism, Confucianism and Buddhism. Short performances of *dìxì* – an ancient form of local drama – are regularly held in the **Yǎnwǔtáng** (演武堂) throughout the day.

Other local idiosyncrasies include distinct colloquialisms: the local expression for a thief is a *yèmāozi* (night cat). Several *kèzhàn* (inns) in the village can put you up for the night for around ¥50, a delightful option for a bucolic evening. To reach Tiānlóng, hop on a bus for Píngbà (平坝; ¥13, 30 minutes, every 20 minutes, 7.20am to 7pm) from Ānshùn's south bus station and at the drop off take a minivan (¥10 to ¥15) to Tiānlóng.

Around a 20-minute walk from Tiānlóng, the astonishing temple of **Wǔlóng Sì** (伍龙寺) emerges surreally from the summit of **Tiāntáishān** (admission ¥25), a bit like Colditz Castle. A refreshing hike through the trees takes you to the summit, where you can explore the various rooms of the temple. In a hall at the rear, a figure of Guanyin lithely sits, illuminated by a guttering candle; a further hall displays exhibits relating to local *dìxì* theatre. Afterwards, climb to the Dàyuètái terrace to gaze out over the glorious countryside.

When descending from the temple keep an eye out for a small shrine along a narrow trail where a statue of one of the 18 *luóhàn* sits grumpily all alone. His skinny frame is the result of generosity in giving food to others; he also bestows good fortune on all. Further below rises a 21m-high and 500-year-old gingko tree, festooned with ribbons, while other trails disappear into the trees.

YÚNFĒNG BĀZHÀI 云峰八寨

Yúnfēng Bāzhài is a scattering of traditional villages about 20km northeast of Ānshùn. Introduced by the mildly interesting **Tunpu Culture Museum** (屯堡文化博物馆; Túnpǔ Wénhuà Bówùguǎn; through ticket ¥50; ⊙8am-6pm), which serves as the point of entry, the village of Yúnshān (云山), at the top of a steep set of steps from the road away from the museum, is a gem. Hung with bright yellow dried corncobs and red lanterns, protected by a wall and a main gate and overlooked by the Yúnjiù Shān (Cloud Vulture Mountain), the settlement is a charming and unruffled portrait of rural Guìzhōu. At the heart of the almost deserted village stands a rickety **Money God Temple** (Cáishén Miào), opposite an ancient pavilion.

If you want to spend the night, a couple of *kèzhàn* can put you up. Whatever you do, don't miss the chance to walk up to **Yúnjiù Temple** (云鹫寺; Yúnjiù Sì) at the top of Yúnjiù Shān for some of the most extraordinary views in Guìzhōu. You can walk virtually all around the top of the temple for a sublime and unparalleled panorama of fields and peaks ranging off into the distance. In spring, flowering bright yellow rapeseed plants (*yóucàihuā*) add vibrant splashes of colour.

From Yúnshān it's a 15-minute walk along the road to the village of **Běnzhài** (本寨), also at the foot of Yúnjiù Shān. With its old pinched alleyways, high walls, carved wood lintels, stone lions and ancient courtyard residences, Běnzhài is brim-full of history.

To reach Yúnfēng Bāzhài, take a bus (¥5, 40 minutes, every 25 minutes, 7am to 6pm) from Ānshùn's west bus station. The last bus from Yúnfēng Bāzhài to Ānshùn leaves at 6.20pm, passing through Běnzhài. Coming from Tiānlóng, hop on a bus from the main road to Qīyǎnqiáo (七眼桥; ¥4, 20 minutes) and then hop on a motorbike (¥10) for the 10-minute journey to the museum and the villages.

Wēiníng 威宁

♪0857 / POP 57,000

A dusty, scrappy place with a manic energy epitomised by the orange motorised rickshaws that career around town, Wēiníng is one of the top spots in the world for that most sedate of hobbies, birdwatching. The jewel-like Cǎohǎi Lake sits close to the city centre and draws twitchers to observe wintering migratory birds, especially the rare

TRADITIONAL GARMENTS

The assortment of clothing among Guìzhōu's minorities provides travellers with a daily visual feast. Clothes are as much a social and ethnic denominator as pure decoration. They also indicate whether or not a woman is married, and provide clues to a woman's wealth and skills at weaving and embroidery.

Many women in remote areas still weave their own hemp and cotton cloth. Some families, especially in Dong areas, still ferment their own indigo paste as well, and you will see this for sale in traditional markets. Many women will not attend festivals in the rain for fear that the dyes in their fabrics will run. Methods of producing indigo are greatly treasured and kept secret, but are increasingly threatened by the introduction of artificial chemical dyes.

Embroidery is central to minority costume and is a tradition passed down from mother to daughter. Designs include many important symbols and references to myths and history. Birds, fish and a variety of dragon motifs are popular. The highest quality work is often reserved for baby carriers, and many young girls work on these as they approach marrying age. Older women will often spend hundreds of hours embroidering their own funeral clothes.

Costumes move with the times. In larger towns, Miao women often substitute their embroidered smocks with a good woolly jumper (sweater) and their headdresses look suspiciously like mass-produced pink and yellow Chinese towels.

black-necked crane. Called 'Sun City' by Chinese for its abundant rays, and historically an important route linking north Yúnnán and Sìchuān, Wēiníng is home to a large population of Hui (Muslim), Miao and Yi; a big market held every three or four days sees the town thronged with people from the surrounding minority villages.

Sights & Activities

Căohăi Lake   LAKE
(草海湖; Căohăi Hú; Grass Sea Lake) Guìzhōu's largest highland lake and southwest China's most significant wetland, Căohăi Lake has a fragile history, having been drained during both the Great Leap Forward and the Cultural Revolution in hopes of producing farmland. It didn't work and the lake was refilled in 1980. Government tinkering with water levels in ensuing years impacted the local environment and villagers' livelihoods; officials have since enlisted locals to help with the lake's protection in an effort to remedy both problems. The 20 sq km freshwater wetland has been a national nature reserve since 1992, but many environmental problems remain.

Black-necked cranes are the main attraction, but among the other 180 or so protected bird species are black and white storks, golden and imperial eagles, white-tailed sea eagles, Eurasian cranes and white spoonbills. The prime time to see them is from November to March.

Lovely trails explore much of the lake, but the best way for a close-up of the birds is to cruise around the lake on a punt. Buy tickets at the **ticket office** (per boat 1/2/3hr ¥120/240/360; ⏰8.30am-5.30pm) at the end of the path leading to the lake, rather than from the touts lurking nearby.

To get to the lake it's a 45-minute walk southwest of central Wēiníng or a five-minute taxi ride (¥5).

Sleeping & Eating

For budget rooms, try the *zhāodàisuǒ* (guesthouse) in the bus station area, where you should be able to net a room for around ¥50.

With a large population of Hui, Muslim *yángròu fěn* (lamb rice noodles) and *niúròu fěn* (beef rice noodles) places are all over town, especially around the bus station area. A local delicacy is dragonfly lava, consumed fried.

Hēijǐnghè Bīnguǎn   HOTEL $$
(黑颈鹤宾馆; ☎623 6888; Jianshe Donglu; s & d ¥188-308; ❄@) Cramped rooms and cold in the winter, this is the self-proclaimed top choice in town. Don't expect too much, especially in cheaper rooms. To get here, turn right out of the bus station; it's a block ahead on the left, set back from the road. Discounts of 30% available.

Căohăi Jiàrì Jiǔdiàn   HOTEL $$
(草海假日酒店; ☎623 1881; Caohai Lu; 草海路; s, d & tr per person ¥358-388; ❄) Right by the

lake, rooms here are big and comfortably furnished, and service has improved markedly. It's still not worth the price, but discounts (of 50% to 60%) make things more tolerable.

ⓘ Information

There's no place to change money in Wēiníng. An ICBC ATM on Jianshe Donglu, west of the Héjǐnghè Bīnguǎn, takes foreign cards, but bring extra cash just in case. Opposite the bus station, above the China Mobile shop, there's an **internet cafe** (per hr ¥2; ⊘24hr).

ⓘ Getting There & Away

Wēiníng is a seven-hour bus ride from Guìyáng (¥90, 9am and noon). You can also get here from Ānshùn's south bus station (¥90, 10am). First take a bus to Shuǐchéng (水城; ¥55, 3½ hours, every 50 minutes from 8.30am to 5.30pm), then transfer to a Wēiníng-bound bus (¥30, two hours, hourly from 7.50am).

Leaving Wēiníng, you can backtrack to Guìyáng (¥90, 9am, noon, 6pm) or take a bus south to Xuānwēi in Yúnnán (¥50, five hours, seven daily from 7.30am to 3.30pm). From Wēiníng, there is also a daily sleeper bus to Kūnmíng (¥108, 11 hours, 5pm).

Alternatively, take a bus to Zhāotōng (¥30, three hours, 8am, 1pm, 3.30pm), from where you can hop over to Xīchāng in southern Sìchuān and connect with the Kūnmíng–Chéngdū train line.

NORTHERN GUÌZHŌU

This is where things get a bit wild. Few foreigners venture north of Guìyáng; those that do will find that already incomprehensible accents get broader, roads more rugged and that a stray *lǎowài* (foreigner) can stop the traffic. Way up on the Sìchuān border, Chìshuǐ and its surrounding valleys, waterfalls and national parks are virgin territory for travellers, and utterly gorgeous. It's a good-looking and little-travelled route into southern Sìchuān.

Chìshuǐ   赤水

☑0852 / POP 50,000

Plonked on the border with Sìchuān, Chìshuǐ was once a riverine node for the transport of salt. Some 230 million years before that this was all ocean and today it's the gateway to some of the least-seen natural delights in the southwest. Just outside town are deep gorges and valleys flanked by towering cliffs hewn out of red sandstone – a World Heritage–listed feature known as *dānxiá* – a profusion of waterfalls, as well as luxuriant bamboo and fern forests that date to the Jurassic Era.

While the locals are extremely friendly, there's nothing of intrinsic interest in Chìshuǐ itself, but it's the logical base for exploring the surrounding sights. The town sits on the east bank of the Chìshuǐ River (Chìshuǐ Hé). Cross the town's main bridge (Chìshuǐ Dàqiáo) to the other side and you're in Jiǔzhī (九支) in Sìchuān.

Note that you cannot change money in either Chìshuǐ or Jiǔzhī, so bring extra cash with you.

🛏 Sleeping

You can find basic rooms for ¥50 in places opposite the bus station on Renmin Donglu.

Chìshuǐ Yuán Bīnguǎn   HOTEL $$
(赤水源宾馆; ☑288 7798; 18 Renmin Beilu; 人民北路18号; s & d ¥388-488; ❄@⊜) A short walk from the bus station, this hotel is the town stalwart and remains popular with tour groups. Rooms are large and perfectly fine, if rather old-fashioned, with plain bathrooms. Expect discounts, if it's not booked out. Discounts of 30% to 50% are the norm.

Chìshuǐ Kǎiyuè Bīnguǎn   HOTEL $$
(赤水凯悦宾馆; ☑288 9888; West Inner Huanlu; 西内环路; s & d ¥398-598; ❄@) This place has clean budget rooms, with ADSL connections. Not all have sit-down toilets, so check them first. Discounts of around 60%.

Zhōngyuè Dàjiǔdiàn   HOTEL $$
(中悦大酒店; ☑282 3888; 22 Nanzheng Jie; 南正街22号; s & d ¥478-548; ❄@) The posh option with comfy rooms, proper showers and helpful staff, although they seem a little alarmed by foreigners, and discounts (30%) even in summer.

🍴 Eating

Popular restaurants are scattered in the area around Hebin Zhonglu, near the Chìshuǐ River. The main drag of Renmin Xilu has hole-in-the-wall eateries serving noodle and rice dishes, dumplings and the ever-present pigs' trotters. There are also streetfood stalls and supermarkets close to the bus station. A few hotpot places are scattered along Renmin Beilu.

CELEBRATING WITH THE LOCALS, GUÌZHŌU-STYLE

Minority celebrations are lively events that can last for days at a time, and often include singing, dancing, horse racing and buffalo fighting.

One of the biggest is the **lúshēng festival**, held in either spring or autumn, depending on the village. The *lúshēng* is a reed instrument used by the Miao people. Other important festivals include the **dragon boat festival**, **hill-leaping festival** and '**sharing the sister's meal festival**' (equivalent to Valentine's Day in the West). The **Miao new year** is celebrated on the first four days of the 10th lunar month in Kǎilǐ, Guàdīng, Zhōuxī and other Miao areas. The **fertility festival** is celebrated only every 13 years (the next one's due in 2016).

All minority festivals follow the lunar calendar and so dates vary from year to year. They will also vary from village to village and shaman to shaman. CITS in Kǎilǐ can provide you with a list of local festivals.

ℹ️ Information

A 24-hour ATM is on the corner of Renmin Xilu, close to the bus station, and takes foreign cards (but don't rely on it). There is an internet cafe or two on Renmin Xilu and Renmin Beilu. The post office is on Nanzheng Jie.

ℹ️ Getting There & Around

Chìshuǐ has two bus stations. The qìchē kèyùnzhàn (汽车客运站) on Renmin Xilu handles most local destinations:

Chéngdū ¥110, five hours, three daily (7.50am, 9.40am and 2.45pm)

Chóngqìng ¥100, five hours, seven daily (6am to 5pm)

Shízhàngdòng ¥10.50, 1½ hours, six daily (7.10am to 4.35pm)

Sìdònggōu ¥5.50, every 20 minutes (from 6.30am)

Zūnyì ¥110, eight hours, two daily (6.35am and 10.10am)

For Guìyáng (¥150, eight hours, 6.55am and 8.50am) and Jīnshāgōu (¥11.50, 1½ hours, 9.30am and 3.55pm), you need the **Lǚyóu Chēzhàn** (旅游车站; Nan Jiao Lu) by the river, a ¥5 cab ride from Renmin Xilu. There are also two buses a day to Zūnyì (¥110, eight hours, 6.35am and 10.10am) from here.

Taxi flagfall is ¥3.

Around Chìshuǐ

It's hard to imagine a more dramatic landscape. The locals claim the region has 4000 waterfalls, and some are spectacular, but everywhere you look they're gushing into the rivers that run red from the colour of the earth (Chìshuǐ means 'red water') and which cut through valleys and gorges covered in lush foliage. If that wasn't enough, there are huge forests of bamboo and alsophila plants, giant ferns that date back 200 million years and were once the food of dinosaurs.

As sights are scattered, consider hiring a taxi or minibus to scoop them all up. Expect to pay ¥200 to ¥400 per day, depending on your bargaining skills. To see the waterfalls at their fullest and loudest, come during the rainy season (May to October).

SHÍZHÀNGDÒNG WATERFALL 十丈洞瀑布

A mere metre or so shorter than the much better-known, and visited, Huángguǒshù Falls, the 76m-high, **Shízhàngdòng Waterfall** (Shízhàngdòng Pùbù; admission ¥40; ☺8am-4pm) explodes in a sea of spray as it plunges. You can stand 100m away and still get drenched if the wind is right.

About 40km from Chìshuǐ, six buses a day (¥10.50, 1½ hours) run here from the bus station on Renmin Xilu starting at 7.10am. The bus will drop you in Shízhàngdòng village, from where it's a short walk to the ticket office. From there, it's a 30- to 40-minute walk up a hard road to the turn-off to the waterfall, or you can ride there on a buggy (single/return ¥10/20). Another, more pleasant walk, stretches to the falls on the other side of the river. Doing the complete circuit takes three to four hours. Try to visit before noon during the low season as a hydroelectric dam upriver slows the water after that time. The waterfall is also known as Chìshuǐ Waterfall (Chìshuǐ Dàpùbù).

Around 9km from the waterfall, **Yànzǐyán National Forest Park** (Yànzǐyán Guójiā Sēnlín Gōngyuán; admission ¥25; ☺8am-5pm) is famed for its *dānxiá* (red rock) formations.

An attractive hike cuts through the trees to an imposing red *dānxiá* cliff face featuring an impressive cascade. The bus to Shízhàngdòng Waterfall from Chìshuǐ passes by the park.

SÌDÒNGGŌU 四洞沟

This 4.5km long valley (admission ¥30; ☺8am-5pm) around 15km from Chìshuǐ is forested with ancient ferns, as well as being dotted with gushing cataracts. Paths follow both sides of a river, as minifalls gush down over them, and take you past four 'proper' waterfalls. The biggest and most impressive is the last one, the 60m-high White Dragon Pond Waterfall (Báilóngtán Pùbù). The cool thing here is that you can get really close to the falls, including being able to walk behind one. It takes about three hours to do the circuit, although there are plenty of trails leading off the main paths that will provide fun and games for intrepid hikers.

Sìdònggōu is the most touristy of Chìshuǐ's sights, but still not overly crowded, even in summer. Minibuses run here from the bus station on Chìshuǐ's Renmin Xilu (¥5.50, 30 minutes) and return when they have at least seven people on board.

Buses to Sìdònggōu from Chìshuǐ pass by the town of Dàtóng (大同), which has an attractive and historic old town (*gǔzhèn*) quarter.

JĪNSHĀGŌU NATURE RESERVE 金沙沟自然保护区

By far the least-visited of the sights in the area, this reserve (Jīnshāgōu Zìrán Bǎohùqū) was established to protect the alsophila ferns that grow in abundance here. It's also the site of a bamboo forest, known as the Bamboo Sea (竹海; Zhúhǎi; admission ¥25; ☺8am-5pm), where you can trek through the trees in almost total isolation. The paths get very slippery when wet and mosquitoes are everywhere, so come armed with repellent.

To get here, catch the buses heading to Jīnshāgōu village from Chìshuǐ's Lǚyóu Chēzhàn (¥11.50, 1½ hours). From there, you'll have to negotiate with the locals for a motorbike or minibus ride to the park entrance, which is another 20 minutes away. Expect to pay ¥30 to ¥40 each way. Make sure to arrange a pick-up for your return; very little transport hangs around the park.

RED ROCK GORGE 红石野谷

Dotted with small waterfalls that make for a vivid contrast with the red sandstone *dānxiá* cliffs of the gorge (Hóngshí Yěgǔ; admission ¥30; ☺8am-5pm), also known as Yángjiāyán, there are impressive photo opportunities here, particularly if the sun is shining, when the red earth really stands out.

Minibuses run the 16km journey here from the bus station on Chìshuǐ's Renmin Xilu (¥6, 40 minutes, five daily from 8am to 4.30pm).

Yúnnán

POP 46 MILLION

Includes »

Kūnmíng 635
Around Kūnmíng 643
Jiànshuǐ 646
Yuányáng Rice
Terraces 648
Dàlǐ 651
Shāxī 657
Lìjiāng 659
Tiger Leaping Gorge 667
Shangri-la (Zhōngdiàn) .. 671
Téngchōng 681
Ruìlì 684
Xīshuāngbǎnnà Region .. 687
Jǐnghóng 688

Best Hikes

» Tiger Leaping Gorge (p667)
» Nù Jiāng Valley (p680)
» Xīshuāngbǎnnà Minority Villages (p690)
» Yǔbēng Village (p678)
» Cāng Shān (p656)

Best Natural Sights

» Lúgū Lake (p670)
» Báishuǐtái (p676)
» Yùlóng Xuěshān (p666)
» Swallow's Cavern (p648)
» Kawa Karpo (p678)

Why Go?

Perhaps more than any other province in China, Yúnnán (云南) boasts the highest degrees of diversity, both in people and landscapes. Its extraordinary sights and peoples have made it one of the trendiest destinations for China's exploding domestic tourist industry.

More than half of the country's ethnic minority groups reside here, providing an unexpected glimpse into China's mix of humanity. Then there's the hugely varied splendour of the land – dense jungle sliced by the Mekong River in the south, soul-recharging glimpses of the sun over rice terraces in the southeastern regions, and snow-capped mountains as you edge towards Tibet.

With everything from laid-back villages and spa resorts to multiday mountain treks and excellent cycling routes, Yúnnán appeals to all tastes. Transportation links are good so getting around is a breeze but you'll need time to see it all – whatever time you've set aside for Yúnnán, double it.

When to Go
Kūnmíng

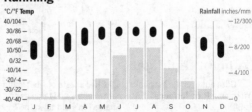

Apr Prepare to get soaked in Xīshuāngbǎnnà during the Dai water-splashing festival.

Jul & Aug Head for the mountains and glaciers around Déqīn.

Dec & Jan Escape China's winter chill and head for Kūnmíng, the city of eternal spring.

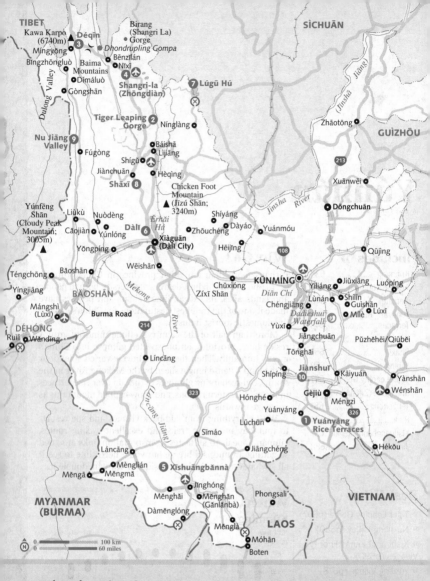

Yúnnán Highlights

1 Gaze out over the magical **Yuányáng Rice Terraces** (p648)

2 Test your legs and lungs trekking **Tiger Leaping Gorge** (p667)

3 Marvel at the peaks (and glacier) around **Déqīn** (p677)

4 Steal a taste of Tibet in the narrow alleys and temples of **Shangri-la's old town** (p671)

5 Look for elephants and hike to minority villages in the jungle of **Xīshuāngbǎnnà** (p687)

6 Kick back in the cafes and bars of **Dàlǐ** (p651)

7 Laze around the shores of stunning **Lúgū Lake** (p670)

8 See how time has stood still in the former Tea-Horse Trail oasis of **Shāxī** (p657)

9 Get way off the map in the remote **Nù Jiāng Valley** (p679)

10 Check out the classic architecture in **Jiànshuǐ** (p646)

History

With its remote location, harsh terrain and diverse ethnic make-up, Yúnnán was once considered a backward place populated by barbarians.

The early Han emperors held tentative imperial power over the southwest and forged southern Silk Road trade routes to Burma. From the 7th to mid-13th centuries, though, two independent kingdoms, the Nanzhao and Dàlǐ, ruled and dominated the trade routes from China to India and Burma. It wasn't until the Mongols swept through that the southwest was integrated into the Chinese empire as Yúnnán. Even so, it remained an isolated frontier region, more closely aligned with Southeast Asia than China.

Today, Yúnnán is still a strategic jumping-off point to China's neighbours. Despite its geographical isolation, much of the province has modernised rapidly in recent years.

Climate

With its enormous range of geomorphology – 76.4m above sea level near Vietnam to 6740m in the Tibetan plateau (averaging around 2000m) – Yúnnán's diverse climate is part of its appeal. In the frozen northwestern region around Déqīn and Shangri-la, winters reach chilling lows of -12°C, but in the subtropical climate of Xīshuāngbǎnnà you can still walk around in a T-shirt in January.

Dàlǐ has an ideal temperature year-round, never dipping below 4°C in winter or above 25°C in summer, while the capital Kūnmíng has a pleasant climate where it can be downright springlike in the winter months and it's never too hot in the summer.

Language

In addition to Mandarin, the other major languages spoken in Yúnnán belong to the Tibeto-Burman family (eg the Naxi language) and the Sino-Tibetan family (eg the Lisu language).

ℹ Getting There & Around

AIR Kūnmíng is served by all Chinese airlines and has daily flights to most cities. International destinations are increasing all the time; in 2012 Kūnmíng opened a US$3.6 billion airport, the fourth-largest in the country. Lìjiāng is also well-connected to a number of Chinese cities.

BOAT In the past it was possible to travel by boat from Jǐnghóng in the south to Thailand. However, recent security threats have stopped boat travel.

> ### PRICE INDICATORS
>
> The following price indicators are used in this chapter:
>
> **Sleeping**
>
> | | |
> |---|---|
> | $ | less than ¥160 |
> | $$ | ¥160 to ¥300 |
> | $$$ | more than ¥300 |
>
> **Eating**
>
> | | |
> |---|---|
> | $ | less than ¥20 |
> | $$ | ¥20 to ¥50 |
> | $$$ | more than ¥50 |

BUS Expressways link Kūnmíng with Dàlǐ, east to Guìzhōu and Guǎngxī, southwest past Bǎoshān to Ruìlì and past Jǐnghóng to the Laos border. An expressway is also being built from Kūnmíng to Hékǒu on the Vietnam border and beyond to Hanoi.

TRAIN Railways link Yúnnán to Guìzhōu, Guǎngxī, Sìchuān and beyond. In Yúnnán itself, development of the railways has been slower than elsewhere, due mostly to topographical interference. A daily train links Dàlǐ and Lìjiāng and a link onward to Shangri-la is under construction.

CENTRAL YÚNNÁN

Kūnmíng 昆明

☏0871 / POP 3 MILLION

Kūnmíng, known as the 'Spring City' for its equable climate, is one of China's most laid-back and liveable cities, and it's very much an enjoyable place to spend a few days. Indeed, 'hurry up' doesn't seem to exist in the local vernacular. Sure, as with other cities, the face of Kūnmíng is constantly changing and many old neighbourhoods have been torn down to make way for shopping malls. Yet the peaceful nature of the place hasn't gone away and it continues to attract large numbers of young Westerners who come to study Chinese.

For short-term visitors, Kūnmíng has some intriguing temples and historic structures, while grand parks are nearby and the legendary Stone Forest is only a day trip away.

Kūnmíng

Map labels:

Yúnnán University

Yuántōng Temple 圆通寺

Wenhua Xiang

Qingyun Jie

Wenlin Jie

Cuihu Beilu

Cuihu Xilu

Green Lake Park

Yuantong Jie

Huashan Xilu

Qianju Jie

Airport Shuttle Bus

Cuihu Nanlu 翠湖南路

Huashan Nanlu

Renmin Xilu

Daguan Jie

Dongfeng Xilu 东风西路

Ru'an Jie

Minsheng Jie

Renmin Zhonglu

Weiyuan Jie

Huguo Lu

Longjing Jie

Zhengyilu 正义路

Yúnnán Provincial Museum

Chongyun Jie

Nánchéng Mosque

Nanping Jie

Xinwen Lu

Guotang Lu

Wuyi Lu 五一路

Xiangyan Jie

Baoshan Jie

Jinmabiji Sq

Jinbi Lu 金碧路

Xiba Lu

Chuàng Kù (The Loft)

Houxin Jie

Xichang Lu

Dongsi Jie

Shulin Jie

West Pagoda

Watsons

East Pagoda

永宁街

Huancheng Xilu

Qingnian Lu

Panlong River

YÚNNÁN KŪNMÍNG

History

The region of Kūnmíng has been inhabited for 2000 years, but it wasn't until WWII that the city really began to expand, when factories were established and refugees, fleeing from the Japanese, started to pour in from eastern China. As the end point of the famous Burma Road, a 1000km-long haul from Lashio in Myanmar (Burma), the city played a key role in the Sino-Japanese war. Renmin Xilu marks the tail end of the road.

Kūnmíng

⊙ Top Sights
Chuàng Kù (The Loft)..............................A5
East Pagoda...D5
Green Lake Park....................................B1
Nánchéng Mosque................................ C4
West Pagoda C5
Yuántōng Temple D1
Yúnnán Provincial Museum.................B4

🛏 Sleeping
1 Camellia Hotel...................................F3
  Camellia Youth Hostel..................(see 1)
2 Green Lake Hotel C2
3 Hump Hostel C5
4 Kūnmíng Cloudland Youth
    Hostel A4
5 Kūnmíng Hotel F3
6 Kunming Upland Youth Hostel C2
7 Kūnmíng Youth Hostel......................B2
  Lost Garden Guesthouse............(see 2)
8 Yúndà Bīnguǎn.................................B1

✗ Eating
9 1910 La Gare du Sud........................D5
10 As You Like......................................B1
11 Carrefour Supermarket D4
12 Déhóng Ruǎnjiā Dǎiwèi Yuán A5
13 Hóng Dòu Yuán B1
14 Salvador's A1
15 Yùquánzhài Vegetarian
    Restaurant....................................D1
16 Zhènxīng Fàndiàn............................F3

☕ Drinking
17 Halfway House A2
18 Kūndū Night Market.........................A4
19 Moondog...B4
20 The Mask...A4

🛍 Shopping
21 Flower & Bird Market C4
22 Fú Lín Táng C3
23 Mandarin Books & CDs.....................A1
24 Tiānfú Famous Teas.........................E4

YÚNNÁN KŪNMÍNG

Following the war the city returned to being overlooked and isolated. When China opened to the West, however, tourists noticed the province, and Kūnmíng used its gateway status to the rest of Yúnnán to become one of the loveliest cities in southwest China.

⊙ Sights & Activities

Yuántōng Temple   BUDDHIST TEMPLE
(圆通寺; Yuántōng Sì; Yuantong Jie; admission ¥6, surrounding park ¥10; ⊙8am-5.20pm) This temple is the largest Buddhist complex in Kūnmíng and a draw for pilgrims. It's more than 1000 years old and has been refurbished many times; the latest renovations were going on at the time of writing. To the

rear, a hall has been added, with a statue of Sakyamuni, a gift from Thailand's king. The good vegetarian restaurant (p640) here is to the left of the temple entrance.

Green Lake Park PARK
(翠湖公园; Cuìhú Gōngyuán; Cuihu Nanlu; ⏰6am-10pm) Come here to people-watch, practise taichi or just hang with the locals and stroll. The roads along the park are lined with wannabe trendy cafes, teahouses and shops. In November, everyone in the city awaits the return of the local favourites, red-beaked seagulls; it's a treat watching people, er, 'flock' to the park when the first one shows up.

FREE Yúnnán Provincial Museum MUSEUM
(云南省博物馆; Yúnnán Shěng Bówùguǎn; 118 Wuyi Lu; ⏰9am-4.30pm Tue-Sun) Set inside a 1950s era building, Yúnnán's provincial museum has recently undergone renovations and its interior is sparkling throughout. The museum has reasonable exhibitions on Diān Chí (Lake Dian) prehistoric and early cultures but the highlight is the section on Yúnnán's minorities, with excellent displays of ethnic costumes and musical instruments.

Chuàng Kù (The Loft) ART GALLERIES
West of downtown in a disused factory area known as Chuàng Kù (创库艺术主题社区; The Loft) are a small number of galleries and cafes featuring modern Chinese artists and photographers. **Yuánshēng Art Space** (源生坊; Yuánshēngfáng; ☎419 5697; 101 Xiba Lu; ⏰9am-1.30am) is a gallery-bar-restaurant-theatre focusing on the province's ethnic groups. The cornerstone of sorts is **TCG Nordica** (诺地卡; Nuòdìkǎ; ☎411 4691; http://en.tcgnordica.com; 101 Xiba Lu; ⏰5-11.30pm Mon, 11.30am-11pm Tue-Sat, noon-4pm Sun), best described as a gallery-exhibition hall-cultural centre – with, oddly, a restaurant serving Scandinavian and Chinese food. The English-speaking folks who run the exhibit have even started running trips to Miao minority villages. Not many taxi drivers know this place as The Loft; ask to go to 101 Xiba Lu.

Tang-Dynasty Pagodas HISTORIC SITES
These pagodas won't give you a 'wow!' moment, but there's a photogenic atmosphere around them, with old men getting haircuts, slurping tea and playing their endless mah jong games, south of Jinbi Lu. **West Pagoda** (西寺塔; Xīsì Tǎ; Dongsi Jie; admission free; ⏰9am-5pm) has surroundings a tad livelier; and **East Pagoda** (东寺塔; Dōngsì Tǎ; 63 Shulin

Jie; ⏰9am-5pm) smacks of a new edifice – it was rebuilt in the 19th century after either a Muslim revolt or an earthquake (foreign and Chinese sources conflict).

Nánchéng Mosque MOSQUE
(南城清真古寺; Nánchéng Qīngzhēn Gǔsì; 51 Zhengyi Lu) Originally built more than 400 years ago, this mosque was ripped down in 1997 in order to build a larger version, which looks vaguely like a bad Las Vegas casino. And sadly, that's now about it for the area's once-thriving Muslim neighbourhood (ripped down *in toto* in 2007).

🛏 Sleeping

Lost Garden Guesthouse BOUTIQUE GUESTHOUSE $$
(一丘田园客栈; Yìqiū Tiányuán Kèzhàn; ☎511 1127; www.lostgardenguesthouse.com; 7 Yiqiu Tian; 一丘田7号; dm ¥40-45, s ¥120-220, d ¥150-220; ☷) A relaxing garden oasis amid white-brick apartment blocks, this boutique guesthouse has nouveau Dàlǐ decor with wood furniture, antiques and a chi-chi lounge. A bonus is the cafe, which serves surprisingly good Western meals. On the downside, there is a noisy school across the road (ask for a room towards the back) and the wi-fi is unreliable. It's tricky to locate: start by walking up the little alley to the right of Green Lake Hotel, take the first left and look for the sign pointing left. Call ahead for instructions.

Green Lake Hotel HOTEL $$$
(翠湖宾馆; Cuìhú Bīnguǎn; ☎515 8888; www.greenlakehotel.com; 6 Cuihu Nanlu; 翠湖南路6号; d from ¥1680; ❀❁@❂) Proud but subdued, this gentle giant of Kūnmíng *hôtellerie* history has a fabulous location, opposite Green Park, and has kept up with modernity, doing so tastefully and with top-notch service. The panorama from the top floors is worth the price alone. Discounts of 30% available.

Kūnmíng Cloudland Youth Hostel HOSTEL $
(昆明大脚氏青年旅社; Kūnmíng Dàjiǎoshì Qīngnián Lǚshè; ☎410 3777; cloudland2005@126.com; 23 Zhuantang Lu; 篆塘路23号; dm ¥30-40, r without/with bathroom ¥110/150; @☷) This well-established Kūnmíng hostel attracts a steady flow of Western and Chinese travellers, drawn primarily by the knowledgeable and friendly staff. Rooms are clean and tastefully furnished with big comfortable beds although the common areas could use a bit of maintenance. It's located on a hard

to spot alley off Xichang Lu. To get here from the train or long-distance bus station, take city bus 64 and get off at the *Yúnnán Daily News* stop (云南日报社站).

Kūnmíng Upland Youth Hostel   HOSTEL $

(昆明倾城青年旅社; Kūnmíng Qīngchéng Qīngnián Lǚshè; ☎337 8910; uplandhostel@gmail. com; 92 Huashan Xilu; 华山西路92号; 8-bed dm ¥35, s/d ¥120/160; @🛜) This brand new place aims to impress with its sharp red and black decor, dimly lit bar and multiple lounges. Rooms have wood furnishings and dorms come with big lockers and power outlets. It has a helpful English-speaking staff and good location near Green Lake. It's just off Huashan Xilu on a little ally called Da Mei Yuan Xiang, near the back entrance of the landmark Green Lake Hotel.

Hump Hostel   HOSTEL $

(驼峰客栈; Tuófēng Kèzhàn; ☎364 0359; www. thehumphostel.com; Jinmabiji Sq, Jinbi Lu; 金碧路金马碧鸡广场; dm ¥35-40, r without/with bathroom ¥90/150; @🛜) You'll hear about Kūnmíng's most notorious hostel long before you arrive. Students, socialites and party animals love the place due to its close proximity to dozens of bars, karaoke joints and restaurants. Bring some earplugs as all this activity could keep you up at night. The hostel itself has a busy bar and terrace that's popular for late night carousing.

Camellia Youth Hostel   HOSTEL $

(茶花国际青年旅舍; Cháhuā Guójì Qīngnián Lǚshè; ☎837 4638; newcamellia@gmail.com; 96 Dongfeng Donglu; 东风东路96号; dm ¥40, s & d ¥135; ⊝@🛜) Part of the same complex as the Camellia Hotel, this sedate hostel has a small garden cafe and good access to transport booking agents in the compound. Rooms are simple but comfortable (dorms have ensuite bathrooms), although the bathrooms and plumbing are due for an upgrade. Internet is available in the lobby.

Camellia Hotel   HOTEL $$

(茶花宾馆; Cháhuā Bīnguǎn; ☎316 3000; www. kmcamelliahotel.com; 96 Dongfeng Donglu; 东风东路96号; s & d ¥388; ✳@🛜) This old travellers' hub has some faded 1970s decor, a musty lobby and a mix of old rooms and some newly renovated ones. The older Class C standard rooms sometimes go for as low as ¥160 while refurbished ones cost around ¥240. There are a number of travel agents onsite that can help organise trips around Yúnnán and beyond. Discounts of 30% available.

Kūnmíng Hotel   HOTEL $$$

(昆明饭店; Kūnmíng Fàndiàn; ☎316 2063; www. kunminghotel.com.cn; 52 Dongfeng Donglu; 东风东路52号; s & d ¥780, ste ¥1419; ⊝✳@🛜) In business since the 1950s, this city landmark has gone through extensive renovations and posits itself as a five-star hotel. It's not the Ritz but it does have a professional staff and comfortable rooms, which are a good deal with the 30% discounts sometimes given. It offers a free airport shuttle and wi-fi is available in the lobby.

Yúndà Bīnguǎn   HOTEL $$

(云大宾馆; Yúnnán University Hotel; ☎503 4179; fax 503 4172; Wenhua Xiang; 文化巷; d & tw ¥298-468; ✳@) Conveniently close to the restaurant--bar hub of Wenhua Xiang and Wenlin Jie, the Yúndà's rooms are not exciting but do the job. The hotel is divided into two, with the cheaper rooms in the wing across the road from the main entrance. Discounts of 40% available.

🍴 Eating

Kūnmíng is home to all of Yúnnán's fabulous foods. Regional specialities are *qìguōjī* (汽锅鸡; herb-infused chicken cooked in an earthenware steampot and imbued with medicinal properties depending on the spices used – *chóngcǎo;* 虫草; caterpillar fungus, or pseudo-ginseng is one); *xuānwēi huǒtuǐ* (宣威火腿; Yúnnán ham); *guòqiáo mǐxiàn* (过桥米线; across-the-bridge noodles); *rǔbǐng* (辱饼; goat's cheese); and various Muslim beef and mutton dishes.

For all manner of foreign restaurants, including Korean, Japanese and Thai, head to Wenhua Xiang. For self-catering, try **Carrefour Supermarket** (家乐福超级市场; Jiālèfú; Nanping Jie), a branch of the popular French chain.

TOP CHOICE 1910 La Gare du Sud   CHINESE YÚNNÁN $$

(火车南站; Huǒchē Nánzhàn; ☎316 9486; dishes from ¥22; ⊙11am-9pm; 🚇) Offering Yúnnán specialities in a pleasant neo-colonial–style atmosphere, this place is now a fave with both expats – it's the kind of place foreign students take their parents when they come to visit – and cashed-up locals. It's hidden down an alley off Chongshan Lu, south of Jinbi Lu.

Salvador's   WESTERN $$

(萨尔瓦多咖啡馆; Sà'ěrwǎduō kāfēiguǎn; 76 Wenhua Xiang; sandwiches from ¥15, mains from ¥25; ⊙8am-11pm; 🚇) Always busy with travellers

ACROSS-THE-BRIDGE NOODLES

Yúnnán's best-known dish is 'across-the-bridge noodles' (过桥米线; guòqiáo mǐxiàn). You are provided with a bowl of very hot soup (stewed with chicken, duck and spare ribs) on which a thin layer of oil is floating, along with a side dish of raw pork slivers (in classier places this might be chicken or fish), vegetables and egg, and a bowl of rice noodles. Diners place all of the ingredients quickly into the soup bowl, where they are cooked by the steamy broth. Prices generally vary from ¥10 to ¥25, depending on the side dishes. It's usually worth getting these, because with only one or two condiments the soup lacks zest.

It is said the dish was created by a woman married to an imperial scholar. He decamped to an isolated island to study and she got creative with the hot meals she brought to him every day after crossing the bridge. This noodle dish was by far the most popular and christened 'across-the-bridge noodles' in honour of her daily commute.

and foreign students, Salvador's is now a Kūnmíng staple. With a Mexican/Mediterranean food theme, as well as solid breakfasts, good coffee and a decent range of teas, it caters for all hours of the day. In the evening you can hang around the bar and watch as Kūnmíng's beautiful people parade along Wenhua Xiang.

As You Like
ENGLISH BAKERY **$$**
(有佳面包店; Yǒujiā miànbāo diàn; 5 Tianjundian Xiang, off Wenlin Jie; pizzas from ¥30, salads from ¥15; ⊙11am-10.30pm Tue-Sun; 🌐) Cute cubbyhole bakery run by a British-Chinese couple. They make excellent pizza, salads and various artisan breads, all from local organic produce. It's an adventure to find – as you walk east on Wenlin Jie (coming from Wenhua Xiang) take the first left up the narrow alley after the Dune Cafe.

Hóng Dòu Yuán
CHINESE YÚNNÁN **$**
(红豆圆; 142 Wenlin Jie; dishes from ¥10; ⊙11am-9pm) An old-school Chinese eatery, with cigarette butts on the floor, a duck-your-head stairway and plastic-film-covered tables, this is a real locals' hang-out on cosmopolitan Wenlin Jie. The food is excellent and will draw you back. Try regional specialities like the táozá rǔbǐng (fried goat's cheese and Yúnnán ham) and liáng bái ròu (peppery, tangy beef). Picture menu.

Déhóng Ruǎnjiā Dǎiwèi Yuán
CHINESE YÚNNÁN **$**
(德宏阮家傣味园; ☎412 8519; 101 Xiba Lu; dishes from ¥12; ⊙9am-9pm) Inside The Loft complex, this fine place serves up authentic, sour and spicy Dai cuisine in a laid-back atmosphere. Try the fantastic barbecued fish, and accompany it with a few glasses

of the rice wine stored in giant vats awaiting your attention. There's a small outside area and a picture menu.

Yùquánzhāi Vegetarian Restaurant
VEGETARIAN **$**
(玉泉斋餐厅; Yùquánzhāi Cāntīng; 22 Yuantong Jie; dishes from ¥18; ⊙10am-9pm) Popular with locals, monks and expats, head here for dishes that look and taste like meat but aren't. We like the Endless Buddha Force (assorted vegies and tofu), but all the dishes here are worth sampling.

Zhènxīng Fàndiàn
CHINESE YÚNNÁN **$**
(振兴饭店; Yúnnán Typical Local Food Restaurant; cnr Baita Lu & Dongfeng Donglu; dishes from ¥12; ⊙24hr) A good introduction to Kūnmíng fare, especially for guòqiáo mǐxiàn, and handy for late-night eats. Pay upfront at the desk where the grumpy middle-aged ladies sit.

🍷 Drinking

Foreigners congregate in the bars on and around Wenhua Xiang, while Jinmabiji Sq is home to many Chinese-style bars and karaoke joints. The Kūndū Night Market area is also a club and bar zone.

The Mask
BAR
(脸谱酒吧; Liǎnpǔ jiǔbā; 14 Kundu Night Market; ⊙8pm-late) In the heart of the Kundu night area, this popular bar is run by a pair of expats from Australia and Italy. It's well-known for putting on great live acts and hosting top DJs.

Halfway House
BAR
(半山咖啡; Bànshān Kāfēi; Kunshi Lu; ⊙10.30am-3am) This multilevel bar attracts a fair mix

of Western students and local Chinese youth who come to mingle, play cards and roll some dice. There's live music here every week. Just off Dongfeng Xilu, it's hard to spot. The nearest landmark is the 'Bai Hui Shang Chang' bus stop across the road.

Moondog BAR
(月亮狗; Yuèliàng Gǒu; 138-5 Wacang Nanlu; ⊙8pm-late) An expat-Chinese run dive bar with excellent fine art events that tends to gather hipsters, artists and travellers.

Shopping
Yúnnán specialities are marble and batik from Dàlǐ, jade from Ruìlì, minority embroidery, musical instruments and spotted-brass utensils.

Some functional items that make good souvenirs include large bamboo water pipes for smoking angel-haired Yúnnán tobacco; and local herbal medicines, such as Yúnnán Báiyào (Yúnnán White Medicine), which is a blend of more than 100 herbs and is highly prized by Chinese throughout the world.

Yunnanese tea is an excellent buy and comes in several varieties, from bowl-shaped bricks of smoked green tea called *tuóchá*, which have been around since at least Marco Polo's time, to leafy black tea that rivals some of India's best.

Tiānfú Famous Teas TEA
(天福茗茶; Tiānfú Míngchá; cnr Shangyi Jie & Beijing Lu; ⊙8.30am-10.30pm) This place offers most types of teas grown in Yúnnán, including the famed pǔ'ěr tea.

Mandarin Books & CDs BOOKS
(五华书苑; Wǔhuá Shūyuàn; 52 Wenhua Xiang; ⊙9.30am-9.30pm) For guidebooks, novels, magazines and a selection of travel writing in English and other languages, try Mandarin.

❶ Information
For any and all information on the city, check out www.gokunming.com (it also covers parts of the rest of Yúnnán).

Maps (¥8) are available from the train/bus station areas and in hotels, but they're not much use to non-Chinese speakers.

Dangers & Annoyances
Kūnmíng is one of the safest cities in China but, as always, take special precautions near the train and long-distance bus stations. Reports of pickpockets are not unheard of, and there have been a number of victims of druggings and robberies on overnight sleeper buses.

Internet Access
Every hotel and cafe frequented by travellers offers internet (网吧) or wi-fi, usually for free. The city has many internet cafes, charging ¥2 to ¥4 per hour.

Medical Services
Richland International Hospital (瑞奇德国际医院; Ruìqídé Guójì Yīyuàn; ☑574 1988; Beijing Lu) Most of the doctors are Chinese but English is spoken here. Standards are generally good and prices are reasonable (consultations start from ¥30). It's on the bottom three floors of the Shàngdū International building; Yanchang Xian extension near Jinxing Flyover. A taxi ride here from the city centre will cost under ¥20.

Watsons (屈臣士; Qū Chén Shì; Dongsi Jie; ⊙9am-10pm) Western cosmetics and basic medicines. Other branches around town.

Yán'ān Hospital (延安医院; Yán'ān Yīyuàn; ☑317 7499, ext 311; 1st fl, block 6, Renmin Donglu) Has a foreigners' clinic.

Money
Some banks other than Bank of China have ATMs which should accept international cards.

Bank of China (中国银行; Zhōngguó Yínháng; 448 Renmin Donglu; ⊙9am-noon & 2-5pm) All necessary services and has an ATM. Branches are at Dongfeng Xilu and Huancheng Nanlu.

ONE-STOP SHOPPING

The **Flower & Bird Market** (花鸟市场; Huāniǎo Shìchǎng; Tongdao Jie), also known as *lǎo jiē* (old street), has shrunk dramatically in recent years and is now ominously hemmed in by encroaching modernity. Nor are flowers and birds the main draw here any more. Instead, strollers peruse stalls chock-full of jewellery, endless curios, knick-knacks and doo-das (the contents of someone's back hall often enough), some occasionally fine rugs and handmade clothing, and a hell of a lot of weird stuff.

One block west of the intersection of Guanghua Jie and the pedestrian-only Zhengyi Lu sits **Fú Lín Táng** (福林堂), the city's oldest pharmacy, which has been dishing out the *sānqì* (the legendary Yunnanese cure-all root mixed into tea; about ¥20 to ¥100 per gram) since 1857.

Post

China Post (国际邮局; Zhōngguó Yóuzhèng; 223 Beijing Lu) The main international office has poste restante and parcel service (per letter ¥3, ID required). It is also the city's Express Mail Service (EMS) and Western Union agent. Another branch on Dongfeng Donglu.

Tourist Information

Many of the popular backpacker hotels and some of the cafes can assist with travel queries. **Tourist Complaint & Consultative Telephone** (316 4961) Where you can complain about, or report, dodgy tourist operations.

Travel Agencies

Wonders of Yunnan (331 1690; www.wondersofyunnan.com; 488 Huangchang Dong Lu, rm 212) This small travel outfit runs tours around Yúnnán. English- and Dutch-speaking guides are available.

Visa extensions

Public Security Bureau (PSB; 公安局; Gōng'-ānjú; 301 7878; 399 Beijing Lu; 9-11:30am & 1-5pm Mon-Fri) To visit the givers of visa extensions, head southeast off Government Sq to the corner of Shangyi Jie and Beijing Lu. Another **office** (571 7001; Jinxing Lu) is off Erhuan Beilu in northern Kūnmíng; take bus 3, 25 or 57.

ⓘ Getting There & Away

Air

Kūnmíng's new airport (completed in 2012) is the fourth largest in China and includes direct services to/from North America, Europe and Australia. International flights to Asian cities include Hong Kong (¥1550), Vientiane (¥1800), Yangon (¥2000) and Kuala Lumpur (¥3088).

China Eastern Airlines/Civil Aviation Administration of China (CAAC; Zhōngguó Mínháng; 28 Tuodong Lu; 8.30am-7.30pm) issues tickets for any Chinese airline but the office only offers discounts on certain flights.

Daily flights from Kūnmíng:

Běijīng ¥1820
Chéngdū ¥1010
Chóngqìng ¥730
Guǎngzhōu ¥1260
Lhasa ¥1960
Shànghǎi ¥1900
Xī'ān ¥1280

Destinations within Yúnnán:

Bǎoshān ¥810
Jǐnghóng ¥1150
Lìjiāng ¥940
Mángshì/Déhóng ¥1000
Shangri-la ¥1150
Xiàguān/Dàlǐ ¥760

Bus

Kūnmíng's five bus stations are located on the outskirts of the city.

Buses departing the **south bus station** (彩云北路南客运站; cǎiyún běilù nán kèyùnzhàn):

Jiànshuǐ ¥81, 3½ hours, every 30 minutes (8am to 8.30pm)
Jǐnghóng ¥220–253, nine to 10 hours, every 30 minutes (8.10am to 10.30pm); buses leaving after 12.30pm are sleeper style
Yuányáng ¥132–142, seven hours, three daily (10.20am, 7.30pm, 8.20pm)

Buses departing the **west bus station** (马街西客运站; mǎjiē xī kèyùnzhàn):

Bǎoshān ¥175–213, nine hours, every hour (8.30am to 10.30pm)
Chǔxióng ¥46–53, two to three hours, every 15 minutes (8.30am to 5.30pm)
Dàlǐ ¥138, four to five hours, every hour (8.50am to 7.20pm); plus two night buses ¥113, seven hours (9.10pm and 10.10pm)
Lìjiāng ¥170–190 (standard service), 10 hours, hourly (8am to 8.30pm); plus two night buses, ¥185, (10pm and 11pm); plus several 'super-express' buses with wide seats and lunch for ¥230.
Ruìlì ¥257–273, 12 hours, seven daily (8.30am to 9pm)
Shangri-la ¥214, 12 hours, one daily (9am); plus three night buses ¥204 (7pm, 8pm and 9pm).
Téngchōng ¥241, 12 hours, one daily (9am); plus five night buses, ¥222 (7pm to 9pm)

Buses departing the **east bus station** (白沙河东客运站; báishāhé dōng kèyùnzhàn):

Hékǒu ¥141, eight hours, four daily (9.40am to 12.40pm)
Shílín ¥35 to ¥40, two hours, every 30 minutes (7am to noon); usually departs when full.

Allow plenty of time to get to the bus stations (60 to 90 minutes). Bus 154 runs to the south bus station from the train station, as does bus 80 to the west bus station and bus 60 to the east bus station. A taxi will cost ¥35 to ¥45.

Train

You can buy train tickets up to 10 days in advance. The following prices are for hard-sleeper, middle berths on the fastest train:

Běijīng ¥578
Chéngdū ¥257
Éméi town ¥234
Guǎngzhōu ¥353
Guìyáng ¥162
Liùpánshuǐ ¥109
Shànghǎi ¥509
Xī'ān ¥399

BORDER CROSSING: GETTING TO LAOS & VIETNAM

Getting to Laos

A daily bus from Kūnmíng to Vientiane (¥587) leaves from the south bus station, at 6pm, reaching its destination 30 hours later. Alternatively, take a bus to Móhàn on the border with Laos, these depart at 8.30pm, cost ¥320 and take about 18 to 20 hours.

Getting to Vietnam

Apart from getting on a plane, the only way to get to Vietnam from Kūnmíng for now is by bus. Buses run from Kūnmíng's east bus station to the border town of Hékǒu (¥143), departing at 9.40pm.

Official proceedings at this border crossing can be frustrating (and officials have been known to confiscate Lonely Planet guides because they show Taiwan as a different country to China). Just keep your cool.

On the Chinese side, the border checkpoint is technically open from 8am to 11pm but don't bank on anything after 6pm. Set your watch when you cross the border – the time in China is one hour later than in Vietnam. Visas are unobtainable at the border crossing.

Within Yúnnán, four daily trains run to Dàlǐ (seat ¥50 to ¥65, hard sleeper ¥83 to ¥89, eight hours). The K9614 (8.28am), K9610 (10am), K9622 (11.10pm) and K9626 (11.39pm). Travel agents book these out well in advance, so it can be tough to get a berth at short notice.

For Lìjiāng (seat ¥90, hard sleeper ¥142 to ¥152, nine hours) there are two night trains, the K9606 (9.58pm) and the K9602 (10.28pm).

Getting Around

A subway is under construction and the first line is scheduled to open in 2013.

To/From the Airport

The new airport is located 25km northeast of the city. An airport bus (¥25) runs there from Xíyì Bīnguǎn (西驿宾馆), formerly called the Nánjiāng Bīnguǎn. There are also airport buses travelling from the train station and the old airport. A subway is planned to start running in 2013. A taxi will average ¥100 to the dead centre of town.

Bicycle

Most hostels and a few hotels rent bikes for around ¥15 to ¥20 per day.

Bus

Bus 63 runs from the east bus station to the Camellia Hotel and on to the main train station. Bus 2 runs from the train station to Government Sq (Dongfeng Guangchang) and then past the west bus station. Fares range from ¥1 to ¥4. The main city buses have no conductors and require exact change.

Around Kūnmíng

There are some grand sights within a 15km radius of Kūnmíng, but getting to most of them is time-consuming and you'll find most of them extremely crowded (weekdays are best to avoid the crowds).

If you don't have much time, the Bamboo Temple (Qióngzhú Sì) and Xī Shān (Western Hills) are the most interesting. Both have decent transport connections. Diān Chí (Lake Dian) has terrific circular-tour possibilities of its own.

BAMBOO TEMPLE 筇竹寺

This serene **temple** (Qióngzhú Sì; admission ¥10; ⊙8am-7pm) is definitely one to be visited by sculptors as much as by those interested in temple collecting. Raised during the Tang dynasty, it was rebuilt in the 19th century by master Sichuanese sculptor Li Guangxiu and his apprentices, who fashioned 500 *luóhàn* (arhats - disciples of the Buddha or noble ones).

Li and his mates pretty much went gonzo in their excruciating, eight-year attempt to represent human existence in statuary – a fascinating mix of superb realism and head-scratching exaggerated surrealism. How about the 70-odd surfing Buddhas riding the waves on a variety of mounts: blue dogs, giant crabs, shrimp, turtles and unicorns? And try this: count the arhats one by one to the right until you reach your age – that arhat is the one that best details your inner self. Note that photography is prohibited inside the temples.

Around Kūnmíng

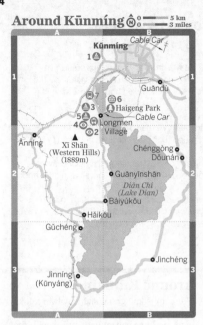

Kūnmíng

Around Kūnmíng

◎ Sights
1 Bamboo Temple	A1
2 Dragon Gate	A2
3 Huátíng Temple	A1
4 Sānqīng Gé	A1
5 Tàihuá Temple	A1
6 Yúnnán Nationalities Museum	B1

ⓘ Transport
7 Gāyáo Bus Station	A1

So lifelike are the sculptures that they were considered in bad taste by Li Guangxiu's contemporaries (some of whom no doubt appeared in caricature), and upon the project's completion he disappeared into thin air.

The temple is about 12km northwest of Kūnmíng. First take bus 2 from Renmin Rd to Huáng tǔ pō (黄土坡) bus stop then change to the C61 bus (¥2, 40 minutes). A taxi to the temple will cost around ¥60.

DIĀN CHÍ 滇池

The shoreline of Diān Chí (Lake Dian), located to the south of Kūnmíng, is dotted with settlements, farms and fishing enterprises. The western side is hilly, while the eastern side is flat country. The southern end of the lake, particularly towards the southeast, is industrial.

The lake is elongated – about 40km from north to south – and covers an area of 300 sq km. Plying the waters are *fānchuán* (pirate-sized junks with bamboo-battened canvas sails). The area around the lake is mainly for scenic touring and hiking, and there are some fabulous aerial views from the ridges at Dragon Gate in Xī Shān.

XĪ SHĀN 西山

This cool, forested mountain range on the western side of Diān Chí makes for a great day trip from Kūnmíng. The range is full of walking trails (some very steep sections), quiet temples, gates and lovely forests. But avoid the weekends when Kūnmíngites come here in droves.

It's a steepish approach from the north side. The hike from the Gāoyáo bus station, at the foot of the hills, to Dragon Gate takes 2½ hours, though most people take a connecting bus from Gāoyáo to the top section.

Alternatively, it is possible to cycle to the hills from the city centre in about an hour – to vary the trip, consider doing the return route across the dikes of upper Diān Chí.

At the foot of the climb, about 15km from Kūnmíng, is **Huátíng Temple** (华亭寺; Huátíng Sì; admission ¥6; ☉8am-6pm), a country temple of the Nanzhao kingdom believed to have been constructed in the 11th century. It's one of the largest in the province and its numerous halls are decorated with arhats.

The road from Huátíng Temple winds 2km from here up to the Ming-dynasty **Tàihuá Temple** (太华寺; Tàihuá Sì; admission ¥6; ☉8am-6pm). The temple courtyard houses a fine collection of flowering trees, including magnolias and camellias.

Sānqīng Gé (三清阁), near the top of the mountain, was a country villa of a Yuan-dynasty prince, and was later turned into a temple dedicated to the three main Taoist deities (*sānqīng* refers to the highest level of Taoist 'enlightenment').

From near here you can catch a **chairlift** (one way/return ¥25/40) if you want to skip the final ascent to the summit. Alternatively, a tourist tram takes passengers up to the Dragon Gate for ¥5.

Near the top of the mountain, is **Dragon Gate** (龙门; Lóng Mén; admission ¥40), a group of grottoes, sculptures, corridors and pavilions that were hacked from the cliff between 1781 and 1835 by a Taoist monk and coworkers, who must have been hanging up there by their fingertips.

To get here, take bus 5 (¥1) from the Kūnmíng Hotel to the terminus at Liǎngjiāhé, and then change to bus 6 (¥1), which will take you to Gāoyáo bus station at the foot of the hills. Alternatively, minibuses (¥6) run from opposite Liǎngjiāhé and drop passengers at spots along the way.

Returning, you could also take the cable car across to Hǎigěng Park for ¥40. From there, take the 94 bus or a taxi for the 3km or so to the Yúnnán Nationalities Village, opposite the Yúnnán Minorities Museum, where you can catch bus 44 (¥1, 40 minutes) to Kūnmíng's main train station.

YÚNNÁN NATIONALITIES MUSEUM 云南民族博物馆

On the northeast corner of the lake, the **Yúnnán Nationalities Museum** (Yúnnán Mínzú Bówùguǎn; www.ynnmuseum.com; admission free; ⊙9.30am-4.20pm Tue-Sun) is reputedly the largest minorities museum in China, even if it doesn't have a whole lot on display. But the ground floor exhibition of costumes is comprehensive and comes with proper English captions.

Across the road is the **Yúnnán Nationalities Village** (云南民族村; Yúnnán Mínzú Cūn; admission ¥90; ⊙8.30am-10pm). Here you can walk through a tacky re-creation of an old Kūnmíng street to reach the 'village', where all-smiling, all-dancing minorities perform for mostly domestic tour groups. Skip it and head to Xīshuāngbǎnnà for the real thing instead.

Buses 24 and 44 (¥1) run to both the museum and village from the main train station.

Shílín 石林

📍0871

A conglomeration of utterly bizarre but stunning karst geology and a hell of a lot of tourists, **Shílín** (Stone Forest; admission ¥175), about 120km southeast of Kūnmíng, is equal parts tourist trap and natural wonderland. A massive collection of grey limestone pillars split and eroded by wind and rainwater (the tallest reaches 30m high), the place was, according to legend, created by immortals who smashed a mountain into a labyrinth for lovers seeking privacy.

Yes, it's packed to the gills, every single rock is affixed with a cheesy poetic moniker,

Sani women can be persistent in sales, and it's all pricey as hell. Yet, idyllic, secluded walks are within 2km of the centre and by sunset or moonlight Shílín becomes otherworldly. To avoid the crowds, arrive early and avoid weekends.

Shílín can easily be visited as a day trip from Kūnmíng, and it doesn't have much in the way of budget accommodation. But if you want to stay the night, the rooms at **Shílín Bìshǔyuán Bīnguǎn** (石林避暑园宾馆; 📞771 1088; d/tr ¥300/360) are quiet and have good views over Shílín, double rooms regularly get knocked down to around ¥160.

Near the main entrance is a cluster of restaurants and snack bars that are open from dawn to dusk. Check all prices before you order, as overcharging is not uncommon.

Sani song and dance evenings are organised when there are enough tourists. Shows normally start at around 8pm at a stage next to the minor stone forest but there are sometimes extra performances. There are also Sani performances at the same location during the day between 2pm and 3pm.

During the July/August **torch festival**, wrestling, bullfighting, singing and dancing are held at a natural outdoor amphitheatre by Hidden Lake south of Shílín.

Buses to Shílín (¥35, two hours, every 30 minutes, 7am to 7pm) leave from Kūnmíng's east bus station.

Hēijǐng 黑井

📍0878

Time-warped **Hēijǐng** (admission ¥30) has for centuries been known for its production of salt and is still an important producer of the 'white gold'. Upscale restaurants in Kūnmíng still come here to purchase salt, believing it to be of better quality than the mass-produced stuff. Hēijǐng has retained much of its period architecture and is a great place to wander for a day or two, marvelling at the old gates, temples and shady narrow alleys.

A small tourist information office near the first bridge can point the way to the various sites.

◉ Sights

The admission fee at the main gate (a few kilometres before the village) includes admission to **Dàlóng Cí** (大龙祠; the clan meeting hall) and **Gǔyán Fáng** (古盐坊; an old salt production facility). The latter offers brief descriptions of the history of salt production, you can find it by walking east from the village for about 15 minutes. A few old salt wells can also be inspected, look out for the **Black Cow Well** (黑牛井; Hēiniú Jǐng), just south of Dàlóng Cí.

Should you tire of salty attractions just take a stroll around some of the back alleys and admire the temples, gates and old homes. Weekends get packed out with day trippers from Kūnmíng but the rest of the week its just the locals going about their business.

There's pleasant **walking** to be done in the hills behind the town too. An obvious path leads up to **Feilai Temple** (飞来寺; Fēilái Sì), then along the ridge line past some tombs before descending to the village. Plan on two to three hours for this walk.

🛌 Sleeping

Wu Family Courtyard INN $$
(武家大院; Wǔjiā Dàyuàn; ☑489 0358; s/d ¥150/220) The best-known place in town was once owned by local salt magnate Wu Weiyang, who was summarily executed by communist forces in 1949. It's got oodles of faded grandeur but for the price you'd expect a bit more renovation – little seems to have changed since Mr Wu was around.

Wang Family Courtyard INN $
(王家大院; Wángjiā Dàyuàn; ☑489 0506; r ¥35) This is the cheapest place in town (if not all of Yúnnán). It's a simple place and a little run down but there are fine views over the river.

ℹ️ Getting There & Away

Getting to Hēijǐng is tricky. The best option is local train No 6162 (¥15, five hours), departing Kūnmíng at 7.43am and arriving at 1.35pm. The train stops a couple of kilometres from the village but horse-drawn buggies are available to take passengers to town. Going the other way the No 6161 departs at 11.20am and reaches Kūnmíng at 6pm.

The alternative is to take the bus from Kūnmíng (or Dàlǐ) to the county capital Chǔxióng (楚雄). These buses stop at the main bus station from where you'll have to take a taxi (¥7) to the east bus station (东站), from where there are buses to Hēijǐng (¥13) every hour between 9am and 3.50pm. Buses return on a similar schedule, the final departure at 2.30pm.

Jiànshuǐ 建水

☑0873 / POP 17,400

Jiànshuǐ is a charming town of old buildings, an enormous Confucian temple, a cave laden with swallows, and some of the best steampot cooking and barbecue you'll find in Yúnnán. The architecture is constantly being 'facelifted', but still retains much of its distinct character, and the locals, who are a mix of Han, Hui and Yi, are extremely friendly.

Known in ancient times as Bùtóu or Bādiàn (巴甸), Jiànshuǐ's history dates back to the Western Jin period, when it was under the auspices of the Ningzhou kingdom. It was handed around to other authorities until its most important days as part of the Tonghai Military Command of the Nanzhao kingdom. The Yuan dynasty established what would eventually become the contemporary town.

◉ Sights

Classic architecture surrounds you in Jiànshuǐ, and not just in the old-style back alleys. Virtually every main street has a historically significant traditional structure. The architecture here is especially intriguing because of the obvious mixture of central plains and local styles. Many old buildings, despite official decrees positing them as state treasures, have been co-opted for other purposes and the trick – and the great fun – is trying to find them.

Note that you can buy a ¥133 **through ticket** (通票; tōngpiào) that gets you into the Confucian Temple, the Zhu Family Garden and Swallow's Cavern. It's on sale at any of those places.

Confucian Temple CONFUCIAN
(文庙; Wénmiào; Linan Lu; admission ¥60; ⊙8am-6.30pm) Jiànshuǐ's famous temple was modelled after the temple in Confucius' hometown of Qūfù (Shāndōng province) and finished in 1285; it covers 7.5 hectares and is the third-largest Confucian temple in China. (Some locals employ a flurry of Byzantine mathematics to prove it's the largest; either way, Xué Lake, around which it sits, uses the Chinese word for 'sea' in its name!)

The temple has operated as a school for nearly 750 years and was so successful that more than half of all Yúnnán's successful candidates in imperial examinations during this period came from Jiànshuǐ. Many of the names of buildings in Jiànshuǐ use the ideogram *wén,* or 'literacy'.

Zhu Family Garden
HISTORIC SITE

(朱家花园; Zhūjiā Huāyuán; Hanlin Jie; admission ¥50; ⊙8am-8pm) This spacious 20,000 sq m complex, a fascinating example of Qing-era one-upping-the-Joneses, comprises ancestral buildings, family homes, ponds and lovely gardens, and took 30 years to build (it's now partially converted into an atmospheric inn with Qing-style rooms for ¥480). The Zhu family made its name through its mill and tavern, and dabbled in everything from tin in Gèjiù to opium in Hong Kong, eventually falling victim to the political chaos following the 1911 revolution.

Cháoyáng Gate
HISTORIC SITE

(朝阳搂; Cháoyáng Lóu) Guarding the centre of town, Cháoyáng Gate, an imposing Ming edifice, was modelled on the Yellow Crane Tower in Wǔhàn and the Yuèyáng Tower in Húnán, and bears more than a passing resemblance to the Gate of Heavenly Peace in Běijīng. There's no charge to walk up into the gate and admire the building and views; you'll find a wonderful traditional teahouse, often with local musicians playing.

Zhǐlín Sì
BUDDHIST MONASTERY

(指林寺) The largest preserved wooden structure in Yúnnán, this monastery was built during the latter stages of the Yuan dynasty; its distinctive design feature is the brackets between columns and crossbeams.

🛏 Sleeping

Huáqīng Jiǔdiàn
HOTEL $$

(华清酒店; ☎766 6166; 46 Hanlin Jie; 翰林街 46号; s & d ¥280-468; ❄@) Decorated in a neo-Qing-dynasty style, the rooms here are nicely set up and come with lovely, small terraces. Prices usually come down to around ¥170. The attached cafe-bar next door is an OK place for a coffee or evening drink.

Lín'ān Inn
INN $

(临安客栈; Lín'ān Kèzhàn; ☎765 5866; 32 Hanlin Jie; 翰林街32号; d & tw ¥198-218; ❄@🖥) A prime location in the heart of the old town, but the biggest draw is the great communal outside area, which is very pleasant in the evening. Regular discounts make this a budget choice (usually down to ¥160), but the rooms are a big step up from the cheapies. They'll cook for you too.

Jiànshuǐ Youth Hostel
HOSTEL $

(建水国际青年旅舍; Jiànshuǐ Guójì Qīngnián Lǚshè; ☎765 2451; yhajianshui@yahoo.com; 77 Yongning Jie; 永宁街77号; dm ¥25, tw/tr ¥70/110; @🖥) This reliable backpacker hangout has clean rooms around a courtyard and helpful English-speaking staff. It rents bikes for ¥15 per day. To find it from Lin'an Lu, walk south on Guan Di Miao Jie and after 75m look for the sign pointing left.

🍴 Eating

Jiànshuǐ is legendary for its *qìguō* (汽锅), a stew made in the county's famed earthenware pots and often infused with medicinal herbs. The cook may make use of the local speciality, *cǎoyá* (草牙; grass sprouts), also known as elephant's tooth grass root, which tastes like bamboo. Only found in Jiànshuǐ County, it's often used in broth or fried with liver or pork. Vegetarians might find a place that will substitute tofu. You'll also find places serving delicious *liáng miàn,* or cold rice noodles served with sesame paste and tofu balls cooked on a grill.

Then there's glorious Jiànshuǐ barbecue (建水烧烤; Jiànshuǐ *shāokǎo*). Cubbyhole restaurants are filled with braziers roasting meats, vegies, tofu and perhaps goat's cheese. A perfect night out is a roasted meal under the Jiànshuǐ stars with friends. Try the intersection of Hanlin Jie and Lin'an Lu for barbecue places.

ℹ Information

There are **internet cafes** (山城网吧; wǎngbā; per hr ¥2.50; ⊙24hr) on Yongning Jie, just south of Lin'an Lu, and on Hanlin Jie next to the Huáqīng Jiǔdiàn. There are a few ICBC ATMs around town that take foreign cards.

ℹ Getting There & Away

Jiànshuǐ has a couple of bus stations. The main one is 3km north of Cháoyáng Gate. For very local destinations, you need to head to the second small (regional) bus station a few minutes' walk west at the corner of Chaoyang Beilu and Beizheng Jie.

From the main station, there are buses continually leaving for Yuányáng (¥30, 2½ hours), but these go to Nánshà. For Xīnjiē and the rice terraces, there is one daily bus (¥41, four hours, 11.34am).

Frequent buses head to Kūnmíng (¥78, every 25 minutes, three to four hours, 7am to 7.35pm). Hékǒu-bound travellers have three morning buses (¥63 to ¥75, five hours, 7.26am, 8.16am, 10.57am). Sleepers to Jīnghóng (¥177, 12 to 17 hours) depart at 1.30pm and 4.30pm.

Around Jiànshuǐ

SWALLOW'S CAVERN   燕子洞

This freak of nature and ornithology is halfway between Jiànshuǐ and Gèjiù. The karst formations (the largest in Asia) are a lure, but what you'll want to see are the hundreds of thousands of swallows flying around in spring and summer. The **cave** (Yànzǐ Dòng; admission ¥80; ☉9am-5pm) is split into two – one high and dry, the other low and wet. The higher cave is so large that a three-storey pavilion and a tree fit inside. Plank walkways link up; the Lú River runs through the lower cave for about 8km and you can tour the caverns in 'dragon-boats'.

There's no direct bus, but the ones bound for Méngzì, Kāiyuán or Gèjiù which don't take the expressway pass the cavern (¥10, one hour).

TWIN DRAGON BRIDGE   双龙桥

This bridge (Shuānglóng Qiáo) across the confluence of the Lú and Tàchōng Rivers is 5km from the western edge of town. One of the 10 oldest in China, the bridge features 17 arches, so many that it took two periods of the Qing dynasty to complete the project. To get there, take minibus 4 from Jiànshuǐ's second bus station (¥2). Note that you have to ask the driver to tell you where to get off and then point you in the right direction. Bus 4 continues to **Huánglóng Sì** (黄龙寺), a small temple.

Yuányáng Rice Terraces   元阳梯田

☑ 0873 / POP 22,700

Picture hilltop villages, the only things visible above rolling fog and cloud banks, an artist's palette of colours at sunrise and sunset, spirit-recharging treks through centuries-old rice-covered hills, with a few water buffalo eyeing you contentedly nearby. Yes, it's hard not to become indulgent when describing these *tītián* (rice terraces), hewn from the rolling topography by the Hani throughout the centuries. They cover roughly 12,500 hectares and are one of Yúnnán's most stunning sights.

Yuányáng is actually split into two: Nánshā, the new town, and Xīnjiē, the old town an hour's bus ride up a nearby hill. Either can be labelled Yuányáng, depending on what map you use. Xīnjiē is the one you want, so make sure you get off there.

XĪNJIĒ   新街

Xīnjiē is a bit grubby, but it's a very friendly place and easy to use as a base of operations. The bus station is a minute's walk from Titian Sq, the town's hub.

◎ Sights & Activities

The terraces around dozens of outlying villages have their own special characteristics, often changing with the daylight. Bilingual maps are available at all hotels in town. Bear in mind that the *tītián* are at their most extraordinary in winter when they are flooded with water which the light bounces off in spectacular fashion.

Duōyīshù (多依树), about 25km from Xīnjiē, has the most awesome sunrises and is the one you should not miss. **Quánfúzhuāng** (全福庄) is a less-crowded alternative and has easy access down to the terraces. For sunsets, **Bádá** (八达) and **Měngpǐn** (勐品), also known as **Lǎohǔzuǐ** (老虎嘴), can be mesmerising.

Commercialisation has come to the *tītián* and there are now charges for the most popular spots. A combined ¥60 ticket gets you to Duōyīshù, Bádá and Quánfúzhuāng. For Měngpǐn/Lǎohǔzuǐ, the entrance fee is ¥30.

Buses run to all the villages from the bus station, but you are much better off arranging your own transport, or hooking up with other travellers to split the cost of a sunrise-sunset drive. Minibuses and motorrickshaws congregate around the Yúntī Shùnjié Dàjiǔdiàn and on the street west of the bus station. Expect to pay ¥400 in peak season for a minibus. Less comfortable motorrickshaws can be got for ¥150 to ¥200.

Several **markets** are worth visiting; check with Window of Yuányáng for up-to-the-minute schedules.

⊨ Sleeping & Eating

There are a number of places surrounding the bus station where rooms can be found for ¥30 to ¥100, depending on the level of comfort you desire. There are restaurants surrounding Titian Sq. Try **Liù Jūn Fàndiàn** (六军饭店; dishes from ¥12; ☉8am-10pm), on the corner of the square closest to the bus station.

Yúntī Shùnjié Dàjiǔdiàn   HOTEL $$
(云梯顺捷大酒店; ☑562 4858; Xīnjiē; s/tr ¥198/268) Just off Titian Sq and a few minutes from the bus station, this place has clean, compact rooms. Discounts bring the price down to ¥100; a good deal.

Yuányáng Rice Terraces

Map Distances
Xīnjiē to Nánshā.................30km
Xīnjiē to Lóngshùbà...............4km
Xīnjiē to Qìngkǒu.................6km
Xīnjiē to Mēngpīn/Lǎohǔzuǐ.18km
Xīnjiē to Bádá..................16km
Xīnjiē to Duōyīshù...............25km

Sunny Guesthouse GUESTHOUSE $
(多依树阳光客栈; Duōyīshù Yángguāng Kèzhàn; 159 8737 1311; sunny_guesthouse@163.com; 10-/4-bed dm ¥30/40, d ¥80) This simple guesthouse has a collection of basic rooms with shared bathroom and shower. Dorm room walls are flimsy but some of the private rooms have excellent views. It has a good vibe and travellers eat together around a communal table. You'll need to wander through Duōyīshù's Pǔgāolǎo village a bit to find it.

Jacky's Guesthouse GUESTHOUSE $
(水云间客栈; Shuǐ Yún Jiān Kèzhàn; 135 2973 2170; jackyguesthouse@gmail.com; d ¥160) Located in the heart of Duōyīshù's Pǔgāolǎo village, this new guesthouse has eight double rooms all with private bathroom, most with excellent views of the terraces, but there are no dorms. Owner Jacky speaks English and runs daily walking tours for ¥300 to ¥400. Meals are ¥30.

ℹ Information

Agricultural Bank of China (中国农业银行; Zhōngguó Nóngyè Yínháng) Has an ATM that takes foreign cards. To find it, head down the stairs by the entrance to the Yúntī Shùnjié Dàjiǔdiàn and walk on for a couple of minutes; it's on the left-hand side.

Internet cafe (山城网吧; wǎngbā; per hr ¥2.50-3; 24hr) There are places close to the bus station and on Titian Sq near the Yúntī Shùnjié Dàjiǔdiàn.

Window of Yuányáng (562 3627; www.windowofyuanyang.com; @) Do visit this place, down the steps from the main square (on the 2nd floor of a building on your right). Staff here work in sustainable economic development in local villages. Volunteers are very friendly and helpful. Great locally produced items are here, too (not to mention coffee!).

ℹ Getting There & Away

There are three buses daily from Kūnmíng to Yuányáng (¥136, seven hours, three daily at 9am, 4.30pm and 6.30pm); these return at 10.20am, 7.30pm and 8.20pm. Other destinations include Hékǒu (¥64, four hours) at 7.30am and 10.10am.

You could forge on to Xīshuāngbǎnnà by taking the 7.30am bus to Lǜchūn (¥39, four hours), where you'll pray to get the Jiāngchéng bus at noon (¥36, five hours). If you miss it, try for a Sīmáo bus. By the time you arrive in Jiāngchéng, there'll be no more buses for the day, but you can stay the night and buses to Jǐnghóng (¥54, 8½ hours) start running at 6am.

Alternatively, backtrack to Jiànshuǐ (¥41, four hours, six daily from 10.20am to 4.30pm) and catch the twice-daily Jǐnghóng sleepers (¥177, 12 to 17 hours, 1.30pm and 4.30pm) from there.

From Xīnjiē, local buses leave when full to Duōyīshù's Pǔgāolǎo village for around ¥20.

Xiàguān 下关

0872 / POP 158,000

Xiàguān, an easy-going city on the southwest shore of Ěrhǎi Hú (Erhai Lake), serves as a transport hub for travellers headed to Dàlǐ, a few kilometres further up the highway. Confusingly, Xiàguān is sometimes referred to as Dàlǐ (大理) on tickets, maps and buses.

There is no reason to stay in Xiàguān and you only need to come here in order to catch a bus or train.

ℹ Information

Bank of China (Zhōngguó Yínháng; Jianshe Donglu) Changes money and travellers cheques, and has an ATM that accepts all major credit cards.

Public Security Bureau (PSB; 公安局; Gōng'ānjú; 214 2149; Tai'an Lu; 8-11am & 2-5pm Mon-Fri) Handles all visa extensions for Xiàguān and Dàlǐ. Take bus 8 from Dàlǐ and ask to get off at the Shi Ji Middle School (世纪中学; Shìjì Zhōngxué).

ℹ Getting There & Away

AIR Xiàguān's airport is 15km from the town centre. Buy air tickets online or at an agency in Old Dàlǐ. No public buses run to the airport; taxis will cost ¥50 from Xiàguān or ¥100 from Dàlǐ. Three flights daily leave for Kūnmíng (¥760) and one or two to Xīshuāngbǎnnà (¥990).

BUS Xiàguān has five bus stations which can confuse things. The Dàlǐ express bus station (kuàisù kèyùnzhàn) is on Nan Jian Lu. The second main station used by travellers is Xīngshèng bus station (also called gāo kuài kèyùnzhàn), located down the road from the express bus station. To find it, walk out of the express bus station, turn right and walk downhill, cross the big intersection to Xingsheng Lu and walk for 100m. The third station of interest is the north bus station (běi kèyùnzhàn) on Dali Lu, which is reached by bus 8 (¥2) or a ¥10 taxi ride.

Remember that when departing, the easiest way to Kūnmíng or Lìjiāng is to get a bus from Old Dàlǐ (see p654). The following departures are from the Dàlǐ express bus station (kuàisù kèyùnzhàn):

Chǔxióng ¥67, 2½ hours, every 30 minutes (7am and 6.40pm)

Kūnmíng ¥103–148, five hours, every 30 minutes (7.45am to 6pm)

Liùkù ¥72–96, five hours, six buses (7.40am to 3pm)

Ruìlì ¥192, eight hours, two buses (8.30am and 8.30pm)

The following departures are from the Xīngshèng bus station (gāo kuài kèyùnzhàn):

Bǎoshān ¥65, 2½ hours, every 40 minutes (7.50am to 7.20pm)

Jǐnghóng ¥200, 16 hours, two daily (9am and 11am)

Kūnmíng ¥146–148, five hours, every 30 minutes (7.20am to 7.30pm)

Lìjiāng ¥53–79, three hours, five daily (9.20am, 10am, 1.30pm, 4.30pm and 7pm)

Mángshì (Lùxī) ¥116, six to eight hours, one daily (8pm)

Téngchōng ¥128, six hours, three daily (10am, 1pm and 8pm)

Yúnlóng (Nuòdèng) ¥42, three hours, seven daily (7.30am to 11.30am)

Departures from the north bus station (běi kèyùnzhàn) include:

Jiànchuān (for Shāxī) ¥45, three hours, every 30 minutes (8am to 3.30pm)

Shangri-la ¥84, eight hours, every 30 minutes (6.30am to noon)

If you want to head to Wēishān, you must go to the southwest bus station (xī nán kèyùnzhàn). For destinations on the east side of the lake such as Shuānglàng and Wāsè, head to the east bus station next to the train station.

Buses to Old Dàlǐ (¥3, 35 minutes) leave from outside the Xīngshèng bus station. Bus 8 (¥3, 35 minutes) runs from the train station to the centre of Xiàguān to Dàlǐ's West Gate. If you want to be sure, ask for Dàlǐ gǔchéng (Dali old city).

Tickets for nearly all destinations can be booked in Dàlǐ and this is often the easiest way

to do it as it will save you a trip to Xiàguān (although you will pay a small service fee).

TRAIN There are four trains from Kūnmíng's main train station at 8.30am, 10am, 11.10pm and 11.40pm, arriving in Xiàguān about seven hours later. Returning to Kūnmíng, trains leave Xiàguān (hard seat/sleeper, ¥65/89) at 8.46am, 10.42am, 9.22pm and 9.49pm. There are two trains daily to Lìjiāng (¥35, two hours) at 9.16am and 4.55pm.

Wēishān 巍山

☑0872 / POP 20,700

Some 55km or so south of Xiàguān, Wēishān is the heart of a region populated by Hui and Yi. It was once the nucleus of the powerful Nanzhao kingdom, and from here the Hui rebel Du Wenxiu led an army in revolt against the Qing in the 19th century. Today, it's an attractive small town of narrow streets lined with wooden houses, with drum towers at strategic points and a lovely backdrop of the surrounding hills.

The town's central point is the unmistakable **Gǒngcháng Lóu** (拱长楼; Gǒngcháng Tower). South from Gǒngcháng Lóu you'll come to **Mēnghuà Old Home** (蒙化老家; Mēnghuà Lǎojiā; admission ¥8; ⏱8am-9pm), the town's best-preserved slice of architecture.

Línyè Bīnguǎn (林业宾馆; ☑612 0761; 24 Xi Xin Jie; 西新街24号; s & d ¥60-80; ⌖) is a hop, skip and a jump from Gǒngcháng Lóu and has big, newly decorated rooms. It's a ¥5 ride from the bus station in a motor-rickshaw.

The only restaurants in the town are cubbyhole eateries. Head north or south of Gǒngcháng Lóu to find most of them. You may see people indulging in a local Yi speciality, baked tea.

Xiàguān's south bus station has buses (¥16, 1½ hours) to Wēishān from 6am to 6pm.

Wēibǎo Shān 巍宝山

Eminently worthy **Wēibǎo Shān** (Wēibǎo Mountain; admission ¥60), about 10km south of Wēishān, has a relatively easy hike to its peak at around 2500m. During the Ming and Qing dynasties it was the zenith of China's Taoism, and you'll find some superb Taoist murals; the most significant are at **Wénchāng Gōng** (文昌宫; Wénchāng Palace; No 3 on the entrance ticket) and **Chángchún Cave** (长春洞; Chángchún Dòng; No 1 on the entrance ticket). Birders in particular love the mountain; the entire county is a node on an international birding flyway.

There are no buses here. Head to the street running east of Gǒngcháng Lóu in Wēishān to pick up a microvan to the mountain. Expect to pay ¥60 for the round trip; you'll need the driver to wait for you.

Dàlǐ 大理

☑ 0872 / POP 40,000

Dàlǐ, the original funky banana-pancake backpacker hang-out in Yúnnán, was once *the* place to chill, with its stunning location sandwiched between mountains and Ěrhǎi Hú (Ěrhǎi Lake). Loafing here for a couple of weeks was an essential Yúnnán experience.

During the past decade the Chinese tourist market discovered Dàlǐ and the scene changed accordingly. Today, Chinese-style snack shops now outnumber the places slinging banana pancakes. Still, Dàlǐ has not succumbed to the tourist mania that infected nearby Lìjiāng and remains a reasonably relaxed destination, with the local population still a part of daily life.

Surrounding Dàlǐ there are fascinating possibilities for exploring, especially by bicycle and in the mountains above the lake, or you can do what travellers have done for years – eat, drink and be merry.

History

Dàlǐ lies on the western edge of Ěrhǎi Hú at an altitude of 1900m, with a backdrop of the imposing 4000m-tall Cāng Shān (Green Mountains). For much of the five centuries in which Yúnnán governed its own affairs, Dàlǐ was the centre of operations, and the old city retains a historical atmosphere that is hard to come by in other parts of China.

The main inhabitants of the region are the Bai, who number about 1.5 million and are thought to have settled the area some 3000 years ago. In the early 8th century they succeeded in defeating the Tang imperial army before establishing the Nanzhao kingdom, which lasted until the Mongol hordes arrived in the mid-13th century.

◉ Sights

Three Pagodas   HISTORIC SITES
(三塔寺; Sān Tǎ Sì; adult incl Chongsheng Temple ¥121; ☉7am-7pm) Absolutely *the* symbol of the town/region, these pagodas 2km north of the north gate are among the oldest standing structures in southwestern China.

The tallest of the three, **Qiānxún Pagoda**, has 16 tiers that reach a height of 70m. It was originally erected in the mid-9th century by

engineers from Xī'ān. It is flanked by two smaller 10-tiered pagodas, each of which are 42m high. While the price is cheeky considering you can't go inside the pagodas, **Chóngshèng Temple** (Chóngshèng Sì) behind them has been restored and converted into a relatively worthy museum.

FREE Dàlǐ Museum   MUSEUM
(大理博物馆; Dàlǐ Shì Bówùguǎn; Fuxing Lu; ☉8.30am-5.30pm) The museum houses a small collection of archaeological pieces relating to Bai history, including some fine figurines. English descriptions are lacking.

Catholic Church   CHURCH
(off Renmin Lu) Also worth checking is Dàlǐ's Catholic Church. It dates back to 1927 and is a unique mix of Bai-style architecture and classic European church design. Mass is held here at 9am every Sunday.

🎊 Festivals & Events

Third Moon Fair   CULTURAL
Merrymaking – along with endless buying, selling and general horse-trading (but mostly merrymaking) – takes place during the third moon fair (*sānyuè jiē*), which begins on the 15th day of the third lunar month (usually April) and ends on the 21st day.

Three Temples Festival   CULTURAL
The three temples festival (*ràosān líng*) is held between the 23rd and 25th days of the fourth lunar month (usually May). The first day involves a trip from Dàlǐ's south gate to Sacred Fountainhead Temple (Shèngyuán Sì) in Xǐzhōu. Here travellers stay up until dawn, dancing and singing, before moving on to Jīnguì Temple (Jīnguì Sì) and returning by way of Mǎjiǔyì Temple (Mǎjiǔyì) on the final day.

Torch Festival   CULTURAL
The torch festival (*huǒbǎ jiē*) is held on the 24th day of the sixth lunar month (normally July) and is likely to be the best photo op in the province. Flaming torches are paraded at night through homes and fields. Locals throw pine resin at the torches causing minor explosions everywhere. According to one local guesthouse owner, 'it's total madness'.

🛏 Sleeping

There's heaps of accommodation in Dàlǐ, but the popular places often fill up quickly during peak summer months.

Dàlǐ

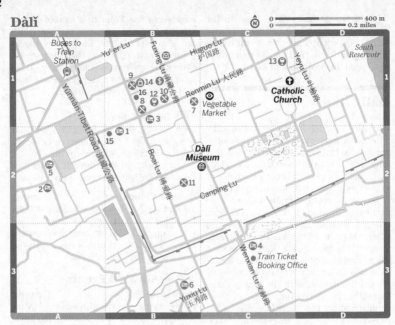

Dàlǐ

◉ Top Sights
Catholic Church C1
Dàlǐ Museum C2

🛏 Sleeping
1 Bird Bar & Nest B2
2 Five Elements A2
3 Four Seasons International
   Youth Hostel B1
4 Friends Guesthouse C3
5 Jade Emu A2
6 Jim's Tibetan Hotel B3

✖ Eating
7 Méi Zǐ Jǐng B1

8 Sweet Tooth B1
9 The Bakery No. 88 .... B1
10 The Good Panda B1
11 Yī Rán Táng B2

🍷 Drinking
12 Bad Monkey B1
13 Daliba Vodka C1

🛍 Shopping
14 Mandarin Books & CDs B1

ⓘ Information
15 Climb Dali B2
16 Dàlǐ Bicycling Club B1

TOP CHOICE ▶ Jade Emu   HOSTEL **$**

(金玉缘中澳国际青年旅舍; Jīnyùyuán Zhōng'ào Guójì Qīngnián Lǚshè; ☑ 267 7311; http://jade-emu. com; West Gate Village; 西门村; dm without/with bathroom ¥25/30, s & d ¥130-160; @ 🛜) This Aussie-owned and run venture smack in the shadow of Cāng Shān (a five-minute walk from the old town) sets the standard for hostels in Dàlǐ. The staff here know what travellers want, the attention to detail is impressive and the rooms are clean and

well-maintained. This is also a good place to arrange bus tickets and tours at fair prices. Around the corner, sister establishment **Jade Roo** copes with the overflow of travellers, with similar but slightly cheaper rooms.

Five Elements   HOSTEL **$**

(五行国际客栈; Wǔ Xíng Guójì Kèzhàn; ☑ 130 9985 0360; www.5elementschina.com; West Gate Village; 西门村; dm ¥20-40, d without/with bathroom ¥80/100; @ 🛜) This place has a popular following with budget Western backpackers, thanks to the low prices and friendly vibe. Rooms are clean, if somewhat bland, and there is a nice courtyard and garden where the manager grows organic vegies. All manner of tours and services are available.

Four Seasons International Youth Hostel
HOSTEL $

(春夏秋冬国际青年旅舍; Chūn Xià Qiū Dōng Guójì Qīngnián Lǚshè; ☑138 8725 3949; yhafs@ yahoo.cn; 46 Boai Lu; 博爱路46号; dm ¥30-35, d ¥100-160; @🤶) Located in the heart of Dàlǐ, this hostel is just steps away from all kinds of facilities, cafes and restaurants. Rooms are clean and well-maintained but avoid the ones overlooking the street as they can get noisy. Wi-fi is in the lobby and ADSL in the rooms.

Jim's Tibetan Hotel
HOTEL $$

(吉姆和平酒店; Jímǔ Hépíng Jiǔdiàn; ☑267 7824; www.china-travel.nl; 13 Yuxiu Lu; 玉秀路13 号; d ¥300, tr ¥400; @🤶) The rooms here are the most distinctive in Dàlǐ, packed with antique Chinese-style furniture and managing to be both stylish and cosy. The bathrooms too are a cut above the competition. There's a garden, rooftop terrace, restaurant and bar. Travel services and tours can be booked.

Bird Bar & Nest
HOTEL $

(鸟吧鸟窝; Niǎobā Niǎowō; ☑266 1843; www.bird bardali.com; 22 Renmin Lu; 人民路22号; s with shared bathroom ¥80, d ¥130-280; @🤶) Set around an attractive tree- and plant-filled garden, the handful of rooms here attract a good mix of local and foreign travellers, as well as vacationing Kūnmíng expats. Rooms are spacious and the English-speaking staff is helpful.

Friends Guesthouse
GUESTHOUSE $

(大理古城三友客栈; Dàlǐ Gǔchéng Sānyǒu Kèzhàn; ☑266 2888; www.friendsdali.com; 2 Wenxian Lu; 文献路2号; dm ¥35, s & d ¥100; @🤶) The choice for budget digs in the old town, this place has always been super busy (and friendly) and has clean and comfortable facilities.

✗ Eating

Bai food makes use of local flora and fauna – many of which are unrecognisable! Province wide, ěr kuài (饵块) are flattened and toasted rice 'cakes' with an assortment of toppings (or plain). Rǔshàn (乳扇; 'milk fan') may not sound appetising, but this 'aired' yogurt/milk mixture (it ends up as a long, thin sheet) is a local speciality and is often fried or melted atop other foods. This is distinct from rǔbǐng (goat's cheese). Given Ěrhǎi Hú's proximity, try shāguō yú (沙锅鱼), a claypot fish casserole/stew made from salted Ěrhǎi Hú carp – and, as a Bai touch, magnolia petals. Local tastes also ensure that when ordering beef the fat-to-meat ratio is typically 50–50.

TOP CHOICE The Good Panda
CHINESE YÚNNÁN $

(妙香园; 81 Renmin Lu; dishes from ¥6; ☉9am-10.30pm; 🍴) On a touristy street with mostly, Western-style restaurants, this small gem is a local favourite. It's a great place for classic local dishes like Dàlǐ-style sizzling beef (tiěbǎn niúròu) and crispy carp (jiànchuān gānshāo yú), plus Yúnnán and Sichuan meals. There's a limited English menu, but you can also point at the vegetables that look best. The patio is an excellent spot for people watching.

TOP CHOICE The Bakery No. 88
WESTERN $$

(88号西点店; Bāshíbā Hào Xīdiǎndiàn; 52 Boai Lu; dishes from ¥20; ☉8am-10pm; 🤶🍴) A clean, well-lit, smoke-free haven of tranquility with excellent sandwiches, pastas and soups all prepared with local produce. It's locally famous for its breads and cakes so don't leave town without trying some.

Méi Zi Jǐng
CHINESE YÚNNÁN $$

(梅子井; 130 Renmin Lu; dishes ¥15-40; ☉11am-9pm) This charmingly authentic Bai restaurant is composed of three grey-brick courtyards each containing small seating nooks where locals cram together and feast on traditional local cuisine. The nonsensical menu includes a few mystery dishes ('Sewing kit fried lily', anyone?), but the 'braised chicken' or 'wild mushroom' dishes are both fine starting points. It's tucked off Renmin Lu opposite the vegetable market.

Sweet Tooth
CAFE $

(甜point屋; Tiándiǎn Wū; 52 Boai Lu; dishes from ¥10; ☉8.30am-10.30pm; 🍴@) Owned and run by a culinary arts graduate, the homemade ice cream and desserts here are simply inspiring. There's also fine coffee and proper English tea. As an added bonus, profits from the cafe benefit the hearing impaired.

Yī Rán Táng
VEGETARIAN $

(一然堂; 20 Honglong Alley; dishes ¥5; ☉11.30am-1pm & 5.30-7pm; 🍴) An altruistic, Buddhist-inspired, all-vegetarian buffet where you pay ¥5 for a bowl of rice and whatever dishes the cooks have come up with on the day.

Drinking

The Western-style restaurants double as bars.

Daliba Vodka BAR
(大理巴; Dàlǐ Bā; 143 Renmin Lu; ⊙5.30pm-late)
Worth trying is this cool bar off the main strip, with a great selection of homemade flavoured vodkas, including Sichuan hotpot!

Bad Monkey BAR
(坏猴子; Huài Hóuzi; Renmin Lu; ⊙9am-late) The eternally happening, Brit-run, Bad Monkey brews its own beers in the nearby mountains, has regular live music and endless drink specials. The Monkey also serves good pub grub (burgers and shepherd's pie) and expats swear by the Sunday roast (7.30pm) for ¥45 (including a glass of wine).

Shopping

Dàlǐ is famous for its marble blue and white batik printed on cotton and silk.

The centre of town has a profusion of clothes shops. Most shopkeepers can also make clothes to your specifications – which will come as a relief when you see how small some of the items of ready-made clothing are.

A few more-or-less useful maps (¥12) can be picked up at hostels and restaurants around town. You can also find them at **Mandarin Books & CDs** (五华书苑; Wǔhuá Shūyuàn; Huguo Lu), along with guidebooks and novels in Chinese, English, French and German.

Information

On hikes around Cāng Shān there have been several reports of robbery of solo walkers. On the overnight sleeper bus from Kūnmíng, a bag is often pinched or razored. Bags in the luggage hold are also not safe.

All hostels and many hotels offer travel advice, arrange tours and book tickets for onward travel. There are also numerous travel agencies and cafes that will book bus tickets and offer all manner of tours. They can be expensive unless you can get a group together.

Internet cafes can be found along all the main streets (¥2 to ¥2.50 per hour), but all hostels and hotels also offer internet access.

Bank of China (中国银行; Zhōngguó Yínháng; Fuxing Lu) Changes cash and travellers cheques, and has an ATM that accepts all major credit cards.

China Minority Travel (china-travel.nl) Henriette, a Dutch expat, can offer a long list of trips, including tours to Muslim markets and Yi minority markets as well as through remote areas of Yúnnán and overland travel to Lhasa from Shangri-la when it is allowed. Check her website for contact details.

Climb Dàlǐ (20 Renmin Lu; ☎131 5064 4701; info@climbdali.com) This outfit runs active adventures around Dàlǐ, including rock climbing, mountaineering, kayaking and rafting trips. It also has a bouldering wall, and a pizza/sandwich restaurant called Goodfellas. Contact Adam Kritzer.

China Post (中国邮政; Zhōngguó Yóuzhèng; cnr Fuxing Lu & Huguo Lu; ⊙8am-8pm)

Public Security Bureau (PSB; 公安局; Gōng'ānjú; ☎214 2149; Dàlǐ Rd, Xiàguān; ⊙8-11am & 2-5pm Mon-Fri) Visas cannot be renewed in Dàlǐ, so you'll have to head to Xiàguān (see p649 for Xiàguān PSB details).

Tibet Motorcycle Adventures (☎151 8499 9452; http://tibetmoto.com) Motorbikes can be rented for ¥250 per day including gas. If you get stuck they will send a car to pick you up. Contact Hendrik Heyne.

Getting There & Away

The golden rule: most buses advertised to Dàlǐ actually go to Xiàguān. Coming from Lìjiāng, Xiàguān-bound buses stop at the eastern end of Dàlǐ to let passengers off before continuing on to the north bus station.

From Kūnmíng's west bus station there are numerous buses to Dàlǐ (¥103 to ¥142, four to five hours, every 20 minutes from 7.30am to 7.30pm). Heading north, it's easiest to pick up a bus on the roads outside the west or east gates; buy your ticket in advance from your guesthouse or a travel agent and they'll make sure you get on the right one. (You could hail one yourself to save a surcharge but you're not guaranteed a seat.)

From the old town (near West Gate Village) you can catch a 30-seat bus to Kūnmíng for ¥110, it runs three or four times a day, departing 9am, 10.30am, 11.30am, 1.30pm and 4.30pm.

Buses run regularly to Shāpíng (¥12), Xǐzhōu (¥10) and other local destinations from outside the west gate.

An official train ticket booking office is located outside the south gate (close to Friends Guesthouse) at 12 Wenxian Lu.

Getting Around

From Dàlǐ, a taxi to Xiàguān airport takes 45 minutes and costs around ¥100; to Xiàguān's train station it costs ¥50.

Bikes are the best way to get around (¥20 to ¥40 per day). Try **Dàlǐ Bicycle Club** (41 Boai Lu; ⊙7.30am-8pm), which has solid bikes and offers loads of other travel services.

Buses (¥2, 30 minutes, marked 大理) run between the old town and Xiàguān from as early as 6.30am; wait along the highway and flag one down. Bus 8 runs between Dàlǐ and central Xiàguān (¥2, 30 minutes) on the way to the train station every 15 minutes from 6.30am.

Around Dàlǐ

Travellers have a **market** to go to nearly every day of the week. Every Monday at **Shāpíng** (沙坪), about 30km north of Dàlǐ, there is a colourful Bai market (Shāpíng Gǎnjí). From 10am to 2.30pm you can buy everything from food products and clothing to jewellery and local batik.

Regular buses to Shāpíng (¥12, one hour) leave from just outside the west gate. By bike, it will take about two hours at a good clip.

Markets also take place in **Shuānglàng** (双廊; Tuesday), **Shābā** (沙巴; Wednesday), **Yòusuǒ** (右所; Friday morning, the largest in Yúnnán) and **Jiāngwěi** (江尾; Saturday). **Xīzhōu** (喜州) and **Zhōuchéng** (州城) have daily morning and afternoon markets, respectively. **Wāsè** (挖色) also has a popular market every five days with trading from 9am to 4.30pm. Thanks to the lack of boats, travellers now have to slog to Xiàguān's east bus station for buses to Wāsè.

Many cafes and hotels in Dàlǐ offer tours or can arrange transportation to these markets for around ¥150 for a half day.

ĚRHǍI HÚ   洱海湖

Ěrhǎi Hú (Ear-Shaped Lake) dominates the local psyche. The seventh-biggest freshwater lake in China, it sits at 1973m above sea level and covers 250 sq km; it's also dotted with trails perfect for bike rides and villages to visit. It's a 50-minute walk, a 15-minute bus ride or a 10-minute downhill zip on a bike from Dàlǐ.

Cáicūn (才村), a pleasant little village east of Dàlǐ (¥1 on bus 2), is the nexus of lake transport. Sadly, putt-putt local ferries are a distant memory. All boat travel is now on 'official' vessels. Expect to pay ¥150 for a three-hour trip. That said, ask around at cafes and guesthouses – something may turn up.

On the east side of the lake the beautiful lakeside town of **Shuānglàng** (双廊) is an increasingly popular destination in its own right. The town is a labyrinth of winding old alleys and traditional homes sitting on a little peninsula that juts into the lake. Just offshore is **Nanzhao Fēngqíng Dǎo** (南诏风

情岛; Nánzhào Customs Island), which has gardens, parks a 17.5m tall marble statue of Avalokiteshvara (Chenresig) aka Guanyin, and a hotel. Boats to the island cost ¥50, the price includes admission.

There are several guesthouses in the town, including the **Sky & Sea Lodge** (海地生活; Hǎidì Shēnghuó; ☎0872-246 1762; www.skysealodge.org; dm ¥30-40, d ¥100-280; ☎), with excellent lake views. You can't take a taxi here so you'll have to walk about 10–15 minutes through the village, ask locals to point the way. There is also a basic guesthouse on the island with beds for ¥60.

The other east side highlight, close to Wāsè, is **Pǔtuó Dǎo** (普陀岛; Pǔtuó Island) and **Lesser Pǔtuó Temple** (小普陀寺; Xiǎopǔtuó Sì), set on an extremely photogenic rocky outcrop.

Roads now encircle the lake so it is possible to do a loop (or partial loop) of the lake by mountain bike. A new bike path goes from Cáicūn to Tǎo Yuán Port, which makes

Dàlǐ & Ěrhǎi Hú

a great day trip (but most travellers turn around at Xīzhōu). Some hard-core cyclists continue right around the lake (the full loop is around 98km). The lack of boats means you're looking at an overnight stay or an extremely long ride in one day.

CĀNG SHĀN 苍山

This range of gorgeous peaks rises imposingly above Dàlǐ and offers the best legwork in the area. Most travellers head first for **Zhōnghé Temple** (中和寺; Zhōnghé Sì), on the side of **Zhōnghé Shān** (中和山; Zhōnghé Mountain; admission ¥30; ⊙8am-6pm). At the temple, be careful of imposter monks passing out incense and then demanding ¥200 for a blessing.

You can hike up the mountain, a sweaty two to three hours for those in moderately good shape (but note the warning that there have been several reports of robbery of solo walkers). Walk about 200m north of the old chairlift base (no longer working) to the riverbed (often dry). Follow the left bank for about 50m and walk through the cemetery, then follow the path zigzagging under the chairlift. When you reach some stone steps, you know you are near the top. This is but one of several paths to the temple.

Branching out from either side of Zhōnghé Temple is a trail that winds along the face of the mountains, taking you in and out of steep, lush valleys and past streams and waterfalls. From the temple, it's a nice 11km walk south to **Gǎntōng Temple** (感通寺; Gǎntōng Sì), **Qīngbì Stream** (清碧溪; Qīngbì Xī) and/or **Guānyīn Pavilion** (观音堂; Guānyīn Táng), from where you can continue to the road and pick up a Dàlǐ-bound bus. The path, called **Jade Belt Road** (玉带路; Yùdài Lù), is paved and easily walkable.

There's also a **cable car** (one way/return ¥50/80) between Qīngbì Stream and Gǎntōng Temple.

Alternatively, take the new **cable car** (return ¥230) up to the **Horse Washing Pond** (洗马潭; Xǐ Mǎ Tán), high in the mountain range, where Kublai Khan set up his base in the late 13th century.

You can loaf in basic luxury at 2950m near Zhōnghé Temple at **Higherland Inn** (高地旅馆; Gāodì Lǚguǎn; ☑266 1599; www.higherland.com; dm ¥30, d ¥80-120). If you want to get away from the crowds in Dàlǐ, this is the place to do it. The hostel has fabulous views, regular barbecues and only a handful of rooms, which means it's an incredibly relaxing place to stay.

XĪZHŌU 喜洲

A trip to the old town of Xīzhōu for a look at its well-preserved Bai architecture is lovely. You can catch a local bus from the west gate in Dàlǐ (¥10) or take a taxi (¥60) to make the 18km trip, but a bicycle trip with an overnight stop in Xīzhōu (there's accommodation in town) is also a good idea.

The best place to stay is the American-run **Linden Centre** (喜林苑; Xǐ Lín Yuàn; ☑0872-245 2988; www.linden-centre.com; d/ste incl breakfast ¥980/1480; @� a traditional Chinese style home turned boutique hotel with 14 rooms, each decked out in antique furniture and modern bathrooms. There are fine views of the surrounding fields from the upper floors. The hotel runs walking tours (per person ¥150) of the village.

From here, the interesting town of **Zhōuchéng** (州城) is 7km further north; it too has basic accommodation.

Nuòdèng 诺邓

☑0872

This anachronistic hamlet, oft-lauded as the 'thousand-year-old' village, has one of the highest concentrations of Bai in Yúnnán and some of the best preserved buildings in the entire province. Off the main tourist routes, Nuòdèng has managed to preserve traditional village life, with ponies and donkeys clomping up the steep flagstone streets past traditional mud-brick buildings with ornate gates, many of which date back to the Ming and Qing dynasties. Nuòdèng's economy was once based on the salt trade and was part of the old Tea Horse trail that stretched from Tibet to Burma.

⊙ Sights

After crossing the bridge at the bottom of the village you'll see one of the original **salt wells**, located inside a wooden shed. The town is built upon a steep hill and winding up through the alleys you'll reach an impressive **Confucian Temple** (孔庙; Kǒng Miào), which today serves as the village primary school (check out the detailed frescoes still visible on the ceiling). Further uphill is the picturesque 16th-century **Yuhuang Pavillion** (玉皇阁; Yùhuáng Gé).

Village life is centred on the small market square; a good place to catch some sun and gab with the local elders. Wandering around you'll likely be invited into a few homes for tea, an opportunity you should not pass up.

On the way to Nuòdèng village from Yúnlóng, the **Bi River** is forced by the surrounding hills into a serpentine roll that from above looks remarkably like a yin-yang symbol, or **Tàijítú** (太极图). You won't notice this natural phenomenon from ground level; you need to go up to a viewing platform on the nearby hill. The road to the pavilion is 7km of endless switchbacks, a tedious and tiring hike, or you could hire a rickshaw to take you there for ¥20.

🛏 Sleeping & Eating

Fùjiǎ Liúfāngyuàn   INN **$**
(复甲留方苑; ☑552 5032; dm ¥15, d ¥50; @) A wonderful Bai courtyard guesthouse with a lush garden of bougainvillea. The pit toilets are a little basic but overall it's a friendly and comfortable place to stay. For an additional ¥5 the owners will show you around their personal museum of local artefacts. The guesthouse is your best bet for meals and you can eat dinner with the family for ¥15.

ℹ Getting There & Away

Buses (¥42, three to four hours, six daily from 7.30am to 11.30am) leave from Xiàguān's long-distance bus station to the county seat Yúnlóng (云龙), from where you can take a three-wheel rickshaw (¥15 to ¥20) the final 7km to Nuòdèng. Buses back to Xiàguān leave on a similar schedule, the final departure is at 3pm. Heading north, there is a daily bus (¥33, five to six hours, 8am) to Jiànchuān. For Liùkù there are six buses (¥52, four to five hours) between 7am and 1pm. Minibuses assemble near the bus station in Yúnlóng, with occasional departures (when full) to these destinations.

Shāxī   沙溪
☑0872

The tiny hamlet of Shāxī, 120km northwest of Dàlī, lies in a time warp, every step harkening back to the clippety-clop of horses' hooves and shouts of traders.

Shāxī was a crucial node on one of the old Tea-Horse Roads that stretched from Yúnnán to India. Only three caravan oases remain, Shāxī being the best preserved and the only one with a surviving market (held on Fridays).

The village's wooden houses, courtyards and narrow, winding streets make it a popular location for period Chinese movies and TV shows, but this is still a wonderfully sleepy place where nightlife means sitting out under the canopy of stars and listening to the frogs croaking in the rice paddies.

⊙ Sights

Sideng Jie (寺登街) is the ancient town street leading off the main road. It's about 300m downhill to the multifrescoed **Xìngjiào Sì** (兴教寺; Xìngjiào Temple), the only Ming-dynasty Bai Buddhist temple. It's currently used as an exhibit hall for town restoration projects but the city hopes to restore it as a functioning temple. On the opposite side of the courtyard is the **Three Terraced Pavilion** (魁星阁; Kuíxīnggé), which has a prominent theatrical **stage** (古戏台; gǔxìtái), something of a rarity in rural China. There is a small museum here, ask the guard at the temple for the key. The absolute highlight, however, is the **Ōuyáng Courtyard** (欧阳大院; Ōuyáng Dàyuàn), a superb example of three-in-one Bai folk architecture in which one wall protected three yards/residences. During the Ming-era, this was considered a 'five-star' hotel, it has exceptional wood carvings on the second floor. At the time of writing admission to sights in town were free (although this may change).

Exit the east gate and head south along the **Huì River** (惠江; Huì Jiāng) for five minutes, cross the ancient **Yùjīn Qiáo** (玉津桥; Yùjīn Bridge), and you're walking the same trail as the horse caravans. (If you look hard enough, you'll still be able to see hoofprints etched into the rock, or so the locals claim.)

Otherwise, the main activity around town is walking. The guesthouses in town have maps that can get you started and keep you busy for days.

🛏 Sleeping & Eating

A number of old courtyard homes on and off Sideng Jie have been converted into upmarket inns; there are also places offering beds from ¥20.

Some of the inns on Sideng Jie operate as cafes and restaurants, or try the hole-in-the-wall places on the village's main road.

Horsepen 46   INN **$**
(马圈46客栈; Mǎjuàn Sìshíliù Kèzhàn; ☑472 2299; www.horsepen46.com; 46 Sideng Jie; 寺登街46号; dm ¥25, r ¥60-120; @☎) This popular YHA-guesthouse has cute rooms of different sizes and shapes surrounding a sunny little courtyard. There's a laid-back traveller vibe here with folks lounging around, reading books and then eating dinner together at a communal table (¥20). The helpful English-speaking staff can organise hikes in the area, as well as rock climbing and kayaking.

Tea and Horse Caravan Trail Inn
INN $

(古道客栈; Gǔdào Kèzhàn; ☎472 1051; 83 Sideng Jie; 寺登街83号; s & d without/with bathroom ¥50/120) The cheap rooms at this friendly place are basic and clean, but the more expensive ones are a significant step up and come with comfy beds and big bathrooms, as well as being set around a pleasant garden area. Discounts of 30% available.

Old Theatre Inn
BOUTIQUE INN $$

(戏台会馆; Xìtái Huìguǎn; ☎472 2296; reservations @shaxichina.com; Duànjiādēng Village; 段家登; r incl breakfast ¥250; @🐾) This quaint boutique guesthouse has been fashioned out of a 200-year-old Chinese theatre and inn. It has been lovingly restored with modern rooms and a cafe that has retained the original flavour of the place. It's located 3km north of Shāxī, you can rent a bike here for ¥20 to get you around.

Karma Cafe
CAFE $

(卡玛聚; Kǎ Mǎ Jù; Sideng Jie; dishes from ¥12; ⏱8am-10pm; 📶) With a dash of old Shāxī atmosphere, this is a relaxing place to unwind after a long day. The menu offers decent Western meals and a few expensive Chinese and Tibetan dishes. The Western-style breakfast with French toast, eggs and yogurt is recommended.

Orange
CHINESE $

(桔子饭店; Júzi Fàndiàn; Xīn Chéng; ⏱7am-10.30pm; 📶) Located in the new town, this local favorite serves traditional Bai and Chinese cuisine. It's good for noodles and dumpling soup, or you can point at the vegies in the fridge and get a stir-fry.

ℹ Getting There & Away

From Jiànchuān, there are hourly buses (¥10, one hour) to/from Shāxī, or catch a shared minivan ride that also stops at Shíbǎo Shān. Moving on you'll have to go back to Jiànchuān. There are frequent buses to Dàlǐ (¥37) between 6.30am and 6pm. To Lìjiāng (¥21) there are buses at 8am, 9.30am, 11.30am, 1.30pm and 3.30pm. To Kūnmíng (¥157) they're at 9.30am and 6pm, and to Shangri-la (¥53) at 8.30am and 9.30am.

Shíbǎoshān   石宝山

Strewn with temples, old-growth cypress forest and waterfalls, Stone Treasure Mountain Grottoes (石宝山石窟; Shíbǎoshān Shíkū; admission ¥50; ⏱8.30am-5pm), a few kilometres north of Shāxī, makes for an excellent half-day trip.

From Shāxī you can head for Stone Bell Temple (石钟寺; Shízhōng Sì), which includes some of the best Bai stone carvings in southern China and offers insights into life at the Nanzhao court of the 9th century. (And some, er, rather racy sculptures of female genitalia.) It's possible to walk to Stone Bell Temple via Shādēng Village (沙登箐; Shādēng Qìng) in about three hours. To get there from Shāxī, walk 1.5km north, turn left at the sign (pointing to Shādēng Qìng) and

---

THE TEA-HORSE ROAD

Less well-known than the Silk Road, but equally important in terms of trade and the movement of ideas, people and religions, the Tea-Horse Road (茶马古道; Chámǎgǔdào) linked southwest China with India via Tibet. A series of caravan routes, rather than a single road, which also went through parts of Sìchuān, Burma, Laos and Nepal, the trails started deep in the jungle of Xīshuāngbǎnnà. They then headed north through Dàlǐ and Lìjiāng and into the thin air of the Himalayan mountains on the way to the Tibetan capital Lhasa, before turning south to India and Burma.

Although archaeological finds indicate that stretches of the different routes were in use thousands of years ago, the road really began life in the Tang dynasty (AD 618–907). An increased appetite for tea in Tibet led to an arrangement with the Chinese imperial court to barter Yúnnán tea for the prized horses ridden by Tibetan warriors. By the Song dynasty (AD 960–1279), 20,000 horses a year were coming down the road to China, while in 1661 alone some 1.5 million kilos of tea headed to Tibet.

Sugar and salt were also carried by the caravans of horses, mules and yaks. Buddhist monks, Christian missionaries and foreign armies utilised the trails as well to move between Burma, India and China. In the 18th century the Chinese stopped trading for Tibetan horses and the road went into a slow decline. Its final glory days came during WWII, when it was a vital conduit for supplies from India for the allied troops fighting the Japanese in China. The advent of peace and the communist takeover of 1949 put an end to the road.

walk another 1km to the foot of the mountain. The path up the mountain is obvious, there are several temples, grottoes and stone carvings between the village and Stone Bell Temple.

On the far side of Shíbǎo Shān (12km from Stone Bell) is the impressive **Bǎoxiāng Temple** (宝相寺; Bǎoxiāng Sì), a dramatic temple complex built into the side of a cliff constructed during the Song dynasty. Bǎoxiāng Temple is best visited by car from Shāxī, a taxi will cost ¥150. The road to Bǎoxiāng goes through the main gate of the Shíbǎo Shān park, where you will have to buy a ticket. From the gate to the temple is 6km. Note that if you just walk to Stone Bell from Shāxī you won't go through the main gate but you can buy an 'unofficial' ticket for around ¥25 (you may need to bargain).

NORTHWEST YÚNNÁN

Lìjiāng 丽江

☑ 0888 / POP (OLD TOWN) 40,000

How popular is this timelocked, if touristified, place? Lìjiāng's maze of cobbled streets, rickety (or rickety-looking, given gentrification) wooden buildings and gushing canals suck in around *five million* people a year. So thick are the crowds in the narrow alleys that most days it can feel like all five million have arrived at once.

But remember the 80/20 rule: 80% of the tourists will be in 20% of the places. Get up early enough and more often than not you'll avoid the crowds. And when they do appear, that's the cue to hop on a bike and cycle out to one of the nearby villages.

A Unesco World Heritage site since 1997, Lìjiāng is a city of two halves: the old town and the very different and modern new town. The old town is where you'll be spending your time and it's a jumble of lanes that twist and turn. If you get lost (and most do), head upstream and you'll make your way back to the main square.

◉ Sights

Note that a ¥80 'protection fee' is sold at most guesthouses and provides free entry to Black Dragon Pool. Proof of payment of this fee is required at some other sites, such as Jade Dragon Snow Mountain.

Old Town HISTORIC AREA

The old town (古城) is dissected by a web of arterylike canals that once brought the city's drinking water from Yuquan Spring, in what is now Black Dragon Pool Park. Several wells and pools are still in use around town (but hard to find). Where there are three pools, these were designated into pools for drinking, washing clothes and washing vegetables. A famous example of these is the **White Horse Dragon Pool** (白马龙潭; Báimǎlóng Tán; ⏲7am-10pm) in the deep south of the old town, where you can still see the odd local washing their vegies after buying them in the market.

The focus of the old town is the busy **Old Market Square** (四方街; Sìfāng Jiē). Once the haunt of Naxi traders, they've long since made way for tacky souvenir stalls. However, the view up the hill and the surrounding lanes are still extraordinary.

Now acting as sentinel of sorts for the town, the **Looking at the Past Pavillion** (望古楼; Wànggǔ Lóu; admission ¥15; ⏲7am-9pm) has a unique design using dozens of four-storey pillars – culled from northern Yúnnán old-growth forests.

A must-see is **Zhongyi Market** (忠义市场; Zhōngyì Shìchǎng; ⏲6am-5pm) where locals sell produce, copper items and livestock. If you are craving a slice of old Lìjiāng this is where you'll find it.

Black Dragon Pool Park SCENIC AREA

(黑龙潭公园; Hēilóngtán Gōngyuán; Xin Dajie; admission free with ¥80 town entrance ticket; ⏲7am-8.30pm) On the northern edge of town is the Black Dragon Pool Park; its view of Yùlóng Xuěshān (Jade Dragon Snow Mountain) is the most obligatory photo shoot in southwestern China. The **Dōngbā Research Institute** (东巴文化研究室; Dōngbā Wénhuà Yánjiūshì; ⏲8am-5pm Mon-Fri) is part of a renovated complex on the hillside here. You can see Naxi cultural artefacts and scrolls featuring a unique pictograph script.

Trails lead up **Xiàng Shān** (Elephant Hill) to a dilapidated gazebo and then across a spiny ridge past a communications centre and back down the other side, making a nice morning hike, but note the warning on p663.

The **Museum of Naxi Dongba Culture** (纳西东巴文化博物馆; Nàxī Dōngbā Wénhuà Bówùguǎn; admission free; ⏲9am-5pm) is at the park's northern entrance and is a decent introduction to traditional Naxi lifestyle and religion, complete with good English captions.

YÚNNÁN LÌJIĀNG

Lìjiāng

400 m
0.2 miles

See Enlargement

To Panba
Hostel
(200m)

Jinhong Lu

Chongren Xiang

Wuyi Jie

OLD TOWN

Qiyi Jie

Mao Square

Buses to Yùlóng
Xuěshān

Yuyuan Lu

Waterwheel

Xin Dajie

Yu
River

Dong Dajie

Xinhua Jie

**Mu Family
Mansion**

Main entrance
to the Old Town

Belief
Supermarket

Bus 6 to
Baisha
village

Minzu Lu 民主路

**Looking at
the Past
Pavilion**

Shīzi Shān
(Lion Hill)

**White Horse
Dragon Pool**

1

3

Fuhui Lu 福慧路

Shangri-la Dadao

To Long-Distance
Bus Station (600m)

NEW TOWN

200 m
0.1 miles

Express Bus
Station

CAAC

Jinhong Lu

**OLD
TOWN**

Wenzhi Xiang

15

14

16

2

6

7

Chongren Xiang

Wuyi Jie

8

5

9

Xinyi Jie

10

Jishan Xiang

11

Mishi Xiang

17

12

13

Xinhua Jie

Dong Dajie

Yu River

Xinhua Jie

**Old Market
Square**

Qiyi Jie 七一街

0   200 m
0   0.1 miles

Lìjiāng

◎ **Top Sights**
Looking at the Past
Pavilion..E3
Mu Family Mansion...............................F4
Old Market Square................................F3
White Horse Dragon Pool....................E4

◎ **Sights**
1 Zhongyi Market.................................E4

⌂ **Sleeping**
2 Blossom Hill......................................C3
3 Crowne Plaza Lijiang E4
4 Garden Inn G2
5 Lijiang International Youth
Hostel B3
6 Mama Naxi's Guesthouse 1...............C3

7 Mama Naxi's Guesthouse 3.................C4
8 Zen Garden Hotel B3

⊗ **Eating**
9 Ama Yi Naxi Snacks B3
10 Lamu's House of Tibet.......................A2
11 N's Kitchen A3
12 Prague Coffee A3
13 Sakura Good Food Square..................A3
14 Tiān Hé Cāntīng C3

◎ **Drinking**
15 Freshnam C3
16 Stone The Crows................................C3

◎ **Entertainment**
17 Naxi Orchestra.....................................A3

Note that the pool has dried up in recent years and without water some visitors are disappointed with this site; ask at your guesthouse first if the pool has water before deciding whether or not to visit.

Mu Family Mansion   HISTORIC SITE
(木氏土府; Mùshì Tǔsǐfǔ; admission ¥60; ◎8.30am-5.30pm) The former home of a Naxi chieftain, the Mu Family Mansion was heavily renovated (more like built from scratch) after the devastating earthquake that struck Lìjiāng in 1996. Mediocre captions do a poor job of introducing the Mu family but many travellers find the beautiful grounds reason enough to visit.

✯✯ Festivals & Events

Fertility Festival   FERTILITY
The 13th day of the third moon (late March or early April) is the traditional day to hold this festival.

Torch Festival   FIRE
July brings the torch festival (Huǒbǎ Jié), also celebrated by the Bai in the Dàlǐ region and the Yi all over the southwest. The origin of this festival can be traced back to the intrigues of the Nanzhao kingdom, when the wife of a man burned to death by the king eluded the romantic entreaties of the monarch by leaping into a fire.

⌂ Sleeping

Throw a stick and you'll hit a Naxi guesthouse in the old town. There are well over a thousand places to stay in the old city, with more appearing all the time. Most have less that 10 rooms. In peak seasons (especially holidays), prices double (or more).

TOP CHOICE Blossom Hill   BOUTIQUE HOTEL $$$
(花间堂客栈; Huājiān Táng Kèzhàn; ☑516 9709; www.blossomhillinn.com; 97 Wenzhi Xiang; 文治巷97号; d ¥480-580, ste ¥800; @?) A lovingly restored boutique inn with classic decor that befits this World Heritage city. Rooms come with handcrafted wood furnishings, antiques and artistic touches like flowers floating in water-filled brass bowls. The large, modern bathrooms with wooden tubs are superb and common areas include a little library and a movie room. A sophisticated Italian restaurant is attached to the inn.

TOP CHOICE Garden Inn   GUESTHOUSE $
(紫藤花园客栈; Zǐténg Huāyuán Kèzhàn; ☑151 0887 3494; 7 Wenming Xiang, Wuyi Jie, Yishang; 义尚村五一街文明巷7号; dm ¥30, s & d ¥100-150; @?) This popular backpacker hangout has a collection of bright and airy rooms, some with nice views of the city. There's a big lounge where you can try Western or Chinese meals, and a sunny outdoor area where travellers gather throughout the day. The inn has a friendly and knowledgeable English-speaking staff, DIY laundry and does tour bookings.

Panba Guesthouse   HOSTEL $
(潘巴家院青年旅舍; Pānbā Jiāyuán Qīngnián Lǚshè; ☑511 9077; panba.hostel@gmail.com; 63 Wenming Xiang, Wuyi Jie, Yishang; 义尚村五一街文明巷63号; dm ¥35-45, r ¥140; @?) At the

KEEPING THE GOOD FORTUNE

An interesting local historical tidbit has it that the original Naxi chieftain, whose former home is the Mu Family Mansion, would not allow the old town to be girdled by a city wall because drawing a box around the Chinese character of his family name would change the character from *mù* (wood) to *kún* (surrounded, or hard pressed).

quiet eastern end of Wuyi Jie, this increasingly popular place is a 15-minute walk from the centre of the old town – a good distance from the tour group madness. The rooms are a decent size and come with shared balconies and modern bathrooms, while the solicitous staff get rave reviews. Book ahead.

Zen Garden Hotel HOTEL $$$
(瑞和园酒店; Ruìhé Yuán Jiǔdiàn; ☑518 9799; www.zengardenhotel.com; 36 Xingren Lane, Wuyi Jie; 五一街兴仁下段36号; d/ste ¥500/1200; @) As befits its name, this is a serene, hushed establishment. Run by a Naxi teacher and decorated with help from her artist brother, the furniture and design in the communal areas is tremendous, even if the rooms themselves are a little more functional than their price suggests.

Mama Naxi's Guesthouse GUESTHOUSE $
(古城香格韵客栈; Gǔchéng Xiānggéyùn Kèzhàn; ☑510 7713; 70 Wangjia Zhuang Lane, Wuyi Jie; 五一街文化巷70号; dm ¥25-30, s & d ¥60-150; @ 🛜) The energetic Mama operates two guesthouses near each other, named '1' and '3' ('2' is in Dàlǐ). Head to '3' at 70 Wangjia Zhuang Lane for dorms, cramped but clean standard rooms, information-gathering, socialising and cheap eats. It's a bit loud when a Naxi wedding is taking place at the next-door wedding hall. '1', at 78 Wangjia Zhuang Lane (☑510 0700), is dorm-free and more peaceful.

Crowne Plaza Lijiang HOTEL $$$
(丽江和府假日酒店; Lìjiāng Héfǔ Jiàrì Jiǔdiàn; ☑558 8888; www.crowneplaza.cn; 276 Xianghe Lu; 祥和路276号; d from ¥1438; @ 🛜 ♒) The best hotel Lìjiāng can offer, a magical space with lofty ceilings, little gardens and epic views of the Jade Dragon Mountain. Other amenities include two restaurants (including a Brazilian barbecue), a swimming pool, day spa and children's play room.

Lijiang International Youth Hostel HOSTEL $
(丽江老谢车马店; Lìjiāng Lǎoxiè Chēmǎdiàn; ☑518 0124; 44 Mishi Xiang, Xinyi Jie; 新义街密士巷44号; dm ¥25, s & d ¥50-120, tr ¥150-180; @ 🛜) The dorms here are big (eight and 12 beds) and a bit run down, the rooms generic, but there's a great bar/communal area and the staff are helpful.

 ## Eating

There are many, many eateries around the old town, and almost every menu will have both Chinese and Western dishes.

Bābā is the Lìjiāng local speciality – thick flatbreads of wheat, served plain or stuffed with meat, vegetables or sweets. There are always several 'Naxi' items on menus, including the famous 'Naxi omelette' and 'Naxi sandwich' (goat's cheese, tomato and fried egg between two pieces of local *bābā*). Try locally produced *qīng méi jiǔ*, a plum-based wine with a 500-year history – it tastes like a decent semisweet sherry.

Sakura Good Food Square CHINESE YÚNNÁN $
(樱花美食广场; Yīnghuā Měishí Guǎngchǎng; Qiyi Jie; ⊙10am-late) Snackers should not miss the open-air food market where vendors sell appetising bite-size treats, some of which are native to Lìjiāng. Try the *Nàxī kǎo qiézi* (纳西烤茄子; Naxi grilled eggplant) served in a boat-shaped crust, *tǔ dòu bǐng* (土豆饼; Naxi potato pancake), and *Nàxī kǎolà cháng* (纳西烤腊肠; Naxi grilled, salty sausage) made with pork, fat and pepper. For dessert, try the delightful *Naxi nuomi tuán* (纳西糯米团) a sticky rice ball stuffed with either *hóngdòushā* (红豆沙; red bean), *shūcài* (蔬菜; vegetable) or *ròu* (肉; meat).

Ama Yi Naxi Snacks CHINESE YÚNNÁN $$
(阿妈意naxi饮食院; Āmāyì Nàxī Yǐnshí Yuàn; Wuyi Jie; dishes from ¥22; ⊙11am-9.30pm) The name doesn't do justice to the small but very authentic selection of Naxi cuisine on offer at this calm courtyard restaurant. There's fantastic mushroom dishes, as well as *zhútǒng fàn*, rice that comes packed in bamboo. It's down an alley off Wuyi Jie, close to the Stone Bridge.

Lamu's House of Tibet TIBETAN $$
(西藏屋西餐馆; Xīzàngwū Xīcāntīng; 56 Xinyi Jie; dishes from ¥20; ⊙7am-midnight; 🍴 🛜) Friendly Lamu has been serving up smiles and hearty Tibetan and international fare for more than a decade. Climb the little wooden staircase to the second floor dining area, a great spot for people watching, and try

the excellent Naxiburger, a pasta or steak. There's also a good selection of paperback books to thumb through.

Prague Coffee WESTERN, CHINESE YÚNNÁN $$
(布拉格咖啡; Bùlágé Kāfēi; 80 Mishi Xiang; dishes from ¥20; ⊙9am-11pm; 🖥🛜) Quaint Western-style cafe with a cosy upstairs nook, jazz music and a collection of English-language books and guidebooks for sale. The Western breakfasts, pastas and burgers are all good but they also do tasty Chinese, Japanese and even Naxi dishes (you can special order a Naxi goat cheese sandwich).

Tiān Hé Cāntīng CHINESE YÚNNÁN $
(天和餐厅; 139 Wuyi Jie; dishes from ¥10; ⊙7am-11pm) It's hard to find a neighbourhood-style restaurant in the old town, or one that doesn't also serve Western food, but this place hits the spot with a mix of Naxi dishes and Chinese staples like dumplings, hotpots and *gōng bǎo jī dīng*.

N's Kitchen WESTERN $$
(二楼小厨; Èrlóu Xiǎochú; 17 Jishan Xiang, Xinyi Jie; dishes from ¥22; ⊙9am-9pm; 🖥@🛜) Clamber up the steep stairs for one of the best breakfasts in town, a monster burger and a cheery welcome, although prices are slightly higher than most Western restaurants. It's a good source of travel info too and can arrange bus tickets.

🍷 Drinking

Xinhua Jie, just off Old Market Square, is packed out with Chinese-style drinking dens.

Freshnam BAR, CAFE
(119 Wuyi Jie; ⊙11am-late) Amenable to Western tastes is expat hang-out, Freshnam, a Korean-run bar-cafe that has nightly live music.

Stone the Crows BAR
(134-2 Wenzhi Xiang; ⊙7pm-late) Worth checking is the Irish-owned Stone the Crows, an endearingly ramshackle bar with cheap beers and good company. If you are walking east on Wuyi Jie it's one alley before Freshnam.

☆ Entertainment

Naxi Orchestra MUSIC
(纳西古乐会; Nàxī Gǔyuè Huì; Naxi Music Academy; tickets ¥120-160; ⊙performances 8pm) One of the few things you can do in the evening in Lìjiāng is attend performances of this orchestra inside a beautiful building in the old town. Not only are all two dozen or so members Naxi, but they play a type of Taoist temple music (known as *dòngjīng*) that has been lost elsewhere in China. The pieces they perform are said to be faithful renditions of music from the Han, Song and Tang dynasties, and are played on original instruments. Local historian of note Xuan Ke often speaks for the group at performances.

❶ Information

Crowded, narrow streets are a pickpocket's heaven. Solo women travellers have been mugged when walking alone at night in isolated areas of historic Lìjiāng. Xiàng Shān (Elephant Hill) in Black Dragon Pool Park (Hēilóngtán Gōngyuán) has been the site of quite a few robberies.

Lìjiāng's cafes and backpacker inns are your best source of information on the area. There are no internet cafes in the old town, but all hostels and hotels have internet access and/or wi-fi, as do virtually all the cafes in town.

There are also dozens of tour operators in the old town, but these cater to tour groups and they often tack on high service fees for booking tickets. Your best bet is to book trips through a guesthouse such as Garden Inn. You could also get in touch with Lìjiāng-based guide **Keith Lyons** (📞137 6900 1439; keithalyons@gmail.com), who runs tours in the area.

Bank of China (中国银行; Zhōngguó Yínháng; Yuyuan Lu; ⊙9am-5pm) This branch has an ATM and is convenient for the old town. There are other banks around town with ATMs too.

China Post (中国邮政; Zhōngguó Yóuzhèng; Minzhu Lu; ⊙8am-8pm) Offers EMS (Express Mail Service). Another post office is in the old town just north of Old Market Sq.

NAXI SCRIPT

The Naxi created a written language more than 1000 years ago using an extraordinary system of pictographs – the only hieroglyphic language still in use. The most famous Naxi text is the Dongba classic *Creation*, and ancient copies of it and other texts can still be found in Lìjiāng, as well as in the archives of some US universities. The Dongba were Naxi shamans who were caretakers of the written language and mediators between the Naxi and the spirit world. The Dongba religion, itself an offshoot of Tibet's pre-Buddhist Bon religion, eventually developed into an amalgam of Tibetan Buddhism, Islam and Taoism.

Useful phrases in the Naxi language are *nuar lala* (hello) and *jiu bai sai* (thank you).

THE NAXI

Lìjiāng has been the base of the 286,000-strong Naxi (纳西; also spelt Nakhi and Nahi) minority for about the last 1400 years. The Naxi descend from ethnically Tibetan Qiang tribes and lived until recently in matrilineal families. Since local rulers were always male it wasn't truly matriarchal, but women still seemed to run the show.

The Naxi matriarchs maintained their hold over the men with flexible arrangements for love affairs. The *azhu* (friend) system allowed a couple to become lovers without setting up joint residence. Both partners would continue to live in their respective homes; the boyfriend would spend the nights at his girlfriend's house but return to live and work at his mother's house during the day. Any children born to the couple belonged to the woman, who was responsible for bringing them up. The man provided support, but once the relationship was over, so was the support. Children lived with their mothers and no special effort was made to recognise paternity. Women inherited all property and disputes were adjudicated by female elders.

There are strong matriarchal influences in the Naxi language. Nouns enlarge their meaning when the word for 'female' is added; conversely, the addition of the word for 'male' will decrease the meaning. For example, 'stone' plus 'female' conveys the idea of a boulder; 'stone' plus 'male' conveys the idea of a pebble.

YÚNNÁN LÌJIĀNG

Public Security Bureau (PSB; 公安局; Gōng'ānjú; ☎518 8437; 110 Taihe Jie, Xianghelicheng District; ☺8.30-11.30am & 2.30-5.30pm Mon-Fri) Reputedly very speedy with visa extensions. Located on the west side of the Government Building. A taxi here will cost ¥15 from the city centre.

ⓘ Getting There & Away

Air

Lìjiāng's airport is 28km east of town. Tickets can be booked at **CAAC** (中国民航; Zhōngguó Mínháng; cnr Fuhui Lu & Shangrila Dadao; ☺8.30am-9pm). Most hotels in the Old Town also offer an air-ticket booking service.

From Lìjiāng there are oodles of daily flights to Kūnmíng (¥940), as well as daily flights to:

Běijīng ¥2410

Chéngdū ¥880

Chóngqìng ¥1000

Guǎngzhōu ¥1790

Shànghǎi ¥2430

Shēnzhèn ¥1630

Xīshuāngbǎnnà ¥1060

Bus

The **main long-distance bus station** (客运站; kèyùnzhàn) is south of the old town; to get there, take bus 8 or 11 (¥1; the latter is faster) from along Minzhu Lu.

Chéngdū ¥317, 24 hours, one daily (1pm)

Jiànchuān ¥22, two to three hours, seven daily (8.20am to 5.15pm)

Kūnmíng ¥170–190 (standard service), 10 hours, hourly (8am to 2.30pm); plus two night buses, ¥185, (both departing at 8.30pm).

There are also several 'super-express' buses, with wide seats and lunch included for ¥230.

Lúgū Hú ¥77, seven hours, two daily (8.30am and 9am)

Nínglàng ¥30, five hours, 14 daily (8am to 3.30pm)

Pānzhīhuā ¥100, eight hours, eight daily (7.10am to 4pm), change here for Chéngdū.

Qiáotóu ¥30, two hours, one daily (7.50am); Lìjiāng to Shangri-la buses also stop here.

Shangri-la ¥63–69, five hours, hourly (7.30am to 5pm)

Xiàguān ¥53–79, three hours, every 30 minutes (7.10am to 6.30pm)

Xīshuāngbǎnnà ¥276–333, 18 hours, one daily (7.30am)

In the north of town, the **express bus station** (高快客运站; gāo kuài kèyùnzhàn; Shangrila Dadao) is where many of the above buses originate, but it's usually more convenient to catch your bus from the long-distance bus station.

Train

There are two trains daily to Dàlǐ at 8.30am and 3.40am (¥35, two hours) and three trains to Kūnmíng (hard sleeper ¥142 to ¥152, soft sleeper ¥223 to ¥227, nine hours) at 8.30am, 8.50pm and 9.50pm. More trains are added in the high season.

ⓘ Getting Around

Buses to the airport (¥20) leave from outside the CAAC office 100 minutes before flight departures.

Taxis start at ¥7 in the new town and are not allowed into the old town. Bike hire is available at most hostels (¥30 per day).

Around Lìjiāng

It is possible to see most of Lìjiāng's environs on your own, but a few agencies offer half- or full-day tours, starting from ¥200, plus fees.

There are a number of monasteries around Lìjiāng, all Tibetan in origin and belonging to the Karmapa (Red Hat) sect. Most were extensively damaged during the Cultural Revolution and there's not much monastic activity nowadays.

Jade Peak Monastery (玉峰寺; Yùfēng Sì; admission ¥30) is on a hillside about 5km past Báishā. The last 3km of the track requires a steep climb. The monastery sits at the foot of Yùlóng Xuěshān (5500m) and was established in 1756. The monastery's main attraction nowadays is the **Camellia Tree of 10,000 Blossoms** (Wànduǒ Shānchá). Ten thousand might be something of an exaggeration, but locals claim that the tree produces at least 4000 blossoms between February and April. A monk on the grounds risked his life to keep the tree secretly watered during the Cultural Revolution.

Lìjiāng is also famed for its **temple frescoes**, most of which were painted during the 15th and 16th centuries by Tibetan, Naxi, Bai and Han artists; many were restored during the later Qing dynasty. They depict various Taoist, Chinese and Tibetan Buddhist themes and can be found on the interior walls of temples in the area. The Cultural Revolution did lots of ravaging here, keep in mind.

Frescoes can be found in Báishā and on the interior walls of **Dàjué Palace** (Dàjué Gōng) in the village of Lóngquán.

Báishā 白沙

Báishā is a small village on the plain north of Lìjiāng, near several old temples, and is one of the best day trips out of Lìjiāng, especially if you have a bike. Before Kublai Khan made it part of his Yuan empire (1271–1368), Báishā was the capital of the Naxi kingdom.

The 'star' attraction of Báishā is **Dr Ho Shi Xiu**, a legendary herbalist who was propelled to fame by the travel writer Bruce Chatwin when he mythologised him in a 1986 *New Yorker* story as the 'Taoist physician in the Jade Dragon Mountains of Lìjiāng'.

A sprightly 89 at the time of writing and still treating the ill every day with herbs collected from the nearby mountains, Dr Ho is very chatty (he speaks English, German and Japanese) and is happy to regale visitors with the secrets of good health and longevity.

Lìjiāng & Around

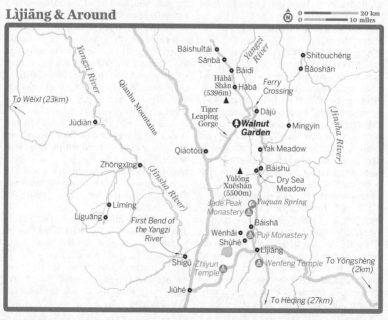

On the same street as Dr Ho you'll find a number of small cafes and restaurants including **Country Road Café** (Xiāng Cūn Lù; dishes from ¥12; ⏰7.30am-7.30pm; 🛜), a rustic cafe that makes Western, Chinese and Naxi dishes. The English-speaking owner Rosey can offer travel information.

The only place to stay in the village is **White Sand Inn** (百沙天净沙; Báishā tiānjìng shā; ☎531 8950; 31 Sān Yuán Cūn Yī Shè; 三元村一社31号; dm ¥35, r ¥140-180; 🛜) a well-maintained little guesthouse with an English-speaking owner.

There are a couple of frescoes worth seeing in town and the surrounding area. The best can be found in Báishā's **Dàbǎojī Palace** (大宝积宫; Dàbǎojī Gōng; admission ¥15; ⏰8.30am-5.30pm), and at the neighbouring **Liúlí Temple** (琉璃殿; Liúlí Diàn) and **Dàdìng Gé** (大定阁).

Báishā is a one-hour bike ride from Lìjiāng. Otherwise, take the No. 6 bus (¥1) from Minzhu Lu, near the pedestrian bridge. It returns to Lìjiāng regularly.

Shùhé Old Town 束河古城

More rustic and tranquil than Lìjiāng, Shùhé Old Town (Shùhé Gǔchéng) is attracting increasing numbers of travellers looking to escape the crowds. A former staging post on the Tea-Horse Road that's just 4km from Lìjiāng, Shùhé can be done as a day trip, or makes a tempting alternative base for exploring the region.

Although there's little in the way of sights, the cobblestoned alleys and streets south of its main square are very picturesque and much more peaceful at night than Lìjiāng. Head for the original section of town, which is sandwiched between the Jiùdǐng and Qīnglóng Rivers and nestles beneath the foothills of Yùlóng Xuěshān. The first part of town, identified by a large Chinese-style gate, is actually completely new (though it looks old), built for the purposes of tourism in the early 2000s (this section of town is actually owned by a private company).

The **K2 Hostel** (K2国际青年旅舍; K2 Guójì Qīngnián Lǚshè; ☎513 0110; www.k2yha.com; 1 Guailiu Xiang, Kangpu Lu; 康普路拐柳巷1号; dm ¥25-30, s & d ¥108-138; @) has become the go-to place in town. The dorms are a bit cramped but there is a big communal area and a friendly English-speaking staff. To get there, don't enter the town's main gate, but take the road to the right, which leads on to Kangpu Lu after five minutes. There are many other guesthouses, cafes and restaurants on and off Renlin Jie, the heart of the 'old town', and around the main square. For meals, try **Nomad Cafe** (卓尔巴; Zhuó ěrbā; ☎513 6627; nomad.lijiang@gmail.com; 35 Long Quan Lu; 龙泉路35号; dishes from ¥20; 🛜) an excellent vegetarian restaurant run by a Dutch cyclist. The cafe also has some reasonably plush rooms (¥85).

Getting to Shùhé is easy from Lìjiāng, with regular minibuses (¥2) running from the corner of Fuhui Lu and Shangri-la Dadao.

Yùlóng Xuěshān 玉龙雪山

Also known as Mt Satseto, **Yùlóng Xuěshān** (Jade Dragon Snow Mountain; adult ¥105, protection fee ¥80) soars to some 5500m. Its peak was first climbed in 1963 by a research team from Běijīng and now, at some 35km from Lìjiāng, it is regularly mobbed by hordes of Chinese tour groups and travellers.

Buses from Lìjiāng arrive at a parking area where you can purchase tickets for the various cable cars and chairlifts that ascend the mountain. This is also where the **Impression Lìjiāng** (admission ¥190-260; ⏰daily 1pm) show is held, a mega song-and-dance performance. Note that if you are going to the performance you will also have to pay the park admission fees. Close to the parking area is **Dry Sea Meadow** (干海子; Gānhǎizǐ), a good spot for photographing the mountain.

A cable car (¥172) ascends the mountain to an elevation of 4506m, from here you can walk up another 200m to a viewing point to see the glacier near the peak. It can often get chilly near the top so bring warm clothes. You will also have to pay ¥20 for the bus ticket to the base of the cable car.

Back down at the parking lot you can switch to a bus that goes to **Blue Moon Lake** (蓝月谷; Lányuè Gǔ) and **White Water River** (白水河; Bái Shuǐ Hé), where a walking trail leads along the river up to the lake (the round-trip walk takes about 90 minutes). The cable car bus ticket is also good for the bus to the lake.

A 10-minute drive past Blue Moon Lake is **Yak Meadow** (牦牛坪; Máoniúpíng), where a chairlift (¥60, plus ¥20 bus ticket) pulls visitors up to an altitude of 3500m.

In summer, when crowds for the cable car are long (up to two hours wait), most travellers just do the trip to the lake and Yak Meadow.

JOSEPH ROCK

Yúnnán has always been a hunting ground for famous, foreign plant-hunters such as Kingdon Ward and Joseph Rock (1884–1962). Rock lived in Lìjiāng between 1922 and 1949, becoming the world's leading expert on Naxi culture and local botany.

Born in Austria, the withdrawn autodidact taught himself eight languages, including Sanskrit. After becoming the world's foremost authority on Hawaiian flora, the US Department of Agriculture, Harvard University and later *National Geographic* (he was their famed 'man in China') sponsored Rock's trips to collect flora for medicinal research. He devoted much of his life to studying Naxi culture, which he feared was being extinguished by the dominant Han culture.

Rock sent more than 80,000 plant specimens from China – two were named after him – along with 1600 birds and 60 mammals. His caravans stretched for half a mile, and included dozens of servants, including a cook trained in Austrian cuisine, a portable darkroom, trains of pack horses, and hundreds of mercenaries for protection against bandits, not to mention the gold dinner service and collapsible bathtub.

Rock lived in Yùhú village (called Nguluko when he was there), outside Lìjiāng. Many of his possessions are now local family heirlooms.

The *Ancient Nakhi Kingdom of Southwest China* (1947) is Joseph Rock's definitive work. Immediately prior to his death, his Naxi dictionary was finally prepared for publishing.

Minibuses (¥20) leave from near the intersection of Minzhu Lu and Fuhui Lu in Lìjiāng. Returning to Lìjiāng, buses leave fairly regularly but check with your driver to find out what time the last bus will depart.

Tiger Leaping Gorge 虎跳峡
🎵 0887

Gingerly stepping along a trail swept with scree to allow an old fellow with a donkey to pass; resting atop a rock, exhausted, looking up to see the fading sunlight dance between snow-shrouded peaks, then down to see the lingering rays dancing on the rippling waters a thousand metres away; feeling utterly exhilarated. That pretty much sums up **Tiger Leaping Gorge** (Hǔtiào Xiá; admission ¥65), the unmissable trek of southwest China.

One of the deepest gorges in the world, it measures 16km long and is a giddy 3900m from the waters of the Jīnshā River (Jīnshā Jiāng) to the snowcapped mountains of Hābā Shān (Hābā Mountain) to the west and Yùlóng Xuěshān to the east, and, despite the odd danger, it's gorgeous almost every single step of the way.

The gorge hike is not to be taken lightly. Even for those in good physical shape, it's a workout. The path constricts and crumbles; it certainly can wreck the knees. When it's raining (especially in July and August), landslides and swollen waterfalls can block the paths, in particular on the low road. (The best time to come is May and the start of June, when the hills are afire with plant and flower life.)

A few people – including a handful of foreign travellers – have died in the gorge. During the past decade, there have also been cases of travellers being assaulted on the trail. As always, it's safer in all ways not to do the hike alone.

Check with cafes and lodgings in Lìjiāng or Qiáotóu for trail and weather updates. Most have fairly detailed gorge maps; just remember they're not to scale and are occasionally out of date.

Make sure you bring plenty of water on this hike – 2L to 3L is ideal – as well as plenty of sunscreen and lip balm.

🏃 Activities

There are two trails: the higher (the older route) and the lower, which follows the new road and is best avoided, unless you enjoy being enveloped in clouds of dust from passing tour buses and 4WDs. While the scenery is stunning wherever you are in the gorge, it's absolutely sublime from the high trail. Make sure you don't get too distracted by all that beauty, though, and so miss the arrows that help you avoid getting lost on the trail.

It's six hours to Běndìwān, eight hours to Middle Gorge (Tina's Guesthouse), or nine hours to Walnut Garden. It's much more fun, and a lot less exhausting, to do the trek

Tiger Leaping Gorge

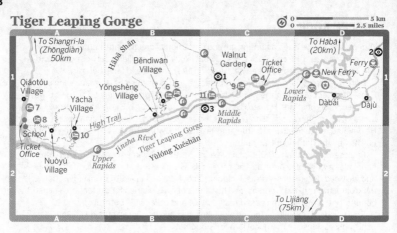

Tiger Leaping Gorge

◎ Sights

1 Bamboo Forest	C1
2 Pagoda	D1
3 Tiger Leaping Stone	C1

🛏 Sleeping

4 Chateau de Woody	C1
5 Five Fingers Mountain Guesthouse	B1
6 Halfway Guesthouse	B1
7 Jane's Guesthouse	A1
8 Naxi Family Guesthouse	A1
9 Sean's Spring Guesthouse	C1
10 Tea Horse Guesthouse	A2
11 Tina's Guesthouse	C1

over two days. By stopping overnight at one of the many guesthouses along the way, you'll have the time to appreciate the magnificent vistas on offer at almost every turn of the trail.

Ponies can be hired (their owners will find you) to take you to the gorge's highest point for between ¥100 and ¥150; it's not uncommon to see three generations of a family together, with the oldies on horseback and the young ones panting on foot behind them.

The following route starts at **Jane's Guesthouse**. Walk away from **Qiáotóu** (桥头), past the school, for five minutes or so, then head up the paved road branching to the left; there's an arrow to guide you. After about 2.5km on the road the gorge trail proper starts and the serious climbing

begins. Note that locals may try and hit you up for an additional 'fee' at this point, which they will claim is reward for them keeping the trail litter-free.

The toughest section of the trek comes after **Nuòyú** (诺余) village, when the trail winds through the 28 agonising bends, or turns, that lead to the highest point of the gorge. Count on five hours at normal pace to get through here and to reach **Yāchà** (牙叉) village. It's a relatively straightforward walk on to **Běndìwān** (本地湾). About 1½ hours on from there, you begin the descent to the road on slippery, poor paths. Watch your step here; if you twist an ankle, it's a long hop down.

After the path meets the road at **Tina's Guesthouse**, there's a good detour that leads down 40 minutes to the middle rapids and **Tiger Leaping Stone**, where a tiger is once said to have leapt across the Yangzi, thus giving the gorge its name. Locals charge ¥10 to go down the path. At the bottom of this insanely steep trail locals charge another ¥10 for one viewpoint but another spot is free. From one of the lower rest points another trail (¥10) heads downstream for a one-hour walk to **Walnut Garden** (核桃园).

Most hikers stop at Tina's, have lunch, and head back to Qiáotóu. Those continuing to Walnut Garden can take the trail along the river or use an alternative trail that keeps high where the path descends to Tina's, crosses a stream and a 'bamboo forest' before descending into Walnut Garden. If you are deciding where to spend the night, Walnut Garden is more attractive than Tina's.

YÚNNÁN TIGER LEAPING GORGE

It's possible to continue to the village of **Dàjù** (大具), about two hours' walk, from where there are buses back to Lìjiāng. The walk includes crossing the river on a ferry (¥20). However, one must now pay an additional ¥105 to take the road from Dàjù to Lìjiāng, because the road passes through Yùlóng Xuěshān (Jade Dragon Snow Mountain), so few bother to go this route nowadays.

🛏 Sleeping & Eating
QIÁOTÓU

Jane's Guesthouse　　　GUESTHOUSE $
(峡谷行客栈; Xiágǔ Xíng Kèzhàn; ☏880 6570; dm ¥25, s & d ¥60-100; @🛜) This two-storey place with tidy, clean rooms is where many people start their trek. The breakfasts here make for good walking fuel and it has left-luggage facilities (¥5 a bag).

IN THE GORGE
The following list of accommodation options along the way (listed in the order that you'll come to them) is not exhaustive. In the unlikely event that everywhere is full, basic rooms will be available with a local. We've never heard of anyone who had to sleep rough in the gorge.

All the guesthouses double as restaurants and shops, where you can pick up bottled water and snacks along the way.

Naxi Family Guesthouse　　　GUESTHOUSE $
(纳西客栈; Nàxī Kèzhàn; ☏880 6928; dm ¥30, s & d ¥70-120) Taking your time to spend a night here instead of double-timing it to Walnut Garden isn't a bad idea. It's an incredibly friendly, well-run place (organic vegies and wines), set around a pleasant courtyard.

Tea Horse Guesthouse　　　GUESTHOUSE $
(茶马客栈; Chámǎ Kèzhàn; ☏139 8871 7292; dm ¥30, s & d ¥120-200) Just after Yāchà village, this bigger place has a great 'Naxi mama' running things, and even has a small spa and massage parlour where aching limbs can be eased.

Halfway Guesthouse　　　GUESTHOUSE $$
(中途客栈; Zhōngtú Kèzhàn, Běndìwān; ☏139 8870 0522; dm ¥30, s & d ¥200) Once a simple home to a guy collecting medicinal herbs and his family, this is now a busy-busy operation. The vistas here are awe-inspiring and perhaps the best of any lodging in the gorge; the view from the communal toilets is worth the price of a bed alone.

Five Fingers Mountain Guesthouse　　　GUESTHOUSE $
(五指客栈; Wǔzhǐ Kèzhàn; ☏139 8877 6286; dm ¥30, r with share bathroom ¥60) An endearingly rustic place, where chickens run around and you're part of the family during your stay. The 200m climb up from the road to get here is a killer after five hours of walking, though.

Tina's Guesthouse　　　GUESTHOUSE $
(中峡旅店; Zhōngxiá Lǚdiàn; ☏820 2258; tina999@live.cn; dm ¥30, r ¥120-280) It's a bit concrete-blocky and lacks the charm and friendliness of other places on the mountain, but there are lots of beds and the location is perfect for those too knackered to make it to Walnut Garden. Pricier rooms have excellent views. Tina organises daily transport to Lìjiāng and Shangri-la.

Sean's Spring Guesthouse　　　GUESTHOUSE $$
(山泉客栈; Shānquán Kèzhàn; ☏820 2223, 158 9436 7846; www.tigerleapinggorge.com; dm ¥30, r ¥60-360) One of the original guesthouses on the trail, and still the spot for lively evenings and socialising. It's run by the eponymous Sean, a true character. There's a variety of rooms, some recently refurbished, and the best have great views of Yùlóng Xuěshān.

Chateau de Woody　　　GUESTHOUSE $
(山白脸旅馆; Shānbáiliǎn Lǚguǎn; ☏139 8871 2705; dm ¥20, s & d ¥60-80) This old-school gorge guesthouse has rooms with good views and modern bathrooms that make for a good deal. Across the road, the less-attractive modern extension has rooms for the same price.

ℹ Getting There & Away
From the Lìjiāng long-distance bus station, buses run to Shangri-la every 40 minutes (7.30am to 5pm; 2¼ hours) and pass through Qiáotóu (¥30). In peak seasons you may have to pay all the way to Shangri-la (¥70).

Most travellers get a minivan (¥35) to the start of the walking track, organised through their guesthouse in Lijiāng. The minivan can deliver extra luggage to the guesthouse of your choice (usually Tina's or Jane's).

Returning to Lijiāng from Qiáotóu, buses start passing through from Shangri-la at around 10am. The last one rolls through at around 5.30pm. The last bus to Shangri-la passes through at around 7pm. Tina's Guesthouse also organises one or two buses a day to both Lìjiāng and Shangri-la.

At the time of writing, there were no buses to Báishuǐtái from Lìjiāng. There are two buses a day from Shangri-la to Báishuǐtái (¥24, three hours, 9.10am & 2pm).

Tiger Leaping Gorge to Báishuǐtái

An adventurous add-on to the gorge trek is to continue north all the way to Hābā (哈巴) village and the limestone terraces of **Báishuǐtái** (白水台; admission ¥30; p676). This turns it into a four-day trek from Qiáotóu and from here you can travel on to Shangri-la. From Walnut Garden to **Hābā**, via **Jiāngbiān** (江边), is a seven to eight hour walk. From here to the Yi village of **Sānbà** (三坝), close to Báishuǐtái, is about the same, following trails. You could just follow the road and hitch with the occasional truck or tractor, but it's longer and less scenic. The best way would be to hire a guide in Walnut Garden for ¥150–300 per day (English-speaking guides charge more). For ¥250 per day you should be able to get a horse and guide. The turn-off to Hābā starts 6km down the road from Walnut Grove, up the hill where you see 'Welcome to Tibet Guest-house' painted on the retaining wall.

In Hābā most people stay at the **Hābā Snow Mountain Inn** (哈巴雪山客栈; Hābā Xuěshān Kèzhàn; ☎0887 886 6596; dm ¥30, d ¥100; @), which has older dorms and new double rooms. The enthusiastic host can organise guides to lead you up **Hābā Mountain** (哈巴山, Hābā Shān), a two-day trek, or to **Black Lake** (黑海, Hēi Hǎi), a nine-hour round trip hike.

If you are travelling by vehicle, from Tina's to Sānbà (¥45, three hours) there is a daily 1pm bus but you have to book in advance. From Sānbà to Shangri-la there is also a daily bus (¥50, three hours) at 1pm. Minivans frequently ply these routes so flagging down a ride isn't too tough.

If you plan to hike the route alone, assume you'll need all provisions and equipment for extremes of weather. Ask for local advice before setting out.

Lúgū Hú   泸沽湖

☎0888

Straddling the remote Yúnnán–Sìchuān border, this **lake** (admission ¥100) remains a laid-back, idyllic place that makes for a great getaway, even with a rise in domestic tourism. The ascent to the lake, which sits at 2690m, is via a spectacular switchback road and the first sight of the 50 sq km body of water, surrounded by lushly forested slopes, will take your breath away.

Villages are scattered around the outskirts of the lake, with **Luòshuǐ** (洛水) the biggest and most developed, and the one where the bus will drop you. As well as guesthouses, and a few cafes with English menus and Western food, there are the inevitable souvenir shops. Nevertheless, it's hardly a boomtown, with the dominant night-time sound being the lapping of the lake.

Most travellers move quickly to **Lǐgé** (里格), 9km further up the road, tucked into a bay on the northwestern shore of the lake. Although guesthouses make up most of the place, along with restaurants serving succulent, but pricey, barbecue, the sights and nights here are lovely. If you want a less touristy experience, then you need to keep village-hopping around the lake to the Sìchuān side. At the moment, top votes for alternative locations are **Luòwǎ** (洛瓦) and **Wǔzhīluó** (五支罗).

The area is home to several Tibetan, Yi and Mosu (a Naxi subgroup) villages. The Mosu are the last practising matriarchal society in the world and many other Naxi customs lost in Lìjiāng are still in evidence here.

The best times to visit the lake are April to May, and September to October, when the weather is dry and mild. It's usually snowbound during the winter months.

◉ Sights & Activities

From Luòshuǐ and Lǐgé you can punt about with local Mosu by dugout canoe – known by the Mosu as 'pig troughs' (zhūcáo). Expect to head for **Lǐwùbǐ Dǎo** (里务比岛), the largest island (and throw a stone into Sìchuān). The second-largest island is **Hēiwǎé Dǎo** (黑瓦俄岛). Boat-trip prices vary wildly. If you're in a group of six to eight people, it's around ¥30 per person.

FREE **Mosu Folk Custom Museum**   MUSEUM
(摩俗民族博物馆; Mósú Mínzú Bówùguǎn; Luòshuǐ; ☉9am-8pm) This museum in Luòshuǐ is set within the traditional home of a wealthy Mosu family, and the obligatory guide will show you around and explain how the matriarchal society functions. There is also an interesting collection of photos taken by Joseph Rock in the 1920s.

Zhǎměi Temple   MONASTERY
(扎美寺; Zhǎměi Sì) On the outskirts of Yǒngníng, this is a Tibetan monastery with at least 20 lamas in residence. Admission is free, but a donation is expected. A private

minivan costs ¥10 per person for the half-hour ride, or you could opt to walk the 20km or so through pleasant scenery.

🛏 Sleeping & Eating

Hotels and guesthouses line the lakeside in Luòshuǐ and Lǐgé, with doubles from around ¥50. Most have attached restaurants that serve traditional Mosu foods, including preserved pig's fat and salted sour fish – the latter being somewhat tastier than the former. Of the two places, Lǐgé is really the place to go for fantastic barbecue.

Yàsé Dába Lǚxíngzhě Zhījiā   HOTEL $$
(雅瑟达吧旅行者之家; ☏588 1196; Lǐgé; d with shared bathroom ¥100, d with private bathroom ¥240-280; @ 🖥) All the rooms at this Lǐgé retreat come with decent views, but the ones on the 2nd floor are tremendous. In the restaurant, try Lúgū Hú fish (泸沽湖鱼; *lúgū hú yú*) or sausage (香肠; *xiāngcháng*).

Húsī Teahouse   HOSTEL $
(湖思茶屋; Húsī Cháwū; ☏139 8886 1858; www. husihostel.com; Luòshuǐ; dm ¥30, r ¥88-248; @ 🖥) The granddaddy of all Lúgū Hú backpacker joints, this place in Luòshuǐ is a multistorey complex of dorms and private rooms, some with excellent lake views. There is a big lounge with computers, books and wi-fi and a restaurant serving Chinese food and mediocre Western meals. The English-speaking staff are helpful.

Lao Shay Youth Hostel   HOSTEL $
(老谢车马店; Lǎoxiè Chēmǎdiàn; ☏588 1555; www.laoshay.com; Lǐgé; dm ¥30, s, d & tr ¥50-198; @) This YHA has a friendly English-speaking staff and a prime location smack in the middle of Lǐgé. The best rooms have lake views and you can rent a bike for ¥30 a day.

Zhāxī Cāntīng   BARBECUE $$
(扎西餐厅; ☏588 1055; Lǐgé; meals from ¥20) Owned by a burly Mosu chap named Zhaxi, this lively restaurant and barbecue joint is a great place to experience local cuisine. A Singapore-run teashop upstairs has good lake views and Hong, the English-speaking owner, is a fount of information.

ℹ Getting There & Away

Lìjiāng's express bus station has two direct buses a day to the lake (¥77, seven hours, 8.30am and 9am) but buy your ticket at least one day in advance as it's often sold out.

Alternatively, you can go to Nínglàng (宁蒗; ¥30, five hours, 13 buses daily, 8am to 3.30pm), from where there's a daily bus to the lake (¥40, three to four hours, 12.30pm), as well as numerous minivans that wait outside the bus station.

For Lǐgé you'll have to change for a minibus in Luòshuǐ (¥15). Hitching may be quicker or you could hire a bike.

Leaving Luòshuǐ, the direct buses to Lìjiāng leave daily at 10am, noon and 3.30pm. Again, tickets should be bought at least a day in advance. Note that the 3.30pm bus comes from Sìchuān so the departure time is not exact. There are also two buses to Nínglàng at 10am and noon. From Nínglàng, there are plenty of buses to Lìjiāng.

For Sìchuān, there's a daily bus to Xīchàng (西昌; ¥120, nine hours, 10.30am).

Shangri-la (Zhōngdiàn)
香格里拉（中甸）

☏0887 / POP 120,000

Shangri-la, previously known as Zhōngdiàn (also with the Tibetan name Gyalthang), is where you begin to breathe in the Tibetan world. That's if you can breathe at all, given its altitude (3200m).

Home to one of Yúnnán's most rewarding monasteries, Shangri-la is also the last stop in Yúnnán before a rough five- or six-day journey to Chéngdū via the Tibetan townships and rugged terrain of western Sìchuān.

Arriving at the central bus station does not give the impression that you have arrived in 'Shangri-la' as the modern part of town feels like a typically ugly, medium-sized Chinese city. It's only when you take a bus to the 'old town' that Shangri-la reveals its charms. Tourism is growing here but its still an easy place to kick back for a few days.

Plan your visit for between April and October. During winter the city practically shuts down and transportation is often halted completely by snowstorms.

In mid- to late June, the town hosts a horse-racing festival that sees several days of dancing, singing, eating and, of course, horse racing. Accommodation is tight at this time.

⊙ Sights

Shangri-la is a wonderful place for getting off the beaten track, with plenty of trekking and horse-riding opportunities, as well as little-visited monasteries and villages. However, the remote sights are difficult to do independently given the lack of public transport.

Shangri-la (Zhōngdiàn)

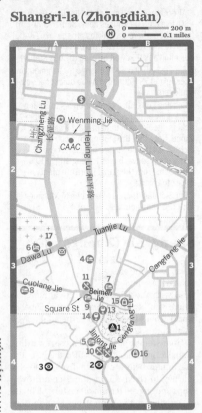

0 — 200 m
0 — 0.1 miles

Shangri-la (Zhōngdiàn)

◎ Sights
1 Guīshān Sì..................................B4
2 Shangri-la Thangka Academy...........A4
3 Zhùangjīn Tǒng.........................A4

🛏 Sleeping
4 Dragoncloud Guesthouse A3
5 Kersang Relay Station....................A4
6 Kevin's Trekker Inn......................A3
7 Olive Bistro & Inn.......................B3
8 Tavern..................................A3
9 The Compass.............................A3

✗ Eating
10 Arro Khampa!...........................A4
11 Somewhere Else.........................A3
12 Tara Gallery Café & Bar................B4

◎ Drinking
13 Namaste................................B3
14 Raven..................................A4

🛍 Shopping
15 Dropenling.............................B3
16 Yunnan Mountain Handicraft
    Center...............................B4

ⓘ Information
Haiwei Trails ....(see 14)
17 Khampa Caravan........................A3

YÚNNÁN SHANGRI-LA (ZHŌNGDIÀN)

Ganden Sumtseling Gompa
MONASTERY
(松赞林寺; Sōngzànlín Sì; admission ¥115; ⊙7am-7pm) About an hour's walk north of town is this 300-year-old Tibetan monastery complex with around 600 monks. Extensive rebuilding has robbed the monastery of some of its charm, but it remains the most important in southwest China and is definitely worth the visit. Bus 3 runs here from anywhere along Changzheng Lu (¥1). From the main gate where the tickets are sold you can catch a tourist bus to the monastery. If you don't mind hiking its possible to visit for free by walking to the left side of the ticket office, up the hill parallel to the paved road and down to a lake with the monastery on the other side (a 30-minute walk).

Old Town
HISTORIC AREA
After checking out the monastery, everyone just wanders about the old town, specifically **Square Street** (Sifang Jie); from this branches a spider web of cobbled lanes and renovated buildings (some say tacky, others say cool). You'll also see white stupas everywhere. Lording over the old town is **Guīshān Sì** (龟山寺; Guīshān Temple), a reconstructed temple home to a few monks that conduct morning prayers. Next to the temple is **Zhùangjīng Tǒng**, the world's biggest prayer wheel standing at 21m high and containing 100,000 small prayer wheels. At least six people are needed to give it a spin.

On the far side of Guishan Temple it's worth visiting the **Shangri-la Thangka Academy** (唐卡学会; Tángkǎ Xuéhuì; ☎888 1612; www.thangkaacademy.com; 31 Jinlong Jie), where *thangka* master Lobsang Khudup trains young monks in painting and Buddhist philosophy. The academy also offers classes for tourists, costing around ¥180 per day; a real bargain considering the price includes room and board. You can also participate in a three-day village homestay for ¥240.

Bǎijī Sì
BUDDHIST TEMPLE

For even better views, head to this delightfully named and little-visited temple (百鸡寺; 100 Chickens Temple). The temple has three monks inside and dozens of chickens wandering around outside. To get there, walk along the narrow paths behind Kersang's Relay Station, past the deserted temple, continue uphill and you'll see it on the left.

🛏 Sleeping

Despite Shangri-la's often glacial night temperatures, many guesthouses are neither heated nor have 24-hour hot water. Most dorms in town are fairly basic too.

⭐ TOP CHOICE Kersang's Relay Station
INN $$

(格桑藏驿; Gésāng Zàng Yì; ☏822 3118; www.kersangs.com; 1 Yamenlang, Jinlong Jie; 衙门廊1号、金龙街; dm ¥40; r without bathroom ¥100, r with bathroom ¥140-260; 🛜) This friendly, Tibetan-run place, popular with Western travellers, has cosy rooms with modern bathrooms, Tibetan prayer flags fluttering in the courtyard and movie nights a couple times a week. The old wooden house keeps the rooms better insulated compared to other concrete hotels.

Dragoncloud Guesthouse
GUESTHOUSE $

(龙行客栈; Lóngxíng Kèzhàn; ☏828 9250; www.dragoncloud.cn; 94 Beimen Jie, Jiantang Zhen; 建塘镇北门街94号; dm ¥40, d ¥100-160; @🛜) Set around a courtyard, the dorms are spacious if rudimentary, while the standard rooms come with modern bathrooms. There are a few basic doubles that are cheaper. During bouts of chill, you'll love the fireplace in the common area, which also has a pool table.

Kevin's Trekker Inn
GUESTHOUSE $

(龙门客栈; Lóngmén Kèzhàn; ☏822 8178; www.kevintrekkerinn.com; 138 Dawa Lu; 达娃路138号; dm ¥30-50, r ¥120-150; @🛜) Kevin, a Yúnnánese Bai, and his wife are charming, and a good source of local knowledge. Their guesthouse has a cosy lounge but rooms are a little boxy and can get cold at night. It's located just off Dawa Lu behind the Long Xiang Inn.

Olive Bistro & Inn
INN $

(橄榄枝客栈; Gǎnlǎnzhī kèzhàn; ☏888 1144; www.theolive.asia; 7 Chilang Shuo; 池廊硕7号; dm/d ¥40/120; @🛜) This cosy, 12-room hotel is a touch warmer than others in the old town (rooms are inside, not around a courtyard) and they have wall heaters in the rooms. Rooms are clean and nicely decorated. It's in a small alley opposite the Olive Bistro.

SHANGRI-LA – FACT & FICTION

At first it seemed like a typically overstated tourist campaign: 'Shangri-la Found'. Only they weren't kidding. In November 1997 'experts' had established with 'certainty' that the fabled 'Shangri-la' of James Hilton's 1933 bestseller *Lost Horizon* was, indeed, in Déqīn County.

Hilton's novel (later filmed by Frank Capra and starring Ronald Coleman and Jane Wyatt) tells the story of four travellers who are hijacked and crash-land in a mountain utopia ruled by a 163-year-old holy man. This 'Shangri-la' is in the Valley of the Blue Moon, a beautiful fertile valley backed by a perfect pyramid peak, Mt Karakul.

The claim is based primarily on the fact that Déqīn's Kawa Karpo peak resembles the 'pyramid-shaped' landmark of Mt Karakul. Also, the county's blood-red valleys with three parallel rivers fit a valley from *Lost Horizon*.

One plausible theory is that Hilton, writing the novel in northwest London, based his descriptions of Shangri-la on articles by Joseph Rock that he had read in *National Geographic* magazine, detailing Rock's expeditions to remote parts of Lìjiāng and Déqīn. Hilton's invented place name 'Shangri-la' may have been a corruption of the word *Shambhala*, a mystical Buddhist paradise.

After Déqīn staked its claim to the name Shangri-la rival bids popped up around Yúnnán. Cízhōng in Wēixī County pointed out that its Catholic churches and Tibetan monasteries live side by side in the valley. Meanwhile, Dàochéng, just over the border in Sìchuān, had a strong bid based around the pyramid peak of its mountain Channa Dorje and the fact that Rock wrote about the region in several articles.

Cynics have had a field day with this and the resulting hijacking of the concept, part of which was to establish tourism as an industry to replace logging, which had been banned.

Shangri-la is at its heart surely a metaphor. As a skinny-dipping Jane Wyatt says in the film version of the book: 'I'm sure there's a wish for Shangri-la in everyone's heart…'

The Compass
INN $$

(舒灯库乐; Shūdēng kùlè; ☎822 3638; www.the
compass.asia; 3 Chilang Gang; 池廊冈3号; s/d
without bathroom ¥120/180, s/d with bathroom
¥320/380; ☎) This place has excellent two-
storey suites with four-poster beds, a little
kitchenette and lots of space to spread out.
Unfortunately, the rooms with shared bath-
rooms are very loud at night (they are next
to a nightclub), so avoid them. The cafe
(Western and Asian dishes) has a warm fire-
place and some of the best food in town.

Tavern
INN $

(仁和客栈; Rénhé kèzhàn; ☎888 1147; chris
tinhe@hotmail.com; 47 Cuolang Jie; 措廊街47号;
dm ¥35, d without/with bathroom ¥80/150; @☎)
Decorated with Mao and Che Guevara post-
ers, lots of plastic plants and Buddha stat-
ues, this place has a creative and colourful
atmosphere. Rooms are a bit small and ram-
shackle but showers are clean. It's a popular
crashpad for budget backpackers.

✖ Eating & Drinking

There are dozens of places to eat offering
Tibetan, Indian, Western and Chinese food.

Tara Gallery Café & Bar
TIBETAN $$

(No 29 Old Town; dishes from ¥20-60; ☺10am-
10pm; ☎☎) This upmarket restaurant,
bar and cafe (and art gallery) is a lovely,
thoughtfully designed space, and includes
a plant-filled 2nd-floor terrace. The menu
is a tantalising mix of Tibetan, Indian and
Yúnnán dishes; the seven-course Tibetan set
meal (¥80) is a feast. It's also a relaxing spot
for a coffee or an evening drink. The owner
Utara is very friendly.

Somewhere Else
WESTERN $$

(他乡咖啡厅; Tāxiāng Kāfēi Tīng; Sifeng Jie; dishes
from ¥16-34; ☺9am-6pm Mon-Sat; ☎☎@) A
Canadian- and Dutch-run cafe serving fill-
ing Western breakfasts, smoothies and
sandwiches. It's a nice open space with a
fireplace for keeping warm and the location
is just about perfect, with windows over-
looking 'Dancing Square'. A good place to
get some travel info and plan the direction
of your plunge.

Arro Khampa!
TIBETAN $$

(阿若康巴; Āruò Kāngbā; 27 Jinlong Jie; dishes
from ¥35-58; ☺10am-10pm; ☎☎) A French and
Chinese couple own this cosy restaurant
but the food is Tibetan. The yak is excellent,
either baked or curried, and there are tasty
momos. A special Tibetan hotpot costs ¥98.

Raven
BAR

(乌鸦酒吧; Wūyā Jiǔbā; 19 Beimen Jie; ☺10.30am-
late) Owned by a Londoner, and with the
comfy feel of a local boozer, this is the one
place in Shangri-la where you'll find English
beers (along with decent coffee and proper
English tea). Lounge on the sofas downstairs, or hit the pool table on the 2nd floor.

Namaste
BAR

(南玛瑟德; Nánmāsèdé; Yamenlang, Jinlong Jie;
☺7pm-late) A fully local Tibetan nightclub,
you'll turn a few heads upon entering. Come
here to see Tibetans getting there funk on,
we even saw a Buddhist monk chilling out
behind the bar. It can get a bit rough here,
knife fights are not unheard of so don't let
down your guard.

🛍 Shopping

Dropenling
HANDICRAFTS

(卓番林; Zhuó fāng lín; ☎823 2292; www.tibet
craft.com; 18 Cengfang Lu; 达娃路18号) Excellent
array of Tibetan handicrafts made with a
Western taste, including bags, cushions, toys
and ornaments.

Yunnan Mountain Handicraft Center
HANDICRAFTS

(云南山地手工艺品中心; Yúnnán Shāndì
Shǒugōng Yìpǐn Zhōngxīn; ☎822 7742; www.ymhf
shangrila.com; 1 Jinlong Jie; 金龙街1号) Fair-
trade handicraft shop that sells locally
produced products including pottery, clothing, jewellery, carpets, Nixi black pottery
and more.

ℹ Information

Altitude sickness is a real problem here and
most travellers need at least a couple of days to
acclimatise. Brutal winter weather can bring the
town to a complete standstill, so try to plan your
visit for between March and October.

There are no internet cafes in the old town, but
all hostels and hotels and most cafes have wi-fi
or internet.

Bank of China (中国银行; Zhōngguó Yínháng;
Heping Lu) Has a 24-hour ATM and changes US
dollars.

Haiwei Trails (www.haiweitrails.com; Raven,
Beimen Jie) Foreign-run, it has a good philosophy towards local sustainable tourism, with
over a decade of experience.

Khampa Caravan (康巴商道探险旅行社;
Kāngbā Shāngdào Tànxiǎn Lǚxíngshè; ☎828
8648; www.khampacaravan.com; 2nd flr, cnr
Dawa Lu & Changzheng Lu; ☺9am-noon &
2-5.30pm Mon-Fri, 9am-noon Sat) Tibetan-run,
this well-established outfit organises some

excellent short or longer adventures that get good feedback, and specialises in arranging travel into Tibet. The company also runs a lot of sustainable development programs within Tibetan communities. See www.shangrilaassociation.org for more details.

Getting There & Away

Note that some air and bus tickets may refer to Shangri-la as Zhōngdiàn.

Air

There are up to four flights daily to Kūnmíng (¥1150), a daily flight to Chéngdū (¥1000), and a daily flight to Lhasa (¥2480) in peak season. Flights for other domestic destinations also leave from the airport but are completely irregular and destinations change from week to week. You can enquire about your destination or buy tickets at **CAAC** (中国民航; Zhōngguó Mínháng; Wenming Jie). If booking on www.elong.com you need to type in 'Diqing' for the city name.

Train

A railway is being built from Lìjiāng to Shangri-la and is expected to be finished by 2014.

Bus

Destinations from Shangri-la:

Bǎishuǐtái ¥24, three hours, two daily (9.10am and 2pm)

Dàochéng ¥120, 11 hours, one daily (7.30am)

Déqīn ¥53–65, six to seven hours, three daily (8.20am, 9.20am and noon)

Dōngwàng ¥50, seven to eight hours, one daily (7.30am)

Kūnmíng ¥205–238, 12 hours, four daily (9am, 5pm, 7pm and 8pm)

Lìjiāng ¥63–69, five hours, hourly (8am to 6pm)

Xiàguān ¥79–90, seven hours, every 30 minutes (7am to 12.30pm, then 7.30pm and 8pm)

Xiāngchéng ¥85, eight hours, one daily (8am)

If you're up for the bus-hopping trek to Chéngdū, in Sìchuān, you're looking at a minimum of three to four days' travel at some very high altitudes – you'll need warm clothes. Note that for political reasons this road may be closed at any time of the year (if the ticket seller at the bus says 'come back tomorrow', it's closed indefinitely for sure).

If you get on the road, the first stage of the trip is to Xiāngchéng in Sìchuān. From Xiāngchéng, your next destination is Lǐtáng, though if roads are bad you may be forced to stay overnight in Dàochéng. From Lǐtáng, it's on to Kāngding, from where you can make your way west towards Chéngdū.

Note that roads out of Shangri-la can be temporarily blocked by snow at any time from November to March. Bring a flexible itinerary.

ℹ Getting Around

To/From the Airport

The airport is 5km from town and is sometimes referred to as Díqíng or Deqen – there is currently no airport at Déqīn. A taxi or minivan between the airport and Shangri-la will cost between ¥30 and ¥50. Otherwise, try to call your hotel to arrange a pick-up.

To/From the Bus Station

From outside the bus station take local bus No 1 (¥1) to the old town (古城, gǔchéng). The bus station is 2km north of the old town, straight up Changzheng Lu.

Around Shangri-la

The following is but a thumbnail sketch; many other sights – mountains, meadows, ponds, *chörtens* (Tibetan stupas) etc – await your exploration. Just note that virtually everything either has or will have a pricey admission fee (those pesky chairlifts, especially).

Some 7km northwest of town you'll find the seasonal **Nàpà Hǎi** (纳帕海; Nàpà Lake; unofficial admission ¥40), surrounded by a large grassy meadow. Between September and March there's myriad rare species, including the black-necked crane. Outside of these months, the lake dries up and you can see large numbers of yaks and cattle grazing on the meadow. It makes a nice bike ride. Note that the unofficial admission fee is enforced by a small, rock wielding Tibetan villager, who is not afraid to pelt you with stones if you don't pay his bogus entry fee.

Approximately 15km southeast of Shangri-la is the **Tiānshēng Bridge** (天生桥; Tiānshēng Qiáo; admission ¥20, hot springs ¥80; ◎9am-11pm). Local Tibetans believe that the sulphur-rich water can cure any number of skin ailments and other health issues. There is a co-ed swimming pool and a natural sauna (inside a cave) that is divided into male and female sections. It's possible to cycle here in about two hours or you could take a taxi (¥100 round trip).

Another 10km past the hot spring is the **Great Treasure Temple** (大宝寺; Dàbǎo Sì; admission ¥5), one of the earliest Buddhist temples in Yúnnán.

EMERALD PAGODA LAKE & SHǓDŪ HǍI　　碧塔海、属都海

Some 25km east of Shangri-la, the bus to Sānbà can drop you along the highway for **Emerald Pagoda Lake** (Bìtǎ Hǎi; admission ¥190), which is also known as Pǔdácuò

GETTING TO TIBET

At the time of writing, it was possible to enter Tibet overland from Shangri-la but only by joining a pricey guided tour. If you're tempted to bypass the tour group thing and try and sneak in, then think again. There were at least 11 checkpoints operating on the road between Shangri-la and Lhasa in 2012; you will be caught, fined, detained and escorted to Chéngdū by a secret service officer.

It is possible to fly to Lhasa from Shangri-la, but flights are cheaper from elsewhere (Kūnmíng and Chéngdū), and you'll need to be part of an organised group with all the necessary permits. By far the best people to talk to about Tibet travel in Shangri-la are at **Khampa Caravan** (康巴商道探险旅行社; Kāngbā Shāngdào Tànxiǎn Lǚxíngshè; ✆828 8648; www.khampacaravan.com).

In Kūnmíng, **Mr Chen's Tour** (陈先生旅游; Chénxiānshēng Lǚyóu; ✆316 6105; Room 105, Camellia Hotel, 154 Dongfeng Lu) has been organising Tibet travel for years, although some travellers report that his sales pitch is better than his trips.

(普达错), a Mandarinised-version of its Tibetan name. The lake is 8km down a trail (a half-hour by pony), and while the ticket price is laughably steep, there are other (free) trails to the lake. A bike is useful for finding them; taxis will drop you at the ticket office.

Pony trips can be arranged at the lake. An intriguing sight in summer is the comatose fish that float unconscious for several minutes in the lake after feasting on azalea petals.

The whopping entrance fee is also due to the inclusion of **Shǔdū Hú**, another lake approximately 10km to the north. The name means 'Place Where Milk is Found' in Tibetan because its pastures are reputedly the most fertile in northwestern Yúnnán.

Getting to the lake(s) is tricky. You usually have to catch the bus to Sānbà, get off at the turn-off and hitch. Getting back you can wait (sometimes interminably) for a bus or hike to one of the entrances or main road and look out for taxis – but there may be none. A taxi will cost around ¥300 to ¥400 for the return trip, including Shǔdū Hú.

BÁISHUǏTÁI   白水台

Báishuǐtái is a limestone deposit plateau 108km southeast of Shangri-la, with some breathtaking scenery and Tibetan villages en route. For good reason it has become probably the most popular backdoor route between Lìjiāng and Shangri-la. The **terraces** (admission ¥30) – think of those in Pamukkale in Turkey or Huánglóng in Sìchuān – are lovely, but can be tough to access if rainfall has made trails slippery.

A couple of guesthouses at the nearby towns of **Báidì** and **Sānbà** have rooms with beds from ¥30 to ¥40.

From Shangri-la there is a daily bus to Báishuǐtái at 9.10am (¥25, three hours). One adventurous option is to hike or hitch all the way from Báishuǐtái to Tiger Leaping Gorge (p670). A taxi from Shangri-la is ¥600.

SHANGRI-LA TO DÉQÌN

The road to Déqìn from Shangri-la takes around six hours with a hired jeep. This time will be cut down once the new road is complete (expected by 2014). The halfway point is **Bēnzǐlán** (奔子栏), 80km past Shangri-la, a small city where bikers could spend the night in one of the simple hotels along the main road. About 22km past Bēnzǐlán is the picturesque **Dhondrupling Gompa** (东竹林寺; Dōngzhúlín Sì), just off the main road. Past Bēnzǐlán the road climbs steeply into the mountains with endless hairpin turns until you reach Déqìn.

If you are travelling in winter, remember you are crossing some serious ranges – three times above 5000m – and at any time from mid-October to late spring, heavy snows can close the roads. Pack sensibly and plan for a snowbound emergency.

Déqìn   德钦

✆0887 / POP 60,100

Mellifluously named Déqìn (that last syllable seems to ring, doesn't it?) lies in some of the most ruggedly gorgeous scenery in China. Snuggly cloud-high at an average altitude of 3550m, it rests in the near embrace of one of China's most magical mountains, **Kawa Karpo** (梅里雪山; often referred to as Méilǐ Xuěshān). At 6740m, it is Yúnnán's highest peak and straddles the Yúnnán–Tibet border.

A true border town, Déqīn is one of Yúnnán's last outposts before Tibet, but from here you could also practically hike east to Sìchuān or southwest to Myanmar (Burma). Díqìng Prefecture was so isolated that it was never really controlled by anyone until the PLA (People's Liberation Army) arrived in force in 1957.

More than 80% of locals are Tibetan, though a dozen other minorities also live here, including one of the few settlements of non-Hui Muslims in China. The town, though, is seriously unattractive and a little rough – the local police impose a midnight curfew. Confusingly, Déqīn is the name of the city and county; both are incorporated by the Díqìng Tibetan Autonomous Prefecture (迪庆藏族自治州).

Most people make immediate tracks for Fēilái Sì. All buses and minivans hang around the main street that runs through town and the bus station is just a little office on the hairpin bend.

For Shangri-la, buses leave three times daily from Déqīn (¥56 to ¥68, six to seven hours) at 8am, 9am and 12.30pm. There is also a daily bus to Lìjiāng (¥258, 10 to 11 hours) at 7.30am and to Kūnmíng (¥258, 18 to 19 hours) at 11am.

Around Déqīn

The long ride to Déqīn is really just the start of your journey. The main reason to come here is to spend time in the valleys below Kawa Karpo and most access is on foot, so you'll need to book at least three or four days to make the most of your journey.

Note that entry to the below sights requires buying a **Meili Snow Mountain National Park** (梅里雪山国家公园; Mĕilĭ Xuĕshān Guó Jiā Gōng Yuăn; ¥228-230) entry ticket. There are three ticket options: one includes three observation points and the glacier (¥228), another ticket is the same three observation points and Yŭbēng village (¥230), and the third is just three observation points (¥150).

If you want to go to the glacier and Yŭbēng village you should buy the full ticket plus a ¥85 supplement for the village. A student card nets a 50% discount.

FĒILÁI SÌ   飞来寺

Approximately 10km southwest of Déqīn is the small but interesting Tibetan **Fēilái Temple** (Fēilái Sì), or Naka Zhashi (or Trashi)

Gompa in Tibetan, devoted to the spirit of Kawa Karpo. There's no charge but leave a donation. No photos are allowed inside the tiny hall.

Everyone comes here for the sublime views – particularly the sunrises – of the Méilĭ Xuĕshān range, including 6740m-high Kawa Karpo (also known as Méilĭ Xuĕshān or Tàizi Shān) and the even more beautiful peak to the south, 6054m-high **Miacimu** (神女; Shénnŭ in Chinese), whose spirit is the female counterpart of Kawa Karpo. Joseph Rock described Miacimu as 'the most glorious peak my eyes were ever privileged to see...like a castle of a dream, an ice palace of a fairy tale'. Locals come here to burn juniper incense to the wrathful spirit of the mountain.

Sadly, weather often as not does not cooperate, shrouding the peaks in mist. Winter is your best shot at a sunrise photo op. A ticket office near the platform sells tickets (¥228) for Fēilái Sì and other sites.

The 'town' is actually just an ugly strip of concrete shops, hotels and restaurants along the main road. Across the road, the government has unsportingly set up a wall, blocking the view of the mountains (just walk downhill 200m for the same view).

Most backpackers stay at **Feeling Village Youth Hostel** (觉色滇乡国际青年旅舍; Juésè Diānxiāng Guójì Qīngnián Lûshè; ☎0887-841 6133; dm ¥40, d without/with bathroom ¥100/¥120; @🛜), which has simple but clean rooms and a cosy lounge. No English is spoken but it's a good place to meet up with other travellers to swap info or share a ride. It's set back from the main road; look for the sign turning right up the little alley at the bottom of the village.

Next door, the **Míngzhū Hotel** (明珠酒店; Míngzhū Jiŭdiàn; ☎841 4688; r ¥130-150; @🛜) has better private rooms, some with good mountain views, but not all rooms have working electric blankets so check this before you settle in.

Lots of places on the main road serve Chinese and Western meals.

To get here from Déqīn a taxi will cost you ¥30. Alternatively, head out onto the road and try to flag down any vehicle that's heading your way.

MÍNGYŎNG GLACIER   明永冰川

Tumbling off the side of Kawa Karpo peak is the 12km-long **Míngyŏng Glacier** (Míngyŏng Bīngchuān). At over 13 sq km,

YŪBĒNG & KAWA KARPO HIKES

The best reason to visit Déqīn is the chance to hike to the foot of Kawa Karpo. The main destination is **Yūbēng** (雨崩) village from where you can make day hikes to mountain meadows, lakes and the fabulous **Yūbēng Waterfall** (雨崩神瀑; Yūbēng Shénpù).

The five-hour trek to Yūbēng starts at the **Xīdāng** (西当) hot spring, about 3km past Xīdāng village. The drive from Fēilái Sì takes one hour and 40 minutes and a taxi will cost ¥150. You could also hike all the way here from Fēilái Sì using local roads and paths. Another possibility is a 3pm minibus from Déqīn to Xīdāng (¥15) that returns the next morning at 8am, or one of the private minibuses that leave when full from near the bus stand. There is a ¥5 entrance fee for Yūbēng but when you show your receipt at your guesthouse you'll get ¥5 discount off your bill.

Yūbēng consists of two sections. You first arrive in 'Upper Yūbēng', which contains most guesthouses, then the trail continues another 1km to 'Lower Yūbēng'. **Lobsang Trekker Lodge** (藏巴乐之家; Zàngbālè Zhījiā; ☎139 8879 7053; http://lobsangtrekkerlodge. webs.com; dm/d ¥30/200), in Upper Yūbēng, is a popular place that offers meals, comfortable rooms, modern bathrooms and good traveller info (English is spoke here). In Lower Yūbēng, the **Mystic Waterfall Lodge** (神瀑客栈; Shénpù Kèzhàn; ☎0887-841 1082; dm/d ¥25/100) is a friendly place with an English-speaking owner.

From Yūbēng village, loads of treks lie out there. It's a three- to four-hour trip on foot or horseback to the waterfall. Or, you could head south to a picturesque lake (it's around 4350m high and not easy to find, so take a guide). Guides cost around ¥150 per day. Supplies (food and water) are pricey in Yūbēng so stock up in Fēilái Sì.

Leaving the village, trekkers will often hike to **Nínóng** (尼农) village by the Mekong River, a four- to five-hour hike that definitely requires a guide (and a good sense of balance as its very steep in some sections). If you are prone to vertigo, head back to Xīdāng instead. Arrange a pick-up in Nínóng or ask around for a taxi, if you are stuck walk 6km to Xīdāng where there is more transport.

Then there's the legendary Kawa Karpo *kora*, a 12-day pilgrim circumambulation of Méilí Xuěshān. However, half of it is in the Tibetan Autonomous Region, so you'll need a permit to do it; and you'll definitely need a guide.

it is not only the lowest glacier in China (around 2200m high) but also an oddity – a monsoon marine glacier, which basically translates as having an ecosystem that couldn't possibly be more diverse: tundra, taiga, broadleaf forest and meadow.

The mountain has been a pilgrimage site for centuries and you'll still meet a few Tibetan pilgrims, some of whom circumambulate the mountain over seven days in autumn. Surrounding villages are known as 'heaven villages' because of the dense fog that hangs about in spring and summer.

The trail to the glacier leads up from Míngyǒng's central square. After 70 minutes of steady uphill walking you will reach the Tibetan **Tàizǐ Miào** (太子庙), a small temple where there are snack and drink stalls. A further 30 minutes along the trail is **Lotus Temple** (莲花庙; Liánhuā Miào), which offers fantastic views of the glacier framed by prayer flags and *chörten*. Horses can also be hired to go up to the glacier (¥150).

If you're coming from Yūbēng, you could also hike to Míngyǒng from Xīdāng in around three hours if you hoof it.

Míngyǒng village consists of only a couple hotels, restaurants and shops. You can overnight in the simple **Renqin Hotel** (仁钦酒店; Rénqín Jiǔdiàn; ☎139 8871 4330; dm/d ¥20/80; @☎) which also serves meals.

From Déqīn, one daily bus (¥15) departs at 3pm. In addition private minibuses to Míngyǒng leave regularly from the bridge near the market at the top end of town (¥16, one to two hours, 8am to 3pm or 4pm). You can also try to rent a car through your accommodation.

The road from Déqīn descends into the dramatic Mekong Gorge. Six kilometres before Míngyǒng the road crosses the Mekong River and branches off to Xīdāng. Nearby is a small temple, the Bǎishūlín Miào, and a *chörten*. There is a checkpoint here where you will need to show your national park ticket (or buy one for around ¥213).

NÙ JIĀNG VALLEY

The 320km-long Nù Jiāng Valley (怒江大峡谷) is one of Yúnnán's best-kept secrets. The Nù Jiāng (known as the Salween in Myanmar; its name in Chinese means 'Raging River') is the second-longest river in Southeast Asia and one of only two undammed rivers in China. Sandwiched between the Gāolígòng Shān and Myanmar to the west, Tibet to the north and the imposing Bìluó Shān to the east, the gorge holds nearly a quarter of China's flora and fauna species, and half of China's endangered species. The valley also has an exotic mix of Han, Nu, Lisu, Drung and Tibetan nationalities, and even the odd Burmese trader. And it's simply stunning – all of it.

Getting there is a pain. On a map, it seems a stone's throw from Déqīn in the province's northwest. Nope. All traffic enters via the Bǎoshān region. Once there, you trundle eight hours up the valley, marvelling at the scenery, and then head back the way you came. Plans have been announced to blast a road from Gòngshān in the northern part of the valley to Déqīn, and another from the village of Bǐngzhōngluò even further north into Tibet. Given the immense topographical challenges, these plans are a long way off.

Liùkù 六库

☎ 0886 / POP 17, 800

Liùkù is the lively, pleasant capital of the prefecture. Divided by the Nù Jiāng River, it's the main transport hub of the region, although it's of little intrinsic interest. You may have to register with a police checkpoint about 5km before entering the town.

🛏 Sleeping & Eating

There are many places on Chuancheng Lu in the centre of town starting from ¥80, although the cheapies tend to be a bit scruffy and geared towards travelling Chinese businessmen.

To eat, head to the riverbank, south of Renmin Lu, where loads of outdoor restaurants cook great barbecued fish.

Nùjiāng Géruì Shāngwù Jiǔdiàn　HOTEL $$
(怒江格瑞商务酒店; ☎388 8885; 123 Chuancheng Lu; 穿城路123号; s & d ¥138-240; ❄@) One of the better options, this solid midrange place has ADSL internet and free breakfast. It can get a bit busy at night when

a gaggle of scantily clad 'hostesses' stand by the door to welcome patrons to karaoke upstairs. After crossing the bridge it's one block uphill from Renmin Lu.

Lín Méng Bīnguǎn　HOTEL $
(林萌宾馆; ☎326 6188; Renmin Lu; 人民路; s & d ¥80) A cheap option with simple rooms and a friendly young staff. Cross the bridge, make the first left onto Renmin Lu, and look for the entrance through a mobile (cell) phone shop.

❶ Information

Bank of China (中国银行; Zhōngguó Yínháng) Located uphill from the bus station.

Internet cafe (网吧; wǎngbā; per hr ¥3) There is an internet cafe near the main pedestrian bridge, in a little shopping mall, opposite the Shèng Bǎo Lù Hotel.

❶ Getting There & Away

The bus station is inconveniently located south of downtown and across the river (a ¥15 taxi ride).

Bǎoshān ¥45–58, three to four hours, every 30 minutes (7.30am to 4pm)

Bǐngzhōngluò ¥85, nine hours, one daily (7am)

Fúgòng ¥44, four hours, hourly (7.20am to 4.40pm)

Gòngshān ¥75, eight hours, four daily (6.40am, 11.30am, 12.30pm and 1pm)

Kūnmíng ¥205–255, 11 to 12 hours, six daily (8.30am, 11am, 6pm, 7pm, 8pm and 8.30pm)

Téngchōng ¥70, six hours, four daily (7am, 8am, 10am and 11am)

Xiàguān ¥72–96, five hours, every 40 minutes (8am to 3pm and 9pm)

Fúgòng 副攻

TRANSPORT HUB

Hemmed in by steep cliffs on all sides, Fúgòng offers some of the best scenery in the valley, even if the town itself is somewhat scruffy and forgettable. Fúgòng is roughly halfway up the valley and a reasonable place to break up the journey if it's late.

There are decent rooms at the no-name hotel in the bus station for ¥100. Across the street is the slightly better **Fúgòng Bīnguǎn** (副攻宾馆; ☎349 2900; s & d ¥130), which has fancy flat panel TVs and ADSL internet (though we could not get it to work). An **internet cafe** (per hr ¥3; ◷10am-midnight) is next to the bus station.

THE NÙ JIĀNG DAM

In 2003 Unesco named the Nù Jiāng Valley a World Heritage site, calling it one of the world's most precious ecosystems of its kind. Then, almost simultaneously, the Chinese government announced plans for a series of 13 dams along the Nù Jiāng. The project would theoretically produce more electricity than even the Three Gorges Dam.

Opposition was immediate. Unesco warned that such a project could warrant the area's delisting; it was joined in its opposition to the project by more than 70 international environmental groups. Local opposition was also fierce; more than 50 prominent Chinese (from pop stars to business billionaires) spoke out against the dams. In a very rare example of people power succeeding in China, the government has since backed away from the plan, with Premier Wen Jiabao ordering more studies on the scheme's potential impact. Local politicians, though, remain keen for the project to go ahead and the area's future remains highly uncertain.

ℹ️ Getting There & Away

There are twice-hourly buses to Liùkù (¥40, four hours) between 7.20am and 4.20pm. To Bīngzhōngluò you'll have to wait for the bus from Liùkù to pass by, which happens around 11am. Otherwise, you could take a bus to Gòngshān (¥32, seven daily from 9am to 5pm), or ask around for a share taxi on the street outside the station. They commence around 8.30am.

Bīngzhōngluò 丙中洛
📞 0886

The main reason to come to the Nù Jiāng Valley is to visit this isolated, friendly **village** (admission ¥100, students ¥50), set in a beautiful, wide and fertile bowl. Just 35km south of Tibet and close to Myanmar, it's a great base for hikes into the surrounding mountains and valleys. The area is at its best in spring and early autumn. Don't even think about coming in the winter.

Potential short hops include heading south along the main road for 2km to the impressive 'first bend' of the Nù Jiāng River, or north along a track more than 15km long that passes a 19th-century church and several villages (the road starts by heading downhill from Road to Tibet Guesthouse).

Longer three- or four-day treks include heading to the Tibetan village of **Dímáluò** (迪麻洛) and then onto the village of **Yŏnzhī** (永芝). From Yŏnzhī it's another two hours walk to the main road from where you can hitch a ride to Déqīn. It is a demanding trek that can really only be done from late May until September as the 3800m pass is too difficult to cross in heavy snow.

A guide is pretty much essential. Tibetan trek leader Alou comes highly recommended. He's based at his guesthouse, although he's often away on treks so email him first. Treks usually runs around ¥200 per day. Note that there are no villages en route to Yŏnzhī so you'll need to carry all your own food and sleep in basic huts along the way (porters can be hired for around ¥100 per day).

Another pricier option is Peter, a Lemao guide, who offers treks for ¥250 a day. You can find him at **Nù Jiāng Baini Travel** (📞139 8853 9641; yangindali@yahoo.co.uk) on the main street. He speaks English and is a good source of local information, and he also rents mountain bikes for ¥50 a day.

Most hotels in town have wi-fi and Peter has internet access at his shop for ¥3 per hour.

🛏️ Sleeping & Eating

TOP CHOICE 📍 **Road to Tibet Guesthouse**   GUEST HOUSE $
(📞358 1168, 189 0886 1168; dm ¥30, s & d ¥80; 📶) Most backpackers end up at this place, located on the street heading downhill from the main road. Beds are hard but it's a clean place with a helpful English-speaking owner and excellent communal dinners. The owner, Alou, also has a simple guesthouse in his home village of Dímáluò, a good destination for a day hike.

Yù Dòng Bīnguǎn   HOTEL $
(玉洞宾馆; 📞358 1285; s & d ¥80-180; 📶) A nice budget hotel option run by a friendly chain-smoking, pot-bellied chap. Rooms are clean and well-maintained and the ones in the back have good views of the valley.

ℹ️ Getting There & Away

There is one direct bus a day from Liùkù to Bīngzhōngluò (¥85, nine hours, 7am). It returns from opposite the Yù Dòng Bīnguǎn at 8am.

Otherwise, take a bus to Gòngshān, where you can transfer to one of the regular buses that go back and forth to Bǐngzhōngluò (¥10, 1½ hours) until 5pm or 6pm.

From Gòngshān, there are 10 daily buses to Liùkù from 6.10am to 1pm.

Dúlóng Valley 独龙江

Separated from the Nù Jiāng Valley by the high Gāolígòng Shān range and only reached by road in 1999, this is one of the remotest valleys in China and is home to the tiny Dulong ethnic group, whose women still tattoo their faces. The Dulong River actually flows out of China into Myanmar, where it eventually joins the Irrawaddy. There is a county guesthouse (xiàn zhāodàisǔo) in the capital **Dúlóngjiāng**.

No buses run into the valley. You'll have to hire a minivan from Gòngshān for the rough 96km trip to Dúlóngjiāng. At the time of writing the road was being upgraded which may improve access. However, there is a checkpoint en route so you'll need to ask in Bǐngzhōngluò if foreigners are allowed into the area. Once you reach the valley, most travel is on foot. All travel is dicey in rainy weather and the road is closed if there's snow.

BĂOSHĀN REGION

Scrunched up against Myanmar (Burma) and bisected by the wild Nù Jiāng, the Bǎoshān region (保山) is a varied landscape that includes thick forests, dormant volcanoes and hot springs.

The eponymous capital is unremarkable; lovely Téngchōng (and its environs) is where it's at. The Téngchōng area is peppered with minority groups whose villages lie in and around the ancient fire mountains.

As early as the 4th and 5th centuries BC (two centuries before the northern routes through central Asia were established), the Bǎoshān area was an important stop on the southern Silk Road – the Sìchuān–India route. The area did not come under Chinese control until the Han dynasty. In 1277 a huge battle was waged in the region between the 12,000 troops of Kublai Khan and 60,000 Burmese soldiers and their 2000 elephants. The Mongols won and went on to take Pagan.

Téngchōng 腾冲

📞0875

With 20 volcanoes in the vicinity, lots of hot springs and great trekking potential, there's plenty to explore in this neck of the woods. And the city itself is a bit of an oddity – one of the few places in China that, though much of the old architecture has been demolished, remains a pleasant place to hang out, with oodles of green space (you can actually smell the flowers!) and a friendly, low-key populace.

👁 Sights & Activities

Much of the old-time architecture is now gone, but some OK places for a random wander are still to be found.

Markets MARKETS
The backstreets running off Yingjiang Xilu sport a couple of small markets with splashes of colour and activity in the mornings. Walking along Fengshan Lu from Feicui Lu, the first side street on the left has a small **produce market** (产品市场; chǎnpǐn shìchǎng). Further down on the right is a large, covered **jade market** (珠宝玉器交易中心; zhūbǎo yùqì jiāoyì zhōngxīn), where you can sometimes see the carving process. Walk east along Yingjiang Xilu and you will come across a larger **produce market** on your right.

Diéshuǐ Waterfall WATERFALL
(叠水瀑布; Diéshuǐ Pùbù; admission ¥30) In the western suburbs of town, beside the **Xiānlè Temple** (仙乐寺; Xiānlè Sì), this is a good place for a picnic. The area makes a nice destination for a bike ride and you could easily combine it with a trip to **Héshùn** (和顺), a picturesque village 4km outside Téngchōng.

🛏 Sleeping & Eating

There's no shortage of places to stay: bargain hard at any hotel.

There are many hole-in-the-wall eateries and barbecue places along Feicui Lu and elsewhere around town. At night, food stalls set up in the centre of town off Fengshan Lu.

TOP CHOICE Téngchōng
International Youth Hostel HOSTEL $
(腾冲国际青年旅舍; Téngchōng Guójì Qīngnián Lǚshè; 📞519 8677; 44494841@qq.com; Yuquanyuan; 玉泉园; dm ¥40, d ¥138-150; ❀@☎) Fronting a redone outdoor shopping plaza just off the main road, this airy hostel is a relaxed place with English-speaking staff and lots of space

Téngchōng

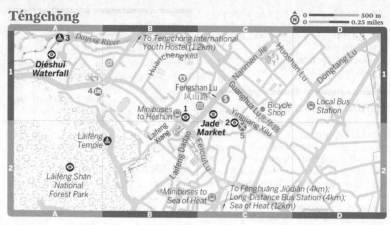

Téngchōng

◉ Top Sights
Diéshuǐ Waterfall................................A1
Jade Market......................................C1

◉ Sights
1 Produce Market B1
2 Produce Market C2
3 Xiānle Temple.................................A1

◉ Sleeping
4 Xīnghuá Dàjiǔdiàn...........................A1

◉ Eating
5 Jùngé Lín Western Restaurant C2

to lounge around. Private bedrooms are spotless but dorms are scruffy and unkempt – the staff expect guests to make their own beds and clean up the dorms (when we noted the dorm floors were dirty they handed us a mop!). It's a ¥13 taxi ride from the long-distance bus station. A YHA card nets you a small discount.

Xīnghuá Dàjiǔdiàn HOTEL $$
(兴华大酒店; ☑513 2688; 7 Tuánpō Xiǎoqū; 团坡小区7号; s & d ¥200; ☀) There are alarming, tiger-pattern carpets here, but the rooms themselves are comfortable, if generic. The location, northeast of Láifēng Shān National Forest Park, is handy in what is a spread-out town. No internet.

Jùngé Lín Western Restaurant WESTERN, THAI $$
(俊格林西餐厅; Jùngé Lín Xī Cāntīng; 188 Buxing Jiē; mains from ¥20; ☉10am-11.30pm; ☑) A Chinese-run place that attempts Western

dishes (steaks, salads, pasta) with varying degrees of success plus some Thai dishes and simple Chinese options.

① Information

Bank of China (中国银行; Zhōngguó Yínháng; cnr Fengshan Lu & Yingjiang Xilu) Has a 24-hour ATM and will change cash and travellers cheques. There are other ATMs around town that take foreign cards too.

China Post (国际邮局; Zhōngguó Yóuzhèng; Fengshan Lu) Serves as post and telephone office.

Internet cafe (网吧; wǎngbā; 100m north of Xīnghuá Dàjiǔdiàn; per hr ¥3)

Public Security Bureau (PSB; 公安局; Gōng'ānjú; Yingjiang Xilu; ☉8.30-11.30am & 2.30-5.30pm Mon-Fri) Can help with visa extensions.

① Getting There & Away

Air
Téngchōng's airport 12km south of town has a daily flight to Kūnmíng (¥1070).

Bus
The city's long-distance bus station is in the south of town.

Bǎoshān ¥52, three hours, every 40 minutes (7.50am to 7pm)

Kūnmíng (express) ¥234–248, 11 hours, 11 daily (9am–8.10pm)

Lìjiāng (sleeper) ¥180, 10 hours, one daily (8pm)

Liùkù ¥70, six hours, four daily (8am, 9am, 10am, 11am)

Xiàguān ¥128, six hours, two daily (10.30am and noon); (sleeper) ¥154, six to seven hours, one daily (7.30pm)

Téngchōng's local bus station (客运站; kèyùn zhàn) has frequent departures to local destinations.

Mángshì ¥33, two to three hours, nine daily (7.30am to 4.30pm)

Ruìlì ¥84, four hours, nine daily (7am to 3.50pm)

Buses to local destinations north of Téngchōng, such as Mǎzhàn, Gùdōng, Ruìdiàn, Diàntān or Zìzhì, either leave from, or pass through, Huoshan Lu in the northeast of town. There's also an old local bus station on Dongfang Lu.

ⓘ Getting Around

Téngchōng's environs make for some fine bike riding. You can hire a bike from a shop on Guanghua Lu or from the Téngchōng International Youth Hostel (both ¥20 per day).

Bus 2 runs from the town centre to the long-distance bus station. Taxis charge ¥5 to hop around town.

Around Téngchōng

Getting out to the sights is a bit tricky. Catching buses part of the way and hiking is one possibility, while some of the closer attractions can be reached by bicycle.

Some highlights of the region are the traditional villages that are scattered between Téngchōng and Yúnfēng Shān (Cloudy Peak Mountain). The relatively plentiful public transport along this route means that you can jump on and off minibuses to go exploring as the whim takes you.

HÉSHÙN
和顺

Southwest of Téngchōng, **Héshùn** (admission ¥80; ⏰8am-7pm) is well worth a visit. It has been set aside as a retirement village for overseas Chinese, but it's of more interest as a quiet, traditional Chinese village with cobbled streets. There are some great old buildings in the village, providing lots of photo opportunities. The village also has a small **museum** (博物馆; bówùguǎn) and a famous old **library** (图书馆; túshūguǎn). You can avoid buying a ticket by walking through the fields around the village (but you won't be able to go to the museum or library where the tickets are checked). Get off the bus at a gas station 1.2km before the village, cross the street and walk along the path near the base of the hill (on your left).

The newish **Héshùn International Youth Hostel** (和顺国际青年旅舍; Téngchōng Guójì Qīngnián Lûshè; ☎515 8398; Cunjiawan; 寸家湾;

dm ¥20, d ¥50-100; @) in the village (by the big banyan tree) is pleasant and set around a small courtyard.

Bus No 6 (which stops near the Téngchōng Youth Hostel) goes to Héshùn or you can take a minibus (¥3) from the corner of Feicui Lu and Laifeng Xiang. It's an easy bicycle ride out to the village but the ride back is an uphill slog.

YÚNFĒNG SHĀN
云峰山

A Taoist mountain dotted with 17th-century temples and monastic retreats, **Yúnfēng Shān** (Cloudy Peak Mountain; admission ¥60) is 47km north of Téngchōng. It's possible to take a **cable car** (one way/return ¥90/160), close to the top from where it's a 20-minute walk to **Dàxióng Bǎodiàn** (大雄宝殿), a temple at the summit. **Lǔzǔ Diàn** (鲁祖殿), the temple second from the top, serves up solid vegetarian food at lunchtime. It's possible to stay here the night in dirty dorm rooms (per person ¥20). It's a quick walk down but it can be hard on the knees. You can walk up the mountain in about 2½ hours.

To get to the mountain, go to Huoshan Lu in Téngchōng and catch a bus to Gùdōng (¥15), and then a microbus from there to the turn-off (¥10). From the turn-off you have to hitch, or you could take the lovely walk past the village of Héping (和平) to the pretty villages just before the mountain. From the parking lot a golf cart (¥5) takes you to the entrance. Hiring a vehicle from Téngchōng to take you on a return trip will cost about ¥300.

VOLCANOES

Téngchōng County is renowned for its volcanoes, and although they have been behaving themselves for many centuries, the seismic and geothermal activity in the area indicates that they won't always continue to do so. The closest volcano to Téngchōng is **Mǎ'ān Shān** (马鞍山; Saddle Mountain), around 5km to the northwest. It's just south of the main road to Yíngjiāng.

Around 22km to the north of town, near the village of **Mǎzhàn**, is the most accessible cluster of **volcanoes** (admission ¥45). The main central volcano is known as **Dàkōng Shān** (大空山; Big Empty Hill), which pretty much sums it up, and to the left of it is the black crater of **Hēikōng Shān** (黑空山; Black Empty Hill). You can haul yourself up the steps for views of the surrounding lava fields (long dormant).

Minibuses run frequently to Mǎzhàn (¥5) from along Huoshan Lu, or take a Gùdōng-bound minibus. From Mǎzhàn town it's a 10-minute walk or you can take a motor-tricycle (¥5) to the volcano area. Once you are in the area there is a fair bit of walking to get between the sights, or you can hitch rides.

SEA OF HEAT   热海

The intriguingly named **Sea of Heat** (Rèhǎi; admission ¥60, pool access ¥268; ⊗8am-11pm) is a steamy cluster of hot springs, geysers and streams (but no actual sea, per se). Located about 12km southwest of Téngchōng, it's essentially an upmarket resort, with a few outdoor hot springs, a nice warm-water swimming pool along with indoor baths. Even if you don't pay the steep price to enter the pools it's possible to just wander along the stone paths admiring the geo-thermal activity. Some of the springs here reach temperatures of 102°C (don't swim in these ones!).

The rooms at the **Yǎng Shēng Gé** (养生阁; ✆586 9700; s & d ¥1600, ste ¥3600) all come with their very own mini-spa complete with water piped from the hot springs. It's close to the ticket office.

Microbuses leave for the Sea of Heat (¥6) when full from the Rehai Lu turn-off in the south of Téngchōng.

DÉHÓNG PREFECTURE

Déhóng Prefecture (德宏州; Déhóng Zhōu and Jingpo Autonomous Prefecture) juts into Myanmar in the far west of Yúnnán. Once a backwater of backwaters, as trade grew, the region saw tourists flock in to experience its raucous border atmosphere.

That's dimmed quite a bit, but most Chinese tourists in Déhóng are still here for the trade from Myanmar that comes through Ruìlì and Wǎndīng; Burmese jade is a popular commodity and countless other items are spirited over the border.

The most obvious minority groups in Déhóng are the Burmese (who are normally dressed in their traditional saronglike *longyi*), Dai and Jingpo – known in Myanmar as the Kachin – a minority group long engaged in armed struggle against the Myanmar government). For information on etiquette for visiting temples in the region see p694.

Ruìlì   瑞丽

☑ 0692

Back in the 1980s this border town was a no-torious haven for drug and gem smugglers, prostitution and various other iniquities. The government cleaned it up in the 1990s and today you're more likely to stumble into a shopping mall than a den of thieves. Still, Ruìlì has an edge to it, thanks to a thriving gem market operated largely by Burmese and Pakistani traders. And with its palm tree-lined streets, bicycle rickshaws and steamy climate, Ruìlì has a distinctly laid-back, Southeast Asian feel.

The minority villages nearby are also good reason to come and it's worth getting a bicycle and heading out to explore. Another draw for travellers is Myanmar, which lies only a few kilometres away. Though individual tourists are not allowed to cross freely, organising permits to take you through the sensitive border area is becoming easier.

◉ Sights

Think atmosphere rather than aesthetics. The huge **market** (市场; *shìchǎng*) in the west of town is one of the most colourful and fun in Yúnnán; a real swirl of ethnicities, including Dai, Jingpo, Han and Burmese, as well as the odd Bangladeshi and Pakistani trader. Get here in the morning, when the stalls are lined with Burmese smokes, tofu wrapped in banana leaves, dodgy pharmaceuticals from Thailand, clothes, you name it. It's also a good place to grab lunch at one of the many snack stalls.

Also great for people-watching is Ruìlì's ever-expanding **jade market** (珠宝街; *zhūbǎo jiē*), the centre of town in all senses. Burmese jade sellers run most of the shops here and for a while you may even forget you are still in China.

☷ Sleeping

There are lots of hotels in Ruìlì, although prices here seem a little higher compared to other cities in Yúnnán. Only top-end places will likely have internet access.

Ruìlì Bīnguǎn   HOTEL $$
(瑞丽宾馆; ✆410 0899; 25 Jianshe Lu; 建设路25号; s & d ¥220; ❀@☎) This place, garishly painted orange and gold, is perhaps the best in town for comfort and facilities, although you'll need to bargain hard and smile a lot to get the price down. Rooms have ADSL inter-

net and there is wi-fi in the lobby. The staff are friendly and can sell maps (¥10) of town and the surrounding area.

Zhōngruì Bīnguǎn　　　HOTEL **$**
(中瑞宾馆; ☑410 0556; cnr Renmin Lu & Nanmao Jie; 南卯街; s & d ¥320; ❀) A central location and decently kept rooms with only mildly stained walls make this a reasonable option in the budget category. Discounts regularly available; you can usually get a room for around ¥120.

Bāshí Jiǔdiàn　　　HOTEL **$**
(巴石酒店; ☑412 9088; cnr Renmin Lu & Nanmao Jie; 南卯街; s & d ¥160; ❀) The staff here have been struck down by the stultifying, steamy atmosphere of Ruìlì and slumber most of the time. You can normally grab one of the big rooms for ¥50 as long as you don't mind the threadbare carpets, rogue hairballs and overall neglected appearance.

✗ Eating & Drinking

Street stalls set up all over town come nightfall; just follow your nose.

TOP CHOICE **Bo Bo's Cold Drinks Shop**　　CAFE **$**
(步步冷饮店; Bùbù Lěngyǐndiàn; Xi'nan Lu; dishes from ¥5; ❂8am-1am; ❂❂) Busy from early to late, the *longyi*-clad Burmese waiters at this Ruìlì institution hustle as they serve up fantastic fruit juices, Burmese-style milky tea, ice cream and cakes, as well as simple but tasty rice and noodle dishes. English is spoken here and wi-fi is available.

Huáfēng Market　　　STREET MARKET **$**
(华丰市场; Huáfēng Shìchǎng; off Jiegang Lu; ❂6pm-late) An outdoor food court that thrives once darkness descends, come here for Burmese and Chinese food, including superb barbecue dishes, and the odd Thai delicacy. The food is all on display, so just pick and point.

❶ Information

Bank of China (中国银行; Zhōngguó Yínháng; Nanmao Jie) Provides all the usual services and will cash travellers cheques for US dollars if you're headed to Myanmar. There are other ATMs around town that take foreign cards. You can also change/find US dollars at the jade market.

China Post (国际邮局; Zhōngguó Yóuzhèng; cnr Mengmao Lu & Renmin Lu)

Internet cafe (网吧; wǎngbā; cnr Nanmao Jie & Jiegang Lu; per hr ¥3; ❂24hr) At the time of writing, foreigners weren't allowed to use Ruìlì's internet cafes. If you have a wi-fi enabled device try Bo Bo's Cold Drinks Shop.

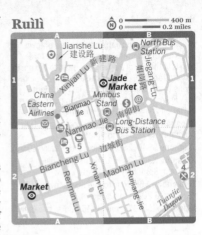

Ruìlì

◎ Top Sights
Jade Market B1
Market A2

▣ Sleeping
1 Bāshí Jiǔdiàn A1
2 Ruìlì Bīnguǎn A1
3 Zhōngruì Bīnguǎn A2

✗ Eating
4 Huáfēng Market B2

◎ Drinking
5 Bo Bo's Cold Drinks Shop A2

Public Security Bureau (PSB; 公安局; Gōng'ānjú; Jianshe Jie; ❂8.30-11.30am & 2.30-5.30pm)

❶ Getting There & Away

An expressway from Bǎoshān to Ruìlì was being built at the time of writing, which will link Ruìlì to Xiàguān and on to Kūnmíng. The first five hours or so out of Ruìlì are still on older roads that pass through villages (and checkpoints), then you get on the highway for a speedy finish to Xiàguān.

Air

Daily flights come from Kūnmíng via Mángshì, a two-hour drive away. You can buy tickets at **China Eastern Airlines** (东方航空公司; Dōngfāng Hángkōng Gōngsī; ☑411 1111; Renmin Lu; ❂8.30am-6pm). Shuttle buses leave daily from the office, three hours before scheduled flights (¥60). You can also use the ticket office to book and reconfirm return flights – do so early.

YÚNNÁN RUÌLÌ

Bus

Ruìlì has a long-distance bus station (长途客运站; chángtú kèyùn zhàn) in the centre of town and a north bus station, really more of a forecourt, at the top of Jiegang Lu. Head to the north bus station (汽车北站; qìchē běizhàn) if you're trying to get to Mángshì (¥35, last bus 6pm – they leave when full); for everything else, you're better off going to the long-distance station.

Bǎoshān ¥94, six to seven hours, every 30 to 40 minutes (7.30am to 4pm)

Jǐnghóng ¥340, 24 to 26 hours, one daily (10am)

Kūnmíng ¥300, 14 to 15 hours, four daily (9.30am, 3pm, 6pm and 8pm)

Téngchōng ¥65, four to five hours, every 40 minutes (6.30am to 12.20pm)

Xiàguān ¥150–170, nine to 10 hours, two daily (9am and 8pm)

For local destinations, minibuses leave from opposite the main bus station, or you can just flag one down in the street. Destinations include Wǎndīng (¥10), the border checkpoint at Jiěgào (¥10) and the village of Nóngdào (¥8). Buses to Zhāngfèng (¥11, one hour) leave from Xinjian Lu.

ⓘ Getting Around

The most interesting day trips require a bicycle. Ask at your accommodation about the best place to rent one.

A flat rate for a taxi ride inside the city should be ¥5, and up for negotiation from there. There are also cheaper motor and cycle rickshaws.

Around Ruìlì

Most of the sights around Ruìlì can be explored by bicycle. It's worth making detours down the narrow paths leading off the main roads to visit minority villages. The people are friendly, and there are lots of photo opportunities. The *Tourism and Traffic Map of Ruìlì*, available from the Xīnhuá bookshop on Renmin Lu, shows major roads and villages.

The shortest ride is to turn left at the corner north of China Post and continue out of Ruìlì into the little village of **Měngmǎo**. There are half a dozen Shan temples scattered about; the fun is in finding them.

GOLDEN DUCK PAGODA   弄安金鸭塔

In the outskirts of town to the southwest, on the main road, this pagoda (Nòng'ān Jīnyā Tǎ) is an attractive stupa set in a temple courtyard. It was established to mark the arrival of a pair of golden ducks that brought good fortune to what was previously an uninhabited marshy area.

TEMPLES

Just past Golden Duck Pagoda is a crossroads and a small wooden temple. The road to the right (west) leads to the villages of **Jiěxiàng** (姐相) and **Nóngdǎo** (弄岛), and on the way are a number of small temples, villages and stupas. None are spectacular but the village life is interesting and there are often small markets near the temples.

The first major Dai temple is **Hǎnshā Zhuāng Temple** (喊沙奘寺; Hǎnshā Zhuāng Sì), a fine wooden structure with a few resident monks. It's set a little off the road and a green tourism sign marks the turn-off. The surrounding Dai village is interesting.

A few kilometres further on is **One Village Two Countries** (一寨两国寺; Yízhài Liǎngguó; admission ¥20; ⊙9am-6pm), a low-key tourist attraction where you can stand on the border between China and Myanmar. There are a few eating stalls and some unusual gimmicks – Kayan women show off their brass neck rings while nearby a daredevil Burmese chap wrestlers alligators.

Another 20 minutes or so further down the road, look out for a blue and gold roofed traditional building on the right side of the road. Turn right here and follow the narrow paved road through the fields to **Léizhuāngxiāng** (雷装相), Ruìlì's oldest stupa, dating back to the middle of the Tang dynasty.

JIĚGÀO BORDER CHECKPOINT   姐告边检点

On land jutting into Myanmar, Jiěgào is the main checkpoint for a steady stream of cross-border traffic. It's a bustling place, with plenty of traders doing last-minute shopping in the many shops and goods outlets. Tourists saunter right up to the border and snap photos in front of the large entry gate. While not a 'must-see' it is fun for border-holics to peek through the gates to Myanmar and dream of a day tourists can cross overland.

To get here, continue straight ahead from Golden Duck Pagoda, cross the Myanmar bridge over Ruìlì Jiāng and you will come to Jiěgào, about 7km from Ruìlì.

Shared red taxis (¥5) with signs for Jiěgào (姐告) drive around the centre of Ruìlì from dawn until late at night. These are different from Ruìlì's typical maroon-coloured taxis.

GOLDEN PAGODA   姐勒金塔

A few kilometres to the east of Ruìlì on the road to Wǎndīng is the Golden Pagoda (Jiělè Jīntǎ), a fine structure that dates back 200 years.

BORDER CROSSING: GETTING TO MYANMAR (BURMA)

At the time of writing it was not possible for third country nationals to travel across the border at Jiěgào. The only way to go is by air from Kūnmíng. Visas are available at the embassy in Běijīng (see p986) or in Kūnmíng at the Myanmar consulate (p987). In Kūnmíng visas cost ¥185, take four days to process and are good for a maximum 28-day visit

The situation remains fluid so it's worth asking Kūnmíng-based travel agents if crossing the border overland is possible. Several agents based at the **Camellia Hotel** (茶花宾馆; Cháhuā Bīnguǎn; www.kmcamelliahotel.com; 96 Dongfeng Donglu) specialise in trips to Myanmar. At the time of writing there were daily flights to Yangon on China Eastern Airlines for ¥2000 or to Mandalay for ¥2600.

XĪSHUĀNGBǍNNÀ REGION

North of Myanmar and Laos, Xīshuāngbǎnnà is the Chinese approximation of the original Thai name of Sip Sawng Panna (12 Rice-Growing Districts). The Xīshuāngbǎnnà region (西双版纳), better known as Bǎnnà, has become China's mini-Thailand, attracting tourists looking for sunshine, water-splashing festivals and epic jungle treks.

Still, Xīshuāngbǎnnà rarely feels overwhelmed by visitors – even the capital, Jǐnghóng, is basically an overgrown town.

Environment

Xīshuāngbǎnnà has myriad plant and animal species, although recent scientific studies have shown the tropical rainforest areas of Bǎnnà are now acutely endangered. The jungle areas that remain contain a handful of tigers, leopards and golden-haired monkeys. The number of elephants has doubled to 250, up 100% from the early 1980s; the government now offers compensation to villagers whose crops have been destroyed by elephants, or who assist in wildlife conservation. In 1998 the government banned the hunting or processing of animals, but poaching is notoriously hard to control.

People

About one-third of the million-strong population of this region are Dai; another third or so are Han Chinese and the rest are a conglomerate of minorities that include the Hani, Lisu and Yao, as well as lesser-known hill tribes such as the Aini (a subgroup of the Hani), Jinuo, Bulang, Lahu and Wa.

Xīshuāngbǎnnà Dai Autonomous Prefecture, as it is known officially, is subdivided into the three counties of Jǐnghóng, Měnghǎi and Měnglà.

Climate

The region has two seasons: wet and dry. The wet season is between June and August, when it rains ferociously, although not every day. From September to February there is less rainfall, but thick fog descends during the late evening and doesn't lift until 10am or even later.

November to March sees temperatures average about 19°C. The hottest months of the year are from April to September, when you can expect an average of 25°C.

✴✴ Festivals & Events

During festivals, booking same-day airline tickets to Jǐnghóng can be extremely difficult. Hotels in Jǐnghóng town are booked solid and prices usually triple. Most people end up commuting from a nearby Dai village. Festivities take place all over Xīshuāngbǎnnà, so you might be lucky further away from Jǐnghóng.

Tanpa Festival   CULTURAL
In February, young boys are sent to the local temple for initiation as novice monks.

Tan Jing Festival   CULTURAL
Held between February and March participants honour Buddhist texts housed in local temples.

Water-Splashing Festival   CULTURAL
Held in mid-April, the water-splashing festival washes away the dirt, sorrow and demons of the old year and brings in the happiness of the new. Jǐnghóng celebrates it from 13 to 15 April but dates in the surrounding villages vary. Although the festival lasts three days, the actual splashing only occurs on 15 April. Foreigners earn special attention, so prepare to be drenched all day.

Xīshuāngbǎnnà

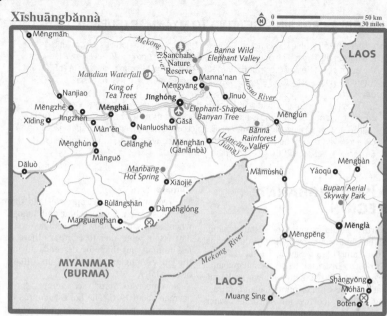

Mēngmǎn
Mekong River
Sanchahe Nature Reserve
Banna Wild Elephant Valley
LAOS
Mandian Waterfall
Manna'nan
King of Tea Trees
Mēngyǎng
Nanjiao
Jǐnghóng
Jinuò
Mēngzhē
Mēnghǎi
Elephant-Shaped Banyan Tree
Mēnglún
Xīdìng
Jǐngzhēn
Màn'ēn
Gāsǎ
Nanluoshan
Bānnà Rainforest Valley
Mēnghùn
Gēlǎnghé
Mēnghǎn (Gǎnlǎnbà)
Làncāng Jiāng
Liùshù River
Màngùo
Dǎluò
Manbang Hot Spring
Xiǎojiē
Mǎmùshù
Mēngbàn
Yáoqū
Bupan Aerial Skyway Park
Bùlǎngshān
Dàměnglóng
Manguanghan
Mekong River
Mēngpēng
Mēnglà
MYANMAR (BURMA)
LAOS
Shàngyòng
Mòhān
Muang Sing
Bòtēn

0 / 50 km
0 / 30 miles

Closed-Door Festival CULTURAL

The farming season, July to October, is the time for the closed-door festival (傣族关门节), when marriages or festivals are banned. Traditionally, this is also the time of year that men aged 20 or older are ordained as monks for a period of time. The season ends with the **Open-Door Festival**, when everyone lets their hair down again to celebrate the harvest.

Tan Ta Festival CULTURAL

This festival is held during a 10-day period of October or November, with temple ceremonies, rocket launches from special towers and hot-air balloons. The rockets, which often contain lucky amulets, blast into the sky; those who find the amulets are assured of good luck.

Jǐnghóng 景洪

📞 0691 / POP 520,000

Jǐnghóng – the 'City of Dawn' in local Dai language – is the capital of Xīshuāngbǎnnà Prefecture, but don't take that too seriously. It's a drowsy Mekong River jungle town as much as a city. Buildings are going up, neophyte tour groups run around in all directions (great people-watching fun, actually) but it's still a perfect representation of laid-back Bǎnnà.

In the summer, the low season, prepare yourself for searing heat and a sapping humidity that puts the entire city into an extended slow motion. If you've acclimatised to higher and nippier elevations in Yúnnán, you'll probably find yourself needing lots of midday siestas. During the winter months, though, the temperature is just perfect.

◉ Sights & Activities

Tropical Flower & Plants Garden GARDENS
(热带花卉园; Rèdài Huāhuìyuán; 99 Jinghong Xilu; admission ¥40; ⏰7.30am-6pm) This terrific botanic garden, west of the town centre, is one of Jǐnghóng's better attractions. Admission gets you into a series of gardens where you can view over 1000 different types of plant life. Take the path on the left-hand side as you enter the gardens to head towards the lovely tropical rainforest area.

Peacock Lake Park PARK
The artificial lake in the centre of town isn't much, but the small park (孔雀湖公园; Kǒngquè Hú Gōngyuán) next to it is pleasant. The English Language Corner takes place here every Sunday evening, so this is a great opportunity to exchange views or to engage with the locals practising their English.

Blind Massage School MASSAGE
(盲人按摩; Mángrén Ànmó; cnr Mengle Dadao & Jingde Lu; ⊙8am-midnight) Jǐnghóng's oft-recommended Blind Massage School offers hour-long massages for ¥50. Staff are extremely kind and travellers give it terrific reports. Head down the lane off Mengle Dadao and climb the stairs on your left up to the 2nd floor.

🛏 Sleeping

Manting Lu is lined with cheapies, where you can find bearable rooms from ¥50. Outside of festival season, big discounts are normally on offer all over town.

**Many Trees
International Youth Hostel** HOSTEL $
(曼丽翠国际青年旅舍; Mànlìcuì Gúojì Qīngnián Lǚshè; ☎212 6210; 5 Manyun Xiang; 嘎兰中路曼允巷5号; dm ¥30-35, d ¥85-95; ❋ ⍟) Jǐnghóng's first hostel offers smallish dorms that have ensuite bathrooms. The doubles are a good deal for the price. There's wi-fi throughout and a cosy communal area. It's down an alley off Galan Zhonglu.

**Mekong River
International Youth Hostel** HOSTEL $
(湄公河国际青年旅舍; Méigōng Hé Gúojì Qīngnián Lǚshè; ☎229 8000; 6 Menglong Lu; 勐龙路6号景兰国际G幢; dm ¥30, d ¥128; ❋ @ ⍟) This centrally located hostel has a utilitarian

feel and some big barren rooms. It's a little scruffy and the dorm beds are rock hard but otherwise it's a very convenient base. It's popular with Chinese backpackers but some English is spoken.

North Bank Youth Hostel HOSTEL $
(北岸青年旅舍; Běi Àn Qīngnián Lǚshè; ☎221 9177; D9 Yijingwan, Jingliang Lu; 景亮路怡景湾D9; dm ¥35, s ¥80, d ¥90-130; ❋ @ ⍟) Located across the river on the north bank of the Mekong (hence the name), this hostel is a solid 25-minute walk from the centre of town. If you don't mind the walk to town, it's a peaceful spot located inside a residential compound, with a big airy lobby, clean rooms and reliable wi-fi. It's difficult to find the first time so have your taxi driver call the hostel for directions.

Popular Holiday Hotel HOTEL $$
(假日时尚酒店; Jiàrì Shíshàng Jiǔdiàn; ☎213 9001; 104 Galan Zhonglu; 嘎兰中路104号; d ¥358; ❋ @) Standing out from the three-star pack by virtue of its sizeable, light, clean and modern rooms, many of which come with computers, the optimistic name of this place is well justified. Ignore the listed prices; you should be able to get a room for ¥100 to ¥120 outside of festival time.

King Land Hotel HOTEL $$$
(鲸兰大酒店; Jīnglán Jiǔdiàn; ☎216 6999; www.newtgh.com; 6 Jingde Lu; 景德路6号; d US$160;

YÚNNÁN JǏNGHÓNG

HIKING IN XĪSHUĀNGBǍNNÀ

Hikes around Xīshuāngbǎnnà used to be among the best in China – you'd be invited into a local's home to eat, sleep and drink *mǐjiǔ* (rice wine). Increasing numbers of visitors have changed this in places. Don't automatically expect a welcome mat and a free lunch just because you're a foreigner, but remember that throwing your money around could change the local economy.

If you do get invited into someone's home, try to establish whether payment is expected. If it's not, leave an offering (ask at the backpacker cafes to find out what's considered appropriate) or leave modest gifts such as candles, matches, rice etc – even though the family may insist on nothing.

Also take care before heading off. It's a jungle out there, so go prepared, and make sure somebody knows where you are and when you should return. In the rainy season you'll need to be equipped with proper hiking shoes and waterproof gear. At any time you'll need water purification tablets, bottled water or a water bottle able to hold boiled water, as well as snacks and sunscreen.

Seriously consider taking a guide. You won't hear much Mandarin Chinese on the trail, let alone any English. Expect to pay around ¥250 to ¥300 per day.

Forest Café (☎0691 898 5122; www.forest-cafe.org) in Jǐnghóng is a great place to start. Sarah, the owner, has years of experience leading treks and comes recommended. The **Mekong Café** (湄公咖啡; Méigōng Kāfē; Menglong Lu) can also organise treks. Nearby, the **Měiměi Café** (☎0691 216 1221; www.meimei-cafe.com) doesn't organise treks but does have lots of details in binders so you can find your own way.

✳@✉) Sporting two enormous elephants at its entrance, this is one of Jǐnghóng's unmistakable landmarks. It has a super central location, four-star standard rooms and a swimming pool. Amenities here include the Lao consulate and Lao airlines office. Discounts of 60% available.

Eating

The Dai restaurants along Menghun Lu and the excellent Dai barbecue restaurants off Manting Lu are where you'll find the locals and the most authentic and tastiest food in town (as well as at the night markets that pop up all over town).

Dai dishes include barbecued fish, eel or beef cooked with lemongrass or served with peanut and tomato sauce. Vegetarians can order roast bamboo shoots prepared in the same fashion. Other specialities include fried river moss (better than it sounds and excellent with beer), spicy bamboo-shoot soup and *shāokǎo* (skewers of meat wrapped in banana leaves and grilled over wood fires).

Měiměi Café
WESTERN $$

(美美咖啡厅; Měiměi Kāfēitīng; Menglong Lu; dishes from ¥15-35; ⊙8.30am-1am; ⊕⊚) You'll find it and you'll eat here. This is the original of all the Western-style cafes in town and still the best, thanks to its menu of burgers and sandwiches, pizza and pasta, and foreigner-friendly Chinese and Thai dishes. The owner Orchid is a great source of local info.

Luō Luō Bīng Wū
NOODLES $

(啰啰冰屋; 96 Xuanwei Dadao; dishes from ¥5; ⊙7.30am-10pm) A buzzing local spot, Jǐnghóngers flock here for the cheap and tasty rice noodle and fried rice dishes, as well as fruit juices, shakes and Taiwanese-style shaved ice desserts that are perfect for cooling off. There's also an open-air area out back.

Thai Restaurant
THAI $

(泰国餐厅; Tàiguó Cāntīng; Manting Lu; mains from ¥12; ⊙8am-9.30pm) If you're not making the trek overland to Southeast Asia, get

MINORITY GROUPS OF XĪSHUĀNGBǍNNÀ

The Dai (傣族) are Hinayana Buddhists (as opposed to China's majority Mahayana Buddhists) who first appeared 2000 years ago in the Yangzi Valley and were subsequently driven south to here by the Mongol invasion of the 13th century. The common dress for Dai women is a straw hat or towel-wrap headdress, a tight, short blouse in a bright colour, and a printed sarong with a belt of silver links. Some Dai men tattoo their bodies with animal designs, and betel-nut chewing is popular. Many Dai youngsters get their teeth capped with gold. Dai language is quite similar to Lao and northern Thai dialects. Some Dai phrases include *douzao li* (hello), *yindi* (thank you) and *goihan* (goodbye).

The Jinuo people (基诺族), sometimes known as the Youle, were officially 'discovered' as a minority in 1979 and are among the smallest groups – numbering between 12,000 and 18,000. They call themselves 'those who respect the uncle' and are thought to possibly have descended from the Qiang. The women wear a white cowl, a cotton tunic with bright horizontal stripes and a tubular black skirt. Earlobe decoration is an elaborate custom – the larger the hole and the more flowers it can contain, the more beautiful the woman is considered. Teeth are sometimes painted black with the sap of the lacquer tree, for both beauty and to protect from teeth decay.

The Bulang people (布朗族) live mainly in the Bùlǎng, Xídìng and Bādá mountains of Xīshuāngbǎnnà. They keep to the hills farming cotton, sugarcane and pǔ'ěr tea, one of Yúnnán's most famous exports. Men traditionally tattoo their arms, legs, chests and stomachs while women wear vibrant headdresses decorated with flowers. Avid betel-nut chewers, the women believe black teeth are beautiful.

The Hani (哈尼族, also known in adjacent countries as the Akha) are closely related to the Yi as a part of the Tibeto-Burman group; the language is Sino-Tibetan but uses Han characters for the written form. They are mostly famed for their river valley rice terraces, especially in the Red River valley, between the Āiláo and Wúliàng Shān, where they cultivate rice, corn and the occasional poppy. Hani women (especially the Aini, a subgroup of the Hani) wear headdresses of beads, feathers, coins and silver rings, some of which are made with French (Vietnamese), Burmese and Indian coins from the turn of the century.

Jǐnghóng

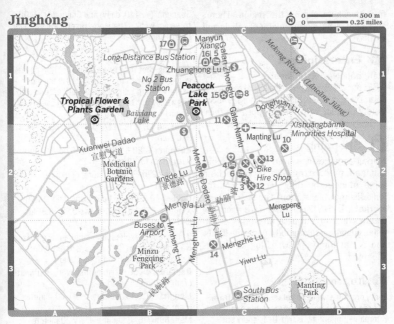

Jǐnghóng

⦿ Top Sights
Peacock Lake Park B1
Tropical Flower & Plants Garden A1

⊕ Activities, Courses & Tours
1 Blind Massage School C2
2 Forest Café B2
3 Mekong Cafe C2

🛏 Sleeping
4 King Land Hotel C2
5 Many Trees International Youth
   Hostel C1
6 Mekong River International
   Youth Hostel C2
7 North Bank Youth Hostel D1

8 Popular Holiday Hotel C1

⊗ Eating
9 Banna Cafe C2
10 Dai BBQ restaurants C2
11 Lūo Lūo Bīng Wū C1
12 Měiměi Café C2
13 Thai Restaurant C2
14 Wàngtiānshù Deli C3

⊙ Entertainment
15 Měngbālā Nàxī Arts Theatre C1

🛍 Shopping
16 Jade Market C1
17 Market B1

your Thai fix at this ever-reliable open-air restaurant. It's not the most upmarket Thai place in town, but it's certainly the most popular and there's a huge range of dishes to choose from.

Banna Cafe WESTERN $$
(版纳咖啡; Bǎnnà Kāfēi; 1 Manting Lu; breakfast from ¥25; ⊗7am-late; 🖳) A good place for breakfast, this friendly, Akha-owned cafe

also has a small terrace that is ideal for a sundowner or late-evening libation while watching the world go by.

Wàngtiānshù Deli WESTERN $$
(望天树美食; Wàngtiānshù Měishí; 111 Mengzhe Lu; dishes ¥12-30; ⊗8.30am-10.30pm; 🖳) Swiss-owned deli with European bread, home-made ice cream and lots of other goodies, in-cluding French wine and cheese, you won't

find anywhere else in the region. There's also a small but decent menu of salads and steaks.

 Entertainment

Měngbālā Nàxī Arts Theatre　　THEATRE
(蒙巴拉纳西艺术宫; Měngbālā Nàxī Yìshùgōng; Galan Zhonglu; tickets ¥190; ⏲8.10pm & 9.45pm) Wildly popular with tour groups, this theatre has nightly song and dance shows.

Shopping

Market groupies can head to the fabulous fish and produce **market** tucked behind some modern buildings across from the long-distance bus station. The nearby **Jade Market** (玉市场; Yù Shìzhǎng; Zhuanghong Lu) features lots of Burmese and other South Asians hawking their goods alongside locals, and is fun for people-watching as well as shopping.

Information

Every once in a while we get reports from travellers regarding drug and rob incidents on the Kūnmíng–Jǐnghóng bus trip. Be friendly but aware, accept nothing, and never leave your stuff unattended when you hop off for a break.

Bank of China (中国银行; Zhōngguó Yínháng; Xuanwei Dadao) Changes travellers cheques and foreign currency, and has an ATM machine. There are other branches on Galan Zhonglu and Minhang Lu.

China Post (国际邮局; Zhōngguó Yóuzhèng; cnr Mengle Dadao & Xuanwei Dadao; ⏲8am-8.30pm) You can make international calls from here.

Internet cafes (山城网吧; wǎngbā; Manting Lu; per hr ¥3) There are many internet cafes along this street.

Public Security Bureau (PSB; 公安局; Gōng'ānjú; 13 Jingde Lu; ⏲8-11.30am & 3-5.30pm Mon-Fri) Has a fairly speedy visa-extension service.

Xīshuǎngbǎnnà Minorities Hospital (西双版纳民族医院; Xīshuǎngbǎnnà Mínzú Yīyuàn; ☏213 0123; Galan Nanlu) The best bet for having an English speaker available.

Getting There & Away
Air

There are several flights a day to Kūnmíng (¥1150) but in April (when the water-splashing festival is held) you'll need to book tickets several days in advance to get either in or out.

In peak seasons you can hop on one or two flights daily to Dàlǐ (¥990) and/or Lìjiāng (¥1060), along with semiregular flights to Shànghǎi (¥2440, daily) and Chéngdū (¥1400, three per week). There are travel agents all over town selling tickets.

Bus

The **long-distance bus station** (长途客运站; chángtú kèyùnzhàn; Minhang Lu) is the most useful for long-distance destinations, and also has a daily bus to Luang Nam Tha in Laos (¥78, seven hours, 10.40am).

Jiànshuǐ ¥177, 12 to 17 hours, two daily (7pm and 8pm)

Kūnmíng ¥220–253, nine to 10 hours, nine daily (8am to 10pm)

Lìjiāng ¥276–333, 18 hours, one daily (9.30pm)

Ruìlì ¥340, 24 to 26 hours, one daily (9am)

Xiàguān ¥200, 16 hours, two daily (8.30am and 10am)

If you want to explore Xīshuāngbǎnnà, go to the No 2 bus station (第二客运站; dì'èr kèyùnzhàn), also known as the Bǎnnà bus station.

Gǎnlǎnbà ¥8.50, 40 minutes, every 30 minutes (7am to 7pm)

Měnghǎi ¥15, 45 minutes, every 20 minutes (7am to 7.20pm)

Měnghùn ¥16, 1½ hours, every 20 minutes (7am to 6.40pm)

Měnglà ¥44, two hours 30 minutes, every 30 minutes (6.30am to 6.20pm)

Měnglún ¥17, 1½ hours, every 20 minutes (7am to 6pm)

Měnyǎng ¥10, 40 minutes, half-hourly (8am to 6pm)

Sānchàhé ¥15, one hour, 10 daily (7.30am to 5pm)

Sīmáo ¥55, two hours, every 30 minutes (6.30am to 7pm)

For buses to Dàměnglóng, head to the south bus station (客运南站; kèyùn nánzhàn), which also has departures to Kūnmíng.

If you want to get to the Yuányáng Rice Terraces, first you'll have to take a bus to Jiāngchéng (江城; ¥56, nine to 10 hours, 6.30am or 9.15am), stay there overnight and then hop on another bus to Lùchūn (绿春; ¥34, five hours), a nice Hani town with a good market, before hopping on a bus to Yuányáng (¥34, four hours). You could also take a bus from the main station to Jiànshuǐ (18 hours) and catch a bus to Yuányáng, this route is longer but involves less changes.

Getting Around

The No 1 bus (¥2) runs to the airport, 5km south of the city, from a stop on Mengla Lu near the corner with Minhang Lu. A taxi will cost around ¥20 but expect to be hit up for up to three times that amount during festivals.

BORDER CROSSING: GETTING TO THAILAND

Not that long ago travellers could travel by cargo boat or ferry to Thailand; the journey took anywhere from seven to 15 hours. However, river traffic was halted on the Mekong in October 2011 after 13 Chinese sailors were massacred on their cargo vessels, in drug-related violence. At the time of research the only way to reach Thailand directly was to fly (twice weekly to Bangkok, ¥1700–2100 one-way). However, you could ask about hitching a ride on a cargo boat, these leave from Guǎnlěi (关累), about 75km southeast of Jǐnghóng. Make enquiries at the cafes in Jǐnghóng for the latest schedule. The only other way to go is to first head into Laos and then skip over the Thai border.

Jǐnghóng is small enough that you can walk to most destinations, but a bike makes life easier and can be rented through most accommodation for ¥25 to ¥30 a day or from the **bike shop** (🕗8.30am-10pm) on Manting Lu.

A taxi anywhere in town costs ¥6.

Around Jǐnghóng

Trekking (or busing) to the endless minority villages is the draw. You can spend weeks, but even with limited time most destinations in Xīshuāngbǎnnà are only two or three hours away by bus. Note that to get to the most isolated villages, you'll often first have to take the bus to a primary (and uninteresting) village and stay overnight there, since only one bus per day – if that – travels to the tinier villages.

Market addicts can rejoice – it's an artist's palette of colours in outlying villages. The most popular markets seem to be the Thursday market in Xīdìng, then Měnghùn, followed by Měnghǎi.

Many villages can be reached by bike from Jǐnghóng. The most famous trek has always been the two- to three-hour ride to Měnghǎn (Gǎnlǎnbà); the ride can be hairy with traffic and pollution, but the village surroundings are sublime.

Take note: it can feel like every second village begins with the prefix 'Meng' and it isn't unheard of for travellers to end up at the wrong village entirely because of communication problems. Have your destination written down in script before you head off.

SĀNCHÀHÉ
NATURE RESERVE   三岔河自然保护区
This nature reserve (Sānchàhé Zìrán Bǎohùqū), 48km north of Jǐnghóng, is one of five enormous forest reserves in southern Yúnnán. It has an area of nearly 1.5 million hectares; seriously, treat it with respect – you get off-trail here, you won't be found. The

madding crowds head for **Bǎnnà Wild Elephant Valley** (版纳野象谷; Bǎnnà Yěxiànggǔ; admission ¥65), named after the 50 or so wild elephants that live in the valley. The elephants are very retiring and rare are the travellers who have actually seen any of them. You will see monkeys, though, and it's worth a visit if you want to see something of the local forest. A 2km-long **cable car** (one way/return ¥50/70) runs over the tree tops from the main entrance into the heart of the park, as does an elevated walkway.

There is no accommodation in the park; it's best to stay in Jǐnghóng. There are 10 buses daily to Sānchàhé (¥15, 1½ hours, 7.30am to 5pm).

MĚNGYǍNG   勐养
The much photographed **Elephant-Shaped Banyan Tree** (象形榕树; Xiàngxíng Róngshù) is the reason most people visit Měngyǎng, 34km northeast of Jǐnghóng on the road to Sīmáo. It's also a centre for the Hani, Floral-Belt Dai and Lahu, one of the poorest minorities in the region.

From Měngyǎng it's another 19km southeast to Jīnuò (基诺), which is home base for the Jinuo minority.

MĚNGHǍN (GǍNLǍNBÀ)   勐罕(橄榄坝)
A few years ago, Měnghǎn (or Gǎnlǎnbà as it's sometimes referred to) was a grand destination – you'd bike here and chill. Sadly, much of the main attraction – the lovely, friendly, somnolent village itself – has basically been roped off as a quasi minority theme park (and a pricey one at that) with tour buses, cacophonic dancing – the usual. That said, the environs of the village are still wondrous.

👁 Sights
Dai Minority Park   ANCIENT VILLAGE
(傣族园; Dǎizúyuán; 📞0691 250 4099; Manting Lu; admission ¥100) This was once the part of town that everyone in this region came

ETIQUETTE IN DAI TEMPLES

Around Dai temples the same rules apply as elsewhere: dress appropriately (no sleeveless tops or shorts); take off shoes before entering; don't take photos of monks or the inside of temples without permission; leave a donation if you do take any shots and consider leaving a token donation even if you don't – unlike in Thailand, these Buddhists receive no government assistance. It is polite to *wai* the monks as a greeting and remember to never rub anyone's head, raise yourself higher than a Buddha figure or point your feet at anyone. (This last point applies to secular buildings too. If you stay the night in a Dai household, it is good form to sleep with your feet pointing towards the door.)

to experience – especially for its classic temples and Dai families hosting visitors in their traditional homes. (It's now the aforementioned 'theme park'.) Tourists can spend the night in villagers' homes and partake in water-splashing 'festivals' twice a day. To join the splash party you need to pay an additional ¥40. Despite the artificial nature of it all, some travellers have loved the experience.

For wonderful scenery along rivers and rice paddies, travellers recommend heading to the south of town, crossing the Mekong by ferry (¥2 with a bike), and then heading left (east). The last ferry returns at 7pm.

🛌 Sleeping & Eating

Beds in a Dai home within the park will cost between ¥40 and ¥60 per person. Food is extra. Beds are traditional Dai mats and are usually very comfortable. Most homes will also have showers for you. Restaurants inside the park are pricey and firmly aimed at tour groups.

ℹ️ Getting There & Away

Buses to Měnghǎn leave from Jǐnghóng's No 2 bus station (¥8.50, every 20 minutes, 7.15am to 7pm). From Měnghǎn's bus station, there are buses back to Jǐnghóng (¥8.50) every 20 minutes and two buses a day to Měnglún (¥9.50, one hour, 10am and 2pm).

It's possible to cycle from Jǐnghóng to Měnghǎn in a brisk two hours or a leisurely three hours, although the traffic can be heavy.

ℹ️ Getting Around

You can rent a mountain bike from one of several bicycle shops along Manting Lu (¥20 per day).

MĚNGLÚN   勐仑

East of Měnghǎn, Měnglún sports the **Tropical Plant Gardens** (热带植物园; Rèdài Zhíwùyuán; admission ¥80; ⏰7.30am-midnight). The gardens are gorgeous and get some high marks from visitors.

To get there, turn left out of the bus station and then take the first left. Follow the road downhill and bear right and you'll reach the ticket office, which is just before a footbridge across the Mekong.

Your best bet for a clean bed in town is the **Chūnlín Bīnguǎn** (春林宾馆; ☑0691 871 5681; d ¥60), which is close to the gardens' entrance.

From Jǐnghóng's No 2 bus station there are buses to Měnglún (¥16, 90 minutes, every 20 minutes, 6.30am to 6.20pm). Alternatively, Měnglún can be combined with a day trip to Měnghǎn.

From Měnglún, there are buses to Měnglà (¥24, 2½ hours, every 20 minutes, 8am to 6pm) and Jǐnghóng (¥16, 75 minutes, every 20 minutes, 6.30am to 7pm).

MĚNGLÀ   勐腊

Měnglà is the first (or last) main city for travellers headed to/from Laos. It has a few palm-tree-lined streets and some garish orange-coloured buildings designed with local architecture in mind, but little in the way of sights. Depending on bus condition/road traffic/arrival time, you may be stuck here for the night (the border is another 45km away). If you need a hotel, try the **Jīnqiáo Dàjiǔdiàn** (金桥大酒店; ☑0691 812 4946; d ¥60-100, tr ¥90; ▣), convenient for the north bus station just up the hill.

Měnglà has two bus stations. The northern long-distance bus station has buses to Kūnmíng (¥287, two or three buses daily, 8.30am to 11.30am). The No 2 bus station is in the southern part of town.

Buses from Měnglà's No 2 station:

Jǐnghóng ¥44, every 30 minutes (6.30am to 6.30pm)

Měnglún ¥20 to ¥25, every 20 minutes (6.40am to 7.30pm)

Móhān ¥15, every 20 minutes (8am to 6pm)

DÀMĚNGLÓNG   大勐龙

Dàměnglóng (just the latter two characters, 'Měnglóng', are written on buses) is a scrappy place with drowsy folks lolling about the dusty streets. Sights include some decent pagodas, but mostly you're here to traipse or bike through endless villages (ask about bike hire at the Huá Jié Bīnguǎn).

About 55km south of Jǐnghóng and a few kilometres from the Myanmar border, the border crossing point (not open for foreigners) with Myanmar has been designated as the entry point for a planned highway linking Thailand, Myanmar and China, which should really liven things up around here if it ever gets built.

◉ Sights

White Bamboo Shoot Pagoda   BUDDHIST PAGODA

(曼飞龙塔; Mànfēilóng Tǎ; admission ¥10) Surrounded by jungle (watch out for stray snakes!), this pagoda dates back to 1204 and is Dàměnglóng's premier attraction. According to the legend, this pagoda's temple was built on the location of a hallowed footprint left behind by Sakyamuni Buddha, who is said to have visited Xīshuāngbǎnnà. If you have an interest in ancient footprints you can look for it in a niche below one of the nine stupas. The temple has been extensively renovated in recent years.

If you're in the area late October or early November, check the precise dates of the **Tan Ta Festival**. At this time, White Bamboo Shoot Pagoda is host to hundreds of locals whose celebrations include dancing, rocket launchings, paper balloons and so on.

The pagoda is easy to get to: just walk back along the main road towards Jǐnghóng for 2km until you reach a small village with a temple on your left. From here there's a path up the hill, it's about a 20-minute walk. There's often no one around to collect the entry fee. A motor-rickshaw from Dàměnglóng is ¥10.

FREE Black Pagoda   BUDDHIST PAGODA

Just above the centre of town is a Dai monastery with a steep path beside it leading up to the Black Pagoda (黑塔; Hēi Tǎ) – you'll notice it when entering Dàměnglóng. The pagoda itself is actually gold, not black. Take a stroll up and have a chat with the five young monks in residence. The views of Dàměnglóng and surrounding countryside are more interesting than the temple itself.

🛏 Sleeping & Eating

Huá Jié Bīnguǎn   HOTEL $

(华杰宾馆; ☎0691 274 2588; d ¥60) Not very prepossessing, but the best option in town. To get here, turn right out of the bus station, then left up the hill and it's on the left-hand side, set back from the road.

There are simple Dai barbecue places scattered around the village. Try the ones close to the Black Pagoda.

❶ Getting There & Away

Buses to Dàměnglóng (¥17, 90 minutes, every 15 minutes, 6.30am to 6.30pm) leave from Jǐnghóng's south bus station. Remember, the 'Da' character is sometimes not displayed. Buses for the return trip run on the same schedule.

MĚNGHǍI   勐海

This modern town is another potential base for exploring the countryside, although it's not as pleasant a place as Jǐnghóng. Grab a bike and head north for the most interesting pagodas and villages.

BORDER CROSSING: GETTING TO LAOS

On-the-spot visas for Laos can be obtained at the border. The price will depend on your nationality (generally US$35 to US$40). You can also pick one up at the **Lao Consulate** (◷8.30am-11.30am & 1.30-4pm) located on the ground floor of the King Land Hotel Jǐnhóng.

The **Chinese checkpoint** (☎0691 812 2684; ◷8am-5.30pm) is generally not much of an ordeal. Don't forget that Laos is an hour behind China.

A daily bus runs to Luang Nam Tha in Laos from Jǐnghóng (¥78, seven hours, 10.40am). Along with the bus to Vientiane from Kūnmíng (which leaves Kūnmíng at 5pm when there are enough passengers; ¥486), it stops at Měnglà, but you're not guaranteed a seat.

No matter what anyone says, there should be no 'charge' to cross. Once your passport is stamped (double-check all stamps), you can jump on a tractor or truck to take you 3km into Laos for around ¥5. Whatever you do, go early, in case things wrap up early on either side. There are guesthouses on both the Chinese and Lao sides; people generally change money on the Lao side.

If you're passing through Měnghǎi, it's worth visiting the huge daily **produce market** that attracts members of the hill tribes. The best way to find it is to follow the early-morning crowds.

Buses run from Jǐnghóng's No 2 bus station to Měnghǎi (¥15, 45 minutes, every 20 minutes, 7am to 7.20pm). They return every 20 minutes or so too.

MĚNGHÙN
勐混

This quiet little village, about 26km southwest of Měnghǎi, has a colourful **Sunday market**. The town begins buzzing around 7am and the action lingers on through to midday. The swirl of hill tribes-people alone, with the women sporting fancy leggings, headdresses, earrings and bracelets, makes the trip worthwhile. Some travellers love it, while others decry the 'foreignisation' of locals.

There are several guesthouses, though none are remarkable. For ¥50 you get a double with bathroom and TV, but no air-con.

Buses departing from Jǐnghóng for Měnghùn (¥16, 90 minutes, every 20 minutes, 7am to 6.40pm) run from the No 2 bus station.

From Měnghùn, minibuses run regularly to Měnghǎi (¥6, one hour), Xīdìng (¥12, 1½ hours, 7.10am and 4pm) and throughout the day to Jǐnghóng.

XĪDÌNG
西定

This sleepy hillside hamlet comes alive every Thursday for its weekly **market**, one of the best in the region (7am to 11am). At other times you'll find Xīdìng almost deserted. If you want to see the market at its most interesting, you'll really have to get here the night before. There's a small hostel located inside the newly built bus station, with four- or six-bed dorms with beds costing ¥50.

To get here by public transport you can catch one of the two direct buses from Měnghǎi (¥15, 10.40am and 3.30pm); going the other way you can catch the bus back to Měnghǎi at 8am and 12.10pm. There are also twice daily buses from Xīdìng to Měnghùn (¥11, 7.20am and 1pm). If you miss the bus you can always get a ride on a motorbike (¥30), a spectacular if hair-raising experience.

JǏNGZHĒN
景真

In the village of Jǐngzhēn, about 14km west of Měnghǎi, is the **Octagonal Pavilion** (八角亭; Bājiǎo Tíng; admission ¥10; ☺8am-6pm), first built in 1701. The original structure was severely damaged during the Cultural Revolution but renovated in 1978 and the ornate decoration is still impressive. The temple also operates as a monastic school. The paintings on the wall of the temple depict scenes from the Jataka, the life history of Buddha.

Frequent minibuses from the bus station in Měnghǎi go via Jǐngzhēn (¥6 to ¥8, 30 minutes).

Sìchuān

POP 84 MILLION

Includes »

Chéngdū	701
Éméi Shān	714
Lèshān	718
Lángzhōng	720
Zìgòng	722
Bamboo Sea	726
Kāngdìng (Dartsendo)	727
Dānbā (Rongtrak)	729
Sìchuān–Tibet Hwy	730
Sōngpān	739
Jiǔzhàigōu National Park	742

Best Hiking

» Yàdīng Nature Reserve (p738)

» Kāngdìng (p727)

» Tǎgōng (p731)

» Jiǔzhàigōu National Park (p742)

» Éméi Shān (p714)

» Bamboo Sea (p726)

Best History & Culture

» Chéngdū (p701)

» Zìgòng (p722)

» Lángzhōng (p720)

» Gānzī (p732)

» Dānbā (p729)

Why Go?

Like the theatre performances of *biànliǎn* (face-changing) that originated here, Sìchuān (四川) is a land of many guises. Capital Chéngdū is quick to show its modern China face, but you don't have to venture far to see a more traditional pose. The countryside is scattered with ancient villages and teahouses, while mist-shrouded mountains creak with wooden monasteries. Central Sìchuān is also home to the giant panda, the most famous face in China.

Head north, though, and you find a Chinese province posing as a region of alpine valleys and forested hills dotted with blue-green lakes and wonderful hiking trails. The hiking becomes spectacularly good as you venture west to witness Sìchuān's fabulous impression of Tibet. This is Kham, one of old Tibet's three traditional provinces: a vast landscape of high-plateau grasslands and glacial mountains where Tibetan culture still thrives and where you're almost certain to have your most challenging, yet most memorable, experiences.

When to Go
Chéngdū

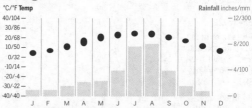

Mar–May Prime time for Chéngdū. Not too humid, no summer rains yet; peach blossoms.

Jul & Aug Good time to visit the Tibetan areas – weather's warm and horse festivals abound.

Jun–Oct Head north to turquoise lakes, warm camping and stunning autumn forests.

Sìchuān Highlights

1 Join Tibetans on a pilgrimage trek around the stunning holy mountain of **Yàdīng Nature Reserve** (p738)

2 Sleep in a monastery on the beautiful forested slopes of **Éméi Shān** (p714)

3 Get eye to eye with China's cuddliest national icon at Chéngdū's **Giant Panda Breeding Research Base** (p701)

4 Go camping along alpine-esque valleys as part of the ecotourism program at **Jiǔzhàigōu National Park** (p742)

5 Stay with Tibetan nomads on the gorgeous high-plateau grasslands around **Tǎgōng** (p731)

6 Feel Lilliputian at **Lèshān** (p718) as you stand beside the toenails of the world's largest Buddha statue

7 Visit ancient salt mines, dinosaur fossils and some of the best teahouses in China at the unusual riverside city of **Zìgòng** (p722)

8 Horse trek in the woods and mountains around the laid-back village of **Sōngpān** (p739)

9 Stay in a Qing-dynasty courtyard and wander the alleyways in the ancient town of **Lángzhōng** (p720)

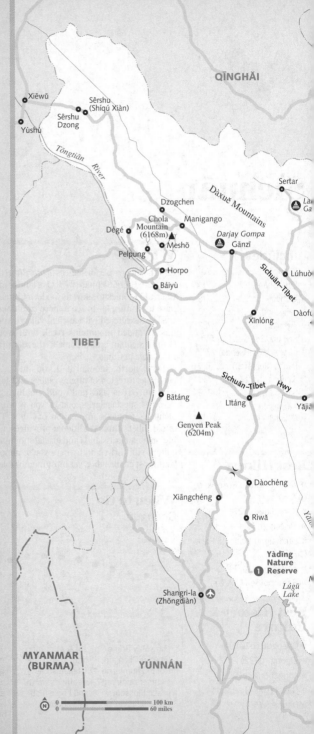

PRICE INDICATORS

The following price indicators are used in this chapter:

Sleeping

$	less than ¥200
$$	¥200 to ¥600
$$$	more than ¥600

Eating

$	less than ¥30
$$	¥30 to ¥50
$$$	more than ¥50

History

Sìchuān's early history was turbulent. The region was the site of various breakaway kingdoms, ever skirmishing with central authority, but it was finally wrestled into control and established as the capital of the Qín empire in the 3rd century BC. It was here that the kingdom of Shu (a name by which the province is still known) ruled as an independent state during the Three Kingdoms period (AD 220–80).

During the Warring States period (475–221 BC), local governor and famed engineer Li Bing managed to harness the flood-prone Mín River (岷江; Mín Jiāng) on the Chuānxī plain with his revolutionary weir system; the Dūjiāngyàn Irrigation Project (p712) still supplies Chéngdū with water, and still protects locals from floods, 2200 years after it was constructed! It's one reason why this part of China is known for being so fertile.

Another more recent factor was the efforts of Zhao Ziyang, governor of Sìchuān in 1975 and the province's first Communist Party secretary. After the tragic mistakes made during the Great Leap Forward, when an estimated one-tenth of Sìchuān's population starved to death, Ziyang became the driving force behind agricultural and economic reforms that put Sìchuān back on the map. His 'Responsibility System', whereby plots of land were let out to individual farmers on the proviso that a portion of the crops be sold back to the government, was so successful it became the national model. This fertile land continues to produce more than 10% of the nation's grain, soybeans, pork and other crops.

Tragedy struck the region on 12 May 2008, when an earthquake measuring 7.9 on the Richter scale hit the province's central region. According to some sources, it killed more than 88,000 people, many of them schoolchildren, and left millions more injured or homeless.

The rebuilding effort in such a remote, mountainous region has taken a number of years. The main road linking Chéngdū with tourist Jiǔzhàigōu took four years to re-open, but bus passengers on that route will now see the region is dotted with a number of brand new towns and villages.

Language

Sichuanese is a Mandarin dialect, but the pronunciation is different enough that it's often difficult for those who speak standard Chinese to understand. Two words visitors will often hear are *yàodé* (pronounced 'yow-day', meaning 'yes' or 'ok') and *méidé* (pronounced 'may-day', meaning 'no').

In addition to Mandarin, Sìchuān's other major languages belong to the Tibeto-Burman family and are spoken by Tibetans and the Yi.

ℹ Information

At the time of research, almost all internet cafes (网吧; *wǎngbā*) in Sìchuān province were following a frustrating new rule, which insists they swipe a Chinese ID card before allowing customers to use the internet, effectively excluding all foreigners. We've still included some internet cafes in this chapter and on our maps in case the rule is lifted by the time you get here. Try asking at a few: *néng shàngwǎng ma?* (Can I use the internet?), but don't make any plans around being able to get online at any of them.

Note, most of the hotels and hostels we list in this chapter have some sort of internet facility.

ℹ Getting There & Around

AIR Chéngdū's airport is the largest in southwest China. Other smaller airports in Sìchuān that are useful for tourists include Jiǔzhàigōu, in the north, and Kāngdìng, in the west.

BUS Speedy expressways in eastern and southern Sìchuān make short trips of many destinations from Chéngdū.

Heading north of Chéngdū or anywhere west of Kāngdìng is a different story altogether. Road and weather conditions deteriorate rapidly and landslides that block the way are common. The scenery, though, can be spectacular.

TRAIN Chéngdū is the main railway hub in China's southwest, with trains to pretty much anywhere, including Lhasa.

CENTRAL SÌCHUĀN

The province's modern yet laid-back capital city, Chéngdū, is where most travellers start their Sìchuān explorations, and it makes a great base for trips out to the region's top sights. This area is dotted with quaint old towns and villages, while lush, forested mountains make for great hiking, especially at Éméi Shān. Nearby Lèshān houses the world's largest Buddha statue, and then, of course, there are the pandas; practically impossible to see in the wild, they are made accessible here by some excellent wildlife reserves.

Chéngdū   成都

☑028 / POP 4.1 MILLION

On the face of it, Chéngdū has little appeal: it's flat, with no distinguishing natural features; the weather's grey and drizzly for much of the year; and the traffic's appalling. Yet somehow everyone comes away satisfied. Perhaps it's the wonderful teahouses found in the city's many parks and temples. Maybe it's the fabulous food, or the decent nightlife scene. It could simply be the pandas, of course. Who knows? Chances are, though, you'll be able to find out for yourself. Chéngdū is the transport hub for the whole of the region, so most travellers pass through this modern, fast-growing, yet surprisingly relaxed city at least once during their forays into China's southwest.

History

Chéngdū has seen the rise and fall of nearly a dozen independent kingdoms or dynasties since its founding in 316 BC; agricultural potential and strategic geography were key to its political power. Yet throughout history it has been equally well known for culture – not by accident did the Tang-dynasty poet Du Fu brush his strokes here.

Two walls were constructed in the Qin dynasty (221–206 BC) to create two adjacent city sections, both lying north of Brocade River (锦江; Jǐn Jiāng). Sadly, nothing remains of either after they were levelled in 1644 by rebel Zhang Xianzhong, who occupied the city, razed it to the ground, murdered most of its residents and then founded his own kingdom.

There's also nothing left of the once vast imperial palace, built in the Ming dynasty (1368–1644) on the site where Tianfu Sq and the Mao statue now stand. It covered 380,000 sq metres, more than half the size of Běijīng's Forbidden City, and one-fifth of Chéngdū's total area at the time, but was destroyed during the Cultural Revolution, the last of its magnificent gates finally disappearing in 1979.

These days the city is split by the Brocade River, a reminder of the city's silk brocade industry, which thrived during the Eastern Han dynasty (AD 25–220); from Chéngdū, the southern Silk Road guided caravans to the known world.

By the time of the Tang dynasty (AD 618–907), the city had become a cornerstone of Chinese society. Three hundred years later, during the Song dynasty, Chéngdū began to issue the world's first paper money.

◉ Sights

Giant Panda Breeding Research Base   WILDLIFE RESERVE

(大熊猫繁育基地; Dàxióngmāo Fányù Jīdì; www. panda.org.cn; adult/student ¥58/28; ⊙8am-6pm) One of Chéngdū's most popular tourist attractions, this reserve, 18km north of the city centre, is the easiest way to catch a glimpse of Sìchuān's most famous residents outside of a zoo. The enclosures here are large and kept in good condition.

Home to nearly 50 giant and red pandas, the base focuses on getting these sexually reluctant creatures to breed; March to May is the 'falling in love period', wink wink. If you visit in autumn or winter, you may see tiny newborns in the nursery.

Try to visit the base in the morning, when the pandas are most active. Feeding takes place around 9.30am, although you'll see them eating in the late afternoon, too. During the middle of the day they spend most of their time sleeping, particularly during the height of midsummer, when they sometimes disappear into their (air-conditioned) living quarters.

Take bus 60 (¥2, one hour, frequent services 7am to 8pm), a little wooden tourist bus, from outside Traffic Inn to Shulong Lu Longqing Lukou (蜀龙路龙青路口) bus stop, from where the panda base is a 400m walk (come back on yourself and turn right). Alternatively, from North Train Station, you can take bus 69 (¥2, 20 minutes, 6am to 8pm) to Zhāojué Sì Bus Station (昭觉寺公交站; Zhāojué Sì Gōngjiāozhàn) from where bus 87 (¥2, 20 minutes, 6.30am to 8.30pm) runs to the gate of the panda base. All youth hostels run trips here, too.

Chéngdū

0 ————— 1 km
0 ————— 0.5 miles

To Giant Panda Breeding
Research Base (12km)

Sha River

Bei Erhuan Lu 北二环路

North Train Station
北火车站

North
Railway
Station

44
46
45

1 Huanlu Bei
4 Duan
一环路北四段

42

3

Jiefang Lu 解放路

X 13

Xing Hui
Rd West
星辉西路

Renmin Beilu

Renmin
North
Road
人民北路

28

35

Wenshū
Temple

8

17

9

Hongxing Lu

Taisheng Nanlu 泰升南路

Bei Dajie 北大街

Xinhua Dadao 新华大道

Shuwa St 树蛙街

Wenwu
Road
文庙路

Fu River (Fu He)

Renmin Zhonglu

36

Shuncheng St 顺城天街

X 12

Xi-Yulong Jie

Luomashi

Dongchenggen Jie

Bei Yihuan Lu 北一环路

Shawan Lu 沙湾路

To Chádiānzi
bus station (5km)

Qinglong Jie

Xiaotong
Xiang
小通巷

Xi Dajie

Changshun Zhongjie

Shang to Ren Lu

7

Kuan
Xiangzi

Tonghuimen

Tomb of
Wáng Jiàn

Yongling Lu 永陵路

Chengdu
University
of TCM
中医药大学

Xi'an Lu

Shi'er Qiao Lu

Qintai Lu
Culture
Park

30

Tonghuimen

Xi Yihuan Lu

Yingmenkou Lu

Qingyang Dadao

Qinghua Jie

To Jīnshā Museum (2km)

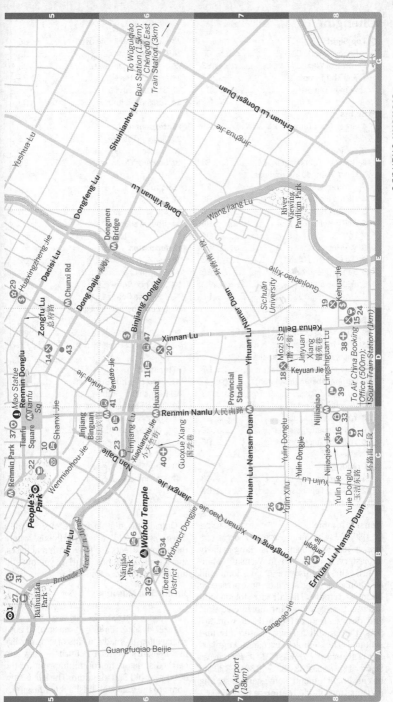

Chéngdū

◎ Top Sights

People's Park...................................... C5
Tomb of Wáng Jiàn............................. B3
Wénshū Temple D3
Wǔhóu Temple B6

◎ Sights

1 Green Ram Temple............................... A5

🛏 Sleeping

2 Chéngdū Grand Hotel D1
3 Hello Chéngdū International
    Youth Hostel....................................E2
4 Holly's Hostel..................................... B6
5 Jǐnjiāng Hotel......................................C6
6 Jīnlǐ Hotel B6
7 Loft... B4
8 Mix Hostel D3
9 Old Chéngdū Club............................. D3
10 Sam's Guesthouse.............................. C5
    Traffic Hotel......................................(see 11)
11 Traffic Inn...D6

❌ Eating

12 Chén Mápó Dòufu............................... D4
13 Chóngqìng Bāyé...................................E3
14 Chuànchuànxiāng Restaurants D5
15 Huí Zhī Fèng..D8
    Kampa Tibetan Restaurant...........(see 4)
16 Sultan C8
17 Vegetarian Restaurant....................... D3
18 Yángyáng Cānguǎn D7
19 Yùlín Chuànchuàn Xiāng......................E8
20 Yùlín Chuànchuàn Xiāng......................D6

◎ Drinking

21 Bookworm C8
22 Hè Míng Teahouse C5

23 Lǎo Nánmén Teahouse C6
24 Le Cafe Panam(e) D8
25 New Little Bar B8
26 Old Little Bar B7
27 Sǎnhuā Lóu B5
28 Tónghú Teahouse D3

◎ Entertainment

29 Jǐnjiāng Theatre E5
30 Shǔfēng Yǎyùn Teahouse B4
31 Shǔfēng Yǎyùn Teahouse B5

◎ Shopping

32 Sanfo B6
33 Sanfo C8
34 Tibetan shops B6

ⓘ Information

35 Bank D2
36 Bank of China.....................................C4
37 Chéngdū Entry & Exit
    Service Centre C5
38 Global Doctor Chéngdū
    Clinic..D8
39 US Consulate D8
40 West China Hospital SCU...................C6

ⓘ Transport

41 Airport Shuttle Bus D6
42 Běimén Bus Station E2
43 China Southern Airlines......................D5
44 Intercity Trains Ticket
    Office..D1
45 North Train Station Bus
    Station...D1
46 Train Ticket Office..............................D1
47 Xīnnánmén Bus Station......................D6

Wénshū Temple BUDDHIST TEMPLE
(文殊院; Wénshū Yuàn; Renmin Zhonglu; admission ¥5; ⊙6am-9pm) This Tang-dynasty monastery is dedicated to Wénshū (Manjushri), the Bodhisattva of Wisdom, and is Chéngdū's largest and best-preserved Buddhist temple. The air is redolent with incense, there's a low murmur of chanting, and despite frequent crowds of worshippers, there's still a sense of serenity and solitude. The temple's excellent **vegetarian restaurant** (文殊院素宴厅; Wénshūyuàn Sùyàn Tīng; dishes ¥8-48; ⊙10.30am-8.30pm) has an English menu, some garden seating and an atmospheric **teahouse** next door.

Outside the temple is one of Chéngdū's three rebuilt 'old' neighbourhoods, where the narrow streets are lined with teahouses, snack stalls and shops. Touristy, yes, but still fun for a quick wander.

Jīnshā Site Museum MUSEUM
(金沙遗址博物馆; Jīnshā Yízhǐ Bówùguǎn; www.jinshasitemuseum.com; 227 Qingyang Dadao; 青羊达到227号; admission ¥80; ⊙8am-6pm) In 2001 archaeologists made a historic discovery in Chéngdū's western suburbs – they unearthed a major site containing ruins of the 3000-year-old Shu kingdom. The site is now home to the excellent Jīnshā Site Museum.

This expansive complex includes one building showing the excavation site itself and another beautifully displaying many of the objects that were excavated from the area. Like the earlier discoveries at Sānxīngduī, the 6000-plus relics found here, which date from 1200 to 600 BC, include both functional and decorative items, from pottery and tools to jade artefacts, stone carvings and ornate gold masks. There's also a large number of elephant tusks that were unearthed here.

Take bus 82 from near Xīnnánmén bus station, passing Wǔhóu Temple and Green Ram Temple en route. Subway Line 2, once finished, will also go close.

Tomb of Wáng Jiàn
MAUSOLEUM

(王建墓; Wángjiàn Mù; 10 Yongling Lu; 永陵路 10号; admission ¥20; ⊙8am-6pm) The only mausoleum excavated in China so far that features an aboveground tomb chamber, this slightly creepy vault honours Wang Jian (847–918), a general who came to power after the AD 907 collapse of the Tang dynasty and became emperor of the Shu kingdom. The tomb itself is decorated with carvings of 24 musicians all playing different instruments, considered to be the best surviving record of a Tang-dynasty musical troupe, while the statue of Wang Jian at the back of the tomb is thought to be the only existing lifelike sculpture of an ancient Chinese king. Take bus 54 from North Train Station bus station.

FREE People's Park
PARK

(人民公园; Rénmín Gōngyuán; ⊙6.30am-10pm) Particularly on weekends, People's Park is filled with locals dancing, singing, strolling and practising taichi. There's a small, willow tree-lined boating lake and a number of teahouses: **Hè Míng Teahouse** (p708) is the most popular.

Green Ram Temple
TAOIST

(青羊宫; Qīngyáng Gōng; admission ¥10; ⊙8am-6pm) Located alongside **Culture Park** (Wénhuà Gōngyuán; ⊙7am-10pm), this is Chéngdū's oldest and most extensive Taoist temple. It dates from the Zhou dynasty, although most of what you see is Qing. A highlight is the unusually squat, eight-sided pagoda, built without bolts or pegs.

Wǔhóu Temple
TEMPLE

(武侯祠; Wǔhóu Cí; admission ¥60; ⊙8am-6pm) Located in **Nánjiāo Park** (Nánjiāo Gōngyuán; ⊙6am-10pm) and surrounded by gardens with mossy cypresses draped over walkways, this temple honours several figures from the Three Kingdoms period, including Emperor Liu Bei and legendary military strategist Zhuge Liang, who was immortalised in one of the classics of Chinese literature, *Romance of the Three Kingdoms (Sān Guó Yǎnyì)*. Just east of the temple is **Jǐnlǐ Gǔjiē** (锦里古街), one of Chéngdū's three reconstructed *ye-olde* districts, crammed with souvenir junk stalls and local snacks.

🛏 Sleeping

TOP CHOICE Hello Chéngdū International Youth Hostel
HOSTEL $

(老沈青年旅舍; Lǎoshěn Qīngnián Lǚshè; ☎8196 7573, 8335 5322; www.gogosc.com; 211 Huanlu Bei 4 Duan; 一环路北四段211号; dm from ¥40, s without/with bathroom ¥90/135, d from ¥170; ❄❀@🛜) Formerly Sim's Cozy Garden Hostel, this used to be one of the best hostels in China, never mind Chéngdū, but it has lost some of its finesse since the legendary Sim and Maki sold up. It's still a fabulous space, though, sprawling its way around two garden courtyards, making it ideal if you have kids in tow. Rooms are simple but clean and the facilities are everything you'd expect from a top-class hostel; bike rental (¥10 to ¥15), wi-fi, a decent cafe, DVD hire and good travel advice. Take bus 28 from Xīnnánmén bus station or bus 34 from North Train Station. The bus stop to get off at is called Yihuan Lu Beisiduan (一环路北四段).

TOP CHOICE Mix Hostel
HOSTEL $

(驴友记青年旅舍; Lǘyǒujì Qīngnián Lǚshè; ☎8322 2271; www.mixhostel.com; 23 Xinghui Rd West; 星辉西路23号; dm/s/d from ¥35/88/98; ❄@🛜) More homely than other Chéngdū hostels, Mix is tucked away behind a bamboo-guarded entranceway and exudes a lovely laid-back atmosphere, making it more of a peaceful retreat than a party-all-night hostel; a vibe which extends to the lazy teahouses that can be found on the riverside nearby. Not particularly central, but only a short walk from the metro, so it's easy to plug yourself into the city-centre action. It has a cafe, wi-fi (lobby area only), bike rental (¥10) and trustworthy travel advice.

Traffic Inn
HOSTEL $

(交通青年旅舍; Jiāotōng Qīngnián Lǚshè; ☎8545 0470; www.trafficinnhostel.com; 6 Linjiang Zhonglu; 临江中路6号; dm ¥45, r without/with bathroom ¥110/180; ❄@🛜) Rooms without private bathrooms are best value here, with stripped-wood furniture, tiled flooring and loads of space. The mosaic-tiled shared shower rooms are spotless. Dorms and rooms with private bathrooms are housed in the adjoining **Traffic Hotel** (交通酒店; Jiāotōng Jiǔdiàn; ☑8545 1017), a good-quality Chinese budget hotel, which has plenty of its own rooms – also spotless, although with less character – going for ¥120 (twins) or ¥50 (fan-cooled singles) after discounts. There's good wi-fi connection in all rooms, staff members are helpful and the location, close to Xīnnánmén bus station, is extremely convenient for day trips. Bike rental costs ¥30.

Jǐnlǐ Hotel
HOTEL $$

(锦里客栈; Jǐnlǐ Kèzhàn; ☑6631 1335; 11 Zhangwu Jie; 武侯祠大街章武街11号; s/d ¥480/560; ✴) If you don't mind the touristy surroundings on the Jǐnlǐ shopping street near Wǔhóu Temple, this upmarket inn, off Wuhouci Dajie and set in two courtyard-style buildings, is a fun place to stay. Rooms mix traditional Chinese wooden furnishings with modern touches such as puffy white duvets and wide-screen TVs. Discounts of around 40%.

Jǐnjiāng Hotel
HOTEL $$$

(锦江宾馆; Jǐnjiāng Bīnguǎn; ☑8550 6050; www. jjhotel.com; 80 Renmin Nanlu; 人民南路二段 80号; r from ¥1700, discounted to ¥1119; ✴@✴) Jǐnjiāng was Sìchuān's first-ever five-star hotel and, up until the late '70s, its nine-storey block was the tallest building in Chéngdū. There are more luxurious hotels in the city these days, but this one retains a certain charm that the bigger international chains lack. Guests are greeted by a string quartet in the lobby and staff members are both courteous and well turned out; especially the red-uniformed bell hops.

Loft
HOSTEL $$

(四号工厂青年旅馆; Sìhào Gōngchǎng Qīngnián Lǚguǎn; ☑8626 5770; www.lofthostel.com; 4 Shangtongren Lu, Xiaotong Xiang; 小通巷上同 仁路4号; dm/s/d/tr ¥50/120/220/300; ✴@✴) Chic boutique meets urban youth hostel at this trendy converted printing factory. Loft is a hostel for grown-ups, with a delightful cafe and an arty vibe – exposed brickwork, black-tiled bathrooms, gritty central courtyard. There's also free internet, bike rental and solid travel advice.

Holly's Hostel
HOSTEL $$

(九龙鼎青年客栈; Jiǔlóngdǐng Qīngnián Kèzhàn; ☑8554 8131; hollyhostelcn@yahoo.com; 246 Wuhouci Dajie; 武侯祠大街246号; dm ¥35-50, d ¥260 & ¥280, discounted to ¥120 & ¥160; ✴@✴) Prepare for your trip out west by first plugging yourself in to Chéngdū's small Tibetan community, which centres on this district. Holly's is cute and friendly, has wi-fi throughout, bike rental (¥20) and a neat rooftop cafe.

Sam's Guesthouse
HOSTEL $

(山姆客栈; Shānmǔ Kèzhàn; ☑8611 8322; www. hostelchengdu.com; 130 Shanxi Jie; 陕西街130号; dm/r ¥60/160; ✴@✴) The traveller vibe isn't as strong here as at other hostels, but the attraction, apart from the central location, is that rooms are housed inside the beautiful 300-year-old **Shǎnxī Guild Hall** (陕西会馆; Shǎnxī Huìguǎn), which also contains, within its courtyard, the pricey but delightful **Shǎnxī Teahouse** (tea from ¥40; ⏰24hr). Rooms are old-fashioned but spacious, and come with free wi-fi. Reception is in an office on the main road. Bike rental costs ¥15.

Old Chéngdū Club
HOTEL $$$

(成都会馆; Chéngdū Huìguǎn; ☑8695 6688; www .oldchengduclub.com.cn; 28 Wuyuegong Jie; 五岳 宫街28号; r from ¥1000; ✴@✴✴) Exclusive and luxurious, this members' club, on the doorstep of Wénshū Temple, also accepts guests in its dozen or so rooms, although it's largely aimed at domestic tourists so English-language skills are surprisingly poor. The complex comprises a number of Ming dynasty–style courtyard buildings (although it isn't genuinely old itself), and rooms are filled with attractive Chinese furnishings and artwork. Guests have access to all the club facilities, including four restaurants (Chinese, Japanese, Korean and Western), a wine bar and a lovely indoor swimming pool. Reservations are essential.

Chéngdū Grand Hotel
HOTEL $$

(成都大酒店; Chéngdū Dàjiǔdiàn; ☑8317 3888; 29 North Renmin; 人民北路二段29号; d & tw ¥400-580, discounted to ¥240-280; ✴@) This 23-storey old-school Chinese hotel with decent, internet-enabled rooms makes a comfortable choice if you need to be near the train station.

🍴 Eating

One popular Chéngdū speciality is **chuàn-chuàn xiāng**, the skewers' version of the famous Chóngqìng hotpot (huǒguō), and just as spicy. *Chuànchuotouàn xiāng* is a quintessential Chéngdū eating experience and there are restaurants all over the city, including a bunch of pocket-sized ones on Shuwa Street (暑袜街; Shuwa Jie).

Several monasteries, including Wénshū Temple and Green Ram Temple, have vegetarian restaurants (dishes ¥7 to ¥20) that are generally open only for lunch.

TOP CHOICE **Yùlín Chuànchuàn Xiāng** HOTPOT $$
(玉林串串香; 2-3 Kehua Jie; 科华街2-3号; pots ¥20-25, skewers short/long ¥0.20/¥1.50; ⏰10am-2am) *Chuànchuàn xiāng*, is Chéngdū's version of the Chóngqìng hotpot, and this lively open-fronted branch of the popular Yùlín chain is packed in the evenings with a hungry student crowd from nearby Sìchuān University. First, choose the broth you want to cook your skewers in: either *hóng guō* (红锅; spicy; ¥20) or *yuānyang guō* (鸳鸯锅; half-spicy, half-clear split pot; ¥25). Then grab whatever skewers you fancy from a side room before cooking them yourself at your table. Staff will count up how many skewers you've eaten at the end of your meal. The garlic and chilli dipping sauce is ¥3 extra. There's another, slightly smaller branch near youth hostel Traffic Inn, which is equally good.

Yángyáng Cānguǎn SICHUANESE $
(杨杨餐馆; 32 Jinyuan Xiang; 锦苑巷32号; mains ¥15-40; ⏰11.30am-2pm & 5-9pm; 📷) Clean, comfortable place to sample good-quality, inexpensive Sichuanese food. The Chinese menu (*zhōngwén càidān*) has photos, but the English menu (*yīngwén càidān*) has neither prices nor photos, so you may want to use a combination of the two.

Chén Mápó Dòufu SICHUANESE $$
(陈麻婆豆腐; 2nd fl, 197 Xi Yulong Jie; mains ¥20-50; ⏰11.30am-2.30pm & 5.30-9pm) This plush branch of the famous chain is a great place to sample *mápó dòufu* (small/large ¥12/20) – soft, fresh bean curd with a fiery sauce of garlic, minced beef, salted soybean, chilli oil and Sìchuān pepper. It's one of Sìchuān's most famous dishes and this restaurant's speciality. Photo menu.

Chóngqìng Bāyé CHINESE $$$
(重庆巴爷; 2nd fl, cnr Jiefang Lu & Zhangjia Xiang; 解放路二段张家巷口，二楼; mains ¥12-25, pots ¥38-128; ⏰9am-11pm) Specialises in *gānguō* (干锅, literally 'dry pot'), a sizzling pot of spicy delights. Favourite concoctions include *chāojí huānlà xiā* (超级欢辣虾; shrimp), *zhúsǔn jībāo* (竹笋鸡煲) chicken and bamboo shoots), *xiānglà páigǔ* (香辣排骨; pork ribs) and *xiānglà yāchún* (香辣鸭唇; duck beak). Pots cost ¥78, ¥98 or ¥128. With rice

(米饭; *mǐfàn*), a ¥78 pot is enough for two or three people. There are non-spicy versions (清的; *qīngde*; ¥68), which come in a fragrant broth, and if you're eating solo, order the pot for one (单人的; *dānrénde*; ¥38). The menu, which is Chinese only, also includes regular Sichuanese dishes. For dessert, don't miss the *mǐjiǔ tāngyuán* (米酒汤圆; sweet glutinous rice balls; ¥10). No English sign.

Kampa Tibetan Restaurant TIBETAN $
(康巴藏餐; Kāngbā Zàngcān; off 246 Wuhouci Dajie; 武侯祠大街246号附18; dishes ¥10-30; ⏰8am-11pm; 📷) Small, friendly Tibetan-run restaurant next to Holly's Hostel serving authentic Tibetan favourites such as *tsampa* (roasted barley flour), *thukpa* (noodles in a soup), *momo* (Tibetan dumplings) and butter tea. English menu.

Sultan MIDDLE EASTERN $$
(苏坦; Sūtǎn; 1 Yulin Nanjie, Dushi Jin'an Bldg; 玉林南街1号; mains ¥30-70; ⏰11am-11pm; 📶📷) Friendly, easygoing Middle Eastern restaurant with lamb kebabs, hummus, warm naan and homemade yoghurt. You could linger over dark Turkish coffee (¥30; there's free wi-fi), sit outside on the patio, or lounge in a private room piled with cushions and puff on a fruit-flavoured *sheesha* pipe (¥50). The entrance is on a side road just off Yulin Nanjie.

Tónghú Teahouse SICHUANESE $
(铜壶茶园; Tónghú Cháyuán; 5 Da'anxi Binhe Lu; 大安西滨河路; mains ¥12-32; ⏰noon-2pm & 6pm-midnight) This delightful riverside teahouse also does food during lunch and dinner times. It's standard Sichuanese fare (including our top five Sichuanese dishes) plus *yúxiāng qiézi* (鱼香茄子; sweet and spicy aubergine; ¥12) and a tasty fish dish called *ruǎndù yú* (软渡鱼; ¥48).

Huì Zhī Fèng
BARBECUE **$$**

(惠之凤; Blue Caribbean Plaza, cnr Kehua Beilu & Kehua Jie; 科华北路143号蓝色加勒比广场; mains ¥10-30; ⏱11am-midnight; 🔲) Chéngdū's answer to teppanyaki and a great place to fill up before drinks on Kehua Jie. There are tables outside, but it's also fun to sit inside around the giant horseshoe-shaped hotplate and watch the chef griddle the dishes you've just ordered. Part of the menu has been translated into English, although our favourite – the bacon-wrapped mushrooms (培根卷; *péigēn juǎn;* ¥25) – isn't on the English version. Two dishes per person is usually enough.

Drinking

Sìchuān represents teahouse culture better than anywhere else in China. The art of tea-drinking dates back 3000 years, and Sìchuān's teahouses have long been the centres of neighbourhood social life. They were, and still are, where people gossiped, played cards, watched opera performances, had haircuts and even had their ear wax removed! Today you'll find crowded teahouses all over Chéngdū, particularly in the city's parks and temple grounds. There are also some pleasant ones on the banks of the city's rivers. Tea is generally bought by the cup (¥10 to ¥20) and is topped up for free as often as you like. See our tea menu for help with ordering a brew.

There's a decent number of bars and cafes here, too. For the latest on Chéngdū's night-life scene, pick up one of the city's expat magazines: *Chengdoo* (www.gochengdoo.com/en) or *More Chengdu* (www.morechengdu.com).

Hè Míng Teahouse
TEAHOUSE

(鹤鸣茶馆; Hèmíng Cháguǎn; People's Park; tea ¥10-25; ⏱7am-9pm) Always busy, but rarely overcrowded, this is one of Chéngdū's most pleasant and popular spots to while away an afternoon over a bottomless cup of flower tea. The tea menu is in English. Having your ears cleaned (¥20) is optional.

Tónghú Teahouse
TEAHOUSE

(铜壶茶园; Tónghú Cháyuán; 5 Da'anxi Binhe Lu; 大安西滨河路; tea per cup ¥10-15; ⏱9am-midnight) Relaxing riverside teahouse with outdoor seating overlooking a rushing weir. See our tea menu for help with ordering a brew. Also does beer.

Old Little Bar
BAR

(小酒馆(玉林店); Xiǎo Jiǔguǎn (Yùlín Diàn); 55 Yulin Xilu; 玉林西路55号; beer from ¥10; ⏱6pm-2am) Reportedly set up by China's rock legend Cui Jian, this is Chéngdū's most established rock bar. It no longer has live performances – go to New Little Bar for that – but is still a cool place to hang out with music-loving locals.

New Little Bar
LIVE MUSIC

(小酒馆(芳沁店); Xiǎo Jiǔguǎn (Fāngqìn Diàn); ☎8515 8790; Fangqin Jie, behind 47 Yongfeng Lu; 永丰路47号芳沁街; beer from ¥10; ⏱6pm-2am) This small pub-like venue is *the* place in Chéngdū to catch local bands performing live. Bands play every Friday and Saturday, and occasionally on weekdays, usually from 8pm. Live music carries a cover charge of around ¥30, depending on who's playing. Check expat magazine *Chengdoo* for monthly line-ups.

Bookworm
CAFE

(老书虫; Lǎo Shūchóng; ☎8552 0177; www.chengdubookworm.com; 2-7 Yujie Donglu, 28 Renmin Nanlu; 人民南路28号、玉洁东路2-7号; ⏱9am-1am) This excellent bookstore-cafe, with branches in Běijīng and Sūzhōu, is a peaceful spot for a drink or a coffee (from ¥20). It also does decent Western food (mains ¥30 to ¥70; open 9am to 11pm). You can buy or borrow books from its extensive library, and it often hosts author talks and other events. Check the website for a schedule.

Lǎo Nánmén Teahouse
TEAHOUSE

(老南门茶苑; Lǎo Nánmén Cháyuàn; Binjiang Xi Lu; 滨江西路; tea per cup ¥10 to ¥20; ⏱9am-7pm) A small but popular riverside tea garden, which is open until 11pm in summer, this pleasant locals' favourite is located beside a rushing weir and serves all the usual teas. No English menu, so check our tea menu (p709) for help with ordering a cuppa.

Sǎnhuā Lóu
TEAHOUSE

(散花楼; Binjiang Xi Lu; 1 Qingyang Zhengjie; 青羊正街1号; tea per cup ¥10 to ¥20; ⏱7am-11pm) Housed in a reconstructed, but highly attractive, four-storey pagoda, this unusual teahouse overlooks the river and Bǎihuātán Park, where there are yet more teahouses.

Le Cafe Panam(e)
BAR

(巴黎酒吧; Bālí Jiǔbā; 2nd fl, Blue Caribbean Plaza, cnr Kehua Beilu & Kehua Jie; 科华北路143号蓝色加勒比广场2层; beer from ¥10; ⏱5pm-4am) Originally French-run and super chic, Panam(e) is now run by Chinese management and is more popular with local drink-

TEA MENU

NAME	PRONUNCIATION	TRANSLATION	TYPE	ORIGIN
普洱	pǔ'ěr	–	Green (post-fermented)	Yúnnán (Pǔ'ěr county)
铁观音	tiě guānyīn	Iron Buddha	Oolong	Fújiàn
苦荞茶	kǔqiáo chá	Buckwheat	Herbal	Yúnnán
菊花	júhuā	Chrysanthemum	Flower	China-wide
花毛峰	huāmáofēng	Jasmine	Flower	Sìchuān
竹叶青	zhúyèqīng	Bamboo-leaf	Green	Sìchuān (Éméi Shān)

ers than Western expats these days. Still one of the coolest of a number of drinking venues in and around Blue Caribbean Plaza, though.

☆ Entertainment

Chéngdū is the home of Sìchuān opera, which dates back more than 250 years. It's nothing like Western opera; many performances feature slapstick, glass-shattering songs, men dressed as women, gymnastics and even fire breathing. An undoubted highlight is 'face-changing' (变脸; biànliǎn) in which performers swap masks, seemingly by magic.

Shǔfēng Yǎyùn Teahouse SÌCHUĀN OPERA
(蜀风雅韵; Shǔfēng Yǎyùn; ☏8776 4530; www.shufengyayun.com; Culture Park; tickets ¥150-260) This famous 100-year-old theatre-cum-teahouse now has two venues; the biggest, best and cheapest is located inside Culture Park, and puts on excellent shows that include music, puppetry, comedy, Sìchuān opera and the province's famed face-changing performances. Shows run nightly from 8pm to 9.30pm. If you come at around 7.30pm you can watch performers putting on their make-up. Kids can even have their own faces painted (from ¥150). Very similar performances are held at the same times at the slightly smaller, newer venue (¥200 to ¥320), just outside the east gate of the park. Beware the ticket tout at the smaller venue who sometimes tells tourists the venue inside the park is closed.

Jǐnjiāng Theatre SÌCHUĀN OPERA
(锦江剧场; Jǐnjiāng Jùchǎng; ☏8666 6891; 54 Huaxingzheng Jie; 华兴正街54号; tickets ¥180-480; ◷8pm-9.10pm) There are similar mixed-performance shows held daily at this renowned opera theatre. The adjoining **Yuèlái Teahouse** (悦来茶楼; Yuèlái Chálóu; tea ¥8-20; ◷8.30am-6pm), a locals' favourite, holds wonderfully informal performances on its small stage every Saturday from 2pm to 4.30pm. Tickets for the teahouse shows cost ¥20 to ¥35.

🔒 Shopping

There are fancy-pants **shopping centres** dotted around the city, but the highest concentration of them is found around the part-pedestrianised area east of Tianfu Sq, between Zongfu Lu and Dong Dajie.

Southeast of Wǔhóu Temple is a small **Tibetan neighbourhood**. While it's not evident in the architecture, it is in the prayer flags, colourful scarves, beads and brass goods for sale. It's an interesting area for wandering.

Outdoor clothing and equipment are a big buy in Chéngdū, as many people head to Tibet or the western mountains. Quality varies and fakes abound.

Sanfo OUTDOOR EQUIPMENT
(三夫户外; Sānfū Hùwài; 243 Wuhouci Dajie; 武侯词大街243号; ◷10am-9.30pm) Good-quality trekking and camping equipment. There's another branch (32 Renmin Nanlu; 人民南路32号) by Nijiaqiao metro station.

ℹ Information

Internet Access

All hotels and cafes we've reviewed here have internet access for laptop users. Most youth hostels and some top-end hotels also have computer terminals for guests. Internet cafes (网吧; wǎngbā) are plentiful, but most insist on swiping a Chinese ID card before use. The one on the 2nd floor of the Xīnnánmén bus station building sometimes waives the rule.

Medical Services

Global Doctor Chéngdū Clinic (环球医生成都诊所; Huánqiú Yīshēng Chéngdū Zhěnsuǒ; ☑8528 3660, 24hr helpline 139 8225 6966; 2nd fl, 9-11 Lippo Tower Bldg, 62 Kehua Beilu; 科华北路62号力宝大夏2层9-11号; ⊗8.30am-noon & 1.30-6pm Mon-Fri) English-speaking doctors and a 24-hour English-language helpline. Consultation is ¥600. Out-of-hours visit costs ¥1000.

West China Hospital SCU (四川大学华西医院; Sìchuān Dàxué Huáxī Yīyuàn; ☑8542 2777; 37 Guoxue Xiang; 国学巷37号) The Huáxī hospital complex is Chéngdū's largest and gets good reports from expats. Foreigners should head for **Jīnkǎ Yīyuàn** (金卡医院), a department within **Inpatient Building No 4** (第四住院大楼; dìsì zhùyuàn dàlóu) – to your right as you enter the complex – where most doctors and some staff members speak English.

Money

Most ATMs now accept foreign cards. We've marked some convenient ones on the map.

Bank of China (中国银行; Zhōngguó Yínháng; 35 Renmin Zhonglu, 2nd Section; 人民中路二段35号; ⊗8.30am-5.30pm Mon-Fri, to 5pm Sat & Sun) Changes money and travellers cheques, and offers cash advances on credit cards.

Visas

Chéngdū Entry & Exit Service Centre (成都市出入境接待中心; Chéngdūshì Chūrùjìng Jiēdài Zhōngxīn; ☑8640 7067; 2 Renmin Xilu; 人民西路2号; ⊗9am-noon & 1.30-5pm Mon-Fri) Foreign affairs office on 3rd floor; extends visas in five working days. North of Tianfu Sq.

Travel Agencies

Skip the gazillion Chinese travel agencies around town and head straight to the travel desk at one of Chéngdū's many excellent youth hostels. You can book anything from panda research centre visits to full-blown multiweek trips across Tibet.

ⓘ Getting There & Away

Air

You can fly from Chéngdū to pretty much any other major Chinese city, while there are international flights to Bangkok, Kuala Lumpur, Singapore, Los Angeles, Vancouver, London, Amsterdam, Sydney, Melbourne, New Delhi, Bangalore and Seoul.

Many travellers choose to fly from here to Lhasa. Those without much time on their hands, but a bit of extra cash, might consider flying to smaller destinations within Sìchuān, such as Kāngdìng or Jiǔzhàigōu.

The best websites for cheap flights are www.elong.com, www.ctrip.com and www.travelzen.com.

If for some reason you can't book online, you could try the following airline offices:

Air China Chéngdū Booking Office (国航世界中心; Guóháng Shìjiè Zhōngxīn; ☑nationwide bookings 95583; 1 Hangkong Lu; 人民南路4段航空路1号; ⊗8.30am-5.30pm) By Tongzilin metro station, Line 1; off Renmin Nanlu.

China Southern Airlines (中国南方航空; Zhōngguó Nánfāng Hángkōng; ☑8666 3618; 278 Shangdong Dajie; ⊗8.30am-5.30pm)

Bus

The main bus station for tourists is Xīnnánmén (新南门), officially called the tourism passenger transport centre. The other two most useful are Chádiànzi (茶店子) and Běimén (北门). However, be prepared to be dropped at other bus stations when arriving in Chéngdū. If you're dropped at Shíyángchǎng bus station (石羊场公交站; Shíyángchǎng gōngjiāozhàn), you can take local bus 28 (¥2) to Xīnnánmén bus station, Běimén bus station (for Hello Chéngdū International Youth Hostel) or North Train Station.

Destinations from Xīnnánmén include the following:

Bamboo Sea ¥118, five hours, two daily (9.10am and 3.30pm)

Dānbā ¥133, nine hours, one daily (6.30am*)

Éméi Shān ¥43, 2½ hours, every 20 minutes (7.20am to 7.20pm)

Hóngyǎ (for Liǔ Jiāng) ¥41, two hours, every 45 minutes (7.40am to 5pm)

Jiǔzhàigōu ¥145 to ¥222, 10 hours, two daily (7.43am & 8.30am**)

Kāngdìng ¥123 to ¥133, seven hours, hourly (7.10am to 2.10pm)

Lèshān ¥47, two hours, every 20 minutes (7.30am to 4pm)

Pínglè ¥30, two hours, every 30 minutes (7.30am to 4pm)

Sānxīngduī ¥16, two hours, one daily (8.30am)

Yǎ'ān (for Bìfēngxiá) ¥50, two hours, every 30 minutes (7am to 7.30pm)

* This is a Dàofú-bound bus, via Dānbā and Bàměi. You must buy a ticket to Bàměi (¥153) and then ask the driver nicely for a ¥20 refund because you want to get off early at Dānbā.

** Extra morning buses are laid on in July and August. Note, all Jiǔzhàigōu buses go via Sōngpān (eight hours), but you have to pay full fare even if you get off at Sōngpān.

Following are some of the destinations from Chádiànzi:

Jiǔzhàigōu ¥120 to ¥170, nine hours, three daily (7.20am, 8am and 9am)

Sōngpān ¥95, seven hours, two daily (6.30am and 8.30am)

Destinations from Běimén include the following:

Lángzhōng ¥98, five hours, every 40 minutes (6.30am to 6.30pm)

Yíbīn ¥94 to ¥107, four hours, hourly (7.20am to 6.30pm)

Zìgòng ¥81, three hours, hourly (7am to 8pm)

Train

Chéngdū's two main train stations are **Chéngdū North Train Station** (火车北站; huǒchē běizhàn) and the newer **Chéngdū East Train Station** (火车东站; huǒchē dōngzhàn), both of which have metro stations. The ticket office of the north station is in a separate building on your right as you approach the station. High-speed train tickets for Chóngqìng and Qīngchéng Shān should be bought at the adjacent **intercity trains ticket office** (城际列车售票处; chéngjì lièchē shòupiàochù). The new high-speed rail link to Lèshān may also be running by the time you read this.

Hotels and hostels can book tickets, for a small fee.

Destinations from East Station include Wǔhàn (¥313, 16 hours) and Guìlín (¥194, 25 hours), with a high-speed link to Shànghǎi reported to be coming soon.

Sample destinations from North Station:

Běijīng West sleeper ¥401/439/391/458, 29/27/31/30 hours, four daily (9.50am, 7.54pm, 10.30pm and 11.59pm)

Chóngqìng 2nd/1st class ¥98/117, two hours, hourly (8am to 9pm)

Éméi Shān seat ¥24, 2½ hours, nine daily (10am to 8pm)

Kūnmíng sleeper ¥240, 19 to 22 hours, six daily (8.40am to 7.20pm)

Lhasa sleeper ¥671, 44 hours, one daily (8.55pm)

Xī'ān seat/sleeper ¥113/195, 13 to 17 hours, 10 daily (9.50am to 10.30pm)

Xīníng West sleeper ¥290, 24/20 hours, two daily (12.01pm and 8.55pm)

Yíbīn seat/sleeper ¥51/97, six to eight hours, seven daily (8.31am to 11.48pm)

Zìgòng seat/sleeper ¥41/87, 4½ to six hours, seven daily (8.31am to 11.48pm)

ⓘ Getting Around

To/From the Airport

Shuāngliú Airport is 18km west of the city. Bus 303 (¥10, 45 minutes, 6am to 10pm) is an airport shuttle (机场大巴; jīchǎng Dàbā) that shadows flight times and travels from Yándào Jiē (盐道街) to the airport. Bus 300 runs a slower service between the airport and the North Train Station, running the length of Renmin Lu, but it stops at every bus stop en route.

A taxi between the airport and the centre costs ¥50 to ¥70, depending on how bad the traffic is. Most guesthouses offer airport pick-up services for slightly more than the taxi fare.

Bicycle

Chéngdū is nice and flat, although the traffic can be a strain on cyclists. Youth hostels rent out bikes for around ¥15 to ¥30 per day. Make sure you use a lock.

Bus

You can get almost anywhere in Chéngdū by bus, as long as you can decipher the labyrinthine bus routings. Stops are marked in Chinese and English, and some have posted route maps for the buses that stop there. Fares within the city are usually ¥2.

Useful routes:

Bus 16 North Train Station–Renmin Lu–South Train Station

Bus 1 City centre–Wǔhóu Temple

Bus 81 Mao statue–Green Ram Temple

Bus 28 Shíyángchǎng bus station–Xīnnánmén bus station–Běimén bus station–North Train Station

Bus 82 Chádiànzi bus station–Jīnshā Museum–Wǔhóu Temple–Xīnnánmén bus station

Bus 69 North Train Station bus station–Zhāojué Sì bus station

Tourist Bus 87 Zhāojué Sì bus station–Panda Breeding Base

Tourist Bus 60 Traffic Inn–Panda Breeding Base

Metro

Line 1 links the North and South Train Stations and runs the length of Renmin Lu. The east–west running Line 2 links Chéngdū East Train Station with the centre of the city, meeting Line 1 at Tianfu Sq before continuing west to Chádiànzì bus station. Line 3, which will run to the Panda Breeding Base, and Line 4, for Chéngdū West Train Station, are due to be completed by 2015. Journeys cost ¥2 to ¥4. Signs, maps and ticket machines are bilingual.

Taxi

Taxis are ¥8 or ¥9 for the first 2km, then ¥1.90 per kilometre after that.

Around Chéngdū

SĀNXĪNGDUĪ MUSEUM　　　三星堆

The striking exhibits at the **Sānxīngduī Museum** (Sānxīngduī Bówùguǎn; admission ¥82, audio guide ¥10; ☉8.30am-6pm, last entry 5pm) highlight archaeological finds that some Chinese archaeologists regard as even more important than Xī'ān's Terracotta Warriors.

Throughout the 20th century, farmers around the town of Guǎnghàn, 40km north of Chéngdū, continually unearthed intriguing pottery shards and other dirt-encrusted detritus. However, war, the lack of funds and other challenges prevented anyone from taking these discoveries seriously. Finally, in 1986, archaeologists launched a full-scale excavation and made a startling discovery: they unearthed a major site dating from the Shu kingdom, considered the cradle of Chinese civilisation, in the upper reaches of the Yangzi River (Cháng Jiāng).

The museum houses two buildings' worth of artefacts from this period, but the stars of its collections are dozens and dozens of bronze masks – so sophisticated that they wouldn't look out of place in a modern art gallery, yet they were crafted more than 4000 years ago.

One morning bus runs here direct from Chéngdū's Xīnnánmén bus station. Alternatively, there are regular buses from Chéngdū's Zhāojué Sì station to Guǎnghàn (¥16, 45 minutes, 7am to 8pm), from where you can catch local bus 6 (¥1.50, 20 minutes) for the remaining 10km to the site. The direct bus back to Chéngdū leaves at 4.10pm, but only goes as far as Zhāojué Sì station.

QĪNGCHÉNG SHĀN 青城山

Covered in dripping-wet forests, the lush holy mountain of **Qīngchéng Shān** (Azure City Mountain; admission ¥90) has been a Taoist retreat for more than 2000 years. Its beautiful trails are lined with ginkgo, plum and palm trees as well as caves, pavilions and gorgeous, centuries-old wooden temples, some of which you can stay overnight in.

The weather is generally better than at Éméi Shān, so the views are less likely to be obscured by mist, and with a summit of only 1600m, it's also a far easier climb: four hours up and down. There's a detailed map of the trails on the back of your entrance ticket and signs are in English, too.

If you want to stay the night, two or three temples on the mountain welcome guests, including the fabulous **Shàngqīng Temple** (Shàngqīng Gōng; d with bathroom ¥180-280), a Qing-dynasty rebuild of the original Jin-dynasty temple set in the forest near the top of the mountain; it has a restaurant (dishes ¥15 to ¥25) and a teahouse (tea from ¥5). The cheapest rooms (¥40 to ¥100) are supposed to be reserved for pilgrims, but you may be able to land one if you ask sweetly.

Snack stands are scattered along the mountain trails.

The new high-speed rail link means the mountain is now even more popular with Chéngdū day-trippers, who can crowd some trails, particularly those near the entry and exit to the cable car (one way/return ¥35/60). Some travellers prefer heading instead to **Hòushān** (后山; Rear Mountain), a more peaceful, less touristy part of the range, 15km northwest of Qīngchéng Shān proper. There are around 20km of pathways here – expect a hike to the summit, where you'll find **Báiyún Temple** (白云寺; Báiyún Sì), to take around six hours; half that if you use the cable cars (¥30). Near the top is **Báiyún Ancient Village** (白云古寨; Báiyún Gǔzhài), where you can find basic guesthouses (客栈; kèzhàn). **Yòuyī Village** (又一村; Yòuyī Cūn), less than half way up the mountain, also has a few guesthouses. There are loads of teahouses and restaurants by the main gate. Buses to Hòushān (¥10, 25 minutes) leave from Qīngchéng Shān Train Station when full. They pass Qīngchéng Shān's main gate en route, but won't stop for passengers here if there are no spare seats.

To get to Qīngchéng Shān take the high-speed rail link from Chéngdū's North Train Station (¥15, 50 minutes, 7am to 8pm, last train back 8.30pm). Bus 101 (¥2, five minutes) links the train station to the mountain.

Consider getting off the train one stop before Qīngchéng Shān to visit the **Dūjiāngyàn Irrigation Project** (都江堰水利工程; Dūjiāngyàn Shuǐlì Gōngchéng; admission ¥90; ◦8am-6pm); take bus 4 (¥2, 20 minutes, last stop). Constructed in the 3rd century BC to tame the fast-flowing Mín River, the irrigation system is a Unesco World Heritage site located in a beautifully scenic area with forested hills, ancient temples, hilltop pagodas and, of course, rushing rivers. To the right of the entrance gate is a tourist centre, which has a map and a scale model of the area. Beside this, the decorative **South Bridge** (南桥; Nán Qiáo) has teahouses and restaurants on either side of it.

From here you can take Bus 101 to Qīngchéng Shān (¥2.50, 40 minutes, last stop).

BĪFĒNGXIÁ PANDA BASE 碧峰峡大熊猫基地

It's always fun to see pandas, of course, but the highlight of a trip here is the fabulous two-hour walk along a deep, forested river gorge in order to get to the **Bìfēngxiá Panda Base** (Bìfēngxiá Dàxióngmāo Jīdì; admission ¥118; ⊙8.30-11.30am & 1.30-4.30pm).

Established in 2003 under the direction of the Giant Panda Research Centre at Wòlóng, this base originally focused more on research than on tourism. However, after the Wòlóng Nature Reserve was severely damaged in the 2008 earthquake, all of its surviving pandas were moved to Bìfēngxiá, and this reserve began to receive an influx of tourists. It's now home to more than 80 pandas, the world's largest collection of captive pandas. At the time of research, the plan was to move some of the pandas back to Wòlóng once it had been rebuilt, sometime in 2014.

The Bìfēngxiá area is very spread out and spans a deep gorge with rivers, waterfalls and generally stunning forest scenery. The **panda centre** (☑0835 231 8145) is on the opposite side of the park from the entrance (there's a zoo, too, which you can skip). The ticket office is inside the building marked 'Deep Ecological Paradise of Bifeng Gorge', in the main car park where the minibuses drop you. Pick up a free map from the **tourist information office** here, too. There's also free bag storage.

To get to the panda centre, 3km away from the ticket office, there's a free bus. But missing out on the hike would be a mistake. Turn left out of the ticket office then take the free lift (请云梯; qǐngyúntī) down 50 storeys to the foot of the gorge. Carry straight on to meet up with the bus, or cross the bridge to start your two-hour hike along the gorge and up the other side to the panda base. It's perfect picnic territory, but there are enough noodle and snack stalls along the way for you to not need to bring supplies.

There's more walking to be done on trails inside the panda centre, where the pandas are kept in OK enclosures similar to those at Chéngdū's Giant Panda Breeding Research Base. There's also an oh-so-cute 'panda kindergarten' enclosure.

You could see Bìfēngxiá in a day trip from Chéngdū, but there are plenty of sleeping options, too. The pick of the bunch, **Xiǎoxītiān Mínlǚcūn** (小西天民旅村; ☑135 5155 6417; tw/tr/qu ¥80/100/120; ❄🌐), is at the end of the two-hour walk, just before you reach the panda base, and has simple rooms set around a courtyard. A handful of other guesthouses, teahouses and restaurants are located by the entrance to the panda base.

ⓘ Getting There & Away

You need to go via the town of Yǎ'ān. Buses from Chéngdū terminate at Yǎ'ān's xīmén bus station (西门车站; xīmén chēzhàn), but you should get off just before, at the **tourist bus station** (旅游车站; lǚyóu chēzhàn), where you'll find minibuses (¥5) waiting to take you the final 18km to the panda base. The last bus back to Chéngdū from the tourist bus station leaves at 6.30pm. From Yǎ'ān you can get to various other destinations without having to go back to Chéngdū.

Buses from Yǎ'ān's xīmén bus station:

Éméi Town ¥50, 2½ hours, four daily (8.15am, 10am, 12.10pm, 2pm)

Kāngdìng ¥73, 4½ hours, five daily (8am to 2.30pm)

Lèshān ¥55, 2½ hours, six daily (8.35am to 4.30pm)

A pedicab between Yǎ'ān's two bus stations costs ¥8.

PÍNGLÈ 平乐

A popular subject of paintings for Chinese art students, this ancient riverside village was originally a way-station on the southern Silk Road more than 2000 years ago. Modern life is encroaching, as are sellers of tourist trinkets (and water pistols!), but enough old-town life remains for a pleasant day-long excursion from Chéngdū, and there's plenty of fun to be had paddling in the river here.

Many of the wooden buildings in the **old town** (古镇; gǔzhèn) have been rebuilt recently, but some still date back to the Ming and Qing dynasties. Locals still live in a few of them, although more and more are being turned into small guesthouses and restaurants, as tourist numbers rise. The town's most venerable inhabitants are its banyan trees, a dozen of which are more than 1000 years old. Don't miss the cutest of old stone passageways, called Fúhuì Street Water Gate (福惠街水门; Fúhuì Jiē Shuǐmén), which leads down to a river pathway where you can lounge on a bamboo chair and drink tea (¥15 to ¥30).

There are plenty of teahouses across the river, too, and on this side you can wander away from the water for a rural stroll in the decidedly untouristy surrounding farmland, which includes some small tea plantations.

There are several small inns on both sides of the river – look for signs saying 客栈 (kèzhàn; guesthouse) or 住宿 (zhùsù; lodgings) – although for most visitors a day trip will be sufficient. **Gǔbù Kèzhàn** (古埠客栈; ☑153 9764 0708; 32 Changqing Jie; 长庆

街32号; r ¥198 & ¥238, discounted to ¥80 & ¥100) has nice little rooms with river views; turn left when you reach the river. Noodle joints (look for the character 面; *miàn*) and small restaurants are everywhere. Some have photo menus.

Be aware that buses to Pínglè usually stop first at the small town of Qiónglái (邛崃), about 15 minutes before Pínglè. Don't get off here by mistake. Once in Pínglè, walk out of the bus station and turn right for the river. Buses returning from Pínglè to Chéngdū's Xīnnánmén bus station leave at 9.30am, noon, 1pm, 2pm, 3pm, 4pm, 4.30pm and 5.30pm.

LIǓ JIĀNG 柳江

The lovely pastoral setting is the main attraction of this gorgeous village tucked away in the central Sìchuān countryside. The **old town** (古镇; *gǔzhèn*), with its narrow alleyways, wooden courtyard buildings and ancient banyan trees, straddles both sides of the Yángcūn River (杨村河; Yángcūn Hé) in a picture-perfect setting. In fact, after recent renovations, it's almost too perfect (it's sometimes tough to pick out genuine old buildings here, although there are some), and at weekends it becomes overrun by tourists all craving a piece of rural charm. Nevertheless, this is still a lovely spot for a lazy lunch, an afternoon in a teahouse or a dip in the river. If you want to stay the night, the charming **Wàngjiāng Kèzhàn** (望江客栈; ☑139 0903 6203; 38 Liujiang Jie; 柳江街38号; r ¥60-80) has creaky wooden floorboards, simple but clean rooms with shared bathrooms, and river views. There's a pleasant terrace overlooking the river, where you can have tea (¥10 to ¥20) or Sichuanese food (mains ¥12 to ¥40).

There's some excellent walking to be done in the surrounding countryside. Look for wooden signboards in the old town with maps of walking trails on them (Chinese only). One fine option is the 3.5km uphill hike to Hóujiā Shānzhài (侯家山寨). The start of the road here is over the other side of the river from where the bus normally drops passengers off, and at the far end of the old town, and it's marked by a wooden archway with the characters 寨山家侯. Once you've found that, just follow the road and signs past mooing cows, ploughing farmers, rice terraces, bamboo clumps and small tea plantations. On the road near the top is **Tiàowàng Wǎwū** (眺望瓦屋; ☑130 8838

1221; r ¥80, dishes from ¥5), a large renovated wooden courtyard building with simple twin rooms, friendly owners and fabulous views. You can grab a bowl of noodles (面; *miàn*) here or whatever rice dishes (饭; *fàn*) it happens to be cooking that day.

To reach Liǔ Jiāng, take a bus from Xīnnánmén bus station to Hóngyǎ (洪雅) then change for Liǔ Jiāng (¥9, one hour, every 15 minutes until 5.30pm). The last bus from Hóngyǎ to Chéngdū is 5.30pm. There are also regular buses from Hóngyǎ to Éméi Shān, Lèshān and Yǎ'ān.

Éméi Shān 峨眉山

☑0833

A cool, misty retreat from the Sìchuān basin's sweltering heat, stunning **Éméi Shān** (adult/student ¥150/80) is one of China's four most famous Buddhist mountains (the others are Pǔtuóshān, Wǔtái Shān and Jiǔhuá Shān). Here you'll find fabulous forested mountain scenery, ramshackle wooden temples and macaques demanding tribute for safe passage. There's also the wonderful opportunity to spend the night in one of the many monasteries that dot the mountain range.

Only a few remnants of Éméi Shān's original templework remain. Glittering **Jīndǐng Temple** (Jīndǐng Sì), for example, with its brass tiling engraved with Tibetan script, was completely gutted by fire. Other temples suffered the same fate, and all were looted to various degrees during the war with Japan and the Cultural Revolution. Some do still go back a few years, though, with **Wànnián Temple**, the oldest, clocking in at a very respectable 1100 years old.

The waves of pilgrims, hawkers and, most of all, tourists during peak season eliminate much solitude, but the crowds hover largely around the areas closest to the cable cars and the major temples. Away from them, the pathways, lined with fir, pine and cedar trees, make for peaceful hiking. Lofty crags, cloud-kissing precipices, butterflies and azaleas together form a nature reserve, and the mountain joins Lèshān, Jiǔzhàigōu and Dūjiāngyàn Irrigation Project on Unesco's list of World Heritage Sites in Sìchuān.

When to Go

The best time to visit is May to October. Avoid the national holidays, when the number of visitors reaches epic proportions. July and August are also busy.

Snowfall generally begins around November on the upper slopes. In winter you can hire iron soles with spikes to deal with encrusted ice and snow.

Some average temperatures:

	JAN	APR	JUL	OCT
Éméi town	7°C	21°C	26°C	17°C
Summit	6°C	3°C	12°C	-1°C

⊙ Sights

Bàoguó Temple　　　BUDDHIST MONASTERY
(报国寺; Bàoguó Sì; Declare Nation Temple; admission ¥8) Constructed in the 16th century, this temple (550m) features beautiful gardens of rare plants, as well as a 3.5m-high porcelain Buddha dating back to 1415, which is housed near the Sutra Library. You don't need the Éméi Shān entrance ticket to get here.

Qīngyīn Pavilion　　　BUDDHIST TEMPLE
(清音阁; Qīngyīn Gé) Named 'Pure Sound Pavilion' after the soothing sounds of the waters coursing around rock formations, this temple (710m) is built on an outcrop in the middle of a fast-flowing stream. Rest in one of the small pavilions here while you appreciate the natural 'music'.

Ecological Monkey Zone　　　WILDLIFE AREA
Between Qīngyīn Pavilion and Hóngchūn Píng (Venerable Trees Terrace) is the first place most hikers encounter the mountain's infamous monkeys. Despite the area's 'ecological' moniker, attendants here alternately feed the monkeys and, when they get too aggressive, chase them away with sticks and slingshots.

Wànnián Temple　　　BUDDHIST MONASTERY
(万年寺; Wànnián Sì; Long Life Monastery; admission ¥10) Reconstructed in the 9th century, Wànnián Temple (1020m) is the oldest surviving Éméi temple. It's dedicated to the man on the white elephant, the Bodhisattva Pǔxián (also known as Samantabhadra), the Buddhist Lord of Truth and protector of the mountain. This 8.5m-high **statue** cast in copper and bronze dates from AD 980 and weighs an estimated 62,000kg. If you can manage to rub the elephant's hind leg, good luck will be cast upon you. The statue is housed in **Brick Hall**, a domed building with small stupas on it and the only building left unharmed in a 1945 fire.

Elephant Bathing Pool　　　BUDDHIST MONASTERY
(洗象池; Xǐxiàng Chí) According to legend, Elephant Bathing Pool (2070m) is where Pǔxián flew his elephant in for a big scrub, but today there's not much of a pool to speak of. Being almost at the crossroads of both major trails, the temple here is sometimes crowded with pilgrims.

Jīndǐng Temple　　　BUDDHIST TEMPLE
(金顶寺; Jīndǐng Sì; Golden Summit Temple) The magnificent Jīndǐng Temple is at the Golden Summit (Jīn Dǐng; 3077m), commonly referred to as the mountain's highest peak. Covered with glazed tiles and surrounded by white marble balustrades, it's a modern renovation, but is quite striking. In front of the temple, the unmissable 48m-tall golden statue **multi-dimensional Samantabhadra** (十方普贤; Shífāng Pǔxián) honours mountain protector Pǔxián and was added in 2006.

The mountain's highest point (3099m) is actually nearby **Wànfó Dǐng** (Ten Thousand Buddha Summit), but it has been closed to visitors for some years now.

Fúhǔ Temple　　　BUDDHIST MONASTERY
(伏虎寺; Fúhǔ Sì; Crouching Tiger Monastery; admission ¥6) Located about 1km from Bàoguó Temple, Fúhǔ Temple (630m) is hidden deep within the forest. It houses a 7m-high copper pagoda inscribed with Buddhist images and texts.

Xiānfēng Temple　　　BUDDHIST MONASTERY
(仙峰寺; Xiānfēng Sì; Immortal Peak Monastery) Somewhat off the beaten track, this well-looked-after monastery (1752m) is backed by rugged cliffs and surrounded by fantastic scenery.

🛏 Sleeping
ON THE MOUNTAIN
Almost all the temples on the mountain (with the notable exception of Jīndǐng Temple at the summit) offer cheap lodgings in dormitory-style accommodation with shared bathrooms but usually no showers. Some also have guesthouse-quality private rooms, sometimes with private bathrooms.

Xiānfēng Temple　　　MONASTERY $
(仙峰寺; Xiānfēng Sì; dm & tw without bathroom ¥30-260, tw with bathroom ¥280) This remote temple, with a lovely forested location backed by rugged cliffs, is set around a large shaded front courtyard and has a peaceful atmosphere. There's

Émei Shān

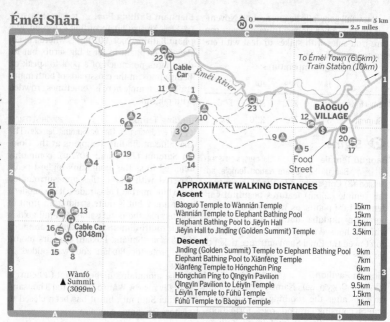

APPROXIMATE WALKING DISTANCES

Ascent

Bàoguó Temple to Wànnián Temple	15km
Wànnián Temple to Elephant Bathing Pool	15km
Elephant Bathing Pool to Jiēyǐn Hall	1.5km
Jiēyǐn Hall to Jīndǐng (Golden Summit) Temple	3.5km

Descent

Jīndǐng (Golden Summit) Temple to Elephant Bathing Pool	9km
Elephant Bathing Pool to Xiānfēng Temple	7km
Xiānfēng Temple to Hóngchūn Píng	6km
Hóngchūn Píng to Qīngyīn Pavilion	6km
Qīngyīn Pavilion to Léiyīn Temple	9.5km
Léiyīn Temple to Fúhǔ Temple	1.5km
Fúhǔ Temple to Bàoguó Temple	1km

Émei Shān

Sights

1 Báilóngdòng	B1
2 Chū Temple	B1
3 Ecological Monkey Zone	B2
4 Elephant Bathing Pool	A2
5 Fúhǔ Temple	D2
6 Huáyán Dǐng	B1
7 Jiēyǐn Monastery	A2
8 Jīndǐng (Golden Summit) Temple	A3
9 Léiyīn Temple	C2
10 Qīngyīn Pavilion	C1
11 Wànnián Temple	B1

Sleeping

12 Bàoguó Temple	D1

13 Cableway Company Hotel	A2
14 Hóngchūn Píng (Venerable Trees Terrace)	B2
15 Jīndǐng Dàjiǔdiàn	A3
16 Tàizǐ Píng	A3
17 Teddy Bear Hotel	D2
18 Xiānfēng Temple	B2
19 Yùxiān Temple	B2

Transport

20 Bàoguó Bus Station	D2
21 Léidòngpíng Bus Depot	A2
22 Wànnián Bus Depot	B1
23 Wǔxiǎnggǎng Bus Depot	C1

a good range of rooms from dorms to pricier twins with showers. Approximate walking time from foot/summit is six/four hours.

Yùxiān Temple MONASTERY $
(遇仙寺; Yùxiān Sì; dm/tw from ¥30/80) Scenery wise this is one of the most spectacular places to stay – at 1680m the views are stunning here. And considering how small the temple is, there's also a large choice of rooms, from basic dorms to private twins. It is very

remote here, though, so could feel a little eerie if you're staying on your own. From foot/summit is seven/three hours.

Hóngchūn Píng MONASTERY $
(洪椿坪; dm ¥30-40, tw ¥45-80) Arguably the smartest of the temples (1120m) with accommodation, this place is another with a nice courtyard, making it a comfortable choice to spend time in. Rooms are simple but decent. From foot/summit it is three/seven hours.

Tàizǐ Píng
MONASTERY $

(太子坪; dm ¥30-40) What this quiet, ramshackle wooden temple lacks in comfort, it gains in charm. Expect extremely basic three-bed dorms with a cold-water sink for washing. From foot/summit is nine hours/one hour.

There are also two bog-standard hotels on the mountain: **Jīndǐng Dàjiǔdiàn** (金顶大酒店; ☎509 8088/77; r from ¥480, discounted to ¥380) where foot/summit is 9½ hours/30 minutes away away; and **Cableway Company Hotel** (索道公司招待所; Suǒdào Gōngsī Zhāodàisuǒ; ☎155 2030 0955; tr/tw ¥150/260) at 2540m, where foot/summit is 8½/1½ hours – it was being renovated at the time of research.

IN BÀOGUÓ VILLAGE

Teddy Bear Hotel
HOSTEL $$

(玩具熊酒店; Wánjùxióng Jiǔdiàn; ☎559 0135, 138 9068 1961; www.teddybear.com.cn; 43 Baoguo Lu; dm ¥35, r ¥80-260; ❈@🛜) This 'backpacker central' place has cute, well-maintained rooms and English-speaking staff. The left-luggage service is free, as are the walking sticks and maps of the mountain trails, and there are massages available when you make it back down the mountain. There's internet access via a cable in some rooms, wi-fi in others and computer terminals in the lobby cafe, which does decent coffee, plus Chinese and Western food. Call Andy, the manager, for a free pick-up from Émèi town.

Bàoguó Temple
MONASTERY $

(报国寺; Bàoguó Sì; Declare Nation Temple; dm/r ¥40/120; ❈) If you don't have time to get up the mountain when you arrive, you can still stay in a monastery. Bàoguó Temple, hidden among the trees, is one of the largest and most atmospheric here, and has simple but clean and spacious rooms with three single beds in each. There's a large common shower area and a dining hall (meals ¥15). Accommodation is run by the friendly Patrick Yang (☎137 0813 1210), who speaks English.

Eating

On the mountain, most temples have small dining halls, but you're never very far from one of the many trailside food stalls that dot the mountain. Most serve simple noodle (面; *miàn*) or rice (饭; *fàn*) dishes as well as instant noodles (方便面; *fāngbiàn miàn*), tea and snacks.

In Bàoguó Village, restaurants and supermarkets abound. Haochi Jie (好吃街; Food Street) is crammed with places to eat, many with outdoor seating. The menu contains various Sichuanese dishes (¥15 to ¥40) and has English translations.

ℹ️ Information

Agricultural Bank of China (农业银行; Nóngyè Yínháng; ⏰9am-5pm) Has foreign exchange desk and foreign-friendly ATM. The ATM by Bàoguó bus station also accepts foreign cards.

ÉMÉI SHĀN HIKING ROUTES

There are numerous options for tackling Émèi Shān with various combinations of buses, cable cars, hiking trails and monastery stop-offs. Below are four popular ones. Note, these estimated walking times do not include breaks, which you will obviously need.

» **One day** Make use of buses and cable cars by taking a bus to Wànnián Temple (45 minutes), then hiking to the top (four hours) with the help of both cable cars before walking down to Léidòngpíng bus depot (1½ hours) and taking a bus back to Bàoguó Village (90 minutes).

» **Two days** Take the bus to Wànnián bus depot (45 minutes) then hike up via Chū Temple to the summit (five to six hours). On the way down, turn right a short distance past Elephant Bathing Pool and take the more scenic path, via Xiānfēng Temple, back to Wànnián bus depot (eight hours).

» **Two days** Take the bus to Léidòngpíng (1½ hours) then walk to the top (one to two hours) before making your long descent to Bàoguó Village (10 hours) via an overnight stay in a monastery.

» **Three days** Ditch the buses completely and simply hike up and down the whole mountain (about 20 hours in total). To mix things up, go via Wànnián Temple on the way up and via Xiānfēng Temple on the way down. While you're on the way down, start preparing yourself mentally for at least three to four days of jelly legs.

Internet Most accommodation in Bàoguó Village has internet access for guests, but the nearest internet cafes (网吧; *wǎngbā*) are around 2km downhill towards Éméi town.

ⓘ Getting There & Away

The town of Éméi (峨眉山市; Éméi Shān Shì) lies 6.5km east of the mountain Éméi Shān and is the transport hub for the mountain. Almost all buses to Éméi Shān terminate here – at the Éméi Shān passenger traffic centre (峨眉山客运中心; Éméi Shān kèyùn zhōngxīn), directly opposite Éméi Train Station (峨眉火车站; Éméi Huǒchēzhàn). From here, it's a ¥20 cab to Bàoguó Village. Alternatively, take local bus 1 (¥1) to Pēnshuǐ Chí (喷水池) bus stop, then take Bus 5 (¥1.50) from across the square to Bàoguó (报国).

Note, while it's not possible to travel direct to Bàoguó from most long-distance destinations, some long-distance buses do leave from Bàoguó.

Buses from Bàoguó bus station include:

Chéngdū ¥50, 2½ hours, frequent services (8am to 6pm)

Chóngqìng ¥130, six hours, two daily (6.40am & 11am)

Lèshān ¥11, 45 minutes, every 30 minutes (8am to 5.30pm)

Yíbīn ¥86, six hours, one daily (6.50am)

Buses from Éméi Shān passenger traffic centre include:

Kāngdìng ¥120, seven hours, one daily (9.50am)

Yǎ'ān ¥51, three hours, four daily (7.45am, 9.30am, 12.30pm & 2.20pm)

Zìgòng ¥51, three hours, frequent (7.40am to 5.10pm)

Train

Chéngdū seat ¥24, 2½ hours, five daily (6.01am to 10.31am, then 9.16pm)

Kūnmíng sleeper ¥216, 17 hours, four daily (3.42pm, 4.57pm, 5.16pm and 9.47pm)

Xī'ān sleeper ¥224, 19½ hours, one daily (10.31am)

ⓘ Getting Around

Bàoguó (报国) Village is your gateway to the mountain. Buses from the village bus station travel to three bus depots on the mountain: **Wǔxiǎngǎng** (五显冈; 20 minutes), about a 20-minute walk below Qīngyīn Pavilion; **Wànnián** (万年; one hour), below Wànnián Temple; and **Léidòngpíng** (雷洞坪; two hours), a few minutes' walk from Jīngdíng cable car.

There are two ticket types. Both are returns. The ¥40 ticket is for the lower two depots. The ¥90 ticket is for Léidòngpíng. If you return via a different depot you may have to pay a small surcharge to make up the difference.

Buses run frequently from around 6am to 5pm (7am to 4pm in winter). The last buses back down the mountain leave at 6pm (5pm in winter).

Lèshān 乐山

☑ 0833 / POP 156,000

With fingernails bigger than the average human, the world's tallest Buddha draws plenty of tourists to this relaxed riverside town. It's an easy day trip from Chéngdū or a convenient stopover en route to or from Éméi Shān.

⊙ Sights

Grand Buddha   BUDDHIST

(大佛; Dàfó; adult ¥90; ☉ 7.30am-6.30pm Apr-early Oct, 8am-5.30pm early Oct-Mar) Lèshān's pride and joy is the serene, 1200-year-old Grand Buddha carved into a cliff face overlooking the confluence of the Dàdù River (大渡河; Dàdù Hé) and the Mín River. And at 71m tall, he's definitely big. His ears stretch for 7m, his shoulders span 28m, and each of his big toes is 8.5m long.

A Buddhist monk called Haitong conceived the project in AD 713, hoping that the Buddha would calm the swift rivers and protect boatmen from lethal currents. The huge project wasn't completed until 90 years after Haitong's death but eventually, just as he had once wished, the river waters calmed. Locals say it was the Grand Buddha's calming effect. Sceptics say it was due to the lengthy construction process in which surplus rocks from the sculpting filled the river hollows.

Inside the body, hidden from view, is a water-drainage system to prevent weathering, although Dàfó is showing his age and soil erosion is an ongoing problem.

To fully appreciate the Buddha's magnitude, get an up-close look at his head, then descend the steep, winding stairway for the Lilliputian view. Avoid visiting on weekends or holidays, when traffic on the staircase can come to a complete standstill.

Admission to the Buddha includes access to a number of caves and temples on the grounds and to the **Máhàoyá Tombs Museum** (麻浩崖墓博物馆; Máhàoyámù Bówùguǎn), which has a modest collection of tombs and burial artefacts dating from the Eastern Han dynasty (AD 25–220).

Also included in the ticket price is **Wūyóu Temple** (乌尤寺; Wūyóu Sì), which, like the Grand Buddha, dates from the Tang dynasty,

Lèshān

◎ **Top Sights**
　Grand Buddha B3

◎ **Sights**
　1 Máhàoyá Tombs Museum B4
　2 Oriental Buddhist Theme Park B4
　3 Wūyóu Temple B4

🛏 **Sleeping**
　4 Jiāzhōu Hotel A2
　5 Jīntáoyuán Dàjiǔdiàn B3

🍴 **Eating**
　6 Xiàogōngzuǐ Bàbā B3
　7 Yang's Restaurant A2

🍷 **Drinking**
　8 Teahouses B2

ℹ **Information**
　9 People's Hospital A2

ℹ **Transport**
　10 Lèshān Dock B3

with Ming and Qing renovations. This monastery also contains calligraphy, painting and artefacts, but the highlight is the hall of 1000 terracotta arhat (Buddhist celestial beings, similar to angels) displaying an incredible variety of postures and facial expressions – no two are alike. Also inside the **Luóhàn Hall**, where the arhat are housed, is a fantastic statue of **Avalokiteshvara**, the Sanskrit name of the Goddess of Mercy (Guanyin in Chinese).

One sight on the grounds that requires a separate ticket is the recently constructed **Oriental Buddhist Theme Park** (东方佛都; Dōngfāng Fódū; admission ¥70), housing 3000 Buddha statues and figurines from around Asia, including a 170m-long reclining Buddha, one of the world's longest.

Bus 13 (¥1) travels from Xiàobà bus station and loops through the town centre before crossing the river to reach the Grand Buddha Scenic Area and Wūyóu Temple.

You could walk across, too, up and down both sides of the river, passing numerous teahouses en route.

🏇 Tours

Tour boats (游船; yóuchuán; 30-min round trip ¥70; ⏱7.30am to 6.30pm) leave regularly from Lèshān dock (乐山港; Lèshān gǎng), passing by the cliffs for panoramic views of the Grand Buddha (hovering in front for about 10 minutes), which reveal two guardians in the cliff side, not visible from land.

The affable **Mr Yang** (☎159 8438 2528; richardyangmin@yahoo.com.cn; Yang's Restaurant, 2f 186 Baita Jie) has been guiding foreign tourists round Lèshān since the 1970s. He arranges a village visit as a half-day trip that includes a calligraphy demonstration, an old-town tour and a visit to a villager's home. He charges ¥200 per person including transport, lunch and his services as an English-speaking guide.

🛏 Sleeping

Jiāzhōu Hotel　　　　　　　　　　HOTEL $$
(嘉州宾馆; Jiāzhōu Bīnguǎn; ☎213 9888; 85 Baita Jie; 白塔街85号; r incl breakfast from ¥360; ❄@) Rooms aren't as grand as the lobby suggests, but this place is more upmarket than most and makes for a comfortable stay. Third-floor rooms and above have

internet connection for laptop users, and many rooms, even some of the cheapies, have river views. Standard twins often go for ¥220.

Jīntáoyuán Dàjiǔdiàn HOTEL $$
(金桃源大酒店; ☑210 7666; 136 Binjiang Lu; 滨江路南段136号; d from ¥456, discounted to ¥160; ❄ @) Smart, clean and by the river. Has internet connection for laptops. No English sign, although the word 'Hotel' is written on the Chinese sign.

✕ Eating

Xiàogōngzuǐ Bàbā SICHUANESE $
(肖公嘴坝吧; Binhe Lu; 滨河路; mains from ¥25; ☉9am-midnight; 🄳) One of a cluster of cafe-restaurants with terrace seating on the riverbank here (walk down the steps from the road). Perfect for tea (from ¥10) or fresh coffee (from ¥25) during the day, or a riverside beer (from ¥8) come evening. The restaurant opens from 11am to 2pm and from 6pm to 11pm and does barbecue skewers plus Sichuanese main courses.

Yang's Restaurant SICHUANESE $
(杨家餐厅; Yángjiā Cāntīng; 2f 186 Baita Jie; 白塔街186号2层; dishes ¥15-30; ☉6-9pm; 🄳) Lèshān veteran Mr Yang runs this small restaurant in the living room of his home. He serves simple but tasty local food and may regale you with tales of his life while you eat.

❶ Information

Bank of China (中国银行; Zhōngguó Yínháng; 16 Renmin Nanlu) Answers all your money-changing needs.

China Post (中国邮政; Zhōngguó Yóuzhèng; 62 Yutang Jie)

Internet cafe (网吧; wǎngbā; per hr ¥2; ☉24hr) Opposite Yang's Restaurant; 2nd floor.

People's Hospital (人民医院; Rénmín Yīyuàn; ☑211 9310, after-hr emergencies 211 9328; 222 Baita Jie) Has some English-speaking doctors. Pharmacies cluster round the entrance.

Public Security Bureau (PSB; 省公安厅外事科; Gōng'ānjú; ☑518 2555; 148 Fenghuang Lu Zhongduan; 凤凰路中段148号; ☉9am-noon & 1-5pm Mon-Fri) Visa extensions in five days. Take Bus 6 (¥1) from the centre.

❶ Getting There & Around

Bus

Lèshān has three main bus stations. Buses from Chéngdū's Xīnnánmén station usually arrive at Xiàobà bus station (肖坝车站; Xiàobà chēzhàn), but central bus station (乐山客运中心车站;

Lèshān kèyùn zhōngxīn chēzhàn) is bigger and has more frequent services to more destinations. You may also be dropped at Liányùn bus station (联运车站; Liányùn chēzhàn). Note, if you're heading to Éméi Shān, it's better to use Xiàobà bus station as buses from there go all the way to Bàoguó (¥11, 45 minutes, every 30 minutes, 7.30am to 5pm).

Services from central bus station include:

Chéngdū ¥49 to ¥51, two hours, every 20 minutes (7.10am to 5.10pm)

Chóngqìng ¥110 to ¥132, six hours, hourly (7.10am to 5.10pm)

Éméi town ¥8, 30 minutes, every 15 minutes (7am to 6.30pm)

Kāngdìng ¥119, seven hours, one daily (9.30am)

Yǎ'ān ¥54, 2½ hours, six daily (9am to 4.40pm)

Zìgòng ¥42, three hours, hourly (8.30am to 5.10pm)

Local buses cost ¥1. Some handy routes:

Bus 1 Xiàobà bus station–Jiāzhōu Hotel–town centre–Liányùn bus station

Bus 6 Xiàobà bus station–town centre–PSB

Bus 13 Xiàobà bus station–town centre–Grand Buddha–Wūyóu Temple

Bus 9 Central bus station–town centre–Lèshān dock

Train

The new 37-minute high-speed rail link from Chéngdū to Lèshān may be ready by the time you read this.

Lángzhōng 阆中

☑0817 / POP 112,000

Seemingly endless black-tile roofs with swooping eaves overlooking the narrowest of alleys; flagstone streets lined with tiny shops; temples atop misty hills above a river. If you're looking for fast disappearing 'old China', hop on a bus to the town of Lángzhōng, Sìchuān's capital city for 17 years during the Qing dynasty and home to the province's largest grouping of extant traditional architecture.

◎ Sights

You'll want to base yourself in the **old town** (古镇; gǔzhèn) here. Most attractions have an English-language overview sign, however inside, English captions vary from some to none. Many people are happy just wandering the alleys and gaping at the architecture – a blend of North China quadrangle and South China garden styles.

There's some good exploring to be done across the river, south of the old town. At the foot of one hill, and among other Buddhist statuary and caves, sits the sedate-looking **Grand Buddha** (大佛寺; Dàfó Sì). From the old town, walk down to the river, turn left and keep going past the second road bridge. Then cross the river on a small passenger boat (¥2).

For bird's-eye views of the town's rooftops and lanes, climb to the top of either of three towers: **Huáguāng Lóu** (华光楼; Dadong Jie; admission ¥15), just past the Fēng Shuǐ Museum and rebuilt in 1867, **Zhōngtiān Lóu** (中天楼; Wumiao Jie; admission ¥10), a 2006 rebuild on the way to Zhāng Fēi Temple, or **South Gate** (南门楼; Nánmén Lóu; admission free), a 2010 rebuild on Nan Jie, a street running parallel with Dadong Jie.

A ¥80 combination ticket admits you to the towers and the three attractions listed below.

Zhāng Fēi Temple
TEMPLE

(张飞庙; Zhāngfēi Miào; Xi Jie; admission ¥40) This temple is the tomb of and shrine to local boy Zhang Fei, a respected general during the kingdom of Shu, who administered the kingdom from here. It's on Xi Jie (西街), a continuation of Wumiao Jie (武庙街).

Fēng Shuǐ Museum
MUSEUM

(风水馆; Fēngshuǐ Guǎn; Dadong Jie; admission ¥20) This museum includes a model of the town, illustrating its feng shui–inspired design. A helpful English-speaking guide is sometimes available here. It's next to Tiānyī Youth Hotel on Dadong Jie (大东街), and is free for hotel guests.

Gòng Yuàn
HISTORIC BUILDING

(贡院; Xuedao Jie; admission ¥35) Among the best-preserved imperial examination halls in China. On Xuedao Jiē (学道街), which is parallel to Wumiao Jie, one block north.

🛏 Sleeping

There are dozens of renovated courtyard guesthouses. Look out for signs saying 客栈 (kèzhàn; guesthouse) or 住宿 (zhùsù; lodgings).

TOP CHOICE Tiānyī Youth Hotel
GUESTHOUSE $

(天一青年旅舍; Tiānyī Qīngnián Lûshè; ✆622 5501; 100 Dadong Jie; 大东街100号; d/tw without bathroom ¥98-138, with bathroom ¥288; ❄@✆) If you want to improve your geomancy, settle into this great value courtyard inn beside the Fēng Shuǐ Museum. Each of the stylish doubles (typically discounted to ¥135) is inspired by a feng shui element: earth, wood, fire, metal or water. The shared-bathroom twins and doubles (which go for ¥80) are simpler but still crisp and clean, with lots of natural wood.

Ancient Hotel
COURTYARD HOTEL $$

(杜家客栈; Dùjiā Kèzhàn; ✆622 4436; 63 Xiaxin Jie; 下新街63号; r from ¥480, discounted to ¥160; ❄@) Large, multicourtyard wooden building next to the Museum of Water Culture. The nicest rooms are set around a back courtyard with an open-air stage (performances 8pm to 10pm), and go for ¥280. Turn right off Dadong Jie just before the Huáguāng Lóu tower.

Lǐ Family Courtyard
COURTYARD HOTEL $$

(李家大院; Lǐjiā Dàyuàn; ✆623 6500; 47 Wumiao Jie; 武庙街47号; r from ¥368, discounted to ¥128) Previously a lovely place to stay, but closed for wholesale renovation when we were last here.

🍴 Eating

Famed local fare includes *zhāngfēi niúròu* (张飞牛肉; preserved water-buffalo beef; from ¥20 per packet), which makes a great bus-journey snack.

Míngzhōu Yǐnshí
NOODLES $

(名州饮食; 6 Shanghua Jie; 上华街6号; noodles ¥5-7; ⏱8.30am-10pm) Small, friendly noodle joint run by Grace, a local English teacher, and her husband. No English menu, but Grace speaks good English. If she's teaching when you visit, just go for the *niúròu miàn* (牛肉面; beef noodles; ¥5 to ¥7) and you won't leave disappointed. Shanghua Jie is a continuation of Dadong Jie, and this place is just up from the Huáguāng Lóu tower.

☆ Entertainment

North Sìchuān Shadow Puppetry
THEATRE

(川北皮影; Chuānběi Píyǐng; ✆623 8668; 67-69 Wumiao Jie; 武庙街67-69号; tickets ¥20; ⏱8-10pm) Informal but fun 20-minute performances of north Sìchuān shadow puppetry are held in the small open-air courtyard here. It's a couple of doors past Lǐ Family Courtyard.

ⓘ Information

You can pick up **street maps** (地图; dìtú; ¥5) at some shops in the old town or at some tourist sights. Multilingual signs and maps are posted throughout the old town's streets.

THE WAY TO XĪ'ĀN

For those on their way to Xī'ān from Jiǔzhàigōu, the most direct way to get there overland is via the mid-sized town of **Guǎngyuán** (广元), which is on the main Chéngdū–Xī'ān train line.

China's only female emperor, Wu Zetian, was born in Guǎngyuán during the Tang dynasty, and she is feted among the temples, pavilions and 1000-odd statues lining the cliffs at **Huángzé Temple** (皇泽寺; Huángzé Sì; admission ¥50).

The train station and long-distance bus station are beside each other. If you need to stay the night, **Tiānzhào Hotel** (天墨马瑞卡酒店; Tiānzhào Mǎruìkǎ Jiǔdiàn; ☑0839 366 8888; 212 Jinlun Nanlu; 金轮南路212号; r from ¥168 @) has extremely smart rooms. Turn right out of the train station and it's on your right. Huángzé Temple is about a 750m walk beyond the hotel.

Selected buses from Guǎngyuán
Chéngdū ¥140, four hours, one daily (9am*)
Xī'ān ¥142, six hours, two daily (10am and 1.30pm)
Lángzhōng ¥56, three hours, every two hours (6am to 4.50pm)
Jiǔzhàigōu ¥88, 8½ hours, two daily (6am and 4.10pm)
* more frequent buses for Chéngdū leave from Guǎngyuán's South Hill bus station (南山站; Nánshān Zhàn)

Selected Trains from Guǎngyuán
Chéngdū seat ¥47, five hours, 22 daily
Xī'ān seat ¥76, 10 hours, 10 daily (2.41pm to 3.43am)

Bank of China ATM (cnr Dadong Jie & Neidong Jie) At the top end of Dadong Jie; is foreign-card friendly.

Internet cafe (网吧; wǎngbā; per hr ¥3; ⊙8am-midnight) On Maojia Xiang (毛家巷) off Bailishu Jiē (百里树街), a lane just outside the old town running parallel to Dadong Jie.

ⓘ Getting There & Away

Buses from Chéngdū's Běimén bus station arrive at kèyùn zhōngxīn qìchēzhàn (客运中心汽车站), the main bus station here, which also serves Chóngqìng (¥105, five hours, 7.20am, 8.40am, 9.40am, 10.50am and 2pm). Buses returning to Chéngdū (¥98, four hours) leave regularly between 6.40am and 5.30pm.

Lángzhōng also has a smaller bus station, Bāshíjiǔ Duì (89队), which serves Guǎngyuán (¥56, three hours, 8am, 9am, noon and 2.30pm), from where you can catch trains north to Xī'ān or buses west to Jiǔzhàigōu (see the boxed text). A local bus, labelled simply 89队 (Bāshíjiǔ Duì; ¥2, 20 minutes), connects the two stations and goes via the old town (ask to get off at Huáguāng Lóu, then walk up towards the tower for Dadong Jie).

From the smaller bus station, it's easiest just to walk to the old town. Turn left out of the station, then after a couple of blocks turn right onto Tianshanggong Jie (天上宫街) and keep walking straight. Dadong Jie will be on your left. Wumiao Jie will be straight on.

SOUTHERN SÌCHUĀN

Not often on the radar of foreign tourists, steamy southern Sìchuān is for those who prefer things a little offbeat. Quirky sights here include dinosaur fossils, ancient cliff-face hanging coffins and a bamboo forest. It's also home to some of China's very best teahouses.

Zìgòng   自贡

☑0813 / POP 693,000

This intriguing, rarely visited riverside city has been an important centre of Chinese salt production for almost 2000 years. Remnants of that industry make up part of an unconventional list of sights that includes the world's deepest traditional salt well and Asia's first dinosaur museum. Zìgòng is also the undisputed king of Sìchuān teahouses, so there's plenty of opportunity to while away the hours here if you fancy putting your feet up for a day.

◎ Sights

Salt Industry History Museum MUSEUM (盐业历史博物馆; Yányè Lìshǐ Bówùguǎn; 89 Dongxing Si; 东兴寺89号; admission ¥22; ⊙8.30am-5pm) This absorbing museum, housed in a beautiful 270-year-old guild hall, is devoted to the region's salt industry and does an excellent job of telling the story through old photographs, good English captions and a modest collection of exhibits. The building itself, though, built by Shaanxi salt merchants in 1736, threatens to steal the show with its cool stone courtyards, intricate woodcarvings and wonderful swooping eaves.

To get here from the hotels, walk down the hill and turn left onto Jiefang Lu (解放路). The museum will be on your right after about 500m.

Shēnhǎi Salt Well
SALT WELL

(燊海井; Shēnhǎi Jǐng; 289 Da'an Jie; 大安街289号; admission ¥22; ⊙8.30am-5pm) This 1001m-deep artesian salt well was the world's deepest well when it was built in 1835 and it remains the deepest salt well ever drilled using the traditional mining technique of percussion drilling.

Many of the original parts, including a 20m-high wooden derrick that towers above the tiny 20cm-wide mouth of the well, are still intact, and the well still operates as a salt provider, although on a much smaller scale than before. Nine salt cauldrons are still in operation and visitors can see them bubbling away beside rows of the 2ft-high blocks of salt that came from them.

There are excellent English captions explaining how bamboo was once used for brine pipes, how buffaloes used to turn the heavy winch (an electric motor is used these days) and how tofu was added to the brine to help separate impurities.

Take bus 5 or 35 (¥1, 10 minutes) from opposite the Róngguāng Business Hotel. Bus 5 terminates here. Bus 35 continues to the Dinosaur Museum.

Dinosaur Museum
MUSEUM

(恐龙馆; Kǒnglóng Guǎn; 238 Dashan Pu, Da'an District; 大安区大山铺238号; admission ¥42; ⊙8.30am-5.30pm) Built on top of an excavation site, which has one of the world's largest concentrations of dinosaur fossils, this museum has a fine collection of reassembled skeletons as well as half-buried dinosaur bones left in situ for visitors to see.

Dinosaur fossils started being discovered here in 1972 and their high numbers baffled archaeologists at first. It is now believed the skeletons were dumped here en masse from other sites in the region by huge floods.

Take bus 35 (¥1, 25 minutes) from opposite Róngguāng Business Hotel.

🛏 Sleeping

Róngguāng Business Hotel
HOTEL $$

(容光商务酒店; Róngguāng Shāngwù Jiǔdiàn; ☑211 9999; 25 Ziyou Lu; 自由路25号; r incl breakfast from ¥388, discounted to ¥120; ✳@) Large, smart rooms with friendly staff, internet access for laptop users and free-to-use computers along with a free buffet breakfast, distinguish this hotel. Smaller doubles go for ¥100. Take bus 1 or 35 from the bus station, or 34 from the train station.

Xióngfēi Holiday Hotel
HOTEL $$$

(雄飞假日酒店; Xióngfēi Jiàrì Jiǔdiàn; ☑211 8888; 193 Jiefang Lu; 解放路193号; r incl breakfast from ¥860, discounted to ¥389; ✳@) For a bit more class, try this upmarket place a few doors down from Róngguāng Business Hotel.

🍴 Eating & Drinking

Evenings here are all about shāokǎo (烧烤; barbecue skewers), with stalls spilling onto the pavement around Róngguāng Business Hotel as well as elsewhere around town. Our favourite sets up outside Bank of China from around 8pm (skewers ¥1 to ¥4). Zìgòng locals love their rabbit meat (兔子肉; tùzi ròu) and the skewers on offer include rabbit.

If you fancy a break from fiery Sìchuān cuisine, try the small dumplings restaurant, just up the hill from Róngguāng Business Hotel, which does delicious Tiānjīn-style xiǎolóng bāo (小龙包; steamed dumplings, per basket ¥6) and xīfàn (稀饭; rice porridge, ¥1) and is open from 6.30am to 8pm. Look for the stacks of bamboo baskets.

🔝 CHOICE Huánhóu Palace
TEAHOUSE $

(桓侯宫; Huánhóu Gōng; Zhonghua Lu; 中华路; tea ¥4-8; ⊙7am-9pm) This fabulous teahouse is located inside an 1868 butchers' guild hall. Its dramatic stone facade leads into an enchanting, tree-shaded, open courtyard which houses an old stone stage and is surrounded on all sides by the beautifully carved wooden structure of the former guild hall. It's up to your left as you walk towards the salt museum from the hotels.

🔝 CHOICE Wángyé Temple
TEAHOUSE $

(王爷庙; Wángyé Miào; Binjiang Lu; 滨江路; tea ¥5-15; ⊙8.30am-11pm) Housed within the ochre-coloured walls of a 100-year-old temple, this is also one of the coolest teahouses you'll find anywhere in Sìchuān. Perched above the Fǔxī River (釜溪河; Fǔxī Hé), it sits opposite the still-active Fǎzàng Temple (法藏寺; Fǎzàng

Sì). The pair was built to ensure safe passage for cargo boats transporting salt downstream. Now locals hang out here, drink tea, play cards and admire the river view. From the hotels, walk down to the river, turn left and follow the river for about 750m.

ⓘ Information

Bank of China (中国银行; Zhōngguó Yínháng; Ziyou Lu) Foreign-friendly ATM next to Róngguāng Business Hotel.

Internet cafe (网吧; wǎngbā; per hr ¥2; ⊘24hr) Up an alley beside the bank.

ⓘ Getting There & Around

Bus

Destinations include:

Chéngdū ¥79, 3½ hours, every 45 minutes (6.30am to 8.30pm)

Chóngqìng ¥75, 3½ hours, every 45 minutes (6.40am to 8.30pm)

Dàzú ¥52, three hours, two daily (8.30am and 2.50pm)

Éméi Shān ¥50, 3½ hours, hourly (6.10am to 2.30pm)

Lèshān ¥43, three hours, hourly (6.30am to 5pm)

Yíbīn ¥27, one hour, every 30 minutes (7.30am to 7pm)

LOCAL BUSES To get to the hotels we list, walk out of the bus station, turn right and walk 200m to the first bus stop. Then take bus 1 or 35 (¥1) five or six stops to Shízì Kǒu (十字口) bus stop. The hotels are down the hill a bit from the bus stop and across the road. From the train station, take bus 34 or 37 (¥1) to Bīnjiāng Lù (滨江路) bus stop. From there, walk back 200m and turn left up Ziyou Lu.

Train

Chéngdū seat ¥41, five hours, six daily (4.52am to 10am)

Chóngqìng seat ¥51/29, seven hours, two daily (9.11am/2.59pm)

Kūnmíng sleeper ¥208, 16 to 18 hours, three daily (1.58am, 2.11pm & 7.55pm)

Yíbīn seat ¥7 to ¥13, 1½ to 2½hours, nine daily (8.42am to 9.43pm)

Yíbīn 宜宾

Overlooking the confluence of the Mín and Jīnshā rivers, which become the mighty Yangzi River once they merge, Yíbīn was throughout history a town of great strategic military importance. These days it's a relatively modern, mid-sized city, which acts as a travel hub for trips to the Bamboo Sea and the Hanging Coffins.

Turn right out of Jīngmào Hotel, and right again to reach the **river confluence**, accessed through the reconstructed **Shuǐ Dōng Mén** (水东门; East Water Gate), which has a teahouse on top of it. Further down and off to the right is a genuinely old city-wall **gateway**, plus remnants of the original **ancient city wall**, leading towards a modern public square where locals dance come evening. Up from the square are more city-wall remains plus **Guanying Jie** (冠英街), a street of courtyard homes, dating from the Qing-dynasty.

Good value **Jīngmào Hotel** (经贸宾馆; Jīngmào Bīnguǎn; ☑0831-513 7222; 108 Minzhu Lu; 民主路108号; tw ¥140-260; ⊛@) gives 10% to 20% discounts and has internet access for laptops or rooms with computers for an extra ¥20. On the 2nd floor of the building next to Jīngmào Hotel is an **internet cafe** (per hr ¥2; ⊘24hr). There are foreign-friendly **ATMs** by Xùfǔ Shāngchéng bus stop.

The lively **night market** (东街; Dong Jie) includes stalls serving *diǎndiǎn màocài* (点点冒菜; skewers boiled in a spicy sauce). Turn left out of the hotel and Dong Jie is on your left. In the daytime, look for *ránmiàn* (然面), a delicious fried noodle dish and a local favourite.

ⓘ Getting There & Around

Bus

Most travellers arrive at Gāokè bus station (高客站; Gāokè zhàn). Take bus 4 (¥1 to¥2, 15 minutes) into town and get off at Xùfǔ Shāngchéng (叙府商城) bus stop on Renmin Lu (人民路). Turn right at the lights ahead of you and Jīngmào Hotel will be on your left.

Continue on bus 4 to get to Nánkè bus station (南客站; Nánkè zhàn) for buses to the Bamboo Sea (竹海; Zhúhǎi; ¥22, 1½ hours, 9.30am, 10am and 4.30pm) and the Hanging Coffins in Luòbiāo (洛表; ¥32, three hours, 2.05pm). If you miss the direct buses to the Bamboo Sea, go via Chángníng (长宁; ¥16, one hour, every 15 minutes from 7am to 7.30pm). If the direct Luòbiāo bus isn't convenient, go via Gǒngxiàn (珙县; ¥17, one hour, every 20 minutes from 6am to 7pm).

Consider visiting the Hanging Coffins from the Bamboo Sea, as buses from Chángníng go to Gǒngxiàn.

Buses from Gāokè bus station include:

Chéngdū ¥107, four hours, frequent services (7.20am to 7pm)

Chóngqìng ¥110, four hours, frequent services (7.10am to 7pm)

Éméi Shān ¥72, 4½ hours, two daily (12.10pm and 1.10pm)

SÌCHUĀN'S MYSTERIOUS HANGING COFFINS

Travellers looking to get off the beaten track might want to consider a trip to the remote corner of southeast Sìchuān, home to one of the province's most unusual and most mysterious sights: the Hanging Coffins of the ancient Bo people. The origins and eventual disappearance of the Bo continue to baffle archaeologists. It is thought they may be distant relatives of the Tujia, who can still be found scattered around the Three Gorges area, particularly in southwestern Húběi and northwestern Húnán. However, almost everything we know about the Bo has been gleaned from the sites of their coffins, which can still be found resting on wooden stakes, hammered into the side of cliffs up to 1000 years ago.

We know, for instance, from crude paintings found on some of the cliff faces, that the Bo were keen horsemen with a sharp social divide. Adult skeletons that have been recovered have also shown that the Bo knocked out their own teeth while still alive, although exactly why they practised this custom is still unknown.

There are hanging coffins at a few sites in this part of China, but at Luòbiǎo (洛表) the **hanging coffins** (悬棺; xuánguān; admission ¥20; ⊙8am-6pm) are found in greater numbers than elsewhere and are reasonably accessible.

At one time there were more than 300 coffins here, although about one-third have fallen to the ground as their support stakes gradually rotted away.

There's a small, free-to-enter museum just inside the site entrance with old photos, burial artefacts and a coffin (with a skeleton still inside it!). About 100m on, you'll find a large collection of coffins with steps leading up to a better vantage point. You can also climb up into a huge cave here. About 2km further on is another impressive collection of coffins.

Locals say the area is at its most photogenic first thing in the morning as the sun rises opposite the cliffs, so you may want to consider arriving the evening before and staying the night. **Bóxiānjū Bīnguǎn** (僰仙居宾馆; ☎0831-441 0169; r without/with computer ¥60/80; ❀@), two doors down from the bus station, is friendly and good value. The coffins are Luòbiǎo's only tourist sight but you could fill any spare time with walks around the fabulous surrounding countryside.

Getting There & Away

One of the reasons this place is so rarely visited is that it's a pain in the neck to get to. First you need to get to the grim coal-mining town of Gǒngxiàn (珙县), which you can reach on buses from either Yíbīn or from Chángníng (¥10.50, one hour, frequent services from 6.20am to 6.20pm) near the Bamboo Sea. At Gǒngxiàn, catch a bus to Luòbiǎo (¥20, 2½ hours, every 20 minutes from 5.50am to 5.10pm), from where you can walk (40 minutes; take the right fork) or take a motorcycle taxi (¥5) to the entrance. The last bus back to Gǒngxiàn leaves at 5.20pm.

To continue into Guìzhōu province, there are regular buses from Gǒngxiàn to Lúzhōu (泸州; ¥37.50, 6am to 4.40pm), where you can change for Chìshuǐ (赤水). For Yúnnán province, you can go from Gǒngxiàn to Wēixìn (威信; ¥50, 6.20am and 1.05pm), then on to Kūnmíng.

Selected buses from Gǒngxiàn:

Chéngdū ¥106, five hours, hourly (7am to 7pm)

Chóngqìng ¥110, five hours, hourly (7.30am to 2.30pm)

Yíbīn ¥17, one hour, every 15 minutes (6am to 6.15pm)

Lèshān ¥61, four hours, hourly (8.20am to 5.30pm)

Zìgòng ¥25, one hour, frequent services (7.30am to 7pm)

Train

Bus 11 (¥1) links the train station with Gāokè bus station and passes by the end of Renmin Lu.

Trains leaving from Yíbīn Train Station (火车站; huǒchē zhàn) include:

Chéngdū seat ¥51, 6½ to 7½ hours, three daily (6.02am, 8.08am and 8.30am)

Kūnmíng sleeper ¥195, 15 to 16 hours, three daily (4.02am, 4.09pm and 9.25pm)

Zìgòng seat ¥7 to ¥13, 1½ hours, seven daily (6.02am to 3.39pm)

Bamboo Sea 蜀南竹海

Swaths of swaying bamboo forest, well-marked walking trails and a handful of charming lakes and waterfalls make south Sìchuān's Bamboo Sea, or **Shǔnán Zhúhǎi** (adult ¥112), a worthwhile detour for those heading south.

There are more than 30 types of bamboo across this 120 sq km national park and the scenery is gorgeous enough to have attracted many a TV and film director.

The villages of Wànlǐng (万岭), near the west gate, and Wànlǐ (万里), near the east gate, are the main settlements inside the park and your best bet for a base. Both have walking options nearby, but one possibility is to hike between the two. It's about 11km if you follow the road the whole way, but various loops within scenic areas mean you'll probably end up walking a lot further. Expect to take at least half a day. Two possible cable car (索道; *suǒdào*) rides can shorten the walking distances considerably, and are a great way to see the forest from another angle.

From Wànlǐng it takes about 20 minutes to reach **Guānguāng cable car** (观光索道; Guānguāng Suǒdào; one way/return ¥30/40; 25 minutes; ◎8am-5pm), which takes you over some stunning bamboo forests. There's a pleasant, one-hour streamside walk (with plenty of paddling opportunities), which loops around the forest just beyond the entrance to the cable car. Once you've ridden the cable car, turn right as you exit to reach **Dàxiágǔ cable car** (大峡谷索道; Dàxiágǔ Suǒdào; one way/return ¥20/30; 10 minutes; ◎8.30am-5.30pm), which crosses a dramatic gorge and leads into another scenic area with a number of trails, some of which pass by two lakes. Leaving this area, head for Sānhé Jiè (三合界), a junction where you can find accommodation. Turn right here for the final 30-minute walk to Wànlǐ village.

Two waterfalls near Wànlǐ are worth a look. To get to **Rainbow Falls** (七彩飞瀑; Qīcǎi Fēipù), either follow the lake by the village or turn right before it and walk along the road for about 1km to the signposted main gate. You can continue down past these falls to **Golden Dragon Falls** (金龙瀑布; Jīnlóng Pùbù). This is off the tourist maps so is pretty quiet, although you sometimes have to pay ¥10 to an enterprising old man for right of passage. You can climb back up to the main road through a wonderfully peaceful bamboo forest.

If you're hiking you'll pass numerous guesthouses and hotels along the way. In Wànlǐng, try **Chéngbīnlóu Jiǔdiàn** (承宾楼酒店; ☑0831-498 0104; s/tw ¥180/200, discounted to ¥100/120; ※⑤). A couple of rooms have wifi. Wànlǐ is smaller, but has plenty of accommodation. For somewhere more tranquil walk 1km beyond Wànlǐ to **Zhúyùn Shānzhuāng** (竹韵山庄; ☑497 9001, 138 9092 5673; r from ¥360), opposite the main gate to Rainbow Falls. Spotless rooms with private bathroom were going for ¥80 when we were here; ¥100 to ¥200 at weekends.

All guesthouses and hotels do food, too. It's generally pretty good, although more expensive than outside the park. Alternatively, look out for one of the cheap noodle restaurants in Wànlǐng or Wànlǐ. Yíbīn's speciality *ránmiàn* (然面) is popular, as is *zhúsūn miàn* (竹荪面; noodles with a type of mushroom that resembles bamboo).

❶ Getting There & Around

There's a map on the back of your entrance ticket, and you can get hold of maps in the park, but the easiest to use and most detailed maps are the ones drawn on wooden boards throughout the park. Take a photo of one to guide you. All the main sights are signposted, too.

Motorbike taxis can take you between the two main villages (around ¥50, 45 minutes) if you decide not to walk.

Bus

Buses into the park stop at the west gate to allow you to get off and buy your entrance ticket, before passing through Wànlǐng and then terminating at Wànlǐ.

There are two direct buses from Wànlǐ back to Yíbīn (¥22, two hours, 7am and 1pm). Both pass Wànlǐng (30 minutes) and, if you ask, will drop you at the junction for Chángníng (one hour), where you can change for Gǒngxiàn to get to the Hanging Coffins. Smaller local buses shuttle regularly between Wànlǐng and Chángníng (¥5, 6am to 7pm).

WESTERN SÌCHUĀN

West of Chéngdū, green tea becomes butter tea, gumdrop hills morph into jagged snowy peaks and *nǐ hǎo!* steps aside for *tashi-delek!* Welcome to Tibet, in all but name.

This part of Sìchuān makes up a large chunk of what Tibetans refer to as Kham (in Chinese 康巴; Kāngbā), one of old Tibet's three traditional provinces, and home to the Khampas, a Tibetan ethnic group known for being fierce warriors.

Western Sìchuān experiences up to 200 freezing days per year, but summers can be blistering by day and the high altitude invites particularly bad sunburn as well as the risk of altitude sickness.

Kāngdìng (Dartsendo) 康定

📞 0836 / POP 82,000

Coming from the Chéngdū area, there are two main gateways into Tibetan Sìchuān. One option is Dānbā, but by far the most popular is Kāngdìng, and for many travellers this is the first taste of the Tibetan world.

The town has long been a trade centre between Chinese and Tibetan cultures and you'll find elements of both here.

Set in a steep river valley at the confluence of the raging Zhéduō and Yǎlā Rivers (known as the Dar and Tse in Tibetan), with the towering Gònggā Shān (7556m) beyond, Kāngdìng is famous throughout China for a popular love song inspired by the town's surrounding scenery.

👁 Sights & Activities

Monasteries
MONASTERIES

There are four main monasteries in Kāngdìng. The central **Ānjué Temple** (安觉寺; Ānjué Sì; Ngachu Gompa in Tibetan) dates back to 1652 but was largely rebuilt recently.

Nánwú Temple (南无寺; Nánwú Sì) belongs to the Gelugpa (Yellow Hat) sect of Tibetan Buddhism and is the most active monastery in the area. Walk south along the main road, cross the river and keep going for about 200m until you see a rusty old sign (in traditional Chinese characters: 南無寺) for the monastery on your right. Follow that track uphill, beside a stream, and the monastery will be on your right.

Nearby, about 100m further along the main road, is **Jīngāng Temple** (金刚寺; Jīngāng Sì), a 400-year-old Nyingma monastery set around a lawned courtyard. Turn right at the sign for Knapsack Inn.

The area's fourth monastery, **Pǎomǎ Temple** (跑马寺; Pǎomǎ Sì; entrance ¥50) is halfway up **Pǎomǎ Shān**.

Hiking
HIKING

Three small mountains loom over Kāngdìng and make rewarding day hikes. The most famous, and easiest to ascend, is **Pǎomǎ Shān** (跑马山), which you can climb or take a **cable car** (索道; suǒdào; one way/return ¥20/30)

halfway up for excellent views of the town and the surrounding mountains and valleys. The stepped path takes you past oodles of prayer flags, en route to Pǎomǎ Temple. To go any further you have to pay ¥50, but you can loop north for free and descend on another path.

More natural (no concrete steps here!) and free of charge, is **Jiǔlián Shān** (九连山), the hill up behind Zhilam Guesthouse. A two-hour climb brings you to a small grassland plateau (perfect for picnics) where horses and yaks sometimes graze.

Guōdá Shān (郭达山) looms large at the eastern end of town and takes a full day to climb up and down. From the top you can see the glacial peaks of Gònggā Shān. Ask staff at Zhilam Hostel for details of how to find the trail.

The trailhead for the five- to seven-day pilgrims' circuit of holy **Gònggā Shān** (贡嘎山) is only a half-hour drive from Kāngdìng. Staff at Zhilam can advise you on how to do the trek independently, and can rent out any camping equipment you may need, but we recommend taking a guide for this trek. Zhilam can put you in touch with one of the best Tibetan guides in this area. He doesn't speak English, but is used to guiding foreign trekkers on the circuit. He charges ¥220 per day.

🎊 Festivals & Events

Kāngdìng's biggest annual festival, the **Walking Around the Mountain Festival** (Zhuànshānjié), takes place on Pǎomǎ Shān on the eighth day of the fourth lunar month (normally in May) to commemorate the birthday of the Historical Buddha, Sakyamuni. White and blue Tibetan tents cover the hillside and there's wrestling, horse racing and visitors from all over western Sìchuān.

LOAD UP WITH CASH

At the time of research it was impossible to change money or travellers cheques, get advances on credit cards or use ATMs with foreign bank cards anywhere in western Sìchuān apart from Kāngdìng. Most other towns have a branch of the Agricultural Bank of China, but despite the VISA signs, the ATMs at these branches rarely accept foreign cards.

Kāngdìng (Dardo)

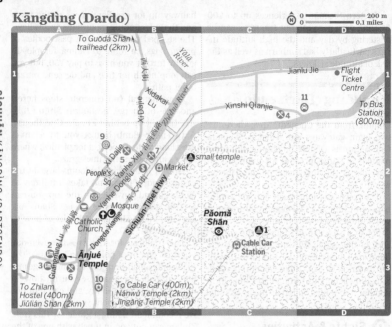

🛏 Sleeping

TOP CHOICE **Zhilam Hostel** HOSTEL $

(汇道客栈; Huìdào Kèzhàn; ☎283 1100; www.zhilam hostel.com; Bái Tǔkǎn Cūn; 白土坎村; dm/r from ¥35/160; @🛜) Run by an accommodating American couple with two young children, this fabulous, family-friendly, hillside hostel makes an excellent base while you're in Kāngdìng. Does decent Western food, dishes out reliable travel advice and rents out camping gear. It's a winding 10-minute walk up the hill beside Yōngzhū Hotel.

Yōngzhū Hotel GUESTHOUSE $

(拥珠驿栈; Yōngzhū Yìzhàn; ☎283 2381, 159 8373 8188; dm/r ¥35/120; 🛜) Hidden in a lane beside Kāngdìng Hotel, this small, friendly guesthouse has comfortable, well-kept rooms, decorated with colourful Tibetan furnishings and built around an inner atrium. There are electric blankets in all rooms, and 24-hour hot water throughout.

Kāngdìng Hotel HOTEL $$

(康定宾馆; Kāngdìng Bīnguǎn; ☎283 2077; 25 Guangming Lu; 光明路25号; r incl breakfast from ¥480; ❋@🛜) For something more comfortable, this decent midranger, right beside Ānjué Temple, had standard twins going for ¥238 when we stayed.

🍴 Eating & Drinking

On mild evenings, **barbecue stalls** set up around the northeast corner of People's Sq.

TOP CHOICE **Mǎlāyà Tibetan Restaurant** TIBETAN $$

(玛拉亚藏餐; Mǎlāyà Zàngcān; Yanhe Donglu; 沿河东路; dishes from ¥15; ⏱9.30am-midnight; 📶) Friendly Tibetan-run restaurant-cum-teahouse serving authentic Tibetan dishes and lashings of butter tea. The menu is in English, but if you need inspiration, try the yak meat burger (which is a meat stew topped with flatbread) or the very filling curry (beef and potato on rice). Located on the 6th floor, above the hard-to-miss fast-food joint Dico's. You'll find similarly authentic food and a similar atmosphere at the slightly more expensive Ä'Rè Tibetan Restaurant.

Mágē Miàn NOODLES $

(麻哥面; noodles ¥5-10; ⏱24hr) The best noodles in Kāngdìng. Don't miss its speciality mágē noodles (麻哥面; ma'gē miàn), topped with a spicy mincemeat sauce and served fresh in small (一两; yīliǎng; ¥5), medium (二两; èr liǎng; ¥8) or large (三两; sānliǎng; ¥10) bowls.

Tibetan Culture Dew TEAHOUSE

(西藏雨; Xīzàng Yǔ; Yanhe Xilu; 沿河西路; ⏱11am-midnight; 📶) Hang out with the butter

Kāngdìng (Dardo)

◎ Top Sights
Ānjué Temple A3
Pǎomǎ Shān C3

◎ Sights
1 Pǎomǎ Temple C3

⬛ Sleeping
2 Kāngdìng Hotel A3
3 Yǒngzhū Hotel A3

✖ Eating
4 Ā'Rè Tibetan Restaurant C1
5 Barbecue Stalls B2
6 Mágē Miàn A3
7 Mǎlāyà Tibetan Restaurant B2

◎ Drinking
8 Tibetan Culture Dew A2

ⓘ Information
9 Liáoliáo internet café A2
10 PSB A3

ⓘ Transport
11 Minibuses to Tǎgòng D1

tea-sipping locals at this lovely teahouse with a rustic stone and wood interior decorated with colourful Tibetan prayer flags.

☆ Entertainment

Come about 7pm, there's only one place to go. Every evening, dozens if not hundreds of locals descend on People's Sq for one of the biggest daily get-togethers of formation dancing we've ever seen.

ⓘ Information

ATM (自动柜员机; Zìdòng Guìyuán Jī; Yanhe Donglu) China Construction Bank ATM. One of a few around town that takes foreign cards.

Liáoliao internet café (聊聊网吧; Liáoliao wǎngbā; per hr ¥5; ⊘24hr) Staff will let you register with their Chinese ID cards if you smile sweetly.

Public Security Bureau (PSB; 公安局; Gōng'ānjú; ☏281 1415; Dongda Xiaojie; ⊘8.30am–noon & 2.30-5.30pm) Visa-extension service in three working days. First-time extensions only.

ⓘ Getting There & Away

Air
Kāngdìng Airport is 43km west of town and has daily flights to Chéngdū (¥1180, 8.55am) and thrice-weekly fights to Chóngqìng (¥1550,

8.50am Tuesday, Thursday & Saturday). Buy tickets online or from the **flight ticket centre** (机场售票中心; Jīchǎng Shòupiào Zhōngxīn; ☏287 1111; 28 Jianlu Jie; 箭炉街28号; ⊘8.30am-5.30pm). Discounts bring prices down to around ¥850 and ¥1000. The airport shuttle bus (¥27) leaves from outside the ticket centre at 6.20am.

Bus

The bus station is a 10-minute walk from the centre (¥7 cab). Shared minibuses to all destinations listed here leave from outside the bus station. Buses to Tǎgōng (¥50 to ¥80) and Gānzī (around ¥200) leave from Xinshi Qianjie. Remember: private hire – *bāochē* (包车); shared vehicle – *pīnchē* (拼车).

Bātáng ¥144.50, 12 hours, one daily (6am)

Chéngdū ¥120 to ¥140, eight hours, hourly (6am to 4pm)

Dānbā ¥44.50, three hours, two daily (7.30am and 3.30pm)

Dàocháng ¥135, 12 hours, one daily (6am)

Dégé ¥180, 16 hours, one daily (6am)

Éméi Shān ¥115, seven hours, one daily (6.30am)

Gānzī ¥113, 11 hours, one daily (6am)

Lèshān ¥113, seven hours, one daily (7am)

Lǐtáng ¥90, eight hours, one daily (6am)

Yǎ'ān ¥72, 4½ hours, every hour (6am to 4pm)

Dānbā (Rongtrak)　丹巴

☏0836 / POP 58,200

This friendly town, set in a dramatic gorge overlooking the confluence of three rivers, makes a nice alternative to Kāngdìng as a gateway into or out of Tibetan Sìchuān.

The town itself is dusty and nondescript, but the hills surrounding Dānbā contain clusters of fascinating ancient watchtowers and a number of picturesque Tibetan villages, some offering homestays.

◎ Sights

Qiāng Watchtowers　RUINS
These ancient stone towers (羌族碉楼; Qiāngzú diāolóu), nestled incongruously among village homes on hillsides overlooking the Dàdù River, were built by the Qiang people between 700 and 1200 years ago. The towers range from 20m to 60m in height and were used as places of worship and to store valuable goods as well as to signal warnings of would-be attackers. They were built with a number of inner wooden storeys, which have since disintegrated, and entrances that were some metres above ground. One

enterprising family in Suōpō (梭坡), the nearest village to Dānbā with watchtowers, has rebuilt the wooden levels of the tower next to their home and allows visitors to climb up the inside from their rooftop, for a small fee of course (¥15). Don't worry about finding them. They, or a 'friend' of theirs, will find you.

To get to Suōpō, turn left out of Zhāxī Zhuōkāng Backpackers Hostel and walk along the river for about 30 minutes. Turn down the track beside the small police station, then cross the suspension bridge and keep walking up to the village. Look for stone steps under some large trees up to your left, just after you reach the village's first couple of buildings. These steps lead to the nearest towers.

Tibetan Villages   VILLAGES

There are a number of pretty Tibetan villages (藏寨; Zàngzhài) in the hills round here but Dānbā's pride and joy is Jiǎjū (甲居; admission ¥30), 7km northwest of town and perched on top of a multi-switchback track that winds its way up a steep river gorge. With its fruit trees, charming Tibetan stone houses and remote location, Jiǎjū often sucks in travellers for a day or two.

One of a number of stone houses that have been converted into a homestay is the excellent **Liǎngkē Shù** (两棵树; ☎880 7199, 135 6868 5278; dm inc meals ¥60), with simple dormitories, traditional Tibetan furniture, a pleasant central courtyard and stunning views. The owner can arrange trips into the fabulous surrounding countryside. To get here, take a shared minivan (¥5) from the Bāměi end of Dānbā. A private taxi costs ¥40 one way.

Another popular homestay village is **Zhōnglù** (中路; admission ¥20), 13km from town (taxi ¥80).

🛏 Sleeping

Zhāxī Zhuōkāng
Backpackers Hostel   HOTEL $
(扎西卓康青年旅舍; Zhāxī Zhuōkāng Qīngnián Lǚshè; ☎352 1806; 35 Sanchahe Nanlu; 三岔河南路35号; dm ¥25, tw without/with bathroom ¥60/80; @🛜) Despite being more hotel than youth hostel, this place is still traveller central in Dānbā. Rooms are decidedly average, but you'll receive a friendly welcome and there are free internet terminals and wi-fi throughout. It's a 25-minute walk from the bus station (walk down to the river, turn right and keep going) or ¥5 in a cab.

🍴 Eating & Drinking

Small restaurants by the bus station open early for breakfast noodles (面; miàn) or dumplings (小龙包子; xiǎolóng bāozi).

Wǎnglǎo Wǔ   SICHUANESE $$
(王老五; dishes ¥20-50; ⊙noon-9pm) Across the street from Zhāxī Zhuōkāng Backpackers Hostel, this decent 2nd-floor Sichuanese restaurant rustles up all the usual Sìchuān favourites (p707) plus some tasty cured-pork dishes. Try the cured pork with green chillies (腊肉青椒; làròu qīngjiāo, ¥30). Photo menu.

Base Camp of Photographer Cafe   CAFE
(大本营咖啡; Dàběngōng Kāfēi; opposite bus station; 车站对面; ⊙1-11pm; @🛜) Fresh coffee (¥25), Chinese tea (from ¥10), internet, wi-fi and ceiling-to-floor windows offering the best river view of any town centre cafe we can remember. Turn right out of the bus station and look for the large painted English sign on the left.

ℹ Getting There & Away

For Tǎgōng, take a minibus (¥60, three hours) from the west end of town, via Bāměi (¥40, two hours). Bus destinations include:

Chéngdū ¥146.50, nine hours, three daily (6.15am, 6.20am and 6.30am)

Gānzī ¥100.50, nine hours, one daily (6.30am)

Kāngdìng ¥46.50, five hours, two daily (6.30am and 3pm)

Mǎ'ěrkāng ¥46, six hours, one daily (7.30am)

Sìchuān–Tibet Highway (Northern Route)

The famous Sìchuān–Tibet Hwy splits in two just west of Kāngdìng. The northern route is 300km longer than the southern route, and is generally less travelled. You'll pass awesome high-plateau grasslands and numerous traditional Tibetan communities, often attached to a local monastery.

Crossing Chola Mountain, the highest pass (5050m) this side of Lhasa, takes you to Dégé and the border with the TAR (Tibetan Autonomous Region), or Tibet proper. You can also take this route to head north into Qīnghǎi province via Sěrshu. And it's possible to travel between Gānzī and Lǐtáng via Xīnlóng.

You *must* come prepared with warm clothing; even in midsummer, it can be very cold at higher elevations. Remember that bus services can be erratic – this is no place to be in a hurry.

TĂGŌNG (LHA GANG) 塔公

☏0836 / POP 8000

The small Tibetan village of Tăgōng and its beautiful surrounding grasslands offer plenty of excuses to linger. As well as an important monastery and a fascinating nearby nunnery, there's also horse trekking, hiking and Tibetan homestays.

Take time to adjust to the altitude if you're coming from lower terrain to the east.

◉ Sights

Tăgōng Monastery BUDDHIST MONASTERY
(塔公寺; Tăgōng Sì; admission ¥20) The story goes that when Princess Wencheng, the Chinese bride-to-be of Tibetan king Songtsen Gampo, was on her way to Lhasa in the 7th century, a precious statue of Jowo Sakyamuni Buddha toppled off one of the carts in her entourage. A replica of the statue was carved on the spot where it landed and a temple then built around it. You'll find the statue in the right-hand hall here. The original, which is the most revered Buddha image in all of Tibet, is housed in Lhasa's Jokhang Temple.

Also note the beautiful 1000-armed Chenresig (Avalokiteshvara) in the hall to the left. And don't miss the impressive collection of over 100 *chörtens* (Tibetan stupas) behind the monastery.

🏃 Activities

Horse riding (per person per day 1/2/3 people ¥420/310/290) and guided **grassland hikes** (per person per day ¥200) can be arranged through Khampa Cafe & Arts Centre. It's an extra ¥60 per person with meals and accommodation. They can also point you in the right direction if you want to hike out into the grasslands on your own. One popular option is the two-hour hike to **Héping Făhuì** (和平法会), the largest nunnery in the area.

Khampa Cafe also rents out camping equipment (tent per day ¥30), mountain bikes (per day ¥40) and motorbikes (per day ¥130).

🎊 Festivals

Like many places in this part of Tibetan Sìchuān, Tăgōng holds an annual **horse-racing festival** *(sàimǎhuì)* during the fifth lunar month (usually early July).

🛏 Sleeping & Eating

The three most popular places to stay are each located along one side of the main square outside Tăgōng Monastery; to your left as you face the monastery. All transport drops passengers by this square.

Angela at Khampa Cafe & Arts Centre can arrange **Tibetan homestays** (per person per night ¥60) out in the grasslands.

TOP CHOICE **Khampa Cafe & Arts Centre** GUESTHOUSE $$
(☏136 8449 3301; http://definitelynomadic.com; r¥160) Run by Angela, a super-helpful American woman, and her Tibetan husband Djarga, this is the most comfortable place to stay in Tăgōng. There are no private bathrooms, but the bedrooms are large, bright and exceptionally clean. The top-floor **cafe** (dishes ¥10-30; ⊙8.30am-11pm) is also the best hangout in town and *the* place to come for info on hiking, camping and the like. Wi-fi (per hour ¥10, available 8.30am to 3.30pm) is available via a modem, which staff can lend to you.

TOP CHOICE **Jya Drolma and Gayla's Guesthouse** GUESTHOUSE $
(☏286 6056; dm ¥25, tw without bathroom ¥50) Bedrooms here – even the dorms – are a riot of golds, reds and blues, with elaborately painted ceilings and walls. There are common toilets on each floor and one shower with 24-hour hot water. No English spoken, but a very friendly welcome.

Snowland Guesthouse GUESTHOUSE $
(雪城旅社; Xuěchéng Lǚshè; ☏286 6098; tagong sally@yahoo.com; dm from ¥15, s/d ¥60/80) This long-standing backpacker hang-out offers a cheaper option for budget travellers. Rooms are much more basic than those at Khampa and have less character than Gayla's but this is still an OK choice. Sally, who runs the place, speaks a bit of English. The attached **Sally's Kham Restaurant** (mains ¥10-20; ⊙8am-10pm) does a selection of simple, well-priced Tibetan, Chinese and Western dishes plus butter tea and beer.

ℹ Getting There & Away

A bus from Gānzī to Kāngdìng (¥40, two hours) passes Tăgōng Monastery at about 7.30am, but it's usually full. Alternatively, take a shared minivan (¥50 to ¥80). Note, you might struggle to find fellow passengers after about 10am.

To get to Lǐtáng, take the Kāngdìng bus or a shared minivan to Xīndūqiáo (新都桥; ¥20 to ¥40, one hour), from where you can flag down the Kāngdìng–Lǐtáng bus (¥64, seven hours), which passes by at around 9am, or a minivan (¥80 to ¥100).

For Dānbā, take a shared minivan to Bāměi (八美; ¥20, one hour), then switch minivans (¥30, two hours).

SÌCHUĀN SÌCHUĀN–TIBET HIGHWAY (NORTHERN ROUTE)

For Gānzī (¥80, eight hours) you can try to snag a seat on the bus from Kāngdìng, which passes here between 9am and 10am, or try to arrange a shared minivan (¥100 to ¥150).

GĀNZĪ (GARZÊ)　　　甘孜
☎ 0836 / POP 61,400

This dusty but lively market town in a picturesque valley surrounded by snowcapped mountains is the capital of the Gānzī Autonomous Prefecture and is populated mostly by Tibetans. It's easy to spend a couple of days here exploring the beautiful countryside, which is scattered with Tibetan villages and large monasteries. Photo opportunities abound.

◎ Sights & Activities

Gānzī Temple　　　BUDDHIST TEMPLE
(甘孜寺; Gānzī Sì; Garzê Gompa in Tibetan; admission ¥15) North of the town's Tibetan quarter is the region's largest monastery, dating back more than 500 years and glimmering with blinding quantities of gold. Encased on the walls of the main hall are hundreds of small golden Sakyamunis. In a smaller hall just west of the main hall is an awe-inspiring statue of Jampa (Maitreya or Future Buddha), dressed in a giant silk robe. The views into the mountains from here are fantastic.

The monastery is about a 25- to 30-minute walk from the bus station. Turn left out of the station and just keep going.

Hot Springs　　　HOT SPRINGS
(温泉; wēnquán; per room ¥10; ◎8am-midnight) Perfect after a day of hiking in the surrounding hills, Ganzi's hot springs are a short walk past the turning for Hotel Himalaya. When you see the road Xinqu Lu (新区路) on your left, turn right down the alley opposite and follow it downhill until the smell of sulphur overwhelms you. Each room has a hot tub. Towels (浴巾; yùjīn) can be provided.

⬛ Sleeping & Eating

Hotel Himalaya　　　HOTEL $
(喜马拉雅宾馆; Xīmǎlāyǎ Bīnguǎn; ☎752 1878; Dongda Jie; 东大街; r ¥150) Run by a Ganzi local who studied medicine in Germany and who speaks English, this is the most comfortable and cleanest place in town. Rooms are large, bright and come with attached bathrooms featuring sit-down toilets and hot-water showers. Turn left out of the bus station, then first right up Chuanzang Lu. Dongda Jie is then on your left after a couple of hundred metres.

Hóng Fú Guesthouse　　　GUESTHOUSE $
(鸿福旅馆; Hóngfú Lǚguǎn; ☎752 5330; Chuanzang Lu; 川藏路; r ¥40) Nowhere near as comfortable as Himalaya, but it's hard not to love this place. Tibetan-run, and housed in a traditional Tibetan wooden building, Hong Fu has very basic but neat and tidy twin rooms, which go for ¥20 per bed. Shared toilets only, and no showers, but, as the owners say, the hot springs are just up the road, and only cost ¥10. Turn left out of the bus station, take the first left and you'll soon see a sign on your right for Long Da Guesthouse (same prices; not as good). Walk towards that and you'll see Hong Fu just before it, on your left.

Jīntàiyáng Bīnguǎn　　　HOTEL $
(金太阳宾馆; ☎752 2444; Chuanzang Lu; 川藏路; r ¥150, discounted to ¥100; ◉) If you need wi-fi, this standard midrange hotel does the trick. Left out the bus station, first right and it's on your left through an archway. No English sign.

[TOP CHOICE] Tibetan Restaurant　　　TIBETAN $
(印度藏餐; Yìndù Zàngcān; 2nd fl, off Chuanzang Lu; 川藏路后边; dishes ¥10-35; ◎6am-11pm; ▣) Small, friendly Tibetan teahouse serving an excellent range of Tibetan food. Has a well-translated English menu, including some photos. Turn left out of the bus station, take the first left and follow the sign under the archway into a small square. Then look for the steps in the far corner that lead up to the 2nd floor.

ⓘ Information

Turn left out of the bus station and take the second road on your right; there's an **internet cafe** (网吧; wǎngbā; per hr ¥4; ◎24hr) on the 2nd floor.

ⓘ Getting There & Away

Minivans congregate outside the bus station. Destinations, and rough prices, include:

Dégé ¥100, six to seven hours

Lǐtáng ¥100, six to seven hours

Mǎnígāngē ¥50, two to three hours

Xīnlóng ¥30, two to three hours

Scheduled bus services run to the following destinations:

Chéngdū ¥226, 18 hours, one daily (6am)

Dānbā ¥101, nine hours, one daily (6.30am)

Kāngdìng ¥117 and ¥129, 11 hours, two daily (both at 6.30am)

Sěrshu ¥102, six hours, one daily (6.30am)

TALAM KHANG GUESTHOUSE

Travellers who are sick of staying in dusty market towns, and only seeing this area's drop-dead-gorgeous scenery through the window of a bus, will adore **Talam Khang Guesthouse** (大金寺旅馆; Dàjīn Sì Lǚguǎn; camping/dm/d/tw ¥30/40/100/200).

A 10-minute walk from **Darjay Gompa** (pronounced dah-jee gompa), one of the area's largest and most revered monasteries, the small temple of Talam Khang is home to three friendly monks who welcome guests to share their mudbrick wood-beamed living quarters set among the prettiest scenery you can imagine – snowcapped mountains to one side, rolling grasslands and a river to the other. Climb up onto the roof for 360-degree views and to plot your next hike to one of the nearby villages, monasteries or mountains.

The dormitories are in the temple building itself, next to the rooms the monks live in. They are very basic, but full of character. Doubles and twins, with sinks for washing but no hot water, are housed in two small modern blocks at each side of the courtyard, which has room for pitching tents.

The lack of hot water needn't worry you as there are free-to-use, open-air **hot springs** (温泉; wēnquán) five minutes' walk away over the other side of the river. Locals use them to wash themselves, their children, their clothes and sometimes even their motorbikes, but there's plenty of room for everyone, so squeeze in.

For an extra ¥50 per person you get three simple meals a day at 8.30am, 1pm and 7pm. There's also a small **shop** (⊘8am-9pm) on the main road outside the monastery, which sells drinks, snacks and instant noodles.

To get to the guesthouse from Darjay Gompa, walk for 10 minutes along the only track that leads away from the back entrance of the monastery.

Darjay Gompa is around 30km west of Ganzi, on the road to Derge. It'll cost around ¥30 to get to here in a shared minivan; at least ¥50 in a private taxi. Keen hikers could consider walking here but it will take a whole day. Walk to **Beri Gompa**, an attractive golden-roofed monastery 8km west of Ganzi, and just keep going. Hitching is another option.

MǍNÍGĀNGĒ (MANIGANGO) 马尼干戈
☎0836

There's not much going on in this dusty two-street town halfway between Gānzī and Dégé. The surrounding hills offer wonderful hiking opportunities, though, and the stunning turquoise lake, Yilhun Lha-tso, is nearby. The large monastery, Dzogchen Gompa, is also within striking distance, on the road north to Yùshù.

🛏 Sleeping & Eating

Fēnglíngdù Kèzhàn GUESTHOUSE $
TOP CHOICE
(风陵渡客栈; ☎150 0248 8791; beds ¥20; 🛜) Cosy, welcoming guesthouse run by Lorna, a friendly young woman who speaks a bit of English. There are only a few rooms: a couple of dorms and a couple of private rooms, but the price is the same; ¥20 per person. No showers, although you can have a bucket of hot water if you wish, and toilets are communal, but clean. There's wi-fi in the evening, and a nice travellers' vibe on account of the young Chinese backpackers who tend to stay here. It's 200m down from Manigange Pani Hotel, on the left. Look for the English 'guesthouse' sign.

Manigange Pani Hotel HOTEL $
(马尼干戈帕尼酒店; Mǎnígāngē Pàní Jiǔdiàn; dm ¥25, tw without/with bathroom ¥80/160) This OK hotel is the town's centre of gravity, with its car park used as the unofficial bus station and its buffet-style restaurant the most popular lunch stop for passing motorists. Sleeping-wise there are rooms for everyone; from dirt-cheap five-bed dorms to decent twins with private bathrooms, and hot water (evenings only), that go for ¥130 when it's quiet. The **restaurant** (vegetable/meat dishes ¥15/20; ⊘7am-11pm) has an easy-to-order, choose and point buffet with surprisingly good results.

Gāoyuán Jíyàng Zàngcān TIBETAN TEAHOUSE $
(高原吉祥藏餐; dishes from ¥10; ⊘8am-10pm) Tiny Tibetan teahouse run by a friendly woman who once walked to India to meet

EATING TIBETAN

ENGLISH	TIBETAN PRONUNCIATION	TIBETAN SCRIPT	CHINESE PRONUNCIATION	CHINESE SCRIPT
Butter tea	*bo-cha*	བོད་ཇ།	*sūyóu chá*	酥油茶
Nnoodles	*thuk-pa*	ཐུག་པ།	*zàngmiàn*	藏面
Rice, potato and yak-meat stew	*shemdre*	ཤ་འབྲས།	*gālí niúròu fàn*	咖喱牛肉饭
Roasted barley flour	*tsampa*	རྩམ་པ།	*zānbā*	糌粑
Tibetan yoghurt	*sho*	ཞོ།	*suānnǎi*	酸奶
Yak-meat dumplings	*sha-momo*	ཤ་མོག་མོག	*niúròu bāozi*	牛肉包子
Vegetable dumplings	*tse-momo*	ཚལ་མོག་མོག	*sùcài bāozi*	素菜包子

the Dalai Lama (25 days, in case you're wondering). She whips up warming pots of butter tea, as well as *tsampa, thukpa* and beef soup (牛肉汤; *niúròu tāng*). Opposite Fēnglíngdù Kèzhàn.

Information

An **internet cafe** (网吧; wǎngbā; per hr ¥5; ⏲noon-11pm) is 100m along the lane opposite Manigange Pani Hotel.

Getting There & Away

A daily bus to Dégé (¥50, three to four hours) passes through Manigango at about 11am, but is often full. Going the other way, there are usually some empty seats on the Gānzī-bound bus (¥35, three to four hours), which passes by at 9am to 10am. Catch both from Manigange Pani Hotel. A bus from Gānzī, heading for Sěrshu (¥80, seven hours), passes by the main crossroads at around 8.30am.

Plenty of minibuses congregate outside Manigange Pani Hotel waiting to scoop up bus-less passengers.

XĪNLÙ HǍI (YILHUN LHA-TSO) 新路海

The fabulous turquoise-blue waters of this holy alpine **lake** (admission ¥20), 13km southwest of Manigango, are the main reason most travellers stop in this area.

The stunning lake is bordered by *chörten* and dozens of rock carvings, and is then framed by snowcapped mountains. You can walk an hour or two up the left (east) side of the lakeshore for views of the nearby glacier.

This is also a great place to camp – some travellers have even slept in caves here although you'll need to be totally self-sufficient. Monks from surrounding monasteries sometimes camp here during the summer in colourful Tibetan nomad tents.

To get here, either nab a seat in a Dégé-bound minibus (¥20), hitch a ride or hike; turn right out of Manigange Pani Hotel and keep going. The lake is a five-minute walk from the main road, along a signposted track. Motorbikes (¥20) wait to take you back to Manigango.

DÉGÉ (DERGE) 德格

☎0836 / POP 58,600

Your bumpy bus rides just got bumpier. Dégé is cut off from the rest of western Sìchuān by the towering Chola Mountain (6168m), and to get here from the east you will probably have to endure a highly uncomfortable, slightly scary three-hour minibus ride along a dirt track that goes up and over the 5050m-high Tro La (Chola) Pass. Here, Tibetans on board will throw coloured prayer paper out the window and chant something that you can only hope will help carry you all to safety.

Unless you've managed to secure the correct permits to enter the rarely travelled Chamdo prefecture of Tibet proper, the main reason you'll have made the arduous trek out here is to see Dégé's famous printing monastery, one of this region's stellar sights.

◉ Sights

TOP CHOICE Bakong Scripture Printing Press & Monastery BUDDHIST MONASTERY

(德格印经院; Dégé Yìnjīngyuàn; www.degeparkhang.org; admission ¥50; ⊙8.30am-noon & 2-6.30pm) This striking 18th-century monastery houses one of western Sìchuān's star attractions: a fascinating printing press that still uses traditional woodblock printing methods and which houses an astonishing 70% of Tibet's literary heritage.

There are more than 217,000 engraved blocks of Tibetan scriptures here from all the Tibetan Buddhist orders, including Bön. These texts include ancient works about astronomy, geography, music, medicine and Buddhist classics, including two of the most important Tibetan sutras. A history of Indian Buddhism comprising 555 woodblock plates is the only surviving copy in the world (written in Hindi, Sanskrit and Tibetan).

Within the monastery, dozens of workers hand produce more than 2500 prints to order each day, as ink, paper and blocks fly through the workers' hands at lightning speed. In one side room you'll find an older crowd of printers who produce larger and more complex prints of Tibetan gods on paper or coloured cloth.

You can also examine storage chambers, paper-cutting rooms and the main hall of the monastery itself, protected from fire and earthquakes by the guardian goddess Drölma (Tara). There are some nice murals in the two ground-floor chapels, so bring a torch.

You aren't allowed to take photos in the storerooms or the main hall, but the workers were happy for us to snap away while they worked frantically to meet their quota.

To get here, turn right out of the bus station, then left over the bridge and keep walking up the hill.

Other Monasteries BUDDHIST MONASTERIES

If you continue following the road up the hill beyond the printing house, you'll reach the huge, recently renovated 1000-year-old **Gonchen Monastery**. High in the mountains to the south and east of Dégé are several other monasteries, including **Pelpung Gompa**, **Dzongsar Gompa** and **Pewar Gompa**.

🛏 Sleeping & Eating

Héxié Hotel HOTEL $

(和谐旅馆; Héxié Lǚguǎn; ☑822 6111; Chamashang Jie; 茶马上街; dm/tw ¥40/80; 🛜) A friendly Tibetan-run hotel with a homely feel to it. Spacious carpeted rooms come with coat stand, hot-water flask and pine-wood table and chairs, while the comfy beds have clean sheets and warm puffy duvets. There's even wi-fi! Bathrooms are shared but have 24-hour hot-water showers. Turn left out of the bus station and it's on your left after a few hundred metres.

Golden Yak Hotel HOTEL $

(金牦牛酒店; Jīnmáoniú Jiǔdiàn; ☑822 5188; beside the bus station; 车站旁边; r ¥180, discounted to ¥80) Conveniently located right by the bus station, Golden Yak has large, comfortable twins and doubles with ensuite bathrooms. Note, showers are solar heated so if the weather's rubbish, the water's cold.

Kāngbā Zàngcān TIBETAN $

(康巴藏餐; Chamashang Jie; 茶马上街; dishes ¥10-20; ⊙noon-midnight) Tibetan teahouse serving authentic Tibetan food, plus tea and beer. There's no menu, but here's a sample of what's on offer: yak pie (牛肉饼; niúròu bǐng; ¥20), yak-meat momos (¥1 per dumpling), thukpa (¥12), tsampa (¥5), butter tea (¥10) and Tibetan yoghurt (¥5). No English sign. No English spoken. Turn left out of the bus station and it's on your right; on the 2nd floor.

There are several small Chinese restaurants and **noodle shops** near the bus station.

ℹ Information

To get to the **internet cafe** (网吧; wǎngbā; per hr ¥3; ⊙8.30am-midnight) turn right out of the bus station, left over the bridge and down steps to your right. The entrance is just past the pool hall.

ℹ Getting There & Away

Just one daily eastbound bus leaves from here, at 7am, heading for Kāngdìng (¥183, next-day arrival) via Manigango (¥41, three hours), Gānzī (¥68, six hours) and Lúhuò, where it stops for the night. Otherwise, there are minibuses.

Foreigners aren't allowed to take public transport west from here into Tibet proper.

SHÍQÚ (SÊRSHU) 石渠
☑0836 / POP 60,000

There are two places commonly called Shíqú (in Tibetan; Sêrshu): the traditional monastery town of Sêrshu Dzong to the west and the modern(ish) county town of Sêrshu (Shíqú Xiàn), 30km to the east, which has more lodgings and transport connections.

While you'll probably stop in Shíqú Xiàn en route between Manigango and Yùshù in Qīnghǎi, the huge monastery of Sêrshu Dzong and its intensely Tibetan village is far more interesting.

It's home to hundreds of monks and has two assembly halls, a Maitreya chapel, several modern chapels and a *shedra,* with a *kora* (holy hike) encircling the lot. The road west from here towards Qīnghǎi is classic yak and nomad country, passing several long *mani* (prayer) walls and dozens of black yak-hair tents in summer.

🛏 Sleeping & Eating

In Sêrshu Dzong you can stay at the basic **monastery guesthouse** (色须寺刚京饭店; sèxū sì gāngjīng fàndiàn; dm ¥10-20, tw per bed ¥40-50). There also are plenty of small restaurants – noodle joints as well as Tibetan teahouses – on and off the main road.

Gésà'ěr Jiǔdiàn　　　　　　GUESTHOUSE $
(格萨尔酒店; tw/tr per bed ¥20, d ¥50) In Shíqú Xiàn, this Tibetan-run place has acceptable cheapies, although the shared bathroom is nothing more than a row of pit toilets. Coming from the direction of Manigango, take the first left after the post office and look for the big green building. Reception is on the 2nd floor along with a very popular Tibetan restaurant.

Shangdeenyma Hotel　　　　　HOTEL $$
(香德尼玛大酒店; Xiāngdénímǎ Dàjiǔdiàn; ☑862 2888; tw/d/tr ¥242/246/288) In Shíqú Xiàn the only place we could find with showers is housed in an imposing Tibetan-style building set back from the main street. The cheaper triples and doubles have common bathrooms and go for ¥180. The standard twins with private bathrooms go for ¥200. Make sure the hot water is working before splashing out for a room.

Tibetan restaurant　　　　　TIBETAN $
(dishes ¥8-35; ⊙10am-11pm) The most comfortable place to get your fix of momo, *tsampa* and butter tea in Shíqú Xiàn is the Gésà'ěr Jiǔdiàn's colourful Tibetan restaurant.

❶ Getting There & Away

The small bus station at the far east end of Shíqú Xiàn has a 7am bus to Gānzī (¥99, eight hours), via Manigango (¥77, four hours).

The bus to Yùshù (¥40, five hours, 8am) leaves from the even smaller bus station at the far west end of town.

The Yùshù-bound buses will let you off at Sêrshu Dzong. Alternatively, it's ¥20 in a shared minivan.

There are sometimes through buses that stop here, and at Sêrshu Dzong, en route between Gānzī and Yùshù, but times are inconsistent, and they don't always run.

Sìchuān–Tibet Highway (Southern Route)

Travel here takes you through vast grasslands dotted with Tibetan block homes and contentedly grazing yaks, while majestic peaks tower beyond. Journeying along this 2140km route is slightly easier than taking the northern route, but it's still not for the faint-hearted; road conditions can be pretty poor, and altitude is just as much a factor here as it is further north. However, Kāngdìng–Lǐtáng–Xiāngchéng–Shangri-la has become a popular route into Yúnnán province.

As in the rest of western Sìchuān, warm clothing is a must here, and be on the lookout for signs of altitude sickness.

LǏTÁNG (LITHANG)　　　　　理塘
☑ 0836 / POP 51,300

Lǐtáng claims to be the world's highest town. It isn't. That accolade is shared by Wēnquán in Qīnghǎi province and La Rinconada in Peru, both of which stand at a wheeze-inducing 5100m. Nevertheless, at a dizzying altitude of 4014m, Lǐtáng is still exceptionally high.

The surrounding scenery will certainly leave you breathless, and there are great opportunities to get out and see it – whether by horse, motorbike or simply hiking – making this a decent place to spend a couple of days.

Lǐtáng is famed as the birthplace of the seventh and 10th Dalai Lamas, but the town's large monastery, Chöde Gompa, is the most absorbing sight.

◉ Sights & Activities

Chöde Gompa　　　　　MONASTERY
(长青春科尔寺; Chángqīngchūn Kē'ěr Sì) At the northern end of town, the large Chöde Gompa is a Tibetan monastery built for the third Dalai Lama. Inside is a statue of Sakyamuni that is believed to have been carried from Lhasa by foot. Don't miss climbing onto the roof of the furthest right of the three main halls for great views of the Tibetan homes leading up to the monastery and the grasslands and mountains beyond. Monks climb up here every day to sound the temple's long horns. To get here, walk past the post office, turn left at the end of the road, then take the first right.

Báitǎ Gōngyuán　　　　　CHÖRTEN
Worshippers seem to be perpetually circling Báitǎ Gōngyuán (白塔公园) as they recite

ROUGH ROADS

The roads in western Sìchuān are notoriously bad, but at the time of research they were in the midst of a massive, three-year resurfacing project, which had reduced parts of them to a mud bath. Travel times were sometimes double what they should have been, and after heavy rain some stretches were impassable. The project is due to be completed in 2014 (so they say). Until then, try to get the latest travel time information from hostels in the area. The times we've listed are pre-resurfacing times.

mantras and spin prayer wheels. You can join the locals hanging out in the surrounding park. Turn left out of the bus station and just keep walking.

If you keep walking past Báitǎ Gōngyuán, there are **hot springs** (温泉; wēnquán; admission ¥15) 4km west of the centre.

Outdoor Activities OUTDOORS

Hiking opportunities abound. The hills behind the monastery are one fine option. You could also attempt the two-day *kora* around Zāgá Shénshān (扎嘎神山), a holy mountain three hours' hike south of town. You'll need a tent. For more details, talk to Mr Zheng at Tiān Restaurant. Potala Inn, meanwhile, can help organise **horse trekking**.

Lǐtáng has a **sky burial** site behind the monastery. If you do attend a sky burial, be sure to remember exactly what you are watching, and treat the ceremony, and all those involved, with the utmost respect. For more details, ask Mr Zheng at Tiān Restaurant.

🎎 Festivals & Events

One of the biggest and most colourful Tibetan festivals, the Lǐtáng Horse Festival, is an annual event that includes horse racing, stunt riding, dance competitions and an arts and crafts fair. It is usually held over several days from 1 August.

🛏 Sleeping

Potala Inn HOSTEL $
(布达拉大酒店; Bùdálā Dàjiǔdiàn; ☑532 2533, 135 5198 9029; dm/tw ¥35/320, tr without bathroom ¥150; @🛜) Run by a warm, English-speaking Tibetan woman called Medok, this large hostel has a mixed bag of rooms, ranging from basic bunk-bed dorms to Tibetan-style twins with private bathroom. Offers hiking trips, horse trekking and sky-burial and free internet and wi-fi in the lobby area. One downside is the badly thought-out communal toilets, which are effectively out of action if anyone is using the one communal shower. Turn left from the bus station and it's on the right, set back from the main street.

Lǐtáng International Youth Guesthouse HOTEL $$
(理塘国际青年酒店; Lǐtáng Guójì Qīngnián Jiǔdiàn; ☑532 4666) Just opening when we were here, this place has tidy twins and doubles with attached bathrooms that were going for ¥160 because the hot water had yet to be connected, but will probably go for ¥200 to ¥300 once everything's ready. Next right after Potala Inn turning.

Night of Grassland GUESTHOUSE $$
(草原之夜; Cǎoyuán Zhīyè; ☑532 2655, 189 9047 3777; tw ¥200-260; 🛜) Smart twin rooms, with wi-fi and attached bathroom, set around a garden courtyard. Popular with the overland 4x4 crew, so worth calling ahead (although little English spoken). Turn left out of the bus station then left after the Potala Inn turning. Signposted in English.

🍴 Eating

TOP CHOICE Tiān Restaurant CHINESE, WESTERN $
(天天饭食; Tiāntiān Fànshí; ☑135 4146 7941; 108 Xingfu Donglu; 幸福东路108号; mains ¥10-30; ⏰9am-11pm) Long-standing travellers' haven run by the ever-friendly, English-speaking ace chef Mr Zheng. Food is a good mix of Chinese, Tibetan and Western; there's also coffee and reliable travel advice. Turn left out of the bus station and it's on the left.

Tibetan Special Dishes TIBETAN $
(藏人特餐; Zàngrénjiā Tècān; Xingfu Donglu; 幸福东路; mains from ¥15; ⏰8am-10pm; 📷) For more-authentic Tibetan food, try this simple place run by a friendly guy from Tǎgōng. He doesn't speak English, but has an English menu. It's between the bus station and Tiān Restaurant, on the left.

ℹ Information

China Post (中国邮政; Zhōngguó Yóuzhèng; Tuanjie Lu; ⏰9-11.30am & 2-5.30pm) Turn left out of the bus station, then right at main roundabout crossroads.

Internet cafe (网吧; wǎngbā; Tuanjie Lu; per hr ¥5; ⏰8.30am-midnight) Next to post office.

WORTH A TRIP

YÀDĪNG NATURE RESERVE

The magnificent **Yàdīng Nature Reserve** (亚丁风景区; Yàdīng Fēngjǐngqū; admission ¥150) centres on three sacred snow-capped mountains, which form a holy trinity around forested valleys, wonderfully clear rivers and glacier-fed lakes. It is, quite simply, one of China's most stunning pieces of scenery, but it's also been a highly revered region for local Tibetans for more than 800 years. For them, each of the three peaks, whose Tibetan names mean 'wisdom', 'power' and 'compassion', represent bodhisattvas, and joining Buddhist pilgrims on the 30km, 12-hour *kora* (holy hike) around the highest peak can be a hugely rewarding experience.

The three mountains – Chenresig, Chana Dorje and Jampelyang – are all around 6000m high, and even the hiking trails are around 4000m above sea level, so be sure to have acclimatised properly before you set off on a trek.

The *kora* is around 6032m **Chenresig** (仙乃日; Xiānnǎirì), the tallest of the three peaks, and takes about 12 hours (although Tibetan pilgrims do it in less than eight hours). To avoid one very long day of walking, we recommend camping halfway round, although you'll have to bring all your own gear and supplies. The path is easy to follow as long as you remember to keep the mountain to your right, and to always take the right-hand turn when there's a choice of paths.

If you don't have the time or the energy for the full *kora*, you can do some shorter walks within the reserve. There are also short horse rides available, as well as electric carts that shuttle visitors up to, and back from, the Luòróng Grassland area.

The main entrance is at a small settlement called **Lónglóng Bà** (龙龙坝). From here you can hike to the 800-year-old **Changgu Monastery** (中古寺; Zhōnggǔ Sì; 3km; one hour), then to the **Luòróng Grasslands** (洛绒牛场; Luòróng Niúchǎng; 6km, two hours), which offer incredible views of all three peaks and is as far as most domestic tourists go. From here, you can continue to **Milk Lake** (牛奶海; Niúnǎi Hǎi; 5km, three hours), which is a 30-minute walk from the stunning **Five-colour Lake** (五色海; Wǔsè Hǎi) and approximately halfway round the mountain.

The best times to visit the reserve are May to June and September to early October.

Getting There & Away

Take a shared minivan (per person ¥50, three hours) from **Dàochéng** to the entrance at Lónglóng Bà.

Tickets for the reserve are bought 35km before Lónglóng Bà, at the small town of **Rìwǎ** (日瓦). Your driver will know to stop here en route. Three kilometres before Lónglóng Bà is **Yàdīng Village** (亚丁村; Yàdīng Cūn), where there are a number of simple guesthouses if you want to make an early start on the *kora*. There is sometimes a free shuttle bus from Yàdīng Village to **Lónglóng Bā**, but if you're not planning to stop in Yàdīng Village, ask your driver to take you all the way to Lónglóng Bà from Dàochéng.

❶ Getting There & Away

It's normally easy to bag Kāngdìng or Xīndūqiáo bus tickets but the other buses are through buses, so are often full by the time they reach Lǐtáng. Minivans (around ¥10 to ¥20 more expensive than buses) hang around outside the bus station to save the day. The quickest way north to Gānzī (¥110; around five hours) is to take a minivan via Xīnlóng. No public buses ply this route.

Public buses:

Bātáng ¥63, 3½ hours, one daily (around 3pm)

Dàochéng ¥48, four hours, one daily (around 1.30pm)

Kāngdìng ¥87, eight hours, one daily (6.30am)

Xiāngchéng ¥65, five hours, one daily (around 1.30pm)

Xīndūqiáo ¥63, six hours, one daily (6.30am)

DÀOCHÉNG (DABPA)   稻城
☑0836

Although the small town centre is fairly modern these days, Dàochéng still packs bags of rural charm and makes a lovely base from which to explore the magnificent Yàdīng Nature Reserve. Even if you don't visit Yàdīng, you could easily rest up for a couple of days here, walking or cycling around the hills and barley fields, which are scattered with Tibetan monasteries.

Sleeping

Freedom Inn Youth Hostel   HOTEL $

(自由驿; Zìyóuyì; ☏189 9047 6036, 130 5645 2058; www.inoat.com; dm/tw/tr ¥25/60/80; ☞) Dexi Jie (德西街), the quiet lane directly opposite Here Cafe, is the nicest place to base yourself. Three hostels in particular are worth checking out. Our favourite is Freedom Inn, managed by the same friendly crew that run Here Cafe. Large, clean rooms with ensuite bathrooms are excellent value, and there's wi-fi and a pleasant garden courtyard. Take the second right off Dexi Jie.

Also recommended are **Yàdīng Back-packers Hostel** (亚丁人社区; Yàdīng Rén Shèqū; ☏135 0829 5808; www.yading.net; dm/tw ¥30/120; @☞), where small rooms are set around the courtyard of a beautiful Tibetan blockhouse (first right off Dexi Jie); and **Dé Jí Zàng Jiā Hostel** (德吉藏家客栈; Déjí Zàngjiā Kèzhàn; ☏133 3079 0114, 150 7086 9707; dm/tw ¥25/90; @☞), similar to Yàdīng Back-packers (on the left, at 3 Dexi Jie).

Eating

TOP CHOICE Here Cafe   CAFE $

(高原反映咖啡馆; Gāoyuán Fǎnyìng Kāfēiguǎn; ☏572 8667; mains ¥15-30; ☉9am-midnight; ☞) This wonderfully rustic cafe, housed in a Tibetan blockhouse, is ground zero for travellers in Dàochéng. It does great coffee (from ¥25), plenty of beer (from ¥15) and a small range of very tasty dishes. It also has free wi-fi. The manager speaks a bit of English; other staff more so. All are friendly, and happy to dish out advice on how best to visit the surrounding countryside, including Yàdīng Nature Reserve. The cafe is on your left as you enter the town, 100m before the bus station.

Information

You can rent **bicycles** (per day ¥15) from a place on the right-hand side of Dexi Jie, the lane opposite Here Cafe. Look for the sign reading 自行车出租行 (zìxíngchē chūzū háng; bike rental).

Getting There & Away

Two buses leave daily at 6am. One goes to Chéngdū (¥245, 20 hours), via Lǐtáng (three hours) and Kāngdìng (¥135, 10 hours). The other goes southwest to Shangri-la (Zhōngdiàn; ¥114, 10 hours) in Yúnnán province, via Xiāngchéng (three hours). You can buy tickets from 2pm the day before, although you cannot buy tickets to Lǐtáng or Xiāngchéng until the morning the bus leaves. Minivans (per person ¥60) are more common for these two destinations.

Minivans are the only option for Yàdīng Nature Reserve (¥50, three hours).

XIĀNGCHÉNG (CHAKTRENG)   乡城
☏0836

If you want to break your journey into or out of Yúnnán province, then this small but modern town makes a comfortable stop. There's an attractive **monastery** (admission ¥15) at the top end of the town, commanding fine views.

Friendly **Seven Lake Hotel** (七湖宾馆; Qīhú Bīnguǎn; ☏582 5059; tw without/with bathroom ¥40/70; ☞), just up from the bus station on the left, has simple but well-priced rooms and a top-floor teahouse and bar with wi-fi.

Further up on your right, just before the town square, **Jiǎozi Diàn** (饺子店; dishes from ¥7; ☉7.30am-7.30pm) specialises in boiled dumplings (水饺; shuǐjiǎo; per jīn (500g; ¥26); half a jīn (bàn jīn) is plenty, but also does a killer bowl of **gàn bànmiàn** (干拌面; mincemeat dry noodles; ¥7 to ¥9).

Getting There & Away

Two buses leave daily at 6am. One goes south to Shangri-la (Zhōngdiàn; ¥85, eight hours). The other is for Kāngdìng (¥151.50, 12 hours), but note you won't be sold tickets on this bus for Lǐtáng even though it's en route. You need to take a shared minivan instead (¥80, four to five hours). A shared minivan to Dàochéng (three hours) is around ¥60.

NORTHERN SÌCHUĀN

Hiking, or even camping, in the stunning Jiǔzhàigōu National Park or heading out on horseback around Sōngpān are how most travellers experience the carpets of alpine forest, swaths of grasslands, icy lakes and snow-topped mountains of northern Sìchuān. You can also travel north from here into Gānsù, Shaanxi or even Qīnghǎi, or loop round towards western Sìchuān via Dānbā.

Sōngpān   松潘
☏0837 / POP 71,650

Horse trekking into the woods and mountains is the main attraction of this laid-back, historic town, but the hiking's also good and there's a reasonably strong backpacker vibe, which makes Sōngpān a good place to catch up on the latest travel tales.

Note, in midwinter (December to March) Sōngpān shuts down almost completely. Many guesthouses and restaurants, including Emma's Kitchen, are closed then. However, horse trekking is still possible.

Sōngpān

Sōngpān

◎ Sights

 1 Covered Bridge A3
 2 Covered Bridge A3
 3 East Gate..B2
 4 Guānyīn Gé A3
 5 North Gate..A1
 6 South Gate..A3
 7 South Gate..A3
 8 West Gate A1

⊕ Activities, Courses & Tours

 9 Qíqílè Mǎduì A3
 10 Shùnjiāng Horse Treks.......................B1

▣ Sleeping

 11 Old House Hotel B1
 12 Shùnjiāng Guesthouse.......................B1
 13 Sun River International Hotel.............A1

⊗ Eating

 14 Emma's Kitchen B1
 15 Muslim restaurants A2
 16 Shèngdì Zàngjiālè A3
 17 Song in the Mountain B1

◎ Drinking

 18 Teahouses A3

⊕ Transport

 19 Bus Station B1

Sights

Sōngpān's part-rebuilt **town wall** may be less than 10 years old but its **ancient gates** are original Ming-dynasty structures going back some 600 years. Note the horse carvings at the foot of the two south gates, half swallowed up by the ever-rising level of the road. The only original part of the **old wall** is by the rebuilt West Gate, which overlooks the town from its hillside perch.

Two wooden **covered bridges** (古松 桥; Gǔsōng Qiáo), the bases of which are genuinely old, span the Mín River. On the western side of the river is **Guānyīn Gé** (观音阁), a small temple near the start of a hillside trail that offers good views over Sōngpān.

Activities

Horse Trekking   HORSE TREKKING

One of the most popular ways to experience the idyllic mountain forests and emerald-green lakes surrounding Sōngpān is by joining up with a horse trek. Guides take you through pristine valleys and forests aboard a not-so-big, very tame horse. Many people rate this experience as a highlight of their travels in this region.

Shùnjiāng Horse Treks (顺江旅游马 队; Shùnjiāng Lǚyóu Mǎduì; ☎723 1201, 139 0904 3501) have been offering horse treks to foreign tourists for years (despite slightly ropey English-language skills). On offer is anything from one- to 14-day treks and trips can be tailored to suit you.

One of the most popular treks is a three- or four-day trek to **Ice Mountain** (雪玉顶; Xuěyùdǐng), a spectacular trip through unspoilt scenery.

Rates are ¥200 to ¥230 per person per day, all-inclusive. The guides take care of everything: you won't touch a tent pole or a cooking pot unless you want to. The only additional charge is entrance to the different sites and national parks visited on some of the trips, but you'll be warned of these before you set out.

The majority of travellers seem happy with their services, but we do sometimes receive reports of apathetic guides showing a lack of environmental awareness. For comparison, you may want to also make enquiries with the less-established but well-run **Qíqílè Mǎduì** (骑奇乐马队; ☎723 4138, 135 6879 2936; per day per person ¥200), although they are less accustomed to dealing with foreign tourists.

Hiking

The surrounding hills are equally good for hiking. One option is to hike up to the only remaining part of the original town wall, by **West Gate**. It takes around one hour. There are three paths up, meaning you can complete a round trip. One starts beside the stream north of North Gate. Another leads up the hill from the post office, while a third is accessed via Guānyīn Gé temple. It's also possible to hike for about two hours to **Shàngníbā Monastery** (上泥巴寺庙; Shàngníbā Sìmiào) in the eastern hills. Ask at Emma's Kitchen for more details.

🛏 Sleeping

Shùnjiāng Guesthouse GUESTHOUSE $
(顺江自助旅馆; Shùnjiāng Zìzhù Lǚguǎn; ☑723 1064, 139 0904 3501; Shunjiang Beilu; 顺江北路; dm¥30, d/tw¥80; ☎) The owners of Shùnjiāng Horse Treks company run this simple guesthouse with decent rooms around an open courtyard. It can be freezing here in cold weather, but bathrooms have heat lamps and 24-hour hot water, and beds come with electric blankets. Rates tend to double in July and August.

Old House Hotel GUESTHOUSE $
(古韵客栈; Gǔyùn Kèzhàn; ☑723 1368; Shunjiang Beilu; 顺江北路; dm/s/tw ¥30/80/100; @☎) Right by the bus station, this attractive old-style, three-storey wooden building has small but clean rooms off an interior courtyard. English-speaking staff, 24-hour hot water and wi-fi. Again, rates tend to double during the summer holidays.

Sun River International Hotel HOTEL $$
(太阳河国际大酒店; Tàiyánghé Guójì Dàjiǔdiàn; ☑723 5000; Shunjiang Beilu; 顺江北路; d/tw ¥600/680, discounted to ¥200/280; ☎) Dark, gloomy corridors lead to decent enough spacious midrange rooms.

🍴 Eating

To see where Sōngpān's large Huí Muslim population gets its fix of noodles, head to **Xiashuiguan Muslim Street** (下水塭清真街) where you'll find a cluster of small **Muslim restaurants** (dishes ¥10-15; ⊗8am-9.30pm) with English signs but no English menus. Typical offerings include *Lánzhōu lāmiàn* (兰州拉面; Lánzhōu pulled noodles), *gān bànmiàn* (干拌面; minced-meat dry noodles), *dāoxiāo miàn* (刀削面; knife-sliced noodles) and *yángzá tāng* (羊杂汤; sheep innards soup).

TOP CHOICE **Emma's Kitchen** CAFE, RESTAURANT $$
(小欧洲西餐厅; Xiǎo Ōuzhōu Xīcāntīng; Shunjiang Beilu; ☑723 1088, 131 0837 2888, emmachina@hotmail.com; mains ¥15-50; ⊗8am-late; @☎) Sōngpān's main travellers' hang-out is this laid-back cafe that serves fresh coffee, pizza and other Western fare, along with a number of Chinese dishes. Emma is exceedingly helpful and can sort out almost anything from laundry or train tickets to packed lunches for your horse trek. Also has internet (per hour ¥6) and CD burning (per disk ¥15). At the time of research, Emma had plans to convert the back of the cafe into a few guestrooms. Email her for the latest.

WORTH A TRIP

HUÁNGLÓNG NATIONAL PARK

A trip to **Huánglóng National Park** (黄龙景区; Huánglóng Jǐngqū; www.huanglong.com; Yellow Dragon Valley; adult ¥200; ⊗7am-6pm) is essentially a very expensive three-hour walk up and down one small valley. The valley, however, is stunning, and its terraced, coloured limestone ponds of blues, turquoises, yellows and greens are exquisite. It's certainly worth the trip if you've got the cash. And it's perfect picnic territory. The best time to come is between May and October, and preferably in July and August.

By the park entrance is a modern **visitor centre** with restaurant, teahouse and free left-luggage room. You can pick up a free English-language leaflet with a map of the park here, too. There are a couple of expensive tour-group hotels by the entrance, but most people day trip it from Sōngpān or Jiǔzhàigōu.

It's reasonably easy to snag a lift in a bus or minvan from here to Jiǔzhàigōu. For Sōngpān, you'll probably have to find a lift to Chuānzhǔ Sì (川主寺; ¥25, one hour), from where you can take a shared taxi to Sōngpān (¥10). Note, there's an airport shuttle bus to Jiǔzhàigōu (¥100), which stops here for long enough for passengers to tour the park.

A couple of doors along, **Song in the Mountain Restaurant**, run by the helpful Sarah Yang, has a similar menu (minus the fresh coffee) with slightly cheaper prices.

Shèngdì Zàngjiālè TIBETAN $
(圣地藏家乐; mains ¥10-35; ☺7am-9pm; 🏠) An OK range of Tibetan dishes served inside traditional tents or at open-air tables set around a tree-shaded riverside garden.

 Drinking

Along the Mín River (岷江; Mín Jiāng), on the southern edge of town, are several small **teahouses** (tea ¥5-10; ☺8am-6pm) where you can while away the afternoon with the locals.

 Information

Agricultural Bank of China (中国农业银行; Nóngyè Yínháng; Shunjiang Beilu) Foreign-friendly ATM.
China Post (中国邮政; Zhōngguó Yóuzhèng; Shunjiang Beilu; ☺9-11.30am & 2-5.30pm)
Public Security Bureau (PSB; 公安局; Gōng'ānjú; ☎723 3778; Shunjiang Beilu; ☺8.30am-noon & 3-6pm) Can usually renew visas in one day.

ⓘ Getting There & Around
Air
See the Jiŭzhàigōu section (p745) for information on flying to this area. There's no public transport between Sōngpān and the airport. A taxi should be around ¥100.

TIBET'S NO-GO REGIONS

At the time of research, foreigners were forbidden from travelling overland from Sìchuān into Tibet proper because Tibet's far eastern prefecture of Chamdo, which borders Sìchuān, was completely off limits. Likewise, the north Sìchuān prefecture of Ābà has, for a long time now, been off limits. During March (which contains some politically sensitive anniversaries), and usually April, too, Tibet is often completely closed to foreigners. This temporary closure has in recent years extended to Sìchuān's Gānzī prefecture, too. Check the China and Tibet branches of Lonely Planet's online forum, **Thorn Tree** (www.lonelyplanet.com/thorntree), for the latest information.

Bus
Buses leaving **Sōngpān bus station** (客运站; kèyùnzhàn) include:
Chéngdū ¥92 to ¥121, eight hours, three daily (6am, 6.30am and 7am)
Huánglóng National Park ¥28, two hours, two daily (6am and 2pm)
Jiŭzhàigōu ¥32, 2½ hours, two daily (9am and 1pm)
Mǎ'ěrkāng ¥105 to ¥120, seven hours, one daily (6.20am)
Zöigě ¥46, three hours, two daily (10am and 2.30pm)

Jiŭzhàigōu National Park
九寨沟风景名胜区
☑0837 / POP 62,000

The stunning Unesco World Heritage Site of **Jiŭzhàigōu National Park** (Jiŭzhàigōu Fēngjǐng Míngshèngqū; Nine Village Valley National Park; www.jiuzhai.com; admission May–mid-Nov ¥220, mid-Nov–Apr ¥80, shuttle bus ¥90; ☺7am-6pm) is one of Sìchuān's star attractions. More than two million people visit the park every year to gawp at its famous bluer-than-blue lakes, its rushing waterfalls and its deep green trees backed by snowy mountain ranges.

Add into the mix kilometres of well-maintained boardwalk trails and ecotourism camping trips and you'll begin to get a feel for Jiŭzhàigōu's charms.

The best time to visit is September through to November, when you're most likely to have clear skies and (particularly in October) blazing autumn colours to contrast with the turquoise lakes. Summer is the busiest but also rainiest time. Spring can be cold but still pleasant, and winter, if you're prepared for frigid temperatures, brings dramatic ice-coated trees and frozen-in-place waterfalls (as well as lower prices).

Peak-time tickets for students and over-60s are ¥110. Over-70s and children under six can enter for free.

Jiŭzhàigōu means 'Nine Village Valley' and refers to the region's nine Tibetan villages. According to legend, Jiŭzhàigōu was created when a jealous devil caused the goddess Wunosemo to drop her magic mirror, a present from her lover the warlord god Dage. The mirror dropped to the ground and shattered into 118 shimmering turquoise lakes.

◉ Sights

Lakes & Waterfalls   LAKES
The main road follows Zéchāwā River (Zéchāwā Hé) up Shùzhēng Valley, as it runs past Héyè Village (Héyè Cūn) to **Sparkling Lake** (火花海; Huǒhuā Hǎi), the first in a series of lakes filled by the **Shùzhēng Waterfall** (树正瀑布; Shùzhēng Pùbù).

A walking trail begins north of Sparkling Lake and runs along the eastern edge of the river up to **Nuòrìlǎng Waterfall** (诺日朗瀑布; Nuòrìlǎng Pùbù). Here, the road branches in two, with the eastern road leading to **Long Lake** (长海; Cháng Hǎi) and **Five-Coloured Pool** (五彩池; Wǔcǎi Chí); and the western road to **Swan Lake** (天鹤海; Tiān'é Hǎi). The western route has a greater concentration of attractions, most of which are accessible from the quiet forest trail leading from **Mirror Lake** (镜海; Jìnghǎi) to **Panda Lake** (熊猫海; Xióngmāo Hǎi). Views from this trail are particularly good, especially of the waterfall known as **Pearl Shoals** (珍珠滩瀑布; Zhēnzhūtān Pùbù).

The eastern route is almost better done by bus as the narrow road sees a great deal of traffic and there are fewer 'sights'. Nevertheless, the two lakes at the far end, Long Lake and Five-Coloured Pool, are both well worth a visit.

From the park entrance to Nuòrìlǎng Waterfall is about 14km. It's a further 17.5km along the western road to Swan Lake and another couple of kilometres on to the **Virgin Forest**, which is as far as the road goes. On the eastern route it's about 18km from Nuòrìlǎng Waterfall to Long Lake.

Zhārú Temple   TEMPLE
The first official site inside the park proper is the Tibetan Zhārú Temple (扎如寺; Zhārú Sì; Zaru Gompa in Tibetan), in the Zhārú Valley. The bus doesn't stop here, but it's only a short walk from the ticket office; turn left at the first fork off the main road.

🏃 Activities

As part of the park's **ecotourism program** (☏773 7811; ecotourism@jiuzhai.com; visitors centre; 1-/2-/3-day hikes ¥560/1360/1960) visitors can now hike along and even camp inside the Zhārú Valley, just east of the main tourist valley. This is an extremely rare opportunity in China and numbers are strictly limited so it's highly advisable to email or phone ahead, especially if you want to camp. Prices include English-speaking guides, all camping equip-

Jiǔzhàigōu

◉ **Top Sights**
  Zhārú Temple.........................B1

🛏 **Sleeping**
1 Jiǔzhàigōu Grand Hotel.....................B1
2 Uncle Jiang's Family Guesthouse..................A1

🍴 **Eating**
3 Ābù Lǔzī.........................A1

🍷 **Drinking**
4 Star Cafe.........................B1

ℹ **Information**
5 Park Entrance.........................A1
6 Visitors Centre & Tickets...................A1

ℹ **Transport**
7 Bus Station.........................B1
8 Nuòrìlǎng Bus Station.....................A3

ment and main meals (although you may want to bring along some fruit and snacks), but do not include the park entrance fee. The multiday hikes include time to visit the main park without a guide after your hike. Check the park website or ask at the visitors centre (游客中心; yóukè zhōngxīn) for more details.

For those who like to do things on their own, there are great **hiking** opportunities all over this area, although be sure to steer clear of the national park itself. One option is to hike around the hills near Zhuo Ma's homestay; Zhuo Ma can advise you on where's good. She also arranges short **horse treks** (2hr; ¥180) from the village, and helps run **Tibetan cookery classes** (2-3hr; per person incl a meal ¥150) at Ābù Lǔzī restaurant.

🛏 Sleeping

There's an almost endless supply of hotels around Péngfēng Village (彭丰村; Péngfēng Cūn), so don't worry if the options listed here are full. Staying inside the park is not allowed.

TOP CHOICE Zhuo Ma's HOMESTAY $
(卓玛; Zhuómǎ; ☎135 6878 3012; www.zhuoma jiuzhaigou.hostel.com; per person ¥180) A genuine Tibetan homestay, this beautifully decorated wood cabin in a tiny village about 10km up the valley from the main park has six simple rooms and a wonderfully accommodating family. The lovely Zhuo Ma speaks some English and is on hand to welcome foreign guests. Her mother (*amma*) is the host and cooks the meals. There's a common bathroom with shower, and prices include three meals a day, and pick-up from the bus station (otherwise it's around ¥50 in a taxi).

If you're coming from Sōngpān you could ask the driver to drop you on the main road at Shānsì Village (山四寨; Shānsì Zhài). Zhuo Ma's is about a 15-minute walk up a dirt track from there. Any problems, just call Zhuo Ma.

Uncle Jiang's Family Guesthouse HOSTEL $
(九寨人家青年旅舍; Jiǔzhài Rénjiā Qīngnián Lǔshè; ☎777 4455; www.jzrjhostel.com; Péngfēng Village; 彭丰村; Péngfēng Cūn; dm/tw ¥30/80; @🛜) There are five or six run-of-the-mill youth hostels within 100m of each other in Péngfēng Village. This one is the furthest from the park entrance, but has the best hostel vibe, with friendly staff and a decent cafe-restaurant area in the lobby. Expect prices to rise to ¥100/180 (dorms/twins) from July to October.

Jiǔzhàigōu Grand Hotel HOTEL $$$
(九寨沟贵宾楼饭店; Jiǔzhàigōu Guìbīnlóu Fàndiàn; ☎773 9066, 773 5555; r incl breakfast from ¥696, discounted to ¥200) You can't beat the location, just beside the park entrance gate. The rooms themselves are fairly average midrange units, but they're large and many have views of either the mountains or the small river that runs alongside the hotel. Expect to pay at least ¥480 from July to October.

🍴 Eating & Drinking

Péngfēng Village is stuffed full with cheap Sichuanese restaurants. There's also a cluster along the pleasant riverside walkway called Bianbian Jie. Inside the park you can buy pricey snacks and drinks. Otherwise, there's a restaurant (also pricey) at the Nuòrìlǎng junction.

TOP CHOICE Ābù Lǔzī TIBETAN $$
(阿布鲁孜; Ābù Lǔzī Fēngqíng Zàngcānba; ☎139 9042 1118, 135 6878 3012; www.abuluzi.com; Péngfēng Village; 彭丰村; Péngfēng Cūn; dishes from ¥35; ⏰11am-11pm; 🅿) The most genuine Tibetan restaurant in Jiǔzhàigōu, this excellent place, run by the same family

---

HOW TO 'DO' JIǓZHÀIGŌU

» **Start early** Get into the park as close to the 7am opening as you can. Not only will you have more time, but you'll also beat the later-sleeping tour groups.

» **Go up first** Since much of the most spectacular scenery is in the park's higher reaches, you'll see the highlights first if you take the (hop-on,-hop-off) bus to the top and walk or ride down. Head first to either Long Lake or Swan Lake, work your way down to the Nuòrìlǎng junction, then go up the other fork. Later in the day you can see the lakes between Nuòrìlǎng and the entrance.

» **Get out of the bus** Walking trails run throughout the park, and by walking, you'll steer clear of the biggest crowds. The walking trails are generally on the opposite side of the lakes from the road, so you'll have more peace and quiet, too.

» **Pack a lunch** Dining options inside the park are limited and expensive. If you bring your own food, you can picnic away from the hordes.

THE ROAD TO GĀNSÙ

Those heading north into Gānsù province will need to bus-hop their way from Sōngpān. First stop is **Zöigě** (若尔盖; Ruò'ěrgài), a small, dusty Tibetan town set among the remote plateau grasslands and with a distinct frontier-town feel to it. The grasslands here burst into life with wildflowers in late summer, and it's possible to arrange horse trekking, although facilities aren't as good as in Sōngpān, and English-language skills among those organising them are pretty much nonexistent.

Shǔguāng Bīnguǎn (曙光宾馆; ☎0837-229 2988; tw ¥100) has decent rooms with private bathroom. Turn left out of the bus station and walk 100m. There are plenty of eating options on this road (Shuguang Jie) too.

Zöigě buses go to Sōngpān (¥42, three hours, 10am and 2.30pm) and Lángmùsì (¥21, two hours, 2.30pm), an enchanting monastery town that straddles the Sìchuān–Gānsù border and from where you can catch onward transport towards Lánzhōu.

Be aware that altitudes are high out here (Zöigě is at 3500m) and temperatures often plummet to uncomfortable levels. In winter, snow sometimes renders roads unpassable, so buses can be sporadic.

behind Zhuo Ma's homestay – Zhuo Ma's brother, Ke Zhu, is a trained chef – has an extensive menu of delicious Tibetan dishes. **Tibetan cookery classes** (¥150) are also held here.

Star Cafe　　　　　　　　　　CAFE $
(太白楼; Tàibái Lóu; ☎773 9839; 23 Bianbian Jie; 边边街23号; mains ¥20-45; ☺11.30am-midnight; ☎◉) The coolest hang-out in town, Star Cafe has a decent selection of fresh coffee (from ¥20), beer (from ¥15) and wine, plus a good range of international dishes (¥20 to ¥45). There's also wi-fi and patio seating by the river.

ⓘ Information

An **ATM** (自动柜员机; Zìdòng Guìyuán Jī) at the park entrance accepts foreign cards, as does the China Construction Bank (near the bus station) and Agricultural Bank of China (in Péngfēng Village), where you can also change cash. There is a number of **internet cafes** (网吧; wǎngbā) in Péngfēng Village.

The park has an excellent English-language website at www.jiuzhai.com. You can also get information from the visitors centre at the park entrance.

ⓘ Getting There & Around
Air
More than a dozen daily flights link Chéngdū with Jiǔzhàigōu Airport (officially called Jiǔhuáng Airport). Other direct flights include Běijīng, Shànghǎi, Hángzhōu, Chóngqìng, Kūnmíng and Xī'ān.

Buses to Jiǔzhàigōu (¥45, 1½ hours) meet arriving flights. A taxi from the airport is about ¥200.

There's also an airport bus that stops first at Huánglóng National Park, waiting long enough for passengers to tour the park, and then continues on to Jiǔzhàigōu (¥100).

Bus
Buses leaving from **Jiǔzhàigōu bus station** (汽车站; qìchēzhàn) include those listed below. Note, you can travel to western Sìchuān, via Mǎ'ěrkāng and Dānbā, without having to go to Chéngdū.
Chéngdū ¥145 to ¥220, 10 hours, four daily (6am, 7am, 7.30am and 8am)
Chóngqìng ¥200, 12 hours, one daily (7.30am)
Guǎngyuán ¥88, eight hours, one daily (6.30am)
Huánglóng National Park ¥45, three hours, two daily (7am and 7.30am)
Lánzhōu ¥237, 11 hours, one daily (7am)
Mǎ'ěrkāng ¥150, nine hours, one daily (8am)
Sōngpān ¥33, two hours, one daily (7.30am)

KOKORDIMAGES.COM / GETTY IMAGES ©

1. Tiān'ānmén Square, Běijīng (p60)

The symbolic centre of the Chinese universe, Tiān'ānmén Square is the world's largest public square.

2. Yùyuán Gardens, Shànghǎi (p185)

A charming example of Ming-dynasty garden design.

3. Chinese opera (p102)

Chinese opera's colourful blend of singing, mime, dancing and acrobatics can be seen at Húguǎng Guild Hall, Běijīng.

4. Bamboo Sea, Sìchuān (p726)

A national park with swaying bamboo forest, walking trails and waterfalls.

KINGWU / GETTY IMAGES ©

FELIX HUG / GETTY IMAGES ©

1. Rice terraces, Guǎngxī (p593)

The rice terraces around Guìlín provide excellent hiking opportunities within an archetypal Chinese landscape.

2. Golden Summit, Éméi Shān (p714)

Golden Summit is the highest point on Mt Emei, one of China's four most famous Buddhist mountains.

3. Lama Temple, Běijīng (p67)

Worshippers burn incense at Běijīng's unmissable Lama Temple during Chinese New Year.

FENG WEI PHOTOGRAPHY / GETTY IMAGES ©

LONELY PLANET / GETTY IMAGES ©

1. Grand Buddha, Lèshān (p718)

Seventy-one metres tall and 1200 years old, the Grand Buddha is carved into the cliff face overlooking the Dàdù River.

2. Jade Market, Hong Kong (p478)

Some 450 stalls in Kowloon sell all varieties and grades of jade, so make sure you know your nephrite from your jadeite.

3. Zhuang ethnic minority, Guǎngxī (p585)

The Zhuang, China's largest minority group, make up 32% of Guǎngxī's population.

KEREN SU / GETTY IMAGES ©

JOHN W BANAGAN / GETTY IMAGES ©

West Lake, Zhèjiāng (p251)

...very definition of classical beauty ...hina, West Lake is lined by willow, ... and peach trees and crossed by ... moon bridges.

2. Giant panda cub, Sìchuān (p701)

Sìchuān's capital Chéngdū is home to China's national icon at the Giant Panda Breeding Research Base.

3. Lìjiāng, Yúnnán (p659)

A Unesco World Heritage Site, Lìjiāng is a maze of cobbled streets, wooden buildings and gushing canals.

Chóngqìng

POP 28 MILLION / CITY POP 7 MILLION

Includes »

Chóngqìng City 756
Dàzú Buddhist Caves ... 766
Zhōngshān 767
Láitān 768
Sōngji 769

Best for History

» Dàzú Buddhist Caves (p766)

» Fishing Town Fortress (p768)

» Chóngqìng's city gates (p757)

Best for Scenery

» Three Gorges (p770)

» Fishing Town Fortress (p768)

» Zhōngshān (p767)

Why Go?

Dominated by its namesake capital city, the municipality of Chóngqìng (重庆) is a relatively new creation, having split from Sìchuān province in the 1990s. But the area it now covers has played a significant role throughout Chinese history, and is still a region of fantastic natural beauty.

Thanks to the mighty Yangzi River (Cháng Jiāng), which powers its way through here, this region has long been one of strategic military importance, with many a famous battle fought on its muddy waters; waters so powerfully persistent that they carved out one of China's greatest natural wonders, the magnificent Three Gorges.

Humans too have left their indelible mark, with a panoply of ancient Buddhist sculptures, dozens of seemingly lost-in-time villages and, of course, the megalopolis that is Chóngqìng; one of the fastest-growing and most alluring cities in all of China.

When to Go
Chóngqìng

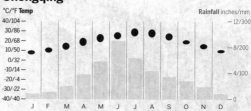

Apr & May Winter chill has lifted; full force of summer sweatbox yet to arrive, but still rainy.

Jul & Aug It's hot; temperatures top 40°C and Chóngqìng City resembles a steam bath.

Sep & Oct Like spring: manageable temperatures; a good time to explore the countryside.

Chóngqìng Highlights

1 Shift down a gear or two as you float past the awe-inspiring Three Gorges on board a **Yangzi River Cruise** (p770)

2 Gasp in wonder at the exquisite ancient artwork of the **Dàzú Buddhist Caves** (p766)

3 Hike the ruins of **Fishing Town Fortress** (p768), one of China's greatest battlefields

4 Tuck into the world's most mouth-numbing **hotpot** (p762) at Yèfù Huǒguō

5 Pull up a stool and sample the delights of *shāokǎo*, Chóngqìng's no-nonsense **streetside barbeques** (p761)

6 See traditional wooden stilt housing in the ancient riverside village of **Zhōngshān** (p767)

7 Track down the last few remains of **Chóngqìng's ancient city wall** (p757)

8 Wander the cobblestones, or just chill in a teahouse in the Ming dynasty village of **Sōngji** (p769)

PRICE INDICATORS

The following price indicators are used in this chapter:

Sleeping

$	less than ¥200
$$	¥200 to ¥500
$$$	more than ¥500

Eating

$	less than ¥40
$$	¥40 to ¥80
$$$	more than ¥80

History

Stone tools unearthed along the Yangzi River valleys show that humans lived in this region two million years ago. The ancient Ba kingdom ruled from here more than 2000 years before subsequent Qin, Sui and Southern Song dynasty rulers took over. From 1938 to 1945, Chóngqìng city (previously known as Chungking) became the Kuomintang's wartime capital. It was here that representatives of the Chinese Communist Party (CCP), including Zhou Enlai, acted as 'liaisons' between the Kuomintang and the communists headquartered at Yán'ān, in Shaanxi province.

Refugees from all over China flooded into the city during WWII. More followed when the construction of Three Gorges Dam forced more than one million people to be relocated.

In 1997 Chóngqìng separated from Sìchuān province and became a municipality under the direct control of the central government.

The city became the focus of attention in 2012 for its role in one of modern China's biggest political scandals, when Gu Kailai, the wife of Chóngqìng's Communist Party boss Bo Xilai, was convicted of murdering British businessman Neil Heywood. Allegations of corruption, extortion and even espionage surrounded the case. Bo was stripped of his office and eventually expelled from the Communist Party, although at the time of research he had yet to face any criminal trial himself.

Language

In addition to standard Mandarin Chinese, Chóngqìng residents also speak Sichuanese. It's a Mandarin dialect, but pronunciation is different enough that it's often difficult for those who speak standard Chinese to understand. Two words visitors will often hear are *yàodé* (pronounced 'yow-day', meaning 'yes' or 'ok') and *méidé* (pronounced 'may-day', meaning 'no').

Chóngqìng City 重庆市

The one-time capital of the ancient Ba kingdom, Chóngqìng City – once a walled river fortress – is now one of the fastest-growing cities on earth. Billions of yuan have gone into its development, launching a major construction surge that shows no sign of slowing, but despite rampant modern development, a gritty old-China atmosphere remains around the river docks and the fascinating hillside alleyways that link them to the rest of the city.

Chóngqìng is sometimes mistakenly referred to as the biggest city in the world. It isn't. Figures for the whole municipality's population edge the 30 million mark, but these are made up of a number of towns and cities. The city of Chóngqìng itself has a mere seven million inhabitants, for now.

◉ Sights & Activities

Arhat Temple   BUDDHIST TEMPLE
(罗汉寺; Luóhàn Sì; Map p758; Luohan Si Jie; 罗汉寺街; admission ¥10; ☺8am-6pm) Built around 1000 years ago, this still-active temple is now sandwiched between skyscrapers. A notable feature is the corridor flanked by intricate rock carvings found just after you enter the complex, but the main attraction here is **Arhat Hall** (罗汉堂; Luóhàn Táng), off to your right just after the corridor, which contains 500 terracotta arhats (a Buddhist term for those who have achieved enlightenment and who pass to nirvana at death). Between the stone-carvings corridor and the temple proper there is a reasonably priced **vegetarian restaurant** (dishes ¥12-35; ☺10am-5pm) with a photo menu.

Húguǎng Guild Hall   MUSEUM
(湖广会馆; Húguǎng Huìguǎn; Map p758; ☎6393 0287; Dongshuimen Zhengjie; 东水门正街; admission ¥30; ☺9am-6pm, tickets not sold after 5pm) You could spend several hours poking around the beautifully restored buildings in this gorgeous museum complex, which once served as a community headquarters for immigrants from the Hú (Húnán and Húběi) and Guǎng (Guǎngdōng and Guǎngxī) prov-

inces who arrived in Chóngqìng several hundred years ago. There are rooms filled with artwork and furniture, a **temple**, a **teahouse** and several stages for Chinese **opera performances**. Free-to-watch rehearsals of Yuèjù (an operatic style originating from Zhèjiāng province) and Jīngjù (Běijīng Opera) are held every Thursday and Saturday, usually between 3pm and 6pm.

Ancient City Gates   RUIN

(古城门; Gǔchéngmén) Sadly, only fragments remain of Chóngqìng's once magnificent Ming dynasty city wall, which stretched 8km around the Jiěfàngbēi peninsula and which was more than 30m tall in places. Of the 17 gates which punctuated the wall before demolition began in 1927, two are still standing. The charming, moss-hewn **Dōngshuǐ Mén** (东水门; Map p758) is on a pathway beside the Yangtze River Hostel. Larger, and partly restored is **Tōngyuán Mén** (通远门; Map p758), a short walk from Exit 1 of Qixinggang metro station. You can walk along the wall for a short stretch at both locations. If you're interested in seeing how the wall once encircled the old city, look for the carved map of ancient Chóngqìng on the public square at Cháotiānmén (Map p758), itself once a city gate.

Cíqìkǒu Ancient Town   OLD TOWN

(磁器口古镇; Cíqìkǒu Gǔzhèn; off Map p757; Cíqìkǒu) The opportunity to glimpse slices of old Chóngqìng makes it worth riding out to this part of town, on the Jiālíng River west of the centre. Most of the buildings, many dating to the late Ming dynasty, have been restored for tourists, and the main drag can feel like a carnival, especially on weekends, but away from the central street, a living, working village remains. You can easily lose yourself in its narrow lanes, peeking into homes and tiny storefronts. And there's plenty to eat here, both in the alleys and overlooking the river.

It's also worth poking your head inside **Bǎolún Sì** (宝轮寺; admission ¥5; ⊙7am-6pm), one of Cíqìkǒu's only remaining temples. Its main building is more than 1000 years old. The quiet alley the temple is on, Heng Jie (横街), is one of the most pleasant places to explore, and contains a string of cute **cafes** with wi-fi and fresh coffee.

Cíqìkǒu has its own metro station on Line 1.

Yangzi River Cable Car   CABLE CAR

(长江索道; Chángjiāng suǒdào; Map p758; one-way ¥5; ⊙7am-10pm) A ride on the creaky old Yangzi River cable car is slightly disconcerting, but gives you a wonderful bird's-eye view of the murky waters and the cityscape beyond. It drops you off near the riverside

Chóngqìng City

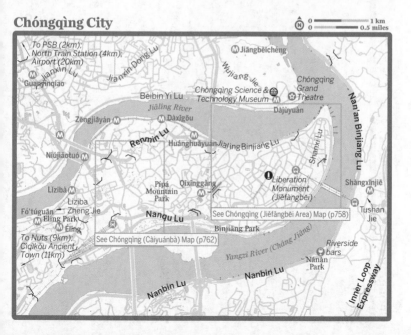

Chóngqìng (Jiěfàngbēi Area)

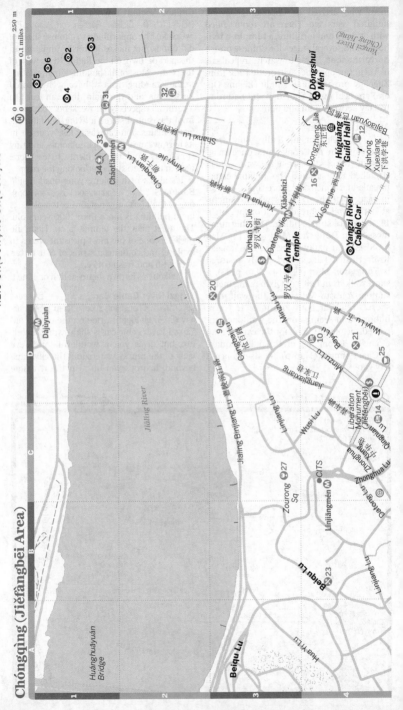

Yangzi River (Cháng Jiāng)

Dòngshuǐ Mén

Húguǎng Guild Hall

Yangzi River Cable Car

Xiahong Xuexiang 下洪学巷

Dongzheng Jie 东正街

Baliaoyuan

Xi San Jie 西三街

Shanxi Lu 陕西路

Xinyi Jie 新义街

Chaoqian Lu 朝千路

Cháotiānmén

Datong Jie Xiaoshizi 打铜街

Luohan Si Jie 罗汉寺街

Arhat Temple 罗汉寺

Xinhua Lu 新华路

Minzu Lu 民族路

Cangbai Lu 沧白路

Bayi Lu 八一路

Wuyi Lu 五一路

Jialing Binjiang Lu 嘉陵滨江路

Linjiang Lu 临江路

Jiangjiaxiang 江家巷

Minzu Lu 民族路

Liberation Monument (Jiěfàngbēi) 解放碑

Zhonghua Lu 中华路

Xinhua Lu 新华路

Qingnian Lu 青年路

Damog Lu 大约路

Zhonghua Lu 中华路

CITS

Linjiāngmén 临江门

Zourong Sq 邹容

Jialing River

Dàjùyuàn

Huánghuāyuán Bridge

Běiqū Lu

Beiqu Lu

Hua Yi Lu

Linjiang Lu 临江路

250 m
0.1 miles

bar and restaurant strip on Nan'an Binjiang Lu (p763). The cable car is by Exit 5 of Xiǎoshízì station on Line 1.

FREE **Three Gorges Museum** MUSEUM
(三峡博物馆; Sānxiá Bówùguǎn; Map p762; 236 Renmin Lu; ⊙9am-4pm) This sleek museum showcases the history of settlement in the Chóngqìng region. A 1st-floor exhibition on the Three Gorges includes a model of the dam, and you can learn more about southwest China's minority cultures through their clothing and artwork. Some exhibits have better English captions than others, but the artefacts are well presented throughout. Take metro Line 2 to Zēngjiāyán station, exit A.

🛏 Sleeping

If you fancy splashing the cash, the **Marriott** (www.marriott.com) and **Intercontinental** (www.ichotelsgroup.com/intercontinental) are both located centrally.

TOP CHOICE **Yangtze River Hostel** HOSTEL **$**
(玺院青年旅舍; Xǐyuàn Qīngnián Lǚshè; Map p758; ☎6310 4270; www.chongqinghostels.com; 80 Changbin Lu; 朝天门长滨路80号; dm/s/d from ¥40/90/160; ✱@⚧) Overlooking the Yangzi River and backing onto one of the remaining stretches of Chóngqìng's ancient city wall, this friendly, well-run hostel is a smart choice if you don't mind climbing steps to walk into town. Rooms are bright and clean, and female-only dorms are available. There's a pool table and a restaurant-cafe in the lobby area as well as another lovely cafe upstairs. They provide reliable travel advice without giving it the hard sell, making this a good place to book your Yangzi River cruises.

Urban Trails Youth Hostel HOSTEL **$**
(玺院解放碑青年旅舍; Xǐyuàn Jiěfàngbēi Qīngnián Lǚshè; Map p758; ☎6303 3925; 115 Xinmin Jie; 新民街115号; dm/s/d ¥35/90/140, tw ¥140; ✱@⚧) This ordinary white-tiled budget hotel was recently converted into a youth hostel and taken under the wing of Yangtze River Hostel. It's still very un-hostel-like – no fresh coffee, no Western breakfasts, no travel desk – but the rooms are clean and comfortable, staff members are very friendly and helpful and it's located on an alluring alleyway. Narrow, winding, stone-paved Xinmen Jie is full of old Chóngqìng flavours with remnants of old stones walls and, if you look hard enough, a couple of old stilt houses (see boxed text, p761).

Chóngqìng (Jiěfàngbēi Area)

◎ **Top Sights**

Arhat Temple...............................E3
Dōngshuǐ Mén G4
Húguǎng Guild Hall.....................F4
Tōngyuàn Mèn A5
Traditional Stilt Housing C6
Yangzi River Cable Car.................E4

◎ **Sights**

1 18 Steps Lane Viewing
   Platform C6
2 Cháotiāngōng Cruise Boat G1
3 Cháotiānmén Cruise Boat G1
4 Cháotiānmén Sq G1
5 Jīnbì Huánggōng Cruise Boat G1
6 Mǎn Jiāng Hóng Cruise Boat........G1
7 Traditional Stilt Housing B5

🛏 **Sleeping**

8 Harbour Plaza D5
9 Hóngyádòng Dàjiǔdiàn..............D3
10 Intercontinental D4
11 JW Marriott C5
12 Sunrise Míngqīng Hostel..........F4
13 Urban Trails Youth Hostel A5
14 Xīnhuá Hotel C4
15 Yangtze River Hostel.................G3

✖ **Eating**

16 Evening shāokǎo barbecues F4
17 Evening shāokǎo barbecues B5
18 Evening shāokǎo barbecues D5

19 Late-night shāokǎo barbecues.............C5
20 Liúyīshǒu Huǒguō E3
21 Shùnfēng 123 ....D4
22 Uncle B6
23 Yèfù Huǒguō B4
24 Zhào'èr Huǒguō E5

🍷 **Drinking**

25 Cafe Lavazza............................D4
26 Caffe Molinari...........................D5
27 Cici Park C3
28 Dè Yì Shì Jiè C5

✪ **Entertainment**

29 Chóngqìng Sìchuān Opera
   House A5

🛍 **Shopping**

Hóngyádòng Dàjiǔdiàn ....(see 9)

ℹ **Information**

30 24-hr Pharmacy.........................C5
Harbour Plaza Travel Centre ....(see 8)

ℹ **Transport**

31 Cháotiānmén Bus Stop G1
32 Cháotiānmén Long-distance
   Bus Station.............................G2
33 Chóngqìng Ferry Port ticket
   hall F1
34 Three Gorges Ferry Port F1

Hóngyádòng Dàjiǔdiàn HOTEL $$
(洪崖洞大酒店; Map p758; ☑6399 2888; 56
Cangbai Lu; 沧白路56号; s/d from ¥618/778, with
river view ¥678/878, discounted to s/d ¥368/448,
with river view ¥388/498; ❄@) This huge com-
plex hugging the cliff side overlooking the
Jiālíng River comes with restaurants, bars,
shopping streets, a theatre and this pretty
decent hotel. The whole complex is new, and
the rooms are clean and modern, but it's
been built in the style of Chóngqìng's once
ubiquitous stilt buildings so some find it a lit-
tle twee. The river views are superb, though.

Harbour Plaza HOTEL $$$
(重庆海逸酒店; Chóngqìng Hǎiyì Jiǔdiàn; Map
p758; ☑6370 0888; www.harbour-plaza.com/hpcq;
Wuyi Lu; 五一路; r from ¥1300, discounted to ¥618;
❄@❄) Rooms are spacious and elegant in
this smart, centrally located hotel, and come
with wide-screen TV, fridge, safe and internet

connection (¥80 per day). Otherwise, decent bathrooms come with a very small tub
which doubles as a shower. The travel desk
on the 3rd floor can help with Yangzi River
cruises.

Sunrise Míngqīng Hostel COURTYARD HOTEL $
(尚悦明清客栈; Shàngyuè Míngqīng Kèzhàn;
Map p758; ☑6393 1579; www.srising.com; 23
Xiahong Xuexiang (down steps from 26 Jiefang
Donglu); 下洪学巷23号 (解放东路26中对
面); dm/d from ¥69/239, discounted to ¥49/159;
❄@❄) Facing the western wall of Húguǎng
Guild Hall, this recently renovated Qing dynasty courtyard hotel lacks the atmosphere
of a youth hostel (probably because there's
no restaurant, cafe or bar), but is nonetheless a gorgeous place to stay. Rooms
are beautifully decorated with dark-wood
furniture and have cute bathrooms, and
it's fun getting here, down the steep alley

off Jiefang Donglu. The surrounding area, with its wonderful old-Chóngqìng flavours, has been slated for demolition so the neighbourhood may resemble a building site by the time you get here.

Perfect Time Youth Hostel
HOSTEL **$**

(纯真年代青年旅舍; Chúnzhēn Niándài Qīngnián Lǚshè; ☑6547 7008; www.hostelchongqing.com; 2 Zhong Jie, Cíqikǒu; 磁器口正街2号; dm/s/tw ¥35/80/160; ❋@🛜) If you fancy the charms of Cíqìkǒu rather than the city centre, this friendly hostel has helpful staff and a lovely cafe terrace overlooking the river. At the end of the main tourist strip.

Xīnhuá Hotel
HOTEL **$$**

(新华酒店; Xīnhuá Jiǔdiàn; Map p758; ☑6355 7777; 9 Qingnian Lu; 青年路9号; tw from ¥828, discounted to ¥398; ❋@) Elegant, low-lit interior with spacious, well-equipped rooms (TV, fridge, safe) and good-sized bathrooms with separate shower and tub. A stone's throw from Liberation Monument so about as central as it gets.

✕ Eating

Chóngqìng is all about hotpot (火锅; huǒguō): a fiery cauldron of head-burning làjiāo (辣椒; chillies) and mouth-numbing huājiāo (花椒; Sìchuān peppers) into which is dipped deliciously fresh ingredients, from vegetables and tofu to all types of fish and meat. It's a dish best sampled with a group of friends. Indeed, hotpot restaurants tend to be among the liveliest you'll find. But don't underestimate a hotpot's bite. This part of China is renowned for spicy food, and it doesn't come spicier than hotpot.

How hot you go is up to you – bù là (不辣; not spicy, but in Chóngqìng this will still be spicy), wēi là (微辣; mildly spicy), zhōng là (中辣; medium spicy), zuì là (最辣; very spicy) and jiā má jiā là (加嘛加辣; extra, extra spicy).

Another great thing to sample in Chóngqìng is shāokǎo (烧烤; barbeque skewers), the perfect point-and-eat street food. Just choose your skewers, hand them over and wait for them to come back spiced and grilled. Select from dòufu pí (豆腐皮; tofu skin), xiǎo mántou (小馒头; mini steamed rolls), niángāo (年糕; sticky rice cake), qiézi (茄子; eggplant/aubergine), and jiǔcài (韭菜; leek) among other ingredients.

We've marked some of our favourite shāokǎo barbeque spots on the map, but there are others all over the city. Most shāokǎo places in Chóngqìng also do bowls of pigs brain (脑花; nǎohuā) as a side dish. We dare you.

Noodles are another firm favourite in Chóngqìng. See boxed text, p764.

TOP CHOICE Shùnfēng 123
SICHUANESE **$$**

(顺风123; Shùnfēng Yāo Èr Sān; Map p758; Dàbùhuì Shopping Centre, West Bldg, 3rd fl, Jiěfàngbēi; 大部会西楼商厦三楼; dishes ¥10-50; ⏱10am-9pm) Mouth-wateringly good, high-quality Sichuanese food, and some pan-Asian dishes too, at the Jiěfàngbēi branch of one of Chóngqìng's best-value high-end restaurants. Everything is tasty, but we loved the jiāowáng chánzuǐ tù (椒王馋嘴兔; rabbit and peppers; ¥38) and the shānhú xiā (珊瑚虾; coral shrimp; ¥36). For dessert, don't miss the mìzhì chāshāo sū (秘制叉烧酥; secret recipe meat-filled pastries; ¥3 each). Enter through a lift accessed from Bayi Lu (八一路). Photo menu.

CHÓNGQÌNG'S STILT HOUSING

Once a striking feature of the Chóngqìng skyline, stilt houses (吊脚楼; diàojiǎo lóu) were, in many ways, the predecessor to the modern skyscraper; sprawling vertically rather than horizontally to save space. Their design also served to keep family units in close quarters despite the uneven terrain of hilly Chóngqìng. They were built on a bamboo or fir frame that was fitted into bore holes drilled into the mountainside, and their thin walls were stuffed with straw and coated with mud to allow for cooling ventilation in a city that swelters in summer.

Modernisation has turned stilt housing into a symbol of poverty, and as a result it has all but disappeared in the city centre. A wonderful exception is the tall, rickety-looking wooden building to your left as you stand at the top of the 18 Steps Lane viewing platform (Map p758). You can also see two small stilt houses in Xinmin Jie, not far from Urban Trails Youth Hostel. And many stilt houses still survive in the villages around Chóngqìng municipality, with some fine examples in the alleyways of Sōngji and particularly by the river in Zhōngshān.

Chóngqìng (Càiyuánbà)

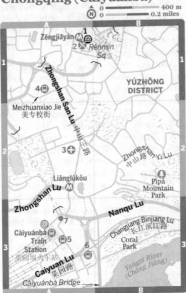

N 0 — 400 m
0 — 0.2 miles

Chóngqìng (Càiyuánbà)

◎ Sights
1 Three Gorges Museum A1

✪ Eating
2 Made in Kitchen A1

ℹ Information
3 Global Doctor Chóngqìng Clinic..........A2

ℹ Transport
4 Airport Shuttle Bus..............................A1
5 Càiyuánbà Bus Station A3
6 Càiyuánbà Old Station A3
7 Escalator entrance A3

Zhào'èr Huǒguō HOTPOT $

(赵二火锅; Map p758; 128 Jiefang Donglu, 3rd fl; 解放东路128号世纪龙门大厦三楼; dipping ingredients ¥4-20; ⊙11.30am-2pm & 5.30-9pm) They say if you only try one hotpot in Chóngqìng it should be Zhào'èr's. It is rightly lauded. There are various pots to choose from: The nine-sectioned pot (九宫锅; jiǔgōng guō) allows you to separate the flavours of your raw ingredients (ideal if one of you is vegetarian), although the broth is shared, while the two-sectioned yuānyang guō (鸳鸯锅), which costs an extra ¥28, has a clear broth that is separated

completely from the spicy one. You may be asked if you want your broth spicy (红的; hóngde) or clear (青的; qīngde) and therefore spiceless. Assuming you opt for spicy, you need to say how spicy; mild (微辣; wēi là), medium (中辣; zhōng là) or very spicy (特辣; tè là). We highly advise you plump for mild! As well as all the usual hotpot raw ingredients (see boxed text opposite), the speciality here is fresh lamb tripe (鲜毛肚; xiān máodǔ). The water spinach (空心菜; kōngxīn cài) is also particularly good. No English sign or menu.

Yèfù Huǒguō HOTPOT $

(夜富火锅; Map p758; Beiqu Lu, 15 Linjiangmen; 临江门15号北区路; ingredients ¥3-15; ⊙9am-4am) Seats are of the plastic stool variety, and if you're fussy about hygiene you might want to consider somewhere else, but if you truly love hotpot, welcome to heaven. This place is widely regarded as the most mouth-numbing hotpot in Chóngqìng. They pile in the chillies, of course, but what they use more of here than anywhere else are Sìchuān peppercorns; expect your head to be buzzing as you leave. Unless you're hardcore, insist on wēi là (微辣; mildly spicy), although even that will be *very* spicy. The delicious xiànzhá sūròu (现炸酥肉; deep-fried pork) is already cooked. Everything else needs to be dunked. From Línjiāngmén metro station (临江门), walk along Beiqu Lu, following the road right, left, and it's on your left up a small flight of stairs (blue sign).

Uncle CANTONESE $

(表叔; Biǎo Shū; Map p758; Riyueguang Zhongxin Sq, 89 Minquan Lu; 民权路89号日月光中心广场; mains ¥20-40; ⊙11am-11pm; 🚇) If your body needs a break from Chóngqìng's fiery chillies, head to this Guǎngzhōu restaurant chain, modelled on a type of Hong Kong teahouse-cum-canteen. It's young, friendly, brightly lit and serves a good variety of tasty Cantonese dishes – lots of soups as well as noodle and rice meals. Portions are hearty, meaning most dishes are meals in themselves. It's at the back of a public square, under the giant TV screen. English menu.

Made in Kitchen CHINESE WESTERN $$$

(厨房制造; Chúfáng Zhìzào; Map p762; ☎6363 6228; Three Gorges Museum, 236 Renmin Lu; 人民路236号三峡博物馆; dishes ¥30-130; ⊙11am-10.30pm; 🚇) Fine dining with tip-top service and a fabulous menu, including excellent steak and a good choice of imported wines (from ¥200). Has a pan-Asian menu as well as a Western-food menu. Located underneath the Three Gorges Museum; the entrance is down to the left as you face the museum entrance. Metro Line 2 to Zēngjiāyán station, Exit A.

Liúyīshǒu Huǒguō
HOTPOT $

(刘一手火锅; Map p758; 46 Cangbai Lu, 3rd fl; 沧白路46号南国丽景大厦3楼; dipping ingredients ¥6-20; ⏰10am-midnight) The hotpot here is decent enough, and the atmosphere is congenial, but the real attraction is the view; dine on Chóngqìng's signature dish as you gaze out across the Jiālíng River. You'll be pushed to find a river-view table at peak eating times, so perhaps come earlier or later than you'd usually eat. Take the lift to the right of Motel 168. No English.

Drinking & Entertainment

As well as the places listed below, there are also cafes and bars at the Hóngyádòng hotel complex (p760), overlooking the Jiālíng River, plus a string of riverside bars (酒吧; *jiǔbā;* Map p757), cafes and restaurants on Nan'an Binjiang Lu (南岸滨江路); take the cable car over the Yangzi, then walk down to the river and turn left. From there, walk 15 minutes along the river or hop on any bus for one stop. The cable car stops running at 10pm.

Dé Yǐ Shì Jiè (得以世界; Map p758) is a public square surrounded by tacky bars, karaoke joints and the city's biggest nightclubs.

For traditional **teahouses**, head to Cíqìkǒu Ancient Town (p757) and look for signs for 茶园 (*cháyuán;* tea garden).

TOP CHOICE Cici Park
BAR

(西西公园; Map p758; Xīxī Gōngyuán; 2 Linjiang Lu; beer from ¥15; ⏰7pm-4am) The most laid-back bar in Chóngqìng, Cici's has chilled-out music and loungey, bohemian furnishings with outdoor seating on the square too. Beers are affordable, mixers start at ¥25 and there's local plum wine (梅子酒; *méizi jiǔ;* ¥10) that comes in a cute bottle with a thimble cup. It's on a big open square on the roof of a small shopping complex whose frontage has been made to look like the long-disappeared decorative archway, Línjiāng Pái (临江牌).

Nuts
LIVE MUSIC

(坚果; Jiānguǒ Jùlèbù; off Map p757; www.douban.com/host/nutsclub, in Chinese; Shazhong Lu, Shāpíngbà district; 沙坪坝区沙中路; beer from ¥5; ⏰8pm-2am) This pint-sized club is the best place to see local bands playing live. It's right by Chóngqìng University so gets a decent crowd in. Live music tends to be weekends only, from 8pm to 10pm, and usually carries a ¥30 cover charge. At other times there are DJs. You can walk here from Shāpíngbà metro station; straight along Hanyu Lu (汉榆路) then left down Shazhong Lu (沙中路); 20 minutes.

Caffe Molinari
CAFE

(魔力咖啡; Mólì Kāfēi; Map p758; cnr Food St & Zourong Lu; 邹容路好吃街; espresso ¥18, ice cream ¥16; ⏰9.30am-11.30pm) A tree-shaded street-side terrace cafe adding a touch of Italian gelaterie to the centre of Chóngqìng's modern shopping district. **Cafe Lavazza** (Map p758), on the other side of Zourong Lu, does similar fare for similar prices.

Chóngqìng Sìchuān Opera House
THEATRE

(重庆市川剧院; Chóngqìngshì Chuānjùyuàn; Map p758; ☑6371 0153; 76 Jintang Jie; 金汤街)

HOTPOT MENU

The best hotpot restaurants are entirely local affairs so you have about as much chance of finding an English menu as you have of being able to eat the thing without your nose running. As with many dishes in Chóngqìng, the first thing to establish when ordering hotpot is how hot you want it (see p761). Then you'll be given a menu checklist of raw ingredients that you will later cook in your pot. Here are some of our favourites for you to look out for on the menu:

» *yángròu juǎn* (羊肉卷; wafer-thin lamb slices)

» *féi niúròu* (肥牛肉; beef slices)

» *xiān máodǔ* (鲜毛肚; fresh tripe, usually lamb)

» *xiān yācháng* (鲜鸭肠; strips of duck intestine)

» *lǎo dòufu* (老豆腐; tofu slabs)

» *ǒu piàn* (藕片; slices of lotus root)

» *xiān huánghuā* (鲜黄花; chrysanthemum stalks)

» *tǔ dòu* (土豆; potato slices)

» *bǎi cài* (百菜; cabbage leaves)

» *mù'ěr* (木耳; mushroom)

» *kōngxīn cài;* (空心菜; water spinach)

CHÓNGQÌNG CHÓNGQÌNG CITY

CHÓNGQÌNG NOODLES

Chongqingers are particular fond of noodles and you'll find noodle joints all over the region. They rarely have English menus or signs – just look for the character 面 (*miàn*; noodles) and you're good to go.

Specialities here include *xiǎomiàn* (小面) – or *málà xiǎomiàn* (麻辣小面) – which is common for breakfast despite being very spicy, and *liángmiàn* (凉面) which are delicious despite being served cold. Noodles in Chóngqìng are served by the *liǎng* (两; 50g). Two-*liǎng* (二两; *èr liǎng*) or three-*liǎng* (三两; *sān liǎng*) portions are most common. Expect to pay between ¥5 and ¥10 for a bowl. Remember; *wǒ néng chī làde* (I like my food spicy); *bù yào tài là* (not too spicy, please).

Noodles Menu

麻辣小面; *málà xiǎomiàn;* spicy noodles

凉面; *liángmiàn;* cold noodles

牛肉面; *niúròu miàn;* beef noodles

鸡蛋面; *jīdàn miàn;* egg noodles

酸辣粉; *suānlà fěn;* tangy glass noodles

肥肠面; *féicháng miàn;* pig intestine noodles

76号; tickets ¥15-20; ⊘2pm) Holds a 2½-hour performance of Sìchuān opera every Saturday afternoon.

Shopping

For top-name brands, head to the glitzy shopping malls around the Liberation Monument (解放碑; Jiěfàngbēi; Map p758). For souvenirs, try the unashamedly touristy 3rd floor of **Hóngyádòng** (56 Cangbai Lu; 沧白路56号), below the hotel of the same name, or head to Cíqìkǒu Ancient Town (p757).

Information

Internet Access

There are internet cafes all over the city, including three or four by Càiyuánbà Train Station. Look for the characters 网吧 (*wǎngbā*).

Huīhuī Wǎngbā (辉辉网吧; Map p758; 1st fl, 20-40 Zhonghua Xiang; 中华巷20-40号1层; per hr ¥3; ⊘24hr)

Medical Services

24-hour pharmacy (药店; Yàodiàn; Map p758; 63 Minquan Lu; 民权路63号; ⊘24hr) Western medicine, ground floor; Chinese medicine, 1st floor.

Global Doctor Chóngqìng Clinic (环球医生重庆诊所; Huánqiú Yīshēng Chóngqìng Zhěnsuǒ; Map p762; ☑8903 8837; Suite 701, 7th fl, Office Tower, Hilton Hotel, 139 Zhongshan Sanlu; 中山三路139号希尔顿酒店商务楼7层701室; ⊘9am-5pm Mon-Fri) A 24-hour emergency service is available by dialling the general clinic number.

Money

ATMs are everywhere, and most accept foreign cards. We've marked a couple on our map.

HSBC (汇丰银行; Huìfēng Yínháng; Map p758; Minquan Lu; 民权路; ⊘9am-5pm Mon-Fri) Only small, but has money-exchange facility.

ICBC (Industrial & Commercial Bank of China; 工商银行; Gōngshāng Yínháng; Map p758; 解放碑民族路; ⊘9am-6pm) On Minzu Lu beside the Liberation Monument. Has a dedicated money-exchange facility.

Post & Telephone

China Post (中国邮政; Zhōngguó Yóuzhèng; Minquan Lu; 民权路; Map p758; ⊘9am-7pm) You can top up your Chinese phone and buy SIM cards at the China Mobile store (open 9am to 9pm) on the 1st floor.

Public Security Bureau

PSB (公安局; Gōng'ānjú; off Map p757; ☑6396 1994; 555 Huanglong Lu; 黄龙路555号; ⊘9am-noon & 1-5pm) Extends visas. Accessed from Ziwei Zhilu (紫薇支路). Take metro Line 3 to Tángjiā Yuànzi (唐家院子). Leave from exit 2, go up the escalator, turn left then first right, then keep going until you see the large building with flags on your right (10 minutes).

Travel Agencies

Yangtze River Hostel (p759) can arrange tours of all types (including Three Gorges cruises) and has better English-language speakers than the travel agencies and ticket offices around town. They charge minimal commission.

Harbour Plaza Travel Centre (海逸旅游中心; Hǎiyì Lǚyóu Zhōngxīn; Map p758; ☑6373 5664; 3rd fl, Harbour Plaza, Wuyi Lu; ⊘8am-10pm) Staff here are helpful, speak OK English and can book air tickets and arrange Three Gorges cruises.

Getting There & Away

Air

Chóngqìng's Jiāngběi Airport (重庆江北飞机场) is 25km north of the city centre, and connected to the metro system. As always, it's easiest to book online. Try www.ctrip.com or www.

elong.net. Alternatively, buy tickets at the **China International Travel Service** (CITS; 中国国际旅行社; Zhōngguó Guójì Lǚxíngshè; Map p758; ☎6383 9777; 8th fl, 151 Zourong Lu; 邹容路151号; ⊙9.30am-5.30pm Mon-Fri). Some English is spoken. Because of the high-speed rail link, there are no longer flights between Chóngqìng and Chéngdū. Direct flights include:

Běijīng ¥1120, 2½ hours
Kúnmíng ¥550, 70 minutes
Shànghǎi ¥920, 2½ hours
Xī'ān ¥470, 90 minutes
Wǔhàn ¥500, 90 minutes

Boat

Chóngqìng is the starting point for hugely popular cruises down the Yangzi River through the magnificent Three Gorges. For all the details, see p770.

Bus

Chóngqìng has several long-distance bus stations, but most buses use Càiyuánbà bus station (菜园坝汽车站; Càiyuánbà qìchēzhàn; Map p762) beside the main (old) train station. Destinations include:

Chéngdū 成都 (in Sìchuān) ¥104 to ¥114, four hours, every hour (8am to 6.50pm)
Chìshuǐ 赤水 (in Guìzhōu) ¥66 to ¥72, 4½ hours, four daily (8.40am, 12.30pm, 3.20pm and 6.30pm)
Dàzú 大足 ¥55, 2½ hours, every hour (7am to 9pm)
Héchuān 合川 ¥30, 90 minutes, every 30 minutes (6.30am to 8.30pm)
Jiāngjīn 江津 ¥25, 70 minutes, every 30 minutes (6.40am to 8pm); leaves from Càiyuánbà Old Station (Map p762)
Sōngji 松溉 ¥43, two hours, one daily (1.20pm)
Wànzhōu 万州 ¥114, 3½ hours, hourly (8am to 6.15pm)
Yíbīn 宜宾 (in Sìchuān) ¥90 to ¥99, three to four hours, hourly (6.35am to 8.30pm)
Yǒngchuān 永川 ¥36, 90 minutes, every 20 minutes (6.30am to 9.20pm)

Buses for Fèngjié (¥163, five hours, four daily, 8.30am, 11.30am, 3.30pm and 7pm) from where you can catch the Three Gorges hydrofoil or ferry, leave from Lóngtóusì bus station (龙头寺汽车站; Lóngtóusì qìchēzhàn), which is on metro Line 3 (station name: 龙头寺; Lóngtóusì).

Train

New, faster trains, including the D class 'bullet' train to and from Chéngdū, use Chóngqìng's new North Station (重庆北站; Chóngqìng Běizhàn; off Map p757), but some others, such as the train to Kūnmíng use the older train station at Càiyuánbà (菜园坝; Map p762).

Destinations include:

Běijīng West 北京西 hard sleeper ¥391, 23 to 31 hours, five daily (9.45am, 11.21am, 1.41pm, 8.32pm and 11.50pm)
Chéngdū East 成都东 hard seat ¥98, two to 2½ hours, 12 daily (8am to 9.27pm)
Guìlín 桂林 hard sleeper ¥164, 20 hours, one daily (8.43pm)
Kūnmíng 昆明 hard sleeper ¥246, 19 hours, two daily (9.10am and 2.11pm)
Lhasa 拉萨 hard sleeper ¥712, 45 hours, every other day (8.11pm)
Shànghǎi 上海 hard sleeper ¥428, 28 hours, two daily (7.46am and 3.19pm)
Xī'ān 西安 hard sleeper ¥179, 10 to 11 hours, five daily (9.16am, 11.02am, 11.48am, 5.35pm and 8.11pm)

CITY RIVER CRUISES

Chóngqìng looks best from the water, especially at night when the city flashes with neon. The so-called **Two-river Cruises** (两江游船; *liǎngjiāng yóuchuán*) last for around two hours and leave every afternoon (2pm to 3pm) and evening (7pm to 8pm) from Cháotiānmén Dock (Map p758), and can be a fun way of getting an alternative view of this unique metropolis. There are a number of boats offering the same service. The difference in prices reflects the quality and age of the boats. The four boats listed below were the most popular at the time of research. Although there are cruises every day, not all the boats run every day. The boats have no English signs and very little English is spoken on board. You can eat on board, although menus are in Chinese only, and the food is pretty expensive (dishes ¥30 to ¥80). Prices listed below are for evening cruises, which are much more popular (and more worthwhile). Expect to get tickets for as little as ¥25 or ¥35 for an afternoon cruise. Buy your tickets from the end of the jetty leading to the boat in question.

Cruise Boats

Cháotiāngōng 朝天宫 (¥128), **Cháotiānmén** 朝天门 (¥148), **Jīnbì Huánggōng** 金碧皇宫 (¥138), **Mǎn Jiāng Hóng** 满江红 (¥88)

ℹ Getting Around

Airport

Metro Line 3 goes from the airport (机场; *jīchǎng*) into town (¥6, 45 minutes, 6.22am to 10.30pm). Note, the metro is signposted as 'Light Rail' (轻轨; *qīngguǐ*) at the airport.

The **airport shuttle bus** (机场大巴; jīchǎng dàbā; ¥15, 45 minutes) meets all arriving planes and takes you to Meizhuanxiao Jie (美专校街), a small road off Zhongshan Sanlu (中山三路), via a couple of stops in the north of the city. Bus 461 goes from Zhongshan Sanlu to Cháotiānmén (朝天门). To get to the metro, turn left onto Zhongshan Sanlu and go straight over the large roundabout. Niújiǎotuó (牛角沱) station will be on your left.

Shuttle buses going to the airport run from 6am to 8pm.

A taxi is around ¥50.

Bus

Local bus fares are ¥1 or ¥2. Useful routes:

Bus 105 North Train Station–Línjiāngmén (near Liberation Monument)

Bus 120 Cháotiānmén–Càiyuánbà Train Station

Bus 141 North Train Station–Cháotiānmén

Bus 419 North Train Station–Càiyuánbà Train Station

Bus 461 Cháotiānmén–Zhongshan Sanlu (for airport bus)

Bus 462 Zhongshan Sanlu (airport bus)–Liberation Monument

Metro

Chóngqìng's part-underground, part-sky train **metro system** (轨道; guǐdào; per trip ¥2-6, roughly 6.30am-10.30pm) links the Jiěfàngbēi peninsula with parts of the city, including the airport and the two train stations. Signs are bilingual but, unhelpfully, the metro map is in Chinese characters only.

The metro station for Càiyuánbà Train Station is called Liǎnglùkǒu (两路口) and is accessed via one of the world's longest escalators (大扶梯; *dà fútī*; ¥2).

Taxi

Fares start at ¥5. A taxi from Jiěfàngbēi to Nuts nightclub should cost around ¥35. It's around ¥50 to the airport.

Dàzú Buddhist Caves   大足石窟

The fabulous rock carvings of Dàzú (Dàzú Shíkū) are a Unesco World Heritage site and one of China's four great Buddhist cave sculpture sites, along with those at Dūnhuáng, Luòyáng and Dàtóng. The Dàzú sculptures are the most recent of the four, but the artwork here is arguably the best.

Scattered over roughly 40 sites are thousands of cliff carvings and statues (with Buddhist, Taoist and Confucian influences), dating from the Tang dynasty (9th century) to the Song dynasty (13th century). The main groupings are at Treasured Summit Hill and North Hill.

◉ Sights

Treasured Summit Hill   ROCK CARVINGS
(宝顶山; Bǎodǐng Shān; admission ¥135, combination ticket with North Hill ¥170; ◉8.30am-6pm) Of all the stunning sculptures at this site, the centrepiece is a 31m-long, 5m-high reclining Buddha depicted entering nirvana, with the torso sunk into the cliff face. Next to the Buddha, with a temple built around her for protection, is a mesmerising gold Avalokiteshvara (or Guanyin, the Goddess of Mercy), which was undergoing extensive renovation at the time of research. Her 1007 individual arms fan out around her, entwined and reaching for the skies. Each hand has an eye, the symbol of wisdom. It is believed these sculptures were completed over roughly 70 years, between 1174 and 1252.

Treasured Summit Hill differs from other cave sites in that it incorporates some of the area's natural features – a sculpture next to the reclining Buddha, for example, makes use of an underground spring.

The site is about 15km northeast of Dàzú town and is accessed on shuttle buses (¥3, 20 minutes, until 7pm) that leave from Dōngguānzhàn bus stop. Dàzú has two bus stations; old and new. Buses from Chóngqìng drop you at Dàzú's old bus station (老站; *lǎozhàn*). Buses from Chéngdū drop you at Dàzú's new bus station (新站; *xīnzhàn*). From either, take bus 101 (¥1) or a ¥10 cycle rickshaw ride to get to Dōngguānzhàn bus stop.

Once at the site, it's a 10-minute walk from where the bus drops you off, past numerous restaurants, guesthouses and souvenir stalls, to the entrance to the sculptures. Buses returning from Treasured Summit Hill run until 6pm.

North Hill   ROCK CARVINGS
(北山; Běi Shān; admission ¥90, combination ticket with Treasured Hill Summit ¥170; ◉8.30am-6pm) This site, originally a military camp, contains some of the region's earliest carvings. The dark niches hold several hundred stat-

THE TOUGHEST PORTERS IN CHINA

Ever since the first Chóngqìng-ers couldn't bear the thought of carrying their buckets of water from the river up to their cliff-side homes, there's been a need for a special kind of porter. A porter who can lift more than his bodyweight and lug that load up and down hills all day long. A porter who can't use a trolley like in other cities, or a bike or a rickshaw, but instead works on foot using only the cheapest of tools: a bamboo pole, or 'bangbang', and a length of rope.

Known as the Bangbang Army, these porters have been bearing the city's weights on their shoulders for hundreds of years, but their numbers really exploded in the 1990s when the government began resettling millions who lived along the Yangzi River. Many came from the countryside with little education and no relevant skills, and soon became part of the 100,000-strong workforce. Unregulated and poor, 'bangbang' porters earn around ¥30 per day to work in one of China's hottest, hilliest cities, lugging heavy loads up and down steep hills. When you consider some of the wealth that's been pumped into the city in recent years (just look across the river at the Grand Theatre), it's perhaps surprising that this age-old trade still thrives. But for now, at least, the Bangbang Army continues to be an integral feature of the alleyway-riddled areas that link this fast modernising city to its old docks.

ues. The collection is smaller than at Treasured Summit Hill and some are in poor condition, but it is still well worth a visit.

The pleasant, forested North Hill is about a 30-minute hike – including many steps – from Dàzú town; turn left out of the old bus station and keep asking the way. It's ¥15 in a taxi.

South Hill ROCK CARVINGS
(南山; Nán Shān; admission ¥5; ☺8.30am-6pm) This modest site really only has one set of carvings, but makes a nice appetiser before you delve into the main courses at North Hill and Treasured Summit Hill. It's behind the old bus station and takes around 15 minutes to walk to. It's ¥10 in a taxi.

Other Sights ROCK CARVINGS
Those with a particular interest in Buddhist rock carvings might like to try to get out to the almost never visited carvings at **Stone Gate Hill** (石门山; Shímén Shān), 19km southeast of Dàzú, or those at **Stone Seal Hill** (石篆山; Shízhuàn Shān), 20km southwest of town. You'll have to take a taxi. The truly adventurous might like to catch a bus to the tiny town of Shíyáng (石羊), just over the border in Sìchuān province, which has a rarely visited collection of Song dynasty Buddhist rock carvings and is about as untouristy as it gets. Buses to Shíyáng leave from Dàzú's old bus station. When you get there, keep asking for **Pílú Dòng** (毗卢洞; Buddha Vaironcana Cave); it's walking distance. From Shíyáng, you can continue by bus to Chéngdū.

🛏 Sleeping

The hotel attached to Jīnfúyuán Restaurant (金福源酒店; Jīnfúyuán Jiǔdiàn; ☑4372 4666; r ¥80-100) is about 50m from Dàzú's old station (turn left) and makes a handy base for your sculpture-seeking adventures.

ℹ Getting There & Away

Buses from Dàzú old station:

Chóngqìng ¥55, 2½ hours, every 30 minutes (6.30am to 6pm)

Shíyáng ¥10, one hour, every 40 minutes (7.20am to 5.40pm)

Yǒngchuān (for Sōngjī) ¥22, 90 minutes, every 45 minutes (7.10am to 5.40pm)

Buses from Dàzú new station:

Chéngdū ¥94 to ¥106, four hours, four daily (7.15am, 8.55am, 9.50am and 2pm)

Héchuān (for Láitān) ¥20 to ¥25, 2½ hours, four daily (7.50am, 11.20am, 2pm and 5.10pm)

Lèshān ¥106, 4½ hours, one daily (7.20am)

Zìgòng ¥54, 3½ hours, two daily (8am and 1.30pm)

Zhōngshān 中山

Chóngqìng's once-ubiquitous stilt-style homes are an endangered species these days, but visit this gorgeous riverside village and you'll find plenty of them to gawp at. The old town (古镇; gǔzhèn) is essentially one long street lined with wooden homes on stilts above the riverbank. Walk down to the river and look up at the houses to see their support structures. You can also hike along the other side of the river.

FISHING TOWN FORTRESS

Famed throughout China for being one of the great ancient battlefields, the 700-year-old **Fishing Town Fortress** (钓鱼城; Diàoyú Chéng; admission ¥60) is surrounded by rushing rivers on three sides and perched on top of a 300m-tall rocky mountain. This was the last stand of the Southern Song dynasty and famously, in the 13th century, the fortress withstood the mighty Mongol armies for an incredible 36 years, during which time an estimated 200 battles were fought here. Mongol leader Mongke Khan was killed in one of them, forcing the Mongol armies to retreat and, ultimately, preventing them from continuing their planned conquest towards Africa.

The fortress was protected by an 8km-long, 30m-tall double wall, punctuated with eight gate towers. Much of the outer wall and all the main gates remain today; some partly restored, others crumbling away. There is little here in terms of facilities (bring a picnic) but it's a fascinating and peaceful place to walk around; narrow stone pathways lead you through the forest, past Buddhist rock carvings, gravestones, bamboo groves, ponds, caves, the wall and its gateways and some fabulous lookout points. There's a map on the back of your ticket, but sights not to miss include the serene 11m-long, 1000-year-old **Sleeping Buddha** (卧佛; Wòfó), cut into the overhang of a cliff, **Hùguó Temple** (护国寺; Hùguó Sì), dating from the Tang dynasty, although largely rebuilt, and the **Imperial Cave** (黄洞; Huángdòng), an ancient drainage passage with steps leading down to it, clinging to the outside of the fort wall.

To reach the fortress, take a bus from Chóngqìng to Héchuān, then take local bus 111 (walk out of Héchuān bus station, cross the road and turn left) to Diàoyúchéng (¥2.50, 40 minutes), which is the last stop. You may be herded onto another bus 111 as you leave the outskirts of town. The last bus back to Chóngqìng from Héchuān is at 6pm.

Many residents of these old houses have turned their front rooms into storefronts. While some hawk souvenir trinkets, others sell locally made products such as chilli sauce or jugs of rice wine. Popular snacks include squares of smoked tofu (烟熏豆腐; *yānxūn dòufu*; ¥1), and sweet doughy rice cakes filled with ground nuts.

Above the river are several restaurants (dishes ¥10 to ¥60) and teahouses. There's even a small bar (at No 63). And there are at least half a dozen guesthouses (rooms ¥30 to ¥80); look for signs saying 住宿 (*zhùsù*; lodgings). Most are small, but clean and have a shared shower room. Some rooms have cracking river views. If you're stuck for choice, try the guesthouse run by Mrs Zhao – **Zhào Shìkè** (赵世客; ☎138 8320 9407; r ¥30-60). She doesn't speak English but is welcoming. A couple of doors down **Yì Xiān Lóu** (逸仙楼; dishes ¥5-50) does decent food (no English menu). Look for *gǔzhèn lǎolàròu* (古镇老腊肉; cured pork fried with green chillies; ¥30), *héshuǐ dòufu* (河水豆腐; river water tofu; ¥5) and *yě cài* (野菜; a type of spinach grown in the hills here; literally 'wild veg'; ¥10).

To get here from Chóngqìng, change buses at Jiāngjīn (江津), from where buses leave for Zhōngshān (¥12, two hours, roughly every 30 minutes from 5.30am to 4.45pm). The last bus back to Jiāngjīn is at 4.20pm. The last bus from Jiāngjīn back to Chóngqìng is at 7pm. You can also head south into Guìzhōu province from Jiāngjīn, via Zūnyì (遵义; ¥110, 3½ hours, 8.35am and 2.35pm), or north to the caves at Dàzú (大足; ¥53, two hours, 11.30am and 2.10pm).

Láitán   涞滩

The main attraction in this ancient walled village overlooking the Qú River is a towering **Buddha** (二佛寺; Èrfó Sì; admission ¥20) carved into a hillside and surrounded by more than 1000 mini-statues. The Buddha dates to the 12th or 13th century. At roughly 14m tall, it pales in comparison to the giant Buddha at Lèshān, but it's still quite impressive – and far less visited.

A short walk from the Buddha is the village **temple** (admission ¥5), which is still in use.

Allow time to wander around the village, which is more than 1000 years old, checking out the small shops and eateries. Láitán *mǐjiǔ* (米酒; rice wine) is a local speciality.

Although it is possible to visit Láitán in a day trip from Chóngqìng, some people might like to stay the night within the village walls at the neat and tidy **Huílóng Kèzhàn** (回笼客栈; ☏023-4256 1999; r ¥128). There's nothing special about the guesthouse itself (although it's clean and well looked after), but staying here gives you the chance to experience the nontouristy side of this ancient village, once all the day-trippers have left.

From Chóngqìng, change buses at Héchuān. You'll be dropped at the town centre bus station, called *kèyùn zǒngzhàn* (客运总站). Turn right out of this station and take local bus 202 (¥1) to the larger bus station on the edge of town, called *kèyùn zhōngxīn zhàn* (客运中心站); it's the last stop. From there, there are three direct buses to Láitān (¥10, 50 minutes, 10.10am, 1.35pm and 4.10pm) as well as regular buses to Lóngshì (¥9.50, 45 minutes). From Lóngshì, minibuses (¥2, five minutes) leave for Láitān from outside the bus station.

The last buses back to Chóngqìng from Héchuān are 6pm (from *kèyùn zǒngzhàn*) and 6.30pm (from *kèyùn zhōngxīn zhàn*).

Sōngjì 松溉

Cobblestone alleyways housing temples, teahouses, old gateways and some wonderful courtyard homes are perfect for aimless strolls in this still-lived-in Ming dynasty village on the banks of the Yangzi River.

If you're looking for a focus, seek out the **Chén Family Compound** (陈家大院; Chén Jiā Dàyuàn; admission ¥2), the historic home of the village's most prominent family. This sprawling structure once contained more than 100 rooms. What remains of the compound is much smaller, but its walls are extensively decorated with family photos and memorabilia. Actor Joan Chen (Bernardo Bertolucci's *The Last Emperor* and Ang Lee's *Lust, Caution*) is the family member best known outside China.

On a bluff above the river, about a 20-minute walk from the old town, is the **Dōngyù Temple** (东狱庙; Dōngyù Miào), home to a 9.5m-tall Buddha and some gruesome dioramas depicting various hells (impaling, scalding, having your tongue ripped out).

Sōngshān Bīnguǎn (松山宾馆; ☏023-4954 6078; r from ¥80; ❄) has smart clean doubles, some with river views. Nearby **Gǔzhèn Jiǔdàwǎn** (古镇九大碗; dishes ¥15-30; ⏰9am-8pm) is a nicely renovated old courtyard that has been turned into a restaurant-cum-teahouse. There's a selection of Chinese teas here plus a well-priced menu of mostly Sichuanese dishes. To guide yourself around the lanes, take a photo of the large wooden bilingual map at the entrance to the old town (古镇; *gǔzhèn*), just down towards the river from where the bus drops you.

There's one direct bus from Chóngqìng (¥43, two hours, 1.20pm). Otherwise, catch a bus to Yǒngchuān, from where minibuses to Sōngjì (¥9, 70 minutes) leave every 20 minutes. The last bus back to Yǒngchuān leaves Sōngjì at about 5.30pm. The last bus from Yǒngchuān to Chóngqìng leaves at 6.50pm.

Cruising the Yangzi

Includes »

The Three Gorges 770

Chóngqìng to
Wànzhōu 771

Wànzhōu to Yíchāng 772

Luxury Cruises 773

Tourist Boats 774

Passenger Ships 774

Hydrofoil 774

Why Go?

Travel in China is often a terrestrial and sedentary experience, with agonising bus rides, colossal freeways, traffic jams, dusty mountain roads, marathon train journeys and daily victories hard won over stupefying distances. So the Yangzi Cruise – on China's longest and most scenically impressive river – enjoys special significance as a trip where the destination is irrelevant compared to the greater drama of the journey. It's an occasion to put the travel schedule on ice, hang up one's hat and admire an astonishing panorama sliding past.

When to Go

December–March The low season; rates are cheaper and the journey is more serene.

April & May The best weather, but the highest prices and rowdiest crowds.

October & November Cooler climes but the crowds are back.

The Three Gorges

Few river panoramas have inspired as much awe as the Three Gorges (三峡; Sānxiá). Well-travelled Tang dynasty poets and men of letters have gone weak-kneed before them. Voluble emperors and hard-boiled communist party VIPs have been rendered speechless. Flotillas of sightseers have mega-pixelled their way from Chóngqìng to Yíchāng. For as long as many Yangzi boat hands can remember, the Three Gorges have been a member of the prestigious China Tour triumvirate, rubbing shoulders with the Terracotta Warriors and the Great Wall.

Yet the gorges these days get mixed press. Some travellers have their socks well and truly blown away; others arrive in Yíchāng scratching their heads and wondering what all the fuss was about. The route's natural scenery is certainly far more dramatic than its historical sights, often crammed with historical allusions obscure to all but

FAST FACTS

» The Three Gorges Dam is the world's largest artificial generator of electric power from a renewable source.

» The Three Gorges Dam is designed to withstand an earthquake of 7 on the Richter scale.

» Plans for the Three Gorges Dam date from 1919, when Sun Yatsen (Sun Zhongshan) saw its huge potential for power generation.

» The Yangzi River will deposit more than 500 million tonnes of silt every year into the reservoir behind the dam.

» The Yangzi River has caused hundreds of catastrophic floods, including the disastrous inundation of 1931, in which an estimated 145,000 people died.

Chinese minds; temples and so forth along the way can be crowded, while uniform riverine towns and settlements are modern-looking rather than twee and charming. To some, the gorges' dramatic appearance can become rather repetitive, especially overlong Xīlíng Gorge (Xīlíng Xiá). The reservoir built up behind the Three Gorges Dam – a body of water almost the length of England – has certainly taken its toll as much more is now inundated.

But if you don't expect to swoon at every bend in the river, journeying downriver is a stimulating and relaxing adventure, not least because of the change of pace and perspective.

The River

The journey puts you adrift on China's mightiest – and the world's third-longest – river, the gushing 6300km Yangzi River (长江; Cháng Jiāng). Starting life as trickles of snow melt in the Tănggŭlā Shān of southwestern Qīnghǎi, the river then spills from Tibet, swells through seven Chinese provinces, sucks in water from hundreds of tributaries and powerfully rolls into the Pacific Ocean north of Shànghǎi.

The Effects of the Three Gorges Dam

The dwarfing chasms of rock, sculpted over aeons by the irresistible volume of water, are the Yangzi River's most fabled stretch. Yet the construction of the controversial and record-breaking Three Gorges Dam (三峡大坝; Sānxiá Dàbà) cloaked the gorges in as much uncertainty as their famous mists: have the gorges been humbled or can they somehow shrug off the rising waters?

In brief, the gorges have been undoubtedly affected by the rising waters. The peaks are not as towering as they once were, nor are the flooded chasms through which boats travel as narrow and pinched. The effect is more evident to seasoned boat hands or repeat visitors. For first-timers the gorges still put together a dramatic show.

THE ROUTE

Apocryphally the handiwork of the Great Yu, a legendary architect of the river, the gorges – Qútáng, Wū and Xīlíng – commence just east of Fèngjié in Chóngqìng province and level out west of Yíchāng in Húběi province, a distance of around 200km. The principal route for those cruising the Yangzi River is therefore between the cities of Chóngqìng and Yíchāng.

The route can be travelled in either direction, but most passengers journey downstream from Chóngqìng.

If you buy your ticket from an agency, ensure you're not charged upfront for the sights along the way, as you may not want to visit them all and some of the entrance fees are as steep as the surrounding inclines. The only ticket really worth buying in advance is for the popular Little Three Gorges tour, which is often full (see p772).

Chóngqìng to Wànzhōu 重庆–万州

The initial stretch is slow-going and unremarkable, although the dismal view of factories gradually gives way to attractive terraced countryside and the occasional small town.

Yangzi River (Cháng Jiāng)

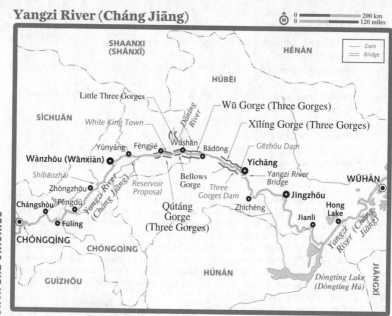

Passing the drowned town of Fúlíng (涪陵), the first port of call is at **Fēngdū** (丰都), 170km from Chóngqìng city. Long nicknamed the City of Ghosts (鬼城; Guǐchéng), the town is just that: inundated in 2009, its residents were moved across the river. This is the stepping-off point for crowds to clamber up **Míng Shān** (名山; admission ¥60; cable car ¥20), with its theme-park crop of ghost-focused temples.

Drifting through the county of Zhōngzhōu, the boat takes around three hours to arrive at **Shíbǎozhài** (石宝寨; Stone Treasure Stockade; admission ¥80; ⊙8am-4pm) on the northern bank of the river. A 12-storey, 56m-high wooden pagoda built on a huge, river-water-encircled rock bluff, the structure dates to the reign of Qing dynasty emperor Kangxi (1662–1722). Your boat may stop for rapid expeditions up to the tower and for climbs into its interior.

Most morning boats moor for the night at partially inundated **Wànzhōu** (万州; also called **Wànxiàn**). Travellers aiming to get from A to B as fast as possible while taking in the gorges can skip the Chóngqìng to Wànzhōu section by hopping on a three-hour bus and then taking either the hydrofoil or a passenger ship from the Wànzhōu jetty.

Wànzhōu to Yíchāng 万州–宜昌

Boats departing from Wànzhōu soon pass the relocated **Zhāng Fēi Temple** (张飞庙; Zhāngfēi Miào; admission ¥20), where short disembarkations may be made. **Yúnyáng** (云阳), a modern town strung out along the northern bank of the river, is typical of many utilitarian settlements. Boats drift on past ragged islets, some carpeted with small patchworks of fields, and alongside riverbanks striated with terraced slopes, rising like green ribbons up the inclines.

The ancient town of **Fèngjié** (奉节), capital of the state of Kui during the periods known as the 'Spring and Autumn' (722–481 BC) and 'Warring States' (475–221 BC), overlooks Qútáng Gorge, the first of the three gorges. The town – where most ships and hydrofoils berth – is also the entrance point to half-submerged **White King Town** (白帝城; Báidìchéng; admission ¥50), where the King of Shu, Liu Bei, entrusted his son and kingdom to Zhu Geliang, as chronicled in *The Romance of the Three Kingdoms*.

Qútáng Gorge (瞿塘峡; Qútáng Xiá), also known as Kui Gorge (夔峡; Kuí Xiá), rises dramatically into view, towering into huge vertiginous slabs of rock, its cliffs jutting out in jagged and triangular chunks. The shortest and narrowest of the three gorges, 8km-long Qútáng Gorge is over almost as abruptly as it starts, but is considered by many to be the most awe-inspiring. The gorge offers a dizzying perspective onto huge strata despite having some of its power robbed by the rising waters. On the northern bank is **Bellows Gorge** (风箱峡; Fēngxiāng Xiá), where nine coffins were discovered, possibly placed here by an ancient tribe.

After Qútáng Gorge the terrain folds into a 20km stretch of low-lying land before boats pull in at the riverside town of **Wūshān** (巫山), situated high above the river. Many boats stop at Wūshān for five to six hours so passengers can transfer to smaller tour boats for trips along the **Little Three Gorges** (小三峡; Xiǎo Sānxiá; tickets ¥150-200) on the **Dàníng River** (大宁河; Dàníng Hé). The landscape is gorgeous, and some travellers insist that the narrow gorges are more impressive than their larger namesakes.

Back on the Yangzi River, boats pull away from Wūshān to enter the penultimate **Wū Gorge**, under a bright-red bridge. Some of the cultivated fields on the slopes overhanging the river reach almost illogical angles.

Wū Gorge (巫峡; Wū Xiá) – the Gorge of Witches – is stunning, cloaked in green and carpeted in shrubs, its sides frequently disappearing into ethereal layers of mist. About 40km in length, its towering cliffs are topped by sharp, jagged peaks on the northern bank. A total of 12 peaks cluster on either side, including **Goddess Peak** (神女峰; Shénnǚ Fēng) and **Peak of the Immortals** (集仙峰; Jíxiān Fēng). If you're fortunate, you'll catch the sunrise over Goddess Peak.

Boats continue floating eastward out of Wū Gorge and into Húběi province, past the mouth of **Shénnóng Stream** (神农溪; Shénnóng Xī) and the town of **Bādōng** (巴东) on the southern bank, along a 45km section before reaching the last of the three gorges.

At 80km, **Xīlíng Gorge** (西陵峡; Xīlíng Xiá) is the longest and perhaps least impressive gorge; sections of the gorge in the west have been submerged. Note the slow-moving cargo vessels, including long freight ships loaded with mounds of coal, ploughing downriver to Shànghǎi. The gorge was traditionally the most hazardous, where hidden shoals and reefs routinely holed vessels, but it has long been tamed, even though river traffic slows when the fog reduces visibility.

Apart from some of the top-end luxury cruises, most tour boats no longer pass through the monumental **Three Gorges Dam**. The passenger ferries and hydrofoils tend to finish (or begin) their journey at **Tàipíng Creek Port** (太平溪港; Tàipíngxī Gǎng), upstream from the dam. From here, two types of shuttle bus wait to take you into Yíchāng (one hour). One is free and takes you to the old ferry port (老码头; lǎo mǎtóu) in the centre of town. The other costs ¥10 and drops you at Yíchāng East Train Station (火车东站; Huǒchē Dōngzhàn). Ordinary tourist boats tend to use **Máopíng Port** (茅坪港; Máopíng Gǎng), from where you can at least see the dam, and which is also connected to Yíchāng via shuttle buses.

BOATS

There are four categories of boats: luxury cruises, tourist boats, passenger ships and hydrofoil.

Luxury Cruises   豪华游轮

The most luxurious passage is on international-standard cruise ships *(háohuá yóulún)*, where maximum comfort and visibility accompany a leisurely agenda. Trips typically depart Chóngqìng mid-evening and include shore visits to all the major sights

---

BEST TOP-END CRUISES

Viking River Cruises (www.vikingrivercruises.com) Very luxurious cruise, offering five-day cruises from Chóngqìng to Wǔhàn, as part of a larger 12-day tour of China; complete tour UK£1995.

Century Cruises (www.centuryrivercruises.com) Claims to be the most luxurious cruise service on the Yangzi. Ships are new, service is first class and facilities are top notch. Chóngqìng to Yíchāng tickets booked through Harbour Plaza Travel Centre (p764) start at ¥3150.

Victoria Cruises (www.victoriacruises.com) Comfortable four- to five-day trips between Chóngqìng and Yíchāng; Older boats than Century, but also has excellent English-speaking guides. From ¥2950, through Harbour Plaza Travel Centre (p764).

(Three Gorges Dam, Little Three Gorges et al), allowing time to tour the attractions (often secondary to the scenery). Cabins have air-con, TV (perhaps satellite), fridge/minibar and sometimes more. These vessels are aimed specifically at Western tourists and are ideal for travellers with time, money and negligible Chinese skills. The average duration for such a cruise is three nights and three to four days.

Tourist Boats 普通游轮

Typically departing from Chóngqìng at around 9pm, ordinary tourist cruise ships (pǔtōng yóulún) usually take just under 40 hours to reach Yíchāng (including three nights on board). Some boats stop at all the sights; others stop at just a few (or even none at all). They are less professional than the luxury tour cruises and are aimed more at domestic travellers (Chinese food, little spoken English). Cabins in all classes are fairly basic, but come with AC and a TV and usually have an attached bathroom with a shower. It is possible to book packages that take you first by bus from Chóngqìng to Wànzhōu, where you board a vessel for the rest of the trip. This reduces the journey by one night.

In theory, you can buy tickets on the day of travel, but booking one or two days in advance is recommended. Fares tend to be similar whether you buy them from an agency or direct from the ticket hall, but it's worth shopping around to check. If buying a ticket through an agent, ensure you know exactly what the price includes.

Special class (特等; tèděng) ¥1750, two-bed cabin

1st class (一等; yīděng) ¥950, two-bed cabin

2nd class (二等; èrděng) ¥610 to ¥630, four-bed cabin

3rd class (三等; sānděng) ¥510 to ¥530, six-bed cabin

Passenger Ships 客船

Straightforward passenger ships (kè chuán) are cheap, but can be disappointing because you sail through two of the gorges in the dead of night. Stops are frequent, but hasty, and they pass by the tourist sights. Journeys between Chóngqìng and Yíchāng take around 36 hours; between Fēngjié and Yíchāng,

around 12 hours. Toilets are shared, and soon get pretty grotty. There are no showers, but there are sinks and power sockets in the twin cabins (as well as TVs, which usually don't work). Meals on board are decent and cheap (¥10 per meal!) but there is no choice of dishes, so take along your own food and drinks in case you don't like what's on offer.

Eastbound boats leave Chóngqìng at 10pm and Fēngjié at 6pm. For westbound journeys, shuttle buses, which connect with the boats, leave Yíchāng's old ferry port at 4.30pm and 8pm, although the 8pm trip only goes as far as Fēngjié.

Tickets can usually be bought on the day of travel.

Chóngqìng to Yíchāng fares:

1st class (一等; yīděng) ¥830, twin cabin

2nd class (二等; èrděng) ¥540 to ¥560, twin cabin

3rd class (三等; sānděng) ¥440 to ¥460, four- to six-bed dorm

4th class (四等; sìděng) ¥300 to ¥330, eight-bed dorm

Fēngjié to Yíchāng fares:

1st class ¥343

2nd class ¥212

3rd class ¥147

4th class ¥119

Hydrofoil 快艇

Yangzi River hydrofoils (kuài tǐng) are a dying breed. There are now just three per day and they only run between Fēngjié and Yíchāng. Regular buses, though, connect Fēngjié with Chóngqìng (¥165, five hours, 7am to 6.30pm) so this is still a quick and reasonably convenient way of seeing the Three Gorges.

Hydrofoils are passenger vessels and are not geared towards tourists, so there's no outside seating. Visibility is OK (albeit through perspex windows), but if you stand by the door you can get a good view. Food and refreshments are served on board, but the food isn't great. Hydrofoils make regular but very brief stops at towns along the river for embarkation and disembarkation.

At the time of research, times of departure and prices for tickets bought at the relevant port's official ticket office were as follows (note, the Yíchāng times of departure are for the free shuttle buses which leave from

Yíchāng's old port before connecting with the hydrofoils which leave from a newer port 45km upstream):

Yíchāng to Fèngjié ¥240, four to five hours (7.20am, 9.50am and 1.20pm)

Fèngjié to Yíchāng ¥230, four to five hours (8.30am, 11am and 2pm)

If you get stuck for the night in Fèngjié, **Fènggǎng Bīnguǎn** (奉港宾馆; ☏023-5683 4333; r from ¥80), attached to the ferry port, has large clean rooms, some with river views. Run by a friendly family, but no English spoken; no English sign.

TICKETS

In Chóngqìng or Yíchāng, most hotels, hostels and travel agents can sell you a trip on either the luxury cruise ships or the ordinary tourist boats. In either city, passenger ferry tickets have to be bought at the ferry port ticket halls, which also sell ordinary tourist boat tickets. For the hydrofoil, you can buy westbound tickets in Yíchāng from the Three Gorges Tourist Centre, at the old ferry port. Eastbound tickets must be bought at the ticket hall in Fèngjié, where the hydrofoil starts its journey. You can no longer buy hydrofoil tickets in Chóngqìng.

The price of your ticket will include the one-hour shuttle bus ride to/from the old ferry port in the centre of Yíchāng from/to one of the two newer ferry ports, about 45km upstream, where almost all boats now leave from or terminate at.

Chóngqìng

Harbour Plaza Travel Centre Specialises in luxury cruises, but also sells ordinary tourist boat tickets. Staff are friendly and speak OK English. See p764.

Yangtze River Hostel Mostly sells tickets for the ordinary tourist boats, but can arrange luxury cruises too. Excellent English skills. See p759.

Chóngqìng Ferry Port ticket hall (重庆港售票大厅; Chóngqìnggǎng Shòupiào Dàtīng; Map772; ◷7am-10pm) Cheapest place to buy ordinary tourist boat tickets, and the only place that sells passenger ferry tickets. No English spoken.

Yíchāng

China International Travel Service (CITS; 中国国际旅行社; Zhōngguó Guójì Lǚxíngshè; ☏0717-625 3088; Yunji Lu; ◷8.30am-5.30pm) Sells luxury cruises to Chóngqìng (from ¥2800), tourist boat tickets to Chóngqìng (¥930 to ¥1020) and hydrofoil tickets to Fèngjié (¥450). Some English spoken. It's 500m from Yílíng Hotel, walking away from the river. From Yíchāng Hotel, turn right out of the hotel, then first left and it's on your left after 500m.

Three Gorges Tourist Centre (三峡游客中心; Sānxiá Yóukè Zhōngxīn; ☏0717-622 2143; Yanjiang Dadao; 沿江大道; ◷7am-8pm) Commission-free, so cheaper than CITS. Sells hydrofoil tickets to Fèngjié (¥240) plus passenger ferry tickets to various destinations between Yíchāng and Chóngqìng. Minimal English spoken, but staff members are young and helpful. Enter the modern tourist centre (no English sign) and head to the ticket counters at the far right of the building.

Yangtze River International Travel (宜昌长江国际旅行社; Yíchāng Chángjiāng Guójì Lǚxíngshè; ☏0717-692 1808; ◷7am-8pm) Slightly cheaper than CITS for ordinary tourist-boat tickets to Chóngqìng (from ¥880). Also sells luxury cruises. Housed inside the Three Gorges Tourist Centre, but has a separate desk beside the passenger-boat ticket counters.

Fèngjié

Fèngjié Ferry Port ticket hall (奉节港售票厅; Fèngjié Gǎng Shòupiàotīng; Map772) Sells passenger ferry tickets in either direction, plus hydrofoil tickets to Yíchāng (¥230). Don't expect to be able to board tourist boats from here because tickets are usually sold out in Chóngqìng or Yíchāng.

Wǔhàn

Pathfinder Youth Hostel Sells tickets for westbound trips from Yíchāng, which include the bus from Wǔhàn to Yíchāng. See p419.

Xīnjiāng

POP 21.5 MILLION

Includes »

Ürümqi	779
Turpan	784
Hāmì (Kumul)	787
Kashgar	790
Karakoram Highway	796
Yarkand	798
Hotan	800
Cherchen	802
Bù'ěrjīn	803
Kanas Lake Nature Reserve	804
Yīníng	806

Best Bazaars

» Sunday market, Hotan (p800)

» Livestock market, Kashgar (p790)

» Sunday bazaar, Kuqa (p789)

» Sunday market, Yarkand (p799)

Best Off The Beaten Track

» Shipton's Arch (p792)

» Hémù Trek to Kanas Lake (p804)

» Hiking around Muztagh Ata (p796)

» Sūbāshí ruins (p790)

Why Go?

The old Chinese proverb 'Heaven is high and the Emperor is far away' could well have been spoken about Xīnjiāng (新疆), China's far-flung and restive western frontier. Xīnjiāng and distant Běijīng have been at odds since time immemorial, but the cultural differences between the two are just what make this province so attractive to travellers. Central Asian culture is still very much alive in this Uighur homeland, from the irresistible smell of teahouse kebabs to the sound of the call to prayer from the neighbourhood mosque. There is much to entice Silk Road travellers here, including ruined desert cities, camel treks, bustling bazaars and a fascinating mix of peoples. Equally awesome are the landscapes, ranging from the scorching sands of the Taklamakan Desert to the cool forests and lakes of the Tiān Shān (Heavenly Mountains). A journey to Chinese Turkestan is above all a trip into the past, along desert tracks that for centuries served as the superhighways of the Asian continent.

When to Go

Ürümqi

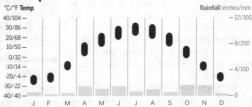

Mar Nauryz (New Year) festivals held in Kazakh and Kyrgyz villages.

Aug Celebrate the grape-harvest festival in Turpan.

Sep Autumnal colours at Kanas Lake and Hémù.

History

By the end of the 2nd century BC the expanding Han dynasty had pushed its borders west into what is now Xīnjiāng. Military garrisons protected the fledgling trade routes, as silk flowed out of the empire in return for the strong Ferghana horses needed to fight nomadic incursions from the north. Chinese imperial rule waxed and waned over the centuries, shrinking after the collapse of the Han and reasserting itself during the 7th-century Tang, though central control was

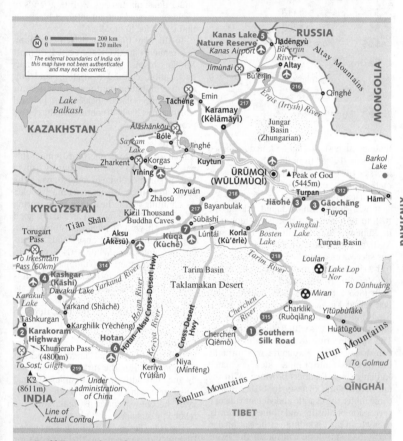

Xīnjiāng Highlights

1 Follow the footprints of Marco Polo along the **Southern Silk Road** (p798), a string of ancient cities on the fringes of the Taklamakan Desert

2 Overnight in a yurt and attend a Tajik wedding amid the dramatic mountain scenery of the **Karakoram Highway** (p796)

3 Explore the ancient ruined cities of **Jiāohé**

(p787) and **Gāochāng** (p787), near the laid-back oasis town of Turpan

4 Haggle for a fat-tailed sheep at the timeless Sunday livestock market at **Kashgar** (p790)

5 Trek by foot or horse over the spectacular Altai mountains from Hémù to **Kanas Lake Nature Reserve** (p804)

6 Explore the story of Central Asian silk in **Hotan** (p800), from cocoon-spun thread at a silk workshop to shopping for *atlas* cloth in the city's fascinating bazaars.

7 Pause on the Northern Silk Road at **Kuqa** (p788), for its authentic bazaar and nearby Buddhist ruins

PRICE INDICATORS

The following price indicators are used in this chapter:

Sleeping

$	less than ¥170
$$	¥170 to ¥280
$$$	more than ¥280

Eating

$	less than ¥20
$$	¥20 to ¥35
$$$	more than ¥35

tenuous at best. A Uighur kingdom based at Khocho thrived from the 8th century and oversaw the Central Asian people's transformation from nomads to farmers and from Manichaeans to Buddhists.

It was during Kharakhanid rule in the 10th to 12th centuries that Islam took hold in Xīnjiāng. In 1219, Yīlí (Ili), Hotan and Kashgar fell to the Mongols and their various successors controlled the whole of Central Asia until the mid-18th century, when the Manchu army marched into Kashgar.

In 1865 a Kokandi officer named Yaqub Beg seized Kashgaria, proclaimed a short-lived independent Turkestan, and made diplomatic contacts with Britain and Russia. The Manchu army eventually returned and two decades later Kashgaria was formally incorporated into China's newly created Xīnjiāng (New Frontier) province. With the fall of the Qing dynasty in 1911, Xīnjiāng came under the chaotic and violent rule of a succession of Muslim and Chinese warlords, over whom the Kuomintang (the Nationalist Party) had very little control. In the 1930s and 1940s there were two attempts in Kashgar and Ili respectively to establish an independent state of Eastern Turkestan, but both were short-lived.

Since 1949, China's main social goal in Xīnjiāng has been to keep a lid on ethnic separatism while flooding the region with Han settlers. The Uighurs once composed 90% of Xīnjiāng's population; today they make up less than 50%. China's 'Develop the West' campaign has used the region's oil resources to ramp up the local economy but the increased arrival of Han settlers has only exacerbated ethnic tensions. In 2008

street protests and bomb attacks rocked the province and in 2009 communal violence between Han and Uighur civilians in downtown Ürümqi led to around 200 deaths and 1700 injuries, according to Chinese police reports. The whole province came under quasi-martial law, with thousands of Uighurs arrested and an internet black-out that lasted for 10 months.

To this day Uighur and Han communities remain effectively segregated in most Xīnjiāng towns. As long as economic marginalisation, cultural restrictions and ethnic discrimination continue to fuel Uighur resentment, isolated incidents of political violence look likely to continue in the restive province.

Climate

Xīnjiāng's climate is one of extremes. Turpan is the hottest spot in the country – up to 47°C in summer (June to August), when the Tarim and Jungar Basins aren't much cooler. As daunting as the heat may seem, spring (April and May) is not a particularly good time to visit, with frequent sandstorms making travel difficult and dust clouds obscuring the landscape. Winters (November to March) see the mercury plummet below 0°C throughout the province, although March is a good time to catching some festivals. Late May through June and September through October (especially) are the best times to visit.

Language

Uighur, the traditional lingua franca of Xīnjiāng, is part of the Turkic language family and thus fairly similar to other regional languages, such as Uzbek, Kazakh and Kyrgyz. The one exception is Tajik, which is related to Persian.

The Han Chinese in Xīnjiāng don't speak Uighur. Vice versa, many Uighurs can't, or won't, speak Mandarin. Now learning Mandarin is mandatory in Uighur-language schools (but not the other way round), and is exclusively used in universities, nominally to provide more economic opportunities to the Uighurs. But resistance to Sinicisation is steadfast, out of concerns the Uighur culture and tradition will be diluted.

ⓘ Getting There & Away

You can fly between Xīnjiāng and most domestic cities, Central Asia and a couple of cities further afield, including Moscow and Tehran; for details, see p788.

There are overland border crossings with Pakistan (Khunjerab Pass), Kyrgyzstan (Irkeshtam and Torugart Passes) and Kazakhstan (Korgas, Ālāshānkǒu, Tǎchéng and Jímùnǎi). The Qolma Pass to Tajikistan may conceivably open to foreign travel in the coming years. All of these border crossings are by bus, except Ālāshānkǒu, China's only rail link to Central Asia.

Heading back into mainland China, the obvious route is the train following the Silk Road through Gānsù. More rugged approaches are the mountain roads from Charklik to Qīnghǎi, and Karghilik to Ali (Tibet).

❶ Getting Around

The railway from Gānsù splits near Turpan, with one branch heading west through Ūrūmqi to Yīníng and Kazakhstan, and the other going southwest to Kashgar and Hotan.

Distances are large in Xīnjiāng and buses are often sleepers. On-board entertainment usually includes kung fu film marathons cranked to the hilt. Shared taxis run along many of the bus routes, taking up to half as long and costing twice as much as buses. Shared taxis only depart when full.

Flying around the province can save a lot of time and tickets are often discounted by up to 60%. Flights are sometimes cancelled for lack of passengers or due to bad weather.

CENTRAL XĪNJIĀNG

Ūrūmqi 乌鲁木齐

📶 0991 / POP 1.7 MILLION

Ūrūmqi's close to two million residents live in a city that sprawls 20km across a fertile plain in the shadow of the Tiān Shān. Highrise apartments and tower blocks form a modern skyline that will soon dash any thoughts of spotting wandering camels and ancient caravanserais.

As a fast-growing Central Asian hub the city does business with traders from Běijīng to Baku and plays host to an exotic mix of people, including burly Kazakh and Russian 'biznezmen' from the former Soviet Union. Cyrillic signs and fragrant corner kebab stands add a Central Asian feel, though in reality over 75% of Ūrūmqi's inhabitants are Han Chinese.

Ūrūmqi is not a historic city, but the provincial museum is excellent and there are some interesting Uighur districts. If you find yourself hanging around for a Kazakh or Kyrgyz visa, consider a side trip to Tiān Chí or Turpan, or possibly both.

⦿ Sights & Activities

TOP CHOICE Xīnjiāng Autonomous Region Museum MUSEUM

(新疆自治区博物馆; Xīnjiāng Zìzhìqū Bówùguǎn; 132 Xibei Lu; admission free; ⦿10am-6pm Tue-Sun) Xīnjiāng's massive provincial museum is a must for Silk Road aficionados. The highlight is the locally famous 'Loulan Beauty', one of the 3800-year-old desert-mummified bodies of Indo-European ancestry that became symbols of Uighur independence in the 1990s. Other exhibits include some amazing silk and sculpture from Astana and an introduction to all of the province's minorities. A free English audiotour is available for a ¥100 deposit. From the Hóngshān Intersection, take bus 7 or 912 for four stops and ask to get off at the museum (bówùguǎn).

Èrdàoqiáo Market BAZAAR

(二道桥市场; Èrdàoqiáo Shìchǎng; Jiefang Nanlu) The Èrdàoqiáo Market and nearby International Bazaar (Guójì Dàbāzhá) have undergone extensive 'redevelopment' in recent years and are now aimed more at Chinese tour groups than Uighur traders. Planted in the bazaar is a replica of the Kalon Minaret from Bukhara in Uzbekistan (though the 12th-century original doesn't have an elevator inside it). The surrounding streets are worth a stroll for their Uighur markets and snack stalls.

WHICH TIME IS IT?

Making an appointment in Xīnjiāng is not just a matter of asking what time, but also 'which time?' All of China officially runs on Běijīng time (Běijīng shíjiān). Xīnjiāng, several time zones removed from Běijīng, however, runs duelling clocks: while the Chinese tend to stick to the official Běijīng time, the locals set their clocks to unofficial Xīnjiāng time (Xīnjiāng shíjiān), two hours behind Běijīng time. Thus 9am Běijīng time is 7am Xīnjiāng time. Most government-run services, such as the bank, post office, bus station and airlines, run on Běijīng time, generally operating from 10am to 1.30pm and from 4pm to 8pm to cater to the time difference. Unless otherwise stated, we use Běijīng time in this chapter.

Ürümqi

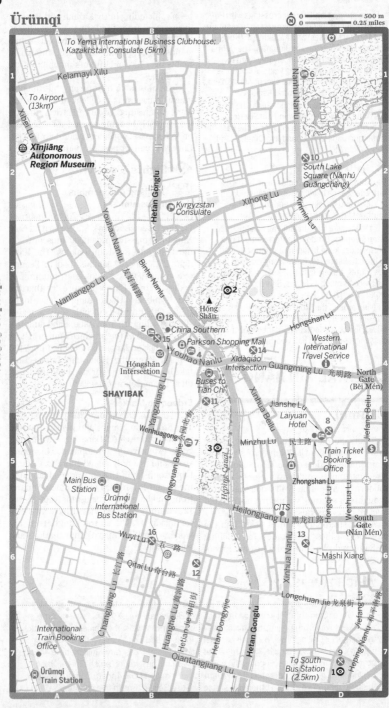

To Yema International Business Clubhouse;
Kazakhstan Consulate (5km)

Kelamayi Xilu

To Airport
(13km)

Xidai Lu

Xīnjiāng
Autonomous
Region Museum

Hetan Gönglu

Youhao Nanlu

Nanliangpo Lu

Binhe Nanlu

Kyrgyzstan
Consulate

Xihong Lu

Xinmin Lu

Nanhu Nanlu

6

South Lake
Square (Nánhú
Guǎngchǎng)

10

2

Hóng
Shān

Hongshan Lu

18

China Southern

5

15

Parkson Shopping Mall

4

14

Western
International
Travel Service

Hóngshān
Intersection

Youhao Nanlu

Xīdàqiáo
Intersection

Guangming Lu 光明路

North
Gate
(Běi Mén)

SHAYIBAK

Buses to
Tian Chi

Yangzijiang Lu

Xinhua Beilu

Jianshe Lu

Laiyuan
Hotel

8

Jiefang Beilu

11

Wenhuagong
Lu

7

3

Minzhu Lu 民主路

17

Train Ticket
Booking
Office

Gongyuan Beijie 公园北街

Zhongshan Lu

Main Bus
Station

Ürümqi
International
Bus Station

Heping Canal

Heilongjiang Lu 黑龙江路

CITS

Hongqi Lu

Wenhua Lu

South
Gate
(Nán Mén)

Wuyi Lu 五一路

16

13

Qitai Lu 奇台路

12

Mashi Xiang

Xinhua Nanlu

Changjiang Lu 长江路

Huanghe Lu 黄河街

Hetianjie 和田街

Hetan Dongyijie

Longchuan Jie 龙泉街

International
Train Booking
Office

Hetan Gonglu

Heping Nanlu 和平南路

Jiefang Nanlu

Ürümqi
Train Station

Qiantangjiang Lu

9

To South
Bus Station
(2.5km)

1

Ürümqi

⊙ **Top Sights**

Xīnjiāng Autonomous Region
  Museum A2

⊙ **Sights**

1 Èrdàoqiáo Market D7
2 Hóngshān Park.................................... C3
3 People's Park....................................... C5

⊜ **Sleeping**

4 Màitián International Youth
  Hostel B4
5 Pea Fowl Mansions............................. B4
6 Silver Birches International
  Youth Hostel.................................. D1
7 Super 8.. B5

⊗ **Eating**

8 Aroma D5
9 Carrefour D7
10 Carrefour D2
11 Fubar C4
12 May Flower B6
13 Texas Cafe D6
14 The Vine Cafe...................................... C4
15 Tiānfǔ Zhèngcài.................................. B4
16 Wǔyī Night Market............................. B6

⊙ **Shopping**

17 Foreign Languages
  Bookshop C5
18 Outdoor Gear B4

Hóngshān Park   PARK
(红山公园; Hóngshān Gōngyuán; admission ¥10; ☉dawn-dusk) More of an amusement park, but with good city views, particularly from the 18th-century hilltop pagoda. The main southern entrance is to the north of the Xīdàqiáo Intersection.

People's Park   PARK
(人民公园; Rénmín Gōngyuán; admission ¥5; ☉7.30am-dusk) A green oasis, with north and south entrances.

🛏 Sleeping

Màitián International Youth Hostel   HOSTEL $
(麦田国际青年旅舍; Màitián Guójì Qīngnián Lüshè; ☑459 1488; www.xjmaitian.com; 726 Youhao Nanlu; 友好南路726号; dm ¥45-60, r ¥150; @🛜) On the east side of the Parkson Shopping Mall, centrally located Màitián has simple doubles and dorms, some with private bathrooms, and a pleasant common area/bar. The shared bathrooms are pretty grotty, but the rooms do get a regular cleaning. Book ahead in summer. Private rooms are discounted from November to mid-April.

Silver Birches International Youth Hostel   HOSTEL $
(白桦林国际青年旅舍; Báihuàlín Guójì Qīngnián Lüshè; ☑488 1428; www.yhaxinjiang.com; 186 Nanhu Nanlu; 南湖南路186号; dm ¥40-60, tw ¥160; @🛜) The English-speaking staff at this hostel are very friendly and can help organise trips and onward transport. It's a bit out of the centre but rooms are modern and it has a peaceful location beside a park. Take bus

104 from Rénmín Guǎngchǎng or bus 537 from the railway station and get off at South Lake Sq (Nánhú Guǎngchǎng).

Pea Fowl Mansions   HOTEL $$
(孔雀大厦; Kǒngquè Dàshà; ☑452 2988; 489 Youhao Nanlu; 友好南路489号; tw from ¥260; ※) If you can overlook the peeling paint, loose wallpaper and scruffy hallways, the irresistibly useful location makes this a decent choice. Discounts of 40% are usually available. It's right by Hóngshān Intersection, the drop-off point for airport buses.

Yema International Business Clubhouse   HOTEL $$$
(野马国际商务会馆; Yěmǎ Guójì Shāngwù Huìguǎn; ☑768 8888; 158 Kunming Lu; 昆明路158号; d incl breakfast ¥318-698; ※@🛜) This elegant and surprisingly stylish modern hotel has an art gallery, wine bar and restaurant, mixing traditional Chinese design with urban chic. It even has its own zoo out the back with rare animals including Przewalski horses (wild horses indigenous to Central Asia). There is a range of rooms, from less expensive Japanese-style doubles to larger rooms in the main tower. The hotel is located north of the city, next to the Kazakhstan embassy.

Super 8   HOTEL $$
(速8酒店; Sùbā Jiǔdiàn; ☑559 0666; www.super8.com.cn; 140 Gongyuan Beijie; 公园北街140号; tw ¥268-308; ※🛜) Quietly located behind People's Park, this is the best of the budget chain hotels, representing good value with its ultra-neat rooms, modern bathrooms and free Chinese-style breakfast.

✖ Eating & Drinking

TOP CHOICE **May Flower** UIGHUR $$$

(五月花; Wǔyuèhuā; cnr Wuyi Lu & Hetian Jie; meals ¥25-55; ⊙11am-midnight) From the delicious Uighur cuisine to the pleasant fauxcourtyard setting, May Flower is a feast for the senses. Try the speciality, *polo* (rice pilaf; *zhuāfàn*), along with a few sticks of shish kebab and a glass of pomegranate juice, then sit back and enjoy the traditional live music (8pm).

Aroma MALTESE $$$

(啊诺玛西餐厅; Ā'nuòmǎ Xīcāntīng; 196 Jianshe Lu; meals ¥40-100; ⊙noon-midnight; 🖱) A Maltese chef who somehow washed up in Ürümqi runs this cosy and warm bistro. Pizzas, pastas and risottos are local favourites, or sink your teeth into a tasty steak. Most of the ingredients are either home-grown or homemade. It's opposite the Laiyuan Hotel.

The Vine Cafe CAFE $$

(德蔓咖啡; Démàn Kāfēi; ☎230 4831; 20th fl, Times Square Apartments, Xīdàqiáo; 西大桥时代广场公寓楼20层; coffee ¥15-25, meals ¥25-60; ⊙1.30-10.30pm Tue-Sun; 🖱🖱) Run by friendly Arlette from Curaçao, this fine cafe brings you savoury West Indian cuisine in a coffeehouse atmosphere. Dishes are flavourful and the cheesecake is divine, but portions are more suited to a light snack than a full meal. The new location in an office block is uninspiring, so ring ahead in case it's moved again.

Tiānfǔ Zhēngcài SHANGHAINESE $

(天府蒸菜; ☎459 5913; 17 Lanxiuyuan Xijie; 揽秀园西街; mains Y15-40) A cosy and friendly neighbourhood place just northwest of the Hóngshān Intersection, featuring tasty eastern Chinese dishes. Try the Shanghai-style braised meatballs (*hóngshāo shīzi tóu*; 红烧狮子头) or tiger skin peppers with braised eggplant (*hǔpí làzi shāoqiézi*; 虎皮辣子烧茄子). It's at the end of a side alley beside the Bingtuan Hotel.

Fubar PUB $$$

(福吧; Fúbā; 40 Gongyuan Beijie; beer ¥25, mains ¥35-65; ⊙11am-2am; 🛜🖱) Fubar is run by an Irish expat who is happy to pull a pint for bedraggled Silk Road travellers. The menu consists of classic pub grub, with tasty pizzas, burgers and bottles of imported beer (¥35 to ¥50). Young expat teachers and volunteers congregate here, making this a good place to get the skinny on activities around Ürümqi. It's on a street of bars and clubs if you want to make a big night of it.

Texas Cafe TEX-MEX $$$

(德克萨斯西餐厅; Dékèsàsī Xīcāntīng; www.texascafe.weebly.com; 55 Mashi Xiang; meals ¥35-70; ⊙1-11pm, closed Tue; 🖱) This Lone Star–inspired place serves great Tex-Mex treats including nachos, fajitas, burritos and steaks. It's hidden down an alley of vine trellises so be persistent. The owner is a native Texan, so you know it's authentic.

Wǔyī Night Market SNACKS $

(五一夜市; Wǔyī Yèshì; Wuyi Lu; ⊙8-11pm) This animated night market is worth a visit for its shish kebabs and handmade noodles. Bus 51 from Hóngshān Intersection to south bus station stops at its entrance on Changjiang Lu.

Carrefour SUPERMARKET $

(加乐福; Jiālèfú) The branches of this French supermarket chain, notably in Èrdàoqiáo Market and near Silver Birches International Youth Hostel, are good for produce and both have excellent value cafeterias.

🔒 Shopping

Foreign Languages Bookshop BOOKS

(外文书店; Wàiwén Shūdiàn; Xinhua Beilu; ⊙10.30am-8pm) Just south of Minzhu Lu.

Outdoor Gear OUTDOOR EQUIPMENT

(山泽户外用品; Shānzé Hùwài Yòngpǐn; 70 Youhao Nanlu) Sells tents, sleeping bags, stoves and gas canisters. Also rents sleeping bags and tents.

ℹ️ Information

Bank of China (中国银行; Zhōngguó Yínháng; cnr Jiefang Beilu & Dongfeng Lu; ⊙10am-6.30pm Mon-Fri, 11am-3.30pm Sat & Sun) Can handle most transactions and has an ATM (and at other branches).

China International Travel Service (CITS; 中国国际旅行社; Zhōngguó Guójì Lǚxíngshè; ☎282 1428; www.xinjiangtour.com; 33 Renmin Lu; ⊙10am-7.30pm Mon-Fri) This office runs standard tours around the province and can supply a driver and English-speaking guide.

China Post (中国邮政; Zhōngguó Yóuzhèng; Hóngshān Intersection; ⊙10am-10pm)

Green Power Internet Cafe (绿色动力网吧; Lǜsè Dònglì Wǎngbā; 190 Wuyi Lu; per hr ¥4; ⊙24hr)

Public Security Bureau (PSB; 公安局; Gōng'ānjú; ☎281 0452, ext 3456; Kelamayi Donglu; ⊙10am-1.30pm & 4-6pm Mon-Fri) Not much hassle extending visas here.

Western International Travel Service (大西部国际旅行社; Dàxībù Gúojì Lǚxíngshè; ☏885 0256; Bógédá Bīnguǎn, 253 Guangming Lu) This agency has the best rates around for trips to Kanas Lake.

❶ Getting There & Away

Air

International flights include Almaty (Kazakhstan), Bishkek and Osh (Kyrgyzstan), Baku (Azerbaijan), Tbilisi (Georgia), Istanbul (Turkey), Islamabad (Pakistan), Moscow (Russia), Dushanbe (Tajikistan), Tashkent (Uzbekistan) and Tehran (Iran). Some of these are seasonal and many are suspended without warning.

You can get to Ürümqi from almost anywhere in China. Destinations within Xīnjiāng include Altay (Ālètài), Hotan (Hétián), Kashgar (Kāshí), Kuqa (Kùchē), Tǎchéng and Yíníng. **China Southern** (南方空收票处; Nánfāng Hángkōng Shòupiàochù; ☏95539; 576 Youhao Nanlu) has the most flights to and around Xīnjiāng, with a central booking office in the Southern Airlines Pearl International Hotel.

Bus

Two long-distance bus stations in Ürümqi serve northern and southern destinations. The **main bus station** (碾子沟长途汽车站; niǎnzigōu chángtú qìchēzhàn; Heilongjiang Lu) has sleeper buses to the following:

Bù'ěrjīn ¥150 to ¥160, 13 hours, two daily (11.15am and 8.10pm)

Hāmì ¥119 to ¥139, one daily (8.30pm)

Yíníng ¥160 to ¥170, 11 to 14 hours, almost hourly (9am to 9pm)

Bus 2 runs from the train station to Hóngshān, passing Heilongjiang Lu on the way.

The **south bus station** (nánjiāo kèyùnzhàn) has frequent departures to the following:

Hotan ¥370 to ¥390, 20 hours, crossing the Taklamakan Desert.

Kashgar ¥253 to ¥264, 24 hours

Kuqa ¥140 (¥230 to ¥280 sleeper), 10 to 14 hours

Turpan ¥36 to ¥45, 2½ hours, every 20 minutes

There is also a once-daily bus that travels to Cherchen (¥280 to ¥300, 16 hours) on the southern Silk Road, departing at 7pm. A seat in a private car to Turpan costs ¥85 and takes around two hours.

BRT bus 2 runs between Xīdàqiáo and the south bus station, bus 51 or 7 will get you there from Hóngshān Intersection, and bus 104 will get you here from the South Lake Square.

Train

The **train booking office** (huǒchē shòupiàochù; 225 Jianshe Lu, next to Laiyuan Hotel; commission ¥5; ◷8.30am-10pm) in the city centre has much shorter queues than the main southern train station. Destinations (hard/soft sleeper):

Běijīng (T70) ¥652/1006, 42 hours (8.03pm)

Chéngdū (K454) ¥552/854, 49 hours (2.05pm)

BORDER CROSSING: GETTING TO KAZAKHSTAN

If you have a Kazakhstan visa, you can go to Almaty (upper/lower bunk ¥440/460, 24 hours) in Kazakhstan by the daily 7pm bus departing from **Ürümqi international bus station** (☏587 8637; 乌鲁木齐国际运输汽车站; Wūlǔmùqí guójì yùnshū qìchēzhàn), behind the main bus station. Expect delays of several hours at the Korgas customs posts. A longer but more pleasant trip is to break the journey in Yíníng.

Trains currently depart Ürümqi twice weekly for Almaty, Kazakhstan (K9795, via Ālāshānkǒu) on Monday and Saturday at midnight. The journey takes a slow 32 hours, six of which are spent at Chinese and Kazakh customs. Tickets cost ¥919 to ¥948 and can only be purchased in the lobby of the Yà'ōu Jiǔdiàn (next to the train station), at the **booking office** (往阿拉木图火车票售票处; wǎng ālāmùtú huǒchēpiào shòupiàochù; ◷10am-1pm & 3.30-6pm Sat, Mon, Wed & Thu). There is also a Monday service (9797) to the Kazakh capital of Astana. Another option is to take local train 5802 to Ālāshānkǒu (12 hours, hard/soft sleeper ¥123/187), departing Ürümqi at 10.05pm, and arrange your own onward transport at the border.

At the time of research you could get a 30-day tourist visa at the Kazakhstan consulate in Ürümqi (see p988). Visas take five days to be issued, cost ¥140 (paid into the local China Construction Bank) and you need one passport photo and copy of your passport and China visa. Visas generally specify your entry date into Kazakhstan. To get to the consulate take bus No 52 or BRT 1 from Hóngshān Intersection to the Jīngguǎn Xuéyuàn (经管学院) stop.

Dūnhuáng (K728) ¥240/374, 15 hours (7.51pm)

Hāmì (K9782) ¥149/224, 7¼ hours (11.56pm)

Kashgar (K9786) ¥345/529, 26 hours (9.50am)

Kuqa (5806) ¥126/200, 16 hours (10.10pm)

Lánzhōu (T296) ¥390/600, 21 hours (2.54pm); one of many options.

Shànghǎi (T54) ¥699/1079, 44 hours (5.20pm)

Xī'ān (1044) ¥287/494, 34 hours (11.46pm)

Yīníng (5815) ¥151/234, 11 hours (9.10pm)

Yīníng (K9789) ¥157/245, 10½ hours (10.54pm)

ⓘ Getting Around

The airport is 16km northwest of the centre; a taxi costs about ¥40. An airport bus (¥10) runs straight south through town via Hóngshān Intersection to the train station, departing when full. In the city centre, an airport shuttle (¥10, free for China Southern passengers) leaves from the Southern Airlines Pearl International Hotel on the hour from 6am to 10pm. You'll need to arrive 10 minutes early to get a seat.

The fastest and most useful buses are the BRT (Bus Rapid Transit) expresses, which dodge traffic by having their very own bus lanes. BRT 1 runs from the railway station to Hóngshān Intersection and then north up Beijing Nanlu. BRT 3 runs from the south bus station up Jiefang Lu to Hóngshān Intersection and then similarly north. Fares are a flat ¥1. See www.chinabrt.org for a route map.

Other useful buses (¥1) include bus 7, which runs up Xinhua Lu from the southern bus station through the Xīdàqiáo and Hóngshān Intersections, and bus 52 from the train station to Hóngshān Intersection.

Tiān Chí 天池

Two thousand metres up in the Tiān Shān range is **Tiān Chí** (Heaven Lake; admission ¥170), a small, long, steely-blue lake nestled below the view-grabbing 5445m Peak of God (Bógédá Fēng). Scattered across the Swiss-style, spruce-covered slopes are Kazakh yurts and lots of sheep. It was a paradise described in Vikram Seth's wonderful travelogue *From Heaven Lake*, but it's seriously overhyped now; hundreds of day-tripping local tourists almost drown out the strains of 'We Are the World' that are piped from plastic tree trunks. There is still some beautiful backcountry here but you need to make some serious effort these days to have a meaningful experience.

To escape the hordes, horse treks offer stunning views of the Tiān Shān range. Horse guides will find you once you arrive at the lake or arrange a trek at the yurt camps. From the main viewpoint signed hiking paths lead up into the mountains, including 9.3km to Mǎwěi Shān (Horse Tail Mountain), which is also reached by road. A circuit leads around the lake in about four hours but the strenuous western side has some serious ups and downs. There are temples to explore on both the east and west shores. Regardless of the temperature in Ürümqi, take warm clothes and rain gear, as the weather can be unpredictable.

In late May, Kazakhs set up yurts around the lake for tourists (¥100 per person with three meals); **Rashit** (☏138 9964 1550; www.rashityurt.com) is the most popular host for backpackers. Alternatively, you can camp here. It's best to bring food as there is not much in the area. The yurt owners sometimes require ID, so make sure to bring your passport.

Tourist buses to the Tiān Chí car park leave Ürümqi around 9am from the north gate of People's Park, giving you around three hours at the lake. Most stop at major hotels to pick up passengers before leaving town. In the low season they may not run at all. The return fare is ¥40 and the trip takes about 2½ hours one way. From the ticket office everyone boards a bus to a parking lot just before the lake.

Turpan 吐鲁番

☏ 0995 / POP 57,900

Turpan (Tǔlǔfān) is China's Death Valley. At 154m below sea level, it's the second-lowest depression in the world and the hottest spot in China. In July and August temperatures soar above 40°C, forcing the local population and visiting tourists into a state of semi-torpor.

Despite the heat, the ground water and fertile soil of the Turpan depression has made this a veritable oasis in the desert, evidenced by the nearby centuries-old remains of ancient cities, imperial garrisons and Buddhist caves.

The town of Turpan itself is a fairly recent creation but it has an extremely mellow vibe. Recovering from a day's sightseeing over a cold Xinjiang beer under the grape vines on a warm summer evening is one of the joys of travelling through the province.

⊙ Sights

Emin Minaret
MINARET

(额敏塔; Émǐn Tǎ; admission ¥30; ☉dawn-dusk)
Emin Hoja, a Turpan general, founded this
splendid Afghan-style structure in 1777. Also
known as Sūgōng Tǎ after Emin's son Sulei-
man, its bowling pin shape is decorated with
a dozen brick motifs, including flowers and
waves. You can't climb the minaret itself so
many travellers are satisfied with snapping a
photograph from the entrance without paying the admission fee.

Biking or strolling the 3km to get there
is half the fun, the dusty, tree-lined Uighur
streets an evocative – and fascinating –
glimpse into old Turpan. If the heat is too
much, hop on bus 6 eastbound from the corner of Gaochang Lu and Laocheng Lu and
walk the last 500m.

FREE Turpan Museum
MUSEUM

(吐鲁番博物馆; Tǔlǔfān Bówùguǎn; Laocheng Lu;
☉10.30am-6.30pmTue-Sun) Xīnjiāng's second-
largest museum houses a rich collection of
relics recovered from archaeological sites
across the Turpan Basin, and there are also
dinosaur fossils and a couple of local mummies. Pop in here before signing up for a
tour; the photos of nearby sites might help
you decide which ones to visit.

🛏 Sleeping

Tǔlǔfān Bīnguǎn
HOTEL $

(吐鲁番宾馆; ☎856 8888; tlfbg@126.com; 2
Qingnian Nanlu; 青年南路2号; dm ¥50, d incl
breakfast ¥160-200; ❄@) The white-tile exterior of the old-school Turpan Hotel is uninspiring, but things improve when you enter
the Arabian Nights–style lobby. The subterranean triple-bed dorms are musty but cool
and come with a shower. The pricier double
rooms are cleaner and newer than the old-
fashioned cheapies. Bike hire and internet
access are bonuses, though the swimming
pool is drier than the Taklamakan Desert.

Tiānhé Bīnguǎn
HOTEL $$

(天河宾馆; ☎862 6999; 969 Laocheng Lu; d ¥188;
❄@) The spacious, modern and clean rooms
here come with a computer, making them
easily the best value in town, though you
might have to gently persuade them to take
foreigners. Discounts of 20% are standard.

Transportation Hotel
HOTEL $$

(交通宾馆; Jiāotōng Bīnguǎn; ☎625 8688; 230
Laocheng Xilu; 老城西路230号; tw ¥480; ❄)
Small but comfortable, modern rooms make

Turpan

⊙ Top Sights
Turpan Museum..................................B2

🛏 Sleeping
1 Tiānhé Bīnguǎn..................................A2
2 Transportation Hotel.........................A2
3 Tǔlǔfān Bīnguǎn................................B2
4 Xīzhōu Dàjiǔdiàn...............................B1

⊗ Eating
5 Bazaar...A2
6 Hanzada Restaurant A2
John's Information Café.............(see 3)
7 Night Market.....................................A2
8 Restaurants......................................B2

ⓘ Transport
9 Long-Distance Bus Station.................A2

this a super-convenient option next to the
bus station. Rates come with breakfast. Discounts of 60% are standard.

Xīzhōu Dàjiǔdiàn
HOTEL $$$

(西州大酒店; ☎855 4000; 8 Qingnian Beilu; 青
年北路8号; tw incl breakfast ¥460; ❄@) A clean
and friendly option, with an ugly pink and
white exterior. Some rooms have internet-
enabled computers. Discounts of 20%.

🍴 Eating

There are several Uighur food stalls hidden
in the **bazaar** opposite the bus station. The
string of restaurants that set up tables un-
der the vine trellises on **Qingnian Lu** are a
fine place to savour a cold drink and bowl of
laghman (pulled noodles; ¥15).

Night Market
MARKET **$**

(夜市; yèshì; Gaochang Lu; dishes from ¥10; ⊙7pm-midnight) Come dusk dozens of stalls set up shop by the fountains to the west of the main central square. Grab a cold beer and choose from fried fish, *shāguō* (casseroles), goat's feet soup and cumin-scented kebabs.

Hanzada Restaurant
UIGHUR **$$**

(韩扎达豪华餐厅; Hánzādá Háohuá Cāntīng; Gaochang Lu; mains Y15-40) Popular with locals for its ornate Central Asian decor (think painted alabaster and chintzy chandeliers) and diner-style booths. The picture menu helps sort out the noodles from the *polo* and *dàpánjī* (Hui-style spicy chicken, potatoes and peppers), all of which are excellent.

John's Information Café
INTERNATIONAL **$**

(☎150 2626 8966; Qingnian Nanlu; dishes from ¥12; ⊙7am-10pm, May-Oct; @⊡) This backpacker refuge has a quiet location in the backyard of the Tǔlǔfān Bīnguǎn. Western and Chinese dishes are offered and the ice-cream sundae is a treat in Turpan's blistering heat. There is little in the way of traveller information.

ⓘ Information

Bank of China (中国银行; Zhōngguó Yínháng; Laocheng Lu; ⊙9.30am-12.30pm & 4.30-7.30pm) Changes cash and travellers cheques.

China Post (中国邮政; Zhōngguó Yóuzhèng; Laocheng Lu; ⊙10am-8pm) West of the Bank of China.

Internet Cafe (网吧; wǎngbā; 2 Qingnian Nanlu; per hr ¥10) The lobby of the Tǔlǔfān Bīnguǎn is one of the only places in town to allow internet access to foreigners.

Public Security Bureau (PSB; 公安局; Gōng'ānjú; Gaochang Lu) North of the city centre; will likely refer you to the capital.

ⓘ Getting There & Away

The nearest train station is at Dàhéyán (大河沿), 54km north of Turpan. You can buy tickets in Turpan at the **train booking office** (火车售票处; huǒchē shòupiàochù; Laocheng Xilu; commission ¥5; ⊙9am-1pm, 3.30-8pm), located inside a China Mobile office. The fastest train to Kashgar (¥320/490, 23 hours) is the K9786, departing at midnight.

From the **long-distance bus station** (长途汽车站; chángtú qìchēzhàn; Laocheng Lu), minibuses to Dàhéyán (¥11, one hour) run approximately every 30 minutes between 8.30am and 7.30pm. If you miss the last bus, shared taxis run to Dàhéyán (per person ¥20) from a lot behind the bus station, near the night market.

Buses to Ürümqi (¥45, 2½ hours) run every 20 minutes between 8am and 8pm, or take a shared taxi from near the night market (¥80 per seat). There is one daily sleeper bus at 3pm to Kashgar (¥292 to ¥320, 22 hours). A bus to Hāmì (¥89, seven hours) departs at 10.30am. For Dūnhuáng (¥160, 12 hours) in Gānsù take the 8pm sleeper bus.

ⓘ Getting Around

Public transport around Turpan is by taxi, minibus or bicycle. Bicycles (about ¥5 per hour), available from John's Information Café, are convenient for the town and the Emin Minaret.

Around Turpan

Some of Turpan's surrounding sights are fascinating and others are a waste of time. Turpan's long-distance bus station has buses going to a couple of the spots, but it won't save you much. The easiest way to see them is on a customised day tour – don't worry, local drivers *will* find you. Several travellers have recommended English-speaking **Tahir** (☎150 2626 1388; tahirtour8@yahoo.com). For four people, figure on paying ¥60 to ¥70 per person. You'll be gone for the day, so don't underestimate the desert heat. Essential survival gear includes a water bottle, sunscreen, sunglasses and a hat.

You can safely bypass the **Astana Graves** (阿斯塔那古墓区; Āsītǎnà Gǔmùqū; admission ¥20), since the most interesting finds of this imperial cemetery are in museums in Ürümqi and Turpan. Some buses stop at **Grape Valley** (葡萄沟; Pútáo Gōu; admission ¥60) for lunch, but there are grapevines all around Turpan, none of which charge admission.

Other underwhelming add-ons include visits to a **karez** (坎儿井; kǎn'érjǐng; admission ¥40), a museum dedicated to the uniquely Central Asian–style system of underground aqueducts, and **Aydingkul Lake** (艾丁湖; Àidīng Hú; admission ¥10), the second-lowest lake in the world. Be forewarned that it's more of a muddy, salt-encrusted flat than a lake.

Near Bezeklik Caves and Tuyoq are the **Flaming Mountains** (火焰山; Huǒyàn Shān; admission ¥40), the midday appearance of which is aptly compared to multicoloured tongues of fire. The Flaming Mountains were immortalised in the Chinese classic *Journey to the West*, when Sun Wukong (the Monkey King) used his magic fan to extinguish the blaze. There's no need to pay the entry fee, as you can see the mountains anywhere on the roadside from Hāmì or Gāochāng.

JIĀOHÉ RUINS 交河故城

Also called Yarkhoto, **Jiāohé** (admission ¥40) was established by the Chinese as a garrison town during the Han dynasty. It's one of the world's largest (6500 residents lived here), oldest (1600 years old) and best-preserved ancient cities, impressive in its scale rather than detail. Get an overview of the site at the central governor's complex then continue along the main road past a large monastery to a 10m-tall pagoda surrounded by 100 smaller pagoda bases.

The ruins are 8km west of Turpan. Take bus No 101 (¥1) to its terminus at the Xīnchéng (新城) crossroads and then take a microbus (¥4) to the ruins (Jiāohé Gùchéng). It's possible to cycle here from Turpan.

TUYOQ 吐峪沟

Set in a green valley fringed by the Flaming Mountains, the mud-constructed village **Tuyoq** (Tǔyùgōu; admission ¥30) offers a glimpse of 'traditional' Uighur life and architecture (traditional as long as you overlook the entry fee and gate). Tuyoq has been a pilgrimage site for Muslims for centuries, and the devout claim that seven trips here equal one trip to Mecca. On the hillside above the village (near the road) is the *mazar*, or *tomb* (admission ¥20), said to hold the first Uighur to convert to Islam and still an object of pilgrimage. Don't leave town without trying some of the locally produced mulberry juice or dried berries (¥10), available near the tomb entrance.

Up the gorge is a series of Buddhist caves dating back to the 3rd century AD (thus the earliest discovered Buddhist caves in Xīnjiāng), though they were closed at the time of research.

Tuyoq is often looped into a tour with the Flaming Mountains and Bezeklik Caves.

GĀOCHĀNG (KHOCHO) RUINS 高昌故城

Originally settled in the 1st century BC, **Gāochāng** (admission ¥40) rose to power in the 7th century during the Tang dynasty. Also known as Khocho, or sometimes Karakhoja, Gāochāng became the Uighur capital in AD 850 and was a major staging post on the Silk Road until it burnt in the 14th century. Texts in classical Uighur, Sanskrit, Chinese and Tibetan have all been unearthed here, as well as evidence of a Nestorian church and a significant Manichaean community – a dualistic Persian religion that borrowed figures from Christianity, Buddhism and Hinduism.

Though the earthen city walls, once 12m thick, are clearly visible, not much else is left standing other than a large Buddhist monastery in the southwest. To the north, adjacent to an adobe pagoda, is a two-storey structure (half underground), purportedly the ancient palace.

BEZEKLIK CAVES 柏孜克里克千佛洞

This **cave complex** (Bózīkèlīkè Qiānfó Dòng; admission ¥20) has a fine location and interesting history, though the caves are essentially empty. The site is famous for having many of its distinctive murals cut out of the rock face by German archaeologists in 1905. Bezeklik means 'Place of Paintings' in Uighur.

Hāmì (Kumul) 哈密

☑ 0902 / POP 365,000

Hāmì, with its famously sweet melons, was a much-anticipated stop on the Silk Road for ancient travellers. Marco Polo suggested one possible reason why: according to local custom men allowed passing caravanmen to spend the night with their wives. No such tradition exists today but Hāmì is still worth a stop; there are enough sights to keep you busy for a day and the town is a convenient halfway point between Turpan and Dūnhuáng.

A **Bank of China** (中国银行; Zhōngguó Yínháng; Guangchang Beilu) is located just north of the main square (Shídài Guǎngchǎng).

◉ Sights

All four of the following sights are together, near the main bus station and 5km south of the train station; a taxi between the two is about ¥10.

Hāmì Kings Mausoleum TOMBS

(哈密王陵; Hāmì Wánglíng; Huancheng Lu; admission ¥40; ⊙9.30am-7.30pm) The main site in Hāmì is this peaceful complex of tombs containing the nine generations of Hāmì kings who ruled the region from 1697 to 1930. The green-tiled main tomb is of the seventh king Muhammed Bixir, with family members and government ministers housed in Mongolian-style buildings to the side.

FREE Hāmì Museum MUSEUM

(哈密博物馆; Hāmì Bówùguǎn; Huancheng Lu; ⊙9.30am-noon & 4-7.30pm; ⊙Tue-Sun) Across from the Hāmì Kings Mausoleum, this mildly interesting museum spotlights mummies and dinosaurs found in the region, including a cool fossilised nest of dinosaur eggs.

Kumul Muqam Heritage Centre MUSEUM
(哈密木卡姆传承中心; Hāmì Mùkǎmǔ Chuán-chéng Zhōngxīn; admission ¥15; ◎9am-1pm & 4-7pm) This eye-catching building focuses specifically on *muqam,* the classical form of Uighur music. Groups of four or more are usually treated to a short concert (¥25).

Mansion of the Hāmì Kings HISTORIC SITE
(哈密回王府; Hāmì Huíwáng Fǔ; admission ¥40; ◎9am-8pm) Opposite the Heritage Centre is a tacky reconstruction of an earlier palace destroyed in the Muslim uprising of the 1930s. It's not really worth the admission price.

🛏 Sleeping & Eating

Jiāngnán Bīnguǎn HOTEL $
(江南宾馆; ☎231 2112; Qianjin Xilu; d ¥120) The cheapest of the dozen or so decent hotels around the train station. The simple but clean rooms make it the best budget choice.

Jiǔchóngtiān Bīnguǎn HOTEL $$
(九重天宾馆; ☎231 5656; 4 Tianshan Beilu; d ¥188-208; ❅@) A definite step up, with clean and fresh rooms, some with computers. With your back to the train station, it's 50m straight ahead, on the right.

ℹ Getting There & Away

Long-distance buses depart from the south bus station (nánjiāo kèyùnzhàn), located 200m east of the Hāmì Kings Mausoleum. Apart from the buses below there are also shared taxis to Turpan (¥300) and Ūrūmqi (¥400) and a dozen daily trains, as well as daily flights to Ūrūmqi (¥1180).

Dūnhuáng ¥85, 9am

Jiǔquán ¥130, 9am

Turpan ¥89, six hours, 10am

Ūrūmqi ¥125 to ¥140, nine hours; 11am, 1pm and 8pm

Local bus No 3 runs from the train station to the south bus station and museum via the central bus station.

Around Hāmì

BARKOL LAKE 巴里坤湖
If the summer heat of Hāmì is unbearable, take a day trip out to the cooler climes of Barkol Lake (Bālǐkūn Hú), on the north side of the Tiān Shān. Kazakh herders set up their yurts here in summer and offer horse riding for ¥10 per hour.

To reach the yurts, first take a bus from Hāmì's **central bus station** (中心车站; zhōngxīn chēzhàn; cnr Jianguo Beilu & Guangchang Beilu) to Bālǐkūn town (¥25, three hours, hourly between 8.30am and 5.30pm). From Bālǐkūn it's 16km to the yurts. A return taxi starts at ¥50.

Along the route from Hāmì, keep an eye out for the remains of ancient beacon towers slowly disintegrating by the roadside.

Kuqa 库车

☑ 0997 / POP 77,000

Part of an excellent triangular itinerary with Kashgar and Hotan, Kuqa (Kùchē) is well worth a couple of days for its interesting bazaars and excursions to the surrounding desert ruins.

The once thriving city-state, then known as Qiuci, was a major centre of Buddhism and was famed in Tang-era China for its music and dancers. Here Kumarajiva (AD 344–413), the first great translator of Buddhist sutras from Sanskrit into Chinese, was born to an Indian father and Kuqean princess, before later being abducted to central China to manage translations of the Buddhist canon. When the 7th-century monk Xuan Zang passed through nearby Subashi, he recorded that two enormous 30m-high Buddha statues flanked Kuqa's western gate, and that the nearby monasteries held over 5000 monks.

The bus station is east of town on Tianshan Lu, and the train station is a further 5km southeast.

⊙ Sights

Qiuci Palace MUSEUM
(库车王府; Kùchē Wángfǔ; Linjilu Jie; 林基路街; admission ¥55; ◎9am-8.30pm) Located in the old town, 3.5km west of the centre, is the newly restored (ie rebuilt) Qiuci Palace, the residence of the kings of Qiuci until the early 20th century. The museum has a good collection of Buddhist frescoes, some from the nearby Kumtura and Simsim caves, and there are human remains from the surrounding desert ruins. Behind the museum, the ancestral hall displays the history of the Qiuci kings and photos of the life of the last king, Dawud Mahsut, now an elderly local party official. Nearby is an impressive section of Qing-dynasty city wall.

Take bus 3 on Tianshan Lu and get off as the road curves into Linjilu Jie.

Sunday Bazaar
BAZAAR

Every Sunday a large **bazaar** (老成巴扎; Lǎochéng Bāzā) is held about 2.5km west of the modern town, next to a bridge over the Kuqa River on Renmin Lu. It doesn't quite rival Kashgar's, but you won't find any tour buses here. A small livestock market also takes place here on Fridays.

The charming nearby **Rasta Mosque** (热斯坦清真寺; Rèsītǎn Qīngzhēn Sì) draws a throng of worshippers at Friday lunchtime. North of here, through the old town, is the large but less animated **Great Mosque** (清真大寺; Qīngzhēn Dàsì; admission ¥15), built in 1931 on the site of a 16th-century original.

To get here from the new town, take buses 1 or 3 from Tianshan Lu.

Maulana Ashiddin Mazar
TOMB

(默拉纳额什丁麻扎; Mòlànà Éshídīng Mázā) This timeless green-tiled mosque and tomb of a 13th-century Arabian missionary is surrounded by a sea of graves and overflows with worshippers at Friday lunchtime prayers. It's a 10-minute walk from the Kùchē Bīnguǎn, along mulberry-tree-lined Wenhua Lu.

Ten minutes' walk from the mazar, located just off the junction of Tianshan Xilu and Wenhua Lu, are the extremely faint ruins of **Old Qiúcí** (龟兹故城; Qiúcí Gùchéng).

🛏 Sleeping & Eating

Jiāotōng Bīnguǎn
HOTEL $

(交通宾馆; Traffic Hotel; 🖀712 2682; 194 Tianshan Lu; 天山路194号; d with/without bathroom from ¥120/80; ❇) Located next to the bus station, this place has a range of acceptable rooms, from decent budget doubles with common squat toilets and showers to spacious doubles with tiled floors (¥160). Hot water runs after 9pm.

Kùchē Bīnguǎn
HOTEL $$

(库车宾馆; 🖀712 2901; 17 Jiefang Beilu; old/new block tw ¥180/280; ❇) Kuqa's main hotel has fresh rooms with plush carpets in the new block and scruffier but acceptable rooms in the quiet old block. Rates include breakfast. It's located near the city centre. Catch a taxi here.

TOP CHOICE Uchar Darvaza Bazaar
MARKET $

(乌恰农货市场; Wūqià Nónghuò Shìchǎng) The best place for Uighur food is this food street at the junction of Tianshan Zhonglu and Youyi Lu. Kebabs, noodles and *samsas* (baked mutton pies) are all served hot and fresh, though our favourites are the chicken kebabs served with sombrero-sized local nan bread. Some stalls start to close at 9pm, others only set up from 10pm.

ℹ Information

Bank of China (中国银行; Zhōngguó Yínháng; 25 Tianshan Donglu; ⏱9.30am-6.30pm Mon-Fri) East of the centre, with an ATM. Travellers cheques are not accepted.

Xīnxīn Wǎngbā (新新网吧; cnr Wenhua Lu & Youyi Lu; per hr ¥3; ⏱24 hr)

ℹ Getting There & Away

AIR The new airport 35km west of the city has daily flights to Ürümqi (¥1120). A taxi there costs ¥30.

BUS The bus station has a variety of sleepers heading east to Ürümqi (¥207 to ¥262, 12 hours). For Kashgar (¥150, 16 hours) you have to wait for a sleeper from Ürümqi to pass and hope that it has berths. There are hourly connections to Aksu (¥50, four hours), where you can connect to Kashgar. Two sleepers depart for Hotan (¥180 to ¥190, eight hours) at noon and 4pm.

TRAIN The train station is southeast of the centre at the end of the No 6 bus line. A taxi costs ¥10. The fast K9787 to Kashgar (hard/soft sleeper ¥183/276) leaves inconveniently at 2.20am. More convenient trains to Ürümqi (hard seat/sleeper ¥116/200) include the 5808 at 6.43pm and the fast K9788 at 11.52pm (soft sleeper ¥326).

ℹ Getting Around

Taxi rides are a standard ¥5 per trip, with pedicabs, tractors and donkey carts around half this.

Around Kuqa

KIZIL THOUSAND BUDDHA CAVES
克孜尔千佛洞

Seventy-five kilometres northwest of Kuqa are the Kizil Thousand Buddha Caves (Kèzī'ěr Qiānfó Dòng; admission ¥55; ⏱daylight), an important site in the development of Serindian Buddhist art, with murals dating from as early as the 3rd century. Kizil is clearly influenced by Central Asian art and may in turn have inspired grottoes further east such as the Mògāo Caves at Dūnhuáng.

Of the more than 230 caves here, only six are open to the public at any one time, and only a couple of these have any real murals. Several of the caves were stripped by German archaeologist Albert Von le Coq, while the others have been defaced by both Muslims and Red Guards. If you have spare time, consider the hike through the desert canyon to the spring Qiānlèi Quán (千泪泉).

A return taxi from Kuqa will cost around ¥200 and takes 90 minutes each way. Add on stops in Sūbāshí and the 13.5m-tall Han-dynasty **watchtower** (烽火台; fēnghuǒtái; admission Y15) at Kizilgah for just ¥240.

SŪBĀSHÍ RUINS   苏巴什故城

The best of Kuqa's surrounding ruins is **Sūbāshí** (admission ¥25; ⊘daylight), a Buddhist complex that thrived from the 3rd to 13th centuries. Most people visit the west complex, with its large central *vihara* (monastery) and two large pagodas. For an adventure, hike across the Kuqa River to the dramatic but little-visited eastern complex (admission Y25). A return taxi to Sūbāshí, 23km northeast of Kuqa, costs about ¥60; you'll need to pay extra waiting time if you want to visit the eastern ruins.

SOUTHWEST XĪNJIĀNG – KASHGARIA

The Uighurs' heartland is Kashgaria, the rough-but-mellifluous-sounding historical name for the western Tarim Basin. Consisting of a ring of oases lined with poplar trees, it was a major Silk Road hub and has bristled with activity for more than 2000 years, with the weekly bazaars remaining the centre of life here to this day.

Kashgar   喀什

♪ 0998 / POP 350,000

Locked away in the westernmost corner of China, physically closer to Tehran and Damascus than to Běijīng, Kashgar (Kāshí) has been the epicentre of regional trade and cultural exchange for more than two millennia.

In recent years modernity has swept through Kashgar like a sandstorm. The roads, rail and planes that now connect the city to the rest of China have brought waves of Han migrant workers and huge swaths of the old city have been bulldozed in the name of economic 'progress'.

Yet, in the face of these changes, the spirit of Kashgar lives on. Uighur craftsmen and artisans still hammer and chisel away in side alleys, traders haggle over deals in the boisterous bazaars and donkey carts still trundle their way through the suburbs. And the Sunday livestock market is the real deal, no matter how many tour buses roll up.

So soak it in for a few days, eat a few kebabs, chat with the local carpet sellers, and prepare your trip along the southern Silk Road to Hotan, over the Torugart or Irkeshtam Passes to Kyrgyzstan or south along the stunning Karakoram Hwy to Pakistan.

⊙ Sights

Grand (Sunday) Bazaar   BAZAAR

(大巴扎; Dàbāzhā; Yengi Bazaar; Aizirete Lu; 艾孜热特路; ⊘daily) Kashgar's main bazaar is open every day but really kicks it up a gear on Sundays. Step carefully through the jam-packed entrance and allow your five senses to guide you through the market; the pungent smell of cumin, the sight of scorpions in a jar, the sound of *muqam* music from tinny radios, the taste of hot *samsas* (baked mutton dumplings) and the feel of soft sheepskin caps are seductive, and overwhelming. A section on the northern side of the market contains everything of interest to foreign visitors, including the spice market, musical instruments, fur caps, kitschy souvenirs and carpets. A taxi to the market is ¥5.

Sunday Livestock Market   BAZAAR

(动物市场; Dòngwù Shìchǎng; Mal Bazaar; ⊘8am-6pm Sun) No visit to Kashgar is complete without a trip to the Livestock Bazaar. Since it only occurs once a week you'll need to plan accordingly. The day begins with Uighur farmers and herders trekking into the city from nearby villages. By lunchtime just about every sellable sheep, camel, horse, cow and donkey within 50km has been squeezed through the bazaar gates. Trading is swift and boisterous between the old traders; animals are carefully inspected and haggling is done with finger motions. Happy buyers then stuff the sheep in the back of a taxi or truck and lurch away. It's dusty, smelly, crowded and totally wonderful. Keep an ear out for the phrase '*Bosh-bosh!*' ('Coming through!') or you risk being ploughed over by a cartload of fat-tailed sheep.

In 2012 the market relocated to the north-western suburbs. A taxi here costs ¥15; it's a good idea to pay it to wait for your return. Alternatively take bus No 8 to People's Hospital and then jump on a motorised pedicab (¥2). Tour buses usually arrive in the morning so consider an early afternoon visit. A few simple stalls offer hot *samsas* if you get peckish.

If you miss the Sunday Market, don't despair: there are plenty of other markets in Xīnjiāng to visit. Try the Sunday market in Hotan or Kuqa, the Monday market in Upal or the Tuesday market in Charbagh.

Kashgar

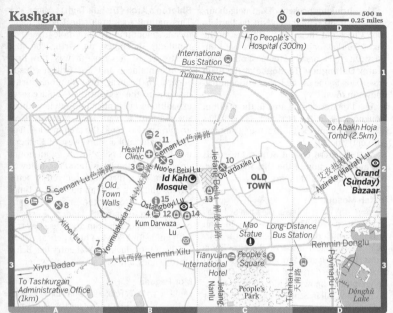

Kashgar

◉ Top Sights

Grand (Sunday) Bazaar	D2
Id Kah Mosque	B2

◉ Sights

1	Ostangboyi Tea House	B2

◉ Sleeping

2	Chini Bagh Hotel	B2
3	Eden Hotel	B2
4	Kashgar Old Town Youth Hostel	B2
5	Sahar Hotel	A2
6	Sèmǎn Bīnguǎn	A2
7	Yambu Hotel	A3

◉ Eating

8	Altun Orda	A2
	John's Cafe	(see 6)
9	Karakorum Cafe	B2
10	Night Market	C2
11	Pakistan Cafe	B2

◉ Shopping

12	Ahmed Carpet Shop	B2
13	Ilhas Supermarket	C2
14	Uighur Musical Instrument Factory	B2

◉ Information

15	Kashgar Guide	B2
	Old Road Tours	(see 6)
	Uighur Tours	(see 2)

Old Town

OLD TOWN

Sprawling on both sides of Jiefang Lu are alleys lined with Uighur workshops and adobe houses right out of an early-20th-century picture book. Houses range in age from 50 to 500 years old and the lanes twist haphazardly through neighbourhoods where Kashgaris have lived and worked for centuries. It's a great place for strolling, peeking through gates, chatting up the locals and admiring the craftsmen as they bang on tin and chase copper.

Sadly, the Chinese government has shown little affection for the old town and has spent the past two decades knocking it down, block by block. During our short stay we witnessed dozens of old homes bulldozed.

The shrinking pockets of old neighbourhoods that do remain tend to be hard to spot. Check out the streets southeast of the Night Market or the craft stalls on Kum Darwaza street, north of the post office. The nearby **Ostangboyi Teahouse** at the main crossroads in town is one of the last traditional teahouses in town.

Avoid the residential area to the north of Dōnghú Park by the ferris wheel, as it has been turned into a tourist trap complete with entry ticket.

At the eastern end of Seman Lu stands a 10m-high section of the **Old Town walls**, which are at least 500 years old.

Id Kah Mosque
MOSQUE

(艾提尕尔清真寺; Ài Tígǎ'ěr Qīngzhēn Sì; Id Kah Sq; admission ¥20) The yellow-tiled Id Kah Mosque, which dates from 1442, is the spiritual and physical heart of the city. Enormous, its courtyard and gardens can hold 20,000 people during the annual Qurban Baiyram (also known as Eid, or Id) celebrations, which fall in September or October for the next few years.

Non-Muslims may enter, but not during prayer time. Dress modestly, including a headscarf for women. Take off your shoes if entering carpeted areas and be discreet when taking photos.

The stalls outside the mosque are a good place to pick up a striped *khalat* (cloak) or traditional Uighur *doppi* (skullcap).

Abakh Hoja Tomb
TOMB

(香妃墓; Xiāngfēimù; Abakh Hoja Maziri; admission ¥30; ☉daylight) On the northeastern outskirts of town is the Abakh Hoja Tomb (1640), covered in splendidly mismatched glazed tiles and best known among Uighurs as the resting place of Abakh Hoja, famed 17th-century Sufi and political leader. Purportedly among others interred is Iparhan, his granddaughter. Known to the Chinese as Xiang Fei (Fragrant Concubine), she was either the beloved but homesick concubine of the Emperor Qianlong and thus a symbol of national unity (the Chinese version), or a Uighur resistance leader who was captured and taken to Beijing where she died broken-hearted (Uighur version). Don't miss the ornately carved pillars of the separate winter, summer and Friday mosques. Take bus 20 from People's Square heading east until the last stop, then walk 500m. A taxi is ¥10.

Shipton's Arch (Tushuk Tagh)
NATURAL ARCH

This natural rock arch (the Uighur name means 'mountain with a hole in it') is reputedly the tallest on earth. The first Westerner to describe it was the British mountaineer and last British consul-general in Kashgar, Eric Shipton, during his visit to the region in 1947. Successive expeditions attempted to find it without success until a team from *National Geographic* rediscovered the arch in 2000. The arch, located 80km northwest of Kashgar, is a half-day excursion involving an hour's drive towards the Irkeshtam Pass, followed by 20km on a dirt track (currently being paved) and then a 30-minute hike, at times scrambling through the narrowest part of the gorge over small ladders. Kashgar-based tour operators can arrange a day trip with guide for ¥800 to ¥1000 per car. There is talk of introducing a ¥30 entry fee. Bring sturdy shoes, a fleece, snacks and water.

Mor Pagoda
RUINS

(莫尔佛塔; Mù'ěr Fótǎ; admission ¥15; ☉daylight) At the end of a 45km drive northeast of town are the ruins of Ha Noi, a Tang-dynasty town built in the 7th century and abandoned in the 12th century. Little remains apart from an enigmatic pyramid-like structure and the impressive four-tiered Mor Pagoda. A round trip taxi, including waiting time, costs ¥100 to ¥150.

☞ Tours

Uighur Tour, Old Road Tours, and Kashgar Guide organise four-day treks around Muztagh Ata, overnighting in tents, yurts or villages, as well as overnight camel tours into the dunes fringing the Taklamakan Desert around Davakul Lake or Yarkand (see the Information section p795). For a real challenge, consider biking the Karakoram Hwy.

🛏 Sleeping

Accommodation can be tighter on the days preceding the Sunday Market.

Eden Hotel
HOTEL $$

(海尔巴格大饭店; Hǎiěrbāgé Dàfàndiàn; ☑266 4444; www.xjeden.com; 148 Seman Lu; d ¥198-218 ❄@) The quiet rooms and excellent location (next to Chini Bagh) of this midrange hotel make it the best value in town. The staff speak English and there's an excellent attached Turkish restaurant. Rates include a good breakfast.

Chini Bagh Hotel
HOTEL $$

(其尼瓦克宾馆; Qíníwǎkè Bīnguǎn; ☎298 2103; 144 Seman Lu; dm ¥70, tw ¥180-280; ❀@) The Chini Bagh, immortalised in William Dalrymple's travelogue *In Xanadu*, is located on the grounds of the former British consulate (1901–1951). Its several buildings contain an eclectic collection of rooms, from three-bed dorms to a new five-star complex. The best standard rooms are in the main building, though renovations are planned for all rooms. The central location is convenient for the old town. Visit the Chinese restaurant behind the north block to see the old consulate building.

Sèmǎn Bīnguǎn
HOTEL $

(色满宾馆; ☎258 2129; 337 Seman Lu; tw without bathroom ¥60, tw ¥150-220; @) A labyrinthine complex with myriad rooms. The cheapest doubles are just about acceptable, but the common toilets and showers could do with a clean. More expensive (but garish) ensuite rooms are next to the former Russian consulate out the back. The staff are very friendly and helpful.

Kashgar Old Town Youth Hostel
HOSTEL $

(喀什老城青年旅舍; Kāshí Lǎochéng Qīngnián Lǚshè; ☎282 3262; www.pamirinn.com; 233 Ostangboyi Lu; 吾斯塘博依路233号; dm ¥35, r without bathroom ¥90; @📶) Nestled in the old city, this atmospheric place is set around a courtyard where overlanders hang out on *shyrdaks* (Kyrgyz-style felt carpets), swapping stories and travel info. The rooms are bare, the toilets simple and the beds are rock hard, but staff speak English and there's cheap laundry and free internet access.

Màitián Youth Hostel
HOSTEL $

(麦田国际青年旅舍; Màitián Guójì Qīngnián Lǚshè; ☎262 0595; www.yhaks.com; Renmin Donglu Nan 1 Xiang; 人民东路南一巷; dm ¥35-45, tw with bathroom ¥80; ❀@) This hostel east of East Lake (Dōnghú) is fresh, piney and modern, and popular with Chinese backpackers, but has an uninspiring location in the modern part of town. Bus 28 from Id Kah Mosque and the train station takes you there; get off on the east side of the bridge, then head south for 300m down the alley named Renmin Donglu Nan 1 Xiang.

Yambu Hotel
HOTEL $$

(金座大饭店; Jīnzuò Dàfàndiàn; ☎258 8888; 198 Renmin Xilu; d ¥588; ❀@) A good bet for affordable, modern and spacious midrange comfort (rates are generally discounted

by 60%) but check a couple of rooms as standards vary. As ever, the back rooms are quietest.

Sahar Hotel
BUDGET HOTEL $

(色哈尔宾馆; Sèhāʾěr Bīnguǎn; ☎258 1122; 348 Seman Lu; d ¥70-80) A friendly but dowdy hotel whose customers are mostly Pakistani, Tajik and Uighur traders. The hotel offers some of the cheapest ensuite rooms available to foreigners, though they are pretty simple. Rooms on the 3rd floor are best.

✗ Eating

Kashgar is one of the best places in Xīnjiāng to try the full gamut of Uighur food.

▣TOP CHOICE Night Market
MARKET $

(夜市; yèshì; Ou'erdaxike Lu; meals from ¥10; ☯8pm-midnight Xīnjiāng time) The night market across Jiefang Beilu from the Id Kah Mosque is a great place to sample local fare. Among the goodies are fried fish, chickpeas, kebabs, fried dumplings known as *hoshan* and bubbling vats of goat's head soup. Top off a meal with a glass of tart pomegranate juice or freshly churned vanillascented ice cream.

Karakorum Café
CAFE $$

(87 Seman Lu; mains ¥20-48; ☯9am-11.30pm; 📶▣) Smart-looking but slightly sterile cafe serving Western-style breakfasts, sandwiches, desserts and coffee (¥10–28) in an oasis of delicious quiet. The bathroom should win an award as the cleanest in Xīnjiāng.

Altun Orda
UIGHUR $$

(金噢尔达食菜; Jīnʾàoʾěrdà Shícài; Xibei Lu; dishes from ¥25) Perfect for a celebration or last Kashgar meal, Altun Orda is a sumptuously decorated Uighur restaurant famous for its roasted mutton (¥78), *gosh nan* (meat pie) and *mirizlig samsa* (pastry with raisins and almonds). There are branches across Xīnjiāng.

Pakistan Cafe
PAKISTANI $

(Seman Lu; mains ¥10-14) This simple, familyrun place outside the Chini Bagh Hotel is a fine place to chat with the fascinating mix of visiting Afghans, Tajiks and Pakistanis over a cup of milky masala chai. The menu is limited to whatever happens to be on the stove at the time but generally includes *keema* (minced lamb), *chapatis* (unleavened bread), mutton curry and *dal* (lentil curry). The nearby Shwarma Restaurant offers similar fare a couple of doors down.

UIGHUR FOOD

Uighur cuisine includes all the trusty Central Asian standbys, such as kebabs, *polo* (pilau rice) and *chuchura* (dumplings), but has benefited from Chinese influence to make it the most enjoyable region of Central Asia in which to eat.

Uighurs boast endless varieties of *laghman* (pulled noodles; *lāmiàn* in Chinese), though the usual topping is a combination of mutton, peppers, tomatoes, eggplant and garlic shoots. *Suoman* are torn noodle squares fried with tomatoes, peppers, garlic and meat, with *suoman goshsiz* the vegetarian variety. *Suoman* can be quite spicy, so ask for *lazasiz* (without peppers) if you prefer a milder version.

Kebabs are another staple and are of a much better standard than the ropey *shashlyk* of the Central Asian republics. *Jiger* (liver) kebabs are the low-fat variety. *Tonor* kebabs are larger and baked in an oven *tonor* (tandoori) style. True kebab connoisseurs insist on *kovurgah kebab* or *bel kebab*, made from rib and waist meat respectively. Most are flavoured with *zir* (cumin).

Nan (breads) are a favourite staple and irresistible when straight out of the oven and sprinkled with poppy seeds, sesame seeds or fennel. They make a great plate for a round of kebabs, especially the Hotanese variety, which are more than 2ft wide. Most Uighur restaurants serve small cartons of delicious *ketik* (yoghurt) to accompany your meal.

Other snacks include *serik ash* (yellow, meatless noodles), *nokot* (chickpeas), *pintang* (meat and vegetable soup) and *gang pan* (rice with vegetables and meat). Most travellers understandably steer clear of *opke*, a broth of bobbing goat's heads and coiled, stuffed intestines.

Samsas (baked mutton dumplings) are available everywhere, but the meat-to-fat ratio varies wildly. Hotan and Kashgar offer huge meat pies called *daman* or *gosh girde*.

For dessert try *morozhenoe* (vanilla ice cream churned in iced wooden barrels), *kharsen meghriz* (fried dough balls filled with sugar, raisins and walnuts, also known as *chiker koimak*) or *dogh* (sometimes known as *doghap*), a delicious mix of shaved ice, syrup, yoghurt and iced water. As with all ice-based food, try the latter at your own risk. *Tangzaza* are triangles of glutinous rice wrapped in bamboo leaves covered in syrup. Anyone else hungry yet?

Anyone with a sweet tooth should look for carts selling *matang* (walnut fruit loaf), and *sokmak*, a delicious paste of walnuts, raisins, almonds and sugar, sold by the 500g jar (¥20–30) at honey and nut stalls. It's fine to ask for a free sample.

Xīnjiāng is justly famous for its fruit, whether it be *uruk* (apricots), *uzum* (grapes), *tawuz* (watermelon), *khoghun* (sweet melon) or *yimish* (raisins). The best grapes come from Turpan; the sweetest melons from Hāmì. Markets groan with the stuff from July to September.

Meals are washed down with *kok chai* (green tea), often laced with nutmeg or rose petals. The one local beer worth going out of your way for is bottled Xinjiang Black Beer, a dark lager-style brew.

John's Cafe INTERNATIONAL $$
(约翰中西餐厅; Yuēhàn Zhōngxī Cāntīng; www.johncafe.net; 337 Seman Lu; mains from ¥20; ⊗May-Oct; 🖥) In the courtyard of Sèmǎn Bīnguǎn, this is a popular backpacker hangout, offering both Western (pricey) and Chinese (cheaper) dishes. Management also arrange local tours.

 Shopping

For serious shopping go to the Old Town, ready to bargain. Kum Darwaza Lu is the best starting point, at least until threatened redevelopment changes the place. The Grand Bazaar has a decent selection but prices tend to be higher. Hats, teapot sets, copper and brass ware, kebab skewers and Uighur knives are among the best souvenirs.

Grand (Sunday) Bazaar MARKET
(大巴扎; Dàbāzhā; Aizirete Lu; ⊗daily) Most carpet dealers display their wares at the Sunday Market pavilion. The rugs here are made of everything from silk to synthetics and finding traditional designs can be difficult. The brightly coloured felt Kyrgyz-style *shyrdaks* are a good buy; don't pay more than ¥450 for a large one. Be careful when you shop.

Ahmed Carpet Shop
CARPETS

(☑283 1557; 49 Kum Darwaza Lu) Ahmed and his son run this Old Town carpet shop, offering a good selection of antique and new carpets, *gilims* and *shyrdaks* from across Central Asia.

Uighur Musical Instrument Factory
MUSICAL INSTRUMENTS

(272 Kum Darwaza Lu) You'll find long-necked stringed instruments here running the gamut from souvenirs to collectors' items. If any traditional performances are on, owner Mohammed will know where to find them. There are several places with the same name on the same street.

Ilhas Supermarket
SUPERMARKET

(伊合拉斯超市; Yīhélāsī Chāoshì; ☺10am-midnight; Jiefang Beilu) An excellent choice of Turkish and Central Asian goods underneath the Id Kah plaza.

ℹ Information

Travellers have lost money or passports to pick-pockets at the Sunday Market, so keep yours tucked away.

Kashgar is the most conservative corner of Xīnjiāng and the one place where you will see women's faces obscured by headscarves or veils. Some foreign women walking the streets alone have been sexually harassed. It is wise for women travellers to dress as would be appropriate in any Muslim country, covering arms and legs.

Internet Access
Effendi Internet Cafe (阿凡提网吧; Āfántí Wǎngbā; 87 Seman Lu; per hr ¥3; ☺24hr) Above the Karakorum Cafe.

Laundry
Angel Dry Cleaners (天使干洗店; Tiānshǐ Gānxǐdiàn; Seman Lu; ☺10am-11.30pm) Laundry service just north of the Chini Bagh Hotel.

Medical Services
Health Clinic (诊所; zhěnsuǒ; Seman Lu) The Chini Bagh Hotel can put you in touch with this English-speaking clinic.

People's Hospital (人民医院; Rénmín Yīyuàn; Jiefang Beilu) North of the river.

Money
Bank of China (中国银行; Zhōngguó Yínháng; People's Sq; ☺9.30am-1.30pm & 4-7pm) Changes travellers cheques and cash and has a 24-hour ATM. You can also sell yuan back into US dollars at the foreign-exchange desk if you have exchange receipts; this is a good idea if you are headed to Tashkurgan, where the bank hours are erratic.

Post
China Post (中国邮政; Zhōngguó Yóuzhèng; 40 Renmin Xilu; ☺9.30am-8pm) The 2nd floor handles all foreign letters and packages.

Public Security Bureau
(PSB; 公安局; Gōng'ānjú; 111 Youmulakexia Lu; ☺9.30am-1.30pm & 4-8pm) Visa extensions take three to four days, dependent on the political climate.

Travel Agencies
Ablimit 'Elvis' Ghopar (☑138 9913 6195; elvis ablimit@yahoo.com) Local English-speaking Uighur carpet dealer Elvis organises city-wide cultural trips, with a special emphasis on Uighur classical music and the Kashgar carpet market. Find him at the Saqiya Teahouse near Id Gah Mosque.

Kashgar Guide (☑295 1029; www.kashgarguide. com, www.xinjiangtravel.com; 407 Ostangboyi Lu) Run by Imam Husan, opposite the Kashgar Old Town Youth Hostel. It organises transport and excursions, and can link you up with other budget-minded travellers to help share costs.

Old Road Tours (☑220 4012, 138 9913 2103; www.oldroadtours.com; 337 Seman Lu) One of the best, run by Abdul Wahab and operating out of the Sèmàn Bīnguǎn.

Uighur Tours (☑298 1073; www.kashgartours. com; 144 Seman Lu) Ali Tash runs this recommended agency based in the Chini Bagh Hotel.

ℹ Getting There & Away

It's imperative when you buy tickets in Kashgar to verify 'which time' the ticket is for (see p779). It should be Běijīng time, but this isn't always the case.

AIR A dozen daily flights depart for Ürümqi (¥1800). A handy **air ticket agent** (Xīnjiāng Jīchǎng Jítuán Jīpiào Dàishòuchù; ☑296 6666; 8 Renmin Donglu) is located at the Tiānyuán International Hotel.

BUS Domestic buses use the **long-distance bus station** (地区客运站; dìqū kèyùnzhàn; Tiannan Lu). There are six buses for Hotan (¥92 to ¥128, seven to 10 hours) between 9am and 9pm, but it's more enjoyable to stop off in Yengisar (¥13, 1½ hours), Yarkand (¥32 to ¥40, three hours) or Karghilik (¥41 to ¥54, four hours). Buses to these towns run at least hourly. Faster shared taxis also run to all these places for twice the bus fare; a ticket office just inside the entrance sells tickets.

Sleeper buses to Ürümqi (¥265 to ¥285, 22 hours) depart from the **international bus station** every 45 minutes between 10am and 8.30pm. There are also sleepers to Kuqa (¥157 to ¥172, 12 hours) every two hours between noon and 8pm.

TRAIN Daily trains to Ürümqi depart at 8.18am and 2.44pm (train 9788) and take 32 and 24 hours, respectively. Sleeper tickets on the faster train cost ¥345/529. Train 5826 from Ürümqi continues to Hotan (10 hours) at 10.30am, stopping at Yengisar (two hours), Yarkand (four hours) and Karghilik (5½ hours) en route. You can buy tickets from the **train booking office** (huǒchē shòupiàochù; Tiannan Lu; commission ¥5; ☺9.30am-1pm & 3-8pm) at the long-distance bus station.

❶ Getting Around

TO/FROM THE AIRPORT The airport is 13km northeast of the town centre. One shuttle bus (¥10) meets all incoming flights. Just tell the driver your destination in town. A taxi should cost ¥15 but drivers often ask for double this. Bus 2 goes directly to the airport from People's Square and Id Kah Mosque.

BICYCLE Mountain bikes can sometimes be hired at the Chini Bagh Hotel for ¥50 per day. The **Giant Bike Shop** (捷安特自行车; Jié'āntè Zìxíngchē; ☐640 1616; 37 Jiangkang Lu) also rents bikes for ¥50 per day. It's located 1.5km south of town opposite the Three Fortune Hotel (三运宾馆; Sānyùn Bīnguǎn).

BUS Useful bus routes are buses 2 (Jiefang Lu north to the international bus station and the airport), 9 (international bus station to the Chini Bagh Hotel and Sèmǎn Bīnguǎn), 20 (China Post to Abakh Hoja Tomb) and 28 (Id Kah Mosque to the train station). The fare is ¥1.

TAXI Taxis are metered and the flag fall is ¥5. Nowhere in town should cost more than ¥14.

Karakoram Highway 中巴公路

The Karakoram Hwy (KKH; Zhōngbā Gōnglù) over the Khunjerab Pass (4800m) is one of the world's most spectacular roads and China's gateway to Pakistan. For centuries this route was used by caravans plodding down the Silk Road. Khunjerab means 'valley of blood' – local bandits used to take advantage of the terrain to slaughter merchants and plunder caravans.

Facilities en route are being gradually improved, but take warm clothing, food and drink on board with you – once stowed on the bus roof it will be unavailable on the journey. Check the state of the highway well ahead of time.

In 2010 a massive landslide on the Pakistani side blocked a river and created a new 20km-long lake that submerged the highway, causing disaster for the people of the Hunza Valley and big headaches for travellers. Check Lonely Planet's Thorn Tree (www.lonelyplanet.com/thorntree) for updates.

Even if you don't plan to go to Pakistan, it's still worth heading up the highway at least to Tashkurgan. It's possible to do a day trip to Karakul Lake and back but it's much better to spend a night or two up in these gorgeous mountains. Some travellers hire bikes in Kashgar, get a lift up to Tashkurgan and cycle back for an exciting three-day journey.

During times of political tension foreigners need a permit from a travel agent to get past the checkpoint at Ghez. This was the case in 2011, but not in 2012, so check in advance with a Kashgar travel agency.

KASHGAR TO TASHKURGAN

Travelling up the KKH to Tashkurgan is a highlight of Kashgaria. The journey begins with a one-hour drive through the Kashgar oasis to **Upal** (Wùpà'ěr in Chinese), where most vehicles stop for breakfast, especially during the interesting Monday market. The renovated **Tomb of Mahmud Kashgari** (admission ¥30), a beloved local 11th-century scholar, traveller and writer, is a potential excursion but it's far from unmissable. The tomb is about 2.5km from the market on the edge of Upal hill.

Two hours from Kashgar you enter the canyon of the Ghez River (Ghez Darya in Uighur), with its dramatic claret-red sandstone walls. Ghez itself is a major checkpoint; photographing soldiers or buildings is strictly prohibited. At the top of the canyon, 3½ hours above the plain, you pop out into a huge wet plateau ringed with mountains of sand, part of the Sarikol Pamir, and aptly called Kumtagh (Sand Mountain) by locals.

Soon Kongur Mountain (Gōnggé'ěr Shān; 7719m) rises up on the left side of the road, followed by heavily glaciered Muztagh Ata (Mùshìtǎgé Shān; 7546m). The main stopping point for views is **Karakul Lake**, a glittering mirror of glacial peaks 194km from Kashgar. From here you can hike into the hills or circumnavigate the lake. Kashgar Guide and Old Road Tours (p795) can organise five-day trekking tours around the lake to Subash village or the Muztagh Ata base camp (4500m), overnighting in tents, villages and Kyrgyz yurts along the way. The trek (US$50 to US$70 per day) includes food, permits, guide and even a camel to haul your gear. Avoid the obvious fenced tourist centre, which has a ¥50 entry fee, restaurant (mains ¥40 to ¥80), concrete yurt accommodation (¥50) and touristy horse rides (¥50). More authentic accommodation is available at the southern end of the lake.

BORDER CROSSING: GETTING TO KYRGYZSTAN, PAKISTAN & TAJIKISTAN

To Kyrgyzstan

There are two passes into Kyrgyzstan: the Torugart Pass, which leads to Bishkek, and the Irkeshtam Pass, which goes to Osh. Getting to Osh (¥570, two days) is straightforward, with a sleeper bus leaving Kashgar's **international bus station** (国际汽车站; guójì qìchēzhàn; Jiefang Beilu) at 9am on Mondays (and perhaps Thursday if demand warrants it). Another option is to take a shared taxi from the station to Uluk Chat (¥30 per seat) and change there. Hiring a car to Irkeshtam through an agency costs around ¥700. Road construction in 2012 should speed up the trip.

Crossing the Torugart requires more red tape, for which you will need a travel agency's help: see p795. You will need to have pre-arranged transport on the Kyrgyz side, which travel agents can arrange with their contacts in Naryn or Bishkek. Rates for a Chinese 4WD to meet/drop you off at Torugart Pass average US$225, which includes transportation, guide and permits (minimum two-day processing). A car/minibus all the way to Naryn is US$420/490 for up to three/six people. Vehicles need a special permit to travel to the border. The border is technically open year round but closed at weekends.

Kyrgyzstan visas are available from the consulate in Ürümqi (see p988). Visa fees depend on the speed of service (ranging from same day to a week). Bring one passport photo and a copy of your passport and visa and arrive early because the consulate is only open for two hours a day. You have to pay the visa fee at a nearby branch of the Bank of China.

To Pakistan

Buses to/from Sost (¥370, two days) in Pakistan leave Kashgar's **international bus station** (国际汽车站; guójì qìchēzhàn; Jiefang Beilu) daily at noon. However, if there are fewer than 10 passengers the bus may not depart until the following day. The 500km trip stops overnight at Tashkurgan, where customs procedures are conducted. If you are already in Tashkurgan, the fare to Sost is ¥225. You can also hire a car from one of the tour outfits in Kashgar.

To Tajikistan

The 4362m Qolma (Kulma) Pass linking Kashgar with Murghab (via Tashkurgan), opened in 2004 to local traders. As of 2012 it was still closed to foreign travellers, though there is renewed talk of opening the pass as a full international crossing.

The journey climbs to a pass offering fine views, then meanders through high mountain pastures dotted with grazing camels and yaks, before passing the turn-off to the Qolma Pass (currently closed to foreigners). The final major town on the Chinese side is **Tashkurgan** at 3600m. You could easily kill a couple of hours wandering the streets and visiting the small museum at the **Folk Culture Centre** (admission ¥30; ☺10am-5pm) at the central crossroads (marked by the eagle statue).

On the outskirts of town, close to the river, is **Tashkurgan Fort** (石头城; Shítóuchéng, admission ¥30), whose 1400-year-old stone (tash) fortifications (kurgan) give the town its name. The ruins were one of the filming locations for the movie *Kite Runner*. The boggy valley below is dotted with Tajik yurts in summer and offers some spectacular views back towards the fort.

Some travellers head up to the Khunjerab Pass for a photo opportunity on the actual border. Note that you need a border permit (available in Kashgar) and a guide, which most tour agencies can arrange.

Officially, the border opens daily between 1 May and 31 October. However, the border can open late or close early depending on conditions at the Khunjerab Pass. The Chinese customs and immigration formalities are done at Tashkurgan (technically 3km down the road towards Pakistan). Then it's 126km to the last checkpost at Khunjerab

Pass, the actual border, where your documents are checked again before you head into Pakistan. Pakistan immigration formalities are performed at Sost. In late 2011 Pakistani visas were *no longer available* to tourists on arrival (and visas are difficult to get in Běijīng), so the safest option is to arrive in China with a visa obtained in your home country. Check the current situation as this could change.

🛌 Sleeping

Jiāotōng Bīnguǎn   HOTEL **$**

(交通宾馆; ☏0998-342 1192; dm ¥50, d ¥140-160) The bus station hotel has fresh and modern doubles and dorms with simple shared bathrooms. Bus passengers en route to Sost generally overnight here.

Crown Inn   HOTEL **$$$**

(皇冠大酒店; Huángguān Dàjiǔdiàn; ☏0998-342 2888; www.crowninntashkorgan.com; 1 Pami'er Lu; d with breakfast ¥580; @🖘) This plush Singaporean-run hotel offers comfortable, bright rooms and a good restaurant (mains ¥48 to ¥108).

❶ Getting There & Away

From Kashgar daily buses run to Tashkurgan from the long-distance bus station, leaving at 10am, 11am and noon (¥51, six hours). Shared taxis also depart from the city's **Tashkurgan Administration Office** (塔什库尔干办事处; Tǎshíkù'ěrgān Bànshìchù; 166 Xiyu Dadao Lu; 西域大道166号), in the west of town.

Three buses depart Tashkurgan for Kashgar (¥51) between 8.30am and 10am; if you miss them, a shared taxi costs ¥100 per person. The bus to Sost (¥250) leaves Tashkurgan at 10am.

From Kashgar it's 118km to the Ghez checkpoint, 194km to Karakul Lake, 283km to Tashkurgan and 380km to the Pakistani border.

A car to Karakul Lake and back costs around ¥800 through a Kashgar travel agency.

SOUTHERN SILK ROAD

The Silk Road east of Kashgar splits into two threads in the face of the Taklamakan Desert, the second largest sandy desert in the world. The northern thread follows the modern road and railway to Kuqa and Turpan. The southern road charts a more remote course between desert sands and the towering Pamir and Kunlun mountain ranges.

There are no jaw-dropping sights here, but the off-the-grid journey takes you about as far into the Uighur heartland as you can get. It's possible to visit the southern towns as a multiday trip from Kashgar before crossing the Taklamakan Desert to Ürümqi, or as part of a rugged backdoor route into Tibet or Qīnghǎi.

For wonderfully detailed but somewhat dated information on the southern Silk Road check out www.centralasiatraveler.com.

Yengisar   英吉沙

The tiny town of Yengisar (Yīngjíshā) is synonymous with knife production. A lesser-known but more sensitive fact is it's the birthplace of the Uighur's icon of nationalism, Isa Yusuf Alptekin (1901–95), the leader of the First East Turkestan Republic in Kashgar who died in exile in Istanbul.

There are dozens of knife shops here, most of them strung along the highway; ask for the 'knife factories' (小刀厂; xiǎodāochǎng in Chinese; pichak chilik karakhana in Uighur). Each worker makes the blade, handle and inlays himself, using only the most basic of tools. To get there from the main bus station, hop in a taxi (¥5) for the 3km trip to the knife shops. They are right on the main road, so you'd even pass them on the way to Yarkand. Note that knives are prohibited in check-in luggage, so you'll have to ship them home.

Buses pass through the town regularly en route to Yarkand (¥28, 1½ hours) and Kashgar (¥13, 1½ hours).

Yarkand   莎车

At the end of a major trade route from British India, over the Karakoram Pass from Leh, Yarkand (Shāchē) was for centuries an important caravan town and regional centre for the trade in cashmere wool. This traditional and conservative town is well worth a stop.

Modern Yarkand is split into a Chinese new town and a Uighur old town to its east. Take a right upon exiting the bus station to get to the main avenue. Once there, take another right and flag down any public bus, which will take you past the Shāchē Bīnguǎn, 1km east of the bus station; the old town and the Altun Mosque complex are 1km further.

⊙ Sights

Altun Mosque Complex   MOSQUE, CEMETERY
(阿勒屯清真寺; Ālètún Qīngzhēn Sì) Yarkand's main sights are clustered around its charming central 18th-century mosque. Next to the

mosque in the modern square is the **Mausoleum of Ammanisahan** (admission ¥15), commemorating a 16th-century local Uighur queen and musician famed for her work collecting Uighur *muqam* music. Behind the tomb is the central **mazar** (tomb) of her husband Sultan Sayid Khan, the founder of the Yarkand dynasty of rulers (1514–1682). The surrounding sprawling cemetery is home to several other impressive shrines, with white flags marking the graves of *pir* (holy men). There are normally groups of elderly Uighurs praying here.

Old Town NEIGHBOURHOOD
The old town to the east of the Altun Mosque is well worth a stroll; craftsmen still work their wares with ball-peen hammers and grindstones and several workshops churn out traditional Uighur instruments. To get here take the dirt lane headed east, just south of the Altun Sq, and keep going. Eventually you'll link up with Laocheng Lu and can return west back to the new town.

Yarkand has a **Sunday Market** a block north of the Altun Mosque, though it's considerably smaller than those of Kashgar or Hotan.

🛏 Sleeping & Eating

There are several good restaurants by Altun Sq, including the Altun Handan Restaurant, with traditional Uighur food and decor.

Xīnshèng Bīnguǎn HOTEL $$
(新盛宾馆; ☑852 7555; 4 Xincheng Lu; 新城路 4号; tw ¥180; @🅪) This place has clean and modern rooms with internet cables in the rooms, making it a good choice. Rates come with breakfast. It's on the main road, just beside the gates of the Shāchē Bīnguǎn.

Subhi Altun Hotel HOTEL $
(苏碧怡阿勒屯宾馆; Sūbìyí Ālètún Bīnguǎn; ☑851 2222; cnr A'letun Lu & Laocheng Lu; 阿勒 屯路和老城路的十字路口; tw/tr ¥138/238) This Uighur hotel has clean rooms, a little rough at the edges, but with a perfect location across from the Altun Mosque complex. Unmarried couples and alcohol are frowned upon.

Altun Kasir Restaurant UIGHUR $
(金宫美食; Jīngōng Měishí; Xincheng Lu; mains ¥12-25) A friendly and pleasant place five minutes' walk west of the Subhi Altun Hotel, and fronted by a row of green shrubbery. The picture menu makes life easier.

ℹ Getting There & Away

Buses leave half-hourly to Kashgar (¥40, three hours), Yengisar (¥28, 1½ hours) and Karghilik (¥12, 1½ hours). Three buses daily take the expressway to Hotan (¥58, five hours), and six leave for Ürümqi (¥310 to ¥340, 25 hours). Faster shared taxis also depart when full to Kashgar (¥60), Yengisar (¥40) and Karghilik (¥25).

Karghilik 叶城

Karghilik (Yèchéng) is of importance to travellers as the springboard to the fantastically remote Hwy 219, the Xīnjiāng–Tibet highway that leads to Ngari (Ali) in far west Tibet.

The main attraction in town is the 15th-century **Friday Mosque** (Jama Masjid) and the surrounding adobe-walled backstreets of the old town.

The town of **Charbagh**, located 10 minutes' drive towards Yarkand, has a large market on Tuesday.

🛏 Sleeping & Eating

The paranoid PSB assumes all foreigners are trying to sneak into Tibet and so limit you to one of the following options.

There are busy Uighur eateries outside the Friday Mosque and 24-hour food stalls across from the bus station.

Jiāotōng Bīnguǎn HOTEL $
(交通宾馆; ☑728 5540; 1 Jiaotong Lu; r ¥120-150; ❄) The Traffic Hotel has a quiet back block with reasonably clean ensuite rooms and a front building with much grimmer rooms with shared bathroom (¥80–¥100).

Qiáogēlǐfēng Dēngshān Bīnguǎn HOTEL $$
(乔戈里峰登山宾馆; 9180 Líng-gōnglǐ; 零公里9180号; r ¥130-190; ❄🅪) The 'K2 Hotel' is the better place to stay but the location isn't great if you're only passing through. Board bus 2 outside the bus station or take a taxi for ¥10. It's 6km from the bus station.

ℹ Getting There & Away

Buses to Yarkand (¥10) and Kashgar (¥34, four hours) leave every half-hour until 8.30pm. Every two hours until 8.30pm there is a bus to Hotan (¥34, five hours), or take a faster shared taxi for ¥85 per seat.

The newly paved 1100km road to Ali, in western Tibet, branches off from the main Kashgar–Hotan road 6km east of Karghilik. The only way to (legally) take the highway is by organising a Land Cruiser tour with an agent in Lhasa. See Lonely Planet's *Tibet* guide for details.

Hotan 和田

✈ 0903 / POP 130,000

Hotan has long been known as the epicentre of the central Asian and Chinese jade trade. Locally unearthed jade artefacts have been dated to around 5000 BC and it is believed that Hotan (Hétián; also known as Khotan) attracted Chinese traders along the Jade Road even before they headed westward to open up the Silk Road. In 5th century AD the Hotanese were also the first to learn the secret of Chinese silkmaking, and later established themselves as the region's foremost carpet weavers.

Hundreds of shops across town continue to offer a huge selection of local jade. In the old days prospectors would feel for river stones in the moonlight using only their bare feet; these days mechanical dredgers dig for jade on an industrial scale.

Today Hotan is largely a Chinese city, but it still has some fascinating old neighbourhoods and markets and retains a cultural authenticity that is increasingly hard to find in Kashgar. What makes the 500km-long slog from Kashgar really worthwhile is the fantastic Sunday Market, the largest and least visited in Xīnjiāng.

Beijing Xilu is the main east–west axis running past the enormous main square (Tuánjié Guǎngchǎng), with its paternalistic statue of Mao looking down on an undersized Uighur craftsman.

◉ Sights

Sunday Market   MARKET

(星期天市场) Hotan's most popular attraction is its weekly Sunday market. The covered market bustles every day of the week but on Sundays it swamps the northeast part of town, reaching fever pitch between noon and 2pm Xīnjiāng time. The most interesting parts to head for are the *doppi* (skullcap) bazaar, the colourful *atlas* (tiedyed, handwoven silk) cloth to the right of the main entrance and the *gilim* (carpet) bazaar, across the road. Nearby Juma Lu (加买路) is worth a stroll for its traditional medicine and spice shops.

The small but authentic Sunday livestock bazaar is about 2km further east, near the Jade Dragon Kashgar River on Donghuan Beilu; take bus 10, 5 or 101 to the junction then walk 500m north.

FREE Carpet Factory   HANDICRAFTS CENTRE

(地毯厂; dìtǎn chǎng; ☉10am-7pm) On the eastern bank of the Jade Dragon Kashgar River is this large factory (*gilim karakhana* in Uighur). It's primarily set up for group visits but you can look around the various halls when open. Even with up to 10 weavers, one sq mt of wool carpet takes 20 days to complete. To get here, take bus 5 from Hotan bus station and get off at the last stop.

Silk Workshop   HANDICRAFTS CENTRE

(丝绸手工工艺; sīchóu shǒugōng gōngyì; ☉10am-7.30pm) Past the carpet factory, northeast of Hotan, is the small town of Jíyà (吉亚乡), a traditional centre for silk production. Visitors can wander the recently renovated workshop (*atlas karakhana* in Uighur) to see how the silk is spun from silk cocoons, then dyed and woven, all using traditional methods. A return trip by taxi to the workshop, taking in the carpet factory, costs ¥80. Buses run frequently to Jíyà (¥2) from inside Hotan's east bus station.

Mazar of Imam Asim   TOMB

A few kilometres beyond Jíyà lies the tomb complex of Imam Asim (Tomb of Four Imams). It's a popular pilgrimage site, particularly during May, and you'll likely see groups of Uighurs praying and chanting at the desert shrine, which is slowly being engulfed by the Taklamakan Desert. The best day to visit is Thursday, when a pilgrim market springs up by the roadside, about 2km before the tomb, and buses run direct to the site from Hotan's east bus station. At other times buses to Jíyà drop you 3km from the site, from where you should be able to hire a motorised cart.

FREE Hotan Cultural Museum   MUSEUM

(和田博物馆; Hétián Bówùguǎn; Beijing Xilu; ☉9.45am-1pm & 4-7.30pm, closed Wed) West of the centre is the regional museum. The main attractions are a fine painted wooden coffin and two 1500-year-old Indo-European mummies unearthed from the nearby Imam Musa Kazim Cemetery. There are also some

SILK

Prices for *atlas* vary wildly depending on whether the cloth is pure silk or a satin mix, whether it's handmade (coarser) or machine made (softer and glossier but not as nice) and whether it uses natural or chemical dyes. A 6m-long piece of pure silk costs up to ¥500, with real silk scarves around ¥100 to ¥180.

Hotan

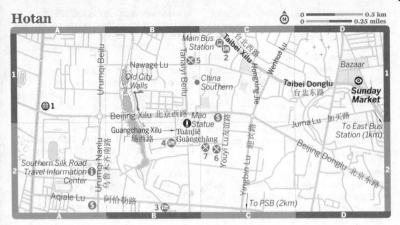

fascinating finds from ancient Niya, including a large wooden pillar, a 2000-year-old bow and arrow and wooden tablets engraved with Indian-influenced Kharoshthi script. Take buses 2 or 6 from the town centre to get here (bus 6 runs from the bazaar).

Melikawat Ruins　ARCHAEOLOGICAL SITE
(玛利克瓦特古城; Mǎlìkèwǎtè Gǔchéng; admission ¥10) The deserts around Hotan are peppered with the faint remains of abandoned cities. The most interesting are those of Melikawat, 25km south of town, a Tang-dynasty settlement with wind-eroded walls, Buddhist stupas and the remains of pottery kilns. Some scholars believe Melikawat was a capital city of the Yutian state (206 BC–AD 907), an Indo-European civilisation that thrived during the height of the Silk Road. A taxi should cost about ¥100 to Melikawat.

Rawaq Pagoda　ARCHAEOLOGICAL SITE
The 9m-tall Rawaq Pagoda is an intriguing but remote sight, about 50km north of Hotan, then 8km off the Cross-Desert Highway. You'll need to buy a ticket (¥200 to ¥450) in advance to visit. Contact the **Cultural Department** (Wénhuàjú; ☑0903-618 2018) at Hotan Museum for information on this and other specialised archaeological sites.

🛏 Sleeping

Tarim Hotel　HOTEL $$
(塔里木大饭店; Tǎlǐmù Dàfàndiàn; ☑206 7777; 135 Aqiale Xilu; 阿恰勒西路135号; d ¥198; ❄@) New four-star hotel with fresh, modern rooms, some with computers (add ¥20), that make it the best value midrange choice. It's a block southwest of the main square.

Hotan

◎ Top Sights

Sunday Market......................................D1

◎ Sights

1 Hotan Cultural Museum.......................A1

🛏 Sleeping

2 Jiāotōng Bīnguǎn................................C1
3 Tarim Hotel...B2
4 Yùdū Dàjiǔdiàn....................................B2

◎ Eating

5 Arom Restaurant.................................B1
6 Marco's Dream Cafe.............................C2
7 Uighur Night Market............................C2

Yùdū Dàjiǔdiàn　HOTEL $$
(玉都大酒店; ☑202 3456; 11 Guangchang Lu; 广场路11号; tw ¥238) The three-star 'Jade Capital' has spacious and modern rooms, with a useful location on the west side of the main square. You can buy air tickets in the lobby.

Jiāotōng Bīnguǎn　HOTEL $
(交通宾馆; ☑203 2700; Taibei Xilu; 台北西路; d with/without bathroom ¥160/100; ❄) The bus station hotel is worn out and overpriced but it's the only real budget option. The shared bathrooms are awful, so consider the en suite rooms or do without.

🍴 Eating

Uighur Night Market　MARKET $
(维族人夜市; Wéizúrén Yèshì; Guangchang Donglu; ◎7pm-midnight) On the southeast corner of the square; a good place to grab such goodies as *tonur kebab* (whole roast sheep)

and *chuchvara* (meat dumplings in broth), topped off with sweet *tangzaza* (sticky rice with syrup and yoghurt).

Marco's Dream Cafe
CAFE **$**

(马克驿站; Mǎkè Yìzhàn; www.marcodream cafe.blogspot.com; 57 Youyi Lu; mains ¥18-30; ⊙1.30-9.30pm Tue-Sun; 🔊) This Malaysian-run restaurant serves a nice range of southeast Asian dishes, including curried chicken, plus cakes and coffee (¥6 to ¥10). The friendly English-speaking owners can provide excellent travel advice.

Arom Restaurant
UIGHUR **$**

(cnr Tanaiyi Beilu & Nawage Lu; mains ¥14) Locals recommend this place for the best *polo* in town, served succulent and moist with delicious yoghurt. Alternatively head to the branch across the road for good-value set meals (¥15).

🛈 Information

Bank of China (中国银行; Zhōngguó Yínháng; cnr Urumqi Nanlu & Aqiale Lu; ⊙9.30am-1.30pm & 4-8pm Mon-Fri) Cashes travellers cheques, in the southwest of town.

China Construction Bank (中国建设银行; Zhōngguó Jiànshè Yínháng; cnr Beijing Lu & Youyi Lu; ⊙9.30am-1pm & 4-6.30pm Mon-Fri) Has ATMs that accept foreign cards.

China International Travel Service (CITS; 中国国际旅行社; Zhōngguó Guójì Lǚxíngshè; 🗷251 6090; 3F, 23 Tunken Lu) Located to the south off Urumqi Nanlu. Can arrange tours to a silk factory, as well as expensive excursions to the ruins at Yotkan and Melikawat.

Public Security Bureau (PSB; 公安局; Gōng'ānjú; 691 Yingbin Lu; ⊙10am-1pm & 4.30-7.30pm Mon-Fri) Can extend visas in one day. Take bus 3 to its terminus at the corner of Yingbin Lu and Tunken Lu in the southern suburbs.

Southern Silk Road Travel Information Center (🗷137 7929 1939; www.southernsilkroadtour. com; treklab@gmail.com; Wulumuqi Nanlu) Local guide Kurbanjan runs private tours along the southern Silk Road from the Hétián Bīnguǎn.

🛈 Getting There & Away

AIR There are a dozen flights daily between Hotan and Ürümqi (¥1680). The airport is 10km southwest of town; a taxi there costs ¥20.

BUS & CAR There are two bus stations in Hotan. Most buses leave from the main station on Taibei Xilu, from where there are nine buses to Kashgar (¥128, seven to 10 hours) from 9.30am to 10pm. These buses also stop at Karghilik (¥52, five hours) and Yarkand (¥71, six hours).

Buses to Ürümqi (¥257 to ¥387, 25 hours) head straight across the desert on one of two cross-desert highways. A daily bus to Kuqa (¥168 to ¥185, eight hours) departs at 2pm and 8pm.

Shared taxis also run to Karghilik (¥90), Yarkand (¥120) and Kashgar (¥200).

To continue east along the southern Silk Road, head to the east bus station (东郊客运站; dōngjiāo kèyùnzhàn) 2km east of downtown. One bus (sometimes a sleeper, sometimes a normal bus) leaves at 10.30am for Cherchen (¥124 to ¥160, 10 hours) and there are buses every two hours to Niya (¥63, four hours).

TRAIN The railway line from Kashgar reached Hotan in 2011. A single daily train leaves at 10.20am for Ürümqi (hard/soft sleeper ¥241/390, 36 hours), via Kashgar (hard seat ¥34, 9 hours).

🛈 Getting Around

Bus 101 runs from the main bus station on Taibei Xilu, past the Sunday Market to the east bus station, 1km away. Metered taxis cost around ¥8 within town; figure on ¥15 to the train station and ¥30 to the airport.

Cherchen
且末

☑ 0996 / POP 60,000

The next major stop along the southern Silk Road is Cherchen (Qiěmò), 580km away via the townships of Keriya (于田; Yútián) and Niya (民丰; Mínfēng). The road initially passes the towering Kunlun Mountains that mark the border with Tibet to the south, before crossing impressive sand dunes and then stony desert for the last 300km to Cherchen.

From Cherchen bus station head right (north) along Aita Lu to the first set of traffic lights at Wenhua Lu: continue straight for the Hóngzǎo Shāngwù Bīnguǎn and museum. Take a right at the next block on Sichou Lu (Silk Road!) for the Kūnyù Bīnguǎn. A taxi/cart to the hotels costs ¥10/3.

To visit the main sights outside Cherchen go first to the Cherchen Museum as you need to take a guide with you to unlock the gates. Guides can help arrange a taxi.

◉ Sights

FREE **Cherchen Museum**
MUSEUM

(且末县博物馆; Qiěmò Xiàn Bówùguǎn; ⊙9.30am-1.30pm, 4-7.30pm) Relics from Cherchen's main sights are on display at this new regional museum, alongside displays ranging from yetis in the Altun Tagh mountains to the travels of explorer Sven Hedin. It's in the northwest of town, by the huge new government square.

Toghraklek Manor
HISTORIC BUILDING

(托乎拉克庄园; Tuōhūlākè Zhuāngyuán; admission ¥20) Cherchen's main sight is this fine example of early-20th century Kashgarian architecture, built in 1911 for a local warlord. It's 2.5km west of town.

Zaghunluq Ancient Mummy Tomb
TOMB

(扎滚鲁克古墓群景点; Zāgǔnlǔkè Gǔmùqún Jǐngdiǎn; admission ¥30) This 2600-year-old tomb contains a dozen or so naturally mummified bodies, still sporting shreds of colourful clothing. The site is a further 4km west of the Toghraklek Manor, on the edge of the desert. Figure on ¥50 for a taxi to both sites.

🛏 Sleeping

Hóngzǎo Shāngwù Bīnguǎn
HOTEL $

(红枣商务宾馆; ☑761 1888; Aita Lu; 埃塔路; r ¥138-158; ❄@) Clean, fresh and spacious rooms make this the best value option, next to the bazaar, though some bathrooms are cleaner than others. The pricier rooms come with computers.

Jiāotōng Bīnguǎn
HOTEL $

(交通宾馆; ☑762 7088; d with/without bathroom ¥100/60; ❄@) If you are just transiting overnight the bus station hotel has small but acceptable rooms, the best with computers (extra ¥20).

Yùdū Bīnguǎn
HOTEL $$$

(玉都宾馆; ☑762 5150; old/new block d incl breakfast ¥150/488) Party cadres live it up in this government-run option next to the (currently defunct) airport. There's a four-star main building and a much cheaper and run-down old block, both set in spacious and quiet grounds.

Kūnyù Bīnguǎn
HOTEL $

(昆玉宾馆; ☑762 6555; Tuanjie Beilu; d ¥120-140) Decent option next to the central town square.

ℹ Getting There & Away

There is a sleeper bus at 7pm to Ürümqi (¥280 to ¥300, 16 hours) and a 10am and 7pm bus to Korla (¥170, six hours); both of these go via the Cross-Desert Hwy. There is no bus service to Kuqa. The bus to Hotan (¥127 to Y177, 10 hours) leaves at 10am and is normally a sleeper bus. A daily 10am bus (¥61, four hours) continues 350km east to Charklik.

Charklik
若羌

Charklik (Ruòqiāng; not to be confused with Karghilik further west) is a soulless, modern Chinese city, but there are several ancient ruined cities nearby. The most famous is remote **Lóulán** (楼兰), located some 260km northeast of Charklik, but you'll probably have to join a very pricey group tour to visit as permits can run into the thousands of dollars. The ruined fortress and stupa of **Miran** (米兰) is closer, located just 7km southeast of the modern town of Miran (which is 85km northwest of Charklik). It's also cheaper – group permits cost around ¥400 to ¥500. Contact CITS (www.xinjiangtour.com) in Ürümqi for help with the paperwork.

If you get stuck in town, the **Yínhǎi Bīnguǎn** (银海宾馆; ☑0996-710 5018; Shengli Lu; d ¥120; ❄) is a clean and good value option, 100m south of the bus station.

From Charklik you can complete the Taklamakan loop by taking a bus to Korla (¥94, six hours, every two hours) Alternatively, you can continue east over the mountains to Golmud in Qīnghǎi (¥230, 12 hours) on a daily 6pm sleeper bus. If for some reason that's not running, you'll have to take the daily bus to Yītūnbùlākè/Shímiánkuàng (¥96, 10am) and then change for the short hop to Huātùgōu, to catch one of two daily buses to Golmud (¥104, six hours).

NORTHERN XĪNJIĀNG

This region of thick evergreen forests, rushing rivers and isolated mountain ranges is historically home to pastoral nomads. It was closed to foreigners until the 1990s, due to the proximity of the sensitive Russian, Mongolian and Kazakhstan borders.

Bù'ěrjīn
布尔津

☑ 0906 / POP 60,000

Bù'ěrjīn, 620km north of Ürümqi, marks the end of the desert-like Jungar Basin and the beginning of the lusher sub-Siberian birch forests and mountains to the north. The town's population is mainly Kazakh, but there are also Russians, Han, Uighurs and Tuvans.

If you have some time to kill, stroll to the southern limits of town to the Erqis (Irtysh) River, where dozens of stone *balbals* (Turkic grave markers) line the river embankment.

From here the river flows eventually into the Arctic Ocean; the only major river in China to do so. In summer, you'll be confronted with swarms of biting insects around dusk, so stock up on insect repellent.

Sleeping & Eating

Hotel rates peak between July and September and are discounted by up to 70% at other times.

Shénxiān Wān Dàjiǔdiàn
HOTEL $

(神仙湾大酒店; ☎652 1325; 5 Shenhu Lu; 神湖路5号; tw ¥140) The Immortal Bay Hotel has clean rooms and an efficient staff that are willing to negotiate the price. From the bus station, turn left and then right at the first intersection. It's about 200m down on the left.

Burqin Tourist Hotel
HOTEL $$$

(布尔津旅游宾馆; Bù'ěrjīn Lǚyóu Bīnguǎn; ☎651 0099; 4 Wolongwan Xilu; 卧龙湾西路4号; d from ¥488; ☺May-Nov) Large, dependable hotel with two-, three- and four-star blocks. Rooms are generally discounted by up to 65%.

Jiàn'ān Bīnguǎn
HOTEL $

(建安宾馆; ☎652 0688; Wenming Lu; 文明路; d ¥120-200) This cheapie opposite the bus station doesn't have official permission but will accept foreigners, making it the best budget value in town. The three wings offer different grades of rooms.

Night Market
MARKET $

(河夜市; Hérí Yèshì; Hebin Lu; mains from ¥10; ☺7pm-midnight) Specialising in grilled fish, fresh yoghurt and *kvas* (a yeasty brew popular in Russia), this riverside night market makes for very atmospheric dining. To find it, walk south on Youyifeng Lu and keep going until the street dead ends: it's on the right. A second night market is in the alley (Meishi Jie) opposite People's Hospital (人民医院; Rénmín Yīyuàn), between Youyifeng Lu and Kanasi Lu.

ⓘ Information

Industrial & Commercial Bank of China (ICBC; Zhōngguó Gōngshāng Yínháng; Huancheng Nanlu; ☺10am-1.30pm & 4-6.30pm) Couldn't change money at time of research but plans to in the future.

Tiānhé Wǎngbā (天和网吧; Meishi Jie; ☺9am-midnight; per hr ¥3) Internet cafe located at the western end of the smaller night market.

Public Security Bureau (PSB; 公安局; Gōng'ānjú; cnr Yueliangwan Lu & Youyifeng Lu)

ⓘ Getting There & Away

AIR Nearby Altay has an airport with year-round daily flights to/from Ürümqi (¥1180).

BUS There are both day (¥148, 10 hours) and night buses (¥170 to ¥180, 12 hours) to Ürümqi. Hourly buses run to Altay (Ālètài; ¥20 to ¥24, 1½ hours) between 10am and 7pm. Six buses a day run to Jímùnǎi (¥20, two hours) on the border with Kazakhstan.

SHARED TAXI Faster shared taxis run from outside the bus station to Ürümqi (¥250 per seat) and Altay (¥40).

TRAIN The overnight K9791 train departs Ürümqi at 8pm for Běitún (北屯; 12½ hours; ¥183/276). From here a limited number of shared taxis make the 90km ride on to Bù'ěrjīn (¥40), or take bus No 1 to Běitún bus station (¥10) and change there. Buy your return train tickets in advance as there is currently no ticket office in Bù'ěrjīn.

Kanas Lake Nature Reserve 哈纳斯湖自然保护区

Stunning Kanas Lake is a long finger of water nestled in the southernmost reaches of the Siberian taiga ecosystem, pinched in between Mongolia, Russia and Kazakhstan. Most of the local inhabitants are Kazakh or Tuvan. Chinese tourists (and the occasional foreigner) descend on the place like locusts in summer, but with a little effort it's just about possible to escape the crowds. Many come hoping for a cameo by the Kanas Lake Monster, China's Nessie, who has long figured in stories around yurt campfires to scare the kids. She appears every year or two, bringing loads of journalists and conspiracy hounds.

The whole area is only accessible from mid-May to mid-October, with ice and snow making transport difficult at other times. The gorgeous autumn colours peak around mid-September.

◉ Sights & Activities

About 160km from Bù'ěrjīn the road comes to an end at Jiǎdēngyù, basically a collection of hotels near the entrance to the **Kanas Lake Nature Reserve** (Hānàsī Hú Zìrán Bǎohùqū; adult/student ¥150/120). Buy a ticket and board a tourist bus (per person ¥80, unlimited rides), which carries you 16km up the canyon to a tourist base. The journey includes three photo stops along the way, including Crouching Dragon Bay (卧龙湾; Wòlóng Wān), Moon Bay (月亮湾; Yuèliàng Wān) and Immortal Bay (神仙湾; Shénxiān Wān).

At the tourist base you can change buses to take you the final 2km to Kanas Lake. The old Tuvan village lines the road, just past the tourist base. (The new Tuvan village is 2km to the west, across the river.) From the final stop it's a five-minute walk to the lake. At the lakeshore you can take a speedboat ride (¥120, 40 minutes) halfway up the lake. A boardwalk along the shore takes you 4.5km up the side of the lake to a vantage point. It's also possible to walk downstream from the dock along the river. The bus terminus is also the starting point for white-water-rafting trips (¥200, 40 minutes), which operate until mid-August.

A great day hike is to the lookout point, **Guānyú Pavilion** (观鱼亭; Guānyú Tíng; 2030m). It's a long, ambling walk from the village; from the lookout there are superb panoramas of the lake and nearby grasslands. It's possible to reach the pavilion by horse – horsemen in the village offer the trip for ¥150 (plus another ¥150 for the guide). The easiest way up is by bus (¥30 one way) from the new Tuvan village. The bus gets close to the top, from where you walk 1066 steps (20 minutes) to the pavilion.

The entry ticket and bus ticket are good for two days. Once you are in the park, no one checks your ticket, so you can stay as long as you like and use the hop on, hop off bus service to get between the lake and village.

A more adventurous route to the reserve is a two-day horse trek from the valley of **Hémù** (禾木; student/adult ¥48/60, plus ¥100 bus fee), 70km southeast of Kanas Lake, via Karakol (Black Lake, or Héi Hú). It's not all that cheap: a guide is ¥200 per day, horse rental is ¥150 per day, and you also have to pay for the guide's horse. You can save money by trekking in on foot. From Hémù it's a seven- to 10-hour walk to Karakol, where Kazakh yurts offer accommodation between June and October. After a night at the lake, walk along the south shore and then continue west for six to seven hours to the old Tuvan village. On day two you won't find much water on the trail, so load up at Black Lake before setting off. The bus fee is waived if you enter this way, but someone may track you down and charge you for an admission ticket.

You can reach Hémù by bus from Bù'ěrjīn but it's faster to get a shared taxi; just make sure it will take you all the way to the village and not just to the gate where you pay the admission fee, which is some 20km before the village. The road to Hémù was being upgraded in 2012. A bus (¥200) is also available from the main Kanas Lake gate at Jiǎdēngyù; the price includes the admission ticket to Hémù.

☞ Tours

The four-day trip out of Ürümqi with Western International Travel Service (p782) is an excellent deal. For around ¥700 you get an air-con minibus (10 hours), two nights in Bù'ěrjīn, a park entrance ticket and one night's lodging at the lake. This company operates some of the facilities and activities in the park, including the rafting and boating trips.

🛏 Sleeping & Eating

The best place to stay is at a homestay in the old or the new Tuvan village. There are several homestays but none have signs, so you'll have to ask around. The homestays are basic, usually just a spare bedroom. You'll pay between ¥50 and ¥100 for a bed depending on the season, plus about ¥20 to ¥30 per meal.

One option is the guesthouse owned by a Tuvan man, **Banzan** (☑135 6518 7064), who lives about 200m past the school (学校; xuéxiào) in the old Tuvan village near the main road about 2km before the lake. Banzan's family are performers, so you may get to see some traditional singing and dancing. Look for the fading green sign with the picture of a man playing the flute.

In the new village across the river, ask for **Hadala Beka** (☑137 7905 4663), who has a guesthouse with three rooms. To find it on your own, first go to the new village, walk down the main road and look for the large solar panels on your left. The guesthouse is on the far side of the solar panels.

If you need running water and flush toilets, there are plenty of hotels at the tourist base. Try the **Lánhú Bīnguǎn** (Blue Lake Hotel; 蓝湖宾馆; ☑0906-632 6008; r ¥200-480), located in a yurt-shaped building near the bus parking lot.

Food in the reserve is expensive and monotonous; bring your own supplies.

In Hémù, you can stay at the **AHA International Youth Hostel** (阿哈国际青年旅社; ☑0991-886 8118; www.yhakanas.com; dm ¥60, d ¥120), a rustic wood-cabin hostel and comfortable base for exploring the village and nearby mountains.

ℹ Getting There & Away

See the Tours section also.

AIR Kanas airport, 50km south of the reserve, has flights to and from Ürümqi (¥1460, one hour) in July and August only. A shuttle (¥40) meets all incoming flights.

BUS There is no public bus to the main gate at Jiǎdēngyù, but two buses per day go to Hémù (¥50, four hours) at 10am and 4pm. The buses leave outside the bus station at Bù'ěrjīn and the village school in Hémù respectively.

TAXI A share taxi to Jiǎdēngyù from Bù'ěrjīn is ¥80 per person, though passengers can be hard to find before June. Rates to Hémù cost the same. Taxi drivers will look for you at Bù'ěrjīn's bus station.

Yīníng 伊宁

☏ 0999 / POP 300,000

Located on the historic border between the Chinese and Russian empires, Yīníng (Yili, or Gulja) has long been subject to a tug-of-war between the two sides. The city was occupied by Russian troops between 1872 and 1881, and in 1962 there were major Sino-Soviet clashes along the Ili River (Yīlí Hé). There are no unmissable sights here but it's a pleasant, untouristed stop on route to Sayram Lake or Kazakhstan.

The bus station is 3km from the centre at the northwest end of Jiefang Lu, the main thoroughfare through town. An **internet café** (绿色心情网吧; ◷24hr) is located on the south side of People's Sq.

◉ Sights

The heart of the city is **People's Square** (Rénmín Guǎngchǎng), a popular place to fly kites. The south side is lined with ice cream, fruit and kebab stands.

From the square's southwest corner continue south into the Uighur old town, past the 260-year-old **Shānxī Mosque** (陕西大寺) and workshops making traditional-style leather Uighur boots. Look for the old **Uzbek Masjid** (Uzbek mosque), then head through backstreets west to Jiefang Nanlu and the modern Saudi-style **Baytullah Mosque**.

⿓ Sleeping & Eating

Yīlí Bīnguǎn HOTEL $$

(伊犁宾馆; ☏802 3799; 8 Yingbin Lu; 迎宾路 8; tw ¥160-388; ❉) Yili's former Soviet consulate is full of character and super-quiet if not booked out by a group of Maotai-slurping visiting party officials. A bust of Lenin greets you at the entrance, beyond which is a forest of chirping birds and 1950s Russian dachas. The Zixiangge Coffee Club, just inside the gate, offers fancy Western-style meals (mains ¥50 to ¥100) and quiet internet access.

V8 Shāngwù Jiǔdiàn HOTEL $

(V8 商务酒店; ☏819 8555; Jiefang Lu; d ¥128-148; ❉@) The new bus station hotel offers immaculate and excellent value rooms with flat-screen TVs, internet-enabled computers and gold carpets. Hopefully management will maintain the place and not hike prices as it becomes popular.

Cháishì Kuàicān UIGHUR $

(柴氏快餐; Yingbin Lu; mains ¥8-15) We came back again and again to this cafeteria just outside the Yīlí Bīnguǎn. The *laghman* and noodles with egg and tomato are excellent, as are the various set meals that come served in a wooden bucket of rice (木桶饭; *mùtǒngfàn*). Wash it all down with a glass of Russian-style kvass (格瓦斯; *gēwǎsī*), a fermented, slightly alcoholic drink made from bread.

Riverside Restaurants UIGHUR $

Just to the south of town is a line of open-air restaurants where you can sit and watch the mighty Ili River (Ili Daria in Uighur, Yīlí Hé in Chinese) slide by over a bottle of honey-flavoured kvass. To get there, hop on bus 2, get off at the last stop and cross the bridge over the river.

ℹ Getting There & Away

From the **main bus station** (zhōu kèyùnzhàn) there are buses to Ürümqi (¥150 to ¥180, nine to 12 hours) and Bólè (¥53, four hours, hourly), and sleepers to Korla (¥200 to ¥220, 18 hours). Buses also run every 30 minutes for the Kazakh border at Korgas (¥20, 90 minutes). Buses 1, 101 and 12 run from the centre to the bus station.

Buses to Almaty (¥250, 12 hours) depart at 7.30am from an unpromising parking lot on Yingayati Lu, east of Renmin Sq. Buy your ticket the day before and expect to spend hours at customs. You must have a Kazakhstan visa.

There are two daily trains to Ürümqi (11 hours), the 5816 (hard/soft sleeper ¥151/234) at 7.42pm and the K9790 (hard/soft sleeper ¥162/245) at 9.50pm. The station is 8km northwest of the city centre; buses 10, 16, 201 and 401 go there or take a taxi for ¥15. There's a useful **train ticket office** (◷8.30am-5.30pm & 6-8pm; commission ¥5) on Shengli Beilu, a block north from the east side of People's Square.

TUGLUGH TIMUR KHAN MAUSOLEUM

Fans of medieval history and Timurid architecture will enjoy making a half-day detour from Yīníng to this unassuming blue-tiled **tomb** (吐虎鲁克铁木尔汗麻扎; tǔhǔlǔkè tiěmùěrhán māzā; admission ¥15). Tuglugh was the 14th-century khan of eastern Chaghatai (or Mughalistan), an offshoot of the Mongol empire centered on the surrounding city of Almaliq, itself once a major medieval Central Asian trade centre. The tomb is covered with an intricate web of blue majolica tiles and incised terracotta that recalls tombs from Samarkand. Nothing remains of Almaliq.

To get here take a minibus or shared taxi from outside Yīníng bus station to Qīngshuǐhé (清水河), then walk a couple of hundred metres to shared taxi No 61 for the short transfer to Liùshíyī Tuán (六十一团; ¥10 per seat). The tomb is easily visited en route to the Kazakh border at Korgas.

There are several flights a day to Ürümqi (¥1320); tickets are available from the **Xinjiang Airport Group** (☎ 803 1888), by the gate of the Yīlí Bīnguǎn. The airport is 5km north of town (¥10 taxi).

Sayram Lake　　塞里木湖

Vast Sayram Lake (Sàilǐmù Hú), 120km north of Yīníng and 90km west of Bólè, is an excellent spot to get a taste of the Tiān Shān range (Tengri Tagh in Kazakh). The lake is especially colourful during June and July, when the alpine flowers are in full bloom.

While there is some food around, the selection is pricey and limited, so take what you need. In the height of summer, there are Kazakh yurts (about ¥40 per night including three meals) scattered around the lake willing to take boarders. Admission to the lake is ¥40.

By bus, Sayram Lake is two hours from Bólè or three hours from Yīníng; any bus passing between the two cities can drop you by the lake. They usually stop at its southwestern corner, where you'll find horses for hire and plenty of yurt accommodation in summer. Coming from Yīníng, the last section of road is a spectacular series of mountain bridges and tunnels.

Gānsù

POP 26.4 MILLION

Includes »

Lánzhōu	810
Xiàhé	815
Hézuò	820
Lángmùsì	821
Wǔwēi	823
Zhāngyè	825
Mǎtí Sì	826
Jiāyùguān & Around	827
Dūnhuáng	829
Tiānshuǐ	836
Píngliáng	838

Best Landscapes

» Yǎdān National Park (p835)

» Singing Sands (p835)

» Road to Bǐnglíng Sì (p814)

» Gānjiā Grasslands (p820)

» Lángmùsì (p821)

Best Buddhist Sites

» Mògāo Caves (p833)

» Zhāngyè Great Buddha Temple (p825)

» Yúlín Grottoes (p836)

» Labrang Monastery (p816)

» Milarepa Palace (p820)

Why Go?

Synonymous with the Silk Road, the slender province of Gānsù flows east to west along the Hèxī Corridor, the gap through which all manner of goods once streamed from China to Central Asia. The constant flow of commerce left Buddhist statues, beacon towers, forts, chunks of the Great Wall and ancient trading towns in its wake.

Gānsù (甘肃) offers an entrancingly rich cultural and geographic diversity. Historians immerse themselves in Silk Road lore, art aficionados swoon before the wealth of Buddhist paintings and sculptures, while adventurers hike to glaciers, ride camels through the desert and tread along paths well worn by Tibetan nomads. The ethnic diversity is equally astonishing: in Línxià, the local Hui Muslims act as though the silk route lives on; in Xiàhé and Lángmùsì a pronounced Tibetan disposition holds sway, while other minority groups such as the Bao'an and Dongxiang join in the colourful minority patchwork.

When to Go
Lánzhōu

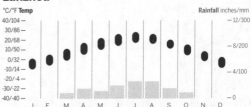

| Feb & Mar Join the Tibetan pilgrims for the magnificent Monlam Festival in Xiàhé. | Apr & May Before the full heat of summer switches on. | Sep & Oct For crisp northern Gānsù autumnal colours, blue skies and cooler climes. |

History

Although the Qin dynasty had a toehold on eastern Gānsù, the first significant push west along the Hèxī Corridor came with the Han dynasty. An imperial envoy, Chang Ch'ien, was dispatched to seek trading partners and returned with detailed reports of Central Asia and the route that would become known as the Silk Road. The Han extended the Great Wall through the Hèxī Corridor, expanding their empire in the process. As trade along the Silk Road grew, so did the small way stations set up along its route; these grew into towns and cities that form the major population centres of modern Gānsù. The stream of traders from

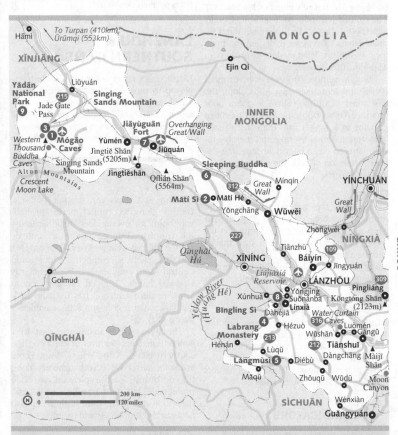

Gānsù Highlights

❶ Peruse the astonishing **Mògāo Caves** (p833)

❷ Relax and explore the venerable Buddha Caves at the Horse Hoof Monastery, **Mǎtí Sì** (p826)

❸ Camp beneath the stars amid the vast dunes of the **Singing Sands Mountain** (p835) near Dūnhuáng

❹ Go with the Tibetan flow around the **Labrang Monastery** (p816) *kora* in Xiàhé

❺ Hike to your heart's content through the fantastic scenery around **Lángmùsì** (p821)

❻ Stand head-to-head with the vast **Sleeping Buddha** (p825) of Zhāngyè

❼ Feel the Gobi wind in your hair as you stand on the ramparts of **Jiāyùguān Fort** (p827) in Jiāyùguān

❽ Ride through a mesmerising terraced landscape on the road to **Bǐnglíng Sì** (p814)

❾ Walk in a dried-out desert lake and marvel at the eroded landforms at **Yǎdān National Park** (p835)

lands east and west also left their mark in the incredible diversity of modern Gānsù. The Buddhist grottoes at Mògāo, Màijī Shān and elsewhere are testament to the great flourishing of religious and artistic schools along the Silk Road.

The mixing of cultures in Gānsù eventually led to serious tensions, which culminated in the Muslim rebellions of 1862 to 1877. The conflict left millions dead and virtually wiped out Gānsù's Muslim population. Ethnic tensions have never really left the province as the pro-Tibetan demonstrations in Xiàhé in 2008 illustrate.

Though remote from the investment banks and manufacturing hubs along the east coast of China, Gānsù is not a poor province. Gross Domestic Product has been growing at a higher rate than the already blistering national average and massive investments in clean energy are fuelling the transformation of both the natural and urban landscapes.

Climate

Gānsù rarely sees any rain outside of the southern regions, and dust storms can whip up, particularly in the spring, so it's good to come prepared with face masks and even antibiotic eye drops. Winters are nippy from November to March. Summer temperatures in the desert regions can top 40°C.

Language

Gānsù has its own group of regional Chinese dialects, loosely known as Gansuhua (part of the northwestern Lanyin Mandarin family). On the borders of Qīnghǎi and Sìchuān there is a significant Tibetan population speaking the Tibetan Amdo dialect.

PRICE INDICATORS

The following price indicators are used in this chapter:

Sleeping

$	less than ¥150
$$	¥150 to ¥500
$$$	more than ¥500

Eating

$	less than ¥30
$$	¥30 to ¥80
$$$	more than ¥80

ⓘ Getting There & Around

Lánzhōu has flights around the country; other airports such as Dūnhuáng and Jiāyùguān only have a handful of flights to major cities, with fewer flights in the winter.

Both trains and buses are handy for connecting the province's Silk Road sights. For southern Gānsù you are largely at the mercy of (sometimes painfully slow) buses.

LÁNZHŌU & SOUTHERN GĀNSÙ

Lánzhōu is a major transportation hub employed by most travellers as a springboard for elsewhere. The Tibetan-inhabited areas around Xiàhé and Lángmùsì are the principal enticements – perfect stopovers for overlanders heading to or from Sìchuān.

Lánzhōu 兰州

♪ 0931 / POP 2.17 MILLION

Roughly at China's cartographic bullseye, Gānsù's elongated capital marks the halfway point for overlanders trekking across the country. Growing up on a strategic stretch of the Yellow River (Huáng Hé), and sitting between competing Chinese and Central Asian empires, Lánzhōu frequently changed hands. Trapped between mountains, modern Lánzhōu has frequent bad-air days when a grey sun sets anaemically over a hazy city.

The city sprawls in an inelegant east–west concrete melange for over 20km along the southern banks of the Yellow River. There are some attractive neighbourhoods along the northwest, and a pleasant riverside promenade, but most travellers will spend their time around the train station, home to an assortment of hotels and eateries.

◉ Sights

FREE **Gānsù Provincial Museum** MUSEUM (甘肃省博物馆; Gānsù Shěng Bówùguǎn; Xijin Xilu; ⊙9am-5pm Tue-Sun) This sparkling museum has an intriguing collection of Silk Road artefacts, including inscribed Han-dynasty wooden tablets used to relay messages along the Silk Road. The graceful Eastern Han (25 BC–AD 220) bronze horse galloping upon the back of a swallow is known as the Flying Horse of Wǔwēi. Unearthed at Léitái, it has been reproduced across northwestern China. Among other items on view are

GĀNSÙ LÁNZHŌU

Lánzhōu

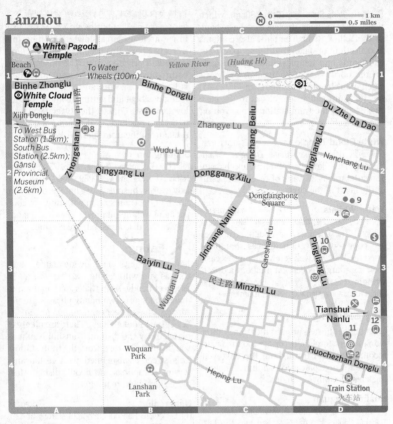

Lánzhōu

◎ Top Sights
White Cloud Temple..............................A1
White Pagoda Temple..........................A1

◎ Sights
1 Water Wheels D1

🛏 Sleeping
2 Huálián Bīnguǎn...................................D4
3 Jǐnjiāng Inn..D3
4 JJ Sun Hotel...D2

✕ Eating
5 Hézhèng Lù Night Market
   Entrance..D3

🔒 Shopping
6 Chénghuáng Miào B1

ℹ Information
7 Gānsù Airport Booking
   Office..D2

ℹ Transport
8 Bus 111 to South Bus
   Station A2
9 China Eastern Airlines.........................D2
10 East Bus Station...................................D3
11 Main Long-Distance Bus
   Station D4
12 Tiānshuǐ Bus Station...........................D4

Persian coins, some lovely Bodhisattva statues from Tiāntīshān and a collection of dinosaur skeletons. Bus 1, which departs from the train station, goes here.

FREE **White Pagoda Temple** BUDDHIST TEMPLE
(白塔寺; Báitǎ Sì) This temple, originally built during the Yuan dynasty (1206–1368), stands near the zenith of **White Pagoda Park**

(白塔山; Báitǎ Shān; ⊙6.30am-8.30pm), which winds up the near treeless northern bank of the Yellow River. The park also contains a collection of fake traditional pavilions, courtyards and temples. Enter from a gate on the north side of Zhōngshān Bridge or catch a **cable car** (up/down/return ¥35/25/45) on the south side a few blocks to the east. Bus 34 from the train station drops you off near the cable car.

White Cloud Temple
TAOIST TEMPLE

(白云观; Báiyún Guàn; Binhe Zhonglu; ⊙7am-5.30pm) This largely rebuilt Qing-dynasty Taoist temple is an oasis of reverential calm at the heart of the city.

Water Wheels
WATER WHEELS

(水车园; Shuǐchē Yuán; admission ¥6; ⊙8am-6.30pm) These massive wooden structures are copies of irrigation devices that once lined the Yellow River. A few kilometres east, look for a larger collection of about a dozen **wheels** (兰州水车博览园; Lánzhōu Shuǐchē Bólǎn Yuán; admission ¥10; ⊙8am-10pm).

🛏 Sleeping

Most budget hostels around the train station won't accept foreigners (or are too dreary to recommend) and throughout the city even many midrange places are off limits, including some nationwide chains.

Huálián Bīnguǎn
HOTEL $$

(华联宾馆; ☑499 2000; www.lzhlbg.com; 7-9 Tianshui Nanlu; 天水南路7-9号; d/tw ¥319/399; ❄@) This 360-room monster has comfortable updated rooms with broadband internet, a restaurant and a big lobby with a travel agency. The staff are friendly, but you'll have to put up with some traffic noise if you get a lower floor. The hotel is directly opposite the train station and has an English sign outside reading 'Lanzhou Mansions'. Expect discounts of 50%.

JJ Sun Hotel
HOTEL $$$

(锦江阳光酒店; Jǐnjiāng Yángguāng Jiǔdiàn; ☑880 5511; www.jjsunhotel.com; 589 Donggang Xilu; 东岗西路589号; tw/d ¥800/900; ❄@) This good four-star choice has well-groomed, spacious and affordable rooms. There's a pleasant wood-panelled restaurant on the 2nd floor. Discounts of 40% are usual.

Lánzhōu Huàr Youth Hostel
HOSTEL $

(兰州花儿国际青年旅舍; Lánzhōu Huà'er Guójì Qīngnián Lǚshè'; ☑9925 9808; Zone D, Lánzhōu Creative Industry Park, 704 Duan Jia Tan Lu; 兰州市城关区段家滩路704号兰州文化创意产业园D区; dm/d without bathroom ¥35/135; 🛜) Set in a warehouse area slowly morphing into a creative park, this friendly hostel has large dorm and private rooms. The unsegregated bathrooms are spic and span, and there is laundry, wi-fi, and an open loft area for lounging about and getting to know your fellow travellers. Contact the hostel if you want to catch a bus here, as it requires a transfer. A taxi from the train station costs ¥10.

Jǐnjiāng Inn
HOTEL $$

(锦江之星; Jǐnjiāng Zhīxīng; ☑861 7333; Tianshui Nanlu; 天水路; tw ¥219-289; ❄❄@) Neat and tidy express business-style hotel around 1km north of the train station with unfussy, compact and well-maintained rooms and snappy service. No discounts, but great value.

🍴 Eating

Lánzhōu enjoys nationwide fame (take that as you will) for its *niúròumiàn* (牛肉面), beef noodle soup that's spicy enough to make you snort. Two handy phrases are '*jiā ròu*' (加肉; add beef) and '*bùyào làjiāo*' (不要辣椒; without chillies). There are plenty of places to try the dish on Tianshui Nanlu as you head up the road from the train station. This street is also lined with restaurants serving dumplings and noodle dishes. Most places have picture menus.

Néngrénjù
HOTPOT $$

(能仁聚; 216 Tianshui Lu; hotpot starting at ¥20; ⊙11am-10pm; 🗐) At this tasty Běijīng-style *shùan yángròu* (涮羊肉; traditional lamb hotpot) the pot of broth costs ¥20, after which you can add sliced mutton (¥30), greens (¥10) and various other dishes. If you go solo expect to spend at least ¥50. The restaurant is about 100m past the intersection with Minzhu Lu.

Hézhèng Lù Night Market
MARKET $

(和政路夜市场入口; Hézhèng Lù Yèshìchǎng Rùkǒu) This bustling somewhat ramshackle market, extending from Tianshui Lu to Pingliang Lu, is terrific for savouring the flavours of the northwest. The mix of Hui, Han and Uighur stalls offer everything from goat's head soup to steamed snails, *ròujiābǐng* (肉夹饼; mutton served inside a 'pocket' of flat bread), lamb dishes seasoned with cumin, *dàpánjī* (大盘鸡; large plate of spicy chicken, noodles and potatoes), Sìchuān hole-in-the-wall outfits, dumplings, spare-rib noodles and more.

🛍 Shopping

TOP CHOICE **Chénghuáng Miào** ANTIQUES
(城隍庙; City God Temple; 202 Zhangye Lu) Jesus would probably not approve but this stately former house of Taoist worship has been turned into one of Lánzhōu's best shopping venues. Vendors sell everything from Mao kitsch, to calligraphy, tea sets, exotic stones and some truly beautiful pottery, woodwork and antiquities. The temple is set back on the north side of Zhangye Lu (a pedestrian-only road) about 500m east of Zhongshan Lu.

ℹ Information

Bank of China (中国银行; Zhōngguó Yínháng; Tianshui Lu; ⊙8.30am-noon & 2.30-5.30pm Mon-Fri) Has an ATM and changes travellers cheques on the 2nd floor.

Internet cafe (网吧; wǎngbā; per hr ¥3; ⊙24hr) On the 2nd floor, to the right of Huálián Bīnguǎn.

Public Security Bureau (PSB; 公安局; Gōng'ānjú; ☎871 8610; 482 Wudu Lu; ⊙8.30-11.30am & 2.30-5.30pm Mon-Fri) The foreign-affairs branch is on the 2nd floor. Visa extensions take several days; one photo required.

Western Travel Agency (西部旅行社; Xībù Lǚxíngshè; ☎882 0529; 486 Donggang Xilu) On the 2nd floor of the west wing of Lánzhōu Fàndiàn at the corner of Donggang Xilu and Tianshui Nanlu. Offers tours around Lánzhōu (as far south as Xiàhé) and ticket bookings.

ℹ Getting There & Away

Air

Among other cities, Lánzhōu has flights to Běijīng (¥1340), Dūnhuáng (¥1380), Jiāyùguān (¥1080), Kūnmíng (¥1410), Shànghǎi (¥1750) and Xī'ān (¥600).

Gānsù Airport Booking Office (甘肃机场售票中心; Gānsù Jīchǎng Shòupiào Zhōngxīn; ☎888 9666; 616 Donggang Xilu; ⊙8.30am-6pm) Can book all air tickets at discounted prices.

Bus

Lánzhōu has several bus stations, all with departures for Xīníng. The **main long-distance bus station** (长途车站; chángtú chēzhàn; Pingliang Lu) is now just a ticket office, outside which you catch a shuttle bus 30 minutes before departure for the **east bus station** (汽车东站; qìchē dōngzhàn; Pingliang Lu). Most bus journeys back into Lánzhōu end up at the east bus station; if you want to rough it on a sleeper to Zhāngyè or Jiāyùguān, buy a ticket directly at that station.

A new bus station had opened at the time of writing 150m east of the train station on Huochezhan Donglu. It offers most of the same routes as the main long-distance and east bus stations.

For journeys to the south of Gānsù head to the **south bus station** (汽车南站; qìchē nánzhàn; Langongping Lu).

From the main long-distance bus station:

Píngliáng ¥119, five hours, hourly (7am to 6pm)

Tiānshuǐ ¥75.50, four hours, every 30 minutes (7am to 6pm)

Wǔwēi ¥62.5, four hours, once daily (8.50am)

Xīníng ¥59, three hours, every 30 minutes (7.10am to 8.10pm)

Yínchuān ¥124, six hours, seven per day (7am to 8pm)

The following services depart from the south bus station:

Hézuò ¥74, four hours, every 20 minutes (8am to 5pm)

Lángmùsì ¥117, eight hours, two daily (8.40am and 9.40am)

Línxià ¥35, three hours, every 30 minutes (7am to 7pm)

Xiàhé ¥75, four hours, five daily (7am to 3pm)

The **west bus station** (汽车西站; qìchē xīzhàn; Xijin Xilu) has frequent departures to Liújiāxiá (¥19.50, 2½ hours, 7am to 6pm) if you are heading to Bǐnglíng Sì.

Hidden off the main street, the **Tiānshuǐ bus station** (天水汽车站; Tiānshuǐ Qìchēzhàn; Tianshui Lu) has buses for eastern Gānsù, including Luòmén (¥55, four hours, hourly). To find the station, look for a large WC sign and turn right into the narrow alley.

Train

Lánzhōu is the major rail link for trains heading to and from western China. In summer buy your onward tickets a couple of days in advance to guarantee a sleeper berth. For Xīníng you are probably better off taking a bus, as service is more frequent and Xīníng's train station has moved to the outskirts of town. For Dūnhuáng make sure to get a train to the town itself and not Liǔyuán, a time-wasting 180km away. For details on trains to Lhasa, see p893.

There are frequent trains to the following:

Dūnhuáng hard/soft sleeper ¥246/383, 13 hours (two per day direct to Dūnhuáng at 5.50pm and 7.10pm; the rest go to Liǔyuán)

Jiāyùguān hard/soft seat ¥103/160, seven to eight hours; hard/soft sleeper ¥179/275, 11 hours

Ürümqi hard/soft sleeper ¥365/574, 24 hours

Wǔwēi hard/soft seat ¥44/72, 3½ hours

Xī'ān hard/soft sleeper ¥164/252, nine hours

Zhāngyè hard/soft seat ¥76/119, five to six hours

THE BUDDHA CAVES & POTATO TERRACES OF BĬNGLÍNG SÌ

With its relative inaccessibility, **Bĭnglíng Sì** (炳灵寺; admission ¥50) is one of the few Buddhist grottoes in China to have survived the tumultuous 20th century unscathed. Which is a good thing, as during a period spanning 1600 years, sculptors dangling from ropes carved 183 niches and sculptures into the porous rock of steep canyon walls. Today the cliffs are isolated by the waters of the Liújiāxiá Reservoir (Liújiāxiá Shuǐkù) on the Yellow River and hemmed in by a ring of dramatic rock citadels. The cave art can't compare to Dūnhuáng but the setting and the remarkable terraced landscaped you pass getting here make Bĭnglíng Sì an unmissable day trip from Lánzhōu.

As with other Silk Road grottoes, wealthy patrons, often traders along the route west, sponsored the development of Bĭnglíng Sì, which reached its height during the prosperous Tang dynasty. The star of the caves is the 27m-high seated **statue of Maitreya**, the future Buddha, but some of the smaller, sway-hipped Bodhisattvas and guardians, bearing an obvious Indian influence, are equally exquisite.

As you loop around past the Maitreya cave, consider hiking 2.5km further up the impressive canyon to a small **Tibetan monastery**. There might also be jeeps running the route.

You can visit Bĭnglíng Sì as a day trip from Lánzhōu or en route to Línxià. The caves are reached via the town of Liújiāxiá either by boat or taxi. Frequent buses from Lánzhōu's west bus station (¥19.50, 2½ hours) run to Liújiāxiá and will drop you off a short walk from the boat ticket office (1km before Liújiāxiá itself) or at the town's main bus station, where you can hire a taxi. Try to catch the earliest buses possible from Lánzhōu (starting at 7am) to avoid getting stuck on the way back. The last return bus to Lánzhōu leaves at 6.30pm.

The going rate for a covered speedboat (seating up to eight people) is ¥700 for the one-hour journey. The boat ticket office is good at hooking up independent travellers with small groups; expect to pay around ¥100 per person in this case.

Surprisingly, the much more scenic route to the caves is by taxi (¥250 return). Out of Liújiāxiá, the road runs high into the rugged hills above the reservoir, and for 90 minutes you will twist and turn, dip and rise through a wonderland of potato-growing terraces laddering and layering every slope, mound, outcrop and ravine. The final descent to the green-blue reservoir, with its craggy backdrop, is sublime.

If heading to Línxià after the caves, there are frequent buses from the station at Liújiāxiá.

ℹ️ Getting Around

Lánzhōu's streets are filled with vehicles these days and traffic jams are common. Give yourself plenty of time to get around, especially if you have a morning bus or train to catch. The airport is 70km north of the city. Airport buses leave hourly from 5am to 7pm in front of **China Eastern Airlines** (东方航空公司; Dōngfāng Hángkōng Gōngsī; 586 Donggang Xilu). The trip costs ¥30 and takes 60 minutes. A taxi costs around ¥150 though you might be able to find a shared taxi across the street from where the airport buses leave.

Useful bus routes:

Buses 1 and 6 From the train station to the west bus station via Xiguan Shizi.

Bus 111 From Zhongshan Lu (at the Xiguan Shizi stop; 去汽车南站的111路公交车) to the south bus station.

Buses 7 and 10 From the train station up the length of Tianshui Nanlu before heading west and east, respectively.

Public buses cost ¥1; taxis are ¥7 for the first 3km. A taxi from the train station to the south bus station costs ¥15.

Línxià 临夏

TRANSPORT HUB
☑ 0930 / POP 198,600

Han China runs out of steam and hits the buffers here in this overt stronghold of Chinese Islam. Línxià isn't quite a destination in itself, but many travellers break up the trip to or from Xiàhé or points in Qīnghǎi.

🛏️ Sleeping & Eating

As you walk out of the bus station onto Jiefang Lu, you'll find both sides lined with small noodle restaurants and decent budget hotels all asking around ¥68 to ¥88 for a room without a bathroom and ¥158 to ¥188 for one with.

About 1km north of the train station (head right as you exit), on the west (left) of Zhongxin Guangchang (中心广场; Centre Sq) look for a night market with rows of vendors selling lamb kebabs (¥1 each) and *shā guō* (砂锅; mini hotpots; ¥10).

Jīnhé Bīnguǎn
HOTEL **$**

(锦河宾馆; ☑631 1301; Qian He Yanlu; tw without/ with bathroom ¥88/168; ❄@) In this alcohol-free hotel, rooms sport a relaxed modern design with just a few carpet stains to spoil the effect. From the south bus station exit, turn right and walk 300m to the first big intersection. Cross and turn left down Qian He Yanlu. The hotel is about 50m down.

ⓘ Information

Bank of China (中国银行; Zhōngguó Yínháng; Jiefang Lu; ⏰8.30am-5pm Mon-Fri) is 400m up Jiefang Lu to the right as you exit the south bus station. There's a 24-hour ATM here and you can change travellers cheques.

ⓘ Getting There & Away

Línxià has three long-distance bus stations: south (nánzhàn), west (xīzhàn) and east (dōngzhàn). You may be dropped off at the west bus station but it is of little use otherwise. Bus 6 links the south and the west bus stations, or a taxi is ¥5.

From the east bus station:

Dōngxiāng ¥7, one hour, frequent
Liújiāxiá ¥16, three hours, frequent

From the south bus station:

Hézuò ¥30, two hours, every 30 minutes
Lánzhōu ¥34, three hours, every 20 minutes
Xiàhé ¥31, 2½ hours, every 30 minutes (6.30am to 5pm)
Xīníng ¥64, eight hours, one daily (6am)

One interesting side route is to the Mèngdá Nature Reserve in Qīnghǎi. The fastest way here is a bus to Dàhéjiā (see boxed text below), followed by a taxi for the last 15km.

If you're on the slow road to Qīnghǎi, buses to Xúnhuà (¥50, 3½ hours, 8am to 3.30pm) leave every hour or two from a courtyard behind the Tiānhé Fàndiàn (天河饭店) hotel. To get here, walk about 300m from the south bus station (turning right as you exit) to the first intersection and then turn right and walk 350m to the hotel. From Xúnhuà you'll find onward transport to Xīníng or Tóngrén.

Xiàhé
夏河

☑0941 / POP 70,000

The alluring monastic town of Xiàhé attracts an astonishing band of visitors: backpack-laden students, insatiable wanderers, shaven-headed Buddhist nuns, Tibetan nomads in their most colourful finery, camera-toting tour groups and dusty, itinerant beggars. Most visitors are rural Tibetans, whose purpose is to pray, prostrate themselves and seek spiritual fulfilment at holy Labrang Monastery (Lābǔléng Sì).

GĀNSÙ XIÀHÉ

MINORITY COMMUNITIES AROUND LÍNXIÀ

Spilling over a ridge high above Línxià and home to both Hui and Dongxiang minorities, the little market town of **Suǒnánbà** (锁南坝; population 12,000) has a single street that's a hive of activity, with locals trading wares and occasional shepherds shooing flocks about.

The town is sometimes also called Dōngxiāng (东乡) after the surrounding county. The Dongxiang people speak an Altaic language and are believed to be descendants of 13th-century immigrants from Central Asia, moved forcibly to China after Kublai Khan's Middle East conquest.

Dàhéjiā (大河家; population 4500), with sweeping views over the Yellow River, towering red cliffs and (in summer) verdant green terraces, is equally a kaleidoscope of colour. The surrounding area is home to a significant population of Bao'an (保安族), Muslims who speak a Mongolic language. The Bao'an are famed for producing knives and share cultural traits with the Hui and Dongxiang. Their Mongol roots come out during summer festivals, when it is possible to see displays of wrestling and horse riding.

To Suǒnánbà, frequent minibuses (¥7, one hour) head up on the pleasant journey past terraced fields from Línxià's east bus station.

You can visit Dàhéjiā when travelling on the road between Línxià and Xīníng. Most buses between the two will stop here. From Línxià you can also catch a frequent minibus (¥25, three hours) from the station called *chéngjiāo qìchē zhàn* (城郊汽車站) on the outskirts of town.

Xiàhé

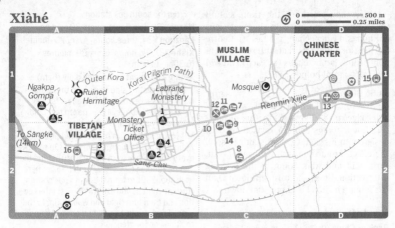

Xiàhé

◎ Sights

1 Barkhang	B1
2 Dewatsang Chapel	B2
3 Gòngtáng Chörten	A2
4 Hall of Hayagriva	B2
5 Nunnery	A1
6 Thangka Display Terrace	A2

⊜ Sleeping

7 Labrang Baoma Hotel	C1
8 Labrang Red Rock International Hostel	C2
9 Overseas Tibetan Hotel	C2
10 Tara Guesthouse	C2
11 White Stupa Hotel	C1

⊗ Eating

Cesar Restaurant	(see 12)
Everest Cafe	(see 9)
12 Nomad Restaurant	C1

ⓘ Information

13 Déshèngtáng Pharmacy	D1
14 OT Travels & Tours	C2

ⓘ Transport

15 Bus Station	D1
16 Buses to Dájiǔtǎn	A2

In a beautiful mountain valley at 2920m above sea level, Xiàhé has a certain rhythm about it and visitors quickly tap into its fluid motions. The rising sun sends pilgrims out to circle the 3km *kora* (pilgrim path) that rings the monastery. Crimson-clad monks shuffle into the temples to chant morning prayers.

It's easy to get swept up in the action, but some of the best moments come as you set your own pace, wandering about town or in the splendid encircling mountains.

The Xiàhé area was long part of the Tibetan region of Amdo. As a microcosm of southwestern Gānsù, the three principal ethnic groups are represented here. In rough terms, Xiàhé's population is 50% Tibetan, 40% Han and 10% Hui. Labrang Monastery marks the division between Xiàhé's mainly Han and Hui Chinese eastern quarter and the scruffy Tibetan village to the west.

Despite Xiàhé's ostensible tranquillity, these ethnic groups don't necessarily mix peacefully. The Tibetan community maintains a strong solidarity with their brethren on the plateau, and demonstrations and rioting here in the wake of the 2008 riots in Lhasa led to the region being closed for nearly two years.

◎ Sights

Labrang Monastery   MONASTERY
(拉卜楞寺; Lābǔléng Sì; admission ¥40) With its endless squeaking prayer wheels (3km in total length), hawks circling overhead and the deep throb of Tibetan trumpets resonating from the surrounding hills, Labrang is a monastery in the entire sense of the word.

In addition to the chapels, residences, golden-roofed temple halls and living quarters for the monks, Labrang is also home to six *tratsang* (monastic colleges or institutes), exploring esoteric Buddhism, theology, medicine, astrology and law. Many of the chapel halls are illuminated in a yellow glow by yak-butter lamps, their strong-smelling fuel scooped out from voluminous tubs. Even if Tibet is not on your itinerary, the monastery sufficiently conveys the esoteric mystique of its devout persuasions, leaving indelible impressions of a deeply sacred domain.

Labrang Monastery was founded in 1709 by Ngagong Tsunde (E'angzongzhe in Chinese), the first-generation Jamyang (a line of reincarnated Rinpoches or living Buddhas ranking third in importance after the Dalai and Panchen lamas), from nearby Gānjiā. The monastery is one of the six major Tibetan monasteries of the Gelugpa order (Yellow Hat sect of Tibetan Buddhism). The others are Ganden, Sera and Drepung monasteries near Lhasa; Tashilhunpo Monastery in Shigatse; and Kumbum (Tǎ'ěr Sì; p872) near Xīníng, Qīnghǎi.

At its peak, Labrang housed nearly 4000 monks, but their ranks greatly declined during the Cultural Revolution. Numbers are recovering, and are currently restricted to 1800 monks, drawn from Qīnghǎi, Gānsù, Sìchuān and Inner Mongolia.

Main Buildings

The only way to visit the interior of the most important buildings is with a tour, which generally includes the Institute of Medicine, the Manjushri Temple, the Serkung (Golden Temple) and the main Prayer Hall (Grand Sutra Hall), plus a museum of relics and yak-butter sculptures. English **tours** (per person ¥40) of the monastery leave the ticket office (售票处; Shòupiàochù) around 10.15am and 3.15pm; take the morning tour if you can, as there's more to see. An alternative is to latch on to a Chinese tour. Even better is to show up at around 6am or 7am to be with the monks. At dusk the hillside resonates with the throaty sound of sutras being chanted behind the wooden doors.

Other Buildings

The rest of the monastery can be explored by walking the *kora* (see boxed text, p818). Although many of the temple halls are padlocked shut, there are a couple of separate smaller chapels you can visit, though one never knows when they will be closed for unexplained reasons. Some charge admission, though again, if no one is staffing the ticket booth just go in.

The three-storey **Barkhang** (admission ¥10) is the monastery's traditional printing press. With rows upon rows of more than 20,000 wood blocks for printing, it's well worth a visit, and photos are allowed. The Barkhang is off the main road down a small side lane. Ask your guide for the latest opening hours.

The **Hall of Hayagriva** (马头明王殿; Mǎtóu Míngwáng Diàn; Hall of Horsehead Buddha), destroyed during the Cultural Revolution, was reopened in 2007. A repository of vivid and bright murals, the hall also encapsulates a startlingly fierce 12m-high effigy of Hayagriva – a wrathful manifestation of the usually calm Avalokiteshvara (Guanyin) – with six arms and three faces. The hall is down a side lane almost directly across from the lane to the Barkhang.

With an interior splashed with murals and illuminated by a combination of yak-butter lamps and electric light bulbs by the thousand, the 31m-tall **Gòngtáng Chörten** (贡唐宝塔; Gòngtáng Bǎotǎ; admission ¥20) is a perennial favourite with visitors. Head up to the roof for views across a landscape dotted with the port-red figures of monks. At the rear of the stupa look for a **Sleeping Buddha** (卧佛; Wòfó), which depicts Sakyamuni on the cusp of entering nirvana. Both the stupa and the chapel below are accessed by gates that face the river. If you follow the *kora* path you will pass by them.

The **Dewatsang Chapel** (德哇仓文殊佛殿; Déwācāng Wénshū Fódiàn; admission ¥10), built in 1814, ranges over four floors and houses a vast 12m-statue of Manjushri (Wenshu) and thousands of Buddhas in cabinets around the walls.

Access to the rest of the monastery area is free, and you can easily spend several hours just walking around and soaking up the atmosphere in the endless maze of mud-packed walls. The Tibetan greeting in the local Amdo dialect is *'Cho day mo?'* (How do you do?) – a great icebreaker.

The best morning views of the monastery come from the **Thangka Display Terrace**, a popular picnic spot, or the forested hills south of the main town.

Nunnery
BUDDHIST

This nunnery (尼姑庵; *ani gompa* in Tibetan, *nigū'ān* in Chinese) is on the hill above the Tibetan part of town. The higher *kora* path begins just to the left of here.

☞ Tours

Lohsang at OT Travels & Tours and the staff at Tara Guesthouse are both excellent resources for information and tours of the surrounding area.

GĀNSÙ XIÀHÉ

WALK LIKE A TIBETAN

Following the 3km *kora* (pilgrim path) encircling Labrang Monastery is perhaps the best approach to grasping its layout, scale and significance. Lined with long rows of squeaking prayer wheels, whitewashed *chörtens* (Tibetan stupas) and chapels, the *kora* passes Gòngtáng Chörten and Dewatsang Chapel. Tibetan pilgrims with beads in their hands and sunhats on their heads, old folk, mothers with babies and children, shabby nomads and more walk in meditative fashion clockwise along the path (called *zhuǎnjìngdào*, 'scripture-turning way' in Chinese), rotating prayer wheels as they go. Look also for the tiny meditation cells on the northern hillside.

For a short hike, the more strenuous outer *kora* path takes about an hour and climbs high above the monastery. To reach the start, head past the monastery's western edges and about one block into the Tibetan village look for a large signpost (in Tibetan but it's the only one around) on the right. Follow the alley up, and make your way to the ridge, where you wind steeply uphill to a collection of prayer flags and the ruins of a hermitage. The views of the monastery open up as you go along. At the end of the ridge there's a steep descent into town.

✢ Festivals & Events

Festivals are central to the calendar for both the devotional monks and the nomads who stream into town from the grasslands in multicoloured splendour. Tibetans use a lunar calendar, so dates for individual festivals vary from year to year.

Monlam (Great Prayer) Festival BUDDHIST
This festival starts three days after the Tibetan New Year, which is usually in February or early March. On the morning of the 13th day of the festival, more than 100 monks carry a huge *thangka* (sacred painting on cloth) of the Buddha, measuring more than 30m by 20m, and unfurl it on the hill facing the monastery. This is accompanied by spectacular processions and prayer assemblies.

On the 14th day there is an all-day session of Cham dances performed by 35 masked dancers, with Yama, the lord of death, playing the leading role. On the 15th day there is an evening display of butter lanterns and sculptures. On the 16th day the Maitreya statue is paraded around the monastery.

During the second month (usually starting in March or early April) there are several interesting festivals, with a procession of monastery relics on the seventh day.

🛏 Sleeping

Overseas Tibetan Hotel HOTEL $
(华侨饭店; Huáqiáo Fàndiàn; ☑712 2642; www.overseastibetanhotel.com; 77 Renmin Xijie; 人民西街77号; dm ¥50, d ¥200-300; @ 🛜) Well-run and bustling place, owned by the energetic and bouncy Jesuit-educated Lohsang, a likeable Tibetan with faultless English who runs the *kora* most mornings. The winter of 2012 saw a complete renovation of the guesthouse including the adoption of solar power to ensure 24/7 hot showers. Services include internet access (¥5) in the lobby, the Everest Cafe (with free wi-fi), bike hire (per day ¥20), laundry and a travel agency.

Labrang Red Rock International Hostel HOSTEL $
(拉卜楞红石国际青年旅馆; Lābùléng Hóngshí Guójì Qíngnián Lǚguǎn; ☑712 3698; 253 Yagetang; 雅鸽搪253号; 8-/4-bed dm ¥40/45, d ¥120; @) This Tibetan-themed, very quiet hostel has varnished pine-wood rooms, solar-powered hot showers, internet, a restaurant and bar area, and a beautiful display of *thangka*. Doubles are clean and spacious, and YHA card holders get a discount. To get here, walk past the Tara Guesthouse, turn left and then left again at the last street before the river.

Tara Guesthouse GUESTHOUSE $
(卓玛旅社; Zhuōmǎ Lǚshè; ☑712 1274; 268 Yagetang; 雅鸽搪268号; dm ¥15, s/tw without bathroom ¥30-40/¥60-100, d with bathroom ¥180; 🛜) This long-running budget place is run by monks from Sìchuān and has frugal dorms, small, comfortable *kang* rooms (shared shower room, no phone), and larger doubles with private bathrooms. Lower-floor rooms are arranged around a courtyard while those on the upper floors have bright common sitting areas. The attached restaurant serves some of the best *momo* (Tibetan dumplings; ¥15) around. English is spoken at the front desk.

Labrang Baoma Hotel
HOTEL $$

(拉卜楞宝马宾馆; Lābǔléng Bǎomǎ Bīnguǎn; 712 1078; www.labranghotel.com; 77 Renmin Xijie; 人民西街77号; 5-bed dm ¥35, r from ¥480; @) Pleasant and vibrantly colourful hotel with friendly staff, nice interior Tibetan-style courtyard and comfortable en suite doubles. Discounts of 50% are common.

White Stupa Hotel
HOTEL $$

(曲登嘎布宾馆; Qūdēng Gābù Bīnguǎn; 712 2866; Renmin Xijie; 人民西街; d/tw ¥168/288; @) Directly across from the Overseas Tibetan Hotel, this friendly place has clean bright rooms with en suite bathrooms and broadband internet. Expect discounts of 20%.

Eating & Drinking

For those of you who can't make it to Tibet, Xiàhé provides an opportunity to develop an appetite for the flavours of the Land of Snows, whether it's *momo, tsampa* (a porridge of roasted barley flour), yak-milk yoghurt or throat-warming glasses of the local firewater. Most hotels and guesthouses have their own attached restaurants, and it seems the entire 2nd floor of the main street is all eateries; finding an English menu in this crowd is not hard.

TOP CHOICE Gesar Restaurant
TIBETAN $

(dishes ¥8-35;) This simple, family-run restaurant on the 1st floor of the same building as the Nomad Restaurant, takes care to bring out tasty dishes with very fresh ingredients (the yoghurt is the best around). There's a long selection of real vegetarian dishes, as well as stews, traditional Tibetan staples such as *momo, tsampa* and fried bread, and a decent à la carte Western breakfast menu.

Nomad Restaurant
TIBETAN $$

(牧民齐全饭庄; Mùmín Qíquán Fànzhuāng; dishes ¥5-35;) From the commanding views of the monastery and *kora* route of this 3rd-floor perch, get into the swing of things with some hot yak milk, boiled yak meat (¥58), a bowl of *tsampa*, a plate of *momo* and a volatile shot of Nomad barley alcohol. Western breakfast items, fruit shakes and a good range of Chinese dishes round out the menu.

Everest Cafe
CAFE $

(77 Renmin Xijie; 人民西街77号; dishes ¥15-40; 7am-late;) Attached to the Overseas Tibetan Hotel, this is a popular spot for set Western breakfasts (¥25), lunch or a late-night beer.

Shopping

Xiàhé is an excellent place to look for Tibetan handicrafts, so why not don a cowboy hat or a Tibetan trilby, enshroud yourself in a *chuba* (Tibetan cloak), light up some juniper incense, wrap your head in a furry yellow monk's hat, jump into a pair of monk's boots, flap a prayer flag or shell out for brocaded silks, *thangka*, Tibetan-style tents or a silver teapot? Stacks of handicraft shops line the upper part of the main road, before the monastery walls, and some painting shops are found off the lower *kora* route alongside the river.

ⓘ Information

Free wi-fi is becoming increasingly common in restaurants, and the Overseas Tibetan Hotel has computers for ¥5 per hour in the lobby. Internet cafes around town require Chinese ID, though some will allow you to use their ID. Try the **internet cafe** (网吧; wǎngbā; per hr ¥3) in the far back left corner of the modern plaza across from China Post.

China Post (中国邮政; Zhōngguó Yóuzhèng; 8am-6pm)

Déshèngtáng Pharmacy (德盛堂药店; Déshèngtáng Yàodiàn) Western, Chinese and Tibetan medicine; just west of China Post.

Industrial & Commercial Bank of China (ICBC; 工商银行; Gōngshāng Yínháng) Has an ATM and changes US dollars but not travellers cheques.

OT Travels & Tours (1390 9419 888; amdolosang@hotmail.com) This reliable travel agency at the Overseas Tibetan Hotel can arrange cars and guides to nearby sights, and also specialises in overland tours from Lánzhōu, Xīníng and Chéngdū to Xiàhé.

ⓘ Getting There & Away

There is no airport in Xiàhé, nor do trains run there, but it's regularly serviced by bus. Most travellers head on to either Lánzhōu or Sìchuān; the road less travelled takes you over the mountains to Tóngrén in Qīnghǎi.

The following bus services depart from Xiàhé:

Hézuò ¥14.50, one hour, every 30 minutes (6.30am to 5.30pm)

Lángmùsì ¥72, four hours, one daily (7.40am)

Lánzhōu ¥75, four hours, four daily (6.30am, 7.30am, 8.30am and 2.30pm)

Línxià ¥31, two hours, every 30 minutes (6am to 5.30pm)

Tóngrén ¥31, 2½ hours, one daily (7.30am)

Xīníng ¥78, seven hours, one daily (6.10am)

If you can't get a direct ticket to/from Lánzhōu, take a bus to Línxià or Hézuò and change there. If you are heading to Xīníng, note that buses run there every 40 minutes from Tóngrén.

GĀNSÙ XIÀHÉ

ⓘ Getting Around

Hotels and restaurants hire bikes for ¥20 per day. Taxis cost ¥1 to ¥2 per seat for a short trip around town, including to the bus station and monastery.

Around Xiàhé

SĀNGKĒ GRASSLANDS 桑科草原

Expanses of open grassland dotted with Tibetans and their grazing yak herds highlight a trip to the village of **Sāngkē** (桑科), 14km from Xiàhé. Development has turned the area into a small circus, complete with touristy horse rides and fake tourist yurts, but there is good hiking in the nearby hills and you can keep going to more distant and pristine grasslands in the direction of Amchog. You can cycle up to Sāngkē in about one hour. A taxi costs ¥50 return. Note that the grasslands are best in the summer months.

GĀNJIĀ GRASSLANDS 甘加草原

The Gānjiā Grasslands (Gānjiā Cǎoyuán), 34km from Xiàhé, aren't as pretty as at Sāngkē but there is more to explore. From Xiàhé the bumpy road crosses the Naren-Ka pass before quickly descending into wide grasslands dotted with herds of sheep and backed by ever-more dramatic mountain scenery. Past Gānjiā Xiàn village, a side road climbs 12km to **Nekhang** (白石崖溶洞; Báishí Yá Róng dòng; admission ¥20), a cave complex where pilgrims lower themselves down ropes and ladders into two sacred underground chambers. A Dutch traveller fell to his death here in 2006, and to prevent the same fate we advise avoiding this place.

Just up the road from the caves is **Trakkar Gompa** (白石崖寺; Báishíyá Sì; admission ¥15), a monastery of 90 monks set against a stunning backdrop of vertical rock formations. From Trakkar it's a short drive to the 2000-year-old Han-dynasty village of **Bājiǎo** (八角; Karnang in Tibetan; admission ¥10). The remarkable 12-sided walls here still shelter a small living community. From the village it's a short 5km diversion to the renovated **Tseway Gompa** (佐海寺; Zuǒhǎi Sì; admission ¥20), one of the few Bön monasteries in Gānsù. Make sure you circumnavigate any holy site counterclockwise in the Bön fashion. There are great views of Bājiǎo from the ridge behind the monastery.

A four- to five-hour return trip to the Gānjiā Grasslands costs around ¥180 for a taxi from Xiàhé. If you want an English-speaking driver and guide (which will cost more), contact OT Travels & Tours.

Hiking

It's possible to hike over several days from the Gānjiā Grasslands to 4636m-high **Dálǐjiā Shān** (达里加山; Dálǐjiā Mountain), but you will need to be well equipped. Summer is the best season for such treks as you have more daylight hours and warmer weather. There are also treks between Tibetan villages and around **Dàowéi Tibetan Village** (道帏藏族乡; Dàowéi Zàngzú Xiāng; also called Guru).

OT Travels & Tours in Xiàhé (see p819) can advise on these and other trips and arrange a car for four people for ¥350 and an English-speaking guide (for another ¥350); they can also arrange fun camping trips for overnighting on the grasslands.

Hézuò 合作

📞 0941 / POP 76,000

The booming regional capital of Gānnán (甘南) prefecture, Hézuò is a transit point for travellers plying the excellent overland route between Gānsù and Sìchuān provinces. The city is also the sight of the incredible Milarepa Palace, a bewitching Tibetan temple ranging spectacularly over nine floors.

Hézuò is a fairly compact town, with a large public square (文化广场; Wenhua Guangchang) roughly halfway between the two bus stations. You'll find banks with ATMs around the square. Most taxi rides around town cost ¥2.

◎ Sights

Milarepa Palace BUDDHIST TEMPLE
(九层佛阁; Sekhar Gutok; Jiǔcéng Fógé; admission ¥20; ◷7am-6pm) About 2km from the bus station along the main road towards Xiàhé is this towering temple, ringed by prayer wheels. The port-coloured building is highly unusual in the Tibetan world in that different spiritual leaders from varying sects are worshipped on each floor. The ground-floor hall is a powerful spectacle: a galaxy of Bodhisattvas, Buddhist statues and celestial figures gloomily illuminated by yak-butter lamps. Climb upstairs to a further rich display of lamas and living Buddhas on the 2nd floor. More deities muster on the 4th floor and an unsettling array of fearsome, blue and turquoise tantric effigies awaits on the 6th floor. Make your way to the 8th floor for further effigies of Sakyamuni and Guanyin, and views over the hills and town. The town's main monastery,

Tso Gompa (admission free; ⊘8am-6pm), is next door. A taxi here costs ¥2 to ¥3 from the central main bus station.

🛏 Sleeping & Eating

There are restaurants around the public square, and also around the bus stations. Across the road from the entrance to the central main station, look for a **Muslim restaurant** (dishes ¥4-10) with a picture menu outside. Try the *gānbǎnmiàn* (干板面; ¥10), a type of spaghetti bolognese with hand-pulled noodles.

With Xiàhé just an hour to the north there is little reason to stay here, and cheap hotels are loath to take foreigners. If you get stuck, the **Gānnán Fàndiàn** (甘南饭店; ☎821 4733; Maqu Xilu; 玛曲西路; tw ¥180-260, discounts of 20%; ❄❀@) has decent, clean and bright doubles with shower and internet; it's on the southwest corner of the public square.

❶ Getting There & Away

Hézuò is where buses from Zöigê (Ruò'ěrgài), in Sìchuān, and Lángmùsì and Xiàhé meet. There is a train booking office just outside the central bus station (though no trains pass through here).

Services from the central main bus station (长途汽车站; chángtú qìchēzhàn):

Lánzhōu ¥74, four hours, every 30 minutes
Línxià ¥30, 1½ hours, every 30 minutes
Xiàhé ¥14.50, 1½ hours, every 30 minutes

From the south bus station (汽车南站; qìchē nán zhàn):

Lángmùsì ¥33 to ¥50, three hours, three daily (7am, 10.20am and 12.20pm)
Zöigê ¥78, 3½ hours, one daily (7.30am)

A taxi between the two bus stations costs ¥2 per person, or take bus 1 (¥1).

Lángmùsì   郎木寺

📞 0941 / POP 3000

Straddling the border between Sìchuān and Gānsù is Lángmùsì (Taktsang Lhamo in Tibetan), an expanding and modernising alpine Amdo Tibetan village nestled among steep grassy meadows, evergreen forests of slender pine trees brushing the sky, crumbling stupas, piles of *mani* stones and snow-clad peaks. Lovely and moist compared to the lowlands, Lángmùsì is a delightful place, surrounded by countless red and white monastery buildings, flapping prayer flags and the mesmerising sound of monks chanting at twilight.

The White Dragon River (白龙江; Báilóng Jiāng) divides the town into two and the Sìchuān side has quickly become the far nicer part to stay in. From where the bus drops you off on the scruffy main street, walk up the road about three blocks and then turn left. The well-paved street runs a few blocks up to the Kerti monastery and is lined with a range of hostels, hotels and eateries.

◉ Sights

Kerti Gompa   MONASTERY
(格尔底寺; Géěrdí Sì; admission valid 3 days ¥30) Rising up on the Sìchuān side of the river is this monastery – otherwise dubbed the Sìchuān Monastery – built in 1413, home to around 700 monks, and composed of five temples and colleges. A short walk from the monastery stand small pavilions built over a brook whose waters power a round-the-clock revolving of prayer wheels housed inside (the *ne plus ultra* of holiness)! Just across from the entrance is a small **Hui Muslim village** with yellow houses and central mosque. The best time to visit the monastery is in the morning (7am to 8am and 10.30am to 1pm) and late afternoon (6pm to 8pm).

Serti Gompa   MONASTERY
(赛赤寺; Sàichì Sì; admission ¥30) On the Gānsù side, higher up the hill, is this smaller monastery with golden- and silver-roofed halls. The monastery dates from 1748 and is simply referred to as Gānsù Monastery. The best time to visit is in the morning (7am to 8am and 10.30am to 1pm) and late afternoon (6pm to 8pm). At all times of day the views are lovely from up here.

🏃 Activities

Hiking

Bountiful hiking opportunities radiate in almost every direction. For reasonably priced guides for all-day or overnight treks, including **Huágàishén Shān** (华盖神山; 4200m), see the horse-trekking companies on the following page.

Southwest of Kerti Gompa is **Namo Gorge** (纳摩大峡谷; Nàmó Dàxiágǔ), which makes for a superlative two- to three-hour (return) hike. The gorge contains several sacred grottoes, one dedicated to the Tibetan goddess Palden Lhamo, the other known as the **Fairy Cave** (仙女洞; Xiānnǚ Dòng), which gives the town its Tibetan name (*lángmù* meaning fairy). Cross rickety bridges flung over the gushing stream, trek past piles of *mani* stones and prayer flags, and hike on into a splendid ravine. After about 30 minutes of clambering over rocks you reach a grassy plain surrounded by towering peaks.

Another popular trek is the hike along the White Dragon River to the **river's source** (白龙江源头; Báilóng Jiāng Yuántóu), where Chinese hikers go in search of *chóngcǎo* (虫草), a coveted herb used in Chinese medicine.

A lovely walk heads out over the hills along a narrow paved road from the stupa at Serti Gompa to the small village of **Jíkēhé Cūn** (吉科合村). This hike can be combined with the White Dragon River source. When you reach the village, simply follow the loop and then head down a dirt path towards the valley below. Watch out for local dogs.

For some glorious open views over Xiàhé, trek up the coxcomblike **Red Stone Mountain** (红石崖; Hóngshí Yá). To start, turn right one street down (heading out of Lángmùsì) past the intersection where the bus drops you off.

Horse Trekking

The mountain trails around Lángmùsì offer spectacular riding opportunities. There are two outfits in town offering similar one- to four-day treks overnighting at nomads' tents and with the option of climbing nearby peaks along the way. **Lángmùsì Tibetan Horse Trekking** (☑667 1504; www.langmusi. net), across from the Black Tent Cafe, is the more established outfit. Horse rental per day is ¥260 for a single traveller; ¥200 for two or more. In addition to guide, food and sleeping bags, trips include a package on no-mad culture.

Wind Horse Trekking (郎木寺白戌马队; ☑151 0944 1588), opposite the China Telecom office on the main road, offers similar packages starting at ¥180 per day (bring your own sleeping bag).

Both companies have friendly English-speaking staff and are good sources of travel information.

Biking

With long, rambling and relatively quiet highways nearby, and many dirt tracks snaking into the hills, Lángmùsì is well worth exploring on two wheels. In addition to biking up to Red Stone Mountain and to the source of the White Dragon River, two distant lakes,

both around 40km from town, are popular destinations. See Lángmùsì Tibetan Horse Trekking for details and also **bike rentals** (per day ¥60-80).

⭐ Festivals & Events

If you are in the area in late July, head out to Mǎqǔ (玛曲) to see the **annual horse races**. The dates change each year, so try contacting the Lángmùsì Bīnguǎn hotel to find out when it is being held. Mǎqǔ is 67km west of Lángmùsì. Travellers cafes and hotels in Lángmùsì can arrange transport to the town.

🛏 Sleeping

Jiǎ Zhōu Guesthouse HOSTEL $
(假周旅馆; Jiǎzhōu Lǚguǎn; ☑138 9396 8011; jiazhouguesthouse.wordpress.com; dm/d/tw without bathroom ¥30/60/80; 🛜) With its wild west boarding house exterior, Tibetan-styled interiors and English-speaking host, this guesthouse is a solid budget choice on the road to Kerti Gompa. Rooms are small but tidy and open onto a balcony overlooking the street. There's an attached restaurant and bar with outdoor seating and free wi-fi.

Lángmùsì Hotel HOTEL $$$
(朗木寺大酒店; Lángmùsì Dà Jiǔdiàn; ☑667 1555; langmusihotel@yahoo.com.cn; d ¥666-699, tr ¥700, discounts of up to 70%) This friendly four-storey hotel is the most upscale in Lángmùsì and offers very pleasant, clean and spacious rooms in either standard or Tibetan styling. It's on the road towards Kerti Gompa, literally across from the ticket booth.

Yǒng Zhōng Hotel HOTEL $$
(永忠賓館; Yǒngzhōng Bīnguǎn; ☑667 1032; tw ¥180-220; ❄🌐) On the Sìchuān side of town, just down from Kerti Gompa, is this pleasant family-run hotel with small, bright, modern rooms all with air-con and 24-hour hot water. There's also a free computer with internet downstairs in the shop where you access the hotel. Expect discounts of 30%.

Lángmùsì Bīnguǎn HOTEL $
(郎木寺宾馆; ☑667 1086; tibetanyakboy@ yahoo.co.uk; dm ¥30, d/tw with shower ¥160-180, discounts of 30%) Just up the side road from where the bus drops you off is this friendly English-speaking place with basic three-bed dorms, and clean en suite rooms that are starting to show a bit of wear and tear.

Nomads Youth Hostel   HOSTEL $

(旅朋青年旅社; Lǚpéng Qīngnián Lǚshè; ☑667 1460; dm ¥30, tw ¥60-80; @☎) Popular with Chinese backpackers, this friendly place on the main street has scruffy and basic dorms, doubles with shared toilet, homey foyer and bar. Can arrange treks.

✖ Eating

English menus are common in this town, and practically every backpacker-oriented guesthouse and hostel has its own attached restaurant-bar serving a combination of Western, Tibetan and Chinese dishes. On the Sìchuān side of town you'll find a dozen pleasant small restaurants serving Sìchuānese, Yúnnánese and Tibetan dishes. For cheap noodles, head to the Muslim restaurants across from the entrance to Kerti Gompa.

Talo Restaurant   TIBETAN, BREAKFAST $$

(达老餐厅; Dálǎo Cāntīng; dishes ¥10-38; ☺7.30am-9pm; ☎▣) Decorated with yak skulls, prayer flags and *thangka,* this friendly upstairs Tibetan restaurant has a good breakfast menu (dishes ¥4 to ¥12) embracing pancakes, apple rings and omelettes, plus a host of Tibetan and Chinese staples.

TOP CHOICE Black Tent Cafe   TIBETAN, CAFE $$

(黑帐篷咖啡; Hēi Zhànpeng Kāfēi; dishes ¥25-50; ☺8am-10pm; ☎▣) Great service, a funky Tibetan-style interior, rooftop seating and a good little menu offering Western and Tibetan dishes are just some of the highlights of this 2nd-floor cafe run by the folks at Lángmùsì Tibetan Horse Trekking. Our only complaint is the price of beer: ¥12 for a small can! The cafe is just up the side street from the intersection where the bus drops you off.

ⓘ Information

There is nowhere to change money and no ATMs that accept foreign cards. Wi-fi is widely available at hostels and cafes. The **PSB** (公安局; Gōngānjú) is just down from the Lángmùsì Hotel.

ⓘ Getting There & Away

There's one daily bus to Zöigê (Ruò'ěrgài; ¥28, 2½ hours) at 7am which arrives with time to connect with the bus to Sōngpān. There are three daily buses to Hézuò (¥38, three hours), departing at 6.30am, 7.20am and noon. The one daily bus to Xiàhé (¥72) leaves at 2pm. Note that while there is a daily bus from Lánzhōu to Lángmùsì, there is no return bus. For the latest schedule see www.langmusi.net.

HÈXĪ CORRIDOR

Bound by the Qílián Shān range to the south and the Mǎzōng (Horse's Mane) and Lóngshǒu (Dragon's Head) ranges to the north, the narrow strip of land that is Hèxī Corridor (河西走廊; Héxī Zǒuláng), around which the province is formed, was once the sole western passage in and out of the Middle Kingdom.

Wǔwēi   武威

☑0935 / POP 509,000

Wǔwēi stands at the strategic eastern end of the Hèxī Corridor. It was from here, two millennia prior, that the emperors of China launched their expeditionary forces into the unknown west, eventually leading them to Jiāyùguān and beyond. Temples, tombs and traditional gates hint at Wǔwēi's Silk Road past, while the rapidly modernising city has some pleasant squares and pedestrian streets.

Wǔwēi is compact enough that with the exception of Hǎizàng Temple you can walk to all the sights in an afternoon. Most travellers base themselves in the southern part of town near the rebuilt South Gate (南门). The city's main square, Wenhua Guangchang (文化广场; Culture Sq), is about 1km directly north of the gate on Bei Dajie. A pedestrian-only street runs west of the square.

⊙ Sights

The following sights are written in the order you would approach them starting from the South Gate.

Confucius Temple   TEMPLE

(文庙; Wénmiào; admission ¥30; ☺8am-6pm) This Ming-era temple is divided into Confucian Temple and Wénchāng Hall sections. Both display some fine examples of traditional architecture, with the former fronted by the grand wooden **Língxīng Gate**. There are also quiet gardens and stele-filled pavilions. The most important stele features the extinct Xīxià language carved into one side and a Chinese translation on the other: a sort of Rosetta stone, the stele has allowed researchers to understand the once unintelligible Xīxià texts. The stele is now housed in a small **museum** (☺8.30am-6pm) on the left side of the square as you exit the temple; your ticket for the Confucius Temple allows you inside. To reach the temple, head east from the South Gate along pleasant Mingqing Fanggu Wenhua Jie to the square at the end (about 600m).

Kumarajiva Pagoda
BUDDHIST PAGODA

(罗什佛塔; Luóshísì Tǎ) Located 400m north of Wenhua Guangchang off Bei Dajie, this pagoda is a brick structure originally dating to 488. Dedicated to the great translator of Buddhist sutras (whose tongue was buried beneath the pagoda), the pagoda was toppled during the great earthquake in 1927 and rebuilt. Pilgrims circumambulate the pagoda in clockwise fashion.

Léitái Sì
HISTORIC SITE

(雷台寺; Lei Tai Dong Lu; admission ¥45; ⊙8am-6pm) The pride and joy of the city, the bronze **Flying Horse of Wǔwēi** (飞马) was discovered here in 1969 and has since been adopted as the unofficial symbol of Gānsù. It was found in a secret tomb beneath this temple, built on top of steep earthen ramparts. While it's a thrill to explore a 2000-year-old tomb, there is precious little inside. The Flying Horse is now displayed in the Gānsù Provincial Museum (p810).

The site is 1.2km north of Wenhua Guangchang. Turn right at Lei Tai Dong Lu. Note that you'll need your passport to enter the park where the tomb is located.

Hǎizàng Temple
BUDDHIST

(海藏寺; Hǎizàng Sì; admission ¥10; ⊙6am-6pm) A short trip on bus 5 (¥2) or taxi (¥15 to ¥20) outside town takes you to the entrance of a shabby **park** (admission ¥2), at the back of which is this temple, a fascinating active monastery. The **Three Sages Hall** (Sānshèng Diàn) contains a 'hermaphroditic Guanyin' (it's at the back of the temple). Dating to the Ming dynasty, the raised **Wúliàng Palace** (Wúliàng Diàn) was once used to store sutras but now houses a reclining Buddha in a glass cabinet. In addition to a venerably old post-and-beam interior (check out the fading carvings and paintings on the main posts), an absorbing feature is the minute pavilion to the right of the entrance containing a **well** whose 'magic waters' (神水; shénshuǐ) are said to connect by subterranean streams to a Holy Lake (圣湖; Shènghú) in the Potala Palace in Lhasa. Drinking the well water is said to cure myriad ailments.

🛏 Sleeping & Eating

The best place to situate yourself is around the South Gate. Mingqing Fanggu Wenhua Jie extends east from the gate and is an attractive street lined with restaurants, coffee shops and a KTV or two.

Zǐ Yún Gé Hotel
HOTEL $$

(紫云阁酒店; Zǐyúngé Jiǔdiàn; ☎225 3888; Mingqing Fanggu Wenhua Jie; 明清仿古文化街; s/d/tr ¥198/280/218; ❋@) Just east of the South Gate, this great hotel has bright, comfortable and spacious rooms with showers and new furnishings. You can often net a standard double for around ¥140.

Wǔwēi Nánchéngmén Bīnguǎn
HOTEL $

(武威南城门宾馆; ☎231 9999; 62 Nan Dajie; tr without bathroom ¥108, d/tw with bathroom ¥138/158; @) Almost touching the northwest side of the South Gate is this friendly hotel with small tidy rooms sporting disproportionally spacious bathrooms. The hotel entrance is down a short alley. Discounts of 15% to 20% are usually available.

Wángjiā Jiǎozi Guǎn
DUMPLINGS $

(王家饺子馆; Wenmiao Guangchang; dumplings ¥12-24; ⊙6.30am-10.30pm) In the square across from the Confucius Temple sits this satisfying dumpling shop with a picture menu. Try a plate of guōtiē (锅贴; fried dumplings).

❶ Information

There's a **Bank of China** (中国银行; Zhōngguó Yínháng) on the west end of the pedestrian shopping street (步行商业街; Buxing Shangye Jie) where you can change money. There's also a branch with a 24-hour ATM behind the Zǐ Yún Gé Hotel. Internet cafes in Wǔwēi require Chinese ID.

❶ Getting There & Around

Bus

Express buses run from the long-distance bus station (长途汽车站), 1.5km southwest of Wenhua Guangchang to:

Jiāyùguān ¥96, seven hours, two daily (7.30am and 9.30am)

Lánzhōu ¥65, four hours, every 30 minutes (7am to 6pm)

Zhāngyè ¥58, four, every 30 minutes (7.30am to 6pm)

Train

The station is 3.5km southwest of Wenhua Guangchang; the two are connected by buses 1 and 2 (¥1). Taxis start at ¥4 and most rides around town are around ¥4 to ¥7. There are frequent trains to the following:

Dūnhuáng hard/soft sleeper ¥195/302, 10 hours (two per day directly to Dūnhuáng at 9.21pm and 10.46pm; other trains drop you off at Liǔyuán)

Jiāyùguān hard/soft seat ¥70/108, five to six hours

Lánzhōu hard/soft seat ¥47/72, 3½ hours

Zhāngyè hard/soft seat ¥41/61, three hours

Zhāngyè 张掖

☎ 0936 / POP 260,000

Most people use this mid-size Silk Road town as a jumping-off base for the unique cliff temples at nearby Mǎtí Sì. But budget at least the afternoon here. There's a colossal Buddha ensconced inside one of China's best preserved wooden temples that deserves an extended visit.

The main road through town (as far as the traveller is concerned) is divided into Xi (West) Dajie and Dong (East) Dajie, depending which direction it radiates from the drum tower. Jianfu Jie intersects with Xi Dajie a few blocks from the drum tower and heading north takes you to a pleasant eating street while south leads to the Great Buddha Temple and Wooden Pagoda.

◉ Sights

Great Buddha Temple BUDDHIST TEMPLE
(大佛寺; Dàfó Sì; admission ¥41; ⊙8am-6pm) Originally dating to 1098 (Western Xia dynasty), this behemoth of a temple contains an astonishing 35m-long sleeping Buddha – China's largest of this variety – surrounded by mouldering clay arhats (Buddhists who have achieved enlightenment) and Qing-dynasty murals. Until the 1960s, small children would clamber into the huge Buddha and play around inside his tummy.

Apart from the statue, take a good look at the main hall and the woodwork, including the doors and the exquisite brackets supporting the roof eaves. This is one of the few wooden structures from this era still standing in China and there is a wealth of traditional symbols to examine. There are also several other temples and halls to explore, as well as the impressive white **earth stupa** (土塔; tǔ tǎ) dating from the Ming dynasty, when this vast temple complex was called Hóngrén Temple (弘仁寺; Hóngrén Sì).

The temple is off Jianfu Jie across a large square. From Xi Dajie head south about 1km.

Wooden Pagoda BUDDHIST PAGODA
(木塔; Muta Jianfu Jie; admission ¥5; ⊙8am-noon & 2.30-6pm) In the town's main square stands this brick and wooden structure. Though first built in AD 528, the present structure is a thorough reconstruction from 1926.

🛏 Sleeping & Eating

For meals, head 300m west of the drum tower and look for Mingqing Jie (明清街),

an alley of faux-Qing architecture lined with dozens of clean, friendly restaurants with picture menus. There is also a **food court** on the northeast side of the drum tower beside the China Construction Bank.

Gānzhōu Hotel HOTEL $$
(甘州宾馆; Gānzhōu Bīnguǎn; ☎888 8822; 373 Nan Dajie; d & tw ¥399; ❋ @) A solid if entirely generic midrange hotel with bright modern rooms, courteous staff and a good location just 150m south of the drum tower. Discounts of up to 50% make this a great choice when the average stained and fading no-star in town charges only slightly less.

Húáyì Bīnguǎn HOTEL $
(华谊宾馆; ☎824 2118; Dong Dajie; d without bathroom ¥40, d/tw ¥90/98; ❋ @) You get what you pay for with the cheapest rooms, but otherwise this is a surprisingly clean and tidy budget hotel with rooms showing a minimum of wear and tear. In-room broadband internet is a definite bonus, as is the location just east of the drum tower.

ⓘ Information

There's an **internet cafe** (网吧; wǎngbā; 3rd fl; per hr ¥3) on the southwest corner of the drum tower intersection. The **Bank of China** (中国银行; Zhōngguó Yínháng) on Dong Dajie can change travellers cheques and has a 24-hour ATM.

ⓘ Getting There & Around

Bus

The town has three bus stations, in the south, east and west. The west bus station (xīguǎn zhàn) has the most frequent departures. In addition to the following there are also buses to Xīníng and Golmud.

Dūnhuáng ¥180, 12 hours, one per day (6.30pm)

Jiāyùguān ¥50.50, four hours, hourly (9.30am to 5.10pm)

Lánzhōu ¥128, eight hours, hourly (7am to 1.30pm, sleepers after that)

Wǔwēi ¥56, four hours, every 30 minutes (7.20am to 5pm)

Train

The **train booking office** (12 Oushi Jie; 欧式街 12号; ⊙8am-6pm) is near a Marco Polo statue (the great explorer spent a year in town). To get here walk west of the drum tower and turn right (north) at Oushi Jie.

Dūnhuáng hard/soft sleeper ¥145/223, 7½ hours (two daily at 12.19am and 2.04am; day trains all go to Liǔyuán)

Jiāyùguān hard/soft seat ¥38/57, two to three hours

Lánzhōu hard/soft seat ¥76/119, six to seven hours

A taxi to/from the train station is ¥10, or take bus 1 (¥1). The station is 7km northeast of the city centre. From either bus station to the hotels costs ¥4 to ¥5. Bus 4 runs past the west bus station from Dong or Xi Dajie.

Mǎtí Sì   马蹄寺

Carved into the cliff sides in foothills of the grand Qílián Mountains (Qílián Shān), the venerable Buddhist grottoes of Mǎtí Sì make for a fine short getaway from the hectic small towns along the Hèxī Corridor. There's excellent hiking in the nearby hills, and a decent range of simple accommodation and food in the nearby village from May to September. Come in July to see the mountain valleys carpeted in blue wildflowers.

👁 Sights & Activities

Horse riding is a popular activity. Prices are fixed up to ¥200 for a four-hour ride. Note it costs ¥20 just to enter into the general village/grotto scenic area.

Mǎtí Sì   CAVES, BUDDHIST
(马蹄寺) Mǎtí Sì translates as Horse Hoof Monastery, a reference to a legendary event in which a heavenly horse left a hoof imprint in a grotto. Between the 5th and 14th centuries a series of caves were almost as miraculously built in sheer sandstone cliffs and filled with carvings, temples and meditation rooms. The caves are reached via twisting staircases, balconies, narrow passages and platforms that will leave your head spinning.

The grottoes are not in one area but spread over many sections. The most accessible are the **Thousand Buddhas Caves** (千佛洞石窟; Qiān Fó Dòng Shíkū; admission ¥35) just past the entrance gate to the scenic area. Within this complex is the Pǔguāng Temple where you'll find the relic of the horse foot imprint. The **Mǎtí Sì North Caves** (马蹄寺北洞; Mǎtísì Běi Dòng; admission ¥35) are just above the village (2km up the road from the Thousand Buddhas Caves). Other collections of grottoes are scattered about the cliff faces, as are utilitarian caves that were formerly used as dwellings by local people.

Both or neither of the main caves may be open if you arrive outside May to September.

Hiking

There are several good day hikes around Mǎtí Sì, including the five-hour loop through pine forest and talus fields to the **Línsōng Waterfall** (临松瀑布; Línsōng Pùbù) and back down past **Sword Split Stone** (剑劈石; Jiànpīshí). For unrivalled panoramas, take the elevatorlike ascent of the ridge starting across from the white chörten just above the village at Sānshísāntiān Shíkū (三十三天石窟).

🛏 Sleeping & Eating

If you're adequately prepared for camping, some overnight trips are possible. The tiny village also has several basic guesthouses. Call **Mr Hua** (☏130 859 2081; tw ¥60) to book at a friendly family-run place and arrange a pick-up at Mǎtí Hé. Decent meals can be had at a couple of village restaurants or head up into the fields towards the mountains to one of several large comfortable tents serving Tibetan-style fare (including butter-milk tea and *tsampa*).

ℹ Getting There & Away

Buses leave every 30 minutes from Zhāngyè's south bus station for the crossroads village of Mǎtí Hé (马蹄河; ¥9.50, 1½ hours, 6.40am to 5.40pm), from where you can catch a minibus or taxi (¥30) for the final 7km or so.

Direct buses to Mǎtí Sì depart at 7.35am, 8.25am and 9.15am from May to September. The last bus back to Mǎtí Hé or possibly Zhāngyè leaves before 5pm. Check with locals on the exact time.

A one-way taxi from Zhāngyè will cost around ¥80.

WORTH A TRIP

THE RAINBOW ROCKS OF ZHĀNGYÈ

Multicoloured rock formations, known in China as **Dānxiá rocks** (张掖丹霞; Zhāngyè Dānxiá), have been getting a bit of attention recently after six well-known formations in the south were inscribed as Unesco World Heritage sites. If you are renting a taxi to go to Mǎtí Sì, consider taking a side trip to Zhāngyè's spectacularly colourful examples. The swirling rainbow palette and the scale of the formations is astonishing.

From Zhāngyè a taxi to both Mǎtí Sì and the rocks will cost around ¥200.

Jiāyùguān & Around 嘉峪关

0937 / POP 170,000

You approach Jiāyùguān through the forbidding lunar landscape of north Gānsù. It's a fitting setting, as Jiāyùguān marks the symbolic end of the Great Wall, the western gateway of China proper and, for imperial Chinese, the beginning of the back of beyond. One of the defining points of the Silk Road, a Ming-dynasty fort was erected here in 1372 and Jiāyùguān came to be colloquially known as the 'mouth' of China, while the narrow Hèxī Corridor, leading back towards the *nèidì* (inner lands), was dubbed the 'throat'.

You'll need plenty of imagination to conjure up visions of the Silk Road, as modern Jiāyùguān is a city of straight roads and identikit blocks, almost as if airlifted into position from North Korea. But the Jiāyùguān Fort is an essential part of Silk Road lore and most certainly worth a visit.

Sights

With the exception of the Wèi Jìn Tombs, all the sites below are covered by a single entrance ticket to the Jiāyùguān Fort. A taxi to all the sights (including the tombs), which are all outside town, is likely to cost ¥200 for the half-day. Just to the sites covered by the fort ticket will cost ¥100 to ¥150 depending on how long you stay to look at things.

Jiāyùguān Fort FORTRESS
(嘉峪关城楼; Jiāyùguān Chénglóu; admission ¥100; 8am-6pm) One of the classic images of western China, the fort guards the pass between the snowcapped Qílián Shān peaks and the Hēi Shān (Black Mountains) of the Mǎzōng Shān range.

Built in 1372, the fort was christened the 'Impregnable Defile Under Heaven'. Although the Chinese often controlled territory far beyond the Jiāyùguān area, this was the last major stronghold of imperial China – the end of the 'civilised world', beyond which lay only desert demons and the barbarian armies of Central Asia.

Towards the eastern end of the fort is the **Gate of Enlightenment** (光化楼; Guānghuá Lóu) and in the west is the **Gate of Conciliation** (柔远楼; Róuyuǎn Lóu), from where exiled poets, ministers, criminals and soldiers would have ridden off into oblivion. Each gate dates from 1506 and has 17m-high towers with upturned flying eaves and double gates that would have been used to trap invading armies. On the inside are horse lanes leading up to the top of the inner wall. On the west-facing side of the Gate of Enlightenment are the shadowy remains of **slogans** praising Chairman Mao, blasted by the desert winds. A further prolix quote from Mao stands out in yellow paint on the south wall of **Wénchāng Pavilion** (文昌阁; Wénchāng Gé).

Jiāyùguān

0 200 m
0 0.1 miles

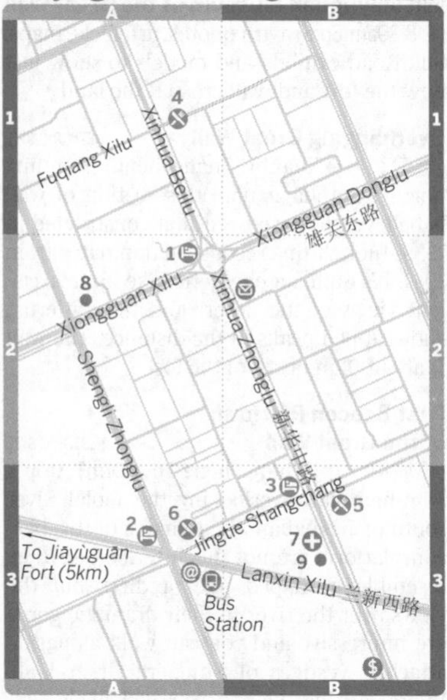

Jiāyùguān

Sleeping
1 Jiāyùguān Bīnguǎn ... A2
2 Jīnyè Bīnguǎn ... A3
3 Liángshijú Zhāodàisuǒ ... B3

Eating
4 Fùqiáng Market Entrance ... A1
5 Jìngtiě Xiǎochīchéng ... B3
6 Yuàn Zhōng Yuàn ... A3

Information
7 People's No 1 Hospital ... B3

Transport
8 Bicycle Hire ... A2
9 Train Booking Office ... B3

Near the fort entrance gate is the excellent **Jiāyùguān Museum of the Great Wall** (⊙8.30am-6pm), with photos, artefacts, maps, Silk Road exhibits and models to show just how the fort and wall crossed the land.

Overhanging Great Wall
HISTORIC SITE

(悬壁长城; Xuánbì Chángchéng) Running north from Jiāyùguān, this section of wall is believed to have been first constructed in 1539, though this reconstruction dates from 1987. It's quite an energetic hike up to excellent views of the desert and the glittering snowcapped peaks in the distance. The wall is about 9km north of the fort.

First Beacon Platform of the Great Wall
HISTORIC SITE

(长城第一墩; Chángchéng Dìyī Dūn) Atop a 56m-high cliff overlooking the Tǎolài River south of Jiāyùguān, the remains of this beacon platform are not much to look at (they resemble a shaped pile of dirt), but the views over the river in their dramatic gorge are impressive and you can walk alongside attached vestiges of Ming-era Great Wall. When visiting, your driver will likely first drop you off at a **subterranean viewing platform** (labelled the 'Underground Valley' and featuring a glass-bottomed platform that extends out over the canyon) about 150m from the beacon platform.

Wèi Jìn Tombs
TOMB

(新城魏晋墓; Xīnchéng Wèijìnmù; admission ¥31; ⊙8.30am-7.30pm) These tombs date from approximately AD 220–420 (the Wei and Western Jin periods) and contain extraordinarily fresh brick wall paintings (some ineptly retouched) depicting scenes from everyday life, from making tea to picking mulberries for silk production. There are literally thousands of tombs in the desert 20km east of Jiāyùguān, but only one is currently open to visitors, that of a husband and wife. The small **museum** is also worth a look. A taxi here will cost around ¥70 so it's worth paying a little more (¥100) to also visit **Yěmáwān Bǎo Yízhǐ** (野麻湾堡遗址), a former walled town with dramatically crumbling remains. Nearby are some unrestored sections of the Great Wall dotting farm fields and free to access.

🛏 Sleeping

Kānghuī Hotel
HOTEL $$

(康辉宾馆; Kānghuī Bīnguǎn; ✆620 3456; www.jygcct.com; tw/tr ¥208/288; ❉@) Wide windows, high ceilings and very spacious rooms (and bathrooms) are highlights at this tidy business hotel in the centre of town. The place was undergoing renovation at the time of writing and prices were expected to rise about ¥20. Discounts of 30% are typical.

Jīnyè Bīnguǎn
HOTEL $

(金叶宾馆; ✆620 1333; 12 Lanxin Xilu; 兰新西路 12号; d/tr without shower ¥100/180, tw/tr ¥200; ❉@) The en suite rooms are a bit of a tight squeeze but overall good value at this hotel with a useful location by the bus station. The cheapest rooms are a bit tatty and the shared bathrooms could be cleaner. Expect discounts of 40%.

Jiāyùguān Bīnguǎn
HOTEL $$$

(嘉峪关宾馆; ✆620 1588; 1 Xinhua Beilu; 新华北路1号; d/tw from ¥669/768; ❉@) Room interiors come from the standard design catalogue for modern three-star hotels, and include computers with broadband internet access. Other services include a restaurant serving Western-style food, a spa, ticket agent and attentive staff. Discounts of 30% to 40% are common.

Liángshijú Zhāodàisuǒ
GUESTHOUSE $

(粮食局招待所; ✆682 1544; 2nd fl, 24 Xinhua Zhonglu; s/tw/tr without shower ¥45/58/60, tw ¥78) This clean and well-run guesthouse is central and good value.

🍴 Eating

For breakfast ask or look around for small shops selling *bāozi* (包子; steamed meat- or vegie-filled buns) and *dòujiāng* (豆浆; soya milk).

TOP CHOICE Yuàn Zhōng Yuàn Restaurant
SICHUANESE $$

(苑中苑酒店; Yuànzhōngyuàn Jiǔdiàn; Jingtie Shangchang; dishes ¥12-48; ⊙9am-9pm) Directly across from the bus station on the far side of a small park is this pleasant Sìchuān restaurant nice enough for a first date. Try its *gōngbǎo jīdīng* (宫保鸡丁; spicy chicken and peanuts), *tiěbǎn dòufu* (铁板豆腐; fried tofu) or a *yúxiāng ròusī* (鱼香肉丝; stir-fried pork and vegie strips) good for a single diner.

Fùqiáng Market
MARKET $

(富强市场; Fùqiáng Shìchǎng) For a fast, hot meal in the evenings, especially barbecued lamb washed down with beer, try the food stalls at this market, north of the traffic circle.

JULY 1ST GLACIER

About 90km southwest of Jiāyùguān, this **glacier** (七一冰川; Qīyī Bīngchuān; admission ¥101) sits high in the Qílián Shān range at 4300m. In summer it's a great place to come to escape the heat of the desert below. If you arrive in the spring or autumn, expect a very cold and forbidding place.

From the ticket office base the 5km-long trail starts out in alpine scrub before running along the rocky borders of the glacial moraine. The views are stupendous in any direction. Expect three to four hours to reach the glacier, scramble up to the closest icy tongue, snap a few pictures, and return. Note that while the sign at the ticket office says you are at 3800m, that is almost certainly wrong by at least 500m. Coming from Jiāyùguān (at 1500m altitude) you should have minimum problem with the altitude.

The glacier is reached via the train to the iron-ore town of **Jìngtiěshān** (镜铁山; tickets ¥4.50), departing from Jiāyùguān's train station at 7am. It's a scenic 2½-hour ride up a deep river canyon and at the station there may be a minibus to take you up the final 20km to the glacier ticket office. Otherwise try to bargain for a ride in a worker's truck. Either way expect to pay at least ¥50 each way, more if you are the only traveller.

The return train to Jiāyùguān leaves Jìngtiěshān at 5pm, allowing you plenty of time to do this hike as a day trip. If you have a group, consider renting a taxi in Jiāyùguān (¥600 to ¥800). In all cases come prepared with food, water, and warm and wet weather gear.

Jìngtiě Xiǎochīchéng MARKET $
(镇铁小吃城; Jìngtiě Market; ⊙10am-10pm) At this busy market, off Xinhua Zhonglu, load up on lamb kebabs, *ròujiāmó* (肉夹馍), wonton soup, dumplings, roast duck and more.

❶ Information

The **Bank of China** (中国银行; Zhōngguó Yínháng) south of the Lanxin Xilu intersection on Xinhua Zhonglu has an ATM and can change money. Look for an **internet cafe** (网络; wǎngbā; per hr ¥3; ⊙24hr) beside the bus station.

❶ Getting There & Away

Jiāyùguān has an airport with flights to Běijīng, Shànghǎi and Lánzhōu but most people arrive by bus or train.

Bus

Doubling as a billiards hall, Jiāyùguān's bus station (汽车站; qìchēzhàn) is by a busy four-way junction on Lanxin Xilu, next to the main budget hotels.

Dūnhuáng ¥73, five hours, four daily (9am to 2.30pm)

Lánzhōu ¥160, 12 hours, three daily sleepers

Wǔwēi ¥95, seven hours, five daily (two in the morning, three in the afternoon)

Zhāngyè ¥50, four hours, hourly (6.40am to 4.20pm)

Train

Most trains to Dūnhuáng stop at Liǔyuán (180km away). Direct trains are few and not well scheduled.

Lánzhōu hard/soft seat ¥103/160, seven to eight hours; hard/soft sleeper ¥179/275, nine hours

Ürümqi hard/soft sleeper ¥246/384, 15 hours

Zhāngyè hard/soft seat ¥38/57, two to three hours

Purchase tickets at the **train booking office** (火车站售票处; huǒchēzhàn shòupiàochù; 28 Xinhua Zhonglu; ⊙8am-noon & 1-4pm Mon-Fri, to 3.30pm Sat & Sun) near the **People's No 1 Hospital** (第一人民医院; Dìyī Rénmín Yīyuàn; Xinhua Zhonglu), next to the China Construction Bank. Note that you can't buy tickets here for Jìngtiěshān (for the July 1st Glacier) but must purchase these directly at the station.

Jiāyùguān's train station (火车站) is southwest of the town centre. Bus 1 runs here from Xinhua Zhonglu (¥1). A taxi costs under ¥10.

❶ Getting Around

The Jiǔgāng Bīnguǎn West Building rents bikes (出租自行车; chūzū zìxíngchē) for ¥30 per day from 9.30am (¥400 deposit). Bus 1 (¥1) runs from the train station to the bus station. A taxi to the airport (25 minutes) costs ¥50.

Dūnhuáng 敦煌

☑ 0937 / POP 187,000

The fertile Dūnhuáng oasis has long been a refuge for weary Silk Road travellers. Most visitors stayed long enough only to swap a camel and have a feed; but some settled down and built the forts, towers and magnificent cave temples that are now scattered over

Dūnhuáng

N 0 — 200 m
0 — 0.1 miles

Dūnhuáng

Sleeping
1 Charley Johng's Hostel B2
2 Dūnhuáng Legend Hotel..................A1
3 Fēitiān Bīnguǎn A2
4 Gōngyì Měishù Zhāodàisuǒ.............A1

Eating
5 Bǔ Jì Lǘ Ròu Huáng Miànguǎn..........B2
6 Charley Johng's Cafe......................A2
7 Oasis Cafe.....................................B2
8 Shāzhōu Night Market B1

Entertainment
9 Dūnhuáng Theatre...........................A1

Information
Fēitiān Travel Service..................(see 3)

Transport
10 Air Ticket Office B1
11 Minibus Stand A2
12 Train Booking Office......................B2
13 Train Booking Office......................B1

the surrounding area. These sites, along with some dwarfing sand dunes and desertscapes, make Dūnhuáng a magnificent place to visit.

Despite its remoteness, per capita income in Dūnhuáng is among the highest in China, thanks to a recent push into wind and solar energy production (see boxed text, p833). The town is now thoroughly modern, but there's no doubt it has maintained its distinction. With clean tree-lined streets, slow-moving traffic, bustling markets, budget hotels, cafes and souvenir shops, it also has remained as much an oasis for the weary traveller as ever.

Sights

Though relatively small, Dūnhuáng is a great walking town with wide sidewalks and endless narrow alleys opening up into squares, markets and the lives of ordinary citizens. The riverside is worth a visit if only to see if you are brave enough to cross to the platforms in the middle of the stream.

FREE Dūnhuáng Museum MUSEUM

(敦煌博物馆; Dūnhuáng Bówùguǎn; Mingshan Lu; ⊙8am-6.30pm) Outside of town on the road to the dunes is this newly opened museum that takes you on an artefact-rich journey through the Dūnhuáng area (from prehistoric to Qing-dynasty times) via hallways designed to make you feel as if you were in a cave. You can easily walk here in 15 minutes from the centre of town. Bring your passport for admission.

Sleeping

Competition among Dūnhuáng's hotels is fierce, and you should get significant discounts (50% or more) outside of summer.

There are a dozen or so smaller business-type hotels along Mingshan and Yangguan Zhonglu. They tend to be around ¥200 in the off-season and ¥300 to ¥400 in the height of summer.

TOP CHOICE Charley Johng's Hostel HOSTEL $

(梦驼铃青年旅舍; Mèng Tuólíng Qīngnián Lǚshè; ☑138 9376 3029; dhzhzh@163.com; 3F, 11 Qingcheng; 情城11号楼3楼; dm/d ¥35/120; @☎) The latest in the Charley Johng backpacking empire is this well-run, well-placed and well-appointed hostel literally in the night market area behind the mosque. Reception and rooms are on the 3rd floor (so you avoid the market smells), where you'll also find a wide inner courtyard, laundry and English travel information. Dorm rooms are clean and basic while the doubles are spacious and have their own powerful showers. The hostel is down a small alley so drop by Charley Johng's Cafe first for directions.

Silk Road Dūnhuáng Hotel HOTEL $$$

(敦煌山庄; Dūnhuáng Shānzhuāng; ☑888 2088; www.dunhuangresort.com; Dunyue Lu; 敦月路; dm ¥80, d ¥350-1200; ☀@☎) Around 2km from Singing Sands Mountain, this four-star resort is tastefully designed with Central Asian rugs, a cool stone floor and Chinese antiques. Four-bed dorms are in the student building way round the back, and the cheaper doubles (with bathrooms) are in the

'Professional Quarters'. The hotel's rooftop restaurant has without doubt the best outdoor perch in Dūnhuáng. A taxi from town costs ¥10, or take minibus 3 (¥1). There are off-season discounts of 20% to 40%.

Dune Guesthouse
HOSTEL $

(月泉山庄青年旅舍; Yuèquán Shānzhuāng Qīngnián Lûshè; ☎138 9376 3029; dhzhzh@163. com; dm ¥30, r & cabins with shared bathroom ¥100) Nearly at the base of the Singing Sands Mountain, and surrounded by flowering gardens and grapevines, this chilled-out backpackers' retreat is superbly located. Cabins are set among the fruit trees; doubles and dorms around the central courtyard. All rooms share showers and toilets (it would be nice if the latter were kept a bit cleaner). A taxi here is ¥15, or catch minibus 3 to the terminus, walk north (back towards town) a short way, take the first turn left on the other side of the road past the vines and follow the signs. The guesthouse is run by the folks at Charley Johng's Cafe, so make enquiries there first.

Dūnhuáng Legend Hotel
HOTEL $$$

(敦煌飞天大酒店; Dūnhuáng Fēitiān Dàjiǔdiàn; ☎885 3888; www.dhlegendhotel.com; Mingshan Lu; 鸣山路; d & tw from ¥888; ❄@) Rooms at this four-star (clearly slipping down the rankings if anyone was counting) Chinese-oriented hotel are spacious and well furnished. In summer they are good value when discounts bring the rates down to about ¥500, and other very basic two-stars in town are charging not much less.

Gōngyì Měishù Zhāodàisuǒ
GUESTHOUSE $

(工艺美术招待所; ☎884 0919; Yangguan Zhonglu; 阳关中路; s & tw without bathroom ¥80) This very basic guesthouse is in a courtyard opposite the China Life Insurance Company. As you enter the courtyard look left for the blue sign with red characters. Rooms are on the 3rd floor and ¥50 in the off-season. Note the guesthouse has bathrooms but no showers.

Mògāo Hotel
HOTEL $$

(莫高宾馆; Mògāo Bīnguǎn; ☎885 1777; 12 Mingshan Lu; 鸣山路12号; d/tw from ¥308/428; ❄@🛜) With its excellent location downtown near restaurants and shops, this is one of the better options for the single traveller who wants a private room. There's in-room broadband and wi-fi in the lobby. Off-season the smaller doubles go for around ¥188.

Fēitiān Bīnguǎn
HOTEL $$

(飞天宾馆; ☎882 2337; www.fttravel.cn; 22 Mingshan Lu; 鸣山路22号; d/tw ¥428/458; ❄@) This long-standing two-star hotel has a good location on one of Dūnhuáng's major streets. Rooms are small but tidy and well lit.

✗ Eating

There are restaurants large and small all over Dūnhuáng, many with English or picture menus. For *niúrò miàn* (牛肉面; beef noodles) head to any number of restaurants along Xiyu Lu.

Several Western travellers' cafes can be found in town with dishes in the ¥10 to ¥20 mark. In addition to providing internet access and bike hire, these are good spots to exchange information with other travellers.

Shāzhōu Night Market
MARKET $$

(沙洲夜市; Shāzhōu Yèshì; ⏰morning-late) Extending from Yangguan Lu south to Xiyu Lu, this market is both a place to eat and to socialise. Off Yanguang Lu are dozens of well-organised stalls with English signs explaining what they sell: expect Sìchuān, Korean noodles, dumplings, claypot, barbecue including *ròujiāmó* (肉夹馍) and Lánzhōu noodles. Also look out for cooling cups of *xìngpíshuǐ* (杏皮水; apricot juice; ¥5).

There is also an evening-only open-air seating area nearby with singing, music bands and roast lamb by the platter or skewer. Along with the seated areas along Fanggu Shangye Yitao Jie, this is the most expensive place to eat barbecued meat. For a better deal try the alleys radiating east. The same lamb skewer that costs ¥8 in the main areas will cost ¥3 to ¥5 here.

⌜TOP⌝ Zhāixīng Gé
⌞CHOICE⌟ CHINESE, INTERNATIONAL $$

(摘星阁; Silk Road Dūnhuáng Hotel; Dunyue Lu; dishes ¥18-38; ⏰7am-1pm & 4.30pm-midnight; 🅿) Part of the Silk Road Dūnhuáng Hotel, this superb rooftop restaurant is ideal for a meal (the Western buffet breakfast is well regarded by travellers) or a sundowner gazing out over the golden sand dunes with someone you love. Dishes are priced reasonably and not much more than places in town. Try the Uighur bread or the surprisingly good thick-crust pizza.

Bǔ Jì Lú Ròu Huáng Miànguǎn
DONKEY MEAT $$

(卜记驴肉黄面馆; Shazhou Nanlu; dishes ¥12-38, set meals from ¥35; ⏰10am-10pm) Donkey meat with yellow noodles is a local speciality and this is one popular place to try it. The restaurant has a banquet hall feel but prices are fine for one or two people. If you've never had it, donkey tastes like roast beef and set meals are served with noodle dishes topped with tofu.

Charley Johng's Cafe BREAKFAST, CHINESE $
(风味餐館; Fēngwèi Cānguǎn; Mingshan Lu; dishes ¥6-20; ⊙8.30am-10pm 📱) Tasty Western-style breakfast items including scrambled eggs, muesli with yoghurt, and pancakes are available all day either à la carte or as a set. There are also sandwiches, and a host of Chinese dishes such as stir-fries and dumplings.

🍷 Drinking

The alley behind Charley Johng's Hostel has a row of stylish cafes with couch seating and free wi-fi that also serve as bars in the evening. In summer the Silk Road Dūnhuáng Hotel hosts a **beer garden** at the entrance to the grounds, while their stylish rooftop **Zhāixīng Gé** (⊙4.30pm-midnight) offers peerless views over the desert to go with a beer or a glass of local red wine.

Oasis Cafe CAFE
(绿洲咖啡館; Lǜzhōu Kāfēiguǎn; Fanggu Shangye Yitiao Jie; ⊙2-11pm Tue-Sun; 🛜📱) Surely the best smoothies and milkshakes (blueberry, peach, kiwifruit and more; ¥14) in northwest China and some of the finest coffee, too. With excellent homemade hamburgers and pizza, you can spend a long time relaxing at this chilled-out spot run by an Oklahoman.

☆ Entertainment

There are often night-time opera and other music performances in the square behind Charley Johng's Hostel. This is also a good place to go if you have children, as there are several large free play areas.

Dūnhuáng Goddess (敦煌神女; Dūnhuáng Shénnǚ; tickets ¥220; ⊙8.30pm) is an 80-minute acrobatic dramatisation of stories on the walls of the Mògāo Caves. It's held at the **Dūnhuáng Theatre** (敦煌大剧院; Dūnhuáng Dàjùyuàn); English subtitles are provided.

ℹ Information

Ask at any of the Western cafes in town for tourist info; they can also help with tours from camel rides to overnight camping excursions. Wi-fi is widely available in cafes, high-speed internet in hotel rooms, and there's an **internet cafe** (网吧; Wǎngbā; cnr Mingshan Lu & Xiyu Lu; per hr ¥4; ⊙24hr).

Bank of China (中国银行; Zhōngguó Yínháng; Yangguan Zhonglu; ⊙8am-noon & 2-6pm Mon-Fri) Has a 24-hour ATM and changes travellers cheques.

Fēitiān Travel Service (飞天旅行社; Fēitiān Lǚxíngshè; 📞138 3070 6288, 885 2318; Fēitiān Bīnguǎn, Mingshan Lu) Can arrange buses to Mògāo, local tours and car hire.

Public Security Bureau (PSB; 公安局; Gōng'ānjú; 📞886 2071; Yangguan Zhonglu; ⊙8am-noon & 3-6.30pm Mon-Fri) Two days needed for visa extension.

ℹ Getting There & Away

Air

Apart from November to March, when there are only flights to/from Lánzhōu and Xī'ān, there are regular flights to/from Běijīng (¥1880), Lánzhōu (¥1380), Shànghǎi (¥2460), Ürümqi (¥710) and Xī'ān (¥1680).

Seats can be booked at the **air ticket office** (⊙8.30am-6.30pm) in the lobby of the **Yóuzhèng Bīnguǎn** hotel (邮政宾馆), west of China Post.

Bus

Dūnhuáng's new station (汽车站; qìchēzhàn) is on Sanwei Lu (a five-minute walk to downtown) has buses to the following:

Golmud ¥99, nine hours, two daily (9am and 7.30pm)

Jiāyùguān ¥72, five hours, three daily (10.10am, 10.45am and 12.50pm)

Lánzhōu ¥226, 17 hours, three daily (11am, 3pm and 5pm), all sleepers

Liǔyuán (柳园) ¥20, eight per day (7.30am to 6.30pm)

Ürümqi ¥198, 14 hours, one daily (7pm), sleeper. May stop in Turpan.

Train

Dūnhuáng's station is 10km east of town but for some destinations, such as Běijīng West and Ürümqi, you'll have to leave from Liǔyuán Station, a crazy 180km away.

Lánzhōu hard/soft sleeper ¥246/383, 14 hours (two per day at 9.32am and 6.58pm; more trains leave from Liǔyuán Station)

Turpan (from Liǔyuán Station) hard/soft sleeper ¥164/252, eight to nine hours

Ürümqi (from Liǔyuán Station) hard/soft sleeper ¥195/302, 11 hours

To purchase tickets to Lánzhōu, head to the **train booking office** (火车票发售点; huǒchē piào Fāshòu diǎn; ⊙8am-noon & 1-4pm) behind the mosque. For tickets to Ürümqi head to the **train booking office** (铁路售票处; tiělù shòupiàochù; ⊙8.30am-8pm) on Yangguan Lu. Both charge a ¥5 commission.

THE WINDY ROAD TO A CLEANER CHINA

Unless you sleep the entire way, the road from Jiāyùguān to Dūnhuáng will likely impress you as much for the endless spinning turbines as the stark desert landscape. In 2011 the windswept northern region was the site of nearly two dozen energy farms, and 5000 (and growing) individual turbines. At the industry centre in Jiǔquán (southeast of Jiāyùguān) dozens of companies are yearly cranking out several thousand more.

Once the cradle of China's oil industry, Gānsù had been experimenting with wind power since 1996. During the first decade, installed capacity barely rose to 100MW (1GW is the capacity of a large coal or nuclear power plant). Then in 2005, the Chinese government announced it would push into clean energy in a massive way (forced in part by its rapidly deteriorating environment), pledging US$700 billion for development over the next decade. By 2020, Běijīng declared, 15% of the country's energy would be produced by wind, solar, biomass and hydropower.

In 2007 the National Development and Reform Commission approved construction of a 10GW wind farm in Gānsù. Similar large-scale wind farms were then approved in Xīnjiāng, Inner Mongolia, Jílín and Héběi, and recently, work began on offshore farms in Jiāngsū and Shāndōng and slow-wind farms in the south of China. An industry was born overnight and by 2011 nationwide capacity had reached 62GW and was growing by 20GW a year!

The pace of change has been breathtaking. From 2006 to 2010, the wind industry experienced triple-digit growth, and from an initial six green energy companies the number rose to more than 100. But rapid progress brought troubles. Installed capacity, for example, was far outpacing the rate at which it could be absorbed by the national electric grid. There were also serious issues with nonstandard installation of turbines, poor component quality and equipment malfunction. In 2012 Premier Wen Jiabao declared that the government needed to rein in its 'blind' expansion of the industry and strengthen overall planning.

According to China's current wind-power development plan, no more than 15GW of installed capacity will be connected annually to the grid. To facilitate this, $US590 billion will also go towards expanding and modernising China's electrical transmission system.

China is determined to become a global leader in green energy production, but within its borders heavily polluting coal thermal plants will still generate most of the country's electricity for decades. Coal production is expected to increase, for example, from 3.2 to 4 billion tonnes by 2020 as the nation literally adds another 1000GW of capacity (which incredibly is the current *total* capacity of the US).

Long-term projections have wind potentially accounting for 30% of all new installed capacity after 2020 and up to one-third of all capacity by 2050. With an equally strong push into solar, hydro and nuclear, China's electrical production could one day become among the cleanest in the world.

GĀNSÙ AROUND DŪNHUÁNG

ℹ️ Getting Around

Dūnhuáng's airport is 13km east of town; taxis cost ¥25. The train station is on the same road as the airport and costs a similar amount. Bus 1 runs to the train station from Mingshan Lu from 7.30am to 9pm.

If you are heading to Liǔyuán Train Station (for trains to Ürümqi), catch a bus or a shared taxi (per person ¥45) from out front of the bus station on Sanwei Lu. Give yourself at least three hours to get to Liǔyuán station (including waiting for the taxi to fill up with other passengers).

Taxis around town start at ¥5.

You can hire bikes from the travellers' cafes for ¥5 per hour. Getting to some of the outlying sights by bike is possible, but hard work at the height of summer.

Around Dūnhuáng

Most people visit the Mògāo Caves in the morning, followed by the Míngshā Shān sand dunes in the late afternoon. Note that it can be above 40°C in the desert during the summer so go prepared with water, a sunhat and snacks.

MÒGĀO CAVES   莫高窟

The Mògāo Caves (Mògāo Kū) are, simply put, one of the greatest repositories of Buddhist art in the world. At its peak, the site housed 18 monasteries, more than 1400 monks and nuns, and countless artists, translators and calligraphers. Wealthy traders and important officials were the primary

SILK ROAD RAIDERS

In 1900 the self-appointed guardian of the Mògāo Caves, Wang Yuanlu, discovered a hidden library filled with tens of thousands of immaculately preserved manuscripts and paintings, dating as far back as AD 406.

It's hard to describe the exact magnitude of the discovery, but stuffed into the tiny room were texts in rare Central Asian languages, military reports, music scores, medical prescriptions, Confucian and Taoist classics, and Buddhist sutras copied by some of the greatest names in Chinese calligraphy – not to mention the oldest printed book in existence, the *Diamond Sutra* (AD 868). In short, it was an incalculable amount of original source material regarding Chinese, Central Asian and Buddhist history.

Word of the discovery quickly spread and Wang Yuanlu, suddenly the most popular bloke in town, was courted by rival archaeologists Auriel Stein and Paul Pelliot, among others. Following much pressure to sell the cache, Wang Yuanlu finally relented and parted with an enormous hoard of treasure. During his watch close to 20,000 of the cave's priceless manuscripts were whisked off to Europe for the paltry sum of £220.

Still today, Chinese intellectuals bitter at the sacking of the caves deride Stein, Pelliot and other 'foreign devils' for making off with a national treasure. Defenders of the explorers point out that had the items been left alone they may have been lost during the ensuing civil war or the Cultural Revolution.

donors responsible for creating new caves, as caravans made the long detour past Mògāo to pray or give thanks for a safe journey through the treacherous wastelands to the west. The traditional date ascribed to the founding of the first cave is AD 366.

The caves fell into disuse after the collapse of the Yuan dynasty and were largely forgotten until the early 20th century, when they were 'rediscovered' by a string of foreign explorers (see boxed text above).

Entrance to the caves (low/high season ¥100/180; ⊘8.15am-6pm May-Oct, 9.15am-5.30pm Nov-Apr, tickets sold till 1hr before closing) is strictly controlled – it's impossible to visit them on your own. The general admission ticket grants you a two-hour tour (display great interest at the start as your guide has the discretion to make this longer) of around 10 caves, including the infamous Library Cave (cave 17) and a related exhibit containing rare fragments of manuscripts in classical Uighur and Manichean. Excellent English-speaking guides are available (and included in the admission price) at 9am, noon and 2pm, and you should be able to arrange tours in other languages as well.

Of the 492 caves, 20 'open' caves are rotated fairly regularly, so recommendations are useless, but tours always include the two big Buddhas, 34.5m and 26m tall respectively. It's also possible to visit some of the more unusual caves for ¥100 to ¥500 per cave. Note that in some of the caves later frescoes may cover earlier wall paintings.

Photography is strictly prohibited everywhere within the fenced-off caves area. And if it's raining, snowing or sand storming, the caves will be closed.

After the tour it's well worth visiting the Dūnhuáng Research Centre, where eight more caves, each representative of a different period, have been flawlessly reproduced, along with selected murals. The 15-minute video on the paintings in cave 254 is also worth watching.

If you have a special interest in the site, check out the International Dūnhuáng Project (http://idp.bl.uk), an online database of digitalised manuscripts from the Library Cave at Mògāo.

◉ Sights

Northern Wei, Western Wei & Northern Zhou Caves
CAVES, BUDDHIST

The earliest caves are distinctly Indian in style and iconography. All contain a central pillar, representing a stupa (symbolically containing the ashes of the Buddha), which the devout would circle in prayer. Paint was derived from malachite (green), cinnabar (red) and lapis lazuli (blue), expensive minerals imported from Central Asia.

The art of this period is characterised by its attempt to depict the spirituality of those who had transcended the material world through their asceticism. The Wei statues are slim, ethereal figures with finely chiselled features and comparatively large heads. The Northern Zhou figures have ghostly white eyes. Don't be fooled by the thick, black modernist strokes – it's the oxidisation of lead in the paint, not some forerunner of Picasso.

Sui Caves
CAVES, BUDDHIST

The Sui dynasty (AD 581–618) began when a general of Chinese or mixed Chinese-Tuoba origin usurped the throne of the northern Zhou dynasty and reunited northern and southern China for the first time in 360 years.

The Sui dynasty was short-lived and very much a transition between the Wei and Tang periods. This can be seen in the Sui caves: the graceful Indian curves in the Buddha and Bodhisattva figures start to give way to the more rigid style of Chinese sculpture.

Tang Caves
CAVES, BUDDHIST

During the Tang dynasty (AD 618–907), China pushed its borders westward as far as Lake Balkash in today's Kazakhstan. Trade expanded and foreign merchants and people of diverse religions streamed into Cháng'ān, the Tang capital.

This was Mògāo's high point. Painting and sculpture techniques became much more refined, and some important aesthetic developments, notably the sex change (from male to female) of Guanyin and the flying *apsaras,* took place. The beautiful murals depicting the Buddhist Western Paradise offer rare insights into the court life, music, dress and architecture of Tang China.

Some 230 caves were carved during the Tang dynasty, including two impressive grottoes containing enormous, seated Buddha figures. Originally open to the elements, the statue of Maitreya in cave 96 (believed to represent Empress Wu Zetian, who used Buddhism to consolidate her power) is a towering 34.5m tall, making it the world's third-largest Buddha. The Buddhas were carved from the top down using scaffolding, the anchor holes of which are still visible.

Post-Tang Caves
CAVES, BUDDHIST

Following the Tang dynasty, the economy around Dūnhuáng went into decline, and the luxury and vigour typical of Tang painting began to be replaced by simpler drawing techniques and flatter figures. The mysterious Western Xia kingdom, which controlled most of Gānsù from 983 to 1227, made a number of additions to the caves at Mògāo and began to introduce Tibetan influences.

ⓘ Getting There & Away

The Mògāo Caves are 25km (30 minutes) southeast from Dūnhuáng. The first green bus (one way ¥8) leaves at 8am or 9am (and possibly other times depending on the season, so enquire at the Western cafes) from the intersection across from the Dūnhuáng Hotel; buses return at noon, 2pm and 4pm. A return taxi costs from ¥100 to ¥150 for a day, whereas you can usually find a taxi willing to just take you back to Dūnhuáng from the caves for ¥40.

Some people ride out to the caves on a bicycle, but be warned that half the ride is through total desert – hot work in summer.

SINGING SANDS MOUNTAIN & CRESCENT MOON LAKE 鸣沙山、月牙泉

Six kilometres south of Dūnhuáng at **Singing Sands Mountain** (Míngshā Shān; admission ¥120; ☉6am-9pm), the desert meets the oasis in most spectacular fashion. From here it's easy to see how Dūnhuáng gained its moniker 'Shāzhōu' (Town of Sand). The climb to the top of the dunes – the highest peak swells to 1715m – is sweaty work, but the view across the undulating desert sands and green poplar trees below is awesome. Hire a pair of bright orange shoe protectors (防沙靴; *fángshāxuē*; ¥10) or just shake your shoes out later.

At the base of the colossal dunes is a famous yet underwhelming pond, **Crescent Moon Lake** (Yuèyáquán). The dunes are a no-holds-barred tourist playpen, with camel rides (per person ¥80) as well as dune buggies, 'dune surfing' (sand sliding), paragliding (jumping off the dunes with a chute on your back) and even microlighting. But if your sole interest is in appreciating the dunes in peace, it's not hard to hike away from the action.

You can ride a bike to the dunes in around 20 minutes. Minibus 3 (¥1) shuttles between Dūnhuáng and the dunes from 7.30am to 9pm, departing from Mingshan Lu. A taxi costs ¥15 one way.

Western cafes in Dūnhuáng offer overnight camel trips to the dunes; Charley Johng's charges ¥400 per person for the ride and an overnight stay in a tent. There are also five- to eight-day expeditions out to the Jade Gate Pass, Liǔyuán and even as far as Lop Nor in the deserts of Xīnjiāng.

YĂDĀN NATIONAL PARK & JADE GATE PASS 雅丹国家地质公园、玉门关

The weird, eroded desert landscape of **Yǎdān National Park** (Yǎdān Guójiā Dìzhì Gōngyuán; incl tour ¥80) is 180km northwest of Dūnhuáng, in the middle of the Gobi Desert's awesome

GĀNSÙ AROUND DŪNHUÁNG

nothingness. A former lake bed that eroded in spectacular fashion some 12,000 years ago, the strange rock formations provided the backdrop to the last scenes of Zhang Yimou's film *Hero*. The desert landscape is dramatic, but you can only tour the site on a group minibus, so there's little scope to explore on your own.

To get to Yǎdān you have to pass by (and buy a ticket to) the **Jade Gate Pass** (Yùmén Guān; admission ¥40), 102km from Dūnhuáng. Both this and the **South Pass** (阳关; Yáng Guān), 78km west of Dūnhuáng, were originally military stations, part of the Han dynasty series of beacon towers that extended to the garrison town of Lóula'n in Xīnjiāng. For caravans travelling westward, the Jade Gate marked the beginning of the northern route to Turpan, while the South Pass was the start of the southern route through Miran. The Jade Gate derived its name from the important traffic in Khotanese jade.

The entry fee includes a small museum (with scraps of real Silk Road silk); a nearby section of Han-dynasty Great Wall built in 101 BC and impressive for its antiquity and lack of restoration; and the ruined city walls of **Hécāng Chéng**, 15km away on a side road.

The best way to get here is to take one of two daily **minibus tours** (per person for 7am departure ¥76, for 2pm departure ¥86), which you can book through Charley Johng's Cafe or Hostel. The 10- to 12-hour tours include a stop at the Jade Gate Pass and the **Western Thousand Buddha Caves** (西千佛洞; Xī Qiānfó Dòng; admission ¥20; ◷8.30am-6.30pm), 35km west of Dūnhuáng, where there are 16 caves hidden in the cliff face of the Dǎng Hé gorge, ranging from the Northern Wei to the Tang dynasties.

YÚLÍN GROTTOES
榆林窟

About 180km south of Dūnhuáng, the 40-plus **caves** (Yúlín Kū; admission ¥45, ◷9am-5pm, tickets sold till 1hr before closing) of the Yúlín Grottoes face each other across a narrow canyon. The interior art spans a 1500-year period, from the Northern Wei to the Qing dynasty. Many show a distinctive Tibetan influence.

While the art at the Mògāo Caves is considered higher quality, the frescoes here are better preserved; there is little of the oxidation and thickening of painted lines so prevalent at Mògāo. It's also intriguing to observe the original carved interior tunnels that formerly connected the caves.

The only way to get out here is to rent a minivan (¥400) for the half-day. Excellent English guides are available on-site for ¥15.

EASTERN GĀNSÙ

Most travellers speed through eastern Gānsù, catching mere glimpses from the train window as they shuttle between Lánzhōu and Xī'ān. This is a shame because the area contains some spectacular Silk Road remnants at Màijī Shān that are well worth stopping for.

Tiānshuǐ
天水

☏0938 / POP 450,000

Tiānshuǐ's splendid Buddhist caves at nearby Màijī Shān entice a consistent flow of visitors to this otherwise bland provincial town. Or is that two towns? Modern Tiānshuǐ is actually two very separate districts 15km apart: there is the railhead sprawl, known as Màijī Qū (麦积区; formerly Běidào), and the central commercial area to the west, known as Qínzhōu Qū (秦州区) and where you'll arrive if coming in by bus. The two sections are lashed together by a long freeway that runs through a hilly corridor.

Màijī Shān is 35km south of the train station.

◉ Sights

Tiānshuǐ's main draw are the grottoes at Màijī Shān. Within walking distance of the Tiānshuǐ Dàjiǔdiàn hotel are two temples worth checking out if you have time to kill.

Fúxī Temple
BUDDHIST TEMPLE

(伏羲庙; Fúxī Miào; off Jiefang Lu, Qínchéng; admission ¥30; ◷8am-6pm) This Ming-dynasty temple was founded in 1483, and more recently cracked during the Sìchuān earthquake of 2008. The main hall is a grand post and beam structure with intricate wooden lattice door panels: look for traditional symbols such as bats, dragons, peonies, cranes and swastikas. On the ceiling bright original paintings of the 64 hexagrams (varying combinations of the eight trigrams used in the *I Ching*) draw the eye upwards.

Yùquán Temple
TAOIST TEMPLE

(玉泉观; Yùquán Guàn; Renmin Xilu, Qínchéng; adult/student ¥20/10; ◷8am-6pm) Ascending in layers up the hillside above Qínchéng, this Taoist temple has been a place of worship since the Tang dynasty. Most of the buildings have been restored in recent decades, but this is still a pleasant, green and rambling shrine with a number of ancient cypress trees.

🛏 Sleeping

Tiānshuǐ has plenty of accommodation in both parts of town.

QÍNZHŌU QŪ

Tiānshuǐ Dàjiǔdiàn HOTEL **$**

(天水大酒店; ☏828 9999; 1 Qinzhou Dazhong Nanlu; 秦州大众南路1号; d/This popular hotel is a solid choice in the Qínzhōu Qū district. The bus to Màijī Shān is just 200m south and restaurants abound. Standard en suite rooms and those with shared bathrooms are pretty much identical in cleanliness, size and furnishings, and are usually discounted up to 40%.

MÀIJĪ QŪ

New Leaf Inn HOTEL **$**

(辛叶酒店; Xīn Yè Jiǔdiàn; ☏261 8808; Longchang Lu; 陇昌路; d & tw ¥138; ☀@) This small business hotel has clean bright rooms with IKEA-style furnishings. The hotel is about 200m east (left as you exit) of the train station on the far side of Longchang Lu.

Wànhuì Zhāodàisuǒ GUESTHOUSE **$**

(万汇招待所; ☏492 7976; Longchang Lu; 陇昌路; s & d without bathroom ¥40, tw ¥90) This serviceable guesthouse is about 100m west (right as you exit) of the train station. Look for the China Post office and then continue down a few more doors. Reception's on the 3rd floor.

🍴 Eating

Tiānshuǐ is famed for its *miànpí* (面皮) noodles, which can be found everywhere. In Qínzhōu, good claypot, Sìchuān and noodle snack stalls, as well as fruit and nut sellers can be found around the Tiānshuǐ Dàjiǔdiàn.

Tasty *ròujiāmó* (肉夹馍) and other fine snack food in Màijī Qū fill Erma Lu, a pedestrian mall two blocks directly south of the train station. One place to try is **Běidào Qīngzhēn Lǎozìhào Niúròu Miànguǎn** (北道清真老字号牛肉面馆; Erma Lu; dishes ¥4-12; ⏰24hr).

Get a ticket from the kiosk out front and collect your beef noodles *(niúròumiàn)* and flatbread *(shāobǐng)* from the kitchen window. The noodles are infused with dollops of scarlet-red chilli oil, and you can point for side dishes of spicy cabbage, cucumber and other vegetables.

There's no English sign, but it's nearly opposite an ICBC bank.

ℹ Information

There's a **Bank of China** (中国银行; Zhōngguó Yínháng) with a 24-hour ATM three blocks directly south from the train station almost at the river. An **internet cafe** (网吧; wǎngbā; per hr ¥2.50; ⏰24hr) can be found on the 2nd floor heading up to the Wànhuì Zhāodàisuǒ in Màijī Qū.

ℹ Getting There & Away

Bus

Buses from the long-distance bus station in Qínzhōu:

Gāngǔ ¥15, 90 minutes, every 15 minutes

Huīxiàn ¥35, three hours, hourly (7.20am to 6pm)

Lánzhōu ¥74, four hours, every 20 minutes (7.20am to 7pm)

Línxià ¥99, seven hours, one daily (6.30am)

Luòmén ¥25, two hours, three daily (7am, 11am and 2.30pm)

Píngliáng ¥65, five hours, hourly (7am to 3pm)

Train

Tiānshuǐ is on the Xī'ān–Lánzhōu rail line; there are dozens of daily trains in either direction.

Lánzhōu hard/soft seat ¥52/81, four hours

Xī'ān hard/soft seat ¥51/78, five hours

ℹ Getting Around

Taxis shuttle passengers between Qínzhōu (from both the city bus station 200m south of Tiānshuǐ Dàjiǔdiàn and also from the long-distance bus station) and the train station in Màijī Qū. It costs ¥10 per person (¥40 for the whole taxi). Alternatively, take the much slower bus 1 or 6 (¥3, 40 minutes).

Around Tiānshuǐ

MÀIJĪ SHĀN 麦积山

Set among wild and lush green hills southeast of Tiānshuǐ, the riveting grottoes of Màijī Shān (Haystack Mountain) hold some of China's most famous Buddhist rock carvings.

◎ Sights

Màijī Shān CAVES, BUDDHIST

(admission ¥70; ⏰8am-6pm) The cliff sides are riddled with niches and statues carved principally during the Northern Wei and Zhou dynasties (AD 386–581), with later additions. Vertigo-inducing catwalks and steep spiral stairways cling to the cliff face, affording close-ups of the art. Within the hard-to-miss Sui-dynasty trinity of Buddha and bodhisattvas is the largest statue on the mountain:

GĀNSÙ AROUND TIĀNSHUǏ

the cave's central effigy of Buddha tops out at 15.7m. When the statue was restored three decades ago, a handwritten copy of the *Sutra of Golden Light* was discovered within the Buddha's fan.

It's not certain just how the artists managed to clamber so high; one theory is that they created piles from blocks of wood reaching to the top of the mountain before moving down, gradually removing them as they descended.

A considerable amount of pigment still clings to many of the statues – a lot of which are actually made of clay rather than hewn from rock – although you frequently have to climb up steps to peer at them through tight mesh grills. Also in many caves there is no natural illumination, so the figures of the Bodhisattvas sit hunched in the gloom or the frescoes are indiscernible. Much, though, is clearly visible and most of the more impressive sculptures decorate the upper walkways, especially at cave 4. A number of the statues were slightly damaged by the Sìchuān earthquake of 2008 but have been repaired.

The entire undertaking is rounded off with a crescent of hawker stalls and a row of food stalls selling delicious spicy cold noodle dishes as well as teas and soft drinks.

An English-speaking guide charges ¥70 for the day. It's possible to view normally closed caves (eg cave 133) for an extra fee of ¥500 per group.

The admission ticket includes entry to **Ruìyìng Monastery** (瑞应寺; Ruìyìng Sì), at the base of the mountain, which acts as a small museum of selected statues. Across the lot from the monastery is the start of a trail to a **botanic garden** (zhíwùyuán; admission free with ticket), which allows for a shortcut back to the entrance gate through the forest.

You can also climb **Xiāngjī Shān** (香积山). For the trailhead, head back towards the food stall area you passed on the way in and look for a sign down a side road to the left.

🛌 Sleeping

There are several places where you can spend the night, including cabins within the botanical gardens at the **Hotel Arboretum** (植物园山庄; Zhíwùyuán Shānzhuāng; ☎223 1025; zwyszhotel@126.com; cabins ¥386). There are also simple **guesthouses** (¥40 to ¥50) in the village about 1km before the entrance gate. Just wander in and your intentions will be clear.

ⓘ Getting There & Away

Green bus 34 (¥5, 40 minutes) leaves every 10 minutes from in front of the Tiānshuǐ train station. The first bus leaves at 6am and the last returns around 6pm. The bus may drop you at the crossroads, 5km before the site, from where a taxi van will cost ¥5 per seat to the ticket office.

Bus 5 leaves from the bus terminal just south of the Tiānshuǐ Dàjiǔdiàn in Qínzhōu at 8.30am and returns at 2.30pm. Taxis wait for passengers (per person ¥30) at the same location most of the morning.

From the ticket office at Màijī Shān you can walk the last 2km to 3km to the caves or take the **tour buggy** (guāngguān chē; return ¥15).

Píngliáng 平凉

☑ 0933 / POP 106,800

A booming Chinese mid-sized town, Píngliáng is a logical base for visits to the nearby holy mountain of Kōngtóng Shān. The train station is in the northeastern part of town and the main bus station in the far western part. Xi Dajie is the main street in town and where you'll find hotels, restaurants and banks.

◉ Sights

Kōngtóng Shān TEMPLES

(崆峒山; admission ¥120; ⊙7am-5pm) Kōngtóng Shān is one of the 12 principal peaks in the Taoist universe. It was first mentioned by the philosopher Zhuangzi (399–295 BC), and illustrious visitors have included none other than the Yellow Emperor. Numerous paths lead over the hilltop past dozens of picturesque (though entirely restored) temples to the summit at over 2100m. While the mountain is an enchanting place to hike, those looking for much genuine historical artefacts or ambience will be disappointed.

From the north gate visitor centre (pick up a free map here to orientate yourself) catch a bus to **Zhōngtái** (¥32) or **Xiāngshān** (¥48), both essentially small visitor areas on the mountain with paths radiating out to lookouts and temples.

Kōngtóng Shān is 11km west of Píngliáng. A taxi costs ¥20, or you can catch bus 16 (¥1) on Xi Dajie and then transfer to bus 13 (¥2) when you reach Kongtong Dadao. Bus 13 drops you off right in front of the main visitor centre before continuing on to the East Gate. At the end of your visit you can walk down from Zhōngtái to the East Gate and catch bus 13 back to town.

🛏 Sleeping & Eating

Just around the corner from Hóngyùn Bīnguǎn, look for the Sìzhōng Alley market (Sìzhōng Xiàng shìchǎng). There are numerous restaurants here, and more food stalls serving noodles, spicy hotpot, barbecued meats, as well as fresh fruit.

Hóngyùn Bīnguǎn   HOTEL **$**
(鸿运宾馆; ✆822 6399; Xi Dajie; 西大街; d/tw without bathroom ¥128/158, tw ¥188; ✳@) The hotel has a friendly guesthouse atmosphere and surprisingly pleasant rooms reached by a very narrow staircase. All rooms have computers and broadband internet, and there are discounts of up to 30%.

Píngliáng Bīnguǎn   HOTEL **$$$**
(平凉宾馆; ✆821 9485; Xi Dajie; 西大街; tw ¥588; ✳@) The top hotel in town is just off the main road in a large complex. Expect discounts up to 40%.

ℹ Getting There & Away

Bus

The following services depart from Píngliáng's main bus station, in the western part of town on Lai Yuan Lu:

Gùyuán ¥24, 1½ hours, frequent

Lánzhōu ¥105, five hours, hourly (6.30am to 5.30pm)

Tiānshuǐ ¥65, seven hours, one daily (9am)

Xī'ān ¥88, six hours, every 40 minutes (6.20am to 6pm)

For Tiānshuǐ there are more frequent departures from the east bus station (qìchē dōngzhàn).

Train

It's better to take a bus to Xī'ān as trains either leave or arrive at very inconvenient hours. There's one sleeper train daily to Lánzhōu (hard/soft sleeper ¥97/151, 11 hours) leaving at 9.18pm.

Bus 1 (¥2) runs from the train station to Xi Dajie. A taxi costs ¥10. From Xi Dajie to the bus station costs ¥4 or take bus 16 (¥1).

Níngxià

POP 6.4 MILLION

Includes »

Yínchuān 842
Zhōngwèi 847
Gùyuán 850

Best Historic Sites

» Western Xia Tombs (p845)
» Hèlán Shān rock carvings (p846)
» Xūmí Shān (p850)
» Shuǐ Dòng Gōu (p846)

Best Temples

» Qīngzhēn Dà Sì (p849)
» Gāo Temple (p847)
» Guǎngzōng Sì (p847)
» Yánfú Sì (p846)

Why Go?

With its raw landscape of dusty plains and stark mountains, sliced in two by the Yellow River (Huáng Hé), there is a distinct *Grapes of Wrath* feel to Níngxià (宁夏). Outside the cities, it's a timeless landscape where farmers till the yellow earth just like their ancestors did.

Yet Níngxià was once the frontline between the empires of the Mongols and the Han Chinese and there is a host of historic sites here, ranging from little-seen Buddhist statues to the royal tombs of long-past dynasties, as well as ancient rock carvings that predate any emperor. And as the homeland of the Muslim Hui ethnic minority, Níngxià is culturally unique, too.

Then there's the chance to camp out under the desert sky, or float down the Yellow River on a traditional raft. Best of all, Níngxià sees few foreign visitors so it seems like you have the place all to yourself.

When to Go
Yínchuān

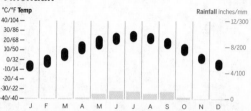

Aug Annual wolf berry festival in Zhōngníng County (east of Zhōngwèi).

Oct It's cooling down and time to play Lawrence of Arabia in the little-visited Tengger Desert.

Nov The Yellow River festival in Yínchuān features concerts and folk dancing.

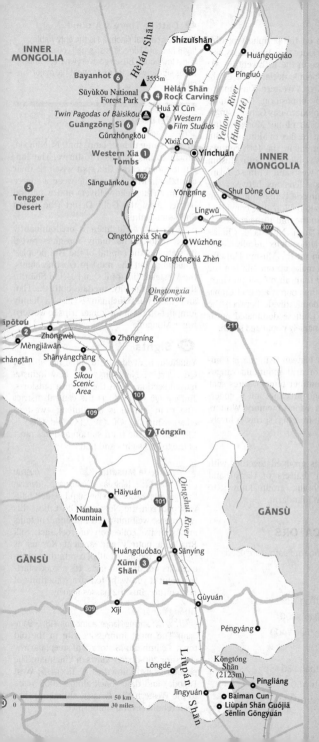

Níngxià Highlights

1 Visit the imperial **Western Xia Tombs** (p845) outside Yínchuān, a rare reminder of this long-extinct culture

2 Raft down the Yellow River or slide down the sand dunes at desert playground **Shāpōtóu** (p848)

3 Explore the little-seen Buddhist grottoes with hundreds of statues at **Xūmí Shān** (p850)

4 Check out the utterly unique rock carvings at **Hèlán Shān** (p850), which date back thousands of years

5 Hop on a camel and trek into the **Tengger Desert** (p849) for an overnight stay

6 Investigate Mongol culture at lonely sites around **Bayanhot** (p846), **Guǎngzōng Sì** (p847) and **Yánfú Sì** (p846)

7 Get way off the beaten track at Tóngxīn's marvellous Ming-era **Great Mosque** (p849)

History

Níngxià had been on the periphery of Chinese empires ever since the Qin dynasty, but it took centre stage in the 10th century AD when the Tangut people declared the establishment of the Xixia (Western Xia) empire in the face of Song opposition. The empire was composed of modern-day Gānsù, Níngxià, Shaanxi and western Inner Mongolia, but it soon collapsed in the face of Mongol might.

The Mongol retreat in the 14th century left a void that was filled by both Muslim traders from the west and Chinese farmers from the east. Tensions between the two resulted in Níngxià being caught up in the great Muslim Rebellion that convulsed northwest China in the mid-19th century.

Once part of Gānsù, Níngxià is China's smallest province, although technically it is an autonomous region for the Muslim Hui ethnic minority, who make up one-third of the population, rather than an official province. It remains one of the poorest areas of China, with a sharp economic divide between the more fertile, Han Chinese–dominated north and the parched, sparsely populated south.

Climate

Part of the Loess Plateau, Níngxià is composed primarily of arid mountain ranges and highlands. Summer temperatures soar during the day, and precipitation is generally no more than a fond memory. Winters are long and often freezing; spring is lovely, though blustery.

Language

Níngxià's dialect is grouped together with the northwestern dialects of Gānsù and Qīnghǎi, an umbrella group known to linguists as Lanyin Mandarin.

PRICE INDICATORS

The following price indicators are used in this chapter:

Sleeping

$	less than ¥250
$$	¥250 to ¥400
$$$	more than ¥400

Eating

$	less than ¥30
$$	¥30 to ¥50
$$$	more than ¥50

ℹ Getting There & Around

Níngxià's capital Yínchuān is the only viable flight hub, but Níngxià is so small you can cross it in a few hours. Buses go everywhere, sometimes slowly, while trains connect the major cities.

Yínchuān 银川

☑ 0951 / POP 510.379

In the sun-parched land that is Níngxià, Yínchuān has managed to thrive. The Tangut founders chose this spot wisely as their capital, planting the city between a source of water (the Yellow River) and a natural barrier from the Gobi Desert (the Hèlán Shān mountains).

Modern-day Yínchuān is predominantly Han, although its many mosques reveal its status as the capital of the Hui peoples' homeland. But the most interesting sights, the Western Xia Tombs and Hèlán Shān to the west of the city, predate both the Han and the Hui. Yínchuān is also a handy jumping-off point for longer trips to western Inner Mongolia.

◉ Sights

Yínchuān is divided into three parts. Xīxià Qū (西夏区; New City), the new industrialised section, is on the western outskirts. Jīnfèng Qū (金凤区) is the central district (the train station is on Jīnfèng's western edge). Xìngqìng Qū (兴庆区; Old City) is 12km east of the train station and has most of the town's sights and hotels.

FREE Níngxià Museum MUSEUM
(宁夏博物馆; Níngxià Bówùguǎn; Renmin Guangchang; ◉9am-5pm Tue-Sun) Located halfway between the New and Old Cities, this cavernous, well-mounted museum contains an extensive collection of rock art, Silk Road–era pottery and ancient Korans as well as the requisite hall of communist propaganda and Mao fun facts. It's a good starting point if you want to learn something of Hui culture. Bus 102 passes nearby.

Chéngtiānsì Tǎ PAGODA
(承天寺塔; Jinning Nanjie; admission ¥18; ◉9am-5pm) The most impressive site in the old town – climb the 13 storeys of steep, narrow stairs for 360-degree views of Yínchuān. The pagoda is also known as Xī Tǎ (西塔; West Pagoda) and dates back almost 1000 years to the Western Xia dynasty, although it has been rebuilt several times since.

Hǎibǎo Tǎ
PAGODA

(海宝塔; Minzu Beijie; admission ¥10; ⊗9am-5pm) This fifth-century pagoda is set on the grounds of a well-maintained monastery. Also known as Běi Tǎ (北塔; North Pagoda), the nine-storey pagoda was toppled by an earthquake in 1739 and rebuilt in 1771 in the original style. Visitors are no longer able to climb it. Take minibus 20 north on Jinning Beijie for five stops to the Běitǎ Lùkǒu (北塔路口) and then walk north for 15 minutes.

🛏 Sleeping

There's no shortage of places to stay in the Old City, but the accommodation is a mostly uninspired mix of chain hotels and over-priced, old-school two- and three-star joints. Nor are there any hostels in Yínchuān (or anywhere in Níngxià). But if you're willing to splash out, then the quality of hotels improves dramatically.

Carnation Chain Hotel
HOTEL $

(康乃馨连锁酒店; Kāngnǎixīn Liánsuǒ Jiǔdiàn; ✆602 0788; 16 Yuhuange Nanjie; 玉皇阁南街16号; d¥248-278, discounts of 30%; ❄@) With its cheerful bright yellow walls, welcoming staff and compact and clean modern rooms, this is one of the best deals in the Old City. All rooms come with computers, while the more expensive ones have heart-shaped beds for romantics. Discounts even in high season take the prices below ¥200.

Níngfēng Bīnguǎn
HOTEL $$$

(宁丰宾馆; ✆609 0222; www.ningfenghotel.com; 6 Jiefang Dongjie; 解放东街6号; d¥688, discounts of 20%; ❄@) A solid choice which is as comfortable as many more expensive hotels in

Yínchuān

⊚ Top Sights
Chéngtiānsì Tǎ B2

🛏 Sleeping
1 Carnation Chain Hotel...........................D1
2 Háo Jiā Fàndiàn D2
3 Jīnjiāng Inn..C1
4 Níngfēng Bīnguǎn B1

⊗ Eating
5 Bái Gōng..D2
6 Dà Mǎ Jiǎozi Guǎn C1
7 Hóng Yuán Shuài C1
8 Xiānhè Lóu D2
9 Xiānhè Lóu D2

ⓘ Transport
10 Minibus 20 ....B1

Yínchuān and better located. Rooms are big and well organised, and the bathrooms are nice and up-to-date. There's a Chinese restaurant on site and a few of the helpful staff can speak some English.

Kempinski Hotel
HOTEL $$$

(凯宾斯基饭店; Kǎibīnsījī Fàndiàn; ✆516 5888; www.kempinski.com/yinchuan; 160 Beijing Zhong-lu; 北京中路160号; d¥1786, discounts of 10%; ◉❄@❄❄) Yínchuān's luxury option comes with all the trimmings: huge, comfy beds, posh bathrooms and efficient staff, as well as a swimming pool, spa and a German-themed restaurant that has excellent, if expensive, beer. You should be able to score a bigger discount outside the peak summer season (when it is advisable to book ahead).

Jǐnjiāng Inn HOTEL $$
(锦江之星旅馆; Jǐnjiāng Zhīxīng Lǚguǎn; ☑602 9966; www.jinjianginns.com; 15 Gulou Beijie; 鼓楼北街15号; d ¥269; ❀@☎) Ever-reliable chain hotel that has spotless modern rooms with broadband access (wi-fi in the lobby) and a great location just north of the Drum Tower.

Háo Jiā Fàndiàn HOTEL $$
(豪珈饭店; ☑385 8998; 192 Liqun Dongjie; 利群东街192号; d & tw ¥398, discounts of 50%; ❀@) It's a little gloomy here, but the rooms themselves are reasonably sized and come with OK bathrooms. The generous discounts make it a decent deal.

✕ Eating & Drinking

Like the rest of northwest China, noodles are a staple here. Every restaurant serves them and in many places in Níngxià they will be all you can find to eat.

TOP CHOICE Xiānhè Lóu CHINESE $
(仙鹤楼; 204 Xinhua Dongjie; dishes from ¥10; ☺24hr) You can't go wrong at this landmark restaurant which never closes and caters for both big spenders and those on a budget. You could splash out on the pricey fish dishes or the great *kǎoyángpái* (烤羊排; barbecued ribs), but you can also get a huge plate of beef noodles for just ¥10. Cold dishes are on display, as is the production line of *shuǐjiǎo* (boiled ravioli-style dumplings) which are a house speciality. They are sold by the *jīn* but a half *jīn* (¥18) is normally enough for two people. There's another smaller **branch** which shuts at 10pm around the corner on Zhongshan Nanjie. Picture menu.

Dà Mā Jiǎozi Guǎn DUMPLINGS $
(大妈饺子馆; 32 Jiefang Dongjie; dumplings from ¥15; ☺11am-10.30pm) Popular joint dedicated to Chinese dumplings. They come by the *jīn*, but you can order a half *jīn*, and there are all sorts of beef, lamb and vegie options. There are plenty of cold dishes, soups and meat and fish dishes available, too, as well as the inevitable noodle choices. Picture menu.

Bái Gōng DIM SUM $$
(白宫; 82 Yuhuange Nanjie; dim sum from ¥15; ☺24hr) Waiters here push around carts piled high with all forms of delicious steamed dumplings, as well as more esoteric nibbles like spicy chicken feet. It offers good vari-ety for solo travellers, but you may need to order a few to quench your appetite. You can also choose a wide range of more expensive dishes from the picture menu.

Hóng Yuán Shuài NOODLES $
(红元帅; 75 Jiefang Dongjie; noodles from ¥11; ☺7am-9pm) Succumb to the inevitable and join the hordes of locals slurping tasty big bowls of noodles at this busy place. Point and choose at what others are eating; cold dishes (¥4) are on display for you.

ℹ Information

Bank of China (中国银行; Zhōngguó Yínháng; 170 Jiefang Xijie; ☺8am-noon & 2.30-6pm) You can change travellers cheques and use the ATM at this main branch. Other branches change cash only.

China Comfort International Travel Service (CCT; 康辉旅游; Kāng Huī Lǚyóu; ☑504 5678; www.chinasilkroadtour.com; 317 Jiefang Xijie; ☺8.30am-noon & 2.30-6pm Mon-Fri) Organises desert trips, rafting and permits for Éjìnà Qí.

China Post (中国邮政; Zhōngguó Yóuzhèng; cnr Jiefang Xijie & Minzu Beijie)

Internet cafe (网吧; wǎngbā; Chaoyang Xiang; per hr ¥3; ☺24hr) On the left-hand side of the road as you walk south from Jiefang Dongjie and on the 2nd floor.

Public Security Bureau (PSB; 公安局; Gōng'ānjú; 472 Beijing Donglu; ☺8.30am-noon & 2.30-6.30pm Mon-Fri) For visa extensions. Take bus 3 from the Drum Tower.

ℹ Getting There & Away

Air

Flights connect Yínchuān with Běijīng (¥1090), Chéngdū (¥1110), Guǎngzhōu (¥1320), Shànghǎi (¥900), Ürümqi (¥1080) and Xī'ān (¥360). Buy tickets at www.ctrip.com or www.elong.net.

Bus

The main bus station (南门汽车站; nánmén qìchēzhàn) is 5km south of Nanmen Sq on the road to Zhōngwèi.

Bus departure times from the long-distance bus station:

Bayanhot ¥30, two to three hours, half-hourly (6.30am to 6pm)

Gùyuán (express) ¥90, four to five hours, half-hourly (7.30am to 6pm)

Lánzhōu ¥140, six hours, two daily (7.20am and 3.40pm)

Xī'ān ¥181, eight to 10 hours, five daily (8.30am to 6.30pm)

THE HUI

The Hui (回族) are perhaps China's most unusual ethnic minority; the only people to be designated as one solely because of their religious beliefs. Nor do they have their own language, speaking only Mandarin, while they are scattered throughout every province of the country with nearly 80% of the 10 million–odd Hui living outside their official homeland.

Their origins date back more than 1000 years to the time of the Silk Road, when trade thrived between China and the Middle East and Central Asia. Arab traders intermarried with the local women and now most Hui are ethnically indistinguishable from the Han Chinese. What marks them out is their adherence to Islam.

Most Hui men wear white skullcaps, while many women don headscarves. The more educated can read and speak Arabic, a result of studying the Koran in its original language. For many young Hui, learning Arabic is the path to a coveted job as a translator for the Chinese companies on the east coast doing business in the Middle East.

Although the Hui can be found all over China, they are most numerous in the north-west provinces of Gānsù, Níngxià and Shaanxi. True to their origins as traders and caravanserai operators, many Hui are still engaged in small businesses, especially the running of restaurants.

Yán'ān ¥136, eight to nine hours, five daily (8am to 5.30pm)

Zhōngwèi (express) ¥53, two to three hours, hourly (8am to 5.30pm)

If you're heading north to Inner Mongolia, you need the northern bus station (北门车站; běimén chēzhàn). Bus 316 (¥1) trundles between it and the main bus station.

The express buses (kuàikè) to Zhōngwèi and Gùyuán are far quicker than the much slower local buses that stop at every village along the way.

Train

Yínchuān is on the Lánzhōu–Běijīng railway line, which runs via Hohhot (11 hours) and Dàtóng (13 hours) before reaching Běijīng (19 hours). If you're heading for Lánzhōu (hard/soft sleeper ¥131/195, eight hours), the handy overnight K915 train leaves at 10.40pm. For Xī'ān (14 hours), try train 2653 (hard/soft sleeper ¥195/302) leaving at 5.06pm.

The train station is in Xīxià Qū, about 12km west of the Old City centre. Book sleeper tickets well in advance.

🛈 Getting Around

The airport is 25km from the Old City centre; buses (¥15) leave from in front of the Civil Aviation Administration of China office on Changcheng Donglu, just south of Nanmen Sq. A taxi to/from the airport costs around ¥50.

Between 6am and 11.30pm bus 1 (¥1) runs from the long-distance bus station to Nanmen Sq in the Old City, along Jiefang Jie and then on to the train station in Xīxià Qū. Count on a mini-

mum 40- to 50-minute trip. Taxis cost ¥7 for the first 3km. A taxi between the train station and the Old City costs ¥20 to ¥30.

Around Yínchuān

WESTERN XIA TOMBS   西夏王陵

The **Western Xia Tombs** (Xīxià Wánglíng; admission ¥60; ☺8am-7pm), which look like giant beehives, are Níngxià's most famous sight. The first tombs were built a millennium ago by Li Yuanhao, the founder of the Western Xia dynasty. There are nine imperial tombs, plus 200 lesser tombs, in an area of 50 sq km. The one you'll see is Li Yuanhao's, a 23m-tall tomb originally constructed as an octagonal seven-storey wooden pagoda. All that remains is the large earthen core. Permits, usually organised through local tour operators, are required to visit other tombs in the area.

The examples of Buddhist art in the good site **museum** (☺8am-5.30pm) offer a rare glimpse into the ephemeral Western Xia culture, and point to clear artistic influences from neighbouring Tibet and Central Asia. There are also many fascinating artefacts excavated from Li Yuanhao's tomb.

The tombs are 33km west of Yínchuān. A return taxi costs around ¥150 (including waiting time). You could take bus 2 to its terminus in Xīxià Qū and then take a cheaper taxi (¥25 each way) from there. The site is also on the road towards Bayanhot, if you are headed that way.

HÈLÁN SHĀN 贺兰山

The rugged Hèlán Mountains have long proved an effective barrier against both nomadic invaders and the harsh Gobi winds. They were the preferred burial site for Xixia monarchs, and the foothills are today peppered with graves and honorific temples.

☉ Sights

Rock Carvings ARCHAEOLOGICAL SITE

(贺兰山岩画; Hèlánshān Yánhuà; admission ¥70; ☉8am-6.30pm) By far the most significant sight here are the ancient rock carvings, thought to date back 10,000 years. There are more than 2000 pictographs depicting animals, hunting scenes and faces, including one (so local guides like to claim) of an alien, and they are the last remnants of the early nomadic tribes who lived in the steppes north of China.

The ticket price includes entry to the world's only museum dedicated to ancient rock art and a ride in a golf cart to the valley containing the rock carvings. Don't miss the image of the Rastafarian-like sun god (climb the steps up the hill on the far side of the valley).

Twin Pagodas of Bàisìkǒu PAGODA

(拜寺口双塔; Bàisìkǒu Shuāngtǎ; admission ¥10; ☉8am-6.30pm) About 10km west of the rock carvings are the Twin Pagodas of Bàisìkǒu. You can't climb the pagodas, but they're an impressive sight against the backdrop of the barren mountains: 13 and 14 storeys high and decorated with intricate animal faces and Buddha statuettes.

Sūyùkǒu National Forest Park PARK

(苏峪口国家森林公园; Sūyùkǒu Guójiā Sēnlín Gōngyuán; admission ¥60; ☉7am-5pm) Halfway between the pagodas and the rock carvings is the Sūyùkǒu National Forest Park. It's a good place to start exploring the mountains themselves. You can hike up the trails from the car park or take the cable car (up/down ¥50/30) straight up to cool pine-covered hills.

Western Film Studios FILM LOCATION

(镇北堡西部影城; Zhènběibǎo Xībù Yǐngchéng; admission ¥80; ☉8am-6pm) On the way back to Yínchuān you can stop at the Western Film Studios, where the famed Chinese movie *Red Sorghum* was shot, as well as countless other films and TV shows. Hugely popular with Chinese tour groups, who swarm all over it in the summer, it's fun to explore the fake fortress and recreations of old Ming and Qing streets.

ⓘ Getting There & Away

The only way to get around the Hèlán Shān sites is by taxi. The cheapest way to do it is to take bus 17 from the Yínchuān train station to the Western Film Studios (¥5) and then hire a taxi from there (¥100). Alternatively, you can hire a minibus from the train station for ¥200 return to do the loop of the sights. You could combine that with a visit to the Western Xia Tombs for around ¥300.

SHUĬ DÒNG GŌU 水洞沟

The archaeological site of Shuǐ Dòng Gōu (admission ¥60, ¥130 for through ticket; ☉8am-6pm), 25km east of Yínchuān, right on the border with Inner Mongolia, has been turned into something of an adventure theme park. The site is divided into two parts; the first is a museum that resembles Jabba the Hut's bunker and which contains the Palaeolithic-era relics first uncovered here in 1923.

From there, it's a golf cart ride to an unrestored section of the Great Wall dating back to the Ming dynasty. Then it's a walk, boat trip, donkey- and camel-cart ride to a fortress with an elaborate network of underground tunnels once used by Chinese soldiers defending the Great Wall. The renovated tunnels include trap doors, false passages and booby traps.

The catch is that the admission price to Shuǐ Dòng Gōu only lets you into the site itself. Everything else – the museum, fort and all transport – costs extra, making this an expensive day out. Unless you fancy an 8km walk around the complex, the cheapest way to do it is to buy the through ticket (通票; *tōngpiào*) for ¥130.

Five buses a day run past Shuǐ Dòng Gōu (¥10) from Yínchuān's main bus station, starting at 8.20am. To return, wait by the highway and flag down any passing Yínchuān-bound bus.

BAYANHOT 阿拉善左旗

Bayanhot (known to the Chinese as Ālāshàn Zuǒqí) is not actually in Níngxià; it's across the border in Inner Mongolia. But the most convenient way to access Bayanhot is from Yínchuān, and a visit here is a good introduction to both Mongol culture and the vast deserts and high blue skies of far western Inner Mongolia.

The original Mongol town was centred on the small 18th-century temple Yánfú Sì (延福寺; admission ¥5; ☉8am-noon & 3-6pm). Completed in 1742, it once housed 200 lamas; around 30 are resident here now.

Next door is the local museum **Ālāshàn Bówùguǎn** (阿拉善博物馆; admission ¥40; ⊙9am-5.30pm), the former home of the local prince, the Alashan Qin Wang. A well-restored, Qing-era complex of buildings and courtyards, there are photos of the last prince (1903–68) and his family, plus some of their personal effects.

Bayanhot means 'Rich City' in Mongolian and there's a thriving jade trade here. Numerous shops deal in it and there's a small market in front of the museum. Bargain hard if you're in a buying mood.

Frequent buses depart from Yínchuān's main bus station for Bayanhot (¥30, two to three hours) between 6.30am and 6pm. If you want to travel further west into Inner Mongolia from Bayanhot there are two buses a day to Éjìnà Qí (¥104, eight hours) at 8am and 8.20am. One daily bus goes to Ālāshàn Yòuqí (¥121, six hours) at 7.10am. Note: you need a permit to travel to Éjìnà Qí, which can be arranged by travel agents in Yínchuān.

AROUND BAYANHOT

Once one of the most magnificent monasteries in Inner Mongolia, **Guǎngzōng Sì** (广宗寺; admission ¥80; ⊙8am-6pm) has a stunning setting in the mountains 38km south of Bayanhot. At its height, some 2000 monks lived here. So important was the monastery that the main prayer hall, Gandan Danjaling Sum, contains the remains of the sixth Dalai Lama inside the golden stupa that dominates it.

Tragically, the monastery was demolished during the Cultural Revolution; a 1957 photo in the main prayer hall gives you an idea of how big it once was. The temples have since been rebuilt, but in the last couple of years a hotel, yurt restaurants and a supremely tacky shopping street have been added to the complex to entice domestic tour groups here.

There are good walking trails in the mountains behind the complex; take the path to the right of the main temple and follow it for one hour to a grassy plateau with fantastic views.

From Bayanhot, a taxi to the monastery and then back to the highway (where you can flag down any Yínchuān-bound bus) is ¥120. On your way back to Yínchuān, look out for the crumbling, yet still mighty, remains of the Great Wall at **Sānguānkǒu** (三关口). Some sections are up to 10m high and 3m wide.

Zhōngwèi 中卫

☎0955 / POP 1 MILLION

With its wide streets and relaxed feel, Zhōngwèi easily wins the prize for Níngxià's best-looking and friendliest city. It's an ideal base for a trip up the Yellow River or further afield into the Tengger Desert (Ténggélǐ Shāmò).

◉ Sights

Gāo Temple   TEMPLE
(高庙; Gāo Miào; Gulou Beijie; admission ¥30; ⊙7.30am-7pm) One of the more extraordinary temples you'll find in China, this eclectic shrine has at various times catered to the needs of Buddhism, Confucianism and Taoism. It's still a funky mishmash of architectural styles, but the revitalised Buddhist deities have muscled out the original Taoists and Confucians.

The real oddity here is the former **bomb shelter**, built beneath the temple during the Cultural Revolution, which has been converted into a Buddhist hell-haunted house. The eerie, dimly lit tunnels contain numerous scenes of the damned having their tongues cut out, being sawn in half or stoked in the fires of hell, while their screams echo all around. Great stuff.

⌁ Sleeping

A number of hotels in Zhōngwèi won't accept foreigners.

Zhōngwèi Dàjiǔdiàn   HOTEL $$
(中卫大酒店; ☎702 5555; 66 Gulou Beijie; 鼓楼北街66号; d & tw ¥368; ☀@) Big, surprisingly comfortable rooms with decent-sized beds and modern showers are on offer here. Outside peak season, discounts are normally available.

Zhōnghuī Shāngwù Bīnguǎn   HOTEL $
(中辉商务宾馆; ☎701 0808; 61 Changcheng Dongjie; 长城东街61号; d & tw ¥98-148; ☀@) The rooms have seen some wear and tear and could be cleaner, but the price is great, the staff amenable and the location very convenient. The more expensive rooms come with computers; the cheaper ones lack air-con.

Fēngmào Yuán Jiǔdiàn   HOTEL $$
(丰茂源酒店; ☎709 1555; 65 Changcheng Dongjie; 长城东街65号; tw ¥298, discounts of 25%; ☀@) A standard two-star joint but one with reasonably sized, clean rooms.

Zhōngwèi

Zhōngwèi

◎ Sights
1 Gāo Temple A1

🛏 Sleeping
2 Fēngmào Yuán Jiǔdiàn B1
3 Zhōnghuī Shāngwù Bīnguǎn B1
4 Zhōngwèi Dàjiǔdiàn B1

✗ Eating
5 Hóng Yùn Lái Hàn Cāntīng A1
6 Night Market A2

✗ Eating & Drinking

On summer nights, with the lit-up Drum Tower acting as a beacon, the locals eat and drink alfresco at numerous locations around the centre of town.

Night Market   MARKET $
(夜市; Yèshì; off Xinglong Beijie; dishes ¥7-20) A Dante's Inferno of flaming woks and grills, the night market is made up of countless stalls in the alleys running left off Xinglong Beijie (which is lined with Chinese-style bars). There are tonnes of cheap eats. Two favourites to check out are *ròujiāmó* (肉夹馍; fried pork or beef stuffed in bread, sometimes with green peppers and cumin) and *shāguō* (砂锅; mini hotpot).

Hóng Yùn Lái Hàn Cāntīng   CHINESE $
(鸿运来汉餐厅; 52 Changcheng Xijie; dishes from ¥14; ⊙9am-9.30pm) Solid restaurant serving up northern Chinese classics, as well as claypot dishes and the inevitable noodle options. Small picture menu.

ℹ Information

Bank of China (中国银行; Zhōngguó Yínháng; cnr Gulou Beijie & Gulou Dongjie; ⊙9am-5pm) One of many around town.

China Post (中国邮政; Zhōngguó Yóuzhèng; Gulou Xijie)

Internet cafe (网吧; wǎngbā; 121 Changcheng Dongjie; per hr ¥2.50; ⊙9am-1am) About 200m east of the Fēngmào Yuán Jiǔdiàn (p847).

Níngxià Desert Travel Service (宁夏沙漠旅行社; Níngxià Shāmò Lǚxíngshè; ☎702 7776, 186 0955 9777; www.nxdesert.com) Pricey but professional outfit for camel and rafting trips (see p849). Contact the English-speaking manager Billy.

Public Security Bureau (PSB; 公安局; Gōng'ānjú; ☎706 0597; Silou Dong Nanjie; ⊙8.30am-noon & 2.30-5pm) About 4km south of the Drum Tower.

ℹ Getting There & Away

Bus

The long-distance bus station (长途汽车站; chángtú qìchēzhàn) is 2.5km east of the Drum Tower, on the southern side of Gulou Dongjie. Take bus 1 or a taxi (¥4). Frequent buses to Yínchuān (¥53, three hours) leave every half-hour from 6.30am to 6pm. There are five buses a day to Tóngxīn starting from 9am (¥26, 2½ hours) and two express buses daily to Gùyuán (¥70, four hours, 10am and 2.30pm).

Buses to Xī'ān (¥180, eight hours, 6pm) run every other day from in front of the train station. There's also a daily night bus to Lánzhōu (¥80, four hours), which departs from the Drum Tower at 10pm.

Train

You can reach Yínchuān in 2½ hours (¥25). It's five hours to Lánzhōu (hard seat/hard sleeper ¥47/101) and 12 hours to Xī'ān (hard/soft sleeper ¥170/254). For Gùyuán (¥33, 3½ hours) take the Xī'ān train.

Around Zhōngwèi

SHĀPŌTÓU   沙坡头
The desert playground of **Shāpōtóu** (admission ¥90; ⊙7.30am-6.30pm), 17km west of Zhōngwèi, lies on the fringes of the Tengger Desert at the dramatic convergence of sand dunes, the Yellow River and lush farmlands. It's based around the Shāpōtóu Desert Research Centre, which was founded in 1956 to battle the ever-worsening problem of desertification in China's northwest.

These days, though, Shāpōtóu is almost an amusement park. You can zipline (¥80) or hang-glide (¥100) on a wire across the Yellow River or go sand-sledding (¥30) or bungee jumping (¥160).

It's also a good place to raft the churning Yellow River. The traditional mode of transport on the river for centuries was the *yángpí fázi* (leather raft), made from sheep or cattle skins soaked in oil and brine and then inflated. At Shāpōtóu you can roar upstream on a speedboat and return on a traditional raft. Prices range from ¥80 to ¥240, depending on how far you go. You can also combine the boat/raft ride with a camel ride (¥110).

Shāpō Shānzhuāng (沙坡山庄; ☎0955-768 9073; r ¥268; ☯Apr-Oct) is a basic but comfortable hotel near the dunes. Meals are available.

Buses (¥4) run between Zhōngwèi and Shāpōtóu from 7.30am to 6.30pm. You can pick them up on Changcheng Xijie about 200m past the Gāo Temple on the opposite side of the road. Taxis cost ¥30/50 one way/return.

TENGGER DESERT 腾格里沙漠

If you fancy playing Lawrence of Arabia, make a trip out to the Tengger Desert, a mystical landscape of shifting sand dunes and the occasional herd of two-humped camels. Shāpōtóu lies on the southern fringe, but it's definitely worth heading deeper into the desert to avoid the crowds. The sun is fierce out here, so you'll need a hat, sunglasses and plenty of water. Nights are cool, so bring a warm layer.

Níngxià Desert Travel Service in Zhōngwèi (see p848) offers overnight camel treks through the desert, with a visit to the Great Wall by car, for ¥500 per person per day for a group of four. The price includes transport, food and guide. Ask your guide to bring along a sand sled for a sunset surfing session. Drinking beers around the campfire under a starry sky tops off the experience. The desert trek can be combined with a rafting trip down the Yellow River.

WORTH A TRIP

TÓNGXĪN 同心

South of Zhōngwèi, the Han Chinese–dominated cities of northern Níngxià give way to the Hui heartland. Journeying here takes you deep into rural Níngxià, through villages of mud-brick houses where the minarets of the numerous mosques tower over the endless cornfields.

Of all the mosques in Níngxià, the most hallowed is Tóngxīn's **Qīngzhēn Dà Sì** (清真 大寺; Great Mosque; admission free). Dating back to the 14th century, although the present mosque was built in 1573 and then renovated in 1791, it was the only one of Níngxià's 1000-odd mosques to avoid the ravages of the Cultural Revolution. As such, it's a near-perfect example of Ming-era and Qing-era temple architecture. Not until you get up close and notice the crescents that top the pagoda roofs does it become apparent that it's a mosque. Enclosed by high brick walls, stone stairs lead up to a courtyard complex where the prayer hall is flanked by intricate wooden carvings.

That the mosque survived the wrath of the Red Guards is solely because of Tóngxīn's impeccable revolutionary history. Mao Zedong himself visited Qīngzhēn Dà Sì when he passed through in June 1936 on the Long March. Tóngxīn was also the site of one of the last battles between the Red Army and the Nationalist forces in September 1949. Just south of the mosque is a museum commemorating these events, although it was closed at the time of writing.

Unsurprisingly, Tóngxīn has a very strong Muslim feel. There are always students in residence at the mosque training to be imams and they will greet you with a *salaam alaikum* and show you around. Tóngxīn is also one of the few places in China outside of southern Xīnjiāng where you'll see women in veils and covered from head to toe in black.

Qīngzhēn Dà Sì is on the south side of town, a ¥5 taxi ride from the bus station on Jingping Jie. There are frequent express buses between Tóngxīn and Yínchuān (¥52, three hours), making a long day trip possible. The last bus back to Yínchuān leaves at 4pm. You could also visit from Zhōngwèi (¥26, 2½ hours), or stop for a couple of hours if you are heading further south to Gùyuán (¥26, two hours). If you get stuck here, try the **Huí Chūn Bīnguǎn** (回春宾馆; ☎0953-803 1888; d ¥138; ✸) opposite the bus station.

Gùyuán & Around 固原

☎0954

An expanding but still small and very new city, Gùyuán makes a convenient base for exploring little-visited southern Níngxià. Few foreigners make it down here, so expect some attention from the overwhelmingly Hui locals. Make sure to bring cash, too; precious few ATMs in this part of the world accept foreign cards.

◉ Sights & Activities

Xūmí Shān   CAVE

(须弥山; admission ¥50; ⊙8am-6.30pm) These Buddhist grottoes (Xūmí is the Chinese transliteration of the Sanskrit *sumeru*, or Buddhist paradise) some 50km northwest of Gùyuán are southern Níngxià's must-see sight.

Cut into the five adjacent sandstone hills are 132 caves housing more than 300 Buddhist statues dating back 1400 years, from the Northern Wei to the Sui and Tang dynasties. Cave 5 contains the largest statue, a colossal Maitreya (future Buddha), standing 20.6m high. Further uphill, the finest statues are protected by the Yuánguāng Temples (caves 45 and 46; sixth century) and Xiàngguó (cave 51; seventh century), where you can walk around the interior and examine the artwork up close – amazingly, the paint on several of the statues is still visible in places.

To reach the caves, take a bus from Gùyuán to Sānyíng (三营; ¥7, one hour). They depart from Wenhua Xilu, by the two big hospitals opposite the night market. From Sānyíng you'll have to hire a taxi for the 40km return trip (¥100 including waiting time) to Xūmí Shān.

Liùpán Shān Guójiā Sēnlín Gōngyuán   PARK

(六盘山国家森林公园; Liùpán Mountain National Forest Park; admission ¥65; ⊙7am-5pm) Those on the trail of Genghis Khan will want to visit southern Níngxià's other highlight Liùpán Shān, where some believe the great man died in 1227. Legend has it that he fell ill and came here to ingest medicinal plants native to the area, but perished on its slopes (it's much more likely he died elsewhere).

The mountain is now a protected area. A walking trail leads 3km up a side valley to a waterfall. About 5km further up the main valley is a clearing with some stone troughs and tables that locals say was used by the Mongols during their stay.

To get here, take a bus from Gùyuán's main bus station to Jīngyuán (泾源; ¥16, one hour) and then hire a taxi for the final 18km to the reserve (¥80 return). A return taxi from Gùyuán will cost ¥200.

Gùyuán Museum   MUSEUM

(固原博物馆; Gùyuán Bówùguǎn; Xicheng Jie; ⊙9am-4.30pm Tue-Sun) For such an out-of-the-way place, Gùyuán's museum is rather good, with Neolithic-era artefacts, Tangut ceramics and some fine figurines from the Northern Wei dynasty. Decent English captions, too.

🛏 Sleeping & Eating

Délóng Business Hotel   HOTEL $$

(德龙商务酒店; Délóng Shāngwù Jiǔdiàn; ☎286 3918; Wenhua Xilu; 文化西路; tw ¥260, discounts of 40%; ✳@) Friendly, helpful staff and good-sized rooms with modern bathrooms make this the pick of the hotels along Wenhua Xilu.

Liùpánshān Bīnguǎn   HOTEL $

(六盘山宾馆; ☎202 1666; 77 Zhongshan Nanjie; 中山南街77号; d & tw ¥196, discounts of 30%; ✳@) The rooms at this long-standing hotel look their age these days, but they are quiet and it still makes a decent base. Foreigners will be directed to the rear annexe, where there's also a restaurant.

Night Market   MARKET $

This alley of food stalls (小吃城; Xiǎochī Chéng) runs till very late and specialises in delicious mini hotpot (砂锅), as well as *shāokǎo* (barbecue) and noodles. Dishes start at ¥11 and are on display, so you can pick and choose. It's down a covered arcade off Wenhua Xilu and directly opposite two big hospitals.

❶ Getting There & Away

Gùyuán is on the Zhōngwèi–Bǎojī railway line, with trains to Xī'ān (hard/soft sleeper ¥118/175, eight hours), Yínchuān (hard seat/sleeper ¥54/108, six hours) and Lánzhōu (hard sleeper ¥92, 9½ hours), but sleeper tickets are near impossible to get and the majority of trains depart in the middle of the night. To get to the train station you'll need to take bus 1 or a taxi (¥5).

Buses from the long-distance bus station:

Lánzhōu ¥95, nine hours, one daily (8am)

Tiānshuǐ ¥65, seven hours, one daily (6.30am)

Tóngxīn ¥26, 2½ hours, hourly (9.45am to 4.40pm)

Xī'ān ¥101, seven hours, hourly (7am to 1.30pm)

Yínchuān ¥90, four hours, every half-hour (7am to 6.10pm)

Zhōngwèi ¥70, two daily (10.10am and 3pm)

Inner Mongolia

POP 24.9 MILLION

Includes »

Hohhot..........................853
Shàngdū (Xanadu)........857
Bāotóu.........................858
Genghis Khan
Mausoleum..................859
Cave Temple.................859
Hǎilā'ěr.........................860
Mǎnzhōulǐ....................863

Best Natural Wonders

» Hūlúnbèi'ěr Grasslands (p860)

» Badain Jaran Desert (p860)

» Ā'ěrshān National Forest Park (p863)

» Hūlún Hú (p863)

Best Temples

» Cave Temple (p859)

» Wǔdāng Lamasery (p859)

» Wǔtǎ Pagoda (p853)

» Ganjur Monastery (p863)

Why Go?

Mongolia. The word alone stirs up visions of nomadic herders, thundering horses and, of course, the warrior-emperor Genghis Khan. The Mongols conquered half the known world in the 13th century and while their empire is long gone, visitors are still drawn to this magical land wrapped up in both myth and legend.

Travellers heading north of the Great Wall half expect to see the Mongol hordes galloping along. The reality is quite different as 21st-century Inner Mongolia (内蒙古; Nèi Měnggǔ) is a wholly different place from Mongolia itself. The more-visited south of the province is industrialised and very much within the realm of China's modern economic miracle. The Mongolia of your dreams exists off the tourist route, amid the shimmering sand dunes of the Badain Jaran Desert or the vast grasslands in the north. Some effort is required to reach these areas but the spectacular scenery makes it worthwhile.

When to Go
Hohhot

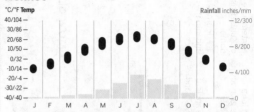

| Jul Hohhot and other regions host the annual Naadam festival. | Aug & Sep The best time to see the grasslands and ride Mongolia's famed horses. | Oct The poplar trees change colours at Éjìnà Qí. |

Inner Mongolia Highlights

1 Saddle up and go for a horse ride around the glorious grasslands near **Hǎilā'ěr** (p860)

2 Wander amid the ancient walls of **Shàngdū** (p857) and

contemplate the lost greatness of Kublai Khan's pleasure dome

3 Journey across the desert and into the mountains to

explore the legendary **Cave Temple** (p859)

4 Mount a camel and set off across the dunes of the **Badain Jaran Desert** (p860)

5 Mingle with the Chinese-speaking ethnic Russians at the unique village of **Shi Wěi** (p862) near the Russian border

6 Listen to the groaning chants of Mongolian monks at the colourful monasteries of **Dà Zhāo** (p854) and **Xilitú Zhāo** (p854) in Hohhot

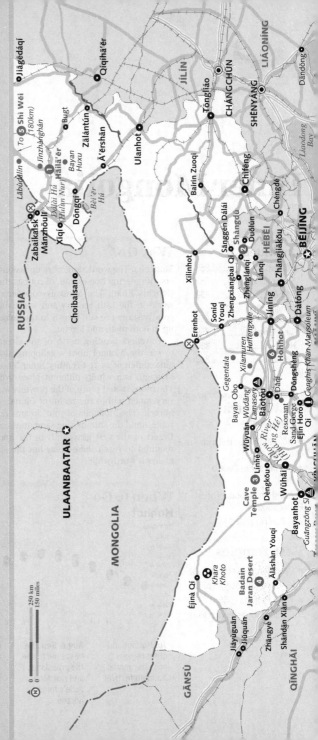

History

The nomadic tribes of the northern steppes have always been at odds with the agrarian Han Chinese, so much so that the Great Wall was built to keep them out. But it acted more like a speed bump than an actual barrier to the Mongol hordes.

Genghis Khan and grandson Kublai rumbled through in the 13th century, and after conquering southern China in 1279 Kublai Khan became the first emperor of the Yuan dynasty. But by the end of the 14th century the Mongol empire had collapsed, and the Mongols again became a collection of disorganised roaming tribes. It was not until the 18th century that the Qing emperors finally gained full control of the region.

A divide-and-conquer policy by the Qing led to the creation of an 'Inner' and 'Outer' Mongolia. The Qing opened up Inner Mongolia to Han farmers, and waves of migrants came to cultivate the land. Outer Mongolia was spared this policy and, with backing from the USSR, it gained full independence in 1921.

Now, Mongolians make up only 15% of Inner Mongolia's population. Most of the other 85% are Han Chinese, with a smattering of Hui, Manchu, Daur and Ewenki.

Inner Mongolia's economy has boomed in recent years thanks to extensive mining of both coal and rare earth minerals. That growth has come at great environmental cost. The mines have swallowed up pastureland at alarming rates and desertification is the root cause of the dust storms that envelop Běijīng each spring. Only the far north of the region has escaped heavy industrialisation and the economy here is largely based on cattle ranching and tourism.

Climate

Siberian blizzards and cold air currents rake the Mongolian plains from November to March. June to August brings pleasant temperatures, but the west is scorching hot during the day.

The best time to visit is between July and September, particularly to see the grasslands, which are green only in summer. Make sure you bring warm, windproof clothing, as even in midsummer it's often windy, and evening temperatures can dip to 10°C or below.

Language

The Mongolian language is part of the Altaic linguistic family, which includes the Central Asian Turkic languages and the now defunct

PRICE INDICATORS

The following price indicators are used in this chapter:

Sleeping

$	less than ¥250
$$	¥250 to ¥400
$$$	more than ¥400

Eating

$	less than ¥30
$$	¥30 to ¥50
$$$	more than ¥50

Manchurian. Although the vertical Mongolian script (written left to right) adorns street signs, almost everyone speaks standard Mandarin.

ℹ Getting There & Away

Inner Mongolia borders Mongolia and Russia. There are border crossings at Erenhot (Mongolia) and Mǎnzhōulǐ (Russia), which are stopovers on the Trans-Mongolian and Trans-Manchurian Railways, respectively. To Mongolia, you can also catch a local train to Erenhot, cross the border and take another local train to Ulaanbaatar (with the appropriate visa). Possible air connections include Hohhot to Ulaanbaatar or Hǎilā'ěr to Choibalsan (eastern Mongolia).

Hohhot 呼和浩特

☏ 0471 / POP 817,529

Founded by Altan Khan in the 16th century, the capital of Inner Mongolia is an increasingly prosperous city. Hohhot (known in Mandarin as Hūhéhàotè) means 'Blue City' in Mongolian, a reference to the arching blue skies over the grasslands. Streets are attractively tree-lined (although the roads are traffic-snarled) and there are a handful of interesting temples and pagodas in the town – enough to keep you busy for a day or two before heading to the hinterlands.

⊙ Sights

Wǔtǎ Pagoda   PAGODA

(五塔寺; Wǔtǎ Sì; Wutasi Houjie; admission ¥35; ⊙8am-6pm) This striking, Indian-influenced, five-tiered pagoda was completed in 1732. Its main claim to fame is the Mongolian star chart around the back, though the engraving

Hohhot

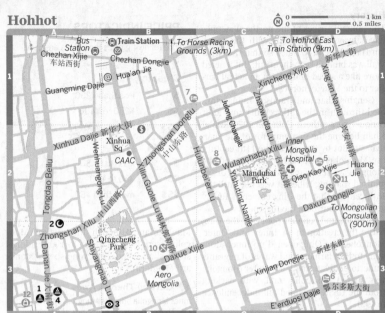

of the Diamond Sutra (in Sanskrit, Tibetan and Mongolian), extending around the entire base of the structure, is in much better condition. Bus 1 runs by the pagoda.

Dà Zhào
MONASTERY

(大召; Danan Jie; admission ¥35; ⊙8am-7pm) Dà Zhào is a large, well-maintained lamasery (monastery for lamas) that is still used as a temple. In the sacred main prayer hall you may come upon groups of Mongol monks chanting and praying (usually at 9am).

Xílìtú Zhào
MONASTERY

(席力图召; Danan Jie; admission ¥30; ⊙7.30am-6.30pm) Across the main boulevard is this simpler, more peaceful monastery, the purported stomping ground of Hohhot's 11th Living Buddha (he actually works elsewhere). Monks chant at 9am and 3pm.

FREE Inner Mongolia Museum
MUSEUM

(内蒙古博物院; Nèi Měnggǔ Bówùyuàn; Xinhua Dongdajie; ⊙9am-5.30pm Tue-Sun) This massive museum has a distinctive sloping roof supposed to resemble the vast steppes of Mongolia. It's one of the better provincial museums, with everything from dinosaurs and Genghis Khan to space-age rockets. Take bus 3 from Xinhua Dajie or pay ¥14 for a cab.

Great Mosque
MOSQUE

(清真大寺; Qīngzhēn Dàsì; 28 Tongdao Beilu) North of the old town is the Great Mosque. Built in the Chinese style, it dates from the Qing dynasty and was being brushed-up at the time of writing. You can look around as long as you don't enter the prayer hall.

Guānyīn Sì
TEMPLE

(观音寺) Close to Dà Zhào and at the end of a restored Qing-era shopping street, is the enormous new temple complex Guānyīn Sì with an oversized stupa (佛塔), which the locals circumambulate.

✦ Festivals & Events

Naadam
TRADITIONAL, SPORTS

The week-long summer festival known as Naadam features traditional Mongolian sports such as archery, wrestling and horse racing. It takes place at Gegentala in July and is very popular with domestic tour groups.

⌇ Sleeping

TOP CHOICE Āndá Guesthouse
GUESTHOUSE $

(安达旅馆; Āndá Lǚguǎn; ☏691 8039, 159 475 19807; andaguesthouse@hotmail.com; Qiao Kao Xijie; 桥靠西街; dm/d ¥60/180; @ ☎) Now the go-to place for backpackers in Hohhot, thanks

Hohhot

⊙ Sights
1 Dà Zhào A3
2 Great Mosque A3
3 Wǔtǎ Pagoda B3
4 Xílìtú Zhào A3

🛌 Sleeping
5 Āndá Guesthouse D2
6 Bīnyuè International Hostel D3
7 Jǐnjiāng Inn B1
8 Nèi Měnggǔ Fàndiàn C2

🍴 Eating
9 Wūzhūmùqìn Nǎichágǔan Sì
   Fēndiàn D2
10 Xiǎoféiyáng Huǒguōchéng B3
11 Xīnjiāng Hóngliǔ Zhuāngyuán D2

🛍 Shopping
12 Souvenir Shops A3

to its friendly, English-speaking, mostly Mongolian staff and cosy atmosphere; the Anda has compact dorms and decent-sized, bright doubles. The dorm bathrooms especially could be cleaner, but there's a small lounge, kitchen facilities and a cute courtyard. The staff are eager to show off Mongolian culture and can organise trips to the grasslands, as well as to the Kubuqi Desert and the Great Wall. Finding the place can be difficult; call ahead and get a pick-up from the train station. If you want to search for it, start by taking bus 2, 37 or 61 to the Inner Mongolia Hospital (内蒙古医院大楼A座; Nèi Měnggǔ Yīyuàn Dàlóu A zuò), then walk west for six minutes on Qiao Kao Xijie. It's down an unmarked alley almost opposite the northern end of Huang Jie. Look for the blue sign.

Bīnyuè International Hostel HOSTEL $
(宾悦国际青年旅舍; Bīnyuè Guójì Qīngnián Lǚshè; ☑660 5588; fax 431 0808; 52 Zhaowuda Lu; 昭乌达路52号; dm ¥60, d & tw ¥180-200; ❄@) More like an old-fashioned hotel than a true hostel, Bīnyuè caters overwhelmingly to domestic travellers. The doubles and twins here are actually comfortable and good value. Some of the dorms too come with their own bathrooms and broadband connections, although the beds are hard. From the train station, take bus 34 southeast to Normal University (师范大学; Shīfàn Dàxué). The hostel is behind the big hotel of the same name.

Nèi Měnggǔ Fàndiàn HOTEL $$$
(内蒙古饭店; Inner Mongolia Hotel; ☑693 8888; www.nmghotel.com; Wulanchabu Xilu; 乌兰察布西路; d ¥660-1480; ❄@🌐❄) Despite competition from upmarket Western chains, this 14-storey high-rise is still the nicest hotel you'll find in Hohhot, featuring fine, recently updated rooms with big, comfy beds, a pool and health centre. You can dine Mongolian-style in concrete yurts out back. Some staff speak English. Prices drop outside the peak summer season.

Jǐnjiāng Inn HOTEL $
(锦江之星旅馆; Jǐnjiāng Zhīxīng Lǚguǎn; ☑666 8111; www.jinjianginns.com; 61 Xinhua Dajie; 新华大街61号; d ¥249; ❄@) Big branch of the ultra-efficient chain hotel that has spotless, if somewhat bland, rooms that come with free broadband access.

🍴 Eating

Mongolia's notable culinary contribution is *huǒguō* (火锅; hotpot), a refined version, so the story goes, of the stew originally cooked in soldiers' helmets. *Yángròu* (羊肉; mutton), *miàn* (面; noodles), *dòufu* (豆腐; tofu), *mógu* (蘑菇; mushrooms) and other vegies are added to the bubbling cauldron.

For an excellent selection of Mongolian and Chinese restaurants, head down to Huang Jie (黄街; Yellow Street), which is lined with about 40 small eateries. There are a few Mongolian music bars nearby; ask at Āndá Guesthouse (p854) for the latest hot spot.

TOP CHOICE Wūzhūmùqìn
Nǎichágǔan Sì Fēndian MONGOLIAN $
(乌珠穆沁奶茶馆四分店; Wūzhūmùqìn Tea Restaurant Fourth Branch; Huang Jie; meals from ¥25; ⊙7am-midnight) This small restaurant serves Mongol 'soul food', including juicy *jiǎozi* (蒙古饺子; dumplings), *makhtai shul* (肉汤; meat soup) and *suutai tsai* (奶茶; salty milk tea), along with hunks of lamb on the bone and beef (served by the *jīn*). Look for the large yellow and blue sign above the door.

Xiǎoféiyáng
Huǒguōchéng MONGOLIAN HOTPOT $$$
(小肥羊火锅城; Little Fat Sheep Hotpot City; Xilin Guole Lu; for 2 people from ¥60; ⊙11am-1.30am; 📶) Giant branch of the popular and reliable Inner Mongolian chain serving Mongolia's most famous culinary export. Decent cuts of lamb and beef, a wide choice of fresh vegies and mushrooms and a fun atmosphere.

BORDER CROSSING: GETTING TO MONGOLIA

Two direct trains run between Hohhot and Ulaanbaatar (hard/soft sleeper ¥970/1480), the Mongolian capital, on Monday and Friday at 10.05pm. The same train stops in Erenhot (二连浩特; Èrliánhàotè; hard seat/hard sleeper ¥36/82, eight hours), at the Mongolian border. Erenhot is listed on Chinese train timetables as Èrlián (二连).

There are also five daily buses to Erenhot (¥89, six hours), leaving between 8am and 1.30pm. From here you can catch a jeep across the border (about ¥50) and continue to Ulaanbaatar on the daily 5.50pm local train.

Aero Mongolia (空蒙古; Kōng Měnggǔ; ☎138 4818 7711; www.aeromongolia.mn; 36 Daxue Xijie) flies from Hohhot to Mongolia on Monday, Wednesday and Friday for ¥1445. The schedule changes in winter. The office is in the Xuéfǔ Kāngdū building, tower A, Room 806 (学府康都A座806号).

If you need a visa, head for the **Mongolian consulate** (蒙古领事馆; Měnggǔ Lǐngshìguǎn; 5 Dongying Nanjie; 东影南街5马; ⊙8.30am-12.30pm Mon, Tue & Thu). Most travellers can get a 30-day visa, although some are only given 21 days. The visa costs ¥260 and takes four days to process. A rush visa (¥495) can be obtained the following day. US citizens do not need a visa to visit Mongolia. To find the consulate, travel east on Daxue Dongjie, turn left on Dongying Nanjie and look for the consulate 200m on the left.

Note that there is also a consulate in **Erenhot** (Měnggǔ Lǐngshì; ⊙8.30am-4.30pm Mon-Fri). To find the consulate from the bus station, walk half a block east to the T-junction and head left. Walk north along this road (Youyi Beilu) for 10 minutes until you see the red, blue and yellow Mongolian flags on your left. A 30-day rush tourist visa (¥495) can be obtained the next day.

Xīnjiāng Hóngliǔ Zhuāngyuán
CHINESE XĪNJIĀNG $$

(新疆红柳庄园; Huang Jie; meals from ¥35; ⊙11.30am-2am) With an outdoor area that's busy until the wee hours and smoke billowing off the giant grill, this place specialises in Uighur cuisine from the far western province of Xīnjiāng. The chunky and succulent lamb kebabs (¥7) – nothing like the scrawny, fatty ones sold by street vendors – are especially good. Dishes are pricier than in other Uighur eateries, but the food is authentic and tasty. Picture menu.

🔒 Shopping

Souvenir Shops
SOUVENIRS

(表记店铺; Biǎojì Diànpù) To the west of Dà Zhào monastery, this Qing-era street is packed with souvenir stalls selling fake Mongolian tat, jade, Buddhist and Mao memorabilia. South of Dà Zhào is a kitschy open-air shopping plaza done up as a *hútòng* (narrow alley), which was being expanded at the time of writing and attracts hordes of tour groups.

ℹ Information

Bank of China (中国银行; Zhōngguó Yínháng; Xinhua Dajie) Has a 24-hour ATM available.

China Post (中国邮政; Zhōngguó Yóuzhèng; Chezhan Dongjie) To the left as you exit the train station.

Internet cafe (网吧; wǎngbā; Xilin Guole Lu; per hr ¥4; ⊙24hr) Large internet cafe about 200m south of the train station.

Public Security Bureau (PSB; 公安局; Gōng'ānjú; Chilechuan Dajie; ⊙8.30am-noon & 2.30-5pm Mon-Fri) For visa extensions and other enquiries, the foreign-affairs bureau is to the left of the main building, outside the gated compound.

ℹ Getting There & Away

Air

Daily flight destinations (routes are reduced in winter) include Běijīng (¥500), Xī'ān (¥830), Hǎilā'ěr (¥1000), Mǎnzhōulǐ (¥860), Chìfēng (¥780), Xilinhot (¥400) and Shànghǎi (¥1350). Book flights on www.elong.net or www.ctrip.com.

Bus

Hohhot's main bus station (长途汽车站; chángtú qìchēzhàn) is next door to the train station.

Bāotóu ¥40, two hours, every 30 minutes (6.40am to 7.30pm)

Běijīng ¥150, six to eight hours, 15 daily (7.25am to 9pm)

Dàtóng ¥80, four hours, hourly (6.30am to 7.20pm)

Dōngshèng ¥63, three hours, every 30 minutes (6.30am to 7.20pm)

Train

From Hohhot, express trains go to the following:

Bāotóu ¥25, two hours, 16 daily

Běijīng hard/soft sleeper ¥170/254, 10 hours, 13 daily

Dàtóng hard seat/hard sleeper ¥39/93, four hours, 10 daily

Xilinhot hard/soft sleeper ¥170/254, 11 hours, one daily

Yínchuān hard/soft sleeper ¥175/264, 10 hours, six daily

Sleeper tickets are hard to come by in July and August; hotel travel desks can book them for a ¥30 commission.

❶ Getting Around

Useful bus routes include bus 1, which runs from the train station to the old part of the city, via Zhongshan Xilu; bus 33, which runs east on Xinhua Dajie from the train station; and bus 5, which plies the length of Xilin Guole Lu. Tickets for local buses are ¥1.

Hohhot's airport is 15km east of the city. The airport bus (¥10) leaves from **Civil Aviation Administration of China** (CAAC; 中国民航; Zhōngguó Mínháng; ☎696 4103; Xilin Guole Lu). A taxi will cost about ¥35 on the meter (flag fall ¥6).

Around Hohhot

In the middle of the fields, 7km east of the airport (about 22km from Hohhot), is **Bái Tǎ** (白塔; White Pagoda; admission ¥35), a striking seven-storey octagonal tower built during the Liao dynasty. A steep, double-barrelled stair-

case leads to a small shrine room at the top. Few travellers come here so you will feel like you have the place to yourself. A taxi from Hohhot will cost around ¥60 to ¥70 return.

About 110km north of Hohhot is the grassland area of **Xilamuren** (Xīlāmùrén), with dozens of yurt camps that cater mainly to the Chinese market. Nearby mining operations have accelerated infrastructure development, so don't come this way if you are looking for a true wilderness experience. Xilamuren is worth considering if you want to try your luck on a Mongolian horse, but if you are hoping for a taste of traditional Mongolian life you'll need to look elsewhere.

If you want to avoid the tourist camps at Xilamuren, **Āndá Guesthouse** (p854) in Hohhot can set you up at the home of a local family; day trips start from ¥290 (including one meal) or ¥390 for an overnight trip (including three meals). Horse riding is an extra ¥90 per hour.

There are more yurt camps at **Gegentala** (Gěgěntǎlā) and **Huitengxile** (Huīténgxīlè). Both are two to 2½ hours from Hohhot, but are even less authentic than Xilamuren and very crowded with domestic tour groups.

Shàngdū (Xanadu) 上都

Explorer Marco Polo made it his final stop and poet Samuel Taylor Coleridge immortalised it in Western minds as the ultimate pleasure palace. Today Xanadu, or **Shàngdū** (元上都遗址; Yuán Shàngdū Yízhǐ; admission ¥30;

ZHAMSU: A GRASSLANDS LIFE

Mongolian Zhamsu, now 50, has spent his entire life living in the grasslands of Xilamuren (p857).

What was your life like growing up? My parents were nomad herders. We lived in a *ger* (yurt). We had more than 300 sheep, 10 cows and 10 horses. I started to help herding when I was seven. Life was hard, but it was less complicated.

How different are the grasslands now? There are more people and fewer animals. The government has banned herding in our area until 2016 to protect the grasslands. So now I live in a house and our *ger* is for tourists to stay in. I still have 20 sheep, but only for the guests to eat, and a few horses for people to ride.

Is Mongolian culture still strong in Inner Mongolia? Not really. Fewer children speak Mongolian now and many young people move to the cities. They speak Mandarin and accept Chinese culture because they think that will lead to a better life. It's only in the grasslands that you can experience traditional Mongolian culture.

Will you ever move to the city? No, I can't imagine how I'd survive. I feel comfortable on the grasslands. I've lived with animals every day for the last 50 years. How could I live without them?

8am-6pm), is little more than a vast prairie with vague remnants of once mighty walls, but it is still a legendary destination thanks to its glory days as one of the most storied cities on earth.

Conceived by Kublai Khan, grandson of Genghis and the first Yuan emperor, as his summer capital, Shàngdū's lifespan was relatively brief. Construction of the city started in 1252 and lasted four years, but it was overrun and destroyed by Ming forces in 1369.

Listed as a World Heritage Site by Unesco in June 2012, Shàngdū actually consisted of three distinct cities: an outer city, imperial city and the palace city. All that is visible now are the outer and inner walls. From the ticket yurt, it's about 1.5km to the outer walls (a golf buggy will take you for ¥10). From there, you can walk another 500m to the inner ramparts. Paths through the wildflower-covered grassland that has swallowed up the city offer the chance for pleasant strolls and reflective musings on the vagaries of history.

Although Shàngdū signifies distant wonders in the Western imagination, in truth it's not that isolated (275km northwest of Běijīng). But it does feel remote, partly because of the huge empty prairie it sits in, and also because getting here requires some effort.

From Hohhot, a number of daily trains make the eight-hour run to Sānggēn Dálái (桑根达来). The best option is the K2052 (hard seat/hard sleeper ¥73/137), which leaves from Hohhot's posh east train station at 11.15am. Shared taxis (¥40 per person) will be waiting to carry you a further 80km south to the small city of Lánqí (蓝旗). From Lánqí it's about a 20km taxi ride (¥150 return) down a mostly abysmal road to Shàngdū. Heading to Hohhot, take the K1814 train at 10.20am from Sānggēn Dálái.

Lánqí's **Xanadu Museum** (上都博物馆; Shàngdū Bówùguǎn; admission ¥20; ⊙8am-5pm Tue-Sun) is worth visiting for the scale models that give a good impression of the sheer ambition of Shàngdū, as well as for relics from the site, including ceramics and statues.

Shàngdū's newfound status as a World Heritage site means Lánqí's hotels are hideously overpriced (but expect big discounts outside the peak summer season). The **Jiādì Shāngwù Bīnguǎn** (佳帝商务宾馆; Shangdu Dajie; 上都大街; tw ¥200) is the most acceptable of the cheaper options. On Shangdu Dajie, you'll also find restaurants and a branch of the ICBC bank with an ATM that takes foreign cards.

Bāotóu 包头

TRANSPORT HUB

Unlovely but booming Bāotóu sprawls across more than 20km of dusty landscape, much of it industrialised and polluted. However, if you're heading to the Wǔdāng Lamasery and Genghis Khan's Mausoleum, or further west to the Cave Temple, you'll likely have to pass through and maybe stop a night.

Bāotóu is divided into eastern and western sections. The eastern district (Dōnghé) is the place to stay; if you're arriving by train make sure to get off at the East Bāotóu train station (Bāotóu dōngzhàn) and not the west station.

🛏 Sleeping & Eating

Head to Nanmenwai Dajie for a selection of hotels, restaurants, banks and internet cafes within walking distance of the East Bāotóu train station and a short hop in a cab (¥6) from the east bus station, around which you can find cheap rooms for around ¥100.

Xīhú Fàndiàn HOTEL $$
(West Lake Hotel; ☑414 4444; 10 Nanmenwai Dajie; 南门外大街10号; d ¥288; ❄@) A five-minute walk from the train station, this friendly place has plenty of clean, comfortable rooms with modern bathrooms. They're nearly always far cheaper than the advertised price, offering discounts of 30% to 40%. There's an internet cafe directly opposite.

ⓘ Getting There & Away

Air
Flights connect Bāotóu with Běijīng (¥590). Buy tickets at www.elong.net.

The airport is 2km south of the East Bāotóu train station. A taxi there is ¥15, but ¥30 if you're coming from it.

Bus
Bus 17 (¥1) runs from East Bāotóu bus station (东和汽车站; dōnghé qìchēzhàn) to Nanmenwai Dajie.

Dōngshèng ¥34, two hours, every 30 minutes (6.30am to 6.30pm)

Hohhot ¥40, three hours, every 30 minutes (6.30am to 7.30pm)

Yán'ān (Shaanxi) ¥174, eight hours, one daily (11.50am)

Yúlín (Shaanxi) ¥92, five hours, eight daily (6.30am to 4.30pm)

Train
Frequent trains between Hohhot and Bāotóu (¥25, two hours) stop at both the east and west stations.

Běijīng hard/soft sleeper ¥175/264, 10 to 13 hours, 11 daily

Lánzhōu hard/soft sleeper ¥231/352, 16 hours, three daily

Tàiyuán hard/soft sleeper ¥175/264, 10 hours, three daily

Yínchuān hard/soft sleeper ¥137/205, seven hours, six daily

Wǔdāng Lamasery 五当召

Lying on the pilgrim route from Tibet to Outer Mongolia, this handsome, Tibetan-style **monastery** (Wǔdāng Zhào; admission ¥60; ⊙8am-6.30pm) saw considerable foot traffic from the time of its establishment in 1749. At its height it was the largest monastery in Inner Mongolia, housing 1200 monks belonging to the Gelugpa sect of Tibetan Buddhism. Around 50 monks are resident here these days, but the monastery's numerous outlying buildings, now occupied by local villagers, are a reminder of how important Wǔdāng once was. At the time of writing, the immediate area around the monastery was being spruced up, an indication that the domestic tour group hordes are preparing to descend.

The monastery is 67km northeast of Bāotóu. To get here, take bus 7 (¥10, one hour) from the bus parking lot in front of East Bāotóu's train station to Shíguǎi (石拐), 40km from Bāotóu. From Shíguǎi hire a taxi to the monastery (¥80 return). The last bus back to Bāotóu from Shíguǎi leaves around 6pm.

Genghis Khan Mausoleum 成吉思汗陵园

Located 130km south of Bāotóu in the middle of absolutely nowhere is the **Genghis Khan Mausoleum** (Chéngjí Sīhán Língyuán; admission ¥110; ⊙7am-7.30pm), China's tribute to the great Mongol warlord.

The first thing to know about this place is that old Genghis was not buried here. Instead, the mausoleum's existence is justified by an old Mongol tradition of worshipping Genghis Khan's personal effects, including his saddle, bow and other items. Kublai Khan established the cult and handed over care for the objects to the Darhats, a Mongol clan. Darhat elders kept the relics inside eight white tents, which could be moved in times of warfare.

In the early 1950s, the government decided to build a permanent site for the relics and constructed this impressive triple-

GENGHIS' GRAVE

The great Genghis left stern instructions that his burial place be kept secret. Legend has it that the slaves who built his tomb were massacred afterwards by soldiers, who were then subsequently killed themselves to prevent anyone knowing the location of his grave. Archaeologists hunting for Genghis' final resting place have been further hampered by a reputed curse that has supposedly struck some down. Most historians assume that after his death (and no one knows where that occurred) in 1227, Genghis' body was taken back to Mongolia and buried near his birthplace in Khentii Aimag close to the Onon River.

domed building. By then, most of the relics had been lost or stolen (everything you'll see here is a replica). But even today, some of the guards at the site still claim descent from the Darhat clan.

The mausoleum, which the locals refer to as Chénglíng (成陵), is 25km south of Ejin Horo Qi (伊金霍洛旗; Yījīn Huòluò Qí), which is abbreviated to just 'Yi Qi'. From there, you catch a bus (¥12, 30 minutes) that will let you off at a small tourist village with a handful of shops and hotels. You'll then have to catch a taxi (¥15) the final 5km to the mausoleum.

From Bāotóu there are two buses a day (¥42, 6.10am and 8.30am) to Ejin Horo Qi. Otherwise, there are buses every half hour from 6.30am to 6.30pm to Dōngshèng (also known by its Mongolian name Ordos), from where frequent buses (¥12, one hour) connect with Ejin Horo Qi. Coming from Hohhot, there are buses to Dōngshèng every 40 minutes or so from 6.30am to 7.20pm (¥63, four hours).

To return, take a cab back to the main highway and flag down any Dōngshèng-bound bus. Buses should pass by regularly till about 5pm.

Cave Temple 阿桂庙

The remote, little-visited **Cave Temple** (Āguì Miào; admission free; ⊙7am-6pm) is one of the oldest monasteries in Inner Mongolia. The journey here takes you out into the wild, through isolated farm country that

WORTH A TRIP

INNER MONGOLIA'S FAR WEST

The golden deserts, shimmering lakes and ruined cities of western Inner Mongolia are fantastic places for adventures far from the beaten track. Visiting them, though, requires some logistical help.

One destination is **Khara Khoto** (Black City; in Chinese Hēichéng; 黑城; admission ¥10; ⏱8am-7pm), a ruined Tangut city built in 1032 and captured by Genghis Khan in 1226 (his last great battle). Khara Khoto continued to thrive under Mongol occupation, but in 1372 an upstart Ming battalion starved the city of its water source, killing everyone inside. Six hundred years of dust storms nearly buried the city, until the Russian explorer PK Kozlov excavated and mapped the site, and recovered hundreds of Tangut-era texts (kept at the Institute of Oriental Manuscripts in St Petersburg). Located about 25km southeast of Éjìnà Qí (额济纳旗), the allure here is the remoteness of the site and surrounding natural beauty. A great time to visit is late September to early October when the poplar trees are changing colours; but be warned that every hotel room in Éjìnà Qí will be booked out at this time.

The second tourist drawcard in these parts is the remote but stunning **Badain Jaran Desert** (巴丹吉林沙漠; Bādānjílín Shāmò), a mysterious landscape of desert lakes, Buddhist temples and towering dunes. The dunes here are the tallest in the world, some topping 380m (incredibly, the same height as the Empire State Building). The closest town in the region, Ālāshàn Yòuqí (阿拉善右旗), is a 30-minute drive from the dunes. **Badanjilin Travel Service** (☎0483-602 1618, 0483-602 6555; www.badanjilin.cn), in the town, organises camel treks (from ¥80 to ¥120 per hour) and jeep tours for ¥1000 per day with English-speaking guides. They can also organise a car to Khara Khoto for ¥1600 return. Chéngdū-based **Navo Tours** (☎028-8611 7722; www.navo-tour.com) runs five-day tours here (three days of which is in the desert) starting from Lánzhōu with English-speaking guides for ¥9800 per person.

This part of Inner Mongolia is highly militarised (China's space city is nearby) and travel permits are required for the road between Jiǔquán and Éjìnà Qí, as well as Khara Khoto itself and the Badain Jaran Desert. Travel agents need at least three days to organise the necessary permits.

The closest rail links are Jiǔquán and Zhāngyè in Gānsù province. However, public transport between Gānsù and Inner Mongolia is limited. A daily bus travels between Ālāshàn Yòuqí and Shāndān Xiàn (山丹县), but the best connections start with other Inner Mongolian towns such as Bayanhot. There are daily buses from Bayanhot to both Éjìnà Qí and Ālāshàn Yòuqí.

gives way to semi-desert where camel herds roam, before you head the final 6km up a rough road in the Yinshan Mountains.

Taking its name from two caves that you can climb up to, construction of the monastery began in the mid-17th century and was expanded in 1831 by the famed Outer Mongolian monks, Danzan Ravjaa. The temples were destroyed during the Cultural Revolution but have since been rebuilt. At the time of writing, more renovations were taking place.

Look out for the most holy relic, a statue of Padmasambhava in the main hall, said to be fashioned by Padmasambhava himself. About 20 monks live here and one will probably guide you around the cave temples (and may offer you a bowl of mutton soup if you arrive in time for lunch).

The monastery is 90km from the city of Dèngkǒu (磴口) and the only way to get here is by taxi (¥250 including waiting time), which takes around 1½ hours.

The easiest way to reach Dèngkǒu is to take a bus (¥75, four hours) from Bāotóu to the small city of Línhé (临河). From there, very frequent buses run from 6.30am to Dèngkǒu (¥17, one hour). Back in Línhé, there are hourly buses to Yínchuān in nearby Níngxià from 7am to 3.10pm (¥90, four hours).

Hǎilā'ěr　　海拉尔
☑0470 / POP 240,369

Hǎilā'ěr is the largest city in northern Inner Mongolia and a busy, ordinary place. But surrounding it are the Hūlúnbèi'ěr Grasslands, a vast expanse of prairie that begins just outside the city and rolls northwards towards the Russian and Mongolian borders, seemingly forever. Superbly lush in July and August, the grasslands are a fantastic sight and *the* place in Inner Mongolia to saddle up a horse.

In the immediate area around Hǎilā'ěr are several tourist yurt camps where you can eat, listen to traditional music and sometimes stay the night. Although they're not places where Mongolians actually live, you can still learn a bit about Mongolian culture, and the wide-open grasslands are a splendid setting. For a more authentic (and far more rustic) experience, you need to travel further away, although staying with local families in the grasslands is not easy to organise unless you speak a bit of Mandarin (or Mongolian).

Hǎilā'ěr's main square is on Zhongyang Dajie, near Xingan Lu. Hotels and services are conveniently located near the main square. Buxing Jie, a pedestrian street just off Zhongyang Dajie, contains a few souvenir shops run by Mongolians. Meeting the owners is a good way to tap into the Mongolian community. Just past Buxing Jie is a mostly deserted, sad re-creation of a Qing-dynasty *hútòng*, completed in 2010.

Sights

FREE Ewenki Museum   MUSEUM

(鄂温克博物馆; Èwēnkè Bówùguǎn; ⊙8.30am-noon & 2.30-5.30pm) Roughly 20,000 Ewenki people live in northern Inner Mongolia, most in the Hūlúnbèi'ěr Grasslands surrounding Hǎilā'ěr. You can glimpse some of their history and culture at this well-mounted modern museum. The Ewenki have traditionally been herders, hunters and farmers; they are one of the few peoples in China to raise reindeer.

The museum is on the southeastern edge of town. Bus 3 (¥1) runs here from the main square; a taxi will cost ¥35 to ¥40 return. The museum is on the road to the Bayan Huxu Grasslands, so you could stop here on your way out of town.

Underground Fortress   FORTRESS

(海拉尔要塞遗址; Hǎilā'ěr Yàosài Yízhǐ; admission ¥60; ⊙8.30am-6pm) In the mid-1930s, during the Japanese occupation of Manchuria, this network of tunnels was constructed by the Japanese army in the grasslands north of Hǎilā'ěr. The site now contains a museum, a monument, and old tanks and artillery guns to climb on. Inside the freezing, spooky tunnels you can peek into 'rooms' where soldiers bunked and a hospital was located.

The site is 4km northwest of the train station and you'll need an hour to see everything. A taxi between the tunnels and the town centre costs about ¥20. If you want the taxi to wait, then a round trip will be around ¥100. Bus 2 runs close to the fortress from the centre of town, but you'll still have to walk uphill for a mile to reach it. Alternatively, the tunnels are on the road to Jīnzhànghán, so you might negotiate a stop here en route.

Festivals & Events

Naadam   TRADITIONAL, SPORTS

The Hǎilā'ěr Naadam (sports festival) is held annually in July on the grasslands just north of town. You'll see plenty of wrestling, horse racing and archery. The city is flooded with tour groups at this time, making it difficult to find a room, and hotel prices double (or more).

Sleeping & Eating

Hǎilā'ěr has a mostly undistinguished, over-priced selection of hotels. For real cheapies, with cell-like, windowless rooms for ¥60 to ¥80, try the alley directly opposite the entrance to the long-distance bus station on the other side of the road.

On summer nights, Buxing Jie and the surrounding alleys become a hub of outdoor *shāokǎo* (barbecue) places that are good for a beer and meeting the locals.

Tiānxìn Room Two   HOTEL $

(天信客房二部; Tiānxìn Kèfáng Èrbù; ☑835 3675; 7 Tianxin Xiaoqu; 天信小区7号; d ¥220; ✳ @) This annexe to the more expensive Tiānxìn Business Hotel (天信商务酒店; Tiānxìn Shāngwù Jiǔdiàn) has clean, decent-sized rooms with modern bathrooms, even if the staff can be grumpy and the place itself is tatty. The location is good and central: down a small lane 100m south of the main roundabout, just off Buxing Jie. Tell taxi drivers to take you to the Tiānxìn Business Hotel and it's 50m south of there.

Bèi'ěr Dàjiǔdiàn   HOTEL $$

(贝尔大酒店; Bèi'ěr Hotel; ☑835 8455; 36 Zhongyang Dajie; 中央大街36号; d ¥300-480; ✳ @) With a large, bright lobby, welcoming staff and well-maintained rooms, this is the number-one midrange choice in town. It's advisable to book ahead here, especially in July and August.

Jīnchuān Dòuhuāzhuāng HOTPOT $$$
(金川豆花庄; ☎834 6555; Xi Dajie; 2 people from ¥75; ☺10am-11pm) Big and bustling hotpot favourite with the locals; you can choose from a wide selection of meat, seafood and veggie options, as well as opting to make your broth less or more spicy. No English or picture menu, but the friendly waitresses will help you out. It's on the corner of Xi Dajie and Bei Xiejie, close to Zhongyang Dajie.

Moongun Choloo MONGOLIAN $
(Tianxin Xiaoqu; dumplings from ¥20; ☺7am-9pm) Down an alley off Buxing Jie (and around the corner from Tiānxìn Room Two), this authentic Mongolian cafe serves fresh yoghurt, *buuz* (dumplings) and *airag* (fermented mare's milk). It's a good place to meet Buriat Mongols.

❶ Information

Bank of China (中国银行; Zhōngguó Yínháng; cnr Xingan Donglu & Zhongyang Dajie) Next door to Bèi'ěr Dàjiǔdiàn in the centre of town.

China Post (中国邮政; Zhōngguó Yóuzhèng; cnr Zhongyang Dajie & Yueju Xilu) Post and telephone office.

Internet cafe (网吧; wǎngbā; lower level, cnr Zhongyang Dajie & Xingan Xilu; per hr ¥3) Diagonally opposite the Bèi'ěr Dàjiǔdiàn.

Public Security Bureau (PSB; 公安局; Gōng'ānjú; Alihe Lu) Opposite CITS in Hédōng district on the east side of the river.

❶ Getting There & Away

Hǎilā'ěr's small airport has direct daily flights to Běijīng (¥1150, two hours) and Hohhot (¥1000, 2¼ hours). Go to www.elong.net or www.ctrip.com to book flights.

EZ Nis (☎130 3041 2081; www.eznisairways.com), a Mongolian airline, flies to Mongolia two or three times per week, stopping in Choibalsan (¥680) and Ulaanbaatar (¥1458). If you plan to fly to Ulaanbaatar you can just buy the ticket online. If you want to stop in Choibalsan you need to get special permission from Mongolian immigration. EZ Nis can organise this in two days (email its office in Ulaanbaatar).

From the **long-distance bus station** (长途汽车站; chángtú qìchēzhàn; Jiaxinzi Lu, off Chezhan Jie), there are regular buses to Mǎnzhōulǐ (¥41, three hours) between 7.30am and 6pm.

Several daily trains go to Mǎnzhōulǐ (¥29, two to three hours). There are daily trains between Hǎilā'ěr and Hā'ěrbīn (hard/soft sleeper ¥125/192, 11 hours), Qíqíhā'ěr (¥137/205, eight hours) and Běijīng (¥418/642, 29 hours).

The train station is in the northwestern part of town. A taxi to the city-centre hotels is ¥12.

❶ Getting Around

There is no airport bus, but you can take a taxi to the airport for around ¥30. At the airport, though, taxi sharks wait for new arrivals and ask ¥60 to get into town.

Bus 7 runs from the train station past the bus station to Bèi'ěr Dàjiǔdiàn. Bus 1 runs from Hédōng to the train station. Taxi fares start at ¥6.

Around Hǎilā'ěr

JĪNZHÀNGHÀN GRASSLANDS 金帐汗草原

Set along a winding river about 40km north of Hǎilā'ěr, this grasslands camp (Jīnzhànghàn Cǎoyuán; ☎133 2700 0919; ☺Jun-early Oct) has a spectacular setting, even if it is designed for tourists. You can occupy an hour or so looking around and sipping milk tea, spend the day horse riding (per hour ¥200) or hiking, or come for an evening of dinner, singing and dancing.

If you want to stay the night, you can sleep in one of the yurts (per person ¥100). There's no indoor plumbing but there is a toilet hut. To get here, you'll have to hire a taxi from Hǎilā'ěr (about ¥300 return).

About 2km before the main camp there are a couple of unsigned family-run camps. Prices for food, accommodation and horse rental are about half what you pay at Jīnzhànghàn, but they are rather less organised.

SHÌ WĚI 室韦

A small Russian-style village of log cabins located right on the Éérgùnà River, which marks the border with Russia, Shì Wěi is deep within the glorious grasslands. North of Hǎilā'ěr, there are few permanent settlements, just the yurts of herders with their flocks of sheep and cows and strings of Mongolian ponies. Closer to the border, the rolling prairie becomes more wooded, as spindly white pine trees appear.

Shì Wěi itself has been discovered by the domestic tourist hordes and is no longer the backwater it once was, although very few foreigners make it up here. But it's still fun to ride a horse along the riverbank (and at ¥40 per half hour, it's as good a deal for a horse ride as you'll get in Inner Mongolia these days), while gazing at the Russian village on the opposite bank.

Even more fascinating are the locals. Decades of intermarriage between the Russians and Chinese mean most are a unique blend of the two nationalities; some could easily pass for Russians.

Many families have turned their homes into guesthouses and/or restaurants. While some will charge ¥200 or more, you can still get a room in a private house for around ¥50 to ¥100. Try Natascha (☎130 8851 4335) who has clean rooms for ¥50 in a separate annexe behind her house on the main drag. She and her husband will show you the family photos, which reveal how the local Russians and Chinese have intermingled over the generations.

To reach Shì Wěi from Hǎilā'ěr, first travel to Lābùdálín (拉布达林; ¥36, two hours); buses leave every 30 minutes from 6.30am to 5.30pm. From Lābùdálín (sometimes called Éěrgùnà) there are two buses per day heading to Shì Wěi (¥35, three hours), departing at 9.30am and 3.30pm. Buses return to Lābùdálín at 8.30am and 9am. A taxi from Lābùdálín and back is ¥300.

SOUTH OF HǍILĀ'ĚR

The road south from Hǎilā'ěr leads 170km southwest to Dōngqí (东旗), known as Zuun Khoshuu in Mongolian. While in town you may spot dusty traders from Mongolia (the town is just 25km north of the border). Dōngqí is listed on maps as Xīnbā'ěr Hǔ Zuǒqí (新巴尔虎左旗).

About 18km northwest of Dōngqí is the renovated **Ganjur Monastery** (甘珠尔). Founded in 1771, the monastery was the largest in Hulunbuir Banner (*banner* is a Qing-era administrative term; similar to a county). Today it is home to 13 monks and situated in very scenic surrounds. A basic **yurt camp** (蒙古包宿营; ménggǔbāo sùyíng; per night ¥100) is located near the gate of the monastery.

Heading west from the monastery, the road leads through vast grasslands (with the occasional yurt-dwelling herder family) for about 105km to Xīqí (西旗), which Mongols refer to as Baruun Khoshuu. The small city is inhabited largely by Barga people (a Mongolian clan). From here it's 23km on a rough track to the shores of Dálài Hú (Dálài Lake), where you'll find more yurt camps at a beach called **Huángjīn Hǎi'àn** (黄金海岸). Foreigners need a permit for Xīqí. Note that on maps, Xīqí is listed as Xīnbā'ěr Hǔ Yòuqí (新巴尔虎右旗).

Buses run every 50 minutes from 7am to 5.30pm between Hǎilā'ěr and Dōngqí (¥30, three hours). Travel between Dōngqí and Xīqí is best done in a taxi so you can stop at the lake, monastery and yurts en route. It is around ¥100 between the towns, plus another ¥100 for a trip to the lake.

A YURT BY ANY OTHER NAME…

'Yurt', the common name for traditional Mongolian tents, is a Turkish word. The Mongolian word is *ger,* and the Chinese call them '*Měnggǔ bāo*' – literally 'Mongolian buns' – perhaps because the white structures with their conical tops resemble puffy steamed breads.

Alternatively, if you are heading east, the back roads lead from Dōngqí to Ā'ěrshān. A bus (¥43, three hours) leaves at 8.10am, or you could take a direct bus from Hǎilā'ěr (¥81, five hours) at 6.30am or 8.40am. There is good hiking in the hills around Ā'ěrshān (阿尔山). From the town you could hire a taxi (¥400 return) to take you into the beautiful **Ā'ěrshān National Forest Park** (阿尔山国家森林公园; Ā'ěrshān Guójiā Sēlín Gōngyuán; admission ¥180 May-Oct, ¥150 Nov-Apr). Ā'ěrshān is about 190km southeast of Dōngqí and 370km from Hǎilā'ěr. It is connected by train to Ulanhot (Wūlánhàotè).

Mǎnzhōulǐ   满洲里

☎0470 / POP 57,316

This laissez-faire border city, where the Trans-Siberian Railway crosses from China to Russia, is a pastel-painted boomtown of shops, hotels and restaurants catering to the Russian market. Unless you look Asian, expect shopkeepers to greet you in Russian. Mǎnzhōulǐ is modernising at lightning speed, but a few Russian-style log houses still line Yidao Jie.

Mǎnzhōulǐ is small enough to get around on foot. From the train station to the town centre, it's a 10-minute walk. Turn right immediately as you exit the station, then right again to cross the footbridge. You'll come off the bridge near the corner of Yidao Jie and Zhongsu Lu.

⊙ Sights

Besides the Russian traders, Mǎnzhōulǐ's main attraction is **Hūlún Hú** (呼伦湖; admission ¥30), one of the largest lakes in China. Called Dalai Nuur (Ocean Lake) in Mongolian, it unexpectedly pops out of the grasslands like an enormous inland sea. You can hire a horse (¥100 per 30 minutes) or a quad bike (¥100 per 20 minutes), take a boat ride

BORDER CROSSING: GETTING TO RUSSIA

Buses to Zabaikalsk (¥72), over the Russian border, depart eight times daily between 7.40am and 1.30pm, but they tend to be much slower than the private cars (because the Chinese traders on your bus will take ages to get through customs). In Mănzhōulǐ you could ask around for a ride from a Russian trader (Russians get through faster). Otherwise, take a taxi to the border (¥40), 9km from town, and get a ride across from there with a Russian driver.

(¥10 per 20 minutes) or simply stroll along the rocky lakeshore. The only way to get to Hūlún Hú, 39km southeast of Mănzhōulǐ, is to hire a taxi (about ¥200 return).

Halfway between the city and the Russian border is a bizarre **park** filled with giant Russian *matryoshka* dolls, many with portraits of famous historical figures, from Albert Einstein to Michael Jordan. The largest doll is a Russian-style restaurant. Next to the park is a **museum** of Russian art.

🛏 Sleeping

There are a huge number of hotels and guesthouses in Mănzhōulǐ, all within walking distance of each other. Signs are in Russian – гостиница (pronounced 'gastinitsa') is the Russian word for 'hotel'. Likewise, there are plenty of restaurants (ресторан in Russian), so just wander around a bit and see what takes your fancy.

TOP CHOICE Fēngzéyuán Lǚdiàn   GUESTHOUSE $
(丰泽源旅店; ☎225 4099, 139 4709 3443; Yidao Jie; 一道街; tw ¥200; @🛜) Located inside a restored Russian log cabin (painted yellow and green), this friendly (and cheap for Mănzhōulǐ) guesthouse has large, clean rooms. Coming off the pedestrian bridge from the train station it's the first building in front of you, next to the statue of Zhou Enlai. Don't confuse this with the nearby Jīxiáng Lǚguǎn, which looks very similar but is closer to the road and more expensive.

Shangri-La   HOTEL $$$
(香格里拉大酒店; Xiānggélǐlā; ☎396 8888; 99 Liudao Jie; 六道街99号; d ¥1388, ste ¥4588; ❄✳@🛜🏊) Nothing indicates Mănzhōulǐ's soaring status more than this new outpost

of the Shangri-La chain; it's surely the most remote of its hotels in China, if not all Asia. Geared towards visitors from across the border and local business types – the restaurants are Chinese and Russian – the efficient, smiling staff will drum up someone who can speak English. The very comfortable rooms offer views over the surrounding grasslands, and there's a swimming pool and spa too.

Chénglín Bīnguǎn   HOTEL $$
(城林宾馆; ☎623 8866; Sidao Jie; 四道街; tw & d ¥280; @) Solid hotel with decent-sized rooms that come with computers. It's a block east of the main square at Sidao Jie and Haiguan Lu.

🍴 Eating

Barguuzin   BURIAT $
(巴图敖其尔; Bātú Áoqí'ěr; ☎622 0121; cnr Erdao Jie & Zhongsu Lu; mains from ¥18; ⏰6.30am-midnight) Run by Buriat Mongols, this popular place specialises in Mongolian and Russian cuisine and does good salads and soups. It's on two levels, one below the street: look for the blue sign on Erdao Jie. Picture menu.

ℹ Information

Bank of China (中国银行; Zhōngguó Yínháng; Yidao Jie) Near the junction with Haiguan Lu.

China International Travel Service (CITS; 中国国际旅行社; Zhōngguó Guójì Lǚxíngshè; ☎622 8319; 35 Erdao Jie; ⏰8-11.30am & 2-4pm Mon-Fri) On the 1st floor of Guójì Fàndiàn (International Hotel). Sells train tickets for Chinese cities.

China Post (中国邮政; Zhōngguó Yóuzhèng; cnr Haiguan Jie & Sidao Jie) Post and telephone office.

Internet cafe (网吧; wǎngbā; Yidao Jie; per hr ¥3; ⏰24hr) About 50m east of the Jīxiáng Lǚguǎn.

Public Security Bureau (PSB; 公安局; Gōng'ānjú; cnr Sandao Jie & Shulin Lu)

ℹ Getting There & Around

Mănzhōulǐ has a small airport on the edge of town; a taxi to the airport will take about 15 minutes (¥40). There are daily flights to Běijīng (¥1560, 2¼ hours) and, in summer, to Hohhot (¥860, 2½ hours).

You can reach Mănzhōulǐ by train from Hǎilā'ěr (¥29, three to 3½ hours), Ha'ěrbīn (hard/soft sleeper ¥222/338, 12 to 16 hours) or Qíqíha'ěr (hard/soft sleeper ¥175/264, 11 hours).

There are 12 buses a day to Hǎilā'ěr (¥41, three hours, 7am to 5.30pm) from the main bus station on Wudao Jie. Taxis charge ¥10 for most trips around town.

Qīnghǎi

POP 5.6 MILLION

Includes »

Xīníng 867
Tóngrén (Repkong) 873
Guìdé 875
Yùshù (Jyekundo) 877
Golmud 880

Best Monasteries & Temples

» Kumbum Monastery (p872)
» Yòuníng Sì (p872)
» Rongwo Gonchen Gompa (p874)
» Princess Wencheng Temple (p879)

Best Natural Sights

» Amnye Machen (p876)
» Mèngdá Nature Reserve (p875)
» Zālíng Lake (p878)
» Nangchen County (p879)

Why Go?

Big, bold and beautifully barren, Qīnghǎi (青海), larger than any European country, occupies a vast swathe of the north-eastern chunk of the Tibetan plateau. In fact, as far as Tibetans are concerned, this isn't China at all; it's Amdo, one of old Tibet's three traditional provinces. Much of what you'll experience here will feel more Tibetan than Chinese; there are monasteries galore, yaks by the hundred and nomads camped out across high-altitude grasslands.

Rough-and-ready Qīnghǎi, which means Blue Sea in Chinese, is classic off-the-beaten-track territory, often with a last frontier feel to it. Travelling around is both inconvenient and uncomfortable, and you can go for days without meeting another tourist. But those wonderful moments of solitude, those middle-of-nowhere high-plateau vistas and the chance to discover some of the more remote communities of China's ethnic minorities make the long bus rides, the cold weather and the often head-achingly high altitude well worth bearing.

When to Go

Xīníng

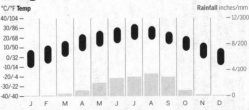

Jan & Feb
Tibetan New Year (Losar), with lots of pilgrims and celebrations at monasteries.

Jul–Sep
Grasslands at their greenest; landscape dotted with nomad tents.

Sep
Safest and most comfortable time for hiking around Mt Amnye Machen.

Qīnghǎi Highlights

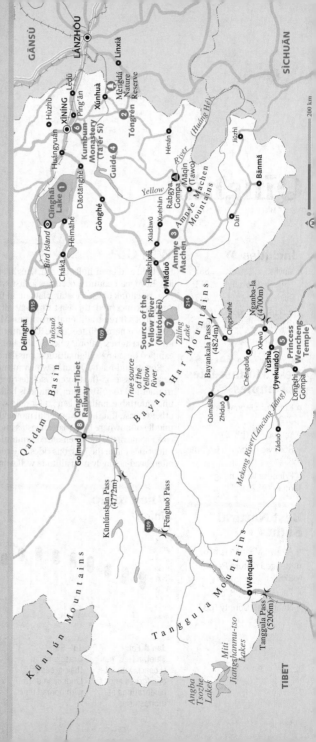

1 Birdwatch on the shores of **Qīnghǎi Lake** (p873), the largest in China

2 Buy a Tibetan *thangka* straight from the artist's easel in **Tóngrén** (p873)

3 Trek on **Amnye Machen** (p876), eastern Tibet's most sacred mountain

4 Turn the world's largest prayer wheel near the walled Old Town of **Guìdé** (p875)

5 Sidestep the web of prayer flags on a hike around the hills beside **Princess Wencheng Temple** (p879)

6 Join the pilgrims and monks at **Kumbum Monastery** (p872), one of the six great monasteries in the Tibetan world

7 Venture across the Qīnghǎi–Tibet plateau to the **source of the Yellow River** (p873)

8 Take one of the world's great train rides, the **Qīnghǎi–Tibet Railway** (p871) to Lhasa, at Xīníng or Golmud

History

The northern Silk Road passed through what is now Qīnghǎi province, and in 121 BC the Han dynasty established a military base near modern Xīníng to counter Tibetan raids on trading caravans.

During the Yarlung dynasty, a time of great expansion of Tibetan power and influence, Qīnghǎi was brought directly under Lhasa's control. After the collapse of the dynasty in AD 842, local rulers filled the ensuing power vacuum, some nominally acting as vassals of Song dynasty emperors.

In the 13th century all of Qīnghǎi was incorporated into the Yuan empire under Genghis Khan. During this time the Tǔ began to move into the area around Hùzhù, followed a century or so later by the Salar Muslims into Xúnhuà.

After the fall of the Yuan dynasty, local Mongol rulers and the Dalai Lamas in Lhasa wrestled for power. The Qing emperors restored the region to full Chinese control, setting it up as a prefecture with more or less the same boundaries as today. As in the past, however, they left administrative control in the hands of local elites.

Qīnghǎi officially became a province of China in 1929 during the republican era, though at the time it was under the de facto control of the Muslim Ma clan. Qīnghǎi was again made a province in 1949 with the establishment of the People's Republic of China.

In the late 1950s an area near Qīnghǎi Lake (Qīnghǎi Hú) became the centre of China's nuclear weapons research program. During the next 40 years, at least 30 tests were held at a secret base, the Qīnghǎi Mine.

In April 2010, Yùshù, a Tibetan town in remote southwest Qīnghǎi, was devastated by a 7.1-magnitude earthquake. Thousands of people died – some say tens of thousands – but the rebuilding effort has been swift.

Language

Most of the population in Qīnghǎi speaks a northwestern Chinese dialect similar to that spoken in Gānsù. Most Tibetans here speak the Amdo dialect. It's possible to travel almost everywhere using Mandarin.

🛈 Getting There & Around

Most people arrive by train, usually into Xīníng, but after that train lines are limited, so long-distance buses are the order of the day. In more remote areas you'll often have no option but to hire a private vehicle or hitch. Off-the-beaten-track overland routes include south into Sìchuān, at Aba or Shíqú, and north into Gānsù or Xīnjiāng from Golmud. Routes southwest into Tibet are even more remote but are often closed to foreigners.

PRICE INDICATORS

The following price indicators are used in this chapter:

Sleeping

$	less than ¥150
$$	¥150 to ¥300
$$$	more than ¥300

Eating

$	less than ¥30
$$	¥30 to ¥50
$$$	more than ¥50

Xīníng 西宁

📞 0971 / POP 1.2 MILLION

Perched on the eastern edge of the Tibetan plateau, this lively provincial capital makes a perfect springboard from which to dive into the surrounding sights and on to the more remote regions of Qīnghǎi and beyond. The food and lodging are good, the air is fresh, and the populace is an interesting mix of Muslim (Huí, Salar and Uighur), Tibetan and Han Chinese.

⊙ Sights

Tibetan Culture Museum MUSEUM
(藏文化博物馆; Zàng Wénhuà Bówùguǎn; admission ¥60; ⊙9.30am-5pm) Previously known as the Tibetan Medicine Museum, this unusual place still focuses on traditional Tibetan medicine and includes old medical instruments, bags, scrolls and, in the astronomy section, a very large sand mandala. The highlight, though, is the incredible 618m-long *thangka* (Tibetan sacred art) scroll – the world's longest – which charts pretty much the whole of Tibetan history. Completed in 1997 it's by no means an ancient relic, but it is unfeasibly long. It took 400 artists four years to complete and is ingeniously displayed in a relatively small hall. Bus 34 (¥1) comes here from West Gate. Bus 1 also goes close. A taxi's about ¥15 from the centre.

QĪNGHĂI XĪNÍNG

Xīníng

0 — 500 m
0 — 0.25 miles

To Xīníng West Train Station (10km)

Train Station (closed for renovations)

Huzı hu Lu

17

Shengli Lu 胜利路

14

To Civil Aviation Administration of China (1.5km)

Bayi Lu 八一路

Qilian Lu

Binhe Nanlu

Wuyi Lu

Qiyi Lu 七一街

Dongguan Dajie 东关大街

10

3

Gonghe Lu 北大街

5

Nan Xiaojie

Huayuan Lu

Ledu Lu

12

Xiao Xinjie 小新街

4

11

Xidu Dajie 西都大街

'Bar Street'

9

Yima Jie

6

7

Wenmiao Square

Dong Dajie 东大街

8

Hongjuesi Jie

Qīnghăi Red Cross Hospital

Bel Dajie

Datong Ji

2

Nan Dajie

1

6

Jiancai Xiang

'To Běichán St (2km)'

Changjiang Lu 长江路

Xi Dajie 西大街

Nanguan Jie 南关街

Kunlun Zhonglu 昆仑中路

Qunli Lu 群力路

Nanshan Hu

13

Central Square

Huanshi Lu

Nanshan Lu

15

16

Xīníng

◉ **Sights**
1 City Wall C4
2 Golden Stupa Temple C3
3 Great Mosque.......................................E3

🛏 **Sleeping**
4 Chéng Lín Hotel.......................................C2
5 Jǐnjiāng Inn.......................................C2
6 Lete Youth Hostel C4
7 Sunshine Pagoda International
    Youth Hostel C2

🍽 **Eating**
    Black Tent.......................................(see 7)
8 Mo Jia Jie Market.......................................C3
9 Qīnghǎi Tǔ Huǒguō C2
10 Zhènyà Niúròu Miàn E3

🍷 **Drinking**
11 Greenhouse.......................................C4

🛍 **Shopping**
12 Amdo Café.......................................D4
13 Shuǐjǐng Xiàng Market.......................................A2
14 Tibetan Market F3

ℹ **Information**
    Snow Lion Tours.......................................(see 4)
    Tibetan Connections.......................................(see 6)

🚍 **Transport**
15 Shared Taxis to Guìdé A3
16 Taxis to Kumbum Monastery A3
17 Xīníng Bus Station.......................................G3

QĪNGHǍI XĪNÍNG

Běichán Sì TEMPLE
(北禅寺; ⊗8am-4pm) The main temple at the foot of this barren hillside is nothing special but halfway up the steep climb to the top you pass cave temples and shrines that are thought to be 1700 years old. A pagoda, and great views of the city, await you at the top. Turn left after you pass under the railway line and follow the road round to the temple entrance, or take a ¥6 cab.

FREE **Qīnghǎi Provincial Museum** MUSEUM
(青海省博物馆; Qīnghǎi Shěng Bówùguǎn; Xinning Sq, 58 Xiguan Dajie; 新宁广场西关大街58号; ⊗9am-4.30pm Mon-Sat) Scaled down in recent years, but still has some nice pieces recovered from excavations in Qīnghǎi. The Tibetan carpet exhibition is worth seeing. Bus 1 goes here, or take bus 22 from Dongguan Dajie.

Great Mosque MOSQUE
(清真大寺; Qīngzhēn Dàsì; 25 Dongguan Dajie; admission ¥15; ⊗7am-8pm) About one-third of Xīníng's population is Muslim and there are more than 80 mosques across the city. But this is the big one. In fact, it's one of the largest mosques in China. Friday lunchtime prayers regularly attract 50,000 worshippers who spill out onto the streets before and afterwards. And during Ramadan as many as 300,000 come here to pray. The mosque was first built during the late 14th century and has since been restored. It's also worth visiting at night when the whole building is lit up with flashing neon lights. Non-Muslims can't enter the main prayer hall, but can stroll around the grounds.

FREE **Golden Stupa Temple** BUDDHIST TEMPLE
(金塔寺; Jīntǎ Sì; 19 Hongjuesi Jie; 宏觉寺街19号; ⊗8am-4pm) Small temple named after long-destroyed golden *chörten* (Tibetan stupa). Used as a place of study by monks at Kumbum Monastery.

City Wall RUIN
(城墙; Chéngqiáng; Kunlun Zhonglu; 昆仑中路) One or two isolated sections of Xīníng's old city wall still remain, the most accessible being this short stretch on Kunlun Zhonglu.

🛏 Sleeping

Lete Youth Hostel HOSTEL $$
(理体青年旅舍; Lǐtǐ Qīngnián Lǚshè; ☑820 2080; www.xnlete.com; 16th fl, Bldg No 5, International Village Apartments, 2-32 Jiancai Xiang; 建材巷国际村公寓5号楼16层; dm ¥30-35, d without/with bathroom ¥120/180; @🛜) This friendly hostel has the best backpacker vibe in Xīníng and is a great place to get the low-down on travelling in Qīnghǎi and on to Tibet. The modern, multifloor layout includes cafe/bar, wide-screen TVs, laundry, kitchen and a small terrace that you can sleep out on in summer (¥35). Rooms are clean, bright and spacious, although the shared bathrooms are falling apart at the seams. Staff members speak good English and the travel agency Tibetan Connections is two floors up.

**Sunshine Pagoda
International Youth Hostel** HOSTEL $
(塔顶阳光国际青年旅舍; Tǎdǐng Yángguāng Guójì Qīngnián Lǚshè; ☑821 5571; www.tdyg-inn.com; 3rd fl, Wenmiao Sq, off Wenhua Jie; 文华

FULL HOUSE

Scoring a hotel room in Xīníng during the summer months can be surprisingly difficult, especially for foreigners as there is a shortage of places that will accept them. Book your room or dorm bed as early as possible, preferably one week in advance.

街文庙广场3层; dm/s/d ¥50/105/120; @☏) More popular with Chinese travellers than Westerners, this OK hostel is in the thick of the action if it's drinking you're after. Rooms are basic but tidy and there's a cosy cafe area.

Qīnghǎi Sāngzhū Youth Hostel HOSTEL $$
(青海桑珠国际青年旅舍; Qīnghǎi Sāngzhū Guójì Qīngnián Lǚshè; ☏359 4118; www.qhhostel.com; 94 Huzhu Zhonglu; 互助中路94号; dm ¥40-55, d ¥218, tr ¥240; @☏) This spacious hostel has a big lounge decorated with Tibetan artwork and clean rooms with comfortable beds. English is spoken and there's plenty of traveller information posted on the walls. On the downside, it's a few kilometres from the centre of town so you'll need to take a bus or taxi to get anywhere. Catch bus 32 or 33 on Dong Dajie, heading east. Once the bus turns onto Huzhu Lu it's another two stops (about 2km down the road).

Chéng Lín Hotel HOTEL $$
(成林大厦; Chénglín Dàshà; ☏491 1199; Dong Dajie; 东大街; tw/d ¥260/280; ✷) Spacious, well-turned-out rooms with en suite shower come with dark-wood furniture, TV and kettle and are great value after discounts. No internet in the rooms, but there's an internet cafe (per hour ¥2 to ¥4) on the 3rd floor. Limited English.

Jīnjiāng Inn HOTEL $$$
(锦江之星; Jǐnjiāng Zhīxīng; ☏492 5666; www.jinjianginns.com; Dongda Jie; 东大街; d incl breakfast ¥329; ✷@) This reliable chain hotel is in the heart of the city and has clean rooms and a helpful staff. Book well in advance in summer.

✗ Eating

Xīníng has a great range of food. Try the Tibetan district around the train station for cheap Tibetan fare. For Muslim food head to Dongguan Dajie, near the Great Mosque, or the northern stretch of Nan Xiaojie.

For snacks, try one of the cheap barbecue places (烧烤; *shāokǎo*) on Xiao Xinjie that stay open until the early hours, or head to **Mo Jia Jie Market** (墨家街市场; Mòjiājiā Shìchǎng) where you can also sample a local favourite: *niàng pí* (酿皮; spicy cold noodles; ¥4).

Black Tent TIBETAN $$
(黑帐房藏餐吧; Hēizhàngfáng Zàngcānbā; 3rd fl; 18 Wenmiao Sq, 文庙广场18号3层; dishes ¥15-40; ☉10am-10pm; 🗉) Authentic Tibetan nosh, including *tsampa* (roasted barley; ¥18), *momo* (dumplings; ¥22) and yak-butter yoghurt (¥12) as well as some tasty Nepalese dishes. Also serves yak-butter tea (per pot ¥24) and Qīnghǎi's favourite local tipple, barley wine (青稞酒; *qīngkē jiǔ*).

Qīnghǎi Tǔ Huǒguō HOTPOT $$$
(青海土火锅; 31 Yinma Jie; pots ¥58/78/98; ☉11am-10pm) Unlike its fiery Chóngqìng cousin, Qīnghǎi's chilli-less hotpot, which comes in attractive copper pots, won't burn your head off when you eat it. This place has three different pot sizes, all of which include 10 different ingredients. If you can read Chinese, you can add more from the menu. The ¥58 version is plenty for two or three people. Dipping sauces – either *xiānglà* (香辣; chilli) or *suànní* (蒜泥; garlic) – are ¥2 extra.

Zhènyà Niúròu Miàn MUSLIM $
(震亚牛肉面; 24 Dongguan Dajie; noodles ¥5/6.50; ☉9am-10pm) Join the local Muslim population for their noodle fix at this busy place by the Great Mosque. There's no menu, but there are only two dishes: *niúròu miàn* (牛肉面; beef noodles; ¥5) and *gān bànmiàn* (干拌面; mincemeat noodles; ¥6.50). *Suān tāng* (酸汤; a small peppery soup) comes free.

🍷 Drinking

If you like your bars to come with loud music, neon lights, booth seating and scantily clad waitresses head to Xīníng's so-called **bar street** (酒吧街; jiǔ bā jiē; beer from ¥6); three floors of bars, cafes and restaurants are set around Wenmiao Sq (文庙广场; Wénmiào Guǎngchǎng) off Wenhua Jie. For a more mellow evening, stroll along Xiadu Dajie, which has about a dozen cafes.

Greenhouse CAFE
(古林房咖啡; Gǔlínfáng Kāfēi; 222-22 Xiadu Dajie; 夏都大街222-22号; coffee from ¥13; ☉8am-10.30pm; ☏) Rustic split-level wood interior with smoothies and the best coffee in town.

🔒 Shopping

In the lively Tibetan market (西藏市场; Xīzàng Guǎngchǎng) near the train station you'll find stall after stall selling traditional fabrics and clothing.

Amdo Café   HANDICRAFTS
(安多咖啡屋; Ānduō Kāfēiwū; ☑821 3127; 19 Ledu Lu; ⊙9am-8pm Mon-Sat; ☎) Profits from the lovely handmade Tibetan gifts (from ¥20) sold here go back to the local craftswomen. There's also decent coffee (from ¥10).

Shuǐjǐng Xiàng Market   SOUVENIRS
(水井巷商场; Shuǐjǐng Xiàng Shāngchǎng; ⊙9am-6pm) Lively market running north–south between Xi Dajie and Nanguan Jie.

ℹ Information

Bank of China (中国银行; Zhōngguó Yínháng; ⊙9am-5pm Mon-Fri, 10am-4pm Sat & Sun) Branches on Dongguan Dajie, Dong Dajie and next to CAAC on Bayi Lu change cash and travellers cheques and have foreign-friendly ATMs.

Post office (中国邮政; Zhōngguó Yóuzhèng; cnr Xi Dajie & Nan Dajie; ⊙8.30am-6pm)

Public Security Bureau (PSB; 公安局; Gōng'ānjú; 35 Bei Dajie; ⊙8.30-11.30am & 2.30-5.30pm Mon-Fri) Can extend visas.

Qīnghǎi Red Cross Hospital (青海红十字医院; Qīnghǎi Hóngshízì Yīyuàn; ☑824 7545; Nan Dajie) English-speaking doctors available. Outpatients (门诊部; ménzhěn bù) has a 24-hour pharmacy (药店; yàodiàn).

Snow Lion Tours (☑816 3350; www.snowlion tours.com; Cheng Lin Mansion, office 1212, 7 Dongdajie Lu) Run by knowledgeable English-speaking Tibetan guy; arranges treks, camping with nomads and Tibet permits. The office is located in the same building as the Chéng Lín Hotel.

Tiāntángniǎo Internet (天堂鸟网络; Tiāntángniǎo wǎngluò; Dong Dajie; per hr ¥2-3.50; ⊙24hr) Second and 3rd floors.

Tibetan Connections (☑820 3271; www. tibetanconnections.com; Jian Cai Xiang, 18th fl, International Village Bldg 5) Tibetan-managed agency organising treks, camp-outs and cultural tours in Qīnghǎi, as well as Lhasa train tickets and permits. Above Lete Youth Hostel.

ℹ Getting There & Away

Air

Flights include Běijīng (¥1600), Chéngdū (¥990), Shànghǎi (¥1860), Yùshù (¥1390), Golmud (¥1420, daily) and Xī'ān (¥660). There are no direct flights to Lhasa. You must fly via Chéngdū.

The **Civil Aviation Administration of China** (CAAC; 中国民航; Zhōngguó Mínháng; ☑813 3333; 32 Bayi Xilu; ⊙8.30am-5.30pm) has a booking office on the eastern edge of town.

Bus

Destinations from Xīníng bus station (车站; chēzhàn):

Bānmǎ ¥173, 15 hours, one daily (4pm)

Golmud ¥160, 12 hours, three daily (2pm, 5pm and 6pm)

Huāshíxiá ¥107, 10 hours, six daily

Lánzhōu ¥59, three hours, every 30 minutes (7.20am to 6pm)

Mǎqìn (Tawo) ¥126, 12 hours, eight daily (10.30am, 11.30am and 12.30pm are express buses)

Tóngrén ¥34, four hours, every 30 minutes (7.30am to 5pm)

Xiàhé ¥78, six hours, one daily (7.15am)

Xúnhuà ¥32, five hours, every 30 minutes (7.20am to 4.50pm)

Yùshù sleeper ¥206, 16 to 17 hours, six daily

Zhāngyè ¥102, five hours one daily (8am). In addition there are slower buses (¥75) taking seven hours, departing at 7am, 9am, 12.15pm and 6.30pm.

Minivan & Shared Taxi

Minivans depart to some of the same destinations one can reach by bus. They leave when full so you won't know how long you have to wait around, but once they go the trip will be shorter than the bus ride. These vehicles typically leave between 8am and 2pm.

Golmud ¥175, 10 hours, departs from opposite the bus station

Guìdé ¥50, 2½ hours, departs the northern side of the intersection on Kunlun Zhonglu (near the bridge)

Mǎqìn (Tawo) ¥175, 10 hours, departs from opposite the bus station

Tóngrén ¥60, 2½ hours, departs from corner of Bayi Lu and Delingha Lu

Train

At the time of writing the Xīníng train station (火车站; huǒchē zhàn) was closed for renovations and was not expected to reopen until 2013 or 2014. In the meantime, trains start/stop at the west train station (西火车站; xī huǒchē zhàn), about 10km west of the city centre.

Lhasa-bound trains pass through Xīníng (hard/soft sleeper ¥504/796, 24 hours, eight daily from 3.04pm to 10pm) on their way towards the now world-famous Qīnghǎi–Tibet Railway stretch of China's rail network, but the K9801 (3.04pm) actually starts here, so is

ℹ️ TRAIN TICKET TRAVAILS

Train tickets can be purchased at the main **post office** (中国邮政; Zhōngguó Yóuzhèng; cnr Xi Dajie & Nan Dajie; ⏰8.30am-6pm) on the 2nd floor, which saves a long trip to the train station. Be aware that in the summer months tickets to most destinations sell out immediately and the only way to get one is through a travel agent (who may be able to score you a ticket from the mafia).

usually easier to get tickets for. You will, of course, need all your Tibet papers in order. Other destinations from Xīníng include:

Běijīng sleeper ¥416, 22 to 24 hours, two daily (12.20am and 3.40pm)

Chéngdū sleeper ¥300, 25 and 20½ hours, two daily (9.20am and 9.35am)

Golmud seat/sleeper ¥111/202, 9½ hours, 10 daily (3.04pm to 10pm)

Lánzhōu seat/sleeper ¥38/89, 2½ hours, 11 daily (8am to 10.20pm)

Xī'ān seat/sleeper ¥120/216, 10½ to 12½ hours, seven daily (5.49am to 10.15pm)

ℹ️ Getting Around

The airport is 27km east of the city. Shuttle buses (¥21, 30 minutes) leave roughly 1½ hours before flights from the CAAC office on Bayi Lu. Coming from the airport, this bus travels along Qiyi Lu as it moves through the city, eventually terminating a half block from Central Sq.

Bus 2 (¥1) runs from the bus station and along Dongguan Dajie to Central Sq before heading north to the west train station, a 40-minute ride. Taxis are ¥6 for the first 3km and ¥1.20 per kilometre thereafter.

Around Xīníng

KUMBUM MONASTERY (TǍ'ĚR SÌ)

塔尔寺

One of the great monasteries of the Gelugpa (Yellow Hat) sect of Tibetan Buddhism, the **Kumbum Monastery** (Tǎ'ěr Sì; admission ¥80; ⏰8.30am-6pm) is in the small town of Huángzhōng (湟中), 26km south of Xīníng. It was built in 1577 on hallowed ground – the birthplace of Tsongkhapa, founder of the Gelugpa sect.

It's of enormous historical significance, and hundreds of monks still live here but, perhaps because it's such a big tourist attraction for this part of Qīnghǎi, the atmosphere pales into comparison with other monasteries in Amdo. The artwork and architecture, however, remain impressive.

Nine temples are open, each with their own characteristics. The most important is the **Grand Hall of Golden Tiles** (大金瓦殿; Dàjīnwǎ Diàn), where an 11m-high *chörten* marks the spot of Tsongkhapa's birth. You'll see pilgrims walking circuits of the building and outside the entrance. Also worth seeking out is the **Yak Butter Scripture Temple** (酥油画馆; Sūyóuhuà Guǎn) which houses sculptures of human figures, animals and landscapes carved out of yak butter.

Shared taxis (拼车; *pīnchē*; ¥15 per seat, 30 minutes) leave from the southwest (and southeast) corner of Kunlun Bridge (昆仑桥) to Huángzhōng (湟中). In addition, a slow bus (¥3, 50 minutes) comes by this intersection en route to the monastery – there is no number so look for 塔尔寺–藏文化路–西宁 in the windshield. An express bus (¥5.40, every 20 minutes) also leaves from a short distance bus station (西宁路客运站; xíníng lù kèyùnzhàn) just north of Xīníng Sq (near the Qīnghǎi Provincial Museum). You can reach this local bus station by taking bus 25 from Dong Dajie.

YÒUNÍNG SÌ

佑宁寺

Well known throughout the Tibetan world, but rarely visited by tourists, this sprawling 17th-century hillside monastery in the Hùzhù Tǔzú (互助土族) Autonomous County is also considered one of the greats of the Gelugpa order.

Famous for its academies of medicine and astrology, its scholars and its living Buddhas (*tulku*), Yòuníng Sì (Rgolung in Tibetan) was instrumental in solidifying Gelugpa dominance over the Amdo region. The monastery was founded by the Mongolian 4th Dalai Lama, and over time became a religious centre for the local Tǔ (themselves a distant Mongolian people). At its height, more than 7000 monks resided here; these days there are probably less than 200, all of whom are Tǔ.

The monastery lies at the edge of a forested valley, and many chapels perch wondrously on the sides of a cliff face. Give yourself a couple of hours to explore the whole picturesque area.

The easiest way to the monastery is to take a bus to Píng'ān (¥5, one hour, six per hour), then hire a taxi (one way/return ¥50/90, 30 minutes). It is possible to bus it from Píng'ān, but it involves a lot of waiting: take a bus bound for Hùzhù (互助) but get off at the turn-off for Yòuníng Sì (Yòuníng Sì lùkŏu) then wave down a bus to the monastery. The monastery is about 25km north of Píng'ān.

BIRTHPLACE OF THE 14TH DALAI LAMA 达赖故居

About 30km southeast of the town of Píng'ān, in the remote, sleepy village of Taktser (红崖村; Hóngyá Cūn), set in a ring of high snow-brushed mountains, is the birthplace of the 14th Dalai Lama (Dálài gùjū). The building is open to foreign visitors only when there are no political tensions in Tibet, and it's been closed to foreigners during March and April in recent years because of a number of sensitive dates during those months.

Assuming you are allowed in, you'll be able to visit the room where his Holiness was born (marked by a golden *chörten*), as well as a restored chapel that contains his former bed and throne. A side room displays some old family photos, including those of the Dalai Lama's parents, brothers and sister .

The Dalai Lama last visited here in 1955 en route to Běijīng to meet with Chairman Mao. The previous (13th) Dalai Lama paused here en route to Labrang just long enough to predict his own next reincarnation. You can spot the building (No 055) by its large wooden gate tied with *katags* (white ceremonial scarves).

Take a bus to Píng'ān (¥5, one hour), then take a cab (¥150 return, 50 minutes).

Tóngrén (Repkong) 同仁

📞 0973

For several centuries now, the villages outside the monastery town of Tóngrén (Repkong in Tibetan) have been famous for producing some of the Tibetan world's best *thangkas* and painted statues, so much so that an entire school of Tibetan art is named after the town. Visiting the Wútún Sì monastery not only gives you a chance to meet the artists, but also to purchase a painting or two, fresh off the easel.

Tóngrén is set on the slopes of the wide and fertile Gu-chu river valley. The local populace is a mix of Tibetans and Tŭ. The valley and surrounding hills are easily explored on foot.

Everywhere is walking distance from the junction by Repkong Bridge (热贡桥; Règòng Qiáo). With your back to the bridge, take the first right to the bus station (50m), the second right to Tóngrén Holiday Hotel (500m), go straight for Zhongshan Lu and turn left for Rongwo Gonchen Gompa (750m).

QĪNGHĂI TÓNGRÉN (REPKONG)

BIRDWATCHING AT QĪNGHĂI LAKE

China's largest lake, Qīnghăi Lake (青海湖; Qīnghăi Hú; Lake Kokonor; elevation 3600m) has become an over-touristy big-draw destination for large tour groups, but birdwatchers may still enjoy a trip here.

Bird Island (鸟岛; Niăo Dăo; admission ¥115), on the western side of the lake, about 300km from Xīníng, is worth visiting from March to early June. The island (now in fact a peninsula) is the breeding ground for thousands of wild geese, gulls, cormorants, sandpipers, extremely rare black-necked cranes and other bird species. Perhaps the most interesting are the bar-headed geese that migrate over the Himalaya to spend winter on the Indian plains, and have been spotted flying at altitudes of 10,000m.

Every travel agency in Xīníng offers trips to Qīnghăi Lake. At the time of research, Tibetan Connections was offering a two-day camping trip for ¥700 (transport costs only). You could get to the lake much more cheaply if you hired a private minivan or taxi from Xīníng with a group of travellers.

The closest accommodation to Bird Island is **Niăo Dăo Bīnguăn** (鸟岛宾馆; 📞 0970-865 5098; r with breakfast from ¥380). You are still 16km from the island here, but you should be able to hire a taxi (¥50 return). Camping is another option.

A new, backpacker-friendly place to stay in the area is **Muming Zhijia International Youth Hostel** (牧民之家国际青年旅舍; Mùmín Zhìjiā Guójì Qīngnián Lǚshè; 📞 0974-851 9511; muminzhijiahostel@163.com; dm ¥40-55; @ 📶), a cosy guesthouse with lake views, *kang*-style beds and bikes for rent (¥60 to ¥70). Water comes in fits and starts. If you have your own tent you can pitch it here for ¥5. To get here from Xīníng, take a bus to Hātú (哈图; ¥31, three hours) and ask the driver to let you off near An Zhí Farm (安置农场; Anzhí Nóngchăng).

◉ Sights

Rongwo Gonchen Gompa MONASTERY

(隆务寺; Lóngwù Sì; Dehelong Nanlu; 德合隆南路; admission ¥50) Tóngrén's main monastery is a huge and rambling maze of renovated chapels and monks' residences, dating from 1301. It's well worth a wander, and you'll need one or two hours to see everything. Your ticket includes entry into six main halls, although you may be able to take a peek inside others, too. There are more than 500 resident monks and every day dozens of them go into the courtyard outside the Hall of Bodhisattva Manjusri to take part in animated, hand-clapping debates. There's a map in English on a wooden board just inside the main gate.

Wútún Sì MONASTERY

Sengeshong village, 6km from Tóngrén, is the place to head if you're interested in Tibetan art. There are two monasteries, collectively known as **Wútún Sì** (吾屯寺), that are divided into an **Upper (Yango) Monastery** (上寺; Shàng Sì; admission ¥30), closest to town, and a **Lower (Mango) Monastery** (下寺; Xià Sì; admission ¥30). The monks will show you around whatever chapels happen to be open and then take you to a showroom or workshop. The resident artists are no amateurs – commissions for their work come in all the way from Lhasa, and prices aren't cheap. Artwork at the Upper Monastery is of an exceptionally high quality, but expect to pay hundreds of rénmínbì for the smallest *thangka*, thousands for a poster-sized one and tens or even hundreds of thousands for the largest pieces. Remember, though, that an A4-sized *thangka* takes one artist at least a month to complete, and larger pieces take two artists up to a year to finish. Just outside the Lower Monastery there are more showrooms and you'll find cheaper versions here (from ¥300), although the quality is still high.

The Lower Monastery is easily recognisable by eight large *chörten* out front. While there, check out the 100-year-old Jampa Lhakhang (Jampa Temple) and the new chapels dedicated to Chenresig and Tsongkhapa.

The Upper Monastery includes a massive modern *chörten* as well as the old *dukhang* (assembly hall) and the new chapel dedicated to Maitreya (Shampa in Amdo dialect). The interior murals here (painted by local artists) are superb.

To get here, take a minibus (¥2 per seat) from the intersection just uphill from Tóngrén bus station ticket office. The walk back from here is pleasant.

Gomar Gompa MONASTERY

(郭麻日寺; Guōmárì Sì; admission ¥10) Across the Gu-chu river valley from Wútún Sì is the mysterious 400-year-old Gomar Gompa, a charming monastery that resembles a medieval walled village. There are 130 monks in residence living in whitewashed mud-walled courtyards and there are a few temples you can visit. The huge *chörten* outside the monastery entrance was built in the 1980s and is the biggest in Amdo. You can climb it, but remember to always walk clockwise. There are photos of the 14th Dalai Lama at the top.

To get here, turn left down a side road as you pass the westernmost of the eight *chörten* outside Wútún Sì's Lower Monastery. Follow the road 1km across the river and turn right at the end on a main road. Then head up the track towards the giant *chörten*. Further up the valley is **Gasar Gompa**, marked by its own distinctive eight *chörtens*. Note that women may not be allowed into the Gomar Gompa or Gasar Gompa.

🛏 Sleeping & Eating

Règòng Sìhéjí Bīnguǎn HOTEL $$

(热贡四合吉宾馆; ☑879 7988; 14 Dehelong Nanlu; 德合隆南路14号; d from ¥160) This well-placed hotel is on the main road about 200m before the monastery. The colourful lobby leads up through startling gold hallways to bright and clean rooms with flat-screen TVs and well-maintained bathrooms.

Hépíng Bīnguǎn HOTEL $

(和平宾馆; ☑872 4188; Maixiu Lu; 麦秀路; d from ¥120) Offers large clean rooms overlooking a car park. Good value for money and they usually knock the price down to ¥100. From the bridge walk on the main road towards the monastery and make the first right turn; the hotel is down the street on the left.

Tóngrén Holiday Hotel HOTEL $$

(同仁假日宾馆; Tóngrén Jiàrì Bīnguǎn; ☑872 8277; Dehelong Beilu; 德合隆北路; d & tw from ¥198) This place is modern and has fairly clean and spacious rooms but they are overpriced and staff may not be willing to negotiate the price, except perhaps in the off season. An internet cafe is on the 1st floor. It's next to the main square in the northern part of town.

TOP CHOICE Homely Teahouse TIBETAN $
(温馨茶艺; Wēnxīn Cháyì; Dehelong Nanlu; dishes ¥8-14; ⏰8am-midnight; 🖊) This authentic Tibetan restaurant – with a yak skull hanging on the wall and plastic flowers throughout – serves *momo*, yoghurt and noodle soup and a range of beers and teas. It's located in a cosy two-storey wood-panelled building with excellent views of the valley, towards the end of the main road before the monastery.

ℹ Information

China Construction Bank ATM (建设银行; Jiànshè Yínháng; Zhongshan Lu; 中山路) Foreign-card friendly.

Internet cafe (网吧; wǎngbā; per hr ¥3; ⏰24hr) Inside China Telecom building, about 150m west of the bridge on the north side of the road (next to Telecom Hotel).

ℹ Getting There & Around

The scenery on the road from Xīníng is awesome as it follows a tributary of the Yellow River through steep-sided gorges, but the way out to Xiàhé is even better, passing dramatic red rock scenery and the impressive Gartse Gompa, where local Tibetan herders board the bus to sell fresh yoghurt. For Xiàhé and Línxià, try to buy your ticket one day in advance. Faster share taxis to Xiàhé (¥50) and Xīníng (¥60) wait at the intersection near the bridge

Buses from Tóngrén bus station include the following:

Línxià ¥38, three hours, one daily (8am)

Xiàhé ¥26, three hours, one daily (8am)

Xīníng ¥34, four hours, every 40 minutes (7am to 4.20pm)

Xúnhuà ¥16, two hours, four daily (9.30am, 11am, 1pm and 3pm)

Around Tóngrén

A nice side trip from Tóngrén is to Xúnhuà (循化), a tidy town in the Xúnhuà Salar Autonomous County, about 75km northeast of Tóngrén. The Salar Muslims have their origins in Samarkand and speak an isolated Turkic language, giving the region a Central Asian feel (and cuisine).

About 30km from Xúnhuà is Heaven Lake (Tiān Chí) at **Mèngdá Nature Reserve** (孟达国家自然保护区; Mèngdá Guójiā Zìrán Bǎohùqū; admission ¥90; ⏰7am-6pm). The tiny lake is sacred for both Salar Muslims and Tibetan Buddhists, and is much hyped locally. There are, in truth, more picturesque lakes around Qīnghǎi, but the road to the

reserve – which follows the coppery-green Yellow River as it cuts its way through a fantastically scenic gorge of rust-red cliffs – is worth the trip alone. You'll find stunning photo opportunities around every turn.

From the main gate of the reserve you can ride horses (¥50, 30 minutes) to the lake or take a gas-powered buggy (free) to a small parking area, then walk the rest of the way.

To get to the reserve you'll need to hire a taxi from outside Xúnhuà bus station. Expect to pay at least ¥120 return, including waiting time. There are plenty of noodle restaurants opposite the bus station. *Miàn piàn* (面片; noodle squares; ¥5) is a local favourite. If you get stuck here, **Jiāotōng Bīnguǎn** (交通宾馆; ☎0972-881 2615; d/tw ¥160/240), beside the bus station, has comfortable rooms often discounted to less than ¥100.

There are four buses a day back to Tóngrén (¥16, 2½ hours, 9am, 11am, 1pm and 2pm), five to Línxià (¥30, three hours, 7.30am, 8.40am, 9.50am, noon and 2.30pm) and buses every 30 minutes to Xīníng (¥32, 3½ hours, 7am to 4pm). Share taxis to Xīníng (¥50, 2½ hours) wait outside the bus station.

Guìdé 贵德

☎0974

As the Yellow River (黄河; Huáng Hé) flows down from the Tibetan Plateau it makes a series of sharp bends as it powers its way past historical Guìdé. Sitting on the riverbank here at sunset, with a beer in hand, is a great way to end the day. The old town (古城; gǔchéng), still largely enclosed within its crumbling 10m-high mud walls, also makes for a pleasant stroll and is a good base for your stay. But changes are afoot. In 2011 the government

HIKING ON SACRED MT AMNYE MACHEN

The 6282m peak of Machen Kangri, or **Mt Amnye Machen** (阿尼玛卿山; Ānímǎqīng Shān), is Amdo's most sacred mountain – it's eastern Tibet's equivalent to Mt Kailash in western Tibet. Tibetan pilgrims travel for weeks to circumambulate the peak, believing it to be home to the protector deity Machen Pomra. The circuit's sacred geography and wild mountain scenery make it a fantastic, though adventurous, trekking destination.

The full circuit takes around 11 days (including transport to/from Xīníng), though tourists often limit themselves to a half circuit. Several monasteries lie alongside the route.

With almost all of the route above 4000m, and the highest pass hitting 4600m, it's essential to acclimatise before setting off, preferably by spending a night or two at nearby Măqìn (Tawo; 3760m). You can make a good excursion 70km north of town to **Rabgya Gompa** (拉加寺; Lājiā Sì), an important branch of Tibet's Sera Monastery. The best months to trek are May to October, though be prepared for snow early and late in the season.

Most trekkers will be on an organised tour. See p871 for travel agencies that can arrange trips, including English-speaking Tibetan guides. Expect to pay around US$140 per person per day, all-inclusive.

If you decide to head out on your own, take the bus to Huāshíxiá (花石峡) and then hitch a ride to Xiàdàwǔ (下大吾), or hire a vehicle for ¥300 to ¥400. In Xiàdàwǔ the starting point for the *kora* (holy hike) path is at Guru Gompa (格日寺; Gérì Sì), and from here follow the road east. After three days the road peters out near Xuĕshān (雪山) from where you can hitch a ride to Măqìn (Tawo). If you intend to continue past Xuĕshān you'll need to ask a local to show you the *kora* footpath. In Xiàdàwǔ, a guide costs ¥120 to ¥150 per day, and it's about the same price for a packhorse or yak.

knocked down most buildings in the old town with a plan to redevelop the place into a major tourist attraction, complete with five-star hotels and a golf course. Get here soon before it's discovered by the masses.

◉ Sights & Activities

Jade Emperor Temple　　　　TEMPLE
(玉皇阁; Yùhuáng Gé; admission ¥60; ⊘8.30am-6pm) The focal point of the old town is this small temple complex, built in 1592. It includes a three-storey pagoda, which can be climbed for good views, and a Confucius Temple (文庙; Wén Miào).

Museum of Guìdé County　　　MUSEUM
(admission free with temple ticket; ⊘8.30am-6pm) The square beside the temple contains the small museum, which houses a handful of interesting Ming and Qing artefacts recovered from the local area, but lacks English captions. Near the museum, a small shop rents out bikes for ¥8 per hour.

Tibetan Prayer Wheel　　　　RELIGIOUS
(中华福运轮; Zhōnghuá Fúyùnlún) Around the back of the old town a dirt track leads down to the Yellow River and a large suspension bridge. From the bridge, turn left and walk about 1.2km to an enormous new gold-plated Tibetan prayer wheel, which is turned with the aid of rushing water from the Yellow River. The prayer wheel is 27m tall, 10m in diameter and weighs 200 tonnes, earning it a spot in the *Guinness World Records* as the world's largest prayer wheel. Inside the wheel are 200 copies of the Kangyur text and the base contains a large prayer hall. Near the wheel is a museum of Tibetan artefacts.

Continuing upstream for another 2km you'll come across a huge, recently built wooden **water wheel** (水车; shuǐchē) by a paved riverbank.

Hot Springs　　　　HOT SPRINGS
(温泉; wēnquán) If your legs need a rest after all that walking, hop in a taxi (¥15 to ¥20 one way) to Guìdé's hot springs, known locally as *rèshuǐ gōu* (热水沟), which are a 13km-drive from town past some mightily impressive barren scenery. Here you can join the local Tibetans for a free outdoor bath. There are several guesthouses here where you can enter the pools for a fee of ¥20.

🛏 Sleeping & Eating

The old farmers'-style courtyard guesthouses (农家院; nóngjiā yuàn) in Guìdé have been razed by government order and it's likely that in the coming years new hotels and guesthouses will appear in the old town.

Yŏuzhèng Bīnguǎn
HOTEL $$

(邮政宾馆; ☎855 0601; r ¥180) Located just outside the main gate to the old town is this decent option with 24-hour hot water and comfortable beds.

Qīng Xiāng Yuán Farmhouse
HOTEL $

(清香源农庄; Qīngxiāngyuán Nóngzhuāng; ☎855 4271; bed per person ¥30; dishes ¥10-60) Just behind the old town walls, on the corner of the road leading down to the river, this is a restaurant that manages to convert some of its dining areas into bedrooms. The big dining table in your room may feel a bit awkward, like a group is about to come in for dinner.

Khawa Chain Tibetan Restaurant
TIBETAN $

(卡哇坚藏餐; kǎwǎjiān zàngcān; dishes ¥10-60) A Tibetan-style place with *momo*, hearty soups and sizzling meat platters. It's on the main road in the old town.

ℹ Information

There are internet cafes (网吧; *wǎngbā*) on Yingbingo Xilu and Bei Dajie.

China Construction Bank ATM (建设银行; Jiànshè Yínháng; 14 Yingbin Xilu; 迎宾西路) Accepts foreign cards. Turn left from the bus station and keep going.

ℹ Getting There & Around

The old town is 1.5km from the bus station. Turn left out of the station on Yingbin Xilu, then left again along Xi Jie and left once more down Bei Dajie and it will be directly in front of you. Three-wheel motorised rickshaws ply the streets of Guídé. Most short trips cost ¥5.

There are regular buses back to Xīníng (¥25, 3½ hours, from 7.30am to 5.45pm). A bus to Mǎqin (Tawo; ¥87) travels on even days, departing at 9am.

Yùshù (Jyekundo)
玉树

☎0976 / POP 28,000

Up until the spring of 2010, Yùshù (Jyekundo is the name of the town itself while Yùshù is the prefecture) and its surrounding areas gained notoriety as one of Qīnghǎi's best new adventure-travel destinations. Yùshù, with its remote location and hardy Tibetan population, was dotted with dozens of impressive monasteries, famous pilgrim sites and gorgeous wooded valleys that cried out for exploration. All that changed on 14 April 2010, when a 7.1-magnitutude earthquake devastated the town, killing 2698 people (although some believe the true figure across the whole region to be more like 20,000).

After the earthquake most of Jyekundo's buildings were pulled down and an army of construction workers arrived to rebuild the city. Locals were housed in government-issued blue tents, giving the place the look and feel of a refugee camp (and a very dusty, noisy one at that). There are plenty of basic restaurants around but other facilities used by travellers – including hotels, banks and internet cafes – are in short supply.

Although the pace of rebuilding has been quick, we recommend travellers avoid Yùshù until the reconstruction phase is mostly complete; that could happen by around 2014 (but 2015 is a better bet if you are making travel plans). You should check the latest, either with hostels in Xīníng, or online through Lonely Planet's Thorn Tree forum (www.lonelyplanet.com/thorntree).

◎ Sights & Activities

Jyekundo
Dondrubling Monastery
MONASTERY

(Jiégǔ Sì) First built in 1398, the Jyekundo Dondrubling Monastery suffered heavy damage from the earthquake (the main prayer hall was completely destroyed and a number of resident monks were killed). At the time of research it was being rebuilt, albeit with concrete and other modern materials and probably won't be completed for a few more years. It's dramatically located in a ridge perched above town. You can walk here from town via the atmospheric **mani lhakhang** (chapel containing a large prayer wheel).

Central Square
SQUARE

(格萨广场; Gesa Guangchang) Yùshù's central square includes a large statue of King Gesar of Ling, a revered Tibetan warrior-god whose epic deeds are remembered in the world's longest epic poem of the same name. At the time of research the square was undergoing massive renovation and the statue had been taken down.

✿ Festivals & Events

Yùshù's spectacular three-day **horse festival** (25 to 28 July) has not been held since the earthquake, so double-check the latest before you make this part of your itinerary.

THE SOURCE OF THE YELLOW RIVER

For an adventurous side trip into remote Qīnghǎi, and a chance to experience some stunning, barren, high-plateau scenery, head towards **Zālíng Lake** (扎陵湖; Zālíng Hú), where it's possible to find the source of arguably China's most revered waterway, the Yellow River (黄河源头; Huánghé Yuántóu).

The scenery around the two lakes here, and en route, is awesome. Wildlife you may spot includes fox, marmot, eagle, antelope and, of course, plenty of yaks. There's nowhere to stay or eat, so most people visit the lake as a day trip from the two-street town of Mǎduō (玛多). It is possible to camp here in the summer but you'll need to be completely self-sufficient.

Remember this area, including Mǎduō (4260m), is over 4000m high so altitude sickness is a real risk. Consider coming from Yùshù (3680m) rather than Xīníng (2275m) so you don't have to ascend too much in one go.

In Mǎduō it's easy to find Landcruisers to take you to the lake and back (¥800 per vehicle; three hours one way). Just left of Mǎduō bus station is **Liángyóu Bīnguǎn** (粮油宾馆; ☎0975-834 5048; r ¥180-298; @) with clean, simple rooms and shared bathroom.

Note, the widely accepted source of the Yellow River, which is marked by an engraved stone tablet, is actually just the most accessible of a number of sources. Locals refer to it as *niutóubēi* (牛头碑). If you want to get to the very-hard-to-find true source of the Yellow River you'll need a two-day round trip from Mǎduō (sleeping in the 4WD) and it will cost around ¥3000 per vehicle, assuming you can find a driver willing to take you.

The bus back to Xīníng from Mǎduō leaves at 7.30am.

🛏 Sleeping & Eating

The earthquake wiped out most hotels in Yùshù and those that have sprung up since are mostly either temporary buildings or brothels (or both). The situation may well have improved by the time you read this and most taxi drivers will know the better places to stay. There are hundreds of restaurants around town, mostly housed in temporary tents.

Sān Jiāng Yuán International Hotel   HOTEL **$$**
(三江源国际大酒店; Sān Jiāng Yuán Guójì Dàjiǔdiàn; ☎189 0976 1988, 139 9736 8378; d without/with bathroom ¥180/240) A temporary building made of white metal siding, located on the outskirts of town on the way to Xīnzhài (新寨). Despite the impermanence of the place, rooms have TV and (cold) running water. The hotel has an attached restaurant.

ℹ Getting There & Away

Air

Yùshù Bātáng Airport is 25km south of town. There are two daily flights to Xīníng (¥1390), with continuing service to Xī'ān.

Bus

There is a temporary bus station 10km from Jyekundo, on the road past the village of Xīnzhài. Daily buses depart for Xīníng (¥206, six daily, 17 hours). You could stop at places along the way, such as Mǎduō (¥70). A second bus station has a daily bus for Chéngdū (¥450, 29 hours) departing at 9.30am and a daily bus to Shíqú (Sêrshu; ¥40) leaving at 8am; this station is about 1km past Xīnzhài village.

In addition to the temporary bus stands there are two minivan stands in town that handle long-distance routes. One is on the main road through town, just outside the new hospital. From here you can catch minivans to Nangchen (¥60, four to five hours) and Xīníng (¥230, 14 hours), both departing when full.

A second minivan stand has vehicles departing when full for Gānzī (¥180, 13 hours) and Kāngdìng (¥330, 20 hours), both in Sìchuān. To reach this minivan stand, walk north along the main road until you reach the T-intersection and turn right. The minivan stand is about 400m down this road.

Note that the bus stations are temporary and could change locations by the time you read this.

ℹ Getting Around

A local bus (¥1) trundles between Yùshù and Xīnzhài village but it only seems to move once or twice an hour. Shared minivans (¥10) travel from the bus station to the town centre, departing when full. Taxis are prevalent around town and fares start at ¥10, rising steeply if you head anywhere out of town. A taxi to the airport is ¥50.

Around Yùshù

SENG-ZE GYANAK MANI WALL 嘛尼石城

Just outside Yùshù, on the road to Xiēwǔ, is what is thought to be the world's largest *mani* wall, the Seng-ze Gyanak Mani (Mǎní Shíchéng). *Mani* walls are piles of stones with Buddhist mantras carved or painted on them. Founded in 1715, the Seng-ze Gyanak Mani is said to now consist of an estimated two billion mantras, piled one on top of the other over hundreds of square metres. It's an astonishing sight that grows more and more marvellous as you circumambulate the wall with the pilgrims, turn dozens of prayer wheels, and head into the pile itself for a moment of quiet reflection.

Seng-ze Gyanak Mani suffered heavy damage from the Yùshù earthquake and at the time of research reconstruction work was ongoing. Despite the work it's still a popular pilgrimage site and is worth a visit. The wall is 3km east of Yùshù in Xīnzhài village.

PRINCESS WENCHENG TEMPLE 文成公主庙

History credits the Tang dynasty Chinese Princess Wencheng as being instrumental in converting her husband and Tibetan king, Songtsen Gampo, to Buddhism in the 7th century. In a valley 20km south of Yùshù, a famous temple (Wénchéng Gōngzhǔ Miào) marks the spot where the princess (and possibly the king) paused for a month en route from Xī'ān to Lhasa.

The inner chapel has a rock carving of Vairocana (Nampa Namse in Tibetan), the Buddha of primordial wisdom, allegedly dating from the 8th century. To the left is a statue of King Songtsen Gampo.

The temple, which suffered minor damage from the Yùshù earthquake, is small, and few linger in it long, but allow time to explore the nearby hills. Here a sprawling spider's web of blue, red, yellow, white and pink prayer flags runs up the slopes, down the slopes and over the ravine, covering every inch of land, and is one of the most extraordinary sights imaginable.

A steep trail (a popular *kora* route for pilgrims) ascends from the end of the row of eight *chörtens* to the left of the temple. At the end of the trail head up the grassy side valley for some great hiking and stunning open views.

A taxi here from Yùshù costs about ¥60. It's just off the road to the airport so you could stop here on your way to catching a flight.

NANGCHEN 囊谦
📞 0976 / ELEV 3680M

The scenic county of Nangchen (Nángqiān), a former Tibetan kingdom, is the end of the line for most travellers. Further south of here is the Qīnghǎi–Tibet border, with roads to Riwoche and Chamdo, but any attempt to go here without the proper permits (and guide and driver) will land you in hot water.

⊙ Sights

Most visit just for the drive from Yùshù to the little county capital of Sharda (3550m). Four monasteries are scattered about town. The most recognisable is **Sajiya Gompa** (萨迦寺; Sàjiā Sì) perched on the hill above town like an old manor. You can hike even further up the hill behind the *gompa* for excellent views of the valley. In the town centre is **Jiaba Gompa** (加巴寺; Jiābā Sì) where Tibetans young and old appear each morning to turn prayer wheels and circumambulate the temple.

MONASTERIES AROUND YÙSHÙ

The road from Yùshù to Xiēwǔ is dotted with monasteries set among beautiful landscapes, perfect for hiking. Worth visiting is **Sebda Gompa** (赛巴寺; Sàibā Sì), about 15km from Yùshù. The main assembly hall at the monastery is impressive, but most surprising is the new chapel featuring a huge 18m statue of Guru Rinpoche, with smaller statues of his various manifestations on either side. The adjacent **ethnographic museum** (admission ¥10) has some offbeat gems like traditional clothing, swords and stuffed animals. If you have more time you can explore the ruins of the old monastery on the ridge behind the *gompa* or do some great hiking in the opposite valley.

At Xiēwǔ village, by the turn-off to Shíqú, is the Sakyapa-school **Drogon Gompa** (歇武寺; Xiēwǔ Sì). Atop the hill is the scary *gönkhang* (protector chapel), adorned with snarling stuffed wolves and Tantric masks. Only men may enter this chapel.

Minivans ply the route between Yùshù and Xiēwǔ from where you should be able to get onward transport to Shíqú.

For a good excursion from town, travel 70km south on a rough road to the stunning **Gar Gompa** (尕尔寺; Gǎ'ěr Sì), nestled on the ridge of a forested mountain. Wildlife is prevalent in the area, including blue sheep and monkeys. It's a popular spot for birdwatchers. A taxi from Sharda costs about ¥500 return.

🛏 Sleeping & Eating

Kāngbā Jiǔdiàn HOTEL $$
(康巴酒店; ☎187 0976 1333; Xingfu Lu; d without/with bathroom ¥180/288; ☎) Has a bright lobby and decent double rooms that usually get knocked down to ¥150/200. The shared bathrooms are wretched so consider a room with attached bathroom (but running water is sporadic in either case). A smattering of English is spoken and wi-fi is available in the lobby. Its sign says 'Khampa Teahouse and Restaurant'.

Náng Qiàn Bīnguǎn HOTEL $
(囊谦宾馆; ☎887 3333; Xingfu Lu; r ¥80) This is a grim place with tatty shared rooms that don't have a bathroom. There are some en suite doubles, but the owner was not letting them out when we visited.

Niǔ Ròu Miàn Dàwáng NOODLES $
(牛肉面大王; Xingfu Lu; dishes ¥10-20; ⊗8am-10pm) A popular place for noodles. Try the zhá jiàng miàn (炸酱面), a sort of spaghetti with meat sauce. It's a couple of doors down from Kāngbā Jiǔdiàn.

ℹ Information

Agricultural Bank of China (农业银行; Nóngyè Yínháng; Xingfu Lu) Near the main intersection but not all foreign cards work here, so don't count on getting cash if you're relying on ATMs.

Guide A useful local Tibetan guide in Sharda is English-speaking **Namdrak** (☎153 0976 1019; namdraktsaka@yahoo.com), who can organise trips to nearby sites and Gar Gompa.

Internet cafe Cafes (网吧; wǎngbā) are on Xingfu Lu, reached by walking through the alley next to a bank (opposite Kāngbā Jiǔdiàn). You can also use wi-fi at the Kāngbā Jiǔdiàn.

ℹ Getting There & Away

Bus & Taxi
From the bus station on the main road, one daily bus goes to Xīníng (¥264, 20 to 24 hours) departing at 10am. Book at least one day in advance.

For Yùshù (¥60, three to five hours) most locals travel by shared taxis, which assemble on the main road near the hotels. Major road construction was ongoing at the time of research.

Golmud

TRANSPORT HUB

For three decades **Golmud** (格尔木; Gé'ěrmù) had faithfully served overlanders as the last jumping-off point before Lhasa. Bedraggled backpackers hung around the city's truck depot trying to negotiate a lift to the 'Roof of the World'. But since the completion of the Qīnghǎi–Tibet railway, this lonesome backwater has become even less important as most Tibet travellers board the train elsewhere and blow right through town. Today it's mostly of use by travellers trying to get between Lhasa and Dūnhuáng (in Gānsù) or Huātǔgōu (en route to Xīnjiāng).

If you are stuck here for the night, try the centrally located **Dōngfāng Bīnguǎn** (东方宾馆; ☎0979-841 0011; r ¥178-218), which has clean but unremarkable standard rooms that come equipped with an ADSL cable for laptop carriers. Slightly pricier rooms come with computers.

Both Bayi Lu and Kunlun Lu are lined with restaurants. Around the train station you can find Muslim places dishing out gānbàn miàn (干拌面; spaghetti-style noodles with meat sauce; ¥6) or niúròu miàn (牛肉面; beef noodles; ¥5).

ℹ Getting There & Away

Note that if you are heading for Dūnhuáng you'll need a special permit (旅行证; lǚxíng zhèng; ¥50) when boarding the bus. Permits are available from the **Public Security Bureau** (PSB; 公安局; Gōng'ānjú; 6 Chaidamu Lu; ⊗8am-noon & 2.30-5pm Mon-Fri). The PSB can also extend visas. We've also heard reports that the PSB only allows tourists to stay one night in Golmud.

There are two daily buses to Dūnhuáng (¥102, seven to eight hours, 9am and 6pm) from the **main bus station** (☎0979-845 3688). The evening one is a sleeper. Likewise, there are two daily buses to Huātǔgōu (¥104, six hours, 10am and noon), the second again being a sleeper. From Huātǔgōu you can catch buses to Charklik (Ruòqiāng) in Xīnjiāng. Three buses depart for Xīníng (¥160, 12 to 14 hours, 4pm, 5pm and 7pm). There is also a sleeper bus to Charklik (Ruòqiāng) (¥224, 10 hours, 1pm).

Trains to Lhasa (¥368, 15 hours, seven daily) tend to pass through Golmud late in the evening or at night; you'll need your Tibet permit to be in order to board it. Other destinations include Xīníng (¥191, 10 hours, 10 daily) and Lánzhōu (¥242, 12 hours, six daily).

Tibet

POP 3 MILLION

Includes »

Lhasa 884
Around Lhasa 893
The Friendship
Highway 894
Western Tibet 902

Best Monasteries

» Drepung (p887)
» Ganden (p893)
» Samye (p894)
» Sakya (p898)

Best Views

» Everest's north face from Rongphu Monastery (p899)
» Nam-tso from Tashi Dor (p893)
» Yamdrok-tso from the Kamba-la (p894)
» Samye Monastery from Hepo Ri (p894)

Why Go?

For centuries Tibet has held the imagination of spiritual seekers, mountain adventurers and intrepid travellers. For today's travellers the 'roof of the world' continues to promise breathtaking high-altitude scenery, awe-inspiring monasteries, epic road trips and a unique Himalayan culture that remains vibrant after a half-century of assault and repression. As you travel around Tibet, meeting crimson-robed monks and wild-haired pilgrims, you'll quickly find that the colour, humour and religious devotion of the immensely likeable Tibetan people is as much of a highlight as the big sights.

Tibet is changing fast, with ambitious new construction and transport projects unveiled seemingly every month. Moreover, the political tensions of recent years have resulted in strict travel restrictions on foreigners throughout the autonomous region. Despite all this, the magic of old Tibet is still there – you just to have to work a bit harder to find it these days.

When to Go
Lhasa

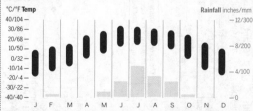

Mar This politically sensitive month brings closures and permit problems; avoid.

May–Sep High season: warm weather, some rain in July/August, and good hiking.

Apr & mid-Oct–Nov A good time to visit, with fewer crowds and warm days.

Tibet Highlights

1 Rub shoulders with Tibetan pilgrims in the holy city of **Lhasa** (p885)

2 Wonder at the murals of angels and demons in the 108 chapels of the

Gyantse Kumbum (p895), an architectural wonder

3 Erase the sins of a lifetime on the three-day pilgrim circuit around sacred **Mt Kailash** (p903)

4 Rouse yourself from a yak-wool tent or monastery guesthouse to catch first light at **Everest Base Camp** (p899)

5 Ride the planet's highest rails across the roof of the

world on the **Qīnghǎi–Tibet Railway** (p893) to Lhasa

6 Explore the mandala-shaped chapels and stupas at **Samye Monastery** (p894), Tibet's first monastery

7 Hire a vehicle for the week-long trip along the **Friendship Highway** (p894) from Lhasa to Kathmandu, one of Asia's great road trips

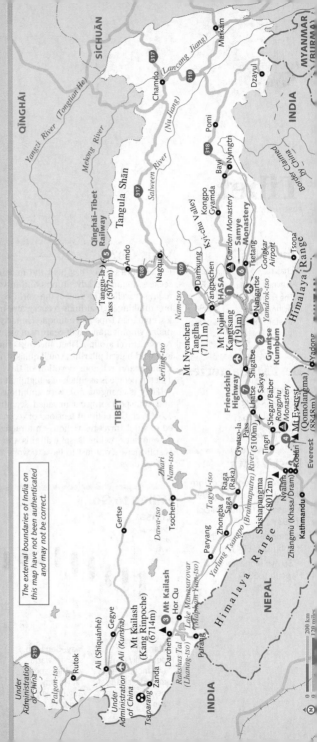

The external boundaries of India on this map have not been authenticated and may not be correct.

History

Recorded Tibetan history began in the 7th century AD, when the Tibetan armies began to assemble a great empire. Under King Songtsen Gampo, the Tibetans occupied Nepal and collected tribute from parts of Yúnnán. Shortly afterwards the Tibetan armies moved north and took control of the Silk Road and the great trade centre of Kashgar, even sacking the imperial Chinese city of Cháng'ān (present-day Xī'ān).

Tibetan expansion came to an abrupt halt in 842 with the assassination of anti-Buddhist King Langdarma; the region subsequently broke into independent feuding principalities. The increasing influence of Buddhism ensured that the Tibetan armies would never again leave their high plateau.

By the 7th century, Buddhism had spread through Tibet, though it had taken on a unique form, as it adopted many of the rituals of Bön (the indigenous pre-Buddhist belief system of Tibet). The prayer flags, pilgrimage circuits and sacred landscapes you'll see across modern Tibet all have their roots in the Bön religion.

From the 13th century, power politics began to play an increasing role in religion. In 1641 the Gelugpa ('Yellow Hat' order) used the support of Mongol troops to crush the Sakyapa, their rivals. It was also during this time of partisan struggle that the Gelugpa leader adopted the title of Dalai Lama (Ocean of Wisdom), given to him by the Mongols. From here on out, religion and politics in Tibet became inextricably entwined and both were presided over by the Dalai Lama.

With the fall of the Qing dynasty in 1911, Tibet entered a period of de facto independence that was to last until 1950. In this year a resurgent communist China invaded Tibet, claiming it was 'liberating' over one million Tibetans from feudal serfdom and bringing it back into the fold of the motherland.

Increasing popular unrest in response to Chinese land reform resulted in a full-blown revolt in 1959, which was crushed by the People's Liberation Army (PLA). Amid popular rumours of a Chinese plot to kidnap him, the Dalai Lama fled to India. He was followed by an exodus of 80,000 of Tibet's best and brightest, who now represent the Tibetan government-in-exile from Dharamsala, India.

The Dalai Lama, who has referred to China's policies on migration as 'cultural genocide', is resigned to pushing for autonomy rather than independence, though

PRICE INDICATORS

The following price indicators are used in this chapter:

Sleeping

$	less than ¥180
$$	¥180 to ¥400
$$$	more than ¥400

Eating

$	less than ¥30
$$	¥30 to ¥80
$$$	more than ¥80

even that concession has borne little fruit. The Chinese for their part seem to be waiting for him to die, positioning themselves to control the future politics of reincarnation. The Dalai Lama's tireless insistence on a non-violent solution to the Tibet problem led to him winning the Nobel Peace Prize in 1989, but despite global sympathy for the Tibetan cause, few nations are willing to raise the issue and place new business deals with China's rising economic superpower at risk.

The Chinese are truly baffled by what they perceive as the continuing ingratitude of the Tibetans. They claim that Tibet pre-1950 was a place of abject poverty and feudal exploitation. China, they say, has brought roads, schools, hospitals, airports, factories and rising incomes.

Many Tibetans, however, cannot forgive the destruction in the 1950s and 1960s of hundreds of monasteries and shrines, the restrictions on religious expression, the continued heavy military presence, economic exploitation and their obvious second-class status within their own land. Riots and protests in the spring of 2008 brought this simmering dissatisfaction out into the open, as Lhasa erupted into full-scale riots and protests spread to other Tibetan areas in Gānsù, Sìchuān and Qīnghǎi provinces. The Chinese response was predictable: arrest, imprisonment and an increased police presence in many monasteries. The increasing desperation felt by many Tibetans has led to a spate of self-immolations by Tibetans across the region, including two in Lhasa's Barkhor Circuit in 2012. At the time of writing, riot police armed with fire extinguishers patrolled much of Lhasa's old town.

TIBET

As immigration and breakneck modernisation continue, the government is gambling that economic advances will diffuse the Tibetans' religious and political aspirations. It's a policy that has so far been successful in the rest of China. Whether it will work in Tibet remains to be seen.

Climate

Most of Tibet is a high-altitude desert plateau at more than 4000m. Days in summer (June to September) are warm, sunny and generally dry but temperatures drop quickly after dark. It's always cool above 4000m and often freezing at night, though thanks to the Himalayan rain shadow there is surprisingly little snow in the 'Land of Snows'. Sunlight is very strong at these altitudes, so bring plenty of high-factor sunscreen and lip balm.

Language

Most urban Tibetans speak Mandarin in addition to Tibetan. Even in the countryside you can get by with basic Mandarin in most restaurants and hotels, since they are normally run by Mandarin-speaking Han or Hui Chinese. That said, Tibetans are extremely pleased when foreign visitors at least greet them in Tibetan, so it's well worth learning a few phrases (see p1023).

❶ Getting There & Away

NEPAL ROUTE The 865km road connecting Lhasa with Kathmandu is known as the Friendship Hwy. Currently the only means of transport for foreigners is a rented vehicle.

When travelling from Nepal to Lhasa, foreigners generally arrange transport and permits through agencies in Kathmandu. Be careful with whom you organise your trip – the vast majority of complaints about Tibet that we receive have been about budget trips from Kathmandu. The most common option is a seven-day overland budget tour, which runs two or three times a week and costs from US$350, plus visa fees and return flight costs (around US$400). There are also fly-in, fly-out options, with Kathmandu–Lhasa flights operating four times a week.

Regardless of what the agency says, you will probably end up with travellers from other companies. Accommodation en route is pretty simple. Most agencies advertising in Thamel are agents only; they don't actually run the trips and so will probably just shrug if there's a complaint. Better agencies in Kathmandu include the following:

Ecotrek (☑01-4424112; www.ecotrek.com.np, www.ecotreknepal.com; Thamel)

Explore Nepal Richa Tours & Travel (☑01-4423064; 2nd fl, Namche Bazaar Bldg, Tri Devi Marg, Thamel)

Green Hill Tours (☑01-4700803; Thamel)

Royal Mount Trekking (☑01-4241452; www.royaltibet.com; Durbar Marg)

Tashi Delek Nepal Treks & Expeditions (☑01-4410746; www.tashidelektreks.com.np; Thamel)

Whatever you do, when coming from Nepal do *not* underestimate the sudden rise in elevation; altitude sickness is very common. It is especially not recommended to visit Everest Base Camp within a few days of leaving Kathmandu. Heading to Nepal, you will arrange 4WD hire as part of your Tibet tour.

QĪNGHǍI ROUTE Now that the railway connects Lhasa with Qīnghǎi, there is no reason to suffer the long ride on the sleeper bus from Golmud. Bear in mind that it is much harder to get train tickets *to* Lhasa than *from* Lhasa, so flying in and taking a train out makes sense.

OTHER ROUTES Between Lhasa and Sìchuān, Yúnnán and Xīnjiāng provinces are some of the wildest, highest and most remote routes in the world. It's generally possible to enter and leave Tibet via these routes if you are travelling with an expensive organised tour and have the proper permits. In 2012 permits were impossible to obtain for overland routes through eastern Tibet, but these may reopen soon.

❶ Getting Around

These days almost all foreigners travel around Tibet in a rented 4WD. Public buses outside Lhasa are off limits for foreigners, and bus stations generally won't sell you a ticket.

As for cycling – it's possible, but currently expensive, as you still need a guide and transport, even if you're not travelling in it! For experienced cyclists, the Lhasa–Kathmandu trip is one of the world's great rides.

Lhasa ल्हासा 拉萨

☑089 / POP 400,000 / ELEV 3650M

Lhasa is the traditional, political and spiritual centre of the Tibetan world. Despite rampant Chinese-led modernisation, Tibet's premodern and sacred heritage survives in the form of the grand Potala Palace (former seat of the Dalai Lama); the ancient Jokhang Temple (Tibet's first and most holy); the great monastic towns of Sera, Drepung and Ganden; and the city's countless other smaller temples, hermitages, caves, sacred rocks, pilgrim paths and prayer-flag–bedecked hilltops.

Lhasa is a comfortable travellers' destination these days. There are dozens of good budget and midrange hotels and no shortage of excellent inexpensive restaurants.

Lhasa

English is not widely spoken, but you'll have no trouble in the more popular hotels, restaurants, cafes and travel agencies. Lhasa is also currently the only place in Tibet where you have a certain freedom to explore without your guide, plus it's cheaper here than the rest of Tibet because you don't need to hire transport.

Lhasa divides clearly into a sprawling Chinese section to the west and a much smaller but infinitely more interesting Tibetan old town in the east, centred on the wonderful Barkhor area. The latter is easily the best place to be based, though at the time of research the oppressive military patrols, riot squads and undercover police in the Barkhor region gave the old town a darker than normal atmosphere.

☉ Sights & Activities

In addition to the main sights and activities listed here, Lhasa's old town is well worth exploring for its backstreet temples, craft shops and interesting Muslim neighbourhood.

TOP CHOICE Barkhor PILGRIM CIRCUIT
(བར་སྐོར་; 八廓; Bākuò; Map p887) It's impossible not to be swept up in the wondrous tide of humanity that is the Barkhor, a *kora* (pilgrim circuit) that winds clockwise around the Jokhang Temple. You'll swear it possesses some spiritual centrifugal force, as every time you approach within 50m, you somehow get sucked right in and gladly wind up making the whole circuit again! The crowd of pilgrims is captivating. Braided-haired Khambas from eastern Tibet swagger in huge *chubas* (cloaks) with

ornate daggers; and Amdowa nomads from the northeast wear ragged sheepskins or, for women, incredibly ornate braids and coral headpieces. It's the perfect place to start your explorations of Lhasa, and the last spot you'll want to see before you bid the city farewell.

There are a couple of small temples that are worth exploring just off the circuit. From the northern side follow the alley south to the **Meru Nyingba Monastery**, a charming place that is normally packed with pilgrims. On the way back to the circuit pop into the orange-walled **Jampa Lhakhang** with its huge, two-storey statue of Maitreya (Jampa in Tibetan).

Lhasa

☉ Top Sights
Barkhor D2
Norbulingka A2
Potala Palace C2

☉ Sights
1 Chagpo Ri Rock Carvings B2
2 Potala South Entrance C2
3 Potala Ticket Booking Office C2
4 Tibet Museum A2

ℹ Information
5 Nepali Consulate-General A2
6 Norbulingka Ticket Office A2

ℹ Transport
7 CAAC C2
8 City Train Ticket Office B2
9 Western (Main) Bus Station A2

TOP CHOICE Jokhang Temple TEMPLE

(ཇོ་ཁང; 大昭寺; Dàzhāo Sì; Map p887; admission ¥85; ⊙9am-1pm, 2-6pm) The 1300-year-old Jokhang Temple is the spiritual heart of Tibet: the continuous movement of awestruck pilgrims prostrating themselves outside are testament to its timeless allure.

The Jokhang was originally built to house an image of Buddha brought to Tibet by King Songtsen Gampo's Nepalese wife. However, another image, the Jowa Sakyamuni, was later moved here by the king's other wife (the Chinese Princess Wencheng), and it is this image that gives the Jokhang both its name and spiritual potency: Jokhang means 'chapel of the Jowo' and the central golden Buddha here is the most revered in all of Tibet.

The two-storeyed Jokhang is definitely best visited in the morning, though the crowds of yak-butter-spooning pilgrims can be thick. Access is possible in the afternoon but the upper-floor chapels are shut and there are no pilgrims.

TOP CHOICE Potala Palace PALACE

(པོ་ཏ་ལ; 布达拉宫; Bùdálā Gōng; Map p885; admission May-Oct ¥200, Nov-Apr ¥100; ⊙9.30am-3pm before 1 May, 9am-3.30pm after 1 May, interior chapels close 4.30pm) The magnificent Potala Palace, once the seat of the Tibetan government and the winter residence of the Dalai Lamas, is Lhasa's cardinal landmark. Your first sight of its towering, maroon and white fortress-like walls is a moment you'll remember for a long time.

An architectural wonder even by modern standards, the palace rises 13 storeys from 130m-high Marpo Ri (Red Hill) and contains more than a thousand rooms. Pilgrims and tourists alike shuffle down through the three storeys, trying to take in the thousands of statues and stupas in the magnificent chapels and prayer halls.

The first recorded use of the site dates from the 7th century AD, when King Songtsen Gampo built a palace here. Construction of the present structure began during the reign of the fifth Dalai Lama in 1645 and took divisions of labourers and artisans more than 50 years to complete. It is impressive enough to have caused Zhou Enlai to send his own troops to protect it from the Red Guards during the Cultural Revolution.

The layout of the Potala Palace includes the rooftop **White Palace** (the eastern part of the building), used for the living quarters of the Dalai Lama, and the central **Red Palace**, used for religious functions. The most stunning chapels of the Red Palace house the jewel-bedecked golden *chörten* (Tibetan stupa) tombs of several previous Dalai Lamas. The apartments of the 13th and 14th Dalai Lamas, in the White Palace, offer a more personal insight into life in the palace. Grand aesthetics and history aside, however, one can't help noticing that today it is essentially an empty shell, notably missing its main occupant, the Dalai Lama, and a cavernous memorial to what once was.

Tickets for the Potala are limited. The day before you wish to visit, your guide will take your passport and reserve a time slot for the next day. The next day, be at the south entrance 30 minutes before the time on the voucher (tour groups use the southeast entrance).

After a security check, follow the other visitors to the stairs up into the palace. Halfway up you'll pass the actual ticket booth. Note that if you arrive later than the time on your voucher (or if you forget your voucher) you can be refused a ticket. Photography isn't allowed inside the chapels. After exiting the Potala on the north side you can walk part of the Potala *kora*.

Sera Monastery MONASTERY

(སེ་ར་དགོན; 色拉寺; Sèlā Sì; admission ¥55; ⊙9am-5pm) About 5km north of central Lhasa, this monastery was founded in 1419 by a disciple of Tsongkhapa and was, along with Drepung Monastery, one of Lhasa's two great Gelugpa monasteries.

About 600 monks are now in residence, well down from an original population of around 5000. The half-dozen main colleges feature spectacular prayer halls and chapels, though many were under renovation in 2012. Equally interesting is the monk debating that takes place from 3.30pm to 5pm in a garden next to the assembly hall in the centre of the monastery (not Sunday). As at Drepung, there's a fine hour-long *kora* path around the exterior of the monastery.

A taxi to Sera costs ¥10 from the old town, or it's a 30-minute bicycle ride from central Lhasa. There is a ¥15 to ¥30 fee per chapel for photography, and it's ¥850 for video.

From Sera Monastery it's possible to take a taxi or walk northwest for another hour to little-visited **Pabonka Monastery**. Built in the 7th century by King Songtsen Gampo, this is one of the most ancient Buddhist sites in the Lhasa region.

Barkhor Area

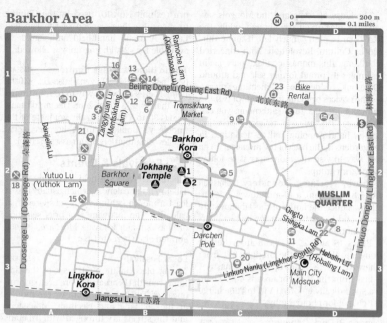

Barkhor Area

◎ Top Sights

Barkhor Kora...................................B2
Jokhang Temple..............................B2
Lingkhor Kora.................................A3

◎ Sights

1 Jampa Lhakhang B2
2 Meru Nyingba Monastery B2

◉ Activities, Courses & Tours

3 Tenzin Blind Massage Centre.........A1

⬡ Sleeping

4 Banak Shol Hotel D1
5 Barkhor Namchen House C2
6 Dhood Gu Hotel............................B1
7 Gorkha Hotel B3
8 Heritage Hotel D3
9 House of Shambhala......................C1
10 Kyichu Hotel A1
11 Rama Kharpo................................D3

12 Yabshi Phunkhang B1
13 Yak Hotel B1

⊗ Eating

14 Dunya Restaurant B1
15 New Mandala Restaurant...............A2
16 Pentoc Tibetan Restaurant............B1
17 Tashi I...B1
18 Tibet Steak House........................A2
19 Woeser Zedroe Tibetan
    Restaurant..................................A2

◎ Drinking

20 Ani Sangkhung Nunnery
    Teahouse....................................C3
   Dunya Bar.........................(see 14)
21 Summit Café A2

⬡ Shopping

22 Dropenling...................................D3
23 Outlook Outdoor Equipment C1

Drepung Monastery   MONASTERY
(འབྲས་སྤུངས་; 哲蚌寺; Zhébàng Sì; admission ¥50;
☉9.30am-5.30pm) A 1½-hour-long *kora* around
this 15th-century monastery, 8km west of the
old town, is among the highlights of Tibet.
Along with Sera and Ganden monasteries,

Drepung functioned as one of the three 'pillars of the Tibetan state' and was purportedly the largest monastery in the world, with around 7000 resident monks at its peak. Drepung means 'rice heap', a reference to the white buildings dotting the hillside.

The kings of Tsang and the Mongols savaged the place regularly, though, oddly, the Red Guards pretty much left it alone during the Cultural Revolution. With concerted rebuilding, this monastic village once again resembles its proud former self and around 600 monks reside here. At lunchtime you can see the novices bringing in buckets of *tsampa* and yak-butter tea. In the afternoons you can often see Tibetan-style religious debating (lots of hand slapping and gesticulating) in the gardens at the back of the monastery. The best way to visit the monastery is to follow the pilgrim groups.

Nearby **Nechung Monastery** (admission ¥10; ☺8.30am-5pm), a 10-minute walk downhill, was once the home of the Tibetan state oracle and is worth a visit for its bloodcurdling murals.

Buses 18 and 25 (¥2) run from Beijing Donglu to the foot of the Drepung hill, from where a coach (¥1) runs up to the monastery. A taxi from the Barkhor area is ¥30. There is a sporadically enforced ¥10 to ¥20 charge per chapel for photography.

Chagpo Ri Rock Carvings   HISTORIC SITE
(Map p885; Deji Zhonglu; admission ¥10; ☺dawn-dusk) Throughout the day pilgrims prostrate themselves in front of this splinter of rock and its hundreds of painted rock carvings, some 1000 years old. Nearby are several stone carvers who have built a huge *chörten* from *mani* (prayer) stones carved onsite. The little-known site is well worth a visit. The carvings are on the southern flank of Chagpo Ri, southwest of the Potala.

Norbulingka   PALACE
(ནོར་བུ་གླིང་ཀ; 罗布林卡; Luóbùlínkǎ; Map p885; Minzu Lu; admission ¥60; ☺9am-6pm) About 3km west of the Potala Palace is the Norbulingka, the former summer residence of the Dalai Lama. The pleasant park contains several palaces and chapels, the highlight of which is the **New Summer Palace** (Takten Migyü Podrang), built by the current (14th) Dalai Lama. It's debatable whether it's worth the entry fee.

FREE Tibet Museum   MUSEUM
(འབྲོག་མཚོ་ལྟར; 西藏博物馆; Xīzàng Bó-wùguǎn; Map p885; Minzu Nanlu; ☺10am-5.30pm Tue-Sun) This museum has some interesting displays, if you can filter out the Chinese propaganda. The multiple halls cover everything from weapons to musical instruments, featuring some fine ancient *thangkas* (Tibetan sacred paintings). Look for the 18th-century golden

urn (exhibit No 310) used by the Chinese to recognise their version of the Panchen Lama. A useful hand-held audio guide is available for ¥20. Photography is allowed.

Tenzin Blind Massage Centre   MASSAGE
(Map p887; ☑634 7591; Zangyiyuan Lu; ☺10am-11pm) There's no better way to recover from a trip than with a Chinese or Tibetan oil massage (¥80 to ¥100) from the graduate of the impressive Braille Without Borders (www.braillewithoutborders.org) massage school.

✹✹ Festivals & Events

Tibetan festivals are held according to the Tibetan lunar calendar, which usually lags at least a month behind the West's Gregorian calendar. The following is a brief selection of Lhasa's major festivals. Most are also celebrated elsewhere in Tibet.

Losar Festival   RELIGIOUS
Taking place in the first week of the first lunar month (February), there are performances of Tibetan opera, prayer ceremonies at the Jokhang and Nechung Monastery, and the streets are thronged with Tibetans dressed in their finest.

Saga Dawa   RELIGIOUS
The 15th day (full moon) of the fourth lunar month (May/June) sees huge numbers of pilgrims walking the Lingkhor pilgrim circuit.

Worship of the Buddha   RELIGIOUS
During the second week of the fifth lunar month (June), the parks of Lhasa, in particular the Norbulingka, are crowded with picnickers.

Drepung Festival   RELIGIOUS
The 30th day of the sixth lunar month (July) is celebrated with the hanging at dawn of a huge *thangka* at Drepung Monastery. Lamas and monks perform opera in the main courtyard.

Shötun Festival   RELIGIOUS
The first week of the seventh lunar month (August) sees the unveiling of a giant *thangka* at Drepung Monastery, then moves down to Sera and down to the Norbulingka for performances of *lhamo* (Tibetan opera) and some epic picnics.

Palden Lhamo   RELIGIOUS
The 15th day of the 10th lunar month (being November) has a procession around the Barkhor circuit bearing Palden Lhamo, protective deity of the Jokhang Temple.

Tsongkhapa Festival
RELIGIOUS

Much respect is shown to Tsongkhapa, the founder of the Gelugpa order, on the anniversary of his death on the 25th day of the lunar month during December. Check for processions and monk dances at the monasteries at Ganden, Sera and Drepung.

🛏 Sleeping

Lhasa has a good range of accommodation for all budgets. Rates depend on visitor numbers but generally peak in July and August, with discounts of at least 20% at other times. A cluster of top-end hotels are planned to open in Lhasa in the coming years, including Intercontinental and Shangri-La properties.

TOP CHOICE Kyichu Hotel
HOTEL $$

(吉曲饭店; Jíqǔ Fàndiàn; Map p887; ☑633 1541; www.kyichuhotel.com; 149/18 Beijing Donglu; r standard/deluxe from ¥380/500; ❋@🖘) The Kyichu is a well-run place that's popular with repeat travellers to Tibet. Rooms are modern and pleasant, with Tibetan carpets, but the real selling points are the excellent service and peaceful garden courtyard (with wi-fi and espresso coffee). The garden-view rooms at the back are the quietest. Reservations are essential and discounts are available in winter. Credit cards accepted.

Yak Hotel
HOTEL $$

(亚宾馆; Yà Bīnguǎn; Map p887; ☑630 0008; 100 Beijing Donglu; dm ¥50, d ¥450-650, r VIP ¥880; ❋@🖘) Once a backpacker favourite, the Yak is still one of Lhasa's most popular hotels, but it's now firmly midrange and most popular with French and Dutch tour groups. Best value are the Tibetan-style back-block rooms, normally discounted to ¥300. The deluxe rooms overlooking the street are larger but noisier. Reservations are recommended. The included rooftop breakfast is excellent.

Rama Kharpo
HOTEL $

(热玛嘎布宾馆; Rèmǎ Gâbù Bīnguǎn; Map p887; ☑634 6963; www.lhasabarkhor.com; 5 Ongto Shingka Lam; dm ¥40-50, d/tr ¥160/220; ❋🖘) This easily missed place is in the old town near the Muslim quarter. Both dorm and en suite rooms are comfortable and the dark, but pleasant cafe is a sociable meeting place, serving beer and simple food. Breakfast is included in rates. It's a popular budget option.

Banak Shol
HOTEL $

(八郎学宾馆; Bālángxué Bīnguǎn; Map p887; ☑632 3829; 8 Beijing Donglu; dm ¥50, d ¥120-150) Re-

DON'T MISS

LHASA'S PILGRIM CIRCUITS

Lhasa's four main *koras* (pilgrim circuits) are well worth walking, especially during the Saga Dawa festival, when the distinction between tourist and pilgrim can become very fine. Remember always to proceed clockwise.

» **Nangkhor** Encircles the inner precincts of the Jokhang.

» **Barkhor** Traces the outskirts of the Jokhang.

» **Lingkhor** You can join the 8km-long circuit anywhere, but the most interesting section is from the southeastern old town to the Potala Palace.

» **Potala Kora (Tsekhor)** An almost continuous circuit of prayer wheels, *chörtens* (Tibetan stupas), rock paintings and chapels encircles the Potala Palace. Stop for sweet tea en route at the charming teahouse by the three white *chörtens* on the northwest corner.

vamped in 2012, this Lhasa old-timer is once again a good budget option. The clean, fresh and spacious carpeted dorms with two to five beds are great value (the unrenovated rooms are less pleasant) and the new shower block is sparkling clean. The knackered ensuite rooms were awaiting renovation in 2013.

Dhood Gu Hotel
HOTEL $$

(敦固宾馆; Dūngù Bīnguǎn; Map p887; ☑632 2555; www.dhodgu-hotel.com; 19 Shasarsu Lu; 冲赛康夏莎苏19号; s/d/ste incl breakfast ¥450/530/650; @🖘) Staff are a little cool at this three-star Nepalese-run hotel, but the old-quarter location and ornate Tibetan-style decor are great, even if rooms are a little small. Rates (with breakfast) are overpriced without the standard discount of 25%. Head to the rooftop bar for Potala views.

House of Shambhala
BOUTIQUE HOTEL $$$

(香巴拉府; Xiāngbālā Fǔ; Map p887; ☑632 6533; www.shambhalaserai.com; 7 Jiri Erxiang; 吉日二巷 7号; d incl breakfast ¥675-900; @🖘) It can take a bit of hunting to locate Lhasa's first boutique hotel, but once you see the mustard-coloured exterior and impressive wooden doors in the old town, you'll know you're there. The hotel's 10 rooms sport a funky Tibetan design, with liberal use of wood, stone and antique furnishings; upper-floor rooms

VISITING MONASTERIES & TEMPLES

Most monasteries and temples extend a warm welcome to foreign guests. Please maintain this good faith by observing the following courtesies:

» Always circumambulate monasteries, chapels and other religious objects clockwise, thus keeping shrines and *chörtens* (Tibetan stupas) to your right.

» Don't touch or remove anything on an altar and don't take prayer flags or *mani* (prayer) stones.

» Don't take photos during a prayer meeting. At other times always ask permission to take a photo, especially when using a flash. The larger monasteries charge photography fees, though some monks will allow you to take a quick photo for free. If they won't, there's no point getting angry – you don't know what pressures they may be under.

» Don't wear shorts or short skirts in a monastery, and take your hat off when you go into a chapel.

» Don't smoke in a monastery.

» If you have a guide, try to ensure that he or she is Tibetan, as Chinese guides invariably know little about Tibetan Buddhism or monastery history.

» Be aware that women are generally not allowed in protector chapels (*gönkhang*).

are best. From the fabulous rooftop terrace the views over the old quarter can really take you back in time. A 16-room annexe, the **Shambhala Palace**, is hidden deeper in the old town and is cheaper, with rooms from ¥350 to ¥500.

Barkhor Namchen House GUESTHOUSE $
(八廓龙乾家庭旅馆; Bākuò Lóngqián Jiātíng Lǚguǎn; Map p887; ☑679 0125; www.tibetnam chen.com; dm/d ¥35/85; @☎) This small backstreet Tibetan-style guesthouse is a good budget choice. The old-town location is near perfect, the staff are friendly, and the Asian-style bathrooms and communal hot showers are clean enough. Rooms are fairly small and some have limited natural light (ask for an upper-floor room), but you can head to the good rooftop sitting room for fine views.

Gorkha Hotel HOTEL $$
(郭尔喀饭店; Guò'ěrkā Fàndiàn; Map p887; ☑627 1992; 45 Linkuo Nanlu; 林廓南路45号; r/ste ¥380/450; @) This atmospheric Nepali–Tibetan venture housed the Nepali consulate in the 1950s and still boasts traditional architecture. Rooms vary, so look at a few (the suites are perfect for families). It's in the south of the old town, near several lovely old temples. It's somewhat overpriced.

Heritage Hotel HOTEL $$
(古艺酒店; Gǔyì Jiǔdiàn; Map p887; ☑691 1333; 11 Chaktsalgang Lu; d ¥300-360; ✳☎) Nice, stylish rooms in the old town, with helpful staff and a good Nepali restaurant onsite.

✗ Eating

The staple diet in Tibet is *tsampa* (porridge of roasted barley flour) and *bö cha* (yak-butter tea). Tibetans mix the two in their hands to create doughlike balls. *Momos* (dumplings filled with vegetables or yak meat) and *thugpa* (noodles with meat) are also local comfort food. Variations include *thanthuk* (fried noodle squares) as well as *shemdre* (rice, potato and yak-meat curry). For a Chinese–Tibetan menu reader, see p734.

Lhasa is filled with restaurants serving a range of excellent Nepalese, Chinese, Tibetan and Western dishes. Unless noted otherwise, the places listed here are open for breakfast, lunch and dinner.

 New Mandala Restaurant NEPALI $$
(新满斋餐厅; Xīnmǎnzhāi Cāntīng; Map p887; Zangyiyuan Lu; dishes ¥20-35; ⊘) The Nepali set meals here are excellent and the rooftop is a great place to savour the views of the Barkhor over a cold Lhasa Beer. The menu is the standard mix of Western, Nepali and Chinese food.

Tashi I INTERNATIONAL $
(Map p887; cnr Zangyiyuan Lu & Beijing Donglu; dishes ¥10-25; ⊘8am-10pm; ⊘) This old standard feels like a slice of old Tibet and is a mellow place to hang out. The newly revamped menu is strong on breakfasts and vegetable dishes. Try the *bobi* (chapattilike unleavened bread), which comes with seasoned cream cheese and fried vegetables or meat.

Tibet Steak House INTERNATIONAL $$

(西藏牛排餐厅; Xīzàng Niúpái Cāntīng; Map p887; Yuthok Lu; dishes ¥15-45; ☺8am-10pm; ☺) This well-run restaurant serves a mix of excellent Continental and Nepali food in modern and fresh surroundings. The Indian dishes are particularly good (we recommend the chicken butter masala). It's run by the old Snowlands Restaurant, long a Lhasa favourite, which is planning a new restaurant on Zangyiyuan Lu.

Woeser Zedroe
Tibetan Restaurant TIBETAN $

(光明泽缀藏餐馆; Guāngmíng Zézhuì Zàngcānguǎn; Map p887; Zangyiyuan Lu; mains ¥10-30; ☺lunch & dinner; ☺) This is where visiting and local Tibetans come to fill up after a visit to the Jokhang. Add some pleasant traditional seating and a perfect location to the Tibetan vibe and it's a logical lunch stop. The *momos* are recommended, especially the fried yak meat or cheese varieties.

Pentoc Tibetan Restaurant TIBETAN $

(Map p887; dishes ¥10-20; ☺) For something authentically Tibetan, charming English-speaking Pentoc runs this local teahouse restaurant. It's a good place to try homemade Tibetan standards, such as *momos, thugpa, shemdre* (rice, potato and yak meat), plus butter tea and *chang* (barley beer). It's 20m down an alleyway off Beijing Donglu, on the left.

Dunya INTERNATIONAL $$

(Map p887; ☎633 3374; www.dunyarestaurant.com; 100 Beijing Donglu; dishes ¥45-65; ☺) With its classy decor, wide-ranging dishes and interesting Indonesian-inspired specials, this foreign-run eatery is popular with travellers who need something reassuringly familiar. Sandwiches, yak burgers and pizzas are all good.

Drinking

Tibetans consume large quantities of *chang* (a tangy alcoholic drink derived from fermented barley) and *bö cha*. The other major beverage is *cha ngamo* (sweet milky tea). Hole-in-the-wall Tibetan teahouses can be found all over the old town.

TOP CHOICE Ani Sangkhung
Nunnery Teahouse TEAHOUSE

(Map p887; 29 Linkuo Nanlu; tea ¥2-8; ☺8am-5pm) If you're exploring the old town and need a break, make a beeline for this bustling teahouse in the courtyard of Lhasa's most important (and most politically active) nunnery. The location and atmosphere are superb.

Summit Café CAFE

(顶峰咖啡店; Dǐngfēng Kāfēidiàn; Map p887; coffee ¥17-27; ☺7.30am-10pm; @☺☺) Off Zangyiyuan Lu, the courtyard of the Shangbala Hotel is the place to head for Lhasa's best espresso hit. There's cosy seating, wi-fi, excellent coffee and great desserts.

Dunya Bar BAR

(Map p887; www.dunyarestaurant.com; 100 Beijing Donglu; bottled beers ¥15; ☺noon-midnight; ☺) This classy bar above the restaurant of the same name has a balcony and screens sports events.

Shopping

Whether it's prayer wheels, *thangkas*, sunhats or imported muesli, you shouldn't have a problem finding it in Lhasa. The Barkhor circuit is especially good for buying spiritual souvenirs and pilgrim accessories, with stalls selling prayer flags, amulets, turquoise jewellery, Tibetan boots, cowboy hats, yak butter and juniper incense. Most of this stuff is massproduced in Nepal. Haggle, haggle, haggle.

Dropenling HANDICRAFTS

(Map p887; ☎633 0898; www.tibetcraft.com; 11 Chaktsalgang Lu; ☺10am-7pm) Wander through the Tibetan old town to this excellent shop established to bolster local handicrafts in the face of Nepali and Chinese imports. Quality and prices are top end. The shop is a little hard to find, but as you get nearer you'll see signs pointing the way. You can watch local craftspeople at work in the courtyard or take a two-hour walking tour (¥30) of old-town craft workshops. A branch showroom is due to open at the entrance to Barkhor Square.

Outlook
Outdoor Equipment OUTDOOR EQUIPMENT

(Kàn Fēngyún Biànhuàn Yuǎnjìng; Map p887; ☎634 5589; 11 Beijing Donglu) The best of many local shops selling Chinese-made Gore-Tex jackets, fleeces, sleeping bags, stoves, tents and mats, and it also rents out equipment.

Information
Embassies

Nepalese Consulate-General (尼泊尔领事馆; Níbó'ěr Lǐngshìguǎn; Map p885; ☎0891-681 3965; www.nepalembassy.org.cn; 13 Luobulingka Beilu; ☺10am-noon Mon-Fri) Issues visas in 24 hours. The current fee for a 15-/30-/90-day visa is ¥175/280/700. Bring a visa photo. Chinese tourists have to get their visas here; foreigners will find it easier to obtain visas on the spot at Kodari, the Nepalese border town.

Internet Access

The Summit Café, and Rama Kharpo and Kyichu hotels offer the most convenient free wi-fi for patrons. A couple of internet cafes operate on Beijing Donglu near the Banak Shol hotel.

Medical Services

120 Emergency Centre (急救中心; Jíjiù Zhōngxīn; Map p885; ✆633 2462; 16 Lingkhor Beilu) Part of People's Hospital. Consultations cost around ¥150.

Military Hospital (西藏军区总医院; Xīzàng Jūnqū Zǒngyīyuàn; ✆625 3120; Niangre Beilu) Best for emergency surgery.

Money

Bank of China (中国银行; Zhōngguó Yínháng; Map p885; Linkuo Xilu; ⏰9am-6pm Mon-Sat, 10.30am-4pm Sun) Credit-card advances, bank transfers, foreign exchange and a 24-hour ATM.

Bank of China (branch) (中国银行; Zhōngguó Yínháng; Map p887; Beijing Donglu; ⏰10am-4.30pm Mon-Fri, 11am-3.30pm Sat & Sun) The most conveniently located bank changes cash and travellers cheques, and has an ATM. It's between the Banak Shol and Kirey hotels.

Post

China Post (中国邮政; Zhōngguó Yóuzhèng; Map p885; Beijing Donglu; ⏰9am-8pm) East of the Potala Palace.

Public Security Bureau

Lhasa City PSB (PSB; 拉萨市公安局; Lāsà Shì Gōng'ānjú; Map p885; ✆624 8154; 17 Linkuo Beilu; ⏰9am-12.30pm & 3.30-6pm Mon-Fri) Visa extensions are hard to obtain here, so do it somewhere else if possible. If you do get one, it will only be given a day or two before your visa expires, and only if you are on a tour.

ⓘ Getting There & Away

Air

It's generally possible to buy flights to Lhasa online on sites such as www.expedia.com, www.ctrip.com and www.elong.net. Most airline offices won't sell you a ticket to Lhasa without a permit, though many local travel agencies will.

Leaving Lhasa is a lot simpler, as tickets can be purchased (and changed) without hassle from the **Civil Aviation Administration of China** (CAAC; 中国民航; Zhōngguó Mínháng; Map p885; ✆682 5430; 1 Niangre Lu; ⏰9am-7pm). Credit cards are not accepted. Flight connections continue to all major destinations in China. Note that tickets to Chéngdū and Chóngqìng in particular are often discounted by up to 30%.

Flights to/from Lhasa include the following destinations:

Ali ¥2600, three weekly
Běijīng ¥2630, daily
Chéngdū ¥1700, 10 daily
Chóngqìng ¥1830, daily
Guǎngzhōu (via Chóngqìng) ¥2700, daily
Kathmandu ¥3076 (US$379 from Kathmandu), three weekly
Kūnmíng (via Zhōngdiàn) ¥2160, daily
Shànghǎi Pǔdōng (via Xī'ān) ¥2960, daily
Xī'ān ¥1850, four weekly
Xīníng ¥1810, six weekly
Zhōngdiàn ¥1580, seven weekly (summer only)

Bus

Foreigners are currently not allowed to travel around Tibet by public transport and so the bus station will not sell you a ticket. Should this change, there are buses from the long-distance station to Shigatse, Gyantse and beyond.

Train

You can buy train tickets up to 10 days in advance at the Lhasa **train station ticket office** (⏰7am-10pm) on the southwest edge of town or at the central **city ticket office** (火车票代售处; huǒchēpiào dàishòuchù; Map p885; Deji Zhonglu; ⏰8am-5.30pm). Trains to Lhasa arrive in the evening. Departures from Lhasa include the following. All are daily unless noted.

Běijīng West (T28), 42 hours, 1.45pm
Chéngdū (T24), 44 hours, every other day, 7.57am
Chóngqìng (T224), 45 hours, every other day, 12.45pm
Guǎngzhōu (T266), 58 hours, 12.05pm
Lánzhōu (K918), 26 hours, 8.20am
Shànghǎi (T166), 48 hours, 11.25am
Xīníng (K918, K9802), 23 hours, 8.20am

ⓘ Getting Around

To/From the Airport

Gongkar airport is 65km south of Lhasa. Almost all tourists are picked up by their guide as part of their tour.

Airport buses (¥25, 75 minutes) leave up to 10 times a day between 7.30am and 1.30pm from in front of the CAAC building. The bus is free if you purchased your air ticket at the CAAC office.

A taxi to the airport costs between ¥150 and ¥200.

Bicycle

A good option for getting around Lhasa once you have acclimatised is to hire a bike. There are a couple of bike-rental places (¥5 per hour) opposite the Banak Shol hotel.

Bus

Buses (¥2) travel frequently between Běijīng Donglu and western Lhasa.

THE WORLD'S HIGHEST TRAIN RIDE

Since starting in 2006 the Qīnghǎi–Tibet Railway has been the world's highest train ride. With the line topping the 5072m Tanggu-la Pass and with 80% of the Golmud to Lhasa stretch above 4000m, the railway is an impressive piece of engineering. Its 160km of bridges and elevated track were built over permafrost, so sections of cooling pipes were inserted to help keep the boggy ground frozen in summer. The cost? A cool US$4.1 billion, and with extensions to Shigatse currently under construction, this figure is set to grow. The Chinese are rightfully proud of this engineering marvel, while many Tibetans aren't quite so sure. The railway brings cheaper (Chinese-made) goods and greater economic growth to the Tbetan Autonomous Region (TAR), but it also increases Han migration, delivering one million passengers to Lhasa every year. What the line does best is staple Tibet ever more firmly to the rest of China.

At the time of writing, foreigners needed a copy of their Tibet Tourism Bureau (TTB) permit to buy a ticket. On board passengers have access to piped-in oxygen, although the cabins are not actually pressurised. Soft-sleeper berths come with TVs, and speakers in each cabin make periodic travel announcements about sights along the way. Schedules are designed to let passengers take in the best scenery during daylight hours.

Train departure times and fares to Lhasa (hard seat/hard sleeper/soft sleeper) from the following cities are listed below, but are subject to change. Note that tickets can be very hard to get in July and August, when many agencies impose a surcharge of around ¥200 to get tickets to Lhasa. Check www.chinatibettrain.com for the latest schedules. Services run daily unless noted:

Běijīng West (T27), ¥389/767/1216, 44 hours, departure 8.09pm

Chéngdū (T22/23), ¥331/671/1065, 44 hours, every other day, 9pm

Chóngqìng (T222/3), ¥355/754/1168, 44 hours, every other day, 7.55pm

Guǎngzhōu (T264/5), ¥451/869/1472, 56 hours, 12.19pm (change trains in Xīníng)

Lánzhōu (K917), ¥242/524/825, 27 hours, 12.13pm

Shànghǎi (T164/5), ¥406/797/1266, 48 hours, 7.52pm

Xīníng (K917, K9803), ¥226/495/783, 27 hours, 11.50am

Taxi

Taxis charge a standard ¥10 to anywhere within the city. Few Chinese drivers know the Tibetan names for even the major sites. Bicycle rickshaws should charge around ¥5 for short trips but require some extended haggling *before* you set off.

Around Lhasa

GANDEN MONASTERY དགའ་ལྡན། 甘丹寺

About 40km east of Lhasa, this **monastery** (Gāndān Sì; admission ¥45; ☉dawn-dusk), founded in 1417 by Tsongkhapa, was the first Gelugpa monastery. Still the order's heart and soul, it's the one out-of-Lhasa sight to choose if your time is limited. Two *koras* offer astounding views over the braided Kyichu Valley and you'll probably meet more pilgrims here than anywhere else.

Some 400 monks have returned since the monastery was destroyed during the Cultural Revolution and extensive reconstruction has been under way for some time now,

alongside a watchful police presence. There is a ¥20 fee per chapel for photography; ¥1500 for video.

Pilgrim buses leave for Ganden Monastery (¥35 return) around 6am from the corner of Yuthok Lam and Duosenge Lu, returning around 1.30pm. Tourists can sometimes take the bus if their guide accompanies them.

NAM-TSO གནམ་མཚོ། 纳木错

The waters of sacred **Nam-tso** (Nàmùcuò; adult ¥120) shimmer with an almost transcendent turquoise, framed by strings of prayer flags and snowcapped mountain peaks. Geographically part of the Changtang Plateau, the huge lake is bordered to the north by the Tǎngǔlā Shān range and to the southeast by 7111m Nyenchen Tanglha peak.

The scenery is breathtaking but so is the altitude: at 4730m it's 1100m higher than Lhasa. Do not rush here but instead count on a week in Lhasa at the minimum to avoid acute mountain sickness (AMS).

GANDEN TO SAMYE HIKE

One of the most popular treks in Tibet is the four- to five-day hike from Ganden Monastery to Samye Monastery, an 80km wilderness walk connecting two of Tibet's most important monasteries. It begins less than 50km from Lhasa and takes you over the high passes of the Shuga-la (5250m) and Chitu-la (5100m). Along the way are subalpine lakes, dwarf forests and meadows, all at high altitude, so it shouldn't be underestimated.

The situation for getting permits for hiking is the same as for normal travel in Tibet. Some agencies will let you arrange your own ad hoc trek (ie horse or yak hire and food), as long as you take a guide and arrange transport to and from the trailheads; others require a fully supported trek. **Wind Horse Adventure** (☎0891-683 3009; www.windhorsetibet.com; Lhasa) is one of the most professional trekking agencies in Lhasa, though it's not the cheapest. For further details of this trek and others in the Everest, Tsurphu and Shalu regions, see the trekking chapter of Lonely Planet's *Tibet* guide.

Most travellers head for **Tashi Do Monastery** in the southeastern corner of the lake. There are some fine walks up to the summits of the twin hills, as well as a short but pilgrim-packed *kora*. Half a dozen charmless metal **guesthouses** (d ¥80-180, q ¥200) offer food and accommodation between April and October; the best options are the Holy Lake Namtso Guesthouse or Sheep Hotel. Bedding is provided but nights here can be very cold. The paucity of toilets and lack of running water are an ecoli outbreak waiting to happen.

Nam-tso is 195km north of Lhasa, a four-hour paved drive over the 5190m Largen-la (*la* means 'pass'). It's much better to visit as an overnight, rather than a day trip. Even if independent travel returns, there is no public transport to the lake.

SAMYE MONASTERY བསམ་ཡས་དགོན་པ 桑耶寺
About 170km southeast of Lhasa, set amongst the sand dunes on the north bank of the Yarlung Tsangpo (Brahmaputra) River is **Samye Monastery** (Sāngyē Sì; admission ¥40; ☉7.30am-6pm), the first monastery in Tibet. Founded in AD 775 by King Trisong Detsen, Samye is famed not just for its pivotal role in the introduction of Buddhism to Tibet, but its unique mandala design: the main hall, or Ütse, represents Mt Meru, the centre of the universe, while the outer temples represent the oceans, continents, subcontinents and other features of the Buddhist cosmology.

The **Monastery Guesthouse** (桑耶寺宾馆; Sāngyē Sì Bīnguǎn; ☎0891-783 6666; tr without bathroom ¥120, d with bathroom ¥180), just outside the northeast corner of the monastery walls has the best ensuite doubles in town and clean and fresh triples without a shower. The **Friendship Snowland Restaurant** (☎136-1893 2819; meals ¥14-40; ☉8am-midnight), outside the east gate, serves good Chinese and Tibetan dishes, banana pancakes and milky tea in a cosy Tibetan atmosphere. Dorm rooms (¥50) with real mattresses (not foam) are available upstairs. There are several other decent accommodation options nearby, including the friendly **Dawa Guesthouse** (达瓦家庭旅馆; Dáwǎ Jiātíng Lǚguǎn; ☎799 5171; dm ¥30).

If you are heading to Everest Base Camp or the Nepal border, a visit here will only add one day to your itinerary. You may have to detour briefly to the nearby town of Tsetang (泽当; Zédāng) for your guide to pick up a required travel permit. One good option is to take the paved road to Samye via Tsetang and then return via the remoter north bank road and interesting Dorje Drak Monastery.

The Friendship Highway

The 865km route between Kathmandu and Lhasa, known as the Friendship Hwy, offers without a doubt one of the world's great overland routes. At times sublime, at times unnerving, at times headache-inducing (the highest point is the Gyatso-la pass at 5100m), it's the yellow-brick road of Tibet, leading to some of the most magical destinations on the plateau.

For the sake of simplicity, we've included the side route from Lhasa to Shigatse via Yamdrok-tso and Gyantse in this section. This is the route most travellers take between the two towns and it's by far the more scenic and attraction-packed.

YAMDROK-TSO ཡར་འབྲོག་མཚོ 羊卓雍错
On the direct road between Gyantse and Lhasa, you'll probably catch your first sight of coiling **Yamdrok-tso** (Yángzhuó Yōngcuò; admission ¥40) from the summit of the Kam-

ba-la pass (4794m). The lake lies several hundred metres below the road, and in clear weather is a fabulous shade of deep turquoise. Far in the northwest distance is the huge massif of Mt Nojin Kangtsang (7191m).

The small town of **Nangartse** along the way is essentially a lunch stop, with popular buffets (¥35 to ¥40) at the Lhasa and Yak restaurants, and most people overnight in Gyantse. A 20-minute detour or a two-hour walk from Nangartse brings you to **Samding Monastery** (admission ¥20), a charming place with scenic views of the surrounding area and lake.

From Nangartse to Gyantse you cross the 4960m Karo-la, site of the highest battle in British imperial history during the Younghusband invasion of 1903–04, where glaciers spill off the side peaks beside a popular **viewpoint** (admission ¥50). Avoid the ridiculous 'admission fee' by stopping further below the pass.

GYANTSE

ᢢᢑᢈᢩᢠ 江孜

☑0892 / ELEV 3980M

The traditional town of Gyantse (Jiāngzī) is famed for its monumental nine-tiered *chörten,* long considered one of Tibet's architectural wonders. Historically, the town was at the centre of a thriving trans-Himalayan wood and wool trade, and Gyantse carpets were considered the best in Tibet. These days, Gyantse remains one of the less Chinese-influenced settlements, and wandering the backstreets around the monastery affords a rare picture of traditional urban Tibetan life.

◉ Sights & Activities

Gyangtse has a great horse-racing and archery festival from 20 to 26 July, featuring traditional Tibetan fun and games like rock-lifting, yak-racing and tug-of-war.

Pelkhor Chöde Monastery MONASTERY
(白居寺; Báijūsì; admission ¥60; ⊘9am-7pm, some chapels closed 1-3pm) The high red-walled compound of this monastery, founded in 1418, once encircled 15 monasteries from three different orders of Tibetan Buddhism. The surviving assembly hall (straight ahead as you enter the compound) is worth a lingering visit for the fine murals, statues and butter-lamp-lit atmosphere. Just beside the assembly hall is the spectacular 15th-century **Gyantse Kumbum**.

Gyantse Dzong FORT
(☑817 2116; admission ¥40; ⊘8.30am-8.30pm) The Gyantse Dzong towers above Gyantse on a finlike outcrop, and has outstanding views of the Pelkhor Chöde Monastery and surrounding valley. The fort was taken by the British in 1904 during their invasion of Tibet. Renovations in 2012 have spruced up the anti-imperialist displays. Entry is via the gate north of the main intersection, or drive up from the back side.

🛏 Sleeping

Gyantse is a popular stop for 4WD tours and has a decent range of accommodation and food along north–south Yingxiong Nanlu.

TOP CHOICE **Yeti Hotel** HOTEL $$
(雅迪花园酒店; Yǎdí Huāyuán Fàndiàn; ☑817 5555; www.yetihoteltibet.com; 11 Weiguo Lu; d incl breakfast ¥520; @🛜) The revamped Yeti is an excellent midrange option, with 24-hour hot water, clean carpeted rooms, reliable wi-fi and a pleasant lobby restaurant, serving everything from yak steak to pizza. Discounts of 50% available.

Jiànzàng Hotel HOTEL $$
(建藏饭店; Jiànzàng Fàndiàn; ☑817 3720; jianzang hotel@yahoo.com.cn; 14 Yingxiong Nanlu; 英雄南路 14号; q per bed ¥50, d ¥260-380) Long a popular place with 4WD groups, the smallish but modern rooms come with bathroom and the new blocks offer 24-hour hot water (the quads are less reliable). The 2nd-floor Tibetan-style restaurant is a decent option for breakfast or a cup of tea. The manager featured in the BBC documentary *A Year in Tibet*.

🍴 Eating

Yak Restaurant INTERNATIONAL $$
(亚美食餐厅; Yà Měishí Cāntīng; Yingxiong Nanlu; mains ¥15-35; ⊘7am-11pm; 🖥) The Yak offers backpacker treats such as French toast, yak burgers, sizzlers (dishes served on a hot, sizzling plate) and Western breakfasts. The owner prides herself on her French cuisine, so have a go at the yak-liver pâté or yak bourguignon.

DON'T MISS

GYANTSE KUMBUM

The one unmissable sight in Gyantse, the spectacular Gyantse Kumbum (literally '100,000 Images Stupa') is the largest *chörten* in Tibet. A pilgrim path spirals up the inside of the monumental nine-tiered structure, passing 108 chapels, each filled with masterful original murals. Bring a torch (flashlight) to examine them in detail.

TIBET THE FRIENDSHIP HIGHWAY

Tashi Restaurant NEPALI $$

(扎西餐厅; Zhàxī Cāntīng; Yingxiong Nanlu; mains ¥20-40; 7.30am-11pm;) This Nepali-run place is the best bet for an Indian curry, though it also has the usual range of Western breakfasts, Italian and Chinese food. The decor is Tibetan but the Bollywood movies and Nepali music give it a subcontinental vibe.

Gyantse Kitchen TIBETAN $$

(江孜厨房; Jiāngzī Chúfáng; Shanghai Zhonglu; dishes ¥15-40; 7am-midnight;) This local favourite serves all the usual suspects but also has a special menu of Tibetan dishes (tip: you can save money by ordering from the Chinese-language menu). It's opposite the huge Gyantse Hotel. The friendly Tibetan owner donates a portion of his income to support poor families in Gyantse.

ℹ Getting There & Away

Most people visit Gyantse as part of a trip to the Nepal border, Mt Everest, or out west to Mt Kailash. Should the permit situation change, there are plenty of minibuses (1½ hours) and taxis (one hour) for the 90km trip between Shigatse and Gyantse.

SHIGATSE 日喀则

📞0892 / POP 80,000 / ELEV 3850M

Shigatse (Rìkàzé) is the second-largest city in Tibet, and like Lhasa has two distinct faces: a Tibetan one and a Chinese one. The Tibetan section, running northeast of the high-walled Tashilhunpo Monastery, is filled with whitewashed compounds, dusty alleys and prayer-wheel-spinning pilgrims. The modern Chinese section has all the charm of a shopping mall but is where you'll find most restaurants and hotels and other life-support systems. With a new airport and a train line due to arrive by 2014, Shigatse looks set to grow even further.

History

As the traditional capital of the central Tsang region, Shigatse was long a rival with Lhasa for political control of the country. The Tsang kings and later governors exercised their power from the imposing heights of the (recently rebuilt) Shigatse Dzong. Since the time of the Mongol sponsorship of the Gelugpa order, Shigatse has been the seat of the Panchen Lamas, the second-highest-ranking lamas in Tibet. Their centre was and remains the Tashilhunpo Monastery.

◎ Sights

Tashilhunpo Monastery MONASTERY

(扎什伦布寺; Zhāshílúnbù Sì; admission ¥80; 9am-7pm) The seat of the Panchen Lama and one of Tibetan culture's six great Gelugpa institutions (along with Drepung, Sera and Ganden monasteries in Lhasa; as well as Kumbum and Labrang in Qīnghǎi and Gānsù provinces, respectively). Built in 1447 by a nephew of Tsongkhapa, the monastery is the size of a small village, and lends itself to a half-day or more of exploration and discovery.

In addition to the mesmerising statue of Jampa (Maitreya) Buddha (at nearly 27m high it's the largest gilded statue in the world) in the Temple of the Maitreya, the monastery is famed for the opulent tombs of the fourth and 10th Panchen Lamas. The former saw 85kg of gold and masses of jewels used in its construction.

TIBET THE FRIENDSHIP HIGHWAY

ALTITUDE SICKNESS

Altitude sickness (or acute mountain sickness, AMS) is no joke and it is quite common to discover that the nice travellers you met on the way into Lhasa have left the next day, sick as a dog (or worse) from the change in altitude. While medicines such as Diamox can certainly help, it's best to avoid shocking your system, by rising in altitude gradually.

Most people experience only minor symptoms (headaches, breathlessness) when flying in to Lhasa (3600m), as long as they take things easy for their first couple of days. The key is to ascend gradually, preferably less than 300m to 500m per day. Spend up to a week in and around Lhasa before heading to higher elevations like Nam-tso or Western Tibet and don't even think about heading straight to Everest Base Camp (5150m) from Kathmandu (1300m): you need at least two or three nights along the way, in places such as Nyalam (3750m) and Tingri (4250m).

If you are really concerned about AMS, spend some time at higher elevations in western Sìchuān or Nepal before travelling to Lhasa.

See p1014 for more information.

Shigatse

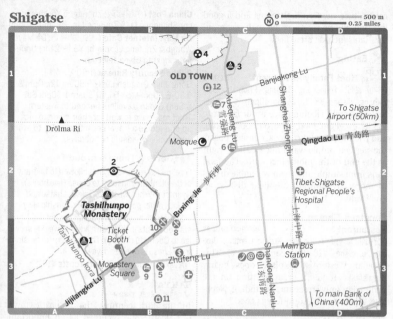

An hour-long *kora* starts at the southwest corner of the outer wall and heads up for views of the monastery and city. Descend to the pedestrian street or continue along the hill to the Potala-like Shigatse Dzong (fortress). The recently rebuilt structure is currently empty but a museum/gallery is planned.

🛏 Sleeping

Gang Gyan Orchard Hotel　　　HOTEL **$$**
(日喀则刚坚宾馆; Rìkāzé Gāngjiān Bīnguǎn; 📞882 0777; 77 Zhufeng Lu; dm ¥50, d with bathroom ¥180) Right next to the traditional-carpet factory and just 100m from Tashilhunpo Monastery, the location here can't be beat. Rooms are large and comfortable, though rooms facing the courtyard are quieter than the noisy road. The shared bathrooms are clean but the hot water supply isn't the most reliable.

Tenzin Hotel　　　HOTEL **$**
(旦增宾馆; Dànzēng Bīnguǎn; 📞882 2018; 8 Bangjiakong Lu; 帮加孔路8号; dm ¥40, d with/without bathroom ¥160/120; ❄) This place has long been popular with travellers. The courtyard can be a bit noisy but the decent rooms, old-town location and views from the restaurant more than compensate. The shared bathrooms usually have 24-hour hot water. The restaurant is a good place to hang out but only opens from June to August.

Shigatse

◎ Top Sights
　　Tashilhunpo Monastery B2

◎ Sights
　1　Chörten A3
　2　Festival Thangka Wall B2
　3　Mani Lhakhang C1
　4　Shigatse Dzong C1

🛏 Sleeping
　5　Gang Gyan Orchard Hotel B3
　6　Tashi Chotar Hotel C2
　7　Tenzin Hotel C1

✕ Eating
　8　Songtsen Tibetan Restaurant B3
　9　Third Eye Restaurant B3
　10　Tibet Family Restaurant B3

🛍 Shopping
　11　Tibet Gang Gyen Carpet
　　　Factory B3
　12　Tibetan Market C1

Tashi Chotar Hotel　　　HOTEL **$$$**
(扎西曲塔大酒店; Zhāxī Qǔtǎ Dàjiǔdiàn; 📞883 0111; www.zxqthotel.com; 2 Xueqiang Lu; d/tr ¥480/680; ❄@) New and comfortable four-star place with Tibetan decor, internet

cables, nice modern bathrooms and a good location. Single rooms come with a computer. Rates include breakfast.

✗ Eating

⌧TOP CHOICE Tibet Family Restaurant   TIBETAN $
(丰盛餐厅; Fēngshèng Cāntīng; Phuntsho Serzikhang; dishes ¥8-20; ◉8am-10pm; ▣) This teahouse-style Tibetan place is our favourite for its excellent food, nice outdoor seating and friendly clientele of locals. It also boasts the perfect people-watching location, right at the end of the monastery *kora*. The food runs from simple and fresh vegetable dishes to more adventurous yak-meat dishes, all great value.

Songtsen Tibetan Restaurant   INTERNATIONAL $$
(松赞西藏餐厅; Sōngzàn Xīzàng Cāntīng; Buxing Jie; dishes ¥20-40; ◉8am-10pm; ▣) This popular Western-style place does hearty breakfasts. It has a great location on the pedestrian-only street and the Indian, Nepalese, Tibetan or Western fare is good.

Third Eye Restaurant   NEPALI $$
(雪莲餐厅; Xuělián Cāntīng; Zhufeng Lu; dishes ¥10-30; ◉9am-10pm; ▣) One of three solid Nepali-run restaurants in town, serving a huge range of decent Western dishes and Indian curries.

🛍 Shopping

The **Tibetan market** in front of the Tenzin Hotel is a good place to pick up souvenirs such as prayer wheels, rosaries and *thangkas*. There are also dozens of souvenir and craft shops along the pedestrian-only street (Buxing Jie). Bargain hard.

Tibet Gang Gyen Carpet Factory   CARPETS
(西藏刚坚地毯厂; Xīzàng Gāngjiān Dìtǎn Chǎng; www.tibetgang-gyencarpet.com; 9 Zhufeng Lu; ◉9am-1pm & 3-7pm Mon-Sat) This Tibetan-French joint venture hires and trains impoverished women to weave high-quality 100% Tibetan wool carpets. You can watch carpets being made on the premises and the factory will ship internationally.

ℹ Information

The cheapest places to make calls are the many private telephone booths around town.

Bank of China (中国银行; Zhōngguó Yínháng; Shanghai Zhonglu; ◉9am-6pm Mon-Sat, 10am-4pm Sun) Changes travellers cheques and cash; with a 24-hour ATM. A more convenient branch on Zhufeng Lu changes cash and has an ATM.

China Post (中国邮政; Zhōngguó Yóuzhèng; cnr Shandong Lu & Zhufeng Lu; ◉9am-6.30pm)

Dà Mǎyǐ Internet Cafe (大蚂蚁网吧; Dà Mǎyǐ Wǎngbā; Zhufeng Lu; per hr ¥5; ◉24hr) Upper floor, next to China Telecom.

Public Security Bureau (PSB; 公安局; Gōng'ānjú; Qingdao Lu; ◉9.30am-12.30pm & 3.30-6.30pm Mon-Fri, 10.30am-1.30pm Sat & Sun) Group travellers headed to western Tibet may have to wait for their guide to pick up or endorse a travel permit here. Try to avoid lunchtime, weekends or holidays.

ℹ Getting There & Around

Foreigners are currently not allowed to take any of the plentiful transport to Lhasa (five hours), Gyantse (1½ hours), Saga, Sakya, Lhatse and various other points along the Friendship Hwy.

Shigatse's new airport, 50km east of the city, started flights in 2012 with a twice-weekly service to Chéngdū (¥1910). The train line extension from Lhasa is due to arrive in 2014.

A taxi anywhere in Shigatse costs ¥10.

SAKYA   ས་སྐྱ་ 萨迦
☑0892 / ELEV 4280M

In the 13th century, the monastic town of Sakya (Sàjiā) emerged as an important centre of scholarship. Less than a century later the Sakya lamas, with Mongol military support, became the short-lived rulers of all Tibet. Still today the local colouring of buildings – ash grey with red and white vertical stripes – symbolises both the Rigsum Gonpo (the trinity of Bodhisattvas) and Sakya authority. For travellers the magnificent, brooding monastery, the visiting bands of pilgrims and the surrounding traditional village make Sakya a real highlight. It's one of our favourites and well worth an overnight stay.

◉ Sights

Sakya Monastery   MONASTERY
(admission ¥45; ◉9am-6pm) The main Sakya Monastery, built in 1268, is a massive, fortresslike compound, with high defensive walls. Inside, the dimly lit assembly hall exudes a sanctity few others can rival, including one of Tibet's great libraries (extra ¥10). The northern section of the monastery, on the other side of the Trum-chu (Trum River), has been mostly reduced to picturesque ruins, though restoration work is ongoing and it's worth exploring the *kora* path.

🛏 Sleeping & Eating

Manasarovar Sakya Hotel   HOTEL $$
(神湖萨迦宾馆; Shénhú Sàjiā Bīnguǎn; ☑824 2222; Gesang Zhonglu; dm/d/tr ¥30/280/380)

There is a mix of rooms in the best hotel in town; the ones that overlook the road are probably best. The thick walls keep the place cold and dark but rooms are comfortable and there's hot water from 7pm to 10pm. The six-bed dorm rooms are OK; one includes a bathroom. There are superb views from the hotel's rooftop and good Western dishes in the rather charmless restaurant. Accommodation discounts of 20% to 30%.

Sakya Lowa Family Hotel   GUESTHOUSE $
(萨迦镇鲁娃家庭旅馆; Sàjiā Zhèn Lǔwā Jiātíng Lǚguǎn; ☑824 2156; 35 Baogang Beilu; per person ¥50-60) The Lowa is a cosy, family-run guesthouse with basic but clean rooms set around a central courtyard. Walls are brightly painted and accented with traditional motifs, but there are no showers and only shared pit toilets. It's around the corner from the Manasarovar Sakya Hotel, on the road to the northern monastery.

Sakya Monastery Restaurant   TIBETAN $
(萨迦寺餐厅; Sàjiā Sì Cāntīng; dishes ¥7-15; ◷8am-9pm) This atmospheric monastery restaurant is always full of pilgrims chowing down on excellent *momos* and steaming glasses of *cha ngamo*.

ℹ Getting There & Away

Sakya is 25km off the Friendship Hwy. Most people stay overnight at Sakya en route to the Everest region. There is one daily minibus between Shigatse and Sakya.

RONGPHU MONASTERY & EVEREST BASE CAMP   རོང་ཕུ་དགོན་པ་ ཇོ་མོ་གླང་མའི་གངས་ལ
绒布寺、珠峰

Before heading to the Nepal border, or as part of a five-day excursion from Lhasa, many travellers make the diversion to iconic **Everest Base Camp** (EBC; 5150m). The clear vistas (if you are lucky) up a glacial valley to the sheer North Face are far superior to anything you'll see in Nepal. Everest is known locally as Chomolungma (sometimes spelt Qomolangma), or as Zhūfēng in Chinese. Because EBC is a prime target for political protests, the Chinese army maintains a strong presence up here.

Vehicles can drive on a gravel road to **Rongphu Monastery** (admission ¥25), at 5000m reputedly the highest in the world, and then proceed just a few kilometres more to a ramshackle collection of nomad tents set near a China Post kiosk (the highest post office in the world). From here it's a one-hour walk (recommended if you aren't suffering from the altitude) or shuttle-bus ride (¥25) up a winding dirt road to EBC. Tourists are not allowed to visit the expedition tents of actual base camp.

Food and lodging are pretty limited up here (though the mobile phone reception is great!). The friendly **Monastery Guesthouse** (dm ¥40, tw without bathroom ¥160-200) at Rongphu has simple rooms but a cosy restaurant with Everest views. The ugly two-star hotel nearby is laughably overpriced. Another option is to stay in one of the **nomad tents** (per person ¥60) clustered around 5km before EBC. The tents are surprisingly warm and comfortable (those yak-dung stoves put out a fantastic amount of heat!) but even so, a sleeping bag is an excellent idea. Simple meals (¥20 to ¥25) and even canned beer are available but the shared toilets will haunt you. Keep your belongings locked in your vehicle.

EBC is about 90km off the Friendship Hwy on a dirt road over the 5050m Pang-la. Before you set off you'll need to stop in **Baber** (白坝; Báibā or New Tingri; 4250m) – or Old Tingri if coming from Nepal – to pay the Qomolangma National Park entrance fee of ¥400 per vehicle, plus ¥180 per passenger. Clarify with your agency whether you are expected to pay for both your vehicle and your guide (¥180).

If you need to spend the night in Baber ,the **Kangjong/Snowland Hotel** (雪域宾馆; Xuěyù Bīnguǎn; ☑136 3892 5738; dm ¥40, d with bathroom ¥180-200; @) is one of several good options, with modern rooms. The attached Tibetan-style **restaurant** (dishes ¥25-40) serves tasty hot meals and is a cosy place to kick back with a thermos of sweet tea. The hotel is in the middle of town at the crossroads to Shegar.

If you are headed from Everest to the Nepal border, note that the dirt road to Tingri via Zombuk village and the Lamna-la offers a handy shortcut.

TINGRI TO ZHĀNGMÙ   དིངྲི་འབྲམ
樟木 定日

The huddle of mudbrick buildings that comprises the old village of **Tingri** (Dìngrì; 4250m) now spreads about a kilometre down the Friendship Hwy. The views of the towering Himalayan peaks of Mt Everest (8848m) and Cho Oyu (8153m) across the sweeping plain make up for the truck-stop feel.

TIBET TRAVEL RESTRICTIONS

Troubled Tibet is essentially part of China, yet in many ways separate from it. Travel regulations here are much more restrictive than the rest of the nation; tourists currently need to arrange a guided tour in order to visit any place in the Tibetan Autonomous Region (TAR).

Authorities would say this is for tourists' protection, though it has more to do with foreigners' tendency to sympathise with the Tibetan cause and bear witness to political tensions. If you want to explore Tibetan areas independently by foot or public transport, you are currently better off heading to the Tibetan areas of Sìchuān and Qīnghǎi.

Travel regulations are in constant flux in Tibet and travel infrastructure is changing at head-spinning speed. Be sure to check current regulations with travel companies and check the designated Tibet branch of the **Lonely Planet Thorn Tree** (http://thorntreelone lyplanet.com). Tibet can completely close to foreigners without warning, as it did for several months in 2012.

At the time of research:

» Foreign travellers need a Tibet Tourism Bureau (TTB) permit to get into Tibet and an Alien Travel Permit (and other permits) to travel outside Lhasa.

» To get these permits you need to prebook an itinerary, a guide for your entire stay and transport for outside Lhasa with an agency, before travelling to Tibet.

» In 2012 new requirements required groups to be a minimum of five people, all of the same nationality, making it that bit more difficult for individual travellers to cobble together a group. Tibetan travel agencies can sometimes help travellers get around these restrictions. Lonely Planet's Thorn Tree has a dedicated page to finding travel companions. These restrictions could well relax in 2013.

» To get on a plane or train to Lhasa you generally need to show your TTB permit. For the plane you need the original, so your agency will courier that to you at an address in China (normally a hostel). A printout/copy is currently acceptable for the train.

» You don't need to book transport for your time in Lhasa but you do need to visit the main monasteries with a guide.

» For travel outside Lhasa you will need to prearrange transport hire (normally a 4WD). You cannot travel outside Lhasa independently and cannot take public transport.

» Most agencies charge around ¥600 for permits, ¥250 per day for a guide and anywhere from US$80 to US$150 per day for 4WD hire (not per person). Many agencies let you book your own accommodation.

» Agencies can only apply for permits 15 days before departure, so there is invariably a last-minute rush to get permits posted to you in time. This obviously complicates booking flight and train tickets; we recommend booking a fully refundable ticket if possible.

» Travel from Nepal to Tibet brings its own complications, since foreigners can only travel on a group visa (a separate piece of paper), which is only valid from two to three weeks

Ruins on the hill overlooking Tingri are all that remain of the **Tingri Dzong**. This fort was destroyed in a late-18th-century Nepalese invasion. Many more ruins on the plains between Shegar and Nyalam shared the same history.

There are several Tibetan guesthouses and restaurants on the main highway, including the **Tingri Snowland Hotel** (定日雪域饭店; Dìngrì Xuěyù Fàndiàn; ☑152 0802 7313; dm/d/tr ¥30/80/105) in the far west of the strip, which has basic but clean rooms and simple common hot showers (¥10). Also good is the **Héhū Bīnguǎn** (合呼宾馆; ☑136 4892 2335; dm ¥30-50, d with bathroom ¥260), a new place in the centre with good mattresses in the pricier dorms and some en suite rooms with carpet and toilet (but no hot water).

From Tingri down to Zhāngmù on the Nepal border is an easy half-day's drive of just under 200km. If you are coming the other way you should break the trip into two days to aid acclimatisation. The highest point along the paved road is the Tongla pass (4950m), 95km from Tingri, from where you can see a horizon of 8000m Himalayan peaks.

and is almost impossible to extend. If you already have a Chinese visa in your passport it will be cancelled. Group visas in Kathmandu cost US$58 and take 10 days, or you can pay US$118 for express service. US citizens pay a surcharge.

The companies listed here can arrange tours and permits for Tibet and are used to dealing with individual travellers. See www.tibetgreenmap.com for other responsible Tibetan tour operators.

Lhasa

» **Namchen Tours** (☑634 5009; www.tibetnamchen.com) Based at Barkhor Namchen House in Lhasa's old town. Contact Doko.

» **Shigatse Travels** (☑633 0489; www.shigatsetravels.com; Yak Hotel, 100 Beijing Donglu) Higher-end tours.

» **Spinn Café** (☑136 5952 3997; www.cafespinn.com; 135 Beijing Donglu) Clear and transparent; contact Kong.

» **Tibet Highland Tours** (☑691 2080, 189 0899 0100; www.tibethighlandtours.com; tibetan intibet@yahoo.cn; Zangyiyuan Lu) Contact Tenzin.

Other Cities in China

» **Leo Hostel** (☑10-8660 8923; www.leohostel.com; 52 Dazhalan Xijie, Qiánmén, Běijīng) See p92.

» **Mix Hostel** (☑028-8322 2271; www.mixhostel.com/tibet.htm; 23 Renjiawan, Xinghui Xilu, Chéngdū) See p705.

» **Hello Chéngdū International Youth Hostel** (☑8196 7573, 8335 5322; www.gogosc.com) Popular agency and hostel (p705) in Chéngdū.

» **Snow Lion Tours** (☑971-816 3350, 134 3932 9243; www.snowliontours.com; Office 1212, Chenglin Mansion, 7 Dongdajie Lu, Xīníng) Contact Wangden Tsering.

» **Tibetan Connections** (☑135 1973 7734; www.tibetanconnections.com; 16th fl, Bldg No 5, International Village Apartments, 2-32 Jiancai Xiang, Xīníng) Recommended.

» **Wind Horse Adventure Tours** (☑971-636 3008; www.windhorseadventuretours.com; Qinghai International Business Centre, 12th fl, 27 Kunlun Zhonglu, Xīníng) Contact Tashi Phuntsok. Linked to Tibetan Connections.

For overland trips from Yúnnán, consult companies such as **Khampa Caravan** (www.khampacaravan.com), p674, and **Haiwei Trails** (www.haiweitrails.com), p674, in Zhōngdiàn, and **China Minority Travel** (www.china-travel.nl) in Dàlǐ, p654.

See also our Itineraries chapter for a permit-free alternative way to see Tibetan lands in Qīnghǎi and Sìchuān.

The one-street town of Nyalam (Nièlāmù) is about 30km from the Nepal border and a usual overnight spot for 4WD trips from Nepal. Like all other hotels in town, the new **Snowlands Hotel** (雪域宾馆; Xuěyù Bīnguǎn; ☑0892-827 2777; r without bathroom ¥280) is well overpriced but its rooms are the best in town, with shared hot-water bathrooms down the hall. Rates include breakfast. It can get booked up with Indian groups returning from Kailash.

After Nyalam, the road drops like a stone into a lush, deep forested gorge (trees!) lined with spectacular waterfalls, many of which are hundreds of metres high. You can feel the air getting thicker as you descend towards the subcontinent.

ZHĀNGMÙ
འགྲམ་ 樟木
☑0892 / ELEV 2250M

The frenetic border town of Zhāngmù (Khasa in Nepalese, Dram in Tibetan) hangs from the forested slopes above the tortuous final kilometres of the Friendship Hwy. The smells of curry and incense float in the air, and the babbling sound of fast-flowing streams cuts through the piercing squeals of truck brakes. After time on the barren high plateau, it's either a feast for the senses, or an unwelcome assault on the meditative mood you've been cultivating for the past weeks.

🛏 Sleeping & Eating

Cáiyuán Bīnguǎn   HOTEL $$
(财缘宾馆; ☑874 5888; d ¥360; ❀) Midrange Land Cruiser groups like this modern, new place for its clean, good quality rooms, en suite bathrooms and decent breakfasts, though it's somewhat overpriced. There's hot water in the evenings.

Lucien Sunny Youth Hostel   HOSTEL $
(路晟阳光青年旅舍; Lùshèng Yángguāng Qīngnián Lǚshè; ☑874 2299; 49 Yingbin Lu; dm ¥35-45, d ¥150-170) The best value in town is this friendly Chinese youth hostel. The private rooms are clean and bright, with homey duvets and pebble-floor showers, though the dim dorms are not so good, with a bathroom divided only by a curtain.

Sherpa Hotel   HOTEL $$
(夏尔巴酒店; Xià'ěrbā Jiǔdiàn; ☑874 2098; d with/without bathroom ¥230/120) The pink painted rooms are clean (if a little small) at this friendly hotel and hot water is available most of the time. The back rooms that face the valley are quietest and afford spectacular views. The Nepali curries in the restaurant are some of the best in town (dishes ¥15 to ¥40).

ℹ Information

Bank of China (中国银行; Zhōngguó Yínháng; ⊙9.30am-1pm & 3.30-6pm Mon-Fri, 10.30am-3pm Sat & Sun) Changes cash and travellers cheques into yuán, and also yuán into US dollars, euros or UK pounds. It doesn't deal in Nepalese rupees; for those go to the money-changers that operate openly around town.

Western Tibet

Tibet's far wild west, known in Tibetan as Ngari, has few permanent settlers, but is nevertheless a lodestone to a billion pilgrims from three major religions (Buddhism, Hinduism and Jainism). They are drawn to the twin spiritual power places of Mt Kailash and Lake Manasarovar, two of the most legendary and far-flung destinations in the world.

Ngari is a blunt, expansive realm of salt lakes, Martian-style deserts, grassy steppes and snowcapped mountains. It's a mesmerising landscape, but also intensely remote: a few tents and herds of yaks may be all the signs of human existence one comes across in half a day's drive. The recent paving of the southern road to Kailash has made the weeklong drive from Lhasa a lot more comfortable and it's now even possible to fly back from Ali.

Warm clothes are essential on any trip to the region, even in summer, and a sleeping bag is recommended. The three-day *kora* around Mt Kailash can be done without a tent but bringing one will give you added flexibility and comfort.

Accommodation along the way ranges from basic guesthouses to chilly hotel rooms. Few have attached bathrooms but most towns have at least one public bathhouse. Most towns now have well-stocked supermarkets, internet cafes and Chinese restaurants, though it's still worth bringing along a few treats, such as peanuts, chocolate bars and dehydrated food from home.

The only places to change money in Ngari are banks in Ali, and it's much easier to change US dollars as cash rather than travellers cheques. It's best just to bring what you expect to spend in renminbi.

CHINA'S REMOTEST ROAD

Highway 219, the 1100km-long road between Ngari (Ali) in western Tibet and Karghilik (Yèchéng) in Xīnjiāng, crosses probably the world's remotest mountain terrain. The road is so remote that back in the late 1950s it took India an entire year to realise that China had built a road across what it considered its own territory (!), leading to a 1962 war between the two giants. The good news for travellers is that paving of the epic road was finally completed in 2012, making for a much smoother ride, including a potentially epic bike route.

Consider the route a three-day drive, with overnight stops in guesthouses at Domar, Sānshílí Yíngfáng and Yèchéng. Highlights of the trip include the monastery at old Rutok, the turquoise waters of Pangong-tso stretching into Ladakh, the sheer emptiness of Aksai-Chin and rare views of the jagged Kunlun Mountains. All the normal Tibet travel restrictions apply, so you need to organise Land Cruiser, guide and permits through an agency in Lhasa (or Kashgar). We advise you to start from Tibet, as the altitude gain from Karghilik (1230m) is particularly dangerous unless you are well acclimatised.

BORDER CROSSING: GETTING TO NEPAL

After a passport check at Zhāngmù, your 4WD will take you 8km down switchbacks to **Chinese immigration** (⊙10am-5pm, sometimes closed 1.30-3.30pm), next to the Friendship Bridge and Nepal border post at Kodari. If for some reason you don't have transport, orange and blue taxis run this stretch for ¥10 per person.

At **Nepali immigration** (⊙8.30am-4pm) in Kodari, you can get a visa for the same price as in Lhasa (US$25/40/100 for a 15-/30-/90-day visa, or the equivalent in rupees). If you don't have a passport photo you'll be charged an extra US$5. Nepal is 2¼ hours behind Chinese time.

There are four daily buses to Kathmandu (Rs 230 to Rs 350, 4½ hours) – the last bus at 1.30pm is express – or take a bus to Barabise (Rs 75 to Rs 125, three hours, last bus 5pm) and change. The easier option is to share a private vehicle with other travellers (Rs 3000 per car, or Rs 800 per seat; four to five hours). You'll struggle to find a driver after 5pm.

For further information, head to shop.lonelyplanet.com to purchase a downloadable PDF of the Kathmandu chapter from Lonely Planet's *Nepal* guide.

When to Go

May, June and from mid-September to early October are probably the best times for travel in the region. The summer months of July and August see the bulk of the rain, though it's still very limited. The Drölma-la pass on the Mt Kailash *kora* is usually blocked with snow from late October or early November until early April. The festival of Saga Dawa during May or June brings hundreds of pilgrims and tourists to the mountain.

Permits

You'll need a fistful of permits to visit Ngari: a TTB permit, Alien Travel Permit, military permit, foreign affairs permit etc. The travel agency that organises your 4WD trip will need around two weeks to arrange these.

ℹ Getting There & Away

Four-wheel-drive trips to Mt Kailash require a minimum 14 days. Add on three days to explore the Guge Kingdom at Tsaparang. One good option is to exit at Zhāngmù, detouring from Saga to the Friendship Hwy via the lake of Peiku-tso. For details of the remoter and longer return route via the northern highway, see Lonely Planet's *Tibet* guide.

LHATSE TO KAILASH

From Lhasa most travellers take the faster, direct southern route to Ngari. It's a two- or three-day trip along the paved Friendship Hwy to the town of **Lhatse** (拉孜; Lāzī), where there are several hotels, including the friendly **Lhatse Tibetan Farmers Hotel** (拉孜农民旅馆; Lāzī Nóngmín Lǚguǎn; ☑832 2333; dm ¥30, d with bathroom ¥120-150), which features new ensuite rooms out back and a cosy Tibet-style restaurant.

Turning off the Friendship Hwy just after Lhatse, Hwy 219 continues on a mostly paved road to the hamlet of **Raga**, near where the lesser-travelled northern route branches north. There are simple **guesthouses** (dm ¥30) in Raga but most groups continue 60km west to the larger military town of **Saga** (萨噶; Sàgá), which has internet cafes and hot public showers. The **Sàgá Bīnguǎn** (萨噶宾馆; ☑0892-820 2888; d with bathroom ¥360-420; ✳@) is at the town crossroads and has hot showers and Western bathrooms. Tibetan guesthouses such as the cosy **Bo Tie The Clan Hotel** (Bodo Dronkhang; 博扎家族旅馆; Bózhá Jiāzú Lǚguǎn; dm per bed ¥30) are a 10-minute walk (800m) north of the centre.

It's possible to reach Darchen in one long day (490km) from Saga, though many groups split the scenic ride into two days. This also helps with the acclimatisation process. After Lhatse the altitude never drops below 4000m.

In grubby **Paryang** (帕羊; Pàyáng), the **Shishapangma Hotel** (希夏邦马宾馆; Xīxiàbāngmǎ Bīnguǎn; dm/d per bed ¥40/100) is popular with Indian pilgrims. The central **Tashi Hotel** (扎西旅馆; Zhāxī Lǚguǎn; dm ¥30) is a smaller, simpler Tibetan-style place. From Paryang to Darchen is 245km.

MT KAILASH ᠊᠊ 冈仁波斋峰

Known in Tibetan as Kang Rinpoche, or 'Precious Jewel of Snow', the hulking pyramidal-shaped Mt Kailash (Gāng Rénbōzhāi Fēng; 6714m) seldom needs to be pointed out to travellers: it just dominates the landscape. For Buddhists, Kailash is the abode of Demchok, a wrathful manifestation of Sakyamuni. For Hindus it is the domain of Shiva, the Destroyer and Transformer.

WORTH A TRIP

THE LOST KINGDOM OF GUGE

One worthwhile detour from Darchen is to the surreal ruins of the Guge Kingdom at **Tsaparang** (admission ¥200). The ruins, which seem to grow like a honeycomb out of the barren hills, were once the centre of one of Tibet's most prosperous kingdoms. The tunnels and caves are great fun to explore and the chapels offer superb examples of Kashmiri-influenced mural art. A trip here will add three days to your itinerary, but is worth it to see some outstanding scenery and one of Asia's little-known wonders.

From Darchen it's a day's drive to **Zanda** (札达; Zhádá), the nearest town to Tsaparang (18km away), and home to spectacular Thöling Monastery.

It's not hard to see why Kailash became associated long ago with the myth of a great mountain. More surprising is that this mountain was said to be the source of the four major rivers of Asia: and most astonishing that the legends are more or less true. The drainage system around Kailash and Lake Manasarovar is in fact the source of the Karnali (a major tributary of the Ganges), the Brahmaputra, Indus and Sutlej Rivers. A visit to Kailash puts you squarely in one of the geographical and spiritual centres of the world.

🏃 Activities

Many pilgrims are often happy enough just to gaze at the southern face of Kailash (scarred in such a way that it resembles a swastika – a Buddhist and Hindu symbol of spiritual strength). But for Tibetans and most foreign travellers the purpose of coming here is to complete a *kora* around the mountain.

The *kora* begins in grubby **Darchen** (塔尔钦; Tǎ'ěrqīn; 4560m), and takes (on average) three days to complete (though most Tibetans do it in one 15-hour day). The *kora* is not a climb to the top, but a walk around the central peak. The highest point is the 5630m Drölma-la Pass, though no point is below 4600m.

The first day is a 20km walk (six to seven hours) from Darchen to Dira-puk Monastery. The ascent is minimal, which allows you to take your time and enjoy the otherworldly landscape of the Lha-chu river valley. The second day is the hardest, as it involves the ascent to the Drölma-la pass, the steep descent down the pass to the Lham-chu Khir river val-

ley, and hike to the Zutul-puk Monastery. Expect to take eight hours to complete this 18km stretch. The final day is a simple 14km (three hours) walk back to Darchen. Fit walkers can cover the *kora* in two days if they wish.

Any reasonably fit and acclimatised person should be able to complete the three-day walk, but come prepared with warm and waterproof clothing and equipment. Local guides and porters are available in Darchen for ¥120 a day. Larger groups often hire yaks to carry their supplies.

Travellers must normally register with the **Public Security Bureau** (PSB; 公安局; Gōng'ānjú) in Darchen. There is a ¥200 joint Kailash and Manasarovar entry fee.

🛏 Sleeping & Eating

At the end of each day's walk there is accommodation (¥40 to ¥60) at the local monasteries or in a nearby guesthouse, though it's advisable to carry a tent if walking during July and August or the popular Saga Dawa festival. Instant noodles, tea and beer are available at nomad tents along the way, but bring hot drinks and snacks with you.

Most travellers spend a night in Darchen before the *kora*. Guesthouses offer basic accommodation (no running water, outdoor pit toilets). There are a couple of supermarkets and a public shower; internet might be available by the time you read this.

Pilgrim Hotel (朝圣宾馆; Cháoshèng Bīnguǎn; dm¥60) donates part of its profits to local monasteries; and **Lhasa Holyland Guesthouse** (拉萨圣地康桑旅馆; Lāsà Shèngdì Kāngsāng Lǚguǎn; ☏139-8907 0818; d ¥80-120) houses the local PSB office.

Darchen Aid the Poor Programme Hotel (塔尔青利民扶贫宾馆; Tǎ'ěrqīng Lìmín Fúpín Bīnguǎn; mains ¥10-25) is a cosy Tibetan-style restaurant and our favourite place to eat; it also has decent rooms.

LAKE MANASAROVAR མ་ཕམ་གཡུ་མཚོ 玛旁雍错

After their *kora*, most travellers head to Lake Manasarovar (Mǎpáng Xióngcuò) or Mapham Yum-tso (Victorious Lake) to rest and gaze at the sapphire-blue waters and perfect snow-capped mountain backdrop. The lake is the most venerated in Tibet, and has its own five-day *kora*, accessible by jeep track.

Picturesque **Chiu village**, sight of the Chiu Monastery, overlooks the northwestern shore of the lake, and here you'll find a half-dozen identical friendly **guesthouses** (dm ¥50), some right down at the water's edge. Basic meals are available.

Understand China

>

CHINA TODAY 906

Inequality in China is among the most extreme in the world: the urban middle class is growing rapidly, but most of China remains rural and poor.

HISTORY 909

China has, for much of its history, been in conflict either internally or with outsiders.

PEOPLE OF CHINA.......................... 930

The Chinese are an exceptionally proud people: proud of their civilisation and history, their written language and of their inventions and achievements.

RELIGION & BELIEFS 934

Religious belief in China is generally marked by great tolerance: although each faith is distinct, some crossover exists between Buddhism, Taoism and Confucianism.

CHINESE CUISINE 941

Food plays a central and prominent role in both Chinese society and the national psyche.

ARTS & ARCHITECTURE..................... 953

China is custodian of one of the world's richest cultural and artistic legacies.

CHINA'S LANDSCAPES...................... 967

China is home to the world's highest mountain range, one of the planet's hottest deserts and a colossal web of waterways.

MARTIAL ARTS OF CHINA 977

Chinese martial arts are deeply impregnated with religious and philosophical values – and perhaps a touch of magic.

population per sq km

BĚIJĪNG KŪNMÍNG SHÀNGHĂI

🚶 ≈ 300 people

China Today

China Superpower?

For decades, the world has been hypnotised by China's meteoric rise. Gazing into the statistics, it's all too easy to see an emergent superpower, a picture made more compelling by a West crippled through austerity measures, high unemployment and rescue packages. Books such as *When China Rules the World* by Martin Jacques triumphantly declare the establishment of a new world order. As if to prove the point, China leaped past Japan to become the world's second largest economy in 2011 with a purchasing power parity (PPP) GDP topping a whopping US$11.4 trillion.

China is hoovering up majority stakes in household Western firms, diligently extracting resources in Africa and aiming at the moon in an ambitious space programme. By the end of 2012, China was expected to have more high-speed rail lines than the rest of the world combined. In 2010, China overtook the US as the world's largest energy consumer.

Behind the hype, however, China still sees itself as a developing nation. China has colossal latent power by virtue of its size and population, but these dimensions hamper equal growth and generate complications. Development remains unwieldy and piecemeal: the Pǔdōng skyline is striking, but China's per capita GDP puts it roughly on a level with East Timor, one of Asia's poorest nations.

Sabre rattlers (and neighbouring countries) see a rising military superpower. The rapidly growing Chinese military budget topped US$100 billion in 2012, but it remains dwarfed by the colossal US$740 billion defence spending of the US. In fact, China's domestic security budget (US$111 billion) exceeds investment in defence, suggesting an obsession with internal, rather than external, threats.

» Population:
1.34 billion

» GDP (PPP):
$11.44 trillion

» GDP per
capita: $8500

» Labour force:
795.5 million

» Unemploy-
ment: 6.5%

» Highest point:
Mt Everest
(8848m)

» Annual
alcohol con-
sumption (per
person): 5.2L

Top Books

Dreaming in Chinese (Deborah Fallows) Insightful observations of living among Chinese people and learning Mandarin in China.

The Rape of Nanking (Iris Chang) Puts into perspective China's deep-rooted ambivalence towards its island neighbour, Japan.

Diary of a Madman & Other Stories (Lu Xun) Astonishing tales from the father of modern Chinese fiction.

belief systems
(% of population)

70	22
Atheist	Buddhist

4	1-2	1-2
Christian	Taoist	Muslim

if China were 100 people

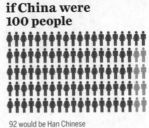

92 would be Han Chinese
8 would be ethnic minorities, eg Zhuang, Manchu, Uighur etc

Challenges

The sky is the limit for China, say many pundits. Naysayers see the start of a hangover as exports contract, overcapacity increases and the property market slides. Less partisan economists discern a levelling out and an adjustment to lower – but still vigorous compared to the West – growth rates. Whatever the scenario, China faces manifold challenges.

Inequality in China is among the most severe on the planet. Factoring in undisclosed income the wealthiest 10% of Chinese may earn 65 times that of the poorest 10%, according to *Bloomberg Businessweek*.

The urban middle class is rapidly expanding, but most of the wealth belongs to a narrow band of plutocrats. The wealth of incoming President Xi Jinping's family reportedly runs into hundreds of millions of US dollars, while outgoing Wen Jiabao's family amassed an astonishing US$2.7 billion, according to a bombshell report by the *New York Times*. The relatives of disgraced Chóngqìng party chief Bo Xilai – expelled from the Communist Party and from China's top legislature amid allegations of corruption in 2012 – amassed riches exceeding US$160 million. As wages in China rise, the days of infinite cheap labour may also be ending. More money in workers' pockets stimulates domestic demand, however, which China must do to break its dependence on exports and develop a more sustainable economic model. Encouraging the Chinese to spend more is tricky, though, as income earners save much of their earnings to compensate for insufficient social-security safety nets.

The Hu Jintao era ended in 2012, and China prepared for a change in leadership with Xi Jinping set to succeed Hu as party secretary and president. Some see Xi Jinping as a potential reformer who will grapple with China's manifest challenges; others sense a more cautious man and a tenure that could see vested interests protected and the status quo upheld.

Top Films

Still Life (Jia Zhangke; 2005) Bleak and hauntingly beautiful portrayal of a family devastated by the construction of the Three Gorges Dam.

Raise the Red Lantern (Zhang Yimou; 1991) The exquisitely fashioned tragedy from the sumptuous palette of the Fifth Generation.

In the Mood for Love (Wong Kar-Wai; 2000) Seductive, stylishly costumed and slow burning Hong Kong romance.

Dissent & Nationalism

The Hu Jintao era took pains to stress social 'harmony', as part of China's formula of a 'peaceful rise'. It is perhaps not surprising that this policy coincided with a period of great social stress.

In its quest for harmony, Běijīng has become less tolerant of dissent. Lawyers, human-rights advocates and democracy activists who attempt to organise resistance to Běijīng's authority routinely face charges of endangering national security. Běijīng reacted with venom to Liu Xiaobo's Nobel Peace Prize in 2010 after he had been sentenced to 11 years in prison for his democratic agenda in Charter 08, a manifesto initially signed by hundreds of Chinese intellectuals and human-rights activists calling for greater political democratic reforms.

Outspoken artist Ai Weiwei has become another sharp thorn in the side of the government. Ai was arrested in 2011 and charged with tax evasion, a charge the artist claims is politically motivated and has, to date, unsuccessfully appealed against.

To shore up support and divert criticism abroad, the Communist Party has long fostered nationalism, which can explode with sudden ferocity. The violent riots over the disputed Diaoyu Islands in 2012 revealed the depth of anti-Japanese sentiment in China, feelings that can be difficult to control once stirred.

China's resurgence is returning it to the prominence it enjoyed for much of its history. It is clear that China considers its moment has arrived, and that it must oppose attempts – whether by the West or Japan – to prevent it taking centre stage in the region.

Dos & Don'ts

» Never, ever fight to settle the bill if your Chinese host is determined to pay.

» Take off your shoes when visiting a Chinese person's home, or offer to.

» Never give a clock as a gift as it has morbid overtones.

Myths

» The Chinese are all hard-working: for sure, but don't expect service with a smile at the train station ticket office.

» The Chinese are communists: some are, more aren't.

» You can see the Great Wall from space: motorways would be more visible as they're far wider.

» Fortune cookies are Chinese: originally Japanese, then popularised in the US, you won't find them in China.

History

The epic sweep of China's history paints a perhaps deceptive impression of long epochs of peace periodically convulsed by break-up, internecine division or external attack. Yet for much of its history China has been in conflict either internally or with outsiders. Although China's size and shape has also continuously changed – from tiny beginnings by the Yellow River (Huáng Hé) to the subcontinent of today – an uninterrupted thread of history runs from its earliest roots to the full flowering of Chinese civilisation. Powerful links connect the Chinese of today with their ancestors 5000 or 6000 years ago, creating the longest-lasting complex civilisation on earth.

> Ban Zhao was the most famous woman scholar in early China. Dating from the late 1st century AD, her work *Lessons for Women* advocated chastity and modesty as favoured female qualities.

From Oracle Bones to Confucius

The earliest 'Chinese' dynasty, the Shang, was long considered apocryphal. However, archaeological evidence – cattle bones and turtle shells in Hénán covered in mysterious scratches, recognised by a scholar as an early form of Chinese writing – proved that a society known as the Shang developed in central China from around 1766 BC. The area it controlled was tiny – perhaps 200km across – but Chinese historians have argued that the Shang was the first Chinese dynasty. By using Chinese writing on 'oracle bones', the dynasty marked its connection with the Chinese civilisation of the present day.

Sometime between 1050 and 1045 BC, a neighbouring group known as the Zhou conquered Shang territory. The Zhou was one of many states competing for power in the next few hundred years, but developments during this period created some of the key sources of Chinese culture that would last till the present day. A constant theme of the first millennium BC was conflict, particularly the periods known as the 'Spring and Autumn' (722–481 BC) and 'Warring States' (475–221 BC).

The Chinese world in the 5th century BC was both warlike and intellectually fertile, in a way similar to ancient Greece during the same period. From this disorder emerged the thinking of Confucius (551–479

TIMELINE

c 4000 BC

Archaeological evidence for the first settlements along the Yellow River (Huáng Hé). Even today, the river remains a central cultural reference point for the Chinese.

c 1700 BC

Craftsmen of the Shang dynasty master the production of bronzeware, in one of the first examples of multiple production in history. The bronzes were ritual vessels.

c 600 BC

Laotzu (Laozi), founder of Taoism, is supposedly born. The folk religion of Taoism coexisted with later introductions such as Buddhism, a reflection of Chinese religion's syncretic, rather than exclusive, nature.

BC), whose system of thought and ethics underpinned Chinese culture for 2500 years (see p155). A wandering teacher, Confucius gave lessons in personal behaviour and statecraft, advocating an ordered and ethical society obedient towards hierarchies. Confucius' desire for an ordered and ethical world seems a far cry from the warfare of the time he lived in.

Early Empires

The Warring States period ended decisively in 221 BC. The Qin kingdom conquered other states in the central Chinese region and Qin Shi Huang declared himself emperor. The first in a line of rulers that would last until 1912, later histories portrayed Qin Shi Huang as particularly cruel and tyrannical, but the distinction is dubious as the ensuing Han dynasty (206 BC–AD 220) adopted many of the short-lived Qin's practices of government.

Qin Shi Huang oversaw vast public works projects, including walls built by some 300,000 men, connecting defences into what would become the Great Wall. He unified the currency, measurements and written language, providing the basis for a cohesive state.

Establishing a trend that would echo through Chinese history, a peasant, Liu Bang (256–195 BC), rose up and conquered China, founding the Han dynasty. The dynasty is so important that the name Hàn (汉; 漢) still refers to ethnic Chinese. Critical to the centralisation of power, Emperor Wu (140–87 BC) institutionalised Confucian norms in government. Promoting merit as well as order, he was the first leader to experiment with examinations for entry into the bureaucracy, but his dynasty was plagued by economic troubles, as estate owners controlled more and more land. Indeed, the issue of land ownership would be a constant problem throughout Chinese history, to today. Endemic economic problems and the inability to exercise control over a growing empire led to

> Evidence from Han tombs suggests that a popular item of cuisine was a thick vegetable and meat stew, and that flavour enhancers such as soy sauce and honey were also used.

---

551 BC

The birth of Confucius. Collected in *The Analects*, his ideas of an ethical, ordered society that operated through hierarchy and self-development would dominate Chinese culture until the early 20th century.

KRZYSZTOF DYDYNSKI / GETTY IMAGES ©

» Confucius statue

214 BC

Emperor Qin indentures thousands of labourers to link existing city walls into one Great Wall, made of tamped earth. The stone-clad bastion dates from the Ming dynasty.

c 100 BC

The Silk Road between China and the Middle East means that Chinese goods become known in places as far off as Rome.

the collapse and downfall of the Han. Social problems included an uprising by Taoists (known as the Yellow Turbans). Upheaval would become a constant refrain in later Chinese dynasties.

Han trade along the Silk Road demonstrated clearly that China was fundamentally a Eurasian power in its relations with neighbouring peoples. To the north, the Xiongnu (a name given to various nomadic tribes of Central Asia) posed the greatest threat to China. Diplomatic links were also formed with Central Asian tribes, and the great Chinese explorer Zhang Qian provided the authorities with information on the possibilities of trade and alliances in northern India. During the same period, Chinese influence percolated into areas that would later become known as Vietnam and Korea.

Disunity Restored

Between the early 3rd and late 6th centuries AD, north China witnessed a succession of rival kingdoms vying for power while a potent division formed between north and south. Riven by warfare, the north was controlled by non-Chinese rule, most successfully by the northern Wei dynasty (386–534), founded by the Tuoba, a northern people who embraced Buddhism and left behind some of China's finest Buddhist art, including the famous caves outside Dūnhuáng (p833). A succession of rival regimes followed until nobleman Yang Jian (d 604) reunified China under the fleeting Sui dynasty (581–618). His son Sui Yangdi contributed greatly to the unification of south and north through construction of the Grand Canal, which was later extended and remained the empire's most important communication route between south and north until the late 19th century. After instigating three unsuccessful incursions onto Korean soil, resulting in disastrous military setbacks, Sui Yangdi faced revolt on the streets and was assassinated in 618 by one of his high officials.

The Tang: China Looks West

The Tang rule (618–907) was an outward-looking time, when China embraced the culture of its neighbours – marriage to Central Asian people or wearing Indian-influenced clothes was part of the era's cosmopolitan élan – and distant nations that reached China via the Silk Road. The Chinese nostalgically regard the Tang as their cultural zenith and Chinatowns around the world are called Tángrénjiē (Tang People Streets) to this day. The output of the Tang poets is still regarded as China's finest, as is Tang sculpture, while its legal code became a standard for the whole East Asian region.

The Tang was founded by the Sui general Li Yuan, his achievements consolidated by his son Taizong (r626–49). Cháng'ān (modern Xī'ān) became the world's most dazzling capital, with its own cosmopolitan foreign quarter, a population of a million, a market where merchants from as far away as Persia mingled with locals and an astonishing city wall

So far, some 7000 soldiers in the famous Terracotta Army have been found near Xī'ān. The great tomb of the first emperor still remains unexcavated, although it is thought to have been looted soon after it was built.

TERRACOTTA ARMY

c 100 BC	AD 755–763	874	c 1000
Buddhism first arrives in China from India. This religious system ends up thoroughly assimilated into Chinese culture and is now more powerful in China than in its country of origin.	An Lushan rebels against the Tang court. Although his rebellion is put down, the court cedes immense military and fiscal power to provincial leaders, a recurring problem through Chinese history.	The Huang Chao rebellion breaks out, which will help reduce the Tang empire to chaos and lead to the fall of the capital in 907.	The major premodern inventions – paper, printing, gunpowder, compass – are commonly used in China. The economy begins to commercialise and create a countrywide market system.

CONFUCIUS TEMPLES 文庙

Confucian temples (wénmiào) are typically lethargic and neglected shrines. This, however, is part of their appeal: they are peaceful, unhurried and often silent.

Confucius Temple, Qūfù (p157) The mother of all patriarchal temples, in Qūfù, Confucius' birthplace.

Confucius Temple, Běijīng (p69) China's second largest Confucius temple and a haven of peace in Běijīng.

Confucius Temple, Jiànshuǐ (p646) Locals insist it's China's biggest temple.

Confucius Temple, Píngyáo (p347) Housing Píngyáo's oldest building in one of China's most magnificent old towns.

Confucius Temple, Xīngchéng (p306) Said to be the oldest temple in China's northeast.

that eventually enveloped 83 sq km. The city exemplified the Tang devotion to Buddhism, with some 91 temples recorded in the city in 722, but a tolerance of and even absorption with foreign cultures allowed alien faiths a foothold, including Nestorian Christianity, Manichaeism, Islam, Judaism and Zoroastrianism.

Taizong was succeeded by a unique figure: Chinese history's sole reigning woman emperor, Wu Zetian (r 690–705). Under her leadership the empire reached its greatest extent, spreading well north of the Great Wall and far west into inner Asia. Her strong promotion of Buddhism, however, alienated her from the Confucian officials and in 705 she was forced to abdicate in favour of Xuanzong, who would preside over the greatest disaster in the Tang's history: the rebellion of An Lushan.

Xuanzong appointed as generals members of minorities from the frontiers, in the belief that they were so far removed from the political system and society that ideas of rebellion or coups would not enter their minds. Nevertheless, it was An Lushan, a general of Sogdian-Turkic parentage, who took advantage of his command in north China to make a bid for imperial power. The fighting lasted from 755 to 763, and although An Lushan was defeated, the Tang's control over China was destroyed forever. It had ceded huge amounts of military and tax-collecting power to provincial leaders to enable them to defeat the rebels, and in doing so dissipated its own power. This was a permanent change in the relationship between the government and the provinces; prior to 755, the government had an idea of who owned what land throughout the empire, but after that date the central government's control was permanently weakened. Even today, the dilemma has not been fully resolved.

The features of the largest Buddhist statue in the Ancestor Worshipping Cave at the Lóngmén Caves outside Luòyáng are supposedly based on Tang female emperor Wu Zetian, a famous champion of Buddhism.

1215	1286	1298–99	1368
Genghis Khan conquers Běijīng as part of his creation of a massive Eurasian empire under Mongol rule. The Mongols overstretch themselves, however, and neglect good governance.	The Grand Canal is extended to Běijīng. Over time, the canal becomes a major artery for the transport of grain, salt and other important commodities between north and south China.	Marco Polo writes his famous account of his travels to China. Inconsistencies in his story have led some scholars to doubt whether he ever went to China at all.	Zhu Yuanzhang founds the Ming dynasty and tries to impose a rigid Confucian social order on the entire population. However, China is now too commercialised for the policy to work.

In its last century, the Tang withdrew from its former openness, turning more strongly to Confucianism, while Buddhism was outlawed by Emperor Wuzong from 842 to 845. The ban was later modified, but Buddhism never regained its previous power and prestige. The Tang decline was marked by imperial frailty, growing insurgencies, upheaval and chaos.

The Song: Conflict & Prosperity

Further disunity – the fragmentary-sounding Five Dynasties or Ten Kingdoms period – followed the fall of the Tang until the northern Song dynasty (960–1127) was established. The Song dynasty existed in a state of constant conflict with its northern neighbours. The northern Song was a rather small empire coexisting with the non-Chinese Liao dynasty (which controlled a belt of Chinese territory south of the Great Wall that now marked China's northern border) and less happily with the western Xia, another non-Chinese power that pressed hard on the northwestern provinces. In 1126 the Song lost its capital, Kāifēng, to a third non-Chinese people, the Jurchen (previously an ally against the Liao). The Song was driven to its southern capital of Hángzhōu for the period of the southern Song (1127–1279), yet the period was culturally rich and economically prosperous.

The full institution of a system of examinations for entry into the Chinese bureaucracy was brought to fruition during the Song. At a time when brute force decided who was in control in much of medieval Europe, young Chinese men sat tests on the Confucian classics, obtaining office if successful (most were not). The system was heavily biased towards the rich, but was remarkable in its rationalisation of authority, and lasted for centuries.

A Chinese woodblock-printed copy of the *Diamond Sutra*, kept in the British Library, is the earliest dated printed book, created in 868. Visit the library website to turn the pages of the sutra online.

RUINS

Many of China's historical artefacts may be in a state of perpetual ruin, but some vestiges get top-billing:

Ruins of the Church of St Paul in Macau (p513) China's most sublime architectural wreck.

Jiànkòu Great Wall (p115) No other section of the Great Wall does the tumble-down look in such dramatic fashion.

Great Fountain Ruins (p72) Sublime tangle of Jesuit-designed stonework in the Summer Palace.

Xanadu (p857) A vivid imagination is required to conjure up impressions of Kublai Khan's pleasure palace.

Ming City Wall Ruins Park (p74) Běijīng's last section of Ming city wall.

1406	1557	c 1600	1644
Ming Emperor Yongle begins construction of the 800 buildings of the Forbidden City. This complex, along with much of the Great Wall, shows the style and size of late-imperial architecture.	The Portuguese establish a permanent trade base in Macau, the first of the European outposts that will eventually lead to imperialist dominance of China until the mid-19th century.	The period of China's dominance as the world's greatest economy begins to end. By 1800 European economies are industrialising and clearly dominant.	Běijīng falls to peasant rebel Li Zicheng and the last Ming emperor Chongzhen hangs himself in Jǐngshān Park; the Qing dynasty is established.

The classical texts set for the examinations became central to the transmission of a sense of elite Chinese culture, even though in later centuries the system's rigidity failed to adapt to social and intellectual change.

China's economy prospered during the Song rule, as cash crops and handicraft products became far more central to the economy, and a genuinely China-wide market emerged, which would become even stronger during the Ming and Qing dynasties. The sciences and arts also flourished under the Song, with intellectual and technical advances across many disciplines. Kāifēng emerged as an eminent centre of politics, commerce and culture.

The cultural quirk of foot binding appears to have emerged during the Song. It is still unknown how the custom of binding up a girl's feet in cloths so that they would never grow larger than the size of a fist began, yet for much of the next few centuries, it became a Chinese social norm.

Mongols to Ming

The fall of the Song reinforced notions of China's Eurasian location and growing external threats. Genghis Khan (1167–1227) was beginning his rise to power, turning his sights on China; he took Běijīng in 1215, destroying and rebuilding it; his successors seized Hángzhōu, the southern Song capital, in 1276. The court fled and, in 1279, southern Song resistance finally expired. Kublai Khan, grandson of Genghis, now reigned over all of China as emperor of the Yuan dynasty. Under Kublai, the entire population was divided into categories of Han, Mongol and foreigner, with the top administrative posts reserved for Mongols, even though the examination system was revived in 1315. The latter decision unexpectedly strengthened the role of local landed elites: since elite Chinese could not advance in the bureaucracy, they decided to spend more time tending their large estates instead. Another innovation was the use of paper money, although overprinting created a problem with inflation.

The Mongols ultimately proved less able at governance than warfare, their empire succumbing to rebellion within a century and eventual vanquishment. Ruling as Ming emperor Hongwu, Zhu Yuanzhang established his capital in Nánjīng, but by the early 15th century the court had begun to move back to Běijīng, where a hugely ambitious reconstruction project was inaugurated by Emperor Yongle (r 1403–24), building the Forbidden City and devising the layout of the city we see today.

Although the Ming tried to impose a traditional social structure in which people stuck to hereditary occupations, the era was in fact one of great commercial growth and social change. Women became subject to stricter social norms (for instance, widow remarriage was frowned upon) but female literacy also grew. Publishing, via woodblock technology, burgeoned and the novel appeared.

To show that he was familiar with classical Chinese culture, emperor Kangxi sponsored a great encyclopaedia of Chinese culture, which is still read by scholars today.

Two Nestorian monks smuggled silkworms out of China in 550 AD, disclosing the method of silk production to the outside world.

1689	1793	1823	1839
The Treaty of Nerchinsk is signed, delineating the border between China and Russia: this is the first modern border agreement in Chinese history, as well as the longest lasting.	British diplomat Lord Macartney visits Běijīng with British industrial products, but is told by the Qianlong emperor that China has no need of his products.	The British are swapping roughly 7000 chests of opium annually – with about 140 pounds of opium per chest, enough to supply one million addicts – compared to 1000 chests in 1773.	The Qing official Lin Zexu demands that British traders at Guǎngzhōu hand over 20,000 chests of opium, leading the British to provoke the First Opium War in retaliation.

DIRTY FOREIGN MUD

Although trade in opium had been banned in China by imperial decree at the end of the 18th century, the *cohong* (local merchants' guild) in Guǎngzhōu helped ensure that the trade continued, and fortunes were amassed on both sides. When the British East India Company lost its monopoly on China trade in 1834, imports of the drug increased to 40,000 chests a year.

In 1839, the Qing government sent Imperial Commissioner Lin Zexu to stamp out the opium trade once and for all. Lin successfully blockaded the British in Guǎngzhōu and publicly burned the 'foreign mud' in Hǔmén. Furious, the British sent an expeditionary force of 4000 men from the Royal Navy to exact reparations and secure favourable trade arrangements.

What would become known as the First Opium War began in June 1840 when British forces besieged Guǎngzhōu and forced the Chinese to cede five ports to the British. With the strategic city of Nanking (Nánjīng) under immediate threat, the Chinese were forced to accept Britain's terms in the Treaty of Nanking.

The treaty abolished the monopoly system of trade, opened the 'treaty ports' to British residents and foreign trade, exempted British nationals from all Chinese laws and ceded the island of Hong Kong to the British 'in perpetuity'. The treaty, signed in August 1842, set the scope and character of the unequal relationship between China and the West for the next half-century.

Emperor Yongle, having usurped power from his nephew, was keen to establish his own legitimacy. In 1405 he launched the first of seven great maritime expeditions. Led by the eunuch general Zheng He (1371–1433), the fleet consisted of more than 60 large vessels and 255 smaller ones, carrying nearly 28,000 men. The fourth and fifth expeditions departed in 1413 and 1417, and travelled as far as the present Middle East. The great achievement of these voyages was to bring tribute missions to the capital, including two embassies from Egypt. Yet ultimately, they were a dead end, motivated by Yongle's vanity to outdo his father, not for the purpose of conquest nor the establishment of a settled trade network. The emperors after Yongle had little interest in continuing the voyages, and China dropped anchor on its global maritime explorations.

The Great Wall was re-engineered and clad in brick while ships also arrived from Europe, presaging an overseas threat that would develop from entirely different directions. Traders were quickly followed by missionaries, and the Jesuits, led by the formidable Matteo Ricci, made their way inland and established a presence at court. Ricci learned fluent Chinese and spent years agonising over how Christian tenets could be made attractive in a Confucian society with very different norms. The

1842

The Treaty of Nánjīng concludes the first Opium War. China is forced to hand over Hong Kong island to the British and open up five Chinese ports to foreign trade.

1856

Hong Xiuquan claims to be Jesus' younger brother and starts the Taiping uprising. With the Nian and Muslim uprisings, the Taiping greatly undermines the authority of the Qing dynasty.

» Victoria Harbour, Hong Kong

HUW JONES / GETTY IMAGES ©

FOREIGN CONCESSIONS & COLONIES

China's coastline is dotted with a string of foreign concession towns that ooze charm and a sensation of 19th and early 20th century grandeur.

Shànghǎi, French Concession (p185) Shànghǎi's most stylish concession goes to the French.

Gǔlàng Yǔ, Xiàmén (p277) Thoroughly charming colonial remains on a beautiful island setting.

Qīngdǎo (p161) Wander the German district for cobbled streets and Teutonic architecture.

Hong Kong (p463) Outstanding ex-colonial cachet on the Guǎngdōng coast.

Macau (p511) An unforgettable cocktail of Cantonese and Portuguese flavour.

Shāmiàn Island (p541) Gentrified and leafy lozenge of Guǎngzhōu sand, decorated with a handsome crop of buildings and streets.

Portuguese presence linked China directly to trade with the New World, which had opened up in the 16th century. New crops, such as potatoes, maize, cotton and tobacco, were introduced, further stimulating the commercial economy. Merchants often lived opulent lives, building fine private gardens (as in Sūzhōu) and buying delicate flowers and fruits.

The Ming was eventually undermined by internal power struggles. Natural disasters, including drought and famine, combined with a menace from the north: the Manchu, a nomadic warlike people, saw the turmoil within China and invaded.

The Qing: the Path to Dynastic Dissolution

After conquering just a small part of China and assuming control in the disarray, the Manchu named their new dynasty the Qing (1644–1911). Once ensconced in the (now torched) Forbidden City, the Manchu realised they needed to adapt their nomadic way of life to suit the agricultural civilisation of China. Threats from inner Asia were neutralised by incorporating the Qing homeland of Manchuria into the empire, as well as that of the Mongols, whom they had subordinated. Like the Mongols before them, the conquering Manchu found themselves in charge of a civilisation whose government they had defeated, but whose cultural power far exceeded their own. The result was quite contradictory: on the one hand, Qing rulers took great pains to win the allegiance of high officials and cultural figures by displaying a familiarity and respect for traditional Chinese culture; on the other hand, the Manchu rulers were at great pains to remain distinct. They enforced strict rules of social

1882

Shànghǎi is electrified by the British-founded Shanghai Electric Company. Shànghǎi's first electricity-producing plant generates 654kw and the Bund is illuminated by electric light the following year.

1898

Emperor Guangxu permits major reforms, including new rights for women, but is thwarted by the Dowager Empress Cixi, who has many reformers arrested and executed.

1898

The New Territories adjoining Kowloon in Hong Kong are leased to the British for 99 years, eventually returning, along with the rest of Hong Kong, in 1997.

» The Bund, Shànghǎi

separation between the Han and Manchu, and tried to maintain – not always very successfully – a culture that reminded the Manchu of their nomadic warrior past. The Qing flourished most greatly under three emperors who ruled for a total of 135 years: Kangxi, Yongzheng and Qianlong.

Much of the map of China that we know today derives from the Qing period. Territorial expansion and expeditions to regions of Central Asia spread Chinese power and culture further than ever. The expansion of the 18th century was fuelled by economic and social changes. The discovery of the New World by Europeans in the 15th century led to a new global market in American food crops, such as chillies and sweet potatoes, allowing food crops to be grown in more barren regions, where wheat and rice had not flourished. In the 18th century, the Chinese population doubled from around 150 million to 300 million people.

Historians now take very seriously the idea that in the 18th century China was among the most advanced economies in the world. The impact of imperialism would help commence China's slide down the table, but the seeds of decay had been sown long before the Opium Wars of the 1840s. Put simply, as China's size expanded, its state remained too small. China's dynasty failed to expand the size of government to cope with the new realities of a larger China.

War & Reform

For the Manchu, the single most devastating incident was not either of the Opium Wars, but the far more destructive anti-Qing Taiping Rebellion of 1850–64, an insurgency motivated partly by a foreign credo (Christianity). Established by Hakka leader Hong Xiuquan, the Heavenly Kingdom of Great Peace (Taiping Tianguo) banned opium and intermingling between the sexes, made moves to redistribute property and was fiercely anti-Manchu. The Qing eventually reconquered the Taiping capital at Nánjīng, but upwards of 20 million Chinese died in the uprising.

The events that finally brought the dynasty down, however, came in rapid succession. Foreign imperialist incursions continued and Western powers nibbled away at China's coastline; Shànghǎi, Qīngdǎo, Tiānjīn, Gǔlàng Yǔ, Shàntóu, Yāntái, Wēihǎi, Níngbō and Běihǎi would all either fall under semicolonial rule or enclose foreign concessions. Hong Kong was a British colony and Macau was administered by the Portuguese. Attempts at self-strengthening – involving attempts to produce armaments and Western-style military technology – were dealt a brutal blow by the Sino-Japanese War of 1894–95. Fought over control of Korea, it ended with the humiliating destruction of the new Qing navy. Not only was Chinese influence in Korea lost, but Taiwan was ceded to Japan.

RAILWAYS

The first railroad in China was the Woosung Railway, which opened in 1876, running between Shànghǎi and Wusong; it operated for less than a year before being dismantled and shipped to Taiwan.

1900	1904–05	1905	1908
The Hanlin Academy in Běijīng – centre of Chinese learning and literature – is accidentally torched by Chinese troops during the Boxer Rebellion, destroying its priceless collection of books.	The Russo–Japanese War is fought entirely on Chinese territory. The victory of Japan is the first triumph by an Asian power over a European one.	Major reforms in the late Qing, including the abolition of the 1000-year-long tradition of examinations in the Confucian classics to enter the Chinese bureaucracy.	Two-year-old Puyi ascends the throne as China's last emperor. Local elites and new classes such as businessmen no longer support the dynasty, leading to its ultimate downfall.

In the 18th century, the Chinese used an early form of vaccination against smallpox that required not an injection, but instead the blowing of serum up the patient's nose.

Japan itself was a powerful Asian example of reform. In 1868 Japan's rulers, unnerved by ever-greater foreign encroachment, had overthrown the centuries-old system of the Shōgun, who acted as regent for the emperor. An all-out program of modernisation, including a new army, constitution, educational system and railway network was undertaken, all of which gave Chinese reformers a lot to ponder.

One of the boldest proposals for reform, which drew heavily on the Japanese model, was the program put forward in 1898 by reformers including the political thinker Kang Youwei (1858–1927). However, in September 1898 the reforms were abruptly halted, as the Dowager Empress Cixi, fearful of a coup, placed the emperor under house arrest and executed several of the leading advocates of change. Two years later, Cixi made a decision that helped to seal the Qing's fate. In 1900 north China was convulsed by attacks from a group of peasant rebels whose martial arts techniques led them to be labelled the Boxers, and who wanted to expel the foreigners and kill any Chinese Christian converts. In a major misjudgement, the dynasty declared in June that it supported the Boxers. Eventually, a multinational foreign army forced its way into China and defeated the uprising which had besieged the foreign Legation Quarter in Běijīng. The imperial powers then demanded huge financial compensation from the Qing. In 1902 the dynasty reacted by implementing the Xinzheng (New Governance) reforms. This set of reforms, now half-forgotten in contemporary China, looks remarkably progressive, even set against the standards of the present day.

Ping pong (pīngpāngqiú) may be China's national sport (guóqiú), but it was invented as an after-dinner game by British Victorians who named it wiff-waff and first used a ball made from champagne corks.

The Cantonese revolutionary Sun Yatsen (1866–1925) remains one of the few modern historical figures respected in both China and Taiwan. Sun and his Revolutionary League made multiple attempts to undermine Qing rule in the late 19th century, raising sponsorship and support from a wide-ranging combination of the Chinese diaspora, the newly emergent middle class, and traditional secret societies. In practice, his own attempts to end Qing rule were unsuccessful, but his reputation as a patriotic figure dedicated to a modern republic gained him high prestige among many of the emerging middle-class elites in China, though much less among the key military leaders.

The end of the Qing dynasty arrived swiftly. Throughout China's southwest, popular feeling against the dynasty had been fuelled by reports that railway rights in the region were being sold to foreigners. A local uprising in the city of Wǔhàn in October 1911 was discovered early, leading the rebels to take over command in the city and hastily declare independence from the Qing dynasty. Within a space of days, then weeks, most of China's provinces did likewise. Provincial assemblies across China declared themselves in favour of a republic, with Sun Yatsen (who was not even in China at the time) as their candidate for president.

1911	1912	1915	1916
Revolution spreads across China as local governments withdraw support for the dynasty, and instead support a republic under the presidency of Sun Yatsen (fundraising in the US at the time).	Yuan Shikai, leader of China's most powerful regional army, goes to the Qing court to announce that the game is up: on 12 February the last emperor, six-year-old Puyi, abdicates.	Japan makes the '21 demands', which would give it massive political, economic and trading rights in parts of China. Europe's attention is distracted by WWI.	Yuan Shikai tries to declare himself emperor. He is forced to withdraw and remain president, but dies of uremia later that year. China splits into areas ruled by rival militarists.

OLD TOWNS & VILLAGES 古镇

For strong shades of historic China, make a beeline for the following old towns *(gǔzhèn)*:

Píngyáo (p346) The best preserved of China's ancient walled towns.

Fènghuáng (p458) Exquisite riverside setting, pagodas, temples, covered bridges and ancient city wall.

Hóngcūn (p381) Gorgeous Huīzhōu village embedded in the lovely south Ānhuī countryside.

Tiánluókēng Tǔlóu Cluster (p282) Overnight in a photogenic Hakka roundhouse.

Shāxī (p657) Flee modern China along Yúnnán's ancient Tea-Horse Road.

Zhènyuǎn (p621) Slot into low gear and admire the peaks, temples and age-old alleys of this riverside Guìzhōu town.

The Republic: Instability & Ideas

The Republic of China lasted less than 40 years on the mainland (1912–1949) and continues to be regarded as a dark chapter in modern Chinese history, when the country was under threat from what many described as 'imperialism from without and warlordism from within'. Yet there was also breathing room for new ideas and culture. In terms of freedom of speech and cultural production, the republic was a much richer time than any subsequent era in Chinese history. Yet the period was certainly marked by repeated disasters, rather like the almost contemporaneous Weimar Republic in Germany.

Sun Yatsen returned to China and only briefly served as president, before having to make way for militarist leader Yuan Shikai. In 1912 China held its first general election, and it was Sun's newly established Kuomintang (Nationalist; Guómíndǎng, literally 'Party of the National People') party that emerged as the largest grouping. Parliamentary democracy did not last long, as the Kuomintang itself was outlawed by Yuan, and Sun had to flee into exile in Japan. However, after Yuan's death in 1916, the country split into rival regions ruled by militarist warlord-leaders. Supposedly 'national' governments in Běijīng often controlled only parts of northern or eastern China and had no real claim to control over the rest of the country. Also, in reality, the foreign powers still had control over much of China's domestic and international situation. Britain, France, the US and the other Western powers showed little desire to lose those rights, such as extraterritoriality and tariff control.

The oldest surviving brick pagoda in China is the Sōngyuè Pagoda, on Sōng Shān in Hénán province, dating to the early sixth century.

The city of Shànghǎi became the focal point for the contradictions of Chinese modernity. By the early 20th century, Shànghǎi was a wonder not just of China, but of the world, with skyscrapers, art deco apartment

1925	1926	1927	1930s
The shooting of striking factory workers on 30 May in Shànghǎi by foreign-controlled police inflames nationalist passions, giving hope to the Kuomintang party, now regrouping in Guǎngzhōu.	The Northern Expedition: Kuomintang and communists unite under Soviet advice to bring together China by force, then establish a Kuomintang government.	The Kuomintang leader Chiang Kaishek turns on the communists in Shànghǎi and Guǎngzhōu, having thousands killed and forcing the communists to turn to a rural-based strategy.	Cosmopolitan Shànghǎi is the world's fifth-largest city (and the largest city in the Far East), supporting a polyglot population of four million people.

HISTORY BOOKS

» *The City of Heavenly Tranquillity: Beijing in the History of China* (Jasper Becker; 2009). Becker's authoritative and heartbreaking rendering of Běijīng's transformation from magnificent Ming capital to communist–capitalist hybrid.

» *The Penguin History of Modern China: The Fall and Rise of a Great Power 1850– 2008* (Jonathan Fenby; 2008).Highly readable account of the paroxysms of modern Chinese history

» *China, A History* (John Key; 2008). An accessible and well-written journey through Middle Kingdom history.

blocks, neon lights, women (and men) in outrageous new fashions, and a vibrant, commercially minded, take-no-prisoners atmosphere. The racism that accompanied imperialism was visible every day, as Europeans kept themselves separate from the Chinese. Yet the glamour of modernity was undeniable too, as workers flocked from rural areas to make a living in the city, and Chinese intellectuals sought out French fashion, British architecture and American movies. In the prewar period, Shànghǎi had more millionaires than anywhere else in China, yet its inequalities and squalor also inspired the first congress of the Chinese Communist Party (CCP).

The militarist government that held power in Běijīng in 1917 provided 96,000 Chinese who served on the Western Front in Europe, not as soldiers but digging trenches and doing hard manual labour. This involvement in WWI led to one of the most important events in China's modern history: the student demonstrations of 4 May 1919.

Double-dealing by the Western Allies and Chinese politicians who had made secret deals with Japan led to an unwelcome discovery for the Chinese diplomats at the Paris Peace Conference in 1919. Germany had been defeated, but its Chinese territories – such as Qīngdǎo – were not to be returned to China but would instead go to Japan. Five days later, on 4 May 1919, some 3000 students gathered in central Běijīng, in front of the Gate of Heavenly Peace, and then marched to the house of a Chinese government minister closely associated with Japan. Once there, they broke in and destroyed the house. This event, over in a few hours, became a legend.

The student demonstration came to symbolise a much wider shift in Chinese society and politics. The May Fourth Movement, as it became known, was associated closely with the New Culture, underpinned by the electrifying ideas of 'Mr Science' and 'Mr Democracy'. In literature, a May Fourth generation of authors wrote works attacking the Confucian-

1930	1931	1932	1935
Chiang's Kuomintang government achieves 'tariff autonomy': for the first time in nearly 90 years, China regains the power to tax imports freely, an essential part of fiscal stability.	Japan invades Manchuria (northeast China), provoking an international crisis and forcing Chiang to consider anti-Japanese, as well as anticommunist, strategies.	War breaks out in the streets of Shànghǎi in February–March, a sign that conflict between the two great powers of East Asia, China and Japan, may be coming soon.	Mao Zedong begins his rise to paramount power at the conference at Zūnyì, held in the middle of the Long March to the northwest, on the run from the Kuomintang.

ism that they felt had brought China to its current crisis, and explored new issues of sexuality and self-development. The CCP, later mastermind of the world's largest peasant revolution, was created in the intellectual turmoil of the movement, many of its founding figures associated with Peking University, such as Chen Duxiu (dean of humanities), Li Dazhao (head librarian) and the young Mao Zedong, a mere library assistant.

The Northern Expedition

After years of vainly seeking international support for his cause, Sun Yat-sen found allies in the newly formed Soviet Russia. The Soviets ordered the fledgling CCP to ally itself with the much larger 'bourgeois' party, the Kuomintang. Their alliance was attractive to Sun: the Soviets would provide political training, military assistance and finance. From their base in Guǎngzhōu, the Kuomintang and CCP trained together from 1923, in preparation for their mission to reunite China.

Sun died of cancer in 1925. The succession battle in the party coincided with a surge in antiforeign feeling that accompanied the May Thirtieth Incident when 13 labour demonstrators were killed by British police in Shànghǎi on 30 May 1925. Under Soviet advice, the Kuomintang and CCP prepared for their 'Northern Expedition', the big 1926 push north that was supposed to finally unite China. In 1926–27, the Soviet-trained National Revolutionary Army made its way slowly north, fighting, bribing or persuading its opponents into accepting Kuomintang control. The most powerful military figure turned out to be an officer from Zhèjiāng named Chiang Kaishek (1887–1975). Trained in Moscow, Chiang moved steadily forward and finally captured the great prize, Shànghǎi, in March 1927. However, a horrific surprise was in store for his communist allies. The Soviet advisers had not impressed Chiang and he was convinced their intention was to take power in alliance with the Kuomintang as a prelude to seizing control themselves. Instead, Chiang struck first. Using local thugs and soldiers, Chiang organised a lightning strike by rounding up CCP activists and union leaders in Shànghǎi and killing thousands of them.

Kuomintang Rule

Chiang Kaishek's Kuomintang government officially came to power in 1928 through a combination of military force and popular support. Marked by corruption, it suppressed political dissent with great ruthlessness. Yet Chiang's government also kick-started a major industrialisation effort, greatly augmented China's transport infrastructure and successfully renegotiated what many Chinese called 'unequal treaties' with Western powers. In its first two years, the Kuomintang doubled the length of highways in China and increased the number of students studying engineering. The government never really controlled more

EUNUCHS

The Tang saw the first major rise to power of eunuchs. Often from ethnic minority groups, they were brought to the capital and given positions within the imperial palace. In many dynasties they had real influence

1937

The Japanese and Chinese clash at Wanping, near Běijīng, on 7 July, sparking the conflict that the Chinese call the 'War of Resistance', which only ends in 1945.

1938

Former prime minister Wang Jingwei announces he has gone over to Japan. He later inaugurates a 'restored' Kuomintang government with Japan holding the whip hand over government.

LONELY PLANET / GETTY IMAGES ©

» Sculpture depicting the 'War of Resistance' against Japan

HISTORIC CITIES

At the centre of things, China's cities have seen dynasties rise, topple and fall, leaving them littered with dynastic vestiges and age-old artefacts.

Běijīng (p50) Heritage, history and imperial grandeur, with the Great Wall to boot.

Xī'ān (p356) The granddaddy of China's old towns, enclosed by an intact Ming-dynasty wall with the Terracotta Warriors in the suburbs.

Hángzhōu (p249) Possibly China's best-looking city, with oodles of charm and history in spades.

Nánjīng (p223) Supreme city walls and imposing imperial Ming vestiges.

than a few (very important) provinces in the east, however, and China remained significantly disunited. Regional militarists continued to control much of western China; the Japanese invaded and occupied Manchuria in 1931; and the communists re-established themselves in the northwest.

In 1934 Chiang Kaishek launched his own ideological counter-argument to communism: the New Life Movement. This was supposed to be a complete spiritual renewal of the nation, through a modernised version of traditional Confucian values, such as propriety, righteousness and loyalty. The New Life Movement demanded that the renewed citizens of the nation must wear frugal but clean clothes, consume products made in China rather than seek luxurious foreign goods, and behave in a hygienic manner. Yet Chiang's ideology never had much success. Against a background of massive agricultural and fiscal crisis, prescriptions about what to wear and how to behave lacked popular appeal.

Chiang Kaishek's New Life Movement and the Chinese Communist Party ideology were attempts to mobilise society through renewal of the individual. But only the communists advocated class war.

The new policies did relatively little to change the everyday life for the population in the countryside, where more than 80% of China's people lived. Some rural reforms were undertaken, including the establishment of rural cooperatives, but their effects were small. The Nationalist Party also found itself unable to collect taxes in an honest and transparent way.

The Long March

The communists had not stood still and after Chiang's treachery, most of what remained of the CCP fled to the countryside. A major centre of activity was the communist stronghold in impoverished Jiāngxī province, where the party began to try out systems of government that would eventually bring them to power. However, by 1934, Chiang's previously ineffective 'extermination campaigns' were making the CCP's position in Jiāngxī untenable, as the Red Army found itself increasingly encircled

1939	**1941**	**1941**	**1943**
On 3–4 May Japanese carpet bombing devastates the temporary Chinese capital of Chóngqìng. From 1938 to 1943, Chóngqìng is one of the world's most heavily bombed cities.	In the base area at Yán'ān (Shaanxi), the 'Rectification' program begins, remoulding the Communist Party into an ideology shaped principally by Mao Zedong.	The Japanese attack the US at Pearl Harbor. China becomes a formal ally of the US, USSR and Britain in WWII, but is treated as a secondary partner at best.	Chiang Kaishek negotiates an agreement with the Allies that, when Japan is defeated, Western imperial privileges in China will end forever, marking the twilight of Western imperialist power in China.

by Nationalist troops. The CCP commenced its Long March, travelling over 6400km. Four thousand of the original 80,000 communists who set out eventually arrived, exhausted, in Shaanxi (Shǎnxī) province in the northwest, far out of the reach of the Kuomintang. It seemed possible that within a matter of months, however, Chiang would attack again and wipe them out.

The approach of war saved the CCP. There was growing public discontent at Chiang Kaishek's seeming unwillingness to fight the Japanese. In fact, this perception was unfair. The Kuomintang had undertaken retraining of key regiments in the army under German advice, and also started to plan for a wartime economy from 1931, spurred on by the Japanese invasion of Manchuria. However, events came to a head in December 1936, when the Chinese militarist leader of Manchuria (General Zhang Xueliang) and the CCP kidnapped Chiang. As a condition of his release, Chiang agreed to an openly declared United Front: the Kuomintang and communists would put aside their differences and join forces against Japan.

War & the Kuomintang

China's status as a major participant in WWII is often overlooked or forgotten in the West. The Japanese invasion of China, which began in 1937, was merciless, with the notorious Nánjīng Massacre (also known as the Rape of Nánjīng; see p225) just one of a series of war crimes committed by the Japanese Army during its conquest of eastern China. The government had to operate in exile from the far southwestern hinterland of China, as its area of greatest strength and prosperity, China's eastern seaboard, was lost to Japanese occupation.

In China itself, it is now acknowledged that both the Kuomintang and the communists had important roles to play in defeating Japan. Chiang, not Mao, was the internationally acknowledged leader of China during this period, and despite his government's multitude flaws, he maintained resistance to the end. However, his government was also increasingly trapped, having retreated to Sìchuān province and a temporary capital at Chóngqìng. Safe from land attack by Japan, the city still found itself under siege, subjected to some of the heaviest bombing in the war. From 1940, supply routes were cut off as the road to Burma was closed by Britain, under pressure from Japan, and Vichy France closed connections to Vietnam. Although the US and Britain brought China on board as an ally against Japan after Pearl Harbor on 7 December 1941, the Allied 'Europe First' strategy meant that China was always treated as a secondary theatre of war. Chiang Kaishek's corruption and leadership qualities were heavily criticised, and while these accusations were not groundless, without Chinese Kuomintang armies (which kept

Paul French's *Midnight in Peking* (2012) is a gripping true-crime murder mystery examining the death of Pamela Werner in 1937 Peking.

Toilet paper was first used in China, as early as the 6th century AD, when it was used by the wealthy and privileged for sanitary purposes.

1946	1949		1950
Communists and the Kuomintang fail to form a coalition government, plunging China back into civil war. Communist organisation, morale and ideology all prove key to the communist victory.	Mao Zedong stands on top of the Gate of Heavenly Peace in Běijīng on 1 October, and announces the formation of the PRC, saying 'The Chinese people have stood up'.		China joins the Korean War, helping Mao to consolidate his regime with mass campaigns that inspire (or terrify) the population.

» Mao Zedong, Běijīng

one million Japanese troops bogged down in China for eight years), the Allies' war in the Pacific would have been far harder. The communists had an important role as guerrilla fighters, but did far less fighting in battle than the Kuomintang.

The real winners from WWII, however, were the communists. They undertook important guerrilla campaigns against the Japanese across northern and eastern China, but the really key changes were taking place in the bleak, dusty hill country centred on the small town of Yán'ān, capital of the CCP's largest stronghold. The 'Yán'ān way' that developed in those years solidified many CCP policies: land reform involving redistribution of land to the peasants, lower taxes, a self-sufficient economy, ideological education and, underpinning it all, the CCP's military force, the Red Army. By the end of the war with Japan, the communist areas had expanded massively, with some 900,000 troops in the Red Army, and party membership at a new high of 1.2 million.

Above all, the war with Japan had helped the communists come back from the brink of the disaster they had faced at the end of the Long March. The Kuomintang and communists then plunged into civil war in 1946 and after three long years the CCP won. On 1 October 1949 in Běijīng, Mao declared the establishment of the People's Republic of China.

Chiang Kaishek fled to the island of Formosa (Taiwan), which China had regained from Japan after WWII. He took with him China's gold reserves and the remains of his air force and navy, and set up the Republic of China (ROC), naming his new capital Taipei (台北, Táiběi).

> Traditionally the dragon (lóng) was associated with the emperor and the male principle while the phoenix (fènghuáng) was a symbol of the empress and the female principle.

Mao's China

Mao's China desired, above all, to exercise ideological control over its population. It called itself 'New China', with the idea that the whole citizenry, down to the remotest peasants, should find a role in the new politics and society. The success of Mao's military and political tactics also meant that the country was, for the first time since the 19th century, united under a strong central government.

Most Westerners – and Western influences – were swiftly removed from the country. The US refused to recognise the new state at all. However, China had decided, in Mao's phrase, to 'lean to one side' and ally itself with the Soviet Union in the still-emerging Cold War. The 1950s marked the high point of Soviet influence on Chinese politics and culture. However, the decade also saw rising tension between the Chinese and the Soviets, fuelled in part by Khrushchev's condemnation of Stalin (which Mao took, in part, as a criticism of his own cult of personality). Sino–Soviet differences were aggravated with the withdrawal of Soviet technical assistance from China, and reached a peak with intense border clashes during 1969. Relations remained frosty until the 1980s.

> Mao Zedong is one of the most intriguing figures of 20th-century history. Philip Short's *Mao: A Life* (1999) is the most detailed and thoughtful recent account of his life in English.

1957	1958	1962	1966
A brief period of liberalisation under the 'Hundred Flowers Movement'. However, criticisms of the regime lead Mao to crack down and imprison or exile thousands of dissidents.	The Taiwan Straits Crisis. Mao's government fires missiles near islands under the control of Taiwan in an attempt to prevent rapprochement between the US and USSR in the Cold War.	The Great Leap Forward causes mass starvation. Politburo members Liu Shaoqi and Deng Xiaoping reintroduce limited market reforms, which will lead to their condemnation during the Cultural Revolution.	The Cultural Revolution breaks out, and Red Guards demonstrate in cities across China. The movement is marked by a fetish for violence as a catalyst for transforming society.

Mao's experiences had convinced him that only violent change could shake up the relationship between landlords and their tenants, or capitalists and their employees, in a China that was still highly traditional. The first year of the regime saw some 40% of the land redistributed to poor peasants. At the same time, some one million or so people condemned as 'landlords' were persecuted and killed. The joy of liberation was real for many Chinese, but campaigns of terror were also real and the early 1950s were no golden age.

As relations with the Soviets broke down in the mid-1950s, the CCP leaders' thoughts turned to economic self-sufficiency. Mao, supported by Politburo colleagues, proposed the policy known as the Great Leap Forward (Dàyuèjìn), a highly ambitious plan to harness the power of socialist economics to boost production of steel, coal and electricity. Agriculture was to reach an ever-higher level of collectivisation. Family structures were broken up as communal dining halls were established: people were urged to eat their fill, as the new agricultural methods would ensure plenty for all, year after year.

However, the Great Leap Forward was a horrific failure. Its lack of economic realism caused a massive famine and at least 20 million deaths; historian Frank Dikötter posits a much larger minimum figure of 45 million deaths in his *Mao's Great Famine* (2010). Yet the return to a semi-market economy in 1962, after the Leap had comprehensively ended, did not dampen Mao's enthusiasm for revolutionary renewal. This led to the last and most fanatical of the campaigns that marked Mao's China: the Cultural Revolution of 1966–76.

Cultural Revolution

Mao had become increasingly concerned that post-Leap China was slipping into 'economism' – a complacent satisfaction with rising standards of living that would blunt people's revolutionary fervour. Mao was particularly concerned that the young generation might grow up with a dimmed spirit of revolution. For these reasons, Mao decided upon a massive campaign of ideological renewal, in which he would attack his own party.

Still the dominant figure in the CCP, Mao used his prestige to undermine his own colleagues. In summer 1966, prominent posters in large, handwritten characters appeared at prominent sites, including Peking University, demanding that figures such as Liu Shaoqi (president of the PRC) and Deng Xiaoping (senior Politburo member) must be condemned as 'takers of the capitalist road'. Top leaders suddenly disappeared from sight, only to be replaced by unknowns, such as Mao's wife Jiang Qing and her associates, later dubbed the 'Gang of Four'. Meanwhile, an all-pervasive cult of Mao's personality took over. One million youths at a

Ding Ling's novel *The Sun Shines on the Sanggan River* (1948) gives a graphic account of the violence, as well as the joy, that greeted land reform (ie redistribution) in China in the early 1950s.

During the Cultural Revolution, some 2.2 billion Chairman Mao badges were cast. Read *Mao's Last Revolution* (2006) by Roderick MacFarquhar and Michael Schoenhals for the history; see Zhang Yimou's film *To Live* (1994) to understand the emotions.

1972	1973	1976	1980
US President Richard Nixon visits China, marking a major rapprochement during the Cold War, and the start of full diplomatic relations between the two countries.	Deng Xiaoping returns to power as deputy premier. The modernising faction in the party fights with the Gang of Four, who support the continuing Cultural Revolution.	Mao Zedong dies, aged 83. The Gang of Four are arrested by his successor and put on trial, where they are blamed for all the disasters of the Cultural Revolution.	The one-child policy is enforced. The state adopts it as a means of reducing the population, but at the same time imposes unprecedented control over the personal liberty of women.

SLOGANEERING

In communist China, political slogans were always one of the first instruments to hand in the propaganda department's ample tool chest. Typically painted in vermillion letters on walls, banners or posters, communist slogans were punchy, formulaic, systematic and unsophisticated. Their language was forthright and simple, appealing directly to the masses. The emphasis on rote learning in Chinese education gave slogans added authority and easy memorability while their appearance everywhere reinforced the ever-presence and watchfulness of the communist state. During the Cultural Revolution they became increasingly violent and intimidating. Slogans from this period survive fitfully around China, including in the following places, although many have either been scrubbed out or buried beneath cement or plaster.

» Nánjiēcūn (p401): literally everywhere
» Chuāndǐxià (p111): on external house walls in the village
» 798 Art District, Běijīng (p67): throughout the district
» Huā'è Lóu (p568): Hakka roundhouse in eastern Guǎngdōng
» Jiāyùguān Fort (p827): in yellow letters and ghostly shadows on buildings and walls

time, known as Red Guards, would flock to hear Mao in Tiān'ānmén Sq. Posters and pictures of Mao were everywhere. The Red Guards were not ashamed to admit that their tactics were violent. Immense violence permeated throughout society: teachers, intellectuals and landlords were killed in their thousands.

While Mao initiated and supported the Cultural Revolution, it was also genuinely popular among many young people (who had less to lose). However, police authority effectively disappeared, creative activity came to a virtual standstill and academic research was grounded.

The Cultural Revolution could not last. Worried by the increasing violence, the army forced the Red Guards off the streets in 1969. The early 1970s saw a remarkable rapprochement between the US and China: the former was desperate to extricate itself from the quagmire of the Vietnam war; the latter terrified of an attack from the now-hostile USSR. Secretive diplomatic manoeuvres led, eventually, to the official visit of US President Richard Nixon to China in 1972, which began the reopening of China to the West. Slowly, the Cultural Revolution began to cool down, but its brutal legacy survives today. Many of those guilty of murder and violence re-entered society with little or no judgment while today's CCP discourages open analysis and debate of the 'decade of chaos'.

1987	1988	1989	1997
The Last Emperor, filmed in the Forbidden City, collects an Oscar for Best Picture, and marks a new openness in China towards the outside world.	The daring series *River Elegy (Héshāng)* is broadcast on national TV. It is a devastating indictment of dictatorship and Mao's rule in particular, and is banned in China after 1989.	Hundreds of civilians are killed by Chinese troops in the streets around Tiān'ānmén Sq. No official reassessment has been made, but rumours persist of deep internal conflict within the party.	Hong Kong is returned to the People's Republic of China. Widespread fears that China will interfere directly in its government prove wrong, but politics become more sensitive to Běijīng.

Reform

Mao died in 1976, to be succeeded by the little-known Hua Guofeng (1921–2008). Within two years, Hua had been outmanoeuvred by the greatest survivor of 20th-century Chinese politics, Deng Xiaoping. Deng had been purged twice during the Cultural Revolution, but after Mao's death he was able to reach supreme leadership in the CCP with a radical program. In particular, Deng recognised that the Cultural Revolution had been highly damaging economically to China. Deng enlisted a policy slogan originally invented by Mao's pragmatic prime minister, Zhou Enlai – the 'Four Modernisations'. The party's task would be to set China on the right path in four areas: agriculture, industry, science and technology, and national defence.

To make this policy work, many of the assumptions of the Mao era were abandoned. The first highly symbolic move of the 'reform era' (as the post-1978 period is known) was the breaking down of the collective farms. Farmers were able to sell a proportion of their crops on the free market, and urban and rural areas were also encouraged to establish small local enterprises. 'To get rich is glorious,' Deng declared, adding, 'it doesn't matter if some areas get rich first.' As part of this encouragement of entrepreneurship, Deng designated four areas on China's coast as Special Economic Zones (SEZs), which would be particularly attractive to foreign investors.

Politics was kept on a much shorter rein than the economy, however. Deng was relaxed about a certain amount of ideological impurity, but some other members of the leadership were concerned by the materialism in reform-era China. They supported campaigns of 'antispiritual pollution', in which influences from the capitalist world were condemned. Yet inevitably the overall movement seemed to be towards a freer, market-oriented society.

The new freedoms that the urban middle classes enjoyed created the appetite for more. After student protests demanding further opening up of the party in 1985–86, the prime minister (and relative liberal) Hu Yaobang was forced to resign in 1987 and take responsibility for allowing social forces to get out of control. He was replaced as general secretary by Zhao Ziyang, who was more conservative politically, although an economic reformer. In April 1989 Hu Yaobang died, and students around China used the occasion of his death to organise protests against the continuing role of the CCP in public life. At Peking University, the breeding ground of the May Fourth demonstrations of 1919, students declared the need for 'science and democracy', the modernising watchwords of 80 years earlier, to be revived.

In spring 1989 Tiān'ānmén Sq was the scene of an unprecedented demonstration. At its height, nearly a million Chinese workers and students, in a rare cross-class alliance, filled the space in front of the

RED SORGHUM

One product of the new freedom of the 1980s was a revived Chinese film industry. *Red Sorghum*, the first film directed by Zhang Yimou, was a searingly erotic film of a type that had not been seen since 1949.

2001

China joins the World Trade Organization, giving it a seat at the top table that decides global norms on economics and finance.

2004

The world's first commercially operating Maglev train begins scorching a trail across Shànghǎi's Pǔdōng District, reaching a top speed of 431km/hour.

» Maglev high-speed train, Shànghǎi (p219)

CHRISTOPHER HERWIG / GETTY IMAGES ©

Gate of Heavenly Peace, with the CCP profoundly embarrassed to have the world's media record such events. By June 1989 the numbers in the square had dwindled to only thousands, but those who remained showed no signs of moving. Martial law was imposed and on the night of 3 June and early hours of 4 June, tanks and armoured personnel carriers were sent in. The death toll in Běijīng has never been officially confirmed, but it seems likely to have been in the high hundreds or even more. Hundreds of people associated with the movement were arrested, imprisoned or forced to flee to the West.

For some three years, China's politics were almost frozen, but in 1992 Deng, the man who had sent in the tanks, made his last grand public gesture. That year, he undertook what Chinese political insiders called his 'southern tour', or *nánxún*. By visiting Shēnzhèn, Deng indicated that the economic policies of reform were not going to be abandoned. The massive growth rates that the Chinese economy has posted ever since have justified his decision. Deng also made another significant choice: grooming Jiang Zemin – the mayor of Shànghǎi, who had peacefully dissolved demonstrations in Shànghǎi in a way that the authorities in Běijīng had not – as his successor by appointing him as general secretary of the party in 1989.

21st century China

From 2002, President Hu Jintao and Prime Minister Wen Jiabao made efforts to deal with growing regional inequality and the poverty scarring rural areas. China's lopsided development continued, however, despite a huge programme to develop the western regions, and help balance them with the booming east and south coast cities. By 2009, an inflow of US$325 billion had dramatically boosted GDP per capita in the western regions but a colossal prosperity gap survived and significant environmental challenges – from desertification to water shortages and soil erosion – persisted.

The question of political reform found itself shelved, partly because economic growth was bringing prosperity to so many, albeit in uneven fashion. Property prices – especially in the richer eastern coastal provinces – were rocketing and the export and investment-driven economy was thriving. For many, the first decade of the 21st century was marked by spectacular riches for some – the number of dollar billionaires doubled in just two years – and property prices began moving dramatically beyond the reach of the less fortunate. This period coincided with the greatest migration of workers to the cities the world has ever seen.

China responded to the credit crunch of 2007 and the downturn in Western economies with a stimulus package of US$586 billion between 2008 and 2009. Property and infrastructure construction enjoyed spec-

Life stories in China went through unimaginable transformations in the early 20th century. Henrietta Harrison's *The Man Awakened from Dreams* (2005) and Robert Bickers' *Empire Made Me* (2003) grippingly describe these changes for a rural scholar and a Shànghǎi policeman.

2006	**2008**	**2008**	**2008**
The Three Gorges Dam is completed. Significant parts of the landscape of western China are lost beneath the waters, but energy is also provided for the expanding Chinese economy.	Běijīng hosts the 2008 Summer Olympic Games and Paralympics. The Games go smoothly and are widely considered to be a great success in burnishing China's image overseas.	Violent riots in Lhasa, Tibet, again put the uneasy region centre stage. Protests spread to other Tibetan areas in Gānsù, Sìchuān and Qīnghǎi provinces.	A huge 8.0 magnitude earthquake convulses Sìchuān province, leaving 87,000 dead or missing and rendering millions homeless.

HISTORY MUSEUMS

» Hong Kong Museum of History (p477) One of the former British territory's best museums: a colourful narrative supported by imaginative displays.

» Shànghǎi History Museum (p194) Excellent chronicle of Shànghǎi's colourful journey from 'Little Sūzhōu' to 'Whore of the Orient' and beyond.

» Macau Museum (p513) The ex-Portuguese territory's fascinating history brought vividly to life.

» Shaanxi History Museum (p359) Eye-opening and informative chronicle of ancient Chang'an.

tacular growth, buffering China from the worst effects of the downturn, but the export sector contracted as demand dried up overseas. A barrage of restrictions on buying second properties attempted to flush speculators from the market and tame price rises. These policies partially worked but millions of flats across China lay empty – bought by investors happy to see prices rise – and entire ghost towns (such as Ordos in Inner Mongolia, built on the back of the coal rush) had already risen from the ground.

Despite resilient and ambitious planning (the high-speed rail network was massively expanded, the space programme set itself bold targets, some of the world's tallest buildings were flung up), the Chinese economy remained fundamentally imbalanced. Skewed towards the export industry and high-investment projects, it needed to build itself more securely on domestic demand to sustain long-term growth and protect itself from global downturns. Some analysts also sensed that the stimulus package had prompted an even greater over-capacity and over-investment in the Chinese economy, the world's second largest after overtaking Japan in 2011.

As a permanent member of the UN Security Council and in its quest for economic and diplomatic influence in Africa and South America, China has a powerful international role. It is, however, hesitant to assume a more influential position in international affairs. China's preference for remaining neutral but business-like may also be tested: crises such as the ever-volatile North Korean situation, Iran's nuclear ambitions, the Syrian conflict, the scramble for mineral resources in Africa, and energy resources around the globe, mean that China is having to make hard choices about which nations it decides to favour. Relations with the neighbours have become pricklier as China has grown in stature and territorial disputes with India, Japan, the Philippines and Vietnam have increasingly occupied the agenda.

The Soviets withdrew all assistance from the PRC in 1960, leaving the great bridge across the Yangzi River at Nánjīng half-built. It became a point of pride for Chinese engineers to finish the job without foreign help.

2009	2010	2011	2012
July riots in Ürümqi leave hundreds dead as interethnic violence flares between Uighurs and Han Chinese. Běijīng floods the region with soldiers and implements a 10-month internet blackout.	A huge 7.1-magnitude earthquake in the Qīnghǎi region of the far west flattens the remote town of Yùshù in April, killing thousands.	Two high-speed trains collide in July near Wēnzhōu in Zhèjiāng province, killing 40 people, the first fatal high-speed rail crash in China.	After the heaviest rainfall in 60 years, Běijīng is inundated with epic summer floods; 77 people are killed by the floodwaters and 65,000 evacuated.

People of China

Despite being the world's most populous nation – the stamping ground of roughly one-fifth of humanity – China is often regarded as being largely homogenous, at least from a remote Western perspective. This is probably because Han Chinese – the majority ethnic type in this energetic and bustling nation – constitute over nine-tenths of the population. But like Chinese cuisine, and of course the nation's mystifying linguistic Babel, you only have to cover a bit more mileage and turn a few extra corners to come face-to-face with a colourful mix of ethnicities.

Ethnicity

Han Chinese

The Naxi created a written language more than 1000 years ago using an extraordinary system of pictographs – the only hieroglyphic language still in use today.

Han Chinese (Han zu) – the predominant clan among China's 56th recognised ethnic group – make up the lion's share of China's people, 92% of the total figure. When we think of China – from its writing system to its visual arts, calligraphy, history, literature, language and politics – we tend to associate it with Han culture.

The Han Chinese are distributed throughout China but are predominantly concentrated along the Yellow River, Yangzi River and Pearl River basins. Taking their name from the Han dynasty, the Han Chinese themselves are not markedly homogenous. China was ruled by non-Han Altaic (Turk, Tungusic or Mongolian) invaders for long periods, most demonstrably during the Yuan dynasty (Mongols) and the long Qing dynasty (Manchu), but also under the Jin, the Liao and other eras. This Altaic influence is more evident in northern Chinese with their larger and broader frames and rounder faces, compared to their slighter and thinner southern Han Chinese counterparts, who are physically more similar to the southeast Asian type. Shànghǎi Chinese for example are notably more southern in appearance; with their rounder faces, Běijīng Chinese are quite typically northern Chinese. With mass migration to the cities from rural areas and the increased frequency of marriage between Chinese from different parts of the land, these physical differences are likely to diminish slightly over time.

Farwest China (www.farwestchina.com) is a useful website and blog covering the people, culture and landscapes of Xīnjiāng in China's northwest.

The Han Chinese display further stark differences in their rich panoply of dialects, which fragments China into a frequently baffling linguistic mosaic, although the promotion of Mandarin (Hànyǔ – or 'language of the Han') has blurred this considerably. The common written form of Chinese using characters (Hànzi – or 'characters of the Han'), however, binds all dialects together.

The Non-Han Chinese

A glance at the map of China reveals that the core heartland regions of Han China are central fragments of modern-day China's huge expanse.

The colossal regions of Tibet, Qīnghǎi, Xīnjiāng, Inner Mongolia and the three provinces of the northeast (Manchuria – Hēilóngjiāng, Jílín and Liáoníng) are all historically non-Han regions, areas of which remain essentially non-Han today.

Many of these regions are peopled by some of the remaining 8% of the population: China's 55 other ethnic minorities, known collectively as *shǎoshù mínzú* (少数民族; minority nationals). The largest minority groups in China include the Zhuang (壮族), Manchu (满族; Man zu), Miao (苗族), Uighur (维吾尔族; Weiwu'er zu), Yi (彝族), Tujia (土家族), Tibetan (藏族; Zang zu), Hui (回族), Mongolian (蒙古族; Menggu zu), Buyi (布依族), Dong (侗族), Yao (瑶族), Korean (朝鲜族; Chaoxian zu), Bai (白族), Hani (哈尼族), Li (黎族), Kazak (哈萨克族; Hasake zu) and Dai (傣族). Population sizes differ dramatically, from the sizeable Zhuang in Guǎngxī to small numbers of Menba (门巴族) in Tibet. Ethnic labelling can be quite fluid: the roundhouse-building Hakka (客家; Kejia) were once regarded as a separate minority, but are today considered Han Chinese.

China's minorities tend to cluster along border regions, in the northwest, the west, the southwest, the north and northeast of China, but are also distributed throughout the country. Some people are found in just one area (such as the Hani in Yúnnán); others, such as the Muslim Hui (p842), live all over China.

Wedged into the southwest corner of China between Tibet, Myanmar (Burma), Vietnam and Laos, fecund Yúnnán province alone is home to more than 20 ethnic groups, making it one of the most ethnically diverse provinces in the country. See that chapter for an introduction to the minority peoples of the region.

The Chinese Character

Shaped by Confucian principles, the Chinese are thoughtful and discreet, subtle but also pragmatic. Conservative and rather introverted, they favour dark clothing over bright or loud colours while their body language is usually reserved and undemonstrative, yet attentive.

The Chinese can be both delightful and mystifyingly contradictory. One moment they will give their seat to an elderly person on the bus or help someone who is lost, and the next moment they will entirely ignore an old lady who has been knocked over by a motorbike.

Particularly diligent, the Chinese are inured to the kind of hours that may prompt a workers' insurrection elsewhere. This is partly due to a traditional culture of hard work but is also a response to the absence of social-security safety nets and an anxiety regarding economic and political uncertainties. The Chinese impressively save much of what they earn, emphasising the virtue of prudence. Despite this restraint, however, wastefulness can be astounding when 'face' is involved: mountains of food are often left on restaurant dining tables, particularly if important guests are present.

PEOPLE OF CHINA THE CHINESE CHARACTER

BILLIONAIRES

Around 35% of Omega watch sales occur in China while the nation is second only to the United States in its number of dollar billionaires.

CHINA DEMOGRAPHICS

» Population: 1.34 billion
» Birth rate: 12.31 births per 1000 people
» Percentage of people over 65 years of age: 8.9%
» Urbanisation rate: 2.3%
» Sex ratio (under age of 15): 1.17 (boys to girls)
» Life expectancy: 74.8 years

CHINA'S 'ONE-CHILD POLICY'

The 'one-child policy' (actually a misnomer) was railroaded into effect in 1979 in a bid to keep China's population to one billion by the year 2000; the latest government estimate claims the population will peak at 1.5 billion in 2033. The policy was harshly implemented at first but rural revolt led to a softer stance; nonetheless, it generated much bad feeling between local officials and the rural population.

All non-Han minorities are exempt from the one-child policy. Han Chinese parents who were both single children can have a second child. Rural families are now allowed to have two children if the first child is a girl, but some have upwards of three or four kids. Additional children often result in fines and families having to shoulder the cost of education themselves, without government assistance. Official stated policy opposes forced abortion or sterilisation, but allegations of coercion continue as local officials strive to meet population targets.

Families who do abide by the one-child policy will often go to great lengths to make sure their child is male. In parts of China, this has resulted in a serious imbalance of the sexes – in 2010, 118 boys were born for every 100 girls. In some provinces the imbalance has been even higher. By 2020, potentially around 35 million men may be unable to find spouses.

Another consequence of the policy is a rapidly ageing population, with a projected one-third of the populace over the age of sixty by 2040.

As women can have a second child abroad, this led to large numbers of mainland women giving birth in Hong Kong (where the child also qualified for Hong Kong citizenship). The Hong Kong government is attempting to use new legislation to curb this phenomenon, dubbed 'birth tourism', as government figures revealed that almost half of babies born in the territory in 2010 were born to mainland parents.

In recent years signals have emerged that the one-child policy may be relaxed or revised in some provinces and cities.

MANCHU

Despite their culture once ruling China during the Qing dynasty (1644–1911), possibly fewer than 70 native speakers of the Manchu language survive today.

Chinese people are deeply generous. Don't be surprised if a person you have just met on a train invites you for a meal in the dining carriage; they will almost certainly insist on paying, grabbing the bill from the waitress at blinding speed and tenaciously fighting off your attempts to pay.

The Chinese are also an exceptionally dignified people. They are proud of their civilisation and history, their written language and their inventions and achievements. This pride rarely comes across as arrogance, however, and can be streaked with a lack of self-assurance. The Chinese may, for example, be very gratified by China's newfound world status, but may squirm at the mention of food safety.

The modern Chinese character has been shaped by recent political realities, and while Chinese people have always been reserved and circumspect, in today's China they can appear even more prudent. Impressive mental gymnastics are performed to detour contentious domestic political issues, which can make the mainland Chinese appear complicated, despite their reputation for being straightforward.

Women in China

Equality & Emancipation

Chairman Mao once said that women hold up half the sky and when Liu Yang became the first Chinese woman in space in 2012, his words took on a new meaning.

Women in today's China officially share complete equality with men; however, as with other nations that profess sexual equality, the reality is often far different. Chinese women do not enjoy strong political representation and the Chinese Communist Party remains a largely patriarchal organisation. Iconic political leaders from the early days of the Chinese Communist Party were men and the influential echelons of the party persist as a largely male domain. Only a handful of the great scientists celebrated in a long photographic mural at Shànghǎi's Science and Technology Museum are women.

The Communist Party after 1949 tried to outlaw old customs and put women on equal footing with men. It abolished arranged marriages and encouraged women to get an education and join the workforce. Women were allowed to keep their maiden name upon marriage and leave their property to their children. In its quest for equality during this period however, the Communist Party seemed to 'desexualise' women, fashioning instead a kind of idealised worker/mother/peasant paradigm.

Chinese Women Today

High-profile, successful Chinese women are very much in the public eye, but the relative lack of career opportunities for females in other fields also suggests a continuing bias against women in employment.

Women's improved social status today has meant that more women are putting off marriage until their late 20s or early 30s, choosing instead to focus on education and career opportunities. This has been enhanced by the rapid rise in house prices, further encouraging women to leave marriage (and having children) till a later age. Premarital sex and co-habitation before marriage are increasingly common in larger cities and lack the stigma they had several years ago.

Some Chinese women are making strong efforts to protect the rights of women in China, receiving international attention in the process. In 2010 the Simone de Beauvoir prize for women's freedom was awarded to Guo Jianmei, a Chinese lawyer and human rights activist, and filmmaker and professor Ai Xiaoming. Guo Jianmei also received the International Women of Courage Award in 2011.

Rural Women in China

A strong rural-urban divide exists. Urban women are far more optimistic and freer, while women from rural areas, where traditional beliefs are at their strongest, fight an uphill battle against discrimination. Rural Chinese mores are heavily biased against females, where a marked preference for baby boys exists. China's women are more likely to commit suicide than men (in the West it is the other way around), while the suicide rate for rural Chinese women is around five times the urban rate.

China has almost 90 cities with populations of five to 10 million people and more than 170 cities with between one and five million people.

PEOPLE OF CHINA WOMEN IN CHINA

Religion & Beliefs

Despite the seemingly pragmatic nature of the Chinese people, ideas have always possessed a particular volatility and potency in the Middle Kingdom. It may have become alloyed with consumerism in today's China, but communism itself was a forceful ideology that briefly assumed supreme authority over the minds of China's citizens. The Taiping Rebellion of the 19th century fused Christianity with revolutionary principles of social organisation, almost sweeping away the Qing dynasty in the process and leaving 20 million dead in its horrifying 20-year spasm. The momentary incandescence of the Boxer Rebellion (1899–1901) drew upon a volatile cocktail of martial-arts practices and superstition, blended with xenophobia. The chaos of the Cultural Revolution is another reminder of what may happen in China when ideas assume the full supremacy and stature they seek.

The Chinese Communist Party (CCP) today remains fearful of ideas and beliefs that challenge its authority. Proselytising is not permitted, religious organisation is regulated and organisations such as Falun Gong (p935) can be banned outright. Despite these constraints, worship and religious practice is generally permitted and China's spiritual world provides a vivid and colourful backdrop to contemporary Chinese life.

The death of a young toddler, who was run over twice and ignored by nearly 20 passers-by in Fóshān in 2011, prompted a passionate debate about morals in modern Chinese society.

Religion Today

China has always had a pluralistic religious culture, and although statistics in China are a slippery fish, an estimated 400 million Chinese today adhere to a particular faith. The CCP made strident efforts after 1949 to supplant religious worship with the secular philosophy of communism but since the abandonment of principles of Marxist–Leninist collectivism, this policy has significantly waned.

Religion is enjoying an upswing as the people return to religion for spiritual solace at a time of great change, dislocation and uncertainty. The hopeless, poor and destitute may turn to religion as they feel abandoned by communism and the safety nets it once assured. Yet the educated and prosperous are similarly turning to religion for a sense of guidance and direction in a land many Chinese suspect has become morally bereft.

Religious belief in China has traditionally been marked by tolerance. Although the faiths are quite distinct, some convergence exists between Buddhism, Taoism and Confucianism, and you may discover shrines where all three faiths are worshipped.

Guanyin, the Buddhist Goddess of Mercy, finds her equivalent in Tianhou (Mazu), the Taoist goddess and protector of fisher folk, and the two goddesses can seem almost interchangeable. Other symbioses exist: elements of Taoism and Buddhism can be discerned in the thinking of some Chinese Christians, while the Virgin Mary finds a familiar toehold in the Chinese psyche owing to her physical similarity with Guanyin.

Buddhism

Although not an indigenous faith, Buddhism (Fó Jiào) is the religion most deeply associated with China and Tibet. Although Buddhism's authority had long ebbed, the faith still exercises a powerful influence over the spiritual persona of China. Many Chinese may not be regular temple-goers but they possess an interest in Buddhism; they may merely be 'cultural Buddhists', with a strong affection for Buddhist civilisation.

Chinese towns with any history usually have several Buddhist temples, but the number is well down on pre-1949 figures. The small Héběi town of Zhèngdìng, for example, has four Buddhist temples, but at one time had eight. Běijīng once had hundreds of Buddhist temples, compared to the 20 or so you can find today.

Some of China's greatest surviving artistic achievements are Buddhist in inspiration. The largest and most ancient repository of Chinese, Central Asian and Tibetan Buddhist artwork can be found at the Mogao Caves in Gānsù, while the carved Buddhist caves at both Lóngmén and Yúngāng are spectacular pieces of religious and creative heritage.

Beyond Tibet, China has four sacred Buddhist mountains, each one the home of a specific Bodhisattva. The two most famous mountains are Wǔtái Shān and Éméi Shān, respectively ruled over by Wenshu and Puxiang.

RELIGION & BELIEFS BUDDHISM

Origins

Founded in ancient India around the 5th century BC, Buddhism teaches that all of life is suffering, and that the cause of this anguish is desire, itself rooted in sensation and attachment. Suffering can only be overcome by following the eightfold path, a set of guidelines for moral behaviour, meditation and wisdom. Those who have freed themselves from suffering and the wheel of rebirth are said to have attained nirvana or enlightenment. The term Buddha generally refers to the historical founder of Buddhism, Siddhartha Gautama, but is also sometimes used to denote those who have achieved enlightenment.

Siddhartha Gautama left no writings; the sutras that make up the Buddhist canon were compiled many years after his death.

Buddhism in China

Like other faiths such as Christianity, Nestorianism, Islam and Judaism, Buddhism originally reached China via the Silk Road. The earliest recorded Buddhist temple in China proper dates back to the 1st century AD, but it was not until the 4th century when a period of warlordism coupled with nomadic invasions plunged the country into disarray, that Buddhism gained mass appeal. Buddhism's sudden growth during this

SACRED MOUNTAIN

FALUN GONG

Falun Gong – a practice that merges elements of *qìgōng*-style regulated breathing and standing exercises with Buddhist teachings, fashioning a quasi-religious creed in the process – literally means 'Practice of the Dharma Wheel'. Riding a wave of interest in *qìgōng* systems in the 1990s, Falun Gong claimed as many as 100 million adherents in China by 1999. The technique was banned in the same year after over 10,000 practitioners stood in silent protest outside Zhōngnánhǎi in Běijīng, following protests in Tiānjīn when a local magazine published an article critical of Falun Gong. The authorities had been unnerved by the movement's audacity and organisational depth, construing Falun Gong as a threat to the primacy of the CCP. The movement was branded a cult (*xiéjiao*) and a robust, media-wide propaganda campaign was launched against practitioners, forcing many to undergo 're-education' in prison and labour camps. After the ban, the authorities treated Falun Gong believers harshly and reports surfaced of adherents dying in custody. The UK Chinese Embassy website (www.chinese-embassy.org.uk) contains propaganda articles on the 'Falun Gong Cult'. Although comments on the articles are invited, there seems to be no messages from readers.

Taoist temple, Sik Sik Yuen Wong Tai Sin, Hong Kong (p479)

period is often attributed to its sophisticated ideas concerning the afterlife (such as karma and reincarnation), a dimension unaddressed by either Confucianism or Taoism. At a time when existence was especially precarious, spiritual transcendence was understandably popular.

As Buddhism converged with Taoist philosophy (through terminology used in translation) and popular religion (through practice), it went on to develop into something distinct from the original Indian tradition. The most famous example is the esoteric Chan school (Zen in Japanese), which originated sometime in the 5th or 6th century, and focused on attaining enlightenment through meditation. Chan was novel not only in its unorthodox teaching methods, but also because it made enlightenment possible for laypeople outside the monastic system. It rose to prominence during the Tang and Song dynasties, after which the centre of practice moved to Japan. Other major Buddhist sects in China include Tiantai (based on the teachings of the Lotus Sutra) and Pure Land, a faith-based teaching that requires simple devotion, such as reciting the Amitabha Buddha's name, in order to gain rebirth in paradise. Today, Pure Land Buddhism is the most common.

China's oldest surviving Buddhist temple is the White Horse Temple in Luòyáng; other Buddhist temples may well have existed but have since vanished.

Buddhist Schools

Regardless of its various forms, most Buddhism in China belongs to the Mahayana school, which holds that since all existence is one, the fate of the individual is linked to the fate of others. Thus, Bodhisattvas – those who have already achieved enlightenment but have chosen to remain on earth – continue to work for the liberation of all other sentient beings. The most popular Bodhisattva in China is Guanyin, the Goddess of Mercy.

Ethnic Tibetans and Mongols within China practise a unique form of Mahayana Buddhism known as Tibetan or Tantric Buddhism (Lǎma Jiào). Tibetan Buddhism, sometimes called Vajrayana or 'thunderbolt vehicle', has been practised since the early 7th century AD and is influenced by Tibet's pre-Buddhist Bon religion, which relied on priests or shamans to placate spirits, gods and demons. Generally speaking, it is much more mystical than other forms of Buddhism, relying heavily on mudras (ritual postures), mantras (sacred speech), yantras (sacred art) and secret initiation rites. Priests called lamas are believed to be reincarnations of highly evolved beings; the Dalai Lama is the supreme patriarch of Tibetan Buddhism.

Taoism

A home-grown philosophy-cum-religion, Taoism is also perhaps the hardest of all China's faiths to grasp. Controversial, paradoxical, and – like the Tao itself – impossible to pin down, it is a natural counterpoint to rigid Confucianist order and responsibility.

The Chinese verb for 'to know' is *zhīdào* (知道), literally 'know the *dao*' or 'to know the way', indicating a possible Taoist etymology.

Taoism predates Buddhism in China and much of its religious culture connects to a distant animism and shamanism, despite the purity of its philosophical school. In its earliest and simplest form, Taoism draws from *The Classic of the Way and Its Power* (Taote Jing; Dàodé Jīng), penned by the sagacious Laotzu (Laozi; c 580–500 BC) who left his writings with the gatekeeper of a pass as he headed west on the back of an ox. Some Chinese believe his wanderings took him to a distant land in the west where he became Buddha.

The Classic of the Way and Its Power is a work of astonishing insight and sublime beauty. Devoid of a god-like being or deity, Laotzu's writings instead endeavour to address the unknowable and indescribable principle of the universe, which he calls Dao (*dào;* 道), or 'the Way'. This way is the way or method by which the universe operates, so it can be understood to be a universal or cosmic principle.

GUANYIN 观音

The boundlessly compassionate countenance of Guanyin, the Buddhist Goddess of Mercy, can be encountered in temples across China. The goddess (more strictly a Bodhisattva or a Buddha-to-be) goes under a variety of aliases: Guanshiyin (literally 'Observing the Cries of the World') is her formal name, but she is also called Guanzizai, Guanyin Dashi and Guanyin Pusa, or, in Sanskrit, Avalokiteshvara. Known as Kannon in Japan and Guanyam in Cantonese, Guanyin shoulders the grief of the world and dispenses mercy and compassion. Christians will note a semblance to the Virgin Mary in the aura surrounding the goddess, which at least partially explains why Christianity has found a slot in the Chinese consciousness.

In Tibetan Buddhism, her earthly presence manifests itself in the Dalai Lama, and her home is the Potala Palace (p886) in Lhasa. In China, her abode is the island of Pǔtuóshān (p265) in Zhèjiāng province, the first two syllables of which derive from the name of her palace in Lhasa.

In temples throughout China, Guanyin is often found at the very rear of the main hall, facing north (most of the other divinities, apart from Weituo, face south). She typically has her own little shrine and stands on the head of a big fish, holding a lotus in her hand. On other occasions, she has her own hall, often towards the rear of the temple.

The goddess (who in earlier dynasties appeared to be male rather than female) is often surrounded by little effigies of the *luóhàn* (or *arhat;* those freed from the cycle of rebirth), who scamper about; the Guānyīn Pavilion (p656) outside Dàlǐ is a good example of this. Guanyin also appears in a variety of forms, often with just two arms, but sometimes also in a multi-armed form (as at the Pǔníng Temple in Chéngdé; p136). The 11-faced Guanyin, the fierce horse-head Guanyin, the Songzi Guanyin (literally 'Offering Son Guanyin') and the Dripping Water Guanyin are just some of her myriad manifestations. She has traditionally been a favourite subject for *déhuà* (white-glazed porcelain) figures, which are typically very elegant.

NATIONALISM

In today's China, '-isms' (主义; *zhǔyì* or 'doctrines') are often frowned upon. Any *zhǔyì* may suggest a personal focus that the CCP would prefer people channel into hard work instead. 'Intellectualism' is suspect as it may clash with political taboos. 'Idealism' is non-pragmatic and potentially destructive, as Maoism showed.

Many argue that China's one-party state has reduced thinking across the spectrum via propaganda and censorship, dumbing-down and an educational system that emphasises patriotic education. This has, however, helped spawn another '-ism': nationalism.

Nationalism is not restricted to Chinese youth but it is this generation – with no experience of the Cultural Revolution's terrifying excesses – which most closely identifies with its message. The *fènqīng* (angry youth) have been swept along with China's rise; while they are no lovers of the CCP, they yearn for a stronger China that can stand up to 'foreign interference' and dictate its own terms.

The CCP actively encourages strong patriotism, but is nervous about its transformation into nationalism and its potential for disturbance. Much nationalism in the PRC has little to do with the CCP but everything to do with China; while the CCP has struggled at length to identify itself with China's civilisation and core values, it has been only partially successful. With China's tendency to get quickly swept along by passions, nationalism is an often unseen but quite potent force in today's China.

The opening lines of *The Classic of the Way and Its Power* confess, however, that the treatise may fail in its task: 道可道非常道，名可名非常名; 'The way that can be spoken of is not the real way, the name that can be named is not the true name'. Despite this disclaimer, the 5000-character book, completed in terse classical Chinese, somehow communicates the nebulous power and authority of 'the Way'. The book remains the seminal text of Taoism, and Taoist purists see little need to look beyond its revelations.

One of Taoism's most beguiling precepts, *wúwéi* (inaction) champions the allowing of things to naturally occur without interference. The principle is enthusiastically pursued by students of Taiji Quan, Wuji Quan and other soft martial arts (p977) who seek to equal nothingness in their bid to lead an opponent to defeat himself.

Confucius Institutes around the world aim to promote Chinese language and culture internationally, while simultaneously developing its economic and cultural influences abroad.

CONFUCIUS INSTITUTES

Confucianism

The very core of Chinese society for the past two millennia, Confucianism (Rújiā Sīxiǎng) is a humanist philosophy that strives for social harmony and the common good. In China, its influence can be seen in everything from the emphasis on education and respect for elders to the patriarchal role of the government.

Confucianism is based upon the teachings of Confucius (Kǒngzǐ; see p155), a 6th-century-BC philosopher who lived during a period of constant warfare and social upheaval. While Confucianism changed considerably throughout the centuries, some of the principal ideas remained the same – namely an emphasis on five basic hierarchical relationships: father-son, ruler-subject, husband-wife, elder-younger, and friend-friend. Confucius believed that if each individual carried out his or her proper role in society (ie, a son served his father respectfully while a father provided for his son, a subject served his ruler respectfully while a ruler provided for his subject, and so on) social order would be achieved. Confucius' disciples later gathered his ideas in the form of short aphorisms and conversations, forming the work known as *The Analects* (Lúnyǔ).

Early Confucian philosophy was further developed by Mencius (Mèngzǐ) and Xunzi, both of whom provided a theoretical and practical foundation for many of Confucius' moral concepts. In the 2nd century BC,

Confucianism became the official ideology of the Han dynasty, thereby gaining mainstream acceptance for the first time. This was of major importance and resulted in the formation of an educated elite that served both the government as bureaucrats and the common people as exemplars of moral action. During the rule of the Tang dynasty an official examination system was created, which, in theory, made the imperial government a true meritocracy. However, this also contributed to an ossification of Confucianism, as the ideology grew increasingly mired in the weight of its own tradition, focusing exclusively on a core set of texts.

Nonetheless, influential figures sporadically reinterpreted the philosophy – in particular Zhu Xi (1130–1200), who brought in elements of Buddhism and Taoism to create Neo Confucianism (Lǐxué or Dàoxué) – and it remained a dominant social force up until the 1911 Revolution toppled the imperial bureaucracy. In the 20th century, intellectuals decried Confucian thought as an obstacle to modernisation and Mao further levelled the sage in his denunciation of 'the Four Olds'. But feudal faults notwithstanding, Confucius' social ethics have again resurfaced in government propaganda where they lend authority to the leadership's emphasis on 'harmony' (héxié).

Christianity

The explosion of interest in Christianity (Jīdūjiào) in China over recent years is unprecedented except for the wholesale conversions that accompanied the tumultuous rebellion of the pseudo-Christian Taiping in the 19th century.

Christianity first arrived in China with the Nestorians, a sect from ancient Persia that split with the Byzantine Church in 431 AD, who arrived in China via the Silk Road in the 7th century. A celebrated tablet – the Nestorian Tablet – in Xī'ān records their arrival. Much later, in the 16th century, the Jesuits arrived and were popular figures at the imperial court, although they made few converts.

Large numbers of Catholic and Protestant missionaries established themselves in the 19th century, but left after the establishment of the People's Republic of China in 1949. One such missionary, James Hudson Taylor from Barnsley in England, immersed himself in Chinese culture and is credited with helping to convert 18,000 Chinese Christians and building 600 churches during his 50 years in China in the 19th century.

In today's China, Christianity is a burgeoning faith perhaps uniquely placed to expand due to its industrious work ethic, associations with first-world nations and its emphasis on human rights and charitable work.

Some estimates point to as many as 100 million Christians in China. However, the exact population is hard to calculate as many groups – outside the four official Christian organisations – lead a strict underground existence (in what are called 'house churches') out of fear of a political clampdown.

Islam

Islam (Yīsīlán Jiào) in China dates to the 7th century, when it was first brought to China by Arab and Persian traders along the Silk Road. Later, during the Mongol Yuan dynasty, maritime trade increased, bringing new waves of merchants to China's coastal regions, particularly the port cities of Guǎngzhōu and Quánzhōu. The descendants of these groups – now scattered across the country – gradually integrated into Han culture, and are today distinguished primarily by their religion. In Chinese, they are referred to as the Hui.

Other Muslim groups include the Uighurs, Kazaks, Kyrgyz, Tajiks and Uzbeks, who live principally in the border areas of the northwest. It is estimated that 1.5% to 3% of Chinese today are Muslim.

RELIGION & BELIEFS CHRISTIANITY

Believing he was the son of God and brother of Jesus Christ, Hakka rebel Hong Xiuquan led the bloody and tumultuous pseudo-Christian Taiping Rebellion against the Qing dynasty from 1856 to 1864.

David Aikman's *Jesus in Beijing: How Christianity Is Transforming China and Changing the Global Balance of Power* (2003) predicts almost one third of Chinese turning to Christianity within 30 years.

Communism & Maoism

Ironically (or perhaps intentionally), Mao Zedong, while struggling to uproot feudal superstition and religious belief, sprung to godlike status in China via a personality cult. In the China of today, Mao retains a semi-deified aura.

Communism sits awkwardly with the economic trajectory of China over the past 30 years. Once a philosophy forged in the white-hot crucible of civil war, revolution and the patriotic fervour to create a nation free from foreign interference, communism had largely run its credible course by the 1960s. By the death of Mao Zedong in 1976, the political philosophy had repeatedly brought the nation to catastrophe, with the Hundred Flowers Movement, the Great Leap Forward and the disastrous violence of the Cultural Revolution.

Communism remains the official guiding principle of the CCP. However, young communist aspirants are far less likely to be ideologues than pragmatists seeking to advance within the party structure. In real terms, many argue that communism has become an adjunct to the survival of the CCP.

Chinese Communism owes something to Confucianism. Confucius' philosophy embraces the affairs of man and human society and the relationship between rulers and the ruled, rather than the supernatural world. Establishing a rigid framework for human conduct, the culture of Confucianism was easily requisitioned by communists seeking to establish authority over society.

With the collapse of the Soviet Union in 1989, Běijīng became aware of the dangers of popular power and sought to maintain the coherence and strength of the state. This has meant that the CCP still seeks to impose itself firmly on the consciousness of Chinese people through patriotic education, propaganda, censorship, nationalism and the building of a strong nation.

Communism also has considerable nostalgic value for elderly Chinese who bemoan the loss of values in modern-day China and pine for the days when they felt more secure and society was more egalitarian. Chairman Mao's portrait still hangs in abundance across China, from drum towers in Guǎngxī province to restaurants in Běijīng, testament to a generation of Chinese who still revere the communist leader. Until his spectacular fall from power in 2012, Chinese politician and Chóngqìng party chief Bo Xilai launched popular Maoist-style 'red culture' campaigns in Chóngqìng, which included the singing of revolutionary songs and the mass-texting of quotes from Mao's *Little Red Book*.

Animism

Around 3% of China's population is animist, a primordial religious belief akin to shamanism. Animists see the world as a living being, with rocks, trees, mountains and people all containing spirits that need to live in harmony. If this harmony is disrupted, restoration of this balance is attempted by a shaman who is empowered to mediate between the human and spirit world. Animism is most widely believed by minority groups and exists in a multitude of forms, some of which have been influenced by Buddhism and other religions.

Kāifēng in Hénán province is home to the largest community of Jews in China. The religious beliefs and customs of Judaism (Yóutài Jiào) have died out, yet the descendants of the original Jews still consider themselves Jewish.

During the Cultural Revolution, many Christian churches around China served as warehouses or factories, and were gradually rehabilitated in the 1980s.

Chinese Cuisine

Cooking plays a central role in both Chinese society and the national psyche. When Chinese people meet, a common greeting is '*Nǐ chīfàn le ma?*' – 'Have you eaten yet?' Work, play, romance, business and the family all revolve around food. Catalysts for all manner of enjoyment, meals are occasions for pleasure and entertainment, to clinch deals, strike up new friendships and rekindle old ones. To fully explore this tasty domain on home soil, all you need is a visa, a pair of chopsticks, an explorative palate and a passion for the unusual and unexpected.

Real Chinese Food

Because it so skilfully exported its cuisine abroad, your very first impressions of China were probably via your taste buds. Chinatowns the world over teem with the aromas of Chinese cuisine, ferried overseas by China's versatile and hard-working cooks. Sundays see flocks of diners filling Chinatowns to 'yum cha' and feast on dim sum. Chinese food is a wholesome and tasty point of contact between an immigrant Chinese population and everyone else.

But what you see – and taste – abroad is usually just a wafer-thin slice of a very hefty and wholesome pie. Chinese cuisine in the West is lifted from the cookbook of an emigrant community that largely originated from China's southern seaboard. In a similar vein, the sing-song melodies of Cantonese were the most familiar of China's languages in Chinatowns, even though the dialect finds little purchase in China beyond Hong Kong, Macau, Guǎngdōng and parts of Guǎngxī. So although you may be hard pressed to avoid dim sum and *cha siu* in your local Chinatown, finding more 'obscure' specialities from elsewhere in China can be either a challenge or an expensive proposition. The 'Peking duck' at your local restaurant, for example, is at best a distant relative of the fowl fired up over fruit-tree wood in the ovens of Běijīng *kǎoyādiàn* (roast duck restaurants).

To get an idea of the size of its diverse menu, remember that China is not that much smaller than Europe. Just as Europe is a patchwork of different nation states, languages, cultural traditions and climates, China is also a smorgasbord of dialects, languages, ethnic minorities and extreme geographic and climatic differences, despite the common Han Chinese cultural overlays.

The sheer size of the land, the strength of local culture and differences in geography and altitude means there can be little in common between the cuisines of Xīnjiāng and Tibet, even though they are adjacent to each other. Following your nose (and palate) around China is one of the exciting ways to journey the land, so pack a sense of culinary adventure along with your travelling boots!

Search on www.
bbcgoodfood.com
for a mouth-
watering selec-
tion of Chinese
recipes and full
instructions on
throwing together
some classic and
less known dishes
from around
China.

Zòngzi (dump-
lings made of
glutinous rice
wrapped in
bamboo or reed
leaves) are eaten
during the Dragon
Boat festival.

Regional Cooking

The evolution of China's wide-ranging regional cuisines has been influenced by the climate, the distribution of crop and animal varieties, the type of terrain, proximity to the sea and the influence of neighbouring nations and the import of ingredients and aromas. Naturally sea fish and seafood is prevalent in coastal regions of China, while in Inner Mongolia and Xīnjiāng there is a dependence on meat such as beef and lamb.

Another crucial ingredient was history. The flight of the Song court south of the Cháng Jiāng (Yangzi River) from northern Jurchen invaders in the 12th century helped develop China's major regional cuisines. This process was further influenced by urbanisation, itself made possible by the commercialisation of agriculture and food distribution, which saw the restaurant industry emerge and the further consolidation of regional schools. Further impetus came from the merchants and bureaucrats who travelled the land and from improved communications, such as the Grand Canal.

Many Chinese regions lay claim to their own culinary conventions, which may overlap and cross-fertilise each other. The cooking traditions of China's ethnic minorities aside, Han cooking has traditionally been divided into eight schools (中华八大菜系; *zhōnghuá bādàcàixì*):

> Spanish traders in the early Qing dynasty first introduced red chilli pepper to China. Not only a spice, chillies are also a rich source of vitamins A and C.

» **Chuān** (Sìchuān cuisine) 川

» **Huī** (Ānhuī cuisine) 徽

» **Lǔ** (Shāndōng cuisine) 鲁

» **Mǐn** (Fújiàn cuisine) 闽

» **Sū** (Jiāngsū cuisine) 苏

» **Xiāng** (Húnán cuisine) 湘

» **Yuè** (Cantonese/Guǎngdōng cuisine) 粤

» **Zhè** (Zhèjiāng cuisine) 浙

FOODCOLLECTION / GETTY IMAGES ©

Qié zhī yú piàn – a fish, tomato and capsicum dish

TRAVEL YOUR TASTE BUDS

China is such a gourmand's paradise you won't know when to stop. In the north, fill up on a tasty dish of wontons *(húndún)* stuffed with juicy leeks and minced pork, or Mongolian hotpot *(Ménggǔ huǒguō)*, a hearty brew of mutton, onions and cabbage.

Locals from China's arid northwest can pop a bowl of noodles topped with sliced donkey meat *(lǘròu huáng miàn)* under your nose or sizzling lamb kebobs *(kǎo yángròu)* in your fingers. Stop by Xīān for warming bowls of mutton broth and shredded flat bread *(yángròu pàomó)*. A bowl of Lánzhōu hand-pulled noodles *(lā miàn)* is a meal in itself.

In case you're pining for something sweet and savoury, head to Shànghǎi for delicious honey-smoked carp *(mìzhī xūnyú)* or a tongue-tingling plate of hot and sour squid *(suānlà yóuyú)*. Cleanse your palate with a glass of heady Shàoxīng yellow wine *(Shàoxīng huángjiǔ)* or the more delicate flavours of Dragonwell tea *(lóngjǐng chá)*. It may not exactly give you wings, but a dish of Huángshān braised pigeon *(Huángshān dùngē)* will definitely give you the stamina to clamber up the misty inclines of Huángshān.

Some like it hot, and little comes hotter than the fiery flavours of Sìchuān. Begin with mouth-numbing mapo tofu *(mápó dòufu)*, followed by the celebrated spicy chicken with peanuts *(gōngbǎo jīdīng)*. If the smoke still isn't coming out of your ears, fish smothered in chilli *(shuǐzhǔ yú)* should have you breathing fire. Alternatively, test your mettle with a volcanic Chóngqìng hotpot.

In the south, relax with morning dim sum in Guǎngzhōu or a bowl of Cantonese snake soup *(shé gēng)* in one of the city's boisterous night markets. While in Macau, taste the Macanese dish *porco à alentejana*, a mouthwatering casserole of pork and clams.

Although each school is independent and well defined, it is possible to group these eight culinary traditions into **Northern**, **Southern**, **Western** and **Eastern** cooking.

A common philosophy lies at the heart of Chinese cooking, whatever the school. Most vegetables and fruits are yin foods, generally moist and soft, possessing a cooling effect while nurturing the feminine aspect. Yang foods – fried, spicy or with red meat – are warming and nourish the masculine side. Any meal should harmonise flavours and achieve a balance between cooling and warming foods.

Northern Cooking

With **Shāndōng** cooking (鲁菜; *lǔcài*) – the oldest of the eight regional schools – at its heart, northern cooking also embraces Běijīng, northeastern (Manchurian) and Shānxī cuisine, creating the most time-honoured and most central form of Chinese cooking.

In the dry north Chinese wheat belt an accent falls on millet, sorghum, maize, barley and wheat rather than rice (which requires lush irrigation by water to cultivate). Particularly well suited to the harsh and hardy winter climate, northern cooking is rich and wholesome (northerners partially attribute their taller size, compared to southern Chinese, to its effects). Filling breads – such as *mántou* (馒头) or *bǐng* (饼; flat breads) – are steamed, baked or fried while noodles may form the basis of any northern meal (although the ubiquitous availability of rice means it can always be found). Northern cuisine is frequently quite salty, and appetising dumplings (饺子; *jiǎozi*) are widely eaten, usually boiled and sometimes fried.

In 2010, diners in China were appalled to discover that one in 10 meals cooked in Chinese restaurants was prepared with cooking oil dredged up from sewers and drains.

As Běijīng was the principal capital through the Yuan, Ming and Qing dynasties, Imperial cooking is a chief characteristic of the northern school. Peking duck is Běijīng's signature dish, served with typical northern ingredients – pancakes, spring onions and fermented bean paste. You can find it all over China, but it's only true to form in the capital, roasted in ovens fired up with fruit-tree wood.

With China ruled from 1644 to 1911 by non-Han Manchurians, the influence of northeast cuisine (*dōngběi cài*) has naturally permeated northern cooking, dispensing a legacy of rich and hearty stews, dense breads, preserved foods and dumplings.

Meat roasting is also more common in the north than in other parts of China. Meats in northern China are braised until falling off the bone, or slathered with spices and barbecued until smoky. Pungent garlic, chives and spring onions are used with abandon and are also used raw.

The nomadic and carnivorous diet of the Mongolians also infiltrates northern cooking, most noticeably in the Mongolian hotpot and the Mongolian barbecue. Milk from nomadic herds of cattle, goats and horses has also crept into northern cuisine, as yoghurts (*suānnǎi*) for example.

Hallmark northern dishes:

PINYIN	SCRIPT	ENGLISH
Běijīng kǎoyā	北京烤鸭	Peking duck
jiāo zhá yángròu	焦炸羊肉	deep-fried mutton
jiǎozi	饺子	dumplings
mántou	馒头	steamed buns
qīng xiāng shāo jī	清香烧鸡	chicken wrapped in lotus leaf
ròu bāozi	肉包子	steamed meat buns
sān měi dòufu	三美豆腐	sliced bean curd with Chinese cabbage
shuàn yángròu	涮羊肉	lamb hotpot
sì xǐ wánzi	四喜丸子	steamed and fried pork, shrimp and bamboo shoot balls
yuán bào lǐ jí	芫爆里脊	stir-fried pork tenderloin with coriander
zào liū sān bái	糟溜三白	stir-fried chicken, fish and bamboo shoots

Streets around China reek with the powerful and popular aromas of stinky tofu (*chòu dòufu*), a form of fermented tofu with an aroma pitched somewhere between unwashed socks and rotting vegetation.

STINKY TOFU

Southern Cooking

The southern Chinese – particularly the Cantonese – historically spearheaded successive waves of immigration overseas, leaving aromatic constellations of Chinatowns around the world. Consequently, Westerners most often associate this school of cooking with China.

Typified by **Cantonese** cooking (粤菜; *yuècài*), southern cooking lacks the richness and saltiness of northern cooking, instead coaxing more subtle aromas to the surface. The Cantonese astutely believe that good cooking does not require much flavouring, for it is the *xiān* (natural freshness) of the ingredients that mark a truly high-grade dish. Hence the near obsessive attention paid to the freshness of ingredients in southern cuisine.

The hallmark Cantonese dish is dim sum (点心; Mandarin: *diǎnxīn*). Yum cha (literally 'drink tea') – another name for dim sum dining – in Guǎngzhōu and Hong Kong can be enjoyed on any day of the week. Dishes – often in steamers – are wheeled around on trolleys so you can see what you want to order. Well-known dim sum dishes include *guōtiē* (a kind of fried dumpling), *shāomài* (a kind of open pork dumpling), *chāshāobāo* (pork-filled bun) and *chūnjuǎn* (spring rolls). The extravagantly named *fèngzhuǎ* (phoenix claw) is the name for the ever-popular steamed chicken's feet. *Xiǎolóngbāo* (steamed dumplings) are often sold in dim sum restaurants but are traditionally from Shànghǎi.

The local regard for Cantonese food is evident in a popular Chinese saying: 'Be born in Sūzhōu, live in Hángzhōu, eat in Guǎngzhōu and die in Liúzhōu'. Sūzhōu was famed for its good-looking people, Hángzhōu was a lovely place to live in, Guǎngzhōu was the best place to eat while Liǔzhōu was famed for the wood of its coffins!

Fújiàn cuisine (闽菜; *mǐncài*) is another important southern cooking style, with its emphasis on light flavours and, due to the province's proximity to the East China Sea, seafood.

Hakka cuisine from the disparate and migratory Hakka people (Kèjiāzú) is another feature of southern Chinese cooking, as is the food of Cháozhōu in eastern Guǎngdōng.

Rice is the primary staple of southern cooking. Sparkling paddy fields glitter across the south; the humid climate, plentiful rainfall and well-irrigated land means that rice has been farmed in the south since the Chinese first populated the region during the Han dynasty (206 BC–AD 220).

Southern-school dishes include the following:

> You will be charged for a wrapped up hand-cleaning wipe if you open it at your restaurant table; if you don't use it, it should not appear on your bill.

PINYIN	SCRIPT	ENGLISH
bái zhuó xiā	白灼虾	blanched prawns with shredded scallions
dōngjiāng yánjú jī	东江盐焗鸡	salt-baked chicken
gālí jī	咖喱鸡	curried chicken
háoyóu niúròu	蚝油牛肉	beef with oyster sauce
kǎo rǔzhū	烤乳猪	crispy suckling pig
mì zhī chāshāo	密汁叉烧	roast pork with honey
shé ròu	蛇肉	snake
tángcù lǐjí/gǔlǎo ròu	糖醋里脊/咕老肉	sweet and sour pork fillets
tángcù páigǔ	糖醋排骨	sweet and sour spare ribs

Western Cooking

The cuisine of landlocked Western China, a region heavily dappled with ethnic shades and contrasting cultures, welcomes the diner to the more scarlet end of the culinary spectrum. The trademark ingredient of the western school is the fiercely hot red chilli, a potent firecracker of a herb that floods dishes with an all-pervading spiciness. Aniseed, coriander, garlic and peppercorns are thrown in for good measure to add extra pungency and bite.

The standout cuisine of the western school is fiery **Sìchuān** (川菜; *chuāncài*) food, one of China's eight regional cooking styles, renowned for its eye-watering peppery aromas. One of the herbs that differentiates Sìchuān cooking from other spicy cuisines is the use of 'flower pepper' *(huājiāo)*, a numbing peppercorn-like herb that floods the mouth with an anaesthetising fragrance in a culinary effect termed *málà* (numb and hot). A Sìchuān dish you can find cooked up by chefs across China is the delicious sour cabbage fish soup (酸菜鱼; *suāncàiyú*; wholesome fish chunks in a spicy broth). The Chóngqìng hotpot is a force to be reckoned with but must be approached with a stiff upper lip (and copious amounts of liquid refreshment). If you want a hotpot pitched between spicy and mild, select a *yuanyang* hotpot (*yuānyāng huǒguō*), a vessel divided yin-yang style into two different compartments for two different soup bases.

Sìchuān restaurants are everywhere in China, swarming around train stations, squeezed away down food streets or squished into street markets with wobbly stools and rickety tables parked out front.

Another of China's eight regional schools of cooking, dishes from **Húnán** (湘菜; *xiāngcài*) are similarly pungent, with a heavy reliance on chilli. Unlike Sìchuān food, flower pepper is not employed and instead spicy flavours are often sharper, fiercer and more to the fore. Meat, particularly in Húnán, is marinated, pickled or otherwise processed before cooking, which is generally by stir or flash-frying.

For the lowdown on Muslim Uighur cuisine from China's northwest, see the boxed text (p794) in the Xinjiang chapter. For a Chinese–Tibetan menu reader, see p734.

Other western-school dishes:

PINYIN	SCRIPT	ENGLISH
bàngbàng jī	棒棒鸡	shredded chicken in a hot pepper and sesame sauce
Chóngqìng huǒguō	重庆火锅	Chóngqìng hotpot
dāndan miàn	担担面	spicy noodles
gānshāo yán lǐ	干烧岩鲤	stewed carp with ham and hot and sweet sauce
huíguō ròu	回锅肉	boiled and stir-fried pork with salty and hot sauce
málà dòufu	麻辣豆腐	spicy tofu
Máoshì Hóngshaōròu	毛氏红烧肉	Mao Family Braised Pork
shuǐ zhǔ niúròu	水煮牛肉	spicy fried and boiled beef
shuǐzhǔyú	水煮鱼	fried and boiled fish, garlic sprouts and celery
suāncàiyú	酸菜鱼	sour cabbage fish soup
yú xiāng ròusī	鱼香肉丝	fish-flavour pork strips
zhàcài ròusī	榨菜肉丝	stir-fried pork or beef tenderloin with tuber mustard

Eastern Cooking

The eastern school of Chinese cuisine derives from a fertile region of China, slashed by waterways and canals, glistening with lakes, fringed by a long coastline and nourished by a subtropical climate. Jiāngsū province itself is the home of **Jiāngsū** cuisine (苏菜; *sūcài*) – one of the core regions of the eastern school – and is famed as the 'Land of Fish and Rice', a tribute to its abundance of food and produce. The region was also historically prosperous and in today's export-oriented economy, the eastern provinces are among China's wealthiest. This combination of riches and bountiful food created a culture of epicurism and gastronomic enjoyment.

South of Jiāngsū, **Zhèjiāng** cuisine (浙菜; *zhècài*) is another cornerstone of Eastern cooking. The Song dynasty saw the blossoming of the restaurant industry here; in Hángzhōu, the southern Song-dynasty capital, restaurants and teahouses accounted for two-thirds of the city's business during a splendidly rich cultural era. At this time, one of Hángzhōu's most famous dishes – *dōngpō ròu* (named after the celebrated poet and governor of Hángzhōu, Su Dongpo) – achieved fame.

Generally more oily and sweeter than other Chinese schools, the eastern school revels in fish and seafood, reflecting its geographical proximity to major rivers and the sea. Fish is usually *qīngzhēng* (清蒸; steamed) but can be stir-fried, pan-fried or grilled. Hairy crabs *(dàzháxiè)* are a Shànghǎi speciality between October and December. Eaten with soy, ginger and vinegar and downed with warm Shàoxīng wine, the best crabs come from Yangcheng Lake. The crab is believed to increase the body's *yīn* (coldness), so *yáng* (warmth) is added by imbibing lukewarm rice wine with it. It is also usual to eat male and female crabs together.

As with Cantonese food, freshness is a key ingredient in the cuisine, and sauces and seasonings are only employed to augment essential flavours. Stir-frying and steaming are also used, the latter with Shànghǎi's famous *xiǎolóngbāo,* steamer buns filled with nuggets of pork or crab swimming in a scalding meat broth. Learning how to devour these carefully without the meat juice squirting everywhere and scalding the roof of your mouth (or blinding your neighbour) requires some – quite enjoyable – practice.

With a lightness of flavour, **Ānhuī** cuisine (徽菜; *huīcài*) – one of China's eight principle culinary traditions and firmly in the eastern cooking sphere – puts less emphasis on seafood. Braising and stewing of vegetables and wildlife from its mountainous habitats is a pronounced feature of this regional cuisine.

China's best soy sauce is also produced in the eastern provinces, and the technique of braising meat using soy sauce, sugar and spices was perfected here. Meat cooked in this manner takes on a dark mauve hue auspiciously described as 'red', a colour associated with good fortune.

Famous dishes from the eastern school include the following:

According to Greenpeace China, 57 billion disposable chopsticks are manufactured in China annually, the equivalent of 3.8 million trees.

CHOPSTICKS

CHINESE CUISINE REGIONAL COOKING

PINYIN	SCRIPT	ENGLISH
gōngbào jīdīng	宫爆鸡丁	spicy chicken with peanuts; kung pao chicken
háoyóu niúròu	蚝油牛肉	beef with oyster sauce
hóngshāo páigǔ	红烧排骨	red-braised spare ribs
hóngshāo qiézi	红烧茄子	red-cooked aubergine
hóngshāo yú	红烧鱼	red-braised fish
huǒguō	火锅	hotpot
húntùn tāng	馄饨汤	wonton soup
jiācháng dòufu	家常豆腐	'homestyle' tofu
jiǎozi	饺子	dumplings
jīdànmiàn	鸡蛋面	noodles and egg
qīngjiāo ròupiàn	青椒肉片	pork and green peppers
shāguō dòufu	沙锅豆腐	bean curd casserole
suānlàtāng	酸辣汤	hot and sour soup
tiěbǎn niúròu	铁板牛肉	sizzling beef platter
xīhóngshì chǎojīdàn	西红柿炒鸡蛋	fried egg and tomato
xīhóngshì jīdàntāng	西红柿鸡蛋汤	egg and tomato soup
xīhóngshì niúròu	西红柿牛肉	beef and tomato
yúxiāng qiézi	鱼香茄子	fish-flavoured aubergine

Home-Style Dishes

Besides China's regional cuisines, there is a tasty variety of *jiācháng cài* (home-style) dishes you will see all over the land, cooked up in restaurants and along food streets.

These include:

PINYIN	SCRIPT	ENGLISH
jiāng cōng chǎo xiè	姜葱炒蟹	stir-fried crab with ginger and scallions
mìzhī xūnyú	蜜汁熏鱼	honey-smoked carp
níng shì shànyú	宁式鳝鱼	stir-fried eel with onion
qiézhī yúkuài	茄汁鱼块	fish fillet in tomato sauce
qīng zhēng guìyú	清蒸鳜鱼	steamed Mandarin fish
sōngzǐ guìyú	松子鳜鱼	Mandarin fish with pine nuts
suānlà yóuyú	酸辣鱿鱼	hot and sour squid
xiǎolóngbāo	小笼包	steamer buns
yóubào xiārén	油爆虾仁	fried shrimp
zhá hēi lǐyú	炸黑鲤鱼	fried black carp
zhá yúwán	炸鱼丸	fish balls

Dining: the Ins & Outs

Chinese Restaurants

Chinese eateries come in every conceivable shape, size and type: from shabby, hole-in-the-wall noodle outfits with flimsy PVC furniture, blaring TV sets and well-worn plastic menus to gilded banquet-style restaurants where elegant cheongsam-clad waitresses will show you to your seat, straighten your chopsticks and bring you a warm hand towel and a gold-embossed wine list.

In between are legions of very serviceable midrange restaurants serving cuisine from across China.

As dining in China is such a big, sociable and often ostentatious affair, many Chinese banqueting-style restaurants have huge round tables, thousand-candle-power electric lights and precious little sense of intimacy or romance. Over-attentive and ever-present staff can add to the discomfort for foreigners.

Organic (*yǒujī*) food is experiencing considerable growth and popularity in China, partly as a result of concerns about food safety but also as a reflection of growing incomes.

Dining Times

The Chinese eat early. Lunch usually commences from around 11.30am, either self-cooked or a takeaway at home, or in a street-side restaurant. Dinner kicks off from around 6pm. Reflecting these dining times, some restaurants open at around 11am to close for an afternoon break at about 2.30pm before opening again at around 5pm and closing in the late evening.

Menus

In Běijīng, Shànghǎi and other large cities, you may be proudly presented with an English menu (英文菜谱; *Yīngwén càipǔ*). In smaller towns and out in the sticks, don't expect anything other than a Chinese-language menu and a hovering waitress with no English language skills. The best is undoubtedly the ever-handy photo menu. If you like the look of what other diners are eating, just point (我要那个; *wǒ yào nèi gè;* 'I want that' – a very handy phrase). Alternatively, pop into the kitchen and point out the meats and vegetables you would like to eat. See the Language chapter (p1016) at the back of the book for handy phrases you can use for ordering food and drink.

Desserts & Sweets

The Chinese do not generally eat dessert, but fruit – typically watermelon *(xīguā)* or oranges *(chéng)* – often concludes a meal. Ice cream can be ordered in some places, but in general sweet desserts *(tiánpǐn)* are consumed as snacks and are seldom available in restaurants.

Table Manners

Chinese meal times are generally relaxed affairs with no strict rules of etiquette. Meals can commence in a Confucian vein before spiralling into total Taoist mayhem, fuelled by incessant toasts with *báijiǔ* (a white spirit) or beer and furious smoking by the men.

It is quite common for banquets and dinners in China to finish abruptly, as everyone stands up and walks away in unison with little delay.

Meals typically unfold with one person ordering on behalf of a group. When a group dines, a selection of dishes is ordered for everyone to share rather than individual diners ordering a dish just for themselves. As they arrive, dishes are placed communally in the centre of the table or on a lazy Susan, which may be revolved by the host so that the principal guest gets first choice of whatever dish arrives. Soup may appear midway through the meal or at the end. Rice often arrives at the end of the meal; if you would like it earlier, just ask.

It is good form to fill your neighbours' tea cups or beer glasses when they are empty. To serve yourself tea or any other drink without serving others first is bad form, and appreciation to the pourer is indicated by gently tapping the middle finger on the table.

When your teapot needs a refill, signal this to the waiter by simply taking the lid off the pot.

LONELY PLANET / GETTY IMAGES ©

Tea ceremony

It's best to wait until someone announces a toast before drinking your beer; if you want to get a quick shot in, propose a toast to the host. The Chinese do in fact toast each other much more than in the West, often each time they drink. A formal toast is conducted by raising your glass in both hands in the direction of the toastee and crying out *gānbēi*, literally 'dry the glass', which is the cue to drain your glass in one hit. This can be quite a challenge if your drink is 65% *báijiǔ*, and your glass is rapidly refilled to the meniscus after you drain it, in preparation for the next toast which may rapidly follow.

Smokers can light up during the meal, unless they are in the no-smoking area of a restaurant. Depending on the restaurant, smokers may smoke through the entire meal. If you are a smoker, ensure you hand around your cigarettes to others as that is standard procedure.

Don't use your chopsticks to point at people or gesticulate with them and never stick your chopsticks upright in bowls of rice (it's a portent of death).

Last but not least, never insist on paying for the bill if someone else is tenaciously determined to pay – usually the person who invited you to dinner. By all means offer, but then raise your hands in mock surrender when resistance is met; to pay for a meal when another person is determined to pay is to make them lose face.

Chinese toothpick etiquette is similar to that found in other Asian nations: one hand excavates with the toothpick, while the other hand shields the mouth.

Chinese diners will often slurp their noodles quite noisily, which is not considered to be impolite.

Street Food

Snacking your way around China is a fine way to sample the different flavours of the land while on the move. Most towns have a street market or a night market (夜市; *yèshì*) for good-value snacks and meals so you can either take away or park yourself on a wobbly stool and grab a beer. Street markets such as Kāifēng's boisterous night market abound with choices you may not find in restaurants. Vocal vendors will be forcing their tasty creations on you but you can also see what people are buying and what's being cooked up, so all you have to do is join the queue and point.

Eating with Kids

Similar to travelling with children in China, dining out with kids can be a challenge. Budget eateries won't have kids' menus; nor will they have booster seats. Smarter restaurants may supply these but it can be touch and go. In large cities you will be able to find more restaurants switched on to the needs of families, especially Western restaurants that may have a play area, kids' menu, activities, booster seats and other paraphernalia.

Breakfast

Breakfast in China is generally light, simple and over and done with quickly. The meal may merely consist of a bowl of rice porridge (粥; *zhōu*) or its watery cousin, rice gruel (稀饭; *xīfàn*). Pickles, boiled eggs, steamed buns, fried peanuts and deep-fried dough sticks (油条; *yóutiáo*) are also popular, washed down with warm soybean milk. Breakfast at your Chinese hotel may consist of some or all of these. Coffee is rarely drunk at breakfast time, unless the family is modern, urban and middle class, but it's easy to find cafes, especially in large towns. Sliced bread (面包; *miànbāo*) was once rare but is increasingly common, as is butter (黄油; *huángyóu*).

Traditionally one of the seven necessities of daily life in China, tea was once employed as a form of currency in the Middle Kingdom.

The world's fifth largest producer of wine in 2010, China may become the world's sixth largest consumer of wine by 2014.

Vegetarianism

If you'd rather chew on a legume than a leg of lamb, it can be hard going trying to find truly vegetarian dishes. China's history of famine and poverty means the consumption of meat has always been a sign of status, and is symbolic of health and wealth. Eating meat is also considered to enhance male virility, so vegetarian men raise eyebrows. Partly because of this, there is virtually no vegetarian movement in China, although Chinese people may forgo meat for Buddhist reasons. For the same reasons, they may avoid meat on certain days of the month but remain carnivorous at other times.

The Chinese word for tea (*chá*) has colloquially entered numerous different languages, including English (UK), Portuguese, Greek and Russian. The word 'tea' itself comes from the Fújiàn dialect for tea.

You will find that vegetables are often fried in animal-based oils, while vegetable soups are often made with chicken or beef stock, so simply choosing vegetable items on the menu is ineffective. In Běijīng and Shànghǎi you will, however, find a generous crop of vegetarian restaurants to choose from alongside outfits such as Element Fresh (p208), which has a decent range of healthy vegetarian options.

Out of the large cities, your best bet may be to head to a sizeable active Buddhist temple or monastery, where Buddhist vegetarian restaurants are often open to the public. Buddhist vegetarian food typically consists of 'mock meat' dishes created from tofu, wheat gluten, potato and other vegetables. Some of the dishes are almost works of art, with vegetarian ingredients sculpted to look like spare ribs or fried chicken. Sometimes the chefs go to great lengths to create 'bones' from carrots and lotus roots.

If you want to say 'I am a vegetarian' in Chinese, the phrase to use is 我吃素 (*wǒ chī sù*).

Tea

An old Chinese saying identifies tea as one of the seven basic necessities of life, along with firewood, oil, rice, salt, soy sauce and vinegar. The Chinese were the first to cultivate tea, and the art of brewing and drinking tea has been popular since Tang times (AD 618–907).

China has three main types of tea: green tea (*lǜ chá*), black tea (*hóng chá*) and *wūlóng* (a semifermented tea, halfway between black and green tea). In addition, there are other variations, including jasmine (*cháshuǐ*) and chrysanthemum (*júhuā chá*). Some famous regional teas of China are Fújiàn's *tiě guānyīn*, *pú'ěrh* from Yúnnán and Zhèjiāng's *lóngjǐng* tea. Eight-treasure tea (*bābǎo chá*) consists of rock sugar, dates, nuts and tea combined in a cup; it makes a delicious treat. Tea is to the Chinese what fine wine is to the French: a beloved beverage savoured for its fine aroma, distinctive flavour and pleasing aftertaste.

Alcoholic Drinks

Beer

If tea is the most popular drink in China, then beer (啤酒; *píjiǔ*) is surely second. Many towns and cities have their own brewery and label, although a remarkable feat of socialist standardisation ensures a striking similarity in flavour and strength. You can drink bathtubs of the stuff and still navigate a straight line. If you want your beer cold, ask for *liáng de* (凉的), and if you want it truly arctic, call for *bīngzhèn de* (冰镇的).

TIPPING

Tipping is never done at cheap restaurants in mainland China. Smart, international restaurants will encourage tipping but it is not obligatory and it's uncertain whether waiting staff receive their tips at the end of the night. Hotel restaurants automatically add a 15% service charge and some high-end restaurants may do the same.

The best-known beer is Tsingtao, made with Láo Shān mineral water, which lends it a sparkling quality. It's originally a German beer since the town of Qīngdǎo (formerly spelled 'Tsingtao') was once a German concession and the Chinese inherited the brewery (see the boxed text, p164), which dates to 1903, along with Bavarian beer-making ways.

Several foreign beers are also brewed in China. If you crave variety, many of the bars listed in this book should have a selection of foreign imported beers; prices will be high, however.

Also look out for black beer from Xīnjiāng and dark beers from other local breweries (eg Reeb beer in Shànghǎi), which offer more bite. Rather more alternative beers include Inner Mongolian milk beer and pineapple beer from Běijīng.

China's huge market for fine wines has seen an explosion in the market for empty bottles. Empty bottles of Chateau Lafite Rothschild 1982 are especially prized by fraudsters who refill bottles with inferior vintages for resale.

Wine

Surging demand for imported wines saw China and Hong Kong emerge as the world's largest consumer of Bordeaux wines in 2011. Expensive French reds (hóngjiǔ) are treasured in a fashionable market that was only finding its feet a mere 15 years ago. Wine has become the drink of choice among an increasingly sophisticated business class eager to appear discerning and flamboyant. Unfortunately this also means you can pay way over the odds at restaurants in Shànghǎi or Běijīng for imported wines. White wine consumption is increasingly associated with female drinkers in China.

China has also cultivated vines and produced wine for an estimated 4000 years, and Chinese wines are generally cheaper than imports from abroad. The provinces of Xīnjiāng and Níngxià in the distant northwest of China are famous for their vineyards.

Spirits

The word 'wine' gets rather loosely translated – many Chinese 'wines' are in fact spirits. Maotai, a favourite of Chinese drinkers, is a very expensive spirit called báijiǔ made from sorghum (a type of millet) and used for toasts at banquets. The cheap alternative is Erguotou, distilled in Běijīng but available all over China; look out for the Red Star (Hongxing) brand. Báijiǔ ranges across the alcohol spectrum from milder forms to around 65% proof. Milder rice wine is intended mainly for cooking rather than drinking but can be drunk warm like sake.

Arts & Architecture

China is custodian of one of the world's richest cultural and artistic legacies. Until the 20th century, China's arts were deeply conservative and resistant to change but in the last hundred years revolutions in technique and content have fashioned a dramatic transformation. Despite this evolution, China's arts – whatever the period – remain united by a common aesthetic that taps into the very soul and essence of the nation.

Aesthetics

In reflection of the Chinese character (p931), Chinese aesthetics have traditionally been marked by restraint and understatement, a preference for oblique references over direct explanation, vagueness in place of specificity and an avoidance of the obvious in place of a fondness for the veiled and subtle. Traditional Chinese aesthetics sought to cultivate a more reserved artistic impulse, principles that compellingly find their way into virtually every Chinese art form, from painting to sculpture, ceramics, calligraphy, film, poetry, literature and beyond.

As one of the central strands of the world's oldest civilisation, China's aesthetic traditions are tightly woven into the Chinese cultural identity. For millennia, Chinese aesthetics were highly traditionalist and, despite coming under the influence of occupiers from the Mongols to the Europeans, defiantly conservative. It was not until the fall of the Qing dynasty in 1911 and the appearance of the New Culture Movement that China's great artistic traditions began to rapidly transform. In literature the stranglehold of classical Chinese loosened to allow breathing space for *báihuà* (colloquial Chinese) and a progressive new aesthetic began to flower, ultimately leading to revolutions in all of the arts, from poetry to painting, theatre and music.

It is hard to square China's great aesthetic traditions with the devastation inflicted upon them since 1949. Confucius advocated the edifying role of music and poetry in shaping human lives, but 5th-century philosopher Mozi was less enamoured with them, seeing music and other arts as extravagant and wasteful. The communists took this a stage further, enlisting the arts as props in their propaganda campaigns, and permitting the vandalism and destruction of much traditional architecture and heritage. Many of China's traditional skills (such as martial arts lineages) and crafts either died out or went into decline during the Cultural Revolution. Many of the arts have yet to recover fully from this deterioration, even though opening up and reform prompted a vast influx of foreign artistic concepts.

BIRD'S NEST

Consultant designer of the Bird's Nest, Chinese artist Ai Weiwei later distanced himself from the stadium, saying it was a 'pretend smile' of bad taste.

Calligraphy

Although calligraphy (书法; *shūfǎ*) has a place among most languages that employ alphabets, the art of calligraphy in China is taken to unusual heights of intricacy and beauty. Although Chinese calligraphy is beautiful in its own right, the complex infatuation Chinese people have for their written language helps elucidate their great respect for the art of calligraphy.

To understand how perfectly suited written Chinese is for calligraphy, it is vital to grasp how written Chinese works. A word in English represents a sound alone; a written character in Chinese combines both sound and a picture. Indeed, the sound element of a Chinese character – when present – is often auxiliary to the presentation of a visual image, even if abstract.

Furthermore, although some Chinese characters were simplified in the 1950s as part of a literacy drive, most characters have remained unchanged for thousands of years. As characters are essentially images, they inadequately reflect changes in spoken Chinese over time. A phonetic written language such as English can alter over the centuries to reflect changes in the sound of the language. Being pictographic, Chinese cannot easily do this, so while the spoken language has transformed over the centuries, the written language has remained more static.

This helps explain why Chinese calligraphy is the trickiest of China's arts to comprehend for Western visitors, unless they have a sound understanding of written Chinese. The beauty of a Chinese character may be partially appreciated by a Western audience, but for a full understanding it is also essential to understand the meaning of the character in context.

There are five main calligraphic scripts – seal script, clerical script, semicursive script, cursive script and standard script – each of which reflects the style of writing of a specific era. Seal script, the oldest and most complex, was the official writing system during the Qin dynasty and has been employed ever since in the carving of the seals and name chops (stamps carved from stone) that are used to stamp documents. Expert calligraphers have a preference for using full-form characters (*fántǐzì*) rather than their simplified variants (*jiǎntǐzì*).

> The most abstract calligraphic form is grass or cursive script (*cǎoshū*), a highly fluid style of penmanship which even Chinese people have difficulty reading.

Painting

Traditional Painting

Unlike Chinese calligraphy, no 'insider' knowledge is required for a full appreciation of traditional Chinese painting. Despite its symbolism, obscure references and occasionally abstruse philosophical allusions, Chinese painting is highly accessible. For this reason, traditional Chinese paintings – especially landscapes – have long been treasured in the West for their beauty.

As described in Xie He's 6th century AD treatise, the *Six Principles of Painting*, the chief aim of Chinese painting is to capture the innate essence or spirit (*qì*) of a subject and endow it with vitality. The brush line, varying in thickness and tone, was the second principle (referred to as the 'bone method') and is the defining technique of Chinese painting. Traditionally, it was imagined that brushwork quality could reveal the artist's moral character. As a general rule, painters were less concerned with achieving outward resemblance (that was the third principle) than with conveying intrinsic qualities.

Early painters dwelled on the human figure and moral teachings, while also conjuring up scenes from everyday life. By the time of the Tang dynasty, a new genre, known as landscape painting, had begun to flower.

> The five fundamental brushstrokes necessary to master calligraphy can be found in the character 永, which means eternal or forever.

BEST ART MUSEUMS AND GALLERIES

» **Shànghǎi Museum** (p181) An outstanding collection of traditional Chinese art and antiquities.

» **Poly Art Museum** (p66) Inspiring displays of traditional bronzes and Buddhist statues.

» **Rockbund Art Museum** (p180) Forward-thinking museum of contemporary art, just off the Bund.

» **Hong Kong Museum of Art** (p478) First-rate display of antiquities, paintings, calligraphy and contemporary Hong Kong art.

» **M50** (p192) Contemporary art in a converted Shànghǎi industrial zone.

» **798 Art District** (p79) Běijīng's premier art zone, housed in a former electronics factory.

» **Propaganda Poster Art Centre** (p192) Shànghǎi treasure trove of propaganda art from the communist golden age.

» **Beaugeste** (p191) Tiny Shànghǎi gallery dedicated to contemporary photography.

Reaching full bloom during the Song and Yuan dynasties, landscape painting meditated on the surrounding environment. Towering mountains, ethereal mists, open spaces, trees and rivers, and light and dark were all exquisitely presented in ink washes on silk. Landscape paintings attempted to capture the metaphysical and the absolute, drawing the viewer into a particular realm where the philosophies of Taoism and Buddhism found expression. Humanity is typically a small and almost insignificant subtext to the performance. The dream-like painting sought to draw the viewer in rather than impose itself on them.

On a technical level, the success of landscapes depended on the artists' skill in capturing light and atmosphere. Blank, open spaces devoid of colour create light-filled voids, contrasting with the darkness of mountain folds, filling the painting with qì and vaporous vitality. Specific emotions are not aroused but instead nebulous sensations permeate. Painting and classical poetry often went hand in hand, best exemplified by the work of Tang-dynasty poet/artist Wang Wei (699–759).

For in-depth articles and reviews of contemporary Chinese arts and artists, click on www.newchinese art.com, run by the Shànghǎi-based gallery Art Scene China.

Modern Art
Socialist-Realism

After 1949, classical Chinese techniques were abandoned and foreign artistic techniques imported wholesale. Washes on silk were replaced with oil on canvas and China's traditional obsession with the mysterious and ineffable made way for concrete attention to detail and realism.

By 1970 Chinese artists had aspired to master the skills of socialist-realism, a vibrant communist-endorsed style that drew from European neoclassical art, the lifelike canvases of Jacques-Louis David and the output of Soviet Union painters. Saturated with political symbolism and propaganda, the blunt artistic style was produced on an industrial scale.

The entire trajectory of Chinese painting – which had evolved in glacial increments over the centuries – had been redirected virtually overnight. Vaporous landscapes were substituted with hard-edged panoramas. Traditional Taoist and Buddhist philosophy was overturned and humans became the master of nature. Dreamy vistas were out; smoke stacks, red tractors and muscled peasants were in.

Propaganda Art

Another art form that found a fertile environment during the Mao era was the propaganda poster. Mass produced from the 1950s onwards and replicated in their thousands through tourist markets across China today, the colourful Chinese propaganda poster was a further instrument of social control in a nation where aesthetics had become subservient to communist orthodoxy.

With a prolific range of themes from chubby, well-fed Chinese babies to the Korean War, the value of physical education, the suppression of counterrevolutionary activity and paeans to the achievements of the Great Leap Forward or China as an earthly paradise, propaganda posters were mass-produced and ubiquitous. The golden age of poster production ran through to the 1980s, only declining during Deng Xiaoping's tenure and the opening up of China to the West.

The success of visual propaganda lay in its appeal to a large body of illiterate or semiliterate peasants. The idealism, revolutionary romanticism and vivid colouring of Chinese propaganda art brought hope and vibrancy to a time that was actually often colourless and drab while adding certainty to an era of great hardship and struggle.

Post-Mao

It was only with the death of Mao Zedong in September 1976 that the shadow of the Cultural Revolution – when Chinese aesthetics were conditioned by the threat of violence – began its retreat and the individual artistic temperament was allowed to thrive afresh.

Painters such as Luo Zhongli employed the realist techniques gleaned from China's art academies to depict the harsh realities etched in the faces of contemporary peasants. Others escaped the suffocating confines of socialist realism to navigate new horizons. A voracious appetite for Western art brought with it fresh concepts and ideas, while the ambiguity of exact meaning in the fine arts offered a degree of protection from state censors.

One group of artists, the Stars, found retrospective inspiration in Picasso and German Expressionism. The ephemeral group had a lasting impact on the development of Chinese art in the 1980s and 1990s, paving the way for the New Wave movement that emerged in 1985. New Wave artists were greatly influenced by Western art, especially the iconoclastic Marcel Duchamp. In true nihilist style, the New Wave artist Huang Yongping destroyed his works at exhibitions, in an effort to escape from the notion of 'art'. Political realities became instant subject matter as performance artists wrapped themselves in plastic or tape to symbolise the repressive realities of modern-day China.

Beyond Tiān'ānmén

The Tiān'ānmén Square protests in 1989 fostered a deep-seated cynicism that permeated artworks with loss, loneliness and social isolation. An exodus of artists to the West commenced. This period also coincided with an upsurge in the art market as investors increasingly turned to artworks and money began to slosh about.

Much post-1989 Chinese art dwelled obsessively on contemporary socioeconomic realities, with consumer culture, materialism, urbanisation and social change a repetitive focus. More universal themes became apparent, however, as the art scene matured. Meanwhile, many artists who left China in the 1990s have returned, setting up private studios and galleries. Government censorship remains, but artists are branching out into other areas and moving away from overtly political content and China-specific concerns.

ASTEROID BLET

Discovered by amateur astronomer William Kwong Yu Yeung in 2001, the main belt asteroid – 83598 Aiweiwei – was named after Chinese artist Ai Weiwei in 2001.

Cynical realists Fang Lijun and Yue Minjun fashioned grotesque portraits that conveyed hollowness and mock joviality, tinged with despair. Born in the late 1950s, Wang Guangyi took pop art as a template for his ironic pieces, fused with propaganda art techniques from the Cultural Revolution.

Born just before the Cultural Revolution in 1964 and heavily influenced by German expressionism, Zeng Fanzhi explored the notions of alienation and isolation – themes commonly explored by Chinese artists during this period – in his *Mask* series from the 1990s. Introspection is a hallmark of Zeng's oeuvre. In 2008 Christie's in Hong Kong sold Zeng Fanzhi's painting *Mask Series 1996 No. 6* (featuring masked members of China's communist youth organisation, the Young Pioneers) for US\$9.7 million, which is the highest price yet paid for a contemporary Chinese artwork.

Also born in the early 1960s, Zhang Dali is another artist who gave expression to social change and the gulf between rich and poor, especially the circumstances of the immigrant worker underclass in Běijīng.

Contemporary Directions

Most artists of note and aspiration gravitate to Běijīng (or Shànghǎi perhaps) to work.

Ai Weiwei, who enjoys great international fame partly due to his disobedient stand, best exemplifies the dangerous overlap between artistic self-expression, dissent and conflict with the authorities. Arrested in 2011 and charged with tax evasion, Ai Weiwei gained further publicity for his temporary *Sunflower Seeds* exhibition at the Tate Modern in London. Ai's Shànghǎi studio was torn down in January 2011, a move the artist said was prompted by his activism. Local authorities said the building was 'illegal'.

Ceramics

China's very first vessels – dating back more than 8000 years – were simple handcrafted earthenware pottery, primarily used for religious purposes. The invention of the pottery wheel during the late Neolithic period, however, led to a dramatic technological and artistic leap.

Over the centuries, Chinese potters perfected their craft, introducing many new exciting styles and techniques. The spellbinding artwork of the Terracotta Warriors in Xī'ān reveals a highly developed level of technical skill achieved by Qin-dynasty craftsmen. Periods of artistic development, under the cosmopolitan Tang dynasty, for example, prompted further stylistic advances. The Tang dynasty 'three-colour ware' is a much admired type of ceramic from this period, noted for its vivid yellow, green and white glaze. Demand for lovely blue-green celadons grew in countries as distant as Egypt and Persia.

In 2010 a Qing-dynasty Chinese vase sold for £53.1 million after being discovered in the attic of a house in north-west London and put up for auction.

The Yuan dynasty saw the first development of China's standout 'blue and white' *(qīnghuā)* porcelain. Cobalt blue paint, from Persia, was applied as an underglaze directly to white porcelain with a brush, the vessel was covered with another transparent glaze, and fired. This technique was perfected during the Ming and such ceramics became hugely popular all over the world, eventually acquiring the name 'China-ware', whether produced in China or not.

Although many kilns were established over China, the most famous was at Jǐngdézhèn in Jiāngxī province, where royal porcelain was fired up.

During the Qing dynasty, porcelain techniques were further refined and developed, showing superb craftsmanship and ingenuity. British and European consumers dominated the export market, displaying an insatiable appetite for Chinese vases and bowls decorated with flowers and

Poet Li Po depicted on a Qing-dynasty plate

landscapes. Stunning monochromatic ware is another hallmark of the Qing, especially the ox-blood vases, imperial yellow bowls and enamel-decorated porcelain. The Qing is also notable for its elaborate and highly decorative wares.

Jǐngdézhèn remains an excellent place to visit ceramic workshops and purchase various types of ceramic wares, from Mao statues to traditional glazed urns. The Shànghǎi Museum has a premier collection of porcelain, while several independent retailers in Běijīng and Shànghǎi also sell more modish and creative pieces.

Sculpture

The earliest sculpture in China dates to the Zhou and Shang dynasties, when small clay and wooden figures were commonly placed in tombs to protect the dead and guide them on their way to heaven.

With the arrival of Buddhism, sculpture turned towards spiritual figures and themes, with sculptors frequently enrolled in huge carving projects for the worship of Sakyamuni. Influences also arrived along the Silk Road from abroad, bringing styles from as far afield as Greece and Persia, via India. The magnificent Buddhist caves at Yúngāng in Shānxī province date back to the 5th century and betray a noticeable Indian influence.

Chisellers also began work on the Lóngmén Caves in Hénán province at the end of the 5th century. The earliest effigies are similar in style to those at Yúngāng, revealing further Indian influences and more otherworldliness in their facial expressions. Later cave sculptures at Lóngmén were completed during the Tang dynasty and reveal a more Chinese style.

The most superlative examples are at the Mògāo Caves at Dūnhuáng in Gānsù province, where well-preserved Indian and central Asian–style sculptures, particularly of the Tang dynasty, carry overtly Chinese characteristics – many statues feature long, fluid bodies and have warmer, more refined facial features.

The *I Ching* (Yìjīng; Book of Changes) is the oldest Chinese text and is used for divination. It is comprised of 64 hexagrams, composed of broken and continuous lines, that represent a balance of opposites (yin and yang), the inevitability of change and the evolution of events.

The Shànghǎi Museum has a splendid collection of Buddhist sculpture, as does Capital Museum and the Poly Art Museum, both in Běijīng.

Beyond China's grottoes, other mesmerising Chinese sculpture hides away in temples across China. The colossal statue of Guanyin in Pǔníng Temple in Chéngdé is a staggering sight, carved from five different types of wood and towering over 22m in height. Shuānglín Temple outside Píngyáo in Shānxī province is famed for its painted statues from the Song and Yuan dynasties.

Literature

Classical Novels

Until the early 20th century, classical literature (古文; *gǔwén*) had been the principal form of writing in China for thousands of years. A breed of purely literary writing, classical Chinese employed a stripped-down form of written Chinese that did not reflect the way people actually spoke or thought. Its grammar differed from the syntax of spoken Chinese and it employed numerous obscure Chinese characters.

Classical Chinese maintained divisions between educated and uneducated Chinese, putting literature beyond the reach of the common person and fashioning a cliquey lingua franca for Confucian officials and scholars.

Classical novels evolved from the popular folk tales and dramas that entertained the lower classes. During the Ming dynasty they were penned in a semivernacular (or 'vulgar') language, and are often irreverently funny and full of action-packed fights.

Probably the best-known novel outside China is *Journey to the West* (Xīyóu Jì) – more commonly known as *Monkey*. Written in the 16th century, it follows the misadventures of a cowardly Buddhist monk (Tripitaka; a stand-in for the real-life pilgrim Xuan Zang) and his companions – a rebellious monkey, lecherous pig-man and exiled monster-immortal – on a pilgrimage to India. In 2007 a Chinese director collaborated with Damon Albarn of the virtual band Gorillaz to transform the story into a circus opera that has played to considerable international acclaim.

The 14th-century novel *The Water Margin/Outlaws of the Marsh/All Men are Brothers* (Shuǐhǔ Zhuàn) is, on the surface, an excellent tale of honourable bandits and corrupt officials along the lines of Robin Hood. On a deeper level, though, it is a reminder to Confucian officials of their right to rebel when faced with a morally suspect government (at least one emperor officially banned it).

Modern Literature
Early-20th-Century Writing

Classical Chinese maintained its authority over literary minds until the early 20th century, when it came under the influence of the West.

Torch-bearing author Lu Xun wrote his short story *Diary of a Madman* in 1918. It was revolutionary stuff. Apart from the opening paragraph, Lu's seminal and shocking fable is written in colloquial Chinese.

For Lu Xun to write his short story in colloquial Chinese was explosive, as readers were finally able to read language as it was spoken. *Diary of a Madman* is a haunting and unsettling work and from this moment on, mainstream Chinese literature would be written as it was thought and spoken: Chinese writing had been instantly revolutionised.

Other notable contemporaries of Lu Xun include Ba Jin (*Family;* 1931), Mao Dun (*Midnight;* 1933), Lao She (*Rickshaw Boy/Camel Xiangzi;* 1936) and the modernist playwright Cao Yu (*Thunderstorm*). Lu Xun and Ba Jin translated a great deal of foreign literature into Chinese.

Published by the Chinese University of Hong Kong Research Centre for Translation, *Renditions* is an excellent journal of Chinese literature in English translation covering works from classical Chinese to modern writing.

Wolf Totem (2009) by Jiang Rong is an astonishing look at life on the grasslands of Inner Mongolia during the Cultural Revolution and the impact of modern culture on an ancient way of life.

ARTS & ARCHITECTURE LITERATURE

NON-NATIVE TONGUES

Beyond translations of famous Chinese works, an accessible corpus of literature exists from Chinese émigrés conceiving works in English and French.

» *Wild Swans* (Jung Chang; 1992) Prize-winning autobiographical saga about three generations of Chinese women struggling to survive the tumultuous events of 20th-century China. Chang is also the co-author of the controversial best-selling biography *Mao: The Unknown Story* (2005).

» *Ocean of Words* (1996), *Waiting* (1999), *The Bridegroom* (2000), *The Crazed* (2002), *War Trash, A Free Life* (2007) The most prolific of the diaspora writers, Ha Jin has won both the National Book Award (USA) and the PEN/Faulkner Award (among others).

» *A Thousand Years of Good Prayers* (Yiyun Li; 2006) Prize-winning short stories depicting the lives of everyday Chinese caught up in the changes of the past two decades.

» *Death of a Red Heroine* (2000), *A Loyal Character Dancer* (2002), *When Red is Black* (2004), *A Case of Two Cities* (2006), *Red Mandarin Dress* (2007), *The Mao Case* (2009) Qiu Xiaolong's insightful Inspector Chen novels feature a literary-minded cop and a vivid street-level portrayal of changing Shànghǎi.

» *The People's Republic of Desire* (Annie Wang; 2006) A candid exploration of sexuality in modern Běijīng.

» *On the Smell of an Oily Rag* (Yu Ouyang; 2008) Clever cross-cultural observances from a Chinese émigré living in Australia.

Contemporary Writing

A growing number of contemporary voices have been translated into English, but far more exist in Chinese only. The provocative Nobel Prize–winning Mo Yan (*Life and Death are Wearing Me Out;* 2008), Yu Hua (*To Live;* 1992) and Su Tong (*Rice;* 1995) have written momentous historical novels set in the 20th century; all are excellent, though their raw, harrowing subject matter is not for the faint of heart.

The Book and the Sword by Jin Yong/Louis Cha (2004) is China's most celebrated martial-arts novelist's first book. The martial-arts genre (*wǔxiá xiǎoshuō*) is a direct descendant of the classical novel.

Zhu Wen mocks the get-rich movement in his brilliantly funny short stories, published in English as *I Love Dollars and Other Stories of China* (2007). It's a vivid and comic portrayal of the absurdities of everyday China.

'Hooligan author' Wang Shuo (*Please Don't Call Me Human;* 2000) is one of China's best-selling authors with his political satires and convincing depictions of urban slackers. Alai (*Red Poppies;* 2002), an ethnic Tibetan, made waves by writing in Chinese about early-20th-century Tibetan Sìchuān – whatever your politics, it's both insightful and a page-turner. Émigré Ma Jian (*Red Dust;* 2004) writes more politically critical work; his debut was a Kerouacian tale of wandering China as a spiritual pollutant in the 1980s. China's most renowned dissident writer, Gao Xingjian, won the Nobel Prize for Literature in 2000 for his novel *Soul Mountain,* an account of his travels along the Yangzi after being misdiagnosed with lung cancer. All of his work has been banned in the PRC since 1989.

Controversial blogger Han Han (http://blog.sina.com.cn/twocold) catapulted himself into the literary spotlight with his novel *Triple Door,* a searing critique of China's educational system.

In his novel *Banished,* poet, essayist, short-story writer and blogger Han Dong reaches to his own experiences during the Cultural Revolution for inspiration. Winner of the Man Asian Literary Prize in 2010, Bi Feiyu's *Three Sisters* is a poignant tale of rural China during the political chaos of the early 1970s. In *Northern Girls,* Sheng Keyi illuminates the prejudices and bigotries of modern Chinese society in her story of a Chinese girl arriving as an immigrant worker in Shēnzhèn.

For a taste of contemporary Chinese short-story writing with both English and Chinese, buy a copy of *Short Stories in Chinese: New Penguin Parallel Text* (2012). *The Picador Book of Contemporary Chinese Fiction* (2006) brings together a range of different contemporary voices and themes into one accessible book.

Film

Early Cinema

The moving image in the Middle Kingdom dates to 1896, when Spaniard Galen Bocca unveiled a film projector and blew the socks off wide-eyed crowds in a Shànghǎi teahouse. Shànghǎi's cosmopolitan verve and exotic looks would make it the capital of China's film industry, but China's very first movie – *Conquering Jun Mountain* (an excerpt from a piece of Běijīng opera) – was actually filmed in Běijīng in 1905.

Shànghǎi opened its first cinema in 1908. In those days, cinema owners would cannily run the film for a few minutes, stop it and collect money from the audience before allowing the film to continue. The golden age of Shànghǎi film-making came in the 1930s when the city had over 140 film companies. Its apogee arrived in 1937 with the release of *Street Angel*, a powerful drama about two sisters who flee the Japanese in northeast China and end up as prostitutes in Shànghǎi; and *Crossroads*, a clever comedy about four unemployed graduates. Japanese control of China eventually brought the industry to a standstill and sent many film-makers packing.

Communist Decline

China's film industry was stymied after the Communist Revolution, which sent film-makers scurrying to Hong Kong and Taiwan, where they played key roles in building up the local film industries that flourished there. Cinematic production in China was co-opted to glorify communism and generate patriotic propaganda. The days of the Cultural Revolution (1966–76) were particularly dark. Between 1966 and 1972, just eight movies were made on the mainland, as the film industry was effectively shut down.

Resurgence

It wasn't until two years after the death of Mao Zedong, in September 1978, that China's premier film school – the Běijīng Film Academy – reopened. Its first intake of students included Zhang Yimou, Chen Kaige and Tian Zhuangzhuang, who are considered masterminds of the celebrated 'Fifth Generation'.

The cinematic output of the Fifth Generation signalled an escape from the dour, colourless and proletarian Mao era, and a second glittering golden age of Chinese film-making arrived in the 1980s and 1990s with their lush and lavish tragedies. A bleak but beautifully shot tale of a Chinese Communist Party cadre who travels to a remote village in Shaanxi province to collect folk songs, Chen Kaige's *Yellow Earth* aroused little interest in China but proved a sensation when released in the West in 1985.

It was followed by Zhang's *Red Sorghum*, which introduced Gong Li and Jiang Wen to the world. Gong became the poster girl of Chinese cinema in the 1990s and the first international movie star to emerge from the mainland. Jiang, the Marlon Brando of Chinese film, has proved both a durable leading man and an innovative, controversial director of award-winning films such as *In the Heat of the Sun* and *Devils on the Doorstep*.

The 2010 remake of the *Karate Kid*, starring Jackie Chan, is set in Běijīng and authentically conveys the city despite having nothing to do with karate.

Rich, seminal works such as *Farewell My Concubine* (1993; Chen Kaige) and *Raise the Red Lantern* (1991; Zhang Yimou) were garlanded with praise, receiving standing ovations and winning major film awards. Their directors were the darlings of Cannes; Western cinemagoers were entranced. Many Chinese cinema-goers also admired their artistry, but some saw Fifth Generation output as pandering to the Western market.

In 1993 Tian Zhuangzhuang made the brilliant *The Blue Kite*. A heartbreaking account of the life of one Běijīng family during the Cultural Revolution, it so enraged the censors that Tian was banned from making films for a decade.

Each generation charts its own course and the ensuing Sixth Generation – graduating from the Běijīng Film Academy post-Tiān'ānmén Square protests – was no different.

Sixth Generation film directors eschewed the luxurious beauty of their forebears, and sought to capture the angst and grit of modern urban Chinese life. Their independent, low-budget works put an entirely different and more cynical spin on mainland Chinese film-making, but their darker subject matter and harsh film style (frequently in black and white) left many Western viewers cold.

Independent film-making found an influential precedent with Zhang Yuan's 1990 debut *Mama*. Zhang is also acclaimed for his candid and gritty documentary-style *Beijing Bastards* (1993).

Meanwhile, *The Days,* directed by Wang Xiaoshui, follows a couple drifting apart in the wake of the Tiān'ānmén Square protests. Wang also directed the excellent *Beijing Bicycle* (2001), inspired by De Sica's *Bicycle Thieves*.

> In 2011 an ink and brush painting by artist Qi Baishi (1864–1957) sold for ¥425 million (US$65 million) at auction.

Contemporary Film

Jia Zhangke has emerged as the most acclaimed of China's new filmmakers. His meditative and compassionate look at the social impact of the construction of the Three Gorges Dam on local people, *Still Life* (2006), scooped the Golden Lion at the 2006 Venice Film Festival.

In mainstream cinema, many Chinese films are highly commercially motivated, frequently epic in scale and aimed at the China/Hong Kong/Taiwan market.

Historical *wuxia* (martial arts) cinema is enduringly popular in China and typified much film-making in the noughties, with larger-than-life films like *Hero* (2002; Zhang Yimou), *House of Flying Daggers* (2004; Zhang Yimou) and *The Banquet* (2006; Feng Xiaogang) leading the way. Epic historical war dramas such as *Red Cliff* (2008 and 2009; John Woo) and *The Warlords* (2007; Peter Chan) belong to a similar genre. The Hong Kong director Wong Kar-wai is particularly notable for seductively filmed classics such as *In the Mood for Love* (2000) and *2046* (2004).

In a protectionist move, Běijīng caps the number of foreign films that can be shown annually in cinemas to around 20. The film industry in China still has to outmanoeuvre taboos with directors walking on eggshells (even oblique criticism of the authorities remains professionally hazardous).

> Major art festivals include Běijīng's 798 International Art Festival, China International Gallery Exposition and Běijīng Biennale, the Shànghǎi Biennale, Guǎngzhōu Triennial and Hong Kong's one-day Clockenflap festival.

Chinese Opera

Contemporary Chinese opera, of which the most famous is Běijīng opera (京剧; *Jīngjù*), has a continuous history of some 900 years. Evolving from a convergence of comic and ballad traditions in the Northern Song period, Chinese opera brought together a disparate range of forms: acrobatics, martial arts, poetic arias and stylised dance.

Operas were usually performed by travelling troupes who had a low social status in traditional Chinese society. Chinese law forbade mixed-sex performances, forcing actors to act out roles of the opposite sex. Opera troupes were frequently associated with homosexuality in the public imagination, contributing further to their lowly social status.

Formerly, opera was performed mostly on open-air stages in markets, streets, teahouses or temple courtyards. The shrill singing and loud percussion were designed to be heard over the public throng, prompting American writer PJ O'Rourke to say it was 'as if a truck full of wind chimes collided with a stack of empty drums during a birdcall contest'.

Opera performances usually take place on a bare stage, with the actors taking on stylised stock characters who are instantly recognisable to the audience. Most stories are derived from classical literature and Chinese mythology, and tell of disasters, natural calamities, intrigues or rebellions.

As well as Běijīng opera, other famous Chinese operatic traditions include Cantonese opera (p544), Kunqu (from the Jiāngnán region), Min opera (from Fújiàn) and Shànghǎi opera.

Architecture

Traditional Architecture

Four principal styles governed traditional Chinese architecture: imperial, religious, residential and recreational. The imperial style was naturally the most grandiose, overseeing the design of buildings employed by successive dynastic rulers; the religious style was employed for the construction of temples, monasteries and pagodas; while the residential and recreational style took care of the design of houses and private gardens.

Whatever the style, Chinese buildings traditionally followed a similar basic ground plan, consisting of a symmetrical layout oriented around a central axis – ideally running north–south, to conform with basic feng shui (*fēngshuǐ*) dictates and to maximise sunshine – with an enclosed courtyard (*yuàn*) flanked by buildings on all sides.

In many aspects, imperial palaces are glorified courtyard homes (south-facing, a sequence of courtyards, side halls and perhaps a garden at the rear) completed on a different scale. Apart from the size, the main dissimilarity would be guard towers on the walls and possibly a moat, imperial yellow roof tiles, ornate dragon carvings (signifying the emperor), the repetitive use of the number nine and the presence of temples.

Many residential quarters of the well-to-do and temples or halls within imperial palaces were protected by a spirit wall (*yǐngbì*) at their entrance, designed to thwart bad spirits, but also to put a stop to prying eyes. Despite the loss of countless spirit walls, China remains dotted with them, often obsolete as the buildings they once shielded have vanished. Dàtóng's Nine Dragon Screen is a spectacular example.

For a taste of Kazakh folk music from northwest Xinjiang province, listen to *Eagle* by Mamer, an intriguing collection of songs described as 'Chinagrass' by their composer.

ART DECO IN SHÀNGHǍI

Fans of art deco must visit Shànghǎi. The reign of art deco is one of the city's architectural high-water marks and the city boasts more art deco buildings than any other city, from the drawing boards of the French firm Leonard, Veysseyre and Kruze, and others. Largely emptied of foreigners in 1949, Shànghǎi mostly kept its historic villas and buildings intact, including its fabulous art deco monuments. The Peace Hotel, Bank of China building, Cathay Theatre, Green House, Paramount Ballroom, Broadway Mansions, Liza Building, Savoy Apartments, Picardie Apartments and Majestic Theatre are all art deco gems. For a comprehensive low-down on the style, hunt down a copy of *Shanghai Art Deco* by Deke Erh and Tess Johnston.

Behind the entrance in palaces and wealthier residential buildings stood a public hall; behind this was the private living quarters, erected around another courtyard with a garden; most buildings were constructed as one-storey edifices. A sense of harmony prevailed over the entire design, ordered by symmetry and a certain reserve, which also meant that no one particular structure took precedence. Compounds were enlarged simply by adding more courtyards.

Religious Architecture

Chinese Buddhist, Taoist and Confucian temples tend to follow a strict, schematic pattern. All temples are laid out on a north–south axis in a series of halls, with the main door of each hall facing south.

With their sequence of halls and buildings interspersed with breezy open-air courtyards, Chinese temples are very different from Christian churches. The roofless courtyards allow the weather to permeate within the temple and permits qì (气; spirit) to circulate, dispersing stale air and allowing incense to be burned.

Buddhist Temples

Once you have cracked the logic of Buddhist temples, you can discover how most temples conform to a pattern. The first hall and portal to the temple is generally the Hall of Heavenly Kings, where a sedentary, central statue of the tubby Bodhisattva Maitreya is flanked by the ferocious Four Heavenly Kings. Behind is the first courtyard, where the Drum Tower and Bell Tower may rise to the east and west, and smoking braziers may be positioned.

The main hall is often the Great Treasure Hall sheltering glittering statues of the past, present and future Buddhas, seated in a row. This is the main focal point for worshippers at the temple. On the east and west interior wall of the hall are often 18 luóhàn (arhat – a Buddhist who has achieved enlightenment) in two lines, either as statues or paintings. In some temples, they gather in a throng of 500, housed in a separate hall. A statue of Guanyin (the Goddess of Mercy) frequently stands at the rear of the main hall, facing north, atop a fish's head or a rocky outcrop. The goddess may also have her own hall and occasionally presents herself with a huge fan of arms, in her 'Thousand Arm' incarnation. The awesome effigy of Guanyin in the Mahayana Hall at Pǔníng Temple in Chéngdé is the supreme example.

The rear hall may be where the sutras (Buddhist scriptures) were once stored, in which case it will be called the Sutra Storing Building.

A dark and Gothic image in the West, the bat is commonly used in Chinese porcelain, wood designs, textiles and artwork as it is considered a good luck omen.

BATTLE OF THE BUDDHAS

China's largest ancient Buddha gazes out over the confluence of the waters of the Dàdù River and the Mín River at Lèshān in Sìchuān. When the even bigger Buddha at Bamyan in Afghanistan was demolished by the Taliban, the Lèshān Buddha enjoyed instantaneous promotion to the top spot as the world's largest. The Buddha in the Great Buddha Temple at Zhāngyè in Gānsù province may not take it lying down, though: he is China's largest 'housed reclining Buddha'. Chinese children once climbed inside him to scamper about within his cavernous tummy.

Lounging around in second place is the reclining Buddha in the Mògāo Caves, China's second largest. The vast reclining Buddha at Lèshān is a whopping 170m long and the world's largest 'alfresco' reclining Buddha. Bristling with limbs, the Thousand Arm Guanyin statue in the Pǔníng Temple's Mahayana Hall in Chéngdé also stands up to be counted: she's the largest wooden statue in China (and possibly the world). Not to be outdone, Hong Kong fights for its niche with the Tian Tan Buddha Statue, the world's 'largest outdoor seated bronze Buddha statue'.

ZHAN TIAN / GETTY IMAGES ©

Buddhist monastery, Gānsù

A pagoda may rise above the main halls or may be the only surviving fragment of an otherwise destroyed temple. Conceived to house the remains of Buddha and later other Buddhist relics, pagodas also contained sutras, religious artefacts and documents.

Taoist Temples

Taoist shrines are more nether-worldly than Buddhist shrines, although the basic layout echoes Buddhist temples. They are decorated with a distinct set of motifs, including the *bāguà* (eight trigrams) formations, reflected in eight-sided pavilions and halls, and the Taiji yin/yang *(yīn/yáng)* diagram. Effigies of Laotzu, the Jade Emperor and other characters popularly associated with Taoist myth, such as the Eight Immortals and the God of Wealth, are customary.

Taoist door gods, similar to those in Buddhist temples, often guard temple entrances; the main hall is usually called the Hall of the Three Clear Ones, devoted to a triumvirate of Taoist deities.

Taoist monks (and nuns) are easily distinguished from their shaven-headed Buddhist confrères by their long hair, twisted into topknots, straight trousers and squarish jackets.

Confucian Temples

Confucian temples bristle with steles celebrating local scholars, some supported on the backs of *bìxì* (mythical tortoise-looking dragons). A statue of Kongzi (Confucius) usually resides in the main hall, overseeing rows of musical instruments and flanked by disciples. A mythical animal, the *qílín* (a statue exists at the Summer Palace in Běijīng), is commonly seen. The *qílín* was a chimera that only appeared on earth in times of harmony. The largest Confucian temple in China is at Qūfù in Shāndōng, Confucius' birthplace.

Modern Architecture

Architecturally speaking, anything goes in today's China. You only have to look at the Pǔdōng skyline to find a melange of competing designs, some dramatic, inspiring and novel, others rash. The skyline represents a nation brimming over with confidence, zeal and money.

If modern architecture in China is regarded as anything post-1949, then China has ridden a rollercoaster ride of styles and fashions. In Běijīng, stand between the Great Hall of the People (1959) and the National Centre for the Performing Arts (2008) and weigh up how far China travelled in 50 years. Interestingly, neither building has clear Chinese motifs. The same applies to the form of Běijīng's CCTV Building, where a continuous loop through horizontal and vertical planes required some audacious engineering.

While many of China's interior provinces lack the cash to build anything too daring or grandiose, the coastal areas are an architect's dreamland – no design is too outrageous, zoning laws have been scrapped, and the labour force is large and inexpensive. Planning permission can be simple to arrange – often all it requires is sufficient *guānxì* (connections).

Many of the top names in international architecture – IM Pei, Rem Koolhaas, Norman Foster, Kengo Kuma, Jean-Marie Charpentier, Herzog & de Meuron – have all designed at least one building in China in the past decade. Other impressive examples of modern architecture include the National Stadium (aka the 'Bird's Nest'), the National Aquatics Center (aka the 'Water Cube') and Běijīng South train station, all in Běijīng; and the art deco–esque Jīnmào Tower, the towering Shànghǎi World Financial Center, Tomorrow Square and the Shànghǎi Tower in Shànghǎi. In Hong Kong, the glittering 2 International Finance Center on Hong Kong Island and the International Commerce Center in Kowloon are each prodigious examples of modern skyscraper architecture.

In China, tower blocks are only built to last for 25 to 30 years. In 2009 a newlybuilt Shànghǎi tower block collapsed, killing one worker and raising further concerns about quality control.

BUILT TO LAST?

Gardens

Originally conceived as either imperial parks or as private compounds attached to residences, Chinese gardens differ in philosophy to European garden design. Like an ink painting, Chinese garden design was rooted in the Chinese notion of the natural world and humankind's place within it. Chinese gardens aimed to echo nature in miniature, from mountains and hills to lakes, ponds and vegetation. Colours are frequently subdued while gardens are typically small, enclosed and restrained.

There is a focus on the arrangements of rocks and rockeries, the placing of ponds and the use of foliage, small trees and shrubs. Pavilions, walkways, corridors and bridges incorporate the human world, but these are never overbearing features.

The landscapes of a traditional Chinese painting are central to a successful garden. Windows may be found strategically placed to frame a particular view, and in private compounds, plants were grown against a backdrop of whitewashed walls, which recalled the empty space of a painting. Mountains *(shān)* and water *(shuǐ)* are essential components of traditional paintings, and find themselves replicated in garden design through rockeries and fish-filled ponds. The play of light is similarly a vital ingredient, playing off water surfaces, reflecting from white walls and casting shadows.

Another important feature of gardens is symbolism. Plants were chosen as much for their symbolic meaning as their beauty (the pine for longevity, the peony for nobility), and the giant eroded rocks suggest mountains as well as the changing, indefinable nature of the Tao. Likewise, the names of gardens and halls are often literary allusions to ideals expressed in classical poetry.

Gardens were particularly prevalent in southeastern China south of the Yangzi River, notably in Hángzhōu and Sūzhōu.

China's Landscapes

The Land

The world's third-largest country – on a par size-wise with the USA – China covers an immense 9.5 million sq km, only surpassed in area by Russia and Canada. Straddling natural environments as diverse as subarctic tundra in the north and tropical rainforests in the south, this massive land embraces the world's highest mountain range and one of its hottest deserts in the west, to the steamy, typhoon-lashed coastline of the South China Sea. Fragmenting this epic landscape is a colossal web of waterways, including one of the world's mightiest rivers – the Yangzi (长江; Cháng Jiāng).

Mountains

China has a largely mountainous and hilly topography, commencing in precipitous fashion in the vast and sparsely populated Qīnghǎi–Tibetan plateau in the west and levelling out gradually towards the fertile, well-watered, populous and wealthy provinces of eastern China.

This mountainous disposition sculpts so many of China's natural scenic wonders, from the glittering Dragon's Backbone Rice Terraces of Guǎngxī to the exhilaration of Mt Everest, the stunning beauty of Jiǔzhàigōu National Park in Sìchuān, the ethereal peaks of misty Huángshān in Ānhuī, the vertiginous inclines of Huà Shān in Shaanxi (Shǎnxī), the divine karst geology of Yángshuò in Guǎngxī and the volcanic drama of Heaven Lake in Jílín.

Averaging 4500m above sea level, the Qīnghǎi–Tibetan region's highest peaks thrust up into the Himalayan mountain range along its southern rim. The Himalayas, on average about 6000m above sea level, include 40 peaks rising dizzyingly to 7000m or more. Also known as the planet's 'third pole', this is where the world's highest peak, Mt Everest – called Zhūmùlǎngmǎfēng by the Chinese – thrusts up jaggedly from the Tibet–Nepal border. Low temperatures, high winds and intense solar radiation are regional characteristics.

This vast high-altitude region (Tibet alone constitutes one-eighth of China's landmass) is home to an astonishing 37,000 glaciers, the third-largest mass of ice on the planet after the Arctic and Antarctic. This enormous body of frozen water ensures that the Qīnghǎi–Tibetan region is the source of many of China's largest rivers, including the Yellow (Huáng Hé), Mekong (Láncāng Jiāng), and Salween (Nù Jiāng) Rivers and, of course, the mighty Yangzi, all of whose headwaters are fed by snowmelt from here. Global warming, however, is inevitably eating into this glacial volume, although experts argue over how quickly they are melting.

It is predicted that China will have around half a million electric, hybrid, fuel-cell or alternatively fuelled vehicles on the streets by 2015.

China Dialogue (www.china dialogue.net) is a resourceful dual-language website that seeks to promote debate on China's immense environmental challenges.

MOUNTAINS, MYTH & MAGIC

Steeped in legend and superstition and infused with spirits and deities, China's mountains have long been cherished by devout bands of Taoists and Buddhists who erected temples and founded monastic communities on their slopes. Mt Kailash and many other peaks in Tibet are powerfully associated with Buddhist divinities and Bodhisattvas, drawing legions of pilgrims and worshippers to complete a *kora* (pilgrim path) around their slopes. Outside Tibet, each of China's five sacred Buddhist mountains has its ruling Bodhisattva, whose presence permeates their shrines, gullies and peaks. In Pǔtuóshān it is the merciful Guanyin (see the boxed text, p937) who is worshipped; in Wǔtái Shān, erudite Wenshu (Manjushri) is the presiding deity. Huà Shān, Sōng Shān, Wǔdāng Shān and other Taoist peaks are famed for the recluses who retreated to their crags and caves to cultivate 'internal power' and devise esoteric martial-arts skills (p977).

Tibet is also an immense storehouse of mineral wealth, helping to clarify its Chinese name (西藏; Xīzàng; 'Western Treasure House'). Deep within the mountains of Tibet lie enormous deposits of gold, copper, uranium, lithium, lead and other valuable minerals and ores.

This mountain geology further corrugates the rest of China, continuously rippling the land into spectacular mountain ranges. There's the breathtaking 2500km-long Kunlun range, the mighty Karakoram mountains on the border with Pakistan, the Tiān Shān range in Xīnjiāng, the Tanggula range on the Qīnghǎi–Tibetan plateau, the Qinling mountains and the Greater Khingan range (Daxingan Ling) in the northeast.

Deserts

China contains head-spinningly huge – and growing – desert regions that occupy almost one-fifth of the country's landmass, largely in its mighty northwest. These are inhospitably sandy and rocky expanses where summers are torturously hot and winters bone-numbingly cold. North towards Kazakhstan and Kyrgyzstan from the plateaus of Tibet and Qīnghǎi lies Xīnjiāng's Tarim Basin, the largest inland basin in the world. This is the location of the mercilessly thirsty Taklamakan Desert – China's largest desert and the world's second largest mass of sand after the Sahara Desert. China's biggest shifting salt lake, Lop Nur (the site of China's nuclear bomb tests) is also here.

The World Health Organisation estimates that air pollution causes more than 650,000 fatal illnesses per year in China, while more than 95,000 die annually from consuming polluted drinking water.

The harsh environment shares many topographical features in common with the neighbouring nations of Afghanistan, Kyrgyzstan and Kazakhstan, and is almost the exact opposite of China's lush and well-watered southern provinces. But despite the scorching aridity of China's northwestern desert regions, their mountains (the mighty Tiān Shān, Altai, Pamir and Kunlun ranges) contain vast supplies of water, largely in the form of snow and ice.

Northeast of the Tarim Basin is Ürümqi, the world's furthest city from the sea. The Tarim Basin is bordered to the north by the lofty Tiān Shān range – home to the glittering mountain lake of Tiān Chí – and to the west by the mighty Pamirs, which border Pakistan. Also in Xīnjiāng is China's hot spot, the Turpan Basin, known as the 'Oasis of Fire' and entered in the record books as China's lowest-lying region and the world's second-deepest depression after the Dead Sea in Israel. China's most famous desert is, of course, the Gobi, although most of it lies outside the country's borders.

The Silk Road into China steered its epic course through this entire region, ferrying caravans of camels laden with merchandise, languages, philosophies, customs and peoples from the far-flung lands of the Middle East. Today the region is rich in fossil fuels, containing one-third of China's known gas and oil reserves as well as vast and unexploited coal deposits and a growing number of sizeable wind farms, especially in Gānsù (see boxed text p833).

East of Xīnjiāng extend the epic grasslands and steppes of Inner Mongolia – China's largest production centre for mining rare earth metals and the nation's largest coal-producing region – in a huge and elongated belt of land that stretches to the erstwhile Manchuria.

Rivers & Plains

The other major region comprises roughly 45% of the country and contains 95% of the population. This densely populated part of China descends like a staircase from west to east, from the high plateaus of Tibet and Qīnghǎi to the fertile but largely featureless plains and basins of the great rivers that drain the high ranges. As a general rule of thumb, as you head east towards the seaboard, provinces become wealthier.

These plains are the most important agricultural areas of the country and the most heavily populated. It's hard to imagine, but the plains have largely been laid down by siltation from the Yangzi and other great rivers throughout many millennia. The process continues: the Yangzi alone deposits millions of tonnes of silt annually and land at the river mouth is growing at a rate of 100m a year. Hardly any significant stands of natural vegetation remain in this area, although several mountain ranges are still forested and provide oases for wildlife and native plants.

At about 5460km long and the second-longest river in China, the Yellow River (黄河; Huánghé) is touted as the birthplace of Chinese civilisation and has been fundamental in the development of Chinese society. The mythical architect of China's rivers, the Great Yu, apocryphally noted 'Whoever controls the Yellow River controls China'. Because of heavy siltation, the river bed in some reaches rises high above the north China plains (outside Kāifēng, the river is some 10m above ground level).

In 2012, the last of the Three Gorges Dam's huge turbines was connected to the energy grid, meaning the dam now supplies 11% of China's hydroelectric power generation.

SOUTH–NORTH WATER DIVERSION PROJECT

Water is the lifeblood of economic and agricultural growth, but as China only possesses around 7% of the world's water resources (with almost 20% of its population), the liquid is an increasingly precious resource.

North China is a region of low rainfall and faces a grim water crisis. Farmers are draining aquifers that have taken thousands of years to accumulate, while Chinese industry is using three to 10 times more water per unit of production than developed nations. Meanwhile, water usage in large cities such as Běijīng and Tiānjīn continues to climb as migrants move in from rural areas. By some estimates, the aquifers of north China may only survive for another 30 years.

To combat the water crisis, the CCP embarked on the construction of the US$62 billion South–North Water Diversion Project, a vast network of rivers, canals and lakes lashing north and south. The logic is to divert surplus water from the Yangzi River to the dwindling and long overexploited Yellow River.

There are concerns that pollution in the Yangzi River waters will become progressively concentrated as water is extracted, while Yangzi cities such as Nánjīng and Wǔhàn are increasingly anxious they will be left with less water. Alarm has also arisen at the pollution in channels – including the Grand Canal, which links Hángzhōu with north China – earmarked to take the diverted waters. There are worries that these polluted reaches are almost untreatable, making elements of the project unviable.

Critics also argue that the project, which will involve the mass relocation of hundreds of thousands of people, will not address the fundamental issue of China's water woes – the absence of policies for the sustainable use of water as a precious resource.

China's longest river, the Yangzi (the 'Long River'), is one of the longest rivers in the world. Its watershed of almost 2 million sq km – 20% of China's land mass – supports 400 million people. Dropping from its source high on the Tibetan plateau, it runs for 6300km to the sea, of which the last few hundred kilometres is across virtually flat alluvial plains.

The Yangzi has been an important thoroughfare for humans for centuries, used throughout China's history for trade and transport; it even has its own unique wildlife, but this has been threatened by the controversial, power-generating Three Gorges Dam. The dam is partly designed to thwart the Yangzi's propensity to flood – floodwaters that have historically inundated millions of hectares and destroyed hundreds of thousands of lives.

Since becoming a net oil importer in 1993, China imported more than five million barrels of oil per day in 2011, a figure only surpassed by the European Union and the US.

Fields & Agriculture

China's hills and mountains may sculpt a dramatic and sublime backdrop for travellers, but they have long been a massive agricultural headache for farmers. Small plots of land are eked out in patchworks of land squashed between hillsides or rescued from mountain cliffs and ravines, in the demanding effort to feed 20% of the world's population with just 10% of its arable land.

Astonishingly, only 15% of China's land can be cultivated so hillside gradients and inclines are valiantly levelled off, wherever possible, into bands of productive terraced fields. Many home gardens in suburban China are dedicated to crops while every available patch of land elsewhere is requisitioned for small-scale agricultural use, from idle land beneath flyovers to strips of earth alongside pavements. The result is an irregularly-shaped patchwork of small fields and plots, frequently covered with plastic sheeting to retain moisture, and a scarcity of land put to common use (eg football pitches). Because of the division of agricultural land into so many small plots, large-scale mechanisation (which would improve efficiency) is difficult.

HARALD SUND / GETTY IMAGES ©

Karst mountains and agricultural villages, Guǎngxi province (p585)

THE SHAPE OF THINGS TO COME

Huge targets for satellite calibration, vast fractal antennas, massive missile shooting ranges or the handiwork of alien civilisations, no one seemed to have a plausible explanation for the colossal geometric forms in west China that sent rumours fizzing about the internet in 2011. The bizarre shapes – some up to a mile in length – range from immense concentric circles to gigantic grids and networks of crazy lines, all clearly visible on Google Maps. Distributed over Gānsù and Xīnjiāng provinces, at least one is in the region of Dūnhuáng in Gānsù province. As some of the shapes were discovered in the vicinity of Lop Nur (China's nuclear testing ground), conspiracy theorists were quick to speculate feverishly. Some claimed the huge grids could be superimposed onto the road layouts of Washington DC and other US cities (indicating a military purpose), while others asserted the Chinese had acquired alien technology. To date, no convincing explanation has been made (although one giant shape was identified as the world's largest potash fertiliser plant).

Wildlife

China's size, diverse topography and climatic disparities support an astonishing range of habitats for a variety of animal life. Scattered from steamy tropical rainforests in the deep southwest to subarctic wilderness in the far north, from the precipitous mountains of Tibet to the low-lying deserts of the northwest and the huge Yangzi River, China's wild animals comprise nearly 400 species of mammal (including some of the world's rarest and most charismatic species), more than 1300 bird species, 424 reptile species and more than 300 species of amphibian. The Tibetan plateau alone is the habitat of more than 500 species of birds, while half of the animal species in the northern hemisphere can be found in China.

It is unlikely you will see many of these creatures in their natural habitat unless you are a specialist, or have a lot of time, patience, persistence, determination and luck. If you go looking for large animals in the wild on the off chance, your chances of glimpsing one are virtually nil. But there are plenty of pristine reserves within relatively easy reach of travellers' destinations such as Chéngdū and Xī'ān. More and more visitors are including visits to protected areas as part of their itinerary for a look at China's elusive wildlife residents – outside of China's rather pitiful zoos.

Mammals

China's towering mountain ranges form natural refuges for wildlife, many of which are now protected in parks and reserves that have escaped the depredations of loggers and dam-builders. The barren high plains of the Tibetan plateau are home to several large animals, such as the *chiru* (Tibetan antelope), Tibetan wild ass, wild sheep and goats, and wolves. In theory, many of these animals are protected but in practice poaching and hunting still threaten their survival.

The beautiful and retiring snow leopard, which normally inhabits the highest parts of the most remote mountain ranges, sports a luxuriant coat of fur against the cold. It preys on mammals as large as mountain goats, but is unfortunately persecuted for allegedly killing livestock.

The Himalayan foothills of western Sìchuān support the greatest diversity of mammals in China. Aside from giant pandas, other mammals found in this region include the panda's small cousin – the raccoon-like red panda – as well as Asiatic black bears and leopards. Among the grazers are golden takin, a large goatlike antelope with a yellowish coat and a reputation for being cantankerous, argali sheep and various deer species, including the diminutive mouse deer.

The sparsely populated northeastern provinces abutting Siberia are inhabited by reindeer, moose, bears, sables and Manchurian tigers.

Chángqīng Nature Reserve in Shaanxi province is well worth a visit for its relatively unspoilt montane forest and the chance to see giant pandas in the wild. Find out more at www.cqpanda.com.

Overall, China is unusually well endowed with big and small cats. The world's largest tiger, the Manchurian Tiger *(Dōngběihǔ)* – also known as the Siberian Tiger (see p323) – only numbers a few hundred in the wild, its remote habitat being one of its principal saviours. Three species of leopard can be found, including the beautiful clouded leopard of tropical rainforests, plus several species of small cat, such as the Asiatic golden cat and a rare endemic species, the Chinese mountain cat.

Rainforests are famous for their diversity of wildlife, and the tropical south of Yúnnán province, particularly the area around Xīshuāngbǎnnà, is one of the richest in China. These forests support Indo-Chinese tigers and herds of Asiatic elephants.

The wild mammals you are most likely to see are several species of monkey. The large and precocious Père David's macaque is common at Éméi Shān in Sìchuān, where bands often intimidate people into handing over their picnics; macaques can also be seen on Hǎinán's Monkey Island. Several other monkey species are rare and endangered, including the beautiful golden monkey of Fànjìng Shān and the snub-nosed monkey of the Yúnnán rainforests. But by far the most endangered is the Hǎinán gibbon, numbering just a few dozen individuals on Hǎinán island thanks to massive forest clearance.

The giant panda *(xióngmāo* – literally 'bear cat') is western Sìchuān's most famous denizen, but the animal's solitary nature makes it elusive for observation in the wild, and even today, after decades of intensive research and total protection in dedicated reserves, sightings are rare. A notoriously fickle breeder (the female is only on heat for a handful of days each spring), there are approximately 1600 pandas in the Chinese wilds according to World Wildlife Fund. Interestingly, the panda has the digestive tract of a carnivore (like other bears), but has become accustomed to exclusively eating bamboo shoots and leaves. However, the panda's digestive tract is unable to efficiently break down plant matter so the mammal needs to consume huge amounts to compensate and spends much of its time eating, clearing one area of bamboo before moving on to another region.

WIND FARMS

Birds

Most of the wildlife you'll see in China will be birds, and with more than 1300 species recorded, including about 100 endemic or near-endemic species, China offers some fantastic birdwatching opportunities. Spring is usually the best time, when deciduous foliage buds, migrants return from their wintering grounds and nesting gets into full swing. **BirdLife International** (www.birdlife.org/regional/asia), the worldwide bird conservation organisation, recognises 12 Endemic Bird Areas (EBAs) in China, nine of which are wholly within the country and three of which are shared with neighbouring countries.

Although the range of birds is huge, China is a centre of endemicity for several species and these are usually the ones that visiting birders will seek out. Most famous are the pheasant family, of which China boasts 62 species, including many endemic or near-endemic species.

Other families well represented in China include the laughing thrushes, with 36 species; parrotbills, which are almost confined to China and its near neighbours; and many members of the jay family. The crested ibis is a pinkish bird that feeds on invertebrates in the rice paddies, and was once found from central China to Japan.

Among China's more famous large birds are cranes, and nine of the world's 14 species have been recorded here. In Jiāngxī province, on the lower Yangzi, a vast series of shallow lakes and lagoons was formed by stranded overflow from Yangzi flooding. The largest of these is Póyáng Lake, although it is only a few metres deep and drains during winter. Vast numbers of waterfowl and other birds inhabit these swamps year-round, including ducks, geese, herons and egrets. Although it is difficult to reach and infrastructure for birdwatchers is practically non-existent, birders are increasingly drawn to the area in winter, when many of the lakes dry up and attract flocks of up to five crane species, including the endangered, pure white Siberian crane.

Parts of China are now well-established on the itineraries of global ecotour companies. **Bird Watching China** (www.birdwatchingchina.com) specialises in arranging birdwatching and photography tours to China; the **China Bird Watching Network** (www.chinabirdnet.org) has useful links to birdwatching societies across China.

Recommended destinations include Zhālóng Nature Reserve, one of several vast wetlands in Hēilóngjiāng province. Visit in summer to see breeding storks, cranes and flocks of wildfowl before they fly south for the winter. Běidàihé, on the coast of the Bohai Sea, is well known for migratory birds. Other breeding grounds and wetlands include Qīnghǎi Hú in Qīnghǎi, Cǎohǎi Lake in Guìzhōu, Jiǔzhàigōu in Sìchuān and Mai Po Marsh in Hong Kong. For the latter, the **Hong Kong Bird Watching Society** (www.hkbws.org.hk) organises regular outings and publishes a newsletter in English.

Most birdwatchers and bird tours head straight for Sìchuān, which offers superb birding at sites such as Wòlóng. Here, several spectacular pheasants, including golden, blood and kalij pheasants, live on the steep forested hillsides surrounding the main road. As the road climbs up, higher-altitude species such as eared pheasants and the spectacular Chinese monal may be seen. Alpine meadows host smaller birds, and the rocky scree slopes at the pass hold partridges, the beautiful grandala and the mighty lammergeier (bearded vulture), with a 2m wingspan.

Reptiles & Amphibians

Native to China, the Chinese alligator – known as the 'muddy dragon' – is one of the smallest of the world's crocodilians, measuring only 2m in length, and is harmless to humans. Owing to habitat clearance and intense pressure to turn its wetlands to agriculture along the lower Yangzi, fewer than 150 of these reptiles survive in the wild. A captive breeding program has been successful, and a number of the rare reptiles have been tagged and released back into the wild from a reserve in Ānhuī.

The cold, rushing rivers of the southwestern mountains are home to the world's largest amphibian, the giant salamander. This enormous amphibian can reach 180cm in length and feeds on small aquatic animals. Unfortunately, it is now critically endangered in the wild and, like so many other animals, hunted for food.

One of the aims of the Three Gorges Dam is to help prevent flooding on the Yangzi River. The river has caused hundreds of catastrophic floods, including the disastrous inundation of 1931, in which an estimated 145,000 died.

THE YANGZI DOLPHIN

The Yangzi floodway was big enough to favour the evolution of distinct large river creatures, including the Yangzi dolphin (baiji) and Chinese alligator, both now desperately endangered. The Yangzi dolphin, one of just a few freshwater dolphin species in the world (others occur in the Ganges and Amazon River systems) and by far the rarest, migrated to the Yangzi River from the Pacific Ocean more than 20 million years ago and adapted itself to its freshwater habitat. The dolphin largely lost the use of its eyes in the gloomy Yangzi waters and instead steered a course through the river using a form of sonar.

From being quite commonplace – around 6000 dolphins still lived in the Yangzi River during the 1950s – numbers fell drastically during the three decades of explosive economic growth from the 1970s, and the last confirmed sighting was in 2002. The creature is a victim – one of many – of human activity in the region, succumbing to drowning in fishing nets and lethal injuries from ships' propellers.

More than 300 other species of frog and salamander occur in China's waterways and wetlands, and preying on them is a variety of snakes, including cobras and vipers. One of China's more unusual national parks is Snake Island, near Dàlián in Liáoníng province. This 800-hectare dot in the Bohai Sea is uninhabited by people, but supports an estimated 130,000 Pallas' pit vipers, an extraordinary concentration of snakes that prey on migrating birds that land on the island every spring and autumn in huge numbers. By eating several birds each season, the snakes can subsist on lizards and invertebrates for the rest of the year until migration time comes round again.

Plants

China is home to more than 32,000 species of seed plant and 2500 species of forest tree, plus an extraordinary plant diversity that includes some famous 'living fossils' – a diversity so great that Jílín province in the semifrigid north and Hǎinán province in the tropical south share few plant species. Many reserves still remain where intact vegetation ecosystems can be seen firsthand, but few parts of the country have escaped human impact. Deforestation continues apace in many regions and vast areas are under cultivation with monocultures such as rice.

In 2010, six of China's *dānxiá* (eroded reddish sandstone rock), karst-like geological formations, were included in Unesco's World Heritage List. The list includes Chìshuǐ (p630) in Gùizhōu province. The rocks can also be seen outside Zhāngyè in Gānsù.

Apart from rice, the plant probably most often associated with China and Chinese culture is bamboo, of which China boasts some 300 species. Bamboos grow in many parts of China, but bamboo forests were once so extensive that they enabled the evolution of the giant panda, which eats virtually nothing else, and a suite of small mammals, birds and insects that live in bamboo thickets. Most of these useful species are found in the subtropical areas south of the Yangzi, and the best surviving thickets are in southwestern provinces such as Sìchuān.

Many plants commonly cultivated in Western gardens today originated in China, among them the ginkgo tree, a famous 'living fossil' whose unmistakable imprint has been found in 270 million-year-old rocks. The unique and increasingly rare dove tree or paper tree, whose greatly enlarged white bracts look like a flock of doves, grows only in the deciduous forests of the southwest.

Deciduous forests cover mid-altitudes in the mountains, and are characterised by oaks, hemlocks and aspens, with a leafy understorey that springs to life after the winter snows have melted. Among the more famous blooms of the understorey are rhododendrons and azaleas, and many species of each grow naturally in China's mountain ranges. Best viewed in spring, some species flower right through summer; one of the best places to see them is at Sìchuān's Wòlóng Nature Reserve. Both rhododendrons and azaleas grow in distinct bands at various heights on the mountain sides, which are recognisable as you drive through the reserve to the high mountain passes. At the very highest elevations, the alpine meadows grazed by yaks are often dotted with showy and colourful blooms.

Deforestation has levelled huge tracts of China's once vast and beautiful primeval forests. At the end of the 19th century, 70% of China's northeast was still forest. Unsustainable clear-cutting in the 20th century – especially during the Great Leap Forward – was not banned there until the mid-1980s, by which time only 5% of old-growth woodland remained. Logging controls were more strictly enforced after the floods of 1998, when deforestation was identified as contributing to the floodwaters. Since then a vigorous replanting campaign was launched to once again cover huge tracts of China with trees, but these cannot restore the rich biodiversity that once existed.

A growing number of international wildlife travel outfits arrange botanical expeditions to China, including UK-based **Naturetrek** (www.naturetrek.co.uk), which arranges tours to Yúnnán and Sìchuān.

Endangered Species

Almost every large mammal you can think of in China has crept onto the endangered species list, as well as many of the so-called 'lower' animals and plants. The snow leopard, Indo-Chinese tiger, chiru antelope, crested ibis, Asiatic elephant, red-crowned crane and black-crowned crane are all endangered.

Deforestation, pollution, hunting and trapping for fur, body parts and sport are all culprits. The Convention on International Trade in Endangered Species of Wild Fauna and Flora (CITES) records legal trade in live reptiles and parrots, and high numbers of reptile and wildcat skins. The number of such products collected or sold unofficially is anyone's guess.

Despite the threats, a number of rare animal species cling to survival in the wild. Notable among them are the Chinese alligator in Ānhuī, the giant salamander in the fast-running waters of the Yangzi and Yellow Rivers, the Yangzi River dolphin in the lower and middle reaches of the river (although there have been no sightings since 2002), and the pink dolphin of the Hong Kong islands of Sha Chau and Lung Kwu Chau. The giant panda is confined to the fauna-rich valleys and ranges of Sìchuān, but your best chances for sighting one is in Chéngdū's Giant Panda Breeding Research Base (p701).

Intensive monoculture farmland cultivation, the reclaiming of wetlands, river damming, industrial and rural waste, and desertification are reducing unprotected forest areas and making the survival of many of these species increasingly precarious. Although there are laws against killing or capturing rare wildlife, their struggle for survival is further complicated as many remain on the most-wanted lists for traditional Chinese medicine and dinner delicacies.

In Tibet, the chiru antelope has long been hunted for a fleece that provides a lucrative type of wool. Despite conservation efforts, poaching still continues in an area that is hard to effectively monitor due to its size and a lack of human resources.

The Environment

China may be vast, but with two-thirds of the land either mountain, desert or uncultivable, the remaining third is overwhelmed by the people of the world's most populous nation. For social, economic and political reasons, China is experiencing its – and the world's – most rapid period of urbanisation in history. All this means the city can impinge in inescapable fashion. For the first time in its history, China's city dwellers outnumbered rural residents in 2011, with an urbanisation rate set to increase to 65% by 2050. In the same year, it was announced that nine urban areas in Guǎngdōng province would congeal into a single metropolitan area, twice the size of Wales, 26 times the size of London, supporting a population of 42 million. The speed of development – and the sheer volume of poured concrete – is staggering. During the next 15 years, China is expected to build urban areas equal in size to 10 New York Cities.

Beyond urban areas, deforestation and overgrazing have accelerated the desertification of vast areas of China, particularly in the western provinces. Deserts now cover almost one-fifth of the country and China's dustbowl is the world's largest, swallowing up 200 sq km of arable land every month.

For decades China neglected the environment as it was costly to protect and slowed the pace of economic development; environmental concerns were parked on the back-burner to be dealt with once the national economy had developed. China embarked on a course of development first, clean up later. The World Bank calculates the annual cost of pollution alone in China at almost 6% of the national GDP; when all forms of environmental damage are incorporated, the figure leaps as high as 12%, meaning China's final environmental costs may overshadow economic growth.

In 2010 China overtook the USA as the world's largest energy consumer; in the same year the nation replaced Japan as the world's second-largest economy and is tipped to overtake the USA by 2030 (some say by 2020).

TOP BOOKS ON CHINA'S ENVIRONMENT

» *When a Billion Chinese Jump* (2010) Jonathan Watts' sober and engaging study of China's environmental issues.

» *The River Runs Black: The Environmental Challenge to China's Future* (2010; 2nd edition) Elizabeth Economy's frightening look at the unhappy marriage between breakneck economic production and environmental degradation.

» *The China Price: The True Cost of Chinese Competitive Advantage* (2008) Alexandra Harney's telling glimpse behind the figures of China's economic rise.

» *China's Water Crisis* (2004) Ma Jun rolls up his sleeves to examine the sources of China's water woes.

» *Mao's War Against Nature* (2001) Judith Shapiro looks at the ideological clash between communism and the environment.

A Greener China?

China is painfully aware of its accelerated desertification, growing water shortages, shrinking glaciers, acidic rain, contaminated rivers, caustic urban air and polluted soil. The government is keenly committed, on a policy level, to the development of greener and cleaner energy sources. China's leaders are also seeking to devise a more sustainable and less wasteful economic model for the nation's future development.

There is evidence of ambitious and bold thinking: in 2010 China announced it would pour billions into developing electric and hybrid vehicles; Běijīng committed itself to overtaking Europe in renewable energy investment by 2020; wind farm construction (in Gānsù, for example) continues apace (p833); and China leads the world in production of solar cells. It aims to reduce energy use per unit of GDP by more than 15% before 2015.

China's Bayan Obo Mining District in Inner Mongolia produces roughly half of the world's rare earth metals, elements essential for the production of mobile phones, high-definition TVs, computers, wind turbines and other products.

While China's system of governance allows it to railroad bold initiatives, it also encourages a reliance on technological 'solutions' and huge engineering programs to combat environmental problems. For example, China is seeking to answer its water crisis by diverting Yangzi River waters to thirsty north China, when other solutions may be a more sustainable policy.

Some greener initiatives, such as the Three Gorges Dam, sport green credentials in some areas (no greenhouse gases, renewable energy source, small carbon footprint) but are environmentally unsound in others (water-polluting, seismic effects, local climate change). In 2012, China finally responded to the US Embassy's publication of atmospheric pollution figures for Běijīng by insisting foreign governments stop releasing data.

Public protests – sometimes violent – against polluting industries have proliferated in recent years across China and have scored a number of notable victories, including the 2012 demonstrations in Shífāng (Sìchuān), which led to the cancellation of a planned US$1.6 billion copper smelting facility.

One of China's main energy quandaries is coal. China's coal-fired growth comes at a time when the effort to tackle global warming has become a chief global priority. Coal is cheap, easy to extract and remains China's primary energy source, accounting for almost 70% of power requirements. China extracts more coal than any other nation and possesses the world's third-largest deposits. Huge untapped reserves in the northwest await exploitation, vast coalfields in Inner Mongolia are being mined and the economics of coal use in China make it a very cheap and reliable fuel source.

Domestic demand for coal leapt almost 10% in 2011 compared to an increase of 2.7% for crude oil in the same year. Coal is not only dirty but an unrenewable resource. Experts predict China may hit 'peak coal' – the point of maximum production, after which the industry will fall into decline – as early as 2020, or even earlier.

Martial Arts of China

Unlike Western fighting arts – Savate, kickboxing, boxing, wrestling etc – Chinese martial arts are deeply impregnated with religious and philosophical values. And, some might add, a morsel or two of magic. Many eminent exponents of *gōngfū* (功夫) – better known in the West as kungfu – were devout monks or religious recluses who drew inspiration from Buddhism and Taoism and sought a mystical communion with the natural world. Their arts were not leisurely pursuits but were closely entangled with the meaning and purpose of their lives.

Often misinterpreted, *gōngfū* teaches an approach to life that stresses patience, endurance, magnanimity and humility. For those who truly take to the Chinese martial arts, it's a rewarding journey with a unique destination. When two people discover they share an interest in martial arts, it's the cue for an endless exchange of techniques and anecdotes.

Styles & Schools
China lays claim to a bewildering range of martial-arts styles, from the flamboyant and showy, inspired by the movements of animals or insects (such as Praying Mantis Boxing) to schools more empirically built upon the science of human movement (eg Wing Chun). Some pugilists stress a mentalist approach, although others put their money on physical power. On the outer fringes are the esoteric arts, abounding with metaphysical feats, arcane practices and closely guarded techniques.

Many fighting styles were once secretively handed down for generations within families and it is only relatively recently that outsiders have been accepted as students. Some schools, especially the more obscure of styles, have been driven to extinction partly due to their exclusivity.

Some styles also found themselves divided into competing factions, each laying claim to the original teachings and techniques. Such styles may exist in a state of schism, where the original principles have become either distorted or lost. Other styles though have become part of the mainstream and flourished; Wing Chun in particular has been elevated into a globally recognised art, largely due to its associations with Bruce Lee.

Unlike Korean and Japanese arts such as Taekwondo or Karate-do, there is frequently no international regulatory body that oversees the syllabus, tournaments or grading requirements for China's individual martial arts. Consequently students of China's myriad martial arts may be rather unsure of where they stand or what level they have attained. With no standard syllabus, it is often down to the individual teacher to decide what to teach students, and how quickly.

Several Chinese styles of *gōngfū* include drunken sets, where the student mimics the supple movements of an inebriate.

Iron Shirt (*tiěshān*) is an external *gōngfū* *qìgōng* training exercise that circulates and concentrates the *qì* in certain areas to protect the body from impacts during a fight.

Hard School

Although there is considerable blurring between the two camps, Chinese martial arts are often distinguished between hard and soft schools. Typically aligned with Buddhism, the hard or 'external' (外家; *wàijiā*) school tends to be more vigorous, athletic and focussed on the development of power. Many of these styles are related to Shaolin Boxing and the Shàolín Temple in Hénán province.

Shàolín Boxing is forever associated with Bodhidharma, an ascetic Indian Buddhist monk who visited the Shàolín Temple and added a series of breathing and physical exercises to the Shàolín monk's sedentary meditations. The Shàolín monk's legendary endeavours and fearsome physical skills became known throughout China and beyond. Famous external schools include Báiméi Quán (White Eyebrow Boxing) and Cháng Quán (Long Boxing).

Praying Mantis master Fan Yook Tung once killed two stampeding bulls with an iron-palm technique.

Soft School

Usually inspired by Taoism, the soft or 'internal' Chinese school (内家; *nèijiā*) develops pliancy and softness as a weapon against hard force. Taichi (Tàijí Quán) is the best known soft school, famed for its slow and lithe movements and an emphasis on cultivating *qì* (energy). Attacks are met with yielding movements that smother the attacking force and lead the aggressor off balance. The road to Taichi mastery is a long and difficult one, involving a re-education of physical movement and suppression of one's instinct to tense up when threatened (see p426). Other soft schools include the circular moves of Bāguà Zhăng and the linear boxing patterns of Xíngyì Quán, based on five basic punches – each linked to one of the five elements of Chinese philosophy – and the movements of 12 animals.

Forms

Most students of Chinese martial arts – hard or soft – learn forms (套路; *tàolu*), a series of movements linked together into a pattern, which embody the principal punches and kicks of the style. In essence, forms are unwritten compendiums of the style, to ensure passage from one generation to the next. The number and complexity of forms varies from style to style: taichi may only have one form, although it may be very lengthy (the long form of the Yang style takes around 20 minutes to perform). Five Ancestors Boxing has dozens of forms, while Wing Chun only has three empty-hand forms.

Zhang Sanfeng, the founder of taichi, was supposedly able to walk more than 1000 li (around 350 miles) a day; others say he lived for more than 200 years!

Qìgōng

Closely linked to both the hard and especially the soft martial-arts schools is the practice of *qìgōng*, a technique for cultivating and circulating *qì* around the body. *Qì* can be developed for use in fighting to protect the body, as a source of power or for curative and health-giving purposes.

Qì can be developed in a number of ways – by standing still in fixed postures or with gentle exercises, meditation and measured breathing techniques. Taichi itself is a moving form of *qìgōng* cultivation while at the harder end of the spectrum a host of *qìgōng* exercises aim to make specific parts of the body impervious to attack.

Bāguà Zhăng

One of the more esoteric and obscure of the soft Taoist martial arts, Bāguà Zhăng (八卦掌; Eight Trigram Boxing, also known as Pa-kua) is also one of the most intriguing. The Bāguà Zhăng student wheels around in a circle, rapidly changing direction and speed, occasionally thrusting out a palm strike.

COURSES, BOOKS & FILMS

Martial-arts courses can be found in abundance across China, from Běijīng, Hong Kong, Shànghǎi, Wǔdāng Shān in Húběi, Yángshuò in Guǎngxī and the Shàolín Temple in Hénán. See under Courses in these sections for more.

Try to track down a copy of John F Gilbey's *The Way of a Warrior,* a tongue-in-cheek, expertly written and riveting account of the Oriental fighting arts. *Meditations on Violence: A Comparison of Martial Arts Training & Real World Violence* by Sgt Rory Miller is a graphic, illuminating and down-to-earth book on violence and its consequences that is also well worth reading.

For metaphysical pointers, soft-school adherents can dip into Laotzu's terse but inspiring *The Classic of the Way and Its Power* (p937). For spectacular (if implausible) Wing Chun moves and mayhem, watch *Ip Man* (2008), starring the indefatigable Donnie Yen.

Bāguà Zhǎng draws its inspiration from the trigrams (an arrangement of three broken and unbroken lines) of the classic *Book of Changes* (Yìjīng or I Ching), the ancient oracle used for divination. The trigrams are typically arranged in circular form and it is this pattern that is traced out by the Bāguà Zhǎng exponent. Training commences by just walking the circle so the student gradually becomes infused with its patterns and rhythms.

A hallmark of the style is the exclusive use of the palm, not the fist, as the principal weapon. This may seem curious and perhaps even ineffectual, but in fact the palm can transmit a lot of power – consider a thrusting palm strike to the chin, for example. The palm is also better protected than the fist as it is cushioned by muscle. The fist also has to transfer its power through a multitude of bones that need to be correctly aligned to avoid damage while the palm sits at the end of the wrist. Consider hitting a brick wall as hard as you can with your palm (and then imagine doing it with your fist!).

The student must become proficient in the subterfuge, evasion, speed and unpredictability that are hallmarks of Bāguà Zhǎng. Force is generally not met with force, but deflected by the circular movements manifested in students through their meditations upon the circle. Circular forms – arcing, twisting, twining and spinning – are the mainstay of all movements, radiating from the waist.

Despite being dated by historians to the 19th century, Bāguà Zhǎng is quite probably a very ancient art. Beneath the Taoist overlay, the movements and patterns of the art suggest a possibly animistic origin, which gives the art its timeless rhythms.

> The linear movements and five punches of the internal Chinese martial art Body-Mind Boxing (Xíngyì Quán) possibly evolved from spear-fighting techniques.

Wing Chun

Conceived by a Buddhist nun called Ng Mui from the Shàolín Temple, who taught her skills to a young girl called Wing Chun (詠春), this is a fast and dynamic system of fighting that promises quick results for novices. Wing Chun (Yǒng Chūn) was the style that taught Bruce Lee how to move and, although he ultimately moved away from it to develop his own style, Wing Chun had an enormous influence on the Hong Kong fighter and actor.

Wing Chun emphasises speed rather than strength. Evasion, rapid strikes and low kicks are the hallmarks of the style. Forms are simple and direct, dispensing with the pretty flourishes that clutter other styles.

The art can perhaps best be described as scientific. There are none of the animal forms that make other styles so exciting and mysterious. Instead, Wing Chun is built around its centre line theory, which draws an imaginary line down the human body and centres all attacks and blocks along that line. The line runs through the sensitive regions: eyes, nose, mouth, throat, heart, solar plexus and groin and any blow on these points is debilitating and dangerous.

The three empty hand forms – which look bizarre to non-initiates – train arm and leg movements that both attack and defend this line. None of the blocks stray beyond the width of the shoulders, as this is the limit of possible attacks, and punches follow the same theory. Punches are delivered with great speed in a straight line, along the shortest distance between puncher and punched. All of this gives Wing Chun its distinctive simplicity.

A two-person training routine called *chi sau* (sticky hands) teaches the student how to be soft and relaxed in response to attacks, as pliancy generates more speed. Weapons in the Wing Chun arsenal include the lethal twin Wing Chun butterfly knives and an extremely long pole, which requires considerable strength to handle with skill.

Survival Guide

DIRECTORY A-Z 982

Accommodation........ 982

Activities 985

Business Hours 985

Children 985

Customs Regulations ... 985

Discount Cards......... 986

Electricity 986

Embassies &
Consulates 986

Gay & Lesbian
Travellers 988

Insurance.............. 988

Internet Access......... 988

Language Courses...... 989

Legal Matters 989

Money................. 989

Passports.............. 990

Post................... 991

Public Holidays......... 991

Safe Travel............. 991

Telephone 992

Visas.................. 992

Volunteering 995

Weights & Measures 995

TRANSPORT 996

GETTING
THERE & AWAY 996

Entering China 996

Air.................... 996

Land 998

River 1000

Sea 1000

GETTING AROUND..... 1000

Air 1000

Bicycle 1001

Boat 1001

Bus 1002

Car & Motorcycle...... 1002

Local Transport........ 1003

CHINA BY TRAIN ..1004

The Chinese
Train Network 1004

Trains 1004

Travelling by Train 1005

Ticket Types 1005

Ticketing 1007

Internet Resources 1009

HEALTH 1010

BEFORE YOU GO........1010

Insurance..............1010

Vaccinations 1010

Medical Checklist.......1010

Websites 1011

Further Reading 1011

IN CHINA.............. 1011

Availability of
Health Care............1011

Infectious Diseases 1011

Traveller's Diarrhoea 1013

Environmental Hazards..1014

Women's Health........1015

Traditional
Chinese Medicine.......1015

LANGUAGE 1016

Directory A-Z

Accommodation

From rustic homesteads, homestays, youth hostels, student dormitories, guesthouses, courtyard lodgings, boutique hotels and historic residences to five-star towers, China's accommodation choice is impressive, on a national level. The choice varies enormously, however, between regions and cities. Top-tier cities such as Běijīng, Shànghǎi, Hángzhōu and Hong Kong sport a rich variety of accommodation options but other towns may have a poor supply, despite being inundated with visitors. In fact, many travellers decide where to visit in China on the strength of the local accommodation choice.

Rooms & Prices

ROOMS

All rooms in this book come with private bathroom or shower room, unless otherwise stated. Rooms are generally easy to procure, but phone ahead to reserve a room in popular tourist towns (such as Hángzhōu), especially for weekend visits.

Most rooms in China fall into the following categories:

Double rooms (双人房、标准间; *shuāng rén fáng* or *biāozhǔn jiān*) In most cases, these are twins, ie with two beds.

Single rooms (单间; *dānjiān*).

Large-bed rooms (大床房; *dàchuáng fáng*) With a large single bed.

Suites (套房; *tàofáng*) Available at most midrange and top-end hotels.

Dorms (多人房; *duōrénfáng*) Usually, but not always, available at youth hostels (and at a few hotels).

Business rooms (商务房; *shāngwù fáng*) Usually equipped with computers.

PRICES

Accommodation in this book is divided by price category, identified by the symbols $ (budget), $$ (midrange) or $$$ (top end); accommodation prices vary across China, so refer to each chapter for that region's budget breakdown, identified at the start of the chapter.

Prices listed in this book are the rack rate, which generally reflects the most you are expected to pay. However, at most times of the year discounts are in effect which can range from 10% to 60%; bargain for the best rate at reception. Rooms reach their maximum price during the big holiday periods at the start of May and October each year. In some towns (such as Hángzhōu), there may be a pricier weekend rate (Friday and Saturday). International credit cards are generally only acceptable at midrange hotels and above, always have cash in case.

You usually have to check out by noon. If you check out between noon and 6pm you will be charged 50% of the room price; after 6pm you have to pay for another full night.

Restrictions & Hassles

Note that quite a number of hotels in China will say they do not accept foreigners. This can be a source of great frustration when you discover cheaper guesthouses are off-limits to non-Chinese and you find yourself steered towards more expensive lodgings, restricting foreigners to midrange and top-end hotels. All hotels listed in this book accept foreign guests.

Booking

Booking online can help you secure a room and obtain a good price, but remember you should be able to bargain down the price of your room at hotel reception (except at youth hostels and the cheapest hotels) or over the phone. To secure accommodation,

---

BOOK YOUR STAY ONLINE

For more accommodation reviews by Lonely Planet authors, check out http://hotels.lonelyplanet.com. You'll find independent reviews, as well as recommendations on the best places to stay. Best of all, you can book online.

PRACTICALITIES

» There are four types of plugs – three-pronged angled pins, three-pronged round pins, two flat pins or two narrow round pins. Electricity is 220 volts, 50 cycles AC.

» The standard English-language newspaper is the (censored) *China Daily* (www.chinadaily.com.cn). China's largest circulation Chinese-language daily is the *People's Daily (Rénmín Rìbào)*. It has an English-language edition on www.english.peopledaily.com.cn. Imported English-language newspapers can be bought from five-star hotel bookshops.

» Listen to the **BBC World Service** (www.bbc.co.uk/worldservice/tuning) or **Voice of America** (www.voa.gov); however, the websites can be jammed. Chinese Central TV (CCTV) has an English-language channel – CCTV9. Your hotel may have ESPN, Star Sports, CNN or BBC News 24.

» China officially subscribes to the international metric system, but you will encounter the ancient Chinese weights and measures system that features the *liǎng* (tael; 37.5g) and the *jīn* (catty; 0.6kg). There are 10 *liǎng* to the *jīn*.

always plan ahead and book your room in advance during the high season. Airports at major cities often have hotel-booking counters that offer discounted rates.

Useful accommodation websites:

Ctrip (☑800 820 6666; www.english.ctrip.com)

Elong (☑800 810 1010; www.elong.com)

Checking In

At check-in you will need your passport; a registration form will ask what type of visa you have. For most travellers, the visa will be L; for a full list of visa categories, see p992. A deposit (押金; *yājīn*) is required at most hotels; this will be paid either with cash or by providing your credit-card details. If your deposit is paid in cash, you will be given a receipt and this will be returned to you when you check out.

Camping

There are few places where you can legally camp and as most of China's flat land is put to agricultural use, you will largely be limited to remote, hilly regions. Camping is more feasible in wilder and less populated parts of west China. In certain destinations with camping possibilities, travel agencies and hotels

will arrange overnight camping trips or multiday treks, in which case camping equipment will be supplied.

Courtyard Hotels

Largely confined to Běijīng, courtyard hotels have rapidly mushroomed. Arranged around traditional *sìhéyuàn* (courtyards), rooms are on ground level. Courtyard hotels are charming and romantic, but are often expensive and rooms are small, in keeping with the dimensions of courtyard residences. Facilities will be limited so don't expect a swimming pool, gym or subterranean garage.

Business Chain Hotels

Dotted around much of China, budget business chain hotels can sometimes be a decent alternative to old-school two- and three-star hotels, with rooms around the ¥150 to ¥200 mark. In recent years, however, their once-pristine facilities have sometimes come to resemble the threadbare clunkers they aimed to replace. Still, their sheer ubiquitousness means you can usually find accommodation (but look at the rooms first). They often have membership/loyalty schemes which make rooms cheaper. Brands include:

Home Inn (www.homeinns.com)

Jinjiang Inn (www.jinjianginns.com)

Motel 168 (www.motel168.com)

Guesthouses

The cheapest of the cheap are China's ubiquitous guesthouses (招待所; *zhāodàisuǒ*). Often found clustering near train or bus stations but also dotted around cities and towns, not all guesthouses accept foreigners and Chinese skills may be crucial in securing a room. Rooms (doubles, twins, triples, quads) are primitive and grey, with tiled floors and possibly a shower room or shabby bathroom; showers may be communal.

Other terms for guesthouses:

» 旅店 (*lǚdiàn*)
» 旅馆 (*lǚguǎn*)
» 有房 means rooms available
» 今日有房 means rooms available today
» 住宿 (*zhùsù*) means accommodation

Homesteads

In more rural destinations, small towns and villages, you should be able to find a homestead (农家; *nóngjiā*) with a small number of rooms in the region of ¥50 (bargaining is possible); you will not need to register. The owner will be more than happy to cook up meals for you as well. Showers and toilets are generally communal.

Hostels

If you're looking for efficiently run budget accommodation, turn to China's youth hostel sector. **Hostelling International** (☎020-8751 3731; www.yhachina.com) hostels are generally well run; other private youth hostels scattered around China are unaffiliated and standards at these may be variable. Book ahead in popular towns as rooms can go fast.

Superb for meeting likeminded travellers, youth hostels are typically staffed by youthful English-speakers who are also well informed on local sightseeing and transport. The foreigner-friendly vibe in youth hostels stands in marked contrast to many Chinese hotels. Double rooms in youth hostels are frequently better than midrange equivalents, often just as comfortable and better located and they may be cheaper (but not always). Many offer wi-fi, while most have at least one internet terminal (free perhaps, free for 30 minutes or roughly ¥5 to ¥10 per hour). Laundry, book-lending, kitchen facilities, bike rental, lockers, noticeboard, bar and cafe should all be available, as well as possibly pool, ping pong, DVDs, PlayStation and other forms of entertainment. Soap, shower gel and toothpaste are generally not provided, although you can purchase them at reception.

Dorms usually cost between ¥40 and ¥55 (discounts of around ¥5 for members). They typically come with bunk beds but may have standard beds. Most dorms won't have an ensuite shower, though some do; they should have air-con. Many hostels also have doubles, singles, twins

and maybe even family rooms; prices vary but are often around ¥150 to ¥250 for a double, again with discounts for members. Hostels can arrange ticketing or help you book a room in another affiliated youth hostel. Book ahead (online if possible) as rooms are frequently booked out, especially at weekends or the busy holiday periods.

Hotels

Hotels vary wildly in quality within the same budget bracket. The star rating system employed in China can also be misleading: hotels may be awarded four or five stars when they are patently a star lower in ranking. The best rule of thumb is to choose the newest hotel in each category as renovations can be rare. Deficiencies may not be immediately apparent, so explore and inspect the overall quality of the hotel; viewing the room up front pays dividends.

China has few independent hotels of real distinction, so it's generally advisable to select chain hotels that offer a proven standard of international excellence. Shangri-La, Marriott, Hilton, St Regis, Ritz-Carlton, Marco Polo and Hyatt all have a presence in China and can

generally be relied upon for high standards of service and comfort.

Note that:

» English skills are often poor, even in some five-star hotels.

» Most rooms are twins rather than doubles, so be clear if you specifically want a double.

» Virtually all hotel rooms, whatever the price bracket, will have air-conditioning and a TV.

» Very cheap rooms may have neither telephone nor internet access.

» Wi-fi is increasingly common in hostels and midrange and up hotels (but might be only in the lobby).

» Late-night telephone calls from 'masseurs' are still common in budget and lower midrange hotels.

» All hotel rooms are subject to a 10% or 15% service charge.

» Practically all hotels will change money for guests, and most midrange and top-end hotels accept credit cards.

» A Western breakfast may be available, certainly at four-star establishments.

» The Chinese method of designating floors is the same as that used in the USA, but

HOTEL DISCOUNTS

Always ignore the rack rate and ask for the discounted price or bargain for a room, as discounts usually apply everywhere but youth hostels (except for hostel members) and the cheapest accommodation; you can do this in person at reception, or book online. Apart from during the busy holiday periods (the end of April and first few days of May, the first week of October and Chinese New Year), rooms should be priced well below the rack rate and are rarely booked out. Discounts of 10% to 60% off the tariff rate (30% is typical) are the norm, available by simply asking at reception, by phoning in advance to reserve a room or by booking online at Ctrip (http://english.ctrip.com). We have listed both the rack rate and the discount you should expect to receive at each hotel, where these apply.

HOTEL TIPS

» Ask your hotel concierge for a local map
» The standard of English is often better at youth hostels than at midrange or some high-end hotels
» Your hotel can help with ticketing, for a commission
» See the Accommodation section of the Language chapter for a handy primer of Chinese phrases
» Almost every hotel has a left-luggage room, which should be free if you are a guest in the hotel
» Always bargain for a room

different from, say, that used in Australia. What would be the ground floor in Australia is the 1st floor in China, the 1st is the 2nd, and so on.

In China, hotels are called:
» *bīnguǎn* (宾馆)
» *dàfàndiàn* (大饭店)
» *dàjiǔdiàn* (大酒店)
» *fàndiàn* (饭店)
» *jiǔdiàn* (酒店)

Temples & Monasteries

Some temples and monasteries (especially on China's sacred mountains) provide accommodation. They are cheap, but ascetic, and may not have running water or electricity.

University Accommodation

Some universities provide cheap and basic accommodation either in their foreign-student dormitory buildings (留学生楼; *liúxuéshēng lóu*) or more expensive rooms at their experts' building (专家楼; *zhuānjiā lóu*), where visiting teachers often stay.

Activities

Grab copies of expat magazines in Běijīng, Hong Kong, Guǎngzhōu and Shànghǎi for information on activities such as golf, running, horse riding, cycling, football, cricket, hiking and trekking, swimming, ice skating, skiing, skateboarding, waterskiing and rock climbing.

Business Hours

China officially has a five-day working week. Saturday and Sunday are public holidays.
» Banks, offices and government departments open Monday to Friday (roughly 9am until 5pm or 6pm), possibly closing for two hours in the middle of the day; many banks are also open Saturdays and maybe Sundays.
» Post offices are generally open seven days a week.
» Museums generally stay open on weekends and may shut for one day during the week.
» Travel agencies and foreign-exchange counters in tourist hotels are usually open seven days a week.
» Department stores, shopping malls and shops are open daily from 10am to 10pm.
» Internet cafes are typically open 24 hours, but some open at 8am and close at midnight.
» Restaurants open from around 10.30am to 11pm; some shut at around 2pm and reopen at 5pm or 6pm.
» Bars open in the late afternoon, shutting around midnight or later.

Children

More comfortable in the large cities of Hong Kong, Běijīng and Shànghǎi, children are likely to feel out of place in smaller towns and in the wilds. With the exception of Hǎinán, China has a dreary selection of beaches. Ask a doctor specialising in travel medicine for information on recommended immunisations for your child.

Practicalities

» Baby food, nappies and milk powder: widely available in supermarkets.
» Restaurants: few have baby chairs.
» Train travel: children shorter than 1.4m can get a hard sleeper for 75% of the full price or a half-price hard seat. Children shorter than 1.1m ride free, but you have to hold them the entire journey.
» Air travel: infants under the age of two fly for 10% of the full airfare, while children between the ages of two and 11 pay half the full price for domestic flights and 75% of the adult price for international flights.
» Sights and museums: many have children's admission prices, for children under 1.1m or 1.3m in height.
» Always ensure your child carries ID in case they get lost.

For more information on travelling with children, consult the following:
» *Travel with Children* (Brigitte Barta et al)
» *Take the Kids Travelling* (Helen Truszkowski)
» *Adventuring with Children* (Nan Jeffrey)
» *Travels with Baby: The Ultimate Guide for Planning Trips with Babies, Toddlers, and Preschool-Age Children* (Shelly Rivoli)
» *Take-Along Travels with Baby: Hundreds of Tips to Help During Travel with Your Baby, Toddler, and Pre-schooler* (Shelly Rivoli)

Customs Regulations

Chinese customs generally pay tourists little attention. 'Green channels' and 'red channels' at the airport are clearly marked. You are not allowed to import or export illegal drugs, or animals and plants (including seeds). Pirated DVDs and CDs are illegal exports from China – if found they will be confiscated. You can take Chinese medicine up to a value of ¥300 when you depart China.

Duty free, you're allowed to import:
» 400 cigarettes or the equivalent in tobacco products.
» 1.5L of alcohol.
» 50g of gold or silver.
» A camera, video camera and similar items for personal use only.

As well:
» Importation of fresh fruit and cold cuts is prohibited.
» You can legally only bring in or take out ¥6000 in Chinese currency, although there are no restrictions on foreign currency (but declare any cash exceeding US$5000 or its equivalent in another currency).

Objects considered antiques require a certificate and a red seal to clear customs when leaving China. Anything made before 1949 is considered an antique, and if it was made before 1795 it cannot legally be taken out of the country. To get the proper certificate and red seal, your antiques must be inspected by the **State Administration of Cultural Heritage** (Guójiā Wénwù Jú; www.sach. gov.cn, Chinese only; ☎010-5988 1572; 10 Chaoyangmen Beidajie) in Běijīng.

Discount Cards

Seniors over the age of 65 are frequently eligible for a discount, so make sure you take your passport when visiting sights as proof of age.

An International Student Identity Card (ISIC; €12) can net students half-price discounts at many sights (but you may have to insist).

Electricity

220V/50Hz

220V/50Hz

Embassies & Consulates

Embassies

There are two main embassy compounds in Běijīng – Jiànguóménwài and Sānlǐtún (Map p76). Embassies are open from 9am to noon and 1.30pm to 4pm Monday to Friday, but visa departments are often only open in the morning. For visas, you need to phone to make an appointment.

Australia (☎010-5140 4111; www.china.embassy.gov.au; 21 Dongzhimenwai Dajie)

Canada (☎010-5139 4000; fax 010-6532 4072; www.canadainternational.gc.ca; 19 Dongzhimenwai Dajie)

France (☎010-8531 2000; fax 010-8531 2020; www.ambafrance-cn.org; 60 Tianze Lu)

Germany (☎010-8532 9000; fax 010-6532 5336; www.peking.diplo.de; 17 Dongzhimenwai Dajie)

India (☎010-8531 2500; fax 010-8531 2515; www.indianembassy.org.cn; 5 Liangmaqiao Beijie)

Ireland (☎010-6532 2691; fax 010-6532 6857; www.embassyofireland.cn; 3 Ritan Donglu)

Kazakhstan (☎010-6532 6182; fax 010-6532 6183; 9 Sanlitun Dongliujie)

Laos (☎010-6532 1224; fax 010-6532 6748; 11 Sanlitun Dongsijie)

Mongolia (☎010-6532 1203; fax 010-6532 5045; www.mongolembassychina.org; 2 Xiushui Beijie)

Myanmar (☎010-6532-0359; fax 010-6532-0408; www.myanmarembassy.com/chinese; 6 Dongzhimenwai Dajie)

Nepal (☎010-6532 1795; fax 010-6532 3251; www.nepalembassy.org.cn; 1 Sanlitun Xiliujie)

Netherlands (☎010-8532 0200; fax 010-8532 0300; www.hollandinchina.org; 4 Liangmahe Nanlu)

New Zealand (☎010-8532 7000; fax 010-6532 4317; www.nzembassy.com/china; 1 Ritan Dong Erjie)

North Korea (☎010-6532 1186; fax 010-6532 6056; 11 Ritan Beilu)

Pakistan (☎010-6532 2504/2558; fax 010-6532 2715; 1 Dongzhimenwai Dajie)

Russia (☎010-6532 1381; fax 010-6532 4851; www.russia.org.cn; 4 Dongzhimen Beizhongjie)

South Korea (☎010-8531 0700; fax 010-8531 0726; 20 Dongfang Donglu)

UK (☎010-5192 4000; fax 010-5192 4239; http://ukinchina.fco. gov.uk; 11 Guanghua Lu)

USA (☎010-8531 3000; fax 010-8531 4200; http://beijing. usembassy-china.org.cn; 55 Anjialou Lu)

Vietnam (☎010-6532 1155; fax 010-6532 5720; www.vnem ba.org.cn; 32 Guanghua Lu)

Consulates

CHÉNGDŪ

France (☎028-6666 6060; 30th fl, Times Sq, 2 Zongtongfu Lu)

Germany (☎028-8528 0800; 25th fl, Western Tower, 19 Renmin Nanlu 4th Section)

Pakistan (☎028-8526 8316; 8th fl, Western Tower, 19 Renmin Nanlu 4th Section)

USA (☎028-8558 3992; 4 Lingshiguan Lu)

CHÓNGQÌNG

Canada (☎023-6373 8007; Suite 1705, 17th fl, Metropolitan Tower, 68 Zourong Lu)

UK (☎023-6369 1500; Suite 2801, 28th fl, Metropolitan Tower, 68 Zourong Lu)

ERENHOT

Mongolia (Ménggǔ Lǐngshìguǎn; see p856 for details)

GUĂNGZHŌU

Australia (☎020-3814 0111; fax 020-3814 0112; 12th fl, Development Centre, 3 Linjiang Dadao)

Canada (☎020-8611 6100; fax 020-8611 6196; Room 801, China Hotel Office Tower, Liuhua Lu)

France (☎020-2829 2000; fax 020-2829 2045; Room 810, 8th fl, Main Tower, Guǎngdōng International Hotel, 339 Huanshi Donglu)

Germany (☎020-8313 0000; fax 020-8516 8133; 14th fl, Main Tower, Yuèhǎi Tiānhé Bldg, 208 Tianhe Lu)

India (☎020-8550 1501; Room 1401-1402, 14th fl, HNA Tower, 8 Linhe Zhonglu)

Netherlands (☎020-3813 2200; fax 020-3813 2299; http://guangzhou.nlconsulate. org; Teem Tower, 208 Tianhe Lu)

New Zealand (☎020-8667 0253; Room 1055, China Hotel Office Tower, Liuhua Lu)

Russia (☎020-8518 5001; 26a Fāzhǎn Zhōngxīn Bldg, 3 Linjiang Dadao)

UK (☎020-8314 3000; fax 020-8332 7509; 2nd fl, Main Tower, Guǎngdōng International Hotel, 339 Huanshi Donglu)

USA (☎020-8121 8000; fax 020-8121 8428; 5th fl, Tiānyù Garden, 136-142 Linhe Zhonglu)

HOHHOT

Mongolia (Ménggǔ Lǐngshìguǎn; 5 Dongying Nanjie; ⊙8.30am-12.30pm Mon, Tue, Thu)

HONG KONG

Australia (☎852-2827 8881; 23rd fl, Harbour Centre, 25 Harbour Rd, Wan Chai)

Canada (☎852-3719 4700; 12-14th fl, One Exchange Sq, 8 Connaught Pl, Central)

France (☎852-3752 9900; 26th fl, Tower II, Admiralty Centre, 18 Harcourt Rd, Admiralty)

Germany (☎852-2105 8777; 21st fl, United Centre, 95 Queensway, Admiralty)

India (☎852-3970 9900; www. cgihk.gov.in; 26A United Centre, 95 Queensway, Admiralty)

Ireland (☎852-2527 4897; 1408 Two Pacific Pl, 88 Queensway, Admiralty)

Japan (☎852-2522 1184; www.hk.emb-japan.go.jp; 46-47th fl, One Exchange Sq, 8 Connaught Pl, Central)

Laos (☎852-2544 1186; 14th fl, Arion Commercial Centre, 2-12 Queen's Rd West, Sheung Wan)

Nepal (☎852-2369 7813; www.nepalconsulatehk.org; 715 China Aerospace Tower, Concordia Plaza, 1 Science Museum Rd, Tsim Sha Tsui)

Netherlands (☎852-2522 5127; Room 5702, 57th fl, Cheung Kong Centre, 2 Queen's Rd, Central)

New Zealand (☎852-2525 5044; Room 6501, 65th fl, Central Plaza, 18 Harbour Rd, Wan Chai)

Russia (☎852-2877 7188; 21st fl, Sun Hung Kai Centre, 30 Harbour Rd, Wan Chai)

UK (☎852-2901 3000; 1 Supreme Court Rd, Admiralty)

USA (☎852-2523 9011; 26 Garden Rd, Central)

Vietnam (☎852-2591 4510; vnconsul@netvigator.com; 15th fl, Great Smart Tower, 230 Wan Chai Rd, Wan Chai)

JĪNGHÓNG

Laos (1st fl, King Land Hotel, 6 Jingde Lu; ⊙8.30-11.30am & 1.30-4pm)

KŪNMÍNG

Laos (☎0871-316 8916; Ground fl, Kūnmíng Diplomat Compound, 6800 Caiyun Beilu)

Myanmar (☎0871-816 2810; 99 Yingbin Lu, Guāndù District Consular Zone)

Thailand (☎0871-316 8916; fax 0871-316 6891; Ground fl, South Wing, Kūnmíng Hotel, 145 Dongfeng Donglu)

Vietnam (☎0871-352 2669; Kai Wah Plaza Hotel, 157 Beijing Lu)

LHASA

Nepal (☎0891-681 3965; www.nepalembassy.org.cn; 13 Norbulingka Beilu; ⊙10am-noon Mon-Fri) On a side street between the Lhasa Hotel and Norbulingka.

QĪNGDĂO

Japan (☎0532-8090 0001; fax 0532-8090 0009; 59 Xiang gang Donglu)

South Korea (☎0532-8897 6001; fax 0532-8897 6005; 8 Qinling Lu)

SHÀNGHĂI

Australia (☎021-2215 5200; www.shanghai.china.embassy. gov.au; 22nd fl, CITIC Sq, 1168 West Nanjing Rd)

Canada (☎021-3279 2800; www.shanghai.gc.ca; 8th fl, 1788 West Nanjing Rd)

France (☎021-6103 2200; www.consulfrance-shanghai. org; Suite 201, 2nd fl, Hǎitōng Securities Bldg, 689 Guangdong Rd)

Germany (☎021-3401 0106; www.shanghai.diplo.de; 181 Yongfu Rd)

India (☎021-6275 8881; 1008 Shànghǎi International Trade Centre, 2201 West Yan'an Rd)

Ireland (☎021-6279 8729; 700a Shànghǎi Centre, 1376 West Nanjing Rd)

Japan (☎021-5257 4766; www.shanghai.cn.emb-japan.go.jp; 8 Wanshan Rd)

Nepal (☎021-6272 0259; 16a, 669 West Beijing Rd)

Netherlands (☎021-2208 7288; 10th fl, Tower B, Dawning-Center, 500 Hongbaoshi Rd)

New Zealand (☎021-5407 5858; Room 1605-1607A, 16th fl, The Centre, 989 Changle Rd)

Russia (☎021-6324 8383; fax 021-6324 2682; 20 Huangpu Rd)

UK (☎021-3279 2000; fax 021-6279 7651; Room 319, 3rd fl, Shànghǎi Centre, 1376 West Nanjing Rd)

USA (http://shanghai.usembassy-china.org.cn) French Concession (☎021-6279 7662; 1469 Middle Huaihai Rd); Jing'ān (☎021-3217 4650, after-hour emergency number for US citizens 021-3217-4650; 8th fl, Westgate Tower, 1038 West Nanjing Rd)

SHĚNYÁNG

France (☎024-2319 0000; fax 024-2319 0001; 34 Nanshisan Weilu)

North Korea (☎024-8690 3451; fax 024-8690 3482; 37 Beiling Dajie) North Korea visas are more likely to be obtained at the North Korean embassy in Běijīng.

Russia (☎024-2322 3927; fax 024-2322 3907; 31 Nanshisan Weilu)

South Korea (☎024-2385 3388; 37 Nanshisan Weilu)

USA (☎024-2322 1198; fax 024-2323 1465; 52 Shisi Weilu)

ÜRÜMQI

Kazakhstan (Hāsàkèsītǎn Lǐngshìguǎn; ☎0991-369 1444; 216 Kunming Lu; ⏲9am-1pm Mon-Fri) If you're applying for a visa, show up early and don't expect calls to be taken.

Kyrgyzstan (38 Hetan Beilu; ⏲noon-2pm Mon-Fri) There's a small blue door to the side of the Aipai (Central Asian) Hotel. Visas (¥475) take one week, or more for express of three days or same day. Bring one passport photo and a copy of your passport and visa (pay at the nearby Bank of China and arrive before opening time to get it done). You can also get a visa once you've arrived at Bishkek airport.

WŬHÀN

France (☎027-6579 7900; fax 027-8577 8426; Rooms 1701-1708, Wǔhàn International Trade Center, 568 Jianshe Dadao)

Gay & Lesbian Travellers

Greater tolerance exists in the big cities than in the more conservative countryside, but even in urban areas, gay and lesbian visitors should be quite discreet. You will often see Chinese same-sex friends holding hands or putting their arms around each other, but this usually has no sexual connotation.

Spartacus International Gay Guide (Bruno Gmunder Verlag) Best-selling guide for gay travellers, also available as an iPhone App.

Utopia (www.utopia-asia.com/tipschin.htm) Tips on travelling in China and a complete listing of gay bars nationwide.

Insurance

Carefully consider a travel-insurance policy to cover theft, loss, trip cancellation and medical eventualities. Travel agents can sort this out for you, although it is often cheaper to find good deals with an insurer online or with a broker. Worldwide travel insurance is available at www.lonelyplanet.com/travel_services. You can buy, extend and claim online anytime – even if you're already on the road.

Some policies specifically exclude 'dangerous activities' such as scuba diving, skiing and even trekking. Check that the policy covers ambulances or an emergency flight home.

Paying for your airline ticket with a credit card often provides limited travel accident insurance – ask your credit-card company what it's prepared to cover.

You may prefer a policy that pays doctors or hospitals directly rather than reimbursing you for expenditures after the fact. If you have to claim later, ensure you keep all documentation.

See also the Insurance section (p1010) in the Health chapter.

Internet Access

China's relationship with the internet is notoriously prickly. Wi-fi accessibility in hotels, cafes, restaurants and bars is generally OK, especially in the big cities. For those using internet cafes, however, problems exist. You will need ID to get online at most internet cafes yet some cities and towns (often provincial capitals or large towns) insist on seeing Chinese ID, barring foreigners from getting online. The best option is to bring a wi-fi enabled mobile phone or laptop or use your hotel computer or broadband internet connection rather than be at the mercy of internet cafes not accepting foreigners.

Up to 10% of websites are traditionally inaccessible in China due to censorship; access to some newspapers articles and other links can suddenly vanish. Social networking sights such as Facebook and Twitter are inaccessible in China; YouTube is also inaccessible.

Internet cafes are listed under the Information section for destinations throughout the book. In large cities and towns, the area around the train station generally has internet cafes.

Rates at internet cafes range from around ¥2 to ¥5 per hour; small deposits are usually required. Opening hours are usually 24 hours.

Youth hostels should have internet access in common areas; if access is not gratis, rates will be around ¥5 per hour. Throughout this book the internet icon (@) is used in hotel reviews to indicate the presence of an internet cafe or a terminal where you can get online; wi-fi areas are indicated with a wi-fi icon (📶).

Language Courses

Learning Chinese in China is big business. Weigh up fees and syllabus carefully and check online reviews – some schools are pricey and may use teaching methods unsuited to Westerners. Consider where you would like to study: the Běijīng accent and setting has obvious cachet, but a course in a setting such as Yángshuò can be delightful.

Legal Matters

Anyone under the age of 18 is considered a minor; the minimum age for driving a car is 18. The age of consent for marriage is 22 for men and 20 for women. There is no minimum age restricting the consumption of alcohol or use of cigarettes.

China's laws against the use of illegal drugs are harsh, and foreign nationals have been executed for drug offences (trafficking in more than 50g of heroin can result in the death penalty); in 2009 a British citizen was executed for smuggling drugs (despite protestations that he was mentally impaired). The Chinese criminal justice system does not always ensure a fair trial and defendants are not presumed innocent until proven guilty. Note that China conducts more judicial executions than the rest of the world put together – up to 10,000 per year (27 per day) according to some estimates. If arrested, most foreign citizens have the right to contact their embassy.

Money

Consult the Need to Know chapter (p22) for a table of exchange rates.

The Chinese currency is the renminbi (RMB), or 'people's money'. The basic unit of RMB is the yuan (元; ¥), which is divided into 10 jiao (角), which is again divided into 10 fen (分). Colloquially, the yuan is referred to as *kuài* and jiao as *máo* (毛). The fen has so little value these days that it is rarely used.

The Bank of China issues RMB bills in denominations of ¥1, ¥2, ¥5, ¥10, ¥20, ¥50 and ¥100. Coins come in denominations of ¥1, 5 jiao, 1 jiao and 5 fen. Paper versions of the coins remain in circulation.

Hong Kong's currency is the Hong Kong dollar (HK$). The Hong Kong dollar is divided into 100 cents. Bills are issued in denominations of HK$10, HK$20, HK$50, HK$100, HK$500 and HK$1000. Copper coins are worth 50c, 20c and 10c, while the $5, $2 and $1 coins are silver and the $10 coin is nickel and bronze. The Hong Kong dollar is pegged to the US dollar at a rate of US$1 to HK$7.80, though it is allowed to fluctuate a little.

Macau's currency is the pataca (MOP$), which is divided into 100 avos. Bills are issued in denominations of MOP$10, MOP$20, MOP$50, MOP$100, MOP$500 and MOP$1000. There are copper coins worth 10, 20 and 50 avos and silver-coloured MOP$1, MOP$2, MOP$5 and MOP$10 coins. The pataca is pegged to the Hong Kong dollar at a rate of MOP$103.20 to HK$100. In effect, the two currencies are interchangeable and Hong Kong dollars, including coins, are accepted in Macau. Chinese renminbi is also accepted in many places in Macau at one-to-one. You can't spend patacas anywhere else, however, so use them before you leave Macau. Prices quoted in this book are in yuan unless otherwise stated.

ATMs

Bank of China and the Industrial & Commercial Bank of China (ICBC) 24-hour ATMs are plentiful, and you can use Visa, MasterCard, Cirrus, Maestro Plus and American Express to withdraw cash. All ATMs accepting international cards have dual language ability. The network is largely found in sizeable towns and cities. If you plan on staying in China for a long period, it is advisable to open an account at a bank with a nationwide network of ATMs, such as the Bank of China. HSBC and Citibank ATMs are available in larger cities. Keep your ATM receipts so you can exchange your yuan when you leave China.

The exchange rate on ATM withdrawals is similar to that for credit cards, but there is a maximum daily withdrawal amount. Note that banks can charge a withdrawal fee for using the ATM network of another bank, so check with your bank before travelling.

ATMs are listed in the Information sections of destinations throughout this book. To have money wired from abroad, visit Western Union or Moneygram (www.moneygram.com).

Credit Cards

In large tourist towns, credit cards are relatively straightforward to use, but don't expect to be able to use them everywhere, and always carry enough cash; the exception is in Hong Kong, where international credit cards are accepted almost everywhere

COSTS IN CHINA

Although the days when China was very cheap are a nostalgic memory – and some prices can be eye-watering – you can still experience China affordably with judicious planning. Admission prices to many big-ticket sights can leap way above inflation, while other once-free sights may suddenly impose access fees. The practice of keeping admission costs low to encourage travellers to spend on other parts of the local economy (hotels, restaurants, shops) has made little headway in China. Other admission prices (The Forbidden City, for example) can be extremely good value, however, and an increasing number of museums are free.

Transport in China remains reasonably priced, but colossal distances between sights means this all stacks up, especially if you fly. When choosing destinations, weigh up transport costs, the latest admission fees, journey times and accommodation prices. As prices can jump without warning, find out the latest ticket price before heading to far-off and difficult to reach destinations.

You can empty your wallet dining at expensive restaurants, but you can still feed yourself cheaply at the budget end; note however that prices in city and town supermarkets are comparable to, and often pricier, than those in the West. Accommodation remains affordable and often cheap, but some cheap hotels and guesthouses will not take foreigners (see p982). Bars are increasingly pricey, but buying beer from small shops is very inexpensive.

(although some shops may try to add a surcharge to offset the commission charged by credit companies, which can range from 2.5% to 7%). Check to see if your credit card company charges a foreign transaction fee (usually between 1% and 3%) for purchases in China.

Where they are accepted, credit cards often deliver a slightly better exchange rate than banks. Money can also be withdrawn at certain ATMs in large cities on credit cards such as Visa, Master-Card and Amex. Always carry cash for purchasing train tickets.

Moneychangers

It's best to wait till you reach China to exchange money as the exchange rate will be better. Foreign currency and travellers cheques can be changed at border crossings, international airports, branches of the Bank of China, tourist hotels and some large department stores; hours of operation for foreign-exchange counters are 8am to 7pm (later at hotels). Top-end hotels will generally change money for hotel guests only. The official

rate is given almost everywhere and the exchange charge is standardised, so there is little need to shop around for the best deal.

Australian, Canadian, US, UK, Hong Kong and Japanese currencies and the euro can be changed in China. In some backwaters, it may be hard to change lesser-known currencies; US dollars are still the easiest to change.

Keep at least a few of your exchange receipts. You will need them if you want to exchange any remaining RMB you have at the end of your trip.

Tipping

Almost no one in China (including Hong Kong and Macau) asks for tips. Tipping used to be refused in restaurants, but nowadays many midrange and top-end eateries include their own (often huge) service charge; cheap restaurants do not expect a tip. Taxi drivers throughout China do not ask for or expect tips.

Travellers Cheques

With the prevalence of ATMs across China, travellers cheques are not as useful

as they once were and cannot be used everywhere, so always ensure you carry enough ready cash. You should have no problem cashing travellers cheques at tourist hotels, but they are of little use in budget hotels and restaurants. Most hotels will only cash the cheques of guests. If cashing them at banks, aim for larger banks such as the Bank of China or ICBC.

Stick to the major companies such as Thomas Cook, Amex and Visa. In big cities travellers cheques are accepted in almost any currency, but in smaller destinations, it's best to stick to big currencies such as US dollars or UK pounds. Keep your exchange receipts so you can change your money back to its original currency when you leave.

Passports

You must have a passport (护照; *hùzhào*) on you at all times; it is the most basic travel document and all hotels will insist on seeing it for check-in. It is now mandatory to present your passport when buying train tickets; you will also need it for using internet cafes that accept foreigners.

The Chinese government requires that your passport be valid for at least six months after the expiry date of your visa. You'll need at least one entire blank page in your passport for the visa.

Take an ID card with your photo in case you lose your passport and make photocopies of your passport: your embassy may need these before issuing a new one. You should also report the loss to the local Public Security Bureau (PSB).

Long-stay visitors should register their passport with their embassy.

Post

The international postal service is generally efficient, and airmail letters and postcards will probably take between five and 10 days to reach their destinations. Domestic post is swift – perhaps one or two days from Guǎngzhōu to Běijīng. Intracity post may be delivered the same day it's sent.

China Post operates an express mail service (EMS) that is fast, reliable and ensures that the package is sent by registered post. Not all branches of China Post have EMS.

Major tourist hotels have branch post offices where you can send letters, packets and parcels. Even at cheap hotels you can usually post letters from the front desk. Larger parcels may need to be sent from the town's main post office for a contents check and a customs form will be attached to the parcel.

In major cities, private carriers such as **United Parcel Service** (☑800 820 8388; www.ups.com), **DHL** (Dūnháo; ☑800 810 8000; www.cn.dhl.com), **Federal Express** (Liánbāng Kuàidì; ☑800 988 1888; http://fedex.com/cn) and **TNT Skypak**

(☑800 820 9868; www.tnt.com/express/zh_cn) have a pick-up service as well as drop-off centres; call their offices for details.

If you are sending items abroad, take them unpacked with you to the post office to be inspected; an appropriate box or envelope will be found for you. Most post offices offer materials for packaging (including padded envelopes, boxes and heavy brown paper), for which you'll be charged. Don't take your own packaging as it will probably be refused. If you have a receipt for the goods, put it in the box when you're mailing it, since the parcel may be opened again by customs further down the line.

Public Holidays

The People's Republic of China has a number of national holidays. Some of the following are nominal holidays that do not result in leave. It's not a great idea to arrive in China or go travelling during the big holiday periods as hotels prices reach their maximum and transport can become very tricky.

New Year's Day 1 January

Chinese New Year 31 January 2014, 19 February 2015; a week-long holiday for most.

International Women's Day 8 March

Tomb Sweeping Festival 5 April; a popular three-day holiday period.

International Labour Day 1 May; for many it's a three-day holiday.

Youth Day 4 May

International Children's Day 1 June

Dragon Boat Festival 12 June 2013, 2 June 2014, 20 June 2015

Birthday of the Chinese Communist Party 1 July

Anniversary of the Founding of the People's Liberation Army 1 August

Moon Festival end of September

National Day 1 October; the big one, a week-long holiday.

Safe Travel

Crime

Travellers are more often the victims of petty economic crime, such as theft, than serious crime. Foreigners are natural targets for pickpockets and thieves – keep your wits about you and make it difficult for thieves to get at your belongings. Incidences of crime increase around the Chinese New Year, but be vigilant at all times.

High-risk areas in China are train and bus stations, city and long-distance buses (especially sleeper buses), hard-seat train carriages and public toilets.

Take a money belt for your cash, passport and credit cards.

Travelling solo – especially if you are female – carries obvious risks; it's advisable

GOVERNMENT TRAVEL ADVICE

The following government websites offer travel advisories and information on current hot spots.

Australian Department of Foreign Affairs & Trade (☑1300 139 281; www.smarttraveller.gov.au)

British Foreign & Commonwealth Office (☑0845-850-2829; www.fco.gov.uk/countryadvice)

Canadian Department of Foreign Affairs & International Trade (☑800-267 6788; www.dfait-maeci.gc.ca)

US State Department (☑888-407 4747; http://travel.state.gov)

to travel with someone else or in a small group. Even in Běijīng, single women taking taxis have been taken to remote areas and robbed by taxi drivers, so don't assume anywhere is safe.

LOSS REPORTS

If something of yours is stolen, report it immediately to the nearest Foreign Affairs Branch of the Public Security Bureau (PSB; 公安局; Gōng'ānjú). Staff will ask you to fill in a loss report before investigating the case.

A loss report is crucial so you can claim compensation if you have travel insurance. Be prepared to spend many hours, perhaps even several days, organising it. Make a copy of your passport in case of loss or theft.

Scams

Con artists are widespread. Well-dressed girls flock along Shànghǎi's East Nanjing Rd, the Bund and Běijīng's Wangfujing Dajie, asking single men to photograph them on their mobile phones before dragging them to expensive cafes or Chinese teahouses, leaving them to foot monstrous bills. 'Poor' art students haunt similar neighbourhoods, press-ganging foreigners into art exhibitions where they are coerced into buying trashy art.

Taxi scams at Běijīng's Capital Airport are legendary; always join the queue at the taxi rank and insist that the taxi driver uses his or her meter. Try to avoid pedicabs and motorised three wheelers wherever possible; we receive a litany of complaints against pedicab drivers who originally agree on a price and then insist on an alternative figure (sometimes 10 times the sum) once you arrive at the destination.

Be alert at all times if you decide to change money or buy tickets (such as train tickets, see p1004) on the black market, which we can't recommend.

Always be alert when buying unpriced goods (which is a lot of the time): foreigners are frequently ripped off. Always examine your restaurant bill carefully for hidden extras and if paying by credit card ensure there are no extra charges.

Transport

Traffic accidents are the major cause of death in China for people aged between 15 and 45, and the World Health Organization (WHO) estimates there are 600 traffic deaths per day. On long-distance buses, you may find there are no seatbelts or the seatbelts are virtually unusable through neglect, inextricably stuffed beneath the seat. Outside of the big cities, taxis are unlikely to have rear seatbelts fitted.

Your greatest danger in China will almost certainly be crossing the road, so develop 360-degree vision and a sixth sense. Crossing only when it is safe to do so could perch you at the side of the road in perpetuity, but don't imitate the local tendency to cross without looking. Note that cars frequently turn on red lights in China, so the green 'walk now' man does not mean it is safe to cross.

Telephone
Mobile Phones

A mobile phone should be the first choice for calls. If you have the right phone (eg Blackberry, iPhone, Android) and are in a wi-fi zone, **Skype** (www.skype.com) and **Viber** (www.viber.com) can make calls either very cheap or free. China Mobile outlets and some newspaper kiosks can sell you a SIM card, which will cost from ¥60 to ¥100 depending on the phone number (numbers with eights in them are more expensive, numbers with fours are cheaper) and will include ¥50 of credit. When this runs out, you can top up by buying a credit-charging card (chōngzhí kǎ)

from China Mobile outlets and some newspaper stands. Ensure your mobile is unlocked for use in China. Buying a mobile phone in China is also an option as they are generally inexpensive. Cafes, restaurants and bars in larger towns and cities are frequently wi-fi enabled.

Landlines

If making a domestic call, look out for very cheap public phones at newspaper stands (报刊亭; bàokāntíng) and hole-in-the-wall shops (小卖部; xiǎomàibù); you make your call and then pay the owner. Domestic and international long-distance phone calls can also be made from main telecommunications offices and 'phone bars' (话吧; huàbā). Cardless international calls are expensive and it's far cheaper to use an internet phone (IP) card. Public telephone booths are rarely used now in China but may serve as wi-fi hot spots (as in Shànghǎi).

Area codes for all cities, towns and destinations appear in the relevant chapters.

Phonecards

Beyond Skype or Viber, using an IP card on your mobile or a landline phone is much cheaper than calling direct, but they can be hard to find outside the big cities. You dial a local number, punch in your account number, followed by a pin number and finally the number you wish to call. English-language service is usually available. Some IP cards can only be used locally, while others can be used nationwide, while still others are no good for international calls, so it is important to buy the right card (and check the expiry date).

Visas
Applying for Visas
FOR CHINA

Apart from visitors on visa-free transit stays (p994) in Běijīng and Shànghǎi,

VISA TYPES

There are eight categories of visas (for most travellers, an L visa will be issued).

TYPE	ENGLISH NAME	CHINESE NAME
C	flight attendant	*chéngwù* 乘务
D	resident	*dìngjū* 定居
F	business or student	*fǎngwèn* 访问
G	transit	*guòjìng* 过境
J	journalist	*jìzhě* 记者
L	travel	*lǚxíng* 旅行
X	long-term student	*liúxué* 留学
Z	working	*gōngzuò* 工作

citizens of Japan, Singapore, Brunei and San Marino, all visitors to China require a visa, which covers the whole of China, although there remain restricted areas that require an additional permit from the PSB. Permits are also required for travel to Tibet (see boxed text, p900), a region that the authorities can suddenly bar foreigners from entering.

Your passport must be valid for at least six months after the expiry date of your visa (nine months for a double-entry visa) and you'll need at least one entire blank page in your passport for the visa. For children under the age of 18, a parent must sign the application form on their behalf.

At the time of writing, the visa application process had become more rigorous and applicants were required to provide the following:

» A copy of your flight confirmation showing onward/return travel.

» For double-entry visas, you need to provide flight confirmation showing all dates of entry and exit.

» If staying at a hotel in China you must provide confirmation from the hotel (this can be cancelled later if you stay elsewhere).

» If staying with friends or relatives, you must provide a

copy of the information page of their passport, a copy of their China visa and a letter of invitation from them.

At the time of writing, prices for a standard single-entry 30-day visa were as follows:

» UK£30 for UK citizens
» US$130 for US citizens
» US$30 for citizens of other nations

Double-entry visas:

» UK£45 for UK citizens
» US$130 for US citizens
» US$45 for all other nationals

Six-month multiple-entry visas:

» UK£90 for UK citizens
» US$130 for US citizens
» US$60 for all other nationals

A standard 30-day single-entry visa can be issued in four to five working days. In many countries, the visa service has been outsourced from the Chinese embassy to a **Chinese Visa Application Service Centre** (www.visaforchina.org), which levies an extra administration fee. In the case of the UK, a single-entry visa costs UK£30, but the standard administration charge levied by the centre is an additional UK£36 (three-day express UK£48, postal service UK£54). In some countries, such as the UK, France, the US and Canada, there

is more than one service centre nationwide. Visa Application Service Centres are open Monday to Friday.

A standard 30-day visa is activated on the date you enter China, and must be used within three months of the date of issue. Sixty-day and 90-day travel visas are harder to get. To stay longer, you can extend your visa in China.

Visa applications require a completed application form (available from the embassy, visa application service centre or downloaded from its website) and at least one photo (normally 51mm x 51mm). You generally pay for your visa when you collect it. A visa mailed to you will take up to three weeks. In the US and Canada, mailed visa applications have to go via a visa agent, at extra cost. In the US, many people use the **China Visa Service Center** (☑ in the USA 800 799 6560; www.mychinavisa.com), which offers prompt service. The procedure takes around 10 to 14 days. **CIBT** (www.uk.cibt.com) offers a global network and a fast and efficient turnaround.

Hong Kong is a good place to pick up a China visa. **China Travel Service** (CTS; 广州中国旅行社; Zhōngguó Lǚxíngshè) will be able to obtain one for you, or you can apply directly to the **Visa Office of the People's Republic of China** (☑852-3413 2300; www.fmcoprc.gov.hk/eng; 7th fl, Lower Block, China Resources Centre, 26 Harbour Rd, Wan Chai; ☺9am-noon & 2-5pm Mon-Fri).

Be aware that American and UK passport holders must pay considerably more for their visas. You must supply two photos. Prices for China visas in Hong Kong are as follows:

» **Standard visa** One-/two-/three-day processing time HK$500/400/200

» **Double-entry visa** One-/two-/three-day processing time HK$600/500/300

VISA-FREE TRANSITS

Citizens from 45 nations (including the US, Australia, Canada, France, Brazil and the UK) can now stay in Běijīng for 72 hours without a visa as long as they are in transit to other destinations outside China, have a third-country visa and an air ticket out of Běijīng (they are not allowed to venture beyond Běijīng). Similarly, citizens from the same nations can also transit through Shànghǎi for 72 hours visa-free, with the same conditions.

» **Multiple-entry six-month visa** One-/two-/three-day processing time HK$800/700/500

» **Multiple-entry (one, two, three year)** HK$1100, 1000, 800

Five-day cash-only visas (¥160 for most nationalities, ¥469 for British, US citizens excluded) are available at the **Luóhú border crossing** (Lo Wu; ⊗9am-10.30pm) between Hong Kong and Shēnzhèn, valid for Shēnzhèn only. The same visa is also available at **Huánggǎng** (⊗9am-1pm & 2.30-5pm) and **Shékǒu** (⊗8.45am-12.30pm & 2.30-5.30pm).

Three-day visas are also available at the **Macau–Zhūhǎi border** (¥160 for most nationalities, ¥469 for British, US citizens excluded; ⊗8.30am-12.15pm, 1-6.15pm & 7-10.30pm). US citizens have to buy a visa in advance in Macau or Hong Kong.

Be aware that political events can suddenly make visas more difficult to procure or renew.

When asked about your itinerary on the application form, list standard tourist destinations; if you are considering going to Tibet or western Xīnjiāng, just leave it off the form. The list you give is not binding. Those working in media or journalism may want to profess a different occupation; otherwise, a visa may be refused or a shorter length of stay than that requested may be given.

FOR HONG KONG

At the time of writing, most visitors to Hong Kong, including citizens of the EU, Australia, New Zealand, the USA and Canada, could enter and stay for 90 days without a visa. British passport holders get 180 days, while South Africans are allowed to stay 30 days visa-free. If you require a visa, apply at a Chinese embassy or consulate before arriving. If you visit Hong Kong from China, you will need a double-entry, multiple-entry visa or a new visa to re-enter China.

FOR MACAU

Most travellers, including citizens of the EU, Australia, New Zealand, the USA, Canada and South Africa, can enter Macau without a visa for between 30 and 90 days. Most other nationalities can get a 30-day visa on arrival, which will cost MOP$100/50/200 per adult/child under 12/family. If you're visiting Macau from China and plan to re-enter China, you will need to be on a multiple-entry or double-entry visa.

Visa Extensions

FOR CHINA

The Foreign Affairs Branch of the local PSB deals with visa extensions.

First-time extensions of 30 days are usually easy to obtain on single-entry tourist visas; a further extension of a month may be possible, but you may only get another week. Travellers report generous extensions in provincial towns, but don't bank on this. Popping across to Hong Kong to apply for a new tourist visa is another option.

Extensions to single-entry visas vary in price, depending on your nationality. At the time of writing, US travellers paid ¥185, Canadians ¥165, UK citizens ¥160 and Australians ¥100. Expect to wait up to five days for your visa extension to be processed.

The penalty for overstaying your visa in China is up to ¥500 per day. Some travellers have reported having trouble with officials who read the 'valid until' date on their visa incorrectly. For a one-month travel (L) visa, the 'valid until' date is the date by which you must enter the country (within three months of the date the visa was issued), not the date upon which your visa expires.

FOR HONG KONG

For tourist-visa extensions, inquire at the **Hong Kong Immigration Department** (☑852-2852 3047; www.immd.gov.hk; 2nd fl, Immigration Tower, 7 Gloucester Rd, Wan Chai; ⊗8.45am-4.30pm Mon-Fri, 9-11.30am Sat). Extensions (HK$160) are not readily

MEASUREMENT CONVERSIONS

METRIC	CHINESE	IMPERIAL
1m (mǐ)	3 chǐ	3.28 ft
1km (gōnglǐ)	2 lǐ	0.62 miles
1L (gōngshēng)	1 shēng	0.22 gallons
1kg (gōngjīn)	2 jīn	2.20 pounds

granted unless there are extenuating circumstances such as illness.

FOR MACAU

If your visa expires, you can obtain a single one-month extension from the **Macau Immigration Department** (☑853-2872 5488; Ground fl, Travessa da Amizade; ☺9am-5pm Mon-Fri).

Residence Permits

The 'green card' is a residence permit, issued for English teachers, foreign expats and long-term students who live in China. Green cards are issued for a period of six months to one year and must be renewed annually. Besides needing all the right paperwork, you must also pass a health exam, for which there is a charge. Families are automatically included once the permit is issued, but there is a fee for each family member. If you lose your card, you'll pay a hefty fee to have it replaced.

Volunteering

Large numbers of Westerners work in China with international development charities such as **VSO** (www. vso.org.uk), which can provide you with useful experience and the chance to learn Chinese.

Global Vision International (GVI; www.gvi.co.uk) Teaching in China.

Global Volunteer Network (www.globalvolunteernetwork. org) Connecting people with communities in need.

Joy in Action (JIA; www. joyinaction.org) Establishing work camps in places in need in south China.

World Teach (www. worldteach.org) Volunteer teachers.

Weights & Measures

The metric system is widely used in China. However, traditional Chinese weights and measures persist, especially in local markets. Fruit and vegetables are weighed by the *jīn* (500g). Smaller weights (for dumplings, tea etc) are measured in *liǎng* (50g).

Transport

GETTING THERE & AWAY

Flights, cars and tours can be booked online at www.lonely planet.com.

Entering China

No particular difficulties exist for travellers entering China. The main requirements are a passport that's valid for travel for six months after the expiry date of your visa and a visa (see p992); however note that documents required for visa application have become more rigorous. As a rule, visas for most nationalities cannot be obtained at the border (apart from five-day visas for Shēnzhèn at the Hong Kong–Shēnzhèn border and three-day visas at the Zhūhǎi–Macau border; US citizens excluded on both counts). In general, visas are not required for Hong Kong or Macau; if you enter Hong Kong or Macau from China and wish to re-enter China, you'll need either a multiple-entry visa or a new visa. For travel to Tibet, see the boxed text on p900. Chinese immigration officers are scrupulous and highly bureaucratic, but not overly officious. Travellers arriving in China will receive a health declaration form and an arrivals form to complete.

Air

Airports

Hong Kong, Běijīng and Shànghǎi are China's principal international air gateways. From 2012, China Southern commenced flights between London Heathrow and Báiyún International Airport in Guǎngzhōu.

Báiyún International Airport (Xīnbáiyún Jīchǎng; ☎020-3606 6999-3) In Guǎngzhōu; receiving an increasing number of international flights.

Capital Airport (Shǒudū Jīchǎng; ☎010-6454 1100; http://en.bcia.com.cn) Běijīng's international airport; three terminals.

Hong Kong International Airport (☎852-2181 8888; www.hongkongairport.com) Located at Chek Lap Kok on Lantau island, in the west of the territory.

Hóngqiáo Airport (Hóngqiáo Jīchǎng; ☎021-6268 8899/3659) In Shànghǎi's west; domestic flights, some international connections.

Pǔdōng International Airport (Pǔdōng Guójì Jīchǎng; ☎021-96990) In Shànghǎi's east; international flights.

Airlines Flying to/ from China

The following list comprises airlines flying into Běijīng, Hong Kong, Shànghǎi, Guǎngzhōu, Kūnmíng and Macau; for all other cities, see the relevant destination section.

Aeroflot Russian Airlines (www.aeroflot.ru)

Air Canada (www.aircanada.ca)

Air China (www.airchina.com)

Air France (www.airfrance.com)

Air Koryo (☎in Běijīng 010-6501 1557)

Air Macau (www.airmacau.com.mo)

Air New Zealand (www.airnewzealand.com)

AirAsia (www.airasia.com)

Alitalia (www.alitalia.com)

All Nippon Airways (www.ana.co.jp) Also flies to Dàlián, Qīngdǎo, Shěnyáng, Tiānjīn and Xiàmén.

American Airlines (www.aa.com)

Asiana Airlines (www.flyasiana.com) Also flies to Chángchūn, Chéngdū, Chóngqìng, Guǎngzhōu, Guìlín, Hāěrbīn, Nánjīng, Xī'ān and Yāntái.

Austrian Airlines (www.aua.com)

British Airways (www.britishairways.com)

Cathay Pacific (www.cathaypacific.com)

China Airlines (www.china-airlines.com)

China Eastern Airlines (www.ce-air.com)

China Southern Airlines (www.cs-air.com)

Delta Air Lines (www.delta.com)

Dragonair (www.dragonair.com)

El Al Israel Airlines (www.elal.co.il)

Emirates Airline (www.emirates.com)

Ethiopian Airlines (www.flyethiopian.com)

EVA Airways (www.evaair.com)

Garuda Indonesia (www.garuda-indonesia.com)

Hong Kong Airlines (www.hkairlines.com)

Iran Air (www.iranair.com)

Japan Airlines (www.jal.com) Also flies to Qīngdǎo, Dàlián and Xiàmén.

Kenya Airways (www.kenya-airways.com)

KLM (www.klm.nl)

Korean Air (www.koreanair.com) Also flies to Qīngdǎo and Shěnyáng.

Lao Airlines (☑in Kūnmíng 0871-312 5748; www.laoairlines.com)

Lufthansa Airlines (www.lufthansa.com)

Malaysia Airlines (www.malaysia-airlines.com.my)

MIAT Mongolian Airlines (www.miat.com)

Nepal Airlines (www.nepalairlines.com.np)

Pakistan International Airlines (www.piac.com.pk)

Philippine Airlines (www.philippineairlines.com)

Qantas Airways (www.qantas.com.au)

Qatar Airways (www.qatarairways.com)

Royal Jordanian Airlines (www.rj.com)

Scandinavian Airlines (www.sas.dk)

Shanghai Airlines (www.shanghai-air.com)

Silk Air (www.silkair.com)

Singapore Airlines (www.singaporeair.com)

Swiss International Airlines (www.swiss.com)

Thai Airways International (www.thaiairways.com)

Tiger Airways (www.tigerairways.com)

Trans Asia Airways (www.tna.com.tw)

United Airlines (www.ual.com)

Uzbekistan Airways (www.uzairways.com)

Vietnam Airlines (www.vietnamair.com.vn)

Virgin Atlantic (www.virgin-atlantic.com)

Tickets

The cheapest tickets to Hong Kong and China exist on price comparison websites or in discount agencies in Chinatowns around the world. Budget and student-travel agents offer cheap tickets, but the real bargains are with agents that deal with the Chinese, who regularly return home. Airfares to China peak between June and September.

The cheapest flights to China are with airlines requiring a stopover at the home airport, such as Air France to Běijīng via Paris, or Malaysia Airlines to Běijīng via Kuala Lumpur.

The best direct ticket deals are available from China's international carriers, such as China Eastern Airlines, Air China or China Southern Airlines.

Beyond internet travel websites – Expedia (www.expedia.com) and Travelocity (www.travelocity.com) for example – flight comparison websites weigh up the best prices from airline websites, travel agents, search engines and other online sources and are highly versatile, but tend to quote similar fares. They include the following:

Fly.com (www.fly.com)

Kayak (www.kayak.co.uk)

Momondo (www.momondo.com)

Travelsupermarket (www.travelsupermarket.com)

Skyscanner (www.skyscanner.net)

Australia

From Australia, Hong Kong is a popular gateway to China. However, fares from Australia to Hong Kong are generally not that much cheaper than fares to Běijīng or Shànghǎi. Qantas, China Eastern, Air China, China Southern and Cathay Pacific all fly direct to Běijīng, Shànghǎi, Hong Kong or Guǎngzhōu. The cheapest flights go via Jakarta, Manila, Bangkok or Kuala Lumpur.

Canada

From Canada, fares to Hong Kong are often higher than those to Běijīng. Air Canada has daily flights to Běijīng and Shànghǎi from Vancouver. Air Canada, Air China and China Eastern Airlines sometimes run supercheap fares.

Continental Europe

Generally, there is little variation in airfare prices from the main European cities. The major airlines and travel agents usually have a number of deals on offer,

CLIMATE CHANGE & TRAVEL

Every form of transport that relies on carbon-based fuel generates CO_2, the main cause of human-induced climate change. Modern travel is dependent on aeroplanes, which might use less fuel per kilometre per person than most cars but travel much greater distances. The altitude at which aircraft emit gases (including CO_2) and particles also contributes to their climate change impact. Many websites offer 'carbon calculators' that allow people to estimate the carbon emissions generated by their journey and, for those who wish to do so, to offset the impact of the greenhouse gases emitted with contributions to portfolios of climate-friendly initiatives throughout the world. Lonely Planet offsets the carbon footprint of all staff and author travel.

so shop around. **STA Travel** (www.statravel.com) and **Nouvelles Frontières** (www.nouvelles-frontieres.fr) have branches throughout Europe.

Japan

Daily flights operate between Tokyo and Běijīng, as well as regular flights between Osaka and Běijīng. Daily flights link Shànghǎi to Tokyo and Osaka, and there are flights from Japan to other major cities in China, including Guǎngzhōu, Dàlián and Qīngdǎo. Try **STA Travel** (☑in Tokyo 03-5391 2922; www.statravel.co.jp).

New Zealand

Air New Zealand has flights to Hong Kong, Shànghǎi and China Southern flies daily to Guǎngzhōu.

Flight Centre (☑0800 24 35 44; www.flightcentre.co.nz)
STA Travel (☑0800 474 400; www.statravel.co.nz)

Singapore

Chinatown Point Shopping Centre on New Bridge Rd has a good selection of travel agents. **STA Travel** (☑6737 7188; www.statravel.com.sg) has three offices in Singapore.

UK & Ireland

British Airways flies to Hong Kong, Běijīng and Shànghǎi; Virgin Atlantic flies to Shànghǎi; China Eastern flies to Shànghǎi and Hong Kong; and Cathay Pacific flies to Hong Kong. The cheapest flights include KLM to China via Amsterdam, Air France via Paris, or Singapore Airlines via Singapore.

Travel agents in London's Chinatown dealing with flights to China include:
Jade Travel (☑020-7734 7726; www.jadetravel.co.uk; 5 Newport Pl)
Omega Travel (☑020-7439 7788; www.omegatravel.ltd.uk; 53 Charing Cross Rd)
Reliance Tours Ltd (☑0800 018 0503; www.reliance-tours.co.uk; 12-13 Little Newport St)

USA

Airlines flying either to Shànghǎi or Běijīng from the US include Air China, American, China Eastern, Delta Airlines, Hainan Airlines and United Airlines. Airlines flying direct to Hong Kong include American Airlines, Delta Airlines, United Airlines and Cathay Pacific. The cheapest tickets to Hong Kong are offered by Chinese-run bucket shops in San Francisco, Los Angeles and New York.

Vietnam

Air China flies between Ho Chi Minh City and Běijīng, Guǎngzhōu, Shànghǎi and Hong Kong. Vietnam Airlines flies from Hanoi to Shànghǎi, Guǎngzhōu, Běijīng and Hong Kong. China Southern Airlines flights are via Guǎngzhōu.

Land

China shares borders with Afghanistan, Bhutan, India, Kazakhstan, Kyrgyzstan, Laos, Mongolia, Myanmar (Burma), Nepal, North Korea, Pakistan, Russia, Tajikistan and Vietnam; the borders with Afghanistan, Bhutan and India are closed. There are also official border crossings between China and its special administrative regions, Hong Kong (see p500 and p500) and Macau (see p531).

Lonely Planet *China* guides can be confiscated by officials, primarily at the Vietnam–China border.

Kazakhstan

Border crossings from Ürümqi to Kazakhstan are via border posts at Korgas, Ālāshànkǒu, Tǎchéng and Jímùnǎi (see p788). Ensure you have a valid Kazakhstan visa (obtainable, at the time of writing, in Ürümqi, or from Běijīng) or China visa. See the Xīnjiāng chapter for further details.

Apart from Ālāshànkǒu, which links China and Kaza-

khstan via train, all other border crossings are by bus; you can generally get a bike over, however. Two trains weekly (32 hours) run between Ürümqi and Almaty (p783), and one train per week runs to Astana.

Remember that borders open and close frequently due to changes in government policy; additionally, many are only open when the weather permits. It's always best to check with the **Public Security Bureau** (PSB; Gōng'ānjú) in Ürümqi for the official line.

Kyrgyzstan

There are two routes between China and Kyrgyzstan: one between Kashgar and Osh, via the Irkeshtam Pass; and one between Kashgar and Bishkek, via the dramatic 3752m Torugart Pass. See p797 for details.

Laos

From the Měnglà district in China's southern Yúnnán province, you can enter Laos via Boten in Luang Nam Tha province, while a daily bus runs between Vientiane and Kūnmíng and also from Jǐnghóng to Luang Nam Tha in Laos (see p643).

On-the-spot visas for Laos are available at the border, the price of which depends on your nationality (although you cannot get a China visa here). See the Yúnnán chapter (p643) for more details.

Mongolia

From Běijīng, the Trans-Mongolian Railway trains and the K23 trains (see p108) run to Ulaanbaatar. Two trains weekly run between Hohhot and Ulaanbaatar, and there are also regular buses between Hohhot and the border town of Erenhot (Èrlián). Mongolian visas on the Chinese side can be acquired in Běijīng, Hohhot and Erenhot. See the Inner Mongolia chapter (p856) for more details.

Myanmar (Burma)

The famous Burma Road runs from Kūnmíng in Yúnnán province to the Burmese city of Lashio. The road is open to travellers carrying permits for the region north of Lashio, although you can legally cross the border in only one direction – from the Chinese side (Jiěgào) into Myanmar; however, at the time of writing the border was not open to foreign travellers and flying in was the only option. See p687 for more details. Myanmar visas can only be arranged in Kūnmíng or Běijīng.

Nepal

The 865km road connecting Lhasa with Kathmandu is known as the Friendship Highway (p894), currently only traversable by rented vehicle (for foreign travellers). It's a spectacular trip across the Tibetan plateau, the highest point being Gyatso-la Pass (5100m).

Visas for Nepal can be obtained in Lhasa, or at the border at Kodari. See p903 for practical information about the journey and the border crossing.

When travelling from Nepal to Tibet, foreigners still have to arrange transport through tour agencies in Kathmandu. Access to Tibet can, however, be restricted for months at a time without warning.

North Korea

Visas for North Korea are difficult to arrange, and at the time of writing it was impossible for US and South Korean citizens. Those interested in travelling to North Korea from Běijīng should contact Nicholas Bonner or Simon Cockerell at **Koryo Tours** (☎010-6416 7544; www.koryogroup.com; 27 Beisanlitun Nan, Běijīng).

Four international express trains (K27 and K28) run between Běijīng train station and Pyongyang.

Pakistan

The exciting trip on the Karakoram Hwy (p796), said to be the world's highest public international highway, is an excellent way to get to or from Chinese Central Asia. There are buses from Kashgar for the two-day trip to the Pakistani town of Sost via Tashkurgan when the pass is open; see the Xīnjiāng chapter (p796) for more details.

Russia

At the time of writing, the train from Hā'ěrbīn East to Vladivostok was no longer running but you could take the train to Suífēnhé and take an onward connection there.

The Trans-Mongolian (via Erenhot) and Trans-Manchurian (via Hā'ěrbīn) branches of the Trans-Siberian Railway run from Běijīng to Moscow; see p1006 for more information.

There are also border crossings 9km from Mǎnzhōulǐ (see p856) and at Hēihé.

Tajikistan

At the time of writing, the Qolma (Kulma) Pass, linking Kashgar with Murghab, was not yet open to foreign travellers. See p797 for more information.

Vietnam

Visas are unobtainable at border crossings; Vietnam visas can be acquired in Běijīng (p986), Kūnmíng (p987), Hong Kong (p987) and Nánníng (p604). Chinese visas can be obtained in Hanoi.

FRIENDSHIP PASS

China's busiest border with Vietnam is at the obscure Vietnamese town of Dong Dang, 164km northeast of Hanoi. The closest Chinese town to the border is Píngxiáng in Guǎngxī province, about 10km north of the actual border gate. See p610 for information about the border crossing, and for transport between Píngxiáng and Vietnam.

Seven Hanoi-bound buses run from Nánníng via the Friendship Pass; twice-weekly trains (T5 and T6) connect Běijīng and Hanoi (via Nánníng) while Border Yúnnán daily train (T8701 and T8702) links Hanoi with Nánníng.

HÉKǑU

The Hékǒu–Lao Cai border crossing is 468km from Kūnmíng and 294km from Hanoi. At the time of writing, the only way to reach Vietnam via Hékǒu was by bus from Kūnmíng; see p643.

INTERNATIONAL TRAIN ROUTES

In addition to the Trans-Siberian and Trans-Mongolian rail services, the following routes can be travelled by train:

» Hung Hom station in Kowloon (Jiǔlóng; Hong Kong; www.throughtrain.kcrc.com; p501) to Guǎngzhōu, Shànghǎi, Běijīng.

» Pyongyang (North Korea) to Běijīng (p108)

» Almaty (Kazakhstan) to Ürümqi (p783)

» Astana (Kazakhstan) to Ürümqi (p783)

» Běijīng to Ulaanbaatar (p108)

» Běijīng to Hanoi (p108)

For more information and advice on international trains from Běijīng, see the box on international trains (p108) in the Běijīng chapter.

MONG CAI

A third, but little-known border crossing is at Mong Cai in the northeast corner of the country, just opposite the Chinese city of Dōngxīng and around 200km south of Nánníng.

River

At the time of writing, fast ferries from Jǐnghóng in Yúnnán to Chiang Saen in Thailand had been suspended; see p693 for more information.

Sea

Japan

There are weekly ferries between Osaka and Kōbe and Shànghǎi (see p220). From Tiānjīn (Tánggū), a weekly ferry runs to Kōbe in Japan; see p127. There are also twice-weekly boats from Qīngdǎo to Shimonoseki; see p169.

Check in two hours before departure for international sailings.

South Korea

International ferries connect the South Korean port of Incheon with Wēihǎi, Qīngdǎo (p169), Yāntái (p175), Tiānjīn (Tánggū; p127), Dàlián (p301) and Dāndōng (p306). There are also boats between Qīngdǎo and Gunsan (p169).

In Seoul, tickets for any boats to China can be bought from the **International Union Travel Agency** (☎822-777 6722; Room 707, 7th fl, Daehan Ilbo Bldg, 340 Taepyonglo 2-ga, Chung-gu). In China, tickets can be bought cheaply at the pier, or from **China International Travel Service** (CITS; Zhōngguó Guójì Lüxíngshè) for a very steep premium.

To reach the International Passenger Terminal from Seoul, take the Seoul-Incheon commuter train (metro Line 1 from the city centre) and get off at the Dongincheon station. The train journey takes 50 minutes. From Dongincheon station it's either a 45-minute walk or five-minute taxi ride to the ferry terminal.

GETTING AROUND

For travel around China by train, see the China by Train chapter (p1004).

Air

Despite being a land of vast distances, it's quite straightforward to navigate your way terrestrially around China by rail and bus if you have time. The high-speed rail network in particular has vastly expanded over the last decade, shrinking journey times and competing with airlines.

China's air network is extensive and growing. The civil aviation fleet is expected to triple in size over the next two decades, up to 56 new airports have been planned for construction and scores more are to be expanded or upgraded. Air safety and quality have improved considerably, but the speed of change generates its own problems: a serious shortage of qualified personnel to fly planes means China will need a reported 18,000 new pilots by 2015.

Shuttle buses usually run from **Civil Aviation Administration of China** (CAAC; Zhōngguó Mínháng) offices in towns and cities throughout China to the airport, often running via other stops; see the Getting Around sections of relevant chapters. For domestic flights, arrive at the airport one hour before departure.

Remember to keep your baggage receipt label on your ticket as you will need to show it when you collect your luggage. Planes vary in style and comfort. You may get a hot meal, or just a small piece of cake and an airline souvenir. On-board announcements are delivered in Chinese and English.

Airlines in China

The CAAC is the civil aviation authority for numerous airlines which include:

Sea Routes

0 250 km
0 150 miles

BĚIJĪNG • Dāndōng

Tiānjīn (Tánggū) • Dàlián

NORTH KOREA

SEA OF JAPAN

Yāntái • Wēihǎi

SEOUL • Incheon

SOUTH KOREA

Qīngdǎo • Gunsan

CHINA

YELLOW SEA

JAPAN
Nagasaki
To Kōbe, Shimonoseki

Shànghǎi

To Osaka and Kōbe

Air China (⏺in China 95583; www.airchina.com.cn)

Chengdu Airlines (⏺in Chengdu 028-6666 8888; www.chengduair.cc)

China Eastern Airlines (⏺in Shànghǎi 95530; www.ceair.com)

China Southern Airlines (⏺in Guǎngzhōu 4006 695 539; www.csair.com/en) Serves a web of air routes, including Běijīng, Shànghǎi, Xī'ān and Tiānjīn.

Hainan Airlines (⏺in Hǎinán 950712; www.hnair.com)

Shandong Airlines (⏺400-60-96777; www.shandongair.com.cn)

Shanghai Airlines (⏺in Shànghǎi 95530; www.ceair.com) Owned by China Eastern Airlines.

Shenzhen Airlines (⏺in Shēnzhèn 95080; www.shenzhenair.com)

Sichuan Airlines (⏺in Chéngdū 4008 300 999; www.scal.com.cn)

Spring Airlines (⏺in Shànghǎi 800 820 6222; www.china-sss.com) Has connections between Shànghǎi and tourist destinations such as Qīngdǎo, Guìlín, Xiàmén and Sānyà.

Tianjin Airlines (⏺in Tiānjīn 950710; www.tianjin-air.com)

Some of the above airlines also have subsidiary airlines. Not all Chinese airline websites have English-language capability. Airline schedules and airfares are listed within the relevant chapters.

The CAAC publishes a combined international and domestic timetable in both English and Chinese in April and November each year. This timetable can be bought at some airports and CAAC offices in China. Individual airlines also publish timetables, which you can buy from ticket offices throughout China.

Tickets

Except during major festivals and holidays, tickets are easy to purchase, with an oversupply of airline seats. Purchase tickets from branches of the CAAC nationwide, airline offices, travel agents or the travel desk of your hotel; travel agents will usually offer a better discount than airline offices. Discounts are common, except when flying into large cities such as Shànghǎi and Běijīng on the weekend, when the full fare can be the norm; prices quoted in this book are the full fare. For cheap flights, visit www.elong.com, www.Ctrip.com or www.travelzen.com (note that some users have reported difficulty using foreign credit cards on Ctrip). Fares are calculated according to one-way travel, with return tickets simply costing twice the single fare. If flying from Hong Kong or Macau to mainland China, note that these are classified as international flights; it is much cheaper to travel overland into Shēnzhèn, Zhūhǎi or Guǎngzhōu and fly from there.

You can use credit cards at most CAAC offices and travel agents. Departure tax is included in the ticket price.

Bicycle

Bikes (自行车; zìxíngchē) are an excellent method for getting around China's cities and tourist sights. They can also be invaluable for exploring the countryside surrounding towns such as Yángshuò.

Hire

A growing number of cities – Hángzhōu for example – have foreigner-friendly bike hire networks with docking stations dotted around the town. You will need to show your passport and hand over a sizeable deposit (around ¥300) but usage fees are generally very good value, with a cost structure that generally encourages shorter journeys (sometimes free for the first hour). Otherwise the best places to try are youth hostels which rent out bicycles, as do many hotels, although the latter are more expensive. Bicycle-hire outlets that cater to travellers are listed in destination chapters.

Bikes can be hired by the day or by the hour and it is also possible to hire for more than one day. Rental rates vary depending on where you find yourself, but rates start at around ¥10 to ¥15 per day in cities such as Běijīng.

Touring

Cycling through China allows you to go when you want, to see what you want and at your own pace. It can also be an extremely cheap, as well as a highly authentic, way to see the land.

You will have virtually unlimited freedom of movement but, considering the size of China, you will need to combine your cycling days with trips by train, bus, boat, taxi or even planes, especially if you want to avoid particularly steep regions, or areas where the roads are poor or the climate is cold.

A basic packing list for cyclists includes a good bicycle-repair kit, sunscreen and other protection from the sun, waterproofs, fluorescent strips and camping equipment. Ensure you have adequate clothing, as many routes will be taking you to considerable altitude. Road maps in Chinese are essential for asking locals for directions.

Bikechina (www.bikechina.com) arranges tours and is a good source of information for cyclists coming to China.

Boat

Boat services within China are limited, especially with the growth of high-speed rail and expressways. They're most common in coastal areas, where you are likely to use a boat to reach offshore islands such as Pǔtuóshān or Hǎinán, or the islands off Hong Kong. The Yāntái–Dàlián ferry will probably survive because it saves hundreds of kilometres of overland travel.

The best-known river trip is the three-day boat ride along the Yangzi (Cháng Jiāng) from Chóngqìng to Yíchāng (p770). The Lí River (Lí Jiāng) boat trip from Guìlín to Yángshuò (p589) is a popular tourist ride.

Hong Kong employs an out-and-out navy of vessels that connects with the territory's myriad islands, and a number of boats run between the territory and other parts of China, including Macau, Zhūhǎi, Shékǒu (for Shēnzhèn) and Zhōngshān. See p463 for details.

Boat tickets can be purchased from passenger ferry terminals or through travel agents.

Bus

Long-distance bus (长途公 共汽车; chángtú gōnggòng qìchē) services are extensive and reach places you cannot reach by train; with the increasing number of intercity highways, journeys are getting quicker.

Buses & Stations

Routes between large cities sport larger, cleaner and more comfortable fleets of private buses, some equipped with toilets and hostesses handing out snacks and mineral water; shorter and more far-flung routes still rely on rattling minibuses into which as many fares as possible are crammed. Buses often wait until they fill up before leaving, or (exasperatingly) trawl the streets looking for fares.

Sleeper buses (卧铺客 车; wòpù kèchē) ply popular long-haul routes, costing around double the price of a normal bus service. Bunks can be short, however, and buses are claustrophobic and impossible to escape if there is a fire.

Bus journey times given throughout this book should be used as a rough guide only. You can estimate times for bus journeys on nonhighway routes by calculating the distance against a speed of 25km per hour.

All cities and most towns have one or more longdistance bus stations (长途 汽车站; chángtú qìchēzhàn), generally located in relation to the direction the bus heads in. Most bus stations have a leftluggage counter. In many cities, the train station forecourt doubles as a bus station.

Tickets

Tickets are getting more expensive as fuel prices increase but are cheaper and easier to get than train tickets; turn up at the bus station and buy your ticket there and then. The earlier you buy, the closer to the front of the bus you will sit, although you may not be able to buy tickets prior to your day of travel.

Tickets can be hard to procure during national holiday periods.

Dangers & Annoyances

Breakdowns can be a hassle, and some rural roads and provincial routes (especially in the southwest, Tibet and the northwest) remain in bad condition. Precipitous drops, pot holes, dangerous road surfaces and reckless drivers mean accidents remain common. Long-distance journeys can also be cramped and noisy, with Hong Kong films and cacophonous karaoke looped on overhead TVs. Drivers continuously lean on the horn (taking an MP3 player is crucial for one's sanity). Note the following when travelling by bus.

» Seat belts are a rarity in many provinces.

» Take plenty of warm clothes on buses to highaltitude destinations in winter. A breakdown in frozen conditions can prove lethal for those unprepared.

» Take a lot of extra water on routes across areas such as the Taklamakan Desert.

Car & Motorcycle

Hiring a car in China has always been complicated or impossible for foreign visitors and in mainland China is currently limited to Běijīng and Shànghǎi, cities that both have frequently gridlocked roads. Throw in the dangers, complexity of Chinese roads for first-time users and the costs of driving in China and it makes more sense to use the subway/metro system and taxis, both of which are cheap and efficient in Běijīng and Shànghǎi. Hiring a car with a driver from your hotel is possible, but it's generally far cheaper and more convenient to hire a taxi (p1003) for the day instead.

Driving Licence

To drive in Hong Kong and Macau, you will need an International Driving Permit. Foreigners can drive motorcycles if they are residents in China and have an official Chinese motorcycle licence. International driving permits are generally not accepted in China.

Hire

Běijīng Capital Airport has a **Vehicle Administration Office** (车管所; chēguǎnsuǒ; ☎010-6453 0010; ☉9am-6pm Mon-Sun) where you can have a temporary three-month driving licence issued (an international driver's licence is insufficient). This will involve checking your driving licence and a simple medical exam (including an eyesight test). You will need this licence before you can hire a car from **Hertz** (☎400-888-1336; www.hertzchina. com), which has branches at Capital Airport. Check out the Hertz office (☎021-6085 1900; Terminal 2; ☉8am-8pm Mon-Fri & 9am-6pm Sat-Sun) at Shànghǎi's Pǔdōng International Airport for how to obtain a temporary licence in Shànghǎi. There are also branches in both central Běijīng and Shànghǎi. Hire cars from Hertz start from ¥230 per day (up to 150km per day; ¥20,000 deposit). **Avis** (☑400 882 1119) also has a growing network around China, with car rental starting from ¥200 per day (¥5000 deposit). See the Hong Kong and Macau chapters for details on car hire in each of those territories.

Road Rules

Cars in China drive on the right-hand side of the road. Even skilled drivers will be unprepared for China's roads: in the cities, cars lunge from all angles and chaos abounds.

Local Transport

Long-distance transport in China is good, but local transport is less efficient, except for cities with metro systems. The choice of local transport is diverse but vehicles can be slow and overburdened, and the network confusing for visitors. Hiring a car is often impractical, while hiring a bike can be inadequate. Unless the town is small, walking is often too tiring. On the plus side, local transport is cheap, taxis are usually ubiquitous and affordable, and metro systems continue to rapidly expand in large tourist towns.

Bus

With extensive networks, buses are an excellent way to get around town, but foreign travellers rarely use them. Ascending a bus, point to your destination on a map and the conductor (seated near the door) will sell you the right ticket. The conductor will usually tell you where to disembark, provided they remember. In conductor-less buses, you put money in a slot near the driver as you embark.

» Fares are very cheap (usually ¥1 to ¥2) but buses may be packed.

» Navigation is tricky for non-Chinese speakers as bus routes at bus stops are generally listed in Chinese, without Pinyin.

» In Běijīng and Shànghǎi and other large tourist towns, stops will be announced in English.

» Always have change ready if there is no conductor on the bus.

» Buses with snowflake motifs are air-conditioned.

» Traffic can make things slow.

Subway, Metro & Light Rail

Going underground or using light rail is fast, efficient and cheap; most networks are either very new or relatively recent and can be found in a rapidly growing number of cities, including Běijīng, Shànghǎi, Sūzhōu, Xī'ān, Hángzhōu, Tiānjīn, Chéngdū, Shēnzhèn, Wǔhàn and Hong Kong.

Taxi

Taxis (出租汽车; *chūzū qìchē*) are cheap and easy to find. Taxi rates per kilometre are clearly marked on a sticker on the rear side window of the taxi; flag fall varies from city to city and depends upon the size and quality of the vehicle. Rates are listed in the Getting Around section of destinations.

Most taxis have meters but they may only be switched on in larger towns and cities. If the meter is not used (on an excursion out of town, for example, or when hiring a taxi for the day or half-day), negotiate a price before you set off and write the fare down. If you want the meter used, ask for *dǎbiǎo* (打表). Also ask for a receipt (发票; *fāpiào*); if you leave something in the taxi, the taxi number is printed on the receipt so it can be located.

Note that:

» Congregation points include train and long-distance bus stations, but usually you can just flag taxis down.

» Taxi drivers rarely speak any English so have your destination written down in characters.

» If you have communication problems, consider using your mobile to phone your hotel for staff to interpret.

» You can hire taxis on a daily or half-day basis, often at reasonable rates (always bargain).

» To use the same driver again, ask for his or her card (名片; *míngpiàn*).

» In many provinces, taxis often cover long-distance bus routes. They generally charge around 30% to 50% more but are much faster. You need to wait for four passengers.

Other Local Transport

A variety of ramshackle transport options exist across China; always agree on a price in advance (preferably have it written down).

» **Motor pedicabs** are enclosed three-wheeled vehicles (often the same price as taxis).

» **Pedicabs** are pedal-powered versions of motor pedicabs.

» **Motorbike** riders also offer lifts in some towns for what should be half the price of a regular taxi. You must wear a helmet – the driver will provide one.

China by Train

Trains are the best way to travel long distance around China in reasonable speed and comfort. They are also adventurous, exciting, fun, practical and efficient, and ticket prices are reasonable to boot. Colossal investment over recent years has put high-speed rail at the heart of China's rapid modernisation drive. You really don't have to be a trainspotter to find China's railways a riveting subculture and you get to meet the Chinese people at their most relaxed and sociable.

The Chinese Train Network

One of the world's most extensive rail networks, passenger railways penetrate every province in China and high-speed connections are suddenly everywhere. In line with China's frantic economic development and the pressures of transporting 1.4 billion people across the world's third-largest nation, expansion of China's rail network over the past decade has been mindboggling.

The network was due to total 110,000km by the end of 2012.

The railway to Lhasa in Tibet began running in 2006, despite scepticism that it could ever be laid, so you can climb aboard a train in Běijīng or Shànghǎi and alight in Tibet's capital (although ticket scarcity for trains into Lhasa means it's easier to fly in and take the train out). Lines are poking further into Tibet, with a line to Shigatse expected by 2014. Thousands of miles of track are laid every year and new express trains have been zipping across China since 2007, shrinking once daunting distances. State-of-the-art train stations are ceaselessly appearing, many to serve high-speed links.

With the advent of high-speed D, G and C class express trains, getting between major cities is increasingly

a breeze (albeit far more expensive than regular fast trains). In 2011, an ultra-high-speed railway was unveiled between Běijīng and Shànghǎi, compressing the journey to around five hours. A high-speed link should connect Běijīng and Xī'ān by 2014. High-speed rail has put the squeeze on numerous domestic air routes and the punctuality of trains sees far fewer delays than airports.

A fatal high-speed train crash in Wēnzhōu in 2011 that killed 40 people was blamed on flawed equipment and management errors. The accident attracted a lot of public attention, particularly when compared to Japan's high-speed network (operating without a single fatality since the 1960s). After the crash, expansion of the (loss-making) high-speed program was scaled back, but the network continues to grow.

For international trains to and from China, see the Transport chapter (p999).

Trains

Chinese train numbers are usually (but not always) prefixed by a letter, designating the category of train.

High Speed Trains

The fastest, most luxurious and expensive intercity trains are the streamlined, high-speed C, D and G trains, which rapidly shuttle between major cities, such as Běijīng and Tiānjīn and Běijīng and Shànghǎi.

REGULAR TRAINS

TYPE	PINYIN	CHINESE	TOP SPEED
Z class (express)	zhídá	直达	160km/h
T class	tèkuài	特快	140km/h
K class	kuàisù	快速	120km/h

HIGH-SPEED TRAINS

TYPE	PINYIN	CHINESE	TOP SPEED
C class	Chéngjì	城际	350km/h
D class	Dòngchē	动车	250km/h
G class	Gāotiě	高铁	350km/h

High-speed C class trains are currently limited to the route between Běijīng and Tiānjīn. D class trains were the first high-speed trains to appear and breathlessly glide around China at high speed, offering substantial comfort and regular services. D class temperature-regulated 1st-class carriages have mobile and laptop chargers, seats are two abreast with ample legroom and TV sets. Second-class carriages have five seats in two rows. Doors between carriages open with electric buttons. G class trains are faster than D class trains and lines include Běijīng to Shànghǎi, Wǔhàn to Guǎngzhōu and Zhèngzhōu to Xī'ān. Luggage space on G class trains is very limited. The Shànghǎi Maglev is China's fastest train with a top speed of 431km/h, but the route is limited to a 30km section between Pǔdōng International Airport and Longyang Rd metro station.

Less fast express classes include the overnight Z class trains, while further down the pecking order are T and K class trains, which are older and more basic.

There are also numbered trains that do not commence with a letter; these are pǔkuài (普快) or pǔkè (普客) trains, with a top speed of around 120km/h.

Travelling by Train

Trains are generally highly punctual in China and are usually a safe way to travel. Train stations are often conveniently close to the centre of town. Travelling on sleeper berths at night means you can frequently arrive at your destination first thing in the morning, saving a night's hotel accommodation. Think ahead, get your tickets early and you can sleep your way around a lot of China.

On entering a large station (eg Shànghǎi South Train Station), you will have to find the correct waiting room number, displayed on an illuminated screen as you walk in.

Trolleys of food and drink are wheeled along carriages during the trip, but prices are high and the selection is limited. You can also load up on mineral water and snacks at stations, where hawkers sell items from platform stalls. Long-distance trains should have a canteen carriage (餐厅车厢; cāntīng chēxiāng); they are sometimes open through the night.

In each class of sleeper, linen is clean and changed for each journey; beds are generally bedbug-free. Staff rarely speak English, except sometimes on the high-speed express trains.

If taking a sleeper train, you will be required to exchange your paper ticket for a plastic or metal card with your bunk number on it. The conductor then knows when you are due to disembark, and will awake you in time to return your ticket to you. Hold on to your paper ticket for possible inspection at the train station exit.

Some do's and don'ts regarding train travel:

» Don't leave it till the very last minute to board your train, as queues outside the main train station entrance can be shocking.

» You are required to pass your bags through a security scanner at the train station entrance.

» On long train trips, load up with snacks, food and drinks for the journey.

» On a non-sleeper, ask a member of staff or a fellow passenger to tell you when your station arrives.

» If you are a light sleeper, take earplugs on sleepers as there's usually a snorer.

Ticket Types

It is possible to upgrade (补票; bǔpiào) your ticket once aboard your train. If you have a standing ticket, for example, find the conductor and upgrade to a hard seat, soft seat, hard sleeper, soft sleeper (if there are any available) or different class.

Soft Sleeper

Soft sleepers are a very comfortable way to travel and work perfectly as mobile hotels; tickets cost much more than hard-sleeper tickets and often sell out, however, so book early. Soft sleepers vary between trains and the best are on the more recent D and Z class trains. All Z class trains are soft-sleeper trains, with very comfortable, up-to-date berths. A few T class trains also offer two-berth compartments, with their own toilet. Tickets on upper berths are slightly cheaper than lower berths. Expect to share with total strangers. If you are asleep, an attendant will wake you to prepare you to disembark so you will have plenty of time to ready your things.

Soft sleeper carriages contain:

» Four air-conditioned bunks (upper and lower) in a closed compartment.

» Bedding on each berth and a lockable door to the carriage corridor.

TRAVELLING THE TRANS-SIBERIAN RAILWAY

Rolling out of Europe and into Asia, through eight time zones and over 9289km of taiga, steppe and desert, the Trans-Siberian Railway and its connecting routes constitute one of the most famous and most romantic of the world's great train journeys.

There are, in fact, three railways. The 'true' **Trans-Siberian** line runs from Moscow to Vladivostok. But the routes traditionally referred to as the Trans-Siberian Railway are the two branches that veer off the main line in eastern Siberia for Běijīng.

Since the first option excludes China, most readers of this book will be choosing between the **Trans-Mongolian** and the **Trans-Manchurian** railway lines. The Trans-Mongolian route (Běijīng to Moscow, 7865km) is faster, but requires an additional visa and another border crossing – on the plus side, you also get to see some of the Mongolian countryside. The Trans-Manchurian route is longer (Běijīng to Moscow, 9025km).

See Lonely Planet's *Trans-Siberian Railway* for further details.

Routes

TRANS-MONGOLIAN RAILWAY

Trains offer deluxe two-berth compartments (with shared shower), 1st-class four-berth compartments and 2nd-class four-berth compartments. Tickets for 2nd-class/deluxe compartments cost from around ¥4049/6527 to Moscow, ¥1430/2250 to Ulaanbaatar and ¥3000/4800 to Novosibirsk. Ticket prices are cheaper if you travel in a group.

» From Běijīng: train K3 leaves Běijīng Train Station on its five-day journey to Moscow at 7.45am every Wednesday, passing through Dàtóng, Ulaanbaatar and Novosibirsk, arriving in Moscow the following Monday at 1.58pm.

» From Moscow: train K4 leaves at 9.35pm on Tuesdays, arriving in Běijīng Train Station the following Monday at 2.04pm. Departure and arrival times may fluctuate slightly.

TRANS-MANCHURIAN RAILWAY

Trains have 1st-class two-berth compartments and 2nd-class four-berth compartments; prices are similar to those on the Trans-Mongolian Railway.

» From Běijīng: train K19 departs Běijīng Train Station at 11pm on Saturday arriving in Moscow (via Manzhōulǐ) the following Friday at 5.58pm.

» From Moscow: train K20 leaves Moscow at 11.55pm on Saturday, arriving at Běijīng Train Station the following Friday at 5.32am. Departure and arrival times may fluctuate slightly.

» Meals, flat-screen TVs and power sockets on some routes.

» A small table and stowing space for your bags.

» Each compartment is equipped with its own hot-water flask, filled by an attendant.

Hard Sleeper

Hard sleepers are available on slower and less modern T, K and N class trains, as well as trains without a letter prefix. As with soft sleeper, they serve very nicely as an overnight hotel.

There is a small price difference between the numbered berths, with the lowest bunk (下铺; *xiàpù*) the most expensive and the highest bunk (上铺; *shàngpù*) the cheapest. The middle bunk (中铺; *zhōngpù*) is good, as all and sundry invade the lower berth to use it as a seat during the day, while the top one has little headroom and puts you near the speakers. As with soft sleepers, an attendant will wake you well in advance of your station.

Hard-sleeper tickets are the most difficult of all to buy; you almost always need to buy these a few days in advance. Expect:

» Doorless compartments with half a dozen bunks in three tiers.

» Sheets, pillows and blankets on each berth.

» A no-smoking policy.

» Lights and speakers out at around 10pm.

» Each compartment is equipped with its own hot-water flask, filled by an attendant.

» Trolleys passing by selling food and drink.

» A rack above the windows for stowing your baggage.

Seats

Soft-seat class is more comfortable but not nearly as common as hard-seat class. First-class (一等; *yīděng*) and 2nd-class (二等; *èrděng*) soft seats are available in D, C and G class high-speed trains.

Visas

Travellers will need Russian and Mongolian visas for the Trans-Mongolian Railway, as well as a Chinese visa. These can often be arranged along with your ticket by travel agents such as China International Travel Service (CITS).

Mongolian visas – either two-day transit visas (¥180) or 30-day tourist visas (¥270) – take three to five days to process. Urgent visas can be arranged in one day for a surcharge. A transit visa is easy to get (present a through ticket and a visa for your onward destination). The situation regarding visas changes regularly, so check with a Mongolian embassy or consulate. All Mongolian embassies shut for the week of National Day (Naadam), which officially falls around 11 to 13 July.

Russian transit visas (one-week/three-day/one-day process US$50/80/120) are valid for 10 days if you take the train, but will only give you three or four days in Moscow at the end of your journey. You need one photo, your passport and the exact amount in US dollars. You will also need a valid entry visa for a third country plus a through ticket from Russia to the third country. You can also obtain a 30-day Russian tourist visa, but the process is complicated.

Buying Tickets

Book well in advance (especially in summer); in Běijīng tickets can be conveniently purchased and booked in advance in central Běijīng from **CITS** (Zhōngguó Guójì Lǚxíngshè; www.cits.net; ☑010-6512 0507; Běijīng International Hotel, 9 Jianguomen Neidajie), for a mark-up. **Monkey Shrine** (www.monkeyshrine.com; Youyi Youth Hostel, 43 Beisanlitun Lu) in Běijīng also arranges trips, and has an informative website with a downloadable brochure. There's another **branch** (☑852-2723 1376; Liberty Mansion, Kowloon) in Hong Kong.

Abroad, tickets (and sometimes visas) can be arranged through an agency:

Intourist UK (www.intouristuk.com)
Russia Experience (☑0845 521-2910; www.trans-siberian.co.uk)
Trans-Sputnik Nederland (www.trans-sputnik.nl)
Vodkatrain (www.vodkatrain.com)

Useful Websites

The Man in Seat 61 (www.seat61.com/Trans-Siberian) Reams of information on travelling the Trans-Siberian Railway.

First-class comes with TVs, mobile phone and laptop charging points, and seats arranged two abreast.

Second-class soft seats are also very comfortable; staff are very courteous throughout. Overcrowding is not permitted. On older trains, soft-seat carriages are often double-decker, and are not as plush as the faster and more modern high-speed express trains.

Hard-seat class is not available on the faster and plusher C, D and G class trains, and is only found on T and K class trains and trains without a number prefix; a handful of Z class trains have hard seat. Hard-seat class generally has padded seats, but it's hard on your sanity; often unclean and noisy, and painful on the long haul.

Since hard seat is the only class most locals can afford, it's packed to the gills.

You should get a ticket with an assigned seat number; if seats have sold out, ask for a standing ticket, which gets you on the train, where you may find a seat or can upgrade; otherwise you will have to stand in the carriage or between carriages (with the smokers).

Hard-seat sections on China's newer trains are air-conditioned and less crowded.

Ticketing
Buying Tickets

The Achilles heel of China's overburdened rail system, buying tickets can be a pain.

Most tickets are one way only, with prices calculated per kilometre and adjustments made depending on class of train, availability of air-con, type of sleeper and bunk positioning.

Some tips on buying train tickets:

» Never aim to get a hard-sleeper (or increasingly, soft-sleeper) ticket on the day of travel – plan ahead.

» Most tickets can be booked in advance between

two and 10 days prior to your intended date of departure.

» Buying tickets for hard-seat carriages at short notice is usually no hassle, but it may be a standing ticket rather than a numbered seat.

» Tickets are only purchasable with cash.

» You will need your passport when buying a ticket (the number is printed on your ticket) at all train ticket offices.

» Most automated ticket machines (eg at Shànghǎi Train Station) require Chinese ID and your passport will not work; you will need to queue at the ticket window.

» Tickets for hard sleepers are usually obtainable in major cities, but are trickier to buy in quiet backwaters.

» As with air travel, buying tickets around the Chinese New Year and the 1 May and 1 October holiday periods can be very hard, and prices increase on some routes.

» Tickets on many routes (such as to Lhasa) can be very hard to get in July and August so prepare to take a flight to distant destinations.

» Expect to queue for up to half an hour or more for a train ticket at the station.

» Try to use train ticket offices outside of the station

(addresses are listed through the book).

» Avoid black market tickets: your passport number must be on the ticket.

» There are no refunds for lost train tickets.

Your ticket will display:

» The train number.

» The name of your departure and destination stations in Chinese and Pinyin.

» The time and date of travel.

» Your carriage and seat (or berth) number.

» The ticket price.

» Your passport number (second from bottom).

CHINA TRAIN ROUTES

ROUTE	DURATION	FARE (SEAT/SLEEPER)
Běijīng West–Liǔyuán (for Dūnhuáng)	24hr	Hard/soft sleeper ¥458/705
Běijīng West–Guìlín	23hr	Hard seat/sleeper ¥242/438
Běijīng–Hāěrbīn	9hr	2nd/1st class ¥267/333
Běijīng South–Hángzhōu	6½hr	2nd/1st class ¥631/1058
Běijīng West–Kūnmíng	38hr	Hard seat/sleeper ¥320/578
Běijīng West–Lhasa	44hr	Hard/soft sleeper ¥766/1189
Běijīng South–Qīngdǎo	4½hr	2nd/1st class ¥315/475
Běijīng South–Shànghǎi	5hr	2nd/1st class ¥555/935
Běijīng South–Tiānjīn	33min	2nd/1st class ¥55/66
Shànghǎi Hóngqiáo–Hángzhōu	1hr	2nd/1st class ¥78/124
Shànghǎi–Hong Kong	18½hr	Hard seat/sleeper ¥226/409
Shànghǎi–Lhasa	48hr	Hard seat/sleeper ¥406/845
Shànghǎi–Nánjīng	1½hr	2nd/1st class ¥135/230
Shànghǎi Hóngqiáo–Wǔhàn	6hr	2nd/1st class ¥265/317
Shànghǎi Hóngqiáo–Xiàmén	8hr	2nd/1st class ¥339/408
Shànghǎi–Xī'ān	14hr	Hard sleeper/soft sleeper ¥333/511
Chéngdū–Chóngqìng North	2hr	2nd/1st class ¥98/117
Guǎngzhōu South–Shēnzhèn North	40min	2nd/1st class ¥75/100
Hohhot–Yínchuān	10hr	Hard/soft sleeper ¥175/264
Kūnmíng–Chéngdū	20hr	2nd/1st class ¥143/263
Lánzhōu–Ürümqi	21hr	Hard seat/hard sleeper ¥215/390
Ürümqi–Kashgar	24hr	Hard/soft sleeper ¥345/529
Wǔhàn–Guǎngzhōu South	4hr	2nd/1st class ¥445/710
Xī'ān–Zhèngzhōu	2hr	2nd/1st class ¥230/370
Xī'ān North–Ürümqi	34hr	Hard/soft sleeper ¥287/494

TRAIN TICKETS

TICKET TYPE	PINYIN	CHINESE
soft sleeper	*ruǎnwò*	软卧
hard sleeper	*yìngwò*	硬卧
soft seat	*ruǎnzuò*	软座
hard seat	*yìngzuò*	硬座
standing ticket	*wúzuò* or *zhànpiào*	无座\站票

Ticket Offices

Ticket offices (售票厅; *shòupiàotīng*) at train stations are usually to one side of the main train station entrance. Automated ticket machines operate on few routes and usually don't accept foreign passports as ID. At large stations there should be a window manned by someone with basic English skills.

Alternatively, independent train ticket offices usually exist elsewhere in town where tickets can be purchased for a ¥5 commission without the same kind of queues; these are listed throughout the book. Larger post offices may also sell train tickets.

Your hotel will also be able to rustle up a ticket for you for a commission, and so can a travel agent.

Telephone booking services exist, but operate only in Chinese.

You can buy tickets online at www.12306.cn but the website is Chinese language only and you will need a Chinese bankcard. It's cheaper to buy your ticket at the station, but tickets can be bought online at:

Travel China Guide (www.travelchinaguide.com)

China Trip Advisor (www.chinatripadvisor.com)

China Train Timetable (www.china-train-ticket.com)

For trains from Hong Kong to Shànghǎi, Guǎngzhōu or Běijīng, tickets can be ordered online at no mark-up from **KCRC** (www.mtr.com.hk).

You can also find English-language train timetables on these websites, as printed timetables for the entire country (¥7), published every April and October, are only available in Chinese.

To get a refund (退票; *tuìpiào*) on an unused ticket, windows exist at large train stations where you can get 80% of the ticket value back.

Internet Resources

Seat 61 (www.seat61.com/China.htm)

Travel China Guide (www.travelchinaguide.com)

Tielu (www.tielu.org, in Chinese)

China Tibet Train (www.chinatibettrain.com)

Health

China is a reasonably healthy country to travel in, but some health issues should be noted. Pre-existing medical conditions and accidental injury (especially traffic accidents) account for most life-threatening problems, but becoming ill in some way is not unusual. Outside of the major cities, medical care is often inadequate, and food and waterborne diseases are common. Malaria is still present in some parts of the country, and altitude sickness can be a problem, particularly in Tibet.

In case of accident or illness, it's best just to get a taxi and go to hospital directly.

The following advice is a general guide only and does not replace the advice of a doctor trained in travel medicine.

BEFORE YOU GO

» Pack medications in their original, clearly labelled containers.

» If you take any regular medication, bring double your needs in case of loss or theft.

» Take a signed and dated letter from your physician describing your medical conditions and medications (using generic names).

» If carrying syringes or needles, ensure you have a physician's letter documenting their medical necessity.

» If you have a heart condition, bring a copy of your ECG taken just prior to travelling.

» Get your teeth checked before you travel.

» If you wear glasses, take a spare pair and your prescription.

In China you can buy some medications over the counter without a doctor's prescription, but not all, and in general it is not advisable to buy medications locally without a doctor's advice. Fake medications and poorly stored or out-of-date drugs are also common, so try and take your own.

Insurance

» Even if you are fit and healthy, don't travel without health insurance – accidents happen.

» Declare any existing medical conditions you have (the insurance company *will* check if your problem is pre-existing and will not cover you if it is undeclared).

» You may require extra cover for adventure activities such as rock climbing or skiing.

» If you're uninsured, emergency evacuation is expensive; bills of more than US$100,000 are not uncommon.

» Ensure you keep all documentation related to any medical expenses you incur.

Vaccinations

Specialised travel-medicine clinics stock all available vaccines and can give specific recommendations for your trip. The doctors will consider your vaccination history, the length of your trip, activities you may undertake and underlying medical conditions, such as pregnancy.

» Visit a doctor six to eight weeks before departure, as most vaccines don't produce immunity until at least two weeks after they're given.

» Ask your doctor for an International Certificate of Vaccination (otherwise known as the 'yellow booklet'), listing all vaccinations received.

» The only vaccine required by international regulations is yellow fever.

Proof of vaccination against yellow fever is only required if you have visited a country in the yellow-fever zone within the six days prior to entering China. If you are travelling to China directly from South America or Africa, check with a travel clinic as to whether you need a yellow-fever vaccination.

Medical Checklist

Recommended items for a personal medical kit:

» Antibacterial cream, eg mucipirocin

» Antibiotics for diarrhoea, including norfloxacin, ciprofloxacin or azithromycin for bacterial diarrhoea; or tinidazole for giardia or amoebic dysentery

» Antibiotics for skin infections, eg amoxicillin/clavulanate or cephalexin

» Antifungal cream, eg clotrimazole

» Antihistamine, eg cetrizine for daytime and promethazine for night-time

» Anti-inflammatory, eg ibuprofen

» Antiseptic, eg Betadine

» Antispasmodic for stomach cramps, eg Buscopan

» Decongestant, eg pseudoephedrine

» Diamox if going to high altitudes

» Elastoplasts, bandages, gauze, thermometer (but not mercury), sterile needles and syringes, safety pins and tweezers

» Indigestion tablets, such as Quick-Eze or Mylanta

» Insect repellent containing DEET

» Iodine tablets to purify water (unless you're pregnant or have a thyroid problem)

» Laxative, eg coloxyl

» Oral-rehydration solution (eg Gastrolyte) for diarrhoea, diarrhoea 'stopper' (eg loperamide) and antinausea medication (eg prochlorperazine)

» Paracetamol

» Permethrin to impregnate clothing and mosquito nets

» Steroid cream for rashes, eg 1% to 2% hydrocortisone

» Sunscreen

» Thrush (vaginal yeast infection) treatment, eg clotrimazole pessaries or Diflucan tablet

» Urinary infection treatment, eg Ural

Websites

Centers for Disease Control & Prevention (CDC; www.cdc.gov)
Lonely Planet (www.lonely planet.com)

HEALTH ADVISORIES

It's usually a good idea to consult your government's travel-health website before departure, if one is available.

Australia (www.dfat.gov.au/travel)
Canada (www.travelhealth.gc.ca)
New Zealand (www.mfat.govt.nz/travel)
UK (www.dh.gov.uk) Search for travel in the site index.
USA (www.cdc.gov/travel)

MD Travel Health (www.mdtravelhealth.com) Provides complete travel-health recommendations for every country; updated daily.
World Health Organization (WHO; www.who.int/ith) Publishes the excellent *International Travel & Health*, revised annually and available online at no cost.

Further Reading

Healthy Travel – Asia & India (Lonely Planet) Handy pocket size, packed with useful information.
Traveller's Health by Dr Richard Dawood.
Travelling Well (www.travel lingwell.com.au) by Dr Deborah Mills.

IN CHINA

Availability of Health Care

Good clinics catering to travellers can be found in major cities. They are more expensive than local facilities but you may feel more comfortable dealing with a Western-trained doctor who speaks your language. These clinics usually have a good understanding of the best local hospital facilities and close contacts with insurance companies should you need evacuation.

Self-treatment may be appropriate if your problem is minor (eg traveller's diarrhoea), you are carrying the relevant medication and you cannot attend a clinic. If you think you may have a serious disease, especially malaria, do not waste time – get to the nearest quality facility. To find the nearest reliable medical facility, contact your insurance company or your embassy. Hospitals are listed in the Information section in cities and towns throughout the book.

Infectious Diseases

Dengue

This mosquito-borne disease occurs in some parts of southern China. There is no vaccine so avoid mosquito bites. The dengue-carrying mosquito bites day and night, so use insect-avoidance measures at all times. Symptoms include high fever, severe headache and body ache. Some people develop a rash and diarrhoea. There is no specific treatment – just rest and paracetamol. Do not take aspirin. See a doctor to be diagnosed and monitored.

Hepatitis A

A problem throughout China, this food-and-waterborne virus infects the liver, causing jaundice (yellow skin and eyes), nausea and lethargy. There is no specific treatment for hepatitis A; you just need to allow time for the liver to heal. All travellers to China should be vaccinated.

RECOMMENDED VACCINATIONS

The World Health Organization (WHO) recommends the following vaccinations for travellers to China:

Adult diphtheria and tetanus (ADT) Single booster recommended if you've not received one in the previous 10 years. Side effects include a sore arm and fever. An ADT vaccine that immunises against pertussis (whooping cough) is also available and may be recommended by your doctor.

Hepatitis A Provides almost 100% protection for up to a year; a booster after 12 months provides at least another 20 years' protection. Mild side effects such as a headache and sore arm occur in 5% to 10% of people.

Hepatitis B Now considered routine for most travellers. Given as three shots over six months; a rapid schedule is also available. There is also a combined vaccination with hepatitis A. Side effects are mild and uncommon, usually a headache and sore arm. Lifetime protection results in 95% of people.

Measles, mumps and rubella (MMR) Two doses of MMR is recommended unless you have had the diseases. Occasionally a rash and a flulike illness can develop a week after receiving the vaccine. Many adults under 40 require a booster.

Typhoid Recommended unless your trip is less than a week. The vaccine offers around 70% protection, lasts for two to three years and comes as a single shot. Tablets are also available; however, the injection is usually recommended as it has fewer side effects. A sore arm and fever may occur. A vaccine combining hepatitis A and typhoid in a single shot is now available.

Varicella If you haven't had chickenpox, discuss this vaccination with your doctor.

The following immunisations are recommended for travellers spending more than one month in the country or those at special risk:

Influenza A single shot lasts one year and is recommended for those over 65 years of age or with underlying medical conditions such as heart or lung disease.

Japanese B encephalitis A series of three injections with a booster after two years. Recommended if spending more than one month in rural areas in the summer months, or more than three months in the country.

Pneumonia A single injection with a booster after five years is recommended for all travellers over 65 years of age or with underlying medical conditions that compromise immunity, such as heart or lung disease, cancer or HIV.

Rabies Three injections in all. A booster after one year will then provide 10 years' protection. Side effects are rare – occasionally a headache and sore arm.

Tuberculosis A complex issue. High-risk adult long-term travellers are usually recommended to have a TB skin test before and after travel, rather than vaccination. Only one vaccine is given in a lifetime. Children under five spending more than three months in China should be vaccinated.

Pregnant women and children should receive advice from a doctor who specialises in travel medicine.

Hepatitis B

The only sexually transmitted disease that can be prevented by vaccination, hepatitis B is spread by contact with infected body fluids. The long-term consequences can include liver cancer and cirrhosis. All travellers to China should be vaccinated.

Japanese B Encephalitis

A rare disease in travellers; however, vaccination is recommended if you're in rural areas for more than a month during summer months, or if spending more than three months in the country. No treatment available; one-third of infected people die, another third suffer permanent brain damage.

Malaria

Malaria has been nearly eradicated in China; it is not generally a risk for visitors to the cities and most tourist areas. It is found mainly in rural areas in the southwestern region bordering Myanmar, Laos and Vietnam, principally Hǎinán, Yúnnán and Guǎngxī. More limited risk exists in the remote rural areas of Fújiàn, Guǎngdōng, Guìzhōu and Sìchuān. Generally, medication is only advised if you are visiting rural Hǎinán, Yúnnán or Guǎngxī.

To prevent malaria:

» Avoid mosquitoes and take antimalaria medications (most people who catch malaria are taking inadequate or no antimalaria medication).

» Use an insect repellent containing DEET on exposed skin (natural repellents such as citronella can be effective, but require more frequent application than products containing DEET).

» Sleep under a mosquito net impregnated with permethrin.

» Choose accommodation with screens and fans (if it's not air-conditioned).

» Impregnate clothing with permethrin in high-risk areas.

» Wear long sleeves and trousers in light colours.

» Use mosquito coils.

» Spray your room with insect repellent before going out for your evening meal.

Rabies

An increasingly common problem in China, this fatal disease is spread by the bite or lick of an infected animal, most commonly a dog. Seek medical advice immediately after any animal bite and commence postexposure treatment. The pretravel vaccination means the post-bite treatment is greatly simplified.

If an animal bites you:

» Gently wash the wound with soap and water, and apply an iodine-based antiseptic.

» If you are not prevaccinated, you will need to receive rabies immunoglobulin as soon as possible, followed by a series of five vaccines over the next month. Those who

have been prevaccinated require only two shots of vaccine after a bite.

» Contact your insurance company to locate the nearest clinic stocking rabies immunoglobulin and vaccine. Immunoglobulin is often unavailable outside of major centres, but it's crucial that you get to a clinic that has immunoglobulin as soon as possible if you have had a bite that has broken the skin.

Schistosomiasis (Bilharzia)

This disease occurs in the central Yangzi River (Cháng Jiāng) basin, carried in water by minute worms that infect certain varieties of freshwater snail found in rivers, streams, lakes and, particularly, behind dams. The infection often causes no symptoms until the disease is well established (several months to years after exposure); any resulting damage to internal organs is irreversible. Effective treatment is available.

» Avoid swimming or bathing in fresh water where bilharzia is present.

» A blood test is the most reliable way to diagnose the disease, but the test will not show positive until weeks after exposure.

Typhoid

Typhoid is a serious bacterial infection spread via food and water. Symptoms include headaches, a high and slowly progressive fever, perhaps accompanied by a dry cough and stomach pain. Vaccination is not 100% effective, so still be careful what you eat and drink. All travellers spending more than a week in China should be vaccinated.

Traveller's Diarrhoea

Between 30% and 50% of visitors will suffer from traveller's diarrhoea within two weeks of starting their trip. In most cases, the ailment is caused by bacteria and responds promptly to treatment with antibiotics.

Treatment consists of staying hydrated; rehydration solutions such as Gastrolyte are best. Antibiotics such as norfloxacin, ciprofloxacin or azithromycin will kill the bacteria quickly. Loperamide is just a 'stopper' and doesn't cure the problem; it can be helpful, however, for long bus rides. Don't take loperamide if you have a fever, or blood in your stools. Seek medical attention if you do not respond to an appropriate antibiotic.

DRINKING WATER

Follow these tips to avoid becoming ill.

» Never drink tap water.

» Bottled water is generally safe – check the seal is intact at purchase.

» Avoid ice.

» Avoid fresh juices – they may have been watered down.

» Boiling water is the most efficient method of purifying it.

» The best chemical purifier is iodine. It should not be used by pregnant women or those with thyroid problems.

» Water filters should also filter out viruses. Ensure your filter has a chemical barrier such as iodine and a pore size of less than 4 microns.

» Eat only at busy restaurants with a high turnover of customers.

» Eat only freshly cooked food.

» Avoid food that has been sitting around in buffets.

» Peel all fruit, cook vegetables and soak salads in iodine water for at least 20 minutes.

Amoebic Dysentery

Amoebic dysentery is actually rare in travellers and is overdiagnosed. Symptoms are similar to bacterial diarrhoea – fever, bloody diarrhoea and generally feeling unwell. Always seek reliable medical care if you have blood in your diarrhoea. Treatment involves two drugs: tinidazole or metronidazole to kill the parasite in your gut, and then a second drug to kill the cysts. If amoebic dysentery is left untreated, complications such as liver or gut abscesses can occur.

Giardiasis

Giardiasis is a parasite relatively common in travellers. Symptoms include nausea, bloating, excess gas, fatigue and intermittent diarrhoea. 'Eggy' burps are often attributed solely to giardia, but are not specific to the parasite. Giardiasis will eventually go away if left untreated, but this can take months. The treatment of choice is tinidazole, with metronidazole a second option.

Intestinal Worms

These parasites are most common in rural, tropical areas. Some may be ingested in food such as undercooked meat (eg tapeworms) and some enter through your skin (eg hookworms). Infestations may not show up for some time, and although they are generally not serious, some can cause severe health problems later if left untreated. Consider having a stool test when you return home.

Environmental Hazards

Air Pollution

Air pollution is a significant problem in many Chinese cities. People with underlying respiratory conditions should seek advice from their doctor prior to travel to ensure they have adequate medications in case their condition worsens. Take treatments such as throat lozenges, and cough and cold tablets.

Altitude Sickness

There are bus journeys in Tibet, Qīnghǎi and Xīnjiāng where the road goes above 5000m. Acclimatising to such extreme elevations takes several weeks at least, but most travellers come up from sea level very fast – a bad move! Acute mountain sickness (AMS) results from a rapid ascent to altitudes above 2700m. It usually commences within 24 to 48 hours of arriving at altitude, and symptoms include headache, nausea, fatigue and loss of appetite (feeling much like a hangover).

If you have altitude sickness, the cardinal rule is that you must not go higher as you are sure to get sicker and could develop one of the more severe and potentially deadly forms of the disease: high-altitude pulmonary oedema (HAPE) and high-altitude cerebral oedema (HACE). Both are medical emergencies and, as there are no rescue facilities similar to those in the Nepal Himalaya, prevention is the best policy.

AMS can be prevented by 'graded ascent'; it is recommended that once you are above 3000m you ascend a maximum of 300m daily with an extra rest day every 1000m. You can also use a medication called Diamox as a prevention or treatment for AMS, but you should discuss this first with a doctor experienced in altitude medicine.

Diamox should not be taken by people with a sulphur drug allergy.

If you have altitude sickness, rest where you are for a day or two until your symptoms resolve. You can then carry on, but ensure you follow the graded-ascent guidelines. If symptoms get worse, descend immediately before you are faced with a life-threatening situation. There is no way of predicting who will suffer from AMS, but certain factors predispose you to it: rapid ascent, carrying a heavy load, and having a seemingly minor illness such as a chest infection or diarrhoea. Make sure you drink at least 3L of noncaffeinated drinks daily to stay well hydrated. The sun is intense at altitude so take care with sun protection.

Heat Exhaustion

Dehydration or salt deficiency can cause heat exhaustion. Take time to acclimatise to high temperatures, drink sufficient liquids and avoid physically demanding activity.

Salt deficiency is characterised by fatigue, lethargy, headaches, giddiness and muscle cramps; salt tablets may help, adding extra salt to your food is better.

Hypothermia

Be particularly aware of the dangers of trekking at high altitudes or simply taking a long bus trip over mountains. In Tibet it can go from being mildly warm to blisteringly cold in minutes – blizzards can appear from nowhere.

Progress from very cold to dangerously cold can be rapid due to a combination of wind, wet clothing, fatigue and hunger, even if the air temperature is above freezing. Dress in layers; silk, wool and some artificial fibres are all good insulating materials. A hat is important, as a lot of heat is lost through the head. A strong, waterproof outer layer (and a space blanket for emergencies) is essential.

Carry basic supplies, including food containing simple sugars, and fluid to drink.

Symptoms of hypothermia are exhaustion, numb skin (particularly the toes and fingers), shivering, slurred speech, irrational or violent behaviour, lethargy, stumbling, dizzy spells, muscle cramps and violent bursts of energy.

To treat mild hypothermia, first get the person out of the wind and/or rain, remove their clothing if it's wet, and replace it with dry, warm clothing. Give them hot liquids – not alcohol – and high-calorie, easily digestible food. Early recognition and treatment of mild hypothermia is the only way to prevent severe hypothermia, a critical condition that requires medical attention.

Insect Bites & Stings

Bedbugs don't carry disease but their bites are very itchy. Treat the itch with an antihistamine.

Lice inhabit various parts of the human body, most commonly the head and pubic areas. Transmission is via close contact with an affected person. Lice can be difficult to treat, but electric lice combs/detectors can be effective (pick one up before travelling); otherwise you may need numerous applications of an antilice shampoo such as permethrin. Pubic lice (crab lice) are usually contracted from sexual contact.

Ticks are contracted by walking in rural areas, and are commonly found behind the ears, on the belly and in armpits. If you have had a tick bite and experience symptoms such as a rash, fever or muscle aches, see a doctor. Doxycycline prevents some tick-borne diseases.

Women's Health

Pregnant women should receive specialised advice before travelling. The ideal time to travel is in the second trimester (between 14 and 28 weeks), when the risk of pregnancy-related problems is at its lowest and pregnant women generally feel at their best. During the first trimester, miscarriage is a risk; in the third trimester, complications such as premature labour and high blood pressure are possible. Travel with a companion and carry a list of quality medical facilities for your destination, ensuring you continue your standard antenatal care at these facilities. Avoid rural areas with poor transport and medical facilities. Most of all, ensure travel insurance covers all pregnancy-related possibilities, including premature labour.

Malaria is a high-risk disease in pregnancy. The World Health Organization recommends that pregnant women do not travel to areas with chloroquine-resistant malaria.

Traveller's diarrhoea can quickly lead to dehydration and result in inadequate blood flow to the placenta. Many drugs used to treat various diarrhoea bugs are not recommended in pregnancy. Azithromycin is considered safe.

Heat, humidity and antibiotics can all contribute to thrush. Treatment is with antifungal creams and pessaries such as clotrimazole. A practical alternative is a single tablet of fluconazole (Diflucan). Urinary tract infections can be precipitated by dehydration or long bus journeys without toilet stops; bring suitable antibiotics.

Supplies of sanitary products may not be readily available in rural areas. Birth-control options may be limited, so bring adequate supplies of your own form of contraception.

Traditional Chinese Medicine

Traditional Chinese Medicine (TCM) views the human body as an energy system in which the basic substances of qì (气; vital energy), jīng (精; essence), xuè (血; blood) and tǐyè (体液; body fluids, blood and other organic fluids) function. The concept of yīn (阴) and yáng (阳) is fundamental to the system. Disharmony between yīn and yáng or within the basic substances may be a result of internal causes (emotions), external causes (climatic conditions) or miscellaneous causes (work, exercise, stress etc). Treatment includes acupuncture, massage, herbs, diet and qì gōng (气功), which seeks to bring these elements back into balance. Treatments can be particularly useful for treating chronic diseases and ailments such as fatigue, arthritis, irritable bowel syndrome and some chronic skin conditions.

Be aware that 'natural' does not always mean 'safe'; there can be drug interactions between herbal medicines and Western medicines. If using both systems, ensure you inform both practitioners what the other has prescribed.

WANT MORE?

For in-depth language information and handy phrases, check out Lonely Planet's *China Phrasebook*. You'll find it at **shop .lonelyplanet.com**, or you can buy Lonely Planet's iPhone phrasebooks at the Apple App Store.

Language

Discounting its many ethnic minority languages, China has eight major dialect groups: Pǔtōnghuà (Mandarin), Yue (Cantonese), Wu (Shanghainese), Minbei (Fuzhou), Minnan (Hokkien-Taiwanese), Xiang, Gan and Hakka. These dialects also divide into subdialects.

It's the language spoken in Běijīng which is considered the official language of China. It's usually referred to as Mandarin, but the Chinese themselves call it Pǔtōnghuà (meaning 'common speech'). Pǔtōnghuà is variously referred to as Hànyǔ (the Han language), Guóyǔ (the national language) or Zhōngwén or Zhōngguóhuà (Chinese). With the exception of the western and southernmost provinces, most of the population speaks Mandarin (although it may be spoken there with a regional accent). In this chapter, we have included Mandarin, Cantonese, Tibetan, Uighur and Mongolian.

MANDARIN

Writing

Chinese is often referred to as a language of pictographs. Many of the basic Chinese characters are in fact highly stylised pictures of what they represent, but around 90% are compounds of a 'meaning' element and a 'sound' element.

A well-educated, contemporary Chinese person might use between 6000 and 8000 characters. To read a Chinese newspaper you need to know 2000 to 3000 characters, but 1200 to 1500 would be enough to get the gist.

Theoretically, all Chinese dialects share the same written system. In practice, Cantonese adds about 3000 specialised characters of its own and many of the dialects don't have a written form at all.

Pinyin & Pronunciation

In 1958 the Chinese adopted Pinyin, a system of writing their language using the Roman alphabet. The original idea was to eventually do away with Chinese characters. However, tradition dies hard, and the idea was abandoned.

Pinyin is often used on shop fronts, street signs and advertising billboards. Don't expect all Chinese people to be able to use Pinyin, however. In the countryside and the smaller towns you may not see a single Pinyin sign anywhere, so unless you speak and read Chinese you'll need a phrasebook with Chinese characters.

Below we've provided Pinyin alongside the Mandarin script.

Vowels

a	as in 'father'
ai	as in 'aisle'
ao	as the 'ow' in 'cow'
e	as in 'her' (without 'r' sound)
ei	as in 'weigh'
i	as the 'ee' in 'meet' (or like a light 'r')
	as in 'Grrr!' after c, ch, r, s, sh, z or zh)
ian	as the word 'yen'
ie	as the English word 'yeah'
o	as in 'or' (without 'r' sound)
ou	as the 'oa' in 'boat'
u	as in 'flute'
ui	as the word 'way'
uo	like a 'w' followed by 'o'
yu/ü	like 'ee' with lips pursed

Consonants

c	as the 'ts' in 'bits'
ch	as in 'chop', but with the tongue curled up and back
h	as in 'hay', but articulated from further back in the throat
q	as the 'ch' in 'cheese'
sh	as in 'ship', but with the tongue curled up and back
x	as the 'sh' in 'ship'
z	as the 'ds' in 'suds'
zh	as the 'j' in 'judge' but with the tongue curled up and back

The only consonants that occur at the end of a syllable are n, ng and r.

In Pinyin, apostrophes are occasionally used to separate syllables in order to prevent ambiguity, eg the word píng'ān can be written with an apostrophe after the 'g' to prevent it being pronounced as pín'gān.

Tones

Mandarin is a language with a large number of words with the same pronunciation but a different meaning. What distinguishes these homophones (as these words are called) is their 'tonal' quality – the raising and the lowering of pitch on certain syllables. Mandarin has four tones – high, rising, falling-rising and falling, plus a fifth 'neutral' tone that you can all but ignore. Tones are important for distinguishing meaning of words – eg the word ma has four different meanings according to tone, as shown below. Tones are indicated in Pinyin by the following accent marks on vowels:

high tone	mā (mother)
rising tone	má (hemp, numb)
falling-rising tone	mǎ (horse)
falling tone	mà (scold, swear)

Basics

When asking a question it is polite to start with qǐng wèn – literally, 'May I ask?'.

Hello.	你好。	Nǐhǎo.
Goodbye.	再见。	Zàijiàn.
How are you?	你好吗?	Nǐhǎo ma?
Fine. And you?	好。你呢?	Hǎo. Nǐ ne?
Excuse me. (to get attention)	劳驾。	Láojià.
(to get past)	借光。	Jièguāng.
Sorry.	对不起。	Duìbùqǐ.
Yes./No.	是。/不是。	Shì./Bùshì.
Please ...	请……	Qǐng ...
Thank you.	谢谢你。	Xièxie nǐ.
You're welcome.	不客气。	Bù kèqi.

KEY PATTERNS – MANDARIN

To get by in Mandarin, mix and match these simple patterns with words of your choice:

How much is (the deposit)?
(押金)多少? (Yājīn) duōshǎo?

Do you have (a room)?
有没有(房)? Yǒuméiyǒu (fáng)?

Is there (heating)?
有(暖气)吗? Yóu (nuǎnqì) ma?

I'd like (that one).
我要(那个)。 Wǒ yào (nàge).

Please give me (the menu).
请给我(菜单)。 Qǐng gěiwǒ (càidān).

Can I (sit here)?
我能(坐这儿)吗? Wǒ néng (zuòzhèr) ma?

I need (a can opener).
我想要(一个开罐器)。 Wǒ xiǎngyào (yīge kāiguàn qì).

Do we need (a guide)?
需要(向导)吗? Xūyào (xiàngdǎo) ma?

I have (a reservation).
我有(预订)。 Wǒ yǒu (yùdìng).

I'm (a doctor).
我(是医生)。 Wǒ (shì yīshēng).

What's your name?
你叫什么名字? Nǐ jiào shénme míngzi?

My name is ...
我叫…… Wǒ jiào ...

Do you speak English?
你会说英文吗? Nǐ huìshuō Yīngwén ma?

I don't understand.
我不明白。 Wǒ bù míngbái.

Accommodation

Do you have a single/double room?
有没有(单人/套)房? Yǒuméiyǒu (dānrén/tào) fáng?

How much is it per night/person?
每天/人多少钱? Měi tiān/rén duōshǎo qián?

campsite	露营地	lùyíngdì
guesthouse	宾馆	bīnguǎn
hostel	招待所	zhāodàisuǒ
hotel	酒店	jiǔdiàn
air-con	空调	kōngtiáo
bathroom	浴室	yùshì
bed	床	chuáng
cot	张婴儿床	zhāng yīng'ér chuáng
window	窗	chuāng

Signs – Mandarin

入口	Rùkǒu	**Entrance**
出口	Chūkǒu	**Exit**
问讯处	Wènxùnchù	**Information**
开	Kāi	**Open**
关	Guān	**Closed**
禁止	Jìnzhǐ	**Prohibited**
厕所	Cèsuǒ	**Toilets**
男	Nán	**Men**
女	Nǚ	**Women**

Directions

Where's (a bank)?
(银行) 在哪儿？ (Yínháng) zài nǎr?

What's the address?
地址在哪儿？ Dìzhǐ zài nǎr?

Could you write the address, please?
能不能请你 Néngbunéng qǐng nǐ
把地址写下来？ bǎ dìzhǐ xiě xiàlái?

Can you show me where it is on the map?
请帮我找它在 Qǐng bāngwǒ zhǎo tā zài
地图上的位置。 dìtú shàng de wèizhi.

Go straight ahead.
一直走。 Yìzhí zǒu.

Turn left.
左转。 Zuǒ zhuǎn.

Turn right.
右转。 Yòu zhuǎn.

at the traffic lights	在红绿灯	zài hónglǜdēng
behind	背面	bèimiàn
far	远	yuǎn
in front of ...	……的前面	... de qiánmian
near	近	jìn
next to	旁边	pángbiān
on the corner	拐角	guǎijiǎo
opposite	对面	duìmiàn

Eating & Drinking

What would you recommend?
有什么菜可以 Yǒu shénme cài kěyǐ
推荐的? tuījiàn de?

What's in that dish?
这道菜用什么 Zhèdào cài yòng shénme
东西做的? dōngxi zuòde?

That was delicious.
真好吃。 Zhēn hǎochī.

The bill, please!
买单! Mǎidān!

Cheers!
干杯! Gānbēi!

I'd like to reserve 我想预订 Wǒ xiǎng yùdìng
a table for ... 一张…… yìzhāng ...
的桌子。 de zhuōzi.

  (eight) o'clock （八）点钟 (bā) diǎn zhōng
  (two) people （两个）人 (liǎngge) rén

I don't eat ... 我不吃…… Wǒ bùchī ...
  fish 鱼 yú
  nuts 果仁 guǒrén
  poultry 家禽 jiāqín
  red meat 牛羊肉 niúyángròu

Key Words

appetisers	凉菜	liángcài
bar	酒吧	jiǔbā
bottle	瓶子	píngzi
bowl	碗	wǎn
breakfast	早饭	zǎofàn
cafe	咖啡屋	kāfēiwū
chidren's menu	儿童菜单	értóng càidān
(too) cold	（太）凉	(tài) liáng
dinner	晚饭	wǎnfàn
dish (food)	盘	pán
food	食品	shípǐn
fork	叉子	chāzi
glass	杯子	bēizi
halal	清真	qīngzhēn
highchair	高凳	gāodèng
hot (warm)	热	rè
knife	刀	dāo
kosher	犹太	yóutài
local specialties	地方小吃	dìfāng xiǎochī
lunch	午饭	wǔfàn
main courses	主菜	zhǔ cài
market	菜市	càishì
menu (in English)	（英文）菜单	(Yīngwén) càidān
plate	碟子	diézi
restaurant	餐馆	cānguǎn
(too) spicy	（太）辣	(tài) là
spoon	勺	sháo
vegetarian food	素食食品	sùshí shípǐn

Meat & Fish

beef	牛肉	niúròu
chicken	鸡肉	jīròu
duck	鸭	yā
fish	鱼	yú

LANGUAGE MANDARIN

lamb	羊肉	yángròu
pork	猪肉	zhūròu
seafood	海鲜	hǎixiān

Fruit & Vegetables

apple	苹果	píngguǒ
banana	香蕉	xiāngjiāo
bok choy	小白菜	xiǎo báicài
carrot	胡萝卜	húluóbo
celery	芹菜	qíncài
cucumber	黄瓜	huángguā
'dragon eyes'	龙眼	lóngyǎn
fruit	水果	shuǐguǒ
grape	葡萄	pútáo
green beans	扁豆	biǎndòu
guava	石榴	shíliu
lychee	荔枝	lìzhī
mango	芒果	mángguǒ
mushroom	蘑菇	mógū
onion	洋葱	yáng cōng
orange	橙子	chéngzi
pear	梨	lí
pineapple	凤梨	fènglí
plum	梅子	méizi
potato	土豆	tǔdòu
radish	萝卜	luóbo
spring onion	小葱	xiǎo cōng
sweet potato	地瓜	dìguā
vegetable	蔬菜	shūcài
watermelon	西瓜	xīguā

Other

bread	面包	miànbāo
butter	黄油	huángyóu
egg	蛋	dàn
herbs/spices	香料	xiāngliào
pepper	胡椒粉	hújiāo fěn
salt	盐	yán

Question Words – Mandarin

How?	怎么?	Zěnme?
What?	什么?	Shénme?
When?	什么时候	Shénme shíhòu?
Where?	哪儿?	Nǎr?
Which?	哪个	Nǎge?
Who?	谁?	Shuí?
Why?	为什么?	Wèishénme?

soy sauce	酱油	jiàngyóu
sugar	砂糖	shātáng
tofu	豆腐	dòufu
vinegar	醋	cù
vegetable oil	菜油	càiyóu

Drinks

beer	啤酒	píjiǔ
Chinese spirits	白酒	báijiǔ
coffee	咖啡	kāfēi
(orange) juice	(橙)汁	(chéng) zhī
milk	牛奶	niúnǎi
mineral water	矿泉水	kuàngquán shuǐ
red wine	红葡萄酒	hóng pútáo jiǔ
rice wine	米酒	mǐjiǔ
soft drink	汽水	qìshuǐ
tea	茶	chá
(boiled) water	(开)水	(kāi) shuǐ
white wine	白葡萄酒	bái pútáo jiǔ
yoghurt	酸奶	suānnǎi

Emergencies

Help!	救命!	Jiùmìng!
I'm lost.	我迷路了。	Wǒ mílù le.
Go away!	走开!	Zǒukāi!

There's been an accident.
出事了。 Chūshì le.

Call a doctor!
请叫医生来! Qǐng jiào yīshēng lái!

Call the police!
请叫警察! Qǐng jiào jǐngchá!

I'm ill.
我生病了。 Wǒ shēngbìng le.

It hurts here.
这里痛。 Zhèlǐ tòng.

Where are the toilets?
厕所在哪儿? Cèsuǒ zài nǎr?

Shopping & Services

I'd like to buy ...
我想买…… Wǒ xiǎng mǎi ...

I'm just looking.
我先看看。 Wǒ xiān kànkan.

Can I look at it?
我能看看吗? Wǒ néng kànkan ma?

I don't like it.
我不喜欢。 Wǒ bù xǐhuan.

Numbers – Mandarin

1	一	yī
2	二/两	èr/liǎng
3	三	sān
4	四	sì
5	五	wǔ
6	六	liù
7	七	qī
8	八	bā
9	九	jiǔ
10	十	shí
20	二十	èrshí
30	三十	sānshí
40	四十	sìshí
50	五十	wǔshí
60	六十	liùshí
70	七十	qīshí
80	八十	bāshí
90	九十	jiǔshí
100	一百	yībǎi
1000	一千	yīqiān

How much is it?
多少钱？ Duōshǎo qián?

That's too expensive.
太贵了。 Tàiguì le.

Can you lower the price?
能便宜一点吗？ Néng piányi yīdiǎn ma?

There's a mistake in the bill.
帐单上 Zhàngdān shàng
有问题。 yǒu wèntí.

ATM	自动取款机	zìdòng qǔkuǎn jī
credit card	信用卡	xìnyòng kǎ
internet cafe	网吧	wǎngbā
post office	邮局	yóujú
tourist office	旅行店	lǚxíng diàn

Time & Dates

What time is it?
现在几点钟？ Xiànzài jǐdiǎn zhōng?

It's (10) o'clock.
（十）点钟。 (Shí) diǎn zhōng.

Half past (10).
（十）点三十分。 (Shí) diǎn sānshífēn.

morning	早上	zǎoshang
afternoon	下午	xiàwǔ
evening	晚上	wǎnshàng

yesterday	昨天	zuótiān
today	今天	jīntiān
tomorrow	明天	míngtiān
Monday	星期一	xīngqī yī
Tuesday	星期二	xīngqī èr
Wednesday	星期三	xīngqī sān
Thursday	星期四	xīngqī sì
Friday	星期五	xīngqī wǔ
Saturday	星期六	xīngqī liù
Sunday	星期天	xīngqī tiān
January	一月	yīyuè
February	二月	èryuè
March	三月	sānyuè
April	四月	sìyuè
May	五月	wǔyuè
June	六月	liùyuè
July	七月	qīyuè
August	八月	bāyuè
September	九月	jiǔyuè
October	十月	shíyuè
November	十一月	shíyīyuè
December	十二月	shí èryuè

Transport
Public Transport

boat	船	chuán
bus (city)	大巴	dàbā
bus (intercity)	长途车	chángtú chē
plane	飞机	fēijī
taxi	出租车	chūzū chē
train	火车	huǒchē
tram	电车	diànchē

I want to go to ...
我要去…… Wǒ yào qù ...

Does it stop at (Hāěrbīn)?
在(哈尔滨)能下 Zài (Hāʻěrbīn) néng xià
车吗？ chē ma?

At what time does it leave?
几点钟出发？ Jǐdiǎnzhōng chūfā?

At what time does it get to (Hángzhōu)?
几点钟到 Jǐdiǎnzhōng dào
(杭州)？ (Hángzhōu)?

Can you tell me when we get to (Hángzhōu)?
到了(杭州) Dàole (Hángzhōu)
请叫我，好吗？ qǐng jiào wǒ, hǎoma?

I want to get off here.
我想这儿下车。 Wǒ xiǎng zhèr xiàchē.

When's the ... (bus)?	······(车) 几点走?	... (chē) jídiǎn zǒu?
first	首趟	Shǒutàng
last	末趟	Mòtàng
next	下一趟	Xià yītàng

A ... ticket to (Dàlián).	一张到 (大连)的 ······票。	Yīzhāng dào (Dàlián) de ... piào.
1st-class	头等	tóuděng
2nd-class	二等	èrděng
one-way	单程	dānchéng
return	双程	shuāngchéng

aisle seat	走廊的 座位	zǒuláng de zuòwèi
cancelled	取消	qǔxiāo
delayed	晚点	wǎndiǎn
platform	站台	zhàntái
ticket office	售票处	shòupiàochù
timetable	时刻表	shíkè biǎo
train station	火车站	huǒchēzhàn
window seat	窗户的 座位	chuānghu de zuòwèi

Driving & Cycling

bicycle pump	打气筒	dǎqìtóng
child seat	婴儿座	yīng'érzuò
diesel	柴油	cháiyóu
helmet	头盔	tóukuī
mechanic	机修工	jīxiūgōng
petrol	汽油	qìyóu
service station	加油站	jiāyóu zhàn

I'd like to hire a ...	我要租 一辆······	Wǒ yào zū yīliàng ...
4WD	四轮驱动	sìlún qūdòng
bicycle	自行车	zìxíngchē
car	汽车	qìchē
motorcycle	摩托车	mótuochē

Does this road lead to ...?
这条路到······吗?   Zhè tiáo lù dào ... ma?

How long can I park here?
这儿可以停多久?   Zhèr kěyǐ tíng duōjiǔ?

The car has broken down (at ...).
汽车是(在······)坏的。 Qìchē shì (zài ...) huài de.

I have a flat tyre.
轮胎瘪了。   Lúntāi biě le.

I've run out of petrol.
没有汽油了。   Méiyou qìyóu le.

CANTONESE

Cantonese is the most widely used Chinese language in Hong Kong, Macau, Guǎngdōng, parts of Guǎngxī and the surrounding region. Cantonese speakers use Chinese characters, but pronounce many of them differently from a Mandarin speaker. Also, Cantonese adds about 3000 characters of its own to the character set. Several systems of Romanisation for Cantonese script exist, and no single one has emerged as an official standard. In this chapter we use Lonely Planet's pronunciation guide, designed for maximum accuracy with minimum complexity.

Pronunciation

In Cantonese, the ng sound can appear at the start of a word. Words ending with the consonant sounds p, t, and k are clipped. Many speakers, particularly young people, replace the n with an l at the start of a word – eg náy (you) often sounds like láy. Where relevant, our pronunciation guide reflects this change.

The vowels are pronounced as follows: a as the 'u' in 'but', ai as in 'aisle' (short), au as the 'ou' in 'out', ay as in 'pay', eu as the 'er' in 'fern', eui as eu followed by i, ew as in 'blew' (short, with lips tightened), i as the 'ee' in 'deep', iu as the 'yu' in 'yuletide', o as in 'go', oy as in 'boy', u as in 'put', ui as in French oui.

Tones in Cantonese fall on vowels (a, e, i, o, u) and on n. The same word pronounced with different tones can have a different meaning, eg gwàt (dig up) vs gwàt (bones). There are six tones, divided into high- and low-pitch groups. High-pitch tones involve tightening the vocal muscles to get a higher note, while lower-pitch tones are made by relaxing the vocal chords to get a lower note. Tones are indicated with the following accent marks: à (high), á (high rising), à̠ (low falling), á̠ (low rising), a̠ (low), a (level – no accent mark).

Basics

Hello.	哈佬。	hàa·ló
Goodbye.	再见。	joy·gin
How are you?	你幾好 啊嗎?	láy gáy hó à maa
Fine.	幾好。	gáy hó
Excuse me.	對唔住。	deui·ng·jew
Sorry.	對唔住。	deui·ng·jew
Yes./No.	係。/不係。	hai/ng·hai
Please ...	唔該······	ng·gòy ...
Thank you.	多謝。	dàw·je

What's your name?
你叫乜嘢名?   láy giu màt·yé méng aa

My name is ...
我叫……   ngáw giu ...

Do you speak English?
你識唔識講   láy sìk·ǹg·sìk gáwng
英文啊？   yìng·mán aa

I don't understand.
我唔明。   ngáw ǹg mìng

Accommodation

campsite	營地	yìng·day
guesthouse	賓館	bàn·gún
hostel	招待所	jiù·doy·sáw
hotel	酒店	jáu·dim
Do you have a ... room?	有冇…… 房？	yáu·mó ... fáwng
double	雙人	sèung·yàn
single	單人	dàan·yàn
How much is it per ...?	一……幾多 錢？	yàt ... gáy·dàw chín
night	晚	máan
person	個人	gaw yàn

Directions

Where's ...?	……喺邊度？	... hái bìn·do
What's the address?	地址係？	day·jí hai
left	左邊	jáw·bìn
on the corner	十字路口	sap·ji·lo·háu
right	右邊	yau·bìn
straight ahead	前面	chìn·min
traffic lights	紅綠燈	hùng·luk·dàng

Eating & Drinking

What would you recommend?
有乜嘢好介紹？   yáu màt·yé hó gaai·siu

That was delicious.
真好味。   jàn hó·may

I'd like the bill, please.
唔該我要埋單。   ǹg·gòy ngáw yiu màai·dàan

Cheers!
乾杯！   gàwn·bùi

I'd like to book a table for ...	我想 訂張檯， ……嘅	ngáw séung deng jèung tóy ... ge
(eight) o'clock	(八) 點鐘	(bàat) dím·jùng
(two) people	(兩)位	(léung) ái

Numbers – Cantonese

1	一	yàt
2	二	yi
3	三	sàam
4	四	say
5	五	ńg
6	六	luk
7	七	chàt
8	八	baat
9	九	gáu
10	十	sap
20	二十	yi·sap
30	三十	sàam·sap
40	四十	say·sap
50	五十	ńg·sap
60	六十	luk·sap
70	七十	chàt·sap
80	八十	baat·sap
90	九十	gáu·sap
100	一百	yàt·baak
1000	一千	yàt·chìn

bar	酒吧	jáu·bàa
bottle	樽	jèun
breakfast	早餐	jó·chàan
cafe	咖啡屋	gaa·fè·ngùk
dinner	晚飯	máan·faan
fork	叉	chàa
glass	杯	bùi
knife	刀	dò
lunch	午餐	ńg·chàan
market	街市 (HK)	gàai·sí
	市場 (China)	sí·chèung
plate	碟	díp
restaurant	酒樓	jáu·làu
spoon	羹	gàng

Emergencies

Help!	救命！	gau·meng
I'm lost.	我蕩失路。	ngáw dawng·sàk·lo
Go away!	走開！	jáu·hòy

Call a doctor!
快啲叫醫生！   faai·dì giu yì·sàng

Call the police!
快啲叫警察！   faai·dì giu gíng·chaat

I'm sick.
我病咗。   ngáw beng·jáw

Shopping & Services

I'd like to buy ...
我想買······   ngáw séung máai ...

How much is it?
幾多錢?   gáy·dàw chín

That's too expensive.
太貴啦。   taai gwai laa

There's a mistake in the bill.
帳單錯咗。   jeung·dàan chaw jáw

internet cafe	網吧	máwng·bàa
post office	郵局	yàu·gúk
tourist office	旅行社	léui·hàng·sé

Time & Dates

What time is it?	而家 幾點鐘?	yi·gàa gáy·dím·jùng
It's (10) o'clock.	(十)點鐘。	(sap)·dím·jùng
Half past (10).	(十)點半。	(sap)·dím bun

morning	朝早	jiù·jó
afternoon	下晝	haa·jau
evening	夜晚	ye·máan
yesterday	寢日	kàm·yat
today	今日	gàm·yat
tomorrow	听日	tìng·yat

Transport

boat	船	sèwn
bus	巴士 (HK)	bàa·sí
	公共	gùng·gung
	汽車 (China)	hay·chè
train	火車	fáw·chè

A ... ticket to (Panyu).	一張去 (番禺)嘅 ······飛。	yàt jèung heui (pùn·yèw) ge ... fày
1st-class	頭等	tàu·dáng
2nd-class	二等	yi·dáng
one-way	單程	dàan·chìng
return	雙程	sèung·chìng

At what time does it leave?
幾點鐘出發?   gáy·dím jùng chèut·faa

Does it stop at ...?
會唔會喺······停呀?   wuí·ng·wuí hái ... tìng aa

At what time does it get to ...?
幾點鐘到······?   gáy·dím jùng do ...

TIBETAN

Tibetan is spoken by around six million people, mainly in Tibet. In urban areas almost all Tibetans also speak Mandarin.

Most sounds in Tibetan are similar to those found in English, so if you read our coloured pronunciation guides as if they were English, you'll be understood. Note that â is pronounced as the 'a' in 'ago', ö as the 'er' in 'her', and ü as the 'u' in 'flute' but with a raised tongue. A vowel followed by n, m or ng indicates a nasalised sound (pronounced 'through the nose'). A consonant followed by h is aspirated (accompanied by a puff of air).

There are no direct equivalents of English 'yes' and 'no' in Tibetan. Although it may not be completely correct, you'll be understood if you use la ong for 'yes' and la men for 'no'.

Hello.	བཀྲ་ཤིས་བདེ་ལེགས།	ta·shi de·lek
Goodbye.		
(if staying)	ག་ལེར་ཕེབས།	ka·lee pay
(if leaving)	ག་ལེར་བཞུགས།	ka·lee shu
Excuse me.	དགོངས་དག	gong·da
Sorry.	དགོངས་དག	gong·da
Please.	ཐུགས་རྗེ་གནང་གིས།	tu·jay·sig
Thank you.	ཐུགས་རྗེ་ཆེ།	tu·jay·chay

How are you?
ཁྱེད་རང་སྐུ་གཟུགས་ བདེ་པོ་ཡིན་པས།   kay·ràng ku·su de·po yin·bay

Fine. And you?
བདེ་པོ་ཡིན། ཁྱེད་རང་ཡང་ སྐུ་གཟུགས་བདེ་པོ་ཡིན་པས།   de·bo·yin kay·ràng·yâng ku·su de·po yin·bay

What's your name?
ཁྱེད་རང་གི་མཚན་ལ་ ག་རེ་རེད།   kay·ràng·gi tsen·là kâ·ray·ray

My name is ...
ངའི་མིང་ལ་ ... རེད།   ngay·ming·la ... ray

Do you speak English?
ཁྱེད་རང་དབྱིན་ཇི་སྐད་ ཤེས་ཀྱི་ཡོད་པས།   kay·ràng in·ji·kay shing·gi yö·bay

I don't understand.
ཧ་གོ་མ་སོང་།   ha ko ma·song

How much is it?
གོང་ག་ཚོད་རེད།   gong kâ·tsay ray

Where is ...?
... ག་བར་ཡོད་རེད།   ... ka·bah yö·ray

UIGHUR

Uighur is spoken all over Xīnjiāng. In China, Uighur is written in Arabic script. The phrases in this chapter reflect the Kashgar dialect.

In our pronunciation guides, stressed syllables are indicated with italics. Most consonant sounds in Uighur are the same as in English, though note that h is pronounced with a puff of air. The vowels are pronounced as follows: a as in 'hat', aa as the 'a' in 'father', ee as in 'sleep' (produced back in the throat), o as in 'go', ŏ as the 'e' in 'her' (pronounced with rounded lips), u as in 'put', and ü as the 'i' in 'bit' (with the lips rounded and pushed forward). Stressed syllables are in italics.

Basics

Hello.	ئەسسالامۇ	as·saa·laa·mu
	ئەلەيكۇم.	a·lay·kom
Goodbye.	خەير ـ خوش.	hayr·hosh
Excuse me.	گۆرۇڭچەككە	ka·chü·rüng ga
	قانداق	kaan·daak
	باردۇ؟	baar·i·du
Sorry.	گۆرۇڭچەك.	ka·chü·rüng
Yes.	ھەئە.	ee·a·a
No.	ياق.	yaak
Please.	مەرھەممەت.	ma·ree·am·mat
Thank you.	رەخمەت سىزگە.	rah·mat siz·ga

How are you?

| قانداق | kaan·daak |
| ئەھۋالىڭىز؟ | a·ee·vaa·li·ngiz |

Fine. And you?

| ياخشى، سىزچۇ؟ | yaah·shi siz·chu |

What's your name?

| سىزنىڭ | siz·ning |
| ئىسمىڭىز نىمە؟ | is·mi·ngiz ni·ma |

My name is ...

| مىنىڭ ئىسمىم ... | mi·ning is·mim ... |

Do you speak English?

| سىز ئىنگگىلىزچە | siz ing·gi·lis·ka |
| بىلەمسىز؟ | bi·lam·siz |

I don't understand.

| چۈشەنمىدىم. | man chu·shan·mi·dim |

How much is it?

| قانچە پۇل؟ | kaan·cha pool |

Where is ...?

| ... نەدە؟ | ... na·da |

MONGOLIAN

Mongolian has an estimated 10 million speakers. The standard Mongolian in the Inner Mongolia Autonomous Region of China is based on the Chahar dialect and written using a cursive script in vertical lines (ie from top to bottom), read from left to right. So if you want to ask a local to read the script in this section, just turn the book 90 degrees clockwise. Our coloured pronunciation guides, however, should simply be read the same way you read English.

Most consonant sounds in Mongolian are the same as in English, though note that r in Mongolian is a hard, trilled sound, kh is a throaty sound like the 'ch' in the Scottish loch, and z is pronounced as the 'ds' in 'lads'. As for the vowels, ē is pronounced as in 'there', ô as in 'alone', ŏ as 'e' with rounded lips, öö as a slightly longer ŏ, u as in 'cut' and ŭ as in 'good'.

In the pronunciation guides, stressed syllables are in italics.

Basics

Hello.

sēn bēn nô

Goodbye.

ba·yur·tē

Excuse me./Sorry.

ôch·lē·rē

Yes.

teem

No.

oo·gway

Thank you.

ba·yur·laa

How are you?

sēn bēn nô

Fine. And you?

sēn sēn
sēn nô

What's your name?

tan·nē al·dur

My name is ...

min·nee nur ...

Do you speak English?

ta ang·gul hul
mu·tun nô

I don't understand.

bee oil·og·sun·gway

How much is it?

hut·tee jôs vē

Where's ...?

... haa bēkh vē

GLOSSARY

apsara – Buddhist celestial being
arhat – Buddhist, especially a monk, who has achieved enlightenment and passes to nirvana at death

běi – north; the other points of the compass are *dōng* (east), *nán* (south) and *xī* (west)
biānjiè – border
biéshù – villa
bīnguǎn – hotel
bìxì – mythical tortoiselike dragon
Bodhisattva – one worthy of nirvana who remains on earth to help others attain enlightenment
Bön – pre-Buddhist indigenous faith of Tibet
bówùguǎn – museum

CAAC – Civil Aviation Administration of China
cadre – Chinese government bureaucrat
cāntīng – restaurant
cǎoyuán – grasslands
CCP – Chinese Communist Party
chau – land mass
chéngshì – city
chí – lake, pool
chop – carved name seal that acts as a signature
chörten – Tibetan *stupa*
CITS – China International Travel Service
cūn – village

dàdào – boulevard
dàfàndiàn – large hotel
dàjiē – avenue
dàjiǔdiàn – large hotel
dǎo – island
dàpùbù – large waterfall
dàqiáo – large bridge
dàshà – hotel, building
dàxué – university
déhuà – white-glazed porcelain
dìtiě – subway

dōng – east; the other points of the compass are *běi* (north), *nán* (south) and *xī* (west)
dòng – cave
dòngwùyuán – zoo

fàndiàn – hotel, restaurant
fēng – peak
fēngjǐngqū – scenic area

gé – pavilion, temple
gompa – monastery
gōng – palace
gōngyuán – park
gōu – gorge, valley
guān – pass
gùjū – house, home, residence

hǎi – sea
hǎitān – beach
Hakka – Chinese ethnic group
Han – China's main ethnic group
hé – river
hú – lake
huáqiáo – overseas Chinese
Hui – ethnic Chinese Muslims
huǒchēzhàn – train station
huǒshān – volcano
hútòng – a narrow alleyway

jiāng – river
jiǎo – unit of *renminbi*; 10 jiǎo equals 1 *yuán*
jiàotáng – church
jīchǎng – airport
jiē – street
jié – festival
jīn – unit of weight; 1 *jīn* equals 600g
jīngjù – Beijing opera
jìniànbēi – memorial
jìniànguǎn – memorial hall
jiǔdiàn – hotel
jū – residence, home
junk – originally referred to Chinese fishing and war vessels with square sails; now applies to various types of boating craft

kang – raised sleeping platform
KCR – Kowloon–Canton Railway
kora – pilgrim circuit
Kuomintang – Chiang Kaishek's Nationalist Party; now one of Taiwan's major political parties

lama – a Buddhist priest of the Tantric or Lamaist school; a title bestowed on monks of particularly high spiritual attainment
lílòng – Shànghǎi alleyway
lín – forest
líng – tomb
lìshǐ – history
lóu – tower
LRT – Light Rail Transit
lù – road
lǚguǎn – guesthouse
luóhàn – Buddhist, especially a monk, who has achieved enlightenment and passes to nirvana at death; see also *arhat*

mah jong – popular Chinese game for four people; played with engraved tiles
mǎtou – dock
mén – gate
ménpiào – entrance ticket
Miao – ethnic group living in Guìzhōu
miào – temple
MTR – Mass Transit Railway
mù – tomb

nán – south; the other points of the compass are *běi* (north), *dōng* (east) and *xī* (west)

páilou – decorative archway
Pinyin – the official system for transliterating Chinese script into roman characters
PLA – People's Liberation Army
Politburo – the 25-member supreme policy-making

authority of the Chinese Communist Party

PRC – People's Republic of China

PSB – Public Security Bureau; the arm of the police force set up to deal with foreigners

pùbù – waterfall

qì – life force
qiáo – bridge
qìchēzhàn – bus station

rénmín – people, people's
renminbi – literally 'people's money'; the formal name for the currency of China, the basic unit of which is the *yuán*; shortened to RMB

sampan – small motorised launch
sānlún mótuōchē – motor tricycle
sānlúnchē – pedal-powered tricycle
SAR – Special Administrative Region

sēnlín – forest
shān – mountain
shāngdiàn – shop, store
shěng – province, provincial
shì – city
shí – rock
shìchǎng – market
shíkū – grotto
shíkùmén – literally 'stone-gate house'; type of 19th-century Shànghǎi residence
shòupiàochù – ticket office
shuǐkù – reservoir
sì – temple, monastery
sìhéyuàn – traditional courtyard house
stupa – usually used as reliquaries for the cremated remains of important *lamas*

tǎ – pagoda
thangka – Tibetan sacred art
tíng – pavilion

wān – bay
wǎngbā – internet café

wēnquán – hot springs

xī – west; the other points of the compass are *dōng* (east), *běi* (north) and *nán* (south)
xī – small stream, brook
xiá – gorge
xiàn – county
xuěshān – snow mountain

yá – cliff
yán – rock or crag
yóujú – post office
yuán – basic unit of *renminbi*
yuán – garden

zhào – lamasery
zhāodàisuǒ – guesthouse
zhíwùyuán – botanic gardens
zhōng – middle
Zhōngguó – China
zìrán bǎohùqū – nature reserve

behind the scenes

SEND US YOUR FEEDBACK

We love to hear from travellers – your comments keep us on our toes and help make our books better. Our well-travelled team reads every word on what you loved or loathed about this book. Although we cannot reply individually to postal submissions, we always guarantee that your feedback goes straight to the appropriate authors, in time for the next edition. Each person who sends us information is thanked in the next edition – the most useful submissions are rewarded with a selection of digital PDF chapters.

Visit **lonelyplanet.com/contact** to submit your updates and suggestions or to ask for help. Our award-winning website also features inspirational travel stories, news and discussions.

Note: We may edit, reproduce and incorporate your comments in Lonely Planet products such as guidebooks, websites and digital products, so let us know if you don't want your comments reproduced or your name acknowledged. For a copy of our privacy policy visit lonelyplanet.com/privacy.

OUR READERS

Many thanks to the travellers who used the last edition and wrote to us with helpful hints, useful advice and interesting anecdotes:

A Joao Aleluia, Mark Allison, Christine Amrhein **B** Richard Balsik, Marieke Blaakmeer, Nick Botham, Cam Bowman, Julia Broska, Dorian Burt **C** Eulalia Calveras, Jamie Carstairs, Javier Castro Guinea, Igor Chabrowski, Sonny Chan, Anirban Chatterjee, Christina Cheng, Gabriel Chew, Alison Clark, Mate Cobrnic, Susan Cofer Jones, Meodi Cohen & Yossi Margoninsky, Philip Corthout, Christine Counsell, Pippa Curtis **D** Bertrand Daigneault, Antonio De Biase, Marianne De Swart, Wolfgang Deuster, Christine Doyle, Clemens Dürrschmid **E** Jenna Eakins, Ros Edwards, Amir Eltanan, Jos Emmerik, Richard Emms **F** Caroline Fink, Mark Fisher, Jordan Flory, Yuji Fujimoto **G** Marcelo Gareca, Anja Gatzsche, Ferran Gonzalez-Franquesa, Tim Grady, Jeff Grigor **H** Stephanie Hancock, Grace Harris, Nicholas Harris, Elvira Hautvast, Tom Hay, Desmond Hennelly, Daniel Holz, Dana Howell **J** Bruce Jackson, Ralpha Jacobson, Wenchi Jin, Jim Jodie, Gary Jones, Marco Jonker **K** Marleen Kaag, Tobias Kalenscher, Magnus Köhler, Björn Krämer, Uta Kreimeier **L** Martin Lægård Poulsen, Lisanne Lee, Pieter Lerou, David Levin, Yoni Levin, Daniel Lidonnici, Peter Lin, Harris Lindenfeld, Louise Linder & Rombout Kampen, Sarah Linten, Paul Lippevelt, Mary Longenbaker, Eladio Lopez, Leonardo Losoviz **M** Anne Mahon, Alex Matos, Deborah McGrouther, Andreas Messerli, Alphee Michelot, Yuval Mizrakli & Naama Melumad, Sander Molenaar, Elena Morara, Julie & Cameron Muir **N** Rachel Nachtrieb, Amar Nanda, Urša & Klemen Naveršnik, Eric Neemann, Francisco Javier Núñez **O** Oonagh O'Hare, Suzanne O'Keefe, Liz O'Sullivan, Onur Oznar **P** John Paer, Stefano Pelli, Alex Phillips, Caroline Pitt, Wai Poc, Ernesto Priarollo **R** James Robinson, Jairo Romero, Marian Rosenberg, Shai Roth **S** Nickolay Salo, Jonas Schulze, Lucy Schumer, Giovanni Segre, Inbal Shani, Gerald Slocock, Jim Smith, Jonathan Spars, Alexandra Staley, Karoline Steinbacher, Victoria Steven, Vilhelm Stokstad **T** Shohei Takashiro, Annie Taylor Chen, Twan Ten Haaf, Bart Ter Haar Romeny, Paulien Ter Meulen, Jean-Claude Thelen, Yanagi Tsuyoshi, Simon Tunderman **U** Manouk Uijtdehaag, Viktoria Urbanek, Hanna Van Egmond, Joris Van Der Mijnsbrugge **V** Sarah Van Beek, Lotte Van Ekert, Karine Van Malderen, Yvonne Van Sambeek & Jan Neels, Benny Verbercht **W** Jess Watt, Marco Weber, Michael Weigh, Nigel West, James & Tamara Wharton, Timo Wiese, Jon Winkels, Alexandra Winter, Elizabeth Wright, Candice Wu **Y** Foo Yee Ling **Z** Jean Zimmermann

AUTHOR THANKS

Damian Harper

Thanks first and foremost to Dai Min, Dai Lu, Li Jianjun, Katarina Nilsson, the resourceful authors of the Sanlian/Lonely Planet *Guizhou* guide (Yi Xiaochun, Wu Yaoyao and Dong Yi), Edward Li and Maggie Zhang. Thanks also to everyone else I bumped into along the way and gratitude as ever to the warm and hospitable folk of China.

Piera Chen

A warm thank you to Ulysses Hwang, Yangyi, Reeve Wong and Carmen Ng for their generosity and wonderful company. Thanks also to Jeremy Chan, Andrew Kwong and Herman Lee for precious, electronically transmitted wisdom. To Mr Kong Xianzhu and all the cab drivers who have enriched my journey and this book with their humour and local knowledge, xièxiè. And as always, much love and gratitude to my husband, Sze Pang-cheung.

Chung Wah Chow

Sincerest thanks to Sean Yap, Cui Qun, Sun Hui and Li Yang, authors of Lonely Planet's domestic guide series, for their in-depth knowledge of respective regions. To Winter Wong, Xing Xing, Lola Liu, Eugenia Lo, Josh Stenberg and Ben Potter, for their company and insider tips on Jiāngsū. To Huang Song, Raynne Ong, Peter Li and Au Oi Sing, for invaluable help and sharing of thoughts on Fújiàn. My eternal thanks to Haider Kikabhoy. Your love and support make it all possible.

David Eimer

Special gratitude goes to Li Xinying for her invaluable help. Thanks to Damian Harper for his support and patience, as well as to Emily Wolman, Barbara Delissen and Mark Griffiths at Lonely Planet. As ever, thanks to the many people who provided tips along the way, whether knowingly or unwittingly.

Tienlon Ho

Many thanks to Jin Liu, Emma, Marcus Murphy, Neil Bhullar and Daniel McCrohan for helping me on this journey. Special thanks goes to Lijie Han who generously lent a hand in this and other projects. I am especially grateful to AJ Wang who never met a challenge he couldn't crack. Thank you Ken Ho, Wenhuei Ho and Tienfong Ho for their incomparable knowledge and enthusiasm, and to Jon Adams who did the dishes and made me laugh, among many other things.

Robert Kelly

A warm thanks to everyone who helped make this one of my best trips ever. Emily Wolman and Damian Harper at Lonely Planet, you guys are great as always. Elizabeth, your hospitality (and banana bread) are legendary for good reasons. Deepest thanks also to the friends who held the fort down while I was away. And finally: to Tania Simonetti for being in the right place at the right time in a sandstorm.

Michael Kohn

Countless folks helped at every step of the journey. Special thanks to Mei (Lìjiāng), Dave Shaw (Dàlǐ), Shirley (Shāxī), Steven (Jǐnghóng), Hendrik Heyne and Tenzin (Shangri-la), Lina and Jane (Kūnmíng), Tsomo (Xīníng) and to Chris, Wendy, Jane and Bobby (Xī'ān). Cheers to some of my fellow travel mates, Oscar Robinson, Clare Johnson, Kimberly Hagner, Nicole Mahnert and Matan Kavel. At Lonely Planet thanks, as always, to Emily Wolman and Damian Harper.

Shawn Low

As always thanks to the CE: Emily for believing and more importantly, hiring! Cheers also to CA: Damian (yet another one done and dusted! We'll find time for that beer one day). Thanks to the LP crew who are working on this: eds, cartos, MEs, MCs, LDs etc. I've been behind the scenes and know how hard you all work. Much love to Wyn-Lyn: can't wait for our future adventures together.

Bradley Mayhew

Thanks to Ali Tash and Abdul Wahab for lots of great information in Kashgar. Bhutti and Tenzin in Lhasa were lifesavers in getting me around Tibet despite all the restrictions. Cheers to Malong for his Běijīng crashpad.

Daniel McCrohan

Thanks to all the travellers I met on the road, for tips, recommendations and good company. For expert advice and insiders' info, thank you to Iain Shaw, Gil Miller, David Goodman-Smith, Kevin Li (all Běijīng), Jamin York, Angela Lankford, Kris Rubesh, Kieran Fitzgerald (all Sìchuān), Roger Geden (Húběi) and Gong Ying (Chóngqìng). A big nǐ hǎo to my mum and the rest of my family and friends in the UK; love you all. Extra special love, as always, to my amazing wife Taotao and our two little angels.

Christopher Pitts

As always, thanks to everyone who offered valuabe insight or who provided company along the way. In Shànghǎi, much gratitude is due to Gerald and May Neumann for their hospitality and great suggestions. Thanks as well to Miranda Yao, Wang Xinhai, Laure Romeyer, Claudio Valsecchi, Sandy Chu, Lynn Ye, Caroline and Antoine Lebouc, and Sam Maurey (Shànghǎi), and You Shaojun, Tingting, Kangkang, Meiling, Su, Little Book and Rose for turning what could have been an overwhelming Qīngmíng Festival in Wùyuán into a fun-filled trip. Special thanks also to Shànghǎi co-author Damian Harper, and to Emily Wolman, Barbara Delissen, Annelies Mertens, Mark Griffiths and all those who work behind the scenes. And love to Perrine, Elliot and Celeste, who provide more inspiration than they'll ever know.

ACKNOWLEDGMENTS

Climate map data adapted from Peel MC, Finlayson BL & McMahon TA (2007) 'Updated World Map of the Köppen-Geiger Climate Classification', Hydrology and Earth System Sciences, 11, 163344.

Illustrations pp58-9 and pp186-7 by Michael Weldon.

Cover photograph: Army of Terracotta Warriors, Xī'ān, Shaanxi (Shǎnxī), John W Banagan/Getty Images.

This Book

This 13th edition of Lonely Planet's *China* was researched and written by a team of stellar authors, led by Damian Harper, who also coordinated and contributed to the last two editions. This guidebook was commissioned in Lonely Planet's Oakland office, and produced by the following:

Commissioning Editors Emily K Wolman, Kathleen Munnelly

Coordinating Editor Amanda Williamson

Coordinating Cartographer Andrew Smith

Coordinating Layout Designer Frank Deim

Managing Editors Barbara Delissen, Annelies Mertens, Martine Power

Managing Cartographers Alison Lyall, Diana Von Holdt

Managing Layout Designer Chris Girdler

Assisting Editors Janet Austin, Kate Kiely, Anne Mulvaney, Alan Murphy, Joanne Newell, Kristin Odjik, Monique Perrin, Simon Williamson

Assisting Cartographers Mick Garrett, Joelene Kowalski, Samantha Tyson, Robert Townsend

Cover Research Naomi Parker

Internal Image Research Nicholas Colicchia, Aude Vauconsant

Language Content Branislava Vladisavljevic

Thanks to Shahara Ahmed, Melanie Dankel, Ryan Evans, Justin Flynn, Larissa Frost, Mark Griffiths, Corey Hutchison, Tim Lu, Trent Paton, Raphael Richards, Jessica Rose, Kerrianne Southway, Gina Tsarouhas, Gerard Walker, Juan Winata

index

798 Art District 79

A

accommodation 982-5, 1017-18, 1022
  see also individual locations
acrobatics
  Běijīng 101, 102
  Dūnhuáng 832
  Guǎngzhōu 540
  Shànghǎi 211
activities 985
  birdwatching 331, 628-30, 650-1, 675, 873, 972-3
  boat trips 27, 288, 475, 542, 557, 589, 608, 622, 719, 773-5, 765, 814, 849
  caving 455
  cycling 87, 330-1, 572, 592, 595, 599, 655-6, 683, 796, 822, 1001, **21**
  hiking 29, 170-1, 247, 342, 387-8, 391, 402-3, 430, 438-40, 442, 480, 482, 509, 523, 557-8, 593, 616, 633, 650-1, 667-8, 678, 680, 689, 697, 717, 726, 727, 731, 737, 738, 741, 743-4, 796, 805, 820, 821-2, 826, 876, 894, **509**
  horse riding 731, 737, 740, 784, 805, 822, 862
  mountain climbing 577-8
  Plank Walk 369
  rafting 455-6, 654, 805
  rock climbing 75, 479, 595, 654
  skiing 310, 316, 329
  surfing 33, 581
  swimming 87, 267, 297-8, 419, 589, 600, 602, 684
  table tennis 87
air travel 996-8
airports 996
  Běijīng Capital Airport 23
  Hong Kong International Airport 23
  Shànghǎi Pǔdōng International Airport 23

000 Map pages
000 Photo pages

altitude sickness 896, 1014
ancient settlements 27
  Bànpō neolithic village 366
  Hóngcūn 381
  Jiǎngtóuzhōu 592-3
  Jiāohé ruins 787
  Luótiáncūn 434-5
  Píngyáo 15, 346-50, **346**, **15**, **27**
  tǔlóu 19, 270, 280-3, 566-7, **18**
  Wǔfū 289
  Wùyuán 437-8
  Xiàméi 288
  Xīdì 380-1
  Yúyuán 265
Ānhuī 44, 375-95, **376**
  climate 377
  costs 377
  highlights 376
  Huángshān 385-90, **386**
  Huīzhōu Villages 380-5
  travel seasons 375
  travel to/from 377
  travel within 377
  Túnxī 377-80, **378**
  weather 375
animism 940
Ānshùn 624-6, **626**
architecture 963-6
  concession-era 122-4, 161-5, 185-92, 277, 384, 418-9, 467, 512, 541
  Huīzhōu 384
  imperial 26, 55-60, 84-7, 133, 135, 292-3, 356-64, 827-8, **56**, **6**
  Lǐngnán 544-5
  modern 26, 75, 78, 81-2, 194, 195, 467, 499, 519
Army of Terracotta Warriors 12, 364-5, 911, **12**
art deco 963
arts & architecture 544, 953-66
atlas 800
ATMs 989

B

Badain Jaran Desert 860
Bāguà villages 557
Bāguà Zhǎng 978-9
Bái Tǎ 857
Bai Third Moon Festival 31, 510, 651
Báishā 665-6
Báishuǐtái 670, 676
Bakong Scripture Printing Press & Monastery 735
Bamboo Sea 632, 726, **746-7**
Bamboo Temple 643-4
Bank of China Building 470-1
Bàojīng 624

Bǎoshān region 681-4
Bāotóu 858-9
Bǎoxiàng Temple 659
Barkhor 885
Bāshā 620
Bayanhot 846-7
bazaars, see markets
beaches
  Běidàihé 142
  Běihǎi 605
  Bó'áo 578-9
  Dàlián 297
  Dōngjiāo Coconut Plantation 575
  Hǎinán 569
  Hong Kong 475
  Macau 522
  Pǔtuóshān 267
  Qīngdǎo 164-5
  Sānyà 581-2, **21**
  Shāndōng 144
  Shíméi Bay 580
  Sun & Moon Bay 580
  Xīngchéng 307
  Yángjiāng 554
  Yāntái 173
  Yuè Liàng Wān 576
beer 951-2
Běidàhú Ski Resort 316
Běidàihé 142
Běihǎi 605-8, **606**
Běijícūn (North Pole Village) 332-3
Běijīng 16, 50-112, **52-3**, **56**, **83**, **746**, **748**
  accommodation 50, 88-93
  activities 87
  Běihǎi Park & Xīchéng North **80**
  city walls 74
  climate 50, 51, 54
  costs 51
  courses 88
  Dōngchéng Central **62-3**
  drinking 99-100
  Drum Tower & Dōngchéng North **68-9**
  eating 50, 93-9
  entertainment 100-2
  food 95, 98
  Forbidden City 6, 55-60, **56**, **6**
  highlights 52-3
  history 51
  hútòng 16, 71, 96, 101, **71**, **16**
  internet access 104
  itineraries 54
  language 54
  maps 104
  markets 103
  medical services 104
  PSB 105

Sānlǐtún & Cháoyáng **76**
shopping 102-4
sights 54-87
Summer Palace 84-7, **86**
Temple of Heaven Park & Dōngchéng South **73**
Tiān'ānmén Square 60-1, **746**
tourist information 105
travel seasons 50
travel to/from 105-7
travel within 107, 109
walking tour 71
weather 50
beliefs 934-40
bicycle hire schemes 259
Bǐfēngxiá Panda Base 712-13
Big Goose Pagoda 359
Big Lìkēng 438
Bīngyù Valley 303
Bīngzhōngluò 680-1
birdwatching 331, 972-3
    Nàpà Hǎi 675
    Qīnghǎi Lake 873
    Wēibǎo Shān 650-1
    Wēiníng 628-30
Bó'áo 578-80
boat travel
    travel to/from China 220, 1000
    travel within China 1001-2
boat trips 27
    Bǐnglíng Sì 814
    Chóngqìng City 765
    Huāshān cliff murals 608
    Lèshān 719
    Lí River 14, 27, 589, 599, **14**, **503**
    Nine Twists River 288
    Pearl River 542
    Qīngyuǎn 557
    Shànghǎi 198, 199
    Star Ferry 475
    Yangzi River 8, 35, 770-5, **772**, **9**
    Yellow River 849
    Zhènyuǎn 622
books 906, 959-61, 976
    Diamond Sutra 914
    Encyclopaedia of Chinese culture 914
    martial arts 979
    Mao: A Life 924
    Midnight in Peking 923
    The Rape of Nanjing 228
    The Sun Shines on the Sanggan River 925
border crossings 998-1000
    Japan 127, 169
    Kazakhstan 783
    Kyrgyzstan 797
    Laos 643, 695
    Mongolia 856
    Myanmar (Burma) 686, 687
    Nepal 903
    Pakistan 797
    Russia 328, 864
    South Korea 127, 169, 175, 301, 306
    Taiwan 280
    Tajikistan 797
    Thailand 693
    Tibet 676
    Vietnam 604, 609, 643
Buddhism 935-7, 964-5
budget 22
Bù'ěrjīn 803-4
Bund 8, 180, **182-3**, **8**, **186-7**
business hours 985

C

Cài Family Former Residence 579
calligraphy 954
canal towns
    Lìjiāng 659-661, **753**
    Lùzhí 243-4
    Mùdú 244-5
    Qībǎo 197
    Sūzhōu 234-9
    Tai O 482
    Tónglǐ 242-3
    Wūzhèn 261-2
    Zhōuzhuāng 245-6
    Zhūjiājiǎo 220, **3**
Cāng Shān 656
Cāngyán Shān 132-3
Cantonese language 1021-3
Cǎo'àn Manichaean Temple 287
Cǎohǎi Lake 629
car travel 23, 1002-3
    driver's licence 1002
casinos 528
Cave Temple 859-60
caves
    Bezeklik Caves 787
    Bǐnglíng Sì 814
    Dàzú Buddhist Caves 766-7
    Dripping Water Cave 451
    dwellings 351
    Gānjiā grasslands 820
    Gǔyájū 112
    Hǎikǒu Volcanic Cluster Geopark 575
    Kizil Thousand Buddha Caves 789-90
    Lǐjiāshān 351
    Lónggōng Cave 626-7
    Lóngmén Caves 407-9, **39**
    Luómèi Lotus Cave 610
    Màijī Shān 837-8
    Mǎtí Sì 826
    Mògāo Caves 833-5
    Pǔtuóshān 267
    Seven Star Crags Park 555
    Swallow's Cavern 648
    Ten Thousand Buddha Cave 372
    Wǔdàlián Chí 331
    Wǔlíngyuán 455
    Xūmí Shān 850
    Yúngāng Caves 16, 338-9, **16**
    Zhījīn Cave 627
caving 455
cell phones 23
Central Mid-Levels Escalator 467
ceramics 440, 550, 957-8, **958**
Chángbái Shān 310-13
Changbai Waterfall 311
Chángchūn 316-18, **317**
Chángshā 446-51, **447**
Cháozhōu 563-5, **564**
Charklik 803
Chen Clan Ancestral Hall 539
Chen Family Compound 769
Chen Tingjing 353
Chéngdé 133-8, **134**
Chéngdū 701-11, **702-3**
Chéngkǎn 383
Chéngyáng Wind & Rain Bridge 594
Cherchen 802-3
Chìkǎn 553
children, travel with 198, 985
China Shànghǎi International Arts Festival 199
Chinese Communist Party (CCP)
    history 177, 920, 921, 922-3
    museums & historical sites 191-2, 372, 432, 442, 446, 448, 541
Chinese opera 495, 539, 709, 962, 963-4, **747**
    Běijīng 81, 102
    Chóngqìng 757
    Guǎndōng 538, 539-40, 545, 564
    Hong Kong 481, 495
    Jiāngsū 231, 238-9, 241
    Sìchuān 709
    Shaanxi 362
    Shànghǎi 211, 212
    Tibet 888
Chìshuǐ 630-1
Chöde Gompa 736
Chóngqìng 46, 754-69, **755**
    climate 756
    costs 756
    highlights 755
    history 756
    travel seasons 754
    weather 754

Chóngqìng City 756-66, **757**, **758-9**, **762**

Chóngshàn Temple 343

Chóngwǔ 286

chorten
Báitǎ Gōngyuán 736-7
Gomar Gompa 874
Gòngtáng Chörten 817
Gyantse Kumbum 895
Kumbum Monastery 872
Potala Palace 14, 886, 889, **14**
Tǎgōng Monastery 731
Wǔtún Sì 874

Christianity 939

Chuāndǐxià 111-12

churches & cathedrals 940
Běijīng 66
Hā'ěrbīn 322
Hángzhōu 254
Hong Kong 474, 478
Lúshān 442
Macau 513-4
Píngyáo 15, 346-50, **346**, **15**
Qīngdǎo 163-4
Shànghǎi 197
Tiānjīn 123

city walls
Běijīng 74
Chóngwǔ 286
Dàtóng 337
Fènghuáng 460
Guìlín 587
Guóyù 352
Jìmíngyì 142-3
Jīngzhōu 423
Kāifēng 413
Nánjīng 229
Píngyáo 15, 347, **15**, **27**
Shàngdū (Xanadu) 858
Sōngpān 740
Xī'ān 357
Xīngchéng 306-7
Xīníng 869
Zhàoqìng 555
Zhèngdìng 130
Zhènyuǎn 622

climate 22, **22** see also *individual regions*

Coloane 522-3

communism 940

concession-era architecture
Gǔlàng Yǔ 277
Hànkǒu 418
Hong Kong 467

Macau 512
Qīngdǎo 161-5
Shāmiàn Island 541
Shànghǎi 180, 185-7, 190
Tiānjīn 122-4
Wǔhàn 418-9

Confucianism 938-9

Confucius 155, 909-10

Confucius Forest 159

Confucius Mansion 158-9

Confucius Temple (Qūfù) 157-8, 508

consulates 987-8

costs 990
Ānhuī 377
Běijīng 51
Chóngqìng 756
Fújiàn 272
Gānsù 810
Guǎngdōng 535
Guǎngxī 587
Guìzhōu 613
Hǎinán 571
Héběi 122
Hēilóngjiāng 321
Hénán 398
Hong Kong 466
Húběi 418
Húnán 446
Inner Mongolia 853
Jiāngsū 223
Jiāngxī 432
Jílín 310
Liáoníng 292
Macau 514
Níngxià 842
Qīnghǎi 867
Shaanxi (Shǎnxī) 356
Shāndōng 146
Shànghǎi 177
Shānxī 336
Sìchuān 700
Tiānjīn 122
Tibet 883
Xīnjiāng 778
Yúnnán 635
Zhèjiāng 249

courses
Buddhist philosophy 672
cooking 85, 88, 198, 596, 744
culture 88
language 88, 595, 989
martial arts 88, 198, 425-6, 482, 595, 979
painting 672
tea 85
traditional Chinese medicine 85
volunteering 595

credit cards 989-90

cuisine, see food

cultural events
Bai Third Moon Festival 31, 510, 651
Confucius' Birthday 33
Miao New Year 33
Monlam Great Prayer Festival 30, 510, 818
Walking Around the Mountain Festival 31

Cultural Revolution 925-6

currency 22

customs 985-6

cycling
Běijīng 87
Ěrhǎi Hú 655-6
Guǎngxī 592, 595, 599
Hǎinán 572, **21**
Hong Kong 484
Karakoram Highway 796
Lángmùsì 822
Macau 523
Téngchōng 683
tours 1001
Wǔdàlián Chí 330-1
Yángshuò 595, 599

D

Dai New Year 31

Dai Temple 150-1

Dàlǐ 651-5, **652**

Dàlián 296-301, **298**, **302**

Dàlián International Beer Festival 31-2, 300

Dàlián oil disaster 297

Dàměnglóng 694-5

Dānbā (Rongtrak) 729-30

Dāndōng 303-6, **305**

dangers 991-2, 1002, see also scams

Dǎngjiācūn 370-1

dānxiá 826

Dàochéng (Dabpa) 738-9

Dàoyùnlóu 565

Dàpéng Fortress 561

Dàtóng 336-8, **337**

Dàzú Buddhist Caves 766-7

Dégé (Derge) 734-5

Déhāng 457-8

Déhóng Prefecture 684-6

demographics 931

Dēngfēng 401-4

Déqīn 676-7

Déshèngbǎo 339

Détiān Waterfall 608-9

Diān Chí 644-5

diàojiǎolóu 460, 624

diāolóu 11, 552, **11**

Dinosaur Museum 723

discounts 984, 986

Dōngjiāo coconut plantation 575
Dragon Boat Festival 31, 510, **510**
Dragon's Backbone Rice Terraces 10, 593-4, **10**
Drepung Monastery 887-8
drinking 1018-19, 1022
driving 23, 1002-3
Dūjiāngyàn irrigation project 712
Dúlóng Valley 681
Dūnhuáng 20, 829-33, **830**, **20**
dynasties
  Han 910-11
  Ming 914-16
  Qing 916-18, 932
  Song 913-14
  Tang 911-13
  Wei 911
  Yuan 914

E
economy 906
embassies 986-7
Éméi Shān 714-17, **716**, **749**
emergencies 23, 1019, 1022
environmental issues 297, 969, 975-6
Ěrhǎi Hú 655-6, **655**
ethnic minorities 29, 631, 645, 907, 931, **750**
  Bai 656-7, 658-9, 661
  Bao'an 815
  Bulang 690
  Dai 690, 693-4
  Dong 457, 616, 620-1, 629
  Dongxiang 815
  Dulong 681
  Ewenki 861
  Hakka 280-1, 443, 565, 566
  Hani 690
  Hui 815, 845
  Jinuo 690
  Korean 314
  Li 577
  Miao 457-8, 577, 616, 618-20, 629
  Mǐnnán (Fujianese) 280-1
  Mosu 670-1
  Naxi 659, 662, 663, 930
etiquette 25, 694, 890
Everest Base Camp 899, **28**
exchange rates 23, 467, 513

F
Falun Gong 935
Fànjìngshān 625
feng shui 499
Fènghuáng 21, 458-62, **459**, **21**
Fertility Festival 661

festivals & events 30-3, 510, 962, **32**, **510** see also cultural events, individual festivals, sporting events
  aurora borealis 332
  beer 31-2
  Closed-door Festival 688
  Dàlǐ 651
  Dàlián International Beer Festival 30
  ethnic minorities 631
  Flower 31
  food 33
  Guìzhōu 631
  Hong Kong 484
  Ice & Snow Festival 30, 325, 510, **510**
  Kurban Bairam 33
  Lǐtáng Horse Festival 737
  literature 30
  Macau 523
  Monlam Great Prayer Festival 30, 510, 818
  Naadam 854, 861
  Nánjīng 230
  Qīngdǎo 164
  Qiántáng River Tide Observing Festival 33
  Qūfù 159
  Shànghǎi 199
  Sūzhōu 239
  Tan Ta Festival 688, 695
  Third Moon Fair 31, 510, 651
  Three Temples Festival 651
  Tibet 888-9
  Torch Festival 651
  Walking Around the Mountain Festival 727
  Water-splashing Festival 687
  Xiàmén 273-4
  Xīshuāngbǎnnà region 687-8
  Yángguān 260
  Yúnnán 661
film locations
  2046 524
  Avatar 455
  Crouching Tiger, Hidden Dragon 381, 382
  Enter the Dragon 481
  Hero 836
  Judou 382
  Kite Runner 797
  Last Emperor 316, 926
  Let the Bullets Fly 552
  Lost Horizon (Shangri-La) 673
  Painted Veil 601
  Raise the Red Lantern 345
  Western Film Studios 846
films 371, 474, 907, 927, 961-2, 979
Fishing Town Fortress 768

Flaming Mountains 786
Fódīng Mountain 267
food 11, 28, 504, 764, 941-52, **504-5**, **942**, **11** see also individual regions
  Fújiàn 276
  Guǎngzhōu 545
  Hǎinán 574, 575
  hotpot 763, 504
  Kūnmíng 640
  language 1018-19, 1022
  menus 95
  noodles 504, 764
  Peking duck 504
  regional cooking 942-8
  Shànghǎi 205
  Sìchuān 707
  Tibetan 734
  Uighur 794
Forbidden City 6, 55-60, **6**, **58-9**
foreign concessions, see concession-era architecture
Formula 1 31
Fóshān 550-1
Fragrant Hills Park 88
Fred Yeung 479
frescoes
  Báishā 666
  Lìjiāng 665
  Lóngxīng Temple 130
  Yúlín Grottoes 836
  Yúngāng Caves 16, 338-9, **16**
Friendship Highway 894-902
Friendship Pass 609, 999
Fúgòng 679-80
Fújiàn 43, 270-89, **271**
  climate 272
  costs 272
  highlights 271
  history 272
  language 272
  tǔlóu 280-3
  travel seasons 270
  travel to/from 272
  travel within 272
  weather 270
  Xiàmén 272-7, **274**
Fúlǐ 600
Fúzhōu 287-8
Fūzǐ Temple 228

G
Ganden Monastery 893
Ganden Sumtseling Gompa 672
Gānjiā grasslands 820
Gānsù 47, 808-39, **809**
  climate 810
  costs 810

Gānsù *continued*
Dūnhuáng 829-33, **830**
highlights 809
history 809-10
language 810
Lánzhōu 810-14, **811**
travel seasons 808
travel to/from 810
travel within 810
weather 808
Xiàhé 815-20, **816**
Gānsù Provincial Museum 810-11
Gānzī (Garzê) 732
Gāo Temple 847
gay travellers 988
Genghis Khan 850, 859, 912, 914
geography 967-76
Giant Panda Breeding Research
Base 701
Golden Duck Pagoda 686
Golmud 880
Gomar Gompa 874
graffiti 479
Grand Buddha 12, 718-19, **13**, **750-1**
Grand Canal 238
Grand (Sunday) Bazaar 20, 790-6,
20, **39**
Great Wall Marathon 31
Great Wall, the 6, 26, 113-19, 506, **114**,
2, **7**, **506-7**
accommodation 89, 115, 117, 118
Bādálǐng 118-19
Déshèngbǎo 339
eating 116, 117, 118
Great Wall Museum 139
hikes 119
history 113-14
Huánghuā Chéng 116-17, 506
Jade Gate Pass 836
Jiànkòu 115-16, 506
Jiāyùguān Fort 506, 827-9, **827**
Jīnshānlǐng 117-18, 506
Jiǔménkǒu Great Wall 141
Miáojiāng Great Wall 621
Mùtiányù 6, 115
Sānguānkǒu 847
Tiger Mountain Great Wall 304-5
Zhuāngdàokǒu 117, 506
guàiwu 310
Guāndì Temple 135
Guǎngdōng 45, 533-68, **534**
costs 535
Guǎngzhōu 535-50, **536**, **540**
highlights 534

history 535
Kāipíng 552-4
language 535
Shēnzhèn 558-61, **560**
travel seasons 533
weather 533
Guǎngjì Bridge 563
Guǎngxī 46, 585-610, **586**
Běihǎi 605-7, **606**
costs 587
Dragon's Backbone Rice Terraces
593-4
Guìlín 587-92, **588**
highlights 586
history 587
language 587
travel seasons 585
weather 585
Yángshuò 595-9, **596**
Guǎngzhōu 535-50, **536-7**, **540**
Guǎngzhōu Opera House 538
Guǎngzōng Sì 847
Guānlù 382
Guanyin 937
Guia Fort 518-19
Guìdé 875-7
Guìlín 587-92, **588**
Guìyáng **614**
Guìzhōu 46, 611-32, **612**
Ānshùn 624-6, **626**
climate 613
costs 613
Guìyáng 613-6, **614**
highlights 612
history 613
language 613
Lónggōng Caves 626-8
travel seasons 611
travel to/from 613
travel within 613
weather 611
Gǔlàng Yǔ 277-80, **274**
Guōdòng 264-5
Guōliàngcūn 409-10
Guóyǔ 352
Gyantse 895-6
Gyantse Kumbum 895

H
Hā'ěrbīn 321-8, **322**
Hǎikǒu 571-5, **573**
Hǎikǒu Volcanic Cluster Geopark 575
Hǎilā'ěr 860-2
Hǎinán 21, 45, 569-84, **570**, **21**
activities 569
beaches 569
Central Highlands 576-8

climate 571
costs 571
East Coast 578-80
Hǎikǒu 571-5, **573**
highlights 570
history 570-1
language 571
Sānyà 581-4, **582**
travel seasons 569
travel to/from 571
travel within 571
weather 569
Hāmì (Kumul) 787-8
Han people 930
Hánchéng 370-1
hanging coffins 441, 725
Hanging Monastery 340
Hángzhōu 249-60, **250-1**
Happy Valley Racecourse 471
health 1010-15
altitude sickness 896, 1014
books 1011
insurance 1010
vaccinations 1010, 1012
websites 1011
Heaven Lake 311
Héběi 12, 128-43, **121**
Chéngdé 133-9, **134**
climate 122
costs 122
highlights 121
language 122
Shānhǎiguān 139-41, **139**
travel seasons 120
travel to/from 122
travel within 122
weather 120
Héféi 392-5, **393**
Hēijīng 645-6
Hēilóngjiāng 44, 319-33, **320**
activities 319
climate 321
costs 321
Hā'ěrbīn 321-8, **322**
highlights 320
history 321
language 321
travel seasons 319
travel to/from 321
travel within 321
weather 319
Wǔdàlián Chí 330-2
Hénán 44, 396-415, **397**
climate 398
costs 398
highlights 397
history 398

Kāifēng 410-415, **412**
  language 398
  Lóngmén Caves 407-9
  Luòyáng 404-7, **406**
  travel seasons 396
  travel to/from 398
  travel within 398
  weather 396
Héng Shān 452-3
Héshùn 683
Hézuò 820-1
high-speed trains 1004-5
Highway 219 902
hiking 29, **509**
  Bamboo Sea 726, **746-7**
  Bīngzhōngluò 680
  Dēngfēng 402-3
  Dragon's Backbone Rice Terraces
    10, 593-4, **10**
  Éméi Shān 717, **749**
  Ganden to Samye 509, 894
  Gānjiā grasslands 820
  Hong Kong 480, 482, 509, **509**
  Huángshān 12, 385-90, 509, **386,
    12, 509**
  Jiāngxī 430
  Jiǔhuá Shān 391
  Jiǔzhàigōu National Park 19, 742-5,
    743, 19
  Kǎilǐ 616
  Kanas Lake Nature Reserve 805
  Kāngdìng (Dartsendo) 727
  Karakoram Highway 796
  Kawa Karpo 678
  Lángmùsì 821-2
  Láo Shān 170-1
  Lǐtáng (Lithang) 737
  Lúshān 442
  Macau 523
  Mǎtí Sì 826
  Mt Amnye Machen 876
  Nánlíng National Forest Park
    557-8
  Sāngkē grasslands 820
  Sānqīng Shān 438-40
  Sìchuān 697, 731
  Sōngpān 741
  Tiger Leaping Gorge 8, 509, 667-9,
    668, 8
  Wēibǎo Shān 650-1
  Wǔtái Shān 342
  Wùyuán 438
  Xīshuāngbǎnnà region 689
  Yàdīng Nature Reserve 738
  Yángshuò 509
  Yúbēng 678
  Yúnnán 633
  Zhèjiāng 247

history 909-29
  CCP 920, 921, 922-3
  Cultural Revolution 925-6
  Japanese occupation 923-4
  Kuomintang rule 921-4
  museums 928
  Soviet relations 921, 924-5
  WWII 923-4
Hohhot 853-7, **854**
Hong Kong 19, 45, 463-502, **464-5,
  18, 483, 509, 751**
  accommodation 463, 484-9
  activities 482
  climate 466
  costs 466
  drinking 493-4
  eating 463, 489-93
  entertainment 494-6
  exchange rates 467
  festivals & events 484
  food 490
  highlights 464-5
  history 466
  internet access 498-9
  itineraries 471
  Kowloon **476**
  language 466-7
  medical services 499
  Sheung Wan, Central & Admiralty
    468-9
  shopping 496-8
  sights 467-82
  tourist information 499
  tours 484
  travel seasons 463
  travel to/from 500-1
  travel within 501-2
  Wan Chai & Causeway Bay **472**
  weather 463
  Yau Ma Tei **474**
Hong Kong Heritage Museum 481
Hóngcūn 381
Hóngjiāng Old Town 462
horse riding
  Jīnzhànghán grasslands 862
  Kanas Lake Nature Reserve
    805
  Lángmùsì 822
  Lǐtáng (Lithang) 737
  Sōngpān 740
  Tǎgōng 731
  Tiān Shān 784
Hotan 800-2, **801**
hot springs, see natural springs
HSBC Building 499
Huà Shān 368-70, **369**
Huángguǒshù Falls 627
Huánglóng National Park 741

Huángshān 12, 385-90, 509, **386,
  12, 509**
Huángyáo 601
Huàshān cliff murals 608
Húběi 44, 416-29, **417**
  climate 418
  costs 418
  highlights 417
  history 418
  language 418, 425
  travel seasons 416
  weather 416
  Wǔdāng Shān 424-7
  Wǔhàn 418-22, **420**
Hui villages 12
Humble Administrator's Garden 234
Húnán 45, 444-62, **445**
  climate 446
  Chángshā 446-51, **447**
  costs 446
  Fènghuáng 458-62, **459**
  highlights 445
  history 446
  language 446
  travel seasons 444
  travel to/from 446
  travel within 446
  weather 444
  Wǔlíngyuán 453-7, **454**
Húnán County No 1 Teachers' Training
  School 446
Huǒmài Village 610
hútòng 16, 71, 96, 101, **71, 16**

I
Ice & Snow Festival 30, 325, 510, **510**
immigration 996
imperial architecture 26
  Bìshǔ Shānzhuāng 133, 135
  Forbidden City 6, 55-60, **56, 6**
  Imperial Palace 292-3
  Jiāyùguān Fort 506, 827-9, **827**
  Summer Palace 84-7, **86**
  Xī'ān 356-64
Imperial Palace 292-3
Imperial Palace of Manchu State
  (Puppet Emperor's Palace) 316
Imperial Tombs 367
Inner Mongolia 47, 851-64, **852**
  climate 853
  costs 853
  Hǎilā'ěr 860-2
  highlights 852
  history 853
  Hohhot 853-7, **854**
  language 853
  travel seasons 851

Inner Mongolia *continued*
  travel to/from 853
  travel within 853
  weather 851
insurance 988
International Beer Festival 165
International Climbing Festival 153
internet access 23, 988-9
internet resources 23, 480
Ip Man 551
Islam 939
itineraries 34-41, **34-41**
  Běijīng to Mongolia 41
  'big ticket' 37
  coastal China 37
  east–south rural towns 38
  northeast China 41
  northern China 34
  Qīnghǎi to Sìchuān 40
  Silk Road 36
  southwest China 38
  Tibet fringes 40
  Yangzi River 35

J
Jade Market 478
Japanese border crossings 127, 169
Japanese Germ Warfare Experimental Base 324
Japanese occupation 293, 316, 324, 861
Jí'ǎn 313-15
Jí'ǎn Museum 315
Jiāngjūnfén (General's Tomb) 314
Jiànshuǐ 646-7
Jiāngsū 43, 221-46, **222**
  climate 223
  costs 223
  highlights 222
  history 223
  Nánjīng 223-33, **224-5**
  Sūzhōu 234-42, **236**
  travel seasons 221
  travel to/from 223
  travel within 223
  weather 221
Jiāngtóuzhōu 592-3
Jiāngxī 45, 430-43, **431**
  climate 432
  costs 432
  highlights 431
  history 432
  language 432

Nánchāng 432-4, **433**
  travel seasons 430
  travel to/from 432
  travel within 432
  weather 430
Jiāyùguān Fort 506, 827-9, **827**
Jiěgào border checkpoint 686
Jílín 43, 308-18, **309**
  Chángbái Shān 310-3,
  climate 310
  costs 310
  highlights 309
  history 309-10
  language 310
  travel seasons 308
  travel to/from 310
  travel within 310
  weather 308
Jìluè Huáng Temple 563
Jīmíng Temple 228
Jīmíngyì 141-3
Jǐ'nán 146-9, **147**
Jīnchéng 352
Jǐnghóng 688-93, **691**
Jìngpò Hú 329-30
Jìngzhēn 696
Jīngzhōu 422-3
Jīnjiānglǐ 552
Jīnmào Tower 194
Jīnzhànghán grasslands 862
Jiǔhuá Shān 390-2
Jiǔménkǒu Great Wall 141
Jiǔzhàigōu National Park 19, 742-5,
  743, **19**
Jokhang Temple 886
July 1st Glacier 829

K
Kāifēng 410-15, **412**
Kǎilǐ 616-18, **617**
Kāipíng 552-4
Kanas Lake Nature Reserve 804-6
Kāngdìng (Dartsendo) 727-9, **728**
Karakoram Highway 796-8
Karghilik 799
Kashgar 20, 790-6, **791**, **20**, **39**
Kawa Karpo 676, 677-8
Kazakhstan border crossing 783
Khara Khoto 860
Kinmen (Taiwan) 279
Kizil Thousand Buddha Caves 789-90
Koguryo 313-14
Kǒng Xiànzhū 539
kora
  Barkhor 885, 889
  Chenresig 738
  Drepung Monastery 887-8

Ganden Monastery 893
Kawa Karpo 678
Labrang Monastery 16, 508, 816-17,
  16, **965**
Mt Amnye Machen 876
Mt Kailash 10, 903-4, **10**
Potala 14, 886, 889, **14**
Princess Wencheng Temple 879
Sera Monastery 886
Tashilhunpo Monastery 896-7
Kumbum Monastery 872
Kūnmíng 635-43, **636-7**, **644**
Kuomintang rule 921-4
Kuqa 788-9
Kurban Bairam 33
Kyrgyzstan border crossing 797

L
Labrang Monastery 16, 508, 816-17,
  16, **965**
Láitān 768-9
lakes
  Barkol Lake 788
  Crescent Moon Lake 835
  Emerald Pagoda Lake 675-6
  Guìlín 587-8
  Heaven Lake 311
  Hūlún Hú 863-4
  Jiǔzhàigōu National Park 19, 742-5,
    743, **19**
  Lake Manasarovar 904
  Lúgū Hú 670-1
  Nam-tso 893-4
  Nàpà Hǎi 675
  Qīnghǎi Lake 873
  Sayram Lake 807
  Shǔdū Hú 676
  Tiān Chí 784
  Xīnlù hǎi (Yilhun Lha-tso) 734
  Yamdrok-tso 894-5
Lángdé 619
Lángmùsì 821-3
language 22, 24, 1016-26
  accommodation 1017-18, 1022
  Cantonese 1021-3
  courses 595, 989
  drinking 1018-19
  emergencies 1019, 1022
  Macau 512
  Mandarin 1016-21
  Mongolian 1024
  Naxi 663
  Tibet 884, 1023
  transport 1020-21
  Uighur 1024
Lángzhōng 720-2
Lantern Festival 30
Lánzhōu 810-14, **811**

Láo Shān 170-1
Laotian border crossings 643, 695
lava fields, *see also* volcanoes
  Hǎikǒu Volcanic Cluster Geopark 575
  Lóngmén 'Stone Village' 331
  Shí Hǎi 331
  Téngchōng 683-4
legal matters 989
Léishān 619
lesbian travellers 988
Lèshān 718-20, **719**
Lèyè 610
Lhasa 14, 884-93, **885, 887, 14**
Lí River 14, 27, 589, 599, **14, 503**
Li Zicheng 374
Liáoníng 43, 290-307, **291**
  climate 292
  costs 292
  highlights 291
  history 292
  language 292
  travel seasons 290
  travel to/from 292
  travel within 292
  weather 290
Lìjiāng 659-64, **660, 665, 753**
Lǐngnán culture 544-5, 550
Língshuǐ 112
Língyán Shān 245
Língyǐn Temple 253
Línxià 814-15
Lǐtáng (Lithang) 736-8
literature 959-61
Little Lǐkēng 437
Liǔ Jiāng 714
Liùkù 679
Lónggōng Cave 626-7
Lónghǔ Shān 440-1
Lónglǐ 620
Lóngnán 443
Lord Bao 394
Lu Xun 263
Lúgū Hú 670-1
Luómèi Lotus Cave 610
Luótiáncūn 434-5
Luòyáng 404-7, **405**
Lúshān 441-3
Lǚshùn 301-3
Lùzhí 243-4

M

Macau 45, 511-32, **512**
  activities 523
  casinos 528
  central Macau **520**
  Coloane Island **524**
  costs 514
  drinking 527-8
  eating 511, 526-7
  entertainment 528-9
  exchange rates 513
  festivals & events 523
  highlights 512
  history 512
  internet access 530
  itineraries 515
  language 512
  Macau Peninsula **516-17**
  medical services 530
  shopping 529-30
  sights 512-23
  sleeping 523-6
  Taipa Island **522**
  tourist information 530-1
  tours 523
  travel seasons 511
  travel to/from 531
  travel within 531
  weather 511
Màijī Shān 837-8
Mandarin language 1016-21
Mǎnígàngē (Manigango) 733-4
Mǎnzhōulǐ 863-4
Mao Zedong 448, 924-6
  childhood house 451
  memorial hall 64-5
  museum 451
  school 451
Maoism 940
Marco Polo 912
Maritime Silk Road Museum of Guǎngdōng 554
markets
  Běijīng 103
  Guǎngxī 591
  Hángzhōu 257
  Hong Kong 475, 478, 481
  Hotan 800
  Kashgar 20, 790-6, **791, 20, 39**
  Kuqa 789
  Qīngdǎo 167
  Téngchōng 681
  Tiānjīn 124
  Ürümqi 779
  Xī'ān 363
  Xīnjiāng 776
  Yúnnán 641, 655, 659, 684
martial arts 977-80
  courses 88, 198, 425-6, 482, 595, 979
  Shàolín Temple 402-3
  taichi 17, 426, **17**
  Wing Chun 551
Mátáng 619-20
Mǎtí Sì 826
mausoleums & memorials, *see also* tombs
  Cemetery of Noblemen at Yushan 315
  Genghis Khan Mausoleum 859
  Hill 203 303
  Mausoleum of Ammanisahan 799
  Mausoleum of General Yue Fei 253
  Mausoleum of the Nanyue King 541
  Memorial Hall of the Nánjīng Massacre 225-6
  Revolutionary Martyrs' Mausoleum 128
  Sun Yatsen Mausoleum 227
  Tomb of Wáng Jiàn 705
medical services 1011
Meili Snow Mountain National Park pass 677
Méizhōu 566-8
Mencius 158
Mènghǎi 695-6
Mènghǎn 693-4
Mènghùn 696
Mènglà 694
Mènglún 694
Mèngyǎng 693
Miacimu 677
Miáojiāng Great Wall 621
Mid-autumn Festival 33
Ming city walls (Nánjīng) 229
Ming Palace ruins 227
Ming Tombs 110-11
Míng Xiàolíng Tomb 226-7
Míngshì Tiányuán 609
Míngyǒng glacier 677-8
Mǐzhǐ 374
mobile phones 23, 992
modern architecture 26
  Bird's Nest & Water Cube 75, 78
  CCTV Building 75
  HSBC Building 467, 499
  Jīnmào Tower 194
  National Centre for the Performing Arts 81-2
  Oriental Pearl Tower 195
  Pier 8 519
  Shànghǎi World Financial Center 194
  World Expo 2010 site 194-5
Mògānshān 260-1
Mògāo Caves 20, 833-5, **20**
Mògāo Caves manuscripts 834
Mòhé 332
money 22, 23, 25, 989-90, *see also* costs, *individual regions*
moneychangers 990
Mongolian border crossing 856
Mongolian language 1024

Monlam Great Prayer Festival 30, 510, 818
Moon Hill 600-1
mosques
Guǎngzhōu 542
Hā'ěrbīn 324
Jamia Mosque 475
Jǐ'nán 146
Kāifēng 414
Kashgar 792
Kowloon Mosque & Islamic Centre 480
Kūnmíng 638
Kuqa 789
Nuí Jiē Mosque 82
Quánzhōu 284
Tóngxīn 849
Turpan 785
Xī'ān 357
Xīníng 869
Yarkand 798-9
Yíníng 806
mountain biking, see cycling
mountain climbing
Qī Xiān Lǐng (Seven Fairy Mountain) 577-8
Wǔzhǐshān (Five Finger Mountain) 577
Mt Amnye Machen 876
Mt Kailash 10, 903-4, **10**
Mu Family Mansion 661, 662
Mǔdānjiāng 328-9
Mùdú 244-5
museum passes
Běijīng 66
Hong Kong 478
Macau 512
museums & galleries 28, 929, 955
18 September History Museum 293
798 Art District 79
AFA 515
Army of Terracotta Warriors 12, 364-5, 911, **12**
Běijīng museum pass 66
Běijīng Police Museum 65
Běijīng Railway Museum 75
Buddhism Museum 267
Bund History Museum 180
Capital Museum 81
Chángshā Municipal Museum 446
Changyu Wine Culture Museum 173
China Art Museum 67
China Science & Technology Museum 78
China Silk Museum 254

China Tea Museum 254
Chinese Navy Museum 165
Chinese Sex Culture Museum 243, 244
Chuàng Kù (The Loft) 638
Confucius Mansion 158-9
Cultural Revolution Museum 566
Dàlǐ Museum 651
Dinosaur Museum 723
Dūnhuáng Museum 830
Eastern Zhou Royal Horse & Carriage Museum 404
Ewenki Museum 861
FCY Tung Maritime Museum 197
Forest of Stelae Museum 357
Gānsù Provincial Museum 810-11
Governor's House Museum 163
Great Wall Museum 139
Guǎngdōng Museum of Art 541
Guǎngdōng Overseas Chinese Museum 541
Guǎngxī Provincial Museum 601
Guǎngzhōu Museum of Art 542
Gùyuán Museum 850
Hǎinán Museum 571
Héběi Provincial Museum 128
Hēilóngjiāng Science & Technology Museum 325
Hénán Provincial Museum 398
Hong Kong Heritage Museum 481
Hong Kong Museum of Art 478
Hong Kong Museum of History 477
Hong Kong museum pass 478
Hotan Cultural Museum 800-1
Húběi Museum of Art 418
Húběi Provincial Museum 418
Húguāng Guild Hall 756-7
Húnán Provincial Museum 447-8
Hundred Beds Museum 262
Imperial Examinations History Museum 228
Imperial Palace of Manchu State (Puppet Emperor's Palace) 316
Inner Mongolia Museum 854
Japanese Germ Warfare Experimental Base 324
Jiāngsū 221
Jīngzhōu Museum 423
Jīnshā Site Museum 704-5
Jǐnxiùzhuāng Puppet Museum 284
Jockey Club Creative Arts Centre 479-80
Kāifēng Museum 413
Liáoníng Provincial Museum 293
Liúlí China Museum 191
Luòyáng Museum 404
Lúshān Museum 442
Lǔshùn Museum 302
M50 192

Macau Museum 513
Macau Museum of Art 515
Macau museum pass 512
Mao's Childhood House 451
Maritime Museum 284, 518
Maritime Silk Road Museum of Guǎngdōng 554
Memorial Hall of the Lǐngnán School of Painting 539
Memorial Museum of Generalissimo Sun Yatsen's mansion 539
Minorities Museum 616
Mínshēng Art Museum 197
Mosu Folk Custom Museum 670
Municipal Museum 165
Museum of Comrade Mao 451
Museum of Naxi Dongba Culture 659
Museum to Commemorate US Aggression 304
Nán'ān School 451
Nánjīng Museum 228-9
National Museum of China 61, 64
Natural History Museum 75
New Guǎngdōng Museum 535
Níngxià Museum 842
OCT Contemporary Art Terminal 559
Pawnshop Museum 514
Peace Gallery 201
Poly Art Museum 66
Propaganda Poster Art Centre 192
Qiuci Palace 788
Revolution of 1911 Museum 419
Rìshēngchāng Financial House Museum 347
Rockbund Art Museum 180
Salt Industry History Museum 722-3
Sānxīngduī Museum 711-12
Science & Technology Museum 195
Shaanxi History Museum 359
Shaanxi (Shǎnxī) 354
Shànghǎi Art Museum 185
Shànghǎi History Museum 194
Shànghǎi Museum 181
Shànghǎi Museum of Contemporary Art 185
Shànghǎi Post Museum 180
Shànghǎi Urban Planning Exhibition Hall 181
Shānxī Museum 343
Shēnzhèn Museum 558
Site of the 1st National Congress of the CCP 191-2
Sun Yatsen Memorial House 521
Sun Yatsen Museum 471
Sūzhōu Museum 234
Sūzhōu Silk Museum 237

000 Map pages
000 Photo pages

Taiping Heavenly Kingdom History Museum 229-30
Three Gorges Museum 759
Tibetan Culture Museum 867
Tousewe Museum 197
Turpan Museum 785
Wàncuìlóu Museum 377
Whampoa Military Academy 541
Wǔdāng Museum of China 424-5
Xanadu Museum 858
Xī'ān Museum 359-60
Xiányáng City Museum 366
Xīnhài Revolution Museum 541
Xīnjiāng Autonomous Region Museum 779
Yán'ān Revolution Museum 372
Yāntái Folk Custom Museum 172
Yāntái Museum 172
Yúnnán Provincial Museum 638
Muslim quarter (Xī'ān) 356-7
Mùtǎ 340
Myanmar (Burma) border crossings 686, 687
myths 908

N

Naadam Festival 31
Nam-tso 893-4
Nánchāng 432-4, **433**
Nangchen 879-80
Nánjiēcūn 401
Nánjīng 223-33, **224-5**
Nánjīng International Plum Blossom Festival 230
Nánlíng National Forest Park 557-8
Nánníng 601-4, **602**
Nánpíng 382
Nánwān Monkey Islet 580
Nánxún 262-3
Nàpà Hǎi 675
nationalism 908, 938
national parks, see also nature reserves, parks & gardens
　Ā'ěrshān National Forest Park 863
　Chángbái Shān 310-13
　Huánglóng National Park 741
　Jiǔzhàigōu National Park 19, 742-5, **743**, **19**
　Liùpán Shān Guójiā Sēnlín Gōngyuán 850
　Meili Snow Mountain National Park 677
　Nánlíng National Forest Park 557-8
　Wǔdàlián Chí 330
　Yādān National Park 835-6
　Zhāngjiājiè National Forest Park 455
natural springs
　Chángbái Shān 311
　Darjay Gompa 733

Gānzī (Garzê) 732
Guìdé 876
Huángshān 12, 387, 509, **386**, **12**, **509**
Huáqīng 365
Jǐ'nán 146
Láo Shān 170-1
Lǐtáng (Lithang) 737
Qī Xiān Lǐng (Seven Fairy Mountain) 578
Sea of Heat 684
Tiānshēng Bridge 675
nature reserves, see also national parks, parks & gardens
　Cǎohǎi Lake 629
　Changqing Nature Reserve 971
　Dīnghú Shān 556-7
　Fànjìngshān 625
　Hǎikǒu Volcanic Cluster Geopark 575
　Horqin National Nature Reserve 331
　Jīnshāgōu Nature Reserve 632
　Kanas Lake Nature Reserve 804-6
　Lèyè Geopark 610
　Lóngruì Nature Reserve 608
　Mèngdá Nature Reserve 875
　Mòmògé National Nature Reserve 331
　Sānchàhé Nature Reserve 693
　Suǒxī Valley Nature Reserve 455
　Tiānzǐ Shān Nature Reserve 455
　Tónggǔ Lǐng 576
　Wǔzhǐshān (Five Finger Mountain) 577
　Xiànghǎi National Nature Reserve 331
　Yàdīng Nature Reserve 738
　Zhālóng Nature Reserve 331
Naxi 664
　language 662, 663
　music 663
Nepalese border crossing 903
New Guǎngdōng Museum 535
Nine Dragon Screen 337
Níngxià 47, 840-50, **841**
　climate 842
　costs 842
　highlights 841
　language 842
　travel seasons 840
　travel to/from 842
　travel within 842
　weather 840
　Western Xia Tombs 845-7
　Yínchuān 842-5, **843**
Norbulingka 888
North Korea 303-4
Nù Jiāng Dam 680
Nù Jiāng Valley 679-81
Nuòdèng 656-7

O

one-child policy 932
Opium Wars 915
Organ Museum 278
overseas Chinese 552, 553

P

Pakistani border crossing 797
parks & gardens 966, see also national parks, nature reserves
　Běijīng 65-6, 72-5, 78-80, 88
　Chángchūn 316
　Chángshā 447
　Chéngdū 705
　Guǎngzhōu 541-2
　Guìlín 588-9
　Gǔlàng Yǔ 278
　Hā'ěrbīn 322-3
　Héféi 393
　HK 473, 474
　Hong Kong 471, 480-1
　Jiāngsū 221, 229
　Jǐ'nán 146
　Jìnghóng 688
　Kāifēng 413
　Luòyáng 405
　Macau 519
　Nánníng 602
　Qīngdǎo 165
　Seven Star Crags Park 555
　Shěnyáng 293
　Shíjiāzhuāng 128
　Sūzhōu 234-5, 238-9
　Yùyuán Gardens 185, **746-7**
　Zhàoqìng 555-6
passports 990
Peak Tram 467
Pénglái Pavilion 174
Peony Festival 404
phonecards 992
Pínglè 713-14
Píngliáng 838-9
pingtán 239
Píngxiáng 608
Pingyáo 15, 346-50, **346**, **15**, **27**
planning
　calendar of events 30-3
　China's regions 42-7
　itineraries 34-41
　travel seasons 30-3
Po Lin Monastery 482
population 930-3
population density 906
porcelain 440, 550, 957-8, **958**
postal services 991
Potala Palace 14, 886, 889, **14**
prayer wheels 876
Prime Minister Chen's Castle 353

Princess Wencheng Temple 879
public holidays 991
Pǔníng Temple 136, 508, **508**
Pǔtuóshān 265-9, **266**
Puyi 316

Q

Qī Xiān Lǐng (Seven Fairy Mountain) 577-8
Qiántáng River Tide Observing Festival 33, 260
Qiao Family Courtyard 345
Qībǎo 197
Qīkǒu 350-2
Qin Shi Huang 366, 371
Qīngchéng Shān 712
Qīngdǎo 161-70, **162**
Qīngdǎo International Beer Festival 32
Qīnghǎi 47, 865-80, **866**
    costs 867
    highlights 866
    history 867
    language 867
    Tóngrén 873-5
    travel seasons 865
    travel to/from 867
    travel within 867
    weather 865
    Xīníng 867-72, **868**
Qīnghǎi Lake 873
Qīnghǎi–Tibet Railway 893
Qīnghuá 437
Qīnglóng Dòng 621
Qīngyán 616
Qīngyuán 437
Qīngzhēn Dà Sì 849
Qīxiá Temple 233
Qíyún Shān 380
Quánzhōu 284-6, **285**
Qūfù 156-61, **157**

R

rafting
    Dàlǐ 654
    Kanas Lake Nature Reserve 805
    Wǔlíngyuán 455
Ráopíng 565
Rape of Nánjīng, the 228
Red Rock Gorge 632
religion 907, 934-40
rock carvings
    Dàzú Buddhist Caves 766-7
    Hèlán Shān 846

---

000 Map pages
000 Photo pages

Lhasa 888
Màijī Shān 837-8
    Princess Wencheng Temple 879
rock climbing
    Běijīng 75
    Dàlǐ 654
    Hong Kong 479
    Yángshuò 595
Rock, Joseph 667
Rongphu Monastery 899
Rongwo Gonchen Gompa 874
Ruìlì 684-6, **685**
ruins 913
    Charklik 803
    Chóngqìng City 757
    Church of St Paul 513
    Gāochāng (Khocho) ruins 787
    Jiāohé ruins 787
    Kāifēng Synagogue 413-14
    Khara Khoto 860
    Melikawat ruins 801
    Ming palace ruins 227
    Mor Pagoda 792
    Qiāng watchtowers 729-30
    Tsaparang 904
    Wandu Mountain City 315
Russian border crossings 328, 864

S

sacred sights 28, 935, 968
    Éméi Shān 714-17, **749**
    Gyantse Kumbum 895
    Héng Shān 452-3
    Huà Shān 368-70
    Huángshān 12, 385-90, 509, **386**, **12**, **509**
    Jiǔhuá Shān 390-2
    Kawa Karpo 676, 677-8
    Labrang Monastery 16, 508, 816-17, **16**, **965**
    Mt Amnye Machen 876
    Mt Kailash 10, 903-4, **10**
    Pǔníng Temple 136, 508, **508**
    Qīngchéng Shān 712
    Sōng Shān 401
    Tài Shān 20, 153-6, **153**, **20**
    Tashilhunpo Monastery 896-7
    Wǔdāng Shān 425
    Wǔtái Shān 340-3
    Yàdīng Nature Reserve 738
safety 991-2, see also dangers, scams
Sage's Birthday 159
Sakya 898-9
Samye Monastery 894
Sānchàhé Nature Reserve 693
sand dunes 860
Sāngkē grasslands 820
Sānjiāng 594-5

Sānqīng Shān 438-40
Sānxīngduī Museum 711-12
Sānyà 581-4, **582**
scams 102, 109, 501, 992, see also dangers, safety
scenery 29
scenic areas
    Bamboo Sea 726, **746-7**
    Dàwān Lake 264
    Déhāng 458
    Elephant's Trunk Hill 441
    Láo Shān 171
    Lìjiāng 659-70
    Línggǔ Temple 227
    Lónghǔ Shān 440-1
    Mǎtí Sì 826
    Míng Xiàolíng 226-7
    Mògānshān 260
    Penha Hill 515
    Tài Shān 20, 153-6, **153**, **20**
    Tiānmén Shān 455
    Tiānzhù Peak 156
    Wànxiān Mountains 409
    Wéizhōu 607
    Wǔlíngyuán 454-5
    Wǔyí Shān 288
    Yuánjiājiè 455
    Yùquánxī 458
    Zuǒ River 607-8
sculpture 958-9
Sea of Heat 684
Seng-ze Gyanak *mani* wall 879
Sera Monastery 886
Shaanxi (Shǎnxī) 44, 354-74, **355**
    costs 356
    highlights 355
    history 356
    Huà Shān 368-70, **369**
    language 356
    travel seasons 354
    travel to/from 356
    travel within 356
    weather 354
    Xī'ān 356-64, **358**
shadow puppets 721
Shāndōng 42, 144-75, **145**
    climate 145
    costs 146
    highlights 145
    history 145
    Jǐ'nán 146-9, **147**
    language 145-6
    Qūfù 156-61, **156**
    Tài Shān 153-6, **153**
    travel seasons 144
    travel to/from 146
    travel within 146
    weather 144

Shàngdū (Xanadu) 857-8
Shànghǎi 8, 11, 43, 176-220, **178-9**, 8, **11**, **32**, **186-7**, **746-7**
accommodation 176, 199-205
activities 212
Bund & People's Square **182-3**
children, travel with 198
climate 176, 177
costs 177
courses 198
drinking 209-11
eating 176, 205-9
entertainment 211-13
festivals & events 199
food 205
French Concession **188-9**
highlights 178-9
history 177
internet access 215
itineraries 181
medical services 215-16
PSB 216
Pǔdōng **194**
Shànghǎi Railway Station **196**
shopping 191, 213-15
sights 177, 180-97
tourist information 216
tours 198-9
travel seasons 176
travel to/from 217-18
travel within 218-19
weather 176
West Nanjing Road **193**
Shànghǎi International Literary Festival 199
Shànghǎi Museum 181
Shànghǎi World Financial Center 194
Shangri-la (Zhōngdiàn) 671-5, **672**
Shānhǎiguān 139-41, **139**
Shàntóu 566, **567**
Shǎnxī 44, 334-53, **335**
climate 336
costs 336
Dàtóng 336-8, **337**
highlights 335
history 336
language 336
Píngyáo 346-50, **346**
travel seasons 334
travel to/from 336
travel within 336
weather 334
Wǔtái Shān 340-3, **341**
Shàolín Temple 402-3
Sháoshān 451-2
Shàoxīng 263

Shāpōtóu 848-9
Shāxī 657-8
Shēnhǎi Salt Well 723
Shénnóngjià 427-8
Shěnyáng 292-6, **294**
Shēnzhèn 558-61, **560**
Shèxiàn 385
Shi Family Residence 127
Shì Wéi 862-3
Shíbǎoshān 658-9
Shigatse 896-9, **897**
Shíjiāzhuāng 128-30, **129**
Shílín 645
Shíméi Bay 580
Shipton's Arch (Tushuk Tagh) 792
Shíqiáo 619
Shíqú (Sêrshu) 735-6
Shítouchéng 601
Shùhé Old Town 666
Shuǐ Dòng Gōu 846
Shuǐyù Cūn 112
Siberian Tiger Park 323
Siberian tigers 323, 324
Sìchuān 46, 697-745, **698-9**
Bamboo Sea 726
Chéngdū 701-11, **702-3**
costs 700
Éméi Shān 714-8, **716**
highlights 698-9
history 700
internet access 700
Kāngdìng 727-9, **728**
language 700
Sichuān–Tibet Highway 730-9
travel seasons 697
travel to/from 700
travel within 700
weather 697
Sìchuān–Tibet Highway
Northern Route 730-6
Southern Route 736-9
Sìdònggōu 632
silk, see atlas
Silk Road 15, 36, 798-803, **36**, **15**
Singing Sands Mountain 835
Sīxī 438
ski resorts
Běidàhú 316
Chángbái Shān 310, 329
sky burial 737
Sky Ladder 409
smoking 493
Sōng Shān 401
Sōngji 769
Sōngpān 739-42, **740**
South Korean border crossings 127, 169, 175, 301, 306
Soviet Martyrs Cemetery 302

sporting events
Dragon Boat Festival 31, 510, **510**
dragon boat races 623, **510**
Formula 1 31, 199
Great Wall Marathon 31
Lǐtáng Horse Festival 32
Naadam Festival 31
Shangri-la Horse Racing Festival 31
surf competition 33
Xiàmén International Marathon 273
Spring Festival 30, 510
Stanley Market 475
Star Ferry 19, 475, **19**
stilt houses (diàojiǎolóu) 761, 767, **21**
St Lazarus Church District 513-14
Summer Palace 84-7, **86**
Sun & Moon Bay 580
Sun Yatsen 918
former residence 192
mausoleum 227
memorial hall 88
memorial house 521
museum 471, 539
Sunday Livestock Market 790
surfing 33, 581
Sūzhōu 234-42, **236**
Sūzhōu Silk Festival 239
Swallow's Cavern 648
synagogues
Hā'ěrbīn New Synagogue 323-4
Kāifēng Synagogue 413-4
Ohel Leah Synagogue 195-6, 475
Ohel Moishe Synagogue 195-6

T

Tǎchuānǎ 381-2
Tǎgōng (Lha Gang) 731-2
cycling 731
hiking 731
horse riding 731
Tai O 482
Tài Shān 20, 153-6, **153**, **20**
central route 154-5
Tiānzhú Peak route 156
western route 155-6
Tài'ān 150-3, **150**
taichi 17, 426, **17**
Táihuái Temple cluster 341
Taipa 521-2
Taiwanese border crossing 280
Tàiyuán 343-5, **343**
Tajikistan border crossing 797
Taktser 873
Tángmó 383-4
Taoism 937-8
Tashilhunpo Monastery 896-7

tea 103, 709, 951, **949**
  China Tea Museum 254
  Fāngcūn Tea Market 548
  Museum of Tea Ware 471
  Xiǎoqī 437
Tea-Horse Road 658
telephone services 23, 992
Temple of Heaven 72-5, 508, **73**, **508**
Temple of Sumeru, Happiness & Longevity 136-7
Temple of the Cave Host 265
Temple Street Night Market 478
temples & monasteries 508, 964-5, **14**, **508**
  A-Ma Temple 515
  Arhat Temple 756
  Bakong Scripture Printing Press & Monastery 735
  Bamboo Temple 643-4
  Bānruò Temple 316
  Bàoguó Temple 715
  Bàopǔ Taoist Temple 255
  Bǎoxiāng Temple 659
  Bǐfēng Temple 352
  Big Goose Pagoda 359
  Black Dragon Temple 351
  Black Pagoda 695
  Cave Temple 859-60
  Chángchūn Temple 419
  Chénghuáng Temple 370, 398
  Chénxiānggé Nunnery 185
  Chi Lin Nunnery 478-9
  Chöde Gompa 736
  Confucian Temple (Jiànshuǐ) 646
  Confucian Temple (Shànghǎi) 185
  Confucian Temple (Sūzhōu) 237
  Confucius Temple (Běijīng) 69-70
  Confucius Temple (Hā'ěrbīn) 325
  Confucius Temple (Hánchéng) 370
  Confucius Temple (Hángzhōu) 253
  Confucius Temple (Píngyáo) 347
  Confucius Temple (Qūfù) 157-8, 508
  Confucius Temple (Wǔwēi) 823
  Confucius Temple (Xīngchéng) 307
  Confucius Temple (Zhèngzhōu) 398
  Courtyard of Eastern Culture 579
  Dài Temple 150-1
  Darjay Gompa 733
  Dōnglín Temple 624
  Dōngyuè Temple 75
  Drepung Monastery 887-8
  Eight Outer Temples 135
  Elephant Bathing Pool 715

  etiquette 694, 890
  Fǎmén Temple 366
  Fǎyǔ Temple 267
  Fǎyuán Temple 83
  Fēilái Temple 677
  Five Officials Memorial Temple 572
  Fújiàn 270
  Fúwén Miào 624
  Fúxī Temple 836
  Ganden Monastery 893
  Ganden Sumtseling Gompa 672
  Gānzī Temple 732
  Gāo Temple 847
  Golden Duck Pagoda 686
  Gomar Gompa 874
  Great Bell Temple 86-7
  Great Buddha Temple 825
  Green Ram Temple 705
  Guāndì Temple 284
  Guānghuì Temple 131
  Guāngxiào Temple 542
  Guǎngzōng Sì 847
  Guīyuán Temple 418-19
  Gyantse Kumbum 895
  Hǎihuì Temple 353
  Hanging Monastery 340
  Hóngfú Temple 613
  Huàchéng Sì 391
  Huáyán Temple 336-7
  Inner Mongolia 851
  Jade Buddha Temple 192
  Jade Peak Monastery 665
  Jīluè Huáng Temple 563
  Jǐndǐng Temple 715
  Jìng'ān Temple 193
  Jìngcí Temple 253
  Jǐnjiāng Pagoda 304
  Jokhang Temple 508, 886
  Jyekundo Dondrubling Monastery 877
  Kāiyuán Temple 131, 284
  Kerti Gompa 821
  Khalsa Diwan Sikh Temple 474
  Kōngtóng Shān 838
  Kumbum Monastery 872
  Kun Iam Temple 519
  Labrang Monastery 16, 508, 816-17, **16**, **965**
  Lama Temple 67, **748**
  Léifēng Pagoda 253
  Línggǔ Temple 227
  Língyǐn Temple 253
  Línjì Temple 131
  Lónghuá Temple 197
  Lóngxīng Temple 130
  Man Mo Temple 467, 481
  Mencius Temple 158
  Miàoyīng Temple 82

  Milarepa Palace 820-1
  Míngjiào Temple 393
  Monastery of Deep Compassion 123
  Na Tcha Temple 514
  Nánpǔtuó Temple 273
  Nányuè Temple 452-3
  Níngxià 840
  North Temple Pagoda 237
  Pak Tai Temple 473
  Pearl Pagoda 242
  Plum Monastery 555
  Po Lin Monastery 482
  Potala Palace 14, 886, 889, **14**
  Princess Wencheng Temple 879
  Pǔjì Temple 267
  Pǔlè Temple 137
  Pǔníng Temple 136, 508, **508**
  Pǔtuózōngchéng Temple 136
  Qīnghǎi 865
  Qīnglóng Dòng 621
  Qīngxū Guàn 347
  Qīngyīn Pavilion 715
  Quánfú Temple 246
  Rénshòu Temple 551
  Residence of the Celestial Masters 441
  Rongphu Monastery 899
  Rongwo Gonchen Gompa 874
  Sakya Monastery 898
  Samye Monastery 894
  Sera Monastery 886
  Serti Gompa 821
  Shàngqīng Palace 441
  Shàngqīng Temple 712
  Shànhuà Temple 337
  Shǎnxī 334
  Shàolín Temple 402-3
  Shuānglín Temple 350
  Sik Sik Yuen Wong Tai Sin Temple 479
  Six Harmonies Pagoda 254
  Stone Bell Temple 658-9
  Sun & Moon Twin Pagodas 588
  Tǎgōng Monastery 731
  Táihuái Temple Cluster 341
  Tāngdì Miào 352
  Tashilhunpo Monastery 896-7
  Tǎyuàn Temple 341
  Temple of Bliss 324
  Temple of Heaven 72-5, 508, **73**, **508**
  Temple of Mystery 238
  Temple of the Chief Minister 411
  Temple of the Eight Immortals 360
  Temple of the Six Banyan Trees 542
  Ten Thousand Buddhas Monastery 481
  Three Pagodas 651

000 Map pages
000 Photo pages

Tianhou Temple 163
Tiānníng Temple 130-1
Tibet 881
Tin Hau Temple 478
Treasure Pagoda 372
Tsing Shan Monastery 481
Twin Pagoda Temple 343
Wànnián Temple 715
Wénshū Temple 704
White Bamboo Shoot Pagoda 695
White Cloud Temple 82
White Horse Temple 409
Wǔdāng Lamasery 859
Wǔhóu Temple 705
Wǔtǎ Pagoda 853-4
Wútún Sì 874
Xiangshan Temple 408-9
Xiàntōng Temple 341-2
Xīnguóchán Temple 146
Yán Temple 159
Yǒngzuò Temple 343
Yòuníng Sì 872-3
Yuánjué Pagoda 370
Yuántōng Temple 637-8
Yùquán Temple 836
Yùshù 879
Zhǐlín Sì 647
Zhìyuán Temple 391
Zhōnghé Temple 656
Zǔ Miào 550
Téngchōng 681-3, **682**
Tengger Desert 849
Terracotta Warriors 12, 364-5, 911, **12**
Thai border crossing 693
thangka 873-4
Three Gorges 8, 428, 759, 770-1, **8**
Tiān Chí 784
Tiān'ānmén Square 60-1, **746**
Tiānjīn 42, 122-7, **121**, **124**
    accommodation 125
    climate 122
    costs 122
    eating & drinking 125-6
    highlights 121
    history 122
    language 122
    medical services 126
    PSB 126
    sights 122-4
    tours 125
    travel seasons 120
    travel to/from 122, 126-7
    travel within 122, 127
    weather 120
Tiānlóng 627-8
Tiānpíng Shān 245
Tiānshuǐ 836-7
Tiāntáishān 628

Tibet 47, 881-904, **882**
    borders 742
    climate 884
    costs 883
    festivals & events 888-9
    Friendship Highway, the 894-902
    food 734
    highlights 882
    history 883-4
    language 884
    Lhasa 884-93, **885**, **887**
    Mt Kailash 903-4
    tours 676, 900-1
    travel seasons 881
    travel to/from 884, 900-1
    travel within 884, 900-1
    weather 881
Tibetan border crossing 676
Tibetan Culture Museum 867
Tibetan language 1023
Tiěxī 624
Tiger Leaping Gorge 8, 667-9, **668**, 8
time zones 779
tipping 25, 951, 990
Tomb of Emperor Jingdi 367
Tomb of Qin Shi Huang 366
Tomb Sweeping Day 159
tombs, *see also* mausoleums & memorials
    Abakh Hoja Tomb 792
    Bai Juyi's Graveyard 408-9
    Hāmì Kings Mausoleum 787
    Huang Taiji 293
    imperial tombs 367
    Jiāngjūnfén 314
    Lord Bao's Tomb 394
    Maulana Ashiddin Mazar 789
    Mazar of Imam Asim 800
    Ming Tombs 110-11
    Míng Xiàolíng Tomb 226-7
    Su Xiaoxiao's Tomb 252
    Sun Yatsen Mausoleum 227
    Tomb of Emperor Jingdi 367
    Tomb of Qin Shi Huang 366
    Tuglugh Timur Khan Mausoleum 807
    Wèi Jin Tombs 828
    Western Xia Tombs 845
    Xióngjiā Zhǒng 424, 427
Tōngdào Dong Minority Autonomous County 457
Tónggǔ Lǐng 576
Tónglǐ 242-3
Tóngrén (Repkong) 873-5
Tóngxīn 849
Torch Festival 661
tours 25, 198
    birdwatching 973
    boat 125, 198, 199, 239, 254

bus 119, 199, 377, 484, 836
camel 792, 849, 860
cycling 198, 199, 1001
Great Wall, the 114-15, 116, 118, 119
Guǎngzhōu Opera House 538
Guiyáng 614
hiking 616
Hong Kong 484
horse riding 740
Kanas Lake Nature Reserve 805
Karakoram Highway 796
Labrang Monastery 16, 816-17, **16**, **965**
Lèshān 719
Lí River 14, 27, 589, 599, **14**, **503**
motorcycle 198
Muztagh Ata 792
rafting 456, 654, 805
Shànghǎi 198-99
skiing 316, 329
Tiānjīn 125
Tibet 900-1
tǔlóu 19, 270, 280-3, 566-7, **18**
Wǔlíngyuán 456
Xiàhé 817
Xī'ān 367-8
Yǎdān National Park 836
traditional Chinese medicine 253, 1015
train travel 23, 1004-9, *see also individual locations*
    international trains 108, 999
    internet resources 1009
    Qīnghǎi 872
    Qīnghǎi–Tibet Railway 893
    Tibet 107
    Trans-Siberian Railway 1006-7
    travel to/from China 999
transport 992, 996-1003
    language 1020-21
    train travel 1004-9
Trans-Siberian Railway 1006-7
travel to/from China 996-1000
travel within China 1000-3
travellers cheques 990
trekking, *see* hiking
Tsingtao beer 164
tǔlóu 19, 270, 280-3, 566-7, **18**
Túnxī 377-80, **378**
Turpan 784, **785**
Tuyoq 787

U
Uighur language 1024
Underground Forest 330
Underground Fortress 861

Unesco World Heritage sites
dānxiá 826, 974
Dàzú Buddhist caves 766-7
diāolóu 11, 552, **11**
Dūjiāngyàn irrigation project 712
Éméi Shān 714-17, **715**, **749**
Macau 512-21
Hóngcūn 381
Huángshān 12, 385-90, 509, **386**, **12**, **509**
Ji'ān 313-15
Jīluè Huáng Temple 563
Jiǔzhàigōu National Park 19, 742-5, **743**, 19
Lèshān 718-20, **719**
Lìjiāng 659-64, **660**, **665**, **753**
Lóngmén caves 407-9, **39**
Ming Tombs 110-11
Nù Jiāng Valley 679-81
Shàngdū (Xanadu) 857
Shàolín Temple 402-3
Tài Shān 20, 153-6, **153**, **20**
tǔlóu 19, 270, 280-3, 566-7, **18**
Wǔdāng Shān 424-7
Wǔlíngyuán 453-7
Xīdì 380-1
urban cities 27
Ürümqi 779-84, **780**

V

vegetarian travellers 951
Victor Sassoon 201
Vietnamese border crossings 604, 609, 643
visas 23, 992-5, 996
volcanoes, see also lava fields
Hǎikǒu Volcanic Cluster Geopark 575
Lǎohēi Shān 331
Téngchōng 683-4
Underground Forest 330
Wǔdàlián Chí 330-1
volunteering 995

W

Walking Around the Mountain Festival 31
walking tours
Bund 186-7, **186-7**
Forbidden City 58-9, **58-9**
Hong Kong 483, **483**
hútòng (Běijīng) 71, **71**
Wang Family Courtyard 350

000 Map pages
000 Photo pages

water wheels 812, 876
waterfalls
Changbai 311
Déhàng 458
Détiān 608-9
Diàoshuǐlóu 330
Diéshuǐ 681
Huángguǒshù 627
Jiǔzhàigōu National Park 19, 742-5, **743**, 19
Shízhàngdòng 631
White Dragon Pond 632
Yǔbēng 678
waterfront
Avenida da República 515
Bund 8, 180, **182-3**, **8**, **186-7**
Hànkǒu Bund 418
Riverside Plaza 315
Tsim Sha Tsui East Promenade 477
Xiàmén 273
Water-splashing Festival 687
weather 22, see also individual regions
Wēibǎo Shān 650-1
weights & measurements 994, 995
wéilóngwū 566-7
Wēiníng 628-30
Wēishān 650
Wéizhōu Island 607
West Lake 251-2
Western Film Studios 846
Western Xia Tombs 845
White Cloud Hills 550
White Horse Temple 409
wildlife 971-4
wildlife parks
Bìfēngxiá Panda Base 712-13
Ecological Monkey Zone 715
Giant Panda Breeding Research Base 701
Mai Po Marsh Nature Reserve 480
Siberian Tiger Park 323
wildlife reserves, see wildlife parks
wind farms 833
Wing Chun 979-80
Wòlóng Valley 438
women in China 932-3
women's health 1015
Wong Fei Hung 551
woodblock printing 415
Wǔdàlián Chí 330-2
Wǔdāng Lamasery 859
Wǔdāng Shān 425-8
Wǔfú 289
Wǔhàn 418-22, **420**
Wǔlíngyuán 453-7, **454**
Wǔtái Shān 340-3
Wùtún Sì 874

Wūwēi 823-4
Wǔyì 264
Wǔyí Shān 288-9
Wùyuán 435-8, **436**
Wūzhèn 261-2
Wǔzhǐshān City (Tōngshí) 576-7
Wǔzhǐshān (Five Finger Mountain) 577

X

Xanadu Museum 858
Xī Shān 644-5
Xiàguān 649-50
Xiàhé 815-20, **816**
Xiàméi 288
Xiàmén 272-7, **274**
Xī'ān 356-64, **358**
Xiǎoqī 437
Xīdì 380-1
Xīdīng 696
Xījiāng 618-19
Xīlāmùrén 857
Xīncūn 580
Xīngchéng 306-7
Xīngpíng 599-600
Xīníng 867-72, **868**
Xīnjiāng 46, 776-807, **777**
climate 778
costs 778
highlights 777
history 777-8
Hotan 800-2, **801**
Kashgar 790-6, **791**
Kuqa 788-9
language 778
travel seasons 776
travel to/from 778-9
travel within 778-9
Ürümqi 779-84, **780**
weather 776
Xīnjiāng Autonomous Region Museum 779
Xīnlù hǎi (Yilhun Lha-tso) 734
Xióngjiā Zhōng 427
Xīshuāngbǎnnà region 687-96, **688**
Xīzhōu 656
Xúnpǔ Village 286

Y

Yàdīng Nature Reserve 738
Yamdrok-tso 894-5
Yán'ān 372-3
Yánbiān Korean Autonomous Prefecture 314
Yáncūn 438
Yángjiāng 554-5, **556**
Yángměi 604-5

Yángshuò 14, 595-9, **596**, **600**
Yangzi dolphin 973
Yangzi River 8, 35, 770-5, **772**, **9**
Yangzi River Bridge 230
Yánjí 313
Yāntái 171-5, **172**
Yarkand 798-9
Yellow River 878
Yengisar 798
Yíbīn 724-5
Yíchāng 428-9
Yínchuān 842-5, **843**
Yīníng 806-7
Yòuníng Sì 872-3
Yuányáng Rice Terraces 17, 648-9, **649**, **17**, **748-9**
Yuè Liàng Wān 576
Yùjiācūn 132
Yúliáng 385
Yúlín 373-4
Yúlín Grottoes 836
Yùlóng River 600
Yùlóng Xuěshān 666-7
Yúnfēng Bāzhài 628
Yúnfēng Shān 683
Yúngāng Caves 16, 338-9, **16**
Yúnnán 46, 633-96, **634**
    climate 635
    costs 635

Dàlǐ 651-5, **652**
    highlights 634
    hiking 633
    history 635
    Kūnmíng 635-43, **636-7**
    language 635
    Lìjiāng 659-65, **660**
    travel seasons 633
    travel to/from 635
    travel within 635
    weather 633
    Yuányáng Rice Terraces 648-9, **649**
yurt camps 857, 861, 862, 863
Yùshù (Jyekundo) 877-8
Yúyuán 265

Z
Zhang Family Compound 263
Zhāngbì Cūn 350
Zhāngbì Underground Castle 350
Zhāngjiājiè 453-7
Zhāngmù 901-2
Zhāngyè 825-6
Zhàoqìng 555-6
Zhàoxīng 620
Zhàozhōu Bridge 133
Zhèjiāng 43, 247-69, **248**, **752**
    climate 249

    costs 249
    Hángzhōu 249-60, **250-1**
    highlights 248
    history 249
    language 249
    Pǔtuóshān 265-9, **266**
    travel seasons 247
    travel to/from 249
    travel within 249
    weather 247
    Wūzhèn 261-2
Zhèngdìng 130-2
Zhèngzhōu 398-400, **399**
Zhènyuán 621-4, **622**
Zhījīn Cave 627
Zhōnghé Temple 656
Zhōngshān 767-8
Zhōngwèi 847-8, **848**
Zhōngyuè Temple 403
Zhōuzhuāng 245-6
Zhùangjīng Tōng 672
Zhūhǎi 561-3, **562**
Zhūjiājiǎo 220, **3**
Zhūjiāyù 149-50
Zhūxiàn Zhèn 415
Zìgòng 722-4
Zìlì 552

how to use this book

These symbols will help you find the listings you want:

- 👁 Sights
- 🏊 Beaches
- 🏃 Activities
- 🥢 Courses
- 👣 Tours
- 🎊 Festivals & Events
- 🛏 Sleeping
- 🍴 Eating
- 🍷 Drinking
- ⭐ Entertainment
- 🛍 Shopping
- ℹ Information/Transport

Look out for these icons:

TOP CHOICE	Our author's recommendation
FREE	No payment required
🍃	A green or sustainable option

Our authors have nominated these places as demonstrating a strong commitment to sustainability – for example by supporting local communities and producers, operating in an environmentally friendly way, or supporting conservation projects.

These symbols give you the vital information for each listing:

- ☎ Telephone Numbers
- ⊙ Opening Hours
- Ⓟ Parking
- ⊖ Nonsmoking
- ✳ Air-Conditioning/Heating
- @ Internet Access
- 📶 Wi-Fi Access
- 🏊 Swimming Pool
- 📖 Vegetarian Selection
- 📄 English-Language Menu
- 👪 Family-Friendly
- 🐾 Pet-Friendly
- 🚌 Bus
- ⛴ Ferry
- Ⓜ Metro
- Ⓢ Subway
- 🚃 Tram
- 🚆 Train

Reviews are organised by author preference.

Map Legend

Sights
- Beach
- Buddhist
- Castle
- Christian
- Hindu
- Islamic
- Jewish
- Monument
- Museum/Gallery
- Ruin
- Winery/Vineyard
- Zoo
- Other Sight

Activities, Courses & Tours
- Diving/Snorkelling
- Canoeing/Kayaking
- Skiing
- Surfing
- Swimming/Pool
- Walking
- Windsurfing
- Other Activity/Course/Tour

Sleeping
- Sleeping
- Camping

Eating
- Eating

Drinking
- Drinking
- Cafe

Entertainment
- Entertainment

Shopping
- Shopping

Information
- Bank
- Embassy/Consulate
- Hospital/Medical
- Internet
- Police
- Post Office
- Telephone
- Toilet
- Tourist Information
- Other Information

Transport
- Airport
- Border Crossing
- Bus
- Cable Car/Funicular
- Cycling
- Ferry
- Monorail
- Parking
- Petrol Station
- Taxi
- Train/Railway
- Tram
- Underground Train Station
- Other Transport

Routes
- Tollway
- Freeway
- Primary
- Secondary
- Tertiary
- Lane
- Unsealed Road
- Plaza/Mall
- Steps
- Tunnel
- Pedestrian Overpass
- Walking Tour
- Walking Tour Detour
- Path

Geographic
- Hut/Shelter
- Lighthouse
- Lookout
- Mountain/Volcano
- Oasis
- Park
- Pass
- Picnic Area
- Waterfall

Population
- Capital (National)
- Capital (State/Province)
- City/Large Town
- Town/Village

Boundaries
- International
- State/Province
- Disputed
- Regional/Suburb
- Marine Park
- Cliff
- Wall

Hydrography
- River, Creek
- Intermittent River
- Swamp/Mangrove
- Reef
- Canal
- Water
- Dry/Salt/Intermittent Lake
- Glacier

Areas
- Beach/Desert
- Cemetery (Christian)
- Cemetery (Other)
- Park/Forest
- Sportsground
- Sight (Building)
- Top Sight (Building)

Tienlon Ho
Shāndōng, Húnán

Tienlon grew up in Worthington, Ohio, where the best Chinese food was always at her house. She's moved around a lot since then but keeps mostly to places where it's easy to find live seafood and mangosteens, including Shànghǎi, Hong Kong, Bangkok, Singapore, New York, and currently San Francisco where she writes about food, travel and other things. She previously worked on Lonely Planet's *Southwest China* guide. You can find her at tienlon.com.

Robert Kelly
Liáoníng, Jílín, Hēilóngjiāng, Hǎinán, Gānsù

Born in Vancouver, Canada, Robert first landed in China in the mid-1980s, and has been a regular visitor since 2003. For the past 16 years Robert has lived in Taiwan, where he is currently working on a documentary about the loss of traditional Taoist temple arts. On his sixth trip to China for Lonely Planet Robert covered the boggy north, the tropical south, and the Silk Road province of Gānsù. For an art and adventure lover, it doesn't get much better than that.

Michael Kohn
Shaanxi, Yúnnán, Qīnghǎi

After studying journalism at the University of California, Michael launched a career as a foreign correspondent, reporting for a handful of media outlets including the BBC and Reuters. His first trip to China was in 1994 when he visited Běijīng and Tibet on a university study program. This is his third tour of duty for Lonely Planet's *China*, having researched Gānsù, Xīnjiāng, Inner Mongolia and Níngxià in earlier editions. Michael is based in Ulaanbaatar. His work can be read online at www.michaelkohn.us.

Shawn Low
Ānhuī, Hénán, Guǎngxī

Shawn grew up in hot, humid, food-crazy Singapore but later made his way further south to less hot, less humid, food-crazy Melbourne (Australia, not Florida). He's spent the past six years working for Lonely Planet as an editor, commissioning editor, author, TV host and travel editor. When not exploring his love-hate relationship with China, Shawn finds time to eat and drink his way through other parts of Asia. Find him on Twitter @shawnlow and all other social media @shawn_low.

Bradley Mayhew
Xīnjiāng, Tibet

Bradley has been drawn to China's borderlands since travelling to Kashgar and Lhasa 20 years ago, while studying Chinese at Oxford University. Bradley wrote first editions of Lonely Planet's guides to *Southwest China* and *Shanghai* and is the coordinating author of *Tibet*, *Bhutan*, *Central Asia* and *Nepal*. He recently starred in a five-part Arte/SWR TV documentary retracing the route of Marco Polo from Venice across Iran and Afghanistan to Kublai Khan's summer capital at Xanadu in inner Mongolia. See what he's currently up to at www.bradleymayhew.blogspot.com.

Read more about Bradley at:
lonelyplanet.com/members/nepalibrad

Daniel McCrohan
Běijīng, The Great Wall, Húběi, Sìchuān, Chóngqìng, Cruising the Yangzi

Daniel has been in China since 2005 and currently lives with his wife and children in a courtyard home, tucked away down an alley behind Běijīng's Drum Tower. He has written more than a dozen Lonely Planet guidebooks on China and India, is the creator of the smartphone app *Beijing on a Budget*, and is the co-host of the Lonely Planet television series *Best in China*. Find out more on his website: daniel mccrohan.com or follow him on Twitter @danielmccrohan.

Read more about Daniel at:
lonelyplanet.com/members/danielmccrohan

Christopher Pitts
Shànghǎi, Jiāngxī

Chris started his university years studying classical Chinese poetry before a week in 1990s Shànghǎi (en route to school in Kūnmíng) abruptly changed his focus to the idiosyncrasies of modern China. Several years in Asia memorising Chinese characters got him hooked, and he returns whenever he can to immerse himself in one of the world's most fascinating languages. He's written for Lonely Planet's *China* since 2004 and is also co-author of the *Shanghai* guide. Visit him online at www.christopherpitts.net.

OUR STORY

A beat-up old car, a few dollars in the pocket and a sense of adventure. In 1972 that's all Tony and Maureen Wheeler needed for the trip of a lifetime – across Europe and Asia overland to Australia. It took several months, and at the end – broke but inspired – they sat at their kitchen table writing and stapling together their first travel guide, *Across Asia on the Cheap*. Within a week they'd sold 1500 copies. Lonely Planet was born.

Today, Lonely Planet has offices in Melbourne, London and Oakland, with more than 600 staff and writers. We share Tony's belief that 'a great guidebook should do three things: inform, educate and amuse'.

OUR WRITERS

Damian Harper

Coordinating Author, Shànghǎi, Zhèjiāng, Guìzhōu

After graduating with a degree in Chinese in the days when it was still an unfashionably exotic choice, Damian relocated to Hong Kong to see out the last year of British rule. Since undertaking a leg-busting nine-province journey for the sixth edition of this book in 1997, Damian has tumble-weeded his way around China, working on multiple editions of *China*, *Shanghai* and *Beijing*, contributing to *Hong Kong* and *China's Southwest* and road-testing incalculable hotel beds, hole-in-the-wall menus and wayside watering holes.

Read more about Damian at:
lonelyplanet.com/members/damianharper

Piera Chen

Hong Kong, Macau, Guǎngdōng

Piera's acquaintance with Guǎngdōng began when she was a teenager living in Hong Kong. Some of her family had settled in southern China, so it was here that she learnt how to smoke, ride a bike and coax a water leech away – skills that came in handy during her research trips for this book. Piera has worked on Lonely Planet titles *Hong Kong*, *Hong Kong Encounter* and the previous edition of *China*.

Read more about Piera at:
lonelyplanet.com/members/pierachen

Chung Wah Chow

Jiāngsū, Fújiàn, Hong Kong

Born with restless feet, Chung Wah has travelled extensively both in her native Hong Kong and elsewhere, and is forever returning to China for trips ranging from village stays in Yúnnán to upriver treks in Qīnghǎi. She contributed to the previous two editions of this book and co-authored Lonely Planet's *Hong Kong*. In this edition, she (un)covered the coastal beauty of southern China and fell for the region's sublime culture and seafood. She considers herself a resident tourist in Hong Kong.

Read more about Chung Wah at:
lonelyplanet.com/members/cwchow

David Eimer

Běijīng, Tiānjīn & Héběi, Shǎnxī, Níngxià, Inner Mongolia

David first came to China in 1988, when cars and foreigners were both in short supply. After spells working as a journalist in LA and his native London, David spent seven years living in Běijīng. His travels have taken him to almost every province in the Middle Kingdom. David has co-authored the last three editions of both the *China* and *Beijing* guides. Now based in Bangkok, he contributes to a variety of newspapers and magazines in the UK.

OVER PAGE | MORE WRITERS

Published by Lonely Planet Publications Pty Ltd
ABN 36 005 607 983
13th edition – May 2013
ISBN 978 1 74220 138 2
© Lonely Planet 2013   Photographs © as indicated 2013
10 9 8 7 6 5 4 3 2 1
Printed in Singapore